U0886248

2014年

Import and Export Tariff of the People's Republic of China and a Declaration Guidebook

中华人民共和国海关进出口税则

及申报指南

汉英文对照版（附光盘）

进出口关税税率　出口退税率　十位商品编码　监管证件　海关申报要素

Import & Export Tariff Rates　Export Tax Rebate Rate　Ten HS Code　Control Documents　Customs Declare Elements

中华人民共和国海关进出口税则及申报指南编委会 编

Compiled by the Editorial Committee of the Import and Export Tariff of the People's Republic of China and a Declaration Guidebook

中国商务出版社

CCTP CHINA COMMERCE AND TRADE PRESS

图书在版编目（CIP）数据

2014年中华人民共和国海关进出口税则及申报指南 / 中华人民共和国海关进出口税则及申报指南编委会编. -- 北京：中国商务出版社，2013.12

ISBN 978-7-5103-0979-3

Ⅰ. ①2… Ⅱ. ①中… Ⅲ. ①海关税则-中国-指南 Ⅳ. ①F752.50-62

中国版本图书馆 CIP 数据核字（2013）第 292485 号

2014年中华人民共和国海关进出口税则及申报指南
2014 NIAN ZHONGHUARENMINGONGHEGUO HAIGUAN JINCHUKOU SHUIZE JI SHENBAO ZHINAN
中华人民共和国海关进出口税则及申报指南编委会 编

出 版：中国商务出版社
发 行：北京中商图出版物发行有限责任公司
社 址：北京市东城区安定门外大街东后巷28号
邮 编：100710
电 话：010-64515141（编辑三室）
010-84493090（作者服务电话）
010-84493089
网 址：www.cctpress.com
邮 箱：cctp@cctpress.com
印 刷：三河市鑫汇源印装厂
开 本：889毫米×1194毫米 1/16
印 张：77.5 字 数：2568千字
版 次：2014年1月第1版 2014年1月第1次印刷
书 号：ISBN 978-7-5103-0979-3
定 价：280.00元

前　言

为进一步发挥关税调控在促进发展、调整结构、深化改革、改善民生方面的积极作用，自 2014 年 1 月 1 日起，我国将进一步调整进出口关税税则，主要涉及最惠国税率、年度暂定税率、协定税率、特惠税率以及税则税目等方面。

本书根据经国务院批准 2014 年对外发布的《中华人民共和国进出口税则》，增加了海关申报用十位进出口商品编码;国家税务总局发布的出口退税率，结合国家相关部委的进出口相关监管证件规定编辑《中华人民共和国海关进出口税则及申报指南》。本书主要内容包括税则号列、商品名称及备注、出口退税率、进口增值税率、进口最惠国税率、年度暂定税率、进口商品协定税率、计量单位和进出口监管条件等内容。采用各项税率、税目对照形式，查阅方便，便于读者使用；是海关监管、企业报关、退税的必备工具图书，具有很高的操作性；是指导进出口单位办理进口征税、出口退税的重要参考书。

适用读者：海关管理部门、外经贸主管部门、报关、物流公司、进出口企业、税务代理机构以及其他从事进出口研究的相关机构。

本书编委会

2014 年 1 月

使用和编辑说明

根据国务院批准的，2014 年《中华人民共和国进出口税则》以及 2014 年以来财政部、国家税务总局出口退税率，结合海关申报十位商品编码和进出口商品的监管证件以及海关规范申报目录等内容，我们编纂本书。

为了读者便于查阅，现将《海关进出口税则》和附录说明如下：

第一部分《海关进出口税则》

《海关进出口税则》包括进口关税征税率、出口退（免）税率、进出口监管证件对照速查表，是本书的核心部分：

第一列是“税则号列”即“商品编号”，其前八位代码与《税则》中的税则号列统一；第九位和第十位代码与进口环节税、进口暂定税率和贸易管制的要求统一。

“税则号列”有*标志的：表示该项商品实施年度进口暂定税率，凡从世界组织成员国或与中国有双边互惠协议的国家或地区进口货物，按进口暂定税率征税。

该项目商品实施出口商品暂定税率，见《出口商品暂定税率表》。

第二列是“商品名称及备注”即该进出口商品的名称和描述。它是《税则》和《统计商品目录》中的货品名称缩减而来。括号内的文字是对该商品的补充描述。

第三列是“进口税率”，分为最惠国进口税率（%）、普通进口税率（%）和年度进口暂定税率（%）。

最惠国进口税率：

原产于共同适用最惠国待遇条款的世界贸易组织成员的进口货物，原产于与中国签订含有相互给予最惠国待遇条款的双边贸易协定的国家或地区的进口的货物，以及原产于中国境内的进口货物，适用于最惠国税率。

普通进口税率：

原产于适用最惠、协定和特惠税率国家或地区以外的国家或地区的进口货物，以及原产地不明的进口货物适用于普通税率。

年度进口暂定税率：

适用普通税率的进口货物，不适用暂定税率。适用最惠税率的进口货物有暂定税率的，应当适用暂定税率。适用协定、特惠税率的进口货物有暂定税率的，适用从低税率。

第四列是“出口退税”，即出口退税率（%），该数据为 2014 年国家出口退税文库正在使用的最新退税率。

由于国家出口退税率是根据国际和国内经济形势随时调整的，因此，在本书出版后出口退税率进行调整的，按最新颁布的规定执行。

第五列是“增值税率”，即该项商品的进口环节增值税率为13%或17%。

第六列是“计量单位”。

第七列是“监管条件”，该栏目的代码表示该商品在一般贸易进出口时需要提交的监管证件。

第二部分 出口商品关税、暂定税率和特别关税税率表

第三部分 《附表》部分是本书的重要组成部分，本书共编辑了十个附表，分别是：

附表1 2014年进口商品消费税税率表

附表2 非全税目信息技术产品税率表

附表3 计量单位换算表

附表4 2014年进口商品从量税及复合税税率表

附表5 中华人民共和国进境物品完税价格表

附表6 2014年进口关税与进口环节代征税（增值税）计税常数表

附表7 关税配额商品进口税率表

附表8 2014年进口关税与进口环节代征税（消费税及增值税）计税常数表

附表9 2014年进口商品协定税目税率表

协定税率：

原产于与中国签订含有关税优惠条款的区域性贸易协定的国家或地区的进口货物，适用协定税率。

目前适用协定税率的国家或地区为原产于文莱、柬埔寨、印度尼西亚、老挝、马来西亚、缅甸、菲律宾、新加坡、泰国、越南、韩国、斯里兰卡、孟加拉、印度、巴基斯坦、智利、新西兰、哥斯达黎加、中国香港、中国澳门和中国台湾的部分进口货物。

附表10 2014年进口商品特惠税目税率表

特惠税率：

根据中国与有关国家或地区签署的贸易或关税优惠协定、双边换文情况以及国务院有关决定，对埃塞俄比亚、贝宁、布隆迪、厄立特里亚、吉布提、刚果、几内亚、几内亚比绍、科摩罗、利比里亚、马达加斯加、马里、马拉维、毛里塔尼亚、莫桑比克、卢旺达、塞拉利昂、苏丹、坦桑尼亚、多哥、乌干达、赞比亚、莱索托、乍得、中非、阿富汗、孟加拉国、尼泊尔、东帝汶、也门、萨摩亚、瓦努阿图、赤道几内亚、安哥拉、塞内加尔、尼日尔、索马里、老挝、缅甸和柬埔寨，共40个联合国认定的最不发达国家实施特惠税率。

第四部分 2014年申报指南

（一）海关进出口货物报关单填制规范

（二）进出口通关申报系统常用代码表及说明

第五部分 2014年海关进出口商品规范申报目录

To the User

According to the Regulations of the People's Republic of China on Import and Export Duties (2014) and the export rebate rate made by the Ministry of Finance and the State Administration of Taxation since 2014, based on the HS Code recognized by the Customs and the regulations by relevant departments on import and export commodities, we hereby compiled this book.

To facilitate readers' inquiry, the Customs Tariff of Import and Export and its appendixes are stated as follows:

Part 1 Customs Tariff of Import and Export

The Customs Tariff of Import and Export includes the import tariff rates, the export rebate (exemption) rates and the comparison and quick check table on the import & export supervision certificates, which are the core part of this book:

The first column is "Tariff Code" i.e. "HS Code", the first eight numbers of which conform to the tariff code in the Regulations and the ninth and tenth number conform to the import linkage tax, temporary import tax rate, and requirements by the trade rstrictions.

The commodity with the tariff code marked with "*" is levied by the annual temporary import and export tax rates (Please see attachment). All the commodities that are imported from the members of the WTO or the countries or regions that have bilateral reciprocal agreements are levied by the temporary import tax rates.

Please see the Table on Tempary Tax Rates on Export Commodities for the tempary tax rates on the export commodities.

The second column is "Name and Remarks", that is, the names and descriptions of the import and export commodities. It's the abbreviation for the names of the commodities in the Regulations and the Commodity Classification.

The third column is "Export Rebate Rate" (%), which is the latest rate used by the state export rebate rate library in 2014.

Since the export rebate rate is adjusted according to the international and domestic economic situation at any time, the latest export rebate rate issued by the state will be executed after the book is published.

The fourth column is "Import Tax Rate", which includes MFN import tax rate (%) and commom import tax rate (%).

Import tariff rates for the most favored nations:

The import tariff rates for the most favored nations apply to the import goods that are originally produced in the members of the World Trade Organization (WTO) jointly applicable to the most favored nation treatment clauses, the import goods originally produced in the countries or territories that sign the bilateral trade agreements with China containing the clauses of granting the other party the most favored nation treatment, and import goods originally produced in the Chinese territory.

Common import tariff rates:

The common import tariff rates apply to the import goods originally produced in the countries or territories other than the aforesaid countries or territories, and import goods whose origins are unidentifiable.

Tentative tax rates on import commodities:

If there are tentative tax rates for import goods applicable to the most favored nation tariff rates, the tentative tax rates shall apply; if there are tentative tax rates for import goods applicable to the conventional tariff rates or preferential tariff rates, the tariff rates shall apply, whichever are lower; and the tentative tax rates do not apply to import goods applicable to common tax rates. If there are tentative tax rates for the export goods applicable to the export tax rates, the tentative tax rates shall apply.

The tentative tax rates are valid only in the specific year.

Column 5 is "Value-added Tax Rate" that means the import VAT rate of the commodity is 13% or 17%.

Column 6 is the "Measuring Unit".

Column 7 is the "Supervision Condition". The code in this column means the supervision certificate that shall be submitted for commodities imported or export under the general trade.

Part 2 Export Commodity Tariff, Tentative Tax Rate and Specific Tariff Rates in 2014

Part 3 Appendixes is an important part of this book. This book contains nine appendixes, which are:

Appendix 1 Consumption Tax on Import Goods 2014

Appendix 2 Duty Rate on Specific Information Technology Products

Appendix 3 Conversion Table

Appendix 4 Specific and Compound Duty Rate on Import Goods 2014

Appendix 5 Import Tariff Rates for Entry Goods of the People's Republic of China

Appendix 6 Table of Import Tariff and Import Tax (Value Added Tax) in 2014

Appendix 7 Tariff Quota Rate on Import Goods

Appendix 8 Table of Import Tariff and Import Tax (Consumption Tax & Value Added Tax) in 2014

Appendix 9 Conventional tax rates on Import Goods 2014

Conventional tax rates

The conventional tax rates apply to the import goods originally produced in the countries or territories that sign regional trade agreements with China containing the tariff preference clauses.

The conventional tax rates are currently applicable to part of the import goods originally produced in Brunei, Cambodia, Indonesia, Laos, Malaysia, Burma, Philippines, Singapore, Thailand, Vietnam, Korea, Sri Lanka, Bangladesh, India, Pakistan, Chile, New Zealand, Costa Rica, China Hong Kong, China Macao and China Taiwan.

Appendix 10 Special Preferential Tariff Rates on Import Goods 2014

Preferential tax rates:

According to the preferential trade or tariff agreements and bilateral exchange of notes signed between China and other countries or regions, as well as the decisions made by the State Council, the preferential tax rates are implemented to a total of 40 least developed countries confirmed by the UN including Ethiopia, Benin, Burundi, Eritrea, Djibouti, Congo, Guinea, Guinea Bissau, Comoros, Liberia, Madagascar , Mali, Malawi, Mauritania, Mozambique, Rwanda, Sierra Leone, Sudan, Tanzania, Togo, Uganda, Zambia, Lesotho, Chad, Central Africa, Afghanistan, Bangladesh, Nepal, East Timor, Yemen, Samoa, Vanuatu, Equatorial Guinea, Angola, Senegal, Niger, Somalia, Laos, Myanmar, and Cambodia.

Part 4 Declaration Guide 2014

(I) Filling Specifications for Customs Declaration on Import and Export Goods

(II) Table of Codes Often Used in Import & Export Customs Clearance and Declaration System and Notes

Part 5 Customs Required Catalogue for the Declaration of Import and Export Goods 2014

《海关进出口商品规范申报目录》使用说明

进出口企业在填报海关进出口商品报关单的“商品名称、规格型号”栏目时，应当按照本《规范申报目录》中所列商品申报要素的内容填报。为方便读者使用《规范申报目录》，特作说明如下：

一、《海关进出口商品规范申报目录》（以下简称《目录》）采用了与《中华人民共和国进出口税则》一致的结构，所列商品按照类、章层次排列。为了准确理解对商品规范申报的要求，在相关章前对该章的共性问题用“注解”加以说明。《目录》的“税则号列”栏及对应的“商品名称”栏所列内容分别与《税则》的“税则号列”栏所列相应编码及“商品名称”栏所列相应内容相同。

二、《目录》正文由“税则号列”、“商品名称”、“申报要素”栏组成。其中，在“申报要素”栏中，用“A”代表“归类要素”，用“B”代表“价格要素”，用“C”代表“审单及其他要素”，用“例”代表“说明举例”。

税则号列	商品名称	申报要素（A:归类要素 B:价格要素 C:审单及其他要素）及说明举例
0208.1020	---冻兔肉、兔头除外	A:1.品名;2.制作或保存方法（冻）。B:3.包装规格

三、《目录》属于结构性目录，其中所列商品按照不同位数编码所代表的层次进行排列，当某一层次编码商品所要求的申报要素与上一层次编码商品的申报要素相同时，则该商品的“税则号列”、“商品名称”、“申报要素”就不列示在本书中。此时应使用上一层次编码商品的申报要素内容，例如：

税则号列	商品名称	申报要素（A:归类要素 B:价格要素 C:审单及其他要素）及说明举例
01.02	牛	A:1.品名;2.是否改良种用
	-家牛:	
0102.2100	--改良种用	
	-水牛:	
0102.3100	--改良种用	

商品编码0102.2100和0102.3100的“申报要素”与上一层级01.02相同的，编码0102.2100和0102.3100所列商品对应的内容就不列在本书中，他们的“申报要素”与上一层级编码01.02所列商品申报要素相同。

编者

2014年1月

《海关进出口商品规范申报目录》电子版 免费赠送回执单

单位公章：

单位名称		联系人	
单位地址		电话	
电子邮箱		手机	
备注			

注：请加盖单位公章，发送电子邮件至 shuizeshouhou@163.com ，我们将通过电子邮件及时为您发送。

总目录

Contents

目　录

INDEX

归类总规则

货品在本协调制度中的归类，应遵循以下规则：

规则一　类、章及分章的标题，仅为查找方便而设；具有法律效力的归类，应按品目条文和有关类注或章注确定，如品目、类注或章注无其他规定，则按以下规则确定。

规则二　（一）品目所列货品，应视为包括该项货品的不完整品或未制成品，只要在报验时该项不完整品或未制成品具有完整品或制成品的基本特征。还应视为包括该项货品的完整品或制成品（或按本款规则可作为完整品或制成品归类的货品）在报验时的未组装件或拆散件。

（二）品目中所列材料或物质，应视为包括该种材料或物质与其他材料或物质混合或组合的物品。品目所列某种材料或物质构成的货品，应视为包括全部或部分由该种材料或物质构成的货品。由一种以上材料或物质构成的货品，应按规则三归类。

规则三　当货品按规则二（二）或由于其他原因看起来可归入两个或两个以上品目时，应按以下规则归类：

（一）列名比较具体的品目，优先于列名一般的品目。但是，如果两个或两个以上品目都仅述及混合或组合货品所含的某部分材料或物质，或零售的成套货品中的部分货品，即使其中某个品目对该货品描述得更为全面、详细，这些货品在有关品目的列名应视为同样具体。

（二）混合物、不同材料构成或不同部件组成的组合物以及零售的成套货品，如果不能按照规则三（一）归类时，在本款可适用的条件下，应按构成货品基本特征的材料或部件归类。

（三）货品不能按照规则三（一）或（二）归类时，应按号列顺序归入其可归入的最末一个品目。

规则四　根据上述规则无法归类的货品，应归入与其最相类似的货品的品目。

规则五　除上述规则外，本规则适用于下列货品的归类：

（一）制成特殊形状，适用于盛装某一或某套物品并适合长期使用的照相机套、乐器盒、枪套、绘图仪器盒、项链盒及类似容器，如果与所装物品同时报验，并通常与所装

GENERAL RULES FOR THE INTERPRETATION OF THE HARMONIZED SYSTEM

Classification of goods in the nomenclature shall be governed by the following principles:

1. The titles of sections, Chapters and sub-Chapters are provided for ease of reference only; for legal purposes, classification shall be determined according to the terms of the headings and any relative Section or Chapter Notes and Provided such headings or Notes do not otherwise require, according to the following provisions.

2. （a）Any reference in a heading to an article shall be taken to include a reference to that article incomplete or unfinished, provided that, as presented, the incomplete or unfinished article has the essential character of the complete or finished article.it shall also be taken to include a reference to that article complete or finished（or falling to be classified as complete or finished by virtue of this Rule）, presented unassembled or disassembled.

（b）Any reference in a heading to a material or substance shall be taken to include a reference to mixtures or combinations of that material or substance with other materials or substances. Any reference to goods of a given material or substance shall be taken to include a reference to goods consisting wholly or partly of such material or substance. The classification of goods consisting of more than one material or substance shall be according to the principles of Rule 3.

3. When by application of Rule 2（b）or for any other reason, goods are, prima facie, classifiable under two or more headings, classification shall be effected as follows:

（a）The heading which provides the most specific description shall be preferred to headings providing a more general description. However, when two or more headings each refer to part only of the materials or substances contained in mixed or composite goods or to part only of the items in a set put up for retail sale, those headings are to be regarded as equally specific in relation to those goods, even if one of them gives a more complete or precise description of the goods.

（b）Mixtures, composite goods consisting of different materials or made up of different components, and goods put up in sets for retail sale, which cannot be classified by reference to 3（a）, shall be classified as if they consisted of the material or component which gives them their essential character, insofar as this criterion is applicable.

（c）When goods cannot be classified by reference to 3（a）or 3（b）, they shall be classified under the heading which occurs last in numerical order among those which equally merit consideration.

4. Goods which cannot be classified in accordance with the above rules shall be classified under the heading appropriate to the goods to which they are most akin.

5. In addition to the foregoing provisions, the following rules shall apply in respect of the goods referred to therein:

（a）Camera cases, musical instrument cases, gun cases, drawing instrument cases, necklace cases and similar containers, specially shaped or fitted to contain a specific article or set of articles, suitable for long-term use and presented with the articles for which they are

物品一同出售的，应与所装物品一并归类。但本款不适用于本身构成整个货品基本特征的容器。

（二）除规则五（一）规定的以外，与所装货品同时报验的包装材料或包装容器，如果通常是用来包装这类货品的，应与所装货品一并归类。但明显可重复使用的包装材料和包装容器不受本款限制。

规则六　货品在某一品目项下各子目的法定归类，应按子目条文或有关的子目注释以及以上各条规则（在必要的地方稍加修改后）来确定，但子目的比较只能在同一数级上进行。除条文另有规定的以外，有关的类注、章注也适用于本规则。

intended, shall be classified with such articles when of a kind normally sold therewith. This rule does not, however, apply to containers which give the whole its essential character.

(b) Subject to the provisions of rule 5 (a) above, packing materials and packing containers presented with the goods therein shall be classified with the goods if they are of a kind normally used for packing such goods. However, this provision is not binding when such packing materials or packing containers are clearly suitable for repetitive use.

6. For legal purposes, the classification of goods in the subheadings of a heading shall be determined according to the terms of those subheadings and any related Subheading Notes and, *mutatis mutandis*, to the above Rules, on the understanding that only subheadings at the same level are comparable. For the purposes of this rule the relative section and Chapter Notes also apply, unless the context otherwise requires.

第一类
活动物；动物产品

注释：

一、本类所称的各属种动物，除条文另有规定的以外，均包括其幼仔在内。

二、除条文另有规定的以外，本税则所称干的产品，均包括经脱水、蒸发或冷冻干燥的产品。

SECTION Ⅰ
LIVE ANIMALS; ANIMAL PRODUCTS

Section Notes:

1. Any reference in this Section to a particular genus or species of an animal, except where the context otherwise requires, includes a reference to the young of that genus or species.
2. Except where the context otherwise requires, throughout the Nomenclature any reference to "dried" products also covers products which have been dehydrated, evaporated or freezedried.

第一章
活动物

注释：

本章包括所有活动物，但下列各项除外：

一、品目 03.01、03.06、03.07 或 03.08 的鱼、甲壳动物、软体动物及其他水生无脊椎动物；

二、品目 30.02 的培养微生物及其他产品；以及

三、品目 95.08 的动物；

Chapter 1
Live animals

Chapter Notes:

This Chapter covers all live animals except:

1. Fish and crustaceans, molluscs and other aquatic invertebrates, of heading 03.01, 03.06 , 03.07 or 03.08
2. Cultures of micro-organisms and other products of heading 30.02; and
3. Animals of heading 95.08.

税则号列 Tariff Item	商品名称及备注	进口税率			出口退税	增值税率	计量单位	监管条件	Article Description
		最惠	普通	暂定					
01.01	马、驴、骡：								**Live horses, asses, mules and hinnies:**
	-马：								-Horses:
0101.2100	--改良种用	0	0			13	千克/头		--Pure-bred breeding
0101 2100.10	改良种用濒危野马	0	0			13	千克/头	AFEB	Endangered wild horses, pure-bred breeding
0101 2100.90	其他改良种用马	0	0		5	13	千克/头	AB	Other horses, pure-bred breeding
0101.2900	--其他	10	30			13	千克/头		--Other
0101 2900.10	非改良种用濒危野马	10	30			13	千克/头	AFEB	Endangered wild horses, non pure-bred breeding
0101 2900.90	非改良种用其他马	10	30		5	13	千克/头	AB	Horses, non pure-bred breeding
	-驴：								-Asses :
0101.3010	---改良种用	0	0			13	千克/头		---Pure-bred breeding
0101 3010.10	改良种用的濒危野驴	0	0			13	千克/头	AFEB	Endangered wild asses, pure-bred breeding
0101 3010.90	改良种用的其他驴	0	0		5	13	千克/头	AB	Other asses, pure-bred breeding
0101.3090	---其他	10	30			13	千克/头		---Other
0101 3090.10	非改良种用濒危野驴	10	30			13	千克/头	AFEB	Endangered wild asses, non pure-bred breeding
0101 3090.90	非改良种用其他驴	10	30		5	13	千克/头	AB	Other asses, non pure-bred breeding

税则号列 Tariff Item	商品名称及备注	进口税率 最惠	普通	暂定	出口退税	增值税率	计量单位	监管条件	Article Description
0101.9000	-其他	10	30		5	13	千克/头	AB	-Other
01.02	牛:								**Live bovine animals:**
	-家牛:								-Cattle :
0102.2100	--改良种用	0	0		5	13	千克/头	AB	--Pure-bred breeding
0102.2900	--其他	10	30		5	13	千克/头	4xAB	--Other
	-水牛:								-Buffalo :
0102.3100	--改良种用	0	0			13	千克/头		--Pure-bred breeding
0102 3100.10	改良种用濒危水牛	0	0			13	千克/头	ABEF	Endangered buffalo, pure-bred breeding
0102 3100.90	改良种用其他水牛	0	0		5	13	千克/头	AB	Other buffalo, pure-bred breeding
0102.3900	--其他	10	30			13	千克/头		--Other
0102 3900.10	非改良种用濒危水牛	10	30			13	千克/头	4ABEFx	Endangered buffalo, non pure-bred breeding
0102 3900.90	非改良种用其他水牛	10	30		5	13	千克/头	4ABx	Other buffalo, non pure-bred breeding
	-其他:								-Other :
0102.9010	---改良种用	0	0			13	千克/头		---Pure-bred breeding
0102 9010.10	改良种用濒危野牛	0	0			13	千克/头	AFEB	Endangered wild bovine, pure-bred breeding
0102 9010.90	其他改良种用牛	0	0		5	13	千克/头	AB	Other bovine, pure-bred breeding
0102.9090	---其他	10	30			13	千克/头		---Other
0102 9090.10	非改良种用濒危野牛	10	30			13	千克/头	4xABFE	Endangered wild bovine, non pure-bred breeding
0102 9090.90	非改良种用其他牛	10	30		5	13	千克/头	4xAB	Other bovine, non pure-bred breeding
01.03	猪:								**Live swine:**
0103.1000	-改良种用	0	0		5	13	千克/头		-Pure-bred breeding
0103 1000.10	改良种用的鹿豚、姬猪	0	0		5	13	千克/头	AFEB	*Babyrousa*, Porcula Salvania, pure-bred breeding
0103 1000.90	其他改良种用的猪	0	0		5	13	千克/头	AB	Other live swine, pure-bred breeding
	-其他:								-Other:
	--重量在50千克以下:								--Weighing less than 50kg:
0103.9110	---重量在10千克以下	10	50		5	13	千克/头		---Weighing less than 10kg
0103 9110.10	重量在10千克以下的其他野猪(改良种用的除外)	10	50		5	13	千克/头	4xABFE	Other wild swine, weighing less than 10kg（other than pure-bred breeding）
0103 9110.90	重量在 10 千克以下的其他猪(改良种用的除外)	10	50		5	13	千克/头	4xAB	Other live swine, weighing less than 10kg（other than pure-bred breeding）
0103.9120	---重量在10千克及以上，但在50二克以下	10	50		5	13	千克/头		---Weighing 10kg or more, but less than 50kg
0103 9120.10	10≤重量<50 千克的其他野猪(改良种用的除外)	10	50		5	13	千克/头	4xABFE	Other wild swine, weighing 10kg or more, but less than 50kg（other than pure-bred breeding）
0103 9120.90	10≤重量<50 千克的其他猪(改良种用的除外)	10	50		5	13	千克/头	4xAB	Other live swine, weighing 10kg or more, but less than 50kg（other than pure-bred breeding）
0103.9200	--重量在50千克及以上	10	50		5	13	千克/头		--Weighing 50kg or more
0103 9200.10	重量在50千克及以上的其他野猪(改良种用的除外)	10	50		5	13	千克/头	4xABFE	Other wild live swine, weighing 50kg or more（other than pure-bred breeding）
0103 9200.90	重量在50千克及以上的其他猪(改良种用的除外)	10	50		5	13	千克/头	4xAB	Other live swine, weighing 50kg or more（other than pure-bred breeding）
01.04	绵羊、山羊:								**Live sheep and goats**:
	-绵羊:								-Sheep:
0104.1010	---改良种用	0	0		5	13	千克/头	AB	---Pure-bred breeding
0104.1090	---其他	10	50		5	13	千克/头	AB	---Other
	-山羊:								-Goats:
0104.2010	---改良种用	0	0		5	13	千克/头	AB	---Pure-bred breeding
0104.2090	---其他	10	50		5	13	千克/头	AB	---Other
01.05	家禽，即鸡、鸭、鹅、火鸡及珍珠鸡:								**Live poultry, that is to say, fowls of the species *Gallus domesticus*, ducks, geese, turkeys and guinea fowls**:
	-重量不超过185克:								-Weighing not more than 185g:
	--鸡:								--Fowls of the species *Gallus domesticus*:
0105.1110	---改良种用	0	0		5	13	千克/只	AB	---Pure-bred breeding
0105.1190	---其他	10	50		5	13	千克/只	AB	---Other
	--火鸡:								--Turkeys:
0105.1210	---改良种用	0	0		5	13	千克/只	AB	---Pure-bred breeding
0105.1290	---其他	10	50		5	13	千克/只	AB	---Other

税则号列 Tariff Item	商品名称及备注	进口税率 最惠	进口税率 普通	进口税率 暂定	出口退税	增值税率	计量单位	监管条件	Article Description
	--鸭:								--Ducks:
0105.1310	---改良种用	0	0		5	13	千克/只	AB	---Pure-bred breeding
0105.1390	---其他	10	50		5	13	千克/只	AB	---Other
	--鹅:								--Geese :
0105.1410	---改良种用	0	0		5	13	千克/只	AB	---Pure-bred breeding
0105.1490	---其他	10	50		5	13	千克/只	AB	---Other
	--珍珠鸡:								--Guinea fowls :
0105.1510	---改良种用	0	0		5	13	千克/只	AB	---Pure-bred breeding
0105.1590	---其他	10	50		5	13	千克/只	AB	---Other
	-其他:								-Other:
	--鸡:								--Fowls of the species *Gallus domesticus*:
0105.9410	---改良种用	0	0		5	13	千克/只	4xAB	---Pure-bred breeding
0105.9490	---其他	10	50		5	13	千克/只	4xAB	---Other
	--其他:								--Other:
0105.9910	---改良种用	0	0		5	13	千克/只	AB	---Pure-bred breeding
	---其他:								---Other:
0105.9991	----鸭	10	50		5	13	千克/只	AB	----Ducks
0105.9992	----鹅	10	50		5	13	千克/只	AB	----Geese
0105.9993	----珍珠鸡	10	50		5	13	千克/只	4xAB	----Guinea fowls
0105.9994	----火鸡	10	50		5	13	千克/只	AB	----Turkeys
01.06	**其他活动物:**								**Other live animals:**
	-哺乳动物:								-Mammals:
	--灵长目:								--Primates:
0106.1110	---改良种用	0	0		5	13	千克/只	AFEB	---Pure-bred breeding
0106.1190	---其他	10	50		5	13	千克/只	AFEB	---Other
	--鲸、海豚及鼠海豚(鲸目哺乳动物);海牛及儒艮(海牛目哺乳动物);海豹、海狮及海象(鳍足亚目哺乳动物):								--Whales, dolphins and porpoises（*mammals of the order Cetacea*）; manatees and dugongs（*mammals of the order Sirenia*）;seals,sea lions and walruses (mammals of the suborder Pinnipedia) :
	---鲸、海豚及鼠海豚(鲸目哺乳动物);海牛即儒艮(海牛目哺乳动物):								---Whales, dolphins and porpoises（*mammals of the order Cetacea*）; manatees and dugongs（*mammals of the order Sirenia*）:
0106.1211 暂	----改良种用	10	50	0	5	13	千克/只	AFEB	----Pure-bred breeding
0106.1219	----其他	10	50		5	13	千克/只	AFEB	----Other
	---海豹、海狮及海象(鳍足亚目哺乳动物):								---seals,sea lions and walruses (mammals of the suborder Pinnipedia) :
0106.1221	----改良种用	0	0		5	13	千克/只	AFEB	----Pure-bred breeding
0106.1229	----其他	10	50		5	13	千克/只	ABEF	----Other
	--骆驼及其他骆驼科动物:								--Camels and other camelides (Camelidae):
0106.1310	---改良种用	0	0			13	千克/只		---Pure-bred breeding
0106 1310.10	改良种用濒危骆驼及其他濒危骆驼科动物(包括人工驯养、繁殖的)	0	0			13	千克/只	ABFE	Other endangered camels, pure-bred breeding, and other endangered camelides (including domesticated and artificially propagated)
0106 1310.90	其他改良种用骆驼及其他骆驼科动物	0	0		5	13	千克/只	AB	Other camels and other camelides (Camelidae), pure-bred breeding
0106.1390	---其他	10	50			13	千克/只		---Other
0106 1390.10	其他濒危骆驼及其他濒危骆驼科动物(包括人工驯养、繁殖的)	10	50			13	千克/只	AFEB	Other endangered camels and other endangered camelides (including domesticated and artificially propagated)
0106 1390.90	其他骆驼及其他骆驼科动物	10	50		5	13	千克/只	AB	Other camels and other camelides (Camelidae)
	--家兔及野兔:								--Rabbits and hares :
0106.1410	---改良种用	0	0			13	千克/只		---Pure-bred breeding
0106 1410.10	改良种用濒危野兔(包括人工驯养、繁殖的)	0	0			13	千克/只	ABEF	Endangered hares, pure-bred breeding (including domesticated and artificially propagated)
0106 1410.90	改良种用家兔及其他改良种用野兔	0	0		5	13	千克/只	AB	Rabbits and hares, pure-bred breeding
0106.1490	---其他	10	50			13	千克/只		---Other

税则号列 Tariff Item	商品名称及备注	进口税率			出口退税	增值税率	计量单位	监管条件	Article Description
		最惠	普通	暂定					
0106 1490.10	其他濒危野兔(包括人工驯养、繁殖的)	10	50			13	千克/只	AFEB	Other endangered hares (including domesticated and artificially propagated)
0106 1490.90	其他家兔及野兔	10	50		5	13	千克/只	AB	Other rabbits and hares
	--其他:								--Other:
0106.1910	---改良种用	0	0			13	千克/只		---Pure-bred breeding
0106 1910.10	其他改良种用濒危哺乳动物(包括人工驯养、繁殖的)	0	0			13	千克/只	ABFE	Other endangered mammals, pure-bred breeding (including domesticated and artificially propagated)
0106 1910.90	其他改良种用哺乳动物	0	0		5	13	千克/只	AB	Other homebred mammals, pure-bred breeding
0106.1990	---其他	10	50			13	千克/只		---Other
0106 1990.10	其他濒危哺乳动物(包括人工驯养、繁殖的)	10	50			13	千克/只	AFEB	Other endangered mammals (including domesticated and artificially propagated)
0106 1990.90	其他哺乳动物	10	50		5	13	千克/只	AB	Other mammals
	-爬行动物（包括蛇及龟鳖）:								-Reptiles（including snakes and turtles）:
	---改良种用:								---Pure-bred breeding:
0106.2011	----鳄鱼苗	0	0		5	13	千克/只	AFEB	----Crocodiles for cultivation
0106.2019	----其他	0	0		5	13	千克/只	FEAB	----Other
0106.2020	---食用	10	50		5	13	千克/只		---For human consumption
0106 2020.10	食用蛇(包括人工驯养、繁殖的)	10	50		5	13	千克/只	AFEB	Snakes, for human consumption (including domesticated and artificially propagated)
0106 2020.20	食用龟鳖(包括人工驯养、繁殖的)	10	50		5	13	千克/只	ABFE	Turtles, for human consumption (including domesticated and artificially propagated)
0106 2020.90	其他食用爬行动物(包括人工驯养、繁殖的)	10	50		5	13	千克/只	FEAB	Other reptiles, for human consumption (including domesticated and artificially propagated)
0106.2090	---其他	10	50		5	13	千克/只	FEAB	---Other
	-鸟:								-Birds:
	--猛禽:								--Birds of prey:
0106.3110	---改良种用	0	0		5	13	千克/只	AFEB	---Pure-bred breeding
0106.3190	---其他	10	50		5	13	千克/只	ABFE	---Other
	--鹦形目（包括普通鹦鹉、长尾鹦鹉、金刚鹦鹉及美冠鹦鹉）:								--Psittaciformes（including parrots, parakeets, macaws and cockatoos）:
0106.3210	---改良种用	0	0		5	13	千克/只		---Pure-bred breeding
0106 3210.10	改良种用虎皮鹦鹉	0	0		5	13	千克/只	AB	Budgerigar, pure-bred breeding
0106 3210.20	改良种用鸡尾鹦鹉	0	0		5	13	千克/只	AB	Cockatiel（*Nymphicus hollandicus*）, pure-bred breeding
0106 3210.90	改良种用其他鹦形目的鸟(包括人工驯养、繁殖的)	0	0		5	13	千克/只	ABFE	Other birds, psittaciformes, pure-bred breeding (including domesticated and artificially propagated)
0106.3290	---其他	10	50		5	13	千克/只		---Other
0106 3290.10	非改良种用虎皮鹦鹉	10	50		5	13	千克/只	AB	Budgerigar, non pure-bred breeding
0106 3290.20	非改良种用鸡尾鹦鹉	10	50		5	13	千克/只	AB	Cockatiel（*Nymphicus hollandicus*）, non pure-bred breeding
0106 3290.90	非改良种用其他鹦形目的鸟(包括人工驯养、繁殖的)	10	50		5	13	千克/只	ABFE	Other birds, psittaciformes (including domesticated and artificially propagated) non pure-bred breeding
	--鸵鸟；鸸鹋:								--Ostriches ; emus (Dromaius novaehollandiae):
0106.3310	---改良种用	0	0			13	千克/只		---Pure-bred breeding
0106 3310.10	改良种用濒危鸵鸟(包括人工驯养、繁殖的)	0	0			13	千克/只	ABFE	Endangered ostriches,pure-bred breeding(including domesticated and artificially propagated)
0106 3310.90	其他改良种用鸵鸟和改良种用鸸鹋	0	0		5	13	千克/只	AB	Other Ostriches and emus (Dromaius novaehollandiae) , pure-bred breeding
0106.3390	---其他	10	50			13	千克/只		---Other
0106 3390.10	其他濒危鸵鸟(包括人工驯养、繁殖的)	10	50			13	千克/只	ABFE	Other endangered ostriches (including domesticated and artificially propagated)
0106 3390.90	其他鸵鸟、鸸鹋	10	50		5	13	千克/只	AB	Other ostriches;emus
	--其他:								--Other:
0106.3910	---改良种用	0	0			13	千克/只		---Pure-bred breeding
0106 3910.10	其他濒危改良种用的鸟(包括人工驯养、繁殖的)	0	0			13	千克/只	ABFE	Other endangered birds, purebred breeding (including domesticated and artificially propagated)
0106 3910.90	其他改良种用的鸟	0	0		5	13	千克/只	AB	Bred breeding birds
	---食用:								---For human consumption:

税则号列 Tariff Item	商品名称及备注	进口税率			出口退税	增值税率	计量单位	监管条件	Article Description
		最惠	普通	暂定					
0106.3921	----乳鸽	10	50		5	13	千克/只	AB	----Squabs
0106.3923	----野鸭	10	50		5	13	千克/只	FEAB	----Teals
0106.3929	----其他	10	50			13	千克/只		----Other
0106 3929.10	其他食用濒危鸟(包括人工驯养、繁殖的)	10	50			13	千克/只	ABFE	Other endangered birds (including domesticated and artificially propagated)
0106 3929.90	其他食用鸟	10	50		5	13	千克/只	AB	Other homebred birds for human consumption
0106.3990	---其他	10	50			13	千克/只		---Other
0106 3990.10	其他濒危鸟(包括人工驯养、繁殖的)	10	50			13	千克/只	ABFE	Other endangered wild bird including domesticated and artificially propagated
0106 3990.90	其他鸟	10	50		5	13	千克/只	AB	Other homebred birds
	-昆虫:								-Insects :
	--蜂:								--Bees:
0106.4110	---改良种用	0	0		5	13	千克/只	AB	---Pure-bred breeding
0106.4190	---其他	10	50		5	13	千克/只		---Other
0106 4190.01[暂]	赤眼蜂	10	50	0	5	13	千克/只	ABS	Trichogramma
0106 4190.90	其他蜂	10	50		5	13	千克/只	AB	Other bees
	--其他:								---Other :
0106.4910	---改良种用	0	0			13	千克/只		---Pure-bred breeding
0106 4910.10	其他改良种用濒危昆虫(包括人工驯养、繁殖的)	0	0			13	千克/只	ABFE	Other endangered insects, pure-bred breeding (including domesticated and artificially propagated)
0106 4910.90	其他改良种用非濒危昆虫	0	0		5	13	千克/只	AB	Other non-endangered insects, pure-bred breeding
0106.4990	---其他	10	50			13	千克/只		---Other
0106 4990.01[暂]	捕食螨	10	50	0	5	13	千克/只	ABS	Predatory mite
0106 4990.10	其他濒危昆虫(包括人工驯养、繁殖的)	10	50			13	千克/只	ABFE	Other endangered insects (including domesticated and artificially propagated)
0106 4990.90	其他非濒危昆虫	10	50		5	13	千克/只	AB	Other non-endangered insects
	-其他:								-Other:
	---改良种用:								---Pure-bred breeding:
0106.9011	----蛙苗	0	0			13	千克/只		----Tadpole and young frogs
0106 9011.10	改良种用濒危蛙苗	0	0			13	千克/只	ABFE	Endangered tadpole and young frogs,pure-bred breeding
0106 9011.90	其他改良种用蛙苗	0	0		5	13	千克/只	AB	Other tadpole and young frogs, pure-bred breeding
0106.9019	----其他					13	千克/只		----Other
0106 9019.10	其他改良种用濒危动物(包括人工驯养、繁殖的)	0	0			13	千克/只	ABFE	Other endangered wild animals, pure-bred breeding (including domesticated and artificially propagated)
0106 9019.90	其他改良种用动物	0	0		5	13	千克/只	AB	Other homebred animals, pure-bred breeding
0106.9090	---其他	10	50			13	千克/只		---Other
0106 9090.10	其他濒危动物(包括人工驯养、繁殖的)	10	50			13	千克/只	ABFE	Other endangered wild animals (including domesticated and artificially propagated)
0106 9090.90	其他动物	10	50		5	13	千克/只	AB	Other homebred animals

第二章 肉及食用杂碎

Chapter 2 Meat and edible meat offal

注释：

本章不包括：

一、品目02.01至02.08或02.10的不适合供人食用的产品；

二、动物的肠、膀胱、胃（品目05.04）或动物血（品目05.11、30.02）；或

三、品目02.09所列产品以外的动物脂肪（第十五章）。

Chapter Notes:

This Chapter does not cover:

1. Products of the kinds described in headings 02.01 to 02.08 or 02.10, unfit or unsuitable for human consumption ;
2. Guts, bladders or stomachs of animals（heading 05.04）or animal blood（heading 05.11 or 30.02）; or
3. Animal fat, other than products of heading 02.09（Chapter 15）.

税则号列 Tariff Item	商品名称及备注	进口税率			出口退税	增值税率	计量单位	监管条件	Article Description
		最惠	普通	暂定					
02.01	鲜、冷牛肉：								**Meat of bovine animals, fresh or chilled:**
0201.1000	-整头及半头	20	70		5	13	千克		-Carcasses and half-carcasses
0201 1000.10	整头及半头鲜或冷藏的野牛肉	20	70		5	13	千克	4ABEFx	Meat of wild bovine animals, carcasses and half-carcasses, fresh or chilled
0201 1000.90	其他整头及半头鲜或冷藏的牛肉	20	70		5	13	千克	4ABx	Other meat of bovine animals, carcasses and half-carcasses, fresh or chilled
0201.2000	-带骨肉	12	70		5	13	千克		-Other cuts with bone in
0201 2000.10	鲜或冷藏的带骨野牛肉	12	70		5	13	千克	47ABEFx	Meat of wild bovine animals, with bone in, fresh or chilled
0201 2000.90	其他鲜或冷藏的带骨牛肉	12	70		5	13	千克	47ABx	Other meat of bovine animals, with bone in, fresh or chilled
0201.3000	-去骨肉	12	70			13	千克		-Boneless
0201 3000.10	鲜或冷藏的去骨野牛肉	12	70		5	13	千克	47ABEFx	Meat of wild bovine animals, boneless, fresh or chilled
0201 3000.90	其他鲜或冷藏的去骨牛肉	12	70		13	13	千克	47ABx	Other meat of bovine animals, boneless, fresh or chilled
02.02	冻牛肉：								**Meat of bovine animals, frozen:**
0202.1000	-整头及半头	25	70		5	13	千克		-Carcasses and half-carcasses
0202 1000.10	冻藏的整头及半头野牛肉	25	70		5	13	千克	4ABEFx	Meat of wild bovine animals, carcasses and half-carcasses, frozen
0202 1000.90	其他冻藏的整头及半头牛肉	25	70		5	13	千克	4ABx	Other meat of bovine animals, carcasses and half-carcasses, frozen
0202.2000	-带骨肉	12	70		5	13	千克		-Other cuts with bone in
0202 2000.10	冻藏的带骨野牛肉	12	70		5	13	千克	47ABEFx	Meat of wild bovine animals, with bone in, frozen
0202 2000.90	其他冻藏的带骨牛肉	12	70		5	13	千克	47ABx	Other meat of bovine animals, with bone in, frozen
0202.3000	-去骨肉	12	70			13	千克		-Boneless
0202 3000.10	冻藏的去骨野牛肉	12	70		5	13	千克	47ABEFx	Meat of wild bovine animals, boneless, frozen
0202 3000.90	其他冻藏的去骨牛肉	12	70		13	13	千克	47ABx	Other meat of bovine animals, boneless, frozen
02.03	鲜、冷、冻猪肉：								**Meat of swine, fresh, chilled or frozen:**
	-鲜或冷的：								-Fresh or chilled:
	--整头及半头：								--Carcasses and half-carcasses:
0203.1110	---乳猪	20	70		5	13	千克		---Sucking pig
0203 1110.10	鲜或冷藏整头及半头野乳猪肉	20	70		5	13	千克	4ABEFx	Meat of wild sucking pig, carcasses and half-carcasses, fresh or chilled
0203 1110.90	其他鲜或冷藏的整头及半头乳猪肉	20	70		5	13	千克	4ABx	Meat of sucking pig, carcasses and half-carcasses, fresh or chilled
0203.1190	---其他	20	70		5	13	千克		---Other
0203 1190.10	其他鲜或冷藏整头及半头野猪肉	20	70		5	13	千克	4ABEFx	Other meat of wild swine, carcasses and half-carcasses, fresh or chilled
0203 1190.90	其他鲜或冷藏的整头及半头猪肉	20	70		5	13	千克	4ABx	Other meat of swine, carcasses and half-carcasses, fresh or chilled
0203.1200	--带骨的前腿、后腿及其肉块	20	70		5	13	千克		--Hams, shoulders and cuts thereof, with bone in
0203 1200.10	鲜或冷的带骨野猪前腿、后腿及肉块	20	70		5	13	千克	47ABEFx	Hams, shoulders and cuts of wild swine, with bone in, fresh or chilled

税则号列 Tariff Item	商品名称及备注	进口税率 最惠	普通	暂定	出口退税	增值税率	计量单位	监管条件	Article Description
0203 1200.90	鲜或冷的带骨猪前腿、后腿及其肉块	20	70		5	13	千克	47ABx	Hams, shoulders and cuts of wild swine, with bone in, fresh or chilled
0203.1900	--其他	20	70		5	13	千克		--Other
0203 1900.10	其他鲜或冷藏的野猪肉	20	70		5	13	千克	47ABEFx	Other meat of wild swine, fresh or chilled
0203 1900.90	其他鲜或冷藏的猪肉	20	70		5	13	千克	47ABx	Other meat of swine, fresh or chilled
	-冻的:								-Frozen:
	--整头及半头:								--Carcasses and half-carcasses:
0203.2110	---乳猪	12	70		5	13	千克		---Sucking pig
0203 2110.10	冻整头及半头野乳猪肉	12	70		5	13	千克	4ABEFx	Meat of wild sucking pig, carcasses and half-carcasses, frozen
0203 2110.90	冻整头及半头乳猪肉	12	70		5	13	千克	4ABx	Meat of sucking pig, carcasses and half-carcasses, frozen
0203.2190	---其他	12	70		5	13	千克		---Other
0203 2190.10	其他冻整头及半头野猪肉	12	70		5	13	千克	47ABEFx	Other meat of wild swine, carcasses and half-carcasses, frozen
0203 2190.90	其他冻整头及半头猪肉	12	70		5	13	千克	47ABx	Other meat of swine, carcasses and half-carcasses, frozen
0203.2200	--带骨的前腿、后腿及其肉块	12	70		5	13	千克		--Hams, shoulders and cuts thereof, with bone in
0203 2200.10	冻带骨野猪前腿、后腿及肉	12	70		5	13	千克	47ABEFx	Hams, shoulders and cuts of wild swine, with bone in, frozen
0203 2200.90	冻藏的带骨猪前腿、后腿及其肉块	12	70		5	13	千克	47ABx	Hams, shoulders and cuts of wild swine, with bone in, frozen
0203.2900	--其他	12	70		5/13	13	千克		--Other
0203 2900.10	冻藏野猪其他肉	12	70		5/13	13	千克	47ABEFx	Other meat of wild swine, frozen
0203 2900.90	其他冻藏猪肉	12	70		5/13	13	千克	47ABx	Other meat of swine, frozen
02.04	**鲜、冷、冻绵羊肉或山羊肉:**								**Meat of sheep or goats, fresh, chilled or frozen:**
0204.1000	-鲜或冷的整头及半头羔羊	15	70		5	13	千克	7AB	-Carcasses and half-carcasses of lamb, fresh or chilled
	-其他鲜或冷的绵羊肉:								-Other meat of sheep, fresh or chilled:
0204.2100	--整头及半头	23	70		5	13	千克	7AB	--Carcasses and half-carcasses
0204.2200	--带骨肉	15	70		5	13	千克	7AB	--Other cuts with bone in
0204.2300	--去骨肉	15	70		5	13	千克	7AB	--Boneless
0204.3000	-冻的整头及半头羔羊	15	70		5	13	千克	7AB	-Carcasses and half-carcasses of lamb, frozen
	-其他冻的绵羊肉:								-Other meat of sheep, frozen:
0204.4100	--整头及半头	23	70		5	13	千克	7AB	--Carcasses and half-carcasses
0204.4200	--带骨肉	12	70		5	13	千克	7AB	--Other cuts with bone in
0204.4300	--去骨肉	15	70		13	13	千克	7AB	--Boneless
0204.5000	-山羊肉	20	70		13	13	千克	7AB	-Meat of goats
02.05	**鲜、冷、冻马、驴、骡肉:**								**Meat of horses, asses, mules or hinnies, fresh, chilled or frozen:**
0205.0000	鲜、冷、冻马、驴、骡肉	20	70			13	千克		Meat of horses, asses, mules or hinnies, fresh, chilled or frozen
0205 0000.10	鲜、冷或冻的濒危野马、野驴肉	20	70			13	千克	ABFE	Meat of endangered wild horses, asses, fresh, chilled or frozen
0205 0000.90	鲜、冷或冻的马、驴、骡肉	20	70		5	13	千克	AB	Other meat of horses, asses, mules or hinnies, fresh, chilled or frozen
02.06	**鲜、冷、冻牛、猪、绵羊、山羊、马、驴、骡食用杂碎:**								**Edible offal of bovine animals, swine, sheep, goats, horses, asses, mules or hinnies, fresh, chilled or frozen:**
0206.1000	-鲜、冷牛杂碎	12	70		5	13	千克	4ABx	-Of bovine animals, fresh or chilled
	-冻牛杂碎:								-Of bovine animals, frozen:
0206.2100	--舌	12	70		5	13	千克	47ABx	--Tongues
0206.2200	--肝	12	70		5	13	千克	47ABx	--Livers
0206.2900	--其他	12	70		5	13	千克	47ABx	--Other
0206.3000	-鲜、冷猪杂碎	20	70		5	13	千克	4ABx	-Of swine, fresh or chilled
	-冻猪杂碎:								-Of swine, frozen:
0206.4100	--肝	20	70		5	13	千克	47ABx	--Livers
0206.4900	--其他	12	70		5	13	千克	47ABx	--Other

税则号列 Tariff Item	商品名称及备注	进口税率 最惠	普通	暂定	出口增值退税税率		计量单位	监管条件	Article Description
0206.8000	-其他鲜或冷杂碎	20	70		5	13	千克		-Other, fresh or chilled
0206 8000.10	鲜或冷的羊杂碎	20	70		5	13	千克	AB	Edible offal of sheep or goats, fresh or chilled
0206 8000.90	鲜或冷的马、驴、骡杂碎	20	70		5	13	千克	AB	Edible offal of horses, asses, mules or hinnies, fresh or chilled
0206.9000	-其他冻杂碎	18	70		5	13	千克		-Other, frozen
0206 9000.10	冻藏的羊杂碎	18	70		5	13	千克	7AB	Edible offal of sheep or goats, frozen
0206 9000.90	冻藏的马、驴、骡杂碎	18	70		5	13	千克	AB	Edible offal of horses, asses, mules or hinnies, frozen
02.07	税目01.05所列家禽的鲜、冷、冻肉及食用杂碎：								**Meat and edible offal, of the poultry of heading No. 01.05, fresh, chilled or frozen:**
	-鸡：								-Of fowls of the species *Gallus domesticus*:
0207.1100	--整只，鲜或冷的	20	70		5	13	千克	4xAB	--Not cut in pieces, fresh or chilled
0207.1200	--整只，冻的	1.3元/kg	5.6元/kg		5	13	千克	4x7AB	--Not cut in pieces, frozen
	--块及杂碎，鲜或冷的：								--Chicken cut and offal,frozen:
	---块：								---Cut:
0207.1311	----带骨的	20	70		13	13	千克	4xAB	----With bone
0207.1319	----其他	20	70		13	13	千克	4xAB	----Other
	---杂碎：								---Offal:
0207.1321	----翼(不包括翼尖)	20	70		13	13	千克	4xAB	----Midjoint wing
0207.1329	----其他	20	70		5	13	千克	AB4x	----Other
	--块及杂碎，冻的：								--Cuts and offal, frozen:
	---块：								---Cut:
0207.1411	----带骨的	0.6元/kg	4.2元/kg		13	13	千克	7AB4x	----With bone
0207.1419	----其他	0.7元/kg	9.5元/kg		13	13	千克	7AB4x	----Other
	---杂碎：								---Offal:
0207.1421	----翼(不包括翼尖)	0.8元/kg	8.1元/kg		13	13	千克	7AB4x	----Midjoint wing
0207.1422	----鸡爪	1元/kg	3.2元/kg		5	13	千克	7AB4x	----Chicken claw
0207.1429	----其他	0.5元/kg	3.2元/kg		5	13	千克	7AB4x	----Other
	-火鸡：								-Of turkeys:
0207.2400	--整只，鲜或冷的	20	70		5	13	千克	AB	--Not cut in pieces, fresh or chilled
0207.2500	--整只，冻的	20	70		5	13	千克	AB	--Not cut in pieces, frozen
0207.2600	--块及杂碎，鲜或冷的	20	70		5/13	13	千克	AB	--Cuts and offal, fresh or chilled
0207.2700	--块及杂碎，冻的	10	70		5/13	13	千克	AB	--Cuts and offal, frozen
	-鸭：								-Of ducks ;
0207.4100	--整只，鲜或冷的	20	70		5	13	千克	AB	--Not cut in pieces, fresh or chilled
0207.4200	--整只，冻的	20	70		5	13	千克	AB	--Not cut in pieces, frozen
0207.4300	--肥肝，鲜或冷的	20	70		5	13	千克	AB	--Fatty livers, fresh or chilled
0207.4400	--其他，鲜或冷的	20	70		5/13	13	千克	AB	--Other, fresh or chilled
0207.4500	--其他，冻的	20	70		5/13	13	千克	AB	--Other, frozen
	-鹅：								-Of geese:
0207.5100	--整只，鲜或冷的	20	70		5	13	千克	AB	--Not cut in pieces, fresh or chilled
0207.5200	--整只，冻的	20	70		5	13	千克	AB	--Not cut in pieces, frozen
0207.5300	--肥肝，鲜或冷的	20	70		5	13	千克	AB	--Fatty livers, fresh or chilled
0207.5400	--其他，鲜或冷的	20	70		5/13	13	千克	AB	--Other, fresh or chilled
0207.5500	--其他，冻的	20	70		5/13	13	千克	AB	--Other, frozen
0207.6000	-珍珠鸡	20	70		5/13	13	千克	AB	-Of guinea fowls
02.08	其他鲜、冷、冻肉及食用杂碎：								**Other meat and edible meat offal, fresh, chilled or frozen:**
	-家兔或野兔的：								-Of rabbits or hares:
0208.1010	---鲜、冷家兔肉，兔头除外	20	70		5/13	13	千克	AB	---Meat of rabbits, fresh or chilled, excluding head
0208.1020	---冻家兔肉，兔头除外	20	70		5/13	13	千克	AB	---Meat of rabbits, frozen, excluding head
0208.1090	---其他	20	70			13	千克		---Other

税则号列 Tariff Item	商品名称及备注	进口税率 最惠	进口税率 普通	进口税率 暂定	出口退税	增值税率	计量单位	监管条件	Article Description
0208 1090.10	鲜、冷或冻濒危野兔肉及其食用杂碎（不包括兔头）	20	70			13	千克	ABFE	Meat and edible meat offal of endangered hares, fresh, chilled or frozen, excluding head
0208 1090.90	鲜、冷或冻家兔食用杂碎	20	70		5	13	千克	AB	Edible offal of rabbits, fresh, chilled or frozen
0208.3000	-灵长目的	23	70		5	13	千克	ABFE	-Of primates
0208.4000	鲜、冷或冻的鲸、海豚及鼠海豚(鲸目哺乳动物)的；鲜、冷或冻的海牛及儒艮（海牛目哺乳动物）的；鲜、冷或冻的海豹、海狮及海象(鳍足亚目哺乳动物)的肉及食用杂碎(鲜、冷或冻的鲸、海豚、鼠海豚、海牛、儒艮、海豹、海狮及海象的肉及食用杂碎)	23	70		5	13	千克	ABFE	-Of whales, dolphins and porpoises (mammals of the order Cetacea); of manatees and dugongs (mammals of the order Sirenia) ;of seals, sea lions and walruses (mammals of the suborder Pinnipedia) , fresh, chilled or frozen
0208.5000	-爬行动物（包括蛇及龟鳖）的	23	70		5	13	千克	ABFE	-Of reptiles（including snakes and turtles）
0208.6000	-骆驼及其他骆驼科动物的	23	70			13	千克		-Of camels and other camelids (Camelidae)
0208 6000.10	鲜、冷或冻的濒危野生骆驼及其他濒危野生骆驼科动物的肉及食用杂碎	23	70			13	千克	ABFE	Other meat and edible meat offal of endangered camels and other endangered camelids (Camelidae), fresh, chilled or frozen
0208 6000.90	其他鲜、冷或冻骆驼及其他骆驼科动物的肉及食用杂碎	23	70		5	13	千克	AB	Other meat and edible meat offal of camels and other camelids (Camelidae), fresh, chilled or frozen
	-其他:								-Other:
0208.9010	---乳鸽的	20	70		5	13	千克	AB	---Of squabs
0208.9090	---其他	23	70			13	千克		---Other
0208 9090.10	其他鲜、冷或冻的濒危野生动物肉	23	70			13	千克	ABFE	Other meat of endangered wild animals,fresh, chilled or frozen
0208 9090.90	其他鲜、冷或冻肉及食用杂碎	23	70		5	13	千克	AB	Other meat and edible offal, fresh, chilled or frozen
02.09	**未炼制或用其他方法提取的不带瘦肉的肥猪肉、猪脂肪及家禽脂肪，鲜、冷、冻、干、熏、盐腌或盐渍的:**								**Pig fat free of lean meat and poultry fat not rendered or otherwise extracted, fresh, chilled, frozen, salted, in brine, dried or smoked:**
0209.1000	-猪的	20	70		5	13	千克	AB	-Of pigs
0209.9000	-其他	20	70		5	13	千克	AB	-Other
02.10	**肉及食用杂碎，干、熏、盐腌或盐渍的；可供食用的肉或杂碎的细粉、粗粉:**								**Meat and edible meat offal, salted, in brine, dried or smoked; edible flours and meals of meat or meat offal:**
	-猪肉:								-Meat of swine:
	—带骨的前腿、后腿及其肉块:								--Hams, shoulders and cuts thereof, with bone in:
0210.1110	---带骨的腿	25	80		5	13	千克		---Hams and shoulders,with bone in
0210 1110.10	干、熏、盐制的带骨鹿豚、姬猪腿	25	80		5	13	千克	ABFE	Hams and shoulders of *Babyrousa*, Porcula Salvania, with bone in, salted, in brine, dried or smoked
0210 1110.90	其他干、熏、盐制的带骨猪腿	25	80		5	13	千克	AB	Other hams and shoulders of swine, with bone in, salted, in brine, dried or smoked
0210.1190	---其他	25	80		5	13	千克		---Other
0210 1190.10	干、熏、盐制带骨鹿豚、姬猪腿肉块	25	80		5	13	千克	ABFE	Cuts of *Babyrousa*, Porcula Salvania, with bone in, salted, in brine, dried or smoked
0210 1190.90	其他干、熏、盐制的带骨猪腿肉	25	80		5	13	千克	AB	Other meat of hams and shoulders, with bone in, salted, in brine, dried or smoked
0210.1200	--腹肉（五花肉）	25	80		5	13	千克		--Bellies（streaky）and cuts thereof
0210 1200.10	干、熏、盐制的鹿豚、姬猪腹肉（指五花肉）	25	80		5	13	千克	ABFE	Bellies（streaky）and cuts of *Babyrousa*, Porcula Salvania, salted, in brine, dried or smoked
0210 1200.90	其他干、熏、盐制的猪腹肉（指五花肉）	25	80		5	13	千克	AB	Other bellies（streaky）and cuts of swine, salted, in brine, dried or smoked
0210.1900	--其他	25	80		5	13	千克		--Other
0210 1900.10	干、熏、盐制的鹿豚、姬猪其他肉	25	80		5	13	千克	ABFE	Other meat of *Babyrousa*, Porcula Salvania, salted, in brine, dried or smoked
0210 1900.90	其他干、熏、盐制的其他猪肉	25	80		5	13	千克	AB	Other meat of swine, salted, in brine, dried or smoked
0210.2000	-牛肉	25	80			13	千克		--Meat of bovine animals

税则号列 Tariff Item	商品名称及备注	进口税率 最惠	普通	暂定	出口退税	增值税率	计量单位	监管条件	Article Description
0210 2000.10	干、熏、盐制的濒危野牛肉	25	80			13	千克	ABFE	Meat of endangered wild bovine animals, salted, in brine, dried or smoked
0210 2000.90	干、熏、盐制的其他牛肉	25	80		5	13	千克	AB	Meat of other bovine animals, salted, in brine, dried or smoked
	-其他，包括可供食用的肉或杂碎的细粉、粗粉：								-Other, including edible flours and meals of meat and meat offal:
0210.9100	--灵长目的	25	80		5	13	千克	ABFE	--Of primates
0210.9200	--鲸、海豚及鼠海豚（鲸目哺乳动物）的；海牛及儒艮（海牛目哺乳动物）的；海豹、海狮及海象（鳍足亚目哺乳动物）的	25	80		5	13	千克	ABFE	--Of whales, dolphins and porpoises (mammals of the order Cetacea）;of manatees and dugongs（mammals of the order Sirenia）; of seals, sea lions and walruses (mammals of the suborder Pinnipedia)
0210.9300	--爬行动物（包括蛇及龟鳖）的	25	80		5	13	千克	ABFE	--Of reptiles（including snakes and turtles）
0210.9900	--其他	25	80			13	千克		--Other
0210 9900.10	干、熏、盐制其他濒危动物肉及杂碎(包括可供食用的肉或杂碎的细粉、粗粉)	25	80			13	千克	ABFE	Meat and edible offal of other endangered wild animals, salted, in brine, dried or smoked（including edible flours and meals of meat and meat offal）
0210 9900.90	干、熏、盐制的其他肉及食用杂碎(包括可供食用的肉或杂碎的细粉、粗粉)	25	80		5	13	千克	AB	Other meat and edible offal salted, in brine, dried or smoked（including edible flours and meals of meat and meat offal）

第三章 鱼、甲壳动物、软体动物及其他水生无脊椎动物

Chapter 3 Fish and crustaceans, molluscs and other aquatic invertebrates

注释：

一、本章不包括：

（一）品目 01.06 的哺乳动物；

（二）品目 01.06 的哺乳动物的肉（品目 02.08 或 02.10）；

（三）因品种或鲜度不适合供人食用的死鱼（包括鱼肝及鱼卵）、死甲壳动物、死软体动物及其他死水生无脊椎动物（第五章）；不适合供人食用的鱼、甲壳动物、软体动物、其他水生无脊椎动物的粉、粒（品目 23.01）；或

（四）鲟鱼子酱及用鱼卵制成的鲟鱼子酱代用品（品目 16.04）。

二、本章所称"团粒"，是指直接挤压或加入少量黏合剂制成的粒状产品。

Chapter Notes:

1. This Chapter does not cover:

(a) Mammals of heading 01.06;

(b) Meat of mammals of heading 01.06 (heading 02.08 or 02.10);

(c) Fish (including livers and roes thereof) or crustaceans, molluscs or other aquatic invertebrates, dead and unfit or unsuitable for human consumption by reason of either their species or their condition (Chapter 5); flours, meals or pellets of fish or of crustaceans, molluscs or other aquatic invertebrates, unfit for human consumption (heading 23.01); or

(d) Caviar or caviar substitutes prepared from fish eggs (heading 16.04).

2. In this Chapter, the term "pellets" means products which have been agglomerated either directly by compression or by the addition of a small quantity of binder.

税则号列 Tariff Item	商品名称及备注	进口税率			出口退税	增值税率	计量单位	监管条件	Article Description
		最惠	普通	暂定					
03.01	活鱼：								**Live fish:**
	-观赏鱼：								-Ornamental fish:
0301.1100	--淡水鱼	17.5	80			13	千克		--Freshwater
0301 1100.10	观赏用濒危淡水鱼	17.5	80			13	千克	ABFE	Endangered ornamental freshwater fish
0301 1100.90	观赏用其他淡水鱼	17.5	80		5	13	千克	AB	Other ornamental freshwater fish
0301.1900	--其他	17.5	80			13	千克		--Other
0301 1900.10	观赏用濒危非淡水鱼	17.5	80			13	千克	ABFE	Endangered ornamental non-freshwater fish
0301 1900.90	其他观赏用非淡水鱼	17.5	80		5	13	千克	AB	Other ornamental non-freshwater fish
	-其他活鱼：								-Other live fish:
	--鳟鱼(河鳟、虹鳟、克拉克大麻哈鱼、阿瓜大麻哈鱼、吉雨大麻哈鱼、亚利桑那大麻哈鱼、金腹大麻哈鱼)：								--Trout (*Salmo trutta, Oncorhynchus my kiss, Oncorhynchus clarki, Oncorhynchus aguabonita, Oncorhynchus gilae, Oncorhynchus apache and Oncorhynchus chrysogaster*):
0301.9110	---鱼苗	0	0		5	13	千克	AB	---Fry
0301.9190	---其他	10.5	40		5	13	千克	AB	---Other
	--鳗鱼（鳗鲡属）：								--Eels (*Anguilla spp.*):
0301.9210	---鱼苗	0	0			13	千克		---Fry
0301 9210.10	花鳗鲡鱼苗	0	0			13	千克	ABE	Fry of marbled eels (*Anguilla marmorata*)
0301 9210.20	欧洲鳗鲡鱼苗	0	0			13	千克	ABEF	European fry eels
0301 9210.90	其他鳗鱼（鳗鲡属）苗	0	0			13	千克	AB	Other fry eels
0301.9290	---其他	10	40		5	13	千克		---Other
0301 9290.10	花鳗鲡	10	40		5	13	千克	ABE	Marbled eels (*Anguilla marmorata*)
0301 9290.20	欧洲鳗鲡	10	40		5	13	千克	ABEF	European eels
0301 9290.90	其他活鳗鱼（鳗鲡属）	10	40		5	13	千克	AB	Other live eels
	--鲤科鱼（西鲤、黑鲫、草鱼、鲢属、鲮属、青鱼）：								--Carp (Cyprinus carpio, Carassius carassius, Ctenopharyngodon idellus, Hypophthalmichthys spp., Cirrhinus spp., Mylopharyngodon piceus):
0301.9310	---鱼苗	0	0		5	13	千克	AB	---Fry
0301.9390	---其他	10.5	40		5	13	千克	AB	---Other
	--大西洋及太平洋蓝鳍金枪鱼：								--Atlantic and Pacific bluefin tunas (Thunnus thynnus, Thunnus orientalis):
0301.9410	---鱼苗	0	0		5	13	千克	AB	---Fry
	---其他：								---Other

税则号列 Tariff Item	商品名称及备注	进口税率			出口退税	增值税率	计量单位	监管条件	Article Description
		最惠	普通	暂定					
0301.9491	----大西洋蓝鳍金枪鱼	10.5	40		5	13	千克	AB	----Atlantic bluefin tunas (Thunnus thynnus)
0301.9492	----太平洋蓝鳍金枪鱼	10.5	40		5	13	千克	AB	----Pacific bluefin tunas (Thunnus orientalis)
	--南方蓝鳍金枪鱼:								--Southern bluefin tunas（*Thunnus maccoyii*）:
0301.9510	---鱼苗	0	0		5	13	千克	AB	---Fry
0301.9590	---其他	10.5	40		5	13	千克	AB	---Other
	--其他:								--Other:
	---鱼苗:								---Fry:
0301.9911	----鲈鱼	0	0		5	13	千克	AB	----Of perches
0301.9912	----鲟鱼	0	0		5	13	千克	ABFE	----Of sturgeon
0301.9919	----其他	0	0			13	千克		----Other
0301 9919.10	其他濒危鱼苗	0	0			13	千克	ABFE	Other endangered fry
0301 9919.90	其他鱼苗	0	0		5	13	千克	AB	Other fry
	---其他:								---Other:
0301.9991	----罗非鱼	10.5	40		5	13	千克	AB	----Tilapia
0301.9992	----鲀	10.5	40		5	13	千克	AB	----Puffer fish
0301.9993	----其他鲤科鱼	10.5	40			13	千克		----Other Carps
0301 9993.10	活的濒危鲤科鱼	10.5	40			13	千克	ABFE	Endangered live Carp
0301 9993.90	活的其他鲤科鱼[鲤科鱼(西鲤、黑鲫、草鱼、鲢属、鲮属、青鱼)除外]	10.5	40		5	13	千克	AB	Other live Carp，other than Carp (Cyprinus carpio , Carassius carassius , Ctenopharyngodon idellus , Cirrhinus spp. Mylopharyngodon piceus)
0301.9999	----其他	10.5	40			13	千克		----Other
0301 9999.10	其他濒危活鱼	10.5	40			13	千克	ABFE	Other endangered live fish
0301 9999.90	其他活鱼	10.5	40		5	13	千克	AB	Other live fish
03.02	**鲜、冷鱼，但品目03.04的鱼片及其他鱼肉除外:**								**Fish, fresh or chilled, excluding fish fillets and other fish meat of heading No.03.04:**
	-鲑科鱼，但鱼肝及鱼卵除外:								-Salmonidae, excluding livers and roes:
0302.1100	--鳟鱼(河鳟、虹鳟、克拉克大麻哈鱼、阿瓜大麻哈鱼、吉雨大麻哈鱼、亚利桑那大麻哈鱼、金腹大麻哈鱼)	12	40		5	13	千克	AB	--Trout（Salmo trutta, Oncorhynchus my kiss, Oncorhynchus clarki, Oncorhynchus aguabonita, Oncorhynchus gilae, Oncor hynchus apache and Oncohynchus chrysogaster）
0302.1300	--大麻哈鱼〔红大麻哈鱼、细磷大麻哈鱼、大麻哈鱼（种）、大鳞大麻哈鱼、银大麻哈鱼、马苏大麻哈鱼、玫瑰大麻哈鱼〕	10	40		5	13	千克	AB	---Pacific salmon（Oncorhynchus nerka, Oncorhynchus gorbuscha, Oncorhynchus keta, Oncorhynchus tschawytscha, Oncorhynchus kisutch, Oncorhynchus masou and Oncorhynchus rhodurus）
	--大西洋鲑鱼及多瑙哲罗鱼:								---Atlantic salmon (Salmo salar) and Danube salmon (Hucho hucho):
0302.1410	---大西洋鲑鱼	10	40		5	13	千克	AB	---Atlantic salmon (Salmo salar)
0302.1420	---多瑙哲罗鱼	10	40		5	13	千克	AB	---Danube salmon (Hucho hucho)
0302.1900	--其他	12	40		5	13	千克		--Other
0302 1900.10	鲜或冷川陕哲罗鲑(鱼肝及鱼卵除外)	12	40		5	13	千克	ABE	*Hucho bleekeri*, fresh or chilled（excluding livers and roes）
0302 1900.20	鲜或冷秦岭细鳞鲑(鱼肝及鱼卵除外)	12	40		5	13	千克	ABE	Brachymystax lenck（*Tslinling lenok*）, fresh or chilled（excluding livers and roes）
0302 1900.90	其他鲜或冷鲑科鱼(鱼肝及鱼卵除外)	12	40		5	13	千克	AB	Other salmon, fresh or chilled,（excluding livers and roes）
	-比目鱼(鲽科、鲆科、舌鳎科、鳎科、菱鲆科、刺鲆科)，但鱼肝及鱼卵除外:								-Flat fish（Pleuronectidae, Bothidae, Cynoglossidae, soleidae, Scophthalmidae and Citharidae）, excluding livers and roes:
0302.2100	--庸鲽鱼	12	40		5	13	千克	AB	--Halibut（Reinhardtius hippoglossoides, Hippoglossus hippoglossus, Hippoglossus stenolepis）
0302.2200	--鲽鱼	12	40		5	13	千克	AB	--Plaice（*Pleuronectes platessa*）
0302.2300	--鳎鱼	12	40		5	13	千克	AB	--Sole（*Solea spp.*）
0302.2400	--大菱鲆（瘤棘鲆）	12	40		5	13	千克	AB	---Turbots (Psetta maxima)
0302.2900	--其他	12	40		5	13	千克	AB	--Other
	-金枪鱼（金枪鱼属）、鲣鱼或狐鲣(鲣)，但鱼肝及鱼卵除外:								-Tunas（of the genus Thunnus）, skipjack or stripe-bellied bonito(Euthynnus（*Katsuwonus*）pelamis)excluding livers and roes:
0302.3100	--长鳍金枪鱼	12	40		5	13	千克	AB	--Albacore or longfinned tunas（*Thunnus alalunga*）

税则号列 Tariff Item	商品名称及备注	进口税率			出口退税	增值税率	计量单位	监管条件	Article Description
		最惠	普通	暂定					
0302.3200	--黄鳍金枪鱼	12	40		5	13	千克	AB	--Yellowfin tunas（*Thunnus albacares*）
0302.3300	--鲣鱼或狐鲣	12	40		5	13	千克	AB	--Skipjack or stripe-bellied bonito
0302.3400	--大眼金枪鱼	12	40		5	13	千克	AB	--Bigeye tunas（*Thunnus obesus*）
	--大西洋及太平洋蓝鳍金枪鱼:								---Atlantic and Pacific bluefin tunas (Thunnus thynnus, Thunnus orientalis):
0302.3510	---大西洋蓝鳍金枪鱼	12	40		5	13	千克	ABU	---Atlantic bluefin tunas(Thunnus thynnus)
0302.3520	---太平洋蓝鳍金枪鱼	12	40		5	13	千克	AB	---Pacific bluefin tunas (Thunnus orientalis)
0302.3600	--南方蓝鳍金枪鱼	12	40		5	13	千克	AB	--Southern bluefin tunas(Thunnus maccoyii)
0302.3900	--其他	12	40		5	13	千克	AB	--Other
	-鲱鱼(大西洋鲱鱼、太平洋鲱鱼)、鳀鱼(鳀属)、沙丁鱼(沙丁鱼、沙瑙鱼属)、小沙丁鱼属、黍鲱或西鲱、鲭鱼〔大西洋鲭、澳洲鲭(鲐)、日本鲭(鲐)〕、对称竹荚鱼、新西兰竹荚鱼及竹荚鱼(竹荚鱼属)、军曹鱼及剑鱼,但鱼肝及鱼卵除外:								-Herrings（Clupea harengus, Clupea pallasii）, anchovies (Engraulis spp.), sardines (Sardina pilchardus, Sardinops spp.), sardinella (Sardinella spp.), brisling or sprats (Sprattus sprattus), mackerel (Scomber scombrus, Scomber australasicus, Scomber japonicus), jack and horse mackerel (Trachurus spp.), cobia (Rachycentron canadum) and swordfish (Xiphias gladius), excluding livers and roes:
0302.4100	--鲱鱼（大西洋鲱鱼、太平洋鲱鱼）	12	40		5	13	千克	AB	--Herrings（Clupea harengus, Clupea pallasii）
0302.4200	--鳀鱼（鳀属）	12	40		5	13	千克	AB	--Anchovies (Engraulis spp.)
0302.4300	--沙丁鱼（沙丁鱼、沙瑙鱼属）、小沙丁鱼属、黍鲱或西鲱	12	40		5	13	千克	AB	--Sardines (Sardina pilchardus, Sardinops spp.), sardinella (Sardinella spp.), brisling or sprats (Sprattus sprattus)
0302.4400	--鲭鱼〔大西洋鲭、澳洲鲭(鲐)、日本鲭（鲐）〕	12	40		5	13	千克	AB	--Mackerel (Scomber scombrus, Scomber australasicus, Scomber japonicus)
0302.4500	--对称竹荚鱼、新西兰竹荚鱼及竹荚鱼（竹荚鱼属）	12	40		5	13	千克	AB	--Jack and horse mackerel (Trachurus spp.)
0302.4600	--军曹鱼	12	40		5	13	千克	AB	--Cobia (Rachycentron canadum)
0302.4700	--剑鱼	12	40		5	13	千克	ABU	--Swordfish (Xiphias gladius)
	-犀鳕科、多丝真鳕科、鳕科、长尾鳕科、黑鳕科、无须鳕科、深海鳕科及南极鳕科鱼,但鱼肝及鱼卵除外:								-Fish of the families Bregmacerotidae, Euclichthyidae, Gadidae, Macrouridae, Melanonidae , Merlucciidae, Moridae and Muraenolepididae, excluding livers and roes:
0302.5100	--鳕鱼（大西洋鳕鱼、格陵兰鳕鱼、太平洋鳕鱼）	12	40		5	13	千克	AB	--Cod (Gadus morhua, Gadus macrocephalus, Gadus ogac)
0302.5200	--黑线鳕鱼（黑线鳕）	12	40		5	13	千克	AB	--Haddock (Melanogrammus aeglefinus)
0302.5300	--绿青鳕鱼	12	40		5	13	千克	AB	--Coalfish (pollachius virens)
0302.5400	--狗鳕鱼(无须鳕属、长鳍鳕属)	12	40		5	13	千克	AB	--Hake (Merluccius spp. , Urophycis spp.)
0302.5500	--狭鳕鱼	12	40		5	13	千克	AB	--Alaska Pollack (Theragra chalcogramma)
0302.5600	--蓝鳕鱼（小鳍鳕、南蓝鳕）	12	40		5	13	千克	AB	--Blue whitings (Micromesistius poutassou, Micromesistius australis)
0302.5900	--其他	12	40		5	13	千克	AB	--Other
	-罗非鱼（口孵非鲫属）、鲶鱼（(鱼芒)鲶属、鲶属、胡鲶属、真鮰属）、鲤科鱼（西鲤、黑鲫、草鱼、鲢属、鲮属、青鱼）、鳗鱼（鳗鲡属）、尼罗河鲈鱼（尼罗尖吻鲈）及黑鱼（鳢属），但鱼肝及鱼卵除外:								-Tilapias (Oreochromis spp.), catfish (Pangasius spp. , Silurus spp. , Clarias spp. , Ictalurus spp.), carp (Cyprinus carpio, Carassius carassius , Ctenopharyngodon idellus , Hypophthalmichthys spp. , Cirrhinus spp. , Mylopharyngodon piceus), eels (Anguillaspp.), Nile perch (Lates niloticus) and snakeheads (Channa spp.), excluding livers and roes :
0302.7100	--罗非鱼（口孵非鲫属）	12	40		5	13	千克	AB	--Tilapias (Oreochromis spp.)
0302.7200	--鲶鱼（(鱼芒)鲶属、鲶属、胡鲶属、真鮰属）	12	40		5	13	千克	AB	--Catfish (Pangasius spp. , Silurus spp. , Clarias spp. , Ictalurus spp.)
0302.7300	--鲤科鱼（西鲤、黑鲫、草鱼、鲢属、鲮属、青鱼）	12	40		5	13	千克	AB	--Carp (Cyprinus carpio , Carassius carassius , Ctenopharyngodon idellus , Hypophthalmichthys spp. , Cirrhinus spp. , Mylopharyngdon piceus)
0302.7400	--鳗鱼（鳗鲡属）	12	40		5	13	千克		--Eles (Anguilla spp.)
0302 7400.10	鲜或冷花鳗鲡(鱼肝及鱼卵除外)	12	40		5	13	千克	ABE	Marbled eels, fresh or chilled，excluding livers and rose

税则号列 Tariff Item	商品名称及备注	进口税率			出口退税	增值税率	计量单位	监管条件	Article Description
		最惠	普通	暂定					
0302 7400.20	鲜或冷的欧洲鳗鲡(鱼肝及鱼卵除外)	12	40		5	13	千克	ABEF	European eels, fresh or chilled， excluding livers and rose
0302 7400.90	其他鲜或冷鳗鱼（鳗鲡属）(鱼肝及鱼卵除外)	12	40		5	13	千克	AB	Other eels, fresh or chilled， excluding livers and rose
0302.7900	--其他	12	40		5	13	千克		--Other
0302 7900.01	鲜或冷尼罗河鲈鱼（尼罗尖吻鲈）(鱼肝及鱼卵除外)	12	40		5	13	千克	AB	Nile perch (Lates niloticus) , fresh or chilled， excluding livers and rose
0302 7900.90	鲜或冷的黑鱼（鳢属）(鱼肝及鱼卵除外)	12	40		5	13	千克	AB	Snakeheads (Channa spp.), fresh or chilled， excluding livers and rose
	-其他鱼，但鱼肝及鱼卵除外:								-Other fish , excluding livers and rose :
0302.8100	--角鲨及其他鲨鱼	12	40		5	13	千克		--Dogfish and other sharks
0302 8100.10	鲜或冷濒危鲨鱼(鱼肝及鱼卵除外)	12	40		5	13	千克	ABEF	Whale shark（*Rhincodon*）, man-eater shark (*careharodon*), basking shark (*Cetorhinus*),fresh or chilled
0302 8100.90	鲜或冷其他鲨鱼(鱼肝及鱼卵除外)	12	40		5	13	千克	AB	Other dogfish and other sharks, fresh or chilled， excluding livers and rose
0302.8200	--魟鱼及鳐鱼（鳐科）	12	40		5	13	千克	AB	--Rays and skates (Rajidae)
0302.8300	--南极犬牙鱼（南极犬牙鱼属）	12	40		5	13	千克	ABU	--Toothfish (Dissostichus spp.)
0302.8400	--尖吻鲈鱼(舌齿鲈属)	12	40		5	13	千克	AB	--Seabass (Dicentrarchus spp.)
0302.8500	--菱羊鲷(鲷科)	12	40		5	13	千克	AB	--Seabream (Sparidae)
	--其他:								--Other :
0302.8910	---带鱼	12	40		5	13	千克	AB	---Scabbard fish（*Trichiurus*）
0302.8920	---黄鱼	12	40		5	13	千克	AB	---Yellow croaker（*Pseudosicaena*）
0302.8930	---鲳鱼	12	40		5	13	千克	AB	---Butterfish（*Pamus*）
0302.8940	---鲀	12	40		5	13	千克	AB	---Puffer fish
0302.8990	---其他	12	40			13	千克		---Other
0302 8990.01	鲜或冷其他鲈鱼(鱼肝及鱼卵除外)	12	40		5	13	千克	AB	Other Perch, fresh or chilled, excluding livers and rose
0302 8990.10	其他未列名濒危鲜或冷鱼(鱼肝及鱼卵除外)	12	40			13	千克	ABFE	Other endangered fish, fresh or chilled， excluding livers and rose
0302 8990.90	其他鲜或冷鱼(鱼肝及鱼卵除外)	12	40		5	13	千克	AB	Other fish, fresh or chilled， excluding livers and rose
0302.9000	-鱼肝及鱼卵	12	50			13	千克		-Livers and roes
0302 9000.10	鲜或冷濒危鱼种的肝及鱼卵	12	50			13	千克	ABFE	Livers and roes of endangered fish, fresh or chilled
0302 9000.90	其他鲜或冷鱼肝及鱼卵	12	50		5	13	千克	AB	Other livers and roes of fish, fresh or chilled
03.03	**冻鱼，但品目03.04的鱼片及其他鱼肉除外:**								**Fish, frozen, excluding fish fillets and other fish meat of heading No.03.04:**
	-鲑科鱼，但鱼肝及鱼卵除外:								-Salmonidae , excluding livers and roes:
0303.1100	--红大麻哈鱼	10	40		13	13	千克	AB	--Sockeye salmon（red salmon）（*Oncorhynchus nerka*）
0303.1200	--其他大麻哈鱼〔细磷大麻哈鱼、大麻哈鱼（种）、大鳞大麻哈鱼、银大麻哈鱼、马苏大麻哈鱼、玫瑰大麻哈鱼〕	10	40		13	13	千克	AB	--Other Pacific salmon (Oncorhynchus gorbuscha, Oncorhynchus keta, Oncorhynchus tschawytscha, Oncorhynchus kisutch, Oncorhynchus masou and Oncorhynchus rhodurus)
0303.1300	--大西洋鲑鱼及多瑙哲罗鱼	10	40		13	13	千克	AB	--Atlantic salmon (Salmo salar) and Danube salmon (Hucho hucho)
0303.1400	--鳟鱼(河鳟、虹鳟、克拉克大麻哈鱼、阿瓜大麻哈鱼、吉雨大麻哈鱼、亚利桑那大麻哈鱼、金腹大麻哈鱼)	12	40		13	13	千克	AB	--Trout (Salmo trutta , Oncorhynchus mykiss , Oncorhynchus clarki , Oncorhynchus aguabonita , Oncorhynchus gilae , Oncorhynchus apache and Oncorhynchus chrysogaster)
0303.1900	--其他	10	40		13	13	千克		--Other
0303 1900.10	冻川陕哲罗鲑（鱼肝及鱼卵除外）	10	40		13	13	千克	ABE	*Hucho bleekeri,* frozen， excluding livers and rose
0303 1900.20	冻秦岭细鳞鲑（鱼肝及鱼卵除外）	10	40		13	13	千克	ABE	Tslinling lenok, frozen， excluding livers and rose
0303 1900.90	其他冻鲑科鱼（鱼肝及鱼卵除外）	10	40		13	13	千克	AB	Other Salmonidae, frozen， excluding livers and rose
	-罗非鱼（口孵非鲫属）、鲶鱼（（鱼芒)鲶属、鲶属、胡鲶属、真鮰属）、鲤科鱼（西鲤、黑鲫、草鱼、鲢属、鲮属、青鱼）、鳗鱼（鳗鲡属）、尼罗河鲈鱼（尼罗尖吻鲈）及黑鱼（鳢属），但鱼肝及鱼卵除外:								-Tilapias (Oreochromis spp.) , catfish (Pangasius spp. , Silurus spp. , Clarias spp. , Ictalurus spp.) , carp (Cyprinus carpio, Carassius carassius , Ctenopharyngodon idellus , Hypophthalmichthys spp. , Cirrhinus spp. , Mylopharyngodon piceus) , eels (Anguilla spp.) , Nile perch (Lates niloticus) and snakeheads (Channa spp.) , excluding livers and rose :

税则号列 Tariff Item	商品名称及备注	进口税率 最惠	普通	暂定	出口退税	增值税率	计量单位	监管条件	Article Description
0303.2300	--罗非鱼（口孵非鲫属）	10	40		13	13	千克	AB	--Tilapias (Oreochromis spp.)
0303.2400	--鲶鱼（(鲶芒)鲶属、鲶属、胡鲶属、真鮰属）	10	40		13	13	千克	AB	--Catfish (Pangasius spp. , Silurus spp. , Clarias spp. , Ictalurus spp.)
0303.2500	--鲤科鱼（西鲤、黑鲫、草鱼、鲢属、鲮属、青鱼）	10	40		13	13	千克	AB	--Carp (Cyprinus carpio , Carassius carassius , Ctenopharyngodon idellus , Hypophthalmichthys spp. , Cirrhinus spp. , Mylopharyngdon piceus)
0303.2600	--鳗鱼（鳗鲡属）	12	40		13	13	千克		--Eels (Anguilla spp.)
0303 2600.10	冻花鳗鲡（鱼肝及鱼卵除外）	12	40		13	13	千克	ABE	Marbled eels, frozen, excluding livers and rose
0303 2600.20	冻欧洲鳗鲡（鱼肝及鱼卵除外）	12	40		13	13	千克	ABEF	European eels, frozen, excluding livers and rose
0303 2600.90	其他冻鳗鱼（鳗鲡属）（鱼肝及鱼卵除外）	12	40		13	13	千克	AB	Other eels, frozen， excluding livers and rose
0303.2900	--其他	10	40		13	13	千克		--Other
0303 2900.01	冻尼罗河鲈鱼(尼罗尖吻鲈)(鱼肝及鱼卵除外)	10	40		13	13	千克	AB	Snakeheads (Channa spp.) , frozen，excluding livers and rose
0303 2900.90	冻黑鱼（鳢属）（鱼肝及鱼卵除外）	10	40		13	13	千克	AB	Greenland halibut, frozen， excluding livers and rose
	-比目鱼（鲽科、鲆科、舌鳎科、鳎科、菱鲆科、刺鲆科），但鱼肝及鱼卵除外:								-Flatfish（*Pleuronectidae, Bothidae, Cynoglossidae, Soleidae, Scophthalmidae and Citharidae*）, excluding livers and roes:
	--庸鲽鱼:								--Halibut（*Reinhardtius hippoglossoides, Hippoglossus hippoglossus, Hippoglossus stenolepis*）:
0303.3110 暂	---格陵兰庸鲽鱼	10	40	5	13	13	千克	AB	---Greenland halibut
0303.3190	---其他	10	40		13	13	千克	AB	---Other
0303.3200 暂	--鲽鱼	12	40	2	13	13	千克	AB	--Plaice（*Pleuronectes platessa*）
0303.3300	--鳎鱼	12	40		13	13	千克	AB	--Sole（*Solea spp.*）
0303.3400	--大菱鲆（瘤棘鲆）	10	40		13	13	千克	AB	--Turbots (Psetta maxima)
0303.3900	--其他	10	40		13	13	千克	AB	--Other
	-金枪鱼（金枪鱼属）、鲣鱼或狐鲣（鲣），但鱼肝及鱼卵除外:								-Tunas（of the genus Thunnus）, skipjack or stripe-bellied bonito(Euthynnus（*Katsuwonus*）pelamis), excluding livers and roes:
0303.4100	--长鳍金枪鱼	12	40		13	13	千克	AB	--Albacore or longfinned tunas（*Thunnus alalunga*）
0303.4200	--黄鳍金枪鱼	12	40		13	13	千克	AB	--Yellowfin tunas（*Thunnus albacares*）
0303.4300	--鲣鱼或狐鲣	12	40		13	13	千克	AB	--Skipjack or stripe-bellied bonito
0303.4400	--大眼金枪鱼	12	40		13	13	千克	ABU	--Bigeye tunas（*Thunnus obesus*）
	--大西洋及太平洋蓝鳍金枪鱼:								--Atlantic and Pacific bluefin tunas (Thunnus thynnus , Thunnus orientalis):
0303.4510	---大西洋蓝鳍金枪鱼	12	40		13	13	千克	ABU	---Atlantic bluefin tunas (Thunnus thynnus , Thunnus orientalis)
0303.4520	---太平洋蓝鳍金枪鱼	12	40		13	13	千克	AB	---Pacific bluefin tunas (Thunnus thynnus)
0303.4600	--南方蓝鳍金枪鱼	12	40		13	13	千克	AB	--Southern bluefin tunas(Thunnus orientalis)
0303.4900	--其他	12	40		13	13	千克	AB	--Other
	-鲱鱼（大西洋鲱鱼、太平洋鲱鱼）、沙丁鱼（沙丁鱼、沙瑙鱼属）、小沙丁鱼属、黍鲱或西鲱、鲭鱼〔大西洋鲭、澳洲鲭(鲐)、日本鲭（鲐）〕、对称竹荚鱼、新西兰竹荚鱼及竹荚鱼(竹荚鱼属)、军曹鱼及剑鱼，但鱼肝及鱼卵除外:								-Herrings（Clupea harengus, Clupea pallasii）, sardines (Sardina pilchardus, Sardinops spp.), sardinella (Sardinella spp.), brisling or sprats (Sprattus sprattus), mackerel (Scomber scombrus, Scomber australasicus, Scomber japonicus), jack and horse mackerel (Trachurus spp.), cobia (Rachycentron canadum) and swordfish (Xiphias gladius), excluding livers and roes:
0303.5100 暂	--鲱鱼(大西洋鲱鱼、太平洋鲱鱼)	10	40	2	13	13	千克	AB	--Herrings（*Clupea harengus, Clupea pallasii*）
0303.5300	--沙丁鱼(沙丁鱼、沙瑙鱼属)、小沙丁鱼属、黍鲱或西鲱	12	40		13	13	千克	AB	--Sardines (Sardina pilchardus, Sardinops spp.), sardinella (Sardinella spp.), brisling or sprats (Sprattus sprattus)
0303.5400	--鲭鱼〔大西洋鲭、澳洲鲭(鲐)、日本鲭（鲐）〕	10	40		13	13	千克	AB	--Mackerel (Scomber scombrus, Scomber australasicus, Scomber japonicus)
0303.5500	--对称竹荚鱼、新西兰竹荚鱼及竹荚鱼(竹荚鱼属)	10	40		13	13	千克	AB	--Jack and horse mackerel (Trachurus spp.)
0303.5600	--军曹鱼	10	40		13	13	千克	AB	--Cobia (Rachycentron canadum)

税则号列 Tariff Item	商品名称及备注	进口税率			出口退税	增值税率	计量单位	监管条件	Article Description
		最惠	普通	暂定					
0303.5700	--剑鱼	10	40		13	13	千克	ABU	--Swordfish (Xiphias gladius)
	-犀鳕科、多丝真鳕科、鳕科、长尾鳕科、黑鳕科、无须鳕科、深海鳕科及南极鳕科鱼，但鱼肝及鱼卵除外:								-Fish of the families Bregmacerotidae, Euclichthyidae, Gadidae, Macrouridae, Melanonidae , Merlucciidae, Moridae and Muraenolepididae, excluding livers and roes :
0303.6300[暂]	--鳕鱼（大西洋鳕鱼、格陵兰鳕鱼、太平洋鳕鱼）	10	40	2	13	13	千克	AB	--Cod (Gadus morhua, Gadus macrocephalus, Gadus ogac)
0303.6400	--黑线鳕鱼（黑线鳕）	12	40		13	13	千克	AB	--Haddock (Melanogrammus aeglefinus)
0303.6500	--绿青鳕鱼	12	40		13	13	千克	AB	--Coalfish (pollachius virens)
0303.6600	--狗鳕鱼(无须鳕属、长鳍鳕属)	12	40		13	13	千克	AB	--Hake (Merluccius spp. , Urophycis spp.)
0303.6700	--狭鳕鱼	10	40		13	13	千克	AB	--Alaska Pollack (Theragra chalcogramma)
0303.6800	--蓝鳕鱼（小鳍鳕、南蓝鳕）	10	40		13	13	千克	AB	--Blue whitings (Micromesistius poutassou, Micromesistius australis)
0303.6900	--其他	10	40		13	13	千克	AB	--Other
	-其他鱼，但鱼肝及鱼卵除外:								-Other fish , excluding livers and roes :
0303.8100	--角鲨及其他鲨鱼	12	40		13	13	千克		--Dogfish and other sharks
0303 8100.10	冻濒危鲨鱼(鱼肝及鱼卵除外)	12	40		13	13	千克	ABFE	Endangered shark, frozen, excluding livers and roes
0303 8100.90	冻其他鲨鱼(鱼肝及鱼卵除外)	12	40		13	13	千克	AB	Other sharks, frozen, excluding livers and roes
0303.8200	--魟鱼及鳐鱼（鳐科）	10	40		13	13	千克	AB	--Rays and skates (Rajidae)
0303.8300	--南极犬牙鱼（南极犬牙鱼属）	10	40		13	13	千克	ABU	--Toothfish (Dissostichus spp.)
0303.8400	--尖吻鲈鱼(舌齿鲈属)	12	40		13	13	千克	AB	--Seabass (Dicentrarchus spp.)
	--其他:								--Other :
0303.8910	---带鱼	10	40		13	13	千克	AB	---Scabbard fish（*Trichiurus*）
0303.8920	---黄鱼	10	40		13	13	千克	AB	---Yellow croaker（*Pseudosicaena*）
0303.8930	---鲳鱼	10	40		13	13	千克	AB	---Butterfish（*Pamus*）
0303.8990	---其他	10	40			13	千克		---Other
0303 8990.01	其他冻鲈鱼(鱼肝及鱼卵除外)	10	40		13	13	千克	AB	Other perch, frozen, excluding livers and roes
0303 8990.10	其他未列名濒危冻鱼(鱼肝及鱼卵除外)	10	40			13	千克	ABFE	Other endangered fish frozen, not elsewhere specified or included, excluding livers and roes
0303 8990.90	其他未列名冻鱼(鱼肝及鱼卵除外)	10	40		13	13	千克	AB	Other fish frozen, not elsewhere specified or included, excluding livers and roes
0303.9000	-鱼肝及鱼卵	10	50			13	千克		-Livers and roes
0303 9000.10	冻濒危鱼种的肝及鱼卵	10	50			13	千克	ABFE	Livers and roes of endangered fish, frozen
0303 9000.90	其他冻鱼肝及鱼卵	10	50		13	13	千克	AB	Other livers and roes, frozen
03.04	**鲜、冷、冻鱼片及其他鱼肉（不论是否绞碎）：**								**Fish fillets and other fish meat（whether or not minced）, fresh, chilled or frozen:**
	-鲜或冷的罗非鱼（口孵非鲫属）、鲶鱼（(鱼芒)鲶属、鲶属、胡鲶属、真鮰属）、鲤科鱼（西鲤、黑鲫、草鱼、鲢属、鳙属、青鱼）、鳗鱼（鳗鲡属）、尼罗河鲈鱼(尼罗尖吻鲈)及黑鱼(鳢属)的鱼片:								-Fresh or chilled fillets of tilapias (Oreochromis spp.), catfish (Pangasius spp. , Silurus spp. , Clarias spp. , Ictalurus spp.), carp (Cyprinus carpio, Carassius carassius, Ctenopharyngodon idellus, Hypophthalmichthys spp. , Cirrhinus spp. , Mylopharyngodon piceus), eels (Anguilla spp.), Nile perch (Lates niloticus) and snakeheads (Channa spp.) :
0304.3100	--罗非鱼（口孵非鲫属）	12	70		5	13	千克	AB	--Tilapias (Oreochromis spp.)
0304.3200	--鲶鱼（(鱼芒)鲶属、鲶属、胡鲶属、真鮰属）	12	70		5	13	千克	AB	--Catfish (Pangasius spp. , Silurus spp. , Clarias spp. , Ictalurus spp.)
0304.3300	--尼罗河鲈鱼（尼罗尖吻鲈）	12	70		5	13	千克	AB	--Nile Perch (Lates niloticus)
0304.3900	--其他	12	70		5	13	千克		--Other
0304 3900.10	鲜或冷的花鳗鲡鱼片	12	70		5	13	千克	ABE	Marbled eels fillet, fresh or chilled
0304 3900.20	鲜或冷的欧洲鳗鲡鱼片	12	70		5	13	千克	ABEF	European eels fillet, fresh or chilled
0304 3900.90	鲜或冷的鲤科鱼（西鲤、黑鲫、草鱼、鲢属、鳙属、青鱼）、其他鳗鱼（鳗鲡属）及黑鱼（鳢属）的鱼片	12	70		5	13	千克	AB	Carp fillet, fresh or chilled (Cyprinus carpio, Carassius carassius, Ctenopharynngodon idellus, Hypophthalmichthys spp. , Cirrhinus spp. , Mylopharyngodon piceus)

税则号列 Tariff Item	商品名称及备注	进口税率 最惠	普通	暂定	出口退税	增值税率	计量单位	监管条件	Article Description
	-鲜或冷的其他鱼片:								-Fresh or chilled fillets of other fish :
0304.4100	--大麻哈鱼〔红大麻哈鱼、细磷大麻哈鱼、大麻哈鱼（种）、大鳞大麻哈鱼、银大麻哈鱼、马苏大麻哈鱼、玫瑰大麻哈鱼〕、大西洋鲑鱼及多瑙哲罗鱼	12	70		5	13	千克	AB	--Pacific salmon（Oncorhynchus nerka, Oncorhynchus gorbuscha, Oncorhynchus keta, Oncorhynchus tschawytscha, Oncorhynchus kisutch, Oncorhynchus masou and Oncorhynchus rhodurus）、Atlantic salmon (Salmo salar) and Danube salmon (Hucho hucho)
0304.4200	--鳟鱼(河鳟、虹鳟、克拉克大麻哈鱼、阿瓜大麻哈鱼、吉雨大麻哈鱼、亚利桑那大麻哈鱼、金腹大麻哈鱼)	12	70		5	13	千克	AB	--Trout (Salmo trutta , Oncorhynchus mykiss , Oncorhynchus clarki , Oncorhynchus aguabonita , Oncorhynchus gilae , Oncorhynchus apache and Oncorhynchus chrysogaster)
0304.4300	--比目鱼（鲽科、鲆科、舌鳎科、鳎科、菱鲆科、刺鲆科）	12	70		5	13	千克	AB	--Flat fish (Pleuronectidae, Bothidae, Cynoglossidae,Soleidae, Scophthalmidae and Citharidae)
0304.4400	--犀鳕科、多丝真鳕科、鳕科、长尾鳕科、黑鳕科、无须鳕科、深海鳕科及南极鳕科鱼	12	70		5	13	千克	AB	--Fish of the families Bregmacerotidae, Euclichthyidae, Gadidae, Macrouridae, Melanonidae , Merlucciidae, Moridae and Muraenolepididae
0304.4500	--剑鱼	12	70		5	13	千克	ABU	--Swordfish (Xiphias gladius)
0304.4600	--南极犬牙鱼(南极犬牙鱼属)	12	70		5	13	千克	ABU	--Toothfish (Dissostichus spp.)
0304.4900	--其他	12	70			13	千克		--Other
0304 4900.10	鲜或冷的其他濒危鱼的鱼片	12	70			13	千克	ABFE	Fillets of other endangered fish, fresh or chilled
0304 4900.90	鲜或冷的其他鱼的鱼片	12	70		5	13	千克	AB	Fillets of other fish, fresh or chilled
	-其他，鲜或冷的:								-Other, fresh or chilled :
0304.5100	--罗非鱼（口孵非鲫属）、鲶鱼（（鱼芒)鲶属、鲶属、胡鲶属、真鮰属）、鲤科鱼（西鲤、黑鲫、草鱼、鲢属、鲮属、青鱼）、鳗鱼（鳗鲡属）、尼罗河鲈鱼（尼罗尖吻鲈）及黑鱼（醴属）	12	70		5	13	千克		--Tilapias (Oreochromis spp.) , catfish (Pangasius spp. , Silurus spp. , Clarias spp. , Ictalurus spp.) , carp (Cyprinus carpio, Carassius carassius , Ctenopharyngodon idellus , Hypophthalmichthys spp. , Cirrhinus spp. , Mylopharyngodon piceus) , eels (Anguillaspp.) , Nile perch (Lates niloticus) and snakeheads (Channa spp.)
0304 5100.10	鲜或冷的花鳗鲡（不论是否绞碎）	12	70		5	13	千克	ABE	Marbled eels, fresh or chilled（ whether or not minced）
0304 5100.20	鲜或冷的欧洲鳗鲡的鱼肉（不论是否绞碎）	12	70		5	13	千克	ABEF	Fillets of european eels, fresh or chilled（ whether or not minced）
0304 5100.90	鲜或冷的罗非鱼(口孵非鲫属)、鲶鱼（（鱼芒)鲶属、鲶属、胡鲶属、真鮰属）、鲤科鱼（西鲤、黑鲫、草鱼、鲢属、鲮属、青鱼）、其他鳗鱼（鳗鲡属）、尼罗河鲈鱼(尼罗尖吻鲈)及黑鱼(醴属)的鱼肉(不论是否绞碎)	12	70		5	13	千克	AB	Tilapias (Oreochromis spp.) , catfish (Pangasius spp. , Silurus spp. , Clarias spp. , Ictalurus spp.) , carp (Cyprinus carpio, Carassius carassius , Ctenopharyngodon idellus , Hypophthalmichthys spp. , Cirrhinus spp. , Mylopharyngodon piceus) , eels (Anguillaspp.) , Nile perch (Lates niloticus) and snakeheads (Channa spp.), fresh or chilled（ whether or not minced）
0304.5200	--鲑科鱼	12	70		5	13	千克	AB	--Salmonidae
0304.5300	--犀鳕科、多丝真鳕科、鳕科、长尾鳕科、黑鳕科、无须鳕科、深海鳕科及南极鳕科鱼	12	70		5	13	千克	AB	--Fish of the families Bregmacerotidae, Euclichthyidae, Gadidae, Macrouridae, Melanonidae , Merlucciidae, Moridae and Muraenolepididae
0304.5400	--剑鱼	12	70		5	13	千克	ABU	--Swordfish (Xiphias gladius)
0304.5500	--南极犬牙鱼（南极犬牙鱼属）	12	70		5	13	千克	ABU	--Toothfish (Dissostichus spp.)
0304.5900	--其他	12	70			13	千克		--Other
0304 5900.10	鲜或冷的其他濒危鱼的鱼肉(不论是否绞碎)	12	70			13	千克	ABEF	Meat of endangered fish, fresh or chilled（ whether or not minced）
0304 5900.90	鲜或冷的其他鱼的鱼肉(不论是否绞碎)	12	70		5	13	千克	AB	Other fish meat, fresh or chilled（ whether or not minced）
	-冻的罗非鱼（口孵非鲫属）、鲶鱼（（鱼芒)鲶属、鲶属、胡鲶属、真鮰属）、鲤科鱼（西鲤、黑鲫、草鱼、鲢属、鲮属、青鱼）、鳗鱼(鳗鲡属)、尼罗河鲈鱼(尼罗尖吻鲈）及黑鱼（鳢属）的鱼片:								-Forzen fillets of tilapias (Oreochromis spp.), catfish (Pangasius spp. , Silurus spp. , Clarias spp. , Ictalurus spp.), carp (Cyprinus carpio, Carassius carassius, Ctenopharyngodon idellus, Hypophthalmichthys spp. , Cirrhinus spp. , Mylopharyngodon piceus), eels (Anguilla spp.), Nile perch (Lates niloticus) and snakeheads (Channa spp.):

税则号列 Tariff Item	商品名称及备注	进口税率 最惠	进口税率 普通	进口税率 暂定	出口退税	增值税率	计量单位	监管条件	Article Description
0304.6100	--罗非鱼（口孵非鲫属）	10	70		13	13	千克	AB	--Tilapias (Oreochromis spp.)
	--鲶鱼（（鱼芒）鲶属、鲶属、胡鲶属、真鮰属）：								--Catfish (Pangasius spp. , Silurus spp. , Clarias spp. , Ictalurus spp.):
	---叉尾鮰鱼（真鮰属）：								---Ictalurus (Ictalurus spp.)
0304.6211	----斑点叉尾鮰鱼	10	70		13	13	千克	AB	----Channel catfish（Ictalurus Punctatus）
0304.6219	----其他	10	70		13	13	千克	AB	----Other
0304.6290	---其他	10	70		13	13	千克	AB	---Other
0304.6300	--尼罗河鲈鱼（尼罗尖吻鲈）	10	70		13	13	千克	AB	--Nile Perch (Lates niloticus)
0304.6900	--其他	10	70		13	13	千克		--Other
0304 6900.10	冻的花鳗鲡鱼片	10	70		13	13	千克	ABE	Forzen fillets of Marbled eels
0304 6900.20	冻的欧洲鳗鲡鱼片	10	70		13	13	千克	ABEF	Forzen fillets of European eels
0304 6900.90	冻的鲤科鱼（西鲤、黑鲫、草鱼、鲢属、鲮属、青鱼）、其他鳗鱼（鳗鲡属）及黑鱼（鳢属）的鱼片	10	70		13	13	千克	AB	Forzen fillets of carp (Cyprinus carpio, Carassius carassius, Ctenopharyngodon idellus, Hypophthalmichthys spp. , Cirrhinus spp. , Mylopharyngodon piceus),
	-冻的犀鳕科、多丝真鳕科、鳕科、长尾鳕科、黑鳕科、无须鳕科、深海鳕科及南极鳕科鱼的鱼片：								-Frozen fillets of fish of the families Bregmacerotidae, Euclichthyidae, Gadidae, Macrouridae, Melanonidae, Merlucciidae, Moridae and Muraenolepididae :
0304.7100	--鳕鱼（大西洋鳕鱼、格陵兰鳕鱼、太平洋鳕鱼）	10	70		13	13	千克	AB	--Cod (Gadus morhua, Gadus macrocephalus, Gadus ogac)
0304.7200	--黑线鳕鱼（黑线鳕）	10	70		13	13	千克	AB	--Haddock (Melanogrammus aeglefinus)
0304.7300	--绿青鳕鱼	10	70		13	13	千克	AB	--Coalfish (Pollachius virens)
0304.7400	--狗鳕鱼(无须鳕属、长鳍鳕属)	10	70		13	13	千克	AB	--Hake (Merluccius spp. , Urophycis spp.)
0304.7500	--狭鳕鱼	10	70		13	13	千克	AB	--Alaska Pollack (Theragra chalcogramma)
0304.7900	--其他	10	70		13	13	千克	AB	--Other
	-其他冻鱼片：								-Forzen fillets of other fish :
0304.8100	--大麻哈鱼〔红大麻哈鱼、细磷大麻哈鱼、大麻哈鱼（种）、大鳞大麻哈鱼、银大麻哈鱼、马苏大麻哈鱼、玫瑰大麻哈鱼〕、大西洋鲑鱼及多瑙哲罗鱼	10	70		13	13	千克	AB	--Pacific salmon（Oncorhynchus nerka, Oncorhynchus gorbuscha, Oncorhynchus keta, Oncorhynchus tschawytscha, Oncorhynchus kisutch, Oncorhynchus masou and Oncorhynchus rhodurus）, Atlantic salmon (Salmo salar) and Danube salmon (Hucho hucho)
0304.8200	--鳟鱼(河鳟、虹鳟、克拉克大麻哈鱼、阿瓜大麻哈鱼、吉雨大麻哈鱼、亚利桑那大麻哈鱼、金腹大麻哈鱼)	10	70		13	13	千克	AB	--Trout (Salmo trutta , Oncorhynchus mykiss , Oncorhynchus clarki , Oncorhynchus aguabonita , Oncorhynchus gilae , Oncorhynchus apache and Oncorhynchus chrysogaster)
0304.8300	--比目鱼（鲽科、鲆科、舌鳎科、鳎科、菱鲆科、刺鲆科）	10	70		13	13	千克	AB	--Flat fish (Pleuronectidae, Bothidae, Cynoglossidae, Soleidae, Scophthalmidae and Citharidae)
0304.8400	--剑鱼	10	70		13	13	千克	ABU	--Swordfish (Xiphias gladius)
0304.8500	--南极犬牙鱼(南极犬牙鱼属)	10	70		13	13	千克	ABU	--Toothfish (Dissostichus spp.)
0304.8600	--鲱鱼（大西洋鲱鱼、太平洋鲱鱼）	10	70		13	13	千克	AB	--Herrings（Clupea harengus, Clupea pallasii）
0304.8700	--金枪鱼(金枪鱼属)、鲣鱼或狐鲣(鲣)	10	70		13	13	千克	AB	--Tunas（of the genus Thunnus）, skipjack or stripe-bellied bonito (Euthynnus （*Katsuwonus*）pelamis)
0304.8900	--其他	10	70			13	千克		-Other
0304 8900.10	冻的其他濒危鱼片	10	70			13	千克	ABEF	Fillets of other endangered fish, frozen
0304 8900.90	冻的其他鱼片	10	70		13	13	千克	AB	Other fish fillets, frozen
	-其他，冻的：								-Other, frozen :
0304.9100	--剑鱼	10	70		13	13	千克	ABU	--Swordfish（*Xiphias gladius*）
0304.9200	--南极犬牙鱼（南极犬牙鱼属）	10	70		13	13	千克	ABU	--Toothfish（Dissostichus spp.）
0304.9300	--罗非鱼（口孵非鲫属）、鲶鱼（（鱼芒）鲶属、鲶属、胡鲶属、真鮰属）、鲤科鱼（西鲤、黑鲫、草鱼、鲢属、鲮属、青鱼）、鳗鱼（鳗鲡属）、尼罗河鲈鱼（尼罗尖吻鲈）及黑鱼（鳢属）	10	70		13	13	千克		--Tilapias (Oreochromis spp.), catfish (Pangasius spp. , Silurus spp. , Clarias spp. , Ictalurus spp.), carp (Cyprinus carpio, Carassius carassius , Ctenopharyngodon idellus , Hypophthalmichthys spp. , Cirrhinus spp. , Mylopharyngodon piceus) , eels (Anguilla spp.) , Nile perch (Lates niloticus) and snakeheads (Channa spp.)

税则号列 Tariff Item	商品名称及备注	进口税率 最惠	普通	暂定	出口退税	增值税率	计量单位	监管条件	Article Description
0304 9300.10	冻的花鳗鲡鱼肉(不论是否绞碎)	10	70		13	13	千克	ABE	Marbled eels, frozen, (whether or not minced)
0304 9300.20	冻的欧洲鳗鲡鱼肉(不论是否绞碎)	10	70		13	13	千克	ABEF	European eels, frozen, (whether or not minced)
0304 9300.90	冻的罗非鱼(口孵非鲫属)、鲶鱼((鱼芒)鲶属、鲶属、胡鲶属、真鮰属)、鲤科鱼(西鲤、黑鲫、草鱼、鲢属、鳙属、青鱼)、其他鳗鱼(鳗鲡属)、尼罗河鲈鱼(尼罗尖吻鲈)及黑鱼(鳢属)鱼肉(不论是否绞碎)	10	70		13	13	千克	AB	Meat of Tilapias (Oreochromis spp.) , catfish (Pangasius spp. , Silurus spp. , Clarias spp. , Ictalurus spp.) , carp (Cyprinus carpio, Carassius carassius , Ctenopharyngodon idellus , Hypophthalmichthys spp. , Cirrhinus spp. , Mylopharyngodon piceus) , eels (Anguilla spp.) , Nile perch (Lates niloticus) and snakeheads (Channa spp.), frozen (whether or not minced)
0304.9400	--狭鳕鱼	10	70		13	13	千克	AB	--Alaska Pollack (Theragra chalcogramma)
0304.9500	--犀鳕科、多丝真鳕科、鳕科、长尾鳕科、黑鳕科、无须鳕科、深海鳕科及南极鳕科鱼,狭鳕鱼除外	10	70		13	13	千克	AB	--Fish of the families Bregmacerotidae, Euclichthyidae, Gadidae, Macrouridae, Melanonidae , Merlucciidae, Moridae and Muraenolepididae, other than Alaska Pollack (Theragra chalcogramma)
0304.9900	--其他	10	70			13	千克		--Other
0304 9900.10	濒危鱼类其他冻鱼肉(不论是否绞碎)	10	70			13	千克	ABFE	Other meat of endangered fish, (whether or not minced) , frozen
0304 9900.90	其他冻鱼肉(不论是否绞碎)	10	70		13	13	千克	AB	Other fish meat, (whether or not minced) , frozen
03.05	**干、盐腌或盐渍的鱼;熏鱼,不论在熏制前或熏制过程中是否烹煮;适合供人食用的鱼的细粉、粗粉及团粒:**								**Fish dried, salted or in brine; smoked fish, whether or not cooked before or during the smoking process; flours,meals and pellets of fish, fit for human consumption:**
0305.1000	-适合供人食用的鱼的细粉、粗粉及团粒	10	80		13/15	13	千克	AB	-Flours, meals and pellets of fish, fit for human consumption
0305.2000	-干、熏、盐腌或盐渍的鱼肝及鱼卵	10	80			13	千克		-Livers and roes, dried, smoked, salted or in brine
0305 2000.10	干、熏、盐制的濒危鱼种肝、卵	10	80			13	千克	ABFE	Livers and roes of endangered fish, dried, smoked, salted or in brine
0305 2000.90	其他干、熏、盐制的鱼肝及鱼卵	10	80		13/15	13	千克	AB	Other Livers and roes of fish, dried, smoked, salted or in brine
	-干、盐腌或盐渍的鱼片,但熏制的除外:								-Fish fillets, dried, salted or in brine, but not smoked:
0305.3100	--罗非鱼(口孵非鲫属)、鲶鱼((鱼芒)鲶属、鲶属、胡鲶属、真鮰属)、鲤科鱼(西鲤、黑鲫、草鱼、鲢属、鳙属、青鱼)、鳗鱼(鳗鲡属)、尼罗河鲈鱼(尼罗尖吻鲈)及黑鱼(鳢属)	10	80		13/15	13	千克		--Tilapias (Oreochromis spp.) , catfish (Pangasius spp. , Silurus spp. , Clarias spp. , Ictalurus spp.) , carp (Cyprinus carpio, Carassius carassius , Ctenopharyngodon idellus , Hypophthalmichthys spp. , Cirrhinus spp. , Mylopharyngodon piceus) , eels (Anguilla spp.) , Nile perch (Lates niloticus) and snakeheads (Channa spp.)
0305 3100.10	干、盐腌或盐渍的花鳗鲡鱼片(熏制的除外)	10	80		13/15	13	千克	ABE	Marbled eels fillets, dried, salted or in brine, but not smoked
0305 3100.20	干、盐腌或盐渍的欧洲鳗鲡鱼片(熏制的除外)	10	80		13/15	13	千克	ABEF	European eels fillets, dried, salted or in brine, but not smoked
0305 3100.90	干、盐腌或盐渍的罗非鱼(口孵非鲫属)、鲶鱼((鱼芒)鲶属、鲶属、胡鲶属、真鮰属)、鲤科鱼(西鲤、黑鲫、草鱼、鲢属、鳙属、青鱼)、其他鳗鱼(鳗鲡属)、尼罗河鲈鱼(尼罗尖吻鲈)及黑鱼(鳢属)的鱼片(熏制的除外)	10	80		13/15	13	千克	AB	Tilapias (Oreochromis spp.) , catfish (Pangasius spp. , Silurus spp. , Clarias spp. , Ictalurus spp.) , carp (Cyprinus carpio, Carassius carassius , Ctenopharyngodon idellus , Hypophthalmichthys spp. , Cirrhinus spp. , Mylopharyngodon piceus) , eels (Anguilla spp.) , Nile perch (Lates niloticus) and snakeheads (Channa spp.), dried, salted or in brine, but not smoked
0305.3200	--犀鳕科、多丝真鳕科、鳕科、长尾鳕科、黑鳕科、无须鳕科、深海鳕科及南极鳕科鱼	10	80		13/15	13	千克	AB	--Fish of the families Bregmacerotidae, Euclichthyidae, Gadidae, Macrouridae, Melanonidae , Merlucciidae, Moridae and Muraenolepididae
0305.3900	--其他	10	80			13	千克		--Other
0305 3900.10	干、盐腌或盐渍的濒危鱼类的鱼片(熏制的除外)	10	80			13	千克	ABEF	Fillets of endangered fish, dried, salted or in brine, but not smoked
0305 3900.90	其他干、盐腌或盐渍的鱼片(熏制的除外)	10	80		13/15	13	千克	AB	Fish fillets, dried, salted or in brine, but not smoked

税则号列 Tariff Item	商品名称及备注	进口税率			出口退税	增值税率	计量单位	监管条件	Article Description
		最惠	普通	暂定					
	-熏鱼，包括鱼片，但食用杂碎除外:								-Smoked fish, including fillets, other than edible fish offal :
	--大麻哈鱼〔红大麻哈鱼、细磷大麻哈鱼、大麻哈鱼（种）、大鳞大麻哈鱼、银大麻哈鱼、马苏大麻哈鱼、玫瑰大麻哈鱼〕、大西洋鲑鱼及多瑙哲罗鱼:								--Pacific salmon（Oncorhynchus nerka, Oncorhynchus gorbuscha, Oncorhynchus keta, Oncorhynchus tschawytscha, Oncorhynchus kisutch, Oncorhynchus masou and Oncorhynchus rhodurus）, Atlantic salmon (Salmo salar) and Danube salmon (Hucho hucho) :
0305.4110	---大西洋鲑鱼	14	80		13	13	千克	AB	---Atlantic salmon
0305.4120	---大麻哈鱼及多瑙哲罗鱼	14	80		13	13	千克	AB	---Pacific salmon and Danube salmon
0305.4200	--鲱鱼（大西洋鲱鱼、太平洋鲱鱼）	16	80		13	13	千克	AB	--Herrings（*Clupea harengus, Clupea pallasii*）
0305.4300	--鳟鱼（河鳟、虹鳟、克拉克大麻哈鱼、阿瓜大麻哈鱼、吉雨大麻哈鱼、亚利桑那大麻哈鱼、金腹大麻哈鱼）	14	80		13	13	千克	AB	--Trout (Salmo trutta , Oncorhynchus mykiss , Oncorhynchus clarki , Oncorhynchus aguabonita , Oncorhynchus gilae , Oncorhynchus apache and Oncorhynchus chrysogaster)
0305.4400	--罗非鱼（口孵非鲫属）、鲶鱼（（鱼芒)鲶属、鲶属、胡鲶属、真鮰属）、鲤科鱼（西鲤、黑鲫、草鱼、鲢属、鲮属、青鱼）、鳗鱼（鳗鲡属）、尼罗河鲈鱼（尼罗尖吻鲈）及黑鱼（鳢属）	14	80		13	13	千克		--Tilapias (Oreochromis spp.) , catfish (Pangasius spp. , Silurus spp. , Clarias spp. , Ictalurus spp.) , carp (Cyprinus carpio, Carassius carassius , Ctenopharyngodon idellus , Hypophthalmichthys spp. , Cirrhinus spp. , Mylopharyngodon piceus) , Eels (Anguilla spp.) , Nile perch (Lates niloticus) and snakeheads (Channa spp.)
0305 4400.10	熏制花鳗鲡及鱼片(食用杂碎除外)	14	80		13	13	千克	ABE	Smoked marbled eels and its fillets， other than edible fish offal
0305 4400.20	熏制欧洲鳗鲡及鱼片(食用杂碎除外)	14	80		13	13	千克	ABEF	Smoked European eels and its fillets， other than edible fish offal
0305 4400.90	熏制罗非鱼（口孵非鲫属）、鲶鱼（（鱼芒）鲶属、鲶属、胡鲶属、真鮰属）、鲤科鱼（西鲤、黑鲫、草鱼、鲢属、鲮属、青鱼）、其他鳗鱼（鳗鲡属）、尼罗河鲈鱼（尼罗尖吻鲈）及黑鱼（鳢属）及鱼片(食用杂碎除外)	14	80		13	13	千克	AB	Smoked Tilapias (Oreochromis spp.) , catfish (Pangasius spp. , Silurus spp. , Clarias spp. , Ictalurus spp.) , carp (Cyprinus carpio, Carassius carassius , Ctenopharyngodon idellus , Hypophthalmichthys spp. , Cirrhinus spp. , Mylopharyngodon piceus) , Eels (Anguilla spp.) , Nile perch (Lates niloticus) and snakeheads (Channa spp.)， other than edible fish offal
0305.4900	--其他	14	80			13	千克		--Other
0305 4900.20	熏制其他濒危鱼及鱼片(食用杂碎除外)	14	80			13	千克	ABEF	Smoked endangered fish and its fillets， other than edible fish offal
0305 4900.90	其他熏鱼及鱼片(食用杂碎除外)	14	80		13	13	千克	AB	other smoked fish and its fillets， other than edible fish offal
	-干鱼（不包括食用杂碎），不论是否盐腌，但熏制的除外:								-Dried fish, other than edible fish offal, whether or not salted but not smoked :
0305.5100	--鳕鱼（大西洋鳕鱼、格陵兰鳕鱼、太平洋鳕鱼）	16	80		13	13	千克	AB	--Cod (Gadus morhua, Gadus macrocephalus, Gadus ogac)
	--其他:								--Other:
0305.5910	---海龙、海马	2	20		13	13	千克	FEAB	---Pipefish and hippocampi
0305.5990	---其他	16	80			13	千克		---Other
0305 5990.10	其他濒危干鱼，食用杂碎除外(不论是否盐腌,但熏制的除外)	16	80			13	千克	AFEB	Other endangered fish, dried,（whether or not salted but not smoked）
0305 5990.90	其他干鱼，食用杂碎除外(不论是否盐腌,但熏制的除外)	16	80		13	13	千克	AB	Other fish, dried,（whether or not salted but not smoked）
	-盐腌及盐渍的鱼（不包括食用杂碎），但干或熏制的除外:								-Fish, salted but not dried or smoked and fish in brine, other than edible fish offal :
0305.6100	--鲱鱼（大西洋鲱鱼、太平洋鲱鱼）	16	80		13	13	千克	AB	--Herrings（*Clupea harengus, Clupea pallasii*）
0305.6200	--鳕鱼（大西洋鳕鱼、格陵兰鳕鱼、太平洋鳕鱼）	16	80		13	13	千克	AB	--Cod（Gadus morhua, Gadus Macrocephalus, Gadus ogac）
0305.6300	--鳀鱼	16	80		13	13	千克	AB	--Anchovies（Engraulis spp.）

税则号列 Tariff Item	商品名称及备注	进口税率 最惠	普通	暂定	出口退税	增值税率	计量单位	监管条件	Article Description
0305.6400	--罗非鱼（口孵非鲫属）、鲶鱼（(鱼芒)鲶属、鲶属、胡鲶属、真鮰属）、鲤科鱼（西鲤、黑鲫、草鱼、鲢属、鳙属、青鱼）、鳗鱼（鳗鲡属）、尼罗河鲈鱼（尼罗尖吻鲈）及黑鱼（鳢属）	16	80		13	13	千克		--Tilapias (Oreochromis spp.) , catfish (Pangasius spp. , Silurus spp. , Clarias spp. , Ictalurus spp.) , carp (Cyprinus carpio, Carassius carassius , Ctenopharyngodon idellus , Hypophthalmichthys spp. , Cirrhinus spp. , Mylopharyngodon piceus) , Eels (Anguilla spp.) , Nile perch (Lates niloticus) and snakeheads (Channa spp.)
0305 6400.10	盐腌及盐渍的花鳗鲡，食用杂碎除外(干或熏制的除外)	16	80		13	13	千克	ABE	Marbled eels, salted or in brine, other than edible fish offal but not dried or smoked and fish in brine
0305 6400.20	盐腌及盐渍的欧洲鳗鲡，食用杂碎除外(干或熏制的除外)	16	80		13	13	千克	ABEF	European eels, salted or in brine, other than edible fish offal, but not dried or smoked and fish in brine
0305 6400.90	盐腌及盐渍的罗非鱼（口孵非鲫属）、鲶鱼（(鱼芒)鲶属、鲶属、胡鲶属、真鮰属）、鲤科鱼（西鲤、黑鲫、草鱼、鲢属、鳙属、青鱼）、其他鳗鱼（鳗鲡属）、尼罗河鲈鱼（尼罗尖吻鲈）及黑鱼（鳢属），食用杂碎除外(干或熏制的除外)	16	80		13	13	千克	AB	Tilapias (Oreochromis spp.) , salted or in brine, catfish (Pangasius spp. , Silurus spp. , Clarias spp. , Ictalurus spp.) , carp (Cyprinus carpio, Carassiuscarassius , Ctenopharyngodon idellus , Hypophthalmichthys spp. , Cirrhinus spp. , Mylopharyngodon piceus) , Eels (Anguilla spp.) , Nile perch (Lates niloticus) and snakeheads (Channa spp.), other than edible fish offal, but not dried or smoked and fish in brine
	--其他:								--Other:
0305.6910	---带鱼	16	80		13	13	千克	AB	---Scabber fish（*Trichurius*）
0305.6920	---黄鱼	16	80		13	13	千克	AB	---Yellow croaker（*Pseudosicaena*）
0305.6930	---鲳鱼	16	80		13	13	千克	AB	---Butterfish（*Pampus*）
0305.6990	---其他	16	80			13	千克		---Other
0305 6990.10	盐腌及盐渍的其他濒危鱼，食用杂碎除外(干或熏制的除外)	16	80			13	千克	ABFE	Other endangered fish, salted or in brine （but not dried nor smoked）
0305 6990.90	盐腌及盐渍的其他鱼，食用杂碎除外(干或熏制的除外)	16	80		13	13	千克	AB	Other fish, salted or in brine（but not dried nor smoked）
	-鱼鳍、鱼头、鱼尾、鱼鳔及其他可食用杂碎:								-Fish fins, heads, tails, maws and other edible fish offal :
0305.7100	--鲨鱼翅	15	80		13	13	千克		--Shark fins
0305 7100.10	濒危鲨鱼鱼翅(不论是否干制、盐腌、盐渍和熏制)	15	80		13	13	千克	ABEF	Endangered sharks' fins,whether or not dried, salted or in brine
0305 7100.90	其他鲨鱼鱼翅(不论是否干制、盐腌、盐渍和熏制)	15	80		13	13	千克	AB	Other Shark fins, whether or not dried, salted or in brine
0305.7200	--鱼头、鱼尾、鱼鳔	16	80			13	千克		--Fish heads, tails and maws
0305 7200.10	濒危鱼的鱼头、鱼尾、鱼鳔(不论是否干制、盐腌、盐渍和熏制)	16	80			13	千克	ABEF	Endangered Fish heads, tails and maws, whether or not dried, salted or in brine
0305 7200.90	其他鱼的鱼头、鱼尾、鱼鳔(不论是否干制、盐腌、盐渍和熏制)	16	80		13	13	千克	AB	Other Fish heads, tails and maws, whether or not dried, salted or in brine
0305.7900	--其他	16	80			13	千克		--Other
0305 7900.10	其他濒危可食用鱼杂碎(不论是否干制、盐腌、盐渍和熏制)	16	80			13	千克	ABEF	Other edible endangered fish offal, whether or not dried, salted or in brine
0305 7900.90	其他可食用鱼杂碎(不论是否干制、盐腌、盐渍和熏制)	16	80		13	13	千克	AB	Other edible fish offal, whether or not dried, salted or in brine
03.06	带壳或去壳的甲壳动物，活、鲜、冷、冻、干、盐腌或盐渍的；熏制的带壳或去壳甲壳动物，不论在熏制前或熏制过程中是否烹煮；蒸过或用水煮过的带壳甲壳动物，不论是否冷、冻、干、盐腌或盐渍的；适合供人食用的甲壳动物的细粉、粗粉及团粒:								**Crustaceans, whether in shell or not,live, fresh, chilled, frozen, dried, salted or in brine; smoked crustaceans, whether in shell or not, whether or not cooked before or during the smoking process; crustaceans, in shell, cooked by steaming or by boiling in water, whether or not chilled, frozen, dried, salted or in brine; flours, meals and pellets of crustaceans, fit for human consumption :**
	-冻的:								-Frozen:
0306.1100	--岩礁虾和其他龙虾（真龙虾属、龙虾属、岩龙虾属）	10	70		13	13	千克	AB	--Rock lobster and other sea crawfish (Palinurus spp., Panulirus spp., Jasus spp.)
0306.1200	--鳌龙虾（鳌龙虾属）	10	70		13	13	千克	AB	--Lobsters(Homarus spp.)
	--蟹:								--Crabs:
0306.1410	---梭子蟹	10	70		13	13	千克	AB	---Swimming crab

税则号列 Tariff Item	商品名称及备注	进口税率 最惠	普通	暂定	出口退税	增值税率	计量单位	监管条件	Article Description
0306.1490	---其他	10	70		13	13	千克	AB	---Other
0306.1500	--挪威海螯虾	16	70		13	13	千克	AB	--Norway lobsters (Nephrops norvegicus)
	--冷水小虾及对虾(长额虾属、褐虾):								--Cold-water shrimps and prawns (Pandalus spp. , Crangon crangon) :
	---冷水小虾:								---Cold-water shrimps :
0306.1611	----虾仁	8	70		13	13	千克	AB	----Shelled
0306.1612	----北方长额(虾仁除外)	5	70		13	13	千克	AB	---- Northem pandalus（*Pandalus*）excluding Shelled
0306.1619	----其他	5	70		13	13	千克	AB	----Other
	---冷水对虾:								---Cold-water prawns (Crangon crangon):
0306.1621	----虾仁	8	70		13	13	千克	AB	----Shelled
0306.1629	----其他	5	70		13	13	千克	AB	----Other
	--其他小虾及对虾:								--Other shrimps and prawns :
	---小虾:								---Shrimps :
0306.1711	----虾仁	8	70		13	13	千克	AB	---Shelled
0306.1719	----其他	5	70		13	13	千克	AB	----Other
	---对虾:								---Prawns:
0306.1721	----虾仁	8	70		13	13	千克	AB	----Shelled
0306.1729	----其他	5	70		13	13	千克	AB	----Other
	--其他,包括适合供人食用的甲壳动物的细粉、粗粉及团粒:								--Other, including flours, meals and pellets of crustaceans, fit for human consumption:
	---淡水小龙虾:								---Freshwater crawfish:
0306.1911	----虾仁	16	70		13	13	千克	AB	----Shelled
0306.1919	----其他	16	70		13	13	千克	AB	----Other
0306.1990	---其他	16	70		13	13	千克	AB	---Other
	-未冻的:								-Not frozen:
	--岩礁虾和其他龙虾（真龙虾属、龙虾属、岩龙虾属）:								--Rock lobster and other sea crawfish (Palinurus spp., Panulirus spp., Jasus spp.):
0306.2110	---种苗	0	0		13	13	千克	AB	---For cultivation
0306.2190	---其他	15	70		13	13	千克	AB	---Other
	--螯龙虾（螯龙虾属）:								--Lobsters (Homarus spp.) :
0306.2210	---种苗	0	0		13	13	千克	AB	---For cultivation
0306.2290	---其他	15	70		13	13	千克	AB	---Other
	--蟹:								--Crabs:
0306.2410	---种苗	0	0		13	13	千克	AB	---For cultivation
	---其他:								---Other:
0306.2491	----中华绒螯蟹	14	70		13	13	千克	AB	----Freshwater crabs, live
0306.2492	----梭子蟹	14	70		13	13	千克	AB	----Swimming crab
0306.2499	----其他	14	70		13	13	千克	AB	----Other
	--挪威海螯虾:								--Norway lobsters (Nephrops norvegicus):
0306.2510	---种苗	0	0		13	13	千克	AB	---For cultivation
0306.2590	---其他	14	70		13/15	13	千克	AB	---Other
	--冷水小虾及对虾(长额虾属、褐虾):								--Cold-water shrimps and prawns (Pandalus spp. , Crangon crangon):
0306.2610	---种苗	0	0		13	13	千克	AB	---For cultivation
0306.2620	---鲜、冷对虾	15	70		13	13	千克	AB	---Cold-water prawns, fresh or chilled
0306.2690	---其他	12	70		13	13	千克		---Other
0306 2690.01	鲜、冷的冷水小虾	12	70		13	13	千克	AB	Cold-water shrimps, fresh or chilled
0306 2690.90	其他活、干、盐腌或盐渍的带壳或去壳冷水对虾、冷水小虾(包括熏制的带壳或去壳的,不论在熏制前或熏制过程中是否烹煮;蒸过或用水煮过的带壳的)	12	70		13	13	千克	AB	Other cold-water shrimps and prawns, live, dried, salted or in brine, whether in shell or not (including smoked in shell or not, regardless of whether or not cooked smoked before or during the smoking process; steamed or boiled in shell)
	--其他小虾及对虾:								--Other shrimps and prawns:
0306.2710	---种苗	0	0		13	13	千克	AB	---For cultivation
0306.2720	---鲜、冷对虾	15	70		13	13	千克	AB	---Prawns, fresh or chilled
0306.2790	---其他	12	70		13	13	千克		---Other

税则号列 Tariff Item	商品名称及备注	进口税率 最惠	进口税率 普通	进口税率 暂定	出口退税	增值税率	计量单位	监管条件	Article Description
0306 2790.01	其他鲜、冷小虾	12	70		13	13	千克	AB	Other shrimps and prawns, fresh or chilled
0306 2790.90	其他活、干、盐腌或盐渍的带壳或去壳小虾及对虾(包括熏制的带壳或去壳的，不论在熏制前或熏制过程中是否烹煮；蒸过或用水煮过的带壳的)	12	70		13	13	千克	AB	Other shrimps and prawns, live, dried, salted or in brine, whether in shell or not (including smoked in shell or not, regardless of whether or not cooked smoked before or during the smoking process; steamed or boiled in shell)
	--其他，包括适合供人食用的甲壳动物的细粉、粗粉及团粒：								--Other, including flours, meals and pellets of crustaceans, fit for human consumption:
0306.2910	---种苗	0	0		13	13	千克	AB	---For cultivation
0306.2990	---其他	14	70		13/15	13	千克	AB	---Other
03.07	**带壳或去壳的软体动物，活、鲜、冷、冻、干、盐腌或盐渍的；熏制的带壳或去壳的软体动物，不论在熏制前或熏制过程中是否烹煮；适合供人食用的软体动物的细粉、粗粉及团粒：**								**Molluscs, whether in shell or not, live,fresh, chilled, frozen, dried, salted or in brine; smoked molluscs, whether in shell or not, whether or not cooked before or during the smoking process; flours, meals and pellets of molluscs, fit for human consumption :**
	-牡蛎（蚝）：								-Oysters:
	--活、鲜或冷的：								--Live, fresh or chilled :
0307.1110	---种苗	0	0		5	13	千克	AB	---For cultivation
0307.1190	---其他	14	70		5	13	千克	AB	---Other
0307.1900	--其他	14	70		5	13	千克	AB	--Other
	-扇贝，包括海扇：								-Scallops, including queen scallops, of the genera Pecten, Chlamys or Placopecten:
	--活、鲜或冷的：								--Live, fresh or chilled:
0307.2110	---种苗	0	0		5	13	千克		---For cultivation
0307 2110.10	大珠母贝种苗	0	0		5	13	千克	ABE	Pearl oysters（Pinctada maxima）, for cultivation
0307 2110.90	其他扇贝种苗（包括海扇种苗）	0	0		5	13	千克	AB	Other scallops, for cultivation,（including queen scallops）
0307.2190	---其他	14	70		5	13	千克		---Other
0307 2190.10	其他活、鲜、冷大珠母贝	14	70		5	13	千克	ABE	Other pearl oysters（Pinctada maxima）, live, fresh or chilled
0307 2190.90	其他活、鲜、冷扇贝(包括海扇，种苗除外)	14	70		5	13	千克	AB	Other scallops live, fresh or chilled,（including queen scallops not for cultivation）
0307.2900	--其他	14	80		13	13	千克		--Other
0307 2900.10	其他冻、干、盐腌或盐渍的大珠母贝(包括熏制的带壳或去壳的，不论在熏制前或熏制过程中是否烹煮)	14	80		13	13	千克	ABE	Other pearl oysters（Pinctada maxima）, frozen, dried, salted or in brine, smoked molluscs, whether in shell or not, whether or not cooked before or during the smoking process
0307 2900.90	其他冻、干、盐腌或盐渍的扇贝(包括海扇；包括熏制的带壳或去壳的，不论在熏制前或熏制过程中是否烹煮)	14	80		13	13	千克	AB	Other scallops, frozen, dried, salted or in brine（including queen scallops）, smoked molluscs, whether in shell or not, whether or not cooked before or during the smoking process
	-贻贝：								-Mussels（*Mytilus spp., Perna spp.*）:
	--活、鲜或冷的：								--Live, fresh or chilled:
0307.3110	---种苗	0	0		5	13	千克	AB	---For cultivation
0307.3190	---其他	14	70		5	13	千克		---Other
0307 3190.01	鲜、冷贻贝	14	70		5	13	千克	AB	Mussels, fresh or chilled
0307 3190.90	其他活贻贝	14	70		5	13	千克	AB	Other mussels, live
0307.3900	--其他	14	70		13	13	千克		--Other
0307 3900.01	冻贻贝	14	70		13	13	千克	AB	Mussels, frozen
0307 3900.90	其他干、盐腌或盐渍的贻贝(包括熏制的带壳或去壳的，不论在熏制前或熏制过程中是否烹煮)	14	70		13	13	千克	AB	Other mussels, dried, salted or in brine, smoked molluscs, whether in shell or not, whether or not cooked before or during the smoking process
	-墨鱼及鱿鱼：								-Cuttle fish（*Sepia of ficinalis, Rossia macrosoma, Sepiola spp.*）and squid（*Ommastrephes spp., Loligo spp., Nototodarus spp., Sepioteuthis spp.*）:
	--活、鲜或冷的：								--Live, fresh or chilled:

税则号列 Tariff Item	商品名称及备注	进口税率			出口退税	增值税率	计量单位	监管条件	Article Description
		最惠	普通	暂定					
0307.4110	---种苗	0	0		5	13	千克	AB	---For cultivation
0307.4190	---其他	12	70		5	13	千克	AB	---Other
0307.4900	--其他	12	70		13	13	千克	AB	--Other
	-章鱼:								-Octopus（*Octopus spp.*）:
0307.5100	--活、鲜或冷的	17	70		5	13	千克	AB	--Live, fresh or chilled
0307.5900	--其他	17	70		13	13	千克	AB	--Other
	-蜗牛及螺，海螺除外:								-Snails, other than sea snails:
0307.6010	---种苗	0	0			13	千克		---For cultivation
0307 6010.10	濒危蜗牛及螺种苗，海螺除外	0	0			13	千克	ABFE	Endangered snails, for cultivation (other than sea snails)
0307 6010.90	其他蜗牛及螺种苗，海螺除外	0	0		5	13	千克	AB	Other snails, for cultivation (other than sea snails)
0307.6090	---其他	14	70			13	千克		---Other
0307 6090.10	其他濒危蜗牛及螺，海螺除外	14	70			13	千克	ABFE	Other endangered snails, for cultivation (other than sea snails)
0307 6090.90	其他活、鲜、冷、冻、干、盐腌或盐渍的蜗牛及螺，海螺除外(包括熏制的带壳或去壳的，不论在熏制前或熏制过程中是否烹煮)	14	70		5	13	千克	AB	Other snails (other than sea snails), live,fresh, chilled, frozen, dried, salted or in brine, smoked molluscs, whether in shell or not, whether or not cooked before or during the smoking process
	-蛤、乌蛤及舟贝(蚶科、北极蛤科、乌蛤科、斧蛤科、缝栖蛤科、蛤蜊科、中带蛤科、海螂科、双带蛤科、截蛏科、竹蛏科、砗磲科、帘蛤科):								-Clams, cockles and arkshells (families Arcidae, Arcticidae, Cardiidae, Donacidae, Hiatellidae, Mactridae, Mesodesmatidae, Myidae, Semelidae, Solecurtidae, Solenidae, Tridacnidae and Veneridae) :
	--活、鲜或冷的:								--Live, fresh or chilled :
0307.7110	---种苗	0	0		5	13	千克		---For cultivation
0307 7110.10	活、鲜、冷砗磲的种苗	0	0		5	13	千克	ABEF	Tridacnidae for cultivation, live, fresh or chilled
0307 7110.90	活、鲜、冷蛤、乌蛤及舟贝（蚶科、北极蛤科、乌蛤科、斧蛤科、缝栖蛤科、蛤蜊科中带蛤科、海螂科、双带蛤科、截蛏科、竹蛏科、帘蛤科）的种苗	0	0		5	13	千克	AB	Clams, cockles and ark shells (families Arcidae, Arcticidae, Cardiidae,Donacidae, Hiatellidae, Mactridae, Mesodesmatidae, Myidae, Semelidae, Solecurtidae, Solenidae, Tridacnidae and Veneridae) for cultivation , live, fresh or chilled
	---其他:								---Other :
0307.7191	----蛤	14	70		5	13	千克	AB	----Clams
0307.7199	----其他	14	70		5	13	千克		----Other
0307 7199.10	活、鲜、冷砗磲	14	70		5	13	千克	ABEF	Tridacnidae, live, fresh or chilled
0307 7199.90	活、鲜、冷乌蛤及舟贝（蚶科、北极蛤科、乌蛤科、斧蛤科、缝栖蛤科、蛤蜊科中带蛤科、海螂科、双带蛤科、截蛏科、竹蛏科、帘蛤科）	14	70		5	13	千克	AB	Clams, cockles and ark shells (families Arcidae, Arcticidae, Cardiidae, Donacidae, Hiatellidae, Mactridae, Mesodesmatidae, Myidae, Semelidae, Solecurtidae, Solenidae, Tridacnidae and Veneridae), live, fresh or chilled
	--其他:								--Other :
0307.7910	---蛤	10	70		13	13	千克	AB	---Clams
0307.7990	---其他	10	70		13/15	13	千克		---Other
0307 7990.10	冻、干、盐制砗磲（包括熏制的带壳或去壳的，不论在熏制前或熏制过程中是否烹煮）	10	70		13/15	13	千克	ABEF	Tridacniae, frozen, dried, salted or in brine (including shell or smoked, regardless of whether or not cooked smoked before or during the smoking process)
0307 7990.90	冻、干、盐制乌蛤及舟贝（蚶科、北极蛤科、乌蛤科、斧蛤科、缝栖蛤科、蛤蜊科、中带蛤科、海螂科、双带蛤科、截蛏科、竹蛏科、帘蛤科）（包括熏制的带壳或去壳的，不论在熏制前或熏制过程中是否烹煮）	10	70		13/15	13	千克	AB	Clams, cockles and ark shells (families Arcidae, Arcticidae, Cardiidae, Donacidae, Hiatellidae, Mactridae, Mesodesmatidae, Myidae, Semelidae, Solecurtidae, Solenidae, Tridacnidae and Veneridae), frozen, dried, salted or in brine whether in shell or not, whether or not cooked before or during the smoking process
	-鲍鱼（鲍属）:								-Abalone (Haliotis spp.) :
	--活、鲜或冷的:								--Live, fresh or chilled :
0307.8110	---种苗	0	0		5	13	千克	AB	---For cultivation
0307.8190	---其他	14	80		5	13	千克	AB	---Other
0307.8900	--其他	10	80		13	13	千克	AB	--Other

税则号列 Tariff Item	商品名称及备注	进口税率			出口退税	增值税率	计量单位	监管条件	Article Description
		最惠	普通	暂定					
	-其他，包括适合供人食用的细粉、粗粉及团粒:								-Other, including flours, meals and pellets, fit for human consumption:
	--活、鲜或冷的:								--Live, fresh or chilled:
0307.9110	---种苗	0	0			13	千克		---For cultivation
0307 9110.10	活、鲜、冷的濒危软体动物的种苗	0	0			13	千克	AFEB	Endangered molluscs, for cultivation（other than crustaceans, for cultivation）,live, fresh or chilled
0307 9110.90	其他活、鲜、冷的软体动物的种苗	0	0		5	13	千克	AB	Other molluscs, for cultivation（other than crustaceans, for cultivation）,live, fresh or chilled
0307.9190	---其他	14	70			13	千克		---Other
0307 9190.10	其他活、鲜、冷的濒危软体动物	14	70			13	千克	ABEF	Other endangered molluscs, live, fresh or chilled
0307 9190.90	其他活、鲜、冷的软体动物	14	70		5	13	千克	AB	Other molluscs, live, fresh or chilled
0307.9900	--其他	10	70			13	千克		--Other
0307 9900.10	其他冻、干、盐腌或盐渍的濒危软体动物(包括供人食用的软体动物粉、团粒,甲壳动物除外;包括熏制的带壳或去壳的,不论在熏制前或熏制过程中是否烹煮)	10	70			13	千克	ABEF	Other endangered molluscs, frozen, dried, salted or in brine, whether in shell or not, whether or not cooked before or during the smoking process; flours, meals and pellets of molluscs, fit for human consumption, other than crustaceans
0307 9900.90	其他冻、干、盐腌或盐渍软体动物(包括供人食用的软体动物粉、团粒,甲壳动物除外;包括熏制的带壳或去壳的,不论在熏制前或熏制过程中是否烹煮)	10	70		13/15	13	千克	AB	Other molluscs, frozen, dried, salted or in brine，whether in shell or not, whether or not cooked before or during the smoking process; flours, meals and pellets of molluscs, fit for human consumption, other than crustaceans
03.08	**不属于甲壳动物及软体动物的水生无脊椎动物，活、鲜、冷、冻、干、盐腌或盐渍的；熏制的不属于甲壳动物及软体动物的水生无脊椎动物，不论在熏制前或熏制过程中是否烹煮；适合供人食用的不属于甲壳动物及软体动物的水生无脊椎动物的细粉、粗粉及团粒:**								**Aquatic invertebrates other than crustaceans and molluscs, live, fresh, chilled, frozen, dried, salted or in brine; smoked aquatic invertebrates other than crustaceans and molluscs, whether or not cooked before or during the smoking process; flours, meals and pellets of aquatic invertebrates other than crustaceans and molluscs, fit for human consumption :**
	-海参（仿刺参、海参纲）:								-Sea cucumbers (Stichopus japonicus, Holothurioidea):
	--活、鲜或冷的:								--Live, fresh or chilled :
0308.1110	---种苗	0	0		5	13	千克		---For cultivation
0308 1110.10	活、鲜或冷的暗色刺参的种苗	0	0		5	13	千克	ABEF	Isostichopus fuscus for cultivation, live, fresh or chilled
0308 1110.90	活、鲜或冷的其他海参(仿刺参、海参纲)的种苗	0	0		5	13	千克	AB	Other sea cucumbers (Stichopus japonicus, Holothurioidea) for cultivation，live, fresh or chilled
0308.1190	---其他	14	70		5	13	千克		---Other
0308 1190.10	活、鲜或冷的暗色刺参	14	70		5	13	千克	ABEF	Isostichopus fuscus, live, fresh or chilled
0308 1190.90	活、鲜或冷的其他海参(仿刺参、海参纲)	14	70		5	13	千克	AB	Other sea cucumbers (Stichopus japonicus, Holothurioidea)，live, fresh or chilled
0308.1900	--其他	10	80		13	13	千克		--Other
0308 1900.10	其他冻、干、盐腌或盐渍暗色刺参（包括熏制的，不论在熏制前或熏制过程中是否烹煮；适合供人食用的细粉、粗粉及团粒）	10	80		13	13	千克	ABEF	Other Isostichopus fuscus, frozen, dried, salted or in brine(including smoked, regardless of whether or not cooked smoked before or during the smoking process; flours, meals and pellets suitable for human consumption)
0308 1900.90	其他冻、干、盐腌或盐渍的海参（仿刺参、海参纲）(包括熏制的，不论在熏制前或熏制过程中是否烹煮；适合供人食用的细粉、粗粉及团粒)	10	80		13	13	千克	AB	Other sea cucumbers (Stichopus japonicus, Holothurioidea), frozen, dried, salted or in brine (including smoked, regardless of whether or not cooked smoked before or during the smoking process; flours, meals and pellets suitable for human consumption)
	-海胆(球海胆属、拟球海胆、智利海胆、食用正海胆):								-Sea urchins (Strongylocentrotus spp. , Paracentrotus lividus, Loxechinus albus, Echichinus esculentus):
	--活、鲜或冷的:								--Live, fresh or chilled :
0308.2110	---种苗	0	0		5	13	千克	AB	---For cultivation
0308.2190	---其他	14	70		5	13	千克	AB	---Other

税则号列 Tariff Item	商品名称及备注	进口税率			出口退税	增值税率	计量单位	监管条件	Article Description
		最惠	普通	暂定					
0308.2900	--其他	10	70		13/15	13	千克	AB	--Other
	-海蜇(海蜇属):								-Jellyfish (Rhopilema spp.):
	---活、鲜或冷的:								---Live, fresh or chilled :
0308.3011	----种苗	0	0		5	13	千克	AB	----For cultivation
0308.3019	----其他	14	70		5	13	千克	AB	----Other
0308.3090	---其他	10	70		13/15	13	千克	AB	---Other
	-其他:								-Other :
	---活、鲜或冷的:								---Live, fresh or chilled :
0308.9011	----种苗	0	0			13	千克		----For cultivation
0308 9011.10	活、鲜或冷的其他濒危水生无脊椎动物的种苗(甲壳动物及软体动物除外)	0	0			13	千克	ABFE	Endangered Aquatic invertebrates for cultivation,live, fresh or chilled, other than crustaceans and molluscs
0308 9011.90	活、鲜或冷的其他水生无脊椎动物的种苗(甲壳动物及软体动物除外)	0	0		5	13	千克	AB	Other Aquatic invertebrates for cultivation,live, fresh or chilled, other than crustaceans and molluscs
0308.9012	----沙蚕，种苗除外	14	70		5	13	千克	AB	----Clamworm, other than those for cultivation
0308.9019	----其他	14	70			13	千克		----Other
0308 9019.10	活、鲜或冷的其他濒危水生无脊椎动物(甲壳动物及软体动物除外)	14	70			13	千克	ABFE	Other endangered Aquatic invertebrates,live, fresh or chilled, other than crustaceans and molluscs
0308 9019.90	活、鲜或冷的其他水生无脊椎动物(甲壳动物及软体动物除外)	14	70		5	13	千克	AB	Other Aquatic invertebrates,live, fresh or chilled, other than crustaceans and molluscs
0308.9090	---其他	10	70			13	千克		---Other
0308 9090.10	其他冻、干、盐制濒危水生无脊椎动物，包括供人食用的水生无脊椎动物粉、团粒（甲壳动物及软体动物除外；包括熏制的，不论在熏制前或熏制过程中是否烹煮；适合供人食用的细粉、粗粉及团粒）	10	70			13	千克	ABFE	Other endangered Aquatic invertebrates, frozen, dried, salted or in brine，including flours, meals and pellets of aquatic invertebrates for human consumption(other than crustaceans and molluscs; including smoked, regardless of whether or not cooked smoked before or during the smoking process; flours, meals and pellets suitable for human consumption)
0308 9090.90	其他冻、干、盐制水生无脊椎动物，包括供人食用的水生无脊椎动物粉、团粒（甲壳动物及软体动物除外；包括熏制的，不论在熏制前或熏制过程中是否烹煮；适合供人食用的细粉、粗粉及团粒）	10	70		13/15	13	千克	AB	Other Aquatic invertebrates, frozen, dried, salted or in brine，including flours, meals and pellets of aquatic invertebrates for human consumption(other than crustaceans and molluscs; including smoked, regardless of whether or not cooked smoked before or during the smoking process; flours, meals and pellets suitable for human consumption)

第四章
乳品；蛋品；天然蜂蜜；其他食用动物产品

注释：

一、所称"乳"，是指全脂乳及半脱脂或全脱脂的乳。

二、品目 04.05 所称：

（一）"黄油"，仅指从乳中提取的天然黄油、乳清黄油及调制黄油（新鲜、加盐或酸败的，包括罐装黄油），按重量计乳脂含量在 80%及以上，但不超过 95%，乳的无脂固形物最大含量不超过 2%，以及水的最大含量不超过 16%。黄油中不含添加的乳化剂，但可含有氯化钠、食用色素、中和盐及无害乳酸菌的培养物。

（二）"乳酱"是一种油包水型可涂抹的乳状物，乳脂是该制品所含的唯一脂肪，按重量计其含量在 39%及以上，但小于 80%。

三、乳清经浓缩并加入乳或乳脂制成的产品，若同时具有下列三种特性，则视为乳酪归入品目 04.06：

（一）按干重计乳脂含量在 5%及以上的；

（二）按重量计干质成分至少为 70%，但不超过 85%的；以及

（三）已成型或可以成型的。

四、本章不包括：

（一）按重量计乳糖含量（以干燥无水乳糖计）超过 95%的乳清制品（品目 17.02）；或

（二）白蛋白（包括按重量计干质成分的乳清蛋白含量超过 80%的两种或两种以上的乳清蛋白浓缩物）（品目 35.02）及球蛋白（品目 35.04）。

子目注释：

一、子目 0404.10 所称"改性乳清"，是指由乳清成分构成的制品，即全部或部分去除乳糖、蛋白或矿物质的乳清、加入天然乳清成分的乳清及由混入天然乳清成分制成的产品。

二、子目0405.10所称"黄油"，不包括脱水黄油及印度酥油（子目0405.90）。

Chapter 4
Dairy products; birds' eggs; natural honey; edible products of animal origin, not elsewhere specified or included

Chapter Notes:

1.The expression "milk" means full cream milk or partially or completely skimmed milk.

2.For the purposes of heading 04.05:

（a）The term "butter" means natural butter, whey butter or recombined butter（fresh, salted or rancid, including canned butter）derived exclusively from milk, with a milkfat content of 80% or more but not more than 95% by weight, a maximum milk solids-not-fat content of 2% by weight and a maximum water content of 16% by weight. Butter does not contain added emulsifiers, but may contain sodium chloride, food colours, neutralising salts and cultures of harmless lactic-acid-producing bacteria.

（b）The expression "dairy spreads" means a spreadable emulsion of the water-in-oil type, containing milkfat as the only fat in the product, with a milkfat content of 39% or more but less than 80% by weight.

3.Products obtained by the concentration of whey and with the addition of milk or milkfat are to be classified as cheese in heading 04.06 provided that they have the three following characteristics:

（a）A milkfat content, by weight of the dry matter, of 5% or more;

（b）A dry matter content, by weight, of at least 70% but not exceeding 85%; and

（c）They are moulded or capable of being moulded.

4.This Chapter does not cover:

（a）Products obtained from whey, containing by weight more than 95% lactose, expressed as anhydrous lactose, calculated on the dry matter（heading 17.02）; or

（b）Albumins（including concentrates of two or more whey proteins, containing by weight more than 80% whey proteins, calculated on the dry matter）（heading 35.02）or globulins （heading 35.04）.

Subheading Notes:

1. For the purposes of subheading 0404.10, the expression "modified whey" means products consisting of whey constituents, that is, whey from which all or part of the lactose, proteins or minerals have been removed, whey to which natural whey constituents have been added, and products obtained by mixing natural whey constituents.

2. For the purposes of subheading 0405.10 the term "butter" does not include dehydrated butter or ghee（subheading 0405.90）

税则号列 Tariff Item	商品名称及备注	进口税率			出口退税	增值税率	计量单位	监管条件	Article Description
		最惠	普通	暂定					
04.01	未浓缩及未加糖或其他甜物质的乳及奶油：								**Milk and cream, not concentrated nor containing added sugar or other sweetening matter:**
0401.1000	-按重量计脂肪含量不超过 1%	15	40		5/15	17	千克	7AB	-Of a fat content, by weight, not exceeding 1%
0401.2000	-按重量计脂肪含量超过 1%，但不超过 6%	15	40		5/15	17	千克	7AB	-Of a fat content, by weight, exceeding 1% but not exceeding 6%
0401.4000	-按重量计脂肪含量超过 6%，但不超过 10%	15	40		5/15	17	千克	7AB	-Of a fat contect, by weight, exceeding 6% but not exceeding 10%

税则号列 Tariff Item	商品名称及备注	进口税率 最惠	普通	暂定	出口退税	增值税率	计量单位	监管条件	Article Description
0401.5000	-按重量计脂肪含量超过10%"	15	40		5/15	17	千克	7AB	-Of a fat contect, by weight, exceeding 10%
04.02	**浓缩、加糖或其他甜物质的乳及奶油：**								**Milk and cream, concentrated or containing added sugar or other sweetening matter:**
0402.1000	-粉状、粒状或其他固体形状，按重量计脂肪含量不超过1.5%	10	40		15	17	千克	7AB	-In powder, granules or other solid forms, of a fat content, by weight, not exceeding 1.5%
	-粉状、粒状或其他固体形状，按重量计脂肪含量超过1.5%:								-In powder, granules or other solid forms, of a fat content, by weight, exceeding1.5%:
0402.2100	----未加糖或其他甜物质	10	40		15	17	千克	7AB	--Not containing added sugar or other sweetening matter
0402.2900	--其他	10	40		15	17	千克	7AB	--Other
	-其他:								-Other:
0402.9100	--未加糖或其他甜物质	10	90		5/15	17	千克	AB	--Not containing added sugar or other sweetening matter
0402.9900	--其他	10	90		5/15	17	千克	AB	--Other
04.03	**酪乳、结块的乳及奶油、酸乳、酸乳酒及其他发酵或酸化的乳和奶油，不论是否浓缩、加糖、加其他甜物质、加香料、加水果、加坚果或加可可：**								**Buttermilk, curdled milk and cream, yogurt, kephir and other fermented or acidified milk and cream, whether or not concentrated or containing added sugar or other sweetening matter or flavoured or containing added fruit, nuts or cocoa:**
0403.1000	-酸乳	10	90		15	17	千克	AB	-Yogurt
0403.9000	-其他	20	90		15	17	千克	AB	-Other
04.04	**乳清，不论是否浓缩、加糖或其他甜物质；其他品目未列名的含天然乳的产品，不论是否加糖或其他甜物质：**								**Whey, whether or not concentrated or containing added sugar or other sweetening matter; products consisting of natural milk constituents, whether or not containing added sugar or other sweetening matter, not elsewhere specified or included:**
0404.1000暂	-乳清及改性乳清，不论是否浓缩、加糖或其他甜物质	6	30	2	15	17	千克	AB	-Whey and modified whey, whether or not concentrated or containing added sugar or other sweetening matter
0404.9000	-其他	20	90		15	17	千克	AB	-Other
04.05	**黄油及其他从乳中提取的脂和油；乳酱：**								**Butter and other fats and oils derived from milk; dairy spreads:**
0405.1000	-黄油	10	90		15	17	千克	AB	-Butter
0405.2000	-乳酱	10	90		15	17	千克	AB	-Dairy spreads
0405.9000	-其他	10	90		15	17	千克	AB	-Other
04.06	**乳酪及凝乳：**								**Cheese and curd:**
0406.1000	-鲜乳酪(未熟化或未固化的)，包括乳清乳酪；凝乳	12	90		15	17	千克	AB	-Fresh（unripened or uncured）cheese, including whey cheese, and curd
0406.2000	-各种磨碎或粉化的乳酪	12	90		15	17	千克	AB	-Grated or powdered cheese, of all kinds
0406.3000	-经加工的乳酪，但磨碎或粉化的除外	12	90		15	17	千克	AB	-Processed cheese, not grated or powdered
0406.4000	-蓝纹乳酪和娄地青霉生产的带有纹理的其他乳酪	15	90		15	17	千克	AB	-Blue-veined cheese and other cheese containing veins produced by penicillium roqueforti
0406.9000	-其他乳酪	12	90		15	17	千克	AB	-Other cheese
04.07	**带壳禽蛋，鲜、腌制或煮过的：**								**Birds' eggs, in shell, fresh, preserved or cooked:**
	-孵化用受精禽蛋:								-Fertilised eggs for incubation :
0407.1100	--鸡的	0	0			13	千克/个		--Of fowls of the species Gallus domesticus
0407 1100.10	孵化用受精的濒危鸡的蛋	0	0			13	千克/个	AFEB	Fertilised endangered eggs for incubation
0407 1100.90	孵化用受精的其他鸡的蛋	0	0		5	13	千克/个	AB	Fertilised other eggs for incubation
0407.1900	--其他	0	0			13	千克/个		--Other
0407 1900.10	其他孵化用受精濒危禽蛋	0	0			13	千克/个	AFEB	Other fertilised endangered eggs for incubation
0407 1900.90	其他孵化用受精禽蛋	0	0		5	13	千克/个	AB	Other fertilized eggs for incubation
	-其他鲜蛋:								-Other fresh eggs :
0407.2100	--鸡的	20	80		5	13	千克/个	AB	--Of fowls of the species Gallus domesticus
0407.2900	--其他	20	80			13	千克/个		--Other
0407 2900.10	其他鲜的带壳濒危禽蛋	20	80			13	千克/个	ABFE	Other endangered fresh eggs, in shell
0407 2900.90	其他鲜的带壳禽蛋	20	80		5	13	千克/个	AB	Other fresh eggs, in shell

税则号列 Tariff Item	商品名称及备注	进口税率 最惠	普通	暂定	出口退税	增值税率	计量单位	监管条件	Article Description
	-其他:								-Other :
0407.9010	---咸蛋	20	90		5	13	千克/个	AB	---Salted eggs
0407.9020	---皮蛋	20	90		5	13	千克/个	AB	---Lime-preserved eggs
0407.9090	---其他	20	90			13	千克/个		---Other
0407 9090.10	其他腌制或煮过的带壳濒危野鸟蛋	20	90			13	千克/个	ABFE	Other endangered wild bird egg, in shell, preserved or cooked
0407 9090.90	其他腌制或煮过的带壳禽蛋	20	90		5/15	13	千克/个	AB	Other bird egg, in shell, preserved or cooked
04.08	**去壳禽蛋及蛋黄，鲜、干、冻、蒸过或水煮、制成型或用其他方法保藏的，不论是否加糖或其他甜物质：**								**Birds' eggs, not in shell, and egg yolks, fresh, dried, cooked by steaming or by boiling in water, moulded, frozen or otherwise preserved, whether or not containing added sugar or other sweetening matter:**
	-蛋黄:								-Egg yolks:
0408.1100	--干的	20	90		5/15	13	千克	AB	--Dried
0408.1900	--其他	20	90		5	13	千克	AB	--Other
	-其他:								-Other:
0408.9100	--干的	20	90		5/15	13	千克	AB	--Dried
0408.9900	--其他	20	90		5/15	13	千克	AB	--Other
04.09	**天然蜂蜜：**								**Natural honey:**
0409.0000	天然蜂蜜	15	80		5	13	千克	AB	Natural honey
04.10	**其他品目未列名的食用动物产品：**								**Edible products of animal origin, not elsewhere specified or included:**
0410.0010	---燕窝	25	80		5	17	千克	AB	---Salanganes' nests
	---蜂产品:								---Bee products:
0410.0041	----鲜蜂王浆	15	70		5	13	千克	AB	----Pure royal jelley
0410.0042	----鲜蜂王浆粉	15	70		5	17	千克	AB	----Pure royal jelley, in powder
0410.0043	----蜂花粉	20	70		5	17	千克	AB	----Bee pollen
0410.0049	----其他	20	70		5	17	千克	AB	----Other
0410.0090	---其他	20	70			17	千克		---Other
0410 0090.10	其他税号未列名濒危野生动物产品（食用）	20	70			17	千克	ABFE	Other edible products of endangered wild animal origin, not elsewhere specified or included
0410 0090.90	其他税号未列名的食用动物产品	20	70		5	17	千克	AB	Other edible products of animal origin, not elsewhere specified or included

第五章
其他动物产品

Chapter 5
Products of animal origin, not elsewhere specified or included

注释：

一、本章不包括：

（一）食用产品（整个或切块的动物肠、膀胱和胃以及液态或干制的动物血除外）；

（二）生皮或毛皮（第四十一章、第四十三章），但品目05.05的货品及品目05.11的生皮或毛皮的边角废料仍归入本章；

（三）马毛及废马毛以外的动物纺织原料（第十一类）；或

（四）供制帚、制刷用的成束、成簇的材料（品目96.03）。

二、仅按长度而未按发根和发梢整理的人发，视为未加工品，归入品目05.01。

三、本税则所称"兽牙"，是指象、河马、海象、一角鲸和野猪的长牙、犀角及其他动物的牙齿。

四、本税则所称"马毛"，是指马科、牛科动物的鬃毛和尾毛。

Chapter Notes:

1. This Chapter does not cover:

(a) Edible products (other than guts, bladders and stomachs of animals, whole and pieces thereof, and animal blood, liquid or dried);

(b) Hides or skins (including furskins) other than goods of heading 05.05 and parings and similar waste of raw hides or skins of heading 05.11 (Chapter 41 or 43);

(c) Animal textile materials, other than horsehair and horsehair waste (Section XI); or

(d) Prepared knots or tufts for broom or brush making (heading 96.03).

2. For the purposes of heading 05.01, the sorting of hair by length (provided the root ends and tip ends respectively are not arranged together) shall be deemed not to constitute working.

3. Throughout the Nomenclature, elephant, hippopotamus, walrus, narwhal and wild boar tusks, rhinoceros horns and the teeth of all animals are regarded as "ivory".

4. Throughout the Nomenclature, the expression "horse-hair" means hair of the manes or tails of equine or bovine animals.

税则号列 Tariff Item	商品名称及备注	进口税率 最惠	普通	暂定	出口退税	增值税率	计量单位	监管条件	Article Description
05.01	**未经加工的人发，不论是否洗涤；废人发：**								**Human hair, unworked, whether or not washed or scoured; waste of human hair:**
0501.0000	未经加工的人发，不论是否洗涤；废人发	15	90		15	17	千克	9B	Human hair, unworked, whether or not washed or scoured; waste of human hair
05.02	**猪鬃、猪毛；獾毛及其他制刷用兽毛；上述鬃毛的废料：**								**Pigs', hogs' or boars' bristles and hair; badger hair and other brush making hair; waste of such bristles or hair:**
	-猪鬃、猪毛及其废料：								-Pigs', hogs' or boars' bristles and hair and waste thereof:
0502.1010	---猪鬃	20	90		5/15	13	千克	AB	---Bristles
0502.1020	---猪毛	20	90		5/15	13	千克	AB	---Hair
0502.1030	---废料	20	90		5	13	千克	9B	---Waste
	-其他：								-Other:
	---獾毛及其他制刷用兽毛：								---Badger hair and other brush making hair:
0502.9011	----山羊毛	20	90		5/15	13	千克	AB	----Goat hair
0502.9012	----黄鼠狼尾毛	20	90		5/15	13	千克	ABEF	----Weasel tail hair
0502.9019	----其他	20	90			13	千克		----Other
0502 9019.10	濒危獾毛及其他制刷用濒危兽毛	20	90			13	千克	ABFE	Endangered badger hair and other endangered animal's brush making hair
0502 9019.90	其他獾毛及其他制刷用兽毛	20	90		5/15	13	千克	AB	Other badger hair and other brush making hair
0502.9020	---废料	20	90			13	千克		---Waste
0502 9020.10	濒危獾毛及其他制刷濒危兽毛废料	20	90			13	千克	BEF	Waste of endangered badger hair and other endangered animal's brush making hair
0502 9020.90	其他獾毛及其他制刷用兽毛的废料	20	90		5	13	千克	9B	Waste of other badger hair and other brush making hair
05.04	**整个或切块的动物（鱼除外）的肠、膀胱及胃，鲜、冷、冻、干、熏、盐腌或盐渍的：**								**Guts, bladders and stomachs of animals (other than fish ,whole and pieces thereof,fresh, chilled,frozen,salted,in brine,dried or smoked:**

税则号列 Tariff Item	商品名称及备注	进口税率 最惠	进口税率 普通	进口税率 暂定	出口退税	增值税率	计量单位	监管条件	Article Description
	---肠衣:								---Casings:
0504.0011	——盐渍猪肠衣(猪大肠头除外)	20	90		13	13	千克	AB	----Hog casings, salted（excluding hog fat-ends）
0504.0012	----盐渍绵羊肠衣	18	90		13	13	千克	AB	----Sheep casings, salted
0504.0013	----盐渍山羊肠衣	18	90		13	13	千克	AB	----Goat casings, salted
0504.0014	----盐渍猪大肠头	20	90		13	13	千克	AB	----Hog fat-ends, salted
0504.0019	----其他	18	90		13	13	千克	AB	----Other
	---胃:								----Gizzard:
0504.0021	----冷、冻的鸡胗	1.3元/kg	7.7元/kg		5	13	千克	7AB	----Cold, frozen gizzard
0504.0029	----其他	20	90		5	13	千克	AB	----Other
0504.0090	----其他	20	80		5	13	千克	AB	---Other
05.05	**带有羽毛或羽绒的鸟皮及鸟体其他部分；羽毛及不完整羽毛（不论是否修边）、羽绒，仅经洗涤、消毒或为了保藏而作过处理，但未经进一步加工；羽毛或不完整羽毛的粉末及废料**								**Skins and other parts of birds, with their feathers or down; feathers and parts of feathers Whether or not with trimmed edges and down, not further worked than cleaned, disinfected or treated for preservation; powder and waste of feathers or parts of feathers:**
0505.1000[暂]	-填充用羽毛；羽绒	10	100	5		13	千克		-Feathers of a kind used for stuffing; down
0505 1000.10[暂]	填充用濒危野生禽类羽毛、羽绒(仅经洗涤、消毒等处理，未进一步加工)	10	100	5		13	千克	ABFE	Feathers or down of endangered wild birds, of a kind used for stuffing（not further worked than cleaned, disinfected or treated for preservation）
0505 1000.90[暂]	其他填充用羽毛；羽绒(仅经洗涤、消毒等处理，未进一步加工)	10	100	5	5/15	13	千克	AB	Feathers of a kind used for stuffing; down (not further worked than cleaned, disinfected or treated for preservation)
	-其他:								-Other:
0505.9010	---羽毛或不完整羽毛的粉末及废料	10	35		5	13	千克	9AB	---Powder and waste of feathers or parts of feathers
0505.9090	---其他	10	90			13	千克		---Other
0505 9090.10	其他濒危野生禽类羽毛、羽绒(包括带有羽毛或羽绒的鸟皮及鸟体的其他部分)	10	90			13	千克	AFEB	Feathers and down of other endangered wild birds including skins and other parts of birds, with their feathers or down
0505 9090.90	其他羽毛、羽绒(包括带有羽毛或羽绒的鸟皮及鸟体的其他部分)	10	90		5/15	13	千克	AB	Other feathers and down including skins and other parts of birds,with their feathers or down
05.06	**骨及角柱，未经加工或经脱脂、简单整理（但未切割成形）、酸处理或脱胶；上述产品的粉末及废料:**								**Bones and horn-cores, unworked, defatted, simply prepared but not cut to shape , treated with acid or degelatinized; powder and waste of these products:**
0506.1000	-经酸处理的骨胶原及骨	12	50			17	千克	AB	-Ossein and bones treated with acid
	-其他:								-Other:
	---骨粉、骨废料:								---Powder and waste of bones:
0506.9011	----含牛羊成分的	12	35			17	千克		----Of bovine and sheep
0506 9011.10	含牛羊成分的骨废料(未经加工或仅经脱脂等加工的)	12	35			17	千克	9AB	Waste of bones, of bovine or sheep, unworked, defatted, simply prepared
0506 9011.90	含牛羊成分的骨粉(未经加工或仅经脱脂等加工的)	12	35			17	千克	AB	Powder of bones, of bovine and sheep （unworked, defatted, simply prepared）
0506.9019	----其他	12	35			17	千克		----Other
0506 9019.10	其他骨废料(未经加工或仅经脱脂等加工的)	12	35			17	千克	9AB	Other waste of bones（unworked, defatted, simply prepared）
0506 9019.90	其他骨粉(未经加工或仅经脱脂等加工的)	12	35			17	千克	AB	Other powder of bones（ unworked,defatted, simply prepared）
0506.9090	---其他	12	50			13	千克		----Other
0506 9090.11	已脱胶的虎骨(指未经加工或经脱脂等加工的)	12	50			13	千克	89	Tiger-bone, degelatinized（unworked, defatted, simply prepared）
0506 9090.19	未脱胶的虎骨(指未经加工或经脱脂等加工的)	12	50			13	千克	89	Tiger-bone, not degelatinized,（unworked, defatted, simply prepared）
0506 9090.21	已脱胶的豹骨(指未经加工或经脱脂等加工的)	12	50			13	千克	ABFE	Leopardbone, degelatinized（ unworked, defatted, simply prepared）

税则号列 Tariff Item	商品名称及备注	进口税率			出口退税	增值税率	计量单位	监管条件	Article Description
		最惠	普通	暂定					
0506 9090.29	未脱胶的豹骨(指未经加工或经脱脂等加工的)	12	50			13	千克	ABFE	Leopardbone, not degelatinized（unworked, defatted, simply prepared）
0506 9090.31	已脱胶的濒危野生动物的骨及角柱(不包括虎骨、豹骨，指未经加工或经脱脂等加工的)	12	50			13	千克	AFEB	Bones and horn-cores of endangered wild animals,degelatinized unworked, defatted, simply prepared excluding tiger-bone, leopard-bone
0506 9090.39	未脱胶的濒危野生动物的骨及角柱(不包括虎骨、豹骨，指未经加工或经脱脂等加工的)	12	50			13	千克	AFEB	Bones and horn-cores of endangered wild animals, not degelatinized(unworked, defatted, simply prepared excluding tiger-bone, leopard-bone
0506 9090.91	已脱胶的其他骨及角柱(不包括虎骨、豹骨，指未经加工或经脱脂等加工的)	12	50			13	千克	AB	Bones and horn-cores of other animals, degelatinized other than tiger-bone, leopard-bone, unworked, defatted, simply prepared
0506 9090.99	未脱胶的其他骨及角柱(不包括虎骨、豹骨，指未经加工或经脱脂等加工的)	12	50			13	千克	AB	Bones and horn-cores of other animals, not degelatinized（other than tigerbone, leopard-bone, unworked, defatted, simply prepared）
05.07	**兽牙、龟壳、鲸须、鲸须毛、角、鹿角、蹄、甲、爪及喙，未经加工或仅简单整理但未切割成形；上述产品的粉末及废料：**								**Ivory, tortoise-shell, whalebone and whalebone hair, horns, antlers, hooves, nails, claws and beaks, unworked or simply prepared but not cut to shape; powder and waste of these products:**
0507.1000	-兽牙；兽牙粉末及废料	10	30			13	千克		-Ivory; ivory powder and waste
0507 1000.10	犀牛角	10	30		5	13	千克	89	Rhinocerus horn（*cornu rhinocerotis*）
0507 1000.20	其他濒危野生兽牙、兽牙粉末及废料	10	30			13	千克	AFEB	Ivory, ivory powder and waste of other endangered wild animals
0507 1000.30	其他兽牙	10	30		5	13	千克	AB	Other Ivory
0507 1000.90	其他兽牙粉末及废料	10	30		5	13	千克	9AB	Ivory, ivory powder and waste of other animals
	-其他：								-Other:
0507.9010	---羚羊角及其粉末和废料	3	14		5	13	千克	ABFE	---Antelope horns and powder or waste thereof
0507.9020	---鹿茸及其粉末	11	30		5	13	千克	ABFE	---Pilose antlers and powder thereof
0507.9090	---其他	10	50		5	13	千克	AFEB	---Other
05.08	**珊瑚及类似品，未经加工或仅简单整理但未经进一步加工；软体动物壳、甲壳动物壳、棘皮动物壳、墨鱼骨，未经加工或仅简单整理但未切割成形，上述壳、骨的粉末及废料**								**Coral and similar materials, unworked or simply prepared but not otherwise worked; shells of molluscs, crustaceans or echinoderms and cuttle-bone, unworked or simply prepared but not cut to shape, powder and waste thereof:**
0508.0010	---粉末及废料	12	35			13	千克		---Powder and waste
0508 0010.10	珊瑚及濒危水产品的粉末、废料(包括介、贝、棘皮动物壳、不包括墨鱼骨的粉末、废料)	12	35			13	千克	AFEB	Powder and waste of coral and endangered aquatic products（including shells of molluscs, crustaceans or echinoderms and cuttle-bone）
0508 0010.90	其他水产品壳、骨的粉末及废料(包括介、贝壳、棘皮动物壳，墨鱼骨的粉末及废料)	12	35		5	13	千克	AB	Powder and waste of other aquatic products（including shells of mol luscs, crustaceans or echinoderms and cuttlebone）
0508.0090	---其他	12	50			13	千克		---Other
0508 0090.10	珊瑚及濒危水产品的壳、骨(包括介、贝、棘皮动物的壳，不包括墨鱼骨)	12	50			13	千克	AFEB	Shells and bone of coral and endangered aquatic products, including shells of molluscs, crustaceans or echinoderms and cuttle-bone
0508 0090.90	其他水产品的壳、骨(包括介、贝、棘皮动物的壳，墨鱼骨)	12	50		5	13	千克	AB	Shells and bone of other aquatic product, including shells of molluscs, crustaceans or echinoderms and cuttle-bone
05.10	**龙涎香、海狸香、灵猫香及麝香；斑蝥；胆汁，不论是否干制；供配制药用的腺体及其他动物产品，鲜、冷、冻或用其他方法暂时保藏的**								**Ambergris, castoreum, civet and musk; cantharides; bile, whether or not dried; glands and other animal products used in the preparation of pharmaceutical products, fresh, chilled, frozen or otherwise provisionally preserved:**
0510.0010	---黄药	3	14		5	13	千克		---Bezoar
0510 0010.10	牛黄	3	14		5	13	千克	8A	Calculus bovis
0510 0010.20	猴枣	3	14		5	13	千克	QAFEB	Monkey bezoar (rhesus macague bezoar)
0510 0010.90	其他黄药（不包括牛黄）	3	14		5	13	千克	AFEB	Other bezoar（excluding calculus bovis）

税则号列 Tariff Item	商品名称及备注	进口税率 最惠	普通	暂定	出口退税	增值税率	计量单位	监管条件	Article Description
0510.0020	---龙涎香、海狸香、灵猫香	7	50		5	13	千克	AFEB	---Ambergris, castoreum and civet
0510.0030	---麝香	7	20			13	千克	8AF	---Musk
0510.0040	---斑蝥	7	50		5	13	千克	QAB	---Cantharides
0510.0090	---其他	6	20			13	千克		---Other
0510 0090.10	其他濒危野生动物胆汁及其他产品（不论是否干制；鲜、冷、冻或用其他方法暂时保藏的）	6	20			13	千克	AFEB	Bile and other endangered wild animals, products whether or not dried, fresh, chilled, frozen or otherwise provisionally preserved
0510 0090.90	胆汁，配药用腺体及其他动物产品（不论是否干制；鲜、冷、冻或用其他方法暂时保藏的）	6	20		5	13	千克	AB	Bile, glands and other animal products used in the preparation of pharmaceutical products, whether or not dried, fresh, chilled, frozen or otherwise provisionally preserved
05.11	**其他品目未列名的动物产品；不适合供人食用的第一章或第三章的死动物：**								**Animal products not elsewhere specified or included; dead animals of Chapter 1 or 3, unfit for human consumption:**
0511.1000	-牛的精液	0	0			13	千克		-Bovine semen
0511 1000.10	濒危野生牛的精液	0	0			13	千克	ABFE	Endangered wild bovine semen
0511 1000.90	其他牛的精液	0	0		5	13	千克	AB	Other bovine semen
	-其他：								-Other:
	--鱼、甲壳动物、软体动物、其他水生无脊椎动物的产品；第三章的死动物：								--Products of fish or crustaceans, molluscs or other aquatic invertebrates; dead animals of Chapter 3:
	---鱼的：								---Fish:
0511.9111 暂	----受精鱼卵	12	35	0		13	千克		----Fertilized fish eggs
0511 9111.10 暂	濒危鱼的受精卵	12	35	0		13	千克	ABFE	Fertilized eggs of endangered fish
0511 9111.90 暂	其他受精鱼卵	12	35	0	5	13	千克	AB	Other fertilized fish eggs
0511.9119	----其他	12	35			13	千克		----Other
0511 9119.10	濒危鱼的非食用产品（包括鱼肚）	12	35			13	千克	ABFE	Endangered fish products（including fish maw）, unfit for human consumption
0511 9119.90	其他鱼的非食用产品（包括鱼肚）	12	35		5	13	千克	AB	Other fish products（including fish maw）unfit for human consumption
0511.9190	---其他	12	35			13	千克		---Other
0511 9190.10	濒危水生无脊椎动物产品(包括甲壳动物、软体动物、第三章死动物)	12	35			13	千克	ABFE	Products of endangered aquatic invertebrates（including crustaceans, molluscs; dead animals of Chapter 3）
0511 9190.90	其他水生无脊椎动物产品(包括甲壳动物、软体动物、第三章死动物)	12	35		5	13	千克	AB	Products of other aquatic Invertebrates （including crustaceans, molluscs; dead animals of Chapter 3）
	--其他：								--Other:
0511.9910	---动物精液(牛的精液除外)	0	0			13	千克		---Animal semen, other than bovine semen
0511 9910.10	濒危野生动物精液(牛的精液除外)	0	0			13	千克	AFEB	Endangered wild animals semen （other than bovine semen）
0511 9910.90	其他动物精液(牛的精液除外)	0	0		5	13	千克	AB	Other animals semen（other than bovine semen）
0511.9920	---动物胚胎	0	0			13	千克		---Animal embryo
0511 9920.10	濒危野生动物胚胎	0	0			13	千克	AFEB	Endangered wild animals embryo
0511 9920.90	其他动物胚胎	0	0		5	13	千克	AB	Other animals embryo
0511.9930	---蚕种	0	0		5	13	千克	AB	---Silkworm graine
0511.9940	---马毛及废马毛，不论是否制成有或无衬垫的毛片	15	90		5/15	13	千克		---Horsehair and horsehair waste, whether or not put up as a layer with or without supporting material
0511 9940.10	废马毛(不论是否制成有或无衬垫的毛片)	15	90		5/15	13	千克	9B	Horsehair waste, whether or not put up as a layer with or without supporting material
0511 9940.90	其他马毛(不论是否制成有或无衬垫的毛片)	15	90		5/15	13	千克	AB	Other horsehair, whether or not put up as a layer with or without supporting material
0511.9990	---其他	12	35			13	千克		---Other
0511 9990.10	其他税号未列名濒危野生动物产品(包括不适合供人食用的第一章的死动物)	12	35			13	千克	AFEB	Endangered wild animal, products not elsewhere specified or included（excluding dead animals of Chapter 1, unfit for human consumption）
0511 9990.90	其他税号未列名的动物产品(包括不适合供人食用的第一章的死动物)	12	35		5	13	千克	AB	Other animal products, not elsewhere specified or included（excluding dead animals of Chapter 1, unfit for human consumption）

第二类
植物产品

注释：

本类所称"团粒"，是指直接挤压或加入按重量计比例不超过3%的黏合剂制成的粒状产品。

SECTION Ⅱ
VEGETABLE PRODUCTS

Section Notes:

In this Section the term "pellets" means products which have been agglomerated either directly by compression or by the addition of a binder in a proportion not exceeding 3% by weight.

第六章
活树及其他活植物；鳞茎、根及类似品；插花及装饰用簇叶

注释：

一、除品目06.01的菊苣植物及其根以外，本章只包括通常由苗圃或花店供应为种植或装饰用的活树及其他货品（包括植物秧苗）；但不包括马铃薯、洋葱、青葱、大蒜及其他第七章的产品。

二、品目06.03、06.04的各种货品，包括全部或部分用这些货品制成的花束、花篮、花圈及类似品，不论是否有其他材料制成的附件。但这些货品不包括品目97.01的拼贴画或类似的装饰板。

Chapter 6
Live trees and other plants; bulbs, roots and the like; cut flowers and ornamental foliage

Chapter Notes:

1. Subject to the second part of heading 06.01, this Chapter covers only live trees and goods (including seedling vegetables) of a kind commonly supplied by nursery gardeners or florists for planting or for ornamental use; nevertheless it does not include potatoes, onions, shallots, garlic or other products of Chapter 7.
2. Any reference in heading 06.03 or 06.04 to goods of any kind shall be construed as including a reference to bouquets, floral baskets, wreaths and similar articles made wholly or partly of goods of that kind, account not being taken of accessories of other materials. However, these headings do not include collages or similar decorative plaques of heading 97.01.

税则号列 Tariff Item	商品名称及备注	进口税率 最惠	普通	暂定	出口退税	增值税率	计量单位	监管条件	Article Description
06.01	鳞茎、块茎、块根、球茎、根颈及根茎，休眠、生长或开花的；菊苣植物及其根，但品目12.12的根除外：								**Bulbs, tubers, tuberous roots, corms, crowns and rhizomes, dormant, in growth or in flower; chicory plants and roots other than roots of heading No.12.12:**
	-休眠的鳞茎、块茎、块根、球茎、根颈及根茎：								-Bulbs, tubers, tuberous roots, corms, crowns and rhizomes, dormant:
0601.1010	---番红花球茎	4	14		5	13	个/千克	AB	---Stigma croci corms
	---百合球茎：								---Lily corms:
0601.1021	----种用	0	0			13	个/千克	AB	----seed
0601.1029	----其他	5	40			13	个/千克	AB	----Other
	---其他：								---Other:
0601.1091	----种用	0	0			13	个/千克		----Seed
0601 1091.10	种用休眠的兰花块茎（包括球茎、根颈及根茎）	0	0		5	13	个/千克	AFEB	Orchid tubers, corms, crowns and rhizomes, dormant, seed
0601 1091.91	种用休眠其他濒危植物鳞茎等（包括球茎、根颈、根茎、鳞茎、块茎、块根）	0	0			13	个/千克	ABFE	Bulbs of endangered plants, dormant, seed (including corms, crowns, rhizomes, tubers, tuberous roots)
0601 1091.99	种用休眠的其他鳞茎、块茎、块根（包括球茎、根颈及根茎）	0	0		5	13	个/千克	AB	Other bulbs, tubers, tuberous roots, dormant, seed (including corms, crowns and rhizomes)
0601.1099	----其他	5	40			13	个/千克		----Other
0601 1099.10	其他休眠的兰花块茎（包括球茎、根颈及根茎）	5	40		5	13	个/千克	AFEB	Other orchid tubers, corms, crowns and rhizomes, dormant
0601 1099.91	其他休眠濒危植物鳞茎等（包括球茎、根颈、根茎、鳞茎、块茎、块根）	5	40			13	个/千克	AFEB	Bulbs of other endangered plants, dormant (including corms, crowns, rhizomes, tubers, tuberous roots)
0601 1099.99	其他休眠的其他鳞茎、块茎、块根（包括球茎、根颈及根茎）	5	40		5	13	个/千克	AB	Other bulbs, tubers, tuberous roots, corms, crowns and rhizomes, dormant, seed
0601.2000	-生长或开花的鳞茎、块茎、块根、球茎、根颈及根茎；菊苣植物及其根	15	80			13	个/千克		-Bulbs, tubers, tuberous roots, corms, crowns and rhizomes, in growth or in flower; chicory plants and roots

税则号列 Tariff Item	商品名称及备注	进口税率			出口退税	增值税率	计量单位	监管条件	Article Description
		最惠	普通	暂定					
0601 2000.10	生长或开花的兰花块茎（包括球茎、根颈及根茎）	15	80		5	13	个/千克	AFEB	Orchid tubers, corms, crowns and rhizomes, in growth or in flower
0601 2000.20	生长或开花的仙客来鳞茎	15	80		5	13	个/千克	AFEB	Cyclamen bulbs, in growth or in flower
0601 2000.91	生长或开花的其他濒危植物鳞茎等（包括球茎、根颈、根茎、鳞茎、块茎、块根、菊苣植物）	15	80			13	个/千克	AFEB	Bulbs corms, crowns, rhizomes, tubers, tuberous roots of other endangered plants; chicory plants in growth or in flower
0601 2000.99	生长或开花的其他鳞茎及菊苣植物（包括块茎、块根、球茎、根颈及根茎，品目 12.12 的根除外）	15	80		5	13	个/千克	AB	Other bulbs and chicory plants, in growth or in flower（including tubers, tuberous roots, corms, crowns, rhizomes, other than roots of heading No. 12.12）
06.02	**其他活植物（包括其根）、插枝及接穗；蘑菇菌丝：**								**Other live plants（including their roots）cuttings and slips; mushroom spawn:**
0602.1000	-无根插枝及接穗	0	0			13	株/千克		-Unrooted cuttings and slips
0602 1000.10	濒危植物的无根插枝及接穗	0	0			13	株/千克	ABFE	Unrooted cuttings and slips of endangered plants
0602 1000.90	其他无根插枝及接穗	0	0		5	13	株/千克	AB	Other unrooted cuttings and slips
	-食用水果或食用坚果的树、灌木，不论是否嫁接：								-Trees, shrubs and bushes, grafted or not, of kinds which bear edible fruit or nuts:
0602.2010	---种用苗木	0	0			13	株/千克	AB	---Seedlings
0602.2090	---其他	10	80		5	13	株/千克	AB	---Other
	-杜鹃，不论是否嫁接：								-Rhododendrons and azaleas, grafted or not:
0602.3010	---种用	0	0		5	13	株/千克	AB	---Seedlings
0602.3090	---其他	15	80		5	13	株/千克	AB	---Other
	-玫瑰，不论是否嫁接：								-Roses, grafted or not:
0602.4010	---种用	0	0		5	13	株/千克	AB	---Seedlings
0602.4090	---其他	15	80		5	13	株/千克	AB	---Other
	-其他：								-Other:
0602.9010	---蘑菇菌丝	0	0		5	13	千克	AB	---Mushroom spawn
	---其他：								---Other:
0602.9091	----种用苗木	0	0			13	株/千克		----Seedlings
0602 9091.10	种用兰花	0	0			13	株/千克	AFEB	Orchid, seedlings
0602 9091.20	种用红豆杉苗木	0	0			13	株/千克	AFEB	Species with yew, seedlings
0602 9091.91	其他濒危植物种用苗木	0	0			13	株/千克	AFEB	Other endangered plants, seedlings
0602 9091.99	其他种用苗木	0	0			13	株/千克	AB	Other seedlings
0602.9092	----兰花	10	80		5	13	株/千克	ABFE	----Orchid
0602.9093	----菊花	10	80		0/5	13	株/千克	AB	----Chrysanthemum
0602.9094	----百合	10	80			13	株/千克		----Lily
0602 9094.10	芦荟（种用除外）	10	80		5	13	株/千克	ABEFQ	Aloes(barbabos aloe), other than seedlings
0602 9094.90	其他百合（种用除外）	10	80			13	株/千克	AB	Other lily, other than seedlings
0602.9095	----康乃馨	10	80		5	13	株/千克	AB	----Carnation
0602.9099	----其他	10	80			13	株/千克		----Other
0602 9099.10	苏铁(铁树)类	10	80		5	13	株/千克	ABFE	Cycas revoluta（Sago cycas）
0602 9099.20	仙人掌(包括仙人球、仙人柱、仙人指)	10	80		5	13	株/千克	ABFE	Cactus（Echpi-nopsis tubiflora, carnegiea gigantia, schumbegera bridgesli）
0602 9099.30	红豆杉(种用除外)	10	80			13	株/千克	ABFE	Chinese yew (other than seedlings)
0602 9099.91	其他濒危活植物（种用除外）	10	80			13	株/千克	AFEB	Other endangered live plants（other than seedlings）
0602 9099.99	其他活植物（种用除外）	10	80		5	13	株/千克	AB	Other live plants（other than seedlings）
06.03	**制花束或装饰用的插花及花蕾，鲜、干、染色、漂白、浸渍或用其他方法处理的：**								**Cut flowers and flower buds of a kind suitable for bouquets or for ornamental purposes, fresh, dried, dyed, bleached, impregnated or otherwise prepared:**
	-鲜的：								-Fresh:
0603.1100	--玫瑰	10	100		5	13	千克/枝	AB	--Roses
0603.1200	--康乃馨	10	100		5	13	千克/枝	AB	--Carnations
0603.1300	--兰花	10	100		5	13	千克/枝	ABEF	--Orchids
0603.1400	--菊花	10	100		5	13	千克/枝	AB	--Chrysanthemums
0603.1500	--百合花（百合属）	10	100		5	13	千克/枝	AB	--Lilies (Lilium spp.)
0603.1900	--其他	10	100			13	千克/枝		--Other

税则号列 Tariff Item	商品名称及备注	进口税率 最惠	普通	暂定	出口退税	增值税率	计量单位	监管条件	Article Description
0603 1900.10	鲜的濒危植物插花及花蕾(制花束或装饰用的)	10	100			13	千克/枝	ABFE	Cut endangered flowers and flower buds of a kind suitable for bouquets or for ornamental purposes, fresh
0603 1900.90	其他鲜的插花及花蕾(制花束或装饰用的)	10	100		5	13	千克/枝	AB	Other cut flowers and flower buds of a kind suitable for bouquets or for ornamental purposes, fresh
0603.9000	-其他	23	100			17	千克/枝		-Other
0603 9000.10	干或染色等加工濒危植物插花及花蕾(制花束或装饰用的,鲜的除外)	23	100			17	千克/枝	ABFE	Cut flowers and flower buds of endangered plants, of a kind suitable for bouquets or for ornamental purposes, dried or dyed, other than fresh
0603 9000.90	其他干或染色等加工的插花及花蕾(制花束或装饰用的,鲜的除外)	23	100		5	17	千克/枝	AB	Other cut flowers and flower buds, of a kind suitable for bouquets or for ornamental purposes, dried or dyed, other than fresh
06.04	**制花束或装饰用的不带花及花蕾的植物枝、叶或其他部分、草、苔藓及地衣,鲜、干、染色、漂白、浸渍或用其他方法处理的:**								**Foliage, branches and other parts of plants, without flowers or flowerbuds, and grasses, mosses and lichens, being goods of a kind suitable for bouquets or for ornamental purposes, fresh, dried, dyed, bleached, impregnated or otherwise prepared:**
	-鲜的:								-Fresh :
0604.2010	---苔藓及地衣	23	100		5	13	千克	AB	---Mosses and lichens
0604.2090	---其他	10	100			13	千克		---Other
0604 2090.10	其他鲜濒危植物枝、叶或其他部分,草(枝、叶或其他部分是指制花束或装饰用并且不带花及花蕾)	10	100			13	千克	ABFE	Foliage, branches and other parts of endangered plants, without flowers or flowerbuds, being goods of a kind suitable for bouquets or for ornamental purposes
0604 2090.90	其他鲜植物枝、叶或其他部分,草(枝、叶或其他部分是指制花束或装饰用并且不带花及花蕾)	10	100		5	13	千克	AB	Foliage, branches and other parts of plants, without flowers or flowerbuds, being goods of a kind suitable for bouquets or for ornamental purposes
	-其他:								-Other:
0604.9010	---苔藓及地衣	23	100		5	13	千克	AB	---Mosses and lichens
0604.9090	---其他	10	100			17	千克		--Other
0604 9090.10	其他染色或经加工濒危植物枝、叶或其他部分,草(枝、叶或其他部分是指制花束或装饰用并且不带花及花蕾)	10	100			17	千克	ABFE	Foliage, branches and other parts of endangered plants, without flowers or flowerbuds, being goods of a kind suitable for bouquets or for ornamental purposes, dyed, bleached, impregnated or otherwise prepared
0604 9090.90	其他染色或加工的植物枝、叶或其他部分,草(枝、叶或其他部分是指制花束或装饰用并且不带花及花蕾)	10	100		5	17	千克	AB	Foliage, branches and other parts of plants, without flowers or flowerbuds, being goods of a kind suitable for bouquets or for ornamental purposes, dyed, bleached, impregnated or otherwise prepared

第七章 食用蔬菜、根及块茎

Chapter 7 Edible vegetables and certain roots and tubers

注释：

一、本章不包括品目12.14的草料。

二、品目07.09、07.10、07.11及07.12所称"蔬菜"，包括食用的蘑菇、块菌、油橄榄、刺山柑、菜葫芦、南瓜、茄子、甜玉米、辣椒、茴香菜、欧芹、细叶芹、龙蒿、水芹、甜茉乔栾那。

三、品目07.12包括干制的归入品目07.01至07.11的各种蔬菜，但下列各项除外：

（一）作蔬菜用的脱荚干豆（品目07.13）；

（二）品目11.02至11.04所列形状的甜玉米；

（三）马铃薯细粉、粗粉、粉末、粉片、颗粒及团粒（品目11.05）；

（四）用品目07.13的干豆制成的细粉、粗粉及粉末（品目11.06）。

四、本章不包括辣椒干及辣椒粉（品目09.04）。

Chapter Notes:

1. This Chapter does not cover forage products of heading 12.14.
2. In headings 07.09, 07.10, 07.11 and 07.12 the word "vegetables" includes edible mushrooms, truffles, olives, capers, marrows, pumpkins, aubergines, sweet corn（Zea mays var. saccharate）, fruits of the genus Capsicumor of the genus Pimenta,fennel, parsley, chervil, tarragon, cress and sweet marjoram（Majorana hortensis or Origanum majorana）.
3. Heading 07.12 covers all dried vegetables of the kinds falling in headings 07.01 to 07.11, other than:

（a）Dried leguminous vegetables, shelled（heading 07.13）;

（b）Sweet corn in the forms specified in headings 11.02 to 11.04;

（c）Flour, meal, powder, flakes, granules and pellets of potatoes（heading 11.05）;

（d）Flour, meal and powder of the dried leguminous vegetables of heading 07.13（heading 11.06）.

4. However, dried or crushed or ground fruits of the genus Capsicum or of the genus Pimenta are excluded from this Chapter（heading 09.04）.

税则号列 Tariff Item	商品名称及备注	进口税率			出口退税	增值税率	计量单位	监管条件	Article Description
		最惠	普通	暂定					
07.01	鲜或冷藏的马铃薯：								**Potatoes, fresh or chilled:**
0701.1000	-种用	13	70			13	千克	AB	-Seeds
0701.9000	-其他	13	70			13	千克	AB	-Other
07.02	鲜或冷藏的番茄：								**Tomatoes, fresh or chilled:**
0702.0000	鲜或冷藏的番茄	13	70			13	千克	AB	Tomatoes, fresh or chilled
07.03	鲜或冷藏的洋葱、青葱、大蒜、韭葱及其他葱属蔬菜：								**Onions, shallots, garlic, leeks and other alliaceous vegetables, fresh or chilled:**
	-洋葱及青葱：								-Onions and shallots:
0703.1010	---洋葱	13	70			13	千克	AB	---Onions
0703.1020	---青葱	13	70			13	千克	AB	---Shallots
	-大蒜：								-Garlic:
0703.2010	---蒜头	13	70			13	千克	AB	---Garlic bulbs
0703.2020	---蒜苔及蒜苗（青蒜）	13	70			13	千克	AB	---Garlic stems, garlic seedlings
0703.2090	---其他	13	70			13	千克	AB	---Other
	-韭葱及其他葱属蔬菜：								-Leeks and other alliaceous vegetables:
0703.9010	---韭葱	13	70			13	千克	AB	---Leeks
0703.9020	---大葱	13	70			13	千克	AB	---Scallion
0703.9090	---其他	13	70			13	千克	AB	---Other
07.04	鲜或冷藏的卷心菜、菜花、球茎甘蓝、羽衣甘蓝及类似的食用芥菜类蔬菜：								**Cabbages, cauliflowers, kohlrabi, kale and similar edible brassicas, fresh or chilled:**
0704.1000	-菜花及硬花甘蓝	10	70			13	千克		-Cauliflowers and headed broccoli
0704 1000.01	鲜、冷硬花甘蓝	10	70			13	千克	AB	Headed broccoli, fresh or chilled
0704 1000.02	鲜、冷花椰菜(花椰菜也叫菜花)	10	70			13	千克	AB	Broccoli (cauliflowers), fresh or chilled
0704.2000	-抱子甘蓝	13	70			13	千克	AB	-Brussels sprouts
	-其他：								-Other:
0704.9010	---卷心菜	13	70			13	千克	AB	---Cabbages(*Brassica oleraceavar.capitata*)
0704.9020	---西兰花	13	70			13	千克	AB	---Broccolis(*Brassica oleraceavar.italica*)
0704.9090	---其他	13	70			13	千克		---Other
0704 9090.01	鲜、冷其他甘蓝	13	70			13	千克	AB	Other Cabbage, fresh or chilled
0704 9090.90	鲜或冷藏的其他食用芥菜类蔬菜	13	70			13	千克	AB	Other edible brassicas juncea, fresh or chilled
07.05	鲜或冷藏的莴苣及菊苣：								**Lettuce（*lactuca sativa*）and chicory （*Cichorium spp.*）, fresh or chilled:**

税则号列 Tariff Item	商品名称及备注	进口税率 最惠	普通	暂定	出口退税	增值税率	计量单位	监管条件	Article Description
	-莴苣:								-Lettuce:
0705.1100	--结球莴苣（包心生菜）	10	70			13	千克	AB	--Cabbage lettuce（head lettuce）
0705.1900	--其他	10	70			13	千克	AB	--Other
	-菊苣:								-Chicory:
0705.2100	--维特罗夫菊苣	13	70			13	千克	AB	--Witloof chicory（*Cichoriym intybus var. foliosum*）
0705.2900	--其他	13	70			13	千克	AB	--Other
07.06	**鲜或冷藏的胡萝卜、萝卜、色拉甜菜根、婆罗门参、块根芹、小萝卜及类似的食用根茎:**								**Carrots, turnips, salad beetroot, salsify, celeriac, radishes and similar edible roots, fresh or chilled:**
0706.1000	-胡萝卜及萝卜	13	70			13	千克		-Carrots and turnips
0706 1000.01	鲜、冷胡萝卜	13	70			13	千克	AB	Carrots, fresh or chilled
0706 1000.90	鲜或冷藏的萝卜	13	70			13	千克	AB	Turnips, fresh or chilled
0706.9000	-其他	13	70			13	千克	AB	-Other
07.07	**鲜或冷藏的黄瓜及小黄瓜:**								**Cucumbers and gherkins, fresh or chilled:**
0707.0000	鲜或冷藏的黄瓜及小黄瓜	13	70			13	千克	AB	Cucumbers and gherkins, fresh or chilled
07.08	**鲜或冷藏的豆类蔬菜，不论是否脱荚:**								**Leguminous vegetables, shelled or unshelled, fresh or chilled:**
0708.1000	-豌豆	13	70			13	千克	AB	-Peas（*Pisum sativum*）
0708.2000	-豇豆属及菜豆属	13	70			13	千克	AB	-Beans（*Vigna spp., Phaseolus spp.*）
0708.9000	-其他豆类蔬菜	13	70			13	千克	AB	-Other leguminous vegetables
07.09	**鲜或冷藏的其他蔬菜:**								**Other vegetables, fresh or chilled:**
0709.2000	-芦笋	13	70			13	千克	AB	-Asparagus
0709.3000	-茄子	13	70			13	千克	AB	-Aubergines（egg-plants）
0709.4000	-芹菜，但块根芹除外	10	70			13	千克	AB	-Celery other than celeriac
	-蘑菇及块菌:								-Mushrooms and truffles:
0709.5100	--伞菌属蘑菇	13	90			13	千克	AB	--Mushrooms of the genus Agaricus
	--其他:								--Other:
0709.5910	---松茸	13	90			13	千克	ABE	---Sungmo
0709.5920	---香菇	13	90			13	千克	AB	---Shiitake
0709.5930	---金针菇	13	90			13	千克	AB	---Winter mushroom
0709.5940	---草菇	13	90			13	千克	AB	---Paddy Straw mushroom
0709.5950	---口蘑	13	90			13	千克	AB	---Tricholoma mongolicum Imai
0709.5960	---块菌	13	90		5	13	千克	AB	---Truffle
0709.5990	---其他	13	90			13	千克	AB	---Other
0709.6000	-辣椒，包括甜椒	13	70			13	千克	AB	-Fruits of the genus *Capsicum* or of the genus *Pimenta*
0709.7000	-菠菜	13	70			13	千克	AB	-Spinach, New Zealand spinach and orache spinach（garden spinach）
	-其他:								-Other:
0709.9100	--洋蓟	13	70		5	13	千克	AB	--Globe artichokes
0709.9200	--油橄榄	13	70		5	13	千克	AB	--Olives
0709.9300	--南瓜、笋瓜及瓠瓜（南瓜属）	13	70			13	千克	AB	--Pumpkins, squash and gourds (Cucurbita spp.)
	--其他:								--Other :
0709.9910	---竹笋	13	70			13	千克		---Bamboo shoots
0709 9910.10	鲜或冷藏的酸竹笋	13	70			13	千克	ABE	Pickled bamboo shoots, fresh or chilled
0709 9910.90	鲜或冷藏的其他竹笋	13	70			13	千克	AB	Other pickled bamboo shoots, fresh or chilled
0709.9990	---其他	13	70			13	千克		---Other
0709 9990.01	鲜或冷藏的丝瓜	13	70			13	千克	AB	Loofah(Lufla) , fresh or chilled
0709 9990.02	鲜或冷藏的青江菜	13	70			13	千克	AB	Spoon cabbage, fresh or chilled
0709 9990.03	鲜或冷藏的小白菜	13	70			13	千克	AB	Bok Choy, fresh or chilled
0709 9990.04	鲜或冷藏的苦瓜	13	70			13	千克	AB	Balsam pear, fresh or chilled
0709 9990.05	鲜或冷藏的山葵	13	70			13	千克	AB	Wasabi Japanese Horse-radish, fresh or chilled
0709 9990.10	鲜或冷藏的莼菜	13	70			13	千克	ABE	Water shield, fresh or chilled
0709 9990.90	鲜或冷藏的其他蔬菜	13	70			13	千克	AB	Other vegetables, fresh or chilled
07.10	**冷冻蔬菜（不论是否蒸煮）：**								**Vegetables（uncooked or cooked by steaming or boiling in water）, frozen:**
0710.1000	-马铃薯	13	70		0/5	13	千克	AB	-Potatoes

税则号列 Tariff Item	商品名称及备注	进口税率 最惠	进口税率 普通	进口税率 暂定	出口退税	增值税率	计量单位	监管条件	Article Description
	-豆类蔬菜，不论是否脱荚:								-Leguminous vegetables, shelled or unshelled:
0710.2100	--豌豆	13	70		0/5	13	千克	AB	--Peas（*Pisum sativum*）
	--豇豆属及菜豆属:								--Beans（*Vigna spp., Phaseolus spp.*）:
0710.2210	---红小豆（赤豆）	13	70		0/5	13	千克	AB	---Small red（*Adzuki*）beans（*Phaseolus or Vigna angularis*）
0710.2290	---其他	13	70		0/5	13	千克	AB	---Other
0710.2900	--其他	13	70		0/5	13	千克	AB	--Other
0710.3000	-菠菜	13	70		0/5	13	千克	AB	-Spinach, New Zealand spinach and orache spinach（garden spinach）
0710.4000	-甜玉米	10	70		0/5	13	千克	AB	-Sweet corn
	-其他蔬菜:								-Other vegetables:
0710.8010	---松茸	13	70		0/5	13	千克	ABE	---Sungmo
0710.8020	---蒜苔及蒜苗(青蒜)	13	70		0/5	13	千克	AB	---Garlic stems, garlic seedlings
0710.8030	---蒜头	13	70		0/5	13	千克	AB	---Garlic bulbs
0710.8040	---牛肝菌	13	70		0/5	13	千克	AB	---Boletus
0710.8090	---其他	13	70		0/5	13	千克		---Other
0710 8090.10	冷冻的大蒜瓣（不论是否蒸煮）	13	70		0/5	13	千克	AB	Garlic bulblet（uncooked or cooked by steaming or boiling in water）, frozen
0710 8090.20	冷冻的香菇（不论是否蒸煮）	13	70		0/5	13	千克	AB	Shiitake Mushroom（uncooked or cooked by steaming or boiling in water）,frozen
0710 8090.30	冷冻莼菜（不论是否蒸煮）	13	70		0/5	13	千克	ABE	Water shield（uncooked or cooked by steaming or boiling in water）, frozen
0710 8090.90	冷冻的未列名蔬菜(不论是否蒸煮)	13	70		0/5	13	千克	AB	Vegetables, not elsewhere specified or included（uncooked or cooked by steaming or boiling in water）, frozen
0710.9000	-什锦蔬菜	10	70		0/5	13	千克	AB	-Mixtures of vegetables
07.11	暂时保藏（例如，使用二氧化硫气体、盐水、亚硫酸水或其他防腐液）的蔬菜，但不适于直接食用的:								**Vegetables provisionally preserved（for example, by sulphur dioxide gas, in brine, in suphur water or in other preservative solutions）, but unsuitable in that state for immediate consumption:**
0711.2000	-油橄榄	13	70		5	13	千克	AB	-Olives
0711.4000	-黄瓜及小黄瓜	13	70		5	13	千克	AB	-Cucumbers and gherkins
	-蘑菇及块菌:								-Mushrooms and truffles:
	--伞菌属蘑菇:								--Mushrooms of the genus *Agaricus*:
	---盐水的:								---In brine:
0711.5112	----白蘑菇	13	90		5	13	千克	AB	----White mushroom
0711.5119	----其他	13	90		5	13	千克	AB	----Other
0711.5190	---其他	13	90		5	13	千克	AB	---Other
	--其他:								--Other:
	---盐水的:								---In brine:
0711.5911	----松茸	13	90		5	13	千克	EAB	----Sungmo
0711.5919	----其他	13	90		5	13	千克		----Other
0711 5919.10	盐水的香菇（不适于直接食用的）	13	90		5	13	千克	AB	Shiitake mushroom in brine (but unsuitable in that state for immediate consumption)
0711 5919.90	盐水的其他非伞菌属蘑菇及块菌（不适于直接食用的）	13	90		5	13	千克	AB	Other mushroom and truffles in brine, not the genus *Agaricus* (but unsuitable in that state for immediate consumption)
0711.5990	---其他	13	90		5	13	千克		---Other
0711 5990.10	暂时保藏的香菇(用二氧化硫气体等物质处理，但不适于直接食用的)	13	90		5	13	千克	AB	Shiitake mushroom provisionally preserved by sulphur dioxide gas or in other preservative solutions, but unsuitable in that state for immediate consumption
0711 5990.90	暂时保藏的蘑菇及块菌(用二氧化硫气体等物质处理，但不适于直接食用的)	13	90		5	13	千克	AB	Mushrooms and truffles provisionally preserved by sulphur dioxide gas or in other preservative solutions, but unsuitable in that state for immediate consumption
	-其他蔬菜；什锦蔬菜:								-Other vegetables; mixtures of vegetables:
	---盐水的:								---In brine:
0711.9031	----竹笋	13	70		5	13	千克		----Bamboo shoots

税则号列 Tariff Item	商品名称及备注	进口税率			出口退税	增值税率	计量单位	监管条件	Article Description
		最惠	普通	暂定					
0711 9031.10	盐水酸竹笋（不适于直接食用的）	13	70		5	13	千克	ABE	Pickled bamboo shoots in brine(unsuitable in that state for immediate consumption)
0711 9031.90	其他盐水竹笋(不适于直接食用的)	13	70		5	13	千克	AB	Other bamboo shoots in brine(unsuitabl in that state for immediate consumption)
0711.9034	----大蒜	13	70		5	13	千克		----Garlic
0711 9034.10	盐水简单腌制的大蒜头、大蒜瓣（无论是否去皮，但不适于直接食用）	13	70		5	13	千克	AB	Garlic bulbs or garlic bulblet, in brine, (whether or not skinned but unsuitable in that state for immediate consumption)
0711 9034.90	盐水简单腌制的其他大蒜(不含蒜头、蒜瓣，无论是否去皮，但不适于直接食用）	13	70		5	13	千克	AB	Other garlic in brine (whether or not skinned, but unsuitable in that state for immediate consumption), excluding garlic bulbs, garlic bulblet
0711.9039	----其他	13	70		5	13	千克	AB	----Other
0711.9090	---其他	13	90		5	13	千克	AB	---Other
07.12	**干蔬菜，整个、切块、切片、破碎或制成粉状，但未经进一步加工的：**								**Dried vegetables, whole, cut, sliced, broken or in powder, but not further prepared:**
0712.2000	-洋葱	13	80		0/5	13	千克	AB	-Onions
	-蘑菇、木耳、银耳及块菌：								-Mushrooms, wood ears（*Auricularia spp.*）, jelly fungi（*Tremella spp.*）and truffles:
0712.3100	--伞菌属蘑菇	13	80		0/5	13	千克	AB	--Mushrooms of the genus *Agaricus*
0712.3200	--木耳	13	100		0/5/15	13	千克	AB	--Wood ears（*Auricularia spp.*）
0712.3300	--银耳	13	90		0/5/15	13	千克	AB	--Jelly fungi（*Tremella spp.*）
	--其他:								--Other:
0712.3910	---香菇	13	100		0/5/15	13	千克	AB	---Shiitake
0712.3920	---金针菇	13	100		0/5	13	千克	AB	--Winter mushroom
0712.3930	---草菇	13	100		0/5	13	千克	AB	---Paddy straw mushroom
0712.3940	---口蘑	13	100		0/5	13	千克	AB	---Tricholoma mongolicum Imai
0712.3950	---牛肝菌	13	100		0/5	13	千克	AB	---Boletus
0712.3990	---其他	13	100		0/5	13	千克		---Other
0712 3990.10	干制松茸（整个、切块、切片、破碎或制成粉状，但未经进一步加工的）	13	100		0/5	13	千克	ABE	Dried sungmo (whole, cut, sliced, broken or in powder, but not further prepared)
0712 3990.90	其他干制蘑菇及块菌（整个、切块、切片、破碎或制成粉状，但未经进一步加工的）	13	100		0/5	13	千克	AB	Other dried mushrooms and truffles (whole, cut, sliced, broken or in powder, but not further prepared)
	-其他蔬菜；什锦蔬菜：								-Other vegetables; mixtures of vegetables:
0712.9010	---笋干丝	13	80			13	千克		---Bamboo shoots
0712 9010.10	酸竹笋干丝	13	80			13	千克	ABE	Dried pickled bamboo shoots
0712 9010.90	其他笋干丝	13	80			13	千克	AB	Other bamboo shoots
0712.9020	---紫萁(薇菜干)	13	80		0/5	13	千克	AB	---Osmund
0712.9030	---金针菜(黄花菜)	13	80		0/5	13	千克	AB	---Day lily flowers
0712.9040	---蕨菜	13	80		0/5	13	千克	AB	---Wild brake
0712.9050	---大蒜	13	80			17	千克		---Garlic
0712 9050.10	干燥或脱水的大蒜头、大蒜瓣（无论是否去皮）	13	80			17	千克	AB	Dried or dewatered garlic bulbs or garlic bulblet (whether or not skinned)
0712 9050.90	干燥或脱水的其他大蒜(不含蒜头、蒜瓣，无论是否去皮）	13	80		0/5/15	17	千克	AB	Other dried or dewatered garlic（other than garlic bulbs and garlic bulblet, whether or not skinned）
0712.9060	---甜椒	13	80		0/5	13	千克	AB	---Capsicum annuum Var. grossum
	---其他:								---Other:
0712.9091	----辣根	13	80		0/5	13	千克	AB	----Horseradish
0712.9099	---其他	13	80		0/5	13	千克		---Other
0712 9099.10	干莼菜（整个、切块、切片、破碎或制成粉状，但未经进一步加工的）	13	80		0/5	13	千克	ABE	Dried water shield(whole, cut, sliced,broken or in powder, but not further prepared)
0712 9099.90	干制的其他蔬菜及什锦蔬菜(整个、切块、切片、破碎或制成粉状，但未经进一步加工的）	13	80		0/5	13	千克	AB	Other dried vegetables; dried mixtures of vegetables (whole, cut, sliced, broken or in powder, but not further prepared)

税则号列 Tariff Item	商品名称及备注	进口税率			出口退税	增值税率	计量单位	监管条件	Article Description
		最惠	普通	暂定					
07.13	脱荚的干豆，不论是否去皮或分瓣：								**Dried leguminous vegetables, shelled, whether or not skinned or split:**
	-豌豆：								-Peas（*Pisum sativum*）：
0713.1010	---种用	0	0			13	千克	AB	---Seed
0713.1090	---其他	5	20			13	千克	AB	---Other
	-鹰嘴豆：								-Chickpeas（*garbanzos*）：
0713.2010	---种用	0	0		5	13	千克	AB	---Seed
0713.2090	---其他	7	20		5	13	千克	AB	---Other
	-豇豆属及菜豆属：								-Beans（*Vigna spp., Phaseolus spp.*）：
	--绿豆：								--Beans of the species *Vigna mungo*（*L.*）*Hepper or Vigna radiata*（*L.*）*Wilczek*:
0713.3110	---种用	0	0		5	13	千克	AB	---Seed
0713.3190	---其他	3	11		5	13	千克	AB	---Other
	--红小豆（赤豆）：								--Small red（*Adzuki*）beans（*Phaseolus or Vigna angularis*）：
0713.3210	---种用	0	0		5	13	千克	AB	---Seed
0713.3290	---其他	3	14		5	13	千克	AB	---Other
	--芸豆：								--Kidney beans, including white pea beans（*Phaseolus vulgaris*）：
0713.3310	---种用	0	0			13	千克	AB	---Seed
0713.3390	---其他	7.5	20			13	千克	AB	---Other
0713.3400	--巴姆巴拉豆	7	20		5	13	千克	AB	--Bambara beans (Vigna subterranea or Voandzeia subterranea)
0713.3500	--牛豆（豇豆）	7	20		5	13	千克	AB	---Cow peas (Vigan unguiculata)
0713.3900	--其他	7	20			13	千克	AB	--Other
	-扁豆：								-Lentils:
0713.4010	---种用	0	0			13	千克	AB	---Seed
0713.4090	---其他	7	20			13	千克	AB	---Other
	-蚕豆：								-Broad beans（*Vicia fabavar. Major*）and horse beans（*Vicia fabavar. equina, Vicia fabavar. Minor*）：
0713.5010	---种用	0	0		5	13	千克	AB	---Seed
0713.5090	---其他	7	20		5	13	千克	AB	---Other
	-木豆（木豆属）：								-Pigeon peas (Cajanus cajan):
0713.6010	---种用	0	0		5	13	千克	AB	---Seed
0713.6090	---其他	7	20		5	13	千克	AB	---Other
	-其他：								-Other:
0713.9010	---种用干豆	0	0			13	千克	AB	---Seed
0713.9090	---其他	7	20			13	千克	AB	---Other
07.14	鲜、冷、冻或干的木薯、竹芋、兰科植物块茎、菊芋、甘薯及含有高淀粉或菊粉的类似根茎，不论是否切片或制成团粒；西谷茎髓：								**Manioc, arrowroot, salep, Jerusalem artichokes, sweet potatoes and similar roots and tubers with high starch or inulin content, fresh, chilled, frozen or dried, whether or not sliced or in the form of pellets; sago pith:**
	-木薯：								-Manioc（cassava）：
0714.1010	---鲜的	10	30		5	13	千克	AB	---Fresh
0714.1020	---干的	5	30		5	13	千克	AB	---Dried
0714.1030	---冷或冻的	10	80		5	13	千克	AB	---Chilled or frozen
	-甘薯：								-Sweet potatoes:
	---鲜的：								---Fresh:
0714.2011	----种用	0	50			13	千克	AB	----For cultivation
0714.2019	----其他	13	50			13	千克	AB	----Other
0714.2020	---干的	13	50			13	千克	AB	---Dried
0714.2030	---冷或冻的	13	80			13	千克	AB	---Chilled or frozen
0714.3000	-山药	13	50			13	千克	AB	-Yams (Dioscorea spp.)
0714.4000	-芋头（芋属）	13	50			13	千克		-Taro (Colocasia spp.)

税则号列 Tariff Item	商品名称及备注	进口税率 最惠	普通	暂定	出口退税	增值税率	计量单位	监管条件	Article Description
0714 4000.01	鲜、冷芋头（芋属）（不论是否切片或制成团粒；芋头又称芋艿，为天南星科芋属植物。分旱芋、水芋）	13	50			13	千克	AB	Fresh, chilled taro, whether or not sliced or in the form of pellets (taros are also called yunai, belong to Colocasia Schott of the Araceae, classified into ground taros and river taros)
0714 4000.90	冻、干的芋头（芋属）（不论是否切片或制成团粒；芋头又称芋艿，为天南星科芋属植物。分旱芋、水芋）	13	50			13	千克	AB	Frozen, dried taro, whether or not sliced or in the form of pellets(taros are also called yunai, belong to Colocasia Schott of the Araceae, classified into ground taros and river taros)
0714.5000	-箭叶黄体芋(黄肉芋属)	13	50		5	13	千克	AB	-Yautia (Xanthosoma spp.)
	-其他:								-Other:
0714.9010	---荸荠	13	50			13	千克	AB	---Water chestnut
	---藕:								---Lotus（*Nelumbo nucifera*）rootstock:
0714.9021	----种用	0	0			13	千克	AB	----For cultivation
0714.9029	----其他	13	50			13	千克	AB	----Other
0714.9090	---其他	13	50			13	千克		---Other
0714 9090.10	鲜、冷、冻、干的兰科植物块茎	13	50			13	千克	ABFE	Tubers of the Orchidaceae, fresh, chilled, frozen or dried
0714 9090.91	含高淀粉或菊粉其他濒危类似根茎（包括西谷茎髓，不论是否切片或制成团粒，鲜、冷、冻或干的）	13	50			13	千克	ABFE	Other endangered similar roots and tubers with high starch or inulin ontent, fresh, chilled, frozen or dried, whether or not sliced or in pellets; sago pith
0714 9090.99	含有高淀粉或菊粉的其他类似根茎（包括西谷茎髓，不论是否切片或制成团粒，鲜、冷、冻或干的）	13	50			13	千克	AB	Other similar roots and tubers with high starch or inulin content, fresh, chilled, frozen or dried, whether or not sliced or in pellets; sago pith

第八章
食用水果及坚果；柑橘属水果或甜瓜的果皮

Chapter 8
Edible fruit and nuts; peel of citrus fruit or melons

注释：

一、本章不包括非供食用的坚果或水果。

二、冷藏的水果和坚果应按相应的鲜果品目归类。

三、本章的干果可以部分复水或为下列目的进行其他处理，但必须保持干果的特征：

（一）为保藏或保持其稳定性（例如，经适度热处理或硫化处理、添加山梨酸或山梨酸钾）；

（二）为改进或保持其外观（例如，添加植物油或少量葡萄糖浆）。

Chapter Notes:

1. This Chapter does not cover inedible nuts or fruits.
2. Chilled fruits and nuts are to be classified in the same headings as the corresponding fresh fruits and nuts.
3. Dried fruit or dried nuts of this Chapter may be partially rehydrated, or treated for the following purposes:

(a) For additional preservation or stabilisation (for example, by moderate heat treatment, sulphuring, the addition of sorbic acid or potassium sorbate);

(b) To improve or maintain their appearance (for example, by the addition of vegetable oil or small quantities of glucose syrup) .provided that they retain the character of dried fruit or dried nuts.

税则号列 Tariff Item	商品名称及备注	进口税率			出口退税	增值税率	计量单位	监管条件	Article Description
		最惠	普通	暂定					
08.01	鲜或干的椰子、巴西果及腰果，不论是否去壳或去皮：								**Coconuts, Brazil nuts and cashew nuts, fresh or dried, whether or not shelled or peeled:**
	-椰子：								-Coconuts:
0801.1100	--干的	12	80		5	13	千克	AB	--Desiccated
0801.1200	--未去内壳（内果皮）	12	80		5	13	千克	AB	--In the inner shell (endocarp)
	--其他：								--Other:
0801.1910	---种用	0	0		5	13	千克	AB	---Seedlings
0801.1990	---其他	12	80		5	13	千克	AB	---Other
	-巴西果：								-Brazil nuts:
0801.2100	--未去壳	10	80		5	13	千克	AB	--In shell
0801.2200	--去壳	10	80		5	13	千克	AB	--Shelled
	-腰果：								-Cashew nuts:
0801.3100[暂]	--未去壳	20	70	10	5	13	千克	AB	--In shell
0801.3200	--去壳	10	70		5	13	千克	AB	--Shelled
08.02	鲜或干的其他坚果，不论是否去壳或去皮：								**Other nuts, fresh or dried, whether or not shelled or peeled:**
	-扁桃仁：								-Almonds:
0802.1100[暂]	--未去壳	24	70	10	5	13	千克	AB	--In shell
0802.1200	--去壳	10	70		5	13	千克	AB	--Shelled
	-榛子：								-Hazelnuts or filberts(*Corylus spp*):
0802.2100	--未去壳	25	70		5	13	千克	AB	--In shell
0802.2200	--去壳	10	70		5	13	千克	AB	--Shelled
	-核桃：								-Walnuts:
0802.3100	--未去壳	25	70		5	13	千克	AB	--In shell
0802.3200	--去壳	20	70		5	13	千克	AB	--Shelled
	-栗子：								-Chestnuts（*Castanea spp.*）:
	--未去壳：								--In shell :
0802.4110	---板栗	25	70		5	13	千克	AB	---Chestnuts
0802.4190[暂]	---其他	25	70	20	5	13	千克	AB	---Other
	--去壳：								---Shelled :
0802.4210	---板栗	25	70		5	13	千克	AB	---Chestnuts
0802.4290[暂]	---其他	25	70	20	5	13	千克	AB	---Other
	-阿月浑子果（开心果）：								-Pistachios :
0802.5100[暂]	--未去壳	10	70	5	5	13	千克	AB	--In shell
0802.5200[暂]	--去壳	10	70	5	5	13	千克	AB	---Shelled
	-马卡达姆坚果（夏威夷果）：								-Macadamia nuts :
	--未去壳：								--In shell :

税则号列 Tariff Item	商品名称及备注	进口税率			出口退税	增值税率	计量单位	监管条件	Article Description
		最惠	普通	暂定					
0802.6110	---种用	0	70		5	13	千克	AB	---Seed
0802.6190	---其他	24	70		5	13	千克	AB	---Other
0802.6200	--去壳	24	70		5	13	千克	AB	--Shelled
0802.7000	-可乐果（可乐果属）	24	70		5	13	千克	AB	-Kola nuts (Cola spp.)
0802.8000	-槟榔果	10	30		5	13	千克		-Areca nuts
0802 8000.01	鲜的槟榔果(不论是否去壳或去皮)	10	30		5	13	千克	AB	Fresh betel nut (whether or not shelled or peeled)
0802 8000.90	干的槟榔果(不论是否去壳或去皮)	10	30		5	13	千克	AB	Dry betel nut (whether or not shelled or peeled)
	-其他:								-Other:
0802.9020[暂]	---白果	25	70	20	5	13	千克	ABE	---Gingko nuts
0802.9030	---松子仁	25	70			13	千克		---Pine-nuts, shelled
0802 9030.10	鲜或干的红松子仁	25	70			13	千克	ABE	Korean pine-nuts, shelled, fresh or dried
0802 9030.20	鲜或干的其他濒危松子仁	25	70			13	千克	ABEF	Other endangered pine-nuts, shelled, fresh or dried
0802 9030.90	鲜或干的其他松子仁	25	70		5	13	千克	AB	Other pine-nuts, shelled, fresh or dried
0802.9090	---其他	24	70			13	千克		---Other
0802 9090.10	鲜或干的榧子、红松子(不论是否去壳或去皮)	24	70		5	13	千克	ABE	Chinese torreya or pine-nuts, fresh or dried, whether or not shelled or peeled
0802 9090.20	鲜或干的其他濒危松子(不论是否去壳或去皮)	24	70			13	千克	ABEF	Endangered pine-nuts, fresh or dried, whether or not shelled or peeled
0802 9090.30	鲜或干的巨籽棕（海椰子）果仁	24	70		5	13	千克	ABEF	Palm seed (Double coconut), fresh or dried
0802 9090.90	鲜或干的其他坚果(不论是否去壳或去皮)	24	70		5	13	千克	AB	Other nuts, fresh or dried, whether or not shelled or peeled
08.03	**鲜或干的香蕉，包括芭蕉：**								**Bananas, including plantains, fresh or dried:**
0803.1000	-芭蕉	10	40		5	13	千克	AB	-Plantains
0803.9000	-其他	10	40		5	13	千克	AB	-Other
08.04	**鲜或干的椰枣、无花果、菠萝、鳄梨、番石榴、芒果及山竹果：**								**Dates, figs, pineapples, avocados, guavas, mangoes and mangosteens, fresh or dried:**
0804.1000	-椰枣	15	40		5	13	千克	AB	-Dates
0804.2000	-无花果	30	70		5	13	千克	AB	-Figs
0804.3000	-菠萝	12	80		5	13	千克		-Pineapples
0804 3000.01	鲜菠萝	12	80		5	13	千克	AB	Pineapples, fresh
0804 3000.90	干菠萝	12	80		5	13	千克	AB	Pineapples, dried
0804.4000	-鳄梨	25	80		5	13	千克	AB	-Avocados
	-番石榴、芒果及山竹果:								-Guavas, mangoes and mangosteens:
0804.5010	---番石榴	15	80		5	13	千克		---Guavas
0804 5010.01	鲜番石榴	15	80		5	13	千克	AB	Guavas, fresh
0804 5010.90	干番石榴	15	80		5	13	千克	AB	Guavas, dried
0804.5020	---芒果	15	80		5	13	千克		---Mangoes
0804 5020.01	鲜芒果	15	80		5	13	千克	AB	Mangoes, fresh
0804 5020.90	干芒果	15	80		5	13	千克	AB	Mangoes, dried
0804.5030	---山竹果	15	80		5	13	千克	AB	---Mangosteens
08.05	**鲜或干的柑橘属水果：**								**Citrus fruit, fresh or dried:**
0805.1000	-橙	11	100		5	13	千克	AB	-Oranges
	-柑橘；杂交柑橘:								-Mandarins（including tangerines and satsumas）; clementines, wilkings and similar citrus hybrids:
0805.2010	---蕉柑	12	100		5	13	千克	AB	---Chiao-Kan
0805.2020	---阔叶柑橘	12	100		5	13	千克	AB	---Latifolia Citrus
0805.2090	---其他	12	100		5	13	千克	AB	---Other
0805.4000	-葡萄柚，包括柚	12	100		5	13	千克		-Grapefruit, including pomelos
0805 4000.01	鲜葡萄柚，包括鲜柚	12	100		5	13	千克	AB	Grapefruit, fresh（including pomelo, fresh）
0805 4000.90	干葡萄柚，包括干柚	12	100		5	13	千克	AB	Grapefruit, dried（including pomelo, dried）
0805.5000	-柠檬及酸橙	11	100		5	13	千克	AB	-Lemons（*Citrus limon, Citrus limonum*） and limes（*Citrus aurantifolia*）
0805.9000	-其他	30	100		5	13	千克	AB	-Other
08.06	**鲜或干的葡萄：**								**Grapes, fresh or dried:**
0806.1000	-鲜的	13	80		5	13	千克	AB	-Fresh

税则号列 Tariff Item	商品名称及备注	进口税率 最惠	普通	暂定	出口退税	增值税率	计量单位	监管条件	Article Description
0806.2000	-干的	10	80		5	13	千克	AB	-Dried
08.07	**鲜的甜瓜（包括西瓜）及木瓜：**								**Melons（including watermelons）and papaws（papayas）, fresh:**
	-甜瓜，包括西瓜：								-Melons（including watermelons）:
0807.1100	--西瓜	25	70		5	13	千克	AB	--Watermelons
	--其他：								--Other:
0807.1910	---哈密瓜	12	70		5	13	千克	AB	---Hami melons
0807.1920	---罗马甜瓜及加勒比甜瓜	12	70		5	13	千克	AB	---Cantaloupe and Calia melons
0807.1990	--其他	12	70		5	13	千克	AB	--Other
0807.2000	-木瓜	25	70		5	13	千克	AB	-Papaws（papayas）
08.08	**鲜的苹果、梨及榅桲：**								**Apples, pears and quinces, fresh:**
0808.1000	-苹果	10	100		5	13	千克	AB	-Apples
	-梨：								-Pears :
0808.3010	---鸭梨及雪梨	12	100		5	13	千克	AB	---Ya pears, Hsueh pears
0808.3020	---香梨	12	100		5	13	千克	AB	---Xiang pears
0808.3090	---其他	10	100		5	13	千克	AB	---Other
0808.4000	-榅桲	16	100		5	13	千克	AB	-Quinces
08.09	**鲜的杏、樱桃、桃（包括油桃）、梅及李：**								**Apricots, cherries, peaches（including nectarines）, plums and sloes, fresh:**
0809.1000	-杏	25	70		5	13	千克	AB	-Apricots
	-樱桃：								-Cherries :
0809.2100	--欧洲酸樱桃	10	70		5	13	千克	AB	--Sour cherries (Prunus cerasus)
0809.2900	--其他	10	70		5	13	千克	AB	--Other
0809.3000	-桃，包括油桃	10	70		5	13	千克	AB	-Peaches, including nectarines
0809.4000	-梅及李	10	70		5	13	千克		-Plums and sloes
0809 4000.01	鲜梅	10	70		5	13	千克	AB	Plums, fresh
0809 4000.90	鲜李子	10	70		5	13	千克	AB	Sloes, fresh
08.10	**其他鲜果：**								**Other fruit, fresh:**
0810.1000	-草莓	14	80		5	13	千克	AB	-Strawberries
0810.2000	-木莓、黑莓、桑葚及罗甘莓	25	80		5	13	千克	AB	-Raspberries, blackberries, mulberries and loganberries
0810.3000	-黑、白或红的穗醋栗（加仑子）及醋栗	25	80		5	13	千克	AB	-Black, white or red currants and gooseberries
0810.4000	-蔓越橘及越橘	30	80		5	13	千克	AB	-Cranberries, bilberries and other fruits of the genus Vaccinium
0810.5000	-猕猴桃	20	80		5	13	千克	AB	-Kiwifruit
0810.6000	-榴莲	20	80		5	13	千克	AB	-Durian
0810.7000	-柿子	20	80		5	13	千克	AB	-Persimmons
	-其他：								-Other:
0810.9010	---荔枝	30	80		5	13	千克	AB	---Lychee
0810.9030	---龙眼	12	80		5	13	千克	AB	---Longan
0810.9040	---红毛丹	20	80		5	13	千克	AB	---Rambutan
0810.9050	---番荔枝	20	80		5	13	千克	AB	---Sugar apple
0810.9060	---杨桃	20	80		5	13	千克	AB	---Carambola
0810.9070	---莲雾	20	80		5	13	千克	AB	---Wax apple
0810.9080	---火龙果	20	80		5	13	千克	AB	---Dragon fruit
0810.9090	---其他	20	80		5	13	千克		---Other
0810 9090.01	鲜枣	20	80		5	13	千克	AB	Jujube (Chinese Date), fresh
0810 9090.02	鲜枇杷	20	80		5	13	千克	AB	Loquat, fresh
0810 9090.10	鲜的翅果油树果	20	80		5	13	千克	ABE	Fruit of Elaeagnus mollis Diels, fresh
0810 9090.90	其他鲜果	20	80		5	13	千克	AB	Other fruit, fresh
08.11	**冷冻水果及坚果，不论是否蒸煮、加糖或其他甜物质：**								**Fruit and nuts, uncooked or cooked by steaming or boiling in water, frozen, whether or not containing added sugar or other sweetening matter:**
0811.1000	-草莓	30	80		5	13	千克	AB	-Strawberries
0811.2000	-木莓、黑莓、桑葚、罗甘莓、黑、白或红的穗醋栗(加仑子)及醋栗	30	80		5	13	千克	AB	-Raspberries, blackberries, mulberries, loganberries, black, white or red currants and gooseberries
	-其他：								-Other:

税则号列 Tariff Item	商品名称及备注	进口税率 最惠	进口税率 普通	进口税率 暂定	出口退税	增值税率	计量单位	监管条件	Article Description
0811.9010	---栗子，未去壳	30	80		5	13	千克	AB	---Chestnuts, in shell
0811.9090	---其他	30	80			13	千克		---Other
0811 9090.10	冷冻的白果	30	80		5	13	千克	ABE	Ginkgo, frozen
0811 9090.21	冷冻的红松子(不论是否去壳或去皮)	30	80		5	13	千克	ABE	Korean pine-nuts, forzen, whether or not shelled or peeled
0811 9090.22	冷冻的其他濒危松子(不论是否去壳或去皮)	30	80			13	千克	ABEF	Other endangered pine-nuts, forzen, whether or not shelled or peeled
0811 9090.30	冷冻的榧子	30	80		5	13	千克	ABE	Chinese torreya-nuts, frozen
0811 9090.40	冷冻的翅果油树果	30	80		5	13	千克	ABE	Fruit of Elaeagus mollis Diels, frozen
0811 9090.50	冷冻的巨籽棕（海椰子）果仁	30	80		5	13	千克	ABEF	Palm seed (Double coconut), frozen
0811 9090.90	其他未列名冷冻水果及坚果	30	80		5	13	千克	AB	Other fruit and nuts, frozen, not elsewhere specified or included
08.12	**暂时保藏（例如，使用二氧化硫气体、盐水、亚硫酸水或其他防腐液）的水果及坚果，但不适于直接食用的：**								**Fruit and nuts, provisionally preserved (for example, by sulphur dioxide gas, in brine, in sulphur water or in other preservative solutions）, but unsuitable in that state for immediate consumption:**
0812.1000	-樱桃	30	80		5	13	千克	AB	-Cherries
0812.9000	-其他	25	80			13	千克		-Other
0812 9000.10	暂时保存的白果(用二氧化硫气体、盐水等物质处理，但不适于直接食用的)	25	80		5	13	千克	ABE	Ginkgo, provisionally preserved by sulphur dioxide gas or in brine, or in other preservative solutions, but unsuitable in that state for immediate consumption
0812 9000.21	暂时保存的红松子(用二氧化硫气体、盐水等物质处理，但不适于直接食用的)	25	80		5	13	千克	ABE	Korean pine-nuts, provisionally preserved by sulphur dioxide gas or in brine, or in other preservative solutions, but unsuitable in that state for immediate consumption
0812 9000.22	暂时保存的其他濒危松子(用二氧化硫气体、盐水等物质处理，但不适于直接食用的)	25	80			13	千克	ABEF	Other endangered pine-nuts, provisionally preserved by sulphur dioxide gas or in brine, or in other preservative solutions, but unsuitable in that state for immediate consumption
0812 9000.30	暂时保存的榧子(用二氧化硫气体、盐水等物质处理，但不适于直接食用的)	25	80		5	13	千克	ABE	Chinese toreeya-nuts, provisionally preserved by sulphur dioxide gas or in brine, or in other preservative solutions, but unsuitable in that state for immediate consumption
0812 9000.40	暂时保存的翅果油树果(用二氧化硫气体、盐水等物质处理，但不适于直接食用的)	25	80		5	13	千克	ABE	Fruit of Elaeagus mollis Diels, provisionally preserved by sulphur dioxide gas or in brine, or in other preservative solutions, but unsuitable in that state for immediate consumption
0812 9000.50	暂时保存的巨籽棕（海椰子）果仁(用二氧化硫气体，盐水等物质处理，但不适于直接食用的)	25	80		5	13	千克	ABEF	Palm seed (Double coconut), provisionally preserved by sulphur dioxide gas or in brine, or in other preservative solutions, but unsuitable in that state for immediate consumption
0812 9000.90	暂时保存的其他水果及坚果(用二氧化硫气体、盐水等物质处理，但不适于直接食用的)	25	80		5	13	千克	AB	Other fruit and nuts, provisionally preserved by sulphur dioxide gas or in brine, or in other preservative solutions, but unsuitable in that state for immediate consumption
08.13	**品目 08.01 至 08.06 以外的干果；本章的什锦坚果或干果：**								**Fruit, dried, other than that of headings No.08.01 to 08.06; mixtures of nuts or dried fruits of this Chapter:**
0813.1000	-杏	25	70		5	13	千克	AB	-Apricots
0813.2000	-梅及李	25	70		5	13	千克	AB	-Prunes
0813.3000	-苹果	25	70		5	13	千克	AB	-Apples
	-其他:								-Other fruit:
0813.4010	---龙眼干、肉	20	70		5	13	千克	AB	---Longans and longan pulps
0813.4020	---柿饼	25	70		5	13	千克	AB	---Persimmons
0813.4030	---红枣	25	70		5	13	千克	AB	---Red jujubes
0813.4040	---荔枝干	25	70		5	13	千克	AB	---Preserved litchi

税则号列 Tariff Item	商品名称及备注	进口税率			出口退税	增值税率	计量单位	监管条件	Article Description
		最惠	普通	暂定					
0813.4090	---其他	25	70		5	13	千克		---Other
0813 4090.10	翅果油树干果	25	70		5	13	千克	ABE	Fruit of *Elaeagus mollis Diels*, dried
0813 4090.90	其他干果（品目 08.01 至 08.06 的干果除外）	25	70		5	13	千克	AB	Other fruit, dried, other than that of headings No.08.01 to 08.06
0813.5000	-本章的什锦坚果或干果	18	70		5	13	千克	AB	-Mixtures of nuts or dried fruits of this Chapter
08.14	**柑橘属水果或甜瓜（包括西瓜）的果皮，鲜、冻、干或用盐水、亚硫酸水或其他防腐液暂时保藏的：**								**Peel of citrus fruit or melons（including watermelons), fresh, frozen, dried or provisionally preserved in brine, in sulphur water or in other preservative solutions:**
0814.0000	柑橘属水果或甜瓜(包括西瓜)的果皮，鲜、冻、干或用盐水、亚硫酸水或其他防腐液暂时保藏的	25	70		5	13	千克	AB	Peel of citrus fruit or melons（including watermelons）, fresh, frozen, dried or provisionally preserved in brine, in sulphur water or in other preservative solutions

第九章 咖啡、茶、马黛茶及调味香料

Chapter 9 Coffee, tea, mate and spices

注释：

一、品目 09.04 至 09.10 所列产品的混合物，应按下列规定归类：

（一）同一品目的两种或两种以上产品的混合物仍应归入该品目；

（二）不同品目的两种或两种以上产品的混合物应归入品目 09.10。

品目 09.04 至 09.10 的产品[或上述（一）或（二）项的混合物]如添加了其他物质，只要所得的混合物保持了原产品的基本特性，其归类应不受影响。基本特性已经改变的，则不应归入本章；构成混合调味品的，应归入品目 21.03。

二、本章不包括荜澄茄椒或品目12.11的其他产品。

Chapter Notes:

1.Mixtures of the products of headings 09.04 to 09.10 are to be classified as follows:

(a) Mixtures of two or more of the products of the same heading are to be classified in that heading;

(b) Mixtures of two or more of the products of different headings are to be classified in heading 09.10.

The addition of other substances to the products of headings 09.04 to 09.10[or to the mixtures referred to in paragraph (a) or (b) above]shall not affect their classification provided the resulting mixtures retain the essential character of the goods of those headings. Otherwise such mixtures are not classified in this Chapter, those constituting mixed condiments or mixed seasonings are classified in heading 21.03.

2.This Chapter does not cover Cubeb pepper(Piper cubeba) or other products of heading 12.11.

税则号列 Tariff Item	商品名称及备注	进口税率 最惠	普通	暂定	出口退税	增值税率	计量单位	监管条件	Article Description
09.01	**咖啡，不论是否焙炒或浸除咖啡碱；咖啡豆荚及咖啡豆皮；含咖啡的咖啡代用品：**								**Coffee, whether or not roasted or decaffeinated; coffee husks and skins; coffee substitutes containing coffee in any proportion:**
	-未焙炒的咖啡:								-Coffee, not roasted:
0901.1100	--未浸除咖啡碱	8	50		5	17	千克	AB	--Not decaffeinated
0901.1200	--已浸除咖啡碱	8	50		5	17	千克	AB	--Decaffeinated
	-已焙炒的咖啡:								-Coffee, roasted:
0901.2100	--未浸除咖啡碱	15	80		15	17	千克	AB	--Not decaffeinated
0901.2200	--已浸除咖啡碱	15	80		15	17	千克	AB	--Decaffeinated
	-其他:								-Other:
0901.9010	---咖啡豆荚及咖啡豆皮	10	30		5	17	千克	AB	---Coffee husks and skins
0901.9020	---含咖啡的咖啡代用品	30	80		15	17	千克	AB	---Coffee substitutes containing coffee
09.02	**茶，不论是否加香料：**								**Tea, whether or not flavoured:**
	-绿茶（未发酵），内包装每件净重不超过 3 千克:								-Green tea (not fermented) in immediate packings of a content not exceeding 3kg:
0902.1010	---花茶	15	100		5/15	13	千克	AB	---Flavoured
0902.1090	---其他	15	100		5/15	13	千克	AB	---Other
	-其他绿茶（未发酵）:								-Other green tea (not fermented) :
0902.2010	---花茶	15	100		5/15	13	千克	AB	---Flavoured
0902.2090	---其他	15	100		5/15	13	千克	AB	---Other
	-红茶（已发酵）及半发酵茶，内包装每件净重不超过 3 千克:								-Black tea (fermented) and partly fermented tea, in immediate packings of a content not exceeding 3 kg:
0902.3010	---乌龙茶	15	100		5/15	13	千克	AB	---Oolong tea
0902.3020	---普洱茶	15	100		5/15	13	千克	AB	---Pu-er tea
0902.3090	---其他	15	100		5/15	13	千克	AB	---Other
	-其他红茶(已发酵)及半发酵茶:								-Other black tea (fermented) and other partly fermented tea:
0902.4010	---乌龙茶	15	100		5/15	13	千克	AB	---Oolong tea
0902.4020	---普洱茶	15	100		5/15	13	千克	AB	---Pu-er tea
0902.4090	---其他	15	100		5/15	13	千克	AB	---Other
09.03	**马黛茶：**								**Mate:**
0903.0000	马黛茶	10	100		15	13	千克	AB	Mate
09.04	**胡椒；辣椒干及辣椒粉：**								**Pepper of the genus *Piper*; dried or crushed or ground fruits of the genus *Capsicum or of the genus Pimenta:***
	-胡椒:								-Pepper:
0904.1100	--未磨	20	70		5	13	千克		--Neither crushed nor ground

税则号列 Tariff Item	商品名称及备注	进口税率 最惠	普通	暂定	出口退税	增值税率	计量单位	监管条件	Article Description
0904 1100.10	毕拨	20	70		5	13	千克	QAB	Piper
0904 1100.90	未磨胡椒（毕拨除外）	20	70		5	13	千克	AB	Pepper of the genus *piper*, neither crushed nor ground （other than piper）
0904.1200	--已磨	20	70		15	13	千克	AB	--Crushed or ground
	-辣椒:								-Fruits of the genus *Capsicum* or of the genus *Pimenta* :
0904.2100	--干，未磨	20	70			13	千克	AB	---Dried, neither crushed nor ground
0904.2200	--已磨	20	70		15	13	千克	AB	---Crushed or ground
09.05	香子兰豆:								**Vanilla:**
0905.1000	-未磨	15	50		5	13	千克	AB	-Neither crushed nor ground
0905.2000	-已磨	15	50		5	13	千克	AB	-Crushed or ground
09.06	肉桂及肉桂花:								**Cinnamon and cinnamon-tree flowers:**
	-未磨:								-Neither crushed nor ground:
0906.1100	--锡兰肉桂	5	50		5	13	千克	AB	--Cinnamon（*Cinnamomum zeylanicum Blume*）
0906.1900	--其他	5	50		5	13	千克	AB	--Other
0906.2000	-已磨	15	50		15	13	千克	QAB	-Crushed or ground
09.07	丁香（母丁香、公丁香及丁香梗）：								**Cloves（whole fruit, cloves and stems）:**
0907.1000	-未磨	3	14		5	13	千克	QAB	-Neither crushed nor ground
0907.2000	-已磨	3	14		5	13	千克	QAB	-Crushed or ground
09.08	肉豆蔻、肉豆蔻衣及豆蔻:								**Nutmeg, mace and cardamoms:**
	-肉豆蔻:								-Nutmeg :
0908.1100	--未磨	8	30		5	13	千克	QABE	--Neither crushed nor ground
0908.1200	--已磨	8	30		5	13	千克	QABE	-Crushed or ground
	-肉豆蔻衣:								-Mace :
0908.2100	--未磨	8	30		5	13	千克	ABE	--Neither crushed nor ground
0908.2200	--已磨	8	30		5	13	千克	ABE	-Crushed or ground
	-豆蔻:								-Cardamoms :
0908.3100	--未磨	3	14		5	13	千克	QABE	--Neither crushed nor ground
0908.3200	--已磨	3	14		15	13	千克	QABE	--Crushed or ground
09.09	茴芹子、八角茴香、小茴香子、芫荽子、枯茗子及贳蒿子；杜松果:								**Seeds of anise, badian, fennel, coriander, cumin or caraway; juniper berries:**
	-芫荽子:								-Seeds of coriander :
0909.2100	--未磨	15	50		5	13	千克	AB	--Neither crushed nor ground
0909.2200	--已磨	15	50		15	13	千克	AB	-Crushed or ground
	-枯茗子:								-Seeds of cumin :
0909.3100	--未磨	15	50		5	13	千克	AB	--Neither crushed nor ground
0909.3200	--已磨	15	50		15	13	千克	AB	--Crushed or ground
	-茴芹子或八角茴香、贳蒿子或小茴香子；杜松果:								-Seeds of anise, badian, caraway or fennel; juniper berries :
	--未磨:								--Neither crushed nor ground :
0909.6110	---八角茴香	20	90		5	13	千克	QAB	---Badian
0909.6190	---其他	15	50		5	13	千克		---Other
0909 6190.10	未磨的小茴香子；未磨的杜松果	15	50		5	13	千克	QAB	Unground fennel; unground juniper berries
0909 6190.90	未磨的茴芹子；未磨的贳蒿子	15	50		5	13	千克	AB	Unground seeds of anise ; unground seeds of caraway
	--已磨:								--Crushed or ground
0909.6210	---八角茴香	20	90		15	13	千克	QAB	---Badian
0909.6290	---其他	15	50		15	13	千克		---Other
0909 6290.10	已磨的小茴香子；已磨的杜松果	15	50		15	13	千克	QAB	Fenmel or juniper berries, crushed or ground
0909 6290.90	已磨的茴芹子；已磨的贳蒿子	15	50		15	13	千克	AB	Seeds of anise or caraway, crushed or ground
09.10	姜、番红花、姜黄、麝香草、月桂叶、咖喱及其他调味香料:								**Ginger, saffron, turmeric (*cnrcuma*), thyme, bay leaves, curry and other spices:**
	-姜:								-Ginger :
0910.1100	--未磨	15	50			13	千克	AB	--Neither crushed nor ground
0910.1200	--已磨	15	50		5	13	千克	AB	--Crushed or ground
0910.2000	-番红花	2	14		5/15	13	千克	QAB	-Saffron

税则号列 Tariff Item	商品名称及备注	进口税率			出口退税	增值税率	计量单位	监管条件	Article Description
		最惠	普通	暂定					
0910.3000	-姜黄	15	50		5	13	千克	QAB	-Turmric（*curcuma*）
	-其他调味香料:								-Other spices:
0910.9100	--本章注释一（二）所述的混合物	15	50		15	17	千克	AB	--Mixtures referred to in Note 1（b） to this Chapter
0910.9900	--其他	15	50		5/15	17	千克	AB	--Other

第十章 谷 物

Chapter 10 Cereals

注释：

一、(一) 本章各品目所列产品必须带有谷粒，不论是否成穗或带杆。

(二) 本章不包括已去壳或经其他加工的谷物。但去壳、碾磨、磨光、上光、半熟或破碎的稻米仍应归入品目10.06。

二、品目10.05不包括甜玉米（第七章）。

子目注释：

所称“硬粒小麦”，是指硬粒小麦属的小麦及以该属具有相同染色体数目（28）的小麦种间杂交所得的小麦。

Chapter Notes:

1. (a) The products specified in the headings of this Chapter are to be classified in those headings only if grains are present, whether or not in the ear or on the stalk.

(b) The Chapter does not cover grains which have been hulled or otherwise worked. However, rice, husked, milled, polished, glazed parboiled or broken remains classified in heading 10.06.

2. Heading 10.05 does not cover sweet corn（Chapter 7）.

Subheading Note:

The term “durum wheat” means wheat of the Triticum durum species and the hybrids derived from the inter-specific crossing of Triticum durum which have the same number（28）of chromosomes as that species.

税则号列 Tariff Item	商品名称及备注	进口税率 最惠	普通	暂定	出口退税	增值税率	计量单位	监管条件	Article Description
10.01	小麦及混合麦：								**Wheat and maslin:**
	-硬粒小麦：								-Durum wheat :
1001.1100	--种用		180			13	千克		--Seed
1001 1100.01	种用硬粒小麦(配额内)	1	180			13	千克	4xABty	Durum wheat seed (in quota)
1001 1100.90	种用硬粒小麦(配额外)	65	180			13	千克	4xABy	Durum wheat seed (out-of-quota)
1001.1900	--其他		180			13	千克		--Other
1001 1900.01	其他硬粒小麦(配额内)	1	180			13	千克	4xABty	Other durum wheat (in quota)
1001 1900.90	其他硬粒小麦(配额外)	65	180			13	千克	4xABy	Other durum wheat (out-of-quota)
	-其他：								-Other:
1001.9100	--种用		180			13	千克		---Seed
1001 9100.01	其他种用小麦及混合麦(配额内)	1	180			13	千克	4xABty	Other wheat seed and maslin seed (in quota)
1001 9100.90	其他种用小麦及混合麦(配额外)	65	180			13	千克	4xABy	Other wheat seed and maslin seed (out-of-quota)
1001.9900	--其他		180			13	千克		---Other
1001 9900.01	其他小麦及混合麦(配额内)	1	180			13	千克	4xABty	Other wheat and maslin (in quota)
1001 9900.90	其他小麦及混合麦(配额外)	65	180			13	千克	4xABy	Other wheat and maslin (out-of-quota)
10.02	黑麦：								**Rye:**
1002.1000	-种用	0	0			13	千克	AB	---Seed
1002.9000	-其他	3	8			13	千克	AB	---Other
10.03	大麦：								**Barley:**
1003.1000	-种用	0	160			13	千克	AB	---Seed
1003.9000	-其他	3	160			13	千克	AB	---Other
10.04	燕麦：								**Oats:**
1004.1000	-种用	0	0			13	千克	AB	---Seed
1004.9000	-其他	2	8			13	千克	AB	---Other
10.05	玉米：								**Maize（corn）:**
1005.1000	-种用		180			13	千克		-Seed
1005 1000.01	种用玉米（配额内）	1	180			13	千克	4xAByt	Maize（corn）seed（in-quota）
1005 1000.90	种用玉米（配额外）	20	180			13	千克	4xABy	Maize（corn）seed（out-of-quota）
1005.9000	-其他		180			13	千克		-Other
1005 9000.01	其他玉米（配额内）	1	180			13	千克	4xAByt	Other maize（corn）（in-quota）
1005 9000.90	其他玉米（配额外）	65	180			13	千克	4xABy	Other maize（corn）（out-of-quota）
10.06	稻谷、大米：								**Rice:**
	-稻谷：								-Rice in husk（paddy or rough）:
	---种用：								---Seed:
1006.1011	----籼米		180			13	千克		----Long grain
1006 1011.01	种用籼米稻谷（配额内）	1	180			13	千克	4xAByt	Rice in husk, long grain, seed（in-quota）
1006 1011.90	种用籼米稻谷（配额外）	65	180			13	千克	4xABy	Rice in husk, long grain, seed（out-of-quota）
1006.1019	----其他		180			13	千克		----Other

税则号列 Tariff Item	商品名称及备注	进口税率 最惠	普通	暂定	出口退税	增值税率	计量单位	监管条件	Article Description
1006 1019.01	其他种用稻谷（配额内）	1	180			13	千克	4xAByt	Other rice in husk, seed（in-quota）
1006 1019.90	其他种用稻谷（配额外）	65	180			13	千克	4xABy	Other rice in husk, seed（out-of-quota）
	---其他:								---Other:
1006.1091	----籼米		180			13	千克		----Long grain
1006 1091.01	其他籼米稻谷（配额内）	1	180			13	千克	4xAByt	Other rice in husk, long grain,（in-quota）
1006 1091.90	其他籼米稻谷（配额外）	65	180			13	千克	4xABy	Other rice in husk, long grain,(out-of-quota)
1006.1099	----其他		180			13	千克		----Other
1006 1099.01	其他稻谷（配额内）	1	180			13	千克	4xAByt	Other rice in husk（in-quota）
1006 1099.90	其他稻谷（配额外）	65	180			13	千克	4xABy	Other rice in husk（out-of-quota）
	-糙米:								-Husked（brown）rice:
1006.2010	---籼米		180			13	千克		---Long grain
1006 2010.01	籼米糙米（配额内）	1	180			13	千克	4xAByt	Husked（brown）rice, long grain,（in quota）
1006 2010.90	籼米糙米（配额外）	65	180			13	千克	4xABy	Husked（brown）rice, long grain,（out of quota）
1006.2090	---其他		180			13	千克		---Other
1006 2090.01	其他糙米（配额内）	1	180			13	千克	4xAByt	Other husked（brown）rice（in-quota）
1006 2090.90	其他糙米（配额外）	65	180			13	千克	4xABy	Other husked(brown）rice,(out-of-quota)
	-精米，不论是否磨光或上光:								-Semi-milled or wholly milled rice, whether or not polished or glazed:
1006.3010	---籼米		180			13	千克		---Long grain
1006 3010.01	籼米精米[不论是否磨光或上光（配额内）]	1	180			13	千克	4xAByt	Semi-milled or wholly milled rice,long grain, whether or not polished or glazed (in-quota)
1006 3010.90	籼米精米[不论是否磨光或上光（配额外）]	65	180			13	千克	4xABy	Semi-milled or wholly milled rice,long grain, whether or not polished or glazed (out-of-quota)
1006.3090	---其他		180			13	千克		---Other
1006 3090.01	其他精米[不论是否磨光或上光（配额内）]	1	180			13	千克	4xAByt	Other semi-milled or wholly milled rice, whether or not polished or glazed（in-quota）
1006 3090.90	其他精米[不论是否磨光或上光（配额外）]	65	180			13	千克	4xABy	Other semi-milled or wholly milled rice, whether or not polished or glazed（out-of-quota）
	-碎米:								-Broken rice:
1006.4010	---籼米		180			13	千克		---Long grain
1006 4010.01	籼米碎米（配额内）	1	180			13	千克	4xAByt	Broken rice, long grain（in-quota）
1006 4010.90	籼米碎米（配额外）	65	180			13	千克	4xABy	Broken rice, long grain（out-of-quota）
1006.4090	---其他		180			13	千克		---Other
1006 4090.01	其他碎米（配额内）	1	180			13	千克	4xAByt	Other broken rice（in-quota）
1006 4090.90	其他碎米（配额外）	65	180			13	千克	4xABy	Other broken rice（out-of-quota）
10.07	**食用高粱:**								**Grain sorghum:**
1007.1000	-种用	0	0			13	千克	AB	---Seed
1007.9000	-其他	2	8			13	千克	AB	---Other
10.08	**荞麦、谷子及加那利草子；其他谷物:**								**Buckwheat, millet and canary seed; other cereals:**
1008.1000	-荞麦	2	8			13	千克	AB	-Buckwheat
	-谷子:								-Millet :
1008.2100	--种用	2	8			13	千克	AB	--Seed
1008.2900	--其他	2	8			13	千克	AB	--Other
1008.3000	-加那利草子	2	8		5	13	千克	AB	-Canary seed
	-直长马唐（马唐属）:								-Fonio (Digitaria spp.)
1008.4010	---种用	0	0			13	千克	AB	---Seed
1008.4090	---其他	3	8			13	千克	AB	---Other
	-昆诺阿藜:								-Quinoa (Chenopodium quinoa) :
1008.5010	---种用	0	0			13	千克	AB	---Seed
1008.5090	---其他	3	8			13	千克	AB	---Other
	-黑小麦:								-Triticale :
1008.6010	---种用	0	0			13	千克	AB	---Seed
1008.6090	---其他	3	80			13	千克	AB	---Other
	-其他谷物:								-Other cereals:
1008.9010	---种用	0	0			13	千克	AB	---Seed
1008.9090	---其他	3	8			13	千克	AB	---Other

第十一章
制粉工业产品；麦芽；淀粉；菊粉；面筋

注释：

一、本章不包括：

（一）作为咖啡代用品的焙制麦芽（品目 09.01 或 21.01）；

（二）品目 19.01 的经制作的细粉、粗粒、粗粉或淀粉；

（三）品目 19.04 的玉米片及其他产品；

（四）品目 20.01、20.04 或 20.05 的经制作或保藏的蔬菜；

（五）药品（第三十章）；或

（六）具有芳香料制品或化妆盥洗品性质的淀粉（第三十三章）。

二、（一）下表所列谷物碾磨产品按干制品重量计，如果同时符合以下两个条件，应归入本章；但是，整粒、滚压、制片或磨碎的谷物胚芽均归入品目 11.04：

1. 淀粉含量（按修订的尤艾斯旋光法测定）超过表列第（2）栏的比例；以及

2. 灰分含量（除去任何添加的矿物质）不超过表列第（3）栏的比例。

否则，应归入品目 23.02。

（二）符合上述规定归入本章的产品，如果用表列第（4）或第（5）栏规定孔径的金属丝网筛过筛，其通过率按重量计不低于表列比例的，应归入品目 11.01 或 11.02。

否则．应归入品目 11.03 或 11.04。

谷　物 （1）	淀粉含量 （2）	灰分含量 （3）	通过下列孔径筛子的比率	
			315 微米 （4）	500 微米 （5）
小麦及黑麦	45%	2.5%	80%	—
大麦	45%	3%	80%	—
燕麦	45%	5%	80%	—
玉米及高粱	45%	2%	—	90%
大米	45%	1.6%	80%	—
荞 麦	45%	4%	80%	—

三、税目 11.03 所称“粗粒”及“粗粉”，是指谷物经碾碎所得的下列产品：

（一）玉米产品，用 2 毫米孔径的金属丝网筛过筛，通过率按重量计不低于 95% 的；

（二）其他谷物产品，用 1.25 毫米孔径的金属丝网筛过筛，通过率按重量计不低于 95％的。

Chapter 11
Products of the milling industry; malt; starches; inulin; wheat gluten

Chapter Notes:

1. This Chapter does not cover:

（a）Roasted malt put up as coffee substitutes（heading 09.01 or 21.01）;

（b）Prepared flours, groats, meals or starches of heading 19.01;

（c）Corn flakes or other products of heading 19.04;

（d）Vegetables, prepared or preserved, of heading 20.01, 20.04 or 20.05;

（e）Pharmaceutical products（Chapter 30）; or

（f）Starches having the character of perfumery; cosmetic or toilet preparations（Chapter 33）.

2.（a）Products from the milling of the cereals listed in the table below fall in this Chapter if they have, by weight on the dry product（However, germ of cereals, whole, rolled, flaked or ground is always classified in heading 11.04.）:

（ⅰ）A starch content（determined by the modified Ewers polarimetric method）exceeding that indicated in Column（2）; and

（ⅱ）An ash content（after deduction of any added minerals）not exceeding that indicated in Column（3）.

Otherwise, they fall in heading 23.02.

（b）Products falling in this Chapter under the above provisions shall be classified in heading 11.01 or 11.02 if the percentage passing through a woven metal wire cloth sieve with the aperture indicated in Column（4）or（5）is not less,by weight, than that shown against the cereal concerned. Otherwise, they fall in heading 11.03 or 11.04.

Cereal （1）	Starch content （2）	Ash content （3）	Rate of passage through a sieve with an aperture of	
			315 micrometres（microns） （4）	500 micrometres（microns） （5）
Wheat and rye	45%	2.5%	80%	—
Barley	45%	3%	80%	—
Oats	45%	5%	80%	—
Mai（corn）and grain Sorghum	45%	2%	—	90%
Rice	45%	1.6%	80%	—
Buckwheat	45%	4%	80%	—

3. For the purposes of heading 11.03, the terms “groats” and “meal” mean products obtained by the fragmentation of cereal grains, of which:

（a）In the case of maize（corn）products, at least 95% by weight passes through a woven metal wire cloth sieve with an aperture of 2mm;

（b）In the case of other cereal products, at least 95% by weight passes through a woven metal wire cloth sieve with an aperture of 1.25mm.

税则号列 Tariff Item	商品名称及备注	进口税率 最惠	普通	暂定	出口退税	增值税率	计量单位	监管条件	Article Description
11.01	**小麦或混合麦的细粉：**								**Wheat or maslin flour:**
1101.0000	小麦或混合麦的细粉		130			13	千克		Wheat or maslin flour
1101 0000.01	小麦或混合麦的细粉（配额内）	6	130			13	千克	4ABtxy	Wheat or maslin flour（in-quota）
1101 0000.90	小麦或混合麦的细粉（配额外）	65	130			13	千克	4ABxy	Wheat or maslin flour（out-of-quota）
11.02	**其他谷物细粉，但小麦或混合麦的细粉除外：**								**Cereal flours other than of wheat or maslin:**
1102.2000	-玉米细粉		130			13	千克		-Maize (corn) flour
1102 2000.01	玉米细粉（配额内）	9	130			13	千克	4ABtxy	Maize (corn) flour (in-quota)
1102 2000.90	玉米细粉（配额外）	40	130			13	千克	4ABxy	Maize (corn) flour (out-of-quota)
	-其他：								-Other:
	---大米细粉：								---Rice flour:
1102.9011	----籼米的		130			13	千克		----Of long grain
1102 9011.01	籼米大米细粉（配额内）	9	130			13	千克	4ABtxy	Rice flour of long grain（in-quota）
1102 9011.90	籼米大米细粉（配额外）	40	130			13	千克	4ABxy	Rice flour of long grain（out-of-quota）
1102.9019	----其他		130			13	千克		----Other
1102 9019.01	其他大米细粉（配额内）	9	130			13	千克	4ABtxy	Other rice flour（in-quota）
1102 9019.90	其他大米细粉（配额外）	40	130			13	千克	4ABxy	Other rice flour（out-of-quota）
1102.9090	---其他	5	14			13	千克	AB	---Other
11.03	**谷物的粗粒、粗粉及团粒：**								**Cereal groats, meal and pellets:**
	-粗粒及粗粉：								-Groats and meal:
1103.1100	--小麦的		130			13	千克		--Of wheat
1103 1100.01	小麦粗粒及粗粉（配额内）	9	130			13	千克	4ABtxy	Groats and meal of wheat（in-quota）
1103 1100.90	小麦粗粒及粗粉（配额外）	65	130			13	千克	4ABxy	Groats and meal of wheat（out-of-quota）
1103.1300	--玉米的		130			13	千克		--Of maize（corn）
1103 1300.01	玉米粗粒及粗粉（配额内）	9	130			13	千克	4ABtxy	Groats and meal of maize(corn) (in-quota)
1103 1300.90	玉米粗粒及粗粉（配额外）	65	130			13	千克	4ABxy	Groats and meal of maize(corn) (out-of-quota)
	--其他：								--Other:
1103.1910	---燕麦的	5	14			13	千克	AB	---Of oats
	---大米的：								---Of rice:
1103.1921	----籼米的		70			13	千克		----Of long grain
1103 1921.01	籼米大米粗粒及粗粉（配额内）	9	70			13	千克	4ABtxy	Groats and meal of rice, long grain(in-quota)
1103 1921.90	籼米大米粗粒及粗粉（配额外）	10	70			13	千克	4ABxy	Groats and meal of rice, long grain(out-of-quota)
1103.1929	----其他		70			13	千克		----Other
1103 1929.01	其他大米粗粒及粗粉（配额内）	9	70			13	千克	4ABtxy	Groats and meal of other rice（in-quota）
1103 1929.90	其他大米粗粒及粗粉(配额外)	10	70			13	千克	4ABxy	Groats and meal of other rice（out-of-quota）
1103.1990	---其他	5	14			13	千克	AB	---Other
	-团粒：								-Pellets:
1103.2010	---小麦的		180			13	千克		---Of wheat
1103 2010.01	小麦团粒（配额内）	10	180			13	千克	4ABtxy	Pellets wheat（in-quota）
1103 2010.90	小麦团粒（配额外）	65	180			13	千克	4ABxy	Pellets wheat（out-of-quota）
1103.2090	---其他	20	50			13	千克	AB	---Of other cereals
11.04	**经其他加工的谷物(例如，去壳、滚压、制片、制成粒状、切片或粗磨），但品目 10.06 的稻谷、大米除外；谷物胚芽，整粒、滚压、制片或磨碎的：**								**Cereal grains otherwise worked（for example, hulled, rolled, flaked, pearled, sliced or kibbled）, except rice of heading No. 10.06; germ of cereals, whole, rolled, flaked or ground:**
	-滚压或制片的谷物：								-Rolled or flaked grains:
1104.1200	--燕麦的	20	50			17	千克	AB	--Of oats
	--其他：								--Other:
1104.1910	---大麦的	20	50			17	千克	AB	---Of barley
1104.1990	---其他	20	50			17	千克		---Other
1104 1990.10	滚压或制片的玉米	20	50			17	千克	4ABxy	Rolled or flaked maize(corn)
1104 1990.90	滚压或制片的其他谷物	20	50			17	千克	AB	Rolled or flaked other grains
	-经其他加工的谷物(例如，去壳、制成粒状、切片或粗磨)：								-Other worked grains（for example, hulled, pearled, sliced or kibbled）:
1104.2200	--燕麦的	20	50			17	千克	AB	--Of oats
1104.2300	--玉米的		180			13	千克		--Of maize corn

税则号列 Tariff Item	商品名称及备注	进口税率 最惠	进口税率 普通	进口税率 暂定	出口退税	增值税率	计量单位	监管条件	Article Description
1104 2300.01	经其他加工的玉米（配额内）	10	180			13	千克	4ABtxy	Other worked maize（corn）（in-quota）
1104 2300.90	经其他加工的玉米（配额外）	65	180			13	千克	4ABxy	Other worked maize（corn）（out-of-quota）
	--其他:								--Other:
1104.2910	---大麦的	65	114			13	千克	AB	---Of barley
1104.2990	---其他	20	50			13	千克	AB	---Other
1104.3000	-谷物胚芽，整粒、滚压、制片或磨碎的	20	50			17	千克	AB	-Germ of cereals, whole, rolled, flaked or ground
11.05	**马铃薯的细粉、粗粉、粉末、粉片、颗粒及团粒:**								**Flour, meal, powder, flakes, granules and pellets of potatoes:**
1105.1000	-细粉、粗粉及粉末	15	50		15	17	千克	AB	-Flour, meal and powder
1105.2000	-粉片、颗粒及团粒	15	50		15	17	千克	AB	-Flakes, granules and pellets
11.06	**用品目 07.13 的干豆或品目 07.14 的西谷茎髓及植物根茎、块茎制成的细粉、粗粉及粉末；用第八章的产品制成的细粉、粗粉及粉末:**								**Flour, meal and powder of the dried leguminous vegetables of heading No.07.13, of sago or of roots or tubers of headingNo. 07.14; or of the products of Chapter 8:**
1106.1000	-用品目 07.13 的干豆制成的	10	30		15	17	千克	AB	-Of the dried leguminous vegetables of heading No. 07.13
1106.2000	-用品目 07.14 的西谷茎髓及植物根茎、块茎制成的	20	50		15	17	千克	AB	-Of sago or of roots or tubers of heading No. 07.14
1106.3000	-用第八章的产品制成的	20	80		5/15	17	千克	AB	-Of the products of Chapter 8
11.07	**麦芽，不论是否焙制:**								**Malt, whether or not roasted:**
1107.1000	-未焙制	10	50		15	17	千克	AB	-Not roasted
1107.2000	-已焙制	10	50		15	17	千克	AB	-Roasted
11.08	**淀粉；菊粉:**								**Starches; inulin:**
	-淀粉:								-Starches:
1108.1100	--小麦淀粉	20	50			17	千克	AB	--Wheat starch
1108.1200	--玉米淀粉	20	50			17	千克	AB	--Maize（corn）starch
1108.1300	--马铃薯淀粉	15	50		15	17	千克	AB	--Potato starch
1108.1400	--木薯淀粉	10	50		15	17	千克	AB	--Manioc（cassava）starch
1108.1900	--其他	20	50		15	17	千克	AB	--Other starches
1108.2000	-菊粉	20	50		15	17	千克	AB	-Inulin
11.09	**面筋，不论是否干制:**								**Wheat gluten, whether or not dried:**
1109.0000	面筋，不论是否干制	18	80		15	17	千克	AB	Wheat gluten, whether or not dried

第十二章
含油子仁及果实；杂项子仁及果实；工业用或药用植物；稻草、秸秆及饲料

注释：

一、品目12.07主要包括棕榈果及棕榈仁、棉子、蓖麻子、芝麻、芥子、红花子、罂粟子、牛油树果，但不包括品目08.01或08.02的产品及油橄榄（第七章或第二十章）。

二、品目12.08不仅包括未脱脂的细粉和粗粉，而且包括部分或全部脱脂以及用其本身的油料全部或部分复脂的细粉和粗粉。但不包括品目23.04至23.06的残渣。

三、甜菜子、草子及其他草本植物种子、观赏用花的种子、蔬菜种子、林木种子、果树种子、巢菜子（蚕豆除外）、羽扇豆属植物种子，可一律视为种植用种子，归入品目12.09。

但下列各项即使作种子用，也不归入品目12.09：

（一）豆类蔬菜或甜玉米（第七章）；
（二）第九章的调味香料及其他产品；
（三）谷物（第十章）；或
（四）品目12.01至12.07或12.11的产品。

四、品目12.11主要包括下列植物或这些植物的某部分：罗勒、琉璃苣、人参、海索草、甘草、薄荷、迷迭香、芸香、鼠尾草及苦艾。

但品目12.11不包括：

（一）第三十章的药品；
（二）第三十三章的芳香料制品及化妆盥洗品；或
（三）品目38.08的杀虫剂、杀菌剂、除草剂、消毒剂及类似产品。

五、品目12.02的“海草及其他藻类”不包括：

（一）品目21.02的已死的单细胞微生物；
（二）品目30.02的培养微生物；或
（三）品目31.01或31.05的肥料。

子目注释：

子目1205.10所称“低芥子酸油菜子”，是指所获取的固定油中芥子酸含量按重量计低于2%，以及所得的固体成分每克葡萄糖苷酸（酯）含量低于30微摩尔的油菜子。

Chapter 12
Oil seeds and oleaginous fruits; miscellaneous grains, seeds and fruit; industrial or medicinal plants; straw and fodder

Chapter Notes:

1. Heading 12.07 applies, *inter alia*, to palm nuts and kernels, cotton seeds, castor oil seeds, sesamum seeds, mustard seeds, safflower seeds, poppy seeds and shea nuts (karite nuts). It does not apply to products of heading 08.01 or 08.02 or to olives (Chapter 7 or Chapter 20).

2. Heading 12.08 applies not only to non-defatted flours and meals but also to flours and meals which have been partially defatted or defatted and wholly or partially refatted with their original oils. It does not, however, apply to residues of headings 23.04 to 23.06

3. For the purposes of heading12.09, beet seeds, grass and other herbage seeds, seeds of ornamental flowers, vegetable seeds, seeds of forest trees, seeds of fruit trees, seeds of vetches (other than those of the species *vicia faba*) or of lupines are to be regarded as “seeds of a kind used for sowing”.

Heading 12.09 does not, however, apply to the following even if for sowing:

(a) Leguminous vegetables or sweet corn (Chapter 7);
(b) Spices or other products of Chapter 9;
(c) Cereals (Chapter 10); or
(d) Products of headings 12.01 to 12.07 or 12.11.

4. Heading 12.11 applies, *inter alia*, to the following plants or parts thereof: basil, borage, ginseng, hyssop, liquorice, all species of mint, rosemary, rue, sage and wormwood.

Heading 12.11 does not, however, apply to:

(a) Medicaments of Chapter 30;
(b) Perfumery, cosmetic or toilet preparations of Chapter 33;or
(c) Insecticides, fungicides, herbicides, disinfectants or similar products of heading 38.08

5 For the purposes of heading 12.12, the term “seaweeds and other algae” does not include:

(a) Dead single-cell micro-organisms of heading 21.02;
(b) Cultures of micro-organisms of heading 30.02; or
(c) Fertilisers of heading 31.01 or 31.05.

Subheading Notes:

For the purposes of subheading 1205.10, the expression “low erucic acid rape or colza seeds” means rape or colza seeds yielding a fixed oil which has an erucic acid content of less than 2% by weight and yielding a solid component which contains less than 30 micromoles of glucosinolates per gram.

税则号列 Tariff Item	商品名称及备注	进口税率			出口退税	增值税率	计量单位	监管条件	Article Description
		最惠	普通	暂定					
12.01	大豆，不论是否破碎：								**Soya beans, whether or not broken:**
1201.1000	-种用	0	180			13	千克	7AB	-Seed
	-其他:								-Other:
1201.9010	---黄大豆	3	180			13	千克	7AB	---Yellow soya beans

税则号列 Tariff Item	商品名称及备注	进口税率 最惠	进口税率 普通	进口税率 暂定	出口退税	增值税率	计量单位	监管条件	Article Description
1201.9020	---黑大豆	3	180			13	千克	7AB	---Black soya beans
1201.9030	---青大豆	3	180			13	千克	7AB	---Green soya beans
1201.9090	---其他	3	180			13	千克	7AB	----Other
12.02	未焙炒或未烹煮的花生，不论是否去壳或破碎：								**Ground-nuts, not roasted or otherwise cooked, whether or not shelled or broken:**
1202.3000	-种用	0	0			13	千克	AB	-Seed
	-其他:								-Other :
1202.4100	--未去壳	15	70			13	千克	AB	--In shell
1202.4200	--去壳，不论是否破碎	15	70			13	千克	AB	---Shelled, whether or not broken
12.03	干椰子肉：								**Copra:**
1203.0000	干椰子肉	15	30		5	13	千克	AB	Copra
12.04	亚麻子，不论是否破碎：								**Linseed, whether or not broken:**
1204.0000	亚麻子不论是否破碎	15	70		5	13	千克	AB	Linseed, whether or not broken
12.05	油菜子，不论是否破碎：								**Rape or colza seeds, whether or not broken:**
	-低芥子酸油菜子:								-Low erucic acid rape or colza seeds:
1205.1010	---种用	0	80			13	千克	7AB	---Seed
1205.1090	---其他	9	80		5	13	千克	7AB	---Other
	-其他:								-Other:
1205.9010	---种用	0	80			13	千克	7AB	---Seed
1205.9090	---其他	9	80		5	13	千克	7AB	---Other
12.06	葵花子，不论是否破碎：								**Sunflower seeds, whether or not broken:**
1206.0010	---种用	0	0		5	13	千克	AB	---Seed
1206.0090	---其他	15	70		5	13	千克	AB	---Other
12.07	其他含油子仁及果实，不论是否破碎：								**Other oil seeds and oleaginous fruits, whether or not broken:**
	-棕榈果及棕榈仁:								-Palm nuts and kernels:
1207.1010	---种用	0	0			13	千克		---Seed
1207 1010.10	种用濒危棕榈果及棕榈仁	0	0			13	千克	ABEF	Endangered palm fruit and palm kernel, seed
1207 1010.90	其他种用棕榈果及棕榈仁	0	0		5	13	千克	AB	Other palm fruit and palm kernel, seed
1207.1090	---其他	10	70			13	千克		---Other
1207 1090.10	其他濒危棕榈果及棕榈仁(不论是否破碎)	10	70			13	千克	ABEF	Other endangered palm fruit and palm kernel (wether broken or not)
1207 1090.90	其他棕榈果及棕榈仁(不论是否破碎)	10	70		5	13	千克	AB	Other palm fruit and palm kernel (whether broken or not)
	-棉子:								-Cotton seeds:
1207.2100	--种用	0	0		5	13	千克	AB	---Seed
1207.2900	--其他	15	70		5	13	千克	AB	---Other
	-蓖麻子:								-Castor oil seeds :
1207.3010	---种用	0	0		5	13	千克	AB	---Seed
1207.3090	---其他	15	70		5	13	千克	AB	---Other
	-芝麻:								-Sesamum seeds:
1207.4010	---种用	0	0		5	13	千克	AB	---Seeds for cultivation
1207.4090	---其他	10	70		5	13	千克	AB	---Other
	-芥子:								-Mustard seeds:
1207.5010	---种用	0	0		5	13	千克	AB	---Seeds for cultivation
1207.5090	---其他	15	70		5	13	千克	AB	---Other
	-红花子:								-Safflower (*Carthamus tinctorius*) seeds :
1207.6010	---种用	0	0		5	13	千克	AB	---Seed
1207.6090	---其他	20	70		5	13	千克	AB	---Other
	-甜瓜的子:								-Melon seeds :
1207.7010	---种用	0	0			13	千克	AB	---Seed
	---其他:								---Other :

税则号列 Tariff Item	商品名称及备注	进口税率			出口退税	增值税率	计量单位	监管条件	Article Description
		最惠	普通	暂定					
1207.7091	----黑瓜子	20	80		5	13	千克	AB	----Black watermelon seeds
1207.7092	----红瓜子	20	80		5	13	千克	AB	----Red watermelon seeds
1207.7099	----其他	30	70		5	13	千克	AB	----Other
	-其他:								-Other:
1207.9100	--罂粟子	20	70		5	13	千克	AB	--Poppy seeds
	--其他:								--Other:
1207.9910	---种用	0	0		5	13	千克	AB	---Seed
	---其他:								---Other:
1207.9991	----牛油树果	20	70		5	13	千克	AB	----Shea nuts（karite nuts）
1207.9999	----其他	10	70		5	13	千克	AB	----Other
12.08	**含油子仁或果实的细粉及粗粉，但芥子粉除外：**								**Flours and meals of oil seeds or oleaginous fruits, other than those of mustard:**
1208.1000	-大豆粉	9	70			17	千克	AB	-Of soya beans
1208.9000	-其他	15	80		15	17	千克	AB	-Other
12.09	**种植用的种子、果实及孢子：**								**Seeds，fruit and spores, of a kind used for sowing:**
1209.1000	-糖甜菜子	0	0		5	13	千克	AB	-Sugar beet seed
	-饲料植物种子:								-Seeds of forage plants:
1209.2100	--紫苜蓿子	0	0			13	千克	AB	--Lucerne（alfalfa）seed
1209.2200	--三叶草子	0	0			13	千克	AB	--Clover（*Trifblium spp.*）seed
1209.2300	--羊茅子	0	0			13	千克	AB	--Fescue seed
1209.2400	--草地早熟禾子	0	0			13	千克	AB	--Kentucky blue grass（*Poa pratensis L.*）seed
1209.2500	--黑麦草种子	0	0			13	千克	AB	--Rye grass(*Lolium multiflorum lam.,Lolium perenne L.*)seed
	--其他:								--Other:
1209.2910	---甜菜子，糖甜菜子除外	0	0		5	13	千克	AB	---Beet seed, excluding sugar beet seed
1209.2990	---其他	0	0			13	千克	AB	---Other
1209.3000	-草本花卉植物种子	0	0			13	千克		-Seeds of herbaceous plants cultivated principally for their flowers
1209 3000.10	濒危草本花卉植物种子	0	0			13	千克	AFEB	Seeds of endangered herbaceous plants cultivated principally for their flowers
1209 3000.90	其他草本花卉植物种子	0	0			13	千克	AB	Other seeds of herbaceous plants cultivated principally for their flowers
	-其他:								-Other:
1209.9100	--蔬菜种子	0	0			13	千克	AB	--Vegetable seeds
1209.9900	--其他	0	0			13	千克		--Other:
1209 9900.10	其他种植用濒危种子、果实及孢子	0	0			13	千克	AFEB	Other planting used endangered seeds, fruits and spores
1209 9900.90	其他种植用的种子、果实及孢子	0	0			13	千克	AB	Other seeds, fruits and spores used for planting
12.10	**鲜或干的啤酒花，不论是否研磨或制成团粒；蛇麻腺：**								**Hop cones, fresh or dried, whether or not ground, powdered or in the form of pellets; lupulin:**
1210.1000	-啤酒花，未经研磨也未制成团粒	20	50		15	17	千克	AB	-Hop cones, neither ground nor powdered nor in the form of pellets
1210.2000	-啤酒花，经研磨或制成团粒；蛇麻腺	10	50		15	17	千克	AB	-Hop cones, ground, powdered or in the form of pellets; lupulin
12.11	**主要用作香料、药料、杀虫、杀菌或类似用途的植物或这些植物的某部分（包括子仁及果实），鲜或干的，不论是否切割、压碎或研磨成粉：**								**Plants and parts of plants（including seeds and fruits), of a kind used primarily in perfumery,in pharmacy or for insecticidal, fungicidal or similar purposes, fresh or dried, whether or not cut, crushed or powdered:**
	-人参:								-Ginseng roots:
1211.2010	---西洋参	7.5	70		5	13	千克	AQBFE	---American ginseng
1211.2020	---野山参（西洋参除外）	20	90		5	13	千克	ABEF	---Wild ginseng（other than American ginseng）

税则号列 Tariff Item	商品名称及备注	进口税率			出口退税	增值税率	计量单位	监管条件	Article Description
		最惠	普通	暂定					
	---其他:								---Other:
1211.2091	----鲜的	20	50		5	13	千克	AB	----Fresh
1211.2099	----其他	20	50		5	13	千克	ABQ	----Other
1211.3000	-古柯叶	9	50		5	13	千克		-Coca leaf
1211 3000.10	药用古柯叶(不论是否切割、压碎或研磨成粉)	9	50		5	13	千克	ABW	Coca leaf, used in pharmacy, whether or not cut, crushed or powdered
1211 3000.20	做香料用古柯叶(不论是否切割、压碎或研磨成粉)	9	50		5	13	千克	AB	Coca leaf, used in perfumery, whether or not cut, crushed or powdered
1211 3000.90	杀虫杀菌用古柯叶(不论是否切割、压碎或研磨成粉)	9	50		5	13	千克	AB	Coca leaf, used for insecticidal or fungicidal, whether or not cut, crushed or powdered
1211.4000	-罂粟秆	9	50		5	13	千克		-Poppy straw
1211 4000.10	药用罂粟秆(不论是否切割、压碎或研磨成粉)	9	50		5	13	千克	AB	Poppy straw,used in pharmacy, whether or not cut, crushed or powdered
1211 4000.20	做香料用罂粟秆(不论是否切割、压碎或研磨成粉)	9	50		5	13	千克	AB	Poppy straw, used in perfumery, whether or not cut, crushed or powdered
1211 4000.90	杀虫杀菌用罂粟秆(不论是否切割、压碎或研磨成粉)	9	50		5	13	千克	AB	Poppy straw, used in insecticidal or fungicidal, whether or not cut, crushed or powdered
	-其他:								-Other:
	---主要用作药料的植物及其某部分:								---Of a kind used primarily in pharmacy:
1211.9011	----当归	6	30		5	13	千克	AQB	----Radix angelicae sinensis
1211.9012	----(三七)田七	6	20		5	13	千克	AQB	----Radix pseudoginseng
1211.9013	----党参	6	20		5	13	千克	AQB	----Radix codonopsitis
1211.9014	----黄连	6	20		5	13	千克	AQB	----Rhizoma coptidis
1211.9015	----菊花	6	20		0/5	13	千克	AQB	----Flos chrysanthemi
1211.9016	----冬虫夏草	6	20		5	13	千克	AQBE	----Cordyceps sinensis
1211.9017	----贝母	6	20		5	13	千克	AQB	----Bulbs fritillariae thunbergii
1211.9018	----川芎	6	20		5	13	千克	AQB	----Rhizoma ligustici
1211.9019	----半夏	6	20		5	13	千克	AQB	----Rhizoma pinelliae
1211.9021	----白芍	6	20		5	13	千克	AQB	----Radix paeoniae lactifiorae
1211.9022	----天麻	6	20		5	13	千克	AQBFE	----Rhizoma gastrodiae
1211.9023	----黄芪	6	30		5	13	千克	AQB	----Radix astragali
1211.9024	----大黄、籽黄	6	20		5	13	千克	AQB	----Rhubarb
1211.9025	----白术	6	20		5	13	千克	AQB	----Rhizoma atractylodis macrocephalae
1211.9026	----地黄	6	20		5	13	千克	AQB	----Radix rehmanniae
1211.9027	----槐米	6	20		5	13	千克	AQB	----Flos sophorae
1211.9028	----杜仲	6	20		5	13	千克	ABQ	----Cortex eucommiae
1211.9029	----茯苓	6	20		5	13	千克	AQB	----Poria
1211.9031	----枸杞	6	30		5	13	千克	AQB	----Fructus lycii
1211.9032	----大海子	6	20		5	13	千克	AQB	----Bantaroi seeds
1211.9033	----沉香	3	20		5	13	千克	AQFEB	----Aloes wood
1211.9034	----沙参	6	20		5	13	千克	AQB	----Adenophora axilliflora
1211.9035	----青蒿	6	20			13	千克	AB	----Southernwood
1211.9036[暂]	----甘草	6	30	0	5	13	千克	AQB4xy	----Liquorice roots
1211.9037	----黄芩	6	20		5	13	千克	ABQ	----Radix astragali
1211.9038	----椴树(欧椴)花及叶	6	30		5	13	千克		---- Linden (European linden) flower and leaf
1211 9038.10	海南椴、紫椴(籽椴)花及叶(不论是否切割、压碎或研磨成粉)	6	30		5	13	千克	ABEQ	Hainan linden, Tilia amurensis (seed linden) flowers and leaves, whether or not cut, crushed or powdered
1211 9038.90	其他椴树(欧椴)花及叶	6	30		5	13	千克	ABQ	Other linden (European linden) flowers and leaves
1211.9039	----其他	6	20			13	千克		----Other
1211 9039.10	药料用麻黄草粉	6	20		5	13	千克	23AQB	Ephedra powder, used in pharmacy
1211 9039.20	药料用麻黄草	6	20		5	13	千克	8AQ	Ephedra sinica, used in pharmacy

税则号列 Tariff Item	商品名称及备注	进口税率 最惠	普通	暂定	出口退税	增值税率	计量单位	监管条件	Article Description
1211 9039.30	大麻	6	20		5	13	千克	AWB	Hemp (Cannabis sativa)
1211 9039.40	罂粟壳	6	20		5	13	千克	AWB	Poppy shell
1211 9039.50	鲜或干的木香（不论是否切割、压碎或研磨成粉）	6	20		5	13	千克	ABFE	Costustoot, fresh or dried, whether or not cut, crushed or powdered
1211 9039.60	鲜或干的黄草及枫斗(石斛)（不论是否切割、压碎或研磨成粉）	6	20		5	13	千克	ABFE	Herba dendrobii and Dendrobium, fresh or dried, whether or not cut, crushed or powdered
1211 9039.70	鲜或干的苁蓉（不论是否切割、压碎或研磨成粉）	6	20		5	13	千克	ABFE	Cistanche, fresh or dried, whether or not cut, crushed or powdered
1211 9039.80	鲜或干的红豆杉皮、枝叶等（不论是否切割、压碎或研磨成粉）	6	20		5	13	千克	ABFE	Bark, branch and leaf of Taxaceae, fresh or dried, whether or not cut, crushed or powdered
1211 9039.91	其他主要用作药料鲜或干濒危植物（包括其某部分，不论是否切割、压碎或研磨成粉）	6	20			13	千克	ABFE	Other endangered plants and parts of plants, of a kind used primarily in pharmacy, fresh or dried, whether or not cut, crushed or powdered
1211 9039.92	加纳籽、车前子壳粉、育亨宾皮（包括其某部分，不论是否切割、压碎或研磨成粉）	6	20		5	13	千克	AB	Griffonia seed, plantago seed powder, yohimbine bark , and its part, whether or not cut, crushed or powdered
1211 9039.93	恰特草(Catha edulis Forssk;包括其某部分,不论是否切割、压碎或研磨成粉)	6	20		5	13	千克	ABI	Catha edulis Forssk, whether or not cut, crushed or powdered
1211 9039.99	其他主要用作药料的鲜或干的植物（包括其某部分，不论是否切割、压碎或研磨成粉）	6	20		5	13	千克	ABQ	Other plants and parts of plants, of a kind used primarily in pharmacy, fresh or dried, whether or not cut, crushed or powdered
1211.9050	---主要用作香料的植物及其某部分	8	50			13	千克		---Of a kind used primarily in perfumery
1211 9050.10	香料用麻黄草粉	8	50		5	13	千克	23AB	Ephedra powder, of a kind used in perfumery
1211 9050.20	香料用麻黄草	8	50		5	13	千克	8A	Ephedra sinica, of a kind used in perfumery
1211 9050.30	香料用沉香木及拟沉香木(包括其某部分,不论是否切割、压碎或研磨成粉)	8	50		5	13	千克	ABFE	Eaglewood and Agalloch eaglewood, and parts of them, of a kind used in perfumery, whether or not cut, crushed or powdered
1211 9050.91	其他主要用作香料的濒危植物（包括其某部分，不论是否切割、压碎或研磨成粉）	8	50			13	千克	ABFE	Other endangered plants and parts of plants, of a kind used in perfumery, whether or not cut, crushed or powdered
1211 9050.99	其他主要用作香料的植物(包括其某部分，不论是否切割、压碎或研磨成粉）	8	50		5	13	千克	AB	Other plants and parts of plants, of a kind used in perfumery, whether or not cut, crushed or powdered
	---其他:								---Other:
1211.9091	----鱼藤根、除虫菊	3	11		5	13	千克	ABS	----Derris roots and pyrethrum
1211.9099	----其他	9	30			13	千克		----Other
1211 9099.10	其他用麻黄草粉	9	30		5	13	千克	23AB	Other ephedra powder
1211 9099.20	其他用麻黄草	9	30		5	13	千克	8A	Other ephedra sinica
1211 9099.91	其他鲜或干杀虫、杀菌用濒危植物（不论是否切割、压碎或研磨成粉）	9	30			13	千克	ABFE	Other endangered plants of a kind used for insecticidal or fungicidal, fresh or dried, whether or not cut, crushed or powdered
1211 9099.99	其他鲜或干的杀虫、杀菌用植物（不论是否切割、压碎或研磨成粉）	9	30		5	13	千克	AB	Other plants, of a kind used for insecticidal or fungicidal, fresh or dried, whether or not cut, crushed or powdered
12.12	**鲜、冷、冻或干的刺槐豆、海草及其他藻类、甜菜及甘蔗，不论是否碾磨；主要供人食用的其他品目未列名的果核、果仁及植物产品（包括未焙制的菊苣根）：**								**Locust beans, seaweeds and other algae, sugar beet and sugar cane, fresh,chilled, frozen or dried, whether or not ground; fruit stones and kernels and other vegetable products（including unroasted chicory roots of the variety Cichorium intybus sativum）of a kind used primarily for human consumption, not elsewhere specified or included:**
	-海草及其他藻类:								-Seaweeds and other algae:
	--适合供人食用的:								--Fit for human consumption :

税则号列 Tariff Item	商品名称及备注	进口税率			出口退税	增值税率	计量单位	监管条件	Article Description
		最惠	普通	暂定					
1212.2110	---海带	20	70			13	千克	AB	---Sea tangle
1212.2120	---发菜	20	70		5	13	千克	8A	---Black moss
	---裙带菜:								---Pinnatifida:
1212.2131	----干的	15	70		5	13	千克	AB	----Dried
1212.2132	----鲜的	15	70		5	13	千克	AB	----Fresh
1212.2139	----其他	15	70		5	13	千克	AB	----Other
	---紫菜:								---Laver:
1212.2141	----干的	15	70			13	千克	AB	----Dried
1212.2142	----鲜的	15	70			13	千克	AB	----Fresh
1212.2149	----其他	15	70			13	千克	AB	----Other
	---麒麟菜:								---Eucheuma：
1212.2161	----干的	15	70		5	13	千克	AB	----Dried
1212.2169	----其他	15	70		5	13	千克	AB	----Other
	---江蓠:								---Gracilaria：
1212.2171	----干的	15	70		5	13	千克	AB	----Dried
1212.2179	----其他	15	70		5	13	千克	AB	----Other
1212.2190[暂]	---其他	15	70	2	5	13	千克	AB	---Other
1212.2900[暂]	--其他	15	70	2	5	13	千克	AB	--Other
	-其他:								-Other:
1212.9100	--甜菜	20	70		5	13	千克	AB	--Sugar beet
1212.9200	--刺槐豆	20	70		5	13	千克	AB	--Locust beans (carob)
1212.9300	--甘蔗	20	70		5	13	千克	AB	--Sugar cane
1212.9400	--菊苣根	20	70		5	13	千克	AB	--Chicory roots
	--其他:								--Other:
	---杏、桃（包括油桃）、梅或李的核及核仁:								---Apricot, peach（including nectarine）or plum stones and kernels:
1212.9911	----苦杏仁	20	80		5	13	千克	QAB	----Bitter apricot kernels
1212.9912	----甜杏仁	20	80		5	13	千克	AB	----Sweet apricot kernels
1212.9919	----其他	20	80		5	13	千克	AB	----Other
	---其他:								---Other:
1212.9993	----白瓜子	20	80		5	13	千克	AB	----Pumpkin seeds
1212.9994	----莲子	20	80		5	13	千克	AB	----Lotus seeds（*Semen Nelurnbinis*）
1212.9996	----甜叶菊叶	30	70		5	13	千克	AB	----Stevia leaf
1212.9999	----其他	30	70			13	千克		----Other
1212 9999.10	其他供人食用濒危植物产品(包括未焙制的菊苣根，包括果核、仁等)	30	70			13	千克	ABFE	Other endangered vegetable products,including fruit stones and kernels（including unroasted chicory roots of the variety *Cichorium intybus sativum*）, for human consumption
1212 9999.90	其他供人食用果核、仁及植物产品(包括未焙制的菊苣根)	30	70		5	13	千克	AB	Other vegetable products, including fruit stones and kernels（including unroasted chicory roots of the variety *Cichorium intybus sativum*）, for human consumption
12.13	未经处理的谷类植物的茎、秆及谷壳，不论是否切碎、碾磨、挤压或制成团粒:								**Cereal straw and husks, unprepared, whether or not chopped, ground, pressed or in the form of pellets:**
1213.0010	---未经处理的稻草的茎、秆	12	35		5	13	千克	AB	---Cereal straw, unprepared
1213.0090	---其他	12	35		5	13	千克	AB	---Other
12.14	芜菁甘蓝、饲料甜菜、饲料用根、干草、紫苜蓿、三叶草、驴喜豆、饲料羽衣甘蓝、羽扇豆、巢菜及类似饲料，不论是否制成团粒:								**Swedes, manigolds, fodder roots, hay,lucerne（alfalfa）, clover, sainfoin,forage kale, lupines, vetches and similar forage products, whether or not in the form of pellets:**
1214.1000	-紫苜蓿粗粉及团粒	5	35			13	千克	AB	-Lucerne（alfalfa）meal and pellets

税则号列 Tariff Item	商品名称及备注	进口税率 最惠	进口税率 普通	进口税率 暂定	出口退税	增值税率	计量单位	监管条件	Article Description
1214.9000	-其他	9	35			13	千克		-Other
1214 9000.01[暂]	其他紫苜蓿（粗粉及团粒除外）	9	35	7		13	千克	AB	Other alfalfa (other than meals and pellets)
1214 9000.02[暂]	以除紫苜蓿外的禾本科和豆科为主的多种混合天然饲草	9	35	4		13	千克	AB	Multi forage products based on Gramineous and leguminous plants,other than alfalfa
1214 9000.90	芜菁甘蓝、饲料甜菜、其他植物饲料(包括饲料用根、干草、三叶草、驴喜豆等，不论是否制成团粒)	9	35			13	千克	AB	Cabbage phalerata, Fodder beet, Feed (including feed use of other plant root, Hay, Clover, Sainfoin beans, whether or not the form of pellets)

第十三章 虫胶；树胶、树脂及其他植物液、汁

Chapter 13 Lac; gums, resins and other vegetable saps and extracts

注释：

品目 13.02 主要包括甘草、除虫菊、啤酒花、芦荟的浸膏及鸦片，但不包括：

一、按重量计蔗糖含量在 10% 以上或制成糖食的甘草浸膏（品目 17.04）；

二、麦芽膏（品目 19.01）；

三、咖啡精、茶精、马黛茶精（品目 21.01）；

四、构成含酒精饮料的植物汁、液（第二十二章）；

五、樟脑、甘草甜及品目 29.14 或 29.38 的其他产品；

六、按重量计生物碱含量不低于 50%的罂粟秆的浓缩物（品目 29.39）；

七、品目 30.03 或 30.04 的药品及品目 30.06 的血型试剂；

八、 鞣料或染料的浸膏（品目 32.01 或 30.03）；

九、精油、浸膏、净油、香膏、提取的油树脂或精油的水馏液及水溶液；饮料制造业用的以芳香物质为基料的制剂（第三十三章）；或

十、天然橡胶、巴拉塔胶、古塔波胶、银胶菊胶、糖胶树胶或类似的天然树胶（品目40.01）。

本国注释：

子目 1302.1100 的鸦片，我国禁止进口。

Chapter Notes:

Heading 13.02 applies, *inter alia*, to liquorice extract and extract of pyrethrum, extract of hops, extract of aloes and opium. The heading does not apply to:

（a） Liquorice extract containing more than 10% by weight of sucrose or put up as confectionery（heading 17.04）;

（b）Malt extract（heading 19.01）;

（c）Extracts of coffee, tea or mate（heading 21.01）;

（d）Vegetable saps or extracts constituting alcoholic beverages（Chapter 22）;

（e）Camphor, glycyrrhizin or other products of heading 29.14 or 29.38;

（f）Concentrates of poppy straw containing not less than 50% by weight of alkaloids（heading 29.39）;

（g）Medicaments of heading 30.03 or 30.04 or bloodgrouping reagents（heading 30. 06）;

（h）Tanning or dyeing extracts（heading 32.01 or 32.03）;

（ij）Essential oils, concretes, absolutes, resinoids, extracted oleoresins, aqueous distillates or aqueous solutions of essential oils or preparations based on odoriferous substances of a kind used for the manufacture of beverages（Chapter 33）; or

（k）Natural rubber, balata, gutta-percha, guayule, chicle or similar natural gums（heading 40.01）.

National note:

Opium of Subheading No. 1302.1100 is subject to import ban.

税则号列 Tariff Item	商品名称及备注	进口税率 最惠	普通	暂定	出口退税	增值税率	计量单位	监管条件	Article Description
13.01	虫胶；天然树胶、树脂、树胶脂及油树脂（例如，香树脂）：								**Lac; natural gums, resins, gum-resins and oleoresins（for example, balsams）:**
1301.2000	-阿拉伯胶	15	40		5	13	千克	AB	-Gum Arabic
	-其他:								-Other:
1301.9010	---胶黄耆树胶（卡喇杆胶）	15	40		5	13	千克	AB	---Gum tragacanth
1301.9020	---乳香、没药及血竭	3	17		5	13	千克	ABQ	---Olibanum, myrrh and dragon's blood
1301.9030	---阿魏	3	17		5	13	千克	AB	---Asafoetida
1301.9040	---松脂	15	45			13	千克		---Pine-resin
1301 9040.10	濒危松科植物的松脂	15	45			13	千克	ABE	Pine-resin of endangered plants of pinaceae
1301 9040.90	其他松脂	15	45		5	13	千克	AB	Other pine-resin
1301.9090	---其他	15	45			13	千克		---Other
1301 9090.10	龙血树脂、大戟脂、愈疮树脂	15	45		5	13	千克	ABFE	Resin of dracaena draco, resin of euph orbia, resin of lignum vitae
1301 9090.20	大麻脂	15	45		5	13	千克	ABW	Cannabis resin
1301 9090.91	其他濒危植物的天然树胶、树脂［包括天然树胶、树脂及其他油树脂（例如，香树脂）］	15	45			13	千克	ABFE	Other natural gums, resins, gum-resins and oleoresins（for example, balsams）of endangered plants
1301 9090.99	其他天然树胶、树脂［包括天然树胶、树脂及其他油树脂（例如，香树脂）］	15	45		5	13	千克	AB	Other natural gums, resins, natural gum-resins and other oleoresins（for example, balsams）
13.02	植物液汁及浸膏；果胶、果胶酸盐及果胶酸酯；从植物产品制得的琼脂、其他胶液及增稠剂，不论是否改性：								**Vegetable saps and extracts; pectic substances, pectinates and pectates; agar and other mucilages and thickeners, whether or not modified, derived from vegetable products:**

税则号列 Tariff Item	商品名称及备注	进口税率			出口退税	增值税率	计量单位	监管条件	Article Description
		最惠	普通	暂定					
	-植物液汁及浸膏:								-Vegetable saps and extracts:
1302.1100	--鸦片	0	0		15	0	千克	9BW	--Opium
1302.1200[暂]	--甘草的	6	20	0	15	17	千克	4xABy	--Of liquorice
1302.1300	--啤酒花的	10	80		15	17	千克	AB	--Of hops
	--其他:								--Other:
1302.1910	---生漆	20	90		5	17	千克	AB	---Crude lacquer
1302.1920	---印楝素	3	11		5	17	千克	ABS	---Azadirachtin
1302.1930	---除虫菊的或含鱼藤酮植物根茎的	3	11		15	17	千克	ABS	---Of pyrethrum or of the roots of plants containing rotenone
1302.1940	---银杏的	20	80		15	17	千克	ABE	---Of ginkgo
1302.1990	---其他	20	80			17	千克		---Other
1302 1990.01[暂]	苦参碱	20	80	3	15	17	千克	ABS	Matrine
1302 1990.11	供制农药用麻黄浸膏粉	20	80		15	17	千克	23AB	Ephedra extracts powder used in pesticide
1302 1990.12	供制农药用麻黄浸膏	20	80		15	17	千克	23AB	Ephedra extracts used in pesticide
1302 1990.13	供制农药用的濒危植物液汁及浸膏	20	80			17	千克	ABFE	Endangered vegetable saps and extracts used in pesticide
1302 1990.19	供制农药用的其他植物液汁及浸膏	20	80		15	17	千克	AB	Other vegetable saps and extracts used in pesticide
1302 1990.91	供制医药用麻黄浸膏粉	20	80		15	17	千克	Q23AB	Ephedra extract powder used in pharmacy
1302 1990.92	供制医药用麻黄浸膏	20	80		15	17	千克	Q23AB	Ephedra extracts used in pharmacy
1302 1990.93	其他麻黄浸膏粉	20	80		15	17	千克	23AB	Other ephedra extract powder
1302 1990.94	其他麻黄浸膏	20	80		15	17	千克	23AB	Other ephedra extracts
1302 1990.95	红豆杉液汁及浸膏	20	80		15	17	千克	ABFE	Saps and extracts of Chinese yew
1302 1990.96	黄草汁液及浸膏	20	80		15	17	千克	ABFE	Saps and extracts of Herba dendrobii
1302 1990.97	其他濒危植物液汁及浸膏	20	80			17	千克	ABFE	Saps and extracts of other endangered vegetables
1302 1990.99	其他植物液汁及浸膏	20	80		15	17	千克	AB	Other vegetable saps and extracts
1302.2000	-果胶、果胶酸盐及果胶酸酯	20	80		15	17	千克	AB	-Pectic substances, pectinates and pectates
	-从植物产品制得的胶液及增稠剂，不论是否改性:								-Mucilages and thickeners, whether or not modified, derived from vegetable products:
1302.3100	--琼脂	10	80		15	17	千克	AB	--Agar
1302.3200	--从刺槐豆、刺槐豆子或瓜尔豆制得的胶液及增稠剂，不论是否改性	15	80		15	17	千克	AB	--Mucilages and thickeners, whether or not modified, derived from locust beans, locust bean seeds or guar seeds
	--其他:								--Other:
	---海草及其他藻类制品:								---Preparations of seaweeds and other algae:
1302.3911	----卡拉胶	15	80		15	17	千克	AB	----Carrageenan
1302.3912	----褐藻胶	15	80		15	17	千克	AB	----Algin
1302.3919	----其他	15	80		15	17	千克	AB	----Other
1302.3990	---其他	15	80			17	千克		---Other
1302 3990.10	未列名濒危植物胶液及增稠剂	15	80			17	千克	ABFE	Mucilages and thickeners, derived from endangered vegetable products, not elsewhere specified or included
1302 3990.90	其他未列名植物胶液及增稠剂	15	80		15	17	千克	AB	Mucilages and thickeners, derived from other vegetable products, not elsewhere specified or included

第十四章
编结用植物材料；其他植物产品

Chapter 14
Vegetable plaiting materials; vegetable products not elsewhere specified or included

注释：

一、本章不包括归入第十一类的下列产品：

主要供纺织用的植物材料或植物纤维，不论其加工程度如何；或经过处理使其只能作为纺织原料用的其他植物材料。

二、品目 14.01 主要包括竹（不论是否劈开、纵锯、切段、圆端、漂白、磨光、染色或进行不燃处理）、劈开的柳条、芦苇及类似品和藤心、藤丝、藤片。但不包括木片条（品目 44.04）。

三、品目14.04不包括木丝（品目44.05）及供制帚、制刷用成束、成簇的材料（品目96.03）。

Chapter Notes:

1. This Chapter does not cover the following products which are to be classified in Section XI:
Vegetable materials or fibres of vegetable materials of a kind used primarily in the manufacture of textiles, however prepared, or other vegetable materials which have undergone treatment so as to render them suitable for use only as textile materials.
2. Heading 14.01 applies, *inter alia*, to bamboos（whether or not split,sawn lengthwise, cut to length, rounded at the ends, bleached, rendered non-inflammable, polished or dyed）, split osier, reeds and the like, to rattan cores and to drawn or split rattans. The heading does not apply to chipwood（heading 44.04）.
3. Heading 14.04 does not apply to wood wool（heading 44.05）and prepared knots or tufts for broom or brush making（heading 96. 03）.

税则号列 Tariff Item	商品名称及备注	进口税率			出口退税	增值税率	计量单位	监管条件	Article Description
		最惠	普通	暂定					
14.01	主要作编结用的植物材料(例如竹、藤、芦苇、灯芯草、柳条、酒椰叶，已净、漂白或染色的谷类植物的茎秆，椴树皮)：								**Vegetable materials of a kind used primarily for plaiting（for example, bamboos, rattans, reeds, rushes, osier, raffia, cleaned, bleached or dyed cereal straw, and lime bark）:**
1401.1000	-竹	10	70		5	13	千克		-Bamboos
1401 1000.10	酸竹	10	70		5	13	千克	ABE	Acidosasa chinensis
1401 1000.90	其他竹	10	70		5	13	千克	AB	Other bamboos
1401.2000	-藤	10	35			13	千克		-Rattans
1401 2000.10	濒危藤	10	35			13	千克	ABFE	Endangered rattans
1401 2000.90	其他藤	10	35		5	13	千克	AB	Other rattans
	--其他:								-Other:
1401.9010	---谷类植物的茎秆(麦秸除外)	10	70		5	13	千克	AB	---Cereal straw（other than wheat straw）
1401.9020	---芦苇	10	70		5	13	千克	AB	---Reeds
	---灯芯草属:								---Rushes:
1401.9031	----蔺草	10	70		5	13	千克	AB4xy	----Mat rush
1401.9039	----其他	10	70		5	13	千克	AB	----Other
1401.9090	----其他	10	70		5	13	千克	AB	---Other
14.04	其他品目未列名的植物产品:								**Vegetable products not elsewhere specified or included:**
1404.2000	-棉短绒	4	30		5	13	千克	AB	-Cotton linters
	-其他:								-Other:
1404.9010	---主要供染料、鞣料用的植物原料	5	45		5	13	千克	AB	---Raw vegetable materials of a kind used primarily in dyeing or tanning
1404.9090	---其他	15	70		5	13	千克	AB	---Other

第三类
动、植物油、脂及其分解产品；精制的食用油脂；动、植物蜡

第十五章
动、植物油、脂及其分解产品；精制的食用油脂；动、植物蜡

注释：

一、本章不包括：

（一）品目 02.09 的猪脂肪及家禽脂肪；

（二）可可脂、可可油（品目 18.04）；

（三）按重量计品目 04.05 所列产品的含量超过15%的食品（通常归入第二十一章）；

（四）品目 23.01 的油渣或品目 23.04 至 23.06 的残渣；

（五）第六类的脂肪酸、精制蜡、药品、油漆、清漆、肥皂、芳香料制品、化妆盥洗品、磺化油及其他货品；或

（六）从油类提取的油膏（品目 40.02）。

二、品目 15.09 不包括用溶剂提取的橄榄油（品目 15.10）。

三、品目 15.18 不包括变性的油、脂及其分离品，这些货品应归入其相应的未变性油、脂及其分离品的品目。

四、皂料、油脚、硬脂沥青、甘油沥青及羊毛脂残渣，归入品目 15.22。

子目注释：

子目1514.11及1514.19所称“低芥子酸菜子油”，是指按重量计芥子酸含量低于2%的固定油。

SECTION Ⅲ
ANIMAL OR VEGETABLE FATS AND OILS AND THEIR CLEAVAGE PRODUCTS; PREPARED EDIBLE FATS; ANIMAL OR VEGETABLE WAXES

Chapter 15
Animal or vegetable fats and oils and their cleavage products; prepared edible fats; animal or vegetable waxes

Chapter Notes:

1. This Chapter does not cover:

（a）Pig fat or poultry fat of heading 02.09;

（b）Cocoa butter, fat or oil（heading 18.04）;

（c）Edible preparations containing by weight more than 15% of the products of heading 04.05（generally Chapter 21）;

（d）Greaves（heading 23.01）or residues of headings 23.04 to 23.06;

（e）Fatty acids, prepared waxes, medicaments, paints, varnishes, soap, perfumery, cosmetic or toilet preparations, sulphonated oils or other goods of Section Ⅵ; or

（f）Factice derived from oils（heading 40.02）.

2.Heading 15.09 does not apply to oils obtained from olives by solvent extraction（heading 15.10）.

3.Heading 15.18 does not cover fats or oils or their fractions, merely denatured, which are to be classified in the heading appropriate to the corresponding undenatured fats and oils and their fractions.

4.Soap-stocks, oil foots and dregs, stearin pitch, glycerol pitch and wool grease residues fall in heading 15.22.

Subheading Note:

For the purposes of subheadings 1514.11 and 1514.19, the expression “low erucic acid rape or colzaoil” means the fixed oil which has an erucic acid content of less than 2% by weight .

税则号列 Tariff Item	商品名称及备注	进口税率			出口退税	增值税率	计量单位	监管条件	Article Description
		最惠	普通	暂定					
15.01	**猪脂肪（包括已炼制的猪油）及家禽脂肪，但品目 02.09 及 15.03 的货品除外：**								**Pig fat（including lard）and poultry fat, other than that of heading No.02.09 or 15. 03:**
1501.1000	-猪油	10	35		15	17	千克	AB	-Lard
1501.2000	-其他猪脂肪	10	35		15	17	千克	AB	-Other pig fat
1501.9000	-其他	10	35		15	17	千克	AB	-Other
15.02	**牛、羊脂肪，但品目 15.03 的货品除外：**								**Fats of bovine animals, sheep or goats, other than those of heading No.15.03:**
1502.1000[暂]	-牛、羊油脂	8	30	4	15	17	千克	AB	---Tallow
1502.9000[暂]	-其他	8	70	4	5	17	千克	AB	---Other
15.03	**猪油硬脂、液体猪油、油硬脂、食用或非食用脂油，未经乳化、混合或其他方法制作：**								**Lard stearin, lard oil, oleostearin, oleooil and tallow oil, not emulsified or mixed or otherwise prepared:**
1503.0000	猪油硬脂、液体猪油、油硬脂、食用或非食用脂油，未经乳化、混合或其他方法制作	10	30		15	17	千克	AB	Lard stearin, lard oil, oleostearin, oleooil and tallow oil, not emulsified ormixed or otherwise prepared
15.04	**鱼或海生哺乳动物的油、脂及其分离品，不论是否精制，但未经化学改性：**								**Fats and oils and their fractions, of fish or marine mammals, whether or not refined, but not chemically modified:**

税则号列 Tariff Item	商品名称及备注	进口税率 最惠	普通	暂定	出口退税	增值税率	计量单位	监管条件	Article Description
1504.1000	-鱼肝油及其分离品	12	30		15	17	千克	AB	-Fish-liver oils and their fractions
1504.2000	-除鱼肝油以外的鱼油、脂及其分离品	12	50		15	17	千克	AB	-Fats and oils and their fractions, of fish, other than liver oils
1504.3000	-海生哺乳动物的油、脂及其分离品	14.4	50			17	千克		-Fats and oils and their fractions, of marine mammals
1504 3000.10	濒危哺乳动物的油、脂及其分离品（仅指海生）	14.4	50			17	千克	ABFE	Fats and oils and their fractions, of endangered marine mammals
1504 3000.90	其他海生哺乳动物油、脂及其分离品	14.4	50		15	17	千克	AB	Other fats and oils and their fractions of marine mammals
15.05	**羊毛脂及从羊毛脂制得的脂肪物质（包括纯净的羊毛脂）：**								**Wool grease and fatty substances derived therefrom（including lanolin）:**
1505.0000	羊毛脂及从羊毛脂制得的脂肪物质（包括纯净的羊毛脂）	20	70		15	17	千克	AB	Wool grease and fatty substances derived therefrom（including lanolin）
15.06	**其他动物油、脂及其分离品，不论是否精制，但未经化学改性:**								**Other animal fats and oils and their fractions, whether or not refined, but not chemically modified:**
1506.0000	其他动物油、脂及其分离品，不论是否精制，但未经化学改性	20	70			17	千克		Other animal fats and oils and their fractions, whether or not refined, but not chemically modified
1506 0000.10	其他濒危动物为原料制取的脂肪（包括河马、熊、野兔、海龟为原料的及海龟蛋油）	20	70			17	千克	ABFE	Fats made of materials of other endangered animals（including hippo, bear, hare, green turtle and green turtle egg）
1506 0000.90	其他动物油、脂及其分离品（不论是否精制，但未经化学改性）	20	70		15	17	千克	AB	Other animals fats and oils and their fractions, whether or not refined, but not chemically modified
15.07	**豆油及其分离品，不论是否精制，但未经化学改性:**								**Soya-bean oil and its fractions, whether or not refined, but not chemically modified:**
1507.1000	-初榨的，不论是否脱胶	9	190			13	千克	7AB	-Crude oil whether or not degummed
1507.9000	-其他	9	190			13	千克	7AB	-Other
15.08	**花生油及其分离品，不论是否精制，但未经化学改性:**								**Ground-nut oil and its fractions, whether or not refined, but not chemically modified:**
1508.1000	-初榨的	10	100			13	千克	AB	-Crude oil
1508.9000	-其他	10	100			13	千克	AB	-Other
15.09	**油橄榄油及其分离品，不论是否精制，但未经化学改性:**								**Olive oil and its fractions, whether or not refined, but not chemically modified:**
1509.1000	-初榨的	10	30			13	千克	7AB	-Virgin
1509.9000	-其他	10	30			17	千克	7AB	-Other
15.10	**其他橄榄油及其分离品，不论是否精制，但未经化学改性，包括掺有品目 15.09 的油或分离品的混合物:**								**Other oils and their fractions, obtained solely from olives, whether or not refined, but not chemically modified, including blends of these oils or fractions with oils or fractions of heading No.15.09:**
1510.0000	其他橄榄油及其分离品，不论是否精制，但未经化学改性，包括掺有品目 15.09 的油或分离品的混合物	10	30			17	千克	7AB	Other oils and their fractions, obtained solely from olives, whether or not refined, but not chemically modified, including blends of these oils or fractions with oils or fractions of heading No.15.09
15.11	**棕榈油及其分离品，不论是否精制，但未经化学改性:**								**Palm oil and its fractions, whether or not refined, but not chemically modified:**
1511.1000	-初榨的	9	60			13	千克	7AB	-Crude oil
	--其他:								--Other:
1511.9010	---棕榈液油（熔点 19℃-24℃）	9	60			13	千克	7AB	---Palm olein（melting point19℃-24℃）
1511.9020	---棕榈硬脂（熔点 44℃-56℃）	8	60			13	千克		---Palm stearin（melting point 44℃-56℃）
1511 9020.01[暂]	固态棕榈硬脂（50℃≤熔点≤56℃）（未经化学改性）	8	60	2		13	千克	7AB	Palm stearin（melting point 50℃-56℃, not chemically modified)
1511 9020.90	棕榈硬脂（44℃≤熔点＜50℃，未经化学改性）	8	60			13	千克	AB	Palm stearin（melting point 44℃-50℃,not chemicallly modified)
1511.9090	---其他	9	60			17	千克	7AB	---Other
15.12	**葵花油、红花油或棉子油及其分离品，不论是否精制，但未经化学改性:**								**Sunflower-seed, safflower or cottonseed oil and fractions thereof, whether or not refined, but not chemically modified:**

税则号列 Tariff Item	商品名称及备注	进口税率 最惠	普通	暂定	出口退税	增值税率	计量单位	监管条件	Article Description
	-葵花油或红花油及其分离品:								-Sunflower-seed or safflower oil and fractions thereof:
1512.1100	--初榨的	9	160			13	千克	AB	--Crude oil
1512.1900	--其他	9	160			17	千克	AB	--Other
	-棉子油及其分离品:								-Cotton-seed oil and its fractions:
1512.2100	--初榨的，不论是否去除棉子酚	10	70			13	千克	AB	--Crude oil, whether or not gossypol has been removed
1512.2900	--其他	10	70			17	千克	AB	--Other
15.13	**椰子油、棕榈仁油或巴巴苏棕榈果油及其分离品，不论是否精制，但未经化学改性:**								**Coconut（copra）, palm kernel or babassu oil and fractions thereof, whether or not refined, but not chemically modified:**
	-椰子油及其分离品:								-Coconut（copra）oil and its fractions:
1513.1100	--初榨的	9	40			13	千克	AB	--Crude oil
1513.1900	--其他	9	40			13	千克	AB	--Other
	-棕榈仁油或巴巴苏棕榈果油及其分离品:								-Palm kernel or babassu oil and fractions thereof:
1513.2100	--初榨的	9	40			13	千克	AB	--Crude oil
1513.2900	--其他	9	40			17	千克	AB	--Other
15.14	**菜子油或芥子油及其分离品，不论是否精制，但未经化学改性:**								**Rape, colza or mustard oil and fractions thereof, whether or not refined, but not chemically modified:**
	-低芥子酸菜子油及其分离品:								-Low erucic acid rape of colza oil and its fractions:
1514.1100	--初榨的	9	170			13	千克	7AB	--Crude oil
1514.1900	--其他	9	170			13	千克	7AB	--Other
	-其他:								-Other:
	--初榨的:								--Crude oil:
1514.9110	---菜子油	9	170			13	千克	7AB	---Rape oil
1514.9190	---芥子油	9	170			13	千克	7AB	---Mustard oil
1514.9900	--其他	9	170			17	千克	7AB	--Other
15.15	**其他固定植物油、脂（包括希蒙得木油）及其分离品，不论是否精制，但未经化学改性:**								**Other fixed vegetable fats and oils (including jojoba oil）and fractions thereof, whether or not refined, but not chemically modified:**
	-亚麻子油及其分离品:								-Linseed oil and its fractions:
1515.1100	--初榨的	15	30			13	千克	AB	--Crude oil
1515.1900	--其他	15	30			17	千克	AB	--Other
	-玉米油及其分离品:								-Maize（corn）oil and its fractions:
1515.2100	--初榨的	10	160			13	千克	AB	--Crude oil
1515.2900	--其他	10	160			17	千克	AB	--Other
1515.3000	-蓖麻油及其分离品	10	70		5	17	千克	AB	-Castor oil and its fractions
1515.5000	-芝麻油及其分离品	12	20			13	千克	AB	-Sesame oil and its fractions
	-其他:								-Other:
1515.9010	---希蒙得木油（霍霍巴油）及其分离品	20	70		5	17	千克	AB	---Jojoba oil and its fractions
1515.9020	---印楝油及其分离品	20	70		5	17	千克	ABS	--Neem oil and its fractions
1515.9030	---桐油及其分离品	20	70		5	17	千克	AB	---Tung oil and its fractions
1515.9090	---其他	20	70			17	千克		---Other
1515 9090.10	红松籽油（不论是否精制，但未经化学改性）	20	70			17	千克	ABE	Pine nut oil (whether or not refined, but not chemically modified)
1515 9090.90	其他固定植物油、脂及其分离品（不论是否精制，但未经化学改性）	20	70			17	千克	AB	Other fixed vegetable fats and oils and fractions thereof, (whether or not refined, but not chemically modified)
15.16	**动、植物油、脂及其分离品，全部或部分氢化、相互酯化、再酯化或反油酸化，不论是否精制，但未经进一步加工:**								**Animal or vegetable fats and oil and fractions thereof, partly or wholly hydrogenated, interesterified, reesterified or elaidinized, whether or not refined, but not further prepared:**
1516.1000	-动物油、脂及其分离品	5	70		15	17	千克	AB	-Animal fats and oils and fractions thereof
1516.2000	-植物油、脂及其分离品	25	70			17	千克	AB	-Vegetable fats and oils and fractions thereof

税则号列 Tariff Item	商品名称及备注	进口税率			出口退税	增值税率	计量单位	监管条件	Article Description
		最惠	普通	暂定					
15.17	**人造黄油；本章各种动、植物油、脂及其分离品混合制成的食用油、脂或制品，但品目15.16的食用油、脂及其分离品除外：**								**Margarine; edible mixtures or preparations of animal or vegetable fats or oils or of fractions of different fats or oils of this Chapter, other than ediblefats or oils or their fractions of heading No.15.16:**
1517.1000	-人造黄油，但不包括液态的	30	80			17	千克	AB	-Margarine, excluding liquid margarine
	-其他：								-Other:
1517.9010	---起酥油	25	70				千克		---Shortening
1517 9010.01	动物油脂制造的起酥油（品目15.16的食用油、脂及其分离品除外）	25	70		15	17	千克	AB	Shortening, made of animal fats or oils (other than edible fats or oils,or their fractions of heading No.15.16)
1517 9010.90	植物油脂制造的起酥油（品目15.16的食用油、脂及其分离品除外）	25	70			13	千克	AB	Shortening, made of vegetable oils (other than edible fats or oils, or their fractions of heading No.15.16)
1517.9090	---其他	25	70				千克		---Other
1517 9090.01	其他混合制成的动物质食用油脂或制品（品目15.16的食用油、脂及其分离品除外）	25	70		15	17	千克	AB	Edible mixtures of animal fats or oils or products (other than edible fats or oil or their fractions of heading No.15.16)
1517 9090.90	其他混合制成的植物质食用油脂或制品（品目15.16的食用油、脂及其分离品除外）	25	70			13	千克	AB	Edible mixtures of vegetable fats or oils or products (other than edible fats or oil or their fractions of heading No.15.16)
15.18	**动、植物油、脂及其分离品，经过熟炼、氧化、脱水、硫化、吹制或在真空、惰性气体中加热聚合及用其他化学方法改性的，但品目15.16的产品除外；本章各种油、脂及其分离品混合制成的其他品目未列名的非食用油、脂或制品：**								**Animal or vegetable fats and oils and fractions thereof, boiled, oxidized, dehydrated, sulphurized, blown, polymerized by heat in vacuum or in inert gas or otherwise chemically modified, excluding those of heading No.15.16; inedible mixtures or preparations of animal or vegetable fats or oils or of fractions of different fats or oils of this Chapter, not elsewhere specified or included:**
1518.0000	动、植物油、脂及其分离品，经过熟炼、氧化、脱水、硫化、吹制或在真空、惰性气体中加热聚合及用其他化学方法改性的，但品目15.16的产品除外；本章各种油、脂及其分离品混合制成的其他品目未列名的非食用油、脂或制品	10	70		15	17	千克	AB	Animal or vegetable fats and oils and fractions thereof, boiled, oxidized, dehydrated, sulphurized, blown, polymerized by heat in vacuum or in inert gas or otherwise chemically modified, excluding those of heading No.15.16; inedible mixtures or preparations of animal or vegetable fats or oils or of fractions of different fats or oils of this Chapter, not elsewhere specified or included
15.20	**粗甘油；甘油水及甘油碱液：**								**Glycerol, crude; glycerol waters and glycerol lyes:**
1520.0000暂	粗甘油，甘油水及甘油碱液	20	50	6	15	17	千克	AB	Glycerol, crude; glycerol waters and glycerol lyes
15.21	**植物蜡（甘油三酯除外）、蜂蜡、其他虫蜡及鲸蜡，不论是否精制或着色：**								**Vegetable waxes（other than triglycerides）, beeswax, other insect waxes and spermaceti, whether or not refined or coloured:**
1521.1000	-植物蜡	20	80		15	17	千克		-Vegetable waxes
1521 1000.10	小烛树蜡	20	80		15	17	千克	ABEF	candelilla wax
1521 1000.90	其他植物蜡	20	80		15	17	千克	AB	other vegetable waxes
	-其他：								-Other:
1521.9010	---蜂蜡	20	80		15	17	千克	AB	---Beeswax
1521.9090	---其他	20	80		15	17	千克		---Other
1521 9090.10	鲸蜡（不论是否精制或着色）	20	80		15	17	千克	AFEB	Spermaceti, whether or not refined or coloured
1521 9090.90	其他虫蜡（不论是否精制或着色）	20	80		15	17	千克	AB	Other insect waxs, whether or not refined or coloured
15.22	**油鞣回收脂；加工处理油脂物质及动、植物蜡所剩的残渣：**								**Degras; residues resulting from the treatment of fatty substances of animal or vegetable waxes:**
1522.0000	油鞣回收脂；加工处理油脂物质及动、植物蜡所剩的残渣	20	50		15	17	千克	9	Degras; residues resulting from the treatment of fatty substances of animal or vegetable waxes

第四类
食品；饮料、酒及醋；烟草、烟草及烟草代用品的制品

注释：

本类所称“团粒”，是指直接挤压或加入按重量计比例不超过 3%的黏合剂制成的粒状产品。

SECTION Ⅳ
PREPARED FOODSTUFFS; BEVERAGES, SPIRITS AND VINEGAR; TOBACCO AND MANUFACTURED TOBACCO SUBSTITUTES

Chapter Note:

In this Section the term “pellets” means products which have been agglomerated either directly by compression or by the addition of a binder in a proportion not exceeding 3% by weight.

第十六章
肉、鱼、甲壳动物，软体动物及其他水生无脊椎动物的制品

注释：

一、本章不包括用第二章、第三章及品目 05.04 所列方法制作或保藏的肉、食用杂碎、鱼、甲壳动物、软体动物或其他水生无脊椎动物。

二、本章的食品按重量计必须含有 20%以上的香肠、肉、食用杂碎、动物血、鱼、甲壳动物、软体动物或其他水生无脊椎动物及其混合物。对于含有两种或两种以上前述产品的食品，则应按其中重量最大的产品归入第十六章的相应品目。但本条规定不适用于品目 19.02 的包馅食品和品目 21.03 及 21.04 的食品。

子目注释：

一、子目 1602.10 的“均化食品”，是指用肉、食用杂碎或动物血经精细均化制成供婴幼儿食用或营养用的零售包装食品（每件净重不超过 250 克）。为了调味、保藏或其他目的，均化食品中可以加入少量其他配料，还可以含有少量可见的肉粒或食用杂碎粒。归类时该子目优先于品目 16.02 的其他子目。

二、品目16.04或16.05项下各子目所列的是鱼、甲壳动物、软体动物及其他水生无脊椎动物的俗名，它们与第三章中相同名称的鱼、甲壳动物、软体动物及其他水生无脊椎动物种类范围相同。

Chapter 16
Preparations of meat, of fish or of crustaceans, molluscs or other aquatic invertebrates

Chapter Notes:

1. This Chapter does not cover meat, meat offal, fish, crustaceans, molluscs or other aquatic invertebrates, prepared or preserved by the processes specified in Chapter 2 or 3 or heading 05.04.
2. Food preparations fall in this Chapter provided that they contain more than 20% by weight of sausage, meat, meat offal, blood, fish or crustaceans, molluscs or other aquatic invertebrates, or any combination thereof. In cases where the preparation contains two or more of the products mentioned above, it is classified in the heading of Chapter 16 corresponding to the component or components which predominate by weight. These provisions do not apply to the stuffed products of heading 19.02 or to the preparations of heading 21.03 or 21.04.

Subheading Notes:

1. For the purposes of subheading 1602.10, the expression “homogenised preparations” means preparations of meat,meat offal or blood, finely homogenised, put up for retail sale as infant food or for dietetic purposes, in containers of a net weight content not exceeding 250g. For the application of this definition no account is to be taken of small quantities of any ingredients which may have been added to the preparation for seasoning, preservation or other purposes.These preparations may contain a small quantity of visible pieces of meat or meat offal. This subheading takes precedence over all other subheadings of heading 16.02.
2. The fish, crustaceans, molluscs and other aquatic invertebrates specified in the subheadings of heading16.04 or 16.05 under their common names only, are of the same species as those mentioned in Chapter 3 under the same name.

税则号列 Tariff Item	商品名称及备注	进口税率 最惠	普通	暂定	出口退税	增值税率	计量单位	监管条件	Article Description
16.01	肉、食用杂碎或动物血制成的香肠及类似产品；用香肠制成的食品：								**Sausages and similar products, of meat, meat offal or blood; food preparations based on these products:**
1601.0010	---用天然肠衣做外包装的香肠及类似产品	15	90			17	千克		---Sausages and similar products, with a natural casing
1601 0010.10	濒危野生动物肉，杂碎，血制天然肠衣香肠（含品目 02.08 的野生动物，包括类似品）	15	90			17	千克	ABFE	Sausages and similar products of meat, meat offal or blood of endangered wild animals, coated with natural casings（including wild animals of heading No.02.08）
1601 0010.90	其他动物肉，杂碎及血制天然肠衣香肠（包括类似品）	15	90		15	17	千克	AB	Sausages and similar products of meat,meat offal or blood of other aminals, with natural casing

税则号列 Tariff Item	商品名称及备注	进口税率 最惠	普通	暂定	出口退税	增值税率	计量单位	监管条件	Article Description
1601.0020	---其他香肠及类似产品	15	90			17	千克		---Other saucages and similar products
1601 0020.10	濒危野生动物肉，杂碎，血制其他肠衣香肠（含品目 02.08 的野生动物，包括类似品）	15	90			17	千克	ABFE	Sausages and similar products of meat, meal offal or blood of endangered wild animals, with other casing,（including wild animals of heading No.02.08）
1601 0020.90	其他动物肉，杂碎及血制其他肠衣香肠（包括类似品）	15	90		15	17	千克	AB	Sauages and simiple products of meat,meat offal or blood of other animals, with other casing
1601.0030	---用香肠制成的食品	15	90			17	千克		---Food preparations based on sausages and similar produts
1601 0030.10	用含濒危野生动物成分的香肠制的食品（含品目 02.08 的野生动物）	15	90			17	千克	ABFE	Food preparations based on sauagses, with composition of endangered wild animals（including endangered wild animals of heading No.02.08）
1601 0030.90	用含其他动物成分的香肠制的食品	15	90		5/15	17	千克	AB	Food preparation based on sauages, with composition of other animals
16.02	**其他方法制作或保藏的肉、食用杂碎或动物血：**								**Other prepared or preserved meat, meat offal or blood:**
1602.1000	-均化食品	15	90			17	千克		-Homogenized preparations
1602 1000.10	含濒危野生动物成分的均化食品（指用肉、食用杂碎或动物血经精细均化制成，零售包装）	15	90			17	千克	ABFE	Homogenized preparations with compositions of endangered wild animals（homogenized meat, meat offal or blood, put up for retail sale）
1602 1000.90	其他动物肉或食用杂碎的均化食品（指用肉、食用杂碎或动物血经精细均化制成，零售包装）	15	90		15	17	千克	AB	Homogenized preparations of other animals（homogenized meat, meat offal or blood, put up for retail sale）
1602.2000	-动物肝	15	90			17	千克		-Of liver of any animal
1602 2000.10	制作或保藏的濒危动物肝(第 2、3 章所列方法制作或保藏的除外)	15	90			17	千克	ABEF	Prepared preserved endangered liver of any animal (other than that of chapter 2,3)
1602 2000.90	制作或保藏的其他动物肝(第 2、3 章所列方法制作或保藏的除外)	15	90		15	17	千克	AB	Prepared preserved other liver of any animal (other than that of chapter 2,3)
	-品目 01.05 的家禽的：								-Of poultry of heading No.01.05:
1602.3100	--火鸡的	15	90		15	17	千克	AB	--Of turkeys
	--鸡的：								--Of fowls of the species *Gallus domesticus*:
1602.3210	---罐头	15	90		15	17	千克	AB	---In airtight containers
	---其他：								---Other:
1602.3291	----鸡胸肉	15	90		15	17	千克	AB	----Chicken breast filets
1602.3292	----鸡腿肉	15	90		15	17	千克	AB	----Chicken leg meat
1602.3299	----其他	15	90		15	17	千克	AB	----Other
	--其他：								--Other:
1602.3910	---罐头	15	90		15	17	千克	AB	---In airtight containers
	---其他：								---Other:
1602.3991	----鸭的	15	90		5/15	17	千克	AB	----Of duck
1602.3999	----其他	15	90		15	17	千克	AB	----Other
	-猪的：								-Of swine:
1602.4100	--后腿及其肉块	15	90		15	17	千克		--Hams and cuts thereof
1602 4100.10	制作或保藏鹿豚，姬猪后腿及肉块	15	90		15	17	千克	ABFE	Hams and cuts of Babyrous, Porcula salvania, prepared or preserved
1602 4100.90	制作或保藏的猪后腿及其肉块	15	90		15	17	千克	AB	Hams and cuts of swine prepared or preserved
1602.4200	--前腿及其肉块	15	90		15	17	千克		--Shoulders and cuts thereof
1602 4200.10	制作或保藏鹿豚，姬猪前腿及肉块	15	90		15	17	千克	ABFE	Shoulders and cuts of Babyrousa, Porcula salvania, prepared or preserved
1602 4200.90	制作或保藏的猪前腿及其肉块	15	90		15	17	千克	AB	Shoulders and cuts of swine, prepared or preserved
	--其他，包括混合的肉：								---Other, including mixtures:
1602.4910	---罐头	15	90		15	17	千克		---In airtight containers
1602 4910.10	其他含鹿豚、姬猪肉及杂碎的罐头	15	90		15	17	千克	ABFE	Other meat, meat offal of Babyrousa Porcula salvania, canned
1602 4910.90	其他猪肉及杂碎的罐头	15	90		15	17	千克	AB	Other meat, meat offal of swine, cannned
1602.4990	---其他	15	90		15	17	千克		---Other
1602 4990.10	制作或保藏其他鹿豚，姬猪肉、杂碎（包括血等）	15	90		15	17	千克	ABFE	Meat, meat offal or blood of *Babyrousa Porcula*, prepared or preserved

税则号列 Tariff Item	商品名称及备注	进口税率			出口退税	增值税率	计量单位	监管条件	Article Description
		最惠	普通	暂定					
1602 4990.90	制作或保藏的其他猪肉，杂碎，血	15	90		15	17	千克	AB	Meat, meat offal or blood of swine,prepared or preserved
	-牛的：								-Of bovine animals:
1602.5010	---罐头	12	90			17	千克		---In airtight containers
1602 5010.10	含濒危野牛肉的罐头	12	90			17	千克	ABFE	Meat of endangered wild bovine animals, cannned
1602 5010.90	其他牛肉及牛杂碎罐头（含野牛肉的除外）	12	90		15	17	千克	AB	Other meat, meat offal of bovine animals, cannned (other than meat of wild bovine animals)
1602.5090	---其他	12	90			17	千克		---Other
1602 5090.10	其他制作或保藏濒危野牛肉、杂碎（包括血等）	12	90			17	千克	ABFE	Other meat, meat offal or blood of endangered wild bovine animals, prepared or preserved
1602 5090.90	其他制作或保藏的牛肉，杂碎，血	12	90		15	17	千克	AB	Other meat, meat offal or blood of bovine animals, prepared or preserved
	-其他，包括动物血的食品：								-Other, including preparations of blood of any animal:
1602.9010	---罐头	15	90			17	千克		---In airtight containers
1602 9010.10	其他濒危野生动物肉及杂碎罐头	15	90			17	千克	ABFE	Other meat, meat offal of endangered wild animal, canned
1602 9010.90	其他肉及杂碎罐头	15	90		15	17	千克	AB	Other meat, meat offal of other animals, cannned
1602.9090	---其他	15	90			17	千克		---Other
1602 9090.10	制作或保藏其他濒危野生动物肉（包括杂碎、血）	15	90			17	千克	ABFE	Other meat, meat offal or blood of endangered wild animals, prepared or preserved
1602 9090.90	经制作或保藏的其他肉、杂碎及血	15	90		15	17	千克	AB	Other meat, meat offal or blood of other animals, prepared or preserved
16.03	**肉、鱼、甲壳动物、软体动物或其他水生无脊椎动物的精及汁：**								**Extracts and juices of meat, fish or crustaceans, molluscs or other aquatic invertebrates:**
1603.0000	肉、鱼、甲壳动物、软体动物或其他水生无脊椎动物的精及汁	23	90			17	千克		Extracts and juices of meat, fish or crustaceans, molluscs or other aquatic invertebrates
1603 0000.10	含濒危野生动物及鱼类成分的肉（指品目 02.08 及子目 0301.92 野生动物及鱼类）	23	90			17	千克	ABFE	Meat with compositions of endangered wild animals and fish of heading No.02.08 or of subheading 0301.92
1603 0000.90	肉及水产品的精、汁（水产品指鱼、甲壳动物、软体动物或其他水生无脊椎动物）	23	90		15	17	千克	AB	Extracts and juices of meat, fish or crustaceans, molluscs or other aquatic invertebrates
16.04	**制作或保藏的鱼；鲟鱼子酱及鱼卵制的鲟鱼子酱代用品：**								**Prepared or preserved fish; caviar and caviar substitutes prepared from fish eggs:**
	-鱼，整条或切块，但未绞碎：								-Fish, whole or in pieces, but not minced:
	--鲑鱼：								--Salmon:
1604.1110	---大西洋鲑鱼	12	90		15	17	千克	AB	---Atlantic salmon
1604.1190	---其他	12	90		15	17	千克		---Other
1604 1190.10	制作或保藏的川陕哲罗鲑鱼（整条或切块，但未绞碎）	12	90		15	17	千克	ABE	*Hucho bleekeri Ts*, prepared or preserved, whole or in pieces, but not minced
1604 1190.20	制作或保藏的秦岭细鳞鲑鱼（整条或切块，但未绞碎）	12	90		15	17	千克	AEB	Tslinling lenok （*Brachymystax lenck*）, prepared or preserved, whole or in pieces, but not minced
1604 1190.90	制作或保藏的其他鲑鱼	12	90		15	17	千克	AB	Other salmon, prepared or preserved
1604.1200	--鲱鱼	12	90		15	17	千克	AB	--Herrings
1604.1300	--沙丁鱼、小沙丁鱼属、黍鲱或西鲱	5	90		15	17	千克	AB	--Sardines , sardinella, brisling or sprats
1604.1400	--金枪鱼、鲣鱼及狐鲣（狐鲣属）	5	90		15	17	千克	AB	--Tunas, skipjack or bonito
1604.1500	--鲭鱼	12	90		15	17	千克	AB	--Mackerel
1604.1600	--鳀鱼	12	90		15	17	千克	AB	--Anchovies
1604.1700	--鳗鱼	12	90		15	17	千克		--Eels
1604 1700.10	制作或保藏的花鳗鲡(整条或切块,但未绞碎)	12	90		15	17	千克	ABE	The produced or stored anguilla marmorata (the whole or dice, but not minced)
1604 1700.20	制作或保藏的欧洲鳗鲡(整条或切块，但未绞碎)	12	90		15	17	千克	ABEF	The produced or stored European eel(the whole or dice, but not mined)
1604 1700.90	其他制作或保藏的鳗鱼(整条或切块，但未绞碎)	12	90		15	17	千克	AB	Other produced or stored conger (the whole or dice, but not mined)

税则号列 Tariff Item	商品名称及备注	进口税率 最惠	普通	暂定	出口退税	增值税率	计量单位	监管条件	Article Description
	--其他:								--Other:
1604.1920	---罗非鱼	12	90		15	17	千克	AB	---Tilapia
	---叉尾鮰鱼:								---Ictalurus:
1604.1931	----斑点叉尾鮰鱼	12	90		15	17	千克	AB	----Channel catfish(Ictalurus punctatus)
1604.1939	----其他	12	90		15	17	千克	AB	----Other
1604.1990	---其他	12	90			17	千克		---Other
1604 1990.10	制作或保藏的濒危鱼类（整条或切块，但未绞碎）	12	90			17	千克	AFEB	Endangered fish, prepared or preserved, whole or in pieces, but not minced
1604 1990.90	制作或保藏的其他鱼（整条或切块，但未绞碎）	12	90		15	17	千克	AB	Other fish, prepared or preserved, whole or in pieces, but not minced
	-其他制作或保藏的鱼:								-Other prepared or preserved fish:
	---罐头:								---In airtight containers:
1604.2011	----鱼翅	12	90		15	17	千克		----Shark's fin
1604 2011.10	濒危鲨鱼鱼翅罐头	12	90		15	17	千克	ABFE	Endangered shark's fins, tinned
1604 2011.90	其他鲨鱼鱼翅罐头	12	90		15	17	千克	AB	Other shark's fins, tinned
1604.2019	----其他	12	90			17	千克		----Other
1604 2019.10	非整条或切块的濒危鱼罐头（鱼翅除外）	12	90			17	千克	ABFE	Endangered fish, not whole nor in pieces, tinned （other than shark's fins）
1604 2019.90	非整条或切块的其他鱼罐头（鱼翅除外）	12	90		15	17	千克	AB	Other fish, not whole nor in pieces, tinned, other than shark's fins
	---其他:								---Other:
1604.2091	----鱼翅	12	90		15	17	千克		----Shark's fin
1604 2091.10	制作或保藏的濒危鲨鱼鱼翅(非整条、非切块、非罐头)	12	90		15	17	千克	ABFE	Endangered shark's fins, prepared or preserved, not whole nor in pieces, not tinned
1604 2091.90	制作或保藏其他鲨鱼鱼翅(非整条、非切块、非罐头)	12	90		15	17	千克	AB	Other shark's fins, prepared or preserved, not whole nor in pieces, not tinned
1604.2099	----其他	12	90			17	千克		----Other
1604 2099.10	其他制作或保藏的濒危鱼（非整条、非切块、非罐头，鱼翅除外）	12	90			17	千克	ABFE	Prepared or preserved endangered fish, not whole nor in pieces, not tinned, other than shark's fins
1604 2099.90	其他制作或保藏的鱼（非整条、非切块、非罐头，鱼翅除外）	12	90		15	17	千克	AB	Other prepared or preserved fish, not whole nor in pieces, not tinned, other than shark's fins
	-鲟鱼子酱及鲟鱼子酱代用品:								-Caviar and caviar substitutes :
1604.3100	--鲟鱼子酱	12	90		15	17	千克	ABFE	--Caviar
1604.3200	--鲟鱼子酱代用品	12	90		15	17	千克	AB	--Caviar substitutes
16.05	**制作或保藏的甲壳动物、软体动物及其他水生无脊椎动物:**								**Crustaceans, molluscs and other aquatic invertebrates, prepared or preserved:**
1605.1000	-蟹	5	90		15	17	千克	AB	-Crab
	-小虾及对虾:								-Shrimps and prawns :
1605.2100	--非密封包装	5	90		15	17	千克	AB	--Not in airtight container
1605.2900	--其他	5	90		15	17	千克	AB	--Other
1605.3000	-龙虾	5	90		15	17	千克	AB	-Lobster
	-其他甲壳动物:								-Other crustaceans:
	---淡水小龙虾:								---Freshwater crawfish:
1605.4011	----虾仁	5	90		15	17	千克	AB	----Shelled
1605.4019	----其他	5	90		15	17	千克	AB	----Other
1605.4090	---其他	5	90		15	17	千克	AB	---Other
	-软体动物:								-Molluscs :
1605.5100	--牡蛎（蚝）	5	90		15	17	千克	AB	--Oysters
1605.5200	--扇贝，包括海扇	5	90		15	17	千克		--Scallops, including queen scallops
1605 5200.10	制作或保藏的大珠母贝	5	90		15	17	千克	ABE	Produced or preserved Pinctada maxima
1605 5200.90	其他制作或保藏的扇贝，包括海扇	5	90		15	17	千克	AB	Other produced or preserved scallop, including sea fan
1605.5300	--贻贝	5	90		15	17	千克	AB	--Mussels
1605.5400	--墨鱼及鱿鱼	5	90		15	17	千克	AB	--Cuttle fish and squid
1605.5500	--章鱼	5	90		15	17	千克	AB	--Octopus
	--蛤、鸟蛤及舟贝:								--Clams, cockles and arkshells :
1605.5610	---蛤	5	90		5/15	17	千克	AB	---Clams

税则号列 Tariff Item	商品名称及备注	进口税率 最惠	普通	暂定	出口退税	增值税率	计量单位	监管条件	Article Description
1605.5620	---乌蛤及舟贝	5	90		15	17	千克		---Cockles and arkshells
1605 5620.10	制作或保藏的砗磲	5	90		15	17	千克	ABEF	Produced or preserved tridacna
1605 5620.90	其他制作或保藏的乌蛤及舟贝	5	90		15	17	千克	AB	Other produced or preserved cockle and arkshells
1605.5700	--鲍鱼	5	90		15	17	千克	AB	--Abalone
1605.5800	--蜗牛及螺，海螺除外	5	90			17	千克		--Snails, other than sea snails
1605 5800.10	制作或保藏的濒危蜗牛及螺，海螺除外	5	90			17	千克	ABFE	Produced or preserved endangered snail and spiral shell, other than snails
1605 5800.90	其他制作或保藏的蜗牛及螺，海螺除外	5	90		15	17	千克	AB	Other produced or preserved snail and spiral shell, other than snails
1605.5900	--其他	5	90			17	千克		--Other
1605 5900.10	其他制作或保藏的濒危软体动物	5	90			17	千克	ABFE	Other produced or preserved endangered mollusc
1605 5900.90	其他制作或保藏的软体动物	5	90		15	17	千克	AB	Other produced or preserved mollusc
	-其他水生无脊椎动物:								-Other aquatic invertebrates :
1605.6100	--海参	5	90		15	17	千克		--Sea cucumbers
1605 6100.10	制作或保藏的暗色刺参	5	90		15	17	千克	ABFE	Produced or preserved dark stichopus japonicus
1605 6100.90	其他制作或保藏的海参	5	90		15	17	千克	AB	Other produced or preserved sea cucumber
1605.6200	--海胆	5	90		15	17	千克	AB	--Sea urchins
1605.6300	--海蜇	15	90		5/15	17	千克	AB	--Jelly-fish
1605.6900	--其他	5	90			17	千克		--Other
1605 6900.10	其他制作或保藏的濒危水生无脊椎动物	5	90			17	千克	ABFE	Other produced or preserved endangered aquatic invertebrate
1605 6900.90	其他制作或保藏的水生无脊椎动物	5	90		15	17	千克	AB	Other produced or preserved aquatic invertebrate

第十七章 糖及糖食

Chapter 17 Sugars and sugar confectionery

注释：

本章不包括：

一、含有可可的糖食（品目 18.06）；

二、品目 29.40 的化学纯糖（蔗糖、乳糖、麦芽糖、葡萄糖及果糖除外）及其他产品；或

三、第三十章的药品及其他产品。

子目注释：

一、子目1701.12、1701.13 及1701.14 所称"原糖"，是指按重量计干燥状态的蔗糖含量对应的旋光读数低于99.5° 的糖。

二、子目1701.13仅包括非离心甘蔗糖，其按重量计干燥状态的蔗糖含量对应的旋光读数不低于69° 但低于93° 。该产品仅含肉眼不可见的不规则形状天然他形微晶，外被蜜糖残余及其他蔗糖成分。

Chapter Notes:

This Chapter does not cover:

(a) Sugar confectionery containing cocoa (heading18. 06);

(b) Chemically pure sugars (other than sucrose, lactose, maltose, glucose and fructose) or other products of heading 29. 40; or

(c) Medicaments or other products of Chapter 30.

Subheading Note:

1. For the purposes of subheadings 1701.12 ,1701.13 and 1701.14 "raw sugar"means sugar whose content of sucrose by weight, in the dry state, corresponds to a polarimeter reading of less than 99.5°.

2. Subheading 1701.13 covers only cane sugar obtained without centrifugation, whose content of sucrose by weight, in the dry state, corresponds to a polarimeter reading of 69° or more but less than 93° ,The product contains only natural anhedral microcystals, of irregular shape, not visible to the naked eye, which are surrounded by residues of molasses and other constituents of sugar cane.

税则号列 Tariff Item	商品名称及备注	进口税率			出口退税	增值税率	计量单位	监管条件	Article Description
		最惠	普通	暂定					
17.01	**固体甘蔗糖、甜菜糖及化学纯蔗糖：**								**Cane or beet sugar and chemically pure sucrose, in solid form:**
	-未加香料或者着色剂的原糖：								-Raw sugar not containing added flavouring or colouring matter:
1701.1200	--甜菜糖		125		15	17	千克		--Beet sugar
1701 1200.01	未加香料或着色剂的甜菜原糖［按重量计干燥状态的糖含量低于旋光读数 99.5 度（配额内）］	15	125		15	17	千克	ABt	Raw beet sugar, without added flavouring or colouring matter, a polarimeter reading of less than 99.5° by weight of sugar, in the dry state (in-quota)
1701 1200.90	未加香料或着色剂的甜菜原糖［按重量计干燥状态的糖含量低于旋光读数 99.5 度（配额外）］	50	125		15	17	千克	AB	Raw beet sugar, without added flavouring or colouring matter, a polarimeter reading of less than 99.5° by weight of sugar, in the dry state (out-of-quota)
1701.1300	--本章子目注释二所述的甘蔗糖		125		15	17	千克		--Cane sugar specified in Subheading note 2 to this chapter
1701 1300.01	未加香料或着色剂的本章子目注释二所述的甘蔗原糖［按重量计干燥状态的蔗糖含量对应旋光读数不低于 69 度，但低于 93 度（配额内）］	15	125		15	17	千克	ABt	Raw cane sugar described in note2 of this chapter without added flavouring or colouring matter,a polarimeter reading of not less than 69 degree, less than 93 degree by weight of sugar, in the dry state (in-quota)
1701 1300.90	未加香料或着色剂的本章子目注释二所述的甘蔗原糖［按重量计干燥状态的蔗糖含量对应旋光读数不低于 69 度，但低于 93 度（配额外）］	50	125		15	17	千克	AB	Raw cane sugar described in note2 of this chapter without added flavouring or colouring matter,a polarimeter reading of not less than 69 degree, less than 93 degree by weight of sugar, in the dry state (out-of- quota)
1701.1400	--其他甘蔗糖		125		15	17	千克		--Other cane sugar
1701 1400.01	未加香料或着色剂其他甘蔗原糖［按重量计干燥状态的糖含量低于旋光读数99.5度(配额内)］	15	125		15	17	千克	ABt	Other raw cane sugar without added flavouring or colouring matter, (a polarimeter reading of less than 99.5 degree by weight of sugar, in the dry state (in quota))
1701 1400.90	未加香料或着色剂其他甘蔗原糖［按重量计干燥状态的糖含量低于旋光读数99.5度(配额外)］	50	125		15	17	千克	AB	Other raw cane sugar without added flavouring or colouring matter, (a polarimeter reading of less than 99.5 degree by weight of sugar, in the dry state (out of quota))
	-其他：								-Other:

税则号列 Tariff Item	商品名称及备注	进口税率			出口退税	增值税率	计量单位	监管条件	Article Description
		最惠	普通	暂定					
1701.9100	--加有香料或着色剂		125		15	17	千克		--Containing added flavouring or colouring matter
1701 9100.01	加有香料或着色剂的糖[指甘蔗糖、甜菜糖及化学纯蔗糖（配额内）]	15	125		15	17	千克	ABt	Suger (referring to cane or beet sugar and chemically pure sucrose), containing added flavouring or colouring matter（in-quota）
1701 9100.90	加有香料或着色剂的糖[指甘蔗糖、甜菜糖及化学纯蔗糖（配额外）]	50	125		15	17	千克	AB	Suger (referring to cane or beet sugar and chemically pure sucrose), containing added flavouring ,colouring matter (out-of-quota)
	--其他:								--Other:
1701.9910	---砂糖		125		15	17	千克		---Granulated sugar
1701 9910.10	砂糖（配额内）	15	125		15	17	千克	ABt	Granulated sugar（in-quota）
1701 9910.90	砂糖（配额外）	50	125		15	17	千克	AB	Granulated sugar (out-of-quota)
1701.9920	---绵白糖		125		15	17	千克		---Superfine sugar
1701 9920.01	绵白糖（配额内）	15	125		15	17	千克	BAt	Superfine sugar（in-quota）
1701 9920.90	绵白糖（配额外）	50	125		15	17	千克	BA	Superfine sugar (out-of-quota)
1701.9990	---其他		125		15	17	千克		---Other
1701 9990.01	其他精制糖（配额内）	15	125		15	17	千克	ABt	Other refined sugar（in-quota）
1701 9990.90	其他精制糖（配额外）	50	125		15	17	千克	AB	Other refined sugar（out-of-quota）
17.02	**其他固体糖，包括化学纯乳糖、麦芽糖、葡萄糖及果糖；未加香料或着色剂的糖浆；人造蜜，不论是否掺有天然蜂蜜；焦糖：**								**Other sugars, including chemically pure lactose, maltose, glucose and fructose, in solid form; sugar syrups not containing added flavouring or colouring matter; artificial honey, whether or not mixed with natural honey; caramel:**
	-乳糖及乳糖浆:								-Lactose and lactose syrup:
1702.1100	--按重量计干燥无水乳糖含量在99%及以上	10	80		15	17	千克	AB	--Containing by weight 99% or more lactose, expressed as anhydrous lactose, calculated on the dry matter
1702.1900	--其他	10	80		15	17	千克	AB	--Other
1702.2000	-槭糖及槭糖浆	30	80		15	17	千克	AB	-Maple sugar and maple syrup
1702.3000	-葡萄糖及葡萄糖浆，不含果糖或按重量计干燥状态的果糖含量在20%以下	30	80		15	17	千克	BA	-Glucose and glucose syrup, not containing fructose or containing in the dry state less than 20% by weight of fructose
1702.4000	-葡萄糖及葡萄糖浆，按重量计干燥状态的果糖含量在20%及以上，但在50%以下，转化糖除外	30	80		15	17	千克	BA	-Glucose and glucose syrup, containing in the dry state at least 20% but less than 50% by weight of fructose, excluding invert sugar
1702.5000	-化学纯果糖	30	80		15	17	千克	AB	-Chemically pure fructose
1702.6000	-其他果糖及果糖浆，按重量计干燥状态的果糖含量在50%以上，转化糖除外	30	80		15	17	千克	BA	-Other fructose and fructose syrup, containing in the dry state more than 50% by weight of fructose, excluding invert sugar
1702.9000	-其他，包括转化糖及其他按重量计干燥状态的果糖含量为50%的糖及糖浆混合物	30	80		15	17	千克		-Other, including invert sugar and other sugar and sugar syrup blends containing in the dry state more than 50% by weight of fructose
1702 9000.10	人造蜜	30	80		15	17	千克	AB	Honey substitute
1702 9000.90	其他固体糖，焦糖（包括转化糖及按重量计干燥状态果糖含量50%的糖、糖浆）	30	80		15	17	千克	AB	Other sugars in solid form, caramel, including invert sugar, (containing in the dry state 50% by weight of fructose）
17.03	**制糖后所剩的糖蜜：**								**Molasses resulting from the extraction or refining or sugar:**
1703.1000	-甘蔗糖蜜	8	50		15	17	千克	ABP	-Cane molasses
1703.9000	-其他	8	50		15	17	千克	ABP	-Other
17.04	**不含可可的糖食（包括白巧克力）：**								**Sugar confectionery（including white chocolate）, not containing cocoa:**
1704.1000	-口香糖，不论是否裹糖	12	50		15	17	千克	AB	-Chewing gum, whether or not sugarcoated
1704.9000	-其他	10	50		15	17	千克	AB	-Other

第十八章 可可及可可制品

Chapter 18 Cocoa and cocoa preparations

注释：

一、本章不包括品目04.03、19.01、19.04、19.05、21.05、22.02、22.08、30.03、30.04的制品。

二、品目18.06包括含有可可的糖食及注释一以外的其他含可可的食品。

Chapter Notes:

1.This Chapter does not cover the preparations of heading 04.03,19.01, 19.04, 19.05, 21.05, 22.02, 22.08, 30.03, or 30.04.

2.Heading 18.06 includes sugar confectionery containing cocoa and, subject to Note 1 to this Chapter, other food preparations containing cocoa.

税则号列 Tariff Item	商品名称及备注	进口税率			出口退税	增值税率	计量单位	监管条件	Article Description
		最惠	普通	暂定					
18.01	**整颗或破碎的可可豆，生的或焙炒的：**								**Cocoa beans, whole or broken, raw or roasted:**
1801.0000[暂]	整颗或破碎的可可豆，生的或焙炒的	8	30	2	5/15	17	千克	AB	Cocoa beans, whole or broken, raw or roasted
18.02	**可可荚、壳、皮及废料：**								**Cocoa shells, husks, skins and other cocoa waste:**
1802.0000	可可荚、壳、皮及废料	10	30		5	17	千克	AB	Cocoa shells, husks, skins and other cocoa waste
18.03	**可可膏，不论是否脱脂：**								**Cocoa paste, whether or not defatted:**
1803.1000	-未脱脂	10	30		15	17	千克	AB	-Not defatted
1803.2000	-全脱脂或部分脱脂	10	30		15	17	千克	AB	-Wholly or partly defatted
18.04	**可可脂、可可油：**								**Cocoa butter, fat and oil:**
1804.0000	可可脂、可可油	22	70		15	17	千克		Cocoa butter, fat and oil
1804 0000.10	可可脂	22	70		15	17	千克	AB	Cocoa butter
1804 0000.90	可可油	22	70		15	17	千克	AB	Cocoa fat and oil
18.05	**未加糖或其他甜物质的可可粉：**								**Cocoa powder, not containing added sugar or other sweetening matter:**
1805.0000	未加糖或其他甜物质的可可粉	15	40		15	17	千克	AB	Cocoa powder, not containing added sugar or other sweetening matter
18.06	**巧克力及其他含可可的食品：**								**Chocolate and other food preparations containing cocoa:**
1806.1000	-加糖或其他甜物质的可可粉	10	50		15	17	千克	AB	-Cocoa powder, containing added sugar or other sweetening matter
1806.2000	-其他重量超过2千克的块状或条状含可可食品，或液态、膏状、粉状、粒状或其他散装形状的含可可食品，容器包装或内包装每件净重超过2千克的	10	50		15	17	千克	AB	-Other preparations in blocks, slabs or bars weighing more than 2kg or in liquid, paste, powder, granular or other bulk form in containers or immediate packings, of a content exceeding 2kg
	-其他块状或条状的含可可食品：								-Other, in blocks, slabs or bars:
1806.3100	--夹心	8	50		15	17	千克	AB	--Filled
1806.3200	--不夹心	10	50		15	17	千克	AB	--Not filled
1806.9000	-其他	8	50		15	17	千克	AB	-Other

第十九章
谷物、粮食粉、淀粉或乳的制品；糕饼点心

Chapter 19
Preparations of cereals, flour, starch or milk; pastrycook's products

注释：

一、本章不包括：

（一）按重量计含香肠、肉、食用杂碎、动物血、鱼、甲壳动物，软体动物、其他水生无脊椎动物及其混合物超过 20%的食品（第十六章），但品目 19.02 的包馅食品除外；

（二）用粮食粉或淀粉制的专作动物饲料用的饼干及其他制品（品目 23.09）；或

（三）第三十章的药品及其他产品。

二、品目 19.01 所称：

（一）“粗粒”是指第十一章的谷物粗粒；

（二）“细粉”及“粗粉”，是指：

1. 第十一章的谷物细粉及粗粉；以及

2. 其他章所列植物的细粉、粗粉及粉末，但不包括干蔬菜、马铃薯和干豆类的细粉、粗粉及粉末（应分别归入品目 07.12、11.05 和 11.06）。

三、品目 19.04 不包括按重量计全脱脂可可含量超过 6%或用巧克力完全包裹的食品或品目 18.06 的其他含可可食品（品目 18.06）。

四、品目19.04所称“其他方法制作的”，是指制作或加工程度超过第十章或第十一章各品目或注释所规定范围的。

Chapter Notes:

1. This Chapter does not cover:

（a）Except in the case of stuffed products of heading 19.02,food prepara-tions containing more than 20% by weight of sausage, meat, meat offal, blood, fish or crustaceans, molluscs or other aquatic invertebr-ates, or any combination thereof（Chapter 16）;

（b）Biscuits or other articles made from flour or from starch, specially prepared for use in animal feeding（heading23.09）; or

（c）Medicaments or other products of Chapter 30.

2. For the purposes of heading 19.01:

（a）The term “groats” means cereal groats of Chapter 11;

（b）The terms “flour” and “meal” mean:

（ i ）Cereal flour and meal of Chapter 11, and

（ ii ）Flour, meal and power of vegetable origin of any Chapter, other than flour, meal or powder of dried vegetables（heading 07.12）, of potatoes（heading 11.05）or of dried leguminous vegetables（heading 11.06）.

3. Heading 19.04 does not cover preparations containing more than 6% by weight of cocoa calculated on a totally defatted basis or completely coated with chocolate or other food preparations containing cocoa of heading 18.06（heading 18.06）.

4. For the purposes of heading 19.04, the expression “otherwise prepared” means prepared or processed to an extent beyond that provided for in the headings of or Notes to Chapter 10 or 11.

税则号列 Tariff Item	商品名称及备注	进口税率 最惠	进口税率 普通	进口税率 暂定	出口退税	增值税率	计量单位	监管条件	Article Description
19.01	**麦精；细粉、粗粒、粗粉、淀粉或麦精制的其他品目未列名的食品，不含可可或按重量计全脱脂可可含量低于 40%；品目 04.01 至 04.04 所列货品制的其他品目未列名的食品，不含可可或按重量计全脱脂可可含量低于 5%：**								**Malt extract; food preparations of flour, groats, meal, starch or malt extract, not containing cocoa or containing less than 40% by weight of cocoa calculated on a totally defatted basis, not elsewhere specified or included; food preparations of goods of headings No.04.01 to 04.04, not containing cocoa or containing less than 5% by weight of cocoa calculated on a totally defatted basis, not elsewhere specified or included:**
	-供婴幼儿食用的零售包装食品:								-Preparations for infant use, put up for retail sale:
1901.1010 暂	---配方奶粉（供婴幼儿食用的零售包装配方奶粉(按重量计全脱脂可可含量＜5%乳品制)	15	40	5	15	17	千克	7AB	---Powdered formulas （Formula milk powder prepared for infant use, put up for retail sale(Cocoa contents:＜5% of dairy products)
1901.1090 暂	---其他	15	40	5	15	17	千克	AB	---Other
1901.2000	-供烘焙品目 19.05 所列面包糕饼用的调制品及面团	25	80		5/15	17	千克	AB	-Mixes and doughs for the preparation of bakers' wares of heading No.19.05
1901.9000 暂	-其他	10	80	5	15	17	千克	AB	-Other
19.02	**面食，不论是否煮熟、包馅（肉馅或其他馅）或其他方法制作，例如，通心粉、面条、汤团、馄饨、饺子、奶油面卷；古斯古斯面食，不论是否制作：**								**Pasta, whether or not cooked or stuffed（with meat or other substances） or otherwise prepared, such as spaghetti, macaroni, noodles, lasagne, gnocchi, ravioli, cannelloni; couscous, whether or not prepared:**
	-生的面食，未包馅或未经其他方法制作:								-Uncooked pasta, not stuffed or otherwise prepared:
1902.1100	--含蛋	15	80		5	17	千克	AB	--Containing eggs

税则号列 Tariff Item	商品名称及备注	进口税率			出口退税	增值税率	计量单位	监管条件	Article Description
		最惠	普通	暂定					
1902.1900	--其他	15	80		5/15	17	千克	AB	--Other
1902.2000	-包馅面食，不论是否烹煮或经其他方法制作	15	80		5/15	17	千克	AB	-Stuffed pasta, whether or not cooked or otherwise prepared
	-其他面食:								-Other pasta:
1902.3010	---米粉干	15	80		5	17	千克	AB	---Rice vermicelli, cooked
1902.3020	---粉丝	15	80		15	17	千克	AB	---Bean vermicelli, cooked
1902.3030	---即食或快熟面条	15	80		5/15	17	千克	AB	---Instant noodle
1902.3090	---其他	15	80		5/15	17	千克	AB	---Other
1902.4000	-古斯古斯面食	25	80		5/15	17	千克	AB	-Couscous
19.03	**珍粉及淀粉制成的珍粉代用品，片、粒、珠、粉或类似形状的:**								**Tapioca and substitutes therefor prepared from starch, in the form of flakes, grains, pearls, siftings or in similar forms:**
1903.0000	珍粉及淀粉制成的珍粉代用品，片、粒、珠、粉或类似形状的	15	80		15	17	千克	AB	Tapioca and substitutes therefor prepared from starch, in the form of flakes, grains, pearls, siftings or in similar forms
19.04	**谷物或谷物产品经膨化或烘炒制成的食品（例如，玉米片）；其他品目未列名的预煮或经其他方法制作的谷粒(玉米除外)，谷物片或经其他加工的谷粒(细粉、粗粒及粗粉除外)：**								**Prepared foods obtained by the swelling or roasting of cereals or cereal products（for example, corn flakes）; cereals（other than maize（corn）in grain form or in the form of flakes or other worked grains（except flour, groats and meal）, precooked or otherwise prepared, not elsewhere specified or included:**
1904.1000	-谷物或谷物产品经膨化或烘炒制成的食品	25	80		15	17	千克	AB	-Prepared foods obtained by the swelling or roasting of cereals or cereal products
1904.2000	-未烘炒谷物片制成的食品及未烘炒的谷物片与烘炒的谷物片或膨化的谷物混合制成的食品	30	80		15	17	千克	AB	-Prepared foods obtained from unroasted cereal flakes or from mixtures of unroasted cereal flakes and roasted cereal flakes or swelled cereals
1904.3000	-碾碎的干小麦	30	80		15	17	千克	AB	-Bulgur wheat
1904.9000	-其他	30	80		15	17	千克	AB	-Other
19.05	**面包、糕点、饼干及其他烘焙糕饼，不论是否含可可；圣餐饼、装药空囊、封缄、糯米纸及类似制品:**								**Bread, pastry, cakes, biscuits and other bakers' wares, whether or not containing cocoa; communion wafers, empty cachets of a kind suitable for pharmaceutical use, sealing wafers, rice paper and similar products:**
1905.1000	-黑麦脆面包片	20	80		15	17	千克	AB	-Crispbread
1905.2000	-姜饼及类似品	20	80		15	17	千克	AB	-Gingerbread and the like
	-甜饼干；华夫饼干及圣餐饼:								-Sweet biscuits; waffles and wafers:
1905.3100	--甜饼干	15	80		15	17	千克	AB	--Sweet biscuits
1905.3200	--华夫饼干及圣餐饼	15	80		15	17	千克	AB	--Waffles and wafers
1905.4000	-面包干、吐司及类似的烤面包	20	80		15	17	千克	AB	-Rusks, toasted bread and similar toasted products
1905.9000	-其他	20	80		15	17	千克	AB	-Other

第二十章 蔬菜、水果、坚果或植物其他部分的制品

注释：

一、本章不包括：

（一）用第七章、第八章或第十一章所列方法制作或保藏的蔬菜、水果或坚果；

（二）按重量计含香肠、肉、食用杂碎、动物血、鱼、甲壳动物、软体动物、其他水生无脊椎动物及其混合物超过20%的食品（第十六章）；

（三）品目19.05的烘焙糕饼及其他制品；或

（四）品目21.04的均化混合食品。

二、品目20.07及20.08不包括制成糖食的果冻、果膏、糖衣杏仁或类似品（品目17.04）及巧克力糖食（品目18.06）。

三、品目20.01、20.04及20.05仅酌情包括用本章注释一（一）以外的方法制作或保藏的第七章或品目11.05、11.06的产品(第八章产品的细粉、粗粉除外)。

四、干重量在7%及以上的番茄汁归入品目20.02。

五、品目20.07所称“烹煮制成的”，是指在常压或减压状态下，通过减少产品中的水分或其他方法增加产品黏稠度的热处理制得的。

六、品目20.09所称“未发酵及未加酒精的水果汁”，是指按容量计酒精浓度（标准见第二十二章注释二）不超过0.5%的水果汁。

子目注释：

一、子目2005.10所称“均化蔬菜”，是指蔬菜经精细均化制成供婴幼儿食用或营养用的零售包装食品（每件净重不超过250克）。为了调味、保藏或其他目的，均化蔬菜中可以加入少量其他配料，还可以含有少量可见的蔬菜粒。归类时，子目2005.10优先于品目20.05的其他子目。

二、子目2007.10所称“均化食品”，是指果实经精细均化制成供婴幼儿食用或营养用的零售包装食品（每件净重不超过250克）。为了调味、保藏或其他目的，均化食品中可以加入少量其他配料，还可以含有少量可见的果粒。归类时，子目2007.10优先于税目20.07的其他子目。

三、子目2009.12、2009.21、2009.31、2009.41、2009.61及2009.71所称“白利糖度值”是指在20℃时直接从白利糖度计读取的度数或从折射计直接读取的以蔗糖百分比含量计的折射

Chapter 20 Preparations of vegetables, fruit, nuts or other parts of plants

Chapter Notes:

1. This Chapter does not cover:

(a) Vegetables, fruit or nuts, prepared or preserved by the processes specified in Chapter 7, 8 or 11;

(b) Food preparations containing more than 20% by weight of sausage, meat, meat offal, blood, fish or crustaceans, molluscs or other aquatic invertebrates, or any combination thereof (Chapter 16);

(c) Bakers' wares and other products of heading 19.05; or

(d) Homogenised composite food preparations of heading21.04.

2. Headings 20.07 and 20.08 do not apply to fruit jellies, fruit pastes, sugar-coated almonds or the like in the form of sugar confectionery (heading 17.04) or chocolate confectionery (heading18.06).

3. Headings 20.01, 20.04 and 20.05 cover, as the case may be,only those products of Chapter 7 or of heading 11.05 or 11.06 (other than flour, meal and powder of the products of Chapter 8) which have been prepared or preserved by processes other than those referred to in Note 1 (a).

4 .Tomato juice the dry weight content of which is 7% or more is to be classified in heading 20.02.

5. For the purposes of heading 20.07 the expression "obtained by cooking" means obtained by heat treatment at atmospheric pressure or under reduced pressure to increase the viscosity of a product through reduction of water content or other means

6. For the purposes of heading 20.09, the expression "juices,unfermented and not containing added spirit" means juices of an alcoholic strength by volume (see Note 2 to Chapter 22) not exceeding 0.5% vol.

Subheading Notes:

1. For the purposes of subheading 2005.10, the expression "homogenised vegetables" means preparations of vegetables, finely homogenised, put up for retail sale as infant food or for dietetic purposes, in containers of a net weight content not exceeding 250g.For the application of this definition no account is to be taken of small quantities of any ingredients which may have been added to the preparation for seasoning, preservation or other purposes.These preparations may contain a small quantity of visible pieces of vegetables. Subheading 2005.10 takes precedence over all other subheadings of heading 20.05.

2. For the purposes of subheading 2007.10, the expression "homogenised preparations" means preparations of fruit, finely homogenised, put up for retail sale as infant food or for dietetic purposes, in containers of a net weight content not exceeding 250g. For the application of this definition no account is to be taken of small quantities of any ingredients which may have been added to the preparation for seasoning, preservation or other purposes. These preparations may contain a small quantity of visible pieces of fruit. Subheading 2007.10 takes precedence over all other subheadings of heading 20.07.

3. For the purposes of subheadings 2009.12, 2009.21, 2009.31, 2009.41,2009.61 and 2009.71, the expression "Brix value" means the direct reading of degrees Brix obtained from a Brix hydrometer or of refractive index expressed in terms of percentage sucrose content

率，在其他温度下读取的数值应折算为 20℃时的数值。

obtained from a refractometer, at a temperature of 20℃ or corrected for 20℃ if the reading is made at a different temperature.

税则号列 Tariff Item	商品名称及备注	进口税率			出口退税	增值税率	计量单位	监管条件	Article Description
		最惠	普通	暂定					
20.01	**蔬菜、水果、坚果及植物的其他食用部分，用醋或醋酸制作或保藏的：**								**Vegetables, fruit, nuts and other edible parts of plants, prepared or preserved by vinegar or acetic acid:**
2001.1000	-黄瓜及小黄瓜	25	70		5/15	17	千克	AB	-Cucumbers and gherkins
	-其他:								-Other:
2001.9010	---大蒜	25	70		5/15	17	千克		---Garlic
2001 9010.10	用醋或醋酸腌制的大蒜头、大蒜瓣（无论是否加糖或去皮）	25	70		5/15	17	千克	AB	Garlic heads and garlic bulblet, prepared by vinegar or acetic acid, whether or not added sugar or skinned
2001 9010.90	用醋或醋酸腌制的其他大蒜(不含蒜头、蒜瓣，无论是否加糖或去皮）	25	70		5/15	17	千克	AB	Other garlic prepared by vinegar or acetic acid, whether or not added sugars or skinned（other than garlic heads and garlic bulblet）
2001.9090	---其他	25	70		5	17	千克		---Other
2001 9090.10	用醋或醋酸制作或保藏的松茸	25	70		5	17	千克	ABE	Sungmo, prepared or preserved by vinegar or acetic acid
2001 9090.20	用醋或醋酸制作或保藏的酸竹笋	25	70		5	17	千克	ABE	Pickled bamboo shoots, prepared or preserved by vinegar or acetic acid
2001 9090.30	用醋或醋酸制作或保藏的芦荟	25	70		5	17	千克	ABFE	Aloe, prepared or preserved by vinegar or acetic acid
2001 9090.40	用醋或醋酸制作或保藏的仙人掌植物	25	70		5	17	千克	ABFE	Cactus, prepared or preserved by vinegar or acetic acid
2001 9090.50	用醋或醋酸制作或保藏的莼菜	25	70		5	17	千克	ABE	Water shield, prepared or preserved by vinegar or acetic acid
2001 9090.90	用醋制作的其他果、菜及食用植物（包括用醋酸制作或保藏的）	25	70		5/15	17	千克	AB	Vegetables, fruit and other edible parts of plants, prepared or preserved by vinegar or acetic acid
20.02	**番茄，用醋或醋酸以外的其他方法制作或保藏的：**								**Tomatoes prepared or preserved otherwise than by vinegar or acetic acid:**
	-番茄，整个或切片：								-Tomatoes, whole or in pieces:
2002.1010	---罐头	19	80		15	17	千克	AB	---In airtight containers
2002.1090	---其他	25	70		5/15	17	千克	AB	---Other
	-其他:								-Other:
	---番茄酱罐头:								---Tomato paste, in airtight containers:
2002.9011	----重量不超过 5kg 的	20	80		15	17	千克	AB	----Weighing not more than 5kg
2002.9019	——重量超过 5kg 的	20	80		15	17	千克	AB	----Weighing more than 5kg
2002.9090	---其他	18	70		5/15	17	千克	AB	---Other
20.03	**蘑菇及块菌，用醋或醋酸以外的其他方法制作或保藏的：**								**Mushrooms and truffles,prepared or preserved otherwise than by vinegar or acetic acid:**
	-伞菌属蘑菇:								-Mushrooms:
	---罐头:								---In airtight containers:
2003.1011	----小白蘑菇	25	90		15	17	千克	AB	----Small white agaric
2003.1019	----其他	25	90		15	17	千克	AB	----Other
2003.1090	---其他	25	90		5/15	17	千克	AB	---Other
	-其他:								-Other:
2003.9010	---罐头	25	90		15	17	千克		---In airtight containers
2003 9010.10	非用醋制作的香菇罐头[用醋或醋酸以外其他方法制作或保藏的（非伞菌属蘑菇）]	25	90		15	17	千克	AB	Shiitake, tinned, prepared or preserved otherwise than by vinegar or acetic acid（non-agaric mushrooms）
2003 9010.20	非用醋制作的松茸罐头(用醋或醋酸以外其他方法制作或保藏的）	25	90		15	17	千克	ABE	Sungmo, tinned, prepared or preserved otherwise than by vinegar or acetic acid
2003 9010.90	非用醋制作的其他蘑菇罐头[用醋或醋酸以外其他方法制作或保藏的（非伞菌属蘑菇）]	25	90		15	17	千克	AB	Other shiitake, tinned, prepared or preserved otherwise than by vinegar or acetic acid（non-agaric mushrooms）
2003.9090	---其他	25	90		5/15	17	千克		---Other
2003 9090.10	非用醋制作的其他香菇[用醋或醋酸以外其他方法制作或保藏的（非伞菌属蘑菇）]	25	90		5/15	17	千克	AB	Other shiitake, prepared or preserved otherwise than by vinegar or acetic acid（non-agaric mushrooms）
2003 9090.20	非用醋制作的其他松茸（用醋或醋酸以外其他方法制作或保藏的）	25	90		5/15	17	千克	ABE	Other sungmo, prepared or preserved otherwise than by vinegar or acetic acid

税则号列 Tariff Item	商品名称及备注	进口税率			出口退税	增值税率	计量单位	监管条件	Article Description
		最惠	普通	暂定					
2003 9090.90	非用醋制作的其他蘑菇[用醋或醋酸以外其他方法制作或保藏的（非伞菌属蘑菇）]	25	90		5/15	17	千克	AB	Other mushrooms, prepared or preserved otherwise than by vinegar or acetic acid（non-agaric mushrooms）
20.04	**其他冷冻蔬菜，用醋或醋酸以外的其他方法制作或保藏的，但品目20.06的产品除外：**								**Other vegetables prepared or preserved otherwise than by vinegar or acetic acid, frozen, other than products of heading No.20.06:**
2004.1000	-马铃薯	13	70		5/15	17	千克	AB	-Potatoes
2004.9000	-其他蔬菜及什锦蔬菜	25	70		5/15	17	千克		-Other vegetables and mixtures of vegetables
2004 9000.10	非用醋制作的冷冻松茸	25	70		5/15	17	千克	ABE	Sungmo, frozen, not prepared by vinegar
2004 9000.20	非用醋制作的冷冻酸竹笋	25	70		5/15	17	千克	ABE	Pickled bamboo shoots, frozen, not prepared by vinegar
2004 9000.30	非用醋制作的冷冻芦荟	25	70		5/15	17	千克	ABFE	Aloe, frozen, not prepared by vinegar
2004 9000.40	非用醋制作的冷冻仙人掌植物	25	70		5/15	17	千克	ABFE	Cactus, frozen, not prepared by vinegar
2004 9000.90	非用醋制作的其他冷冻蔬菜(品目20.06的货品除外)	25	70		5/15	17	千克	AB	Other vegetables, frozen, not prepared by vinegar, frozen（other than products of heading No.20.06）
20.05	**其他未冷冻蔬菜，用醋或醋酸以外的其他方法制作或保藏的，但品目20.06的产品除外：**								**Other vegetables prepared or preserved otherwise than by vinegar or acetic acid, not frozen, other than products of heading No.20.06:**
2005.1000	-均化蔬菜	25	70		15	17	千克	AB	-Homogenized vegetables
2005.2000	-马铃薯	15	70		5/15	17	千克	AB	-Potatoes
2005.4000	-豌豆	25	70		5/15	17	千克	AB	-Peas（*Pisum sativum*）
	-豇豆属及菜豆属:								-Beans（*Vigna spp.*, *Phaseolus spp.*）:
	--脱荚的:								--Beans, Shelled:
	---罐头:								---In airtight containers:
2005.5111	----赤豆馅	25	80		15	17	千克	AB	----Red bean paste
2005.5119	----其他	25	80		15	17	千克	AB	----Other
	---其他:								---Other:
2005.5191	----赤豆馅	25	70		15	17	千克	AB	----Red bean paste
2005.5199	----其他	25	70		5/15	17	千克	AB	----Other
	--其他:								--Other:
2005.5910	---罐头	25	80		15	17	千克	AB	---In airtight containers
2005.5990	---其他	25	70		5/15	17	千克	AB	---Other
	-芦笋:								-Asparagus:
2005.6010	---罐头	25	80		15	17	千克	AB	---In airtight containers
2005.6090	---其他	25	70		5/15	17	千克	AB	---Other
2005.7000	-油橄榄	10	70		5/15	17	千克	AB	-Olives
2005.8000	-甜玉米	10	80		5/15	17	千克	AB	-Sweet corn（*Zea mays var. Saccharata*）
	-其他蔬菜及什锦蔬菜:								-Other vegetables and mixtures of vegetables:
	--竹笋:								--Bamboo shoots:
2005.9110	---竹笋罐头	25	80		15	17	千克		---Bamboo shoots, in airtight containers
2005 9110.10	非用醋制作的酸竹笋罐头	25	80		15	17	千克	ABE	Bamboo shoots, pickled, tinned, prepared otherwise than by vinegar
2005 9110.90	非用醋制作的其他竹笋罐头	25	80		15	17	千克	AB	Other bamboo shoots, tinned, prepared otherwise than by vinegar
2005.9190	---其他	25	70		5/15	17	千克		---Other
2005 9190.10	非用醋制作的酸竹笋	25	70		5/15	17	千克	ABE	Bamboo shoots, pickled, prepared otherwise than by vinegar
2005 9190.90	非用醋制作的其他竹笋	25	70		5/15	17	千克	AB	Other bamboo shoots, prepared otherwise than by vinegar
	--其他:								--Other:
2005.9920	---蚕豆罐头	25	80		15	17	千克	AB	---Broad beans, in airtight containers
2005.9940	---榨菜	25	70		5/15	17	千克	AB	---Hot pickled mustard tubers
2005.9950	---咸蕨菜	25	70		5/15	17	千克	AB	---Chueh tsai（fiddle-head）, salted
2005.9960	---咸藠头	25	70		5/15	17	千克	AB	---Scallion, salted
	---其他:								---Other:
2005.9991	----罐头	25	70		15	17	千克	AB	----in airtight containers
2005.9999	----其他	25	70		5/15	17	千克		----Other

税则号列 Tariff Item	商品名称及备注	进口税率 最惠	普通	暂定	出口退税	增值税率	计量单位	监管条件	Article Description
2005 9999.10	非用醋制作的仙人掌	25	70		5/15	17	千克	ABFE	Cactus, prepared otherwise than by vinegar
2005 9999.20	非用醋制作的芦荟	25	70		5/15	17	千克	ABFE	Aloe, prepared otherwise than by vinegar
2005 9999.90	非用醋制作的其他蔬菜及什锦蔬菜	25	70		5/15	17	千克	AB	Other vegetables and mixtures of vegetables, prepared otherwise than by vinegar
20.06	**糖渍蔬菜、水果、坚果、果皮及植物的其他部分（沥干、糖渍或裹糖的）：**								**Vegetables, fruit, nuts, fruit-peel and other parts of plants, preserved by sugar（drained, glace or crystallized）:**
2006.0010	---蜜枣	30	90		15	17	千克	AB	---Preserved jujubes
2006.0020	---橄榄	30	90		15	17	千克	AB	---Preserved olives
2006.0090	---其他	30	90		15	17	千克		---Other
2006 0090.10	糖渍制松茸	30	90		15	17	千克	ABE	Sungmo, preserved by sugar
2006 0090.90	其他糖渍蔬菜、水果、坚果、果皮（包括糖渍植物的其他部分）	30	90		15	17	千克	AB	Other vegetables, fruit, nuts, fruitpeel and other parts of plants, preserved by sugar
20.07	**烹煮的果酱、果冻、柑橘酱、果泥及果膏，不论是否加糖或其他甜物质：**								**Jams, fruit jellies, marmalades, fruit or nut puree and fruit or nut pastes, being cooked preparations, whether or not containing added sugar or other sweetening matter:**
2007.1000	-均化食品	30	80		15	17	千克	AB	-Homogenized preparations
	-其他:								-Other:
2007.9100	--柑橘属水果的	30	80		15	17	千克	AB	--Citrus fruit
	--其他:								-Other:
2007.9910	---罐头	5	80		15	17	千克	AB	---In airtight containers
2007.9990	---其他	5	80		15	17	千克	AB	---Other
20.08	**用其他方法制作或保藏的其他品目未列名水果、坚果及植物的其他食用部分，不论是否加酒、加糖或其他甜物质：**								**Fruit, nuts and other edible parts of plants, otherwise prepared, or preserved, whether or not containing added sugar or other sweetening matter or spirit, not elsewhere specified or included:**
	-坚果、花生及其他子仁，不论是否混合:								-Nuts, ground-nuts and other seeds, whether or not mixed together:
	--花生:								--Ground-nuts:
2008.1110	---花生米罐头	30	90		15	17	千克	AB	---Ground-nut kernels, in airtight containers
2008.1120	---烘焙花生	30	80		15	17	千克	AB	---Roasted ground-nuts
2008.1130	---花生酱	30	90		15	17	千克	AB	---Ground-nut butter
2008.1190	---其他	30	80		5/15	17	千克	AB	---Other
	--其他，包括什锦坚果及其他子仁:								--Other, including mixtures:
2008.1910	---核桃仁罐头	20	90		15	17	千克	AB	---Walnut meats, in airtight containers
2008.1920	---其他果仁罐头	13	90		15	17	千克	AB	---Other nuts, in airtight containers
	---其他:								---Other:
2008.1991	----栗仁	10	80		5/15	17	千克	AB	----Chestnut seed
2008.1992	----芝麻	10	80		5/15	17	千克	AB	----Sesame
2008.1999	----其他	10	80			17	千克		----Other
2008 1999.10	其他方法制作或保藏的红松子仁（用醋或醋酸以外其他方法制作或保藏的）	10	80			17	千克	ABE	Korean pine-nuts, prepared or preserved otherwise than by vinegar or acetic acid
2008 1999.90	未列名制作或保藏的坚果及其他子仁（用醋或醋酸以外其他方法制作或保藏的）	10	80		5/15	17	千克	AB	Nuts and other seeds, prepared or preserved otherwise than by vinegar or acetic acid, not elsewhere specified or included
	-菠萝:								-Pineapples:
2008.2010	---罐头	15	90		15	17	千克	AB	---In airtight containers
2008.2090	---其他	15	80		5/15	17	千克	AB	---Other
	-柑橘属水果:								-Citrus fruit:
2008.3010	---罐头	20	90		15	17	千克	AB	---In airtight containers
2008.3090	---其他	20	80		5/15	17	千克	AB	---Other
	-梨:								-Pears:
2008.4010	---罐头	20	90		15	17	千克	AB	---In airtight containers
2008.4090	---其他	20	80		5/15	17	千克	AB	---Other

税则号列 Tariff Item	商品名称及备注	进口税率 最惠	进口税率 普通	进口税率 暂定	出口退税	增值税率	计量单位	监管条件	Article Description
2008.5000	-杏	20	90		5/15	17	千克	AB	-Apricots
	-樱桃:								-Cherries:
2008.6010	---罐头	20	90		15	17	千克	AB	---In airtight containers
2008.6090	---其他	20	90		5/15	17	千克	AB	---Other
	-桃，包括油桃:								-Peaches including nectarines:
2008.7010	---罐头	10	90		15	17	千克	AB	---In airtight containers
2008.7090	---其他	20	80		5/15	17	千克	AB	---Other
2008.8000	-草莓	15	90		5/15	17	千克	AB	-Strawberries
	-其他，包括子目号 2008.19 以外的什锦果实:								-Other, including mixtures other than those of subheading No.2008.19:
2008.9100	--棕榈芯	5	80		5/15	17	千克	AB	--Palm hearts
2008.9300	--蔓越橘（大果蔓越橘、小果蔓越橘、越橘）	15	80		5/15	17	千克	AB	--Cranberries (Vaccinium macrocarpon, Vaccinium oxycoccos, Vaccinium vitis-idaea)
2008.9700	--什锦果实	10	80		5/15	17	千克	AB	--Mixtures
	--其他:								--Other:
2008.9910	---荔枝罐头	20	90		15	17	千克	AB	---Lychee can
2008.9920	---龙眼罐头	15	80		15	17	千克	AB	---Longan can
	---海草及其他藻类制品:								---Preparations of seaweeds and other algae:
2008.9931	----调味紫菜	15	90		15	17	千克	AB	---Seasoned laver
2008.9932	----盐腌海带	15	80		5/15	17	千克	AB	---Sea tangle,salted
2008.9933	----盐腌裙带菜	15	80		5/15	17	千克	AB	---Pinnatifida, salted
2008.9939	----其他	15	80		5/15	17	千克	AB	---Other
2008.9940	---清水荸荠（马蹄）罐头	25	80		15	17	千克	AB	---Water chestnut, in airtight containers
2008.9990	---其他	15	80		5/15	17	千克	AB	---Other
20.09	**未发酵及未加酒精的水果汁（包括酿酒葡萄汁）、蔬菜汁，不论是否加糖或其他甜物质:**								**Fruit juices (including grape must) and vegetable juices, unfermented and not containing added spirit, whether or not containing added sugar or other sweetening matter:**
	-橙汁:								-Orange juice:
2009.1100	--冷冻的	7.5	90		15	17	千克	AB	--Frozen
2009.1200	--非冷冻的，白利糖度值不超过 20	30	90		15	17	千克	AB	--Not frozen, of a Brix value not exceeding 20
2009.1900	--其他	30	90		15	17	千克	AB	--Other
	-葡萄柚（包括柚）汁:								-Grapefruit (including pomelo) juice:
2009.2100	--白利糖度值不超过 20 的	15	90		15	17	千克	AB	--Of a Brix value not exceeding 20
2009.2900	--其他	15	90		15	17	千克	AB	--Other
	-其他未混合的柑橘属水果汁:								-Juice of any other single citrus fruit:
	--白利糖度值不超过 20 的:								--Of a Brix value not exceeding 20:
2009.3110	---柠檬汁	18	90		15	17	千克	AB	---Lemon juice
2009.3190	---其他	18	90		15	17	千克	AB	---Other
	--其他:								--Other:
2009.3910	---柠檬汁	18	90		15	17	千克	AB	---Lemon Juice
2009.3990	---其他	18	90		15	17	千克	AB	---Other
	-菠萝汁:								-Pineapple juice:
2009.4100	--白利糖度值不超过 20 的	10	90		15	17	千克	AB	--Of a Brix value not exceeding 20
2009.4900	--其他	10	90		15	17	千克	AB	--Other
2009.5000	-番茄汁	30	80		15	17	千克	AB	-Tomato juice
	-葡萄汁，包括酿酒葡萄汁:								-Grape juice (including grape must) :
2009.6100	--白利糖度值不超过 30 的	20	90		15	17	千克	AB	--Of a Brix value not exceeding 30
2009.6900	--其他	20	90		15	17	千克	AB	--Other
	-苹果汁:								-Apple juice:
2009.7100	--白利糖度值不超过 20 的	20	90		15	17	千克	AB	-Of a Brix value not exceeding 20
2009.7900	--其他	20	90		15	17	千克	AB	--Other
	-其他未混合的水果汁或蔬菜汁:								-Juice of any other single fruit or vegetable:
2009.8100	--蔓越橘汁（大果蔓越橘、小果蔓越橘、越橘）	20	90		15	17	千克	AB	--Cranberries (Vaccinium macrocarpon, Vaccinium oxycoccos, Vaccinium vitis-idaea) juice
	--其他:								--Other :

税则号列 Tariff Item	商品名称及备注	进口税率			出口退税	增值税率	计量单位	监管条件	Article Description
		最惠	普通	暂定					
	---水果汁:								---Fruit juice:
2009.8912	----芒果汁	20	90		15	17	千克	AB	----Mango juice
2009.8913	----西番莲果汁	20	90		15	17	千克	AB	----Passion-fruit juice
2009.8914	----番石榴果汁	20	90		15	17	千克	AB	----Guva juice
2009.8915	----梨汁	20	90		15	17	千克	AB	---- Pears juice
2009.8919	----其他	20	90		15	17	千克	AB	----Other
2009.8920	---蔬菜汁	20	80		15	17	千克	AB	---Vegetable juice
	-混合汁:								-Mixtures of juices:
2009.9010	---水果汁	20	90		15	17	千克	AB	---Of fruit juices
2009.9090	---其他	20	80		15	17	千克	AB	---Other

第二十一章
杂 项 食 品

Ch
Miscellaneou

注释：

一、本章不包括：

（一）品目07.12的什锦蔬菜；

（二）含咖啡的焙炒咖啡代用品（品目09.01）；

（三）加香料的茶（品目09.02）；

（四）品目09.04至09.10的调味香料或其他产品；

（五）按重量计含香肠、肉、食用杂碎、动物血、鱼、甲壳动物、软体动物、其他水生无脊椎动物及其混合物超过20%的食品（第十六章），但品目21.03或21.04的产品除外；

（六）品目30.03或30.04的药用酵母及其他产品；或

（七）品目35.07的酶制品。

二、上述注释一（二）所述咖啡代用品的精汁归入品目21.01。

三、品目21.04所称"均化混合食品"，是指两种或两种以上的基本配料，例如，肉、鱼、蔬菜或果实等，经精细均化制成供婴幼儿食用或营养用的零售包装食品（每件净重不超过250克）。为了调味、保藏或其他目的，可以加入少量其他配料，还可以含有少量可见的小块配料。

Chapter Notes:

1. This Chapter does not cover:

(a) Mixed vegetables of heading 07.12;

(b) Roasted coffee substitutes containing coffee in any proportio 09.01);

(c) Flavoured tea (heading 09.02);

(d) Spices or other products of headings 09.04 to 09.10;

(e) Food preparations, other than the products described in heading 21.03 or 21.04, containing more than 20% by weight of sausage, meat, meat offal, blood, fish or crustaceans, molluscs or other aquatic invertebrates, or any combination thereof (Chapter 16);

(f) Yeast put up as a medicament or other products of heading 30.03 or 30.04; or

(g) Prepared enzymes of heading 35. 07.

2. Extracts of the substitutes referred to in Note 1(b) above are to be classified in heading 21.01.

3. For the purposes of heading 21. 04, the expression "homogenised composite food preparations" means preparations consisting of a finely homogenised mixture of two or more basic ingredients such as meat, fish, vegetables, fruit or nuts, put up for retail sale as infant food or for dietetic purposes, in containers of a net weight content not exceeding 250g. For the application of this definition, no account is to be taken of small quantities of any ingredients which may be added to the mixture for seasoning, preservation or other purposes. Such preparations may contain a small quantity of visible pieces of ingredients.

税则号列 Tariff Item	商品名称及备注	进口税率			出口退税	增值税率	计量单位	监管条件	Article Description
		最惠	普通	暂定					
21.01	**咖啡、茶、马黛茶的浓缩精汁及以其为基本成分或以咖啡、茶、马黛茶为基本成分的制品；烘焙菊苣和其他烘焙咖啡代用品及其浓缩精汁：**								**Extracts, essences and concentrates,of coffee, tea or mate and preparations with a basis of these products or with a basis of coffee, tea or mate; roasted chicory and other roasted coffee substitutes, and extracts, essences and concentrates thereof:**
	-咖啡浓缩精汁及以其为基本成分或以咖啡为基本成分的制品：								-Extracts, essences and concentrates of coffee, and preparations with a basis of these extracts, essences or concentrates or with a basis of coffee:
2101.1100	--浓缩精汁	17	130		15	17	千克	AB	--Extracts, essences and concentrates
2101.1200	--以浓缩精汁或咖啡为基本成分的制品	30	130		15	17	千克	AB	--Preparations with a basis of extracts, essences or concentrates or with a basis of coffee
2101.2000	-茶、马黛茶浓缩精汁及以其为基本成分或以茶、马黛茶为基本成分的制品	32	130		15	17	千克	AB	-Extracts, essences and concentrates, of tea or mate, and preparations with abasis of these extracts, essences or concentrates or with a basis of tea or mate
2101.3000	-烘焙菊苣和其他烘焙咖啡代用品及其浓缩精汁	32	130		15	17	千克	AB	-Roasted chicory and other roasted coffee substitutes, and extracts, essences and concentrates thereof
21.02	**酵母（活性或非活性）；已死的其他单细胞微生物（不包括品目30.02的疫苗）；发酵粉：**								**Yeasts (active or inactive); other singlecell micro-organisms, dead (but not including vaccines of heading No.30.02); prepared baking powders:**
2102.1000	-活性酵母	25	80		15	17	千克	AB	-Active yeasts
2102.2000	-非活性酵母；已死的其他单细胞微生物	25	70		15	13	千克	AB	-Inactive yeasts; other singlecell microorganisms, dead
2102.3000	-发酵粉	25	70		15	17	千克	AB	-Prepared baking powders

									Article Description
	调味汁及其制品；混合调味品；芥子粉及其调制品：								**Sauces and preparations therefor; mixed condiments and mixes seasonings; mustard flour and meal and prepared mustard:**
3.1000	-酱油	28	90	15	15	17	千克	AB	-Soya sauce
103.2000	-番茄沙司及其他番茄调味汁	15	90		15	17	千克	AB	-Tomato ketchup and other tomato sauces
2103.3000	-芥子粉及其调制品	15	70		15	17	千克	AB	-Mustard flour and meal and prepared mustard
	-其他：								-Other:
2103.9010	---味精	21	130			17	千克	AB	---Gourmet powder
2103.9020	---别特酒（Aromatic bitters），按体积计酒精含量 44.2%～49.2%，按重量计含1.5%～6%的香料、各种配料以及4%～10%的糖	21	90		15	17	千克	AB	---Aromatic bitters, 44.2%-49.2% of which is alcoholic strength by volume, 1.5%-6% of which is spiles and various ingredients by weight and 4% -10% of which is sugar by weight
2103.9090	---其他	21	90		5/15	17	千克	AB	---Other
21.04	**汤料及其制品；均化混合食品：**								**Soups and broths and preparations therefor; homogenized composite food preparations:**
2104.1000	-汤料及其制品	15	90		15	17	千克	AB	-Soups and broths and preparations therefor
2104.2000	-均化混合食品	32	90		15	17	千克	AB	-Homogenized composite food preparations
21.05	**冰淇淋及其他冰制食品，不论是否含可可：**								**Ice cream and other edible ice, whether or not containing cocoa:**
2105.0000	冰淇淋及其他冰制食品，不论是否含可可	19	90		15	17	千克	AB	Ice cream and other edible ice, whether or not containing cocoa
21.06	**其他品目未列名的食品：**								**Food preparations not elsewhere specified or included:**
2106.1000	-浓缩蛋白质及人造蛋白物质	10	90		15	17	千克	AB	-Protein concentrates and textured protein substances
	-其他：								-Other:
2106.9010	---制造碳酸饮料的浓缩物	35	100		15	17	千克	AB	---Beverage bases
2106.9020	---制造饮料用的复合酒精制品	20	180		15	17	千克	AB	---Compound alcoholic preparations of a kind used for the manufacture of beverages
2106.9030	---蜂王浆制剂	3	80			17	千克		---Royal jelly, put up as tonic essences
2106 9030.1(	含濒危植物成分的蜂王浆制剂	3	80			17	千克	ABFE	Royal jelly, put up as tonic essences containing composition of endangered plants
2106 9030.9(	其他蜂王浆制剂	3	80		15	17	千克	AB	Other royal jelly, put up as tonic essences
2106.9040	---椰子汁	10	90		15	17	千克	AB	---Coconut juice
2106.9050	---海豹油胶囊	20	90			17	千克		--- Seal oil capsules
2106 9050.10	濒危海豹油胶囊	20	90			17	千克	ABEF	Endangered seal oil capsules
2106 9050.90	其他海豹油胶囊	20	90		15	17	千克	AB	Other seal oil capsules
2106.9090	---其他	20	90			17	千克		---Other
2106 9090.01[暂]	乳蛋白部分水解配方、乳蛋白深度水解配方、氨基酸配方、无乳糖配方特殊婴幼儿奶粉	20	90	5	15	17	千克	AB	Special infant milk powder of partial hydrolysis formular of lactoprotein, deep hydrolysis formula of lactoprotein, amino acid formular
2106 9090.10	含濒危动植物成分的其他税号未列名食品	20	90			17	千克	ABEF	Other food preparations, containing endangered plants, not elsewhere specified or included
2106 9090.90	其他税号未列名的食品	20	90		5/15	17	千克	AB	Other food preparations, not elsewhere specified or included

第二十二章
饮料、酒及醋

Chapter 22
Beverages, spirits and vinegar

注释：

一、本章不包括：

（一）本章的产品（品目 22.09 的货品除外）经配制后，用于烹饪而不适于作为饮料的制品（通常归入品目 21.03）；

（二）海水（品目 25.01）；

（三）蒸馏水、导电水及类似的纯净水（品目 28.53）；

（四）按重量计浓度超过 10%的醋酸（品目 29.15）；

（五）品目 30.03 或 30.04 的药品；或

（六）芳香料制品及盥洗品（第三十三章）。

二、本章及第二十章和第二十一章所称“按容量计酒精浓度”，应是温度在 20℃时测得的浓度。

三、品目 22.02 所称“无酒精饮料”，是指按容量计酒精浓度不超过 0.5%的饮料。含酒精饮料应分别归入品目 22.03 至 22.06 或品目 22.08。

子目注释：

子目2204.10所称“汽酒”，是指温度在20℃时装在密封容器中超过大气压力3巴及以上的酒。

Chapter Notes:

1. This Chapter does not cover:

(a) Products of this Chapter (other than those of heading22.09) prepared for culinary purposes and thereby rendered unsuitable for consumption as beverages (generally heading21.03);

(b) Sea water (heading 25.01);

(c) Distilled or conductivity water or water of similar purity (heading 28.53);

(d) Acetic acid of a concentration exceeding 10% by weight of acetic acid (heading 29.15);

(e) Medicaments of heading 30.03 or 30.04; or

(f) Perfumery or toilet preparations (Chapter 33).

2.For the purposes of this Chapter and of Chapters 20 and 21, the “alcoholic strength by volume” shall be determined at a temperature of20℃.

3.For the purposes of heading 22.02, the term “non-alcoholic beverages” means beverages of an alcoholic strength by volume not exceeding 0.5% vol. Alcoholic beverages are classified in headings 22.03 to 22.06 or heading 22.08 as appropriate.

Subheading Note:

For the purposes of subheading 2204.10, the expression “sparkling wine” means wine which, when kept at a temperature of 20℃ in closed containers, has an excess pressure of not less than 3 bars.

税则号列 Tariff Item	商品名称及备注	进口税率 最惠	进口税率 普通	进口税率 暂定	出口退税	增值税率	计量单位	监管条件	Article Description
22.01	**未加糖或其他甜物质及未加味的水，包括天然或人造矿泉水及汽水；冰及雪：**								**Waters, including natural or artificial mineral waters and aerated waters,not containing added sugar or other sweetening matter or flavoured; ice and snow:**
	-矿泉水及汽水：								-Mineral waters and aerated waters:
2201.1010	---矿泉水	20	90			17	升/千克	AB	---Mineral waters
2201.1020	---汽水	20	90		15	17	升/千克	AB	---Aerated waters
	-其他：								-Other:
2201.9010	---天然水	10	30			17	千升/千克	AB	---Natural waters
2201.9090	---其他	10	30			17	千升/千克	AB	---Other
22.02	**加味、加糖或其他甜物质的水，包括矿泉水及汽水，其他无酒精饮料，但不包括品目 20.09 的水果汁或蔬菜汁：**								**Waters, including mineral waters and aerated waters, containing added sugar or other sweetening matter or flavoured, and other non-alcoholic beverages, not including fruit or vegetable juices of heading No.20.09:**
2202.1000	-加味、加糖或其他甜物质的水，包括矿泉水及汽水	20	100			17	升/千克		-Waters, including mineral waters and aerated waters, containing added sugar or other sweetening matter or flavoured
2202 1000.10	含濒危动植物成分的加味、加糖或其他甜物质的水（包括矿泉水及汽水）	20	100			17	升/千克	ABEF	Waters, containing added sugar or other sweetening matter or flavoured, and containing endangered plants composition
2202 1000.90	其他加味、加糖或其他甜物质的水（包括矿泉水及汽水）	20	100		15	17	升/千克	AB	Other waters, containing added sugar or other sweetening matter or flavoured
2202.9000	-其他	35	100			17	升/千克		-Other
2202 9000.11	含濒危动植物成分散装无酒精饮料（不包括品目 20.09 的水果汁或蔬菜汁）	35	100			17	升/千克	ABEF	Non-alcoholic beverages, in bulk (other than fruit juices and vegetable juices of heading No.20.09), containing endangered plant compostion
2202 9000.19	其他散装无酒精饮料（不包括品目 20.09 的水果汁或蔬菜汁）	35	100		15	17	升/千克	AB	Other non-alcoholic beverage, in bulk (other than fruit juices and vegetable juices of heading No.20.09)

税则号列 Tariff Item	商品名称及备注	进口税率			出口退税	增值税率	计量单位	监管条件	Article Description
		最惠	普通	暂定					
2202 9000.91	含濒危动植物成分其他包装无酒精饮料(不包括品目20.09的水果汁或蔬菜汁)	35	100			17	升/千克	ABEF	Non-alcoholic beverages, in other packing, containing endangered plants compostion (other than fruit juices and vegetable juices of heading No.20.09)
2202 9000.99	其他包装无酒精饮料(不包括品目20.09的水果汁或蔬菜汁)	35	100		15	17	升/千克	AB	Non-alcoholic beverages, in other packing (other than fruit juices and vegetable juices of heading No.20.09)
22.03	**麦芽酿造的啤酒:**								**Beer made from malt:**
2203.0000	麦芽酿造的啤酒	0	7.5元/L		15	17	升/千克	AB	Beer made from malt
22.04	**鲜葡萄酿造的酒，包括加酒精的;品目20.09以外的酿酒葡萄汁:**								**Wine of fresh grapes, including fortified wines; grape must other than that of heading No.20.09:**
2204.1000	-汽酒	14	180		15	17	升/千克	AB	-Sparkling wine
	-其他酒;加酒精抑制发酵的酿酒葡萄汁:								-Other wine; grape must with fermentation prevented or arrested by the addition of alcohol:
2204.2100	--装入2升及以下容器的	14	180		15	17	升/千克	AB	--In containers holding 2L or less
2204.2900	--其他	20	180		15	17	升/千克	AB	--Other
2204.3000	-其他酿酒葡萄汁	30	90		15	17	升/千克	AB	-Other grape must
22.05	**味美思酒及其他加植物或香料的用鲜葡萄酿造的酒:**								**Vermouth and other wine of fresh grapes flavoured with plants or aromatic substances:**
2205.1000	-装入2升及以下容器的	65	180		15	17	升/千克	AB	-In containers holding 2L or less
2205.9000	-其他	65	180		15	17	升/千克	AB	-Other
22.06	**其他发酵饮料(例如，苹果酒、梨酒、蜂蜜酒);其他品目未列名的发酵饮料的混合物及发酵饮料与无酒精饮料的混合物:**								**Other fermented beverages (for example, cider, perry, mead); mixtures of fermented beverages and mixtures of fermented beverages and non-alcoholic beverages, not elsewhere specified or included:**
2206.0010	---黄酒	40	180		15	17	升/千克	AB	---Yellow rice wine
2206.0090	---其他	40	180		15	17	升/千克	AB	---Other
22.07	**未改性乙醇，按容量计酒精浓度在80%及以上;任何浓度的改性乙醇及其他酒精:**								**Undenatured ethyl alcohol of an alcoholic strength by volume of 80% vol or higher; ethyl alcohol and other spirits, denatured, of any strength:**
2207.1000	-未改性乙醇，按容量计酒精浓度在80%及以上	40	100			17	升/千克	ABG	-Undenatured ethyl alcohol of an alcoholic, strength by volume of 80% vol or higher
2207.2000[暂]	-任何浓度的改性乙醇及其他酒精	30	80	5		17	升/千克		-Ethyl alcohol and other spirits, denatured of any strength
2207 2000.10[暂]	任何浓度的改性乙醇	30	80	5		17	升/千克	ABG	Ethyl alcohol, denatured, of any strength
2207 2000.90[暂]	任何浓度的其他酒精	30	80	5		17	升/千克	ABG	Other spirits, of any strength
22.08	**未改性乙醇，按容量计酒精浓度在80%以下;蒸馏酒、利口酒及其他酒精饮料:**								**Undenaturated ethyl alcohol of an alcoholic strength by volume of less than 80% vol; spirits, liqueurs and other spirituous beverages:**
2208.2000	-蒸馏葡萄酒制得的烈性酒	10	180		15	17	升/千克	AB	-Spirits obtained by distilling grape wine or grape marc
2208.3000	-威士忌酒	10	180		15	17	升/千克	AB	-Whiskies
2208.4000	-朗姆酒及蒸馏已发酵甘蔗产品制得的其他烈性酒	10	180		15	17	升/千克	AB	-Rum and other spirits obtained by distilling fermented sugarcaneproducts
2208.5000	-杜松子酒	10	180		15	17	升/千克	AB	-Gin and geneva
2208.6000	-伏特加酒	10	180		15	17	升/千克	AB	-Vodka
2208.7000	-利口酒及柯迪尔酒	10	180		15	17	升/千克	AB	-Liqueurs and cordials
	-其他:								-Other:
2208.9010	---龙舌兰酒	10	180		15	17	升/千克		---Tequila, Mezcal
2208 9010.10	濒危龙舌兰酒	10	180		15	17	升/千克	ABEF	Tequila, Mezcal, containing endangered plants
2208 9010.90	其他龙舌兰酒	10	180		15	17	升/千克	AB	Other Tequilal, Mezca
2208.9020	---白酒	10	180		15	17	升/千克	AB	---Chinese distilled spirits
2208.9090	---其他	10	180			17	升/千克		---Other
2208 9090.01	酒精浓度在80%以下的未改性乙醇	10	180		15	17	升/千克	AB	Undenatured ethyl alcohol of an alcoholic strength by volume of less than 80% vol
2208 9090.21	含濒危野生动植物成分的薯类蒸馏酒	10	180			17	升/千克	ABEF	Potato spirits containing endangered wild animals and plants
2208 9090.29	其他薯类蒸馏酒	10	180		15	17	升/千克	AB	Other spirits obtained by distilling potatoes

税则号列 Tariff Item	商品名称及备注	进口税率			出口增值退税税率	计量单位	监管条件	Article Description
		最惠	普通	暂定				
2208 9090.91	含濒危野生动植物成分的其他蒸馏酒及酒精饮料	10	180		17	升/千克	ABEF	Other spirits and spirituous beverages containing endangered wild animals and plants
2208 9090.99	其他蒸馏酒及酒精饮料	10	180		15　17	升/千克	AB	Other spirits , spirituous beverages
22.09	**醋及用醋酸制得的醋代用品：**							**Vinegar and substitutes for vinegar obtained from acetic acid:**
2209.0000[暂]	醋及用醋酸制得的醋代用品	20	70	15	15　17	升/千克	AB	Vinegar and substitutes for vinegar obtained from acetic acid

第二十三章 食品工业的残渣及废料；配制的动物饲料

Chapter 23 Residues and waste from the food industries; prepared animal fodder

注释：

品目23.09包括其他品目未列号的配制动物饲料，这些饲料是由动、植物原料加工而成的，并且已改变了原料的基本特性，但加工过程中的植物废料、植物残渣及副产品除外。

子目注释：

子目2306.41所称“低芥子酸油菜籽”，是指第十二章子目注释一所定义的菜子。

Chapter Notes:

Heading 23.09 includes products of a kind used in animal feeding,not elsewhere specified or included, obtained by processing vegetable or animal materials to such an extent that they have lost the essential characteristics of the original material, other than vegetable waste, vegetable residues and by-products of such processing.

Subheading Note:

For the purposes of subheading 2306.41, the expression “low erucic acid rape or colza seeds” means seeds as defined in Subheading Note 1 to Chapter 12.

税则号列 Tariff Item	商品名称及备注	进口税率			出口退税	增值税率	计量单位	监管条件	Article Description
		最惠	普通	暂定					
23.01	**不适于供人食用的肉、杂碎、鱼、甲壳动物、软体动物或其他水生无脊椎动物的渣粉及团粒；油渣：**								**Flours, meals and pellets, of meat or meat offal, of fish or of crustaceans,molluscs or other aquatic invertebrates, unfit, for human consumption;greaves:**
	-肉、杂碎的渣粉及团粒；油渣：								-Flours, meals and pellets, of meat or meat offal; greaves:
	---肉骨粉：								---Flours and meals, of meat bones:
2301.1011	----含牛羊成分的	2	11		15	13	千克	AB	----Of bovine and sheep
2301.1019	----其他	2	11		15	13	千克	AB	----Other
2301.1020	---油渣	5	50			13	千克	AB	--Greaves
2301.1090	---其他	5	30			13	千克	AB	---Other
	-鱼、甲壳动物、软体动物或其他水生无脊椎动物的渣粉及团粒：								-Flours, meals and pellets, of fish or of crustaceans, molluscs or other aquatic invertebrates:
2301.2010	---饲料用鱼粉	2	11			13	千克	AB	---Flours and meals of fish, of a kind used in animal feeding
2301.2090	---其他	5	30			13	千克	AB	---Other
23.02	**谷物或豆类植物在筛、碾或其他加工过程中所产生的糠、麸及其他残渣，不论是否制成团粒：**								**Bran, sharps and other residues, whether or not in the form of pellets, derived from the sifting, milling or other working of cereals or of leguminous plants:**
2302.1000	-玉米的	5	30			13	千克	AB	-Of maize（corn）
2302.3000	-小麦的	3	30			13	千克	AB	-Of wheat
2302.4000	-其他谷物的	5	30			13	千克	AB	-Of other cereals
2302.5000	-豆类植物的	5	30			13	千克	AB	-Of leguminous plants
23.03	**制造淀粉过程中的残渣及类似的残渣，甜菜渣、甘蔗渣及制糖过程中的其他残渣，酿造及蒸馏过程中的糟粕及残渣，不论是否制成团粒：**								**Residues of starch manufacture and similar residues, beet-pulp, bagasses and other waste of sugar manufacture, brewing or distilling dregs and waste, whether or not in the form of pellets:**
2303.1000	-制造淀粉过程中的残渣及类似的残渣	5	30			13	千克	AB	-Residues of starch manufacture and similar residues
2303.2000	-甜菜渣、甘蔗渣及制糖过程中的其他残渣	5	30		0/5	13	千克	AB	-Beet-pulp, bagasses and other waste of sugar manufacture
2303.3000	-酿造及蒸馏过程中的糟粕及残渣	5	30			13	千克		-Brewing or distilling dregs and waste
2303 3000.10	玉米酒糟	5	30			13	千克	AB	Corn distillers solubles
2303 3000.90	其他酿造及蒸馏过程中的糟粕及残渣	5	30			13	千克	AB	Other dross and residues during the process of brewing and distillation
23.04	**提炼豆油所得的油渣饼及其他固体残渣，不论是否碾磨或制成团粒：**								**Oil-cake and other solid residues, whether or not ground or in the form of pellets, resulting from the extraction of soyabean oil:**
2304.0010	---油渣饼	5	30		13	13	千克	7AB	---Oil-cake
2304.0090	---其他	5	30		13	13	千克	7AB	---Other

税则号列 Tariff Item	商品名称及备注	进口税率 最惠	进口税率 普通	进口税率 暂定	出口退税	增值税率	计量单位	监管条件	Article Description
23.05	**提炼花生油所得的油渣饼及其他固体残渣，不论是否碾磨或制成团粒：**								**Oil-cake and other solid residues, whether or not ground or in the form of pellets, resulting from the extraction of ground nutoil:**
2305.0000	提炼花生油所得的油渣饼及其他固体残渣，不论是否碾磨或制成团粒	5	30			13	千克	AB	Oil-cake and other solid residues, whether or not ground or in the form of pellets, resulting from the extraction of groundnut oil
23.06	**品目23.04或23.05以外的提炼植物油脂所得的油渣饼及其他固体残渣，不论是否碾磨或制成团粒：**								**Oil-cake and other solid residues, whether or not ground or in the form of pellets, resulting from the extraction of vegetable fats or oils, other than those of heading No.23.04 or 23.05:**
2306.1000	-棉子的	5	30		13	13	千克	AB	-Of cotton seeds
2306.2000	-亚麻子的	5	30		13	13	千克	AB	-Of linseed
2306.3000	-葵花子的	5	30		13	13	千克	AB	-Of sunflower seeds
	-油菜子的：								-Of rape or colza seeds:
2306.4100	--低芥子酸的	5	30		13	13	千克	AB	--Of low erucic acid rape or colza seeds
2306.4900	--其他	5	30		13	13	千克	AB	--Other
2306.5000	-椰子或干椰肉的	5	30		13	13	千克	AB	-Of coconut or copra
2306.6000	-棕榈果或棕榈仁的	5	30			13	千克		-Of palm nuts or kernels
2306 6000.10	濒危棕榈果或濒危棕榈仁油渣饼及固体残渣(品目23.04或23.05以外提炼植物油脂所得的)	5	30			13	千克	ABEF	Endangered palm nuts or endangered palm kernel oil cake and solid residues (other than those of heading 23.04 or 23.05)
2306 6000.90	其他棕榈果或其他棕榈仁油渣饼及固体残渣(品目23.04或23.05以外提炼植物油脂所得的)	5	30		13	13	千克	AB	Other palm nuts or palm kernel oil cake and solid residues (other than those of heading 23.04 or 23.05)
2306.9000	-其他	5	30		0/13/15	13	千克	AB	-Other
23.07	**葡萄酒渣；粗酒石：**								**Wine lees; argol:**
2307.0000	葡萄酒渣；粗酒石	5	30			13	千克	AB	Wine lees; argol
23.08	**动物饲料用的其他品目未列名的植物原料、废料、残渣及副产品，不论是否制成团粒：**								**Vegetable materials and vegetable waste, vegetable residues and by-products, whether or not in the form of pellets, of a kind used in animal feeding, not elsewhere specified or included:**
2308.0000	动物饲料用的其他品目未列名的植物原料、废料、残渣及副产品，不论是否制成团粒	5	35		0/5/15	13	千克	AB	Vegetable materials and vegetable waste, vegetable residues and by-products, whether or not in the form of pellets, of a kind used in animal feeding, not elsewhere specified or included
23.09	**配制的动物饲料：**								**Preparations of a kind used in animal feeding:**
	-零售包装的狗食或猫食：								-Dog or cat food, put up for retail sale:
2309.1010	---罐头	15	90		13	13	千克	AB	---In airtight containers
2309.1090	---其他	15	90		13	13	千克	AB	---Other
	-其他：								-Other:
2309.9010	---制成的饲料添加剂	5	14		13/15	17	千克	AB	---Preparations for use in making the complete feeds or supplementary feeds
2309.9090[暂]	---其他	6.5	14	4	13	13	千克	AB	---Other

第二十四章 烟草、烟草及烟草代用品的制品

Chapter 24 Tobacco and manufactured tobacco substitutes

注释：

本章不包括药用卷烟（第三十章）。

子目注释：

子目2403.11 所称‘水烟料’，是指由烟草和甘油混合而成用水烟筒吸用的烟草，不论是否含有芳香油及提取物、糖蜜或糖，也不论是否用水果调味，但供在水烟筒中吸用的非烟草产品除外。

Chapter Notes:

This Chapter does not cover medicinal cigarettes（Chapter 30）.

Subheading Note:

For the purposes of Subheading 2403.11, the expression "water pipe tobacco" means tobacco intended for smoking in a water pipe and which consists of a mixture of tobacco and glycerol, whether or not containing aromatic oils and extracts, molasses or sugar, and whether or not flavoured with fruit. However, tobacco-free products intended for smoking in a water pipe are excluded from this Subheading.

税则号列 Tariff Item	商品名称及备注	进口税率			出口退税	增值税率	计量单位	监管条件	Article Description
		最惠	普通	暂定					
24.01	烟草；烟草废料：								**Unmanufactured tobacco; tobacco refuse:**
	-未去梗的烟草：								-Tobacco, not stemmed/stripped:
2401.1010	---烤烟	10	70		5/15	17	千克	7AB	---Flue-cured
2401.1090	---其他	10	70		5	17	千克	7AB	---Other
	-部分或全部去梗的烟草：								-Tobacco, partly or wholly stemmed/ stripped:
2401.2010	---烤烟	10	70		5/15	17	千克	7AB	---Flue-cured
2401.2090	---其他	10	70		15	17	千克	7AB	---Other
2401.3000	-烟草废料	10	70		5/15	17	千克	AB7	-Tobacco refuse
24.02	烟草或烟草代用品制成的雪茄烟及卷烟：								**Cigars, cheroots, cigarillos and cigarettes, of tobacco or of tobacco substitutes:**
2402.1000	-烟草制的雪茄烟	25	180			17	千克/千支	7AB	-Cigars, cheroots and cigarillos, containing tobacco
2402.2000	-烟草制的卷烟	25	180			17	千克/千支	7AB	-Cigarettes containing tobacco
2402.9000	-其他	25	180			17	千克/千支		-Other
2402 9000.01	烟草代用品制的卷烟	25	180			17	千克/千支	7AB	Cigarettes, of tobacco substitutes
2402 9000.09	烟草代用品制的雪茄烟	25	180			17	千克/千支	7AB	Gigars, cheroots and cigarillos, of tobacco substitutes
24.03	其他烟草及烟草代用品的制品；"均化"或"再造"烟草；烟草精汁：								**Other manufactured tobacco and manufactured tobacco substitutes; "homogenized" or "reconstituted" tobacco; tobacco extracts and essences:**
	-供吸用的烟草，不论是否含有任何比例的烟草代用品：								-Smoking tobacco, whether or not containing tobacco substitutes in any proportion :
2403.1100	--本章子目注释所述的水烟料	57	180		15	17	千克	7AB	--Water pipe tobacco specified in subheading note 1 of this Chapter
2403.1900	--其他	57	180		15	17	千克	7AB	--Other
	-其他：								-Other:
2403.9100	--"均化"或"再造"烟草	57	180		15	17	千克		--"Homogenized" or "reconstituted" tobacco
2403 9100.10[暂]	再造烟草	57	180	40	15	17	千克	AB7	Reconstituted tobacco
2403 9100.90	均化烟草	57	180		15	17	千克	AB7	Homogenized tobacco
2403.9900	--其他	57	180		15	17	千克		--Other
2403 9900.10	烟草精汁	57	180		15	17	千克	7AB	Tobacco extracts and essences
2403 9900.90	其他烟草及烟草代用品的制品	57	180		15	17	千克	AB	Other manufactured tobacco and manufactured tobacco substitutes

第五类
矿　产　品

第二十五章
盐；硫磺；泥土及石料；石膏料、石灰及水泥

注释：

一、除条文及注释四另有规定的以外，本章各品目只包括原产状态的矿产品，或只经过洗涤（包括用化学物质清除杂质而未改变产品结构的）、破碎、磨碎、研粉、淘洗、筛分以及用浮选、磁选和其他机械物理方法（不包括结晶法）精选过的货品，但不得经过焙烧、煅烧、混合或超过品目所列的加工范围。

本章产品可含有添加的抗尘剂，但所加剂料并不使原产品改变其一般用途而适合于某些特殊用途。

二、本章不包括：

（一）升华硫磺、沉淀硫磺及胶态硫磺（品目28.02）；

（二）土色料，按重量计三氧化二铁含量在70%及以上（品目28.21）；

（三）第三十章的药品及其他产品；

（四）芳香料制品及化妆盥洗品（第三十三章）；

（五）长方砌石、路缘石、扁平石（品目68.01）、镶嵌石或类似石料（品目68.02）及铺屋顶、饰墙面或防潮用的板岩（品目68.03）；

（六）宝石或半宝石（品目71.02或71.03）；

（七）每颗重量不低于2.5克的氯化钠或氧化镁培养晶体（光学元件除外）（品目38.24）；氯化钠或氧化镁制的光学元件（品目90.01）；

（八）台球用粉块（品目95.04）；或

（九）书写或绘画用粉笔及裁缝划粉（品目96.09）。

三、既可归入品目25.17又可归入本章其他品目的产品，应归入品目25.17。

四、品目25.30主要包括：未膨胀的蛭石、珍珠岩及绿泥石；不论是否煅烧或混合的土色料；天然云母氧化铁；海泡石（不论是否磨光成块）；琥珀；模制后未经进一步加工的片、条、杆或类似形状的粘聚海泡石及粘聚琥珀；黑玉；菱锶矿（不论是否煅烧），但不包括氧化锶；陶器；砖或混凝土的碎块。

SECTION V
MINERAL PRODUCTS

Chapter 25
Salt; sulphur; earths and stone; plastering materials, lime and cement

Chapter Notes:

1. Except where their context or Note 4 to this Chapter otherwise requires, the headings of this Chapter cover only products which are in the crude state or which have been washed (even with chemical substances eliminating the impurities without changing the structure of the product), crushed, ground, powdered,levigated, sifted, screened, concentrated by flotation, magnetic separation or other mechanical or physical processes (except crystallisation), but not products which have been roasted,calcined, obtained by mixing or subjected to processing beyond that mentioned in each heading.

   The products of this Chapter may contain an added anti-dusting agent, provided that such addition does not render the product particularly suitable for specific use rather than for general use.

2. This Chapter does not cover:

   (a) Sublimed sulphur, precipitated sulphur or colloidal sulphur (heading 28.02);

   (b) Earth colours containing 70% or more by weight of combined iron evaluated as Fe_2O_3 (heading 28.21);

   (c) Medicaments or other products of Chapter 30;

   (d) Perfumery, cosmetic or toilet preparations (Chapter 33);

   (e) Setts, curbstones or flagstones (heading 68.01); mosaic cubes or the like (heading 68.02); roofing, facing or damp course slates (heading 68.03);

   (f) Precious or semi-precious stones (heading 71.02 or 71.03);

   (g) Cultured crystals (other than optical elements) weighing not less than 2.5g each, of sodium chloride or of magnesium oxide, of heading 38.24; optical elements of sodium chloride or of magnesium oxide (heading 90.01);

   (h) Billiard chalks (heading 95.04); or

   (ij) Writing or drawing chalks or tailors'chalks (heading96.09).

3. Any products classifiable in heading 25.17 and any other heading of the Chapter are to be classified in heading 25.17.

4. Heading 25.30 applies, *inter alia*, to: vermiculite, perlite and chlorites, unexpanded; earth colours, whether or not calcined or mixed together; natural micaceous iron oxides; meerschaum (whether or not in polished pieces); amber; agglomerated meerschaum and agglomerated amber, in plates, rods, sticks or similar forms, not worked after moulding; jet; strontianite (whether or not calcined), other than strontium oxide; broken pieces of pottery, brick or concrete.

税则号列 Tariff Item	商品名称及备注	进口税率			出口退税	增值税率	计量单位	监管条件	Article Description
		最惠	普通	暂定					
25.01	盐（包括精制盐及变性盐）及纯氯化钠，不论是否为水溶液，也不论是否添加抗结块剂或松散剂；海水：								**Salt (including table salt and denatured salt) and pure sodium chloride, whether or not in aqueous solution or containing added anticaking or freeflowing agents; sea water:**

税则号列 Tariff Item	商品名称及备注	进口税率 最惠	普通	暂定	出口退税	增值税率	计量单位	监管条件	Article Description
	---盐:								---Salt:
2501.0011	----食用盐	0	0		13	13	千克	AB	----Edible salt
2501.0019	----其他	0	0		13	17	千克	AB	----Other
2501.0020	---纯氯化钠	3	35		13	17	千克		---Pure sodium chloride
2501.0030	---海水	0	0			17	千克		---Sea water
25.02	**未焙烧的黄铁矿:**								**Unroasted iron pyrites:**
2502.0000[暂]	未焙烧的黄铁矿	3	20	1		17	千克		Unroasted iron pyrites
25.03	**各种硫磺，但升华硫磺、沉淀硫磺及胶态硫磺除外:**								**Sulphur of all kinds, other than sublimed sulphur, precipitated sulphur and colloidal sulphur:**
2503.0000[暂]	各种硫磺，但升华硫磺、沉淀硫磺及胶态硫磺除外	3	17	1		17	千克	AB	Sulphur of all kinds, other than sublimed sulphur, precipitated sulphur and colloidal sulphur
25.04	**天然石墨:**								**Natural graphite:**
	-粉末或粉片:								-In powder or in flakes:
2504.1010[暂]	---粉片（磷片状天然石墨）	3	30	1		17	千克		---In flakes（natural graphite in flakes）
	---其他:								---Other:
2504.1091	----球化石墨	3	30		13	17	千克		----Spheroidized graphite
2504.1099	----其他	3	30			17	千克		----Other
2504.9000	-其他	3	30			17	千克		--Other
25.05	**各种天然砂，不论是否着色，但第二十六章的含金属矿砂除外:**								**Natural sands of all kinds, whether or not coloured, other than metal-bearing sands of Chapter 26:**
2505.1000[暂]	-硅砂及石英砂	3	40	1		17	千克	48xy	-Silica sands and quartz sands
2505.9000[暂]	-其他	3	40	1		17	千克		-Other
2505 9000.10[暂]	标准砂（不论是否着色，第二十六章的金属矿砂除外）	3	40	1		17	千克	4xy	Standard sand, whether or not coloured, other than metal-bearing sands of Chapter 26:
2505 9000.90[暂]	其他天然砂（不论是否着色，第二十六章的金属矿砂除外）	3	40	1		17	千克	48xy	Other natural sands, whether or not coloured, other than metal-bearing sands of Chapter 26:
25.06	**石英（天然砂除外）；石英岩，不论是否粗加修整或仅用锯或其他方法切割成矩形（包括正方形）的板、块:**								**Quartz（other than natural sands）; quartzite, whether or not roughly trimmed or merely cut, by sawing or otherwise, into blocks or slabs of a rectangular（including square）shape:**
2506.1000[暂]	-石英	3	40	1		17	千克		-Quartz
2506.2000[暂]	--石英岩	3	40	1		17	千克		-Quartzite
25.07	**高岭土及类似土，不论是否煅烧:**								**Kaolin and other kaolinic clays, whether or not calcined:**
2507.0010[暂]	---高岭土	3	50	1		17	千克		---Kaolin
2507.0090[暂]	---其他	3	50	1		17	千克		---Other
25.08	**其他黏土（不包括品目 68.06 的膨胀黏土）、红柱石、蓝晶石及硅线石，不论是否煅烧；富铝红柱石；火泥及第纳斯土:**								**Other clays（not including expanded clays of heading No.68.06）, andalusite, kyanite and sillimanite, whether or not calcined; mullite; chamotte or dinas earths:**
2508.1000	-膨润土	3	50			17	千克		-Bentonite
2508.3000[暂]	-耐火黏土	3	20	1		17	千克	4xy	-Fire-clay
2508.4000	-其他黏土	3	50			17	千克		-Other clays
2508.5000	-红柱石、蓝晶石及硅线石	3	40			17	千克		-Andalusite, kyanite and sillimanite
2508.6000	-富铝红柱石	3	40			17	千克		-Mullite
2508.7000	-火泥及第纳斯土	3	20			17	千克		-Chamotte or dinas earths
2508 7000.10	火泥	3	20			17	千克		Chamotte
2508 7000.90	第纳斯土	3	20			17	千克		Dinas earths
25.09	**白垩:**								**Chalk:**
2509.0000	白垩	3	45			17	千克		Chalk
25.10	**天然磷酸钙、天然磷酸铝钙及磷酸盐白垩:**								**Natural calcium phosphates, natural aluminium calcium phosphates and phosphatic chalk:**
	-未碾磨:								-Unground:
2510.1010[暂]	---磷灰石	3	11	0		17	千克	4xy	---Apatite
2510.1090	---其他	3	20			17	千克	4xy	---Other
	-已碾磨:								-Ground:

税则号列 Tariff Item	商品名称及备注	进口税率 最惠	进口税率 普通	进口税率 暂定	出口退税	增值税率	计量单位	监管条件	Article Description
2510.2010[暂]	---磷灰石	3	11	0		17	千克	4xy	---Apatite
2510.2090	---其他	3	20			17	千克	4xy	---Other
25.11	**天然硫酸钡(重晶石);天然碳酸钡(毒重石),不论是否煅烧,但品目28.16的氧化钡除外:**								**Natural barium sulphate（barytes）;natural barium carbonate（witherite）, whether or not calcined, other than barium oxide of heading No.28.16:**
2511.1000[暂]	-天然硫酸钡(重晶石)	3	45	1		17	千克		-Natural barium sulphate（barytes）
2511.2000	-天然碳酸钡(毒重石)	3	45			17	千克		-Natural barium carbonate（witherite）
25.12	**硅质化石粗粉(例如各种硅藻土)及类似的硅质土,不论是否煅烧,其表观比重不超过1:**								**Siliceous fossil meals（for example, kieselguhr, tripolite and diatomite）and similar siliceous earths, whether or not calcined, of an apparent specific gravity of 1 or less:**
2512.0010	---硅藻土	3	40			17	千克	AB	---Kieselguhr
2512.0090	---其他	3	40			17	千克		---Other
25.13	**浮石;刚玉岩;天然刚玉砂;天然石榴石及其他天然磨料,不论是否热处理:**								**Pumice stone; emery; natural corundum, natural garnet and other natural abrasives, whether or not heat-treated:**
2513.1000	-浮石	3	35			17	千克		-Pumice stone
2513.2000	-刚玉岩、天然刚玉砂、天然石榴石及其他天然磨料	3	17			17	千克		-Emery, natural corundum, narural garnet and other natural abrasives
25.14	**板岩,不论是否粗加修整或仅用锯或其他方法切割成矩形(包括正方形)的板、块:**								**Slate, whether or not roughly trimmed or merely cut, by sawing or otherwise, into blocks or slabs of a rectangular（including square）shape:**
2514.0000	板岩,不论是否粗加修整或仅用锯或其他方法切割成矩形(包括正方形)的板、块	3	50			17	千克		Slate, whether or not roughly trimmed or merely cut, by sawing or otherwise, into blocks or slabs of a rectangular（including square）shape
25.15	**大理石、石灰华及其他石灰质碑用或建筑用石,表观比重为2.5及以上,蜡石,不论是否粗加修整或仅用锯或其他方法切割成矩形(包括正方形)的板、块:**								**Marble, travertine, ecaussine and other calcareous monumental or building stone of an apparent specific gravity of 2.5 or more, and alabaster, whether or not roughly trimmed or merely cut,by sawing or otherwise, into blocks or slabs of a rectangular（including square）shape:**
	-大理石及石灰华:								-Marble and travertine:
2515.1100[暂]	--原状或粗加修整	4	80	0		17	千克		--Crude or roughly trimmed
2515.1200[暂]	--用锯或其他方法切割成矩形,包括正方形	4	80	0		17	千克		--Merely cut, by sawing or otherwise, into blocks or slabs of a rectangular（including square）shape
2515.2000[暂]	-其他石灰质碑用或建筑用石;蜡石	3	50	0		17	千克		-Ecaussine and other calcareous monumental or building stone; alabaster
25.16	**花岗岩、斑岩、玄武岩、砂岩以及其他碑用或建筑用石,不论是否粗加修整或仅用锯或其他方法切割成矩形(包括正方形)的板、块:**								**Granite, porphyry, basalt, sandstone and other monumental or building stone, whether or not roughly trimmed or merely cut, by sawing or otherwise, into blocks or slabs of a rectangular（including square）shape:**
	-花岗岩:								-Granite:
2516.1100[暂]	--原状或粗加修整	4	50	0		17	千克	A	--Crude or roughly trimmed
2516.1200[暂]	--仅用锯或其他方法切割成矩形,包括正方形	4	50	0		17	千克	A	--Merely cut, by sawing or otherwise, into blocks or slabs of a rectangular（including square）shape
2516.2000[暂]	-砂岩	3	50	0		17	千克		-Sandstone
2516 2000.01[暂]	原状或粗加修整砂岩	3	50	0		17	千克	A	Crude or roughly trimmed sandstone
2516 2000.90[暂]	矩形(包括正方形)砂岩(用锯或其他方法切割成矩形的板、块)	3	50	0		17	千克		Sandstone,cut by sawing or otherwise, into blocks or slabs of rectangular（including square）
2516.9000[暂]	-其他碑用或建筑用石	3	50	0		17	千克		-Other monumental or building stone
25.17	**通常做混凝土粒料、铺路、铁道路基或其他路基用的卵石、砾石及碎石,圆石子及燧石,不论是否热处理;矿渣、浮渣及类似的工业残渣,不论是否混有本品目第一部分所列的材料;沥青碎石,品目25.15、25.16所列各种石料的碎粒、碎屑及粉末,不论是否热处理:**								**Pebbles, gravel, broken or crushed stone, of a kind commonly used for concrete aggregates, for road metalling or for railway or other ballast, shingle and flint, whether or not heat treated; macadan of slag, dross or similar industrial waste, whether or not incorporating the materials cited in the first part of the heading; tarred macadam; granules, chippings and powder, of stones of heading No.25.15 or 25.16, whether or not heat treated:**
2517.1000	-通常作混凝土粒料、铺路、铁道路基或其他路基用的卵石、砾	4	50			17	千克		-Pebbles, gravel, broken or crushed stone, of a kind commonly used for concrete aggregates, for road

税则号列 Tariff Item	商品名称及备注	进口税率 最惠	普通	暂定	出口退税	增值税率	计量单位	监管条件	Article Description
	石及碎石，圆石子及燧石，不论是否热处理								metalling or for railway or other ballast, shingle and flint, whether or not heat-treated
2517.2000	-矿渣、浮渣及类似的工业残渣，不论是否混有子目号 2517.10 所列的材料	3	50			17	千克	9	-Macadam of slag, dross or similar industrial waste, whether or not incorporating the materials cited in subheading No.2517.10
2517.3000	-沥青碎石	3	50			17	千克	9	-Tarred macadam
	-品目 25.15 及 25.16 所列各种石料的碎粒、碎屑及粉末，不论是否热处理:								-Granules, chippings and powder, stones of heading No.25.15 or No.25.16, whether or not heat-treated:
2517.4100	--大理石	3	50			17	千克		--Of marble
2517.4900	--其他	3	50			17	千克		--Other
25.18	**白云石，不论是否煅烧或烧结、粗加修整或仅用锯或其他方法切割成矩形（包括正方形）的板、块；夯混白云石:**								**Dolomite, whether or not calcined ;including dolomite roughly trimmed or merely cut, by sawing or otherwise, into blocks or slabs of a rectangular（including square） shape; dolomite ramming mix:**
2518.1000 暂	-未煅烧或烧结的白云石	3	40	1		17	千克		-Dolomite, not calcinecd or sintered
2518.2000 暂	-已煅烧或烧结的白云石	3	40	1		17	千克		-Calcined or sintered dolomite
2518.3000 暂	-夯混白云石	3	40	1		17	千克		-Dolomite ramming mix
25.19	**天然碳酸镁（菱镁矿）；熔凝镁氧矿；烧结镁氧矿，不论烧结前是否加入少量其他氧化物；其他氧化镁，不论是否纯净:**								**Natural magnesium carbonate（magnesite）; fused magnesia; dead-burned （sintered） magnesia, whether or not containing small quantities of other oxides added before sintering; other magnesium oxide, whether or not pure:**
2519.1000 暂	-天然碳酸镁(菱镁矿)	3	40	1		17	千克	y4x	-Natural magnesium carbonate（magnesite）
	-其他:								-Other:
2519.9010 暂	---熔凝镁氧矿	3	40	1		17	千克	y4x	---Fused magnesia
2519.9020 暂	---烧结镁氧矿(重烧镁)	3	40	1		17	千克	y4x	---Dead-burned（sintered） magnesia
2519.9030 暂	---碱烧镁(轻烧镁)	3	40	1		17	千克	y4x	---Light-burned magnesia
	---其他:								---Other:
2519.9091	----化学纯氧化镁	3	35			17	千克	AB	----Magnesium oxide, chemically pure
2519.9099	----其他	3	40			17	千克		----Other
2519 9099.10 暂	其他氧化镁含量在70%以上的矿产品	3	40	1		17	千克	4xy	Other mineral products containing by weight more than 70% of magnesium oxide
2519 9099.90	其他氧化镁	3	40			17	千克		Other magnesium oxide
25.20	**生石膏；硬石膏；熟石膏（由煅烧的生石膏或硫酸钙构成），不论是否着色，也不论是否带有少量促凝剂或缓凝剂:**								**Gypsum; anhydrite; plasters（consisting of calcined gypsum or calcium sulphate） whether or not coloured,with or without small quantities of accelerators or retarders:**
2520.1000	-生石膏，硬石膏	5	80			17	千克		-Gypsum; anhydrite
	-熟石膏:								-Plasters:
2520.2010	---牙科用	5	40			17	千克		---For dental use
2520.2090	---其他	5	80			17	千克		---Other
25.21	**石灰石助熔剂；通常用于制造石灰或水泥的石灰石及其他钙质石:**								**Limestone flux; limestone and other calcareous stone, of a kind used for the manufacture of lime or cement:**
2521.0000	石灰石助熔剂；通常用于制造石灰或水泥的石灰石及其他钙质石	5	50			17	千克		Limestone flux; limestone and other calcareous stone, of a kind used for the manufacture of lime or cement
25.22	**生石灰、熟石灰及水硬石灰，但品目 28.25 的氧化钙及氢氧化钙除外:**								**Quicklime, slaked lime and hydraulic lime, other than calcium oxide and hydroxide of heading No.28.25:**
2522.1000	-生石灰	5	80			17	千克		-Quicklime
2522.2000	-熟石灰	5	80			17	千克		-Slaked lime
2522.3000	-水硬石灰	5	80			17	千克		-Hydraulic lime
25.23	**硅酸盐水泥、矾土水泥、矿渣水泥、富硫酸盐水泥及类似的水凝水泥，不论是否着色，包括水泥**								**Portland cement, aluminous cement, slag cement, supersulphate cement and similar hydraulic cements, whether or not coloured or in the form of**

税则号列 Tariff Item	商品名称及备注	进口税率 最惠	普通	暂定	出口退税	增值税率	计量单位	监管条件	Article Description
	熟料：								**clinkers:**
2523.1000	-水泥熟料	8	30			17	千克		-Cement clinkers
	-硅酸盐水泥：								-Portland cement:
2523.2100	--白水泥，不论是否人工着色	6	30			17	千克		--White cement, whether or not artificially coloured
2523.2900	--其他	8	30			17	千克	A	--Other
2523.3000	-矾土水泥	6	30			17	千克		-Aluminous cement
2523.9000	-其他水凝水泥	8	30			17	千克	A	-Other hydraulic cements
25.24	**石棉：**								**Asbestos:**
2524.1000	-青石棉	5	30			17	千克	89	-Crocidolite
	-其他：								-Other:
2524.9010	---长纤维的	5	30			17	千克		---Of long staple
2524 9010.10	长纤维阳起石石棉（包括长纤维铁石棉、透闪石石棉及直闪石石棉）	5	30			17	千克	89	Actinolite asbestos of long staple（including Amosa asbestos, Tremolite asbestos or Anthopyllite asbestos）
2524 9010.90	其他长纤维石棉	5	30			17	千克		Other asbestos of long staple
2524.9090	---其他的	5	35			17	千克		---Others
2524 9090.10	其他阳起石石棉（包括其他铁石棉、透闪石石棉及直闪石石棉）	5	35			17	千克	89	Other actinolite asbestos（including other Amosa asbestos, Tremolite asbestos or Anthopyllite asbestos）
2524 9090.90	其他石棉	5	35			17	千克		Other asbestos
25.25	**云母，包括云母片；云母废料：**								**Mica, including splittings; mica waste:**
2525.1000[暂]	-原状云母及劈开的云母片	5	30	1		17	千克		-Crude mica and mica rifted into sheets or splittings
2525.2000	-云母粉	5	30			17	千克		-Mica powder
2525.3000	-云母废料	5	30			17	千克	AP	-Mica waste
25.26	**天然冻石，不论是否粗加修整或仅用锯或其他方法切割成矩形（包括正方形）的板、块；滑石：**								**Natural steatite, whether or not roughly trimmed or merely cut, by sawing or otherwise, into blocks or slabs or a rectangular(including square)shape; talc:**
	-未破碎及未研粉：								-Not crushed, not powdered:
2526.1010	---冻石	3	50			17	千克		---Natural steatite
2526.1020[暂]	---滑石	3	50	1		17	千克	4xy	---Talc
	-已破碎或已研粉：								-Crushed or powdered:
2526.2010	---冻石	3	50			17	千克		---Natural steatite
2526.2020[暂]	---滑石	3	50	1		17	千克		---Talc
2526 2020.01[暂]	滑石粉（体积百分比 90%及以上的产品颗粒度≤18 微米的）	3	50	1		17	千克	4ABxy	Talc powder (products with the volume percentage exceeding 90% and the particle size less than or equal to 18 microns)
2526 2020.90[暂]	已破碎或已研粉的其他天然滑石	3	50	1		17	千克	4xy	Other natural talc, crushed or powered
25.28	**天然硼酸盐及其精矿（不论是否煅烧），但不包括从天然盐水析离的硼酸盐；天然粗硼酸，含硼酸干重不超过 85%：**								**Natural borates and concentrates thereof（whether or not calcined）, but not including borates separated from natural brine; natural boric acid containing not more than 85% of H_3BO_3 calculated on the dry weight:**
2528.0010[暂]	---天然硼沙及其精矿（不论是否煅烧，不含从天然盐水析离的硼酸盐）	3	30	0		17	千克	A	---Natural sodium borates and concentrates thereof（whether or not calcined, not including borates separated from natural brine）
2528.0090[暂]	---其他	5	30	0		17	千克		---Other
25.29	**长石；白榴石；霞石及霞石正长岩；萤石（氟石）：**								**Felspar; leucite; nepheline and nepheline syenite; fluorspar:**
2529.1000[暂]	-长石	3	50	1		17	千克		-Felspar
	-萤石：								-Fluorspar:
2529.2100	--按重量计氟化钙含量在 97%及以下	3	50			17	千克	4xy	--Containing by weight 97% or less of calcium fluoride
2529.2200	--按重量计氟化钙含量在 97%以上	3	50			17	千克	4xy	--Containing by weight more than 97% of calcium fluoride
2529.3000	-白榴石；霞石及霞石正长岩	5	50			17	千克		-Leucite; nepheline and nepheline syenite

税则号列 Tariff Item	商品名称及备注	进口税率			出口退税	增值税率	计量单位	监管条件	Article Description
		最惠	普通	暂定					
25.30	其他品目未列名的矿产品:								**Mineral substances not elsewhere specified or included:**
	-未膨胀的蛭石、珍珠岩及绿泥石:								-Vermiculite, perlite and chlorites, unexpanded:
2530.1010	---绿泥石	5	30			17	千克		---Chlorites
2530.1020	---未膨胀的蛭石和珍珠岩	5	30			17	千克		---Vermiculite, perlite unexpanded
2530.2000	-硫镁矾矿及泻盐矿(天然硫酸镁)	3	30			17	千克		-Kieserite, epsomite（natural magnesium sulphates）
	-其他:								-Other:
2530.9010	---矿物性药材	3	30			17	千克		---Mineral medicinal substances
2530.9020	---稀土金属矿	0	0			17	千克		---Ores of rare earth metals
2530 9020.10	按重量计中重稀土总含量≥30%的稀土金属矿	0	0			17	千克	4Bxy	Measure the medium heavy tombarthite metal with a total content≥30% by the weight
2530 9020.90	其他稀土金属矿	0	0			17	千克	4Bxy	Other tombarthite metal
	---其他:								---Other:
2530.9091	----硅灰石	3	50			17	千克		----Wollastonite
2530.9099	----其他	3	50			17	千克		----Other
2530 9099.01[暂]	天青石	3	50	1		17	千克		Celestite
2530 9099.02[暂]	锂辉石矿	3	50	0		17	千克		Spodumene
2530 9099.10[暂]	废镁砖	3	50	1		17	千克	49xy	Magnesia waste bricks
2530 9099.20	叶腊石	3	50			17	千克		Pyrophyllite
2530 9099.30[暂]	未煅烧的水镁石	3	50	1		17	千克	4xy	Brucite
2530 9099.92	其他品目未列名氧化镁含量在70%及以上的矿产品	3	50			17	千克		Mineral substances, not elsewhere specified or included, containing by weight more than 70% of magnesium oxide
2530 9099.99	其他矿产品	3	50			17	千克		Other mineral substances

第二十六章
矿砂、矿渣及矿灰

注释：

一、本章不包括：

（一）供铺路用的矿渣及类似的工业废渣（品目25.17）；

（二）天然碳酸镁（菱镁矿），不论是否煅烧（品目25.19）；

（三）主要含有石油的石油储罐的淤渣（品目27.10）

（四）第三十一章的碱性熔渣；

（五）矿物棉（品目68.06）；

（六）贵金属或包贵金属的废碎料；主要用于回收贵金属的含贵金属或贵金属化合物的其他废碎料（品目71.12）；或

（七）通过熔炼所产生的铜锍、镍锍或钴锍（第十五类）。

二、品目26.01至26.17所称“矿砂”，是指冶金工业中提炼汞，品目28.44的金属以及第十四类、第十五类金属的矿物，即使这些矿物不用于冶金工业，也包括在内。但品目26.01至26.17不包括不是以冶金工业正常加工方法处理的各种矿物。

三、品目26.20仅适用于：

（一）在工业上提炼金属或作为生产金属化合物基本原料的矿渣、矿灰及残渣，但焚化城市垃圾所产生的灰、渣除外(品目26.21)；以及

（二）含有砷的矿渣、矿灰及残渣，不论其是否含有金属，用于提取或生产砷或金属及其化合物。

子目注释：

一、子目2620．21所称“含铅汽油的淤渣及含铅抗震化合物的淤渣”，是指含铅汽油及含铅抗震化合物（例如，四乙基铅）储罐的淤渣，主要含有铅、铅化合物以及铁的氧化物。

二、含有砷、汞、铊及其混合物的矿渣、矿灰及残渣，用于提取或生产砷、汞、铊及其化合物，归入子目2620.60。

Chapter 26
Ores, slag and ash

Chapter Notes:

1. This Chapter does not cover:

(a) Slag or similar industrial waste prepared as macadam (heading 25.17);

(b) Natural magnesium carbonate (magnesite), whether or not calcined (heading 25.19);

(c) Sludges from the storage tanks of petroleum oils, consisting mainly of such oils (heading 27.10);

(d) Basic slag of Chapter 31;

(e) Slag wool, rock wool or similar mineral wools (heading 68.06);

(f) Waste or scrap of precious metal or of metal clad with precious metal; other waste or scrap containing precious metal or precious metal compounds, of a kind used principally for the recovery of precious metal (heading 71.12); or

(g) Copper, nickel or cobalt mattes produced by any process of smelting (Section XV).

2. For the purposes of headings 26.01 to 26.17, the term“ores”means minerals of mineralogical species actually used in the metallurgical industry for the extraction of mercury, of the metals of heading 28.44 or of the metals of Section XIVorXV, even if they are intended for non-metallurgical purposes. Headings 26.01 to 26.17do not, however, include minerals which have been submitted to processes not normal to the metallurgical industry.

3. Heading 26.20 applies only to:

(a) Slag, ash and residues of a kind used in industry either for the extraction of metals or as a basis for the manufacture of chemical compounds of metals, excluding ash and residues from the incineration of municipal waste (heading 26.21); and

(b) Slag, ash and residues containing arsenic, whether or not containing metals, of a kind used either for the extraction of arsenic or metals or for the manufacture of their chemical compounds.

Subheading Notes:

1. For the purposes of subheading 2620.21, “leaded gasoline sludges and leaded anti-knock compound sludges” mean sludges obtained from storage tanks of leaded gasoline and leaded anti-knock compounds (for example, tetraethyllead), and consisting essentially of lead, lead compounds and iron oxide.

2. Slag, ash and residues containing arsenic, mercury, thallium or their mixtures, of a kind used for the extraction of arsenic or those metals or for the manufacture of their chemical compounds, are to be classified in subheading 2620.60

税则号列 Tariff Item	商品名称及备注	进口税率			出口退税	增值税率	计量单位	监管条件	Article Description
		最惠	普通	暂定					
26.01	铁矿砂及其精矿，包括焙烧黄铁矿： -铁矿砂及其精矿，但焙烧黄铁矿除外： --未烧结：								**Iron ores and concentrates, including roasted iron pyrites:** -Iron ores and concentrates, other than roasted iron pyrites: --Non agglomerated:
2601.1110	---平均粒度小于0.8毫米的	0	0			17	千克	7A	---The average grain size less than 0.8mm

税则号列 Tariff Item	商品名称及备注	进口税率 最惠	普通	暂定	出口退税	增值税率	计量单位	监管条件	Article Description
2601.1120	---平均粒度不小于 0.8 毫米，但不大于 6.3毫米的	0	0			17	千克	7A	---The average grain size not less than 0.8mm,but not more than 6.3mm
2601.1190	---其他	0	0			17	千克	7A	---Other
2601.1200	--已烧结	0	0			17	千克	7A	--Agglomerated
2601.2000	-焙烧黄铁矿	0	0			17	千克	7A	-Roasted iron pyrites
26.02	**锰矿砂及其精矿，包括以干重计含锰量在 20%及以上的锰铁矿及其精矿：**								**Manganese ores and concentrates, including ferruginous manganese ores and concentrates with a manganese content of 20% or more, calculated on the dry weight:**
2602.0000	锰矿砂及其精矿，包括以干重计含锰量在 20%及以上的锰铁矿及其精矿	0	0			17	千克	A	Manganese ores and concentrates, including ferruginous manganese ores and concentrates with a manganese content of 20% or more, calculated on the dry weight
26.03	**铜矿砂及其精矿：**								**Copper ores and concentrates:**
2603.0000	铜矿砂及其精矿	0	0				千克		Copper ores and concentrates
2603 0000.10	铜矿砂及其精矿（黄金价值部分）	0	0			0	千克	7A	Copper ores and concentrates (part of the gold value)
2603 0000.90	铜矿砂及其精矿（非黄金价值部分）	0	0			17	千克	7A	Copper ores and concentrates (part of the non-gold value)
26.04	**镍矿砂及其精矿：**								**Nickel ores and concentrates:**
2604.0000	镍矿砂及其精矿	0	0				千克		Nickel ores and concentrates
2604 0000.01	镍矿砂及其精矿（黄金价值部分）	0	0			0	千克		Nickel ores and concentrates(part of gold value)
2604 0000.90	镍矿砂及其精矿（非黄金价值部分）	0	0			17	千克		Nickel ores and concentrates(part of the non-gold value)
26.05	**钴矿砂及其精矿：**								**Cobalt ores and concentrates:**
2605.0000	钴矿砂及其精矿	0	0				千克		Cobalt ores and concentrates
2605 0000.01	钴矿砂及其精矿（黄金价值部分）	0	0			0	千克		Cobalt ores and concentrates (part of the gold value)
2605 0000.90	钴矿砂及其精矿（非黄金价值部分）	0	0			17	千克		Cobalt ores and concentrates(part of the non-gold value)
26.06	**铝矿砂及其精矿：**								**Aluminium ores and concentrates:**
2606.0000	铝矿砂及其精矿	0	0			17	千克	47xy	Aluminium ores and concentrates
26.07	**铅矿砂及其精矿：**								**Lead ores and concentrates:**
2607.0000	铅矿砂及其精矿	0	0				千克		Lead ores and concentrates
2607 0000.01	铅矿砂及其精矿（黄金价值部分）	0	0			0	千克	A	Lead ores and concentrates (part of the gold value)
2607 0000.90	铅矿砂及其精矿（非黄金价值部分）	0	0			17	千克	A	Lead ores and concentrates(part of the non-gold value)
26.08	**锌矿砂及其精矿：**								**Zinc ores and concentrates:**
2608.0000	锌矿砂及其精矿	0	0			17	千克		Zinc ores and concentrates
2608 0000.01	灰色饲料氧化锌(氧化锌（ZnO）含量大于 80%)	0	0			17	千克	A	Grey zinc oxide feed, containing by weight more than 80% of ZnO
2608 0000.90	其他锌矿砂及其精矿	0	0			17	千克	A	Other zinc ores and concentrates
26.09	**锡矿砂及其精矿：**								**Tin ores and concentrates:**
2609.0000	锡矿砂及其精矿	0	0			17	千克	4xy	Tin ores and concentrates
26.10	**铬矿砂及其精矿：**								**Chromium ores and concentrates:**
2610.0000	铬矿砂及其精矿	0	0			17	千克	A	Chromium ores and concentrates
26.11	**钨矿砂及其精矿：**								**Tungsten ores and concentrates:**
2611.0000	钨矿砂及其精矿	0	0			17	千克	4xy	Tungsten ores and concentrates
26.12	**铀或钍矿砂及其精矿：**								**Uranium or thorium ores and concentrates:**
2612.1000	-铀矿砂及其精矿	0	0			17	千克		-Uranium ores and concentrates
2612.2000	-钍矿砂及其精矿	0	0			17	千克	4xy	-Thorium ores and concentrates
26.13	**钼矿砂及其精矿：**								**Molybdenum ores and concentrates:**
2613.1000	-已焙烧	0	0			17	千克	4xy	-Roasted
2613.9000	-其他	0	0			17	千克	4xy	-Other
26.14	**钛矿砂及其精矿：**								**Titanium ores and concentrates:**
2614.0000	钛矿砂及其精矿	0	0			17	千克		Titanium ores and concentrates
26.15	**铌、钽、钒或锆矿砂及其精矿：**								**Niobium, tantalum, vanadium or zirconium ores and concentrates:**
2615.1000	-锆矿砂及其精矿	0	0			17	千克		-Zirconium ores and concentrates
	-其他：								-Other:

税则号列 Tariff Item	商品名称及备注	进口税率 最惠	普通	暂定	出口退税	增值税率	计量单位	监管条件	Article Description
2615.9010	---水合钽铌原料（钽铌矿富集物）	0	0			17	千克		---Hydrated Tantalum/Niobium materials or enriched materials from Tantalum/Niobium Ore
2615.9090	---其他	0	0			17	千克		---Other
2615 9090.10	铌、钽精矿及其矿砂	0	0			17	千克		Niobium, tantalum concentrates and ores
2615 9090.90	钒矿砂，钒精矿	0	0			17	千克		Vanadium ores and concentrates
26.16	**贵金属矿砂及其精矿：**								**Precious metal ores and concentrates:**
2616.1000	-银矿砂及其精矿	0	0			17	千克		-Silver ores and concentrates
2616.9000	-其他	0	0				千克		-Other
2616 9000.01	黄金矿砂	0	0			0	千克		Gold ores
2616 9000.09	其他贵金属矿砂及其精矿	0	0			17	千克		Other precious metal ores and concentrates
26.17	**其他矿砂及其精矿：**								**Other ores and concentrates:**
	-锑矿砂及其精矿：								-Antimony ores and concentrates:
2617.1010	---生锑(锑精矿，选矿产品)	0	0			17	千克	4xy	---Crude antimony（Antimony concentrates which are mineral products）
2617.1090	---其他	0	0				千克		---Other
2617 1090.01	其他锑矿砂及其精矿（黄金价值部分）	0	0			0	千克	4xy	Other antimony ores and concentrates(part of the gold value)
2617 1090.90	其他锑矿砂及其精矿（非黄金价值部分）	0	0			17	千克	4xy	Other antimony ores and concentrates(part of the non-gold value)
	-其他：								-Other:
2617.9010	---朱砂(辰砂)	3	14			17	千克	X	---Cinnabar
2617.9090	---其他	0	0			17	千克		---Other
26.18	**冶炼钢铁所产生的粒状熔渣（熔渣砂）：**								**Granulated slag（slag sand）from the manufacture of iron or steel:**
2618.0010	---主要含锰	4	35			17	千克		---Containing mainly Manganese
2618 0010.01[暂]	主要含锰的冶炼钢铁产生的粒状熔渣，含锰量＞25 %(包括熔渣砂)	4	35	1		17	千克	AP	Granulous slag (slag sand) from the manufacture of iron or steel, containing mainly Manganese, with more than 25 % of manganese
2618 0010.90	其他主要含锰的冶炼钢铁产生的粒状熔渣(包括熔渣砂)	4	35			17	千克	9A	Other granulous slag (slag sand) from the manufacture of iron or steel, containing mainly Manganese
2618.0090	---其他	4	35			17	千克	9A	---Other
26.19	**冶炼钢铁所产生的熔渣、浮渣(粒状熔渣除外)、氧化皮及其他废料：**								**Slag, dross（other than granulated slag）, scalings and other waste from the manufacture of iron or steel:**
2619.0000	冶炼钢铁所产生的熔渣、浮渣(粒状熔渣除外)、氧化皮及其他废料	4	35			17	千克		Slag, dross（other than granulated slag）,scalings and other waste from the manufacture of iron or steel
2619 0000.10	轧钢产生的氧化皮	4	35			17	千克	AP	Scalings from the rolling of iron or steel
2619 0000.21[暂]	冶炼钢铁所产生的含钒浮渣、熔渣，五氧化二钒含量＞20％(冶炼钢铁所产生的粒状熔渣除外)	4	35	1		17	千克	AP	The dross and slag with vanadium, containing＞20％ Vanadium pentoxide, other than granulated slag, from the manufacture of iron or steel
2619 0000.29	其他冶炼钢铁所产生的含钒浮渣、熔渣(冶炼钢铁所产生的粒状熔渣除外)	4	35			17	千克	AP	Other dross and slag with vanadium, from the manufacture of iron or steel (other than granulated slag from the manufacture of iron or steel
2619 0000.30	含铁大于80%的冶炼钢铁产生的渣钢铁	4	35			17	千克	AP	Slag iron, dross containing more than 80% of iron, from the manufacture of iron or steel
2619 0000.90	冶炼钢铁产生的其他熔渣、浮渣及其他废料（冶炼钢铁所产生的粒状熔渣除外）	4	35			17	千克	9A	Other slag, dross and other waste from the manufacture of iron or steel（other than granulated slag, from the manufacture of iron or steel）
26.20	**含有金属、砷及其化合物的矿渣、矿灰及残渣（冶炼钢铁所产生的灰、渣除外）：**								**Slag, ash and residues (other than from the manufacture of iron or steel) containing metals, arsenic or their compounds:**
	-主要含锌：								-Containing mainly zinc:
2620.1100	--含硬锌	4	35			17	千克	9	--Hard zinc spelter
2620.1900	--其他	4	35			17	千克		--Other
2620 1900.10	含锌大于12%的烧结铅锌冶炼矿渣(用作锌冶炼的原料)	4	35			17	千克	AP	Slag and residues containing more than 12% of zinc (used as a raw material for manufacturing zinc)

税则号列 Tariff Item	商品名称及备注	进口税率			出口退税	增值税率	计量单位	监管条件	Article Description
		最惠	普通	暂定					
2620 1900.90	含其他锌的矿渣、矿灰及残渣(冶炼钢铁所产生灰、渣的除外)	4	35			17	千克	9	Slag, ash and residues containing other zinc (other than those from the manufacture of iron or steel)
	-主要含铅:								-Containing mainly lead:
2620.2100	--含铅汽油的淤渣及含铅抗震化合物的淤渣	4	35			17	千克	9	--Leaded gasoline sludges and leaded anti-knock compound sludges
2620.2900	--其他	4	35			17	千克	9	--Other
2620.3000	-主要含铜	4	35			17	千克	9	-Containing mainly copper
2620.4000	-主要含铝	4	35			17	千克	9	-Containing mainly aluminium
2620.6000	-含砷、汞、铊及其混合物，用于提取或生产砷、汞、铊及其化合物	4	35			17	千克	9	-Containing arsenic, mercury, thallium or their mixtures of a kind used for the extraction of arsenic or those metals or for the manufacture of their chemical compounds
	-其他:								-Other:
2620.9100	--含锑、铍、镉、铬及其混合物	4	35			17	千克	9	--Containing antimony, beryllium, cadmium, chromium or their mixtures
	--其他:								--Other:
2620.9910	---主要含钨	4	35			17	千克	y4x9	---Containing mainly tungsten
2620.9990	---其他	4	35			17	千克		---Other
2620 9990.11[暂]	含其他金属及其化合物的矿渣、矿灰及残渣，五氧化二钒＞20%(冶炼钢铁所产生的除外)	4	35	1		17	千克	AP	Slag, ash and residue containing other metal and its compound, whose vanadium pentoxide＞20%,(other than those from the manufacture of iron or steel)
2620 9990.19	含其他金属及其化合物的矿渣、矿灰及残渣，10%＜五氧化二钒≤20%的(冶炼钢铁所产生的除外)	4	35			17	千克	AP	Slag, ash and residue with other metal, whose vanadium is＞10% but≤20%(other than those from the manufacture of iron or steel)
2620 9990.20	含铜大于10%的铜冶炼转炉渣、其他铜冶炼渣	4	35			17	千克	AP	Slag, ash and residues from the manufacture of copper, containing more than 10% of copper
2620 9990.90	含其他金属及其化合物的矿渣、矿灰及残渣（冶炼钢铁所产生灰、渣的除外）	4	35			17	千克	9	Slag, ash and residues, containing other metals or their compounds（other than those from the manufacture of iron or steel）
26.21	**其他矿渣及矿灰，包括海藻灰(海草灰)；焚化城市垃圾所产生的灰、渣:**								**Other slag and ash, including seaweed ash (kelp); ash and residues from the incineration of municipal waste:**
2621.1000	-焚化城市垃圾所产生的灰、渣	4	35			17	千克	9	-Ash and residues from the incineration of municipal waste
2621.9000	-其他	4	35			17	千克		-Other
2621 9000.10	海藻灰及其他植物灰（包括稻壳灰）	4	35			17	千克	9	Seaweed ash（kelp）and other plant ash, including rice husk ash
2621 9000.90	其他矿渣及矿灰	4	35			17	千克	9	Other slag and ash

第二十七章
矿物燃料、矿物油及其蒸馏产品；沥青物质；矿物蜡

注释：

一、本章不包括：

（一）单独的已有化学定义的有机化合物，但纯甲烷及纯丙烷应归入品目 27.11；

（二）品目 30.03 及 30.04 的药品；或

（三）品目 33.01、33.02 及 38.05 的不饱和烃混合物。

二、品目 27.10 所称“石油及从沥青矿物提取的油类”，不仅包括石油、从沥青矿物提取的油及类似油，还包括那些用任何方法提取的主要含有不饱和烃混合物的油，但其非芳族成分的重量必须超过芳族成分。

然而，它不包括采用减压蒸馏法，在压力转换为 1013 毫巴下的温度 300℃时，以体积计馏出量小于 60%的液体合成聚烯烃（第三十九章）。

三、品目 27.10 所称“废油”，是指主要含石油及从沥青矿物提取的油类(参见本章注释二)的废油，不论其是否与水混合。它们包括：

（一）不再适于作为原产品使用的废油（例如，用过的润滑油、液压油及变压器油）；

（二）石油储罐的淤渣油，主要含废油及高浓度的在生产原产品时使用的添加剂（例如，化学品）；以及

（三）水乳浊液状的或与水混合的废油，例如，浮油、清洗油罐所得的油或机械加工中已用过的切削油。

子目注释：

一、子目 2701.11 所称“无烟煤”，是指含挥发物（以干燥、无矿物质计）不超过 14%的煤。

二、子目 2701.12 所称“烟煤”，是指含挥发物（以干燥、无矿物质计）超过 14%，并且热值（以潮湿、无矿物质计）等于或大于 5833 大卡/千克的煤。

三、子目 2707.10、2707.20、2707.30 及 2707.40 所称“粗苯”、“粗甲苯”、“粗二甲苯”及“萘”，是分别指按重量计苯、甲苯、二甲苯或萘的含量在 50%以上的产品。

四、子目2710.12所称“轻油及其制品”，是指温度在210℃时以体积计馏出量（包括损耗）在90%及以上的产品（以美国标准试验法D86为准）。

五、税目27.10的子目所称‘生物柴油’，是指从动植物油脂（不论是否使用过）得到的用作燃料的脂肪酸单烷基酯。

Chapter 27
Mineral fuels, mineral oils and products of their distillation; bituminous substances; mineral waxes

Chapter Notes:

1. This Chapter does not cover:

（a）Separate chemically defined organic compounds, other than pure methane and propane which are to be classified in heading 27.11;

（b）Medicaments of heading 30.03 or 30.04; or

（c）Mixed unsaturated hydrocarbons of heading 33.01, 33.02 or 38.05

2. References in heading 27.10 to “petroleum oils and oils obtained from bituminous minerals” include not only petroleum oils and oils obtained from bituminous minerals but also similar oils, as well as those consisting mainly of mixed unsaturated hydrocarbons, obtained by any process, provided that the weight of the non-aromatic constituents exceeds that of the aromatic constituents.

However, the references do not include liquid synthetic polyolefins of which less than 60%by volume distils at 300℃, after conversion to 1, 013 millibar when a reduced-pressure distillation method is used（Chapter 39）.

3. For the purposes of heading 27.10, “waste oils” means waste containing mainly petroleum oils and oils obtained from bituminous minerals（as described in Note 2 to this Chapter）, whether or not mixed with water. These include:

（a）Such oils no longer fit for use as primary products（for example, used lubricating oils，used hydraulic oils and used transformer oils）;

（b）Sludge oils from the storage tanks of petroleum oils, mainly containing such oils and a high concentration of additives（for example, chemicals）used in the manufacture of the primary products; and

（c）Such oils in the form of emulsions in water or mixtures with water, such as those resulting from oil spills or storage tank washings, or from the use of cutting oils for machining operations.

Subheading Notes:

1. For the purposes of subheading 2701.11, “anthracite” means coal having a volatile matter limit（on a dry, mineral-matter-free basis）not exceeding 14%.

2. For the purposes of subheading 2701.12,“bituminous coal”means coal having a volatile matter limit(on a dry, mineral-matter-free basis)exceeding 14%and a calorific value limit（on a moist,mineral-matter-free basis）equal to or greater than 5,833 kcal / kg.

3. For the purposes of subheadings 2707.10, 2707.20, 2707.30 and 2707.40, the terms “benzol（benzene）”, “toluol（toluene）”, “xylol（xylenes）”and “naphthalene” apply to products which contain more than 50%by weight of benzene, toluene, xylenes or naphthalene,respectively.

4. For the purposes of subheading 2710.12, “light oils and preparations” are those of which 90% or more by volume（including losses）distil at 210℃（ASTM D86 method）

5. For the purposes of the Subheadings of heading 27.10, the term “biodiesel “ means mono-alkyl esters of fatty acids of a kind used as a fuel, derived from animal or vegetable fats and oils whether or not used.

税则号列 Tariff Item	商品名称及备注	进口税率			出口退税	增值税率	计量单位	监管条件	Article Description
		最惠	普通	暂定					
27.01	**煤；煤砖、煤球及用煤制成的类似固体燃料：**								**Coal; briquettes, ovoids and similar solid fuels manufactured from coal:**
	-煤，不论是否粉化，但未制成型：								-Coal, whether or not pulverized, but not agglomerated:
2701.1100 暂	--无烟煤	3	20	0		17	千克		--Anthracite
2701 1100.10 暂	无烟煤（不论是否粉化，但未制成型）	3	20	0		17	千克	47Axy	Anthracite, whether or not pulverized, but not agglomerated
2701 1100.90 暂	无烟煤滤料	3	20	0		17	千克	7A	Anthracite filtering media
	--烟煤：								--Bituminous coal:
2701.1210 暂	---炼焦煤	3	20	0		17	千克	47Axy	---Coking coal
2701.1290 暂	---其他	6	20	0		17	千克	47Axy	---Other
2701.1900 暂	--其他煤	5	20	0		17	千克	47Axy	--Other coal
2701.2000 暂	-煤砖、煤球及用煤制成的类似固体燃料	5	50	0		17	千克		-Briquettes, ovoids and similar solid fuels manufactured from coal
27.02	**褐煤，不论是否制成型，但不包括黑玉：**								**Lignite, whether or not agglomerated, excluding jet:**
2702.1000	-褐煤，不论是否粉化，但未制成型	3	20			17	千克	4Axy	-Lignite, whether or not pulverized, but not agglomerated
2702.2000	-制成型的褐煤	3	20			17	千克	A	-Agglomerated lignite
27.03	**泥煤（包括肥料用泥煤），不论是否制成型：**								**Peat（including peat litter）, whether or not agglomerated:**
2703.0000	泥煤(包括肥料用泥煤)，不论是否制成型	5	20			17	千克		Peat（including peat litter）, whether or not agglomerated
2703 0000.10	泥炭(草炭)［沼泽（湿地）中，地上植物枯死、腐烂堆积而成的有机矿体（不论干湿）］	5	20			17	千克	8AB	Peat (peat moss), formed by dried or ritten plant in swamp and wetland , whether dry or wet
2703 0000.90	泥煤(包括肥料用泥煤)（不论是否制成型）	5	20			17	千克	AB	Peat（including peat litter）, whether or not agglomerated
27.04	**煤、褐煤或泥煤制成的焦炭及半焦炭，不论是否制成型；甑炭：**								**Coke and semi-coke of coal, of lignite or of peat, whether or not agglomerated; retort carbon:**
2704.0010 暂	---焦炭及半焦炭	5	11	0		17	千克	4xy	---Coke and semi-coke
2704.0090 暂	---其他	5	11	0		17	千克		---Other
27.05	**煤气、水煤气、炉煤气及类似气体，但石油气及其他烃类气除外：**								**Coal gas, water gas, producer gas and similar gases, other than petroleum gases and other gaseous hydrocarbons:**
2705.0000 暂	煤气、水煤气、炉煤气及类似气体，但石油气及其他烃类气除外	5	20	1		13	千克		Coal gas, water gas, producer gas and similar gases, other than petroleum gases and other gaseous hydrocarbons
2705 0000.10 暂	煤气	5	20	1		13	千克	AB	Coal gas
2705 0000.90 暂	水煤气、炉煤气及类似气体(石油气及其他烃类气除外)	5	20	1		13	千克		Water gas, blast furnace gas and other similar gas, (other than petroleum gases and other gaseous hydrocarbons)
27.06	**从煤、褐煤或泥煤蒸馏所得的焦油及其他矿物焦油，不论是否脱水或部分蒸馏，包括再造焦油：**								**Tar distilled from coal, from lignite or from peat, and other mineral tars, whether or not dehydrated or partially distilled, including reconstituted tars:**
2706.0000 暂	从煤、褐煤或泥煤蒸馏所得的焦油及其他矿物焦油，不论是否脱水或部分蒸馏，包括再造焦油	6	30	1		17	千克		Tar distilled from coal, from lignite or from peat, and other mineral tars, whether or not dehydrated or partially distilled, including reconstituted tars
2706 0000.01 暂	含蒽油≥50%及沥青≥40%的“炭黑油”	6	30	1		17	千克		Carbon black oil, containing more than 50% of anthracene oil and more than 40% of pitch
2706 0000.90 暂	其他从煤、褐煤或泥煤蒸馏所得的焦油及矿物焦油（不论是否脱水或部分蒸馏，包括再造焦油）	6	30	1		17	千克	AB	Other tar distilled from coal, from lignite or from peat, and other mineral tars, whether or not dehydrated or partially distilled, including reconstituted tars
27.07	**蒸馏高温煤焦油所得的油类及其他产品；芳族成分重量超过非芳族成分的类似产品：**								**Oils and other products of the distillation of high temperature coal tar; similar products in which the weight of the aromatic constituents exceeds that of the non-aromatic constituents:**
2707.1000	-粗苯	6	20			17	千克	AB	-Benzole
2707.2000	-粗甲苯	6	30			17	千克		-Toluole

税则号列 Tariff Item	商品名称及备注	进口税率 最惠	普通	暂定	出口退税	增值税率	计量单位	监管条件	Article Description
2707.3000[暂]	-粗二甲苯	6	20	2		17	千克		-Xylole
2707.4000	-萘	7	30			17	千克		-Naphthalene
2707.5000[暂]	-其他芳烃混合物，温度在250℃时蒸馏出芳烃含量以体积计（包括损耗）在65%及以上（以美国标准试验法D86为准）	7	30	3		17	千克		-Other aromatic hydrocarbon mixtures of which 65% or more by volume（including losses）distils at 250℃ by the ASTM D86 method
	-其他:								-Other:
2707.9100	--杂酚油	7	30			17	千克		--Creosote oils
	--其他:								--Other:
2707.9910	---酚	7	30			17	千克		---Phenols
2707.9990	---其他	7	30			17	千克		---Other
27.08	**从煤焦油或其他矿物焦油所得的沥青及沥青焦:**								**Pitch and pitch coke, obtained from coal tar or from other mineral tars:**
2708.1000	-沥青	7	35			17	千克		-Pitch
2708.2000	-沥青焦	6	11			17	千克		-Pitch coke
2708 2000.01[暂]	针状沥青焦	6	11	3		17	千克		Needle-shaped pitch coke
2708 2000.90	其他沥青焦	6	11			17	千克		Other pitch coke
27.09	**石油原油及从沥青矿物提取的原油:**								**Petroleum oils and oils obtained from bituminous minerals, crude:**
2709.0000	石油原油及从沥青矿物提取的原油	0	85元/t			17	千克	4x7AByv	Petroleum oils and oils obtained from bituminous minerals, crude
27.10	**石油及从沥青矿物提取的油类，但原油除外；以上述油为基本成分（按重量计不低于70%）的其他品目未列名制品；废油:**								**Petroleum oils and oils obtained from bituminnous minerals, other than crude; preparations not elsewhere specified or included,containing by weight 70% or more of petroleum oils or of oils obtained from bituminous minerals, these oils being the basic constituents of the preparations; waste oils:**
	-石油及从沥青矿物提取的油类（但原油除外）以及以上述油为基本成分（按重量计不低于70%）的其他品目未列名制品，不含有生物柴油，但废油除外:								-Petroleum oils and oils obtained from bituminous minerals（other than crude）and preparations not elsewhere specified or included, containing by weight 70% or more of petroleum oils or of oils obtained from bituminous minerals, these oils being the basic constituents of the preparations, other than those containing biodiesel and other than waste oils :
	--轻油及其制品:								--Light oils and preparations :
2710.1210[暂]	---车用汽油及航空汽油	5	14	1		17	千克/升		---Motor gasoline, aviation gasoline
2710 1210.01[暂]	车用汽油及航空汽油，不含生物柴油(铅含量每升不超过0.013克)	5	14	1		17	千克/升	47ABvy	Motor gasooline, aviation gasoline，other than those containing biodiesel（containing lead not exceeding 0.013g/L）
2710 1210.02[暂]	车用汽油及航空汽油，不含生物柴油(铅含量每升超过0.013克)	5	14	1		17	千克/升	47ABvy	Motor gasoline and aviation gasoline without biodiesel（containing lead exceeding 0.013g/L）
2710.1220[暂]	---石脑油	6	20	0		17	千克/升	47ABvy	---Naphtha
2710.1230	---橡胶溶剂油、油漆溶剂油、抽提溶剂油	6	30			17	千克/升		---Rubber solvent, paint solvent, extractive solvent
	---其他:								---Other :
2710.1291	----壬烯	9	20			17	千克		----Nonene
2710 1291.01[暂]	壬烯，不含生物柴油（碳九异构体混合物含量高于90%）	9	20	4		17	千克	4Ay	Nonene with no biodiesel
2710 1291.90	其他壬烯，不含生物柴油	9	20			17	千克	4Ay	Other nonne with no biodiesel
2710.1299	----其他	9	20			17	千克		----Other
2710 1299.10[暂]	异戊烯同分异构体混合物，不含生物柴油	9	20	5		17	千克	4Ay	Isoamylene isomeride compound, other than those containing biodiesel
2710 1299.90	其他轻油及制品，不含生物柴油(包括按重量计含油≥70%的制品)	9	20			17	千克	4Ay	Other light oil and products, other than those containing biodiesel (including products with oil≥70%, measuring by weight)
	--其他:								--Other:

税则号列 Tariff Item	商品名称及备注	进口税率 最惠	普通	暂定	出口退税	增值税率	计量单位	监管条件	Article Description
	---煤油馏分:								---Kerosene distillages:
2710.1911[暂]	----航空煤油	9	14	0		17	千克/升	47ABvy	----Aviation kerosene
2710.1912	----灯用煤油	9	14			17	千克	47ABvy	----Lamp-kerosene
2710.1919	----其他	6	20			17	千克		----Other
2710 1919.10[暂]	正构烷烃(C9～C13),不含生物柴油	6	20	2		17	千克	4y	Normal paraffin(C9-C13), other than those containing biodiesel
2710 1919.90	其他煤油馏分的油及制品,不含生物柴油	6	20			17	千克	4ABy	Other kerosene distillages oils and preparations, other than those containing biodiesel
	---柴油及其他燃料油:								---Diesel oils and other fuel oils:
2710.1922[暂]	----5-7号燃料油	6	20	1		17	千克/升	7ABv	----Fuel oils No.5- No.7
2710.1923[暂]	----柴油	6	11	1		17	千克/升		----Diesel oil
2710 1923.10[暂]	车用、普通柴油,不含生物柴油	6	11	1		17	千克/升	47ABvy	Diesel oil for automobile, other than those containing biodiesel
2710 1923.90[暂]	其他柴油,不含生物柴油	6	11	1		17	千克/升	7ABv	Other diesel oi, other than those containing biodiesel
2710.1929	----其他	6	20			17	千克/升		----Other
2710 1929.10[暂]	蜡油，不含生物柴油（350℃以下馏出物体积＜20%，550℃以下馏出物体积＞80%）	6	20	0		17	千克/升	7ABv	Paraffin oils, other than those containing biodiesel（which less than 20% by volume distils at below 350℃, more than 80% by volume distils at below 550℃）
2710 1929.90	其他燃料油，不含生物柴油	6	20			17	千克/升	7ABv	Other diesel oils and other fuel oils, without biodiesel
	---润滑油、润滑脂及其他重油:								---Lubricating oils, lubricating greases and other heavy oils:
2710.1991	----润滑油	6	17			17	千克/升	4Axy	----Lubricating grease
2710.1992	----润滑脂	6	17			17	千克/升	4Axy	----Lubricating oils
2710.1993	----润滑油基础油	6	17			17	千克/升	4xy	----Basic oils for lubricating oils
2710.1994	----液体石蜡和重质液体石蜡	6	20			17	千克	AB	----Liquid paraffin and heavy liquid paraffin
2710.1999	----其他	6	20			17	千克/升	B	----Other
2710.2000	-石油及从沥青矿物提取的油类（但原油除外）以及以上述油为基本成分（按重量计不低于70%）的其他税目未列名制品，含有生物柴油＜30%，但废油除外	6	20			17	千克/升	4Ay	-Petroleum oils and oils obtained from bituminous minerals（other than crude）and preparations not elsewhere specified or included, containing by weight 70％ or more of petroleum oils or of oils obtained from bituminous minerals, these oils being the basic constituents of the preparations, containing biodiesel＜30％, other than waste oils
	-废油:								-Waste oils:
2710.9100	--含多氯联苯（PCBs）、多氯三联苯（PCTs）或多溴联苯（PBBs）的	6	20			17	千克	9	--Containing poly chlorinated biphenyls（PCBs）, polychlorinated terphenyls（PCTs）or polybrominated biphenyls（PBBs）
2710.9900	--其他	6	20			17	千克	9	--Other
27.11	**石油气及其他烃类气:**								**Petroleum gases and other gaseous hydrocarbons:**
	-液化的:								-Liquefied:
2711.1100	--天然气	0	20			13	千克	4ABy	--Natural gas
2711.1200[暂]	--丙烷	5	20	1		13	千克	AB	--Propane
	--丁烷:								--Butanes:
2711.1310	---直接灌注香烟打火机及类似打火器用，其包装容器的容积超过300立方厘米	11	80			17	千克		---Liquid or liquefied-gas fuels in containers of a kind used for filling or refilling cigarette or similar lighters and of a capacity exceeding 300cm³
2711.1390[暂]	---其他	5	20	1		13	千克		---Other
2711.1400	--乙烯、丙烯、丁烯及丁二烯	5	20			17	千克		--Ethylene, propylene, butylene and butadiene
2711 1400.10	液化的乙烯	5	20			17	千克	AB	Lequefied ethylene
2711 1400.90	液化的丙烯、丁烯及丁二烯	5	20			17	千克		Lequefied propylene, butene and butadiene
	--其他:								--Other:
2711.1910	---直接灌注香烟打火机及类似打火器用的燃料，其包装容器的容积超过300立方厘米	10	80			17	千克		---Liquid or liquefied-gas fuels in containers of a kind used for filling or refilling cigarette or similar lighters and of a capacity exceeding 300cm³
2711.1990	---其他	3	20			13	千克		---Other
2711 1990.10	其他液化石油气	3	20			13	千克	AB	Other lequefied petroleum gas
2711 1990.90	其他液化烃类气	3	20			13	千克		Other liquified hydrocarbon gas
	-气态的:								-In gaseous state:

税则号列 Tariff Item	商品名称及备注	进口税率 最惠	普通	暂定	出口退税	增值税率	计量单位	监管条件	Article Description
2711.2100	--天然气	0	20			13	千克	AB	--Natural gas
2711.2900	--其他	6	20			13	千克		--Other
2711 2900.10	其他气态石油气	6	20			13	千克	AB	Other gaseous pertroleum gas
2711 2900.90	其他气态烃类气	6	20			13	千克		Other gaseous hydrocarbon gas
27.12	**凡士林；石蜡、微晶石蜡、疏松石蜡、地蜡、褐煤蜡、泥煤蜡、其他矿物蜡及用合成或其他方法制得的类似产品，不论是否着色：**								**Petroleum jelly; paraffin wax, microcrystalline petroleum wax, slack wax, ozokerite, lignite wax, peat wax, other mineral waxes, and similar products obtained by synthesis or by other processes, whether or not coloured:**
2712.1000	-凡士林	8	45			17	千克	AB	-Petroleum jelly
2712.2000	-石蜡，按重量计含油量小于0.75%	8	45			17	千克	4ABx	-Paraffin wax containing by weight less than 0.75% of oil
	-其他:								-Other:
2712.9010	---微晶石蜡	8	45			17	千克	4ABx	---Microcrystalline petroleum wax
2712.9090	---其他	8	45			17	千克		---Other
27.13	**石油焦、石油沥青及其他石油或从沥青矿物提取的油类的残渣：**								**Petroleum coke, petroleum bitumen and other residues of petroleum oils or of oils obtained from bituminous minerals:**
	-石油焦:								-Petroleum coke:
	--未煅烧:								--Not calcined:
2713.1110	---硫的重量百分比小于3%的	3	11			17	千克		---Containing by weight less than 3% of Sulphur
2713.1190	---其他	3	11			17	千克		---Other
	--已煅烧:								--Calcined:
2713.1210	---硫的重量百分比小于0.8%	3	11			17	千克		---Containing by weight less than 0.8% of sulphur
2713.1290	---其他	3	11			17	千克		---Other
2713.2000	-石油沥青	8	35			17	千克		-Petroleum bitumen
2713.9000	-其他石油或从沥青矿物提取的油类的残渣	6	35			17	千克	9	-Other residues of petroleum oils or of oils obtained from bituminous minerals
27.14	**天然沥青（地沥青）、沥青页岩、油页岩及焦油砂；沥青岩：**								**Bitumen and asphalt, natural; bituminous or oil shale and tar sands; asphaltites and asphaltic rocks:**
2714.1000	-沥青页岩、油页岩及焦油砂	6	20			17	千克		-Bituminous or oil shale and tar sands
	-其他:								-Other:
2714.9010 暂	---天然沥青(地沥青)	8	35	4		17	千克		---Natural bitumen and asphalt
2714.9020	---乳化沥青	0	20			17	千克		---Emulsified bitumen and asphalt
2714.9090	---其他	3	20			17	千克		---Other
27.15	**以天然沥青（地沥青）、石油沥青、矿物焦油或矿物焦油沥青为基本成分的沥青混合物（例如，沥青胶黏剂、稀释沥青）：**								**Bituminous mixtures based on natural asphalt, on natural bitumen, on petroleum bitumen, on mineral tar or on mineral tar pitch（for example, bituminous mastics, cut-backs）：**
2715.0000	以天然沥青（地沥青）、石油沥青、矿物焦油或矿物焦油沥青为基本成分的沥青混合物（例如，沥青胶黏剂、稀释沥青）：	8	35			17	千克		Bituminous mixtures based on natural asphalt, on natural bitumen, on petroleum bitumen, on mineral tar or on mineral tar pitch（for example, bituminous mastics, cut-backs）：
27.16	**电力：**								**Electrical energy:**
2716.0000	电力	0	8		13	17	千瓦时		Electrical energy

第六类
化学工业及其相关工业的产品

注释：

一、（一）凡符合品目 28.44 或 28.45 规定的货品（放射性矿砂除外），应分别归入这两个品目而不归入本目录的其他品目。

（二）除上述（一）款另有规定的以外，凡符合品目28.43、28.46或28.52规定的货品，应分别归入以上品目而不归入本类的其他品目。

二、除上述注释一另有规定的以外，凡由于按一定剂量或作为零售包装而可归入品目30.04、30.05、30.06、32.12、33.03、33.04、33.05、33.06、33.07、35.06、37.07或38.08的货品，应分别归入以上品目，而不归入本目录的其他品目。

三、由两种或两种以上单独成分配套的货品，其部分或全部成分属于本类范围以内，混合后则构成第六类或第七类的货品，应按混合后产品归入相应的品目，但其组成成分必须符合下列条件：

（一）其包装形式足以表明这些成分不需经过改装就可一起使用的；

（二）一起报验的；以及

（三）这些成分的属性及相互比例足以表明是相互配用的。

SECTION Ⅵ
PRODUCTS OF THE CHEMICAL OR ALLIED INDUSTRIES

Section Notes:

1.（a）Goods（other than radioactive ores）answering to a description in heading 28.44 or 28.45 are to be classified in those headings and in no other heading of the Nomenclature.

（b）Subject to paragraph（a）above，goods answering to a description in heading 28.43, 28.46 or 28.52 are to be classified in those headings and in no other heading of this Seciton.

2. Subject to Note 1 above，goods classifiable in heading 30.04, 30.05, 30.06, 32.12, 33.03, 33.04, 33.05, 33.06, 33.07, 35.06, 37.07, or 38.08 by reason of being put up in measured doses or for retail sale are to be classified in those headings and in no other heading of the Nomenclature.

3. Goods put up in sets consisting of two or more separate constituents, some or all of which fall in this Section and are intended to be mixed together to obtain a product of Section Ⅵ or Ⅶ, are to be classified in the heading appropriate to that product, provided that the constituents are:

（a）having regard to the manner in which they are put up, clearly identifiable as being intended to be used together without first being repacked;

（b）presented together; and

（c）identifiable, whether by their nature or by the relative proportions in which they are present, as being complementary one to another.

第二十八章
无机化学品；贵金属、稀土金属、放射性元素及其同位素的有机及无机化合物

注释：

一、除条文另有规定的以外，本章各品目只适用于：

（一）单独的化学元素及单独的已有化学定义的化合物，不论是否含有杂质；

（二）上述（一）款产品的水溶液；

（三）溶于其他溶剂的上述（一）款产品，但该产品处于溶液状态只是为了安全或运输所采取的正常必要方法，其所用溶剂并不使该产品改变其一般用途而适合于某些特殊用途；

（四）为了保存或运输需要，加入稳定剂(包括抗结块剂)的上述（一）、（二）、（三）款产品；

（五）为了便于识别或安全起见，加入抗尘剂或着色剂的上述（一）、（二）、（三）、（四）款产品，但所加剂料并不使原产品改变其一般用途而适合于某些特殊用途。

Chapter 28
Inorganic chemicals; organic or inorganic compounds of precious metals, of rare-earth metals, of radioactive elements or of isotopes

Chapter Notes:

1. Except where the context otherwise requires, the headings of this Chapter apply only to:

（a）Separate chemical elements and separate chemically defined compounds, whether or not containing impurities;

（b）The products mentioned in（a）above dissolved in water;

（c）The products mentioned in（a）above dissolved in other solvents, provided that the solution constitutes a normal and necessary method of putting up these products adopted solely for reasons of safety or for transport, and that the solvent does not render the product particularly suitable for specific use rather than for general use;

（d）The products mentioned in（a）,（b）or（c）above with an added stabiliser（including an anti-caking agent）necessary for their preservation or transport;

（e）The products mentioned in（a）,（b）,（c）or（d）above with an added anti-dusting agent or a colouring substance added to facilitate their identification or for safety reasons, provided that the additions do not render the product particularly suitable for specific use rather than for general use.

二、除以有机物质稳定的连二亚硫酸盐及次硫酸盐（品目28.31），无机碱的碳酸盐及过碳酸盐（品目28.36），无机碱的氰化物、氧氰化物及氰络合物（品目28.37），无机碱的雷酸盐、氰酸盐及硫氰酸盐（品目28.42），品目28.43至28.46及28.52的有机产品，以及碳化物（品目28.49）之外，本章仅包括下列碳化合物：

（一）碳的氧化物，氰化氢及雷酸、异氰酸、硫氰酸及其他简单或络合氰酸（品目28.11）；

（二）碳的卤氧化物（品目28.12）；

（三）二硫化碳（品目28.13）；

（四）硫代碳酸盐、硒代碳酸盐、碲代碳酸盐、硒代氰酸盐、碲代氰酸盐、四氰硫基二氨基络酸盐及其他无机碱络合氰酸盐（品目28.42）；

（五）用尿素固化的过氧化氢（品目28.47）、氧硫化碳、硫代羰基卤化物、氰、卤化氰、氨基氰及其金属衍生物（品目28.53），不论是否纯净，但氰氨化钙除外（第三十一章）。

2. In addition to dithionites and sulphoxylates, stabilised with organic substances (heading 28.31), carbonates and peroxocarbonates of inorganic bases (heading 28.36), cyanides, cyanide oxides and complex cyanides of inorganic bases (heading 28.37), fulminates, cyanates and thiocyanates, of inorganic bases (heading 28.42), organic products included in heading 28.43 to 28.46 and 28.52 and carbides (heading 28.49), only the following compounds of carbon are to be classified in this Chapter:

(a) Oxides of carbon, hydrogen cyanide and fulminic, isocyanic, thiocyanic and other simple or complex cyanogen acids (heading 28.11);

(b) Halide oxides of carbon (heading 28.12);

(c) Carbon disulphide (heading 28.13);

(d) Thiocarbonates, selenocarbonates, tellurocarbonates, selenocyanates, tellurocyanates,tetrathio-cyanatodiamminochromates (reineckates) and other complex cyanates, of inorganic bases (heading 28.42);

(e) Hydrogen peroxide, solidified with urea (heading 28.47) ,carbon oxysulphide, thiocarbonyl halides, cyanogen, cyanogen halides and cyanamide and its metal derivatives (heading 28.53) other than calcium cyanamide, whether or not pure (Chapter 31).

三、除第六类注释一另有规定的以外，本章不包括：

（一）氯化钠或氧化镁（不论是否纯净）及第五类的其他产品；

（二）上述注释二所述以外的有机-无机化合物；

（三）第三十一章注释二、三、四或五所述的产品；

（四）品目32.06的用作发光剂的无机产品；品目32.07的搪瓷玻璃料及其他玻璃，呈粉、粒或粉片状的；

（五）人造石墨（品目38.01）；品目38.13的灭火器的装配药及已装药的灭火弹；品目38.24的零售包装的除墨剂；品目38.24的每颗重量不少于2.5克的碱金属或碱土金属卤化物的培养晶体（光学元件除外）；

（六）宝石或半宝石（天然、合成或再造）及这些宝石、半宝石的粉末（品目71.02至71.05），第七十一章的贵金属及贵金属合金；

（七）第十五类的金属（不论是否纯净）、金属合金或金属陶瓷，包括硬质合金（与金属烧结的金属碳化物）；或

（八）光学元件，例如，用碱金属或碱土金属卤化物制成的（品目90.01）。

3. Subject to the provisions of Note 1 to Section VI, this Chapter does not cover:

(a) Sodium chloride or magnesium oxide, whether or not pure, or other products of Section Ⅴ;

(b) Organo-inorganic compounds other than those mentioned in Note 2 above;

(c) Products mentioned in Note 2, 3, 4 or 5 to Chapter 31;

(d) Inorganic products of a kind used as luminophores, of heading 32.06; glass frit and other glass in the form of powder, granules of flakes, of heading 32.07;

(e) Artificial graphite (heading 38.01); products put up as charges for fire-extinguishers or put up in fire-extinguishing grenades, of heading 38.13; ink removers put up in packings for retail sale, of heading 38.24, cultured crystals (other than optical elements) weighing not less than 2.5g each, of the halides of the alkali or alkaline-earth metals, of heading 38.24;

(f) Precious or semi-precious stones (natural, synthetic or reconstructed) or dust or powder of such stones (headings 71.02 to 71.05), or precious metals or precious metal alloys of Chapter 71;

(g) The metals, whether or not pure, metal alloys or cermets, including sintered metal carbides (metal carbides sintered with a metal), of Section XV; or

(h) Optical elements, for example, of the halides of the alkali or alkaline-earth metals (heading 90.01).

四、由本章第二分章的非金属酸和第四分章的金属酸所构成的已有化学定义的络酸，应归入品目28.11。

4. Chemically defined complex acids consisting of a nonmetal acid of sub-Chapter Ⅱ and a metal acid of sub-Chapter Ⅳ are to be classified in heading 28.11.

五、品目 28.26 至 28.42 只适用于金属盐、铵盐及过氧酸盐。

除条文另有规定的以外，复盐及络盐应归入品目 28.42。

5. Headings 28.26 to 28.42 apply only to metal or ammonium salts or peroxysalts.

Except where the context otherwise requires, double or complex salts are to be classified in heading 28.42.

六、品目28.44只适用于：

（一）锝（原子序数43）、钷（原子序数61）、钋（原子序数84）及原子序数大于84的所有化学元素；

（二）天然或人造放射性同位素（包括第十四类及第十五类的贵金属和贱金属的放射性同位素），不论是否混合；

（三）上述元素或同位素的无机或有机化合物，不论是否已有化学定义或是否混合；

（四）含有上述元素或同位素及其无机或有机化合物并且具有某种放射性强度超过74贝克勒尔/克（0.002微居里/克）的合金、分散体（包括金属陶瓷）、陶瓷产品及混合物；

（五）核反应堆已耗尽（已辐照）的燃料元件（释热元件）；

（六）放射性的残渣，不论是否有用。

品目28.44、28.45及本注释所称“同位素”，是指：

1. 单独的核素，但不包括自然界中以单一同位素状态存在的核素；
2. 同一元素的同位素混合物，其中一种或几种同位素已被浓缩，即人工地改变了该元素同位素的自然构成。

七、品目28.48包括按重量计含磷量超过15%的磷化铜（磷铜）。

八、经掺杂用于电子工业的化学元素（例如，硅、硒），如果拉制后未经加工或呈圆筒形、棒形，应归入本章；如果已切成圆片、薄片或类似形状，则归入品目38.18。

子目注释：

一、子目2852.10所称‘已有化学定义’是指符合第二十八章注释一（一）至（五）或第二十九章注释一（一）至（八）规定的汞的无机或有机化合物。

6. Heading 28.44 applies only to:

(a) Technetium (atomic No. 43), promethium (atomic No. 61), polonium (atomic No. 84) and all elements with an atomic number greater than 84;

(b) Natural or artificial radioactive isotopes (including those of the precious metals or of the base metals of Sections XIVandXV), whether or not mixed together;

(c) Compounds, inorganic or organic, of these elements or isotopes, whether or not chemically defined, whether or not mixed together;

(d) Alloys, dispersions (including cermets), ceramic products and mixtures containing these elements or isotopes or inorganic or organic compounds thereof and having a specific radioactivity exceeding 74 Bq/g (0.002μ ci/g);

(e) Spent (irradiated) fuel elements (cartridges) of nuclear reactors;

(f) Radioactive residues whether or not usable.

The term “isotopes”, for the purposes of this Note and of the wording of headings 28.44 and 28.45, refers to:

(i) Individual nuclides, excluding, however, those existing in nature in the monoisotopic state;

(ii) Mixtures of isotopes of one and the same element, enriched in one or several of the said isotopes, that is, elements of which the natural isotopic composition has been artificially modified.

7. Heading 28.48 includes copper phosphide (phosphor copper) containing more than 15% by weight of phosphorus.

8. Chemical elements (for example, silicon and selenium) doped for use in electronics are to be classified in this Chapter, provided that they are in forms unworked as drawn, or in the form of cylinders or rods. When cut in the form of discs, wafers or similar forms, they fall in heading 38.18

Subheading Notes:

1. For the purposes of Subheading 2852.10, the expression “chemically defined” means all organic or inorganic compounds of mercury meeting the requirements of paragraphs (a) to (e) of Note 1 to Chapter 28 or paragraphs (a) to (h) of Note 1 to Chapter 29.

税则号列 Tariff Item	商品名称及备注	进口税率			出口退税	增值税率	计量单位	监管条件	Article Description
		最惠	普通	暂定					
	第一分章　化学元素								I. CHEMICAL ELEMENTS
28.01	氟、氯、溴及碘：								Fluorine, chlorine, bromine and iodine:
2801.1000	-氯	5.5	80			17	千克	AB	-Chlorine
2801.2000	-碘	5.5	30			17	千克	G	-Iodine
	-氟；溴：								-Fluorine; bromine:
2801.3010	---氟	5.5	30			17	千克	AB	---Fluorine
2801.3020 暂	---溴	5.5	30	1		17	千克	AB	---Bromine
28.02	升华硫磺、沉淀硫磺；胶态硫磺：								Sulphur, sublimed or precipitated;colloidal sulphur:
2802.0000 暂	升华硫磺、沉淀硫磺；胶态硫磺	5.5	17	1		17	千克	AB	Sulphur, sublimed or precipitated; colloidal sulphur
28.03	碳（碳黑及其他品目未列名的其他形态的碳）：								Carbon (carbon blacks and other forms of carbon not elsewhere specified or included):
2803.0000	碳（碳黑及其他税号未列名的其他形态的碳）	5.5	35			17	千克		Carbon (carbon blacks and other forms of carbon not elsewhere specified or included)
28.04	氢、稀有气体及其他非金属：								Hydrogen, rare gases and other non-metals:
2804.1000	-氢	5.5	30			17	千克/立方米	AB	-Hydrogen

税则号列 Tariff Item	商品名称及备注	进口税率 最惠	普通	暂定	出口退税	增值税率	计量单位	监管条件	Article Description
	-稀有气体:								-Rare gases:
2804.2100	--氩	5.5	30			17	千克/立方米	AB	--Argon
2804.2900	--其他	5.5	30			17	千克/立方米		--Other
2804.3000	-氮	5.5	30			17	千克/立方米	AB	-Nitrogen
2804.4000	-氧	5.5	80			17	千克/立方米	AB	-Oxygen
2804.5000	-硼；碲	5.5	17			17	千克		-Boron; tellurium
2804 5000.01[暂]	碲	5.5	17	0		17	千克		Tellurium
2804 5000.10	颗粒＜500 微米的硼及其合金（含量≥97%，不论球形、椭球体、雾化、片状、研碎金属燃料）	5.5	17			17	千克	3	Boron and its alloys, granularity＜500μm （containing more than 97% by weight of boron whether in the form of spheroid, ellipsoid, flakes, atomized or pulverized metallic fuel）
2804 5000.20	能量密度＞40MJ/kg 的硼浆（硼溶于溶剂形成的硼浆）	5.5	17			17	千克	3	Boron paste, energy density＞40MJ/kg, boron dissolved in solvent and become boron paste
2804 5000.90	其他硼	5.5	17			17	千克		Other boron
	-硅:								-Silicon:
	-按重量计含硅量不少于99.99%:								--Containing by weight not less than 99.99% of silicon:
	---经掺杂用于电子工业的直径在7.5厘米及以上的单晶硅棒:								---Monocrystals doped for use in electronics, in the form of cylinders or rods, 7.5cm or more in diameter:
2804.6117	----直径在30厘米及以上的	4	11		17	17	千克		----30cm or more in diameter
2804.6119	----其他	4	11			17	千克		----Other
2804.6120	---经掺杂用于电子工业的其他单晶硅棒	4	17			17	千克		---Other monocrystals doped for use in electronics, in the form of cylinders or rods
2804.6190	---其他	4	30			17	千克		---Other
2804 6190.11[暂]	含硅量>99.9999999%的多晶硅废碎料(太阳能级多晶硅除外)	4	30	1		17	千克	AP	Polycrystalline silicon waste or scrap, containing by weight not less than 99.9999999% of silicon (other than Polycrystalline silicon for solar cells)
2804 6190.12	含硅量≥99.9999999%的太阳能级多晶硅	4	30			17	千克		Polycrystalline silicon, containing by weight not less than 99.9999999% of silicon, for solar cells
2804 6190.13	含硅量≥99.9999999%的太阳能级多晶硅废碎料	4	30			17	千克	AP	Polycrystalline silicon waste or scrap, containing by weight of silicon ≥ 99.9999999% for solar cells
2804 6190.19[暂]	其他含硅量>99.9999999%的多晶硅(太阳能级多晶硅除外)	4	30	1		17	千克		Other polycrystalline silicon, containing by weight not less than 99.9999999% of silicon(other than Polycrystalline silicon for solar cells)
2804 6190.91	其他含硅量≥99.99%的硅废碎料(太阳能级多晶硅除外)	4	30			17	千克	AP	Other silicon waste or scrap, containing by weight not less than 99.99% of silicon (other than Polycrystalline silicon for solar cells)
2804 6190.92	含硅量≥99.99%的太阳能级多晶硅	4	30			17	千克		Polycrystalline silicon for solar cells, containing by weight not less than 99.99% of silicon
2804 6190.93	含硅量≥99.99%的太阳能级多晶硅废碎料	4	30			17	千克	AP	Polycrystalline silicon waste or scrap for solar cells, containing by weight not less than 99.99% of silicon
2804 6190.99	其他含硅量≥99.99%的硅(太阳能级多晶硅除外)	4	30			17	千克		Other silicon, containing by weight not less than 99.99% of silicon (other than Polycrystalline silicon for solar cells)
2804.6900	--其他	4	30			17	千克		--Other
	-磷:								-Phosphorus:
2804.7010	---黄磷(白磷)	5.5	30			17	千克	AB	---Yellow phosphorus （white phosphorus）
2804.7090	---其他	5.5	30			17	千克		---Other
2804 7090.10	红磷	5.5	30			17	千克	ABG	Red phosphorus
2804 7090.90	其他磷	5.5	30			17	千克		Other phosphorus
2804.8000	-砷	5.5	30			17	千克	X	-Arsenic

税则号列 Tariff Item	商品名称及备注	进口税率 最惠	普通	暂定	出口退税	增值税率	计量单位	监管条件	Article Description
	-硒:								-Selenium:
2804.9010	---经掺杂用于电子工业的硒晶体棒	4	17			17	千克		---Crystals doped for use in electronics,in the form of cylinders or rods
2804.9090 暂	---其他	5.5	30	0		17	千克		---Other
28.05	**碱金属、碱土金属；稀土金属、钪及钇，不论是否相互混合或相互熔合；汞：**								**Alkali or alkaline-earth metals; rare-earth metals, scandium and yttrium, whether or not intermixed or interalloyed; mercury:**
	-碱金属及碱土金属:								-Alkali metals or alkaline-earth metals:
2805.1100 暂	--钠	5.5	30	1		17	千克	AB	--Sodium
2805.1200 暂	--钙	5.5	30	1		17	千克		--Calcium
2805 1200.10 暂	高纯度钙(金属杂质（除镁外）含量＜1‰，硼含量小于十万分之一)	5.5	30	1		17	千克	3A	High-purity calcium, metal impurity（other than Magnesium）＜ 1‰, containing less than1/10^5 by weight of boron
2805 1200.90 暂	其他钙	5.5	30	1		17	千克		Other calcium
2805.1900 暂	--其他	5.5	30	1		17	千克		--Other
	-稀土金属、钪及钇，不论是否相互混合或相互熔合:								-Rare-earth metals, scandium and yttrium, whether or not intermixed or interalloyed:
	---稀土金属、钪及钇，未相互混合或相互熔合:								---Not intermixed or interalloyed:
2805.3011 暂	----钕	5.5	30	0		17	千克	4Bxy	----Neodymium
2805.3012 暂	----镝	5.5	30	0		17	千克	4Bxy	----Dysprosium
2805.3013 暂	----铽	5.5	30	0		17	千克	4Bxy	----Terbium
2805.3014 暂	----镧	5.5	30	0		17	千克	4Bxy	----Lanthanum
2805.3015 暂	----铈	5.5	30	0		17	千克		----Cerium
2805 3015.10 暂	颗粒＜500 微米的铈及其合金(含量≥97%,不论球形,椭球体,雾化,片状,研碎金属燃料;未相互混合或相互熔合)	5.5	30	0		17	千克	3B	Cerium and its alloys, granularity＜500 μm, containing more than 97% by weight of cerium, whether in the form of spheroid, ellipsoid, flakes, atomized or pulverized metallic fuel
2805 3015.90 暂	其他金属铈(未相互混合或相互熔合)	5.5	30	0		17	千克	4Bxy	Other Cerium metal, not intermixed or interalloyed
2805.3016 暂	----镨	5.5	30	0		17	千克	4Bxy	----Praseodymium
2805.3017 暂	----钇	5.5	30	0		17	千克	4Bxy	----Yttrium
2805.3019 暂	----其他	5.5	30	0		17	千克		----Other
2805 3019.13 暂	金属钐（未相互混合或相互熔合）	5.5	30	0		17	千克	4Bxy	Samarium metal, not intermixed or interalloyed
2805 3019.14 暂	金属铕（未相互混合或相互熔合）	5.5	30	0		17	千克	4Bxy	Europium metal, not intermixed or interalloyed
2805 3019.15 暂	金属钪（未相互混合或相互熔合）	5.5	30	0		17	千克	4Bxy	Scandium metal, not intermixed or interalloyed
2805 3019.90 暂	其他稀土金属（未相互混合或相互熔合）	5.5	30	0		17	千克	4Bxy	Other rare-earth metal, not intermixed or interalloyed
	---稀土金属、钪及钇，相互混合或相互熔合:								---Rare-earth metals, scandium and yttrium, intermixed or interalloyed:
2805.3021 暂	----电池级	5.5	30	0		17	千克		----Battery grade
2805 3021.10 暂	按重量计中重稀土总含量≥30%电池级的稀土金属、钪及钇(已相互混合或相互熔合)	5.5	30	0		17	千克	4Bxy	Measure the medium heavy tombarthite metal, scandium and yttrium of the battery level with total content of tombarthite ≥30% by weight（intermixed or interalloyed）
2805 3021.90 暂	其他电池级的稀土金属、钪及钇(已相互混合或相互熔合)	5.5	30	0		17	千克	4Bxy	The tombarthite metal, scandium and yttrium of other battery level（intermixed or interalloyed）
2805.3029 暂	----其他	5.5	30	0		17	千克		----Other
2805 3029.10 暂	按重量计中重稀土总含量≥30%的其他稀土金属、钪及钇(已相互混合或相互熔合)	5.5	30	0		17	千克	4Bxy	Measure the medium heavy tombarthite metal, scandium and yttrium of other battery level with total content of tombarthite ≥30% by weight（intermixed or interalloyed）
2805 3029.90 暂	其他稀土金属、钪及钇(已相互混合或相互熔合)	5.5	30	0		17	千克	4Bxy	Other tombarthite metal, scandium and yttrium（intermixed or interalloyed）

税则号列 Tariff Item	商品名称及备注	进口税率 最惠	进口税率 普通	进口税率 暂定	出口退税	增值税率	计量单位	监管条件	Article Description
2805.4000	-汞	5.5	17			17	千克	X	-Mercury
	第二分章　无机酸及非金属无机氧化物								**Ⅱ. INORGANIC ACIDS AND INORGANIC; OXYGEN COMPOUNDS OF NON-METALS**
28.06	**氯化氢（盐酸）；氯磺酸：**								**Hydrogen chloride（hydrochloric acid）; chorosulphuric acid:**
2806.1000	-氯化氢(盐酸)	5.5	80			17	千克	23AB	-Hydrogen chloride（hydrochloric acid）
2806.2000	-氯磺酸	5.5	40			17	千克	AB	-Chlorosulphuric acid
28.07	**硫酸；发烟硫酸：**								**Sulphuric acid; oleum:**
2807.0000[暂]	硫酸；发烟硫酸	5.5	35	1		17	千克		Sulphuric acid; oleum
2807 0000.10[暂]	硫酸	5.5	35	1		17	千克	32	Sulphuric acid
2807 0000.90[暂]	发烟硫酸	5.5	35	1		17	千克	AB	Oleum
28.08	**硝酸；磺硝酸：**								**Nitric acid; sulphonitric acids:**
2808.0000	硝酸；磺硝酸	5.5	40			17	千克		Nitric acid; sulphonitric acids
2808 0000.10	红发烟硝酸	5.5	40			17	千克	3A	Red fuming nitric acid
2808 0000.90	磺硝酸及其他硝酸	5.5	40			17	千克		Sulphonitric acids and other nitric acids
28.09	**五氧化二磷；磷酸；多磷酸，不论是否已有化学定义：**								**Diphosphorus pentaoxide; phosphoric acid; polyphosphoric acids, whether or not chemically defined:**
2809.1000	-五氧化二磷	1	8			17	千克	AB	-Diphosphorus pentaoxide
	-磷酸及多磷酸:								-Phosphoric acid and polyphosphoric acids:
	---磷酸及偏磷酸、焦磷酸:								---Phosphoric acid, metaphosphoric acid and pyrophosphoric acid：
2809.2011	----食品级磷酸	1	8			17	千克	AB	----Phosphoric acid, food grade
2809.2019	----其他	1	8			17	千克	B	----Other
2809.2090	----其他	5.5	35			17	千克		----Other
28.10	**硼的氧化物；硼酸：**								**Oxides of boron; boric acids:**
2810.0010	---硼的氧化物	5.5	30			17	千克		---Oxides of boron
2810.0020	---硼酸	5.5	30			17	千克	A	---Boric acids
28.11	**其他无机酸及非金属无机氧化物：**								**Other inorganic acids and other inorganic oxygen compounds of non-metals:**
	-其他无机酸:								-Other inorganic acids:
2811.1100	--氟化氢（氢氟酸）	5.5	35			17	千克	3A	--Hydrofluoric acid
	--其他:								--Other
2811.1910	---氢氰酸	5.5	35			17	千克	23	---Hydrocyanic acid
2811.1920	---硒化氢	5.5	35			17	千克	AB	---Hydrogen selenide
2811.1990	---其他	5.5	35			17	千克		---Other
2811 1990.10	氢碘酸	5.5	35			17	千克	ABG	hydriodic acid
2811 1990.20	砷酸、焦砷酸、偏砷酸	5.5	35			17	千克	X	Arsenic acid, Pyroarsenic acid, Meta-arsenic acid
2811 1990.90	其他无机酸	5.5	35			17	千克	AB	Other inorganic acids
	-其他非金属无机氧化物:								-Other inorganic oxygen compounds of non-metals:
2811.2100	--二氧化碳	5.5	30			17	千克	AB	--Carbon dioxide
	--二氧化硅:								--Silicon dioxide:
2811.2210	---硅胶	5.5	30		9	17	千克	AB	---Silica gel
2811.2290	---其他	5.5	30		9	17	千克	AB	---Other
2811.2900	--其他	5.5	30			17	千克		--Other
2811 2900.10	三氧化二砷、五氧化二砷[亚砷(酸)酐、砒霜、白砒、氧化亚砷、砷(酸)酐、三氧化砷]	5.5	30			17	千克	X	Arsenic trioxide, arsenic pentaoxide（arsenics anhydride arsenous oxide acid anhydride, white arsenic）
2811 2900.20	四氧化二氮	5.5	30			17	千克	3A	Dinitrogen tetroxide
2811 2900.90	其他非金属无机氧化物	5.5	30			17	千克		Other inorganic oxygen compounds of non-metals
	第三分章　非金属卤化物及硫化物								**Ⅲ. HALOGEN OR SULPHUR COMPOUNDS OF NONMETALS**
28.12	**非金属卤化物及卤氧化物：**								**Halides and halide oxides of non-metals:**
	-氯化物及氯氧化物:								-Chlorides and chloride oxides:

税则号列 Tariff Item	商品名称及备注	进口税率 最惠	普通	暂定	出口退税	增值税率	计量单位	监管条件	Article Description
2812.1010[暂]	---氯化亚砜	5.5	30	2		17	千克	23	---Sulphoxide chloride
2812.1020	---氧氯化磷（磷酰氯；三氯氧磷）	5.5	30			17	千克	23	---Phosphorus oxychloride（phosphoryl monochloride, phosphorus oxytrichloride）
2812.1030	---碳酰二氯(光气)	5.5	30			17	千克	23	---Carbonyl dichloride（phosgene）
	---非金属氯化物:								---Other chlorides of non-metals:
2812.1041	----一氯化硫(氯化硫)	5.5	30			17	千克	23	----Sulfur monochloride
2812.1042	----二氯化硫	5.5	30			17	千克	23	----Sulfur dichloride
2812.1043	----三氯化磷	5.5	30			17	千克	23	----Phosphorus trichloride
2812.1044	----三氯化砷	5.5	30			17	千克	23	----Arsenic trichloride
2812.1045	----五氯化磷	5.5	30			17	千克	23	----Phosphorus pentachloride
2812.1049	----其他	5.5	30			17	千克		----Other
2812.1090	---其他	5.5	30			17	千克		---Other
	-其他:								-Other:
	---氟化物及氟氧化物:								----Fluoride and oxyfluoride:
2812.9011	----三氟化氮	5.5	30			17	千克	AB	----Nitrogen trifluoride
2812.9019	----其他	5.5	30			17	千克		----Other
2812 9019.10	三氟化氯	5.5	30			17	千克	3A	Chlorine trifluoride
2812 9019.20	三氟化砷(氟化亚砷)	5.5	30			17	千克	X	Arsenic trifuoride (Arsenic Fluoride)
2812 9019.30	硫酰氟	5.5	30			17	千克	S	Sulfuryl fluoride
2812 9019.90	其他氟化物及氟氧化物	5.5	30			17	千克		Other fluoride
2812.9090	---其他	5.5	30			17	千克		----Other
2812 9090.10	三溴化砷,三碘化砷(溴化亚砷,碘化亚砷)	5.5	30			17	千克	X	Arsenic tribromide, arsenic triiodide (Arsenic Bromide , Arsenous Iodide)
2812 9090.90	其他非金属卤化物及卤氧化物	5.5	30			17	千克		Other non-metal and metalloid halides
28.13	**非金属硫化物；商品三硫化二磷:**								**Sulphides of non-metals; commercial phosphorus trisuiphides:**
2813.1000	-二硫化碳	5.5	30			17	千克	X	-Carbon disulphide
2813.9000	-其他	5.5	30			17	千克		-Other
2813 9000.10	五硫化二磷	5.5	30			17	千克	23	Phosphorus pentasulfide
2813 9000.20	三硫化二磷	5.5	30			17	千克	AB	Phosphorus trisulfide
2813 9000.90	其他非金属硫化物	5.5	30			17	千克		Other sulphides of non-metals
	第四分章　无机碱和金属氧化物、氢氧化物及过氧化物								**Ⅳ. INORGANIC BASES AND OXIDES, HYDROXIDES AND PEROXIDES OF METALS**
28.14	**氨及氨水:**								**Ammonia, anhydrous or in aqueous solution:**
2814.1000[暂]	-氨	5.5	35	0		17	千克	AB	-Anhydrous ammonia
2814.2000[暂]	-氨水	5.5	35	0		17	千克		-Ammonia in aqueous solution
2814 2000.10[暂]	氨水(含量≥10%)	5.5	35	0		17	千克	AB	Ammonia water(containing more than 10%)
2814 2000.90[暂]	其他氨水	5.5	35	0		17	千克		Other ammonia water
28.15	**氢氧化钠（烧碱）；氢氧化钾（苛性钾）；过氧化钠及过氧化钾:**								**Sodium hydroxide(caustic soda); potassium hydroxide(caustic potash);peroxides or sodium or postassium:**
	-氢氧化钠（烧碱）:								-Sodium hydroxide（caustic soda）:
2815.1100	--固体	10	35			17	千克	ABG	--Solid
2815.1200	--水溶液（氢氧化钠浓溶液及液体烧碱）	8	35			17	千克	ABG	--In aqueous solution（soda lye or liquid soda）
2815.2000	-氢氧化钾(苛性钾)	5.5	30		13	17	千克	AB	-Potassium hydroxide（caustic potash）
2815.3000	-过氧化钠及过氧化钾	5.5	30			17	千克	AB	-Peroxides of sodium or potassium
28.16	**氢氧化镁及过氧化镁；锶或钡的氧化物、氢氧化物及过氧化物:**								**Hydroxide and peroxide of magnesium; oxides, hydroxides and peroxides, of strontium or barium:**
2816.1000	-氢氧化镁及过氧化镁	5.5	30			17	千克		-Hydroxide and peroxide of magnesium
2816 1000.10	过氧化镁	5.5	30			17	千克	AB	Peroxide of magnesium
2816 1000.90	氢氧化镁	5.5	30			17	千克		Hydroxide
2816.4000[暂]	-锶或钡的氧化物、氢氧化物及过氧化物	5.5	30	2		17	千克		-Oxides, hydroxides and peroxides, of strontium or barium

税则号列 Tariff Item	商品名称及备注	进口税率			出口退税	增值税率	计量单位	监管条件	Article Description
		最惠	普通	暂定					
28.17	**氧化锌及过氧化锌:**								**Zinc oxide; Zinc peroxide:**
2817.0010	---氧化锌	5.5	40			17	千克	AB	---Zinc oxide
2817.0090	---过氧化锌	5.5	30			17	千克	AB	---Zinc peroxide
28.18	**人造刚玉，不论是否已有化学定义；氧化铝；氢氧化铝:**								**Artificial corundum, whether or not chemically defined; aluminium oxide; aluminium hydroxide:**
	-人造刚玉，不论是否已有化学定义:								-Artificial corundum, whether or not chemically defined:
2818.1010	---棕刚玉	5.5	20			17	千克		---Brown fused alumina
2818.1090	---其他	5.5	20			17	千克		---Other
2818.2000[暂]	-氧化铝，但人造刚玉除外	8	30	0		17	千克	7	-Aluminium oxide, other than artificial corundum
2818.3000	-氢氧化铝	5.5	30			17	千克		-Aluminium hydroxide
28.19	**铬的氧化物及氢氧化物:**								**Chromium oxides and hydroxides:**
2819.1000	-三氧化铬	5.5	20			17	千克	AB	-Chromium trioxide
2819.9000	-其他	5.5	30			17	千克		-Other
28.20	**锰的氧化物:**								**Manganese oxide:**
2820.1000	-二氧化锰	5.5	40			17	千克		-Manganese dioxide
2820.9000	-其他	5.5	30			17	千克		-Other
28.21	**铁的氧化物及氢氧化物；土色料，按重量计三氧化二铁含量在70%及以上:**								**Iron oxides and hydroxides; earth colours containing 70%or more by weight of combined iron evaluated as Fe_2O_3:**
2821.1000	-铁的氧化物及氢氧化物	5.5	30			17	千克		-Iron oxides and hydroxides
2821.2000	-土色料	5.5	45			17	千克		-Earth colours
28.22	**钴的氧化物及氢氧化物；商品氧化钴:**								**Cobalt oxides and hydroxides; commercial cobalt oxides:**
2822.0010[暂]	---四氧化三钴	5.5	30	2	13	17	千克	4xy	---Cobalt tetroxide
2822.0090[暂]	---其他	5.5	30	2		17	千克	4xy	---Other
28.23	**钛的氧化物:**								**Titanium oxides:**
2823.0000	钛的氧化物	5.5	30			17	千克		Titanium oxides
28.24	**铅的氧化物；铅丹及铅橙:**								**Lead oxides; red lead and orange lead:**
2824.1000	-一氧化铅(铅黄、黄丹)	5.5	30			17	千克	X	-Lead monoxide（litharge, massicot）
	-其他:								-Other:
2824.9010	---铅丹及铅橙	5.5	45			17	千克	X	---Red lead and orange lead
2824.9090	---其他	5.5	30			17	千克		---Other
28.25	**肼（联氨）、胲（羟胺）及其无机盐；其他无机碱；其他金属氧化物、氢氧化物及过氧化物:**								**Hydrazine and hydroxylamine and their inorganic salts; other inorganic bases; othermetal oxides, hydroxides and peroxides:**
	-肼（联氨）、胲（羟胺）及其无机盐:								-Hydrazine and hydroxylamine and their inorganic salts:
2825.1010	---水合肼	5.5	30			17	千克		---Hydrazine hydrate
2825 1010.10	纯度70%及以上的水合肼	5.5	30			17	千克	3A	Hydrazine hydrate, Purity of 70% and above
2825 1010.90	纯度70%以下的水合肼	5.5	30			17	千克	AB	Hydrazine hydrate, Purity of 70% and below
2825.1020	---硫酸羟胺	5.5	30			17	千克	AB	---Hydroxylamine sulfate
2825.1090	---其他	5.5	30			17	千克		---Other
	-锂的氧化物及氢氧化物:								-Lithium oxide and hydroxide:
2825.2010	---氢氧化锂	5.5	30			17	千克	AB	---Lithium hydroxide
2825.2090	---其他	5.5	30			17	千克		---Other
	-钒的氧化物及氢氧化物:								-Vanadium oxides and hydroxides:
2825.3010	---五氧化二钒	5.5	30			17	千克	4ABxy	---Divanadium pentaoxide
2825.3090	---其他	5.5	30			17	千克	4xy	---Other
2825.4000[暂]	-镍的氧化物及氢氧化物	5.5	30	2		17	千克		-Nickel oxides and hydroxides
2825.5000	-铜的氧化物及氢氧化物	5.5	30			17	千克		-Copper oxides and hydroxides
2825.6000	-锗的氧化物及二氧化锆	5.5	30			17	千克		-Germanium oxides and zirconium dioxide
2825 6000.01	锗的氧化物	5.5	30			17	千克	4xy	Germanium oxides
2825 6000.90	二氧化锆	5.5	30			17	千克	3	Zirconium dioxide

税则号列 Tariff Item	商品名称及备注	进口税率			出口退税	增值税率	计量单位	监管条件	Article Description
		最惠	普通	暂定					
2825.7000	-钼的氧化物及氢氧化物	5.5	30			17	千克	4xy	-Molybdenum oxides and hydroxides
2825.8000	-锑的氧化物	5.5	30			17	千克	4xBy	-Antimony oxides
	-其他:								-Other:
	---钨的氧化物及氢氧化物:								---Tungsten oxides and hydroxides:
2825.9011	----钨酸	5.5	30			17	千克	4xy	----Tungstic acid
2825.9012	----三氧化钨	5.5	30			17	千克	4xy	----Tungstic oxide
2825.9019	----其他	5.5	30			17	千克		---Other
2825 9019.10	蓝色氧化钨	5.5	30			17	千克	4xy	Blue tungsten trioxide
2825 9019.90	其他钨的氧化物及氢氧化物	5.5	30			17	千克		Other tungsten trioxide and hydroxides
	---铋的氧化物及氢氧化物:								---Bismuth oxides and hydroxides:
2825.9021	---三氧化二铋	5.5	30			17	千克	4ABxy	---Dibismuth trioxide
2825.9029	---其他	5.5	30			17	千克	4ABxy	---Other
	---锡的氧化物及氢氧化物:								---Tin oxides and hydroxides:
2825.9031	---二氧化锡	5.5	30			17	千克	4ABxy	---Tin dioxide
2825.9039	---其他	5.5	30			17	千克	4ABxy	---Other
	---铌的氧化物及氢氧化物:								---Niobium oxides and hydroxides:
2825.9041	----一氧化铌	5.5	30			17	千克	A	----Niobium monoxide
2825.9049	----其他	5.5	30			17	千克	AB	----Other
2825.9090	---其他	5.5	30			17	千克	AB	---Other
	第五分章 无机酸盐、无机过氧酸盐及金属酸盐、金属过氧酸盐								**V. SALTS AND PEROXYSALTS, OFINORGANIC ACIDS AND METALS**
28.26	氟化物；氟硅酸盐、氟铝酸盐及其他氟络盐:								**Fluorides; fluorosilicates，fluoroaluminates and other complex fluorine salts:**
	-氟化物:								-Fluorides:
	--氟化铝:								--Of aluminium:
2826.1210	---无水氟化铝	5.5	30			17	千克	AB	---Aluminium fluoride(anhy-drous)
2826.1290	---其他	5.5	30			17	千克	AB	---Other
	--其他:								--Other
2826.1910	---铵的氟化物	5.5	30			17	千克		---Of ammonium
2826 1910.10	氟化氢铵	5.5	30			17	千克	3A	Ammonium hydrogen fluoride
2826 1910.90	其他铵的氟化物	5.5	30			17	千克		Other ammonium fluorid
2826.1920	---钠的氟化物	5.5	30			17	千克		---Of sodium
2826 1920.10	氟化钠	5.5	30			17	千克	3AB	Sodium fluoride
2826 1920.20	氟化氢钠	5.5	30			17	千克	3A	Sodium hydrogen difluoride
2826 1920.90	其他钠的氟化物	5.5	30			17	千克		Other sodium fluorid
2826.1990	---其他	5.5	30			17	千克		---Other
2826 1990.10	氟化钾	5.5	30			17	千克	3A	Potassium fluoride
2826 1990.20	氟化氢钾	5.5	30			17	千克	3A	Potassium hydrogen fluoride
2826 1990.30	氟化铅，四氟化铅，氟化镉	5.5	30			17	千克	X	Lead fluoride, lead tetrafluoride, cadmium fluoride
2826 1990.90	其他氟化物	5.5	30			17	千克		Other fluorides
2826.3000	-六氟铝酸钠(人造冰晶石)	5.5	30		13	17	千克		-Sodium hexafluoroaluminate（synthetic cryolite）
	-其他:								-Other:
2826.9010	---氟硅酸盐	5.5	30			17	千克		---Fluorosilicates
2826.9090	---其他	5.5	30			17	千克		---Other
2826 9090.10	氟钽酸钾	5.5	30			17	千克		Potassium fluotantalate
2826 9090.30	氟硼酸铅，氟硼酸镉	5.5	30			17	千克	X	Lead fluoborate, cadmium fluoroborate
2826 9090.90	氟铝酸盐及其他氟络盐	5.5	30			17	千克		Fluoroaluminate, Other fluorine complex salt
28.27	氯化物、氯氧化物及氢氧基氯化物；溴化物及溴氧化物；碘化物及碘氧化物:								**Chlorides, chloride oxides and chloride hydroxides; bromides and bromide oxides; iodides and iodide oxides:**
	-氯化铵:								-Ammonium chloride:
2827.1010	---肥料用	4	11			17	千克	G	---For use as fertilizer
2827.1090	---其他	5.5	30			17	千克	G	---Other
2827.2000	-氯化钙	5.5	50		9	17	千克	AB	-Calcium chloride

税则号列 Tariff Item	商品名称及备注	进口税率 最惠	进口税率 普通	进口税率 暂定	出口退税	增值税率	计量单位	监管条件	Article Description
	-其他氯化物:								-Other chlorides:
2827.3100	--氯化镁	5.5	30			17	千克	AB	--Of magnesium
2827.3200	--氯化铝	5.5	30			17	千克		--Of aluminium
2827.3500	--氯化镍	5.5	30			17	千克		--Of nickel
	--其他:								--Other:
2827.3910	---氯化锂	5.5	30			17	千克		---Lithium chloride
2827.3920	---氯化钡	5.5	30			17	千克	AB	---Barium chloride
2827.3930	---氯化钴	5.5	30			17	千克	4ABxy	---Cobalt chloride
2827.3990	---其他	5.5	30			17	千克	AB	---Other
	-氯氧化物及氢氧基氯化物:								-Chloride oxides and chloride hydroxides:
2827.4100	--铜的氯氧化物及氢氧基氯化物	5.5	30			17	千克		--Of copper
	--其他:								--Other:
2827.4910	---锆的氯氧化物及氢氧基氯化物	5.5	30			17	千克		---Of zirconium
2827.4990	---其他	5.5	30			17	千克		---Other
	-溴化物及溴氧化物:								-Bromides and bromide oxides:
2827.5100	--溴化钠及溴化钾	5.5	30			17	千克		--Bromides of sodium or of potassium
2827.5900	--其他	5.5	30			17	千克		--Other
2827.6000	-碘化物及碘氧化物	5.5	30			17	千克	AB	-Iodides and iodide oxides
28.28	**次氯酸盐;商品次氯酸钙;亚氯酸盐;次溴酸盐:**								**Hypochlorites ; commercial calcium hypochlorite ; chlorites ; hypobromites :**
2828.1000	-商品次氯酸钙及其他钙的次氯酸盐	12	80		5	17	千克		-Commercial calcium hypochlorite and other calcium hypochlorites
2828.9000	-其他	5.5	30			17	千克	AB	-Other
28.29	**氯酸盐及高氯酸盐;溴酸盐及过溴酸盐;碘酸盐及高碘酸盐:**								**Chlorates and perchlorates; bromates and perbromates; iodates and periodates:**
	-氯酸盐:								-Chlorates:
2829.1100	--氯酸钠	12	30			17	千克	AB	--Of sodium
	--其他:								--Other:
2829.1910	---氯酸钾(洋硝)	5.5	20			17	千克	9B	---Potassium chlorate
2829.1990	---其他	5.5	30			17	千克		---Other
2829.9000	-其他	5.5	30			17	千克		-Other
2829 9000.10	颗粒＜500微米的球形高氯酸铵	5.5	30			17	千克	3A	Ammonium perchlorate, spheroid, granularity less than 500μm
2829 9000.90	其他高氯酸盐,溴酸盐等(包括过溴酸盐、碘酸盐及高碘酸盐)	5.5	30			17	千克		Other perchlorates; bromates and perbromates; iodates and periodates
28.30	**硫化物;多硫化物,不论是否已有化学定义:**								**Sulphides; polysulphides, whether or not chemically defined:**
	-钠的硫化物:								-Sodium sulphides:
2830.1010	---硫化钠	5.5	40			17	千克	3A	---Sodium sulphide
2830.1090	---其他	5.5	30			17	千克		---Other
	-其他:								-Other:
2830.9020	---硫化锑	5.5	45			17	千克	B	---Antimony sulphide
2830.9030	---硫化钴	5.5	30			17	千克		---Cobalt sulphide
2830.9090	---其他	5.5	30			17	千克		---Other
28.31	**连二亚硫酸盐及次硫酸盐:**								**Dithionites and sulphoxylates:**
	-钠的连二亚硫酸盐及次硫酸盐:								-Of sodium:
2831.1010	---钠的连二亚硫酸盐	5.5	30			17	千克	AB	---Sodium dithionites
2831.1020	---钠的次硫酸盐	5.5	30			17	千克		---Sodium sulphoxylates
2831.9000	-其他	5.5	30			17	千克		-Other
28.32	**亚硫酸盐;硫代硫酸盐:**								**Sulphites; thiosulphates:**
2832.1000	-钠的亚硫酸盐	5.5	30			17	千克		-Sodium sulphites
2832.2000	-其他亚硫酸盐	5.5	30			17	千克	AB	-Other sulphites
2832.3000	-硫代硫酸盐	5.5	30			17	千克		-Thiosulphates

税则号列 Tariff Item	商品名称及备注	进口税率 最惠	普通	暂定	出口退税	增值税率	计量单位	监管条件	Article Description
28.33	硫酸盐；矾；过硫酸盐：								**Sulphates;alums;peroxosulphates (persul-phates):**
	-钠的硫酸盐：								-Sodium sulphates:
2833.1100	--硫酸钠	5.5	40			17	千克	4xy	--Disodium sulphate
2833.1900	--其他	5.5	30			17	千克		--Other
	-其他硫酸盐：								-Other sulphates:
2833.2100	--硫酸镁	5.5	30			17	千克	AB	--Of magnesium
2833.2200	--硫酸铝	5.5	30			17	千克		--Of aluminium
2833.2400	--镍的硫酸盐	5.5	30			17	千克		--Of nickel
2833.2500	--铜的硫酸盐	5.5	30			17	千克		--Of copper
2833.2700	--硫酸钡	5.5	30			17	千克	G	--Of barium
	--其他：								--Other:
2833.2910	---硫酸亚铁	5.5	45			17	千克	AB	---Ferrous sulphate
2833.2920	---铬的硫酸盐	5.5	30			17	千克		---Chromium sulphates
2833.2930	---硫酸锌	5.5	30		5	17	千克	AB	---Zine sulphate
2833.2990	---其他	5.5	30			17	千克		---Other
2833 2990.10	硫酸钴	5.5	30			17	千克	4ABxy	Cobalt sulphate
2833 2990.90	其他硫酸盐	5.5	30			17	千克	AB	Other sulphates
	-矾：								-Alums:
2833.3010	---钾铝矾	5.5	45			17	千克		---Potassium aluminum sulfate
2833.3090	---其他	5.5	30			17	千克		---Other
2833.4000	-过硫酸盐	5.5	30			17	千克		-Peroxosulphates（persulphates）
28.34	亚硝酸盐；硝酸盐：								**Nitrites ；nitrates ：**
2834.1000	-亚硝酸盐	5.5	30			17	千克	AB	-Nitrites
	-硝酸盐：								-Nitrates:
	--硝酸钾：								--Of potassium:
2834.2110[暂]	---肥料用	4	11	1		17	千克	AB	---For use as fertilizer
2834.2190	---其他	5.5	30			17	千克	AB	---Other
	--其他：								--Other:
2834.2910	---硝酸钴	5.5	30			17	千克	AB	---Of cobalt
2834.2990	---其他	5.5	30			17	千克		---Other
2834 2990.01[暂]	硝酸钡	5.5	30	2		17	千克	AB	Barium nitrate
2834 2990.90	其他硝酸盐	5.5	30			17	千克		Other nitrates
28.35	次磷酸盐、亚磷酸盐及磷酸盐；多磷酸盐，不论是否已有化学定义：								**Phosphinates(hypophosphites),phosphonates (phosphites) phosphates and polyphosphates, whether or not chemically defined:**
2835.1000	-次磷酸盐及亚磷酸盐	5.5	20			17	千克		-Phosphinates（hypophosphites）and phosphonates（phosphites）
	-磷酸盐：								-Phosphates:
2835.2200	--磷酸一钠及磷酸二钠	5.5	20			17	千克		--Of mono-or disodium
2835.2400	--钾的磷酸盐	5.5	20			17	千克		--Of potassium
	--正磷酸氢钙(磷酸二钙)：								--Calcium hydrogenorthophosphate(dicalcium phosphate):
2835.2510	---饲料级的	5.5	20			17	千克	AB	---Feed grade
2835.2520	---食品级的	5.5	20		5	17	千克	AB	---Food grade
2835.2590	---其他	5.5	20			17	千克		---Other
2835.2600	--其他磷酸钙	5.5	20			17	千克		--Other phosphates of calcium
	--其他：								--Other:
2835.2910	---磷酸三钠	5.5	20			17	千克	AB	---Trisodium phosphate
2835.2990	---其他	5.5	20			17	千克	A	---Other
	-多磷酸盐：								-Polyphosphates:
	--三磷酸钠(三聚磷酸钠)：								--Sodium triphosphate（sodium tripoly phosphate）：
2835.3110	---食品级的	5.5	20			17	千克	AB	---Food grade
2835.3190	---其他	5.5	20			17	千克		---Other
	--其他：								--Other:
	---六偏磷酸钠：								---Sodium hexametaphosphate :

税则号列 Tariff Item	商品名称及备注	进口税率 最惠	普通	暂定	出口退税	增值税率	计量单位	监管条件	Article Description
2835.3911	----食品级的	5.5	20		5	17	千克	AB	----Food grade
2835.3919	----其他	5.5	20			17	千克		----Other
2835.3990	---其他	5.5	20			17	千克		---Other
28.36	**碳酸盐；过碳酸盐；含氨基甲酸铵的商品碳酸铵：**								**Carbonates;peroxocarbonates(percarbonates);commercial ammonium carbonate containing ammonium carbamate:**
2836.2000	-碳酸钠(纯碱)	5.5	35		9	17	千克	AG	-Disodium carbonate
2836.3000	-碳酸氢钠(小苏打)	5.5	45		9	17	千克	ABG	-Sodium hydrogencarbonate（sodium bicarbonate）
2836.4000	-钾的碳酸盐	5.5	30			17	千克		-Potassium carbonates
2836.5000	-碳酸钙	5.5	45			17	千克	AB	-Calcium carbonate
2836.6000[暂]	-碳酸钡	5.5	40	1		17	千克		-Barium carbonate
	-其他:								-Other:
2836.9100[暂]	--锂的碳酸盐	5.5	30	2		17	千克		--Lithium carbonates
2836.9200[暂]	--锶的碳酸盐	5.5	30	2		17	千克		--Strontium carbonate
	--其他:								--Other:
2836.9910	---碳酸镁	5.5	45			17	千克	AB	---Magnesium carbonate
2836.9930[暂]	---碳酸钴	5.5	30	2		17	千克	4xy	---Cobalt carbonate
2836.9940	---商品碳酸铵及其他铵的碳酸盐	5.5	30			17	千克		---Commercial ammonium carbonate and other ammonium carbonates
2836.9950	---碳酸锆	5.5	30			17	千克	AB	---Zirconium carbonate
2836.9990	---其他	5.5	30		13	17	千克	A	---Other
28.37	**氰化物、氧氰化物及氰络合物：**								**Cyanides, cyanide oxides and complex cyanides ：**
	-氰化物及氧氰化物:								-Cyanides and cyanide oxides:
	--氰化钠及氧氰化钠:								--Of sodium:
2837.1110	---氰化钠	5.5	20			17	千克	X23	---Sodium cyanide
2837.1120	---氧氰化钠	5.5	30			17	千克		---Sodium cyanide oxide
	--其他:								--Other:
2837.1910	---氰化钾	5.5	20			17	千克	23X	---Potassium cyanide
2837.1990	---其他	5.5	30			17	千克		---Other
2837 1990.11	氰化锌，氰化亚铜，氰化铜（氰化高铜）	5.5	30			17	千克	X	Zinc cyanide, cuprous cyanide, copper cyanide (cupric cyanide)
2837 1990.12	氰化镍，氰化钙（氰化亚镍）	5.5	30			17	千克	X	Nickel cyanide, calcium cyanide (Nickel Cyanide)
2837 1990.13	氰化钡，氰化镉，氰化铅	5.5	30			17	千克	X	Barium cyanide, cadium cyanide, lead cyanide
2837 1990.14	氰化钴[氰化钴(Ⅱ)\氰化钴(Ⅲ)]	5.5	30			17	千克	X	Cobalt cyanide［Cobalt cyanide(Ⅱ)\ Cobalt cyanide(Ⅲ)］
2837 1990.90	其他氰化物及氧氰化物	5.5	30			17	千克		Other cyanides and cyanide oxides
2837.2000	-氰络合物	5.5	30			17	千克		-Complex cyanides
2837 2000.11	氰化镍钾，氰化钠铜锌（氰化钾镍，镍氰化钾，铜盐）	5.5	30			17	千克	X	Potassium nickel cyanide, Sodium copper-zinc (potassium nickel cyanide, nickel potassium cyanide, cyanide salt)
2837 2000.12	氰化亚铜(三)钠，氰化亚铜(三)钾（紫铜盐、紫铜矾、氰化铜钠、氰化亚铜钾、亚铜氰化钾）	5.5	30			17	千克	X	Sodium copper cyanide; copper potassium cyanide,(sodium copper cyanide, copper sodium cyanide, sodium copper cyanide, potassiuM tetracyanocuprate (I),copper potassium cyanide)
2837 2000.90	其他氰络合物	5.5	30			17	千克		Other complex cyanide
28.39	**硅酸盐；商品碱金属硅酸盐：**								**Silicates ；commercial alkali metal silicates ：**
	-钠盐:								-Of sodium:
2839.1100	--偏硅酸钠	5.5	40			17	千克		--Sodium metasilicates
	--其他 ：								--Other
2839.1910	---硅酸钠	5.5	30			17	千克	A	---Sodium silicate
2839.1990	---其他钠盐	5.5	30			17	千克		---Other
2839.9000	-其他	5.5	30			17	千克		-Other
2839 9000.01[暂]	锆的硅酸盐	5.5	30	2		17	千克		Zirconium silicate
2839 9000.10	硅酸铅	5.5	30			17	千克	X	Lead silicate
2839 9000.90	其他硅酸盐；商品碱金属硅酸盐	5.5	30			17	千克		Other silicate, commercial alkali metal silicates

税则号列 Tariff Item	商品名称及备注	进口税率			出口退税	增值税率	计量单位	监管条件	Article Description
		最惠	普通	暂定					
28.40	**硼酸盐及过硼酸盐:**								**Borates; peroxoborates（perborates）:**
	-四硼酸钠（精炼硼砂）:								-Disodium tetraborate（refined borax）:
2840.1100[暂]	--无水四硼酸钠	5.5	20	2		17	千克		--Anhydrous
2840.1900[暂]	--其他	5.5	20	2		17	千克		--Other
2840.2000	-其他硼酸盐	5.5	30			17	千克		-Other borates
2840.3000	-过硼酸盐	5.5	30			17	千克		-Peroxoborates（perborates）
28.41	**金属酸盐及过金属酸盐:**								**Salts of oxometanic or peroxometallicacids:**
2841.3000	-重铬酸钠	5.5	20			17	千克	AB	-Sodium dichromate
2841.5000	-其他铬酸盐及重铬酸盐；过铬酸盐	5.5	30			17	千克		-Other chromates and dichromates; peroxochromates
	-亚锰酸盐、锰酸盐及高锰酸盐:								-Manganites, manganates and perman ganates :
2841.6100	--高锰酸钾	5.5	30			17	千克	23AB	--Potassium permanganate
	--其他:								--Other:
2841.6910	---锰酸锂	5.5	30			17	千克		---Lithium manganate
2841.6990	---其他	5.5	30			17	千克		---Other
	-钼酸盐:								-Molybdates:
2841.7010	---钼酸铵	5.5	30			17	千克	4xy	---Ammonium molybdates
2841.7090	---其他	5.5	30			17	千克	4xy	---Other
	-钨酸盐:								-Tungstates（wolframates）:
2841.8010	---仲钨酸铵	5.5	30			17	千克	4xy	---Ammonium paratungstate
2841.8020	---钨酸钠	5.5	30			17	千克	4xy	---Sodium tungstate
2841.8030	---钨酸钙	5.5	30			17	千克	4xy	---Calcium wolframate
2841.8040	---偏钨酸铵	5.5	30			17	千克	4xy	---Ammonium metatungstate
2841.8090	---其他	5.5	30			17	千克		---Other
2841.9000	-其他	5.5	30			17	千克		-Other
2841 9000.01[暂]	钴酸锂	5.5	30	2	13	17	千克		Lithium Cobalt oxide
2841 9000.90	其他金属酸盐及过金属酸盐	5.5	30			17	千克		Other salts of oxometallic or peroxometallic acids
28.42	**其他无机酸盐或过氧酸盐（包括不论是否已有化学定义的硅铝酸盐），但叠氮化物除外:**								**Other Salts of inorganic acids or peroxoacids（including aluminosilicates whether or not chemically defined）, other than azides:**
2842.1000	-硅酸复盐及硅酸络盐，（包括不论是否已有化学定义的硅铝酸盐）	5.5	30			17	千克	AB	-Double or complex silicates, including aluminosilicates whether or not chemically defined
	-其他:								-Other:
	---雷酸盐、氰酸盐及硫氰酸盐 :								---Fulminates, cyanates and thiocyanates
2842.9011	----硫氰酸钠	5.5	30			17	千克	A	----Sodium thiocyanate
2842.9019	----其他	5.5	30			17	千克		----Other
2842 9019.10	其他硫氰酸盐	5.5	30			17	千克	AB	Other thiocyanate
2842 9019.90	雷酸盐及氰酸盐	5.5	30			17	千克		Fulminate and cyanate
2842.9020	---碲化镉	5.5	30			17	千克	X	---Cadmium telluride
2842.9030	---锂镍钴锰氧化物	5.5	30			17	千克	AB	---Lithium nickel cobalt manganese oxides
2842.9040	---磷酸铁锂	5.5	30			17	千克	A	---Lithium Iron Phosphate
2842.9050	---硒酸盐及亚硒酸盐	5.5	30			17	千克	AB	---Selenium and selenite
2842.9090	---其他	5.5	30			17	千克		---Other
2842 9090.13	亚砷酸钠、亚砷酸钾、亚砷酸钙（偏亚砷酸钠）	5.5	30			17	千克	X	Sodium arsenite, Potassium arsenite,Calcium arsenite (Sodium meta-arsenite)
2842 9090.14	亚砷酸锶、亚砷酸钡、亚砷酸铁	5.5	30			17	千克	X	Strontium arsenite, Barium arsenite Ferric arsenite
2842 9090.15	亚砷酸铜、亚砷酸锌、亚砷酸铅（亚砷酸氢铜）	5.5	30			17	千克	X	Copper arsenite, Zinc arsenite, Lead arsenite(Cupric arsenite)
2842 9090.16	亚砷酸锑、砷酸铵、砷酸氢二铵	5.5	30			17	千克	X	Antimony arsenite, Ammonium arsenate, Diammonium hydrogen arsenate
2842 9090.17	砷酸钠、砷酸氢二钠、砷酸二氢钠（砷酸三钠）	5.5	30			17	千克	X	Sodium arsenate ,Sodium arsenate dibasic, Sodium arsenate monobasic(Trisodium Arsenate)
2842 9090.18	砷酸钾、砷酸二氢钾、砷酸镁	5.5	30			17	千克	X	Potassium arsenate, potassium dihydrogen arsenate, Magnesium arsenate
2842 9090.19	砷酸钙、砷酸钡、砷酸铁（砷酸	5.5	30			17	千克	X	Calcium arsenate, Barium arsenate, Ferric arsenate,

税则号列 Tariff Item	商品名称及备注	进口税率 最惠	普通	暂定	出口退税	增值税率	计量单位	监管条件	Article Description
	三钙)								(Tricalcium arsenate)
2842 9090.21	砷酸亚铁、砷酸铜、砷酸锌	5.5	30			17	千克	X	Ferrous arsenate, Cupric arsenate, Zinc arsenate
2842 9090.22	砷酸铅、砷酸锑、偏砷酸钠	5.5	30			17	千克	X	Lead arsenate, Antimony arsenate, Sodium metaarsenate
2842 9090.23	硒化铅、硒化镉	5.5	30			17	千克	X	Lead Selenide, Cadmium selenide
2842 9090.90	其他无机酸盐及过氧酸盐(迭氮化物除外)	5.5	30			17	千克	AB	Other salts of inorganic acids or peroxoacids (other than azides)
	第六分章 杂项产品								**Ⅵ. MISCELLANEOUS**
28.43	**胶态贵金属;贵金属的无机或有机化合物,不论是否已有化学定义;贵金属汞齐:**								**Colloidal precious metals; inorganic or organic compounds of precious metals, whether or not chemically defined; amalgams of precious metals:**
2843.1000	-胶态贵金属	5.5	30			17	克		-Colloidal precious metals
	-银化合物:								-Silver compounds:
2843.2100	--硝酸银	5.5	30			17	克	AB	--Silver nitrate
2843.2900	--其他	5.5	30			17	克		--Other
2843 2900.10	氰化银、氰化银钾、亚砷酸银(银氰化钾、砷酸银)	5.5	30			17	克	X	Silver cyanide, Potassium silver cyanide, Silver arsenite(Potassium silver cyanide, Silver arsenate)
2843 2900.90	其他银化合物(不论是否已有化学定义)	5.5	30			17	克		Other silver compounds, whether or not chemically defined
2843.3000	-金化合物	5.5	30			17	克		-Gold compounds
2843 3000.10	氰化金、氰化金钾等[包括氰化亚金(Ⅰ)钾、氰化亚金(Ⅲ)钾]	5.5	30			17	克	JX	Gold cyanide gold potassium cyanide, including cyanide gold(Ⅰ) potassium, cyanide gold(III) potassium
2843 3000.90	其他金化合物(不论是否已有化学定义)	5.5	30			17	克	J	Other gold compounds, whether or not chemically defined
2843.9000	-其他贵金属化合物;贵金属汞齐	5.5	30			17	克		-Other compounds; amalgams
2843 9000.10	氯化钯	5.5	30			17	克	G	Palladium chloride
2843 9000.20	氯化铂	5.5	30			17	克	4xy	Platinum chloride
2843 9000.30	其他铂化合物	5.5	30			17	克	4xy	Other platinum compounds
2843 9000.90	其他贵金属化合物,贵金属汞齐(不论是否已有化学定义)	5.5	30			17	克	4xy	Other precious metal compounds or precious metals amalgam, or not chemically defined
28.44	**放射性化学元素及放射性同位素(包括可裂变或可转换的化学元素及同位素)及其化合物;含上述产品的混合物及残渣:**								**Radioactive chemical elements and radioactive isotopes (including the fissile or fertile chemical elements and isotopes) and their compounds; mixtures and residues containing these products:**
2844.1000	-天然铀及其化合物;含天然铀或天然铀化合物的合金、分散体(包括金属陶瓷)、陶瓷产品及混合物	5.5	30			17	克/百万贝可	23	-Natural uranium and its compounds; alloys, dispersions (including cermets), ceramic products and mixtures containing natural uranium or natural uranium compouds
2844.2000	-U235浓缩铀及其化合物;钚及其化合物;含U235浓缩铀、钚或它们的化合物的合金、分散体(包括金属陶瓷)、陶瓷产品及混合物	5.5	30			17	克/百万贝可	23	-Uranium enriched in U235 and its compounds; plutonium and its compounds; alloys dispersion (including cermets), ceramic products and mixtures containing uranium enriched in U235, plutonium or compounds of these products
2844.3000	-U235贫化铀及其化合物;钍及其化合物;含U235贫化铀、钍或它们的化合物的合金、分散体(包括金属陶瓷)、陶瓷产品及混合物	5.5	30			17	克/百万贝可	23	-Uranium depleted in U235 and its compounds; thorium and its compounds; alloys, dispersions (including cermets) ,ceramic products and mixtures containing uranium depleted in U235, thorium or compounds of these products
	-除子目号2844.10、2844.20及2844.30以外的放射性元素、同位素及其化合物;含这些元素、同位素及其化合物的合金、分散体(包括金属陶瓷)、陶瓷产品								-Radioactive elements and isotopes and compounds other than those of subheading No.2844.10, 2844.20 or 2844.30; alloys, dispersions (including cermets), ceramic products and mixtures containing these elements, isotopes or compounds radioactive residues:

税则号列 Tariff Item	商品名称及备注	进口税率 最惠	普通	暂定	出口退税	增值税率	计量单位	监管条件	Article Description
	及混合物:								
2844.4010	---镭及镭盐	4	14			17	克/百万贝可		---Radium and its salts
2844 4010.10	镭-226及其化合物、混合物(两用物项管制商品)	4	14			17	克/百万贝可	23	Radium—226 and its compound, mixture (Dual-use items controlled goods)
2844 4010.90	其他镭及镭盐	4	14			17	克/百万贝可	2	Other radium and its salts
2844.4020	---钴及钴盐	4	14			17	克/百万贝可	2	---Cobalt and its salts
2844.4090	---其他	5.5	30			17	克/百万贝可		---Other
2844 4090.10	铀-233及其化合物(包括呈金属、合金、化合物或浓缩物形态的各种材料)	5.5	30			17	克/百万贝可	23	Uranium-233 and its compounds,including metallic, alloys, compounds or concentration materials
2844 4090.20	氚、氚化物和氚的混合物,以及含有上述任何一种物质的产品[氚-氢原子比超过千分之一的,不包括含氚(任何形态)量小于 1.48×10^3GBq的产品]	5.5	30			17	克/百万贝可	23	Tritium, compound of tritide and tritium and products containing any of the above mentioned material(tritium—with hydrogen atoms ratio over 1‰, not including products whose tritium (any form) quantity is less than1.48×10^3GBq)
2844 4090.30	氦-3(3He)、含有氦-3的混合物(不包括氦-3的含量<1g的产品)	5.5	30			17	克/百万贝可	3	Helium -3(3He) , containing the compound with Helium -3(not including products whose helium-3 quantity<1g)
2844 4090.40	发射α粒子,其α半衰期为10天或更长但小于200年的放射性核素(1. 单质; 2. 含有α总活度为37GBq/kg或更大的任何这类放射性核素的化合物; 3. 含有α总活度为37GBq/kg或更大的任何这类放射性核素的混合物; 4. 含有任何上述物质的产品,不包括所含α活度小于3.7GBq的产品)	5.5	30			17	克/百万贝可	23	Emit radionuclide with α granule whose half-life-period is 10 days or longer but less than 200 years (1.Simple substance; 2.Containing compound of radionuclide any of this type with overall α activity of 37GBq/kg or above; 3. Containing mixture of any radionuclide of this type with α overall activity of 37GBq/kg or above; 4. containing products of any of the abovementioned materials, not including products whose α activity is less than 3.7GBq)
2844 4090.90	其他放射性元素、同位素及其化合物(税号2844.10、2844.20、2844.30以外的放射性元素,同位素)	5.5	30			17	克/百万贝可	2	Other radioactive elements and isotopes and compounds, other than those of subheading No.2844.10, 2844.20 or 2844.30
2844.5000	-核反应堆已耗尽(已辐照)的燃料元件(释热元件)	5.5	30			17	克		-Spent (irradiated) fuel elements (cartridges) of nuclear reactors
28.45	**品目28.44以外的同位素;这些同位素的无机或有机化合物,不论是否已有化学定义:**								**Isotopes other than those of heading No.28.44; compounds, inorganic or organic, of such isotopes, whether or not chemically defined:**
2845.1000	-重水(氧化氘)	5.5	30			17	克	3	-Heavy water (deuterium oxide)
2845.9000	-其他	5.5	30			17	克		-Other
2845 9000.10	除重水外的氘及氘化物	5.5	30			17	克	3	Deuterium and deuterides, other than heavy water
2845 9000.20	硼-10同位素及其化合物、混合物(硼-10同位素占硼总量>20%的硼及其化合物、混合物)	5.5	30			17	克	3	Boron-10 and its compounds, the total boron content containing boron-10 more than 20%
2845 9000.30	富集锂-6同位素及其化合物混合物[富集锂-6同位素指锂-6同位素富集度>7.5%(按原子数计)]	5.5	30			17	克	3	Lithium enriched in lithium-6 and its compounds and mixtures[1ithium enriched in lithium-6 refers to enrichment of lithium-6 isotope more than7.5% (atomicity)]
2845 9000.90	其他同位素及其他化合物(品目28.44以外的同位素)	5.5	30			17	克		Other isotopes and other compounds (other than those of heading No.28.44)
28.46	**稀土金属、钇、钪及其混合物的无机或有机化合物:**								**Compounds, inorganic or organic, of rare-earth metals, of yttrium or of scandium or of mixtures of these metals:**
	-铈的化合物:								-Ceric compounds:

税则号列 Tariff Item	商品名称及备注	进口税率			出口退税	增值税率	计量单位	监管条件	Article Description
		最惠	普通	暂定					
2846.1010[暂]	---氧化铈	5.5	30	0		17	千克	4Bxy	---Cerium oxide
2846.1020[暂]	---氢氧化铈	5.5	30	0		17	千克	4Bxy	---Cerium hydroxide
2846.1030[暂]	---碳酸铈	5.5	30	0		17	千克	4Bxy	---Cerium carbonate
2846.1090[暂]	---其他	5.5	30	0		17	千克		---Other
2846 1090.10[暂]	氰化铈	5.5	30	0		17	千克	4BXxy	Cerium cyanide
2846 1090.90[暂]	铈的其他化合物	5.5	30	0		17	千克	4Bxy	Other ceric compounds
	-其他:								-Other:
	---氧化稀土（氧化铈除外）:								---Rare-earth oxides（other than cerium oxide）:
2846.9011[暂]	----氧化钇	5.5	30	0		17	千克	4xBy	----Yttrium oxide
2846.9012[暂]	----氧化镧	5.5	30	0		17	千克	4Bxy	----Lanthanum oxide
2846.9013[暂]	----氧化钕	5.5	30	0		17	千克	4Bxy	----Neodymium oxide
2846.9014[暂]	----氧化铕	5.5	30	0		17	千克	4Bxy	----Eurapium oxide
2846.9015[暂]	----氧化镝	5.5	30	0		17	千克	4Bxy	----Dysprosium oxide
2846.9016[暂]	----氧化铽	5.5	30	0		17	千克	4Bxy	----Terbium oxide
2846.9017[暂]	----氧化镨	5.5	30	0		17	千克	4Bxy	----Praseodymium oxide (sesqui-oxide)
2846.9019[暂]	----其他	5.5	30	0		17	千克		----Other
2846 9019.20[暂]	氧化铒	5.5	30	0		17	千克	4Bxy	Dierbium trioxide
2846 9019.30[暂]	氧化钆	5.5	30	0		17	千克	4Bxy	Gadolinium oxide
2846 9019.40[暂]	氧化钐	5.5	30	0		17	千克	4Bxy	Samarium oxide
2846 9019.70[暂]	氧化镱	5.5	30	0		17	千克	4Bxy	Ytterbium oxide
2846 9019.80[暂]	氧化钪	5.5	30	0		17	千克	4Bxy	Scandium oxide
2846 9019.91[暂]	灯用红粉	5.5	30	0		17	千克	4Bxy	Red power for lighting
2846 9019.92[暂]	按重量计中重稀土总含量≥30%的其他氧化稀土(灯用红粉、氧化铈除外)	5.5	30	0		17	千克	4Bxy	Other rare-earth oxides which containing ≥30% by the weight of heavy rare-earth (other than red powder of lighting, cerium oxide)
2846 9019.99[暂]	其他氧化稀土(灯用红粉、氧化铈除外)	5.5	30	0		17	千克	4Bxy	Other rare-earth oxides(other than red powder of lighting, cerium oxide)
	---氯化稀土:								---Rare-earth chlorides:
2846.9021[暂]	----氯化铽	5.5	30	0		17	千克	4Bxy	----Terbium chloride
2846.9022[暂]	----氯化镝	5.5	30	0		17	千克	4Bxy	----Dysprosium chlorides
2846.9023[暂]	----氯化镧	5.5	30	0		17	千克	4Bxy	----Lanthanum chloride
2846.9024[暂]	----氯化钕	5.5	30	0		17	千克	4Bxy	----Neodymium chloride
2846.9025[暂]	----氯化镨	5.5	30	0		17	千克	4Bxy	----Praseodymium chloride
2846.9026[暂]	----氯化钇	5.5	30	0		17	千克	4Bxy	----Yttrium chloride
2846.9028[暂]	----混合氯化稀土	5.5	30	0		17	千克		----Mixture of rare-earth chlorides
2846 9028.10[暂]	按重量计中重稀土总含量≥30%的混合氯化稀土	5.5	30	0		17	千克	4Bxy	Mixture of rare-earth chloride which containing≥30% by the weight of heavy rare-earth
2846 9028.90[暂]	其他混合氯化稀土	5.5	30	0		17	千克	4Bxy	Other mixture of rare-earth chloride
2846.9029[暂]	----其他	5.5	30	0		17	千克	4Bxy	----Other
	---氟化稀土:								---Rare-earth fluorides:
2846.9031[暂]	----氟化铽	5.5	30	0		17	千克	4Bxy	----Terbium fluoride
2846.9032[暂]	----氟化镝	5.5	30	0		17	千克	4Bxy	----Dysprosium fluoride
2846.9033[暂]	----氟化镧	5.5	30	0		17	千克	4Bxy	----Lanthanum fluoride
2846.9034[暂]	----氟化钕	5.5	30	0		17	千克	4Bxy	----Neodymium fluoride
2846.9035[暂]	----氟化镨	5.5	30	0		17	千克	4Bxy	----Praseodymium fluoride
2846.9036[暂]	----氟化钇	5.5	30	0		17	千克	4Bxy	----Yttrium fluoride
2846.9039[暂]	----其他	5.5	30	0		17	千克	4Bxy	----Other
	---碳酸稀土:								---Rare-earth carbonate:
2846.9041[暂]	----碳酸镧	5.5	30	0		17	千克	4Bxy	----Lanthanum carbonate
2846.9042[暂]	----碳酸铽	5.5	30	0		17	千克	4Bxy	----Terbium carbonate
2846.9043[暂]	----碳酸镝	5.5	30	0		17	千克	4Bxy	----Dysprosium carbonate
2846.9044[暂]	----碳酸钕	5.5	30	0		17	千克	4Bxy	----Neodymium carbonate
2846.9045[暂]	----碳酸镨	5.5	30	0		17	千克	4Bxy	----Praseodymium carbonate
2846.9046[暂]	----碳酸钇	5.5	30	0		17	千克	4Bxy	----Yttrium carbonate

税则号列 Tariff Item	商品名称及备注	进口税率 最惠	进口税率 普通	进口税率 暂定	出口退税	增值税率	计量单位	监管条件	Article Description
2846.9048[暂]	----混合碳酸稀土	5.5	30	0		17	千克		----Mixture of rare-earth carbonate
2846 9048.10[暂]	按重量计中重稀土总含量≥30%的混合碳酸稀土	5.5	30	0		17	千克	4Bxy	Mixture of rare-earth carbonate which containing≥30% by the weight of heavy rare-earth
2846 9048.90[暂]	其他混合碳酸稀土	5.5	30	0		17	千克	4Bxy	Other Mixture of rare-earth carbonate
2846.9049[暂]	----其他	5.5	30	0		17	千克	4Bxy	----Other
	---其他：								---Other:
2846.9091[暂]	----镧的其他化合物	5.5	30	0		17	千克	4Bxy	----Other compounds of lanthanum
2846.9092[暂]	----钕的其他化合物	5.5	30	0		17	千克	4Bxy	----Other compounds of neodymium
2846.9093[暂]	----铽的其他化合物	5.5	30	0		17	千克	4Bxy	----Other compounds of terbium
2846.9094[暂]	----镝的其他化合物	5.5	30	0		17	千克	4Bxy	----Other compounds of dysprosium
2846.9095[暂]	----镨的其他化合物	5.5	30	0		17	千克	4Bxy	----Other compounds of praseodymium
2846.9096[暂]	----钇的其他化合物	5.5	30	0		17	千克		----Other compounds of yttrium
2846 9096.01[暂]	LED 用荧光粉(成分含钇的其他化合物)	5.5	30	0		17	千克	B	Phosphor powder for LED, with composition of other yttrium
2846 9096.90[暂]	钇的其他化合物	5.5	30	0		17	千克	4Bxy	Other compounds of yttrium
2846.9099[暂]	----其他	5.5	30	0		17	千克		----Other
2846 9099.01[暂]	LED 用荧光粉(成分含稀土金属、钪的其他化合物，铈的化合物除外)	5.5	30	0		17	千克	B	Phosphor powder for LED, with composition of rare-earth metal and scandium, (other than Ceric compounds)
2846 9099.10[暂]	按重量计中重稀土总含量≥30%的稀土金属、钪的其他化合物(铈的化合物除外)	5.5	30	0		17	千克	4Bxy	Other compounds of rare-earth metal and Scandium which containing≥30% by the weight of heavy rare-earth (other than Ceric compounds)
2846 9099.90[暂]	其他稀土金属、钪的其他化合物(铈的化合物除外)	5.5	30	0		17	千克	4Bxy	Other compounds of rare-earth metal and scandium (other than Ceric compounds)
28.47	**过氧化氢，不论是否用尿素固化：**								**Hydrogen peroxide, whether or not solidified with urea:**
2847.0000	过氧化氢，不论是否用尿素固化	5.5	30			17	千克	AB	Hydrogen peroxide, whether or not solidified with urea
28.48	**磷化物，不论是否已有化学定义，但不包括磷铁：**								**Phosphides, whether or not chemically defined, excluding ferrophosphorus:**
2848.0000	磷化物，不论是否已有化学定义，但不包括磷铁	5.5	20			17	千克		Phosphides, whether or not chemically defined, excluding ferrophophorus
2848 0000.10	磷化铝，磷化锌	5.5	20			17	千克	S	Aluminium phosphide, zinc phosphide
2848 0000.90	其他磷化物（不论是否已有化学定义，但不包括磷铁）	5.5	20			17	千克		Other phosphides, whether or not chemieally defined, excluding ferrophosphorus
28.49	**碳化物，不论是否已有化学定义：**								**Carbides, whether or not chemically defined:**
2849.1000	-碳化钙	5.5	45			17	千克	AB	-Of calcium
2849.2000	-碳化硅	5.5	30			17	千克	4xy	-Of silicon
	-其他：								-Other:
2849.9010	---碳化硼	5.5	30			17	千克		---Of boron
2849.9020	---碳化钨	5.5	30			17	千克	4xy	---Of tungsten
2849.9090	---其他	5.5	30			17	千克		---Other
28.50	**氢化物、氮化物、叠氮化物、硅化物及硼化物，不论是否已有化学定义，但可归入品目 28.49 的碳化物除外：**								**Hydrides, nitrides, azides, silicides and borides, whether or not chemically defined, other than compounds which are also carbides of heading No.28.49:**
	---氮化物：								---Nitride:
2850.0011	----氮化锰	5.5	30			17	千克		----Manganese nitride
2850.0019	----其他	5.5	30			17	千克		----Other
2850.0090	---其他	5.5	30			17	千克		---Other
2850 0090.10	砷化氢(砷烷、砷化三氢、胂)	5.5	30			17	千克	X	Arsenic hydride（Arsine, Arsenic hydride, Arsenic trihydride）
2850 0090.90	其他氢化物、硅化物等(包括硼化物，可归入品目 28.49 的碳化物	5.5	30			17	千克		Other hydrides, nitrides, azides, silicides and borides, other than compounds which are also carbides of

税则号列 Tariff Item	商品名称及备注	进口税率 最惠	普通	暂定	出口退税	增值税率	计量单位	监管条件	Article Description
	除外)								heading No.28.49
28.52	汞的无机或有机化合物，汞齐除外：								**Compounds, inorganic or organic, of mercury, excluding amalagams**:
2852.1000	-已有化学定义的	5.5	30			17	千克	X	-Chemically defined
2852.9000	-其他	5.5	30			17	千克	X	-Other
28.53	其他无机化合物（包括蒸馏水、导电水及类似的纯净水）；液态空气（不论是否除去稀有气体）；压缩空气；汞齐，但贵金属汞齐除外：								**Other inorganic compounds（including distilled or conductivity water and water of similar purity）; liquid air（whether or not rare gases have been removed）; compressed air; amalgams, other than amalgams of precious metals:**
2853.0010	---饮用蒸馏水	5.5	70			17	千克	AB	--Distilled water for human consumption
2853.0020	---氯化氰	5.5	30			17	千克	23	---Chlorocyanogen, cyanogen chloride
2853.0030	---镍钴锰氢氧化物	6.5	30			17	千克		---Nickel cobalt manganese composite hydroxide
2853.0090	---其他	5.5	30			17	千克		---Other
2853 0090.10	饮用纯净水	5.5	30			17	千克	AB	Purified water for human consumption
2853 0090.21	氰、氰化碘、氰化溴、铅汞齐(包括氰气、碘化氰、溴化氰)	5.5	30			17	千克	X	Cyano, cyanogen iodide, bromine cyanide, Lead amalgam (including cyanogen, cyanogen iodide, cyanogen bromide)
2853 0090.22	砷化锌、砷化镓	5.5	30			17	千克	X	Zinc arsenide, gallium arsenide
2853 0090.30	单氰胺	5.5	30			17	千克		Monocyanamide
2853 0090.90	其他无机化合物、压缩空气等（包括导电水、液态空气、汞齐等，贵金属汞齐除外）	5.5	30			17	千克		Other inorganic compounds, compressed air（including conductivity water, liquid air, amalgams, other than amalgamms of precious metals）

第二十九章 有机化学品

Chapter 29 Organic chemicals

注释：

一、除条文另有规定的以外，本章各品目只适用于：

（一）单独的已有化学定义的有机化合物，不论是否含有杂质；

（二）同一有机化合物的两种或两种以上异构体的混合物（不论是否含有杂质），但无环烃异构体的混合物（立体异构体除外），不论是否饱和，应归入第二十七章；

（三）品目29.36至29.39的产品，品目29.40的糖醚、糖缩醛、糖酯及其盐类和品目29.41的产品，不论是否已有化学定义；

（四）上述（一）、（二）、（三）款产品的水溶液；

（五）溶于其他溶剂的上述（一）、（二）、（三）款的产品，但该产品处于溶液状态只是为了安全或运输所采取的正常必要方法，其所用溶剂并不使该产品改变其一般用途而适合于某些特殊用途；

（六）为了保存或运输的需要，加入稳定剂（包括抗结块剂）的上述（一）、（二）、（三）、（四）、（五）各款产品；

（七）为了便于识别或安全起见，加入抗尘剂、着色剂或气味剂的上述（一）、（二）、（三）、（四）、（五）、（六）各款产品，但所加剂料并不使原产品改变其一般用途而适合于某些特殊用途；

（八）为生产偶氮染料而稀释至标准浓度的下列产品：重氮盐，用于重氮盐、可重氮化的胺及其盐类的耦合剂。

二、本章不包括：

（一）品目15.04的货品及品目15.20的粗甘油；

（二）乙醇（品目22.07或22.08）；

（三）甲烷及丙烷（品目27.11）；

（四）第二十八章注释二所述的碳化合物；

（五）税目30.02的免疫制品；

（六）尿素（品目31.02或31.05）；

（七）植物性或动物性着色料（品目32.03）、合成有机着色料、用作萤光增白剂或发光体的合成有机产品（品目32.04）及零售包装的染料或其他着色料（品目32.12）；

（八）酶（品目35.07）；

（九）聚乙醛、六亚甲基四胺（乌洛托品）及类似物质，制成片、条或类似形状作为燃料用的，以及包装容器的容积不超过300立方厘米的直接灌注香烟打火机及类似打火器用的液体燃料或液化气体燃料（品目

Chapter Notes:

1. Except where the context otherwise requires, the headings of this Chapter apply only to:

（a）Separate chemically defined organic compounds, whether or not containing impurities;

（b）Mixtures of two or more isomers of the same organic compound（whether or not containing impurities）, except mixtures of acyclic hydrocarbon isomers（other than stereoisomers）, whether or not saturated（Chapter 27）;

（c）The products of headings 29.36 to 29.39 or the sugar ethers, sugar acetals and sugar esters, and their salts, of heading 29.40, or the products of heading 29.41, whether or not chemically defined;

（d）The products mentioned in（a）,（b）or（c）above dissolved in water;

（e）The products mentioned in（a）,（b）or（c）above dissolved in other solvents provided that the solution constitutes a normal and necessary method of putting up these products adopted solely for reasons of safety or for transport and that the solvent does not render the product particularly suitable for specific use rather than for general use:

（f）The products mentioned in（a）,（b）,（c）,（d）or（e）above with an added stabiliser(including an anti-caking agent)necessary for their preservation or transport;

（g）The products mentioned in（a）,（b）,（c）,（d）,（e）or（f）above with an added anti-dusting agent or a colouring or odoriferous substance added to facilitate their identification or for safety reasons, provided that the additions do not render the product particularly suitable for specific use rather than for general use;

（h）The following products, diluted to standard strengths, for the production of azo dyes: diazonium salts, couplers used for these salts and diazotisable amines and their salts.

2. This Chapter does not cover:

（a）Goods of heading 15.04 or crude glycerol of heading 15.20;

（b）Ethyl alcohol（heading 22.07 or 22.08）;

（c）Methane or propane（heading 27.11）;

（d）The compounds of carbon mentioned in Note 2 to Chapter 28;

（e）Immunological products of heading 30.02;

（f）Urea（heading 31.02 or 31.05）;

（g）Colouring matter of vegetable or animal origin（heading 32.03）, synthetic organic colouring matter, synthetic organic products of a kind used as fluorescent brightening agents or as luminophores（heading 32.04)or dyes or other colouring matter put up in forms or packings for retail sale（heading 32.12）;

（h）Enzymes（heading 35.07）;

（ij）Metaldehyde, hexamethylenetetramine or similar substances, put up in forms（for example, tablets, sticks or similar forms）for use as fuels, or liquid or liquefied-gas fuels in containers of a kind used for filling or refilling cigarette or similar lighters and of a capacity not exceeding $300cm^3$（heading 36.06）;

36.06）；

（十）灭火器的装配药及已装药的灭火弹（品目38.13）；零售包装的除墨剂（品目38.24）；或

（十一）光学元件，例如，用酒石酸乙二胺制成的（品目90.01）。

三、可以归入本章两个或两个以上品目的货品，应归入有关品目中的最后一个品目。

四、品目29.04至29.06、29.08至29.11及29.13至29.20的卤化、磺化、硝化或亚硝化衍生物均包括复合衍生物，例如，卤磺化、卤硝化、磺硝化及卤磺硝化衍生物。

硝基及亚硝基不作为品目29.29的含氮基官能团。

品目29.11、29.12、29.14、29.18及29.22所称"含氧基"，仅限于品目29.05至29.20的各种含氧基（其特征为有机含氧基）。

五、（一）本章第一分章至第七分章的酸基有机化合物与这些分章的有机化合物构成的酯，应归入有关品目的最后一个品目。

（二）乙醇与本章第一分章至第七分章的酸基有机化合物所构成的酯，应按有关酸基化合物归类。

（三）除第六类注释一及第二十八章注释二另有规定的以外：

1. 第一分章至第十分章及品目29.42的有机化合物的无机盐，例如，含酸基、酚基或烯醇基的化合物及有机碱的无机盐，应归入相应的有机化合物的品目；

2. 第一分章至第十分章及品目29.42的有机化合物之间生成的盐，应按生成该盐的碱或酸（包括酚基或烯醇基化合物）归入本章有关品目中的最后一个品目；以及

3. 除第十一分章或品目29.41的产品外，配位化合物应按该化合物所有金属键（金属—碳键除外）"断开"所形成的片段归入第二十九章有关品目中的最后一个品目。

（四）除乙醇外，金属醇化物应按相应的醇归类（品目29.05）。

（五）羧酸酰卤化物应按相应的酸归类。

六、品目29.30及29.31的化合物是指有机化合物，其分子中除含氢、氧或氮原子外，还含有与碳原子直接连接的其他非金属或金属原子（例如，硫、砷或铅）。

品目29.30（有机硫化合物）及品目29.31（其他有机-无机化合物）不包括某些磺化或卤化衍生物（含复合衍生物）。这些衍生物分子中除氢、

(x) Products put up as charges for fire-extinguisher or put up in fire-extinguishing grenades, of heading 38.13; ink removers put up in packings for retail sale of heading 38.24: or

(l) Optical elements, for example, of ethylenediamine tartrate (heading 90.01)

3. Goods which could be included in two or more of the headings of this Chapter are to be classified in that one of those headings which occurs last in numerical order.

4. In headings 29.04 to 29.06, 29.08 to 29.11 and 29.13 to 29.20,any reference to halogenated, sulphonated, nitrated or nitrosated derivatives includes a reference to compound derivatives, such as sulphohalogenated, nitrohalogenated, nitroslphonated or nitroslphohalogenated derivatives.

Nitro or nitroso groups are not to be taken a "nitrogen-functions" for the purpose of heading 29.29.

For the purposes of headings 29.11, 29.12, 29.14, 29.18 and29.22, "oxygen-function" is to be restricted to the functions (the characteristic organic oxygen-containing groups) referred to in headings 29.05 to 29.20.

5. (a) The esters of acid-function organic compounds of sub-Chapters I to VII with organic compounds of these sub-Chapters are to be classified with that compound which is classified in the heading which occurs last in numerical order in these sub-Chapters.

(b) Esters of ethyl alcohol with acid-function organic compounds of sub-Chapters I to VII are to be classified in the same heading as the corresponding acid-function compounds.

(c) Subject to Note 1 to Section VI and Note 2 to Chapter 28:

(i) Inorganic salts of organic compounds such as acid-, phenol- or enol-function compounds or organic bases of sub-Chapters I to X or heading 29.42, are to be classified in the heading appropriate to the organic compound;

(ii) Salts formed between organic compounds of sub-Chapters Ⅰ to Ⅹ or heading 29.42 are to be classified in the heading appropriate to the base or to the acid (including phenol- or enol-function compounds) from which they are formed, whichever occurs last in numerical order in the Chapter; and

(iii) Co-ordination compounds, other than products classifiable in sub-Chapter Ⅺ or heading 29.41, are to be classified in the heading which occurs last in numerical order in Chapter 29, among those appropriate to fragments formed by "cleaving" of all metal bonds, other than metal-carbon bonds.

(d) Metal alcoholates are to be classified in the same heading as the corresponding alcohols except in the case of ethanol (heading 29.05).

(e) Halides of carboxylic acids are to be classified in the same heading as the corresponding acids.

6. The compounds of headings 29.30 and 29.31 are organic compounds the molecules of which contain, in addition to atoms of hydrogen, oxygen or nitrogen, atoms of other nonmetals or of metals (such as sulphur, arsenic or lead) directly linked to carbon atoms.

Heading 29.30 (organo-sulphur compounds) and heading29.31 (other organo-inorganic compounds) do not include sulphonated or halogenated derivatives (including compound derivatives) which, apart from hydrogen, oxygen and nitrogen,only have directly linked to carbon the atoms of

氧、氮之外，只有具有磺化或卤化衍生物（或复合衍生物）性质的硫原子或卤素原子与碳原子直接连接。

七、品目29.32、29.33及29.34不包括三节环环氧化物、过氧化酮、醛或硫醛的环聚合物、多元羧酸酐、多元醇或酚与多元酸构成的环酯及多元酸酰亚胺。

本条规定只适用于由本条所列环化功能形成环内杂原子的化合物。

八、品目29.37所称：

（一）“激素”包括激素释放因子、激素刺激和释放因子、激素抑制剂以及激素抗体；

（二）“主要用作激素的”，不仅适用于主要起激素作用的激素衍生物及结构类似物，也适用于在本品目所列产品合成过程中主要用作中间体的激素衍生物以及结构类似物。

子目注释：

一、属于本章任一品目项下的一种（组）化合物的衍生物，如果该品目其他子目未明确将其包括在内，而且有关的子目中又无列名为“其他”的子目，则应与该种（组）化合物归入同一子目。

二、第二十九章注释三不适用于本章的子目。

sulphur or of a halogen which give them their nature of sulphonated or halogenated derivatives（or compound derivatives）.

7. Headings 29.32, 29.33 and 29.34 do not include epoxides with a three-membered ring, ketone peroxides, cyclic polymers of aldehydes or of thioaldehydes, anhydrides of polybasic carboxylic acids, cyclic esters of polyhydric alcohols or phenols with polybasic acids, or imides of polybasic acids.

These provisions apply only when the ring-position heteroatoms are those resulting solely from the cyclising function or functions here listed.

8. For the purposes of heading 29.37:

（a）the term “hormones” includes hormone-releasing or hormone-stimulating factors, hormone inhibitors and hormone antagonists（anti-hormones）;

（b）the expression “used primarily as hormones” applies not only to hormone derivatives and structural analogues used primarily for their hormonal effect, but also to those derivatives and structural analogues used primarily as intermediates in the synthesis of products of this heading.

Subheading Notes:

1. Within any one heading of this Chapter, derivatives of a chemical compound（or group of chemical compounds）are to be classified in the same subheading as that compound（or group of compounds）provided that they are not more specifically covered by any other subheading and that there is no residual subheading named “Other” in the series of subheadings concerned.

2. The Note 3 of Chapter 29 does not apply to the subheading of this Chapter.

税则号列 Tariff Item	商品名称及备注	进口税率 最惠	普通	暂定	出口退税	增值税率	计量单位	监管条件	Article Description
	第一分章　烃类及其卤化、磺化、硝化或亚硝化衍生物								**I. HYDROCARBONS AND THEIR HALOGENATED, SULPHONATED, NITRATED OR NITROSATED DERIVATIVES**
29.01	无环烃：								**Acyclic hydrocarbons:**
2901.1000	-饱和	2	30		9	17	千克		-Saturated
	-不饱和：								-Unsaturated:
2901.2100	--乙烯	2	20		9	17	千克	AB	--Ethylene
2901.2200[暂]	--丙烯	2	20	1	9	17	千克	AB	--Propene（propylene）
	--丁烯及其异构体：								--Butene（butylene）and isomers thereof:
2901.2310	---1-丁烯	2	20		9	17	千克	AB	---1-Butene
2901.2320	---2-丁烯	2	20		9	17	千克	AB	---2-Butene
2901.2330	---2-甲基丙烯	2	20		9	17	千克		---2-methyl propylene
	--1,3-丁二烯及异戊二烯：								--Buta-1, 3-diene and isoprene:
2901.2410	---1,3-丁二烯	2	20		9	17	千克	AB	Buta-1, 3-diene
2901.2420	---异戊二烯	2	20		9	17	千克		---Isoprene
	--其他：								--Other:
2901.2910	---异戊烯	2	30		9	17	千克	AB	---Isopentene
2901.2920	---乙炔	2	45		9	17	千克	AB	---Acetylene
2901.2990	---其他	2	30		9	17	千克		---Other
2901 2990.10	诱虫烯	2	30		9	17	千克	S	Muscalure
2901 2990.90	其他不饱和无环烃	2	30		9	17	千克		Other unsaturated acyclic hydrocarbons
29.02	环烃：								**Cyclic hydrocarbons:**
	-环烷烃、环烯及环萜烯：								-Cyclanes, cyclenes and cycloterpenes:
2902.1100	--环已烷	2	30		9	17	千克	AB	--Cyclohexane
	--其他：								--Other:
2902.1910	---蒎烯	2	30		9	17	千克		---Pinene

税则号列 Tariff Item	商品名称及备注	进口税率 最惠	进口税率 普通	进口税率 暂定	出口退税	增值税率	计量单位	监管条件	Article Description
2902.1920	---4-烷基-4'-烷基双环己烷	2	30		9	17	千克		---4-Alkyl-4'-alkylbicyclohexane
2902.1990	---其他	2	30		9	17	千克		---Other
2902 1990.11	1-甲基环丙烯	2	30		9	17	千克	S	1-methyl cyclopropene
2902 1990.12	d-柠檬烯	2	30		9	17	千克		D-limonene
2902 1990.90	其他环烷烃、环烯及环萜烯	2	30		9	17	千克		Other cyclanes, cyclenes and cycloterpenes
2902.2000	-苯	2	20			17	千克	AB	-Benzene
2902.3000	-甲苯	2	30		13	17	千克	23	-Toluene
	-二甲苯:								-Xylenes:
2902.4100	--邻二甲苯	2	20		9	17	千克		--*o*-Xylene
2902.4200	--间二甲苯	2	20		9	17	千克		--*m*-Xylene
2902.4300	--对二甲苯	2	20		13	17	千克		--*p*-Xylene
2902.4400	--混合二甲苯异构体	2	20		13	17	千克		--Mixed xylene isomers
2902.5000	-苯乙烯	2	30		9	17	千克	AB	-Styrene
2902.6000	-乙苯	2	30		9	17	千克	AB	-Ethylbenzene
2902.7000	-异丙基苯	2	30		9	17	千克	AB	-Cumene
	-其他:								-Other:
2902.9010	---四氢萘	2	11		9	17	千克		---Tetrahydronaphthalene（tetralin）
2902.9020	---精萘	2	35		9	17	千克	AB	---Naphthalene
2902.9030	---十二烷基苯	2	30		9	17	千克		---Dodecylbenzene
2902.9040	---4-(4'-烷基环己基)环己基乙烯	2	30		13	17	千克		---4-(4'-alkylcyclohexyl)cyclohexyl ethylene
2902.9090	---其他	2	30		9	17	千克		---Other
2902 9090.10	联苯	2	30		9	17	千克		Biphenyl
2902 9090.90	其他芳香烃	2	30		9	17	千克		Other aromatic hydrocarbons
29.03	**烃的卤化衍生物:**								**Halogenated derivatives of hydrocarbons:**
	-无环烃的饱和氯化衍生物:								-Saturated chlorinated derivatives of acyclic hydrocarbons:
2903.1100	---一氯甲烷及氯乙烷	5.5	30		9	17	千克		--Chloromethane（methyl chloride）and Chloroethane（ethyl chloride）
2903.1200	--二氯甲烷	8	30		9	17	千克		--Dichloromethane（methylene chloride）
2903 1200.01	纯度在99%及以上的二氯甲烷	8	30		9	17	千克	X	Dichloromethane（methylene chloride）,（purity of 99% or more）
2903 1200.90	其他二氯甲烷	8	30		9	17	千克	X	Other dichloromethane（methylene chloride）
2903.1300	--氯仿（三氯甲烷）	10	30		9	17	千克	23X	--Chloroform（trichloromethane）
2903.1400	--四氯化碳	8	30		9	17	千克		--Carbon tetrachloride
2903 1400.10	非用于清洗剂的四氯化碳	8	30		9	17	千克	49Bxy	Carbon tetrachloride, not used in cleaner
2903 1400.90	用于清洗剂的四氯化碳	8	30		9	17	千克	89	Carbon tetrachloride, used in cleaner
2903.1500[暂]	--1，2-二氯乙烷（ISO）	5.5	30	1		17	千克	ABX	--1, 2-Dichloroethane (ISO)（ethylene dichloride）
	--其他:								--Other:
2903.1910	---1，1，1-三氯乙烷（甲基氯仿）	8	30		9	17	千克		---1, 1, 1-Trichloroethane（methylchloro form）
2903 1910.10	1，1，1-三氯乙烷（甲基氯仿）（用于清洗剂的除外）	8	30		9	17	千克	14ABxy	1, 1, 1-Trichloroethane（methylchloro form）（other than used in cleaner）
2903 1910.90	1，1，1-三氯乙烷（甲基氯仿）（用于清洗剂的）	8	30		9	17	千克	18A	1, 1, 1-Trichloroethane（methylchloro form)（used in cleaner）
2903.1990	---其他	5.5	30		9	17	千克		---Other
	-无环烃的不饱和氯化衍生物:								-Unsaturated chlorinated derivatives of acyclic hydrocarbons:
2903.2100[暂]	--氯乙烯	5.5	30	1	9	17	千克	AB	--Vinyl chloride（chloroethylene）
2903.2200	--三氯乙烯	8	30		9	17	千克	X	--Trichloroethylene
2903.2300	--四氯乙烯（全氯乙烯）	5.5	30		9	17	千克	X	--Tetrachloroethylene（perchloroethylene）
	--其他:								--Other:
2903.2910	---3-氯-1-丙烯（氯丙烯）	5.5	30		9	17	千克		---3-Chloro-1-propene（Chloropropene）
2903.2990	---其他	5.5	30		9	17	千克		---Other
2903 2990.10	1，1-二氯乙烯	5.5	30		9	17	千克	X	1, 1-dichloroethylene

税则号列 Tariff Item	商品名称及备注	进口税率 最惠	进口税率 普通	进口税率 暂定	出口退税	增值税率	计量单位	监管条件	Article Description
2903 2990.90	其他无环烃的不饱和氯化衍生物	5.5	30		9	17	千克		Other unsaturated chlorinated derivatives of acyclic hydrocarbons
	-无环烃的氟化、溴化或碘化衍生物:								-Fluorinated, brominated or iodinated derivatives of acyclic hydrocarbons:
2903.3100	--1，2-二溴乙烷（ISO）	5.5	30			17	千克	89	--Ethylene dibromide（ISO）（1, 2- dibromoethane）
	--其他:								--Other:
2903.3910	---1,1,3,3,3-五氟-2-三氟甲基-1-丙烯（全氟异丁烯；八氟异丁烯）	5.5	30		9	17	千克	23	---1, l, 3, 3, 3-Pentafluro-2-triflurometthyl-1-propene（Perfluorolisobutylene, isobutylene octafluoride）
2903.3990	---其他	5.5	30			17	千克		---Other
2903 3990.10	二溴甲烷	5.5	30		9	17	千克	AB	Dibromomethane
2903 3990.20	溴甲烷（别名甲基溴）	5.5	30			17	千克	14ABxy	Methyl bromide
2903 3990.30	碘甲烷	5.5	30		13	17	千克	AB	Methyl iodide
2903 3990.90	其他无环烃的氟化、溴化或碘化衍生物	5.5	30		13	17	千克		Other fluorinated, brominated or iodinated derivatives of acyclic hydrocarbons
	-含有两种或两种以上不同卤素的无环烃卤化衍生物:								-Halogenated derivatives of acyclic hydrocarbons containing two or more different halogens:
2903.7100	--一氯二氟甲烷	5.5	30		13	17	千克	14ABxy	--Chlorodifluoromethane
2903.7200	--二氯三氟乙烷	5.5	30		9	17	千克	14xy	--Dichlorotrifluoroethanes
2903.7300	--二氯一氟乙烷	5.5	30		9	17	千克	14xy	--Dichlorofluoroethanes
2903.7400	--一氯二氟乙烷	5.5	30		9	17	千克	14xy	-Chlorodifluoroethanes
2903.7500	--二氯五氟丙烷	5.5	30		9	17	千克		--Dichloropentafluoropropanes
2903 7500.10	1,1,1,2,2-五氟-3,3-二氯丙烷	5.5	30		9	17	千克	14xy	1,1,1,2,2- Pentafluro -3,3-dicholoropropane
2903 7500.20	1,1,2,2,3-五氟-1,3-二氯丙烷	5.5	30		9	17	千克	14xy	1,1,1,2,3- Pentafluro -1,3-dicholoropropane
2903 7500.90	其他二氯五氟丙烷	5.5	30		9	17	千克	14xy	Other Dichloropentafluoropropane
2903.7600	--溴氯二氟甲烷、溴三氟甲烷及二溴四氟乙烷	5.5	30		9	17	千克		--Bromochlorodifluoromethane, bromotrifluoromethane and dibromotetraf luoroethanes
2903 7600.10	溴氯二氟甲烷 (Halon-1211)	5.5	30		9	17	千克	14xy	Bromo chlorodifluorom ethane (Halon-1211)
2903 7600.20	溴三氟甲烷 (Halon-1301)	5.5	30		9	17	千克	14ABxy	Bromo trifluorom ethane (Halon-1301)
2903 7600.30	二溴四氟乙烷	5.5	30		9	17	千克		Dibromotetrafluoroethane
	--其他，仅含氟和氯的全卤化物:								--Other, perhalogenated derivatives only with fluorine and chlorine :
2903.7710	---三氯氟甲烷	5.5	30		9	17	千克	14ABxy	---Trichlorofluoromethane
2903.7720	---其他仅含氟和氯的甲烷、乙烷及丙烷的全卤化物	5.5	30		9	17	千克		---Other methane ethane and propane perhalogenated derivatives only with fluorine and chlorine
2903 7720.11	二氯二氟甲烷(CFC-12)	5.5	30		9	17	千克	14ABxy	Dichlorodifluoromethane (CFC-12)
2903 7720.12	三氯三氟乙烷,用于清洗剂除外(CFC-113)	5.5	30		9	17	千克	14xy	Trichlorotrifluoroethane,which other than used in cleaning agent (CFC-113)
2903 7720.13	三氯三氟乙烷,用于清洗剂(CFC-113)	5.5	30		9	17	千克	89	Trichlorotrifluoroethane,which used in cleaning agent (CFC-113)
2903 7720.14	二氯四氟乙烷 (CFC-114)	5.5	30		9	17	千克	14ABxy	Dichlorotetrafluoroethane (CFC-114)
2903 7720.15	一氯五氟乙烷 (CFC-115)	5.5	30		9	17	千克	14ABxy	Chloropentafluoroethane (CFC-115)
2903 7720.16	一氯三氟甲烷 (CFC-13)	5.5	30		9	17	千克	14ABxy	Chlorotrifluoromethane (CFC-13)
2903 7720.17	五氯一氟乙烷	5.5	30		9	17	千克		Chloropentafluoroethane
2903 7720.18	四氯二氟乙烷	5.5	30		9	17	千克		Difluorotetrachloroethane
2903 7720.19	七氯一氟丙烷	5.5	30		9	17	千克		Heptachlorofluoropropane
2903 7720.21	六氯二氟丙烷	5.5	30		9	17	千克		Hexachlorodifluoropropanes
2903 7720.22	五氯三氟丙烷	5.5	30		9	17	千克		Pentachlorotrifluoropropane
2903 7720.23	四氯四氟丙烷	5.5	30		9	17	千克		Tetrachlorodifluoroethane
2903 7720.24	三氯五氟丙烷	5.5	30		9	17	千克		Trichloro pentafluoropropane
2903 7720.25	二氯六氟丙烷	5.5	30		9	17	千克		Dichloro-hexafluoropropane
2903 7720.26	一氯七氟丙烷	5.5	30		9	17	千克		Monochlorine heptafluoropropane

税则号列 Tariff Item	商品名称及备注	进口税率 最惠	普通	暂定	出口退税	增值税率	计量单位	监管条件	Article Description
2903.7790	---其他	5.5	30		13	17	千克		---Other
2903.7800	--其他全卤化衍生物	5.5	30		9	17	千克		--Other perhalogenated derivatives
	--其他:								--Other:
2903.7910	---其他仅含氟和氯的甲烷、乙烷及丙烷的卤化衍生物	5.5	30		9	17	千克		---Other methane, ethane and propane halogenated derivatives only with fluorine and chlorine
2903 7910.11	一氟二氯甲烷	5.5	30		9	17	千克	14xy	Dichloromonofluoromethane
2903 7910.12	1,1,1,2-四氟-2-氯乙烷	5.5	30		9	17	千克	14xy	2-Chloro-1,1,1,2-tetrafluoroethane
2903 7910.13	三氟一氯乙烷	5.5	30		9	17	千克	14ABxy	Trifluoroacetic monochloroethane
2903 7910.14	1-氟-1,1-二氯乙烷	5.5	30		9	17	千克	14xy	1,1-Dichoro-1-fluoroethane
2903 7910.15	1,1-二氟-1-氯乙烷	5.5	30		9	17	千克	14xy	1-Chloro-1,1-difluoroethane
2903 7910.90	其他仅含氟和氯的甲烷、乙烷及丙烷的卤化衍生物	5.5	30		9	17	千克	14xy	Other methane, ethane and propane halogenate derivative containing flurorine and chloric
2903.7990	---其他	5.5	30		9	17	千克		---Other
2903 7990.10	二溴氯丙烷(1,2-二溴-3-氯丙烷)	5.5	30		9	17	千克	89	Dibromochloropropane(1,2-dibromo-3-chloropropane)
2903 7990.21	其他仅含溴、氟的甲烷、乙烷和丙烷	5.5	30		9	17	千克	14xy	Other methane,ethane and propane only with bromine and fluorine
2903 7990.29	其他仅含氟和溴的甲烷等卤化衍生物(包括其他仅含氟和溴的乙烷及丙烷的卤化衍生物)	5.5	30		9	17	千克		Other methane,ethane and propane halogenated derivatives only with fluorine and bromine
2903 7990.90	其他无环烃卤化衍生物(含二种或二种以上不同卤素)	5.5	30		9	17	千克		Other halogenated derivatives of acyclic hydrocarbons containing two or more different halogens:
	-环烷烃、环烯烃或环萜烯烃的卤化衍生物:								-Halogenated derivatives of cyclanic,cyclenic or cycloterpenic hydrocarbons :
2903.8100	--1, 2, 3, 4, 5, 6-六氯环已烷[六六六(ISO)],包括林丹(ISO, INN)	5.5	30			17	千克		--1, 2, 3, 4, 5, 6-Hexachlorocyclohexane (HCH (ISO)), including linadne (ISO, INN)
2903 8100.10	林丹(ISO, INN)	5.5	30			17	千克	S	Lindane (ISO, INN)
2903 8100.90	1,2,3,4,5,6-六氯环已烷{六六六(ISO)}(混合异构体)	5.5	30			17	千克	X	1, 2,3,4,5,6-Hexachlorocyclohexane (hexachloro-cyclohexane soprocide ISO)
2903.8200	--艾氏剂(ISO)、氯丹(ISO)及七氯(ISO)	5.5	30			17	千克		-- Aldrin (ISO), chlordane (ISO) and heptachlor (ISO)
2903 8200.10	艾氏剂(ISO)及七氯(ISO)	5.5	30			17	千克	89	Aldrin (ISO) and heptachlor (ISO)
2903 8200.90	氯丹(ISO)(别名八氯化甲桥茚)	5.5	30			17	千克	89	Chlordan (ISO)
2903.8900	--其他	5.5	30			17	千克		--Other
2903 8900.10	毒杀芬	5.5	30			17	千克	89	Toxaphene
2903 8900.30	灭蚁灵	5.5	30			17	千克	89	Mirex
2903 8900.90	其他环烷烃、环烯烃或环萜烯烃的卤化衍生物	5.5	30		13	17	千克		Other Cycloalkanes, cycloolefin or cyc-terpene olefin halogenate dervative
	-芳烃卤化衍生物:								-Halogenated derivatives of aromatic hydrocarbons:
	--氯苯、邻二氯苯及对二氯苯:								--Chlorobenzene, *o*-dichlorobenzene and *p*-dichlorobenzene :
2903.9110	---邻二氯苯	5.5	30		9	17	千克		---*o*-Dichlorobenzene
2903.9190	---其他	5.5	30		9	17	千克		---Other
2903 9190.10	1,4-二氯苯(又称对二氯苯)	5.5	30		9	17	千克	S	1,4-dichlorobenzene
2903 9190.90	氯苯	5.5	30		9	17	千克	AB	Chlorobenzene
2903.9200	--六氯苯(ISO)及滴滴涕(ISO, INN)(六氯苯别名过氯苯,滴滴涕别名[1,1,1-三氯-2,2-双(4-氯苯基)乙烷])	5.5	30			17	千克	89	-- Hexachlorobenzene (ISO) and DDT (ISO) (clofenotane(INN) (hexachlorobenzene alias before chlorobenzene, DDT the alias [1,1,1 - trichloro -2,2 - bis (4 - chlorophenyl) ethane])
	--其他:								--Other :
2903.9910	---对氯甲苯	5.5	30		9	17	千克	AB	---*P*-Chlorotoluene
2903.9920	---3,4-二氯三氟甲苯	5.5	30		9	17	千克		---3, 4-Dichlorotrifluoride toluene

税则号列 Tariff Item	商品名称及备注	进口税率 最惠	普通	暂定	出口退税	增值税率	计量单位	监管条件	Article Description
2903.9930	---4-（4’-烷基苯基）-1-（4’-烷基苯基）-2-氟苯	5.5	30		13	17	千克		---4-(4’-alkylphenyl)-1-(4’-alkylphenyl)-2-fluorobenzene
2903.9990	---其他	5.5	30			17	千克		---Other
2903 9990.10	多氯联苯、多溴联苯	5.5	30		9	17	千克	89	Polychlorinated biphenyl, polybromobiphenyls
2903 9990.30	多氯三联苯(PCT)	5.5	30		9	17	千克	X	Polychlorinated Terphenyls (PCT)
2903 9990.40	稗草烯	5.5	30			17	千克	S	Tavron
2903 9990.90	其他芳烃卤化衍生物	5.5	30		9	17	千克		Other arene halogenate derivative
29.04	烃的磺化、硝化或亚硝化衍生物，不论是否卤化：								**Sulphonated, nitrated or nitrosated derivatives of hydrocarbons, whether or not halogenated:**
2904.1000	-仅含磺基的衍生物及其盐和乙酯	5.5	30		9	17	千克		-Derivatives containing only sulphogroups, their salts and ethyl esters
	-仅含硝基或亚硝基的衍生物：								-Derivatives containing only nitro or only nitroso groups:
2904.2010	---硝基苯	5.5	20		9	17	千克	AB	---Nitrobenzene
2904.2020	---硝基甲苯	5.5	30		9	17	千克		---Nitrotoluene and nitrochlorobenzene
2904.2030	---二硝基甲苯	5.5	20		9	17	千克	AB	---Dinitrotoluene and dinitrochlorobenzene
2904.2040	---三硝基甲苯(TNT)	5.5	40		9	17	千克	AB	---Trinitrotoluene (TNT)
2904.2090	---其他	5.5	30		9	17	千克		---Other
2904 2090.10	六硝基芪	5.5	30		9	17	千克	3	Hexanitrostilbene
2904 2090.20	4-硝基联苯	5.5	30		9	17	千克	X	4-Nitrobiphenyl
2904 2090.90	其他仅含硝基或亚硝基衍生物	5.5	30		9	17	千克		Other derivatives containing only nitro or only nitroso groups
	-其他:								-Other:
	---硝基氯化苯:								---Nitrochlorobenzene：
2904.9011	----邻硝基氯化苯	5.5	30		9	17	千克		----o-Nitrochlorobenzene
2904.9012	----间硝基氯化苯	5.5	30		9	17	千克		----m-Nitrochlorobenzene
2904.9013	----对硝基氯化苯	5.5	30		9	17	千克		----p-Nitrochlorobenzene
2904.9020	---二硝基氯化苯	5.5	20		9	17	千克		---Dinitrochlorobenzene
2904.9030	---三氯硝基甲烷（氯化苦；硝基氯仿）	5.5	30			17	千克	23S	---Trichloronitromethane（chloropicrin, nitrochloroform）
2904.9090	---其他	5.5	30			17	千克		---Other
2904 9090.11	氯硝丙烷	5.5	30			17	千克	S	Sodium chloride Propane
2904 9090.12	四氯硝基苯	5.5	30			17	千克	S	Tecnazene
2904 9090.13	五氯硝基苯	5.5	30			17	千克	S	Quintozine
2904 9090.14	全氟辛基磺酸、全氟辛基磺酸钾、全氟辛基磺酸锂、全氟辛基磺酸铵、全氟辛基磺酰氟	5.5	30			17	千克	X	Perfluorooctane sulfonic acid, Potassium heptadecafluoro-1-octanesulfonate, Ammonium perfluorooctanesulfonate,Perfluoro-1-octanesulfonyl fluoride
2904 9090.90	其他烃的磺化、硝化、亚硝化衍生物（不论是否卤化）	5.5	30		9	17	千克		Other sulphonated, nitrated,nitrosalted derivatives of hydrocarbons, whether or not halogenated
	第二分章　醇类及其卤化、磺化、硝化或亚硝化衍生物								**Ⅱ. ALCOHOLS AND THEIR HALOGENATED, SULPHONATED, NITRATED OR NITROSATED DERIVATIVES**
29.05	无环醇及其卤化、磺化、硝化或亚硝化衍生物：								**Acyclic alcohols and their halogenated, sulphonated, nitrated or nitrosated derivatives:**
	-饱和一元醇:								--Saturated monohydric alcohols:
2905.1100	--甲醇	5.5	30		13	17	千克	AB	--Methanol（methyl alcohol）
	--丙醇及异丙醇:								--Propan-1-ol（propyl alcohol）and propan-2-ol（isopropyl alcohol）:
2905.1210[暂]	---正丙醇	5.5	30	3	9	17	千克	AB	---Propan-1-ol（propyl alcohol）
2905.1220	---异丙醇	5.5	30		9	17	千克	AB	---Propan-2-ol（isopropyl alcohol）
2905.1300	--正丁醇	5.5	30		13	17	千克	AB	--Butan-l-ol（*n*-butyl alcohol）
	--其他丁醇:								--Other butanols:
2905.1410	---异丁醇	5.5	30		9	17	千克		---Isobutanol
2905.1420	---仲丁醇	5.5	30		9	17	千克		---Secbutanol

税则号列 Tariff Item	商品名称及备注	进口税率			出口增值退税税率		计量单位	监管条件	Article Description
		最惠	普通	暂定	出口退税	增值税率			
2905.1430	---叔丁醇	5.5	30		9	17	千克		---Tertiary butanol
	--辛醇及其异构体:								--Octanol（octyl alcohol） and isomers thereof:
2905.1610	---正辛醇	5.5	30		13	17	千克		---n-octanol
2905.1690	---其他	5.5	30		9	17	千克		---Other
2905.1700	--十二醇、十六醇及十八醇	7	30		9	17	千克		--Dodecan-1-ol（lauryl alcohol）, hexade can-1-ol（cetyl alcohol）and octadecan-1-ol（stearyl alcohol）
	--其他:								--Other:
2905.1910	---3,3-二甲基丁-2-醇(频哪基醇)	5.5	30		9	17	千克	23	---3, 3-Dimethyl-2-butanol（pinacolyl alcohol）
2905.1990	---其他	5.5	30		13	17	千克		---Other
2905 1990.10	三十烷醇	5.5	30		13	17	千克	S	Triacontanol
2905 1990.90	其他饱和一元醇	5.5	30		13	17	千克		Other saturated monohydric alcohols
	-不饱和一元醇:								-Unsaturated monohydric alcohols:
	--无环萜烯醇:								--Acyclic terpene alcohols:
2905.2210	---香叶醇、橙花醇（3，7-二甲基-2，6-辛二烯-1-醇）	5.5	30		9	17	千克		---Geraniol, nerol（cis-3, 7-Dimethyl-2, 6-octa-dien-l-ol）
2905.2220	---香茅醇（3，7-二甲基-6-辛烯-1-醇）	5.5	30		9	17	千克		---Citronellol（3, 7-Dimethyl-6-octen-1-ol）
2905.2230	---芳樟醇	5.5	30		13	17	千克	AB	---Linalool
2905.2290	---其他	5.5	30		9	17	千克		---Other
2905.2900	--其他	5.5	30		9	17	千克		--Other
	-二元醇:								-Diols:
2905.3100	--1,2-乙二醇	5.5	30		9	17	千克		--Ethylene glycol（ethanediol）
2905.3200[暂]	--1,2-丙二醇	5.5	30	3	9	17	千克		--Propylene glycol（propane-1, 2-diol）
	--其他:								-Other:
2905.3910	---2,5-二甲基己二醇	4	11		9	17	千克		---2.5-dimethyl hexandiol
2905.3990	---其他	5.5	30		9	17	千克		---Other
2905 3990.01[暂]	1,3-丙二醇	5.5	30	3	9	17	千克	AB	1,3-Propanediol
2905 3990.02	1,4-丁二醇	5.5	30		9	17	千克	AB	1,4-Butanediol
2905 3990.10	驱蚊醇	5.5	30		9	17	千克	S	Ethohexadiol
2905 3990.90	其他二元醇	5.5	30		9	17	千克	AB	Other diatomic alcohols
	-其他多元醇:								-Other polyhydric alcohols:
2905.4100	--2-乙基-2-（羟甲基）丙烷-1,3-二醇（三羟甲基丙烷）	5.5	30		9	17	千克		--2-Ethyl-2-（hydroxymethyl） propane-1, 3-diol（trimethylolpropane）
2905.4200	--季戊四醇	5.5	30		9	17	千克		--Pentaerythritol
2905.4300	--甘露糖醇	8	30		9	17	千克	AB	--Mannitol
2905.4400	--山梨醇	14	40		9	17	千克		--D-glucitol（sorbitol）
2905.4500[暂]	--丙三醇(甘油)	14	50	3	9	17	千克	AB	--Glycerol
	--其他:								--Other:
2905.4910	---木糖醇	5.5	30		9	17	千克	AB	---Xylitol
2905.4990	---其他	5.5	30		9	17	千克		---Other
	-无环醇的卤化、磺化、硝化或亚硝化衍生物:								-Halogenated,sulphonated,nitrated or nitrosated derivatives of acyclic alcohols:
2905.5100	--乙氯维诺（INN）	5.5	30		9	17	千克	I	--Ethchlorvynol（INN）
2905.5900	--其他	5.5	30		9	17	千克		--Other
2905 5900.10	乙氯维诺的盐	5.5	30		9	17	千克	I	Salts of Ethchlorvynol（INN）
2905 5900.20	2-氯乙醇	5.5	30		9	17	千克	3A	2-Chloroethanol
2905 5900.30	溴硝醇	5.5	30		9	17	千克		Bronopol(BAN)
2905 5900.40	鼠甘伏	5.5	30		9	17	千克	S	Gliftor
2905 5900.90	其他无环醇的卤化、磺化等衍生物	5.5	30		9	17	千克		Other halogenated, sulphonated derivatives of acyclic alcohol
29.06	环醇及其卤化、磺化、硝化或亚硝化衍生物:								**Cyclic alcohols and their halogenated, snlphonated, nitrated or nitrosated derivatives:**
	-环烷醇、环烯醇及环萜烯醇:								-Cyclanic, cyclenic or cycloterpenic:

税则号列 Tariff Item	商品名称及备注	进口税率 最惠	进口税率 普通	进口税率 暂定	出口退税	增值税率	计量单位	监管条件	Article Description
2906.1100	--薄荷醇	5	70		13	17	千克		--Menthol
2906.1200	--环己醇、甲基环己醇及二甲基环己醇	5.5	30		9	17	千克		--Cyclohexanol, methylcyclohexanols and dimethylcyctohexanols
2906 1200.10	甲基环己醇	5.5	30		9	17	千克	AB	Methylcyclohexanols
2906 1200.90	环己醇,二甲基环己醇	5.5	30		9	17	千克		Cyclohexanol, dimethyl-cyclohexanol
	--固醇及肌醇:								--Sterols and inositols:
2906.1310[暂]	---固醇	5.5	30	3	9	17	千克		---Sterol
2906.1320	---肌醇	5.5	30		9	17	千克	AB	---Inositol
	--其他:								--Other:
2906.1910	---萜品醇	5.5	30		9	17	千克		---Terpineols
2906.1990	---其他	5.5	30		13	17	千克		---Other
2906 1990.11	5α-雄烷-3α，17α-二醇（阿法雄烷二醇）(包括5α-雄烷-3β，17β-二醇(倍他雄烷二醇))	5.5	30		13	17	千克	L	5α-androstane-3α,17α-diol (including 5α-androstane-3β,17β-diol)
2906 1990.12	雄甾-4-烯-3α，17α-二醇(包括雄甾-4-烯-3α，17β-二醇)	5.5	30		13	17	千克	L	4-Androstenediol (3α,17α) 〔including 4-Androstene-diol (3α,17β)〕
2906 1990.13	雄甾-5-烯-3α，17α-二醇(包括雄甾-5-烯-3α，17β-二醇)	5.5	30		13	17	千克	L	5-Androstenediol (3α,17α) 〔including 5-Androstene-diol (3α,17β)〕
2906 1990.90	其他环烷醇，环烯醇及环萜烯醇	5.5	30		13	17	千克		Other cyclanic, cyclenic or cycloterpenic
	-芳香醇:								-Aromatic:
2906.2100	--苄醇	5	30		9	17	千克		--Benzyl alcohol
	--其他:								--Other:
2906.2910	---2-苯基乙醇	5.5	30		9	17	千克		---2-Phenylethyl alcohol
2906.2990	---其他	5.5	30		9	17	千克		---Other
2906 2990.10	三氯杀螨醇、杀螨醇	5.5	30		9	17	千克	S	Dicofol, chlorfenethol
2906 2990.90	其他芳香醇	5.5	30		9	17	千克		Other aromatic alcohols
	第三分章　酚、酚醇及其卤化、磺化、硝化或亚硝化衍生物								**Ⅲ.PHENOLS, PHENOL-ALCOHOLS, AND THEIR HALOGENATED, SULPHONATED, NITRATED OR NITROSATED DERIVATIVES**
29.07	**酚；酚醇:**								**Phenols; phenol-alcohols:**
	-一元酚:								-Monophenols:
	--苯酚及其盐:								--Phenol（hydroxybenzene）and its salts:
2907.1110	---苯酚	5.5	30		13	17	千克	AB	---Phenol
2907.1190	---其他	5.5	30		9	17	千克		---Other
	--甲酚及其盐:								--Cresol and its salts:
	---甲酚:								---Cresol:
2907.1211[暂]	----间甲酚	5.5	30	3	9	17	千克		----m-Cresol
2907.1212[暂]	----邻甲酚	5.5	30	3	9	17	千克		----o-Cresol
2907.1219	----其他	5.5	30		9	17	千克	AB	----Other
2907.1290	---其他	5.5	30		9	17	千克		---Other
	--辛基酚、壬基酚及其异构体以及它们的盐:								--Octylphenol, nonylphenol and their isomers; salts thereof:
2907.1310	---壬基酚	5.5	30		9	17	千克	X	---Nonylphenol
2907.1390	---其他	5.5	30		9	17	千克		---Other
	--萘酚及其盐:								--Naphthols and their salts:
2907.1510	---2-萘酚（β-萘酚）	5.5	30		9	17	千克		---2-Naphthols（β-naphthol）
2907.1590	---其他	5.5	30		9	17	千克	AB	---Other
	--其他:								--Other:
2907.1910[暂]	---邻仲丁基酚、邻异丙基酚	4	11	2	9	17	千克		---*o*-Sec-butyl phenol, *o*-isopropyl phenol
2907 1910.10[暂]	邻异丙基(苯)酚	4	11	2	9	17	千克	AB	O-isopropyl (benzene) phenol
2907 1910.90[暂]	邻仲丁基酚	4	11	2	9	17	千克		2-(1-methylpropyl)phenol, 2-sec-buty phenol
2907.1990	---其他	5.5	30			17	千克		---Other
2907 1990.11	邻苯基苯酚及其盐	5.5	30			17	千克		O-phenylphenol and its salt

税则号列 Tariff Item	商品名称及备注	进口税率 最惠	普通	暂定	出口退税	增值税率	计量单位	监管条件	Article Description
2907 1990.12	邻烯丙基苯酚及盐	5.5	30			17	千克	S	O-allylphenol and salt
2907 1990.90	其他一元酚	5.5	30		9	17	千克		Other Monophenols
	-多元酚；酚醇:								-Polyphenols; phenol-alcohols:
2907.2100	--间苯二酚及其盐	5.5	30		9	17	千克		--*m*-Dihydroxybenzene（resorcinol）and its salts
2907 2100.01	间苯二酚	5.5	30		9	17	千克		*m*-Dihydroxybenzene（resorcinol）
2907 2100.90	间苯二酚盐	5.5	30		9	17	千克		Salts of *m*-Dihydroxybenzene（resorcinol）
	--对苯二酚及其盐:								--p-Dihydroxybenzene（hydroquinone）and its salts:
2907.2210	---对苯二酚	5.5	30		9	17	千克		---Hydroquinone
2907.2290	---其他	5.5	30		9	17	千克		---Other
2907.2300	--4，4’-异亚丙基联苯酚（双酚A，二苯基酚丙烷）及其盐	5.5	30		9	17	千克		--4, 4’-Isopropylidenediphenol（bisphenol A, diphenylolpropane）and its salts
2907 2300.01	双酚A（4，4-异亚丙基联苯酚）	5.5	30		9	17	千克		Bisphenol-A(4,4’-Isopropylidenediphenol)
2907 2300.90	双酚A的盐（4，4-异亚丙基联苯酚的盐）	5.5	30		9	17	千克		Salts of bisphenol-A (salts of 4,4’- Isopropylidene-diphenol)
	--其他:								--Other:
2907.2910	---邻苯二酚	4	11		9	17	千克		---*o*-Dihydroxybenzene（catechol, pyrocatechol）
2907.2990	---其他	5.5	30			17	千克		---Other
2907 2990.10	毒菌酚	5.5	30			17	千克	S	Hexachlorophene
2907 2990.90	其他多元酚;酚醇	5.5	30		9	17	千克	AB	Other Polyphenols; phenol-alcohols
29.08	**酚及酚醇的卤化、磺化、硝化或亚硝化衍生物:**								**Halogenated, sulphonated, nitrated or nitrosated derivatives of phenols or phenolalcohols:**
	-仅含卤素取代基的衍生物及其盐:								-Derivatives containing only halogen substituents and their salts:
2908.1100	--五氯苯酚（ISO）	5.5	30			17	千克	X	--Pentachlorophenol（ISO）
	--其他:								--Other:
2908.1910	---对氯苯酚	4	11		9	17	千克		---*p*-Chlorophenol
2908.1990	---其他	5.5	30			17	千克		---Other
2908 1990.21	格螨酯	5.5	30			17	千克	S	Genite
2908 1990.22	双氯酚	5.5	30			17	千克	S	Dichlorophene
2908 1990.23	五氯酚钠	5.5	30			17	千克	S	Sodium pentachlorophenate
2908 1990.90	其他仅含卤素取代基的衍生物及盐	5.5	30		9	17	千克		Other derivatives containing only halogen substituents and their salts
	-其他:								-Other:
2908.9100	--地乐酚（ISO）及其盐	5.5	30			17	千克	89	--Dinoseb（ISO）and its salts
2908.9200	--4,6-二硝基邻甲酚[二硝酚（ISO）]及其盐	5.5	30		9	17	千克	89	--4,6-Dinitro-o-cresol (DNOC (ISO)) and its salts
	--其他:								--Other:
2908.9910	---对硝基酚、对硝基酚钠	5.5	30			17	千克		---*p*-Nitrophenol, sodium *p*-nitro-phenolate
2908 9910.10	4-硝基苯酚（对硝基苯酚）	5.5	30		9	17	千克	X	4- Nitrophenol(p-nitrophenol)
2908 9910.90	对硝基苯酚钠	5.5	30			17	千克	S	Sodium para-nitrophenolate
2908.9990	---其他	5.5	30			17	千克		---Other
2908 9990.21	芬螨酯	5.5	30			17	千克	S	Fenson
2908 9990.22	消螨酚	5.5	30			17	千克	S	Dinex
2908 9990.23	戊硝酚	5.5	30			17	千克	S	Dinosam
2908 9990.24	特乐酚	5.5	30			17	千克	S	Dinoterb
2908 9990.90	其他酚及酚醇的卤化等衍生物（包括其磺化、硝化或亚硝化衍生物）	5.5	30		9	17	千克		Other Halogenated, sulphonated, nitrated or nitrosated derivatives of phenols or phenolalcohols
	第四分章　醚、过氧化醇、过氧化醚、过氧化酮、三节环环氧化物、缩醛及半缩醛及其卤化、磺化、硝化或亚硝化衍生物								**Ⅳ. ETHERS, ALCOHOL PEROXIDES, ETHER PEROXIDES, KETONE PEROXIDES, EPOXIDES WITH A THREE-MEMBERED RING, ACETALS AND HEMIACETALS, AND THEIR HALOGENATED, SULPHONATED, NITRATED OR NITROSATED DERIVATIVES**

税则号列 Tariff Item	商品名称及备注	进口税率 最惠	普通	暂定	出口退税	增值税率	计量单位	监管条件	Article Description
29.09	**醚、醚醇、醚酚、醚醇酚、过氧化醇、过氧化醚、过氧化酮（不论是否已有化学定义）及其卤化、磺化、硝化或亚硝化衍生物:**								**Ethers, ether-alcohols, ether-phenols, ether-alcohol-phenols, alcohol peroxides, ether peroxides, ketone peroxides(whether or not chemically defined), and their halogenated, sulphonated, nitrated or nitrosated derivatives:**
	-无环醚及其卤化、磺化、硝化或亚硝化衍生物:								-Acyclic ethers and their halogenated, sulphonated, nitrated or nitrosated derivatives:
2909.1100	--乙醚	5.5	30		9	17	千克	23	--Diethyl ether
	--其他:								--Other:
2909.1910	---甲醚	5.5	30		13	17	千克		---Methyl ether
2909.1990	---其他	5.5	30		13/15	17	千克		---Other
2909 1990.11	八氯二丙醚	5.5	30		13/15	17	千克	S	Octachlorodipropyl ether
2909 1990.12	二氯异丙醚	5.5	30		13/15	17	千克	S	Nemamort（DCIP）
2909 1990.90	其他无环醚及其卤化等衍生物（包括其磺化、硝化或亚硝化衍生物）	5.5	30		13/15	17	千克		Other acyclic ethers and their halogenated, sulphonated, nitrated or nitrosated derivatives
2909.2000	-环烷醚、环烯醚或环萜烯醚及其卤化、磺化、硝化或亚硝化衍生物	5.5	30		9	17	千克		-Cyclanic, cyclenic or cycloterpenie ethers and their halogenated, sulphonated, nitrated or nitrosated derivatives
	-芳香醚及其卤化、磺化、硝化或亚硝化衍生物:								-Aromatic ethers and their halogenated, sulphonated, nitrated or nitrosated derivatives:
2909.3010	---1-烷氧基-4-（4-乙烯基环己基）-2，3-二氟苯	5.5	30		9	17	千克		---1-Alkoxy-4-(4-vinylcyclohexyl)-2,3-difluorobenzene
2909.3090	---其他	5.5	30			17	千克		---Other
2909 3090.11	甲氧滴滴涕、除草醚	5.5	30			17	千克	S	Methoxychlor, nitrofen
2909 3090.12	醚菊酯、苄螨醚、三氟醚	5.5	30		9	17	千克	S	Ethofenprox,halfenprox,trifluoro
2909 3090.13	氯苯甲醚、甲氧除草醚	5.5	30		9	17	千克	S	Chloroneb, chlomethoxyfen
2909 3090.14	三氟硝草醚、草枯醚	5.5	30		9	17	千克	S	Fluordifen, chlonitrofen
2909 3090.15	氟除草醚、乙氧氟草醚	5.5	30		9	17	千克	S	Fluoronitrofen,oxyfluorfen
2909 3090.90	其他芳香醚及其卤化、磺化、硝化衍生物(包括其亚硝化衍生物)	5.5	30		9	17	千克		Other aromatic ethers and their halogenated, sulphonated, nitrated or nitrosated derivatives
	-醚醇及其卤化、磺化、硝化或亚硝化衍生物:								-Ether-alcohols and their halogenated, sulphonated, nitrated or nitrosated derivatives:
2909.4100[暂]	--2,2′-氧联二乙醇(二甘醇)	5.5	30	3	9	17	千克		--2, 2′-Oxydiethanol（diethylene glycol,digol）
2909.4300	--乙二醇或二甘醇的单丁醚	5.5	30		9	17	千克		--Monobutyl ethers of ethylene glycol or of diethylene glycol
2909.4400	--乙二醇或二甘醇的其他单烷基醚	5.5	30		9	17	千克		--Other monoalkylethers of ethylene glycol or of diethylene glycol
	--其他:								--Other:
2909.4910	---间苯氧基苄醇	4	11		9	17	千克		---*m*-Phenoxy benzalcohol
2909.4990	---其他	5.5	30		9	17	千克		---Other
2909.5000	-醚酚、醚醇酚及其卤化、磺化、硝化或亚硝化衍生物	5.5	30		9	17	千克		-Ether-phenols, ether-alcohol-phenols and their halogenated, sulphonated, nitrated or nitrosated derivatives
2909.6000	-过氧化醇、过氧化醚、过氧化酮(含其卤化、磺化、硝化或亚硝化衍生物)	5.5	30		9	17	千克		-Alcohol peroxides, ether peroxides, ketone peroxides and their halogenated, sulphonated, nitrated or nitrosated derivatives
29.10	**三节环环氧化物、环氧醇、环氧酚、环氧醚及其卤化、磺化、硝化或亚硝化衍生物:**								**Epoxides, epoxyalcohols, epoxyphenols and epoxyethers, with a three-membered ring, and their halogenated, sulphonated, nitrated or nitrosated derivatives:**
2910.1000	-环氧乙烷(氧化乙烯)	5.5	30		13	17	千克	X	-Oxirane（ethylene oxide）
2910.2000	-甲基环氧乙烷(氧化丙烯)	5.5	30			17	千克		-Methyloxirane（propylene oxide）
2910.3000	-1-氯-2,3-环氧丙烷(表氯醇)	5.5	30			17	千克		-1-Chloro-2, 3-epoxypropane（epichlorohydrin）
2910.4000	-狄氏剂(ISO、INN)	5.5	30			17	千克	89	-Dieldrin（ISO, INN）

税则号列 Tariff Item	商品名称及备注	进口税率 最惠	普通	暂定	出口退税	增值税率	计量单位	监管条件	Article Description
2910.9000	-其他	5.5	30			17	千克		-Other
2910 9000.10	异狄氏剂	5.5	30			17	千克	89	Endrin
2910 9000.20	灭草环	5.5	30		13	17	千克	S	Tridiphane
2910 9000.90	三节环环氧化物，环氧醇(酚、醚)(包括其卤化、磺化、硝化或亚硝化的衍生物)	5.5	30		13	17	千克		Epoxides, epoxyalcohols, with a three-membered ring, and their halogenated, sulphonated, nitrated or nitrosated derivatives
29.11	**缩醛及半缩醛，不论是否含有其他含氧基，及其卤化、磺化、硝化或亚硝化衍生物：**								**Acetals and hemiacetals, whether or not with other oxygen function, and their halogenated, sulphonated, nitrated or nitrosated derivatives:**
2911.0000	缩醛及半缩醛，不论是否含其他含氧基，及其卤化、磺化、硝化或亚硝化衍生物	5.5	30		9	17	千克		Acetals and hemiacetals, whether or not with other oxygen function, and their halogenated, sulphonated, nitrated or nitrosated derivatives
	第五分章　醛基化合物								**V.　ALDEHYDE-FUNCTION COMPO-UNDS**
29.12	**醛，不论是否含有其他含氧基；环聚醛；多聚甲醛：**								**Aldehydes, whether or not with other oxygen function; cyclic polymers of aldehydes; paraformaldehyde:**
	-不含其他含氧基的无环醛：								-Acyclic aldehydes without other oxygen function:
2912.1100	--甲醛	5.5	30		9	17	千克	AB	--Methanal（formaldehyde）
2912.1200	--乙醛	5.5	30		9	17	千克	X	--Ethanal（acetaldehyde）
2912.1900	--其他	5.5	30		9	17	千克		--Other
2912 1900.01[暂]	乙二醛	5.5	30	3	9	17	千克		Glyoxal
2912 1900.30	丙烯醛	5.5	30		9	17	千克	X	Acrolein
2912 1900.90	其他无环醛(指不含其他含氧基)	5.5	30		9	17	千克		Other acyclic aldehydes without other oxygen function
	-不含其他含氧基的环醛：								-Cyclic aldehydes without other oxygen function:
2912.2100	--苯甲醛	5.5	30		9	17	千克		--Benzaldehyde
	--其他：								--Other:
2912.2910	---铃兰醛(对叔丁基-α-甲基-氧化肉桂醛)	5.5	30		9	17	千克		---Lilial（p-tert-butyl-α-methyl-oxocinn amaldehyde）
2912.2990	---其他	5.5	30		13	17	千克		---Other
	-醛醇、醛醚、醛酚及含其他含氧基的醛：								-Aldehyde-alcohos, aldehyde-e-ethers, aldehy-phenols and aldehydes with other oxygen function:
2912.4100	--香草醛(3-甲氧基-4-羟基苯甲醛)	5.5	30		13	17	千克		--Vanillin（4-hydroxy-3-methox-ybenzaldehyde）
2912.4200	--乙基香草醛	5.5	30		13	17	千克		--Ethylvanillin
	--其他：								--Other :
2912.4910	---醛醇	5.5	30		13	17	千克		---Aldehyde-alcohols
2912.4990	---其他	5.5	30		9	17	千克		---Other
2912.5000	-环聚醛	5.5	30		9	17	千克		-Cyclic polymers of aldehydes
2912 5000.10	四聚乙醛	5.5	30		9	17	千克	S	Metaldehyde
2912 5000.90	其他环聚醛	5.5	30		9	17	千克		Other cyclic polymers of aldehydes
2912.6000	-多聚甲醛	5.5	30		9	17	千克	AB	-Paraformaldehyde
29.13	**品目29.12所列产品的卤化、磺化、硝化或亚硝化衍生物：**								**Halogenated, sulphonated, nitrated or nitrosated derivatives of products of heading No.29.12:**
2913.0000	品目29.12所列产品的卤化、磺化、硝化或亚硝化衍生物	5.5	30		9	17	千克		Halogenated, sulphonated, nitrated or nitrosated derivatives of products of heading No.29.12
2913 0000.10	三氯乙醛	5.5	30		9	17	千克	ABG	Chloral hydrate
2913 0000.90	品目29.12所列产品的其他衍生物(指卤化、磺化、硝化或亚硝化的衍生物)	5.5	30		9	17	千克		Halogenated, sulphonated, nitrated or nitrosated derivatives of articles of heading No.29.12
	第六分章　酮基化合物及醌基化合物								**VI. KETONE-FUNCTION COMPOUNDS AND QUINONEFUNCTION COMPOUNDS**
29.14	**酮及醌，不论是否含有其他含氧基，及其卤化、磺化、硝化或亚硝化衍生物：**								**Ketones and quinones, whether or not with other oxygen function, and their halogenated, sulphonated, nitrated or nitrosated derivatives:**

税则号列 Tariff Item	商品名称及备注	进口税率 最惠	普通	暂定	出口退税	增值税率	计量单位	监管条件	Article Description
	-不含其他含氧基的无环酮:								-Acyclic ketones without other oxygen function:
2914.1100	--丙酮(二甲基甲酮、二甲酮、醋酮、木酮	5.5	20		13	17	千克	23	--Acetone (dimethyl ketone, dimethyl ketone, vinegar ketone, xylulose)
2914.1200	--丁酮[甲基乙基(甲)酮]	5.5	30		9	17	千克	23	--Butanone（methyl ethyl ketone）
2914.1300	--4-甲基-2-戊酮[甲基异丁基(甲)酮]	5.5	30		9	17	千克		--4-Methl1-2-pentanone（isobutylmethyl ketone）
2914.1900	--其他	5.5	30		9	17	千克		--Other
2914 1900.10	频哪酮	5.5	30		9	17	千克	23	Pinacolone
2914 1900.90	其他不含其他含氧基的无环酮	5.5	30		9	17	千克		Other acyclic ketones, without other oxygen function
	-不含其他含氧基的环烷酮、环烯酮或环萜烯酮:								-Cyclanic, cyclenic or cycloterpenic ketones without other oxygen function:
2914.2200	--环已酮及甲基环已酮	5.5	30		9	17	千克	AB	--Cyclohexanone and methylcyclohexanone
2914.2300	--芷香酮及甲基芷香酮	5.5	30		9	17	千克		--Ionones and methylionones
	--其他:								--Other :
2914.2910	---樟脑	5.5	40		9	17	千克	B	---Camphor
2914.2990	---其他	5.5	30		13	17	千克		---Other
	-不含其他含氧基的芳香酮:								-Aromatic ketones without other oxygen function:
2914.3100	--苯丙酮(苯基丙-2-酮)	5.5	30		9	17	千克	23	--Propiophenone（phenyl propan-2-one）
	--其他:								--Other:
2914.3910	---苯乙酮	4	11		9	17	千克		---Acetophenone
2914.3990	---其他	5.5	30			17	千克		---Other
2914 3990.11	杀鼠酮	5.5	30		9	17	千克	S	Duocide
2914 3990.12	鼠完	5.5	30			17	千克	S	Pindone
2914 3990.13	敌鼠	5.5	30		9	17	千克	S	Diphacinone
2914 3990.14	邻氯苯基环戊酮	5.5	30		9	17	千克	23	O-chlorophenyl cyclopentanone
2914 3990.90	其他不含其他含氧基的芳香酮	5.5	30		13	17	千克		Other aromatic ketones without other oxygen function
2914.4000	-酮醇及酮醛	5.5	30			17	千克		-Ketone-alcohols and ketone-aldehydes
2914 4000.10	敌鼠钠	5.5	30			17	千克	S	Diphacinone Sodium
2914 4000.20	3β-羟基-5α-雄烷-17-酮、表睾酮	5.5	30		9	17	千克	L	3β-Hydroxy-5α-androstane-17-ketone,epitestosterone
2914 4000.90	其他酮醇及酮醛	5.5	30		9	17	千克		Other ketoe-alcohol and ketoe-aldehyde
	-酮酚及含有其他含氧基的酮:								-Ketone-phenols and ketones with other oxygen function:
	---酮酚:								---Ketone-phenols:
2914.5011	----覆盆子酮	5.5	30		9	17	千克		----Raspberry ketone
2914.5019	----其他	5.5	30		9	17	千克		----Other
2914.5020	---2-羟基-4-甲氧基二苯甲酮	5.5	30		9	17	千克		---2-Hydroxy-4-methoxy dibenzophenone
2914.5090	---其他	5.5	30		9	17	千克		---Other
2914 5090.11	肟草酮,双炔酰菌胺	5.5	30		9	17	千克	S	Tralkoxydim, Mandipropamid
2914 5090.12	甲氧虫酰肼	5.5	30		9	17	千克	S	Methoxyfenozide
2914 5090.90	含其他含氧基的酮	5.5	30		9	17	千克		etone with other oxygen function
	-醌:								-Quinones:
2914.6100	--蒽醌	5.5	30		9	17	千克		--Anthraquinone
	--其他:								--Other:
2914.6910	---辅酶Q10	5.5	30		9	17	千克		---CoenzymeQ10
2914.6990	---其他	5.5	30		9	17	千克		---Other
2914 6990.10	大黄素甲醚	5.5	30		9	17	千克	S	Physcione
2914 6990.90	其他醌	5.5	30		9	17	千克		Other quinones
2914.7000	-卤化、磺化、硝化或亚硝化衍生物	5.5	30			17	千克		-Halogenated, sulphonated, nitrated or nitrosated derivatives
2914 7000.11	氯鼠酮,表苯草酮、茚草酮	5.5	30			17	千克	S	Chlorophacinone, indanofan
2914 7000.12	二氯萘醌	5.5	30			17	千克	S	Dichlone
2914 7000.13	四氯对醌	5.5	30			17	千克	S	Chloranil

税则号列 Tariff Item	商品名称及备注	进口税率 最惠	进口税率 普通	进口税率 暂定	出口退税	增值税率	计量单位	监管条件	Article Description
2914 7000.14	六氯丙酮	5.5	30			17	千克	S	Hexachloroacetone
2914 7000.15	氯敌鼠钠盐	5.5	30		9	17	千克	S	Chlorophacinone
2914 7000.90	其他酮及醌的卤化、磺化衍生物（包括硝化或亚硝化衍生物）	5.5	30		9	17	千克		Halogenated, sulphonated, nitrated or nitrosated derivatives of other ketones and quinones
	第七分章　羧酸及其酸酐、酰卤化物、过氧化物和过氧酸以及它们的卤化、磺化、硝化或亚硝化衍生物								**Ⅶ.CARBOXYLIC ACIDS AND THEIR ANHYDRIDES, HALIDES, PEROXIDES AND PEROXYACIDS AND THEIR HALOGENATED, SULPHONATED,NITRATED OR NITROSATED DERIVATIVES**
29.15	**饱和无环一元羧酸及其酸酐、酰卤化物、过氧化物和过氧酸，以及它们的卤化、磺化、硝化或亚硝化衍生物:**								**Saturated acyclic monocarboxylic acids and their anhydrides, halides, peroxides and peroxyacids; their halogenated, sulphonated, nitrated or nitrosated derivatives:**
	-甲酸及其盐和酯:								-Formic acid, its salts and esters:
2915.1100	--甲酸	5.5	40		9	17	千克	AB	--Formic acid
2915.1200	--甲酸盐	5.5	30		9	17	千克		--Salts of formic acid
2915.1300	--甲酸酯	5.5	30		9	17	千克		--Esters of formic acid
	-乙酸及其盐；乙酸酐:								-Acetic acid and its salts; acetic anhydride:
	--乙酸:								--Acetic acid:
	---冰乙酸:								---Acetic acid, glacial:
2915.2111	----食品级的	5.5	30		9	17	千克	ABG	----Food grade
2915.2119	----其他	5.5	30		9	17	千克	G	----Other
2915.2190	---其他	5.5	50		9	17	千克		---Other
2915 2190.10	乙酸溶液，80≥含量＞10%	5.5	50		9	17	千克	ABG	Acetic acid solution, 80≥content> 10%
2915 2190.20	乙酸，含量＞80%	5.5	50		9	17	千克	ABG	Acetic acid content> 80%
2915 2190.90	其他乙酸	5.5	50		9	17	千克	ABG	Other acetic acid
2915.2400	--乙酸酐	5.5	50		9	17	千克	23	--Acetic anhydride
	--其他:								--Other:
2915.2910	---乙酸钠	5.5	50		9	17	千克	ABG	---Sodium acetate
2915.2990	---其他	5.5	50		9	17	千克		---Other
2915 2990.11	乙酸铜	5.5	50		9	17	千克		Copper acetate
2915 2990.23	乙酸铅(醋酸铅)	5.5	50		9	17	千克	X	Lead acetate
2915 2990.90	其他乙酸盐	5.5	50		9	17	千克	AB	Salts of other Acetate acid
	-乙酸酯:								-Esters of acetic acid:
2915.3100	--乙酸乙酯	5.5	30		9	17	千克	ABG	-Ethyl acetate
2915.3200	--乙酸乙烯酯	5.5	30		9	17	千克	AB	--Vinyl acetate
2915.3300	--乙酸（正）丁酯	5.5	30		9	17	千克	AB	--*n*-Butyl acetate
2915.3600	--地乐酚(ISO)乙酸酯	5.5	30			17	千克	S	--Dinoseb（ISO）acetate
2915.3900	--其他	5.5	30			17	千克		--Other
2915 3900.11	三氯杀虫酯	5.5	30		13	17	千克	S	Acetofenate
2915 3900.13	特乐酯	5.5	30		13	17	千克	S	Dinoterb acetate
2915 3900.14	灭螨醌	5.5	30			17	千克	S	Acequinocyl
2915 3900.15	红铃虫性诱素	5.5	30		13	17	千克	S	11-hexadecadien-1-yl-acetate
2915 3900.16	种衣酯	5.5	30		13	17	千克	S	Fenitropan
2915 3900.90	其他乙酸酯	5.5	30		13	17	千克	AB	Esters of other acetic acid
2915.4000	--一氯代乙酸、二氯乙酸或三氯乙酸及其盐和酯	5.5	30			17	千克		-Mono-, di-or trichloroacetic acids, their salts and esters
2915 4000.10	一氯醋酸钠	5.5	30			17	千克		Sodium monochloracetate
2915 4000.90	其他一氯代乙酸的盐和酯（包括二氯乙酸或三氯乙酸的盐和酯）	5.5	30		9	17	千克		Other mono-, di-or trichloroacetic acid salts and esters
	-丙酸及其盐和酯:								-Propionic acid, its salts and esters:
2915.5010[暂]	---丙酸	5.5	30	3	9	17	千克	AB	---Propionic acid
2915.5090	---其他	5.5	30		9	17	千克	AB	---Other
2915.6000	-丁酸、戊酸及其盐和酯	5.5	30		9	17	千克		-Butanoic acids, pentanoic acids, their salts and

税则号列 Tariff Item	商品名称及备注	进口税率 最惠	普通	暂定	出口退税	增值税率	计量单位	监管条件	Article Description
									esters
	-棕榈酸、硬脂酸及其盐和酯:								-Palmitic acid, stearic acid, their salts and esters:
2915.7010	---硬脂酸	7	50		9	17	千克	AB	---Stearic acid
2915.7090	---其他	5.5	30		9	17	千克		---Other
2915.9000	-其他	5.5	30			17	千克		-Other
2915 9000.11	茅草枯	5.5	30			17	千克	S	Dalapon
2915 9000.12	抑草蓬	5.5	30			17	千克	S	Erbon
2915 9000.13	四氟丙酸	5.5	30		9	17	千克	S	Flupropanate
2915 9000.20	氟乙酸钠	5.5	30		9	17	千克	89	Sodium fluoroacetate
2915 9000.90	其他饱和无环一元羧酸及其酸酐[(酰卤、过氧)化物,过氧酸及其卤化、硝化、磺化、亚硝化衍生物]	5.5	30		9	17	千克	AB	Other Saturated acyclic monocarboxylic acids and their anhydrides, halides, peroxides and peroxyacids; their halogenated, sulphonated, nitrated or nitrosated derivatives
29.16	**不饱和无环一元羧酸、环一元羧酸及其酸酐、酰卤化物、过氧化物和过氧酸,以及它们的卤化、磺化、硝化或亚硝化衍生物:**								**Unsaturated acyclie monocarboxylic acids, cyclic monocarboxylie acids, their anhydrides, halides, peroxides and peroxyacids; their halogenated, sulphonated, nitrated or nitrosated derivatives:**
	-不饱和无环一元羧酸及其酸酐、酰卤化物、过氧化物和过氧酸以及它们的衍生物:								-Unsaturated acyclic monocarboxylic acids, their anhydrides, halides, peroxides, peroxyacids and their derivatives:
2916.1100	--丙烯酸及其盐	6.5	30		9	17	千克		--Acrylic acid and its salts
	--丙烯酸酯:								--Esters of acrylic acid:
2916.1210	---丙烯酸甲酯	6.5	30		9	17	千克	AB	---Methyl acrylate
2916.1220	---丙烯酸乙酯	6.5	30		9	17	千克	AB	---Ethyl acrylate
2916.1230	---丙烯酸丁酯	6.5	30		9	17	千克		---Butyl acrylate
2916 1230.01	丙烯酸正丁酯	6.5	30		9	17	千克	AB	N-butyl Acrylate
2916 1230.90	丙烯酸异丁酯	6.5	30		9	17	千克	AB	Isobutyl acylate
2916.1240	---丙烯酸异辛酯	6.5	30		9	17	千克		---Isooctyl acrylate
2916.1290	---其他	6.5	30		9	17	千克		---Other
2916.1300	--甲基丙烯酸及其盐	6.5	80		13	17	千克		--Methacrylic acid and its salts
2916 1300.10	甲基丙烯酸	6.5	80		13	17	千克	AB	Methacrylic acid
2916 1300.90	甲基丙烯酸盐	6.5	80		13	17	千克		Salts of methacrylic acid
2916.1400	--甲基丙烯酸酯	6.5	80		13	17	千克		--Esters of methacrylie acid
2916.1500	--油酸、亚油酸或亚麻酸及其盐和酯	6.5	30		9	17	千克		--Oleic, linoleic or linotenic acids, their salts and esters
2916.1600	--乐杀螨(ISO)	6.5	30			17	千克	S	--Binapacryl (ISO)
2916.1900	--其他	6.5	30		9	17	千克		--Other
2916 1900.11	烯虫乙酯	6.5	30		9	17	千克	S	Hydroprene
2916 1900.12	烯虫炔酯	6.5	30		9	17	千克	S	Kinoprene
2916 1900.13	消螨普	6.5	30		9	17	千克	S	Dinocap
2916 1900.90	其他不饱和无环一元羧酸(包括其酸酐,酰卤化物,过氧化物和过氧酸及它们的衍生物)	6.5	30		9	17	千克	AB	Other unsaturated acyclic monocarboxylic acids, their anhydrides, halides, peroxides, peroxyacids and their derivatives
	-环烷一元羧酸、环烯一元羧酸或环萜烯一元羧酸及其酸酐、酰卤化物、过氧化物和过氧酸以及它们的衍生物:								-Cyclanic, cyclenic or cycloterpenic monocarboxylic acids, their anhydrides, halides, peroxides, peroxyacids and their derivatives:
2916.2010	---二溴菊酸、DV 菊酸甲酯	4	11		9	17	千克		---Dibromochrysanthermic acid, DVchrysanthemimono carboxylate
2916.2090	---其他	6.5	30		9	17	千克		---Other
2916 2090.21	苄菊酯、苯醚菊酯(包括右旋苯醚菊酯、富右旋反式苯醚菊酯)	6.5	30		9	17	千克	S	Dimethirn, Phenothrin (including dphenothrin, rich-d-trans-phenothrin)
2916 2090.22	苄烯菊酯、氯菊酯(包括生物氯菊酯)	6.5	30		9	17	千克	S	Butethrin, Permethrin (including Trans-Permethrin)
2916 2090.23	氯烯炔菊酯、联苯菊酯	6.5	30		9	17	千克	S	Chlorempenthrin, Bifenthrin

税则号列 Tariff Item	商品名称及备注	进口税率 最惠	普通	暂定	出口退税	增值税率	计量单位	监管条件	Article Description
2916 2090.24	七氟菊酯、四氟苯菊酯、五氟苯菊酯、七氟甲醚菊酯(包括甲氧苄氟菊酯、氯氟醚菊酯)	6.5	30		9	17	千克	S	Tefluthrin, transfluthrin, fenfluthrin, sevoflurane methothrin (incuding metofluthrin, lambda ethofenprox)
2916 2090.25	戊菊酯、环螨酯	6.5	30		9	17	千克	S	Valerate, cyclopropate
2916 2090.26	四氟甲醚菊酯、烯炔菊酯(包括右旋烯炔菊酯、富右旋反式烯炔菊酯)	6.5	30		9	17	千克	S	Dimefluthrin, empenthrin（including d-empenthrin, rich-d-empenthrin）
2916 2090.27	炔丙菊酯(包括右旋炔丙菊酯、富右旋反式炔丙菊酯)	6.5	30		9	17	千克	S	Prallethrin（including d-prallethrin, rich-d-t-prallethrin）
2916 2090.28	氯丙炔菊酯(包括右旋反式氯丙炔菊酯)	6.5	30		9	17	千克	S	Chlorpromazine acetylene Permethrin（including d-trans-permethrin chlorpromazine acetylene）
2916 2090.90	其他(环烷、环烯、环萜烯)一元羧酸(包括酸酐、酰卤化物、过氧化物和过氧酸及其衍生物)	6.5	30		9	17	千克	AB	Other (cycloalkane, cyclenes, acyclic terpene) monocarboxylic acids (including acid anhydride, etheride, peroxide and peroxy-acid and their derivatives)
	-芳香一元羧酸及其酸酐、酰卤化物、过氧化物和过氧酸以及它们的衍生物:								-Aromatic monocarboxylic acids, their anhydrides, halides, peroxides, peroxyacids and their derivatives:
2916.3100	--苯甲酸及其盐和酯	6.5	30			17	千克		--Benzoic acid, its salts and esters
2916 3100.20	2-(乙酰氧基)苯甲酸	6.5	30			17	千克	S	2-（acetoxy）benzoic acid
2916 3100.90	其他苯甲酸及其盐和酯	6.5	30		9	17	千克	AB	Other benzoic acid and its salts and ester
2916.3200	--过氧化苯甲酰及苯甲酰氯	6.5	30		9	17	千克	AB	--Benzoyl peroxied and benzoyl chloride
2916.3400	--苯乙酸及其盐	6.5	30		9	17	千克		--Phenylacetic acid and its salts
2916 3400.10	苯乙酸	6.5	30		9	17	千克	23	Phenylacetic acid
2916 3400.90	苯乙酸盐	6.5	30		9	17	千克		Phenylacetic acid and its salts
	--其他:								--Other:
2916.3910	---邻甲基苯甲酸	6.5	30		9	17	千克		---*o*-Methylbenzoic acid
2916.3920	---布洛芬	6.5	30		9	17	千克		---Brufen（Ibuprofen）
2916.3990	---其他	6.5	30			17	千克		---Other
2916 3990.12	草芽畏、燕麦酯	6.5	30		9	17	千克	S	2,3,6-TBA,methachlorphenprop
2916 3990.13	5-硝基邻甲氧基苯酸钠	6.5	30			17	千克	S	5- Sodium nitro-o-methoxy-benzene
2916 3990.14	对氯苯氧乙酸及其盐	6.5	30		9	17	千克	S	chlorophenoxyacetic acid and its salts
2916 3990.15	三碘苯甲酸	6.5	30			17	千克	S	Triiodobenzoic acid
2916 3990.16	萘乙酸	6.5	30		9	17	千克	S	Naphthylacetic acid
2916 3990.17	伐草克	6.5	30		9	17	千克	S	Chlorfenac
2916 3990.18	α-萘乙酸及其盐	6.5	30		9	17	千克	S	α-Naphthylacetic acid and its salts
2916 3990.90	其他芳香一元羧酸	6.5	30		9	17	千克		Other aromatic monocarboxylic acids
29.17	**多元羧酸及其酸酐、酰卤化物、过氧化物和过氧酸,以及它们的卤化、磺化、硝化或亚硝化衍生物:**								**Polycarboxylic acids, their anhydrides, halides, peroxides and peroxyacids;their halogennated, sulphonated, nitrated or nitrosated derivatives:**
	-无环多元羧酸及其酸酐、酰卤化物、过氧化物和过氧酸以及它们的衍生物:								-Acyclie polycarboxylic acids, their anhydrides, halides, peroxides, peroxyacids and their derivatives:
	--草酸及其盐和酯:								--Oxalie acid, its salts and esters:
2917.1110	---草酸	6.5	40		9	17	千克		---Oxalic acid
2917.1120	---草酸钴	9	30		9	17	千克	4xy	---Cobalt oxalate
2917.1190	---其他	6.5	30		9	17	千克		---Other
2917.1200	--己二酸及其盐和酯	6.5	30		13	17	千克		--Adipic acid and its salts and esters
2917 1200.01	己二酸	6.5	30		13	17	千克	AB	Adipic acid
2917 1200.90	己二酸盐和酯	6.5	30		13	17	千克	AB	Adipic acid salts and esters
	--壬二酸、癸二酸及其盐和酯:								--Azelaic acid, sebacic acid, their salts and esters:
2917.1310	---癸二酸及其盐和酯	6.5	30		9	17	千克		---Sebacic acid, its salts and esters
2917.1390	---其他	6.5	30		9	17	千克		---Other
2917.1400	--马来酐	6.5	30		9	17	千克		--Maleic anhydride
2917.1900	--其他	6.5	30			17	千克		--Other

税则号列 Tariff Item	商品名称及备注	进口税率 最惠	普通	暂定	出口退税	增值税率	计量单位	监管条件	Article Description
2917 1900.10	驱虫特、硝苯菌酯	6.5	30			17	千克	S	Dibutyl Succinate, meptyldinocap
2917 1900.90	其他无环多元羧酸	6.5	30		9	17	千克		Other acyclic pohycarboxylic acid
	-环烷多元羧酸、环烯多元羧酸、环萜烯多元羧酸及其酸酐、酰卤化物、过氧化物和过氧酸以及它们的衍生物:								-Cyclanic, eyclenic or cycloterpenic polycarboxylic acids, their anhydrides, halides, peroxides, peroxyacids and their derivatives:
2917.2010	---四氢苯酐	4	11		9	17	千克		---Tetrahydrobenzoic anhydride
2917.2090	---其他	6.5	30			17	千克		---Other
2917 2090.10	驱蚊灵	6.5	30			17	千克	S	Dimethyl carbat
2917 2090.90	其他(环烷、环烯、环萜烯)多元羧酸	6.5	30		9	17	千克	AB	Other（Cyclanic, cyclenic or cycloterpenic）polycarboxylic acids
	-芳香多元羧酸及其酸酐、酰卤化物、过氧化物和过氧酸以及它们的衍生物:								-Aromatic polycarboxylic acids, their anhydrides, halides,peroxides, peroxyacids and their derivatives:
2917.3200	--邻苯二甲酸二辛酯	6.5	30		9	17	千克		--Dioctyl orthophthalates
2917.3300	--邻苯二甲酸二壬酯及邻苯二甲酸二癸酯	6.5	30		9	17	千克		--Dinonyl or didecyl orthophthalates
	--其他邻苯二甲酸酯:								--Other esters of orthophthalic acid:
2917.3410	---邻苯二甲酸二丁酯	6.5	30			17	千克		---Dibutyl orthophthalates
2917 3410.10	驱蚊叮	6.5	30			17	千克	S	Dibutyl phthalate
2917 3410.90	其他邻苯二甲酸二丁酯	6.5	30		9	17	千克		Other dibutyl orthophthalate
2917.3490	---其他	6.5	30		9	17	千克		---Other
2917.3500	--邻苯二甲酸酐	6.5	30		9	17	千克	AB	--Phthalic anhydride
	--对苯二甲酸及其盐:								--Terephthalie acid and its salts:
	---对苯二甲酸:								---Terephthalic acid:
2917.3611	----精对苯二甲酸	6.5	30		13	17	千克		----PTA（Purified terephthalic acid）
2917.3619	----其他	6.5	30		9	17	千克		----Other
2917.3690	---其他	6.5	30		9	17	千克		---Other
2917.3700	--对苯二甲酸二甲酯	6.5	30		9	17	千克		--Dimethyl terephthalate
	--其他:								--Other:
2917.3910	---间苯二甲酸	6.5	30		9	17	千克		---M-phthalic acid
2917.3990	---其他	6.5	30		9	17	千克		---Other
2917 3990.11	酞菌酯	6.5	30		9	17	千克	S	Nitrothale-isopropyl
2917 3990.12	氯酞酸甲酯	6.5	30		9	17	千克	S	Chlorthal-dimethyl
2917 3990.13	氯酞酸	6.5	30		9	17	千克	S	Chlorthal
2917 3990.90	其他芳香多元羧酸	6.5	30		9	17	千克		Other aromatic polycarboxylic acid
29.18	**含附加含氧基的羧酸及其酸酐、酰卤化物、过氧化物和过氧酸,以及它们的卤化、磺化、硝化或亚硝化衍生物:**								**Carboxylic acids with additional oxygen function and their anhydrides, halides, peroxides and peroxyacids;their halogenated,sulphonated, nitrated or nitrosated derivatives:**
	-含醇基但不含其他含氧基的羧酸及其酸酐、酰卤化物、过氧化物和过氧酸以及它们的衍生物:								-Carboxylic acids with alcohol function but without other oxygen function, their anhydrides, halides, peroxides, peroxyacids and their derivatives:
2918.1100	--乳酸及其盐和酯	6.5	30		9	17	千克	AB	--Lactic acid, its salts and esters
2918.1200	--酒石酸	6.5	35		9	17	千克	AB	--Tartaric acid
2918.1300	--酒石酸盐及酒石酸酯	6.5	30		9	17	千克	AB	--Salts and esters of tartaric acid
2918.1400	--柠檬酸	6.5	35		13	17	千克	4ABxy	--Citric acid
2918.1500	--柠檬酸盐及柠檬酸酯	6.5	30		13	17	千克	4ABxy	--Salts and esters of citric acid
2918.1600	--葡糖酸及其盐和酯	6.5	30		9	17	千克		--Gluconic acid, its salts and esters
2918.1800	--乙酯杀螨醇(ISO)	6.5	30			17	千克	S	--Chlorobenzilate（ISO）
	--其他:								--Other:
2918.1910	---2,2-二苯基-2-羟基乙酸(二苯羟乙酸;二苯乙醇酸)	6.5	30		9	17	千克	23	---2, 2-Diphenyl-2-hydroxyacetic acid（ahydroxy-diphenylacetic acid, benzilic acid）
2918.1990	---其他	6.5	30			17	千克		---Other
2918 1990.10	二苯乙醇酸甲酯(包括其酸酐、	6.5	30		9	17	千克	23	Methyl benzilate（including their anhydrides, halides,

税则号列 Tariff Item	商品名称及备注	进口税率 最惠	进口税率 普通	进口税率 暂定	出口退税	增值税率	计量单位	监管条件	Article Description
	酰卤化物、过氧化物和过氧酸及其衍生物）								peroxides, peroxyacids and their derivatives）
2918 1990.30	γ-羟基丁酸及其盐	6.5	30		9	17	千克	I	γ-hydroxybutanoic acid and its salts
2918 1990.41	丙酯杀螨醇	6.5	30			17	千克	S	Chlorobenzilate
2918 1990.42	溴螨酯	6.5	30		9	17	千克	S	Bromopropylate
2918 1990.43	芴丁酯	6.5	30		9	17	千克	S	Flurenol-butyl
2918 1990.44	整形醇	6.5	30		9	17	千克	S	Chlorflurenol
2918 1990.90	其他含醇基但不含其他含氧基羧酸（包括其酸酐、酰卤化物、过氧化物和过氧酸及其衍生物）	6.5	30		9	17	千克		Other Carboxylic acids with phenol function but without other oxygen function,(including their anhydrides, etheride, peroxides, peroxyacids and their derivatives)
	-含酚基但不含其他含氧基的羧酸及其酸酐、酰卤化物、过氧化物和过氧酸以及它们的衍生物:								-Carboxylic acids with phenol function but without other oxygen function, their anhydrides, halides, peroxides, peroxyacids and their derivatives:
	--水杨酸及其盐:								--Salicylic acid and its salts:
2918.2110	---水杨酸、水杨酸钠	6.5	20		9	17	千克		---Salicylic acid and sodium salicylate
2918.2190	---其他	6.5	30		9	17	千克		---Other
	--邻乙酰水杨酸及其盐和酯:								--*o*-Acetylsalicylic acid, its salts and esters:
2918.2210	---邻乙酰水杨酸(阿司匹林)	6	20		9	17	千克		---Acetylsalicylic acid
2918.2290	---其他	6.5	30		9	17	千克		---Other
2918.2300	--水杨酸的其他酯及其盐	6.5	30		9	17	千克		--Other esters of salicylic acid and their salts
2918.2900	--其他	6.5	30		9	17	千克	AB	--Other
2918.3000	-含醛基或酮基但不含其他含氧基的羧酸及其酸酐、酰卤化物、过氧化物和过氧酸以及它们的衍生物:	6.5	30		9	17	千克		-Carboxylic acids with aldehyde or ketone function but without other oxygen function, their anhydrides, halides, peroxides, peroxyacids and their derivatives
2918 3000.11	除虫菊素 I、除虫菊素 II	6.5	30		9	17	千克	S	Pyrethrin I, Pyrethrin II
2918 3000.12	瓜叶菊素 I、瓜叶菊素 II	6.5	30		9	17	千克	S	Cinerin I, Cinerin II
2918 3000.13	茉酮菊素 I、茉酮菊素 II	6.5	30		9	17	千克	S	Jasmolin I, Jasmolin II
2918 3000.14	环戊烯丙菊酯	6.5	30		9	17	千克	S	Terallethrin
2918 3000.15	调环酸、抗倒酯、环虫菊酯	6.5	30		9	17	千克	S	Prohexadione-calcium, trinexapac-ethyl, Cyclethrin
2918 3000.16	烯丙菊酯等（包括右旋烯丙菊酯、富右旋反式烯丙菊酯、右旋反式烯丙菊酯）	6.5	30		9	17	千克	S	Allethrin (including d-allethrin,rich-d-t-rans-allethrin,d-t-rans-allethrin）
2918 3000.17	Es-生物烯丙菊酯、生物烯丙菊酯等（包括S-生物烯丙菊酯）	6.5	30		9	17	千克	S	Es-bioallethrin,bioallethrin(including S-bioallethrin)
2918 3000.18	乙酰氟菊酯	6.5	30		9	17	千克	S	Acetyl fluthrinate
2918 3000.90	其他含醛基或酮基不含其他含氧基羧酸(包括酸酐、酰卤化物、过氧化物和过氧酸及其衍生物）	6.5	30		9	17	千克		Other carboxylic acids with aldehyde or ketone function but without other oxygen function, their anhydrides, halides, peroxides, peroxyacids and their derivatives
	-其他:								-Other:
2918.9100	--2，4，5-涕(ISO)(2，4，5-三氯苯氧基乙酸)及其盐或酯	6.5	30			17	千克	89	--2, 4, 5-T（ISO）(2, 4, 5-trichlorophenoxy acetic acid）, its salts and esters
2918.9900	--其他	6.5	30		9	17	千克		--Other
2918 9900.21	2,4-滴、2,4-滴丙酸、2,4-滴丁酸等（包括精 2，4-滴丙酸、苯醚菌酯）	6.5	30		9	17	千克	S	2, 4-d, 2, 4- Dichlorprop-p,2,4-Embutox（including J-2, 4-Dichlorprop-p）
2918 9900.22	2 甲 4 氯、2 甲 4 氯丙酸等（包括精 2 甲 4 氯丙酸）	6.5	30		9	17	千克	S	2-Methyl-4-chlorophenoxyacetic acid, 2-(4-Chloro-2-methylphenoxy) propanoic acid
2918 9900.23	2 甲 4 氯丁酸	6.5	30		9	17	千克	S	(2-Methyl-4-Chlorophenoxy)butyric acid
2918 9900.24	麦草畏、杀草畏	6.5	30		9	17	千克	S	Dicamba, tricamba
2918 9900.25	禾草灵、乳氟禾草灵	6.5	30		9	17	千克	S	Diclofop-methyl, lactofen
2918 9900.26	氟萘禾草灵、甲羧除草醚	6.5	30		9	17	千克	S	Fluoro-naphthalene Diclofop, bifenox
2918 9900.27	三氟羧草醚、乙羧氟草醚	6.5	30		9	17	千克	S	Acifluorfen, Fluoroglycofen
2918 9900.28	氟乳醚、调果酸、座果酸	6.5	30		9	17	千克	S	Ethhoxyfen , cloprop, cloxyfonac

税则号列 Tariff Item	商品名称及备注	进口税率			出口退税	增值税率	计量单位	监管条件	Article Description
		最惠	普通	暂定					
2918 9900.29	增糖酯、S-诱抗素、氯氟草醚乙酯(包括烯虫酯)	6.5	30		9	17	千克	S	Dicamba-methyl, S-abscisic acid, ethhoxyfen-ethyl (including methoprene)
2918 9900.30	调磺酸钙	6.5	30		9	17	千克	S	Adjusted calcium sulfonate
2918 9900.90	其他含其他附加含氧基羧酸(包括其酸酐、酰卤化物、过氧化物和过氧酸及其衍生物)	6.5	30		9	17	千克		Other Carboxylic acids with additional oxygen function and their anhydrides, halides, peroxides and peroxyacids and their derivatives
	第八分章 非金属无机酸酯及其盐以及它们的卤化、磺化、硝化或亚硝化衍生物								**Ⅷ. ESTERS OF INORGANIC ACIDS OF NON-METALS AND THEIR SALTS, AND THEIR HALOGENATED, SULPHONATED, NITRATED OR NITROSATED DERIVATIVES**
29.19	**磷酸酯及其盐，包括乳磷酸盐，以及它们的卤化、磺化、硝化或亚硝化衍生物：**								**Phosphoric esters and their salts, including lactophosphates; their halogenated, sulphonated, nitrated or nitrosated derivatives:**
2919.1000	-三(2,3-二溴丙基)磷酸酯	6.5	30		9	17	千克	89	-Tris（2, 3-dibromopropyl）phosphate
2919.9000	-其他	6.5	30			17	千克		-Other
2919 9000.20	磷酸三丁酯	6.5	30		9	17	千克	3	Tributyl phosphate
2919 9000.31	敌敌钙、敌敌畏	6.5	30		9	17	千克	S	Calvinphos, dichlorovos
2919 9000.32	速灭磷、二溴磷	6.5	30		9	17	千克	S	Mevinphos, naled
2919 9000.33	巴毒磷、杀虫畏	6.5	30			17	千克	S	Crotoxyphos, tetrachlorvinphos
2919 9000.34	毒虫畏、甲基毒虫畏	6.5	30			17	千克	S	Chlorfenvinphos, dimethylvinphos
2919 9000.35	庚烯磷、特普	6.5	30			17	千克	S	Heptenophos, tepp
2919 9000.36	三乙膦酸铝、乙膦酸	6.5	30		9	17	千克	S	Fosetyl-aluminium,phosphonoacetic acid ethyl
2919 9000.37	氯瘟磷、伐草磷	6.5	30			17	千克	S	Phosdiphen, grasskilling phosphate
2919 9000.90	其他磷酸酯及其盐(包括乳磷酸盐)(包括它们的卤化、磺化、硝化或亚硝化衍生物)	6.5	30		9	17	千克	AB	Other phosphoric esters and their salts, including lactophosphates; their halogenated, sulphonated, nitrated or nitrosated derivatives
29.20	**其他非金属无机酸酯(不包括卤化氢的酯)及其盐，以及它们的卤化、磺化、硝化或亚硝化衍生物：**								**Esters of other inorganic acids of nonmetals（excluding esters of hydrogen halides）and their salts; their halogenated, sulphonated, nitrated or nitrosated derivatives:**
	-硫代磷酸酯及其盐以及它们的卤化、磺化、硝化或亚硝化衍生物：								-Thiophosphoric esters（phosphorothioates）and their salts; theirhalogenated, sulphonated, nitrated or nitrosated derivatives:
2920.1100	--对硫磷(ISO)及甲基对硫磷(ISO)	6.5	30			17	千克	X	--Parathion（ISO）and parathion-methyl（ISO）（metyl-parathion）
2920.1900	--其他	6.5	30			17	千克		--Other
2920 1900.12	氯氧磷、虫螨畏	6.5	30			17	千克	S	Chlorethoxyfos,methacrifos
2920 1900.13	杀螟硫磷、除线磷	6.5	30		9	17	千克	S	Fenitrothion, dichlofenthion
2920 1900.14	异氯磷、皮蝇磷	6.5	30		9	17	千克	S	Dicaptan, fenchlorphos
2920 1900.15	溴硫磷、乙基溴硫磷、硝虫硫磷	6.5	30		9	17	千克	S	Bromophos, Bromophos-ethyl, Xiaochongthion
2920 1900.16	甲基增效磷、增效磷	6.5	30		9	17	千克		Methyl phosphorus efficiency, dietholate
2920 1900.17	碘硫磷、苯稻瘟净	6.5	30			17	千克	S	Jodfenphos, inezin
2920 1900.18	甲基立枯磷、克菌磷	6.5	30		9	17	千克	S	Tolclofos-methyl, pyrazophos
2920 1900.19	速杀硫磷、丰丙磷	6.5	30		9	17	千克	S	Heterophos, Aphidan
2920 1900.90	其他硫代磷酸酯及其盐(包括它们的卤化、磺化、硝化或亚硝化衍生物)	6.5	30		9	17	千克		Other thiophosphoric esters（phosphorothioates）and their salts; their halogenated, sulphonated, nitrated or nitrosated derivatives
	-其他：								-Other:
	---亚磷酸酯：								---Phosphites:
2920.9011	----亚磷酸三甲酯	6.5	30		9	17	千克	23	----Trimethyl phosphite
2920.9012	----亚磷酸三乙酯	6.5	30		9	17	千克	23	----Trimethyl phosphite
2920.9013	----亚磷酸二甲酯	6.5	30		9	17	千克	23	----Dimethyl phosphite
2920.9014	----亚磷酸二乙酯	6.5	30		9	17	千克	23	----Diethyl phosphite
2920.9019	----其他	6.5	30		9	17	千克		----Other

税则号列 Tariff Item	商品名称及备注	进口税率 最惠	普通	暂定	出口退税	增值税率	计量单位	监管条件	Article Description
2920.9090	---其他	6.5	30			17	千克		---Other
2920 9090.01 暂	碳酸二苯酯	6.5	30	2	9	17	千克		Diphenyl carbonate
2920 9090.11	硫丹	6.5	30			17	千克	S	Endosulfan
2920 9090.12	治螟磷	6.5	30			17	千克	S	Sulfotepp
2920 9090.13	消螨通	6.5	30			17	千克	S	Dinobuton
2920 9090.14	炔螨特	6.5	30		9	17	千克	S	Propargite
2920 9090.15	浸种磷	6.5	30			17	千克	S	Izopamfos
2920 9090.16	赛松	6.5	30			17	千克	S	Sesone
2920 9090.20	三乙基砷酸酯	6.5	30		9	17	千克	X	Thiethyl arsenate
2920 9090.90	其他无机酸酯(不包括卤化氢的酯)（包括其盐以及它们的卤化、磺化、硝化或亚硝化衍生物）	6.5	30		9	17	千克		Other Esters of other inorganic acids excluding esters of hydrogen halides）and their salts; their halogenated, sulphonated, nitrated or nitrosated derivatives
	第九分章 含氮基化合物								**IX. NITROGEN-FUNCTION COMPOUNDS**
29.21	**氨基化合物:**								**Amine-function compounds:**
	-无环单胺及其衍生物以及它们的盐:								-Acyclic monoamines and their derivatives; salts thereof:
2921.1100	--甲胺、二甲胺或三甲胺及其盐	6.5	30		9	17	千克		--Methylamine, di-or trimethylamine and their salts
2921 1100.10	二甲胺	6.5	30		9	17	千克	23	Dimethylamine
2921 1100.20	二甲胺盐酸盐	6.5	30		9	17	千克	23	Dimethylamine hydrochloride
2921 1100.30	甲胺盐	6.5	30		9	17	千克		Methylamine salt
2921 1100.90	甲胺，三甲胺及其盐	6.5	30		9	17	千克	AB	Methylamine, trimethylamine and their salts
	--其他:								--Other:
2921.1910	---二正丙胺	4	11		9	17	千克	AB	---Di-*n*-propylamine
2921.1920 暂	---异丙胺	6.5	30	2	9	17	千克		---Isopropyl amine
2921.1930	---N,N-二(2-氯乙基)乙胺	6.5	30		9	17	千克	32	---N, N-Bis（2-chloroethyl）ethylamine
2921.1940	---N,N-二(2-氯乙基)甲胺	6.5	30		9	17	千克	32	---N, N-Bis（2-chloroethyl）methylamine
2921.1950	---三(2-氯乙基)胺	6.5	30		9	17	千克	32	---Tri-（2-chloroethyl）amine
2921.1960	---二烷（甲、乙、正丙或异丙）氨基乙基-2-氯及其质子化盐	6.5	30		9	17	千克	23	---N, N-Dialkyl（Me, Et, n-Pr or i-Pr）aminoethyl-2-chlorides and corresponding protonated salts
2921.1990	---其他	6.5	30			17	千克		---Other
2921 1990.11	三乙胺（单一成分，用做点火剂）	6.5	30		9	17	千克	3A	Triethylamine（Single component, used for igniter）
2921 1990.20	二异丙胺	6.5	30		9	17	千克	3	Diisopropylamine
2921 1990.31	2-氨基丁烷	6.5	30			17	千克	S	2-aminobutane
2921 1990.33	胺鲜酯	6.5	30		9	17	千克	S	Diethyl aminoethyl hexanoate
2921 1990.90	其他无环单胺及其衍生物及其盐	6.5	30		9	17	千克		Other acyclic monoamines and its derivatives and its salts
	-无环多胺及其衍生物以及它们的盐:								-Acyclic polyamines and their derivatives; salts thereof:
	--乙二胺及其盐:								--Ethylenediamine and its salts:
2921.2110	---乙二胺	6.5	30		9	17	千克		---Ethylenediamine
2921.2190	---其他	6.5	30		9	17	千克		---Other
	--六亚甲基二胺及其盐:								--Hexamethylenediamine and its salts:
2921.2210	---已二酸已二胺盐(尼龙66盐)	6.5	20		9	17	千克		---Hexamethylene adipamide (nylon-66 salt)
2921.2290	---其他	6.5	30		9	17	千克		---Other
2921.2900	--其他	6.5	30		9	17	千克		--Other
2921.3000	-环烷单胺或多胺、环烯单胺或多胺、环萜烯单胺或多胺及其衍生物以及它们的盐	6.5	30		9	17	千克		-Cyclanic, cyclenic or cycloterpenic monoor polyamines, and their derivatives; salts thereof
2921 3000.10	丙己君及其盐	6.5	30		9	17	千克	I	Propylhexedrine and its salts
2921 3000.30	氨基羧酸环丙烷	6.5	30		9	17	千克	S	1-Aminocy-clopropane-1-carboxylic acid
2921 3000.40	乙撑亚胺	6.5	30		9	17	千克	AB	Ethylenimine
2921 3000.90	其他环(烷、烯、萜烯)单胺或多胺（包括其衍生物及它们的盐）	6.5	30		9	17	千克		Other Cylanic, cyclenic or cycloterpenic monoor polyamines, and their derivatives; salts thereof

税则号列 Tariff Item	商品名称及备注	进口税率			出口退税	增值税率	计量单位	监管条件	Article Description
		最惠	普通	暂定					
	-芳香单胺及其衍生物以及它们的盐:								-Aromatic monoamines and their derivatives; salts thereof:
	--苯胺及其盐:								--Aniline and its salts:
2921.4110	---苯胺	6.5	20		9	17	千克	X	---Aniline
2921.4190	---其他	6.5	30		9	17	千克		---Other
2921.4200	--苯胺衍生物及其盐	6.5	30		9	17	千克		--Aniline derivatives and their salts
2921 4200.12	敌锈钠	6.5	30		9	17	千克	S	Sodium-p-aminobenzensulfonate
2921 4200.13	苯草醚	6.5	30		9	17	千克	S	Aclonifen
2921 4200.90	其他苯胺衍生物及其盐	6.5	30		9	17	千克		Other aniline derivatives and their salts
2921.4300	--甲苯胺及其衍生物以及它们的盐	6.5	30			17	千克		--Toluidines and their derivatives; salts thereof
2921 4300.01	间甲苯胺或对甲苯胺	6.5	30		9	17	千克		m- Toluidines or p-Toluidines
2921 4300.10	氟乐灵	6.5	30		9	17	千克	S	Trifluralin
2921 4300.20	邻甲苯胺	6.5	30		9	17	千克		o-Toluidine
2921 4300.31	溴鼠胺	6.5	30			17	千克	S	Bromethalin
2921 4300.32	乙丁氟灵	6.5	30		9	17	千克	S	Benfluralin
2921 4300.33	氯乙氟灵	6.5	30		9	17	千克	S	Fluchloralin
2921 4300.34	环丙氟灵	6.5	30		9	17	千克	S	Profluralin
2921 4300.35	乙丁烯氟灵	6.5	30		9	17	千克	S	Ethalfluralin
2921 4300.36	地乐灵	6.5	30		9	17	千克	S	Dipropalin
2921 4300.37	氯乙灵	6.5	30		9	17	千克	S	Chlornidine
2921 4300.38	氟节胺	6.5	30		9	17	千克	S	Flumetralin
2921 4300.90	甲苯胺盐、甲苯胺衍生物及其盐	6.5	30		9	17	千克		Toluidines and their derivatives and its salts
2921.4400	--二苯胺及其衍生物以及它们的盐	6.5	30		17	17	千克		--Diphenylamine and its derivatives; salts thereof
2921.4500	--1-萘胺（α-萘胺）、2-萘胺（β-萘胺）及其衍生物以及它们的盐	6.5	30		9	17	千克		--1-Naphthylamine（α-naphthylamine）, 2-naphthylamine（β-naphthylamine）and their derivatives; salts thereof
2921 4500.10	2-萘胺	6.5	30		9	17	千克	X	2-Naphthylamine
2921 4500.90	1-萘胺和2-萘胺的衍生物及盐（包括1-萘胺）	6.5	30		9	17	千克		1-Naphthylamine and 2-Naphthylamine and their derivatives and its salts (including 1naphthy- lamine)
2921.4600	--安非他明（INN）、苄非他明（INN）、右苯丙胺（INN）、乙非他明、芬坎法明（INN）、利非他明、左苯丙胺（INN）、美芬雷司（INN）、苯丁胺（INN）以及它们的盐	6.5	30		9	17	千克		--Amfetamine（INN）, benzfetamine（INN）, dexamfetamine（INN）, etilamfetamine（INN）, fencamfamin(INN), lefetamine(INN), levamfetamine（INN）, mefenorex（INN）and phentermine（INN）; salts thereof
2921 4600.11	安非他明、苄非他明、右苯丙胺（包括它们的盐）	6.5	30		9	17	千克	I	Amfetamine（INN）, benzfetamine（INN）, dexamfetamine（INN）（including their salts）
2921 4600.12	乙非他明、芬坎法明、利非他明（包括它们的盐）	6.5	30		9	17	千克	I	Etilamfetamine(INN), fencamfamin(INN), lefetamine（INN）（including their salts）
2921 4600.13	左苯丙胺、美芬雷司、芬特明（包括它们的盐）	6.5	30		9	17	千克	I	Levamfetamine（INN）, mefenorex（INN）and phentermine（INN）（including their salts）
	--其他:								--Other:
2921.4910	---对异丙基苯胺	4	11		9	17	千克		---*p*-Isopropyl-aniline
2921.4920	---二甲基苯胺	6.5	20		9	17	千克		---Dimethylanilines
2921.4930	---2,6-甲基乙基苯胺	4	11		9	17	千克		---2, 6-Methyl ethyl aniline
2921.4940	---2,6-二乙基苯胺	6.5	20		9	17	千克		---2, 6-Diethylaniline
2921.4990	---其他	6.5	30		9	17	千克		---Other
2921 4990.11	异丙乐灵	6.5	30		9	17	千克	S	Isopropalin
2921 4990.12	仲丁灵	6.5	30		9	17	千克	S	Butralin
2921 4990.13	二甲戊灵	6.5	30		9	17	千克	S	Pendimethalin
2921 4990.20	4-氨基联苯	6.5	30		9	17	千克	X	4 - aminobiphenyl
2921 4990.31	乙环利定、二甲基安非他明（以	6.5	30		9	17	千克	I	Eticyclidine, dimethylamphetamine (and their salts)

税则号列 Tariff Item	商品名称及备注	进口税率 最惠	普通	暂定	出口退税	增值税率	计量单位	监管条件	Article Description
	及它们的盐)								
2921 4990.32	芬氟拉明、右旋芬氟拉明(以及它们的盐)	6.5	30		9	17	千克	I	Fenfluramine,d-fenfluramine (and their salts)
2921 4990.90	其他芳香单胺及衍生物及它们的盐	6.5	30		9	17	千克		other aromatic monoamine and derivants and their salts
	-芳香多胺及其衍生物以及它们的盐:								-Aromatic polyamines and their derivatives; salts thereof:
	--邻-、间-、对-苯二胺、二氨基甲苯及其衍生物以及它们的盐:								--*o*-, *m*-, *p*-Phenylenediamine, diaminotoluenes, and their derivatives; salts thereof:
2921.5110	---邻苯二胺	4	11		9	17	千克		---*o*-Phenylenediamine
2921.5190	---其他	6.5	30			17	千克		---Other
2921 5190.11	氨氟灵	6.5	30		9	17	千克	S	Dinitramine
2921 5190.12	氨氟乐灵	6.5	30		9	17	千克	S	Prodiamine
2921 5190.20	2,4-二氨基甲苯	6.5	30		17	17	千克	X	2, 4 -diaminotoluene
2921 5190.90	间-、对-苯二胺、二氨基甲苯等(包括衍生物及它们的盐)	6.5	30		17	17	千克		*m*-, *p*- phenylene diamine,diaminotoluene (including their derivatives and salts)
2921.5900	--其他	6.5	30			17	千克		--Other
2921 5900.10	三氨基三硝基苯	6.5	30		9	17	千克	3	Triamino trinitrobenzene
2921 5900.20	联苯胺(4,4' -二氨基联苯)	6.5	30		9	17	千克	89	Benzidine（4, 4' - diaminodiphenyl）
2921 5900.31	4,4' -二氨基-3,3' -二氯二苯基甲烷	6.5	30		9	17	千克	X	4, 4' - diamido -3, 3' - dichloroditane
2921 5900.32	3,3' -二氯联苯胺	6.5	30		9	17	千克	X	3, 3' - dichloro-benzidine
2921 5900.33	4,4' -二氨基二苯基甲烷	6.5	30		13	17	千克	X	4, 4' - diaminodiphenylmethane
2921 5900.90	其他芳香多胺及衍生物及它们的盐	6.5	30		13	17	千克		Other aromatic polyamines and derivatives and their salts
29.22	**含氧基氨基化合物:**								**Oxygen-function amino-compounds:**
	-氨基醇(但含有一种以上含氧基的除外)及其醚和酯,以及它们的盐:								-Amino-alcohols, other than those containing more than one kind of oxygen function, their ethers and esters; salts thereof:
2922.1100	--单乙醇胺及其盐:	6.5	30		9	17	千克		--Monoethanolamine and its salts:
2922 1100.01	单乙醇胺	6.5	30		9	17	千克	AB	monoethanolamine
2922 1100.90	单乙醇胺盐	6.5	30		9	17	千克		monoethanolamine salt
2922.1200	--二乙醇胺及其盐	6.5	30		9	17	千克		--Diethanolamine and its salts
2922 1200.01	二乙醇胺	6.5	30		9	17	千克		Diethanolamine
2922 1200.10	全氟辛基磺酸二乙醇胺	6.5	30		9	17	千克	X	Heptadecafluorooctane-1-sulphonic acid 2,2'-Iminodiethanol
2922 1200.90	二乙醇胺盐	6.5	30		9	17	千克		Diethanolamine salt
	--三乙醇胺及其盐:								--Triethanolamine and its salts:
2922.1310	---三乙醇胺	6.5	30		9	17	千克	23AB	---Triethanolamine
2922.1320	---三乙醇胺盐	6.5	30		9	17	千克		---Salts of triethanolamine
2922 1320.20	三乙醇胺盐酸盐	6.5	30		9	17	千克	23	Triethanolamine hydrochloride
2922 1320.90	其他三乙醇胺的盐	6.5	30		9	17	千克		Other salts of triethanolamine
2922.1400	--右丙氧吩(INN)及其盐	6.5	30		9	17	千克	W	--Dextropropoxyphene（INN）and its salts
	--其他:								--Other:
2922.1910	---乙胺丁醇	6.5	30		9	17	千克		---Ethylamino butanol（Ethambutol）
	----二烷(甲、乙、正丙或异丙)氨基乙-2-醇及其质子化盐:								---N, N-Dialkyl-（Me, Et, n-Pr or i-Pr）aminoethane-2-ols and corresponding protonated salts:
2922.1921	----二甲氨基乙醇及其质子化盐	6.5	30		9	17	千克		----N, N-Dimethylaminoethanol and corresponding protonated salts
2922.1922	----二乙氨基乙醇及其质子化盐	6.5	30		9	17	千克		----N, N-Diethylaminoethanol and corresponding protonated salts
2922 1922.10	2-二乙氨基乙醇(或称N,N-二乙基乙醇胺)	6.5	30		9	17	千克	3	2-diethylaminoethanol(N,N-diethyl ethylene diamine）
2922 1922.90	二乙氨基乙醇的质子化盐	6.5	30		9	17	千克		N, N-Diethylaminoethanol and corresponding

税则号列 Tariff Item	商品名称及备注	进口税率			出口退税	增值税率	计量单位	监管条件	Article Description
		最惠	普通	暂定					
									protonated salts
2922.1929	----其他	6.5	30		9	17	千克	23	----Other
2922.1930	---乙基二乙醇胺	6.5	30		9	17	千克	23	---Ethyldiethanolamine
2922.1940	---甲基二乙醇胺	6.5	30		9	17	千克	23	---Methyldiethanolamine
2922.1950	---本芴醇	6.5	30		9	17	千克		---Benflumetol
2922.1990	---其他	6.5	30		9	17	千克		---Other
2922 1990.10	增产胺	6.5	30		9	17	千克	S	Guayule
2922 1990.20	克仑特罗	6.5	30		9	17	千克	L	Clenbuterol
2922 1990.31	醋美沙朵、阿醋美沙朵、阿法美沙朵（以及它们的盐）	6.5	30		9	17	千克	W	Acetylmethadol,alphacetylmethadol,alphamethadol (and their salts)
2922 1990.32	倍醋美沙朵、倍他美沙朵（以及它们的盐）	6.5	30		9	17	千克	W	Betacetylmethadol,betamethadol (and their salts)
2922 1990.33	地美沙朵、地美庚醇、诺美沙朵（以及它们的盐）	6.5	30		9	17	千克	W	Dimenoxadol,dimepheptanol,noracymethadol(and their salts)
2922 1990.90	其他氨基醇及其醚、酯和它们的盐（但含有一种以上含氧基的除外）	6.5	30		9	17	千克		Other alkamine and its ether, ester and their salts （other than those containing more than one kind of Oxygen function）
	-氨基萘酚和其他氨基酚（但含有一种以上含氧基的除外）及其醚和酯，以及它们的盐：								-Amino-naphthols and amino-phenols, other than those containing more than one kind of oxygen function, their ethers and esters; salts thereof:
2922.2100	--氨基羟基萘磺酸及其盐	6.5	30		13	17	千克		--Aminohydroxynaphthalenesulphonic acid and their salts
	--其他：								--Other:
2922.2910	---茴香胺、二茴香胺、氨基苯乙醚及其盐	6.5	30		9	17	千克		---Anisidines, dianisidines, phenetidines, and their salts
2922.2990	---其他	6.5	30		9	17	千克		---Other
2922 2990.11	布苯丙胺、二甲氧基乙基安非他明（以及它们的盐）	6.5	30		9	17	千克	I	Brolamfetamine, (±)-4-ethyl-2,5-dimethoxy- α -methyl phenethylamine (and their salts)
2922 2990.12	二甲氧基安非他明、副甲氧基安非他明（以及它们的盐）	6.5	30		9	17	千克	I	(±)-2,5-Dimethoxy-alpha-methylphenethylamine, P-methoxy-alpha-methylphenethylamine (and their salts)
2922 2990.13	二甲氧基甲苯异丙胺、三甲氧基安非他明（以及它们的盐）	6.5	30		9	17	千克	I	2,5-Dimethoxy-alpha,4-dimethylphenethylamine, (±)-3,4,5-Trimethoxy-alpha-methylphenethylamine (and their salts)
2922 2990.14	2，5-二甲氧基-4-溴苯乙胺、地佐辛（以及它们的盐）	6.5	30		9	17	千克	I	4-Bromo-2,5-dimethoxyphenethylamine, dezocine (and their salts)
2922 2990.15	他喷他多	6.5	30		9	17	千克	I	Tapentadol CAS：175591-23-8
2922 2990.16	2，5-二甲氧基-4-碘苯乙胺	6.5	30		9	17	千克	I	2，5-Dimethoxy-4-iodophenethylamine；CAS：69587-11-7
2922 2990 17	2，5-二甲氧基苯乙胺	6.5	30		9	17	千克	I	2，5-Dimethoxy-phenethylamine；CAS：3600-86-0
2922 2990.90	其他氨基(萘酚、酚)及醚、酯(包括它们的盐，但含有一种以上含氧基的除外)	6.5	30		9	17	千克		Other Amino-naphthols and amino-phenols, other than those containing more than one kind of oxygen function, their ethers and esters; salts thereof
	-氨基醛、氨基酮和氨基醌，但含有一种以上含氧基的除外，以及它们的盐：								-Amino-aldehydes, amino-ketones and amino-quinones, other than those containing more than one kind of oxygen function; salts thereof:
2922.3100	--安非拉酮(INN)、美沙酮(INN)和去甲美沙酮(INN)以及它们的盐	6.5	30		9	17	千克		--Amfepramone（INN）, methadone（INN）and normethadone（INN）;salts thereof
2922 3100.10	安非拉酮及其盐	6.5	30		9	17	千克	I	Amfepramone（INN）and its salts
2922 3100.20	美沙酮、去甲美沙酮及它们的盐	6.5	30		9	17	千克	W	Methadone（INN）, normethadone （INN）and their salts
	--其他：								--Other:
2922.3910	---4-甲基甲卡西酮	6.5	30		9	17	千克	I	---4-Methylmethcathinone
2922.3990	---其他	6.5	30		9	17	千克		---Other

税则号列 Tariff Item	商品名称及备注	进口税率 最惠	普通	暂定	出口退税	增值税率	计量单位	监管条件	Article Description
2922 3990.10	氯胺酮及其盐	6.5	30		9	17	千克	I	Ketamine and its salts
2922 3990.20	灭藻醌	6.5	30		9	17	千克	S	Quinoclamine
2922 3990.30	异美沙酮及其盐	6.5	30		9	17	千克	W	Isomethadone and its salts
2922 3990.40	甲卡西酮及其盐	6.5	30		9	17	千克	I	Methcathinone and its salts
2922 3990.50	4-甲基乙卡西酮（4-MEC）	6.5	30		9	17	千克	I	4-Methylethcathinone;CAS：1225617-18-4
2922 3990.90	其他氨基醛、氨基酮及其盐（包括氨基醌及其盐，但含有一种以上含氧基的除外）	6.5	30		9	17	千克		Other amino-aldehydes, amino-ketones and amino-quinones; salts thereof (other than those containing more than one kind of oxygen function)
	-氨基酸(但含有一种以上含氧基的除外)及其酯，以及它们的盐：								-Amino-acids, other than those containing more than one kind of oxygen function, and their esters; salts thereof:
	—赖氨酸及其酯以及它们的盐：								--Lysine and its esters; salts thereof:
2922.4110	---赖氨酸	5	20		9	17	千克	AB	---Lysine
2922.4190	---其他	6	30		9	17	千克	AB	---Other
	--谷氨酸及其盐：								--Glutamic acid and its salts:
2922.4210[暂]	---谷氨酸	10	90	5	9	17	千克	AB	---Glutamic acid
2922.4220	---谷氨酸钠	10	130			17	千克	AB	---Sodium glutamate
2922.4290	---其他	6.5	30		9	17	千克	AB	---Other
	--邻氨基苯甲酸（氨茴酸）及其盐：								--Anthranilic acid and its salts:
2922.4310	---邻氨基苯甲酸(氨茴酸)	6.5	20		9	17	千克	23	---Anthranilic acid
2922.4390	---其他	6.5	30		9	17	千克		---Other
2922.4400	--替利定(INN)及其盐	6.5	30		9	17	千克	W	--Tilidine（INN） and its salts
	--其他：								--Other:
	---其他氨基酸：								---Amino acids:
2922.4911	----氨甲环酸	6.5	20		13	17	千克	AB	----Tranexamic acid
2922.4919	----其他	6.5	20		13	17	千克		----Other
2922 4919.10	安咪奈丁	6.5	20		13	17	千克	I	Amineptine
2922 4919.90	其他氨基酸	6.5	20		13	17	千克	AB	Other amino acids
	---其他：								---Other:
2922.4991	----普鲁卡因	6	20		9	17	千克		----Procaine
2922.4999	----其他	6.5	30			17	千克		----Other
2922 4999.11	草灭畏	6.5	30		9	17	千克	ABS	Chloramben
2922 4999.12	灭杀威、灭除威、混灭威等（害扑威、速灭威、残杀威、猛杀威）	6.5	30		9	17	千克	ABS	Meobal,XMC,trimethacarb (etrofol,MTMC, propoxur, promecarb)
2922 4999.13	兹克威、灭害威、除害威	6.5	30			17	千克	ABS	Mexacarbate, aminocarb, allyxycarb
2922 4999.14	异丙威	6.5	30		9	17	千克	ABS	Isoprocarb
2922 4999.15	仲丁威、畜虫威、合杀威	6.5	30		9	17	千克	ABS	Fenobucarb,butacarb,bufencarb
2922 4999.16	甲萘威、地麦威、蜱虱威	6.5	30		9	17	千克	ABS	Carbaryl,dimetan,promacyl
2922 4999.17	苯氧威、除线威	6.5	30		9	17	千克	ABS	Fenoxycarb,cloethocarb
2922 4999.18	氨酰丙酸（盐酸盐）	6.5	30		9	17	千克	ABS	Hydrochloride
2922 4999.19	安咪奈丁的盐	6.5	20		13	17	千克	I	Amineptine salt
2922 4999.90	其他氨基酸及其酯及它们的盐（含有一种以上含氧基的除外）	6.5	30		9	17	千克	AB	Other amino-acids, and their esters; salts thereof (other than those containing more than one kind of oxygen function)
	-氨基醇酚、氨基酸酚及其他含氧基氨基化合物：								-Amino-alcohol-phenols, amino-acidphenols and other amino-compounds with oxygen function :
2922.5010	---对羟基苯甘氨酸及其邓钾盐	6.5	30			17	千克	AB	---D-p-hydroxyphenylglycine and its monopotassium salt
2922.5020	---莱克多巴胺和盐酸莱克多巴胺	6.5	30		9	17	千克	89	---Ractopamine and ractopamine hydrochloride
2922.5090	---其他	6.5	30			17	千克		---Other
2922 5090.10	曲马多	6.5	30			17	千克	I	Tramadol
2922 5090.90	其他氨基醇酚、氨基酸酚(包括	6.5	30			17	千克	AB	Other Amino-alcohol-phenols, Amino phenol (Including

税则号列 Tariff Item	商品名称及备注	进口税率 最惠	进口税率 普通	进口税率 暂定	出口退税	增值税率	计量单位	监管条件	Article Description
	其他含氧基氨基化合物)								other amino compounds with oxygroup function)
29.23	**季铵盐及季铵碱；卵磷脂及其他磷氨基类脂，无论是否已有化学定义：**								**Quaternary ammonium salts and hydroxides; leeithins and other phosphoaminolipids, whether or not chemically defined:**
2923.1000	-胆碱及其盐	6.5	30		9	17	千克	AB	-Choline and its salts
2923.2000	-卵磷脂及其他磷氨基类脂	6.5	30		9	17	千克	AB	-Lecithins and other phosphoaminolipids
2923.9000	-其他	6.5	30		9	17	千克		-Other
2923 9000.11	矮壮素	6.5	30		9	17	千克	S	Chlorocholine chloride
2923 9000.12	菊胺酯	6.5	30		9	17	千克	S	Tetramethrin
2923 9000.13	全氟辛基磺酸四乙胺、全氟辛基磺酸双癸基二甲基铵	6.5	30		9	17	千克	X	Heptadecafluorooctane-1-sulphonic acid tetraethylaminium·4-toluenesulfonate
2923 9000.90	其他季铵盐及季铵碱	6.5	30		9	17	千克		Other quaternary ammonium salts and hydroxides
29.24	**羧基酰胺基化合物；碳酸酰胺基化合物：**								**Carboxyamide-function compounds; amidefunction compounds of carbonic acid:**
	-无环酰胺（包括无环氨基甲酸酯）及其衍生物以及它们的盐：								-Aeyclic amides（including acyclic carbamates）and their derivatives; salts thereof:
2924.1100	--甲丙氨酯（INN）	6.5	30		9	17	千克	I	--Meprobamate（INN）
2924.1200	--氟乙酰胺（ISO）久效磷（ISO）及磷胺（ISO）	6.5	30			17	千克		--Fluoroacetamide（ISO）, monocrotophos（ISO）and phosphamidon（ISO）
2924 1200.10	氟乙酰胺（ISO）（氟乙酰胺别名敌蚜胺）	6.5	30			17	千克	89	Fluoroacetamide （ISO）(acetamide,2-fluoro)
2924 1200.90	久效磷（ISO）及磷胺（ISO）	6.5	30			17	千克	X	Monocrotophos（ISO） and phosphamidon （ISO）
	--其他：								--Other:
2924.1910	---二甲基甲酰胺	6.5	30		9	17	千克		---N, N-dimethylformamide
2924.1990	---其他	6.5	30				千克		---Other
2924 1990.12	百治磷	6.5	30			17	千克	S	Dicrotophos
2924 1990.13	溴乙酰胺	6.5	30			17	千克	S	Bromoacetamide
2924 1990.14	霜霉威	6.5	30		9	17	千克	S	Propamocarb
2924 1990.15	叶枯炔	6.5	30			17	千克	S	Cellocidin
2924 1990.16	二丙烯草胺	6.5	30		9	17	千克	S	Allidochlor
2924 1990.17	解草烯	6.5	30		9	17	千克		Solution Humulene
2924 1990.18	驱蚊酯	6.5	30		9	17	千克	S	Dimethyl phthalate
2924 1990.30	甲丙氨酯的盐	6.5	30		9	17	千克	I	Salts of meprobamate（INN）
2924 1990.40	丙烯酰胺	6.5	30		9	17	千克	X	Acrylamide
2924 1990.90	其他无环酰胺(包括无环氨基甲酸酯)（包括其衍生物及其盐）	6.5	30		13	17	千克		Other acyclic amides（including acyclic carbamates）and their derivatives; salts thereof
	-环酰胺（包括环氨基甲酸酯）及其衍生物以及它们的盐：								-Cyclic amides（including cyclic carbamates）and their derivatives; salts thereof:
2924.2100	--酰脲及其衍生物以及它们的盐	6.5	30		9	17	千克		--Ureides and their derivatives; salts thereof
2924 2100.10	氟环脲	6.5	30		9	17	千克	S	Flucycloxuron
2924 2100.90	其他酰脲及其衍生物以及它们的盐	6.5	30		9	17	千克		Other ureides and their derivants and salts thereof
2924.2300	--2-乙酰氨基苯甲酸（N-乙酰邻氨基苯甲酸）及其盐	6.5	30		9	17	千克		--2-Acetamidobenzoic acid（N-acety-lanthranilic acid）and its salts
2924 2300.10	2-乙酰氨基苯甲酸、N-乙酰邻氨基苯酸(包括N-乙酰邻氨基苯甲酸)	6.5	30		9	17	千克	23	2-Acetamidobenzoic acid,N-acetylanthranilic acid（including N-acetylanthranilic acid）
2924 2300.90	2-乙酰氨基苯甲酸的盐	6.5	30		9	17	千克		Salts of 2-N-acetylanthranilic acid
2924.2400	--炔已蚁胺（INN）	6.5	30		9	17	千克	I	--Ethinamate（INN）
	--其他：								--Other:
2924.2910	---对乙酰氨基苯乙醚(非那西丁)	6	30		9	17	千克	Q	---Phenacetin
2924.2920	---对乙酰氨基酚(扑热息痛)	6	30		9	17	千克	Q	---*p*-Acetaminophenol（paracetanol）
2924.2930	---阿斯巴甜	6.5	30		9	17	千克		---Aspartame

税则号列 Tariff Item	商品名称及备注	进口税率 最惠	进口税率 普通	进口税率 暂定	出口退税	增值税率	计量单位	监管条件	Article Description
2924.2990	---其他	6.5	30		9	17	千克		---Other
2924 2990.11	避蚊胺、灭锈胺、叶枯酞、水杨菌胺、氟丁酰草胺(包括苯酰菌胺)	6.5	30		9	17	千克	S	Delphene,mepronil,tecloftalam, trichlamide, beflubutamid (including zoxamide)
2924 2990.12	萘草胺、新燕灵、非草隆、氯炔灵、苄草隆	6.5	30		9	17	千克	S	Napropamide,benzoylpropethyl,fenuron,chlorbufam, cumyluron
2924 2990.13	燕麦灵、苄胺灵、特草灵、特胺灵、环丙酰亚胺	6.5	30		9	17	千克	S	Barban,dichlormate, trebucarb, karbutilate, carpropamid
2924 2990.14	毒草胺、丁烯草胺、二氯乙酰草胺	6.5	30		9	17	千克	S	Propachlor, butenachlor, dichloroacetylthenylchlor
2924 2990.15	萘丙胺、牧草胺、溴丁酰草胺	6.5	30		9	17	千克	S	Naproanilide,tebutam,bromobutide
2924 2990.16	氯甲酰草胺、麦草伏M、麦草伏	6.5	30		9	17	千克	S	Clomeprop, flamprop M, flamprop
2924 2990.17	氯虫酰肼、异丙甲草胺、苯肽胺酸等(包括精异丙甲草胺、缬霉威)	6.5	30		9	17	千克	S	Halofenozide,metolachlor,phthalanillic acid (including s-metolachlor, iprovalicarb)
2924 2990.20	氟酰脲、环丙酰草胺、烯草胺	6.5	30		9	17	千克	S	Novaluron, cyclopropancarboxylic acid, pethoxamid
2924 2990.31	苯胺灵、苯霜灵、丙草胺、敌稗等(包括丙炔草胺、草不隆、草完隆、除虫脲、除幼脲)	6.5	30		9	17	千克	S	Propham,Benalaxyl,Pretilachlor, Propanil etc. (including prynachlor, neburon, noruron, diflubenzuron, dichlorbenzuron)
2924 2990.32	敌草胺、敌草隆、二甲苯草胺等(包括丁草胺、丁酰草胺、二甲草胺、氟苯脲、氟草隆)	6.5	30		9	17	千克	S	Napropamide, Diuron, xylachlor etc. (including Butachlor, chloranocryl, dimethachlor, teflubenzurcn, Fluometuron)
2924 2990.33	庚酰草胺、环丙草胺、环酰草胺、氟啶隆等(包括氟虫脲、氟铃脲、氟酰胺、氟蚁灵、氟幼脲)	6.5	30		9	17	千克	S	Monalide,cypromid, cypromid, chlorfluazuron etc. (including flufenoxuron, Hexaflumuron, flutolanil, nifluridide, penfluron)
2924 2990.34	甲氯酰草胺、甲霜灵、环草隆等(包括环莠隆、甲草胺、甲氧隆、克草胺、枯草隆)	6.5	30		9	17	千克	S	Pentanochlor,Metalaxyl,Siduron etc.(including cycluron,alachlor,metoxuron, ethachlor,Chloroxuron)
2924 2990.35	甲基杀草隆、枯莠隆、邻酰胺等(包括绿麦隆、氯苯胺灵、麦草氟甲酯、麦草氟异丙酯)	6.5	30		9	17	千克	S	Methyldymron,difenoxuron,mebenil, etc. (including chlortoluron, chlorpropham, flamprop-methyl, flamprop-isopropyl)
2924 2990.36	灭草隆、灭幼脲、炔苯酰草胺等(包括麦锈灵、棉胺宁、灭草灵、炔草隆、杀草胺)	6.5	30		9	17	千克	S	Monuron, Chlorbenzuron, Propyzamide etc. (including benodanil, phenisopham, swep, buturon, ethaprochlor)
2924 2990.37	虱螨脲、双苯酰草胺、双酰草胺等(包括杀草隆、杀铃脲、杀螺胺、莎稗磷)	6.5	30		9	17	千克	S	Lufenuron,diphenamid,carbetamide etc. (including daimuron, triflumuron, niclosamide, anilofos)
2924 2990.38	甜菜安、特丁草胺、乙氧苯草胺等(包括甜菜宁、戊菌隆、酰草隆、乙草胺、乙霉威)	6.5	30		9	17	千克	S	Desmedipham,terbuchlor,ethobenzanid etc. (including Phenmedipham,Pencycuron, phenobenzuron, Acetochlor, diethofencarb)
2924 2990.39	乙酰甲草胺、异丙隆、异草完隆等(包括异丙草胺、异丁草胺)	6.5	30		9	17	千克	S	Diethatyl,isoproturon,Isonoruron etc., (including propisochlor,delachlor)
2924 2990.40	炔己蚁胺的盐	6.5	30		9	17	千克	I	Salts of ethinamate (INN)
2924 2990.50	地恩丙胺及其盐	6.5	30		9	17	千克	W	Diampromide and its salts
2924 2990.90	其他环酰胺(包括环氨基甲酸酯)(包括其衍生物,以及它们的盐)	6.5	30		9	17	千克		Other Cyclic amides (including cyclic carbamates) and their derivatives; salts thereof:
29.25	**羧基酰亚胺化合物(包括糖精及其盐)及亚胺基化合物:**								**Carboxyimide-function compounds (including saccharin and its salts) and iminefunction compounds:**
	-酰亚胺及其衍生物以及它们的盐:								-Imides and their derivatives; salts thereof:
2925.1100	--糖精及其盐	9	90		9	17	千克	AB	--Saccharin and its salts
2925.1200	--格鲁米特(INN)	6.5	30		9	17	千克	I	--Glutethimide (INN)
2925.1900	--其他	6.5	30		9	17	千克		--Other
2925 1900.10	格鲁米特的盐	6.5	30		9	17	千克	I	Salts of glutethimide (INN)
2925 1900.21	腐霉利	6.5	30		9	17	千克	S	Procymidone

税则号列 Tariff Item	商品名称及备注	进口税率 最惠	普通	暂定	出口退税	增值税率	计量单位	监管条件	Article Description
2925 1900.22	菌核净、菌核利、甲菌利、乙菌利	6.5	30		9	17	千克	S	Dimetachlone, dichlozolin, myclozolin,chlozolinate
2925 1900.23	氟烯草酸	6.5	30		9	17	千克	S	Flumiclorac
2925 1900.24	胺菊酯（包括右旋胺菊酯、右旋反式胺菊酯、富右旋反式胺菊酯）	6.5	30		9	17	千克	S	Tetramethrin（including d-tetramethrin, d-trans-Tetramethrin, rich-d-t-tetramethrin）
2925 1900.90	其他酰亚胺及其衍生物、盐	6.5	30		9	17	千克		Other imides and their derivatives; salts thereof
	-亚胺及其衍生物以及它们的盐:								-Imines and their derivatives; salts thereof:
2925.2100	--杀虫脒（ISO）	6.5	30			17	千克	89	--Chlordimeform（ISO）
2925.2900	--其他	6.5	30		9	17	千克		--Other
2925 2900.11	杀螨特、杀螨脒	6.5	30		9	17	千克	S	Aramite, Chlorfenamidine
2925 2900.12	单甲脒、伐虫脒、丙烷脒	6.5	30		9	17	千克	S	Semiamitraz, formetanate, Propamidine
2925 2900.13	烯肟菌胺、烯肟菌酯、醚菌酯	6.5	30		9	17	千克	S	Trichlamide, enestroburin, kresoxim-methy
2925 2900.14	双胍辛胺、多果啶、双胍辛胺乙酸盐等（包括双胍三辛烷基苯磺酸盐）	6.5	30		9	17	千克	S	Iminoctadine,Dodine,iminoctadine,triacetate,etc.(including iminoctadine trialbesilate）
2925 2900.15	禾草灭、氟草醚、增产肟	6.5	30		9	17	千克	S	Alloxydim, ethoxyfen-ethyl, heptopargil
2925 2900.16	氯代水杨胺、双胍辛乙酸盐、顺己烯醇	6.5	30		9	17	千克	S	Chlorosalicvlicamide, iminoctadine triacetate, leaf alcohol
2925 2900.20	羟亚胺及其盐	6.5	30		9	17	千克	23	Hydroxylimine and its salts
2925 2900.30	双甲脒	6.5	30		9	17	千克	S	Amitraz
2925 2900.90	其他亚胺及其衍生物，以及它们的盐	6.5	30		9	17	千克		Other imines and their derivatives and their salts
29.26	**腈基化合物:**								**Nitrile-function compounds:**
2926.1000[暂]	-丙烯腈	6.5	30	3	13	17	千克	X	-Acrylonitrile
2926.2000	-1-氰基胍(双氰胺)	6.5	30		13	17	千克		-1-cyanoguanidine（dicyandiamide）
2926.3000	-芬普雷司（INN）及其盐；美沙酮中间体（4-氰基-2-二甲氨基-4，4-二苯基丁烷）	6.5	30		9	17	千克		-Fenproporex（INN）and its salts; methadone（INN）intermediate（4-cyano-2-dimethylamino-4, 4-diphenylbutane）
2926 3000.10	美沙酮中间体（4-氰基-2-二甲氨基-4，4-二苯基丁烷）	6.5	30		9	17	千克	W	Methadone（INN）intermediate（4-cyano-2-dimethylamino-4, 4-diphenylbutane）
2926 3000.20	芬普雷司及其盐	6.5	30		9	17	千克	I	Fenproporex（INN）and its salts
	-其他:								-Other:
2926.9010	---对氯氰苄	4	11		9	17	千克		---*p*-Chlorobenzyl cyanide
2926.9020	---间苯二甲腈	6.5	30		9	17	千克		---*m*-Phthalonitrile
2926.9090	---其他	6.5	30		9	17	千克		---Other
2926 9090.10	甲氰菊酯、S-氰戊菊酯、氯氟氰菊酯(包括氰氟虫腙)	6.5	30		9	17	千克	S	Fenpropathrin,esfenvalerate,cyhalothrin (including metaflumizone)
2926 9090.20[暂]	己二腈	6.5	30	1	9	17	千克		1,4-Dicyanobutan
2926 9090.30	杀灭菊酯乳剂(含量>25%)	6.5	30		9	17	千克	AB	Fenvalerate emulsion(content＞25%)
2926 9090.31	氯氰菊酯、氟氯氰菊酯等（包括高效氯氰菊酯、高效反式氯氰菊酯、高效氟氯氰菊酯）	6.5	30		9	17	千克	S	Cypermethrin, cyfluthrin etc.（including beta-cypermethrin,theta-Cypermethrin, cyfluthrin）
2926 9090.32	杀螟腈、甲基辛硫磷等（包括敌草腈、碘苯腈、辛酰碘苯腈、溴苯腈、辛酰溴苯腈）	6.5	30		9	17	千克	S	Cyanophos, Phoxiom-methyl etc.（including dichlobenil, Ioxynil, Ioxynil octanoate, Bromoxynil, Bromoxynil octanoate）
2926 9090.33	氯辛硫磷、戊氰威、苯醚氰菊酯等（包括稻瘟酰胺、丙螨氰、右旋苯醚氰菊酯）	6.5	30		9	17	千克	S	Chlorphoxim,nitrilacarb,cyphenothrin etc.（including fenoxanil, Propanedinitrile, d-cyphenothrin）
2926 9090.34	戊烯氰氯菊酯、溴氯氰菊酯（包括高效氯氟氰菊酯、精高效氯氟氰菊酯）	6.5	30		9	17	千克	S	Pentmethrin,tralocythrin（including Lambda-cyhalothrin,gamma-cyhalothrin）
2926 9090.35	溴氰菊酯、四溴菊酯、氟丙菊酯	6.5	30		9	17	千克	S	Deltamethrin, tralomerhrin, acrinathrin

税则号列 Tariff Item	商品名称及备注	进口税率			出口退税	增值税率	计量单位	监管条件	Article Description
		最惠	普通	暂定					
2926 9090.36	氟氯苯菊酯、氰戊菊酯、乙氰菊酯	6.5	30		9	17	千克	S	Flumethrin, fenvalerate, Cycloprothrin
2926 9090.37	氟氰戊菊酯、溴氟菊酯、溴灭菊酯	6.5	30		9	17	千克	S	Flucythrinate,brofluthrinate,brofenvalerate
2926 9090.38	氰菌胺、百菌清、霜脲氰、溴菌腈	6.5	30		9	17	千克	S	Zarilamid,chlorothalonil,cymoxanil,bromothalonil
2926 9090.39	氟胺氰菊酯、氰氟草酯、苯氰菊酯（包括富右旋反式苯氰菊酯）	6.5	30		9	17	千克	S	Taufluralinate,cyhalofop-butyl,cyphenothrin（including Rich d-trans-Cyphenothrin）
2926 9090.50	辛硫磷	6.5	30		9	17	千克	S	Phoxim
2926 9090.60	丁氟螨酯	6.5	30		9	17	千克	S	2-methoxyethyl ester
2926 9090.90	其他腈基化合物	6.5	30		9	17	千克		Other nitrile function compounds
29.27	**重氮化合物、偶氮化合物及氧化偶氮化合物：**								**Diazo-, azo-. or azoxy-compounds:**
2927.0000	重氮化合物、偶氮化合物及氧化偶氮化合物	6.5	30		9	17	千克		Diazo-, azo-.or azoxy-compounds
2927 0000.10	敌磺钠(包括氧化偶氮化合物)	6.5	30		9	17	千克	S	Fenaminosulf(including azoxy-compounds)
2927 0000.20	4-二丙基氨基苯重氮氯化锌盐	6.5	30		9	17	千克	AB	4-Dipropylaminobenzenediazonium zinc chloride
2927 0000.90	其他重氮化合物、偶氮化合物等（包括氧化偶氮化合物）	6.5	30		9	17	千克		Other diazo-azo-compounds（including azoxy-compounds）
29.28	**肼（联氨）及胲（羟胺）的有机衍生物：**								**Organic derivatives of hydrazine or of hydroxylamine:**
2928.0000	肼（联氨）及胲（羟胺）的有机衍生物	6.5	20		9	17	千克		Organic derivatives of hydrazine or of hydroxylamine
2928 0000.10	偏二甲肼	6.5	20		9	17	千克	3	Dimethylhydrazine
2928 0000.20	甲基肼	6.5	20		9	17	千克	3A	Methylhydrazine
2928 0000.31	抑食肼、虫酰肼、丁酰肼、联苯肼酯(包括肟菌酯,苯氧菌胺)	6.5	20		9	17	千克	S	Tebufenozide,daminozide, bifenazate((including Trifloxystrobin,Metominostrobin)
2928 0000.32	绿谷隆、溴谷隆、利谷隆、氯溴隆	6.5	20		9	17	千克	S	Monolinuron,metobromuron,linuron, chlorbromuron
2928 0000.33	溴酚肟、乙二肟	6.5	20		9	17	千克	S	Bromofenoxim, glyoxime
2928 0000.34	苯螨特	6.5	20		9	17	千克	S	Benzoximate
2928 0000.35	醌肟腙	6.5	20		9	17	千克	S	Benquinox
2928 0000.36	三甲苯草酮	6.5	20		9	17	千克	S	Tralkoxydim
2928 0000.37	解草胺腈	6.5	20		9	17	千克		Cyometrinil
2928 0000.90	其他肼(联氨)及胲(羟胺)的有机衍生物	6.5	20		9	17	千克		Other Organic derivatives of hydrazine or of hydroxylamine
29.29	**其他含氮基化合物：**								**Compounds with other nitrogen function:**
	-异氰酸酯:								-Isocyanates:
2929.1010	---2，4-和 2，6-甲苯二异氰酸酯混合物(甲苯二异氰酸酯 TDI)	6.5	30		9	17	千克		---Toluene diisocyanate
2929.1020	---二甲苯二异氰酸酯(TODI)	6.5	30		9	17	千克		---*o*-Xylene diisocyanate
2929.1030	---二苯基甲烷二异氰酸酯(纯MDI)	6.5	30		13	17	千克		---Diphenylmethane diisocyanate
2929.1040	---六亚基甲烷二异氰酸酯	6.5	30		9	17	千克		---Hexamethelene diisocyanate
2929.1090	---其他	6.5	30		13	17	千克		---Other
	-其他:								-Other:
2929.9010	---环已基氨基磺酸钠(甜蜜素)	9	90		9	17	千克	AB	---Sodium cyclamate
2929.9020	---二烷（甲、乙、正丙或异丙）氨基膦酰二卤	6.5	30		9	17	千克	23	---N, N-Dialkyl（Me, Et, n-Pr or i-Pr）phosphoramidic dihalides
2929.9030	---二烷（甲、乙、正丙或异丙）氨基膦酸二烷（甲、乙、正丙或异丙）酯	6.5	30		9	17	千克	23	---Dialkyl（Me, Et, n-Pr or i-Pr）N, N-dialkyl（Me, Et, n-Pr or i-Pr）-phosphoramidates
2929.9040	---乙酰甲胺磷	6.5	30		9	17	千克	S	---Acephate
2929.9090	---其他	6.5	30			17	千克		---Other
2929 9090.11	胺丙畏、胺草磷、抑草磷，丁苯草酮等（包括甲基胺草磷）	6.5	30		9	17	千克	S	Propetamphos, amiprophos, butamifos, butroxydim（including amiprophosmethyl）
2929 9090.12	异柳磷、甲基异柳磷、丙胺氟磷	6.5	30			17	千克	S	Isofenphos,isofenphos-methyl,mipafox

税则号列 Tariff Item	商品名称及备注	进口税率 最惠	普通	暂定	出口退税	增值税率	计量单位	监管条件	Article Description
	等								
2929 9090.13	八甲磷、育畜磷、甘氨硫磷等(包括甲氟磷、毒鼠磷、水胺硫磷)	6.5	30		9	17	千克	S	Schradan,crufomate,phosglycin etc.（including dimefox,phosazetin,isocarbophs）
2929 9090.90	其他含氮基化合物	6.5	30		9	17	千克		Compounds with other nitrogen function
	第十分章　有机—无机化合物、杂环化合物、核酸及其盐以及磺（酰）胺								**X. ORGANO-INORGANIC COMPOU-NDS, HETEROCYCLIC COMPOUNDS, NUCLEIC ACIDS AND THEIR SALTS, AND SULPHONAMIDES**
29.30	**有机硫化合物:**								**Organo-sulphur compounds:**
2930.2000	-硫代氨基甲酸盐（或酯）及二硫代氨基甲酸盐	6.5	30		9	17	千克		-Thiocarbamates and dithiocarbamates
2930 2000.11	禾草丹、杀螟丹	6.5	30		9	17	千克	S	Thiobencarb, cartap
2930 2000.12	威百亩、代森钠、丙森锌、福美铁等(包括福美锌、代森福美锌、安百亩)	6.5	30		9	17	千克	S	Metam-sodium,nabam,propineb,ferbam etc.（including ziram, polycarbamate, metam-ammonium）
2930 2000.13	燕麦敌、野麦畏、硫草敌	6.5	30		9	17	千克	S	Diallate,triallate,ethiolate
2930 2000.14	苄草丹、戊草丹、坪草丹、仲草丹	6.5	30		9	17	千克	S	Prosulfocarb,esprocarb,orbencarb,tiocarbazil
2930 2000.15	丁草敌、克草敌、茵草敌、灭草敌等（包括环草敌）	6.5	30		9	17	千克	S	Butylate,pebulate,eradicane,vernolate（including cycloate）
2930 2000.16	硫菌威、菜草畏	6.5	30		9	17	千克	S	Prothiocarb, sulfallate
2930 2000.90	其他硫代氨基甲酸盐(或酯)(包括二硫代氨基甲酸盐)	6.5	30		9	17	千克		Other thiocarbamates（including dithiocarbamates）
2930.3000	-一硫化二烃氨基硫羰、二硫化二烃氨基硫羰及四硫化二烃氨基硫羰	6.5	30		9	17	千克		-Thiuram mono-, di or tetrasulphide
2930 3000.10	福美双	6.5	30		9	17	千克	S	Thiram
2930 3000.90	其他一硫化二烃氨基硫羰等(包括二硫化二烃氨基硫羰及四硫化二烃氨基硫羰)	6.5	30		9	17	千克		Other thiuram mono -, di or tetrasulphide
2930.4000	-甲硫氨酸(蛋氨酸)	6.5	30		13	17	千克	AB	-Methionine
2930.5000	-敌菌丹（ISO）及甲胺磷（ISO）	6.5	30			17	千克		-Captafol（ISO） and methamidophos（ISO）
2930 5000.10	甲胺磷(ISO)	6.5	30			17	千克	X	Methamidophos (ISO)
2930 5000.20	敌菌丹(ISO)	6.5	30			17	千克	S	Coptafol (ISO)
	-其他:								-Other:
2930.9010	---双巯丙氨酸(胱氨酸)	6.5	30		9	17	千克	AB	---Cystine
2930.9020	---二硫代碳酸酯(或盐)[黄原酸酯(或盐)]	6.5	30		9	17	千克		---Dithiocarbonates（xanthates）
2930.9090	---其他	6.5	30			17	千克		---Other
2930 9090.11	烯禾啶，双环磺草酮，氟虫酰胺，氟虫双酰胺	6.5	30		9	17	千克	S	Sethoxydim, benzobicylon, flubendiamide
2930 9090.13	2-氯乙基氯甲基硫醚	6.5	30		9	17	千克	32	2-Chloroethyl Methyl Sulfide
2930 9090.14	二(2-氯乙基)硫醚（即芥子气）	6.5	30		9	17	千克	32	Bis(2-chloroethyl)sulfide (Mustard gas)
2930 9090.15	二(2-氯乙硫基)甲烷	6.5	30		9	17	千克	32	Bis(2-chloroethylthio) methane
2930 9090.16	1,2-二(2-氯乙硫基)乙烷（即倍半芥子气）	6.5	30		9	17	千克	32	1,2-Bis(2-chloroethylthio) ethane (Sesquimustard)
2930 9090.17	1,3-二(2-氯乙硫基)正丙烷	6.5	30		9	17	千克	32	1,3-Bis(2-chloroethylthio)-n-propane
2930 9090.18	1,4-二(2-氯乙硫基)正丁烷	6.5	30		9	17	千克	32	1,4-Bis(2-chloroethylthio)-n-butane
2930 9090.19	1,5-二(2-氯乙硫基)正戊烷	6.5	30		9	17	千克	32	1,5-Bis(2-chloroethylthio)-n-pentane
2930 9090.21	二(2-氯乙硫基甲基)醚	6.5	30		9	17	千克	32	Bis(2-chloroethylthiomethyl) ether
2930 9090.22	二(2-氯乙硫基乙基)醚（即氧芥气）	6.5	30		9	17	千克	32	Bis(2-chloroethylthioethyl) ether (O-Mustard)
2930 9090.23	胺吸膦（硫代磷酸二乙基-S-2-二乙氨基乙酯及烷基化或质子化盐）	6.5	30		9	17	千克	23	Amiton O, O-Diethyl S-2-（diethy lamino） ethyl phosphorothilolate and corresponding alkylated or protonated salts

税则号列 Tariff Item	商品名称及备注	进口税率 最惠	普通	暂定	出口退税	增值税率	计量单位	监管条件	Article Description
2930 9090.24	烷基氨基乙-2-硫醇及相应质子盐	6.5	30		9	17	千克	23	N. N-dialkyl aminoethane-2-thiols and corresponding protonated salts
2930 9090.25	硫二甘醇(二（2-羟乙基）硫醚、硫代双乙醇)	6.5	30		9	17	千克	23	Thiodiglycol: Bis（2-hydroxyethyl）sulfide; thiodiethanol
2930 9090.26	烷基硫代膦酸烷 S-2-二烷氨基乙酯(包括相应烷基化盐、质子化盐，烷基指甲、乙、正丙、异丙基)	6.5	30		9	17	千克	23	Alkyl alkane thiophosphate-S-2-aminoethyl, including cyclo alkane-S-2-dialkane（Me, Et, n-Pr or i-Pr）aminoethyl and corresponding alkylated or protonated salts
2930 9090.27	含一磷原子与甲、乙、丙基结合化合物（不包括地虫磷）	6.5	30		9	17	千克	23	Compounds, containing a phosphorus atom to which is boned one methyl, ethyl or propyl group (other than O-Ethyl S-phenyl ethylphosphonothiolothionate)
2930 9090.28	内吸磷	6.5	30		9	17	千克	X	Demeton
2930 9090.31	4-甲基硫基安非他明	6.5	30		9	17	千克	I	4-Methylthioamfetamine
2930 9090.32	莫达非尼	6.5	30		9	17	千克	I	Modafinil
2930 9090.40[暂]	DL-羟基蛋氨酸	6.5	30	5	9	17	千克	AB	DL-Methionine Hydroxy Analogue
2930 9090.51	甲基硫菌灵、硫菌灵、苯螨醚等（包括乙蒜素、敌灭生、丁酮威、丁酮砜威、棉铃威）	6.5	30		9	17	千克	S	Thiophanate-methyl,thiophanate,phenproxide etc.（including ethylicin, dimexano, butocarboxim, butoxycarboxim, alanycarb）
2930 9090.52	灭多威、涕灭威、乙硫苯威等（包括杀线威、甲硫威、多杀威、涕灭砜威、硫双威）	6.5	30			17	千克	S	Methomyl,aldicarb,ethiofencarb etc.（including oxamyl,methiocarb,toxamate, aldoxycarb, thiodicarb）
2930 9090.53	丁醚脲、久效威、苯硫威等（包括敌螨特、2 甲 4 氯乙硫酯）	6.5	30		9	17	千克	S	Diafenthiuron, thiofanox, fenothiocarb etc.（including chlorfensulphide, MCPAthioethyl）
2930 9090.54	杀虫双、杀虫单、灭虫脲等（包括避虫醇、烯虫硫酯、三氯杀螨砜、杀螨醚、杀螨酯）	6.5	30		9	17	千克	S	Dimehypo,monosultap,chloromethiuron etc.（including 2-(octylthio)-ethano, triprene,tetradifon, chlorbenside, chlorfenson）
2930 9090.55	代森锌、代森锰、代森锰锌等（包括福美胂、福美甲胂、代森铵、代森联）	6.5	30		9	17	千克	S	Zineb, maneb, mancozeb etc.（including asomate, urbacide, amobam, metiram）
2930 9090.56	烯草酮、磺草酮、嗪草酸甲酯、硝磺草酮等（包括苯氟磺胺、甲磺乐灵、氯硫酰草胺、脱叶磷）	6.5	30		9	17	千克	S	Clethodim,sulcotrione,fluthiacet-methyl,mesotrione etc.（including dichlofluanid, nitralin, chlorthiamide, tribuphos ）
2930 9090.57	灭菌丹、克菌丹、杀螨硫醚等（包括氟杀螨、硫肟醚、莠不生）	6.5	30		9	17	千克	S	Folpet,captan,tetrasul etc.（including fiuorbenside, pyriproxyfen, bexide）
2930 9090.58	稻瘟净、异稻瘟净、稻丰散等（包括敌瘟磷）	6.5	30		9	17	千克	S	Kitazin, iprobenfos, phenthoate etc.（including edifenphos）
2930 9090.59	安妥、灭鼠特、二硫氰基甲烷等（包括灭鼠肼、氟硫隆）	6.5	30		9	17	千克	S	Antu,thiosemicarbazide,Methylenedithiocyanate etc.（including promurit, fluothiuron）
2930 9090.61	马拉硫磷、苏硫磷、赛硫磷等（包括丙虫磷、双硫磷、亚砜磷、异亚砜磷）	6.5	30		9	17	千克	S	Malathion,sophamide,amidithion etc.（including propaphos,temephos,oxydemeton-methyl,oxydeprofos）
2930 9090.62	丙溴磷、田乐磷、特丁硫磷等（包括硫丙磷、地虫硫膦、乙硫磷、丙硫磷、甲基乙拌磷）	6.5	30		9	17	千克	S	Profenofos, demephion, terbufos etc.（including sulprofos,fonofos,ethion,prothiofos,thiometon）
2930 9090.63	乐果、益硫磷、氧乐果等（包括甲拌磷、乙拌磷、虫螨磷、果虫磷）	6.5	30		9	17	千克	S	Dimethoate,ethoate-methyl,omethoate etc.（including phorate, disulfoton, chlorthiophos, cyanthoate）
2930 9090.64	氯胺磷、家蝇磷、灭蚜磷等（包括安硫磷、四甲磷、丁苯硫磷、苯线磷、蚜灭磷）	6.5	30		9	17	千克	S	Chloramine phosphorus,acethion,mecarbam etc.（including formothion,mecarphon,fosmethilan, fenamiphos,vamidothion）
2930 9090.65	硫线磷、氯甲硫磷、杀虫磺等（包括砜吸磷、砜拌磷、异拌磷、三硫磷、芬硫磷）	6.5	30		9	17	千克	S	Cadusafos,chlormephos,bensultap etc.（including Oxydemeton-methyl, oxydisulfoton, isothioate, carbophenothion, phenkapton）
2930 9090.66	倍硫磷、甲基内吸磷、乙酯磷等	6.5	30		9	17	千克	S	Fenthion,demeton-S-methyl, acetophos etc.

税则号列 Tariff Item	商品名称及备注	进口税率 最惠	普通	暂定	出口退税	增值税率	计量单位	监管条件	Article Description
	(包括丰索磷、内吸磷、发硫磷)								(including fensulfothion, demeton, prothoate)
2930 9090.67	灭线磷	6.5	30		9	17	千克	S	Phophos (MOCAP)
2930 9090.90	其他有机硫化合物	6.5	30		13	17	千克		Other organo-sulphur compounds
29.31	**其他有机-无机化合物:**								**Other organo-inorganic compounds:**
2931.1000	-四甲基铅及四乙基铅	6.5	30		9	17	千克	X	-Tetramethyl lead and tetraethyl lead
2931.2000	-三丁基锡化合物	6.5	30			17	千克	X	-Tributyltin compounds
	-其他:								-Other:
	---含有磷原子的:								--- Containing phosphorus atoms
2931.9011	----双甘膦	6.5	30			17	千克	AB	---- N-Phosphonomethyl aminodiacetic acid
2931.9019	----其他	6.5	30			17	千克		----Other
2931 9019.11	烷基亚膦酰烷基-2-二烷氨基乙酯(包括相应烷基化盐或质子化盐)	6.5	30		9	17	千克	23	Alkyl phosphonic acid alkyl -2-dialkyl-aminoethyl alkyl - phosphonothiolates (including the corresponding alkylated or protonated salts)
2931 9019.12	氯沙林、氯梭曼(氯沙林即甲基氯膦酸异丙酯,氯梭曼即甲基氯膦酸频那酯)	6.5	30		9	17	千克	23	Chlorosarin, Chlorosoman (Chlorosarin, namely, O-Isopropyl methylphosphonofluoridate, Chlorosoman, namely, O-Pinacolyl methylphosphonofluoridate)
2931 9019.13	烷基氟膦酸烷酯,10碳原子以下(烷基指甲、乙、正丙、异丙基,例如,沙林、梭曼)	6.5	30		9	17	千克	23	O-Alkyl (<=C10), alkyl (Me, Et, n-Pr or i-Pr)-phosphonofluoridates such as sarin and soman)
2931 9019.14	二烷氨基氰膦酸烷酯10碳原子以下(烷基指甲、乙、正丙、异丙基,例如,塔崩)	6.5	30		9	17	千克	23	O-Alkyl (<=C10) N,N-dialkyl (Me, Et, n-Pr or i-Pr) phosphoramidocyanidates l, such as tabun)
2931 9019.15	烷基膦酰二氟(烷基指甲、乙、正丙、异丙基,例如,DF:甲基膦酰二氟)	6.5	30		9	17	千克	23	Alkyl (Me, Et, n-Pr or i-Pr) phosphonyldifluorides, such as DF: Methylphosphonyldifluoride)
2931 9019.16	草甘膦	6.5	30			17	千克	S	Glyphosate
2931 9019.17	草铵膦、草硫膦、杀木膦等(包括双丙氨膦、双丙氨酰膦、增甘膦及其盐)	6.5	30		9	17	千克	S	Glufosinate, Sulfosate, fosamine and so on (Including Bialaphos,Bi-alanyl-phosphine, glyphosine and their salts)
2931 9019.18	三丁氯苄鏻	6.5	30		9	17	千克	S	Phosphan(Chlorphonium)
2931 9019.19	乙烯利	6.5	30		9	17	千克	S	Ethephon
2931 9019.21	敌百虫、氟硅菊酯、毒壤膦等(包括苯硫膦、溴苯膦、苯腈膦、丁酯膦)	6.5	30		9	17	千克	S	Trichlorfon, silafluofen, trichloronant (Including EPN, Leptophos., Cyanofenphos, butonate)
2931 9019.90	其他含磷原子的有机-无机化合物	6.5	30		9	17	千克	AB	Other organo-inorganic compounds, containing phosphorus atoms
2931.9090	---其他	6.5	30			17	千克		---Other
2931 9090.01	六甲基环三硅氧烷(包括八甲基环四硅氧烷,十甲基环五硅氧烷,十二甲基环六硅氧烷)	6.5	30		9	17	千克		Hexamethyl Cyclotrisiloxane (Including octamethylcyclotetrasiloxane,decamethylcyclopentasiloxane, decamethylcyclopentasiloxane)
2931 9090.11	2-氯乙烯基二氯胂	6.5	30			17	千克	23	2-Chlorovinyldichloroarsine
2931 9090.12	二(2-氯乙烯基)氯胂	6.5	30			17	千克	23	Bis(2-chlorovinyl)chloroarsine
2931 9090.13	三(2-氯乙烯基)胂	6.5	30			17	千克	23	Tris(2-chlorovinyl)arsine
2931 9090.14	锆试剂、二甲胂酸等(包括4-二甲氨基偶氮苯-4'-胂酸、卡可基酸、二甲基胂酸钠)	6.5	30			17	千克	X	Zicon, Cacodylie acid (Include 4-Dimethylamino-azobenzene-4'-arsonic acid, cacodylic acid, Sodium dimethyl arsine)
2931 9090.15	4-氨基苯胂酸钠、二氯化苯胂(对氨基苯胂酸钠、二氯苯胂、苯胂化二氯)	6.5	30			17	千克	X	4-Aminophenyl arsinic acid sodium, Dichloride phenylarsonic (arsmin,dichlorophenarsine, Phenylarsine dichloride)
2931 9090.16	蒽醌-1-胂酸、三环锡(普特丹)等(包括月桂酸三丁基锡、醋酸三丁基锡)	6.5	30			17	千克	X	Anthrauinone-1-arsonic acid, cyhexatin (Pute Dan) and so on (Including Tributyltin laurate, Tributyltin acetate)
2931 9090.17	硫酸三乙基锡、二丁基氧化锡等	6.5	30		9	17	千克	X	Triethyltin sulfate, Dibutyltin oxide (Including Dibutyltin

税则号列 Tariff Item	商品名称及备注	进口税率			出口退税	增值税率	计量单位	监管条件	Article Description
		最惠	普通	暂定					
	(包括氧化二丁基锡、乙酸三乙基锡,三乙基乙酸锡)								oxide, Triethyltin acetate, Triethyltin acetate)
2931 9090.18	四乙基锡、乙酸三甲基锡(四乙锡、醋酸三甲基锡)	6.5	30		9	17	千克	X	Tetraethyltin, trimethyltin acid (Tetraethyltin, Trimethyltin acetate)
2931 9090.19	毒菌锡［三苯基羟基锡(含量>20%)］	6.5	30		9	17	千克	X	Fentin hydroxide, Hydroxytriphenyltin (content>20%)
2931 9090.21	乙酰亚砷酸铜、二苯(基)胺氯胂(祖母绿;翡翠绿;醋酸亚砷酸铜,吩吡嗪化氯;亚当氏气)	6.5	30			17	千克	X	Copper acetoarsenite, phenarsazine chloride (Emerald, emerald green, Diphenylamine Chloroarsine)
2931 9090.22	3-硝基-4-羟基苯胂酸(4-羟基-3-硝基苯胂酸)	6.5	30			17	千克	X	3-Nitryl -4-Hydroxyphenyl arsenic acid (4-hydroxy-3-nitrophenylarsonicacid)
2931 9090.23	乙基二氯胂、二苯(基)氯胂(包括二氯化乙基胂、氯化二苯胂)	6.5	30			17	千克	X	Ethyldichloroarsine , Diphenylchloroarsine (Including dichlorioethylarsine, diphenylarsinechloride)
2931 9090.24	甲(基)胂酸、丙(基)胂酸、二碘化苯胂(苯基二碘胂)	6.5	30			17	千克	X	Methyl arsenic acid, Propyl arsonic acid, Phenyldichloroarsine (PDA)
2931 9090.25	苯胂酸,2-硝基苯胂酸等(包括邻硝基苯胂酸、3-硝基苯胂酸、间硝基苯胂酸等)	6.5	30			17	千克	X	Phenylarsonic acid, 2-Nitrophenylarsonic acid (Including O-nitrophenyl arsenic acid, 3-nitrophenylarsonicacid , m-Nitrophenylarsonic acid)
2931 9090.26	4-硝基苯胂酸,2-氨基苯胂酸(对硝基苯胂酸,邻氨基苯胂酸)	6.5	30			17	千克	X	4-Nitrophenyl arsenic acid, 2-aminophenylarsonic acid (p-Nitrophenyl Arsenic Acid, o-Aminbenzene arsonic acid)
2931 9090.27	3-氨基苯胂酸、4-氨基苯胂酸(间氨基苯胂酸、对氨基苯胂酸)	6.5	30			17	千克	X	3-Aminophenylarsonicacid , 4-Aminophenyl arsonic acid (m-,or p-Aminobenzene arsonic acid)
2931 9090.28	三苯锡、三苯基乙酸锡等(包括三苯基氯化锡、三苯基氢氧化锡、苯丁锡、三唑锡)	6.5	30		9	17	千克	S	Fentin hydroxide, Fentin acetate (Including Chlorotriphenyltin, Fentin hydroxide, Fenbutatin oxide, Azocyclotin)
2931 9090.29	田安	6.5	30		13	17	千克	S	Neoasozin (MAFA)
2931 9090.31	乙烯硅	6.5	30		9	17	千克	S	Etacelasil
2931 9090.90	其他有机-无机化合物	6.5	30		13	17	千克	AB	Other organic –non-organic compound
29.32	**仅含有氧杂原子的杂环化合物:**								**Heterocyclic compounds with oxygen heteroatom（s）only:**
	-结构上含有一个非稠合呋喃环（不论是否氢化）的化合物:								-Compounds containing an unfused furan ring（whether or not hydrogenated）in the structure:
2932.1100	--四氢呋喃	6	20		9	17	千克	AB	--Tetrahydrofuran
2932.1200	--2-糠醛	6	20		9	17	千克	B	--2-Furaldehyde（furfuraldehyde）
2932.1300	--糠醇及四氢糠醇	6	20		9	17	千克		--Furfuryl alcohol and tetrahydrofurfuryl alcohol
2932.1900	--其他	6.5	20		9	17	千克		--Other
2932 1900.11	喃烯菊酯、炔呋菊酯等（包括甲呋炔菊酯、溴苄呋菊酯、右旋炔呋菊酯）	6.5	20		9	17	千克	S	Japothrins,furamethrin etc.（including proparthrin, bromethrin, d-t-furamethrin）
2932 1900.12	呋菌胺、酯菌胺、抑霉胺等（包括环菌胺、甲呋酰胺、二甲呋酰胺）	6.5	20		9	17	千克	S	Methuroxam,cyprofuram, etaconazole, etc（including cyclafuramid,fenfuram,furcarbanil）
2932 1900.13	呋氧草醚、环庚草醚、呋草酮等（包括茵多酸）	6.5	20		9	17	千克	S	Furyloxyfen, cinmethylin, flurtamone etc.（including endothall）
2932 1900.14	楝素,呋霜灵等(包括呋菌隆,螺螨酯)	6.5	20		9	17	千克	S	Azadirachtin, furalaxyl etc.（including furophanate, spirodiclofen）
2932 1900.15	苄呋菊酯（包括右旋苄呋菊酯、生物苄呋菊酯）	6.5	20		9	17	千克	S	Resmethrin（including d-resmethrin, bioresmethrin）
2932 1900.20	呋芬雷司	6.5	20		9	17	千克	I	Furfennorex
2932 1900.90	其他结构上有非稠合呋喃环化合物	6.5	20		9	17	千克		Other compounds containing an unfused Furanring in the structure
	-内酯:								-Lactones:
2932.2010	---香豆素、甲基香豆素及乙基	6.5	20		13	17	千克		---Coumarin, methylcoumarins and ethylcoumarins

税则号列 Tariff Item	商品名称及备注	进口税率 最惠	普通	暂定	出口退税	增值税率	计量单位	监管条件	Article Description
	香豆素								
2932.2090	---其他内酯	6.5	20			17	千克		---Other lactones
2932 2090.11	杀鼠灵、克鼠灵、敌鼠灵、溴鼠灵等(包括氯灭鼠灵、氟鼠灵、鼠得克、杀鼠醚)	6.5	20			17	千克	S	Warfarin, coumafuryl, diphacinone, Brodifacoum and so on (Including coumachlor, flocoumafen, Difenacoum and coumatetralyl)
2932 2090.12	赤霉酸	6.5	20		13	17	千克	S	Gibberellic acid
2932 2090.13	蝇毒磷、茴蒿素、溴敌隆、呋酰胺等(包括四氯苯酞、畜虫磷)	6.5	20			17	千克	S	Coumaphos, santonin, bromadiolone, Ofurace (Including phthalide, coumithoate)
2932 2090.14	丁香菌酯	6.5	20		13	17	千克	S	Coumoxystrobin
2932 2090.90	其他内酯	6.5	20		13	17	千克		Other lactone
	-其他:								-Other:
2932.9100	--4-丙烯基-1,2-亚甲二氧基苯(异黄樟脑)	6.5	20		9	17	千克	23	--Isosafrole
2932.9200	--1-(1,3-苯并二噁茂-5-基)丙烷-2-酮	6.5	20		9	17	千克	23	--1-(1, 3- Benzodioxol -5-yl) Propane -2- Ketone
2932.9300	--3,4-亚甲二氧基苯甲醛(胡椒醛)	6.5	20		13	17	千克	23	-- Piperonal
2932.9400	--4-烯丙基-1,2-亚甲二氧基苯(黄樟脑)	6.5	20		13	17	千克	23	--Safrole
2932.9500	--四氢大麻酚(所有的异构体)	6.5	20		9	17	千克	I	--Tetrahydrocannabinols (all isomers)
	--其他:								--Other:
2932.9910	---7-羟基苯并呋喃(呋喃酚)	4	11		9	17	千克		---Furan phenol
2932.9920	--2,2′-双甲氧羰基-4,4′-双甲氧基-5,6,5′,6′-双亚甲二氧基联苯(联苯双酯)	6.5	20		9	17	千克		---Bifendate
2932.9930	---蒿甲醚	6.5	20		13	17	千克		---Artemether
2932.9990	---其他	6.5	20			17	千克		---Other
2932 9990.11	克百威	6.5	20		13	17	千克	S	Carbofuran
2932 9990.12	二氧威、恶虫威、丙硫克百威等(包括丁硫克百威、呋线威)	6.5	20		13	17	千克	S	Dioxocarb, bendiocarb, benfuracarb (including carbosulfan, furathiocarb)
2932 9990.13	因毒磷、敌恶磷、碳氯灵	6.5	20		13	17	千克	S	Endothion, dioxathion, isobenzan
2932 9990.14	增效特、增效砜、增效醚、增效酯等(包括增效环、增效散)	6.5	20		13	17	千克		Bucarpolate, sufoxide, piperonyl butoxide, propylisome etc. (including pipepxonyl cyclrnene, sesamex)
2932 9990.15	吡喃灵、吡喃隆、乙氧呋草黄等(包括呋草黄、氟草肟)	6.5	20		13	17	千克	S	Pyracarbolin,metobenzuron,ethofumesate etc. (including benfuresate, fluxofenim)
2932 9990.16	避蚊酮、苯虫醚、鱼藤酮	6.5	20		13	17	千克	S	Butopyronoxyl,difenolan,rotenone
2932 9990.17	调呋酸、芸苔素内酯	6.5	20		13	17	千克	S	Dikegulac, brassinolide
2932 9990.21	紫杉醇	6.5	20			17	千克	QFE	Taxol
2932 9990.22	三尖杉宁碱	6.5	20		13	17	千克	FE	Cephalomannine
2932 9990.23	十去乙酰基巴卡丁三(红豆杉提取物 10-DAB)	6.5	20		13	17	千克	FE	10-deacetylate-baccatin III, taxus extracts 10-DAB
2932 9990.24	十去乙酰基紫杉醇(红豆杉提取物 10-DAT)	6.5	20			17	千克	FE	10-deacetylate-paclitaxel, taxus extracts 10-DAT
2932 9990.25	巴卡丁三	6.5	20		13	17	千克	FE	Baccatin three
2932 9990.26	7-表紫杉醇	6.5	20			17	千克	FE	7- Epipaclitaxel
2932 9990.27	10-去乙酰 7-表紫杉醇	6.5	20			17	千克	FE	10- Deacetylation -7- Epipaclitaxel
2932 9990.28	7,10-双(三氯乙酰基)-10-去乙酰基巴卡丁三类似物	6.5	20		13	17	千克	EF	Analogues of 7,10-bi-(Trichloroacetyl) -10-deacetylate-baccatin III
2932 9990.29	多烯紫杉醇	6.5	20			17	千克	EF	Docetaxel
2932 9990.31	7,10-双(三氯乙酰基)-多西他赛	6.5	20		13	17	千克	EF	7,10-Bi (trichloro-acetyl)- Docetaxel
2932 9990.40	替苯丙胺及其盐	6.5	20		13	17	千克	I	Tenamfetamine and its salts
2932 9990.51	(1,2-二甲基庚基)羟基四氢甲基二苯吡喃(包括六氢大麻酚)	6.5	20		13	17	千克	I	(1,2-Dimetol)Hydroxytetrahydrobiopterin-DMHP (including Parahexyl)
2932 9990.52	甲羟芬胺、乙芬胺、羟芬胺	6.5	20		13	17	千克	I	5-methoxy-α-methyl- 3,4-(methylenedioxy)

税则号列 Tariff Item	商品名称及备注	进口税率 最惠	普通	暂定	出口退税	增值税率	计量单位	监管条件	Article Description
									phenethylamine,(±)-N-ethyl-alpha-methyl-3,4-(methylenedioxy)phenethylamine,(±)-N-[alpha-methyl-3,4-(methylenedioxy)phenethyl]hydroxylamine
2932 9990.53	二亚甲基双氧安非他明及其盐(MDMA)	6.5	20		13	17	千克	I	(±)-N,alpha-dimethyl-3,4-(methylene-dioxy)phenethylamine and its salts
2932 9990.54	3，4-亚甲二氧基甲卡西酮	6.5	20		13	17	千克	I	3,4-methylenedioxy-N-methylcathinone;CAS：186028-79-5
2932 9990.60	二恶英、呋喃（多氯二苯并对二恶英、多氯二苯并呋喃）	6.5	20		13	17	千克	89	Dioxin, Furan（Polychlorinated dibenzo-p-dioxins , Polychlorinated dibenzofurans）
2932 9990.70	1,4-二噁烷	6.5	20		13	17	千克	X	1, 4-Dioxane
2932 9990.80	二氢黄樟素	6.5	20		13	17	千克	G	Dihydroisosafrole
2932 9990.91	其他濒危植物提取的仅含氧杂原子的杂环化合物	6.5	20			17	千克	EF	Other heterocyclic compounds with oxygen hetero-atom only, distilled from endangered plants
2932 9990.99	其他仅含氧杂原子的杂环化合物	6.5	20		13	17	千克		Other heterocyclic compounds with oxygen hetero-atom（s）only
29.33	**仅含有氮杂原子的杂环化合物：**								**Heterocyclic compounds with nitrogen heteroatom（s）only:**
	-结构上含有一个非稠合吡唑环（不论是否氢化）的化合物：								-Compounds containing an unfused pyrazole ring（whether or not hydrogenated）in the structure:
2933.1100	--二甲基苯基吡唑酮（安替比林）及其衍生物	6.5	20		9	17	千克		--Phenazone（antipyrin）and its derivatives
	--其他：								--Other:
2933.1920	---安乃近	6	20		9	17	千克	Q	---Analgin
2933.1990	---其他	6.5	20		9	17	千克		---Other
2933 1990.11	吡硫磷、吡唑硫磷、敌蝇威、乙虫腈等（包括异索威、吡唑威）	6.5	20		9	17	千克	S	Pyrazothion,pyraclofos,dimetilan, Ethiprole（including Isolan, pyrolan）
2933 1990.12	氟虫腈、唑螨酯、吡螨胺等（包括吡唑醚菌酯）	6.5	20		9	17	千克	S	Fipronil,Fenpyroximate,Tebufenpyrad etc.（including pyraclostrobin ）
2933 1990.13	吡草醚、吡唑草胺、氟氯草胺等（包括野燕枯、苄草唑、吡唑特、吡草酮）	6.5	20		9	17	千克	S	Pyraflufen-ethyl, metazachlor , nipyralofen, etc.（including Difenzoquat, Pyrazoxyfen, pyrazolate, benzofenap）
2933 1990.14	吡唑萘菌胺(包括氟唑菌胺、乙唑螨腈、异丙吡草酯、唑虫酰胺)	6.5	20		9	17	千克	S	Isopyrazam (including Fluorine, pyraclos, Fluazolate, and Tolfenpyrad)
2933 1990.90	其他结构上有非稠合吡唑环化合物	6.5	20		9	17	千克		Other compounds containing an unfused pyrazole ring in the structure
	-结构上含有一个非稠合咪唑环(不论是否氢化)的化合物：								-Compounds containing an unfused imidazole ring（whether or not hydrogenated）in the structure:
2933.2100	--乙内酰脲及其衍生物	6.5	30		9	17	千克		--Hydantoin and its derivatives
2933.2900	--其他	6.5	20		9	17	千克		--Other
2933 2900.11	异菌脲	6.5	20		9	17	千克	S	Iprodione
2933 2900.12	抑霉唑,咪菌腈,咪菌酮,咪鲜胺等（包括克霉唑,咪鲜胺锰盐）	6.5	20		9	17	千克	S	Imazalil,fenapanil,climbazole,prochloraz etc.（including clotrimazole, prochloraz manganese）
2933 2900.13	咪草酸、丁咪酰胺	6.5	20		9	17	千克	S	Imazamethabenz-methyl, isocarbamid
2933 2900.14	果绿啶	6.5	20		9	17	千克	S	Glyodin
2933 2900.15	氟菌唑	6.5	20		9	17	千克	S	Triflumizole
2933 2900.90	其他结构上有非稠合咪唑环化合物	6.5	20		9	17	千克		Other compounds containing an unfused imidazole ring in the structure
	-结构上含有一个非稠合吡啶环（不论是否氢化）的化合物：								-Compounds containing an unfused pyridine ring（whether or not hydrogenated）in the structure:
2933.3100	--吡啶及其盐	6	20		9	17	千克		--Pyridine and its salts
2933 3100.10	吡啶	6	20		9	17	千克	AB	Pyridine
2933 3100.90	吡啶盐	6	20		9	17	千克		Pyridine salts
	--六氢吡啶（哌啶）及其盐：								--Piperidine and its salts:
2933.3210	---六氢吡啶（哌啶）	4	11		9	17	千克	23	---Hexahydropyridine（piperidine）

税则号列 Tariff Item	商品名称及备注	进口税率 最惠	普通	暂定	出口退税	增值税率	计量单位	监管条件	Article Description
2933.3220	---六氢吡啶（哌啶）盐	6.5	20		9	17	千克		--Isoniazidum
2933.3300	--阿芬太尼（INN）、阿尼利定（INN）、苯氰米特(INN)，溴西泮（INN）、地芬诺新（INN）、地芬诺酯（INN）、地匹哌酮（INN）、芬太尼（INN）、凯托米酮（INN）、哌醋甲酯（INN）、喷他左辛（INN）、哌替啶（INN）、哌替啶中间体A（INN）、苯环利定（INN）、苯哌利定（INN）、哌苯甲醇（INN）、哌氰米特（INN）、哌丙吡胺（INN）和三甲利定（INN）以及它们的盐	6.5	20		9	17	千克		--Alfentanil（INN），anileridine（INN），bezitramide（INN），bromazepam（INN），difenoxin（INN），diphenoxylate（INN），dipipanone（INN），fentanyl（INN），ketobemidone（INN），methylphenidate（INN），pentazocine（INN），pethidine（INN），pethidine intermediate A（INN），phencyclidine（INN）（PCP），phenoperidine（INN），pipradrol（INN），piritramide（INN），propiram（INN）and trimeperidine（INN）; salts thereof
2933 3300.11	阿芬太尼、芬太尼（以及它们的盐）	6.5	20		9	17	千克	W	Alfentanil（INN），fentanyl（INN）(and its salts)
2933 3300.12	哌替啶、地芬诺酯（以及它们的盐）	6.5	20		9	17	千克	W	Pethidine（INN），diphenoxylate（INN）(and its salts)
2933 3300.13	哌腈(氰)米特,丙吡兰(哌丙吡胺)(以及它们的盐)	6.5	20		9	17	千克	W	Piridolan（INN），propiram（INN）(and its salts)
2933 3300.21	哌醋甲酯、喷他左辛、溴西泮(以及它们的盐）	6.5	20		9	17	千克	I	Methylphenidate（INN），pentazocine（INN），bromazepam（INN）(and its salts)
2933 3300.22	苯环利定、哌苯甲醇（以及它们的盐）	6.5	20		9	17	千克	I	Phencyclidine（INN）（PCP），pipradrol（INN）(and its salts)
2933 3300.31	地匹哌酮、凯托米酮、地芬诺新（以及它们的盐）	6.5	20		9	17	千克	W	Dipipanone（INN），ketobemidone（INN），difenoxin（INN）(and its salts)
2933 3300.32	哌替啶中间体A、苯哌利定、三甲利定（以及它们的盐）	6.5	20		9	17	千克	W	Pethidine Intermediate A（INN），phenoperidine（INN），trimeperidine（INN）(and its salts)
2933 3300.33	阿尼利定、苯氰米特（以及它们的盐）	6.5	20		9	17	千克	W	Anileridine（INN），bezitramide（INN）(and its salts)
	--其他：								--Other:
2933.3910	---二苯乙醇酸-3-奎宁环酯	6.5	20		9	17	千克	23	---Benzilic acid-3-quinuclidinate
2933.3920	---奎宁环-3-醇	6.5	20		9	17	千克	23	---Quinuclidine-3-ol
2933.3990	---其他	6.5	20		9		千克		---Other
2933 3990.10	甲基吡啶、氰基吡啶、吡啶硫酮锌（包括三甲基吡啶）	6.5	20		9	17	千克		Methylpyridine,cyanopyridine, Pyrithione (including Trimethyl pyridine)
2933 3990.21	精吡氟禾草灵,毒死蜱,二氯氨基吡啶羧酸(包括二氟吡隆,三氟甲吡醚,氯虫苯甲酰胺)	6.5	20		9	17	千克	S	Fluazifop-p-butyl, chlorpyrifos, Dichloro-pyridine carboxylic acid (Diflufenzopyr, trifluoromethane-topiramate-ether, Chlorantraniliprole)
2933 3990.22	百草枯、啶虫脒	6.5	20		9	17	千克	S	Paraquat, acetamiprid
2933 3990.23	精喹禾灵	6.5	20		9	17	千克	S	Quizalofop-p-ethyl
2933 3990.24	喹禾灵、氟吡禾灵、吡氟禾草灵等（包括炔禾灵、氟吡乙禾灵、氟吡胺、卤草啶）	6.5	20		9	17	千克	S	Quizalofop,haloxyfop,fluazifop etc.（including chloroazifop-propyny,haloxyfop-methyl,picolinafe, haloxydine）
2933 3990.25	高效氟吡甲禾灵、氟吡甲禾灵等（包括鼠特灵、灭鼠优、灭鼠安、氟鼠啶）	6.5	20		9	17	千克	S	Haloxyfop-P-methyl, haloxyfop-methyl etc.（including norbormide,pyrinuron, Rodent An, flupropadine）
2933 3990.26	甲基毒死蜱、吡虫啉等（包括吡氯氰菊酯、啶蜱脲、氟啶脲、哒幼酮、吡丙醚）	6.5	20		9	17	千克	S	Chlorpyrifos-methyl,imidacloprid etc.（including fenpirithrin,fluazuron,chlorfluazuron, pyridaben, pyriproxyfen）
2933 3990.27	驱蝇啶、烯啶虫胺	6.5	20		9	17	千克	S	Dipropyl pyridine,nitenpyram
2933 3990.28	咪唑烟酸、甲咪唑烟酸、咪唑乙烟酸等（包括氨氯吡啶酸、三氯吡氧乙酸、氯氟吡氧乙酸、二氯吡啶酸）	6.5	20		9	17	千克	S	Imazapyr,imazapic,imazethapyr etc.（including picloram, trichlopyr,fluroxypyr, clopyralid）

税则号列 Tariff Item	商品名称及备注	进口税率 最惠	进口税率 普通	进口税率 暂定	出口退税	增值税率	计量单位	监管条件	Article Description
2933 3990.29	炔草酸、哌草磷、哌草丹、稗草丹等（包括吡氟酰草胺、氟啶草酮、氟硫草啶、甲氧咪草烟）	6.5	20		9	17	千克	S	Clodinafop-propargyl,piperophos,dimepiperate, pyributicarb etc.（including diflufenican, fluridone, dithiopyr,Imazamox）
2933 3990.30	3-羟基-1-甲基哌啶	6.5	20		9	17	千克	23	3-hydroxy-1-methyl piperidine
2933 3990.40	3-奎宁环酮	6.5	20		9	17	千克	23	3-Quinuclidone
2933 3990.51	甲哌翁、抗倒胺、氯吡脲、吡啶醇	6.5	20		9	17	千克	S	Mepiquatechloride,inabenfide,forchlorfenuron, Pyridinol alcohol
2933 3990.52	啶菌噁唑、苯锈啶、啶斑肟等(包括啶菌腈)	6.5	20		9	17	千克	S	SYP-Z048, Fenpropidin,pyrifenox etc.（including pyridinitril）
2933 3990.53	氟啶胺、氟啶虫酰胺、三氯甲基吡啶	6.5	20		9	17	千克	S	Fluazinam,flonicamid,Nitrapyrin
2933 3990.54	咪唑嗪、丁硫啶、氯苯吡啶、哌丙灵	6.5	20		9	17	千克	S	Triazoxide,buthiobate,parinol,piperlin etc.
2933 3990.55	氟吡菌酰胺	6.5	20		9	17	千克	S	Fluopyram
2933 3990.56	氯啶菌酯	6.5	20		9	17	千克	S	Carbamate
2933 3990.57	氯氨吡啶酸	6.5	20		9	17	千克	S	Aminopyralid
2933 3990.60	啶氧菌酯(包括氟啶虫胺腈、环啶菌胺、四氯虫酰胺、溴氰虫酰胺、玉雄杀、氟吡菌胺)	6.5	20		9	17	千克	S	Picoxystrobin(including sulfoxaflor, Pyridine fungus amines, tetrachloride amides, bromine cyantraniliprole fluopicolide)
2933 3990.71	乙酰阿法甲基芬太尼、烯丙罗定、阿法美罗定(以及它们的盐)	6.5	20		9	17	千克	W	Acetyl-alpha-methylfentanyl,allylprodine,alphameprodine (and their salts)
2933 3990.72	阿法甲基芬太尼、阿法罗定、苄替啶（以及它们的盐）	6.5	20		9	17	千克	W	Alpha-methylfentanyl,alphaprodine,benzethidine (and their salts)
2933 3990.73	倍他羟基芬太尼、倍他羟基-3-甲基芬太尼、倍他美罗定（以及它们的盐）	6.5	20		9	17	千克	W	Beta-hydroxyfentanyl,beta-hydroxy-3-methylf-entanyl, betameprodine (and their salts)
2933 3990.74	倍他罗定、依托利定、羟哌替啶、美他佐辛（以及它们的盐）	6.5	20		9	17	千克	W	Betaprodine,etoxeridine,hydroxypethidine,metazocine (and their salts)
2933 3990.75	3-甲基芬太尼、1-甲基-4-苯基-4-哌啶丙酸酯、诺匹哌酮（以及它们的盐）	6.5	20		9	17	千克	W	3-methylfentanyl,1-Methyl-4-phenyl-4-piperidinol propionate (ester),norpipanone (and their salts)
2933 3990.76	对氟芬太尼、1-苯乙基-4-苯基-4-哌啶乙酸酯(以及它们的盐)	6.5	20		9	17	千克	W	Para-fluorofentanyl,1-Phenethyl-4-phenyl-4-piperidinol acetate (ester) (and their salts)
2933 3990.77	哌替啶中间体B、哌替啶中间体C（以及它们的盐）	6.5	20		9	17	千克	W	Pethidine intermediate B, pethidine intermediate C (and their salts)
2933 3990.78	非那丙胺、非那佐辛、匹米诺定、丙哌利定（以及它们的盐）	6.5	20		9	17	千克	W	Phenampromide,phenazocine,piminodine,porperidine (and their salts)
2933 3990.80	瑞芬太尼及其盐	6.5	20		9	17	千克	W	Remifentanil and its salts
2933 3990.90	其他结构上有非稠合吡啶环化合物	6.5	20		9	17	千克		Other compounds containing an unfused pyrazole ring in the structure
	-结构上含有一个喹啉或异喹啉环系（不论是否氢化）的化合物，但未经进一步稠合的:								-Compounds containing a quinoline or isoquinoline ring-system（whether or not hydrogenated）, not further fused:
2933.4100	--左非诺(INN)及其盐	6.5	20		9	17	千克	W	--Levorphanol（INN）and its salts
	--其他:								--Other:
2933.4910	---环丙氟哌酸	6.5	20		9	17	千克		---Ciprofloxacin
2933.4990	---其他	6.5	20		9	17	千克		---Other
2933 4990.11	丙烯酸喹啉酯、苯氧喹啉	6.5	20		9	17	千克	S	Halacrinate, quinoxyfen
2933 4990.12	咯喹酮	6.5	20		9	17	千克	S	Pyroquilon
2933 4990.13	氯甲喹啉酸、喹草酸、乙氧喹啉	6.5	20		9	17	千克	S	Quinmerac, quinclorac, ethoxyquin
2933 4990.14	二氯喹啉酸	6.5	20		9	17	千克	S	Quinclorac
2933 4990.21	羟蒂巴酚、左美沙芬、左芬啡烷	6.5	20		9	17	千克	W	Drotebanol,levomethorphan,levophenacylmorphan
2933 4990.22	去甲左啡诺、非诺啡烷、消旋甲啡烷、消旋啡烷	6.5	20		9	17	千克	W	Norlevorphanol,phenomorphan,racemethorphan,racemorphan

税则号列 Tariff Item	商品名称及备注	进口税率			出口退税	增值税率	计量单位	监管条件	Article Description
		最惠	普通	暂定					
2933 4990.30	布托啡诺	6.5	20		9	17	千克	I	Butorphanol
2933 4990.90	其他含喹琳或异喹啉环系的化合物（但未进一步稠合的）	6.5	20		9	17	千克		Other compounds containing quinoline or isoquinoline ring-system, no further fused
	-结构上含有一个嘧啶环（不论是否氢化）或哌嗪环的化合物:								-Compounds containing a pyrimidine ring（whether or not hydrogenated）or piperazine ring in the structure:
2933.5200	--丙二酰脲(巴比妥酸)及其盐	6.5	20		9	17	千克		--Malonylurea（barbituric acid）and its salts
2933.5300	--阿洛巴比妥（INN）、异戊巴比妥（INN）、巴比妥（INN）、布他比妥(INN)、正丁巴比妥(INN)、环己巴比妥（INN）、甲苯巴比妥（INN）、戊巴比妥（INN）、苯巴比妥(INN)、仲丁巴比妥(INN)、司可巴比妥（INN）、和乙烯比妥（INN）以及它们的盐	6.5	20		9	17	千克		--Allobarbital（INN）, amobarbital （INN）, barbital（INN）, butalbital（INN）, butobarbital, cyclobarbital（INN）, methylphenobarbital（INN）, pentobarbital（INN）, phenobarbital（INN）, secbutabarbital（INN）, secobarbital（INN）and vinylbital（INN）; salts thereof
2933 5300.11	阿洛巴比妥、仲丁巴比妥（以及它们的盐）	6.5	20		9	17	千克	I	Allobarbital（INN）,secbutabarbital（INN）(and their salts)
2933 5300.12	乙烯比妥,布他比妥,丁巴比妥(以及它们的盐)	6.5	20		9	17	千克	I	Vinylbital（INN）,butalbital（INN）,butobarbital（INN）(and their salts)
2933 5300.13	环己巴比妥、甲苯巴比妥（以及它们的盐）	6.5	20		9	17	千克	I	Cyclobarbital（INN）,methylphenobarbital（INN）(and their salts)
2933 5300.14	司可巴比妥、异戊巴比妥（以及它们的盐）	6.5	20		9	17	千克	I	Secobarbital(INN),amobarbital(INN)(and their salts)
2933 5300.15	戊巴比妥、苯巴比妥、巴比妥(以及它们的盐）	6.5	20		9	17	千克	I	Pentobarbital（INN）,phenobarbital（INN）,Barbital（INN）(and their salts)
2933.5400	--其他丙二酰脲（巴比妥酸）的衍生物以及它们的盐	6.5	20		9	17	千克		--Other derivatives of malonylurea（barbituric acid）; salts thereof
2933.5500	--氯普唑仑（INN）、甲氯喹酮（INN）、甲喹酮（INN)和齐培丙醇（INN）以及它们的盐	6.5	20		9	17	千克		--Loprazolam（INN）, mecloqualone （INN）, methaqualone(INN)and zipeprol(INN); salts thereof
2933 5500.11	甲氯喹酮、甲喹酮（以及它们的盐）	6.5	20		9	17	千克	I	Mecloqualone(INN),methaqualone(INN) (and their salts)
2933 5500.12	氯普唑仑、齐培丙醇（以及它们的盐）	6.5	20		9	17	千克	I	Loprazolam（INN）, zipeprol（INN）(and their salts)
	--其他:								--Other:
2933.5910	---胞嘧啶	6.5	20		9	17	千克		---Cytosine
2933.5990	---其他	6.5	20		9	17	千克		---Other
2933 5990.11	嘧啶磷、甲基嘧啶磷、二嗪磷、双苯嘧草酮等（包括嘧啶氧磷,乙嘧硫磷）	6.5	20		9	17	千克	S	Pyrimithate,pirimiphos-methyl,diazinon,benzfendizone etc.（including midinyanglin,etrimfos）
2933 5990.12	烯腺嘌呤、苄腺嘌呤、丁基嘧啶磷、嘧啶肟草醚等（包括苄氨基嘌呤、羟烯腺嘌呤）	6.5	20		9	17	千克	S	Enadenine, benzylaminopurine, tebupirimfos, pyribenzonxim etc.,including benzyladenine, oxyenadenine）
2933 5990.13	嘧草醚、双草醚、除草啶、环草啶等(包括异草啶、异丙酯草醚、嘧草硫醚、特草啶）	6.5	20		9	17	千克	S	Pyriminobac-methyl,bispyribac-sodium, bromacil, lenacil etc.（including isocil,flupropacil-pyraflufenethyl, pyrithiobac-sodium,terbacil）
2933 5990.14	吡菌磷、嘧霉胺、嘧菌胺、嘧菌酯等（包括嘧菌环胺、嘧菌腙）	6.5	20		9	17	千克	S	Pyrazophos,pyrimethanil,mepanipyrim, Azoxystrobin etc.（including pyrimethanil ferimzone）
2933 5990.15	嘧啶威、抗蚜威、环虫腈、嘧螨醚等（包括嘧螨酯）	6.5	20		9	17	千克	S	Pyramat,Pirimicarb,dicyclanil,pyrimidifen etc.（including fluacrypyrim）
2933 5990.16	氯苯嘧啶醇、环丙嘧啶醇、呋嘧醇等（包括氟苯嘧啶醇）	6.5	20		9	17	千克	S	Fenarimol,ancymidol,flurprimidol etc.（including nuarimol）
2933 5990.17	氟蚁腙、鼠立死	6.5	20		9	17	千克	S	Hydramethylnon, crimidine
2933 5990.18	二甲嘧酚、乙嘧酚、乙嘧酚磺酸酯	6.5	20		9	17	千克	S	Dimethirimol, ethirimol, bupirimate

税则号列 Tariff Item	商品名称及备注	进口税率			出口退税	增值税率	计量单位	监管条件	Article Description
		最惠	普通	暂定					
2933 5990.19	嗪氨灵、咪唑喹啉酸、丙酯草醚	6.5	20		9	17	千克	S	Triforine, imazaquin, pyribambenz propyl
2933 5990.20	氟丙嘧草酯、氯丙嘧啶酸	6.5	20		9	17	千克	S	Butafenacil, chloropropionic orotic acid
2933 5990.30	溴嘧草醚	6.5	20		9	17	千克	S	Ethyl bromide
2933 5990.40	唑嘧菌胺	6.5	20		9	17	千克	S	Ametoctradin
2933 5990.51	依他喹酮	6.5	20		9	17	千克	I	Etaqualone;CAS：7432-25-9
2933 5990.52	苄基哌嗪	6.5	20		9	17	千克	I	Benzylpiperazine;CAS：2759-28-6
2933 5990.90	其他结构上有嘧啶环等的化合物（包括其他结构上有哌嗪环的化合物）	6.5	20		9	17	千克		Other compounds containing pyrimidine ring and piperazine rings in the strcture
	-结构上含有一个非稠合三嗪环（不论是否氢化）的化合物:								-Compounds containing an unfused triazine ring（whether or not hydrogenated）in the structure:
2933.6100	--三聚氰胺(蜜胺)	6.5	20		9	17	千克	A	--Melamine
	--其他:								--Other:
2933.6910	---三聚氰氯	6	20		9	17	千克		---Cyanuric chloride
	---异氰脲酸氯化衍生物:								---Chloroisocyanurate:
2933.6921	----二氯异氰脲酸	6.5	20		9	17	千克	AB	----Dichloroisooyanurate acid
2933.6922	----三氯异氰脲酸	6.5	20		9	17	千克	AB	----Trichloroisocyanurate acid
2933.6929	----其他	6.5	20		9	17	千克		----Other
2933 6929.10	二氯异氰尿酸钠	6.5	20		9	17	千克	AB	Sodium dichloroisocyanurate
2933 6929.90	其他异氰脲酸氯化衍生物	6.5	20		9	17	千克		Other chloroisocyanuric acid derivatives
2933.6990	---其他	6.5	20		9	17	千克		---Other
2933 6990.11	西玛津、莠去津、扑灭津、草达津等（包括特丁津、氰草津、环丙津、甘扑津、甘草津）	6.5	20		9	17	千克	S	Simazine, atrazine, propazine, trietazine etc.（including terbuthylazine, cyanazine, cyprazine, proglinazine, eglinazine-ethyl）
2933 6990.12	西草净、扑草净、敌草净、莠灭净等（包括特丁净、异丙净、异戊乙净、氰草净、氟草净、甲氧丙净）	6.5	20		9	17	千克	S	Simetryn,prometryn,desmetryn,ametryn etc.(including terbutryn,dipropetryn,dimethametryn, cyanatryn, 2-difluoromethylthio-4,6-bis (iso-propylamino)-1,3,5-triazine,methprotryne)
2933 6990.13	扑灭通、仲丁通	6.5	20		9	17	千克	S	Prometon,secbumeton
2933 6990.14	丁嗪草酮、环嗪酮、嗪草酮等(包括苯嗪草酮、乙嗪草酮)	6.5	20		9	17	千克	S	Isomethiozin,hexazinone,metribuzin etc.（including metamitron, ethiozin）
2933 6990.15	灭蚜硫磷、灭蝇胺、吡蚜酮等(包括敌菌灵)	6.5	20		9	17	千克	S	Menazon,cyromazine,pymetrozine etc.（including anilazine）
2933 6990.16	三嗪氟草胺	6.5	20		9	17	千克	S	Triaziflam
2933 6990.90	其他结构上含非稠合三嗪环化合物	6.5	20		9	17	千克		Other compounds containing an unfused triazine ring in the structure
	-内酰胺:								-Lactams:
2933.7100	--6-己内酰胺	9	35		9	17	千克	A	--6-Hexanolactam（epsilon-caprolactam）
2933.7200	--氯巴占(INN)和甲乙哌酮(INN)	9	15		9	17	千克	I	--Clobazam（INN）and methyprylon（INN）
2933.7900	--其他内酰胺	9	20		9	17	千克		--Other lactams
2933 7900.10	氯巴占和甲乙哌酮的盐	9	20		9	17	千克	I	Salts of clobazam（INN）and methyprylon（INN）
2933 7900.20	灭菌磷，螺虫乙酯	9	20		9	17	千克	S	Ditalimfos, spirotetramat
2933 7900.30	佐匹克隆	9	20		9	17	千克	I	Zopiclone；CAS：43200-80-2
2933 7900.90	其他内酰胺	9	20		9	17	千克		Other lactams
	-其他:								-Other:
2933.9100	--阿普唑仑（INN）、卡马西泮（INN）、氯氮卓（INN）、氯硝西泮（INN）、氯拉卓酸（INN）、地洛西泮(INN)、地西泮(INN)、艾司唑仑（INN）、氯氟卓乙酯（INN）、氟地西泮（INN）、氟硝西泮（INN）、氟西泮（INN）、哈拉西泮(INN)、劳拉西泮(INN)、氯甲西泮(INN)、马吲哚(INN)、	6.5	20		9	17	千克		--Alprazolam（INN）, camazepam（INN）, chlordiazepoxide（INN）, clonazepam（INN）, clorazepate, delorazepam （INN）, diazepam（INN）, estazolam（INN）, ethyl loflazepate（INN）, fludiazepam （INN）, flunitrazepam （INN）, flurazepam （INN）,halazepam （INN）, lorazepam（INN）,lormetazepam（INN）, mazindol （INN）, medazepam（INN）, midazolam（INN）, nimetazepam（INN）, nitrazepam （INN）, nordazepam（INN）,

税则号列 Tariff Item	商品名称及备注	进口税率			出口退税	增值税率	计量单位	监管条件	Article Description
		最惠	普通	暂定					
	美达西泮(INN)、咪达唑仑(INN)、硝甲西泮(INN)、去甲西泮(INN)、奥沙西泮(INN)、匹那西泮(INN)、普拉西泮(INN)、吡咯戊酮(INN)、替马西泮(INN)、四氢西泮(INN)和三唑仑(INN)以及它们的盐								oxazepam (INN), pinazepam (INN), prazepam (INN),pyrovalerone (INN); temazepam (INN), tetrazepam (INN) and triazolam (INN); salts thereof
2933 9100.11	阿普唑仑、卡马西泮、氯氮卓(以及它们的盐)	6.5	20		9	17	千克	I	Alprazolam (INN),camazepam (INN),chlordiazepoxide (INN) (and their salts)
2933 9100.12	氯硝西泮、氯拉卓酸、地洛西泮(以及它们的盐)	6.5	20		9	17	千克	I	Clonazepam (INN),clorazepate (INN), delorazepam (INN) (and their salts)
2933 9100.13	地西泮、艾司唑仑、氯氟卓乙酯(以及它们的盐)	6.5	20		9	17	千克	I	Diazepam (INN), estazolam, ethyl Loflazepate (INN) (and their salts)
2933 9100.14	氟地西泮、氟硝西泮、氟西泮(以及它们的盐)	6.5	20		9	17	千克	I	Fludiazepam (INN), Clonazepam (INN), flurazepam (INN) (and their salts)
2933 9100.15	哈拉西泮、劳拉西泮、氯甲西泮(以及它们的盐)	6.5	20		9	17	千克	I	Halazepam (INN), lorazepam (INN), lormetazepam (INN) (and their salts)
2933 9100.16	马吲哚、咪达唑仑、硝西泮(以及它们的盐)	6.5	20		9	17	千克	I	Mazindol (INN), midazolam (INN),nitrazepam (INN) (and their salts)
2933 9100.17	奥沙西泮、匹那西泮、普拉西泮(以及它们的盐)	6.5	20		9	17	千克	I	Oxazepam (INN), pinazepam (INN) prazepam (INN) (and their salts)
2933 9100.18	去甲西泮,三唑仑(以及它们的盐)	6.5	20		9	17	千克	I	Nordazepam (INN), triazolam (INN) (and their salts)
2933 9100.21	硝甲西泮,美达西泮(以及它们的盐)	6.5	20		9	17	千克	I	Nimetazepam (INN),medazepam (INN) (and their salts)
2933 9100.22	吡咯戊酮,替马西泮,四氢西泮(以及它们的盐)	6.5	20		9	17	千克	I	Pyrovalerone (INN), temazepam (INN), tetrazepam (INN) (and their salts)
2933.9900	--其他	6.5	20		9	17	千克		--Other
2933 9900.11	抑芽丹、三唑磷、虫线磷、喹硫磷、唑啶草酮等(包括哒嗪硫磷、亚胺硫磷、氯亚胺硫磷、保棉磷、益棉磷、威菌磷)	6.5	20		9	17	千克	S	Maleic hydrazide,Triazophos,Thionazin,Quinalphos, Azafenidin (including pyridaphenthion, phosmet, dialifos, azinphos-methyl,azinphos-ethyl, triamiphos)
2933 9900.12	氯唑磷、炔咪菊酯,吲哚酮草酯等(包括呋喃虫酰肼、唑蚜威、不育胺、虫螨腈、抗螨唑、四螨嗪)	6.5	20		9	17	千克	S	Isazofos,Imiprothrin, Cinidon ester (including Furan tebufenozide, triazamate, infertility amines, Chlorfenapyr, azole anti-mite, clofentezine)
2933 9900.13	多菌灵、苯菌灵、氰菌灵、麦穗宁、氟哒嗪草酯等(包括咪菌威、丙硫多菌灵、氟氯菌核利、哒菌酮、拌种咯、杀草强)	6.5	20		9	17	千克	S	Carbendazim,benomyl,cypendazole, fuberidazole, flufenpyr-ethyl (including debacarb,albendazole, fluoromide, diclomezine, fenpiclonil,amitrole)
2933 9900.14	三唑酮、哒草敏、三唑醇、唑草酮等(包括四氯喹恶啉、己唑醇、腈苯唑、亚胺唑、四氟醚唑、氟环唑)	6.5	20		9	17	千克	S	Triadimefon,credazine (JMAF),triadimenol, carfentrazone-ethyl etc. (including chlorquinox, hexaconazole,fenbuconazole,Imibenconazole,tertraconazole,epoxiconazole)
2933 9900.15	苄氯三唑醇、戊菌唑、粉唑醇等(包括联苯三唑醇、腈菌唑、环丙唑醇、烯唑醇、戊唑醇、氟硅唑)	6.5	20		9	17	千克	S	Diclobutrazol,penconazole,flutriafol etc. (including bitertanol, myclobutanil, cyproconazole, diniconazole, tebuconazole, flusilazole)
2933 9900.16	环菌唑、叶菌唑、灭菌唑、种菌唑等(包括申嗪霉素、氟喹唑、哒螨灵、喹螨醚、氟草敏、氟咯草酮)	6.5	20		9	17	千克	S	Cyproconazole,metconazole,triticonazole,ipco-nazole etc. (including Doxorubicin hydrochloride fluquinconazole, pyridaben, fenazaquin,no-rflurazon, fluorochloridone)
2933 9900.17	唑草酯、四环唑、恶草酸等(包括喹禾糠酯、哒草特、咯草隆、禾草敌、唑草胺、敌草快、氯草敏)	6.5	20		9	17	千克	S	Carfentrazone-ethyl,tetcyclacis,propaquizafop ect. (including quizalofop-P-tefuryl, pyridate, cisanilide, molinate,cafenstrole,diquat,chloridazon)

税则号列 Tariff Item	商品名称及备注	进口税率			出口退税	增值税率	计量单位	监管条件	Article Description
		最惠	普通	暂定					
2933 9900.18	氟胺草唑、酰胺磺隆、三氟苯唑等（包括吲哚丁酸、溴莠敏、哌壮素、吲熟酯、三唑磺、四唑酰草胺）	6.5	20		9	17	千克	S	Flupoxam,foramsulfuron,fluotrimazole etc.（including Indolebutyric acid(IBA),brompyrazon, piprootanly, ethychlozat（JMAF）,fentrazamide）
2933 9900.19	多效唑、烯效唑、抑芽唑等（包括异麦赛津、叶枯净、叶锈特、吡喃草酮、吲哚乙酸）	6.5	20		9	17	千克	S	Paclobutrazol,uniconazole,triapenthenol（including phenazine oxide, butfizol, tepraloxydim, indoleacetic acid）
2933 9900.21	氯尼他秦	6.5	20		9	17	千克	W	Clonitazene
2933 9900.22	依托尼秦	6.5	20		9	17	千克	W	Etonitazene
2933 9900.23	普罗庚嗪、布桂嗪	6.5	20		9	17	千克	W	Proheptazine,bucinnazine
2933 9900.30	扎莱普隆、唑吡坦（以及它们的盐）	6.5	20		9	17	千克	I	Zaleplon,zolpidem (and their salts)
2933 9900.40	齐帕特罗	6.5	20		9	17	千克	L	Zilpaterol
2933 9900.51	二甲基色胺、二乙基色胺	6.5	20		9	17	千克	I	Dimethyltryptamine,diethyltryptamine
2933 9900.52	乙色胺、咯环利定	6.5	20		9	17	千克	I	Etryptamine,rolicyclidine
2933 9900.53	[1-(5-氟戊基)-1H-吲哚-3-基](2-碘苯基)甲酮	6.5	20		9	17	千克	I	1-[(5-Fluoropentyl)-1H-indol-3-yl]-(2-iodophenyl)methanone；CAS：335161-03-0
2933 9900.54	1-(5-氟戊基)-3-(1-萘甲酰基)-1H-吲哚	6.5	20		9	17	千克	I	1-(5-Fluoropentyl)-3-(1-naphthoyl)indole；CAS：335161-24-5
2933 9900.55	1-戊基-3-(1-萘甲酰基)吲哚	6.5	20		9	17	千克	I	1-Pentyl-3-(1-naphthoyl)indole；CAS：209414-07-3
2933 9900.56	1-丁基-3-(1-萘甲酰基)吲哚	6.5	20		9	17	千克	I	1-Butyl-3-(1-naphthoyl)indole；CAS：208987-48-8
2933 9900.57	2-(2-甲氧基苯基)-1-(1-戊基-1H-吲哚-3-基)乙酮	6.5	20		9	17	千克	I	2-(2-Methoxyphenyl)-1-(1-pentyl-1H-indol-3-yl)ethanone；CAS：864445-43-2
2933 9900.60	(环)四亚甲基四硝胺（俗名奥托金 HMX）	6.5	20		9	17	千克	3	Cyclotetramethylene tetranitramine (HMX)
2933 9900.70	(环)三亚甲基三硝基胺（俗名黑索金 RDX）	6.5	20		9	17	千克	3	Hexahydro-1,3,5-trinitro-1,3,5-triazine (RDX)
2933 9900.80	丁羟咯酮(包括杀雄啉、杀雄嗪酸、双唑草腈、唑酮草酯)	6.5	20		9	17	千克	S	Tepraloxydim (including sintofen, clofencet, pyraclonil and carfentrazone-ethyl)
2933 9900.90	其他仅含氮杂原子的杂环化合物	6.5	20		9	17	千克		Other heterocyclic compounds with nitrogen hetero-atom（s）only
29.34	**核酸及其盐，无论是否已有化学定义；其他杂环化合物：**								**Nucleic acids and their salts; whether or not chemically defined; Other heteroeyclic compounds:**
2934.1000	-结构上含有一个非稠合噻唑环（不论是否氢化）的化合物	6.5	20		9	17	千克		-Compounds containing an unfused thiazole ring（whether or not hydrogenated）in the structure
2934 1000.11	噻螨酮	6.5	20		9	17	千克	S	Hexythiazox
2934 1000.12	噻唑膦、噻唑硫磷	6.5	20		9	17	千克	S	Fosthiazate,colophonate
2934 1000.13	噻唑烟酸、噻唑菌胺	6.5	20		9	17	千克	S	Thiazopyr,ethaboxam
2934 1000.14	氯噻啉、氟螨噻	6.5	20		9	17	千克	S	Imidaclothiz,flubenzimine
2934 1000.15	噻菌灵、噻菌胺、噻丙腈	6.5	20		9	17	千克	S	Thiabendazole,metsulfovax,thiapronil
2934 1000.16	噻呋酰胺、噻虫胺、噻虫嗪、噻虫啉	6.5	20		9	17	千克	S	Thifluzamide, clothianidin, thiamethoxam, thiacloprid
2934 1000.17	辛噻酮、拌种灵	6.5	20		9	17	千克	S	Octhilinone, seedavay
2934 1000.18	稻瘟灵	6.5	20		9	17	千克	S	Isoprothiolane
2934 1000.90	结构上含有非稠合噻唑环的化合物(非稠合噻唑环不论是否氢化)	6.5	20		9	17	千克		Compounds containing an unfused thiazole ring (whether or not hydrogenated)in the structure
2934.2000	-结构上含有一个苯并噻唑环系（不论是否氢化）的化合物，但未经进一步稠合的	6.5	20			17	千克		-Compounds containing in the structure a benzo-thiazole ringsystem（whether or not hydrogenated）, not further fused
2934 2000.11	噻螨威、噻霉酮	6.5	20		9	17	千克	S	Tazimcarb, Benziothiazolinone
2934 2000.12	苯噻硫氰	6.5	20		9	17	千克	S	Benzoth thiocyanate
2934 2000.13	烯丙苯噻唑	6.5	20		9	17	千克	S	Probenazole

税则号列 Tariff Item	商品名称及备注	进口税率 最惠	进口税率 普通	进口税率 暂定	出口退税	增值税率	计量单位	监管条件	Article Description
2934 2000.14	草除灵	6.5	20		9	17	千克	S	Benazolin-ethyl
2934 2000.15	噻唑禾草灵	6.5	20		9	17	千克	S	Fenthiaprop-ethyl
2934 2000.16	苯噻隆	6.5	20		9	17	千克	S	Benzthiazuron
2934 2000.17	甲基苯噻隆	6.5	20		9	17	千克	S	Methabenzthiazuron
2934 2000.18	苯噻酰草胺	6.5	20		9	17	千克	S	Mefenacet
2934 2000.19	苯噻菌酯	6.5	20		13	17	千克	S	Benzothiostrobin
2934 2000.90	其他含一个苯并噻唑环系的化合物	6.5	20		13	17	千克		Other Compounds containing in the structure a benzothiazole ring-system
2934.3000	-结构上含有一个吩噻嗪环系（不论是否氢化）的化合物，但未经进一步稠合的	6.5	20		9	17	千克		-Compounds containing in the structure a phenothiazine ringsystem（whether or not hydrogenated）, not further fused
	-其他:								-Other:
2934.9100	--阿米雷司（INN）、溴替唑仑（INN）、氯噻西泮（INN）、氯恶唑仑（INN）、右吗拉胺（INN）、卤恶唑仑（INN）、凯他唑仑（INN）、美索卡（INN）、恶唑仑（INN）、匹莫林（INN）、苯巴曲嗪（INN）、芬美曲嗪（INN）和舒芬太尼（INN）及它们的盐	6.5	20		9	17	千克		--Aminorex（INN）, brotizolam（INN）, clotiazepam（INN）, cloxazolam（INN）, dextromoramide（INN）, haloxazolam（INN）, ketazolam（INN）, mesocarb（INN）, oxazolam（INN）, pemoline（INN）, phendimet razine（INN）,phenmetrazine（INN）and sufentanil（INN）; salts thereof
2934 9100.11	阿米雷司、溴替唑仑、氯噻西泮（以及它们的盐）	6.5	20		9	17	千克	I	Aminorex（INN）, brotizolam（INN）,clotiazepam（INN）(and their salts)
2934 9100.12	氯恶唑仑、卤沙（恶）唑仑（以及它们的盐）	6.5	20		9	17	千克	I	Cloxazolam（INN）, haloxazolam（INN）(and their salts)
2934 9100.13	凯他唑仑,美索卡,奥沙(恶)唑仑(以及它们的盐)	6.5	20		9	17	千克	I	Ketazolam（INN）, mesocarb（INN）,oxazolam（INN）(and their salts)
2934 9100.14	匹莫林、苯甲曲嗪、芬美曲嗪(以及它们的盐)	6.5	20		9	17	千克	I	Pemoline（INN）, phendimetrazine（INN）, phenmetrazine（INN）（and their salts）
2934 9100.20	右吗拉胺、舒芬太尼（以及它们的盐）	6.5	20		9	17	千克	W	Dextromoramide（INN）, sufentanil（INN）（and their salts）
	--其他:								--Other:
2934.9910	---磺内酯及磺内酰胺	6.5	30		9	17	千克		---Sultones and sultams
2934.9920	---呋喃唑酮	6	20		9	17	千克	A	---Furazolidone
2934.9930	---核酸及其盐	6.5	35		9	17	千克		---Nucleic acids and their salts
2934.9940	---奈韦拉平，依发韦仑，利托那韦及它们的盐	6.5	20		13	17	千克		---Nevirapine, efavirenz, ritonavir and their salts
2934.9950	---克拉维酸及其盐	6.5	20		13	17	千克		---Clavulanic acid and its salts
2934.9960	---7-苯乙酰氨基-3-氯甲基-4-头孢烷酸对甲氧基苄酯、7-氨基头孢烷酸、7-氨基脱乙酰氧基头孢烷酸	6	20		9/15	17	千克		---4-methoxybenzyl 3-chlormethyl-7-(2-phenylacetamido) -3-cephem-4-carboxylate,7-aminocepthalosporianic acid, 7-aminodeacetoxycephalosporanic acid
2934.9990	---其他	6.5	20		9	17	千克		---Other
2934 9990.01	核苷酸类食品添加剂	6.5	20		9	17	千克	AB	Nucleotides food additives
2934 9990.10	恶草酮、氟噻草胺、活化酯、高效二甲吩草胺(包括吡噻菌胺)	6.5	20		9	17	千克	S	Oxadiazon, flufenacet, Activated ester, dimethenamid including Penthiopyrad
2934 9990.21	恶唑磷、蔬果磷、茂硫磷、除害磷等（包括甲基吡恶磷、丁硫环磷、硫环磷、杀扑磷、伏杀硫磷、地胺磷）	6.5	20		9	17	千克	S	Isoxathion,salithion, morphothion, lythidathion etc.（including azamethiphos, fosthietan, phosfolan, methidathion, phosalone, mephosfolan）
2934 9990.22	环线威、杀虫环、杀虫钉、多噻烷等（包括甲基硫环磷、噻嗯菊酯、噻嗪酮、恶虫酮、茚虫威）	6.5	20		9	17	千克	S	Tirpate,thiocyclam,trithialan,polythiacycloalkane etc.（including phosfolan-methyl, kadethrine, buprofezin, metoxadiazone,indoxacarb）
2934 9990.23	恶唑禾草灵、毒鼠硅、噻鼠灵等	6.5	20		9	17	千克	S	Fenoxaprop-ethyl,silatrane,difethialone etc.（including

税则号列 Tariff Item	商品名称及备注	进口税率			出口退税	增值税率	计量单位	监管条件	Article Description
		最惠	普通	暂定					
	（包括福拉比、噻节因、糠菌唑、精恶唑禾草灵）								furametpyr,dimethipin,bromuconazole, fenoxaprop-p-ethyl）
2934 9990.24	代森硫、代森环、福吗啉、咯菌腈等（包括稻瘟酯、烯酰吗啉、噻菌腈、土菌灵、恶霜灵、恶霉灵）	6.5	20		9	17	千克	S	Etem（BSI）,milmeb（BSI）,flumorph,fludioxonil etc.（including pefurazoate, dimethomorph, thicyofen, etridiazole,oxadixyl,hymexazol）
2934 9990.25	噻森铜、丙环唑、乙环唑等（包括恶唑菌酮、金核霉素、呋菌唑、叶枯唑、呋醚唑、苯醚甲环唑）	6.5	20		9	17	千克	S	N、N'-jiacheng-di(5-Amino-1,3,4-thiadiazole-2-thiol) copper, proconazole,etaconazole,etc.（including famoxadone, aureonucleomycin, furconazole, bismerthiazol, furconazole-cis,difenoconazole）
2934 9990.26	嗪草酸、噻氟隆、丁噻隆、异恶隆等（包括噻苯隆、磺噻隆、恶唑隆、异恶草醚、噻吩草胺、二甲吩草胺）	6.5	20		9	17	千克	S	Fluthiacet,thiazfluron,tebuthiuron,isouron etc.（including thidiazuron,ethidimuron, dimefuron, isoxapyrifop,thenychlor, dimethenamid）
2934 9990.27	苯草灭、灭草松、灭草唑等（包括异恶草松、恶嗪草酮、环苯草酮、丙炔氟草胺）	6.5	20		9	17	千克	S	Bentranil,bentazone,methazole etc.（including clomazone,oxaziclomefone, profoxydim, flumioxazin）
2934 9990.28	氟噻乙草酯、丙炔恶草酮、噻草酮等（包括糖氨基嘌呤、苯螨噻、异恶酰草胺、异恶唑草酮）	6.5	20		9	17	千克	S	Fluthiacet-methyl,oxadiargyl,cycloxydim etc.（including suger Aminopurine, triarathene,isoxaben, isoxaflutole）
2934 9990.29	炔丙恶唑草、韩乐宁、噻唑锌等（包括噻菌茂、硅丰环）	6.5	20		9	17	千克	S	Oxadiargyl,ethaboxam,zinc thiazole etc.(including Thiodiazole, silatrane)
2934 9990.31	多抗霉素、灰瘟素	6.5	20		9	17	千克	S	Polyoxin, Gray blasticidin
2934 9990.32	三环唑、氧环唑	6.5	20		9	17	千克	S	Tricyclazole,azaconazole
2934 9990.33	灭螨猛、克杀螨、螨蜱胺	6.5	20		9	17	千克	S	Chinomethionate,thioquinox,tifatol
2934 9990.34	二氰蒽醌、吗菌威	6.5	20		9	17	千克	S	Dithianon,carbamorph
2934 9990.35	十二环吗啉、十三吗啉	6.5	20		9	17	千克	S	Dodemorph,tridemorph
2934 9990.36	杀螺吗啉、丁苯吗啉	6.5	20		9	17	千克	S	Trifenmorph, fenpropimorph
2934 9990.37	喹菌酮、肼菌酮	6.5	20		9	17	千克	S	Oxolinic acid, Hydrazine cycloheximide
2934 9990.38	萎锈灵、氧化萎锈灵	6.5	20		9	17	千克	S	Carboxin,oxycarboxin
2934 9990.39	棉隆、乙烯菌核利	6.5	20		9	17	千克	S	Dazomet,vinclozolin
2934 9990.41	环酯草醚	6.5	20		9	17	千克	S	Pyriftalid
2934 9990.42	噻菌铜	6.5	20		9	17	千克	S	Thiodiazole copper
2934 9990.43	苯唑草酮	6.5	20		9	17	千克	S	Topramezone
2934 9990.44	丁吡吗啉	6.5	20		9	17	千克	S	Pyrimorph
2934 9990.45	环戊噁草酮	6.5	20		9	17	千克	S	Pentoxazone
2934 9990.50	恶唑酰草胺(包括环氧虫啶、噻恩菊酯、双苯恶唑酸 、乙螨唑、异恶氯草酮、唑啉草酯)	6.5	20		9	17	千克	S	Metamifop (including Cycloxaprid, kadethrine, Isoxadifen ethyl ester, Etoxazole, Clomazone and Pinoxaden)
2934 9990.61	甲米雷司及其盐	6.5	20		9	17	千克	I	4-methylaminorex and its salts
2934 9990.62	替诺环定及其盐	6.5	20		9	17	千克	I	Tenocyclidine and its salts
2934 9990.71	硫代芬太尼、阿法甲基硫代芬太尼（以及它们的盐）	6.5	20		9	17	千克	W	Thiofentanyl, Alpha-methylthiofentanyl (and their salts)
2934 9990.72	二乙噻丁、二甲噻丁 、吗苯丁酯、乙甲噻丁（以及它们的盐）	6.5	20		9	17	千克	W	Diethylthiambutene, dimethylthiambutene, dioxaphetylbutyrate,ethylmethylthiambutene (and their salts)
2934 9990.73	呋替啶、左吗拉胺、3-甲基硫代芬太尼（以及它们的盐）	6.5	20		9	17	千克	W	Furethidine,levomoramide,3-methylthiofentanyl (and their salts)
2934 9990.74	吗拉胺中间体、吗哌利定、苯吗庚酮、消旋吗拉胺（以及它们的盐）	6.5	20		9	17	千克	W	Moramide intermediate,morpheridine,phenadoxone, racemoramide (and their salts)
2934 9990.75	亚甲基二氧吡咯戊酮	6.5	20		9	17	千克	I	Methylenedioxypyrovalerone;CAS：687603-66-3
2934 9990.90	其他杂环化合物	6.5	20		9	17	千克		Other heterocyclic compounds
29.35	磺（酰）胺：								**Sulphonamides:**
2935.0010	---磺胺嘧啶	6.5	35		9	17	千克		---Sulphadiazine
2935.0020	---磺胺双甲基嘧啶	6.5	35		9	17	千克	A	---Sulfadimidine

税则号列 Tariff Item	商品名称及备注	进口税率 最惠	进口税率 普通	进口税率 暂定	出口退税	增值税率	计量单位	监管条件	Article Description
2935.0030	----磺胺甲噁唑	6.5	35		9	17	千克		---Sulfamethoxazole
2935.0090	----其他	6.5	35		9	17	千克		---Other
2935 0090.11	氟唑磺隆,氟吡磺隆,磺酰磺隆,氯酯磺草胺等(包括甲酰氨基嘧磺隆,乙氧磺隆,氯磺隆,甲磺隆,苯磺隆,胺苯磺隆)	6.5	35		9	17	千克	S	Flucarbazone,flucetosulfuron, Sulfosulfuron, chlorine esters sulfentrazone,including formamide-sulfometu -ron, ethoxysulfuron,chlorsulfuron, metsulfuron-methyl,tribenuronmethyl, etham- etsulfuron-methyl)
2935 0090.12	醚苯磺隆、噻吩磺隆、醚磺隆、氟啶嘧磺隆等(包括氟胺磺隆、氟磺隆、甲嘧磺隆、氯嘧磺隆、氟嘧磺隆)	6.5	35		9	17	千克	S	Triasulfuron,Thifensulfuron, Cinosulfuron, Fluoride flazasulfuron,including Metsulfuron amine fluoride, Prosulfuron, Methyl-ethyl, Mesotrione, Primisulfuron
2935 0090.13	苄嘧磺隆、吡嘧磺隆、烟嘧磺隆、双氯磺草胺等(包括啶嘧磺隆、砜嘧磺隆、唑嘧磺隆)	6.5	35		9	17	千克	S	Bensulfuron-methyl,pyrazosulfuronethyl, nicosulf-uron,etc.(including flazasulfuron, rimsulfuron, imazosulfuron)
2935 0090.14	四唑嘧磺隆、唑吡嘧磺隆、三氟甲磺隆等(包括氯吡嘧磺隆、酰嘧磺隆、环丙嘧磺隆、甲基二磺隆)	6.5	35		9	17	千克	S	Tetrazole ethyl, zolpidem ethyl, trifluoromethyl metsulfuron(including Topiramate ethyl chloride, ethyl acid, cyproterone ethyl, methyl Tribenuron)
2935 0090.15	氟磺酰草胺、甲磺草胺、嘧苯胺磺隆等(包括唑嘧磺草胺、双氟磺草胺、五氟磺草胺)	6.5	35		9	17	千克	S	Mefluidide, sulfentrazone, Ethyl-aniline-metsulfuron (including flumetsulam, florasulam, Pentafluoropropylene-sulfentrazone)
2935 0090.16	氟磺胺草醚、磺草灵、吲唑磺菌胺等(包括单嘧磺酯、磺草唑胺、三氟啶磺隆钠)	6.5	35		9	17	千克	S	Fomesafen,asulam, Indazole-flusulfamide etc. (including monosulfuron ester, metosulam, Trifloxysulfuron-sodium)
2935 0090.17	磺草膦、氨磺乐灵、三氟啶磺隆、啶磺草胺等(包括甲基碘磺隆钠盐)	6.5	35		9	17	千克	S	Sulcotri-phosphine,oryzalin,Trifloxysulfuron,Pyridine-sulfentrazone (including iodosulfuron methyl sodium)
2935 0090.18	磺菌胺、增糖胺等(包括甲苯氟磺胺、氟虫胺)	6.5	35		9	17	千克	S	Flusulfamide,fluoridamid etc.(including tolylfluanid, sulfluramid)
2935 0090.19	畜蜱磷、伐灭磷、地散磷等(包括磺菌威、氰霜唑)	6.5	35		9	17	千克	S	Cythioate,famphur (ESA) ,bensulide etc.(including methasulfocarb,cyazofamid)
2935 0090.20	环氧嘧磺隆	6.5	35		9	17	千克	S	Oxasulfuron
2935 0090.31	苯嘧磺草胺	6.5	35		9	17	千克	S	Saflufenacil
2935 0090.32	噻酮磺隆	6.5	35		9	17	千克	S	Chlorthalidone Sulfosulfuron
2935 0090.33	N-乙基全氟辛基磺酰胺、N-甲基全氟辛基磺酰胺、N-乙基-N-(2-羟乙基)全氟辛基磺酰胺、N-(2-羟乙基)-N-甲基全氟辛基磺酰胺	6.5	35		9	17	千克	X	Sulfluramid, N—2-Methylindole Perfluorooctanesul-fonamide,2-(1-Pyrrolidinyl)Perfluorooctanesulfonamide ,2-(1-Pyrrolidinyl) N—2-Methylindole Perfluorooctanesul fonamide
2935 0090.90	其他磺(酰)胺	6.5	35		9	17	千克		Other sulphonamides
	第十一分章　维生素原、维生素及激素								**XI. PROVITAMINS, VITAMINS AND HORMONES**
29.36	**天然或合成再制的维生素原和维生素(包括天然浓缩物)及其主要用作维生素的衍生物,上述产品的混合物,不论是否溶于溶剂:**								**Provitamins and vitamins, natural or reproduced by synthesis (including natural concentrates) , derivatives thereof used primarily as vitamins, and intermixtures of the foregoing, whether or not in any solvent:**
	-未混合的维生素及其衍生物:								-Vitamins and their derivatives, unmixed:
2936.2100	--维生素A及其衍生物	4	20		17	17	千克	AB	--Vitamins A and their derivatives
2936.2200	--维生素B_1及其衍生物	4	20		13	17	千克	AB	--Vitamin B1 and its derivatives
2936.2300	--维生素B_2及其衍生物	4	20		13	17	千克	AB	--Vitamin B2 and its derivatives
2936.2400	--D或DL-泛酸(维生素B_3或维生素B_5)及其衍生物	4	20		13	17	千克	AB	--D-or DL-Pantothenic acid (Vitamin B3 or Vitamin B5) and its derivatives
2936.2500	--维生素B_6及其衍生物	4	20		13	17	千克	AB	--Vitamin B6 and its derivatives
2936.2600	--维生素B_{12}及其衍生物	4	20		13	17	千克	AB	--Vitamin B12 and its derivatives
2936.2700	--维生素C及其衍生物	4	20		13	17	千克		--Vitamin C and its derivatives
2936 2700.10	未混合的维生素C原粉(不论是	4	20		13	17	千克	4ABxy	Natural concentrates of Vitamins C, unmixed(whether

税则号列 Tariff Item	商品名称及备注	进口税率 最惠	进口税率 普通	进口税率 暂定	出口退税	增值税率	计量单位	监管条件	Article Description
	否溶于溶剂)								or not in any solvent)
2936 2700.20	未混合的维生素C钙、维生素C钠(不论是否溶于溶剂)	4	20		13	17	千克	4ABxy	Vitamin C calcium, vitamin C sodium , unmixed (whether or not in any solvent)
2936 2700.30	颗粒或包衣维生素C(不论是否溶于溶剂)	4	20		13	17	千克	4ABxy	Vitamin C, coated or particles (whether or not in any solvent)
2936 2700.90	维生素C酯类及其他(不论是否溶于溶剂)	4	20		13	17	千克	4ABxy	Vitamin C esters and others(whether or not in any solvent)
2936.2800	--维生素E及其衍生物	4	20		17	17	千克	AB	--Vitamin E and its derivatives
2936.2900	--其他维生素及其衍生物	4	20		17	17	千克		--Other vitamins and their derivatives
2936 2900.10	胆钙化醇(不论是否溶于溶剂)	4	20		17	17	千克	ABS	Cholecalciferol (whether or not in any solvent)
2936 2900.90	其他未混合的维生素及其衍生物(不论是否溶于溶剂)	4	20		17	17	千克	AB	Other vitamins and their deviants, unmixed, (whether or not in any solvent)
2936.9000	-其他，包括天然浓缩物	4	20		13	17	千克	AB	-Other, including natural concentrates
29.37	**天然或合成再制的激素、前列腺素、血栓烷、白细胞三烯及其衍生物和结构类似物，包括主要用做激素的改性链多肽：**								**Hormones, prostaglandins, thromboaxnes and leukotrienes, natural or reproduced by synthesis ; derivatives and structural analogues thereof, including chain modified polypeptides, used primarily as hormones:**
	-多肽激素、蛋白激素、糖蛋白激素及其衍生物和结构类似物:								-Polypeptide hormones, protein hormones and glycoprotein hormones, their derivatives and structural analogues:
2937.1100	--生长激素及其衍生物和结构类似物	4	20		9	17	千克		--Somatotropin, its derivatives and structural analogues
2937 1100.10	生长激素(GH)	4	20		9	17	千克	L	Somatotropin
2937 1100.90	生长激素的衍生物和结构类似物	4	20		9	17	千克		Derivatives and structural analogues of somatotropin
	--胰岛素及其盐:								--Insulin and its salts:
2937.1210	---重组人胰岛素及其盐	4	20		15	17	千克	L	---Recombinant human insulin and its salts
2937.1290	---其他	4	20		15	17	千克	L	---Other
2937.1900	--其他	4	20		9	17	千克		--Other
2937 1900.13	绒促性素及促黄体生成素	4	20		9	17	千克	L	Chorionic gonadotrophin and luteinizing hormone
2937 1900.15	促皮质素类	4	20		9	17	千克	L	Corticotrophin
2937 1900.90	其他多肽激素及衍生物和结构类似物(包括蛋白激素、糖蛋白激素及其衍生物和结构类似物)	4	20		9	17	千克	Q	Other polypeptide hormones, including protein hormones、glycoprotein hormones, their derivatives and structural analogues
	-甾族激素及其衍生物和结构类似物:								-Steroidal hormones, their derivatives and structural analogues:
2937.2100	--可的松、氢化可的松、脱氢可的松及脱氢皮质甾醇	4	20		9	17	千克	Q	--Cortisone, hydrocortisone, prednisone（dehydrocortisone）and prednisolone（dehydrocortisone）
	--皮质(甾)类激素的卤化衍生物:								--Halogenated derivatives of corticosteroidal hormones:
2937.2210	---地塞米松	4	30		9	17	千克	Q	---Dexamethasone
2937.2290	--其他	4	30		9	17	千克	Q	---Other
	--雌(甾)激素及孕激素:								--Oestrogens and progestogens:
	---动物源的:								---Zoogenic:
2937.2311	----孕马结合雌激素	4	30		9	17	千克	Q	----Progesterone conjugated equine estrogen
2937.2319	----其他	4	30		9	17	千克	Q	----Other
2937.2390	---其他	4	30		9	17	千克		--Other
2937 2390.10	泽仑诺;孕三烯酮;替勃龙(包括四氢孕三烯酮)	4	30		9	17	千克	L	Zeranol,gestrinone,tibolone（including tetrahydrogestrinone）
2937 2390.90	其他雌(甾)激素及孕激素	4	30		9	17	千克	Q	Other oestrogens and progestogens
2937.2900	--其他	4	30		9	17	千克		--Other
2937 2900.11	1-雄烯二醇;1-雄烯二酮(包括雄甾-4-烯-3β，17α-二醇;雄甾-5-烯-3β，17α-二醇)	4	30		9	17	千克	L	Androstenediol,1-androstenedione, including 4-Androstanediol (3β,17α), 5- Androstanediol (3β,17α)）
2937 2900.12	4-雄烯二醇;5-雄烯二酮(包括5α-	4	30		9	17	千克	L	4- Androstanediol,5- Androstenedione(including3α,

税则号列 Tariff Item	商品名称及备注	进口税率 最惠	进口税率 普通	进口税率 暂定	出口退税	增值税率	计量单位	监管条件	Article Description
	雄烷-3α，17β-二醇；5α-雄烷-3β，17α-二醇；勃拉睾酮)								17β-androstanediol; 3β，17α- Androstenedione, bolasterone)
2937 2900.13	勃地酮；卡芦睾酮(包括勃二酮；氯司替勃)	4	30		9	17	千克	L	Boldenone,calusterone（including 1,4-androst adiene-3,17-dione,clostebol）
2937 2900.14	达那唑；脱氢氯甲睾酮(包括普拉睾酮；去氧甲睾酮)	4	30		9	17	千克	L	Danazol,dehydrochlormethyltestosterone（including Prasterone, Deoxy methyltestosterone）
2937 2900.15	双氢睾酮；屈他雄酮（包括表双氢睾酮、乙雌烯醇、氟甲睾酮、甲酰勃龙）	4	30		9	17	千克	L	Dihydrotestosterone, drostanolone,（including epi-dihydrotestosterone, ethylestrenol, fluoxymesterone, formebolone）
2937 2900.16	夫拉扎勃(包括4-羟基睾酮；3α-羟基-5α-雄烷-17-酮)	4	30		9	17	千克	L	Furazabol（including 4- hydroxyl testosterone, 3α-hydroxyl-5α-androstane- 17- ketone）
2937 2900.17	美雄诺龙；美睾酮；美雄酮(包括甲基屈他雄酮)	4	30		9	17	千克	L	Mestanolone,mesterolone,methandienone（including Methyl drostanolone）
2937 2900.18	甲基-1-睾酮；甲睾酮；甲诺睾酮(包括甲二烯诺龙；去甲雄酮)	4	30		9	17	千克	L	Methyl-1-testosterone,methyltestosterone, methylnortestosterone（including diene nandrolone, Norandrosterone）
2937 2900.19	美替诺龙；美雄醇(包括美曲勃龙)	4	30		9	17	千克	L	Metenolone,methandriol（including Methyltrienolone）
2937 2900.21	米勃酮；诺龙；诺勃酮；诺司替勃(包括19-去甲雄烯二酮；诺乙雄龙)	4	30		9	17	千克	L	Mibolerone,nandrolone,norbolethone,norclostebol(including 19-norandrostenedione , norethandrolone)
2937 2900.22	19-去甲胆烷醇酮(包括羟勃龙；氧雄龙)	4	30		9	17	千克	L	19-noretiocholanolone（including oxabolone, oxandrolone）
2937 2900.23	羟甲睾酮；羟甲烯龙(包括前列他唑)	4	30		9	17	千克	L	Oxymesterone, oxymetholone（including prostanozol）
2937 2900.24	奎勃龙；司坦唑醇；司腾勃龙（包括1-睾酮、睾酮、群勃龙）	4	30		9	17	千克	L	Quinbolone, stanozolol, Stenbolone（including 1-Testosterone, Testosterone, trenbolone）
2937 2900.25	7α-羟基-普拉睾酮	4	30		9	17	千克	L	7α- Hydroxy - Prasterone
2937 2900.26	7β-羟基-普拉睾酮	4	30		9	17	千克	L	7β- Hydroxy - Prasterone
2937 2900.27	7-羰基-普拉睾酮	4	30		9	17	千克	L	7- Carbonyl - Prasterone
2937 2900.28	胆烷醇酮	4	30		9	17	千克	L	Aetiocholanolone
2937 2900.31	雄甾-5-烯-3β，17β-二醇	4	30		9	17	千克	L	5 - Androstenediol (3β, 17β)
2937 2900.32	雄甾-4-烯-3，17-二酮	4	30		9	17	千克	L	4 - androstenedione
2937 2900.33	勃雄二醇	4	30		9	17	千克	L	Bolandiol
2937 2900.90	其他甾类激素及其衍生物和结构类似物	4	30		9	17	千克	Q	Other steroid hormones its derivatives and structural analogue
2937.5000	-前列腺素、血栓烷和白细胞三烯(包括它们的衍生物和结构类似物)	4	30		9	17	千克		-Prostaglandins, thromboxanes and leukotrienes, their derivatives and structural analogues
2937.9000	-其他	4	30		9	17	千克		-Other
2937 9000.10	氨基酸衍生物	4	30		9	17	千克	ABQ	Amino acids and its derivatives
2937 9000.90	其他激素及其衍生物和结构类似物	4	30		9	17	千克	Q	Other hormones and its derivatives and structural analogues
	第十二分章　天然或合成再制的苷（配糖物）、植物碱及其盐、醚、酯和其他衍生物								**XII. GLYCOSIDES AND VEGETABLE ALKALOIDS, NATURAL OR REPRODUCED BYSYNTHESIS,AND THEIR SALTS, ETHERS, ESTERS AND OTHER DERIVATIVES**
29.38	**天然或合成再制的苷（配糖物）及其盐、醚、酯和其他衍生物：**								**Glycosides, natural or reproduced by synthesis, and their salts, ethers, esters and other derivatives:**
2938.1000	-芸香苷及其衍生物	6.5	20		9	17	千克	Q	-Rutosideand and its derivatives
	-其他：								-Other:
2938.9010	---齐多夫定、拉米夫定、司他夫定、地达诺新及它们的盐	6.5	20		13	17	千克		---Zidovudine, lamivudine, stavudine, didanosine and their salts
2938.9090	---其他	6.5	20		9	17	千克		---Other
2938 9090.10	甘草酸粉	6.5	20		9	17	千克	y4x	Glycyrrhizic acid powder
2938 9090.20	甘草酸盐类	6.5	20		9	17	千克	4ABxy	Dipotassium glycyrrhizinate

税则号列 Tariff Item	商品名称及备注	进口税率 最惠	普通	暂定	出口退税	增值税率	计量单位	监管条件	Article Description
2938 9090.30	甘草次酸及其衍生物	6.5	20		9	17	千克	y4x	Glycyrrhetic acid and its derivatives
2938 9090.90	其他天然或合成再制的苷及其盐等(包括醚、酯和其他衍生物)	6.5	20		9	17	千克		Other glycosides, natural or reproduced by synthesis, and their salts, ethers, esters and other derivatives
29.39	**天然或合成再制的生物碱及其盐、醚、酯和其他衍生物:**								**Vegetable alkaloids, natural or reproduced by synthesis, and their salts, ethers, esters and other derivatives:**
	-鸦片碱及其衍生物，以及它们的盐:								-Alkaloids of opium and their derivatives; salts thereof:
2939.1100	--罂粟杆浓缩物、丁丙诺啡(INN)、可待因、双氢可待因(INN)、乙基吗啡、埃托啡(INN)、海洛因、氢可酮(INN)、氢吗啡酮(INN)、吗啡、尼可吗啡(INN)、羟考酮(INN)、羟吗啡酮(INN)、福尔可定(INN)、醋氢可酮(INN)和蒂巴因，以及它们的盐	4	50		9	17	千克		--Concentrates of poppy straw; buprenorphine(INN), codeine, dihydrocodeine (INN), ethylmorphine, etorphine (INN), heroin, hydrocodone (INN), hydromorphone (INN), morphine, nicomorphine(INN), oxycodone(INN), oxymorphone (INN), pholcodine (INN), thebacon (INN) and thebaine; salts thereof
2939 1100.11	罂粟杆浓缩物	4	50		9	17	千克	W	Concentrates of poppy straw
2939 1100.12	可待因、双氢可待因、乙基吗啡(以及它们的盐)	4	50		9	17	千克	W	Codeine, dihydrocodeine (INN), ethylmorphine (and their salts)
2939 1100.13	埃托啡、海洛因、氢可酮(以及它们的盐)	4	50		9	17	千克	W	Etorphine (INN), heroin, hydrocodone (INN) (and their salts)
2939 1100.14	氢吗啡酮、吗啡、尼可吗啡(以及它们的盐)	4	50		9	17	千克	W	Hydromorphone (INN), morphine, nicomorphine (INN) (and their salts)
2939 1100.15	羟考酮、羟吗啡酮、福尔可定(以及它们的盐)	4	50		9	17	千克	W	Oxycodone (INN), oxymorphone (INN) pholcodine (INN) (and their salts)
2939 1100.16	醋氢可酮,蒂巴因(以及它们的盐)	4	50		9	17	千克	W	Thebacon (INN) and thebaine (and their salts)
2939 1100.20	丁丙诺啡及其盐	4	50		9	17	千克	I	Buprenorphine and its salts
2939.1900	--其他	4	50		9	17	千克		--Other
2939 1900.10	二氢埃托啡及其盐	4	50		9	17	千克	W	Dihydroetorphine and its salts
2939 1900.21	苄吗啡、可多克辛、地索吗啡、醋托啡(以及它们的盐)	4	50		9	17	千克	W	Benzylmorphine,codoxime,desomorphine, acetorphine (and their salts)
2939 1900.22	双氢吗啡、氢吗啡醇、甲地索啡、甲二氢吗啡(以及它们的盐)	4	50		9	17	千克	W	Dihydromorphine,hydromorphinol,methyldesorphine,methyldihydromorphine (and their salts)
2939 1900.23	美托酮、吗啡-N-氧化物、麦罗啡、去甲吗啡(以及它们的盐)	4	50		9	17	千克	W	Metopon,Morphine-N-oxide,myrophine normorphine (and their salts)
2939 1900.24	醋氢可待因、尼可待因、尼二氢可待因、去甲可待因(以及它们的盐)	4	50		9	17	千克	W	Acetyldihydrocodeine, nicocodine, nicomorphine, norcodeine (and their salts)
2939 1900.25	吗啡甲溴化物及其盐	4	50		9	17	千克	W	Morphine methobromide and its salts
2939 1900.30	纳布啡及其盐	4	50		9	17	千克	I	Nalbuphine and its salts
2939 1900.40	奥列巴文	4	50		9	17	千克	W	Oripavine;CAS：467-04-9
2939 1900.90	其他鸦片碱及其衍生物及它们的盐	4	50		9	17	千克	Q	Other alkaloids of opium and their derivatives; salts thereof
2939.2000	-金鸡纳生物碱及其衍生物，以及它们的盐	4	20		9	17	千克	Q	-Alkaloids of cinchona and their derivatives; salts thereof
2939.3000	-咖啡因及其盐	4	20		9	17	千克		-Caffeine and its salts
2939 3000.10	咖啡因	4	20		9	17	千克	ABI	Caffeine
2939 3000.90	咖啡因的盐	4	20		9	17	千克	ABI	Salts of caffeine
	-麻黄碱类及其盐:								-Ephedrines and their salts:
2939.4100	麻黄碱及其盐	4	20		9	17	千克		--Ephedrine and its salts
2939 4100.10	麻黄碱(麻黄素,盐酸麻黄碱)	4	20		9	17	千克	23Q	Ephedrine (ephedrine, ephedrine hydrochloride)
2939 4100.20	硫酸麻黄碱	4	20		9	17	千克	23Q	Ephedrine sulfate

税则号列 Tariff Item	商品名称及备注	进口税率 最惠	进口税率 普通	进口税率 暂定	出口退税	增值税率	计量单位	监管条件	Article Description
2939 4100.30	消旋盐酸麻黄碱	4	20		9	17	千克	23Q	Racephedrine hydrochloride
2939 4100.40	草酸麻黄碱	4	20		9	17	千克	23Q	Ephedrine oxalate
2939 4100.90	麻黄碱盐	4	20		9	17	千克	Q	Salts of ephedrine
2939.4200	--假麻黄碱（INN）及其盐	4	20		9	17	千克		--Pseudoephedrine（INN） and its salts
2939 4200.10	伪麻黄碱（伪麻黄素，盐酸伪麻黄碱）	4	20		9	17	千克	23Q	Pseudoephedrine(pseudoephedrine, pseudoephedrine hydrochloride)
2939 4200.20	硫酸伪麻黄碱	4	20		9	17	千克	23Q	Pseudoephedrine sulfate
2939 4200.90	假麻黄碱盐（D-2-甲胺基-1-苯基丙醇）	4	20		9	17	千克	Q	Salts of pseudoephedrine (D-2-methyl amino-1-phenylethyl carbinol)
2939.4300	--d-去甲假麻黄碱(INN)及其盐	4	20		9	17	千克	I	--d-Norpseudoephedrine and its salts
2939.4400	--去甲麻黄碱(INN)及其盐	4	20		9	17	千克	23	--Norephedrine and its salts
2939.4900	--其他	4	20		9	17	千克		--Other
2939 4900.10	盐酸甲基麻黄碱	4	20		9	17	千克	Q23	Methylephedrine hydrochloride
2939 4900.20	消旋盐酸甲基麻黄碱	4	20		9	17	千克	Q23	DL-Methylephedrine hydrochloride
2939 4900.90	其他麻黄碱及其盐	4	20		9	17	千克	Q	Other ephedrines and its salts
	-茶碱和氨茶碱及其衍生物，以及它们的盐:								-Theophylline and aminophylline（theophylline-ethylenediamine） and their derivatives; salts thereof:
2939.5100	--芬乙茶碱（INN）及其盐	4	20		9	17	千克	I	--Fenetylline（INN） and its salts
2939.5900	--其他	4	20		9	17	千克	Q	--Other
	-麦角生物碱及其衍生物，以及它们的盐:								-Alkaloids of rye ergot and their derivatives; salts thereof:
2939.6100	--麦角新碱及其盐	4	20		9	17	千克		--Ergometrine（INN） and its salts
2939 6100.10	麦角新碱	4	20		9	17	千克	3Q2	Ergometrine（INN）
2939 6100.90	麦角新碱盐	4	20		9	17	千克	Q	Salts of ergometrine（INN）
2939.6200	-麦角胺(INN)及其盐	4	20		9	17	千克		--Ergotamine（INN） and its salts
2939 6200.10	麦角胺	4	20		9	17	千克	3Q2	Ergotamine（INN）
2939 6200.90	麦角胺盐	4	20		9	17	千克	Q	Salts of ergotamine（INN）
2939.6300	--麦角酸及其盐	4	20		9	17	千克		--Lysergic acid and its salts
2939 6300.10	麦角酸	4	20		9	17	千克	3Q2	Lysergic acid
2939 6300.90	麦角酸盐	4	20		9	17	千克	Q	Salts of lysergic acid
2939.6900	--其他	4	20		9	17	千克		--Other
2939 6900.10	麦角二乙胺及其盐	4	20		9	17	千克	I	Lysergide and its salts
2939 6900.90	其他麦角生物碱及其衍生物（包括它们的盐）	4	20		9	17	千克	Q	Other alkaloids of rye ergot and their derivatives; salts thereof
	-其他:								-Other:
	--可卡因、芽子碱、左甲苯丙胺、去氧麻黄碱（INN）、去氧麻黄碱外消旋体，它们的盐、酯及其他衍生物:								--Cocaine, ecgonine, levometamfetamine, metamfetamine（INN）, metamfetamine racemate; salts, esters and other derivatives thereof:
2939.9110	---可卡因及其盐	4	20		9	17	千克	W	---Cocaine and its salts
2939.9190	---其他	4	20		9	17	千克		---Other
2939 9190.11	左甲苯丙胺（以及它们的盐、酯及其他衍生物）	4	20		9	17	千克	I	Levometamfetamine (and their salts,esters and other derivatives)
2939 9190.12	去氧麻黄碱（以及它们的盐、酯及其他衍生物）	4	20		9	17	千克	I	Metamfetamine（INN）(and their salts, esters and other derivatives)
2939 9190.13	去氧麻黄碱外消旋体（以及它们的盐、酯及其他衍生物）	4	20		9	17	千克	I	Metamfetamine racemate (and their salts, esters and other derivatives)
2939 9190.20	芽子碱及其盐	4	20		9	17	千克	W	Ecgonine and its salts
	--其他:								-Other:
2939.9910	---烟碱及其盐	4	20		9	17	千克		---Nicotine and its salts
2939 9910.10	烟碱	4	20		9	17	千克	ABQ	Nicotine
2939 9910.90	烟碱盐	4	20		9	17	千克	Q	Nicotine salts
2939.9920	---番木鳖碱(士的年)及其盐	4	17		9	17	千克		---Strychnine and its salts

税则号列 Tariff Item	商品名称及备注	进口税率 最惠	进口税率 普通	进口税率 暂定	出口退税	增值税率	计量单位	监管条件	Article Description
2939 9920.10	番木鳖碱	4	17		9	17	千克	ABQ	Strychnine
2939 9920.90	番木鳖碱盐	4	17		9	17	千克	Q	Strychnine salts
2939.9990	---其他	4	20		9	17	千克		---Other
2939 9990.11	卡西酮、麦司卡林（以及它们的盐）	4	20		9	17	千克	I	Cathinone,mescaline (and their salts)
2939 9990.12	赛洛新、赛洛西宾（以及它们的盐）	4	20		9	17	千克	I	Psilocine, psilocybine (and their salts)
2939 9990.90	其他生物碱及其衍生物（包括生物碱的盐、酯及其他衍生物）	4	20		9	17	千克	ABQ	Other Vegetable alkaloids, and their salts, ethers, esters and other derivatives
	第十三分章 其他有机化合物								**Ⅷ OTHER ORGANIC COMPOUNDS**
29.40	**化学纯糖，但蔗糖、乳糖、麦芽糖、葡萄糖及果糖除外；糖醚、糖缩醛、糖酯及其盐，但不包括品目 29.37、29.38、29.39 的产品：**								**Sugars, chemically pure, other than sucrose, lactose, maltose, glucose and fructose; sugar ethers, sugar acetals and sugar esters, and their salts, other than products of heading No.29.37, 29.38 or 29.39:**
2940.0000	化学纯糖，但蔗糖、乳糖、麦芽糖、葡萄糖及果糖除外；糖醚、糖缩醛、糖酯及其盐，但不包括品目 29.37、29.38 及 29.39 的产品	6	30		9	17	千克	ABQ	Sugars, chemically pure, other than sucrose, lactose, maltose, glucose and fructose; sugar ethers, sugar acetals and sugar esters, and their salts, other than products of heading No.29.37, 29.38 or 29.39
29.41	**抗菌素：**								**Antibiotics:**
	-青霉素和具有青霉烷酸结构的青霉素衍生物及其盐:								-Penicillins and their derivatives with a penicillanic acid structure; salts thereof:
	---氨苄青霉素及其盐:								---Ampicillin and its salts:
2941.1011	----氨苄青霉素	6	20		13	17	千克	Q	----Ampicillin
2941.1012	----氨苄青霉素三水酸	6	20		13	17	千克	Q	----Ampicillin trihydrate
2941.1019	----其他	6	20		13	17	千克	Q	----Other
	---其他:								---Other:
2941.1091	----羟氨苄青霉素	4	20		13	17	千克	Q	----Amoxycillin
2941.1092	----羟氨苄青霉素三水酸	4	20		13	17	千克	Q	----Amoxycillin trihydrate
2941.1093	----6-氨基青霉烷酸(6APA)	4	20		13	17	千克		----6-Aminopenicillanic acid
2941.1094	----青霉素 V	4	20		13	17	千克	Q	----Penicillin V
2941.1095	----磺苄青霉素	4	20		13	17	千克	Q	----Sulfobenzylpenicillin
2941.1096	----邻氯青霉素	4	20		13	17	千克	Q	----Cloxacillin
2941.1099	----其他	4	20		13	17	千克	4Qxy	----Other
2941.2000	-链霉素及其衍生物，以及它们的盐	4	20		13	17	千克	Q	-Streptomycins and their derivatives; salts thereof
	-四环素及其衍生物，以及它们的盐:								-Tetracyclines and their derivatives; salts thereof:
	----四环素及其盐:								---Tetracyclines and their salts:
2941.3011	----四环素	4	20		13	17	千克	Q	----Tetracyclines
2941.3012	----四环素盐	4	20		13	17	千克	Q	----Salts of tetracyclines
2941.3020	---四环素衍生物及其盐	4	20		13	17	千克	Q	---Tetracyclines derivatives and their salts
2941.4000	-氯霉素及其衍生物，以及它们的盐	4	20		13	17	千克	Q	-Chloramphenicol and its derivatives; salts thereof
2941.5000	-红霉素及其衍生物，以及它们的盐	4	20		13	17	千克	Q	-Erythromycin and its derivatives; salts thereof
	-其他:								-Other:
2941.9010	---庆大霉素及其衍生物，以及它们的盐	4	20		13	17	千克	Q	---Gentamycin and its derivatives; salts thereof
2941.9020	---卡那霉素及其衍生物，以及它们的盐	4	20		13	17	千克	Q	---Kanamycin and its derivatives; salts thereof
2941.9030	---利福平及其衍生物，以及它	4	20		13	17	千克	Q	---Rifampicin（RFP）; salts thereof

税则号列 Tariff Item	商品名称及备注	进口税率			出口退税	增值税率	计量单位	监管条件	Article Description
		最惠	普通	暂定					
	们的盐								
2941.9040	---林可霉素及其衍生物，以及它们的盐	4	20		13	17	千克	Q	---Lincomycin and its derivatives; salts thereof
	---头孢菌素及其衍生物，以及它们的盐:								---Cephamycin and its derivatives;salts thereof:
2941.9052	----头孢氨苄及其盐	6	20		13	17	千克	Q	---Cefalexin and its salts
2941.9053	----头孢唑啉及其盐	6	20		13	17	千克	Q	----Cefazolin and its salts
2941.9054	----头孢拉啶及其盐	6	20		13	17	千克	Q	----Cefradine and its salts
2941.9055	----头孢三嗪(头孢曲松)及其盐	6	20		13	17	千克	Q	----Ceftriaxone and its salts
2941.9056	----头孢哌酮及其盐	6	20		13	17	千克	Q	----Cefoperazone and its salts
2941.9057	----头孢噻肟及其盐	6	20		13	17	千克	Q	----Cefotaxime and its salts
2941.9058	----头孢克罗及其盐	6	20		13	17	千克	Q	----Cefaclor and its salts
2941.9059	----其他	6	20		13	17	千克		----Other
2941 9059.10	放线菌酮	6	20		13	17	千克	QS	Actidione
2941 9059.90	其他头孢菌素及其衍生物(包括它们的盐)	6	20		13	17	千克	Q	Other cephalosporins and their deviatives (including their salts)
2941.9060	---麦迪霉素及其衍生物，以及它们的盐	6	20		13	17	千克	Q	---Midecamycin and its derivatives; salts thereof
2941.9070	---乙酰螺旋霉素及其衍生物以及它们的盐	4	20		13	17	千克	Q	---Acetyl-spiramycin and its derivatives; salts thereof
2941.9090	---其他	6	20		15	17	千克	Q	---Other
29.42	**其他有机化合物:**								**Other organic compounds:**
2942.0000	其他有机化合物	6.5	30		9	17	千克		Other organic compounds

第三十章
药　　品

注释：

一、本章不包括：

（一）食品及饮料（例如，营养品、糖尿病食品、强化食品、保健食品、滋补饮料及矿泉水），但不包括供静脉摄入用的滋养品（第四类）；

（二）用于帮助吸烟者戒烟的制剂，例如，片剂、咀嚼胶或透皮贴片（税目21.06或38.24）；

（三）经特殊煅烧或精细研磨的牙科用熟石膏（品目25.20）；

（四）适合医药用的精油水馏液及水溶液（品目33.01）；

（五）品目33.03至33.07的制品，不论是否具有治疗及预防疾病的作用；

（六）加有药料的肥皂及品目34.01的其他产品；

（七）以熟石膏为基本成分的牙科月制品（品目34.07）；或

（八）不作治疗及预防疾病用的血清蛋白（品目35.02）。

二、品目30.02所称的“免疫制品”是指直接参与免疫过程调节的多肽及蛋白质（品目29.37的货品除外），例如，单克隆抗体（MAB）、抗体片断、抗体偶联物及抗体片断偶联物、白介素、干扰素（IFN）、趋化因子及特定的肿瘤坏死因子（TNF）、生长因子（GF）、促红细胞生成素及集落刺激因子（CSF）。

三、品目30.03及30.04以及本章注释四（四）所述的非混合产品及混合产品，按下列规定处理：

（一）非混合产品：

1. 溶于水的非混合产品；
2. 第二十八章及第二十九章的所有货品；以及
3. 品目13.02的单一植物浸膏，只经标定或溶于溶剂的。

（二）混合产品：

1. 胶体溶液及悬浮液（胶态硫磺除外）；
2. 从植物性混合物加工所得的植物浸膏；以及
3. 蒸发天然矿质水所得的盐及浓缩物。

四、品目30.06仅适用于下列物品（这些物品只能归入品目30.06而不得归入本税则其他品目）：

（一）无菌外科肠线、类似的无菌缝合材料（包括外科或牙科用无菌可吸收缝线）及外伤创口闭合用的无菌粘合胶布；

（二）无菌昆布及无菌昆布塞条；

（三）外科或牙科用无菌吸收性止血材料；外科或牙科用无菌抗粘连阻隔材料，不论是否可吸收；

Chapter 30
Pharmaceutical products

Chapter Notes:

1. This Chapter does not cover:

(a) Foods or beverages (such as dietetic, diabetic or fortified foods, food supplements, tonic beverages and mineral waters), other than nutritional preparations for intravenous administration (Section Ⅳ);

(b) Preparations, such as tablets, chewing gum or patches (transdermal systems), intended to assist smokers to stop smoking (heading21.06 or 38.04);

(c) Plasters specially calcined or finely ground for use in dentistry (heading 25.20);

(d) Aqueous distillates or aqueous solutions of essential oils, suitable for medicinal uses (heading 33.01);

(e) Preparations of headings 33.03 to 33.07, even if they have therapeutic or prophylactic properties;

(f) Soap or other products of heading 34.01 containing added medicaments;

(g) Preparations with a basis of plaster for use in dentistry (heading 34.07); or

(h) Blood albumin not prepared for therapeutic or prophylactic uses (heading 35.02).

2. For the purposes of heading 30.02, the expression “immunological products” applies to peptides and proteins(other than goods of heading 29.37) which are directly involved in the regulation of immunological processes, such as monoclonal antibodies (MAB), antibody fragments, antibody conjugates and antibody fragment conjugates, interleukins, interferons (IFN), chemokines and certain tumor necrosis factors (TNF), growth factors (GF), hematopoietins and colony stimulating factors (CSF).

3. For the purposes of headings 30.03 and 30.04 and of Note 4 (d) to this Chapter, the following are to be treated:

(a) As unmixed products:

(i) Unmixed products dissolved in water;

(ii) All goods of Chapter 28 or 29; and

(iii) Simple vegetable extracts of heading 13.02, merely standardised or dissolved in any solvent;

(b) As products which have been mixed:

(i) Colloidal solutions and suspensions (other than colloidal sulphur);

(ii) Vegetable extracts obtained by the treatment of mixtures of vegetable materials; and

(iii) Salts and concentrates obtained by evaporating naural mineral waters.

4. Heading 30.06 applies only to the following, which are to be classified in that heading and in no other heading of the Nomenclature:

(a) Sterile surgical catgut, similar sterile suture materials (including sterile absorbable surgical or dental yarns) and sterile tissue adhesives for surgical wound closure;

(b) Sterile laminaria and sterile laminaria tents;

(c) Sterile absorbable surgical or dental haemostatics; sterile surgical or dental adhesion barriers, whether or not absorbable;

（四）用于病人的 X 光检查造影剂及其他诊断试剂，这些药剂是由单一产品配定剂量或由两种以上成分混合而成的；

（五）血型试剂；

（六）牙科粘固剂及其他牙科填料；骨骼粘固剂；

（七）急救药箱、药包；

（八）以激素、品目 29.37 的其他产品或杀精子剂为基本成分的化学避孕药物；

（九）专用于人类或作兽药用的凝胶制品，作为外科手术或体检时躯体部位的润滑剂，或者作为躯体和医疗器械之间的耦合剂；

（十）废药物，即因超过有效保存期等原因而不适合作原用途的药品；以及

（十一）可确定用于造口术的用具，即裁切成型的结肠造口术，回肠造口术、尿道造口术用袋及其具有黏性的片或底盘。

(d) Opacifying preparations for X-ray examinations and diagnostic reagents designed to be administered to the patient, being unmixed products put up in measured doses or products consisting of two or more ingredients which have been mixed together for such uses;

(e) Blood-grouping reagents;

(f) Dental cements and other dental fillings; bone reconstruction cements;

(g) First-aid boxes and kits;

(h) Chemical contraceptive preparations based on hormones, on other products of heading 29.37 or on spermicides;

(ij) Gel preparations designed to be used in human or veterinary medicine as a lubricant for parts of the body for surgical operations or physical examinations or as a coupling agent between the body and medical instruments;

(k) Waste pharmaceuticals, that is, pharmaceutical products which are unfit for their original intended purpose due to, for example, expiry of shelf life; and

(l) Appliances identifiable for ostomy use, that is, colostomy, ileostomy and urostomy pouches cut to shape and their adhesive wafers or faceplates.

税则号列 Tariff Item	商品名称及备注	进口税率 最惠	进口税率 普通	进口税率 暂定	出口退税	增值税率	计量单位	监管条件	Article Description
30.01	**已干燥的器官疗法用腺体及其他器官，不论是否制成粉末；器官疗法用腺体、其他器官及其分泌物的提取物；肝素及其盐；其他供治疗或预防疾病用的其他品目未列名的人体或动物制品：**								**Glands and other organs for organotherapeutic uses, dried, whether or not powdered; extracts of glands or other organs or of their secretions for organotherapeutic uses; heparin and its salts; other human or animal substances prepared for therapeutic or prophylactic uses, not elsewhere specified or included:**
3001.2000	-腺体、其他器官及其分泌物的提取物	3	30			17	千克		-Extracts of glands or other organs or of their secretions
3001 2000.10	其他濒危野生动物腺体、器官（包括分泌物）	3	30			17	千克	AQFEB	Extracts of glands or other organs or of their secretions of endangered wild animals
3001 2000.20	人类的腺体、器官及其分泌物提取物	3	30		15	17	千克	AQB	Human extracts of glands or organs or of their secretions
3001 2000.90	其他腺体、器官及其分泌物提取物	3	30		15	17	千克	AQB	Other extracts of glands or other organs or of their secretions
	-其他:								-Other:
3001.9010	---肝素及其盐	3	30		15	17	千克	Q	---Heparin and its salts
3001.9090	---其他	3	30			17	千克		---Other
3001 9090.10	蛇毒制品（供治疗或预防疾病用）	3	30		15	17	千克	AQFEB	Snake venom substances, prepared for therapeutic or prophylactic uses
3001 9090.91	其他濒危动物制品（供治疗或预防疾病用）	3	30			17	千克	ABFEQ	Other substances of endangered animal, prepared for therapeutic or prophylactic uses
3001 9090.99	其他未列名的人体或动物制品（供治疗或预防疾病用）	3	30		13/15	17	千克	ABQ	Other human or animal substances prepared for therapeutic or prophylactic uses, not elsewhere specified or included
30.02	**人血；治病、防病或诊断用动物血制品；抗血清、其他血份及修饰免疫制品，不论是否修饰或通过生物工艺加工制得；疫苗、毒素、培养微生物（不包括酵母）及类似产品：**								**Human blood; animal blood prepared for therapeutic, prophylactic or diagnostic uses; antisera, other blood fractions and immunological products, whether or not modified or obtained by means of biotechnological processes; vaccines, toxins, cultures of micro-organisms (excluding yeasts) and similar products:**
3002.1000暂	-抗血清、其他血份及免疫制品，不论是否修饰或通过生物工艺	3	20	0	15	17	千克		-Antisera and other blood fractions and immunological products, whether or not modified or obtained by

税则号列 Tariff Item	商品名称及备注	进口税率			出口退税	增值税率	计量单位	监管条件	Article Description
		最惠	普通	暂定					
	加工制得								means of biotechnological processes
3002 1000.11[暂]	促红素（EPO）及其类似物(包括培促红素β；培尼沙肽；达促红素；缺氧诱导因子（HIF）稳定剂类)	3	20	0	15	17	千克	ABL	Erythropoietin (EPO) and its analogs (including erythropoietin beta; Pei Nisha peptide; erythropoietin; hypoxia inducible factor (HIF) stabilizers)
3002 1000.12[暂]	胰岛素样生长因子1（IGF-1）	3	20	0	15	17	千克	ABL	Insulin-like growth factor 1 (IGF-1)
3002 1000.13[暂]	机械生长因子类	3	20	0	15	17	千克	ABL	MGF(mechano growth factors)
3002 1000.14[暂]	成纤维细胞生长因子（FGFs）类	3	20	0	15	17	千克	ABL	Fibroblast growth factors (FGFs)
3002 1000.15[暂]	肝细胞生长因子（HGF）	3	20	0	15	17	千克	ABL	Hepatocyte growth factor (HGF)
3002 1000.16[暂]	血小板衍生生长因子（PDGF）	3	20	0	15	17	千克	ABL	Platelet-derived growth factor (PDGF)
3002 1000.17[暂]	血管内皮生长因子（VEGF）	3	20	0	15	17	千克	ABL	Vascular endothelial growth factor (VEGF)
3002 1000.90[暂]	其他抗血清、其他血份及免疫制品(不论是否通过修饰或生物工艺加工制得)	3	20	0	15	17	千克	AB	Other Antisera, other blood fractions and immunological products, whether or not modified or obtained by means of biotechnological processes
3002.2000[暂]	-人用疫苗	3	20	0	15	17	千克	QAB	-Vaccines for human medicine
3002.3000	-兽用疫苗	3	20		15	17	千克	ABR	-Vaccines for veterinary medicine
	-其他:								-Other:
3002.9010	---石房蛤毒素	3	20		15	17	千克	23Q	---Saxitoxin
3002.9020	---蓖麻毒素	3	20		15	17	千克	23Q	---Ricitoxin
3002.9030	---细菌及病毒	3	20			17	千克/亿株		---Bacteria and Virus
3002 9030.10	两用物项管制细菌及病毒	3	20		15	17	千克/亿株	3AB	Bacteria ,virus under control of sensitive items
3002 9030.20	苏云金杆菌	3	20		13/15	17	千克/亿株	ABS	Bacillus thuringiensis
3002 9030.90	其他细菌及病毒	3	20		15	17	千克/亿株	AB	Other bacteria and virus
3002.9040[暂]	---遗传物质和基因修饰生物体	3	20	0	15	17	千克		---Genetics material and Gene modified Organism
3002 9040.10[暂]	两用物项管制遗传物质和基因修饰生物体	3	20	0	15	17	千克	3AB	Genetics materials and gene-modified organisms under control of sensitive items
3002 9040.90[暂]	其他遗传物质和基因修饰生物体	3	20	0	15	17	千克	AB	Other genetics materials and gene-modified organisms
3002.9090[暂]	---其他	3	20	0		17	千克		---Other
3002 9090.11[暂]	濒危动物血制品	3	20	0		17	千克	ABQFE	Endangered animals blood
3002 9090.19[暂]	其他人血制品、动物血制品	3	20	0	15	17	千克	ABQ	Other human or animal blood products
3002 9090.91[暂]	两用物项管制毒素	3	20	0	15	17	千克	3AB	Toxins under control of sensitive items
3002 9090.99[暂]	人血、其他毒素等[包括培养微生物(不包括酵母)及类似产品]	3	20	0	15	17	千克	AB	Human blood, other toxins, cultures of microorganism （excluding yeasts） and similar products
30.03	**两种或两种以上成分混合而成的治病或防病用药品（不包括品目30.02、30.05或30.06的货品），未配定剂量或制成零售包装：**								**Medicaments（excluding goods of heading No.30.02, 30.05 or 30.06）consisting of two or more constituents which have been mixed together for therapeutic or prophylactic uses, not put up in measured doses or in forms or packings for retail sale:**
	-含有青霉素及具有青霉烷酸结构的青霉素衍生物或链霉素及其衍生物:								-Containing penicillins or derivatives thereof, with a penicillanic acid structure, or streptomycins or their derivatives:
	---青霉素:								---Containing penicillins:
3003.1011	----氨苄青霉素	6	30		15	17	千克	Q	----Ampicillin
3003.1012	----羟氨苄青霉素	6	30		15	17	千克	Q	----Amoxycillin
3003.1013	----青霉素V	6	30		15	17	千克	Q	----Penicillin V
3003.1019	----其他	6	30		15	17	千克	Q	----Other
3003.1090	---其他	6	30		15	17	千克	Q	---Other
	-含有其他抗菌素:								-Containing other antibiotics:
	---头孢菌素:								---Containing cephamycins:
3003.2011	----头孢噻肟	6	30		15	17	千克	Q	----Cefotaxime

税则号列 Tariff Item	商品名称及备注	进口税率 最惠	普通	暂定	出口退税	增值税率	计量单位	监管条件	Article Description
3003.2012	----头孢他啶	6	30		15	17	千克	Q	----Ceftazidime
3003.2013	----头孢西丁	6	30		15	17	千克	Q	----Cefoxitin
3003.2014	----头孢替唑	6	30		15	17	千克	Q	----Ceftezole
3003.2015	----头孢克罗	6	30		15	17	千克	Q	----Cefaclor
3003.2016	----头孢呋辛	6	30		15	17	千克	Q	----Cefuroxime
3003.2017	----头孢三嗪(头孢曲松)	6	30		15	17	千克	Q	----Ceftriaxone
3003.2018	----头孢哌酮	6	30		15	17	千克	Q	----Cefoperazone
3003.2019	----其他	6	30		15	17	千克	Q	----Other
3003.2090	---其他	6	30		15	17	千克	Q	---Other
	-含有激素或品目 29.37 的其他产品，但不含抗菌素:								-Containing hormones or other products of heading 29.37 but not containing antibiotics:
3003.3100	--含有胰岛素	5	30		15	17	千克	Q	--Containing insulin
3003.3900	--其他	6	30		15	17	千克	Q	--Other
	-含有生物碱及其衍生物，但不含抗菌素及品目 29.37 的激素或其他产品:								-Containing alkaloids or derivatives thereof but not containing hormones or other products of heading 29.37 or antibiotics:
3003.4010	---含有奎宁或其盐	5	35		15	17	千克	Q	---Containing quinine or its salts
3003.4090	---其他	5	30		15	17	千克	Q	---Other
	-其他:								-Other:
3003.9010	---含有磺胺类	6	40		15	17	千克	Q	---Containing sulfa drugs
3003.9020	---含有青蒿素及其衍生物	5	30		15	17	千克	Q	---Containing artemisinins and their derivatives
3003.9090	---其他	5	30			17	千克		---Other
3003 9090.10	含紫杉醇的混合药品（未配定剂量或非零售包装，混合指含两种或两种以上成分）	5	30			17	千克	EFQ	Medicaments, with paclitaxel, consisting of two or more constituents, not put up in measured doses or packings for retail sale
3003 9090.20	含其他未列名濒危动植物混合药品（未配定剂量或非零售包装，混合指含两种或两种以上成分）	5	30			17	千克	QFE	Medicaments, containing other two or more constituents of endangered animals, not elsewhere specified or included, not put up in measured doses or in forms of packings for retail sale
3003 9090.90	含其他未列名成分混合药品（未配定剂量或非零售包装，混合指含两种或两种以上成分）	5	30		15	17	千克	Q	Medicaments, containing other two or more constituents, not elsewhere specified or included, not put up in measured doses or in forms of packings for retail sale
30.04	**由混合或非混合产品构成的治病或防病用药品（不包括品目30.02、30.05或30.06的货品），已配定剂量（包括制成皮肤摄入形式的）或制成零售包装:**								**Medicaments（excluding goods of heading No.30.02, 30.05 or 30.06）consisting of mixed or unmixed products for therapeutic or prophylactic uses, put up in measured doses（including those in the form of transdermal administration systems）or in forms of packings for retail sale:**
	-含有青霉素及具有青霉烷酸结构的青霉素衍生物或链霉素及其衍生物:								-Containing penicillins or derivatives thereof, with a penicillanic acid structure, or streptomycins or their derivatives:
	---青霉素:								---Containing penicillins:
3004.1011	----氨苄青霉素制剂	6	30		15	17	千克		----Ampicillin
3004 1011.10	兽用普鲁卡因青霉素、奈夫西林钠制剂(包括制成零售包装)	6	30		15	17	千克	R	Procaine penicillin and Nafcillin sodium formulateons for livestock, in forms of packings for retail sale
3004 1011.90	氨苄青霉素制剂(包括制成零售包装)	6	30		15	17	千克	Q	Ampicillin, in forms of packings for retail sale
3004.1012	----羟氨苄青霉素制剂	6	30		15	17	千克	Q	----Amoxycillin
3004.1013	----青霉素V制剂	6	30		15	17	千克	Q	----Penicillin V
3004.1019	----其他	6	30		15	17	千克	Q	----Other
3004.1090	---其他	6	30		15	17	千克	Q	---Other
	-含有其他抗菌素:								-Containing other antibiotics:
	---头孢菌素:								---Containing cephamycins:
3004.2011	----头孢噻肟制剂	6	30		15	17	千克	Q	---Cefotaxime

税则号列 Tariff Item	商品名称及备注	进口税率			出口退税	增值税率	计量单位	监管条件	Article Description
		最惠	普通	暂定					
3004.2012	----头孢他啶制剂	6	30		15	17	千克	Q	---Ceftazidime
3004.2013	----头孢西丁制剂	6	30		15	17	千克	Q	----Cefoxitin
3004.2014	----头孢替唑制剂	6	30		15	17	千克	Q	----Ceftezole
3004.2015	----头孢克罗制剂	6	30		15	17	千克	Q	----Cefaclor
3004.2016	----头孢呋辛制剂	6	30		15	17	千克	Q	----Cefuroxime
3004.2017	——头孢三嗪(头孢曲松)制剂	6	30		15	17	千克	Q	----Ceftriaxone
3004.2018	----头孢哌酮制剂	6	30		15	17	千克	Q	----Cefoperazone
3004.2019	----其他	6	30		15	17	千克		----Other
3004 2019.11	兽用已配剂量的头孢氨苄、头孢噻呋钠制剂(包括零售包装的制成品)	6	30		15	17	千克	R	Cefalexin and Ceftiofur sodium formulations for livestock, put up in measured doses or in forms of packings for retail sale
3004 2019.12	兽用已配剂量的头孢噻呋晶体,硫酸头孢喹肟制剂(包括零售包装的制成品)	6	30		15	17	千克	R	Ceftiofur crystal and Cefquinome sulphate for livestock, put up in measured doses of in forms or packings for retail sale
3004 2019.90	其他已配剂量头孢菌素制剂(包括零售包装的制成品)	6	30		15	17	千克	Q	Other Cephalosporin preparations, put up in measured doses or in forms of packings for retail sale
3004.2090	---其他	6	30		15	17	千克		---Other
3004 2090.11	兽用已配剂量的土霉素、延胡索酸泰妙菌素、泰拉霉素制剂(包括制成零售包装)	6	30		15	17	千克	R	Terramycin, Tiamulin Fumarate and Tulathromycin for livestock, put up in measured doses or in forms of packings for retail sale
3004 2090.12	兽用已配剂量的氟苯尼考、多拉菌素、硫酸庆大霉素制剂(包括制成零售包装)	6	30		15	17	千克	R	Florfenicol, Doramectin and Gentamicin sulfate for livestock, put up in measured doses or in forms of packings for retail sale
3004 2090.13	兽用已配剂量的硫酸双羟链霉素制剂(包括制成零售包装)	6	30		15	17	千克	R	Streptomycin sulfate for livestock, put up in measured doses or in forms of packings for retail sale
3004 2090.90	已配剂量含有其他抗菌素的药品(包括制成零售包装)	6	30		15	17	千克	Q	Medicaments of other antibiotics, put up in measured doses or in forms of packings for retail sale
	-含有激素或品目 29.37 的其他产品,但不含抗菌素:								-Containing hormones or other products of heading No.29.37 but not containing antibiotics:
	--含有胰岛素:								--Containing insulin:
3004.3110	---含有重组人胰岛素的	5	30		15	17	千克		---Containing recombinant human insulin
3004 3110.10	已配剂量含重组人胰岛素的单方制剂(包括零售包装)	5	30		15	17	千克	L	Single preparations, containing recombinant human insulin, put up in measured doses or packings for retail sale
3004 3110.90	已配剂量含重组人胰岛素的其他药品(不含抗菌素,包括零售包装)	5	30		15	17	千克	Q	Other Medicaments , containing recombinant human insulin, without antibiotics, put up in measured doses or packings for retail sale
3004.3190	---其他	5	30		15	17	千克		---Other
3004 3190.10	其他已配剂量含胰岛素的单方制剂(包括零售包装)	5	30		15	17	千克	L	Other single preparations, containing insulin, put up in measured doses or packings for retail sale
3004 3190.90	其他已配剂量含胰岛素的其他药品(不含抗菌素,包括零售包装)	5	30		15	17	千克	Q	Other Medicaments, , containing insulin, without antibiotics, put up in measured doses or packings for retail sale
3004.3200	--含有皮质甾类激素及其衍生物或结构类似物	5	30		15	17	千克		--Containing corticosteroid hormones, their derivatives and structural analogues
3004 3200.11	已配剂量含 1-雄烯二醇或 1-雄烯二酮的单方制剂(包括其衍生物及结构类似物,包括零售包装)	5	30		15	17	千克	L	Single preparation containing 1-Androstenediol or 1-androstenedione, including their derivatives and structural analogues, put up in measured doses, packings for retail sale
3004 3200.12	已配剂量含甲酰勃龙的单方制剂(包括其衍生物及结构类似物,包括零售包装)	5	30		15	17	千克	L	Single preparation containing formebolone, including their derivatives and structural analogues, put up in measured doses, packings for retail sale
3004 3200.13	已配剂量含雄甾-4-烯-3β,17α-二醇的单方制剂(包括其衍生物及结构类似物,包括零售包装)	5	30		15	17	千克	L	Single preparation containing 4-androstenediol(3β,17α), diol including their derivatives and structural analogues, put up in measured doses, packings for retail sale

税则号列 Tariff Item	商品名称及备注	进口税率			出口退税	增值税率	计量单位	监管条件	Article Description
		最惠	普通	暂定					
3004 3200.14	已配剂量含雄甾-5-烯-3β，17α-二醇的单方制剂（包括其衍生物及结构类似物，包括零售包装）	5	30		15	17	千克	L	Single preparation containing 5- androstenediol（3β,17α）, including their derivatives and structural analogues, put up in measured doses, packings for retail sale
3004 3200.15	已配剂量含 4-雄烯二醇或乙雌烯醇的单方制剂（包括其衍生物及结构类似物，包括零售包装）	5	30		15	17	千克	L	Single preparation with 4-androstenediol and ethylestrenol, including their derivatives and structural analogues, put up in measured doses, packings for retail sale
3004 3200.16	已配剂量含 5-雄烯二酮的单方制剂（包括其衍生物及结构类似物，包括零售包装）	5	30		15	17	千克	L	Single preparation containing 5-androstendione, including their derivatives and structural analogues, put up in measured doses, packings for retail sale
3004 3200.17	已配剂量含5α-雄烷-3α，17β-二醇的单方制剂（包括其衍生物及其结构类似物，包括零售包装）	5	30		15	17	千克	L	Single preparation containing 5a-androstane-3a 17 β adiol, including their derivatives and structural analogues, put up in measured doses, packings for retail sale
3004 3200.18	已配剂量含 5α-雄烷-3β，17α-二醇的单方制剂（包括其衍生物及结构类似物，包括零售包装）	5	30		15	17	千克	L	Single preparation containing 3β,17α-5a-androstane-3a 17a-diol, including their derivatives and structural analogues, put up in measured doses, packings for retail sale
3004 3200.19	已配剂量含勃拉睾酮的单方制剂（包括其衍生物及结构类似物，包括零售包装）	5	30		15	17	千克	L	Single preparation containing bolasterone, including their derivatives and structural analogues, put up in measured doses, packings for retail sale
3004 3200.21	已配剂量含勃地酮的单方制剂（包括其衍生物及结构类似物，包括零售包装）	5	30		15	17	千克	L	Single preparation containing boldenone, including their derivatives and structural analogues, put up in measured doses, packings for retail sale
3004 3200.22	已配剂量含勃二酮的单方制剂（包括其衍生物及结构类似物，包括零售包装）	5	30		15	17	千克	L	Single preparation containing androstadien-3,17-dione , including their derivatives and structural analogues, put up in measured doses, packings for retail sale
3004 3200.23	已配剂量含卡芦睾酮或达那唑的单方制剂（包括其衍生物及结构类似物，包括零售包装）	5	30		15	17	千克	L	Single preparation containing calusterone or danazol, including their derivatives and structural analogues, put up in measured doses, packings for retail sale
3004 3200.24	已配剂量含氯司替勃的单方制剂（包括其衍生物及结构类似物，包括零售包装）	5	30		15	17	千克	L	Single preparation containing clostebol, including their derivatives and structural analogues, put up in measured doses, packings for retail sale
3004 3200.25	已配剂量含脱氢氯甲睾酮的单方制剂（包括其衍生物及结构类似物，包括零售包装）	5	30		15	17	千克	L	Single preparation containing dehydrochlorme-thyltestosterone, including their derivatives and structural analogues, put up in measured doses, packings for retail sale
3004 3200.28	已配剂量含普拉睾酮或屈他雄酮的单方制剂（包括其衍生物及结构类似物，包括零售包装）	5	30		15	17	千克	L	Single preparation containing prasterone or dromostan-olone, including their derivatives and structural analogues, put up in measured doses, packings for retail sale
3004 3200.29	已配剂量含去氧甲睾酮或双氢睾酮的单方制剂（包括其衍生物及结构类似物，包括零售包装）	5	30		15	17	千克	L	Single preparation containing deoxymethyl testosterone or stanolone, and their derivatives and structural analogues, put up in measured doses, packings for retail sale
3004 3200.31	已配剂量含表双氢睾酮或氟甲睾酮的单方制剂（包括其衍生物及结构类似物，包括零售包装）	5	30		15	17	千克	L	Single preparation containing epidihydrotestosterone or fluoxymesterone, and their derivatives and structural analogues, put up in measured doses, packings for retail sale
3004 3200.32	已配剂量含夫拉扎勃的单方制剂（包括其衍生物及结构类似物，包括零售包装）	5	30		15	17	千克	L	Single preparation containing furazabol, and their derivatives and structural analogues, in measured doses, packings for retail sale
3004 3200.33	已配剂量含孕三烯酮或 4-羟基睾酮的单方制剂（包括其衍生物及结构类似物，包括零售包装）	5	30		15	17	千克	L	Single preparation containing gestrinone or 4-hydroxyandrostenedione, and their derivatives and struct- ural analogues, put up in measured doses,

税则号列 Tariff Item	商品名称及备注	进口税率 最惠	进口税率 普通	进口税率 暂定	出口退税	增值税率	计量单位	监管条件	Article Description
									packings for retail sale
3004 3200.34	含 3α-羟基-5α-雄烷-17-酮的单方制剂（包括其衍生物及结构类似物，已配剂量或制成零售包装）	5	30		15	17	千克	L	Single preparation containing 3α-hydroxide-5α-androstane-17-fraxinellone,and their derivatives and structural analogues, put up in measured doses, packings for retail sale
3004 3200.35	已配剂量含美睾酮或美雄酮的单方制剂（包括其衍生物及结构类似物，包括零售包装）	5	30		15	17	千克	L	Single preparation containing mestanolone or Metandienone, and their derivatives and structural analogues, put up in measured doses, packings for retail sale
3004 3200.36	已配剂量含甲基屈他雄酮的单方制剂(包括其衍生物及结构类似物. 包括零售包装)	5	30		15	17	千克	L	Single preparation ontaining17a-Methyl-Drostanolone , and their derivatives, structural analogues, in measured doses, packings for retail sale
3004 3200.37	已配剂量含甲二烯诺龙的单方制剂(包括其衍生物及结构类似物, 包括零售包装)	5	30		15	17	千克	L	Single preparation containing 17α- methyl-17β-hydroxy-estr-4,9(10)-di-3-ketone, including their derivatives and structural analogues, put up in measured doses, packings for retail sale
3004 3200.38	已配剂量含甲基-1-睾酮或甲诺睾酮的单方制剂(包括其衍生物及结构类似物, 包括零售包装)	5	30		15	17	千克	L	Single preparation containing methyl-1-testosterone or methylnortestosterone, and their derivatives and structural analogues, in measured doses, packings for retail sale
3004 3200.39	已配剂量含美曲勃龙的单方制剂(包括其衍生物及结构类似物, 包括零售包装)	5	30		15	17	千克	L	Single preparation containing Methyltrienolone, and their derivatives and structural analogues, put up in measured doses, packings for retail sale
3004 3200.41	已配剂量含美雄诺龙或美替诺龙的单方制剂（包括其衍生物及结构类似物，包括零售包装）	5	30		15	17	千克	L	Single preparation containing mestanolone or methenolone, and their derivatives and structural analogues, put up in measured doses, packings for retail sale
3004 3200.42	已配剂量含美雄醇或甲睾酮或米勃酮的单方制剂（包括其衍生物及结构类似物，包括零售包装）	5	30		15	17	千克	L	Single preparation containing methandriol or methyltestosterone or mibloerone, and their derivatives and structural analogues, put up in measured doses, packings for retail sale
3004 3200.43	已配剂量含诺龙或诺勃酮或诺司替勃的单方制剂（包括其衍生物及结构类似物，包括零售包装）	5	30		15	17	千克	L	Single preparation containing nandrolone or norboletone or norclostebol, and their derivatives and structural analogues, put up in measured doses, packings for retail sale
3004 3200.44	已配剂量含 19-去甲雄烯二酮的单方制剂(包括其衍生物及结构类似物, 包括零售包装)	5	30		15	17	千克	L	Single preparation containing 19-Norandrostendione, and their derivatives and structural analogues, in measured doses, packings for retail sale
3004 3200.45	已配剂量含去甲雄酮或诺乙雄龙的单方制剂（包括其衍生物及结枯类似物，包括零售包装）	5	30		15	17	千克	L	Single preparation containing norandrosterone or norethandrolone, and their derivatives and structural analogues, put up in measured doses, packings for retail sale
3004 3200.46	已配剂量含 19-去甲胆烷醇酮的单方制剂(包括其衍生物及结构类似物, 包括零售包装)	5	30		15	17	千克	L	Single preparation containing19-noretiocholanolone, and their derivatives and structural analogues, put up in measured doses, packings for retail sale
3004 3200.47	已配剂量含羟勃龙或氧雄龙的单方制剂(包括其衍生物及结构类似物, 包括零售包装)	5	30		15	17	千克	L	Single preparation containing oxabolone or oxandrolone, and their derivatives and structural analogues, put up in measured doses, packings for retail sale
3004 3200.48	已配剂量含羟甲睾酮或羟甲烯龙的单方制剂（包括其衍生物及结构类似物，包括零售包装）	5	30		15	17	千克	L	Single preparation containing oxymesterone or oxymetholone, and their derivatives and structural analogues, put up in measured doses, packings for retail sale
3004 3200.49	已配剂量含前列他唑的单方制剂(包括其衍生物及结构类似物, 包括零售包装)	5	30		15	17	千克	L	Single preparation containing17β-hydroxy-5α-androstane〔3,2-c〕pyrazole, and their derivatives and structuralanalogues, put up in measured doses,

税则号列 Tariff Item	商品名称及备注	进口税率			出口退税	增值税率	计量单位	监管条件	Article Description
		最惠	普通	暂定					
									packings for retail sale
3004 3200.51	含奎勃龙或替勃龙或群勃龙的单方制剂(包括其衍生物及结构类似物，已配剂量或制成零售包装)	5	30		15	17	千克	L	Single preparation containing quinbolone or tibolone or trenbolone, and their derivatives and structural analogues, put up in measured doses, packings for retail sale
3004 3200.52	已配剂量含司坦唑醇或司腾勃龙的单方制剂(包括其衍生物及结构类似物，包括零售包装)	5	30		15	17	千克	L	Single preparation containing Stanozolol or stenbolone, and their derivatives and structural analogues, put up in measured doses, packings for retail sale
3004 3200.53	已配剂量含 1-睾酮或睾酮的单方制剂(包括其衍生物及结构类似物，包括零售包装)	5	30		15	17	千克	L	Single preparation containing 1-testosterone or testosterone, and their derivatives and structural analogues, put up in measured doses, packings for retail sale
3004 3200.54	已配剂量含四氢孕三烯酮或泽仑诺的单方制剂(包括其衍生物及结构类似物，包括零售包装)	5	30		15	17	千克	L	Single preparation containing tetrahydrogestrinone or zeranol, and their derivatives and structural analogues, put up in measured doses, packings for retail sale
3004 3200.60	兽用已配剂量倍他米松戊酸酯制剂(包括其衍生物及结构类似物,包括零售包装)	5	30		15	17	千克	R	Betamethasone 17-valerate for livestock, put up in measured doses or in forms of packings for retail sale, including their derivatives and structural analogues
3004 3200.71	已配剂量含雄甾-5-烯-3β，17β-二醇的单方制剂(包括其衍生物及结构类似物,不含抗菌素，包括零售包装)	5	30		15	17	千克	L	Single preparations containing 5 - Androstenediol (3β, 17β- diol (including its derivatives and structural analogues without antibiotics, packings for retail sale)
3004 3200.72	已配剂量含雄甾-4-烯-3,17-二酮的单方制剂(包括其衍生物及结构类似物,不含抗菌素，包括零售包装)	5	30		15	17	千克	L	Single preparations containing 4 – androstenedione-3, 17-dione (including their derivatives and structural analogues, without antibiotics, packings for retail sale)
3004 3200.73	已配剂量含勃雄二醇的单方制剂(包括其衍生物及结构类似物,不含抗菌素，包括零售包装)	5	30		15	17	千克	L	Single preparations containing Bolandiol (including their derivatives and structural analogues without antibiotics, packings for retail sale)
3004 3200.74	已配剂量含 7α-羟基-普拉睾酮的单方制剂(包括其衍生物及结构类似物,不含抗菌素，包括零售包装)	5	30		15	17	千克	L	Single preparation containing 7α-hydroxy-DHEA (including their derivatives and structural analogues, without antibiotics, packings for retail sale)
3004 3200.75	已配剂量含 7β-羟基-普拉睾酮的单方制剂(包括其衍生物及结构类似物,不含抗菌素，包括零售包装)	5	30		15	17	千克	L	Single preparations containing 7β-hydroxy-DHEA (including their derivatives and structural analogues, without antibiotics, packings for retail sale)
3004 3200.76	已配剂量含 7-羰基-普拉睾酮的单方制剂(包括其衍生物及结构类似物,不含抗菌素，包括零售包装)	5	30		15	17	千克	L	Single preparations containing 7-carbonyl Prasterone (including their derivatives and structural analogues, without antibiotics, packings for retail sale)
3004 3200.77	已配剂量含胆烷醇酮的单方制剂(包括其衍生物及结构类似物,不含抗菌素，包括零售包装)	5	30		15	17	千克	L	Single preparations containing Androstane (including their derivatives and structural analogues, without antibiotics, packings for retail sale)
3004 3200.90	已配剂量含其他皮质甾类激素的药品(包括其衍生物及结构类似物，不含抗菌素，包括零售包装)	5	30		15	17	千克	Q	Drugs containing corticosteroid hormone, and their derivatives and structural analogues, without antibiotics, put up in measured doses, packings for retail sale
3004.3900	--其他	5	30		15	17	千克		--Other
3004 3900.11	已配剂量含克仑特罗的单方制剂(包括零售包装)	5	30		15	17	千克	L	Single preparation containing clenbuterol, put up in measured doses, packings for retail sale
3004 3900.22	已配剂量含生长激素(GH)的单方制剂(包括零售包装)	5	30		15	17	千克	L	Single preparation containing growth hormone, in measured doses, packings for retail sale

税则号列 Tariff Item	商品名称及备注	进口税率 最惠	进口税率 普通	进口税率 暂定	出口退税	增值税率	计量单位	监管条件	Article Description
3004 3900.25	已配剂量含绒促性素及促黄体生成素的单方制剂(包括零售包装)	5	30		15	17	千克	L	Single preparation containing gonadotrophins, in measured doses, packings for retail sale
3004 3900.26	已配剂量含促皮质素的单方制剂（包括零售包装）	5	30		15	17	千克	L	Single preparation containing corticotrophins, in measured doses, packings for retail sale
3004 3900.30	兽用血促性素、绒促性素制剂(包括零售包装)	5	30		15	17	千克	R	Serum gonadotrophin and Chorionic Gonadotropin for livestock, in forms of packings for retail sale
3004 3900.90	其他已配剂量含激素或品目29.37产品的药品(不含抗菌素，包括零售包装）	5	30		15	17	千克	Q	Other drugs containing hormones or products of heading No.29.37, without antibiotics, put up in measured doses, packings for retail sale
	-含有生物碱及其衍生物，但不含抗菌素及品目29.37的激素或其他产品:								-Containing alkaloids or derivatives thereof but not containing hormones, other products of heading No.29. 37 or antibiotics:
3004.4010	---含有奎宁或其盐	5	35		15	17	千克	Q	---Containing quinine or its salts
3004.4090	---其他	5	30		15	17	千克		---Other
3004 4090.10	麻黄碱盐类单方制剂［指盐酸（伪）麻黄碱片、盐酸麻黄碱注射剂、硫酸麻黄碱片］	5	30		15	17	千克	23Q	Single preparations, containing ephedrine and its salts（Ephedrine, ephedrine hydrochloride injection or ephedrine sulfate tablet）
3004 4090.20	含可待因及衍生物及盐的复方制剂（已配定剂量或制成零售包装）	5	30		15	17	千克	I	Compound preparations, containing codeine, its derivatives and salts, put up in measured doses, packings for retail sale
3004 4090.31	丁丙诺啡透皮贴剂(包括其衍生物，已配定剂量或制成零售包装)	5	30		15	17	千克	I	Buprenorfin transdermal patch, and its derivatives, put up in measured doses, packings for retail sale
3004 4090.39	其他含生物碱类精神药品的单方制剂(包括其衍生物，已配定剂量或制成零售包装)	5	30		15	17	千克	I	Other single preparations, containing alkaloids spirit drug and its derivatives, put up in measured doses, packings for retail sale
3004 4090.40	含生物碱类麻醉药品的单方制剂（包括其衍生物，已配定剂量或制成零售包装）	5	30		15	17	千克	W	Single preparations, containing alkaloids narcotic drugs and its derivatives, put up in measured doses, packings for retail sale
3004 4090.50	吗啡阿托品注射液	5	30		15	17	千克	W	Morphine and atropine sulfate injection
3004 4090.61	含有氨酚氢可酮片或其盐	5	30		15	17	千克	I	Paracetamol and hydrocodone bitartrate tablet or its salt
3004 4090.62	含有麦角胺咖啡因片/安钠咖或其盐	5	30		15	17	千克	I	Ergotamine and caffeine tablet or caffeine and sodium benzoate or its salt
3004 4090.63	阿桔片、复方甘草片(含阿片粉，已配定剂量或制成零售包装)	5	30		15	17	千克	I	Compound Platycodon and Liquorice tablets with powdered opium, put up in measured doses or in forms of packings for retail sale
3004 4090.70	氨酚双氢可待因片	5	30		15	17	千克	I	Paracetamol and dihydrocodeine tablets
3004 4090.90	已配剂量含有其他生物碱等的药品（不含抗菌素及品目29.37的激素或其他产品，包括零售包装）	5	30		15	17	千克	Q	Drugs containing other alkaloids or derivatives thereof but not containing hormones, other products of heading No.29.37 or antibiotics:
3004.5000	-含有维生素或品目29.36所列产品的其他药品	6	40		15	17	千克	Q	-Other medicaments containing vitamins or other products of heading No.29.36
	-其他:								-Other:
3004.9010	---含有磺胺类	6	40		15	17	千克	Q	---Containing sulfa drugs
3004.9020	---含有联苯双酯	4	30		15	17	千克	Q	---Containing biphenyl dicarbxybte
	---中式成药:								---Medicaments of Chinese type:
3004.9051	----中药酒	3	30			17	千克		----Medicated liquors or wines
3004 9051.10	含濒危动植物成分的中药酒（已配定剂量或零售包装）	3	30			17	千克	FE	Medicated liquors or wines, containing composition endangered animal or vegetables, put up in measured doses, packings for retail sale
3004 9051.90	含其他成分的中药酒（已配定剂量或零售包装）	3	30		15	17	千克		Medicated liquors or wines, containing composition other composition, put up in measured doses, packings for retail sale

税则号列 Tariff Item	商品名称及备注	进口税率 最惠	普通	暂定	出口退税	增值税率	计量单位	监管条件	Article Description
3004.9052	----片仔癀	3	30		15	17	千克	QFE	----Pien Tzu Huang
3004.9053	----白药	3	30		15	17	千克		----Bai Yao
3004 9053.10	含天然麝香的白药(已配定剂量或零售包装)	3	30		15	17	千克	FEQ	Baiyao with natural musk (put up in measured doses, packings for retail sale)
3004 9053.90	含人工麝香的白药(已配定剂量或零售包装)	3	30		15	17	千克	Q	Baiyao with artificial musk (put up in measured doses, packings for retail sale)
3004.9054	----清凉油	3	30		15	17	千克	Q	----Essential balm
3004.9055	----安宫牛黄丸	3	30			17	千克		----Angong niuhuang wan
3004 9055.10	含天然麝香的安宫牛黄丸(已配定剂量或零售包装)	3	30			17	千克	QFE	Angong niuhuang wan containing natural musk (put up in measured doses, packing for retail sale)
3004 9055.90	其他安宫牛黄丸(已配定剂量或零售包装)	3	30		15	17	千克	Q	Other angong niuhuang wan (put up in measured doses, packing for retail sale)
3004.9059	----其他	3	30			17	千克		----Other
3004 9059.10	含濒危动植物成分的中式成药(已配定剂量或零售包装)	3	30			17	千克	QFE	Medicaments of Chinese style, containing endangered animal or vegetables, put up in measured doses, packings for retail sale
3004 9059.90	含其他成分的中式成药(已配定剂量或零售包装)	3	30		15	17	千克	Q	Medicaments of Chinese style, containing other composition, put up in measured doses, packings for retail sale
3004.9060	---含有青蒿素及其衍生物	4	30		17	17	千克	Q	---Containing artemisinins and their derivatives
3004.9090	---其他	4	30			17	千克		---Other
3004 9090.10	含濒危野生动植物成分的药品(已配定剂量或零售包装,不含紫杉醇)	4	30			17	千克	FEQ	Medicaments containing composition of endangered animal or vegetable,without taxinol, put up in measured doses, packings for retail sale
3004 9090.20	含紫杉醇成分的药品(已配定剂量或制成零售包装)	4	30			17	千克	EFQ	Medicaments containing paclitaxel, put up in measured doses, packings for retail sale
3004 9090.30	其他含第29章麻醉药品的单方制剂(已配定剂量或制成零售包装)	4	30		15	17	千克	W	Other single preparations containing narcotic drugs of Chapter 29, put up in measured doses, packings for retail sale
3004 9090.41	地芬诺酯复方制剂(已配定剂量或制成零售包装)	4	30		15	17	千克	I	Compound preparation of Diphenoxylate, put up in measured doses or packings for retail sale
3004 9090.49	其他含第29章精神药品的单方制剂(已配定剂量或制成零售包装)	4	30		15	17	千克	I	Other single preparations containing psychotropic substances of Chapter 29, put up in measured doses or packings for retail sale
3004 9090.50	含右丙氧芬及其盐的复方制剂(已配定剂量或制成零售包装)	4	30		15	17	千克	I	Compound preparations containing propoxyphene and its salts, put up in measured doses, packings for retail sale
3004 9090.60	复方樟脑酊(含阿片酊、樟脑、苯甲酸、八角茴香油等,包括零售包装)	4	30		15	17	千克	W	Compound camphor tineture (Tincture of opium, camphor, Benzoic acid, Anise Oil) , packings for retail sale
3004 9090.71	已配剂量含雄甾-4-烯-3α,17β-二醇的单方制剂(包括零售包装)	4	30		15	17	千克	L	Single preparation,containing 4-Androstenediol -3α, 17β-diol , put up in measured doses, packings for retail sale
3004 9090.72	已配剂量含雄甾-5-烯-3α,17α-二醇的单方制剂(包括零售包装)	4	30		15	17	千克	L	Single preparation,containing 5-Androstenediol -3α, 17α-diol, put up in measured doses, packings for retail sale
3004 9090.73	已配剂量含雄甾-5-烯-3α,17β-二醇的单方制剂(包括零售包装)	4	30		15	17	千克	L	Single preparation,containing 5-Androstenediol -3α, 17β-diol, put up in measured doses, packings for retail sale
3004 9090.74	已配剂量含5α-雄烷-3α,17α-二醇(阿法雄烷二醇)或雄甾-4-烯-3α,17α-二醇的单方制剂(包括零售包装)	4	30		15	17	千克	L	Single preparation,containing α-androstane diol or 4-Androstenediol -3α, 17β-diol, put up in measured doses, packings for retail sale
3004 9090.75	已配剂量含5α-雄烷-3β,17β-二醇(倍他雄烷二醇)的单	4	30		15	17	千克	L	Single preparation, containing 5-Androstenediol -3α, 17β-diol, put up in measured doses, packings for retail

税则号列 Tariff Item	商品名称及备注	进口税率 最惠	进口税率 普通	进口税率 暂定	出口退税	增值税率	计量单位	监管条件	Article Description
	方制剂(包括零售包装)								sale
3004 9090.77	含3β-羟基-5α-雄烷-17-酮的单方制剂(已配剂量或制成零售包装)	4	30		15	17	千克	L	Single preparation, containing 3β-hydroxy-5α-androstane -17-ketone, put up in measured doses, packings for retail sale
3004 9090.78	已配剂量含齐帕特罗的单方制剂(包括零售包装)	4	30		15	17	千克	L	Single preparation, containing zilpaterol, put up in measured doses, packings for retail sale
3004 9090.79	已配剂量含表睾酮的单方制剂(包括零售包装)	4	30		15	17	千克	L	Single preparations containing epitestosterone, put up in measured doses or packings for retail sale
3004 9090.81	兽用已配剂量含右旋糖苷铁、替泊沙林、布他磷制剂(包括零售包装)	4	30		15	17	千克	R	Preparations containing Iron dextran, Tepoxalin and Butafosfan for livestock, put up in measured doses or in forms of packings for retail sale
3004 9090.82	兽用已配剂量含硝碘酚腈、氟尼辛葡甲胺、美洛昔康制剂(包括零售包装)	4	30		15	17	千克	R	Preparations containing Nitroxinil , Flunixin meglumine and meloxicam for livestock, put up in measured doses or in forms of packings for retail sale
3004 9090.90	其他已配定剂量的药品(包括零售包装)	4	30		15	17	千克	Q	Other medicaments, put up in measured doses, packings for retail sale
30.05	**软填料、纱布、绷带及类似物品(例如,敷料、橡皮膏、泥罨剂),经过药物浸涂或制成零售包装供医疗、外科、牙科或兽医用:**								**Wadding, gauze, bandages and similar articles(for example, dressings, adhesive plasters, poultices), impregnated or coated with pharmaceutical substances or put up in forms or packings for retail sale for medical, surgical, dental or veterinary purposes:**
	-胶粘敷料及有胶粘涂层的其他物品:								-Adhesive dressings and other articles having an adhesive layer:
3005.1010	---橡皮膏	5	70		15	17	千克		---Adhesive plasters
3005.1090	---其他	5	35		15	17	千克		---Other
	-其他:								-Other:
3005.9010	---药棉、纱布、绷带	5	70		15	17	千克		---Absorbent cotton, gauze, bandages
3005.9090	---其他	5	35		15	17	千克		---Other
30.06	**本章注释四所规定的医药用品:**								**Pharmaceutical goods specified in Note 4 to this Chapter:**
3006.1000	-无菌外科肠线、类似的无菌缝合材料(包括外科或牙科用无菌可吸收缝线)及外伤创口闭合用的无菌粘合胶布;无菌昆布及无菌昆布塞条;外科或牙科用无菌吸收性止血材料;外科或牙科用无菌抗粘连阻隔材料,不论是否可吸收	5	30		15	17	千克		-Sterile surgical catgut, similar sterile suture materials (including sterile absorbable surgical or dental yarns) and sterile tissue adhesives for surgical wound closure; sterile laminaria and sterile laminaria tents; sterile absorbable surgical or dental haemostatics; sterile surgical or dental adhesion barriers,whether or not absorbable
3006.2000	-血型试剂	3	20		15	17	千克	AB	-Blood-grouping reagents
3006.3000	-X光检查造影剂;用于病人的诊断试剂	4	30		15	17	千克	AB	-Opacifying preparations for Xray examinations; diagnostic reagents designed to be administered to the patient
3006.4000	-牙科粘固剂及其他牙科填料;骨骼粘固剂	5	30		15	17	千克		-Dental cements and other dental fillings;bone reconstruction cements
3006.5000	-急救药箱、药包	5	30		15	17	千克		-First-aid boxes and kits
	-以激素,品目29.37的其他产品或杀精子剂为基本成分的化学避孕药物:								-Chemical contraceptive preparations based on hormones, on other products of heading 29.37 or on spermicides:
3006.6010	---以激素为基本成分的避孕药	0	0				千克	Q	---Contraceptive preparations based on hormones
3006.6090	---其他	0	0				千克	Q	---Other
3006.7000	-专用于人类或作兽药用的凝胶制品,作为外科手术或体检时躯体部位的润滑剂,或者作为躯体和医疗器械之间的耦合剂	6.5	30		15	17	千克		-Gel preparations designed to be used in human or veterinary medicine as a lubricant for parts of the body for surgical operations or physical examinations or as a coupling agent between the body and medical instruments

税则号列 Tariff Item	商品名称及备注	进口税率			出口退税	增值税率	计量单位	监管条件	Article Description
		最惠	普通	暂定					
	-其他:								-Other:
3006.9100	--可确定用于造口术的用具	10	80		15	17	千克		--Appliances identifiable for ostomy use
3006.9200	--废药物	5	30		15	17	千克	9	--Waste pharmaceuticals

第三十一章
肥　料

注释：

一、本章不包括：

（一）品目 05.11 的动物血；

（二）单独的已有化学定义的化合物[符合下列注释二（一）、三（一）、四（一）或五所规定的化合物除外]；或

（三）品目 38.24 的每颗重量不低于 2.5 克的氯化钾培养晶体（光学元件除外）；氯化钾光学元件（品目 90.01）。

二、品目 31.02 只适用于下列货品，但未制成品目 31.05 所述形状或包装：

（一）符合下列任何一条规定的货品：

1. 硝酸钠，不论是否纯净；
2. 硝酸铵，不论是否纯净；
3. 硫酸铵及硝酸铵的复盐，不论是否纯净；
4. 硫酸铵，不论是否纯净；
5. 硝酸钙及硝酸铵的复盐（不论是否纯净）或硝酸钙及硝酸铵的混合物；
6. 硝酸钙及硝酸镁的复盐（不论是否纯净）或硝酸钙及硝酸镁的混合物；
7. 氰氨化钙，不论是否纯净或用油处理；
8. 尿素，不论是否纯净。

（二）由上述（一）款任何货品相互混合的肥料。

（三）由氯化铵或上述（一）或（二）款任何货品与白垩、石膏或其他无肥效无机物混合而成的肥料。

（四）由上述（一）2 或 8 项的货品或其混合物溶于水或液氨的液体肥料。

三、品目 31.03 只适用于下列货品，但未制成品目 31.05 所述形状或包装：

（一）符合下列任何一条规定的货品：

1. 碱性熔渣；
2. 品目 25.10 的天然磷酸盐，已焙烧或经过超出清除杂质范围的热处理；
3. 过磷酸钙（一过磷酸钙、二过磷酸钙或三过磷酸钙）；
4. 磷酸氢钙，按干燥无水产品重量计含氟量不低于 0.2%。

（二）由上述（一）款的任何货品相互混合的肥料，不论含氟量多少。

（三）由上述（一）或（二）款的任何货品与白垩、石膏或其他无肥效无机物混合而成的肥料，不论含氟量多少。

四、品目 31.04 只适用于下列货品，但未制成品目 31.05 所述形状或包装：

（一）符合下列任何一条规定的货品：

Chapter 31
Fertilisers

Chapter Notes:

1. This Chapter does not cover:

(a) Animal blood of heading 05.11;

(b) Separate chemically defined compounds [other than those answering to the descriptions in Note 2 (a), 3 (a), 4 (a) or 5 below]; or

(c) Cultured potassium chloride crystals (other than optical elements) weighing not less than 2.5g each, of heading 38.24;optical elements of potassium chloride (heading 90.01).

2. Heading 31.02 applies only to the following goods, provided that they are not put up in the forms or packages described in heading 31.05:

(a) Goods which answer to one or other of the descriptions given below:

(i) Sodium nitrate, whether or not pure;

(ii) Ammonium nitrate, whether or not pure;

(iii) Double salts, whether or not pure, of ammonium sulphate and ammonium nitrate;

(iv) Ammonium sulphate, whether or not pure;

(v) Double salts (whether or not pure) or mixtures of calcium nitrate and ammonium nitrate;

(vi) Double salts (whether or not pure) or mixtures of calcium nitrate and magnesium nitrate;

(vii) Calcium cyanamide, whether or not pure or treated with oil;

(viii) Urea, whether or not pure.

(b) Fertilisers consisting of any of the goods described in (a) above mixed together.

(c) Fertilisers consisting of ammonium chloride or of any of the goods described in (a) or (b) above mixed with chalk, gypsum or other inorganic non-fertilising substances.

(d) Liquid fertilisers consisting of the goods of subparagraph (a) (ii) or (viii) above, or of mixtures of those goods, in an aqueous or ammoniacal solution.

3. Heading 31.03 applies only to the following goods, provided that they are not put up in the forms or packages described in heading 31.05:

(a) Goods which answer to one or other of the descriptions given below:

(i) Basic slag;

(ii) Natural phosphates of heading 25.10, calcined or further heat-treated than for the removal of impurities;

(iii) Superphosphates (single, double or triple);

(iv) Calcium hydrogenorthophosphate containing not less than 0.2% by weight of fluorine calculated on the dry anhydrous product.

(b) Fertilisers consisting of any of the goods described in (a) above mixed together, but with no account being taken of the fluorine content limit.

(c) Fertilisers consisting of any of the goods described in (a) or (b) above, but with no account being taken of the fluorine content limit, mixed with chalk, gypsum or other inorganic non-fertilising substances.

4. Heading 31.04 applies only to the following goods, provided that they are not put up in the forms or packages described in heading 31.05:

(a) Goods which answer to one or other of the descriptions given below:

1. 天然粗钾盐（例如，光卤石、钾盐镁矾及钾盐）；
2. 氯化钾，不论是否纯净，但上述注释一（三）所述的产品除外；
3. 硫酸钾，不论是否纯净；
4. 硫酸镁钾，不论是否纯净。

（二）由上述（一）款任何货品相互混合的肥料。

五、磷酸二氢铵及磷酸氢二铵（不论是否纯净）及其相互之间的混合物应归入品目31.05。

六、品目31.05所称“其他肥料”，仅适用于其基本成分至少含有氮、磷、钾中一种肥效元素的肥料用产品。

（i）Crude natural potassium salts（for example, carnallite,kainite and sylvite）;

（ii）Potassium chloride, whether or not pure, except as provided in Note 1（c）above;

（iii）Potassium sulphate, whether or not pure;

（iv）Magnesium potassium sulphate, whether or not pure.

（b)Fertilisers consisting of any of the goods described in(a)above mixed together.

5. Ammonium dihydrogenorthophosphate（monoammonium phosphate）and diammonium hydrogenorthophosphate（diammonium phosphate）, whether or not pure, and intermixtures thereof, are to be classified in heading 31.05.

6. For the purposes of heading 31.05, the term “other fertilisers” applies only to products of a kind used as fertilisers and containing, as an essential constituent, at least one of the fertilising elements nitrogen, phosphorus or potassium.

税则号列 Tariff Item	商品名称及备注	进口税率 最惠	进口税率 普通	进口税率 暂定	出口退税	增值税率	计量单位	监管条件	Article Description
31.01	**动物或植物肥料，不论是否相互混合或经化学处理；动植物产品经混合或化学处理制成的肥料：**								**Animal or vegetable fertilizers, whether or not mixed together or chemically treated; fertilizers produced by the mixing or chemical treatment of animal or vegetable products:**
	---未经化学处理：								---Not chemically treated:
3101.0011	----鸟粪	3	11			13	千克	AB	----Guano
3101.0019	----其他	6.5	30			13	千克		----Other
3101 0019.10	未经化学处理的森林凋落物（包括腐叶、腐根、树皮、树叶、树根等森林腐殖质）	6.5	30			13	千克	8AB	Forest litter, not chemically treated, including rotten leaves, rotten roots, bark, leaves,roots and forest humus
3101 0019.90	未经化学处理的其他动植物肥料	6.5	30			13	千克	AB	Other animal and vegetable fertilizer, not chemically treated
3101.0090	---其他	4	11			13	千克		---Other
3101 0090.10	经化学处理的含动物源性成分(如粪、羽毛等)动植物肥料	4	11			13	千克	AB	Animal or vegetable fertilizer, chemically treated, containing composition of animal origin
3101 0090.20	经化学处理的森林凋落物（包括腐叶、腐根、树皮、树叶、树根等森林腐殖质）	4	11			13	千克	8AB	Animal or vegetable litter, chemically treated, including rotten leaves, rotten roots, bark, leaves, roots and forest humus
3101 0090.90	经化学处理的其他动植物肥料	4	11			13	千克	AB	Other animal or vegetable fertilizer, chemically treated
31.02	**矿物氮肥及化学氮肥：**								**Mineral or chemical fertilizers, nitrogenous:**
3102.1000	-尿素，不论是否水溶液		150			13	千克		-Urea, whether or not in aqueous solution
3102 1000.01	尿素（配额内，不论是否水溶液）	4	150			13	千克	tA	Urea, whether or not in aqueous solution, in-quota
3102 1000.90	尿素（配额外，不论是否水溶液）	50	150			13	千克	A	Urea, whether or not in aqueous solution, out-of-quota
	-硫酸铵；硫酸铵和硝酸铵的复盐及混合物：								-Ammonium sulphate; double salts and mixtures of ammonium sulphate and ammonium nitrate:
3102.2100	--硫酸铵	4	11			13	千克	7AB	--Ammonium sulphate
3102.2900	--其他	4	11			13	千克	7	--Other
3102.3000	-硝酸铵，不论是否水溶液	4	11			13	千克	9	-Ammonium nitrate, whether or not in aqueous solution
3102.4000	-硝酸铵与碳酸钙或其他无肥效无机物的混合物	4	11			13	千克	7	-Mixtures of ammonium nitrate with calcium carbonate or other inorganic nonfertilizing substances
3102.5000	-硝酸钠	4	11			13	千克	7AB	-Sodium nitrate
3102.6000	-硝酸钙和硝酸铵的复盐及混合物	4	11			13	千克	7	-Double salts and mixtures of calcium nitrate and ammonium nitrate

税则号列 Tariff Item	商品名称及备注	进口税率			出口退税	增值税率	计量单位	监管条件	Article Description
		最惠	普通	暂定					
3102.8000	-尿素及硝酸铵混合物的水溶液或氨水溶液	4	11			13	千克	7	-Mixtures of urea and ammonium nitrate in aqueous or ammoniacal solution
	-其他，包括上述子目未列名的混合物:								-Other, including mixtures not specified in the foregoing subheadings:
3102.9010	---氰氨化钙	4	11			13	千克	7AB	---Calcium cyanamide
3102.9090	---其他	4	11			13	千克	7	---Other
31.03	**矿物磷肥及化学磷肥:**								**Mineral or chemical fertilizers, phosphatic:**
	-过磷酸钙:								-Superphosphates:
3103.1010[暂]	---重过磷酸钙	4	11	1		13	千克	7A	---Triple superphosphates
3103.1090[暂]	---其他	4	11	1		13	千克	7A	---Other
3103.9000[暂]	-其他	4	11	1		13	千克	7	-Other
31.04	**矿物钾肥及化学钾肥:**								**Mineral or chemical fertilizers, potassic:**
	-氯化钾:								-Potassium chloride:
3104.2020	---纯氯化钾(按重量计氧化钾含量≥99.5%)	3	11			13	千克	7A	---Pure potassium chloride, containing ≥99.5% by weight of hydroxide
3104.2090[暂]	---其他	3	11	1		13	千克	7AB	---Other
3104.3000[暂]	-硫酸钾	3	11	1		13	千克	7A	-Potassium sulphate
	-其他:								-Other:
3104.9010[暂]	---光卤石、钾盐及其他天然粗钾盐	3	11	1		13	千克	7	---Carnallite, sylvite and other crude natural potassium salts
3104.9090[暂]	---其他	3	11	1		13	千克	7	---Other
31.05	**含氮、磷、钾中两种或三种肥效元素的矿物肥料或化学肥料；其他肥料；制成片及类似形状或每包毛重不超过10千克的本章各项货品:**								**Mineral or chemical fertilizers containing two or three of the fertilizing elements nitrogen, phosphorus and potassium; other fertilizers; goods of this Chapter in tablets or similar forms or in packages of a gross weight not exceeding 10kg:**
3105.1000[暂]	-制成片及类似形状或每包毛重不超过10千克的本章各项货品	4	11	1		13	千克		-Goods of this Chapter in tablets or similar forms or in packages of a gross weight not exceeding 10kg
3105 1000.10[暂]	制成片状及类似形状或零售包装的硝酸铵（零售包装每包毛重不超过10千克）	4	11	1		13	千克	9	Ammonium nitrate, in tablets or similar forms or in packages for retail sale, of a gross weight not exceeding 10kg
3105 1000.90[暂]	制成片状及类似形状或零售包装的第31章其他货品(零售包装每包毛重不超过10千克)	4	11	1		13	千克	7	Other goods of the Chapter 31, in tablets or similar forms or in packages for retail sale, of a gross weight not exceeding 10kg
3105.2000	-含氮、磷、钾三种肥效元素的矿物肥料或化学肥料		150			13	千克		-Mineral or chemical fertilizers containing the three fertilizing elements nitrogen, phosphorus and potassium
3105 2000.01	化学肥料或矿物肥料（配额内，含氮、磷、钾三种肥效元素）	4	150			13	千克	At	Mineral or chemical fertilizers containing the three fertilizing elements nitrogen, phosphorus and potassium, in-quota
3105 2000.90	化学肥料或矿物肥料（配额外，含氮、磷、钾三种肥效元素）	50	150			13	千克	A	Mineral or chemical fertilizers containing the three fertilizing elements nitrogen, phosphorus and potassium, out-of-quota
3105.3000	-磷酸氢二铵		150			13	千克		-Diammonium hydrogenorthophosphate（diammonium phosphate）
3105 3000.01	磷酸氢二铵（配额内）	4	150			13	千克	ABt	Diammonium hydrogenorthophosphate（diammonium phosphate), in-quota
3105 3000.90	磷酸氢二铵（配额外）	50	150			13	千克	AB	Diammonium hydrogenorthophosphate（diammonium phosphate), out-of-quota
3105.4000[暂]	-磷酸二氢铵及磷酸二氢铵与磷酸氢二铵的混合物	4	11	1		13	千克	7A	-Ammonium dihydrogenorthophosphate (monoammonium phosphate) and mixtures thereof with diammonium hydrogenorthophosphate（diammonium

税则号列 Tariff Item	商品名称及备注	进口税率			出口退税	增值税率	计量单位	监管条件	Article Description
		最惠	普通	暂定					
									phosphate）
	-其他含氮、磷两种肥效元素的矿物肥料或化学肥料:								-Other mineral or chemical fertilizers containingthe two fertilizing elements nitrogen and phosphorus:
3105.5100[暂]	--含有硝酸盐及磷酸盐	4	11	1		13	千克	7A	--Containing nitrates and phosphates
3105.5900[暂]	--其他	4	11	1		13	千克	7A	--Other
3105.6000[暂]	-含磷、钾两种肥效元素的矿物肥料或化学肥料	4	11	1		13	千克	7A	-Mineral or chemical fertilizers containing the two fertilizing elements phosphorus and potassium
3105.9000[暂]	-其他	4	11	1		13	千克	7A	-Other

第三十二章
鞣料浸膏及染料浸膏；鞣酸及其衍生物；染料、颜料及其他着色料；油漆及清漆；油灰及其他类似胶粘剂；墨水、油墨

注释：

一、本章不包括：

（一）单独的已有化学定义的化学元素及化合物（品目 32.03 及 32.04 的货品、品目 32.06 的用作发光体的无机产品、品目 32.07 所述形状的熔融石英或其他熔融硅石制成的玻璃及品目 32.12 的零售形状或零售包装的染料及其他着色料除外）；

（二）品目 29.36 至 29.39、29.41 及 35.01 至 35.04 的鞣酸盐及其他鞣酸衍生物；或

（三）沥青胶粘剂（品目 27.15）。

二、品目 32.04 包括生产偶氮染料用的稳定重氮盐与偶合物的混合物。

三、品目 32.03、32.04、32.05 及 32.06 也包括以着色料为基本成分的制品（例如，品目 32.06 包括以品目 25.30 或第二十八章的颜料，金属粉片及金属粉末为基本成分的制品）。该制品是用作原材料着色剂的拼料。但以上品目不包括分散在非水介质中呈液状或浆状的制漆用颜料，例如，品目 32.12 的瓷漆及品目 32.07、32.08、32.09、32.10、32.12、32.13 及 32.15 的其他制品。

四、品目 32.08 包括由品目 39.01 至 39.13 所列产品溶于挥发性有机溶剂的溶液（胶棉除外），但溶剂重量必须超过溶液重量的 50%。

五、本章所称“着色料”，不包括作为油漆填料的产品，不论这些产品能否用于水浆涂料的着色。

六、品目 32.12 所称“压印箔”，只包括用以压印诸如书本封面或帽带之类的薄片，这些薄片由以下材料构成：

（一）金属粉（包括贵金属粉）或颜料经胶水、明胶及其他黏合剂凝结而成的；或

（二）金属（包括贵金属）或颜料沉积于任何材料衬片上的。

Chapter 32
Tanning or dyeing extracts; tannins and their derivatives; dyes, pigments and other colouring matter; paints and varnishes; putty and other mastics; inks

Chapter Notes:

1. This Chapter does not cover:

(a) Separate chemically defined elements or compounds (except those of heading 32.03 or 32.04, inorganic products of a kind used as luminophores (heading 32.06), glass obtained from fused quartz or other fused silica in the forms provided for in heading 32.07, and also dyes and other colouring matter put up in forms or packings for retail sale, of heading 32.12);

(b) Tannates or other tannin derivatives of products of headings 29.36 to 29.39, 29.41 or 35.01 to 35.04; or

(c) Mastics of asphalt or other bituminous mastics (heading 27.15).

2. Heading 32.04 includes mixtures of stabilised diazonium salts and couplers for the production of azo dyes.

3. Headings 32.03, 32.04, 32.05 and 32.06 apply also to preparations based on colouring matter (including, in the case of heading 32.06, colouring pigments of heading 25.30 or Chapter 28, metal flakes and metal powders), of a kind used for colouring any material or used as ingredients in the manufacture of colouring preparations. The headings do not apply, however, to pigments dispersed in non-aqueous media, in liquid or paste form, of a kind used in the manufacture of paints, including enamels (heading 32.12), or to other preparations of heading 32.07, 32.08, 32.09, 32.10, 32.12, 32.13 or 32.15.

4. Heading 32.08 includes solutions (other than collodions) consisting of any of the products specified in headings 39.01 to 39.13 in volatile organic solvents when the weight of the solvent exceeds 50% of the weight of the solution.

5. The expression "colouring matter" in this Chapter does not include products of a kind used as extenders in oil paints, whether or not they are also suitable for colouring distempers.

6. The expression "stamping foils" in heading 32.12 applies only to thin sheets of a kind used for printing, for example, book covers or hat bands, and consisting of:

(a) Metallic powder (including powder of precious metal) or pigment, agglomerated with glue, gelatin or other binder; or

(b) Metal (including precious metal) or pigment, deposited on a supporting sheet of any material.

税则号列 Tariff Item	商品名称及备注	进口税率			出口退税	增值税率	计量单位	监管条件	Article Description
		最惠	普通	暂定					
32.01	植物鞣料浸膏；鞣酸及其盐、醚、酯和其他衍生物：								**Tanning extracts of vegetable origin; tannins and their salts, ethers, esters and other derivatives:**
3201.1000	-坚木浸膏	5	35			17	千克		-Quebracho extract
3201.2000	-荆树皮浸膏	6.5	35			17	千克		-Wattle extract
	-其他:								-Other:
3201.9010	---其他鞣料侵膏	6.5	40			17	千克		---Other tanning extracts
3201 9010.10	其他濒危植物鞣料浸膏	6.5	40			17	千克	FE	Other tanning extracts of endangered vegetable origin
3201 9010.90	其他植物鞣料浸膏	6.5	40			17	千克		Other tanning extracts of vegetable origin
3201.9090	---其他	6.5	35			17	千克		---Other

税则号列 Tariff Item	商品名称及备注	进口税率 最惠	普通	暂定	出口退税	增值税率	计量单位	监管条件	Article Description
32.02	**有机合成鞣料；无机鞣料；鞣料制剂，不论是否含有天然鞣料；预鞣用酶制剂：**								**Synthetic organic tanning substances; inorganic tanning substances; tanning preparations, whether or not containing natural tanning substances; enzymatic preparations for pre-tanning:**
3202.1000	-有机合成鞣料	6.5	35			17	千克		-Synthetic organic tanning substances
3202.9000	-其他	6.5	35			17	千克		-Other
32.03	**动植物质着色料（包括染料浸膏，但动物炭黑除外），不论是否已有化学定义；本章注释三所述的以动植物质着色料为基本成分的制品：**								**Colouring matter of vegetable or animal origin（including dyeing extracts but excluding animal black）, whether or not chemically defined; preparations as specified in Note 3 to this Chapter based on colouring matter of vegetable or animal origin:**
	---植物质着色料及以其为基本成分的制品：								---Colouring matter of vegetable origin and preparations based thereon:
3203.0011	----天然靛蓝及以其为基本成分的制品	6.5	80			17	千克	AB	----Natural indigo and preparations based thereon
3203.0019	----其他	6.5	45			17	千克		----Other
3203 0019.10	濒危植物质着色料及制品（制品是指以植物质着色料为基本成分的）	6.5	45			17	千克	ABEF	Colouring matter of endangered vegetable origin and preparations based thereon
3203 0019.90	其他植物质着色料及制品（制品是指以植物质着色料为基本成分的）	6.5	45			17	千克	AB	Other colouring matter of vegetable origin and preparations based thereon
3203.0020	---动物质着色料及以其为基本成分的制品	6.5	50		13	17	千克	A	---Colouring matter of animal origin and preparations based thereon
32.04	**有机合成着色料，不论是否已有化学定义；本章注释三所述的以有机合成着色料为基本成分的制品；用作荧光增白剂或发光体的有机合成产品，不论是否已有化学定义：**								**Synthetic organic colouring matter, whether or not chemically defined;preparations as specified in Note 3 to this Chapter based on synthetic organic colouring matter; synthetic organic products of a kind used as fluorescent brightening agents or as luminophores, whether or not chemically defined:**
	-有机合成着色料及本章注释三所述的以有机合成着色 料为基本成分的制品：								-Synthetic organic colouring matter and preparations based thereon as specified in Note 3 to this Chapter:
3204.1100	--分散染料及以其为基本成分的制品	6.5	35			17	千克	AB	--Disperse dyes and preparations based thereon
3204.1200	--酸性染料（不论是否与金属络合）及以其为基本成分的制品；媒染染料及以其为基本成分的制品	6.5	35			17	千克	AB	--Acid dyes, whether or not premetallized, and preparations based thereon; mordant dyes and preparations based thereon
3204.1300	--碱性染料及以其为基本成分的制品	6.5	35			17	千克	AB	--Basic dyes and preparations based thereon
3204.1400	--直接染料及以其为基本成分的制品	6.5	35			17	千克	AB	--Direct dyes and preparations based thereon
	--瓮染料（包括颜料用的）及以其为基本成分的制品：								--Vat dyes（including those usable in that state as pigments）and preparations based thereon:
3204.1510	---合成靛蓝(还原靛蓝)	6.5	35			17	千克	AB	---Synthetic indigo（reductive indigo）
3204.1590	---其他	6.5	35			17	千克		---Other
3204.1600	--活性染料及以其为基本成分的制品	6.5	35			17	千克		--Reactive dyes and preparations based thereon
3204.1700	—颜料及以其为基本成分的制品	6.5	35			17	千克		--Pigments and preparations based thereon
	--其他，包括由子目号3204.11至3204.19中两个或多个子目所列着色料组成的混合物：								--Other, including mixtures of colouring matter of two or more of the subheadings No. 3204.11 to 3204.19:
	---硫化染料及以其为基本成分的制品：								---Sulphur dyes and preparations based thereon:
3204.1911	----硫化黑（硫化氢）及以其为基本成分的制品	6.5	35			17	千克		----Sulphur black and preparations based thereon

税则号列 Tariff Item	商品名称及备注	进口税率 最惠	普通	暂定	出口退税	增值税率	计量单位	监管条件	Article Description
3204.1919	----其他	6.5	35			17	千克		----Other
3204.1990	---其他	6.5	35			17	千克	AB	---Other
3204.2000	-用作荧光增白剂的有机合成产品	6.5	40			17	千克	A	-Synthetic organic products of a kind used as flourescent brightening agents
	-其他:								-Other:
3204.9010	---生物染色剂及染料指示剂	6.5	20			17	千克		---Biological stains and dye indicators
3204.9090	---其他	6.5	40			17	千克		---Other
32.05	**色淀；本章注释三所述的以色淀为基本成分的制品：**								**Colour lakes; preparations as specified in Note 3 to this Chapter based on colour lakes:**
3205.0000	色淀；本章注释三所述的以色淀为基本成分的制品	6.5	35			17	千克	AB	Colour lakes; preparations as specified in Note 3 to this Chapter based on colour lakes
32.06	**其他着色料；本章注释三所述的制品，但品目32.03、32.04及32.05的货品除外；用作发光体的无机产品，不论是否已有化学定义：**								**Other colouring matter; preparations as specified in Note 3 to this Chapter, other than those of heading No. 32.03, 32.04 or 32.05; inorganic products of a kind used as luminophores, whether or not chemically defined:**
	-以二氧化钛为基本成分的颜料及制品:								-Pigments and preparations based on titanium dioxide:
	--以干物质计二氧化钛含量在80%及以上的:								--Containing 80% or more by weight of titanium dioxide calculated on the dry matter:
3206.1110	---钛白粉	6.5	30			17	千克	4xy	---Titanium White
3206.1190	---其他	6.5	30			17	千克		---Other
3206.1900	--其他	10	30			17	千克		--Other
3206.2000	-以铬化合物为基本成分的颜料及制品	6.5	35			17	千克		-Pigments and preparations based on chromium compounds
	-其他着色料及其他制品:								-Other colouring matter and other preparations:
3206.4100	--群青及以其为基本成分的制品	6.5	35			17	千克		--Ultramarine and preparations based thereon
	--锌钡白及以硫化锌为基本成分的其他颜料和制品:								--Lithopone and other pigments and preparations based on zinc sulphide:
3206.4210	---锌钡白	6.5	30			17	千克		---Lithopone
3206.4290	---其他	6.5	30			17	千克		---Other
	--其他:								--Other:
	---以铋化合物为基本成分的颜料及制品:								---Pigments and preparations based on bismuth compound:
3206.4911	----以钒酸铋为基本成分的颜料及制品	6.5	35			17	千克		---Pigments and preparations based on bismuth vanadate
3206.4919	----其他	6.5	35			17	千克		----Other
3206.4990	---其他	6.5	35			17	千克		---Other
3206.5000	-用作发光体的无机产品	6.5	35			17	千克		-Inorganic products of a kind used as luminophores
32.07	**陶瓷、搪瓷及玻璃工业用的调制颜料、遮光剂、着色剂、珐琅和釉料、釉底料（泥釉）、光瓷釉以及类似产品；搪瓷玻璃料及其他玻璃，呈粉、粒或粉片状的：**								**Prepared pigments, prepared opacifiers and prepared colours, vitrifiable enamels and glazes, engobes（slips）, liquid lustres and similar preparations, of a kind used in the ceramic, enamelling or glass industry; glass frit and other glass, in the form of powder, granules or flakes:**
3207.1000	-调制颜料、遮光剂、着色剂及类似制品	5	50			17	千克		-Prepared pigments, prepared opacifiers,prepared colours and similar preparations
3207.2000	-珐琅和釉料、釉底料（泥釉）及类似制品	5	50			17	千克		-Vitrifiable enamels and glazes, engobes（slips）and similar preparations
3207.3000	-光瓷釉及类似制品	5	50			17	千克		-Liquid lustres and similar preparations
3207.4000	-搪瓷玻璃料及其他玻璃，呈粉、粒或粉片状的	5	50			17	千克		-Glass frit and other glass, in the form of powder, granules or flakes
32.08	**以合成聚合物或化学改性天然聚合物为基本成分的油漆及清漆（包括瓷漆及大漆），分散于或溶于非水介质的；本章注释四所述的溶液：**								**Paints and varnishes（including enamels and lacquers）based on synthetic polymers or chemically modified natural polymers, dispersed or dissolved in a nonaqueous medium; solutions as defined in Note 4 to this Chapter:**

税则号列 Tariff Item	商品名称及备注	进口税率 最惠	进口税率 普通	进口税率 暂定	出口退税	增值税率	计量单位	监管条件	Article Description
3208.1000	-以聚酯为基本成分	10	50			17	千克	A	-Based on polyesters
	-以丙烯酸聚合物或乙烯聚合物为基本成分:								-Based on acrylic or vinyl polymers:
3208.2010	---以丙烯酸聚合物为基本成分	10	50			17	千克		---Based on acrylic polymers
3208 2010.01[暂]	分散于或溶于非水介质的光导纤维用涂料(主要成分为聚胺酯丙烯酸酯类化合物,以丙烯酸聚合物为基本成分)	10	50	6		17	千克	A	Paints varnishes for optial fibers（based on acrylic pdmers）, dispersed or dissolved in a nonaqueous medium
3208 2010.90	其他聚丙烯酸油漆、清漆等（溶于非水质的以丙烯酸聚合物为基本成分，包括瓷漆大漆）	10	50			17	千克	A	Other paints and varnishes（including enamels and lacquers）, based on acrylic polymers, dispersed or dissolved in a nonaqueous medium
3208.2020	---以乙烯聚合物为基本成分	10	50			17	千克	A	---Based on vinyl polymers
	-其他:								-Other:
3208.9010	---以聚胺酯类化合物为基本成分	10	50			17	千克		---Based on polyurethane polymers
3208 9010.01[暂]	分散于或溶于非水介质的光导纤维用涂料(主要成分为聚胺酯丙烯酸酯类化合物,以聚胺酯类化合物为基本成分)	10	50	6		17	千克	A	Paints for optial fibers, based on polyurethane polymers, dispersed or dissolved in a nonaqueous medium
3208 9010.90	其他聚胺酯油漆、清漆等（溶于非水介质以聚胺酯类化合物为基本成分，含瓷漆大漆）	10	50			17	千克	A	Other paints and varnishes（including enamels and lacquers）, based on polyurethane polymers, dispersed or dissolved in a nonaqueous medium
3208.9090	---其他	10	50			17	千克	A	---Other
32.09	**以合成聚合物或化学改性天然聚合物为基本成分的油漆及清漆（包括瓷漆及大漆），分散于或溶于水介质的:**								**Paints and varnishes（including enamels and lacquers）based on synthetic polymers or chemically modified natural polymers, dispersed or dissolved in an aqueous medium:**
3209.1000	-以丙烯酸聚合物或乙烯聚合物为基本成分的	10	50			17	千克	A	-Based on acrylic or vinyl polymers
	-其他:								-Other:
3209.9010	---以环氧树脂为基本成分	10	50			17	千克	A	---Based on epoxy resin
3209.9020	---以氟树脂为基本成分	10	50			17	千克	A	---Based on fluororesin
3209.9090	---其他	10	50			17	千克	A	---Other
32.10	**其他油漆及清漆（包括瓷漆、大漆及水浆涂料）；加工皮革用的水性颜料:**								**Other paints and varnishes（including enamels, lacquers and distempers）; prepared water pigments of a kind used for finishing leather:**
3210.0000	其他油漆及清漆（包括瓷漆，大漆及水浆涂料）；加工皮革用的水性颜料	10	50			17	千克		Other paints and varnishes（including enamels, lacquers and distempers）; prepared water pigments of a kind used for finishing leather
3210 0000.01[暂]	其他光导纤维用涂料	10	50	6		17	千克		Other paints for optical fiber
3210 0000.90	其他油漆及清漆,皮革用水性颜料(包括非聚合物为基料的瓷漆,大漆及水浆涂料)	10	50			17	千克		Other paints and varnishes（including enamels, lacquers and distempers based on nonpolymer）prepared water pigment for leather
32.11	**配制的催干剂:**								**Prepared driers:**
3211.0000	配制的催干剂	10	50			17	千克		Prepared driers
32.12	**制造油漆(含瓷漆)用的颜料(包括金属粉末或金属粉片）分散于非水介质中呈液状或浆状的；压印箔；零售形状及零售包装的染料或其他着色料:**								**Pigments（including metallic powders and flakes）dispersed in non-aqueous media, in liquid or paste form, of a kind used in the manufacture of paints（including enamels）; stamping foils; dyes and other colouring matter put up in forms or packings for retail sale:**
3212.1000	-压印箔	15	80			17	千克		-Stamping foils
3212.9000	-其他	10	50			17	千克		-Other
32.13	**艺术家、学生和广告美工用的颜料、调色料、文娱颜料及类似品，片状、管装、罐装、瓶装、扁盒装以及类似形状或包装的:**								**Artists', students' or signboard painters' colours, modifying tints, amusement colours and the like, in tablets, tubes, jars, bottles, pans or in similar forms or packings:**
3213.1000	-成套的颜料	10	70		13	17	千克		-Colours in sets

税则号列 Tariff Item	商品名称及备注	进口税率			出口退税	增值税率	计量单位	监管条件	Article Description
		最惠	普通	暂定					
3213.9000	-其他	10	70		13	17	千克		-Other
32.14	**安装玻璃用油灰、接缝用油灰、树脂胶泥、嵌缝胶及其他类似胶粘剂；漆工用填料；非耐火涂面制剂，涂门面、内墙、地板、天花板等用：**								**Glaziers' putty, grafting putty, resin cements, caulking compounds and other mastics; painters' fillings; non-refractory surfacing preparations for facades, indoor walls, floors, ceilings or the like:**
	-安装玻璃用油灰、接缝用油灰、树脂胶泥、嵌缝胶及其他类似胶粘剂；漆工用填料:								-Glaziers' putty, grafting putty, resin cements, caulking compounds and other mastics; painters' fillings:
3214.1010	---半导体器件封装材料	9	70			17	千克		---Encapsulation material for semiconductor device
3214.1090	---其他	9	70			17	千克		---Other
3214.9000	-其他	9	70			17	千克		-Other
32.15	**印刷油墨、书写或绘图墨水及其他墨类，不论是否固体或浓缩：**								**Printing ink, writing or drawing ink and other inks, whether or not concentrated or solid:**
	-印刷油墨:								-Printing ink:
3215.1100	--黑色	6.5	45			17	千克	AB	--Black
3215.1900	--其他	6.5	45			17	千克		--Other
	-其他:								-Other:
3215.9010	---书写墨水	6.5	70		13	17	千克		---Writing or drawing inks
3215.9020	---水性喷墨墨水	10	70		13	17	千克		---water-based inkjet inks
3215.9090	---其他	10	70		13	17	千克		---Other

第三十三章 精油及香膏；芳香料制品及化妆盥洗品

Chapter 33 Essential oils and resinoids; perfumery, cosmetic or toilet preparations

注释：

一、本章不包括：

（一）品目 13.01 或 13.02 的天然油树脂或植物浸膏；

（二）品目 34.01 的肥皂及其他产品；或

（三）品目 38.05 的脂松节油、木松节油和硫酸盐松节油及其他产品。

二、品目 33.02 所称“香料”仅指品目 33.01 所列的物质，从这些物质离析出来的香料组分，以及合成芳香剂。

三、品目 33.03 至 33.07 主要包括适合作这些品目所列用途的零售包装产品，不论其是否混合（精油水馏液及水溶液除外）。

四、品目 33.07 所称“芳香料制品及化妆盥洗品”，主要适用于下列产品：香袋；通过燃烧散发香气的制品；香纸及用化妆品浸渍或涂布的纸；隐形眼镜片或假眼用的溶液；用香水或化妆品浸渍、涂布、包覆的絮胎、毡呢及无纺织物；动物用盥洗品。

Chapter Notes:

1. This Chapter does not cover:

（a）Natural oleoresins or vegetable extracts of heading 13.01 or 13.02;

（b）Soap or other products of heading 34.01; or

（c）Gum, wood or sulphate turpentine or other products of heading38.05.

2. The expression “odoriferous substances” in heading 33.02 refers only to the substances of heading 33.01, to odoriferous constituents isolated from those substances or to synthetic aromatics.

3. Headings 33.03 to 33.07 apply, inter alia, to products, whether or not mixed（other than aqueous distillates and aqueous solutions of essential oils）, suitable for use as goods of these headings and put up in packings of a kind sold by retail for such use.

4. The expression “perfumery, cosmetic or toilet preparations” in heading 33.07 applies, inter alia, to the following products:scented sachets; odoriferous preparations which operate by burning; perfumed papers and papers impregnated or coated with cosmetics; contact lens or artificial eye solutions; wadding, felt and nonwovens, impregnated, coated or covered with perfume or cosmetics; animal toilet preparations.

税则号列 Tariff Item	商品名称及备注	进口税率			出口退税	增值税率	计量单位	监管条件	Article Description
		最惠	普通	暂定					
33.01	精油(无萜或含萜)，包括浸膏及净油；香膏；提取的油树脂；用花香吸取法或浸渍法制成的含浓缩精油的脂肪、固定油、蜡及类似品；精油脱萜时所得的萜烯副产品；精油水馏液及水溶液：								**Essential oils（terpeneless or not）, including concretes and absolutes; resinoids; extracted oleoresins; concentrates of essential oils in fats, in fixedoils, in waxes or the like, obtained by enfleurage or maceration; terpenicbyproducts of the deterpenation of essential oils; aqueous distillates and aqueous solutions of essential oils:**
	-柑橘属果实的精油:								-Essential oils of citrus fruit:
3301.1200	--橙油	20	80		9	17	千克	A	--Of orange
3301.1300	--柠檬油	20	80		9	17	千克	A	--Of lemon
	--其他:								--Other:
3301.1910	---白柠檬油(酸橙油)	20	80		9	17	千克	A	---Of lime
3301.1990	---其他	20	80		9	17	千克	A	---Other
	-非柑橘属果实的精油:								-Essential oils other than those of citrus fruit:
3301.2400	--胡椒薄荷油	20	90		9	17	千克	A	--Of peppermint（Mentha piperita）
3301.2500[暂]	--其他薄荷油	15	90	5	13	17	千克	A	--Of other mints
	--其他:								--Other:
3301.2910	---樟脑油	20	90		9	17	千克	ABE	---Of camphor
3301.2920	---香茅油	15	70		9	17	千克	A	---Of citronella
3301.2930	---茴香油	20	80		9	17	千克	A	---Of aniseed
3301.2940	---桂油	20	80		9	17	千克	A	---Of cassia
3301.2950	---山苍子油	20	80		9	17	千克	A	---Of litsea cubeba
3301.2960	---桉叶油	20	80		9	17	千克	AB	---Of eucalyptus
	---其他:								---Other:
3301.2991	----老鹳草油(香叶油)	20	80		9	17	千克	A	----Of geranium
3301.2999	----其他	15	80			17	千克		----Other
3301 2999.10[暂]	黄樟油	15	80	7	9	17	千克	23A	Oil of sassafras
3301 2999.91	其他濒危植物精油（柑桔属果实除外）(包括浸膏及净油)	15	80			17	千克	AFE	Other essential oils other than those of endangered citrus fruit(including concretes and absolutes)

税则号列 Tariff Item	商品名称及备注	进口税率 最惠	进口税率 普通	进口税率 暂定	出口退税	增值税率	计量单位	监管条件	Article Description
3301 2999.99	其他非柑橘属果实的精油（包括浸膏及净油）	15	80		9	17	千克	A	Other essential oils other than those of citrus fruit(including concretes and absolutes)
	-香膏:								-Resinoids:
3301.3010[暂]	---鸢尾凝脂	20	80	10	13	17	千克		---Balsam of irises
3301.3090	---其他	20	80			17	千克		---Other
3301 3090.10	其他濒危植物香膏	20	80			17	千克	FE	Other resinoids of endangered vegetable
3301 3090.90	其他香膏	20	80		9	17	千克		Other resinoids
	-其他:								-Other:
3301.9010	---提取的油树脂	20	80			17	千克		---Extracted oleoresins
3301 9010.10	濒危植物提取的油树脂	20	80			17	千克	FE	Extracted oleoresins of endangered vegetable
3301 9010.90	其他提取的油树脂	20	80		9	17	千克		Other extracted oleoresins
3301.9020	---柑橘属果实的精油脱萜的萜烯副产品	20	80		9	17	千克		---Terpenic byproducts of the deterpenation of essential oils of citrus fruit
3301.9090	---其他	20	80		9	17	千克		---Other
33.02	**工业原料用的混合香料以及以一种或多种香料为基本成分的混合物（包括酒精溶液）；生产饮料用的以香料为基本成分的其他制品:**								**Mixtures of odoriferous substances and mixtures （including alcoholic solutions） with a basis of one or more of these substances, of a kind used as raw materials in industry; other preparations based on odoriferous substances, of a kind used for the manufacture of beverages**:
	-食品或饮料工业用:								-Of a kind used in the food or drink industry:
3302.1010	---生产饮料用的以香料为基本成分的制品，按容量计酒精浓度不超过 0.5%的	15	90		13	17	千克	AB	---Preparations based on odoriferous substances, of a kind used for the manufacture of beverages, alcoholic strength by volume not exceeding 0.5% vol.
3302.1090	---其他	15	130		13	17	千克		---Other
3302 1090.01	生产食品、饮料用混合香料及制品（含以香料为基本成分的混合物，按容量计酒精浓度＞0.5%）	15	130		13	17	千克	A	Mixtures of odoriferous substances and products, of a kind used for the manufacture of beverages and food, alcoholic strength by volume exceeding 0.5%
3302 1090.90	其他生产食品用混合香料及制品（含以香料为基本成分的混合物）	15	130		13	17	千克	A	Mixtures of odoriferous substances, of a kind used for the manufacture of food, preparations based on odoriferous substances
3302.9000	-其他	10	130		13	17	千克		-Other
33.03	**香水及花露水:**								**Perfumes and toilet waters:**
3303.0000	香水及花露水	10	150		13	17	千克/件	AB	Perfumes and toilet waters
33.04	**美容品或化妆品及护肤品（药品除外），包括防晒油或晒黑油；指（趾）甲化妆品:**								**Beauty or make-up preparations and preparations for the care of the skin, (other than medicaments), including sunscreen or sun tan preparations; manicure or pedicure preparations:**
3304.1000	-唇用化妆品	10	150			17	千克/件		-Lip make-up preparations
3304 1000.10	含濒危植物成分唇用化妆品	10	150			17	千克/件	ABEF	Lip make-up preparations,containing endangered plants
3304 1000.90	其他唇用化妆品	10	150		13	17	千克/件	AB	Other lip make-up preparations
3304.2000	-眼用化妆品	10	150			17	千克/件		-Eye make-up preparations
3304 2000.10	含濒危植物成分眼用化妆品	10	150			17	千克/件	ABEF	Eye make-up preparations, containing endangered plants
3304 2000.90	其他眼用化妆品	10	150		13	17	千克/件	AB	Other eye make-up preparations
3304.3000[暂]	-指(趾)甲化妆品	15	150	10	13	17	千克/件	AB	-Manicture or pedicure preparations
	-其他:								-Other:
3304.9100	--粉，不论是否压紧	10	150		13	17	千克/件		--Powders, whether or not compressed
3304 9100.01	痱子粉、爽身粉	10	150		13	17	千克/件	AB	Bath powder (prickly heat power); talcum powder
3304 9100.90	粉,不论是否压紧	10	150		13	17	千克/件	AB	Powders, whether or not compressed
3304.9900	--其他	6.5	150			17	千克/件		--Other
3304 9900.10[暂]	护肤品（包括防晒油或晒黑油，但药品除外）	6.5	150	5	13	17	千克/件	AB	Preparations for the care of the skin(other than medicaments), including sunscreen or sun tan preparations
3304 9900.91	其他含濒危植物成分美容品或化妆品	6.5	150			17	千克/件	ABFE	Beauty or make-up preparations, containing endangered plants

税则号列 Tariff Item	商品名称及备注	进口税率			出口退税	增值税率	计量单位	监管条件	Article Description
		最惠	普通	暂定					
3304 9900.99	其他美容品或化妆品	6.5	150		13	17	千克/件	AB	Other beauty or make-up preparations
33.05	**护发品:**								**Preparations for use on the hair:**
3305.1000	-洗发剂(香波)	6.5	150			17	千克		-Shampoos
3305 1000.10	含濒危植物成分的洗发剂	6.5	150			17	千克	ABFE	Shampoos containing endangered vegetable
3305 1000.90	其他洗发剂(香波)	6.5	150		13	17	千克	AB	Other shampoos
3305.2000[暂]	-烫发剂	15	150	10	13	17	千克	AB	-Preparations for permanent waving or straightening
3305.3000[暂]	-定型剂	15	150	10	13	17	千克	AB	-Hair lacquers
3305.9000	-其他	10	150		13	17	千克	AB	-Other
33.06	**口腔及牙齿清洁剂,包括假牙模膏及粉;清洁牙缝用的纱线(牙线),单独零售包装的:**								**Preparations for oral or dental hygiene, including denture fixative pastes and powders; yarn used to clean between the teeth(dental floss), in individual retail package:**
	-洁齿品:								-Dentifrices:
3306.1010	---牙膏	10	150			17	千克		---Toothpastes
3306 1010.10	含濒危植物成分牙膏	10	150			17	千克	ABEF	Toothpastes containing endangered vegetable
3306 1010.90	其他牙膏	10	150		13	17	千克	AB	Other toothpastes
3306.1090	---其他	10	150		9	17	千克		---Other
3306.2000	-清洁牙缝用的纱线(牙线)	10	70		9	17	千克		-Yarn used to clean between the teeth(dental floss)
3306.9000	-其他	10	70		9	17	千克	AB	-Other
33.07	**剃须用制剂、人体除臭剂、沐浴用制剂、脱毛剂和其他品目未列名的芳香料制品及化妆盥洗品;室内除臭剂,不论是否加香水或消毒剂:**								**Pre-shave,shaving or after-shave preparations, personal deodorants, bath preparations, depilatories and other perfumery, cosmetic or toilet preparations, not elsewhere specified or included; prepared room deodorizers,whether or not perfumed or having disinfectant properties:**
3307.1000	-剃须用制剂	10	150		13	17	千克	AB	-Pre-shave, shaving or after-shave preparations
3307.2000	-人体除臭剂及止汗剂	10	150		13	17	千克	AB	-Personal deodorants and antiperspirants
3307.3000	-香浴盐及其他沐浴用制剂	10	150		13	17	千克	AB	-Perfumed bath salts and other bath preparations
	-室内散香或除臭制品,包括宗教仪式用的香:								-Preparations for perfuming or deodorizing rooms, including odoriferous preparations used during religious rites:
3307.4100	--神香及其他通过燃烧散发香气的制品	10	150		9	17	千克		--Agarbatti and other odoriferous preparations which operate by burning
3307.4900	--其他	10	150		9	17	千克		--Other
3307.9000	-其他	9	150		13	17	千克		-Other

第三十四章
肥皂、有机表面活性剂、洗涤剂、润滑剂、人造蜡、调制蜡、光洁剂、蜡烛及类似品、塑型用膏、“牙科用蜡”及牙科用熟石膏制剂

注释：

一、本章不包括：

（一）用作脱模剂的食用动植物油、脂混合物或制品（品目 15.17）；

（二）单独的已有化学定义的化合物；或

（三）含肥皂或其他有机表面活性剂的洗发剂、洁齿品、剃须膏及沐浴用制剂（品目 33.05、33.06 及 33.07）。

二、品目 34.01 所称“肥皂”，只适用于水溶性肥皂。品目 34.01 的肥皂及其他产品可以含有添加料（例如，消毒剂、磨料粉、填料或药料）。含磨料粉的产品，只有条状、块状或模制形状可以归入品目 34.01。其他形状的应作为“去污粉及类似品”归入品目 34.05。

三、品目 34.02 所称“有机表面活性剂”，是指温度在 20℃时与水混合配成 0.5%浓度的水溶液，并在同样温度下搁置一小时后与下列规定相符的产品：

（一）成为透明或半透明的液体或稳定的乳浊液而未离析出不溶解物质；以及

（二）将水的表面张力降低到每厘米 45 达因及以下。

四、品目 34.03 所称“石油及从沥青矿物提取的油类”，适用于第二十七章注释二所规定的产品。

五、品目 34.04 所称“人造蜡及调制蜡”，仅适用于：

（一）用化学方法生产的具有蜡质特性的有机产品，不论是否为水溶性的；

（二）各种蜡混合制成的产品；

（三）以一种或几种蜡为基本原料并含有油脂、树脂、矿物质或其他原料的具有蜡质特性的产品。

本品目不包括：

（一）品目 15.16、34.02 或 38.23 的产品，不论是否具有蜡质特性；

（二）品目 15.21 的未混合的动物蜡或未混合的植物蜡，不论是否精制或着色；

（三）品目 27.12 的矿物蜡或类似产品，不论是否相互混合或仅经着色；或

（四）混合、分散或溶解于液体溶剂的蜡（品目 34.05、38.09 等）。

Chapter 34
Soap, organic surface-active agents, washing preparations, lubricating preparations, artificial waxes, prepared waxes, polishing or scouring preparations, candles and similar articles, modelling pastes, “detal waxes” and dental preparations with a basis of plaster

Chapter Notes:

1. This Chapter does not cover:

（a）Edible mixtures or preparations of animal or vegetable fats or oils of a kind used as mould release preparations（heading 15.17）;

（b）Separate chemically defined compounds: or

（c）Shampoos, dentifrices, shaving creams and foams, or bath preparations, containing soap or other organic surface-active agents（heading 33.05, 33.06 or 33.07）.

2. For the purposes of heading 34.01, the expression “soap” applies only to soap soluble in water. Soap and the other products of heading 34.01 may contain added substances（for example, disinfectants, abrasive powders, fillers or medicaments）. Products containing abrasive powders remain classified in heading 34.01 only if in the form of bars, cakes or moulded pieces or shapes. In other forms they are to be classified in heading 34.05 as “scouring powders and similar preparations”.

3. For the purposes of heading 34.02, “organic surface-active agents” are products which when mixed with water at a concentration of 0.5% at 20℃ and left to stand for one hour at the same temperature:

（a）Give a transparent or translucent liquid or stable emulsion without separation of insoluble matter; and

（b）Reduce the surface tension of water to 4.5×10^{-2} N/m（45 dyne/cm）or less.

4. In heading 34.03 the expression “petroleum oils and oils obtained from bituminous minerals” applies to the products defined in Note 2 to Chapter 27.

5. In heading 34.04, subject to the exclusions provided below, the expression “artificial waxes and prepared waxes” applies only to:

（a）Chemically produced organic products of a waxy character,whether or not water-soluble;

（b）Products obtained by mixing different waxes;

（c）Products of a waxy character with a basis of one or more waxes and containing fats, resins, mineral substances or other materials.

The heading does not apply to:

（a）Products of heading 15.16, 34.02 or 38.23, even if having a waxy character;

（b）Unmixed animal waxes or unmixed vegetable waxes, whether or not refined or coloured, of heading 15.21;

（c）Mineral waxes or similar products of heading 27.12.whether or not intermixed or merely coloured; or

（d）Waxes mixed with, dispersed in or dissolved in a liquid medium（headings 34.05, 38.09, etc.）

税则号列 Tariff Item	商品名称及备注	进口税率 最惠	普通	暂定	出口退税	增值税率	计量单位	监管条件	Article Description
34.01	肥皂；作肥皂用的有机表面活性产品及制品，条状、块状或模制形状的，不论是否含有肥皂；洁肤用的有机表面活性产品及制品，液状或膏状并制成零售包装的，不论是否含有肥皂；用肥皂或洗涤剂浸渍、涂面或包覆的纸、絮胎、毡呢及无纺织物								**Soap; organic surface-active products and preparations for use as soap, in the form of bars,cakes,moulded pieces or shapes, whether or not containing soap; organic surface-active and preparations for washing the skin, in the form of liquid or cream and put up for retail sale, whether or not containing soap; paper, wadding, felt and nonwovens, impregnated,coated or covered with soap or detergent:**
	-肥皂及有机表面活性产品及制品，条状、块状或模制形状的，以及用肥皂或洗涤剂浸渍、涂面或包覆的纸、絮胎、毡呢及无纺织物：								-Soap and organic surface-active products and preparations, in the form of bars, cakes, moulded pieces or shapes, and paper, wadding, felt and nonwovens, impregnated, coated or covered with soap or detergent:
3401.1100	--盥洗用（包括含有药物的产品）	10	130		13	17	千克	AB	--For toilet use（including medicated products）
	--其他：								--Other:
3401.1910	---洗衣皂	10	80		13	17	千克		---Laundry soap
3401.1990 暂	---其他	15	130	10	13	17	千克		---Other
3401.2000 暂	-其他形状的肥皂	15	130	10	13	17	千克		-Soap in other forms
3401.3000	-洁肤用的有机表面活性产品及制品，液状或膏状并制成零售包装的，不论是否含有肥皂	10	130		13	17	千克	AB	-Organic surface-active products and preparations for washing the skin, in the form of liquid or cream and put up for retail sale,whether or not containing soap
34.02	有机表面活性剂（肥皂除外）；表面活性剂制品、洗涤剂（包括助洗剂）及清洁剂，不论是否含有肥皂，但品目 34.01 的产品除外：								**Organic surface-active agents（other than soap）; surface-active preparations, washing preparations （including auxiliary washing preparations） and cleaning preparations, whether or not containing soap, other than those of heading No. 34.01:**
	-有机表面活性剂，不论是否零售包装：								-Organic surface-active agents, whether or not put up for retail sale:
3402.1100	--阴离子型	6.5	30		13	17	千克		--Anionic
3402.1200	--阳离子型	6.5	30		13	17	千克		--Cationic
3402.1300	--非离子型	6.5	30		13	17	千克		--Non-ionic
3402 1300.10	含有壬基酚聚氧乙烯醚的有机表面活性剂(不论是否零售包装,肥皂除外)	6.5	30		13	17	千克	X	Organic surface-active agents, containing polyoxyethylene nonylphenol ether (whether or not put up for retail sale, other than soap)
3402 1300.90	其他非离子型有机表面活性剂(不论是否零售包装,肥皂除外)	6.5	30		13	17	千克		Other organic non ionic surface-active agents (whether or not put up for retail sale, other than soap)
3402.1900	--其他	6.5	30		13	17	千克		--Other
	-零售包装的制品：								-Preparations put up for retail sale:
3402.2010	---合成洗涤粉	10	80		13	17	千克		---Synthetic detergents in powder form
3402.2090	---其他	10	80		13	17	千克		---Other
3402.9000	-其他	9	80		13	17	千克		-Other
3402 9000.01 暂	十二烷基苯磺酸钙甲醇溶液（非零售包装，十二烷基苯磺酸钙含量高于 70%）	9	80	7	13	17	千克		Methanol solution of calcium dodecyl benzene sulfonate, (containing more than 70% of calcium dodecyl benzosulfonate), not put up for retail sale)
3402 9000.90	非零售包装有机表面活性剂制品（包括洗涤剂及清洁剂，不论是否含有肥皂）	9	80		13	17	千克		Organic surface-active agents, (including washing and cleaning preparations, whether or not containing soap), not put up for retail sale
34.03	润滑剂（包括以润滑剂为基本成分的切削油制剂、螺栓或螺母松开剂、防锈或防腐蚀制剂及脱模剂）及用于纺织材料、皮革、毛皮或其他材料油脂处理的制剂，但不包括以石油或从沥青矿物提取的油类为基本成分（按重量计不低于 70%）的制剂								**Lubricating preparations（including cutting-oil preparations, bolt or nutrelease preparations, anti-rust or anticorosion preparations and mould release preparations, based on lubricants） and preparations of a kind used for the oil or grease treatment of textile materials, leather, furskins or other materials, but excluding preparations containing, as basic constituents, 70% or more by weight of petroleum oils or of oils obtained from bituminous minerals:**

税则号列 Tariff Item	商品名称及备注	进口税率			出口退税	增值税率	计量单位	监管条件	Article Description
		最惠	普通	暂定					
	-含有石油或从沥青矿物提取的油类:								-Containing petroleum oils or oils obtained from bituminous minerals:
3403.1100[暂]	--处理纺织等材料、皮革、毛皮或其他材料的制剂	10	50	8	9	17	千克		--Preparations for the treatment of textile materials, leather, furskins or other materials
3403.1900[暂]	--其他	10	50	8	9	17	千克		--Other
	-其他:								-Other:
3403.9100[暂]	--处理纺织材料、皮革、毛皮或其他材料的制剂	10	50	8	9	17	千克		--Preparations for the treatment of textile materials, leather, furskins or other materials
3403.9900	--其他	10	50		9	17	千克		--Other
34.04	**人造蜡及调制蜡:**								**Artificial waxes and prepared waxes:**
3404.2000	-聚氧乙烯（聚乙二醇）蜡	10	70		9	17	千克		-Of poly（oxyethylene）（polyethyleneglycol）
3404.9000	-其他	10	70			17	千克		-Other
34.05	**鞋靴、家具、地板、车身、玻璃或金属用的光洁剂、擦洗膏、去污粉及类似制品（包括用这类制剂浸渍、涂面或包覆的纸、絮胎、毡呢、无纺织物、泡沫塑料或海绵橡胶），但不包括品目34.04的蜡**								**Polishes and creams for footwear, furniture, floors, coachwork, glass or metal, scouring pastes and powders and similar preparations（whether or not in the form of paper, wadding, felt, nonwovens, cellular plastics or cellular rubber, impregnated, coated or covered with such preparations）, excluding waxes of heading No. 34.04:**
3405.1000	-鞋靴或皮革用的上光剂及类似制品	10	80		9	17	千克		-Polishes, creams and similar preparations for footwear or leather
3405.2000	-保养木制家具、地板或其他木制品用的上光剂及类似制品	10	80		9	17	千克		-Polishes, creams and similar preparations for the maintenance of wooden furniture, floors or other woodwork
3405.3000	-车身用的上光剂及类似制品，但金属用的光洁剂除外	10	80		9	17	千克		-Polishes and similar preparations for coachwork, other than metal polishes
3405.4000	-擦洗膏、去污粉及类似制品	10	80		9	17	千克		-Scouring pastes and powders and other scouring preparations
3405.9000	-其他	10	80		9	17	千克		-Other
34.06	**各种蜡烛及类似品:**								**Candles, tapers and the like:**
3406.0000	各种蜡烛及类似品	10	130			17	千克		Candles, tapers and the like
3406 0000.10	含濒危动物成分的蜡烛及类似品	10	130			17	千克	EF	Candle and tapers and the like, containing composition of endangered animals
3406 0000.90	其他各种蜡烛及类似品	10	130		13	17	千克		Other candles, tapers and the like
34.07	**塑型用膏，包括供儿童娱乐用的在内；通称为“牙科用蜡”或“牙科造形膏”的制品，成套、零售包装或制成片状、马蹄形、条状及类似形状的；以熟石膏（煅烧石膏或硫酸钙）为基本成分的牙科用其他制品**								**Modelling pastes, including those put up for children's amusement; preparations known as “dental wax” or as “dental impression compounds”, put up in sets, in packings for retail sale or in plates, horseshoe shapes, sticks or similar forms; other preparations for ues in dentistry, with a basis of plaster（of calcined gypsum or calcium sulphate）:**
3407.0010	---牙科用蜡及造型膏	6.5	30		9	17	千克		---Preparations of a kind known as “dental wax” or as “dental impression compounds”
3407.0020	---以熟石膏为基本成分的牙科用其他制品	6.5	40		9	17	千克		---Other preparations for use in dentistry, with a basis of plaster
3407.0090	---其他	10	100		9	17	千克		---Other

第三十五章 蛋白类物质；改性淀粉；胶；酶

Chapter 35 Albuminoidal substances; modified starches; glues; enzymes

注释：

一、本章不包括：

（一）酵母（品目21.02）；

（二）第三十章的血份（非治病、防病用的血清白蛋白除外）、药品及其他产品；

（三）预鞣用酶制剂（品目32.02）；

（四）第三十四章的加酶的浸透剂、洗涤剂及其他产品；

（五）硬化蛋白（品目39.13）；或

（六）印刷工业用的明胶产品（第四十九章）。

二、品目 35.05 所称“糊精”，是指淀粉的降解产品，其还原糖含量以右旋糖的干重量计不超过10%。

如果还原糖含量超过 10%，应归入品目 17.02。

Chapter Notes:

1. This Chapter does not cover:

(a) Yeasts (heading 21.02);

(b) Blood fractions (other than blood albumin not prepared for therapeutic or prophylactic uses), medicaments or other products of Chapter 30;

(c) Enzymatic preparations for pre-tanning (heading 32.02);

(d) Enzymatic soaking or washing preparations or other products of Chapter 34;

(e) Hardened proteins (heading 39.13); or

(f) Gelatin products of the printing industry (Chapter 49).

2. For the purposes of heading 35.05, the term “dextrins” means starch degradation products with a reducing sugar content, expressed as dextrose on the dry substance, not exceeding 10%.

Such products with a reducing sugar content exceeding 10%fall in heading 17.02.

税则号列 Tariff Item	商品名称及备注	进口税率			出口退税	增值税率	计量单位	监管条件	Article Description
		最惠	普通	暂定					
35.01	酪蛋白、酪蛋白酸盐及其他酪蛋白衍生物；酪蛋白胶：								**Casein, caseinates and other casein derivatives; casein glues:**
3501.1000	-酪蛋白	10	35		13	17	千克	AB	-Casein
3501.9000	-其他	10	35		13	17	千克	AB	-Other
35.02	白蛋白（包括按重量计干质成分的乳清蛋白含量超过 80%的两种或两种以上的乳清蛋白浓缩物）、白蛋白盐及其他白蛋白衍生物：								**Albumins (including concentrates of two or more whey proteins, containing by weight more than 80% whey proteins, calculated on the dry matter), albuminates and other albumin derivatives:**
	-卵清蛋白：								-Egg albumin:
3502.1100	--干的	10	80		13	17	千克	AB	--Dried
3502.1900	--其他	10	80		13	17	千克	AB	--Other
3502.2000	-乳白蛋白，包括两种或两种以上的乳清蛋白浓缩物	10	35		13	17	千克	AB	-Milk albumin, including concentrates of two or more whey proteins
3502.9000	-其他	10	35		13	17	千克	AB	-Other
35.03	明胶（包括长方形、正方形明胶薄片，不论是否表面加工或着色）及其衍生物；鱼鳔胶；其他动物胶，但不包括品目 35.01 的酪蛋白胶：								**Gelatin (including gelatin in rectangular (including square) sheets, whether or not surface-worked or coloured) and gelatin derivatives; isinglass; other glues of animal origin, excluding casein glues of heading No. 35.01:**
3503.0010	---明胶及其衍生物	12	35		13	17	千克		---Gelatin and gelatin derivatives
3503 0010.01暂	明胶	12	35	5	13	17	千克	AB	Gelatin
3503 0010.90	明胶的衍生物（包括长方形、正方形明胶薄片，不论是否表面加工或着色）	12	35		13	17	千克	AB	Gelatin derivatives, including gelatin in rectangular (including square) sheets, whether or not surface-worked or coloured
3503.0090	---其他	12	50		13	17	千克	AB	---Other
35.04	蛋白胨及其衍生物；其他品目未列名的蛋白质及其衍生物；皮粉，不论是否加入铬矾：								**Peptones and their derivatives; other protein substances and their derivatives, not elsewhere specified or included; hide powder, whether or not chromed:**
3504.0010	---蛋白胨	3	11		13	17	千克	AB	---Peptones

税则号列 Tariff Item	商品名称及备注	进口税率 最惠	普通	暂定	出口退税	增值税率	计量单位	监管条件	Article Description
3504.0090	---其他	8	35		13	17	千克	AB	---Other
35.05	**糊精及其他改性淀粉（例如，预凝化淀粉或酯化淀粉）；以淀粉、糊精或其他改性淀粉为基本成分的胶：**								**Dextrins and other modified starches（for example,pregelatinized or esterified starches）; glues based on starches, or on dextrins or other modified starches:**
3505.1000[暂]	-糊精及其他改性淀粉	12	50	6	13	17	千克	A	-Dextrins and other modified starches
3505.2000	-胶	20	50		13	17	千克	A	-Glues
35.06	**其他品目未列名的调制胶及其他调制黏合剂；适于作胶或黏合剂用的产品，零售包装每件净重不超过1 千克：**								**Prepared glues and other prepared adhesives, not elsewhere specified or included; products suitable for use as glues or adhesives, put up for retail sale as glues or adhesives, not exceeding a net weight of 1 kg:**
3506.1000	-适于作胶或黏合剂用的产品，零售包装每件净重不超过1千克	10	90		13	17	千克		-Products suitable for use as glues or adhesives, put up for retail sale as glues or adhesives, not exceeding a net weight of 1 kg
3506 1000.10	硅酮结构密封胶（零售包装每件净重不超过1千克）	10	90		13	17	千克	A	Structural silicone sealant, put up for retail sale, not exceeding a net weight of 1 kg
3506 1000.90	其他适于作胶或黏合剂的零售产品（零售包装每件净重不超过1千克）	10	90		13	17	千克		Other products suitable for use as glues or adhesives, put up for retail sale as glues or adhesives, not exceeding a net weight of 1 kg
	-其他:								-Other:
	--以橡胶或品目39.01至39.13的聚合物为基本成分的黏合剂:								--Adhesives based on polymers of headings No. 39.01 to 39.13 or on rubber:
3506.9110	---以聚酰胺为基本成分的	10	90		13	17	千克		---Based on polyamide
3506.9120	---以环氧树脂为基本成分的	10	90		13	17	千克		---Based on epoxy resin
3506.9190	---其他	10	90		13	17	千克		---Other
3506 9190.10	非零售，硅酮结构密封胶	10	90		13	17	千克	A	Structural silicone sealant, not put up for retail sale
3506 9190.90	其他橡胶或塑料为基本成分黏合剂［包括以人造树脂（环氧树脂除外）为基本成分的］	10	90		13	17	千克		Other adhesives based on rubber or plastic or artificial resin （other than epoxy resin）
3506.9900	--其他	10	90		13	17	千克		--Other
35.07	**酶；其他品目未列名的酶制品：**								**Enzymes; prepared enzymes not elsewhere specified or included:**
3507.1000	-粗制凝乳酶及其浓缩物	6	30		13	17	千克	AB	-Rennet and concentrates thereof
	-其他:								-Other:
3507.9010	---碱性蛋白酶	6	30		13	17	千克	AB	---Basic proteinase
3507.9020	---碱性脂肪酶	6	30		13	17	千克	AB	---Basic lipase
3507.9090	---其他	6	30		13	17	千克	AB	---Other

第三十六章
炸药；烟火制品；火柴；引火合金；易燃材料制品

Chapter 36
Explosives; pyrotechnic products; matches; pyrophoric alloys; certain combustible preparations

注释：

一、本章不包括单独的已有化学定义的化合物，但下列注释二（一）、（二）所述物品除外。

二、品目 36.06 所称“易燃材料制品”，只适用于：

（一）聚乙醛、六亚甲基四胺（六甲撑四胺）及类似物质，已制成片、棒或类似形状作燃料用的；以酒精为基本成分的固体或半固体燃料及类似的配制燃料；

（二）直接灌注香烟打火机及类似打火器用的液体燃料或液化气体燃料，其包装容器的容积不超过300立方厘米；以及

（三）树脂火炬、引火物及类似品。

Chapter Notes:

1. This Chapter does not cover separate chemically defined compounds other than those described in Note 2（a）or（b）below.

2. The expression “articles of combustible materials” in heading 36.06 applies only to:

（a）Metaldehyde, hexamethylenetetramine and similar substances, put up in forms（for example, tablets, sticks or similar forms）for use as fuels; fuels with as basis of alcohol, and similar prepared fuels, in solid or semi-solid form;

（b）Liquid or liquefied-gas fuels in containers of a kind used for filling or refilling cigarette or similar lighters and of a capacity not exceeding $300cm^3$; and.

（c）Resin torches, firelighters and the like.

税则号列 Tariff Item	商品名称及备注	进口税率			出口退税	增值税率	计量单位	监管条件	Article Description
		最惠	普通	暂定					
36.01	发射药：								**Propellent powders:**
3601.0000	发射药	9	50			17	千克		Propellent powders
3601 0000.10	模压的胶质推进剂	9	50			17	千克	3	Colloidal molded propellant
3601 0000.20	含硝化粘接剂及铝粉＞5%的推进剂	9	50			17	千克	3	Propellant, containing nitrification adhesives and more than 5% of aluminum powder
3601 0000.90	其他发射药	9	50			17	千克		Other propellent powders
36.02	配制炸药，但发射药除外：								**Prepared explosives, other than propellent powders:**
3602.0010	---硝铵炸药	9	50			17	千克		---Based on ammonals nitrate
3602 0010.10	符合特定标准的硝铵炸药（硝胺类物质超过2%，或密度＞1.8g/cm^3、爆速＞8000m/s）	9	50			17	千克	3	Ammonium nitrate explosives meets specific criteria（containing more than 2% of nitramines, density＞1.8g/cm^3, explosion velocity＞8000m/s）
3602 0010.90	其他硝铵炸药,但发射药除外	9	50			17	千克		Other ammonium nitrate explosives, other than propellent powders
3602.0090	---其他	9	50			17	千克		---Other
3602 0090.10	符合特定标准的其他配制炸药（含六硝基芪＞2%，或密度＞1.8 g/cm^3、爆速＞8000 m/s）	9	50			17	千克	3	Other prepared explosives meets specific criteria（containing more than 2% of hexanitrostilbene , density＞1.8g/cm^3,explosion velocity＞8000m/s）
3602 0090.90	其他配制炸药,但发射药除外	9	50			17	千克		Other prepared explosives, other than propellent powders
36.03	**安全导火索；导爆索；火帽或雷管；引爆器；电雷管：**								**Safety fuses; detonating fuses; percussion or detonating caps; igniters; electric detonators:**
3603.0000	安全导火索；导爆索；火帽或雷管；引爆器；电雷管	9	50			17	千克		Safety fuses; detonating fuses; percussion or detonating caps; igniters; electric detonators
3603 0000.10	爆炸桥	9	50			17	千克	3	Exploding bridge
3603 0000.20	爆炸桥丝	9	50			17	千克	3	Exploding bridge filaments
3603 0000.30	冲击片	9	50			17	千克	3	Slapper detonators
3603 0000.40	爆炸箔起爆器	9	50			17	千克	3	Exploding foil initiator
3603 0000.50	使用单个或多个雷管的装置（由单一点火信号同时起爆，不包括仅使用起药的雷管）	9	50			17	千克	3	Devices with one or more detonator（the ignition signal from a single initiation at the same time, other than those used detonating powder only）
3603 0000.60	炸药雷管点火装置（用于引爆上述品目 36.03 各子目列名的爆炸配件的雷管）	9	50			17	千克	3	Explosive detonator ignition （for igniting detonator assembled with parts of subheadings of heading No.36.03
3603 0000.90	其他安全导火索导爆索等引爆器件（包括火帽或雷管、引爆器、	9	50			17	千克		Other Safety fuses; detonating fuses; percussion or detonating caps; igniters; electric detonators

税则号列 Tariff Item	商品名称及备注	进口税率			出口退税	增值税率	计量单位	监管条件	Article Description
		最惠	普通	暂定					
	电雷管）								
36.04	**烟花、爆竹、信号弹、降雨火箭、浓雾信号弹及其他烟火制品：**								**Fireworks, signalling flares, rain rockets, fog signals and other pyrotechnic articles:**
3604.1000	-烟花、爆竹	6	130		13	17	千克	AB	-Fireworks
3604.9000	-其他	6	100		13	17	千克		-Other
36.05	**火柴，但品目 36.04 的烟火制品除外：**								**Matches, other than pyrotechnic articles of heading No. 36.04:**
3605.0000	火柴，但品目 36.04 的烟火制品除外	6	100			17	千克	AB	Matches, other than pyrotechnic articles of heading No. 36.04
36.06	**各种形状的铈铁及其他引火合金；本章注释二所述的易燃材料制品：**								**Ferro-cerium and other pyrophoric alloys in all forms; articles of combustible materials as specified in Note 2 to this Chapter:**
3606.1000	-直接灌注香烟打火机及类似打火器用的液体燃料或液化气体燃料，其包装容器的容积不超过300立方厘米	10	80			17	千克		-Liquid or liquefied-gas fuels in containers of a kind used for filling or refilling cigarette or similar lighters and of a capacity not exceeding $300cm^3$
	--其他：								--Other:
	---铈铁及其他引火合金：								---Ferro-cerium and other pyrophoric alloys:
3606.9011	----已切成形可直接使用	9	80			17	千克		----Cut to shape, for immediate use
3606.9019	----其他	9	50			17	千克		----Other
3606.9090	---其他	9	80			17	千克		---Other

第三十七章 照相及电影用品

Chapter 37 Photographic or cinematographic goods

注释：

一、本章不包括废碎料。

二、本章所称"摄影"，是指光或其他射线作用于感光面上直接或间接形成可见影像的过程。

Chapter Notes:

1. This Chapter does not cover waste or scrap.
2. In this Chapter the word "photographic" relates to the process by which visible images are formed, directly or indirectly, by the action of light or other forms of radiation on photosensitive surfaces

税则号列 Tariff Item	商品名称及备注	进口税率			出口退税	增值税率	计量单位	监管条件	Article Description
		最惠	普通	暂定					
37.01	**未曝光的摄影感光硬片及平面软片，用纸、纸板及纺织物以外任何材料制成；未曝光的一次成像感光平片，不论是否分装：**								**Photographic plates and film in the flat, sensitized, unexposed, of any material other than paper, paperboard or textiles; instant print film in the flat, sensitized, unexposed, whether or not in packs:**
3701.1000[暂]	-X 光用	20	40	10	13	17	千克/平方米		-For X-ray
3701.2000	-一次成像平片	5	40		13	17	千克		-Instant print film
	-其他硬片及软片，任何一边超过 255 毫米:								-Other plates and film, with any side exceeding 255 mm:
	---照相制版用:								---For preparing printing plates or cylinders:
3701.3021	----激光照排片	10	50		13	17	千克/平方米		----Laser phototypesetting film
3701.3022	----PS 版	10	50		13	17	千克/平方米		----Precoated sensitized plate
3701.3024	----CTP 版	10	50		13	17	千克/平方米		----CTP plate
3701.3025	----柔性印刷版	10	50		13	17	千克/平方米		----Flexographic printing plates
3701.3029	----其他	10	50		13	17	千克/平方米		----Other
3701.3090	---其他	20	70		13	17	千克/平方米		---Other
	-其他:								-Other:
3701.9100	--彩色摄影用	22	70		13	17	千克		--For colour photography（polychrome）
	--其他:								--Other:
3701.9920	---照相制版用	10	40		13	17	千克/平方米		---For preparing printing plates or cylinders
3701 9920.01[暂]	石英玻璃基质的未曝光感光硬片	10	40	5	13	17	千克/平方米		Quartz glass plates, unexposed, sensitized
3701 9920.10	超微粒干版	10	40		13	17	千克/平方米		Ultrafine-grain plate
3701 9920.90	照相制版用其他未曝光软片及硬片(非彩色摄影用,边长≤255mm)	10	40		13	17	千克/平方米		Other plates and film, sensitized, unexposed, for preparing printing plates or cylinders, not for colour photography ,of side lengths not exceeding 255mm
3701.9990	其他	25	70		13	17	千克/平方米		---Other
37.02	**成卷的未曝光摄影感光胶片，用纸、纸板及纺织物以外任何材料制成；未曝光的一次成像感光卷片：**								**Photographic film in rolls, sensitized, unexposed, of any material other than paper, paperboard or textiles; instant print film in rolls, sensitized, unexposed:**
3702.1000	-X 光用	10	40		13	17	千克/平方米		-For X-ray
	-无齿孔的其他胶片，宽度不超过 105 毫米:								-Other film, without perforations, of a width not exceeding 105 mm:
	--彩色摄影用:								--For colour photography（polychrome）:
3702.3110	----一次成像卷片	5	40		13	17	个/平方米		---Instant print film

税则号列 Tariff Item	商品名称及备注	进口税率 最惠	进口税率 普通	进口税率 暂定	出口退税	增值税率	计量单位	监管条件	Article Description
3702.3190	---其他	56 元/㎡	433 元/㎡		13	17	个/平方米		---Other
	--其他涂卤化银乳液的:								--Other, with silver halide emulsion:
3702.3210	----一次成像卷片	5	40		13	17	千克/平方米		---Instant print film
3702.3220	---照相制版用	4.5 元/㎡	104/㎡		13	17	千克/平方米		---For preparing printing plates or cylinders
3702.3290	---其他	21 元/㎡	202 元/㎡		13	17	千克/平方米		---Other
	--其他:								--Other:
3702.3920	---照相制版用	12 元/㎡	104 元/㎡		13	17	千克/平方米		---For preparing printing plates or cylinders
3702.3990	---其他	24 元/㎡	202 元/㎡		13	17	千克/平方米		---Other
	-无齿孔的其他胶片，宽度超过105 毫米:								-Other film, without perforations, of a width exceeding 105mm:
3702.4100	--彩色摄影用，宽度超过 610 毫米，长度超过 200 米	7.1 元/㎡	202 元/㎡		13	17	千克/平方米		--Of a width exceeding 610mm and of a length exceeding 200m, for colour photography （polychrome）
	--非彩色摄影用，宽度超过 610 毫米，长度超过 200 米:								--Of a width exceeding 610mm and of a length exceeding 200m, other than for colour photography:
	---照相制版用:								---For preparing printing plates or cylinders:
3702.4221	----印刷电路板制造用光致抗蚀干膜	0.6 元/㎡	110 元/㎡		13	17	千克/平方米		----Wide anticorrosive photographic plate for printed circuit processing
3702.4229	----其他	1.6 元/㎡	110 元/㎡		13	17	千克/平方米		----Other
	---其他:								---Other:
3702.4292	----红色或红外激光胶片	2.4 元/㎡	213 元/㎡		13	17	千克/平方米		----Red or Infrared laser film
3702 4292.01 [暂]	未曝光红色或红外激光胶片(宽长胶卷指宽度>800mm，长度>1000m)	2.4 元/㎡	213 元/㎡	1.05元/㎡	13	17	千克/平方米		Unexposed infrared or helium-neon laser film, of a width exceeding 800mm, of a length exceeding 1000m
3702 4292.90	其他未曝光红色或红外激光胶片（610mm＜宽度≤800mm，200m＜长度≤1000m）	2.4 元/㎡	213 元/㎡		13	17	千克/平方米		Other unexposed infrared or helium-neon laser film, （610mm＜of a width≤800mm，200m＜of a length≤1000m）
3702.4299	----其他	7 元/㎡	213 元/㎡		13	17	千克/平方米		----Other
	--宽度超过 610 毫米，长度不超过 200 米:								--Of a width exceeding 610mm and of a length not exceeding 200m:
	---照相制版用:								---For preparing printing plates or cylinders:
3702.4321	----激光照排片	10 元/㎡	104 元/㎡		13	17	千克/平方米		----Laser phototypesetting film
3702.4329	----其他	3.7 元/㎡	104 元/㎡		13	17	千克/平方米		----Other
3702.4390	---其他	17 元/㎡	202 元/㎡		13	17	千克/平方米		---Other
	--宽度超过 105 毫米，但不超过 610 毫米:								--Of a width exceeding 105mm but not exceeding 610mm:
	---照相制版用:								---For preparing printing plates or cylinders:
3702.4421	----激光照排片	2.0 元/㎡	115 元/㎡		13	17	千克/平方米		----Laser phototypesetting film
3702.4422	----印刷电路板制造用光致抗蚀干膜	5 元/㎡	115 元/㎡		13	17	千克/平方米		----Narrow anticorrosive photographic plate for printed circuit processing
3702.4429	----其他	2.9 元/㎡	115 元/㎡		13	17	千克/平方米		----Other
3702.4490	---其他	27 元/㎡	202 元/㎡		13	17	千克/平方米		---Other

税则号列 Tariff Item	商品名称及备注	进口税率 最惠	进口税率 普通	进口税率 暂定	出口退税	增值税率	计量单位	监管条件	Article Description
	-彩色摄影用的其他胶片:								-Other film, for colour photography（pylychrome）:
3702.5200	--宽度不超过16毫米	95元/㎡	433元/㎡		13	17	米/平方米		--Of a width not exceeding 16mm
3702.5300	--幻灯片用，宽度超过16毫米，但不超过35毫米，长度不超过30米	128元/㎡	433元/㎡		13	17	米/平方米		--Of a width exceeding 16mm but not exceeding 35mm and of a length not exceeding 30m, for slides
	--非幻灯片用，宽度超过16毫米，但不超过35毫米，长度不超过30米:								--Of a width exceeding 16mm but not exceeding 35mm and of a length not exceeding 30m, other than for slides:
3702.5410	---宽度为35毫米，长度不超过2米	18元/㎡	433元/㎡		13	17	米/平方米		---Of a width 35mm and of a length not exceeding 2m
3702.5490	---其他	24元/㎡	433元/㎡		13	17	米/平方米		---Other
	--宽度超过16毫米，但不超过35毫米，长度超过30米:								--Of a width exceeding 16mm but not exceeding 35mm and of a length exceeding 30m:
3702.5520[暂]	---电影胶片	9元/㎡	232元/㎡	6元/㎡	13	17	米/平方米		---Cinematographic film
3702.5590	---其他	27元/㎡	433元/㎡		13	17	米/平方米		---Other
	--宽度超过35毫米:								--Of a width exceeding 35mm:
3702.5620	---电影胶片	13元/㎡	232元/㎡		13	17	米/平方米		---Cinematographic film
3702.5690	---其他	74元/㎡	433元/㎡		13	17	米/平方米		---Other
	-其他:								-Other:
3702.9600	--宽度不超过35毫米，长度不超过30米	21元/㎡	210元/㎡		13	17	米/平方米		--Of a width not exceeding 35mm and of a length not exceeding 30m
3702.9700	--宽度不超过35毫米，长度超过30米	9元/㎡	210元/㎡		13	17	米/平方米		--Of a width not exceeding 35mm and of a length exceeding 30m
3702.9800	--宽度超过35毫米	10元/㎡	210元/㎡		13	17	米/平方米		--Of a width exceeding 35mm
37.03	**未曝光的摄影感光纸、纸板及纺织物:**								**Photographic paper, paperboard and textiles, sensitized, unexposed:**
	-成卷，宽度超过610毫米:								-In rolls of a width exceeding 610 mm:
3703.1010	---感光纸及纸板	18	100		13	17	千克		---Photographic paper and paperboard
3703.1090	---其他	18	70		13	17	千克		---Other
	-其他，彩色摄影用:								-Other, for colour photography（polychrome）:
3703.2010	---感光纸及纸板	35	100		13	17	千克		---Photographic paper and paperboard
3703.2090	---其他	18	70		13	17	千克		---Other
	-其他:								-Other:
3703.9010	---感光纸及纸板	35	100		13	17	千克		---Photographic paper and paperboard
3703.9090	---其他	18	70		13	17	千克		---Other
37.04	**已曝光未冲洗的摄影硬片、软片、纸、纸板及纺织物:**								**Photographic plates, film, paper, paperboard and textiles, exposed but not developed:**
3704.0010	---电影胶片	6.5	30		13	17	千克	Z	---Cinematographic film
3704.0090	---其他	18	70		13	17	千克		---Other
37.05	**已曝光已冲洗的摄影硬片及软片，但电影胶片除外:**								**Photographic plates and film, exposed and developed, other than cinematographic film:**
3705.1000	-供复制胶版用	18	70		13	17	千克		-For offset reproduction
	-其他:								-Other:
3705.9010	---教学专用幻灯片	0	0		13	17	千克		---Lantern slides, for educational use only
	---缩微胶片:								---Microfilms:
3705.9021	----书籍、报刊的	0	0		13	17	千克		----For printed books and newspapers
3705.9029	----其他	4	14		13	17	千克		----Other
3705.9090	---其他	18	70		13	17	千克		---Other
37.06	**已曝光已冲洗的电影胶片，不论是否配有声道或仅有声道:**								**Cinematographic film, exposed and developed, whether or not incorporating sound track or**

税则号列 Tariff Item	商品名称及备注	进口税率			出口退税	增值税率	计量单位	监管条件	Article Description
		最惠	普通	暂定					
									consisting only of sound track:
	-宽度在 35 毫米及以上:								-Of a width of 35mm or more:
3706.1010	---教学专用	0	0		13	17	千克/米	Z	---For educational use only
3706.1090	---其他	5	14		13	17	千克/米	Z	---Other
	-其他:								-Other:
3706.9010	---教学专用	0	0		13	17	千克/米	Z	---For educational use only
3706.9090	---其他	4	14		13	17	千克/米	Z	---Other
37.07	**摄影用化学制剂（不包括上光漆、胶水、黏合剂及类似制剂）；摄影用未混合产品；定量包装或零售包装可立即使用的：**								**Chemical preparations for photographic use (other than varnishes, glues, adhesives and similar preparations); unmixed products for photographic uses, put up in measured portions or put up for retail sale in a form ready for use:**
3707.1000	-感光乳液	8	35		13	17	千克		-Sensitizing emulsions
3707 1000.01[暂]	不含银的感光乳液剂	8	35	4	13	17	千克		Non-silver light-sensitive emulsion agent
3707 1000.90	其他感光乳液	8	35		13	17	千克		Other light-sensitive emulsion agent
	-其他:								-Other:
3707.9010	---冲洗照相胶卷及相片用	16	100		13	17	千克		---For use in developing photographic film and photographs
3707.9020[暂]	---复印机用	10	45	8	13	17	千克		---For use in photo-copying apparatus
3707.9090	---其他	8	35		13	17	千克		---Other

第三十八章 杂项化学产品

注释：

一、本章不包括：

（一）单独的已有化学定义的元素及化合物，但下列各项除外：

1．人造石墨（品目38.01）；

2．制成品目38.08所述的形状或包装的杀虫剂、杀鼠剂、杀菌剂、除草剂、抗萌剂、植物生长调节剂、消毒剂及类似产品；

3．灭火器的装配药及已装药的灭火弹（品目38.13）；

4．下列注释二所规定的检定参照物；

5．下列注释三（一）及三（三）所规定的产品。

（二）化学品与食品或其他营养物质的混合物，配制食品用的（一般归入品目21.06）；

（三）含有金属、砷及其混合物，并符合第二十六章注释三（一）或三（二）的规定的矿渣、矿灰和残渣（包括淤渣，但下水道淤泥除外）（品目26.20）；

（四）药品（品目30.03及30.04）；或

（五）用于提取贱金属或生产贱金属化合物的废催化剂（品目26.20），主要用于回收贵金属的废催化剂（品目71.12），或某种形状（例如，精细粉末或纱网状）的金属或金属合金催化剂（第十四类或第十五类）。

二、（一）品目 38.22 所称的"检定参照物"，是指附有证书的参照物，该证书标明了参照物属性的指标、确定这些指标的方法以及与每一指标相关的确定度，这些参照物用于分析、校准和比较。

（二）除第二十八章和二十九章的产品外，检定参照物在本目录中应优先归入品目38.22。

三、品目38.24包括不归入本协调制度其他品目的下列货品：

（一）每颗重量不小于2.5克的氧化镁、碱金属或碱土金属卤化物制成的培养晶体（光学元件除外）；

（二）杂醇油；骨焦油；

（三）零售包装的除墨剂；

（四）零售包装的蜡纸改正液、其他改正液及改正带（品目96.12的产品除外）；以及

（五）可熔性陶瓷测温器（例如，塞格测温锥）。

四、本目录所称"城市垃圾"，是指从家庭、宾馆、餐馆、医院、商店、办公室等收集来的废物，马路和人行道的垃圾，以及建筑垃圾或拆建垃圾。

Chapter 38 Miscellaneous chemical products

Chapter Notes:

1. This Chapter does not cover:

(a) Separate chemically defined elements or compounds with the exception of the following:

(i) Artificial graphite (heading 38.01);

(ii) Insecticides, rodenticides, fungicides, herbicides, anti-sprouting products and plant-growth regulators, disinfectants and similar products, put up as described in heading 38.08;

(iii) Products put up as charges for fire-extinguishers or put up in fire-extinguishing grenades (heading 38.13);

(iv) Certified reference materials specified in Note 2 below;

(v) Products specified in Note 3 (a) or 3 (c) below;

(b) Mixtures of chemicals with foodstuffs or other substances with nutritive value, of a kind used in the preparation of human foodstuffs (generally heading 21.06);

(c) Slag, ash and residues (including sludges, other than sewage sludge), containing metals, arsenic or their mixtures and meeting the requirements of Note 3 (a) or 3 (b) to Chapter 26 (heading 26.20);

(d) Medicaments (heading 30.03 or 30.04); or

(e) Spent catalysts of a kind used for the extraction of base metals or for the manufacture of chemical compounds of base metals (heading 26.20), spent catalysts of a kind used principally for the recovery of precious metal (heading 71. 12) or catalysts consisting of metals or metal alloys in the form of, for example, finely divided powder or woven gauze (Section XIV or XV).

2. (a) For the purpose of heading 38.22, the expression "certified reference materials" means reference materials which are accompanied by a certificate which indicates the values of the certified properties, the methods used to determine these values and the degree of certainty associated with each value and which are suitable for analytical, calibrating or referencing purposes.

(b) With the exception of the products of Chapter 28 or 29, for the classification of certified reference materials, heading 38.22 shall take precedence over any other heading in the Nomenclature.

3. Heading 38.24 includes the following goods which are not to be classified in any other heading of the Nomenclature:

(a) Cultured crystals (other than optical elements) weighing not less than 2.5g each, of magnesium oxide or of the halides of the alkali or alkaline-earth metals;

(b) Fusel oil; Dippel's oil;

(c) Ink removers put up in packings for retail sale;

(d) Stencil correctors, other correcting fluids and correction tapes (other than those of heading 96.12), put up in packings for retail sale; and

(e) Ceramic firing testers, fusible (for example, Seger cones).

4. Throughout the Nomenclature, "municipal waste" means waste of a kind collected from households, hotels, restaurants, hospitals, shops, offices, etc., road and pavement sweepings, as well as construction and

城市垃圾通常含有大量各种各样的材料，例如，塑料、橡胶、木材、纸张、纺织品、玻璃、金属、食物、破烂家具和其他已损坏或被丢弃的物品，但“城市垃圾”不包括：

（一）已从垃圾中分拣出来的单独的材料或物品，例如，废的塑料、橡胶、木材、纸张、纺织品、玻璃、金属及电池的废品。这些材料或物品应归入本目录中适当品目；

（二）工业废物；

（三）第三十章注释四（十）所规定的废药物；或

（四）本章注释六（一）所规定的医疗废物。

五、品目 38.25 所称“下水道淤泥”，是指经城市污水处理厂处理的淤泥，包括预处理的废料、刷洗污垢和性质不稳定的淤泥。但适合作为肥料用的性质稳定的淤泥除外（第三十一章）。

六、品目 38.25 所称“其他废物”适用于：

（一）医疗废物，即医学研究、诊断、治疗，以及其他内科、外科、牙科或兽医治疗所产生的被污染的废物，通常含有病菌和药物，需作专门处理（例如，脏的敷料、用过的手套及注射器）；

（二）废有机溶剂；

（三）废的金属酸洗液、液压油、制动油及防冻液；以及

（四）化学工业及相关工业的其他废物。

但不包括主要含有石油及从沥青矿物提取的油类的废油（品目 27.10）。

七、品目 38.26 所称的‘生物柴油’，是指从动植物油脂（不论是否使用过）得到的用做燃料的脂肪酸单烷基酯。

demolition waste. Municipal waste generally contains a large variety of materials such as plastics, rubber, wood, paper, textiles, glass, metals, food materials, broken furniture and other damaged or discarded articles. The term “municipal waste” , however, does not cover:

（a）Individual materials or articles segregated from the waste, such as wastes of plastics, rubber, wood, paper, textiles, glass or metals and spent batteries which fall in their appropriate headings of the Nomenclature;

（b）Industrial waste;

（c）Waste pharmaceuticals, as defined in Note 4（k）to Chapter 30; or

（d）Clinical waste, as defined in Note 6（a）below.

5. For the purposes of heading 38.25, “sewage sludge” means sludge arising from urban effluent treatment plant and includes pre-treatment waste, scourings and unstabilised sludge. Stabilised sludge when suitable for use as fertiliser is excluded（Chapter 31）.

6. For the purposes of heading 38.25, the expression “other wastes” applies to:

（a）Clinical waste, that is, contaminated waste arising from medical research, diagnosis, treatment or other medical, surgical, dental or veterinary procedures, which often contain pathogens and pharmaceutical substances and require special disposal procedures（for example, soiled dressings, used gloves and used syringes）;

（b）Waste organic solvents;

（c）Wastes of metal pickling liquors, hydraulic fluids, brake fluids and anti-freezing fluids; and

（d）Other wastes from chemical or allied industries.

The expression “other wastes” does not, however, cover wastes which contain mainly petroleum oils or oils obtained from bituminous minerals（heading 27.10）.

7. For the purposes of heading 38.26, the term “biodiesel” means mono-alkyl esters of fatty acids of a kind used as a fuel, derived from animal or vegetable fats and oils whether or not used.

子目注释：

一、子目 3808.50 仅包括品目 38.08 的货品，含有一种或多种下列物质：艾氏剂（ISO）；乐杀螨（ISO）；毒杀芬（ISO）；敌菌丹（ISO）；氯丹（ISO）；杀虫脒（ISO）；乙酯杀螨醇（ISO）；滴滴涕（ISO，INN）[1，1，1-三氯-2，2-双（4-氯苯基）乙烷]；狄氏剂（ISO，INN）；4，6-二硝基邻甲酚[二硝酚（ISO）]及其盐；地乐酚（ISO）及其盐或酯；1，2-二溴乙烷（ISO）；1，2-二氯乙烷（ISO）；氟乙酰胺（ISO）；七氯（ISO）；六氯苯（ISO）；1，2，3，4，5，6-六氯环已烷[六六六（ISO）]，包括林丹（ISO，INN）；汞化合物；甲胺磷（ISO）；久效磷（ISO）；环氧乙烷（氧化乙烯）；对硫磷（ISO）；甲基对硫磷（ISO）；五氯苯酚（ISO）及其盐或酯；磷胺（ISO）；2，4，5-涕（ISO）（2，4，5-三氯苯氧基乙酸）及其盐或酯；三丁基锡化合物。

子目 3808.50 还包括含有苯菌灵（ISO）、克百威（ISO）及福美双（ISO）混合物的粉状制剂。

二、子目 3825.41 和 3825.49 所称“废有机溶剂”，是指主要含有有机溶剂的废物，不适合再作原产品使用，不论其是否用于回收溶剂。

Subheading Note:

1. Subheading 3808.50 covers only goods of heading 38.08, containing one or more of the following substances: aldrin（ISO）;binapacryl（ISO）; camphechlor（ISO）（toxaphene）;captafol（ISO）; chlordane（ISO）; chlordimeform（ISO）;chlorobenzilate（ISO）; DT（ISO）[clofenotane（INN）,1, 1, 1- trichloro-2, 2-bis（p-chlorophenyl）ethane]; dieldrin（ISO, INN）; 4, 6- dinitro-o-cresol(DNOC(ISO)) or its salts; dinoseb（ISO）, its salts or its esters; ethylene dibromide（ISO）（1, 2-dibromoethane）; ethylene dichloride（ISO）（1, 2-dichloroethane）; fluoroacetamide（ISO）; heptachlor（ISO）; hexachlorobenzene（ISO）;1, 2, 3, 4, 5, 6-hexachlorocyclohexane [HCH（ISO）], including lindane（ISO, INN）; mercury compounds; methamidophos（ISO）; monocrotophos（ISO）; oxirane（ethylene oxide）; parathion（ISO）; parathion-methyl（ISO）（methyl-parathion）; pentachlorophenol（ISO）, its salts or its esters; phosphamidon（ISO）; 2, 4, 5-T（ISO）（2, 4, 5-trichlorophenoxyacetic acid）, its salts or its esters; tributyltin compounds.subheading 3808.50 also covers dustable powder formulations containing a mixture of benomyl (ISO), carbofuran (ISO) and thiram (ISO).

2. For the purposes of subheadings 3825.41 and 3825.49, “waste organic solvents” are wastes containing mainly organic solvents, not fit for further use as presented as primary products, whether or not intended for recovery of the solvents.

税则号列 Tariff Item	商品名称及备注	进口税率 最惠	普通	暂定	出口退税	增值税率	计量单位	监管条件	Article Description
38.01	**人造石墨；胶态或半胶态石墨；以石墨或其他碳为基本成分的糊状、块状、板状制品或半制品：**								**Artificial graphite; colloidal or semicolloidal graphite; preparations based on graphite or other carbon in the form of pastes, blocks, plates or other semi-manufactures:**
3801.1000[暂]	-人造石墨	6.5	30	3		17	千克		-Artificial graphite
3801 1000.10[暂]	核级石墨（纯度高于百万分之五硼当量，密度大于1.50g/cm^3）	6.5	30	3		17	千克	3	Nuclear graphite, (the purity is higher than 5/million boron equivalent, the density is bigger than 1.50g/cm^3)
3801 1000.20[暂]	人造细晶粒整体石墨（20℃下的密度、拉伸断裂应变、热膨胀系数符合特殊要求）	6.5	30	3		17	千克	3	Artificial fine-grained graphite（Density, tensile fracture strain, coefficient of thermal expansion in line with specific requirements at 20℃or below）
3801 1000.90[暂]	其他人造石墨	6.5	30	3		17	千克	3	Other artificial graphite
3801.2000	-胶态或半胶态石墨	6.5	30			17	千克		-Colloidal or semi-colloidal graphite
3801.3000	-电极用碳糊及炉衬用的类似糊	6.5	35			17	千克		-Carbonaceous pastes for electrodes and similar pastes for furnace linings
	-其他								-Other
3801.9010	---表面处理的球化石墨	6.5	35			17	千克	3	---Surface treatment of the spherical graphite
3801.9090	---其他	6.5	35			17	千克	3	---Other
38.02	**活性碳；活性天然矿产品；动物炭黑，包括废动物炭黑：**								**Activated carbon; activated natural mineral products; animal black, including spent animal black:**
	-活性碳：								-Activated carbon:
3802.1010	---木质的	6.5	20			17	千克	G	---Wood based
3802.1090	---其他	6.5	20			17	千克	ABG	---Other
3802.9000	-其他	10	45			17	千克		-Other
3802 9000.10	濒危动物炭黑（包括废动物炭黑）	10	45			17	千克	FE	Endangered animal black（including spent animal black）
3802 9000.90	活性天然矿产品；其他动物炭黑（包括废动物炭黑）	10	45			17	千克		Activated natural mineral products; other animal black（including spent animal black）
38.03	**妥尔油，不论是否精炼：**								**Tall oil, whether or not refined:**
3803.0000	妥尔油，不论是否精炼	6.5	35			17	千克		Tall oil, whether or not refined
38.04	**木浆残余碱液，不论是否浓缩、脱糖或经化学处理，包括木素磺酸盐，但不包括品目38.03的妥尔油：**								**Residual lyes from the manufacture of wood pulp, whether or not concentrated, desugared or chemically treated,including lignin sulphonates, but excluding tall oil of heading No. 38.03:**
3804.0000	木浆残余碱液，不论是否浓缩、脱糖或经化学处理，包括木素磺酸盐，但不包括品目38.03的妥尔油	6.5	35			17	千克		Residual lyes from the manufacture of wood pulp, whether or not concentrated, desugared or chemically treated, including lignin sulphonates, but excluding tall oil of heading No. 38.03
3804 0000.10	未经浓缩、脱糖或经过化学处理的木浆残余碱液（妥尔油除外）	6.5	35			17	千克	9	Residual lyes from the manufacture of wood pulp,not concentrated, not desugared nor chemically treated (excluding tall oil)
3804 0000.90	经浓缩、脱糖或经过化学处理的木浆残余碱液，包括木素磺酸盐（妥尔油除外）	6.5	35			17	千克		Residual lyes from the manufacture of wood pulp, concentrated,desugared or chemically treated, including lignin sulphonates, but excluding tall oil
38.05	**脂松节油、木松节油和硫酸盐松节油及其他萜烯油，用蒸馏或其他方法从针叶木制得；粗制二聚戊烯；亚硫酸盐松节油及其他粗制对异丙基苯甲烷；以α萜品醇为基本成分的松油：**								**Gum, wood or sulphate turpentine and other terpenic oils produced by the distillation or other treatment of coniferous woods; crude dipentene; sulphite turpentine and other crude paracymene; pine oil containing alpha terpineol as the main constituent:**
3805.1000	-脂松节油、木松节油和硫酸盐松节油	6.5	50			17	千克	AB	-Gum, wood or sulphate turpentine oils
	-其他：								-Other:
3805.9010	---松油	6.5	50			17	千克	AB	---Pine oil
3805.9090	---其他	6.5	50			17	千克		---Other
38.06	**松香和树脂酸及其衍生物；松香**								**Rosin and resin acids, and derivatives thereof;**

税则号列 Tariff Item	商品名称及备注	进口税率 最惠	普通	暂定	出口退税	增值税率	计量单位	监管条件	Article Description
	精及松香油；再熔胶：								**rosin spirit and rosin oils; rungums:**
	-松香及树脂酸:								-Rosin and resin acids:
3806.1010	---松香	10	70			17	千克		---Rosin
3806.1020	---树脂酸	10	70			17	千克		---Resin acids
	-松香盐、树脂酸盐及松香或树脂酸衍生物的盐，但松香加合物的盐除外:								-Salts of rosin, of resin acids or of derivatives of rosin or resin acids, other than salts of rosin adducts:
3806.2010	---松香盐及树脂酸盐	6.5	40		13	17	千克		---Salts of rosin, of resin acids
3806.2090	---其他	6.5	40		13	17	千克		---Other
3806.3000	-酯胶	6.5	50			17	千克	AB	-Ester gums
3806.9000	-其他	6.5	40			17	千克		-Other
3806 9000.10	歧化松香及松香衍生物	6.5	40			17	千克		Disproportionated rosin and derivatives thereof
3806 9000.90	其他松香及树脂酸衍生物（包括松香精及松香油；再熔胶）	6.5	40			17	千克		Other rosin and resin acids, and derivatives thereof; (including rosin spirit and rosin oils; rungums)
38.07	**木焦油；精制木焦油；木杂酚油；粗木精；植物沥青；以松香、树脂酸或植物沥青为基本成分的啤酒桶沥青及类似制品:**								**Wood tar; wood tar oils; wood creosote; wood naphtha; vegetable pitch; brewers'pitch and similar preparations based on rosin, resin acids or on vegetable pitch:**
3807.0000	木焦油；精致木焦油；木杂酚油；粗木精；植物沥青；以松香、树脂酸或植物沥青为基本成分的啤酒桶沥青及类似制品	6.5	35			17	千克		Wood tar; wood tar oils; wood creosote;wood naphtha; vegetable pitch; brewers' pitch and similar preparations based on rosin, resin acids or on vegetable pitch
38.08	**杀虫剂、杀鼠剂、杀菌剂、除草剂、抗萌剂、植物生长调节剂、消毒剂及类似产品，零售形状、零售包装或制成制剂及成品（例如，经硫磺处理的带子、杀虫灯芯、蜡烛及捕蝇纸）**								**Insecticides, rodenticides, fungicides, herbicides, anti-sprouting products and plantgrowth regulators, disinfectants and similar products, put up in forms or packings for retail sale or as preparations or articles(for example, sulphurtreated bands, wicks and candles, and fly-papers):**
	-本章子目注释-所规定的货品:								-Goods specified in Subheading Note 1 to this Chapter:
3808.5010	---零售包装	9	35		5	13	千克		---Put up for retail sale
3808 5010.10	零售包装的含有一种第38章子目注释一所列物质的货品	9	35		5	13	千克	S	Goods containing substances specified in subheading Note 1 to Chapter 38, put up for retail sale
3808 5010.90	零售包装含有多种第38章子目注释一所列物质的货品	9	35		5	13	千克	X	Goods containing several kinds of substances specified in subheading Note 1 to Chapter 38, put up for retail sale
3808.5090	---其他	5	11		5	13	千克		---Other
3808 5090.10	非零售包装的含有一种第38章子目注释一所列物质的货品	5	11		5	13	千克	S	Goods containing substances specified in subheading Note 1 to Chapter 38, not put up for retail sale
3808 5090.90	非零售包装含有多种第38章子目注释一所列物质的货品	5	11		5	13	千克	X	Goods containing several kinds of substances specified in subheading Note 1 to Chapter 38, not put up for retail sale
	-其他:								-Other:
	--杀虫剂:								---Insecticides:
	---零售包装:								---Put up for retail sale:
3808.9111	----蚊香	10	80		5	17	千克	AS	----Mosquito smudges
3808.9112	----生物杀虫剂	10	35		5	13	千克	AS	----Biological insecticides
3808.9119	----其他	10	35		5	13	千克	AS	----Other
3808.9190	---其他	6	11		5	13	千克	AS	---Other
	--杀菌剂:								--Fungicides:
3808.9210	---零售包装	9	35		5	17	千克	S	---Put up for retail sale
3808.9290	---其他	6	11		5		千克		---Other
3808 9290.10	非零售包装的医用杀菌剂	6	11		5	17	千克		Medical fungicides, not put up for retail sale
3808 9290.21	经农药杀菌剂浸渍的纸质水果套袋	6	11		5	17	千克	S	Paper bagfor fruit bagging, impregnated by pesticide fungicide
3808 9290.29	非零售包装的其他农用杀菌剂	6	11		5	13	千克	S	Other agricultural fungicides medicine, not put up

税则号列 Tariff Item	商品名称及备注	进口税率 最惠	普通	暂定	出口退税	增值税率	计量单位	监管条件	Article Description
	成药								for retail sale
3808 9290.90	非零售包装的非农用杀菌剂成药（包括非医用杀菌剂）	6	11		5	13	千克		Non-agricultural fungicides medicines and non-medical fungicides, not put up for retail sale
	--除草剂、抗萌剂及植物生长调节剂:								--Herbicides,anti-sprouting products and plant –growth regulators:
	---除草剂:								---Herbicides:
3808.9311	----零售包装	9	35		5	13	千克	AS	----Put up for retail sale
3808.9319	----其他	5	11		5	13	千克		----Other
3808 9319.10	非零售包装百草枯母液	5	11		5	13	千克	AS	Paraquat liquor, not put up for retail sale
3808 9319.90	其他非零售包装的除草剂成药	5	11		5	13	千克	AS	Other herbicides medicine, not put up for retail sale
	---其他:								---Other:
3808.9391	----零售包装	9	35		5	13	千克	S	----Put up for retail sale
3808.9399	----其他	6	14		5	13	千克	S	----Other
3808.9400	--消毒剂	9	35		5		千克		--Disinfectants
3808 9400.10	医用消毒剂	9	35		5	17	千克		Medical disinfectants
3808 9400.20	兽用已配剂量含戊二醛、癸甲溴铵消毒剂等(包括复方煤焦油酸溶液消毒防腐药)	9	35		5	13	千克	R	Glutaraldehyde and decyl bromide disinfectant, etc. for livestock (including disinfectants and antiseptics for compound coal tar acid solution)
3808 9400.90	其他非医用消毒剂	9	35		5	13	千克		Other non-medical disinfectants
	--其他:								--Other:
3808.9910	---零售包装	9	35		5	13	千克	S	---Put up for retail sale
3808.9990	---其他	9	14		5	13	千克	S	---Other
38.09	**纺织、造纸、制革及类似工业用的其他品目未列名的整理剂、染料加速着色或固色助剂及其他产品和制剂（例如，修整剂及媒染剂）：**								**Finishing agents, dye carriers to accelerate the dyeing or fixing of dyestuffs and other products and preparations（for example, dressings and mordants）, of a kind used in the textile, paper, leather or like industries, not elsewhere specified or included:**
3809.1000	-以淀粉物质为基本成分	10	35			17	千克		-With a basis of amylaceous substances
	-其他:								-Other:
3809.9100	--纺织工业及类似工业用	6.5	35			17	千克		--Of a kind used in the textile or like industries
3809.9200	--造纸工业及类似工业用	6.5	35			17	千克		--Of a kind used in the paper or like industries
3809.9300	--制革工业及类似工业用	6.5	35			17	千克		--Of a kind used in the leather or like industries
38.10	**金属表面酸洗剂；焊接用的焊剂及其他辅助剂；金属及其他材料制成的焊粉或焊膏；作焊条芯子或焊条涂料用的制品：**								**Pickling preparations for metal surfaces;fluxes and other auxiliary preparations for soldering, brazing or welding; soldering, brazing or welding powders and pastes consisting of metal and other materials; preparations of a kind used as cores or coatings for welding electrodes or rods:**
3810.1000	-金属表面酸洗剂；金属及其他材料制成的焊粉或焊膏	6.5	35		13	17	千克		-Pickling preparations for metal surfaces; soldering, brazing or welding powders and pastes consisting of metal and other materials
3810.9000	-其他	6.5	35			17	千克		-Other
38.11	**抗震剂、抗氧剂、防胶剂、粘度改良剂、防腐蚀制剂及其他配制添加剂，用于矿物油（包括汽油）或与矿物油同样用途的其他液体：**								**Anti-knock preparations, oxidation inhibitors, gum inhibitors, viscosity improvers, anticorrosive preparations and other prepared additives, for mineral oils（including gasoline） or for other liquids used for the same purposes as mineral oils:**
	-抗震剂:								-Anti-knock preparations:
3811.1100	--以铅化合物为基本成分	6.5	35			17	千克	X	--Based on lead compounds

税则号列 Tariff Item	商品名称及备注	进口税率 最惠	进口税率 普通	进口税率 暂定	出口退税	增值税率	计量单位	监管条件	Article Description
3811.1900	--其他	6.5	35			17	千克		--Other
	-润滑油添加剂:								-Additives for lubricating oils:
3811.2100	--含有石油或从沥青矿物提取的油类	6.5	35			17	千克		--Containing petroleum oils or oils obtained from bituminous minerals
3811.2900	--其他	6.5	35			17	千克		--Other
3811.9000	-其他	6.5	35			17	千克		-Other
38.12	**配制的橡胶促进剂；其他品目未列名的橡胶或塑料用复合增塑剂；橡胶或塑料用抗氧制剂及其他复合稳定剂：**								**Prepared rubber accelerators; compounds plasticizers for rubber or plastics, not elsewhere specified or included; anti-oxidizing preparations and other compound stabilizers for rubber or plastics:**
3812.1000	-配制的橡胶促进剂	6	20		13	17	千克		-Prepared rubber accelerators
3812.2000	-橡胶或塑料用复合增塑剂	6.5	35		5	17	千克		-Compound plasticizers for rubber or plastics
	-橡胶或塑料用抗氧制剂及其他复合稳定剂:								-Anti-oxidizing preparations and other compound stabilizers for rubber or plastics:
3812.3010	---橡胶防老剂	6	20		5	17	千克		---Rubber antioxidants
3812.3090	---其他	6.5	35		5	17	千克		---Other
38.13	**灭火器的装配药；已装药的灭火弹：**								**Preparations and charges for fire-extinguishers; charged fire-extinguishing grenades:**
3813.0010	---灭火器的装配药	6.5	35			17	千克		---Preparations and charges for fire-extinguishers
3813.0020	---已装药的灭火弹	10	70			17	千克		---Charged fire-extinguishing grenades
38.14	**其他品目未列名的有机复合溶剂及稀释剂；除漆剂：**								**Organic composite solvents and thinners, not elsewhere specified or included; prepared paint or varnish removers:**
3814.0000	其他品目未列名的有机复合溶剂及稀释剂；除漆剂	10	50			17	千克		Organic composite solvents and thinners, not elsewhere specified or included; prepared paint or varnish removers
38.15	**其他品目未列名的反应引发剂、反应促进剂、催化剂：**								**Reaction initiators, reaction accelerators and catalytic preparations, not elsewhere specified or included:**
	-载体催化剂:								-Supported catalysts:
3815.1100	--以镍及其化合物为活性物的	6.5	35			17	千克		--With nickel or nickel compounds as the active substance
3815.1200[暂]	--以贵金属及其化合物为活性物的	6.5	35	4		17	千克		--With precious metal or precious metal compounds as the active substance
3815 1200.10[暂]	载铂催化剂（为了从重水中回收氚或为了生产重水而专门设计或制备，用于加速氢和水之间的氢同位素交换反应）	6.5	35	4		17	千克	3	Supported platinum catalyst（for recycling tritium from heavy water or for producing heavy water especially designed or prepared, used for accelerating hydrogen and water, the hydrogen isotope exchange reaction between）
3815 1200.90[暂]	其他以贵金属为活性物的载体催化剂	6.5	35	4		17	千克		Other supported catalysts with precious metal or its compounds as the active substance
3815.1900	--其他	6.5	35			17	千克		--Other
3815.9000	-其他	6.5	35			17	千克		-Other
38.16	**耐火的水泥、灰泥、混凝土及类似耐火混合制品，但品目 38.01 的产品除外：**								**Refractory cements, mortars, concretes and similar compositions, other than products of heading No. 38.01:**
3816.0000	耐火水泥、灰泥及类似耐火材料，耐火混凝土及类似耐火混合制品，但品目 38.01 的产品除外	6.5	35			17	千克		Refractory cements, mortars, concretes and similar compositions, other than products of heading No. 38.01
38.17	**混合烷基苯及混合烷基萘，但品目 27.07 及 29.02 的货品除外：**								**Mixed alkylbenzentes and mixed alkylnaphthalenes, other than those of heading No.27.07 or 29.02:**

税则号列 Tariff Item	商品名称及备注	进口税率 最惠	普通	暂定	出口退税	增值税率	计量单位	监管条件	Article Description
3817.0000	混合烷基苯及混合烷基萘，但税目27.07及29.02的货品除外	6.5	35			17	千克		Mixed alkylbenzenes and alkylnaphthalenes, other than those of heading No.27.07 or 29.02
38.18	**经掺杂用于电子工业的化学元素，已切成圆片、薄片或类似形状；经掺杂用于电子工业的化合物：**								**Chemical elements doped for use in electronics, in the form of discs, wafers or similar forms; chemical compounds doped for use in electronics:**
	---直径在7.5厘米及以上的单晶硅切片：								---Monocrystalline silicon, in the form of discs, wafers or similar form, 7.5 cm or more in diameter:
3818.0011	----直径在15.24厘米及以下的	0	11		13	17	千克/片		----Diameter not exceeding 15.24cm
3818.0019	----其他	0	11		13	17	千克/片		----Other
3818.0090	---其他	0	17		13	17	千克		---Other
38.19	**闸用液压油及其他液压传动用液体，不含石油或从沥青矿物提取的油类，或者按重量计石油或从沥青矿物提取的油类含量低于70%：**								**Hydraulic brake fluids and other prepared liquids for hydraulic transmission, not ontainning or containing lessthan 70% by weight of petroleum oils or oils obtained from bituminous minerals:**
3819.0000	闸用液压油及其他液压传动用液体，不含石油或从沥青矿物提取的油类，或者按重量计石油或从沥青矿物提取的油类含量低于70%	6.5	35			17	千克		Hydraulic brake fluids and other prepared liquids for hydraulic transmission, not containing or containing less than 70% by weight of petroleum oils or oils obtaines from bituminous minerals
38.20	**防冻剂及解冻剂：**								**Anti-freezing preparations and prepared deicing fluids:**
3820.0000	防冻剂及解冻剂	10	35			17	千克		Anti-freezing preparations and prepared deicing fluids
38.21	**制成的供微生物（包括病毒及类似品）或植物、人体、动物细胞生长或维持用的培养基：**								**Prepared culture media for the development or maintenance of micro-organisms（including viruses and the like）or of plant, human or animal cells：**
3821.0000	制成的供微生物(包括病毒及类似品)或植物、人体、动物细胞生长或维持用的培养基	3	11			17	千克		Prepared culture media for the development or maintenance of micro-organisms（including viruses and the like）or of plant, human or animal cells
38.22	**附于衬背上的诊断或实验用试剂及不论是否附于衬背上的诊断或实验用配制试剂，但品目30.02及30.06的货品除外；检定参照物：**								**Diagnostic or laboratory reagents on a backing and prepared diagnostic or laboratory reagents whether or not on a backing, other than those of heading No. 30.02 or 30.06; certified reference materials:**
3822.0010	---附于衬背上的	4	35			17	千克	AB	---On a backing
3822.0090	---其他	5	35			17	千克	AB	---Other
38.23	**工业用单羧脂肪酸；精炼所得的酸性油；工业用脂肪醇：**								**Industrial monocarboxylic fatty acids; acid oils from refining; industrial fatty alcohols:**
	-工业用单羧脂肪酸；精炼所得的酸性油：								-Industrial monocarboxylic fatty acids; acid oils from refining:
3823.1100	--硬脂酸	16	50		13	17	千克		--Stearic acid
3823.1200[暂]	--油酸	16	50	8		17	千克	AB	--Oleic acid
3823.1300	--妥尔油脂肪酸	16	50			17	千克		--Tall oil fatty acids
3823.1900	--其他	16	50			17	千克		--Other
3823 1900.01[暂]	植物酸性油(酸性油仅指精炼所得的)	16	50	5		17	千克		Plant acid oil (refers to the refined acid oil only)
3823 1900.90	其他工业用单羧脂肪酸、酸性油(酸性油仅指精炼所得的)	16	50			17	千克		Other monocarboxylic fatty acids for industrial use and acid oil (refers to the refined acid oil only)
3823.7000[暂]	-工业用脂肪醇	13	50	9		17	千克		-Industrial fatty alcohols
38.24	**铸模及铸芯用黏合剂；其他处未列名的化学工业及其相关工业的化学产品及配制品（包括由天**								**Prepared binders for foundry moulds or cores; chemical products and preparations of the chemical or allied industries（including those**

税则号列 Tariff Item	商品名称及备注	进口税率 最惠	进口税率 普通	进口税率 暂定	出口退税	增值税率	计量单位	监管条件	Article Description
	然产品混合组成的）：								consisting of mixtures of natural products），not elsewhere specified or included:
3824.1000	-铸模及铸芯用黏合剂	6.5	35		5	17	千克		-Prepared binders for foundry moulds or cores
3824.3000	-自身混合或与金属黏合剂混合的未烧结金属碳化物	6.5	35			17	千克		-Non-agglomerated metal carbides mixed together cr with metallic binders
3824 3000.10	混合的未烧结金属碳化钨（包括自身混合或与金属黏合剂混合的）	6.5	35			17	千克	4xy	Non-agglomerated metal carbonized tungsten, mixed together or with metallic binders
3824 3000.90	其他混合的未烧结金属碳化物（包括自身混合或与金属黏合剂混合的）	6.5	35			17	千克		Other non-agglomerated metal carbides, mixed together or with metallic binders
	-水泥，灰泥及混凝土用添加剂:								-Prepared additives for cements, mortars or concretes:
3824.4010	---高效减水剂	6.5	35		13	17	千克		---High efficiency water reducing agent
3824.4090	---其他	6.5	35			17	千克		---Other
3824.5000	-非耐火的灰泥及混凝土	6.5	35			17	千克		-Non-refractory mortars and concretes
3824.6000	-子目号 2905.44 以外的山梨醇	14	40			17	千克		-Sorbitol other than that of subheading No.2905.44
	-含有甲烷、乙烷或丙烷的卤化衍生物的混合物:								-Mixtures containing halogenated derivatives of methane, ethane or propane:
3824.7100	--含全氯氟烃（CFCs）的，不论是否含氢氯氟烃（HCFCs）、全氟烃（PFCs）或氢氟烃（HFCs）	6.5	35			17	千克		--Containing chlorofluorocarbons (CFCs) whether or not containing hydrochloro fluorocarbons (HCFCs), perfluorocarbons (PFCs) or hydrofluorocarbons (HFCs)
3824 7100.11	二氯二氟甲烷和二氟乙烷的混合物（R-500）	6.5	35			17	千克	14ABxy	Mixture of dichlorodifluoromethane and difluoroethane (R-500)
3824 7100.12	一氯二氟甲烷和二氯二氟甲烷的混合物(R-501)	6.5	35			17	千克	14xy	Mixtures of difluorochloromethane and dichlorodifluoromethane (R-501)
3824 7100.13	一氯二氟甲烷和一氯五氟乙烷的混合物(R-502)	6.5	35			17	千克	14ABxy	Mixtures of difluorochloromethane and chloropentafluoroethane (R-502)
3824 7100.14	三氟甲烷和一氯三氟甲烷的混合物（R-503）	6.5	35			17	千克	14ABxy	Mixtures of trifluoromethane and chlorotrfluoromethane (R-503)
3824 7100.15	二氟甲烷和一氯五氟乙烷的混合物（R-504）	6.5	35			17	千克	14xy	Mixtures of difluoromethane and chloropentafluoroethane (R-504)
3824 7100.16	二氯二氟甲烷和一氟一氯甲烷的混合物（R-505）	6.5	35			17	千克	14xy	Mixtures of dichlorodifluoromethane, and a fluoro-chloro-methane (R-505)
3824 7100.17	一氟一氯甲烷和二氯四氟乙烷的混合物（R-506）	6.5	35			17	千克	14xy	Mixtures of a fluoro-chloro-methane and 1,2-dichlorotetrafluoroethane (R-506)
3824 7100.18	二氯二氟甲烷和二氯四氟乙烷的混合物（R-400）	6.5	35			17	千克	14xy	Mixtures of dichlorodifluoromethane, and 1,2-dichlorotetrafluoroethane (R-400)
3824 7100.90	其他含甲烷、乙烷或丙烷的全氯氟烃（CFCs）混合物［不论是否含甲烷、乙烷或丙烷的氢氯氟烃（HCFCs）、全氟烃（PFCs）或氢氟烃（HFCs）］	6.5	35			17	千克		Other mixtures containing chlorofluorocarbons of methane, ethane or propane, whether or not containing HCFCs, PFCs, HFCs of methane, ethane or propane
3824.7200	--含溴氯二氟甲烷、溴三氟甲烷或二溴四氟乙烷的混合物	6.5	35			17	千克		--Containing bromochlorodifluoromethane, bromotrifluoromethane or dibromotetrafluoroethanes
3824.7300	--含氢溴氟烃(HBFCs)的	6.5	35			17	千克		--Containing hydrobromofluorocarbons (HBFCS)
3824.7400	--含氢氯氟烃（HCFCs）的，不论是否含全氟烃（PFCs）或氢氟烃（HFCs），但不含全氯氟烃（CFCs）	6.5	35			17	千克		--Containing hydrochlorofluorocarbons (HCFCS), whether or not containing perfluorocarbons (PFCs) or hydroflourocarbons (HFCs),but not containing chlorofluorocarbons (CFCs)
3824 7400.11	二氟一氯甲烷、二氟乙烷和一氯四氟乙烷的混合物(R-401)	6.5	35			17	千克	14xy	Mixtures of difluorochloromethane, difluoroethane and chlorotetrafluoroethane (R-401)

税则号列 Tariff Item	商品名称及备注	进口税率 最惠	普通	暂定	出口退税	增值税率	计量单位	监管条件	Article Description
3824 7400.12	五氟乙烷、丙烷和二氟一氯甲烷的混合物(R402)	6.5	35			17	千克	14xy	Mixtures of pentafluoroethane, propane and difluorochloromethane (R402)
3824 7400.13	丙烷、二氟一氯甲烷和八氟丙烷的混合物(R403)	6.5	35			17	千克	14xy	Mixtures of propane, difluorochloromethane and perfluoropropane (R403)
3824 7400.14	二氟一氯甲烷、二氟乙烷、一氯二氟乙烷和八氟环丁烷的混合物(R405)	6.5	35			17	千克	14xy	Mixtures of difluorochloromethane, difluoroethane, 1-chloro-1,1-difluoroethane and octafluorocyclobutane(R405)
3824 7400.15	二氟一氯甲烷、2-甲基丙烷（异丁烷）和一氯二氟乙烷的混合物(R406)	6.5	35			17	千克	14xy	Mixtures of difluorochloromethane, 2-methylpropane (isobutane) and 1-chloro-1,1-difluoroethane (R406)
3824 7400.16	五氟乙烷、三氟乙烷和二氟一氯甲烷的混合物(R408)	6.5	35			17	千克	14xy	Mixtures of pentafluoroethane, 1,1,1-trifluoroethane and difluorochloromethane (R408)
3824 7400.17	二氟一氯甲烷、一氯四氟乙烷和一氯二氟乙烷的混合物(R409)	6.5	35			17	千克	14xy	Mixtures of difluorochloromethane, chlorotetrafluoroethane and 1-chloro-1,1-difluoroethane (R409)
3824 7400.18	丙烯、二氟一氯甲烷和二氟乙烷的混合物(R411)	6.5	35			17	千克	14xy	Propylene, difluorochloromethane and difluoroethane (R411)
3824 7400.19	二氟一氯甲烷、八氟丙烷和一氯二氟乙烷的混合物(R412)	6.5	35			17	千克	14xy	Difluorochloromethane, perfluoropropane and 1-chloro-1,1-difluoroethane (R412)
3824 7400.21	二氟一氯甲烷、一氯四氟乙烷、一氯二氟乙烷和 2-甲基丙烷的混合物(R414)	6.5	35			17	千克	14xy	Mixtures of difluorochloromethane, chlorotetrafluoroethane, 1-chloro-1,1-difluoroethane and 2-methylpropane
3824 7400.22	二氟一氯甲烷和二氟乙烷的混合物(R415)	6.5	35			17	千克	14xy	Mixtures of difluorochloromethane and difluoroethane(R415)
3824 7400.23	四氟乙烷、一氯四氟乙烷和丁烷的混合物(R416)	6.5	35			17	千克	14xy	Mixtures of 1,1,1,2-tetrafluoroethane, chlorotetrafluoroethane and n-butane (R416)
3824 7400.24	丙烷、二氟一氯甲烷和二氟乙烷的混合物(R418)	6.5	35			17	千克	14xy	Mixtures of propane, difluorochloromethane and difluoroethane(R418)
3824 7400.25	二氟一氯甲烷和八氟丙烷的混合物(R509)	6.5	35			17	千克	14xy	Mixtures of difluorochloromethane and perfluoropropane (R509)
3824 7400.26	二氟一氯甲烷和一氯二氟乙烷的混合物	6.5	35			17	千克	14xy	Mixtures of difluorochloromethane and 1-chloro-1,1-difluoroethane
3824 7400.90	其他含甲烷、乙烷或丙烷的氢氯氟烃混合物(不论是否含甲烷、乙烷或丙烷的全氟烃或氢氟烃，但不含全氯氟烃)	6.5	35			17	千克	14xy	Other HCFCs mixtures containing methane, ethane or propane (perfluorocarbons or hydrofluorocarbons whether or not containing methane, ethane or propane, but not containing CFCs)
3824.7500	--含四氯化碳的	6.5	35			17	千克		--Containing carbon tetrachloride
3824.7600	--含1,1,1—三氯乙烷(甲基氯仿)的	6.5	35			17	千克		--Containing 1, 1, 1-trichloroethane（methyl chloroform）
3824.7700	--含溴化甲烷(甲基溴)或溴氯甲烷的	6.5	35			17	千克		--Containing bromomethane (methyl bromide) or bromochloro methane
3824.7800	--含全氟烃(PFCs)或氢氟烃（HFCs）的，但不含全氯氟烃（CFCs）或氢氯氟烃（HCFCs）的	6.5	35		13	17	千克		--Containing perfluorocarbons (PFCs) or hydrofluorocarbons (HFCs), but not containing chlorofluorocarbons (CFCs) or hydrochlorofluorocarbons (HCFCs)
3824.7900	--其他	6.5	35			17	千克		--Other
	-含环氧乙烷(氧化乙烯)、多溴联苯（PBBs）、多氯联苯(PCBs)、多氯三联苯(PCTs)或三(2,3—二溴丙基)磷酸酯的混合物及制品:								-Mixtures and preparations containing oxirane (ethylene oxide), polybrominated biphenyls (PBBs), polychlorinated biphenyls (PCBs), polychlorinated terphenyls (PCTs), or tris (2, 3-dibromopropyl) phosphate:
3824.8100	--含环氧乙烷(氧化乙烯)的	6.5	35			17	千克		--Containing oxirane (ethylene oxide)
3824.8200	--含多氯联苯(PCBs)、多氯三联	6.5	35			17	千克	X	--Containing polychlorinated biphenyls (PCBs),

税则号列 Tariff Item	商品名称及备注	进口税率 最惠	进口税率 普通	进口税率 暂定	出口退税	增值税率	计量单位	监管条件	Article Description
	苯(PCTs)或多溴联苯(PBBs)的								polychlorinated terphenyls (PCTs) or polybrominated biphenyls (PBBs)
3824.8300	--含三(2,3—二溴丙基)磷酸酯的	6.5	35			17	千克		--Containing tris (2, 3-dibromopropyl) phosphate
	-其他:								-Other:
3824.9010	---杂醇油	6.5	40			17	千克		---Fusel oil
3824.9020	---除墨剂、蜡纸改正液及类似品	9	80			17	千克		---Ink-removers, stencil correctors and the like
3824.9030	---增炭剂	6.5	35			17	千克		---Carburetant
	---其他:								---Other:
3824.9091	----按重量计含滑石50%以上的混合物	6.5	35			17	千克	4xy	----Mixtures containing more than 50% by weight of talc
3824.9092	----按重量计含氧化镁70%以上的混合物	6.5	35			17	千克	4xy	----Mixtures containing more than 70% by weight of magnesium oxide
3824.9093	----表层包覆钴化合物的氢氧化镍(掺杂碳)	6.5	35		5	17	千克		----Nickel hydroxide, surface coated with a cobalt compound (doping carbon)
3824.9099	----其他	6.5	35			17	千克		----Other
3824 9099.01[暂]	高钛渣(二氧化钛质量百分含量>70%的)	6.5	35	0		17	千克		Titanium-rich slag (containing more than 70% by weight of titanium dioxide)
3824 9099.04	水解物或水解料、DMC(六甲基环三硅氧烷、八甲基环四硅氧烷、十甲基环五硅氧烷、十二甲基环六硅氧烷中任何2种、3种或4种组成的混合物)	6.5	35		13	17	千克		Hydrolyzate or hydrolysis materials, DMC (the mixtures, composed of any 2, 3 or 4 kinds of hexamethylcyclotrisiloxane, octamethylcyclotetrasil-oxane, decamethylcyclopentasiloxane, Dodecamethylcyclohexasiloxane)
3824 9099.05	核苷酸类食品添加剂	6.5	35		5	17	千克	AB	Nucleotide food additives
3824 9099.06[暂]	按重量计氧化锌含量在50%及以上的混合物	6.5	35	3		17	千克		Mixtures containing 50% or more by weight of zinc oxide
3824 9099.10	粗制碳化硅[其中碳化硅含量大于15%(按重量计)]	6.5	35			17	千克	y4x	Crude silicon carbide, containing more than 15% by weight of silicon carbide
3824 9099.20	混胺(二甲胺和三乙胺混合物的水溶液)	6.5	35			17	千克	3	Mixed amine (dimethylamine and triethylamine mixture in aqueous solution)
3824 9099.30	氰化物的混合物	6.5	35			17	千克	X	Mixtures of cyanide
3824 9099.40	膨胀石墨	6.5	35			17	千克	3	Expanded graphite
3824 9099.90	其他编号未列名的化工产品	6.5	35		5	17	千克		Other chemical products, not elsewhere specified or included
38.25	**其他品目未列名的化学工业及其相关工业的副产品;城市垃圾;下水道淤泥;本章注释六所规定的其他废物:**								**Residual products of the chemical or allied industries, not elsewhere specified or included; municipal waste; sewage sludge; other wastes specified in Note 6 to this Chapter:**
3825.1000	-城市垃圾	6.5	35			17	千克	9	-Municipal waste
3825.2000	-下水道淤泥	6.5	35			17	千克	9	-Sewage sludge
3825.3000	-医疗废物	6.5	35			17	千克	9	-Clinical waste
	-废有机溶剂:								-Waste organic solvents:
3825.4100	--卤化物的	6.5	35			17	千克	9	--Halogenated
3825.4900	--其他	6.5	35			17	千克	9	--Other
3825.5000	-废的金属酸洗液、液压油、制动油及防冻液	6.5	35			17	千克	9	-Wastes of metal pickling liquors, hydraulic fluids, brake fluids and antifreeze fluids
	-其他化学工业及相关工业的废物:								-Other wastes from chemical or allied industries:
3825.6100	--主要含有有机成分的	6.5	35			17	千克	9	--Mainly containing organic constituents
3825.6900	--其他	6.5	35			17	千克	9	--Other
3825.9000	-其他	6.5	35			17	千克		-Other
3825 9000.10	浓缩糖蜜发酵液	6.5	35			17	千克	AB	Condensed molasses fermentation solubles
3825 9000.90	其他商品编号未列名化工副产	6.5	35			17	千克	9	Other chemical by-products or waste, not elsewhere

税则号列 Tariff Item	商品名称及备注	进口税率			出口退税	增值税率	计量单位	监管条件	Article Description
		最惠	普通	暂定					
	品及废物								specified or included
38.26	**生物柴油及其混合物，不含或含有按重量计低于70%的石油或从沥青矿物提取的油类：**								**Biodiesel and mixtures thereof, not containing or containing less than 70% by weight of petroleum oils or oils obtained from bituminous minerals :**
3826.0000	生物柴油及其混合物，不含或含有按重量计低于70%的石油或从沥青矿物提取的油类	6.5	35			17	千克/升		Biodiesel and mixtures thereof, not containing or containing less than 70% by weight of petroleum oils or oils obtained from bituminous minerals

第七类

塑料及其制品；橡胶及其制品

注释：

一、由两种或两种以上单独成分配套的货品，其部分或全部成分属于本类范围以内，混合后则构成第六类或第七类的货品，应按混合后产品归入相应的品目，但其组成成分必须同时符合下列条件：

（一）其包装形式足以表明这些成分不需经过改装就可以一起使用的；

（二）一起报验的；以及

（三）这些成分的属性及相互比例足以表明是相互配用的。

二、除品目 39.18 或 39.19 的货品外，印有花纹、文字、图画的塑料、橡胶及其制品，如果所印花纹、字画作为其主要用途，应归入第四十九章。

SECTION Ⅶ

PLASTICS AND ARTICLES THEREOF; RUBBER AND ARTICLES THEREOF

Section Notes:

1.Goods put up in sets consisting of two or more separate constituents, some or all of which fall in this Section and are intended to be mixed together to obtain a product of Section Ⅵ or Ⅶ, are to be classified in the heading appropriate to that product, provided that the constituents are:

(a) Having regard to the manner in which they are put up, clearly identifiable as being intended to be used together without first being repacked;

(b) Presented together; and

(c) Identifiable, whether by their nature or by the relative proportions in which they are present, as being complementary one to another.

2.Except for the goods of heading 39.18 or 39.19, plastics, rubber, and articles thereof, printed with motifs, characters or pictorial representations, which are not merely incidental to the primary use of the goods, fall in Chapter 49.

第三十九章 塑料及其制品

注释：

一、本目录所称“塑料”，是指品目 39.01 至 39.14 的材料，这些材料能够在聚合时或聚合后在外力（一般是热力和压力，必要时加入溶剂或增塑剂）作用下通过模制、浇铸、挤压、滚轧或其他工序制成一定的形状，成形后除去外力，其形状仍保持不变。

本目录所称“塑料”，还应包括钢纸，但不包括第十一类的纺织材料。

二、本章不包括：

（一）品目 27.10 或 34.03 的润滑剂；

（二）品目 27.12 或 34.04 的蜡；

（三）单独的已有化学定义的有机化合物（第二十九章）；

（四）肝素及其盐（品目 30.01）；

（五）品目 39.01 至 39.13 所列的任何产品溶于挥发性有机溶剂的溶液（胶棉除外），但溶剂的重量必须超过溶液重量的 50%（品目 32. 08）；品目 32.12 的压印箔；

（六）有机表面活性剂或品目 34.02 的制剂

（七）再熔胶及酯胶（品目 38.06）；

（八）矿物油（包括汽油）或与矿物油用途相同的其他液体的配制添加剂（品目 38.11）

（九）以第三十九章的聚乙二醇、聚硅氧烷或其他聚合物为基本成分配制的液压用液体（品目 38.19）；

（十）附于塑料衬背上的诊断或实验用试剂（品目 38.22）；

Chapter 39 Plastics and articles thereof

Chapter Notes:

1. Throughout the Nomenclature the expression “plastics” means those materials of headings 39.01 to 39.14 which are or have been capable, either at the moment of polymerisation or at some subsequent stage, of being formed under external influence (usually heat and pressure, if necessary with a solvent or plasticiser) by moulding, casting, extruding, rolling or other process into shapes which are retained on the removal of the external influence.

Throughout the Nomenclature any reference to “plastics” also includes vulcanised fibre.The expression, however, does not apply to materials regarded as textile materials of Section Ⅺ.

2. This Chapter does not cover:

(a) Lubricating preparations of heading 27.10 or 34.03;

(b) Waxes of heading 27.12 or 34.04;

(c) Separate chemically defined organic compounds (Chapter29);

(d) Heparin or its salts (heading 30.01);

(e) Solutions (other than collodions) consisting of any of the products specified in headings 39.01 to 39.13 in volatile organic solvents when the weight of the solvent exceeds 50% of the weight of the solution (heading 32.08); stamping foils of heading 32.12:

(f) Organic surface-active agents or preparations of heading 34.02;

(g) Run gums or ester gums (heading 38.06);

(h) Prepared additives for mineral oils (including gasoline) or for other liquids used for the same purposes as mineral oils (heading 38.11)

(ij) Prepared hydraulic fluids based on polyglycols, silicones or other polymers of Chapter 39 (heading 38.19);

(k) Diagnostic or laboratory reagents on a backing of plastics (heading 38.22);

（十一）第四十章规定的合成橡胶及其制品；

（十二）鞍具及挽具（品目 42.01）；品目 42.02 的衣箱、提箱、手提包及其他容器；

（十三）第四十六章的缏条、编结品及其他制品；

（十四）品目 48.14 的壁纸；

（十五）第十一类的货品（纺织原料及纺织制品）；

（十六）第十二类的物品（例如，鞋靴、帽类、雨伞、阳伞、手杖、鞭子、马鞭及其零件）；

（十七）品目 71.17 的仿首饰；

（十八）第十六类的物品（机器、机械器具或电气器具）；

（十九）第十七类的航空器零件及车辆零件；

（二十）第九十章的物品（例如，光学元件、眼镜架及绘图仪器）；

（二十一）第九十一章的物品（例如，钟壳及表壳）；

（二十二）第九十二章的物品（例如，乐器及其零件）；

（二十三）第九十四章的物品（例如，家具、灯具照明装置、灯箱及活动房屋）；

（二十四）第九十五章的物品（例如，玩具、游戏品及运动用品）；或

（二十五）第九十六章的物品（例如，刷子、钮扣、拉链、梳子、烟斗的嘴及柄、香烟嘴及类似品、保温瓶的零件及类似品、钢笔、活动铅笔）。

三、品目 39.01 至 39.11 仅适用于化学合成的下列货品：

（一）采用减压蒸馏法，在压力转换为 1013 毫巴下的温度 300℃时，以体积计馏出量小于 60% 的液体合成聚烯烃（品目 39.01 及 39.02）；

（二）非高度聚合的苯并呋喃—茚树脂（品目 39.11）；

（三）平均至少有五个单体单元的其他合成聚合物；

（四）聚硅氧烷（品目 39.10）；

（五）甲阶酚醛树脂（品目 39.09）及其他预聚物。

四、所称"共聚物"，包括在整个聚合物中按重量计没有一种单体单元的含量在 95%及以上的各种聚合物。

在本章中，除条文另有规定的以外，共聚物（包括共缩聚物、共加聚物、嵌段共聚物及接枝共聚物）及聚合物混合体应按聚合物中重量最大的那种共聚单体单元所构成的聚合物归入相应品目。在本注释中，归入同一品目的聚合物的共聚单体单元应作为一种单体单元对待。

如果没有任何一种共聚单体单元重量为最大，共聚物或聚合物混合体应按号列顺序归入其可归入的最末一个品目。

五、化学改性聚合物，即聚合物主链上的支链通过化学反应发生了变化的聚合物，应按未改性的聚合物的相应品目归类。本规定不适用于接枝共聚物。

(l) Synthetic rubber, as defined for the purposes of Chapter 40, or articles thereof;

(m) Saddlery or harness (heading 42.01) or trunks, suitcases, handbags or other containers of heading 42.02;

(n) Plaits, wickerwork or other articles of Chapter 46;

(o) Wall coverings of heading 48. 14;

(p) Goods of Section XI (textiles and textile articles);

(q) Articles of Section XII (for example, footwear, headgear, umbrellas, sun umbrellas, walking-sticks, whips, riding-crops or parts thereof);

(r) Imitation jewellery of heading 71.17;

(s) Articles of Section XVI (machines and mechanical or electrical appliances);

(t) Parts of aircraft or vehicles of Section XVII;

(u) Articles of Chapter 90 (for example, optical elements, spectacle frames, drawing instruments);

(v) Articles of Chapter 91 (for example, clock or watch cases);

(w) Articles of Chapter 92 (for example, musical instruments or parts thereof);

(x) Articles of Chapter 94 (for example, furniture, lamps and lighting fittings, illuminated signs, prefabricated buildings);

(y) Articles of Chapter 95 (for example, toys, games, sports requisites); or

(z) Articles of Chapter 96 (for example, brushes, buttons, slide fasteners, combs, mouthpieces or stems for smoking pipes, cigarette-holders or the like, parts of vacuum flasks or the like, pens, propelling pencils).

3. Headings 39.01 to 39.11 apply only to goods of a kind produced by chemical synthesis, falling in the following categories:

(a) Liquid synthetic polyolefins of which less than 60% by volume distils at 300℃, after conversion to 1013 milibars when a reduced-pressure distillation method is used (headings 39.01 and 39.02);

(b) Resins, not highly polymerised, of the coumarone-indene type (heading 39.11);

(c) Other synthetic polymers with an average of at least 5 monomer units;

(d) Silicones (heading 39.10);

(e) Resols (heading 39.09) and other prepolymers.

4. The expression "copolymers" covers all polymers in which no single monomer unit contributes 95% or more by weight to the total polymer content.

For the purposes of this Chapter, except where the context otherwise requires, copolymers (including copolycondensates, co-polyaddition products, block copolymers and graft copolymers) and polymer blends are to be classified in the heading covering polymers of that comonomer unit which predominates by weight over every other single comonomer unit. For the purposes of this Note,constituent comonomer units of polymers falling in the same heading shall be taken together.

If no single comonomer unit predominates, copolymers or polymer blends, as the case may be, are to be classified in the heading which occurs last in numerical order among those which equally merit consideration.

5. Chemically modified polymers, that is those in which only appendages to the main polymer chain have been changed by chemical reaction, are to be classified in the heading appropriate to the unmodified polymer. This

provision does not apply to graft copolymers.

六、品目 39.01 至 39.14 所称“初级形状”，只限于下列各种形状：

（一）液状及糊状，包括分散体（乳浊液及悬浮液）及溶液；

（二）不规则形状的块、团、粉（包括压型粉）、颗粒、粉片及类似的散装形状。

6. In headings 39.01 to 39.14, the expression “primary forms” applies only to the following forms:

(a) Liquids and pastes, including dispersions (emulsions and suspensions) and solutions;

(b) Blocks of irregular shape, lumps, powders (including moulding powders), granules, flakes and similar bulk forms.

七、品目 39.15 不适用于已制成初级形状的单一的热塑材料废碎料及下脚料（品目 39.01 至 39.14）。

7. Heading 39.15 does not apply to waste, parings and scrap of a single thermoplastic material, transformed into primary forms (headings 39.01 to 39.14).

八、品目 39.17 所称“管子”，是指通常用于输送或供给气体或液体的空心制品或半制品(例如，肋纹浇花软管、多孔管)，还包括香肠用肠衣及其他扁平管。除肠衣及扁平管外，内截面如果不呈圆形、椭圆形、矩形(其长度不超过宽度的 1.5 倍)或正几何形，则不能视为管子，而应作为异型材。

8. For the purposes of heading 39.17, the expression “tubes, pipes and hoses” means hollow products, whether semi-manufactures or finished products, of a kind generally used for conveying, conducting or distributing gases or liquids (for example, ribbed garden hose, perforated tubes). This expression also includes sausage casings and other lay-flat tubing. However, except for the last-mentioned, those having an internal cross-section other than round, oval, rectangular (in which the length does not exceed 1.5 times the width) or in the shape of a regular polygon are not to be regarded as tubes, pipes and hoses but as profile shapes.

九、品目 39.18 所称“塑料糊墙品”，适用于墙壁或天花板装饰用的宽度不小于 45 厘米的成卷产品，这类产品是将塑料牢固地附着在除纸张以外任何材料的衬背上，并且在塑料面起纹、压花、着色、印制图案或用其他方法装饰。

9. For the purposes of heading 39.18, the expression “wall or ceiling coverings of plastics” applies to products in rolls, of a width not less than 45 cm, suitable for wall or ceiling decoration, consisting of plastics fixed permanently on a backing of any material other than paper,the layer of plastics (on the face side) being grained, embossed, coloured, design-printed or otherwise decorated.

十、品目 39.20 及 39.21 所称“板、片、膜、箔、扁条”，只适用于未切割或仅切割成矩形(包括正方形)(含切割后即可供使用的)，但未经进一步加工的板、片、膜、箔、扁条(第五十四章的物品除外)及正几何形块，不论是否经过印制或其他表面加工。

10. In headings 39.20 and 39.21, the expression “plates, sheets, film, foil and strip” applies only to plates, sheets, film, foil and strip (other than those of Chapter 54) and to blocks of regular geometric shape, whether or not printed or otherwise surface-worked, uncut or cut into rectangles (including squares) but not further worked (even if when so cut they become articles ready for use).

十一、品目 39.25 只适用于第二分章以前各品目未包括的下列物品：

（一）容积超过 300 升的囤、柜（包括化粪池）、罐、桶及类似容器；

（二）用于地板、墙壁、隔墙、天花板或屋顶等方面的结构件；

（三）槽管及其附件；

（四）门、窗及其框架和门槛；

（五）阳台、栏杆、栅栏、栅门及类似品；

（六）窗板、百叶窗（包括威尼斯式百叶窗）或类似品及其零件、附件；

（七）商店、工棚、仓库等用的拼装式固定大型货架；

（八）建筑用的特色（例如，凹槽、圆顶及鸽棚式）装饰件；以及

（九）固定装于门窗、楼梯、墙壁或建筑物其他部位的附件及架座，例如，球形把手、拉手、挂钩、托架、毛巾架、开关板及其他护板。

11. Heading 39.25 applies only to the following articles, not being products covered by any of the earlier headings of sub-Chapter Ⅱ:

(a) Reservoirs, tanks (including septic tanks), vats and similar containers, of a capacity exceeding 300 L;

(b) Structural elements used, for example, in floors, walls or partitions, ceilings or roofs;

(c) Gutters and fittings thereof;

(d) Doors, windows and their frames and thresholds for doors;

(e) Balconies, balustrades, fencing, gates and similar barriers;

(f) Shutters, blinds (including Venetian blinds) and similar articles and parts and fittings thereof;

(g) Large-scale shelving for assembly and permanent installation,for example, in shops, workshops, warehouses;

(h) Ornamental architectural features, for example, flutings, cupolas, dovecotes; and

(ij) Fittings and mountings intended for permanent installation in or on doors, windows, staircases, walls or other parts of buildings, for example, knobs, handles, hooks, brackets, towel rails, switch-plates and other protective plates.

子目注释：

属于本章任一品目项下的聚合物（包括共聚物）及化学改性聚合物应按下列规则归类：

Subheading Notes:

Within any one heading of this Chapter, polymers (including copolymers) and chemically modified polymers are to be classified according to the following

一、在同级子目中有一个"其他"子目的：

（一）子目所列聚合物名称冠有"聚（多）"的（例如，聚乙烯及聚酰胺-6，6），是指列名的该种聚合物单体单元含量在整个聚合物中按重量计必须占95%及以上。

（二）子目3901.30、3903.20、3903.30及3904.30所列的共聚物，如果该种共聚单体单元含量在整个聚合物中按重量计占95%及以上，即应归入上述子目。

（三）化学改性聚合物如未在其他子目具体列名，应归入列明为"其他"的子目内。

（四）不符合上述（一）、（二）、（三）款规定的聚合物．应按聚合物中重量最大的那种单体单元（与其他各种单一的共聚单体单元相比）所构成的聚合物归入该级其他相应子目。为此，归入同一子目的聚合物单体单元应作为一种单体单元对待。只有在同级子目中的聚合物共聚单体单元才可以进行比较。

二、在同级子目中没有"其他"子目的：

（一）聚合物应按聚合物中重量最大的那种单体单元（与其他各种单一的共聚单体单元相比）所构成的聚合物归入该级相应子目。为此，归入同一子目的聚合物单体单元应作为一种单体单元对待。只有在同级子目中的聚合物共聚单体单元才可以进行比较。

（二）化学改性聚合物应按相应的未改性聚合物的子目归类。

聚合物混合体应按单体单元比例相等、种类相同的聚合物归入相应子目。

三、子目3920.43所称"增塑剂"，包括"次级增塑剂"。

provisions:

(a) Where there is a subheading named "Other" in the same series:

(i) The designation in a subheading of a polymer by the prefix "poly" (for example, polyethylene and polyamide-6, 6) means that the constituent monomer unit or monomer units of the named polymer taken together must contribute 95% or more by weight of the total polymer content.

(ii) The copolymers named in subheadings 3901.30, 3903.20, 3903. 30 and 3904.30 are to be classified in those subheadings, provided that the comonomer units of the named copolymers contribute 95% or more by weight of the total polymer content.

(iii) Chemically modified polymers are to be classified in the subheading named "Other", provided that the chemically modified polymers are not more specifically covered by another subheading.

(iv) Polymers not meeting (a), (b) or (c) above, are to be classified in the subheading, among the remaining subheadings in the series, covering polymers of that monomer unit which predominates by weight over every other single comonomer unit. For this purpose, constituent monomer units of polymers falling in the same subheading shall be taken together. Only the constituent comonomer units of the polymers in the series of subheadings under consideration are to be compared.

(b) Where there is no subheading named "Other" in the same series:

(i) Polymers are to be classified in the subheading covering polymers of that monomer unit which predominates by weight over every other single comonomer unit.For this purpose, constituent monomer units of polymers falling in the same subheading shall be taken together. Only the constituent comonomer units of the polymers in the series under consideration are to be compared.

(ii) Chemically modified polymers are to be classified in the subheading appropriate to the unmodified polymer.

Polymer blends are to be classified in the same subheading as polymers of the same monomer units in the same proportions.

3. For the purposes of subheading 3920.43, the term "plasticisers" includes secondary plasticisers.

税则号列 Tariff Item	商品名称及备注	进口税率 最惠	普通	暂定	出口退税	增值税率	计量单位	监管条件	Article Description
	第一分章 初级形状								Ⅰ. PRIMARY FORMS
39.01	初级形状的乙烯聚合物：								Polymers of ethylene, in primary forms:
3901.1000	-聚乙烯，比重小于0.94	6.5	45		13	17	千克		-Polyethylene having a specific gravity of less than 0.94
3901 1000.01[暂]	初级形状比重<0.94的聚乙烯（进口CIF价高于3800美元/吨）	6.5	45	3	13	17	千克		Polyethylene having a specific gravity of less than 0.94, in primary forms, import CIF price is more than 3500 U.S. dollars / ton
3901 1000.90	初级形状比重<0.94的聚乙烯	6.5	45		13	17	千克		Polyethylene having a specific gravity of less than 0.94, in primary forms
3901.2000	-聚乙烯，比重在0.94及以上	6.5	45		13	17	千克		-Polyethylene having a specific gravity of 0.94 or more
3901 2000.01[暂]	初级形状比重≥0.94的聚乙烯（进口CIF价高于3800美元/吨）	6.5	45	3	13	17	千克		Polyethylene having a specific gravity of 0.94 or more, in primary forms, import CIF price is more than 3500 U.S. dollars / ton
3901 2000.90	初级形状比重≥0.94的聚乙烯	6.5	45		13	17	千克		Polyethylene having a specific gravity of 0.94 or more, in primary forms
3901.3000	-乙烯-乙酸乙烯酯共聚物	6.5	45		5	17	千克		-Ethylene-vinyl acetate copolymers
	-其他：								-Other:

税则号列 Tariff Item	商品名称及备注	进口税率 最惠	普通	暂定	出口退税	增值税率	计量单位	监管条件	Article Description
3901.9010	---乙烯-丙烯共聚物(乙丙橡胶)	6.5	45		5	17	千克		---Ethylene-propylene copolymers
3901.9020	---线型低密度聚乙烯	6.5	45		13	17	千克		---Linearity low density polyethylene
3901.9090	---其他	6.5	45		13	17	千克		---Other
39.02	**初级形状的丙烯或其他烯烃聚合物：**								**Polymers of propylene or of other olefins, in primary forms:**
3902.1000	-聚丙烯	6.5	45		13	17	千克		-Polypropylene
3902 1000.10[暂]	电工级初级形状聚丙烯树脂（灰分含量不大于 30PPM）	6.5	45	3	13	17	千克		Polypropylene of electrical grade, in primary forms, containing not more than 30ppm of ash
3902 1000.90	其他初级形状的聚丙烯	6.5	45		13	17	千克		Other polypropylene in primary forms
3902.2000	-聚异丁烯	6.5	45		5	17	千克	AB	-Polyisobutylene
	-丙烯共聚物:								-Propylene copolymers:
3902.3010	---乙烯-丙烯共聚物(乙丙橡胶)	6.5	45		5	17	千克		---Ethylene-propylene copolymers
3902.3090	---其他	6.5	45		5	17	千克		---Other
3902.9000	-其他	6.5	45		5	17	千克		-Other
3902 9000.10	端羧基聚丁二烯, CTPB（做粘接剂或燃料）	6.5	45		5	17	千克	3	Carboxyl-terminated polybutadiene, of a kind used as adhesive or fuel
3902 9000.20	端羟基聚丁二烯, HTPB（做粘接剂或燃料）	6.5	45		5	17	千克	3	Hydroxyl-terminated polybutadiene, of a kind used as adhesive or fuel
3902 9000.90	其他初级形状的烯烃聚合物	6.5	45		5	17	千克		Polymers of other olefins, in primary forms
39.03	**初级形状的苯乙烯聚合物：**								**Polymers of styrene, in primary forms:**
	-聚苯乙烯:								-Polystyrene:
3903.1100	--可发性的	6.5	45		5	17	千克	AB	--Expansible
	--其他:								--Other:
3903.1910	---改性的	6.5	45		13	17	千克		---Modified
3903.1990	---其他	6.5	45		5	17	千克		---Other
3903.2000	-苯乙烯-丙烯腈（SAN）共聚物	12	45		5	17	千克		-Styrene-acrylonitrile（SAN）copolymers
	-丙烯腈-丁二烯-苯乙烯（ABS）共聚物:								-Acrylonitrile-butadiene-styrene（ABS）copolymers:
3903.3010	---改性的	6.5	45		13	17	千克		---Modified
3903.3090	---其他	6.5	45		5	17	千克		---Other
3903.9000	-其他	6.5	45		5	17	千克		-Other
39.04	**初级形状的氯乙烯或其他卤化烯烃聚合物：**								**Polymers of vinyl chloride or of other halogenated olefins, in primary forms:**
	-聚氯乙烯，未掺其他物质:								-Poly（vinyl chloride）, not mixed with any other substances:
3904.1010	---糊树脂	6.5	45		13	17	千克		---Paste resin
3904.1090	---其他	6.5	45		13	17	千克		---Other
3904 1090.01	聚氯乙烯纯粉（纯指未掺其他物质）	6.5	45		13	17	千克		Pure poly（vinyl chloride） powder, not mixed with any other substances
3904 1090.90	其他初级形状的纯聚氯乙烯（纯指未掺其他物质）	6.5	45		13	17	千克		Other pure poly（vinyl chloride） in primary forms, not mixed with any other substances
	-其他聚氯乙烯								-Other poly (vinyl chloride):
3904.2100	--未塑化	6.5	45		13	17	千克		--Non-plasticized
3904.2200	--已塑化	6.5	45		13	17	千克		--Plasticized
3904.3000	-氯乙烯-乙酸乙烯酯共聚物	9	45		5	17	千克		-Vinyl chloride-vinyl acetate copolymers
3904.4000	-其他氯乙烯共聚物	12	45		5	17	千克		-Other vinyl chloride copolymers
3904.5000	-偏二氯乙烯聚合物	6.5	45		5	17	千克		-Vinylidene chloride polymers
	-氟聚合物:								-Fluoro-polymers:
3904.6100	-聚四氟乙烯	10	45		13	17	千克		--Polytetrafluoroethylene
3904.6900	--其他	6.5	45		13	17	千克		--Other
3904.9000	-其他	10	45		5	17	千克		-Other
39.05	**初级形状的乙酸乙烯酯或其他乙烯酯聚合物；初级形状的其他乙烯基聚合物：**								**Polymers of vinyl acetate or of other vinyl esters, in primary forms; other vinyl polymers in primary forms:**
	-聚乙酸乙烯酯:								-Poly（vinyl acetate）:
3905.1200	--水分散体	10	45		5	17	千克		--In aqueous dispersion

税则号列 Tariff Item	商品名称及备注	进口税率 最惠	普通	暂定	出口退税	增值税率	计量单位	监管条件	Article Description
3905.1900	--其他	10	45		5	17	千克		--Other
	-乙酸乙烯酯共聚物:								-Vinyl acetate copolymers:
3905.2100	-水分散体	10	45		5	17	千克		--In aqueous dispersion
3905.2900	--其他	10	45		5	17	千克		--Other
3905.3000	-聚乙烯醇，不论是否含有未水解的乙酸酯基	14	45		5	17	千克	AB	-Poly（vinyl alcohol）, whether or not containing unhydrolyzed acetate groups
	-其他:								-Other:
3905.9100	--共聚物	10	45		5	17	千克		--Copolymers
3905.9900	--其他	10	45		5	17	千克		--Other
39.06	**初级形状的丙烯酸聚合物:**								**Acrylic polymers in primary forms:**
3906.1000	-聚甲基丙烯酸甲酯	6.5	45		13	17	千克		-Poly（methyl methacrylate）
	-其他:								-Other:
3906.9010	---聚丙烯酰胺	6.5	45		5	17	千克	AB	---Polyacrylamide
3906.9090	---其他	6.5	45			17	千克		---Other
3906 9090.01[暂]	聚丙烯酸钠	6.5	45	3	5	17	千克		Sodium polyacrylate
3906 9090.90	其他初级形状的丙烯酸聚合物	6.5	45		13	17	千克		Other acrylic polymers in primary forms
39.07	**初级形状的聚缩醛、其他聚醚及环氧树脂；初级形状的聚碳酸酯、醇酸树脂、聚烯丙基酯及其他聚酯:**								**Polyacetals, other polyethers and epoxide resins, in primary forms; polycarbonates, alkyd resins, polyallyl esters and other polyesters, in primary forms:**
	-聚缩醛:								-Polyacetals:
3907.1010	---聚甲醛	6.5	45		13	17	千克		---Polyoxymethylene（POM）
3907.1090	---其他	6.5	45		5	17	千克		---Other
	-其他聚醚:								-Other polyethers:
3907.2010[暂]	---聚四亚甲基醚二醇	6.5	45	3	5	17	千克		---Polytetramethylene ether glycol (PTMEG)
3907.2090	---其他	6.5	45		13	17	千克		---Other
3907.3000	-环氧树脂	6.5	45		5	17	千克		-Epoxide resins
3907 3000.01[暂]	初级形状溴质量≥18%或进口CIF价＞3800美元/吨的环氧树脂（如溶于溶剂，以纯环氧树脂折算溴的百分比含量）	6.5	45	4	5	17	千克	A	Epoxide resins, in primary forms（containing ≥18% by weight of bromine or import CIF price is more than 3800 U.S. dollars / ton, if soluting in solvent, pureepoxide resins are converted to content of pecentage of bromine
3907 3000.90	初级形状的环氧树脂（溴重量百分比含量在18%以下）	6.5	45		5	17	千克	AB	Epoxide resins, in primary forms, containing less than 18% by weight of bromine
3907.4000[暂]	-聚碳酸酯	6.5	45	3	13	17	千克		-Polycarbonates
3907.5000	-醇酸树脂	10	45		5	17	千克	AB	-Alkyd resins
	-聚对苯二甲酸乙二酯:								-Poly（ethylene terephthalate）:
	---切片:								---In the form of slices or chips:
3907.6011	----高粘度	6.5	45		13	17	千克		----High viscosity
3907.6019	----其他	6.5	45		13	17	千克		----Other
3907.6090	---其他	6.5	45		13	17	千克		---Other
3907.7000[暂]	-聚乳酸	6.5	45	3	5	17	千克		-Poly(lactic acid)
	-其他聚酯:								-Other polyesters:
3907.9100	--不饱和	6.5	45		5	17	千克		--Unsaturated
	--其他:								--Other:
3907.9910	---聚对苯二甲酸丁二酯	6.5	45		13	17	千克		---PBT（Polybutylene terephthalate）
3907 9910.01	未经增强或改性的初级形状PBT树脂	6.5	45		13	17	千克		PBT resins, in primary forms ,not reinforced or modified
3907 9910.90	其他聚对苯二甲酸丁二酯	6.5	45		13	17	千克		Other PBT（polybutylene terephthalate）
	---其他:								---Other:
3907.9991	----聚对苯二甲酸-己二醇-丁二醇酯	6.5	45		5	17	千克	AB	----ploy(terephthalic acid-hexanediol-butanediol ester)
3907.9999	----其他	6.5	45		5	17	千克	AB	--Other
39.08	**初级形状的聚酰胺:**								**Polyamides in primary forms:**
	-聚酰胺-6、-11、-12、-6,6、-6,9、-6,10或-6,12:								-Polyamide-6, -11, -12, -6,6, -6,9, -6,10 or-6,12:
	---切片:								---In the form of slices or chips:

税则号列 Tariff Item	商品名称及备注	进口税率 最惠	普通	暂定	出口退税	增值税率	计量单位	监管条件	Article Description
3908.1011	----聚酰胺-6,6切片	6.5	45		13	17	千克		----Of polyamide-6,6
3908 1011.01	聚酰胺-6,6切片	6.5	45		13	17	千克		Polyamide -6,6, slices or chips
3908 1011.90	改性聚酰胺-6,6切片(经螺杆二次混炼加入玻璃纤维、矿物质、增韧剂、阻燃剂的改性聚酰胺-6,6切片)	6.5	45		13	17	千克		Modified polyamide -6,6 slices (by adding glass fiber, minerals, toughening agents, flame retardants via screw-secondary mixing)
3908.1012	----聚酰胺-6切片	6.5	45		13	17	千克		----Of polyamide-6
3908.1019	----其他	6.5	45		13	17	千克		----Other
3908 1019.10	尼龙11、尼龙12切片(即聚酰胺-11、-12切片)	6.5	45		13	17	千克		Nylon 11, Nylon 12, slices or chips (polyamide-11,-12)
3908 1019.99	聚酰胺-6,9切片等(包括聚酰胺-6,9、-6,10、-6,12)	6.5	45		13	17	千克		polyamide -6,9 slices or chips, etc. (including polyamide -6,9; -6,10; -6,12)
3908.1090	---其他	6.5	45		5	17	千克		---Other
3908.9000	---其他	10	45		5	17	千克		-Other
39.09	**初级形状的氨基树脂、酚醛树脂及聚氨酯类:**								**Amino-resins, phenolic resins and polyurethanes, in primary forms:**
3909.1000	-尿素树脂;硫脲树脂	6.5	45		5	17	千克		-Urea resins; thiourea resins
3909.2000	-蜜胺树脂	6.5	45		5	17	千克		-Melamine resins
	-其他氨基树脂:								-Other amino-resins:
3909.3010	---聚(亚甲基苯基异氰酸酯)(聚合MDI或粗MDI)	6.5	35		13	17	千克		---Poly(methylene phenyl isocyanate)(polymeric MDI or crude MDI)
3909.3090	---其他	6.5	45		5	17	千克	AB	---Other
3909.4000	-酚醛树脂	6.5	45		5	17	千克	AB	-Phenolic resins
3909.5000	-聚氨基甲酸酯	6.5	45		13	17	千克	AB	-Polyurethanes
39.10	**初级形状的聚硅氧烷:**								**Silicones in primary forms:**
3910.0000	初级形状的聚硅氧烷	6.5	45		13	17	千克		Silicones in primary forms
39.11	**初级形状的石油树脂、苯并呋喃—茚树脂、多萜树脂、多硫化物、聚砜及本章注释三所规定的其他品目未列名产品:**								**Petroleum resins, eonmarone-indene resins, polyterpenes, polysulphides, polysulphones and other products specified in Note 3 to this Chapter, not elsewhere specified or included, in primary forms:**
3911.1000	-石油树脂、苯并呋喃树脂、茚树脂、苯并呋喃-茚树脂及多萜树脂	6.5	45		5	17	千克		-Petroleum resins, coumarone, indene or coumarone-indene resins and polyterpenes
3911.9000	-其他	6.5	45			17	千克		-Other
3911 9000.01[暂]	芳基酸与芳基胺预缩聚物	6.5	45	3	5	17	千克		Prepoly condensate of aryl acid and aryl amine
3911 9000.03[暂]	改性三羟乙基脲酸酯类预缩聚物	6.5	45	3	5	17	千克		Prepoly condensate of modified 3-hydroxyethyl urea esters
3911 9000.04	聚苯硫醚	6.5	45		13	17	千克		Poly (p-phenylene sulfide)
3911 9000.05[暂]	偏苯三酸酐和异氰酸预缩聚物	6.5	45	3	5	17	千克		Prepoly condensate of trimelltic anhydride and isocyanic acid
3911 9000.90	其他初级形状的多硫化物、聚砜等(包括本章注释三所规定的其他编号未列名产品)	6.5	45		13	17	千克		Other polysulphides, polysulphones and other products specified in Note 3 to this Chapter, not elsewhere specified or included, in primary forms
39.12	**初级形状的其他品目未列名的纤维素及其化学衍生物:**								**Cellulose and its chemical derivatives, not elsewhere specified or included, in primary forms:**
	-乙酸纤维素:								-Cellulose acetates:
3912.1100	--未塑化	6.5	40			17	千克		--Non-plasticized
3912 1100.10	初级形状的未塑化二、三醋酸纤维素	6.5	40			17	千克		Cellulose triacetate,cellulose diacetate in primary forms,Non-plasticized
3912 1100.90	初级形状的未塑化其他醋酸纤维素	6.5	40			17	千克		Other cellulose acetates, in primary forms, non-plasticized
3912.1200	--已塑化	6.5	40			17	千克		--Plasticized
3912.2000	-硝酸纤维素(包括胶棉)	6.5	45			17	千克		-Cellulose nitrates(including collodions)
	-纤维素醚:								-Cellulose ethers:
3912.3100	--羧甲基纤维素及其盐	6.5	45			17	千克		--Carboxymethylcellulose and its salts
3912.3900	--其他	6.5	45			17	千克		--Other
3912.9000	-其他	6.5	45			17	千克		-Other
39.13	**初级形状的其他品目未列名的**								**Natural polymers(for example, alginic acid) and**

税则号列 Tariff Item	商品名称及备注	进口税率			出口退税	增值税率	计量单位	监管条件	Article Description
		最惠	普通	暂定					
	天然聚合物（例如，藻酸）及改性天然聚合物（例如，硬化蛋白、天然橡胶的化学衍生物）：								**modified natural polymers(for example, hardened proteins, chemical derivatives of natural rubber), not elsewhere specified or included, in primary forms:**
3913.1000	-藻酸及其盐和酯	10	45			17	千克	AB	-Alginic acid, its salts and esters
3913.9000	-其他	6.5	50		13	17	千克		-Other
39.14	**初级形状的离子交换剂，以品目39.01至39.13的聚合物为基本成分的：**								**In-exchangers based on polymers of headings No. 39.01 to 39.13, in primary forms:**
3914.0000	初级形状的离子交换剂，以品目39.01至39.13的聚合物为基本成分的	6.5	45		5	17	千克		In-exchangers based on polymers of headings No. 39.01 to 39.13, in primary forms
	第二分章　废碎料及下脚料；半制品；制成品								**Ⅱ. WASTE, PARINGS AND SCRAP; SEMI-MANUFACTURES; ARTICLES**
39.15	**塑料的废碎料及下脚料：**								**Waste, parings and scrap, of plastics:**
3915.1000	-乙烯聚合物的	6.5	50			17	千克	AP	-Of polymers of ethylene
3915.2000	-苯乙烯聚合物的	6.5	50			17	千克	AP	-Of polymers of styrene
3915.3000	-氯乙烯聚合物的	6.5	50			17	千克	AP	-Of polymers of vinyl chloride
	-其他塑料的:								-Of other plastics:
3915.9010	---聚对苯二甲酸乙二酯的	6.5	50			17	千克	AP	---Of polyethylene glycol terephthalate
3915.9090	---其他	6.5	50			17	千克	AP	---Other
39.16	**塑料制的单丝（截面直径超过1毫米）、条、杆、型材及异型材，不论是否经表面加工，但未经其他加工：**								**Monofilament of which any cross-sectional dimension exceeds 1 mm, rods, sticks and profile shapes, whether or not surfaceworked but not otherwise worked, of plastics:**
3916.1000	-乙烯聚合物制	10	45		13	17	千克		-Of polymers of ethylene
	-氯乙烯聚合物制 ：								-Of polymers of vinyl chloride:
3916.2010	---异型材	10	45		13	17	千克		---Sections
3916.2090	---其他	10	45		13	17	千克		---Other
	-其他塑料制:								-Of other plastics:
3916.9010	---聚酰胺制	10	45		13	17	千克		---Of polyamides
3916.9090	---其他	10	45		13	17	千克		---Other
39.17	**塑料制的管子及其附件（例如，接头、肘管、法兰）：**								**Tubes, pipes and hoses, and fittings therefor（for example, joints, elbows, flanges）, of plastics:**
3917.1000	-硬化蛋白或纤维素材料制的人造肠衣（香肠用肠衣）	10	50		13	17	千克	A	-Artificial guts（sausage casings）of hardened protein or of cellulosic materials
	-硬管:								-Tubes, pipes and hoses, rigid:
3917.2100	--乙烯聚合物制	10	45		13	17	千克		--Of polymers of ethylene
3917.2200	--丙烯聚合物制	10	45		13	17	千克		--Of polymers of propylene
3917.2300	--氯乙烯聚合物制	10	45		13	17	千克		--Of polymers of vinyl chloride
3917.2900	--其他塑料制	10	45		13	17	千克		--Of other plastics
	-其他管:								-Other tubes, pipes and hoses:
3917.3100	--软管，最小爆破压力为27.6兆帕斯卡	10	45		13	17	千克		--Flexible tubes, pipes and hoses, having a minimum burst pressure of 27.6 MPa
3917.3200	--其他未装有附件的塑料制管子，未经加强也未与其他材料合制	6.5	45		13	17	千克		--Other, not reinforced or otherwise combined with other materials, without fittings
3917.3300	--其他装有附件的管子，未经加强也未与其他材料合制	6.5	45		13	17	千克		--Other, not reinforced or otherwise combined with other materials, with fittings
3917.3900	--其他	6.5	45		13	17	千克		--Other
3917.4000	-管子附件	10	45		13	17	千克		-Fittings
39.18	**块状或成卷的塑料铺地制品，不论是否胶粘；本章注释九所规定的塑料糊墙品：**								**Floor coverings of plastics, whether or not self-adhesive, in rolls or in the form of tiles; wall or ceiling coverings of plastics, as defined in Note 9 to this Chapter:**
	-氯乙烯聚合物制:								-Of polymers of vinyl chloride:
3918.1010	---糊墙品	10	45		13	17	千克		---Wall or ceiling coverings

税则号列 Tariff Item	商品名称及备注	进口税率 最惠	进口税率 普通	进口税率 暂定	出口退税	增值税率	计量单位	监管条件	Article Description
3918.1090	---其他	10	45		13	17	千克		---Other
	-其他塑料制:								-Of other plastics:
3918.9010	---糊墙品	10	45		13	17	千克		---Wall or ceiling coverings
3918.9090	---其他	10	45		13	17	千克		---Other
39.19	**自粘的塑料板、片、膜、箔、带、扁条及其他扁平形状材料，不论是否成卷:**								**Self-adhesive plates, sheets, film, foil, tape, strip and other flat shapes, of plastics, whether or not in rolls:**
	-成卷，宽度不超过20厘米:								-In rolls of a width not exceeding 20 cm:
3919.1010	---丙烯酸树脂类为基本成分	6.5	45		13	17	千克		---Based on acrylic resin
	---其他:								---Other:
3919.1091	----胶囊型反光膜	6.5	45		13	17	千克		----Encapsulant reflective film
3919.1099	----其他	6.5	45		13	17	千克		----Other
	-其他:								-Other:
3919.9010	---胶囊型反光膜	6.5	45		13	17	千克		---Encapsulant reflective film
3919.9090	---其他	6.5	45		13	17	千克		---Other
39.20	**其他非泡沫塑料的板、片、膜、箔及扁条，未用其他材料强化、层压、支撑或用类似方法合制:**								**Other plates, sheets, film, foil and strip, of plastics, non-cellular and not reinforced, laminated, supported or similarly combined with other materials:**
	-乙烯聚合物制:								-Of polymers of ethylene:
3920.1010[暂]	---乙烯聚合物制电池隔膜	6.5	45	3	13	17	千克		---Battery separator , of polymers of ethylene
3920.1090	---其他	6.5	45				千克		---Other
3920 1090.10	农用非泡沫聚乙烯薄膜（未用其他材料强化、层压、支撑或用类似方法合制）	6.5	45			13	千克		Film of polymers of ethylene, non-cellular and not reinforced, laminated, supported or similarly combined with other materials, for agricultural use
3920 1090.90	其他非泡沫乙烯聚合物板、片、膜、箔及扁条（未用其他材料强化、层压、支撑或用类似方法合制，非农用）	6.5	45		13	17	千克		Plates, sheets, film, foil and strip, of polymers of ethylene, non-cellular, not reinforced, laminated, supported or similarly combined with other materials, not for agricultural use
	-丙烯聚合物制:								-Of polymers of propylene:
3920.2010	---丙烯聚合物制电池隔膜	6.5	45		13	17	千克		---Battery separator, of polymers of propylene
3920.2090	---其他	6.5	45				千克		---Other
3920 2090.10	农用非泡沫聚丙烯薄膜（未用其他材料强化、层压、支撑或用类似方法合制）	6.5	45			13	千克		Film of polymers of propylene, non-cellular and not reinforced, laminated, supported or similarly combined with other materials, for agricultural use
3920 2090.90	非泡沫丙烯聚合物板、片、膜、箔及扁条（未用其他材料强化、层压、支撑或用类似方法合制，非农用）	6.5	45		5	17	千克		Plates, sheets, film, foil and strip, of polymers of propylene, non-cellular and not reinforced, laminated, supported or similarly combined with other materials not for agricultural use
3920.3000	-苯乙烯聚合物制	6.5	45		13	17	千克		-Of polymers of styrene
	-氯乙烯聚合物制:								-Of polymers of vinyl chloride:
3920.4300	--按重量计增塑剂含量不小于6%	6.5	45				千克		--Containing by weight not less than 6% of plasticisers
3920 4300.10	农用软质聚氯乙烯薄膜（增塑剂含量≥6%，未用其他材料强化、层压、支撑）	6.5	45			13	千克		Soft polymers of vinyl chloride film, containing by weight not less than 6% of plasticisers, not reinforced, laminated, supported with other materials, for agricultural use
3920 4300.90	氯乙烯聚合物板、片、膜、箔及扁条（增塑剂含量≥6%，未用其他材料强化、层压、支撑）	6.5	45		5	17	千克		Plates, sheets, film, foil and strip, of PVC, containing by weight≥6%of plasticisers, not reinforced, laminated, supported with other materials
3920.4900	--其他	6.5	45				千克		--Other
3920 4900.10	其他农用软质聚氯乙烯薄膜（非泡沫料的，未用其他材料强化、层压、支撑）	6.5	45			13	千克		Other soft PVC film, non-cellular, not reinforced laminated, supported with other materials , for agricultural use
3920 4900.90	其他氯乙烯聚合物板、片、膜、箔及扁条（非泡沫料的，未用其他材料强化、层压、支撑，非农用）	6.5	45		5	17	千克		Other plates, sheets, film, foil and strip, of PVC, non-cellular and not reinorced, laminated, supported or similarly combined with other materials, not for agricultural use

税则号列 Tariff Item	商品名称及备注	进口税率 最惠	进口税率 普通	进口税率 暂定	出口退税	增值税率	计量单位	监管条件	Article Description
	-丙烯酸聚合物制:								-Of acrylic polymers:
3920.5100	--聚甲基丙烯酸甲酯制	6.5	45		13	17	千克		--Of poly（methyl methacrylate）
3920.5900	--其他	6.5	45		13	17	千克		--Other
	-聚碳酸酯、醇酸树脂、聚烯丙酯或其他聚酯制:								-Of polycarbonates, alkyd resins, polyallyl esters or other polyesters:
3920.6100	--聚碳酸酯制	6.5	45		13	17	千克		--Of polycarbonates
3920.6200	--聚对苯二甲酸乙二酯制	6.5	45		13	17	千克		--Of poly（ethylene terephthalate）
3920 6200.01	9≤厚≤15.9微米聚酯薄膜（聚对苯二甲酸乙二酯制，型号XA10AUDIO）	6.5	45		13	17	千克		Polyester film, of ethylene terephthalate, 9μm≤thickness≤15.9μm（Type: XA10AUDIO）
3920 6200.02	5≤厚≤8.9微米聚酯薄膜(聚对苯二甲酸乙二酯制，型号XL07AUTEN）	6.5	45		13	17	千克		Polyester film, of ethylene terephthalate, 5μm≤thickness≤8.9μm（Type: XL07AUTEN）
3920 6200.03	16≤厚≤29.9微米聚酯薄膜(聚对苯二甲酸乙二酯制，型号XB30CAB（N））	6.5	45		13	17	千克		Polyester film, of ethylene terephthalate, 16μm≤thickness≤29.9μm（Type: XB30CAB（N））
3920 6200.04	50≤厚≤99.9微米聚酯薄膜(聚对苯二甲酸乙二酯制，型号XB30CAB（M））	6.5	45		13	17	千克		Polyester film, of ethylene terephthalate, 50μm≤thickness≤99.9μm（Type: XB30CAB（M））
3920 6200.09	其他聚对苯二甲酸乙二酯板、片、膜等（包括箔及扁条，非泡沫料，未用其他材料强化、层压、支撑）	6.5	45		13	17	千克		Other plates, sheets, film, foil and strip, of poly（ethylene terephthalate）, non-cellular and not reinforced, laminated, supported or similarly combined with other materials
3920.6300	--不饱和聚酯制	10	45		13	17	千克		--Of unsaturated polyesters
3920.6900	--其他聚酯制	10	45		13	17	千克		--Of other polyesters
	-纤维素及其化学衍生物制:								-Of cellulose or its chemical derivatives:
3920.7100	--再生纤维素制	6.5	45		13	17	千克		--Of regenerated cellulose
3920.7300	--醋酸纤维素制	6.5	45		13	17	千克		--Of cellulose acetate
3920.7900	--其他纤维素衍生物制	10	45		13	17	千克		--Of other cellulose derivatives
	-其他塑料制:								-Of other plastics:
3920.9100	--聚乙烯醇缩丁醛制	6.5	45		13	17	千克		--Of poly（vinyl butyral）
3920 9100.01 暂	聚乙烯醇缩丁醛膜(厚度不超过3毫米，非泡沫料的，未用其他材料强化、层压、支撑）	6.5	45	3	13	17	千克		Poly（vinyl butyral）film, (of a thickness exceeding 3mm) non-cellular, not reinforced, laminated, supported or similary combind with other materials
3920 9100.90	聚乙烯醇缩丁醛板，片，箔，扁条，及厚度超过3毫米的膜（非泡沫料的，未用其他材料强化、层压、支撑）	6.5	45		13	17	千克		Plates,sheets,foil and strip, of poly（vinyl butyral）, and film(of a thickness exceeding 3mm) non-cellular, not reinforced, supported or similarly combined with other materials
3920.9200	--聚酰胺制	10	45		13	17	千克		--Of polyamides
3920.9300	--氨基树脂制	6.5	45		13	17	千克		--Of amino-resins
3920.9400	--酚醛树脂制	10	45		13	17	千克		--Of phenolic resins
	--其他塑料制:								--Of other plastics:
3920.9910	---聚四氟乙烯制	6.5	45		13	17	千克		---Of polytetrafluoroethylene
3920.9990	---其他塑料制	6.5	45		13	17	千克		---Of other plastics
3920 9990.01 暂	聚酰亚胺膜，厚度≤0.03mm(未用其他材料强化、层压、支撑)	6.5	45	3	13	17	千克		Polyimide film, of a thickness not exceeding 0.03 (not reinforced, laminated, supported)
3920 9990.90	其他非泡沫塑料板，片，膜，箔，扁条(未用其他材料强化、层压、支撑)	6.5	45		13	17	千克		Other plates, sheets, film, foil and strip, of plastics(not reinforced, laminated, supported, supported or similarly combined with other materials)
39.21	**其他塑料板、片、膜、箔、扁条:**								**Other plates, sheets, film, foil and strip, of plastics:**
	-泡沫塑料的:								-Cellular:
3921.1100	--苯乙烯聚合物制	10	45		13	17	千克		--Of polymers of styrene
	--氯乙烯聚合物制:								--Of polymers of vinyl chloride:
3921.1210	---人造革及合成革	9	70		13	17	千克/米		---Combined with textile fabrics
3921.1290	---其他	6.5	45		13	17	千克		---Other
	--氨酯聚合物制:								--Of polyurethanes:

税则号列 Tariff Item	商品名称及备注	进口税率			出口退税	增值税率	计量单位	监管条件	Article Description
		最惠	普通	暂定					
3921.1310	---人造革及合成革	9	70		13	17	千克/米		---Combined with textile fabrics
3921.1390	---其他	6.5	45		13	17	千克		---Other
3921.1400	--再生纤维素制	10	45		13	17	千克		--Of regenerated cellulose
	--其他塑料制:								--Of other plastics:
3921.1910	---人造革及合成革	9	45		13	17	千克/米		---Combined with textile fabrics
3921.1990	---其他	6.5	45		13	17	千克		---Other
	-其他:								-Other:
3921.9020	---聚乙烯嵌有玻璃纤维的板、片	6.5	45		13	17	千克		---Plates, sheets of polyethylene with glass fibres
3921.9030	---聚异丁烯为基本成分的附有人造毛毡的板，片，卷材	6.5	45		13	17	千克		---Plates, sheets, coils of polyisobutylene with man-made felt
3921.9090	---其他	6.5	45		13	17	千克		---Other
3921 9090.01 暂	离子交换膜	6.5	45	5	13	17	千克		Ion (ic) exchange membrane
3921 9090.10	两用物项管制结构复合材料的层压板（用纤维和丝材增强而制成的各种预浸件和预成形件，其中增强材料的比拉伸强度大于 7.62×10^4 米和比模量大于 3.18×10^6 米）	6.5	45		13	17	千克	3	Laminated board made of structure of composite materials under sensitive item control（various prepreg and pre-formed parts reinforced by fibers and threads, the specific tensile strength of reinforcing materials is greater than 7.62×10^4m and specific modulus greater than 3.18×10^6m）
3921 9090.90	未列名塑料板、片、膜、箔、扁条（离子交换膜、两用物项管制结构复合材料的层压板除外）	6.5	45		13	17	千克		Other plates, sheets, film, foil and strip of plastic, not elsewhere specified or included (other than ion (ic) exchange membrane and laminated board made of composite materials under sensitive item control)
39.22	**塑料浴缸、淋浴盘、洗涤槽、盥洗盆、坐浴盆、便盆、马桶座圈及盖、抽水箱及类似卫生洁具:**								**Baths, shower-baths, sinks, washbasins, bidets, lavatory pans, seats and covers, flushing cisterns and similar sanitary ware, of plastics:**
3922.1000	-浴缸、淋浴盘、洗涤槽及盥洗盆	10	80		13	17	千克		-Baths, shower-baths, sinks and wash-basins
3922.2000	-马桶座圈及盖	10	80			17	千克		-Lavatory seats and covers
3922 2000.10	含濒危动物成分的塑料马桶座圈及盖	10	80			17	千克	EF	Lavatory seats and covers, of plastics, containing compositions of endangered animals
3922 2000.90	其他塑料马桶座圈及盖	10	80		13	17	千克		Other lavatory seats and cover of plastics
3922.9000	-其他	10	80		13	17	千克		-Other
39.23	**供运输或包装货物用的塑料制品；塑料制的塞子、盖子及类似品:**								**Articles for the conveyance or packing of goods, of plastics; stoppers, lids, caps and other closures, of plastics:**
3923.1000	-盒、箱（包括板条箱）及类似品	10	80		13	17	千克		-Boxes, cases, crates and similar articles
	-袋及包（包括锥形的）:								-Sacks and bags（including cones）:
3923.2100	--乙烯聚合物制	10	80		13	17	千克		--Of polymers of ethylene
3923.2900	--其他塑料制	10	80		13	17	千克		--Of other plastics
3923.3000	-坛、瓶及类似品	6.5	80		13	17	千克		-Carboys, bottles, flasks and similar articles
3923.4000	-卷轴、纡子、筒管及类似品	10	35		13	17	千克		-Spools, cops, bobbins and similar supports
3923.5000	-塞子、盖子及类似品	10	80		13	17	千克		-Stoppers, lids, caps and other closures
3923.9000	-其他	10	80		13	17	千克		-Other
39.24	**塑料制的餐具、厨房用具、其他家庭用具及卫生或盥洗用具:**								**Tableware, kitchenware, other household articles and hygienic or toilet articles, of plastics:**
3924.1000	-餐具及厨房用具	10	80		13	17	千克	AB	-Tableware and kitchenware
3924.9000	-其他	10	80		13	17	千克	A	-Other
39.25	**其他品目未列名的建筑用塑料制品:**								**Builders'ware of plastics, not elsewhere specified or included:**
3925.1000	-囤、柜、罐、桶及类似容器，容积超过 300 升	10	80		13	17	千克		-Reservoirs, tanks, vats and similar containers, of a capacity exceeding 300L
3925.2000	-门、窗及其框架、门槛	10	80		13	17	千克		-Doors, windows and their frames and thresholds for doors
3925.3000	-窗板、百叶窗（包括威尼斯式百叶窗）或类似制品及其零件	10	80		13	17	千克		-Shutters, blinds（including Venetian blinds） and similar articles and parts thereof

税则号列 Tariff Item	商品名称及备注	进口税率			出口退税	增值税率	计量单位	监管条件	Article Description
		最惠	普通	暂定					
3925.9000	-其他	10	80		13	17	千克		-Other
39.26	**其他塑料制品及品目 39.01 至 39.14 所列其他材料的制品:**								**Other articles of plastics and articles of other materials of headings No. 39.01 to 39.14:**
3926.1000	-办公室或学校用品	10	80		13	17	千克		-Office or school supplies
	-衣服及衣着附件(包括分指手套、连指手套及露指手套):								-Articles of apparel and clothing accessories (including gloves,mittens and mitts):
	---手套（包括分指手套、连指手套及露指手套）:								---Gloves (including gloves, mittens and mitts):
3926.2011	----聚氯乙烯制	10	90		13	17	千克/双		----Of poly (vinyl chloride)
3926.2019	----其他	10	90		13	17	千克/双		----Other
3926.2090	---其他	10	90		13	17	千克		---Other
3926.3000	-家具、车厢或类似品的附件	10	80		13	17	千克		-Fittings for furniture, coachwork or the like
3926.4000	-小雕塑品及其他装饰品	10	100		13	17	千克		-Statuettes and other ornamental articles
	-其他:								-Other:
3926.9010	---机器及仪器用零件	10	35		13	17	千克		---Of a kind for used in machines or instruments
3926.9090	---其他	10	80		13	17	千克		---Other
3926 9090.10	两用物项管制结构复合材料的预成形件和制品（用纤维和丝材增强而制成的各种预浸件和预成形件，其中增强材料的比拉伸强度大于 7.62×10^4 米和比模量大于 3.18×10^6 米）	10	80		13	17	千克	3	Laminated board made of structure of composite materials under sensitive item control（various prepreg and pre-formed parts reinforced by fibers and threads, the specific tensile strength of reinforcing materials is greater than 7.62×10^4m and specific modulus greater than 3.18×10^6m）
3926 9090.90	其他塑料制品（包括品目 39.01 至 39.14 所列材料的制品）	10	80		13	17	千克		Other articles of plastics and articles of other materials of heading No.39.01 to 39.14

第四十章
橡胶及其制品

注释：

一、除条文另有规定的以外，本目录所称“橡胶”，是指不论是否硫化或硬化的下列产品：天然橡胶、巴拉塔胶、古塔波胶、银胶菊胶、糖胶树胶及类似的天然树胶、合成橡胶、从油类中提取的油膏以及上述物品的再生品。

二、本章不包括：

（一）第十一类的货品（纺织原料及纺织制品）；

（二）第六十四章的鞋靴及其零件；

（三）第六十五章的帽类及其零件（包括游泳帽）；

（四）第十六类的硬质橡胶制的机械器具、电气器具及其零件（包括各种电气用品）；

（五）第九十章、第九十二章、第九十四章或第九十六章的物品；或

（六）第九十五章的物品（运动用分指手套、连指手套及露指手套及品目40.11至40.13的制品除外）。

三、品目 40.01 至 40.03 及 40.05 所称“初级形状”，只限于下列形状：

（一）液状及糊状，包括胶乳（不论是否预硫化）及其他分散体和溶液；

（二）不规则形状的块，团、包、粉、粒、碎屑及类似的散装形状。

四、本章注释一和品目 40.02 所称“合成橡胶”，适用于：

（一）不饱和合成物质，即用硫磺硫化能使其不可逆地变为非热塑物质，这种物质能在温度18℃～29℃之间被拉长到其原长度的3倍而不致断裂，拉长到原长度的2倍时，在5分钟内能回复到不超过原长度的1.5倍。为了进行上述试验，可以加入交联所需的硫化活化剂或促进剂；也允许含有注释五（二）2及3所述的物质。但不能加入非交联所需的物质，例如，增量剂、增塑剂及填料；

（二）聚硫橡胶（TM）；以及

（三）与塑料接枝共聚或混合而改性的天然橡胶、解聚天然橡胶以及不饱和合成物质与饱和合成高聚物的混合物，但这些产品必须符合以上（一）款关于硫化、延伸及回复的要求。

五、（一）品目 40.01 及 40.02 不适用于任何凝结前或凝结后与下列物质相混合的橡胶或橡胶混合物：

1. 硫化剂、促进剂、防焦剂或活性剂（为制造预硫胶乳所加入的除外）；

Chapter 40
Rubber and articles thereof

Chapter Notes:

1. Except where the context otherwise requires, throughout the Nomenclature the expression “rubber” means the following products, whether or not vulcanised or hard: natural rubber, balata, guttapercha, guayule, chicle and similar natural gums, synthetic rubber, factice derived from oils, and such substances reclaimed.

2. This Chapter does not cover:

(a) Goods of Section XI (textiles and textile articles);

(b) Footwear or parts thereof of Chapter 64;

(c) Headgear or parts thereof (including bathing caps) of Chapter 65;

(d) Mechanical or electrical appliances or parts thereof of Section XVI (including electrical goods of all kinds), of hard rubber;

(e) Articles of Chapter 90, 92, 94 or 96; or

(f) Articles of Chapter 95 (other than sports gloves, mittens and mitts and articles of headings 40.11 to 40.13).

3. In headings 40.01 to 40.03 and 40.05, the expression “primary forms” applies only to the following forms:

(a) Liquids and pastes (including latex, whether or not pre-vulcanised, and other dispersions and solutions);

(b) Blocks of irregular shape, lumps, bales, powders, granules, crumbs and similar bulk forms.

4. In Note 1 to this Chapter and in heading 40.02, the expression “synthetic rubber” applies to:

(a) Unsaturated synthetic substances which can be irreversibly transform-ed by vulcanisation with sulphur into non-thermoplastic substances which, at a temperature between 18℃ and 29℃, will not break on being extended to three times their original length and will return, after being extended to twice their original length, within a period of five minutes, to a length not greater than one and a half times their original length. For the purposes of this test, substances necessary for the cross-linking, such as vulcanising activators or accelerators, may be added; the presence of substances as provided for by Note 5 (b) (ii) and (iii) is also permitted. However,the presence of any substances not necessary for the cross-linking, such as extenders, plasticisers and fillers, is not permitted;

(b) Thioplasts (TM); and

(c) Natural rubber modified by grafting or mixing with plastics, depolymerized natural rubber, mixtures of unsaturated synthetic substances with saturated synthetic high polymers provided that all the above-mentioned products comply with the requirements concerning vulcanisation, elongation and recovery in (a) above.

5. (a) Headings 40.01 and 40.02 do not apply to any rubber or mixture of rubbers which has been compounded, before or after coagulation, with:

(i) vulcanising agents, accelerators, retarders or activators (other than those added for the preparation of prevulcanised rubber latex）;

2．颜料或其他着色料，但仅为易于识别而加入的除外；

（ii）pigments or other colouring matter, other than those added solely for the purpose of identification;

3．增塑剂或增量剂（用油增量的橡胶中所加的矿物油除外）、填料、增强剂、有机溶剂或其他物质，但以下（二）款所述的除外；

（iii）plasticisers or extenders（except mineral oil in the case of oil-extended rubber）, fillers, reinforcing agents, organic solvents or any other substances, except those permitted under（b）;

（二）含有下列物质的橡胶或橡胶混合物，只要仍具有原料的基本特性，应归入品目40.01或40.02：

（b）The presence of the following substances in any rubber or mixture of rubbers shall not affect its classification in heading 40.01 or 40.02, as the case may be, provided that such rubber or mixture of rubbers retains its essential character as a raw material:

1．乳化剂或防粘剂；

（i）emulsifiers or anti-tack agents;

2．少量的乳化剂分解产品；

（ii）small amounts of breakdown products of emulsifiers;

3．微量的下列物质：热敏剂（一般为制造热敏胶乳用）、阳离子表面活性剂（一般为制造阳性胶乳用）、抗氧剂、凝固剂、碎裂剂、抗冻剂、胶溶剂、保存剂、稳定剂、粘度控制剂或类似的特殊用途添加剂。

（iii）very small amounts of the following: heatsensitive agents (generally for obtaining thermosensitive rubber latexes), cationic surface-active agents(generally for obtaining electropo-sitive rubber latexes), antioxidants, coagulants, crumbling agents, freeze-resisting agents, peptisers, preservatives, stabilisers, viscosity-control agents, or similar special-purpose additives.

六、品目40.04所称“废碎料及下脚料”，是指在橡胶或橡胶制品生产或加工过程中由于切割、磨损或其他原因明显不能按橡胶或橡胶制品使用的废橡胶及下脚料。

6. For the purposes of heading 40.04, the expression “waste, parings and scrap” means rubber waste, parings and scrap from the manufacture or working of rubber and rubber goods definitely not usable as such because of cutting-up, wear or other reasons.

七、全部用硫化橡胶制成的线，其任一截面的尺寸超过5毫米的，应作为带、杆或型材及异型材归入品目40．08。

7. Thread wholly of vulcanised rubber, of which any cross-sectional dimension exceeds 5mm, is to be classified as strip, rods or profile shapes, of heading 40.08.

八、品目40.10包括用橡胶浸渍、涂布、包覆或层压的织物制成的或用橡胶浸渍、涂布、包覆或套裹的纱线或绳制成的传动带、输送带。

8. Heading 40.10 includes conveyor or transmission belts or belting of textile fabric impregnated, coated, covered or laminated with rubber or made from textile yarn or cord impregnated, coated,covered or sheathed with rubber.

九、品目40.01、40.02、40.03、40.05及40.08所称“板”、“片”、“带”，仅指未切割或只简单切割成矩形（包括正方形）的板、片、带及正几何形块，不论是否具有成品的特征，也不论是否经过印制或其他表面加工，但未切割成其他形状或进一步加工。

品目40.08所称“杆”或“型材及异型材”，仅指不论是否切割成一定长度或表面加工，但未经进一步加工的该类产品。

9. In headings 40.01, 40.02, 40.03, 40.05, and 40.08, the expressions “plates”, “sheets” and “strip” apply only to plates, sheets and strip and to blocks of regular geometric shape, uncut or simply cut to rectangular（including square）shape, whether or not having the character of articles and whether or not printed or otherwise surface-worked, but not otherwise cut to shape or further worked.

In heading 40.08 the expressions “rods” and “profile shapes”apply only to such products, whether or not cut to length or surfaceworked but not otherwise worked.

税则号列 Tariff Item	商品名称及备注	进口税率			出口退税	增值税率	计量单位	监管条件	Article Description
		最惠	普通	暂定					
40.01	**天然橡胶、巴拉塔胶、古塔波胶、银胶菊胶、糖胶树胶及类似的天然树胶，初级形状或板、片、带:**								**Natural rubber, balata, gutta-percha, guayule, chicle and similar natural gums, in primary forms or in plates, sheets or strip:**
4001.1000[暂]	-天然胶乳，不论是否预硫化	20	40	（1）	5	17	千克	AB	-Natural rubber latex, whether or not prevulcanized
	-其他形状的天然橡胶:								-Natural rubber in other forms:
4001.2100[暂]	--烟胶片	20	40	（2）	5	17	千克	AB	--Smoked sheets
4001.2200[暂]	--技术分类天然橡胶（TSNR）	20	40	（2）	5	17	千克		--Technically specified natural rubber（TSNR）
4001.2900	--其他	20	40		5	17	千克		--other
4001.3000	-巴拉塔胶、古塔波胶、银胶菊胶、糖胶树胶及类似的天然树胶	20	40		5	17	千克		-Balata, gutta-percha, guayule, chicle and similar natural gums

（1）10%或720元/吨，两者从低；（2）20%或1200元/吨，两者从低

税则号列 Tariff Item	商品名称及备注	进口税率			出口退税	增值税率	计量单位	监管条件	Article Description
		最惠	普通	暂定					
40.02	合成橡胶及从油类提取的油膏，初级形状或板、片、带；品目40.01所列产品与本品目所列产品的混合物，初级形状或板、片、带：								**Synthetic rubber and factice derived from oils, in primary forms or in plates, sheets or strip; mixtures of any products of heading No.40.01 with any product of this heading, in primary forms or in plates, sheets or strip:**
	-丁苯橡胶（SBR）；羧基丁苯橡胶（XSBR）：								-Styrene-butadiene rubber（SBR）; carboxylated styrene-butadiene rubber（XSBR）:
	--胶乳:								--Latex:
4002.1110	---羧基丁苯橡胶	7.5	14		5	17	千克		---Carboxylated styrene-butadiene rubber（XSBR）
4002.1190	---其他	7.5	14		5	17	千克		---Other
	--其他:								--Other:
	---初级形状的:								---In primary forms:
4002.1911	----未经任何加工丁苯橡胶	7.5	14		13	17	千克		----SBR, not worked
4002.1912	----充油丁苯橡胶	7.5	14		5	17	千克		----SBR, oil-filled
4002.1913	----热塑丁苯橡胶	7.5	14		5	17	千克		----SBR, thermo-plasticated
4002.1914	----充油热塑丁苯橡胶	7.5	14		5	17	千克		----SBR, oil-filled and thermo-plasticated
4002.1919	----其他	7.5	14		5	17	千克		----Other
4002.1990	---其他	7.5	35			17	千克		---Other
4002 1990.01	简单处理的丁苯橡胶，热塑或充油热塑丁苯橡胶除外（指为便于运输，对初级形状进行压缩、挤压等简单成型处理）	7.5	35		5	17	千克		Styrene-butadiene rubber (SBR), to facilitate transport, the shape of primary of compression, extrusion and other simple processing）,other than oil-filled and thermo-plasticated SBR
4002 1990.90	其他丁苯橡胶及羧基丁苯橡胶板，片，带（4002199001项下的除外）	7.5	35			17	千克		Other SBR and XSBR in plates, sheets or strip (other than any products of heading No. 40021990.01)
	-丁二烯橡胶（BR）：								-Butadiene rubber（BR）:
4002.2010	---初级形状的	7.5	14		5	17	千克		---In primary forms
4002.2090	---其他	7.5	35			17	千克		---Other
	-异丁烯-异戊二烯（丁基）橡胶（IIR）；卤代丁基橡胶（CIIR或BIIR）：								-Isobutene-isoprene（butyl）rubber（IIR）; halo-isobutene-isoprene rubber（CIIR or BIIR）:
	--异丁烯-异戊二烯（丁基）橡胶（IIR）：								--Isobutene-isoprene（butyl）rubber（IIR）:
4002.3110	---初级形状的	6	14		5	17	千克		---In primary forms
4002.3190	---其他	7.5	35			17	千克		---Other
	--其他:								--Other:
4002.3910	---初级形状的	7.5	14		5	17	千克		---In pimary forms
4002.3990	---其他	7.5	35			17	千克		---Other
	-氯丁二烯（氯丁）橡胶（CR）：								-Chloroprene（chlorobutadiene）rubber（CR）:
4002.4100	--胶乳	7.5	14		5	17	千克		--Latex
	--其他:								--Other:
4002.4910	---初级形状的	7.5	14		5	17	千克		---In primary forms
4002.4990	---其他	7.5	35			17	千克		---Other
	-丁腈橡胶（NBR）：								-Acrylonitrile-butadient rubber（NBR）:
4002.5100	--胶乳	7.5	14		5	17	千克		--Latex
	--其他:								--Other:
4002.5910	---初级形状的	7.5	14		5	17	千克		---In primary forms
4002.5990	---其他	7.5	35			17	千克		---Other
	-异戊二烯橡胶（IR）：								-Isoprene rubber（IR）:
4002.6010	---初级形状的	3	14		5	17	千克		---In primary forms
4002.6090	---其他	5	35			17	千克		---Other
	-乙丙非共轭二烯橡胶（EPDM）：								-Ethylene-propylene-non-conjugated diene rubber（EPDM）:
4002.7010	---初级形状的	7.5	14		5	17	千克		---In primary forms
4002.7090	---其他	7.5	35			17	千克		---Other
4002.8000	-品目40.01所列产品与本品目所列产品的混合物	7.5	35			17	千克		-Mixtures of any product of heading No. 40.01 with any product of this heading
	-其他:								-Other:

税则号列 Tariff Item	商品名称及备注	进口税率 最惠	普通	暂定	出口退税	增值税率	计量单位	监管条件	Article Description
4002.9100	--胶乳	7.5	14			17	千克		--Latex
	--其他:								--Other:
	---其他合成橡胶:								---Other synthetic rubber:
4002.9911	----初级形状的	7.5	14		13	17	千克		---In primary forms
4002.9919	----其他	7.5	35			17	千克		----Other
4002.9990	---其他	4	14			17	千克		---Other
40.03	**再生橡胶，初级形状或板、片、带:**								**Reclaimed rubber in primary forms or in plates, sheets or strip:**
4003.0000	再生橡胶，初级形状或板、片、带	8	30		13	17	千克		Reclaimed rubber in primary forms or in plates, sheets or strip
40.04	**橡胶（硬质橡胶除外）的废碎料、下脚料及其粉、粒:**								**Waste, parings and scrap of rubber（other than hard rubber）and powders and granules obtained therefrom:**
4004.0000	橡胶（硬质橡胶除外）的废碎料、下脚料及其粉、粒	8	30			17	千克		Waste, parings and scrap of rubber（other than hard rubber）and powders and granules obtained therefrom
4004 0000.10	废轮胎及其切块	8	30			17	千克	9	Waste rubber tyres and their cuts
4004 0000.20	硫化橡胶废碎料、下脚料及其粉、粒（硬质橡胶除外）	8	30			17	千克	9	Vulcanized rubber waste and scrap, and powders and granules obtained therefrom（other than hard rubber）
4004 0000.90	未硫化橡胶废碎料、下脚料及其粉、粒	8	30			17	千克	AP	Waste, parings and scrap of rubber and powders and granules obtained therefrom not vulcanized (other than hard rubber)
40.05	**未硫化的复合橡胶，初级形状或板、片、带:**								**Compounded rubber, unvulcanized, in primary forms or in plates, sheets or strip:**
4005.1000	-与碳黑或硅石混合	8	35			17	千克		-Compounded with carbon black or silica
4005.2000	-溶液；子目号 4005.10 以外的分散体	8	35			17	千克		-Solutions; dispersions other than those of sub-heading No. 4005.10
	-其他:								-Other:
4005.9100	--板、片、带	8	35			17	千克		--Plates, sheets and strip
4005.9900	--其他	8	35			17	千克		--Other
40.06	**其他形状（例如，杆、管或型材及异型材）的未硫化橡胶及未硫化橡胶制品（例如，盘、环）:**								**Other forms（for example, rods, tubes and profile shapes）and articles（for example, discs and rings）, or unvulcanized rubber:**
4006.1000	-轮胎翻新用胎面补料胎条	8	35			17	千克		-Camel-back strips for retreading rubber tyres
	-其他:								-Other:
4006.9010	---其他形状的未硫化橡胶	8	35			17	千克		---Other forms of unvulcanized rubber
4006.9020	---未硫化橡胶制品	14	80			17	千克		---Articles of unvulcanized rubber
40.07	**硫化橡胶线及绳:**								**Vulcanized rubber thread and cord:**
4007.0000	硫化橡胶线及绳	14	80		9	17	千克		Vulcanized rubber thread and cord
40.08	**硫化橡胶（硬质橡胶除外）制的板、片、带、杆或型材及异型材:**								**Plates, sheets, strip, rods and profile shapes, of vulcanized rubber other than hard rubber:**
	-海绵橡胶制:								-Of cellular rubber:
4008.1100	--板、片、带	8	35		9	17	千克		--Plates, sheets and strip
4008.1900	--其他	8	35		9	17	千克		--Other
	-非海绵橡胶制:								-Of non-cellular rubber:
4008.2100	--板、片、带	8	35		9	17	千克		--Plates, sheets and strip
4008.2900	--其他	8	35		9	17	千克		--Other
40.09	**硫化橡胶（硬质橡胶除外）制的管子，不论是否装有附件（例如，接头、肘管、法兰）:**								**Tubes, pipes and hoses, of vulcanized rubber other than hard rubber, with or without their fittings（for example, joints, elbows, flanges）:**
	-未经加强或未与其他材料合制:								-Not reinforced or otherwise combined with other materials:
4009.1100	--未装有附件	10.5	40		9	17	千克		--Without fittings
4009.1200	--装有附件	10	40		9	17	千克		--With fittings
	-用金属加强或只与金属合制:								-Reinforced or otherwise combined only with metal:
4009.2100	--未装有附件	10.5	40		9	17	千克		--Without fittings
4009.2200	--装有附件	10	40		9	17	千克		--With fittings
	-用纺织材料加强或只与纺织材								-Reinforced or otherwise combined only with textile

税则号列 Tariff Item	商品名称及备注	进口税率 最惠	普通	暂定	出口退税	增值税率	计量单位	监管条件	Article Description
	料合制:								materials:
4009.3100	--未装有附件	10.5	40		9	17	千克		--Without fittings
4009.3200	--装有附件	10	40		9	17	千克		--With fittings
	-用其他材料加强或与其他材料合制:								-Reinforced or otherwise combined with other materials:
4009.4100	--未装有附件	10.5	40		9	17	千克		--Without fittings
4009.4200	--装有附件	10	40		9	17	千克		--With fittings
40.10	**硫化橡胶制的传动带或输送带及带料:**								**Conveyor or transmission belts or belting, of vulcanized rubber:**
	-输送带及带料:								-Conveyor belts or belting:
4010.1100	--仅用金属加强的	10	35		9	17	千克		--Reinforced only with metal
4010.1200	--仅用纺织材料加强的	10	35		9	17	千克		--Reinforced only with textile materials
4010.1900	--其他	10	35		9	17	千克		--Other
	-传动带及带料:								-Transmission belts or belting:
4010.3100	--梯形截面的环形传动带(三角带),V形肋状的,外周长超过60厘米,但不超过180厘米	8	35		9	17	千克		--Endless transmission belts of trapezoidal cross-section(V-belts), of an outside circumference exceeding 60cm but not exceeding 180cm
4010.3200	--梯形截面的环形传动带(三角带),外周长超过60厘米,但不超过180厘米,V形肋状的除外	8	35		9	17	千克		--Endless transmission belts of trapezoidal cross-section(V-belts), other than V-ribbed, of an outside circumference exceeding 60cm but not exceeding 180cm
4010.3300	--梯形截面的环形传动带(三角带),V形肋状的,外周长超过180厘米,但不超过240厘米	8	35		9	17	千克		--Endless transmission belts of trapezoidal cross-section(V-belts), V-ribbed, of an outside circumference exceeding 180cm but not exceeding 240cm
4010.3400	--梯形截面的环形传动带(三角带),外周长超过180厘米,但不超过240厘米,V形肋状的除外	8	35		9	17	千克		--Endless transmission belts of trapezoidal cross-section(V-belts), other than V-ribbed, of an outside circumference exceeeding 180cm but not exceeding 240cm
4010.3500	--环形同步带,外周长超过60厘米,但不超过150厘米	10	35		9	17	千克		--Endless synchronous, of an outside circumference exceeding 60cm but not exceeding 150cm
4010.3600	--环形同步带,外周长超过150厘米,但不超过198厘米	10	35		9	17	千克		--Endless synchronous belts, of an outside circumference exceeding 150cm but not exceeding 198cm
4010.3900	--其他	8	35		9	17	千克		--Other
40.11	**新的充气橡胶轮胎:**								**New pneumatic tyres, of rubber:**
4011.1000	-机动小客车(包括旅行小客车及赛车)用	10	50		9	17	千克/条		-Of a kind used on motor cars(including station wagons and racing cars)
4011 1000.10	机动小客车用新的充气子午线轮胎(橡胶轮胎,包括旅行小客车及赛车用)	10	50		9	17	千克/条	A	New pneumatic radial-ply tyres of rubbe, used on motor cars(including station wagons and racing cars)
4011 1000.90	机动小客车用新的充气非子午线轮胎(橡胶轮胎,包括旅行小客车及赛车用)	10	50		9	17	千克/条	A	New pneumatic non radial-ply tyres of rubber, of a kind used on motor cars(including station wagons and racing cars)
4011.2000	-客运机动车辆或货运机动车辆用	10	50		9	17	千克/条		-Of a kind used on buses or lorries
4011 2000.11 [暂]	客或货运车用新的充气子午线轮胎(指机动车辆用橡胶轮胎,断面宽度≥30英寸)	10	50	3	9	17	千克/条	A	New pneumatic radial-ply tyres of rubber, used on buses or lorries(of a cross-section width exceeding 30 inch)
4011 2000.19 [暂]	断面宽≥30英寸的客或货车用新非子午线充气橡胶轮胎	10	50	3	9	17	千克/条	A	New pneumatic non radial-ply tyres of rubber, used on buses or lorries, of a cross-section width exceeding 30 inch
4011 2000.91	其他客或货车用新充气子午线轮胎(指机动车辆用橡胶轮胎)	10	50		9	17	千克/条	A	New pneumatic radial-ply tyres of rubber, used on other buses or lorries(referring to tyres used on motor vehicle)
4011 2000.99	客或货车用新的其他非子午线充气橡胶轮胎	10	50		9	17	千克/条	A	Other new pneumatic non radial-ply tyres of rubber, used on buses or lorries
4011.3000	-航空器用	1	11		9	17	千克/条		-Of a kind used on aircraft
4011.4000	-摩托车用	15	80		9	17	千克/条	A	-Of a kind used on motorcycles

税则号列 Tariff Item	商品名称及备注	进口税率 最惠	普通	暂定	出口退税	增值税率	计量单位	监管条件	Article Description
4011.5000	-自行车用	20	80		13	17	千克/条		-Of a kind used on bicycles
	-其他，人字型胎面或类似胎面的:								-Other, having a "herring-bone" or similar tread:
4011.6100	--农业或林业车辆及机器用	17.5	50		9	17	千克/条		--Of a kind used on agricultural or forestry vehicles and machines
4011 6100.11[暂]	断面宽≥24英寸人字形子午线轮胎（新充气橡胶轮胎，含胎面类似人字形的，农林车辆机械用）	17.5	50	6	9	17	千克/条	A	New pneumatic radial-ply tyres of rubber, with "herring-bone" tread, of a cross-section width exceeding 24 inches, of a kind used on agricultural or forestry vehicles and machines
4011 6100.19[暂]	断面宽≥24英寸人字形非子午线轮胎（新充气橡胶轮胎，含胎面类似人字形的，农林车辆机械用）	17.5	50	6	9	17	千克/条	A	New pneumatic non radial-ply tyres of rubber, with "herring-bone" tread, of a cross-section width exceeding 24 inches, of a kind used on agricultural or forestry vehicles and machines
4011 6100.91	其他人字形胎面子午线轮胎（新充气橡胶轮胎，含胎面类似人字形的，农林车辆机械用）	17.5	50		9	17	千克/条	A	Other new pneumatic radial-ply tyres of rubber, with "herring-bone" tread, of a kind used on agricultural or forestry vehicles and machines
4011 6100.99	其他人字形胎面非子午线轮胎（新充气橡胶轮胎，含胎面类似人字形的，农林车辆机械用）	17.5	50		9	17	千克/条	A	Other new pneumatic non radial-ply tyres of rubber, with "herring-bone" tread, of a kind used on agricultural or forestry vehicles and machines
4011.6200	--建筑业或工业搬运车辆及机器用，辋圈尺寸不超过61厘米	17.5	50		9	17	千克/条		--Of a kind used on construction or industrial handling vehicles and machines and having a rim size not exceeding 61cm
4011 6200.11	断面宽≥24英寸人字形子午线轮胎（建筑业、工业用，辋圈≤61厘米，新充气橡胶胎，含类似人字形）	17.5	50		9	17	千克/条	A	New pneumatic radial-ply tyres of rubber, with "herring-bone" tread, of a cross-section width exceeding 24 inches, on construction or industrial uses and having a rim size not exceeding 61cm
4011 6200.19	断面宽≥24英寸人字形非子午线轮胎（建筑业、工业用，辋圈≤61厘米，新充气橡胶胎，含类似人字形）	17.5	50		9	17	千克/条	A	New pneumatic non radial-ply tyres of rubber, with "herring-bone" tread, of a cross-section width exceeding 24 inches, on construction or industrial uses and having a rim size not exceeding 61cm
4011 6200.91	其他人字形胎面子午线轮胎（建筑业、工业用，辋圈≤61厘米，新充气橡胶胎，含类似人字形）	17.5	50		9	17	千克/条	A	Other new pneumatic radial-ply tyres of rubber, with "herring-bone" tread, on construction or industrial uses and having a rim size not exceeding 61cm
4011 6200.99	其他人字形胎面非子午线轮胎（建筑业、工业用，辋圈≤61厘米，新充气橡胶胎，含类似人字形）	17.5	50		9	17	千克/条	A	Other new pneumatic non radial-ply tyres of rubber, with "herring-bone" tread, on construction or industrial uses and having a rim size not exceeding 61cm
4011.6300	--建筑业或工业搬运车辆及机器用，辋圈尺寸超过61厘米	17.5	50		9	17	千克/条		--Of a kind used on construction or industrial handling vehicles and machines and having a rim size exceeding 61cm
4011 6300.11[暂]	断面宽≥24英寸人字形子午线轮胎（建筑业、工业用，辋圈>61厘米，新充气橡胶胎，含类人字形）	17.5	50	8	9	17	千克/条	A	New pneumatic radial-ply tyres of rubber, with "herring-bone" tread, of a cross-section width exceeding 24 inches, on construction or industrial uses and having a rim size exceeding 61cm
4011 6300.19[暂]	断面宽≥24英寸人字形非子午线轮胎（建筑业、工业用，辋圈>61厘米，新充气橡胶胎，含类人字形）	17.5	50	8	9	17	千克/条	A	New pneumatic non radial-ply tyres of rubber, with "herring-bone" tread, of a cross-section width exceeding 24 inches, on construction or industrial uses and having a rim size exceeding 61cm
4011 6300.91	其他人字形胎面子午线轮胎（建筑业、工业用，辋圈>61厘米，新充气橡胶胎，含类人字形）	17.5	50		9	17	千克/条	A	Other new pneumatic radial-ply tyres of rubber, with "herring-bone" tread, on construction or industrial uses and having a rim size exceeding 61cm
4011 6300.99	其他人字形胎面非子午线轮胎（建筑业、工业用，辋圈>61厘米，新充气橡胶胎，含类似人字形）	17.5	50		9	17	千克/条	A	Other new pneumatic non radial-ply tyres of rubber, with "herring-bone" tread, on construction or industrial uses and having a rim size exceeding 61cm
4011.6900	--其他	17.5	50		9	17	千克/条		--Other

税则号列 Tariff Item	商品名称及备注	进口税率 最惠	进口税率 普通	进口税率 暂定	出口退税	增值税率	计量单位	监管条件	Article Description
4011 6900.11[暂]	断面宽≥30英寸人字形子午线轮胎（其他用途，新充气橡胶轮胎，含胎面类似人字形的）	17.5	50	6	9	17	千克/条	A	New pneumatic radial-ply tyres of rubber, with “herring-bone” tread, on other uses, of a cross-section width exceeding 30 inches
4011 6900.19[暂]	断面宽≥30英寸人字形非子午线轮胎（其他用途，新充气橡胶轮胎，含胎面类似人字形的）	17.5	50	6	9	17	千克/条	A	New pneumatic non radial-ply tyres of rubber, with “herring-bone” tread, on other uses, of a cross-section width exceeding 30 inches
4011 6900.91	其他人字形胎面子午线轮胎（其他用途，新充气橡胶轮胎，含胎面类似人字形的）	17.5	50		9	17	千克/条	A	Other new pneumatic radial-ply tyres of rubber, with “herring-bone” tread, on other uses
4011 6900.99	其他人字形胎面非子午线轮胎（其他用途，新充气橡胶轮胎，含胎面类似人字形的）	17.5	50		9	17	千克/条	A	Other new pneumatic non radial-ply tyres of rubber, with “herring-bone” tread, on other uses
	-其他：								-Other:
4011.9200	--农业或林业车辆及机器用	25	50		9	17	千克/条		--Of a kind used on agricultural or forestry vehicles and machines
4011 9200.11[暂]	其他断面宽度≥24英寸子午线轮胎（新充气橡胶轮胎，非人字形胎面，农林车辆机械用）	25	50	6	9	17	千克/条		Other new pneumatic radial-ply tyres of rubber, non “herring-bone” tread, of a cross-section width exceeding 24 inches, used on agricultural or forestry vehicles and machines
4011 9200.19[暂]	其他断面宽≥24英寸非子午线轮胎（新充气橡胶轮胎，非人字形胎面，农林车辆机械用）	25	50	6	9	17	千克/条		Other new pneumatic non radial-ply tyres of rubber, non “herring-bone” tread, of a cross-section width exceeding 24 inches,used on agricultural or forestry vehicles and machines
4011 9200.91	其他新的充气橡胶子午线轮胎（新充气橡胶轮胎，非人字形胎面，农林车辆机械用）	25	50		9	17	千克/条		Other new pneumatic radial-ply tyres of rubber, non “herring-bone” tread, used on agricultural or forestry vehicles and machines
4011 9200.99	其他新的充气橡胶非子午线轮胎（新充气橡胶轮胎，非人字形胎面，农林车辆机械用）	25	50		9	17	千克/条		Other new pneumatic non radial-ply tyres of rubber, non “herring-bone” tread, used on agricultural or forestry vehicles and machines
4011.9300	--建筑业或工业搬运车辆及机器用，辋圈尺寸不超过61厘米	25	50		9	17	千克/条		--Of a kind used on construction or industrial handling vehicles and machines and having a rim size not exceeding 61cm
4011 9300.11	其他断面宽度≥24英寸子午线轮胎（建筑业、工业用，辋圈≤61厘米，新充气橡胶胎，非人字形胎面）	25	50		9	17	千克/条		Other new pneumatic radial-ply tyres of rubber, non “herring-bone” tread, on construction or Industrial uses, of a cross-section width exceeding 24 inches and having a rim size not exceeding 61cm
4011 9300.19	其他断面宽≥24英寸非子午线轮胎（建筑业、工业用，辋圈≤61厘米，新充气橡胶胎，非人字形胎面）	25	50		9	17	千克/条		Other new pneumatic non radial-ply tyres of rubber, non “herring-bone” tread, on construction or industrial uses, of a cross-section width exceeding 24 inches and having a rim size not exceeding 61cm
4011 9300.91	其他新的充气橡胶子午线轮胎（建筑业、工业用，辋圈≤61厘米，新充气橡胶胎，非人字形胎面）	25	50		9	17	千克/条		Other new pneumatic radial-ply tyres of rubber, non “herring-bone” tread, on construction or industrial uses and having a rim size not exceeding 61cm
4011 9300.99	其他新的充气橡胶非子午线轮胎（建筑业、工业用，辋圈≤61厘米，新充气橡胶胎，非人字形胎面）	25	50		9	17	千克/条		Other new pneumatic non radial-ply tyres of rubber non “herring-bone” tread, on construction or industrial uses and having a rim size not exceeding 61cm
4011.9400	--建筑业或工业搬运车辆及机器用，辋圈尺寸超过61厘米	25	50		9	17	千克/条		--Of a kind used on construction or industrial handling vehicles and machines and having a rim size exceeding 61cm
4011 9400.11[暂]	其他断面宽度≥24英寸子午线轮胎（建筑业、工业用，辋圈>61厘米，新充气橡胶胎，非人字形胎面）	25	50	8	9	17	千克/条		Other new pneumatic radial-ply tyres of rubber, non “herring-bone” tread, on construction or industrial uses, of a cross-section width exceeding 24 inches and having a rim size exceeding 61cm
4011 9400.19[暂]	其他断面宽≥24英寸非子午线轮胎（建筑业、工业用，辋圈>	25	50	8	9	17	千克/条		Other new pneumatic non radial-ply tyres of rubber, non “herring-bone” tread, on construction or industrial

税则号列 Tariff Item	商品名称及备注	进口税率 最惠	进口税率 普通	进口税率 暂定	出口退税	增值税率	计量单位	监管条件	Article Description
	61厘米，新充气橡胶胎，非人字形胎面）								uses, of a cross-section width exceeding 24 inches and having a rim size exceeding 61cm
4011 9400.91	其他新的充气橡胶子午线轮胎（建筑业，工业用，辋圈>61厘米，新充气橡胶胎，非人字形胎面）	25	50		9	17	千克/条		Other new pneumatic radial-ply tyres of rubber, non "herring-bone" tread, on construction or industrial uses, having a rim size exceeding 61cm
4011 9400.99	其他新的充气橡胶非子午线轮胎（建筑业、工业用，辋圈>61厘米，新充气橡胶胎，非人字形胎面）	25	50		9	17	千克/条		Other new pneumatic non radial-ply tyres of rubber, non "herring-bone" tread, on construction or industrial uses, having a rim size exceeding 61cm
4011.9900	--其他	25	50		9	17	千克/条		--Other
4011 9900.11[暂]	其他断面宽度≥30英寸子午线轮胎（其他用途，新充气橡胶轮胎，非人字形胎面）	25	50	5	9	17	千克/条		Other new pneumatic radial-ply tyres of rubber, non "herring-bone" tread, on other uses, of a cross-section width exceeding 30 inches
4011 9900.19[暂]	其他断面宽≥30英寸非子午线轮胎（其他用途，新充气橡胶轮胎，非人字形胎面）	25	50	5	9	17	千克/条		Other new pneumatic non radial-ply tyres of rubber, non "herring-bone" tread, on other uses, of a cross-section width exceeding 30 inches
4011 9900.91	其他新的充气橡胶子午线轮胎（其他用途，新充气橡胶轮胎，非人字形胎面）	25	50		9	17	千克/条		Other new pneumatic radial-ply tyres of rubber, non "herring-bone" tread, on other uses
4011 9900.99	其他新的充气橡胶非子午线轮胎（其他用途，新充气橡胶轮胎，非人字形胎面）	25	50		9	17	千克/条		Other new pneumatic non radial-ply tyres of rubber, non "herring-bone" tread, on other uses
40.12	**翻新的或旧的充气橡胶轮胎；实心或半实心橡胶轮胎、橡胶胎面及橡胶轮胎衬带：**								**Retreaded or used pneumatic tyres of rubber; solid or cushion tyres, tyre treads and tyre flaps, of rubber:**
	-翻新轮胎：								-Retreaded tyres:
4012.1100	--机动小客车（包括旅行小客车及赛车）用	20	50		9	17	千克/条	A	--Of a kind used on motor cars,（including station wagons and racing cars）
4012.1200	--机动大客车或货运机动车辆用	20	50		9	17	千克/条	A	--Of a kind used on buses or lorries
4012.1300[暂]	--航空器用	20	50	8	9	17	千克/条		--Of a kind used on aircraft
4012.1900	--其他	20	50		9	17	千克/条		--Other
	-旧的充气轮胎：								-Used pneumatic tyres:
4012.2010	---汽车用	25	50		9	17	千克/条		---Of a kind used on motor cars, buses or lorries
4012 2010.10	汽车用旧的充气橡胶子午线轮胎	25	50		9	17	千克/条	A	Used pneumatic, radial ply tyres of rubber , of a kind used on automobiles
4012 2010.90	汽车用旧的充气橡胶非子午线轮胎	25	50		9	17	千克/条	A	Used pneumatic, non-radial ply tyres of rubber , of a kind used on automobiles
4012.2090	---其他	25	80		9	17	千克/条		---Other
4012 2090.10	其他用途旧的充气橡胶子午线轮胎	25	80		9	17	千克/条		Used pneumatic, radial ply tyres of rubber, on other uses
4012 2090.90	其他用旧的充气橡胶非子午线轮胎	25	80		9	17	千克/条		Used pneumatic, non-radial ply tyres of rubber, on other uses
	-其他：								-Other:
4012.9010[暂]	---航空器用	3	11	1	9	17	千克		---Of a kind used on aircraft
4012.9020	---汽车用	22	50		9	17	千克		---Of a kind used on motor cars, buses or lorries
4012 9020.10	汽车用实心或半实心子午线轮胎	22	50		9	17	千克	A	Solid or cushion radial-ply tyres, of a kind used on automobiles
4012 9020.90	汽车用实心或半实心非子午线轮胎（还包括可互换橡胶胎面及橡胶轮胎衬带）	22	50		9	17	千克	A	Solid or cushion, non radial-ply tyres, of a kind used on automobile （including interchangeable tyre treads and tyre flaps）
4012.9090	---其他	22	50		9	17	千克		---Other
4012 9090.10	其他用实心或半实心子午线轮胎	22	50		9	17	千克		Other Solid or cushion radial-ply tyres, on other uses
4012 9090.90	其他用实心或半实心非子午线轮胎（还包括可互换橡胶胎面及橡胶轮胎衬带）	22	50		9	17	千克		Other solid or cushion, non radial-ply tyres, on other uses（including interchangeable tyre treads and tyre flaps）
40.13	橡胶内胎：								**Inner tubes, of rubber:**

税则号列 Tariff Item	商品名称及备注	进口税率			出口退税	增值税率	计量单位	监管条件	Article Description
		最惠	普通	暂定					
4013.1000	-机动小客车（包括旅行小客车及赛车）、客运、机动车辆或货运机动车辆用	15	50		9	17	千克/条	A	-Of a kind used on motor cars（including station wagons and racing cars）, buses or lorries
4013.2000	-自行车用	15	80		13	17	千克/条		-Of a kind used on bicycles
	-其他:								-Other:
4013.9010[暂]	---航空器用	3	11	1	9	17	千克/条		---Of a kind used on aircraft
4013.9090	---其他	15	50		9	17	千克/条		---Other
40.14	**硫化橡胶（硬质橡胶除外）制的卫生及医疗用品（包括奶嘴），不论是否装有硬质橡胶制的附件：**								**Hygienic or pharmaceutical articles（including teats）, of vulcanized rubber other than hard rubber, with or without fittings of hard rubber:**
4014.1000	-避孕套	0	0			0	千克		-Sheath contraceptives
4014.9000	-其他	17.5	50		9	17	千克	A	-Other
40.15	**硫化橡胶（硬质橡胶除外）制的衣着用品及附件（包括分指手套、连指手套及露指手套）：**								**Articles of apparel and clothing accessories（including gloves, mittens and mitts）, for all purposes, of vulcanized rubber other than hard rubber:**
	-分指手套、连指手套及露指手套:								-Gloves, mittens and mitts:
4015.1100	--外科用	8	30		13	17	千克/双		--Surgical
4015.1900	--其他	18	80		13	17	千克/双		--Other
	-其他:								-Other:
4015.9010	---医疗用	8	30		9	17	千克		---For medical purpose
4015.9090	---其他	15	90		9	17	千克		---Other
40.16	**硫化橡胶（硬质橡胶除外）的其他制品：**								**Other articles of vulcanized rubber other than hard rubber:**
	-海绵橡胶制:								-Of cellular rubber:
4016.1010	---机器及仪器用零件	8	30		9	17	千克		---Of a kind used in machines or instruments
4016.1090	---其他	15	80		9	17	千克		---Other
	-其他:								---Other:
4016.9100	--铺地制品及门垫	18	80		9	17	千克		--Floor coverings and mats
4016.9200	--橡皮擦	18	80		9	17	千克		--Erasers
	--垫片、垫圈及其他密封垫:								--Gaskets、washers and other seals:
4016.9310	---机器及仪器用	8	30		9	17	千克		---Of a kind used in machines or instruments
4016.9390	---其他	15	80		9	17	千克		---Other
4016.9400	--船舶或码头的碰垫，不论是否可充气	18	80		9	17	千克		--Boat or dock fenders, whether or not inflatable
4016.9500	--其他可充气制品	18	80		9	17	千克		--Other inflatable articles
4016 9500.01[暂]	硫化橡胶制液压隔离式蓄能器用胶囊	18	80	9	9	17	千克		Capsules for islated hydraulic accumulators, of vulcanized rubber
4016 9500.90	硫化橡胶制其他可充气制品	18	80		9	17	千克		Other inflatable articles of vulcanized rubber
	--其他:								--Other:
4016.9910	---机器及仪器用零件	8	30		9	17	千克		---Of a kind used in machines or instruments
4016 9910.01[暂]	奶衬(硬质橡胶除外)	8	30	4	9	17	千克		Milk lining (other than hard rubber)
4016 9910.90	硫化橡胶制机器及仪器用其他零件(硬质橡胶除外)	8	30		9	17	千克		Other parts, used in machinery and instruments of vulcanized rubber (other than hard rubber)
4016.9990	---其他	10	80		9	17	千克		---Other
4016 9990.01[暂]	动车组用胶囊，外风挡板(硬质橡胶除外)	10	80	5	9	17	千克		The capsule, of a kind used in EMU, outside air damper (other than hard rubber)
4016 9990.90	其他未列名硫化橡胶制品(硬质橡胶除外)	10	80		9	17	千克		Other articles of vulcanized rubber, not elsewhere specified or included (other than hard rubber)
40.17	**各种形状的硬质橡胶（例如，纯硬质胶），包括废碎料；硬质橡胶制品：**								**Hard rubber（for example, ebonite）in all forms, including waste and scrap; articles of hard rubber:**
4017.0010	---各种形状的硬质橡胶，包括废碎料	8	35		9	17	千克		---Hard rubber in all forms, including waste and scrap
4017 0010.10	各种形状的硬质橡胶废碎料	8	35		9	17	千克	9	Hard rubber waste and scrap in all forms
4017 0010.90	各种形状的硬质橡胶	8	35		9	17	千克		Hard rubber in all forms
4017.0020	---硬质橡胶制品	15	90		9	17	千克		---Articles of hard rubber

第八类
生皮、皮革、毛皮及其制品；鞍具及挽具；旅行用品、手提包及类似容器；动物肠线（蚕胶丝除外）制品

SECTION Ⅷ
RAW HIDES AND SKINS, LEATHER, FURSKINS AND ARTICLES THEREOF; SADDLERY AND HARNESS; TRAVEL GOODS, HANDBAGS AND SIMILAR CONTAINERS; ARTICLES OF ANIMAL GUT（OTHER THAN SILK-WORM GUT）

第四十一章
生皮（毛皮除外）及皮革

Chapter 41
Raw hides and skins（other than furskins）and leather

注释：

一、本章不包括：

（一）生皮的边角废料（品目 05.11）

（二）品目 05.05 或 67.01 的带羽毛或羽绒的整张或部分鸟皮；

（三）带毛生皮或已鞣的带毛皮张（第四十三章）；但下列动物的带毛生皮应归入第四十一章：牛（包括水牛）、马、绵羊及羔羊（不包括阿斯特拉罕、喀拉科尔、波斯羔羊或类似羔羊、印度、中国或蒙古羔羊）、山羊或小山羊（不包括也门、蒙古或西藏的山羊及小山羊）、猪（包括野猪）、小羚羊、瞪羚、骆驼（包括单峰骆驼）、驯鹿、麋、鹿、狍或狗。

二、（一）品目 41.04 至 41.06 不包括经退鞣（包括预鞣）加工的皮（酌情归入品目 41.01 至 41.03）；

（二）品目 41.04 至 41.06 所称“坯革”，包括在干燥前经复鞣、染色或加油（加脂）的皮。

三、本税则所称“再生皮革”，仅指品目 41.15 的皮革。

Chapter Notes:

1.This Chapter does not cover:

（a）Parings or similar waste, of raw hides or skins（heading 05.11）

（b）Birdskins or parts of birdskins, with their feathers or down,of heading 05.05 or 67.01; or

（c）Hides or skins, with the hair or wool on, raw, tanned or dressed（Chapter 43）; the following are, however, to be classified in Chapter 41, namely, raw hides and skins with the hair or wool on, of bovine animals（including buffalo）, of equine animals, of sheep or lambs（except Astrakhan, Broadtail, Caracul, Persian or similar lambs, Indian, Chinese, Mongolian or Tibetan lambs）, of goats or kids（except Yemen, Mongolian or Tibetan goats and kids）, of swine （including peccary）, of chamois, of gazelle, of camels （including dromedaries）of reindeer, of elk, of deer, of roebucks or of dogs.

2.（a）Headings 41.04 to 41.06 do not cover hides and skins which have undergone a tanning（including pre-tanning）process which is reversible（headings 41.01 to 41.03, as the case may be）;

（b）For the purposes of headings 41.04 to 41.06, the term “crust” includes hides and skins that have been retanned, coloured or fat-liquored（stuffed）prior to drying.

3.Throughout the Nomenclature the expression “composition leather” means only substances of the kind referred to in heading 41.15.

税则号列 Tariff Item	商品名称及备注	进口税率 最惠	进口税率 普通	进口税率 暂定	出口退税	增值税率	计量单位	监管条件	Article Description
41.01	生牛皮（包括水牛皮）、生马皮（鲜的、盐腌的、干的、石灰浸渍的、浸酸的或以其他方法保藏，但未鞣制、未经羊皮纸化处理或进一步加工的），不论是否去毛或剖层：								**Raw hides and skins of bovine（including buffalo）or equine animals（fresh, or salted, dried, limed, pickled or otherwise preserved, but not tanned, parchment-dressed or further prepared）, whether or not dehaired or split:**
	-未剖层的整张皮，简单干燥的每张重量不超过 8 千克，干盐腌的不超过 10 千克，鲜的、湿盐腌的或以其他方法保藏的不超过 16 千克：								-Whole hides and skins, unsplit , of a weight per skin not exceeding 8kg when simply dried, 10kg when dry-salted, or 16kg when fresh, wet-salted or otherwise preserved:
	---牛皮：								---Of bovine animals:
4101.2011	----经退鞣处理的	8	17			13	千克/张		----Have undergone a reversible tanning process
4101 2011.10	规定重量退鞣未剖层整张濒危生野牛皮（指每张简单干燥≤8 千克，干盐渍≤10千克，鲜或湿盐≤16 千克）	8	17			13	千克/张	ABFE	Whole raw hides and skins of endangered wild bovine, have undergone a reversible tanning process, of a weight per skin not exceeding 8kg when simply dried, 10kg when dry-salted, or 16kg when fresh, wet-salted

税则号列 Tariff Item	商品名称及备注	进口税率 最惠	进口税率 普通	进口税率 暂定	出口退税	增值税率	计量单位	监管条件	Article Description
4101 2011.90	规定重量未剖层退鞣处理整张生牛皮（包括水牛皮）(指每张,简单干燥≤8 千克,干盐渍≤10 千克,鲜或湿盐≤16 千克)	8	17			13	千克/张	AB	Whole raw hides and skins of bovine, have undergone a reversible tanning process, of a weight per skin not exceeding 8kg when simply dried, 10kg when dry-salted, or 16kg when fresh, wet-salted
4101.2019	----其他	5	17			13	千克/张		----Other
4101 2019.10	规定重量非退鞣未剖层整张濒危生野牛皮(指每张, 简单干燥≤8 千克,干盐渍≤10 千克,鲜或湿盐≤16 千克)	5	17			13	千克/张	ABFE	Whole raw hides and skins of endangered wild bovine, not have undergone a reversible tanning process, of a weight per skin not exceeding 8kg when simply dried, 10kg when dry-salted, or 16kg when fresh, wet-salted
4101 2019.90	规定重量非退鞣未剖层处理整张生牛皮（包括水牛皮）(指每张简单干燥的≤8 千克,干盐渍≤10 千克,鲜或湿盐≤16 千克)	5	17			13	千克/张	AB	Whole raw hides and skins of bovine, not have undergone a reversible tanning process, of a weight per skin not exceeding 8kg when simply dried, 10kg when dry-salted, or 16kg when fresh, wet-salted
4101.2020	---马皮	5	30			13	千克/张		---Of equine animals
4101 2020.10	规定重量未剖层整张濒危生野马皮(指每张, 简单干燥≤8 千克,干盐渍≤10 千克,鲜或湿盐≤16 千克)	5	30			13	千克/张	ABFE	Whole raw hides and skins of endangered wild equine animals, of a weight per skin not exceeding 8kg when simply dried, 10kg when dry-salted, or 16kg when fresh, wet-salted
4101 2020.90	规定重量未剖层整张生马皮(指每张, 简单干燥≤8 千克,干盐渍≤10 千克,鲜或湿盐≤16 千克)	5	30			13	千克/张	AB	Whole raw hides and skins of equine animals, of a weight per skin not exceeding 8kg when simply dried, 10kg when dry-salted, or 16kg when fresh, wet-salted
	-整张皮，重量超过 16 千克: ---牛皮:								-Whole hides and skins, of a weight exceeding 16kg: ---Of bovine animals:
4101.5011	----经退鞣处理的	8.4	17			13	千克/张		----Have undergone a reversible tanning process
4101 5011.10	重>16 千克退鞣整张濒危生野牛皮	8.4	17			13	千克/张	ABFE	Whole raw hides and skins of endangered wild bovine, have undergone a reversible tanning process, of a weight exceeding 16kg
4101 5011.90	重>16 千克退鞣处理整张生牛皮（包括水牛皮）	8.4	17			13	千克/张	AB	Whole raw hides and skins of bovine, have undergone a reversible tanning process, of a weight exceeding 16kg
4101.5019	----其他	5	17			13	千克/张		----Other
4101 5019.10	重>16 千克非退鞣整张濒危生野牛皮	5	17			13	千克/张	ABFE	Whole raw hides and skins of endangered wild bovine, not have undergone a reversible tanning process, of a weight exceeding 16kg
4101 5019.90	重>16 千克非退鞣处理整张生牛皮（包括水牛皮）	5	17			13	千克/张	AB	Whole raw hides and skins of bovine, not have undergone a reversible tanning process, of a weight exceeding 16kg
4101.5020	---马皮	5	30			13	千克/张		---Of equine animals
4101 5020.10	重>16 千克整张濒危生野马皮	5	30			13	千克/张	ABFE	Whole raw hides and skins of endangered equine animals, of a weight exceeding 16kg
4101 5020.90	重>16 千克整张生马皮	5	30			13	千克/张	AB	Whole raw hides and skins of equine animals, of a weight exceeding 16kg
	-其他，包括整张或半张的背皮及腹皮: ---牛皮:								-Other, including butts, bends and bollies: ---Of bovine animals:
4101.9011	----经退鞣处理的	8.4	17			13	千克		----Have undergone a reversible tanning process
4101 9011.10	其他退鞣处理濒危生野牛皮（包括整张或半张的背皮及腹皮）	8.4	17			13	千克	FEAB	Other whole raw hides and skins of endangered wild bovine, have undergone a reversible tanning process, (including butts, bends and bellies)
4101 9011.90	其他退鞣处理生牛皮（包括整张或半张的背皮及腹皮）	8.4	17			13	千克	AB	Other whole raw hides and skins of bovine, have undergone a reversible tanning process,(including butts, bends and bellies)
4101.9019	----其他	5	17			13	千克		----Other
4101 9019.10	其他濒危生野牛皮（包括整张或	5	17			13	千克	FEAB	Other whole raw hides and skins of endangered wild

税则号列 Tariff Item	商品名称及备注	进口税率 最惠	普通	暂定	出口退税	增值税率	计量单位	监管条件	Article Description
	半张的背皮及腹皮）								bovine (including butts, bends and bellies)
4101 9019.90	其他生牛皮（包括整张或半张的背皮及腹皮）	5	17			13	千克	AB	Other whole raw hides and skins of bovine including butts, bends and bellies
4101.9020	---马皮	5	30			13	千克		---Of equine animals
4101 9020.10	其他濒危生野马皮（包括整张或半张的背皮及腹皮）	5	30			13	千克	FEAB	Other whole raw hides and skins of endangered equine animals (including butts, bends and bellies)
4101 9020.90	其他生马皮（包括整张或半张的背皮及腹皮）	5	30			13	千克	AB	Other whole raw hides and skins of equine animals (including butts, bends and bellies)
41.02	**绵羊或羔羊生皮（鲜的、盐渍的、干的、石灰浸渍的、浸酸的或经其他方法保藏，但未鞣制、未经羊皮纸化处理或进一步加工的），不论是否带毛或剖层，但本章注释一（三）所述不包括的生皮除外：**								**Raw skins of sheep or lambs（fresh, or salted, dried, limed, pickled or otherwise preserved, but not tanned, parchmentdressed or further prepared）, whether or not with wool on or split, other than those excluded by Note 1（c）to this chapter:**
4102.1000	-带毛	7	30			13	千克/张	AB	-With wool on
	-不带毛:								-Without wool on:
	--浸酸的:								--Pickled:
4102.2110	---经退鞣处理的	14	30			13	千克/张	AB	---Have undergone a reversible tanning process
4102.2190	---其他	9	30			13	千克/张	AB	---Other
	--其他:								--Other:
4102.2910	---经退鞣处理的	14	30			13	千克/张	AB	---Have undergone a reversible tanning process
4102.2990	---其他	7	30			13	千克/张	AB	---Other
41.03	**其他生皮（鲜的、盐渍的、干的、石灰浸渍的、浸酸的或以其他方法保藏，但未鞣制、未经羊皮纸化处理或进一步加工的），不论是否去毛或剖层，但本章注释一（二）或（三）所述不包括的生皮除外：**								**Other raw hides and skins（fresh, or salted, dried, limed, pickled or otherwise preserved, but not tanned, parchment-dressed or further prepared）, whether or not dehaired or split, other than those excluded by Note 1（b）or 1（c）to this Chapter:**
4103.2000	-爬行动物皮	9	30			13	千克/张	FEAB	-Of reptiles
4103.3000	-猪皮	9	30			13	千克/张		-Of swine
4103 3000.10	生鹿豚、姬猪皮	9	30			13	千克/张	ABFE	Raw hides and skins of *Baby rousa*, *Porcula* salvania
4103 3000.90	生猪皮	9	30			13	千克/张	AB	Raw hides and skins of swine
	-其他:								-Other:
	---山羊板皮:								---Of goats:
4103.9011	----经退鞣处理的	14	35			13	千克/张	AB	----Have undergone a reversible tanning process
4103.9019	----其他	9	35			13	千克/张	AB	----Other
	---其他山羊或小山羊皮:								---Other, of goats or kids:
4103.9021	----经退鞣处理的	14	30			13	千克/张	AB	----Have undergone a reversible tanning process
4103.9029	----其他	9	30			13	千克/张	AB	----Other
4103.9090	---其他	9	30			13	千克/张		---Other
4103 9090.10	其他濒危野生动物生皮［本章注释一（二）或（三）所述不包括的生皮除外］	9	30			13	千克/张	ABEF	Other raw hides and skins of endangered wild animals, other than those excluded by Note 1（b）or 1（c）to this Chapter
4103 9090.90	其他生皮［本章注释一（二）或（三）所述不包括的生皮除外］	9	30			13	千克/张	AB	Other raw hides and skins of animals, other than those excluded by Note 1（b） 1（c）to this Chapter
41.04	**经鞣制的不带毛牛皮（包括水牛皮）、马皮及其坯革，不论是否剖层，但未经进一步加工：**								**Tanned or crust hides and skins of bovine（including buffalo）or equine animals, without hair on, whether or not split, but not further prepared:**
	-湿革（包括蓝湿皮）：								-In the wet state（including wet-blue）:
	--全粒面未剖层革；粒面剖层革：								--Full grains, unsplit; grain splits:
	---牛皮:								---Of bovine animals:
4104.1111 暂	----蓝湿的	7	17	3		17	千克		----Wet-blue
4104 1111.10 暂	蓝湿濒危野牛皮（全粒面未剖或粒面剖层，经鞣制不带毛）	7	17	3		17	千克	ABFE	Tanned or crust hides and skins of endangered wild bovine, wet-blue, without hair on (full grains, unsplit or grain splits)
4104 1111.90 暂	全粒面未剖层或粒面剖层蓝湿	7	17	3		17	千克	AB	Tanned or crust hides and skins of bovine, wet-blue,

税则号列 Tariff Item	商品名称及备注	进口税率			出口退税	增值税率	计量单位	监管条件	Article Description
		最惠	普通	暂定					
	牛皮（经鞣制不带毛）								without hair on (full grains, unsplit or grain splits)
4104.1119	----其他	8	35			17	千克		----Other
4104 1119.10	湿濒危野牛皮（全粒面未剖或粒面剖层，经鞣制不带毛）	8	35			17	千克	EF	Tanned or crust hides and skins of endangered wild bovine, in the wet state, without hair on, full grains, unsplit or grain splits
4104 1119.90	全粒面未剖层或粒面剖层湿牛皮（经鞣制不带毛）	8	35			17	千克		Tanned or crust hides and skins of bovine, in the wet state, without hair on, full grains, unsplit or grain splits
4104.1120	---马皮	5	35			17	千克		---Of equine animals
4104 1120.10	湿濒危野马皮（全粒面未剖或粒面剖层，经鞣制不带毛）	5	35			17	千克	EF	Tanned or crust hides and skins of endangered equine animals, in the wet state, without hair on, full grains, unsplit or grain splits
4104 1120.90	全粒面未剖层或粒面剖层湿马皮（经鞣制不带毛）	5	35			17	千克		Tanned or crust hides and skins of endangered equine animals, in the wet state, without hair on, full grains, unsplit or grain splits
	--其他:								--Other:
	---牛皮:								---Of bovine animals:
4104.1911 暂	----蓝湿的	6	17	3		17	千克		----Wet-blue
4104 1911.10 暂	其他蓝湿濒危野牛皮（经鞣制不带毛）	6	17	3		17	千克	ABFE	Other tanned or crust hides and skins of endangered wild bovine , wet-blue, without hair on
4104 1911.90 暂	其他蓝湿牛皮（经鞣制不带毛）	6	17	3		17	千克	AB	Other tanned or crust hides and skins of bovine, wet-blue, without hair on
4104.1919	----其他	7	35			17	千克		----Other
4104 1919.10	其他湿濒危野牛皮（经鞣制不带毛）	7	35			17	千克	EF	Other tanned or crust hides and skins of endangered wild bovine, without hair on, in the wet state
4104 1919.90	其他湿牛皮（经鞣制不带毛）	7	35			17	千克		Other tanned or crust hides and skins of bovine, without hair on, in the wet state
4104.1920 暂	---马皮	7	35	5		17	千克		---Of equine animals
4104 1920.10 暂	其他湿濒危野马皮（经鞣制不带毛）	7	35	5		17	千克	EF	Other tanned or crust hides and skins of endangered wild equine animals, wet, without hair on
4104 1920.90 暂	其他湿马皮（经鞣制不带毛）	7	35	5		17	千克		Other tanned or crust hides and skins of equine animals, without hair on, in the wet state
	-干革（坯革）:								-In the dry state（crust）:
4104.4100 暂	--全粒面未剖层革；粒面剖层革	5	35	3		17	千克		--Full grain, unsplit; grain splits
4104 4100.10 暂	濒危野牛马干革（全粒面未剖或粒面剖层，经鞣制不带毛）	5	35	3		17	千克	EF	Tanned or crust, dry hides and skins of endangered wild bovine or equine animals,without hair on, full grains, unsplit or grain splits
4104 4100.90 暂	全粒面未剖层或粒面剖层干革（经鞣制不带毛）	5	35	3		17	千克		Tanned or crust, dry hides and skins of animals, without hair on, full grains, unsplit or grain splits
	--其他:								---Other:
4104.4910	---机器带用牛、马皮革	5	20			17	千克		---For machinery belting
4104 4910.10	其他机器带用濒危野牛马皮革（经鞣制不带毛）	5	20			17	千克	FE	Other tanned or crust hides and skins of endangered wild bovine or equine animals,without hair on, for machinery belting
4104 4910.90	其他机器带用牛马皮革（经鞣制不带毛）	5	20			17	千克		Tanned or crust hides and skins of bovine, equine animals, without hair on, for machinery belting
4104.4990	---其他	7	35			17	千克		---Other
4104 4990.10	其他濒危野牛马皮革（经鞣制不带毛）	7	35			17	千克	EF	Other tanned or crust hides and skins of endanger -ed wild bovine or equine animals, without hair on
4104 4990.90	其他牛马皮革（经鞣制不带毛）	7	35			17	千克		Other tanned or crust hides and skins of bovine, equine animals, without hair on
41.05	**经鞣制的不带毛绵羊或羔羊皮及其坯革，不论是否剖层，但未经进一步加工：**								**Tanned or crust skins of sheep or lambs, without wool on, whether or not split, but not further prepared:**
	-湿革（包括蓝湿皮）:								-In the wet state（including wet-blue）:
4105.1010 暂	---蓝湿的	14	50	10		17	千克	AB	---Wet-blue
4105.1090	---其他	10	50			17	千克		---Other

税则号列 Tariff Item	商品名称及备注	进口税率			出口退税	增值税率	计量单位	监管条件	Article Description
		最惠	普通	暂定					
4105.3000	-干革（坯革）	8	50			17	千克		-In the dry state（crust）
41.06	**经鞣制的其他不带毛动物皮及其坯革，不论是否剖层，但未经进一步加工：**								**Tanned or crust hides and skins of other animals, without wool or hair on, whether or not split, but not further prepared:**
	-山羊或小山羊的：								--Of goats or kids:
4106.2100	--湿革（包括蓝湿皮）	14	50			17	千克		--In the wet state（including wet-blue）
4106 2100.01[暂]	蓝湿山羊皮（经鞣制不带毛）	14	50	10		17	千克		Tanned or crust, wet-blue hides and skins of goats, without wool or hair on
4106 2100.90	其他山羊或小山羊湿革（经鞣制不带毛）	14	50			17	千克		Other tanned or crust, wet hides and skins of goats or kids, without wool or hair on
4106.2200	--干革（坯革）	14	50			17	千克		--In the dry state（crust）
	-猪的：								-Of swine:
	--湿革（包括蓝湿皮）：								--In the wet state（including wet-blue）:
4106.3110[暂]	---蓝湿的	14	50	10		17	千克		---Wet-blue
4106 3110.10[暂]	蓝湿鹿豚、姬猪皮（经鞣制不带毛）	14	50	10		17	千克	FEAB	Tanned or crust, wet-blue hides and skins of *Babyrousa*, *Porcula* salvania , without hair on
4106 3110.90[暂]	其他蓝湿猪皮（经鞣制不带毛）	14	50	10		17	千克	AB	Other tanned or crust, wet-blue hides and skins of swine, without hair on
4106.3190	---其他	14	50			17	千克		---Other
4106 3190.10	鹿豚、姬猪湿革（经鞣制不带毛）	14	50			17	千克	EF	Tanned or crust, wet hides and skins of *Babyrousa*, *Porcula* salvania ,without hair on
4106 3190.90	其他猪湿革（经鞣制不带毛）	14	50			17	千克		Other tanned or crust, wet hides and skins of swine, without hair on
4106.3200	--干革（坯革）	14	50			17	千克		--In the dry state（crust）
4106 3200.10	鹿豚、姬猪干革（经鞣制不带毛，坯革）	14	50			17	千克	EF	Tanned, crust or dry hides and skins of *Babyrousa*, *Porcula* salvania , without hair on
4106 3200.90	其他猪干革（经鞣制不带毛，坯革）	14	50			17	千克		Other tannd or crust, dry hides and skins of swine, without hair on
4106.4000	-爬行动物的	14	50			17	千克	FE	-Of reptiles
	-其他：								-Other:
4106.9100	--湿革（包括蓝湿皮）：	14	50			17	千克		--In the wet state（including wet-blue）
4106 9100.10	其他濒危野生动物湿革（经鞣制不带毛）	14	50			17	千克	FE	Tanned or crust, wet hides and skins of other endangered wild animals, without wool or hair on
4106 9100.90	其他动物湿革（经鞣制不带毛）	14	50			17	千克		Tanned or crust, wet hides and skins of other animals, without wool or hair on
4106.9200	--干革（坯革）	14	50			17	千克		--In the dry state（crust）
4106 9200.10	濒危其他野生动物干革（经鞣制不带毛）	14	50			17	千克	FE	Tanned or crust, dry hides and skins of other endangered wild animals, without wool or hair on
4106 9200.90	其他动物干革（经鞣制不带毛）	14	50			17	千克		Tanned or crust, dry hides and skins of other animals, without wool or hair on
41.07	**经鞣制或半硝处理后进一步加工的牛皮革（包括水牛皮革）及马皮革，包括羊皮纸化处理的皮革，不论是否剖层，但品目41.14的皮革除外：**								**Leather further prepared after tanning or crusting, including parchment-dressed leather, of bovine（including buffalo） or equine animals, without hair on, whether or not split, other than leather of heading No.41.14:**
	-整张的：								-Whole hides and skins:
	--全粒面未剖层革：								--Full grains, unsplit:
4107.1110	---牛皮	8	50			17	千克/张		---Of bovine animals
4107 1110.10	全粒面未剖层整张濒危野牛皮（经鞣制或半硝后进一步加工，羊皮纸化处理）	8	50			17	千克/张	FE	Leather further prepared after tanning or crusting, including parchment-dressed leather, of endangered bovine, whole hides and skins, full grains, unsplit
4107 1110.90	全粒面未剖层整张牛皮（经鞣制或半硝后进一步加工，羊皮纸化处理）	8	50			17	千克/张		Leather further prepared after tanning or crusting, including parchment-dressed leather, of bovine, whole hides and skins, full grains, unsplit
4107.1120	---马皮	5	50			17	千克/张		---Of equine animals
4107 1120.10	全粒面未剖层整张濒危野马皮	5	50			17	千克/张	FE	Leather further prepared after tanning or crusting, including

税则号列 Tariff Item	商品名称及备注	进口税率 最惠	普通	暂定	出口退税	增值税率	计量单位	监管条件	Article Description
	（经鞣制或半硝后进一步加工，羊皮纸化处理）								parchment-dressed leather, of endangered wild equine animals, whole hides and skins, full grains, unsplit
4107 1120.90	全粒面未剖层整张马皮（经鞣制或半硝后进一步加工，羊皮纸化处理）	5	50			17	千克/张		Leather further prepared after tanning or crusting, including parchment-dressed leather, of equine animals, whole hides and skins, full grains, unsplit
	--粒面剖层革:								--Grain splits:
4107.1210[暂]	---牛皮	8	50	6		17	千克/张		---Of bovine animals
4107 1210.10[暂]	粒面剖层整张濒危野牛皮（经鞣制或半硝后进一步加工，羊皮纸化处理）	8	50	6		17	千克/张	FE	Leather further prepared after tanning or crusting, including parchment-dressed leather, of endangered wild bovine, whole hides and skins, grain splits
4107 1210.90[暂]	粒面剖层整张牛皮（经鞣制或半硝后进一步加工，羊皮纸化处理）	8	50	6		17	千克/张		Leather further prepared after tanning or crusting, including parchment-dressed leather, of bovine, whole hides and skins, grain splits
4107.1220	---马皮	5	50			17	千克/张		---Of equine animals
4107 1220.10	粒面剖层整张濒危野马皮（经鞣制或半硝后进一步加工，羊皮纸化处理）	5	50			17	千克/张	FE	Leather further prepared after tanning or crusting, including parchment-dressed leather, of endangered wild equine animals, whole hides and skins, grain splits
4107 1220.90	粒面剖层整张马皮（经鞣制或半硝后进一步加工，羊皮纸化处理）	5	50			17	千克/张		Leather further prepared after tanning orcrusting, including parchment-dressed leather, of equine animals, whole hides and skins, grain splits
	--其他:								--Other:
4107.1910	---机器带用	5	50			17	千克/张		---For machinery belting
4107 1910.10	其他机器带用整张濒危野牛马皮革（经鞣制或半硝后进一步加工，羊皮纸化处理）	5	50			17	千克/张	FE	Other leather further prepared after tanning or crusting, including parchment-dressed leather, of endangered wild bovine or equine animals, whole hides and skins, for machinery belting
4107 1910.90	其他机器带用整张牛马皮革（经鞣制或半硝后进一步加工，羊皮纸化处理）	5	50			17	千克/张		Other leather further prepared after tanning or crusting, including parchment-dressed leather, of bevine or equine animals, whole hides and skins, for machinery belting
4107.1990	---其他	7	50			17	千克/张		---Other
4107 1990.10	其他整张濒危野牛马皮革（经鞣制或半硝后进一步加工，羊皮纸化处理）	7	50			17	千克/张	EF	Other leather further prepared after tanning or crusting, including parchment-dressed leather of endangered wild bovine or equine animals, whole hides and skins
4107 1990.90	其他整张牛马皮革（经鞣制或半硝后进一步加工，羊皮纸化处理）	7	50			17	千克/张		Other leather further prepared after tanning or crusting, including parchment-dressed leather, of bovine or equine animals, whole hides and skins
	-其他，包括半张的:								-Other, including sides:
4107.9100	--全粒面未剖层革	5	50			17	千克		--Full grains, unsplit
4107 9100.10	全粒面未剖层非整张濒危野牛马皮（经鞣制或半硝后进一步加工，羊皮纸化处理）	5	50			17	千克	EF	Other leather further prepared after tanning or crusting, including parchment-dressed leather, of endangered wild bovine or equine animals, not whole hides and skins, full grains, unsplit
4107 9100.90	全粒面未剖层非整张革（经鞣制或半硝后进一步加工，羊皮纸化处理）	5	50			17	千克		Leather further prepared after tanning or crusting, including parchment-dressed leather, not whole hides and skins, full grains, unsplit
4107.9200	--粒面剖层革	5	50			17	千克		--Grain splits
4107 9200.10	粒面剖层非整张濒危野牛马皮革（经鞣制或半硝后进一步加工，羊皮纸化处理）	5	50			17	千克	FE	Leather further prepared after tanning or crusting, including parchment-dressed leather, of engangered wild bovine or equine animals, not whole hides and skins, grain splits
4107 9200.90	粒面剖层非整张革（经鞣制或半硝后进一步加工，羊皮纸化处理）	5	50			17	千克		Leather further prepared after tanning or crusting, including parchment-dressed leather, not whole hides and skins, grain splits
	--其他:								--Other:

税则号列 Tariff Item	商品名称及备注	进口税率 最惠	进口税率 普通	进口税率 暂定	出口退税	增值税率	计量单位	监管条件	Article Description
4107.9910	---机器带用	5	50			17	千克		---For machinery belting
4107 9910.10	其他机器带用非整张濒危野牛马皮（经鞣制或半硝后进一步加工，羊皮纸化处理）	5	50			17	千克	FE	Other leather further prepared after tanning or crusting, including parchment-dressed leather of endangered bovine or equine animals, not whole hides and skins, for machinery belting
4107 9910.90	其他机器带用非整张牛马皮革（经鞣制或半硝后进一步加工，羊皮纸化处理）	5	50			17	千克		Other leather further prepared after tanning or crusting, including parchment-dressed leather, of bovine or equine animals, not whole hides and skins, for machinery belting
4107.9990	---其他	7	50			17	千克		---Other
4107 9990.10	其他非整张濒危野牛马皮革（经鞣制或半硝后进一步加工，羊皮纸化处理）	7	50			17	千克	EF	Other leather further prepared after tanning or crusting, including parehment-dressed leather, of endangered wild bovine or equine animals, not whole hides and skins
4107 9990.90	其他非整张牛马皮革（经鞣制或半硝后进一步加工，羊皮纸化处理）	7	50			17	千克		Other leather further prepared after tanning or crusting, including parchment-dressed leather, of bovine or equine animals, not whole hides and skins
41.12	**经鞣制或半硝处理后进一步加工的不带毛的绵羊或羔羊皮革，包括羊皮纸化处理的，不论是否剖层，但品目41.14的皮革除外：**								**Leather further prepared after tanning or crusting, including parchment-dressed leather, of sheep or lamb, without wool on, whether or not split, other than leather of heading No. 41.14:**
4112.0000	经鞣制或半硝处理后进一步加工的不带毛的绵羊或羔羊皮革，包括羊皮纸化处理的，不论是否剖层，但品目41.14的皮革除外：	8	50			17	千克		Leather further prepared after tanning or crusting, including parchment-dressed leather, of sheep or lamb, without wool on, whether or not split, other than leather of heading 41.14:
41.13	**经鞣制或半硝处理后进一步加工的不带毛的其他动物皮革，包括羊皮纸化处理的，不论是否剖层，但品目41.14的皮革除外：**								**Leather further prepared after tanning or crusting, including parchment-dressed leather, of other animals, without wool or hair on, whether or not split, other than leather of heading No. 41.14:**
4113.1000	-山羊或小山羊皮的	14	50			17	千克		-Of goats or kids
4113.2000	-猪皮的	14	50			17	千克		-Of swine
4113 2000.10	加工的鹿豚、姬猪皮革（经鞣制或半硝后进一步加工，不带毛，羊皮纸化处理）	14	50			17	千克	EF	Leather further prepared after tanning or crusting, including parchment-dressed leather, of *Babyrousa*, *Porcula* salvania , without wool or hair on
4113 2000.90	加工的猪皮革（经鞣制或半硝后进一步加工，不带毛，羊皮纸化处理）	14	50			17	千克		Leather further prepared after tanning or crusting, including parchment-dressed leather, of swine, without wool or hair on
4113.3000	-爬行动物皮的	14	50			17	千克	FE	-Of reptiles
4113.9000	-其他	14	50			17	千克		-Other
4113 9000.10	加工的其他濒危野生动物皮革（经鞣制或半硝后进一步加工，不带毛，羊皮纸化处理）	14	50			17	千克	FE	Leather further prepared after tanning or crusting, including parchment-dressed leather, of other endangered wild animals, without wool or hair on
4113 9000.90	加工的其他动物皮革（经鞣制或半硝后进一步加工，不带毛，羊皮纸化处理）	14	50			17	千克		Leather further prepared after tanning or crusting, including parchment-dressed leather, of other animals, without hair on
41.14	**油鞣皮革(包括结合鞣制的油鞣皮革)；漆皮及层压漆皮；镀金属皮革：**								**Chamois（including combination chamois）leather; patent leather and patent laminated leather; metallised leather:**
4114.1000	-油鞣皮革（包括结合鞣制的油鞣皮革）	14	50			17	千克		-Chamois（including combination chamois）leather
4114 1000.10	油鞣其他濒危野生动物皮革(包括结合鞣制的油鞣皮革)	14	50			17	千克	FE	Chamois（including combination chamois）leather of other endangered wild animals
4114 1000.90	油鞣其他动物皮革(包括结合鞣制的油鞣皮革；野生动物皮革除外)	14	50			17	千克		Chamois （including combination chamois）leather of other animals, other than leather of wild animals
4114.2000	-漆皮及层压漆皮；镀金属皮革	10	50			17	千克		-Patent leather and patent laminated leather; metallised leather
41.15	**以皮革或皮革纤维为基本成分**								**Composition leather with a basis of leather or**

税则号列 Tariff Item	商品名称及备注	进口税率 最惠	普通	暂定	出口退税	增值税率	计量单位	监管条件	Article Description
	的再生皮革，成块、成张或成条的，不论是否成卷；皮革或再生皮革的边角废料，不适宜做皮革制品用；皮革粉末：								leather fibre, in slabs, sheets or strip, whether or not in rolls; parings and other waste of leather or of composition leather, not suitable for the manufacture of leather articles; leather dust, powder and flour:
4115.1000	-以皮革或皮革纤维为基本成分的再生皮革，成块、成张或成条，不论是否成卷	14	50			17	千克		-Composition leather with a basis of leather or leather fibre, in slabs, sheets or strip, whether or not in rolls
4115.2000	-皮革或再生皮革的边角废料，不适宜作皮革制品用；皮革粉末	14	50			17	千克		-Parings and other waste of leather or of composition leather, not suitable for the manufacture of leather articles; leather dust, powder and flour
4115 2000.10	皮革废渣、灰渣、淤渣及粉末	14	50			17	千克	9	Waste residue, dust, powder and flour of leather
4115 2000.90	皮革或再生皮革边角料	14	50			17	千克	AP	Parings and other waste of leather or of composition leather

第四十二章
皮革制品；鞍具及挽具；旅行用品、手提包及类似容器；动物肠线（蚕胶丝除外）制品

注释：

一、本章所称的‘皮革’包括油鞣皮革（含结合鞣制的油鞣皮革）、漆皮、层压漆皮和镀金属皮革。

二、本章不包括：

（一）外科用无菌肠线或类似的无菌缝合材料（品目 30.06）；

（二）以毛皮或人造毛皮衬里或作面（仅饰边的除外）的衣服及衣着附件（分指手套、连指手套及露指手套除外）（品目 43.03 或 43.04）；

（三）网线袋及类似品（品目 56.08）；

（四）第六十四章的物品；

（五）第六十五章的帽类及其零件；

（六）品目 66.02 的鞭子、马鞭或其他物品；

（七）袖扣、手镯或其他仿首饰（品目 71.17）；

（八）单独报验的挽具附件或装饰物，例如，马镫、马嚼子、马铃铛及类似品、带扣（一般归入第十五类）；

（九）弦线、鼓面皮或类似品及其他乐器零件（品目 92.09）；

（十）第九十四章的物品（例如，家具、灯具及照明装置）；

（十一）第九十五章的物品（例如，玩具、游戏品及运动用品）；或

（十二）品目 96.06 的钮扣、揿扣、钮扣芯或这些物品的其他零件、钮扣坯。

三、（一）除上述注释二所规定的以外，品目 42.02 也不包括：

1. 非供长期使用的带把手塑料薄膜袋，不论是否印制（品目 39.23）；

2. 编结材料制品（品目 46.02）。

（二）品目 42.02 及 42.03 的制品，如果装有用贵金属、包贵金属、天然或养殖珍珠、宝石或半宝石（天然、合成或再造）制的零件，即使这些零件不是仅作为小配件或小饰物的，只要其未构成物品的基本特征，仍应归入上述税号。但如果这些零件已构成物品的基本特征，则应归入第七十一章。

四、品目 42.03 所称“衣服及衣着附件”，主要适用于分指手套、连指手套及露指手套（包括运动手套及防护手套）、围裙及其他防护用衣着、裤吊带、腰带、子弹带及腕带，但不包括表带（品目 91.13）。

Chapter 42
Articles of leather; saddlery and harness; travel goods, handbags and similar containers; articles of animal gut（other than silk-worm gut）

Chapter Notes:

1. For the purposes of this Chapter, the term "leather" includes chamois (including combination chamois) leather, patent leather, patent laminated leather and metallised leather.

2. This Chapter does not cover:

（a）Sterile surgical catgut or similar sterile suture materials（heading 30.06）;

（b）Articles of apparel or clothing accessories（except gloves, mittens and mitts）, lined with furskin or artificial fur or to which furskin or artificial fur is attached on the outside except as mere trimming（heading 43.03 or 43.04）;

（c）Made up articles of netting（heading 56.08）;

（d）Articles of Chapter 64;

（e）Headgear or parts thereof of Chapter 65;

（f）Whips, riding-crops or other articles of heading 66.02;

（g）Cuff-links, bracelets or other imitation jewellery（heading 71.17）;

（h）Fittings or trimmings for harness, such as stirrups, bits, horse brasses and buckles, separately presented（generally Section XV）;

（ij）Strings, skins for drums or the like, or other parts of musical instruments（heading 92.09）;

（k）Articles of Chapter 94（for example, furniture, lamps and lighting fittings）;

（l）Articles of Chapter 95（for example, toys, games, sports requisites）;or

（m）Buttons, press-fasteners, snap-fasteners, press-studs, button moulds or other parts of these articles, button blanks, of heading 96.06.

3. （a）In addition to the provisions of Note 2 above, heading 42.02 does not cover:

（ i ）Bags made of sheeting of plastics, whether or not printed, with handles, not designed for prolonged use （heading 39.23）;

（ii）Articles of plaiting materials（heading 46.02）.

（b）Articles of headings 42.02 and 42.03 which have parts of precious metal or metal clad with precious metal, of natural or cultured pearls, of precious or semi-precious stones（natural, synthetic or reconstructed）remain classified in those headings even if such parts constitute more than minor fittings or minor ornamentation, provided that these parts do not give the articles their essential character. If, on the other hand, the parts give the articles their essential character, the articles are to be classified in Chapter 71.

4. For the purpose of heading 42.03, the expression "articles of apparel and clothing accessories" applies, *inter alia*, to gloves, mittens and mitts（including those for sport or for protection）, aprons and other protective clothing, braces, belts, bandoliers and wrist straps, but excluding watch straps（heading 91.13）.

税则号列 Tariff Item	商品名称及备注	进口税率			出口退税	增值税率	计量单位	监管条件	Article Description
		最惠	普通	暂定					
42.01	**各种材料制成的鞍具及挽具（包括缰绳、挽绳、护膝垫、口套、鞍褥、马褡裢、狗外套及类似品），适合各种动物用:**								**Saddlery and harness for any animal（including traces, leads, knee pads, muzzles, saddle cloths, saddle bags, dog coats and the like）, of any material:**
4201.0000	各种材料制成的鞍具及挽具(包括缰绳、挽绳、护膝垫、口套、鞍褥、马褡裢、狗外套及类似品），适合各种动物用	20	100			17	千克		Saddlery and harness for any animal（including traces, leads, knee pads, muzzles, saddle cloths, saddle bags, dog coats and the like）, of any material
4201 0000.10	濒危野生动物材料制的鞍具及挽具（适合各种动物用）	20	100			17	千克	FE	Saddlery and harness for any animal, of material of endangered wild animals
4201 0000.90	各种材料制成的鞍具及挽具（野生动物材料制的除外，适合各种动物用）	20	100		13	17	千克		Saddlery and harness for any animal, of any material (other than the material of wild animals)
42.02	**衣箱、提箱、小手袋、公文箱、公文包、书包、眼镜盒、望远镜盒、照相机套、乐器盒、枪套及类似容器；旅行包、食品或饮料保温包、化妆包、帆布包、手提包、购物袋、钱夹、钱包、地图盒、烟盒、烟袋、工具包、运动包、瓶盒、首饰盒、粉盒、刀叉餐具盒及类似容器，用皮革或再生皮革、塑料片、纺织材料、钢纸或纸板制成，或者全部或主要用上述材料或纸包覆制成**								**Trunks, suit-cases, vanity-cases, executivecases, brief-cases, school satchels, spectacle cases, birocular cases, camera cases, musical instrument cases, gun cases, holsters and similar containers; traveling-bags, insulated food or beverages bags, toilet bags, rucksacks, handbags, shopping-bags, wallets, purses, map-cases, cigarett-cases, tobacco- pouches, tool bags, sports bags, bottle-cases, jewellery boxes, powder-boxes, cutlery cases and similar containers, of leather or of composition leather, of sheeting of plastics, of textile materials, of vulcanized fibre or of paperboard, or wholly or mainly covered with such materials or with paper:**
	-衣箱、提箱、小手袋、公文箱、公文包、书包及类似容器:								-Trunks, suit-cases, vanity-cases, executivecases, briefcases, school satchels and similar containers:
	--以皮革、再生皮革作面:								--With outer surface of leather leather:
4202.1110	---衣箱	15	100			17	千克/个		---Trunks or of composition
4202 1110.10	以含濒危野生动物皮革或再生皮革作面的衣箱	15	100			17	千克/个	FE	Trunks with outer surface of leather, of composition leather or patent leather, of endangered wild animals
4202 1110.90	其他以皮革或再生皮革作面的衣箱	15	100		15	17	千克/个		Trunks with outer surface of leather, of composition leather or patent leather
4202.1190	---其他	10	100			17	千克/个		---Other
4202 1190.10	以濒危野生动物皮革或再生皮革作面的箱包(包括提箱、小手袋、公文包、书包及类似容器，但不包括衣箱)	10	100			17	千克/个	FE	Cases(trunks, suit-cases, vanity-cases, executivecases, briefcases, school satchels and similar containers) with outer surface of leather, of composition leather or patent leather, of endangered wild animals
4202 1190.90	其他以皮革或再生皮革作面的箱包(包括提箱、小手袋、公文包、书包及类似容器，但不包括衣箱)	10	100		15	17	千克/个		Cases (trunks, suit-cases, vanity-cases, executive-cases, briefcases, school satchels and similar containers) with outer surface of leather,of composition leather or patent leather
	--以塑料或纺织材料作面:								--With outer surface of plastics or of textile materials:
4202.1210	---衣箱	20	100		15	17	千克/个		---Trunks
4202.1290	---其他	20	100		15	17	千克/个		---Other
4202.1900	--其他	20	100		15	17	千克/个		--Other
	-手提包，不论是否有背带，包括无把手的:								-Handbags, whether or not with shoulder strap, including those without handle:
4202.2100	--以皮革或再生皮革作面	10	100			17	千克/个		--With outer surface of leather or of composition leather
4202 2100.10	以濒危野生动物皮革或再生皮革作面的手提包(不论是否有背带，包括无把手的)	10	100			17	千克/个	FE	Handbags,with outer surface of leather or of composition leather of endangered animals, whether or not with shoulder strap, including those without handle

税则号列 Tariff Item	商品名称及备注	进口税率 最惠	普通	暂定	出口退税	增值税率	计量单位	监管条件	Article Description
4202 2100.90	其他以皮革或再生皮革作面的手提包(不论是否有背带,包括无把手的)	10	100		15	17	千克/个		Handbags,with outer surface of leather or of composition leather, whether or not with shoulder strap, including those without handle
4202.2200	--以塑料片或纺织材料作面	10	100		15	17	千克/个		--With outer surface of plastic sheeting or of textile materials
4202.2900	--其他	20	100		15	17	千克/个		--Other
	-通常置于口袋或手提包内的物品:								-Articles of a kind normally carried in the pocket or in the handbag:
4202.3100	--以皮革或再生皮革作面	10	100			17	千克/个		--With outer surface of leather or of composition leather
4202 3100.10	以濒危野生动物皮革或再生皮革作面的钱包等物品(指通常置于口袋或手提包内的物品)	10	100			17	千克/个	FE	Pocket with outer surface of leather or of composition leather of endangered animals,, whether or not with shoulder strap, including those without handle
4202 3100.90	以皮革或再生皮革作面钱包等物品(指通常置于口袋或手提包内的物品)	10	100		15	17	千克/个		Pocket with outer surface of leather or of composition leather of endangered animals,, whether or not with shoulder strap, including those without handle
4202.3200	--以塑料片或纺织材料作面	20	100		15	17	千克/个		--With outer surface of plastic sheeting or of textile materials
4202.3900	--其他	20	100		15	17	千克/个		--Other
	-其他:								-Other:
4202.9100	--以皮革或再生皮革作面	10	100			17	千克/个		--With outer surface of leather or of composition leather
4202 9100.10	濒危野生动物皮革或再生皮革作面的其他容器	10	100			17	千克/个	FE	Containers with outer surface of leather or of composition leather of endangered animals
4202 9100.90	其他皮革或再生皮革作面其他容器	10	100		15	17	千克/个		Containers with outer surface of leather or of composition leather
4202.9200	--以塑料片或纺织材料作面	10	100		15	17	千克/个		--With outer surface of plastic sheeting or of textile materials
4202.9900	--其他	20	100		15	17	千克/个		--Other
42.03	皮革或再生皮革制的衣服及衣着附件:								**Articles of apparel and clothing accessories, of leather or of composition leather:**
4203.1000	-衣服	10	100			17	千克/件		-Articles of apparel
4203 1000.10	濒危野生动物皮革制的衣服(包括再生野生动物皮革制作的)	10	100			17	千克/件	EF	Articles of apparel of leather or of composition leather, of endangered wild animals
4203 1000.90	皮革或再生皮革制的衣服(野生动物皮革制作的除外)	10	100		13	17	千克/件		Articles of apparel of leather or of composition leather （other than of leather of wild animals）
	-手套,包括连指或露指的:								-Gloves, mittens and mitts:
4203.2100	--专供运动用	20	100			17	千克/双		--Specially designed for use in sports
4203 2100.10	濒危野生动物皮革制的运动手套(包括再生野生动物皮革制作的)	20	100			17	千克/双	FE	Gloves, specially designed for use in sports, of leather or of composition leather, of endangered wild animals
4203 2100.90	皮革或再生皮革制专供运动用手套(包括连指或露指的,野生动物皮革制作的除外)	20	100		13	17	千克/双		Gloves, mittens and mitts, specially designed for use in sports, of leather or of composition leather（other than of leather of wild animals）
	--其他:								--Other:
4203.2910	---劳保手套	20	100			17	千克/双		---Working gloves
4203 2910.10	濒危野生动物皮革制的劳保手套(包括再生野生动物皮革制作的)	20	100			17	千克/双	FE	Working gloves, of leather or of composition leather, of endangered wild animals
4203 2910.90	皮革或再生皮革制的劳保手套(野生动物皮革制作的除外)	20	100		13	17	千克/双		Working gloves, of leather or of composition leather （other than of leather of wild animals）
4203.2990	---其他	20	100			17	千克/双		---Other
4203 2990.10	濒危野生动物皮革制的其他手套(包括再生野生动物皮革制作的)	20	100			17	千克/双	FE	Other gloves, of leather or of composition leather of endangered wild animals
4203 2990.90	皮革或再生皮革制的其他手套(包括连指或露指的)	20	100		13	17	千克/双		Gloves, mittens and mitts, of leather or of composition leather

税则号列 Tariff Item	商品名称及备注	进口税率 最惠	普通	暂定	出口退税	增值税率	计量单位	监管条件	Article Description
	-腰带及子弹带:								-Belts and bandoliers:
4203.3010	---腰带	10	100			17	千克		---Belts
4203 3010.10	濒危野生动物皮革制的腰带(包括再生野生动物皮革制作的)	10	100			17	千克	FE	Belts, of leather or of composition leather, of endangered wild animals
4203 3010.90	其他动物皮革制的腰带(包括再生动物皮革制作的)	10	100		13	17	千克		Belts, of leather or of composition leather ,of other animals
4203.3020	---子弹带	10	100			17	千克		---Bandoliers
4203 3020.10	濒危野生动物皮革制的子弹带(包括再生野生动物皮革制作的)	10	100			17	千克	FE	Bandoliers, of leather or of composition leather, of endangered wild animals
4203 3020.90	其他动物皮革制的子弹带(包括再生动物皮革制作的)	10	100		13	17	千克		Bandoliers, of leather or of composition leather, of other animals
4203.4000	-其他衣着附件	20	100			17	千克		-Other clothing accessories
4203 4000.10	濒危野生动物皮革制的衣着附件(包括再生野生动物皮革制作的)	20	100			17	千克	FE	Clothing accessories, of leather or of composition leather, of endangered wild animals
4203 4000.90	皮革或再生皮革制的其他衣着附件	20	100		13	17	千克		Other clothing accessories, of leather or of composition leather
42.05	**皮革或再生皮革的其他制品:**								**Other articles of leather or of composition leather:**
	-皮革或再生皮革的其他制品:								-Other articles of leather or of composition leather:
4205.0010	---坐具套	12	100			17	千克		---Cover of seat
4205 0010.10	濒危野生动物皮革制的坐具套(包括再生野生动物皮革制作的)	12	100			17	千克	FE	Cover of seats, of leather or of composition leather, of endangered wild animals
4205 0010.90	其他动物皮革制的坐具套(包括再生皮革制作的)	12	100		13	17	千克		Cover of seats, of leather or of composition leather, of other animals
4205.0020	---机器、机械器具或其他专门技术用途的	8	35			17	千克		---Of a kind used in machinery or mechanical appliances or for other technical uses
4205 0020.10	濒危野生动物皮革制工业用皮革或再生皮革制品(工业用指机器、机械器具或其他专门技术用途的)	8	35			17	千克	FE	Articles of leather or of composition leather of endangered wild animals, of a kind used in machinery or mechanial appilances or for other technical uses
4205 0020.90	其他工业用皮革或再生皮革制品(工业用指机器、机械器具或其他专门技术用途的)	8	35		13	17	千克		Other articles of leather or of composition leather, of a kind used in machinery or mechanial appilances or for other technical uses
4205.0090	---其他	12	100			17	千克		---Other
4205 0090.10	濒危野生动物皮革的其他制品(包括再生野生动物皮革制作的)	12	100			17	千克	FE	Other articles, of leather or of composition leather, of endangered wild animals
4205 0090.20	皮革或再生皮革制宠物用品	12	100		13	17	千克	AB	Articles for pets, of leather or of composition leather
4205 0090.90	皮革或再生皮革的其他制品	12	100		13	17	千克		Other articles, of leather or of composition leather
42.06	**肠线(蚕胶丝除外)、肠膜、膀胱或筋腱制品:**								**Articles of gut(other than silkwormgut), of goldbeater's skin, of bladders or of tendons:**
4206.0000	肠线(蚕胶丝除外)、肠膜、膀胱或筋腱制品(不包括外科用无菌肠线或制成乐器弦的肠线)	20	90		5	17	千克		Articles of gut(other than silkwormgut), of goldbeater's skin, of bladders or of tendons(other than sterile catgut for surgical use or catgut of musical chord)

第四十三章
毛皮、人造毛皮及其制品

注释：

一、本税则所称“毛皮”，是指已鞣的各种动物的带毛毛皮，但不包括品目 43.01 的生毛皮。

二、本章不包括：

（一）带羽毛或羽绒的整张或部分鸟皮（品目 05.05 或 67.01）；

（二）第四十一章的带毛生皮[参见该章注释一（三）]；

（三）用皮革与毛皮或用皮革与人造毛皮制成的分指手套、连指手套及露指手套（品目 42.03）；

（四）第六十四章的物品；

（五）第六十五章的帽件及其零件；或

（六）第九十五章的物品（例如，玩具、游戏品及运动用品）。

三、品目 43.03 包括加有其他材料缝合的毛皮和毛皮部分品，以及缝合成衣服、衣服部分品、衣着附件或其他制品的毛皮和毛皮部分品。

四、以毛皮或人造毛皮衬里或作面（仅饰边的除外）的衣服及衣着附件（不包括注释二所述的货品），应分别归入品目 43.03 或 43.04，但毛皮或人造毛皮仅作为装饰的除外。

五、本税则所称“人造毛皮”，是指以毛 、发或其他纤维粘附或缝合于皮革、织物或其他材料之上而构成的仿毛皮，但不包括以机织或针织方法制得的仿毛皮（一般应归入品目 58.01 或 60.01）。

Chapter 43
Furskins and artificial fur; manufactures thereof

Chapter Notes:

1. Throughout the Nomenclature references to “furskins” , other than to raw furskins of heading 43.01, apply to hides or skins of all animals which have been tanned or dressed with the hair or wool on.

2. This Chapter does not cover:

(a)Birdskins or parts of birdskins, with their feathers or down（heading 05.05 or 67.01）;

(b) Raw hides or skins, with the hair or wool on, of Chapter 41（see Note 1（c）to that Chapter）;

(c) Gloves, mittens and mitts consisting of leather and furskin or of leather and artificial fur（heading 42.03）;

(d) Articles of Chapter 64;

(e) Headgear or parts thereof of Chapter 65; or

(f)Articles of Chapter 95（for example, toys, games, sports requisites).

3. Heading 43.03 includes furskins and parts thereof, assembled with the addition of other materials, and furskins and parts thereof, sewn together in the form of garments or parts or accessories of garments or in the form of other articles.

4. Articles of apparel and clothing accessories（except those excluded by Note 2）lined with furskin or artificial fur or to which furskin or artificial fur is attached on the outside except as mere trimming are to be classified in heading 43.03 or 43.04 as the case may be.

5. Throughout the Nomenclature the expression “artificial fur” means any imitation of furskin consisting of wool, hair or other fibres gummed or sewn on to leather, woven fabric or other materials, but does not include imitation furskins obtained by weaving or knitting （generally, heading 58.01 or 60.01）.

税则号列 Tariff Item	商品名称及备注	进口税率			出口退税	增值税率	计量单位	监管条件	Article Description
		最惠	普通	暂定					
43.01	**生毛皮（包括适合加工皮货用的头、尾、爪及其他块、片），但品目 41.01、41.02 或 41.03 的生皮除外：**								**Raw furskins（including heads, tails, paws and other pieces or cuttings, suitable for furriers' use）, other than raw hides and skins of heading No. 41.01, 41.02 or 41.03:**
4301.1000[暂]	-整张水貂皮，不论是否带头、尾或爪	15	100	10		13	千克	AB	-Of mink, whole, with or without head, tail or paws
4301.3000	-下列羔羊的整张毛皮，不论是否带头、尾或爪：阿斯特拉罕、喀拉科尔、波斯羔羊及类似羔羊、印度、中国或蒙古羔羊	20	90			13	千克	AB	-Of lamb, the following: Astrakhan, Broadtail, Caracul, Persian and similar lamb, Indian, Chinese, Mongolian or Tibetan lamb, whole, with or without head, tail or paws
4301.6000[暂]	-整张狐皮，不论是否带头、尾或爪	20	100	15		13	千克/张		-Of fox, whole, with or without head, tail or paws
4301 6000.10[暂]	整张濒危生狐皮（不论是否带头,尾或爪）	20	100	15		13	千克/张	AFEB	Raw furskins of endangered fox, whole (with or without head, tail or paws)
4301 6000.90[暂]	其他整张生狐皮（不论是否带头,尾或爪）	20	100	15		13	千克/张	AB	Other raw furskins of fox, whole (with or without head, tail or paws)
	-整张的其他毛皮，不论是否带头、尾或爪：								-Other furskins , whole , with or without head , tail or paws:
4301.8010	---整张兔皮，不论是否带头、尾或爪	20	90			13	千克/张		---Of rabbit or hare,whole,with or without head, tail or paws

税则号列 Tariff Item	商品名称及备注	进口税率 最惠	进口税率 普通	进口税率 暂定	出口退税	增值税率	计量单位	监管条件	Article Description
4301 8010.10	整张生濒危野兔皮（不论是否带头，尾或爪）	20	90			13	千克/张	AFEB	Raw furskins of endangered rabbit or hare, whole (with or without head, tail or paws)
4301 8010.90	整张生兔皮（不论是否带头，尾或爪）	20	90			13	千克/张	AB	Raw furskins of rabbit or hare, whole (with or without head, tail or paws)
4301.8090	---其他	20	90			13	千克/张		---Other
4301 8090.10	整张的其他生濒危野生动物毛皮（不论是否带头，尾或爪，包括整张濒危生海豹皮）	20	90			13	千克/张	ABEF	Raw furskins of other endangered wild animals, whole (with or without head, tail or paws, including endangered raw sealskin）
4301 8090.90	整张的其他生毛皮（不论是否带头，尾或爪，包括整张生海豹皮）	20	90			13	千克/张	AB	Raw furskins of other animals, whole (with or without head, tail or paws,including raw sealskin）
	-适合加工皮货用的头、尾、爪及其他块、片:								-Heads, tails, paws and other pieces or cuttings, suitable for furriers' use:
4301.9010	---黄鼠狼尾	20	50			13	千克	ABEF	---Weasel tails
4301.9090	---其他	20	90			13	千克		---Other
4301 9090.10	其他濒危野生动物未鞣头尾（加工皮货用，包括爪及其他块、片）	20	90			13	千克	ABFE	Heads or tails（including paws and other pieces or cuttings） of endangered wild animals, not tanned nor dressed, suitable for furriers' use
4301 9090.90	适合加工皮货用的其他未鞣头、尾（包括爪及其他块、片）	20	90			13	千克	AB	Other heads or tails（including paws and other pieces or cuttings） of animals, not tanned nor dressed, suitable for furriers' use
43.02	**未缝制或已缝制（不加其他材料）的已鞣毛皮（包括头、尾、爪及其他块、片），但品目43.03的货品除外：**								**Tanned or dressed furskins（including heads, tails, paws and other pieces or cuttings）, unassembled, or assembled（without the addition of other materials） other than those of heading No. 43.03:**
	-未缝制的整张毛皮，不论是否带头、尾或爪:								-Whole skins, with or without head, tail or paws, not assembled:
4302.1100	--水貂皮	12	130		5	17	千克/张		--Of mink
	--其他:								--Other:
4302.1910	---灰鼠皮、白鼬皮、其他貂皮、狐皮、水獭皮、旱獭皮及猞猁皮	10	130			17	千克/张		---Of grey squirrel, ermine, other marten, fox, otter, marmot and lynx
4302 1910.10	已鞣未缝制的濒危狐皮（兰狐皮，银狐皮除外）	10	130			17	千克/张	EF	Furskins of endangered fox, tanned or dressed, unassembled （other than furskins of blue fox or silver fox）
4302 1910.20	已鞣未缝制的兰狐皮、银狐皮	10	130		5	17	千克/张		Furskins of blue fox or silver fox, tanned or dressed, unassembled
4302 1910.90	已鞣未缝制的其他贵重濒危动物毛皮（灰鼠皮，白鼬皮，其他貂皮，水獭皮，旱獭皮，猞猁皮）	10	130			17	千克/张	EF	Precious furskins of endangered animals(grey squirrel, ermine, other marten, fox, otter, marmot and lynx), tanned or dressed, assembled
4302.1920	---兔皮	10	100			17	千克/张		---Of rabbit or hare
4302 1920.10	已鞣未缝制的整张濒危野兔皮（不论是否带头，尾或爪）	10	100			17	千克/张	FE	Furskins of endangered rabbit and hare, whole, tanned or dressed, unassembled, with or without head, tail or paws
4302 1920.90	已鞣未缝制的整张兔皮（不论是否带头，尾或爪）	10	100		5	17	千克/张		Furskins of rabbit and hare, whole, tanned or dressed, unassembled, with or without head, tail or paws
4302.1930	---下列羔羊皮：阿斯特拉罕、喀拉科尔、波斯羔羊及类似羔羊、印度、中国或蒙古羔羊	20	100		5	17	千克/张		---Of lamb, the following: Astrakhan,Broadtail, Caracul, Persian and similar lamb, Indian, Chinese, Mongolian or Tibetan lamb
4302.1990	---其他	10	100			17	千克/张		---Other
4302 1990.10	已鞣未缝制其他濒危野生动物毛皮	10	100			17	千克/张	EF	Furskins of other endangered wild animals, tanned or dressed, unassembled
4302 1990.90	已鞣未缝制的其他毛皮	10	100		5	17	千克/张		Other furskins of other animals, tanned or dressed, unassembled
4302.2000	-未缝制的头、尾、爪及其他块、片	20	100			17	千克		-Heads, tails, paws and other pieces or cuttings, not assembled
4302 2000.10	已鞣未缝濒危野生动物头，尾，爪等（包括块、片）	20	100			17	千克	EF	Heads, tails, paws and other pieces or cuttings, of endangered wild animals, tanned or dressed, unassembled

税则号列 Tariff Item	商品名称及备注	进口税率 最惠	普通	暂定	出口退税	增值税率	计量单位	监管条件	Article Description
4302 2000.90	已鞣未缝制的头，尾，爪及其他块片	20	100		5	17	千克		Tanned or dressed heads, tails, paws and other pieces or cuttings of other animals, unassembled
	-已缝制的整张毛皮及其块、片:								-Whole skins and pieces or cuttings thereof, assembled:
4302.3010	---灰鼠、白鼬、貂、狐、水獭、旱獭及猞猁的整张毛皮及其块、片	20	130			17	千克		---Of grey squirrel, ermine, other marten, fox, otter, marmot and lynx
4302 3010.10	已鞣已缝制貂皮、狐皮及其块、片（兰狐、银狐、水貂、艾虎的整张毛皮及块，片除外）	20	130		5	17	千克	EF	Whole skins and pieces or cuttings thereof, of marten or fox, tanned or dressed, assembled（other than of blue fox, silver fox, mink, fitch）
4302 3010.90	已鞣已缝制的贵重濒危动物毛皮及其块、片（灰鼠皮，白鼬皮，其他貂皮，水獭皮，旱獭皮，猞猁皮及块，片）	20	130			17	千克	EF	Whole skins and pieces or cuttings thereof of endangered precious animal, tanned or dressed, assembled（of grey squirrel, ermine, other marten, fox, otter, marmot and lynx）
4302.3090	---其他	20	100			17	千克		---Other
4302 3090.10	已鞣缝的其他整张濒危野生毛皮（包括块、片）	20	100			17	千克	EF	Whole skins and pieces or cuttings thereof, of other endangered wild animals, tanned or dressed, assembled
4302 3090.90	已鞣已缝制的其他整张毛皮及块、片	20	100		5	17	千克		Whole skins and pieces or cuttings thereof, of other animals, tanned or dressed, assembled
43.03	**毛皮制的衣服、衣着附件及其他物品:**								**Articles of apparel, clothing accessories and other articles of furskin:**
	-衣服及衣着附件:								-Articles of apparel and clothing accessories:
4303.1010	---毛皮衣服	23	150			17	千克/件		---Articles of apparel
4303 1010.10	濒危野生动物毛皮衣服	23	150			17	千克/件	EF	Articles of apparel of endangered wild animals
4303 1010.90	其他毛皮衣服	23	150		13	17	千克/件		Articles of apparel of other animals
4303.1020	---毛皮衣着附件	18	150			17	千克		---Clothing accessories
4303 1020.10	濒危野生动物毛皮衣着附件	18	150			17	千克	EF	Clothing accessories of endangered wild animals
4303 1020.90	其他毛皮衣着附件	18	150		13	17	千克		Clothing accessories of other animals
4303.9000	-其他	18	150			17	千克		-Other
4303 9000.10	濒危野生动物毛皮制其他物品	18	150			17	千克	EF	Other articles of furskin of endangered wild animals
4303 9000.90	其他毛皮制物品	18	150		13	17	千克		Other articles of furskin of other animals
43.04	**人造毛皮及其制品:**								**Artificial fur and articles thereof:**
4304.0010	---人造毛皮	18	130		13	17	千克		---Artificial fur
4304.0020	---人造毛皮制品	18	150		13	17	千克		---Articles of artificial fur

第九类
木及木制品；木炭；软木及软木制品；稻草、秸秆、针茅或其他编结材料制品；篮筐及柳条编结品

第四十四章
木及木制品；木炭

注释：

一、本章不包括：

（一）主要作香料、药料、杀虫、杀菌或类似用途的木片、刨花、碎木、木粒或木粉（品目 12.11）；

（二）竹或主要作编结用的其他木质材料，呈原木状，不论是否经劈开、纵锯或切段（品目 14.01）；

（三）主要作染料或鞣料用的木片、刨花、木粒或木粉（品目 14.04）；

（四）活性炭（品目 38.02）；

（五）品目 42.02 的物品；

（六）第四十六章的货品；

（七）第六十四章的鞋靴及其零件；

（八）第六十六章的货品（例如，伞、手杖及其零件）；

（九）品目 68.08 的货品；

（十）品目 71.17 的仿首饰；

（十一）第十六类或第十七类的货品（例如，机器零件，机器及器具的箱、罩、壳，车辆部件）；

（十二）第十八类的货品（例如，钟壳、乐器及其零件）；

（十三）火器的零件（品目 93.05）；

（十四）第九十四章的物品（例如，家具、灯具及照明装置、活动房屋）；

（十五）第九十五章的物品（例如，玩具、游戏品及运动用品）；

（十六）第九十六章的物品（例如，烟斗及其零件、钮扣、铅笔），但品目 96.03 所列物品的木身及木柄除外；或

（十七）第九十七章的物品（例如，艺术品）。

二、本章所称“强化木”，是指经过化学或物理方法处理（对于多层粘合木材，其处理应超出一般粘合需要），从而增加了密度或硬度并改善了机械强度、抗化学或抗电性能的木材。

三、品目 44.14 至 44.21 适用于碎料板或类似木质材料板、纤维板、层压板或强化木的制品。

SECTION Ⅸ
WOOD AND ARTICLES OF WOOD; WOOD CHARCOAL; CORK AND ARTICLES OF CORK; MANUFACTURES OF STRAW, OF ESPARTO OR OF OTHER PLAITING MATERIALS; BASKETWARE AND WICKERWORK

Chapter 44
Wood and articles of wood; wood charcoal

Chapter Notes:

1. This Chapter does not cover:

(a) Wood, in chips, in shavings, crushed, ground or powdered, of a kind used primarily in perfumery, in pharmacy, or for insecticidal, fungicidal or similar purposes (heading 12.11);

(b) Bamboos or other materials of a woody nature of a kind used primarily for plaiting, in the rough, whether or not split, sawn lengthwise or cut to length (heading 14.01);

(c) Wood, in chips, in shavings, ground or powdered, of a kind used primarily in dyeing or in tanning (heading 14.04);

(d) Activated charcoal (heading 38.02);

(e) Articles of heading 42.02;

(f) Goods of Chapter46;

(g) Footwear or parts thereof of Chapter 64;

(h) Goods of Chapter 66 (for example, umbrellas and walking-sticks and parts thereof);

(ij) Goods of heading 68.08;

(k) Imitation jewellery of heading 71.17;

(l) Goods of Section ⅩⅥ or Section ⅩⅦ (for example, machine parts, cases, covers, cabinets for machines and apparatus and wheel wrights' wares);

(m) Goods of Section ⅩⅧ (for example, clock cases and musical instruments and parts thereof);

(n) Parts of firearms (heading 93.05);

(o) Articles of Chapter 94 (for example, furniture, lamps and lighting fittings, prefabricated buildings);

(p) Articles of Chapter 95 (for example, toys, games, sports requisites);

(q) Articles of Chapter 96 (for example, smoking pipes and parts thereof, buttons, pencils) excluding bodies and handles, of wood, for articles of heading 96.03; or

(r) Articles, of Chapter 97 (for example, works of art).

2. n this Chapter, the expression "densified wood" means wood which has been subjected to chemical or physical treatment (being, in the case of layers bonded together, treatment in excess of that needed to ensure a good bond), and which has thereby acquired increased density or hardness together with improved mechanical strength or resistance to chemical or electrical agencies.

3. Headings 44.14 to 44.21 apply to articles of the respective descriptions of particle board or similar board, fibreboard, laminated wood or densified wood as they apply to such articles of wood.

四、品目 44.10、44.11 或 44.12 的产品，可以加工成品目 44.09 所述的各种形状，也可以加工成弯曲、瓦楞、多孔或其他形状（正方形或矩形除外），以及经其他任何加工，但未具有其他品目所列制品的特性。

五、品目 44.17 不包括装有第八十二章注释一所述材料制成的刀片、工作刃、工作面或其他工作部件的工具。

六、除上述注释一及其他条文另有规定的以外，本章品目中所称“木”，也包括竹及其他木质材料。

4. Products of heading 44.10, 44.11 or 44.12 may be worked to form the shapes provided for in respect of the goods of heading 44. 09, curved, corrugated, perforated, cut or formed to shapes other than square or rectangular or submitted to any other operation provided it does not give them the character of articles of other headings.

5. Heading 44.17 does not apply to tools in which the blade,working edge, working surface or other working part is formed by any of the materials specified in Note 1 to Chapter 82.

6. Subject to Note 1 above and except where the context otherwise requires, any reference to "wood" in a heading of this Chapter applies also to bamboos and other materials of a woody nature.

子目注释：

一、子目 4401.31 所称‘木屑棒’是指由木材加工业、家具制造业及其他木材加工活动中产生的副产品（例如，刨花、锯末及碎木片）直接压制而成或加入按重量计不超过 3% 的黏合剂后粘聚而成的产品。此类产品成圆柱状，其直径不超过 25 毫米，长度不超过 100 毫米。

二、子目4403.41至4403.49，4407.21至4407.29，4408.31 至 4408.39 及 4412.31 所称“热带木”，是指下列木材：

大叶帽柱木、非洲桃花心木、西非红豆木、箭毒木、阿兰木、圭亚那苦油楝木、非洲甘比山榄木、杜楝木、非洲栎柞木、婆罗双木、美洲轻木、白驼峰楝木、黑驼峰楝木、卡蒂沃木、雪松木、西非褐红椴木、深红色红柳桉木、非洲核桃楝木、阿夫苏木、象牙海岸榄仁木、破布木、吉贝木、丝棉木、乔状黄牛木、安哥拉丛花木、巴西胡桃木、皮蚁木、伊罗科木、拟爱神木、夹竹桃木、巴西红木、绒根木、龙脑香木、开姆帕斯木、羯布罗香木、康多非洲楝木、象牙海岸褐红椴木、象牙海岸翼梧桐木、浅红色红柳安木、非洲榄仁木、南美樟木、圭亚那铁线子木、西印度桃花心木、猴子果木、肖氏夸利亚木、曼孙梧桐木、马来蝴蝶木、巴栲红柳桉木、粗轴坡垒木、茚茄木、斯温漆木、异翅香木、亚洲梨木、非洲银叶木、胶木、非洲白梧桐木、加蓬榄木、蓖麻木、爱里古夷苏木、奥文科尔木、中非蜡烛木、紫檀木、人面子木、危地马拉黑黄檀木、印度黑黄檀木、巴西黑黄檀木、巴西花梨木、巴西柚木、白坚木、鸡骨常山木、印马四出香木、大沃契希亚木、东西亚棱柱木、萨撇列木、萌生木棉木、苏帕楠木、西波木、苏古皮拉木、红椿木、圭亚那考拉玉蕊木、柚木、安哥拉香桃花心木、非洲阿勃木、南美肉豆蔻木、白柳桉木、白色红柳桉木、白色柳桉木、黄色红柳桉木。

Subheading Note:

1. For the purposes of Subheading 4401.31, the expression "wood pellets" means by-products such as cutter shavings, sawdust or chips, of the mechanical wood processing industry, furniture-making industry or other wood transformation activities, which have been agglomerated either directly by compression or by the addition of a binder in a proportion not exceeding 3% by weight. Such pellets are cylindrical, with a diameter not exceeding 25mm and a length not exceeding 100mm.

2. For the purposes of subheadings 4403.41 to 4403.49, 4407.21 to 4407.29, 4408.31 to 4408.39 and 4412.31, the expression "tropical wood" means one of the following types of wood:

Abura, Acajou d'Afrique, Afrormosia, Ako, Alan, Andiroba,Aningré, Avodiré, Azobé, Balau, Balsa, Bossé clair, Bossé foncé, Cativo, Cedro, Dabema, Dark Red Meranti, Dibétou,Doussié, Framiré, Freijo, Fromager, Fuma, Geronggang, Ilomba, Imbuia, Ipé, Iroko, Jaboty, Jelutong, Jequitiba, Jongkong,Kapur, Kempas, Keruing, Kosipo, Kotibé, Koto Light Red Meranti, Limba, Louro, Macaranduba, Mahogany, Makoré, Mandioqueira, Mansonia, Mengkulang, Meranti Bakau, Merawan, Merbau, Merpauh, Mersawa, Moabi, Niangon, Nyatoh, Obeche, Okoumé, Onzabili, Orey, Ovengkol, Ozigo, Padauk, Paldao,Palissandre de Guatemala, Palissandre de Para, Palissandre deRio, Palissandre de Rose, Pau Amarelo, Pau Marfim, Pulai, Punah, Quaruba, Ramin, Sapelli, Saqui-Saqui, Sepetir, Sipo, Sucupira, Suren, Tauari, Teak, Tiama, Tola, Virola, White Lauan, White Meranti, White Seraya, Yellow Meranti.

税则号列 Tariff Item	商品名称及备注	进口税率			出口退税	增值税率	计量单位	监管条件	Article Description
		最惠	普通	暂定					
44.01	**薪柴（圆木段、块、枝、成捆或类似形状）；木片或木粒；锯末、木废料及碎片，不论是否粘结成圆木段、块、片或类似形状：**								**Fuel wood, in logs, in billets, in twigs, in faggots or in similar forms; wood in chips or particles; sawdust and wood waste and scrap, whether or not agglomerated in logs, briquettes, pellets or similar forms:**
4401.1000	-薪柴（圆木段、块、枝，成捆或类似形状）	0	70			17	千克	AB	-Fuel wood, in logs, in billets, in twigs, in faggots or in similar forms
	-木片或木粒:								-Wood in chips or particles:
4401.2100	--针叶木	0	8			17	千克		--Coniferous
4401 2100.10	濒危针叶木木片或木粒	0	8			17	千克	ABFE	Endangered coniferous wood in chips or particles
4401 2100.90	其他针叶木木片或木粒	0	8			17	千克	AB	Other coniferous wood in chips or particles
4401.2200	--非针叶木	0	8			17	千克		--Non-coniferous
4401 2200.10	濒危非针叶木木片或木粒	0	8			17	千克	ABFE	Endangered non-coniferous wood in chips or particles
4401 2200.90	其他非针叶木木片或木粒	0	8			17	千克	AB	Other chips or particles of non-coniferous wood
	-锯末、木废料及碎片，不论是否粘结成圆木段、块、片或类似形状:								-Sawdust and wood waste and scrap, whether or not agglomerated in logs, briquettes, pellets or similar forms:
4401.3100	--木屑棒	0	8			17	千克	ABP	--Wood pellets
4401.3900	--其他	0	8			17	千克	ABP	--Other
44.02	**木炭（包括果壳炭及果核炭），不论是否结块：**								**Wood charcoal（including shell or nut charcoal）, whether or not agglomerated:**
4402.1000	-竹的	10.5	70			17	千克		-Of bamboo
4402.9000	-其他	10.5	70			17	千克		-Other
4402 9000.10	以木材为原料直接烧制的木炭	10.5	70			17	千克	8	Wood charcoal, of wood as raw materials,directly burnt
4402 9000.90	其他木炭（包括果壳炭及果核炭，不论是否结块）	10.5	70			17	千克		Other wood charcoal（including shell or nut charcoal, whether or not agglomerated）
44.03	**原木，不论是否去皮、去边材或粗锯成方：**								**Wood in the rough, whether or not stripped of bark or sapwood, or roughly squared:**
4403.1000	-用油漆、着色剂、杂酚油或其他防腐剂处理	0	8			13	千克/立方米		-Treated with paint, stains, creosote or other preservatives
4403 1000.10	油漆,着色剂等处理的红豆杉原木(包括用杂酚油或其他防腐剂处理)	0	8			13	千克/立方米	8AF	Endangered wood in the rough, treated with paint, stains, creosote or other preservatives
4403 1000.20	油漆,着色剂等处理的其他濒危树种原木(包括用杂酚油或其他防腐剂处理)	0	8			13	千克/立方米	8AF	Paint, coloring agents and other endangered species in the processing of logs (including with creosote or other preservatives)
4403 1000.90	其他油漆、着色剂等处理的原木（包括用杂酚油或其他防腐剂处理）	0	8			13	千克/立方米	8A	Other wood in the rough, treated with paint, stains, creosote or other preservatives
	-其他，针叶木:								-Other, coniferous:
4403.2010	---红松和樟子松	0	8			13	千克/立方米		---Korean pine and Mongolian scotch pine
4403 2010.10	其他红松原木(用油漆、着色剂、杂酚油或其他防腐剂处理的除外）	0	8			13	千克/立方米	8AEF	Other korean pine wood in the rough（other than that treated with paint, stains, creosote or other preservatives）
4403 2010.90	其他樟子松原木（用油漆、着色剂、杂酚油或其他防腐剂处理的除外）	0	8			13	千克/立方米	8A	Other mongolian scotch pine wood in the rough（other than that treated with paint, stains, creosote or other preservatives）
4403.2020	---白松(云杉和冷杉)	0	8			13	千克/立方米		---White pine（spruce and fir）
4403 2020.10	濒危白松、云杉和冷杉原木	0	8			13	千克/立方米	8AF	Endangered white pine（spruce and fir）

税则号列 Tariff Item	商品名称及备注	进口税率 最惠	进口税率 普通	进口税率 暂定	出口退税	增值税率	计量单位	监管条件	Article Description
4403 2020.90	其他白松、云杉和冷杉原木	0	8			13	千克/立方米	8A	Other white pine（spruce and fir）
4403.2030	---辐射松	0	8			13	千克/立方米	8A	---Radiata pine
4403.2040	---落叶松	0	8			13	千克/立方米	8A	---Larch
4403.2050	---花旗松	0	8			13	千克/立方米	8A	---Douglas fir
4403.2090	---其他	0	8			13	千克/立方米		---Other
4403 2090.10	其他红豆杉原木	0	8			13	千克/立方米	8AF	Endangered coniferous wood in the rough
4403 2090.20	其他濒危针叶木原木	0	8			13	千克/立方米	8AF	Other endangered softwood logs
4403 2090.90	其他针叶木原木	0	8			13	千克/立方米	8A	Other coniferous wood in the rough
	-其他，本章子目注释二所列的热带木的:								-Other, of tropical wood specified in subheading note 2 to this Chapter:
4403.4100	--深红色红柳桉木、浅红色红柳桉木及巴栲红柳桉木	0	8			13	千克/立方米	8A	--Dark Red Meranti, Light Red Meranti and Meranti Bakau
	--其他(本章子目注释一所列热带非针叶木):								---Other（of tropical non-contiferous wood specified in subheading note 1 to this chapter）:
4403.4910	---柚木	0	35			13	千克/立方米	8A	---Teak
4403.4920	---奥克曼（奥克榄）	0	35			13	千克/立方米	8A	---Okoume（Aukoumed Klaineana）
4403.4930	---龙脑香木(克隆)	0	35			13	千克/立方米	8A	---Dipterocarpus spp. Keruing
4403.4940	---山樟（香木）	0	35			13	千克/立方米	8A	---Kapur（Dryobalanops spp.）
4403.4950	---印加木（波罗格）	0	35			13	千克/立方米	8A	---Intsia spp.（Mengaris）
4403.4960	---大干巴豆（门格里斯或康派斯）	0	35			13	千克/立方米	8A	---Koompassia spp.（Mengaris or Kempas）
4403.4970	---异翅香木	0	35			13	千克/立方米	8A	---Anisopter spp.
4403.4990	---其他	0	8			13	千克/立方米		---Other
4403 4990.10	其他本章子目注释二濒危热带原木(用油漆,着色剂,杂酚油或其他防腐剂处理的除外)	0	8			13	千克/立方米	8AF	Endangered tropical wood in the rough,specified in Subheading Note 2 to this Chapter（other than that treated with paint, stains, creosote or other preservatives）
4403 4990.90	其他本章子目注释二所列热带原木(用油漆,着色剂,杂酚油或其他防腐剂处理的除外)	0	8			13	千克/立方米	8A	Tropical wood in the rough, specified in subheading Note 2 to this Chapter,other than that treated with paint, stains, creosote or other preservatives
	-其他:								-Other:
4403.9100	--栎木(橡木)	0	8			13	千克/立方米	8A	--Of oak（*Quercus spp.*）
4403.9200	--山毛榉木	0	8			13	千克/立方米	8A	--Of beech（*Fagus spp.*）
	--其他:								--Other:
4403.9910	---楠木	0	35			13	千克/立方米	8A	---Of nan mu（Phoebe）

税则号列 Tariff Item	商品名称及备注	进口税率 最惠	普通	暂定	出口退税	增值税率	计量单位	监管条件	Article Description
4403.9920	---樟木	0	35			13	千克/立方米	8A	---Of camphor wood
4403.9930	---红木	0	35			13	千克/立方米	8AF	---Of rosewood
4403.9940	---泡桐木	0	8			13	千克/立方米	8A	---Of Kiri（Paulownia）
4403.9950	---水曲柳	0	8			13	千克/立方米	8A	---Ash
4403.9960	---北美硬阔叶木（包括樱桃木、黑胡桃木、枫木）	0	8			13	千克/立方米	8A	---North American hard wood（including cherry, walnut, and maple）
4403.9980	---其他未列名的温带非针叶木	0	8			13	千克/立方米		---Other temperate non-coniferous not specified
4403 9980.10	其他未列名温带濒危非针叶木原木（用油漆，着色剂，杂酚油或其他防腐剂处理的除外）	0	8			13	千克/立方米	8AF	Other endangered temperate non-coniferous wood, not specified (other than that treated with paint, stains, creosote or otherpreservatives）
4403 9980.90	其他未列名温带非针叶木原木（用油漆，着色剂，杂酚油或其他防腐剂处理的除外）	0	8			13	千克/立方米	8A	Other temperate non-coniferous wood, not specifi -ed, other than that treated with paint, stains, creosote or other preservatives
4403.9990	---其他	0	8			13	千克/立方米		---Other
4403 9990.11	南美蒺藜木（玉檀木）原木(用油漆，着色剂，杂酚油或其他防腐剂处理的除外)	0	8			13	千克/立方米	8AEF	POLO SANTO (Bulnesia sarmientoi) wood in the rough (other than that treated with paint, stains, creosote or other preservatives)
4403 9990.12	沉香木及拟沉香木原木(用油漆，着色剂，杂酚油或其他防腐剂处理的除外)	0	8			13	千克/立方米	8AEF	Aloewood in the rough (other than that treated with paint, stains, creosote or other preservatives)
4403 9990.19	其他未列名濒危非针叶原木(用油漆，着色剂，杂酚油或其他防腐剂处理的除外)	0	8			13	千克/立方米	8AEF	Other endangered non-coniferous wood in the rough, not specified, other than that treated with paint, stains, creosote or other preservatives
4403 9990.90	其他未列名非针叶原木（用油漆、着色剂、杂酚油或其他防腐剂处理的除外）	0	8			13	千克/立方米	8A	Other non-coniferous wood in the rough, not specified, other than that treated with paint,stains, creosote or other preservatives
44.04	**箍木；木劈条；已削尖但未经纵锯的木桩；粗加修整但未经车圆、弯曲或其他方式加工的木棒，适合制手杖、伞柄、工具把柄及类似品；木片条及类似品：**								**Hoopwood; split poles; piles, pickets and stakes of wood, pointed but not sawn lengthwise; wooden sticks, roughly trimmed but not turned, bent or otherwise worked, suitable for the manufacture of walking-sticks, umbrellas, tool handles or the like; chipwood and the like:**
4404.1000	-针叶木的	8	50			17	千克		-Coniferous
4404 1000.10	濒危针叶木的箍木等及类似品（包括木劈条，棒及类似品）	8	50			17	千克	ABFE	Hoopwood, split poles, wooden sticks and the like, of endangered coniferous wood
4404 1000.90	其他针叶木的箍木等及类似品（包括木劈条，棒及类似品）	8	50			17	千克	AB	Hoopwood, split poles, wooden sticks and the like, of other coniferous wood
4404.2000	-非针叶木的	8	50			17	千克		-Non-coniferous
4404 2000.10	濒危非针叶木箍木等（包括木劈条，棒及类似品）	8	50			17	千克	ABFE	Hoopwood, split poles, wooden sticks and the like, of endangered non-coniferous wood
4404 2000.90	其他非针叶木箍木等（包括木劈条，棒及类似品）	8	50			17	千克	AB	Hoopwood, split poles, wooden sticks and the like, of other non-coniferous wood
44.05	**木丝；木粉：**								**Wood wool; wood flour:**
4405.0000	木丝；木粉	8	40			17	千克	AB	Wood wool; wood flour
44.06	**铁道及电车道枕木：**								**Railway or tramway sleepers（crossties）of wood:**
4406.1000	-未浸渍	0	14			17	立方米/千克	4ABxy	-Not impregnated

税则号列 Tariff Item	商品名称及备注	进口税率			出口退税	增值税率	计量单位	监管条件	Article Description
		最惠	普通	暂定					
4406.9000	-其他	0	14			17	立方米/千克		-Other
4406 9000.10	濒危木已浸渍铁道及电车道枕木	0	14			17	立方米/千克	FE	Railway or tramway sleepers（crossties）of endangered wood, impregnated
4406 9000.90	其他已浸渍的铁道及电车道枕木	0	14			17	立方米/千克		Other railway or tramway sleepers（crossties）of wood, impregnated
44.07	**经纵锯、纵切、刨切或旋切的木材，不论是否刨平、砂光或指榫接合，厚度超过6毫米：**								**Wood sawn or chipped lengthwise, sliced or peeled, whether or not planed, sanded or end-jionted, of a thickness exceeding 6mm:**
	-针叶木：								-Coniferous:
4407.1010	---红松和樟子松	0	14			17	千克/立方米		---Korean pine and Mongolian scotch pine
4407 1010.11	端部接合的红松厚板材（经纵锯、纵切、刨切或旋切的，厚度超过6mm）	0	14			17	千克/立方米	ABEF	Korean pine wood, sawn or chipped lengthwise, sliced or peeled, end-jointed, of a thickness exceeding 6mm
4407 1010.19	端部接合的樟子松厚板材（经纵锯、纵切、刨切或旋切的，厚度超过6mm）	0	14			17	千克/立方米	AB	Mongolian scotch pine wood sawn or chipped lengthwise, sliced or peeled, end-jointed, of a thickness exceeding 6mm
4407 1010.91	非端部接合的红松厚板材(经纵锯、纵切、刨切或旋切的,厚度超过6mm)	0	14			17	千克/立方米	4ABEFxy	Korean pine and Mongolian scotch pine wood, sawn or chipped lengthwise, sliced or peeled, not end-jointed, of a thickness exceeding 6mm
4407 1010.99	非端部接合的樟子松厚板材(经纵锯、纵切、刨切或旋切的,厚度超过6mm)	0	14			17	千克/立方米	4ABxy	Wood sawn or chipped lengthwise, sliced or peeled, not end jointed, of Mongolian scocth pine, of a thinkness exceeding 6mm
4407.1020	---白松(云杉和冷杉)	0	14			17	千克/立方米		---White pine（*spruce and fir*）
4407 1020.11	端部接合的濒危白松(云杉,冷杉)厚板材(经纵锯、纵切、刨切或旋切的,厚度超过6mm)	0	14			17	千克/立方米	ABEF	Wood of endangered white pine(spruce and fir), sawn or chipped lengthwise, sliced or peeled, end-jointed, of a thickness exceeding 6mm
4407 1020.19	端部接合的其他白松(云杉,冷杉)厚板材(经纵锯、纵切、刨切或旋切的,厚度超过6mm)	0	14			17	千克/立方米	AB	Wood of other white pine(spruce and fir), sawn or chipped lengthwise, sliced or peeled, end-jointed, of a thickness exceeding 6mm
4407 1020.91	非端部接合濒危白松(云杉,冷杉)厚板材(经纵锯、纵切、刨切或旋切的,厚度超过6mm)	0	14			17	千克/立方米	4ABEFxy	Wood sawn or chipped lengthwise, sliced or peeled, of endangered white pine(spruce and fir), not end-jointed, of a thickness exceeding 6mm
4407 1020.99	非端部接合其他白松(云杉,冷杉)厚板材(经纵锯、纵切、刨切或旋切的,厚度超过6mm)	0	14			17	千克/立方米	4ABxy	Wood sawn or chipped lengthwise, sliced or peeled, of other white pine(spruce and fir), not endjointed, of a thickness exceeding 6mm
4407.1030	---辐射松	0	14			17	千克/立方米		---Rediata pine
4407 1030.10	端部接合的辐射松厚板材（经纵锯、纵切、刨切或旋切的，厚度超过6毫米）	0	14			17	千克/立方米	AB	Radiata pine wood sawn or chipped lengthwise, sliced or peeled, end-jointed, of a thickness exceeding 6mm
4407 1030.90	非端部接合的辐射松厚板材（经纵锯、纵切、刨切或旋切的，厚度超过6毫米）	0	14			17	千克/立方米	4ABxy	Radiata pine wood sawn or chipped lengthwise, sliced or peeled, not end-jointed, of a thickness exceeding 6mm
4407.1040	---花旗松	0	14			17	千克/立方米		---Douglas fir
4407 1040.10	端部接合的花旗松厚板材（经纵锯、纵切、刨切或旋切的，厚度超过6毫米）	0	14			17	千克/立方米	AB	Radiata pine wood sawn or chipped lengthwise, sliced or peeled, not end-jointed, of a thickness exceeding 6mm
4407 1040.90	非端部接合的花旗松厚板材（经纵锯、纵切、刨切或旋切的，厚度超过6毫米）	0	14			17	千克/立方米	4ABxy	Douglas fir wood sawn or chipped lengthwise, sliced or peeled, not end-jointed, of a thickness exceeding 6mm

税则号列 Tariff Item	商品名称及备注	进口税率			出口退税	增值税率	计量单位	监管条件	Article Description
		最惠	普通	暂定					
4407.1090	----其他	0	14			17	千克/立方米		---Other
4407 1090.11	端部接合其他濒危针叶木厚板材（经纵锯、纵切、刨切或旋切的，厚度超过6毫米）	0	14			17	千克/立方米	FEAB	Other wood of endangered conifer, sawn or chipped lengthwise, sliced or peeled, end-jointed, of a thickness exceeding 6mm
4407 1090.19	端部接合其他针叶木厚板材（经纵锯、纵切、刨切或旋切的，厚度超过6毫米）	0	14			17	千克/立方米	AB	Other wood of conifes sawn or chipped lengthwise, sliced or peeled, end-jointed, of a thickness exceeding 6mm
4407 1090.91	非端部接合其他濒危针叶木厚板材（经纵锯、纵切、刨切或旋切的，厚度超过6mm）	0	14			17	千克/立方米	FEAB4xy	Other wood of endangered conifer,sawn or chipped lengthwise, sliced or peeled, not endjointed, of a thickness exce eding 6mm
4407 1090.99	非端部接合的其他针叶木厚板材（经纵锯、纵切、刨切或旋切的，厚度超过6毫米）	0	14			17	千克/立方米	AB4xy	Other wood of conifes sawn or chipped lengthwise, sliced or peeled, not end-jointed, of a thickness exceeding 6mm
	-本章子目注释二所列的热带木:								-Of tropical wood specified in subheading note 2 to this Chapter:
4407.2100	--美洲桃花心木	0	14			17	千克/立方米		--Mahogany（*Swietenia spp.*）
4407 2100.10	端部接合美洲桃花心木（经纵锯、纵切、刨切或旋切的，厚度超过6毫米）	0	14			17	千克/立方米	FEAB	Mahogany wood sawn or chipped lengthwise, sliced or peeled, end-jointed, of a thickness exceeding 6mm
4407 2100.90	非端部接合美洲桃花心木（经纵锯、纵切、刨切或旋切的，厚度超过6毫米）	0	14			17	千克/立方米	4ABEFxy	Mahogany wood sawn or chipped lengthwise, sliced or peeled, not-endjointed, of a thickness exceeding 6mm
4407.2200	--苏里南肉豆蔻木、巴西胡桃木及美洲轻木	0	14			17	千克/立方米		--Virola, Imbuia and Balsa
4407 2200.10	端部接合的苏里南肉豆蔻木、巴西胡桃木及美洲轻木（经纵锯、纵切、刨切或旋切的，厚度超过6毫米）	0	14			17	千克/立方米	AB	Virola, Imbuia and Balsa wood sawn or chipped lengthwise sliced or peeled, end-jointed, of a thickness exceeding 6mm
4407 2200.90	非端部接合的苏里南肉豆蔻木、巴西胡桃木及美洲轻木（经纵锯、纵切、刨切或旋切的，厚度超过6毫米）	0	14			17	千克/立方米	4ABxy	Virola, Imbuia and Balsa wood sawn or chipped lengthwise, sliced or peeled, not endjoined, of a thickness exceeding 6mm
4407.2500	--深红色红柳桉木、浅红色红柳桉木及巴栲红柳桉木	0	14			17	千克/立方米		--Dark Red Meranti, Light Red Meranti and Meranti Bakau
4407 2500.10	端部接合的红柳桉木板材（指深红色、浅红色及巴栲红柳桉木，厚度超过6毫米）	0	14			17	千克/立方米	AB	Wood sawn or chipped lengthwise, sliced or peeled, of Dark Red Meranti, Light Red Meranti and Meranti Bakau, end-jointed, of a thickness exceeding 6mm
4407 2500.90	非端部接合的红柳桉木板材（指深红色、浅红色及巴栲红柳桉木，经纵锯、纵切、刨切或旋切的，厚度超过6毫米）	0	14			17	千克/立方米	y4xAB	Wood sawn or chipped lengthwise, sliced or peeled, of Dark Red Meranti, Light Red Meranti and Meranti Bakau, not end-jointed, of a thickness exceeding 6mm
4407.2600	--白柳桉木、白色红柳桉木、白色柳桉木、黄色红柳桉木及阿兰木	0	14			17	千克/立方米		--White Lauan, White Meranti, White Seraya, Yellow Meranti and Alan
4407 2600.10	端部接合的白柳桉、其他柳桉木和阿兰木板材（经纵锯、纵切、刨切或旋切的，厚度超过6毫米）	0	14			17	千克/立方米	AB	Wood sawn or chipped lengthwise, sliced or peeled, of White Lauan, White Meranti, White Seraya, Yellow Meranti and Alan, end-jointed, of a thickness exceeding 6mm
4407 2600.90	非端部接合的白柳桉、其他柳桉木和阿兰木板材（经纵锯、纵切、刨切或旋切的，厚度超过6毫米）	0	14			17	千克/立方米	y4xAB	Wood sawn or chipped lengthwise, sliced or peeled, of White Lauan, White Meranti, White Seraya, Yellow Meranti and Alan, not end-jointed, of a thickness exceeding 6mm

税则号列 Tariff Item	商品名称及备注	进口税率 最惠	进口税率 普通	进口税率 暂定	出口退税	增值税率	计量单位	监管条件	Article Description
4407.2700	--沙比利	0	40			17	千克/立方米		--Sapelli
4407 2700.10	端部接合的沙比利木板材(经纵锯、纵切、刨切或旋切的,厚度超过6毫米)	0	40			17	千克/立方米	AB	Sapelli wood sawn or chipped lengthwise, sliced or peeled, end-jointed, of a thickness exceeding 6mm
4407 2700.90	非端部接合的沙比利木板材(经纵锯、纵切、刨切或旋切的,厚度超过6毫米)	0	40			17	千克/立方米	4ABxy	Sapelli wood sawn or chipped lengthwise, sliced or peeled, not end-jointed, of a thickness exceeding 6mm
4407.2800	---伊罗科木	0	14			17	千克/立方米		---Iroko
4407 2800.10	端部接合的伊罗科木板材(经纵锯、纵切、刨切或旋切的,厚度超过6毫米)	0	14			17	千克/立方米	AB	Iroko wood sawn or chipped lengthwise, sliced or peeled, end-jointed, of a thickness exceeding 6mm
4407 2800.90	非端部接合的伊罗科木板材(经纵锯、纵切、刨切或旋切的,厚度超过6毫米)	0	14			17	千克/立方米	4ABxy	Iroko wood sawn or chipped lengthwise, sliced or peeled, not end-jointed, of a thickness exceeding 6mm
	--其他:								--Other:
4407.2910	---柚木	0	40			17	千克/立方米		---Teak
4407 2910.10	端部接合的柚木板材(经纵锯、纵切、刨切或旋切的,厚度超过6毫米)	0	40			17	千克/立方米	AB	Teak wood sawn or chipped lengthwise, sliced or peeled, end-jointed, of a thickness exceeding 6mm
4407 2910.90	非端部接合的柚木板材(经纵锯、纵切、刨切或旋切的,厚度超过6毫米)	0	40			17	千克/立方米	y4xAB	Teak wood sawn or chipped lengthwise, sliced or peeled, not end-jointed, of a thickness exceeding 6mm
4407.2920	---非洲桃花心木	0	40			17	千克/立方米		---Acajou
4407 2920.10	端部接合的非洲桃花心木板材(经纵锯、纵切、刨切或旋切的,厚度超过6毫米)	0	40			17	千克/立方米	AB	Acajou wood sawn or chipped lengthwise, sliced or peeled, end-jointed, of a thickness exceeding 6mm
4407 2920.90	非端部接合的非洲桃花心木板材(经纵锯、纵切、刨切或旋切的,厚度超过6毫米)	0	40			17	千克/立方米	AB	Acajou wood sawn or chipped lengthwise, sliced or peeled, not end-jointed, of a thickness exceeding 6mm
4407.2930	---波罗格	0	40			17	千克/立方米		---Merbau
4407 2930.10	端部接合的波罗格Merban板材(经纵锯、纵切、刨切或旋切的,厚度超过6毫米)	0	40			17	千克/立方米	AB	Merban wood sawn or chipped lengthwise, sliced or peeled, end-jointed, of a thickness exceeding 6mm
4407 2930.90	非端部接合的波罗格Merban板材(经纵锯、纵切、刨切或旋切的,厚度超过6毫米)	0	40			17	千克/立方米	AB	Merban wood sawn or chipped lengthwise, sliced or peeled, not end-jointed, of a thickness exceeding 6mm
4407.2990	---其他	0	14			17	千克/立方米		---Other
4407 2990.11	端部接合拉敏木厚板材(经纵锯、纵切、刨切或旋切的,厚度超过6毫米)	0	14			17	千克/立方米	FEAB	Ramin wood sawn or chipped lengthwise, sliced or peeled, not end-jointed, of a thickness exceeding 6mm
4407 2990.12	端部接合其他未列名本章子目注释二濒危热带木厚板材(经纵锯、纵切、刨切或旋切的,厚度超过6mm)	0	14			17	千克/立方米	FEAB	Other endangered tropical wood, not specified in Subheading Note 2 to this Chapter not specified, sawn or chipped lengthwise, sliced or peeled, end-jointed, of a thickness exceeding 6mm
4407 2990.19	端部接合其他未列名本章子目注释二热带木厚板材(经纵锯、纵切、刨切或旋切的,厚度超过6mm)	0	14			17	千克/立方米	AB	Other tropical wood, not specified in Subheading Note 2 to this Chapter, sawn or chipped lengthwise, sliced or peeled,end-jointed, of a thickness exceeding 6mm
4407 2990.91	非端部接合其他未列名本章子目注释二濒危热带木板材(经纵	0	14			17	千克/立方米	y4xAFEB	Other endangered tropical wood, not specified in Subheading Note 2 to this Chapter, sawn or chipped

税则号列 Tariff Item	商品名称及备注	进口税率 最惠	普通	暂定	出口退税	增值税率	计量单位	监管条件	Article Description
	锯、纵切、刨切或旋切的,厚度超过 6mm)								lengthwise, sliced or peeled, not end-jointed, of a thickness exceeding 6mm
4407 2990.99	非端部接合其他未列名本章子目注释二热带木板材(经纵锯、纵切、刨切或旋切的,厚度超过 6mm)	0	14			17	千克/立方米	y4xAB	Other tropical wood, not specified in Subheading Note 2 to this Chapter, sawn or chipped lengthwise, sliced or peeled, not endjointed, of a thickness exceeding 6mm
	-其他:								-Other:
4407.9100	--栎木(橡木)	0	14			17	千克/立方米		--Of oak（*Ouercus spp.*）
4407 9100.10	端部接合的栎木(橡木)厚板材（经纵锯、纵切、刨切或旋切的,厚度超过 6 毫米）	0	14			17	千克/立方米	AB	Oak（*Ouercus spp.*）wood sawn or chipped lengthwise, sliced or peeled, end-jointed, of a thickness exceeding 6mm
4407 9100.90	非端部接合的栎木(橡木)厚板材（经纵锯、纵切、刨切或旋切的,厚度超过 6 毫米）	0	14			17	千克/立方米	y4xAB	Oak（*Ouercus spp.*）wood sawn or chipped lengthwise, sliced or peeled, not end-jointed, of a thickness exceeding 6mm
4407.9200	--山毛榉木	0	14			17	千克/立方米		--Of beech（*Fagus spp.*）
4407 9200.10	端部接合的山毛榉木厚板材（经纵锯、纵切、刨切或旋切的，厚度超过 6 毫米）	0	14			17	千克/立方米	ABE	Beech（*Fagus spp.*）wood sawn or chipped lengthwise, sliced or peeled, end-jointed, of a thickness exceeding 6mm
4407 9200.90	非端部接合的山毛榉木厚板材（经纵锯、纵切、刨切或旋切的,厚度超过 6 毫米）	0	14			17	千克/立方米	4ABExy	Beech（*Fagus spp.*）wood sawn or chipped lengthwise, sliced or peeled, not end-jointed, of a thickness exceeding 6mm
4407.9300	--枫木	0	14			17	千克/立方米		--Of maple（Acer spp.）
4407 9300.10	端部接合的枫木厚板材（经纵锯、纵切、刨切或旋切，厚度超过 6 毫米）	0	14			17	千克/立方米	AB	Maple wood sawn or chipped lengthwise, sliced or peeled, end-jointed, of a thickness exceeding 6mm
4407 9300.90	非端部接合的枫木厚板材（经纵锯、纵切、刨切或旋切，厚度超过 6 毫米）	0	14			17	千克/立方米	4ABxy	Maple wood sawn or chipped lengthwise, sliced or peeled, not end-jointed, of a thickness exceeding 6mm
4407.9400	--樱桃木	0	14			17	千克/立方米		--Of cherry（*Prunus spp.*）
4407 9400.10	端部接合的樱桃木厚板材（经纵锯、纵切、刨切或旋切，厚度超过 6 毫米）	0	14			17	千克/立方米	AB	Cherry wood sawn or chipped lengthwise, sliced or peeled, end-jointed, of a thickness exceeding 6mm
4407 9400.90	非端部接合的樱桃木厚板材（经纵锯、纵切、刨切或旋切，厚度超过 6 毫米）	0	14			17	千克/立方米	4ABxy	Cherry wood sawn or chipped lengthwise, sliced or peeled, not end-jointed, of a thickness exceeding 6mm
4407.9500	--白蜡木	0	14			17	千克/立方米		--Of ash（*Fraxinus spp.*）
4407 9500.10	端部接合的白蜡木厚板材（经纵锯、纵切、刨切或旋切的，厚度超过 6 毫米）	0	14			17	千克/立方米	AB	Ash wood sawn or chipped lengthwise, sliced or peeled, end-jointed, of a thickness exceeding 6mm
4407 9500.90	非端部接合的白蜡木厚板材（经纵锯、纵切、刨切或旋切的，厚度超过 6 毫米）	0	14			17	千克/立方米	4ABxy	Ash wood sawn or chipped lengthwise, sliced or peeled, not end-jointed, of a thickness exceeding 6mm
	--其他:								--Other:
4407.9910	---樟木、楠木、红木	0	40			17	千克/立方米		---Of camphor-wood, nanmu or rosewood
4407 9910.10	端部接合樟木/楠木/红木厚板材（经纵锯、纵切、刨切或旋切的,厚度超过 6 毫米）	0	40			17	千克/立方米	AFEB	Wood sawn or chipped lengthwise, sliced or peeled of Camphor-wood, Nanmu or Rosewood, end-jointed, of a thickness exceeding 6mm
4407 9910.90	非端部接合樟木/楠木/红木厚板	0	40			17	千克/	y4xAFEB	Wood sawn or chipped lengthwise, sliced or peeled,

税则号列 Tariff Item	商品名称及备注	进口税率 最惠	普通	暂定	出口退税	增值税率	计量单位	监管条件	Article Description
	材（经纵锯、纵切、刨切或旋切的，厚度超过6mm）						立方米		of Camphor-wood, Nanmu or Rosewood, not end-jointed, of a thickness exceeding 6mm
4407.9920	---泡桐木	0	14		13	17	千克/立方米		---Of Paulownia
4407 9920.10	端部接合的泡桐木厚板材（经纵锯、纵切、刨切或旋切的，厚度超过6毫米）	0	14		13	17	千克/立方米	AB	Paulownia wood sawn or chipped lengthwise, sliced or peeled, end-jointed, of a thickness exceeding 6mm
4407 9920.90	非端部接合的泡桐木厚板材（经纵锯、纵切、刨切或旋切的，厚度超过6毫米）	0	14		13	17	千克/立方米	AB	Paulownia wood sawn or chipped lengthwise, sliced or peeled, not end-jointed, of a thickness exceeding 6mm
4407.9930	---北美硬阔叶材（含黑胡桃木）	0	14			17	千克/立方米		---North American hard wood（including walnut）
4407 9930.10	端部接合的北美硬阔叶材厚板材（含黑胡桃木，纵锯纵切刨切或旋切，厚度超过6毫米）	0	14			17	千克/立方米	AB	Wood sawn or chipped lengthwise, sliced or peeled, of North American hard wood, including walnut, end-jointed, of a thickness exceeding 6mm
4407 9930.90	非端部接合的北美硬阔叶材厚板材（含黑胡桃木，纵锯纵切刨切或旋切，厚度超过6毫米）	0	14			17	千克/立方米	AB	Wood sawn or chipped lengthwise, sliced or peeled, of North American hardwood,including walnut, not end-jointed, of a thickness exceeding 6mm
4407.9980	---其他温带非针叶木	0	14			17	千克/立方米		---Other temperate, non-coniferous wood
4407 9980.11	端部接合其他温带濒危非针叶板材（纵锯、纵切、刨切或旋切的，厚度超过6毫米）	0	14			17	千克/立方米	FEAB	Wood sawn or chipped lengthwise, sliced or peeled, of endangered temperate non-coniferous wood, end-jointed, of a thickness exceeding 6mm
4407 9980.19	端部接合的其他温带非针叶厚板材（纵锯、纵切、刨切或旋切的，厚度超过6毫米）	0	14			17	千克/立方米	AB	Wood sawn or chipped lengthwise, sliced or peeled, of temperate non-coniferous wood, end-jointed, of a thickness exceeding 6mm
4407 9980.91	非端部结合其他温带濒危非针叶厚板材（纵锯、纵切、刨切或旋切的，厚度超过6毫米）	0	14			17	千克/立方米	4ABEFxy	Wood sawn or chipped lengthwise, sliced or peeled, of endangered temperate non-coniferous wood, not end-jointed, of a thickness exceeding 6mm
4407 9980.99	非端部接合的其他温带非针叶厚板材（纵锯、纵切、刨切或旋切的，厚度超过6mm）	0	14			17	千克/立方米	4ABxy	Wood sawn or chipped lengthwise, sliced or peeled, of other temperate non-coniferous wood, not end-jointed, of a thickness exceeding 6mm
4407.9990	---其他	0	14			17	千克/立方米		---Other
4407 9990.11	端部接合的南美蒺藜木（玉檀木）厚板材(经纵锯、纵切、刨切或旋切的,厚度超过6mm)	0	14			17	千克/立方米	AFEB	Wood sawn or chipped lengthwise, sliced or peeled, end jointed, of POLO SANTO (Bulnesia sarmientoi), of a thinkness exceeding 6mm
4407 9990.12	端部接合的沉香木及拟沉香木厚板材(经纵锯、纵切、刨切或旋切的,厚度超过6mm)	0	14			17	千克/立方米	AFEB	Endangered wood, sawn or chipped lengthwise, sliced or peeled, end-jointed, of a thickness exceeding 6mm
4407 9990.15	端部接合的其他濒危木厚板材(经纵锯、纵切、刨切或旋切的,厚度超过6mm)	0	14			17	千克/立方米	AFEB	Wood sawn or chipped lengthwise, sliced or peeled, end jointed, of endangered wood, of a thinkness exceeding 6mm
4407 9990.19	端部接合的其他木厚板材（经纵锯、纵切、刨切或旋切的，厚度超过6毫米）	0	14			17	千克/立方米	AB	Other wood sawn or chipped lengthwise, sliced or peeled, end-jointed, of a thickness exceeding 6mm
4407 9990.91	非端部接合的南美蒺藜木（玉檀木）厚板材(经纵锯、纵切、刨切或旋切的,厚度超过6mm)	0	14			17	千克/立方米	y4xAFEB	Endangered wood sawn or chipped lengthwise, sliced or peeled, not end-jointed, of a thickness exceeding 6mm
4407 9990.92	非端部接合的沉香木及拟沉香木厚板材(经纵锯、纵切、刨切或旋切的,厚度超过6mm)	0	14			17	千克/立方米	y4xAFEB	Wood sawn or chipped lengthwise, sliced or peeled, not end jointed, of Aloewood, of a thinkness exceeding 6mm
4407 9990.95	非端部接合的其他濒危木厚板	0	14			17	千克/	y4xAFEB	Wood sawn or chipped lengthwise, sliced or peeled,

税则号列 Tariff Item	商品名称及备注	进口税率 最惠	普通	暂定	出口退税	增值税率	计量单位	监管条件	Article Description
	材(经纵锯、纵切、刨切或旋切的,厚度超过 6mm)						立方米		not-end jointed, of endangered wood, of a thinkness exceeding 6mm
4407 9990.99	非端部接合的其他木厚板材（经纵锯、纵切、刨切或旋切的，厚度超过 6 毫米）	0	14			17	千克/立方米	y4xAB	Other wood sawn or chipped lengthwise, sliced or peeled, not end-jointed ,of a thickness exceeding 6mm
44.08	**饰面用单板（包括刨切积层木获得的单板）、制胶合板或类似多层板用单板以及其他经纵锯、刨切或旋切的木材，不论是否刨平、砂光、拼接或端部接合，厚度不超过 6 毫米**								**Sheets for veneering（including those obtained by slicing laminated wood）, for plywood or for similar laminated wood and other wood, sawn lengthwise, sliced or peeled, whether or not planed, sanded, spliced or end-jointed, of a thickness not exceeding 6mm:**
	-针叶木:								-Coniferous:
	---饰面用单板:								---Veneer sheets:
4408.1011	----用胶合板等多层板制的	8	40			17	千克		----Of laminated plywood
4408 1011.10	胶合板等多层板制濒危针叶木单板（厚度≤6 毫米，饰面用）	8	40			17	千克	ABFE	Sheets for veneering of endangered coniferous wood, of laminated plywood, of a thickness not exceeding 6mm
4408 1011.90	其他胶合板等多层板制针叶木单板（厚度≤6 毫米，饰面用）	8	40			17	千克	AB	Other sheets for veneering of coniferous wood, of laminated plywood, of a thickness not exceeding 6mm
4408.1019	----其他	4	40			17	千克		----Other
4408 1019.10	其他饰面濒危针叶木单板（厚度≤6 毫米）	4	40			17	千克	ABFE	Other veneer sheets of endangered coniferous wood, of a thickness not exceeding 6mm
4408 1019.90	其他饰面针叶木单板（厚度≤6 毫米）	4	40			17	千克	AB	Other sheets for veneering of coniferous wood, of a thickness not exceeding 6mm
4408.1020	---制胶合板用单板	4	17			17	千克		---Sheets for plywood
4408 1020.10	制胶合板用濒危针叶木单板（厚度≤6 毫米）	4	17			17	千克	ABFE	Sheets for plywood of endangered coniferous wood, of a thickness not exceeding 6mm
4408 1020.90	其他制胶合板用针叶木单板（厚度≤6 毫米）	4	17			17	千克	AB	Other sheets for plywood of coniferous wood, of a thickness not exceeding 6mm
4408.1090	---其他	4	30			17	千克		---Other
4408 1090.10	其他濒危针叶木单板材（经纵锯，刨切或旋切的，厚度≤6 毫米）	4	30			17	千克	ABFE	Sheets of endangered coniferous wood, sawn or chipped lengthwise, sliced or peeled, of a thickness not exceeding 6mm
4408 1090.90	其他针叶木单板材（经纵锯，刨切或旋切的，厚度≤6mm）	4	30			17	千克	AB	Sheets of coniferous wood, sawn or chipped lengthwise, sliced or peeled, of a thickness not exceeding 6mm
	-本章子目注释二所列的热带木:								-Of tropical wood specified in Subheading Note 2 to this Chapter:
	--深红色红柳桉木、浅红色红柳桉木及巴栲红柳桉木:								--Dark Red Meranti, Light Red Meranti and Meranti Bakau:
	---饰面用单板:								---Veneer sheets:
4408.3111	----用胶合板等多层板制的	10	40			17	千克	AB	----Of laminated plywood
4408.3119	----其他	4	40			17	千克	AB	----Other
4408.3120	---制胶合板用单板	4	17			17	千克	AB	---Sheets for plywood
4408.3190	---其他	4	30			17	千克	AB	---Other
	--其他:								--Other:
	---饰面用单板:								---Veneer sheets:
4408.3911	----用胶合板等多层板制的	10	40			17	千克		----Of laminated plywood
4408 3911.10	胶合板多层板制饰面桃花心木单板（厚度≤6 毫米）	10	40			17	千克	ABFE	Veneer sheets, of Acajou d'afrique, of laminated plywood, of a thickness not exceeding 6mm
4408 3911.20	胶合板多层板制饰面拉敏木单板（厚度≤6 毫米）	10	40			17	千克	ABFE	Veneer sheets, of Ramin wood, of laminated plywood, of a thickness not exceeding 6mm
4408 3911.30	厚度≤6mm 胶合板多层板制饰面	10	40			17	千克	ABFE	Veneer sheets, of endangered tropical wood, specified

税则号列 Tariff Item	商品名称及备注	进口税率 最惠	普通	暂定	出口退税	增值税率	计量单位	监管条件	Article Description
	濒危木单板(本章子目注释二所列其他热带木)								in Subheading Note 2to this Chapter, of laminated plywood, of a thickness not exceeding 6mm
4408 3911.90	厚度≤6mm胶合板多层板制饰面热带木单板(本章子目注释二所列其他热带木)	10	40			17	千克	AB	Veneer sheets, of tropical wood specified in Subheading Note 2 to this Chapter, of laminated plywood, of a thickness not exceeding 6mm
4408.3919	----其他	4	40			17	千克		----Other
4408 3919.10	其他饰面用桃花心木单板(厚度不超过6毫米)	4	40			17	千克	ABFE	Veneer sheets, of Acajou d'afrique, of a thickness not exceeding 6mm
4408 3919.20	其他饰面用拉敏木单板(厚度不超过6毫米)	4	40			17	千克	ABFE	Veneer sheets, of Ramin wood, of a thickness not exceeding 6mm
4408 3919.30	厚度≤6mm其他濒危热带木制饰面用单板(本章子目注释二所列其他热带木)	4	40			17	千克	ABFE	Veneer sheets, of endangered tropical wood specified in Subheading Note 2 to this Chapter, of a thickness not exceeding 6mm
4408 3919.90	厚度≤6mm其他饰面用单板(本章子目注释二所列其他热带木)	4	40			17	千克	AB	Veneer sheets of tropical wood, specified in Subheading Note 2 to this Chapter, of a thickness not exceeding 6mm
4408.3920	---制胶合板用单板	4	17			17	千克		---Sheets for plywood
4408 3920.10	其他桃花心木制的胶合板用单板(厚度≤6毫米)	4	17			17	千克	ABFE	Other sheets for plywood, of acajou d'afrique, of a thickness not exceeding 6mm
4408 3920.20	其他拉敏木制的胶合板用单板(厚度≤6毫米)	4	17			17	千克	ABFE	Other sheets for plywood of Ramin wood, of a thickness not exceeding 6mm
4408 3920.30	其他濒危热带木制的胶合板用单板(本章子目注释二所列其他热带木,厚度≤6mm)	4	17			17	千克	ABFE	Other sheets for plywood, of endangered tropical wood, specified in Subheading Note 2 to this Chapter, of a thickness not exceeding 6mm
4408 3920.90	其他列名热带木制的胶合板用单板(本章子目注释二所列其他热带木,厚度≤6mm)	4	17			17	千克	AB	Other sheets for plywood, of tropical wood, specified in Subheading Note 2 to this Chapter, of a thickness not exceeding 6mm
4408.3990	---其他	4	30			17	千克		---Other
4408 3990.10	其他桃花心木制的其他单板(本章子目注释二所列其他热带木,厚度≤6mm)	4	30			17	千克	ABFE	Other sheets of other Acajou d'afrique, of tropical wood, specified in Subheading Note 2 to this Chapter, of a thickness not exceeding 6mm
4408 3990.20	其他拉敏木制的其他单板(本章子目注释二所列其他热带木,厚度≤6mm)	4	30			17	千克	ABFE	Other sheets of other Ramin wood, of tropical wood ,specified in Subheading Note 2 to this Chapter, of a thickness not exceeding 6mm
4408 3990.30	其他列名濒危热带木制的其他单板(本章子目注释二所列其他热带木,厚度≤6mm)	4	30			17	千克	ABFE	Other sheets of endangered tropical wood, specified in Subheading Note 2 to this Chapter, of a thickness not exceeding 6mm
4408 3990.90	其他列名的热带木制的其他单板(本章子目注释二所列其他热带木,厚度≤6mm)	4	30			17	千克	AB	Other sheets of tropical wood ,specified in Subheading Note 1 to this Chapter, of a thickness not exceeding 6mm
	-其他:								-Other:
	---饰面用单板:								---Veneer sheets:
4408.9011	----用胶合板等多层板制的	4	40			17	千克		----Of laminated plywood
4408 9011.10	胶合板多层板制饰面濒危木单板(厚度≤6毫米)	4	40			17	千克	ABFE	Veneer sheets of endangered wood, of laminated plywood , of a thickness not exceeding 6mm
4408 9011.90	胶合板多层板制饰面其他木单板(厚度≤6毫米,针叶木、热带木除外)	4	40			17	千克	AB	Veneer sheets of other wood, of laminated plywood, of a thickness not exceeding 6mm (other than coniferous or tropical wood)
4408.9012 暂	----温带非针叶木制	3	40	1		17	千克		----Of temperate non-coniferous wood
4408 9012.10 暂	温带濒危非针叶木制饰面用木单板(厚度≤6毫米,针叶木、热带木除外)	3	40	1		17	千克	ABFE	Veneer sheets of endangered temperate non-coniferous wood, of a thickness not exceeding 6mm (other than coniferous or tropical wood)
4408 9012.90 暂	其他温带非针叶木制饰面用木	3	40	1		17	千克	AB	Veneer sheets of temperate non-coniferous wood, of

税则号列 Tariff Item	商品名称及备注	进口税率 最惠	普通	暂定	出口退税	增值税率	计量单位	监管条件	Article Description
	单板（厚度≤6毫米，针叶木、热带木除外）								a thickness not exceeding 6mm（other than coniferous or tropical wood）
4408.9013	----竹制	4	40			17	千克		----Of bamboo
4408 9013.10	濒危竹制饰面用单板(厚度≤6mm)	4	40			17	千克	ABE	Veneer sheets of endangered bamboo(thinckness≤6mm)
4408 9013.90	其他竹制饰面用单板(厚度≤6mm)	4	40			17	千克	AB	Veneer sheets of other bamboo(thinckness≤6mm)
4408.9019	----其他	3	40			17	千克		----Other
4408 9019.11[暂]	家具饰面用濒危木单板（厚度≤6毫米）	3	40	1		17	千克	ABFE	Veneer sheets of endangered wood, for furniture, of a thickness not exceeding 6mm
4408 9019.19[暂]	其他家具饰面用单板（厚度≤6毫米）	3	40	1		17	千克	AB	Other veneer sheets for furniture, of a thickness not exceeding 6mm
4408 9019.91	其他饰面用濒危木单板（厚度≤6毫米）	3	40			17	千克	ABFE	Other Veneer sheets of endangered wood, of a thickness not exceeding 6mm
4408 9019.99	其他饰面用单板(厚度≤6毫米)	3	40			17	千克	AB	Other Veneer sheets of wood, of a thickness not exceeding 6mm
	---制胶合板用单板:								---Sheets for plywood:
4408.9021	----温带非针叶木制	3	17			17	千克		----Of temperate non-coniferous wood
4408 9021.10	温带濒危非针叶木制胶合板用单板（厚度≤6毫米）	3	17			17	千克	ABFE	Sheets for plywood of endangered temperate non-coniferous wood of a thickness not exceeding 6mm
4408 9021.90	其他温带非针叶木制胶合板用单板（厚度≤6毫米）	3	17			17	千克	AB	Other sheets for plywood of temperate non-coniferous wood, of a thickness not exceeding 6mm
4408.9029	----其他	3	17			17	千克		----Other
4408 9029.11[暂]	其他濒危木制胶合板用旋切单板（厚度≤6毫米）	3	17	1		17	千克	ABFE	Other sheets for plywood of endangered wood, peeled, of a thickness not exceeding 6mm
4408 9029.19	其他濒危木制胶合板用其他单板（厚度≤6毫米，旋切单板除外）	3	17			17	千克	ABFE	Other sheets for plywood of endangered wood , of a thickness not exceeding 6mm, other than peeled sheets
4408 9029.91[暂]	其他木制胶合板用旋切单板（厚度≤6毫米）	3	17	1		17	千克	AB	Other sheets for plywood of wood, peeled, of a thickness not exceeding 6mm
4408 9029.99	其他木制胶合板用其他单板（厚度≤6毫米，旋切单板除外）	3	17			17	千克	AB	Other sheets foe plywood of wood thiekness of a exceeding 6mm, other than peeled
	---其他:								---Other:
4408.9091	----温带非针叶木制	3	30			17	千克		----Of temperate non-coniferous wood
4408 9091.10	温带濒危非针叶木制其他单板材（经纵锯，刨切或旋切的，厚度≤6毫米）	3	30			17	千克	ABFE	Sheets of temperate non-coniferous wood, sawn or chipped lengthwise, sliced or peeled, of a thickness not exceeding 6mm
4408 9091.90	温带非针叶木制其他单板材（经纵锯,刨切或旋切的，厚度≤6毫米）	3	30			17	千克	AB	Other sheets of temperate non-coniferous wood, sawn or chipped lengthwise, sliced or peeled, of a thickness not exceeding 6mm
4408.9099	----其他	3	30			17	千克		----Other
4408 9099.10	其他濒危木制的其他单板材（经纵锯，刨切或旋切的，厚度≤6毫米）	3	30			17	千克	ABFE	Other sheets of endangered wood, sawn or chipped lengthwise, sliced or peeled, of a thickness not exceeding 6mm
4408 9099.90	其他木材,但针叶木热带木除外（经纵锯，刨切或旋切的，厚度≤6毫米）	3	30			17	千克	AB	Other wood, sawn or chipped lengthwise, sliced or peeled(other than coniferous and tropical wood), of a thickness not exceeding 6mm
44.09	**任何一边端或面制成连续形状（舌榫、槽榫、半槽榫、斜角、V形接头、珠榫、缘饰、刨圆及类似形状）的木材（包括未装拼的拼花地板用板条及缘板），不论是否刨平、砂光或端部接合**								**Wood（including strips and friezes for parquet flooring, not assembled）continuously shaped（tongues, grooved, rebated, chamfered, V-jointed, beaded, moulded, rounded or the like）along any of its “edges, ends or faces, whether or not planed, sanded or end-jointed”:**

税则号列 Tariff Item	商品名称及备注	进口税率 最惠	普通	暂定	出口退税	增值税率	计量单位	监管条件	Article Description
	-针叶木:								-Coniferous:
4409.1010	---地板条(块)	7.5	50			17	千克		---Floor board strips
4409 1010.10	一边或面制成连续形状的濒危针叶木制地板条、块(包括未装拼的拼花地板用板条及缘板)	7.5	50			17	千克	ABFE	Floor board strips of endangered coniferous wood (including strips and friezes for parquet flooring, not assembled) continuously shaped along any of its edges or faces
4409 1010.90	一边或面制成连续形状的其他针叶木地板条、块(包括未装拼的拼花地板用板条及缘板)	7.5	50			17	千克	AB	Floor board strips of other coniferous wood (including strips and friezes for parquet flooring, not assembled) continuously shaped along any of its edges or faces
4409.1090	---其他	7.5	50			17	千克		---Other
4409 1090.10	一边或面制成连续形状濒危针叶木材	7.5	50			17	千克	ABFE	Endangered coniferous wood, continuously shaped along any of its edges or faces
4409 1090.90	其他一边或面制成连续形状的针叶木材	7.5	50			17	千克	AB	Coniferous wood, continuously shaped along any of its edges or faces
	-非针叶木:								-Non-coniferous:
	--竹的:								--Of bamboo:
4409.2110	---地板条(块)	4	50			17	千克		---Floor board strips
4409 2110.10	一边或面制成连续形状的濒危竹地板条(块)(包括未装拼的拼花竹地板用板条及缘板)	4	50			17	千克	ABE	Floor board strips of endangered bamboo(including strips and friezes for parquet flooring, not assembled)continuously shaped along any of its edges or faces
4409 2110.90	一边或面制成连续形状的竹地板条(块)(包括未装拼的拼花竹地板用板条及缘板)	4	50		13	17	千克	AB	Floor board strips of bamboo(including strips and friezes for parquet flooring, not assembled) continuously shaped along any of its edges or faces
4409.2190	---其他	4	50			17	千克		---Other
4409 2190.10	一边或面制成连续形状的其他濒危竹材	4	50			17	千克	ABE	Other endangered bamboo continuously shaped along any of its edges or faces
4409 2190.90	一边或面制成连续形状的其他竹材	4	50		13	17	千克	AB	Other bamboo, continuously shaped along any of its edges or faces
	--其他:								--Other:
4409.2910	---地板条(块)	4	50			17	千克		---Floor board strips
4409 2910.10	一边或面制成连续形状的拉敏木地板条、块(包括未装拼的拉敏木拼花地板用板条及缘板)	4	50			17	千克	ABFE	Floor board strips of ramin wood(including strips and friezes for parquet flooring, not assembled) continuously shaped along any of its edges or faces
4409 2910.20	一边或面制成连续形状的桃花心木地板条、块(包括未装拼的桃花心木拼花地板用板条及缘板)	4	50			17	千克	ABFE	Floor board strips of acajou wood(including strips and friezes for parquet flooring, not assembled) continuously shaped along any of its edges or faces
4409 2910.30	一边或面制成连续形状的其他濒危木地板条、块(包括未装拼的其他濒危木拼花地板用板条及缘板)	4	50			17	千克	ABFE	Floor board strips of other endangered wood(including strips and friezes for parquet flooring, not assembled)continuously shaped along any of its edges or faces
4409 2910.90	一边或面制成连续形状的其他非针叶木地板条、块(包括未装拼的其他非针叶木拼花地板用板条及缘板)	4	50			17	千克	AB	Floor board strips of other non-coniferous wood(including strips and friezes for parquet flooring, not assembled)continuously shaped along any of its edges or faces
4409.2990	---其他	4	50			17	千克		---Other
4409 2990.10	一边或面制成连续形状的拉敏木	4	50			17	千克	ABFE	Ramin wood, continuously shaped along any of its edges or faces
4409 2990.20	一边或面制成连续形状的桃花心木	4	50			17	千克	ABFE	Acajou wood, continuously shaped along any of its edges or faces
4409 2990.30	一边或面制成连续形状的其他濒危木	4	50			17	千克	ABFE	Other endangered wood continuously shaped along any of its edges or faces
4409 2990.90	一边或面制成连续形状的其他非针叶木材	4	50			17	千克	AB	Other non-coniferous wood, continuously shaped along any of its edges or faces
44.10	**碎料板、定向刨花板(OSB)及类似板(例如,华夫板),木或其他木质材料制,不论是否用树**								**Particle board, oriented strand board (OSB) and similar board (for example, waferboard) of wood or other ligneous materials, whether or not**

税则号列 Tariff Item	商品名称及备注	进口税率 最惠	进口税率 普通	进口税率 暂定	出口退税	增值税率	计量单位	监管条件	Article Description
	脂或其他有机黏合剂黏合:								agglomerated with resins or other organic binding substances:
	-木制:								-Of wood:
4410.1100	--碎料板	4	40		9	17	千克	AB	--Particle board
4410.1200	--定向刨花板	4	40		9	17	千克	AB	--Oriented standard board（OSB）
4410.1900	--其他	4	40		9	17	千克	AB	--Other
	-其他:								-Other:
	---碎料板:								---Particle board:
4410.9011	----麦稻秸秆制	7.5	40		9	17	千克	AB	----Of wheat or rice straw
4410.9019	----其他	7.5	40		9	17	千克	AB	----Other
4410.9090	---其他	7.5	40		9	17	千克	AB	---Other
44.11	**木纤维板或其他木质材料纤维板，不论是否用树脂或其他有机黏合剂黏合:**								**Fibreboard of wood or other ligneous materials, whether or not bonded with resins or other organic substances:**
	-中密度纤维板:								-Medium density fibreboard（MDF）:
	--厚度不超过5毫米:								--Of a thickness not exceeding 5mm:
	---密度超过每立方厘米0.8克:								---Of a density exceeding 0.8g/cm^3:
4411.1211	----未经机械加工或盖面的	4	40		9	17	千克	AB	----Not mechanically worked or surface covered
4411.1219	----其他	7.5	40		9	17	千克	AB	----Other
	---密度超过每立方厘米0.5克，但未超过每立方厘米0.8克:								---Of a density exceeding 0.5g/cm^3 but not exceeding 0.8g/cm^3:
4411.1221	----辐射松制的	4	40		9	17	千克	AB	----Of rodiata pine
4411.1229	----其他	4	40		9	17	千克	AB	----Other
	---其他:								---Other:
4411.1291	----未经机械加工或盖面的	7.5	40		9	17	千克	AB	----Not mechanically worked or surface covered
4411.1299	----其他	4	40		9	17	千克	AB	----Other
	--厚度超过5毫米，但未超过9毫米:								--Of a thickness exceeding 5mm but not exceeding 9mm:
	---密度超过每立方厘米0.8克:								---Of a density exceeding 0.8g/cm^3:
4411.1311	----未经机械加工或盖面的	4	40		9	17	千克	AB	----Not mechanically worked or surface covered
4411.1319	----其他	7.5	40		9	17	千克	AB	----Other
	---密度超过每立方厘米0.5克，但未超过每立方厘米0.8克:								---Of a density exceeding 0.5g/cm^3 but not exceeding 0.8g/cm^3:
4411.1321	----辐射松制的	4	40		9	17	千克	AB	----Of radiata pine
4411.1329	----其他	4	40		9	17	千克	AB	----Other
	---其他:								---Other:
4411.1391	----未经机械加工或盖面的	7.5	40		9	17	千克	AB	----Not mechanically worked or suface covered
4411.1399	----其他	4	40		9	17	千克	AB	----Other
	---厚度超过9毫米:								--Of a thickness exceeding 9 mm:
	---密度超过每立方厘米0.8克:								---Of a density exceeding 0.8g/cm^3:
4411.1411	----未经机械加工或盖面的	4	40		9	17	千克	AB	----Not mechanically worked or surface covered
4411.1419	----其他	7.5	40		9	17	千克	AB	----Other
	---密度超过每立方厘米0.5克，但未超过每立方厘米0.8克:								---Of a density exceeding 0.5g/cm^3 but not exceeding 0.8g/cm^3:
4411.1421	----辐射松制的	4	40		9	17	千克	AB	----Of radiata pine
4411.1429	----其他	4	40		9	17	千克	AB	----Other
	---其他:								---Other:
4411.1491	----未经机械加工或盖面的	7.5	40		9	17	千克	AB	----Not mechanically worked or surface covered
4411.1499	----其他	4	40		9	17	千克	AB	----Other
	-其他:								-Other:
	--密度超过每立方厘米0.8克:								--Of a density exceeding 0.8g/cm^3:

税则号列 Tariff Item	商品名称及备注	进口税率 最惠	普通	暂定	出口退税	增值税率	计量单位	监管条件	Article Description
4411.9210	---未经机械加工或盖面的	4	40		9	17	千克	AB	---Not mechanically worked or surface covered
4411.9290	---其他	7.5	40		9	17	千克	AB	---Other
	--密度超过每立方厘米 0.5 克，但未超过每立方厘 0.8 克:								--Of a density exceeding 0.5g/cm^3 but not exceeding 0.8g/cm^3:
4411.9310	---辐射松制的	4	40		9	17	千克	AB	---Of radiate pine
4411.9390	---其他	4	40		9	17	千克	AB	---Other
	--密度未超过每立方厘米 0.5 克:								--Of a density not exceeding 0.5g/cm^3:
4411.9410	---密度超过每立方厘米 0.35 克，但未超过每立方厘米 0.5 克	7.5	40		9	17	千克	AB	---Of a density exceeding 0.35g/cm^3 but not exceeding 0.5g/cm^3
	---密度未超过每立方厘米 0.35 克:								---Of a density not exceeding 0.35g/cm^3:
4411.9421	----未经机械加工或盖面的	7.5	40		9	17	千克	AB	----Not mechanically worked or surface covered
4411.9429	----其他	4	40		9	17	千克	AB	----Other
44.12	**胶合板、单板饰面板及类似的多层板:**								**Plywood, veneered panels and similar laminated wood:**
	-竹制的:								-Of bamboo:
	---仅由薄板制的胶合板，每层厚度不超过 6 毫米:								---Plywood consisting solely of sheets of wood, each ply not exceeding 6mm thickness:
4412.1011	----至少有一表层是本章子目注释二所列的热带木	12	30			17	千克/立方米		----With at least one outer ply of tropical wood specified in Subheading Note 2 to this Chapter
4412 1011.11	至少有一表层为濒危热带木薄板制濒危竹胶合板(每层厚度≤6mm,热带木指本章子目注释二所列木材)	12	30			17	千克/立方米	ABFE	With at least one outer ply of endangered tropical wood, plywood consisting solely of sheets of endangered bamboo, each ply not exceeding 6mm thickness, specified in Subheading Note 2 to this Chapter
4412 1011.19	至少有一表层为濒危热带木薄板制其他竹胶合板(每层厚度≤6mm，热带木指本章子目注释二所列木材)	12	30			17	千克/立方米	ABFE	With at least one outer ply of endangered tropical wood, plywood consisting solely of sheets of other bamboo, each ply not exceeding 6mm thickness, specified in Subheading Note 2 to this Chapter
4412 1011.91	至少有一表层是其他热带木薄板制濒危竹胶合板(每层厚度≤6mm,热带木指本章子目注释二所列木材)	12	30			17	千克/立方米	ABEF	With at least one outer ply of other tropical wood, specified in Subheading Note 2 to this Chapter, plywood consisting solely of sheets of endangered bamboo, each ply not exceeding 6 mm thickness
4412 1011.99	至少有一表层是其他热带木薄板制其他竹胶合板(每层厚度≤6mm,热带木指本章子目注释二所列木材)	12	30		9	17	千克/立方米	AB	With at least one outer ply of other tropical wood, specified in subheading Note 2 to this Chapter, plywood consisting solely of sheets of other bamboo, each ply not exceeding 6 mm thickness
4412.1019	----其他	4	30			17	千克/立方米		----Other
4412 1019.11	至少有一表层为濒危非针叶木薄板胶合板(至少有一表层为温带非针叶木制，每层厚度≤6 毫米)	4	30			17	千克/立方米	ABFE	With at least one outer ply of temperate non-coniferous wood, plywood consisting solely of sheets of endangered non-coniferous wood, each ply not exceeding 6 mm thickness
4412 1019.19	其他至少有一表层为非针叶木薄板胶合板(至少有一表层为温带非针叶木制，每层厚度≤6 毫米)	4	30		9	17	千克/立方米	AB	With at least one outer ply of temperate non-coniferous wood, plywood consisting solely of sheets of non-coniferous wood, each ply not exceeding 6mm thickness
4412 1019.21	濒危竹地板层叠胶合而成的多层板(每层厚度≤6 毫米)	4	30			17	千克/立方米	ABE	Plywood with multi-plies of endangered bamboo, each ply not exceeding 6mm thickness
4412 1019.29	其他竹地板层叠胶合而成的多层板(每层厚度≤6 毫米)	4	30		13	17	千克/立方米	AB	Plywood with multi-plies of other bamboo, each ply not exceeding 6mm thickness
4412 1019.91	其他濒危竹胶合板(每层厚度≤6 毫米)	4	30			17	千克/立方米	ABE	Plywood of other endangered bamboo, each ply not exceeding 6mm thickness

税则号列 Tariff Item	商品名称及备注	进口税率 最惠	普通	暂定	出口退税	增值税率	计量单位	监管条件	Article Description
4412 1019.99	其他竹胶合板（每层厚度≤6毫米）	4	30		13	17	千克/立方米	AB	Plywood of other bamboo, each ply not exceeding 6mm thickness
4412.1020	---其他，至少有一表层是非针叶木	10	30			17	千克/立方米		---Other, with at least one outer ply of non-coniferrous wood
4412 1020.11	至少有一表层是濒危非针叶木的濒危竹制多层板（每层厚度≤6毫米）	10	30			17	千克/立方米	ABFE	Laminated wood of endangerd bamboo, with at least one outer ply of endangered non-coniferous wood, each ply not exceeding 6mm thickness
4412 1020.19	至少有一表层是其他非针叶木的其他濒危竹制多层板（每层厚度≤6毫米）	10	30			17	千克/立方米	ABEF	Laminated wood of other endangerd bamboo, with at least one outer ply of other non-coniferous wood, each ply not exceeding 6mm thickness
4412 1020.91	至少有一表层是濒危非针叶木的其他竹制多层板（每层厚度≤6毫米）	10	30			17	千克/立方米	ABEF	Laminated wood of other bamboo, with at least one outer ply of endangered non-coniferous wood, each ply not exceeding 6mm thickness
4412 1020.99	至少有一表层是其他非针叶木的其他竹制多层板（每层厚度≤6毫米）	10	30		9	17	千克/立方米	AB	Laminated wood of other bamboo, with at least one outer ply of other non-coniferous wood, each ply not exceeding 6mm thickness
	---其他:								---Other:
4412.1091	----至少有一层是本章子目注释二所列的热带木	8	30			17	千克/立方米		----With at least one ply of tropical wood specified in Subheading Note 2 to this Chapter
4412 1091.10	至少有一层是热带木的濒危竹制多层板(热带木指本章子目注释二所列木材)	8	30			17	千克/立方米	ABEF	Laminated wood of other endangerd bamboo, with at least one outer ply of tropical wood（specified in Subheading Note 2 to this Chapter）
4412 1091.90	至少有一层是热带木的其他竹制多层板(热带木指本章子目注释二所列木材)	8	30		9	17	千克/立方米	AB	Laminated wood of other bamboo, with at least one outer ply of tropical wood（specified in Subheading Note 2 to this Chapter）
4412.1092	----至少含有一层木碎料板	10	30			17	千克/立方米		----Containing at least one layer of particle board
4412 1092.10	至少含有一层木碎料板的濒危竹制多层板	10	30			17	千克/立方米	ABEF	Laminated wood of endangered bamboo, containing at least one layer of particle board
4412 1092.90	至少含有一层木碎料板的其他竹制多层板	10	30		9	17	千克/立方米	AB	Laminated wood of other bamboo, containing at least one layer of particle board
4412.1099	----其他	4	30			17	千克/立方米		----Other
4412 1099.10	其他濒危竹制多层板	4	30			17	千克/立方米	ABE	Other laminated wood of endangered bamboo
4412 1099.90	其他竹制多层板	4	30		13	17	千克/立方米	AB	Other laminated wood of bamboo
	-其他仅由薄木板制的胶合板（竹制除外），每层厚度不超过6毫米:								-Other plywood consisting solely of sheets of wood (other than bamboo), each ply not exceeding 6mm thickness:
4412.3100	--至少有一表层是本章子目注释二所列的热带木	12	30			17	千克/立方米		--With at least one outer ply of tropical wood specified in Subheading Note 2 to this Chapter
4412 3100.10	至少有一表层为桃花心木薄板制胶合板（每层厚度≤6毫米）	12	30		5	17	千克/立方米	ABFE	Plywood, with at least one outer ply of Acajou d'affrique, each ply not exceeding 6mm thickness
4412 3100.20	至少有一表层为拉敏木薄板制胶合板（每层厚度≤6mm）	12	30		5	17	千克/立方米	ABFE	Plywood, with at least one outer ply of Ramin wood, each ply not exceeding 6mm thickness
4412 3100.30	一表层为濒危热带木薄板制胶合板(每层厚度≤6mm，热带木指本章子目注释二所列木材)	12	30			17	千克/立方米	ABFE	Plywood, with at least one outer ply of tropical wood, each ply not exceeding 6mm thickness, specified in Subheading Note 2 to this Chapter
4412 3100.90	至少有一表层是其他热带木制的胶合板(每层厚度≤6mm,竹制除外,热带木指本章子目注释二所列木材)	12	30		9	17	千克/立方米	AB	Plywood, with at least one outer ply of other tropical wood, specified in subheading Note 2 to this Chapter, each ply not exceeding 6mm thickness

税则号列 Tariff Item	商品名称及备注	进口税率 最惠	普通	暂定	出口退税	增值税率	计量单位	监管条件	Article Description
	一其他，至少有一表层是非针叶木:								--Other, with at least one outer ply of non-coniferous wood:
4412.3210	---至少有一表层是温带非针叶木	4	30			17	千克/立方米		---With at least one outer ply of temperate non-coniferous wood
4412 3210.10	至少有一表层是濒危温带非针叶木薄板制胶合板（每层厚度≤6毫米，竹制除外）	4	30			17	千克/立方米	ABFE	Plywood, with at least one outer ply of endangered temperate non-coniferous wood, each ply not exceeding 6mm thickness (other than of bamboo)
4412 3210.90	至少有一表层是其他温带非针叶木薄板制胶合板（每层厚度≤6毫米，竹制除外）	4	30		9	17	千克/立方米	AB	Plywood, with at least one outer ply of other temperate non-coniferous wood, each ply not exceeding 6mm thickness (other than of bamboo)
4412.3290	---其他	4	30			17	千克/立方米		---Other
4412 3290.10	至少有一表层是濒危其他非针叶胶合板（每层厚度≤6毫米，竹制除外）	4	30			17	千克/立方米	ABEF	Plywood, with at least one outer ply of other endangered non-coniferous wood, each ply not exceeding 6mm thickness (other than of bamboo)
4412 3290.90	至少有一表层是其他非针叶胶合板（每层厚度≤6毫米，竹制除外）	4	30		9	17	千克/立方米	AB	Plywood, with at least one outer ply of other non-coniferous wood, each ply not exceeding 6mm thickness (other than of bamboo)
4412.3900	--其他	4	30			17	千克/立方米		--Other
4412 3900.10	其他濒危薄板制胶合板（每层厚度≤6毫米，竹制除外）	4	30			17	千克/立方米	ABFE	Plywood consisting solely of sheets of endangered wood,each ply not exceeding 6mm thickness (other than of bamboo)
4412 3900.90	其他薄板制胶合板（每层厚度≤6毫米，竹制除外）	4	30		9	17	千克/立方米	AB	Plywood consisting solely of sheets of wood, each ply notexceeding 6mm thickness (other than of bamboo)
	-其他:								--Other:
	--木块芯胶合板，侧板条芯胶合板及板条芯胶合板:								--Blockboard, laminboard and battenboard:
4412.9410	---至少有一表层是非针叶木	10	30			17	千克/立方米		---With at least one outer ply of non-coniferous wood
4412 9410.10	至少有一表层是桃花心木的木块芯胶合板等（还包括侧板条芯胶合板及板条芯胶合板）	10	30		5	17	千克/立方米	ABFE	Blockboard, laminboard and battenboard, with at least one outer ply of acajou board
4412 9410.20	至少有一表层是拉敏木的木块芯胶合板等（还包括侧板条芯胶合板及板条芯胶合板）	10	30		5	17	千克/立方米	ABFE	Blockboard, laminboard and battenboard, with at least one outer ply of Ramin wood
4412 9410.30	至少有一表层是濒危热带木的木块芯胶合板等（还包括侧板条芯胶合板及板条芯胶合板）	10	30			17	千克/立方米	ABFE	Blockboard, laminboard and battenboard, with at least one outer ply of endangered tropical wood
4412 9410.40	至少有一表层是濒危非针叶木的木块芯胶合板等（还包括侧板条芯胶合板及板条芯胶合板）	10	30			17	千克/立方米	ABFE	Blockboard, laminboard and battenboard, with at least one outer ply of endangered non-coniferous wood
4412 9410.90	至少有一表层是非针叶木的木块芯胶合板等（还包括侧板条芯胶合板及板条芯胶合板）	10	30		9	17	千克/立方米	AB	Blockboard, laminboard and battenboard, with at least one outer ply of non-coniferous wood
	---其他:								---Other：
4412.9491	----至少有一层是本章子目注释二所列的热带木	8	30			17	千克/立方米		----With at least one ply of tropical wood specified in Subheading Note 2 to this Chapter
4412 9491.10	至少有一层是濒危热带木的针叶木面木块芯胶合板等(还包括侧板条芯胶合板及板条芯胶合板，热带木指本章子目注释二所列木材)	8	30			17	千克/立方米	ABFE	Blockboard, laminboard and battenboard, with at least one outer ply of endangered tropical coniferous wood, specified in Subheading Note 2 to this Chapter
4412 9491.90	至少有一层是热带木的针叶木面木块芯胶合板等(还包括侧板条	8	30		9	17	千克/立方米	AB	Blockboard, laminboard and battenboard, with at least one outer ply of tropical coniferous wood,

税则号列 Tariff Item	商品名称及备注	进口税率 最惠	普通	暂定	出口退税	增值税率	计量单位	监管条件	Article Description
	芯胶合板及板条芯胶合板，热带木指本章子目注释二所列木材)								specified in Subheading Note2 to this Chapter
4412.9492	----其他，至少含有一层木碎料板	10	30			17	千克/立方米		----Other, containing at least one layer of particle board
4412 9492.10	至少含有一层木碎料板的濒危针叶木面木块芯胶合板等(还包括侧板条芯胶合板及板条芯胶合板)	10	30			17	千克/立方米	ABFE	Blockboard, laminboard and battenboard, with outer ply of endangered coniferous wood, containing at least one layer of particle board
4412 9492.90	至少含有一层木碎料板的针叶木面木块芯胶合板等(还包括侧板条芯胶合板及板条芯胶合板)	10	30		9	17	千克/立方米	AB	Blockboard, laminboard and battenboard, with outer ply of coniferous wood, containing at least one layer of particle board
4412.9499	----其他	4	30			17	千克/立方米		----Other
4412 9499.10	其他濒危针叶木面木块芯胶合板等(还包括侧板条芯胶合板及板条芯胶合板)	4	30			17	千克/立方米	ABEF	Other blockboard, including laminboard and battenboard, with outer ply of endangered coniferous wood
4412 9499.90	其他针叶木面木块芯胶合板等(还包括侧板条芯胶合板及板条芯胶合板)	4	30		9	17	千克/立方米	AB	Other blockboard, including laminboard and battenboard, with outer ply of coniferous wood
	--其他:								--Other:
4412.9910	---至少有一表层是非针叶木	10	30			17	千克/立方米		---With at least one outer ply of non-coniferous wood
4412 9910.10	至少有一表层是桃花心木的多层板	10	30		0/5	17	千克/立方米	ABFE	Laminated wood, with at least one outer ply of Acajou d'afrique
4412 9910.20	至少有一表层是拉敏木的多层板	10	30		0/5	17	千克/立方米	ABFE	Laminated wood, with at least one outer ply of Ramin wood
4412 9910.30	至少有一表层是濒危热带木的多层板	10	30			17	千克/立方米	ABFE	Laminated wood, with at least one outer ply of endangered tropical wood
4412 9910.40	其他至少有一表层是濒危非针叶木的多层板	10	30			17	千克/立方米	ABFE	Other laminated wood, at least one outer ply of endangered non-coniferous wood
4412 9910.90	其他至少有一表层是非针叶木的多层板	10	30		9	17	千克/立方米	AB	Other laminated wood, with at least one outer ply of non-coniferous wood
	---其他:								---Other:
4412.9991	----至少有一层是本章子目注释二所列的热带木	8	30			17	千克/立方米		----With at least one ply of tropical wood specified in Subheading Note 2 to this Chapter
4412 9991.10	其他至少有一层是濒危热带木的针叶木面多层板(热带木指本章子目注释二所列木材)	8	30			17	千克/立方米	ABFE	Other laminated wood, with at least one outer ply of endangered tropical coniferous wood, specified in Sunbheading Note 2 to this Chapter
4412 9991.90	其他至少有一层是热带木的针叶木面多层板(热带木指本章子目注释二所列木材)	8	30		9	17	千克/立方米	AB	Other laminated wood, with at least one outer ply of tropical coniferous wood ,specified in Sunbheading Note 2 to this Chapter
4412.9992	----其他，至少含有一层木碎料板	10	30			17	千克/立方米		----Other, containing at least one layer of particle board
4412 9992.10	其他至少含有一层木碎料板的濒危针叶木面多层板	10	30			17	千克/立方米	ABFE	Laminated wood, with one outer ply of endangered coniferous wood, containing at least one layer of particle board
4412 9992.90	其他至少含有一层木碎料板的针叶木面多层板	10	30		9	17	千克/立方米	AB	Laminated wood, with one outer ply of coniferous wood, containing at least one layer of particle board
4412.9999	----其他	4	30			17	千克/立方米		----Other
4412 9999.10	其他濒危针叶木面多层板	4	30			17	千克/立方米	ABFE	Laminated wood, with one outer ply of endangered coniferous wood
4412 9999.90	其他针叶木面多层板	4	30		9	17	千克/立方米	AB	Laminated wood, with one outer ply of coniferous wood
44.13	强化木，成块、板、条或异型的:								**Densified wood, in blocks, plates, strips or profile shapes:**

税则号列 Tariff Item	商品名称及备注	进口税率 最惠	普通	暂定	出口退税	增值税率	计量单位	监管条件	Article Description
4413.0000	强化木，成块、板、条或异型的	6	20		9	17	千克	AB	Densified wood, in blocks, plates, strips or profile shapes
44.14	**木制的画框、相框、镜框及类似品:**								**Wooden frames for paintings, photographs, mirrors or similar objects:**
4414.0010	---辐射松制的	20	100		5	17	千克	AB	---Of radiate pine
4414.0090	---其他	20	100			17	千克		---Other
4414 0090.10	拉敏木制画框,相框,镜框及类似品	20	100		5	17	千克	ABFE	Ramin wood frames for paintings , photographs , mirrors or similar objects
4414 0090.20	濒危木制画框,相框,镜框及类似品	20	100			17	千克	ABFE	Endangered wood frames for paintings , photographs , mirrors or similar objects
4414 0090.90	其他木制的画框,相框,镜框及类似品	20	100		13	17	千克	AB	Other wooden frames for paintings , photographs , mirrors or similar objects
44.15	**包装木箱、木盒、板条箱、圆桶及类似的包装容器；木制电缆卷筒；木托板、箱形托盘及其他装载用木板；木制的托盘护框:**								**Packing cases, boxes, crates, drums and similar packings, of wood; cabledrums of wood; pallets, box pallets and other load boards, of wood; pallet collars of wood:**
4415.1000	-箱、盒、板条箱、圆桶及类似的包装容器；电缆卷筒	7.5	80			17	千克/件		-Cases, boxes,crates, drums and similar packing; cabledrums
4415 1000.10	拉敏木制木箱及类似包装容器（电缆卷筒）	7.5	80		5	17	千克/件	ABFE	Cases and similar packing, of Ramin wood (*gonystylus. spp.*）;cabledrums
4415 1000.20	濒危木制木箱及类似包装容器（电缆卷筒）	7.5	80			17	千克/件	ABFE	Cases and similar packing, of endangered wood;cabledrums
4415 1000.90	木箱及类似的包装容器,电缆卷筒	7.5	80		9	17	千克/件	AB	Cases and similar packing, of wood; cabledrums
	-木托板、箱形托盘及其他装载用木板；木制的托盘护框:								-Pallets, box pallets and other load boards; pallet collars:
4415.2010	---辐射松制的	7.5	80		5	17	千克/件	AB	---Of radiatat pine
4415.2090	---其他	7.5	80			17	千克/件		---Other
4415 2090.10	拉敏木托板、箱形托盘及装载木板（包括拉敏木制托盘护框）	7.5	80		5	17	千克/件	ABFE	Pallets, box pallets and other load boards, including pallet collars, of Ramin wood
4415 2090.20	濒危木托板、箱形托盘及装载木板（包括濒危木制托盘护框）	7.5	80			17	千克/件	ABFE	Pallets, box pallets and other load boards, including pallet collars, of endangered wood
4415 2090.90	其他木制托板、箱形托盘及其他装载木板（包括其他木制托盘护框）	7.5	80		9	17	千克/件	AB	Pallets, box pallets and other load boards, including pallet collars, of other wood
44.16	**木制大桶、琵琶桶、盆和其他木制箍桶及其零件，包括桶板:**								**Casks, barrels, vats, tubs and other coopers' products and parts thereof, of wood,including staves:**
4416.0010	---辐射松制的	16	80			17	千克	AB	---Of radiatat pine
4416.0090	---其他	16	80			17	千克		---Other
4416 0090.10	拉敏木制大桶、琵琶桶、盆和其他箍桶及其零件(包括拉敏木制桶板)	16	80			17	千克	ABFE	Casks, barrels, vats, tubs and other coopers' products and parts thereof, including staves ,of Ramin wood
4416 0090.20	濒危木制大桶、琵琶桶、盆和其他箍桶及其零件(包括濒危木制桶板)	16	80			17	千克	ABFE	Casks, barrels, vats, tubs and other coopers' products and parts thereof, including staves ,of endangered wood
4416 0090.90	其他木制大桶、琵琶桶、盆和其他箍桶及其零件(包括其他木制桶板)	16	80			17	千克	AB	Casks, barrels, vats, tubs and other coopers' products and parts thereof, including staves ,of other wood
44.17	**木制的工具、工具支架、工具柄、扫帚及刷子的身及柄；木制鞋靴楦及楦头:**								**Tools, tool bodies, tool handles, broom or brush bodies and handles, of wood; boot or shoe lasts and trees, of wood:**

税则号列 Tariff Item	商品名称及备注	进口税率			出口退税	增值税率	计量单位	监管条件	Article Description
		最惠	普通	暂定					
4417.0010	---辐射松制的	16	80			17	千克	AB	---Of radiatat pine
4417.0090	---其他	16	80			17	千克		---Other
4417 0090.10	拉敏木制工具、工具支架、工具柄、扫帚及刷子的身及柄（包括拉敏木制鞋靴楦及楦头）	16	80			17	千克	ABFE	Tools, tool bodies, tool handles, broom or brush bodies and handles, and boot or shoe lasts and trees, of ramin wood
4417 0090.20	濒危木制工具、工具支架、工具柄、扫帚及刷子的身及柄（包括濒危木制鞋靴楦及楦头）	16	80			17	千克	ABFE	Tools, tool bodies, tool handles, broom or brush bodies and handles, and boot or shoe lasts and trees, of endangered wood
4417 0090.90	其他木制工具、工具支架、工具柄、扫帚及刷子的身及柄（包括其他木制鞋靴楦及楦头）	16	80			17	千克	AB	Tools, tool bodies, tool handles, broom or brush bodies and handles, and boot or shoe lasts and trees, of other wood
44.18	**建筑用木工制品，包括蜂窝结构木镶板、已装拼的地板、木瓦及盖屋板：**								**Builders' joinery and carpentry of wood, including cellular wood panels, assembled flooring panels, shingles and shakes:**
	-窗、法兰西式（落地）窗及其框架:								-Windows, French-windows and their frames:
4418.1010	---辐射松制的	4	70		5	17	千克	AB	---Of radiatat pine
4418.1090	---其他	4	70			17	千克		---Other
4418 1090.10	拉敏木制木窗,落地窗及其框架	4	70		5	17	千克	ABFE	Windows, French-windows and their frames of Ramin wood
4418 1090.20	濒危木制木窗,落地窗及其框架	4	70			17	千克	ABFE	Windows, French-windows and their frames of endangered wood
4418 1090.90	其他木制木窗,落地窗及其框架	4	70		9	17	千克	AB	Windows, French-windows and their frames of other wood
4418.2000	-门及其框架和门槛	4	70			17	千克		-Doors and their frames and thresholds
4418 2000.10	拉敏木制的木门及其框架和门槛	4	70		5	17	千克	ABFE	Doors and their frames and thresholds, of ramin wood
4418 2000.20	濒危木制的木门及其框架和门槛	4	70			17	千克	ABFE	Doors and their frames and thresholds, of endangered wood
4418 2000.90	木门及其框架和门槛	4	70		9	17	千克	AB	Doors and their frames and thresholds, of wood
4418.4000	-水泥构件的模板	4	70		9	17	千克	AB	-Shuttering for concrete constructional work
4418.5000	-木瓦及盖屋板	7.5	70		9	17	千克	AB	-Shingles and shakes
4418.6000	-柱及梁	4	70			17	千克		-Posts and beams
4418 6000.10	濒危木制柱和梁	4	70			17	千克	FEAB	Poles and beams, of endangered wood
4418 6000.90	其他木制柱和梁	4	70		9	17	千克	AB	Poles and beams, of other wood
	-已装拼的地板:								-Assembled flooring panels:
4418.7100	--马赛克地板用	4	70			17	千克		--For mosaic floors
4418 7100.10	已装拼的拉敏木制马赛克地板	4	70			17	千克	ABFE	Assembled flooring panels for mosaic floor, of Ramin wood
4418 7100.20	已装拼的其他濒危木制马赛克地板	4	70			17	千克	ABFE	Assembled flooring panels for mosaic floor, of endangered wood
4418 7100.90	已装拼的其他木制马赛克地板	4	70			17	千克	AB	Assembled flooring panels for mosaic floor, of other wood
	--其他，多层的:								--Other, multilayer:
4418.7210	---竹制	4	70		13	17	千克	AB	---Of bomboo
4418.7290	---其他	4	70			17	千克		---Other
4418 7290.10	已装拼的拉敏木制多层地板	4	70			17	千克	ABFE	Assembled flooring panels,multilayer,of Ramin wood
4418 7290.20	已装拼的其他濒危木制多层地板	4	70			17	千克	ABFE	Assembled flooring panels, multilayer, of endangered wood
4418 7290.90	已装拼的其他木制多层地板	4	70			17	千克	AB	Assembled flooring panels,multilayer,of other wood
	--其他的:								--Other:
4418.7910	---竹制	4	70		13	17	千克	AB	---Of bomboo
4418.7990	---其他	4	70			17	千克		---Other
4418 7990.10	已装拼的拉敏木制其他地板	4	70			17	千克	ABFE	Other flooring panels of ramin wood , assembled
4418 7990.20	已装拼的其他濒危木制地板	4	70			17	千克	ABFE	Other flooring panels of endangered wood, assembled
4418 7990.90	已装拼的木制其他地板	4	70			17	千克	AB	Other flooring panels of wood , assembled
	-其他:								-Other:
4418.9010	---竹制	4	70			17	千克		---Of bomboo

税则号列 Tariff Item	商品名称及备注	进口税率 最惠	普通	暂定	出口退税	增值税率	计量单位	监管条件	Article Description
4418 9010.10	濒危竹制其他建筑用木工制品（包括蜂窝结构的木镶板）	4	70			17	千克	ABE	Other builder' s joinery and carpentry of endangered bamboo(including cellular wood panels)
4418 9010.90	其他竹制其他建筑用木工制品（包括蜂窝结构的木镶板）	4	70		9	17	千克	AB	Other builder's joinery and carpentry of other bamboo(including cellular wood panels)
4418.9090	---其他	4	70			17	千克		---Other
4418 9090.10	拉敏木制其他建筑用木工制品（包括蜂窝结构的木镶板）	4	70		5	17	千克	FEAB	Other builders' joinery and carpentry, and cellular wood panels, of ramin wood
4418 9090.20	濒危木制其他建筑用木工制品（包括蜂窝结构的木镶板）	4	70			17	千克	FEAB	Other builders' joinery and carpentry, and cellular wood panels, of endangered wood
4418 9090.90	其他建筑用木工制品（包括蜂窝结构的木镶板）	4	70		9	17	千克	AB	Other builders' joinery and carpentry, and cellular wood panels, of other wood
44.19	**木制餐具及厨房用具:**								**Tableware and kitchenware, of wood:**
	---一次性筷子:								---One-time chopsticks:
4419.0031	----木制	0	100			17	千克	AB	----Of wood
4419.0032	----竹制	0	100			17	千克		----Of bamboo
4419 0032.10	酸竹制一次性筷子	0	100			17	千克	ABE	One-time chopsticks, of bamboo
4419 0032.90	其他竹制一次性筷子	0	100		13	17	千克	AB	One-time chopsticks, of other bamboo
	---其他:								---Other:
4419.0091	----竹制	0	100		13	17	千克	AB	----Of bamboo
4419.0099	----其他	0	100			17	千克		----Other
4419 0099.10	拉敏木制的餐具及厨房用具	0	100		5	17	千克	FEAB	Tableware and kitchenware of ramin wood
4419 0099.20	濒危木制的餐具及厨房用具	0	100			17	千克	FEAB	Tableware and kitchenware of endangered wood
4419 0099.90	其他木制餐具及厨房用具	0	100		9	17	千克	AB	Tableware and kitchenware of other wood
44.20	**镶嵌木（包括细工镶嵌木）；装珠宝或刀具用的木制盒子和小匣子及类似品；木制小雕像及其他装饰品；第九十四章以外的木制家具**								**Wood marquetry and inlaid wood; caskets and cases for jewellery or cutlery, and similar articles, of wood; statuettes and other ornaments, of wood; wooden articles or furniture not falling in Chapter 94:**
	-木制小雕像及其他装饰品:								-Statuettes and other ornaments, of wood:
	---木刻及竹刻:								---Wood or bamboo carvings:
4420.1011	----木刻	0	100			17	千克		---Wood carvings
4420 1011.10	拉敏木制的木刻	0	100		5	17	千克	FEAB	Wood carving, of Ramin wood
4420 1011.20	濒危木制的木刻	0	100			17	千克	FEAB	Wood carving, of endangered wood
4420 1011.90	其他木刻	0	100		9	17	千克	AB	Wood or bamboo carvings
4420.1012	----竹刻	0	100		9	17	千克	AB	----Bamboo carvings
4420.1020	---木扇	0	100			17	千克		---Wooden fans
4420 1020.10	拉敏木制的木扇	0	100		5	17	千克	FEAB	Wooden fans, of Ramin wood
4420 1020.20	濒危木制的木扇	0	100			17	千克	FEAB	Wooden fans, of endangered wood
4420 1020.90	木扇	0	100		9	17	千克	AB	Wooden fans
4420.1090	---其他	0	100			17	千克		---Other
4420 1090.10	拉敏木制其他小雕像及其他装饰品	0	100		5	17	千克	FEAB	Statuettes and other ornaments, of ramin wood
4420 1090.30	沉香木及拟沉香木制其他小雕像及其他装饰品	0	100			17	千克	FEAB	Statuettes and other ornaments, of Eaglewood and Agalloch Eaglewood
4420 1090.40	其他濒危木制其他小雕像及其他装饰品	0	100			17	千克	FEAB	Other Statuettes and other ornaments, of endangered wood
4420 1090.90	其他木制小雕像及其他装饰品	0	100		13	17	千克	AB	Statuettes and other ornaments of other wood
	-其他:								-Other:
4420.9010	---镶嵌木	0	45			17	千克		---Wood marquetry and inlaid wood
4420 9010.10	拉敏木制的镶嵌木	0	45		5	17	千克	FEAB	Ramin wood marquetry and inlaid wood
4420 9010.20	濒危木制的镶嵌木	0	45			17	千克	FEAB	Endangered wood marquetry and inlaid wood
4420 9010.90	镶嵌木	0	45		13	17	千克	AB	Wood marquetry and inlaid wood
4420.9090	---其他	0	100			17	千克		---Other
4420 9090.10	拉敏木盒及类似品，非落地木家	0	100		5	17	千克	FEAB	Caskets,cases and similar articles for jewelry or

税则号列 Tariff Item	商品名称及备注	进口税率			出口退税	增值税率	计量单位	监管条件	Article Description
		最惠	普通	暂定					
	具(前者用于装珠宝或家具;后者不包括第九十四章的家具)								furniture, of ramin wood; ramin wooden articles or furniture not falling, excluding furniture in Chapter 94
4420 9090.20	濒危木盒及类似品,非落地木家具(前者用于装珠宝或家具;后者不包括第九十四章的家具)	0	100			17	千克	FEAB	Caskets,cases and similar articles for jewelry or furniture, of endangered wood; endangered wooden articles or furniture not falling, excluding furniture in Chapter 94
4420 9090.90	木盒子及类似品;非落地式木家具(前者用于装珠宝或家具,后者不包括第九十四章的家具)	0	100		9	17	千克	AB	Caskets,cases and similar articles for jewelry or furniture, of wood; wooden articles or furniture not falling, excluding furniture in Chapter 94
44.21	**其他木制品:**								**Other articles of wood:**
4421.1000	-衣架	0	90			17	千克		-Clothes hangers
4421 1000.10	拉敏木制木衣架	0	90		5	17	千克	FEAB	Clothes hangers of Ramin wood
4421 1000.20	濒危木制木衣架	0	90			17	千克	FEAB	Clothes hangers of endangered wood
4421 1000.90	木衣架	0	90		9	17	千克	AB	Clothes hangers of wood
	-其他:								-Other:
4421.9010	---卷轴、纡子、筒管、缝纫用线轴及类似品	0	35			17	千克		---Spools, cops, bobbins, sewing thread reels and the like
4421 9010.10	拉敏木纡子,筒管,卷轴,线轴及类似品	0	35		5	17	千克	FEAB	Cops, bobbins, spools, sewing thread reels and the like, of Ramin wood
4421 9010.20	濒危木纡子,筒管,卷轴,线轴及类似品	0	35			17	千克	FEAB	Cops, bobbins, spools, sewing thread reels and the like, of endangered wood
4421 9010.90	木卷轴,纡子,筒管,线轴及类似品	0	35		9	17	千克	AB	Spools, cops, bobbins, sewing thread reels and the like, of wood
	---圆签、圆棒、冰果棒、压舌片及类似一次性制品:								---Circle sticks,circle bars,popsicle sticks,spatula and the like:
4421.9021	----木制	0	35			17	千克		----Of wood
4421 9021.10	一次性拉敏木制圆签,圆棒,冰果棒,压舌片(包括类似的一次性制品)	0	35			17	千克	FEAB	Round picks and sticks, sticks for ice-sucker, spatulas and similar one time articles, of ramin wood
4421 9021.20	一次性濒危木制圆签,圆棒,冰果棒,压舌片(包括类似的一次性制品)	0	35			17	千克	FEAB	Round picks and sticks, sticks for ice-sucker, spatulas and similar one time articles, of endangered wood
4421 9021.90	一次性其他木制圆签,圆棒,冰果棒,压舌片(包括类似的一次性制品)	0	35			17	千克	AB	Round picks and sticks, sticks for ice-sucker, spatulas and similar one time articles, of other wood
4421.9022	----竹制	0	35			17	千克		----Of bamboo
4421 9022.10	一次性酸竹制圆签,圆棒,冰果棒,压舌片(包括类似的一次性制品)	0	35			17	千克	ABE	Round picks and sticks, sticks for ice-sucker, spatulas and similar one time articles, of bamboo
4421 9022.90	一次性其他竹制圆签,圆棒,冰果棒,压舌片(包括类似的一次性制品)	0	35		13	17	千克	AB	Round picks and sticks, sticks for icesucker, spatulas and similar one time articles, of other bamboo
4421.9090	---其他	0	90			17	千克		---Other
4421 9090.10	拉敏木制的未列名的木制品	0	90		5	17	千克	FEAB	Articles of Ramin wood, not specified
4421 9090.20	濒危木制的未列名的木制品	0	90			17	千克	FEAB	Articles of endangered wood, not specified
4421 9090.90	未列名的木制品	0	90		13	17	千克	AB	Articles of wood, not specified

第四十五章 软木及软木制品

Chapter 45 Cork and articles of cork

注释：

本章不包括：

一、第六十四章的鞋靴及其零件；

二、第六十五章的帽类及其零件；或

三、第九十五章的物品（例如，玩具、游戏品及运动用品）。

Chapter Notes:

This Chapter does not cover:

（a）Footwear or parts of footwear of Chapter 64;

（b）Headgear or parts of headgear of Chapter 65; or

（c）Articles of Chapter 95（for example, toys, games, sports requisites）

税则号列 Tariff Item	商品名称及备注	进口税率			出口退税	增值税率	计量单位	监管条件	Article Description
		最惠	普通	暂定					
45.01	**未加工或简单加工的天然软木；软木废料；碎的、粒状的或粉状的软木：**								**Natural cork, raw or simply prepared; waste cork; crushed, granulated or ground cork:**
4501.1000[暂]	-未加工或简单加工的天然软木	6	17	1		17	千克	AB	-Natural cork, raw or simply prepared
	-其他:								-Other:
4501.9010	---软木废料	0	17			17	千克	ABP	---Waste cork
4501.9020	---碎的、粒状的或粉状的软木(软木碎、软木粒或软木粉)	0	17			17	千克	AB	---Crushed, granulated or ground cork
45.02	**天然软木，除去表皮或粗切成方形，或成长方块、正方块、板、片或条状（包括作塞子用的方块坯料）：**								**Natural cork, debarked or roughly squared, or in rectangular（including square）blocks, plates, sheets or strip,（including sharp-edged blanks for corks or stoppers）:**
4502.0000	天然软木，除去表皮或粗切成方形，或成长方块、正方块、板、片或条状（包括作塞子用的方块坯料）	8	30			17	千克	AB	Natural cork, debarked or roughly squared, or in rectangular（including square）blocks, plates, sheets or strip,（including sharp-edged blanks for corks or stoppers）
45.03	**天然软木制品：**								**Articles of natural cork:**
4503.1000	-塞子	8	50			17	千克	AB	-Corks and stoppers
4503.9000	-其他	10.5	50			17	千克	AB	-Other
45.04	**压制软木（不论是否使用黏合剂压成）及其制品：**								**Agglomerated cork（with or without a binding substance）and articles of agglomerated cork:**
4504.1000	-块，板，片及条状压制软木（包括任何形状的压制软木的砖、瓦、实心圆柱体、圆片）	8.4	30			17	千克	AB	-Blocks, plates, sheets and strip; tiles of any shape; solid cylinders, including discs
4504.9000	-其他	0	50			17	千克	AB	-Other

第四十六章 稻草、秸秆、针茅或其他编结材料制品；篮筐及柳条编结品

Chapter 46 Manufactures of straw, of esparto or of other plaiting materials; basketware and wickerwork

注释：

一、本章所称“编结材料”，是指其状态或形状适于编结、交织或类似加工的材料，包括稻草、秸秆、柳条、竹、藤、灯芯草、芦苇、木片条、其他植物材料扁条（例如，树皮条、狭叶、酒椰叶纤维或其他从阔叶获取的条）、未纺的天然纺织纤维、塑料单丝及扁条、纸带，但不包括皮革、再生皮革、毡呢或无纺织物的扁条、人发、马毛、纺织粗纱或纱线以及第五十四章的单丝和扁条。

二、本章不包括：

（一）品目 48.14 的壁纸；

（二）不论是否编结而成的线、绳、索、缆（品目 56.07）；

（三）第六十四章和第六十五章的鞋靴、帽类及其零件；

（四）编结而成的车辆或车身（第八十七章）；或

（五）第九十四章的物品（例如，家具、灯具及照明装置）。

三、品目 46.01 所称“平行连结的成片编结材料、缏条或类似的编结材料产品”，是指编结材料、缏条及类似的编结材料产品平行排列连结成片的制品，其连结材料不论是否为纺制的纺织材料。

Chapter Notes:

1. In this Chapter the expression “plaiting materials” means materials in a state or form suitable for plaiting, interlacing or similar processes; it includes straw, osier or willow, bamboos, rattans, rushes, reeds, strips of wood, strips of other vegetable material (for example, strips of bark, narrow leaves and raffia or other strips obtained from broad leaves), unspun natural textile fibres, monofilament and strip and the like of plastics and strips of paper, but not strips of leather or composition leather or of felt or nonwovens, human hair, horsehair, textile rovings or yarns, or monofilament and strip and the like of Chapter 54.

2. This Chapter does not cover:

(a) Wall coverings of heading 48.14;

(b) Twine, cordage, ropes or cables, plaited or not (heading 56.07);

(c) Footwear or headgear or parts thereof of Chapter 64 or 65;

(d) Vehicles or bodies for vehicles of basketware (Chapter 87); or

(e) Articles of Chapter 94 (for example, furniture, lamps and lighting fittings).

3. For the purposes of heading 46.01, the expression “plaiting materials, plaits and similar products of plaiting materials, bound together in parallel strands” means plaiting materials, plaits and similar products of plaiting materials, placed side by side and bound together, in the form of sheets, whether or not the binding materials are of spun textile materials.

税则号列 Tariff Item	商品名称及备注	进口税率			出口退税	增值税率	计量单位	监管条件	Article Description
		最惠	普通	暂定					
46.01	用编结材料编成的缏条及类似产品，不论是否缝合成宽条；平行连结或编结的成片材料、缏条或类似的编结材料产品，不论是否制成品(例如，席子、席料、帘子)								**Plaits and similar products of plaiting materials, whether or not assembled into strips; plaiting materials, plaits and similar products of plaiting materials, bound together in parallel strands or woven, in sheet form, whether or not being finished articles (for example, mats, matting, screens):**
	-植物材料制的席子、席料及帘子:								-Mats, matting and screens of vegetable materials:
4601.2100	--竹制的	9	90		13	17	千克/张	AB	--Of bamboo
4601.2200	--藤制的	9	100		13	17	千克/张	AB	--Of rattan
	--其他:								--Other:
	---草制的:								---Of grass or straw:
4601.2911	----灯心草属材料制的	9	90		13	17	千克/张		----Of rushes
4601 2911.11	蔺草制的提花席、双苜席、垫子（单位面积＞1 平方米，不论是否包边）	9	90		13	17	千克/张	4ABxy	Jacquard mats, clover mats and cushion, of Rush, of per unit area exceeding 1 m², whether or not edged
4601 2911.12	蔺草制的其他席子（单位面积＞1 平方米，不论是否包边）	9	90		13	17	千克/张	4ABxy	Other mats, matting, of Rush, of per unit area exceeding 1 m², whether or not edged
4601 2911.19	蔺草制的其他席子、席料及帘子（单位面积≤1 平方米，不论是否包边）	9	90		13	17	千克/张	AB	Other mats, matting and screens, of Rush, of per unit area not exceeding 1 m², whether or not edged

税则号列 Tariff Item	商品名称及备注	进口税率 最惠	普通	暂定	出口退税	增值税率	计量单位	监管条件	Article Description
4601 2911.90	其他灯心草属材料制的席子等(包括席子、席料、帘子、垫子)	9	90		13	17	千克/张	AB	Other mats, matting and screens, of rush
4601.2919	----其他	9	90		13	17	千克/张	AB	----Other
	---芦苇制的:								---Of reeds:
4601.2921	----苇帘	9	90		13	17	千克/张	AB	----Screens of reeds
4601.2929	----其他	9	90		13	17	千克/张	AB	----Other
4601.2990	---其他	9	90		13	17	千克/张	AB	---Other
	-其他:								-Other:
	--竹制的:								--Of bamboo:
4601.9210	---缏条及类似产品, 不论是否缝合成宽条	9	100		13	17	千克	AB	---Plaits and similar products of plaiting materials, whether or not assembled into strips
4601.9290	---其他	9	90		13	17	千克	AB	---Other:
	--藤制的:								--Of rattan:
4601.9310	---缏条及类似产品,不论是否缝合成宽条	9	100		13	17	千克	AB	---Plaits and similar products of plaiting materials, whether or not assembled into strips
4601.9390	---其他	9	90		13	17	千克	AB	---Other
	--其他植物材料制的:								--Of other vegetable materials:
	---稻草制的:								---Of straw:
4601.9411	----缏条(绳)	10	90		13	17	千克	AB	----Plaits
4601.9419	----其他	10	90		13	17	千克	AB	----Other
	---其他:								---Other:
4601.9491	----缏条及类似产品, 不论是否缝合成宽条	9	100		13	17	千克	AB	----Plaits and similar products of plaiting materials, whether or not assembled into strips
4601.9499	----其他	9	90		13	17	千克	AB	----Other
	--其他:								--Other:
4601.9910	----缏条及类似产品, 不论是否缝合成宽条	9	90		13	17	千克		---Plaits and similar products of plaiting materials, whether or not assembled into strips
4601.9990	---其他	9	90		13	17	千克		---Other
46.02	**用编结材料直接编成或用品目46.01所列货品制成的篮筐、柳条编结品及其他制品;丝瓜络制品:**								**Basketwork, wickerwork and other articles, made directly to shape from plaiting materials or made up from goods of heading No.46.01; articles of loofah:**
	-植物材料制:								-Of vegetable materials:
4602.1100	--竹制的	9	100		13	17	千克	AB	--Of bamboo
4602.1200	--藤制的	9	100		13	17	千克	AB	--Of rattan
	--其他:								--Other:
4602.1910	---草制的	9	100		13	17	千克	AB	---Of grass or straw
4602.1920	---玉米皮制的	9	100		13	17	千克	AB	---Of maize-shuck
4602.1930	---柳条制的	9	100		13	17	千克	AB	---Of osier
4602.1990	---其他	9	100		13	17	千克	AB	---Other
4602.9000	-其他	9	100		13	17	千克		-Other

第十类 木浆及其他纤维状纤维素浆 回收（废碎）纸或纸板；纸、纸板及其制品

SECTION X PULP OF WOOD OR OF OTHER FIBROUS CELLULOSIC MATERIAL; RECOVERED（WASTE AND SCRAP）PAPER OR PAPERBOARD; PAPER AND PAPERBOARD AND ARTICLES THEREOF

第四十七章 木浆及其他纤维状纤维素浆 回收（废碎）纸或纸板

Chapter 47 Pulp of wood or of other fibrous cellulosic material; recovered（waste and scrap）paper or paperboard

注释：

品目 47.02 所称“化学木浆，溶解级”，是指温度在 20℃时浸入含 18%氢氧化钠的苛性碱溶液内，一小时后，按重量计含有 92%及以上的不溶级分的碱木浆或硫酸盐木浆，或者含有 88%及以上的不溶级分的亚硫酸盐木浆。对于亚硫酸盐木浆，按重量计灰分含量不得超过 0.15%。

Chapter Notes:

For the purposes of heading 47.02, the expression “chemical wood pulp, dissolving grades” means chemical wood pulp having by weight an insoluble fraction of 92% or more for soda or sulphate wood pulp or of 88% or more for sulphite wood pulp after one hour in a caustic soda solution containing 18% sodium hydroxide （NaOH）at 20℃, and for sulphite wood pulp an ash content that does not exceed 0.15% by weight.

税则号列 Tariff Item	商品名称及备注	进口税率			出口退税	增值税率	计量单位	监管条件	Article Description
		最惠	普通	暂定					
47.01	机械木浆：								**Mechanical wood pulp:**
4701.0000	机械木浆	0	8			17	千克		Mechanical wood pulp
47.02	化学木浆，溶解级：								**Chemical wood pulp, dissolving grades:**
4702.0000	化学木浆，溶解级	0	8			17	千克		Chemical wood pulp, dissolving grades
4702 0000.01	用于生产粘胶等化学纤维（不含醋酸纤维）的化学木浆，溶解级（浆粕的粘度≧3.7dl/g，且<6.4dl/g，或者≧350ml/g，且<700ml/g，α纤维素含量（R18，硫酸盐法）≧88%，且<95.5%，或者α纤维素含量（R18，亚硫酸盐法）≧87%，且<94%，灰分≦0.15%）	0	8			17	千克		Chemical wood pulp, dissolving grades, for producing chemical fibers such as viscose other than acetate, with pulp viscosity 3.7dl/g or more, less than 6.4dl/g, or with pulp viscosity350ml/g or more, less than 700ml/g; containing cellulose(R18,by Kraft) by weight of 88%or more, less than 95.5%, or containing cellulose (R18,by Kraft) by weight of 87%or more, less than 94%, with ash≦0. 15%
4702 0000.90	其他化学木浆，溶解级	0	8			17	千克		Other chemical wood pulp, dissolving grades
47.03	碱木浆或硫酸盐木浆，但溶解级的除外：								**Chemical wood pulp, soda or sulphate, other than dissolving grades:**
	-未漂白：								-Unbleached:
4703.1100	--针叶木的	0	8			17	千克		--Coniferous
4703.1900	--非针叶木的	0	8			17	千克		--Non-coniferous
	-半漂白的或漂白：								-Semi-bleached or bleached:
4703.2100	--针叶木的	0	8			17	千克		--Coniferous
4703 2100.01	用于生产粘胶等化学纤维（不含醋酸纤维）的漂白针叶木碱木浆或硫酸盐木浆（包括半漂白的，溶解级的除外）（浆粕的粘度≧3.7dl/g，且<6.4dl/g，或者≧350ml/g，且<700ml/g，α纤维素含量（R18，硫酸盐法）≧88%，且<95.5%，灰分≦0.15%）	0	8			17	千克		Bleached coniferous chemical wood pulp, including semi-bleached, , for producing chemical fibers such as viscose other than acetate, with pulp viscosity 3.7dl/g or more, less than 6.4dl/g, or with pulp viscosity350ml/g or more, less than 700ml/g; containing cellulose(R18,by Kraft) by weight of 88%or more, less than 95.5%, or containing cellulose (R18,by Kraft) by weight of 87%or more, less than 94%, with ash≦0. 15%, other than dissolving grades
4703 2100.90	其他漂白针叶木碱木浆或硫酸盐木浆（包括半漂白的，溶解级的除外）	0	8			17	千克		Other chemical wood pulp, including semi-bleached, other than dissolving grades
4703.2900	--非针叶木的	0	8			17	千克		--Non-coniferous

税则号列 Tariff Item	商品名称及备注	进口税率 最惠	普通	暂定	出口退税	增值税率	计量单位	监管条件	Article Description
47.04	亚硫酸盐木浆，但溶解级的除外：								**Chemical wood pulp, sulphite, other than dissolving grades:**
	-未漂白:								-Unbleached:
4704.1100	--针叶木的	0	8			17	千克		--Coniferous
4704.1900	--非针叶木的	0	8			17	千克		--Non-coniferous
	-半漂白的或漂白:								-Semi-bleached or bleached:
4704.2100	--针叶木的	0	8			17	千克		--Coniferous
4704.2900	--非针叶木的	0	8			17	千克		--Non-coniferous
47.05	用机械与化学联合制浆法制得的木浆：								**Wood pulp obtained by a combination of mechanical and chemical pulping processes:**
4705.0000	用机械与化学联合制浆法制的木浆	0	8			17	千克		Wood pulp obtained by a combination of mechanical and chemical pulping processes
47.06	从回收（废碎）纸或纸板提取的纤维浆或其他纤维状纤维素浆：								**Pulps of fibres derived from recovered （waste and scrap） paper or paperboard or of other fibrous cellulosic material:**
4706.1000	-棉短绒纸浆	0	8		13	17	千克		-Cotton linters pulp
4706 1000.01	用于生产粘胶等化学纤维（不含醋酸纤维）的棉短绒浆粕(浆粕的粘度≧3.7dl/g，且<6.4dl/g，或者≧350ml/g，且<700ml/g，α纤维素含量（R18，硫酸盐法）≧88%，且<95.5%，或者α纤维素含量（R18，亚硫酸盐法）≧87%，且<94%，灰分≦0.15%)	0	8		13	17	千克		Cotton linters pulp, dissolving grades, for producing chemical fibers such as viscose other thanacetate, with pulp viscosity 3.7dl/g or more, less than 6.4dl/g, or with pulp viscosity350ml/g or more, less than 700ml/g; containing cellulose(R18,by Kraft) by weight of 88%or more, less than 95.5%, or containing cellulose (R18,by Kraft) by weight of 87%or more, less than 94%, with ash≦0.15%
4706 1000.90	其他棉短绒纸浆	0	8		13	17	千克		Other cotton linters pulp
4706.2000	-从回收（废碎）纸或纸板提取的纤维浆	0	8			17	千克		-Pulps of fibres derived from recovered （waste and scrap） paper or paperboard
4706.3000	-其他,竹浆	0	8			17	千克		-Other, of bamboo
4706 3000.01	用于生产粘胶等化学纤维（不含醋酸纤维）的其他纤维状纤维素竹浆（包括机械浆、化学浆、半化学浆）（浆粕的粘度≧3.7dl/g，且<6.4dl/g，或者≧350ml/g，且<700ml/g，α纤维素含量（R18，硫酸盐法）≧88%，且<95.5%，或者α纤维素含量（R18，亚硫酸盐法）≧87%，且<94%，灰分≦0.15%)	0	8			17	千克		Other bamboo pulp in form of fibers, dissolving grades, for producing chemical fibers such as viscose other than acetate, with pulp viscosity 3.7dl/g or more, less than 6.4dl/g, or with pulp viscosity350ml/g or more, less than 700ml/g; containing cellulose(R18,by Kraft) by weight of 88%or more, less than 95.5%, or containing cellulose (R18,by Kraft) by weight of 87%or more, less than 94%, with ash≦0.15%
4706 3000.90	其他纤维状纤维素竹浆（包括机械浆、化学浆、半化学浆）	0	8			17	千克		Other bamboo pulp in form of fibers including mechanical, chemical or semi-blenched pulp
	-其他:	0	8			17	千克		-Other:
4706.9100	--机械浆	0	8			17	千克		--Mechanical
4706.9200	--化学浆	0	8			17	千克		--Chemical
4706.9300	--用机械和化学联合法制得的浆	0	8			17	千克		--Obtained by a combination of mechanical and chemical processes
47.07	回收（废碎）纸或纸板:								**Recovered (waste and scrap) paper or paperboard:**
4707.1000	-未漂白的牛皮纸或纸板及瓦楞纸或纸板	0	8			17	千克	ABP	-Unbleached kraft paper or paperboard or of corrugated paper or paperboard
4707.2000	-主要由漂白化学木浆制成未经本体染色的其他纸和纸板	0	8			17	千克	ABP	-Other paper or paperboard made mainly of bleached chemical pulp, not coloured in the mass
4707.3000	-主要由机械浆制成的纸或纸板（例如，报纸、杂志及类似印刷品）	0	8			17	千克	ABP	-Paper or paperboard made mainly of mechanical pulp（for example, newspapers, journals and similar printed matter）
4707.9000	-其他,包括未分选的废碎品	0	8			17	千克		-Other, including unsorted waste and scrap
4707 9000.10	回收（废碎）墙（壁）纸、涂蜡纸、浸蜡纸、复写纸（包括未分	0	8			17	千克	9AB	Recoverd (waste and scrap) wallpaper, waxcoated paper or waxed paper and carbon paper (including

税则号列 Tariff Item	商品名称及备注	进口税率			出口退税	增值税率	计量单位	监管条件	Article Description
		最惠	普通	暂定					
	选的废碎品）								unsorted waste and scrap)
4707 9000.90	其他回收纸或纸板（包括未分选的废碎品）	0	8			17	千克	ABP	Other recovered paper or paperboard, including unsorted waste and scrap

第四十八章
纸及纸板：纸浆、纸或纸板制品

注释：

一、除条文另有规定外，本章所称“纸”包括纸板（不考虑其厚度或每平方米重量）。

二、本章不包括：

（一）第三十章的物品；

（二）品目32.12的压印箔；

（三）香纸及用化妆品浸渍或涂布的纸（第三十三章）；

（四）用肥皂或洗涤剂浸渍、覆盖或涂布的纸或纤维素絮纸（品目34.01）和用光洁剂、擦光膏及类似制剂浸渍、覆盖或涂布的纸或纤维素絮纸（品目34.05）；

（五）品目37.01至37.04的感光纸或感光纸板；

（六）用诊断或实验用试剂浸渍的纸（品目38.22）；

（七）第三十九章的用纸强化的层压塑料板，用塑料覆盖或涂布的单层纸或纸板（塑料部分占总厚度的一半以上），以及上述材料的制品，但品目48.14的壁纸除外；

（八）品目42.02的物品（例如，旅行用品）；

（九）第四十六章的物品（编结材料制品）；

（十）纸纱线或纸纱线纺织物（第十一类）；

（十一）第六十四章或第六十五章的物品；

（十二）品目68.05的砂纸或品目68.14的用纸或纸板衬底的云母（但涂布云母粉的纸及纸板归入本章）；

（十三）用纸或纸板衬底的金属箔（通常归入第十四类或第十五类）；

（十四）品目92.09的制品；

（十五）第九十五章的物品（例如，玩具、游戏品及运动用品）；或

（十六）第九十六章的物品[例如，纽扣，卫生巾（护垫）及止血塞、婴儿尿布及尿布衬里]。

三、除注释七另有规定的以外，品目48.01至48.05包括经研光、高度研光、釉光或类似处理、仿水印、表面施胶的纸及纸板；同时还包括用各种方法本体着色或染成斑纹的纸、纸板、纤维素絮纸及纤维素纤维网纸。除品目48.03另有规定的以外，上述品目不适用于经过其他方法加工的纸、纸板、纤维素絮纸或纤维素纤维网纸。

四、本章所称“新闻纸”，是指所含用机械或化学-机械方法制得的木纤维不少于全部纤维重量的50%的未经涂布的报刊用纸，未施胶或微施胶，每面粗糙度[帕克印刷表面粗糙度（1兆帕）]超过2.5微米，每平方米重量不小于40克，但

Chapter 48
Paper and paperboard; articles of paper pulp, of paper or of paperboard

Chapter Notes:

1. For the purposes of this Chapter, except where the context otherwise requires, a reference to “paper” includes references to paperboard （irrespective of thickness or weight per squar meter）.

2. This Chapter does not cover:

（a）Articles of Chapter 30;

（b）Stamping foils of heading 32.12;

（c）Perfumed papers or papers impregnated or coated with cosmetics （Chapter 33）;

（d）Paper or cellulose wadding impregnated, coated or covered with soap or detergent（heading 34.01）, or with polishes, creams or similar preparations（heading 34.05）;

（e）Sensitised paper or paperboard of headings 37.01 to 37.04;

（f）Paper impregnated with diagnostic or laboratory reagents （heading 38.22）;

（g）Paper-reinforced stratified sheeting of plastics, or one layer of paper or paperboard coated or covered with a layer of plastics, （the latter constituting more than half the total thickness）, or articles of such materials, other than wall coverings of heading 48.14（Chapter 39）;

（h）Articles of heading 42.02（for example, travel goods）;

（ij）Articles of Chapter 46（manufactures of plaiting material）;

（k）Paper yarn or textile articles of paper yarn（Section XI）;

（l）Articles of Chapter 64 or Chapter 65;

（m）Abrasive paper or paperboard（heading 68.05）or paper-backed or paperboard-backed mica（heading 68.14）（paper and paperboard coated with mica powder are, however, to be classified in this Chapter）;

（n）Metal foil backed with paper or paperboard（generally to be classified in section XIV or XV）;

（o）Articles of heading 92.09;

（p）Articles of Chapter 95（for example, toys, games, sports requisites）;or

（q）Articles of Chapter 96(for example, buttons, sanitary towels(pads) and tampons, napkins (diapers) and napkin liners for babies).

3. Subject to the provisions of Note 7, headings 48.01 to 48.05 include paper and paperboard which have been subjected to calendering, super-calendering, glazing or similar finishing, false water-marking or surface sizing, and also paper, paperboard, cellulose wadding and webs of cellulose fibres, coloured or marbled throughout the mass by any method. Except where heading 48.03 otherwise requires, these headings do not apply to paper, paperboard, cellulose wadding or webs of cellulose fibres which have been otherwise processed.

4. In this Chapter the expression “newsprint” means uncoated paper of a kind used for the printing of newspapers, of which not less than 50% by weight of the total fibre content consists of wood fibres obtained by a mechanical or chemi-mechanical process, unsized or very lightly sized, having a surface roughness Parker Print Surf（1MPa）on each side exceeding 2.5 micrometre

不超过 65 克。

五、品目 48.02 所称"书写、印刷或类似用途的纸及纸板"、"未打孔的穿孔卡片和穿孔纸带纸"，是指主要用漂白纸浆或用机械或化学-机械方法制得的纸浆制成的纸及纸板，并且符合下列任一标准：

每平方米重量不超过 150 克的纸或纸板：

（一）用机械或化学-机械方法制得的纤维含量在10%及以上，并且

1．每平方米重量不超过 80 克；或

2．本体着色；

（二）灰分含量在8%以上，并且

1．每平方米重量不超过 80 克；或

2．本体着色；

（三）灰分含量在3%以上，亮度在60%及以上；或

（四）灰分含量在3%以上，但不超过8%，亮度低于60%，耐破指数等于或小于2.5千帕斯卡·平方米/克；或

（五）灰分含量在3%及以下，亮度在60%及以上，耐破指数等于或小于2.5千帕斯卡·平方米/克。

每平方米重量超过 150 克的纸或纸板：

（一）本体着色；或

（二）亮度在60%及以上，并且

1．厚度在225微米及以下；或

2．厚度在225微米以上，但不超过508微米，灰分含量在3%以上；或

（三）亮度低于60%，厚度不超过254微米，灰分含量在8%以上。

品目 48.02 不包括滤纸及纸板（含茶袋纸）或毡纸及纸板。

六、本章所称"牛皮纸及纸板"，是指所含用硫酸盐法或烧碱法制得的纤维不少于全部纤维重量的80%的纸及纸板。

七、除品目条文另有规定的以外，符合品目 48.01 至 48.11 中两个或两个以上品目所规定的纸、纸板、纤维素絮纸及纤维素纤维网纸，应按号列顺序归入有关品目中的最末一个品目。

八、品目 48.01 及 48.03 至 48.09 仅适用于下列规格的纸、纸板、纤维素絮纸及纤维素纤维网纸：

（一）成条或成卷，宽度超过36厘米；或

（二）成张矩形（包括正方形），一边超过36厘米，另一边超过15厘米（以未折叠计）。

九、品目 48.14 所称"壁纸及类似品"，仅限于：

（一）适合作墙壁或天花板装饰用的成卷纸张，宽度不小于45厘米，但不超过160厘米：

1．起纹、压花、染面、印有图案或经其他装饰的（例如，植绒），不论是否用透明的防护塑料涂布或覆盖；

2．表面饰有木粒或草粒而凹凸不平的；

(micron), weighing not less than $40g/m^2$ and not more than $65g/m^2$.

5. For the purposes of heading 48.02, the expressions "paper and paperboard, of a kind used for writing, printing or other graphic purposes" and "non perforated punch-cards and punch tape paper" mean paper and paperboard made mainly from bleached pulp or from pulp obtained by a mechanical or chemi-mechanical process and satisfying any of the following criteria:

For paper or paperboard weighing not more than $150g/m^2$:

(a) containing 10% or more of fibres obtained by a mechanical or chemi-mechanical process, and

(i) weighing not more than $80g/m^2$, or

(ii) coloured throughout the mass; or

(b) containing more than 8% ash, and

(i) weighing not more than $80g/m^2$, or

(ii) coloured throughout the mass; or

(c) containing more than 3% ash and having a brightness of 60% or more; or

(d) containing more than 3% but not more than 8% ash, having a brightness less than 60%, and a burst index equal to or less than 2.5 $kPa \cdot m^2/g$; or

(e) containing 3% ash or less, having a brightness of 60% or more and a burst index equal to or less than 2.5 $kPa \cdot m^2/g$.

For paper or paperboard weighing more than $150g/m^2$:

(a) coloured throughout the mass; or

(b) having a brightness of 60% or more, and

(i) a caliper of 225 micrometre (micron) or less; or

(ii) a caliper of more than 225 micrometre (micron) but not more than 508 micrometre (micron) and an ash content of more than 3%; or

(c) having a brightness of less than 60%, a caliper of 254 micrometre (micron) or less and an ash content of more than 8%

Heading 48.02 does not, however, cover filter paper or paperboard (including tea-bag paper) or felt paper or paperboard.

6. In this Chapter "kraft paper and paperboard" means paper and paperhoard of which not less than 80% by weight of the total fibre content consists of fibres obtained by the chemical sulphate or soda processes.

7. Except where the terms of the headings otherwise require, paper,paperboard, cellulose wadding and webs of cellulose fibres answering to a description in two or more of the headings 48.01 to 48.11 are to be classified under that one of such headings which occurs last in numerical order in the Nomenclature.

8. Headings 48.01 and 48.03 to 48.09 apply only to paper, paperboard, cellulose wadding and webs of cellulose fibres:

(a) in strips or rolls of a width exceeding 36cm; or

(b) in rectangular (including square) sheets with one side exceeding 36cm and the other side exceeding 15cm in the unfolded state.

9. For the purposes of heading 48.14, the expression "wallpaper and similar wall coverings" applies only to:

(a) Paper in rolls, of a width of not less than 45cm and not more than 160cm, suitable for wall or ceiling decoration:

(i) Grained, embossed, surface-coloured, design-printed or otherwise surface-decorated (for example, with textile flock), whether or not coated or covered with transparent protective plastics;

(ii) With an uneven surface resulting from the incorporation of particles of wood, straw, etc.;

3. 表面用塑料涂布或覆盖并起纹、压花、染面、印有图案或经其他装饰的；或

(iii) Coated or covered on the face side with plastics, the layer of plastics being grained, embossed, coloured, design-printed or otherwise decorated; or

4. 表面用不论是否平行连结或编织的编结材料覆盖的；

(iv) Covered on the face side with plaiting material, whether or not bound together in parallel strands or woven;

（二）适于装饰墙壁或天花板用的经上述加工的纸边及纸条，不论是否成卷；

(b) Borders and friezes, of paper, treated as above, whether or not in rolls, suitable for wall or ceiling decoration;

（三）由几幅拼成的壁纸，成卷或成张，贴到墙上可组成印制的风景画或图案。

(c) Wall coverings of paper made up of several panels, in rolls or sheets, printed so as to make up a scene, design or motif when applied to a wall.

既可作铺地制品，也可作壁纸的以纸或纸板为底的产品，应归入品目48.23。

Products on a base of paper or paperboard, suitable for use both as floor coverings and as wall coverings, are to be classified in heading 48.23.

十、品目 48.20 不包括切成一定尺寸的活页纸张或卡片，不论是否印制、压花、打孔。

10. Heading 48.20 does not cover loose sheets or cards, cut to size, whether or not printed, embossed or perforated.

十一、品目 48.23 主要适用于提花机或类似机器用的穿孔纸或卡片，以及纸花边。

11. Heading 48.23 applies, inter alia, to perforated paper or paperboard cards for Jacquard or similar machines and paper lace.

十二、除品目 48.14 及 48.21 的货品外，印有图案、文字或图画的纸、纸板、纤维素絮纸及其制品，如果所印图案、文字或图画作为其主要用途，应归入第四十九章。

12. Except for the goods of heading 48.14 or 48.21, paper, paperboard, cellulose wadding and articles thereof, printed with motifs, characters or pictorial representations, which are not merely incidental to the primary use of the goods, fall in Chapter 49.

子目注释：

Subheading Notes:

一、子目 4804.11 及 4804.19 所称“牛皮衬纸”，是指所含用硫酸盐法或烧碱法制得的木纤维不少于全部纤维重量的 80%的成卷机器整饰或上光纸及纸板，每平方米重量超过 115 克，并且最低缪伦耐破度符合下表所示（其他重量的耐破度可参照下表换算）：

重　量 (克／平方米)	最低耐破度 (千帕斯卡)
115	393
125	417
200	637
300	824
400	961

1. For the purposes of subheadings 4804.11 and 4804.19, “kraftliner” means machine-finished or machine-glazed paper and paperboard, of which not less than 80% by weight of the total fibre content consists of wood fibres obtained by the chemical sulphate or soda processes, in rolls, weighing more than 115g/m^2 and having a minimum Mullen bursting strength as indicated in the following table or the linearly interpolated or extrapolated equivalent for any other weight.

Weight (g/ m^2)	Minimum Mullen bursting strength (kpa)
115	393
125	417
200	637
300	824
400	961

二、子目4804.21及4804.29所称“袋用牛皮纸”，是指所含用硫酸盐法或烧碱法制得的木纤维不少于全部纤维重量的80%的成卷机器上光纸，每平方米重量不小于60克，但不超过115克，并且符合下列一种规格：

（一）缪伦耐破指数不小于3.7千帕斯卡·平方米/克，并且横向伸长率大于4.5%，纵向伸长率大于2%；

（二）至少能达到下表所示的最小撕裂度和抗张强度（其他重量的可参照下表换算）：

2. For the purposes of subheadings 4804.21 and 4804.29, “sack kraft paper” means machine-finished paper, of which not less than 80% by weight of the total fibre content consists of fibres obtained by the chemical sulphate or soda processes, in rolls, weighing not less than 60g/m^2 but not more than 115g/ m^2 and meeting one of the following sets of specifications:

(a) Having a Mullen burst index of not less than 3.7 kPa · m^2/g and a stretch factor of more than 4.5% in the cross direction and of more than 2% in the machine direction;

(b) Having minima for tear and tensile as indicated in the following table or the linearly interpolated equivalent for any other weight:

重量	最小撕裂度(毫牛顿)		最小抗张强度(千牛顿/米)	
克/平方米	纵向	纵向加横向	横向	纵向加横向
60	700	1510	1.9	6
70	830	1790	2.3	7.2
80	965	2070	2.8	8.3
100	1230	2635	3.7	10.6
115	1425	3060	4.4	12.3

三、子目 4805.11 所称"半化学的瓦楞纸"，是指所含用机械和化学联合法制得的未漂白硬木纤维不少于全部纤维重量的 65%的成卷纸张，并且在温度为 23℃和相对湿度为 50%时，经过 30 分钟的瓦楞芯纸平压强度测定（CMT30），抗压强度超过 1.8 牛顿/克/平方米。

四、子目 4805.12 包括主要用机械和化学联合法制得的草浆制成的成卷纸张，每平方米重量在 130 克及以上，并且在温度为 23℃和相对湿度为 50%时，经过 30 分钟的瓦楞芯纸平压强度测定（CMT30），抗压强度超过 1.4 牛顿/克/平方米。

五、子目 4805.24 及 4805.25 包括全部或主要由回收（废碎）纸或纸板制得的纸浆制成的纸和纸板。强韧箱纸板也可以有一面用染色纸或漂白或未漂白的非再生浆制得的纸做表层。这些产品缪伦耐破指数不小于 2 千帕斯卡·平方米/克。

六、子目 4805.30 所称"亚硫酸盐包装纸"，是指所含用亚硫酸盐法制得的木纤维超过全部纤维重量的 40%的机器砑光纸，灰分含量不超过 8%，并且缪伦耐破指数不小于 1.47 千帕卡·平方米/克

七、子目 4810.22 所称"轻质涂布纸"，是指双面涂布纸，其每平方米总重量不超过 72 克，每面每平方米的涂层重量不超过 15 克，原纸中所含用机械方法制得的木纤维不少于全部纤维重量的 50%。

Weight g/m^2	Minimmn tear(mN)		Minimum tensile(kN/m)	
	Machine direction	Machine direction plus cross direction	Cross direction	Machine direction plus cross direction
60	700	1510	1.9	6
70	830	1790	2.3	7.2
80	965	2070	2.8	7.3
100	1230	2635	3.7	10.6
115	1425	3060	4.4	12.3

3. For the purposes of subheading 4805.11, "semichemical fluting paper" means paper, in rolls, of which not less than 65% by weight of the total fibre content consists of unbleached hardwood fibres obtained by a combination of mechical and chemical pulping processes, and having a CMT 30（Corrugated Medium Test with 30 minutes of conditioning）crush resistance exceeding 1.8 N/g/m^2 at 50% relative humidity, at 23 ℃.

4. Subheading 4805.12 cover paper, in rolls, made mainly of straw pulp obtained by a combination of mechanical and chemical process, weighing 130 g/m^2 or more, and having a CMT 30（Corrugated Medium Test with 30 minutes of conditioning）crush resistance exceeding 1.4 N/g/m^2 at 50% relative humidity, at 23℃.

5. Subheading 4805.24 and 4805.25 cover paper and paperboard made wholly or mainly of pulp of recovered（waste and scrap）paper or paperboard. Testliner may also have a surface layer of dyed paper or of paper made of bleached or unbleached non-recovered pulp. These products have a Mullen burst index of not less than 2 kPa · m^2/g.

6. For the purposes of subheading 4805.30, "sulphite wrapping paper" means machine-glazed paper, of which more than 40% by weight of the total fibre content consists of wood fibres obtained by the chemical sulphite process, having an ash content not exceeding 8%and having a Mullen burst index of not less than 1.47 kPa · m^2/g.

7. For the purposes of subheading 4810.22, "lightweight coated paper" means paper, coated on both sides, of a total weight not exceeding 72g/m^2, with a coating weight not exceeding 15g/m^2 per side, on a base of which not less than 50% by weight of the total fibre content consists of wood fibres obtained by a mechanical process.

税则号列 Tariff Item	商品名称及备注	进口税率 最惠	普通	暂定	出口退税	增值税率	计量单位	监管条件	Article Description
48.01	成卷或成张的新闻纸:								Newsprint, in rolls or sheets:
4801.0000	成卷或成张的新闻纸	5	30			17	千克		Newsprint, in rolls or sheets
48.02	书写、印刷或类似用途的未经涂布的纸及纸板、未打孔的穿孔卡片纸及穿孔纸带纸，成卷或成张矩形（包括正方形），任何尺寸，但品目 4801 或 4803 的纸除外；手工制纸及纸板								Uncoated paper and paperboard, of a kind used for writing, printing or other graphic purposes, and non perforated punch-cards and punch tape paper,in rolls or rectangular（including square）sheets, of any size, other than paper of heading No.48.01 or 48.03; hand-made paper and paper-board:
	-手工制纸及纸板:								-Hand-made paper and paperboard:
4802.1010	---宣纸	7.5	70		13	17	千克		---Xuan paper
4802.1090	---其他	7.5	70		13	17	千克		---Other

税则号列 Tariff Item	商品名称及备注	进口税率 最惠	普通	暂定	出口退税	增值税率	计量单位	监管条件	Article Description
	-光敏、热敏、电敏纸及纸板的原纸和原纸板:								-Paper and paperboard of a kind used as a base for photo-sensitive, heat-sensitive or electrosensitive paper or paperboard:
4802.2010[暂]	---照相原纸	7.5	40	5		17	千克		---Photo paper base
4802.2090	---其他	7.5	40			17	千克		---Other
4802.4000	-壁纸原纸	7.5	40			17	千克		-Wallpaper base
	-其他纸及纸板,不含用机械或化学-机械方法制得的纤维或所含前述纤维不超过全部纤维重量的10%:								-Other paper and paperboard, not containning fibres obtained by a mechanical or chemimechanical process or of which not more than 10% by weight of the total fibre content consists of such fibres:
4802.5400	--每平方米重量小于40克	7.5	30			17	千克		--Weighing less than 40g/m²
4802.5500	--每平方米重量在40克及以上,但不超过150克,成卷	5	30			17	千克		--Weighing 40g/m² or more but not more than 150g/m², in rolls
4802 5500.10	40<每平方米重≤150g的胶版纸(成卷,机械或化学—机械法制得的纤维含量≤10%)	5	30			17	千克		Offset paper, weighing 40g/m² or more but not more than 150g/m², (in rolls, containing fibres less than 10%, obtained by mechanical or chemimechanical process)
4802 5500.90	40<每平方米重≤150g未涂布中厚纸(书写印刷用,成卷,含机械或化学—机械法制纤维≤10%)	5	30			17	千克		Uncoated paper, weighing 40g/m² or more but not more than 150g/m² used for writing and printing (in rolls, containing fibres less than 10% ,obtained by mechanical or chemi-mechanical process)
4802.5600	--每平方米重量在40克及以上,但不超过150克,一边不越过435毫米,另一边不超过297毫米(以未折叠计)成张的	5	30			17	千克		--Weighing 40g/m² or more but not more than 150g/m², in sheets with one side not exceeding 435mm and the other side not exceeding 297mm in the unfolded state
4802 5600.10	成张40<每平方米重≤150g胶版纸(长≤435mm,宽≤297mm,含机械或化学—机械法制纤维≤10%)	5	30			17	千克		Offset paper, weighing 40g/m² or more but not more than 150g/m², (in sheets with one side not exceeding 435mm and the other side not exceeding 297mm, containing less than 10% of fibres, obtained by mechanical or chemimechanical process)
4802 5600.90	40<每平方米重≤150g未涂布纸,成张(书写印刷,长≤435mm,宽≤297mm,含机械或半化学浆≤10%)	5	30			17	千克		Uncoated paper, weighing 40g/m² or more but not more than 150g/m², used for writing and printing (in sheets with one side not exceeding 435mm and the other side not exceeding 297mm, containing less than 10% of fibres, obtained by mechanical or chemi-mechanical process)
4802.5700	--其他,每平方米重量在40克及以上,但不超过150克	5	30			17	千克		--Other,weighing 40g/m² or more but not more than 150 g/m²
4802 5700.10	其他40<每平方米重≤150g的胶版纸(机械或化学—机械法制得的纤维含量≤10%)	5	30			17	千克		Other offset paper, weighing 40g/m² or more but not more than 150g/m², (containing more than 10% of fibres obtained by mechanical or chemimechanical process)
4802 5700.90	其他40<每平方米重≤150g未涂中厚纸(书写印刷用,含机械或化学—机械法制纤维≤10%)	5	30			17	千克		Other uncoated paper, weighing 40g/m² or more but not more than 150g/m², (used for writing and printing, containing more than 10% of fibres obtained by mechanical or chemi-mechanical process)
4802.5800	--每平方米重量超过150克	5	30			17	千克		--Weighing more than 150g/m²
	-其他纸及纸板,所含用机械或化学-机械方法制得的纤维超过全部纤维重量的10%:								-Other paper and paperboard, of which more than 10% by weight of the total fibre content consists of fibres obtained by a mechanical or chemimechanical process:
	--成卷的:								--In rolls:
4802.6110	---新闻纸	7.5	30			17	千克		---Newsprint
4802.6190	---其他	5	30			17	千克		---Other
4802.6200	--成张的,一边不超过435毫米,另一边不超过297毫米(以未折叠计)	5	30			17	千克		--In sheets with one side not exceeding 435mm and the other side not exceeding 297mm in the unfolded state

税则号列 Tariff Item	商品名称及备注	进口税率 最惠	普通	暂定	出口退税	增值税率	计量单位	监管条件	Article Description
	--其他:								--Other:
4802.6910	---新闻纸	7.5	30			17	千克		---Newsprint
4802.6990	---其他	5	30			17	千克		---Other
48.03	**卫生纸、面巾纸、餐巾纸以及家庭或卫生用的类似纸、纤维素絮纸和纤维素纤维网纸，不论是否起纹、压花、打孔、染面、饰面或印花，成卷或成张的：**								**Toilet or facial tissue stock, towel or napkin stock and similar paper of a kind used for household or sanitary purposes, cellulose wadding and webs of cellulose fibres, whether or not creped, crinkled, embossed, perforated,surface-coloured, surface-decoratd or printed, in rolls or sheets:**
4803.0000	卫生纸、面巾纸、餐巾纸以及家庭或卫生用的类似纸、纤维素絮纸和纤维素纤维网纸，不论是否起纹、压花、打孔、染面、饰面或印花，成卷或成张的	7.5	40			17	千克	A	Toilet or facial tissue stock, towel or napkin stock and similar paper of a kind used for household or sanitary purposes, cellulose wadding and webs of cellulose fibres, whether or not creped, crinkled, embossed,perforated,surface-coloured,surface-decorated or printed, in rolls or sheets
48.04	**成卷或成张的未经涂布的牛皮纸及纸板，但不包括品目 48.02 或 48.03 的货品：**								**Uncoated kraft paper and poperboard,in rolls or sheets, other than that of heading No.48.02 or 48.03:**
	-牛皮挂面纸:								-Krafliner:
4804.1100	--未漂白	5	30			17	千克		--Unbleached
4804 1100.10	每平方米重 115～360 克未漂白、成卷或成张未涂布牛皮挂面纸（紧度不小于 0.68g/ cm³，耐破指数不小于 2.6kpa . m²/g，横向环压指数不小于 7.5N/m · m²/g，横向耐折度不小于 60 次，饱和牛皮纸除外）	5	30			17	千克		Uncoated Krafliner paper, unbleached, in rolls or sheets, weighing more than 115g/m² but less than 360g/m²（tightness more than 0.68g/cm³, burst index not smaller than 2.6kPa • m²/g, crossdirection ring crush Index not smaller than 7.5N/ m • m²/g cross-direction folding endurance not less than 60 times, other than saturated kraft paper）
4804 1100.90	其他未漂白的牛皮挂面纸（成卷或成张的及未经涂布的）	5	30			17	千克		Other uncoated kraft paper, unbleached, in rolls or sheets
4804.1900	--其他	5	30			17	千克		--Other
	-袋用牛皮纸:								-Sack kraft paper:
4804.2100	--未漂白	5	30			17	千克		--Unbleaehed
4804.2900	--其他	5	30			17	千克		--Other
	-其他牛皮纸及纸板,每平方米重量不超过150克:								-Other kraft paper and paperboard weighing 150g/m² or less:
4804.3100	--未漂白	2	30			17	千克		--Unbleached
4804 3100.10	每平方米重 115～150 克未漂白、成卷或成张未涂布其他牛皮纸（紧度不小于 0.68 g/ cm³，耐破指数不小于 2.6kpa · m²/g，横向环压指数不小于 7.5N/m · m²/g，横向耐折度不小于 60 次，饱和牛皮纸除外）	2	30			17	千克		Uncoated Krafliner paper, unbleached, in rolls or sheets, weighing more than 115g/m² but less than 150g/m²（tightness more than 0.68g/cm³, burst index not smaller than 2.6kPa • m²/g, crossdirection ring crush Index not smaller than 7.5N/ m • m²/g cross-direction folding endurance not less than 60 times, other than saturated kraft paper）
4804 3100.90	其他未漂白的其他薄牛皮纸及纸板（薄纸指每平方米重≤150g，成卷或成张未经涂布的）	2	30			17	千克		Other uncoated kraft paper and paperboard, unbleached（weighing 150g/m² or less, in rolls or sheets）
4804.3900	--其他	2	30			17	千克		--Other
	-其他牛皮纸及纸板,每平方米重量超过150克，但小于225克:								-Other kraft paper and paperboard weighing more than 150g/m² but less than 225g/m²:
4804.4100	--未漂白	2	30			17	千克		--Unbleached
4804 4100.10	150＜每平方米重＜225 克未漂白、成卷或成张未涂布其他牛皮纸（紧度不小于 0.68 g/ cm³，耐破指数不小于 2.6kpa · m²/g，横向环压指数不小于 7.5N/m · m²/g，横向耐折度不小于 60 次，饱和牛皮纸除外）	2	30			17	千克		Other uncoated Krafliner paper, unbleached, in rolls or sheets, weighing more than 115g/m² but less than 225g/m²（tightness more than 0.68g/ cm³, burst index not smaller than 2.6kPa • m²/g, crossdirection ring crush Index not smaller than 7.5N/ m • m²/g cross-direction folding endurance not less than 60 times, other than saturated kraft paper）

税则号列 Tariff Item	商品名称及备注	进口税率 最惠	普通	暂定	出口退税	增值税率	计量单位	监管条件	Article Description
4804 4100.90	其他未漂白的其他中厚牛皮纸及纸板（中厚指150克<每平方米重<225克，成卷或成张未涂布的）	2	30			17	千克		Other uncoated kraft paper and paperboard, unbleached（weighing more than 115g/m² but less than 225g/m², in rolls or sheets）
4804.4200	--本体均匀漂白，所含用化学方法制得的木纤维超过全部纤维重量的95%	5	30			17	千克		--Bleached uniformly throughout the mass and of which more than 95% by weight of the total fibre content consists of wood fibres obtained by a chemical process
4804.4900	--其他	2	30			17	千克		--Other
	-其他牛皮纸及纸板，每平方米重量在225克及以上:								Other kraft paper and paperboard weighing 225g/m² or more:
4804.5100	--未漂白	2	30			17	千克		--Unbleached
4804 5100.10	每平方米重225～360克未漂白、成卷或成张未涂布其他牛皮纸（紧度不小于0.68 g/cm³，耐破指数不小于2.6kpa·m²/g，横向环压指数不小于7.5N/m·m²/g，横向耐折度不小于60次，饱和牛皮纸除外）	2	30			17	千克		Other uncoated Kraftliner paper, unbleached, in rolls or sheets, weighing more than 225g/m² but less than 360g/m²（tightness more than 0.68g/ cm³, burst index not smaller than 2.6kPa · m²/g, crossdirection ring crush Index not smaller than 7.5N/ m · m²/g cross-direction folding endurance not less than 60 times, other than saturated kraft paper）
4804 5100.90	其他未漂白的其他厚牛皮纸及纸板（厚纸指每平方米重≥225克，成卷或成张未经涂布的）	2	30			17	千克		Other uncoated kraft paper and paperboard, unbleached（weighing more than 225g/m², in rolls or sheets）
4804.5200	--本体均匀漂白，所含用化学方法制得的木纤维超过全部纤维重量的95%	5	30			17	千克		--Bleached uniformly throughout the mass and of which more than 95% by weight of the total fibre content consists of wood fibres obtained by a chemical process
4804.5900	--其他	2	30			17	千克		--Other
48.05	成卷或成张的其他未经涂布的纸及纸板，加工程度不超过本章注释三所列范围:								**Other uncoated paper and paperboard, in rolls or sheets, not further worked or processed than as specified in Note 3 to this Chapter:**
	-瓦楞原纸:								-Fluting paper:
4805.1100	--半化学的瓦楞原纸	7.5	30			17	千克		--Semi-chemical fluting paper
4805.1200	--草浆瓦楞原纸	7.5	30			17	千克		--Straw fluting paper
4805.1900	--其他	7.5	30			17	千克		--Other
	-强韧箱纸板（再生挂面纸板）:								-Testliner（recycled liner board）:
4805.2400	--每平方米重量在150克及以下	7.5	30			17	千克		--Weighing 150g/m² or less
4805.2500	--每平方米重量超过150克	7.5	30			17	千克		--Weighing more than 150g/m²
4805.3000	-亚硫酸盐包装纸	7.5	30			17	千克		-Sulphite wrapping paper
4805.4000	-滤纸及纸板	7.5	30			17	千克		-Filter paper and paperboard
4805.5000	-毡纸及纸板	7.5	30			17	千克		-Felt paper and paperboard
	-其他:								-Other:
	--每平方米重量在150克及以下:								---Weighing 150g/m² or less:
4805.9110	---电解电容器原纸	7.5	30			17	千克		---Paper base for electrolytic capacitor
4805.9190	---其他	7.5	30			17	千克		---Other
4805.9200	--每平方米重量超过150克，但小于225克	7.5	30			17	千克		--Weighing more than 150g/m² but less than 225g/m²
4805.9300	--每平方米重量在225克及以上	7.5	30			17	千克		--Weighing 225g/m² or more
48.06	成卷或成张的植物羊皮纸、防油纸、描图纸、半透明纸及其他高光泽透明或半透明纸:								**Vegetable parchment, greaseproof papers, tracing papers and glassine and other glazed transparent or translucent papers, in rolls or sheets:**
4806.1000	-植物羊皮纸	7.5	40			17	千克		-Vegetable parchment
4806.2000	-防油纸	7.5	40			17	千克		-Greaseproof papers
4806.3000	-描图纸	7.5	30			17	千克		-Tracing papers
4806.4000 [暂]	-高光泽透明或半透明纸	7.5	40	5		17	千克		-Glassine and other glazed transparent or translucent papers
48.07	成卷或成张的复合纸及纸板（用								**Composite paper and paperboard（made by**

税则号列 Tariff Item	商品名称及备注	进口税率 最惠	进口税率 普通	进口税率 暂定	出口退税	增值税率	计量单位	监管条件	Article Description
	黏合剂黏合各层纸或纸板制成），未经表面涂布或未浸渍，不论内层是否有加强材料：								**sticking flat layers of paper or paperboard together with an adhesive), not surface-coated or impregnated, whether or not internally reinforced, in rolls or sheets:**
4807.0000[暂]	成卷或成张的复合纸及纸板(用黏合剂黏合各层纸或纸板制成)，未经表面涂布或未浸渍，不论内层是否有加强材料	7.5	40	5		17	千克		Composite paper and paperboard (made by sticking flat layers of paper or paperboard together with an adhesive), not surfacecoated or impregnated, whether or not internally reinforced, in rolls or sheets
48.08	**成卷或成张的瓦楞纸及纸板（不论是否与平面纸胶合）、皱纹纸及纸板、压纹纸及纸板、穿孔纸及纸板，但品目4803的纸除外**								**Paper and paperboard, corrugated (with or without glued flat surface sheets), creped, crinkled, embossed or perforated, in rolls or sheets, other than paper of the kind described in heading No.48.03:**
4808.1000	-瓦楞纸及纸板，不论是否穿孔	7.5	30			17	千克		-Corrugated paper and paperboard, whether or not perforated
4808.4000	-皱纹牛皮纸，不论是否压花或穿孔	7.5	40			17	千克		-Kraft paper, creped or crinkled, whether or not embossed or perforated
4808.9000	-其他	7.5	40			17	千克		-Other
48.09	**复写纸、自印复写纸及其他拷贝或转印纸（包括涂布或浸渍的油印蜡纸或胶印版纸），不论是否印制，成卷或成张的：**								**Carbon paper, self-copy paper and other copying or transfer papers (including coated or impregnated paper for duplicator stencils or offset plates), whether or not printed, in rolls or sheets:**
4809.2000	-自印复写纸	7.5	40			17	千克		-Self-copy paper
4809.9000	-其他	7.5	40			17	千克		-Other
48.10	**成卷或成张矩形(包括正方形)的任何尺寸的单面或双面涂布高岭土或其他无机物质(不论是否加粘合剂)的纸及纸板，但未涂布其他涂料，不论是否染面、饰面或印花**								**Paper and paperboard, coated on one or both sides with kaolin (China clay) or other inorganic substances, with or without a binder, and with no othe coating, whether or not surfacecoloured, surface-decorated or printed, in rolls or rectangular(including square)sheets, of any size:**
	-书写、印刷或类似用途的纸及纸板，不含用机械或化学-机械方法制得的纤维或所含前述纤维不超过全部纤维重量的10%:								-Paper and paperboard of a kind used for writing, printing or other graphic purposes, not containing fibres obtained by a mechanical or chemimechanical process or of which not more than 10% by weight of the total fibre content consists of such fibres:
4810.1300	--成卷的	5	40			17	千克		--In rolls
4810 1300.01	成卷的铜版纸（所含用机械或化学—机械法制得的纤维≤10%）	5	40			17	千克		Chrome paper, in rolls, containing not more than 10% of fibres obtained by a mechanical or chemimechanical process
4810 1300.90	涂无机物的其他书写、印刷或类似用途纸及纸板（成卷的，所含用机械或化学—机械法制得的纤维≤10%）	5	40			17	千克		Other paper and paperboard, coated on inorganic substances, used for writing, printing or other graphic purposes, (in rolls, containing not more than 10% of fibres obtained by mechanical or chemimechanical process)
4810.1400	--成张的，一边不超过435毫米，另一边不超过297毫米（以未折叠计）	5	40			17	千克		--In sheets with one side not exceeding 435mm and the other side not exceeding 297mm in the unfolded state
4810 1400.01	成张的铜版纸（一边≤435mm，另一边≤297mm，机械或化学—机械纤维≤10%）	5	40			17	千克		Chrome paper, in sheets with one side not exceeding 435mm and the other side not exceeding 297mm, containing not more than 10% of fibres obtained by mechanical or chemimechanical process)
4810 1400.90	涂无机物的其他成张的书写、印刷的纸及纸板（一边≤435mm，另一边≤297mm，机械或化学—机械纤维≤10%）	5	40			17	千克		Other paper and paperboard, coated on inorganic substances, used for writing and printing (in sheets with one side not exceeding 435mm and the other side not exceeding 297mm, containing not more than 10% of fibres obtained by mechanical or chemi-mechanical process)
4810.1900	--其他	5	40			17	千克		--Other
4810 1900.01	其他铜版纸（所含用机械或化学	5	40			17	千克		Other chrome paper, containing more than 10% of

税则号列 Tariff Item	商品名称及备注	进口税率 最惠	普通	暂定	出口退税	增值税率	计量单位	监管条件	Article Description
	—机械法制得的纤维≤10%)								fibres obtained by mechanical or chemimechanical process)
4810 1900.90	涂无机物的其他书写、印刷用途的纸及纸板(所含用机械或化学—机械法制得的纤维≤10%)	5	40			17	千克		Other paper and paperboard, coated on inorganic substances, used for writing and printing (containing not more than 10% of fibres obtained by mechanical or chemi-mechanical process)
	-书写、印刷或类似用途的纸及纸板,所含用机械或化学-机械方法制得的纤维超过全部纤维重量的10%:								-Paper and paperboard of a kind used for writing, printing or other graphic purposes, of which more than 10% by weight of the total fibre content consists of fibres obtained by a mechanical or chemi-mechanical process:
4810.2200	--轻质涂布纸	5	40			17	千克		--Light-weight coated paper
4810.2900	--其他	5	40			17	千克		--Other
	-牛皮纸及纸板,但书写、印刷或类似用途的除外:								-Kraft paper and paperboard, other than that of a kind used for writing, printing or other graphic purposes:
4810.3100	--本体均匀漂白,所含用化学方法制得的木纤维超过全部纤维重量的95%,每平方米重量不超过150克	5	40			17	千克		--Bleached uniformly throughout the mass and of which more than 95% by weight of the total fibre content consists of wood fibres obtained by a chemical process, and weighing 150g/m² or less
4810 3100.10	涂无机物的白板纸、白卡纸(薄纸指重量≤150克/平方米,含用化学方法制得木纤维)	5	40			17	千克		White paper and paperboard, coated with inorganic substances, weighing 150g/m² or less, containing wood fibres obtained by a chemical process
4810 3100.90	涂无机物的薄漂白牛皮纸及纸板(薄纸指重量≤150 克/平方米,含用化学方法制得的木纤维)	5	40			17	千克		Kraft paper and paperboard, bleached, coated with inorganic substances, weighing 150g/m² or less, containing wood fibres obtained by a chemical process
4810.3200	--本体均匀漂白,所含用化学方法制得的木纤维超过全部纤维重量的 95%,每平方米重量超过150 克	5	40			17	千克		--Bleached uniformly throughout the mass and of which more than 95% by weight of the total fibre content consists of wood fibres obtained by a chemical process, and weighing more than 150g/m²
4810 3200.10	涂无机物的白板纸、白卡纸(厚纸指重量>150 克/平方米,含用化学方法制得的木纤维)	5	40			17	千克		White paper and paperboard, coated with inorganic substances, weighing more than 150g/m², containing wood fibres obtained by a chemical process
4810 3200.90	涂无机物的厚漂白牛皮纸及纸板(厚纸指重量>150 克/平方米,含用化学方法制得的木纤维)	5	40			17	千克		White kraft paper and paperboard, bleached, coated with inorganic substances, weighing more than 150g/m², containing wood fibres obtained by a chemical process
4810.3900	--其他	5	40			17	千克		--Other
	-其他纸及纸板:								-Other paper and paperboard:
4810.9200	--多层的	5	40			17	千克		--Multiply
4810.9900	--其他	7.5	40			17	千克		--Other
48.11	**成卷或成张矩形(包括正方形)的任何尺寸的经涂布、浸渍、覆盖、染面、饰面或印花的纸、纸板、纤维素絮纸及纤维素纤维网纸,但品目 4803、4809 或 4810 的货品除外**								**Paper, paperboard, cellulose wadding and webs of cellulose fibres, coated, impregnated, covered, surface coloured, surface-decorated or printed, in rolls or rectangular (including square) sheets, of any size, other than goods of the kind described in heading No.48.03, 48.09 or 48.10:**
4811.1000	-焦油纸及纸板,沥青纸及纸板	7.5	40			17	千克		-Tarred, bituminised or asphalted paper and paperboard
	-胶粘纸及纸板:								-Gummed or adhesive paper and paperboard:
4811.4100	--自粘的	7.5	40			17	千克		--Self-adhesive
4811.4900	--其他	7.5	40			17	千克		--Other
	-用塑料(不包括黏合剂)涂布、浸渍或覆盖的纸及纸板:								-Paper and paperboard coated, impregnated or covered with plastics (excluding adhesives):
	--漂白的,每平方米重量超过150克:								--Bleached, weighing more than 150 g/m²:

税则号列 Tariff Item	商品名称及备注	进口税率 最惠	普通	暂定	出口退税	增值税率	计量单位	监管条件	Article Description
4811.5110[暂]	---彩色相纸用双面涂塑厚纸	7.5	40	1		17	千克		---Paper coated on both sides with plastics for colour photography
4811.5190	---其他	7.5	40			17	千克		---Other
	--其他:								--Other:
4811.5910	---绝缘纸及纸板	7.5	30			17	千克		---Insulating paper and paperboard
	---其他:								---Other:
4811.5991	----镀铝的	7.5	40			17	千克		----Aluminium plated
4811.5999	----其他	7.5	40			17	千克		----Other
	-压蜡、石蜡、硬脂精、油或甘油涂布、浸渍、覆盖的纸及纸板:								-Paper and paperboard, coated, impregnated or covered with wax, paraffin wax, stearin, oil or glyecrol:
4811.6010	---绝缘纸及纸板	7.5	30			17	千克		---Insulating paper and paperboard
4811.6090	---其他	7.5	40			17	千克		---Other
4811.9000	-其他纸、纸板、纤维素絮纸及纤维素纤维网纸	7.5	40			17	千克		-Other paper, paperboard, cellulose wadding and webs of cellulose fibres
48.12	**纸浆制的滤块、滤板及滤片:**								**Filter blocks, slabs and plates, of paper pulp:**
4812.0000	纸浆制的滤块,滤板及滤片	7.5	40			17	千克		Filter blocks, slabs and plates, of paper pulp
48.13	**卷烟纸，不论是否切成一定尺寸、成小本或管状:**								**Cigarette paper, whether or not cut to size or in the form of booklets or tubes:**
4813.1000	-成小本或管状	7.5	100			17	千克	7	-In the form of booklets or tubes
4813.2000	-宽度不超过5厘米成卷的	7.5	100			17	千克	7	-In rolls of a width not exceeding 5cm
4813.9000	-其他	7.5	100			17	千克	7	-Other
48.14	**壁纸及类似品；窗用透明纸:**								**Wallpaper and similar wall coverings; window transparencies of paper:**
4814.2000	-用塑料涂面或盖面的壁纸及类似品，起纹、压花、着色、印刷图案或经其他装饰	7.5	50		13	17	千克		-Wallpaper and similar wall coverings, consisting of paper coated or covered, on the face side, with a grained, embossed, coloured, design-printed or otherwise decorated layer of plastics
4814.9000	-其他	7.5	50			17	千克		-Other
4814 9000.10	用木粒或草粒等饰面的壁纸	7.5	50			17	千克	A	Wallpape with grain of wood or grass
4814 9000.90	其他壁纸及类似品,窗用透明纸	7.5	50			17	千克		Other wallpaper and similar wall coverings; window transparencies of paper:
48.16	**复写纸、自印复写纸及其他拷贝或转印纸（不包括品目48.09的纸），油印蜡纸或胶印版纸，不论是否盒装:**								**Carbon paper, self-copy paper and other copying or transfer papers （other than those of heading No.48.09）, duplicator stencils and offset plates, of paper, whether or not put up in boxes:**
4816.2000	-自印复写纸	7.5	70			17	千克		-Self-copy paper
	-其他:								-Other:
4816.9010	---热敏转印纸	7.5	40			17	千克		----Heat transfer paper
4816.9090	---其他	7.5	70			17	千克		---Other
48.17	**纸或纸板制的信封、封缄信片、素色明信片及通信卡片；纸或纸板制的盒子、袋子及夹子，内装各种纸制文具:**								**Envelopes, letter cards, plain postcards and correspondence cards, of paper or paperboard; boxes, pouches, wallets and writing compendiums, of paper or paperboard, containing an assortment of paper stationery:**
4817.1000	-信封	7.5	80		13	17	千克		-Envelopes
4817.2000	-封缄信片、素色明信片及通信卡片	7.5	80		13	17	千克		-Letter cards, plain postcards and correspondence cards
4817.3000	-纸或纸板制的盒子、袋子及夹子,内装各种纸制文具	7.5	80		13	17	千克		-Boxes, pouches, wallets and writing compendiums, of paper or paperboard,containing an assortment of paper stationery
48.18	**卫生纸及类似纸，家庭或卫生用纤维素絮纸及纤维素纤维网纸，成卷宽度不超过36厘米或切成一定尺寸或形状的；纸浆、纸、纤维素絮纸或纤维素纤维网纸**								**Toilet paper and similar paper, cellulose wadding or webs of cellulose fibres, of a kind used for household or sanitary purposes, in rolls of a width not exceeding 36cm, or cut to size or shape; handkerchiefs, cleansing tissues, towels,**

税则号列 Tariff Item	商品名称及备注	进口税率			出口退税	增值税率	计量单位	监管条件	Article Description
		最惠	普通	暂定					
	制的手帕、面巾、台布、餐巾、尿布、止血塞、床单及类似的家庭、卫生或医院用品、衣服及衣着附件								**tablecloths, serviettes napkins for babis, tampons, bed sheets and similar household, sanitary or hospital articles, articles of apparel and clothing accessories, of paper pulp, paper, cellulose wadding or webs of cellulose fibres:**
4818.1000	-卫生纸	7.5	80		5	17	千克	A	-Toilet paper
4818.2000	-纸手帕及纸面巾	7.5	90		5	17	千克	A	-Handkerchiefs, cleansing or facial tissues and towels
4818.3000	-纸台布及纸餐巾	7.5	90		5	17	千克	A	-Tablecloths and serviettes
4818.5000	-衣服及衣着附件	7.5	90		13	17	千克	A	-Articles of apparel and clothing accessories
4818.9000	-其他	7.5	90		13	17	千克	A	-Other
48.19	**纸、纸板、纤维素絮纸或纤维素纤维网纸制的箱、盒、匣、袋及其他包装容器；纸或纸板制的卷宗盒、信件盘及类似品，供办公室、商店及类似场所使用的**								**Cartons, boxes, cases, bags and other packing containers, of paper, paperboard, cellulose wadding or webs of cellulose fibres; box files, letter trays and similar articles, of paper or paperboard of a kind used in offices, shops or the like:**
4819.1000	-瓦楞纸或纸板制的箱、盒、匣	5	80		13	17	千克		-Cartons, boxes and cases, of corrugated paper or paperboard
4819.2000	-非瓦楞纸或纸板制的可折叠箱、盒、匣	5	80		13	17	千克		-Folding cartons, boxes and cases, of noncorrugated paper or paperboard
4819.3000	-底宽40厘米及以上的纸袋	7.5	80		13	17	千克		-Sacks and bags, having a base of a width of 40cm or more
4819.4000	-其他纸袋，包括锥形袋	7.5	80		13	17	千克		-Other sacks and bags, including cones
4819.5000	-其他包装容器，包括唱片套	7.5	80		13	17	千克	A	-Other packing containers, including record sleeves
4819.6000	-办公室、商店及类似场所使用的卷宗盒、信件盘、存储盒及类似品	7.5	80		13	17	千克		-Box files, letter trays, storage boxes and simiar articles, of a kind used in offices, shops or the like
48.20	**纸或纸板制的登记本、帐本、笔记本、定货本、收据本、信笺本、记事本、日记本及类似品、练习本、吸墨纸本、活动封面（活页及非活页）、文件夹、卷宗皮、多联商业表格纸、页间夹有复写纸的本及其他文具用品；纸或纸板制的样品簿、粘贴簿及书籍封面**								**Registers, account books, note books, order books, receipt books, letter pads, memorandum pads, diaries and similar articles, exercise books, blotting-pads, binders (loose-leaf or other), folders, file covers, manifold business forms, interleaved carbon sets and other articles of stationery, of paper of paperboard; albums for samples or for collections and book covers, of paper or paperboard:**
4820.1000	-登记本、账本、笔记本、订货本、收据本、信笺本、记事本、日记本及类似品	7.5	80		13	17	千克		-Registers, account books, note books, order books, receipt books, letter pads, memorandum pads, diaries and similar articles
4820.2000	-练习本	7.5	80		13	17	千克		-Exercise books
4820.3000	-活动封面（书籍封面除外）、文件夹及卷宗皮	7.5	80		13	17	千克		-Binders(other than book covers), folders and file covers
4820.4000	-多联商业表格纸、页间夹有复写纸的本	7.5	80		13	17	千克		-Manifold business forms and interleaved carbon sets
4820.5000	-样品簿及粘贴簿	7.5	80		13	17	千克		-Albums for samples or for collections
4820.9000	-其他	7.5	80		13	17	千克		-Other
48.21	**纸或纸板制的各种标签，不论是否印制：**								**Paper or paperboard labels of all kinds, whether or not printed:**
4821.1000	-印制	7.5	50		13	17	千克		-Printed
4821.9000	-其他	7.5	50		13	17	千克		-Other
48.22	**纸浆、纸或纸板（不论是否穿孔或硬化）制的筒管、卷轴、纡子及类似品：**								**Bobbins, spools， cops and similar supports of paper pulp, paper or paperboard (whether or not perforated or hardened):**
4822.1000	-纺织纱线用	7.5	35		13	17	千克		-Of a kind used for winding textile yarn
4822.9000	-其他	7.5	70		13	17	千克		-Other
48.23	**切成一定尺寸或形状的其他纸、纸板、纤维素絮纸及纤维素纤维**								**Other paper, paperboard, cellulose wadding and webs of cellulose fibres, cut to size or shape;**

税则号列 Tariff Item	商品名称及备注	进口税率			出口退税	增值税率	计量单位	监管条件	Article Description
		最惠	普通	暂定					
	网纸；纸浆、纸、纸板、纤维素絮纸及纤维素纤维网纸制的其他物品								**other articles of paper pulp, paper, paperboard, cellulose wadding or webs of cellulose fibres:**
4823.2000	-滤纸及纸板	7.5	30		13	17	千克		-Filter paper and paperboard
4823.4000	-已印制的自动记录器用打印纸卷、纸张及纸盘	7.5	30		13	17	千克		-Rolls, sheets and dials, printed for self-recording apparatus
	-纸或纸板制的盘、碟、盆、杯及类似品:								-Trays, dishes, plates, cups and the like, of paper or paperboard:
4823.6100	--竹浆纸制	7.5	90		13	17	千克	AB	--Of bamboo
	--其他:								--Other:
4823.6910	----非木植物浆制	7.5	90		13	17	千克	AB	--of non-wood plant pulp
4823.6990	---其他	7.5	90		13	17	千克	AB	---Other
4823.7000	-压制或模制纸浆制品	7.5	90		13	17	千克		-Moulded or pressed articles of paper pulp
	-其他:								-Other:
4823.9010	---以纸或纸板为底制成的铺地制品	7.5	90			17	千克		---Floor coverings on a base of paper or of paperboard, whether or not cut to size
4823.9020	---神纸及类似用品	7.5	180		13	17	千克		---Joss paper and the like
4823.9030	---纸扇	7.5	90		13	17	千克		---Paper fans
4823.9090	---其他	7.5	90		13	17	千克		---Other

第四十九章
书籍、报纸、印刷图画及其他印刷品；手稿、打字稿及设计图纸

Chapter 49
Printed books, newspapers, pictures and other products of the printing industry; manuscripts, typescripts and plans

注释：

一、本章不包括：

（一）透明基的照相负片或正片（第三十七章）；

（二）立体地图、设计图表或地球仪、天体仪，不论是否印刷（品目90.23）；

（三）第九十五章的扑克牌或其他物品；或

（四）雕版画、印刷画、石印画的原本（品目97.02），品目97.04的邮票、印花税票、纪念封、首日封、邮政信笺及类似品，以及第九十七章的超过100年的古物或其他物品。

二、第四十九章所称"印刷"，也包括用胶版复印机、油印机印制，在自动数据处理设备控制下打印绘制，压印、冲印、感光复印、热敏复印或打字。

三、用纸以外材料装订成册的报纸、杂志和期刊，以及一期以上装订在同一封面里的成套报纸、杂志和期刊，应归入品目 49.01，不论是否有广告材料。

四、品目 49.01 还包括：

（一）附有说明文字，每页编有号数以便装订成一册或几册的整集印刷复制品，例如，美术作品、绘画；

（二）随同成册书籍的图画附刊；以及

（三）供装订书籍或小册子用的散页、集页或书帖形式的印刷品，已构成一部作品的全部或部分。

但没有说明文字的印刷图画或图解，不论是否散页或书帖形式，应归入品目 49.11。

五、除本章注释三另有规定的以外，品目 49.01 不包括主要做广告用的出版物（例如，小册子、散页印刷品、商业目录、同业公会出版的年鉴、旅游宣传品），这类出版物应归入品目 49.11。

六、品目 49.03 所称"儿童图画书"，是指以图画为主、文字为辅．供儿童阅览的书籍。

Chapter Note:

1.This Chapter does not cover:

（a）Photographic negatives or positives on transparent bases（Chapter 37）;

（b）Maps, plans or globes, in relief, whether or not printed（heading 90.23）;

（c）Playing cards or other goods of Chapter 95; or

（d）Original engravings, prints or lithographs（heading 97.02）, postage or revenue stamps, stamp-postmarks, first-day covers, postal stationery or the like of heading 97.04, antiques of an age exceeding one hundred years or other articles of Chapter 97.

2.For the purposes of Chapter 49, the term "printed" also means reproduced by means of a duplicating machine, produced under the control of an automatic data processing machine, embossed, photographed, photocopied, thermocopied or typewritten

3.Newspapers, journals and periodicals which are bound otherwise than in paper, and sets of newspapers, journals or periodicals comprising more than one number under a single cover are to be classified in heading 49.01, whether or not containing advertising material.

4.Heading 49.01 also covers:

（a）A collection of printed reproductions of, for example, works of art or drawings, with a relative text, put up with numbered pages in a form suitable for binding into one or more volumes;

（b）A pictorial supplement accompanying, and subsidiary to, a bound volume; and

（c）Printed parts of books or booklets，in the form of assembed or separate sheets or signatures, constituting the whole or a part of a complete work and designed for binding.

However, printed pictures or illustrations not bearing a text, whether in the form of signatures or separate sheets, fall in heading 49.11.

5.Subject to Note 3 to this Chapter, heading 49.01 does not cover publications which are essentially devoted to advertising（for example, brochures, pamphlets, leaflets, trade catalogues, year books published by trade associations, tourist propaganda）. Such publications are to be classified in heading 49.11.

6.For the purposes of heading 49.03, the expression "children's picture books" means books for children in which the pictures form the principal interest and the text is subsidiary.

税则号列 Tariff Item	商品名称及备注	进口税率			出口退税	增值税率	计量单位	监管条件	Article Description
		最惠	普通	暂定					
49.01	书籍、小册子、散页印刷品及类似印刷品，不论是否单张：								**Printed books, brochures, leaflets and similar printed matter, whether or not in single sheets:**
4901.1000	-单张的，不论是否折叠	0	0		13	13	千克		-In single sheets, whether or not folded
	-其他：								-Other:
4901.9100	--字典或百科全书及其连续出版的分册	0	0		13	13	千克		--Dictionaries and encyclopaedias, and serial instalments thereof

税则号列 Tariff Item	商品名称及备注	进口税率 最惠	进口税率 普通	进口税率 暂定	出口退税	增值税率	计量单位	监管条件	Article Description
4901.9900	--其他	0	0		13	13	千克		--Other
49.02	**报纸、杂志及期刊，不论有无插图或广告材料：**								**Newspapers, journals and periodicals, whether or not illustrated or containing advertising material:**
4902.1000	-每周至少出版四次	0	0		13	13	千克		-Appearing at least four times a week
4902.9000	-其他	0	0		13	13	千克		-Other
49.03	**儿童图画书、绘画或涂色书：**								**Children's picture, drawing or colouring books:**
4903.0000	儿童图画书,绘画或涂色书	0	0		13	13	千克		Children's picture, drawing or colouring books
49.04	**乐谱原稿或印本，不论是否装订或印有插图：**								**Music, printed or in manuscript, whether or not bound or illustrated:**
4904.0000	乐谱原稿或印本，不论是否装订或印有插图	0	0		13	13	千克		Music, printed or in manuscript, whether or not bound or illustrated
49.05	**各种印刷的地图、水道图及类似图表，包括地图册、挂图、地形图及地球仪、天体仪：**								**Maps and hydrographic or similar charts of all kinds, including atlases, wall maps, topographical plans and globes, printed:**
4905.1000	-地球仪、天体仪	0	0		13	17	千克		-Globes
	-其他:								-Other:
4905.9100	--成册的	0	0		13	17	千克		--In book form
4905.9900	--其他	0	0		13	17	千克		--Other
49.06	**手绘的建筑、工程、工业、商业、地形或类似用途的设计图纸原稿；手稿；用感光纸照相复印或用复写纸誊写的上述物品复制件**								**Plans and drawings for architectural, engineering, industrial, commercial,topographical or similar purposes, being originals drawn by hand; hand-wri- tten text; photographic reproductions on sensitized paper and carbon copies of the foregoing:**
4906.0000	手绘的建筑、工程、工业、商业、地形或类似用途的设计图纸原稿；手稿；用感光纸照相复印或用复写纸眷写的上述物品复制件	0	0		13	17	千克		Plans and drawings for architectural, engineering, industrial, commercial, topographical or similar purposes, being originals drawn by hand; hand-written text; photographic reproduetions on sensitized paper and carbon copies of the foregoing
49.07	**在承认或将承认其面值的国家流通或新发行并且未经使用的邮票、印花税票及类似票证；印有邮票或印花税票的纸品；钞票；空白支票；股票、债券及类似所有权凭证**								**Unused postage, revenue or similar stamps of current or new issue in the country in which they have, or will have, a recognised face value; stamp-impressed paper; banknotes; cheque forms; stock, share or bond certificates and similar documents of title:**
4907.0010	---邮票	7.5	50		13	17	千克		---Postage
4907.0020	---钞票	0	50		13	17	千克		---Banknotes
4907.0030	---证券凭证	0	50		13	17	千克		---Documents of title
4907.0090	---其他	7.5	50		13	17	千克		---Other
4907 0090.01[暂]	特许权使用凭证(包括软件升级许可证、软件用户许可证等，但游戏软件升级许可证、游戏软件用户许可证除外)	7.5	50	0	13	17	千克		Certificate of right of special permission (including software upgrade license , software user License，license of game sofrware upgrades, license of game sofrware users)
4907 0090.90	其他印有邮票等的其他纸品（包括印有印花税票的纸品，特许权使用凭证除外）	7.5	50		13	17	千克		Other stamp-impressed paper (including revenue stamps, other than certificate of right of special permission)
49.08	**转印贴花纸（移画印花法用图案纸）：**								**Transfers（decalcomanias）:**
4908.1000	-釉转印贴花纸（移画印花法用图案纸）	7.5	50		13	17	千克		-Transfers（decalcomanias）, vitrifiable
4908.9000	-其他	7.5	50		13	17	千克		-Other
49.09	**印刷或有图画的明信片；印有个人问候、祝贺、通告的卡片，不论是否有图画、带信封或饰边：**								**Printed or illustrated postcards; printed cards bearing personal greetings, messages or announcements, whether or not illustrated, with or without envelopes or trimmings:**
4909.0010	---印刷或有图画的明信片	7.5	50		13	17	千克		---Printed or illustrated postcards
4909.0090	---其他	7.5	50		13	17	千克		---Other

税则号列 Tariff Item	商品名称及备注	进口税率			出口退税	增值税率	计量单位	监管条件	Article Description
		最惠	普通	暂定					
49.10	印刷的各种日历，包括日历芯:								**Calendars of any kind, printed, including calendar blocks:**
4910.0000	印刷的各种日历，包括日历芯	7.5	50		13	17	千克		Calendars of any kind, printed, including calendar blocks
49.11	其他印刷品，包括印刷的图片及照片:								**Other printed matter, including printed pictures and photographs:**
	-商业广告品、商品目录及类似印刷品:								-Trade advertising material, commercial catalogues and the like:
4911.1010	---无商业价值的	0	0		13	17	千克		---No commercial value
4911.1090	---其他	7.5	50		13	17	千克		---Other
	-其他:								-Other:
4911.9100	--图片、设计图样及照片	7.5	50		13	17	千克		--Pictures, designs and photographs
	--其他:								--Other:
4911.9910	---纸质的	7.5	50		13	17	千克		---Of paper
4911 9910.01 [暂]	印有自动数据处理设备用程序的纸张	7.5	50	0	13	17	千克		Papers printed with programs for automatic data processing equipment
4911 9910.90	其他纸质的印刷品，不包括纸质的图片、设计图样及照片(印有自动数据处理设备用程序的纸张除外)	7.5	50		13	17	千克		Other printed matter, excluding printed pictures, designed drawing and photographs(other than Papers printed with programs for automatic data processing equipment)
4911.9990	---其他	7.5	50		13	17	千克		---Other
4911.9990.90	其他印刷品（印有自动数据处理设备用程序的纸张除外）	7.5	50		13	17	千克		---Other printed matter (other than the papers printed with programs for ADPE)

第十一类
纺织原料及纺织制品

注释：

一、本类不包括：

（一）制刷用的动物鬃、毛（品目05.02）；马毛及废马毛（品目05.11）；

（二）人发及人发制品（品目05.01、67.03或67.04），但通常用于榨油机或类似机器的滤布除外（品目59.11）；

（三）第十四章的棉短绒或其他植物材料；

（四）品目25.24的石棉、品目68.12或68.13的石棉制品或其他产品；

（五）品目30.05或30.06的物品；品目33.06的用于清洁牙缝的纱线（牙线），单独零售包装的；

（六）品目37.01至37.04的感光布；

（七）截面尺寸超过1毫米的塑料单丝和表面宽度超过5毫米的塑料扁条及类似品（例如，人造草）（第三十九章），以及上述单丝或扁条的缏条、织物、篮筐或柳条编结品（第四十六章）；

（八）第三十九章的用塑料浸渍、涂布、包覆或层压的机织物、针织物或钩编织物、毡呢或无纺织物及其制品；

（九）第四十章的用橡胶浸渍、涂布、包覆或层压的机织物、针织物或钩编织物、毡呢或无纺织物及其制品；

（十）带毛皮张（第四十一章或第四十三章）、品目43.03或43.04的毛皮制品、人造毛皮及其制品；

（十一）品目42.01或42.02的用纺织材料制成的物品；

（十二）第四十八章的产品或物品（例如，纤维素絮纸）；

（十三）第六十四章的鞋靴及其零件、护腿、裹腿及类似品；

（十四）第六十五章的发网、其他帽类及其零件；

（十五）第六十七章的货品；

（十六）涂有研磨料的纺织材料（品目68.05）以及品目68.15的碳纤维及其制品；

（十七）玻璃纤维及其制品，但可见底布的玻璃线刺绣品除外（第七十章）；

（十八）第九十四章的物品（例如，家具、寝具、灯具及照明装置）；

（十九）第九十五章的物品（例如，玩具、游戏品、运动用品及网具）；

（二十）第九十六章的物品［例如：刷子、旅行用成套缝纫用具、拉链、打字机色带、卫生巾（护垫）及止血塞、婴儿尿布及尿布衬里］；或

SECTION XI
TEXTILES AND TEXTILE ARTICLES

Section Notes:

1. This Section does not cover:

(a) Animal brush-making bristles or hair (heading 05.02) ;horsehair or horsehair waste (heading 05.11) ;

(b) Human hair or articles of human hair (heading 05.01,67.03 or 67.04) , except straining cloth of a kind commonly used in oil presses or the like (heading 59.11) ;

(c) Cotton linters or other vegetable materials of Chapter 14;

(d) Asbestos of heading 25.24 or articles of asbestos or other products of heading 68.12 or 68.13;

(e) Articles of heading 30.05 or 30.06; yarn used to clean between the teeth(dental floss), in individual retail packages, of heading 33.06;

(f) Sensitised textiles of headings 37.01 to 37.04;

(g) Monofilament of which any cross-sectional dimension exceeds 1mm or strip or the like (for example, artificial straw) of an apparent width exceeding 5mm, of plastics (Chapter39) , or plaits or fabrics or other basketware or wickerwork of such monofilament or strip (Chapter46) ;

(h) Woven, knitted or crocheted fabrics, felt or non-wovens, impregnated, coated, covered or laminated with plastics,or articles thereof, of Chapter 39;

(ij) Woven, knitted or crocheted fabrics, felt or non- wovens, impregnated, coated, covered or laminated with rubber, or articles thereof, of Chapter 40;

(k) Hides or skins with their hair or wool on (Chapter 41 or 43) or articles of furskin, artificial fur or articles thereof,of heading 43.03 or 43.04;

(l) Articles of textile materials of heading 42.01 or 42.02;

(m) Products or articles of Chapter 48 (for example, cellulose wadding) ;

(n) Footwear or parts of footwear, gaiters or leggings or similar articles of Chapter 64;

(o) Hair-nets or other headgear or parts thereof of Chapter 65;

(p) Goods of Chapter 67;

(q) Abrasive-coated textile material (heading 68.05) and also carbon fibres or articles of carbon fibres of heading 68.15;

(r) Glass fibres or articles of glass fibres, other than embroidery with glass thread on a visible ground of fabric (Chapter 70) ;

(s) Articles of Chapter 94 (for example, furniture, bedding,lamps and lighting fittings) ;

(t) Articles of Chapter 95 (for example, toys, games, sports requisites and nets) ;

(u) Articles of Chapter 96 (for example, brushes, travel sets for sewing, slide fasteners, typewriter ribbons, sanitary towels(pads) and tampons, napkins(diapers) and napkin liners for babies) ; or

（二十一）第九十七章的物品。

二、（一）可归入第五十章至第五十五章及品目58.09或59.02的由两种或两种以上纺织材料混合制成的货品，应按其中重量最大的那种纺织材料归类。

当没有一种纺织材料重量较大时，应按可归入的有关品目中最后一个品目所列的纺织材料归类。

（二）应用上述规定时：

1. 马毛粗松螺旋花线（品目 51.10）和含金属纱线（品目 56.05）均应作为一种单一的纺织材料，其重量应为它们在纱线中的合计重量；在机织物的归类中，金属线应作为一种纺织材料；

2. 在选择合适的品目时，应首先确定章，然后再确定该章的有关品目，至于不归入该章的其他材料可不予考虑；

3. 当归入第五十四章及第五十五章的货品与其他章的货品进行比较时，应将这两章作为一个单一的章对待；

4. 同一章或同一品目所列各种不同的纺织材料应作为单一的纺织材料对待。

（三）上述（一）、（二）两款规定亦适用于以下注释三、四、五或六所述纱线。

三、（一）本类的纱线（单纱、多股纱线或缆线）除下列（二）款另有规定的以外，凡符合以下规格的应作为“线、绳、索、缆”：

1. 丝或绢丝纱线，细度在20000分特以上；

2. 化学纤维纱线（包括第五十四章的用两根及以上单丝纺成的纱线），细度在 10000 分特以上；

3. 大麻或亚麻纱线：

（1）加光或上光的，细度在1429分特及以上；或

（2）未加光或上光的，细度在 20000 分特以上。

4. 三股或三股以上的椰壳纤维纱线。

5. 其他植物纤维纱线，细度在20000分特以上。

6. 用金属线加强的纱线。

（二）下列各项不按上述（一）款规定办理：

1. 羊毛或其他动物毛纱线及纸纱线，但用金属线加强的纱线除外；

2. 第五十五章的化学纤维长丝丝束以及第五十四章的未加捻或捻度每米少于5转的复丝纱线；

3. 品目 50.06 的蚕胶丝及第五十四章

（v）Articles of Chapter 97.

2. （a）Goods classifiable in Chapters 50 to 55 or of heading 58.09 or in heading 58.09 or 59.02 and of a mixture of two or more, textile materials are to be classified as if consisting wholly of that one textile material which predominates by weight over any other single textile material.

When no one textile material predominates by weight, the goods are to be classified as if consisting wholly of that one textile material which is covered by the heading which occurs last in numerical order among those which equally merit consideration.

（b）For the purposes of the above rule:

（i）Gimped horsehair yarn（heading 51.10）and metallised yarn（heading 56.05）are to be treated as a single textile material the weight of which is to be taken as the aggregate of the weights of its components; for the classification of woven fabrics, metal thread is to be regarded as a textile material;

（ii）The choice of appropriate heading shall be effected by determining first the Chapter and then the applicable heading within that Chapter, disregarding any materials not classified in that Chapter;

（iii）When both Chapters 54 and 55 are involved with any other Chapter, Chapters 54 and 55 are to be treated as a single Chapter;

（iv）Where a Chapter or a heading refers to goods of different textile materials, such materials are to be treated as a single textile material.

（c）The provisions of paragraphs（a）and（b）above apply also to the yarns referred to in Note 3, 4, 5 or 6 below.

3. （a）For the purposes of this Section, and subject to the exceptions in paragraph（b）below, yarns[single, multiple（folded）or cabled]of the following descriptions are to be treated as “twine, cordage, ropes and cables”:

（i）Of silk or waste silk, measuring more than 20,000 decitex;

（ii）Of man-made fibres（including yarn of two or more monofilaments of Chapter 54）, measuring more than 10,000 decitex;

（iii）Of true hemp or flax:

i）Polished or glazed, measuring 1,429 decitex or more; or

ii）Not polished or glazed, measuring more than 20,000 decitex;

（iv）Of coir, consisting of three or more plies;

（v）Of other vegetable fibres, measuring more than 20,000 decitex; or

（vi）Reinforced with metal thread.

（b）Exceptions:

（i）Yarn of wool or other animal hair and paper yarn, other than yarn reinforced with metal thread;

（ii）Man-made filament tow of Chapter 55 and multifilament yarn without twist or with a twist of less than 5 turns per metre of Chapter 54;

（iii）Silk worm gut of heading 50.06, and monofilaments of

的单丝；

4．品目 56.05 的含金属纱线；但用金属线加强的纱线按上述（一）款 6 项规定办理；以及

5．品目 56.06 的绳绒线、粗松螺旋花线及纵行起圈纱线。

四、（一）除下列（二）款另有规定的以外，第五十章、第五十一章、第五十二章、第五十四章和第五十五章所称“供零售用”纱线，是指以下列方式包装的纱线（单纱、多股纱线或缆线）：

1．绕于纸板、线轴、纱管或类似芯子上，其重量（含线芯）符合下列规定：

（1）丝、绢丝或化学纤维长丝纱线，不超过 85 克；或

（2）其他纱线，不超过 125 克；

2．绕成团、绞或束，其重量符合下列规定：

（1）细度在 3000 分特以下的化学纤维长丝纱线，丝或绢丝纱线，不超过 85 克；

（2）细度在 2000 分特以下的任何其他纱线，不超过 125 克；或

（3）其他纱线，不超过 500 克。

3．绕成绞或束，每绞或每束中有若干用线分开的小绞或小束，每小绞或小束的重量相等，并且符合下列规定：

（1）丝、绢丝或化学纤维长丝纱线，不超过 85 克；或

（2）其他纱线，不超过 125 克。

（二）下列各项不按上述（一）款规定办理：

1．各种纺织材料制的单纱，但下列两种除外：

（1）未漂白的羊毛或动物细毛单纱；以及

（2）漂白、染色或印色的羊毛或动物细毛单纱，细度在 5000 分特以上；

2．未漂白的多股纱线或缆线：

（1）丝或绢丝制的，不论何种包装；或

（2）除羊毛或动物细毛外其他纺织材料制，成绞或成束的；

3．漂白、染色或印色丝或绢丝制的多股纱线或缆线，细度在 133 分特及以下；

4．任何纺织材料制的单纱、多股纱线或缆线：

（1）交叉绕成绞或束的；或

（2）绕于纱芯上或以其他方式卷绕，明显用于纺织工业的（例如，绕于纱管、加捻管、纬纱管、锥形筒管或锭子上的或者绕成蚕茧状以供绣花机使用的纱线）。

Chapter 54;

(iv) Metallised yarn of heading 56.05; yarn reinforced with metal thread is subject to paragraph (a) (vi) above; and

(v) Chenille yarn, gimped yarn and loop wale-yarn of heading 56.06

4. (a) For the purposes of Chapters 50, 51, 52, 54 and 55, the expression "put up for retail sale" in relation to yarn means, subject to the exceptions in paragraph (b) below, yarn [single, multiple (folded) or cabled] put up:

(i) On cards, reels, tubes or similar supports, of a weight (including support) not exceeding:

i) 85g in the case of silk, waste silk or man-made filament; or

ii) 125g in other cases;

(ii) In balls, hanks or skeins of a weight not exceeding:

i) 85g in the case of man-made filament yarn of less than 3,000 decitex, silk or silk waste;

ii) 125g in the case of all other yarns of less than 2, 000 decitex; or

iii) 500g in other cases.

(iii) In hanks or skeins comprising several smaller hanks or skeins separated by dividing threads which render them independent one of the other, each of uniform weight not exceeding:

i) 85g in the case of silk, waste silk or man-made filaments; or

ii) 125g in other cases.

(b) Exceptions:

(i) Single yarn of any textile material, except:

i) Shigle yarn of wool or fine animal hair, unbleached; and

ii) Single yarn of wool or fine animal hair, bleached,dyed of printed, measuring more than 5, 000 decitex;

(ii) Multiple (folded) or cabled yarn, unbleached:

i) Of silk or waste silk, however put up; or

ii) Of other textile material except wool or fine animal hair,in hanks or skeins;

(iii) Multiple (folded) or cabled yarn of silk or waste silk,bleached, dyed or printed, measuring 133 decitex or less; and

(iv) Single, multiple (folded) or cabled yarn of any textile material:

i) In cross-reeled hanks or skeins; or

ii) Put up on supports or in some other manner indicating its use in the textile industry (for example, on cops, twisting mill tubes, pirns, conical bobbins or spindles, or reeled in the form of cocoons for embroidery looms).

五、品目 52.04、54.01 及 55.08 所称“缝纫线”，是指下列多股纱线或缆线：
（一）绕于芯子（例如，线轴、纱管）上，重量（包括纱芯）不超过 1000 克；
（二）作为缝纫线上过浆的；以及
（三）终捻为反手（Z）捻的。

六、本类所称“高强力纱”，是指断裂强度大于下列标准的纱线：
尼龙、其他聚酰胺或聚酯制的单纱 60 厘牛顿/特克斯；
尼龙、其他聚酰胺或聚酯制的多股纱线或缆线 53 厘牛顿/特克斯；
粘胶纤维制的单纱、多股纱线或缆线 27 厘牛顿/特克斯。

七、本类所称“制成的”，是指：
（一）裁剪成除正方形或长方形以外的其他形状的；
（二）呈制成状态，无需缝纫或其他进一步加工（或仅需剪断分隔联线）即可使用的（例如，某些抹布、毛巾、台布、方披巾、毯子）；
（三）裁剪成一定尺寸，至少有一边为带有可见的锥形或压平形的热封边，其余各边经本注释其他各项所述加工，但不包括为防止剪边脱纱而用热切法或其他简单方法处理的织物；
（四）已缝边或滚边，或者在任一边带有结制的流苏，但不包括为防止剪边脱纱而锁边或用其他简单方法处理的织物；
（五）裁剪成一定尺寸并经抽纱加工的；
（六）缝合、胶合或用其他方法拼合而成的（将两段或两段以上同样料子的织物首尾连接而成的匹头，以及由两层或两层以上的织物，不论中间有无胎料，层叠而成的匹头除外）；
（七）针织或钩编成一定形状，不论报验时是单件还是以若干件相连成幅的。

八、对于第五十章至第六十章：
（一）第五十章至第五十五章和第六十章，以及除条文另有规定以外的第五十六章至第五十九章，不适用于上述注释七所规定的制成货品；以及
（二）第五十章至第五十五章及第六十章不包括第五十六章至第五十九章的货品。

九、第五十章至第五十五章的机织物包括由若干层平行纱线以锐角或直角相互层叠，在纱线交叉点用黏合剂或以热粘合法粘合而成的织物。

十、以纺织材料和橡胶线制成的弹性产品归入本类。

十一、本类所称“浸渍”，包括“浸泡”。

十二、本类所称“聚酰胺”，包括“芳族聚酰

5. For the purposes of headings 52.04, 54.01 and 55.08 the expression “sewing thread” means multiple (folded) or cabled yarn:
(a) Put up on supports (for example, reels, tubes) of a weight (including support) not exceeding 1,000g;
(b) Dressed for use as sewing thread; and
(c) With a final “Z” twist.

6. For the purposes of this Section, the expression “high tenacity yarn” means yarn having a tenacity, expressed in cN/tex (centinewton per tex), greater than the following:
Single yarn of nylon or other polyamides, or of polyesters 60cN/tex;
Multiple (folded) or cabled yarn of nylon or other polyamides, or of polyesters 53cN/tex;
Single, multiple (folded) or cabled yarn of viscose rayon 27cN/tex.

7. For the purposes of this Section, the expression “made up” means:
(a) Cut otherwise than into squares or rectangles;
(b) Produced in the finished state, ready for use (or merely needing separation by cutting dividing threads) without sewing or other working (for example, certain dusters, towels, table cloths, scarf squares, blankets);
(c) Cut to size and with at least one heat-sealed edge with a visibly tapered or compressed border and the other edges treated as described in any other subparagraph of this Note, but excluding fabrics the cut edges of which have been prevented from unraveling by hot cutting or by other simple means;
(d) Hemmed or with rolled edges, or with a knotted fringe at any of the edges, but excluding fabrics the cut edges of which have been prevented from unravelling by whipping or by other simple means;
(e) Cut to size and having undergone a process of drawn thread work;
(f) Assembled by sewing, gumming or otherwise (other than piece goods consisting of two or more lengths of identical material joined end to end and piece goods composed of two or more textiles assembled in layers, whether or not padded);
(g) Knitted or crocheted to shape, whether presented as separate items or in the form of a number of items in the length.

8. For the purposes of Chapters 50 to 60:
(a) Chapters 50 to 55 and 60 and, except where the context otherwise requires, Chapters 56 to 59 do not apply to goods made up within the meaning of Note 7 above; and
(b) Chapters 50 to 55 and 60 do not apply to goods of Chapters 56 to 59.

9. The woven fabrics of Chapters 50 to 55 include fabrics consisting of layers of parallel textile yarns superimposed on each other at acute or right angles. These layers are bonded at the intersections of the yarns by an adhesive or by thermal bonding.

10. Elastic products consisting of textile materials combined with rubber threads are classified in this Section.

11. For the purposes of this Section, the expression “impregnated” includes “dipped”.

12. For the purposes of this Section, the expression “polyamides”

胺”。

十三、本类及本税则所称“弹性纱线”是指合成纤维纺织材料制成的长丝纱线（包括单丝），但变形纱线除外。这些纱线可拉伸至原长的三倍而不断裂，并可在拉伸至原长两倍后五分钟内回复到不超过原长度一倍半。

十四、除条文另有规定的以外，各种服装即使成套包装供零售用，也应按各自品号分别归类。本注释所称“纺织服装”，是指品目 61.01 至 61.14 及品目 62.01 至 62.11 所列的各种服装。

子目注释：

一、本类及本税则所用有关名词解释如下：

（一）未漂白纱线

1. 带有纤维自然色泽并且未经漂染（不论是否整体染色）或印色的纱线；或

2. 从回收纤维制得，色泽未定的纱线（本色纱）。

这种纱线可用无色浆料或易褪色染料（可轻易地用肥皂洗去）处理，如果是化学纤维纱线，则整体用消光剂（例如，二氧化钛）进行处理。

（二）漂白纱线

1. 经漂白加工、用漂白纤维制得或经染白（除条文另有规定的以外）（不论是否整体染色）及用白浆料处理的纱线；

2. 用未漂白纤维和漂白纤维混纺制得的纱线；或

3. 用未漂白纱和漂白纱纺成多股纱线或缆线。

（三）着色（染色或印色）纱线

1. 染成彩色（不论是否整体染色，但白色或易褪色除外）或印色的纱线，以及用染色或印色纤维纺制的纱线；

2. 用各色染色纤维混合纺制或用未漂白或漂白纤维与着色纤维混合制得的纱线（夹色纱或混色纱），以及用一种或几种颜色间隔印色而获得点纹印迹的纱线；

3. 用已经印色的纱条或粗纱纺制的纱线；或

4. 用未漂白纱和漂白纱与着色纱纺成的多股纱线或缆线。

上述定义在必要的地方稍作修改后可适用于第五十四章的单丝、扁条或类似产品。

（四）未漂白机织物

用未漂白纱线织成后未经漂白、染色或印花的机织物。这类织物可用无色浆料

includes “aramids”.

13. For the purposes of this Section and, where applicable, throughout the Nomenclature, the expression “elastomeric yarn” means filament yarn, including monofilament, of synthetic textile material, other than textured yarn, which does not break on being extended to three times its original length and which returns, after being extended to twice its original length, within a period of five minutes, to a length not greater than one and a half times its original length.

14. Unless the context otherwise requires, textile garments of different headings are to be classified in their own headings even if put up in sets for retail sale. For the purposes of this Note, the expression “textile garments” means garments of headings 61.01 to 61.14 and headings 62.01 to 62.11.

Subheading Notes:

1. In this Section and, where applicable, throughout the Nomenclature, the following expressions have the meanings hereby assigned to them:

(a) Unbleached yarn which:

(i) has the natural colour of its constituent fibres and has not been bleached, dyed (whether or not in the mass) or printed; or

(ii) is of indeterminate colour (“grey yarn”), manufactured from garnetted stock.

Such yarn may have been treated with a colourless dressing or fugitive dye (which disappears after simple washing with soap) and, in the case of man-made fibres, treated in the mass with delustring agents (for example, titanium dioxide).

(b) Bleached yarn which:

(i) has undergone a bleaching process, is made of bleached fibres or, unless the context otherwise requires, has been dyed white (whether or not in the mass) or treated with a white dressing;

(ii) consists of a mixture of unbleached and bleached fibres; or

(iii) is multiple (folded) or cabled and consists of unbleached and bleached yarns.

(c) Coloured (dyed or printed) yarn which:

(i) is dyed (whether or not in the mass) other than white or in a fugitive colour, or printed, or made from dyed or printed fibres;

(ii) consists of a mixture of dyed fibres of different colours or of a mixture of unbleached or bleached fibres with coloured fibres (marl or mixture yarns), or is printed in one or more colours at intervals to give the impression of dots;

(iii) is obtained from slivers or rovings which have been printed; or

(iv) is multiple (folded) or cabled and consists of unbleached or bleached yarn and coloured yarn.

The above definitions also apply, mutatis mutandis, to monofilament and to strip or the like of Chapter 54.

(d) Unbleached woven fabric

Woven fabric made from unbleached yarn and which has not

或易褪色染料处理。

（五）漂白机织物

1. 经漂白、染白或用白浆料处理（除条文另有规定的以外）的成匹机织物；

2. 用漂白纱线织成的机织物；或

3. 用未漂白纱线和漂白纱线织成的机织物。

（六）染色机织物

1. 除条文另有规定的以外，染成白色以外的其他单一颜色或用白色以外的其他有色整理剂处理的成匹机织物；或

2. 用单一颜色的着色纱线织成的机织物。

（七）色织机织物除印花机织物以外的下列机织物：

1. 用各种不同颜色纱线或同一颜色不同深浅（纤维的自然色彩除外）纱线织成的机织物；

2. 用未漂白或漂白纱线与着色纱线织成的机织物；或

3. 用夹色纱线或混色纱线织成的机织物。不论何种情况，布边或布头的纱线均可忽略不计。

（八）印花机织物

成匹印花的机织物，不论是否用各色纱线织成。用刷子或喷枪，经转印纸转印、植绒或蜡防印花等方法印成花纹图案的机织物亦可视为印花机织物。

上述各类纱线或织物如经丝光工艺处理并不影响其归类。

上述第（四）至（八）项的定义在必要的地方稍加修改后，可适用于针织或钩编织物。

（九）平纹组织

每根纬纱在并排的经纱间上下交错而过，而每根经纱也在并排的纬纱间上下交错而过的织物组织。

二、（一）含有两种或两种以上纺织材料的第五十六章至第六十三章的产品，应根据本类注释二对第五十章至第五十五章或品目58.09的此类纺织材料产品归类的规定来确定归类。

（二）运用本条规定时：

1. 应酌情考虑按归类总规则第三条来确定归类；

2. 对由底布和绒面或毛圈面构成的纺织品，在归类时可不考虑底布的属

been bleached, dyed or printed. Such fabric may have been treated with a colourless dressing or a fugitive dye.

(e) Bleached woven fabric

Woven fabric which:

(i) has been bleached or, unless the context otherwise requires, dyed white or treated with a white dressing, in the piece;

(ii) consists of bleached yarn; or

(iii) consists of unbleached and bleached yarn.

(f) Dyed woven fabric

Woven fabric which:

(i) is dyed a single uniform colour other than white (unless the context otherwise requires) or has been treated with a coloured finish other than white (unless the context otherwise requires), in the piece; or

(ii) consists of coloured yarn of a single uniform colour.

(g) Woven fabric of yarns of different colours

Woven fabric (other than printed woven fabric) which:

(i) consists of yarns of different colours or yarns of different shades of the same colour (other than the natural colour of the constituent fibres);

(ii) consists of unbleached or bleached yarn and coloured yarn; or

(iii) consists of marl or mixture yarns. (In all cases, the yarn used in selvedges and piece ends is not taken into consideration.)

(h) Printed woven fabric

Woven fabric which has been printed in the piece, whether or not made from yarns of differenent colours. (The following are also regarded as printed woven fabrics: woven fabrics bearing designs made, for example, with a brush or spray gun, by means of transfer paper, by flocking or by the batik process.)

The process of mercerisation does not affect the classification of yarns or fabrics within the above categories.

The definitions at (d) to (h) above apply, mutatis mutandis, to knitted or crocheted fabrics.

(ij) Plain weave

A fabric construction in which each yarn of the weft passes alternately over and under successive yarns of the warp and each yarn of the warp passes alternately over and under successive yarns of the weft.

2. (a) Products of Chapters 56 to 63 containing two or more textile materials are to be regarded as consisting wholly of that textile material which would be selected under Note 2 to this Section for the classification of a product of Chapters 50 to 55 consisting of the same textile materials.

(b) For the application of this rule:

(i) where appropriate, only the part which determines the classification under Interpretative Rule 3 shall be taken into account;

(ii) in the case of textile products consisting of a ground fabric

性；

3. 对品目 58.10 的刺绣品及其制品，归类时应只考虑底布的属性，但不见底布的刺绣品及其制品应根据绣线的属性确定归类。

and a pile or looped surface no account shall be taken of the ground fabric;

(iii) in the case of embroidery of heading 58.10 and goods thereof, only the ground fabric shall be taken into account. However, embroidery without visible ground, and goods thereof, shall be classified with reference to the embroidering threads alone.

第五十章 蚕 丝

Chapter 50 Silk

税则号列 Tariff Item	商品名称及备注	进口税率 最惠	普通	暂定	出口退税	增值税率	计量单位	监管条件	Article Description
50.01	适于缫丝的蚕茧：								**Silk-worm cocoons suitable for reeling:**
5001.0010	---适于缫丝的桑蚕茧	6	70		5	17	千克	AB	---Bombyx mori cocoons (Mulberry feeding silk- worm cocoons)
5001.0090	---其他	6	70		5	17	千克	AB	---Other
50.02	生丝（未加捻）：								**Raw silk (not thrown):**
	---桑蚕丝：								---Steam filature silk:
5002.0011	----厂丝	9	80		15	17	千克	AB	----Plant reeled (filature silk)
5002.0012	----土丝	9	80		15	17	千克	AB	----Home reeled
5002.0013	----双宫丝	9	80		15	17	千克	AB	----Doupion
5002.0019	----其他	9	80		15	17	千克	AB	----Other
5002.0020	---柞蚕丝	9	80		15	17	千克	AB	---Tussah silk
5002.0090	---其他	9	80		15	17	千克	AB	---Other
50.03	废丝（包括不适于缫丝的蚕茧、废纱及回收纤维）：								**Silk waste (including cocoons unsuitable for reeling, yarn waste and garnetted stock):**
	---未梳：								---Not carded or combed:
5003.0011	----下茧、茧衣、长吐、滞头	9	70		13	17	千克	AB	----Spoiled cocoon, cocoon outer floss, frison, frigon
5003.0012	----回收纤维	9	70		13	17	千克	AB	----Garnetted Stock
5003.0019	----其他	9	70		13	17	千克	AB	----Other
	---其他：								---Other:
5003.0091	----棉球	9	70		13	17	千克	AB	----Silk tops
5003.0099	----其他	9	70		13	17	千克	AB	----Other
50.04	丝纱线（绢纺纱线除外），非供零售用：								**Silk yarn (other than yarn spun from silk waste) not put up for retail sale:**
5004.0000	丝纱线（绢纺纱线除外），非供零售用	6	90		16	17	千克		Silk yarn (other than yarn spun from silk waste) not put up for retail sale
50.05	绢纺纱线，非供零售用：								**Yarn spun from silk waste, not put up for retail sale:**
5005.0010	---细丝纱线	6	90		16	17	千克		---Spun from noil
5005 0010.10	非供零售用细丝纱线(细丝为主，含丝及绢丝85%及以上纱线)	6	90		16	17	千克		Spun from noil, containing 85% or more by weight of silk or silk waste, not put up for retail sale
5005 0010.90	非供零售用细丝纱线(细丝为主，含丝及绢丝85%以下的纱线)	6	90		16	17	千克		Spun from noil, containing less than 85% by weight of silk or silk waste, not put up for retail sale
5005.0090	---其他	6	90		16	17	千克		---Other
5005 0090.10	非供零售用其他绢纺纱线（含丝及绢丝 85%及以上纱线）	6	90		16	17	千克		Other yarn spun from silk waste, containing 85% or more by weight of silk or silk waste, not put up for retail sale
5005 0090.20	非供零售用其他绢纺纱线（含丝及绢丝 85%以下纱线）	6	90		16	17	千克		Other yarn spun from silk waste, containing less than 85% by weight of silk or silk waste, not put up for retail sale
50.06	丝纱线及绢纺纱线，供零售用；蚕胶丝：								**Silk yarn and yarn spun from silk waste, put up for retail sale; silk-worm gut:**
5006.0000	丝纱线及绢纺纱线，供零售用；蚕胶丝	6	100		16	17	千克		Silk yarn and yarn spun from silk waste, put up for retail sale; silk-worm gut
5006 0000.10	零售用丝纱线，绢纺纱线；蚕胶丝(含丝及绢丝 85%及以上纱线)	6	100		16	17	千克		Silk yarn, yarn spun from silk waste, and silk-worm gut, containing 85% or more by weight of silk or silk waste, put up for retail sale

税则号列 Tariff Item	商品名称及备注	进口税率 最惠	进口税率 普通	进口税率 暂定	出口退税	增值税率	计量单位	监管条件	Article Description
5006 0000.20	零售用丝纱线，绢纺纱线；蚕胶丝（含丝及绢丝 85%以下纱线）	6	100		16	17	千克		Silk yarn, yarn spun from silk waste, and silk-worm gut, containing less than 85% by weight of silk or silk waste, put up for retail sale
50.07	丝或绢丝机织物:								**Woven fabrics of silk or of silk waste:**
	-细丝机织物:								-Fabrics of noil silk:
5007.1010	---未漂白（包括未练白或练白）或漂白	10	130		16	17	米/千克		---Unbleached（unscoured or scoured）or bleached
5007 1010.10	未漂白或漂白的细丝机织物（包括未练白或练白的，含细丝 85%及以上）	10	130		16	17	米/千克		Fabrics of noil silk, unbleached（unscoured or scoured）or bleached (containning 85% or more by weight of noil silk)
5007 1010.20	未漂白或漂白的细丝机织物（包括未练白或练白的，含细丝 85%以下，棉或化纤限内）	10	130		16	17	米/千克		Fabrics of noil silk, unbleached（unscoured or scoured）or bleached, containing less than 85% by weight of noil silk (cotton or man-made fibres limit in)
5007 1010.31	未漂白或漂白的细丝机织物（含未练白或练白，细丝＜85%与精梳羊毛或动物细毛混纺，羊毛限内）	10	130		16	17	米/千克		Fabrics of noil silk, unbleached（unscoured or scoured）or bleached, containing less than 85% by weight of noil silk, mixed with combed wool or combed fine animal hair (wool limit in)
5007 1010.39	未漂白或漂白的细丝机织物（未练白或练白的，含细丝 85%以下，与其他混纺，羊毛限内）	10	130		16	17	米/千克		Fabrics of noil silk, unbleached（unscoured or scoured）or bleached, containing less than 85% by weight of noil silk, mixed with others (wool limit in)
5007 1010.91	未漂白或漂白的细丝机织物（未练白或练白的，含细丝＜85%与精梳羊毛或动物细毛混纺）	10	130		16	17	米/千克		Fabrics of noil silk, unbleached（unscoured or scoured）or bleached, containing less than 85% by weight of noil silk (mixed with combed wool or fine animal hair)
5007 1010.99	未漂白或漂白的细丝机织物（包括未练白或练白的，含细丝 85%以下，与其他混纺）	10	130		16	17	米/千克		Fabrics of noil silk, unbleached（unscoured or scoured）or bleached, containing less than 85% by weight of noil silk (mixed with others)
5007.1090	---其他	10	130		16	17	米/千克		---Other
5007 1090.10	其他细丝机织物（含细丝 85%及以上）	10	130		16	17	米/千克		Other fabrics of noil silk (containing 85% or more by weight of noil silk)
5007 1090.21	其他色织细丝机织物（含细丝 85%以下，棉或化纤限内）	10	130		16	17	米/千克		Other fabrics of noil silk, yarn-dyed, containing less than 85% by weight of noil silk (cotton or man-made fibres limit in)
5007 1090.29	其他非色织细丝机织物（含细丝 85%以下，棉或化纤限内）	10	130		16	17	米/千克		Other woven fabrics of noil silk, not yarn-dyed, containing 85% less than by weight of noil silk, (cotton or man-made fibres limit in)
5007 1090.31	其他细丝机织物（含细丝 85%以下，与精梳羊毛或动物细毛混纺，羊毛限内）	10	130		16	17	米/千克		Other fabrics of noil silk, containing less than 85% by weight of noil silk, mixed with combed wool or fine animal hair (wool limit in)
5007 1090.39	其他细丝机织物(含细丝 85%以下，与其他混纺，羊毛限内)	10	130		16	17	米/千克		Other fabrics of noil silk, containing less than 85% by weight of noil silk, mixed with others (wool limit in)
5007 1090.91	其他细丝机织物（含细丝 85%以下，与精梳羊毛或动物细毛混纺）	10	130		16	17	米/千克		Other fabrics of noil silk, containing less than 85% by weight of noil silk (mixed with combed wool or fine animal hair)
5007 1090.99	其他细丝机织物（含细丝 85%以下，与其他混纺）	10	130		16	17	米/千克		Other woven fabrics of noil silk, containing less than 85% by weight of noil silk(mixed with others)
	-其他机织物，按重量计丝或绢丝（细丝除外）含量在 85%及以上:								-Other fabrics, containing 85% or more by weight of silk or of silk waste other than noil silk:
	---桑蚕丝机织物:								---Of Bornbyx mori silk:
5007.2011	----未漂白（包括未练白或练白）或漂白	10	130		16	17	米/千克		----Unbleached（unscoured or scoured）or bleached
5007.2019	----其他	10	130		16	17	米/千克		----Other
	---柞蚕丝机织物:								---Of tussah silk:
5007.2021	----未漂白（包括未练白或练白）或漂白	10	130		16	17	米/千克		----Unbleached（unscoured or scoured）or bleached
5007.2029	----其他	10	130		16	17	米/千克		----Other

税则号列 Tariff Item	商品名称及备注	进口税率			出口退税	增值税率	计量单位	监管条件	Article Description
		最惠	普通	暂定					
	---绢丝机织物:								---Of silk waste other than noil silk:
5007.2031	----未漂白（包括未练白或练白）或漂白	10	130		16	17	米/千克		----Unbleached（unscoured or scoured）or bleached
5007.2039	----其他	10	130		16	17	米/千克		----Other
5007.2090	---其他	10	130		16	17	米/千克		---Of other silk
5007 2090.10	未漂白或漂白其他丝机织物（包括未练白或练白，按重量计丝或绢丝含量在85%及以上）	10	130		16	17	米/千克		Other fabrics of silk, unbleached（unscoured or scoured）or bleached (containing 85% or more by weight of silk and silk waste)
5007 2090.90	其他丝机织物（按重量计丝或绢丝含量在85%及以上）	10	130		16	17	米/千克		Other fabrics of silk (containing 85% or more by weight of silk and silk waste)
	-其他机织物:								-Other fabrics:
5007.9010	---未漂白（包括未练白或练白）或漂白	10	130		16	17	米/千克		---Unbleached（unscoured or scoured）or bleached
5007 9010.10	未漂白或漂白其他丝机织物（包括未练白或练白，含丝及绢丝85%及以上）	10	130		16	17	米/千克		Other fabrics of silk, unbleached（unscoured or scoured）or bleached (containing 85% or more by weight of silk and silk waste)
5007 9010.20	未漂白或漂白其他丝机织物（包括未练白或练白，含丝及绢丝<85%，与其他混纺的，棉或化纤限内）	10	130		16	17	米/千克		Other fabrics of silk, unbleached（unscoured or scoured）or bleached, containing less than 85% by weight of silk and silk waste, mixed with others (cotton or man-made fibres limit in)
5007 9010.31	未漂白或漂白其他丝机织物（未练白或练白，含丝及绢丝<85%，与精梳羊毛或动物细毛混纺，羊毛限内）	10	130		16	17	米/千克		Other fabrics of silk, unbleached（unscoured or scoured）or bleached ,containing less than 85% by weight of silk and silk waste, mixed with combed wool or fine animals hair (wool limit in)
5007 9010.39	未漂白或漂白其他丝机织物（未练白或练白，含丝及绢丝小于85%，与其他混纺，羊毛限内）	10	130		16	17	米/千克		Other fabrics of silk, unbleached（unscoured or scoured）or bleached, containing less than 85% by weight of silk and spun silk, mixed with others (wool limit in)
5007 9010.91	未漂白或漂白其他丝机织物（未练白或练白，含丝及绢丝小于85%，与精梳羊毛或动物细毛混纺）	10	130		16	17	米/千克		Other fabrics of silk, unbleached（unscoured or scoured）or bleached,containing less than 85% by weight of silk and silk waste (mixed with combed wool or fine animals hair)
5007 9010.99	未漂白或漂白其他丝机织物（未练白或练白，含丝及绢丝85%以下，与其他混纺）	10	130		16	17	米/千克		Other woven fabrics of silk, unbleached（unscoured or scoured）or bleached, containing less than 85% by weight of silk and silk waste (mixed with others)
5007.9090	---其他	10	130		16	17	米/千克		---Other
5007 9090.10	其他丝机织物（含丝及绢丝85%及以上）	10	130		16	17	米/千克		Other fabrics of silk, containing 85% or more by weight of silk and silk waste
5007 9090.21	其他色织丝机织物（含丝及绢丝85%以下，与其他混纺，棉或化学纤维限内）	10	130		16	17	米/千克		Other fabrics of silk, yarn-dyed, containing less than 85% by weight of silk and silk waste, mixed with others (cotton or man-made fibres limit in)
5007 9090.29	其他非色织丝机织物（含丝及绢丝85%以下，与其他混纺，棉或化学纤维限内）	10	130		16	17	米/千克		Other fabrics of silk, not yarn-dyed, containing less than 85% by weight of silk and silk waste mixed with others (cotton or man-made limit in
5007 9090.31	其他丝机织物（含丝及绢丝<85%，与精梳羊毛或动物细毛混纺，羊毛限内）	10	130		16	17	米/千克		Other fabrics of silk, containing less than 85% by weight of silk and silk waste, mixed with combed wool or fine animal hair(wool limit in)
5007 9090.39	其他丝机织物（含丝及绢丝85%以下，与其他混纺，羊毛限内）	10	130		16	17	米/千克		Other fabrics of silk, containing less than 85% by weight of silk and silk waste, mixed with others (wool limit in)
5007 9090.91	其他丝机织物（含丝及绢丝85%以下，与精梳羊毛或动物细毛混纺）	10	130		16	17	米/千克		Other fabrics of silk, containing less than 85% by weight of silk and silk waste (mixed with combed wool or fine animal hair)
5007 9090.99	其他丝机织物（含丝及绢丝85%以下，与其他混纺）	10	130		16	17	米/千克		Other woven fabrics of silk, containing less than 85% by weight of silk and spun silk (mixed with others

第五十一章
羊毛、动物细毛或粗毛；马毛纱线及其机织物

Chapter 51
Wool, fine or coarse animal hair; horsehair yarn and woven fabric

注释：

本税则所称：

一、“羊毛”，是指绵羊或羔羊身上长的天然纤维；

二、“动物细毛”，是指下列动物的毛：羊驼、美洲驼、驼马、骆驼（包括单峰骆驼）、牦牛、安哥拉山羊、西藏山羊、喀什米尔山羊及类似山羊（普通山羊除外）、家兔（包括安哥拉兔）、野兔、海狸、河狸鼠或麝鼠；

三、“动物粗毛”，是指以上未提及的其他动物的毛，但不包括制刷用鬃、毛（品目05.02）以及马毛（品目05.11）。

Chapter Notes:

Throughout the Nomenclature:

1.“Wool” means the natural fibre grown by sheep or lambs;

2.“Fine animal hair” means the hair of alpaca, llama, vicuna, camel,（including dromedary）yak, Angora, Tibetan, Kashmir or similar goats（but not common goats）, rabbit（including Angora rabbit）, hare, beaver, nutria or musk-rat;

3.“Coarse animal hair” means the hair of animals not mentioned above, excluding brush-making hair and bristles（heading 05.02） and horsehair （heading 05.11）.

税则号列 Tariff Item	商品名称及备注	进口税率 最惠	普通	暂定	出口退税	增值税率	计量单位	监管条件	Article Description
51.01	未梳的羊毛:								**Wool, not carded or combed:**
	-含脂羊毛,包括剪前水洗毛:								-Greasy, including fleece-washed wool:
5101.1100	--剪羊毛		50		5	13	千克		--Shorn wool
5101 1100.01	未梳的含脂剪羊毛（配额内）	1	50		5	13	千克	tAB	Greasy shorn wool, not carded or combed, in-quota
5101 1100.90	未梳的含脂剪羊毛（配额外）	38	50		5	13	千克	AB	Greasy shorn wool, not carded or combed, out-of-quota
5101.1900	--其他		50		5	13	千克		--Other
5101 1900.01	未梳的其他含脂羊毛（配额内）	1	50		5	13	千克	tAB	Other greasy wool, not carded or combed, in-quota
5101 1900.90	未梳的其他含脂羊毛（配额外）	38	50		5	13	千克	AB	Other greasy wool, not carded or combed, out-of-quota
	-脱脂羊毛，未碳化:								-Degreased, not carbonized:
5101.2100	--剪羊毛		50		13	17	千克		--Shorn wool
5101 2100.01	未梳的脱脂剪羊毛（未碳化）（配额内）	1	50		13	17	千克	tAB	Shorn wool, not carded or combed(degreased, not carbonized), in-quota
5101 2100.90	未梳的脱脂剪羊毛（未碳化）（配额外）	38	50		13	17	千克	AB	Shorn wool, not carded or combed(degreased, not carbonized), out-of-quota
5101.2900	--其他		50		13	17	千克		--Other
5101 2900.01	未梳的其他脱脂羊毛（未碳化）（配额内）	1	50		13	17	千克	tAB	Other wool, not carded or combed(degreased, not carbonized), in-quota
5101 2900.90	未梳的其他脱脂羊毛（未碳化）（配额外）	38	50		13	17	千克	AB	Other wool, not carded or combed(degreased, not carbonized), out-of-quota
5101.3000	-碳化羊毛		50		13	17	千克		-Carbonized
5101 3000.01	未梳碳化羊毛（配额内）	1	50		13	17	千克	tAB	Wool, not carded or combed, carbonized, in-quota
5101 3000.90	未梳碳化羊毛（配额外）	38	50		13	17	千克	AB	Wool, not carded or combeb, carbonized, out-of-quota
51.02	未梳的动物细毛或粗毛:								**Fine or coarse animal hair, not carded or combed:**
	-细毛:								-Fine animal hair:
5102.1100	--喀什米尔山羊的	9	45			17	千克	AB	--Of kashmir（cashmere）goats
	--其他:								--Other:
5102.1910	---兔毛	9	50			17	千克		---Of rabbit and hare
5102 1910.10	未梳濒危兔毛	9	50			17	千克	ABFE	Fine hair of endangered rabbit and hare, not carded or combed
5102 1910.90	其他未梳兔毛	9	50		5	17	千克	AB	Other fine hair of rabbit and hare, not carded or combed
5102.1920	---其他山羊绒	9	45			17	千克	AB	---Of other goats
5102.1930	---骆驼毛、骆驼绒	9	45			17	千克		---Of camel
5102 1930.10	未梳濒危野生骆驼科动物毛、绒	9	45			17	千克	FEAB	Fine hair of endangered wild camel, not carded or combed
5102 1930.90	其他未梳骆驼毛、绒	9	45		5	17	千克	AB	Other fine hair of camel, not carded or combed
5102.1990	---其他	9	45			17	千克		---Other

税则号列 Tariff Item	商品名称及备注	进口税率			出口退税	增值税率	计量单位	监管条件	Article Description
		最惠	普通	暂定					
5102 1990.10	未梳的其他濒危野生动物细毛	9	45			17	千克	FEAB	Fine hair of other endangered wild animals, not carded or combeb
5102 1990.90	未梳的其他动物细毛	9	45		5	17	千克	AB	Fine hair of other animals, not carded or combeb
5102.2000	-粗毛	9	50			17	千克		-Coarse animal hair
5102 2000.10	未梳的濒危野生动物粗毛	9	50			17	千克	FEAB	Coarse hair of endangered wild animals, not carded or combeb
5102 2000.90	未梳的其他动物粗毛	9	50		5	17	千克	AB	Coarse hair of other animals,not carded or combeb
51.03	**羊毛或动物细毛或粗毛的废料，包括废纱线，但不包括回收纤维:**								**Waste of wool or of fine or coarse animal hair, including yarn waste but excluding garnetted stock:**
	-羊毛或动物细毛的落毛:								-Noils of wool or of fine animal hair:
5103.1010	---羊毛落毛		50		5	17	千克		---Of wool
5103 1010.01	羊毛落毛（配额内）	1	50		5	17	千克	tAB	Noils of wool, in-quota
5103 1010.90	羊毛落毛（配额外）	38	50		5	17	千克	AB	Noils of wool, out-of-quota
5103.1090	---其他	9	50			17	千克		---Other
5103 1090.10	其他濒危野生动物细毛的落毛	9	50			17	千克	FEAB	Other noils of fine hair of endangered wild animal
5103 1090.90	其他动物细毛的落毛	9	50		5	17	千克	ABP	Other noils of fine hair of wild animal
	-羊毛或动物细毛的其他废料:								-Other waste of wool or of fine animal hair:
5103.2010	---羊毛废料	13.5	20		5	17	千克	AB	---Of wool
5103.2090	---其他	9	50			17	千克		---Other
5103 2090.10	其他濒危野生动物细毛废料（包括废纱线，不包括回收纤维）	9	50			17	千克	FEAB	Other waste of fine hair of endangered wild animal, including yarn waste but excluding garnetted stock
5103 2090.90	其他动物细毛废料（包括废纱线，不包括回收纤维）	9	50		5	17	千克	ABP	Other waste of fine hair of other animal, including yarn waste but excluding garnetted stock
5103.3000	-动物粗毛废料	9	50			17	千克		-Waste of coarse animal hair
5103 3000.10	濒危野生动物粗毛废料（包括废纱线，不包括回收纤维）	9	50			17	千克	FEAB	Waste of coarse hair of endangered wild animal, including yarn waste but excluding garnetted stock
5103 3000.90	其他动物粗毛废料（包括废纱线，不包括回收纤维）	9	50		5	17	千克	ABP	Other waste of coarse animal hair, including yarn waste but excluding garnetted stock
51.04	**羊毛或动物细毛或粗毛的回收纤维:**								**Garnetted stock of wool or of fine or coarse animal hair:**
5104.0010	---羊毛的回收纤维	15	20		5	17	千克	AB	---Of wool
5104.0090	---其他	5	50			17	千克		---Other
5104 0090.10	其他濒危野生动物细毛（包括粗毛回收纤维）	5	50			17	千克	FEAB	Garnetted stock of fine or coarse hair of other endangered wild animal
5104 0090.90	其他动物细毛或粗毛的回收纤维	5	50		13	17	千克	ABP	Garnetted stock of fine or coarse of other animal hair
51.05	**已梳的羊毛及动物细毛或粗毛(包括精梳片毛)**								**Wool and fine or coarse animal hair, carded or combed（including combed wool in fragments）:**
5105.1000	-粗梳羊毛		50		13	17	千克		-Carded wool
5105 1000.01	粗梳羊毛（配额内）	3	50		13	17	千克	tAB	Carded wool, in-quota
5105 1000.90	粗梳羊毛（配额外）	38	50		13	17	千克	AB	Carded wool, out-of-quota
	-兰毛条及其他精梳羊毛:								-Wool tops and other combed wool:
5105.2100	--精梳片毛		50		13	17	千克		--Combed wool in fragments
5105 2100.01	精梳羊毛片毛（配额内）	3	50		13	17	千克	tAB	Combed wool in fragments, in-quota
5105 2100.90	精梳羊毛片毛（配额外）	38	50		13	17	千克	AB	Combed wool in fragments, out-of-quota
5105.2900	--其他		50		13	17	千克		--Other
5105 2900.01	羊毛条及其他精梳羊毛（配额内）	3	50		13	17	千克	tAB	Wool tops and other combed wool, in-quota
5105 2900.90	羊毛条及其他精梳羊毛（配额外）	38	50		13	17	千克	AB	Wool tops and other combed wool,out-of-quota
	-已梳动物细毛:								-Fine animal hair, carded or combed:
5105.3100	--喀什米尔山羊的	5	50			17	千克	AB	--Of kashmir（cashmere）goats
	--其他:								--Other:
5105.3910	---兔毛	5	70			17	千克		---Of rabbit or hare
5105 3910.10	已梳濒危兔毛	5	70			17	千克	ABFE	Fine hair of endangered rabbit and hare,carded or combed
5105 3910.90	其他已梳兔毛	5	70		13	17	千克	AB	Other fine hair of rabbit and hare, carded or combed
	---其他山羊绒:								---Of other goats:
5105.3921	----无毛山羊绒	5	50			17	千克	AB	----Dehaired goats wool

税则号列 Tariff Item	商品名称及备注	进口税率 最惠	普通	暂定	出口退税	增值税率	计量单位	监管条件	Article Description
5105.3929	----其他	5	50			17	千克	AB	----Other
5105.3990	---其他	5	50		13	17	千克		---Other
5105 3990.10	其他已梳野生动物细毛	5	50		13	17	千克	ABEF	Other fine wild animal hair, carded or combed
5105 3990.90	其他已梳动物细毛	5	50		13	17	千克	AB	Other fine animal hair, carded or combed
5105.4000	-已梳动物粗毛	5	50			17	千克		-Coarse animal hair, carded or combed
5105 4000.10	其他已梳濒危野生动物粗毛	5	50			17	千克	FEAB	Other coarse endangered wild animal hair, carded or combed
5105 4000.90	其他已梳动物粗毛	5	50		13	17	千克	AB	Other coarse animal hair, carded or combed
51.06	**粗梳羊毛纱线，非供零售用:**								**Yarn of carded wool, not put up for retail sale:**
5106.1000	-按重量计羊毛含量在85%及以上	5	70		16	17	千克		-Containing 85% or more by weight of wool
5106.2000	-按重量计羊毛含量在85%以下	5	70		16	17	千克		-Containing less than 85% by weight of wool
51.07	**精梳羊毛纱线，非供零售用:**								**Yarn of combed wool, not put up for retail sale:**
5107.1000	-按重量计羊毛含量在 85%及以上	5	70		16	17	千克		-Containing 85% or more by weight of wool
5107.2000	-按重量计羊毛含量在85%以下	5	70		16	17	千克		-Containing less than 85% by weight of wool
51.08	**动物细毛（粗梳或精梳）纱线，非供零售用:**								**Yarn of fine animal hair（carded or combed）, not put up for retail sale:**
	-粗梳:								-Carded:
	---按重量计动物细毛含量在85%及以上的:								---Containing 85% or more by weight of fine animal hair:
5108.1011	----山羊绒的	5	70		16	17	千克		----Of goats
5108.1019	----其他	5	70			17	千克		----Other
5108 1019.10	非供零售用粗梳其他濒危动物细毛纱线（按重量计其他动物细毛含量≥85%）	5	70			17	千克	FE	Yarn of fine hair of endangered animals, carded, not put up for retail sale, containing 85% or more by weight of other animal hair
5108 1019.90	非供零售用粗梳其他动物细毛纱线（按重量计其他动物细毛含量≥85%）	5	70		16	17	千克		Yarn of fine animal hair, carded, not put up for retail sale, containing 85% or more by weight of other animal hair
5108.1090	---其他	5	70			17	千克		---Other
5108 1090.10	非供零售用粗梳其他濒危动物细毛纱线（按重量计其他粗梳动物细毛含量＜85%）	5	70			17	千克	FE	Yarn of fine endangered animal hair, carded not put up for retail sale, containing less than 85% by weight of other animal hair
5108 1090.90	非供零售用粗梳其他动物细毛纱线（按重量计其他粗梳动物细毛含量＜85%）	5	70		16	17	千克		Yarn of fine endangered animal hair, carded, not put up for retail sale, containing less than 85% by weight of other animal hair
	-精梳:								-Combed:
	---按重量计动物细毛含量在85%及以上的:								---Containing 85% or more by weight of fine animal hair:
5108.2011	----山羊绒的	5	70		16	17	千克		----Of goats
5108.2019	-----其他	5	70			17	千克		----Other
5108 2019.10	非供零售用精梳其他濒危动物细毛纱线（按重量计其他动物细毛含量≥85%）	5	70			17	千克	FE	Yarn of fine endangered animal hair, combed not put up for retail sale, containing 85% or more by weight of other fine animal hair
5108 2019.90	非供零售用精梳其他动物细毛纱线（按重量计其他动物细毛含量≥85%）	5	70		16	17	千克		Yarn of fine animal hair , combed, not put up for retail sale, containing 85% or more by weight of other fine animal hair
5108.2090	---其他	5	70			17	千克		---Other
5108 2090.10	非供零售用精梳其他濒危动物细毛纱线（按重量计其他精梳动物细毛含量＜85%）	5	70			17	千克	FE	Yarn of fine endangered animal hair, combed, not put up for retail sale, containing less than 85% by weight of other fine animal hair
5108 2090.90	非供零售用精梳其他动物细毛纱线（按重量计其他精梳动物细毛含量＜85%）	5	70		16	17	千克		Yarn of fine animal hair, combed, not put up for retail sale, containing less than 85% by weight of other animal hair
51.09	**羊毛或动物细毛的纱线，供零售用:**								**Yarn of wool or of fine animal hair, put up for retail sale:**
	-按重量计羊毛或动物细毛含量在85%及以上:								-Containing 85% or more by weight of wool or of fine animal hair:

税则号列 Tariff Item	商品名称及备注	进口税率 最惠	进口税率 普通	进口税率 暂定	出口退税	增值税率	计量单位	监管条件	Article Description
	---动物细毛:								---Of fine animal hair:
5109.1011	----山羊绒的	6	80		16	17	千克		----Of goats
5109.1019	----其他	6	80		16	17	千克		----Other
5109.1090	---其他	6	80		16	17	千克		---Other
	-其他:								-Other:
	---动物细毛:								---Of fine animal hair:
5109.9011	----山羊绒的	6	80		16	17	千克		----Of goats
5109.9019	----其他	6	80		16	17	千克		----Other
5109.9090	---其他	6	80		16	17	千克		---Other
51.10	**动物粗毛或马毛的纱线（包括马毛粗松螺旋花线），不论是否供零售用:**								**Yarn of coarse animal hair or of horsehair （including gimped horsehair yarn）, whether or not put up for retail sale:**
5110.0000	动物粗毛或马毛的纱线（包括马毛粗松螺旋花线），不论是否供零售用	6	70			17	千克		Yarn of coarse animal hair or of horse hair(including gimped horsehair yarn), whether or not put up for retail sale
5110 0000.10	濒危动物粗毛的纱线（包括马毛粗松螺旋花线，不论是否供零售用）	6	70			17	千克	FE	Yarn of coarse hair of endangered animal(including gimped horse hair yarn), whether or not put up for retail sale
5110 0000.90	其他动物粗毛或马毛的纱线（包括马毛粗松螺旋花线，不论是否供零售用）	6	70		16	17	千克		Yarn of other coarse hair or of horsehair(including gimped horse hair yarn), whether or not put up for retail sale
51.11	**粗梳羊毛或粗梳动物细毛的机织物:**								**Woven fabrics of carded wool or of carded fine animal hair:**
	-按重量计羊毛或动物细毛含量在85%及以上:								-Containing 85% or more by weight of wool or of fine animal hair:
	--每平方米重量不超过300克:								--Of a weight not exceeding 300g/m²:
	---动物细毛的:								---Of fine animal hair:
5111.1111	----山羊绒的	10	130		16	17	米/千克		----Of goats
5111.1119	----其他	10	130		16	17	米/千克		----Other
5111.1190	---其他	10	130		16	17	米/千克		---Other
	--其他:								--Other:
	---动物细毛的:								---Of fine animal hair:
5111.1911	----山羊绒的	10	130		16	17	米/千克		----Of goats
5111.1919	----其他	10	130		16	17	米/千克		----Other
5111.1990	---其他	10	130		16	17	米/千克		---Other
5111.2000	-其他，主要或仅与化学纤维长丝混纺	10	130		16	17	米/千克		-Other, mixed mainly or solely with manmade filaments
5111 2000.10	与化纤长丝混纺提花、装饰家具布（重量≤140克/平方米或>300克/平方米，羊毛或动物细毛含量<85%）	10	130		16	17	米/千克		Jacquard/decorative cloth, mixed with man-made filaments, of a weight exceeding 300g/m², not exceeding 140g/m², containing less than 85% by weight of wool and fine animal hair
5111 2000.90	与化纤长丝混纺其他粗梳毛机织物（羊毛或动物细毛含量<85%）	10	130		16	17	米/千克		Other woven fabrics of carded wool or of carded animal hair, mixed with man-made filaments, containing less than 85% by weight of wool and fine animal hair
5111.3000	-其他，主要或仅与化学纤维短纤混纺	10	130		16	17	米/千克		-Other, mixed mainly or solely with manmade staple fibres
5111 3000.10	与化纤短纤混纺提花、装饰家具布（重量≤140克/平方米或>300克/平方米，羊或动物细毛含量<85%）	10	130		16	17	米/千克		Jacquard/decorative cloth, mixed with man-made staplefibres, of a weight exceeding 300g/m², not exceeding 140g/m², containing less than 85% by weight of wool and fine animal hair
5111 3000.90	与化纤短纤混纺其他粗梳毛机织物（羊毛或动物细毛含量<85%）	10	130		16	17	米/千克		Other woven fabrics of carded wool or fine animal hair, mixed with man-made staple fibres, containing less than 85% by weight of wool and fine animal hair
5111.9000	-其他	10	130		16	17	米/千克		-Other
5111 9000.11	其他丝与粗梳羊毛或动物细毛混纺(丝及绢丝含量≥30%,	10	130		16	17	米/千克		Other woven fabrics of carded wool or of fine animal hair， mixed with silk, containing 30% or more by

税则号列 Tariff Item	商品名称及备注	进口税率			出口退税	增值税率	计量单位	监管条件	Article Description
		最惠	普通	暂定					
	粗梳羊毛或动物细毛含量＜85%，价值＞＄33/千克）								weight of silk and silk waste, containing less than 85% by weight of carded wool or fine animal hair, of a value exceeding USD33/kg
5111 9000.19	其他丝混纺机织物（丝及绢丝含量≥30%，粗梳羊毛或动物细毛含量＜85%，价值＞＄33/千克）	10	130		16	17	米/千克		Other woven fabrics, mixed with silk, containing 30% or more by weight of silk and silk waste, containing less than 85% by weight of carded wool or of fine animal hair, of a value exceeding USD33/kg
5111 9000.21	其他毛混纺提花/装饰家具布（粗梳羊毛或动物细毛含量＜85%，重量≤140克/平方米或＞300克/平方米）	10	130		16	17	米/千克		Jacquard/decorative cloth, mixed with wool or animals hair, of a weight exceeding 300g/m², not exceeding 140g/m², containing less than 85% by weight of carded wool or of fine animal hair
5111 9000.29	其他毛混纺提花/装饰家具布（粗梳羊毛或动物细毛含量＜85%，重量≤140克/平方米或＞300克/平方米）	10	130		16	17	米/千克		Other jacquard/decorative cloth, mixed with wool or animal hair, containing less than 85% by weight of carded wool or of fine animal hair, of a weight exceeding 300g/m², not exceeding 140g/m²
5111 9000.91	其他机织物（与粗梳羊毛或动物细毛混纺，粗梳羊毛或动物细毛含量＜85%）	10	130		16	17	米/千克		Other woven fabrics， mixed with carded wool or fine animal hair, containing less than 85% by weight of carded wool or of fine animal hair
5111 9000.99	其他机织物（与其他混纺，粗梳羊毛或动物细毛含量＜85%）	10	130		16	17	米/千克		Other woven fabrics, mixed, containing less than 85% by weight of carded wool or of fine animal hair
51.12	**精梳羊毛或精梳动物细毛的机织物:**								**Woven fabrics of combed wool or of combed fine animal hair:**
	-按重量计羊毛和动物细毛含量在85%及以上:								-Containing 85% or more by weight of wool or of fine animal hair:
5112.1100	--每平方米重量不超过200克	10	130		16	17	米/千克		--Of a weight not exceeding 200g/m²
5112 1100.10	重量≤140克/平方米毛提花/装饰家具布（精梳羊毛或动物细毛含量≥85%）	10	130		16	17	米/千克		Jacquard/decorative cloth, of a weight not exceeding 140g/m², containing 85% or more by weight of combed wool or of fine animal hair
5112 1100.90	其他重量≤200克/平方米毛制机织物（精梳羊毛或动物细毛含量≥85%）	10	130		16	17	米/千克		Other woven fabrics of wool, of a weight not exceeding 200g/m², containing 85% or more by weight of combed wool or of fine animal hair
5112.1900	--其他	10	130		16	17	米/千克		--Other
5112 1900.10	重量＞200克/平方米毛提花/装饰家具布（精梳羊毛或动物细毛含量≥85%）	10	130		16	17	米/千克		Jacquard/decorative cloth, of a weight exceeding 200g/m², containing 85% or more by weight of combed wool or of fine animal hair
5112 1900.90	重量＞200克/平方米其他毛制机织物（精梳羊毛或动物细毛含量≥85%）	10	130		16	17	米/千克		Other woven fabrics of wool, of a weight exceeding 200g/m², containing 85% or more by weight of combed wool or of fine animal hair
5112.2000	-其他，主要或仅与化学纤维长丝混纺	10	130		16	17	米/千克		-Other, mixed mainly or solely with manmade filaments
5112 2000.10	与化纤长丝混纺毛制提花、家具布（精梳羊毛或动物细毛含量＜85%，重量≤140克/平方米或＞300克/平方米）	10	130		16	17	米/千克		Jacquard/decorative cloth, mixed with man-made filaments, containing less than 85% by weight of combed wool or of fine animal hair,of a weight ≤140g/m² or weight＞300g/m²
5112 2000.90	与化纤长丝混纺其他毛制机织物（精梳羊毛或动物细毛含量＜85%）	10	130		16	17	米/千克		Other wool woven fabrics, mixed with man-made filaments (containing less than 85% by weight of combed wool or of fine animal hair)
5112.3000	-其他，主要或仅与化学纤维短纤混纺	10	130		16	17	米/千克		-Other, mixed mainly or solely with manmade staple fibres
5112 3000.10	与化纤短纤混纺毛制提花、家具布（精梳羊/动物细毛含量＜85%，重量≤140克/平方米或＞300克/平方米）	10	130		16	17	米/千克		Jacquard/decorative cloth, mixed with man-made staple fibres (containing less than 85% by weight of combed wool or of fine animal hair, of a weight≤ 140g/m² or weight＞300g/m²)
5112 3000.90	与化纤短纤混纺其他毛制机织物（精梳羊毛或动物细毛含量＜	10	130		16	17	米/千克		Other woven fabrics of wool, mixed with man-made staple fibres (containing less than 85% by weight of

税则号列 Tariff Item	商品名称及备注	进口税率 最惠	普通	暂定	出口退税	增值税率	计量单位	监管条件	Article Description
	85%)								combed wool or of fine animal hair)
5112.9000	-其他	10	130		16	17	米/千克		-Other
5112 9000.10	其他丝与毛混纺机织物(精梳羊毛或动物细毛含量＜85%，丝及绢丝含量≥30%，价值＞＄33/千克)	10	130		16	17	米/千克		Other woven fabrics of wool or animal hair, mixed with silk (containing less than 85% by weight of combed wool or of fine animal hair, containing≥ 30% by weight of silk, of a value exceeding USD33/kg)
5112 9000.20	其他精梳毛制提花、装饰家具布(羊毛或动物细毛含量＜85%，重量≤140g/平方米或＞300g/平方米)	10	130		16	17	米/千克		Other jacquard/decorative cloth of combed hair (containing less than 85% by weight of wool or fine animal hair, of a weight≤140g/m² or weight＞300g/m²)
5112 9000.90	其他机织物(精梳羊毛或动物细毛含量＜85%)	10	130		16	17	米/千克		Other woven fabrics (containing less than 85% by weight of combed wool or of fine animal hair)
51.13	**动物粗毛或马毛的机织物:**								**Woven fabrics of coarse animal hair or of horsehair:**
5113.0000	动物粗毛或马毛的机织物	10	130		16	17	米/千克		Woven fabrics of coarse animal hair or of horsehair

第五十二章 棉　花

Chapter 52 Cotton

子目注释：

子目5209.42及5211.42所称“粗斜纹布（劳动布）”，是指用不同颜色的纱线织成的三线或四线斜纹织物，包括破斜纹组织的织物，这种织物以经纱为面，经纱染成一种相同的颜色，纬纱未漂白或经漂白、染成灰色或比经纱稍浅的颜色。

Subheading Note:

For the purposes of subheadings 5209.42 and 5211.42. the expression “denim” means fabrics of yarns of different colours, of 3-thread or 4-thread twill, including broken twill, warp faced, the warp yarns of which are of one and the same colour and the weft yarns of which are unbleached, bleached, dyed grey or coloured a lighter shade of the colour of the warp yarns.

税则号列 Tariff Item	商品名称及备注	进口税率			出口退税	增值税率	计量单位	监管条件	Article Description
		最惠	普通	暂定					
52.01	**未梳的棉花：**								**Cotton, not carded or combed:**
5201.0000	未梳的棉花		125		13	13	千克		Cotton, not carded or combed
5201 0000.01	未梳的棉花（包括脱脂棉花（配额内））	1	125		13	13	千克	t4xAB	Cotton, not carded or combed, including degreased cotton, in-quota
5201 0000.80	未梳的棉花（包括脱脂棉花（关税配额外暂定））	0	0		13	13	千克	4ABex	Cotton, not carded or combed, including degreased cotton（tariff and out-of-quota, interim）
5201 0000.90	未梳的棉花（包括脱脂棉花（配额外））	40	125		13	13	千克	4xAB	Cotton, not carded or combed, including degreased cotton, out-of-quota
52.02	**废棉（包括废棉纱线及回收纤维）：**								**Cotton waste (including yarn waste and garnetted stock):**
5202.1000	-废棉纱线（包括废棉线）	10	30		13	17	千克	AP	-Yarn waste（including thread waste）
	-其他:								-Other:
5202.9100	--回收纤维	10	30		13	17	千克	ABP	--Garnetted stock
5202.9900	--其他	10	30		13	17	千克	ABP	--Other
52.03	**已梳的棉花：**								**Cotton, carded or combed:**
5203.0000	已梳的棉花		125		13	17	千克		Cotton, carded or combed
5203 0000.01	已梳的棉花（配额内）	1	125		13	17	千克	t4xAB	Cotton, carded or combed, in-quota
5203 0000.90	已梳的棉花（配额外）	40	125		13	17	千克	4xAB	Cotton, carded or combed, out-of-quota
52.04	**棉制缝纫线，不论是否供零售用：**								**Cotton sewing thread, whether or not put up for retail sale:**
	-非供零售用:								-Not put up for retail sale:
5204.1100	--按重量计含棉量在85%及以上	5	40		16	17	千克		--Containing 85% or more by weight of cotton
5204.1900	--其他	5	40		16	17	千克		--Other
5204.2000	-供零售用	5	50		16	17	千克		-Put up for retail sale
52.05	**棉纱线（缝纫线除外），按重量计含棉量在85％及以上，非供零售用：**								**Cotton yarn (other than sewing thread), containing 85% or more by weight of cotton, not put up for retail sale:**
	-未精梳纤维纺制的单纱:								-Single yarn, of uncombed fibres:
5205.1100	--细度在714.29分特及以上（不超过14公支）	5	40		16	17	千克		--Measuring 714.29 decitex or more (not exceeding 14 metric number)
5205.1200	--细度在714.29分特以下，但不细于232.56分特（超过14公支，但不超过43公支）	5	40		16	17	千克		--Measuring less than 714.29 decitex but not less than 232.56 decitex (exceeding 14 metric number but not exceeding 43 metric number)
5205.1300	--细度在232.56分特以下，但不细于192.31分特（超过43公支，但不超过52公支）	5	40		16	17	千克		--Measuring less than 232.56 decitex but not less than 192.31 decitex（exceeding 43 metric number but not exceeding 52 metric number）
5205.1400	--细度在192.31分特以下，但不细于125分特(超过52公支，但不超过80公支）	5	40		16	17	千克		--Measuring less than 192.31 decitex but not less than 125 decitex（exceeding 52 metric number but not exceeding 80 metric number）
5205.1500	--细度在125分特以下（超过80公支）	5	40		16	17	千克		--Measuring less than 125 decitex（exceeding 80 metric number）
	-精梳纤维纺制的单纱:								-Single yarn, of combed fibres:
5205.2100	--细度在714.29分特及以上（不超过14公支）	5	40		16	17	千克		--Measuring 714.29 decitex or more（not exceeding 14 metric number）

税则号列 Tariff Item	商品名称及备注	进口税率 最惠	普通	暂定	出口退税	增值税率	计量单位	监管条件	Article Description
5205.2200	--细度在714.29分特以下，但不细于232.56分特（超过14公支，但不超过43公支）	5	40		16	17	千克		--Measuring less than 714.29 decitex but not less than 232.56 decitex（exceeding 14 metric number but not exceeding 43 metric number）
5205.2300	--细度在232.56分特以下，但不细于192.31分特(超过43公支，但不超过52公支)	5	40		16	17	千克		--Measuring less than 232.56 decitex but not less than 192.31 decitex（exceeding 43 metric number but not exceeding 52 metric number）
5205.2400	--细度在192.31分特以下，但不细于125分特(超过52公支，但不超过80公支)	5	40		16	17	千克		--Measuring less than 192.31 decitex but not less than 125 decitex（exceeding 52 metric number but not exceeding 80 metric number）
5205.2600	--细度在125分特以下，但不细于106.38分特（超过80公支，但不超过94公支）	5	40		16	17	千克		--Measuring less than 125 decitex but not less than 106.38 decitex（exceeding 80 metric number but not exceeding 94 metric number）
5205.2700	--细度在106.38分特以下，但不细于83.33分特（超过94公支，但不超过120公支）	5	40		16	17	千克		--Measuring less than 106.38 decitex but not less than 83.33 decitex（exceeding 94 metric number but not exceeding 120 metric nunber）
5205.2800	--细度在83.33分特以下(超过120公支)	5	40		16	17	千克		--Measuring less than 83.33 decitex（exceeding 120 metric number）
	-未精梳纤维纺制的多股纱线或缆线:								-Multiple（folded）or cabled yarn, of uncombed fibres:
5205.3100	--每根单纱细度在714.29分特及以上（每根单纱不超过14公支）	5	40		16	17	千克		--Measuring per single yarn 714.29 decitex or more（not exceeding 14 metric number per single yarn）
5205.3200	--每根单纱细度在714.29分特以下，但不细于232.56分特(每根单纱超过14公支，但不超过43公支)	5	40		16	17	千克		--Measuring per single yarn less than 714.29 decitex but not less than 232.56 decitex（exceeding 14 metric number but not exceeding 43 metric number per single yarn）
5205.3300	--每根单纱细度在232.56分特以下，但不细于192.31分特(每根单纱超过43公支，但不超过52公支)	5	40		16	17	千克		--Measuring per single yarn less than 232.56 decitex but not less than 192.31 decitex（exceeding 43 metric number but not exceeding 52 metric number per single yarn）
5205.3400	--每根单纱细度在192.31分特以下，但不细于125分特(每根单纱超过52公支，但不超过80公支)	5	40		16	17	千克		--Measuring per single yarn less than 192.31 decitex but not less than 125 decitex（exceeding 52 metric number but not exceeding 80 metric number per single yarn）
5205.3500	--每根单纱细度在125分特以下(每根单纱超过80公支)	5	40		16	17	千克		--Measuring per single yarn less than 125 decitex（exceeding 80 metric number per single yarn
	-精梳纤维纺制的多股纱线或缆线:								-Multiple（folded）or cabled yarn, of combed fibres:
5205.4100	--每根单纱细度在714.29分特及以上（每根单纱不超过14公支）	5	40		16	17	千克		--Measuring per single yarn 714.29 decitex or more（not exceeding 14 metric number per single yarn）
5205.4200	--每根单纱细度在714.29分特以下，但不细于232.56分特(每根单纱超过14公支，但不超过43公支)	5	40		16	17	千克		--Measuring per single yarn less than 714.29 decitex but not less than 232.56 decitex（exceeding 14 metric number but not exceeding 43 metric number per single yarn）
5205.4300	—每根单纱细度在232.56分特以下，但不细于192.31分特(每根单纱超过43公支，但不超过52公支)	5	40		16	17	千克		–Measuring per single yarn less than 232.56 decitex but not less than 192.31 decitex（exceeding 43 metric number but not exceeding 52 metric number per single yarn）
5205.4400	—每根单纱细度在192.31分特以下，但不细于125分特(每根单纱超过52公支，但不超过80公支)	5	40		16	17	千克		–Measuring per single yarn less than 192.31 decitex but not less than 125 decitex（exceeding 52 metric number but not exceeding 80 metric number per single yarn）
5205.4600	--每根单纱细度在125分特以下，但不细于106.38分特(每根单纱超过80公支，但不超过94公支)	5	40		16	17	千克		--Measuring per single yarn less than 125 decitex but not less than 106.38 decitex（exceeding 80 metric number but not exceeding 94 metric number per single yarn）

税则号列 Tariff Item	商品名称及备注	进口税率			出口退税	增值税率	计量单位	监管条件	Article Description
		最惠	普通	暂定					
5205.4700	--每根单纱细度在106.38分特以下，但不细于83.33分特（每根单纱超过94公支，但不超过120公支）	5	40		16	17	千克		--Measuring per single yarn less than 106.38 decitex but not less than 83.33 decitex（exceeding 94 metric number but not exceeding 120 metric number per single yarn）
5205.4800	--每根单纱细度在83.33分特以下（每根单纱超过120公支）	5	40		16	17	千克		--Measuring per single yarn less than 83.33 decitex（exceeding 120 metric number per single yarn）
52.06	棉纱线（缝纫线除外），按重量计含棉量在85%以下，非供零售用：								**Cotton yarn（other than sewing thread），containing less than 85% by weight of cotton, not put up for retail sale:**
	-未精梳纤维纺制的单纱：								-Single yarn, of uncombed fibres:
5206.1100	--细度在714.29分特及以上（不超过14公支）	5	40		16	17	千克		--Measuring 714.29 decitex or more（not exceeding 14 metric number）
5206.1200	--细度在714.29分特以下，但不细于232.56分特（超过14公支，但不超过43公支）	5	40		16	17	千克		--Measuring less than 714.29 decitex but not less than 232.56 decitex（exceeding 14 metric number but not exceeding 43 metric number）
5206.1300	--细度在232.56分特以下，但不细于192.31分特（超过43公支，但不超过52公支）	5	40		16	17	千克		--Measuring less than 232.56 decitex but not less than 192.31 decitex（exceeding 43 metric number but not exceeding 52 metric number）
5206.1400	--细度在192.31分特以下，但不细于125分特（超过52公支，但不超过80公支）	5	40		16	17	千克		--Measuring less than 192.31 decitex but not less than 125 decitex（exceeding 52 metric number but not exceeding 80 metric number）
5206.1500	--细度在125分特以下（超过80公支）	5	40		16	17	千克		--Measuring less than 125 decitex（exceeding 80 metric number）
	-精梳纤维纺制的单纱：								-Single yarn, of combed fibres:
5206.2100	--细度在714.29分特及以上（不超过14公支）	5	40		16	17	千克		--Measuring 714.29 decitex or more（not exceeding 14 metric number）
5206.2200	--细度在714.29分特以下，但不细于232.56分特（超过14公支，但不超过43公支）	5	40		16	17	千克		--Measuring less than 714.29 decitex but not less than 232.56 decitex（exceeding 14 metric number but not exceeding 43 metric number）
5206.2300	--细度在232.56分特以下，但不细于192.31分特（超过43公支，但不超过52公支）	5	40		16	17	千克		--Measuring less than 232.56 decitex but not less than 192.31 decitex（exceeding 43 metric number but not exceeding 52 metric number）
5206.2400	--细度在192.31分特以下，但不细于125分特（超过52公支，但不超过80公支）	5	40		16	17	千克		--Measuring less than 192.31 decitex but not less than 125 decitex（exceeding 52 metric number but not exceeding 80 metric number）
5206.2500	--细度在125分特以下（超过80公支）	5	40		16	17	千克		--Measuring less than 125 decitex（exceeding 80 metric number）
	-未精梳纤维纺制的多股纱线或缆线：								-Multiple（folded）or cabled yarn, of uncombed fibres:
5206.3100	--每根单纱细度在714.29分特及以上，（每根单纱不超过14公支）	5	40		16	17	千克		--Measuring per single yarn 714.29 decitex or more（not exceeding 14 metric number per single yarn）
5206.3200	--每根单纱细度在714.29分特以下，但不细于232.56分特（每根单纱超过14公支，但不超过43公支）	5	40		16	17	千克		--Measuring per single yarn less than 714.29 decitex but not less than 232.56 decitex（exceeding 14 metric number but not exceeding 43 metric number per single yarn）
5206.3300	--每根单纱细度在232.56分特以下，但不细于192.31分特（每根单纱超过43公支，但不超过52公支）	5	40		16	17	千克		--Measuring per single yarn less than 232.56 decitex but not less than 192.31 decitex（exceeding 43 metric number but not exceeding 52 metric number per single yarn）
5206.3400	--每根单纱细度在192.31分特以下，但不细于125分特（每根单纱超过52公支，但不超过80公支）	5	40		16	17	千克		--Measuring per single yarn less than 192.31 decitex but not less than 125 decitex（exceeding 52 metric number but not exceeding 80 metric number per single yarn）
5206.3500	--每根单纱细度在125分特以下	5	40		16	17	千克		--Measuring per single yarn less than 125 decitex

税则号列 Tariff Item	商品名称及备注	进口税率 最惠	普通	暂定	出口退税	增值税率	计量单位	监管条件	Article Description
	（每根单纱超过80公支）								(exceeding 80 metric number per single yarn)
	-精梳纤维纺制的多股纱线或缆线：								-Multiple (folded) or cabled yarn, of combed fibres:
5206.4100	--每根单纱细度在714.29分特及以上（每根单纱不超过14公支）	5	40		16	17	千克		--Measuring per single yarn 714.29 decitex or more (not exceeding 14 metric number per single yarn)
5206.4200	--每根单纱细度在714.29分特以下，但不细于232.56分特（每根单纱超过14公支，但不超过43公支）	5	40		16	17	千克		--Measuring per single yarn less than 714.29 decitex but not less than 232.56 decitex (exceeding 14 metric number but not exceeding 43 metric number per single yarn)
5206.4300	--每根单纱细度在232.56分特以下，但不细于192.31分特（每根单纱超过43公支，但不超过52公支）	5	40		16	17	千克		--Measuring per single yarn less than 232.56 decitex but not less than 192.31 decitex (exceeding 43 metric number but not exceeding 52 metric number per single yarn)
5206.4400	--每根单纱细度在192.31分特以下，但不细于125分特（每根单纱超过52公支，但不超过80公支）	5	40		16	17	千克		--Measuring per single yarn less than 192.31 decitex but not less than 125 decitex (exceeding 52 metric number but not exceeding 80 metric number per single yarn)
5206.4500	--每根单纱细度在125分特以下（每根单纱超过80公支）	5	40		16	17	千克		--Measuring per single yarn less than 125 decitex (exceeding 80 metric number per single yarn)
52.07	**棉纱线（缝纫线除外），供零售用：**								**Cotton yarn (other than sewing thread) put up for retail sale:**
5207.1000	-按重量计含棉量在85%及以上	6	50		16	17	千克		-Containing 85% or more by weight of cotton
5207.9000	-其他	6	50		16	17	千克		-Other
52.08	**棉机织物，按重量计含棉量在85%及以上，每平方米重量≤200克：**								**Woven fabrics of cotton, containing 85% or more by weight of cotton, weighing not more than 200g/m²:**
	-未漂白：								-Unbleached:
5208.1100	--平纹机织物，每平方米重量不超过100克	10	70		16	17	米/千克		--Plain weave, weighing not more than 100g/m²
5208 1100.10	未漂白全棉平纹府绸及细平布（每平方米重量不超过100克，含棉85%及以上）	10	70		16	17	米/千克		Plain Poplin and fine plain cloth of cotton, unbleached, weighing not more than 100g/m², containing 85% or more by weight of cotton
5208 1100.20	未漂白全棉平纹机织平布（每平方米重量不超过100克，68号及以下）	10	70		16	17	米/千克		Plain weave cloth of cotton, unbleached, weighing not more than 100g/m², No.68 or below
5208 1100.30	未漂白全棉平纹奶酪布（每平方米重量不超过100克，含棉85%及以上）	10	70		16	17	米/千克		Plain weave cheese cloth, unbleached, weighing not more than 100g/m², containing 85% or more by weight of cotton
5208 1100.40	未漂白全棉平纹印染用布（每平方米重量不超过100克，43~68号）	10	70		16	17	米/千克		Plain cloth of cotton for printing and dyeing, unbleached, weighing not more than 100g/m², No.43-68,
5208 1100.50	未漂白全棉平纹巴里纱及薄细布（每平方米重量不超过100克，69号及以上）	10	70		16	17	米/千克		Plain voiles and muslin of cotton, unbleached, weighing not more than 100g/m², No.69 or above
5208 1100.60	未漂白全棉平纹机织打字布（每平方米重量不超过100克，含棉85%及以上）	10	70		16	17	米/千克		Plain typewriter ribbon of cotton, unbleached, weighing not more than 100g/m², containing 85% or more by weight of cotton
5208 1100.70	未漂白全棉医用纱布（每平方米重量不超过100克，含棉85%及以上）	10	70		16	17	米/千克		Medical gauze of cotton, unbleached, weighing not more than 100g/m², containing 85% or more by weight of cotton
5208.1200	--平纹机织物，每平方米重量超过100克	10	70		16	17	米/千克		--Plain weave, weighing more than 100 g/m²
5208 1200.10	未漂白全棉平纹府绸及细平布（100克<每平方米重量≤200克，含棉85%及以上）	10	70		16	17	米/千克		Plain Poplin and fine cloth of cotton, unbleached weighing more than 100g/m², less than 200g/m², containing 85% or more by weight of cotton
5208 1200.20	未漂白全棉平纹机织平布（100	10	70		16	17	米/千克		Plain weave cloth of cotton, unbleached, weighing

税则号列 Tariff Item	商品名称及备注	进口税率 最惠	进口税率 普通	进口税率 暂定	出口退税	增值税率	计量单位	监管条件	Article Description
	克＜每平方米重量≤200克，68号及以下）								more than 100g/m², less than 200g/m², No.68 or below
5208 1200.30	未漂白全棉平纹奶酪布（100克＜每平方米重量≤200克，含棉85%及以上）	10	70		16	17	米/千克		Plain cheese cloth of cotton, unbleached, weighing more than 100g/m², less than 200g/m², containing 85% or more by weight of cotton
5208 1200.40	未漂白全棉平纹印染用布（100克＜每平方米重量≤200克，43～68号）	10	70		16	17	米/千克		Plain cloth of cotton for printing and dyeing, unbleached, weighing more than 100g/m², less than 200g/m², No.43-68
5208 1200.50	未漂白全棉平纹巴里纱及薄细布（100克＜每平方米重量≤200克，69号及以上）	10	70		16	17	米/千克		Plain voiles and muslin of cotton, unbleached, weighing more than 100g/m², less than 200g/m², No.69 or above
5208.1300	--三线或四线斜纹机织物，包括双面斜纹机织物	10	70		16	17	米/千克		--3-thread or 4-thread twill, including cross twill
5208.1900	--其他机织物	10	70		16	17	米/千克		--Other fabrics
5208 1900.10	未漂白其他全棉机织缎布（每平方米重量≤200克，含棉85%及以上）	10	70		16	17	米/千克		Woven satin cloth of cotton, unbleached, weighing less than 200g/m², containing 85% or more by weight of cotton
5208 1900.20	未漂白其他全棉机织斜纹布（每平方米重量≤200克，含棉85%及以上）	10	70		16	17	米/千克		Woven twill cloth of cotton, unbleached, weighing less than 200g/m²,containing 85% or more by weight of cotton
5208 1900.30	未漂白其他全棉机织牛津布（每平方米重量≤200克，含棉85%及以上）	10	70		16	17	米/千克		Woven oxford cloth of cotton, unbleached, weighing less than 200g/m², containing 85% or more by weight of cotton
5208 1900.90	未漂白其他全棉机织物（每平方米重量≤200克，含棉85%及以上）	10	70		16	17	米/千克		Other woven fabrics of cotton, unbleached, weighing less than 200g/m², containing 85% or moreby weight of cotton
	-漂白：								-Bleached:
5208.2100	--平纹机织物，每平方米重量不超过100克	10	70		16	17	米/千克		--Plain weave, weighing not more than 100g/m²
5208 2100.10	漂白全棉平纹府绸及细平布（每平方米重量≤100克，含棉85%及以上）	10	70		16	17	米/千克	A	Plain Poplin and fine plain cloth of cotton,, bleached, weighing not more than 100g/m², containing 85% or more by weight of cotton
5208 2100.20	漂白全棉平纹机织平布（每平方米重量≤100克，68号及以下）	10	70		16	17	米/千克	A	Plain weave cloth of cotton, bleached, weighing not more than 100g/m², No.68 or below
5208 2100.30	漂白全棉平纹奶酪布（每平方米重量≤100克，含棉85%及以上）	10	70		16	17	米/千克	A	Plain cheese cloth of cotton, bleached, weighing not more than 100g/m², containing 85% or more by weight of cotton, bleached
5208 2100.40	漂白全棉平纹印染用布（每平方米重量≤100克，43～68号）	10	70		16	17	米/千克	A	Plain cloth of cotton for printing and dying, bleached, weighing not more than 100g/m²,, No.43-68
5208 2100.50	漂白全棉平纹巴里纱及薄细布（每平方米重量≤100克，69号及以上）	10	70		16	17	米/千克	A	Plain voiles and muslin of cotton, bleached, weighing not more than 100g/m², No.69 or above
5208 2100.60	漂白全棉医用纱布（每平方米重量≤100克，含棉85%及以上）	10	70		16	17	米/千克	A	Medical gauze of cotton, bleached, weighing not more than 100g/m², containing 85% or more by weight of cotton
5208.2200	--平纹机织物，每平方米重量超过100克	10	70		16	17	米/千克		--Plain weave, weighing more than 100g/m²
5208 2200.10	漂白全棉平纹府绸及细平布（100克＜每平方米重量≤200克，含棉85%及以上）	10	70		16	17	米/千克	A	Plain Poplin and fine cloth of cotton, bleached, weighing more than 100g/m²and less than 200g/m², containing 85% or more by weight of cotton
5208 2200.20	漂白全棉平纹机织平布（100克＜每平方米重量≤200克，68号及以下）	10	70		16	17	米/千克	A	Plain weave cloth of cotton, bleached, weighing more than 100g/m²and less than 200g/m², No.68 or below
5208 2200.30	漂白全棉平纹奶酪布（100克＜	10	70		16	17	米/千克	A	Plain cheese cloth of cotton, bleached, weighing more

税则号列 Tariff Item	商品名称及备注	进口税率 最惠	普通	暂定	出口退税	增值税率	计量单位	监管条件	Article Description
	每平方米重量≤200克，含棉85%及以上）								than 100g/m² and less than 200g/m², containing 85% or more by weight of cotton
5208 2200.40	漂白全棉平纹印染用布（100克<每平方米重量≤200克，43~68号）	10	70		16	17	米/千克	A	Plain cloth of cotton for printing and dyeing, bleached weighing more than 100g/m² and less than 200g/m², No.43-68
5208 2200.50	漂白全棉巴里纱及薄细布（100克<每平方米重量≤200克，69号及以上）	10	70		16	17	米/千克	A	Plain Voiles and muslin of cotton, bleached, weighing more than 100g/m² and less than 200g/m², No.69 or above
5208.2300	--三线或四线斜纹机织物，包括双面斜纹机织物	12	70		16	17	米/千克	A	--3-thread or 4-thread twill, including cross twill
5208.2900	--其他机织物	10	70		16	17	米/千克		--Other fabrics
5208 2900.10	漂白其他全棉机织缎布（每平方米重量不超过200克，含棉85%及以上）	10	70		16	17	米/千克	A	Woven satin cloth of cotton, bleached, weighing not more than 200g/m², containing 85% or more by weight of cotton
5208 2900.20	漂白其他全棉机织斜纹布（每平方米重量不超过200克，含棉85%及以上）	10	70		16	17	米/千克	A	Woven twill cloth of cotton, bleached, weighing not more than 200g/m²,containing 85% or more by weight of cotton
5208 2900.30	漂白其他全棉机织牛津布（每平方米重量不超过200克，含棉85%及以上）	10	70		16	17	米/千克	A	Woven oxford cloth of cotton, bleached, weighing not more than 200g/m², containing 85% or more by weight of cotton
5208 2900.90	漂白其他全棉机织物（每平方米重量不超过200克，含棉85%及以上）	10	70		16	17	米/千克	A	Other woven fabrics of cotton, bleached, weighing not more than 200g/m², containing 85% or more by weight of cotton
	-染色：								-Dyed:
5208.3100	--平纹机织物，每平方米重量不超过100克	10	70		16	17	米/千克		--Plain weave, weighing not more than 100 g/m²
5208 3100.10	染色全棉手工织布（每平方米重量不超过100克，含棉85%及以上）	10	70		16	17	米/千克	A	Handwoven plain cloth of cotton, dyed, weighing not more than 100g/m², containing 85% or more by weight of cotton
5208 3100.91	染色全棉平纹府绸及细平布（每平方米重量不超过100克，含棉85%及以上）	10	70		16	17	米/千克	A	Plain Poplin and fine cloth of cotton, dyed, weighing not more than 100g/m²,containing 85% or more by weight of cotton
5208 3100.92	染色全棉平纹机织平布（每平方米重量不超过100克，68号及以下）	10	70		16	17	米/千克	A	Plain weave cloth of cotton, dyed, weighing not more than 100g/m², No.68 or below
5208 3100.93	染色全棉平纹奶酪布（每平方米重量不超过100克，含棉85%及以上）	10	70		16	17	米/千克	A	Plain cheese cloth of cotton, dyed, weighing not more than 100g/m²,containing 85% or more by weight of cotton
5208 3100.94	染色全棉平纹印染用布（每平方米重量不超过100克，43~68号）	10	70		16	17	米/千克	A	Plain weave cloth of cotton for printing and dyeing, dyed, weighing not more than 100g/m², No.43-68
5208 3100.95	染色全棉巴里纱及薄细布（每平方米重量不超过100克，69号及以上）	10	70		16	17	米/千克	A	Plain Voiles and muslin of cotton, dyed, weighing not more than 100g/m², No.69 or above
5208.3200	--平纹机织物，每平方米重量超过100克	10	70		16	17	米/千克		--Plain weave, weighing more than 100 g/m²
5208 3200.10	染色全棉手工织布（100克<每平方米重量≤200克，含棉85%及以上）	10	70		16	17	米/千克	A	Handwoven cloth of cotton, dyed, weighing more than 100g/m² and less than 200g/m², containing 85% or more by weight of cotton
5208 3200.91	染色全棉平纹府绸及细平布（100克<每平方米重量≤200克，含棉85%及以上）	10	70		16	17	米/千克	A	Plain poplin and fine plain cloth of cotton, dyed, weighing more than 100g/m² and less than 200g/m², containing 85% or more by weight of cotton
5208 3200.92	染色全棉平纹机织平布（100克<每平方米重量≤200克，68号及以下）	10	70		16	17	米/千克	A	Plain weave cloth of cotton, dyed, weighing more than 100g/m² and less than 200g/m², No.68 or below
5208 3200.93	染色全棉平纹奶酪布（100克<	10	70		16	17	米/千克	A	Plain cheese cloth of cotton, dyed, weighing more than

税则号列 Tariff Item	商品名称及备注	进口税率 最惠	普通	暂定	出口退税	增值税率	计量单位	监管条件	Article Description
	每平方米重量≤200克，含棉85%及以上）								100g/m²and less than 200g/m², containing 85% or more by weight of cotton
5208 3200.94	染色全棉平纹印染用布（100克<每平方米重量≤200克，43~68号）	10	70		16	17	米/千克	A	Plain weave cloth of cotton for printing and dyeing, dyed, weighing more than 100g/m²and less than 200g/m², No.43-68
5208 3200.95	染色全棉巴里纱及薄细布（100克<每平方米重量≤200克，69号及以上）	10	70		16	17	米/千克	A	Plain voiles and muslin of cotton, dyed, weighing more than 100g/m²and less than 200g/m², No.69 or above
5208.3300	--三线或四线斜纹机织物，包括双面斜纹机织物	10	70		16	17	米/千克	A	--3-thread or 4-thread twill, including cross twill
5208.3900	--其他机织物	10	70		16	17	米/千克		--Other fabrics
5208 3900.10	染色其他全棉机织缎布（每平方米重量不超过200克，含棉85%及以上）	10	70		16	17	米/千克	A	Woven satin cloth of cotton, dyed, weighing not more than 200g/m²,containing 85% or more by weight of cotton
5208 3900.20	染色其他全棉机织斜纹布（每平方米重量不超过200克，含棉85%及以上）	10	70		16	17	米/千克	A	Woven twill cloth of cotton, dyed, weighing not more than 200g/m², containing 85% or more by weight of cotton
5208 3900.30	染色其他全棉机织牛津布（每平方米重量不超过200克，含棉85%及以上）	10	70		16	17	米/千克	A	Woven oxford cloth of cotton, dyed, weighing not more than 200g/m², containing 85% or more by weight of cotton
5208 3900.90	染色其他全棉机织物（每平方米重量不超过200克，含棉85%及以上）	10	70		16	17	米/千克	A	Other woven fabrics of cotton, dyed, weighing not more than 200g/m², containing 85% or more by weight of cotton
	-色织:								-Of yarns of different colours:
5208.4100	--平纹机织物，每平方米重量不超过100克	10	70		16	17	米/千克		--Plain weave, weighing not more than 100g/m²
5208 4100.10	色织的全棉手工织布（每平方米重量不超过100克，含棉85%及以上）	10	70		16	17	米/千克	A	Handwoven cloth of cotton, yarn-dyed, weighing not more than 100g/m²,containing 85% or more by weight of cotton
5208 4100.90	色织的全棉平纹机织物（每平方米重量不超过100克，含棉85%及以上）	10	70		16	17	米/千克	A	Plain woven fabrics of cotton, and yarn-dyed, weighing not more than 100g/m², containing 85% or more by weight of cotton
5208.4200	--平纹机织物，每平方米重量超过100克	10	70		16	17	米/千克		--Plain weave, weighing more than 100 g/m²
5208 4200.10	色织的全棉手工织布（100克<每平方米重量≤200克，含棉85%及以上）	10	70		16	17	米/千克	A	Handwoven cloth of cotton, yarn-dyed, weighing more than 100 g/m², not more than 200g/m², containing 85% or more by weight of cotton
5208 4200.90	色织的全棉平纹机织物（100克<每平方米重量≤200克，含棉85%及以上）	10	70		16	17	米/千克	A	Plain woven fabrics of cotton, yarn-dyed, weighing more than 100 g/m², not more than 200g/m², containing 85% or more by weight of cotton
5208.4300	--三线或四线斜纹机织物，包括双面斜纹机织物	10	70		16	17	米/千克	A	--3-thread or 4-thread twill, including cross twill
5208.4900	--其他机织物	10	70		16	17	米/千克		--Other fabrics
5208 4900.10	色织的其他全棉提花机织物（每平方米重量≤200克，含棉85%及以上）	10	70		16	17	米/千克	A	Other jacquard weave fabrics of cotton,yarn-dyed, weighing not more than 200g/m², containing 85% or more by weight of cotton
5208 4900.90	色织的其他全棉机织物（每平方米重量≤200克，含棉85%及以上）	10	70		16	17	米/千克	A	Other woven fabrics of cotton, yarn-dyed,weighing not more than 200g/m²,containing 85% or more by weight of cotton
	-印花:								-Printed:
5208.5100	--平纹机织物，每平方米重量不超过100克	10	70		16	17	米/千克		--Plain weave, weighing not more than 100g/m²
5208 5100.10	印花全棉手工织布（每平方米重量≤100克，含棉85%及以上）	10	70		16	17	米/千克	A	Handwoven cloth of cotton, printed, weighing not more than 100g/m², containing 85% or more by weight of cotton
5208 5100.91	印花全棉平纹府绸及细平布（每	10	70		16	17	米/千克	A	Plain Poplin and fine plain cloth of cotton, printed,

税则号列 Tariff Item	商品名称及备注	进口税率 最惠	普通	暂定	出口退税	增值税率	计量单位	监管条件	Article Description
	平方米重量≤100克，含棉85%及以上）								weighing not more than 100g/m², containing 85% or more by weight of cotton
5208 5100.92	印花全棉平纹机织平布（每平方米重量≤100克，68号及以下）	10	70		16	17	米/千克	A	Plain weave cloth of cotton, printed, weighing not more than 100g/m², No.68 or below
5208 5100.93	印花全棉平纹奶酪布（每平方米重量≤100克，含棉85%及以上）	10	70		16	17	米/千克	A	Plain cheese cloth of cotton, printed, weighing not more than 100g/m², containing 85% or more by weight of cotton
5208 5100.94	印花全棉平纹印染用布（每平方米重量≤100克，43~68号）	10	70		16	17	米/千克	A	Plain weave cloth of cotton for printing and dyeing, printed, weighing not more than 100g/m², No.43-68
5208 5100.95	印花全棉平纹巴里纱及薄细布（每平方米重量≤100克，69号及以上）	10	70		16	17	米/千克	A	Plain Voiles and muslin of cotton, printed, weighing not more than 100g/m², No.69 or above
5208.5200	--平纹机织物，每平方米重量超过100克	10	70		16	17	米/千克		--Plain weave, weighing more than 100g/m²
5208 5200.10	印花的全棉手工织布（100克<每平方米重量≤200克，含棉85%及以上）	10	70		16	17	米/千克	A	Handwoven cloth of cotton, printed, weighing more than 100 g/m², not more than 200g/m², containing 85% or more by weight of cotton
5208 5200.91	印花的全棉平纹府绸及细平布（100克<每平方米重量≤200克，含棉85%及以上）	10	70		16	17	米/千克	A	Plain Poplin and fine cloth of cotton, printed, weighing more than 100 g/m², not more than 200g/m², containing 85% or more by weight of cotton
5208 5200.92	印花的全棉平纹机织平布（100克<每平方米重量≤200克，68号及以下）	10	70		16	17	米/千克	A	Plain weave cloth of cotton, printed, weighing more than 100 g/m², not more than 200g/m²,, No.68 or below
5208 5200.93	印花的全棉平纹奶酪布（100克<每平方米重量≤200克，含棉85%及以上）	10	70		16	17	米/千克	A	Plain cheese cloth of cotton, printing, weighing more than 100 g/m², not more than 200g/m², containing 85% or more by weight of cotton
5208 5200.94	印花的全棉平纹印染用布（100克<每平方米重量≤200克，43~68号）	10	70		16	17	米/千克	A	Plain cloth of cotton for printing and dyeing, printed, weighing more than 100 g/m², not more than 200g/m²,No.43-68
5208 5200.95	印花的全棉巴里纱及薄细布（100克<每平方米重量≤200克，69号及以上）	10	70		16	17	米/千克	A	Plain Voiles and muslin of cotton, printed,weighing more than 100 g/m², not more than 200g/m², No.69 or above
	--其他机织物:								--Other fabrics:
5208.5910	---三线或四线斜纹机织物，包括双面斜纹机织物	10	70		16	17	米/千克	A	---3-thread or 4-thread twill, including crosss twill
5208.5990	----其他	10	70		16	17	米/千克		---Other
5208 5990.10	印花其他全棉机织缎布（每平方米重量≤200克，含棉85%及以上）	10	70		16	17	米/千克	A	Woven satin cloth of cotton, printed, weighing not more than 200g/m², containing 85% or more by weight of cotton
5208 5990.20	印花其他全棉机织斜纹布（每平方米重量≤200克，含棉85%及以上）	10	70		16	17	米/千克	A	Woven twill cloth of cotton, printed, weighing not more than 200g/m², containing 85% or more by weight of cotton
5208 5990.30	印花其他全棉机织牛津布（每平方米重量≤200克，含棉85%及以上）	10	70		16	17	米/千克	A	Woven oxford cloth of cotton, printed, weighing not more than 200g/m², containing 85% or more by weight of cotton
5208 5990.90	印花其他全棉机织物（每平方米重量≤200克，含棉85%及以上）	10	70		16	17	米/千克	A	Other woven fabrics of cotton, printed, weighing not more than 200g/m², containing 85% or more by weight of cotton
52.09	**棉机织物，按重量计含棉量在85%及以上，每平方米重量超过200克:**								**Woven fabrics of cotton, containing 85% or more by weight of cotton, weighing more than 200 g/m²:**
	-未漂白:								-Unbleached:
5209.1100	--平纹机织物	10	70		16	17	米/千克		--Plain weave
5209 1100.10	未漂白全棉平纹府绸及细平布（指每平方米重超过200克，含	10	70		16	17	米/千克		Plain Poplin and fine plain cloth of cotton, unbleached, weighing more than 200g/m², containing 85% or more

税则号列 Tariff Item	商品名称及备注	进口税率 最惠	普通	暂定	出口退税	增值税率	计量单位	监管条件	Article Description
	棉85%及以上）								by weight of cotton,
5209 1100.20	未漂白的全棉平纹机织平布（指每平方米重超过200克，含棉85%及以上）	10	70		16	17	米/千克		Plain weave cloth of cotton, unbleached, weighing more than 200g/m², containing 85% or more by weight of cotton
5209 1100.30	未漂白的全棉平纹机织帆布（指每平方米重超过200克，含棉85%及以上）	10	70		16	17	米/千克		Plain weave canvas of cotton, unbleached, weighing more than 200g/m², containing 85% or more by weight of cotton
5209.1200	--三线或四线斜纹机织物，包括双面斜纹机织物	10	70		16	17	米/千克		--3-thread or 4-thread twill, including cross twill
5209.1900	--其他机织物	10	70		16	17	米/千克		--Other fabrics
5209 1900.10	未漂白的其他全棉机织缎布（指每平方米重超过200克，含棉85%及以上）	10	70		16	17	米/千克		Other woven satin cloth of cotton, unbleached, weighing more than200g/m², containing 85% or more by weight of cotton
5209 1900.20	未漂白的其他全棉机织斜纹布（指每平方米重超过200克，含棉85%及以上）	10	70		16	17	米/千克		Other woven twill fabrics of cotton, unbleached, weighing more than 200g/m², containing 85% or more by weight of cotton
5209 1900.30	未漂白的其他全棉机织帆布（指每平方米重超过200克，含棉85%及以上）	10	70		16	17	米/千克		Other woven canvas of cotton, unbleached weighing more than 200g/m², containing 85% or more by weight of cotton
5209 1900.90	未漂白的其他全棉机织物（指每平方米重超过200克，含棉85%及以上）	10	70		16	17	米/千克		Other woven fabrics of cotton, unbleached, weighing more than 200g/m², containing 85% or more by weight of cotton
	-漂白：								-Bleached:
5209.2100	--平纹机织物	12	70		16	17	米/千克		--Plain weave
5209 2100.10	漂白全棉平纹府绸及细平布（指每平方米重超过200克，含棉85%及以上）	12	70		16	17	米/千克		Plain Poplin and fine plain cloth of cotton, bleached, weighing more than 200g/m², containing 85% or more by weight of cotton
5209 2100.20	漂白的全棉平纹机织平布（指每平方米重超过200克，含棉85%及以上）	12	70		16	17	米/千克		Plain weave cloth of cotton, bleached, weighing more than 200g/m², containing 85% or more by weight of cotton
5209 2100.30	漂白的全棉平纹机织帆布（指每平方米重超过200克，含棉85%及以上）	12	70		16	17	米/千克		Plain weave canvas of cotton, bleached, weighing more than 200g/m², containing 85% or more by weight of cotton
5209.2200	--三线或四线斜纹机织物，包括双面斜纹机织物	12	70		16	17	米/千克		--3-thread or 4-thread twill, including cross twill
5209.2900	--其他机织物	12	70		16	17	米/千克		--Other fabrics
5209 2900.10	漂白的其他全棉机织缎布（指每平方米重超过200克，含棉85%及以上）	12	70		16	17	米/千克		Other woven satin cloth of cotton, bleached, weighing more than200g/m², containing 85% or more by weight of cotton
5209 2900.30	漂白的其他全棉机织帆布（指每平方米重超过200克，含棉85%及以上）	12	70		16	17	米/千克		Other woven canvas of cotton, bleached, weighing more than 200g/m², containing 85% or more by weight of cotton
5209 2900.90	漂白的其他全棉机织物（指每平方米重超过200克，含棉85%及以上）	12	70		16	17	米/千克		Other woven fabrics of cotton, bleached, weighing more than 200g/m², containing 85% or more by weight of cotton
	-染色：								-Dyed:
5209.3100	--平纹机织物	10	70		16	17	米/千克		--Plain weave
5209 3100.10	染色全棉手工织布（指每平方米重超过200克，含棉85%及以上）	10	70		16	17	米/千克	A	Handwoven cloth of cotton, dyed, weighing more than 200g/m², containing 85% or more by weight of cotton
5209 3100.91	染色全棉平纹府绸及细平布（指每平方米重超过200克，含棉85%及以上）	10	70		16	17	米/千克	A	Plain Poplin and fine plain cloth of cotton, dyed, weighing more than 200g/m², containing 85% or more by weight of cotton
5209 3100.92	染色的全棉平纹机织平布（指每平方米重超过200克，含棉85%	10	70		16	17	米/千克	A	Plain weave cloth of cotton, dyed, weighing more than 200g/m², containing 85% or more by weight of cotton

税则号列 Tariff Item	商品名称及备注	进口税率 最惠	普通	暂定	出口退税	增值税率	计量单位	监管条件	Article Description
	及以上)								
5209 3100.93	染色的全棉平纹机织帆布(指每平方米重超过200克,含棉85%及以上)	10	70		16	17	米/千克	A	Plain weave canvas of cotton, dyed, weighing more than 200g/m², containing 85% or more by weight of cotton
5209.3200	--三线或四线斜纹机织物,包括双面斜纹机织物	10	70		16	17	米/千克	A	--3-thread or 4-thread twill, including cross twill
5209.3900	--其他机织物	10	70		16	17	米/千克		--Other fabrics
5209 3900.10	染色的其他全棉机织缎布(指每平方米重超过200克,含棉85%及以上)	10	70		16	17	米/千克	A	Other woven satin cloth of cotton, dyed, weighing more than 200g/m², containing 85% or more by weight of cotton
5209 3900.20	染色的其他全棉机织斜纹布(指每平方米重超过200克,含棉85%及以上)	10	70		16	17	米/千克	A	Other woven twill cloth of cotton, dyed, weighing more than 200g/m²,containing 85% by weight of cotton
5209 3900.30	染色的其他全棉机织帆布(指每平方米重超过200克,含棉85%及以上)	10	70		16	17	米/千克	A	Other woven canvas of cotton, dyed, weighing more than 200g/m², containing 85% or more by weight of cotton
5209 3900.90	染色的其他全棉机织物(指每平方米重超过200克,含棉85%及以上)	10	70		16	17	米/千克	A	Other woven fabrics of cotton, dyed, weighing more than 200g/m², containing 85% or more by weight of cotton
	-色织:								-Of yarns of different colours:
5209.4100	--平纹机织物	10	70		16	17	米/千克		--Plain weave
5209 4100.10	色织的全棉手工织布(指每平方米重超过200克,含棉85%及以上)	10	70		16	17	米/千克	A	Handwoven cloth of cotton, yarn-dyed, weighing more than 200g/m²,containing 85% or more by weight of cotton
5209 4100.90	色织的全棉平纹机织物(指每平方米重超过200克,含棉85%及以上)	10	70		16	17	米/千克	A	Plain weave fabrics of cotton, weighing more than 200g/m², containin≥85% by weight of cotton
5209.4200	--粗斜纹布(劳动布)	10	70		16	17	米/千克		--Denim
5209 4200.10	色织全棉蓝粗斜纹布(劳动布)(指每平方米重超过200克,含棉85%及以上)	10	70		16	17	米/千克	A	Blue denim of cotton, yarn-dyed, weighing more than 200g/m², containing 85% or more by weight of cotton
5209 4200.90	色织其他全棉粗斜纹布(劳动布)(指每平方米重超过200克,含棉85%及以上)	10	70		16	17	米/千克	A	Denim of cotton, yarn-dyed, weighing more than 200 g/m², containing 85% or more by weight of cotton
5209.4300	--其他三线或四线斜纹机织物,包括双面斜纹机织物	10	70		16	17	米/千克	A	--Other fabrics of 3-thread or 4-thread twill, including cross twill
5209.4900	--其他机织物	10	70		16	17	米/千克		--Other fabrics
5209 4900.10	色织的其他全棉提花机织物(指每平方米重超过200克,含棉85%及以上)	10	70		16	17	米/千克	A	Other woven jacquad fabrics of cotton, yarn-dyed, weighing more than 200g/m², containing 85% or more by weight of cotton
5209 4900.90	色织的其他全棉机织物(指每平方米重超过200克,含棉85%及以上)	10	70		16	17	米/千克	A	Other woven fabrics of cotton, yarn-dyed, weighing more than 200g/m²,containing 85% or more by weight of cotton
	-印花:								-Printed:
5209.5100	--平纹机织物	10	70		16	17	米/千克		--Plain weave
5209 5100.10	印花全棉手工织布(指每平方米重超过200克,含棉85%及以上)	10	70		16	17	米/千克	A	Handwoven cloth of cotton, printed, weighing more than 200g/m², containing 85% or more by weight of cotton
5209 5100.91	印花全棉平纹府绸及细平布(指每平方米重超过200克,含棉85%及以上)	10	70		16	17	米/千克	A	Plain Poplin and fine plain cloth of cotton, printed, weighing more than 200g/m²,containing 85% or more by weight of cotton
5209 5100.92	印花全棉平纹机织平布(指每平方米重超过200克,含棉85%及	10	70		16	17	米/千克	A	Plain weave cloth of cotton, printed, weighing more than 200g/m², containing 85% or more by weight of cotton

税则号列 Tariff Item	商品名称及备注	进口税率			出口退税	增值税率	计量单位	监管条件	Article Description
		最惠	普通	暂定					
	以上)								
5209 5100.93	印花全棉平纹机织帆布(指每平方米重超过200克,含棉85%及以上)	10	70		16	17	米/千克	A	Plain weave canvas of cotton, printed, weighing more than 200g/m², containing 85% or more by weight of cotton
5209.5200	--三线或四线斜纹机织物,包括双面斜纹机织物	10	70		16	17	米/千克	A	--3-thread or 4-thread twill, including cross twill
5209.5900	--其他机织物	10	70		16	17	米/千克		--Other fabrics
5209 5900.10	印花的其他全棉机织缎布(指每平方米重超过200克,含棉85%及以上)	10	70		16	17	米/千克	A	Other woven satin cloth of cotton, printed, weighing more than 200g/m², containing 85% or more by weight of cotton
5209 5900.20	印花的其他全棉机织斜纹布(指每平方米重超过200克,含棉85%及以上)	10	70		16	17	米/千克	A	Other woven twill cloth of cotton, printed, weighing more than 200g/m², containing 85% or more by weight of cotton
5209 5900.30	印花的其他全棉机织帆布(指每平方米重超过200克,含棉85%及以上)	10	70		16	17	米/千克	A	Other woven canvas of cotton, printed, weighing more than 200g/m², containing 85% or more by weight of cotton
5209 5900.90	印花的其他全棉机织物(指每平方米重超过200克,含棉85%及以上)	10	70		16	17	米/千克	A	Other woven fabrics of cotton, printed, weighing more than 200g/m², containing 85% or more by weight of cotton
52.10	**棉机织物,按重量计含棉量在85%以下,主要或仅与化学纤维混纺,每平方米重量不超过200克:**								**Woven fabrics of cotton, containing less than 85% by weight of cotton, mixed mainly or solely with manmade fibres, weighing not more than 200g/m²:**
	-未漂白:								-Unbleached:
5210.1100[暂]	--平纹机织物	12	90	6	16	17	米/千克		--Plain weave
5210 1100.11[暂]	未漂白与聚酯短纤混纺的棉制府绸(指每平方米重≤200克,含棉85%以下,含平细布)	12	90	6	16	17	米/千克		Plain Poplin and fine cloth of cotton, unbleached, mixed with polyester staple fibres, weight≤200g/m², containing less than 85% by weight of cotton
5210 1100.12[暂]	未漂白与聚酯短纤混纺棉机织平布(指每平方米重≤200克,≤68号,含棉85%以下)	12	90	6	16	17	米/千克		Plain cloth of cotton, mixed with polyester staple fibres, weight≤200g/m²,containing 85% by weight of cotton, unbleached, No.68 or below
5210 1100.13[暂]	未漂白与聚酯短纤混纺棉奶酪布(指每平方米重≤200克,含棉85%以下)	12	90	6	16	17	米/千克		Plain cheese cloth of cotton, unbleached, mixed with polyester staple fibres, weight≤200g/m², containing less than 85% by weight of cotton
5210 1100.14[暂]	未漂白与聚酯短纤混纺棉印染用布(指每平方米重≤200克,43~68号,含棉85%以下)	12	90	6	16	17	米/千克		Plain cloth of cotton for printing and dyeing, unbleached, mixed with polyester staple fibres, weighing not more than 200g/m², containing less than 85% by weight of cotton, No.43-68
5210 1100.15[暂]	未漂白与聚酯短纤混纺棉巴里纱(指每平方米重≤200克,≥69号,含棉85%以下,含薄细布)	12	90	6	16	17	米/千克		Plain Voiles and muslin of cotton, unbleached, mixed with polyester stapie fibres, weighing not more than 200g/m², containing less than 85% by weight of cotton, No.69 or above
5210 1100.91[暂]	未漂白与其他化纤混纺棉府绸(指每平方米重≤200克,含棉85%以下,含细平布)	12	90	6	16	17	米/千克		Plain Poplin and fine cloth of cotton, mixed with other man-made fibres, unbleached, weight≤200g/m², containing less than 85% by weight of cotton,
5210 1100.92[暂]	未漂白与其他化纤混纺棉机织平布(指每平方米重≤200克,≤68号,含棉85%以下)	12	90	6	16	17	米/千克		Plain cloth of cotton, mixed with other man-made fibres, unbleached, weight≤200g/m², containing less than 85% by weight of cotton, No.68 or above
5210 1100.93[暂]	未漂白与其他化纤混纺棉奶酪布(指每平方米重量≤200克,含棉85%以下)	12	90	6	16	17	米/千克		Plain cheese cloth of cotton, mixed with other man-made fibres, unbleached, weight≤200g/m², containing less than 85% by weight of cotton
5210 1100.94[暂]	未漂白与其他化纤混纺棉印染用布(指每平方米重≤200克,43~68号,含棉85%以下)	12	90	6	16	17	米/千克		Cloth of cotton for printing and dyeing, mixed with other man-made fibres, unbleached, weighing not more than 200g/m², containing less than 85% by weight of cotton, No.43-68
5210 1100.95[暂]	未漂白与其他化纤混纺棉巴里	12	90	6	16	17	米/千克		Voiles and muslin of cotton, mixed with man-made fibres,

税则号列 Tariff Item	商品名称及备注	进口税率 最惠	普通	暂定	出口退税	增值税率	计量单位	监管条件	Article Description
	纱（指每平方米重≤200克，≥69号，含棉85%以下，含薄细布）								unbleached, weighing not more than 200g/m², containing less than 85% by weight of cotton No.69 or above
	--其他机织物：								--Other fabrics:
5210.1910 暂	---三线或四线斜纹机织物，包括双面斜纹机织物	12	90	6	16	17	米/千克		---3-thread or 4-thread twill, including cross twill
5210 1910.10 暂	未漂白与聚酯短纤混纺3/4线或双面棉斜纹布（每平方米重≤200克，含棉85%以下）	12	90	6	16	17	米/千克		3 or 4-thread cloth or cross twill cloth of cotton, mixed with polyester staple fibres, unbleached, weighing not more than 200g/m², containing less than 85% by weight of cotton
5210 1910.90 暂	未漂白与其他化纤混纺3/4线或双面棉斜纹布（每平方米重≤200克，含棉85%以下）	12	90	6	16	17	米/千克		3 or 4-thread cloth or cross twill cloth of cotton, mixed with other man-made fibres, unbleached,weight ≤ 200g/m², containing less than 85% of cotton
5210.1990 暂	---其他	12	90	6	16	17	米/千克		---Other
5210 1990.11 暂	其他未漂白与聚酯短纤混纺的缎布（每平方米重≤200克，含棉85%以下）	12	90	6	16	17	米/千克		Other woven satin cloth , mixed with polyester staple fibres, unbleached, weight ≤ 200g/m², containing less than 85% by weight of cotton
5210 1990.12 暂	其他未漂白与聚酯短纤混纺斜纹布（每平方米重≤200克，含棉85%以下）	12	90	6	16	17	米/千克		Other woven twill cloth, mixed with polyester staple fibres, unbleached, weight ≤ 200g/m², containing less than 85% by weight of cotton
5210 1990.13 暂	其他未漂白与聚酯短纤混纺牛津布（每平方米重≤200克，含棉85%以下）	12	90	6	16	17	米/千克		Other woven oxford cloth, mixed with polyester staple fibres, unbleached, weight ≤ 200g/m², containing less than 85% by weight of cotton
5210 1990.19 暂	其他未漂白与聚酯短纤混纺棉布（每平方米重≤200克，含棉85%以下）	12	90	6	16	17	米/千克		Other cloth of cotton, mixed with polyester staple fibres, unbleached, weighing not more than 200g/m², containing less than 85% by weight of cotton
5210 1990.91 暂	其他未漂白与其他化纤混纺缎布（每平方米重≤200克，含棉85%以下）	12	90	6	16	17	米/千克		Other stain cloth, mixed with other man-made fibres, unbleached, weighing not more than 200g/m², containing less than 85% by weight of cotton
5210 1990.92 暂	其他未漂白与其他化纤混纺斜纹布（每平方米重≤200克，含棉85%以下）	12	90	6	16	17	米/千克		Other twill cloth, mixed with other man-made fibres, unbleached, weighing not more than200 g/m², containing less than 85% by weight of cotton
5210 1990.93 暂	其他未漂白与其他化纤混纺牛津布（每平方米重≤200克，含棉85%以下）	12	90	6	16	17	米/千克		Other oxford cloth, mixed with other man-made fibres, unbleached, weighing not more than200g/m², containing less than 85% by weight of cotton
5210 1990.99 暂	其他未漂白与其他化纤混纺棉布（每平方米重≤200克，含棉85%以下）	12	90	6	16	17	米/千克		Other cloth of cotton, mixed with other man-made fibres,unbleached, weighing not more than200g/m², containing less than 85% by weight of cotton
	-漂白：								-Bleached:
5210.2100	--平纹机织物	14	90		16	17	米/千克		--Plain weave
5210 2100.11	漂白与聚酯短纤混纺棉府绸（每平方米重≤200克，含棉85%以下，含细平布）	14	90		16	17	米/千克		Plain Poplin and fine plain cloth of cotton, mixed with plyester staple fibres, bleached, weight≤200g/m², containing less than 85% by weight of cotton
5210 2100.12	漂白与聚酯短纤混纺棉机织平布（每平方米重≤200克，68号及以下，含棉85%以下）	14	90		16	17	米/千克		Plain weave cloth of cotton, mixed with polyester staple fibres, bleached weighing not more than 200g/m², containing less than 85% by weight of cotton, No.68 or below
5210 2100.13	漂白与聚酯短纤混纺棉奶酪布（每平方米重≤200克，含棉85%以下）	14	90		16	17	米/千克		Plain cheese cloth of cotton, mixed with polyester staple fibres, bleached, weight ≤ 200g/m², containing less than 85% by weight of cotton
5210 2100.14	漂白与聚酯短纤混纺棉印染布（每平方米重≤200克，43～68号，含棉85%以下）	14	90		16	17	米/千克		Cloth of cotton for printing and dyeing, mixed with polyester staple fibres, weighing not more than 200g/m², containing less than 85% by weight of cotton, bleached, No.43-48
5210 2100.15	漂白与聚酯短纤混纺棉巴里纱	14	90		16	17	米/千克		Poplin and fine cloth of cotton, mixed with polyester

税则号列 Tariff Item	商品名称及备注	进口税率			出口退税	增值税率	计量单位	监管条件	Article Description
		最惠	普通	暂定					
	（每平方米重≤200克，69号及以上，含棉85%以下，含薄细布）								staple fibres, bleached, weighing not more than 200g/m², containing less than 85% by weight of cotton, No.69 or above
5210 2100.21	漂白与化纤长丝混纺棉府绸（每平方米重≤200克，含棉85%以下，含细平布）	14	90		16	17	米/千克		Poplin and fine plain cloth of cotton, mixed with man-made filaments, bleached, weight≤200g/m², containing less than 85% by weight of cotton
5210 2100.22	漂白与化纤长丝混纺棉机织平布（每平方米重≤200克，68号及以下，含棉85%以下）	14	90		16	17	米/千克		Plain cloth of cotton, mixed with man-made filaments, bleached,weight≤200g/m², containing less than 85% by weight of cotton, No.68 or below
5210 2100.23	漂白与化纤长丝混纺棉奶酪布（每平方米重≤200克,含棉85%以下）	14	90		16	17	米/千克		Plain cheese cloth of cotton, mixed with man-made filaments, bleached, weighing not more than200g/m², containing less than 85% by weight of cotton
5210 2100.24	漂白与化纤长丝混纺棉印染布（每平方米重≤200克，43~68号，含棉85%以下）	14	90		16	17	米/千克		Cotton cloth for printing and dyeing,mixed with man-made filaments, bleached,weight ≤ 200g/m²,containing less than 85% by weight of cotton, No.43-68
5210 2100.25	漂白与化纤长丝混纺棉巴里纱（每平方米重≤200克，69号及以上，含棉85%以下，含薄细布）	14	90		16	17	米/千克		Voiles and muslin of cotton, mixed with man-made filaments, weighing not more than 200g/m², containing less than 85% by weight of cotton, bleached, No.69 or above
5210 2100.91	漂白与其他化纤混纺棉府绸（每平方米重≤200克，含棉85%以下，含细平布）	14	90		16	17	米/千克		Plain Poplin and fine plain cloth of cotton, mixed with other man-made fibres, bleached, weight ≤ 200g/m², containing less than 85% by weight of cotton,
5210 2100.92	漂白与其他化纤混纺棉机织平布（每平方米重≤200克，68号及以下，含棉85%以下）	14	90		16	17	米/千克		Plain weave cloth of cotton, mixed with other man-made fibres, bleached, weighing not more than 200g/m², containing less than 85% by weight of cotton, No.68 or below
5210 2100.93	漂白与其他化纤混纺棉奶酪布（每平方米重≤200克,含棉85%以下）	14	90		16	17	米/千克		Plain cheese cloth of cotton, mixed with other man-made fibres, weight ≤ 200g/m², containing less than 85% by weight of cotton, bleached
5210 2100.94	漂白与其他化纤混纺棉印染布（每平方米重≤200克，43~68号，含棉85%以下）	14	90		16	17	米/千克		Cotton cloth for printing and dying,mixed with other man-made fibres, bleached,weighing not more than 200g/m², containing less than 85% by weight of cotton, No.43-68
5210 2100.95	漂白与其他化纤混纺棉巴里纱（每平方米重≤200克，69号及以上，含棉85%以下，含薄细布）	14	90		16	17	米/千克		Voiles and muslin of cotton, mixed with other man-made fibres, bleached, weighing not more than 200g/m², containing less than 85% by weight of cotton, No.69 or above
	--其他机织物:								--Other fabrics:
5210.2910	---三线或四线斜纹机织物，包括双面斜纹机织物	14	90		16	17	米/千克		---3-thread or 4-thread twill, including cross twill
5210 2910.10	漂白与聚酯短纤混纺3/4线或双面棉斜纹布（每平方米重≤200克，含棉85%以下）	14	90		16	17	米/千克		3 or 4-thread twil and cross twill cloth of cotton, mixed with polyester staple fibres, bleached, weighing not more than 200g/m², containing less than 85% by weight of cotton
5210 2910.20	漂白与化纤长丝混纺3/4线或双面棉斜纹布（每平方米重≤200克，含棉85%以下）	14	90		16	17	米/千克		3 or 4-thread twil and cross twill cloth of cotton, mixed with man-made filaments,weight ≤ 200g/m², containing less than 85% by weight of cotton
5210 2910.90	漂白与其他化纤混纺3/4线或双面棉斜纹布（每平方米重≤200克，含棉85%以下）	14	90		16	17	米/千克		3 or 4-thread twil and cross twill cloth of cotton, mixed with man-made fibres, weight ≤ 200g/m²,containing less than 85% by weight of cotton
5210.2990	---其他	14	90		16	17	米/千克		---Other
5210 2990.11	其他漂白与聚酯短纤混纺缎布	14	90		16	17	米/千克		Other satin cloth, mixed with polyester staple fibres,

税则号列 Tariff Item	商品名称及备注	进口税率			出口退税	增值税率	计量单位	监管条件	Article Description
		最惠	普通	暂定					
	（每平方米重≤200克，含棉85%以下）								bleached, weighing not more than200g/m², containing less than 85% by weight of cotton
5210 2990.12	其他漂白与聚酯短纤混纺斜纹布（每平方米重≤200克，含棉85%以下）	14	90		16	17	米/千克		Other twill cloth, mixed with polyester staple fibres, bleached, weighing not more than 200g/m², containing less than 85% by weight of cotton
5210 2990.13	其他漂白与聚酯短纤混纺牛津布（每平方米重≤200克，含棉85%以下）	14	90		16	17	米/千克		Other oxford cloth, mixed with polyester staple fibres, bleached, weighing not more than200g/m², containing less than 85% by weight of cotton
5210 2990.19	其他漂白与聚酯短纤混纺棉布（每平方米重≤200克，含棉85%以下）	14	90		16	17	米/千克		Other cotton cloth, mixed with polyester staple fibres, bleached, weighing not more than 200g/m², containing less than 85% by weight of cotton
5210 2990.21	其他漂白与化纤长丝混纺缎布（每平方米重≤200克，含棉85%以下）	14	90		16	17	米/千克		Other satin cloth, mixed with man-made filaments, bleached, weighing not more than 200g/m², containing less than 85% by weight of cotton
5210 2990.22	其他漂白与化纤长丝混纺斜纹布（每平方米重≤200克，含棉85%以下）	14	90		16	17	米/千克		Other twill cloth, mixed with man-made filaments, bleached, weighing not more than 200g/m², containing less than 85% by weight of cotton
5210 2990.23	其他漂白与化纤长丝混纺牛津布（每平方米重≤200克，含棉85%以下）	14	90		16	17	米/千克		Other oxford cloth,mixed with manmade filaments, bleached, weighing not more than 200g/m², containing less than 85% by weight of cotton
5210 2990.29	其他漂白与化纤长丝混纺棉布（每平方米重≤200克，含棉85%以下）	14	90		16	17	米/千克		Other cotton cloth,mixed with manmade filaments, bleached, weighing not more than 200g/m², containing less than 85% by weight of cotton
5210 2990.91	其他漂白与其他化纤混纺缎布（每平方米重≤200克，含棉85%以下）	14	90		16	17	米/千克		Other satin cloth, mixed with other manmade fibres, bleached, weighing not more than 200g/m², containing less than 85% by weight of cotton
5210 2990.92	其他漂白与其他化纤混纺斜纹布（每平方米重≤200克，含棉85%以下）	14	90		16	17	米/千克		Other twill cloth, mixed with other manmade fibres, bleached, weighing not more than 200g/m², containing less than 85% by weight of cotton
5210 2990.93	其他漂白与其他化纤混纺牛津布（每平方米重≤200克，含棉85%以下）	14	90		16	17	米/千克		Other oxford cloth, mixed with other man-made fibres, bleached, weighing not more than 200g/m², containing less than 85% by weight of cotton
5210 2990.99	其他漂白与其他化纤混纺棉布（每平方米重≤200克，含棉85%以下）	14	90		16	17	米/千克		Other cloth of cotton, mixed with other man-made fibres, bleached, weighing not more than 200g/m², containing less than 85% by weight of cotton
	-染色：								-Dyed:
5210.3100	--平纹机织物	10	90		16	17	米/千克		--Plain weave
5210 3100.11	染色与聚酯短纤混纺棉府绸（每平方米重≤200克，含棉85%以下，含细平布）	10	90		16	17	米/千克		Poplin of cotton including fine plain cloth, mixed with polyester staple fibres, dyed, weight≤200g/m², containing less than 85% by weight of cotton
5210 3100.12	染色与聚酯短纤混纺棉机织平布（每平方米重≤200克，68号及以下，含棉85%以下）	10	90		16	17	米/千克		Plain weave cloth of cotton, mixed with polyester staple fibres, dyed, weight≤200g/m², containing less than 85% by weight of cotton, No.68 or below
5210 3100.13	染色与聚酯短纤混纺棉奶酪布（每平方米重≤200克，含棉85%以下）	10	90		16	17	米/千克		Plain cheese cloth of cotton, mixed with polyester staple fibres, dyed, weighing not more than200g/m², containing less than 85% by weight of cotton
5210 3100.14	染色与聚酯短纤混纺棉印染布（每平方米重≤200克，43～68号，含棉85%以下）	10	90		16	17	米/千克		Plain cloth of cotton for printing and dying, mixed with polyester staple fibres, dyed, weighing not more than 200g/m², containing less than 85% by weight of cotton, No.43-68
5210 3100.15	染色与聚酯短纤混纺棉巴里纱（每平方米重≤200克，69号及以上，含棉85%以下，含薄细布）	10	90		16	17	米/千克		Voiles and muslin of cotton, mixed with polyester staple fibres,dyed, weighing not more than 200g/m², containing less than 85% by weight of cotton, No.69 or above
5210 3100.21	染色与化纤长丝混纺棉府绸（每	10	90		16	17	米/千克		Poplin of cotton, including fine plain cloth, mixed with

税则号列 Tariff Item	商品名称及备注	进口税率			出口退税	增值税率	计量单位	监管条件	Article Description
		最惠	普通	暂定					
	平方米重≤200克，含棉85%以下，含细平布）								man-made filaments, dyed, weight ≤ 200g/m² containing less than 85% by weight of cotton
5210 3100.22	染色与化纤长丝混纺棉机织平布（每平方米重≤200克，含棉85%以下）	10	90		16	17	米/千克		Plain weave cloth of cotton, mixed with man-made filaments, dyed,weighing not more than 200g/m²,containing less than 85% by weight of cotton
5210 3100.23	染色与化纤长丝混纺棉奶酪布（每平方米重≤200克,含棉85%以下）	10	90		16	17	米/千克		Plain cheese cloth of cotton, mixed with man-made filaments, dyed, weighing not more than 200g/m², containing less than 85% by weight of cotton
5210 3100.24	染色与化纤长丝混纺棉印染布（每平方米重≤200克，43~68号，含棉85%以下）	10	90		16	17	米/千克		Plain cloth of cotton for printing and dyeing, mixed with man-made filaments, dyed, weighing not more than 200g/m², containing less than 85% by weight of cotton, No.43-68
5210 3100.25	染色与化纤长丝混纺棉巴里纱（每平方米重≤200克，69号及以上，含棉85%以下，含薄细布）	10	90		16	17	米/千克		Voiles and muslin of cotton, mixed with man-made filaments, dyed,weighing not more than 200g/m², containing less than 85% by weight of cotton, No.69 or above
5210 3100.91	染色与其他化纤混纺棉府绸（每平方米重≤200克，含棉85%以下，含细平布）	10	90		16	17	米/千克		Poplin of cotton including fine plain cloth, mixed with other man-made fibres, dyed, weight≤200g/m², containing less than 85% by weight of cotton
5210 3100.92	染色与其他化纤混纺棉机织平布（每平方米重≤200克，68号及以下，含棉85%以下）	10	90		16	17	米/千克		Plain weave cloth of cotton, mixed with other man-made fibres, dyed, weighing not more than 200g/m², containing less than 85% by weight of cotton, No.68 or below
5210 3100.93	染色与其他化纤混纺棉奶酪布（每平方米重≤200克,含棉85%以下）	10	90		16	17	米/千克		Plain cheese cloth of cotton, mixed with other man-made fibres, dyed, weight≤200g/m², containing less than 85% by weight of cotton
5210 3100.94	染色与其他化纤混纺棉印染布（每平方米重≤200克，43~68号，含棉85%以下）	10	90		16	17	米/千克		Plain Cloth for printing and dyeing of cotton, mixed with other man-made fibres, dyed, weighing not more than 200g/m², containing less than 85% by weight of cotton, No.43-68
5210 3100.95	染色与其他化纤混纺棉巴里纱（每平方米重≤200克，69号及以上，含棉85%以下，含薄细布）	10	90		16	17	米/千克		Voiles and muslin of cotton, mixed with other man-made fibres, weighing not more than 200g/m², containing less than85% by weight of cotton, dyed, No.69 or above
5210.3200	--三线或四线斜纹机织物，包括双面斜纹机织物	10	90		16	17	米/千克		--3-thread or 4-thread twill, including cross twill
5210 3200.10	染色与聚酯短纤混纺的3/4线斜纹棉布（每平方米重≤200克，含棉85%以下，含双面斜纹布）	10	90		16	17	米/千克		3 or 4-thread twill, or cross twill cloth of cotton mixed with polyester staple fibres, dyed, weighing not more than 200g/m², containing less than 85% by weight of cotton
5210 3200.20	染色与化纤长丝混纺的3/4线斜纹棉布（每平方米重≤200克，含棉85%以下，含双面斜纹布）	10	90		16	17	米/千克		3 or 4-thread twill or cross twill cloth of cotton, mixed with man-made filaments, dyed, weighing not more than 200g/m², containing less than 85% by weight of cotton
5210 3200.90	染色与其他化纤混纺的3/4线斜纹棉布（每平方米重≤200克，含棉85%以下，含双面斜纹布）	10	90		16	17	米/千克		3 or 4-thread twill or cross twill cloth of cotton, mixed with other man-made fibres, dyed, weighing not more than 200g/m², containing less than 85% by weight of cotton
5210.3900	--其他机织物	10	90		16	17	米/千克		--Other fabrics
5210 3900.11	其他染色与聚酯短纤混纺缎布（每平方米重≤200克,含棉85%以下）	10	90		16	17	米/千克		Other satin cloth of cotton, mixed with polyester staple fibres, dyed, weighting not more 200g/m², containing less than 85% by weight of cotton
5210 3900.12	其他染色与聚酯短纤混纺斜纹	10	90		16	17	米/千克		Other twill cloth of cotton, mixed with polyester staple fibres,

税则号列 Tariff Item	商品名称及备注	进口税率 最惠	普通	暂定	出口退税	增值税率	计量单位	监管条件	Article Description
	布（每平方米重≤200克，含棉85%以下）								dyed, weighing not more than 200g/m², containing less than 85% by weight of cotton
5210 3900.13	其他染色与聚酯短纤混纺牛津布（每平方米重≤200克，含棉85%以下）	10	90		16	17	米/千克		Other oxford cloth of cotton, dyed, mixed with polyester staple fibres, weighing not more than 200g/m², containing less than 85% by weight of cotton
5210 3900.19	其他染色与聚酯短纤混纺棉布（每平方米重≤200克，含棉85%以下）	10	90		16	17	米/千克		Other cloth of cotton, mixed with polyester staple fibres, dyed, weighing not more than 200g/m², containing less than 85% by weight of cotton
5210 3900.21	其他染色与化纤长丝混纺缎布（每平方米重≤200克，含棉85%以下）	10	90		16	17	米/千克		Other satin cloth of cotton, mixed with man-made filaments, dyed, weighing not more than 200g/m², containing less than 85% by weight of cotton
5210 3900.22	其他染色与化纤长丝混纺斜纹布（每平方米重≤200克，含棉85%以下）	10	90		16	17	米/千克		Other twill cloth of cotton, mixed with man-made filaments, dyed, weighing not more than 200g/m²,containing less than 85% by weight of cotton
5210 3900.23	其他染色与化纤长丝混纺牛津布（每平方米重≤200克，含棉85%以下）	10	90		16	17	米/千克		Other oxford clothof cotton, mixed with man-made filaments, dyed, weighing not more than 200g/m², containing less than 85% by weight of cotton
5210 3900.29	其他染色与化纤长丝混纺棉布（每平方米重≤200克，含棉85%以下）	10	90		16	17	米/千克		Other cloth of cotton, mixed with man-made filaments, dyed, weighing not more than 200g/m², containing less than 85% by weight of cotton
5210 3900.91	其他染色与其他化纤混纺缎布（每平方米重≤200克，含棉85%以下）	10	90		16	17	米/千克		Other satin cloth of cotton, mixed with other man-made fibres, dyed, weighing not more than 200g/m², containing less than 85% by weight of cotton
5210 3900.92	其他染色与其他化纤混纺斜纹布（每平方米重≤200克，含棉85%以下）	10	90		16	17	米/千克		Other twill cloth of cotton, mixed with other man-made fibres, dyed, weighing not more than 200g/m², containing less than 85% by weight of cotton
5210 3900.93	其他染色与其他化纤混纺牛津布（每平方米重≤200克，含棉85%以下）	10	90		16	17	米/千克		Other oxford cloth of cotton, mixed with other man-made fibres, dyed, weighing not more than 200g/m², containing less than 85% by weight of cotton
5210 3900.99	其他染色与其他化纤混纺棉布（每平方米重≤200克，含棉85%以下）	10	90		16	17	米/千克		Other cloth of cotton, mixed with other man-made fibres, dyed, weighing not more than 200g/m², containing less than 85% by weight of cotton
	-色织:								-Of yarns of different colours:
5210.4100	--平纹机织物	10	90		16	17	米/千克		--Plain weave
5210 4100.10	色织与聚酯短纤混纺棉平纹布（每平方米重≤200克，含棉85%以下）	10	90		16	17	米/千克		Plain weave cloth of cotton, yarn-dyed, mixed with polyester staple fibres, containing less than 85% by weight of cotton, weighing not more than 200g/m²
5210 4100.20	色织与化纤长丝混纺棉平纹布（每平方米重≤200克，含棉85%以下）	10	90		16	17	米/千克		Plain weave cloth of cotton, yarn-dyed, mixed with man-made filaments, containing less than 85% by weight of cotton, weighing not more than 200g/m²
5210 4100.90	色织与其他化纤混纺棉平纹布（每平方米重≤200克，含棉85%以下）	10	90		16	17	米/千克		Plain weave cloth of cotton, yarn-dyed, mixed with other man-made fibres, containing less than 85% by weight of cotton, weighing not more than 200g/m²
	--其他机织物:								--Other fabrics:
5210.4910	---三线或四线斜纹机织物，包括双面斜纹机织物	10	90		16	17	米/千克		---3-thread or 4-thread twill, including cross twill
5210 4910.10	色织与聚酯短纤混纺3/4斜纹棉布（每平方米重≤200克，含棉85%以下，含双面斜纹布）	10	90		16	17	米/千克		3 or 4-thread twill or cross twill cloth of cotton, yarn-dyed, mixed with polyester staple fibres, containing less than 85% by weight of cotton, weighing not more than 200g/m²
5210 4910.20	色织与化纤长丝混纺3/4斜纹棉布（每平方米重≤200克，含棉85%以下，含双面斜纹布）	10	90		16	17	米/千克		3 or 4-thread twill or cross twill cloth of cotton, yarn-dyed, mixed with other man-made fibres, weighing not more than 200g/m², containing lessthan 85% by weight of cotton
5210 4910.90	色织其他化纤混纺3/4斜纹棉布	10	90		16	17	米/千克		3 or 4-thread twill or cross twill cloth of cotton, yarn-

税则号列 Tariff Item	商品名称及备注	进口税率 最惠	进口税率 普通	进口税率 暂定	出口退税	增值税率	计量单位	监管条件	Article Description
	（每平方米重≤200克,含棉85%以下，含双面斜纹布）								dyed,mixed with other man-made fibres, weighing not more than 200g/m², containing less than 85% by weight of cotton
5210.4990	---其他	10	90		16	17	米/千克		---Other
5210 4990.11	色织与聚酯短纤混纺提花布（每平方米重≤200克，含棉85%以下）	10	90		16	17	米/千克		Other jacquard cloth of cotton, yarn-dyed, mixed with polyester staple fibres, weighing not more than 200g/m², containing less than 85% by weight of cotton
5210 4990.19	色织与聚酯短纤混纺其他棉布（每平方米重≤200克,含棉85%以下）	10	90		16	17	米/千克		Other cloth of cotton, yarn-dyed, mixed with polyester staple fibres, weighing not more than 200g/m², containing less than 85% by weight of cotton
5210 4990.20	色织与化纤长丝混纺棉布(每平米重不超过200克,含棉85%以下)	10	90		16	17	米/千克		Other cloth of cotton, yarn-dyed, mixed with man-made filaments, weighing not more than 200g/m², containing less than 85% by weight of cotton
5210 4990.90	色织与其他化纤混纺棉布(每平米重不超过200克,含棉85%以下)	10	90		16	17	米/千克		Other weave of cotton,yarn-dyed, mixed with other man-made fibres, weighing not more than 200g/m², containing less than 85% by weight of cotton
	-印花:								-Printed:
5210.5100	---平纹机织物	10	90		16	17	米/千克		--Plain weave
5210 5100.11	印花与聚酯短纤混纺棉府绸（每平方米重≤200克，含棉85%以下，含细平布）	10	90		16	17	米/千克		Poplin of cotton including fine plain cloth, mixed with polyester staple fibres, printed, weight ≤200g/m², containing less than 85% by weight of cotton
5210 5100.12	印花与聚酯短纤混纺棉机织平布（每平方米重≤200克，68号及以下，含棉85%以下）	10	90		16	17	米/千克		Plain weave cloth of cotton, mixed with polyester staple fibres, printed, weight≤200g/m², containing less than 85% by weight of cotton, No.68 or below
5210 5100.13	印花与聚酯短纤混纺棉奶酪布（每平方米重≤200克,含棉85%以下）	10	90		16	17	米/千克		Cheese cloth of cotton, mixed with polyester staple fibres, printed, containing less than 85% by weight of cotton, weighing not more than 200 g/m²
5210 5100.14	印花与聚酯短纤混纺棉印染布（每平方米重≤200克，43~68号，含棉85%以下）	10	90		16	17	米/千克		Cloth of cotton for printing and dyeing, mixed with polyester staple fibres, printed, weighing not more than 200g/m², containing less than 85% by weight of cotton, No.43-68
5210 5100.15	印花与聚酯短纤混纺棉巴里纱（每平方米重≤200克，69号及以上，含棉85%以下，含薄细布）	10	90		16	17	米/千克		Voiles of cotton including fine thin cloth, mixed with polyester staple fibres, printed, weighing not more than 200g/m², containing less than 85% by weight of cotton, No.69 or above
5210 5100.21	印花与化纤长丝混纺棉府绸（每平方米重≤200克，含棉85%以下，含细平布）	10	90		16	17	米/千克		Poplin of cotton including fine plain cloth, mixed with man-made filaments, printed, weight≤200g/m², containing less than 85% by weight of cotton
5210 5100.22	印花与化纤长丝混纺棉机织平布（每平方米重≤200克，68号及以下，含棉85%以下）	10	90		16	17	米/千克		Plain weave clothof cotton, mixed with man-made filaments, printed, weight≤200g/m², containing less than 85% by weight of cotton, No.68 or below
5210 5100.23	印花与化纤长丝混纺棉奶酪布（每平方米重≤200克,含棉85%以下）	10	90		16	17	米/千克		Cheese cloth of cotton, mixed with man-made filaments,printed, weighing not more than 200g/m², containing less than 85% by weight of cotton
5210 5100.24	印花与化纤长丝混纺棉印染布（每平方米重≤200克，43~68号，含棉85%以下）	10	90		16	17	米/千克		Cloth of cotton for printing and dyeing, mixed with man-made filaments, printed, weight≤200g/m², containing less than85% by weight of cotton, No.43-68
5210 5100.25	印花与化纤长丝混纺棉巴里纱（每平方米重≤200克，69号及以上，含棉85%以下，含薄细布）	10	90		16	17	米/千克		Voiles and muslin of cotton, mixed with man-made filaments, printed,weighing not more than 200g/m², containing less than 85% by weight of cotton, No.69 or above
5210 5100.91	印花与其他化纤混纺棉府绸（每平方米重≤200克，含棉85%以下，含细平布）	10	90		16	17	米/千克		Poplin of cotton including fine plaincloth, mixed with other man-made fibres, printed,weight≤200g/m², containing less than 85% by weight of cotton
5210 5100.92	印花与其他化纤混纺棉机织平	10	90		16	17	米/千克		Plain weave cloth of cotton, mixed with other man-made

税则号列 Tariff Item	商品名称及备注	进口税率 最惠	进口税率 普通	进口税率 暂定	出口退税	增值税率	计量单位	监管条件	Article Description
	布（每平方米重≤200克，68号及以下，含棉85%以下）								fibres, printed, weight≤200 g/m², containing less than 85% by weight of cotton, No.68 or below
5210 5100.93	印花与其他化纤混纺棉奶酪布（每平方米重≤200克，含棉85%以下）	10	90		16	17	米/千克		Cheese cloth of cotton, mixed with other man-made fibres, printed, weight≤200g/m², containing less than 85% by weight of cotton
5210 5100.94	印花与其他化纤混纺棉印染布（每平方米重≤200克，43~68号，含棉85%以下）	10	90		16	17	米/千克		Cloth of cotton for printing and dyeing, mixed with other man-made fibres, printed, weighing not more than 200g/m², containing less than 85% by weight of cotton, No.43-68
5210 5100.95	印花与其他化纤混纺棉巴里纱（每平方米重≤200克，65号及以上，含棉85%以下，含薄细布）	10	90		16	17	米/千克		Voiles and muslin of cotton, mixed with other man-made fibres, printed, weighing not more than 200g/m², containing less than 85% by weight of cotton, No.65 or above
	--其他机织物:								--Other fabrics:
5210.5910	---三线或四线斜纹机织物，包括双面斜纹机织物	10	90		16	17	米/千克		---3-thread or 4-thread twill, including cross twill
5210 5910.10	印花聚酯短纤混纺3/4线斜纹棉布（每平方米重≤200克，含棉85%以下，含双面斜纹布）	10	90		16	17	米/千克		3 or 4-thread twill or cross twill cloth of cotton, mixed with polyester staple fibres, printed, weighing not more than 200g/m²,containing less than 85% by weight of cotton
5210 5910.20	印花化纤长丝混纺3/4线斜纹棉布（每平方米重≤200克，含棉85%以下，含双面斜纹布）	10	90		16	17	米/千克		3 or 4-thread twill or cross twill cloth of cotton, mixed with man-made filaments, printed, weighing not more than 200g/m², containing less than 85% by weight of cotton
5210 5910.90	印花其他化纤混纺3/4线斜纹棉布（每平方米重≤200克，含棉85%以下，含双面斜纹布）	10	90		16	17	米/千克		3 or 4-thread twill or cross twill cloth of cotton, mixed with other man-made fibres,printed, weighing not more than 200g/m², containing less than 85% by weight of cotton
5210.5990	---其他	10	90		16	17	米/千克		---Other
5210 5990.11	其他印花与聚酯短纤混纺缎布（每平方米重≤200克,含棉85%以下）	10	90		16	17	米/千克		Other satin cloth of cotton, mixed with polyester staple fibres, printed,weighing not more than 200g /m², containing less than 85% by weight of cotton
5210 5990.12	其他印花与聚酯短纤混纺斜纹布（每平方米重≤200克，含棉85%以下）	10	90		16	17	米/千克		Other twill cloth of cotton, mixed with polyester staple fibres, printed,weighing not more than 200g /m², containing less than85% by weight of cotton
5210 5990.13	其他印花与聚酯短纤混纺牛津布（每平方米重≤200克，含棉85%以下）	10	90		16	17	米/千克		Other Oxford cloth of cotton,mixed with man-made filaments, printed, weighing not more than 200g /m², containing less than 85% by weight of cotton
5210 5990.19	其他印花与聚酯短纤混纺棉布（每平方米重≤200克,含棉85%以下）	10	90		16	17	米/千克		Other cloth of cotton, mixed with polyester staple fibres, printed, weighing not more than 200g/m², containing less than 85% by weight of cotton
5210 5990.21	其他印花与化纤长丝混纺缎布（每平方米重≤200克,含棉85%以下）	10	90		16	17	米/千克		Other satin cloth of cotton, mixed with man-made filaments, printed, weighing not more than 200g/m², containing less than 85% by weight of cotton
5210 5990.22	其他印花与化纤长丝混纺斜纹布（每平方米重≤200克，含棉85%以下）	10	90		16	17	米/千克		Other twill cloth of cotton, mixed with man-made filaments, printed, weighing not more than 200g/m², containing less than 85% by weight of cotton
5210 5990.23	其他印花与化纤长丝混纺牛津布（每平方米重≤200克，含棉85%以下）	10	90		16	17	米/千克		Other oxford cloth of cotton, mixed with man-made filaments, printed, weighing not more than 200g/m², containing less than 85% by weight of cotton
5210 5990.29	其他印花与化纤长丝混纺棉布（每平方米重≤200克,含棉85%以下）	10	90		16	17	米/千克		Other cloth of cotton, mixed with man-made filaments, printed, weighing not more than 200g/m², containing less than 85% by weight of cotton
5210 5990.91	其他印花与其他化纤混纺缎布	10	90		16	17	米/千克		Other satin cloth of cotton, mixed with other

税则号列 Tariff Item	商品名称及备注	进口税率 最惠	普通	暂定	出口退税	增值税率	计量单位	监管条件	Article Description
	（每平方米重≤200克，含棉85%以下）								man-made fibres, printed, weight≤200g/m², containing less than 85% by weight of cotton
5210 5990.92	其他印花与其他化纤混纺斜纹布（每平方米重≤200克，含棉85%以下）	10	90		16	17	米/千克		Other twill cloth of cotton, mixed with other man-made fibres, printed,weighing not more than 200g/m², containing less than 85% by weight of cotton
5210 5990.93	其他印花与其他化纤混纺牛津布（每平方米重≤200克，含棉85%以下）	10	90		16	17	米/千克		Other oxford cloth of cotton, mixed with other man-made fibres, printed, weight≤200g/m², containing less than85% by weight of cotton
5210 5990.99	其他印花与其他化纤混纺棉布（每平方米重≤200克，含棉85%以下）	10	90		16	17	米/千克		Other cloth of cotton, mixed with other man-made fibrews, printed, weighing not more than 200g /m², containing less than 85% by weight of cotton
52.11	**棉机织物，按重量计含棉量在85%以下，主要或仅与化学纤维混纺，每平方米重量超过200克：**								**Woven fabrics of cotton, containing less than 85% by weight of cotton, mixed mainly or solely with man-made fibres, weighing more than 200g/m²:**
	-未漂白：								-Unbleached:
5211.1100[暂]	--平纹机织物	12	90	6	16	17	米/千克		--Plain weave
5211 1100.11[暂]	未漂白与聚酯短纤混纺棉府绸（每平方米重>200克，含棉85%以下，含细平布）	12	90	6	16	17	米/千克		Poplin of cotton including fine plain cloth, mixed with polyester staple fibres, unbleached, weighing more than 200g/m², containing less than 85% by weight of cotton
5211 1100.12[暂]	未漂白与聚酯短纤混纺棉机织平布（每平方米重>200克，含棉85%以下）	12	90	6	16	17	米/千克		Plain weave cloth of cotton, mixed with polyester staple fibres,unbleached,weighing morethan 200g/m², containing less than 85% by weight of cotton,
5211 1100.19[暂]	未漂白与聚酯短纤混纺棉平纹帆布（每平方米重>200克，含棉85%以下）	12	90	6	16	17	米/千克		Plain canvas of cotton, mixed with polyester staple fibres,unbleached, weighing more than 200g/m², containing less than 85% by weight of cotton
5211 1100.91[暂]	未漂白与其他化纤混纺棉府绸（每平方米重>200克，含棉85%以下，含细平布）	12	90	6	16	17	米/千克		Poplin of cotton including fine plain cloth,mixed with other man-made fibres, unbleached, weight>200g/m², containing less than 85% by weight of cotton
5211 1100.92[暂]	未漂白与其他化纤混纺棉机织平布（每平方米重>200克，含棉85%以下）	12	90	6	16	17	米/千克		Plain weave cloth of cotton, mixed with other man-made fibres, unbleached,weight>200g/m², containing less than 85% by weight of cotton
5211 1100.99[暂]	未漂白与其他化纤混纺棉平纹帆布（每平方米重>200克，含棉85%以下）	12	90	6	16	17	米/千克		Plain canvas of cotton, mixed with other manmade fibres, unbleached, weighingmore than 200g/m², containing less than 85% by weight of cotton
5211.1200[暂]	--三线或四线斜纹机织物，包括双面斜纹机织物	12	90	6	16	17	米/千克		--3-thread or 4-thread twill, including cross twill
5211 1200.10[暂]	未漂白聚酯短纤混纺斜纹棉布（每平方米重>200克，含棉85%以下，3/4线斜纹布，双面斜纹布）	12	90	6	16	17	米/千克		3- or 4-thread twill or cross twill cloth of cotton, mixed with polyester staple fibres, unbleached, weighing more than 200g/m², containing less than 85% by weight of cotton,
5211 1200.90[暂]	未漂白其他化纤混纺斜纹棉布（每平方米重>200克，含棉85%以下，3/4线斜纹布，双面斜纹布）	12	90	6	16	17	米/千克		3- or 4-thread twill or cross twill cloth of cotton, mixed with other man-made fibres, unbleached, weighing more than 200g/m², containing less than 85% by weight of cotton
5211.1900[暂]	--其他机织物	12	90	6	16	17	米/千克		--Other fabrics
5211 1900.11[暂]	未漂白与聚酯短纤混纺其他棉缎布（每平方米重>200克，含棉85%以下）	12	90	6	16	17	米/千克		Other satin cloth of cotton, mixed with polyester staple fibres, unbleached, weight>200g/m², containing less than 85% by weight of cotton
5211 1900.12[暂]	未漂白与聚酯短纤混纺其他棉斜纹布（每平方米重>200克，含棉85%以下）	12	90	6	16	17	米/千克		Other twill cloth of cotton, mixed with polyester staple fibres, unbleached, weight>200g/m², containing less than 85% by weight of cotton
5211 1900.13[暂]	未漂白与聚酯短纤混纺其他棉帆布（每平方米重>200克，含棉85%以下）	12	90	6	16	17	米/千克		Other canvas of cotton, mixed with polyester staple fibres, unbleached, weight>200g/m², containing less than 85% by weight of cotton

税则号列 Tariff Item	商品名称及备注	进口税率 最惠	普通	暂定	出口退税	增值税率	计量单位	监管条件	Article Description
5211 1900.19[暂]	未漂白与聚酯短纤混纺其他棉布(每平方米重>200克，含棉85%以下)	12	90	6	16	17	米/千克		Other cloth of cotton, mixed with polyester staple fibres, unbleached, weighing more than 200g/m², containing less than 85% by weight of cotton
5211 1900.91[暂]	未漂白与其他化纤混纺其他棉缎布(每平方米重>200克，含棉85%以下)	12	90	6	16	17	米/千克		Other satin cloth of cotton, mixed with other man-made fibres, unbleached, weight>200g/m², containing less than 85% by weight of cotton
5211 1900.92[暂]	未漂白与其他化纤混纺其他棉斜纹布(每平方米重>200克，含棉85%以下)	12	90	6	16	17	米/千克		Other twill cloth of cotton, mixed with other man-made fibres, unbleached, weight>200g/m², containing less than 85% by weight of cotton
5211 1900.93[暂]	未漂白与其他化纤混纺其他棉帆布(每平方米重>200克，含棉85%以下)	12	90	6	16	17	米/千克		Other canvas of cotton, mixed with other man-made fibres, unbleached, weight>200g/m², containing less than 85% by weight of cotton
5211 1900.99[暂]	未漂白与其他化纤混纺其他棉布(每平方米重>200克，含棉85%以下)	12	90	6	16	17	米/千克		Other cloth of cotton, mixed with other man-made fibres, unbleached, weighing more than 200g/m², containing less than 85% by weight of cotton
5211.2000	-漂白	14	90		16	17	米/千克		-Bleached
	-染色:								-Dyed:
5211.3100	--平纹机织物	10	90		16	17	米/千克		--Plain weave
5211 3100.11	染色与聚酯短纤混纺棉府绸(每平方米重>200克，含棉85%以下，含细平布)	10	90		16	17	米/千克		Poplin of cotton including fine plain cloth, mixed with polyester staple fibres, dyed, weight>200g/m², containing less than 85% by weight of cotton
5211 3100.12	染色与聚酯短纤混纺机织平布(每平方米重>200克,含棉85%以下)	10	90		16	17	米/千克		Plain weave cloth of cotton, mixed with polyester staple fibres, dyed, weighing more than 200g/m², containing less than 85% by weight of cotton
5211 3100.13	染色与聚酯短纤混纺平纹帆布(每平方米重>200克,含棉85%以下)	10	90		16	17	米/千克		Plain canvas of cotton, mixed with polyester staple fibres, dyed, weighing more than 200g/m², containing less than 85% by weight of cotton
5211 3100.21	染色与化纤长丝混纺棉府绸(每平方米重>200克，含棉85%以下，含细平布)	10	90		16	17	米/千克		Poplin of cotton including fine plain cloth, mixed with man-made filaments,dyed, weight>200g/m², containing less than 85% by weight of cotton
5211 3100.22	染色与化纤长丝混纺机织平布(每平方米重>200克,含棉85%以下)	10	90		16	17	米/千克		Plain weave cloth of cotton, mixed with man-made filaments, dyed, weighing more than 200g/m², containing less than 85% by weight of cotton
5211 3100.23	染色与化纤长丝混纺平纹帆布(每平方米重>200克,含棉85%以下)	10	90		16	17	米/千克		Canvas of cotton, mixed with man-made filaments, dyed, weighing more than 200g/m², containing less than 85% by weight of cotton
5211 3100.91	染色与其他化纤混纺棉府绸(每平方米重>200克，含棉85%以下，含细平布)	10	90		16	17	米/千克		Poplin of cotton including fine plain cloth,mixed with other man-made fibres, dyed, weight>200g/m², containing less than 85% by weight of cotton
5211 3100.92	染色与其他化纤混纺机织平布(每平方米重>200克,含棉85%以下)	10	90		16	17	米/千克		Plain weave cloth of cotton, mixed with other man-made fibres, dyed, weighing more than 200g/m², containing less than 85% by weight of cotton
5211 3100.93	染色与其他化纤混纺平纹帆布(每平方米重>200克,含棉85%以下)	10	90		16	17	米/千克		Canvas of cotton, plain weave, mixed with other man-made fibres, dyed, weighing more than 200g/m², containing less than85% by weight of cotton
5211.3200	--三线或四线斜纹机织物，包括双面斜纹机织物	10	90		16	17	米/千克		--3-thread or 4-thread twill, including cross twill
5211 3200.10	染色聚酯短纤混纺3/4线斜纹棉布(每平方米重>200克，含棉85%以下，含双面斜纹布)	10	90		16	17	米/千克		3 or 4-thread twill or cross twill cloth of cotton, mixed with polyester staple fibres, dyed, weighing more than 200g/m², containing less than 85% by weight of cotton
5211 3200.20	染色化纤长丝混纺3/4线斜纹棉布(每平方米重>200克，含棉85%以下，含双面斜纹布)	10	90		16	17	米/千克		3 or 4-thread twill or cross twill cloth of cotton, mixed with man-made filaments, dyed, weighing more than 200g/m², containing less than 85% by weight of cotton
5211 3200.90	染色其他化纤混纺3/4线斜纹棉布(每平方米重>200克，含棉	10	90		16	17	米/千克		3 or 4-thread twill or cross twill cloth of cotton, mixed with other man-made fibres, dyed, weighing more than

税则号列 Tariff Item	商品名称及备注	进口税率 最惠	普通	暂定	出口退税	增值税率	计量单位	监管条件	Article Description
	85%以下，含双面斜纹布）								200g/m², containing less than 85% by weight of cotton
5211.3900	---其他机织物	10	90		16	17	米/千克		--Other fabrics
5211 3900.11	染色与聚酯短纤混纺的棉缎布（每平方米重>200克，含棉85%以下）	10	90		16	17	米/千克		Satin cloth of cotton, mixed with polyester staple fibres, dyed, weighing more than 200g/m², containing less than 85% by weight of cotton
5211 3900.12	染色与聚酯短纤混纺的棉斜纹布（每平方米重>200克，含棉85%以下）	10	90		16	17	米/千克		Twill cloth of cotton, mixed with polyester staple fibres, dyed, weighing more than 200g/m², containing less than 85% by weight of cotton
5211 3900.13	染色与聚酯短纤混纺的棉帆布（每平方米重>200克，含棉85%以下）	10	90		16	17	米/千克		Canvas of cotton, mixed with polyester staple fibres, dyed, weighing more than 200g/m², containing less than 85% by weight of cotton
5211 3900.19	染色与聚酯短纤混纺其他棉布（每平方米重>200克，含棉85%以下）	10	90		16	17	米/千克		Other cloth of cotton, mixed with polyester staple fibres, dyed, weighing more than 200g/m², containing less than 85% by weight of cotton
5211 3900.21	染色与化纤长丝混纺的棉缎布（每平方米重>200克，含棉85%以下）	10	90		16	17	米/千克		Satin cloth of cotton, mixed with man-made filaments, dyed, weighing more than 200g/m², containing less than 85% by weight of cotton
5211 3900.22	染色与化纤长丝混纺的棉斜纹布（每平方米重>200克，含棉85%以下）	10	90		16	17	米/千克		Twill cloth of cotton, mixed with man-made filaments, dyed, weighing more than 200g/m², containing less than85% by weight of cotton
5211 3900.23	染色与化纤长丝混纺的棉帆布（每平方米重>200克，含棉85%以下）	10	90		16	17	米/千克		Canvas of cotton, mixed with man-made filaments, dyed, weighing more than 200g/m², containing less than 85% by weight of cotton
5211 3900.29	染色与化纤长丝混纺的其他棉布（每平方米重>200克，含棉85%以下）	10	90		16	17	米/千克		Other cloth of cotton, mixed with man-made filaments,dyed, weighing more than 200g/m², containing less than 85% by weight of cotton
5211 3900.91	染色与其他化纤混纺的棉缎布（每平方米重>200克，含棉85%以下）	10	90		16	17	米/千克		Satin cloth of cotton, mixed with other man-made fibres, dyed, weighing more than 200g/m², containing less than 85% by weight of cotton
5211 3900.92	染色与其他化纤混纺的棉斜纹布（每平方米重>200克，含棉85%以下）	10	90		16	17	米/千克		Twill cloth of cotton, mixed with other man-made fibres, dyed, weighing more than 200g/m², containing less than 85% by weight of cotton
5211 3900.93	染色与其他化纤混纺的棉帆布（每平方米重>200克，含棉85%以下）	10	90		16	17	米/千克		Canvas of cotton, mixed with other man-made fibres, dyed,weighing more than 200g/m², containing less than 85% by weight of cotton
5211 3900.99	染色与其他化纤混纺其他棉布（每平方米重>200克，含棉85%以下）	10	90		16	17	米/千克		Other clothof cotton, mixed with other man-made fibres, dyed, weighing more than 200g/m², containing less than85% by weight of cotton
	-色织:								-Of yarns of different colours:
5211.4100	---平纹机织物	10	90		16	17	米/千克		--Plain weave
5211 4100.10	色织与聚酯短纤混纺平纹棉布（每平方米重>200克，含棉85%以下）	10	90		16	17	米/千克		Plain weave cloth of cotton, yarn-dyed, mixed with polyester staple fibres, weighing more than 200g/m², containing less than 85% by weight of cotton
5211 4100.20	色织与化纤长丝混纺平纹棉布（每平方米重>200克，含棉85%以下）	10	90		16	17	米/千克		Plain cloth of cotton, yarn-dyed, mixed with man-made filaments, weighing more than 200g/m², containing less than 85% by weight of cotton
5211 4100.90	色织与其他化纤混纺平纹棉布（每平方米重>200克，含棉85%以下）	10	90		16	17	米/千克		Plain cloth of cotton,yarn-dyed, mixed with other man-made fibres, weighing more than 200g/m², containing less than 85% by weight of cotton
5211.4200	---粗斜纹布（劳动布）	10	90		16	17	米/千克		--Denim
5211 4200.10	色织与化纤混纺蓝色粗斜纹棉布（每平方米重>200克，含棉85%以下）	10	90		16	17	米/千克		Blue denim of cotton, mixed with other man-made fibres,yarn-dyed, weighing more than 200g/m², containing less than 85% by weight of cotton
5211 4200.90	色织与化纤混纺非蓝色粗斜纹棉布（每平方米重>200克，含棉85%以下）	10	90		16	17	米/千克		Non-blue denim of cotton, yarn-dyed, weighing more than 200g/m², containing less than 85% by weight of cotton

税则号列 Tariff Item	商品名称及备注	进口税率 最惠	进口税率 普通	进口税率 暂定	出口退税	增值税率	计量单位	监管条件	Article Description
5211.4300	--其他三线或四线斜纹机织物，包括双面斜纹机织物	10	90		16	17	米/千克		--Other fabrics of 3-thread or 4-thread twill, including cross twill
5211 4300.10	其他色织与聚酯短纤混纺3/4线斜纹棉布(每平米重超过200克,含棉85%以下,含双面斜纹布)	10	90		16	17	米/千克		3 or 4-thread twill or cross twill cloth of cotton, yarn-dyed, mixed with polyester staple fibres, weight＞200g/m², containing＜85% by weight of cotton
5211 4300.20	其他色织与化纤长丝混纺3/4线斜纹棉布(每平米重超过200克,含棉85%以下,含双面斜纹布)	10	90		16	17	米/千克		3 or 4-thread twill or cross twill cloth of cotton, mixed with man-made filaments, yarn-dyed, weighing more than 200g/m², containing less than 85% by weight of cotton
5211 4300.90	其他色织与其他化纤混纺3/4线斜纹棉布(每平米重超过200克,含棉85%以下,含双面斜纹布)	10	90		16	17	米/千克		3 or 4-thread twill or cross twill cloth of cotton, mixed with other man-made fibres, yarn-dyed, weighing more than 200g/m², containing less than 85% by weight of cotton
5211.4900	--其他机织物	10	90		16	17	米/千克		--Other fabrics
5211 4900.11	色织与聚酯短纤混纺的提花布（每平方米重＞200克,含棉85%以下）	10	90		16	17	米/千克		Jacquard cloth, mixed with polyester staple fibres, yarn-dyed, weighing more than 200g/m², containing less than 85% by weight of cotton
5211 4900.19	色织与聚酯短纤混纺其他棉布（每平方米重＞200克,含棉85%以下）	10	90		16	17	米/千克		Other cloth of cotton, mixed with polyester staple fibres, yarn-dyed, weighing more than 200g/m², containing less than 85% by weight of cotton
5211 4900.21	色织与化纤长丝混纺的提花布（每平方米重＞200克,含棉85%以下）	10	90		16	17	米/千克		Jacquard cloth, mixed with man-made filaments, yarn-dyed, weighing more than 200g/m², containing less than 85% by weight of cotton
5211 4900.29	色织与化纤长丝混纺其他棉布（每平方米重＞200克,含棉85%以下）	10	90		16	17	米/千克		Other cloth of cotton, mixed with man-made filaments, yarn-dyed, weighing more than 200g/m², containing less than 85% by weight of cotton
5211 4900.91	色织与其他化纤混纺的提花布（每平方米重＞200克,含棉85%以下）	10	90		16	17	米/千克		Jacquard cloth, mixed with other man-made fibres, yarn-dyed, weighing more than 200g/m², containing less than 85% by weight of cotton
5211 4900.99	色织与其他化纤混纺其他棉布（每平方米重＞200克,含棉85%以下）	10	90		16	17	米/千克		Other cloth of cotton, mixed with other man-made fibres,yarn-dyed, weighing more than 200g/m², containing less than 85% by weight of cotton
	-印花:								-Printed:
5211.5100	--平纹机织物	10	90		16	17	米/千克		--Plain weave
5211 5100.11	印花与聚酯短纤混纺棉府绸（每平方米重＞200克，含棉85%以下，含细平布）	10	90		16	17	米/千克		Poplin of cotton including fine plain cloth, mixed with polyester staple fibres, printed, weight＞200g/m², containing＜85% by weight of cotton
5211 5100.12	印花与聚酯短纤混纺机织平布（每平方米重＞200克,含棉85%以下）	10	90		16	17	米/千克		Plain weave cloth, mixed with polyester staple fibres, printed, weighing more than 200g/m², containing less than 85% by weight of cotton
5211 5100.13	印花与聚酯短纤混纺平纹帆布（每平方米重＞200克,含棉85%以下）	10	90		16	17	米/千克		Plain canvas, mixed with polyester staple fibres, printed, weighing more than 200g/m², containing less than 85% by weight of cotton
5211 5100.21	印花与化纤长丝混纺棉府绸（每平方米重＞200克，含棉85%以下，含细平布）	10	90		16	17	米/千克		Poplin of cotton including fine plain cloth,mixed with man-made filaments, printed, weight＞200g/m², containing＜85% by weight of cotton
5211 5100.22	印花与化纤长丝混纺机织平布（每平方米重＞200克,含棉85%以下）	10	90		16	17	米/千克		Plain weave cloth, mixed with man-made filaments, printed, weighing more than 200g/m², containing less than 85% by weight of cotton
5211 5100.23	印花与化纤长丝混纺平纹帆布（每平方米重＞200克,含棉85%以下）	10	90		16	17	米/千克		Plain canvas, mixed with man-made filaments, printed, weighing more than 200g/m², containing less than 85% by weight of cotton
5211 5100.91	印花与其他化纤混纺棉府绸（每平方米重＞200克，含棉85%以下，含细平布）	10	90		16	17	米/千克		Poplin of cotton including fine plain cloth, mixed with man-made filaments, printed, weight＞200g/m², containing＜85% by weight of cotton

税则号列 Tariff Item	商品名称及备注	进口税率			出口退税	增值税率	计量单位	监管条件	Article Description
		最惠	普通	暂定					
5211 5100.92	印花与其他化纤混纺的机织平布（每平方米重＞200克，含棉85%以下）	10	90		16	17	米/千克		Plain weave cloth, mixed with man-made filaments, printed, weighing more than 200g/m², containing less than 85% by weight of cotton
5211 5100.93	印花与其他化纤混纺平纹帆布（每平方米重＞200克,含棉85%以下）	10	90		16	17	米/千克		Plain canvas, mixed with man-made filaments, printed, weighing more than 200g/m², containing less than 85% by weight of cotton
5211.5200	--三线或四线斜纹机织物，包括双面斜纹机织物	10	90		16	17	米/千克		--3-thread or 4-thread twill, including cross twill
5211 5200.10	印花与聚酯短纤混纺3/4线斜纹棉布（每平方米重＞200克，含棉85%以下，含双面斜纹布）	10	90		16	17	米/千克		3 or 4-thread twill or cross twill cloth of cotton, mixed with polyester staple fibres, printed, weighing more than 200g/m², containing less than 85% by weight of cotton
5211 5200.20	印花与化纤长丝混纺3/4线斜纹棉布（每平方米重＞200克，含棉85%以下，含双面斜纹布）	10	90		16	17	米/千克		3 or 4-thread twill or cross twill cloth of cotton, mixed with man-made filaments, printed, weighing more than 200g/m², containing less than 85% by weight of cotton
5211 5200.90	印花与其他化纤混纺3/4线斜纹棉布（每平方米重＞200克，含棉85%以下，含双面斜纹布）	10	90		16	17	米/千克		3 or 4-thread twill or cross twill cloth of cotton, mixed with other man-made fibres, printed, weighing more than 200g/m², containing less than 85% by weight of cotton
5211.5900	--其他机织物	10	90		16	17	米/千克		--Other fabrics
5211 5900.11	印花与聚酯短纤混纺棉缎布（每平方米重＞200克，含棉85%以下）	10	90		16	17	米/千克		Satin cloth of cotton, mixed with polyester staple fibres, printed, weighing more than 200g/m², containing less than 85% by weight of cotton
5211 5900.12	印花与聚酯短纤混纺斜纹棉布（每平方米重＞200克,含棉85%以下）	10	90		16	17	米/千克		Twill cloth of cotton, mixed with polyester staple fibres, printed, weighing more than 200g/m², containing less than 85% by weight of cotton
5211 5900.13	印花与聚酯短纤混纺棉帆布（每平方米重＞200克，含棉85%以下）	10	90		16	17	米/千克		Canvas of cotton, mixed with polyester staple fibres, printed, weighing more than 200g/m², containing less than 85% by weight of cotton
5211 5900.19	印花与聚酯短纤混纺其他棉布（每平方米重＞200克,含棉85%以下）	10	90		16	17	米/千克		Other cloth of cotton, mixed with polyester staple fibres, printed, weighing more than 200g/m², containing less than 85% by weight of cotton
5211 5900.21	印花与化纤长丝混纺棉缎布（每平方米重＞200克，含棉85%以下）	10	90		16	17	米/千克		Other satin cloth of cotton, mixed with man-made filaments, printed, weighing more than 200g/m², containing less than 85% by weight of cotton
5211 5900.22	印花与化纤长丝混纺斜纹棉布（每平方米重＞200克,含棉85%以下）	10	90		16	17	米/千克		Other twill cloth of cotton, mixed with man-made filaments, printed, weighing more than 200g/m², containing less than 85% by weight of cotton
5211 5900.23	印花与化纤长丝混纺棉帆布（每平方米重＞200克，含棉85%以下）	10	90		16	17	米/千克		Other canvas of cotton, mixed with man-made filaments, printed, weighing more than 200g/m², containing less than 85% by weight of cotton
5211 5900.29	印花与化纤长丝混纺其他棉布（每平方米重＞200克,含棉85%以下）	10	90		16	17	米/千克		Other cloth of cotton, mixed with man-made filaments, printed, weighing more than 200g/m², containing less than 85% by weight of cotton
5211 5900.91	印花与其他化纤混纺棉缎布（每平方米重＞200克，含棉85%以下）	10	90		16	17	米/千克		Other satin cloth of cotton, mixed with other man-made fibres, printed, weighing more than 200g/m², containing less than 85% by weight of cotton
5211 5900.92	印花与其他化纤混纺斜纹棉布（每平方米重＞200克,含棉85%以下）	10	90		16	17	米/千克		Other twill cloth of cotton, mixed with other man-made fibres, printed, weighing more than 200g/m², containing less than 85% by weight of cotton
5211 5900.93	印花与其他化纤混纺棉帆布（每平方米重＞200克，含棉85%以下）	10	90		16	17	米/千克		Other canvas of cotton, mixed with other man-made fibres, printed, weighing more than 200g/m², containing less than 85% by weight of cotton
5211 5900.99	印花与其他化纤混纺其他棉布（每平方米重＞200克,含棉85%以下）	10	90		16	17	米/千克		Other cloth of cotton, mixed with other man-made fibres, printed, weighing more than 200g/m², containing less than 85% by weight of cotton

税则号列 Tariff Item	商品名称及备注	进口税率 最惠	普通	暂定	出口退税	增值税率	计量单位	监管条件	Article Description
52.12	其他棉机织物:								Other woven fabrics of cotton:
	-每平方米重量不超过200克:								-Weighing not more than 200g/m²:
5212.1100[暂]	--未漂白	12	80	6	16	17	米/千克		--Unbleached
5212 1100.11[暂]	未漂白的其他混纺棉布(每平方米重≤200克,与36%及以上精梳羊毛或动物细毛混纺)	12	80	6	16	17	米/千克		Other cloth of cotton, mixed,unbleached, weighing not more than 200g/m², containing 36% or more by weight of combed wool or fine animal hair
5212 1100.19[暂]	未漂白的其他混纺棉布(每平方米重≤200克,与36%以下精梳羊毛或动物细毛混纺)	12	80	6	16	17	米/千克		Other cloth of cotton, mixed,unbleached, weighing not more than 200g/m², containing less than 36% by weight of combed wool or fine animal hair
5212 1100.21[暂]	未漂白的其他混纺棉布(每平方米重≤200克,与36%及以上其他羊毛或动物细毛混纺)	12	80	6	16	17	米/千克		Other cloth of cotton, mixed,unbleached, weighing not more than 200g/m², containing 36% or more by weight other wool or fine animal hair
5212 1100.29[暂]	未漂白的其他混纺棉布(每平方米重≤200克,与其他羊毛或动物细毛混纺)	12	80	6	16	17	米/千克		Other cloth of cotton, mixed with other wool or fine animal hair, unbleached, weighing not more than 200g/m²
5212 1100.30[暂]	未漂白的其他混纺府绸及细平布(每平方米重≤200克,与化纤、羊毛或动物细毛以外其他纤维混纺)	12	80	6	16	17	米/千克		Other poplin of cotton and fine plain cloth, mixed with other fibres, other than man-made fibres, wool or fine animals hair, unbleached, weighing not more than 200g/m²
5212 1100.40[暂]	未漂白的其他混纺棉机织平布(每平方米重≤200克,与化纤、羊毛或动物细毛以外其他纤维混纺)	12	80	6	16	17	米/千克		Other plain weave cloth of cotton,mixed with other fibres other than man-made fibres, wool or fine animals hair, unbleached, weighing not more than 200g/m²
5212 1100.50[暂]	未漂白的其他混纺棉印染布(每平方米重≤200克,与化纤、羊毛或动物细毛以外其他纤维混纺)	12	80	6	16	17	米/千克		Other cloth of cotton for printing and dyeing, mixed with other fibres, other than man-made fibres, wool or fine animals hair, , unbleached, weighing not more than 200g/m²
5212 1100.60[暂]	未漂白其他混纺棉奶酪布,薄细布,巴里纱(每平方米重≤200克,与化纤、羊毛或动物细毛以外其他纤维混纺)	12	80	6	16	17	米/千克		Other cheese cloth and muslin of cotton, mixed with other fibres other than man-made fibres, wool or fine animals hair, unbleached, weighing not more than 200g/m²
5212 1100.70[暂]	未漂白的其他混纺棉缎布(每平方米重≤200克,与化纤、羊毛或动物细毛以外其他纤维混纺)	12	80	6	16	17	米/千克		Other satin cloth of cotton, mixed with other fibres, other than man-made fibres, wool or fine animals hair, unbleached, weighing not more than 200g/m²
5212 1100.81[暂]	未漂白的其他混纺斜纹棉布(每平方米重≤200克,与化纤、羊毛或动物细毛以外其他纤维混纺)	12	80	6	16	17	米/千克		Other twill cloth of cotton, mixed with other fibres, other than man-made fibres, wool or fine animals hair, unbleached, weighing not more than 200g/m²
5212 1100.89[暂]	未漂白的其他混纺棉牛津布(每平方米重≤200克,与化纤、羊毛或动物细毛以外其他纤维混纺)	12	80	6	16	17	米/千克		Other oxford cloth of cotton, mixed with other fibres other than man-made fibres, wool or fine animals hair, , unbleached, weighing not more than 200g/m²
5212 1100.90[暂]	未漂白的其他混纺棉布(每平方米重≤200克,与化纤、羊毛或细毛以外其他纤维混纺)	12	80	6	16	17	米/千克		Other cloth of cotton,mixed with other fibres other than man-made fibres, wool or fine animals hair, unbleached, weighing not more than 200g/m²
5212.1200	--漂白	14	80		16	17	米/千克		--Bleached
5212 1200.11	漂白的其他混纺棉布(每平方米重≤200克,与36%及以上精梳羊毛或动物细毛混纺)	14	80		16	17	米/千克		Other cloth of cotton, mixed, containing 36% or more by weight of combed wool or fine animal hair, bleached, weighing not more than 200g/m²
5212 1200.19	漂白的其他混纺棉布(每平方米重≤200克,与36%以下精梳羊毛或动物细毛混纺)	14	80		16	17	米/千克		Other cloth of cotton, mixed, containing less than 36% by weight of combed wool or fine animal hair, bleached, weighing not more than 200g/m²
5212 1200.20	漂白的其他混纺棉布(每平米重≤200克,与其他羊毛或动物细毛	14	80		16	17	米/千克		Other cloth of cotton, containing, weighing not more than 200g/m²bleached mixed with other fibres other

税则号列 Tariff Item	商品名称及备注	进口税率			出口退税	增值税率	计量单位	监管条件	Article Description
		最惠	普通	暂定					
	混纺）								than man-made fibres and wool or fine animal hair
5212 1200.50	漂白的其他混纺棉印染布（每平方米重≤200克，与除化纤/羊毛/动物细毛其他纤维混纺）	14	80		16	17	米/千克		Cloth of cotton for printing and dyeing, mixed with other fibres, other than man-made fibres, wool or fine animal hair, bleached, weighing not more than 200g/m²
5212 1200.60	漂白其他混纺棉奶酪布、薄细布、纱（每平方米重≤200克，与除化纤/羊毛/动物细毛其他纤维混纺）	14	80		16	17	米/千克		Cheese cloth/fine thin cloth/yarn, mixed with other fibres, other than man-made fibres, wool or fine animal hair, bleached, weighing not more than 200g/m²
5212 1200.71	漂白的其他混纺棉缎布（每平方米重≤200克，与除化纤/羊毛/动物细毛其他纤维混纺）	14	80		16	17	米/千克		Satin cloth of cotton, mixed with other fibres, other than man-made fibres, wool or fine animal hair, bleached, weighing not more than 200g/m²
5212 1200.72	漂白的其他混纺斜纹棉布（每平方米重≤200克，与除化纤/羊毛/动物细毛其他纤维混纺）	14	80		16	17	米/千克		Twill cloth of cotton, mixed with other fibres, other than man-made fibres, wool or fine animal hair, bleached, weighing not more than 200g/m²
5212 1200.79	漂白的其他混纺棉牛津布(每平方米重≤200克，与除化纤/羊毛/动物细毛其他纤维混纺）	14	80		16	17	米/千克		Oxford clothof cotton, mixed with other fibres, other than man-made fibres, wool or fine animal hair, bleached, weighing not more than 200g/m²
5212 1200.90	漂白的其他混纺棉机织物（每平方米重≤200克，与除化纤/羊毛/动物细毛其他纤维混纺）	14	80		16	17	米/千克		Other woven fabrics of cotton, mixed with other fibres, other than man-made fibres, wool or fine animal hair, bleached, weighing not more than 200g/m²
5212.1300	--染色	10	80		16	17	米/千克		--Dyed
5212 1300.11	染色其他混纺棉布（每平方米重≤200克，与36%及以上精梳羊毛/动物细毛混纺）	10	80		16	17	米/千克		Other cloth of cotton, mixed, dyed, weighing not more than 200g/m², containing 36% or more by weight of combed wool or fine animal hair
5212 1300.19	染色其他混纺棉布（每平方米重≤200克，与36%及以下精梳羊毛/动物细毛混纺）	10	80		16	17	米/千克		Other cloth of cotton, mixed, dyed, weighing not more than 200g/m², containing less than 36% by weight, of combed wool or fine animal hair
5212 1300.21	染色其他混纺棉布（每平方米重≤200克，与36%及以上其他羊毛/动物细毛混纺）	10	80		16	17	米/千克		Other cloth of cotton, mixed, dyed, weighing not more than 200g/m², containing 36% or more by weight of other wool or fine animal hair
5212 1300.29	染色其他混纺棉布（每平方米重≤200克，与36%及以下其他羊毛/动物细毛混纺）	10	80		16	17	米/千克		Other cloth of cotton, mixed, dyed, weighing not more than 200g/m², containing less than 36% by weight of wool or fine animal hair
5212 1300.30	染色其他混纺府绸及平细布（每平方米重≤200克，与化纤以外其他纤维混纺）	10	80		16	17	米/千克		Poplin and fine plain cloth, mixed with other fibres, other than man-made fibres, dyed, weighing not more than 200g/m²,
5212 1300.60	染色其他混纺奶酪布，薄细布，巴里纱（每平方米重≤200克，与化纤以外其他纤维混纺）	10	80		16	17	米/千克		Cheese cloth, voiles and muslin, mixed with other fibres, other than man-made fibres, dyed, weighing not more than 200g/m²
5212 1300.71	染色其他混纺棉缎布（每平方米重≤200克，与化纤以外其他纤维混纺）	10	80		16	17	米/千克		Other satin cloth of cotton, mixed with other fibres, other than man-made fibres, dyed, weighing not more than 200g/m²
5212 1300.72	染色其他混纺斜纹棉布（每平方米重≤200克，与化纤以外其他纤维混纺）	10	80		16	17	米/千克		Other twill cloth of cotton, mixed with other fibres, other than man-made fibres, dyed, weighing not more than 200g/m²
5212 1300.79	染色其他混纺棉牛津布（每平方米重≤200克，与化纤以外其他纤维混纺）	10	80		16	17	米/千克		Other oxford cloth of cotton, mixed with other fibres,other than man-made fibres, dyed, weighing not more than 200g/m²
5212 1300.90	染色其他混纺棉布（每平方米重≤200克，与化纤以外其他纤维混纺）	10	80		16	17	米/千克		Other woven fabrics of cotton, mixed with other fibres, other than man-made fibres, weight≤200g/m², dyed
5212.1400	--色织	10	80		16	17	米/千克		--Of yarns of different colours
5212 1400.11	色织其他混纺棉布（每平方米重	10	80		16	17	米/千克		Other woven fabrics of cotton,yarn-dyed, weighing not

税则号列 Tariff Item	商品名称及备注	进口税率 最惠	进口税率 普通	进口税率 暂定	出口退税	增值税率	计量单位	监管条件	Article Description
	≤200克，与36%及以上精梳羊毛/动物细毛混纺）								more than 200g/m², mixed, containing 36% or more by weight of combed wool or fine animal hair
5212 1400.19	色织其他混纺棉布（每平方米重≤200克，与36%及以下精梳羊毛/动物细毛混纺）	10	80		16	17	米/千克		Other cloth of cotton, mixed,yarn-dyed,weighing not more than 200 g/m² containing less than 36% by weight of combed wool or fine animal hair
5212 1400.21	色织其他混纺棉布（每平方米重≤200克，与36%及以上其他羊毛/动物细毛混纺）	10	80		16	17	米/千克		Other cloth of cotton, mixed,yarn-dyed, weighing not more than 200 g/m², containing 36% or more by weight of wool or fine animal hair
5212 1400.29	色织其他混纺棉布（每平方米重≤200克，与36%及以下其他羊毛/动物细毛混纺）	10	80		16	17	米/千克		Other cloth of cotton, yarn-dyed, mixed, containing less than 36% by weight of wool or fine animal hair, weighing not more than 200 g/m²
5212 1400.30	色织其他混纺棉提花布（每平方米重≤200克，与化纤以外其他纤维混纺）	10	80		16	17	米/千克		Other jacquard cloth of cotton, mixed with other fibres, other than man-made fibres, weighing not more than 200 g/m²
5212 1400.90	色织其他混纺棉布（每平方米重≤200克，与化纤以外其他纤维混纺）	10	80		16	17	米/千克		Other cloth of cotton, mixed with other fibres, other than man-made fibres weighing not more than 200 g/m²
5212.1500	--印花	10	80		16	17	米/千克		--Printed
5212 1500.11	印花其他混纺棉布（每平方米重≤200克，与36%及以上精梳羊毛/动物细毛混纺）	10	80		16	17	米/千克		Other cloth of cotton, mixed, printed, weighing not more than 200 g/m², containing 36% or more by weight of combed wool or fine animal hair
5212 1500.19	印花其他混纺棉布（每平方米重≤200克，与36%及以下精梳羊毛/动物细毛混纺）	10	80		16	17	米/千克		Other cloth of cotton, mixed, printed, weighing not more than 200 g/m² containing less than 36% by weight of combed wool or fine animal hair
5212 1500.21	印花其他混纺棉布（每平方米重≤200克，与36%及以上其他羊毛/动物细毛混纺）	10	80		16	17	米/千克		Other woven fabrics of cotton, mixed, printed, weighing not more than 200 g/m²,containing 36% or more by weight of wool or fine animal hair
5212 1500.29	印花其他混纺棉布（每平方米重≤200克，与36%及以下其他羊毛/动物细毛混纺）	10	80		16	17	米/千克		Other woven fabrics of cotton, mixed, printed, weighing not more than 200 g/m², containing less than 36% by weight of wool or fine animal hair
5212 1500.40	印花其他混纺棉机织平布（每平方米重≤200克，与化纤/羊毛/细毛以外其他纤维混纺）	10	80		16	17	米/千克		Plain weave cloth, printed, weighing not more than 200 g/m², mixed with other fibres, other than man-made fibres, wool or fine animals hair
5212 1500.50	印花其他混纺棉印染布（每平方米重≤200克，与化纤/羊毛/细毛以外其他纤维混纺）	10	80		16	17	米/千克		Cloth of cotton for printing and dyeing, weighing not more than 200 g/m², mixed with other fibres other than man-made fibres, wool or fine animals hair, printed
5212 1500.60	印花其他混纺棉奶酪布，薄细布，巴里纱（每平方米重≤200克，与化纤/羊毛/细毛以外其他纤维混纺）	10	80		16	17	米/千克		Cheese cloth, voiles and muslin, mixed with other fibres other than man-made fibres, wool or fine animals hair, weighing not more than 200 g/m², printed
5212 1500.71	印花其他混纺棉缎布（每平方米重≤200克，与化纤/羊毛/细毛以外其他纤维混纺）	10	80		16	17	米/千克		Other satin cloth of cotton, weighing not more than 200 g/m², mixed with other fibres other than man-made fibres, wool or fine animals hair, printed
5212 1500.72	印花其他混纺斜纹棉布（每平方米重≤200克，与化纤/羊毛/细毛以外其他纤维混纺）	10	80		16	17	米/千克		Other twill cloth of cotton, weighing not more than 200 g/m², mixed with other fibres other than man-made fibres wool or fine animals hair,printed
5212 1500.79	印花其他混纺棉牛津布（每平方米重≤200克，与化纤/羊毛/细毛以外其他纤维混纺）	10	80		16	17	米/千克		Other oxford of cotton, weighing not more than 200 g/m², mixed with other fibres,other than man-made fibres, wool or fine animals hair, printed
5212 1500.90	印花其他混纺棉布（每平方米重≤200克，与化纤/羊毛/细毛以外其他纤维混纺）	10	80		16	17	米/千克		Other cloth of cotton, weighing not more than 200 g/m², mixed with other fibres,other than man-made fibres, wool or fine animals hair, printed
	-每平方米重量超过200克：								-Weighing more than 200g/m²:
5212.2100暂	--未漂白	12	80	6	16	17	米/千克		--Unbleached

税则号列 Tariff Item	商品名称及备注	进口税率			出口退税	增值税率	计量单位	监管条件	Article Description
		最惠	普通	暂定					
5212 2100.11[暂]	未漂白其他混纺棉布（每平方米重＞200克，与36%及以上精梳羊毛/动物细毛混纺）	12	80	6	16	17	米/千克		Other cloth of cotton,mixed, unbleached, weighing more than 200 g/m², containing 36% or more by weight of combed wool or fine animal hair
5212 2100.19[暂]	未漂白其他混纺棉布（每平方米重＞200克，与36%及以下精梳羊毛/动物细毛混纺）	12	80	6	16	17	米/千克		Other cloth of cotton,mixed, unbleached, weighing more than 200 g/m²,containing less than 36% by weight of combed wool or fine animal hair
5212 2100.21[暂]	未漂白其他混纺棉布（每平方米重＞200克，与36%及以上其他羊毛/动物细毛混纺）	12	80	6	16	17	米/千克		Other cloth of cotton, unbleached, mixed,weighing more than 200 g/m², containing 36% or more by weight of wool or fine animal hair
5212 2100.29[暂]	未漂白其他混纺棉布（每平方米重＞200克，与36%及以下其他羊毛/动物细毛混纺）	12	80	6	16	17	米/千克		Other woven fabrics of cotton, mixed, unbleached, weighing more than 200 g/m²,containing less than 36% by weight of wool or fine animal hair
5212 2100.30[暂]	未漂白其他混纺府绸及平细布（每平方米重＞200克，与化纤以外其他纤维混纺）	12	80	6	16	17	米/千克		Poplin and fine plain cloth, unbleached, weighing more than 200 g/m², mixed with other fibres, other than man-made fibres
5212 2100.40[暂]	未漂白其他混纺棉机织平布（每平方米重＞200克，与化纤以外其他纤维混纺）	12	80	6	16	17	米/千克		Plain cloth of cotton, unbleached, weighing more than 200 g/m²,mixed with other fibres other than man-made fibres
5212 2100.50[暂]	未漂白其他混纺棉帆布（每平方米重＞200克，与化纤以外其他纤维混纺）	12	80	6	16	17	米/千克		Canvas of cotton, unbleached, weighing more than 200 g/m², mixed with other fibres,other than man-made fibres
5212 2100.60[暂]	未漂白其他混纺棉缎布（每平方米重＞200克，与化纤以外其他纤维混纺）	12	80	6	16	17	米/千克		Other satin cloth of cotton, unbleached, weighing more than 200 g/m²,mixed with other fibres,other than man-made fibres
5212 2100.70[暂]	未漂白其他混纺斜纹棉布（每平方米重＞200克，与化纤以外其他纤维混纺）	12	80	6	16	17	米/千克		Other twill cloth of cotton, unbleached, weighing more than 200 g/m², mixed with other fibres,other than man-made fibres
5212 2100.90[暂]	未漂白其他混纺棉布（每平方米重＞200克，与化纤以外其他纤维混纺）	12	80	6	16	17	米/千克		Other cloth of cotton, unbleached, weighing more than 200 g/m², mixed with other fibres, other than man-made fibres
5212.2200	--漂白	14	80		16	17	米/千克		--Bleached
5212 2200.11	漂白的其他混纺棉布（每平方米重＞200克，与36%及以上精梳羊毛、动物细毛混纺）	14	80		16	17	米/千克		Other cloth of cotton, mixed, bleached, weighing more than 200 g/m², containing 36% or more by weight of combed wool or fine animal hair
5212 2200.19	漂白的其他混纺棉布（每平方米重＞200克，与36%及以下精梳羊毛、动物细毛混纺）	14	80		16	17	米/千克		Other cloth of cotton, weighing more than 200 g/m², mixed,bleached, containing less than 36% by weight of combed wool or fine animal hair
5212 2200.21	漂白的其他混纺棉布（每平方米重＞200克，与36%及以上其他羊毛、动物细毛混纺）	14	80		16	17	米/千克		Other cloth of cotton, weighing more than 200 g/m², mixed, bleached, containing 36% or more by weight of wool or fine animal hair
5212 2200.29	漂白的其他混纺棉布（每平方米重＞200克，与36%及以下其他羊毛、动物细毛混纺）	14	80		16	17	米/千克		Other cloth of cotton, bleached, mixed, weighing more than 200 g/m², containing less than 36% by weight of wool or fine animal hair, bleached
5212 2200.30	漂白的其他混纺府绸及细平布（每平方米重＞200克，与化纤、羊毛、动物细毛以外其他纤维混纺）	14	80		16	17	米/千克		Poplin and fine plain cloth, bleached, weighing more than 200 g/m², mixed with other fibres, other than man-made fibres, wool or fine animals hair,
5212 2200.40	漂白的其他混纺棉机织平布（每平方米重＞200克，与化纤、羊毛、动物细毛以外其他纤维混纺）	14	80		16	17	米/千克		Plain fabrics of cotton, bleached, weighing more than 200 g/m²,mixed with other fibres, other than man-made fibres wool or fine animals hair
5212 2200.50	漂白的其他混纺棉帆布（每平方米重＞200克，与化纤、羊毛、动物细毛以外其他纤维混纺）	14	80		16	17	米/千克		Canvas of cotton, bleached, weighing more than 200 g/m², mixed with other fibres, other than man-made fibres, wool or fine animals hair
5212 2200.60	漂白的其他混纺棉缎布（每平方	14	80		16	17	米/千克		Satin cloth of cotton, bleached, weighing more than

税则号列 Tariff Item	商品名称及备注	进口税率 最惠	普通	暂定	出口退税	增值税率	计量单位	监管条件	Article Description
	米重＞200克，与化纤、羊毛、动物细毛以外其他纤维混纺）								200 g/m², mixed with other fibres, other than man-made fibres, wool or fine animals hair
5212 2200.70	漂白的其他混纺棉斜纹布（每平方米重＞200克，与化纤、羊毛、动物细毛以外其他纤维混纺）	14	80		16	17	米/千克		Twill cloth of cotton, bleached, weighing more than 200 g/m², mixed with other fibres, other than man-made fibres, wool or fine animals hair
5212 2200.90	漂白的其他混纺棉布（每平方米重＞200克，与化纤、羊毛、动物细毛以外其他纤维混纺）	14	80		16	17	米/千克		Cloth of cotton, bleached, weighing more than 200 g/m²,mixed with other fibres, other than man-made fibres, wool or fine animals hair
5212.2300	--染色	10	80		16	17	米/千克		--Dyed
5212 2300.11	染色的其他混纺棉布（每平方米重＞200克，与36%及以上精梳羊毛、动物细毛混纺）	10	80		16	17	米/千克		Other cloth of cotton, dyed, mixed, weighing more than 200 g/m², containing 36% or more by weight of combed wool or fine animal hair
5212 2300.19	染色的其他混纺棉布（每平方米重＞200克，与36%及以下精梳羊毛、动物细毛混纺）	10	80		16	17	米/千克		Other cloth of cotton, dyed, mixed, weighing more than 200 g/m², containing less than 36% by weight of combed wool or fine animal hair,
5212 2300.21	染色的其他混纺棉布（每平方米重＞200克，与36%及以上其他羊毛、动物细毛混纺）	10	80		16	17	米/千克		Other cloth of cotton, mixed, dyed, weighing more than 200 g/m², containing 36% or more by weight of wool or fine animal hair
5212 2300.29	染色的其他混纺棉布（每平方米重＞200克，与36%及以下其他羊毛、动物细毛混纺）	10	80		16	17	米/千克		Other woven fabrics of cotton, dyed, mixed, weighing more than 200 g/m²,containing less tha 36% by weight of wool or fine animal hair
5212 2300.30	染色的其他混纺府绸及细平布（每平方米重＞200克，与化纤、羊毛、动物细毛以外其他纤维混纺）	10	80		16	17	米/千克		Poplin and fine plain cloth, dyed, weighing more than 200 g/m², mixed with other fibres, other than man-made fibres, wool or fine animals hair
5212 2300.40	染色的其他混纺棉机织平布（每平方米重＞200克，与化纤、羊毛、动物细毛以外其他纤维混纺）	10	80		16	17	米/千克		Plain weave cloth of cotton, dyed, weighing more than 200 g/m²,mixed with other fibres, other than man-made fibres, wool or fine animals hair
5212 2300.50	染色的其他混纺棉帆布（每平方米重＞200克，与化纤、羊毛、动物细毛以外其他纤维混纺）	10	80		16	17	米/千克		Canvas of cotton, dyed, weighing more than 200 g/m²,,mixed with other fibres, other than man-made fibres, wool or fine animals hair
5212 2300.60	染色的其他混纺棉缎布（每平方米重＞200克，与化纤、羊毛、动物细毛以外其他纤维混纺）	10	80		16	17	米/千克		Other satin cloth of cotton, dyed, weighing more than 200 g/m²,mixed with other fibres, other than man-made fibres, wool or fine animals hair
5212 2300.70	染色的其他混纺棉斜纹布（每平方米重＞200克，与化纤、羊毛、动物细毛以外其他纤维混纺）	10	80		16	17	米/千克		Other twill cloth of cotton, dyed, weighing more than 200 g/m², mixed with other fibres, other than man-made fibres, wool or fine animals hair
5212 2300.90	染色的其他混纺棉布（每平方米重＞200克，与化纤、羊毛、动物细毛以外其他纤维混纺）	10	80		16	17	米/千克		Other cloth of cotton, dyed, weighing more than 200 g/m², mixed with other fibres, other than man-made fibres, wool or fine animals hair
5212.2400	--色织	10	80		16	17	米/千克		--Of yarns of different colours
5212 2400.11	色织的其他混纺棉布（每平方米重＞200克，与36%及以上精梳羊毛、动物细毛混纺）	10	80		16	17	米/千克		Other cloth of cotton, mixed,yarn-dyed, weighing more than 200 g/m², containing 36% or more by weight of combed wool or fine animal hair
5212 2400.19	色织的其他混纺棉布（每平方米重＞200克，与36%及以下精梳羊毛、动物细毛混纺）	10	80		16	17	米/千克		Other cloth of cotton, mixed,yarn-dyed, weighing more than 200 g/m², containing less than 36% by weight of combed wool or fine animal hair
5212 2400.21	色织的其他混纺棉布（每平方米重＞200克，与36%及以上其他羊毛、动物细毛混纺）	10	80		16	17	米/千克		Other cloth of cotton, mixed,yarn-dyed, weighing more than 200 g/m²,containing 36% or more by weight of combed wool or fine animal hair
5212 2400.29	色织的其他混纺棉布（每平方米重＞200克，与36%及以下其他羊毛、动物细毛混纺）	10	80		16	17	米/千克		Other cloth of cotton, mixed,yarn-dyed, weighing more than 200 g/m², containing less than 36% by weight of combed wool or fine animal hair
5212 2400.30	色织的其他混纺蓝色粗斜纹布（每平方米重＞200克，与化纤、	10	80		16	17	米/千克		Other blue denim of cotton, yarn-dyed, weighing more than 200 g/m², mixed with other fibres, other than

税则号列 Tariff Item	商品名称及备注	进口税率 最惠	普通	暂定	出口退税	增值税率	计量单位	监管条件	Article Description
	羊毛、动物细毛以外其他纤维混纺)								man-made fibres, wool or fine animals hair
5212 2400.40	色织的其他混纺提花布(每平方米重>200克,与化纤、羊毛、动物细毛以外其他纤维混纺)	10	80		16	17	米/千克		Other jacquard cloth of cotton, yarn-dyed,weighing more than 200g/m², mixed with other fibres, other than man-made fibres, wool or fine animals hair
5212 2400.90	色织的其他混纺棉布(每平方米重>200克,与化纤、羊毛、动物细毛以外其他纤维混纺)	10	80		16	17	米/千克		Other cloth of cotton, yarn-dyed, weighing more than 200g/m², mixed with other fibres,other than man-made fibres, wool or fine animals hair
5212.2500	--印花	10	80		16	17	米/千克		--Printed
5212 2500.11	印花的其他混纺棉布(每平方米重>200克,与36%及以上精梳羊毛、动物细毛混纺)	10	80		16	17	米/千克		Other cloth of cotton, mixed, printed, weighing more than 200g/m², containing 36% or more by weight of combed wool or fine animal hair
5212 2500.19	印花的其他混纺棉布(每平方米重>200克,与36%及以下精梳羊毛、动物细毛混纺)	10	80		16	17	米/千克		Other cloth of cotton, mixed, printed, weighing more than 200g/m², containing less than 36% by weight of combed wool or fine animal hair
5212 2500.21	印花的其他混纺棉布(每平方米重>200克,与36%及以上其他羊毛、动物细毛混纺)	10	80		16	17	米/千克		Other cloth of cotton, mixed, printed, weighing more than 200g/m², containing 36% or more by weight of wool or fine animal hair, printed
5212 2500.29	印花的其他混纺棉布(每平方米重>200克,与36%及以下其他羊毛、动物细毛混纺)	10	80		16	17	米/千克		Other clothof cotton, mixed, printed, weighing more than 200g/m², containing less than 36% by weight of wool or fine animal hair, printed
5212 2500.30	印花的其他混纺府绸及细平布(每平方米重>200克,与化纤、羊毛、动物细毛以外其他纤维混纺)	10	80		16	17	米/千克		Poplin and fine plain cloth, printed, weighing more than 200g/m², mixed with other fibres, other than man-made fibres, wool or fine animals hair
5212 2500.40	印花的其他混纺棉机织平布(每平方米重>200克,与化纤、羊毛、动物细毛以外其他纤维混纺)	10	80		16	17	米/千克		Plain weave cloth of cotton, printed, weighing more than 200g/m²,mixed with other fibres, other than man-made fibres wool or fine animals hair
5212 2500.50	印花的其他混纺棉帆布(每平方米重>200克,与化纤、羊毛、动物细毛以外其他纤维混纺)	10	80		16	17	米/千克		Canvas of cotton, printed, weighing more than 200g/m², mixed with other fibres, other than man-made fibres, wool or fine animals hair
5212 2500.60	印花的其他混纺棉缎布(每平方米重>200克,与化纤、羊毛、动物细毛以外其他纤维混纺)	10	80		16	17	米/千克		Other satin cloth of cotton, printed, weighing more than 200g/m², mixed with other fibres, other than man-made fibres, wool or fine animals hair
5212 2500.70	印花的其他混纺棉斜纹布(每平方米重>200克,与化纤、羊毛、动物细毛以外其他纤维混纺)	10	80		16	17	米/千克		Other twill cloth of cotton, printed, weighing more than 200g/m²,mixed with other fibres, other than man-made fibres, wool or fine animals hair
5212 2500.90	印花的其他混纺棉布(每平方米重>200克,与化纤、羊毛、动物细毛以外其他纤维混纺)	10	80		16	17	米/千克		Other cloth of cotton, printed, weighing more than 200g/m²,, mixed with other fibres, other than man-made fibres, wool or fine animals hair

第五十三章
其他植物纺织纤维；纸纱线及其机织物

Chapter 53
Other vegetable textile fibres;paper yarn and woven fabrics of paper yarn

税则号列 Tariff Item	商品名称及备注	进口税率 最惠	普通	暂定	出口退税	增值税率	计量单位	监管条件	Article Description
53.01	**亚麻，生的或经加工但未纺制的；亚麻短纤及废麻（包括废麻纱线及回收纤维）：**								**Flax, raw or processed but not spun;flax tow and waste(including yarn waste and garnetted stock):**
5301.1000	-生的或经沤制的亚麻	6	30		5	17	千克	AB	-Flax, raw or retted
	-破开、打成、栉梳或经其他加工但未纺制的亚麻:								-Flax, broken, scutched, hackled or otherwise processed, but not spun:
5301.2100[暂]	--破开的或打成的	6	30	1	5	17	千克	AB	--Broken or scutched
5301.2900	--其他	6	30		5	17	千克	AB	--Other
5301.3000[暂]	-亚麻短纤及废麻	6	30	1	5	17	千克	AB	-Flax tow and waste
53.02	**大麻，生的或经加工但未纺制的；大麻短纤及废麻（包括废麻纱线及回收纤维）：**								**True hemp（Cannabis sativa L）, raw or processed but not spun; tow and waste of true hemp（including yarn waste and garnetted stock）:**
5302.1000	-生的或经沤制的大麻	6	30		5	17	千克	AB	-True hemp, raw or retted
5302.9000	-其他	6	30		5	17	千克	AB	-Other
53.03	**黄麻及其他纺织用韧皮纤维（不包括亚麻、大麻及苎麻），生的或经加工但未纺制的；上述纤维的短纤及废麻（包括废纱线及回收纤维）：**								**Jute and other textile bast fibres（excluding flax, true hemp and ramie）,raw or processed but not spun; tow and waste of these fibres（including yarn waste and garnetted stock）:**
5303.1000	-生的或经沤制的黄麻及其他纺织用韧皮纤维	5	20		5	13	千克	AB	-Jute and other textile bast fibres, raw or retted
5303.9000	-其他	5	30		5	17	千克	AB	-Other
53.05	**椰壳纤维、蕉麻（马尼拉麻）、苎麻及其他品目未列名的纺织用植物纤维，生的或经加工但未纺制的；上述纤维的短纤、落麻及废料（包括废纱线及回收纤维）：**								**Coconut, abaca（Manila hemp or Musatextilis Nee）, ramie and other vegetable textile fibres, not elsewhere specified or included, raw or processed but not spun; tow, noils and waste of these fibres（including yarn waste and garnetted stock）:**
	---苎麻:								---Remie:
5305.0011	----生的	5	30		5	17	千克	AB	----Raw
5305.0012	----经加工但未纺制的	5	30		5	17	千克	AB	----Processed but not spun
5305.0013	----短纤及废料	5	30		5	17	千克	AB	----Tow and waste
5305.0019	----其他	5	20		5	17	千克	AB	----Other
5305.0020	---蕉麻	3	20		5	17	千克	AB	----Of abaca
	---其他:								---Other:
5305.0091	----西沙尔麻及其他纺织用龙舌兰类纤维	5	30		5	17	千克	AB	----Sisal and other textile fibres of the genus Agave, raw
5305.0092	----椰壳纤维	5	30		5	17	千克	AB	----Of coconut（coir）
5305.0099	----其他	5	30		5	17	千克	AB	----Other
53.06	**亚麻纱线：**								**Flax yarn:**
5306.1000	-单纱	6	50		16	17	千克		-Single
5306.2000[暂]	-多股纱线或缆线	10	50	5	16	17	千克		-Multiple（folded）or cabled
53.07	**黄麻纱线或品目53.03的其他纺织用韧皮纤维纱线：**								**Yarn of jute or of other textile bast fibres of heading No.53.03:**
5307.1000	-单纱	6	35		16	17	千克		-Single
5307.2000	-多股纱线或缆线	6	35		16	17	千克		-Multiple（folded）or cabled
53.08	**其他植物纺织纤维纱线；纸纱线：**								**Yarn of other vegetable textile fibres; paper yarn:**
5308.1000	-椰壳纤维纱线	6	45		16	17	千克		-Coir yarn
5308.2000	-大麻纱线	6	45		16	17	千克		-True hemp yarn
	-其他:								-Other:

税则号列 Tariff Item	商品名称及备注	进口税率 最惠	普通	暂定	出口退税	增值税率	计量单位	监管条件	Article Description
	---苎麻纱线:								---Ramie yarn:
5308.9011	----按重量计苎麻含量在85%及以上的未漂白或漂白纱线	6	50		16	17	千克		----Containing 85% or more by weight of ramie, unbleached or bleached yarn
5308.9012	----按重量计苎麻含量在85%及以上的色纱线	6	50		16	17	千克		----Containing 85% or more by weight of ramie, coloured yarn
5308.9013	----按重量计苎麻含量在85%以下的未漂白或漂白纱线	6	50		16	17	千克		----Containing less than 85% by weight of ramie, unbleached or bleached yarn
5308.9014	----按重量计苎麻含量在85%以下的色纱线	6	50		16	17	千克		----Containing less than 85% by weight of coloured yarn
	---其他:								---Other:
5308.9091	----纸纱线	6	70		16	17	千克		----Paper yarn
5308.9099	----其他	6	45		16	17	千克		----Other
53.09	亚麻机织物:								**Woven fabrics of flax::**
	-按重量计亚麻含量在85%及以上:								-Containing 85% or more by weight of flax:
	--未漂白或漂白:								--Unbleached or bleached:
5309.1110	---未漂白	10	80		16	17	米/千克		---Unbleached
5309.1120	---漂白	10	80		16	17	米/千克		---Bleached
5309.1900	--其他	10	80		16	17	米/千克		--Other
	-按重量计亚麻含量在85%以下:								-Containing less than 85% by weight of flax:
	--未漂白或漂白:								--Unbleached or bleached:
5309.2110	---未漂白	10	80		16	17	米/千克		---Unbleached
5309 2110.11	未漂白与精梳毛混纺的亚麻机织物（亚麻含量在85%以下，含17%以上羊毛或动物细毛）	10	80		16	17	米/千克		Woven fabrics of flax, unbleached, mixed, containing 17% or more by weight of combed wool or fine animal hair, and less than 85% by weight of flax
5309 2110.19	未漂白的其他混纺亚麻机织物（亚麻含量在85%以下，含17%以上羊毛或动物细毛）	10	80		16	17	米/千克		Woven fabrics of flax, unbleached, mixed, containing 17% or more by weight of wool or fine animal hair, and less than 85% by weight of flax
5309 2110.21	未漂白的混纺亚麻府绸及细平布（亚麻含量在85%以下，与棉及化纤混纺，棉限内）	10	80		16	17	米/千克		Poplin and fine plain cloth of flax, mixed with cotton and man-made fibres, unbleached, cotton limit in
5309 2110.22	未漂白的混纺亚麻机织平布（亚麻含量在85%以下，与棉及化纤混纺，棉限内）	10	80		16	17	米/千克		Plain weave cloth of flax, unbleached,containing less than 85% by weight of flax, mixed with cotton and man- made fibres, cotton limit in
5309 2110.23	未漂白的混纺亚麻机织印染用布（亚麻含量在85%以下，与棉及化纤混纺，棉限内）	10	80		16	17	米/千克		Cloth of flax for printing and dyeing, unbleached, mixed with cotton and man-made fibres,containing less than 85% by weight of flax, cotton limit in
5309 2110.24	未漂白的混纺亚麻其他机织物（亚麻含量在85%以下，与棉及化纤混纺，棉限内）	10	80		16	17	米/千克		Other woven fabrics of flax, unbleached,mixed with cotton and man-made fibres, containing less than 85% by weight of flax, cotton limit in
5309 2110.25	未漂白的混纺亚麻府绸及细平布（亚麻含量在85%以下，与棉及化纤混纺，化纤限内）	10	80		16	17	米/千克		Poplin and fine plain cloth of flax, mixed with cotton and man-made fibres, containing less than 85% by weight of flax, man-made fibres limit in
5309 2110.26	未漂白的混纺亚麻机织平布（亚麻含量在85%以下，与棉及化纤混纺，化纤限内）	10	80		16	17	米/千克		Plain weave cloth of flax, unbleached, mixed with cotton and man-made fibres, containing less than 85% by weight of flax, man-made fibres limit in
5309 2110.27	未漂白的混纺亚麻机织印染用布（亚麻含量在85%以下，与棉及化纤混纺，化纤限内）	10	80		16	17	米/千克		Cloth of flax for printing and dyeing, mixed with cotton and man-made fibres, containing less than 85% by weight of flax, man-made fibres limit in
5309 2110.28	未漂白的混纺亚麻其他机织物（亚麻含量在85%以下，与棉及化纤混纺，化纤限内）	10	80		16	17	米/千克		Other woven fabrics of flax, mixed with cotton and man-made fibres, containing less than 85% by weight of flax, man-made fibres limit in
5309 2110.29	未漂白的混纺亚麻其他机织物（亚麻含量在85%以下，与棉及化纤混纺）	10	80		16	17	米/千克		Other woven fabrics of flax, unbleached, mixed with cotton and man-made fibres, containing less than 85% by weight of flax,
5309 2110.91	未漂白的混纺亚麻其他机织物（亚麻含量＜85%，主要或仅与精梳羊毛或动物细毛混纺）	10	80		16	17	米/千克		Other woven fabrics of flax, unbleached, mixed mainly or solely with combed wool or fine animal hair, containing less than 85% by weight of flax,

税则号列 Tariff Item	商品名称及备注	进口税率			出口退税	增值税率	计量单位	监管条件	Article Description
		最惠	普通	暂定					
5309 2110.99	未漂白的混纺亚麻其他机织物（亚麻含量在85%以下）	10	80		16	17	米/千克		Other woven fabrics of flax, unbleached, mixed, containing less than 85% by weight of flax
5309.2120	---漂白	10	80		16	17	米/千克		---Bleached
5309 2120.11	漂白与精梳毛混纺的亚麻机织物（亚麻含量在85%以下，含17%以上羊毛或动物细毛）	10	80		16	17	米/千克		Woven fabrics of flax, mixed, bleached, containing less than 85% by weight of flax, containing 17% or more by weight of combed wool or fine animal hair
5309 2120.19	漂白的其他混纺亚麻机织物（亚麻含量在85%以下，含17%以上羊毛或动物细毛）	10	80		16	17	米/千克		Other woven fabrics of flax, mixed, bleached, containing less than 85% by weight of flax and 17% or more by weight of wool or fine animal hair
5309 2120.21	漂白的混纺亚麻府绸及细平布（亚麻含量在85%以下，与棉及化纤混纺，棉限内）	10	80		16	17	米/千克		Poplin and fine plain cloth of flax, bleached, mixed with cotton and man-made fibres, containing less than 85% by weight of flax, cotton limit in
5309 2120.22	漂白的混纺亚麻机织平布（亚麻含量在85%以下，与棉及化纤混纺，棉限内）	10	80		16	17	米/千克		Plain weave cloth, bleached,mixed with cotton and man-made fibres, containing less than 85% by weight of flax ,cotton limit in
5309 2120.23	漂白的混纺亚麻机织印染用布（亚麻含量在85%以下，与棉及化纤混纺，棉限内）	10	80		16	17	米/千克		Cloth of flax for printing and dyeing, mixed with cotton and man-made fibres, bleached, containing less than 85% by weight of flax, cotton limit in
5309 2120.24	漂白的混纺亚麻其他机织物（亚麻含量在85%以下，与棉及化纤混纺，棉限内）	10	80		16	17	米/千克		Other woven fabrics of flax, bleached, mixed with cotton and man-made fibres, containing less than 85% by weight of flax, cotton limit in
5309 2120.25	漂白的混纺亚麻府绸及细平布（亚麻含量在85%以下，与棉及化纤混纺，化纤限内）	10	80		16	17	米/千克		Poplin and fine plain cloth of flax, mixed with cotton and man-made fibres, containing less than 85% by weight of flax, man-made fibres limit in
5309 2120.26	漂白的混纺亚麻机织平布（亚麻含量在85%以下，与棉及化纤混纺，化纤限内）	10	80		16	17	米/千克		Plain weave cloth, mixed with cotton and man-mace fibres, bleached,containing less than 85% by weight of flax, man-made fibres limit in
5309 2120.27	漂白的混纺亚麻机织印染用布（亚麻含量在85%以下，与棉及化纤混纺，化纤限内）	10	80		16	17	米/千克		Woven fabrics of flax for printing and dyeing, mixed with cotton and man-made fibres, man-made fibres limit in
5309 2120.28	漂白的混纺亚麻其他机织物（亚麻含量在85%以下，与棉及化纤混纺，化纤限内）	10	80		16	17	米/千克		Other woven fabrics of flax, mixed with cotton and man-made fibres, bleached,containing less than 85% by weight of flax,manmade fibres limit in
5309 2120.29	漂白的混纺亚麻其他机织物（亚麻含量在85%以下，与棉及化纤混纺）	10	80		16	17	米/千克		Other woven fabrics of flax, mixed with cotton and man-made fibres, bleached,containing less than 85% by weight of flax,
5309 2120.91	漂白的混纺亚麻其他机织物（亚麻含量<85%，主要或仅与精梳羊毛或动物细毛混纺）	10	80		16	17	米/千克		Other woven fabrics of flax, mixed mainly or solely with combed wool or fine animal hair, bleached, containing less than 85% by weight of flax,
5309 2120.99	漂白的混纺亚麻其他机织物（亚麻含量在85%以下）	10	80		16	17	米/千克		Other woven fabrics of flax, bleached, containing less than 85% by weight of flax
5309.2900	--其他	10	80		16	17	米/千克		--Other
5309 2900.11	其他与精梳毛混纺的亚麻机织物（亚麻含量在85%以下，含17%以上羊毛或动物细毛）	10	80		16	17	米/千克		Other woven fabrics of flax, mixed, containning 17% or more by weight of combed wool or fine animal hair, and less than 85% by weight of flax
5309 2900.19	其他混纺亚麻机织物（亚麻含量在85%以下，含17%以上羊毛或动物细毛）	10	80		16	17	米/千克		Other woven fabrics of flax, mixed, containing 17% or more by weight of wool or fine animal hair, containing less than 85% by weight of flax
5309 2900.21	其他混纺亚麻府绸及细平布（亚麻含量在85%以下，与棉及化纤混纺，棉限内）	10	80		16	17	米/千克		Other poplin and fine plain cloth of flax, mixed with cotton and man-made fibres, containing less than 85% by weight of flax,cotton limit in
5309 2900.22	其他混纺亚麻机织平布（亚麻含量在85%以下，与棉及化纤混纺，棉限内）	10	80		16	17	米/千克		Other plain weave cloth of falx, mixed with cotton and man-made fibres, containing less than 85% by weight of flax, cotton limit in
5309 2900.23	其他混纺亚麻机织印染用布（亚麻含量在85%以下，与棉及化纤混纺，棉限内）	10	80		16	17	米/千克		Other cloth of flax for printing and dyeing, mixed with cotton and man-made fibres, containing less than 85% by weight of flax, cotton limit in

税则号列 Tariff Item	商品名称及备注	进口税率			出口退税	增值税率	计量单位	监管条件	Article Description
		最惠	普通	暂定					
5309 2900.24	其他混纺亚麻其他机织物（亚麻含量在85%以下，与棉及化纤混纺，棉限内）	10	80		16	17	米/千克		Other woven fabrics of flax, mixed with cotton and man-made fibres, containing less than 85% by weight of flax, cotton limit in
5309 2900.25	其他混纺亚麻府绸及细平布（亚麻含量在85%以下，与棉及化纤混纺，化纤限内）	10	80		16	17	米/千克		Poplin and fine plain cloth of flax,mixed with cotton and man-made fibres, containing less than 85% by weight of flax, man-made fibres limit in
5309 2900.26	其他混纺亚麻机织平布（亚麻含量在85%以下，与棉及化纤混纺，化纤限内）	10	80		16	17	米/千克		Plain weave cloth of flax, mixed with cotton and man-made fibres, containing less than 85% by weight of flax, man-made fibres limit in
5309 2900.27	其他混纺亚麻机织印染用布（亚麻含量在85%以下，与棉及化纤混纺，化纤限内）	10	80		16	17	米/千克		Other cloth of flax for printing and dyeing, mixed with cotton and manmade fibres, containing less than85% by weight of flax,man-made fibres limit in
5309 2900.28	其他混纺亚麻其他机织物（亚麻含量在85%以下，与棉及化纤混纺，化纤限内）	10	80		16	17	米/千克		Other woven fabrics of flax, mixed with cotton and man-made fibres, containing less than 85% by weight of flax, man-made fibres limit in
5309 2900.29	其他混纺亚麻其他机织物（亚麻含量在85%以下，与棉及化纤混纺）	10	80		16	17	米/千克		Other woven fabrics of flax, containing less than 85% by weight of flax, mixed with cotton and man-made fibres
5309 2900.91	其他混纺亚麻其他机织物（亚麻含量<85%，主要或仅与精梳羊毛或动物细毛混纺）	10	80		16	17	米/千克		Other woven fabrics of flax, containing less than 85% by weight of flax, mixed mainly or solely with combed wool or fine animal hair
5309 2900.99	其他混纺亚麻机织物（亚麻含量在85%以下）	10	80		16	17	米/千克		Other woven fabrics of flax, mixed, containing less than 85% by weight of flax
53.10	**黄麻或品目53.03的其他纺织用韧皮纤维机织物：**								**Woven fabrics of jute or of other textilebast fibres of heading No.53.03:**
5310.1000	-未漂白	10	40		16	17	米/千克		-Unbleached
5310 1000.11	未漂白黄麻或其他韧皮纤维机织物（宽度不超过150厘米，与精梳羊毛或动物细毛混纺）	10	40		16	17	米/千克		Woven fabrics of jute or of other textilebast fibres, unbleached, of a width not exceeding 150cm, mixed with combed wool or fine animal hair
5310 1000.19	未漂白黄麻或其他韧皮纤维机织物（宽度不超过150厘米，与其他纤维混纺）	10	40		16	17	米/千克		Woven fabrics of jute or of other textilebast fibres, unbleached,of a width not exceeding 150cm, mixed with other fibres
5310 1000.91	未漂白黄麻或其他韧皮纤维机织物（宽度超过150厘米，与精梳羊毛或动物细毛混纺）	10	40		16	17	米/千克		Woven fabrics of jute or of other textilebast fibres, unbleached,of a width exceeding 150cm, mixed with combed wool or fine animal hair
5310 1000.99	未漂白黄麻或其他韧皮纤维机织物（宽度超过150厘米，与其他纤维混纺）	10	40		16	17	米/千克		Woven fabrics of jute or of other textilebast fibres, unbleached, of a width exceeding 150cm, mixed with other fibres
5310.9000	-其他	10	40		16	17	米/千克		-Other
5310 9000.11	其他黄麻机织物，宽度≤150厘米（含品目53.03其他纺织用韧皮纤维布与精梳羊毛或动物细毛混纺）	10	40		16	17	米/千克		Other woven fabrics of jute or of other textilebast fibres of heading No.53.03, of a width not exceeding 150cm, mixed with combed wool or fine animal hair
5310 9000.19	其他黄麻机织物，宽度≤150厘米（含品目53.03的其他纺织用韧皮纤维布，与其他纤维混纺）	10	40		16	17	米/千克		Other woven fabrics of jute or of other textilebast fibres of heading No.53.03, of a width not exceeding 150cm, mixed with other fibres
5310 9000.91	其他黄麻机织物，宽度>150厘米（含品目53.03其他纺织用韧皮纤维布与精梳羊毛或动物细毛混纺）	10	40		16	17	米/千克		Other woven fabrics of jute or of other textilebast fibres of heading No.53.03, of a width exceeding 150cm, mixed with combed wool or fine animal hair
5310 9000.99	其他黄麻机织物，宽度>150厘米（含品目53.03的其他纺织用韧皮纤维布，与其他纤维混纺）	10	40		16	17	米/千克		Other woven fabrics of jute or of other textilebast fibres of heading No.53.03, of a width exceeding 150cm, mixed with other fibres
53.11	**其他纺织用植物纤维机织物；纸纱线机织物：**								**Woven fabrics of other vegetable textile fibres; woven fabrics of paper yarn:**

税则号列 Tariff Item	商品名称及备注	进口税率			出口退税	增值税率	计量单位	监管条件	Article Description
		最惠	普通	暂定					
	---苎麻的:								---Of ramie:
5311.0012	----按重量计苎麻含量在85%及以上的未漂白机织物	10	80		16	17	米/千克		----Containing 85% or more by weight of ramie, unbleached woven fabrics
5311 0012.11	未漂白与精梳毛混纺的苎麻机织物(苎麻含量在85%及以上,含17%以上羊毛或动物细毛)	10	80		16	17	米/千克		Unbleached woven fabrics of ramie, mixed, containing 17% or more by weight of combed wool or fine animal hair, and 85% or more by weight of ramie
5311 0012.19	未漂白苎麻机织物(苎麻含量在85%及以上,含17%以上的羊毛或动物细毛)	10	80		16	17	米/千克		Unbleached woven fabrics of ramie, mixed, containing 17% or more by weight of wool or fine animal hair, containing 85% or more by weight of ramie
5311 0012.21	未漂白的苎麻府绸及细平布(苎麻含量在85%及以上,与棉及化纤混纺,棉限内)	10	80		16	17	米/千克		Unbleached poplin and fine plain cloth of ramie, mixed with cotton and man-made fibres, containing 85% or more by weight of ramie, , cotton limit in
5311 0012.22	未漂白的苎麻机织平布(苎麻含量在85%及以上,与棉及化纤混纺,棉限内)	10	80		16	17	米/千克		Unbleached plain weave cloth of ramie, mixed with cotton and man-made fibres, containing 85% or more by weight of ramie, cotton limit in
5311 0012.23	未漂白的苎麻机织印染用布(苎麻含量在85%及以上,与棉及化纤混纺,棉限内)	10	80		16	17	米/千克		Unbleached woven fabrics of ramie for printing and dyeing, mixed with cotton and man-made fibres, containing 85% or more by weight of ramie, cotton limit in
5311 0012.29	未漂白的苎麻其他机织物(苎麻含量在85%及以上,与棉及化纤混纺,棉限内)	10	80		16	17	米/千克		Unbleached other woven fabrics of ramie, mixed with cotton and man-made fibres, containing 85% or more by weight of ramie, cotton limit in
5311 0012.31	未漂白的苎麻府绸及细平布(苎麻含量在85%及以上,与棉及化纤混纺,化纤限内)	10	80		16	17	米/千克		Unbleached poplin and fine plain cloth of ramie, mixed with cotton and man-made fibres, containing 85% or more by weight of ramie, man-made fibres limit in
5311 0012.32	未漂白的苎麻机织平布(苎麻含量在85%及以上,与棉及化纤混纺,化纤限内)	10	80		16	17	米/千克		Unbleached plain weave cloth of ramie, mixed with cotton and man-made fibres, containing 85% or more by weight of ramie,manmade fibres limit in
5311 0012.33	未漂白的苎麻机织印染用布(苎麻含量在85%及以上,与棉及化纤混纺,化纤限内)	10	80		16	17	米/千克		Unbleached woven fabrics of ramie for printing and dyeing, mixed with cotton and man-made fibres, containing 85% or more by weight of ramie, man-made fibres limit in
5311 0012.39	未漂白的苎麻其他机织物(苎麻含量在85%及以上,与棉及化纤混纺,化纤限内)	10	80		16	17	米/千克		Unbleached other woven fabrics of ramie, mixed with cotton and man-made fibres, containing 85% or more by weight of ramie,manmade fibres limit in
5311 0012.40	未漂白的苎麻其他机织物(苎麻含量在85%及以上,与棉及化纤混纺)	10	80		16	17	米/千克		Unbleached other woven fabrics of ramie, mixed with cotton and man-made fibres, containing 85% or more by weight of ramie
5311 0012.91	未漂白的苎麻其他机织物(苎麻含量在85%及以上,主要/仅与精梳羊毛/细毛混纺)	10	80		16	17	米/千克		Unbleached other woven fabrics of ramie, mixed mainly or solely with combed wool or fine animal hair, containing 85% or more by weight of ramie
5311 0012.99	未漂白的苎麻其他机织物(苎麻含量在85%及以上)	10	80		16	17	米/千克		Unbleached other woven fabrics of ramie, containing 85% or more by weight of ramie
5311.0013	----按重量计苎麻含量在85%及以上的其他机织物	12	80		16	17	米/千克		----Containing 85% or more by weight of ramie, other woven fabrics
5311 0013.11	与精梳毛混纺的苎麻其他机织物(苎麻含量≥85%,含17%以上羊毛或动物细毛)	12	80		16	17	米/千克		Other woven fabrics of ramie, mixed, containing 17% or more by weight of combed wool or fine animal hair, and 85% or more by weight of ramie
5311 0013.19	苎麻其他机织物(苎麻含量≥85%,羊毛/细毛>17%)	12	80		16	17	米/千克		Other woven fabrics of ramie, mixed, containing less than 17% by weight of wool or fine animal hair, and 85% or more by weight of ramie
5311 0013.21	苎麻府绸及细平布(苎麻含量≥85%,与棉及化纤混纺,棉限内)	12	80		16	17	米/千克		Poplin and fine plain cloth of ramie, mixed with cotton and man-made fibres, containing 85% or more by weight of ramie, cotton limit in
5311 0013.22	苎麻机织平布(苎麻含量≥85%,与棉及化纤混纺,棉限内)	12	80		16	17	米/千克		Plain weave cloth of ramie, mixed with cotton and man-made fibres, containing 85% or more by weight of ramie, cotton limit in
5311 0013.23	苎麻机织印染布(苎麻含量≥85%,与棉及化纤混纺,棉限内)	12	80		16	17	米/千克		Cloth of ramie for printing and dyeing, mixed with cotton and man-made fibres, containing 85% or more

税则号列 Tariff Item	商品名称及备注	进口税率 最惠	普通	暂定	出口退税	增值税率	计量单位	监管条件	Article Description
									by weight of ramie, cotton limit in
5311 0013.29	苎麻其他机织物（苎麻含量≥85%，与棉及化纤混纺，棉限内）	12	80		16	17	米/千克		Woven fabrics of ramie, mixed with cotton and man-made fibres, containing 85% or more by weight of ramie, cotton limit in
5311 0013.31	苎麻府绸及细平布（苎麻含量≥85%，与棉及化纤混纺，化纤限内）	12	80		16	17	米/千克		Poplin and fine plain cloth of ramie, mixed with cotton and man-made fibres, containing 85% or more by weight of ramie, man-made fibres limit in
5311 0013.32	苎麻机织平布（苎麻含量≥85%，与棉及化纤混纺，化纤限内）	12	80		16	17	米/千克		Plain weave cloth of ramie, mixed with cotton and man-made fibres, containing 85% or more by weight of ramie, man-made fibres limit in
5311 0013.33	苎麻机织印染布（苎麻含量≥85%，与棉及化纤混纺，化纤限内）	12	80		16	17	米/千克		Cloth of ramie for printing and dyeing, mixed with cotton and man-made fibres, containing 85% or more by weight of ramie, man-made fibres limit in
5311 0013.39	苎麻其他机织物（苎麻含量≥85%，与棉及化纤混纺，化纤限内）	12	80		16	17	米/千克		Other woven fabrics of ramie,mixed with cotton and man-made fibres, containing 85% or more by weight of ramie, man-made fibres limit in
5311 0013.40	苎麻其他机织物（苎麻含量≥85%，与棉及化纤混纺）	12	80		16	'17	米/千克		Other woven fabrics of ramie,mixedwith cotton and man-made fibres, containing 85% or more by weight of ramie
5311 0013.91	苎麻其他机织物（苎麻含量≥85%，主要/仅与精梳羊毛/细毛混纺）	12	80		16	17	米/千克		Other woven fabrics of ramie, mixed mainly or solely with combed wool or fine animal hair, containing 85% or more by weight of ramie
5311 0013.99	苎麻其他机织物（苎麻含量≥85%）	12	80		16	17	米/千克		Other woven fabrics of ramie, containing 85% or more by weight of ramie
5311.0014	----按重量计苎麻含量在85%以下的未漂白机织物	10	80		16	17	米/千克		----Containing less than 85% by weight of ramie, unbleached woven fabrics
5311 0014.11	未漂白与精梳羊毛混纺苎麻机织物（苎麻含量<85%，含17%以上的羊毛/细毛）	10	80		16	17	米/千克		Unbleached woven fabrics of ramie, containing less than 85% by weight of ramie and 17% or more by weight of wool or fine animal hair
5311 0014.19	未漂白苎麻机织物（苎麻含量<85%，含17%以上的羊毛/细毛）	10	80		16	17	米/千克		Unbleached other woven fabrics of ramie, containing 17% or more by weight of wool or fine animal hair, containing less than 85% by weight of ramie
5311 0014.21	未漂白的苎麻府绸及细平布（苎麻含量在85%以下，与棉及化纤混纺，棉限内）	10	80		16	17	米/千克		Unbleached poplin and fine plain cloth of ramie, mixed with cotton and man-made fibres,containing less than 85% by weight of ramie, cotton limit in
5311 0014.22	未漂白的苎麻机织平布（苎麻含量在85%以下，与棉及化纤混纺，棉限内）	10	80		16	17	米/千克		Unbleached plain weave cloth of ramie, mixed with cotton and man-made fibres, containing less than 85% by weight of ramie, cotton limit in
5311 0014.23	未漂白的苎麻机织印染用布（苎麻含量在85%以下，与棉及化纤混纺，棉限内）	10	80		16	17	米/千克		Unbleached cloth of ramie for printing and dyeing, mixed with cotton and man-made fibres, containing less than 85% by weight of ramie, cotton limit in
5311 0014.29	未漂白的苎麻其他机织物（苎麻含量在85%以下，与棉及化纤混纺，棉限内）	10	80		16	17	米/千克		Unbleached other woven fabrics of ramie, mixed with cotton and man-made fibres, containing less than 85% by weight of ramie, cotton limit in
5311 0014.31	未漂白的苎麻府绸及细平布（苎麻含量在85%以下，与棉及化纤混纺，化纤限内）	10	80		16	17	米/千克		Unbleached poplin and fine plain fabrics of ramie, mixed with cotton and man-made fibres,containing less than 85% by weight of ramie, man-made fibres limit in
5311 0014.32	未漂白的苎麻机织平布（苎麻含量在85%以下，与棉及化纤混纺，化纤限内）	10	80		16	17	米/千克		Unbleached plain weave cloth of ramie, mixed with cotton and man-made fibres, containing less than 85% by weight of ramie,man-made fibres limit in
5311 0014.33	未漂白的苎麻机织印染用布（苎麻含量在85%以下，与棉及化纤混纺，化纤限内）	10	80		16	17	米/千克		Unbleached cloth of ramie for printing and dyeing, mixed with cotton and man-made fibres, containing less than 85% by weight of ramie, man-made fibres limit in
5311 0014.39	未漂白的苎麻其他机织物（苎麻含量在85%以下，与棉及化纤混	10	80		16	17	米/千克		Unbleached other woven fabrics of ramie, mixed with cotton and man-made fibres, containing less than 85%

税则号列 Tariff Item	商品名称及备注	进口税率 最惠	普通	暂定	出口退税	增值税率	计量单位	监管条件	Article Description
	纺，化纤限内）								by weight of ramie, man-made fibres limit in
5311 0014.40	未漂白的苎麻其他机织物（苎麻含量在85%以下，与棉及化纤混纺）	10	80		16	17	米/千克		Unbleached other woven fabrics of ramie, mixed with cotton and man-made fibres, containing less than 85% by weight of ramie
5311 0014.91	未漂白的苎麻其他机织物（苎麻含量＜85%，主要或仅与精梳羊毛或动物细毛混纺）	10	80		16	17	米/千克		Unbleached other woven fabrics of ramie, mixed mainly or solely with combed wool or fine animal hair, containing less than 85% by weight of ramie
5311 0014.99	未漂白的苎麻其他机织物（苎麻含量在85%以下）	10	80		16	17	米/千克		Unbleached other woven fabrics of ramie, containing less than 85% by weight of ramie
5311.0015	----按重量计苎麻含量在85%以下的其他机织物	12	80		16	17	米/千克		----Containing less than 85% by weight of ramie, other woven fabrics
5311 0015.11	其他苎麻机织物，含量＜85%（毛重＞17%，主要或仅与精梳羊毛或动物细毛混纺）	12	80		16	17	米/千克		Other woven fabrics of ramie, mixed mainly or solely with combed wool or of fine animal hair, containing less than 85% by weight of ramie and 17% or more by weight of combed wool or fine animal hair
5311 0015.19	其他苎麻机织物（苎麻含量在85%以下，含17%以上羊毛或动物细毛）	12	80		16	17	米/千克		Other woven fabrics of ramie, mixed, containing less than 85% by weight of ramie and 17% or more by weight of wool or fine animal hair
5311 0015.21	苎麻府绸及细平布（苎麻含量在85%以下，与棉及化纤混纺，棉限内）	12	80		16	17	米/千克		Poplin and fine plain fabrics of ramie, mixed with cotton and man-made fibres, containing less than 85% by weight of ramie, cotton limit in
5311 0015.22	苎麻机织平布（苎麻含量在85%以下，与棉及化纤混纺，棉限内）	12	80		16	17	米/千克		Plain weave cloth of ramie, mixed with cotton and man-made fibres, containing less than 85% by weight of ramie, cotton limit in
5311 0015.29	其他苎麻机织物（苎麻含量在85%以下，与棉及化纤混纺，棉限内）	12	80		16	17	米/千克		Other woven fabrics of ramie, mixed with cotton and man-made fibres, containing less than 85% by weight of ramie, cotton limit in
5311 0015.31	苎麻府绸及细平布（苎麻含量在85%以下，与棉及化纤混纺，化纤限内）	12	80		16	17	米/千克		Poplin and fine plain fabrics of ramie, mixed with cotton and man-made fibres, containing less than 85% by weight of ramie, man-made fibres limit in
5311 0015.32	苎麻机织平布（苎麻含量在85%以下，与棉及化纤混纺，化纤限内）	12	80		16	17	米/千克		Plain weave cloth of ramie, mixed with cotton and man-made fibres, containing less than 85% by weight of ramie, man-made fibres limit in
5311 0015.33	苎麻机织印染用布（苎麻含量在85%以下，与棉及化纤混纺，化纤限内）	12	80		16	17	米/千克		Cloth of ramie for printing and dyeing, mixed with cotton and man-made fibres, containing less than 85% by weight of ramie, man-made fibres limit in
5311 0015.39	其他苎麻机织物（苎麻含量在85%以下，与棉及化纤混纺，化纤限内）	12	80		16	17	米/千克		Other woven fabrics of ramie, mixed with cotton and man-made fibres, containing less than 85% by weight of ramie, man-made fibres limit in
5311 0015.91	其他苎麻机织物（苎麻＜85%，主要或仅与精梳羊毛或动物细毛混纺）	12	80		16	17	米/千克		Other woven fabrics of ramie, mixed mainly or solely with combed wool or fine animal hair, containing less than 85% by weight of ramie,
5311 0015.99	其他苎麻机织物（指按重量计苎麻含量在85%以下）	12	80		16	17	米/千克		Other woven fabrics of ramie, containing less than 85% by weight of ramie
5311.0020	---纸纱线的	10	90		16	17	米/千克		---Of paper yarn
5311 0020.10	纸纱线机织物（主要或仅与精梳羊毛或动物细毛混纺）	10	90		16	17	米/千克		Woven fabrics of paper yarn, mixed mainly or solely with combed wool or combed fine animal hair
5311 0020.90	纸纱线机织物	10	90		16	17	米/千克		Woven fabrics of paper yarn
5311.0030	---大麻的	10	50		16	17	米/千克		---Of true hemp
5311.0090	---其他	10	50		16	17	米/千克		---Other
5311 0090.10	其他纺织用植物纤维机织物(含17%以上羊毛或动物细毛)	10	50		16	17	米/千克		Woven fabrics of vegetable fibres, used for other textiles, containing 17% or more by weight of wool and fine animal hai
5311 0090.21	其他纺织用植物纤府绸及细平布（与棉及化纤混纺，棉限内）	10	50		16	17	米/千克		Poplin and fine plain cloth of other vegetable fibres used for textile, mixed with cotton and man-made fibres, cotton limit in
5311 0090.22	其他纺织用植物纤维机织平布（与棉及化纤混纺，棉限内）	10	50		16	17	米/千克		Plain weave cloth of other vegetable fibres, used for textile, mixed with cotton and man-made fibres, cotton

税则号列 Tariff Item	商品名称及备注	进口税率			出口退税	增值税率	计量单位	监管条件	Article Description
		最惠	普通	暂定					
									limit in
5311 0090.29	其他纺织用植物纤维机织物（与棉及化纤混纺，棉限内）	10	50		16	17	米/千克		Woven fabrics of other vegetable fibres, used for textile,mixed with cotton and man-made fibres, cotton limit in
5311 0090.32	其他纺织用植物纤维机织平布（与棉及化纤混纺，化纤限内）	10	50		16	17	米/千克		Plain weave cloth of other vegetable fibres, used for textile, mixed with cotton and man-made fibres, man-made fibres limit in
5311 0090.33	其他纺织用植物纤维机织印染用布（与棉及化纤混纺，化纤限内）	10	50		16	17	米/千克		Cloth of other vegetable fibres for printing and dyeing, used for textile,mixed with cotton and man-made fibres, man-made fibres limit in
5311 0090.39	其他纺织用植物纤维其他机织物（与棉及化纤混纺，化纤限内）	10	50		16	17	米/千克		Woven fabrics of other vegetable fibres, used for textile, mixed with cotton and man-made fibres, man-made fibres limit in
5311 0090.40	其他纺织用植物纤维其他机织物（与棉及化纤混纺）	10	50		16	17	米/千克		Woven fabrics of other vegetable fibres, used for textile,mixed with cotton and man-made fibres
5311 0090.90	其他纺织用植物纤维其他机织物	10	50		16	17	米/千克		Other woven fabrics of other vegetable fibres, used for textile

第五十四章 化学纤维长丝；化学纤维纺织材料制扁条及类似品

Chapter 54 Man-made filaments; strip and the like of man-made textile materials

注释：

一、本税则所称“化学纤维”，是指通过下列任一方法加工制得的有机聚合物的短纤或长丝：

（一）将有机单体物质加以聚合而制成的聚合物，例如，聚酰胺、聚酯、聚烯烃、聚氨基甲酸酯；或通过上述加工得到的聚合物经化学改性制得（例如，聚乙酸乙烯酯水解制得的聚乙烯醇）；或

（二）将天然有机聚合物（例如，纤维素）溶解或化学处理制成聚合物，例如，铜铵纤维或粘胶纤维；或将天然有机聚合物（例如，纤维素、酪蛋白及其他蛋白质或藻酸）经化学改性制成聚合物，例如，醋酸纤维素纤维或藻酸盐纤维。

对于化学纤维，所称“合成”，是指（一）款所述的纤维；所称“人造”，是指（二）款所述的纤维。品目 54.04 或 54.05 的扁条及类似品不视作化学纤维。

对于纺织材料，所称“化学纤维”、“合成纤维”及“人造纤维”，其含义应与上述解释相同。

二、品目 54.02 及 54.03 不适用于第五十五章的合成纤维或人造纤维的长丝丝束。

Chapter Note:

1. Throughout the Nomenclature, the term “man-made fibres” means staple fibres and filaments of organic polymers produced by manufacturing processes, either:

（a）By polymerisation of organic monomers to produce polymers such as polyamides, polyester, polyolefins or polyurethanes, or by chemical modification of polymers produced by this process[（for example, poly（vinyl alcohol）prepared by the hydrolysis of poly（vinyl acetate）]; or

（b）By dissolution or chemical treatment of natural organic polymers（for example, cellulose）to produce polymers such as cuprammonium rayon（cupro）or viscose rayon, or by chemical modification of natural organic polymers （for example, cellulose, casein and other proteins, or alginic acid）, to produce polymers such as cellulose acetate or alginates.

The terms “synthetic” and “artificial” , used in relation to fibres , mean: synthetic: fibres as defined at（a）; artificial: fibres as defined at（b）. Strip and the like of heading 54.04 or 54.05 are not considered to be man-made fibres.

The terms “man-made”, “synthetic” and “artificial” shall have the same meanings when used in relation to“textile materials”.

2. Headings 54.02 and 54.03 do not apply to synthetic or artificial filament tow of Chapter 55.

税则号列 Tariff Item	商品名称及备注	进口税率 最惠	普通	暂定	出口退税	增值税率	计量单位	监管条件	Article Description
54.01	化学纤维长丝纺制的缝纫线，不论是否供零售用：								**Sewing thread of man-made filaments, whether or not put up for retail sale:**
	-合成纤维长丝纺制：								-Of synthetic filaments:
5401.1010	---非供零售用	5	70		16	17	千克		---Not put up for retail sale
5401.1020	---供零售用	5	90		16	17	千克		---Put up for retail sale
	-人造纤维长丝纺制：								-Of artificial filaments:
5401.2010	---非供零售用	5	35		16	17	千克		---Not put up for retail sale
5401.2020	---供零售用	5	90		16	17	千克		---Put up for retail sale
54.02	合成纤维长丝纱线（缝纫线除外），非供零售用，包括细度在 67 分特以下的合成纤维单丝：								**Synthetic filament yarn（other than sewing thread）, not put up for retail sale, including synthetic monofilament of less than 67 decitex:**
	-尼龙或其他聚酰胺纺制的高强力纱：								-High tenacity yarn of nylon or other polyamides:
	--芳香族聚酰胺纺制：								--Of aramids:
5402.1110	---聚间苯二甲酰间苯二胺纺制	5	70		16	17	千克	A	---Of polyisophthaloyl metaphenylene diamine
5402.1120	---聚对苯二甲酰对苯二胺纺制	5	70		16	17	千克	A	---Of poly-p-phenylene terephthalamide
5402.1190	---其他	5	70		16	17	千克	A	---Other
	--其他：								--Other:
5402.1910	---聚酰胺-6（尼龙-6）纺制的	5	70		16	17	千克	A	---Of nylon-6
5402.1920	---聚酰胺-6，6（尼龙-6，6）纺制的	5	70		16	17	千克	A	---Of nylon-6,6
5402.1990	---其他	5	70		16	17	千克	A	---Other
5402.2000	-聚酯高强力纱	5	70		16	17	千克		-High tenacity yarn of polyesters
5402 2000.10	非零售聚酯高强力纱（单丝/未捻或捻度＜5 转/米的复丝单纱）	5	70		16	17	千克	A	High tenacity yarn of polyesters (single filament /multi-filament single yarn not twisted or with a twist of less than 5 turns per meter) not for retail sale

税则号列 Tariff Item	商品名称及备注	进口税率 最惠	进口税率 普通	进口税率 暂定	出口退税	增值税率	计量单位	监管条件	Article Description
5402 2000.20	非零售聚酯高强力纱（捻度≥5转/米的的复丝单纱）	5	70		16	17	千克	A	High tenacity yarn of polyesters, multi-filament single yarn with a twist of 5 or more turns per meter, not for retail sale
5402 2000.90	非零售聚酯高强力多股纱	5	70		16	17	千克	A	High tenacity yarn of polyesters, multiple yarn, not for retail sale
	-变形纱线:								-Textured yarn:
	--尼龙或其他聚酰胺纺制，每根单纱细度不超过50特:								--Of nylon or other polyamides, measuring per single yarn not more than 50 tex:
	---弹力丝:								---Elastic filament:
5402.3111	----聚酰胺-6(尼龙-6)纺制	5	80		16	17	千克	A	----Of nylon-6
5402.3112	----聚酰胺-6,6（尼龙-6,6）纺制	5	80		16	17	千克	A	----Of nylon-6, 6
5402.3113	----芳香族聚酰胺纺制	5	80		16	17	千克	A	----Of aramides
5402.3119	----其他	5	80		16	17	千克	A	----Other
5402.3190	---其他	5	70		16	17	千克	A	---Other
	--尼龙或其他聚酰胺纺制，每根单纱细度超过50特:								--Of nylon or other polyamides, measuring per single yarn more than 50 tex:
	---弹力丝:								---Elastic filament:
5402.3211	----聚酰胺-6(尼龙-6)纺制	5	80		16	17	千克		----Of nylon-6
5402.3212	----聚酰胺-6，6（尼龙-6，6）纺制	5	80		16	17	千克		----Of nylon-6, 6
5402.3213	----芳香族聚酰胺纺制	5	80		16	17	千克		----Of aramides
5402.3219	----其他	5	80		16	17	千克		----Other
5402.3290	---其他	5	70		16	17	千克		---Other
	--聚酯纺制:								--Of polyesters:
5402.3310	---弹力丝	5	90		16	17	千克	A	---Elastic filament
5402.3390	---其他	5	70		16	17	千克	A	---Other
5402.3400	--聚丙烯纺制	5	70		16	17	千克		--Of polypropylene
5402.3900	--其他	5	70		16	17	千克		--Other
	-其他单纱，未加捻或捻度每米不超过50转:								-Other yarn, single, untwisted or with a twist not exceeding 50 turns per metre:
	--弹性纱线:								--Elastomeric:
5402.4410	---氨纶纱线	5	70		16	17	千克		---Of polyurethane
5402.4490	---其他	5	70		16	17	千克	A	---Other
	--其他，尼龙或其他聚酰胺纱线:								---Other,of nylon or other polyamides:
5402.4510	---聚酰胺-6(尼龙-6)纺制的	5	70		16	17	千克		---Of nylon-6
5402.4520	---聚酰胺-6,6(尼龙-6,6)纺制的	5	70		16	17	千克		---Of nylon-6, 6
5402.4530	---芳香族聚酰胺纺制的	5	70		16	17	千克		---Of aramides
5402.4590	---其他	5	70		16	17	千克		---Other
5402.4600	--其他,部分定向聚酯纱线	5	70		16	17	千克	A	--Other, of polyesters, partially oriented
5402.4700	--其他,聚酯纱线	5	70		16	17	千克	A	--Other, of polyesters
5402.4800	--其他,聚丙烯纱线	5	70		16	17	千克		--Other, of polypropylene
	--其他:								--Other:
5402.4910	---断裂强度大于等于22cN/dtex,且初始模量大于等于750cN/dtex的聚乙烯纱线	5	70		16	17	千克		---Of polyethylene (having an breaking strength of 22cN/dtex or more and initial modulus of 750cN/dtex or more)
5402.4990	---其他	5	70		16	17	千克		---Other
5402 4990.01	非弹性氨纶单纱(非供零售用,未加捻或捻度每米不超过50转,缝纫线除外)	5	70		16	17	千克		Non-elastic polyurethane yarn (not used for retail, no twisting or the twisting strength is no more than 50 turns/per meter, except the sewing thread)
5402 4990.90	其他合成纤维长丝单纱(非供零售用,未加捻或捻度每米不超过50转，缝纫线除外)	5	70		16	17	千克		Other synthetic fibre filament single yarn (not used for retail, no twisting or the twisting strength doesn't surpass 50 turns /per meter)
	-其他单纱，捻度每米超过50转:								-Other,yarn, single, with a twist exceeding 50 turns per metre:

税则号列 Tariff Item	商品名称及备注	进口税率 最惠	进口税率 普通	进口税率 暂定	出口退税	增值税率	计量单位	监管条件	Article Description
	--尼龙或其他聚酰胺纱线:								--Of nylon or other polyamides:
5402.5110	---聚酰胺-6(尼龙-6)制	5	70		16	17	千克		---Of nylon-6
5402.5120	---聚酰胺-6，6（尼龙-6，6）纺制的	5	70		16	17	千克		---Of nylon-6, 6
5402.5130	---芳香族聚酰胺纺制的	5	70		16	17	千克		---Of aramides
5402.5190	---其他	5	70		16	17	千克		---Other
5402.5200	--聚酯纱线	5	70		16	17	千克		--Of polyesters
	--其他:								--Other:
5402.5910	---聚丙烯纱线	5	70		16	17	千克		---Of polypropylene
5402.5920	---断裂强度大于等于22cN/dtex,且初始模量大于等于750cN/dtex的聚乙烯纱线	5	70		16	17	千克		---Of polyethylene,of which breaking strength≥22cN/dtex and initial modulus≥750cN/dtex
5402.5990	---其他	5	70		16	17	千克		---Other
	-其他纱线（多股纱线或缆线）:								-Other yarn, multiple（folded）or cabled:
	--尼龙或其他聚酰胺纺制:								--Of nylon or other polyamides:
5402.6110	---聚酰胺-6(尼龙-6)纺制的	5	70		16	17	千克		---Of nylon-6
5402.6120	---聚酰胺-6,6（尼龙-6,6）纺制的	5	70		16	17	千克		---Of nylon-6, 6
5402.6130	---芳香族聚酰胺纺制的	5	70		16	17	千克		---Of aramides
5402.6190	---其他	5	70		16	17	千克		---Other
5402.6200	--聚酯纺制	5	70		16	17	千克		--Of polyesters
	--其他:								--Other:
5402.6910	---聚丙烯纱线	5	70		16	17	千克		---Of polypropylene
5402.6920	---氨纶纱线	5	70		16	17	千克		---Of polyurethane
5402.6990	---其他	5	70		16	17	千克		---Other
54.03	**人造纤维长丝纱线（缝纫线除外），非供零售用，包括细度在67分特以下的人造纤维单丝:**								**Artificial filament yarn（other than sewing thread), not put up for retail sale, including artificial monofilament of less than 67 decitex :**
5403.1000	-粘胶纤维纺制的高强力纱	5	35		16	17	千克		-High tenacity yarn of viscose rayon
5403 1000.10	非零售粘胶纤维高强力纱（单丝/未捻或捻度每米5转以下的复丝单纱，非供零售用）	5	35		16	17	千克		High tenacity yarn of viscose rayon,single filament /multi-filament single yarn, not twisted or with a twist of less than 5 turns per meter, not for retail sale
5403 1000.20	非零售粘胶纤维高强力纱（捻度5转/米及以上的复丝单纱）	5	35		16	17	千克		High tenacity yarn of viscose rayon, multi-filament single yarn, with a twist of 5 or more turns per meter, not for retail sale
5403 1000.90	非零售粘胶纤维高强力多股纱	5	35		16	17	千克		High tenacity yarn of viscose rayon, multiple yarn, not for retail sale
	-其他单纱:								-Other yarn, single:
	--粘胶纤维纺制，未加捻或捻度每米不超过120转:								--Of viscose rayon, untwisted or with a twist not exceeding 120 turns per metre:
5403.3110	---竹制	5	35		16	17	千克		---Of bamboo
5403.3190	---其他	5	35		16	17	千克		---Other
	--粘胶纤维纺制,捻度每米超过120转:								--Of viscose rayon, with a twist exceeding 120 turns per metre:
5403.3210	---竹制	5	35		16	17	千克		---Of bamboo
5403.3290	---其他	5	35		16	17	千克		---Other
	--醋酸纤维纺制:								--Of cellulose acetate:
5403.3310	---二醋酸纤维纺制	5	40		16	17	千克		--Of cellulose diacetate
5403 3310.10	非零售二醋酸纤维单纱（单丝/未捻或捻度每米5转以下的复丝单纱，包括变形纱线）	5	40		16	17	千克	A	Single yarn of cellulose diacetate, single filament /multi-filament single yarn, not twisted or with a twist of less than 5 turns per meter, not for retail sale, including textured filament yarn
5403 3310.20	非零售二醋酸纤维单纱（5转/米≤捻度≤250转/米，包括变形纱线）	5	40		16	17	千克	A	Yarn of cellulose diacetate, single, not for retail sale (5 turns/meter≤twist≤250 turns/meter, including textured filament yarn)
5403 3310.90	非零售二醋酸纤维单纱（捻度超过250转/米）	5	40		16	17	千克	A	Yarn of other cellulose diacetate, single, not for retail sale (with a twist exceeding 250 turns/meter, including textured filament yarn)

税则号列 Tariff Item	商品名称及备注	进口税率 最惠	进口税率 普通	进口税率 暂定	出口退税	增值税率	计量单位	监管条件	Article Description
5403.3390	---其他	5	35		16	17	千克		---Other
5403 3390.10	非零售其他醋酸纤维单纱（单丝/未捻或捻度每米 5 转以下的复丝单纱，非供零售用，包括变形纱线）	5	35		16	17	千克		Other single yarn of cellulose acetate, single filament /multi- filament single yarn, untwisted or with a twist not exceeding 5 turns per meter, not for retail sale, including textured filament yarn
5403 3390.20	非零售其他醋酸纤维单纱(5 转/米≤捻度≤250 转/米，包括变形纱线）	5	35		16	17	千克		Other single yarn of cellulose acetate, including textured filament yarn, 5 turns/m≤twist≤250 tums/m, not for retail sale
5403 3390.90	非零售其他醋酸纤维单纱（捻度超过 250 转/米，包括变形纱线）	5	35		16	17	千克		Other single yarn of cellulose acetate, including textured filament yarn, with a twist exceeding 250 turns/m, not for retail sale
5403.3900	--其他	5	35		16	17	千克		--Other
5403 3900.10	非零售其他人纤长丝单纱（单丝/未捻或捻度每米 5 转以下的复丝单纱，非供零售用，包括变形纱线）	5	35		16	17	千克		Other single yarn of artificial filaments, single filament /multi- filament single yarn, untwisted or with a twist not exceeding 5 turns per meter, not for retail sale, including textured filament yarn,
5403 3900.90	非零售其他人纤长丝单纱（捻度 5 转/米及以上，包括变形纱线）	5	35		16	17	千克		Other single yarn of artificial filaments, including textured filament yarn, with a twist exceeding 5 turns per meter, not for retail sale
	-其他纱线（多股纱线或缆线）:								-Other yarn, multiple （folded） or cabled:
5403.4100	--粘胶纤维纺制	5	35		16	17	千克		--Of viscose rayon
5403.4200	--醋酸纤维纺制	5	35		16	17	千克		--Of cellulose acetate
5403.4900	--其他	5	35		16	17	千克		--Other
54.04	**截面尺寸不超过 1 毫米，细度在 67 分特及以上的合成纤维单丝；表观宽度不超过 5 毫米的合成纤维纺织材料制扁条及类似品（例如，人造草）:**								**Synthetic monofilament of 67 decitex or more and of which no cross-sectional dimension exceeding 1mm; strip and the like （for example, artificial straw） of synthetic textile materials of an apparent width not exceeding 5mm:**
	-单丝:								-Monofilament:
5404.1100	--弹性单丝	5	80		16	17	千克		--Elastomeric
5404 1100.10	细度≥67 分特的涤纶纤维弹性单丝（截面尺寸不超过 1mm，细度＜67 分特的合纤单丝归入品目 54.02）	5	80		16	17	千克		Elastomeric monofilament of polyester of 67 decitex or more, of which no cross-sectional dimension exceeds 1mm, but of less than 67 decitex, classified under in No.54.02)
5404 1100.90	细度≥67 分特的其他合成纤维弹性单丝（截面尺寸不超过 1 mm，细度＜67 分特的合纤单丝归入品目 54.02）	5	80		16	17	千克		Other elastomeric synthetic monofilament of 67 decitex or more,(of which no cross-sectional dimension exceeds 1mm, but of less than 67 decitex, classified in No.54.02)
5404.1200	--其他，聚丙烯单丝	5	80		16	17	千克		--Other, of polypropylene
5404.1900	--其他	5	80		16	17	千克		--Other
5404 1900.10	细度≥67 分特的涤纶纤维单丝（截面尺寸不超过 1 mm，细度＜67 分特的合纤单丝归入品目 54.02）	5	80		16	17	千克		Monofilament of polyester of 67 decitex or more, of which no cross-sectional dimension exceeds 1mm, but of less than 67 decitex, classified in No.5402
5404 1900.90	细度≥67 分特的其他合成纤维单丝（截面尺寸不超过 1 mm，细度＜67 分特的合纤单丝归入品目 54.02）	5	80		16	17	千克		Other synthetic monofilament of 67 decitex or more, (of which no cross-sectional dimension exceeds 1mm, but of less than 67 decitex, classified in No.5402)
5404.9000	-其他	5	80		16	17	千克		-Other
54.05	**截面尺寸不超过 1 毫米，细度在 67 分特及以上的人造纤维单丝；表观宽度不超过 5 毫米的人造纤维纺织材料制扁条及类似品（例如，人造草）:**								**Artificial monofilament of 67 decitex or more and of which no cross-sectional dimension exceeds 1mm; strip and the like （for example, artificial straw） of artificial textile materials of an apparent width not exceeding 5 mm:**

税则号列 Tariff Item	商品名称及备注	进口税率			出口退税	增值税率	计量单位	监管条件	Article Description
		最惠	普通	暂定					
5405.0000	截面尺寸不超过1毫米，细度在67分特及以上的人造纤维单丝；表观宽度不超过5毫米的人造纤维纺织材料制扁条及类似品(例如，人造草)	5	80		16	17	千克		Artificial monofilament of 67 decitex or more and of which no cross-sectional dimension exceeds 1mm; strip and the like（for example, artificial straw）of artificial textile materials of an apparent width not exceeding 5 mm
54.06	**化学纤维长丝纱线（缝纫线除外），供零售用：**								**Man-made filament yarn (other than sewing thread) , put up for retail sale:**
5406.0010	---合成纤维长丝纱线	5	90		16	17	千克		---Synthetic filament yarn
5406.0020	---人造纤维长丝纱线	5	90		16	17	千克		---Artificial filament yarn
54.07	**合成纤维长丝纱线的机织物，包括品目54.04所列材料的机织物：**								**Woven fabrics of synthetic filament yarn, including woven fabrics obtained from materials of heading No. 54.04:**
	-尼龙或其他聚酰胺高强力纱、聚酯高强力纱纺制的机织物:								-Woven fabrics obtained from high tenacity yarn of nylon or other polyamides or of polyesters:
5407.1010	---尼龙或其他聚酰胺高强力纱纺制	10	130		16	17	米/千克	A	---Of nylon or other polyamides
5407.1020	---聚酯高强力纱纺制	10	130		16	17	米/千克		---Of polyesters
5407 1020.10	聚酯高强力纱纺制机织物（重量≤170克/平方米）	10	130		16	17	米/千克	A	Woven fabrics of high tenacity yarn of polyesters, weighing less than170g/m²
5407 1020.90	聚酯高强力纱纺制机织物（重量＞170克/平方米）	10	130		16	17	米/千克	A	Woven fabrics of high tenacity yarn of polyesters, weighing more than 170g/m²
5407.2000	-扁条及类似品的机织物	10	130		16	17	米/千克		-Woven fabrics obtained from strip or the like
5407 2000.10	聚乙烯聚丙烯扁条或类似机织物（宽度在3米以下）	10	130		16	17	米/千克		Woven fabrics of strip or the like of polyethylene or of polypropylene, of a width not exceeding 3m
5407 2000.90	其他合成纤维扁条及类似品机织物	10	130		16	17	米/千克		Other woven fabrics of strip or the like of synthetic fibre
5407.3000	-第十一类注释九所列的机织物	10	130		16	17	米/千克		-Fabrics specified in Note 9 to Section XI
5407 3000.10	平行纱线相互层迭并黏合织物（第十一类注释九所列的机织物，含塑料＞60%）	10	130		16	17	米/千克		Woven fabrics consisting of layers of parallel textile yarn stacked and glued, specified in Note 9 to Section XI, containing＞60% by weight of plastics
5407 3000.20	平行纱线相互层迭并黏合织物（第十一类注释九所列的机织物，含塑料≤60%）	10	130		16	17	米/千克		Woven fabrics consisting of layers of parallel textile yarn stacked and glued, specified in Note 9 to Section XI, containing≤60% by weight of plastics
	-其他机织物，按重量计尼龙或其他聚酰胺长丝含量在85%及以上:								-Other woven fabrics, containing 85% or more by weight of filaments of nylon or other polyamides:
5407.4100	--未漂白或漂白	10	130		16	17	米/千克		--Unbleached or bleached
5407 4100.10	未漂或漂白的打字机带用机织物（尼龙或其他聚酰胺长丝含量≥85%）	10	130		16	17	米/千克		Unbleached or bleached woven fabrics for typewriter ribbon, containing 85% or more by weight of filaments of nylon or of other polyamides
5407 4100.20	未漂白纯尼龙机织物（尼龙含量≥85%）	10	130		16	17	米/千克		Unbleached woven fabrics of nylon, containing 85% or more by weight of filaments of nylon
5407 4100.90	未漂白的或漂白的其他机织物（其他聚酰胺长丝含量≥85%）	10	130		16	17	米/千克		Other unbleached or bleached woven fabrics,containing 85% or more by weight of filaments of other polyamides
5407.4200	--染色	10	130		16	17	米/千克		--Dyed
5407.4300	--色织	10	130		16	17	米/千克		--Of yarns of different colours
5407.4400	--印花	10	130		16	17	米/千克		--Printed
	-其他机织物，按重量计聚酯变形长丝含量在85%及以上:								-Other woven fabrics, containing 85% or more by weight of textured polyester filaments:
5407.5100	--未漂白或漂白	10	130		16	17	米/千克		--Unbleached or bleached
5407 5100.10	未漂白或漂白纯聚酯变形长丝布（聚酯变形长丝含量≥85%，重量≤170克/平方米）	10	130		16	17	米/千克		Unbleached orbleached cloth of textured polyester filaments, containing 85% or more of textured polyester filaments, weighing less than 170g/m²
5407 5100.20	未漂白或漂白纯聚酯变形长丝机织物（聚酯变形长丝含量≥85%，重量大于170克/平方米）	10	130		16	17	米/千克		Unbleached or bleached woven fabrics of textured polyester filaments, containing 85% or more of textured polyester filaments, weighing more than 170g/m²,
5407.5200	--染色	10	130		16	17	米/千克		--Dyed

税则号列 Tariff Item	商品名称及备注	进口税率 最惠	普通	暂定	出口退税	增值税率	计量单位	监管条件	Article Description
5407 5200.10	染色的聚酯变形长丝布,含量≥85%(宽<77厘米,每厘米经纱密70~142根,纬密32~71根)	10	130		16	17	米/千克		Cloth of textured polyester filaments, containing 85% or more of textured polyester filaments, dyed, of a width less than 77cm, warp yarn 70-142/cm, weft yarn 32-71/cm
5407 5200.91	染色的其他聚酯变形长丝机织物(聚酯变形长丝含量≥85%,重量≤170克/平方米)	10	130		16	17	米/千克		Other dyed woven fabrics of textured polyester filaments, containing 85% or more of textured polyester filaments, weighing less than 170g/m²
5407 5200.92	染色的其他聚酯变形长丝机织物(聚酯变形长丝含量≥85%,重量>170克/平方米)	10	130		16	17	米/千克		Other dyed woven fabrics of textured polyester filaments, containing 85% or more of textured polyester filaments, weighing more than 170g/m²
5407.5300	--色织	10	130		16	17	米/千克		--Of yarns of different colours
5407 5300.10	色织的聚酯变形长丝布,含量≥85%(宽<77厘米,每厘米经纱密70~142根,纬密32~71根)	10	130		16	17	米/千克		Woven fabrics of textured polyester filaments, yarn-dyed, containing 85% or more of textured polyester filaments, of a width less than 77cm, warp yarn 70-142/cm, weft yarn 32-71/cm
5407 5300.91	色织的聚酯变形长丝机织物(聚酯变形长丝含量≥85%,重量≤170克/平方米)	10	130		16	17	米/千克		Woven fabrics of textured polyester filaments, yarn-dyed,containing 85% or more of textured polyester filaments, weighing less than 170g/m²
5407 5300.92	色织的聚酯变形长丝机织物(聚酯变形长丝含量≥85%,重量>170克/平方米)	10	130		16	17	米/千克		Woven fabrics of textured polyester filaments, yarn-dyed, containing 85% or more of textured polyester filaments, weighing more than 170g/m²
5407.5400	--印花	10	130		16	17	米/千克		--Printed
5407 5400.10	印花的聚酯变形长丝机织物(聚酯变形长丝含量≥85%,重量≤170克/平方米)	10	130		16	17	米/千克		Woven fabrics of textured polyester filaments, printed, containing 85% or more of textured polyester filaments, weighing 170g/m² or less
5407 5400.20	印花的聚酯变形长丝机织物(聚酯变形长丝含量≥85%,重量>170克/平方米)	10	130		16	17	米/千克		Woven fabrics of textured polyester filaments, printed, containing 85% or more of textured polyester filaments, weighing more than 170g/m²
	-其他机织物,按重量计聚酯长丝含量在85%及以上:								-Other woven fabrics, containing 85% or more by weight of polyester filaments:
5407.6100	--按重量计聚酯非变形长丝含量在85%及以上	10	130		16	17	米/千克		--Containing 85% or more by weight of non- textured polyester filaments
5407 6100.11	染色聚酯非变形长丝布,含量≥85%(宽<77厘米,每厘米经纱密70~142根,纬密32~71根)	10	130		16	17	米/千克		Dyed cloth of non-textured polyester filaments, containing 85% or more of non-textured polyester filaments, of a width less than 77cm, warp yarn 70-142/cm, weft yarn 32-71/cm
5407 6100.12	色织聚酯非变形长丝布,含量≥85%(宽<77厘米,每厘米经纱密70~142根,纬密32~71根)	10	130		16	17	米/千克		Cloth of non-textured polyester filaments, yarn- dyed, containing 85% or more of non-textured polyester filaments, of a width less than 77cm warp yarn 70-142/cm, weft yarn 31-71/cm
5407 6100.20	全聚酯其他非变形长丝机织物(单纱含27根丝,细度75~80分特,捻度900转及以上)	10	130		16	17	米/千克		Woven fabrics of non-textured polyester filaments, a single yarn with 27 threads, 75-80 decitex, with a twist exceeding 900 turns per meter
5407 6100.31	未漂白或漂白聚酯非变形长丝机织物(聚酯非变形长丝含量≥85%,重量>170克/平方米)	10	130		16	17	米/千克		Unbleached or bleached woven fabrics of non- textured polyester filaments, containing 85% or more of non-textured polyester filaments, weighing more than 170g/m²,
5407 6100.32	未漂白或漂白聚酯非变形长丝机织物(聚酯非变形长丝含量≥85%,重量≤170克/平方米)	10	130		16	17	米/千克		Unbleached or bleached woven fabrics of non-textured polyester filaments, containing 85% or more of non-textured polyester filaments, weighing 170g/m² or less
5407 6100.41	染色其他聚酯非变形长丝布(聚酯非变形长丝含量≥85%,重量>170克/平方米)	10	130		16	17	米/千克		Other dyed woven fabrics of nontextured polyester filaments, containing 85% or more of non-textured polyester filaments, weighing more than170g/m²,
5407 6100.42	染色其他纯聚酯非变形长丝布(聚酯非变形长丝含量≥85%,重量≤170克/平方米)	10	130		16	17	米/千克		Other dyed cloth of non-textured pure polyester filaments, containing 85% or more of non-textured polyester filaments, weighing 170g/m²or less
5407 6100.51	色织其他聚酯非变形长丝布(聚	10	130		16	17	米/千克		Other yarn-dyed cloth of non-textured polyester

税则号列 Tariff Item	商品名称及备注	进口税率			出口退税	增值税率	计量单位	监管条件	Article Description
		最惠	普通	暂定					
	酯非变形长丝含量≥85%，重量>170克/平方米）								filaments, containing 85% or more of non-textured polyester filaments, weighing more than 170g/m²
5407 6100.52	色织其他聚酯非变形长丝布（聚酯非变形长丝含量≥85%，重量≤170克/平方米）	10	130		16	17	米/千克		Other yarn-dyed cloth of non-textured polyester filaments, containing 85% or more of non-textured polyester filaments, weighing 170g/m² or less
5407 6100.61	印花其他聚酯非变形长丝布（聚酯非变形长丝含量≥85%，重量>170克/平方米）	10	130		16	17	米/千克		Other printed cloth of nontextured polyester filaments, containing 85% or more of non-textured polyester filaments, weighing more than 170g/m²
5407 6100.62	印花其他聚酯非变形长丝布（聚酯非变形长丝含量≥85%，重量≤170克/平方米）	10	130		16	17	米/千克		Other printed cloth of nontextured polyester filaments, containing 85% or more of non-textured polyester filaments, weighing 170g/m² or less
5407.6900	--其他	10	130		16	17	米/千克		--Other
5407 6900.11	未漂白或漂白其他聚酯长丝布（聚酯长丝含量≥85%，重量>170克/平方米）	10	130		16	17	米/千克		Other unbleached or bleached cloth of polyester filaments, containing 85% or more of polyester filaments, weighing more than170g/m²,
5407 6900.12	未漂白或漂白其他聚酯长丝布（聚酯长丝含量≥85%，重量≤170克/平方米）	10	130		16	17	米/千克		Other unbleached or bleached cloth of polyester filaments, containing 85% or more of polyester filaments, weighing 170g/m² or less
5407 6900.21	染色其他聚酯长丝布（聚酯长丝含量≥85%，重量>170克/平方米）	10	130		16	17	米/千克		Other dyed cloth of polyester filaments, containing 85% or more of polyester filaments, weighing more than 170g/m²,
5407 6900.22	染色其他聚酯长丝布（聚酯长丝含量≥85%，重量≤170克/平方米）	10	130		16	17	米/千克		Other dyed cloth of polyester filaments, containing 85% or more of polyester filaments, weighing 170g/m² or less
5407 6900.31	色织其他聚酯长丝布，含量≥85%（每厘米经纱密70～142根，纬密32～71根）	10	130		16	17	米/千克		Other yarn-dyed cloth of polyester filaments, containing 85% or more of polyester filaments, warp yarn 70-142/cm, weft yarn 32-71/cm
5407 6900.32	色织其他聚酯长丝布（聚酯长丝含量≥85%，重量>170克/平方米）	10	130		16	17	米/千克		Other yarn-dyed cloth of polyester filaments, containing 85% or more of polyester filaments, weighing more than 170g/m²,
5407 6900.33	色织其他聚酯长丝布（聚酯长丝含量≥85%，重量≤170克/平方米）	10	130		16	17	米/千克		Other yarn-dyed cloth of polyester filaments, containing 85% or more of polyester filaments, weighing 170g/m² or less
5407 6900.41	印花其他聚酯长丝布（聚酯长丝含量≥85%，重量>170克/平方米）	10	130		16	17	米/千克		Other printed cloth of polyester filaments, containing 85% or more of polyester filaments, weighing more than 170g/m²,
5407 6900.42	印花其他聚酯长丝布（聚酯长丝含量≥85%，重量≤170克/平方米）	10	130		16	17	米/千克		Other printed cloth of polyester filaments, containing 85% or more of polyester filaments, weighing 170g/m² or less
	-其他机织物，按重量计其他合成纤维长丝含量在85%及以上：								-Other woven fabrics, containing 85% or more by weight of synthetic filaments:
5407.7100	--未漂白或漂白	10	130		16	17	米/千克		--Unbleached or bleached
5407.7200	--染色	10	130		16	17	米/千克		--Dyed
5407.7300	--色织	10	130		16	17	米/千克		--Of yarns of different colours
5407.7400	--印花	10	130		16	17	米/千克		--Printed
	-其他机织物，按重量计其他合成纤维长丝含量在85%以下，主要或仅与棉混纺：								-Other woven fabrics, containing less than 85% by weight of synthetic filaments, mixed mainly or solely with cotton:
5407.8100	--未漂白或漂白	10	130		16	17	米/千克		--Unbleached or bleached
5407 8100.10	未漂白或漂白与棉混纺府绸及细平布（其他合成纤维长丝含量在85%以下）	10	130		16	17	米/千克		Unbleached or bleached poplin and fine plain cloth, mixed with cotton, containing less than 85% of synthetic filaments
5407 8100.20	未漂白或漂白的与棉混纺平布（其他合成纤维长丝含量在85%以下）	10	130		16	17	米/千克		Unbleached or bleached plain cloth, mixed with cotton, containing less than 85% of synthetic filaments
5407 8100.30	未漂或漂白的与棉混纺印染用	10	130		16	17	米/千克		Unbleached or bleached cloth for printing and dyeing,

税则号列 Tariff Item	商品名称及备注	进口税率 最惠	进口税率 普通	进口税率 暂定	出口退税	增值税率	计量单位	监管条件	Article Description
	布(混纺合纤布指按重量计其他合成纤维长丝含量在85%以下)								mixed with cotton, containing less than 85% of synthetic filaments
5407 8100.40	未漂白或漂白与棉混纺缎纹或斜纹布(混纺合纤布指按重量计其他合成纤维长丝含量在85%以下)	10	130		16	17	米/千克		Unbleached or bleached satin cloth or twill cloth, mixed with cotton, containing less than 85% of synthetic filaments
5407 8100.90	未漂白或漂白与棉混纺其他合纤布(混纺合纤布指按重量计其他合成纤维长丝含量在85%以下)	10	130		16	17	米/千克		Other unbleached or bleached cloth of synthetic filaments, mixed with cotton, containing less than 85% of synthetic filaments
5407.8200	--染色	10	130		16	17	米/千克		--Dyed
5407 8200.10	染色的与棉混纺府绸及细平布(混纺合纤布指按重量计其他合成纤维长丝含量在85%以下)	10	130		16	17	米/千克		Dyed poplin and fine plain cloth, mixed with cotton (cloth of synthetic filaments refers to containing less than 85% by weight of other synthetic filaments)
5407 8200.20	染色的与棉混纺平布(混纺合纤布指按重量计其他合成纤维长丝含量在85%以下)	10	130		16	17	米/千克		Dyed plain cloth, mixed with cotton (cloth of synthetic filaments refers to containing less than 85% by weight of other synthetic filaments)
5407 8200.30	染色的与棉混纺印染用布(混纺合纤布指按重量计其他合成纤维长丝含量在85%以下)	10	130		16	17	米/千克		Dyed cloth for printing and dyeing, mixed with cotton (cloth of synthetic filaments refers to containing less than 85% by weight of other synthetic filaments)
5407 8200.40	染色的与棉混纺缎纹或斜纹布(混纺合纤布指按重量计其他合成纤维长丝含量在85%以下)	10	130		16	17	米/千克		Dyed satin cloth or twill cloth, mixed with cotton (cloth of synthetic filaments refers to containing less than 85% by weight of other synthetic filaments)
5407 8200.90	染色的与棉混纺其他合成纤维布(混纺合纤布指按重量计其他合成纤维长丝含量在85%以下)	10	130		16	17	米/千克		Dyed cloth of synthetic filaments, mixed with cotton (cloth of synthetic filaments refers to containing less than 85% by weight of other synthetic filaments)
5407.8300	--色织	10	130		16	17	米/千克		--Of yarns of different colours
5407 8300.10	色织的与棉混纺府绸及细平布(混纺合纤布指按重量计其他合成纤维长丝含量在85%以下)	10	130		16	17	米/千克		Poplin and fine plain cloth of yarns of different colours, mixed with cotton (cloth of synthetic filaments refers to containing less than 85% by weight of other synthetic filaments)
5407 8300.20	色织的与棉混纺平布(混纺合纤布指按重量计其他合成纤维长丝含量在85%以下)	10	130		16	17	米/千克		Plain cloth of yarns of different colours, mixed with cotton (cloth of synthetic filaments refers to containing less than 85% by weight of other synthetic filaments)
5407 8300.30	色织的与棉混纺印染用布(混纺合纤布指按重量计其他合成纤维长丝含量在85%以下)	10	130		16	17	米/千克		Cloth for printing and dyeing of yarns of different colours, mixed with cotton (cloth of synthetic filaments refers to containing less than 85% by weight of other synthetic filaments)
5407 8300.40	色织的与棉混纺缎纹或斜纹布(混纺合纤布指按重量计其他合成纤维长丝含量在85%以下)	10	130		16	17	米/千克		Satin cloth or twill cloth of yarns of different colours, mixed with cotton (cloth of synthetic filaments refers to containing less than 85% by weight of other synthetic filaments)
5407 8300.90	色织的与棉混纺其他合成纤维布(混纺合纤布指按重量计其他合成纤维长丝含量在85%以下)	10	130		16	17	米/千克		Cloth of synthetic filaments of yarns of different colours, mixed with cotton (cloth of synthetic filaments refers to containing less than 85% by weight of other synthetic filaments)
5407.8400	--印花	10	130		16	17	米/千克		--Printed
5407 8400.10	印花的与棉混纺府绸及细平布(混纺合纤布指按重量计其他合成纤维长丝含量在85%以下)	10	130		16	17	米/千克		Printed poplin and fine plain cloth, mixed with cotton (cloth of synthetic filaments refers to containing less than 85% by weight of other synthetic filaments)
5407 8400.30	印花的与棉混纺印染用布(混纺合纤布指按重量计其他合成纤维长丝含量在85%以下)	10	130		16	17	米/千克		Printed cloth for printing and dyeing, mixed with cotton (cloth of synthetic filaments refers to containing less than 85% by weight of other synthetic filaments)
5407 8400.90	印花的与棉混纺其他合成纤维布(混纺合纤布指按重量计其他合成纤维长丝含量在85%以下)	10	130		16	17	米/千克		Printed cloth of synthetic filaments, mixed with cotton (cloth of synthetic filaments refers to containing less than 85% by weight of other synthetic filaments)
	-其他机织物:								-Other woven fabrics:
5407.9100	--未漂白或漂白	10	130		16	17	米/千克		--Unbleached or bleached
5407 9100.11	未漂白或漂白的其他混纺合成	10	130		16	17	米/千克		Other unbleached or bleached cloth of synthetic

税则号列 Tariff Item	商品名称及备注	进口税率 最惠	普通	暂定	出口退税	增值税率	计量单位	监管条件	Article Description
	纤维布（与精梳羊毛或动物细毛≥36%混纺，合纤＜85%）								fibres, mixed, containing 36% or more of combed wool or fine animal hair, and less than 85% of synthetic fibres,
5407 9100.19	未漂白或漂白的其他混纺合成纤维布（合纤含量在85%以下，与其他羊毛或动物细毛36%及以上混纺）	10	130		16	17	米/千克		Other unbleached or bleached cloth of synthetic fibres, mixed, containing 36% or more of wool or fine animal hair, and less than 85% of synthetic fibres
5407 9100.21	未漂白或漂白的其他混纺合成纤维布（与精梳羊毛或动物细毛＜36%混纺，合纤＜85%）	10	130		16	17	米/千克		Other unbleached or bleached cloth of synthetic fibres, mixed, containing less than 36% of combed wool or fine animal hair, and less than 85% of synthetic fibres
5407 9100.29	未漂白或漂白的其他混纺合成纤维布（与其他羊毛或动物细毛＜36%混纺，合纤＜85%）	10	130		16	17	米/千克		Other unbleached or bleached cloth of synthetic fibres, mixed, containing less than 36% of other wool or fine animal hair, and less than 85% of synthetic fibres
5407 9100.30	未漂白或漂白的其他混纺合成纤维布（与人造纤维长丝混纺，合纤含量＜85%）	10	130		16	17	米/千克		Other unbleached or bleached cloth of synthetic fibres,, mixed with artificial filaments, containing less than 85% of synthetic filaments
5407 9100.91	未漂白或漂其他混纺府绸及细平布（合成纤维长丝含量在85%以下，与其他纤维混纺）	10	130		16	17	米/千克		Other unbleached or bleached poplin and fine plain cloth, mixed with other fibres, containing less than 85% of synthetic filaments
5407 9100.92	未漂白或漂白的其他混纺平布（合成纤维长丝含量在85%以下，与其他纤维混纺）	10	130		16	17	米/千克		Other unbleached or bleached plain cloth, mixed with other fibres, containing less than 85% of synthetic filaments
5407 9100.93	未漂白或漂白的其他混纺印染用布（合成纤维长丝含量在85%以下，与其他纤维混纺）	10	130		16	17	米/千克		Other unbleached or bleached cloth for printing and dyeing, mixed with other fibres, containing less than 85% of synthetic filaments
5407 9100.94	未漂白或漂其他混纺缎纹或斜纹布（合成纤维长丝含量在85%以下，与其他纤维混纺）	10	130		16	17	米/千克		Other unbleached or bleached satin or twill cloth, mixed with other fibres, containing less than 85% by weight of synthetic filaments,
5407 9100.99	未漂白或漂白的其他混纺合成纤维布（合成纤维长丝含量在85%以下，与其他纤维混纺）	10	130		16	17	米/千克		Other unbleached or bleached cloth of synthetic fibres , mixed with other fibres, containing less than 85% of synthetic filaments
5407.9200	--染色	10	130		16	17	米/千克		--Dyed
5407 9200.11	染色的其他混纺合成纤维布（与精梳羊毛或动物细毛≥36%混纺，合纤＜85%）	10	130		16	17	米/千克		Other dyed cloth of synthetic fibres, mixed, containing 36% or more of combed wool or fine animal hair, and less than 85% of synthetic fibres
5407 9200.19	染色的其他混纺合成纤维布（与其他羊毛或动物细毛≥36%混纺，合纤＜85%）	10	130		16	17	米/千克		Other dyed cloth of synthetic fibres, mixed, containing 36% or more of wool or fine animal hair, and less than 85% of synthetic fibres
5407 9200.21	染色的其他混纺合成纤维布（与精梳羊毛或动物细毛＜36%混纺，合纤＜85%）	10	130		16	17	米/千克		Other dyed cloth of synthetic fibres, mixed, containing less than 36% of combed wool or fine animal hair, and less than 85% of synthetic fibres
5407 9200.29	染色的其他混纺合成纤维布（与其他羊毛或动物细毛＜36%混纺，合纤＜85%）	10	130		16	17	米/千克		Other dyed cloth of synthetic fibres, mixed, containing less than 36% of wool or fine animal hair, and less than 85% of synthetic fibres
5407 9200.30	染色的其他混纺合成纤维布（与人造纤维长丝或含金属纱线混纺，合纤含量在85%以下）	10	130		16	17	米/千克		Other dyed cloth of synthetic fibres, mixed with artificial filaments or metallic yarn, containing less than 85% of synthetic fibres
5407 9200.91	染色的其他混纺府绸及细平布（合成纤维长丝含量在85%以下，与其他纤维混纺）	10	130		16	17	米/千克		Other dyed poplin and fine plain cloth, mixed with other fibres, containing less than 85% by weight of synthetic filaments
5407 9200.92	染色的其他混纺平布（合成纤维长丝含量在85%以下，与其他纤维混纺）	10	130		16	17	米/千克		Other dyed plain cloth, mixed with other fibres, containing less than 85% by weight of synthetic filaments
5407 9200.93	染色的其他混纺印染用布（合成纤维长丝含量在85%以下，与其	10	130		16	17	米/千克		Other dyed plain cloth for printing and dyeing, mixed with other fibres, containing less than 85% of synthetic

税则号列 Tariff Item	商品名称及备注	进口税率 最惠	进口税率 普通	进口税率 暂定	出口退税	增值税率	计量单位	监管条件	Article Description
	他纤维混纺）								filaments
5407 9200.94	染色的其他混纺缎纹或斜纹布（合成纤维长丝含量在85%以下，与其他纤维混纺）	10	130		16	17	米/千克		Other dyed satin or twill cloth, mixed with other fibres, containing less than 85% of synthetic filaments
5407 9200.99	染色的其他混纺合成纤维布（合成纤维长丝含量在85%以下，与其他纤维混纺）	10	130		16	17	米/千克		Other dyed cloth of synthetic fibres, mixed with other fibres, containing less than 85% by weight of synthetic filaments
5407.9300	--色织	10	130		16	17	米/千克		--Of yarns of different colours
5407 9300.11	色织的其他混纺合成纤维布（与精梳羊毛或动物细毛≥36%混纺，合纤＜85%）	10	130		16	17	米/千克		Other cloth of synthetic fibres, mixed, yarn-dyed, containing 36% or more of combed wool or fine animal hair, and less than 85% of synthetic fibres
5407 9300.19	色织的其他混纺合成纤维布（与其他羊毛或动物细毛≥36%混纺，合纤＜85%）	10	130		16	17	米/千克		Other cloth of synthetic fibres, mixed, yarn-dyed, containing 36% or more of wool or fine animal hair, containing less than 85% of synthetic fibres
5407 9300.21	色织的其他混纺合成纤维布（与精梳羊毛或动物细毛＜36%混纺，合纤＜85%）	10	130		16	17	米/千克		Other cloth of synthetic fibres, mixed, yarn-dyed, containing less than 36% of combed wool or fine animal hair, and less than 85% of synthetic fibres
5407 9300.29	色织的其他混纺合成纤维布（与其他羊毛或动物细毛＜36%混纺，合纤＜85%）	10	130		16	17	米/千克		Other cloth of synthetic fibres, mixed, yarn-dyed, containing less than 36% of wool or fine animal hair, containing less than 85% of synthetic fibres
5407 9300.30	色织其他混纺合纤布，合纤<85%（含化纤长丝≥85%，每厘米经密70～142根，纬密32～71根）	10	130		16	17	米/千克		Other cloth of synthetic fibres, mixed, yarn-dyed, containing less than 85% of synthetic fibres (containing 85% or more of chemical filament fiber warp yarn 70-142/cm, weft yarn 32-71/cm)
5407 9300.40	色织的其他混纺合成纤维布（与人造纤维长丝或含金属纱线混纺，合纤长丝含量＜85%）	10	130		16	17	米/千克		Other cloth of synthetic fibres, yarn-dyed, mixed with artificial filaments or metallic yarn, containing less than 85% of synthetic fibres
5407 9300.91	色织的其他混纺府绸及细平布（合成纤维长丝含量在85%以下，与其他纤维混纺）	10	130		16	17	米/千克		Other yarn-dyed poplin and fine plain cloth, mixed with other fibres, containing less than 85% by weight of synthetic filaments
5407 9300.92	色织的其他混纺平布（合成纤维长丝含量在85%以下，与其他纤维混纺）	10	130		16	17	米/千克		Other yarn-dyed plain cloth, mixed with other fibres, containing less than 85% by weight of synthetic filaments
5407 9300.93	色织的其他混纺印染用布（合成纤维长丝含量在85%以下，与其他纤维混纺）	10	130		16	17	米/千克		Other yarn-dyed plain cloth for printing and dyeing, mixed with other fibres, containing less than 85% of synthetic filaments
5407 9300.94	色织的其他混纺缎纹或斜纹布（合成纤维长丝含量在85%以下，与其他纤维混纺）	10	130		16	17	米/千克		Other yarn-dyed satin or twill cloth, mixed with other fibres, containing less than 85% of synthetic filaments
5407 9300.99	色织的其他混纺合成纤维布（合成纤维长丝含量在85%以下，与其他纤维混纺）	10	130		16	17	米/千克		Other yarn-dyed cloth of synthetic fibres, mixed with other fibres, containing less than 85% by weight of synthetic filaments
5407.9400	--印花	10	130		16	17	米/千克		--Printed
5407 9400.10	印花的其他混纺合成纤维布(与羊毛或动物细毛≥36%混纺，合纤<85%)	10	130		16	17	米/千克		Other printed cloth of synthetic fibres, mixed, containing 36% or more of wool or fine animal hair, and less than 85% of synthetic fibres
5407 9400.20	印花的其他混纺合成纤维布(与羊毛或动物细毛<36%混纺，合纤<85%)	10	130		16	17	米/千克		Other printed cloth of synthetic fibres, mixed, containing less than 36% of wool or fine animal hair, and less than 85% of synthetic fibres
5407 9400.30	印花的其他混纺合成纤维布（与人造纤维长丝或含金属纱线混纺，合纤＜85%）	10	130		16	17	米/千克		Other printed cloth of synthetic fibres, mixed with artificial filaments or metallic yarn, containing less than 85% of synthetic fibres
5407 9400.91	印花的其他混纺府绸及细平布（合成纤维长丝含量在85%以下，与其他纤维混纺）	10	130		16	17	米/千克		Other printed poplin and fine plain cloth, mixed with other fibres, containing less than 85% by weight of synthetic filaments
5407 9400.92	印花的其他混纺平布（合成纤维长丝含量在85%以下，与其他纤	10	130		16	17	米/千克		Other printed plain cloth, mixed with other fibres, containing less than 85% by weight of synthetic

税则号列 Tariff Item	商品名称及备注	进口税率 最惠	普通	暂定	出口退税	增值税率	计量单位	监管条件	Article Description
	维混纺)								filaments
5407 9400.93	印花的其他混纺印染用布(合成纤维长丝含量在85%以下，与其他纤维混纺)	10	130		16	17	米/千克		Other printed plain cloth for printing and dyeing, mixed with other fibres, containing less than 85% of synthetic filaments
5407 9400.94	印花的其他混纺缎纹或斜纹布(合成纤维长丝含量在85%以下，与其他纤维混纺)	10	130		16	17	米/千克		Other printed satin or twill cloth, mixed with other fibres, containing less than 85% of synthetic filaments
5407 9400.99	印花的其他混纺合成纤维布(合成纤维长丝含量在85%以下，与其他纤维混纺)	10	130		16	17	米/千克		Other printed cloth of synthetic fibres, mixed with other fibres, containing less than 85% by weight of synthetic filaments
54.08	**人造纤维长丝纱线的机织物，包括品目54.05所列材料的机织物:**								**Woven fabrics of artificial filament yarn, including woven fabrics obtained from materials of heading No.54.05:**
5408.1000	-粘胶纤维高强力纱的机织物	10	130		16	17	米/千克		-Woven fabrics obtained from high tenacity yarn of viscose rayon
	-其他机织物，按重量计人造纤维长丝、扁条或类似品含量在85%及以上:								-Other woven fabrics, containing 85% or more by weight of artificial filament or strip or the like:
	--未漂白或漂白:								--Unbleached or bleached:
5408.2110	---粘胶长丝制	12	130		16	17	米/千克		---Of yarns of viscose rayon
5408.2120	---醋纤长丝制	12	130		16	17	米/千克		---Of yarns of cellulose acetate
5408.2190	---其他	12	130		16	17	米/千克		---Other
	--染色:								--Dyed:
5408.2210	---粘胶长丝制	10	130		16	17	米/千克		---Of yarns of viscose rayon
5408.2220	---醋纤长丝制	10	130		16	17	米/千克		---Of yarns of cellulose acetate
5408.2290	---其他	10	130		16	17	米/千克		---Other
	--色织:								--Of yarns of different colours:
5408.2310	---粘胶长丝制	10	130		16	17	米/千克		--Of yarns of viscose rayon
5408.2320	---醋纤长丝制	10	130		16	17	米/千克		---Of yarns of cellulose acetate
5408.2390	---其他	10	130		16	17	米/千克		---Other
	--印花:								--Printed:
5408.2410	---粘胶长丝制	10	130		16	17	米/千克		---Of yarns of viscose rayon
5408.2420	---醋纤长丝制	10	130		16	17	米/千克		---Of yarns of cellulose acetate
5408.2490	---其他	10	130		16	17	米/千克		---Other
	-其他机织物:								-Other woven fabrics:
5408.3100	--未漂白或漂白	10	130		16	17	米/千克		--Unbleached or bleached
5408 3100.11	未漂白或漂白人纤长丝机织物(与精梳羊毛或动物细毛≥36%混纺，人纤<85%)	10	130		16	17	米/千克		Unbleached or bleached woven fabrics of artificial filaments, mixed with, containing 36% or more of combed wool or fine animal hair, and less than 85% of artificial fibres
5408 3100.19	未漂白或漂白人纤长丝机织物(与其他羊毛或动物细毛≥36%混纺，人纤<85%)	10	130		16	17	米/千克		Unbleached or bleached woven fabrics of artificial filaments, mixed with,containing 36% or more of wool or fine animal hair, and less than 85% of artificial fibres
5408 3100.21	未漂白或漂白人纤长丝机织物(与精梳羊毛或动物细毛<36%混纺，人纤<85%)	10	130		16	17	米/千克		Unbleached or bleached woven fabrics of artificial filaments, mixed with, containing less than 36% of combed wool or fine animal hair, and less than 85% of artificial fibres
5408 3100.29	未漂白或漂白人纤长丝机织物(与其他羊毛或动物细毛<36%混纺，人纤<85%)	10	130		16	17	米/千克		Unbleached or bleached woven fabrics of artificial filaments, mixed with,containing less than 36% of wool or fine animal hair, and less than 85% of artificial fibres
5408 3100.30	未漂白或漂白人纤长丝机织物(与人纤长丝混纺，人纤长丝含量在85%以下)	10	130		16	17	米/千克		Unbleached or bleached woven fabrics of artificial filaments, mixed with artificial filament, containing less than 85% of artificial filaments
5408 3100.91	未漂白或漂白人纤长丝府绸及细平布(混纺布指按重量计人纤	10	130		16	17	米/千克		Unbleached or bleached poplin and fine plain cloth of artificial filaments (Mixed cloth refers to containing

税则号列 Tariff Item	商品名称及备注	进口税率 最惠	普通	暂定	出口退税	增值税率	计量单位	监管条件	Article Description
	长丝、扁条或类似品含量在85%以下)								less than 85% by weight of artificial filament or strip or the like)
5408 3100.92	未漂白或漂白人纤长丝平布(混纺布指按重量计人纤长丝、扁条或类似品含量在85%以下)	10	130		16	17	米/千克		Unbleached or bleached plain cloth of artificial filaments (Mixed cloth refers to containing less than 85% by weight of artificial filament or strip or the like)
5408 3100.93	未漂白或漂白人纤长丝印染用布(混纺布指按重量计人纤长丝、扁条或类似品含量在85%以下)	10	130		16	17	米/千克		Unbleached or bleached cloth of artificial filaments for printing and dyeing (Mixed cloth refers to containing less than 85% by weight of artificial filament or strip or the like)
5408 3100.94	未漂白或漂白人纤长丝缎纹或斜纹布(混纺布指按重量计人纤长丝、扁条或类似品含量在85%以下)	10	130		16	17	米/千克		Unbleached or bleached satin or twill cloth of artificial filaments (Mixed cloth refers to containing less than 85% by weight of artificial filament or strip or the like)
5408 3100.99	未漂白或漂白人纤长丝其他混纺布(混纺布指按重量计人纤长丝、扁条或类似品含量在85%以下)	10	130		16	17	米/千克		Other unbleached or bleached mixed cloth of artificial filaments (Mixed cloth refers to containing less than 85% by weight of artificial filament or strip or the like)
5408.3200	--染色	10	130		16	17	米/千克		--Dyed
5408 3200.11	染色的人纤长丝机织物(与精梳羊毛或动物细毛≥36%混纺,人纤<85%)	10	130		16	17	米/千克		Dyed woven fabrics of artificial filaments, mixed with, containing 36% or more of combed wool or fine animal hair, and less than 85% of artificial fibres
5408 3200.19	染色的人纤长丝机织物(与其他羊毛或动物细毛≥36%混纺,人纤<85%)	10	130		16	17	米/千克		Dyed woven fabrics of artificial filaments, mixed with,containing 36% or more of wool or fine animal hair, and less than 85% of artificial fibres
5408 3200.21	染色的人纤长丝机织物(与精梳羊毛或动物细毛<36%混纺,人纤<85%)	10	130		16	17	米/千克		Dyed woven fabrics of artificial filaments, mixed with, containing less than 36% of combed wool or fine animal hair, and less than 85% of artificial fibres
5408 3200.29	染色的人纤长丝机织物(与其他羊毛或动物细毛<36%混纺,人纤<85%)	10	130		16	17	米/千克		Dyed woven fabrics of artificial filaments, mixed with,containing less than 36% of wool or fine animal hair, and less than 85% of synthetic fibres
5408 3200.30	染色的人纤长丝机织物(含丝及绢丝30%及以上,每千克价值超过$33,人纤<85%)	10	130		16	17	米/千克		Dyed woven fabrics of artificial filaments, containing 30% or more of silk or silk waste, of a value exceeding $33/kg, containing less than 85% of artificial fibres
5408 3200.40	染色的人纤长丝机织物(与合纤长丝混纺,人纤长丝、扁条或类似品含量在85%以下)	10	130		16	17	米/千克		Dyed woven fabrics of artificial filaments,, mixed with synthetic filament, containing less than 85% by weight of artificial filament or strip or the like
5408 3200.91	染色的人纤长丝府绸或细平布(混纺布指按重量计人纤长丝、扁条或类似品含量在85%以下)	10	130		16	17	米/千克		Dyed poplin and fine plain cloth of artificial filaments (Mixed cloth refers to containing less than 85% by weight of artificial filament or strip or the like)
5408 3200.92	染色的人纤长丝平布(混纺布指按重量计人纤长丝、扁条或类似品含量在85%以下)	10	130		16	17	米/千克		Dyed plain cloth of artificial filaments (Mixed cloth refers to containing less than 85% by weight of artificial filament or strip or the like)
5408 3200.93	染色的人纤长丝印染用布(混纺布指按重量计人纤长丝、扁条或类似品含量在85%以下)	10	130		16	17	米/千克		Dyed cloth of artificial filaments for printing and dyeing (Mixed cloth refers to containing less than 85% by weight of artificial filament or strip or the like)
5408 3200.99	染色的人纤长丝其他机织物(混纺布指按重量计人纤长丝、扁条或类似品含量在85%以下)	10	130		16	17	米/千克		Other dyed woven fabrics of artificial filaments (Mixed cloth refers to containing less than 85% by weight of artificial filament or strip or the like)
5408.3300	--色织	10	130		16	17	米/千克		--Of yarns of different colours
5408 3300.11	色织的人纤长丝机织物(与精梳羊毛或动物细毛≥36%混纺,人纤<85%)	10	130		16	17	米/千克		Yarn-dyed woven fabrics of artificial filaments, mixed with, containing 36% or more of combed wool or fine animal hair, and less than 85% of artificial fibres
5408 3300.19	色织的人纤长丝机织物(与其他羊毛或动物细毛≥36%混纺,人纤<85%)	10	130		16	17	米/千克		Yarn-dyed woven fabrics of artificial filaments, mixed with,containing 36% or more of wool or fine animal hair, and less than 85% of artificial fibres
5408 3300.21	色织的人纤长丝机织物(与精梳	10	130		16	17	米/千克		Yarn-dyed woven fabrics of artificial filaments, mixed

税则号列 Tariff Item	商品名称及备注	进口税率 最惠	普通	暂定	出口退税	增值税率	计量单位	监管条件	Article Description
	羊毛或动物细毛<36%混纺，人纤<85%)								with, containing less than 36% of combed wool or fine animal hair, and less than 85% of artificial fibres
5408 3300.29	色织的人纤长丝机织物（与其他羊毛或动物细毛<36%混纺，人纤<35%）	10	130		16	17	米/千克		Yarn-dyed woven fabrics of artificial filaments, mixed with,containing less than 36% of wool or fine animal hair, and less than 85% of synthetic fibres
5408 3300.30	色织的人纤长丝机织物,人纤<85%（含化纤长丝≥85%，每厘米经密70~142根,纬密32~71根）	10	130		16	17	米/千克		Yarn-dyed woven fabrics of artificial filaments, containing less than 85% of artificial filaments (containing 85% or more of chemical filament fiber warp yarn 70-142/cm, weft yarn 32-71/cm)
5408 3300.40	色织的人纤长丝机织物（含丝及绢丝30%及以上，每千克价值超过$33，人纤<85%）	10	130		16	17	米/千克		Yarn-dyed woven fabrics of artificial filaments, containing 30% or more of silk or silk waste, of a value exceeding $33/kg, containing less than 85% of artificial fibres
5408 3300.50	色织的人纤长丝机织物（与合纤长丝混纺，人纤长丝、扁条或类似品含量在85%以下）	10	130		16	17	米/千克		Yarn-dyed woven fabrics of artificial filaments, mixed with synthetic filament, containing less than 85% of artificial filament or strip or the like
5408 3300.92	色织的人纤长丝平布（混纺布指按重量计人纤长丝、扁条或类似品含量在85%以下）	10	130		16	17	米/千克		Yarn-dyed plain cloth of artificial filaments (Mixed cloth refers to containing less than 85% by weight of artificial filament or strip or the like)
5408 3300.94	色织的人纤长丝缎纹或斜纹布（混纺布指按重量计人纤长丝、扁条或类似品含量在85%以下）	10	130		16	17	米/千克		Yarn-dyed satin or twill cloth of artificial filaments (Mixed cloth refers to containing less than 85% by weight of artificial filament or strip or the like)
5408 3300.99	色织的人纤长丝其他机织物（混纺布指按重量计人纤长丝、扁条或类似品含量在85%以下）	10	130		16	17	米/千克		Other yarn-dyed woven fabrics of artificial filaments (Mixed cloth refers to containing less than 85% by weight of artificial filament or strip or the like)
5408.3400	--印花	10	130		16	17	米/千克		--Printed
5408 3400.10	印花的人纤长丝机织物(与羊毛或动物细毛≥36%混纺,人纤<85%)	10	130		16	17	米/千克		Printed woven fabrics of artificial filaments, mixed with, containing 36% or more of wool or fine animal hair, and less than 85% of artificial fibres
5408 3400.20	印花的人纤长丝机织物(与羊毛或动物细毛<36%混纺,人纤<85%)	10	130		16	17	米/千克		Printed woven fabrics of artificial filaments, mixed with, containing less than 36% of wool or fine animal hair, and less than 85% of artificial fibres
5408 3400.30	印花的人纤长丝机织物（含丝及绢丝30%及以上，每千克超过$33，人纤<85%）	10	130		16	17	米/千克		Printed woven fabrics of artificial filaments, containing 30% or more of silk or silk waste, of a value exceeding $33/kg, containing less than 85% of artificial fibres
5408 3400.40	印花的人纤长丝机织物（与合纤长丝混纺，人纤长丝、扁条或类似品含量在85%以下）	10	130		16	17	米/千克		Printed woven fabrics of artificial filaments, mixed with synthetic filament, containing less than 85% of artificial filament or strip or the like
5408 3400.91	印花的人纤长丝府绸或细平布（混纺布指按重量计人纤长丝、扁条或类似品含量在85%以下）	10	130		16	17	米/千克		Printed poplin and fine plain cloth of artificial filaments (Mixed cloth refers to containing less than 85% by weight of artificial filament or strip or the like)
5408 3400.92	印花的人纤长丝平布（混纺布指按重量计人纤长丝、扁条或类似品含量在85%以下）	10	130		16	17	米/千克		Printed plain cloth of artificial filaments (Mixed cloth refers to containing less than 85% by weight of artificial filament or strip or the like)
5408 3400.93	印花的人纤长丝印染用布（混纺布指按重量计人纤长丝、扁条或类似品含量在85%以下）	10	130		16	17	米/千克		Printed cloth of artificial filaments for printing and dyeing (Mixed cloth refers to containing less than 85% by weight of artificial filament or strip or the like)
5408 3400.94	印花的人纤长丝缎纹或斜纹布（混纺布指按重量计人纤长丝、扁条或类似品含量在85%以下）	10	130		16	17	米/千克		Printed satin or twill cloth of artificial filaments (Mixed cloth refers to containing less than 85% by weight of artificial filament or strip or the like)
5408 3400.99	印花的人纤长丝其他机织物（混纺布指按重量计人纤长丝、扁条或类似品含量在85%以下）	10	130		16	17	米/千克		Other printed woven fabrics of artificial filaments (Mixed cloth refers to containing less than 85% by weight of artificial filament or strip or the like)

第五十五章 化学纤维短纤

Chapter 55 Man-made staple fibres

注释：

品目55.01和55.02仅适用于每根与丝束长度相等的平行化学纤维长丝丝束。前述丝束应同时符合下列规格：

一、丝束长度超过2米；

二、捻度每米少于5转；

三、每根长丝细度在67分特以下；

四、合成纤维长丝丝束，须经拉伸处理，即本身不能被拉伸至超过本身长度的一倍；

五、丝束总细度大于20000分特。

丝束长度不超过2米的归入品目55.03或55.04。

Chapter Notes:

Headings.No. 55.01 and 55.02 apply only to man-made filament tow, consisting of parallel filaments of a uniform length equal to the length of the tow, meeting the following specifications:

1. Length of tow exceeding 2m;
2. Twist less than 5 turns per metre;
3. Measuring per filament less than 67 decitex;
4. Synthetic filament tow only: the tow must be drawn, that is to say, be incapable of being stretched by more than 100% of its length;
5. Total measurement of tow more than 20,000 decitex.

Tow of a length not exceeding 2m is to be classified in heading.No. 55.03 or 55.04.

税则号列 Tariff Item	商品名称及备注	进口税率 最惠	进口税率 普通	进口税率 暂定	出口退税	增值税率	计量单位	监管条件	Article Description
55.01	合成纤维长丝丝束：								**Synthetic filament tow:**
5501.1000	-尼龙或其他聚酰胺制	5	70		16	17	千克		-Of nylon or other polyamides
5501.2000	-聚酯制	5	70		16	17	千克		-Of polyesters
5501.3000	-聚丙烯腈或变性聚丙烯腈制	5	35		16	17	千克		-Acrylic or modacrylic
5501.4000	-聚丙烯制	5	70		16	17	千克		-Of polypropylene
5501.9000	-其他	5	70		16	17	千克		-Other
55.02	人造纤维长丝丝束：								**Artificial filament tow:**
5502.0010	---二醋酸纤维丝束	3	40		16	17	千克	7	---Cellulose diacetate filament tow
5502.0090	---其他	5	35		16	17	千克		---Other
55.03	合成纤维短纤，未梳或未经其他纺前加工：								**Synthetic staple fibres, not carded, combed or otherwise processed for spinning:**
	-尼龙或其他聚酰胺制：								-Of nylon or other polyamides:
	--芳香族聚酰胺纺制：								--Of aromatic polyamides:
5503.1110	---聚间苯二甲酰间苯二胺纺制	5	70		16	17	千克		---Of polyisophthaloyl metaphenylene diamine
5503.1120	---聚对苯二甲酰对苯二胺纺制	5	70		16	17	千克		---Of poly-p-phenylene terephthamide
5503.1190	---其他	5	70		16	17	千克		---Other
5503.1900	--其他	5	70		16	17	千克		--Other
5503.2000	-聚酯制	5	70		16	17	千克		-Of polyesters
5503.3000	-聚丙烯腈或变性聚丙烯腈制	5	35		16	17	千克		-Acrylic or modacrylie
5503.4000	-聚丙烯制	5	70		16	17	千克		-Of polypropylene
	-其他：								-Other:
5503.9010	---聚苯硫醚制	5	70		16	17	千克		---Polyphenylene sulfide short fibre
5503.9090	---其他	5	70		16	17	千克		---Other
55.04	人造纤维短纤，未梳或未经其他纺前加工：								**Artificial staple fibres, not carded, combed or otherwise processed for spinning:**
	-粘胶纤维制：								-Of viscose rayon:
5504.1010	---竹制	5	35		16	17	千克		---Of bamboo
	---木制：								---Of wood:
5504.1021	----阻燃的	5	35		16	17	千克		----Flame resistant
5504.1029	----其他	5	35		16	17	千克		----Other
5504 1029.01[暂]	高湿模量未梳木制非阻燃粘胶纤维（湿强≥2.0cn/dtex，干强≥3.0cn/dtex）（干伸>14%，湿伸>18%，纤度0.89~2.67dtex）	5	35	2	16	17	千克		Non-carded wooden viscose fiber with high wet modulus (wetness strength ≥ 2.0cn/dtex, dryness strength ≥ 3.0cn/dtex) (dry elongation＞14%, wet stretch＞18% denier 0.89dtex ~ 2.67dtex)
5504 1029.90	其他未梳的木制非阻燃粘胶短纤（包括未经其他纺前加工的）	5	35		16	17	千克		Other non-carded wooden viscose staple fiber (including those without additional processing before spinning)

税则号列 Tariff Item	商品名称及备注	进口税率			出口退税	增值税率	计量单位	监管条件	Article Description
		最惠	普通	暂定					
5504.1090	---其他	5	35		16	17	千克		---Other
5504.9000	-其他	5	35		16	17	千克		-Other
55.05	**化学纤维废料（包括落绵、废纱及回收纤维）：**								**Waste（including noils, yarn waste and garnetted stock） of man-made fibres:**
5505.1000	-合成纤维的	5	70		16	17	千克	AP	-Of synthetic fibres
5505.2000	-人造纤维的	5	70		16	17	千克	AP	-Of artificial fibres
55.06	**合成纤维短纤，已梳或经其他纺前加工：**								**Synthetic staple fibres, carded, combed or otherwise processed for spinning:**
	-尼龙或其他聚酰胺制:								-Of aromatic polyamides:
	---芳香族聚酰胺纺制:								---Of nylon or other polyamides :
5506.1011	----聚间苯二甲酰间苯二胺纺制	5	70		16	17	千克		----Of polyisophthaloyl metaphenylene diamine
5506.1012	----聚对苯二甲酰对苯二胺纺制	5	70		16	17	千克		Of poly-p-phenylene terephthamide
5506.1019	----其他	5	70		16	17	千克		----Other
5506.1090	---其他	5	70		16	17	千克		---Other
5506.2000	-聚酯制	5	70		16	17	千克		-Of polyesters
5506.3000	-聚丙烯腈或变性聚丙烯腈制	5	35		16	17	千克		-Acrylic or modacrylic
	-其他:								-Other:
5506.9010	---聚苯硫醚制	5	70		16	17	千克		---Of polyphenylene sulfide
5506.9090	---其他	5	70		16	17	千克		---Other
55.07	**人造纤维短纤，已梳或经其他纺前加工：**								**Artificial staple fibres, carded, combed or otherwise processed for spinning:**
5507.0000	人造纤维短纤，已梳或经其他纺前加工	5	35		16	17	千克		Artificial staple fibres, carded, combed or otherwise processed for spinning
55.08	**化学纤维短纤纺制的缝纫线，不论是否供零售用：**								**Sewing thread of man-made staple fibres, whether or not put up for retail sale:**
5508.1000	-合成纤维短纤纺制	5	90		16	17	千克		-Of synthetic staple fibres
5508 1000.11	非零售用聚丙烯腈短纤缝纫线	5	90		16	17	千克		Sewing thread of acrylic staple fibres, not for retail sale
5508 1000.19	非零售用其他合纤短纤缝纫线	5	90		16	17	千克		Sewing thread of synthetic staple fibres, not for retail sale
5508 1000.90	零售用合成纤维短纤缝纫线	5	90		16	17	千克		Sewing thread of synthetic staple fibres, for retail sale
5508.2000	-人造纤维短纤纺制	5	70		16	17	千克		-Of artificial staple fibres
5508 2000.10	非零售用人造纤维短纤缝纫线	5	70		16	17	千克		Sewing thread of other artificial staple fibres, not for retail sale
5508 2000.90	零售用人造纤维短纤缝纫线	5	70		16	17	千克		Sewing thread of artificial staple fibres, for retail sale
55.09	**合成纤维短纤纺制的纱线（缝纫线除外），非供零售用：**								**Yarn（other than sewing thread）of synthetic staple fibres, not put up for retail sale:**
	-按重量计尼龙或其他聚酰胺短纤含量在85%及以上:								-Containing 85% or more by weight of staple fibres of nylon or other polyamides:
5509.1100	--单纱	5	90		16	17	千克		--Single yarn
5509.1200	--多股纱线或缆线	5	90		16	17	千克		--Multiple（folded） or cabled yarn
	-按重量计聚酯短纤含量在85%及以上:								-Containing 85% or more by weight of polyester staple fibres:
5509.2100	--单纱	5	90		16	17	千克		--Single yarn
5509.2200	--多股纱线或缆线	5	90		16	17	千克		--Multiple（folded） or cabled yarn
5509 2200.10	非零售聚酯短纤多股纱线或缆线（终捻为Z捻，聚酯短纤含量在85%及以上，缝纫线除外）	5	90		16	17	千克		Multiple（folded） or cabled yarn, with a final “Z” twist, containing 85% or more by weight of polyester staple fibres, not for retail sale, other than sewing thread
5509 2200.90	非零售其他聚酯短纤多股纱线缆线（聚酯短纤含量在85%及以上，缝纫线除外）	5	90		16	17	千克		Other multiple（folded）or cabled yarn, containing 85% or more by weight of polyester staple fibres, not for retail sale, other than sewing thread

税则号列 Tariff Item	商品名称及备注	进口税率 最惠	进口税率 普通	进口税率 暂定	出口退税	增值税率	计量单位	监管条件	Article Description
	-按重量计聚丙烯腈或变性聚丙烯腈短纤含量在85%及以上:								-Containing 85% or more by weight of acrylic or modacrylic staple fibres:
5509.3100	--单纱	5	90		16	17	千克		--Single yarn
5509.3200	--多股纱线或缆线	5	90		16	17	千克		--Multiple（folded）or cabled yarn
	-其他纱线，按重量计合成纤维短纤含量在85%及以上:								-Other yarn, containing 85% or more by weight of synthetic staple fibres:
5509.4100	--单纱	5	90		16	17	千克		--Single yarn
5509.4200	--多股纱线或缆线	5	90		16	17	千克		--Multiple（folded）or cabled yarn
	-其他聚酯短纤纺制的纱线:								-Other yarn, of polyester staple fibres:
5509.5100	--主要或仅与人造纤维短纤混纺	5	90		16	17	千克		--Mixed mainly or solely with artificial staple fibres
5509.5200	--主要或仅与羊毛或动物细毛混纺	5	90		16	17	千克		--Mixed mainly or solely with wool or fine animal hair
5509.5300	--主要或仅与棉混纺	5	90		16	17	千克		--Mixed mainly or solely with cotton
5509.5900	--其他	5	90		16	17	千克		--Other
	-其他聚丙烯腈或变性聚丙烯腈短纤纺制的纱线:								-Other yarn, of acrylic or modacrylic staple fibres:
5509.6100	--主要或仅与羊毛或动物细毛混纺	5	90		16	17	千克		--Mixed mainly or solely with wool or fine animal hair
5509.6200	--主要或仅与棉混纺	5	90		16	17	千克		--Mixed mainly or solely with cotton
5509.6900	--其他	5	90		16	17	千克		--Other
	-其他纱线:								-Other yarn:
5509.9100	--主要或仅与羊毛或动物细毛混纺	5	90		16	17	千克		--Mixed mainly or solely with wool or fine animal hair
5509.9200	--主要或仅与棉混纺	5	90		16	17	千克		--Mixed mainly or solely with cotton
5509.9900	--其他	5	90		16	17	千克		--Other
55.10	**人造纤维短纤纺制的纱线（缝纫线除外），非供零售用:**								**Yarn（other than sewing thread）of artificial staple fibres, not put up for retail sale:**
	-按重量计人造纤维短纤含量在85%及以上:								-Containing 85% or more by weight of artificial staple fibres:
5510.1100	--单纱	5	70		16	17	千克		-Single yarn
5510.1200	--多股纱线或缆线	5	70		16	17	千克		--Multiple（folded）or cabled yarn
5510.2000	-其他纱线，主要或仅与羊毛或动物细毛混纺	5	70		16	17	千克		-Other yarn, mixed mainly or solely with wool or fine animal hair
5510.3000	-其他纱线，主要或仅与棉混纺	5	70		16	17	千克		-Other yarn, mixed mainly or solely with cotton
5510.9000	-其他	5	70		16	17	千克		-Other yarn
55.11	**化学纤维短纤纺制的纱线（缝纫线除外），供零售用:**								**Yarn（other than sewing thread）of man-made staple fibres, put up for retail sale:**
5511.1000	-按重量计合成纤维短纤含量在85%及以上	5	90		16	17	千克		-Of synthetic staple fibres, containing 85% or more by weight of such fibres
5511.2000	-按重量计合成纤维短纤含量在85%以下	5	90		16	17	千克		-Of synthetic staple fibres, containing less than 85% by weight of such fibres
5511.3000	-人造纤维短纤纺制	5	90		16	17	千克		-Of artificial staple fibres
55.12	**合成纤维短纤纺制的机织物，按重量计合成纤维短纤含量在85%及以上:**								**Woven fabrics of synthetic staple fibres, containing 85% or more by weight of synthetic staple fibres:**
	-按重量计聚酯短纤含量在85%及以上:								-Containing 85% or more by weight of polyester staple fibres:
5512.1100	--未漂白或漂白	15	130		16	17	米/千克		--Unbleached or bleached
5512 1100.10	未漂或漂白聚酯短纤机织府绸（聚酯短纤含量在85%及以上，包括细平布）	15	130		16	17	米/千克		Poplin and fine plain fabrics, containing 85% or more by weight of polyester staple fibres, unbleached or bleached
5512 1100.20	未漂或漂白聚酯短纤机织平布（聚酯短纤含量在85%及以上）	15	130		16	17	米/千克		Plain fabrics, containing 85% or more by weight of polyester staple fibres, unbleached or bleached

税则号列 Tariff Item	商品名称及备注	进口税率 最惠	普通	暂定	出口退税	增值税率	计量单位	监管条件	Article Description
5512 1100.30	未漂或漂白聚酯短纤印染用布（纯聚酯布指按重量计聚酯短纤含量在85%及以上）	15	130		16	17	米/千克		Woven fabrics for printing and dyeing, containing 85% or more by weight of polyester staple fibres, unbleached or bleached
5512 1100.40	未漂或漂白聚酯短纤平纹奶酪布（聚酯短纤含量在85%及以上，含薄细布、巴里纱）	15	130		16	17	米/千克		Plain weave cheese cloth, including muslin and voiles, containing 85% or more by weight of polyester staple fibres, unbleached or bleached
5512 1100.50	未漂或漂白聚酯短纤机织帆布（纯聚酯布指按重量计聚酯短纤含量在85%及以上）	15	130		16	17	米/千克		Canvas, containing 85% or more by weight of polyester staple fibres, unbleached or bleached
5512 1100.60	未漂或漂白聚酯短纤其他斜纹机织物（聚酯短纤含量在85%及以上，含缎纹）	15	130		16	17	米/千克		Twill weave and satin weave fabrics, containing 85% or more by weight of polyester staple fibres, unbleached or bleached
5512 1100.70	未漂或漂白聚酯短纤牛津布(纯聚酯布指按重量计聚酯短纤含量在85%及以上）	15	130		16	17	米/千克		Oxford fabrics, containing 85% or more by weight of polyester staple fibres, unbleached or bleached
5512 1100.90	未漂或漂白聚酯短纤其他机织物（纯聚酯布指按重量计聚酯短纤含量在85%及以上）	15	130		16	17	米/千克		Other woven fabrics, containing 85% or more by weight of polyester staple fibres, unbleached or bleached
5512.1900	--其他	10	130		16	17	米/千克		--Other
5512 1900.10	聚酯短纤色织机织物(聚酯短纤含量在85%及以上，蓝粗斜纹布及提花织物除外）	10	130		16	17	米/千克		Yarn-dyed woven fabrics, containing 85% or more by weight of polyester staple fibres, other than blue denim and jacquard weave
5512 1900.20	聚酯短纤蓝粗斜纹布(纯聚酯布指按重量计聚酯短纤含量在85%及以上）	10	130		16	17	米/千克		Blue denim, containing 85% or more by weight of polyester staple fibres
5512 1900.31	聚酯短纤其他机织府绸或细平布（纯聚酯布指按重量计聚酯短纤含量在85%及以上）	10	130		16	17	米/千克		Other poplin and fine plain fabrics, containing 85% or more by weight of polyester staple fibres
5512 1900.32	聚酯短纤其他机织平布(纯聚酯布指按重量计聚酯短纤含量在85%及以上）	10	130		16	17	米/千克		Other plain fabrics, containing 85% or more by weight of polyester staple fibres
5512 1900.33	聚酯短纤其他机织印染用布(纯聚酯布指按重量计聚酯短纤含量在85%及以上）	10	130		16	17	米/千克		Other woven fabrics for printing and dyeing, containing 85% or more by weight of polyester staple fibres
5512 1900.34	聚酯短纤其他平纹奶酪布等(聚酯短纤含量在85%及以上，含薄细布，巴里纱）	10	130		16	17	米/千克		Other cheese cloth, including muslin and voiles, containing 85% or more by weight of polyester staple fibres
5512 1900.35	聚酯短纤其他机织帆布(纯聚酯布指按重量计聚酯短纤含量在85%及以上）	10	130		16	17	米/千克		Other canvas, containing 85% or more by weight of polyester staple fibres
5512 1900.36	聚酯短纤其他缎纹或斜纹机织物（纯聚酯布指按重量计聚酯短纤含量在85%及以上）	10	130		16	17	米/千克		Other satin weave or twill weave fabrics, containing 85% or more by weight of polyester staple fibres
5512 1900.37	聚酯短纤其他牛津布(纯聚酯布指按重量计聚酯短纤含量在85%及以上）	10	130		16	17	米/千克		Other oxford fabrics, containing 85% or more by weight of polyester staple fibres
5512 1900.90	聚酯短纤其他机织物(纯聚酯布指按重量计聚酯短纤含量在85%及以上）	10	130		16	17	米/千克		Other woven fabrics, containing 85% or more by weight of polyester staple fibres
	-按重量计聚丙烯腈或变性聚丙烯腈短纤含量在85%及以上:								-Containing 85% or more by weight of acrylic or modacrylic staple fibres:
5512.2100	--未漂白或漂白	13	130		16	17	米/千克		--Unbleached or bleached
5512 2100.10	未漂白或漂白腈纶短纤机织府绸细平布(纯腈纶布指按重量计腈纶短纤含量在85%及以上）	13	130		16	17	米/千克		Poplin and fine plain fabrics, containing85% or more by weight of acrylic or modacrylic staple fibres, unbleached or bleached

税则号列 Tariff Item	商品名称及备注	进口税率 最惠	普通	暂定	出口退税	增值税率	计量单位	监管条件	Article Description
5512 2100.20	未漂白或漂白腈纶短纤机织平布（纯腈纶布指按重量计腈纶短纤含量在85%及以上）	13	130		16	17	米/千克		Plain fabrics, containing 85% or more by weight of acrylic or modacrylic staple fibres, unbleached or bleached
5512 2100.30	未漂白或漂白腈纶短纤机织印染用布（纯腈纶布指按重量计腈纶短纤含量在85%及以上）	13	130		16	17	米/千克		Woven fabrics for printing and dyeing, containing 85% or more by weight of acrylic or modacrylic staple fibres, unbleached or bleached
5512 2100.40	未漂白或漂白腈纶短纤平纹奶酪布等（腈纶短纤含量在85%及以上，含薄细布、巴里纱）	13	130		16	17	米/千克		Cheese cloth, including voiles and muslin, containing 85% or more by weight of acrylic or modacrylic staple fibres, unbleached or bleached
5512 2100.50	未漂白或漂白腈纶短纤机织帆布(纯腈纶布指按重量计腈纶短纤含量在85%及以上)	13	130		16	17	米/千克		Canvas, containing 85% or more by weight of acrylic or modacrylic staple fibres, unbleached or bleached
5512 2100.60	未漂白或漂白腈纶短纤其他斜纹机织物(腈纶短纤含量在85%及以上，含缎纹机织物)	13	130		16	17	米/千克		Other twill weave fabrics, satin weave, containing 85% or more by weight of acrylic or modacrylic staple fibres, unbleached or bleached
5512 2100.70	未漂白或漂白腈纶短纤牛津布（纯腈纶布指按重量计腈纶短纤含量在85%及以上）	13	130		16	17	米/千克		Oxford fabrics, containing 85% or more by weight of acrylic or modacrylic staple fibres, unbleached or bleached
5512 2100.90	未漂白或漂白腈纶短纤其他机织物(纯腈纶布指按重量计腈纶短纤含量在85%及以上)	13	130		16	17	米/千克		Other woven fabrics, containing 85% or more by weight of acrylic or modacrylic staple fibres, unbleached or bleached
5512.2900	--其他	10	130		16	17	米/千克		--Other
5512 2900.10	腈纶短纤色织机织物(腈纶短纤含量在85%及以上，蓝粗斜纹布及提花织物除外)	10	130		16	17	米/千克		Yarn-dyed woven fabrics, containing 85% or more by weight of acrylic or modacrylic staple fibres, other than blue denim and jacquard weave
5512 2900.20	腈纶短纤蓝粗斜纹布(纯腈纶布指按重量计腈纶短纤含量在85%及以上)	10	130		16	17	米/千克		Blue denim, containing 85% or more by weight of acrylic or modacrylic staple fibres
5512 2900.31	腈纶短纤其他机织府绸或细平布(纯腈纶布指按重量计腈纶短纤含量在85%及以上)	10	130		16	17	米/千克		Other poplin and fine plain fabrics, containing85% or more by weight of acrylic or modacrylic staple fibres
5512 2900.32	腈纶短纤其他机织平布(纯腈纶布指按重量计腈纶短纤含量在85%及以上)	10	130		16	17	米/千克		Other plain fabrics, containing 85% or more by weight of acrylic or modacrylic staple fibres
5512 2900.33	腈纶短纤其他机织印染用布(纯腈纶布指按重量计腈纶短纤含量在85%及以上)	10	130		16	17	米/千克		Other woven fabrics for printing and dyeing, containing 85% or more by weight of acrylic or modacrylic staple fibres
5512 2900.34	腈纶短纤其他平纹奶酪布等(腈纶短纤含量在85%及以上，含薄细布、巴里纱)	10	130		16	17	米/千克		Other plain weave cheese cloth, , including voiles and muslin, containing 85% or more by weight of acrylic or modacrylic staple fibres
5512 2900.35	腈纶短纤其他机织帆布(纯腈纶布指按重量计腈纶短纤含量在85%及以上)	10	130		16	17	米/千克		Other canvas, containing 85% or more by weight of acrylic or modacrylic staple fibres
5512 2900.36	腈纶短纤其他缎纹或斜纹机织物(纯腈纶布指按重量计腈纶短纤含量在85%及以上)	10	130		16	17	米/千克		Other satin weave or twill weave fabrics, containing 85% or more by weight of acrylic or modacrylic staple fibres
5512 2900.37	腈纶短纤其他牛津布(纯腈纶布指按重量计腈纶短纤含量在85%及以上)	10	130		16	17	米/千克		Other oxford fabrics, containing 85% or more by weight of acrylic or modacrylic staple fibres
5512 2900.90	腈纶短纤其他机织物(纯腈纶布指按重量计腈纶短纤含量在85%及以上)	10	130		16	17	米/千克		Other woven fabrics, containing 85% or more by weight of acrylic or modacrylic staple fibres
	-其他:								-Other:
5512.9100	--未漂白或漂白	18	130		16	17	米/千克		--Unbleached or bleached

税则号列 Tariff Item	商品名称及备注	进口税率			出口退税	增值税率	计量单位	监管条件	Article Description
		最惠	普通	暂定					
5512 9100.10	未漂白或漂白其他合纤短纤机织府绸（其他合纤短纤含量在85%及以上，含细平布）	18	130		16	17	米/千克		Other poplin, fine plain fabrics, containing 85% or more by weight of synthetic staple fibres, unbleached or bleached
5512 9100.20	未漂白或漂白其他合纤短纤机织平布(其他纯合纤布指按重量计其他合纤短纤含量在85%及以上)	18	130		16	17	米/千克		Other plain fabrics, containing 85% or more by weight of synthetic staple fibres, unbleached or bleached
5512 9100.30	未漂白或漂白其他合纤短纤印染用布(其他纯合纤布指按重量计其他合纤短纤含量在85%及以上)	18	130		16	17	米/千克		Other woven fabrics for printing and dyeing, containing 85% or more by weight of synthetic staple fibres, unbleached or bleached
5512 9100.40	未漂白或漂白其他合纤短纤平纹奶酪布(其他合纤短纤含量在85%及以上，含薄细布、巴里纱)	18	130		16	17	米/千克		Other cheese cloth, including voiles and muslin, containing 85% or more by weight of synthetic staple fibres, unbleached or bleached
5512 9100.50	未漂白或漂白其他合纤短纤机织帆布(其他纯合纤布指按重量计其他合纤短纤含量在85%及以上)	18	130		16	17	米/千克		Other canvas, containing 85% or more by weight of synthetic staple fibres, unbleached or bleached
5512 9100.60	未漂白或漂白其他合纤短纤斜纹机织物(其他合纤短纤含量在85%及以上，含缎纹机织物)	18	130		16	17	米/千克		Twill weave fabrics, satin weave, containing 85% or more by weight of synthetic staple fibres, unbleached or bleached
5512 9100.70	未漂白或漂白其他合纤短纤牛津布（其他纯合纤布指按重量计其他合纤短纤含量在85%及以上)	18	130		16	17	米/千克		Oxford fabrics, containing 85% or more by weight of synthetic staple fibres, unbleached or bleached
5512 9100.90	未漂白或漂白其他合纤短纤其他机织物(其他纯合纤布指按重量计其他合纤短纤含量在85%及以上)	18	130		16	17	米/千克		Other woven fabrics, containing 85% or more by weight of synthetic staple fibres, unbleached or bleached
5512.9900	--其他	10	130		16	17	米/千克		--Other
5512 9900.10	其他合纤短纤色织机织物(其他合纤短纤含量≥85%，蓝粗斜纹布及提花织物除外)	10	130		16	17	米/千克		Other yarn-dyed woven fabrics, containing 85% or more by weight of other synthetic staple fibres, other than blue denim and jacquard weave
5512 9900.20	其他合纤短纤蓝粗斜纹布(其他纯合纤布指按重量计其他合纤短纤含量在85%及以上)	10	130		16	17	米/千克		Other blue denim, containing 85% or more by weight of other synthetic staple fibres
5512 9900.31	其他合纤短纤机织府绸或细平布(其他纯合纤布指按重量计其他合纤短纤含量在85%及以上)	10	130		16	17	米/千克		Other poplin and fine plain fabrics, containing 85% or more by weight of other synthetic staple fibres
5512 9900.32	其他合纤短纤其他机织平布(其他纯合纤布指按重量计其他合纤短纤含量在85%及以上)	10	130		16	17	米/千克		Other plain fabrics, containing 85% or more by weight of other synthetic staple fibres
5512 9900.33	其他合纤短纤其他机织印染用布(其他纯合纤布指按重量计其他合纤短纤含量在85%及以上)	10	130		16	17	米/千克		Other woven fabrics for printing and dying, containing 85% or more by weight of other synthetic staple fibres
5512 9900.34	其他合纤短纤平纹奶酪布等(其他合纤短纤85%及以上，含薄细布、巴里纱)	10	130		16	17	米/千克		Other cheese cloth, including voiles and muslin, containing 85% or more by weight of other synthetic staple fibres
5512 9900.35	其他合纤短纤其他机织帆布(其他纯合纤布指按重量计其他合纤短纤含量在85%及以上)	10	130		16	17	米/千克		Other canvas, containing 85% or more by weight of other synthetic staple fibres
5512 9900.36	其他合纤短纤缎纹或斜纹机织物(其他纯合纤布指按重量计其他合纤短纤含量在85%及以上)	10	130		16	17	米/千克		Other satin or twill weave fabrics, containing 85% or more by weight of other synthetic staple fibres
5512 9900.39	其他合纤短纤其他牛津布(其他纯合纤布指按重量计其他合纤短纤含量在85%及以上)	10	130		16	17	米/千克		Other oxford fabrics, containing 85% or more by weight of other synthetic staple fibres

税则号列 Tariff Item	商品名称及备注	进口税率 最惠	普通	暂定	出口退税	增值税率	计量单位	监管条件	Article Description
5512 9900.90	其他合纤短纤其他机织物(其他纯合纤布指按重量计其他合纤短纤含量在85%及以上)	10	130		16	17	米/千克		Other woven fabrics, containing 85% or more by weight of other synthetic staple fibres
55.13	**合成纤维短纤纺制的机织物，按重量计合成纤维短纤含量在85%以下，主要或仅与棉混纺，每平方米重量不超过170克：**								**Woven fabrics of synthetic staple fibres, containing less than 85% by weight of such fibres, mixed mainly or solely with cotton, of a weight not exceeding 170g/m²:**
	-未漂白或漂白:								-Unbleached or bleached:
	--聚酯短纤纺制的平纹机织物:								--Of polyester staple fibres, plain weave:
5513.1110	---未漂白	16	130		16	17	米/千克		---Unbleached
5513 1110.10	与棉混纺未漂白聚酯短纤平纹府绸(含聚酯短纤85%以下，每平方米重≤170克，含细平布)	16	130		16	17	米/千克		Poplin, fine plain fabrics, mixed with cotton, containing less than 85% by weight of polyester staple fibres, of a weight not exceeding 170g/m², unbleached
5513 1110.20	与棉混纺未漂白聚酯短纤机织平布(混纺为含聚酯短纤85%以下，轻质指每平方米重≤170克)	16	130		16	17	米/千克		Plain fabrics, mixed with cotton, containing less than 85% by weight of polyester staple fibres, of a weight not exceeding 170g/m², unbleached
5513 1110.30	与棉混纺未漂白聚酯短纤平纹印染用布(混纺为含聚酯短纤85%以下，轻质指每平方米重≤170克)	16	130		16	17	米/千克		Woven fabrics for printing and dyeing, plain weave, mixed with cotton, containing less than 85% by weight of polyester staple fibres, of a weight not exceeding 170g/ m², unbleached
5513 1110.40	与棉混纺未漂白聚酯短纤平纹奶酪布(含聚酯短纤85%以下，轻质每平方米重≤170克，含薄细布、巴里纱)	16	130		16	17	米/千克		Plain weave cheese cloth, including voiles and muslin, mixed with cotton, containing less than 85% by weight of polyester staple fibres, of a weight not exceeding 170g/m², unbleached
5513.1120	---漂白	15	130		16	17	米/千克		---Bleached
5513 1120.10	与棉混纺漂白聚酯短纤平纹府绸(含聚酯短纤85%以下，每平方米重≤170克，含细平布)	15	130		16	17	米/千克	A	Poplin, plain weave, including muslin, mixed with cotton, containing less than 85% by weight of polyester staple fibres, of a weight not exceeding 170g/m², bleached
5513 1120.20	与棉混纺漂白聚酯短纤机织平布(混纺为含聚酯短纤85%以下，轻质指每平方米重≤170克)	15	130		16	17	米/千克	A	Plain fabrics, mixed with cotton, containing less than 85% by weight of polyester staple fibres, of a weight not exceeding 170g/m², bleached
5513 1120.30	与棉混纺漂白聚酯平纹印染用布(混纺为含聚酯短纤85%以下，轻质指每平方米重≤170克)	15	130		16	17	米/千克	A	Woven fabrics for printing and dyeing, plain weave, mixed with cotton, containing less than 85% by weight of polyester staple fibres, of a weight not exceeding 170g/m², bleached
5513 1120.40	与棉混纺漂白聚酯短纤平纹奶酪布等(含聚酯短纤85%以下，每平方米重≤170克，含薄细布、巴里纱)	15	130		16	17	米/千克	A	Plain weave cheese cloth, , including voiles and muslin, mixed with cotton, containing less than 85% by weight of polyester staple fibres, of a weight not exceeding 170g/m², bleached
	--聚酯短纤纺制的三线或四线斜纹机织物，包括双面斜纹机织物:								--3-thread or 4-thread twill, including cross twill, of polyester staple fibres:
5513.1210	---未漂白	16	130		16	17	米/千克		---Unbleached
5513.1220	---漂白	18	130		16	17	米/千克		---Bleached
	--其他聚酯短纤纺制的机织物:								--Other woven fabrics of polyester staple fibres:
5513.1310	---未漂白	16	130		16	17	米/千克		---Unbleached
5513 1310.10	与棉混纺未漂聚酯短纤斜纹机织物(含聚酯短纤<85%，轻质指每平方米重≤170克，含缎纹布)	16	130		16	17	米/千克		Twill weave fabrics, satin weave, mixed with cotton, containing less than 85% by weight of polyester staple fibres, of a weight not exceeding 170g/m², unbleached
5513 1310.20	与棉混纺未漂白聚酯短纤牛津布(混纺为含聚酯短纤85%以下，轻质指每平方米重≤170克)	16	130		16	17	米/千克		Oxford fabrics, mixed with cotton, containing less than 85% by weight of polyester staple fibres, of a weight not exceeding 170g/m², unbleacheds

税则号列 Tariff Item	商品名称及备注	进口税率 最惠	普通	暂定	出口退税	增值税率	计量单位	监管条件	Article Description
5513 1310.90	与棉混纺未漂聚酯短纤其他机织物（混纺为含聚酯短纤 85%以下，轻质指每平方米重≤170克）	16	130		16	17	米/千克		Other woven fabrics, mixed with cotton containing less than 85% by weight of polyester staple fibres, of a weight not exceeding 170g/m², unbleached
5513.1320	---漂白	18	130		16	17	米/千克		---Bleached
5513 1320.10	与棉混纺漂白聚酯短纤斜纹机织物（含聚酯短纤 85%以下，轻质指每平方米重≤170 克，含缎纹）	18	130		16	17	米/千克		Twill weave fabrics, satin weave, mixed with cotton, containing less than 85% by weight of polyester staple fibres, of a weight not exceeding 170g/ m², bleached
5513 1320.20	与棉混纺漂白聚酯短纤牛津布（混纺为含聚酯短纤 85%以下，轻质指每平方米重≤170 克）	18	130		16	17	米/千克		Oxford fabrics, mixed with cotton, containing less than 85% by weight of polyester staple fibres, of a weight not exceeding 170g/m², bleached
5513 1320.90	与棉混纺漂白聚酯短纤其他机织物（混纺为含聚酯短纤 85%以下，轻质指每平方米重≤170克）	18	130		16	17	米/千克		Other woven fabrics, mixed with cotton, containing less than 85% by weight of polyester staple fibres, of a weight not exceeding 170g/m², bleached
5513.1900	--其他机织物	18	130		16	17	米/千克		--Other woven fabrics
5513 1900.10	与棉混纺的未漂白或漂白的其他合纤短纤布（其他合短纤＜85%，每平方米重≤170 克，专指府绸或细平布）	18	130		16	17	米/千克		Poplin and muslin, mixed with cotton, containing less than 85% by weight of synthetic staple fibres, of a weight not exceeding 170g/m², unbleached or bleached
5513 1900.20	与棉混纺的未漂白或漂白的其他合纤短纤布（其他合短纤＜85%，每平方米重≤170 克，专指机织平布）	18	130		16	17	米/千克		Plain fabrics, mixed with cotton, containing less than 85% by weight of synthetic staple fibres, of a weight not exceeding 170g/m², unbleached or bleached
5513 1900.30	与棉混纺的未漂白或漂白的其他合纤短纤布（其他合短纤＜85%，每平方米重≤170 克，专指平纹印染用布）	18	130		16	17	米/千克		Other woven fabrics, mixed with cotton, for printing, dyeing, containing less than 85% by weight of synthetic staple fibres, of a weight not exceeding 170g/m², unbleached, bleached
5513 1900.40	与棉混纺的未漂白或漂白的其他合纤短纤布（合短纤＜85%，每平方米重≤170 克，指奶酪布、薄细布、巴里纱）	18	130		16	17	米/千克		Cheese cloth, voiles and muslin, mixed with cotton, containing less than 85% by weight of synthetic staple fibres, of a weight not exceeding 170g/m², unbleached or bleached
5513 1900.50	与棉混纺的未漂白或漂白的其他合纤短纤布（其他合短纤＜85%，每平方米重≤170 克，专指缎纹或斜纹布）	18	130		16	17	米/千克		Other woven fabrics, satin and twill weave, mixed with cotton, containing less than 85% by weight of synthetic staple fibres, of a weight not exceeding 170g/m², unbleached or bleached
5513 1900.60	与棉混纺的未漂白或漂白的其他合纤短纤布（其他合短纤＜85%，每平方米重≤170 克，专指牛津布）	18	130		16	17	米/千克		Other oxford fabrics, mixed with cotton, containing less than 85% by weight of synthetic staple fibres, of a weight not exceeding 170g/m², unbleached or bleached
5513 1900.90	与棉混纺的未漂白或漂白的其他合纤短纤布（其他合短纤＜85%，每平方米重≤170 克，特指其他机织物）	18	130		16	17	米/千克		Other woven fabrics, mixed with cotton, containing less than 85% by weight of synthetic staple fibres, of a weight not exceeding 170g/m², unbleached or bleached
	-染色：								-Dyed:
5513.2100	—聚酯短纤纺制的平纹机织物	10	130		16	17	米/千克		--Of polyester staple fibres, plain weave
5513 2100.10	与棉混纺染色聚酯短纤平纹府绸（含聚酯短纤 85%以下，每平方米重≤170 克，含细平布）	10	130		16	17	米/千克		Poplin, plain weave and muslin, mixed with cotton, containing less than 85% by weight of polyester staple fibres, of a weight not exceeding 170g/m², dyed
5513 2100.20	与棉混纺染色聚酯短纤机织平布（混纺为含聚酯短纤 85%以下，轻质指每平方米重≤170克）	10	130		16	17	米/千克		Plain cloth, mixed with cotton, containing less than 85% by weight of polyester staple fibres, of a weight not exceeding 170g/m², dyed

税则号列 Tariff Item	商品名称及备注	进口税率 最惠	普通	暂定	出口退税	增值税率	计量单位	监管条件	Article Description
5513 2100.30	与棉混纺的染色聚酯短纤平纹印染用布（混纺为含聚酯短纤85%以下，轻质指每平方米重≤170克）	10	130		16	17	米/千克		Woven fabrics for printing and dyeing, mixed with cotton, containing less than 85% by weight of polyester staple fibres, of a weight not exceeding 170g/m², dyed
5513 2100.40	与棉混纺染色聚酯短纤平纹奶酪布等（聚酯短纤85%以下，每平方米重≤170克，含薄细布、巴里纱）	10	130		16	17	米/千克		Plain cheese cloth, including voiles and muslin, mixed with cotton, containing less than 85% by weight of polyester staple fibres, of a weight not exceeding 170g/m², dyed
	--其他聚酯短纤纺制的机织物:								--Other woven fabrics of polyester staple fibres:
5513.2310	---聚酯短纤纺制的三线或四线斜纹机织物，包括双面斜纹机织物	10	130		16	17	米/千克		---3-thread or 4-thread twill, including cross twill, of polyester staple fibres
5513.2390	---其他	10	130		16	17	米/千克		---Other
5513.2900	--其他机织物	10	130		16	17	米/千克		--Other woven fabrics
5513 2900.10	与棉混纺染色其他合纤短纤府绸（其他合短纤<85%，每平方米重≤170克，含细平布）	10	130		16	17	米/千克		Poplin, fine plain fabrics, mixed with cotton, containing less than 85% by weight of synthetic staple fibres, of a weight not exceeding 170g/m², dyed
5513 2900.20	与棉混纺染色其他合纤短纤平布(混纺为含其他合短纤<85%，轻质指每平方米重≤170克)	10	130		16	17	米/千克		Plain fabrics, mixed with cotton, containing less than 85% by weight of synthetic staple fibres, of a weight not exceeding 170g/m², dyed
5513 2900.30	与棉混纺染色其他合纤短纤平纹布（印染用，其他合短纤<85%，指每平方米重≤170克）	10	130		16	17	米/千克		Plain weave for printing and dyeing, mixed with cotton, containing less than 85% by weight of synthetic staple fibres, of a weight not exceeding 170g/m², dyed
5513 2900.40	与棉混纺的染色其他合纤短纤平纹布(合短纤<85%，每平方米重≤170克，指奶酪布、薄细布、巴里纱)	10	130		16	17	米/千克		Cheese cloth, voiles and muslin, mixed with cotton, containing less than 85% by weight of synthetic staple fibres, of a weight not exceeding 170g/m², dyed
5513 2900.50	与棉混纺染色其他合纤短纤斜纹布（其他合短纤<85%，每平方米重≤170克，含缎纹布）	10	130		16	17	米/千克		Twill and satin weave fabrics, mixed with cotton, containing less than 85% by weight of synthetic staple fibres, of a weight not exceeding 170g/m², dyed
5513 2900.60	与棉混纺染色其他合纤短纤牛津布（混纺为含其他合短纤<85%，轻质指每平方米重≤170克）	10	130		16	17	米/千克		Oxford fabrics, mixed with cotton, containing less than 85% by weight of synthetic staple fibres, of a weight not exceeding 170g/m², dyed
5513 2900.90	与棉混纺染色其他合纤短纤其他布（混纺为含其他合短纤<85%，轻质指每平方米重≤170克）	10	130		16	17	米/千克		Other woven fabric, mixed with cotton, containing less than 85% by weight of synthetic staple fibres, of a weight not exceeding 170g/m², dyed
	-色织:								-Of yarns of different colours:
5513.3100	--聚酯短纤纺制的平纹机织物	10	130		16	17	米/千克		--Of polyester staple fibres, plain weave
	--其他机织物:								--Other woven fabrics:
5513.3910	---聚酯短纤纺制的三线或四线斜纹机织物,包括双面斜纹机织物	10	130		16	17	米/千克		---3-thread or 4-thread twill, including cross twill, of polyester staple fibres
5513.3920	---其他聚酯短纤纺制的机织物	10	130		16	17	米/千克		---Other woven fabrics of polyester staple fibres
5513.3990	---其他	10	130		16	17	米/千克		---Other
	-印花:								-Printed:
5513.4100	--聚酯短纤纺制的平纹机织物	10	130		16	17	米/千克		--Of polyester staple fibres, plain weave
5513 4100.10	与棉混纺印花聚酯短纤平纹府绸(含聚酯短纤85%以下，指每平方米重≤170克，含细平布)	10	130		16	17	米/千克		Poplin, plain weave and muslin, mixed with cotton, containing less than 85% by weight of polyester staple fibres, of a weight not exceeding 170g/m², printed
5513 4100.20	与棉混纺印花聚酯短纤机织平	10	130		16	17	米/千克		Plain fabrics, mixed with cotton, containing less than

税则号列 Tariff Item	商品名称及备注	进口税率			出口退税	增值税率	计量单位	监管条件	Article Description
		最惠	普通	暂定					
	布（混纺为含聚酯短纤 85%以下，轻质指每平方米重≤170克）								85% by weight of polyester staple fibres, of a weight not exceeding 170g/m², printed
5513 4100.30	与棉混纺的印花聚酯短纤平纹印染用布（混纺为含聚酯短纤85%以下，轻质指每平方米重≤170克）	10	130		16	17	米/千克		Woven fabrics for printing and dyeing, mixed with cotton, containing less than 85% by weight of polyester staple fibres, of a weight not exceeding 170g/m², printed
5513 4100.40	与棉混印花聚酯短纤平纹奶酪布等（含聚酯短纤<85%，每平方米重≤170克，含薄细布、巴里纱）	10	130		16	17	米/千克		Cheese cloth, voiles and muslin, mixed with cotton, containing less than 85% by weight of polyester staple fibres, of a weight not exceeding 170g/m², printed
	--其他机织物：								--Other woven fabrics:
5513.4910	---聚酯短纤纺制的三线或四线斜纹机织物，包括双面斜纹机织物	10	130		16	17	米/千克		---3-thread or 4-thread twill including cross twill, of polyester staple fibres
5513.4920	---其他聚酯短纤纺制的机织物	10	130		16	17	米/千克		---Other woven fabrics of polyester staple fibres
5513.4990	---其他	10	130		16	17	米/千克		---Other
55.14	**合成纤维短纤纺制的机织物，按重量计合成纤维短纤含量在85%以下，主要或仅与棉混纺的，每平方米重量超过170克：**								**Woven fabrics of synthetic staple fibres, containing less than 85% by weight of such fibres, mixed mainly or solely with cotton, of a weight exceeding 170g/m²:**
	-未漂白或漂白：								-Unbleached or bleached:
	--聚酯短纤纺制的平纹机织物：								--Of polyester staple fibres, plain weave:
5514.1110	---未漂白	16	130		16	17	米/千克		---Unbleached
5514 1110.10	与棉混纺未漂白聚酯短纤平纹府绸（含聚酯短纤85%以下，每平方米重>170克，含细平布）	16	130		16	17	米/千克		Poplin, fine plain fabrics, mixed with cotton, containing less than 85% by weight of polyester staple fibres, of a weight exceeding 170g/m², unbleached
5514 1110.20	与棉混纺未漂白聚酯短纤机织平布（混纺为含聚酯短纤 85%以下，重质指每平方米重>170克）	16	130		16	17	米/千克		Plain fabrics, mixed with cotton, containing less than 85% by weight of polyester staple fibres, of a weight exceeding 170g/m², unbleached
5514 1110.30	与棉混纺未漂白聚酯短纤平纹帆布（混纺为含聚酯短纤 85%以下，重质指每平方米重>170克）	16	130		16	17	米/千克		Canvas, plain weave, mixed with cotton, containing less than 85% by weight of polyester staple fibres, of a weight exceeding 170g/m², unbleached
5514.1120	---漂白	18	130		16	17	米/千克		---Bleached
5514 1120.10	与棉混纺漂白聚酯短纤平纹府绸（聚酯短纤85%以下，每平方米重>170克，含细平布）	18	130		16	17	米/千克		Poplin, fine plain fabrics, mixed with cotton, containing less than 85% by weight of polyester staple fibres, of a weight exceeding 170g/m², bleached
5514 1120.20	与棉混纺漂白聚酯短纤机织平布（混纺为含聚酯短纤 85%以下，重质指每平方米重>170克）	18	130		16	17	米/千克		Plain fabrics, mixed with cotton, containing less than 85% by weight of polyester staple fibres, of a weight exceeding 170g/m², bleached
5514 1120.30	与棉混纺漂白聚酯短纤平纹帆布（混纺为含聚酯短纤 85%以下，重质指每平方米重>170克）	18	130		16	17	米/千克		Canvas, mixed with cotton, containing less than 85% by weight of polyester staple fibres, of a weight exceeding 170g/m², bleached
	--聚酯短纤纺制的三线或四线斜纹机织物，包括双面斜纹机织物：								--3-thread or 4-thread twill, including cross twill, of polyester staple fibres:
5514.1210	---未漂白	16	130		16	17	米/千克		---Unbleached
5514.1220	---漂白	18	130		16	17	米/千克		---Bleached
	--其他机织物：								--Other woven fabrics:
	---聚酯短纤纺制的机织物：								---Woven fabrics of polyester staple fibres:

税则号列 Tariff Item	商品名称及备注	进口税率 最惠	进口税率 普通	进口税率 暂定	出口退税	增值税率	计量单位	监管条件	Article Description
5514.1911	----未漂白	16	130		16	17	米/千克		----Unbleached
5514.1912	----漂白	18	130		16	17	米/千克		----Bleached
5514.1990	---其他	16	130		16	17	米/千克		---Other
	-染色:								-Dyed:
5514.2100	--聚酯短纤纺制的平纹机织物	10	130		16	17	米/千克		--Of polyester staple fibres, plain weave
5514 2100.10	与棉混纺染色聚酯短纤平纹府绸(含细平布，聚酯短纤85%以下，重质指每平方米重＞170克)	10	130		16	17	米/千克		Poplin, plain weave, including fine plain fabrics, mixed with cotton, containing less than 85% by weight of polyester staple fibres, of a weight exceeding 170g/m², dyed
5514 2100.20	与棉混纺染色聚酯短纤机织平布(混纺为含聚酯短纤 85%以下，重质指每平方米重＞170克)	10	130		16	17	米/千克		Plain fabrics, mixed with cotton, containing less than 85% by weight of polyester staple fibres, of a weight exceeding 170g/m², dyed
5514 2100.30	与棉混纺染色聚酯短纤平纹帆布(混纺为含聚酯短纤 85%以下，重质指每平方米重＞170克)	10	130		16	17	米/千克		Canvas, mixed with cotton, containing less than 85% by weight of polyester staple fibres, of a weight exceeding 170g/m², dyed
5514.2200	--聚酯短纤纺制的三线或四线斜纹机织物，包括双面斜纹机织物	10	130		16	17	米/千克		--3-thread or 4-thread twill, including cross twill, of polyester staple fibres
5514.2300	--其他聚酯短纤纺制的机织物	10	130		16	17	米/千克		--Other woven fabrics of polyester staple fibres
5514 2300.10	与棉混纺染色聚酯短纤其他斜纹布(聚酯短纤 85%以下，每平方米重＞170克，含缎纹布)	10	130		16	17	米/千克		Twill weave, satin weave fabrics, mixed with cotton, containing less than 85% by weight of polyester staple fibres, of a weight exceeding 170g/m², dyed
5514 2300.20	与棉混纺染色聚酯短纤其他帆布(混纺为含聚酯短纤 85%以下，重质指每平方米重＞170克)	10	130		16	17	米/千克		Other canvas, mixed with cotton, containing less than 85% by weight of polyester staple fibres, of a weight exceeding 170g/m², dyed
5514 2300.90	与棉混纺染色聚酯短纤其他机织物(混纺为含聚酯短纤 85%以下，重质指每平方米重＞170克)	10	130		16	17	米/千克		Other woven fabrics, mixed with cotton, containing less than 85% by weight of polyester staple fibres, of a weight exceeding 170g/m², dyed
5514.2900	--其他机织物	10	130		16	17	米/千克		--Other woven fabrics
5514 2900.10	与棉混纺染色其他合纤短纤府绸(含细平布，其他合短纤＜85%，重质指每平方米重＞170克)	10	130		16	17	米/千克		Poplin, including fine plain fabrics, mixed with cotton, containing less than 85% by weight of synthetic staple fibres, of a weight exceeding 170g/m², dyed
5514 2900.20	与棉混纺染色其他合纤短纤平布(混纺为含其他合短纤＜85%，重质指每平方米重＞170克)	10	130		16	17	米/千克		Plain fabrics, mixed with cotton, containing less than 85% by weight of synthetic staple fibres, of a weight exceeding 170g/m², dyed
5514 2900.30	与棉混纺染色其他合纤短纤帆布(混纺为含其他合短纤＜85%，重质指每平方米重＞170克)	10	130		16	17	米/千克		Other canvas, mixed with cotton, containing less than 85% by weight of synthetic staple fibres, of a weight exceeding 170g/m², dyed
5514 2900.40	与棉混纺染色其他合纤短纤斜纹布(含缎纹布，其他合短纤＜85%，重质指每平方米重＞170克)	10	130		16	17	米/千克		Other twill weave, satin weave fabrics, mixed with cotton, containing less than 85% by weight of synthetic staple fibres, of a weight exceeding 170g/m², dyed
5514 2900.90	与棉混纺染色其他合纤短纤其他布(混纺为含其他合短纤＜85%，重质指每平方米重＞170克)	10	130		16	17	米/千克		Other woven fabrics, mixed with cotton, containing less than 85% by weight of synthetic staple fibres, of a weight exceeding 170g/m², dyed
	-色织:								-Of yarns of different colours:
5514.3010	---聚酯短纤纺制的平纹机织物	10	130		16	17	米/千克		---Of polyester staple fibres, plain weave
5514.3020	---聚酯短纤纺制的三线或四线	10	130		16	17	米/千克		---3-thread or 4-thread twill, including cross twill, of

税则号列 Tariff Item	商品名称及备注	进口税率 最惠	进口税率 普通	进口税率 暂定	出口退税	增值税率	计量单位	监管条件	Article Description
	斜纹机织物，包括双面斜纹机织物								polyester staple fibres
5514.3030	---其他聚酯短纤纺制的机织物	10	130		16	17	米/千克		---Other woven fabrics of polyester staple fibres
5514.3090	---其他机织物	10	130		16	17	米/千克		---Other woven fabrics
	-印花:								-Printed:
5514.4100	--聚酯短纤纺制的平纹机织物	10	130		16	17	米/千克		--Of polyester staple fibres, plain weave
5514 4100.10	与棉混纺印花聚酯短纤平纹府绸（聚酯短纤85%以下，每平方米重＞170克，含细平布）	10	130		16	17	米/千克		Poplin, fine plain fabrics, mixed with cotton, containing less than 85% by weight of polyester staple fibres, of a weight exceeding 170g/m², printed
5514 4100.20	与棉混纺印花聚酯短纤机织平布（混纺为含聚酯短纤 85%以下，重质指每平方米重＞170克）	10	130		16	17	米/千克		Plain fabrics, mixed with cotton, containing less than 85% by weight of polyenster staple fibres, of a weight exceeding 170g/m², printed
5514 4100.30	与棉混纺印花聚酯短纤平纹帆布（混纺为含聚酯短纤 85%以下，重质指每平方米重＞170克）	10	130		16	17	米/千克		Canvas, mixed with cotton, containing less than 85% by weight of polyester staple fibres, of a weight exceeding 170g/m², printed
5514.4200	--聚酯短纤纺制的三线或四线斜纹机织物，包括双面斜纹机织物	10	130		16	17	米/千克		--3-thread or 4-thread twill, including cross twill, of polyester staple fibres
5514.4300	--其他聚酯短纤纺制的机织物	10	130		16	17	米/千克		--Other woven fabrics of polyester staple fibres
5514 4300.10	与棉混纺印花聚酯短纤其他斜纹布(含缎纹布，聚酯短纤85%以下，重质指每平方米重＞170克）	10	130		16	17	米/千克		Other twill and satin weave fabrics, mixed with cotton, containing less than 85% by weight of polyesterstaple fibres, of a weight exceeding 170g/m², printed
5514 4300.20	与棉混纺印花聚酯短纤其他帆布(混纺为含聚酯短纤 85%以下，重质指每平方米重＞170克）	10	130		16	17	米/千克		Other canvas, mixed with cotton, containing less than 85% by weight of polyester staple fibres, of a weight exceeding 170g/m², printed
5514 4300.90	与棉混纺印花聚酯短纤其他机织物（混纺为含聚酯短纤 85%以下，重质指每平方米重＞170克）	10	130		16	17	米/千克		Other woven fabrics, mixed with cotton, containing less than 85% by weight of polyester staple fibres, of a weight exceeding 170g/m², printed
5514.4900	--其他机织物	10	130		16	17	米/千克		--Other woven fabrics
5514 4900.10	与棉混纺印花其他合纤短纤府绸（含细平布，其他合纤＜85%，重质指每平方米重＞170克）	10	130		16	17	米/千克		Other poplin, and fine plain fabrics, mixed with cotton, containing less than 85% by weight of synthetic staple fibres, of a weight exceeding 170g/m², printed
5514 4900.20	与棉混纺印花其他合纤短纤平布(混纺为含其他合短纤＜85%，重质指每平方米重＞170克）	10	130		16	17	米/千克		Other plain fabrics, mixed with cotton, containing less than 85% by weight of synthetic staple fibres, of a weight exceeding 170g/m², printed
5514 4900.30	与棉混纺印花其他合纤短纤帆布(混纺为含其他合短纤＜85%，重质指每平方米重＞170克）	10	130		16	17	米/千克		Canvas, mixed with cotton, containing less than 85% by weight of synthetic staple fibres, of a weight exceeding 170g/m², printed
5514 4900.40	与棉混纺印花其他合纤短纤斜纹布（含缎纹布，其他合短纤＜85%，重质指每平方米重＞170克）	10	130		16	17	米/千克		Twill and satin weave fabrics, mixed with cotton, containing less than 85% by weight of synthetic staple fibres, of a weight exceeding 170g/m², printed
5514 4900.90	与棉混纺印花其他合纤短纤其他布（混纺为含其他合短纤＜85%，重质指每平方米重＞170克）	10	130		16	17	米/千克		Other woven fabrics, mixed with cotton, containing less than 85% by weight of synthetic staple fibres, of a weight exceeding 170g/m², printed
55.15	**合成纤维短纤纺制的其他机织物:**								**Other woven fabrics of synthetic staple fibres:**
	-聚酯短纤纺制:								-Of polyester staple fibres:
5515.1100	--主要或仅与粘胶纤维短纤混纺	10	130		16	17	米/千克		--Mixed mainly or solely with viscose rayon staple fibres

税则号列 Tariff Item	商品名称及备注	进口税率			出口退税	增值税率	计量单位	监管条件	Article Description
		最惠	普通	暂定					
5515 1100.11	聚酯短纤蓝粗斜纹布(与粘胶纤维短纤混纺，聚酯短纤含量在85%以下)	10	130		16	17	米/千克		Blue denim, mixed with viscose rayon staple fibres, containing less than 85% by weight of polyester staple fibres
5515 1100.19	聚酯短纤其他色织布(短纤含量在85%以下，提花织物除外，与粘胶纤维短纤混纺)	10	130		16	17	米/千克		Yarn-dyed woven fabrics, mixed with viscose rayon staple fibres, containing less than 85% by weight of polyester staple fibres, other than jacquard weave
5515 1100.21	未漂或漂白聚酯短纤府绸或细平布(聚酯短纤含量在85%以下,主要或仅与粘胶纤维短纤混纺)	10	130		16	17	米/千克		Poplin and fine plain fabrics, unbleached or bleached, containing less than 85% by weight of polyester staple fibres, mixed mainly or solely with viscose rayon staple fibres
5515 1100.22	未漂或漂白聚酯短纤其他机织平布(聚酯短纤含量在85%以下,主要或仅与粘胶纤维短纤混纺)	10	130		16	17	米/千克		Plain fabrics, unbleached or bleached, containing less than 85% by weight of polyester staple fibres, mixed mainly or solely with viscose rayon staple fibres
5515 1100.23	未漂或漂白聚酯短纤其他印染用布(聚酯短纤含量在85%以下,主要或仅与粘胶纤维短纤混纺)	10	130		16	17	米/千克		Woven fabrics for printing and dyeing, unbleached or bleached, containing less than 85% by weight of polyester staple fibres, mixed mainly or solely with viscose rayon staple fibres
5515 1100.24	未漂或漂白聚酯短纤奶酪布等(短纤含量<85%，含薄细布、巴里纱，与粘胶纤维短纤混纺)	10	130		16	17	米/千克		Cheese cloth, including voiles and muslin, unbleached or bleached, containing less than 85% by weight of polyester staple fibres, mixed with viscose rayon staple fibres
5515 1100.25	未漂或漂白聚酯短纤机织帆布(聚酯短纤含量在85%以下，主要或仅与粘胶纤维短纤混纺)	10	130		16	17	米/千克		Canvas, unbleached or bleached, containing less than 85% by weight of polyester staple fibres, mixed mainly or solely with viscose rayon staple fibres
5515 1100.26	未漂或漂白聚酯短纤缎纹或斜纹布(聚酯短纤含量在85%以下,主要或仅与粘胶纤维短纤混纺)	10	130		16	17	米/千克		Other satin weave or twill weave fabrics, unbleached or bleached, containing less than 85% by weight of polyester staple fibres, mixed mainly or solely with viscose rayon staple fibres
5515 1100.27	未漂或漂白聚酯短纤牛津布(聚酯短纤含量在85%以下，主要或仅与粘胶纤维短纤混纺)	10	130		16	17	米/千克		Other oxford fabrics, unbleached or bleached, containing less than 85% by weight of polyester staple fibres, mixed mainly or solely with viscose rayon staple fibres
5515 1100.29	未漂或漂白聚酯短纤其他机织物(聚酯短纤含量在85%以下，主要或仅与粘胶纤维短纤混纺)	10	130		16	17	米/千克		Other woven fabrics, unbleached or bleached, containing less than 85% by weight of polyester staple fibres, mixed mainly or solely with viscose rayon staple fibres
5515 1100.31	其他聚酯短纤府绸或细平布(聚酯短纤含量在85%以下，主要或仅与粘胶纤维短纤混纺)	10	130		16	17	米/千克		Other poplin and fine plain fabrics, containing less than 85% by weight of polyester staple fibres, mixed mainly or solely with viscose rayon staple fibres
5515 1100.32	其他聚酯短纤机织平布(聚酯短纤含量在85%以下，主要或仅与粘胶纤维短纤混纺)	10	130		16	17	米/千克		Other plain fabrics, containing less than 85% by weight of polyester staple fibres, mixed mainly or solely with viscose rayon staple fibres
5515 1100.33	其他聚酯短纤机织印染用布(聚酯短纤含量在85%以下，主要或仅与粘胶纤维短纤混纺)	10	130		16	17	米/千克		Other woven fabrics for printing and dyeing, containing less than 85% by weight of polyester staple fibres, mixed mainly or solely with viscose rayon staple fibres
5515 1100.34	其他聚酯短纤奶酪布等(短纤含量<85%，含薄细布、巴里纱，与粘胶纤维短纤混纺)	10	130		16	17	米/千克		Other cheese cloth, voiles and muslin, containing less than 85% by weight of polyester staple fibres, mixed mainly or solely with viscose rayon staple fibres
5515 1100.35	其他聚酯短纤机织帆布(聚酯短纤含量在85%以下，主要或仅与粘胶纤维短纤混纺)	10	130		16	17	米/千克		Other canvas, containing less than 85% by weight of polyester staple fibres, mixed mainly or solely with viscose rayon staple fibres
5515 1100.36	其他聚酯短纤缎纹或斜纹机织物(聚酯短纤含量在85%以下，主要或仅与粘胶纤维短纤混纺)	10	130		16	17	米/千克		Other twill weave or satin weave fabrics, containing less than 85% by weight of polyester staple fibres, mixed mainly or solely with viscose rayon st ple fibres

税则号列 Tariff Item	商品名称及备注	进口税率 最惠	普通	暂定	出口退税	增值税率	计量单位	监管条件	Article Description
5515 1100.37	其他聚酯短纤牛津布(聚酯短纤含量在85%以下，主要或仅与粘胶纤维短纤混纺)	10	130		16	17	米/千克		Other oxford fabrics, containing less than 85% by weight of polyester staple fibres, mixed mainly or solely with viscose rayon staple fibres
5515 1100.39	其他聚酯短纤其他机织物(聚酯短纤含量在85%以下，主要或仅与粘胶纤维短纤混纺)	10	130		16	17	米/千克		Other woven fabrics, containing less than 85% by weight of polyester staple fibres, mixed mainly or solely with viscose rayon staple fibres
5515.1200	--主要或仅与化学纤维长丝混纺	10	130		16	17	米/千克		--Mixed mainly or solely with man-made filaments
5515 1200.11	未漂或漂聚酯短纤府绸或细平布（聚酯短纤含量在85%以下，与化纤长丝混纺）	10	130		16	17	米/千克		Poplin and fine plain fabrics, unbleached or bleached, containing less than 85% by weight of polyester staple fibres, mixed mainly or solely with man-made filaments
5515 1200.12	未漂白或漂白聚酯短纤平布(聚酯短纤含量在85%以下，与化纤长丝混纺)	10	130		16	17	米/千克		Plain fabrics, unbleached or bleached, containing less than 85% by weight of polyester staple fibres, mixed mainly or solely with man-made filaments
5515 1200.13	未漂白或漂白聚酯短纤印染用布（聚酯短纤含量在85%以下，与化纤长丝混纺）	10	130		16	17	米/千克		Woven fabrics for printing and dyeing, unbleached or bleahed, containing less than 85% by weight of polyester staple fibres, mixed mainly or solely with man-made filaments
5515 1200.14	未漂白或漂白聚酯短纤缎纹或斜纹布(聚酯短纤含量在85%以下，与化纤长丝混纺)	10	130		16	17	米/千克		Satin weave or twill weave fabrics, unbleached or bleached, containing less than 85% by weight of polyester staple fibres, mixed mainly or solely with man-made filaments
5515 1200.19	未漂白或漂白聚酯短纤其他机织物（聚酯短纤含量在 85%以下，与化纤长丝混纺）	10	130		16	17	米/千克		Woven fabrics, unbleached or bleached, containing less than 85% by weight of polyester staple fibres, mixed mainly or solely with man-made filaments
5515 1200.21	其他聚酯短纤府绸或细平布(聚酯短纤含量在85%以下，与化纤长丝混纺)	10	130		16	17	米/千克		Other poplin and fine plain fabrics, mixed mainly or solely with man-made filaments, containing less than 85% by weight of polyester staple fibres
5515 1200.22	其他聚酯短纤平布(聚酯短纤含量在 85%以下，与化纤长丝混纺)	10	130		16	17	米/千克		Other plain fabrics, mixed mainly or solely with man-made filaments, containing less than 85% by weight of polyester staple fibres
5515 1200.23	其他聚酯短纤印染用布(聚酯短纤含量在85%以下，与化纤长丝混纺)	10	130		16	17	米/千克		Other woven fabrics for printing and dyeing, mixed mainly or solely with man-made filaments, containing less than 85% by weight of polyester staple fibres
5515 1200.24	其他聚酯短纤缎纹或斜纹机织物（聚酯短纤含量在85%以下，与化纤长丝混纺）	10	130		16	17	米/千克		Other satin weave or twill weave fabrics, mixed mainly or solely with man-made filaments, containing less than 85% by weight of polyester staple fibres
5515 1200.29	其他聚酯短纤其他机织物(聚酯短纤含量在85%以下，与化纤长丝混纺)	10	130		16	17	米/千克		Other woven fabrics, mixed mainly or solely with man-made filaments, containing less than 85% by weight of polyester staple fibres
5515.1300	--主要或仅与羊毛或动物细毛混纺	10	130		16	17	米/千克		--Mixed mainly or solely with wool or fine animal hair
5515 1300.11	未漂白或漂白的聚酯短纤与精梳毛混纺布(含羊毛或动物细毛36%及以上，聚酯短纤含量在85%以下)	10	130		16	17	米/千克		Woven fabrics, mixed, with 36% or more by weight cf combed wool or fine animal hair, and less than 85% by weight of polyester staple fibres, unbleached or bleached
5515 1300.12	未漂白或漂白的聚酯短纤与粗梳毛混纺布(含羊毛或动物细毛36%及以上，聚酯短纤含量在85%以下)	10	130		16	17	米/千克		Woven fabrics, mixed, with 36% or more by weight carded wool or of fine animal hair, and less than 85% by weight of polyester staple fibres, unbleached or bleached
5515 1300.13	未漂白或漂白的聚酯短纤与精梳毛混纺布(含羊毛或动物细毛36%以下，聚酯短纤含量在 85%以下)	10	130		16	17	米/千克		Woven fabrics, mixed, with less than 36% by weight of combed wool or fine anilmal hair, and less than 85% by weight of polyester staple fibres, unbleached or bleached
5515 1300.19	未漂白或漂白的聚酯短纤与粗	10	130		16	17	米/千克		Woven fabrics, mixed, with less than 36% by weight of

税则号列 Tariff Item	商品名称及备注	进口税率			出口退税	增值税率	计量单位	监管条件	Article Description
		最惠	普通	暂定					
	梳毛混纺布(含羊毛或动物细毛＜36%，聚酯短纤含量在85%以下)								carded wool or of fine animal hair, and less than 85% by weight of polyester staple fibres, unbleached or bleached
5515 1300.21	其他聚酯短纤与精梳毛混纺机织物(含羊毛或动物细毛36%及以上，聚酯短纤含量在85%以下)	10	130		16	17	米/千克		Other woven fabrics, mixed, with less than 36% by weight of combed wool or fine animal hair, and less than 85% by weight of polyester staple fibres
5515 1300.22	其他聚酯短纤与粗梳毛混纺机织物(含羊毛或动物细毛36%及以上，聚酯短纤含量在85%以下)	10	130		16	17	米/千克		Other woven fabrics, mixed, with less than 36% by weight carded wool or fine animal hair, and less than 85% by weight of polyester staple fibres
5515 1300.23	其他聚酯短纤与精梳毛混纺机织物(含羊毛或动物细毛＜36%，聚酯短纤含量在85%以下)	10	130		16	17	米/千克		Other woven fabrics, mixed, with less than 36% by weight of combed wool or fine animal hair, and less than 85% by weight of polyester staple fibres
5515 1300.29	其他聚酯短纤与粗梳毛混纺机织物(含羊毛或动物细毛＜36%，聚酯短纤含量在85%以下)	10	130		16	17	米/千克		Other woven fabrics, mixed, with less than 36% by weight of carded wool or fine animal hair, and less than 85% by weight of polyester staple fibres
5515.1900	--其他	10	130		16	17	米/千克		--Other
5515 1900.11	聚酯短纤与其他纤维混蓝粗斜纹布(混纺为以聚酯短纤为主，但聚酯短纤含量在85%以下)	10	130		16	17	米/千克		Blue denim, twill weave, mixed with other fibres, mixed mainly with polyester staple fibers, containing less than 85% by weight of polyester staple fibres
5515 1900.19	聚酯短纤其他色织机织物(聚酯短纤＜85%，提花织物除外，与其他纤维混纺)	10	130		16	17	米/千克		Woven fabrics, mixed with other fibres containing less than 85% by weight of polyester staple fibres, other than jacquard weave
5515 1900.21	未漂白或漂白聚酯短纤其他府绸(聚酯短纤含量在85%以下，与其他纤维混纺，含细平布)	10	130		16	17	米/千克		Poplin and fine plain fabrics, mixed with other fibres, containing less than 85% by weight of polyester staple fibres, unbleached or bleached
5515 1900.22	未漂白或漂白聚酯短纤其他机织平布(聚酯短纤含量在85%以下，与其他纤维混纺)	10	130		16	17	米/千克		Other plain fabrics, mixed with other fibres, unbleached or bleached, containing less than 85% by weight of polyester staple fibres
5515 1900.23	未漂白或漂白聚酯短纤其他机织印染布(聚酯短纤含量在85%以下，与其他纤维混纺)	10	130		16	17	米/千克		Woven fabrics for printing and dyeing, mixed with other fibres, unbleached or bleached, containing less than 85% by weight of polyester staple fibres
5515 1900.24	未漂白或漂白聚酯短纤奶酪布等(短纤含量＜85%，与其他纤维混纺，含薄细布、巴里纱)	10	130		16	17	米/千克		Cheese cloth, including voiles and muslin, mixed with other fibres, unbleached or bleached, containing less than 85% by weight of polyester staple fibres
5515 1900.25	未漂白或漂白聚酯短纤机织帆布(聚酯短纤含量在85%以下，与其他纤维混纺)	10	130		16	17	米/千克		Canvas, mixed with other fibres, unbleached or bleached, containing less than 85% by weight of polyester staple fibres
5515 1900.26	未漂白或漂白聚酯短纤缎纹或斜纹布(聚酯短纤含量在85%以下，与其他纤维混纺)	10	130		16	17	米/千克		Other satin weave or twill weave fabrics, mixed with other fibres, unbleached or bleached, containing less than 85% by weight of polyester staple fibres
5515 1900.27	未漂白或漂白聚酯短纤牛津布(聚酯短纤含量在85%以下，与其他纤维混纺)	10	130		16	17	米/千克		Other oxford fabrics, mixed with other fibres, unbleached or bleached, containing less than 85% by weight of polyesterstaple fibres
5515 1900.29	未漂白或漂白聚酯短纤其他机织物(聚酯短纤含量在85%以下，与其他纤维混纺)	10	130		16	17	米/千克		Other woven fabrics, mixed with other fibres, unbleached or bleached,containing less than 85% by weight of polyester staple fibres
5515 1900.31	其他聚酯短纤府绸或细平布(聚酯短纤含量在85%以下，与其他纤维混纺)	10	130		16	17	米/千克		Other poplin and fine plain fabrics, mixed with other fibres, containing less than 85% by weight of polyester staple fibres
5515 1900.32	其他聚酯短纤机织平布(聚酯短纤含量在85%以下，与其他纤维混纺)	10	130		16	17	米/千克		Other plain fabrics, mixed with other fibres, containing less than 85% by weight of polyester staple fibres
5515 1900.33	其他聚酯短纤机织印染用布(聚酯短纤含量在85%以下，与其他	10	130		16	17	米/千克		Other woven fabrics for printing and dyeing, mixed with other fibres, containing less than 85% by weight

税则号列 Tariff Item	商品名称及备注	进口税率 最惠	普通	暂定	出口退税	增值税率	计量单位	监管条件	Article Description
	纤维混纺）								of polyester staple fibres
5515 1900.34	其他聚酯短纤奶酪布等(短纤含量＜85%，与其他纤维混纺，含薄细布、巴里纱）	10	130		16	17	米/千克		Other cheese cloth, voiles and muslin, mixed with other fibres, containing less than 85% by weight of polyester staple fibres
5515 1900.35	其他聚酯短纤机织帆布(聚酯短纤含量在85%以下，与其他纤维混纺）	10	130		16	17	米/千克		Other canvas, mixed with other fibres, containing less than 85% by weight of polyester staple fibres
5515 1900.36	其他聚酯短纤缎纹或斜纹机织物（聚酯短纤含量在85%以下，与其他纤维混纺）	10	130		16	17	米/千克		Other satin weave or twill weave fabrics, mixed with other fibres containing less than 85% by weight of polyester staple fibres
5515 1900.37	其他聚酯短纤牛津布(聚酯短纤含量在85%以下，与其他纤维混纺）	10	130		16	17	米/千克		Other oxford fabrics, mixed with other fibres, containing less than 85% weight of polyester staple fibres
5515 1900.39	其他聚酯短纤其他机织物(聚酯短纤含量在85%以下，与其他纤维混纺）	10	130		16	17	米/千克		Other woven fabrics, mixed with other fibres, containing less than 85% by weight of polyester staple fibres
	-聚丙烯腈或变性聚丙烯腈短纤纺制:								-Of acrylic or modacrylic staple fibres:
5515.2100	--主要或仅与化学纤维长丝混纺	10	130		16	17	米/千克		--Mixed mainly or solely with man-made filaments
5515 2100.11	未漂白或漂白腈纶短纤府绸或细平布（腈短纤含量在85%以下，主要或仅与化纤长丝混纺）	10	130		16	17	米/千克		Poplin and fine plain fabrics, containing less than 85% by weight of acrylic or modacrylic staple fibres, mixed mainly or solely with man-made filaments, unbleached or bleached
5515 2100.12	未漂白或漂白腈纶短纤平布(腈短纤含量在85%以下，主要或仅与化纤长丝混纺）	10	130		16	17	米/千克		Plain fabrics, containing less than 85% by weight of acrylic or modacrylic staple fibres, mixed mainly or solely with man-made filaments, unbleached or bleached
5515 2100.13	未漂白或漂白腈纶短纤印染用布（腈短纤含量在85%以下，主要或仅与化纤长丝混纺）	10	130		16	17	米/千克		Woven fabrics for printing and dyeing, mixed mainly or solely with man-made filaments, containing less than 85% by weight of acrylic or modacrylic staple fibres, unbleached or bleached
5515 2100.14	未漂白或漂白腈纶短纤缎纹或斜纹布（腈短纤含量在85%以下，主要或仅与化纤长丝混纺）	10	130		16	17	米/千克		Satin weave or twill weave fabrics, mixed mainly or solely with man-made filaments, containing less than 85% by weight of acrylic or modacrylic staple fibres, unbleached or bleached,
5515 2100.19	未漂白或漂白腈纶短纤其他机织物（腈短纤含量在85%以下，主要或仅与化纤长丝混纺）	10	130		16	17	米/千克		Other woven fabrics, mixed mainly or solely with man-made filaments, containing less than 85% by weight of acrylic staple fibres, unbleached or bleached
5515 2100.21	其他腈纶短纤混纺府绸或细平布（腈短纤含量在85%以下，主要或仅与化纤长丝混纺）	10	130		16	17	米/千克		Other poplin and fine plain fabrics, mixed mainly or solely with man-made filaments, containing less than 85% by weight of acrylic staple fibres
5515 2100.22	其他腈纶短纤平布(腈短纤含量在85%以下，主要或仅与化纤长丝混纺）	10	130		16	17	米/千克		Other plain fabrics, mixed mainly or solely with man-made filaments, containing less than 85% by weight of acrylic staple fibres
5515 2100.23	其他腈纶短纤印染用布(腈短纤含量在85%以下，主要或仅与化纤长丝混纺）	10	130		16	17	米/千克		Other woven fabrics for printing and dyeing, mixed mainly or solely with man-made filaments, containing less than 85% by weight of acrylic staple fibres
5515 2100.24	其他腈纶短纤混纺缎纹或斜纹布（腈短纤含量在85%以下，主要或仅与化纤长丝混纺）	10	130		16	17	米/千克		Other satin weave or twill weave fabrics, mixed mainly or solely with man-made filaments, containing less than 85% by weight of acrylic staple fibres
5515 2100.29	其他腈纶短纤混纺其他机织物（腈短纤含量在85%以下，主要或仅与化纤长丝混纺）	10	130		16	17	米/千克		Other woven fabrics, mixed mainly or solely with man-made filaments, containing less than 85% by weight of acrylic staple fibres
5515.2200	--主要或仅与羊毛或动物细毛混纺	12	130		16	17	米/千克		--Mixed mainly or solely with wool or fine animal hair

税则号列 Tariff Item	商品名称及备注	进口税率			出口退税	增值税率	计量单位	监管条件	Article Description
		最惠	普通	暂定					
5515 2200.11	未漂白或漂白的腈纶短纤与精梳毛混纺布(腈短纤含量<85%,含羊毛或动物细毛36%及以上)	12	130		16	17	米/千克		Woven fabrics, mixed, containing less than 85% by weight of acrylic staple fibres, and 36% or more by weight of combed wool or fine animal hair, unbleached or bleached
5515 2200.12	未漂白或漂白的腈纶短纤与粗梳毛混纺布(腈短纤含量<85%,含羊毛或动物细毛36%及以上)	12	130		16	17	米/千克		Woven fabrics, mixed, containing less than 85% by weight of acrylic staple fibres, and 36% or more by weight carded wool or fine animal hair, unbleached or bleached
5515 2200.13	未漂白或漂白的腈纶短纤与精梳毛混纺布(腈短纤含量<85%,含羊毛或动物细毛<36%)	12	130		16	17	米/千克		Woven fabrics, mixed, containing less than 85% by weight of acrylic staple fibres, and less than 36% by weight of combed wool or fine animal hair, unbleached or bleached
5515 2200.19	未漂白或漂白的腈纶短纤与粗梳毛混纺布(腈短纤含量<85%,含羊毛或动物细毛<36%)	12	130		16	17	米/千克		Woven fabrics, mixed, containing less than 85% by weight of acrylic staple fibres, and less than 36% by weight of carded wool or fine animal hair, unbleached or bleache
5515 2200.21	其他腈纶短纤与精梳毛混纺机织物(腈短纤含量<85%,含羊毛或动物细毛36%及以上)	12	130		16	17	米/千克		Other woven fabrics, mixed, containing less than 85% by weight of acrylic staple fibres, and 36% or more by weight of combed wool or fine animal hair
5515 2200.22	其他腈纶短纤与粗梳毛混纺机织物(腈短纤含量<85%,含羊毛或动物细毛36%及以上)	12	130		16	17	米/千克		Other woven fabrics, mixed, containing less than 85% by weight of acrylic staple fibres, and 36% or more by weight carded wool or of fine animal hair
5515 2200.23	其他腈纶短纤与精梳毛混纺机织物(腈短纤含量<85%,含羊毛或动物细毛<36%)	12	130		16	17	米/千克		Other woven fabrics, mixed, containing less than 85% by weight of acrylic staple fibres, and less than 36% by weight of combed wool or fine animal hair
5515 2200.29	其他腈纶短纤与粗梳毛混纺机织物(腈短纤含量<85%,含羊毛或动物细毛<36%)	12	130		16	17	米/千克		Other woven fabrics, mixed, containing less than 85% by weight of acrylic staple fibre, and 36% or more by weight of carded wool or fine animal hair
5515.2900	--其他	10	130		16	17	米/千克		--Other
5515 2900.11	腈纶短纤与其他纤维混蓝粗斜纹布(混纺为以聚丙烯腈短纤为主,腈短纤含量在85%以下)	10	130		16	17	米/千克		Blue denim, twill weave, mixed mainly with acrylic staple fibers, containing less than 85% by weight of acrylic staple fibres
5515 2900.19	其他腈纶短纤色织机织布(腈短纤含量<85%,提花织物除外,与其他纤维混纺)	10	130		16	17	米/千克		Other woven fabrics, mixed, containing less than 85% by weight of acrylic staple fibres, of different collours, other than jacquard weave
5515 2900.21	其他未漂白或漂白的腈纶短纤府绸(腈短纤含量在85%以下,与其他纤维混纺,含细平布)	10	130		16	17	米/千克		Other poplin and fine plain fabrics, mixed with other fibres, unbleached or bleached, containing less than 85% by weight of acrylic staple fibres
5515 2900.22	其他未漂白或漂白的腈纶短纤平布(腈短纤含量在85%以下,与其他纤维混纺)	10	130		16	17	米/千克		Other plain fabrics, mixed with other fibres,unbleached or bleached, containing less than 85% by weight of acrylic staple fibres
5515 2900.23	其他未漂白或漂白的腈纶短纤印染用布(腈短纤含量在85%以下,与其他纤维混纺)	10	130		16	17	米/千克		Other woven fabrics for printing and dyeing, mixed with other fibres, unbleached or bleached, containing less than 85% by weight of acrylic staple fibres
5515 2900.24	其他未漂白或漂白的腈纶短纤奶酪布等(腈短纤含量<85%,与其他纤维混纺,含薄细布、巴里纱)	10	130		16	17	米/千克		Other cheese cloth, voiles and muslin, mixed with other fibres, unbleached or bleached, containing less than 85% by weight of acrylic staple fibres
5515 2900.25	其他未漂白或漂白的腈纶短纤机织帆布(腈短纤含量在85%以下,与其他纤维混纺)	10	130		16	17	米/千克		Other canvas, mixed with other fibres, unbleached or bleached, containing less than 85% by weight of acrylic staple fibres
5515 2900.26	其他未漂白或漂白的腈纶短纤缎纹布(含斜纹机织物,腈短纤	10	130		16	17	米/千克		Other satin weave or twill weave fabrics, mixed with other fibres, unbleached or bleached containing less

税则号列 Tariff Item	商品名称及备注	进口税率 最惠	普通	暂定	出口退税	增值税率	计量单位	监管条件	Article Description
	含量＜85%，与其他纤维混纺）								than 85% by weight of acrylic staple fibres
5515 2900.27	其他未漂白或漂白的腈纶短纤牛津布（腈短纤含量在85%以下，与其他纤维混纺）	10	130		16	17	米/千克		Other oxford fabrics, mixed with other fibres, unbleached or bleached containing less than 85% by weight of acrylic staple fibres
5515 2900.29	其他未漂白或漂白的腈纶短纤其他机织物（腈短纤含量在85%以下，与其他纤维混纺）	10	130		16	17	米/千克		Other woven fabrics, mixed with other fibres, unbleached or bleached containing less than 85% by weight of acrylic staple fibres
5515 2900.31	其他腈纶短纤府绸或细平布（腈短纤含量在85%以下，与其他纤维混纺）	10	130		16	17	米/千克		Other poplin or fine plain fabrics, mixed with other fibres, containing less than 85% by weight of acrylic staple fibres
5515 2900.32	其他腈纶短纤机织平布（腈短纤含量在85%以下，与其他纤维混纺）	10	130		16	17	米/千克		Other plain fabrics, mixed with other fibres, containing less than 85% by weight of acrylic staple fibres
5515 2900.33	其他腈纶短纤机织印染用布（腈短纤含量在85%以下，与其他纤维混纺）	10	130		16	17	米/千克		Other woven fabrics for printing and dyeing, mixed with other fibres, containing less than 85% by weight of acrylic staple fibres
5515 2900.34	其他腈纶短纤奶酪布等（腈短纤含量＜85%，与其他纤维混纺，含薄细布、巴里纱）	10	130		16	17	米/千克		Other cheese cloth, voiles and muslin, mixed with other fibres, containing less than 85% by weight of acrylic staple fibres
5515 2900.35	其他腈纶短纤机织帆布（腈短纤含量在85%以下，与其他纤维混纺）	10	130		16	17	米/千克		Other canvas, mixed with other fibres, containing less than 85% by weight of acrylic staple fibres
5515 2900.36	其他腈纶短纤与其他纤维混牛津布（腈短纤含量在85%以下，与其他纤维混纺）	10	130		16	17	米/千克		Other oxford fabrics, mixed with other fibres, containing less than 85% by weight of acrylic staple fibres
5515 2900.37	其他腈纶短纤缎纹或斜纹机织物（腈短纤含量在85%以下，与其他纤维混纺）	10	130		16	17	米/千克		Other satin weave or twill weave fabrics, mixed with other fibres, containing less than 85% by weight of acrylic staple fibres
5515 2900.39	其他腈纶短纤与其他纤维混机织物（混纺为以聚丙烯腈短纤为主、腈短纤含量在85%以下）	10	130		16	17	米/千克		Other woven fabrics, mixed with other fibres, containing less than 85% by weight of acrylic staple fibres
	-其他机织物:								-Other woven fabrics:
5515.9100	--主要或仅与化学纤维长丝混纺	10	130		16	17	米/千克		--Mixed mainly or solely with man-made filaments
5515 9100.11	未漂白或漂白的其他合纤短府绸（与化纤长丝混纺，合成纤维短纤含量＜85%，含细平布）	10	130		16	17	米/千克		Poplin and fine plain fabrics, mixed mainly or solely with man-made filaments, containing less than 85% by weight of synthetic staple fibres
5515 9100.12	未漂白或漂白的其他合纤短纤平布（与化纤长丝混纺，合成纤维短纤含量在85%以下）	10	130		16	17	米/千克		Plain fabrics, mixed mainly or solely with man-made filaments, containing less than 85% by weight of synthetic staple fibres,unbleached or bleached
5515 9100.13	未漂白或漂白的其他合纤短纤混印染用布（与化纤长丝混纺，合成纤维短纤含量在85%以下）	10	130		16	17	米/千克		Other woven fabrics for printing and dyeing, mixed mainly or solely with man-made filaments, containing less than 85% by weight of synthetic staple fibres, unbleached or bleached
5515 9100.14	未漂白或漂白的其他合纤短纤缎纹布等（与化纤长丝混纺，合成纤维短纤含量＜85%，含斜纹机织物）	10	130		16	17	米/千克		Other satin weave, twill weave fabrics, mixed mainly or solely with man-made filaments, containing less than 85% by weight of synthetic staple fibres, unbleached or bleached
5515 9100.19	未漂白或漂白的其他合纤短纤其他机织物（与化纤长丝混纺，合成纤维短纤含量在85%以下）	10	130		16	17	米/千克		Other woven fabrics, mixed mainly or solely with man-made filaments, containing less than 85% by weight of synthetic staple fibres, unbleached or bleached
5515 9100.21	其他合纤短纤府绸或细平布（与化纤长丝混纺，合成纤维短纤含量在85%以下）	10	130		16	17	米/千克		Other poplin or fine plain fabrics, mixed mainly or solely with man-made filaments, containing less than 85% by weight of synthetic staple fibres

税则号列 Tariff Item	商品名称及备注	进口税率			出口退税	增值税率	计量单位	监管条件	Article Description
		最惠	普通	暂定					
5515 9100.22	其他合纤短纤平布(与化纤长丝混纺，合成纤维短纤含量在85%以下)	10	130		16	17	米/千克		Other plain fabrics, mixed mainly or solely with man-made filaments,containing less than 85% by weight of synthetic staple fibres
5515 9100.23	其他合纤短纤印染用布(与化纤长丝混纺,合成纤维短纤含量在85%以下)	10	130		16	17	米/千克		Other woven fabrics for printing and dyeing, mixed mainly or solely with man-made filaments, containing less than 85% by weight of synthetic staple fibres
5515 9100.24	其他合纤短纤缎纹或斜纹机织物(与化纤长丝混纺，合成纤维短纤含量在85%以下)	10	130		16	17	米/千克		Other satin weave or twill weave fabrics, mixed mainly or solely with man-made filaments, containing less than 85% by weight of synthetic staple fibres
5515 9100.29	其他合纤短纤其他机织物(与化纤长丝混纺,合成纤维短纤含量在85%以下)	10	130		16	17	米/千克		Other woven fabrics, mixed mainly or solely with man-made filaments, containing less than 85% by weight of synthetic staple fibres
5515.9900	--其他	10	130		16	17	米/千克		--Other
5515 9900.11	其他合纤短纤蓝粗斜纹布(合成纤维短纤含量在85%以下，与其他纤维混纺)	10	130		16	17	米/千克		Other blue denim, twill weave, mixed with other fibres, containing less than 85% by weight of synthetic staple fibres
5515 9900.19	其他合纤短纤其他色织机织物(合成纤维短纤含量<85%，与其他纤维混纺，提花织物除外)	10	130		16	17	米/千克		Other yarn-dyed woven fabrics, mixed with other fibres, other than jacquard weave, containing less than 85% by weight of synthetic staple fibres
5515 9900.21	未漂白或漂白的其他合纤短纤府绸(合成纤维短纤含量在85%以下，与其他纤维混纺，含细平布)	10	130		16	17	米/千克		Other poplin and fine plain fabrics, mixed with other fibres, containing less than 85% by weight of synthetic staple fibres, , unbleached or bleached
5515 9900.22	未漂白或漂白的其他合纤短纤其他平布(合成纤维短纤含量在85%以下，与其他纤维混纺)	10	130		16	17	米/千克		Other plain fabrics, mixed with other fibres,unbleached or bleached, containing less than 85% by weight of synthetic staple fibres
5515 9900.23	未漂白或漂白的其他合纤短纤印染用布(合成纤维短纤含量在85%以下，与其他纤维混纺)	10	130		16	17	米/千克		Other woven fabrics for printing and dyeing, mixed with other fibres, containing less than 85% by weight of synthetic staple fibres, unbleached or bleached
5515 9900.24	未漂白或漂白的其他合纤短纤奶酪布等(合纤短纤含量<85%，与其他纤维混纺，含薄细布、巴里纱)	10	130		16	17	米/千克		Other cheese cloth, voiles and muslin, mixed with other fibres, containing less than 85% by weight of synthetic staple fibres, unbleached or bleached
5515 9900.25	未漂白或漂白的其他合纤短纤帆布(合成纤维短纤含量在85%以下，与其他纤维混纺)	10	130		16	17	米/千克		Other canvas, mixed with other fibres, containing less than 85% by weight of synthetic staple fibres, unbleached or bleached
5515 9900.26	未漂白或漂白的其他合纤短纤混纺缎纹布(合成纤维短纤含量<85%，与其他纤维混纺，含斜纹机织物)	10	130		16	17	米/千克		Other satin weave or twill weave fabrics, mixed with other fibres, containing less than 85% by weight of synthetic staple fibres, unbleached or bleached
5515 9900.27	未漂白或漂白的其他合纤短纤牛津布(合成纤维短纤含量在85%以下，与其他纤维混纺)	10	130		16	17	米/千克		Other oxford fabrics, mixed with other fibres, containing less than 85% by weight of synthetic staple fibres, unbleached or bleached
5515 9900.29	未漂白或漂白的其他合纤短纤其他机织物(合成纤维短纤含量在85%以下，与其他纤维混纺)	10	130		16	17	米/千克		Other woven fabrics, mixed with other fibres, containing less than 85% by weight of synthetic staple fibres, unbleached or bleached
5515 9900.31	其他合纤短纤府绸或细平布(合成纤维短纤含量在85%以下，与其他纤维混纺)	10	130		16	17	米/千克		Other poplin or fine plain fabrics, mixed with other fibres, containing less than 85% by weight of synthetic staple fibres
5515 9900.32	其他合纤短纤其他机织平布(合成纤维短纤含量在85%以下，与其他纤维混纺)	10	130		16	17	米/千克		Other plain fabrics, mixed with other fibres, containing less than 85% by weight of synthetic staple fibres
5515 9900.33	其他合纤短纤机织印染用布(合成纤维短纤含量在85%以下，与	10	130		16	17	米/千克		Other woven fabrics for printing and dyeing, mixed with other fibres, containing less than 85% by weight

税则号列 Tariff Item	商品名称及备注	进口税率 最惠	普通	暂定	出口退税	增值税率	计量单位	监管条件	Article Description
	其他纤维混纺)								of synthetic staple fibres
5515 9900.34	其他合纤短纤奶酪布等(合纤短纤含量<85%,与其他纤维混纺,含薄细布、巴里纱)	10	130		16	17	米/千克		Other cheese cloth, voiles and muslin, mixed with other fibres, containing less than 85% by weight of synthetic staple fibres
5515 9900.35	其他合纤短纤机织帆布(合成纤维短纤含量在85%以下,与其他纤维混纺)	10	130		16	17	米/千克		Other canvas, mixed with other fibres, containing less than 85% by weight of synthetic staple fibres
5515 9900.36	其他合纤短纤缎纹或斜纹机织物(合成纤维短纤含量在85%以下,与其他纤维混纺)	10	130		16	17	米/千克		Other satin weave or twill weave fabrics, mixed with other fibres, containing less than 85% by weight of synthetic staple fibres
5515 9900.37	其他合纤短纤其他纤维混牛津布(合成纤维短纤含量在85%以下,与其他纤维混纺)	10	130		16	17	米/千克		Other oxford fabrics, mixed with other fibres, containing less than 85% by weight of synthetic staple fibres
5515 9900.39	其他合纤短纤其他机织物(合成纤维短纤含量在85%以下,与其他纤维混纺)	10	130		16	17	米/千克		Other woven fabrics, mixed with other fibres, containing less than 85% by weight of synthetic staple fibres
55.16	**人造纤维短纤纺制的机织物:**								**Woven fabrics of artificial staple fibres:**
	-按重量计人造纤维短纤含量在85%及以上:								-Containing 85% or more by weight of artificial staple fibres:
5516.1100	--未漂白或漂白	12	130		16	17	米/千克		--Unbleached or bleached
5516.1200	--染色	10	130		16	17	米/千克		--Dyed
5516.1300	--色织	10	130		16	17	米/千克		--Of yarns of different colours
5516.1400	--印花	10	130		16	17	米/千克		--Printed
	-按重量计人造纤维短纤含量在85%以下,主要或仅与化学纤维长丝混纺:								-Containing less than 85% by weight of artificial staple fibres, mixed mainly or solely with man-made filaments:
5516.2100	--未漂白或漂白	12	130		16	17	米/千克		--Unbleached or bleached
5516 2100.10	未漂白或漂白的人纤短纤府绸或细平布(人造纤维短纤含量在85%以下,与化纤长丝混纺)	12	130		16	17	米/千克		Poplin or fine plain fabrics, unbleached or bleached,containing less than 85% by weight of artificial staple fibres, mixed with man-made filaments
5516 2100.20	未漂白或漂白的人纤短纤平布(人造纤维短纤含量在85%以下,与化纤长丝混纺)	12	130		16	17	米/千克		Plain fabrics, unbleached or bleached,containing less than 85% by weight of artificial staple fibres, mixed with man-made filaments
5516 2100.30	未漂白或漂白的人纤短纤印染用布(人造纤维短纤含量在85%以下,与化纤长丝混纺)	12	130		16	17	米/千克		Woven fabrics for printing and dyeing, unbleached or bleached, containing less than 85% by weight of artificial staple fibres, mixed with man-made filaments
5516 2100.40	未漂白或漂白的人纤短纤缎纹或斜纹布(人造纤维短纤含量在85%以下,与化纤长丝混纺)	12	130		16	17	米/千克		Satin weave or twill weave, unbleached or bleached, containing less than 85% by weight of artificial staple fibres, mixed with man-made filaments
5516 2100.90	未漂白或漂白的人纤短纤其他机织物(人造纤维短纤含量在85%以下,与化纤长丝混纺)	12	130		16	17	米/千克		Other woven fabrics, unbleached or bleached, containing less than 85% by weight of artificial staple fibres, mixed with man-made filaments
5516.2200	--染色	10	130		16	17	米/千克		--Dyed
5516 2200.10	染色人纤短纤府绸或细平布(人造纤维短纤含量在85%以下,与化纤长丝混纺)	10	130		16	17	米/千克		Poplin or fine plain fabrics, dyed, containing less than 85% by weight of artificial staple fibres, mixed with man-made filaments
5516 2200.20	染色人纤短纤平布(人造纤维短纤含量在85%以下,与化纤长丝混纺)	10	130		16	17	米/千克		Plain fabrics, dyed, containing less than 85% by weight of artificial staple fibres, mixed with man-made filaments
5516 2200.30	染色人纤短纤印染用布(人造纤维短纤含量在85%以下,与化纤长丝混纺)	10	130		16	17	米/千克		Woven fabrics for printing and dyeing, dyed, containing less than 85% by weight of artificial staple fibres, mixed with man-made filaments
5516 2200.40	染色人纤短纤缎纹或斜纹机织物(人造纤维短纤含量在85%以	10	130		16	17	米/千克		Satin weave or twill weave fabrics, dyed, containing less than 85% by weight of artificial staple fibres,

税则号列 Tariff Item	商品名称及备注	进口税率 最惠	普通	暂定	出口退税	增值税率	计量单位	监管条件	Article Description
	下，与化纤长丝混纺）								mixed with man-made filaments
5516 2200.90	染色人纤短纤其他机织物(人造纤维短纤含量在85%以下，与化纤长丝混纺）	10	130		16	17	米/千克		Other woven fabrics, dyed, containing less than 85% by weight of artificial staple fibres, mixed with man-made filaments
5516.2300	--色织	10	130		16	17	米/千克		--Of yarns of different colours
5516 2300.10	色织人纤短纤府绸和细平布(人造纤维短纤含量在85%以下，与化纤长丝混纺）	10	130		16	17	米/千克		Yarn-dyed poplin and fine plain fabrics, containing less than 85% by weight of artificial staple fibres, mixed with man-made filaments
5516 2300.20	色织人纤短纤平布(人造纤维短纤含量在85%以下，与化纤长丝混纺）	10	130		16	17	米/千克		Yarn-dyed plain fabrics, containing less than 85% by weight of artificial staple fibres, mixed with man-made filaments
5516 2300.30	色织人纤短纤印染用布(人造纤维短纤含量在85%以下，与化纤长丝混纺）	10	130		16	17	米/千克		Yarn-dyed woven fabrics for printing and dyeing, mixed with man-made filaments, containing less than 85% by weight of artificial staple fibres
5516 2300.40	色织人纤短纤缎纹或斜纹机织物(人造纤维短纤含量在85%以下，与化纤长丝混纺）	10	130		16	17	米/千克		Yarn-dyed satin weave or twill weave fabrics, mixed with man-made filaments, containing less than 85% by weight of artificial staple fibres
5516 2300.90	色织人纤短纤其他机织物(人造纤维短纤含量在85%以下，与化纤长丝混纺）	10	130		16	17	米/千克		Yarn-dyed other woven fabrics, mixed with man-made filaments, containing less than 85% by weight of artificial staple fibres
5516.2400	--印花	10	130		16	17	米/千克		--Printed
5516 2400.10	印花人纤短纤府绸或细平布(人造纤维短纤含量在85%以下，与化纤长丝混纺）	10	130		16	17	米/千克		Poplin or fine plain cloth, printed, containing less than 85% by weight of artificial staple fibres, mixed with man-made filaments
5516 2400.20	印花人纤短纤平布(人造纤维短纤含量在85%以下，与化纤长丝混纺）	10	130		16	17	米/千克		Plain fabrics, printed, containing less than 85% by weight of artificial staple fibres, mixed with man-made filaments
5516 2400.30	印花人纤短纤印染用布(人造纤维短纤含量在85%以下，与化纤长丝混纺）	10	130		16	17	米/千克		Woven fabrics for printing and dyeing, printed, containing less than 85% by weight of artificial staple fibres, mixed with man-made filaments
5516 2400.40	印花人纤短纤缎纹或斜纹机织物(人造纤维短纤含量在85%以下，与化纤长丝混纺）	10	130		16	17	米/千克		Satin weave or twill weave fabrics, printed, containing less than 85% by weight of artificial staple fibres, mixed with man-made filaments
5516 2400.90	印花人纤短纤其他布(人造纤维短纤含量在85%以下，与化纤长丝混纺）	10	130		16	17	米/千克		Other woven fabrics, printed, containing less than 85% by weight of artificial staple fibres, mixed with man-made filaments
	-按重量计人造纤维短纤含量在85%以下，主要或仅与羊毛或动物细毛混纺:								-Containing less than 85% by weight of artificial staple fibres, mixed mainly or solely with wool or fine animal hair:
5516.3100	--未漂白或漂白	12	130		16	17	米/千克		--Unbleached or bleached
5516 3100.11	未漂白或漂白人纤短纤与精梳毛混纺布(人造纤维短纤含量<85%，羊毛或动物细毛 36%及以上）	12	130		16	17	米/千克		Woven fabrics, mixed, containing less than 85% by weight of artificial staple fibres, and 36% or more by weight of combed wool or fine animal hair, unbleached or bleached
5516 3100.19	未漂白或漂白人纤短纤与粗梳毛混纺布(人造纤维短纤含量<85%，羊毛或动物细毛 36%及以上）	12	130		16	17	米/千克		Woven fabrics, mixed, containing less than 85% by weight of artificial staple fibres, and 36% or more by weight of carded wool or fine animal hair, unbleached or bleached
5516 3100.21	未漂白或漂白人纤短纤与精梳毛混纺布(人造纤维短纤含量<85%，羊毛或动物细毛<36%）	12	130		16	17	米/千克		Woven fabrics, mixed, containing less than 85% by weight of artificial staple fibres, and less than 36% by weight of combed wool or fine animal hair, unbleached or bleached

税则号列 Tariff Item	商品名称及备注	进口税率 最惠	普通	暂定	出口退税	增值税率	计量单位	监管条件	Article Description
5516 3100.29	未漂白或漂白人纤短纤与粗梳毛混纺布(人造纤维短纤含量<85%，羊毛或动物细毛<36%)	12	130		16	17	米/千克		Woven fabrics, mixed, containing less than 85% by weight of artificial staple fibres, and less than 36% by weight of carded wool or fine animal hair, unbleached or bleached
5516.3200	--染色	10	130		16	17	米/千克		--Dyed
5516 3200.11	染色人纤短纤与精梳毛混纺机织物(人造纤维短纤含量<85%，羊毛或动物细毛36%及以上)	10	130		16	17	米/千克		Woven fabrics, dyed, mixed, containing less than 85% by weight of artificial staple fibres, and 36% or more by weight of combed wool or fine animal hair
5516 3200.19	染色人纤短纤与粗梳毛混纺机织物(人造纤维短纤含量<85%，羊毛或动物细毛36%及以上)	10	130		16	17	米/千克		Woven fabrics, dyed, mixed, containing less than 85% by weight of artificial staple fibres, and 36% or more by weight carded of wool or fine animal hair
5516 3200.21	染色人纤短纤与精梳毛混纺机织物(人造纤维短纤含量<85%，羊毛或动物细毛<36%)	10	130		16	17	米/千克		Woven fabrics, dyed, mixed, containing less than 85% by weight of artificial staple fibres, and less than 36% by weight of combed wool or fine animal hair
5516 3200.29	染色人纤短纤与粗梳毛混纺机织物(人造纤维短纤含量<85%，羊毛或动物细毛<36%)	10	130		16	17	米/千克		Woven fabrics, dyed, mixed, containing less than 85% by weight of artificial staple fibres, and less than 36% by weight of carded wool or fine animal hair
5516.3300	--色织	10	130		16	17	米/千克		--Of yarns of different colours
5516 3300.11	色织人纤短纤与精梳毛混纺机织物(人造纤维短纤含量<85%，羊毛或动物细毛36%及以上)	10	130		16	17	米/千克		Woven fabrics yarn-dyed, mixed, containing less than 85% by weight of artificial staple fibres, and 36% or more by weight of combed wool or fine animal hair
5516 3300.19	色织人纤短纤与粗梳毛混纺机织物(人造纤维短纤含量<85%，羊毛或动物细毛36%及以上)	10	130		16	17	米/千克		Woven fabrics yarn-dyed, mixed, containing less than 85% by weight of artificial staple fibres, and 36% or more by weight of carded wool or fine animal hair
5516 3300.21	色织人纤短纤与精梳毛混纺机织物(人造纤维短纤含量<85%，羊毛或动物细毛<36%)	10	130		16	17	米/千克		Woven fabrics yarn-dyed, mixed, containing less than 85% by weight of artificial staple fibres, and less than 36% by weight of combed wool or fine animal hair
5516 3300.29	色织人纤短纤与粗梳毛混纺机织物(人造纤维短纤含量<85%，羊毛或动物细毛<36%)	10	130		16	17	米/千克		Woven fabrics yarn-dyed, mixed, containing less than 85% by weight of artificial staple fibres, and less than 36% by weight of carded wool or fine animal hair
5516.3400	--印花	10	130		16	17	米/千克		--Printed
5516 3400.11	印花人纤短纤与精梳毛混纺机织物(人造纤维短纤含量<85%，羊毛或动物细毛36%及以上)	10	130		16	17	米/千克		Woven fabrics, printed, mixed, containing less than 85% by weight of artificial staple fibres, and 36% or more by weight of combed wool or fine animal hair
5516 3400.19	印花人纤短纤与粗梳毛混纺机织物(人造纤维短纤含量<85%，羊毛或动物细毛36%及以上)	10	130		16	17	米/千克		Woven fabrics, printed, mixed, containing less than 85% by weight of artificial staple fibres, and 36% or more by weight of carded wool or fine animal hair
5516 3400.21	印花人纤短纤与精梳毛混纺机织物(人造纤维短纤含量<85%，羊毛或动物细毛<36%)	10	130		16	17	米/千克		Woven fabrics, printed, mixed, containing less than 85% by weight of artificial staple fibres, and less than 36% by weight of combed wool or fine animal hair
5516 3400.29	印花人纤短纤与粗梳毛混纺机织物(人造纤维短纤含量<85%，羊毛或动物细毛<36%)	10	130		16	17	米/千克		Woven fabrics, printed, mixed, containing less than 85% by weight of artificial staple fibres, and less than 36% by weight of carded wool or fine animal hair
	-按重量计人造纤维短纤含量在85%以下，主要或仅与棉混纺:								-Containing less than 85% by weight of artificial staple fibres, mixed mainly or solely with cotton:
5516.4100	--未漂白或漂白	12	130		16	17	米/千克		--Unbleached or bleached
5516 4100.10	未漂白或漂白人纤短纤府绸或细平布（人造纤维短纤含量在85%以下，与棉混纺）	12	130		16	17	米/千克		Poplin and fine plain fabrics, unbleached or bleached, mixed with cotton, containing less than 85% by weight of artificial staple fibres
5516 4100.20	未漂白或漂白人纤短纤与棉混纺平布（混纺为以人纤短纤为主，但人造纤维短纤含量在85%以下）	12	130		16	17	米/千克		Plain fabrics, unbleached or bleached, mixed with cotton, and mainly with artificial staple fibers, containing less than 85% by weight of artificial staple fibres
5516 4100.30	与棉混纺的未漂白或漂白人纤短纤印染用布(混纺为以人纤短	12	130		16	17	米/千克		Woven fabrics for printing and dyeing, unbleached or bleached, mixed with cotton, and mainly with artificial

税则号列 Tariff Item	商品名称及备注	进口税率 最惠	普通	暂定	出口退税	增值税率	计量单位	监管条件	Article Description
	纤为主,但人造纤维短纤含量在85%以下)								staple fibres, containing less than 85% by weight of artificial staple fibres
5516 4100.40	未漂白或漂白人纤短纤与棉混纺的奶酪布等(人造纤维短纤含量在85%以下,含薄细布、巴里纱)	12	130		16	17	米/千克		Cheese cloth, voiles and muslin, unbleached or bleached, mixed with cotton, containing less than 85% by weight of artificial staple fibres
5516 4100.50	与棉混纺的未漂白或漂白人纤短纤机织帆布(混纺为以人纤短纤为主,但人造纤维短纤含量在85%以下)	12	130		16	17	米/千克		Canvas, unbleached or bleached, mixed with cotton, and mainly with artificial staple fibres, containing less than 85% by weight of artificial staple fibres
5516 4100.60	与棉混纺的未漂白或漂白人纤短纤缎纹布等(含斜纹布,人造纤维短纤含量在85%以下)	12	130		16	17	米/千克		Satin weave or twill weave fabrics, unbleached or bleached, mixed with cotton, containing less than 85% by weight of artificial staple fibres
5516 4100.70	与棉混纺的未漂白或漂白人纤短纤牛津布(混纺为以人纤短纤为主,但人造纤维短纤含量在85%以下)	12	130		16	17	米/千克		Oxford fabrics, unbleached or bleached, mixed with cotton, and mainly with artificial staple fibres, containing less than 85% by weight of artificial staple fibre
5516 4100.90	与棉混纺的未漂白或漂白人纤短纤其他布(混纺为以人纤短纤为主,但人造纤维短纤含量在85%以下)	12	130		16	17	米/千克		Other woven fabrics, unbleached or bleached, mixed with cotton c and mainly with artificial staple fibres, containing less than 85% by weight of artificial staple fibres
5516.4200	--染色	12	130		16	17	米/千克		--Dyed
5516 4200.10	与棉混纺的染色人纤短纤府绸或细平布(混纺为以人纤短纤为主,但人造纤维短纤含量在85%以下)	12	130		16	17	米/千克		Poplin and fine plain fabrics, dyed, mixed with cotton ,and mainly with artificial staple fibres, containing less than 85% by weight of artificial staple fibres
5516 4200.20	与棉混纺的染色人纤短纤平布(混纺为以人纤短纤为主,但人造纤维短纤含量在85%以下)	12	130		16	17	米/千克		Plain fabrics, dyed, mixed with cotton ,and mainly with artificial staple fibres, containing less than 85% by weight of artificial staple fibres
5516 4200.30	与棉混纺的染色人纤短纤印染用布(混纺为以人纤短纤为主,但人造纤维短纤含量在 85%以下)	12	130		16	17	米/千克		Woven fabrics for printing and dyeing, dyed, mixed with cotton ,and mainly with artificial staple fibres, containing less than 85% by weight of artificial staple fibre
5516 4200.40	与棉混纺的染色人纤短纤奶酪布等(含薄细布、巴里纱,人造纤维短纤含量在85%以下)	12	130		16	17	米/千克		Cheese cloth, voiles and muslin, dyed,mixed with cotton, containing less than 85% by weight of artificial staple fibres
5516 4200.50	与棉混纺的染色人纤短纤机织帆布(混纺为以人纤短纤为主,但人造纤维短纤含量在 85%以下)	12	130		16	17	米/千克		Canvas, dyed, mixed with cotton ,and mainly with artificial staple fibres, containing less than 85% by weight of artificial staple fibres
5516 4200.60	与棉混纺的染色人纤短纤缎纹或斜纹布(混纺为以人纤短纤为主,但人造纤维短纤含量在85%以下)	12	130		16	17	米/千克		Satin weave or twill weave fabrics, dyed, mixed with cotton ,and mainly with artificial staple fibres, containing less than 85% by weight of artificial staple fibres
5516 4200.70	与棉混纺的染色人纤短纤牛津布(混纺为以人纤短纤为主,但人造纤维短纤含量在85%以下)	12	130		16	17	米/千克		Oxford fabrics, dyed, mixed with cotton ,and mainly with artificial staple fibres, containing less than 85% by weight of artificial staple fibres
5516 4200.90	与棉混纺的染色人纤短纤其他机织物(混纺为以人纤短纤为主,但人造纤维短纤含量在85%以下)	12	130		16	17	米/千克		Woven fabrics, dyed, mixed with cotton, and mainly with artificial staple fibres, containing less than 85% by weight of artificial staple fibres
5516.4300	--色织	10	130		16	17	米/千克		--Of yarns of different colours
5516 4300.10	与棉混纺的人纤短纤色织蓝色粗斜纹布(混纺为以人纤短纤为主,但人造纤维短纤含量在85%以下)	10	130		16	17	米/千克		Blue denim, twill weave, yarn-dyed, mixed with cotton ,and mainly with artificial staple fibres, containing less than 85% by weight of artificial staple fibres

税则号列 Tariff Item	商品名称及备注	进口税率 最惠	普通	暂定	出口退税	增值税率	计量单位	监管条件	Article Description
5516 4300.20	与棉混纺人纤短纤色织提花机织物（混纺为以人纤短纤为主，但人造纤维短纤含量在 85%以下）	10	130		16	17	米/千克		Woven fabrics, jacquard weave, yarn-dyed, mixed with cotton ,and mainly with artificial staple fibres, containing less than 85% by weight of artificial staple fibres
5516 4300.90	与棉混纺人纤短纤其他色织机织物（混纺为以人纤短纤为主，但人造纤维短纤含量在 85%以下）	10	130		16	17	米/千克		Woven fabrics, yarns-dyed, mixed with cotton ,and mainly with artificial staple fibres, containing less than 85% by weight of artificial staple fibres
5516.4400	--印花	10	130		16	17	米/千克		--Printed
5516 4400.10	与棉混纺印花人纤短纤府绸或细平布（混纺为以人纤短纤为主，但人造纤维短纤含量在 85%以下）	10	130		16	17	米/千克		Poplin and fine plain fabrics, printed, mixed with cotton ,and mainly with artificial staple fibres, containing less than 85% by weight of artificial staple fibres
5516 4400.20	与棉混纺印花人纤短纤平布(混纺为以人纤短纤为主，但人造纤维短纤含量在 85%以下）	10	130		16	17	米/千克		Plain fabrics, printed, mixed with cotton ,and mainly with artificial staple fibres, containing less than 85% by weight of artificial staple fibres
5516 4400.30	与棉纺的混印花人纤短纤印染用布（混纺为以人纤短纤为主，但人造纤维短纤含量在 85%以下）	10	130		16	17	米/千克		Woven fabrics for printing and dyeing, printed, mixed with cotton ,and mainly with artificial staple fibres, containing less than 85% by weight of artificial staple fibres
5516 4400.40	与棉混纺印花人纤短纤奶酪布等（含薄细布、巴里纱，人造纤维短纤含量在 85%以下）	10	130		16	17	米/千克		Cheese cloth, voiles and muslin, printed, mixed with cotton, containing less than 85% by weight of artificia staple fibres
5516 4400.50	与棉混纺印花人纤短纤机织帆布（混纺为以人纤短纤为主，但人造纤维短纤含量在 85%以下）	10	130		16	17	米/千克		Canvas, printed, mixed with cotton ,and mainly with artificial staple fibres, containing less than 85% by weight of artificial staple fibres
5516 4400.60	印花人纤短纤缎纹或斜纹机织物（与棉混纺，人造纤维短纤含量在 85%以下）	10	130		16	17	米/千克		Woven fabrics, satin weave or twill weave, printed, mixed with cotton, containing less than 85% by weight of artificial staple fibres
5516 4400.70	与棉混纺印花人纤短纤牛津布（混纺为以人纤短纤为主，但人造纤维短纤含量在 85%以下）	10	130		16	17	米/千克		Woven oxford fabrics, printed, mixed with cotton ,and mainly with ariti ficial staple fibres, containing less than 85% by weight of artificial staple fibres
5516 4400.90	与棉混纺印花人纤短纤其他机织物（混纺为以人纤短纤为主，但人造纤维短纤含量在 85%以下）	10	130		16	17	米/千克		Other woven fabrics, printed, mixed with cotton, and mainly with artificial staple fibres, containing less than 85% by weight of artificial staple fibres
	-其他:								-Other:
5516.9100	--未漂白或漂白	12	130		16	17	米/千克		--Unbleached or bleached
5516 9100.10	未漂或漂白人纤短纤府绸或细平布（与其他纤维混纺，人造纤维短纤含量在 85%以下）	12	130		16	17	米/千克		Poplin and fine plain fabrics, unbleached or bleached, mixed with other fibres, containing less than 85% by weight of artificial staple fibres
5516 9100.20	未漂或漂白人纤短纤机织平布（与其他纤维混纺，人造纤维短纤含量在 85%以下）	12	130		16	17	米/千克		Plain fabrics, unbleached or bleached, mixed with other fibres, containing less than 85% by weight of artificial staple fibres
5516 9100.30	未漂或漂白人纤短纤印染用布（与其他纤维混纺，人造纤维短纤含量在 85%以下）	12	130		16	17	米/千克		Woven fabrics for printing and dyeing, unbleached or bleached, mixed with other fibres, containing less than 85% by weight of artificial staple fibres
5516 9100.40	未漂或漂白人纤短纤奶酪布等（与其他纤维混纺，人纤短纤含量<85%，含薄细布、巴里纱）	12	130		16	17	米/千克		Cheese cloth，voiles and muslin, unbleached or bleached, mixed with other fibres, containing less than 85% by weight of artificial staple fibres
5516 9100.50	未漂或漂白人纤短纤机织帆布（与其他纤维混纺，人造纤维短纤含量在 85%以下）	12	130		16	17	米/千克		Canvas, unbleached or bleached, mixed with other fibres, containing less than 85% by weight of artificial staple fibres
5516 9100.60	未漂或漂白人纤短纤缎纹或斜纹布（与其他纤维混纺，人造纤	12	130		16	17	米/千克		Satin weave or twill weave fabrics, unbleached or bleached, mixed with other fibres, containing less than

税则号列 Tariff Item	商品名称及备注	进口税率 最惠	普通	暂定	出口退税	增值税率	计量单位	监管条件	Article Description
	维短纤含量在85%以下)								85% by weight of artificial staple fibres
5516 9100.70	未漂或漂白人纤短纤牛津布(与其他纤维混纺,人造纤维短纤含量在85%以下)	12	130		16	17	米/千克		Oxford fabrics, unbleached or bleached, mixed with other fibres, containing less than 85% by weight of artificial staple fibres
5516 9100.90	未漂或漂白人纤短纤其他机织物(与其他纤维混纺,人造纤维短纤含量在85%以下)	12	130		16	17	米/千克		Other woven fabrics, unbleached or bleached, mixed with other fibres, containing less than 85% by weight of artificial staple fibres
5516.9200	--染色	10	130		16	17	米/千克		--Dyed
5516 9200.10	染色人纤短纤府绸或细平布(与其他纤维混纺,人造纤维短纤含量在85%以下)	10	130		16	17	米/千克		Poplin and fine plain fabrics, dyed, mixed with other fibres, containing less than 85% by weight of artificial staple fibres
5516 9200.20	染色人纤短纤机织平布(与其他纤维混纺,人造纤维短纤含量在85%以下)	10	130		16	17	米/千克		Plain fabrics, dyed, mixed with other fibres, containing less than 85% by weight of artificial staple fibres
5516 9200.30	染色人纤短纤印染用布(与其他纤维混纺,人造纤维短纤含量在85%以下)	10	130		16	17	米/千克		Woven fabrics for printing and dyeing, dyed,mixed with other fibres, containing less than 85% by weight of artificial staple fibres
5516 9200.40	染色人纤短纤奶酪布等(与其他纤维混纺,人纤短纤含量<85%,含薄细布、巴里纱)	10	130		16	17	米/千克		Cheese cloth, voiles and muslin, dyed,mixed with other fibres, containing less than 85% by weight of artificial staple fibres
5516 9200.50	染色人纤短纤机织帆布(与其他纤维混纺,人造纤维短纤含量在85%以下)	10	130		16	17	米/千克		Canvas, dyed, mixed with other fibres, containing less than 85% by weight of artificial staple fibres
5516 9200.60	染色人纤短纤缎纹或斜纹机织物(与其他纤维混纺,人造纤维短纤含量在85%以下)	10	130		16	17	米/千克		Satin weave or twill weave fabrics, dyed, mixed with other fibres, containing less than 85% by weight of artificial staple fibres
5516 9200.70	染色人纤短纤牛津布(与其他纤维混纺,人造纤维短纤含量在85%以下)	10	130		16	17	米/千克		Oxford fabrics, dyed, mixed with other fibres, containing less than 85% by weight of artificial staple fibres
5516 9200.90	染色人纤短纤其他机织物(与其他纤维混纺,人造纤维短纤含量在85%以下)	10	130		16	17	米/千克		Other woven fabrics, dyed, mixed with other fibres, containing less than 85% by weight of artificial staple fibres
5516.9300	--色织	10	130		16	17	米/千克		--Of yarns of different colours
5516 9300.10	人纤短纤色织蓝粗斜纹布(与其他纤维混纺,人造纤维短纤含量在85%以下)	10	130		16	17	米/千克		Blue denim, twill weave, yarn-dyed, mixed with other fibres, containing less than 85% by weight of artificial staple fibres
5516 9300.20	色织人纤短纤提花机织物(与其他纤维混纺,人造纤维短纤含量在85%以下)	10	130		16	17	米/千克		Woven fabrics, jacquard weave, yarn-dyed, mixed with other fibres, containing less than 85% by weight of artificial staple fibres
5516 9300.90	色织人纤短纤其他机织物(与其他纤维混纺,人造纤维短纤含量在85%以下)	10	130		16	17	米/千克		Other woven fabrics, yarn-dyed, mixed with other fibres, containing less than 85% by weight of artificial staple fibres
5516.9400	--印花	10	130		16	17	米/千克		--Printed
5516 9400.10	印花人造纤维短纤府绸或细平布(与其他纤维混纺,按重量计人造纤维短纤含量在85%以下)	10	130		16	17	米/千克		Poplin or fine plain fabrics, printed, mixed with other fibres, containing less than 85% by weight of artificial staple fibres
5516 9400.20	印花人造纤维短纤机织平布(与其他纤维混纺,按重量计人造纤维短纤含量在85%以下)	10	130		16	17	米/千克		Plain fabrics, printed, mixed with other fibres, containing less than 85% by weight of artificial staple fibres
5516 9400.30	印花人造纤维短纤印染用布(与其他纤维混纺,按重量计人造纤维短纤含量在85%以下)	10	130		16	17	米/千克		Woven fabrics for printing and dyeing, printed, mixed with other fibres, containing less than 85% by weight of artificial staple fibres
5516 9400.40	印花人造纤维短纤奶酪布等(含薄细布、巴里纱,与其他纤维混	10	130		16	17	米/千克		Cheese cloth, voiles and muslin, printed, mixed with other fibres, containing less than 85% by weight of

税则号列 Tariff Item	商品名称及备注	进口税率			出口退税	增值税率	计量单位	监管条件	Article Description
		最惠	普通	暂定					
	纺，人纤短纤含量<85%）								artificial staple fibres
5516 9400.50	印花人造纤维短纤机织帆布(与其他纤维混纺,按重量计人造纤维短纤含量在85%以下)	10	130		16	17	米/千克		Canvas, printed, mixed with other fibres, containing less than 85% by weight of artificial staple fibres
5516 9400.60	印花人纤短纤缎纹或斜纹机织物（与其他纤维混纺，按重量计人造纤维短纤含量在85%以下）	10	130		16	17	米/千克		Satin weave or twill weave fabrics, printed, mixed with other fibres, containing less than 85% by weight of artificial staple fibres
5516 9400.70	印花人造纤维短纤牛津布（与其他纤维混纺，按重量计人造纤维短纤含量在85%以下）	10	130		16	17	米/千克		Oxford fabrics, printed, mixed with other fibres, containing less than 85% by weight of artificial staple fibres
5516 9400.90	印花人造纤维短纤其他机织物（与其他纤维混纺,按重量计人造纤维短纤含量在85%以下）	10	130		16	17	米/千克		Other woven fabrics, printed, mixed with other fibres, containing less than 85% by weight of artificial staple fibres

第五十六章
絮胎、毡呢及无纺织物；特种纱线；线、绳、索、缆及其制品

注释：

一、本章不包括：

（一）用各种物质或制剂（例如，第三十三章的香水或化妆品、品目34.01的肥皂或洗涤剂、品目34.05的光洁剂及类似制剂、品目38.09的织物柔软剂）浸渍、涂布、包覆的絮胎、毡呢或无纺织物，其中的纺织材料仅作为承载介质；

（二）品目58.11的纺织产品；

（三）以毡呢或无纺织物为底的砂布及类似品（品目68.05）；

（四）以毡呢或无纺织物为底的粘聚或复制云母（品目68.14）；

（五）以毡呢或无纺织物为底的金属箔（通常归入第十四类或第十五类）；或

（六）品目96.19的卫生巾（护垫）及止血塞、婴儿尿布及尿布衬里和类似品。

二、所称“毡呢”，包括针刺机制毡呢以及纤维本身通过缝编工序增强了抱合力的纺织纤维网状织物。

三、品目56.02及56.03分别包括用各种性质（紧密结构或泡沫状）的塑料或橡胶浸渍、涂布、包覆或层压的毡呢及无纺织物。

品目56.03还包括用塑料或橡胶作粘合材料的无纺织物。

但品目56.02及56.03不包括：

（一）用塑料或橡胶浸渍、涂布、包覆或层压，按重量计纺织材料含量在50%及以下的毡呢或者完全嵌入塑料或橡胶之内的毡呢（第三十九章或第四十章）；

（二）完全嵌入塑料或橡胶之内的无纺织物，以及用肉眼可辨别出两面都用塑料或橡胶涂布、包覆的无纺织物，涂布或包覆所引起的颜色变化可不予考虑（第三十九章或第四十章）；或

（三）与毡呢或无纺织物混制的泡沫塑料或海绵橡胶板、片或扁条，纺织材料仅在其中起增强作用（第三十九章或第四十章）。

四、品目56.04不包括用肉眼无法辨别出是否经过浸渍、涂布或包覆的纺织纱线或品目54.04或54.05的扁条及类似品（通常归入第五十章至第五十五章）；运用本条规定，可不考虑浸渍、涂布或包覆所引起的颜色变化。

Chapter 56
Wadding, felt and nonwovens; special yarns; twine, cordage, ropes and cables and articles thereof

Chapter Notes:

1. This Chapter does not cover:

(a) Wadding, felt or nonwovens, impregnated, coated or covered with substances or preparations (for example, perfumes or cosmetics of Chapter 33, soaps or detergents of heading 34.01, polishes, creams or similar preparations of heading 34.05, fabric softeners of heading 38.09) where the textile material is present merely as a carrying medium;

(b) Textile products of heading 58.11;

(c) Natural or artificial abrasive powder or grain, on a backing of felt or nonwovens (heading 68.05);

(d) Agglomerated or reconstituted mica, on a backing of felt or nonwovens (heading 68.14);

(e) Metal foil on a backing of felt or nonwovens (generally Section XIV or XV); or

(f) Sanitary towels(pads) and tampons, napkins and napkin liners for babies and similar articles of heading 96.19.

2. The term “felt” includes needleloom felt and fabrics consisting of a web of textile fibres the cohesion of which has been enhanced by a stitch-bonding process using fibres from the web itself.

3. Headings 56.02 and 56.03 cover respectively felt and nonwovens, impregnated, coated, covered or laminated with plastics or rubber whatever the nature of these materials (compact or cellular).

Heading 56.03 also includes nonwovens in which plastics or rubber forms the bonding substance.

Headings 56.02 and 56.03 do not, however, cover:

(a) Felt impregnated, coated, covered or laminated with plastics or rubber, containing 50% or less by weight of textile material or felt completely embedded in plastics or rubber (Chapter 39 or 40);

(b) Nonwovens, either completely embedded in plastics or rubber, or entirely coated or covered on both sides with such materials, provided that such coating or covering can be seen with the naked eye with no account being taken of any resulting change of colour (Chapter 39 or 40); or

(c) Plates, sheets or strip of cellular plastics or cellular rubber combined with felt or nonwovens, where the textile material is present merely for reinforcing purposes (Chapter 39 or 40).

4. Heading 56.04 does not cover textile yarn, or strip or the like of heading 54.04 or 54.05, in which the impregnation, coating or covering cannot be seen with the naked eye (usually Chapters 50 to 55); for the purpose of this provision, no account should be taken of any resulting change of colour.

税则号列 Tariff Item	商品名称及备注	进口税率 最惠	进口税率 普通	进口税率 暂定	出口退税	增值税率	计量单位	监管条件	Article Description
56.01	**纺织材料絮胎及其制品；长度不超过 5 毫米的纺织纤维（纤维屑）、纤维粉末及球结：**								**Wadding of textile materials and articles thereof; textile fibres, not exceeding 5mm in length(flock), textile dust and mill neps:**
	-絮胎；其他絮胎制品：								-Wadding; other articles of wadding:
5601.2100	--棉制	10	50		16	17	千克		--Of cotton
5601 2100.10	棉制的成匹絮胎	10	50		16	17	千克		Cotton wadding , into a piece
5601 2100.90	其他棉制的絮胎及絮胎制品	10	50		16	17	千克		Other cotton wadding and its articles
	--化学纤维制：								--Of man-made fibres:
5601.2210	---卷烟滤嘴	12	100		16	17	千克	7	---Cigarette filter tips
5601.2290	---其他	12	100		16	17	千克		---Other
5601 2290.10	化学纤维制的成匹絮胎	12	100		16	17	千克		Wadding of man-made fibres, into a piece
5601 2290.90	化学纤维制的其他絮胎及絮胎制品	12	100		16	17	千克		Other wadding and its article, of man-made fibres
5601.2900	--其他	10	90		16	17	千克		--Other
5601 2900.10	羊毛或动物细毛制絮胎及制品	10	90		16	17	千克		Wadding and its articles, of wool or fine animal hair
5601 2900.90	其他纺织材料制絮胎及制品	10	90		16	17	千克		Wadding and its articles, of other textile materials
5601.3000	-纤维屑、纤维粉末及球结	10	100		16	17	千克		-Textile flock and dust and mill neps
5601 3000.10[暂]	由两种或以上有机聚合物纺制的纤维(横截面为皮芯结构或并列结构或海岛结构，长度不超过5mm)	10	100	5	16	17	千克		Textile fibres spinned by two or more organic polymer, cross-section is structure of skin-core or parallel or island, of a length not exceeding 5mm
5601 3000.90	纺织纤维屑，纤维粉末及球结（纺织纤维长度不超过5mm）	10	100		16	17	千克		Textile flock, dust and mill neps（textile fiber length is not exceeding 5mm）
56.02	**毡呢，不论是否浸渍、涂布、包覆或层压：**								**Felt, whether or not impregnated, coated, covered or laminated:**
5602.1000	-针刺机制毡呢及纤维缝编织物	10	100		16	17	千克		-Needleloom felt and stitch-bonded fibre fabrics
5602 1000.10	毛制针刺机制毡呢及纤维缝编织（不论是否浸渍、涂布、包覆或层压）	10	100		16	17	千克		Needleloom felt and stitch-bonded fibre fabrics, of wool or animal hair（whether or not impregnated, coated, covered, laminated）
5602 1000.90	其他纺织料制针刺机制毡呢等（含缝编织物，不论是否浸渍、涂布、包覆或层压）	10	100		16	17	千克		Needleloom felt and stitch-bonded fibre fabrics, of other textile materials（whether or not impregnated, coated, covered, laminated）
	-其他毡呢，未浸渍、涂布、包覆或层压：								-Other felt, not impregnated, coated, covered or laminated:
5602.2100	--兰毛或动物细毛制	10	100		16	17	千克		--Of wool or fine animal hair
5602.2900	--其他纺织材料制	10	100		16	17	千克		--Of other textile materials
5602.9000	-其他	10	100		16	17	千克		-Other
5602 9000.10	其他纺织材料制其他毡呢（层压）	10	100		16	17	千克		Other laminated felt of other textile materials
5602 9000.91	化学纤维制其他毡呢（浸渍、涂布、包覆）	10	100		16	17	千克		Other felt of man-made fibres, impregnated, coated or covered
5602 9000.99	其他纺织材料制其他毡呢（浸渍、涂布、包覆）	10	100		16	17	千克		Other felt, of other textile materials, impregnated, coated or covered
56.03	**无纺织物，不论是否浸渍、涂布、包覆或层压：**								**Nonwovens, whether or not impregnated, coated, covered or laminated:**
	-化学纤维长丝制：								-Of man-made filaments:
	--每平方米重量不超过25克：								--Weighing not more than 25g/m²:
5603.1110	---经浸渍、涂布、包覆或层压	10	70		16	17	千克		---Impregnated, coated, covered or laminated
5603.1190	---其他	10	130		16	17	千克		---Other
	--每平方米重量超过25克，但不超过70克：								--Weighing more than 25g/m² but not more than 70g/m²:
5603.1210	---经浸渍、涂布、包覆或层压	10	70		16	17	千克		---Impregnated, coated, covered or laminated
5603.1290	---其他	10	130		16	17	千克		---Other

税则号列 Tariff Item	商品名称及备注	进口税率 最惠	普通	暂定	出口退税	增值税率	计量单位	监管条件	Article Description
	--每平方米重量超过70克，但不超过150克:								--Weighing more than 70g/m² but not more than 150g/m²:
5603.1310	---经浸渍、涂布、包覆或层压	10	70		16	17	千克		---Impregnated, coated, covered or laminated
5603.1390	---其他	10	130		16	17	千克		---Other
	--每平方米重量超过150克:								--Weighing more than 150g/m²:
5603.1410	---经浸渍、涂布、包覆或层压	10	70		16	17	千克		---Impregnated, coated, covered or laminated
5603.1490	---其他	10	130		16	17	千克		---Other
	-其他:								-Other:
	--每平方米重量不超过25克:								--Weighing not more than 25g/m²:
5603.9110	---经浸渍、涂布、包覆或层压	10	70		16	17	千克		---Impregnated, coated, covered or laminated
5603.9190	---其他	10	85		16	17	千克		---Other
	--每平方米重量超过25克，但不超过70克:								--Weighing more than 25g/m² but not more than 70g/m²:
5603.9210	---经浸渍、涂布、包覆或层压	10	70		16	17	千克		---Impregnated, coated, covered or laminated
5603.9290	---其他	10	85		16	17	千克		---Other
	--每平方米重量超过70克，但不超过150克:								--Weighing more than 70g/m² but not more than 150g/m²:
5603.9310	---经浸渍、涂布、包覆或层压	10	70		16	17	千克		---Impregnated, coated, covered or laminated
5603.9390	---其他	10	85		16	17	千克		---Other
	--每平方米重量超过150克:								--Weighing more than 150g/m²:
5603.9410	---经浸渍、涂布、包覆或层压	10	70		16	17	千克		---Impregnated, coated, covered or laminated
5603 9410.11	毛制铺地品衬底用物纺织物(浸渍、涂布、包覆或压层，每平方米重＞150克)	10	70		16	17	千克		Floor coverings of wool or animal hair, nonwovens on a backing（impregnated, coated, covered or laminated, weighing more than 150g/m²）
5603 9410.19	其他材料制铺地品衬底用无纺织物(浸渍、涂布、包覆或压层，每平方米重＞150克)	10	70		16	17	千克		Floor coverings of other materials, nonwovens on a backing（impregnated, coated, covered or laminated, weighing more than 150g/m²）
5603 9410.90	其他材料制无纺织物(浸渍、涂布、包覆或压层，每平方米重＞150克)	10	70		16	17	千克		Nonwovens of other materials（impregnate, coated, covered or laminated, weighing more than 150g/m²）
5603.9490	---其他	10	85		16	17	千克		---Other
5603 9490.11	毛制铺地品衬底用无纺织物(每平方米重＞150克)	10	85		16	17	千克		Floor coverings of wool or animal hair, nonwovens on a backing（weighing more than 150g/m²）
5603 9490.19	其他材料制铺地品衬底用无纺织物(每平方米重＞150克)	10	85		16	17	千克		Floor coverings of other materials, nonwovens on a backing（weighing more than 150g/m²）
5603 9490.90	其他材料制无纺织物(每平方米重＞150克)	10	85		16	17	千克		Nonwovens of other materials（weighing more than 150g/m²）
56.04	**用纺织材料包覆的橡胶线及绳；用橡胶或塑料浸渍、涂布、包覆或套裹的纺织纱线及品目54.04或54.05的扁条及类似品:**								**Rubber thread and cord, textile covered; textile yarn, and strip and the like of heading No.54.04 or 54.05, impregnated, coated, covered or sheathed with rubber or plastics:**
5604.1000	-用纺织材料包覆的橡胶线及绳	5	80		16	17	千克		-Rubber thread and cord, textile covered
5604.9000	-其他	5	80		16	17	千克		-Other
5604 9000.10	棉制纱线(用橡胶或塑料浸渍、涂布、包覆、套裹)	5	80		16	17	千克		Cotton yarn（impregnated, coated, covered or sheathed, with rubber or plastics）
5604 9000.20	品目54.04的合成纤维单丝、扁条(用橡胶或塑料浸渍、涂布、包覆、套裹)	5	80		16	17	千克		Monofilament or strip, of synthetic fibre of heading No. 54.04（impregnated, coated, covered or sheathed, with rubber or plastics）
5604 9000.30	品目54.04的人造纤维单丝、扁条(用橡胶或塑料浸渍、涂布、包覆、套裹)	5	80		16	17	千克		Monofilament or strip, of artificial fibre of heading No. 54.04（impregnated, coated, covered or sheathed, with rubber or plastics）
5604 9000.90	其他纺织纱线(用橡胶或塑料浸渍、涂布、包覆、套裹)	5	80		16	17	千克		Other textile yarn（impregnated, coated, covered or sheathed, with rubber or plastics）

税则号列 Tariff Item	商品名称及备注	进口税率 最惠	进口税率 普通	进口税率 暂定	出口退税	增值税率	计量单位	监管条件	Article Description
56.05	**含金属纱线，不论是否螺旋花线，由纺织纱线或品目 54.04 或 54.05 的扁条及类似品与金属线、扁条或粉末混合制得或用金属包覆制得：**								**Metallized yarn, whether or not gimped, being textile yarn, or strip or the like of heading No. 54.04 or 54.05, combined with metal in the form of thread, strip or powder or covered with metal:**
5605.0000	含金属纱线，不论是否螺旋花线，由纺织纱线或品目 54.04 或 54.05 的扁条及类似品与金属线、扁条或粉末混合制得或用金属包覆制得	5	70		16	17	千克		Metallized yarn, whether or not gimped,being textile yarn, or strip or the like of heading No.54.04 or 54.05, combined with metal in the form of thread, strip or powder or covered with metal
5605 0000.10	金属涂层或层压化纤长丝等（扁条及类似品，非螺旋，未加捻或捻度每米低于 5 转）	5	70		16	17	千克		Chemical fiber filament, strip or the like, coated or laminated with metal（not gimped, untwisted or twist less than 5 turns/m）
5605 0000.90	其他含金属纱线，可含螺旋花边（与金属线、扁条或粉末混合制的或用金属包覆制）	5	70		16	17	千克		Other metallized yarn, gimped, combined with metal in the form of thread, strip or powder or covered with metal
56.06	**粗松螺旋花线，品目 54.04 或 54.05 的扁条及类似品制的螺旋花线（品目 56.05 的货品及马毛粗松螺旋花线除外）；绳绒线（包括植绒绳绒线）；纵行起圈纱线：**								**Gimped yarn, and strip and the like of heading No.54.04 or 54.05, gimped (other than those of heading No.56.05 and gimped horsehair yarn); chenille yarn (including flock chenille yarn) ; loopwale yarn:**
5606.0000	粗松螺旋花线，品目 54.04 或 54.05 的扁条及类似品制的螺旋花线（品目 56.05 的货品及马毛粗松螺旋花线除外）；绳绒线（包括植绒绳绒线）；纵行起圈纱线	5	70		16	17	千克		Gimped yarn, and strip and the like of heading No.54.04 or 54.05, gimped（other than those of heading No.56.05 and gimped horsehair yarn）; chenille yarn（including flock chenille yarn）; loopwale yarn
56.07	**线、绳、索、缆，不论是否编织或编结而成，也不论是否用橡胶或塑料浸渍、涂布、包覆或套裹：**								**Twine, cordage, rope and cables, whether or not plaited or braided and whether or not impregnated, coated, covered or sheathed with rubber or plastics:**
	-西沙尔麻或其他纺织用龙舌兰类纤维纺制：								-Of sisal or other textile fibres of the genus Agave:
5607.2100	--包扎用绳	5	50		16	17	千克		--Binder or baler twine
5607 2100.10	剑麻或其他龙舌兰纤维制包扎用绳（农机用，可编织或编结，可用橡胶或塑料浸涂包套）	5	50		16	17	千克		Binder or baler twine of sisal or othertextile fibres of the genus agave, used for agricultural machinery, plaited or braided, impregnated, coated, covered or sheahed, with rubber or plastics
5607 2100.90	剑麻或龙舌兰纤维制其他包扎用绳（农机用，可编织或编结，可用橡胶或塑料浸涂包套）	5	50		16	17	千克		Other binder or baler twine of sisal or other textile fibres of the genus agave, used for agricultural machinery, plaited or braided, impregnated, coated, covered or sheathed, with rubber or plastics
5607.2900	--其他	5	50		16	17	千克		--Other
	-聚乙烯或聚丙烯纺制：								-Of polyethylene or polypropylene:
5607.4100	--包扎用绳	5	100		16	17	千克		--Binder or baler twine
5607 4100.10	宽的非裂膜扁条聚乙烯包扎用绳（可编织或编结，可用橡胶或塑料浸渍、涂布、包覆、套裹）	5	100		16	17	千克		Binder or baler twine of polyethylene, wide and non-cleft film strip (plaited or braided, impregnated, coated, covered or sheathed, with rubber or plastics)
5607 4100.90	其他聚乙烯或聚丙烯制包扎用绳（可编织或编结，可用橡胶或塑料浸渍、涂布、包覆、套裹）	5	100		16	17	千克		Other binder or baler twine of polyethylene or polypropylene（plaited or braided, impregnated, coated, covered or sheathed, with rubber or plastics)
5607.4900	-其他	5	100		16	17	千克		--Other
5607 4900.10	宽非裂膜扁条聚乙烯其他线绳索缆(可编织或编结用橡胶或塑	5	100		16	17	千克		Other twine, cordage, ropes and cables, of polyethylene or polypropylene, wide and non-cleft film

税则号列 Tariff Item	商品名称及备注	进口税率 最惠	普通	暂定	出口退税	增值税率	计量单位	监管条件	Article Description
	料浸涂包套，含聚丙烯制）								strip (plaited or braided, impregnated, coated, covered or sheathed, with rubber or plastics)
5607 4900.20	其他聚乙烯或聚丙烯制线绳索缆（未经编织或编结，可用橡胶或塑料浸渍、涂布、包覆、套裹）	5	100		16	17	千克		Other twine, cordage, ropes and cables of polyethylene or polypropylene (not plaited or not braided, and impregnated, coated, covered or sheathed, with rubber or plastics)
5607 4900.90	其他聚乙烯或聚丙烯制线绳索缆（已编织或编结，可用橡胶或塑料浸渍、涂布、包覆、套裹）	5	100		16	17	千克		Other twine, cordage, ropes and cables of polyethylene or polypropylene (plaited or braided, and impregnated, coated, covered or sheathed, with rubber or plastics)
5607.5000	-其他合成纤维纺制	5	100		16	17	千克		-Of other synthetic fibres
5607 5000.10	其他合纤制未编织或编织线绳索缆（可用橡胶或塑料浸渍、涂布、包覆、套裹）	5	100		16	17	千克		Twine, cordage, ropes and cables of other synthetic fibres（not plaited or not braided, and impregnated, coated-covered or sheathed, with rubber or plastics）
5607 5000.90	其他合纤制已编织或编织线绳索缆（可用橡胶或塑料浸渍、涂布、包覆、套裹）	5	100		16	17	千克		Twine, cordage, ropes and cables of other synthetic fibres, plaited or braided （impregnated, coated, covered or sheathed, with rubber or plastics）
	-其他:								-Other:
5607.9010	---蕉麻（马尼拉麻）或其他硬质（叶）纤维纺制	5	50		16	17	千克		---Of abaca（Manila hemp or *Muse textilis Nee*） or other hard（leaf） fibres
5607.9090	---其他	5	100		16	17	千克		---Other
5607 9090.10	大麻制线、绳、索、缆（可编织或编结，可用橡胶或塑料浸渍、涂布、包覆、套裹）	5	100		16	17	千克		Twine, cordage, ropes and cables of abaca（plaited or braided, impregnated, coated, covered or sheathed, with rubber or plastics）
5607 9090.90	其他纺织材料制线、绳、索、缆（可编织或编结，可用橡胶或塑料浸渍、涂布、包覆、套裹）	5	100		16	17	千克		Twine, cordage, ropes and cables of other textile materials（plaited or braided, impregnated, coated, covered or sheathed, with rubber or plastics）
56.08	**线、绳或索结制的网料；纺织材料制成的渔网及其他网：**								**Knotted netting of twine, cordage or rope; made up fishing nets and other made up nets, of textile materials:**
	-化学纤维材料制:								-Of man-made textile materials:
5608.1100	--制成的渔网	10	50		16	17	千克		--Made up fishing nets
5608 1100.10	化纤材料制成手撒线拉的渔网	10	50		16	17	千克		Hand casting and rope pulling fishing nets of man-made textile materials
5608 1100.90	化纤材料制成其他渔网	10	50		16	17	千克		Other made up fishing nets of man-made textile materials
5608.1900	--其他	12	100		16	17	千克		--Other
5608 1900.10	化纤材料制用拉线收口的诱饵包（罗网及篓状网除外）	12	100		16	17	千克		Bait bag with a drawstring, of man-made textile materials（other than toils or basket-like nets）
5608 1900.90	化纤材料制成的网料和其他网（包括化纤线、绳、索结制的网料，罗网及篓状网除外）	12	100		16	17	千克		Other knotted netting of twine, cordage or rope; made up fishing nets and other made up nets, of man-made textile materials, other than toils or basket-like nets
5608.9000	-其他	10	100		16	17	千克		-Other
5608 9000.11	毛、棉制的渔网	10	100		16	17	千克		Made up fishing nets, of wool or animal hair, or of cotton
5608 9000.19	其他纺织纤维制的渔网	10	100		16	17	千克		Made up fishing nets of other textile materials
5608 9000.91	棉制的其他网及网料（吊床，罗网及篓状网除外）	10	100		16	17	千克		Other made up nets and other knotted netting of twine, cordage or rope, of cotton,（other than hammock, toils or basket-like nets）
5608 9000.92	毛制的其他网及网料（包括棉制的网式吊床，罗网及篓状网除外）	10	100		16	17	千克		Other made up nets and other knotted netting of twine, cordage or rope, of wool or animal hair（including net hammock of cotton, other than toils or basket-like nets）
5608 9000.99	其他纺织纤维制成的其他网及网料（罗网及篓状网除外）	10	100		16	17	千克		Other made up nets and knotted netting of twine, cordage or rope of other textile materials（other than

税则号列 Tariff Item	商品名称及备注	进口税率			出口退税	增值税率	计量单位	监管条件	Article Description
		最惠	普通	暂定					
									toils or basket-shaped nets)
56.09	**用纱线、品目 54.04 或 54.05 的扁条及类似品或线、绳、索、缆制成的其他品目未列名物品：**								**Articles of yarn, strip or the like of heading No.54.04 or 54.05, twine, cordage, rope or cables, not elsewhere specified or included:**
5609.0000	用纱线、品目 54.04 或 54.05 的扁条及类似品或线、绳、索、缆制成的其他品目未列名物品	10	100		16	17	千克		Articles of yarn, strip or the like of heading No. 54.04 or 54.05, twine, cordage, rope or cables, not elsewhere specified or included

第五十七章 地毯及纺织材料的其他铺地制品

Chapter 57 Carpets and other textile floor coverings

注释：

一、本章所称“地毯及纺织材料的其他铺地制品”，是指使用时以纺织材料作面的铺地制品，也包括具有纺织材料铺地制品特征但作其他用途的物品。

二、本章不包括铺地制品衬垫。

Chapter Notes:

1. For the purposes of this Chapter, the term “carpets and other textile floor coverings” means floor coverings in which textile materials serve as the exposed surface of the article when in use and includes articles having the characteristics of textile floor coverings but intended for use for other purposes.
2. This Chapter does not cover floor covering underlays.

税则号列 Tariff Item	商品名称及备注	进口税率 最惠	普通	暂定	出口退税	增值税率	计量单位	监管条件	Article Description
57.01	结织栽绒地毯及纺织材料的其他结织栽绒铺地制品，不论是否制成的：								**Carpets and other textile floor coverings, knotted, whether or not made up:**
5701.1000	-羊毛或动物细毛制	14	130		16	17	千克/平方米		-Of wool or fine animal hair
	-其他纺织材料制：								-Of other textile materials:
5701.9010	---化学纤维制	16	130		16	17	千克/平方米		---Of man-made textile materials
5701.9020	---丝制	14	100		16	17	千克/平方米		---Of silk
5701.9090	---其他	14	100		16	17	千克/平方米		---Other
57.02	机织地毯及纺织材料的其他机织铺地制品，未簇绒或未植绒，不论是否制成的，包括“开来姆”、“苏麦克”、“卡拉马尼”及类似的手织地毯：								**Carpets and other textile floor coverings, woven, not tufted or flocked, whether or not made up, including “Kelem”, “Schumacks”, “Karamanie” and similar handwoven rugs:**
5702.1000	-“开来姆”、“苏麦克”、“卡拉马尼”及类似的手织地毯	14	130		16	17	千克/平方米		-“Kelem”, “Schumacks”, “Karamanie” and similar handwoven rugs
5702.2000	-椰壳纤维制的铺地制品	14	100		16	17	千克/平方米		-Floor coverings of coconut fibres（coir）
	-其他起绒结构的铺地制品，未制成的：								-Other, of pile construction, not made up:
5702.3100	--羊毛或动物细毛制	10	130		16	17	千克/平方米		--Of wool or fine animal hair
5702.3200	--化学纤维制	16	130		16	17	千克/平方米		--Of man-made textile materials
5702.3900	--其他纺织材料制	14	100		16	17	千克/平方米		--Of other textile materials
	-其他起绒结构的铺地制品，制成的：								-Other, of pile construction, made up:
5702.4100	--羊毛或动物细毛制	10	130		16	17	千克/平方米		--Of wool or fine animal hair
5702.4200	--化学纤维制	10	130		16	17	千克/平方米		--Of man-made textile materials
5702.4900	--其他纺织材料制	14	100		16	17	千克/平方米		--Of other textile materials
	-其他非起绒结构的铺地制品，未制成的：								-Other, not of pile construction, not made up:
5702.5010	---羊毛或动物细毛制	14	130		16	17	千克/平方米		---Of wool or fine animal hair
5702.5020	---化学纤维制	16	130		16	17	千克/平方米		---Of man-made textile materials

税则号列 Tariff Item	商品名称及备注	进口税率			出口退税	增值税率	计量单位	监管条件	Article Description
		最惠	普通	暂定					
5702.5090	---其他纺织材料制	14	100		16	17	千克/平方米		---Of other textile materials
	-其他非起绒结构的铺地制品，制成的：								-Other, not of pile construction, made up:
5702.9100	--羊毛或动物细毛制	14	130		16	17	千克/平方米		--Of wool or fine animal hair
5702.9200	--化学纤维制	16	130		16	17	千克/平方米		--Of man-made textile materials
5702.9900	--其他纺织材料制	14	100		16	17	千克/平方米		--Of other textile materials
57.03	**簇绒地毯及纺织材料的其他簇绒铺地制品，不论是否制成的：**								**Carpets and other textile floor coverings, tufted, whether or not made up:**
5703.1000	-羊毛或动物细毛制	14	130		16	17	千克/平方米		-Of wool or fine animal hair
5703.2000	-尼龙或其他聚酰胺制	10	130		16	17	千克/平方米		-Of nylon or other polyamides
5703.3000	-其他化学纤维制	10	130		16	17	千克/平方米		-Of other man-made textile materials
5703.9000	-其他纺织材料制	14	100		16	17	千克/平方米		-Of other textile materials
57.04	**毡呢地毯及纺织材料的其他毡呢铺地制品，未簇绒或未植绒，不论是否制成的：**								**Carpets and other textile floor coverings,of felt, not tufted or flocked,whether or not made up:**
5704.1000	-最大表面面积不超过0.3平方米	14	130		16	17	千克/平方米		-Tiles, having a maximum surface area of 0.3 m²
5704.9000	-其他	10	130		16	17	千克/平方米		-Other
57.05	**其他地毯及纺织材料的其他铺地制品，不论是否制成的：**								**Other carpets and other textile floor coverings, whether or not made up:**
5705.0010	---羊毛或动物细毛制	14	130		16	17	千克/平方米		---Of wool or fine animal hair
5705.0020	---化学纤维制	10	130		16	17	千克/平方米		---Of man-made textile materials
5705.0090	---其他	14	100		16	17	千克/平方米		---Other

第五十八章
特种机织物；簇绒织物；花边；装饰毯；装饰带；刺绣品

注释：

一、本章不适用于经浸渍、涂布、包覆或层压的第五十九章注释一所述的纺织物或第五十九章的其他货品。

二、品目 58.01 也包括因未将浮纱割断而使表面无竖绒的纬起绒织物。

三、品目 58.03 所称“纱罗”，是指经线全部或部分由地经纱和绞经纱构成的织物，其中绞经纱绕地经纱半圈、一圈或几圈而形成圈状，纬纱从圈中穿过。

四、品目 58.04 不适用于品目 56.08 的线、绳、索结制的网状织物。

五、品目 58.06 所称“狭幅机织物”，是指：

（一）幅宽不超过30厘米的机织物，不论是否织成或从宽幅料剪成，但两侧必须有织成的、胶粘的或用其他方法制成的布边；

（二）压平宽度不超过30厘米的圆筒机织物；以及

（三）折边的斜裁滚条布，其未折边时的宽度不超过30厘米。

流苏状的狭幅机织物归入品目58.08。

六、品目 58.10 所称“刺绣品”，除了一般纺织材料绣线绣制的刺绣品外，还包括在可见底布上用金属线或玻璃线刺绣的刺绣品，也包括用珠片、饰珠、纺织材料或其他材料制的装饰用花纹图案所缝绣的贴花织物。该品目不包括手工针绣嵌花装饰毯（品目 58.05）。

七、除品目 58.09 的产品外，本章还包括金属线制的用于衣着、装饰及类似用途的物品。

Chapter 58
Special woven fabrics; tufted textile fabrics; lace; tapestries; trimmings; embroidery

Chapter Notes:

1. This Chapter does not apply to textile fabrics referred to in Note 1 to Chapter 59, impregnated, coated, covered or laminated, or to other goods of Chapter 59.

2. Heading 58.01 also includes woven weft pile fabrics which have not yet had the floats cut, at which stage they have no pile standing up.

3. For the purposes of heading 58.03, “gauze” means a fabric with a warp composed wholly or in part of standing or ground threads and crossing or doup threads which cross the standing or ground threads making a half turn, a complete turn or more to form loops through which weft threads pass.

4. Heading 58.04 does not apply to knotted net fabrics of twine, cordage or rope, of heading 56.08.

5. For the purposes of heading 58.06, the expression “narrow woven fabrics” means:

(a) Woven fabrics of a width not exceeding 30cm, whether woven as such or cut from wider pieces, provided with selvedges (woven, gummed or otherwise made) on both edges;

(b) Tubular woven fabrics of a flattened width not exceeding 30cm; and

(c) Bias binding with folded edges, of a width when unfolded not exceeding 30cm.

Narrow woven fabrics with woven fringes are to be classified in heading 58.08.

6. In heading 58.10, the expression “embroidery” means, inter alia, embroidery with metal or glass thread on a visible ground of textile fabric, and sewn applique work of sequins, beads or ornamental motifs of textile or other materials. The heading does not apply to needlework tapestry (heading 58.05).

7. In addition to the products of heading 58.09, this Chapter also includes articles made of metal thread and of a kind used in apparel, as furnishing fabrics or for similar purposes.

税则号列 Tariff Item	商品名称及备注	进口税率 最惠	普通	暂定	出口退税	增值税率	计量单位	监管条件	Article Description
58.01	**起绒机织物及绳绒织物，但品目 58.02 或 58.06 的织物除外：**								**Woven pile fabrics and chenille fabrics, other than fabrics of heading No.58.02 or 58.06:**
5801.1000	-羊毛或动物细毛制	10	130		16	17	米/千克		-Of wool or fine animal hair
	-棉制：								-Of cotton:
5801.2100	--不割绒的纬起绒织物	12	70		16	17	米/千克		--Uncut weft pile fabrics
5801 2100.10	未漂白不割绒的棉制纬起绒织物(品目 58.02 或 58.06 的织物除外)	12	70		16	17	米/千克		Uncut weft pile fabrics of cotton, unbleached (other than fabrics of heading No. 58. 02 or 58.06)
5801 2100.90	其他不割绒的棉制纬起绒织物(品目 58.02或 58.06 的织物除外)	12	70		16	17	米/千克		Other uncut weft pile fabrics of cotton, unbleached (other than fabrics of heading No. 58.02 or 58.06)
5801.2200	--割绒的灯芯绒	10	70		16	17	米/千克		--Cut corduroy
5801.2300	--其他纬起绒织物	10	70		16	17	米/千克		--Other weft pile fabrics

税则号列 Tariff Item	商品名称及备注	进口税率 最惠	进口税率 普通	进口税率 暂定	出口退税	增值税率	计量单位	监管条件	Article Description
5801 2300.10	未漂白其他棉制纬起绒织物(品目 58.02 或 58.06 的织物除外)	10	70		16	17	米/千克		Other weft pile fabrics of cotton, unbleached (other than fabrics of heading No. 58.02 or 58.06)
5801 2300.90	其他棉制纬起绒织物(品目 58.02 或 58.06 的织物除外)	10	70		16	17	米/千克		Other weft pile fabrics of cotton (other than fabrics of heading No. 58.02 or 58.06)
5801.2600	--绳绒织物	10	70		16	17	米/千克		--Chenille fabrics
5801 2600.10	未漂白棉制绳绒织物(品目 58.02 或 58.06 的织物除外)	10	70		16	17	米/千克		Chenille fabrics of cotton, unbleached (other than fabrics of heading No. 58.02 or 58.06)
5801 2600.90	其他棉制绳绒织物(品目 58.02 或 58.06 的织物除外)	10	70		16	17	米/千克		Other chenille fabrics of cotton (other than fabrics of heading No. 58.02 or 58.06)
	--经起绒织物:								--Warp pile fabrics:
5801.2710	---不割绒的(棱纹绸)	10	70		16	17	米/千克		---uncut (èpinglè)
5801.2720	---割绒的	10	70		16	17	米/千克		---Cut
	-化学纤维制:								-Of man-made fibres:
5801.3100	--不割绒的纬起绒织物	10	130		16	17	米/千克		--Uncut weft pile fabrics
5801.3200	--割绒的灯芯绒	10	130		16	17	米/千克		--Cut corduroy
5801.3300	--其他纬起绒织物	10	130		16	17	米/千克		--Other weft pile fabrics
5801.3600	--绳绒织物	10	130		16	17	米/千克		--Chenille fabrics
	--经起绒织物:								--Warp pile fabrics:
5801.3710	---不割绒的(棱纹绸)	10	130		16	17	米/千克		---uncut (èpinglè)
5801.3720	---割绒的	10	130		16	17	米/千克		---Cut
	-其他纺织材料制:								-Of other textile materials:
5801.9010	---丝及绢丝制	10	130		16	17	米/千克		---Of silk or silk waste
5801.9090	---其他	10	80		16	17	米/千克		---Other
5801 9090.10	亚麻和苎麻起绒机织物及绳绒织物(品目 58.02 或 58.06 的织物除外)	10	80		16	17	米/千克		Chenille fabrics and pile fabrics, of flax and ramie (other than fabrics of heading No. 58.02 or 58.06)
5801 9090.90	其他材料制起绒机织物及绳绒织物(品目 58.02 或 58.06 的织物除外)	10	80		16	17	米/千克		Chenille fabrics and pile fabrics, of other materials (other than fabrics of heading No. 58.02 or 58.06)
58.02	**毛巾织物及类似的毛圈机织物,但品目 58.06 的狭幅织物除外;簇绒织物,但品目 57.03 的产品除外:**								**Terry towelling and similar woven terry fabrics, other than narrow fabrics of heading No. 58.06; tufted textile fabrics, other than products of heading No.57.03:**
	-棉制毛巾织物及类似毛圈机织物:								-Terry towelling and similar woven terry fabrics, of cotton:
5802.1100	--未漂白	12	70		16	17	米/千克		--Unbleached
5802.1900	--其他	10	70		16	17	米/千克		--Other
	-其他纺织材料制的毛巾织物及类似的毛圈机织物:								-Terry towelling and similar woven terry fabrics, of other textile materials:
5802.2010	---丝及绢丝制	12	130		16	17	米/千克		---Of silk or silk waste
5802 2010.10	丝及绢丝毛巾织物及类似毛圈织物(品目 58.06 的狭幅织物除外,含丝 85%及以上)	12	130		16	17	米/千克		Terry towelling and similar woven terry fabrics, of silk or silk waste (other than narrow fabrics of heading No. 58.06, containing 85% or more by weight of silk)
5802 2010.90	丝及绢丝毛巾织物及类似毛圈织物(品目 58.06 的狭幅织物除外,含丝 85%以下)	12	130		16	17	米/千克		Terry towelling and similar woven terry fabrics of silk or silk waste (containing less than 85% by weight of silk, other than narrow fabrics of heading No. 58.06)
5802.2020	---羊毛或动物细毛制	12	130		16	17	米/千克		---Of wool or fine animal hair
5802.2030	---化学纤维制	14	130		16	17	米/千克		---Of man-made fibres
5802.2090	---其他	12	80		16	17	米/千克		---Other
	-簇绒织物:								-Tufted textile fabrics:
5802.3010	---丝及绢丝制	10	130		16	17	米/千克		---Of silk or silk waste
5802 3010.10	丝及绢丝制簇绒织物(品目 57.03 的产品除外,含丝 85%及以上)	10	130		16	17	米/千克		Tufted textile fabrics of silk or silk waste, (other than products of heading No. 57.03, containing 85% or more by weight of silk)
5802 3010.90	其他丝及绢丝制簇绒织物(品目 57.03 的产品除外,含丝 85%以下)	10	130		16	17	米/千克		Other tufted textile fabrics of silk or silk waste (other than products of heading No. 57.03, containing less than 85% by weight of silk)

税则号列 Tariff Item	商品名称及备注	进口税率 最惠	进口税率 普通	进口税率 暂定	出口退税	增值税率	计量单位	监管条件	Article Description
5802.3020	---羊毛或动物细毛制	10	130		16	17	米/千克		---Of wool or fine animal hair
5802.3030	---棉或麻制	10	70		16	17	米/千克		---Of cotton or bast fibres
5802 3030.10	麻制簇绒织物(品目 57.03 的产品除外)	10	70		16	17	米/千克		Tufted textile fabrics of bast fibres (other than products of heading No. 57.03)
5802 3030.90	棉制簇绒织物(品目 57.03 的产品除外)	10	70		16	17	米/千克		Tufted textile fabrics of cotton (other than products of heading No. 57.03)
5802.3040	---化学纤维制	10	130		16	17	米/千克		---Of man-made fibres
5802.3090	---其他纺织材料制	10	80		16	17	米/千克		---Of other textile materials
58.03	**纱罗,但品目 58.06 的狭幅织物除外:**								**Gauze, other than narrow fabrics of heading No.58.06:**
5803.0010	---棉制	10	70		16	17	米/千克		---Of cotton
5803.0020	---丝及绢丝制	10	130		16	17	米/千克		---Of silk or silk waste
5803.0030	---化学纤维制	10	130		16	17	米/千克		---Of man-made fibres
5803.0090	---其他纺织材料制	10	80		16	17	米/千克		---Of other textile materials
58.04	**网眼薄纱及其他网眼织物,但不包括机织物、针织物或钩编织物;成卷、成条或成小块图案的花边,但品目 60.02 的织物除外:**								**Tulles and other net fabrics, not including woven, knitted or crocheted fabrics; lace in the piece, in strips or in motifs, other than fabrics of headings No. 60.02 :**
	-网眼薄纱及其他网眼织物:								-Tulles and other net fabrics:
5804.1010	---丝及绢丝制	10	130		16	17	千克		---Of silk or silk waste
5804 1010.10	丝及绢丝网眼薄纱及其他网眼织物(含丝 85%及以上,不包括机织物,针织物或钩编织物)	10	130		16	17	千克		Tulles and other net fabrics of silk or silk waste, not including woven, knitted or crocheted fabrics, containing 85% or more by weight of silk
5804 1010.90	丝及绢丝网眼薄纱及其他网眼织物(含丝 85%以下,不包括机织物,针织物或钩编织物)	10	130		16	17	千克		Tulles and other net fabrics of silk or silk waste, not including woven, knitted or crocheted fabrics, containing less than 85% by weight of silk
5804.1020	---棉制	10	70		16	17	千克		---Of cotton
5804.1030	---化学纤维制	12	130		16	17	千克		---Of man-made fibres
5804.1090	---其他纺织材料制	10	90		16	17	千克		---Of other textile materials
	-机制花边:								-Mechanically made lace:
5804.2100	--化学纤维制	10	130		16	17	千克		--Of man-made fibres
	--其他纺织材料制:								--Of other textile materials:
5804.2910	---丝及绢丝制	10	130		16	17	千克		---Of silk or silk waste
5804 2910.10	丝及绢丝含量 85%及以上机制花边(成卷成条或成小块图案的,但品目 60.02 的织物除外)	10	130		16	17	千克		Mechanically made lace, in the piece,in strips or in motifs, containing 85% or more by weight of silk or silk waste, other than fabrics of heading No. 60.02
5804 2910.90	丝及绢丝含量 85%以下机制花边(成卷成条或成小块图案的,但品目 60.02 的织物除外)	10	130		16	17	千克		Mechanically made lace, in the piece, in strips or in motifs, containing less than 85% by weight of silk or silk waste, other than fabrics of heading No. 60.02
5804.2920	---棉制	10	70		16	17	千克		---Of cotton
5804.2990	---其他	10	90		16	17	千克		---Other
5804.3000	-手工制花边	10	100		16	17	千克		-Hand-made lace
5804 3000.11	丝含量达 85%及以上制手工制花边(成卷成条或成小块图案的,但品目 60.02 的织物除外)	10	100		16	17	千克		Hand-made lace, in the piece, in strips or in motifs, containing 85% or more by weight of silk, other than fabrics of heading No. 60.02
5804 3000.19	丝含量达 85%以下制手工制花边(成卷成条或成小块图案的,但品目 60.02 的织物除外)	10	100		16	17	千克		Hand-made lace, in the piece, in strips or in motifs, containing less than 85% by weight of silk, other than fabrics of heading No. 60.02
5804 3000.20	棉或化纤制手工制花边(成卷成条或成小块图案的,但品目 60.02 的织物除外)	10	100		16	17	千克		Hand-made lace, in the piece, in strips or in motifs, of cotton or of man-made fibres, other than fabrics of heading No. 60.02
5804 3000.90	其他纺织材料制手工制其他花边(成卷成条或成小块图案的,但品目 60.02 的织物除外)	10	100		16	17	千克		Other hand-made lace, in the piece, in strips or in motifs, of other textile materials, other than fabrics of heading No. 60.02

税则号列 Tariff Item	商品名称及备注	进口税率			出口退税	增值税率	计量单位	监管条件	Article Description
		最惠	普通	暂定					
58.05	"哥白林"、"弗朗德"、"奥步生"、"波威"及类似式样的手织装饰毯，以及手工针绣嵌花装饰毯（例如，小针脚或十字绣），不论是否制成的：								**Hand-woven tapestries of the type Gobelins, Flanders, Aubusson, Beauvais and the like, and needle-worked tapestries（for example, petit point, cross stitch）, whether or not made up:**
5805.0010	---手工针绣嵌花装饰毯	12	130		16	17	平方米/千克		---Needle-worked tapestries
5805 0010.10	毛制非民间工艺针绣嵌花其他装饰毯（不论是否制成的）	12	130		16	17	平方米/千克		Needle-worked tapestries of wool or fine animal hair, non-folk handicraft（whether or not made up）
5805 0010.20	棉制手工针绣嵌花其他装饰毯（不论是否制成的）	12	130		16	17	平方米/千克		Needle-worked tapestries of cotton（whether or not made up）
5805 0010.30	化纤制手工针绣嵌花其他装饰毯（不论是否制成的）	12	130		16	17	平方米/千克		Needle-worked tapestries of man-made fibres（whether or not made up）
5805 0010.90	其他纺织料制手工针绣嵌花装饰毯（不论是否制成的）	12	130		16	17	平方米/千克		Needle-worked tapestries of other textile materials（whether or not made up）
5805.0090	---其他	12	130		16	17	平方米/千克		---Other
5805 0090.10	毛制非民间工艺的手织装饰毯（包括"哥白林"，"弗朗德"，"奥步生"，"波威"及类似式样的）	12	130		16	17	平方米/千克		Hand-woven tapestries of wool or fine animal hair, noncraftsmanship (including the type Gobelins, Flanders, Aubusson, Beauvais and the like)
5805 0090.20	棉制"哥白林"等手织装饰毯(包括"弗朗德"，"奥步生"，"波威"及类似式样的手织装饰毯)	12	130		16	17	平方米/千克		Hand-woven tapestries of the type Gobelins, of cotton (including the type Flanders, Aubusson, Beauvais and the like)
5805 0090.30	化纤制"哥白林"等手织装饰毯(包括"弗朗德"，"奥步生"，"波威"及类似式样的手织装饰毯)	12	130		16	17	平方米/千克		Hand-woven tapestries of the type Gobelins, of man-made fibres (including the type Flanders, Aubusson, Beauvais and the like)
5805 0090.90	其他纺织料制"哥白林"等手织装饰毯（包括"弗朗德"，"奥步生"，"波威"及类似式样的手织装饰毯）	12	130		16	17	平方米/千克		Hand-woven tapestries of the type Gobelins, Flanders, Aubusson, Beauvais and the like, of other textile materials
58.06	狭幅机织物，但品目58.07的货品除外；用黏合剂黏合制成的有经纱而无纬纱的狭幅织物（包扎匹头用带）：								**Narrow woven fabrics, other than goods of heading No.58.07; narrow fabrics consisting of warp without weft assembled by means of an adhesive（bolducs）:**
	-起绒机织物（包括毛巾织物及类似的毛圈织物）及绳绒织物:								-Woven pile fabrics（including terry towelling and similar terry fabris）and chenille fabrics:
5806.1010	---棉或麻制	10	70		16	17	千克		---Of cotton or bast fibres
5806 1010.10	棉制狭幅起绒机织物及绳绒织物（包括狭幅毛巾织物及类似毛圈织物，品目58.07的货品除外）	10	70		16	17	千克		Narrow woven pile fabrics（including terry towelling and similar terry fabris）and chenille fabrics, of cotton (other than goods of heading No. 58.07）
5806 1010.90	麻制狭幅起绒机织物及绳绒织物（包括狭幅毛巾织物及类似毛圈织物，品目58.07的货品除外）	10	70		16	17	千克		Narrow woven pile fabrics（including terry towelling and similar terry fabris） and chenille fabrics, of bast fibres (other than goods of heading No. 58.07)
5806.1090	---其他纺织材料制	10	80		16	17	千克		---Of other textile materials
5806 1090.10	含丝≥85%狭幅起绒及绳绒等织物(包括狭幅毛巾织物及类似毛圈织物，品目58.07的货品除外)	10	80		16	17	千克		Narrow woven pile fabrics（including terry towelling and similar terry fabris）and chenille fabrics, containing 85% or more by weight of silk (other than goods of heading No. 58.07)
5806 1090.20	毛制狭幅起绒织物及绳绒织物（包括狭幅毛巾织物及类似毛圈织物，品目58.07的货品除外）	10	80		16	17	千克		Narrow woven pile fabrics（including terry towelling and similar terry fabris）and chenille fabrics, of wool or fine animal hair (other than goods of heading No. 58.07)
5806 1090.30	化纤制狭幅起绒织物及绳绒织物(包括狭幅毛巾织物及类似毛	10	80		16	17	千克		Narrow woven pile fabrics（including terrytowelling and similar terry fabris） and chenille fabrics of

税则号列 Tariff Item	商品名称及备注	进口税率 最惠	普通	暂定	出口退税	增值税率	计量单位	监管条件	Article Description
	圈织物，品目 58.07 的货品除外）								man-made fibres (other than goods of heading No. 58.07)
5806 1090.90	其他材料狭幅起绒织物及绳绒织物(包括狭幅毛巾织物及类似毛圈织物,品目 58.07 的货品除外）	10	80		16	17	千克		Narrow woven pile fabrics(including terry towelling and similar terry fabris） and chenille fabrics ,of other textile materials（other than goods of heading No. 58.07）
5806.2000	-按重量计弹性纱线或橡胶线含量在5%及以上的其他机织物	10	100		16	17	千克		-Other woven fabrics, containing by weight 5% or more of elastomeric yarn or rubber thread
	-其他机织物:								-Other woven fabrics:
5806.3100	--棉制	10	70		16	17	千克		--Of cotton
5806.3200	--化学纤维制	10	130		16	17	千克		--Of man-made fibres
5806 3200.10	化纤制用于打字机色带狭幅机织物（品目 58.07 的货品除外）	10	130		16	17	千克		Narrow woven fabrics of man-made fibres, used for typewriter ribbon, other than goods of heading No. 58.07
5806 3200.90	化纤制其他狭幅机织物（品目 58.07 的货品除外）	10	130		16	17	千克		Other narrow woven fabrics of man-made fibres, other than goods of heading No. 58.07
	--其他纺织材料制:								--Of other textile materials:
5806.3910	---丝及绢丝制	10	130		16	17	千克		---Of silk or silk waste
5806.3920	---羊毛或动物细毛制	10	130		16	17	千克		---Of wool or fine animal hair
5806.3990	---其他	10	80		16	17	千克		---Other
5806 3990.10	含金属纱线制其他狭幅机织物（品目 58.07 的货品除外）	10	80		16	17	千克		Other narrow woven fabrics, of metallized yarn (other than goods of heading No. 58.07)
5806 3990.90	其他材料制其他狭幅机织物(品目 58.07 的货品除外）	10	80		16	17	千克		Other narrow woven fabrics, of other materials（other than goods of heading No. 58.07）
	-用黏合剂黏合制成的有经纱而无纬纱的织物(包扎匹头用带):								-Fabrics consisting of warp without weft assembled by means of an adhesive（bolducs）:
5806.4010	---棉或麻制	10	70		16	17	千克		---Of cotton or bast fibres
5806.4090	---其他纺织材料制	10	80		16	17	千克		---Of other textile materials
58.07	**非绣制的纺织材料制标签、徽章及类似品,成匹、成条或裁成一定形状或尺寸:**								**Labels, badges and similar articles of textile materials, in the piece, in strips or cut to shape or size, not embroidered:**
5807.1000	-机织	10	100		16	17	千克		-Woven
5807 1000.10	棉制机织非绣制标签(成匹，成条或裁成一定形状或尺寸）	10	100		16	17	千克		Woven labels of cotton, in the piece, in strips or cut to shape or size, not embroidered
5807 1000.20	化纤制机织非绣制标签（成匹，成条或裁成一定形状或尺寸）	10	100		16	17	千克		Woven labels of man-made fibres, in the piece, in strips or cut to shape or size, not embroidered
5807 1000.90	其他纺织材料制机织非绣制标签等(包括徽章及类似品,成匹,成条或裁成一定形状或尺寸）	10	100		16	17	千克		Woven labels, including badges and similar articles, of other textile materials, in the piece, in strips or cut to shape or size, not embroidered
5807.9000	-其他	10	100		16	17	千克		-Other
5807 9000.10	棉制非绣制的标签(成匹，成条或裁成一定形状或尺寸）	10	100		16	17	千克		Labels of cotton in the piece, in strips or cut to shape or size, not embroidered
5807 9000.20	化纤制非绣制的标签(成匹，成条或裁成一定形状或尺寸）	10	100		16	17	千克		Labels of man-made fibres, in the piece, in strips or cut to shape or size, not embroidered
5807 9000.90	其他纺织材料制非绣制的标签等（包括徽章及类似品，成匹，成条或裁成一定形状或尺寸）	10	100		16	17	千克		Labels, including badges and similar articles, of other textile materials, in the piece, in strips or cut to shape or size, not embroidered
58.08	**成匹的编带;非绣制的成匹装饰带,但针织或钩编的除外;流苏、绒球及类似品:**								**Braids in the piece; ornamental trimmings in the piece, without embroidery, other than knitted or crocheted; tassels, pompons and similar articles:**
5808.1000	-成匹的编带	10	100		16	17	千克		-Braids in the piece
5808 1000.10	棉或化纤制成匹的编带	10	100		16	17	千克		Braids of cotton or of man-made fibres, in the piece
5808 1000.20	蕉麻或苎麻制成匹的编带(适合制造或装饰帽类用）	10	100		16	17	千克	A	Braids of abaca or ramie, in the piece（suitable for manufacture or decoration of headgear）
5808 1000.90	其他纺织材料制成匹的编带	10	100		16	17	千克		Braids of other textile materials, in the piece
5808.9000	-其他	10	100		16	17	千克		-Other

税则号列 Tariff Item	商品名称及备注	进口税率			出口退税	增值税率	计量单位	监管条件	Article Description
		最惠	普通	暂定					
5808 9000.10	棉或化纤制非绣制成匹装饰带（针织或钩编的除外）	10	100		16	17	千克		Ornamental trimmings, of cotton or of man-made fibres, in the piece(other than knitted or crocheted)
5808 9000.90	其他非绣制成匹装饰带，流苏等（含绒球及类似品，针织或钩编的除外）	10	100		16	17	千克		Other ornamental trimmings (including tassels, pompons and similar articles) in the piece,without embroidery, other than knitted or crocheted
58.09	**其他品目未列名的金属线机织物及品目 56.05 所列含金属纱线的机织物，用于衣着、装饰及类似用途：**								**Woven fabrics of metal thread and woven fabrics of metallized yarn of heading No.56.05, of a kind used in apparel, as furnishing fabrics or for similar purposes, not elsewhere specified or included:**
5809.0010	---与棉混制	10	90		16	17	米/千克		---Combined with cotton
5809.0020	---与化学纤维混制	10	130		16	17	米/千克		---Combined with man-made fibres
5809.0090	---其他	10	100		16	17	米/千克		---Other
58.10	**成匹、成条或成小块图案的刺绣品：**								**Embroidery in the piece, in strips or in motifs:**
5810.1000	-不见底布的刺绣品	10	130		16	17	千克		-Embroidery without visible ground
	-其他刺绣品：								-Other embroidery:
5810.9100	--棉制	10	130		16	17	千克		--Of cotton
5810.9200	--化学纤维制	10	130		16	17	千克		--Of man-made fibres
5810 9200.10	化学纤维制见底布刺绣标签(成匹，成条或成小块图案)	10	130		16	17	千克		Embroidered labels of man-made fibres, with visible ground, in the piece, in strips or in motifs
5810 9200.90	其他化学纤维制见底布刺绣品(成匹，成条或成小块图案)	10	130		16	17	千克		Embroidery of other man-made fibres, with visible ground, in the piece, in strips or in motifs
5810.9900	--其他纺织材料制	10	130		16	17	千克		--Of other textile materials
5810 9900.10	羊毛或动物细毛制见底布刺绣品（成匹，成条或成小块图案）	10	130		16	17	千克		Embroidery of wool or fine animal hair, with visible ground, in the piece, in strips or in motifs
5810 9900.90	其他纺织材料制见底布刺绣品（成匹，成条或成小块图案）	10	130		16	17	千克		Other embroidery of textile materials, with visible ground, in the piece, in strips or in motifs
58.11	**用一层或几层纺织材料与胎料经绗缝或其他方法组合制成的被褥状纺织品，但品目 58.10 的刺绣品除外：**								**Quilted textile products in the piece,composed of one or more layers of textile materials assembled with padding by stitching or otherwise, other than embroidery of heading No.58.10:**
5811.0010	---丝及绢丝制	10	130		16	17	千克		---Of silk or silk waste
5811.0020	---羊毛或动物细毛制	10	130		16	17	千克		---Of wool or fine animal hair
5811.0030	---棉制	10	80		16	17	千克		---Of cotton
5811 0030.10	未漂白或漂白棉制被褥状纺织品(经绗缝等法用一层或几层织物与胎料组合不含品目 58.10 刺绣品)	10	80		16	17	千克		Quilted textile products of cotton in the piece, composed of one or more layers of textile materials assembled with padding by stitching or otherwise, other than embroidery of heading No. 58.10, unbleached or bleached
5811 0030.90	其他棉制被褥状纺织品(经绗缝等法用一层或几层织物与胎料组合不含品目 58.10 刺绣品)	10	80		16	17	千克		Other quilted textile products of cotton in the piece, composed of one or more layers of textile materials assembled with padding by stitching or otherwise, other than embroidery of heading No. 58.10
5811.0040	---化学纤维制	12	130		16	17	千克		---Of man-made fibres
5811.0090	---其他纺织材料制	10	90		16	17	千克		---Of other textile materials

第五十九章
浸渍、涂布、包覆或层压的纺织物；工业用纺织制品

注释：

一、除条文另有规定的以外，本章所称“纺织物”，仅适用于第五十章至第五十五章、品目 58.03 及 58.06 的机织物、品目 58.08 的成匹编带和装饰带及品目 60.02 至 60.06 的针织物或钩编织物。

二、品目 59.03 适用于：

（一）用塑料浸渍、涂布、包覆或层压的纺织物，不论每平方米重量多少以及塑料的性质如何（紧密结构或泡沫状的），但下列各项除外：

1. 用肉眼无法辨别出是否经过浸渍、涂布、包覆或层压的织物（通常归入第五十章至第五十五章、第五十八章或第六十章），但由于浸渍、涂布、包覆或层压所引起的颜色变化可不予考虑；
2. 温度在15℃～30℃时，用手工将其绕于直径7毫米的圆柱体上会发生断裂的产品（通常归入第三十九章）；
3. 纺织物完全嵌入塑料内或在其两面均用塑料完全包覆或涂布，而这种包覆或涂布用肉眼是能够辨别出的产品（但由于包覆或涂布所引起的颜色变化可不予考虑）（第三十九章）；
4. 用塑料部分涂布或包覆并由此而形成图案的织物（通常归入第五十章至第五十五章、第五十八章或第六十章）；
5. 与纺织物混制而其中纺织物仅起增强作用的泡沫塑料板、片或带（第三十九章）；或
6. 品目58.11的纺织品。

（二）由品目56.04的用塑料浸渍、涂布、包覆或套裹的纱线、扁条或类似品制成的织物。

三、品目 59.05 所称“糊墙织物”，是指以纺织材料作面，固定在一衬背上或在背面进行处理（浸渍或涂布以便于裱糊），适于装饰墙壁或天花板，且宽度不小于 45 厘米的成卷产品。

但本品目不适用于以纺织纤维屑或粉末直接粘于纸上（品目 48.14）或布底上（通常归入品目 59.07）的糊墙物品。

四、品目 59.06 所称“用橡胶处理的纺织物”是指：

Chapter 59
Impregnated, coated, covered or laminated textile fabrics; textile articles of a kind suitable for industrial use

Chapter Notes:

1. Except where the context otherwise requires, for the purposes of this Chapter the expression “textile fabrics” applies only to the woven fabrics of Chapters 50 to 55 and headings 58.03 and 58.06, the braids and ornamental trimmings in the piece of headings 58.08 and the knitted or crocheted fabrics of headings 60.02 to 60.06.

2. Heading 59.03 applies to:

(a) Textile fabrics, impregnated, coated, covered or laminated with plastics, whatever the weight per square metre and whatever the nature of the plastic material (compact or cellular), other than:

(i) Fabrics in which the impregnation, coating, or covering cannot be seen with the naked eye (usually Chapters 50 to 55, 58 or 60); for the purpose of this provision, no account should be taken of any resulting change of colour;

(ii) Products which cannot, without fracturing, be bent manually around a cylinder of a diameter of 7 mm, at a temperature between 15℃ and 30℃ (usually Chapter 39);

(iii) Products in which the textile fabric is either completely embedded in plastics or entirely coated or covered on both sides with such material, provided that such coating or covering can be seen with the naked eye with no account being taken of any resulting change of colour (Chapter 39);

(iv) Fabrics partially coated or partially covered with plastics and bearing designs resulting from these treatments (usually Chapters 50 to 55, 58 or 60);

(v) Plates, sheets or strip of cellular plastics, combined with textile fabric, where the textile fabric is present merely for reinforcing purposes (Chapter 39); or

(vi) Textile products of heading 58.11.

(b) Fabrics made from yarn, strip or the like, impregnated, coated, covered or sheathed with plastics, of heading 56.04.

3. For the purposes of heading 59.05, the expression “textile wall coverings” applies to products in rolls, of a width of not less than 45 cm, suitable for wall or ceiling decoration, consisting of a textile surface which has been fixed on a backing or has been treated on the back (impregnated or coated to permit pasting).

This heading does not, however, apply to wall coverings consisting of textile flock or dust fixed directly on a backing of paper (heading 48.14) or on a textile backing (generally heading 59.07).

4. For the purposes of heading 59.06, the expression “rubberised textile fabrics” means:

（一）用橡胶浸渍、涂布、包覆或层压的纺织物：

1. 每平方米重量不超过1500克；或
2. 每平方米重量超过1500克，按重量计纺织材料含量在50%以上；

（二）由品目56.04的用橡胶浸渍、涂布、包覆或套裹的纱线、扁条或类似品制成的织物；以及

（三）平行纺织纱线经橡胶粘合的织物，不论每平方米重量多少。

但本品目不包括与纺织物混制而其中纺织物仅起增强作用的海绵橡胶板、片或带（第四十章），也不包括品目58.11的纺织品。

（a）Textile fabrics impregnated, coated, covered or laminated with rubber:

（i）Weighing not more than 1,500g/ m^2; or
（ii）Weighing more than 1,500g/m^2 and containing more than 50% by weight of textile material;

（b）Fabrics made from yarn, strip or the like, impregnated, coated, covered or sheathed with rubber, of heading 56.04; and

（c）Fabrics composed of parallel textile yarns agglomerated with rubber, irrespective of their weight per square metre.

This heading does not, however, apply to plates, sheets or strips of cellular rubber, combined with textile fabric, where the textile fabric is present merely for reinforcing purposes（Chapter 40）, or textile products of heading 58.11.

五、品目59.07不适用于：

（一）用肉眼无法辨别出是否经过浸渍、涂布或包覆的织物（通常归入第五十章至第五十五章、第五十八章或第六十章），但由于浸渍、涂布或包覆所引起的颜色变化可不予考虑；

（二）绘有图画的织物（作为舞台、摄影布景或类似品的已绘制的画布除外）；

（三）用短绒、粉末、软木粉或类似品部分覆面并由此而形成图案的织物，但仿绒织物仍归入本品目；

（四）以淀粉或类似物质为基本成分的普通浆料上浆整理的织物；

（五）以纺织物为底的木饰面板（品目44.08）；

（六）以纺织物为底的砂布及类似品（品目68.05）；

（七）以纺织物为底的粘聚或复制云母片（品目68.14）；或

（八）以纺织物为底的金属箔（通常归入第十四类或第十五类）。

5. Heading 59.07 does not apply to:

（a）Fabrics in which the impregnation, coating or covering cannot be seen with the naked eye（usually Chapters 50 to 55, 58 or 60）; for the purpose of this provision, no account should be taken of any resulting change of colour;

（b）Fabrics painted with designs（other than painted canvas being theatrical scenery, studio back-cloths or the like）;

（c）Fabrics partially covered with flock, dust, powdered cork or the like and bearing designs resulting from these treatments; however, imitation pile fabrics remain classified in this heading;

（d）Fabrics starched with normal dressings having a basis of amylaceous or similar substances;

（e）Wood veneered on a backing of textile fabrics（heading 44.08）;

（f）Natural or artificial abrasive powder or grain, on a backing of textile fabrics（heading 68.05）;

（g）Agglomerated or reconstituted mica, on a backing of textile fabrics（heading 68.14）; or

（h）Metal foil on a backing of textile fabrics（generally Section XIV or XV）.

六、品目59.10不适用于：

（一）厚度小于3毫米的纺织材料制传动带料或输送带料；或

（二）用橡胶浸渍、涂布、包覆或层压的织物制成的或用橡胶浸渍、涂布、包覆或套裹的纱线或绳制成的传动带料及输送带料（品目40.10）。

6. Heading 59.10 does not apply to:

（a）Transmission or conveyor belting, of textile material, of a thickness of less than 3 mm; or

（b）Transmission or conveyor belts or belting of textile fabric impregnated, coated, covered or laminated with rubber or made from textile yarn or cord impregnated, coated, covered or sheathed with rubber（heading 40.10）.

七、品目59.11适用于下列不能归入第十一类其他品目的货品：

（一）下列成匹的、裁成一定长度或仅裁成矩形（包括正方形）的纺织产品（具有品目59.08至59.10所列产品特征的产品除外）：

1. 用橡胶、皮革或其他材料涂布、包覆或层压的作针布用的纺织物、毡呢及毡呢衬里机织物，以及其他专门技术用途的类似织物，包括用橡胶浸渍的用于包覆纺锤（织轴）的狭幅丝绒织物。

7. Heading 59.11 applies to the following goods, which do not fall in any other heading of Section XI:

（a）Textile products in the piece, cut to length or simply cut to rectangular（including square）shape（other than those having the character of the products of headings 59.08 to 59.10）, the following only:

（i）Textile fabrics, felt and felt-lined woven fabrics, coated, covered or laminated with rubber, leather or other material, of a kind used for card clothing, and similar fabrics of a kind used for other technical purposes, including narrow fabrics made of velvet impregnated with rubber, for covering weaving spindles（weaving beams）;

2. 筛布；
3. 用于榨油机器或类似机器的纺织材料制或人发制滤布；
4. 用多股经纱或纬纱平织而成的纺织物，不论是否毡化、浸渍或涂布，通常用于机械或其他专门技术用途；
5. 专门技术用途的增强纺织物；
6. 工业上用作填塞或润滑材料的线绳、编带及类似品，不论是否涂布、浸渍或用金属加强。

（二）专门技术用途的纺织制品（品目59.08至59.10的货品除外），例如，造纸机器或类似机器（如制浆机或制石棉水泥的机器）用的环状或装有连接装置的纺织物或毡呢、密封垫、垫圈、抛光盘及其他机器零件。

(ii) Bolting cloth;
(iii) Straining cloth of a kind used in oil presses or the like, of textile material or of human hair;
(iv) Flat woven textile fabrics with multiple warp or weft, whether or not felted, impregnated or coated, of a kind used in machinery or for other technical purposes;
(v) Textile fabrics reinforced with metal, of a kind used for technical purposes;
(vi) Cords, braids and the like, whether or not coated, impregnated or reinforced with metal, of a kind used in industry as packing or lubricating materials.

(b) Textile articles (other than those of headings 59.08 to 59.10) of a kind used for technical purposes for example, textile fabrics and felts, endless or fitted with linking devices, of a kind used in paper-making or similar machines (for example, for pulp or asbestos-cement), gaskets, washers, polishing discs and other machinery parts.

税则号列 Tariff Item	商品名称及备注	进口税率			出口退税	增值税率	计量单位	监管条件	Article Description
		最惠	普通	暂定					
59.01	**用胶或淀粉物质涂布的纺织物，作书籍封面及类似用途的；描图布；制成的油画布；作帽里的硬衬布及类似硬挺纺织物：**								**Textile fabrics coated with gum or amylaceous substances, of a kind used for the outer covers of books or the like; tracing cloth; prepared painting canvas; buckram and similar stiffened textile fabrics of a kind used for hat foundations:**
	-用胶或淀粉物质涂布的纺织物，作书籍封面及类似用途的：								-Textile fabrics coated with gum or amylaceous substances, of a kind used for the outer covers of books or the like:
5901.1010	---棉或麻制	10	80		16	17	千克		---Of cotton or bast fibres
5901 1010.10	胶或淀粉涂布的棉纺织物(作书籍封面，棉织物重≥50%，经漂染印花)	10	80		16	17	千克		Textile fabrics, containing 50% or more by weight of cotton, coated with gum or amylaceous substances, bleached, printed and dyed, used for the outer covers of books or the like
5901 1010.90	胶或淀粉涂布的麻及其他棉纺织（作书籍封面及类似用途的）	10	80		16	17	千克		Textile fabrics of bast fibres and other cotton, coated with gum or amylaceous substances, used for the outer covers of books or the like
5901.1020	---化学纤维制	10	130		16	17	千克		---Of man-made fibres
5901 1020.10	胶或淀粉涂布的涤棉短纤混纺织品(书籍封面及类似用途，聚酯短纤棉混纺漂染织物重>50%)	10	130		16	17	千克		Textile fabrics, containing 50% or more by weight of polyester staple fibres and cotton, coated with gum or amylaceous substances, bleached and dyed, used for the outer covers of books or the like
5901 1020.90	胶或淀粉涂布的其他化纤纺织物（作书籍封面及类似用途的）	10	130		16	17	千克		Other man-made textile fabrics coated with gum or amylaceous substances, used for the outer covers of books or the like
5901.1090	---其他	10	100		16	17	千克		---Other
5901 1090.10	用胶或淀粉涂布的精梳毛纺织物(书籍封面及类似用途，精梳羊毛或动物细毛织物重≥50%)	10	100		16	17	千克		Textile fabrics, containing 50% or more by weight of combed wool or fine animal hair, coated with gum or amylaceous substances, used for the outer covers of books or the like
5901 1090.90	用胶或淀粉涂布的其他纺织物（作书籍封面及类似用途的）	10	100		16	17	千克		Other textile fabrics coated with gum or amylaceous substances, used for the outer covers of books or the like
	-其他：								-Other:
5901.9010	---制成的油画布	10	50		16	17	千克		---Prepared painting canvas
5901 9010.10	精梳毛织物制油画布(精梳羊毛或动物细毛织物重≥50%)	10	50		16	17	千克		Prepared painting canvas containing 50% or more by weight of combed wool or fine animal hair
5901 9010.20	棉制油画布（棉织物重≥50%，经漂白染色印花等加工）	10	50		16	17	千克		Prepared painting canvas of cotton,containing 50% or more by weight of cotton bleached, dyed or printed

税则号列 Tariff Item	商品名称及备注	进口税率			出口退税	增值税率	计量单位	监管条件	Article Description
		最惠	普通	暂定					
5901 9010.30	聚酯短纤与棉混纺织物制油画（织物重≥50%，经漂白染色印花等加工）	10	50		16	17	千克		Prepared painting canvas, mixed with polyester staple fibres and cotton, containing 50% or more by weight, bleached, dyed or printed
5901 9010.90	其他纺织物制成的油画布	10	50		16	17	千克		Prepared painting canvas of other textile fabrics
	---其他:								---Other:
5901.9091	----棉或麻制	10	80		16	17	千克		----Of cotton or bast fibres
5901 9091.10	棉制描图布、帽里硬衬布等（包括类似硬挺纺织物，棉织物重≥50%，经漂染印花）	10	80		16	17	千克		Tracing cloth, buckram and similar stiffened textile fabrics, containing 50% or more by weight ofcotton, bleached, dyed or printed, used for hat foundations
5901 9091.90	麻及其他棉制描图布、帽里硬衬布（包括类似硬挺纺织物）	10	80		16	17	千克		Tracing cloth, buckram and similar stiffened textile fabrics, used for hat foundations, of bast fibres and other cotton
5901.9092	----化学纤维制	10	130		16	17	千克		----Of man-made fibres
5901 9092.10	聚酯短纤与棉混纺织物制描图布（含帽里硬衬类似硬挺纺织物，织物重≥50%，经漂染印）	10	130		16	17	千克		Tracing cloth, buckram and similar stiffened textile fabrics, used for hat foundations, mixed with polyester staple fibres and cotton, containing 50% or more by weight, bleached, dyed, printed
5901 9092.90	其他化纤制描图布，帽里硬衬布等（包括类似硬挺纺织物）	10	130		16	17	千克		Tracing cloth, buckram and similar stiffened textile fabrics, used for hat foundations, of other man-made fibres
5901.9099	----其他	10	100		16	17	千克		----Other
5901 9099.10	精梳毛纺织物制描图布，帽里硬衬（包括类似硬挺纺织物，精梳羊毛或动物细毛织物重≥50%）	10	100		16	17	千克		Tracing cloth, buckram and similar stiffened textile fabrics, used for hat foundations of combed wool or fine animals hair, containing 50% or more by weight
5901 9099.90	其他纺织物制描图布，帽里硬衬布（包括类似硬挺纺织物）	10	100		16	17	千克		Tracing cloth, buckram and similar stiffened other textile fabrics, used for hat foundations
59.02	**尼龙或其他聚酰胺、聚酯或粘胶纤维高强力纱制的帘子布：**								**Tyre cord fabric of high tenacity yarn of nylon or other polyamides, polyesters or viscose rayon:**
	-尼龙或其他聚酰胺制:								-Of nylon or other polyamides:
5902.1010	---聚酰胺-6（尼龙-6）制	10	40		16	17	千克		---Of polyamide-6 (nylon-6)
5902.1020	---聚酰胺-6，6（尼龙-6，6）制	10	40		16	17	千克		---Of polyamide-6,6(nylon-6,6)
5902.1090	---其他	10	40		16	17	千克		---Other
5902.2000	-聚酯制	10	40		16	17	千克		-Of polyesters
5902.9000	-其他	10	40		16	17	千克		-Other
59.03	**用塑料浸渍、涂布、包覆或层压的纺织物，但品目59.02的货品除外：**								**Textile fabrics impregnated, coated, covered or laminated with plastics, other than those of heading No.59.02:**
	-用聚氯乙烯浸渍、涂布、包覆或层压的:								-With poly（vinyl chloride）:
5903.1010	---绝缘布或带	10	40		16	17	千克		---Insulating cloth or tape
5903 1010.10	若干平行化纤纱线黏合绝缘布或带（聚氯乙烯浸渍、涂布、包覆或层压，塑料占60%及以下）	10	40		16	17	千克		Insulating cloth or tape, bonded with layers of parallel textile yarns of man-made fibres, impregnated, coated, covered or laminated with poly, containing 60% or less by weight of plastics
5903 1010.20	聚氯乙烯浸渍涤棉混纺绝缘布或带（聚氯乙烯涂、包、漂、染聚酯短纤棉混纺，塑或胶＜50%）	10	40		16	17	千克		Insulating cloth or tape, mixed with polyester staple fibres and cotton, impregnated, coated, covered or laminated with poly, containing less than 50% by weight of plastics or glue
5903 1010.30	聚氯乙烯浸渍其他化纤绝缘布或带（用聚氯乙烯涂布、包覆或层压，塑或胶≤70%）	10	40		16	17	千克		Insulating cloth or tape, of other man-made fibres, impregnated, coated, covered or laminated with poly, containing less than 70% by weight of plastics or glue
5903 1010.90	用聚氯乙烯浸渍的其他绝缘布或带（包括用聚氯乙烯涂布、包覆或层压的）	10	40		16	17	千克		Other insulating cloth or tape, impregnated, coated, covered or laminated with poly
5903.1020	---人造革	10	70		16	17	千克/米		---Imitation leather
5903 1020.10	若干层平行纱线黏合的化纤人造革（用聚氯乙烯浸渍、涂布、包覆层压，塑料占60%及以下）	10	70		16	17	千克/米		Imitation leather, bonded with layers of parallel textile yarns of man-made fibres, impregnated, coated, covered or laminated with poly, containing 60% or less by weight of plastics

税则号列 Tariff Item	商品名称及备注	进口税率			出口退税	增值税率	计量单位	监管条件	Article Description
		最惠	普通	暂定					
5903 1020.20	用聚氯乙烯浸渍的涤棉织物人造革（聚氯乙烯涂布、漂、印、染聚酯短纤棉混纺，塑或胶<50%）	10	70		16	17	千克/米		Imitation leather, mixed with polyester staple fibres and cotton, impregnated, coated, covered or laminated with poly, containing less than 50% by weight of plastics or glue
5903 1020.30	用聚氯乙烯浸渍的其他化纤人造革（包括用聚氯乙烯涂布、包覆或层压，塑或胶≤70%）	10	70		16	17	千克/米		Imitation leather, of other man-made fibres, impregnated, coated, covered or laminated with poly, containing less than 70% by weight of plastics or glue
5903 1020.40	用聚氯乙烯浸渍的棉织物人造革(聚氯乙烯涂布、包覆或层压，漂、染、印花织物不小于50%）	10	70		16	17	千克/米		Imitation leather of cotton fabrics, impregnated, coated, covered or laminated with poly, bleached, dyed or printed, containing more than 50% by weight of printed fabric
5903 1020.90	用聚氯乙烯浸渍的其他人造革（包括用聚氯乙烯涂布、包覆或层压的）	10	70		16	17	千克/米		Other imitation leather, impregnated, coated, covered or laminated with poly
5903.1090	---其他	10	90		16	17	千克		---Other
5903 1090.10	若干层平行纱线黏合化纤其他织物（聚氯乙烯浸渍涂布、包覆层压，塑料重≤60%）	10	90		16	17	千克		Other textile fabrics, bonded with layers of parallel textile yarns of man-made fibres, impregnated, coated, covered or laminated with poly, containing 60% or less by weight of plastics
5903 1090.21	聚氯乙烯浸渍的其他涤棉混纺织物（聚氯乙烯涂布、漂印染，聚酯短纤棉混纺，塑或胶<50%）	10	90		16	17	千克		Other textile fabrics , mixed with polyester staple fibres and cotton, impregnated, coated, covered or laminated with poly, containing less than 50% by weight of plastics or glue
5903 1090.29	聚氯乙烯浸渍的其他化纤织物（包括用聚氯乙烯涂布包覆层压，塑或胶≤70%）	10	90		16	17	千克		Other textile fabrics of man-made fibres, impregnated, coated, covered or laminated with poly, containing less than 70% by weight of plastics or glue
5903 1090.30	聚氯乙烯浸渍的棉织物(聚氯乙烯涂布包覆层压，漂染印花织物≥50%）	10	90		16	17	千克		Other textile fabrics of cotton, impregnated, coated, covered or laminated with poly, bleached, dyed or printed, containing 50% or more by weight of printed fabrics
5903 1090.40	用聚氯乙烯浸渍的精梳毛织物（聚氯乙烯涂布包覆层压，精梳羊毛或动物细毛≥50%）	10	90		16	17	千克		Other textile fabrics, containing 50% or more by weight of combed wool or fine animal hair impregnated, coated, covered or laminated with poly
5903 1090.90	聚氯乙烯浸渍的其他纺织物(包括用聚氯乙烯涂布、包覆或层压的）	10	90		16	17	千克		Other textile fabrics, impregnated, coated, covered or laminated with poly
	-用聚氨基甲酸酯浸渍、涂布、包覆或层压的:								-With polyurethane:
5903.2010	---绝缘布或带	10	40		16	17	千克		---Insulating cloth or tape
5903 2010.10	若干平行纱线黏合化纤绝缘布或带（聚氨基甲酸酯浸渍涂布、包覆或层压，塑料重≤60%）	10	40		16	17	千克		Insulating cloth or tape, bonded with layers of parallel textile yarns of man-made fibres, impregnated, coated, covered or laminated with polyurethane, containing 60% or less by weight of plastics
5903 2010.20	聚氨基甲酸酯浸渍涤棉绝缘布或带(聚氨基甲酸酯浸涂漂染聚酯短纤棉混纺，塑或胶<50%）	10	40		16	17	千克		Insulating cloth or tape, mixed with polyester staple fibres and cotton, impregnated, coated, covered or laminated with polyurethane, containing less than 50% by weight of plastics or glue
5903 2010.30	聚氨基甲酸酯浸渍其他化纤绝缘布（包括用聚氨基甲酸酯涂布、包覆层压，塑或胶≤70%）	10	40		16	17	千克		Insulating cloth or tape, of other man-made fibres, impregnated, coated, covered or laminated with polyurethane, containing less than 70% by weight of plastics or glue
5903 2010.90	聚氨基甲酸酯浸渍其他绝缘布或带（包括用聚氨基甲酸酯涂布、包覆或层压的）	10	40		16	17	千克		Other insulating cloth or tape, impregnated, coated, covered or laminated with polyurethane
5903.2020	---人造革	10	70		16	17	千克/米		---Imitation leather
5903 2020.10	若干层平行纱线黏合化纤人造革(聚氨基甲酸酯浸渍涂布、包覆层压，塑料≤60%）	10	70		16	17	千克/米		Imitation leather, bonded with layers of parallel textile yarns of man-made fibres, impregnated, coated, covered or laminated with polyurethane, containing 60% or less by weight of plastics

税则号列 Tariff Item	商品名称及备注	进口税率 最惠	普通	暂定	出口退税	增值税率	计量单位	监管条件	Article Description
5903 2020.20	用聚氨基甲酸酯浸渍的涤棉人造革(聚氨基甲酸酯涂布漂染聚酯短纤棉混纺，塑或胶＜50%)	10	70		16	17	千克/米		Imitation leather, mixed with polyester staple fibres and cotton, impregnated, coated, covered or laminated with polyurethane, containing less than 50% by weight of plastics or glue
5903 2020.30	聚氨基甲酸酯浸渍其他化纤人造革（包括用聚氨基甲酸酯涂布、包覆层压，塑或胶≤70%）	10	70		16	17	千克/米		Imitation leather, of other man-made fibres, impregnated, coated, covered or laminated with polyurethane, containing less than 70% by weight of plastics or glue
5903 2020.40	聚氨基甲酸酯浸渍的棉织物人造革(聚氨基甲酸酯涂布、包覆层压，漂染印织物≥50%)	10	70		16	17	千克/米		Imitation leather of cotton fabrics, impregnated, coated, covered or laminated with polyurethane, bleached, dyed or printed, containing more than 50% by weight of printed fabric
5903 2020.90	用聚氨基甲酸酯浸渍的其他人造革（包括用聚氨基甲酸酯涂布、包覆或层压的）	10	70		16	17	千克/米		Other imitation leather, impregnated, coated, covered or laminated with polyurethane
5903.2090	---其他	10	90		16	17	千克		---Other
5903 2090.10	若干层平行纱线粘合化纤其他织物(聚氨基甲酸酯浸渍、涂布、包覆层压，塑料≤60%)	10	90		16	17	千克		Other textile fabrics, bonded with layers of parallel textile yarns of man-made fibres, impregnated, coated, covered or laminated with polyurethane, containing 60% or less by weight of plastics
5903 2090.21	聚氨基甲酸酯浸渍其他涤棉织物(聚氨基甲酸酯涂布漂染聚酯短纤棉混纺，塑或胶＜50%)	10	90		16	17	千克		Other textile fabrics , mixed with polyester staple fibres and cotton, impregnated, coated, covered or laminated with polyurethane, containing less than 50% by weight of plastics or glue
5903 2090.29	聚氨基甲酸酯浸渍其他化纤织物(含聚氨基甲酸酯涂布包覆或层压，塑或胶≤70%)	10	90		16	17	千克		Other textile fabrics of man-made fibres, impregnated, coated, covered or laminated with polyurethane, containing less than 70% by weight of plastics or glue
5903 2090.30	用聚氨基甲酸酯浸渍的棉织物（聚氨基甲酸酯涂布包覆层压，漂染印织物≥50%）	10	90		16	17	千克		Other textile fabrics of cotton, impregnated,coated, covered or laminated with polyurethane, bleached, dyed or printed, containing 50% or more by weight of printed fabrics
5903 2090.41	用聚氨基甲酸酯浸渍的精梳毛织物(聚氨基甲酸酯涂布包覆层压,精梳羊毛或动物细毛≥50%)	10	90		16	17	千克		Other textile fabrics, containing 50% or more by weight of combed wool or fine animal hair impregnated, coated, covered or laminated with polyurethane
5903 2090.49	用聚氨基甲酸酯浸渍的其他毛织物(聚氨基甲酸酯涂布包覆或层压，精梳毛织物除外）	10	90		16	17	千克		Other textile fabrics of wool or animal hair, impregnated, coated, covered or laminated with polyurethane (other than fabrics of combed wool or fine animal hair)
5903 2090.90	用聚氨基甲酸酯浸渍的其他纺织物（包括用聚氨基甲酸酯涂布、包覆或层压的）	10	90		16	17	千克		Other textile fabrics, impregnated, coated, covered or laminated with polyurethane
	-其他:								-Other:
5903.9010	---绝缘布或带	10	40		16	17	千克		---Insulating cloth or tape
5903 9010.10	若干平行化纤纱线黏合绝缘布或带(其他塑料浸渍涂布、包覆或层压，塑料重≤60%)	10	40		16	17	千克		Insulating cloth or tape, bonded with layers of parallel textile yarns of man-made fibres, impregnated, coated, covered or laminated with other plastics, containing 60% or less by weight of plastics
5903 9010.20	其他塑料浸渍涤棉混纺绝缘布或带(塑料浸涂包的漂染聚酯短纤棉混纺，塑料橡胶＜50%)	10	40		16	17	千克		Insulating cloth or tape, mixed with polyester staple fibres and cotton, impregnated, coated, covered or laminated with other plastics, containing less than 50% by weight of plastics or glue
5903 9010.30	其他塑料浸渍其他化纤绝缘布或带(包括用其他塑料涂布、包覆或层压，塑料或橡胶≤70%)	10	40		16	17	千克		Insulating cloth or tape, of other man-made fibres, impregnated, coated, covered or laminated with other plastics, containing less than 70% by weight of plastics or glue

税则号列 Tariff Item	商品名称及备注	进口税率 最惠	进口税率 普通	进口税率 暂定	出口退税	增值税率	计量单位	监管条件	Article Description
5903 9010.90	用其他塑料浸渍的其他绝缘布或带（包括用其他塑料涂布、包覆或层压的）	10	40		16	17	千克		Other insulating cloth or tape, impregnated, coated, covered or laminated with other plastics
5903.9020	---人造革	10	70		16	17	千克/米		---Imitation leather
5903 9020.10	由若干层平行纱线黏合化纤人造革（用其他塑料涂布、包覆或层压，塑料重≤60%）	10	70		16	17	千克/米		Imitation leather, bonded with layers of parallel textile yarns of man-made fibres, impregnated, coated, covered or laminated with other plastics, containing 60% or less by weight of plastics
5903 9020.20	用其他塑料浸渍的涤棉织物人造革（其他塑料涂布、包覆的漂染、印花聚酯短纤棉混纺，塑料或橡胶＜50%）	10	70		16	17	千克/米		Imitation leather, mixed with polyester staple fibres and cotton, impregnated, coated, covered or laminated with other plastics, containing less than 50% by weight of plastics or glue
5903 9020.30	用其他塑料浸渍的其他化纤人造革（包括用其他塑料涂布、包覆的，塑料或橡胶≤70%）	10	70		16	17	千克/米		Imitation leather, of other man-made fibres, impregnated, coated, covered or laminated with other plastics, containing less than 70% by weight of plastics or glue
5903 9020.40	用其他塑料浸渍的棉织物人造革（用其他塑料涂布、包覆或层压，漂染印花织物≥50%）	10	70		16	17	千克/米		Imitation leather of cotton fabrics, impregnated, coated, covered or laminated with other plastics, bleached, dyed or printed, containing more than 50% by weight of printed fabric
5903 9020.90	用其他塑料浸渍的其他人造革（包括用其他塑料涂布、包覆或层压的）	10	70		16	17	千克/米		Other imitation leather, impregnated, coated, covered or laminated with other plastics
5903.9090	---其他	10	90		16	17	千克		---Other
5903 9090.10	若干层化纤平行纱线黏合其他织物（用其他塑料浸渍、涂布、包覆或层压，塑料重≤60%）	10	90		16	17	千克		Other textile fabrics, bonded with layers of parallel textile yarns of man-made fibres, impregnated, coated, covered or laminated with other plastics, containing 60% or less by weight of plastics
5903 9090.21	其他塑料浸渍的其他涤棉混纺织物(其他塑料涂布、漂染印花，聚酯短纤棉混纺，塑料或橡胶＜50%）	10	90		16	17	千克		Other textile fabrics , mixed with polyester staple fibres and cotton, impregnated, coated, covered or laminated with other plastics, containing less than 50% by weight of plastics or glue
5903 9090.29	用其他塑料浸渍的其他化纤织物（包括用其他塑料涂布、包覆或层压的，塑料或橡胶≤70%）	10	90		16	17	千克		Other textile fabrics of man-made fibres, impregnated, coated, covered or laminated with other plastics, containing less than 70% by weight of plastics or glue
5903 9090.30	用其他塑料浸渍的棉织物(用其他塑料涂布、包覆或层压的，漂染印花织物≥50%）	10	90		16	17	千克		Other textile fabrics of cotton, impregnated, coated, covered or laminated with other plastics, bleached, dyed or printed, containing 50% or more by weight of printed fabrics
5903 9090.41	用其他塑料浸渍的精梳毛织物（用其他塑料涂布、包覆或层压的，精梳羊毛或动物细毛≥50%）	10	90		16	17	千克		Other textile fabrics, containing 50% or more by weight of combed wool or fine animal hair impregnated, coated, covered or laminated with other plastics
5903 9090.49	用其他塑料浸渍的其他毛织物（用其他塑料涂布、包覆或层压的，精梳毛织物除外）	10	90		16	17	千克		Other textile fabrics of wool or animal hair, impregnated, coated, covered or laminated with other plastics (other than fabrics of combed wool or fine animal hair)
5903 9090.90	用其他塑料浸渍的其他纺织物（包括用其他塑料涂布、包覆或层压的）	10	90		16	17	千克		Other textile fabrics, impregnated, coated, covered or laminated with other plastics
59.04	**列诺伦（亚麻油地毡），不论是否剪切成形；以织物为底布经涂布或覆面的铺地制品，不论是否剪切成形：**								**Linoleum, whether or not cut to shape; floor coverings consisting of a coating or covering applied on a textile backing, whether or not cut to shape:**
5904.1000	-列诺伦（亚麻油地毡）	14	90		16	17	千克/平方米		-Linoleum
5904.9000	-其他	14	90		16	17	千克/平方米		-Other
59.05	**糊墙织物:**								**Textile wall coverings:**

税则号列 Tariff Item	商品名称及备注	进口税率 最惠	普通	暂定	出口退税	增值税率	计量单位	监管条件	Article Description
5905.0000	糊墙织物	10	80		16	17	千克/平方米		Textile wall coverings
5905 0000.11	以纸衬背的合成短纤制糊墙织物	10	80		16	17	千克/平方米		Textile wall coverings of synthetic staple fibres, as paper lining the back
5905 0000.19	以纸衬背的人造短纤制糊墙织物	10	80		16	17	千克/平方米		Textile wall coverings of artificial staple fibres, as paper lining the back
5905 0000.20	平行纱线固定的糊墙织物(固定在任何其他衬背上的)	10	80		16	17	千克/平方米		Textile wall coverings, fixed by parallel textile yarns, and on other lining the back
5905 0000.31	其他合成短纤制糊墙织物	10	80		16	17	千克/平方米		Textile wall coverings of other synthetic fibres
5905 0000.39	其他人造短纤制糊墙织物	10	80		16	17	千克/平方米		Textile wall coverings of other artificial fibres
5905 0000.90	其他纺织糊墙织物	10	80		16	17	千克/平方米		Textile wall coverings of other fabrics
59.06	**用橡胶处理的纺织物，但品目59.02的货品除外：**								**Rubberized textile fabrics, other than those of heading No.59.02:**
	-宽度不超过20厘米的胶粘带:								-Adhesive tape of a width not exceeding 20cm:
5906.1010	---绝缘带	10	40		16	17	千克		---Insulating tape
5906.1090	---其他	10	100		16	17	千克		---Other
	-其他:								-Other:
5906.9100	--针织或钩编的	10	130		16	17	千克		--Knitted or crocheted
5906 9100.10	用橡胶处理的针织或钩编化纤纺织物（按重量计塑料或橡胶不超过70%，宽＞20cm）	10	130		16	17	千克		Rubberized knitted or crocheted textile fabrics, containing less than 70% by weight of plastics or rubber, of a width exceeding 20cm
5906 9100.90	用橡胶处理的针织或钩编其他纺织物（宽＞20 cm）	10	130		16	17	千克		Rubberized other knitted or crocheted textile fabrics, of a width exceeding 20cm
	--其他:								--Other:
5906.9910	---绝缘布或带	10	40		16	17	千克		---Insulating cloth or tape
5906 9910.10	用橡胶处理的精梳毛纺绝缘布或带（非针织或钩编，精梳羊毛或动物细毛≥50%，宽＞20 cm）	10	40		16	17	千克		Rubberized insulating cloth or tape of combed wool or fine animal hair, which containing 50% or more by weight, not knited or crocheted, of a width exceeding 20cm
5906 9910.20	用橡胶处理的棉织物绝缘布或带（非针织或钩编，漂染印花棉织物≥50%，宽＞20 cm）	10	40		16	17	千克		Rubberized insulating cloth or tape of cotton fabrics , which containing 50% or more by weight, bleached, dyed or printed, not knited or crocheted, of a width exceeding 20cm
5906 9910.31	用橡胶处理聚酯短纤棉混纺绝缘布带（非针织或钩编，漂染印花混纺布≥50%，宽＞20 cm）	10	40		16	17	千克		Rubberized insulating cloth or tape, mixed with polyester staple fibres and cotton, which containing 50% or more by weight, bleached, dyed or printed, not knited or crocheted, of a width exceeding 20cm
5906 9910.39	用橡胶处理的其他化纤绝缘布或带（非针织或钩编，宽＞20 cm，塑料或橡胶≤70%）	10	40		16	17	千克		Rubberized insulating cloth or tape of other man-made fibres, containing less than 70% by weight of plastics or glue, not knited or crocheted, of a width exceeding 20cm
5906 9910.90	用橡胶处理宽＞20 cm其他绝缘布或带（非针织或钩编的，宽＞20 cm）	10	40		16	17	千克		Other rubberized insulating cloth or tape, not knited or crocheted, of a width exceeding 20cm
5906.9990	---其他	10	100		16	17	千克		---Other
5906 9990.10	用橡胶处理的精梳毛纺织物（精梳羊毛或动物细毛≥50%，非针织或钩编的，宽＞20 cm）	10	100		16	17	千克		Rubberized textile fabrics of combed wool or fine animal hair, which containing 50% or more by weight, not knited or crocheted, of a width exceeding 20cm
5906 9990.20	用橡胶处理的其他棉纺织物（非针织或钩编，宽＞20 cm，漂染印花棉织物≥50%）	10	100		16	17	千克		Rubberized other cotton fabrics , which containing 50% or more by weight, bleached, dyed or printed, not knited or crocheted, of a width exceeding 20cm
5906 9990.31	用橡胶处理的聚酯短纤棉混纺	10	100		16	17	千克		Rubberized textile fabrics, mixed with polyester staple

税则号列 Tariff Item	商品名称及备注	进口税率 最惠	普通	暂定	出口退税	增值税率	计量单位	监管条件	Article Description
	织物（非针织或钩编，宽＞20 cm，漂染印花聚酯混纺布≥50%）								fibres and cotton, which containing 50% or more by weight, bleached, dyed or printed, not knited or crocheted, of a width exceeding 20cm
5906 9990.39	用橡胶处理的其他化纤纺织物（非针织或钩编，宽＞20 cm，塑料或橡胶≤70%）	10	100		16	17	千克		Rubberized textile fabrics of other man-made fibres, containing less than 70% by weight of plastics or glue, not knited or crocheted, of a width exceeding 20cm
5906 9990.90	用橡胶处理的其他纺织物(非针织或钩编，宽＞20 cm)	10	100		16	17	千克		Other rubberized textile fabrics, not knited or crocheted, of a width exceeding 20cm
59.07	**用其他材料浸渍、涂布或包覆的纺织物；作舞台、摄影布景或类似用途的已绘制画布：**								**Textile fabrics otherwise impregnated,coated or covered；painted canvas being theatrical scenery, studio backcloths or the like:**
5907.0010	---绝缘布或带	10	40		16	17	千克		---Insulating cloth or tape
5907 0010.10	其他材料浸涂植物纤维绝缘布或带（用橡胶、塑料、浆料以外材料浸渍涂布或包覆，棉除外）	10	40		16	17	千克		Insulating cloth or tape of vegetable fibres, impregnated, coated or covered with other materials other than rubber, plastic, paste（other than cotton）
5907 0010.20	其他材料浸涂的棉制绝缘布或带（用橡胶、塑料、浆料以外材料浸涂或包覆，漂染棉织物≥50%）	10	40		16	17	千克		Insulating cloth or tape of cotton, which containing 50% or more,bleached, dyed or printed, impregnated, coated or covered with other materials other than rubber, plastic, paste
5907 0010.30	其他材料浸涂涤短纤棉混纺绝缘布（橡胶、塑料、浆料以外材料浸涂或包覆,漂染涤棉织物≥50%）	10	40		16	17	千克		Insulating cloth or tape, mixed with fabrics of polyester staple fibres and cotton, which containning 50% or more by weight, bleached or dyed, impreguated, coated or covered with other materials other than rubber, plastic, paste
5907 0010.90	其他材料浸涂其他纺织绝缘布或带（用橡胶、塑料、浆料以外材料浸渍、涂布或包覆）	10	40		16	17	千克		Insulating cloth or tape of other textile fabrics, impregnated, coated or covered with other materials other than rubber, plastic, paste
5907.0020	---已绘制画布	10	50		16	17	千克		---Painted canvas
5907 0020.10	其他材料浸涂植物纤维已绘制画布（用橡胶、塑料、浆料以外材料浸渍、涂布或包覆，棉除外）	10	50		16	17	千克		Painted canvas of vegetable fibres, impregnated, coated or covered with other materials other than rubber, plastic, paste（other than cotton）
5907 0020.20	其他材料浸涂精梳毛已绘制画布（用橡胶、塑料、浆料以外材料浸涂或包覆，精梳羊/动物细毛≥50%）	10	50		16	17	千克		Painted canvas of combed wool or fine animal hair, which containing 50% or more, impregnated, coated or covered with other materials other than rubber, plastic, paste
5907 0020.30	用其他材料浸涂的棉制已绘制画布（用橡胶、塑料、浆料以外材料浸涂或包覆，漂，染棉织物≥50%）	10	50		16	17	千克		Painted canvas of cotton, which containing 50% or more, bleached,dyed or printed, impregnated, coated or covered with other materials other than rubber, plastic, paste
5907 0020.40	其他材料浸涂涤短纤棉混已绘画布（用橡胶、塑料、浆料以外材料浸涂或包覆，漂，染涤短棉织物≥50%）	10	50		16	17	千克		Painted canvas, mixed with fabrics of polyester staple fibres and cotton, which containning 50% or more by weight, bleached or dyed, impreguated, coated or covered with other materials other than rubber, plastic, paste
5907 0020.90	其他材料浸涂其他织物已绘制画布（用橡胶、塑料、浆料以外材料浸渍、涂布或包覆）	10	50		16	17	千克		Painted canvas of other textile fabrics, impregnated, coated or covered with other materials other than rubber, plastic, paste
5907.0090	---其他	10	100		16	17	千克		---Other
5907 0090.10	用其他材料浸涂的植物纤维纺织物（用橡胶、塑料、浆料以外材料浸渍、涂布或包覆，棉除外）	10	100		16	17	千克		Textile fabrics of vegetable fibres, impregnated, coated or covered with other materials other than rubber, plastic, paste（other than cotton）
5907 0090.20	用其他材料浸涂的精梳毛纺织物（用橡胶、塑料、浆料以外材料浸涂或包覆，精梳羊/动物细毛≥50%）	10	100		16	17	千克		Textile fabrics of combed wool or fine animal hair, which containing 50% or more, impregnated, coated or covered with other materials other than rubber, plastic, paste
5907 0090.30	用其他材料浸涂的棉制纺织物（用橡胶、塑料、浆料以外材料	10	100		16	17	千克		Textile fabrics of cotton, which containing 50% or more, bleached or dyed, impregnated, coated or covered with

税则号列 Tariff Item	商品名称及备注	进口税率 最惠	普通	暂定	出口退税	增值税率	计量单位	监管条件	Article Description
	浸涂或包覆，漂，染棉织物≥50%）								other materials other than rubber, plastic, paste
5907 0090.40	用其他材料浸涂的涤短纤棉混纺织物（用橡胶、塑料、浆料以外材料浸涂或包覆，漂，染涤棉织物≥50%）	10	100		16	17	千克		Textile fabrics, mixed with fabrics of polyester staple fibres and cotton, which containning 50% or more by weight, bleached or dyed, impreguated, coated or covered with other materials other than rubber, plastic, paste
5907 0090.90	用其他材料浸涂的其他纺织物（用橡胶、塑料、浆料以外材料浸渍、涂布或包覆）	10	100		16	17	千克		Textile fabrics of other textile fabrics, impregnated, coated or covered with other materials other than rubber, plastic, paste
59.08	**用纺织材料机织、编结或针织而成的灯芯、炉芯、打火机芯、烛芯或类似品；煤气灯纱筒及纱罩，不论是否浸渍：**								**Textile wicks, woven, plaited or knitted, for lamps, stoves, lighters, candles or the like; incandescent gas mantles and tubular knitted gas mantle fabric therefor, whether or not impregnated:**
5908.0000	用纺织材料机织、编结或针织而成的灯芯、炉芯、打火机芯、烛芯或类似品；煤气灯纱筒及纱罩，不论是否浸渍	10	70		16	17	千克		Textile wicks, woven, plaited or knitted,for lamps, stoves, lighters, candles or the like; incandescent gas mantles and tubular knitted gas mantle fabric therefor, whether or not impregnated
59.09	**纺织材料制的水龙软管及类似的管子，不论有无其他材料作衬里、护套或附件：**								**Textile hosepiping and similar textile tubing, with or without lining, armour or accessories of other materials:**
5909.0000	纺织材料制的水龙软管及类似的管子，不论有无其他材料作衬里、护套或附件	8	35		16	17	千克		Textile hosepiping and similar textile tubing, with or without lining, armour or accessories of other materials
59.10	**纺织材料制的传动带或输送带及带料，不论是否用塑料浸渍、涂布、包覆或压层，也不论是否用金属或其他材料加强：**								**Transmission or conveyor belts or belting, of textile material, whether or not impregnated, coated, covered or laminated with plastics, or reinforced with metal or other material:**
5910.0000	纺织材料制的传动带或输送带及带料，不论是否用塑料浸渍、涂布、包覆或压层，也不论是否用金属或其他材料加强	8	35		16	17	千克		Transmission or conveyor belts or belting, of textile material, whether or not impregnated, coated, covered or laminated with plastics, or reinforced with metal or other material
59.11	**本章注释七所规定的作专门技术用途的纺织产品及制品：**								**Textile products and articles, for technical uses, specified in Note 7 to this Chapter:**
	-用橡胶、皮革或其他材料涂布、包覆或层压的作针布用的纺织物、毡呢及毡呢衬里机织物，以及作专门技术用途的类似织物，包括用橡胶浸渍的、用于包覆纺绖（织轴）的狭幅丝绒织物：								-Textile fabrics, felt and felt-lined woven fabrics, coated, covered or laminated with rubber, leather or other material, of a kind used for card clothing, and similar fabrics of a kind used for other technical purposes, including narrow fabrics made of velvet impregnated with rubber, for covering weaving spindles（weaving beams）:
5911.1010	---用橡胶浸渍的、用于包覆纺绖（织轴）的狭幅丝绒织物	8	75		16	17	千克		—Narrow fabrics made of velvet impregnated with rubber, for covering weaving spindles（weaving beams）
5911.1090	---其他	8	35		16	17	千克		---Other
5911.2000	-筛布，不论是否制成的	8	35		16	17	千克		-Bolting cloth, whether or not made up
5911 2000.10	丝制筛布（不论是否制成的）	8	35		16	17	千克		Bolting cloth of silk, whether or not made up
5911 2000.90	其他纺织材料制筛布(不论是否制成的，刻版、筛网、印布除外)	8	35		16	17	千克		Bolting cloth of other textile materials, whether or not made up, other than engraved screen printed fabric
	-环状或装有连接装置的纺织物及毡呢，用于造纸机器或类似机器（例如，制浆机或制石棉水泥的机器）：								-Textile fabrics and felts, endless or fitted with linking devices, of a kind used in paper-making or similar machines （for example, for pulp or asbestos-cement）:
5911.3100	--每平方米重量在650克以下	8	35		16	17	千克		--Weighing less than 650g/m²
5911.3200	--每平方米重量在650克及以上	8	35		16	17	千克		--Weighing 650g/m² or more
5911.4000	-用于榨油机器或类似机器的滤布，包括人发制滤布	8	35		16	17	千克		-Straining cloth of a kind used in oil presses or the like, including that of human hair
5911.9000	-其他	8	35		16	17	千克		-Other

第六十章 针织物及钩编织物

Chapter 60 Knitted or crocheted fabrics

注释：

一、本章不包括：

（一）品目58.04的钩编花边；

（二）品目58.07的针织或钩编的标签、徽章及类似品；或

（三）第五十九章的经浸渍、涂布、包覆或层压的针织物及钩编织物。但经浸渍、涂布、包覆或层压的起绒针织物及起绒钩编织物仍归入品目60.01。

二、本章还包括用金属线制的用于衣着、装饰或类似用途的织物。

三、本税则所称"针织物"，包括由纺织纱线用链式针法构成的缝编织物。

Chapter Notes:

1. This Chapter does not cover:

（a）Crochet lace of heading.No 58.04;

（b）Labels, badges or similar articles, knitted or crocheted, of heading.No 58.07; or

（c）Knitted or crocheted fabrics, impregnated, coated, covered or laminated, of Chapter 59. However, knitted or crocheted pile fabrics, impregnated, coated, covered or laminated, remain classified in heading.No 60.01.

2. This Chapter also includes fabrics made of metal thread and of a kind used in apparel, as furnishing fabrics or for similar purposes.

3. Throughout the Nomenclature any reference to "knitted" goods includes a reference to stitch-bonded goods in which the chain stitches are formed of textile yarn.

税则号列 Tariff Item	商品名称及备注	进口税率 最惠	普通	暂定	出口退税	增值税率	计量单位	监管条件	Article Description
60.01	针织或钩编的起绒织物，包括"长毛绒"织物及毛圈织物：								**Pile fabrics, including "long pile" fabrics and terry fabrics, knitted or crocheted:**
6001.1000	-"长毛绒"织物	10	130		16	17	米/千克		-"Long pile" fabrics
6001 1000.10	毛制针织或钩编的长毛绒织物(羊毛及动物细毛制)	10	130		16	17	米/千克		"Long pile" fabrics of wool and fine animal hair, knitted or crocheted
6001 1000.20	棉制针织或钩编的长毛绒织物	10	130		16	17	米/千克		"Long pile" fabrics of cotton, knitted or crocheted
6001 1000.30	化纤制针织或钩编的长毛绒织物	10	130		16	17	米/千克		"Long pile" fabrics of man-made fibres, knitted or crocheted
6001 1000.90	其他纺材制针织或钩编长毛绒织物	10	130		16	17	米/千克		"Long pile" fabrics of other textile materials, knitted or crocheted
	-毛圈绒头织物：								-Looped pile fabrics:
6001.2100	--棉制	10	70		16	17	米/千克		--Of cotton
6001.2200	--化学纤维制	10	130		16	17	米/千克		--Of man-made fibres
6001.2900	--其他纺织材料制	12	130		16	17	米/千克		--Of other textile materials
6001 2900.10	毛制针织或钩编毛圈绒头织物（羊毛及动物细毛制）	12	130		16	17	米/千克		Looped pile fabrics of wool and fine animal hair,knitted or crocheted
6001 2900.90	其他材料制针织或钩编毛圈绒头布	12	130		16	17	米/千克		Looped pile fabrics of other textile materials, knitted or crocheted
	-其他：								-Other:
6001.9100	--棉制	10	70		16	17	米/千克		-Of cotton
6001.9200	--化学纤维制	10	130		16	17	米/千克		--Of man-made fibres
6001.9900	--其他纺织材料制	12	130		16	17	米/千克		--Of other textile materials
6001 9900.10	丝制针织或钩编其他起绒织物（按重量计含丝及绢丝 85%及以上）	12	130		16	17	米/千克		Other pile fabrics, containing by weight 85% or more of silk or silk waste, knitted or crocheted
6001 9900.20	毛制针织或钩编其他起绒织物（羊毛及动物细毛制）	12	130		16	17	米/千克		Other pile fabrics of wool and fine animal hair, knitted or crocheted
6001 9900.90	其他纺材制针织或钩编起绒织物	12	130		16	17	米/千克		Pile fabrics of other textile materials, knitted or crocheted
60.02	宽度不超过 30 厘米，按重量计弹性纱线或橡胶线含量在 5%及以上的针织物或钩编织物，但品目60.01 的货品除外：								**Knitted or crocheted fabrics of a width not exceeding 30cm, containing by weight 5% or more of elastomeric yarn or rubber thread, other than those of heading 60.01:**
	-按重量计弹性纱线含量在 5%及以上，但不含橡胶线：								-Containing by weight 5% or more of elastomeric yarn but not containing rubber thread:
6002.4010	---棉制	10	70		16	17	米/千克		---Of cotton

税则号列 Tariff Item	商品名称及备注	进口税率 最惠	进口税率 普通	进口税率 暂定	出口退税	增值税率	计量单位	监管条件	Article Description
6002.4020	---丝及绢丝制	10	130		16	17	米/千克		---Of silk or silk waste
6002.4030	---合成纤维制	10	130		16	17	米/千克		---Of synthetic fibres
6002.4040	---人造纤维制	10	130		16	17	米/千克		---Of artificial fibres
6002.4090	---其他	10	130		16	17	米/千克		---Other
	-其他:								-Other:
6002.9010	---棉制	10	70		16	17	米/千克		---Of cotton
6002.9020	---丝及绢丝制	10	130		16	17	米/千克		---Of silk or silk waste
6002.9030	---合成纤维制	10	130		16	17	米/千克		---Of synthetic fibres
6002.9040	---人造纤维制	10	130		16	17	米/千克		---Of artificial fibres
6002.9090	---其他	10	130		16	17	米/千克		---Other
60.03	宽度不超过30厘米的针织或钩编织物，但品目60.01或60.02的货品除外:								**Knitted or crocheted fabrics of a width not exceeding 30cm, other than those of heading No.60.01 or 60.02:**
6003.1000	-羊毛或动物细毛制	10	130		16	17	米/千克		-Of wool or fine animal hair
6003.2000	-棉制	10	70		16	17	米/千克		-Of cotton
6003 2000.10	棉制宽≤30cm 经编织物（按重量计弹性纱线或橡胶线含量＜5%）	10	70		16	17	米/千克		Warp knit fabric of cotton, of a width not exceeding 30cm（containing by weight less than 5% of elastomeric yarn or rubber thread）
6003 2000.90	棉制宽≤30cm 非经编针织或钩编织物(按重量计弹性纱线或橡胶线含量＜5%)	10	70		16	17	米/千克		Not warp knit or knitted or crocheted fabrics of cotton, of a width not exceeding 30cm, containing by weight less than 5% of elastomeric yarn or rubber thread
6003.3000	-合成纤维制	10	130		16	17	米/千克		-Of synthetic fibres
6003 3000.10	合纤制宽小于等于30厘米经编织物(按重量计弹性纱线或橡胶线含量＜5%)	10	130		16	17	米/千克		Warp knit fabric of synthetic fiber, of a width not exceeding 30cm,（containing by weight less than 5% of elastomeric yarn or rubber thread）
6003 3000.90	合纤制宽小于等于30厘米非经编针织或钩编织物(按重量计弹性纱线或橡胶线含量＜5%)	10	130		16	17	米/千克		Not warp knit or knitted or crocheted fabrics of synthetic fiber, of a width not exceeding 30cm, containing by weight less than 5% of elastomeric yarn or rubber thread
6003.4000	-人造纤维制	10	130		16	17	米/千克		-Of artificial fibres
6003 4000.10	人纤制宽小于等于30厘米经编织物(按重量计弹性纱线或橡胶线含量＜5%)	10	130		16	17	米/千克		Warp knit fabric of artificial fibres, of a width not exceeding 30cm,（containing by weight less than 50% of elastomeric yarn or rubber thread）
6003 4000.90	人纤制宽小于等于30厘米非经编织物(按重量计弹性纱线或橡胶线含量＜5%)	10	130		16	17	米/千克		Not warp knit fabrics of artificial fibres, of a width not exceeding 30cm, containing by weight less than 5% of elastomeric yarn or rubber thread
6003.9000	-其他	10	130		16	17	米/千克		-Other
60.04	宽度超过30厘米，按重量计弹性纱线或橡胶线含量在5%及以上的针织物或钩编织物，但品目60.01的货品除外:								**Knitted or crocheted fabrics of a width exceeding 30 cm, containing by weight 5% or more elastomeric yarn or rubber thread, other than those of heading 60.01:**
	-按重量计弹性纱线含量在5%及以上，但不含橡胶线:								-Containing by weight 5% or more of elastomeric yarn but not containing rubber thread:
6004.1010	---棉制	10	70		16	17	米/千克		---Of cotton
6004.1020	---丝及绢丝制	10	130		16	17	米/千克		---Of silk or silk waste
6004.1030	---合成纤维制	10	130		16	17	米/千克		---Of synthetic fibres
6004.1040	---人造纤维制	10	130		16	17	米/千克		---Of artificial fibres
6004.1090	---其他	10	130		16	17	米/千克		---Other
	-其他:								-Other:
6004.9010	---棉制	10	70		16	17	米/千克		---Of cotton
6004.9020	---丝及绢丝制	10	130		16	17	米/千克		---Of silk or silk waste
6004.9030	---合成纤维制	10	130		16	17	米/千克		---Of synthetic fibres
6004.9040	---人造纤维制	10	130		16	17	米/千克		---Of artificial fibres
6004.9090	---其他	10	130		16	17	米/千克		---Other
60.05	经编织物(包括由花边针织机织成的)，但品目60.01至60.04的货品除外:								**Warp knit fabrics（including those made on galloon knitting machines）,other than those of heading 60.01 to 60.04:**
	-棉制:								-Of cotton:
6005.2100	--未漂白或漂白	10	70		16	17	米/千克		--Unbleached or bleached

税则号列 Tariff Item	商品名称及备注	进口税率			出口退税	增值税率	计量单位	监管条件	Article Description
		最惠	普通	暂定					
6005.2200	--染色	10	70		16	17	米/千克		--Dyed
6005.2300	--色织	10	70		16	17	米/千克		--Of yarns of different colours
6005.2400	--印花	10	70		16	17	米/千克		--Printed
	-合成纤维制:								-Of synthetic fibres:
6005.3100	--未漂白或漂白	10	130		16	17	米/千克		--Unbleached or bleached
6005 3100.10	漂白或未漂白合成纤维制经编透孔织物(包括由花边针织机织成的经编织物)	10	130		16	17	米/千克		Warp knit openwork fabrics of synthetic fibers, bleached or unbleached(including those made on galloon knitting machines)
6005 3100.90	漂白或未漂白合成纤维制经编非透孔织物(包括由花边针织机织成的经编织物)	10	130		16	17	米/千克		Warp knit not openwork of synthetic fibers, bleached or unbleached (including those made on galloon knitting machines)
6005.3200	--染色	10	130		16	17	米/千克		--Dyed
6005 3200.10	染色合成纤维制经编透孔织物(包括由花边针织机织成的经编织物)	10	130		16	17	米/千克		Warp knit openwork fabrics of synthetic fibers, dyed (including those made on galloon knitting machines)
6005 3200.90	染色合成纤维制经编非透孔织物(包括由花边针织机织成的经编织物)	10	130		16	17	米/千克		Warp knit not openwork fabrics of synthetic fibers, dyed (including those made on galloon knitting machines)
6005.3300	--色织	10	130		16	17	米/千克		--Of yarns of different colours
6005 3300.10	色织合成纤维制经编透孔织物(包括由花边针织机织成的经编织物)	10	130		16	17	米/千克		Warp knit openwork fabrics of synthetic fibers, of yarns of different colours (including those made on galloon knitting machines)
6005 3300.90	色织合成纤维制经编非透孔织物(包括由花边针织机织成的经编织物)	10	130		16	17	米/千克		Warp knit not openwork fabrics of synthetic fibers, of yarns of different colours (including those made on galloon knitting machines)
6005.3400	--印花	10	130		16	17	米/千克		-Printed
6005 3400.10	印花合成纤维制经编透孔织物(包括由花边针织机织成的经编织物)	10	130		16	17	米/千克		Warp knitted openwork fabrics of synthetic fibers, printed (including those made on galloon knitting machines)
6005 3400.90	印花合成纤维制经编非透孔织物(包括由花边针织机织成的经编织物)	10	130		16	17	米/千克		Warp knitted not openwork fabrics of synthetic fibers, printed (including those made on galloon knitting machines)
	-人造纤维制:								-Of artificial fibres:
6005.4100	--未漂白或漂白	10	130		16	17	米/千克		--Unbleached or bleached
6005 4100.10	漂白或未漂白人造纤维制经编透孔织物(包括由花边针织机织成的经编织物)	10	130		16	17	米/千克		Warp knitted openwork fabrics of artificial fibres, bleached or unbleached (including those made on galloon knitting machines)
6005 4100.90	漂白或未漂白人造纤维制经编非透孔织物(包括由花边针织机织成的经编织物)	10	130		16	17	米/千克		Warp knitted not openwork fabrics of artificial fibres, bleached or unbleached (including those made on galloon knitting machines)
6005.4200	--染色	10	130		16	17	米/千克		--Dyed
6005 4200.10	染色人造纤维制经编透孔织物(包括由花边针织机织成的经编织物)	10	130		16	17	米/千克		Warp knitted openwork fabrics of artificial fibres, dyed (including those made on galloon knitting machines)
6005 4200.90	染色人造纤维制经编非透孔织物(包括由花边针织机织成的经编织物)	10	130		16	17	米/千克		Warp knitted not openwork fabrics of artificial fibres, dyed (including those made on galloon knitting machines)
6005.4300	--色织	10	130		16	17	米/千克		--Of yarns of different colours
6005 4300.10	色织人造纤维制经编透孔织物(包括由花边针织机织成的经编织物)	10	130		16	17	米/千克		Warp knitted openwork fabrics of artificial fibres, dyed (including those made on galloon knitting machines)
6005 4300.90	色织人造纤维制经编非透孔织物(包括由花边针织机织成的经编织物)	10	130		16	17	米/千克		Warp knitted not openwork fabrics of artificial fibres, dyed (including those made on galloon knitting machines)
6005.4400	--印花	10	130		16	17	米/千克		--Printed

税则号列 Tariff Item	商品名称及备注	进口税率			出口退税	增值税率	计量单位	监管条件	Article Description
		最惠	普通	暂定					
6005 4400.10	印花人造纤维制经编透孔织物（包括由花边针织机织成的经编织物）	10	130		16	17	米/千克		Warp knitted openwork fabrics of artificial fibers, printed（including those made on galloon knitting machines）
6005 4400.90	印花人造纤维制经编非透孔织物(包括由花边针织机织成的经编织物)	10	130		16	17	米/千克		Warp knitted not openwork fabrics of artificial fibers, printed（including those made on galloon knitting machines）
	-其他:								-Other:
6005.9010	---羊毛或动物细毛制	12	130		16	17	米/千克		---Of wool or fine animal hair
6005.9090	---其他	12	130		16	17	米/千克		---Of other textile materials
60.06	**其他针织或钩编织物:**								**Other knitted or crocheted fabrics:**
6006.1000	-羊毛或动物细毛制	12	130		16	17	米/千克		-Of wool or fine animal hair
	-棉制:								-Of cotton:
6006.2100	--未漂白或漂白	10	70		16	17	米/千克		--Unbleached or bleached
6006.2200	--染色	10	70		16	17	米/千克		--Dyed
6006.2300	--色织	10	70		16	17	米/千克		--Of yarns of different colours
6006.2400	--印花	10	70		16	17	米/千克		--Printed
	-合成纤维制:								-Of synthetic fibres:
6006.3100	--未漂白或漂白	10	130		16	17	米/千克		--Unbleached or bleached
6006.3200	--染色	10	130		16	17	米/千克		--Dyed
6006.3300	--色织	10	130		16	17	米/千克		--Of yarns of different colours
6006.3400	--印花	10	130		16	17	米/千克		--Printed
	-人造纤维制:								-Of artificial fibres:
6006.4100	--未漂白或漂白	10	130		16	17	米/千克		--Unbleached or bleached
6006.4200	--染色	10	130		16	17	米/千克		--Dyed
6006.4300	--色织	10	130		16	17	米/千克		--Of yarns of different colours
6006.4400	--印花	10	130		16	17	米/千克		--Printed
6006.9000	-其他	12	130		16	17	米/千克		-Other
6006 9000.10	丝及绢丝制其他针织或钩编织物（按重量计含丝及绢丝85%及以上）	12	130		16	17	米/千克		Other fabrics of silk or silk waste, containing by weight 85% or more of silk or silk waste, knitted or crocheted
6006 9000.90	其他纺材制其他针织或钩编织物	12	130		16	17	米/千克		Other fabrics of other textile materials, knitted or crocheted

第六十一章
针织或钩编的服装及衣着附件

注释：

一、本章仅适用于制成的针织品或钩编织品。

二、本章不包括：

（一）品目62.12的货品；

（二）品目63.09的旧衣着或其他旧物品；或

（三）矫形器具、外科手术带、疝气带及类似品（品目90.21）。

三、品目61.03及61.04所称：

（一）“西服套装”，是指面料用相同的织物制成的两件套或三件套的下列成套服装：

——一件人体上半身穿着的外套或短上衣，除袖子外，其面料应由四片或四片以上组成；也可附带一件马甲（西服背心），这件马甲（西服背心）的前片面料应与套装其他各件的面料相同，后片面料则应与外套或短上衣的衬里料相同；以及

——一件人体下半身穿着的服装，即不带背带或护胸的长裤、马裤、短裤（游泳裤除外）、裙子或裙裤。

西服套装各件面料质地、颜色及构成必须相同，其款式也必须相同，尺寸大小还须相互般配，但可以用不同织物滚边（在缝口上缝入长条织物）。

如果数件人体下半身穿着的服装同时报验（例如，两条长裤、长裤与短裤、裙子或裙裤与长裤），构成西服套装下装的应是一条长裤，而对于女式西服套装，应是裙子或裙裤，其他服装应分别归类。

所称“西服套装”，包括不论是否完全符合上述条件的下列配套服装：

1. 常礼服，由一件后襟下垂并下端开圆弧形叉的素色短上衣和一条条纹长裤组成；

2. 晚礼服（燕尾服），一般用黑色织物制成，上衣前襟较短且不闭合，背后有燕尾；

3. 无燕尾套装夜礼服，其中上衣款式与普通上衣相似（可以更为显露衬衣前胸），但有光滑丝质或仿丝质的翻领。

（二）“便服套装”，是指面料相同并作零售包装的下列成套服装（西服套装及品目61.07、61.08或61.09的物品除外）：

——一件人体上半身穿着的服装，但套头衫及背心除外，因为套头衫可在两件套服装中作为内衣，背心也可作为内衣；以及

Chapter 61
Articles of apparel and clothing accessories, knitted or crocheted

Chapter Notes:

1. This Chapter applies only to made up knitted or crocheted articles.

2. This Chapter does not cover:

（a）Goods of heading 62.12;

（b）Worn clothing or other worn articles of heading 63.09; or

（c）Orthopaedic appliances, surgical belts, trusses or the like（heading 90.21）.

3. For the purposes of headings 61.03 and 61.04:

（a）The term “suit” means a set of garments composed of two or three pieces made up, in respect of their outer surface, in identical fabric and comprising:

-One suit coat or jacket the outer shell of which, exclusive of sleeves, consists of four or more panels, designed to cover the upper part of the body, possibly with a tailored waistcoat in addition whose front is made from the same fabric as the outer surface of the other components of the set and whose back is made from the same fabric as the lining of the suit coat or jacket; and

-One garment designed to cover the lower part of the body and consisting of trousers, breeches or shorts（other than swimwear）, a skirt or a divided skirt, having neither braces nor bibs.

All of the components of a “suit” must be of the same fabric construction, colour and composition; they must also be of the same style and of corresponding or compatible size. However, these components may have piping（a strip of fabric sewn into the seam）in a different fabric.

If several separate components to cover the lower part of the body are presented together（for example, two pairs of trousers or trousers and shorts, or a skirt or divided skirt and trousers）, the constituent lower part shall be one pair of trousers or, in the case of women's or girls' suits, the skirt or divided skirt, the other garments being considered separately.

The term “suit” includes the following sets of garments, whether or not they fulfil all the above conditions:

（i）Morning dress, comprising a plain jacket（cutaway）with rounded tails hanging well down at the back and striped trousers;

（ii）Evening dress（tailcoat）, generally made of black fabric, the jacket of which is relatively short at the front, does not close and has narrow skirts cut in at the hips and hanging down behind;

（iii）Dinner jacket suits, in which the jacket is similar in style to an ordinary jacket（though perhaps revealing more of the shirt front）, but has shiny silk or imitation silk lapels.

（b）The term “ensemble” means a set of garments（other than suits and articles of heading 61.07, 61.08 or 61.09）,composed of several pieces made up in identical fabric,put up for retail sale, and comprising:

-One garment designed to cover the upper part of the body, with the exception of pullovers which may form a second upper garment in the sole context of twin sets, and of waistcoats which may also form a second

——一件或两件不同的人体下半身穿着的服装，即长裤、护胸背带工装裤、马裤、短裤（游泳裤除外）、裙子或裙裤。

便服套装各件面料质地、款式、颜色及构成必须相同；尺寸大小也须相互般配。所称“便服套装”，不包括品目 61.12 的运动服及滑雪服。

四、品目 61.05 及 61.06 不包括在腰围以下有口袋的服装、带有罗纹腰带及以其他方式收紧下摆的服装或其织物至少在 10 厘米×10 厘米的面积内沿各方向的直线长度上平均每厘米少于 10 针的服装。品目 61.05 不包括无袖服装。

五、品目 61.09 不包括带有束带、罗纹腰带或其他方式收紧下摆的服装。

六、对于品目 61.11：

（一）所称“婴儿服装及衣着附件”，是指用于身高不超过86厘米幼儿的服装；

（二）既可归入品目 61.11，也可归入本章其他品目的物品，应归入品目 61.11。

七、品目61.12所称“滑雪服”，是指从整个外观和织物质地来看，主要在滑雪（速度滑雪或高山滑雪）时穿着的下列服装或成套服装：

（一）“滑雪连身服”，即上下身连在一起的单件服装；除袖子和领子外，滑雪连身服可有口袋或脚带；或

（二）“滑雪套装”，即由两件或三件构成一套并作零售包装的下列服装：

——一件用一条拉链扣合的带风帽的厚夹克、防风衣、防风短上衣或类似的服装，可以附带一件背心（滑雪背心）；以及

一条不论是否过腰的长裤、一条马裤或一条护胸背带工装裤。

“滑雪套装”也可由一件类似以上（一）款所述的连身服和一件可套在连身服外面的有胎料背心组成。

“滑雪套装”各件颜色可以不同，但面料质地、款式及构成必须相同；尺寸大小也须相互般配。

八、既可归入品目 61.13，也可归入本章其他品目的服装，除品目 61.11 所列的仍归入该品目外，其余的应一律归入品目 61.13。

九、本章的服装，凡门襟为左压右的，应视为男式；右压左的，应视为女式。但本规定不适用于其式样已明显为男式或女式的服装。

无法区别是男式还是女式的服装，应按女式服装归入有关品目。

十、本章物品可用金属线制成。

upper garment; and

-One or two different garments, designed to cover the lower part of the body and consisting of trousers, bib and brace overalls, breeches, shorts (other than swimwear), a skirt or a divided skirt.

All of the components of an ensemble must be of the same fabric construction, style, colour and composition; they also must be of corresponding or compatible size. The term “ensemble” does not apply to track suits or ski suits, of heading 61.12.

4. Headings 61.05 and 61.06 do not cover garments with pockets below the waist, with a ribbed waistband or other means of tightening at the bottom of the garment, or garments having an average of less than 10 stitches per linear centimetre in each direction counted on an area measuring at least 10cm×10cm. Heading 61.05 does not cover sleeveless garments.

5. Heading 61.09 does not cover garments with a drawstring, ribbed waistband or other means of tightening at the bottom of the garment.

6. For the purposes of heading 61.11:

(a) The expression “babies' garments and clothing accessories” means articles for young children of a body height not exceeding 86cm;

(b) Articles which are, prima facie, classifiable both in heading. 61.11 and in other headings of this Chapter are to be classified in heading 61.11.

7. For the purposes of heading 61.12, “ski suits” means garments or sets of garments which, by their general appearance and texture, are identifiable as intended to be worn principally for skiing (cross-country or alpine). They consist either of:

(a) A “ski overall”, that is, a one-piece garment designed to cover the upper and the lower parts of the body; in addition to sleeves and a collar the ski overall may have pockets or footstraps; or

(b) A “ski ensemble”, that is, a set of garments composed of two or three pieces, put up for retail sale and comprising:

-One garment such as an anorak, wind-cheater, wind-jacket or similar article, closed by a slide fastener (zipper), possibly with a waistcoat in addition; and

-One pair of trousers whether or not extending above waist-level, one pair of breeches or one bib and brace overall.

The “ski ensemble” may also consist of an overall similar to the one mentioned in paragraph (a) above and a type of padded, sleeveless jacket worn over the overall.

All the components of a “ski ensemble” must be made up in a fabric of the same texture, style and composition whether or not of the same colour; they also must be of corresponding or compatible size.

8. Garments which are, prima facie, classifiable both in heading 61.13 and in other headings of this Chapter; excluding heading 61.11, are to be classified in heading 61.13.

9. Garments of this Chapter desinged for left over right closure at the front shall be regarded as men's or boys' garments, and those designed for right over left closure at the front as women's or girls' garments. These provisions do not apply where the cut of the garment clearly indicates that it is designed for one or other of the sexes.

Garments which cannot be identified as either men's or boys' garments or as women's or girls' garments are to be classified in the headings covering women's or girls'garments.

10. Articles of this Chapter may be made of metal thread.

税则号列 Tariff Item	商品名称及备注	进口税率 最惠	普通	暂定	出口退税	增值税率	计量单位	监管条件	Article Description
61.01	**针织或钩编的男式大衣、短大衣、斗蓬、短斗蓬、带风帽的防寒短上衣(包括滑雪短上衣)、防风衣、防风短上衣及类似品，但品目61.03的货品除外：**								**Men's or boys' overcoats, car-coats, capes, cloaks, anoraks（including ski-jackets）, wind-cheaters, wind-jackets and similar articles, knitted or crocheted, other than those of heading No.61.03:**
6101.2000	-棉制	17.5	90		16	17	件/千克		-Of cotton
6101 2000.10	棉制针织或钩编男式大衣(包括短大衣、斗篷、短斗篷及类似品，雨衣除外)	17.5	90		16	17	件/千克		Men's or boys' overcoats, car-coats,capes, cloak and similar articles, of cotton, knitted or crocheted, other than rain-coats
6101 2000.21	棉制针织或钩编手工制男式防风衣(包括防寒短上衣、防风短上衣及类似品)	17.5	90		16	17	件/千克		Men's or boys' hand-work wind-cheaters, anoraks, wind-jackets and similar articles, of cotton, knitted or crocheted
6101 2000.29	棉制针织或钩编男式防风衣(包括防寒短上衣、防风短上衣及类似品)	17.5	90		16	17	件/千克		Men's or boys' wind-cheaters, anoraks,wind- jackets and similar articles, of cotton, knitted or crocheted
6101 2000.30	棉制针织或钩编男式雨衣	17.5	90		16	17	件/千克		Men's or boys' raincoats of cotton, knitted or crocheted
6101.3000	-化学纤维制	17.5	130		16	17	件/千克		-Of man-made fibres
6101 3000.11	化纤制针织或钩编男式大衣等(含毛≥23%，包括短上衣、斗篷、短斗篷及类似品，雨衣除外)	17.5	130		16	17	件/千克		Men's or boys'overcoats, car-coats, cloaks and similar articles, containing 23% or more of wool or fine animal hair, of man-made fibres, knitted or crocheted, other than raincoats
6101 3000.19	其他化纤制针织或钩编男式大衣等(包括短大衣、斗篷、短斗篷及类似品，雨衣除外)	17.5	130		16	17	件/千克		Men's or boys'overcoats,car-coats, capes, cloak and similar articles, knitted or crocheted, of other man-made fibres, other than raincoats
6101 3000.21	化纤制针织或钩编手工男式防风衣(含毛≥23%，包括防寒短上衣、防风短上衣及类似品)	17.5	130		16	17	件/千克		Men's or boys' handwork wind-cheaters, anoraks, wind- jackets and similar articles, of man-made fibres, containing 23% or more of wool or fine animal hair, knitted or crocheted
6101 3000.22	化纤制针织或钩编男式防风衣(含毛≥23%,包括防寒短上衣、防风短上衣及类似品)	17.5	130		16	17	件/千克		Men's or boys' wind-cheaters, anoraks, wind- jackets and similar articles, of man-made fibres, containing 23% or more of wool or fine animal hair, knitted or crocheted
6101 3000.23	其他化纤针织钩编手工男式防风衣(包括防寒短上衣、防风短上衣及类似品)	17.5	130		16	17	件/千克		Men's or boys' handwork wind-cheaters, anoraks, wind-jackets and similar articles, of other man- made fibres, knitted or crocheted
6101 3000.29	其他化纤制其他男式防风衣(包括防寒短上衣、防风短上衣及类似品)	17.5	130		16	17	件/千克		Other men's or boys' wind-cheaters, anoraks, wind-jackets and similar articles, of man-made fibres, knitted or crocheted
6101 3000.31	化纤制针织或钩编男式雨衣(按重量计含羊毛或动物细毛≥23%)	17.5	130		16	17	件/千克		Men's or boys' knitted or crocheted raincoats, of man-made fibres, containing 23% or more of wool or fine animal hair
6101 3000.39	化纤制针织或钩编男式雨衣	17.5	130		16	17	件/千克		Men's or boys' raincoats of man-made fibres, knitted or crocheted
	-其他纺织材料制：								-Of other textile materials:
6101.9010	---羊毛或动物细毛制	25	130		16	17	件/千克		---Of wool or fine animal hair
6101 9010.10	毛制针织或钩编非手工制男式防风衣(包括防寒短上衣、防风短上衣及类似品)	25	130		16	17	件/千克		Men's or boys' non-handwork wind-cheaters, anoraks, wind-jackets and similar articles, of wool or fine animal hair, knitted or crocheted
6101 9010.90	毛制针织或钩编其他男大衣、斗篷、防风衣等(包括防寒短上衣、防风短上衣、短大衣、短斗篷及类似品)	25	130		16	17	件/千克		Men's or boys' overcoats, capes, wind-cheaters, anoraks, wind-jackets, carcoats, cloak and similar articles, of wool or fine animal hair, knitted or crocheted
6101.9090	---其他纺织材料制	17.5	130		16	17	件/千克		---Of other textile materials
61.02	**针织或钩编的女式大衣、短大**								**Women's or girls' overcoats, car-coats, capes,**

税则号列 Tariff Item	商品名称及备注	进口税率 最惠	普通	暂定	出口退税	增值税率	计量单位	监管条件	Article Description
	衣、斗蓬、短斗蓬、带风帽的防寒短上衣(包括滑雪短上衣)、防风衣、防风短上衣及类似品，但品目61.04的货品除外：								**cloaks, anoraks（including skijackets）, wind-cheaters, wind-jackets and similar articles, knitted or crocheted, other than those of heading No.61.04:**
6102.1000	-羊毛或动物细毛制	25	130		16	17	件/千克		-Of wool or fine animal hair
6102 1000.10	毛制针织或钩编女式大衣等(包括短大衣、斗篷、短斗篷及类似品，雨衣除外)	25	130		16	17	件/千克		Women's or girls' overcoats, car-coats,capes, cloak and similar articles, of wool or fine animal hair, knitted or crocheted, other than raincoats
6102 1000.21	毛制针织或钩编手工制女式防风衣(包括防寒短上衣、防风短上衣及类似品)	25	130		16	17	件/千克		Women's or girls' non-handwork wind-cheaters, anoraks, wind-jackets and similar articles, of wool or fine animal hair, knitted or crocheted
6102 1000.29	毛制针织或钩编女式防风衣(包括防寒短上衣、防风短上衣及类似品)	25	130		16	17	件/千克		Other women's or girls' wind-cheaters,anoraks, wind-jackets and similar articles, of wool or fine animal hair, knitted or crocheted
6102 1000.30	毛制针织或钩编女式雨衣	25	130		16	17	件/千克		Women's or girls' knitted or crocheted raincoats of wool or fine animal hair
6102.2000	-棉制	17.5	90		16	17	件/千克		-Of cotton
6102 2000.10	棉制针织或钩编女式大衣(包括短大衣、斗篷、短斗篷及类似品，雨衣除外)	17.5	90		16	17	件/千克		Women's or girls' overcoats, car-coats, capes, cloak and similar articles, of cotton, knitted or crocheted, other than rain-coats
6102 2000.21	棉制针织或钩编手工女式防风衣(包括防风短上衣、防寒短上衣及类似品)	17.5	90		16	17	件/千克		Women's or girls' handwork wind-cheaters, anoraks, wind-jackets and similar articles, of cotton, knitted or crocheted
6102 2000.29	棉制针织或钩编女式防风衣(包括防风短上衣、防寒短上衣及类似品)	17.5	90		16	17	件/千克		Other women's or girls' wind-cheaters,anoraks, wind-jackets and similar articles, of cotton, knitted or crocheted
6102 2000.30	棉制针织或钩编女式雨衣	17.5	90		16	17	件/千克		Women's or girls' knitted or crocheted raincoats of cotton
6102.3000	-化学纤维制	17.5	130		16	17	件/千克		-Of man-made fibres
6102 3000.11	化纤制针织或钩编女式大衣等（含毛≥23%，含短大衣、斗篷、短斗篷及类似品，雨衣除外）	17.5	130		16	17	件/千克		Women's or girls' overcoats, car-coats, capes, cloak and similar articles, of man-made fibres, containing 23% or more of wool or fine animal hair, knitted or crocheted, other than raincoats
6102 3000.19	其他化纤制针织或钩编女式大衣（含短大衣、斗篷、短斗篷及类似品，雨衣除外）	17.5	130		16	17	件/千克		Other women's or girls' overcoats, carcoats, capes, cloak and similar articles, of man-made fibres, knitted or crocheted, other than raincoats
6102 3000.21	化纤制针织或钩编手工女式防风衣（含毛≥23%，包括防寒短上衣、防风短上衣及类似品）	17.5	130		16	17	件/千克		Women's or girls' handwork wind-cheaters, anoraks, wind-jackets and similar articles, of man-made fibres, containing 23% or more of wool or fine animal hair, knitted or crocheted
6102 3000.22	化纤制针织或钩编女式防风衣（含毛≥23%,包括防寒短上衣、防风短上衣及类似品）	17.5	130		16	17	件/千克		Women's or girls' wind-cheaters, anoraks, wind-jackets and similar articles, of man-made fibres, containing 23% or more of wool or fine animal hair, knitted or crocheted
6102 3000.23	其他化纤制针织钩编手工女防风衣(包括防寒短上衣、防风短上衣及类似品)	17.5	130		16	17	件/千克		Other women's or girls' handwork wind-cheaters, anoraks, wind-jackets and similar articles, of man-made fibres, knitted or crocheted
6102 3000.29	其他化纤制针织钩编其他女防风衣(包括防寒短上衣、防风短上衣及类似品)	17.5	130		16	17	件/千克		Other women's or girls' wind-cheaters,anoraks, wind-jackets and similar articles, of man-made fibres, knitted or crocheted
6102 3000.31	化纤制针织或钩编女式雨衣(按重量计羊毛及动物细毛≥23%)	17.5	130		16	17	件/千克		Women's or girls' knitted or crocheted raincoats, of man-made fibres, containing 23% or more of wool or fine animal hair
6102 3000.39	化纤制针织或钩编女式雨衣	17.5	130		16	17	件/千克		Women's or girls' knitted or crocheted raincoats of man-made fibres
6102.9000	-其他纺织材料制	20	130		16	17	件/千克		-Of other textile materials

税则号列 Tariff Item	商品名称及备注	进口税率 最惠	普通	暂定	出口退税	增值税率	计量单位	监管条件	Article Description
6102 9000.11	丝及绢丝制针织或钩编女式大衣等（含丝≥70%，包括短大衣、斗篷、短斗篷及类似品，雨衣除外）	20	130		16	17	件/千克		Women's or girls' overcoats, car-coats, capes, cloak and similar articles, knitted or crocheted, containing 70% or more of silk or silk waste, other than raincoats
6102 9000.14	丝及绢丝制针织或钩编女式防风衣(含丝≥70%,包括防寒短上衣、防风短上衣及类似品)	20	130		16	17	件/千克		Women's or girls' wind-cheaters, anoraks, wind-jackets and similar articles, knitted or crocheted, containing 70% or more of silk or silk waste
6102 9000.15	丝及绢丝制针织或钩编女式雨衣（含丝≥70%）	20	130		16	17	件/千克		Women's or girls' knitted or crocheted raincoats, containing 70% or more of silk or silk waste
6102 9000.21	其他纺织材料制针织或钩编女大衣（包括短大衣、斗篷、短斗篷及类似品,雨衣除外,棉限内）	20	130		16	17	件/千克		Women's or girls' overcoats, car-coats,capes, cloak and similar articles, of other textile materials, knitted or crocheted, other than raincoats, cotton limit in
6102 9000.22	其他纺织材料制针织或钩编女大衣（包括短大衣、斗篷、短斗篷及类似品，雨衣除外，羊毛限内）	20	130		16	17	件/千克		Women's or girls' overcoats, car-coats,capes, cloak and similar articles, of other textile materials, knitted or crocheted, other than raincoats, wool limit in
6102 9000.23	其他纺织材料制针织或钩编女大衣（包括短大衣、斗篷、短斗篷及类似品，雨衣除外，化纤限内）	20	130		16	17	件/千克		Women's or girls' overcoats, car-coats, capes, cloak and similar articles, of other textile materials, knitted or crocheted, other than raincoats, man-made fibres limit in
6102 9000.29	其他纺织材料制针织或钩编女大衣（包括短大衣、斗篷、短斗篷及类似品，雨衣除外）	20	130		16	17	件/千克		Women's or girls' overcoats, car-coats,capes, cloak and similar articles, of other textile materials, knitted or crocheted, other than raincoats
6102 9000.31	其他纺织料针织或钩编女式防风衣（包括防寒短上衣、防风短上衣及类似品，棉限内）	20	130		16	17	件/千克		Women's or girls' wind-cheaters, anoraks, wind-jackets and similar articles, of other textile materials, knitted or crocheted, cotton limit in
6102 9000.32	其他纺织料针织或钩编女式防风衣（包括防寒短上衣、防风短上衣及类似品，羊毛限内）	20	130		16	17	件/千克		Women's or girls' wind-cheaters, anoraks, wind-jackets and similar articles, of other textile materials, knitted or crocheted, wool limit in
6102 9000.33	其他纺织料针织或钩编女式防风衣（包括防寒短上衣、防风短上衣及类似品，化纤限内）	20	130		16	17	件/千克		Women's or girls' wind-cheaters, anoraks, windjackets and similar articles, of other textile materials,knitted or crocheted, man-made fibres limit in
6102 9000.39	其他纺织料针织或钩编女式防风衣（包括防寒短上衣、防风短上衣及类似品）	20	130		16	17	件/千克		Other women's or girls' wind-cheaters,anoraks, wind-jackets and similar articles, of other textile materials, knitted or crocheted
6102 9000.41	其他纺材制针织或钩编女式雨衣（棉限内）	20	130		16	17	件/千克		Women's or girls' knitted or crocheted raincoats of other textile materials, cotton limit in
6102 9000.42	其他纺材制针织或钩编女式雨衣（羊毛限内）	20	130		16	17	件/千克		Women's or girls' knitted or crocheted raincoats of other textile materials, wool limit in
6102 9000.43	其他纺材制针织或钩编女式雨衣（化纤限内）	20	130		16	17	件/千克		Women's or girls' knitted or crocheted raincoats of other textile materials, man-made fibres limit in
6102 9000.49	其他纺材制针织或钩编女式雨衣	20	130		16	17	件/千克		Women's or girls' knitted or crocheted raincoats of other textile materials
61.03	**针织或钩编的男式西服套装、便服套装、上衣、长裤、护胸背带工装裤、马裤及短裤（游泳裤除外）：**								**Men's or boys' suits, ensembles, jackets, blazers, trousers, bib and brace overalls, breeches and shorts（other than swimwear）, knitted or crocheted:**
	-西服套装:								-Suits:
6103.1010	---羊毛或动物细毛制	25	130		16	17	套/千克		---Of wool or fine animal hair
6103.1020	---合成纤维制	25	130		16	17	套/千克		---Of synthetic fibres
6103 1020.10	合成纤维制针织或钩编男西服套装（含羊毛或动物细毛23%及以上）	25	130		16	17	套/千克		Men's or boys' knitted or crocheted suits of synthetic fibres, containing 23% or more of wool or fine animal hair
6103 1020.90	其他合成纤维制针织或钩编男式西服套装	25	130		16	17	套/千克		Men's or boys' knitted or crocheted suits, of synthetic fibres

税则号列 Tariff Item	商品名称及备注	进口税率 最惠	普通	暂定	出口退税	增值税率	计量单位	监管条件	Article Description
6103.1090	---其他纺织材料制	17.5	130		16	17	套/千克		---Of other textile materials
6103 1090.11	人造纤维针织或钩编男式西服套装（含羊毛或动物细毛23%及以上）	17.5	130		16	17	套/千克		Men's or boys' knitted or crocheted suits of artificial fibres, containing 23% or more of wool or fine animal hair
6103 1090.19	其他人纤针织或钩编男式西服套装	17.5	130		16	17	套/千克		Men's or boys' knitted or crocheted suits of other artificial fibres
6103 1090.20	棉制针织或钩编男式西服套装	17.5	130		16	17	套/千克		Men's or boys' knitted or crocheted suits of cotton
6103 1090.30	丝及绢丝制针织或钩编男西服套装	17.5	130		16	17	套/千克		Men's or boys' knitted or crocheted suits of silk and silk waste
6103 1090.41	其他纺材制针织或钩编男西服套装（棉限内）	17.5	130		16	17	套/千克		Men's or boys' knitted or crocheted suits of other textile materials, cotton limit in
6103 1090.42	其他纺材制针织或钩编男西服套装（羊毛限内）	17.5	130		16	17	套/千克		Men's or boys' knitted or crocheted suits of other textile materials, wool limit in
6103 1090.43	其他纺材制针织或钩编男西服套装（化纤限内）	17.5	130		16	17	套/千克		Men's or boys' knitted or crocheted suits of other textile materials, man-made fibres limit in
6103 1090.49	其他纺材制针织或钩编男西服套装	17.5	130		16	17	套/千克		Men's or boys' knitted or crocheted suits, of other textile materials
	-便服套装:								-Ensembles:
6103.2200	--棉制	20	90		16	17	套/千克		--Of cotton
6103.2300	--合成纤维制	25	130		16	17	套/千克		--Of synthetic fibres
6103 2300.10	合成纤维制针织或钩编男便服套装（含羊毛或动物细毛23%及以上）	25	130		16	17	套/千克		Men's or boys' knitted or crocheted ensembles of synthetic fibres, containing 23% or more of wool or fine animal hair
6103 2300.91	其他合纤针织或钩编含毛衫或针织衬衫或裤子的男便服套装	25	130		16	17	套/千克		Men's or boys' knitted shirts or trousers ensembles of synthetic fibres, knitted or crocheted, with sweater
6103 2300.99	其他合纤针织或钩编其他男便服套装	25	130		16	17	套/千克		Men's or boys' knitted or crocheted ensembles, of synthetic fibres
	--其他纺织材料制:								--Of other textile materials:
6103.2910	---羊毛或动物细毛制	25	130		16	17	套/千克		---Of wool or fine animal hair
6103.2990	---其他纺织材料制	25	130		16	17	套/千克		---Of other textile materials
6103 2990.10	丝或绢丝制针织或钩编男便服套装（含丝或绢丝70%及以上）	25	130		16	17	套/千克		Men's or boys' knitted or crocheted ensembles, containing 70% or more of silk and silk waste
6103 2990.20	人造纤维制针织或钩编男便服套装	25	130		16	17	套/千克		Men's or boys' knitted or crocheted ensembles, of artificial fibres
6103 2990.31	其他纺织料针织或钩编男便服套装（上装为毛衫，棉限内）	25	130		16	17	套/千克		Men's or boys' knitted or crocheted ensembles, of other textile materials,（the upper garment is a sweater, cotton limit in）
6103 2990.32	其他纺织料针织或钩编男便服套装（上装为毛衫，羊毛限内）	25	130		16	17	套/千克		Men's or boys' knitted or crocheted ensembles of other textile materials（the upper garment is a sweater, wool limit in）
6103 2990.33	其他纺织料针织或钩编男便服套装（上装为毛衫，化纤限内）	25	130		16	17	套/千克		Men's or boys' knitted or crocheted ensembles of other textile materials（the upper garment is a sweater, man-made fibres limit in）
6103 2990.34	其他纺织料针织或钩编男便服套装（上装为毛衫）	25	130		16	17	套/千克		Men's or boys' knitted or crocheted ensembles of other textile materials（the upper garment is a sweater）
6103 2990.35	其他纺织料针织或钩编男便服套装	25	130		16	17	套/千克		Men's or boys' knitted or crocheted ensembles, of other textile materials
	-上衣:								-Jackets and blazers:
6103.3100	--羊毛或动物细毛制	16	130		16	17	件/千克		--Of wool or fine animal hair
6103.3200	--棉制	16	90		16	17	件/千克		--Of cotton
6103.3300	--合成纤维制	19	130		16	17	件/千克		--Of synthetic fibres
6103 3300.10	合成纤维制针织或钩编男式上衣（含羊毛或动物细毛23%及以上）	19	130		16	17	件/千克		Men's or boys' knitted or crocheted jackets and blazers of synthetic fibres, containing 23% or more of wool or fine animal hair

税则号列 Tariff Item	商品名称及备注	进口税率			出口退税	增值税率	计量单位	监管条件	Article Description
		最惠	普通	暂定					
6103 3300.90	其他合纤制针织或钩编男式上衣	19	130		16	17	件/千克		Other men's or boys' knitted or crocheted jackets and blazers, of synthetic fibres
6103.3900	--其他纺织材料制	16	130		16	17	件/千克		--Of other textile materials
6103 3900.10	人造纤维制针织或钩编男式上衣	16	130		16	17	件/千克		Men's or boys' knitted or crocheted jackets and blazers, of artificial fibres
6103 3900.20	丝制针织或钩编男式上衣(含丝及绢丝 70%及以上)	16	130		16	17	件/千克		Men's or boys' knitted or crocheted jackets and blazers, containing 70% or more of silk or silk waste
6103 3900.31	其他纺织料制针织或钩编男式上衣(棉限内)	16	130		16	17	件/千克		Men's or boys' knitted or crocheted jackets and blazers, of other textile materials, cotton limit in
6103 3900.32	其他纺织料制针织或钩编男式上衣(羊毛限内)	16	130		16	17	件/千克		Men's or boys' knitted or crocheted jackets and blazers, of other textile materials, wool limit in
6103 3900.33	其他纺织料制针织或钩编男式上衣(化纤限内)	16	130		16	17	件/千克		Men's or boys' knitted or crocheted jackets and blazers, of other textile materials, man-made fibres limit in
6103 3900.39	其他纺织料制针织或钩编男式上衣	16	130		16	17	件/千克		Men's or boys' knitted or crocheted jackets and blazers, of other textile materials
	-长裤、护胸背带工装裤、马裤及短裤:								-Trousers, bib and brace overalls, breeches and shorts:
6103.4100	--羊毛或动物细毛制	16	130		16	17	条/千克		--Of wool or fine animal hair
6103 4100.10	毛制针织或钩编护胸背带男工装裤(羊毛或动物细毛制)	16	130		16	17	条/千克		Kitted or crocheted bib and brace overalls, of wool or fine animal hair
6103 4100.20	毛制针织或钩编男长裤(羊毛或动物细毛制,包括 8~18 号男童长裤)	16	130		16	17	条/千克		Men's knitted or crocheted trousers, of wool or fine animal hair, including boys' trousers, size 8-18
6103 4100.90	毛制针织或钩编其他男裤(羊毛或动物细毛制,包括马裤、短裤及其他长裤)	16	130		16	17	条/千克		Other men's or boys' knitted or crocheted trousers, breeches and shorts, of wool or fine animal hair
6103.4200	--棉制	16	90		16	17	条/千克		--Of cotton
6103 4200.11	棉制针织或钩编护胸背带男工装裤(保暖)	16	90		16	17	条/千克		Men's or boys' bib and brace overalls （thermal）, of cotton, knitted or crocheted
6103 4200.12	棉针织钩编男童非保暖背带工装裤(2~7 号男童护胸背带工装裤)	16	90		16	17	条/千克	A	Boys' knitted or crocheted bib and brace overalls, of cotton, not thermal, size 2-7
6103 4200.19	棉针织钩编男式非保暖背带工装裤(护胸背带工装裤, 2~7 号男童的除外)	16	90		16	17	条/千克		Men's or boys' bib and brace overalls, of cotton, knitted or crocheted,（other than boys' size 2-7）
6103 4200.21	棉制针织或钩编男童游戏套装长裤(指男童 8~18 号)	16	90		16	17	条/千克	A	Boys' playsuit trousers size 8-18, of cotton, knitted or crocheted
6103 4200.29	棉针织或钩编其他男童游戏套装裤(包括长裤、马裤、短裤)	16	90		16	17	条/千克	A	Other boys' playsuit, including trousers, breeches and shorts, of cotton, knitted or crocheted
6103 4200.30	棉制针织或钩编男长裤(包括 8~18 号男童长裤)	16	90		16	17	条/千克		Men's trousers or boys' trousers, size 8-18, of cotton, knitted or crocheted
6103 4200.90	棉制针织或钩编其他男裤等(包括马裤、短裤及其他长裤)	16	90		16	17	条/千克		Other men's or boys' trousers, breeches and shorts, of cotton, knitted or crocheted
6103.4300	--合成纤维制	17.5	130		16	17	条/千克		--Of synthetic fibres
6103 4300.10	合纤针织或钩编护胸背带男工装裤(含羊毛或动物细毛 23%及以上)	17.5	130		16	17	条/千克		Men's or boys' bib and brace overalls,of synthetic fibres, knitted or crocheted, containing 23% or more of wool or fine animal hair
6103 4300.21	合成纤维制针织或钩编男长裤(含羊毛或动物细毛 23%及以上, 包括 8~18 号男童长裤)	17.5	130		16	17	条/千克		Men's or boys' trousers of synthetic fibres, knitted or crocheted, containing 23% or more of wool or fine animal hair, including boys' trousers, size 8-18
6103 4300.29	合成纤维制针织或钩编其他男裤(含毛 23%及以上,包括马裤、短裤及其他长裤)	17.5	130		16	17	条/千克		Other men's or boys' trousers, breeches and shorts, of synthetic fibres, knitted or crocheted, containing 23% or more of wool or fine animal hair

税则号列 Tariff Item	商品名称及备注	进口税率 最惠	普通	暂定	出口退税	增值税率	计量单位	监管条件	Article Description
6103 4300.91	其他合纤制护胸背带男工装裤（针织或钩编）	17.5	130		16	17	条/千克		Other men's or boys' bib and brace overalls, of synthetic fibres, knitted or crocheted
6103 4300.92	其他合纤制男童游戏套装长裤（针织或钩编，指男童 8～18号）	17.5	130		16	17	条/千克	A	Other boys' playsuit trousers, size 8-18, of synthetic fibres, knitted or crocheted
6103 4300.93	其他合纤制男童游戏套装长裤（针织或钩编，包括马裤、短裤及其他长裤）	17.5	130		16	17	条/千克	A	Other boys' playsuit trousers, including breeches, shorts and other trousers, of synthetic fibres, knitted or crocheted
6103 4300.94	其他合纤制针织或钩编男长裤（包括8～18号男童长裤）	17.5	130		16	17	条/千克		Other men's or boys' trousers, of synthetic fibres, knitted or crocheted, including boys' trousers 8-18
6103 4300.99	其他合纤制针织或钩编其他男裤(包括马裤、短裤及其他长裤)	17.5	130		16	17	条/千克		Other men's or boys' trousers, breeches and shorts, of synthetic fibres, knitted or crocheted
6103.4900	--其他纺织材料制	16	130		16	17	条/千克		--Of other textile materials
6103 4900.11	丝制男式护胸背带工装裤(针织或钩编，丝及绢丝含量在 70%及以上)	16	130		16	17	条/千克		Silk men's bib and brace overalls (knitted or crocheted, of silk or silk waste of 70% and more)
6103 4900.12	丝制针织或钩编男成人长裤、马裤（含 8～18 号男童长裤及马裤，丝及绢丝含量在 70%及以上）	16	130		16	17	条/千克		Men's knitted or crocheted trousers and breeches, containing 70% or more of silk or silk waste, (including boys' trousers and breeches, size 8-17）
6103 4900.13	丝制针织或钩编其他男童长裤、马裤（丝及绢丝含量在 70%及以上）	16	130		16	17	条/千克	A	Boys' knitted or crocheted trousers and breeches, containing 70% or more of silk or silk waste
6103 4900.14	丝制针织或钩编其他男式短裤（丝及绢丝含量在 70%及以上）	16	130		16	17	条/千克		Other men's or boys' knitted or crocheted shorts, containing 70％ or more of silk or silk waste
6103 4900.21	人造纤维制男式护胸背带工装裤（针织或钩编）	16	130		16	17	条/千克		Men's or boys' bib and brace overalls of artificial fibres, knitted or crocheted
6103 4900.22	人纤制针织或钩编男人长裤、马裤（含 8～18 号男童长裤及马裤，含毛 23%及以上）	16	130		16	17	条/千克		Men's knitted or crocheted trousers and breeches of artificial fibres, containing 23% or more of wool or fine animal hair, including boys' trousers and breeches, size 8-18
6103 4900.23	人纤制针织或钩编其他男童长裤、马裤（含毛 23%及以上）	16	130		16	17	条/千克	A	Other boys' trousers and breeches of artificial fibres, containing 23% or more of wool or fine animal hair, knitted or crocheted
6103 4900.24	人纤制针织或钩编男式短裤(含毛 23%及以上)	16	130		16	17	条/千克		Men's or boys' knitted or crocheted shorts of artificial fibres,containing 23% or more of wool or fine animal hair
6103 4900.25	其他人纤制针织或钩编男长裤、马裤(含 8～18 号男童长裤及马裤)	16	130		16	17	条/千克		Other men's trousers and breeches of artificial fibres, knitted or crocheted, including boys' trousers, breeches, size 8-18
6103 4900.26	其他人纤制针织或钩编其他男童长裤（包括马裤）	16	130		16	17	条/千克	A	Other boys' knitted or crocheted trousers and breeches, of artificial fibres
6103 4900.27	其他人纤制针织或钩编其他男短裤	16	130		16	17	条/千克		Other men's or boys' knitted or crocheted shorts of artificial fibres
6103 4900.31	其他纺材制男式护胸背带工装裤（针织或钩编，棉限内）	16	130		16	17	条/千克		Men's or boys' bib and brace overalls, of other textile materials, knitted or crocheted, cotton limit in
6103 4900.32	其他纺材制男式护胸背带工装裤（针织或钩编，羊毛限内）	16	130		16	17	条/千克		Men's or boys' bib and brace overalls, of other textile materials, knitted or crocheted, wool limit in
6103 4900.33	其他纺材制男式护胸背带工装裤（针织或钩编，化纤限内）	16	130		16	17	条/千克		Men's or boys' bib and brace overalls, of other textile materials, knitted or crocheted, man-made fibres limit in
6103 4900.39	其他纺材制男式护胸背带工装裤（针织或钩编）	16	130		16	17	条/千克		Other men's or boys' knitted or crocheted bib and brace overalls, of other textile materials
6103 4900.41	其他纺材制针织或钩编男长裤、马裤（包括 8～18 号男童长裤、马裤，棉限内）	16	130		16	17	条/千克		Men's knitted or crocheted trousers and breeches of other textile materials, including boys' trousers and breeches,size 8-18, cotton limit in

税则号列 Tariff Item	商品名称及备注	进口税率 最惠	普通	暂定	出口退税	增值税率	计量单位	监管条件	Article Description
6103 4900.42	其他纺材制针织或钩编男长裤、马裤（包括8～18号男童长裤、马裤，羊毛限内）	16	130		16	17	条/千克		Men's knitted or crocheted trousers and breeches, of other textile materials, including boys' trousers and breeches,size 8-18, wool limit in
6103 4900.43	其他纺材制针织或钩编男长裤、马裤（包括8～18号男童长裤、马裤，化纤限内）	16	130		16	17	条/千克		Men's t knitted or crocheted trousers and breeches of other textile materials, including boys' trousers and breeches, size 8-18, man-made fibres limit in
6103 4900.49	其他纺材制针织或钩编男长裤、马裤（包括8～18号男童长裤、马裤）	16	130		16	17	条/千克		Men's knitted or crocheted trousers and breeches, of other textile materials, including boys', size 8-18
6103 4900.51	其他纺织材料制其他男童长裤马裤（针织或钩编，棉限内）	16	130		16	17	条/千克	A	Other boys' knitted or crocheted trousers and breeches, of other textile materials, cotton limit in
6103 4900.52	其他纺织材料制其他男童长裤马裤（针织或钩编，羊毛限内）	16	130		16	17	条/千克	A	Other boys' knitted or crocheted trousers and breeches, of other textile materials, wool limit in
6103 4900.53	其他纺织材料制其他男童长裤马裤（针织或钩编，化纤限内）	16	130		16	17	条/千克	A	Other boys' knitted or crocheted trousers and breeches; of other textile materials, man-made fibres limit in
6103 4900.59	其他纺织材料制其他男童长裤马裤（针织或钩编）	16	130		16	17	条/千克	A	Other boys' knitted or crocheted trousers and breeches, of other textile materials
6103 4900.61	其他纺材制针织或钩编男式短裤（棉限内）	16	130		16	17	条/千克		Other men's or boys' knitted or crocheted shorts, of other textile materials, cotton limit in
6103 4900.62	其他纺材制针织或钩编男式短裤（羊毛限内）	16	130		16	17	条/千克		Other men's or boys' knitted or crocheted shorts, of other textile materials, wool limit in
6103 4900.63	其他纺材制针织或钩编男式短裤（化纤限内）	16	130		16	17	条/千克		Other men's or boys' knitted or crocheted shorts, of other textile materials, man-made fibres limit in
6103 4900.69	其他纺材制针织或钩编男式短裤	16	130		16	17	条/千克		Other men's or boys' knitted or crocheted shorts, of other textile materials
61.04	**针织或钩编的女式西服套装、便服套装、上衣、连衣裙、裙子、裙裤、长裤、护胸背带工装裤、马裤及短裤（游泳服除外）：**								**Women's or girls' suits, ensembles,jackets, blazers, dresses, skirts, divided skirts, trousers, bib and brace overalls, breeches and shorts（other than swimwear）, knitted or crocheted:**
	-西服套装:								-Suits:
6104.1300	--合成纤维制	25	130		16	17	套/千克		--Of synthetic fibres
6104 1300.10	合成纤维制针织或钩编女西服套装（含羊毛或动物细毛23%及以上）	25	130		16	17	套/千克		Women's or girls' knitted or crocheted suits, of synthetic fibres, containing 23% or more of wool or fine animal hair
6104 1300.90	其他合纤制针织或钩编女西服套装	25	130		16	17	套/千克		Women's or girls' knitted or crocheted suits of synthetic fibres
	--其他纺织材料制:								--Of other textile materials:
6104.1910	---羊毛或动物细毛制	17.5	130		16	17	套/千克		---Of wool or fine animal hair
6104.1920	---棉制	17.5	90		16	17	套/千克		---Of cotton
6104 1920.10	含裤子的棉针织或钩编女西服套装	17.5	90		16	17	套/千克		Women's or girls' suits of cotton, knitted or crocheted, with trousers
6104 1920.90	不含裤子的棉针织或钩编女西服套装	17.5	90		16	17	套/千克		Women's or girls' suits of cotton, knitted or crocheted, without trousers
6104.1990	---其他	17.5	130		16	17	套/千克		---Other
6104 1990.10	含裤子的其他纺材制针织或钩编女西服套装（棉限内）	17.5	130		16	17	套/千克		Other women's or girls' knitted or crocheted suits , of other textile materials, with trousers, cotton limit in
6104 1990.90	其他纺织材料制针织或钩编女式西服套装（除合成纤维、羊毛或动物细毛、棉以外的其他纺织材料）	17.5	130		16	17	套/千克		Women's or girls' knitted or crocheted suits, of other textile materials, (other than synthetic fibres, wool or fine animal hair, cotton materials)
	-便服套装:								-Ensembles:
6104.2200	--棉制	17.5	90		16	17	套/千克		--Of cotton
6104 2200.10	含针织衬衫或毛衫或裤子棉制针织或钩编女便服套装	17.5	90		16	17	套/千克		Women's or girls' knitted or crocheted suits of cotton, with sweater, knitted shirt or trousers

税则号列 Tariff Item	商品名称及备注	进口税率 最惠	进口税率 普通	进口税率 暂定	出口退税	增值税率	计量单位	监管条件	Article Description
6104 2200.90	其他棉针织或钩编女便服套装	17.5	90		16	17	套/千克		Other women's or girls' knitted or croeheted ensembles of cotton
6104.2300	--合成纤维制	25	130		16	17	套/千克		--Of synthetic fibres
6104 2300.10	合纤制针织或钩编女便服套装（含羊毛23%及以上）	25	130		16	17	套/千克		Women's or girls' knitted or croeheted ensembles, of synthetic fibres, containing 23% or more of wool
6104 2300.91	含针织衬衫或毛衫或裤子其他合纤针织或钩编女便服套装(含毛23%以下）	25	130		16	17	套/千克		Women's or girls' knitted or crocheted suits of other synthetic fibres, with sweater, knitted shirt or trousers, containing less than 23%of animal hair
6104 2300.99	其他合纤针织或钩编其他女便服套装（含毛23%以下）	25	130		16	17	套/千克		Other women's or girls' suits, of synthetic fibres, knitted or crocheted, containing less than 23% of animal hair
	--其他纺织材料制:								--Of other textile materials:
6104.2910	---羊毛或动物细毛制	17.5	130		16	17	套/千克		---Of wool or fine animal hair
6104.2990	---其他	15	130		16	17	套/千克		---Other
6104 2990.21	含针织衬衫或毛衫或裤子人纤制其他女便服套装（针织或编织）	15	130		16	17	套/千克		Other women's or girls' knitted or crocheted suits, of artificial fibres, with knitted shirt, sweater or trousers
6104 2990.29	人纤制其他女便服套装(针织或编织）	15	130		16	17	套/千克		Women's or girls' ensembles, of wool or fine animal hair
6104 2990.31	含针织衬衫或毛衫或裤子其他纺材针织或钩编女便服套装(棉限内）	15	130		16	17	套/千克		Women's or girls' knitted or crocheted suits, of other textile materials, with knitted shirt, sweater or trousers, cotton limit in
6104 2990.32	其他纺材针织或钩编女式便服套装（羊毛限内）	15	130		16	17	套/千克		Women's or girls' knitted or crocheted ensembles, of other textile materials, wool limit in
6104 2990.33	含针织衬衫或毛衫或裤子的其他纺材针织或钩编女便服套装（化纤限内）	15	130		16	17	套/千克		Women's or girls' knitted or crocheted suits, of other textile materials, with knitted shirt, sweater or trousers, man-made fibres limit in
6104 2990.34	含裤子的其他纺材针织或钩编女式便服套装	15	130		16	17	套/千克		Women's or girls' ensembles, of other textile materials, with trousers
6104 2990.39	其他纺材针织或钩编其他女式便服套装	15	130		16	17	套/千克		Other women's or girls' knitted or crocheted ensembles, of synthetic fibres
	-上衣:								-Jackets and blazers:
6104.3100	--羊毛或动物细毛制	16	130		16	17	件/千克		--Of wool or fine animal hair
6104 3100.10	毛制钩编女式上衣	16	130		16	17	件/千克		Women's or girls' crocheted jackets and blazers of wool or fine animal hair
6104 3100.90	毛制针织女式上衣	16	130		16	17	件/千克		Women's or girls' knitted jackets and blazers of wool or fine animal hair
6104.3200	--棉制	16	90		16	17	件/千克		--Of cotton
6104 3200.10	棉制钩编女式上衣	16	90		16	17	件/千克		Women's or girls' crocheted jackets and blazers of cotton
6104 3200.90	棉制针织女式上衣	16	90		16	17	件/千克		Women's or girls' knitted jackets and blazers of cotton
6104.3300	--合成纤维制	19	130		16	17	件/千克		--Of synthetic fibres
6104 3300.11	合成纤维制钩编女上衣(含羊毛或动物细毛23%及以上）	19	130		16	17	件/千克		Women's or girls' crocheted jackets and blazers of synthetic fibres , containing 23% or more of wool or fine animal hair
6104 3300.19	其他合成纤维制钩编女上衣	19	130		16	17	件/千克		Other women's or girls' crocheted jackets and blazers of synthetic fibres
6104 3300.91	合成纤维制针织女上衣(含羊毛或动物细毛23%及以上）	19	130		16	17	件/千克		Women's or girls' knitted jackets and blazers of synthetic fibres, containing 23% or more of wool or fine animal hair
6104 3300.99	其他合成纤维制针织女上衣	19	130		16	17	件/千克		Other women's or girls' knitted jackets and blazers of synthetic fibres
6104.3900	--其他纺织材料制	16	130		16	17	件/千克		--Of other textile materials
6104 3900.11	丝及绢丝制钩编女上衣（含丝70%及以上）	16	130		16	17	件/千克		Women's or girls' crocheted jackets and blazers, containing 70% or more of silk or silk waste

税则号列 Tariff Item	商品名称及备注	进口税率			出口退税	增值税率	计量单位	监管条件	Article Description
		最惠	普通	暂定					
6104 3900.19	丝及绢丝制针织女上衣（含丝70%及以上）	16	130		16	17	件/千克		Women's or girls' knitted jackets and blazers, containing 70% or more of silk or silk waste
6104 3900.21	人造纤维制钩编女上衣	16	130		16	17	件/千克		Women's or girls' crocheted jackets and blazers, of artificial fibres
6104 3900.29	人造纤维制针织女上衣	16	130		16	17	件/千克		Women's or girls' knitted jackets and blazers, of artificial fibres
6104 3900.31	其他纺织材料制钩编女上衣(棉限内)	16	130		16	17	件/千克		Women's or girls' crocheted jackets and blazers of other textile materials, cotton limit in
6104 3900.32	其他纺织材料制钩编女上衣(羊毛限内)	16	130		16	17	件/千克		Women's or girls' crocheted jackets and blazers of other textile materials , wool limit in
6104 3900.33	其他纺织材料制钩编女上衣(化纤限内)	16	130		16	17	件/千克		Women's or girls' crocheted jackets and b!azers of other textile materials, man-made fibres limit in
6104 3900.39	其他纺织材料制钩编女上衣	16	130		16	17	件/千克		Women's or girls' crocheted jackets and blazers, of other textile materials
6104 3900.41	其他纺织材料制针织女上衣(棉限内)	16	130		16	17	件/千克		Women's or girls' knitted jackets and blazers, of other textile materials, cotton limit in
6104 3900.42	其他纺织材料制针织女上衣(羊毛限内)	16	130		16	17	件/千克		Women's or girls' knitted jackets and blazers, of other textile materials, wool limit in
6104 3900.43	其他纺织材料制针织女上衣(化纤限内)	16	130		16	17	件/千克		Women's or girls' knitted jackets and blazers, of other textile materials, man-made fibres limit in
6104 3900.49	其他纺织材料制针织女上衣	16	130		16	17	件/千克		Women's or girls' knitted jackets and blazers of other textile materials, man-made fibres limit in
	-连衣裙:								-Dresses:
6104.4100	--羊毛或动物细毛制	16	130		16	17	件/千克		--Of wool or fine animal hair
6104.4200	--棉制	16	90		16	17	件/千克		--Of cotton
6104.4300	--合成纤维制	17.5	130		16	17	件/千克		--Of synthetic fibres
6104 4300.10	合纤制针织或钩编连衣裙(含羊毛或动物细毛23%及以上)	17.5	130		16	17	件/千克		Knitted or crocheted dresses of synthetic fibres, containing 23% or more of wool or fine animal hair
6104 4300.90	其他合纤制针织或钩编连衣裙	17.5	130		16	17	件/千克		Other knitted or crocheted dresses of synthetic fibres
6104.4400	--人造纤维制	16	130		16	17	件/千克		--Of artificial fibres
6104 4400.10	人纤制针织或钩编连衣裙(含羊毛或动物细毛23%及以上)	16	130		16	17	件/千克		Knitted or crocheted dresses of artificial fibres, containing 23% or more of wool or fine animal hair
6104 4400.90	其他人纤制针织或钩编连衣裙	16	130		16	17	件/千克		Other knitted or crocheted dresses, of artificial fibres
6104.4900	--其他纺织材料制	16	130		16	17	件/千克		--Of other textile materials
6104 4900.10	丝及绢丝制针织或钩编连衣裙（含丝70%及以上）	16	130		16	17	件/千克		Knitted or crocheted dresses, containing 70％ or more of silk or silk waste
6104 4900.91	其他纺织材料制针织或钩编连衣裙（棉限内）	16	130		16	17	件/千克		Knitted or crocheted dresses of other textile materials, cotton limit in
6104 4900.92	其他纺织材料制针织或钩编连衣裙（羊毛限内）	16	130		16	17	件/千克		Knitted or crocheted dresses of other textile materials, wool limit in
6104 4900.93	其他纺织材料制针织或钩编连衣裙（化纤限内）	16	130		16	17	件/千克		Knitted or crocheted dresses of other textile materials, man-made fibres limit in
6104 4900.99	其他纺织材料制针织或钩编连衣裙	16	130		16	17	件/千克		Knitted or crocheted dresses, of other textile materials
	-裙子及裙裤:								-Skirts and divided skirts:
6104.5100	--羊毛或动物细毛制	14	130		16	17	件/千克		--Of wool or fine animal hair
6104.5200	--棉制	14	90		16	17	件/千克		--Of cotton
6104.5300	--合成纤维制	16	130		16	17	件/千克		--Of synthetic fibres
6104 5300.10	合纤制针织或钩编裙子及裙裤（含羊毛或动物细毛23%及以上）	16	130		16	17	件/千克		Knitted or crocheted skirts and divided skirts, containing 23% or more of wool or fine animal hair
6104 5300.90	其他合纤制针织或钩编裙子及裙裤	16	130		16	17	件/千克		Other knitted or crocheted skirts and divided skirts, of synthetic fibres
6104.5900	--其他纺织材料制	14	130		16	17	件/千克		--Of other textile materials
6104 5900.10	丝及绢丝制针织或钩编裙子及裙裤（含丝70%及以上）	14	130		16	17	件/千克		Knitted or crocheted skirts and divided skirts, containing 70% or more of silk or silk waste

税则号列 Tariff Item	商品名称及备注	进口税率			出口退税	增值税率	计量单位	监管条件	Article Description
		最惠	普通	暂定					
6104 5900.21	人纤制针织或钩编裙子及裙裤（含兰毛或动物细毛 23%及以上）	14	130		16	17	件/千克		Knitted or crocheted skirts and divided skirts of artificial fibres, containing 23% or more of wool or animal hair
6104 5900.29	其他人纤制针织或钩编裙子及裙裤	14	130		16	17	件/千克		Other knitted or crocheted skirts and divided skirts of artificial fibres,
6104 5900.91	其他纺材制针织或钩编裙子及裙裤（棉限内）	14	130		16	17	件/千克		Skirts and divided skirts of other textile materials, knitted or crocheted, cotton limit in
6104 5900.92	其他纺材制针织或钩编裙子及裙裤（羊毛限内）	14	130		16	17	件/千克		Skirts and divided skirts of other textile materials, knitted or crocheted, wool limit in
6104 5900.93	其他纺材制针织或钩编裙子及裙裤（化纤限内）	14	130		16	17	件/千克		Skirts and divided skirts of other textile materials, knitted or crocheted, man-made fibres limit in
6104 5900.99	其他纺材制针织或钩编裙子及裙裤	14	130		16	17	件/千克		Skirts and divided skirts of other textile materials, knitted or crocheted
	-长裤、护胸背带工装裤、马裤及短裤:								-Trousers, bib and brace overalls, breeches and shorts:
6104.6100	--羊毛或动物细毛制	16	130		16	17	条/千克		--Of wool or fine animal hair
6104 6100.10	毛制针织或钩编女护胸背带工装裤	16	130		16	17	条/千克		Knitted or crocheted women's or girls' bib and brace overalls, of wool or fine animal hair
6104 6100.20	毛制针织或钩编女长裤、马裤（包括女童 7～16 号）	16	130		16	17	条/千克		Knitted or crocheted women's trousers and breeches （including girls', size 7-16）, of wool or fine animal hair
6104 6100.90	毛制针织或钩编其他女裤(包括短裤及其他女童裤)	16	130		16	17	条/千克		Other knitted or crocheted women's trousers, (including shorts and other girls' trousers), of wool or fine animal hair
6104.6200	--棉制	16	90		16	17	条/千克		--Of cotton
6104 6200.10	棉制针织或钩编护胸背带女工装裤（保暖护胸背带工装裤）	16	90		16	17	条/千克		Knitted or crocheted women's or girls' bib and brace overalls, of cotton, thermal
6104 6200.20	棉针织或钩编非保暖女成人工装裤（护胸背带工装裤）	16	90		16	17	条/千克		Knitted or crocheted women's bib and brace overalls, non thermal, of cotton
6104 6200.30	棉制针织或钩编女童游戏套装长裤(指女童 7～16 号，包括马裤)	16	90		16	17	条/千克	A	Knitted or crocheted girls' playsuit trousers, size 7-16, of cotton, with breeches
6104 6200.40	棉针织或钩编其他女童游戏套装裤(包括马裤、短裤、非保暖护胸背带工装裤及其他长裤)	16	90		16	17	条/千克	A	Other knitted or crocheted girls' playsuit, with breeches, shorts, bib and brace overalls and other trousers, of cotton
6104 6200.50	棉制针织或钩编女长裤、马裤（包括女童 7～16 号）	16	90		16	17	条/千克		Knitted or crocheted women's trousers and breeches （girls', size 7-16）, of cotton
6104 6200.90	棉制针织或钩编其他女裤(包括短裤及其他女童裤)	16	90		16	17	条/千克		Other knitted or crocheted women's and girls' shorts and trousers, of cotton
6104.6300	--合成纤维制	17.5	130		16	17	条/千克		--Of synthetic fibres
6104 6300.10	合成纤维制护胸背带女工装裤（针织或钩编，包括女童护胸背带工装裤）	17.5	130		16	17	条/千克		Knitted or crocheted women's or girls' bib and brace overalls, of synthetic fibres
6104 6300.21	合成纤维制针织或钩编女长裤（含毛或动物细毛 23%及以上，包括女童 7～16 号）	17.5	130		16	17	条/千克		Knitted or crocheted women's trousers and girls', size 7-16, containing 23% or more of wool or fine animal hair, of synthetic fibres
6104 6300.29	合成纤维制针织或钩编其他女裤（含毛或动物细毛 23%及以上，包括长裤、短裤）	17.5	130		16	17	条/千克		Other knitted or crocheted women's or girls' trousers and shorts, containing 23% or more of wool or fine animal hair, of synthetic fibres
6104 6300.91	其他合纤制女童游戏套装长裤、马裤（针织或钩编，指女童 7～16 号）	17.5	130		16	17	条/千克	A	Knitted or crocheted girls' playsuit trousers or breeches, size 7-16, of synthetic fibres
6104 6300.92	其他合成纤维制女童游戏套装裤(针织或钩编，包括短裤及其他长裤)	17.5	130		16	17	条/千克	A	Other knitted or crocheted girls' playsuit, shorts and other trousers, of synthetic fibres

税则号列 Tariff Item	商品名称及备注	进口税率			出口退税	增值税率	计量单位	监管条件	Article Description
		最惠	普通	暂定					
6104 6300.99	其他合成纤维制针织或钩编女裤（包括长裤、马裤、短裤）	17.5	130		16	17	条/千克		Other knitted or crocheted women's or girls' trousers, breeches and shorts, of synthetic fibres
6104.6900	--其他纺织材料制	16	130		16	17	条/千克		--Of other textile materials
6104 6900.11	丝及绢丝制针织或钩编女工装裤（含丝70%及以上）	16	130		16	17	条/千克		Knitted or crocheted women's or girls' bib and brace overalls, containing 70% or more of silk or silk waste
6104 6900.12	丝及绢丝制针织或钩编女长裤、马裤（含丝70%及以上，包括女童7～16号）	16	130		16	17	条/千克		Knitted or crocheted women's trousers, breeches and girls' , size 7-16, containing 70% or more of silk or silk waste
6104 6900.13	丝及绢丝制针织或钩编女短裤（含丝 70%及以上，包括女童7～16号）	16	130		16	17	条/千克		Knitted or crocheted women's shorts, including girls' 7-16, containing 70% or more of silk or silk waste
6104 6900.19	丝及绢丝制针织或钩编其他女长裤（含丝70%及以上）	16	130		16	17	条/千克		Other knitted, crocheted women's or girls' trousers, containing 70% or more of silk or silk waste
6104 6900.21	人造纤维制护胸背带女工装裤（针织或钩编）	16	130		16	17	条/千克		Knitted or crocheted women's or girls' bib and brace overalls, of artificial fibres, knitted or crocheted
6104 6900.22	人造纤维制针织或钩编女长裤、马裤（含毛或动物细毛23%及以上，包括女童7～16号）	16	130		16	17	条/千克		Knitted or crocheted women's trousers and breeches and girls',size 7-16, of artificial fibres, containing 23% or more of wool or fine animal hair
6104 6900.23	人造纤维制针织或钩编其他女裤（含毛或动物细毛 23%及以上，包括长裤、短裤）	16	130		16	17	条/千克		Other knitted or crocheted women's or girls' trousers, shorts of artificial fibres, containing 23% or more of wool or fine animal hair
6104 6900.24	其他人造纤维制女长裤（针织或钩编，包括女童7～16号）	16	130		16	17	条/千克		Knitted or crocheted women's trousers and girls' , size 7-16, of artificial fibres
6104 6900.29	其他人纤制针织或钩编其他女裤（包括长裤、马裤）	16	130		16	17	条/千克		Other knitted or crocheted women's or girls' trousers and breeches, of artificial fibres
6104 6900.31	其他纺材制针织或钩编女工装裤（棉限内）	16	130		16	17	条/千克		Knitted or crocheted women's or girls' bib and brace overalls, of other textile materials, cotton limit in
6104 6900.32	其他纺材制针织或钩编女工装裤（羊毛限内）	16	130		16	17	条/千克		Knitted or crocheted women's or girls' bib and brace overalls,of other textile materials,wool limit in
6104 6900.33	其他纺材制针织或钩编女工装裤（化纤限内）	16	130		16	17	条/千克		Knitted or crocheted women's or girls' bib and brace overalls, of other textile materials, man-made fibres limit in
6104 6900.39	其他纺材制针织或钩编女工装裤	16	130		16	17	条/千克		Knitted or crocheted women's or girls' bib and brace overalls, of other textile materials
6104 6900.41	其他纺织材料制针织或钩编女长裤（棉限内，包括女童7～16号，包括马裤）	16	130		16	17	条/千克		Knitted or crocheted women's trousers and breeches girls', size 7-16, of other textile materials, cotton limit in
6104 6900.42	其他纺织材料制针织或钩编女长裤（羊毛限内，包括女童7～16号，包括马裤）	16	130		16	17	条/千克		Knitted or crocheted women's trousers and breeches and girls', size 7-16, of other textile materials, wool limit in
6104 6900.43	其他纺织材料制针织或钩编女长裤（化纤限内，包括女童7～16号，包括马裤）	16	130		16	17	条/千克		Knitted or crocheted women's trousers and breeches, including girls', size 7-16, of other textile materials, man-made fibres limit in
6104 6900.49	其他纺织材料制针织或钩编女长裤（包括女童7～16号，包括马裤）	16	130		16	17	条/千克		Knitted or crocheted women's trousers and breeches, including girls' , size 7-16, of other textile materials
6104 6900.51	其他纺织材料针织或钩编其他女长裤（棉限内）	16	130		16	17	条/千克		Other women's or girls' trousers, of other textile materials, cotton limit in
6104 6900.52	其他纺织材料针织或钩编其他女长裤（羊毛限内）	16	130		16	17	条/千克		Other knitted or crocheted women's or girls' trousers, of other textile materials, wool limit in
6104 6900.53	其他纺织材料针织或钩编其他女长裤（化纤限内）	16	130		16	17	条/千克		Other knitted or crocheted women's or girls' trousers, of other textile materials, man-made fibres limit in
6104 6900.59	其他纺织材料针织或钩编其他女长裤	16	130		16	17	条/千克		Other knitted or crocheted women's or girls' trousers, of other textile materials
6104 6900.61	其他纺织材料制针织或钩编女短裤（棉限内）	16	130		16	17	条/千克		Other knitted or crocheted women's or girls' shorts, of other textile materials, cotton limit in
6104 6900.62	其他纺织材料制针织或钩编女	16	130		16	17	条/千克		Other knitted or crocheted women's or girls' shorts, of

税则号列 Tariff Item	商品名称及备注	进口税率 最惠	进口税率 普通	进口税率 暂定	出口退税	增值税率	计量单位	监管条件	Article Description
	短裤（羊毛限内）								other textile materials, wool limit in
6104 6900.63	其他纺织材料制针织或钩编女短裤（化纤限内）	16	130		16	17	条/千克		Other knitted or crocheted women's or girls' shorts, of other textile materials, man-made fibres limit in
6104 6900.69	其他纺织材料制针织或钩编女短裤	16	130		16	17	条/千克		Other knitted or crocheted women's or girls' shorts, of other textile materials
61.05	**针织或钩编的男衬衫：**								**Men's or boys' shirts, knitted or crocheted:**
6105.1000	-棉制	16	90		16	17	件/千克		-Of cotton
6105 1000.11	棉制针织或钩编男童游戏套装衬衫（不带缝制领，指男童8～18号）	16	90		16	17	件/千克	A	Knitted or crocheted boys' playsuit shirts,size 8-18, of cotton, without stitched collar
6105 1000.19	棉制其他男童游戏套装衬衫(针织或钩编)	16	90		16	17	件/千克	A	Other knitted or crocheted boys' playsuit shirts, of cotton
6105 1000.91	其他棉制针织或钩编男衬衫(不带缝制领，包括男童8～18号)	16	90		16	17	件/千克		Other knitted or crocheted men's shirts, of cotton, without stitched collar, including boys',size 8-18
6105 1000.99	其他棉制针织或钩编其他男衬衫	16	90		16	17	件/千克		Other knitted or crocheted men's or boys' shirts, of cotton,
6105.2000	-化学纤维制	17.5	130		16	17	件/千克		-Of man-made fibres
6105 2000.11	化纤制针织或钩编男衬衫(含羊毛23%及以上，不带缝制领，包括男童8～18号)	17.5	130		16	17	件/千克		Knitted or crocheted men's shirts of man-made fibres, containing 23% or more of wool, without stitched collar, including boys', size 8-18
6105 2000.19	化纤制针织或钩编其他男衬衫（含羊毛23%及以上）	17.5	130		16	17	件/千克		Other knitted or crocheted men's or boys' shirts, of man-made fibres, containing 23% or more of wool
6105 2000.21	化纤针织或钩编男童游戏套装衬衫（不带缝制领，指男童8～18号）	17.5	130		16	17	件/千克	A	Knitted or crocheted boys' playsuit shirts, size 8-18, of man-made fibres, without stitched collar
6105 2000.29	化纤制其他男童游戏套装衬衫（针织或钩编）	17.5	130		16	17	件/千克	A	Other knitted or crocheted boys' playsuit shirts, of man-made fibres
6105 2000.91	其他化纤制针织或钩编男衬衫（不带缝制领，包括男童8～18号）	17.5	130		16	17	件/千克		Other knitted or crocheted men's shirts, of man-made fibres, without stitched collar, including boys', size 8-18
6105 2000.99	其他化纤制针织或钩编其他男衬衫	17.5	130		16	17	件/千克		Other knitted or crocheted men's or boys' shirts, of man-made fibres
6105.9000	-其他纺织材料制	16	130		16	17	件/千克		-Of other textile materials
6105 9000.11	丝及绢丝制针织或钩编男衬衫（含丝 70%及以上，不带特制领，包括男童8～18号）	16	130		16	17	件/千克		Knitted or crocheted men's shirts, containing 70% or more of silk or silk waste, without stitched collar, including boys', size 8-18
6105 9000.19	丝及绢丝制针织或钩编其他男衬衫（含丝70%及以上）	16	130		16	17	件/千克		Other knitted or crocheted men's or boys' shirts, containing 70% or more of silk or silk waste
6105 9000.21	羊毛或动物细毛制男衬衫(针织或钩编，不带缝制领，包括男童8～18号)	16	130		16	17	件/千克		Knitted or crocheted men's shirts of wool or fine animal hair,without stitched collar, including boys', size 8-18
6105 9000.29	羊毛或动物细毛制其他男衬衫（针织或钩编）	16	130		16	17	件/千克		Other men's or boys' shirts of wool or fine animal hair, knitted or crocheted
6105 9000.31	其他纺织材料制针织或钩编男衬衫（棉限内，不带特制领，包括男童8～18号）	16	130		16	17	件/千克		Other knitted or crocheted men's shirts, of other textile materials,without stitched collar, including boys', size 8-18, cotton limit in
6105 9000.32	其他纺织材料制针织或钩编男衬衫（羊毛限内，不带特制领，包括男童8～18号）	16	130		16	17	件/千克		Knitted or crocheted men's shirts, without stitched collar, including boys', size 8-18, of other textile materials, wool limit in
6105 9000.33	其他纺织材料制针织或钩编男衬衫（化纤限内，不带特制领，包括男童8～18号）	16	130		16	17	件/千克		Knitted or crocheted men's shirts, of other textile materials, without stitched collar, including boys', size 8-18, man-made fibres limit in
6105 9000.39	其他纺织材料制针织或钩编男衬衫（不带特制领，包括男童8～18号）	16	130		16	17	件/千克		Knitted or crocheted men's or boys' shirts, of other textile materials, without stitched collar, including boys', size 8-18

税则号列 Tariff Item	商品名称及备注	进口税率 最惠	普通	暂定	出口退税	增值税率	计量单位	监管条件	Article Description
6105 9000.41	其他纺织材料制针织或钩编男衬衫（棉限内）	16	130		16	17	件/千克		Knitted or crocheted men's or boys' shirts, of other textile materials, cotton limit in
6105 9000.42	其他纺织材料制针织或钩编男衬衫（羊毛限内）	16	130		16	17	件/千克		Knitted or crocheted men's or boys' shirts, of other textile materials, wool limit in
6105 9000.43	其他纺织材料制针织或钩编男衬衫（化纤限内）	16	130		16	17	件/千克		Knitted or crocheted men's or boys' shirts, of other textile materials, man-made fibres limit in
6105 9000.49	其他纺材制针织或钩编其他男衬衫	16	130		16	17	件/千克		Other knitted or crocheted men's or boys' shirts, of other textile materials
61.06	**针织或钩编的女衬衫：**								**Women's or girls' blouses, shirts and shirt blouses, knitted or crocheted:**
6106.1000	-棉制	16	90		16	17	件/千克		-Of cotton
6106 1000.10	棉制针织或钩编女童游戏套装衬衫	16	90		16	17	件/千克	A	Knitted or crocheted girls' playsuit shirts, of cotton
6106 1000.90	棉制针织或钩编其他女衬衫	16	90		16	17	件/千克		Other knitted or crocheted women's or girls' shirts, of cotton
6106.2000	-化学纤维制	17.5	130		16	17	件/千克		-Of man-made fibres
6106 2000.10	化纤制针织或钩编女衬衫(含羊毛23%及以上)	17.5	130		16	17	件/千克		Knitted or crocheted women's or girls' shirts of man-made fibres, containing 23% or more of wool or fine animal hair
6106 2000.20	其他化纤制女童游戏套装衬衫（针织或钩编）	17.5	130		16	17	件/千克	A	Knitted or crocheted girls' playsuit shirts, of man-made fibres
6106 2000.90	其他化纤针织或钩编未列名女衬衫（针织或钩编）	17.5	130		16	17	件/千克		Other knitted or crocheted women's or girls' shirts, of man-made fibres, not specified
6106.9000	-其他纺织材料制	16	130		16	17	件/千克		-Of other textile materials
6106 9000.10	丝及绢丝制针织或钩编女衬衫（含丝 70%及以上）	16	130		16	17	件/千克		Knitted or crocheted women's or girls' shirts, containing 70% or more of silk or silk waste
6106 9000.20	羊毛或动物细毛针织或钩编女衬衫	16	130		16	17	件/千克		Knitted or crocheted women's or girls' shirts, of wool or fine animal hair
6106 9000.31	其他纺织材料制针织或钩编女衬衫（棉限内）	16	130		16	17	件/千克		Knitted or crocheted women's or girls' shirts, of other textile materials, cotton limit in
6106 9000.32	其他纺织材料制针织或钩编女衬衫（羊毛限内）	16	130		16	17	件/千克		Knitted or crocheted women's or girls' shirts, of other textile materials, wool limit in
6106 9000.33	其他纺织材料制针织或钩编女衬衫（化纤限内）	16	130		16	17	件/千克		Knitted or crocheted women's or girls' shirts, of other textile materials, man-made fibres limit in
6106 9000.39	其他纺织材料制针织或钩编女衬衫	16	130		16	17	件/千克		Knitted or crocheted women's or girls' shirts, of other textile materials
61.07	**针织或钩编的男式内裤、三角裤、长睡衣、睡衣裤、浴衣、晨衣及类似品：**								**Men's or boys' underpants, briefe, night-shirts, pyjamas, bathrobes, dressing gowns and similar articles, knitted or crocheted:**
	-内裤及三角裤:								-Underpants and briefs:
6107.1100	--棉制	14	90		16	17	件/千克	A	--Of cotton
6107.1200	--化学纤维制	16	130		16	17	件/千克	A	--Of man-made fibres
	--其他纺织材料制:								--Of other textile materials:
6107.1910	---丝及绢丝制	14	130		16	17	件/千克		---Of silk or silk waste
6107 1910.10	丝及绢丝制男内裤及三角裤(含丝 70%及以上，针织或钩编）	14	130		16	17	件/千克	A	Knitted or crocheted men's or boys' underpants and briefs,containing 70% or more of silk or silk waste
6107 1910.90	其他丝及绢丝制男内裤及三角裤(含丝 70%以下，针织或钩编)	14	130		16	17	件/千克	A	Other knitted or crocheted men's or boys' underpants and briefs, containing less than 70% of silk or silk waste
6107.1990	---其他	14	130		16	17	件/千克		---Other
6107 1990.10	羊毛或动物细毛制男内裤及三角裤（针织或钩编）	14	130		16	17	件/千克	A	Knitted or crocheted men's or boys' underpants and briefs, of wool or fine animal hair
6107 1990.90	其他纺织材料制男内裤及三角裤（针织或钩编）	14	130		16	17	件/千克	A	Knitted or crocheted men's or boys' underpants and briefs,of other textile fibres
	-长睡衣及睡衣裤:								-Nightshirts and pyjamas:

税则号列 Tariff Item	商品名称及备注	进口税率 最惠	普通	暂定	出口退税	增值税率	计量单位	监管条件	Article Description
6107.2100	--棉制	14	90		16	17	件/千克	A	--Of cotton
6107.2200	--化学纤维制	16	130		16	17	件/千克	A	--Of man-made fibres
	--其他纺织材料制:								--Of other textile materials:
6107.2910	---丝及绢丝制	14	130		16	17	件/千克		---Of silk or silk waste
6107 2910.10	丝及绢丝制针织或钩编男睡衣裤(含丝70%及以上，包括长睡衣)	14	130		16	17	件/千克	A	Knitted or crocheted men's or boys' nightshirts, pyjamas,containing 70% or more of silk or silk waste
6107 2910.90	其他丝及绢丝制针织或钩编男睡衣裤(含丝70%以下，包括长睡衣)	14	130		16	17	件/千克	A	Knitted or crocheted men's or boys' nightshirts, pyjamas, containing less than 70% of silk or silk waste
6107.2990	---其他	14	130		16	17	件/千克	A	--- Other
	-其他:								-Other:
6107.9100	--棉制	14	90		16	17	件/千克		--Of cotton
6107 9100.10	棉制针织或钩编其他睡衣裤	14	90		16	17	件/千克	A	Other knitted or crocheted men's or boys' pyjamas, of cotton
6107 9100.90	棉制针织或钩编男浴衣、晨衣等(包括类似品)	14	90		16	17	件/千克	A	Knitted or crocheted men's or boys' bathrobes, dressing gowns and similar articles, of cotton
	--其他纺织材料制:								--Of other textile materials:
6107.9910	---化学纤维制	16	130		16	17	件/千克	A	---Of man-made fibres
6107.9990	---其他	14	130		16	17	件/千克	A	---Other
61.08	**针织或钩编的女式长衬裙、衬裙、三角裤、短衬裤、睡衣、睡衣裤、浴衣、晨衣及类似品:**								**Women's or girls' slips, petticoats,briefs, panties, nightdresses, pyjamas, nèligès, bathrobes, dressing gowns and similar articles, knitted or crocheted:**
	-长衬裙及衬裙:								-Slips and petticoats:
6108.1100	--化学纤维制	16	130		16	17	件/千克		--Of man-made fibres
	--其他纺织材料制:								--Of other textile materials:
6108.1910	---棉制	14	90		16	17	件/千克		---Of cotton
6108.1920	---丝及绢丝制	14	130		16	17	件/千克		---Of silk or silk waste
6108 1920.10	丝及绢丝制女式长衬裙及衬裙(针织或钩编，含丝70%及以上)	14	130		16	17	件/千克		Knitted or crocheted women's or girls' slips and petticoats, containing 70% or more of silk or silk waste
6108 1920.90	其他丝及绢丝制女式长衬裙及衬裙(针织或钩编，含丝70%以下)	14	130		16	17	件/千克		Other knitted or crocheted women's or girls' slips, petticoats, containing less than 70% of silk or silk waste
6108.1990	---其他	14	130		16	17	件/千克		---Other
	-三角裤及短衬裤:								-Briefs and panties:
6108.2100	--棉制	14	90		16	17	件/千克	A	--Of cotton
6108.2200	--化学纤维制	16	130		16	17	件/千克	A	--Of man-made fibres
6108 2200.10	化纤制一次性女三角裤及短衬裤(针织或钩编)	16	130		16	17	件/千克	A	Knitted or crocheted women's or girls' briefs and panties, of man-made fibres, one-off
6108 2200.90	化纤制其他女三角裤及短衬裤(针织或钩编)	16	130		16	17	件/千克	A	Other knitted or crocheted women's or girls' briefs and panties, of man-made fibres
	--其他纺织材料制:								--Of other textile materials:
6108.2910	---丝及绢丝制	14	130		16	17	件/千克		---Of silk or silk waste
6108 2910.10	丝及绢丝制女三角裤及短衬裤(针织或钩编，含丝70%及以上)	14	130		16	17	件/千克	A	Knitted or crocheted women's or girls' briefs and panties, containing 70%or more of silk or silk waste
6108 2910.90	其他丝及绢丝制女三角裤及短衬裤(针织或钩编，含丝70%以下)	14	130		16	17	件/千克	A	Other knitted or crocheted women's or girls' briefs and panties, containing less than 70% of silk or silk waste
6108.2990	---其他	14	130		16	17	件/千克		---Other
6108 2990.10	羊毛制女三角裤及短衬裤(针织或钩编)	14	130		16	17	件/千克	A	Knitted or crocheted women's or girls' briefs and panties,of wool
6108 2990.90	其他纺织材料制女三角裤及短衬裤(针织或钩编)	14	130		16	17	件/千克	A	Knitted or crocheted women's or girls' briefs and panties, of other textile materials

税则号列 Tariff Item	商品名称及备注	进口税率 最惠	普通	暂定	出口退税	增值税率	计量单位	监管条件	Article Description
	-睡衣及睡衣裤:								-Nightdresses and pyjamas:
6108.3100	--棉制	14	90		16	17	件/千克	A	--Of cotton
6108.3200	--化学纤维制	16	130		16	17	件/千克	A	--Of man-made fibres
	--其他纺织材料制:								--Of other textile materials:
6108.3910	---丝及绢丝制	14	130		16	17	件/千克		---Of silk or silk waste
6108 3910.10	丝及绢丝制女睡衣及睡衣裤(针织或钩编，含丝70%及以上)	14	130		16	17	件/千克	A	Knitted or crocheted women's or girls' nightshirts, pyjamas, containing 70% or more of silk or silk waste
6108 3910.90	其他丝及绢丝制女睡衣及睡衣裤(针织或钩编,含丝70%以下)	14	130		16	17	件/千克	A	Other knitted or crocheted women's or girls' nightshirts and pyjamas, containing less than 70％ of silk or silk waste
6108.3990	---其他	14	130		16	17	件/千克		---Other
6108 3990.10	羊毛或动物细毛制女睡衣及睡衣裤（针织或钩编）	14	130		16	17	件/千克	A	Knitted or crocheted women's or girls' nightshirts and pyjamas, of wool or fine animal hair
6108 3990.90	其他纺织材料制女睡衣及睡衣裤（针织或钩编）	14	130		16	17	件/千克	A	Knitted or crocheted women's or girls' nightshirts and pyjamas, of other textile materials
	-其他:								-Other:
6108.9100	--棉制	14	90		16	17	件/千克		--Of cotton
6108 9100.10	棉制针织或钩编女内裤、内衣	14	90		16	17	件/千克	A	Knitted or crocheted women's or girls' briefs, panties and underwear, of cotton
6108 9100.90	其他棉制针织或钩编女浴衣、晨衣等（包括类似品）	14	90		16	17	件/千克	A	Knitted or crocheted women's or girls' bathrobes, dressing gowns and similar articles, of cotton
6108.9200	--化学纤维制	16	130		16	17	件/千克		--Of man-made fibres
6108 9200.10	化纤制针织或钩编女内裤、内衣	16	130		16	17	件/千克	A	Knitted or crocheted women's or girls' briefs, panties and underwear, of man-made fibres
6108 9200.90	其他化纤制针织或钩编女浴衣、晨衣等（包括类似品）	16	130		16	17	件/千克	A	Knitted or crocheted women's or girls' bathrobes, dressing gowns and similar articles, of man-made fibres
6108.9900	--其他纺织材料制	14	130		16	17	件/千克		--Of other textile materials
6108 9900.10	丝及绢丝制制女浴衣、晨衣等（针织或钩编，包括类似品，含丝70%及以上）	14	130		16	17	件/千克	A	Knitted or crocheted women's or girls' bathrobes, dressing gowns and similar articles, containing 70% or more of silk or silk waste
6108 9900.20	羊毛或动物细毛制女浴衣、晨衣等（针织或钩编，包括类似品）	14	130		16	17	件/千克	A	Knitted or crocheted women's or girls' bathrobes, dressing gowns and similar articles, of wool or fine animal hair
6108 9900.90	其他纺织材料制女浴衣、晨衣等（针织或钩编，包括类似品）	14	130		16	17	件/千克	A	Knitted or crocheted women's or girls' bathrobes, dressing gowns and similar articles, of other textile materials
61.09	**针织或钩编的T恤衫、汗衫及其他背心:**								**T-shirts, singlets and other vests, knitted or crocheted:**
6109.1000	-棉制	14	90		16	17	件/千克		-Of cotton
6109 1000.10	棉制针织或钩编T恤衫、汗衫等（内衣式，包括其他背心）	14	90		16	17	件/千克	A	T-shirts, singlets, underwear style, and other vests, of cotton, knitted or crocheted
6109 1000.21	其他棉制针织或钩编男式T恤衫（内衣除外）	14	90		16	17	件/千克	A	Other knitted or crocheted men's or boys' T-shirts, of cotton, other than underwear
6109 1000.22	其他棉制针织或钩编女式T恤衫（内衣除外）	14	90		16	17	件/千克	A	Other knitted or crocheted women's or gifts T-shirts, of cotton, other than underwear
6109 1000.91	其他棉制男式汗衫及其他背心（针织或钩编，内衣除外，包括男童8～18号）	14	90		16	17	件/千克	A	Other knitted or crocheted men's singlets and other vests, including boys', size 8-18, of cotton, other than underwear
6109 1000.92	其他棉制男式汗衫及其他背心（针织或钩编，内衣除外）	14	90		16	17	件/千克	A	Other knitted or crocheted men's or boys' singlets and other vests, of cotton, other than underwear
6109 1000.99	其他棉制女式汗衫及其他背心（针织或钩编，内衣除外）	14	90		16	17	件/千克	A	Other knitted or crocheted women's or girls' singlets and othervests, of cotton, other than underwear
	-其他纺织材料制:								-Of other textile materials:

税则号列 Tariff Item	商品名称及备注	进口税率			出口退税	增值税率	计量单位	监管条件	Article Description
		最惠	普通	暂定					
6109.9010	---丝及绢丝制	14	130		16	17	件/千克		---Of silk or silk waste
6109 9010.11	丝及绢丝针织或钩编T恤衫、汗衫、背心（内衣式，含丝≥70%）	14	130		16	17	件/千克	A	Knitted or crocheted T-shirts, singlets and other vests, underwear, containing 70% or more of silk or silk waste
6109 9010.19	其他丝及绢丝针织或钩编T恤衫、背心（包括汗衫，内衣式，含丝70%以下）	14	130		16	17	件/千克	A	Other knitted or crocheted T-shirts, singlets and other vests, underwear, containing less than 70％ of silk or silk waste
6109 9010.21	丝及绢丝针织钩编汗衫、背心（内衣除外，含丝≥70%，男童8～18号，女童7～16号）	14	130		16	17	件/千克	A	Knitted or crocheted Singlets, vests, including boys', size 8-18, and girls' , size 7-16, , containing 70％ or more of silk or silk waste, other than underwear
6109 9010.29	其他丝及绢丝针织钩编汗衫、背心（内衣除外，含丝＜70%，男童8～18号，女童7～16号）	14	130		16	17	件/千克	A	Other knitted or crocheted singlets, vests, including boys', size 8- 18, and girls', size 7-16, , containing less than 70% of silk or silk waste, other than underwear
6109 9010.91	其他丝及绢丝针织或钩编T恤衫、汗衫（含丝≥70%，包括其他背心）	14	130		16	17	件/千克	A	Other knitted or crocheted T-shirts, singlets and other vests, containing 70% or more of silk or silk waste
6109 9010.99	其他丝及绢丝针织或钩编T恤衫、汗衫（含丝＜70%，包括其他背心）	14	130		16	17	件/千克	A	Other knitted or crocheted T-shirts, singlets and other vests, containing less than 70% of silk or silk waste
6109.9090	---其他	14	130		16	17	件/千克		---Other
6109 9090.11	毛制针织或钩编T恤衫、汗衫等（内衣式，长袖衫）	14	130		16	17	件/千克	A	Knitted or crocheted T-shirts, singlets and other vests, underwear style, long sleeve, of wool or fine animal hair
6109 9090.12	毛制针织或钩编男式T恤衫、汗衫（内衣式，长袖衫除外）	14	130		16	17	件/千克	A	Knitted or crocheted men's or boys' T-shirts, singlets, underwear style, of wool or fine animal hair, other than long sleeve
6109 9090.13	毛制针织或钩编女式T恤衫、汗衫（内衣式，长袖衫除外）	14	130		16	17	件/千克	A	Knitted or crocheted women's or grils' T-shirts, singlets,underwear style, of wool or fine animal hair, other than long sleeve
6109 9090.21	毛制针织或钩编男式其他T恤衫（内衣除外）	14	130		16	17	件/千克	A	Knitted or crocheted men's or boys' T-shirts, of wool or fine animal hair, other than underwear
6109 9090.22	毛制针织或钩编女式其他T恤衫（内衣除外）	14	130		16	17	件/千克	A	Knitted or crocheted women's or girls' T-shirts, of wool or fine animal hair, other than underwear
6109 9090.31	毛制男式汗衫及其他背心(针织或钩编，内衣除外，含男童8～18号)	14	130		16	17	件/千克	A	Knitted or crocheted men's singlets, other vests, and boys', size 8-18, of wool or fine animal hair, other than underwear
6109 9090.32	其他毛制男式汗衫及其他背心（针织或钩编，内衣除外）	14	130		16	17	件/千克	A	Knitted or crocheted men's or boys' singlets, other vests, of wool or fine animal hair, other than underwear
6109 9090.33	其他毛制女式汗衫及其他背心（针织或钩编，内衣除外）	14	130		16	17	件/千克	A	Knitted or crocheted women's or girls singlets and other vests of wool or fine animal hair, other than underwear
6109 9090.40	化纤制针织或钩编内衣	14	130		16	17	件/千克	A	Knitted or crocheted underwear, of man-made fibres
6109 9090.50	化纤制针织或钩编T恤衫(内衣除外)	14	130		16	17	件/千克	A	Other knitted or crocheted T-shirts, of man-made fibres, other than underwear
6109 9090.60	化纤针织或钩编汗衫及其他背心(内衣除外)	14	130		16	17	件/千克	A	Knitted or crocheted singlets, other vests, of man-made fibres, other than underwear
6109 9090.91	其他纺织材料制T恤衫、汗衫等（针织或钩编，内衣式，包括其他背心）	14	130		16	17	件/千克	A	Knitted or crocheted T-shirts, singlets and other vests, of other textile materials, underwear style
6109 9090.92	其他纺材制针织或钩编汗衫及其他背心（内衣除外，包括男童8～18号，女童7～16号）	14	130		16	17	件/千克	A	Knitted or crocheted singlets, and other vests of other textile materials, including boys', size8-18 and girls', size 7-16, other than underwear
6109 9090.93	其他纺材制针织或钩编T恤衫、汗衫(内衣除外,包括其他背心)	14	130		16	17	件/千克	A	Knitted or crocheted T-shirts, singlets and other vests of other textile materials, other than underwear

税则号列 Tariff Item	商品名称及备注	进口税率			出口退税	增值税率	计量单位	监管条件	Article Description
		最惠	普通	暂定					
61.10	**针织或钩编的套头衫、开襟衫、背心及类似品:**								**Jerseys, pullovers, cardigans, waistcoats and similar articles, knitted or crocheted:**
	-羊毛或动物细毛制:								-Of wool or fine animal hair:
6110.1100	--羊毛制	14	130		16	17	件/千克		--Of wool
6110 1100.11	羊毛制手工针织或钩编起绒外穿背心	14	130		16	17	件/千克		Handwork knitted or crocheted piled waistcoats, of wool
6110 1100.19	羊毛制针织或钩编起绒外穿背心	14	130		16	17	件/千克		Knitted or crocheted piled waistcoats, of wool
6110 1100.21	羊毛制手工制起绒男毛衫(针织或钩编)	14	130		16	17	件/千克		Hand-worked knitted or crocheted men's or boys' piled sweater, of wool
6110 1100.29	羊毛针织制或钩编起绒男毛衫	14	130		16	17	件/千克		Knitted or crocheted men's or boys' piled sweater, of wool
6110 1100.31	羊毛制手工制起绒女毛衫(针织或钩编)	14	130		16	17	件/千克		Hand-worked knitted or crocheted women's or girls' piled sweater, of wool
6110 1100.39	羊毛制针织或钩编起绒女毛衫	14	130		16	17	件/千克		Knitted or crocheted women's or girls' piled sweater, of wool
6110 1100.41	羊毛手工制起绒套头衫等(包括开襟衫、背心及类似品,针织或钩编)	14	130		16	17	件/千克		Handwork knitted or crocheted piled pullovers, cardigans, waistcoats and similar articles, of wool
6110 1100.49	羊毛针织或钩编起绒套头衫等(包括开襟衫、背心及类似品)	14	130		16	17	件/千克		Knitted or crocheted piled pullovers, cardigans, waistcoats and similar articles, of wool
6110 1100.51	羊毛手工制非起绒外穿背心(针织或钩编)	14	130		16	17	件/千克		Handwork waistcoats, not piled, knitted or crocheted, of wool
6110 1100.59	羊毛针织或钩编非起绒外穿背心	14	130		16	17	件/千克		Knitted or crocheted waistcoats of wool, not piled
6110 1100.61	其他羊毛手工制非起绒男毛衫(针织或钩编)	14	130		16	17	件/千克		Other handwork knitted or crocheted men's or boys' sweater, of wool, not piled
6110 1100.69	其他羊毛针织或钩编非起绒男毛衫	14	130		16	17	件/千克		Other men's or boys' sweater, of wool, not piled
6110 1100.71	其他羊毛制手工制非起绒女毛衫(针织或钩编)	14	130		16	17	件/千克		Other handwork knitted or crocheted women's or girls' sweater, of wool, not piled
6110 1100.79	其他羊毛针织或钩编非起绒女毛衫	14	130		16	17	件/千克		Other knitted or crocheted women's or girls' sweater, of wool, not piled
6110 1100.91	其他羊毛制手工制非起绒套头衫等(针织或钩编,包括开襟衫、背心及类似品)	14	130		16	17	件/千克		Handwork knitted or crocheted pullovers, cardigans, waistcoats and similar articles, of wool, not piled
6110 1100.99	其他羊毛制非起绒套头衫等(针织或钩编,包括开襟衫、背心及类似品)	14	130		16	17	件/千克		Knitted or crocheted pullovers, cardigans, waistcoats and similar articles, of wool, not piled
6110.1200	--喀什米尔山羊细毛制	14	130		16	17	件/千克		--Of kashmir (cashmere) goats
6110 1200.11	喀什米尔山羊细毛手工起绒男套头衫(针织或钩编,包括开襟衫、外穿背心及类似品)	14	130		16	17	件/千克		Handwork knitted or crocheted Men's or boys' pullovers, cardigans, waistcoats and similar articles, of Kashmir (cashmere) goats, piled
6110 1200.19	喀什米尔山羊细毛制起绒男套头衫(针织或钩编,包括开襟衫、外穿背心及类似品)	14	130		16	17	件/千克		Men's or boys' pullovers, cardigans, waistcoats and similar articles of Kashmir (cashmere) goats, piled, knitted or crocheted
6110 1200.21	喀什米尔山羊细毛手工起绒女套头衫(针织或钩编,包括开襟衫、外穿背心及类似品)	14	130		16	17	件/千克		Women's or girls' handwork pullovers, cardigans, waistcoats and similar articles, of Kashmir (cashmere) goats, piled, knitted or crocheted
6110 1200.29	喀什米尔山羊细毛制起绒女套头衫(针织或钩编,包括开襟衫、外穿背心及类似品)	14	130		16	17	件/千克		Women's or girls' pullovers, cardigans,waistcoats and similar articles, of Ka-shmir (cashmere) goats, piled, knitted or crocheted
6110 1200.31	喀什米尔山羊细毛手工非起绒男套头衫(针织或钩编,包括开襟衫、外穿背心及类似品)	14	130		16	17	件/千克		Handwork knitted or crocheted men's or boys' pullovers, cardigans, waistcoats and similar articles, of Kashmir (cashmere) goats, not piled
6110 1200.39	喀什米尔山羊细毛非起绒男套头衫(针织或钩编,包括开襟衫、	14	130		16	17	件/千克		Knitted or crocheted men's or boys' pullovers, cardigans, waistcoats and similar articles, of Kashmir

税则号列 Tariff Item	商品名称及备注	进口税率 最惠	普通	暂定	出口退税	增值税率	计量单位	监管条件	Article Description
	外穿背心及类似品）								（cashmere） goats, not piled
6110 1200.41	喀什米尔山羊细毛手工非起绒女套头衫（针织或钩编，包括开襟衫、外穿背心及类似品）	14	130		16	17	件/千克		Handwork knitted or crocheted women's or girls' pullovers, cardigans,waistcoats and similar articles, of Kashmir（cashmere） goats, not piled
6110 1200.49	喀什米尔山羊细毛非起绒女套头衫(针织或钩编,包括开襟衫、外穿背心及类似品）	14	130		16	17	件/千克		Knitted or crocheted women's or girls' pullovers, cardigans,waistcoats and similar articles, of Kashmir （cashmere） goats, not piled
	--其他:								--Other:
6110.1910	---其他山羊细毛制	14	130		16	17	件/千克		---Of other goats
6110 1910.11	其他山羊细毛手工起绒男套头衫（针织或钩编，包括开襟衫、背心及类似品）	14	130		16	17	件/千克		Knitted or crocheted handwork men's or boys' pullovers, cardigans, waistcoats and similar articles, of other goats, piled
6110 1910.19	其他山羊细毛制起绒男套头衫（针织或钩编，包括开襟衫、背心及类似品）	14	130		16	17	件/千克		Knitted or crocheted men's or boys' pullovers, cardigans, waistcoats and similar articles, of other goats, piled
6110 1910.21	其他山羊细毛手工起绒女套头衫（针织或钩编，包括开襟衫、背心及类似品）	14	130		16	17	件/千克		Knitted or crocheted women's or girls' handwork pullovers, cardigans, waistcoats and similar articles, of other goats, piled
6110 1910.29	其他山羊细毛制起绒女套头衫（针织或钩编，包括开襟衫、背心及类似品）	14	130		16	17	件/千克		Knitted or crocheted women's or girls' pullovers, cardigans, waistcoats and similar articles, of other goats, piled
6110 1910.31	其他山羊细毛手工非起绒男套头衫(针织或钩编,包括开襟衫、背心及类似品）	14	130		16	17	件/千克		Handwork knitted or crocheted men's or boys' pullovers, cardigans, waistcoats and similar articles, of other goats, not piled
6110 1910.39	其他山羊细毛非起绒男套头衫（针织或钩编，包括开襟衫、背心及类似品）	14	130		16	17	件/千克		Knitted or crocheted men's or boys' pullovers, cardigans, waistcoats and similar articles, of other goats, not piled
6110 1910.41	其他山羊细毛手工非起绒女套头衫(针织或钩编,包括开襟衫、背心及类似品）	14	130		16	17	件/千克		Knitted or crocheted women's or girls' handwork pullovers, cardigans, waistcoats and similar articles, of other goats, not piled
6110 1910.49	其他山羊细毛非起绒女套头衫（针织或钩编，包括开襟衫、背心及类似品）	14	130		16	17	件/千克		Knitted or crocheted women's or girls' pullovers, cardigans, waistcoats and similar articles, of other goats, not piled
6110.1920	---兔毛制	14	130		16	17	件/千克		---Of rabbit and hare
6110 1920.11	兔毛制手工针织或钩编起绒马甲	14	130		16	17	件/千克		Handwork piled waistcoats, knitted or crocheted, of rabbit and hare
6110 1920.19	兔毛制针织或钩编起绒马甲	14	130		16	17	件/千克		Knitted or crocheted waistcoats, piled, of rabbit and hare
6110 1920.21	兔毛制手工针织或钩编起绒男毛衫	14	130		16	17	件/千克		Knitted or crocheted men's or boys' sweater, piled, handwork, of rabbit and hare
6110 1920.29	兔毛制针织或钩编起绒男毛衫	14	130		16	17	件/千克		Knitted or crocheted men's or boys' sweater, piled, of rabbit and hare
6110 1920.31	兔毛制手工针织或钩编起绒女毛衫	14	130		16	17	件/千克		Handwork knitted or crocheted women's or girls' sweater, piled, of rabbit and hare
6110 1920.39	兔毛制针织或钩编起绒女毛衫	14	130		16	17	件/千克		Knitted or crocheted women's or girls' sweater, piled, of rabbit and hare
6110 1920.41	其他兔毛制手工制起绒套头衫等（针织或钩编，包括开襟衫、背心及类似品）	14	130		16	17	件/千克		Other handwork knitted or crocheted pullovers, cardigans, waistcoats and similar articles, piled, of rabbit and hare
6110 1920.49	其他兔毛制起绒套头衫等(针织或钩编，包括开襟衫、背心及类似品）	14	130		16	17	件/千克		Knitted or crocheted pullovers, cardigans, waistcoats and similar articles, piled, of rabbit and hare
6110 1920.51	兔毛制手工制非起绒马甲(针织或钩编）	14	130		16	17	件/千克		Handwork knitted or crocheted waistcoats, not piled, , of rabbit and hare
6110 1920.59	兔毛制针织或钩编非起绒马甲	14	130		16	17	件/千克		Knitted or crocheted waistcoats, not piled,of rabbit and

税则号列 Tariff Item	商品名称及备注	进口税率 最惠	进口税率 普通	进口税率 暂定	出口退税	增值税率	计量单位	监管条件	Article Description
									hare
6110 1920.61	兔毛手工制非起绒男毛衫(针织或钩编)	14	130		16	17	件/千克		Handwork knitted or crocheted men's or boys' sweater, not piled, of rabbit and hare
6110 1920.69	兔毛针织或钩编非起绒男毛衫	14	130		16	17	件/千克		Knitted or crocheted men's or boys' sweater, not piled, of rabbit and hare
6110 1920.71	兔毛制手工制非起绒女毛衫(针织或钩编)	14	130		16	17	件/千克		Handwork knitted or crocheted women's or girls' sweater, not piled, of rabbit and hare
6110 1920.79	兔毛制针织或钩编非起绒女毛衫	14	130		16	17	件/千克		Knitted or crocheted women's or girls' sweater, not piled, of rabbit and hare
6110 1920.91	其他兔毛制手工制非起绒套头衫等(针织或钩编,包括开襟衫、背心及类似品)	14	130		16	17	件/千克		Other handwork knitted or crocheted pullovers, cardigans, waistcoats and similar articles, not piled, of rabbit and hare
6110 1920.99	其他兔毛制非起绒套头衫等(针织或钩编,包括开襟衫、背心及类似品)	14	130		16	17	件/千克		Other knitted or crocheted pullovers, cardigans, waistcoats and similar articles, not piled, of rabbit and hare
6110.1990	---其他	14	130		16	17	件/千克		---Other
6110 1990.11	其他动物细毛制手工起绒马甲(针织或钩编)	14	130		16	17	件/千克		Handwork knitted or crocheted waistcoats, of other fine animal hair, piled
6110 1990.19	其他动物细毛制起绒马甲(针织或钩编)	14	130		16	17	件/千克		Knitted or crocheted waistcoats, of other fine animal hair, piled
6110 1990.21	其他动物细毛手工起绒男毛衫(针织或钩编)	14	130		16	17	件/千克		Handwork knitted or crocheted men's or boys' sweater, of other fine animal hair, piled
6110 1990.29	其他动物细毛制起绒男毛衫(针织或钩编)	14	130		16	17	件/千克		Knitted or crocheted men's or boys' sweater, of other fine animal hair, piled
6110 1990.31	其他动物细毛手工起绒女毛衫(针织或钩编)	14	130		16	17	件/千克		Handwork knitted or crocheted women's or girls' sweater, of other fine animal hair, piled
6110 1990.39	其他动物细毛制起绒女毛衫(针织或钩编)	14	130		16	17	件/千克		Knitted or crocheted women's or girls' sweater, of other fine animal hair, piled
6110 1990.41	其他动物细毛手工起绒套头衫(针织或钩编,包括开襟衫、背心及类似品)	14	130		16	17	件/千克		Handwork knitted or crocheted pullovers and cardigans, waistcoats and similar articles, of other fine animal hair, piled
6110 1990.49	其他动物细毛制起绒套头衫(针织或钩编,包括开襟衫、背心及类似品)	14	130		16	17	件/千克		Knitted or crocheted pullovers, cardigans, waistcoats and similar articles, of other fine animal hair, piled
6110 1990.51	其他动物细毛制手工非起绒马甲(针织或钩编)	14	130		16	17	件/千克		Handwork knitted or crocheted waistcoats of other fine animal hair, not piled
6110 1990.59	其他动物细毛制非起绒马甲(针织或钩编)	14	130		16	17	件/千克		Handwork knitted or crocheted waistcoats of other fine animal hair, not piled
6110 1990.61	其他动物细毛手工非起绒男毛衫(针织或钩编)	14	130		16	17	件/千克		Knitted or crocheted men's or boys' handwork sweater, of other fine animal hair, not piled
6110 1990.69	其他动物细毛非起绒男毛衫(针织或钩编)	14	130		16	17	件/千克		Knitted or crocheted men's or boys' sweater, of other fine animal hair, not piled
6110 1990.71	其他动物细毛手工非起绒女毛衫(针织或钩编)	14	130		16	17	件/千克		Knitted or crocheted women's or girls' handwork sweater, of other fine animal hair, not piled
6110 1990.79	其他动物细毛非起绒女毛衫(针织或钩编)	14	130		16	17	件/千克		Knitted or crocheted women's or girls' sweater, of other fine animal hair, not piled
6110 1990.91	其他动物细毛手工非起绒套头衫(针织或钩编,包括开襟衫、背心及类似品)	14	130		16	17	件/千克		Handwork knitted or crocheted pullovers, cardigans, waistcoats and similar articles, of other fine animal hair, not piled
6110 1990.99	其他动物细毛非起绒套头衫(针织或钩编,包括开襟衫、背心及类似品)	14	130		16	17	件/千克		Knitted or crocheted pullovers, cardigans, waistcoats and similar articles, of other fine animal hair, not piled
6110.2000	-棉制	14	90		16	17	件/千克		-Of cotton
6110 2000.11	棉制儿童游戏套装紧身衫及套	14	90		16	17	件/千克	A	Boys' or girls' playsuit, jerseys, pullover, thin and

税则号列 Tariff Item	商品名称及备注	进口税率 最惠	进口税率 普通	进口税率 暂定	出口退税	增值税率	计量单位	监管条件	Article Description
	头衫(针织起绒,轻薄细针翻领、开领、高领,含亚麻36%以下)								high-gauge, turn-down, open and high-collar, of cotton, knitted, containing less than 36% of flax, piled
6110 2000.12	棉制其他起绒儿童游戏套头衫等(针织钩编,包括开襟衫、背心及类似品,含亚麻36%以下)	14	90		16	17	件/千克	A	Other boys' or girls' playsuit, pullovers, cardigans, waistcoats and similar articles, of cotton, knitted or crocheted, containing less than 36% of flax
6110 2000.20	棉制针织或钩编起绒马甲(毛衫、背心除外)	14	90		16	17	件/千克		Waistcoats of cotton, piled, knitted or crocheted, (other than sweater, vest)
6110 2000.31	棉制针织起绒紧身及套头毛衫(轻薄细针翻领、开领、高领)	14	90		16	17	件/千克		Jerseys or pullovers, piled, of cotton, knitted, thin and high-gauge, turn-down collar, open-collar, high-collar
6110 2000.32	棉制针织起绒男紧身衫及套头衫(轻薄细针翻领、开领、高领,但平床机生产、直接针织成形除外)	14	90		16	17	件/千克		Men's or boys' jerseys, pullovers, piled,of cotton, knitted, thin and high-gauge, turn-down collar, open-collar, high-collar(other than made by flat-bed machine, directly knitted pattern)
6110 2000.33	棉制针织起绒女紧身衫及套头衫(轻薄细针翻领、开领、高领,但平床机生产、直接针织成形除外)	14	90		16	17	件/千克		Women's or girls' jerseys, pullovers, of cotton, knitted, piled, thin and high-gauge, turndown collar, open-collar, high collar(other than made by flat-bed machine, directly knitted pattern)
6110 2000.41	棉制针织或钩编起绒其他毛衫	14	90		16	17	件/千克		Other sweater, of cotton, piled, knitted or crocheted
6110 2000.42	棉制针织或钩编起绒男套头衫等(包括开襟衫、背心及类似品,但平床机生产、直接针织成形除外)	14	90		16	17	件/千克		Men's or boys' pullovers, cardigans, waistcoats and similar articles, of cotton, piled, knitted or crocheted (other than made by flat-bed machine, directly knitted pattern)
6110 2000.43	棉制针织或钩编起绒女套头衫等(包括开襟衫、背心及类似品,但平床机生产、直接针织成形除外)	14	90		16	17	件/千克		Women's or girls' pullovers, cardigans,waistcoats and similar articles, of cotton, piled, knitted or crocheted (other than made by flat-bed machine, directly knitted pattern)
6110 2000.51	其他棉儿童游戏套装紧身及套头衫(针织,非起绒,轻薄细针翻领、开领、高领)	14	90		16	17	件/千克	A	Other boys' or girls' playsuit, jerseys, pullovers, of cotton, thin and high-gauge, turn-down collar, open collar and high collar, not piled, knitted
6110 2000.52	其他棉儿童游戏套装套头衫等(针织或钩编、非起绒,包括开襟衫、背心及类似品)	14	90		16	17	件/千克	A	Other boys'or girls' playsuit, pullovers,cardigans, waistcoats and similar articles, of cotton, not piled, knitted or crocheted
6110 2000.60	其他棉制针织或钩编非起绒马甲(毛衫、背心除外)	14	90		16	17	件/千克		Other waistcoats, of cotton, not piled, knitted or crocheted (other than sweater)
6110 2000.71	棉制针织非起绒男紧身及套头衫等(轻薄细针翻领、开领、高领)	14	90		16	17	件/千克		Men's or boys' jerseys, pullovers, of cotton, thin and high-gauge turn-down, open and high collar, knitted, not piled
6110 2000.72	棉制非起绒男紧身衫及套头衫(轻薄细针翻领、开领、高领,但平床机生产、直接针织成形除外)	14	90		16	17	件/千克		Men's or boys' jerseys, pullovers, of cotton, thin and high-gauge, turn-down collar, open collar, high collar, not piled (other than made by flat-bed machine, directly knitted pattern)
6110 2000.73	棉制针织非起绒女紧身衫及套头衫(轻薄细针翻领、开领、高领,但平床机生产、直接针织成形除外)	14	90		16	17	件/千克		Women's or girls' jerseys, pullovers, of cotton, thin and high-gauge, turn-down, open and high collar, knitted, not piled, knitted(other than made by flat-bed machine, directly knitted pattern)
6110 2000.91	其他棉制针织或钩编非起绒毛衫	14	90		16	17	件/千克		Other sweater, of cotton, not piled, knitted or crocheted
6110 2000.92	其他针织或钩编棉制非起绒男套头衫等(包括开襟衫、背心及类似品,但平床机生产、直接针织成形除外)	14	90		16	17	件/千克		Other men's or boys' pullovers, cardigans, waistcoats and similar articles, not piled, of cotton, knitted or crocheted(other than made by flat-bed machine, directly knitted pattern)
6110 2000.93	棉制针织或钩编女套头衫等(包括开襟衫、背心及类似品,但平床机生产、直接针织成形除外)	14	90		16	17	件/千克		Women's or girls' pullovers, cardigans,waistcoats and similar articles, of cotton, not piled, knitted or crocheted (other than made by flat-bed machine, directly knitted pattern)

税则号列 Tariff Item	商品名称及备注	进口税率 最惠	普通	暂定	出口退税	增值税率	计量单位	监管条件	Article Description
6110 2000.99	其他棉制针织钩编套头衫等（包括开襟衫、背心及类似品）	14	90		16	17	件/千克		Other pullovers, cardigans, waistcoats and similar articles, of cotton, not piled, knitted or crocheted
6110.3000	-化学纤维制	16	130		16	17	件/千克		-Of man-made fibres
6110 3000.11	化纤儿童游戏套装紧身衫及套头衫(针织起绒,轻薄细针翻领、开领、高领，毛＜23%，丝＜30%)	16	130		16	17	件/千克	A	Boys'or girls' playsuit, jerseys, pull-overs, of man-made fibres, thin and high-gauge, turn-down, open and high collar, containing less than 23% of wool, and less than 30% of silk or silk waste, knitted, piled
6110 3000.12	化纤起绒儿童游戏套装及套头衫等(针织或钩编,包括开襟衫、背心及类似品，含毛＜23%，含丝＜30%)	16	130		16	17	件/千克	A	Boys' or girls' playsuit, jerseys, pull-overs, cardigans, waistcoats and similar articles, of man-made fibres, containing less than 23% of wool, and less than 30% of silk or silk waste, knitted or crocheted, piled
6110 3000.21	化纤制针织或钩编起绒马甲(含羊毛或动物细毛23%及以上)	16	130		16	17	件/千克		Waistcoats, piled, of man-made fibres, containing 23% or more of wool or fine animal hair, knitted or crocheted
6110 3000.22	化纤制针织起绒男紧身及套头毛衫(含羊毛或动物细毛23%及以上，轻薄细针翻领、开领、高领)	16	130		16	17	件/千克		Men's or boys' jerseys, pullovers, piled, knitted, containing 23% or more of wool or fine animal hair, thin and high-gauge, turn-down, open and high collar, of man-made fibres
6110 3000.23	化纤制针织或钩编起绒男毛衫（含羊毛或动物细毛 23%及以上）	16	130		16	17	件/千克		Men's or boys' sweater of man-made fibres, piled, containing 23% or more of wool or fine animal hair, knitted or crocheted
6110 3000.24	化纤制针织起绒女紧身及套头毛衫	16	130		16	17	件/千克		Women's or girls' jerseys, pullovers,of man-made fibres, piled, knitted
6110 3000.25	化纤制针织或钩编起绒女毛衫（含羊毛或动物细毛 23%及以上）	16	130		16	17	件/千克		Women's or girls' sweater of man-made fibres, piled, containing 23% or more of wool or fine animal hair, knitted or crocheted
6110 3000.26	其他化纤针织起绒套头衫(含羊毛或动物细毛≥23%，轻薄细针翻领、开领、高领)	16	130		16	17	件/千克		Other pullovers, piled, knitted of man-made fibres, containing 23% or more of wool or fine animal hair, thin and high-gauge, turn-down collar, opencollar, high-collar
6110 3000.29	其他化纤针织或钩编起绒开襟衫等(含羊毛或动物细毛≥23%，包括背心及类似品)	16	130		16	17	件/千克		Other cardigans, waistcoats and similar articles, of man-made fibres, piled, containing 23% or more byweight of wool or fine animal hair, knitted or crocheted
6110 3000.31	其他化纤制针织或钩编起绒马甲	16	130		16	17	件/千克		Other waistcoats, of man-made fibres, piled, knitted or crocheted
6110 3000.32	化纤针织或起绒男紧身及套头毛衫（轻薄细针翻领、开领、高领）	16	130		16	17	件/千克		Men's or boys' jerseys, pullovers, knitted or piled, thin and high-gauge, turn-down collar, open collar, high collar, of man-made fibres
6110 3000.33	其他化纤制针织或钩编起绒男毛衫	16	130		16	17	件/千克		Other men's or boys' sweater, of man-made fibres, knitted or crocheted
6110 3000.34	化纤制针织起绒女紧身及套头毛衫（轻薄细针翻领、开领、高领）	16	130		16	17	件/千克		Women's or girls' jerseys, pullovers, piled, knitted, thin and high-gauge, turn-down collar, open collar, high collar, of man-made fibres
6110 3000.35	其他化纤制针织或钩编起绒女毛衫	16	130		16	17	件/千克		Other women's or girls' sweater, of man-made fibres, piled, knitted or crocheted
6110 3000.36	其他化纤针织起绒男套头衫(轻薄细针翻领、开领、高领，但平床机生产、直接针织成形除外)	16	130		16	17	件/千克		Other men's or boys' pullovers, piled,thin and high-gauge, turn-down,open, high collar, of man-made fibres, knitted or crocheted, other than made by flat-bed machine, directly knitted pattern
6110 3000.37	其他化纤针织或钩编起绒男开襟衫等（包括背心及类似品，但平床机生产、直接针织成形除外）	16	130		16	17	件/千克		Other men's or boys' cardigans, waist-coats and similar articles, piled, of man-made fibres, knitted or crocheted, other than made by flat-bed machine, directly knitted pattern
6110 3000.38	其他化纤起绒针织女套头衫(轻	16	130		16	17	件/千克		Other women's or girls' pullovers, piled,knitted（thin

税则号列 Tariff Item	商品名称及备注	进口税率 最惠	普通	暂定	出口退税	增值税率	计量单位	监管条件	Article Description
	薄细针翻领、开领、高领，但平床机生产、直接针织成形除外）								and high-gauge, turn-down, open, high collar), of man-made fibres, other than made by flat-bed machine, directly knitted pattern
6110 3000.39	其他化纤制针织或钩编女开襟衫等（起绒，包括背心及类似品，但平床机生产、直接针织成形除外）	16	130		16	17	件/千克		Women's or girls' cardigans, waistcoats and similar articles, of man-made fibres, piled, knitted or crocheted, other than made by flat-bed machine, directly knitted pattern
6110 3000.41	化纤其他童游戏套装紧身及套头衫（针织非起绒，轻薄细针翻领、开领、高领）	16	130		16	17	件/千克	A	Other boys' or girls' playsuit, jerseys, pullovers, knitted, not piled, thin and high-gauge, turn-down, open, high collar, of man-made fibres
6110 3000.42	化纤制其他童游戏套装套头衫等（针织/钩编，非起绒，包括开襟衫、背心及类似品）	16	130		16	17	件/千克	A	Other boys' or girls' playsuit, cardigans, waistcoats and similar articles, of man-made fibres, not piled, knitted or crocheted
6110 3000.51	其他化纤制针织或钩编非起绒马甲（含羊毛/动物细毛 23%及以上）	16	130		16	17	件/千克		Other waistcoats, not piled, of man-made fibres, knitted or crocheted, containing 23% or more of wool or fine animal hair
6110 3000.52	化纤针织非起绒男紧身及套头毛衫（含羊毛/动物细毛 23%及以上，轻薄细针翻领、开领高领）	16	130		16	17	件/千克		Men's or boys' jerseys, pullovers, knitted, not piled, of man-made fibres, containing 23% or more of wool or fine animal hair（thin and high-gauge, turn-down, open, high collar）
6110 3000.53	化纤制针织或钩编非起绒男毛衫（含羊毛/动物细毛 23%及以上）	16	130		16	17	件/千克		Men's or boys' sweater, not piled, of man-made fibres, knitted or crocheted, containing 23% or more of wool or fine animal hair
6110 3000.54	化纤制针织非起绒女紧身及套头毛衫（含羊毛/动物细毛 23%及以上，轻薄细针翻领、开领、高领）	16	130		16	17	件/千克		Women's or girls' jerseys, pullovers, containing 23% or more of wool or fine animal hair , thin and high-gauge, turn-down, open, high collar, not piled, knitted, of man-made fibres
6110 3000.57	化纤制针织钩编非起绒女毛衫（含羊毛/动物细毛 23%及以上）	16	130		16	17	件/千克		Women's or girls' sweater, not piled, of man-made fibres, knitted or crocheted, containing 23% or more of wool or fine animal hair
6110 3000.58	其他化纤制针非起绒套头衫（含毛≥23%，非起绒，轻薄细针翻领、开领、高领）	16	130		16	17	件/千克		Other pullovers, of man-made fibres, containing 23% or more of wool or fine animal hair, (thin and high-gauge, turn-down, open and high collar), not piled, knitted
6110 3000.59	其他化纤针织或钩编开襟衫等（含羊毛或动物细毛≥23%，非起绒，包括背心及类似品）	16	130		16	17	件/千克		Other cardingans, waistcoats and similar articles, of man-made fibres,containing23% or more of wool or fine animal hair, not piled, knitted or crocheted
6110 3000.91	其他化纤针织男紧身及套头毛衫（非起绒，轻薄细针翻领、开领、高领）	16	130		16	17	件/千克		Other men's or boys' jerseys, pullovers, of man-made fibres,（thin and high-gauge, turn-down, open and h gh collar）, knitted, not piled
6110 3000.92	其他化纤针织或钩编非起绒男毛衫	16	130		16	17	件/千克		Other men's or boys' sweater, of man-made fibres, not piled, knitted or crocheted
6110 3000.93	化纤针织非起绒女紧身及套头毛衫（轻薄细针翻领、开领、高领）	16	130		16	17	件/千克		Other women's or girls' jerseys, pullovers, not piled, of man-made fibres, knitted（thin and high-gauge turn-down, open and high collar）
6110 3000.94	其他化纤针织或钩编非起绒女毛衫	16	130		16	17	件/千克		Other women's or girls' sweater, of man-made fibres, not piled, knitted or crocheted
6110 3000.95	其他化纤针织非起绒男套头衫（轻薄细针翻领、开领、高领，但平床机生产、直接针织成形除外）	16	130		16	17	件/千克		Other men's or boys' pullovers, not piled, of man-made fibres, knitted, thin and high-gauge, turn-down, open and high collar, other than made by flat-bed machine, directly knitted pattern
6110 3000.96	其他化纤针织或钩编男开襟衫等（非起绒，包括外穿背心及类似品，但平床机生产、直接针织成形除外）	16	130		16	17	件/千克		Other men's or boys' cardigans, waistcoats and similar articles, not piled, of man-made fibres, knitted or crocheted other than made by flat-bed machine, directly knitted pattern

税则号列 Tariff Item	商品名称及备注	进口税率 最惠	普通	暂定	出口退税	增值税率	计量单位	监管条件	Article Description
6110 3000.97	其他化纤制针织非起绒女套头衫（轻薄细针翻领、开领、高领，但平床机生产、直接针织成形除外）	16	130		16	17	件/千克		Other women's or girls' pullovers, not piled, knitted, of man-made fibres, thin and high-gauge, turn-down, open and high collar, other than made by flat-bed machine, directly knitted pattern
6110 3000.98	其他化纤制针织或钩编女开襟衫等（包括外穿背心及类似品，但平床机生产、直接针织成形除外）	16	130		16	17	件/千克		Other women's or girls' cardigans, waistcoats and similar articles, of man-made fibres, knitted or crocheted, other than made by flat-bed machine, directly knitted pattern
6110 3000.99	其他化纤制针织钩编套头衫等（包括开襟衫，背心及类似品）	16	130		16	17	件/千克		Other pullovers, and cardingams, waistcoats and similar articles, of man-made fibres, knitted or crocheted
	-其他纺织材料制:								-Of other textile materials:
6110.9010	---丝及绢丝制	14	130		16	17	件/千克		---Of silk or silk waste
6110 9010.11	丝及绢丝制针织或钩编起绒毛衫等（含丝≥70%，含开衫、马甲）	14	130		16	17	件/千克		Sweater, cardigans and waistcoats, piled, knitted or crocheted, containing 70% or more of silk or silk waste
6110 9010.19	丝及绢丝制针织或钩编起绒毛衫等（含丝＜70%，含开衫、马甲）	14	130		16	17	件/千克		Sweater, cardigans and waistcoats, piled, knitted or crocheted, containing less than 70% of silk or silk waste
6110 9010.91	其他丝及绢丝针织或钩编毛衫等（非起绒，含丝≥70%，含开衫、马甲）	14	130		16	17	件/千克		Other sweater, cardigans and waistcoats, not piled, knitted or crocheted, containing 70% or more of silk or silk waste
6110 9010.99	其他丝及绢丝针织或钩编毛衫等（非起绒，含丝＜70%，含开衫、马甲）	14	130		16	17	件/千克		Other sweater, cardigans and waistcoats, not piled, knitted or crocheted, containing less than 70％ of silk or silk waste
6110.9090	---其他	14	130		16	17	件/千克		---Other
6110 9090.11	其他纺织材料针织或钩编起绒马甲（棉限内，毛衫背心除外）	14	130		16	17	件/千克		Waistcoats of other textile materials, piled, knitted or crocheted, cotton limit in, other than sweater or vest
6110 9090.12	其他纺织材料针织或钩编起绒马甲(羊毛限内,毛衫背心除外)	14	130		16	17	件/千克		Waistcoats, of other textile materials, piled, knitted or crocheted, wool limit in, other than sweater or vest
6110 9090.13	其他纺织材料针织或钩编起绒马甲(化纤限内,毛衫背心除外)	14	130		16	17	件/千克		Waistcoats of other textile materials, piled, knitted or crocheted, man-made fibres limit in, other than sweater or vest
6110 9090.19	其他纺织材料起绒针织或钩编马甲（毛衫背心除外）	14	130		16	17	件/千克		Waistcoats, of other textile materials, piled, knitted or crocheted, other than sweater or vest
6110 9090.21	其他纺材制针织或钩编非起绒马甲（棉限内，毛衫背心除外）	14	130		16	17	件/千克		Waistcoats, of other textile materials,not piled, knitted or crocheted, cotton limit in, other than sweater or vest
6110 9090.22	其他纺材制针织或钩编非起绒马甲(羊毛限内,毛衫背心除外)	14	130		16	17	件/千克		Waistcoats, of other textile materials, not piled, knitted or crocheted, wool limit in, other than sweater or vest
6110 9090.23	其他纺材制针织或钩编非起绒马甲(化纤限内,毛衫背心除外)	14	130		16	17	件/千克		Waistcoats, of other textile materials, not piled, knitted or crocheted, man-made fibres limit in, other than sweater or vest
6110 9090.29	其他纺材制针织或钩编马甲(非起绒，毛衫背心除外）	14	130		16	17	件/千克		Waistcoats, of other textile materials not piled, knitted or crocheted, other than sweater or vest
6110 9090.31	其他纺材制针织或钩编起绒毛衫（棉限内）	14	130		16	17	件/千克		Sweater, of other textile materials, piled, knitted or crocheted, cotton limit in
6110 9090.33	其他纺材制针织或钩编起绒男毛衫（羊毛限内）	14	130		16	17	件/千克		Men's or boys' sweater, of other textile materials, piled, knitted or crocheted, wool limit in
6110 9090.34	其他纺材制针织或钩编起绒女毛衫（羊毛限内）	14	130		16	17	件/千克		Women's or girls' sweater, of other textile materials, piled, knitted or crocheted, wool limit in
6110 9090.35	其他纺材制针织或钩编起绒男毛衫（化纤限内）	14	130		16	17	件/千克		Men's or boys' sweater, of other textile materials, knitted or crocheted, man-made fibres limit in
6110 9090.36	其他纺材制针织或钩编起绒女毛衫（化纤限内）	14	130		16	17	件/千克		Women's or girls' sweater of other textile materials, knitted or crocheted, piled, man-made fibres limit in
6110 9090.39	其他纺材制针织或钩编毛衫(起	14	130		16	17	件/千克		Other sweater, of other textile materials, knitted or

税则号列 Tariff Item	商品名称及备注	进口税率 最惠	普通	暂定	出口退税	增值税率	计量单位	监管条件	Article Description
	绒）								crocheted, piled
6110 9090.41	其他纺材针织或钩编起绒男套头衫等（棉限内，包括开襟衫、马甲及类似品，但平床机生产、直接针织成形除外）	14	130		16	17	件/千克		Men's or boys' pullovers, cardigans, waistcoats and similar articles, of other textile materials, knitted or crocheted, piled, cotton limit in, other than made by flat-bed machine, directly knitted pattern
6110 9090.42	其他纺材针织或钩编起绒女套头衫等（棉限内，包括开襟衫、马甲及类似品，但平床机生产、直接针织成形除外）	14	130		16	17	件/千克		Women's or girls' pullovers, cardigans,waistcoats and similar articles, of other textile materials, knitted or crocheted, piled, cotton limit in, other than made by flat-bed machine, directly knitted pattern
6110 9090.43	其他纺材针织或钩编起绒套头衫等（羊毛限内，包括开襟衫、马甲及类似品）	14	130		16	17	件/千克		Pullovers, cardigans, waistcoats and similar articles, of other textile materials, piled, knitted or crocheted, wool limit in
6110 9090.45	其他纺材针织或钩编起绒男套头衫等(化纤限内,包括开襟衫、马甲及类似品，但平床机生产、直接针织成形除外)	14	130		16	17	件/千克		Men's or boys' pullovers, cardigans, waistcoats and similar articles, of other textile aterials,knitted or crocheted, piled, man-made fibres limit in other than made by flat-bed machine, directly knitted pattern
6110 9090.46	其他纺材针织或钩编起绒女套头衫等(化纤限内,包括开襟衫、马甲及类似品，但平床机生产、直接针织成形除外)	14	130		16	17	件/千克		Women's or girls' pullovers, cardigans, waistcoats and similar articles, of other textile materials, piled, knitted or crocheted, man-made fibres limit in, other than made by flat-bed machine, directly knitted pattern
6110 9090.49	其他纺材针织或钩编套头衫等（起绒，包括开襟衫、马甲及类似品）	14	130		16	17	件/千克		Pullovers, cardigans, waistcoats and similar articles, of other textile materials, piled, knitted or crocheted
6110 9090.51	其他纺材针织或钩编非起绒毛衫（棉限内）	14	130		16	17	件/千克		Sweater, of other textile materials, not piled, knitted or crocheted, cotton limit in
6110 9090.53	其他纺材针织或钩编非起绒男毛衫（羊毛限内）	14	130		16	17	件/千克		Men's or boys' sweater, of other textile materials, not piled, knitted or crocheted, wool limit in
6110 9090.54	其他纺材针织或钩编非起绒女毛衫（羊毛限内）	14	130		16	17	件/千克		Women's or girls' sweater of other textile materials, not piled, knitted or crocheted, wool limit in
6110 9090.57	其他纺材针织或钩编非起绒男毛衫（化纤限内）	14	130		16	17	件/千克		Men's or boys' sweater, of other textile materials, not piled, knitted or crocheted, man-made fibres limit in
6110 9090.58	其他纺材针织或钩编非起绒女毛衫（化纤限内）	14	130		16	17	件/千克		Women's or girls' sweater of other textile materials, not piled, knitted or crocheted, man-made fibres limit in
6110 9090.59	其他纺材针织或钩编毛衫(非起绒)	14	130		16	17	件/千克		Sweater, of other textile materials, not piled, knitted or crocheted
6110 9090.61	其他纺材针织或钩编非起绒男套衫等(包括开襟衫、背心及类似品，但平床机生产、直接针织成形除外)	14	130		16	17	件/千克		Men's or boys' pullovers, cardigans,waistcoats and similar articles, of other textile materials, not piled, knitted or crocheted, cotton limit in, other than made by flat-bed machine, directly knitted pattern
6110 9090.62	其他纺材针织或钩编非起绒女套衫等(包括开襟衫、背心及类似品，但平床机生产、直接针织成形除外)	14	130		16	17	件/千克		Women's or girls' pullovers, cardigans, waistcoats and similar articles, of other textile materials, not piled, knitted or crocheted, cotton limit in
6110 9090.63	其他纺材针织或钩编非起绒套头衫等(羊毛限内,包括开襟衫、背心及类似品)	14	130		16	17	件/千克		Other pullovers, cardigans, waistcoats and similar articles, of other textile materials, not piled, knitted or crocheted wool limit in, other than made by flat-bed machine, directly knitted pattern
6110 9090.65	其他纺材针织或钩编非起绒男套衫等(化纤限内,包括开襟衫、背心及类似品，但平床机生产、直接针织成形除外)	14	130		16	17	件/千克		Men's or boys' pullovers, cardigans, waistcoats and similar articles, of other textile materials, not piled, knitted or crocheted, man-made fibres limit in
6110 9090.66	其他纺材针织或钩编非起绒女套衫等(化纤限内,包括开襟衫、	14	130		16	17	件/千克		Women's or girls' pullovers, cardigans, waistcoats and similar articles, of other textile materials, not piled,

税则号列 Tariff Item	商品名称及备注	进口税率 最惠	普通	暂定	出口退税	增值税率	计量单位	监管条件	Article Description
	背心及类似品，但平床机生产、直接针织成形除外)								knitted or crocheted, man-made fibres limit in, other than made by flat-bed machine, directly knitted pattern
6110 9090.69	其他纺材针织或钩编套头衫等(非起绒，包括开襟衫、背心及类似品)	14	130		16	17	件/千克		Other pullovers, cardigans, waistcoats and similar articles, of other textile materials, not piled, knitted or crocheted
6110 9090.90	其他纺材针织或钩编套头衫等(包括开襟衫、背心及类似品)	14	130		16	17	件/千克		Other pullovers, cardisans, waistcoats and similar articles, of other textile materials, knities or crocheied
61.11	**针织或钩编的婴儿服装及衣着附件:**								**Babies' garments and clothing accessories, knitted or crocheted:**
6111.2000	-棉制	14	90		16	17	千克		-Of cotton
6111 2000.10	棉制针织或钩编婴儿袜	14	90		16	17	千克	A	Knitted or crocheted babies' hosiery, of cotton
6111 2000.20	棉制婴儿分指、连指、露指手套(针制或钩编)	14	90		16	17	千克	A	Knitted or crocheted babies' gloves, mittens and mitts, of cotton
6111 2000.40	棉制针织婴儿外衣、雨衣、滑雪装(针制或钩编，包括夹克类似品)	14	90		16	17	千克	A	Knitted or crocheted babies' coat, raincoat, ski suit, jacked and similar articles, of cotton
6111 2000.50	棉制针织钩编婴儿其他服装	14	90		16	17	千克	A	Other knitted or crocheted babies' garments of cotton
6111 2000.90	棉制针织钩编婴儿衣着附件	14	90		16	17	千克	A	Knitted or crocheted babies' clothing accessories, of cotton
6111.3000	-合成纤维制	16	130		16	17	千克		-Of synthetic fibres
6111 3000.10	合纤制针织或钩编婴儿袜	16	130		16	17	千克	A	Knitted or crocheted babies' hosiery, of synthetic fibres
6111 3000.20	合纤婴儿分指、连指及露指手套(针制或钩编)	16	130		16	17	千克	A	Knitted or crocheted babies' gloves, mittens and mitts, of synthetic fibres
6111 3000.40	合纤婴儿外衣、雨衣、滑雪装(针制或钩编，包括夹克类似服装)	16	130		16	17	千克	A	Knitted or crocheted babies' coat, raincoat, ski suit, jacked and similar articles, of synthetic fibres
6111 3000.50	合纤针织或钩编婴儿其他服装(包括衣着附件)	16	130		16	17	千克	A	Other knitted or crocheted babies' garments, of synthetic fibres
6111 3000.90	合纤针织或钩编婴儿衣着附件	16	130		16	17	千克	A	Knitted or crocheted babies' clothing accessories, of synthetic fibres
	-其他纺织材料制:								-Of other textile materials:
6111.9010	---羊毛或动物细毛制	14	130		16	17	千克	A	---Of wool or fine animal hair
6111.9090	---其他	14	130		16	17	千克		---Other
6111 9090.10	人造纤维针织或钩编婴儿袜	14	130		16	17	千克	A	Knitted or crocheted babies' hosiery, of artificial fibres
6111 9090.90	其他纺织材料制婴儿服装及衣着附件(针织或钩编)	14	130		16	17	千克	A	Knitted or crocheted babies' garments and clothing accessories, of other textile materials
61.12	**针织或钩编的运动服、滑雪服及游泳服:**								**Track suits, ski suits and swimwear, knitted or crocheted:**
	-运动服:								-Track suits:
6112.1100	--棉制	16	90		16	17	套/千克		--Of cotton
6112 1100.11	棉制针织或钩编男式运动套装	16	90		16	17	套/千克		Knitted or crocheted men's or boys' track suits, of cotton
6112 1100.19	棉制针织或钩编女式运动套装	16	90		16	17	套/千克		Knitted or crocheted women's or girls' track suits, of cotton
6112.1200	--合成纤维制	17.5	130		16	17	套/千克		--Of synthetic fibres
6112 1200.21	合纤制针织或钩编男式运动服	17.5	130		16	17	套/千克		Knitted or crocheted men's or boys' track suits, of synthetic fibres
6112 1200.29	合纤制针织或钩编女式运动套装	17.5	130		16	17	套/千克		Knitted or crocheted women's or girls' track suits, of synthetic fibres
6112.1900	--其他纺织材料制	16	130		16	17	套/千克		--Of other textile materials
6112 1900.31	人造纤维制针织或钩编男式运动服	16	130		16	17	套/千克		Knitted or crocheted men's or boys' track suits, of artificial fibres
6112 1900.39	人造纤维制针织或钩编女运动套装	16	130		16	17	套/千克		Knitted or crocheted women's or girls' track suits of artificial fibres
6112 1900.41	羊毛制男式运动套装(针织或钩编含丝 70%以下)	16	130		16	17	套/千克		Knitted or crocheted men's or boys' track suits, of wool, containing less than 70% of silk
6112 1900.49	羊毛制女式运动套装(针织或钩编含丝 70%以下)	16	130		16	17	套/千克		Knitted or crocheted women's or girls' track suits, of wool, containing less than 70% of silk

税则号列 Tariff Item	商品名称及备注	进口税率			出口退税	增值税率	计量单位	监管条件	Article Description
		最惠	普通	暂定					
6112 1900.51	动物细毛制男式运动套装(针织或钩编含丝 70%以下)	16	130		16	17	套/千克		Knitted or crocheted men's or boys' track suits, of other fine animal hair, containing less than 70% of silk
6112 1900.59	动物细毛制女式运动套装(针织或钩编含丝 70%以下)	16	130		16	17	套/千克		Knitted or crocheted women's or girls' track suits, of other fine animal hair, containing less than 70% of silk
6112 1900.61	其他纺织材料制男式运动套装(针织或钩编含丝 70%以下)	16	130		16	17	套/千克		Knitted or crocheted men's or boys' track suits of other textile materials, containing less than 70% of silk
6112 1900.69	其他纺织材料制女式运动套装(针织或钩编含丝 70%以下)	16	130		16	17	套/千克		Knitted or crocheted women's or girls' track suits of other textile materials, containing less than 70% of silk
6112 1900.90	其他纺织材料制运动套装(针织或钩编含丝 70%以上)	16	130		16	17	套/千克		Knitted or crocheted track suits of other textile materials, containing less than 70% of silk
	-滑雪服:								-Ski suits:
6112.2010	---棉制	16	90		16	17	套/千克		---Of cotton
6112.2090	---其他	19	130		16	17	套/千克		---Other
6112 2090.10	羊毛或动物细毛针织或钩编滑雪套装	19	130		16	17	套/千克		Knitted or crocheted ski suits of wool or fine animal hair
6112 2090.21	化学纤维制针织或钩编男式滑雪套装	19	130		16	17	套/千克		Knitted or crocheted men's or boys' ski suits of man-made fibres
6112 2090.29	化学纤维制针织或钩编女式滑雪套装	19	130		16	17	套/千克		Knitted or crocheted women's or girls' ski suits of man-made fibres
6112 2090.90	其他纺织材料针织或钩编滑雪套装	19	130		16	17	套/千克		Knitted or crocheted ski suits of other textile materials
	-男士游泳服:								-Men's or boys' swimwear:
6112.3100	--合成纤维制	17.5	130		16	17	件/千克	A	--Of synthetic fibres
6112.3900	--其他纺织材料制	16	130		16	17	件/千克	A	--Of other textile materials
	-女士游泳服:								-Women's or girls' swimwear:
6112.4100	--合成纤维制	17.5	130		16	17	件/千克	A	--Of synthetic fibres
6112.4900	--其他纺织材料制	16	130		16	17	件/千克	A	--Of other textile materials
61.13	**用品目 59.03、59.06 或 59.07 的针织物或钩编织物制成的服装:**								**Garments, made up of knitted or crocheted fabrics of heading No.59.03, 59.06 or 59.07:**
6113.0000	用税号 59.03、59.06、或 59.07 的针织物或钩编织物制成的服装	16	130		16	17	件/千克		Garments, made up of knitted or crocheted fabrics of heading No.59.03, 59.06 or 59.07
6113 0000.11	用橡胶处理的服装(针织或钩编,织物外表面由橡胶完全覆盖)	16	130		16	17	件/千克		Garments treated with rubber (made up of knitted or crocheted fabrics, surface of fabrics totally covered with rubber)
6113 0000.13	用塑料处理的毛、棉及化纤制服装(针织或钩编,毛指羊毛或动物细毛织物外表面由塑料完全覆盖)	16	130		16	17	件/千克		Garments, of artificial fibres, of wool or fine animal hair, of man-made fibres, treated with plastics (made up of knitted or crocheted fabrics , surface of fabrics totally covered with plastics)
6113 0000.19	用塑料处理的其他纺织材料制服装(针织或钩编,织物外表面由塑料完全覆盖)	16	130		16	17	件/千克		Garments of other textile materials, treated with plastics (made up of knitted or crocheted fabrics, surface of fabrics totally covered with plastics)
6113 0000.21	其他橡胶处理的棉针织或钩编男上衣	16	130		16	17	件/千克		Men's or boys' jacket and blazers of cotton, treated with other rubber, knitted or crocheted
6113 0000.22	其他塑料等处理的棉制针织男上衣(包括钩编,包括用其他材料处理的)	16	130		16	17	件/千克		Men's or boys' jacket and blazers of cotton, treated with other plastics and other materials, knitted or crocheted
6113 0000.23	其他橡胶处理的棉针织或钩编女上衣	16	130		16	17	件/千克		Women's or girls' jacket and blazers of cotton, treated with other rubber, knitted or crocheted
6113 0000.28	其他塑料等处理的棉针织女上衣(包括钩编,包括用其他材料处理的)	16	130		16	17	件/千克		Women's or girls' jacket and blazers of cotton, treated with plastics and other materials, knitted or crocheted
6113 0000.31	其他橡胶处理的纺织材料制男上衣(针织或钩编)	16	130		16	17	件/千克		Men's or boys' jacket and blazers of other textile materials, treated with other rubber, knitted or crocheted

税则号列 Tariff Item	商品名称及备注	进口税率 最惠	普通	暂定	出口退税	增值税率	计量单位	监管条件	Article Description
6113 0000.32	其他塑料等处理的毛制男上衣（针织或钩编，羊毛或动物细毛制，包括用其他材料处理的）	16	130		16	17	件/千克		Men's or boys' jacket and blazers of wool or fine animal hair, treated with plastics and other materials, knitted or crocheted
6113 0000.33	其他塑料等处理的毛、化纤男上衣（针织或钩编，包括用其他材料处理的）	16	130		16	17	件/千克		Men's or boys' jacket and blazers of wool or fine animal hair, of man-made fibres, treated with plastics and other materials, knitted or crocheted
6113 0000.34	其他塑料等处理的纺织材料男上衣（针织或钩编，包括用其他材料处理的）	16	130		16	17	件/千克		Men's or boys' jacket and blazers of other textile materials, treated with plastics and other materials, knitted or crocheted
6113 0000.35	其他橡胶处理的纺织材料制女上衣（针织或钩编）	16	130		16	17	件/千克		Women's or girls' jacket and blazers of other textile materials, treated with other rubber, knitted or crocheted
6113 0000.36	其他塑料等处理的毛制女上衣（针织或钩编，羊毛或动物细毛制，包括用其他材料处理的）	16	130		16	17	件/千克		Women's or girls' jacket and blazers of wool or fine animal hair, treated with plastics and other materials, knitted or crocheted
6113 0000.37	其他塑料等处理的化纤制女上衣（针织或钩编，包括用其他材料处理的）	16	130		16	17	件/千克		Women's or girls' jaeket and blazers of man-made fibres, treated with plastics and other materials, knitted or crocheted
6113 0000.38	其他塑料等处理的纺织料制女上衣（针织或钩编，包括用其他材料处理的）	16	130		16	17	件/千克		Women's or girls' jacket and blazers of other textile materials, treated with plastics and other materials, knitted or crocheted
6113 0000.41	其他橡胶等处理的棉制男式长短裤（针织或钩编）	16	130		16	17	件/千克		Men's or boys' trousers and shorts of cotton, treated with other rubber, knitted or crocheted
6113 0000.42	其他塑料等处理的棉制男式长短裤（针织或钩编，包括用其他材料处理的）	16	130		16	17	件/千克		Men's or boys' trousers and shorts of cotton, treated with plastics and other materials, knitted or crocheted
6113 0000.43	其他橡胶等处理的棉制女式长短裤（针织或钩编）	16	130		16	17	件/千克		Women's or girls' trousers and shorts of cotton, treated with other rubber, knitted or crocheted
6113 0000.44	其他塑料等处理的棉制女式长短裤（针织或钩编，包括用其他材料处理的）	16	130		16	17	件/千克		Women's or girls' trousers and shorts of cotton, treated with plastics and other materials, knitted or crocheted
6113 0000.51	其他橡胶处理纺织材料男长短裤（针织或钩编）	16	130		16	17	件/千克		Men's or boys' trousers and shorts of other textile materials, treated with other rubber， knitted or crocheted
6113 0000.53	其他塑料等处理的毛化纤制男裤（针织或钩编长短裤包括用其他材料处理的）	16	130		16	17	件/千克		Men's or boys' trousers and shorts of wool or fine animal hair, of man-made fibres, treated with plastics and other materials, knitted or crocheted
6113 0000.54	其他塑料等处理纺织材料男长短裤（针织或钩编长、短裤，包括用其他材料处理的）	16	130		16	17	件/千克		Men's or boys' trousers and shorts of other textile materials, treated with plastics and other materials, knitted or crocheted
6113 0000.57	其他橡胶处理纺织材料女长短裤（针织或钩编）	16	130		16	17	件/千克		Women's or girls' trousers and shorts of other textile materials, treated with other rubber, knitted or crocheted
6113 0000.58	其他塑料等处理的毛、化纤制女裤（针织或钩编长、短裤，包括用其他材料处理）	16	130		16	17	件/千克		Women's or girls' trousers and shorts of wool or fine animal hair, of man-made fibres, treated with plastics and other materials, knitted or crocheted
6113 0000.59	其他塑料等处理纺织材料女长短裤（针织或钩编，包括用其他材料处理）	16	130		16	17	件/千克		Women's or girls' trousers and shorts of other textile materials, treated with plastics and other materials, knitted or crocheted
6113 0000.91	其他橡胶处理棉针织或钩编服装	16	130		16	17	件/千克		Other garments of cotton, treated with rubber, knitted or crocheted
6113 0000.92	其他塑料处理棉针织或钩编服装（包括用其他材料处理的）	16	130		16	17	件/千克		Other garments of cotton, treated with plastics and other materials, knitted or crocheted
6113 0000.93	其他橡胶处理纺织材料针织服装（包括钩编服装）	16	130		16	17	件/千克		Other garments of textile materials, treated with rubber, knitted or crocheted

税则号列 Tariff Item	商品名称及备注	进口税率			出口退税	增值税率	计量单位	监管条件	Article Description
		最惠	普通	暂定					
6113 0000.94	其他塑料等处理毛化纤针织服装（包括钩编服装，包括用其他材料处理）	16	130		16	17	件/千克		Other garments of wool or fine animal hair, of man-made fibres, treated with plastics and other materials, knitted or crocheted
6113 0000.98	其他塑料等处理纺织材料针织服装（包括钩编服装，包括用其他材料处理）	16	130		16	17	件/千克		Other garments of textile materials,treated with plastics and other materials, knitted or crocheted
61.14	**针织或钩编的其他服装：**								**Other garments, knitted or crocheted:**
6114.2000	-棉制	16	90		16	17	件/千克		-Of cotton
6114 2000.11	棉制针织或钩编儿童非保暖连身裤	16	90		16	17	件/千克	A	Knitted or crocheted childrens' overall, of cotton, non-thermal
6114 2000.19	棉制针织或钩编其他连身裤	16	90		16	17	件/千克		Knitted or crocheted other overall, of cotton
6114 2000.21	棉制针织或钩编男成人及男童TOPS（指8～18号男童TOPS）	16	90		16	17	件/千克	A	Knitted or crocheted men's TOPS or boys' TOPS(size 8-18), of cotton
6114 2000.22	棉制针织或钩编其他男童TOPS	16	90		16	17	件/千克	A	Knitted or crocheted other boys' TOPS, of cotton
6114 2000.29	棉制针织或钩编女式TOPS	16	90		16	17	件/千克		Knitted or crocheted women's TOPS, of cotton
6114 2000.30	棉制针织或钩编其他运动服	16	90		16	17	件/千克		Knitted or crocheted other sports suits, of cotton
6114 2000.40	棉制针织或钩编夏服、水洗服（包括女成人、女童及男童）	16	90		16	17	件/千克	A	Knitted or crocheted summer wear and wash wear, of cotton (including women's or girls' and boys')
6114 2000.90	棉制针织或钩编其他服装	16	90		16	17	件/千克		Knitted or crocheted other garments, of cotton
6114.3000	-化学纤维制	17.5	130		16	17	件/千克		-Of man-made fibres
6114 3000.11	化纤制针织或钩编连身衣（含羊毛/动物细毛23%及以上）	17.5	130		16	17	件/千克		Overall, of man-made fibres, knitted or crocheted, containing 23% or more of wool or fine animal hair
6114 3000.12	化纤制针织或钩编紧身服及衬衫（含羊毛或动物细毛23%及以上，包括无袖罩衫）	17.5	130		16	17	件/千克		Jerseys and shirts, of man-made fibres, knitted or crocheted, containing 23% or more of wool or fine animal hair, including blouse without sleeve
6114 3000.13	化纤制针织或钩编其他连身衣	17.5	130		16	17	件/千克		Other knitted or crocheted overall, of man-made fibres
6114 3000.19	化纤制针织或钩编紧身服及衬衫（包括无袖罩衫）	17.5	130		16	17	件/千克		Jerseys and shirts, of man-made fibres, knitted or crocheted, including blouse without sleeve
6114 3000.21	化纤针织或钩编男成人及男童TOPS（指8～18号男童TOPS）	17.5	130		16	17	件/千克	A	Knitted or crocheted men's TOPS or boys' TOPS (size 8-18), of man-made fibres
6114 3000.22	化纤针织或钩编其他男童TOPS	17.5	130		16	17	件/千克	A	Other children's TOPS, of man-made fibres, knitted or crocheted
6114 3000.29	化纤针织或钩编女式TOPS	17.5	130		16	17	件/千克		Women's TOPS, of man-made fibres, knitted or crocheted
6114 3000.30	化纤针织或钩编其他运动服	17.5	130		16	17	件/千克		Knitted or crocheted other sports suits, of man-made fibres
6114 3000.40	化纤针织或钩编夏服、水洗服（包括女成人、女童及男童）	17.5	130		16	17	件/千克		Knitted or crocheted summer wear and wash wear, of man-made fibres(including women's or girls' and boys')
6114 3000.90	化纤针织或钩编其他服装	17.5	130		16	17	件/千克		Other knitted or crocheted garments, of man-made fibres
	-其他纺织材料制：								-Of other textile materials:
6114.9010	---羊毛或动物细毛制	16	130		16	17	件/千克		---Of wool or fine animal hair
6114.9090	---其他	16	130		16	17	件/千克		---Other
61.15	**针织或钩编的连裤袜、紧身裤袜、长筒袜、短袜及其他袜类，包括渐紧压袜类(例如用以治疗静脉曲张的长筒袜)和无外绱鞋底的鞋类：**								**Panty hose, tights, stockings, socks and other hosiery, including graduated compression hosiery (for example, stockings for varicose veins) and footwear without applied soles, knitted or crocheted:**
6115.1000	-渐紧压袜类（例如，用以治疗静脉曲张的长筒袜）	16	130		16	17	双/千克		-Graduated compression hosiery（for example, stockings for varicose veins）
	-其他连裤袜及紧身裤袜：								-Other panty hose and tights:
6115.2100	--每根单丝细度在67分特以下的合成纤维制	16	130		16	17	双/千克		--Of synthetic fibres, measuring per single yarn less than 67 decitex
6115.2200	--每根单丝细度在67分特及以	16	130		16	17	双/千克		--Of synthetic fibres, measuring per single yarn 67

税则号列 Tariff Item	商品名称及备注	进口税率 最惠	进口税率 普通	进口税率 暂定	出口退税	增值税率	计量单位	监管条件	Article Description
	上的合成纤维制								decitex or more
	--其他纺织材料制:								--Of other textile materials:
6115.2910	---棉制	14	90		16	17	双/千克		---Of cotton
6115.2990	---其他	14	130		16	17	双/千克		---Other
6115.3000	-其他女士长筒袜或中筒袜,每根单丝细度在67分特以下	14	130		16	17	双/千克		-Other women's full-length or knee-length hosiery, measuring per single yarn less than 67 decitex
6115 3000.21	合纤制针织或钩编女长筒袜(单丝细度在67分特以下)	14	130		16	17	双/千克		Knitted or crocheted women's full-length hosiery of synthetic fibres, measuring per single yarn less than 67 decitex
6115 3000.29	合纤制针织或钩编女中筒袜(单丝细度在67分特以下)	14	130		16	17	双/千克		Knitted or crocheted women's knee-length hosiery of synthetic fibres, measuring per single yarn less than 67 decitex
6115 3000.90	其他材料制女筒袜(单丝细度在67分特以下)	14	130		16	17	双/千克		Knitted or crocheted women's full-length or knee-length hosiery of other textile materials measuring per single yarn less than 67 decitex
	-其他:								-Other:
6115.9400	--羊毛或动物细毛制	14	130		16	17	双/千克		--Of wool or fine animal hair
6115.9500	--棉制	14	90		16	17	双/千克		--Of cotton
6115 9500.11	棉制针织或钩编矫正袜(外科用带压缩刻度)	14	90		16	17	双/千克		Knitted or crocheted orthopedic stockings, with surgical suppressed scale, of cotton
6115 9500.19	棉制针织或钩编短袜及其他袜类	14	90		16	17	双/千克		Knitted or crocheted socks and other hosiery of cotton
6115.9600	--合成纤维制	16	130		16	17	双/千克		--Of synthetic fibres
6115 9600.11	合纤制针织或钩编矫正袜(外科用带压缩刻度)	16	130		16	17	双/千克		Knitted or crocheted orthopedic stockings, with surgical suppressed scale, of synthetic fibres
6115 9600.12	合纤制女长筒袜(针织或钩编,含羊毛或动物细毛23%及以上)	16	130		16	17	双/千克		Knitted or crocheted women's full-length hosiery of synthetic fibres, containing 23% or more of wool or fine animal hair
6115 9600.13	合纤制短袜及其他袜类(针织或钩编,含羊毛或动物细毛23%及以上)	16	130		16	17	双/千克		Knitted or crocheted socks and other hosiery of synthetic fibres, containing 23% or more of wool or fine animal hair
6115 9600.14	其他合纤制女长筒袜(针织或钩编)	16	130		16	17	双/千克		Knitted or crocheted women's full-length hosiery of synthetic fibres
6115 9600.19	其他合纤制短袜及其他袜类(针织或钩编)	16	130		16	17	双/千克		Knitted or crocheted socks and other hosiery of synthetic fibres
6115.9900	--其他纺织材料制	14	130		16	17	双/千克		--Of other textile materials
6115 9900.11	人纤制短袜及其他袜类(针织或钩编,含羊毛或动物细毛23%及以上)	14	130		16	17	双/千克		Knitted or crocheted socks or other hosiery of artificial fibres, containing 23% or more of wool or fine animal hair
6115 9900.19	其他人纤制短袜及其他袜类(针织或钩编)	14	130		16	17	双/千克		Knitted or crocheted socks or other hosiery of artificial fibres
6115 9900.91	其他纺织材料制短袜及其他袜类(针织或钩编,含丝70%及以上)	14	130		16	17	双/千克		Knitted or crocheted socks or other hosiery of other textile materials, containing 70% or more of silk
6115 9900.99	其他纺织材料制短袜及其他袜类(针织或钩编,含丝70%及以下)	14	130		16	17	双/千克		Knitted or crocheted socks or other hosiery of other textile materials, containing less than 70% of silk
61.16	**针织或钩编的分指手套、连指手套及露指手套:**								**Gloves, mittens and mitts, knitted or crocheted:**
6116.1000	-用塑料或橡胶浸渍、涂布或包覆的	14	130		16	17	双/千克		-Impregnated, coated or covered with plastics or rubber
6116 1000.10	塑料或橡胶浸渍的运动手套	14	130		16	17	双/千克		Sports gloves impregnated with plastics or rubber
6116 1000.91	塑料或橡胶浸渍的非运动手套(含塑料或橡胶超过50%及以上)	14	130		16	17	双/千克		Nonsports gloves impregnated, with plastics or rubber, containing 50% or more of plastics or rubber

税则号列 Tariff Item	商品名称及备注	进口税率 最惠	进口税率 普通	进口税率 暂定	出口退税	增值税率	计量单位	监管条件	Article Description
6116 1000.92	塑料或橡胶浸渍的非运动手套（含塑料或橡胶不超过50%，棉限内）	14	130		16	17	双/千克		Nonsports gloves impregnated with plastics or rubber, containing less than 50% of plastics or rubber, cotton limit in
6116 1000.93	塑料或橡胶浸渍的非运动手套（含塑料或橡胶不超过50%，毛限内）	14	130		16	17	双/千克		Nonsports gloves impregnated with plastics or rubber, containing less than 50% of plastics or rubber, wool limit in
6116 1000.94	塑料或橡胶浸渍的其他非运动手套（含塑料或橡胶不超过50%，化纤限内）	14	130		16	17	双/千克		Nonsports gloves impregnated with plastics or rubber, containing less than 50% of plastics or rubber, man-made fibres limit in
6116 1000.99	塑料或橡胶浸渍的其他非运动手套(含塑料或橡胶不超过50%)	14	130		16	17	双/千克		Other nonsports gloves impregnated with plastics or rubber, containing less than 50% of plastics or rubber
	-其他:								-Other:
6116.9100	--羊毛或动物细毛制	14	130		16	17	双/千克		--Of wool or fine animal hair
6116.9200	--棉制	14	90		16	17	双/千克		--Of cotton
6116.9300	--合成纤维制	16	130		16	17	双/千克		--Of synthetic fibres
6116 9300.10	合纤制其他针织或钩编手套(含羊毛或动物细毛23%及以上)	16	130		16	17	双/千克		Knitted or crocheted mittens and mitts, of synthetic fibres, containing 23% or more of wool or fine animal hair
6116 9300.90	合纤制其他针织或钩编手套(含羊毛或动物细毛23%以下)	16	130		16	17	双/千克		Knitted or crocheted mittens and mitts, of synthetic fibres, containing less than 23% of wool or fine animal hair
6116.9900	--其他纺织材料制	14	130		16	17	双/千克		--Of other textile materials
6116 9900.11	人造纤维制其他针织或钩编手套（运动手套）	14	130		16	17	双/千克		Other knitted or crocheted gloves（sports gloves）, of artificial fibres
6116 9900.19	人造纤维制其他针织或钩编手套（非运动手套）	14	130		16	17	双/千克		Other knitted or crocheted gloves（sports gloves）, of artificial fibres
6116 9900.20	丝或绢丝制其他针织或钩编手套（含丝70%及以上）	14	130		16	17	双/千克		Other knitted or crocheted gloves, mittens and mitts of silk or silk waste, containing 70% or more of silk
6116 9900.91	其他纺材制其他针织或钩编手套（棉限内）	14	130		16	17	双/千克		Knitted or crocheted gloves of other textile materials, cotton limit in
6116 9900.92	其他纺材制其他针织或钩编手套（毛限内）	14	130		16	17	双/千克		Knitted or crocheted gloves of other textile materials, wool limit in
6116 9900.93	其他纺材制其他针织或钩编手套（化纤限内）	14	130		16	17	双/千克		Knitted or crocheted gloves of other textile materials, man-made fibres limit in
6116 9900.99	未列名纺材制其他针织或钩编手套	14	130		16	17	双/千克		Other knitted or crocheted gloves of textile materials, not elsewhere specified or included
61.17	**其他制成的针织或钩编的衣着附件；服装或衣着附件的针织或钩编的零件：**								**Other made up clothing accessories, knitted or crocheted; knitted or crocheted parts of garments or of clothing accessories:**
	-披巾、头巾、围巾、披纱、面纱及类似品：								-Shawls, scarves, mufflers, mantillas,veils and the like:
	---动物细毛制:								---Of fine animal hair:
6117.1011	----山羊绒制	14	130		16	17	条/千克		----Of goats
6117.1019	----其他	14	130		16	17	条/千克		----Other
6117.1020	---羊毛制	14	130		16	17	条/千克		----Of wool
6117.1090	---其他	14	130		16	17	条/千克		---Other
	-其他附件:								-Other accessories:
6117.8010	---领带及领结	14	130		16	17	千克/条		---Ties, bow ties and cravats
6117.8090	---其他	14	130		16	17	千克		---Other
6117.9000	-零件	14	130		16	17	千克		-Parts
6117 9000.10	保暖型衬里（针织或钩编）	14	130		16	17	千克		Knitted or crocheted thermal lining
6117 9000.21	毛制针织毛衫的零件(针织或钩编，羊毛或动物细毛)	14	130		16	17	千克		Knitted or crocheted parts of sweaters of wool or fine animal hair
6117 9000.22	毛制针织衬衫的零件(针织或钩编，羊毛或动物细毛)	14	130		16	17	千克		Knitted or crocheted parts of shirts of wool or fine animal hair

税则号列 Tariff Item	商品名称及备注	进口税率			出口退税	增值税率	计量单位	监管条件	Article Description
		最惠	普通	暂定					
6117 9000.23	毛制针织上衣的零件(针织或钩编，羊毛或动物细毛)	14	130		16	17	千克		Knitted or crocheted parts of upper outer garments wool or fine animal hair
6117 9000.24	毛制针织长裤、马裤、短裤的零件(针织或钩编，羊毛或动物细毛)	14	130		16	17	千克		Knitted or crocheted parts of trousers, breeches and shorts, of wool or fine animal hair
6117 9000.29	毛制其他未列名针织服装零件(针织或钩编，羊毛或动物细毛)	14	130		16	17	千克		Knitted or crocheted part of other garments of wool or fine animal hair, not elsewhere specified or included
6117 9000.31	棉制针织毛衫的零件(针织或钩编)	14	130		16	17	千克		Knitted or crocheted parts of sweaters of cotton
6117 9000.32	棉制针织衬衫的零件(针织或钩编)	14	130		16	17	千克		Knitted or crocheted parts of sweaters of cotton
6117 9000.33	棉制针织上衣的零件(针织或钩编)	14	130		16	17	千克		Knitted or crocheted parts of shirts of cotton
6117 9000.34	棉制针织长裤、马裤、短裤的零件(针织或钩编)	14	130		16	17	千克		Knitted or crocheted parts of upper outer garment, of cotton
6117 9000.39	棉制其他未列名针织服装零件(针织或钩编)	14	130		16	17	千克		Knitted or crocheted parts of trousers, breeches and shorts, of cotton
6117 9000.41	化纤制针织毛衫的零件(针织或钩编)	14	130		16	17	千克		Knitted or crocheted parts of sweaters of man-made fibres
6117 9000.42	化纤制针织衬衫的零件(针织或钩编)	14	130		16	17	千克		Knitted or crocheted parts of shirts of man-made fibres
6117 9000.43	化纤制针织上衣的零件(针织或钩编)	14	130		16	17	千克		Knitted or crocheted parts of upper outer garment, of man-made fibres
6117 9000.44	化纤制针织长裤、马裤、短裤零件(针织或钩编)	14	130		16	17	千克		Knitted or crocheted parts of trousers, breeches, shorts, of man-made fibres
6117 9000.49	化纤制其他未列名针织服装零件(针织或钩编)	14	130		16	17	千克		Knitted or crocheted parts of other garments of man-made fibres not elsewhere specified or included
6117 9000.91	其他材料制衣着零件(针织或钩编，含丝70%及以上)	14	130		16	17	千克		Knitted or crocheted parts of garments of other textile materials, containing 70% or more of silk
6117 9000.92	其他材料制针织毛衫的零件(针织或钩编)	14	130		16	17	千克		Knitted or crocheted parts of sweaters of other textile materials
6117 9000.93	其他材料制针织衬衫的零件(针织或钩编)	14	130		16	17	千克		Knitted or crocheted parts of shirts of other textile materials
6117 9000.94	其他材料制针织上衣的零件(针织或钩编)	14	130		16	17	千克		Knitted or crocheted parts of upper outer garments of other textile materials
6117 9000.95	其他材料制长裤、马裤、短裤零件(针织或钩编)	14	130		16	17	千克		Knitted or crocheted parts of trousers, breeches, shorts of other textile materials
6117 9000.99	其他材料制未列名针织服装零件(针织或钩编)	14	130		16	17	千克		Other Knitted or crocheted parts of garments of other textile Materials, not elsewhere specified or included

第六十二章
非针织或非钩编的服装及衣着附件

注释：

一、本章仅适用于除絮胎以外任何纺织物的制成品，但不适用于针织品或钩编织品（品目 62.12 的除外）。

二、本章不包括：

（一）品目 63.09 的旧衣着或其他旧物品；或

（二）矫形器具、外科手术带、疝气带及类似品（品目 90.21）。

三、品目62.03及62.04所称：

（一）“西服套装”，是指面料用完全相同织物制成的两件套或三件套的下列成套服装：

——一件人体上半身穿着的外套或短上衣，除袖子外，应由四片或四片以上面料组成；也可附带一件马甲（西服背心），这件马甲（西服背心）的前片面料应与套装其他各件的面料相同，后片面料则应与外套或短上衣的衬里料相同；以及

——一件人体下半身穿着的服装，即不带背带或护胸的长裤、马裤、短裤（游泳裤除外）、裙子或裙裤。

西服套装各件面料质地、颜色及构成必须完全相同，其款式、尺寸大小也须相互般配，但套装的各件可以有不同织物的滚边（缝入夹缝中的成条织物）。

如果数件人体下半身穿着的服装同时报验（例如，两条长裤、长裤与短裤、裙子或裙裤与长裤），构成西服套装下装的应是一条长裤，而对于女式西服套装，应是裙子或裙裤，其他服装应分别归类。

所称“西服套装”，包括不论是否完全符合上述条件的下列配套服装：

1. 常礼服，由一件后襟下垂并下端开圆弧形叉的素色短上衣和一条条纹长裤组成；
2. 晚礼服（燕尾服），一般用黑色织物制成，上衣前襟较短且不闭合，背后有燕尾；
3. 无燕尾套装夜礼服，其中上衣款式与普通上衣相似（可以更为显露衬衣前胸），但有光滑丝质或仿丝质的翻领。

（二）“便服套装”，是指面料相同并作零售包装的下列成套服装（西服套装及品目 62.07 或 62.08 的物品除外）：

—一件人体上半身穿着的服装，但背心除外，因为背心可作为内衣；以及

Chapter 62
Articles of apparel and clothing accessories, not knitted or crocheted

Chapter Notes:

1. This Chapter applies only to made up articles of any textile fabric other than wadding, excluding knitted or crocheted articles (other than those of heading 62.12).
2. This Chapter does not cover:

(a) Worn clothing or other worn articles of heading 63.09; or

(b) Orthopaedic appliances, surgical belts, trusses or the like (heading 90.21).

3. For the purposes of headings 62.03 and 62.04:

(a) The term "suit" means a set of garments composed of two or three pieces made up, in respect of their outer surface, in identical fabric and comprising:

-One suit coat or jacket the outer shell of which, exclusive of sleeves, consists of four or more panels, designed to cover the upper part of the body, possibly with a tailored waistcoat in addition whose front is made from the same fabric as the outer surface of the other components of the set and whose back is made from the same fabric as the lining of the suit coat or jacket; and

-One garment designed to cover the lower part of the body and consisting of trousers, breeches or shorts (other than swimwear), a skirt or a divided skirt, having neither braces nor bibs.

All of the components of a "suit" must be of the same fabric construction, colour and composition; they must also be of the same style and of corresponding or compatible size. However, these components may have piping (a strip of fabric sewn into the seam) in a different fabric.

If several separate components to cover the lower part of the body are presented together (for example, two pairs of trousers or trousers and shorts, or a skirt or divided skirt and trousers), the constituent lower part shall be one pair of trousers or, in the case of women's or girls' suits, the skirt or divided skirt, the other garments being considered separately.

The term "suit" includes the following sets of garments, whether or not they fulfil all the above conditions:

(i) Morning dress, comprising a plain jacket (cutaway) with rounded tails hanging well down at the back and striped trousers;

(ii) Evening dress (tailcoat), generally made of black fabric, the jacket of which is relatively short at the front, does not close and has narrow skirts cut in at the hips and hanging down behind;

(iii) Dinner jacket suits, in which the jacket is similar in style to an ordinary jacket (though perhaps revealing more of the shirt front), but has shiny silk or imitation silk lapels.

(b) The term "ensemble" means a set of garments (other than suits and articles of heading 62.07 or 62.08) composed of several pieces made up in identical fabric, put up for retail sale, and comprising:

—One garment designed to cover the upper part of the body, with the exception of waistcoats which may also form a second upper garment; and

——一件或两件不同的人体下半身穿着的服装，即长裤、护胸背带工装裤、马裤、短裤（游泳裤除外）、裙子或裙裤。

便服套装各件面料质地、款式、颜色及构成必须相同；尺寸大小也须相互般配。所称"便服套装"，不包括品目 62.11 的运动服及滑雪服。

四、对于品目62.09：

（一）所称"婴儿服装及衣着附件"，是指用于身高不超过86厘米幼儿的服装；

（二）既可归入品目62.09，也可归入本章其他品目的物品，应归入品目62.09；

五、既可归入品目62.10，也可归入本章其他品目的服装，除品目62.09所列的仍归入该品目外，其余的应一律归入品目62.10。

六、品目62.11所称"滑雪服"，是指从整个外观和织物质地来看，主要在滑雪（速度滑雪和高山滑雪）时穿着的下列服装或成套服装：

（一）"滑雪连身服"，即上下身连在一起的单件服装；除袖子和领子外，滑雪连身服可有口袋或脚带；或

（二）"滑雪套装"，即由两件或三件构成一套并作零售包装的下列服装：

——一件用一条拉链扣合的带风帽的厚夹克、防风衣、防风短上衣或类似的服装，可以附带一件背心滑雪背心；以及

——一条不论是否过腰的长裤、一条马裤或一条护胸背带工装裤。

"滑雪套装"也可由一件类似以上（一）款所述的连身服和一件可套在连身服外面的有胎料背心组成。

"滑雪套装"各件颜色可以不同，但面料质地、款式及构成必须相同；尺寸大小也须相互般配。

七、正方形或近似正方形的围巾及围巾式样的物品，如果每边均不超过60厘米，应作为手帕归类（品目62.13）。任何一边超过60厘米的手帕，应归入品目62.14。

八、本章的服装，凡门襟为左压右的，应视为男式；右压左的，应视为女式。但本规定不适用于其式样已明显为男式或女式的服装。

无法区别是男式还是女式的服装，应按女式服装归入有关品目。

九、本章物品可用金属线制成。

—One or two different garments, designed to cover the lower part of the body and consisting of trousers, bib and brace overalls, breeches, shorts（other than swimwear）, a skirt or a divided skirt.

All of the components of an ensemble must be of the same fabric construction, style, colour and composition; they also must be of corresponding or compatible size, The term "ensemble" does not apply to track suits or ski suits, of heading 62.11.

4. For the purposes of heading 62.09:

（a）The expression "babies' garments and clothing accessories"means articles for young children of a body height not exceeding 86 cm;

（b）Articles which are, prima facie, classifiable both in heading 62.09 and in other headings of this Chapter are to be classified in heading 62.09.

5. Garments which are, prima facie, classifiable both in heading 62.10 and in other headings of this Chapter, excluding heading 62.09, are to be classified in heading 62.10.

6. For the purposes of heading 62.11, "ski suits" means garments or sets of garments which, by their general appearance and texture, are identifiable as intended to be worn principally for skiing（cross-country or alpine）. They consist either of:

（a）A"ski overall", that is, a one-piece garment designed to cover the upper and the lower parts of the body; in addition to sleeves and a collar the ski overall may have pockets or footstraps; or

（b）A "ski ensemble", that is, a set of garments composed of two or three pieces, put up for retail sale and comprising:

—One garment such as an anorak, wind-cheater, wind-jacket or similar article, closed by a slide fastener（zipper）, possibly with a waistcoat in addition; and

—One pair of trousers whether or not extending above waist-level, one pair of breeches or one bib and brace overall.

The "ski ensemble" may also consist of an overall similar to the one mentioned in paragraph（a）above and a type of padded, sleeveless jacket worn over the overall.

All the components of a "ski ensemble" must be made up in a fabric of the same texture, style and composition whether or not of the same colour; they also must be of corresponding or compatible size.

7.Scarves and articles of the scarf type, square or approximately square, of which no side exceeds 60cm, are to be classified as handkerchiefs（heading 62.13）. Handkerchiefs of which any side exceeds 60cm are to be classified in heading 62.14.

8. Garments of this Chapter designed for left over right closure at the front shall be regarded as men's or boys' garments, and those designed for right over left closure at the front as women's or girls' garments. These provisions do not apply where the cut of the garment clearly indicates that it is designed for one or other of the sexes.

Garments which cannot be identified as either men's or boys' garments or as women's or girls' garments are to be classified in the headings convering women's or girls' garments.

9. Articles of this Chapter may be made of metal thread.

税则号列 Tariff Item	商品名称及备注	进口税率 最惠	普通	暂定	出口退税	增值税率	计量单位	监管条件	Article Description
62.01	男式大衣、短大衣、斗蓬、短斗蓬、带风帽的防寒短上衣（包括滑雪短上衣）、防风衣、防风短上衣及类似品，但品目62.03的货品除外：								**Men's or boys' overcoats, car-coats,capes, cloaks, anoraks（including ski-jackets）, wind-cheaters, wind-jackets and similar articles, other than those of heading No.62.03:**
	-大衣、雨衣、短大衣、斗篷、短斗篷及类似品：								-Overcoats, raincoats, car-coats, capes,cloaks and similar articles:
6201.1100	--羊毛或动物细毛制	16	130		16	17	件/千克		--Of wool or fine animal hair
6201 1100.10	毛制男式雨衣（羊毛或动物细毛制）	16	130		16	17	件/千克		Men's or boys' raincoats, of wool or fine animal hair
6201 1100.90	毛制男式大衣、斗篷及类似品（含短大衣、短斗篷，羊毛或动物细毛制）	16	130		16	17	件/千克		Men's or boys' overcoats, cloak and similar articles, of wool or fine animal hair（including car-coats, capes）
	--棉制：								--Of cotton:
6201.1210	---羽绒服	16	90		16	17	件/千克		---Padded with feathers or down
6201.1290	---其他	16	90		16	17	件/千克		---Other
6201 1290.10	棉制男式雨衣	16	90		16	17	件/千克		Men's or boys' raincoats of cotton
6201 1290.20	棉制男式连风帽派克大衣等（含带风帽的防寒短上衣、防风衣、防风短上衣及类似品）	16	90		16	17	件/千克		Men's or boys' hooded parka, of cotton （including anoraks, wind-cheaters, windjackets and similar articles）
6201 1290.90	棉制男式大衣、斗篷及类似品（包括短大衣、短斗篷）	16	90		16	17	件/千克		Men's or boys' overcoats, cloak and similar articles, of cotton（including car-coats, capes）
	--化学纤维制：								--Of man-made fibres:
6201.1310	---羽绒服	17.5	130		16	17	件/千克		---Padded with feathers or down
6201.1390	---其他	17.5	130		16	17	件/千克		---Other
6201 1390.10	化纤制男式雨衣	17.5	130		16	17	件/千克		Men's or boys' raincoats of man-made fibres
6201 1390.20	化纤制男式连风帽派克大衣等（羊毛/动物细毛≥36%，带风帽防寒短上衣、防风衣等）	17.5	130		16	17	件/千克		Men's or boys' hooded parka, of man-made fibres（anoraks, wind-cheaters wind-jackets, containing 36% or more of wool or fine animal hair）
6201 1390.30	化纤制男大衣、斗篷及类似品(包括短大衣、短斗篷，含羊毛或动物细毛36%及以上）	17.5	130		16	17	件/千克		Men's or boys' overcoats,cloak and similar articles, of man-made fibres (including car-coats, capes, containing 36% or more of wool or fine animal hair)
6201 1390.40	化纤制男式连风帽派克大衣等（羊毛/动物细毛＜36%，带风帽防寒短上衣/防风衣等）	17.5	130		16	17	件/千克		Men's or boys' hooded parka, of man-made fibres (anoraks, wind-jackets and similar articles, containing less than 36% of wool or fine animal hair）
6201 1390.90	化纤制男大衣、斗篷及类似品（包括短大衣、短斗篷，含羊毛或动物细毛36%以下）	17.5	130		16	17	件/千克		Men's or boys' overcoats, cloak and similar articles, of man-made fibres（including car-coats, capes, containing less than 36% of wool or fine animal hair）
6201.1900	--其他纺织材料制	16	100		16	17	件/千克		--Of other textile materials
6201 1900.10	其他材料制男雨衣	16	100		16	17	件/千克		Men's or boys' raincoats of other textile materials
6201 1900.21	其他材料制男大衣、斗篷及类似品（含短大衣、斗篷、短斗篷，含丝70%及以上）	16	100		16	17	件/千克		Men's or boys' overcoats, cloak and similar articles（including car-coats, capes, containing 70% or more of silk）
6201 1900.29	其他材料制男大衣、斗篷及类似品（含短大衣、斗篷、短斗篷，含丝＜70%）	16	100		16	17	件/千克		Men's or boys' overcoats, cloak and similar articles（including car-coats, capes, containing less than 70% of silk）
6201 1900.30	其他材料制男大衣等，羊毛限内（含短大衣、斗篷、短斗篷）	16	100		16	17	件/千克		Men's or boys' overcoats, of other textile materials, (including car-coats, capes, cloak and similar articles), wool limit in
6201 1900.40	其他材料制男大衣等，棉限内（含短大衣、斗篷、短斗篷）	16	100		16	17	件/千克		Men's or boys' overcoats, of other textile materials, cotton limit in（including car-coats, capes, cloak and similar articles）
6201 1900.50	其他材料制男大衣等，化纤限内（含短大衣、斗篷、短斗篷）	16	100		16	17	件/千克		Men's or boys' overcoats, of other textile materials, man-made fibres limit in（including car-coats, capes, cloak and similar articles）
6201 1900.90	其他材料制男大衣等（含短大衣、斗篷、短斗篷）	16	100		16	17	件/千克		Men's or boys' overcoats, of other textile materials (including car-coats, capes, cloak and similar articles）
	-其他：								-Other:

税则号列 Tariff Item	商品名称及备注	进口税率			出口退税	增值税率	计量单位	监管条件	Article Description
		最惠	普通	暂定					
6201.9100	--羊毛或动物细毛制	16	130		16	17	件/千克		--Of wool or fine animal hair
6201 9100.10	毛制男式有填料无袖上衣(羊毛或动物细毛制)	16	130		16	17	件/千克		Men's or boys' tops, without sleeves, padded, of wool or fine animal hair
6201 9100.20	毛制男式带防寒衬里防风衣(羊毛或动物细毛制，含防风短上衣)	16	130		16	17	件/千克		Men's or boys' wind-cheaters with winter liner, of wool or fine animal hair, including wind-jackets
6201 9100.30	毛制男式带风帽、有填料短上衣(羊毛或动物细毛制，含防风上衣，衬衫式样，特制领)	16	130		16	17	件/千克		Men's or boys' anoraks, padded, of wool or fine animal hair, (including wind-jackets, shirt style, specially made collar）
6201 9100.90	毛制男式其他防寒上衣(羊毛或动物细毛制)	16	130		16	17	件/千克		Other men's or boys' anoraks, of wool or fine animal hair
	--棉制:								--Of cotton:
6201.9210	---羽绒服	16	90		16	17	件/千克		---Padded with feathers or down
6201.9290	---其他	16	90		16	17	件/千克		---Other
6201 9290.10	棉制男式有填料无袖上衣(不带可连接袖子配件)	16	90		16	17	件/千克		Men's or boys' cloaks, without sleeves, padded, of cotton（without accessories of detachable sleeves）
6201 9290.20	棉制男式带防寒衬里防风衣(含防风短上衣)	16	90		16	17	件/千克		Men's or boys' wind-cheaters with winter liner, , of cotton, including wind-jackets
6201 9290.30	棉制男式带风帽、有填料上衣(包括防风上衣，衬衫式样，特制领)	16	90		16	17	件/千克		Men's or boys' anoraks, of cotton, padded, (including wind-jackets, shirt style, specially made collar)
6201 9290.90	棉制男式其他防寒上衣(包括滑雪短上衣、防风短上衣及类似品)	16	90		16	17	件/千克		Other men's or boys' anoraks, of cotton, including ski-jackets, wind-cheaters, wind-jackets and similar articles
	--化学纤维制:								--Of man-made fibres:
6201.9310	---羽绒服	17.5	130		16	17	件/千克		---Padded with feathers or down
6201.9390	---其他	17.5	130		16	17	件/千克		---Other
6201 9390.10	化纤制男式有填料无袖上衣(不带可连接袖子配件)	17.5	130		16	17	件/千克		Men's or boys' cloaks, without sleeves, padded, of man-made fibres（without accessories of detachable sleeves）
6201 9390.20	化纤制男式带风帽防寒短上衣(羊毛或动物细毛36%及以上)	17.5	130		16	17	件/千克		Men's or boys' anoraks, of man-made fibre, containing 36% or more of wool or fine animal hair
6201 9390.30	化纤制男式带防寒衬里防风衣(含防风短上衣)	17.5	130		16	17	件/千克		Men's or boys' wind-cheaters with winter liner, of man-made fibres, including wind-jackets
6201 9390.40	化纤制男式带风帽、有填料上衣(包括防风上衣，衬衫式样，特制领)	17.5	130		16	17	件/千克		Men's or boys' anoraks, of man-made fibres wind-jackets, padded, (including wind-jackets, shirt style, specially made collar)
6201 9390.90	化纤制其他防寒上衣(包括带风帽防寒短上衣、防风短上衣及其他类似品)	17.5	130		16	17	件/千克		Other men's or boys' anoraks, of man-made fibres including wind-cheaters, wind-jackets and similar articles,
6201.9900	--其他纺织材料制	16	100		16	17	件/千克		--Of other textile materials
6201 9900.11	丝制男式带防寒衬里短上衣(含丝70%及以上，含防风上衣、防风短上衣)	16	100		16	17	件/千克		Men's or boys' wind-cheaters, wind-jackets, with winter liner, containing 70% or more of silk
6201 9900.12	丝制男式带特制领、有填料短上衣(含丝70%及以上，含防风上衣，衬衫式样，带风帽)	16	100		16	17	件/千克		Men's or boys' tops, padded, with specially made collar（containing 70% or more by weight of silk, including wind-cheaters, shirt style, with hood）
6201 9900.19	丝制其他防寒上衣(含丝70%及以上)	16	100		16	17	件/千克		Other men's or boys' anoraks of silk, containing 70% or more of silk
6201 9900.21	丝制男式带防寒衬里短上衣(含丝70%以下，含防风上衣，防风短上衣)	16	100		16	17	件/千克		Men's or boys' wind-cheaters with winter liner, including wind-jackets, containing less than 70% by weight of silk
6201 9900.22	丝制男式带特制领、有填料短上衣(含丝70%以下，含防风上衣，衬衫式样，带风帽)	16	100		16	17	件/千克		Men's or boys' tops of silk, padded, with specially made collar（containing less than 70％ by weight of silk, including wind-cheaters, shirt style, with hood）
6201 9900.29	丝制其他防寒上衣(含丝70%以下)	16	100		16	17	件/千克		Other men's or boys' anoraks of silk, containing less than 70% of silk

税则号列 Tariff Item	商品名称及备注	进口税率			出口退税	增值税率	计量单位	监管条件	Article Description
		最惠	普通	暂定					
6201 9900.31	其他材料制男式带风帽防寒短上衣（棉限内，带防寒衬里）	16	100		16	17	件/千克		Men's or boys' anoraks with winter liner, of other textile materials, cotton limit in
6201 9900.32	其他材料制男式带风帽防寒短上衣（羊毛限内，带防寒衬里）	16	100		16	17	件/千克		Men's or boys' anoraks with winter liner, of other textile materials, wool limit in
6201 9900.33	其他材料制男式带风帽防寒短上衣（化纤限内，带防寒衬里）	16	100		16	17	件/千克		Men's or boys' anoraks with winter liner, of other textile materials, man-made fibres limit in
6201 9900.39	其他材料制男式带风帽防寒短上衣（其他纺织材料制，带防寒衬里）	16	100		16	17	件/千克		Men's or boys' anoraks with winter liner, of other textile materials
6201 9900.41	其他材料制男式带风帽短上衣（棉限内，带特制领，有填料，衬衫式样）	16	100		16	17	件/千克		Men's or boys' anoraks, of other textile materials, padded, with specially made collar, shirt style, cotton limit in
6201 9900.42	其他材料制男式带风帽短上衣（羊毛限内，带特制领，有填料，衬衫式样）	16	100		16	17	件/千克		Men's or boys' anoraks, of other textile materials, padded, with specially made collar, shirt style, wool limit in
6201 9900.43	其他材料制男式带风帽短上衣（化纤限内，带特制领，有填料，衬衫式样）	16	100		16	17	件/千克		Men's or boys' anoraks, of other textile materials, padded, with specially made collar, shirt style, man-made fibres limit in
6201 9900.49	其他材料制男式带风帽短上衣（其他材料制，带特制领，有填料，衬衫式样）	16	100		16	17	件/千克		Men's or boys' anoraks, of other textile materials, padded, with specially made collar, shirt style
6201 9900.91	其他材料制男式防寒短上衣（棉限内，含防风衣、防风短上衣类似品）	16	100		16	17	件/千克		Men's or boys' wind-cheaters, of other textile materials, including wind-jackets and similar articles, cotton limit in
6201 9900.92	其他材料制男式防寒短上衣（羊毛限内，含防风衣、防风短上衣类似品）	16	100		16	17	件/千克		Men's or boys' wind-cheaters, of other textile materials, including wind-jackets and similar articles, wool limit in
6201 9900.93	其他材料制男式防寒短上衣（化纤限内，含防风衣、防风短上衣类似品）	16	100		16	17	件/千克		Men's or boys' wind-cheaters, of other textile materials, including wind-jackets and similar articles, man-made fibres limit in
6201 9900.99	其他材料制男式其他防寒短上衣（含防风衣、防风短上衣类似品）	16	100		16	17	件/千克		Other men's or boys' anoraks, of other textile materials, including wind-cheaters, wind-jackets and similar articles
62.02	**女式大衣、短大衣、斗篷、短斗篷、带风帽的防寒短上衣（包括滑雪短上衣）、防风衣、防风短上衣及类似品，但品目62.04的货品除外：**								**Women's or girls' overcoats, car-coats, capes, cloaks, anoraks（including ski-jackets）, wind-cheaters, wind-jackets and similar articles, other than those of heading No.62.04:**
	-大衣、雨衣、短大衣、斗篷、短斗篷及类似品:								-Overcoats, raincoats, car-coats, capes, cloaks and similar articles:
6202.1100	--羊毛或动物细毛制	16	130		16	17	件/千克		--Of wool or fine animal hair
6202 1100.10	毛制女式雨衣（羊毛或动物细毛制）	16	130		16	17	件/千克		Women's or girls' raincoats of wool or fine animal hair
6202 1100.90	毛制女式大衣、斗篷及类似品等（包括短大衣、短斗篷，羊毛或动物细毛制）	16	130		16	17	件/千克		Women's or girls' overcoats, of wool or fine animal hair, including car-coats,capes, cloak and similar articles
	--棉制:								--Of cotton:
6202.1210	---羽绒服	16	90		16	17	件/千克		---Padded with feathers or down
6202.1290	---其他	16	90		16	17	件/千克		---Other
6202 1290.10	棉制女式雨衣	16	90		16	17	件/千克		Women's or girls' raincoats of cotton
6202 1290.20	棉制女式连风帽派克大衣等（含带风帽的防寒短上衣、防风衣、防风短上衣及类似品）	16	90		16	17	件/千克		Women's or girls' hooded parka, of cotton, including wind-cheaters, wind-jackets and similar articles
6202 1290.90	棉制女式大衣、斗篷及类似品（包括短大衣、短斗篷）	16	90		16	17	件/千克		Women's or girls' overcoats of cotton, including car-coats, capes, cloak and similar articles
	--化学纤维制:								--Of man-made fibres:
6202.1310	---羽绒服	19	130		16	17	件/千克		---Padded with feathers or down

税则号列 Tariff Item	商品名称及备注	进口税率			出口退税	增值税率	计量单位	监管条件	Article Description
		最惠	普通	暂定					
6202.1390	---其他	19	130		16	17	件/千克		---Other
6202 1390.10	化纤制女雨衣（含羊毛/动物细毛＜36%，含带风帽防寒上衣、防风衣及类似品）	19	130		16	17	件/千克		Women's or girls' raincoats, anoraks, wind cheaters, wind-jackets, of man-made fibres, containing less than 36% of wool or fine animal hair
6202 1390.20	化纤制女式连风帽派克大衣(含短大衣、短斗篷，含羊毛或动物细毛 36%及以上）	19	130		16	17	件/千克		Women's or girls' hooded parka, wind-cheaters, wind-jackets, of man-made fibres, containing 36% or more of wool or fine animal hair
6202 1390.30	化纤制女大衣、斗篷及类似品（含短大衣、短斗篷，含羊毛或动物细毛 36%及以上）	19	130		16	17	件/千克		Women's or girls' overcoats, of man-made fibres, containing 36% or more of wool or fine animal hair, car-coats, capes, cloak and similar articles
6202 1390.40	化纤制女式连风帽派克大衣(含羊毛/动物细毛<36%，含带风帽防寒上衣、防风衣及类似品）	19	130		16	17	件/千克		Women's or girls' hooded parka, of man-made fibres, containing less than 36% by weight of wool or fine animal hair, including wind-cheaters, wind-jackets and similar articles
6202 1390.90	化纤制女大衣、斗篷及类似品（含短大衣、短斗篷，含羊毛或动物细毛 36%以下）	19	130		16	17	件/千克		Women's or girls' overcoats, of man-made fibres, containing less than 36% of wool or fine animal hair, car-coats,capes, cloak and similar articles
6202.1900	---其他纺织材料制	16	100		16	17	件/千克		---Of other textile materials
6202 1900.10	其他材料制女雨衣	16	100		16	17	件/千克		Women's or girls' raincoats of other materials
6202 1900.21	其他材料制女大衣、斗篷及类似品（含短大衣、短斗篷，含丝 70%及以上）	16	100		16	17	件/千克		Women's or girls' overcoats, of other materials, containing 70% or more of silk, including car-coats, capes, cloak and similar articles
6202 1900.29	其他材料制女大衣、斗篷及类似品（含短大衣、短斗篷，含丝 70%及以下）	16	100		16	17	件/千克		Women's or girls' overcoats, of other materials, containing less than 70% of silk, including carcoats, capes, cloak and similar articles
6202 1900.30	其他材料制女大衣等，羊毛限内（含短大衣、斗篷、短斗篷）	16	100		16	17	件/千克		Women's or girls' overcoats, of other materials, including car-coats,capes, cloak, wool limit in
6202 1900.40	其他材料制女大衣等，棉限内（含短大衣、斗篷、短斗篷）	16	100		16	17	件/千克		Women's or girls' overcoats, of other materials, including car-coats, capes, cloak, cotton limit in
6202 1900.50	其他材料制女大衣等，化纤限内（含短大衣、斗篷、短斗篷）	16	100		16	17	件/千克		Women's or girls' overcoats, of other materials, including car-coats, capes, cloak and similar articles, man-made fibres limit in
6202 1900.90	其他材料制女大衣（含短大衣、斗篷、短斗篷）	16	100		16	17	件/千克		Women's or girls' overcoats, of other textile materials, including car-coats, capes, clock
	-其他：								-Other:
6202.9100	--羊毛或动物细毛制	16	130		16	17	件/千克		--Of wool or fine animal hair
6202 9100.10	毛制女式有填料无袖上衣(羊毛或动物细毛制）	16	130		16	17	件/千克		Women's or girls' cloaks, padded, without sleeves of wool or fine animal hair
6202 9100.20	毛制女式带防寒衬里的短上衣（羊毛或动物细毛制，含防风衣、防风短上衣）	16	130		16	17	件/千克		Women's or girls' wind-cheaters, wind-jackets, with winter liner, of wool or fine animal hair
6202 9100.90	毛制女式其他防寒上衣(羊毛或动物细毛制）	16	130		16	17	件/千克		Other women's or girls' anoraks, of wool or fine animal hair
	--棉制：								--Of cotton:
6202.9210	---羽绒服	16	90		16	17	件/千克		---Padded with feathers or down
6202.9290	---其他	16	90		16	17	件/千克		---Other
6202 9290.10	棉制女式有填料无袖上衣(不带可连接袖子配件）	16	90		16	17	件/千克		Women's or girls' cloaks, padded, without sleeves of cotton（without accessories of detachable sleeves）
6202 9290.20	棉制女式带防寒衬里的短上衣（含防风衣、防风短上衣）	16	90		16	17	件/千克		Women's or girls' wind-cheaters with winter liner, of cotton, including wind-jackets
6202 9290.90	棉制女式其他防寒上衣	16	90		16	17	件/千克		Other women's or girls' anoraks of cotton
	--化学纤维制：								--Of man-made fibres:
6202.9310	---羽绒服	17.5	130		16	17	件/千克		---Padded with feathers or down
6202.9390	---其他	17.5	130		16	17	件/千克		---Other
6202 9390.10	化纤制女式有填料无袖上衣(不带可连接袖子配件）	17.5	130		16	17	件/千克		Women's or girls' cloaks, padded, without sleeves of man-made fibres
6202 9390.20	化纤制女式带风帽防寒短上衣（含羊毛或动物细毛 36%及以上）	17.5	130		16	17	件/千克		Women's or girls' anoraks of man-made fibres, containing 36% or more by weight of wool or fine animal hair

税则号列 Tariff Item	商品名称及备注	进口税率			出口退税	增值税率	计量单位	监管条件	Article Description
		最惠	普通	暂定					
6202 9390.30	化纤制女式带防寒衬里的短上衣（含防风衣、防风短上衣）	17.5	130		16	17	件/千克		Women's or girls' wind-cheaters with winter liner, of man-made fibres, including wind-jackets
6202 9390.90	化纤制女式其他防寒上衣	17.5	130		16	17	件/千克		Other women's or girls' anoraks of man-made fibres
6202.9900	--其他纺织材料制	16	100		16	17	件/千克		--Of other textile materials
6202 9900.11	丝制女式带防寒衬里的短上衣（含丝 70%及以上，含防风衣、防风短上衣）	16	100		16	17	件/千克		Women's or girls' wind-cheaters, wind-jackets, with winter liner, containing 70% or more by weight of silk
6202 9900.19	丝制女式其他防寒上衣（含丝 70%及以上）	16	100		16	17	件/千克		Other women's or girls' anoraks of silk,containing 70% or more by weight of silk
6202 9900.21	丝制女式带防寒衬里的短上衣（含丝 70%以下，含防风衣、防风短上衣）	16	100		16	17	件/千克		Women's or girls' wind-cheaters, wind-jackets, with winter liner, containing less than 70% by weight of silk
6202 9900.29	丝制女式其他防寒上衣（含丝 70%以下）	16	100		16	17	件/千克		Other women's or girls' anoraks of silk, containing less than 70% by weight of silk
6202 9900.31	其他材料制女式带风帽防寒短上衣（棉限内，带防寒衬里）	16	100		16	17	件/千克		Women's or girls' anoraks with winter liner, of other textile materials, cotton limit in
6202 9900.32	其他材料制女式带风帽防寒短上衣（羊毛限内，带防寒衬里）	16	100		16	17	件/千克		Women's or girls' anoraks, wind-jackets, of other textile materials, with winter liner, wool limit in
6202 9900.33	其他材料制女式带风帽防寒短上衣（化纤限内，带防寒衬里）	16	100		16	17	件/千克		Women's or girls' anoraks,of other textile materials,with winter liner, man-made fibres limit in
6202 9900.39	其他材料制女式带风帽防寒短上衣（其他纺织材料制，带防寒衬里）	16	100		16	17	件/千克		Women's or girls' anoraks, of other textile materials, with winter liner
6202 9900.91	其他材料制女式防寒短上衣等（棉限内，含防风衣、防风短上衣及类似品）	16	100		16	17	件/千克		Women's or girls' wind-cheaters, of other textile materials, including wind-jackets and similar articles, cotton limit in
6202 9900.92	其他材料制女式防寒短上衣等（羊毛限内，含防风衣、防风短上衣及类似品）	16	100		16	17	件/千克		Women's or girls' wind-cheaters, of other textile materials, including wind-jackets and similar articles, wool limit in
6202 9900.93	其他材料制女式防寒短上衣等（化纤限内，含防风衣、防风短上衣及类似品）	16	100		16	17	件/千克		Women's or girls' wind-cheaters, of other textile materials, including wind-jackets and similar articles, man-made fibres limit in
6202 9900.99	其他材料制女式其他防寒短上衣等（含防风衣、防风短上衣及类似品）	16	100		16	17	件/千克		Other women's or girls' anoraks, of other textile materials, including wind-cheaters, wind-jackets and similar articles
62.03	**男式西服套装、便服套装、上衣、长裤、护胸背带工装裤、马裤及短裤（游泳裤除外）：**								**Men's or boys' suits, ensembles, jackets, blazers, trousers, bib and brace overalls, breeches and shorts（other than swimwear）:**
	-西服套装:								-Suits:
6203.1100	--羊毛或动物细毛制	17.5	130		16	17	套/千克		--Of wool or fine animal hair
6203.1200	--合成纤维制	17.5	130		16	17	套/千克		--Of synthetic fibres
6203 1200.10	合纤制男式西服套装（含羊毛或动物细毛 36%及以上）	17.5	130		16	17	套/千克		Men's or boys' suits of synthetic fibres, containing 36% or more by weight of wool or fine animal hair
6203 1200.90	其他合纤制男式西服套装	17.5	130		16	17	套/千克		Other men's or boys' suits of synthetic fibres
	--其他纺织材料制:								--Of other textile materials:
6203.1910	----丝及绢丝制	17.5	100		16	17	套/千克		---Of silk or silk waste
6203 1910.10	丝及绢丝制男式西服套装（含丝 70%及以上）	17.5	100		16	17	套/千克		Men's or boys' suits of silk and silk waste, containing 70% or more by weight of silk
6203 1910.90	其他丝及绢丝制男式西服套装（含丝 70%以下）	17.5	100		16	17	套/千克		Other men's or boys' suits of silk and silk waste, containing less than 70% by weight of silk
6203.1990	---其他	17.5	100		16	17	套/千克		---Other
6203 1990.10	棉制男式西服套装	17.5	100		16	17	套/千克		Men's or boys' suits of cotton
6203 1990.21	人造纤维制男式西服套装（含羊毛或动物细毛 36%及以上）	17.5	100		16	17	套/千克		Men's or boys' suits of artificial fibres, containing 36% or more by weight of wool or fine animal hair
6203 1990.29	其他人造纤维制男式西服套装	17.5	100		16	17	套/千克		Men's or boys' suits of other artificial fibres
6203 1990.91	其他材料制男式西服套装（棉限内）	17.5	100		16	17	套/千克		Men's or boys' suits of other textile materials (cotton limit in)

税则号列 Tariff Item	商品名称及备注	进口税率			出口退税	增值税率	计量单位	监管条件	Article Description
		最惠	普通	暂定					
6203 1990.92	其他材料制男式西服套装(毛限内)	17.5	100		16	17	套/千克		Men's or boys' suits of other textile materials (wool limit in)
6203 1990.93	其他材料制男式西服套装(化纤限内)	17.5	100		16	17	套/千克		Men's or boys' suits of other textile materials (man-made fibres limit in)
6203 1990.99	其他材料制其他男式西服套装	17.5	100		16	17	套/千克		Men's or boys' suits of other textile materials
	-便服套装:								-Ensembles:
6203.2200	--棉制	17.5	90		16	17	套/千克		--Of cotton
6203 2200.10	棉制男式便服套装(工业及职业用)	17.5	90		16	17	套/千克		Men's or boys' ensembles of cotton, industrial and occupational use
6203 2200.90	其他棉制男式便服套装	17.5	90		16	17	套/千克		Other men's or boys' ensembles of cotton
6203.2300	--合成纤维制	17.5	130		16	17	套/千克		--Of synthetic fibres
6203 2300.11	合纤制其他男式便服套装(含羊毛或动物细毛≥36%，工业及职业用)	17.5	130		16	17	套/千克		Other men's or boys' ensembles of synthetic fibres, containing 36% or more by weight of wool or fine animal hair, industrial and occupational use
6203 2300.19	合纤制其他男式便服套装(含羊毛或动物细毛≥36%)	17.5	130		16	17	套/千克		Other men's or boys' ensembles of synthetic fibres, containing 36% or more of wool or fine animal hair
6203 2300.91	其他合纤制其他男式便服套装(工业及职业用)	17.5	130		16	17	套/千克		Other men's or boys' ensembles of synthetic fibres, industrial and occupational use
6203 2300.99	其他合纤制其他男式便服套装	17.5	130		16	17	套/千克		Other men's or boys' ensembles of synthetic fibres
	--其他纺织材料制:								--Of other textile materials:
6203.2910	---丝及绢丝制	17.5	130		16	17	套/千克		---Of silk or silk waste
6203 2910.10	丝制男式便服套装(含丝70%及以上)	17.5	130		16	17	套/千克		Men's or boys' ensembles of silk, containing 70% or more by weight of silk
6203 2910.90	丝制其他男式便服套装(含丝70%以下)	17.5	130		16	17	套/千克		Other men's or boys' ensembles of silk, containing less than 70% by weight of silk
6203.2920	---羊毛或动物细毛制	17.5	130		16	17	套/千克		---Of wool or fine animal hair
6203.2990	---其他	17.5	100		16	17	套/千克		---Other
6203 2990.11	人造纤维制其他男式便服套装(工业及职业用)	17.5	100		16	17	套/千克		Other men's or boys' ensembles of artificial fibres, industrial and occupational use
6203 2990.19	人造纤维制其他男式便服套装	17.5	100		16	17	套/千克		Other men's or boys' ensembles of artificial fibres
6203 2990.90	其他材料制其他男式便服套装	17.5	100		16	17	套/千克		Other men's or boys' ensembles of other textile materials
	-上衣:								-Jackets and blazers:
6203.3100	--羊毛或动物细毛制	16	130		16	17	件/千克		--Of wool or fine animal hair
6203 3100.10	毛制男式西服式上衣(羊毛或动物细毛制)	16	130		16	17	件/千克		Men's or boys' suit jackets and blazers, of wool or fine animal hair
6203 3100.90	毛制男式其他上衣(羊毛或动物细毛制)	16	130		16	17	件/千克		Other men's or boys' jackets and blazers, of wool or fine animal hair
6203.3200	--棉制	16	90		16	17	件/千克		--Of cotton
6203 3200.10	棉制工业及职业用男式上衣	16	90		16	17	件/千克		Men's or boys' jackets and blazers of cotton, industrial and occupational use
6203 3200.90	棉制其他男式上衣	16	90		16	17	件/千克		Men's or boys' jackets and blazers of cotton
6203.3300	--合成纤维制	17.5	130		16	17	件/千克		--Of synthetic fibres
6203 3300.11	合成纤维制男式西服式上衣(含羊毛或动物细毛36%及以上，工业及职业用)	17.5	130		16	17	件/千克		Men's or boys' suit-type jacket of synthetic fibres, containing 36% or more by weight of wool or fine animal hair, industrial and occupational use
6203 3300.19	合成纤维制男式西服式上衣(含羊毛或动物细毛36%及以上)	17.5	130		16	17	件/千克		Men's or boys' suit-type jacket of synthetic fibres, containing 36% or more by weight of wool or fine animal hair
6203 3300.21	合成纤维制男式其他上衣(含羊毛或动物细毛36%及以上，工业及职业用)	17.5	130		16	17	件/千克		Other men's or boys' jackets and blazers of synthetic fibres, containing 36% or more of wool or fine animal hair, industrial and occupational use
6203 3300.29	合成纤维制男式其他上衣(含羊毛或动物细毛36%及以上)	17.5	130		16	17	件/千克		Other men's or boys' jackets and blazers of synthetic fibres, containing 36% or more by weight of wool or fine animal hair
6203 3300.91	其他合成纤维制男式上衣(工业及职业用)	17.5	130		16	17	件/千克		Other men's or boys' jackets and blazers of synthetic fibres, industrial and occupational use

税则号列 Tariff Item	商品名称及备注	进口税率			出口退税	增值税率	计量单位	监管条件	Article Description
		最惠	普通	暂定					
6203 3300.99	其他合成纤维制男式上衣	17.5	130		16	17	件/千克		Other men's or boys' jackets and blazers of synthetic fibres
	--其他纺织材料制:								--Of other textile materials:
6203.3910	---丝及绢丝制	16	130		16	17	件/千克		---Of silk or silk waste
6203 3910.10	丝制男式上衣（含丝 70%及以上）	16	130		16	17	件/千克		Men's or boys' jackets and blazers of silk, containing 70% or more by weight of silk
6203 3910.90	丝制男式上衣（含丝 70%以下）	16	130		16	17	件/千克		Men's or boys' jackets and blazers of silk, containing less than 70% by weight of silk
6203.3990	---其他	16	100		16	17	件/千克		---Other
6203 3990.11	人造纤维制男式西服式上衣(含羊毛或动物细毛 36%及以上，工业及职业用）	16	100		16	17	件/千克		Men's or boys' suit-type jacket of artificial fibres, industrial and occupational use, containing 36% or more by weight of wool or fine animal hair
6203 3990.19	人造纤维制男式西服式上衣(含羊毛或动物细毛 36%及以上）	16	100		16	17	件/千克		Men's or boys' suit-type jacket of artificial fibres, containing 36% or more by weight of wool or fine animal hair
6203 3990.21	人造纤维制男式其他上衣(含羊毛或动物细毛 36%及以上，工业及职业用）	16	100		16	17	件/千克		Other men's or boys' jackets and blazers of artificial fibres,containing 36% or more of wool or fine animal hair, industrial and occupational use
6203 3990.29	人造纤维制男式其他上衣(含羊毛或动物细毛 36%及以上）	16	100		16	17	件/千克		Other men's or boys' jackets and blazers of artificial fibres, containing 36% or more by weight of wool or fine animal hair
6203 3990.31	其他人造纤维制男式上衣(工业及职业用）	16	100		16	17	件/千克		Men's or boys' jackets and blazers of artificial fibres, industrial and occupational use
6203 3990.39	其他人造纤维制男式上衣	16	100		16	17	件/千克		Men's or boys' jackets and blazers of artificial fibres
6203 3990.91	其他材料制男式上衣（棉限内）	16	100		16	17	件/千克		Other men's or boys' jackets and blazers of other textile materials (cotton limit in)
6203 3990.92	其他材料制男式上衣（毛限内）	16	100		16	17	件/千克		Other men's or boys' jackets and blazers of other textile materials (wool limit in)
6203 3990.93	其他材料制男式上衣（化纤限内）	16	100		16	17	件/千克		Other men's or boys' jackets and blazers of other textile materials (man-made fibres limit in)
6203 3990.99	其他材料制男式上衣	16	100		16	17	件/千克		Other men's or boys' jackets and blazers of other textile materials
	-长裤、护胸背带工装裤、马裤及短裤:								-Trousers, bib and brace overalls, breeches and shorts:
6203.4100	--羊毛或动物细毛制	16	130		16	17	条/千克		--Of wool or fine animal hair
6203 4100.11	毛制男式护胸背带工装裤（羊毛或动物细毛制，带防寒衬里）	16	130		16	17	条/千克		Men's or boys' bib and brace overalls, of wool or fine animal hair, with winter liner
6203 4100.19	毛制男式护胸背带工装裤(羊毛或动物细毛制）	16	130		16	17	条/千克		Men's or boys' bib and brace overalls, of wool or fine animal hair
6203 4100.21	毛制男式长裤、马裤(羊毛或动物细毛制，带防寒衬里）	16	130		16	17	条/千克		Men's or boys' trousers and breeches, of wool or fine animal hair, with winter liner
6203 4100.22	毛制男式长裤、马裤（羊毛或动物细毛制，含 8~18 号男童）	16	130		16	17	条/千克	A	Men's trousers and breeches, of wool or fine animal hair, including boys', size 8-18
6203 4100.29	毛制其他男童长裤、马裤(羊毛或动物细毛制）	16	130		16	17	条/千克	A	Other boys' trousers and breeches, of wool or fine animal hair
6203 4100.90	毛制男式短裤(羊毛或动物细毛制）	16	130		16	17	条/千克		Men's or boys' shorts of wool or fine animal hair
	--棉制:								--Of cotton:
6203.4210	---阿拉伯裤	16	90		16	17	条/千克		---Arabian trousers
6203 4210.10	棉制男式阿拉伯裤(羽绒和水禽毛≥15%且含绒率≥35%，或含羽绒≥10%）	16	90		16	17	条/千克		Men's or boys' Arabian trousers of cotton, containing15% or more of down and water-fowl hair, 35% or more of down, or containing 10% or more of down fills
6203 4210.90	棉制男式阿拉伯裤	16	90		16	17	条/千克		Men's or boys' Arabian trousers of cotton
6203.4290	---其他	16	90		16	17	条/千克		---Other
6203 4290.11	工业、职业用棉男护胸背带工装裤（羽绒和水禽毛≥15%且含绒率≥35%，或含羽绒≥10%）	16	90		16	17	条/千克		Men's or boys' bib and brace overalls of cotton, industrial and occupational use, containing15% or more of down and water-fowl hair, 35% or more of down, or containing 10% or more of down fills

税则号列 Tariff Item	商品名称及备注	进口税率 最惠	普通	暂定	出口退税	增值税率	计量单位	监管条件	Article Description
6203 4290.12	棉制男式护胸背带工装裤(羽绒和水禽毛≥15%且含绒率≥35%，或含羽绒≥10%)	16	90		16	17	条/千克		Men's or boys' bib and brace overalls of cotton, containing15% or more of down and water-fowl hair, 35% or more of down, or containing 10% or more of down fills
6203 4290.13	棉制其他男成人护胸背带工装裤(带防寒衬里，工业及职业用)	16	90		16	17	条/千克		Other men's bib and brace overalls of cotton, with winter liner, industrial and occupational use
6203 4290.14	棉制其他男成人护胸背带工装裤（带防寒衬里）	16	90		16	17	条/千克		Other men's bib and brace overalls of cotton, with winter liner
6203 4290.15	棉制其他男童护胸背带工装裤（带防寒衬里）	16	90		16	17	条/千克	A	Other boys' bib and brace overalls of cotton, with winter liner
6203 4290.16	棉制其他男成人护胸背带工装裤（工业及职业用）	16	90		16	17	条/千克		Other men's bib and brace overalls, of cotton, industrial and occupational use
6203 4290.17	棉制其他男成人护胸背带工装裤	16	90		16	17	条/千克		Other men's bib and brace overalls of cotton
6203 4290.19	棉制其他男童护胸背带工装裤	16	90		16	17	条/千克	A	Other boys' bib and brace overalls of cotton
6203 4290.21	工业、职业用棉男长裤、马裤(羽绒和水禽毛≥15%且含绒率≥35%，或含羽绒≥10%)	16	90		16	17	条/千克		Men's or boys' working trousers and breeches, industrial and occupational use（containing15% or more of down and water-fowl hair, 35% or more of down, or containing 10% or more of down fills）
6203 4290.29	棉制男式长裤、马裤（羽绒和水禽毛≥15%且含绒率≥35%，或含羽绒≥10%）	16	90		16	17	条/千克		Men's or boys' trousers and breeches of cotton, containing15% or more of down and water-fowl hair, 35% or more of down, or containing 10% or more of down fills
6203 4290.30	棉制男式长裤、马裤（游戏装，带防寒衬里）	16	90		16	17	条/千克		Men's or boys' trousers and breeches, playsuit, of cotton, with winter liner
6203 4290.41	棉制男式长裤、马裤（游戏装，不带防寒衬里，含8~18号男童）	16	90		16	17	条/千克		Men's or boys' trousers and breeches, playsuit, of cotton, without winter liner, including boys', size 8-18
6203 4290.49	棉制其他男童长裤、马裤（游戏装，不带防寒衬里）	16	90		16	17	条/千克	A	Other boys' trousers and breeches, of cotton, playsuit, without winter liner
6203 4290.51	棉制男式长裤、马裤(非游戏装，带防寒衬里，工业及职业用）	16	90		16	17	条/千克		Men's or boys' trousers and breeches, of cotton, with winter liner, industrial and occupational use（other than playsuit）
6203 4290.59	棉制男式长裤、马裤(非游戏装，带防寒衬里)	16	90		16	17	条/千克		Men's or boys' trousers and breeches, of cotton, with winter liner, other than playsuit
6203 4290.61	棉制男成人长裤、马裤(非游戏装，不带防寒衬里，工业及职业用）	16	90		16	17	条/千克		Men's trousers and breeches, of cotton, industrial and occupational use, other than playsuit, without winter liner
6203 4290.62	棉制男式长裤、马裤（非游戏装，不带防寒衬里，含8~18号男童）	16	90		16	17	条/千克	A	Men's trousers and breeches, of cotton, other than playsuit, without winter liner, including boys', size 8-18
6203 4290.69	棉制其他男童长裤、马裤（非游戏装，不带防寒衬里）	16	90		16	17	条/千克	A	Other boys' trousers and breeches of cotton, other than playsuit, without winter liner
6203 4290.91	棉制男式短裤(羽绒和水禽毛≥15%且含绒率≥35%，或含羽绒≥10%)	16	90		16	17	条/千克		Men's or boys' shorts of cotton, containing15% or more of down and water-fowl hair, 35% or more of down, or containing 10% or more of down fills
6203 4290.92	棉制其他男式短裤（游戏装）	16	90		16	17	条/千克		Other men's or boys' shorts of cotton, playsuit
6203 4290.99	棉制其他男式短裤（非游戏装）	16	90		16	17	条/千克		Other men's or boys' shorts of cotton,not playsuit
	--合成纤维制:								--Of synthetic fibres:
6203.4310	---阿拉伯裤	17.5	130		16	17	条/千克		---Arabian trousers
6203 4310.10	合成纤维制男式阿拉伯裤(羽绒和水禽毛≥15%且含绒率≥35%，或含羽绒≥10%)	17.5	130		16	17	条/千克		Men's or boys' Arabian trousers of synthetic fibres, containing15% or more of down and water-fowl hair, 35% or more of down, or containing 10% or more of down fills
6203 4310.90	合成纤维制男式阿拉伯裤	17.5	130		16	17	条/千克		Men's or boys' Arabian trousers of synthetic fibres
6203.4390	---其他	17.5	130		16	17	条/千克		---Other
6203 4390.11	工业、职业用合纤制男护胸背带工裤（羽绒和水禽毛≥15%且含绒率≥35%，或含羽绒≥10%）	17.5	130		16	17	条/千克		Men's or boys' bib and brace overalls of synthetic fibres, industrial and occupation use, containing 15% or more of down and water-fowl hair, 35% or more of down, containing 10% or more of down fills

税则号列 Tariff Item	商品名称及备注	进口税率			出口退税	增值税率	计量单位	监管条件	Article Description
		最惠	普通	暂定					
6203 4390.12	合纤制男式护胸背带工裤(羽绒和水禽毛≥15%且含绒率≥35%,或含羽绒≥10%)	17.5	130		16	17	条/千克		Men's or boys' bib and brace overalls of synthetic fibres, containing15% or more of down and waterfowl hair, 35% or more of down, or containing 10% or more of down fills
6203 4390.13	其他合纤制男成人护胸背带工装裤(带防寒衬里,工业及职业用)	17.5	130		16	17	条/千克		Other men's bib and brace overalls of synthetic fibres, with winter liner, industrial and occupational use
6203 4390.14	其他合纤制男成人护胸背带工装裤(带防寒衬里)	17.5	130		16	17	条/千克		Other men's bib and brace overalls of synthetic fibres, with winter liner
6203 4390.15	其他合纤制男童护胸背带工装裤(带防寒衬里)	17.5	130		16	17	条/千克	A	Other boys' bib and brace overalls of synthetic fibres, with winter liner
6203 4390.16	其他合纤制男成人护胸背带工装裤(工业及职业用)	17.5	130		16	17	条/千克		Other men's bib and brace overalls of synthetic fibres, industrial and occupational use
6203 4390.17	其他合纤制男成人护胸背带工装裤	17.5	130		16	17	条/千克		Other men's bib and brace overalls of synthetic fibres
6203 4390.19	其他合纤制男童护胸背带工装裤	17.5	130		16	17	条/千克	A	Other boys' bib and brace overalls of synthetic fibres
6203 4390.21	工业、职业用合纤制男长裤、马裤(羽绒和水禽毛≥15%且含绒率≥35%,或含羽绒≥10%)	17.5	130		16	17	条/千克		Men's or boys' trousers and breeches of synthetic fibres, containing15% or more of down and waterfowl hair, 35% or more of down, or containing 10% or more of down fills
6203 4390.29	合纤制男式长裤、马裤(羽绒和水禽毛≥15%且含绒率≥35%,或含羽绒≥10%)	17.5	130		16	17	条/千克		Men's or boys' trousers and breeches of synthetic fibres, containing 15% or more of down and waterfowl hair, 35% or more of down, or containing 10% or more of down fills
6203 4390.31	其他合纤制男式长裤、马裤(带防寒衬里,含羊毛或动物细毛36%及以上,工业及职业用)	17.5	130		16	17	条/千克		Men's or boys' trousers and breeches of synthetic fibres, with winter liner,containing 36% or more of wool or fine animal hair,industrial and occupational use
6203 4390.39	其他合纤制男式长裤、马裤(带防寒衬里,含羊毛或动物细毛36%及以上)	17.5	130		16	17	条/千克		Men's or boys' trousers and breeches of synthetic fibres, with winter liner, containing 36% or more of wool or fine animal hair
6203 4390.41	其他合纤制男成人长裤、马裤(不带防寒衬里,含羊毛或动物细毛36%及以上,工业及职业用)	17.5	130		16	17	条/千克		Men's trousers and breeches of synthetic fibres, without winter liner, containing 36% or more of wool or fine animal hair, industrial and occupational use
6203 4390.42	其他合纤制男式长裤、马裤(不带防寒衬里,含羊毛或动物细毛36%及以上,指8~18号男童)	17.5	130		16	17	条/千克		Men's trousers and breeches of synthetic fibres , without winter liner, containing 36% or more of wool or fine animal hair, including boys' size 8-18
6203 4390.49	其他合纤制男童长裤、马裤(不带防寒衬里,含羊毛或动物细毛36%及以上)	17.5	130		16	17	条/千克	A	Boys' trousers and breeches of synthetic fibres, without winter liner, containing 36% or more of wool or fine animal hair
6203 4390.50	其他合纤制男式长裤、马裤(带防寒衬里,游戏装)	17.5	130		16	17	条/千克		Other men's or boys' trousers and breeches of synthetic fibres, with winter liner, playsuit
6203 4390.61	其他合纤制男式长裤、马裤(不带防寒衬里,游戏装,含8~18号男童)	17.5	130		16	17	条/千克	A	Other men's trousers and breeches of synthetic fibres, without winter liner, playsuit, including boys' size 8-18
6203 4390.69	其他合纤制其他男童长裤、马裤(不带防寒衬里,游戏装)	17.5	130		16	17	条/千克	A	Other boys' trousers and breeches of synthetic fibres, without winter liner, playsuit
6203 4390.71	其他合纤制男式长裤、马裤(带防寒衬里,非游戏装和滑雪裤,工业及职业用)	17.5	130		16	17	条/千克		Other men's or boys' trousers and breeches of synthetic fibres, with winter liner, industrial and occupational use, not playsuit or ski trousers
6203 4390.79	其他合纤制男式长裤、马裤(带防寒衬里,非游戏装和滑雪裤)	17.5	130		16	17	条/千克		Other men's or boys' trousers and breeches of synthetic fibres, with winter liner, not playsuit or ski trousers
6203 4390.81	其他合纤制男成人长裤、马裤(不带防寒衬里,非游戏装和滑雪裤,工业及职业用)	17.5	130		16	17	条/千克		Other men's trousers and breeches, industrial and occupational use, of synthetic fibres, not playsuit or ski trousers, without winter liner
6203 4390.82	其他合纤制男童长裤、马裤(不带防寒衬里,非游戏装和滑雪裤,指8~18号男童)	17.5	130		16	17	条/千克	A	Other boy's trousers and breeches, size 8-18, of synthetic fibres(without winter liner, not playsuit or ski trousers)

税则号列 Tariff Item	商品名称及备注	进口税率 最惠	普通	暂定	出口退税	增值税率	计量单位	监管条件	Article Description
6203 4390.89	其他合纤制其他男童长裤、马裤（不带防寒衬里，非游戏装和滑雪裤）	17.5	130		16	17	条/千克	A	Other boys' trousers and breeches of synthetic fibres, without winter liner, not playsuit or ski trousers
6203 4390.91	合纤制男式短裤(羽绒和水禽毛≥15%且含绒率≥35%，或含羽绒≥10%）	17.5	130		16	17	条/千克		Men's or boys' shorts, containing 15% or more of down and water-fowl hair, 35% or more of down, or containing 10% or more of down fills
6203 4390.92	其他合纤制男式短裤（游戏装）	17.5	130		16	17	条/千克		Men's or boys' shorts, playsuit, of synthetic fibres
6203 4390.93	其他合纤制男式短裤（非游戏装）	17.5	130		16	17	条/千克		Other men's or boys' shorts of synthetic fibres, not playsuit
6203 4390.99	其他合纤制男裤	17.5	130		16	17	条/千克		Other men's or boys' trousers of synthetic fibres
	--其他纺织材料制:								--Of other textile materials:
6203.4910	---阿拉伯裤	16	100		16	17	条/千克		---Arabian trousers
6203 4910.10	人纤制男式阿拉伯裤(羽绒和水禽毛≥15%且含绒率≥35%，或含羽绒≥10%）	16	100		16	17	条/千克		Men's or boys' Arabian trousers of artificial fibres, containing 15% or more of down and water-fowl hair, 35% or more of down, or containing 10% or more of down fills
6203 4910.20	人纤制男式阿拉伯裤	16	100		16	17	条/千克		Men's or boys' Arabian trousers of artificial fibres
6203 4910.30	其他材料制男式阿拉伯裤(羽绒和水禽毛≥15%且含绒率≥35%，或含羽绒≥10%）	16	100		16	17	条/千克		Men's or boys' Arabian trousers of other textile materials, containing 15% or more of down and water-fowl hair, 35% or more of down, or containing 10% or more of down fills
6203 4910.90	其他材料制男式阿拉伯裤	16	100		16	17	条/千克		Men's or boys' Arabian trousers of other textile materials
6203.4990	---其他	16	100		16	17	条/千克		---Other
6203 4990.11	人纤制男成人护胸背带工装裤（带防寒衬里）	16	100		16	17	条/千克		Men's bib and brace overalls of artificial fibres, with winter liner
6203 4990.12	人纤制男童护胸背带工装裤(带防寒衬里）	16	100		16	17	条/千克	A	Boys' bib and brace overalls of artificial fibres, with winter liner
6203 4990.13	人纤制男成人护胸背带工装裤	16	100		16	17	条/千克		Men's bib and brace overalls, of artificial fibres
6203 4990.19	人纤制男童护胸背带工装裤	16	100		16	17	条/千克	A	Boys' bib and brace overalls, of artificial fibres
6203 4990.21	人纤制男式长裤、马裤（带防寒衬里，含羊毛或动物细毛36%及以上）	16	100		16	17	条/千克		Men's or boys' trousers and breeches of artificial fibres, with winter liner, containing 36% or more of wool or fine animal hair
6203 4990.22	人纤制其他男式长裤、马裤（不带防寒衬里，含羊毛或动物细毛36%及以上）	16	100		16	17	条/千克		Men's or boys' trousers, breeches of artificial fibre (without winter liner, containing 36% or more of wool or fine animal hair)
6203 4990.23	人纤制男式长裤、马裤（带防寒衬里，游戏装）	16	100		16	17	条/千克		Men's or boys' trousers and breeches of artificial fibres, with winter liner, playsuit
6203 4990.24	人纤制其他男式长裤、马裤（不带防寒衬里，游戏装）	16	100		16	17	条/千克		Men's or boys' trousers and breeches of artificial fibres, playsuit, without winter liner
6203 4990.25	人纤制男式长裤、马裤（带防寒衬里，非游戏装）	16	100		16	17	条/千克		Men's or boys' trousers and breeches of artificial fibres, with winter liner, not playsuits
6203 4990.26	人纤制其他男式长裤、马裤（不带防寒衬里，非游戏装）	16	100		16	17	条/千克		Men's or boys' trousers and breeches, of artificial fibres, without winter liner, not playsuits
6203 4990.27	人纤制男式短裤(含羊毛或动物细毛36%及以上）	16	100		16	17	条/千克		Men's or boys' shorts of artificial fibres, containing 36% or more of wool or fine animal hair
6203 4990.28	人纤制男式短裤（游戏装）	16	100		16	17	条/千克		Men's or boys' shorts of artificial fibres, playsuit
6203 4990.29	人纤制男式短裤（非游戏装）	16	100		16	17	条/千克		Men's or boys' shorts of artificial fibres, not playsuit
6203 4990.31	丝制男式护胸背带工装裤(含丝70%及以上）	16	100		16	17	条/千克		Men's or boys' bib and brace overalls, containing 70% or more of silk
6203 4990.32	丝制男式长裤、马裤（含丝70%及以上，带防寒衬里）	16	100		16	17	条/千克		Men's or boys' trousers and breeches with winter liner, containing 70% or more of silk
6203 4990.33	丝制男式长裤、马裤（含丝70%及以上，不带防寒衬里）	16	100		16	17	条/千克		Men's or boys' trousers and breeches without winter liner, containing 70% or more of silk
6203 4990.34	丝制男式短裤（含丝70%及以上）	16	100		16	17	条/千克		Men's or boys' shorts, containing70% or more of silk
6203 4990.35	丝制男式护胸背带工装裤(含丝70%以下，带防寒衬里）	16	100		16	17	条/千克		Men's or boys' bib and brace overalls with winter lining, containing less than 70% of silk

税则号列 Tariff Item	商品名称及备注	进口税率 最惠	普通	暂定	出口退税	增值税率	计量单位	监管条件	Article Description
6203 4990.36	丝制男式护胸背带工装裤(含丝70%以下，不带防寒衬里)	16	100		16	17	条/千克		Men's or boys' bib and brace overalls without winter liner, containing less than 70% of silk
6203 4990.37	丝制男式长裤、马裤(含丝70%以下，带防寒衬里)	16	100		16	17	条/千克		Men's or boys' trousers and breeches with winter liner, containing less than 70% by weight of silk
6203 4990.38	丝制男式长裤、马裤(含丝70%以下，不带防寒衬里)	16	100		16	17	条/千克		Men's or boys' trousers and breeches without winter liner, containing less than 70% of silk
6203 4990.39	丝制男式短裤(含丝70%以下)	16	100		16	17	条/千克		Men's or boys' shorts, containing less than 70% by weight of silk
6203 4990.41	其他材料制男式长裤、马裤(棉限内，带防寒衬里)	16	100		16	17	条/千克		Men's or boys' trousers and breeches of other textile materials, cotton limit in, with winter liner
6203 4990.42	其他材料制男式长裤、马裤(棉限内、不带防寒衬里)	16	100		16	17	条/千克		Men's or boys' trousers and breeches of other textile materials, cotton limit in, without winter liner
6203 4990.49	其他材料制男式短裤(棉限内)	16	100		16	17	条/千克		Men's or boys' shorts of other textile materials, cotton limit in
6203 4990.51	其他材料制男式长裤、马裤(毛限内，带防寒衬里)	16	100		16	17	条/千克		Men's or boys' trousers and breeches of other textile materials, wool limit in, with winter liner
6203 4990.52	其他材料制男式长裤、马裤(毛限内，不带防寒衬里)	16	100		16	17	条/千克		Men's or boys' trousers and breeches of other textile materials, wool limit in, without winter liner
6203 4990.59	其他材料制男式短裤(毛限内)	16	100		16	17	条/千克		Men's or boys' shorts of other textile materials, wool limit in
6203 4990.61	其他材料制男式长裤、马裤(化纤限内，带防寒衬里)	16	100		16	17	条/千克		Men's or boys' trousers and breeches of other textile materials, with winter liner, man-made fibres limit in
6203 4990.62	其他材料制男式长裤、马裤(化纤限内，不带防寒衬里)	16	100		16	17	条/千克		Men's or boys' trousers and breeches of other textile materials, without winter liner, man-made fibres limit in
6203 4990.69	其他材料制男式短裤(化纤限内)	16	100		16	17	条/千克		Men's or boys' shorts, of other textile materials, man-made fibres limit in
6203 4990.91	其他材料制男式护胸背带工装裤(带防寒衬里)	16	100		16	17	条/千克		Men's or boys' bib and brace overalls, of other textile materials, with winter liner
6203 4990.92	其他材料制男式护胸背带工装裤(不带防寒衬里)	16	100		16	17	条/千克		Men's or boys' bib and brace overalls, of other textile materials, without winter liner
6203 4990.93	其他材料制男式长裤、马裤(带防寒衬里)	16	100		16	17	条/千克		Men's or boys' trousers and breeches of other textile materials, with winter liner
6203 4990.94	其他材料制男式长裤、马裤(不带防寒衬里)	16	100		16	17	条/千克		Men's or boys' trousers and breeches of other textile materials, without winter liner
6203 4990.99	其他材料制男式短裤	16	100		16	17	条/千克		Men's or boys' shorts of other textile materials
62.04	**女式西服套装、便服套装、上衣、连衣裙、裙子、裙裤、长裤、护胸背带工装裤、马裤及短裤(游泳服除外)：**								**Women's or girls' suits, ensembles, jackets, blazers dresses, skirts, divided skirts, trousers, bib and brace overalls, breeches and shorts(other than swimwear)：**
	-西服套装:								-Suits:
6204.1100	--羊毛或动物细毛制	17.5	130		16	17	套/千克		--Of wool or fine animal hair
6204.1200	--棉制	17.5	90		16	17	套/千克		--Of cotton
6204 1200.10	含裤子的棉制女式西服套装	17.5	90		16	17	套/千克		Women's or girls' suits of cotton,including trousers
6204 1200.90	不含裤子的棉制女式西服套装	17.5	90		16	17	套/千克		Women's or girls' suits of cotton, excluding trousers
6204.1300	--合成纤维制	17.5	130		16	17	套/千克		--Of synthetic fibres
6204 1300.10	合纤制女式西服套装(含羊毛或动物细毛36%及以上)	17.5	130		16	17	套/千克		Women's or girls' suits of synthetic fibres, containing36% or more of wool or fine animal hair
6204 1300.90	其他合纤制女式西服套装	17.5	130		16	17	套/千克		Other women's or girls' suits of synthetic fibres
	--其他纺织材料制:								--Of other textile materials:
6204.1910	---丝及绢丝制	17.5	100		16	17	套/千克		---Of silk or silk waste
6204 1910.10	丝及绢丝制女式西服套装(含丝70%及以上)	17.5	100		16	17	套/千克		Women's or girls' suits of silk and silk waste, containing 70% or more
6204 1910.90	其他丝及绢丝制女式西服套装(含丝70%以下)	17.5	100		16	17	套/千克		Women's or girls' suits of silk and silk waste, containing less than 70%
6204.1990	---其他	17.5	100		16	17	套/千克		---Other
6204 1990.11	人造纤维制女式西服套装(含羊毛或动物细毛36%及以上)	17.5	100		16	17	套/千克		Women's or girls' suits of artificial fibres, containing 36% or more by weight of wool or fine animal hair
6204 1990.19	其他人造纤维制女式西服套装	17.5	100		16	17	套/千克		Women's or girls' suits of artificial fibres

税则号列 Tariff Item	商品名称及备注	进口税率 最惠	普通	暂定	出口退税	增值税率	计量单位	监管条件	Article Description
6204 1990.91	含裤子的其他材料制女西服套装（棉限内）	17.5	100		16	17	套/千克		Women's or girls' suits of other textile materials, cotton limit in
6204 1990.92	其他材料制女式西服套装（毛限内）	17.5	100		16	17	套/千克		Women's or girls' suits of other textile materials, wool limit in
6204 1990.93	其他材料制女式西服套装（化纤限内）	17.5	100		16	17	套/千克		Women's or girls' suits of other textile materials, man-made fibres limit in
6204 1990.99	其他材料制其他女式西服套装	17.5	100		16	17	套/千克		Women's or girls' suits of other textile materials
	-便服套服:								-Ensembles:
6204.2100	--羊毛或动物细毛制	17.5	130		16	17	套/千克		--Of wool or fine animal hair
6204.2200	--棉制	17.5	90		16	17	套/千克		--Of cotton
6204 2200.11	含裤子的棉制女式便服套装（工业及职业用）	17.5	90		16	17	套/千克		Women's or girls' ensembles of cotton,industrial and occupational use
6204 2200.19	不含裤子的棉制女式便服套装（工业及职业用）	17.5	90		16	17	套/千克		Women's or girls' ensembles of cotton
6204 2200.91	含裤子的棉制非工业及职业用女式便服套装	17.5	90		16	17	套/千克		Women's or girls' ensembles of cotton, including trousers, non-industrial or occupational use
6204 2200.99	不含裤子的棉制非工业及职业用女式便服套装	17.5	90		16	17	套/千克		Women's or girls' ensembles of cotton, excluding trousers, non-industrial or occupational use
6204.2300	--合成纤维制	20	130		16	17	套/千克		--Of synthetic fibres
6204 2300.11	工业、职业用合纤制女式便服套装（含羊毛或动物细毛≥36%）	20	130		16	17	套/千克		Women's or girls' ensembles of synthetic fibres, containing36% or more of wool or fine animal hair, industrial and occupational use
6204 2300.19	合成纤维制其他女式便服套装（含羊毛或动物细毛≥36%）	20	130		16	17	套/千克		Women's or girls' ensembles of synthetic fibres, containing 36% or more of wool or fine animal hair
6204 2300.91	其他合成纤维制含裤子的女式便服套装	20	130		16	17	套/千克		Women's or girls' ensembles of synthetic fibres, industrial and occupational use
6204 2300.99	其他合成纤维制其他女式便服套装	20	130		16	17	套/千克		Women's or girls' ensembles of synthetic fibres
	--其他纺织材料制:								--Of other textile materials:
6204.2910	---丝及绢丝制	20	130		16	17	套/千克		---Of silk or silk waste
6204 2910.10	丝制女式便服套装（含丝及绢丝≥70%）	20	130		16	17	套/千克		Women's or girls' ensembles, containing 70% or more by weight of silk or silk waste
6204 2910.90	丝制其他女式便服套装（含丝及绢丝＜70%）	20	130		16	17	套/千克		Women's or girls' ensembles, containing less than 70% by weight of silk or silk waste
6204.2990	---其他	14	100		16	17	套/千克		---Other
6204 2990.11	含裤子的人纤制女便服套装	14	100		16	17	套/千克		Women's or girls' ensembles of artificial fibres, including trousers
6204 2990.19	不含裤子的人纤制女便服套装	14	100		16	17	套/千克		Women's or girls' ensembles of artificial fibres, excluding trousers
6204 2990.21	含裤子的其他材料制女式便服套装（棉限内）	14	100		16	17	套/千克		Women's or girls' ensembles of other textile materials, including trousers, cotton limit in
6204 2990.29	不含裤子的其他材料制女式便服套装（棉限内）	14	100		16	17	套/千克		Women's or girls' ensembles of other textile materials, excluding trousers, cotton limit in
6204 2990.30	其他材料制女式便服套装（毛限内）	14	100		16	17	套/千克		Women's or girls' ensembles of other textile materials, wool limit in
6204 2990.41	含裤子的其他材料制女式便服套装（化纤限内）	14	100		16	17	套/千克		Women's or girls' ensembles of other textile materials, including trousers, man-made fibres limit in
6204 2990.49	不含裤子的其他材料制女式便服套装（化纤限内）	14	100		16	17	套/千克		Women's or girls' ensembles, of other textile material, excluding trousers, man-made fibres limit in
6204 2990.91	含裤子的其他材料制女式便服套装	14	100		16	17	套/千克		Women's or girls' ensembles, of other textile material, including trousers
6204 2990.99	不含裤子的其他材料制女式便服套装	14	100		16	17	套/千克		Women's or girls' ensembles of other textile materials, excluding trousers
	-上衣:								-Jackets and blazers:
6204.3100	--羊毛或动物细毛制	16	130		16	17	件/千克		--Of wool or fine animal hair
6204.3200	--棉制	16	90		16	17	件/千克		--Of cotton
6204 3200.10	棉制女式上衣（工业及职业用）	16	90		16	17	件/千克		Women's or girls' jackets and blazers of cotton, industrial and occupational use

税则号列 Tariff Item	商品名称及备注	进口税率 最惠	进口税率 普通	进口税率 暂定	出口退税	增值税率	计量单位	监管条件	Article Description
6204 3200.90	棉制其他女式上衣	16	90		16	17	件/千克		Other Women's or girls' jackets and blazers of cotton
6204.3300	--合成纤维制	17.5	130		16	17	件/千克		--Of synthetic fibres
6204 3300.10	合成纤维制女式上衣(含羊毛或动物细毛36%及以上，工业及职业用)	17.5	130		16	17	件/千克		Women's or girls' jackets and blazers of synthetic fibres, containing 36% or more of wool or fine animal hair, industrial and occupational use
6204 3300.20	合成纤维制其他女式上衣(含羊毛或动物细毛36%及以上)	17.5	130		16	17	件/千克		Women's or girls' jackets and blazers of synthetic fibres, containing 36% or more of wool or fine animal hair
6204 3300.30	合成纤维制女式上衣(工业及职业用)	17.5	130		16	17	件/千克		Women's or girls' jackets and blazers of synthetic fibres, industrial and occupational use
6204 3300.90	合成纤维制其他女式上衣	17.5	130		16	17	件/千克		Other women's or girls' jackets and blazers of synthetic fibres
	--其他纺织材料制:								--Of other textile materials:
6204.3910	---丝及绢丝制	16	130		16	17	件/千克		---Of silk or silk waste
6204 3910.10	丝制女式上衣(含丝及绢丝70%及以上)	16	130		16	17	件/千克		Women's or girls' jackets and blazers of silk, containing 70% or more by weight of silk or silk waste
6204 3910.90	丝制其他女式上衣(含丝及绢丝70%以下)	16	130		16	17	件/千克		Women's or girls' jackets and blazers of silk, containing less than 70% by weight of silk or silk waste
6204.3990	---其他	16	100		16	17	件/千克		---Other
6204 3990.11	人纤制女式上衣(含羊毛或动物细毛≥36%，工业及职业用)	16	100		16	17	件/千克		Women's or girls' jackets and blazers of artificial fibres, containing 36% or more of wool or fine animal hair, industrial and occupational use
6204 3990.12	人纤制其他女式上衣(含羊毛或动物细毛≥36%)	16	100		16	17	件/千克		Women's or girls' jackets and blazers of artificial fibres, containing 36% or more of wool or fine animal hair
6204 3990.13	人纤制女式上衣(工业及职业用)	16	100		16	17	件/千克		Women's or girls' jackets and blazers of artificial fibres, industrial and occupational use
6204 3990.19	人纤制其他女式上衣	16	100		16	17	件/千克		Women's or girls' jackets and blazers, of artificial fibres
6204 3990.91	其他材料制女式上衣(棉限内)	16	100		16	17	件/千克		Women's or girls' jackets and blazers of other textile materials, cotton limit in
6204 3990.92	其他材料制女式上衣(毛限内)	16	100		16	17	件/千克		Women's or girls' jackets and blazers of other textile materials, wool limit in
6204 3990.93	其他材料制女式上衣(化纤限内)	16	100		16	17	件/千克		Women's or girls' jackets and blazers of other textile materials, man-made fibres limit in
6204 3990.99	其他材料制女式上衣	16	100		16	17	件/千克		Women's or girls' jackets and blazers of other textile materials
	-连衣裙:								-Dresses:
6204.4100	--羊毛或动物细毛制	16	130		16	17	件/千克		--Of wool or fine animal hair
6204.4200	--棉制	16	90		16	17	件/千克		--Of cotton
6204.4300	--合成纤维制	17.5	130		16	17	件/千克		--Of synthetic fibres
6204 4300.10	合成纤维制女式连衣裙(含羊毛或动物细毛≥36%)	17.5	130		16	17	件/千克		Women's or girls' dresses of synthetic fibres, containing 36% or moreby weight of wool or fine animal hair
6204 4300.90	合成纤维制其他女式连衣裙	17.5	130		16	17	件/千克		Other women's or girls' dresses of synthetic fibres
6204.4400	--人造纤维制	16	130		16	17	件/千克		--Of artificial fibres
6204 4400.10	人造纤维制女式连衣裙(含羊毛或动物细毛≥36%)	16	130		16	17	件/千克		Women's or girls' dresses of artificial fibres, containing 36% or more of wool or fine animal hair
6204 4400.90	人造纤维制其他女式连衣裙	16	130		16	17	件/千克		Other women's or girls' dresses of artificial fibres
	--其他纺织材料制:								--Of other textile materials:
6204.4910	---丝及绢丝制	16	130		16	17	件/千克		---Of silk or silk waste
6204 4910.10	丝制女式连衣裙(含丝及绢丝70%及以上)	16	130		16	17	件/千克		Women's or girls' dresses of silk, containing 70% or more of silk or silk waste
6204 4910.90	丝制其他女式连衣裙(含丝及绢丝70%以下)	16	130		16	17	件/千克		Other women's or girls' dresses of silk, containing less than 70% by weight of silk or silk waste
6204.4990	---其他	16	100		16	17	件/千克		---Other

税则号列 Tariff Item	商品名称及备注	进口税率 最惠	普通	暂定	出口退税	增值税率	计量单位	监管条件	Article Description
6204 4990.91	其他材料制女式连衣裙（棉限内）	16	100		16	17	件/千克		Women's or girls' dresses of other textile materials, cotton limit in
6204 4990.92	其他材料制女式连衣裙（毛限内）	16	100		16	17	件/千克		Women's or girls' dresses of other textile materials, wool limit in
6204 4990.93	其他材料制女式连衣裙(化纤限内)	16	100		16	17	件/千克		Women's or girls' dresses of other textile materials, man-made fibres limit in
6204 4990.99	其他材料制其他女式连衣裙	16	100		16	17	件/千克		Women's or girls' dresses of other textile materials
	-裙子及裙裤:								-Skirts and divided skirts:
6204.5100	--羊毛或动物细毛制	14	130		16	17	件/千克		--Of wool or fine animal hair
6204.5200	--棉制	14	90		16	17	件/千克		--Of cotton
6204.5300	--合成纤维制	16	130		16	17	件/千克		--Of synthetic fibres
6204 5300.10	合成纤维制女式裙子及裙裤(含羊毛或动物细毛≥36%)	16	130		16	17	件/千克		Women's or girls' skirts and divided skirts, of synthetic fibres, containing 36% or more by weight of wool or fine animal hair
6204 5300.90	合成纤维制其他女式裙子及裙裤	16	130		16	17	件/千克		Women's or girls' skirts and divided skirts, of synthetic fibres
	--其他纺织材料制:								--Of other textile materials:
6204.5910	---丝及绢丝制	14	130		16	17	件/千克		---Of silk or silk waste
6204 5910.10	丝制女式裙子及裙裤（含丝70%及以上）	14	130		16	17	件/千克		Women's or girls' skirts and divided skirts of silk, containing 70% or more by weight of silk
6204 5910.90	其他丝制女式裙子及裙裤(含丝70%以下)	14	130		16	17	件/千克		Women's or girls' skirts and divided skirts of silk, containing less than 70% by weight of silk
6204.5990	---其他	14	100		16	17	件/千克		---Other
6204 5990.11	人造纤维制女式裙子及裙裤（含羊毛或动物细毛36%及以上）	14	100		16	17	件/千克		Women's or girls' skirts and divided skirts, of artificial fibres, containing 36% or more of wool or fine animal hair
6204 5990.19	人造纤维制其他女式裙子及裙裤	14	100		16	17	件/千克		Women's or girls' skirts and divided skirts, of artificial fibres
6204 5990.91	其他材料制女式裙子及裙裤(棉限内)	14	100		16	17	件/千克		Women's or girls' skirts and divided skirts of other textile materials, cotton limit in
6204 5990.92	其他材料制女式裙子及裙裤(毛限内)	14	100		16	17	件/千克		Women's or girls' skirts and divided skirts of other textile materials, wool limit in
6204 5990.93	其他材料制女式裙子及裙裤(化纤限内)	14	100		16	17	件/千克		Women's or girls' skirts and divided skirts of other textile materials, man-made fibres limit in
6204 5990.99	其他材料制其他女式裙子及裙裤	14	100		16	17	件/千克		Women's or girls' skirts and divided skirts of other textile materials
	-长裤、护胸背带工装裤、马裤及短裤:								-Trousers, bib and brace overalls, breeches and shorts:
6204.6100	--羊毛或动物细毛制	16	130		16	17	条/千克		--Of wool or fine animal hair
6204 6100.10	毛制女式护胸背带工装裤及短裤（带防寒衬里）	16	130		16	17	条/千克		Women's or girls' bib and brace overalls, with winter liner, of wool or fine animal hair
6204 6100.90	毛制女式长裤、马裤	16	130		16	17	条/千克		Women's or girls' trousers and breeches, of wool or fine animal hair
6204.6200	--棉制	16	90		16	17	条/千克		--Of cotton
6204 6200.10	棉制女式护胸背带工装裤	16	90		16	17	条/千克		Women's or girls' bib and brace overalls of cotton
6204 6200.21	棉制女式长裤、马裤(羽绒和水禽毛≥15%且含绒率≥35%,或含羽绒≥10%)	16	90		16	17	条/千克		Women's or girls' trousers and breeches of cotton, containing 15% or more of down and water-fowl hair, 35% or more of down, or containing 10% or more of down fills
6204 6200.22	棉制女式长裤、马裤（游戏装）	16	90		16	17	条/千克		Women's trousers and breeches,of cotton, playsuit
6204 6200.29	其他棉制女式长裤、马裤	16	90		16	17	条/千克		Women's or girls' trousers and breeches of cotton
6204 6200.91	棉制女式短裤(羽绒和水禽毛≥15%且含绒率≥35%,或含羽绒≥10%)	16	90		16	17	条/千克		Women's or girls' shorts of cotton, containing 15% or more of down and water-fowl hair, 35% or more of down, or containing 10% or more of down fills
6204 6200.92	棉制女式短裤（游戏装）	16	90		16	17	条/千克		Girls' shorts of cotton（playsuit）
6204 6200.99	其他棉制女式短裤	16	90		16	17	条/千克		Other women's shorts of cotton
6204.6300	--合成纤维制	17.5	130		16	17	条/千克		--Of synthetic fibres
6204 6300.10	合纤制女式护胸背带工装裤	17.5	130		16	17	条/千克		Women's or girls' bib and brace overalls

税则号列 Tariff Item	商品名称及备注	进口税率			出口退税	增值税率	计量单位	监管条件	Article Description
		最惠	普通	暂定					
6204 6300.21	合纤女式长裤、马裤(羽绒和水禽毛≥15%且含绒率≥35%,或含羽绒≥10%)	17.5	130		16	17	条/千克		Women's or girls' trousers and breeches of synthetic fibres, containing 15% or more of down and water-fowl hair, 35% or more of down, or containing 10% or more of down fills
6204 6300.22	合纤制其他女式长裤、马裤(含羊毛或动物细毛36%及以上)	17.5	130		16	17	条/千克		Women's or girls' trousers and breeches of synthetic fibres, containing 36% or more by weight of wool or fine animal hair
6204 6300.23	合纤制女式长裤、马裤(游戏装)	17.5	130		16	17	条/千克		Women's or girls' trousers and breeches, of synthetic fibres (playsuit)
6204 6300.24	合纤制女式长裤、马裤(滑雪裤除外)	17.5	130		16	17	条/千克		Women's or girls' trousers and breeches, of synthetic fibres (other than ski trousers)
6204 6300.29	合纤制女式其他长裤、马裤	17.5	130		16	17	条/千克		Other women's or girls' trousers and breeches, of synthetic fibres
6204 6300.91	合纤制女式短裤(羽绒和水禽毛≥15%且含绒率≥35%,或含羽绒≥10%)	17.5	130		16	17	条/千克		Women's or girls' shorts of synthetic fibres, containing 15% or more of down and water-fowl hair, 35% or more of down, or containing 10% or more of down fills
6204 6300.92	合纤制女式短裤(游戏装)	17.5	130		16	17	条/千克		Other women's shorts of synthetic fibres
6204 6300.99	其他合纤制女式短裤	17.5	130		16	17	条/千克		Other women's or girls' trousers short,of synthetic fibres
6204.6900	--其他纺织材料制	16	100		16	17	条/千克		--Of other textile materials
6204 6900.11	人纤制女式护胸背带工装裤	16	100		16	17	条/千克		Women's bib and brace overalls of artificial fibres
6204 6900.12	人纤制女式长裤、马裤(含羊毛或动物细毛36%及以上)	16	100		16	17	条/千克		Women's trousers and breeches of artificial fibres (containing 36% or more by weight of wool or fine animal hair)
6204 6900.13	人纤制女式短裤(含羊毛或动物细毛36%及以上)	16	100		16	17	条/千克		Women's trousers and shorts, of artificial fibres (containing 36% or more by weight of wool or fine animal hair)
6204 6900.14	人纤制女式长裤、马裤(游戏装)	16	100		16	17	条/千克		Women's or girls' trousers, breeches and shorts, of artificial fibres, playsuit
6204 6900.15	人纤制女式短裤(游戏装)	16	100		16	17	条/千克		Women's trousers and shorts, of artificial fibres, playsuit
6204 6900.16	人纤制女式其他长裤、马裤	16	100		16	17	条/千克		Other women's trousers, breeches of artificial fibres
6204 6900.17	人纤制女式其他短裤	16	100		16	17	条/千克		Women's or girls' other trousers and short, of artificial fibres
6204 6900.21	丝制女式护胸背带工装裤	16	100		16	17	条/千克		Women's or girls' bib and brace overalls, of silk
6204 6900.25	丝制女式其他长裤、马裤、短裤(含丝70%及以上)	16	100		16	17	条/千克		Women's or girls' other trousers, breeches and shorts, of silk, containing 70% or more of silk
6204 6900.26	丝制女式长裤、马裤、短裤(含丝70%以下的游戏装)	16	100		16	17	条/千克		Women's or girls' trousers, breeches and shorts, of silk, containing 70% or more of silk, playsuit
6204 6900.29	丝制女式其他长裤、马裤、短裤(含丝70%以下)	16	100		16	17	条/千克		Women's or girls' other trousers, breeches and shorts, of silk, containing less than 70% of silk
6204 6900.91	其他材料制女式护胸背带工装裤	16	100		16	17	条/千克		Women's or girls' bib and brace overalls of other textile materials
6204 6900.92	其他材料制女长裤、马裤、短裤(游戏装)	16	100		16	17	条/千克		Women's or girls' trousers, breeches and shorts, of other textile materials, playsuit
6204 6900.93	其他材料制女式长裤、马裤、短裤(棉限内)	16	100		16	17	条/千克		Women's or girls' trousers, breeches and shorts of other textile materials, cotton limit in
6204 6900.94	其他材料制女式长裤、马裤、短裤(羊毛限内)	16	100		16	17	条/千克		Trousers, breeches and shorts of other textile materials, wool limit in
6204 6900.95	其他材料制女式长裤、马裤、短裤(化纤限内)	16	100		16	17	条/千克		Women's trousers, breeches and shorts of man-made fibres, man-made fibres limit in
6204 6900.99	其他材料制其他女式长、马、短裤	16	100		16	17	条/千克		Women's or girls' other trousers, breeches and shorts, of other textile materials
62.05	男衬衫:								**Men's or boys' shirts:**
6205.2000	-棉制	16	90		16	17	件/千克		-Of cotton
6205 2000.10	不带特制领的棉制男成人衬衫(含男童8~18号衬衫)	16	90		16	17	件/千克	A	Men's shirts and boys', size 8-18, of cotton, without specially made collar

税则号列 Tariff Item	商品名称及备注	进口税率 最惠	普通	暂定	出口退税	增值税率	计量单位	监管条件	Article Description
6205 2000.91	其他棉制男童游戏套装衬衫(不包括长衬衫)	16	90		16	17	件/千克	A	Boy's shirts of cotton, playsuit, other than long shirts
6205 2000.99	其他棉制男式衬衫	16	90		16	17	件/千克	A	Other men's or boys' shirts, of cotton
6205.3000	-化学纤维制	16	130		16	17	件/千克		-Of man-made fibres
6205 3000.11	不带特制领的化学纤维制男式衬衫(含羊毛或动物细毛36%及以上，含男童8~18号衬衫)	16	130		16	17	件/千克	A	Men's or boys' shirts of man-made fibres, without specially made collar, containing 36% or more of wool or fine animal hair, including boys' , size 8-18
6205 3000.19	不带特制领的化纤制其他男童衬衫(含羊毛或动物细毛36%及以上)	16	130		16	17	件/千克	A	Boys' shirts, of man-made fibres, without specially made collar, containing 36% or more by weight of wool or fine animal hair
6205 3000.91	化学纤维制其他男成人及男童衬衫(不带特制领，男童衬衫指8~18号)	16	130		16	17	件/千克	A	Men's or boys' shirts , of man-made fibres, without specially made collar, including boys', size 8-18
6205 3000.92	化学纤维制其他男童游戏套装衬衫	16	130		16	17	件/千克	A	Other boy's shirts of playsuit, of man-made fibres
6205 3000.99	化纤制其他男成人衬衫	16	130		16	17	件/千克	A	Other men's shirts of man-made fibres
	-其他纺织材料制:								-Of other textile materials:
6205.9010	---丝及绢丝制	16	130		16	17	件/千克		---Of silk or silk waste
6205 9010.11	不带特制领的丝制非针织男式衬衫(含丝70%及以上，含男童8~18号衬衫)	16	130		16	17	件/千克	A	Men's or boys' shirts of silk, without specially made collar, not knitted, containing 70% or more by weight of silk, including boys', size 8-18
6205 9010.19	丝制非针织其他男式衬衫(含丝70%及以上)	16	130		16	17	件/千克	A	Men's or boys' shirts of silk, not knitted, containing 70% or more by weight of silk
6205 9010.21	丝制其他非针织男式衬衫(棉限内，不带特制领的，含男童8~18号衬衫)	16	130		16	17	件/千克	A	Men's or boys' shirts of silk, not knitted, without specially made collar, including boys', size 8-18, cotton limit in
6205 9010.29	丝制其他非针织其他男式衬衫(棉限内)	16	130		16	17	件/千克	A	Men's or boys' shirts of silk, not knitted, cotton limit in
6205 9010.31	丝制其他非针织男式衬衫(羊毛限内，不带特制领的，含男童8~18号衬衫)	16	130		16	17	件/千克	A	Men's or boys' shirts of silk, not knitted, without specially made collar, including boys',size 8-18, wool limit in
6205 9010.39	丝制其他非针织其他男式衬衫(羊毛限内)	16	130		16	17	件/千克	A	Men's or boys' shirts of silk, not knitted, without specially made collar, including boys'size 8-18, wool limit in
6205 9010.41	丝制非针织男式衬衫(化纤限内，不带特制领的，含男童8~18号衬衫)	16	130		16	17	件/千克	A	Men's or boys' shirts of silk, not knitted, without specially made collar, including boys' size 8-18, man-made fibres limit in
6205 9010.49	丝制其他非针织其他男式衬衫(化纤限内)	16	130		16	17	件/千克	A	Men's or boys' shirts of silk, not knitted, man-made fibres limit in
6205 9010.91	未列名丝制非针织男式衬衫(含丝70%以下，不带特制领的，含男童8~18号衬衫)	16	130		16	17	件/千克	A	Men's or boys' shirts of silk, not knitted, containing less than 70% of silk, without specially made collar, including boys', size 8-18, not elsewhere specified
6205 9010.99	未列名丝制非针织其他男式衬衫(含丝70%以下)	16	130		16	17	件/千克	A	Other men's or boys' shirts of silk, not knitted, containing less than 70% by weight of silk, not elsewhere specified or included
6205.9020	---羊毛或动物细毛制	16	100		16	17	件/千克	A	---Of wool or fine animal hair
6205.9090	---其他	16	100		16	17	件/千克		---Other
6205 9090.11	其他纺织材料制男式衬衫(棉限内，不带特制领的，含男童8~18号衬衫)	16	100		16	17	件/千克	A	Men's or boys' shirts of other textile materials, without specially made collar , including boys' size 8-18, cotton limit in
6205 9090.19	其他纺织材料制其他男式衬衫(棉纤限内)	16	100		16	17	件/千克	A	Men's or boys' shirts of other textile materials, cotton or man-made fibres limit in
6205 9090.21	其他纺织材料制男式衬衫(羊毛限内，不带特制领的，含男童8~18号衬衫)	16	100		16	17	件/千克	A	Men's or boys' shirts of other textile materials, without specially made collar, including boys' size 8-18, wool limit in
6205 9090.29	其他纺织材料制其他男式衬衫(羊毛限内)	16	100		16	17	件/千克	A	Men's or boys' shirts of other textile materials, wool or man-made fibres limit in

税则号列 Tariff Item	商品名称及备注	进口税率 最惠	普通	暂定	出口退税	增值税率	计量单位	监管条件	Article Description
6205 9090.31	其他纺织材料制男式衬衫(化纤限内，不带特制领的，含男童8～18号衬衫)	16	100		16	17	件/千克	A	Men's or boys' shirts of other textile materials, without specially made collar, including boys' size 8-18, man-made fibres limit in
6205 9090.39	其他纺织材料制其他男式衬衫(化纤限内)	16	100		16	17	件/千克	A	Men's or boys' shirts of other textile materials, man-made fibres limit in
6205 9090.91	未列名纺织材料制男式衬衫(不带特制领的,含男童8～18号衬衫)	16	100		16	17	件/千克	A	Men's or boys' shirts of other textile materials, without specially made collar, including boys' size 8-18, not elsewhere specified or included
6205 9090.99	未列名纺织材料制其他男式衬衫	16	100		16	17	件/千克	A	Other men's or boys' shirts of other textile materials, not elsewhere specified or included
62.06	女衬衫:								**Women's or girls' blouses, shirts and shirtblouses:**
6206.1000	-丝或绢丝制	16	130		16	17	件/千克		-Of silk or silk waste
6206 1000.11	丝及绢丝制女式衬衫(棉限内，成人及7～16号女童衬衫)	16	130		16	17	件/千克	A	Women's or girls' shirts of silk or silk waste, cotton limit in, including girls' size 7-16
6206 1000.19	丝及绢丝制其他女童衬衫(棉限内)	16	130		16	17	件/千克	A	Other girls' shirts of silk or silk waste,cotton limit in
6206 1000.21	丝及绢丝制女式衬衫(羊毛限内，成人及7～16号女童衬衫)	16	130		16	17	件/千克	A	Women's or girls' shirts of silk or silk waste, wool limit in, including girls' ,size 7-16
6206 1000.29	丝及绢丝制其他女童衬衫(羊毛限内)	16	130		16	17	件/千克	A	Other girls' shirts of silk and silk waste,wool limit in
6206 1000.31	丝及绢丝制女式衬衫(化纤限内，成人及7～16号女童衬衫)	16	130		16	17	件/千克	A	Women's or girls' shirts of silk and silk waste, including girls', size 7-16, man-made fibres limit in
6206 1000.39	丝及绢丝制其他女童衬衫(化纤限内)	16	130		16	17	件/千克	A	Other girls' shirts of silk and silk waste, man-made fibres limit in
6206 1000.41	丝制女成人及7～16号女童衬衫(含丝70%及以上)	16	130		16	17	件/千克	A	Women's shirts of silk, containing 70% or more by weight of silk, including girls', size 7-16
6206 1000.49	其他丝及绢丝制女童衬衫(含丝70%及以上)	16	130		16	17	件/千克	A	Other girls' shirts of silk and silk waste,containing 70% or more by weight of silk
6206 1000.91	丝制女成人及7～16号女童衬衫(含丝70%以下)	16	130		16	17	件/千克	A	Women's shirts of silk, containing less than 70% by weight of silk, including girls', size 7-16
6206 1000.99	其他丝及绢丝制女童衬衫(含丝70%以下)	16	130		16	17	件/千克	A	Other girls' shirts of silk and silk waste, containing less than 70% by weight of silk
6206.2000	-羊毛或动物细毛制	16	130		16	17	件/千克		-Of wool or fine animal hair
6206 2000.10	毛制女成人及7～16号女童衬衫	16	130		16	17	件/千克	A	Women's shirts and girls', size 7-16, of wool or fine animal hair
6206 2000.90	其他羊毛或动物细毛制女童衬衫	16	130		16	17	件/千克	A	Other girls' shirts of wool or fine animal hair
6206.3000	-棉制	16	90		16	17	件/千克		-Of cotton
6206 3000.10	棉制女成人及7～16号女童衬衫	16	90		16	17	件/千克	A	Women's shirts and girls', size 7-16, of cotton
6206 3000.20	棉制女童游戏套装衫(含游戏套装衬衫)	16	90		16	17	件/千克	A	Girls' playsuit of cotton, including shirt of playsuit
6206 3000.90	其他棉制女式衬衫	16	90		16	17	件/千克	A	Other women's or girls' shirts of cotton
6206.4000	-化学纤维制	17.5	130		16	17	件/千克		-Of man-made fibres
6206 4000.11	化学纤维制女成人及女童衬衫(含羊毛或动物细毛36%及以上，成人及7～16号女童衬衫)	17.5	130		16	17	件/千克	A	Women's shirts and girls', size 7-16, of man-made fibres,containing 36% or more by weight of wool or fine animal hair
6206 4000.19	化学纤维制女成人及女童衬衫(含羊毛或动物细毛36%及以上)	17.5	130		16	17	件/千克	A	Other women's or girls' shirts of man-made fibres, containing 36% or more by weight of wool or fine animal hair
6206 4000.20	化纤制女成人及7～16号女童衬衫	17.5	130		16	17	件/千克	A	Women's shirts and girls', size 7-16, of man-made fibres
6206 4000.30	化学纤维制女童游戏套装衫	17.5	130		16	17	件/千克	A	Girls' shirts and playsuit, of man-made fibres
6206 4000.90	其他化学纤维制女式衬衫	17.5	130		16	17	件/千克	A	Other women's or girls' shirts of man-made fibres
6206.9000	-其他纺织材料制	16	100		16	17	件/千克		-Of other textile materials
6206 9000.10	其他纺织材料制女式衬衫(棉限内)	16	100		16	17	件/千克	A	Women's or girls' shirts of other textile materials, cotton limit in

税则号列 Tariff Item	商品名称及备注	进口税率 最惠	普通	暂定	出口退税	增值税率	计量单位	监管条件	Article Description
6206 9000.20	其他纺织材料制女式衬衫(羊毛限内)	16	100		16	17	件/千克	A	Women's or girls' shirts of other textile materials, wool limit in
6206 9000.30	其他纺织材料制女式衬衫(化纤限内)	16	100		16	17	件/千克	A	Women's or girls' shirts of other textile materials, man-made fibres limit in
6206 9000.91	其他纺织材料制女成人及女童衬衫(女童衬衫指7~16号)	16	100		16	17	件/千克	A	Women's shirts and girls', of other textile materials, including girls' size 7-16
6206 9000.99	其他纺织材料制女成人及女童衬衫	16	100		16	17	件/千克	A	Other women's or girls' shirts of other textile materials
62.07	**男式背心及其他内衣、内裤、三角裤、长睡衣、睡衣裤、浴衣、晨衣及类似品:**								**Men's or boys' singlets and other vests, underpants, briefs, nightshirts, pyjamas, bathrobes, dressing gowns and similar articles:**
	-内裤及三角裤:								-Underpants and briefs:
6207.1100	--棉制	14	90		16	17	件/千克	A	--Of cotton
	--其他纺织材料制:								--Of other textile materials:
6207.1910	---丝及绢丝制	14	130		16	17	件/千克		---Of silk or silk waste
6207 1910.10	含丝70%及以上男式内裤及三角裤	14	130		16	17	件/千克	A	Men's or boys' underpants and briefs, containing 70% or more by weight of silk
6207 1910.90	含丝70%以下男式内裤及三角裤	14	130		16	17	件/千克	A	Men's or boys' underpants and briefs, containing less than 70% by weight of silk
6207.1920	---化学纤维制	16	130		16	17	件/千克	A	---Of man-made fibres
6207.1990	---其他	14	100		16	17	件/千克		---Other
6207 1990.10	毛制男式内裤及三角裤	14	100		16	17	件/千克	A	Men's or boys' underpants and briefs of wool or fine animal hair
6207 1990.90	其他材料制男式内裤及三角裤	14	100		16	17	件/千克	A	Men's or boys' underpants and briefs of other textile materials
	-长睡衣及睡衣裤:								-Nightshirts and pyjamas:
6207.2100	--棉制	14	90		16	17	件/千克	A	--Of cotton
6207.2200	--化学纤维制	16	130		16	17	件/千克	A	--Of man-made fibres
	--其他纺织材料制:								--Of other textile materials:
6207.2910	---丝及绢丝制	14	130		16	17	件/千克		---Of silk or silk waste
6207 2910.11	含丝70%及以上男式长睡衣/睡衣裤(含8~18号男童长睡衣/睡衣裤)	14	130		16	17	件/千克	A	Men's or boys' nightshirts and pyjamas, containing 70% or more by weight of silk, including boys', size 8-18
6207 2910.19	含丝70%以下男式长睡衣/睡衣裤(含8~18号男童长睡衣/睡衣裤)	14	130		16	17	件/千克	A	Men's or boys' nightshirts and pyjamas, containing less than 70% by weight of silk, including boys' size 8-18
6207 2910.91	其他含丝≥70%男童长睡衣/睡衣裤	14	130		16	17	件/千克	A	Other boys' nightshirts and pyjamas, containing 70% or more by weight of silk
6207 2910.99	其他含丝<70%男童长睡衣/睡衣裤	14	130		16	17	件/千克	A	Other boys' nightshirts and pyjamas, containing less than 70% by weight of silk
6207.2990	---其他	14	100		16	17	件/千克		---Other
6207 2990.10	毛制男式长睡衣及睡衣裤	14	100		16	17	件/千克	A	Men's or boys' nightshirts and pyjamas, of wool or fine animal hair
6207 2990.91	其他材料制男式长睡衣及睡衣裤(含8~18号男童长睡衣及睡衣裤)	14	100		16	17	件/千克	A	Men's or boys' nightshirts and pyjamas, of other textile materials, including boys' size 8-18
6207 2990.99	其他材料制男童长睡衣及睡衣裤	14	100		16	17	件/千克	A	Boys' nightshirts and pyjamas of other textile materials
	-其他:								-Other:
6207.9100	--棉制	14	90		16	17	件/千克		--Of cotton
6207 9100.11	棉制男式内衣式背心	14	90		16	17	件/千克	A	Men's or boys' vest-type singlets of cotton
6207 9100.12	棉制男式非内衣式背心(男成人及8~18号男童背心)	14	90		16	17	件/千克	A	Men's and boys', singlets of cotton, including boys' size 8-18
6207 9100.19	棉制其他男童非内衣式背心	14	90		16	17	件/千克	A	Other boy's non-vest type singlets of cotton
6207 9100.91	棉制男式浴衣、晨衣及类似品	14	90		16	17	件/千克	A	Men's or boys' bathrobes, dressing gowns and similar articles, of cotton

税则号列 Tariff Item	商品名称及备注	进口税率 最惠	普通	暂定	出口退税	增值税率	计量单位	监管条件	Article Description
6207 9100.92	棉制男式睡衣、睡裤(男成人及8~18号男童背心)	14	90		16	17	件/千克	A	Men's or boys' nightshirts and pyjamas of cotton, Including men's or boy's singlets, boy's size 8-18
6207 9100.99	棉制男式其他内衣(男成人及8~18号男童背心)	14	90		16	17	件/千克	A	Other men's or boys' vests of cotton, including men's and boys' singlets, boys' size 8-18
	--其他纺织材料制:								--Of other textile materials:
6207.9910	---丝及绢丝制	14	130		16	17	件/千克		---Of silk or silk waste
6207 9910.11	丝制男式内衣式背心(含丝70%及以上)	14	130		16	17	件/千克	A	Men's or boys' vest-type singlets of silk, containing 70% or more by weight of silk
6207 9910.19	丝制其他男式内衣式背心	14	130		16	17	件/千克	A	Other men's or boys' vest-type singlets of silk
6207 9910.21	丝制男式非内衣式背心(含丝70%及以上)	14	130		16	17	件/千克	A	Men's or boys' non-vest-type singlets of silk, containing 70% or more by weight of silk
6207 9910.29	丝制其他男式非内衣式背心	14	130		16	17	件/千克	A	Other men's or boys' non-vest-type singlets of silk
6207 9910.91	丝制男睡衣、浴衣、晨衣及类似品(含丝70%及以上)	14	130		16	17	件/千克	A	Men's or boys' bathrobes, dressing gowns and similar articles, containing 70% or more of silk
6207 9910.99	丝制其他男睡衣、浴衣、晨衣(含类似品)	14	130		16	17	件/千克	A	Other men's or boys' pyjamas, bathrobes, dressing gowns and similar articles, of silk
6207.9920	---化学纤维制	16	130		16	17	件/千克		---Of man-made fibres
6207 9920.11	化学纤维制男式内衣式背心	16	130		16	17	件/千克	A	Men's or boys' vest-type singlets, of man-made fibres
6207 9920.12	化学纤维制男式非内衣式背心(男成人及8~18号男童背心)	16	130		16	17	件/千克	A	Men's or boys' non-vests type singlets, of man-made fibres, including men's and boys' singlets, boys' size 8-18
6207 9920.19	化学纤维制其他男式非内衣式背心	16	130		16	17	件/千克	A	Other men's or boys' non-vests type singlets, of man-made fibres
6207 9920.21	化纤制男式浴衣、晨衣(含羊毛或动物细毛36%及以上,含类似品)	16	130		16	17	件/千克	A	Men's or boys' bathrobes, dressing gowns and similar articles, of man-made fibres, containing 36% or more by weight of wool or fine animal hair
6207 9920.29	其他化纤制男浴衣、晨衣(含类似品)	16	130		16	17	件/千克	A	Other men's or boys' bathrobes, dressing gowns and similar articles, of man-made fibres
6207 9920.91	化纤制男睡衣、睡裤(含类似品)	16	130		16	17	件/千克	A	Men's or boys' nightshirts, pyjamas and similar articles, of man-made fibres
6207 9920.99	化纤制男式其他内衣(含类似品)	16	130		16	17	件/千克	A	Other men's or boys' vest and similar articles, of man-made fibres
6207.9990	---其他	14	100		16	17	件/千克		---Other
6207 9990.11	毛制男式内衣式背心	14	100		16	17	件/千克	A	Men's or boys' vest-type singlets, of wool or fine animal hair
6207 9990.12	毛制男式非内衣式背心(男成人及8~18号男童背心)	14	100		16	17	件/千克	A	Men's or boys' non-vest type singlets,of wool or fine animal hair, including boys'size 8-18
6207 9990.13	毛制其他男式非内衣式背心	14	100		16	17	件/千克	A	Other men's or boys' non-vest type singlets of wool or fine animal hair
6207 9990.19	毛制男睡衣、浴衣、晨衣及类似品	14	100		16	17	件/千克	A	Men's or boys' bathrobes, dressing gowns and similar articles, of wool or fine animal hair
6207 9990.91	其他材料制男式内衣式背心	14	100		16	17	件/千克	A	Men's or boys' vest type singlets, of other textile materials
6207 9990.92	其他材料制男式非内衣式背心	14	100		16	17	件/千克	A	Men's or boys' non-vest type singlets, of other textile materials
6207 9990.99	其他材料制男睡衣、浴衣、晨衣(含类似品)	14	100		16	17	件/千克	A	Other men's or boys' bathrobes, dressing gowns and similar articles, of other textile materials
62.08	**女式背心及其他内衣、长衬裙、衬裙、三角裤、短衬裤、睡衣、睡衣裤、浴衣、晨衣及类似品:**								**Women's or girls' singlets and other vests, slips, petticoats, briefs, panties, nightdresses, pyjamas, nègligès, bathrobes, dressing gowns and similar articles:**
	-长衬裙及衬裙:								-Slips and petticoats:
6208.1100	--化学纤维制	16	130		16	17	件/千克		--Of man-made fibres
	--其他纺织材料制:								--Of other textile materials:
6208.1910	---丝及绢丝制	14	130		16	17	件/千克		---Of silk or silk waste
6208 1910.11	丝制女式长衬裙及衬裙(含7~16号女童长衬裙及衬裙,含丝70%及以上)	14	130		16	17	件/千克		Women's slips and petticoats of silk, including girls', size 7-16, containing 70% or more by weight of silk

税则号列 Tariff Item	商品名称及备注	进口税率 最惠	普通	暂定	出口退税	增值税率	计量单位	监管条件	Article Description
6208 1910.19	丝制其他女式长衬裙及衬裙(含7~16号女童长衬裙及衬裙，含丝70%以下)	14	130		16	17	件/千克		Other women'sslips and petticoats of silk, including girls', size 7-16, containing less than 70% by weight of silk
6208 1910.91	丝制女童长衬裙及衬裙(含丝70%及以上)	14	130		16	17	件/千克		Girls' slips and petticoats of silk, containing 70% or more by weight of silk
6208 1910.99	丝制其他女童长衬裙及衬裙(含丝70%以下)	14	130		16	17	件/千克		Girls' slips and petticoats of silk, containing less than 70% by weight of silk
6208.1920	---棉制	14	90		16	17	件/千克		---Of cotton
6208.1990	---其他	14	100		16	17	件/千克		---Other
6208 1990.10	毛制女式长衬裙及衬裙	14	100		16	17	件/千克		Women's or girls' slips and petticoats of wool
6208 1990.90	其他材料制女式长衬裙及衬裙	14	100		16	17	件/千克		Women's or girls' slips and petticoats of other textile materials
	-睡衣及睡衣裤:								-Nightdresses and pyjamas:
6208.2100	--棉制	14	90		16	17	件/千克	A	--Of cotton
6208.2200	--化学纤维制	16	130		16	17	件/千克	A	--Of man-made fibres
	--其他纺织材料制:								--Of other textile materials:
6208.2910	---丝及绢丝制	14	130		16	17	件/千克		---Of silk or silk waste
6208 2910.10	丝及绢丝≥70%女式睡衣及睡衣裤	14	130		16	17	件/千克	A	Women's or girls' nightdresses and pyjamas, containing 70% or more of silk or silk waste
6208 2910.90	丝及绢丝<70%女式睡衣及睡衣裤	14	130		16	17	件/千克	A	Women's or girls' nightdresses and pyjamas, containing less than 70% of silk or silk waste
6208.2990	---其他	14	100		16	17	件/千克		---Other
6208 2990.10	毛制女式睡衣及睡衣裤	14	100		16	17	件/千克	A	Women's or girls' nightdresses and pyjamas, of wool or fine animal hair
6208 2990.90	其他材料制女式睡衣及睡衣裤	14	100		16	17	件/千克	A	Women's or girls' nightdresses and pyjamas of other textile materials
	-其他:								-Other:
6208.9100	--棉制	14	90		16	17	件/千克		--Of cotton
6208 9100.10	棉制女式内衣式背心、三角裤等(包括短衬裤)	14	90		16	17	件/千克	A	Women's or girls' vest-type singlets, briefs, of cotton, including panties
6208 9100.21	棉制女式非内衣式背心(女成人及7~16号女童背心)	14	90		16	17	件/千克	A	Women's or girls' non-vest-type singlets of cotton, including girls', size 7-16)
6208 9100.29	棉制其他女式非内衣式背心	14	90		16	17	件/千克	A	Other women's or girls' non-vest-type singlets of cotton
6208 9100.90	棉制女式浴衣、晨衣及类似品	14	90		16	17	件/千克	A	Women's or girls' bathrobes, dressing gowns and similar articles, of cotton
6208.9200	--化学纤维制	16	130		16	17	件/千克		--Of man-made fibres
6208 9200.10	化纤制女式内衣式背心、三角裤(含短衬裤)	16	130		16	17	件/千克	A	Women's or girls' vest-type singlets briefs of man-made fibres, including panties
6208 9200.21	化纤制女式非内衣式背心(女成人及7~16号女童背心)	16	130		16	17	件/千克	A	Women's or girls' non vest-type singlets of man-made fibres,including girls', size 7-16)
6208 9200.29	化纤制其他女式非内衣式背心	16	130		16	17	件/千克	A	Other women's or girls' non vest-type singlets of man-made fibres
6208 9200.90	化纤制女式浴衣、晨衣及类似品	16	130		16	17	件/千克	A	Women's or girls' bathrobes of man-made fibres, including dressing gowns and similar articles
	--其他纺织材料制:								--Of other textile materials:
6208.9910	---丝及绢丝制	14	130		16	17	件/千克		---Of silk or silk waste
6208 9910.11	丝制女内衣式背心、三角裤等(含丝及绢丝≥70%，包括短衬裤)	14	130		16	17	件/千克	A	Women's or girls' vest-type singlets and briefs, containing 70% or more of silk or silk waste, including panties
6208 9910.19	丝制女内衣式背心、三角裤等(含丝及绢丝<70%，包括短衬裤)	14	130		16	17	件/千克	A	Women's or girls' singlets, briefs, panties, of silk, vest style, containing less than 70% by weight of silk or silk waste
6208 9910.21	丝制女式非内衣式背心(含丝及绢丝70%及以上)	14	130		16	17	件/千克	A	Women's or girls' non vest-type singlets of silk, containing 70% or more of silk or silk waste
6208 9910.29	丝制女式非内衣式背心(含丝70%以下)	14	130		16	17	件/千克	A	Women's or girls' non vest type singlets of silk, containing less than 70% by weight of silk

税则号列 Tariff Item	商品名称及备注	进口税率 最惠	普通	暂定	出口退税	增值税率	计量单位	监管条件	Article Description
6208 9910.91	丝制女式浴衣、晨衣及类似品（含丝及绢丝 70%及以上）	14	130		16	17	件/千克	A	Women's or girls' bathrobes, dressing gowns and similar articles, containing 70% or more by weight of silk or silk waste
6208 9910.99	丝制女式浴衣、晨衣及类似品（含丝及绢丝 70%以下）	14	130		16	17	件/千克	A	Women's or girls' bathrobes, dressing gowns and similar articles, containing less than 70% by weight of silk or silk waste
6208.9990	---其他	14	100		16	17	件/千克		---Other
6208 9990.11	毛制女式内衣式背心、三角裤等(包括短衬裤)	14	100		16	17	件/千克	A	Women's or girls' vest-type singlets and briefs, of wool or fine animal hair, including panties
6208 9990.12	毛制女式非内衣式背心(女成人及 7～16 号女童背心)	14	100		16	17	件/千克	A	Women's non-vest type singlets of wool or fine animal hair including girls' size 7-16
6208 9990.13	毛制其他女式非内衣式背心	14	100		16	17	件/千克	A	Other women's or girls' non-vest type singlets, of wool or fine animal hair
6208 9990.19	毛制女式浴衣、晨衣及类似品	14	100		16	17	件/千克	A	Women's or girls' bathrobes, dressing gowns and similar articles, of wool or fine animal hair
6208 9990.90	其他材料制女式背心、三角裤、短衬裤、浴衣、晨衣及类似品	14	100		16	17	件/千克	A	Women's or girls' vest type singlets, of other textile materials bathrobes, dressing gowns and similar articles
62.09	**婴儿服装及衣着附件：**								**Babies' garments and clothing accessories:**
6209.2000	棉制	14	90		16	17	千克	A	Of cotton
6209.3000	-合成纤维制	16	130		16	17	千克		-Of synthetic fibres
6209 3000.10	合成纤维制婴儿手套、袜子(含分指、连指及露指手套，长袜，短袜及其他袜)	16	130		16	17	千克	A	Babies' gloves and stockings of synthetic fibres, including mittens, mitts, socks and similar articles
6209 3000.20	合成纤维婴儿外衣、雨衣、滑雪装（包括夹克类似服装）	16	130		16	17	千克	A	Babies' coats, raincoats and ski-suits of synthetic fibres（including jackets and similar articles）
6209 3000.30	合成纤维制婴儿其他服装(含裤子、衬衫、裙子、睡衣、内衣等)	16	130		16	17	千克	A	Babies' other garments of synthetic fibres (including trousers, shirt, skirt, pyjamas, underwear）
6209 3000.90	合成纤维制婴儿衣着附件	16	130		16	17	千克	A	Babies' clothing accessories, of synthetic fibres
	-其他纺织材料制:								-Of other textile materials:
6209.9010	---羊毛或动物细毛制	14	130		16	17	千克	A	---Of wool or fine animal hair
6209.9090	---其他纺织材料制	14	100		16	17	千克	A	---Of other textile materials
62.10	**用品目 56.02、56.03、59.03、59.06 或 59.07 的织物制成的服装：**								**Garments, made up of fabrics of heading No.56.02, 56.03, 59.03, 59.06 or 59. 07:**
	-用税号 56.02 或 56.03 的织物制成的服装								-Of fabrics of heading No.56.02 or 56.03:
6210.1010	---羊毛或动物细毛制	16	130		16	17	件/千克		---Of wool or fine animal hair
6210 1010.10	毛制纸衬背或覆盖的无纺布服装(羊毛或动物细毛制，包括毡呢或无纺织物制服装)	16	130		16	17	件/千克		Garments, made up of nonwovens or felt fabrics, paper backed or covered, of wool or fine animal hair
6210 1010.20	毛制一次性或医疗用无纺织物服装（羊毛或动物细毛制）	16	130		16	17	件/千克		Garments, made up of nonwovens fabrics, one-off or for medical use, of wool or fine animal hair
6210 1010.90	毛制其他毡呢或无纺织物服装（羊毛或动物细毛制）	16	130		16	17	件/千克		Garments, made up of other nonwovens or felt fabrics, of wool or fine animal hair
6210.1020	---棉或麻制	16	90		16	17	件/千克		---Of cotton or bast fibres
6210 1020.10	棉或麻制纸衬或覆盖的无纺布服装(包括毡呢或无纺织物制服装)	16	90		16	17	件/千克		Garments, made up of nonwovens or felt fabrics, paper backed or covered, of cotton or bast fibres
6210 1020.20	棉或麻一次性或医用无纺织物服装	16	90		16	17	件/千克		Garments, made up of nonwovens fabrics, one-off or for medical use, of cotton or bast fibres
6210 1020.90	棉或麻制其他毡呢或无纺织物服装	16	90		16	17	件/千克		Other garments, made up of other nonwovens or felt fabrics, of cotton or bast fibres
6210.1030	---化学纤维制	17.5	130		16	17	件/千克		---Of man-made fibres
6210 1030.10	化纤制纸衬背或覆盖的无纺布服装(包括毡呢或无纺织物制服装)	17.5	130		16	17	件/千克		Garments, made up of other nonwovens or felt fabrics, paper backed or covered, of man-made fibres

税则号列 Tariff Item	商品名称及备注	进口税率 最惠	普通	暂定	出口退税	增值税率	计量单位	监管条件	Article Description
6210 1030.20	化纤制一次性或医用无纺织物服装	17.5	130		16	17	件/千克		Garments, made up of nonwovens fabrics, one-off or for medical use, of man-made fibres
6210 1030.90	化纤制其他毡呢或无纺织物服装	17.5	130		16	17	件/千克		Other garments, made up of nonwovens or felt fabrics, of man-made fibres
6210.1090	---其他纺织材料制	16	100		16	17	件/千克		---Of other textile materials
6210 1090.10	其他纺织材料制纸衬背的无纺服装(包括纸覆盖的毡呢或无纺织物制服装)	16	100		16	17	件/千克		Garments, made up of nonwovens or felt fabrics , paper backed or covered, of other textile materials
6210 1090.20	其他材料制一次性或医用无纺服装	16	100		16	17	件/千克		Garments, made up of nonwovens fabrics,one-off or for medical use, of other textile materials
6210 1090.90	其他纺织材料制其他无纺织物服装(包括毡呢制服装)	16	100		16	17	件/千克		Garments, made up of other f nonwovens or felt fabrics, of other textile materials
6210.2000	-子目号 6201.11 至 6201.19 所列类型的其他服装	16	100		16	17	件/千克		-Other garments, of the type described in subheadings 6201.11 to 6201.19
6210 2000.11	用塑料或橡胶处理化纤制男外装(织物外表面由塑料或橡胶完全覆盖的大衣、雨衣、斗篷等)	16	100		16	17	件/千克		Men's or boys' garments of man-made fibres, treated with plastic or rubber; outer surface of fabrics of overcoats, rain-coats, clokes, etc. is completely covered with plastics or rubber
6210 2000.19	其他用塑料或橡胶处理化纤制男外装(含用其他材料处理的织物制大衣、雨衣、斗篷等)	16	100		16	17	件/千克		Other men's or boys' garments of man-made fibres, treated with plastic or rubber; overcoats, raincoats, clokes, of textile fabrics, treated with other materials
6210 2000.21	用塑料或橡胶处理的羊毛制男外装(织物外表面由塑料或橡胶完全覆盖的大衣、雨衣、斗篷等)	16	100		16	17	件/千克		Men's or boys' garments of wool, treated with plastic or rubber; outer surface of fabrics of overcoats, raincoats, clokes, etc. is completely covered with plastics or rubber
6210 2000.29	用塑料或橡胶处理的羊毛制男外装(含用其他材料处理的织物制大衣、雨衣、斗篷等)	16	100		16	17	件/千克		Men's or boys' garments of wool, treated with plastic or rubber; overcoats, raincoats, clokes, etc. of textile fabrics, treated with other materials
6210 2000.31	用塑料或橡胶处理的棉制男外装(织物外表面由塑料或橡胶完全覆盖的大衣、雨衣、斗篷等)	16	100		16	17	件/千克		Men's or boys' garments of cotton, treated with plastic or rubber; outer surface of fabrics of overcoats, raincoats, clokes, etc. is completely covered with plastics or rubber
6210 2000.39	其他用塑料或橡胶等处理棉制男外装(含用其他材料处理的织物制大衣、雨衣、斗篷等)	16	100		16	17	件/千克		Other men's or boys' garments of cotton, treated with plastic or rubber; overcoats,raincoats, clokes, of textile fabrics, treated with other materials
6210 2000.40	用塑料或橡胶处理的其他纺材男外装(织物外表面由塑料或橡胶完全覆盖的大衣、雨衣、斗篷等)	16	100		16	17	件/千克		Men's or boys' garments of other textile materials, treated with plastic or rubber ; outer surface of fabrics of overcoats, raincoats, clokes, etc. is completely covered with plastics or rubber
6210 2000.91	用塑料或橡胶等处理的亚麻制男外装(含用其他材料处理的织物制大衣、雨衣、斗篷等)	16	100		16	17	件/千克		Men's or boys' garments of flax, treated with plastic or rubber; overcoats, raincoats, clokes, etc. of textile fabrics, treated with other materials
6210 2000.99	用塑料等处理的其他纺材制男外装(含用橡胶及其他材料处理的织物制大衣、雨衣、斗篷等)	16	100		16	17	件/千克		Other men's or boys' garments of other textile materials, treated with plastic; overcoats, raincoats, clokes, etc. of textile fabrics, treated with rubber or other materials
6210.3000	-子目号 6202.11 至 6202.19 所列类型的其他服装	16	100		16	17	件/千克		-Other garments, of the type described in subheadings 6202.11 to 6202.19
6210 3000.11	用塑料或橡胶处理化纤制女外装(织物外表面由塑料或橡胶完全覆盖的大衣、雨衣、斗篷等)	16	100		16	17	件/千克		Women's or girls' garments of man-made fibres, treated with plastic or rubber; outer surface of fabrics of overcoats, raincoats, clokes, etc. is completely covered with plastics or rubber
6210 3000.19	其他用塑料或橡胶处理化纤制女外装(含用其他材料处理的织物制大衣、雨衣、斗篷等)	16	100		16	17	件/千克		Other women's or girls' garments of man-made fibres, treated with plastic or rubber; overcoats, raincoats, clokes, etc. of textile fabrics, treated with other materials

税则号列 Tariff Item	商品名称及备注	进口税率 最惠	普通	暂定	出口退税	增值税率	计量单位	监管条件	Article Description
6210 3000.21	用塑料或橡胶处理的羊毛制女外装(织物外表面由塑料或橡胶完全覆盖的大衣、雨衣、斗篷等)	16	100		16	17	件/千克		Women's or girls' outer garments of wool, treated with plastic or rubber ; outer surface of fabrics of overcoats, raincoats, clokes, etc. is completely covered with plastics or rubber
6210 3000.29	用塑料或橡胶处理的羊毛制女外装（含用其他材料处理的织物制大衣、雨衣、斗篷等）	16	100		16	17	件/千克		Women's or girls' garments of wool, treated with plastic or rubber; overcoats, raincoats, clokes of textile fabrics, treated with other materials
6210 3000.31	用塑料或橡胶处理的棉制女外装(织物外表面由塑料或橡胶完全覆盖的大衣、雨衣、斗篷等)	16	100		16	17	件/千克		Women's or girls' garments of cotton, treated with plastic or rubber ; outer surface of fabrics of overcoats, raincoats, clokes, etc. completely covered with plastics or rubber
6210 3000.39	其他用塑料或橡胶等处理棉制女外装（含用其他材料处理的织物制大衣、雨衣、斗篷等）	16	100		16	17	件/千克		Other women's or girls' garments of cotton, treated with plastic or rubber; overcoats, raincoats, clokes, etc. of textile fabrics, treated with other materials
6210 3000.40	用塑料或橡胶处理的其他纺材制女外装(织物外表面由塑料或橡胶完全覆盖的大衣、雨衣、斗篷等)	16	100		16	17	件/千克		Women's or girls' garments of other textile materials, treated with plastic or rubber; outer surface of fabrics of overcoats, raincoats, clokes, etc. is ompletely covered with plastics or rubber
6210 3000.91	用塑料或橡胶等处理的亚麻制女外装(含用其他材料处理的织物制大衣、雨衣、斗篷等)	16	100		16	17	件/千克		Women's or girls' garments of flax, treated with plastic or rubber; overcoats, raincoats, clokes of textile fabrics, treated with other materials
6210 3000.99	用塑料等处理的其他纺材制女外装(含用橡胶及其他材料处理的织物制大衣、雨衣、斗篷等)	16	100		16	17	件/千克		Women's or girls' garments of other textile materials, treated with plastic; overcoats, raincoats, clokes, etc. of textile fabrics,treated with rubber or other materials
6210.4000	-其他男式服装	16	100		16	17	件/千克		-Other men's or boys' garments
6210 4000.11	用塑料或橡胶处理化纤制其他男式服装(织物外表面由塑料或橡胶完全覆盖)	16	100		16	17	件/千克		Men's or boys' garments of man-made fibre, treated with plastic or rubber; outer surface of fabrics is completely covered with plastic or rubber
6210 4000.12	用塑料等处理的化纤制男防风衣(含用橡胶及其他材料处理织物制带风帽防寒短上衣、风衣)	16	100		16	17	件/千克		Men's or boys' wind-cheaters of man-made fibres, treated with plastic; anoraks, wind-jackets, of textile fabrics, treated with rubber or other materials
6210 4000.13	用塑料等处理的化纤制男式长、短裤（滑雪裤除外）	16	100		16	17	件/千克		Men's or boys' trousers and shorts of man-made fibres, treated with plastic (other than ski trousers)
6210 4000.19	用塑料等处理的化纤制其他男式服装(含用橡胶及其他材料处理的织物)	16	100		16	17	件/千克		Other men's or boys' garments of man-made fibres, treated with plastic, including fabrics treated with rubber or other materials
6210 4000.21	用塑料或橡胶处理的毛制其他男外装（织物外表面由塑料或橡胶完全覆盖，羊毛或动物细毛制）	16	100		16	17	件/千克		Other men's or boys' garments of wool or fine animal hair, treated with plastic or rubber; outer surface of fabrics completely covered with plastic or rubber
6210 4000.22	用塑料等处理的毛制男式防风衣(含用橡胶及其他材料处理的织物制带风帽防寒短上衣、风衣)	16	100		16	17	件/千克		Men's or boys' wind-cheaters, of wool or fine animal hair, treated with plastic or rubber;anoraks, wind-jackets, of fabrics, treated with plastic or rubber or other materials
6210 4000.23	用塑料等处理的毛制男式长、短裤(含用橡胶及其他材料处理的毛制男式长、短裤)	16	100		16	17	件/千克		Men's or boys' trousers and shorts, of wool or fine animal hair, treated with plastic or rubber or other materials
6210 4000.29	用塑料等处理的其他男式服装（用橡胶及其他材料处理的织物）	16	100		16	17	件/千克		Other men's or boys' garments, treated with plastic or other materials (fabrics treated with rubber and other materials)
6210 4000.31	用塑料或橡胶处理的棉制其他男外装(织物外表面由塑料或橡胶完全覆盖)	16	100		16	17	件/千克		Men's or boys' garments of cotton, treated with plastic or rubber; outer surface of fabrics is completely covered with plastic or rubber
6210 4000.32	用塑料等处理的棉制男式防风衣(含用橡胶及其他材料处理织物制带风帽防寒短上衣、风衣)	16	100		16	17	件/千克		Men's or boys' wind-cheaters, of cotton treated with plastic; anoraks,wind-jackets, of fabrics, treated with rubber or other materials
6210 4000.33	用塑料等处理的棉制男式长、短	16	100		16	17	件/千克		Men's or boys' trousers and shorts, of cotton treated

税则号列 Tariff Item	商品名称及备注	进口税率 最惠	普通	暂定	出口退税	增值税率	计量单位	监管条件	Article Description
	裤(含用橡胶及其他材料处理的棉制男式长、短裤)								with plastic or rubber or other materials
6210 4000.39	用塑料等处理的棉制其他男式服装(含用橡胶及其他材料处理的织物)	16	100		16	17	件/千克		Other men's or boys' garments of cotton, treated with plastic or rubber or other materials
6210 4000.40	用塑料或橡胶处理其他纺材其他男装	16	100		16	17	件/千克		Other men's or boys' garments of other textile materials
6210 4000.91	用塑料等处理的丝制其他男式服装(含用橡胶及其他材料处理的织物，含丝及绢丝70%及以上)	16	100		16	17	件/千克		Other men's or boys' garments of silk, treated with plastic, containing the fabrics treated with rubber or other textile materials, containing 70% or more of silk or silk waste
6210 4000.92	用塑料等处理其他纺材制男防风衣(含用橡胶及其他材料处理织物制带风帽防寒短上衣、风衣)	16	100		16	17	件/千克		Men's or boys' wind-cheaters, of other textile materials, treated with plastic; including anoraks,wind-cheaters of fabrics, treated with rubber or other materials
6210 4000.93	用塑料等处理其他纺材制男长、短裤(含用橡胶及其他材料处理的其他纺材制男长、短裤)	16	100		16	17	件/千克		Men's or boys' trousers and shorts, of other textile materials, treated with rubber or other materials
6210 4000.99	用塑料等处理的其他纺材制男服装(含用橡胶及其他材料处理的织物)	16	100		16	17	件/千克		Other men's or boys' garments, of other textile materials, treated with plastic, rubber or other materials
6210.5000	-其他女式服装	16	100		16	17	件/千克		-Other women's or girls' garments
6210 5000.11	用塑料或橡胶处理化纤制其他女装(织物外表面由塑料或橡胶完全覆盖)	16	100		16	17	件/千克		Women's or girls' garments of man-made fibres, treated with plastic or rubber; outer surface of fabrics is completely covered with plastic or rubber
6210 5000.12	用塑料等处理的化纤制女防风衣(含用橡胶及其他材料处理织物制带风帽防寒短上衣、风衣)	16	100		16	17	件/千克		Women's or girls' wind-cheaters, of man-made fibres, treated with plastic; including anoraks and wind-cheaters of fabrics, treated with rubber or other materials
6210 5000.13	用塑料等处理的化纤制女式长、短裤(滑雪裤除外)	16	100		16	17	件/千克		Women's or girls' trousers and shorts of man-made fibres, treated with plastic, other than ski trousers
6210 5000.19	用塑料等处理的化纤制其他女服装(含用橡胶及其他材料处理的织物)	16	100		16	17	件/千克		Other women's or girls' garments of man-made fibres, treated with plastic, rubber or other materials
6210 5000.21	用塑料或橡胶处理的毛制其他女外装(织物外表面由塑料或橡胶完全覆盖，羊毛或动物细毛制)	16	100		16	17	件/千克		Other women's or girls' garments of wool or fine animal hair, treated with plastic or rubber; outer surface of fabrics is completely covered with plastic or rubber
6210 5000.22	用塑料等处理的毛制女式防风衣(含用橡胶及其他材料处理织物制带风帽防寒短上衣、风衣)	16	100		16	17	件/千克		Women's or girls' wind-cheaters, of wool or fine animal hair, treated with plastic; including anoraks and wind-cheaters of fabrics, treated with rubber or other materials
6210 5000.23	用塑料等处理的毛制女式长、短裤(含用橡胶及其他材料处理的毛制女式长、短裤)	16	100		16	17	件/千克		Women's or girls' trousers and shorts of wool or fine animal hair, treated with plastic, rubber or other materials
6210 5000.29	用塑料等处理的毛制其他女式服装(含用橡胶及其他材料处理的织物)	16	100		16	17	件/千克		Other women's or girls' garments of wool or fine animal hair, treated with plastic, rubber or other materials
6210 5000.31	用塑料或橡胶处理的棉制其他女外装(织物外表面由塑料或橡胶完全覆盖)	16	100		16	17	件/千克		Other women's or girls' garments of cotton, treated with plastic or rubber; outer surface of fabrics is completely covered with plastic or rubber
6210 5000.32	用塑料等处理的棉制女式防风衣(含用橡胶及其他材料处理织物制带风帽防寒短上衣、风衣)	16	100		16	17	件/千克		Women's or girls' wind-cheaters, of cotton, treated with plastic; including anoraks and wind-cheaters of fabrics, treated with rubber or other materials
6210 5000.33	用塑料等处理的棉制女式长、短	16	100		16	17	件/千克		Women's or girls' trousers and shorts of cotton,

税则号列 Tariff Item	商品名称及备注	进口税率 最惠	普通	暂定	出口退税	增值税率	计量单位	监管条件	Article Description
	裤(含用橡胶及其他材料处理的棉制女式长、短裤)								treated with plastic, rubber or other materials
6210 5000.39	用塑料等处理的棉制其他女式服装(含用橡胶及其他材料处理的棉制其他女式服装)	16	100		16	17	件/千克		Other women's or girls' garments of cotton, treated with plastic or rubber or other materials
6210 5000.40	用塑料或橡胶处理其他纺材其他女装(织物外表面由塑料或橡胶完全覆盖)	16	100		16	17	件/千克		Other women's or girls' garments of other textile materials, treated with plastic or rubber; outer surface of fabrics is completely covered with plastic or rubber
6210 5000.91	用塑料等处理的丝制其他女式服装(含用橡胶及其他材料处理的织物,含丝及绢丝70%及以上)	16	100		16	17	件/千克		Other women's or girls' garments of silk,treated with plastic, containing the fabrics treated with rubber or other textile materials, containing 70% or more of silk or silk waste
6210 5000.92	用塑料等处理其他纺材制女防风衣(含用橡胶及其他材料处理织物制带风帽防寒短上衣、风衣)	16	100		16	17	件/千克		Women's or girls' wind-cheaters, of other textile materials, treated with plastic; including anoraks, wind-cheaters of fabrics, treated with rubber or other materials
6210 5000.93	用塑料等处理其他纺材制女长、短裤(含用橡胶及其他材料处理织物制带风帽防寒短上衣、风衣)	16	100		16	17	件/千克		Women's or girls' trousers and shorts, of other textile materials, treated with plastic; including anoraks, wind-cheaters of fabrics, treated with rubber or other materials
6210 5000.99	用塑料等处理的其他纺材制女服装(含用橡胶及其他材料处理的其他纺材制女服装)	16	100		16	17	件/千克		Other women's or girls' garments, of other textile materials, treated with plastic, rubber or other materials
62.11	**运动服、滑雪服及游泳服;其他服装:**								**Track suits, ski suits and swimwear; other garments:**
	-游泳服:								-Swimwear:
6211.1100	--男式	16	130		16	17	件/千克		--Men's or boys'
6211 1100.10	羊毛或动物细毛制男式游泳服	16	130		16	17	件/千克	A	Men's or boys' swimwear, made of wool or fine animal hair
6211 1100.41	丝制男式游泳服(含丝70%及以上)	16	130		16	17	件/千克	A	Men's or boys' swimwear, made of silk, containing 70% or more by weight of silk
6211 1100.49	丝制男式游泳服(含丝70%以下)	16	130		16	17	件/千克	A	Men's or boys' swimwear, made of silk, containing less than 70% by weight of silk
6211 1100.90	其他纺织材料制男式游泳服	16	130		16	17	件/千克	A	Other men's or boys' swimwear, made of other textile materials
6211.1200	--女式	16	130		16	17	件/千克		--Women's or girls'
6211 1200.10	羊毛或动物细毛制女式游泳服	16	130		16	17	件/千克	A	Women's or girls' swimwear, made of wool or fine animal hair
6211 1200.41	丝制女式游泳服(含丝70%及以上)	16	130		16	17	件/千克	A	Women's or girls' swimwear made of silk, containing 70% or more by weight of silk
6211 1200.49	丝制女式游泳服(含丝70%以下)	16	130		16	17	件/千克	A	Women's or girls' swimwear made of silk, containing less than 70% by weight of silk
6211 1200.90	其他纺织材料制女式游泳服	16	130		16	17	件/千克	A	Women's or girls' swimwear of other textile materials
	-滑雪服:								-Ski suits:
6211.2010	---棉制	16	90		16	17	套/千克		---Of cotton
6211.2090	---其他纺织材料制	19	130		16	17	套/千克		---Of other textile materials
6211 2090.11	含滑雪男裤的羊毛制滑雪套装	19	130		16	17	套/千克		Ski suits made of wool, including men's or boys' ski pants
6211 2090.19	不含滑雪男裤的羊毛制滑雪套装	19	130		16	17	套/千克		Ski suits made of wool, excluding men's or boys' ski pants
6211 2090.21	含滑雪短裤或不防水滑雪裤的化纤制滑雪套装	19	130		16	17	套/千克		Ski suits made of man-made fibres (including ski shorts or non water-proof ski pants)
6211 2090.29	化纤制其他滑雪套装	19	130		16	17	套/千克		Other ski suits made of man-made fibres
6211 2090.90	其他纺织材料制滑雪套装	19	130		16	17	套/千克		Ski suits made of other textile materials
	-其他男式服装:								-Other garments, men's or boys':
	--棉制:								--Of cotton:
6211.3210	---阿拉伯袍	16	90		16	17	件/千克		---Arabian robes

税则号列 Tariff Item	商品名称及备注	进口税率			出口退税	增值税率	计量单位	监管条件	Article Description
		最惠	普通	暂定					
6211.3220	---运动服	16	90		16	17	套/千克		---Track suits
6211 3220.11	棉制男式运动套装(面和衬里的面料相同的运动套装)	16	90		16	17	套/千克		Men's or boys' track suits, made of cotton, same fabrics of outer and lining
6211 3220.19	棉制其他男式运动套装	16	90		16	17	套/千克		Other men's or boys' track suits made of cotton
6211.3290	---其他	16	90		16	17	件/千克		---Other
6211 3290.21	棉制男式连衣服及类似品	16	90		16	17	件/千克		Men's or boys' one-piece garment and similar articles, made of cotton
6211 3290.29	棉制男式连衣裤及类似品	16	90		16	17	件/千克		Men's or boys' overalls and similar articles, made of cotton
6211 3290.30	棉制男式水洗服、夏服、游戏装	16	90		16	17	件/千克		Men's or boys' summer wear, wash wear, playsuit, made of cotton
6211 3290.40	棉制男式工业及职业衣着	16	90		16	17	件/千克		Men's or boys' garments of cotton, industrial and occupational use
6211 3290.51	棉制男式TOPS(男成人及8~18号男童TOPS)	16	90		16	17	件/千克		Men's TOPS and boys' TOPS , size8-18, made of cotton
6211 3290.59	棉制其他男式TOPS	16	90		16	17	件/千克		Other men's or boys' TOPS, made of cotton
6211 3290.60	棉制男式风雪套装及类似服装	16	90		16	17	件/千克		Men's or boys' ski suits and similar articles, made of cotton
6211 3290.91	棉制男衬衫(品目62.05的衬衫除外)	16	90		16	17	件/千克		Men's or boys' shirt (other than the shirt of heading No. 62. 05)
6211 3290.99	棉制男式其他服装(含马甲、上衣)	16	90		16	17	件/千克		Other men's or boys' garments, made of cotton including vests and coats
	--化学纤维制:								--Of man-made fibres:
6211.3310	---阿拉伯袍	17.5	130		16	17	件/千克		---Arabian robes
6211.3320	---运动服	18	130		16	17	套/千克		---Track suits
6211 3320.11	化纤制男式运动套装(面和衬里的面料相同的运动套装)	18	130		16	17	套/千克		Men's or boys' track suits of man-made fibres, same fabrics of outer and lining
6211 3320.19	化纤制其他男式运动套装	18	130		16	17	套/千克		Other men's or boys' track suits of man-made fibres
6211.3390	---其他	17.5	130		16	17	件/千克		---Other
6211 3390.21	化纤制男式连衣服及类似品	17.5	130		16	17	件/千克		Men's or boys' one-piece garment and similar arti-cles, made of man-made fibres
6211 3390.29	化纤制男式连衣裤及类似品	17.5	130		16	17	件/千克		Men's or boys' overalls and similar articles, made of man-made fibres
6211 3390.30	化纤制男式水洗服、夏服、游戏装(含类似服)	17.5	130		16	17	件/千克		Men's or boys' summer wear, wash wear, playsuit and similar articles, made of man-made fibres
6211 3390.91	化纤制男式工业及职业衣着	17.5	130		16	17	件/千克		Men's or boys' garments made of man-madefibres, industrial and occupational use
6211 3390.92	化纤制男式TOPS(男成人及8~18号男童TOPS)	17.5	130		16	17	件/千克		Men's TOPS and boys' TOPS size 8-18, made of man-made fibres
6211 3390.93	化纤制其他男式TOPS	17.5	130		16	17	件/千克		Other men's or boys' TOPS, of man-made fibres
6211 3390.94	化纤制男式风雪套装及类似服装	17.5	130		16	17	件/千克		Men's or boys' ski suits and similar articles, made of man-made fibres
6211 3390.95	化纤制男衬衫(品目62.05的衬衫除外)	17.5	130		16	17	件/千克		Men's or boys' shirt made of man-made fibres(other than the shirt of subheading No.62. 05)
6211 3390.99	化纤制男式其他服装(含马甲,上衣)	17.5	130		16	17	件/千克		Other men's or boys' garments made of man-made fibres, including vests, coats
	--其他纺织材料制:								--Of other textile materials:
6211.3910	---丝及绢丝制	16	130		16	17	件/千克		---Of silk or silk waste
6211 3910.11	丝及绢丝制男运动服(含丝70%及以上)	16	130		16	17	件/千克		Men's or boys' track suits, made of silk, containing 70% or more by weight of silk
6211 3910.19	丝及绢丝制男运动服(含丝70%以下)	16	130		16	17	件/千克		Men's or boys' track suits, made of silk, containing less than 70% by weight of silk
6211 3910.21	丝或绢丝制男连衣裤及类似品(含丝70%及以上)	16	130		16	17	件/千克		Men's or boys' overall and similar articles, made of silk or silk waste, containing 70% or more of silk
6211 3910.29	丝或绢丝制男连衣裤及类似品(含丝70%以下)	16	130		16	17	件/千克		Men's or boys' overall and similar articles of silk, containing less than 70% by weight of silk
6211 3910.91	丝或绢丝制男式TOPS(含丝70%及以上)	16	130		16	17	件/千克		Men's or boys' TOPS made of silk or silk waste, containing 70% or more by weight of silk

税则号列 Tariff Item	商品名称及备注	进口税率			出口退税	增值税率	计量单位	监管条件	Article Description
		最惠	普通	暂定					
6211 3910.92	丝或绢丝制男式 TOPS(含丝 70%以下)	16	130		16	17	件/千克		Men's or boys' TOPS made of silk or silk waste, containing less than 70% by weight of silk
6211 3910.93	丝或绢丝制男式风雪套装(含类似服装，含丝 70%及以上)	16	130		16	17	件/千克		Men's or boys' ski suits and similar articles, of silk or silk waste, containing 70% or more of silk
6211 3910.94	丝或绢丝制男式风雪套装(含类似服装，含丝 70%以下)	16	130		16	17	件/千克		Men's or boys' ski suits and similar articles, of silk or silk waste, containing less than 70% of silk
6211 3910.95	丝或绢丝制男式其他服装(含衬衫、马甲、上衣，含丝 70%及以上)	16	130		16	17	件/千克		Other men's or boys' garments, including shirts, vests, coats, of silk or silk waste, containing 70% or more by weight of silk
6211 3910.99	丝或绢丝制男式其他服装(含衬衫、马甲、上衣，含丝 70%以下)	16	130		16	17	件/千克		Other men's or boys' garments, including shirts, vests, coats, of silk or silk waste, containing less than 70% by weight of silk
6211.3920	---羊毛或动物细毛制	16	130		16	17	件/千克		---Of wool or fine animal hair
6211 3920.10	毛制男式运动套装	16	130		16	17	件/千克		Men's or boys' track suits made of wool or fine animal hair
6211 3920.90	毛制男式其他服装	16	130		16	17	件/千克		Other men's or boys' shirts, made of wool or fine animal hair
6211.3990	---其他	16	100		16	17	件/千克		---Other
6211 3990.10	其他纺织材料制男式运动套装	16	100		16	17	件/千克		Men's or boys' track suits made of other textile materials
6211 3990.20	其他纺织材料制男连衣裤(含类似品)	16	100		16	17	件/千克		Men's or boys' overalls and similar articles, made of other textile materials
6211 3990.91	其他纺织材料制男式水洗服、夏服(含游戏装等类似服装)	16	100		16	17	件/千克		Men's or boys' summer wear, wash wear, playsuit and similar articles, made of other textile materials
6211 3990.92	其他纺织材料制男式 TOPS	16	100		16	17	件/千克		Men's or boys' TOPS, of other textile materials
6211 3990.93	其他纺织材料制男式风雪套装(含类似服装)	16	100		16	17	件/千克		Men's or boys' ski suits and similar articles, made of other textile materials
6211 3990.99	其他纺织材料制男式其他服装(含衬衫、马甲、上衣)	16	100		16	17	件/千克		Other men's or boys' garments, including shirts, vests, coats, made of other textile materials
	-其他女式服装:								-Other garments, women's or girls':
	--棉制:								--Of cotton:
6211.4210	---运动服	16	90		16	17	套/千克		---Track suits
6211 4210.10	棉制女式运动套装(面和衬里的面料相同的运动套装)	16	90		16	17	套/千克		Women's or girls' track suits, made of cotton, and same fabrics of outer and lining
6211 4210.90	棉制其他女式运动套装	16	90		16	17	套/千克		Other Women's or girls' track suits, made of cotton
6211.4290	---其他	16	90		16	17	件/千克		---Other
	--化学纤维制:								--Of man-made fibres:
6211.4310	---运动服	17.5	130		16	17	套/千克		---Track suits
6211 4310.10	化纤制女式运动套装(面和衬里的面料相同的运动套装)	17.5	130		16	17	套/千克		Women's or girls' track suits, made of man-made fibres, same fabrics of outer and lining
6211 4310.90	化纤制其他女式运动套装	17.5	130		16	17	套/千克		Other Women's or girls' track suits, made of man-made fibres
6211.4390	---其他	17.5	130		16	17	件/千克		---Other
	--其他纺织材料制:								--Of other textile materials:
6211.4910	---丝及绢丝制	16	130		16	17	件/千克		---Of silk or silk waste
6211 4910.11	丝或绢丝制女式运动套装(含丝 70%及以上)	16	130		16	17	件/千克		Women's or girls' track suits, made of silk or silk waste, containing 70% or more of silk
6211 4910.19	丝或绢丝制女式运动套装(含丝 70%以下)	16	130		16	17	件/千克		Women's or girls' track suits, made of silk or silk waste, containing less than 70% by weight of silk
6211 4910.21	丝或绢丝制女连衣裤及类似品(含丝 70%及以上)	16	130		16	17	件/千克		Women's or girls' overalls and similar articles, of silk or silk waste, containing 70% or more of silk
6211 4910.29	丝或绢丝制女连衣裤及类似品(含丝 70%以下)	16	130		16	17	件/千克		Women's or girls' overalls and similar articles, of silk or silk waste, containing less than 70% of silk
6211 4910.31	丝或绢丝制女式 TOPS(含丝 70%及以上)	16	130		16	17	件/千克		Women's or girls' TOPS, of silk or silk waste, containing 70% or more of silk
6211 4910.39	丝或绢丝制女式 TOPS(含丝 70%以下)	16	130		16	17	件/千克		Women's or girls' TOPS, of silk or silk waste, containing less than 70% of silk
6211 4910.41	丝或绢丝制女式风雪套装(含类似服装，含丝 70%及以上)	16	130		16	17	件/千克		Women's or girls' ski suits and similar articles, of silk or silk waste, containing 70% or more of silk

税则号列 Tariff Item	商品名称及备注	进口税率 最惠	普通	暂定	出口退税	增值税率	计量单位	监管条件	Article Description
6211 4910.49	丝或绢丝制女式风雪套装(含类似服装，含丝70%以下)	16	130		16	17	件/千克		Women's or girls' ski suits and similar articles, of silk or silk waste, containing less than 70% of silk
6211 4910.51	丝及绢丝制女式其他服装(含衬衫、马甲、上衣、无袖罩衫，含丝70%及以上)	16	130		16	17	件/千克		Other women's or girls' garments, made of silk or silk waste, including shirts, vests, coat, cloaks, containing 70% or more by weight of silk
6211 4910.59	丝及绢丝制女式其他服装(含衬衫、马甲、上衣和无袖罩衫，含丝70%以下)	16	130		16	17	件/千克		Other women's or girls' garments,made of silk or silk waste, including shirts, vests, coats, cloaks, containing less than 70% by weight of silk
6211 4910.91	丝及绢丝制女式其他服装(含丝70%及以上)	16	130		16	17	件/千克		Other women's or girls' garments, made of silk or silk waste, containing 70% or more of silk
6211 4910.99	丝及绢丝制女式其他服装(含丝70%以下)	16	130		16	17	件/千克		Other women's or girls' garments, made of silk or silk waste, containing less than 70% of silk
6211.4990	---其他	16	100		16	17	件/千克		---Other
6211 4990.10	其他纺织材料制女式运动套装	16	100		16	17	件/千克		Other women's or girls' track suits, made of other textile materials
6211 4990.20	其他纺织材料制女连衣裤(含类似品)	16	100		16	17	件/千克		Other women's or girls' overalls and similar articles, made of other textile materials
6211 4990.30	其他纺织材料制女式其他服装(含游戏装、类似服)	16	100		16	17	件/千克		Other women's or girls' garments of other textile materials, including playsuit and similar articles
6211 4990.40	其他纺织材料制女式TOPS	16	100		16	17	件/千克		Women's or girls' TOPS, of other textile materials
6211 4990.50	其他纺织材料制女式风雪套装(含类似服装)	16	100		16	17	件/千克		Women's or girls' ski suits and similar articles, made of other textile materials
6211 4990.90	其他纺织材料制女式其他服装(含衬衫、马甲、上衣、无袖罩衫)	16	100		16	17	件/千克		Other women's or girls' garments, made of other textile materials, including shirts, vests, coats, cloaks
62.12	**胸罩、束腰带、紧身胸衣、吊裤带、吊袜带、束袜带和类似品及其零件，不论是否针织或钩编的:**								**Brassières, girdles, corsets, braces, suspenders, garters and similar articles and parts thereof, whether or not knitted or crocheted:**
	-胸罩:								-Brassières:
6212.1010	---化学纤维制	16	130		16	17	件/千克	A	---Of man-made fibres
6212.1090	---其他纺织材料制	14	100		16	17	件/千克		---Of other textile materials
6212 1090.10	毛制其他胸罩(不论是否针织或钩编)	14	100		16	17	件/千克	A	Brassières of wool, whether or not knitted or crocheted
6212 1090.20	棉制其他胸罩(不论是否针织或钩编)	14	100		16	17	件/千克	A	Brassières of cotton, whether or not knitted or crocheted
6212 1090.31	丝制胸罩(不论是否针织或钩编，含丝70%及以上)	14	100		16	17	件/千克	A	Brassières of silk, whether or not knitted or crocheted, containing 70% or more of silk
6212 1090.39	丝制其他胸罩(不论是否针织或钩编，含丝70%以下)	14	100		16	17	件/千克	A	Brassières of silk, whether or not knitted or crocheted, containing less than 70% of silk
6212 1090.90	其他纺织材料制其他胸罩(不论是否针织或钩编)	14	100		16	17	件/千克	A	Brassières of other textile materials, whether or not knitted or crocheted
	-束腰带及腹带:								-Girdles and panty-girdles:
6212.2010	---化学纤维制	16	130		16	17	件/千克	A	---Of man-made fibres
6212.2090	---其他纺织材料制	14	100		16	17	件/千克		---Of other textile materials
6212 2090.10	毛制束胸带及腹带(不论是否针织或钩编)	14	100		16	17	件/千克	A	Girdles and panty-girdles of wool, whether or not knitted or crocheted
6212 2090.20	棉制束腰带及腹带(不论是否针织或钩编)	14	100		16	17	件/千克	A	Girdles and panty-girdles of cotton whether or not knitted or crocheted
6212 2090.31	丝制束腰带及腹带(不论是否针织或钩编，含丝70%及以上)	14	100		16	17	件/千克	A	Girdles and panty-girdles of silk, whether or not knitted or crocheted, containing 70% or more of silk
6212 2090.39	丝制束腰带及腹带(不论是否针织或钩编，含丝70%以下)	14	100		16	17	件/千克	A	Girdles and panty-girdles of silk, whether or not knitted or crocheted, containing less than 70% of silk
6212 2090.90	其他材料制束胸带及腹带(不论是否针织或钩编)	14	100		16	17	件/千克	A	Girdles and panty-girdles of other textile materials, whether or not knitted or crocheted
	-束腰胸衣:								-Corselettes:
6212.3010	---化学纤维制	16	130		16	17	件/千克	A	---Of man-made fibres

税则号列 Tariff Item	商品名称及备注	进口税率 最惠	普通	暂定	出口退税	增值税率	计量单位	监管条件	Article Description
6212.3090	---其他纺织材料制	14	100		16	17	件/千克		---Of other textile materials
6212 3090.10	毛制紧身胸衣(不论是否针织或钩编)	14	100		16	17	件/千克	A	Corselettes of wool, whether or not knitted or crocheted
6212 3090.20	棉制紧身胸衣(不论是否针织或钩编)	14	100		16	17	件/千克	A	Corselettes of cotton, whether or not knitted or crocheted
6212 3090.31	丝制紧身胸衣(不论是否针织或钩编，含丝70%及以上)	14	100		16	17	件/千克	A	Corselettes of silk, whether or not knitted or crocheted, containing 70% or more of silk
6212 3090.39	丝制其他紧身胸衣(不论是否针织或钩编，含丝70%以下)	14	100		16	17	件/千克	A	Corselettes of silk, whether or not knitted or crocheted, containing less than 70% of silk
6212 3090.90	其他材料制紧身胸衣(不论是否针织或钩编)	14	100		16	17	件/千克	A	Corselettes of other textile materials,whether or not knitted or crocheted
	-其他:								-Other:
6212.9010	---化学纤维制	16	130		16	17	件/千克		---Of man-made fibres
6212.9090	---其他纺织材料制	14	100		16	17	件/千克		---Of other textile materials
6212 9090.10	毛制吊裤带、吊袜带、束袜带等(不论是否针织或钩编,含羊毛与橡胶、塑料制的)	14	100		16	17	件/千克		Braces, suspenders and garters, of wool and plastics or rubber, whether or not knitted or crocheted
6212 9090.20	棉制吊裤带、吊袜带、束袜带等(不论是否针织或钩编,含棉与橡胶、塑料制的)	14	100		16	17	件/千克		Braces, suspenders and garters, of cotton and plastics or rubber, whether or not knitted or crocheted
6212 9090.31	丝制吊裤带、吊袜带、束袜带等(不论是否针织或钩编，含丝70%及以上)	14	100		16	17	件/千克		Braces, suspenders and garters, of silk, containing 70% or more of silk, whether or not knitted or crocheted
6212 9090.39	丝制吊裤带、吊袜带、束袜带等(不论是否针织或钩编，含丝70%以下)	14	100		16	17	件/千克		Braces, suspenders and garters, of silk, containing less than 70% of silk, whether or not knitted or crocheted
6212 9090.90	其他材料制吊裤带、吊袜带等(不论是否针织或钩编，包括束袜带和类似品及其零件)	14	100		16	17	件/千克		Braces, suspenders, garters and similar articles and parts thereof, of other textile materials, whether or not knitted or crocheted
62.13	**手帕:**								**Handkerchiefs:**
	-棉制:								-Of cotton:
6213.2010	---刺绣的	14	90		16	17	条/千克		---Embroidered
6213.2090	---其他	14	90		16	17	条/千克		---Other
	-其他纺织材料制:								-Of other textile materials:
6213.9020	---刺绣的	14	100		16	17	条/千克		---Embroidered
6213.9090	---其他	14	100		16	17	条/千克		---Other
6213 9090.10	化纤制其他手帕	14	100		16	17	条/千克		Other handkerchiefs of man-made fibres
6213 9090.20	麻制其他手帕	14	100		16	17	条/千克		Other handkerchiefs of flax
6213 9090.90	其他材料制手帕	14	100		16	17	条/千克		Handkerchiefs of other textile materials
62.14	**披巾、领巾、围巾、披纱、面纱及类似品:**								**Shawls, scarves, mufflers, mantillas, veils and the like:**
6214.1000	-丝或绢丝制	14	130		16	17	条/千克		-Of silk or silk waste
6214 1000.10	含丝70%及以上的披巾、头巾、围巾(包括披纱、面纱等及类似品)	14	130		16	17	条/千克		Shawls, scarves, mufflers of silk, containing 70% or more by weight of silk or silk waste, including mantillas,veils and the like
6214 1000.90	含丝70%以下的披巾、头巾、围巾(包括披纱、面纱等及类似品)	14	130		16	17	条/千克		Shawls, scarves, mufflers of silk, containing less than 70% by weight of silk or silk waste, including mantillas,veils and the like
	-羊毛或动物细毛制:								-Of wool or fine animal hair:
6214.2010	---羊毛制	14	130		16	17	条/千克		---Of wool
6214.2020	---山羊绒制	14	130		16	17	条/千克		---Of goats
6214.2090	---其他	14	130		16	17	条/千克		---Other
6214.3000	-合成纤维制	16	130		16	17	条/千克		-Of synthetic fibres
6214.4000	-人造纤维制	14	130		16	17	条/千克		-Of artificial fibres
6214.9000	-其他纺织材料制	14	100		16	17	条/千克		-Of other textile materials
6214 9000.10	棉制披巾、头巾及类似品(包括围巾、披纱、面纱)	14	100		16	17	条/千克		Shawls, scarves and mufflers, of cotton, including mantillas,veils and the like
6214 9000.90	其他材料制披巾、头巾及类似品	14	100		16	17	条/千克		Shawls, scarves and mufflers, of other textile

税则号列 Tariff Item	商品名称及备注	进口税率 最惠	普通	暂定	出口退税	增值税率	计量单位	监管条件	Article Description
	（包括围巾、披纱、面纱及类似品）								materials, including mantillas,veils and the like
62.15	领带及领结：								**Ties, bow ties and cravats:**
6215.1000	-丝或绢丝制	14	130		16	17	条/千克		-Of silk or silk waste
6215 1000.11	丝及绢丝制领带及领结(非丝纺织材料含量在50%及以上)	14	130		16	17	条/千克		Ties, bow ties and cravats of silk and silk waste (containing 50% or more of non-silk textile fabrics)
6215 1000.19	丝及绢丝制领带及领结(非丝纺织材料含量在50%以下，外层织物含丝70%及以上)	14	130		16	17	条/千克		Ties, bow ties and cravats of silk and silk waste, containing less than 50% of non-silk textile fabrics, outer fabrics containing 70% or more of silk
6215 1000.90	其他丝及绢丝制领带及领结(非丝纺织材料含量50%以下)	14	130		16	17	条/千克		Ties, bow ties and cravats of other silk and silk waste, containing less than 50% of non-silk textile fabrics
6215.2000	-化学纤维制	16	130		16	17	条/千克		-Of man-made fibres
6215.9000	-其他纺织材料制	14	100		16	17	条/千克		-Of other textile materials
6215 9000.10	毛制领带及领结	14	100		16	17	条/千克		Ties, bow ties and cravats, of wool or fine animal hair
6215 9000.20	棉制领带及领结	14	100		16	17	条/千克		Ties, bow ties and cravats, of cotton
6215 9000.90	其他材料制领带及领结	14	100		16	17	条/千克		Ties, bow ties and cravatsof other textile materials
62.16	分指手套、连指手套及露指手套：								**Gloves, mittens and mitts:**
6216.0000	分指手套、连指手套及露指手套	14	100		16	17	双/千克		Gloves, mittens and mitts
6216 0000.11	非针织物裁剪缝制成的运动手套（已浸渍塑料/橡胶，但含量不超过50%；棉限内；并四指）	14	100		16	17	双/千克		Sports mittens, made up of not-knitted fabrics, impregnated with rubber or plastics and containing less than 50%, cotton limit in
6216 0000.12	非针织物裁剪缝制成的非运动手套（已浸渍塑料/橡胶，但含量不超过50%；棉限内；并四指）	14	100		16	17	双/千克		Non sports mittens, made up of not-knitted fabrics, impregnated with rubber or plastics and containing less than 50%, cotton limit in
6216 0000.13	非针织物裁剪缝制成的运动手套（已浸渍塑料/橡胶，但含量不超过50%；化纤限内；并四指）	14	100		16	17	双/千克		Sports mittens, made up of not-knitted fabrics, impregnated with rubber or plastics and containing less than 50%, man-made fibres limit in
6216 0000.14	非针织物裁剪缝制成的非运动手套（已浸渍塑料/橡胶，但含量不超过50%；化纤限内；并四指）	14	100		16	17	双/千克		Non sports mittens, made up of not-knitted fabrics, impregnated with rubber or plastics and containing less than 50%, man-made fibres limit in)
6216 0000.15	其他非针织物裁剪缝成的运动手套（已浸渍塑料/橡胶，但含量不超过50%；并四指）	14	100		16	17	双/千克		Other sports mittens, made up of not-knitted fabrics, impregnated with rubber or plastics and containing less than 50%,
6216 0000.19	其他非针织物制成的非运动手套（已浸渍塑料/橡胶，但含量不超过50%；并四指）	14	100		16	17	双/千克		Non sports mittens, made up of other not-knitted fabrics, impregnated with rubber or plastics and containing less than 50%,
6216 0000.21	其他浸渍塑料/橡胶非针织运动手套(含棉、化学纤维及其他纺织纤维50%及以上；棉限内)	14	100		16	17	双/千克		Other not-knitted sports gloves, impregnated with rubber or plastics, containing 50% or more of cotton, man-made fibres or other textile fibres, cotton limit in
6216 0000.22	其他浸渍塑料/橡胶非针织非运动手套(含棉、化学纤维及其他纺织纤维50%及以上；棉限内)	14	100		16	17	双/千克		Other not-knitted non-sports gloves, impregnated with rubber or plastics, containing 50% or more of cotton, man-made fibres or other textile fibres, cotton limit in
6216 0000.23	其他浸渍塑料/橡胶非针织运动手套(含棉、化学纤维及其他纺织纤维50%及以上；化纤限内)	14	100		16	17	双/千克		Other not-knitted sports gloves, impregnated with rubber or plastics, containing 50% or more of cotton, man-made fibres or other textile fibres, man-made fibres limit in
6216 0000.24	其他浸渍塑料/橡胶非针织非运动手套(含棉、化学纤维及其他纺织纤维50%及以上；化纤限内)	14	100		16	17	双/千克		Other not-knitted non-sports gloves, impregnated with rubber or plastics, containing 50% or more of cotton, man-made fibres or other textile fibres, man-made fibres limit in
6216 0000.25	未列名浸渍塑料/橡胶非针织运动手套(含棉、化学纤维及其他纺织纤维50%及以上)	14	100		16	17	双/千克		Not-knitted sports gloves, , impregnated with rubber or plastics, containing 50% or more of cotton, man-made fibres or other textile fibres, not elsewhere specified or included
6216 0000.29	未列名浸渍塑料/橡胶非针织非运动手套（含棉、化学纤维及其	14	100		16	17	双/千克		Not-knitted non sports gloves, , impregnated with rubber or plastics, containing 50% or more of cotton,

税则号列 Tariff Item	商品名称及备注	进口税率			出口退税	增值税率	计量单位	监管条件	Article Description
		最惠	普通	暂定					
	他纺织纤维 50%及以上）								man-made fibres or other textile fibres, not elsewhere specified or included
6216 0000.31	棉非针织物制的运动手套（非浸渍塑料、橡胶；含并四指、分四指）	14	100		16	17	双/千克		Not-knitted sports gloves and mittens of cotton, not impregnated with rubber or plastics
6216 0000.39	棉非针织物制的非运动手套（非浸渍塑料、橡胶；含并四指、分四指）	14	100		16	17	双/千克		Not-knitted non sports gloves and mittens of cotton, not impregnated with rubber or plastics
6216 0000.41	化纤制非针织物制的运动手套（非浸渍塑料/橡胶;含并/分四指；含羊毛或动物细毛≥36%）	14	100		16	17	双/千克		Not-knitted sports gloves and mittens of man-made fibres, not impregnated with rubber or plastics, containing 36% or more by weight of wool or fine animal hair
6216 0000.42	化纤制非针织物制的非运动手套（非浸渍塑料/橡胶；含并/分四指；含羊毛或动物细毛≥36%）	14	100		16	17	双/千克		Not-knitted non sports gloves and mittens of man-made fibres, not impregnated with rubber or plastics, containing 36% or more by weight of wool or fine animal hair
6216 0000.43	其他化纤制非针织运动手套（非浸渍塑料、橡胶的；含并四指、分四指）	14	100		16	17	双/千克		Other not-knitted sports gloves and mittens, of man-made fibres, not impregnated with rubber or plastics
6216 0000.49	其他化纤制非针织非运动手套（非浸渍塑料、橡胶的；含并四指、分四指）	14	100		16	17	双/千克		Other not-knitted non-sports gloves and mittens , of man-made fibres, not impregnated with rubber or plastics
6216 0000.51	毛制非针织运动手套（非浸渍塑料、橡胶的；含并四指、分四指）	14	100		16	17	双/千克		Other not-knitted sports gloves and mittens of wool or fine animal hair, not impregnated with rubber or plastics
6216 0000.59	毛制非针织非运动手套（非浸渍塑料、橡胶的；含并四指、分四指）	14	100		16	17	双/千克		Not-knitted sports gloves and mittens of wool or fine animal hair, not impregnated with rubber or plastics
6216 0000.91	其他纺织材料制非针织运动手套（非浸渍塑料、橡胶的；含分指手套、连指手套及露指手套）	14	100		16	17	双/千克		Other not-knitted sports gloves, mittens and mitts of other textile materials, not impregnated with rubber or plastics
6216 0000.99	其他纺织材料制非针织非运动手套（非浸渍塑料、橡胶的；含分指手套、连指手套及露指手套）	14	100		16	17	双/千克		Other not-knitted non sports gloves, mittens and mitts of other textile materials, not impregnated with rubber or plastics
62.17	**其他制成的衣着附件；服装或衣着附件的零件，但品目 62.12 的货品除外：**								**Other made up clothing accessories; parts of garments or of clothing accessories, other than those of heading No.62. 12:**
	-附件:								-Accessories:
6217.1010	---袜子及袜套	14	130		16	17	千克/双		---Stocking, socks and socketes
6217.1020	---和服腰带	14	100		16	17	千克/条		---Kimono belts
6217.1090	---其他	14	100		16	17	千克		---Other
6217 1090.10	毛制服装或衣着附件（指非针织非钩编）	14	100		16	17	千克		Other made up clothing accessories of wool or fine animal hair, not knitted or crocheted
6217 1090.20	棉制服装或衣着附件（指非针织非钩编）	14	100		16	17	千克		Other made up clothing accessories of cotton, not knitted or crocheted
6217 1090.30	化纤制服装或衣着附件（指非针织非钩编）	14	100		16	17	千克		Parts of garments or of clothing accessories of man-made fibres, not knitted or crocheted
6217 1090.41	丝制服装或衣着附件（指非针织非钩编，含丝 70%及以上）	14	100		16	17	千克		Other made up clothing accessories of silk, not knitted or crocheted, containing 70% or more by weight of silk
6217 1090.49	丝制服装或衣着附件（指非针织非钩编，含丝 70%以下）	14	100		16	17	千克		Other made up clothing accessories of silk, not knitted or crocheted, containing less than 70% by weight of silk
6217 1090.90	其他服装或衣着附件（指非针织非钩编）	14	100		16	17	千克		Other made up clothing accessories, not knitted or crocheted
6217.9000	-零件	14	100		16	17	千克		-Parts
6217 9000.11	羊毛或动物细毛制保暖型衬里	14	100		16	17	千克		Thermal lining of wool or fine animal hair
6217 9000.12	毛制非针织或非钩编衬衫的零	14	100		16	17	千克		Parts of shirts, of wool or fine animal hair, not knitted

税则号列 Tariff Item	商品名称及备注	进口税率 最惠	进口税率 普通	进口税率 暂定	出口退税	增值税率	计量单位	监管条件	Article Description
	件								or crocheted
6217 9000.13	毛制非针织或非钩编上衣的零件	14	100		16	17	千克		Parts of jackets and blazers, of wool or fine animal hair, not knitted or crocheted
6217 9000.14	毛制长裤及马裤的零件(指非针织非钩编)	14	100		16	17	千克		Parts of trousers or breeches, of wool or fine animal hair, not knitted or crocheted
6217 9000.19	其他毛制服装或衣着零件(指非针织非钩编)	14	100		16	17	千克		Other parts of garments or of clothing accessories, of wool or fine animal hair, not knitted or crocheted
6217 9000.21	棉制保暖型衬里	14	100		16	17	千克		Thermal lining of cotton
6217 9000.22	棉制非针织非钩编衬衫的零件	14	100		16	17	千克		Parts of shirts, of cotton, not knitted or crocheted
6217 9000.23	棉制非针织非钩编上衣的零件	14	100		16	17	千克		Parts of jackets and blazers, of cotton, not knitted or crocheted
6217 9000.24	棉制长裤及马裤的零件(指非针织非钩编)	14	100		16	17	千克		Parts of trousers or breeches, of cotton, not knitted or crocheted
6217 9000.29	棉制服装或衣着零件(指非针织非钩编)	14	100		16	17	千克		Other parts of garments or of clothing accessories, of cotton, not knitted or crocheted
6217 9000.31	化纤制保暖型衬里	14	100		16	17	千克		Thermal lining, of man-made fibres
6217 9000.32	化纤制非针织非钩编衬衫的零件	14	100		16	17	千克		Parts of shirts, of man-made fibres, not knitted or crocheted
6217 9000.33	化纤制非针织非钩编上衣的零件	14	100		16	17	千克		Parts of jackets and blazers, of man-made fibres, not knitted or crocheted
6217 9000.34	化纤制长裤及马裤的零件(指非针织非钩编)	14	100		16	17	千克		Parts of trousers or breeches, of man-made fibres, not knitted or crocheted
6217 9000.39	化纤制服装或衣着零件(指非针织非钩编)	14	100		16	17	千克		Other parts of garments or of clothing accessories, of man-made fibres, not knitted or crocheted
6217 9000.41	丝制保暖型衬里	14	100		16	17	千克		Thermal lining of silk, not knitted or crocheted
6217 9000.42	丝制服装或衣着零件(指非针织非钩编，含丝 70%及以上)	14	100		16	17	千克		Parts of garments or of clothing accessories of silk, containing 70% or more by weight of silk, not knitted or crocheted
6217 9000.49	丝制服装或衣着零件(指非针织非钩编，含丝 70%以下)	14	100		16	17	千克		Parts of garments or of clothing accessories of silk, containing less than 70% by weight of silk, not knitted or crocheted
6217 9000.91	其他材料制保暖型衬里	14	100		16	17	千克		Thermal lining of other textile materials
6217 9000.92	其他材料制衬衫零件(非针织非钩编)	14	100		16	17	千克		Parts of shirts of other textile materials, not knitted or crocheted
6217 9000.93	其他材料制上衣零件(指非针织非钩编)	14	100		16	17	千克		Parts of jackets and blazers, of other textile materials, not knitted or crocheted
6217 9000.94	其他材料制长裤及马裤的零件(指非针织非钩编)	14	100		16	17	千克		Parts of trousers or breeches, of other textile materials, not knitted or crocheted
6217 9000.99	其他材料制服装或衣着附件(指非针织或非钩编,含各种附件的零件)	14	100		16	17	千克		Parts of garments or of clothing accessories, of other textile materials, not knitted or crocheted

第六十三章
其他纺织制成品；成套物品；旧衣着及旧纺织品；碎织物

注释：

一、第一分章仅适用于各种纺织物制成的物品。

二、第一分章不包括：

（一）第五十六章至第六十二章的货品；或

（二）品目63.09的旧衣着或其他旧物品。

三、品目63.09仅适用于下列货品：

（一）纺织材料制品：

1. 衣着和衣着附件及其零件；
2. 毯子及旅行毯；
3. 床上、餐桌、盥洗及厨房用的织物制品；
4. 装饰用织物制品，但品目57.01至57.05的地毯及品目58.05的装饰毯除外。

（二）用石棉以外其他任何材料制成的鞋帽类。

上述物品只有同时符合下列两个条件才能归入本品目：

1. 必须明显看得出穿用过；以及
2. 必须以散装、捆装、袋装或类似的大包装形式报验。

Chapter 63
Other made up textile articles; sets; worn clothing and worn textile articles; rags

Chapter Notes:

1. Sub-Chapter 1 applies only to made up articles, of any textile fabric.

2. Sub-Chapter 1 does not cover:

(a) Goods of Chapters 56 to 62; or

(b) Worn clothing or other worn articles of heading 63.09.

3. Heading 63.09 applies only to the following goods:

(a) Articles of textile materials:

(ⅰ) Clothing and clothing accessories, and parts thereof;

(ⅱ) Blankets and travelling rugs;

(ⅲ) Bed linen, table linen, toilet linen and kitchen linen;

(ⅳ) Furnishing articles, other than carpets of headings 57.01 to 57. 05 and tapestries of heading 58.05:

(b) Footwear and headgear of any material other than asbestos.

In order to be classified in this heading, the articles mentioned bove must comply with both of the following requirements:

(ⅰ) They must show signs of appreciable wear; and

(ⅱ) They must be presented in bulk or in bales, sacks or similar packings.

税则号列 Tariff Item	商品名称及备注	进口税率 最惠	普通	暂定	出口退税	增值税率	计量单位	监管条件	Article Description
	第一分章　其他纺织制成品								I.OTHER MADE UP TEXTILE ARTICLES
63.01	毯子及旅行毯：								**Blankets and travelling rugs:**
6301.1000	-电暖毯	16	100		16	17	条/千克	A	-Electric blankets
6301.2000	-羊毛或动物细毛制的毯子（电暖毯除外）及旅行毯	16	130		16	17	条/千克		-Blankets (other than electric blankets) and travelling rugs, of wool or of fine animal hair
6301 2000.10	毛制毯子及旅行毯(羊毛或动物细毛制，非电暖的，长度不超过3米)	16	130		16	17	条/千克		Non-electric blankets and travelling rugs, of wool or of fine animal hair, of a length not exceeding 3m
6301 2000.20	其他毛制毯子及旅行毯(羊毛或动物细毛制，非电暖的，长度超过3米)	16	130		16	17	条/千克		Other non-electric blankets and travelling rugs, of wool or of fine animal hair, of a length exceeding 3m
6301.3000	-棉制的毯子(电暖毯除外)及旅行毯	16	90		16	17	条/千克		-Blankets (other than electric blankets) and travelling rugs, of cotton
6301.4000	-合成纤维制的毯子(电暖毯除外)及旅行毯	17.5	130		16	17	条/千克		-Blankets (other than electric blankets) and travelling rugs, of synthetic fibres
6301.9000	-其他毯子及旅行毯	16	90		16	17	条/千克		-Other blankets and travelling rugs
6301 9000.10	人造纤维制的毯子及旅行毯(非电暖的)	16	90		16	17	条/千克		Non-electric blankets and travelling rugs of artificial fibres
6301 9000.20	丝制毯子及旅行毯（非电暖的，含丝及绢丝85%及以上）	16	90		16	17	条/千克		Non-electric blankets and travelling rugs, containing 85% or more by weight of silk or silk waste
6301 9000.90	其他纺织材料制毯子及旅行毯（非电暖的）	16	90		16	17	条/千克		Non-electric blankets and travelling rugs of other textile materials
63.02	床上、餐桌、盥洗及厨房用的织物制品：								**Bed linen, table linen, toilet linen and kitchen linen:**
	-针织或钩编的床上用织物制品:								-Bed linen, knitted or crocheted:
6302.1010	---棉制	14	90		16	17	条/千克		---Of cotton
6302.1090	---其他纺织材料制	14	130		16	17	条/千克		---Of other textile materials
	-其他印花的床上用织物制品:								-Other bed linen, printed:
	--棉制:								--Of cotton:
6302.2110	---床单	14	90		16	17	条/千克		---Bed sheets

税则号列 Tariff Item	商品名称及备注	进口税率			出口退税	增值税率	计量单位	监管条件	Article Description
		最惠	普通	暂定					
6302.2190	---其他	14	90		16	17	条/千克		---Other
6302 2190.10	棉制印花枕套	14	90		16	17	条/千克		Printed pillowcases of cotton
6302 2190.20	棉制印花枕罩	14	90		16	17	条/千克		Printed pillowcovers of cotton
6302 2190.90	其他棉制印花床上用织物制品	14	90		16	17	条/千克		Other printed bed linen of cotton
	--化学纤维制:								--Of man-made fibres:
6302.2210	---床单	16	130		16	17	条/千克		---Bed sheets
6302.2290	---其他	16	130		16	17	条/千克		---Other
6302 2290.10	化纤制印花枕套	16	130		16	17	条/千克		Printed pillowcases of man-made fibres
6302 2290.20	化纤无纺织物制印花床上用织物制品	16	130		16	17	条/千克		Printed bed linen of non-woven of man-made fibres
6302 2290.90	其他化纤制印花床上用织物制品	16	130		16	17	条/千克		Other printed bed linen of man-made fibres
	--其他纺织材料制:								---Of other textile materials:
6302.2910	---丝及绢丝制	14	130		16	17	条/千克		---Of silk or silk waste
6302 2910.10	丝及绢丝制印花床上用织物制品（含丝85%及以上）	14	130		16	17	条/千克		Printed bed linen of silk, containing 85% or more by weight of silk or silk waster
6302 2910.90	丝及绢丝制印花床上用织物制品（含丝85%以下）	14	130		16	17	条/千克		Printed bed linen of silk, containing 85% or more by weight of silk or silk waster
6302.2920	---麻制	14	90		16	17	条/千克		---Of bast fibres
6302 2920.10	亚麻或苎麻制印花床上用织物制品	14	90		16	17	条/千克		Printed bed linen of flax or ramie
6302 2920.90	其他麻制印花床上用织物制品	14	90		16	17	条/千克		Printed bed linen of other bast fibres
6302.2990	---其他	14	100		16	17	条/千克		---Other
	-其他床上用织物制品:								-Other bed linen:
	--棉制:								--Of cotton:
6302.3110	---刺绣的	14	90		16	17	条/千克		---Embroidered
	---其他:								---Other:
6302.3191	----床单	14	90		16	17	条/千克		----Bed sheets
6302.3192	----毛巾被	14	90		16	17	条/千克		----Towelling coverlets
6302.3199	----其他	14	90		16	17	条/千克		----Other
6302 3199.10	棉制其他枕套	14	90		16	17	条/千克		Other pillowcases of cotton
6302 3199.20	其他棉与亚麻混纺床上用织物制品	14	90		16	17	条/千克		Other bed linen of blended fabrics, mixed with cotton and flax
6302 3199.30	棉制其他枕罩	14	90		16	17	条/千克		Pillow cover of cotton
6302 3199.90	棉制其他床上用织物制品	14	90		16	17	条/千克		Other bed linen of cotton
	--化学纤维制:								--Of man-made fibres:
6302.3210	---刺绣的	16	130		16	17	条/千克		---Embroidered
6302.3290	---其他	16	130		16	17	条/千克		---Other
6302 3290.10	化纤制其他床单	16	130		16	17	条/千克		Bed sheets of man-made fibres
6302 3290.20	化纤制其他枕套	16	130		16	17	条/千克		Other pillowcases of man-made fibres
6302 3290.30	其他化纤无纺织物制床上织物制品	16	130		16	17	条/千克		Other bed linen of non-woven fabrics of man-made fibres
6302 3290.90	化纤制其他床上用织物制品	16	130		16	17	条/千克		Other bed linen, of man-made fibres
	--其他纺织材料制:								--Of other textile materials:
6302.3910	---丝及绢丝制	14	130		16	17	条/千克		---Of silk or silk waste
6302 3910.10	丝及绢丝制其他床上用织物制品（含丝85%及以上）	14	130		16	17	条/千克		Other bed linen of silk and silk waste, containing 85% or more by weight of silk
6302 3910.90	丝及绢丝制其他床上用织物制品（含丝85%以下）	14	130		16	17	条/千克		Other bed linen of silk and silk waste, containing less than 85% by weight of silk
	---麻制:								---Of bast fibres:
6302.3921	----刺绣的	14	90		16	17	条/千克		----Embroidered
6302 3921.10	亚麻或苎麻制其他床上用织物制品（刺绣的）	14	90		16	17	条/千克		Other embroidered bed linen of flax or ramie
6302 3921.90	其他麻制其他床上用织物制品（刺绣的）	14	90		16	17	条/千克		Other embroidered bed linen of other bast fibres
6302.3929	----其他	14	90		16	17	条/千克		----Other
6302 3929.10	亚麻或苎麻制其他床上用织物制品	14	90		16	17	条/千克		Other bed linen of flax or ramie

税则号列 Tariff Item	商品名称及备注	进口税率 最惠	普通	暂定	出口退税	增值税率	计量单位	监管条件	Article Description
6302 3929.90	其他麻制其他床上用织物制品	14	90		16	17	条/千克		Other bed linen of other bast fibres
	---其他:								---Other:
6302.3991	----刺绣的	14	100		16	17	条/千克		----Embroidered
6302 3991.10	毛制刺绣床上用织物制品	14	100		16	17	条/千克		Other embroidered bed linen of wool or fine animal hair
6302 3991.90	其他材料制刺绣床上用织物制品	14	100		16	17	条/千克		Other embroidered bed linen of other textile materials
6302.3999	----其他	14	100		16	17	条/千克		----Other
6302 3999.10	毛制非刺绣床上用织物制品	14	100		16	17	条/千克		Other embroidered bed linen of wool or fine animal hair
6302 3999.90	其他材料制其他床上用织物制品	14	100		16	17	条/千克		Other bed linen of other textile materials
	-针织或钩编的餐桌用织物制品:								-Table linen, knitted or crocheted:
6302.4010	---手工制	14	100		16	17	件/千克		---Hand-worked
6302 4010.10	手工棉制餐桌用织物制品(指针织或钩编类的)	14	100		16	17	件/千克		Hand-worked table linen of cotton, knitted or crocheted
6302 4010.20	手工植物纺织纤维制餐桌用制品（指针织或钩编类的）	14	100		16	17	件/千克		Hand-worked table linen of other vegetable textile fibres, knitted or crocheted
6302 4010.90	手工其他纺织材料制餐桌用制品（指针织或钩编类的）	14	100		16	17	件/千克		Other hand-worked table linen of other textile materials, knitted or crocheted
6302.4090	---其他	14	100		16	17	件/千克		---Other
6302 4090.10	棉制餐桌用织物制品(针织或钩编的，非手工)	14	100		16	17	件/千克		Non hand-worked table linen of cotton, knitted or crochetedt
6302 4090.20	植物纺织纤维制的餐桌用织物制品（针织或钩编的，非手工）	14	100		16	17	件/千克		Non hand-worked table linen of other vegetable textile fibres, knitted or crocheted
6302 4090.90	其他纺织材料制餐桌用织物制品（针织或钩编的，非手工）	14	100		16	17	件/千克		Non hand-worked table linen of other textile materials, knitted or crocheted
	-其他餐桌用织物制品:								-Other table linen:
	--棉制:								--Of cotton:
6302.5110	---刺绣的	14	90		16	17	件/千克		---Embroidered
6302.5190	---其他	14	90		16	17	件/千克		---Other
	--化学纤维制:								--Of man-made fibres:
6302.5310	---刺绣的	14	130		16	17	件/千克		---Embroidered
6302.5390	---其他	16	130		16	17	件/千克		---Other
6302 5390.10	化纤无纺织物制餐桌用织物制品	16	130		16	17	件/千克		Table linen of non-woven fabrics of man-made fibres
6302 5390.90	化纤制其他餐桌用织物制品	16	130		16	17	件/千克		Other table linen of man-made fibres
	--其他纺织材料制:								--Of other textile materials:
	---亚麻制:								---Of flax:
6302.5911	----刺绣的	14	90		16	17	件/千克		----Embroidered
6302.5919	----其他	14	90		16	17	件/千克		----Other
6302.5990	---其他	14	100		16	17	件/千克		---Other
6302 5990.10	羊毛或动物细毛制餐桌用织物制品	14	100		16	17	件/千克		Table linen of wool or fine animal hair
6302 5990.90	其他纺织材料制餐桌用织物制品	14	100		16	17	件/千克		Table linen of other textile materials
	-盥洗及厨房用棉制毛巾织物或类似的毛圈织物的制品:								-Toilet linen and kitchen linen, of terry towelling or similar terry fabrics, of cotton:
6302.6010	---浴巾	14	90		16	17	条/千克		---Bath towels
6302 6010.10	棉制针织或钩编毛巾织物浴巾（含类似毛圈织物的制品）	14	90		16	17	条/千克		Cotton toilet linen of terry towelling or similar terry fabrics, knitted or crocheted
6302 6010.90	棉制非针织或非钩编毛巾织物浴巾（含类似毛圈织物的制品）	14	90		16	17	条/千克		Cotton toilet linen of terry towelling or similar terry fabrics, not knitted or crocheted
6302.6090	---其他	14	90		16	17	条/千克		---Other
6302 6090.11	棉制针织或钩编毛巾织物茶巾（包括类似毛圈织物的制品）	14	90		16	17	条/千克		Cotton tea towel of terry towelling or similar terry fabrics, knitted or crocheted
6302 6090.19	棉制非针织或非钩编毛巾织物茶巾（包括类似毛圈织物的制品）	14	90		16	17	条/千克		Cotton tea towel of terry towelling or similar terry fabrics, not knitted or crocheted

税则号列 Tariff Item	商品名称及备注	进口税率 最惠	普通	暂定	出口退税	增值税率	计量单位	监管条件	Article Description
6302 6090.91	棉制其他盥洗及厨房用毛巾制品（包括类似毛圈织物的制品，针织或钩编）	14	90		16	17	条/千克		Other cotton toilet linen and kitchen linen of terry towelling or similar terry fabrics, knitted or crocheted
6302 6090.99	棉制其他盥洗及厨房用毛巾制品（含类似毛圈织物的制品，非针织或非钩编）	14	90		16	17	条/千克		Other cotton toilet linen and kitchen linen of terry towelling or similar terry fabrics, not knitted or crocheted
	-其他:								-Other:
6302.9100	--棉制	14	90		16	17	条/千克		--Of cotton
6302 9100.10	棉制茶巾(毛巾织物或类似毛圈织物的除外）	14	90		16	17	条/千克		Tea towel of cotton, other than terry-towelling or similar terry fabrics
6302 9100.20	棉制毛巾(毛巾织物或类似毛圈织物的除外）	14	90		16	17	条/千克		Towels of cotton, other than terry-towelling or similar terry fabrics
6302 9100.90	棉制其他盥洗及厨房织物制品（毛巾织物或类似毛圈织物的除外）	14	90		16	17	条/千克		Other toilet linen and kitchen linen of cotton, other than terry towelling or similar terry fabrics
6302.9300	--化学纤维制	16	130		16	17	条/千克		--Of man-made fibres
6302 9300.10	化纤无纺织物制盥洗及厨房制品	16	130		16	17	条/千克		Toilet linen and kitchen linen of non-woven fabrics of man-made fibres
6302 9300.90	化纤制其他盥洗及厨房织物制品	16	130		16	17	条/千克		Other toilet linen and kitchen linen of man-made fibres
	--其他纺织材料制:								--Of other textile materials:
6302.9910	---亚麻制	14	90		16	17	条/千克		---Of flax
6302.9990	---其他	14	100		16	17	条/千克		---Other
6302 9990.10	毛制盥洗及厨房用织物制品	14	100		16	17	条/千克		Other toilet linen and kitchen linen of wool or other fine animal hair
6302 9990.90	其他材料制盥洗及厨房织物制品	14	100		16	17	条/千克		Other toilet linen and kitchen linen of other textile materials
63.03	**窗帘（包括帷帘）及帐幔；帘帷或床帷:**								**Curtains（including drapes） and interior blinds; curtain or bed valances:**
	-针织或钩编的:								-Knitted or crocheted:
	--合成纤维制:								--Of synthetic fibres:
6303.1210	---针织的	16	130		16	17	千克		---Knitted
6303 1210.10	合纤制针织百叶窗、卷帘和窗幔	16	130		16	17	千克		Curtains（inclucling drapes） and interior or blinds, curtain or bed valances, of synthetic fibres, knitted
6303 1210.90	其他合纤制针织窗帘等(包括帷帘、帐幔、帘帷及床帷）	16	130		16	17	千克		Other curtains, drapes, interior blinds, curtain and bed valances, of knitted, of synthetic fibres, knitted
6303.1220	---钩编的	16	130		16	17	千克		---Crocheted
6303 1220.10	合纤制钩编百叶窗、卷帘和窗幔	16	130		16	17	千克		Curtains（including drapes）and interior blinds; curtain or bed valances, of synthetic fibres, crocheted
6303 1220.90	其他合纤制钩编的窗帘等(包括帷帘、帐幔、帘帷及床帷）	16	130		16	17	千克		Other curtains（including drapes， interior blinds, curtain and bed valances), of synthetic fibres , crocheted
	--其他纺织材料制:								--Of other textile materials:
	---棉制:								---Of cotton:
6303.1931	----针织的	14	90		16	17	千克		----Knitted
6303.1932	----钩编的	14	90		16	17	千克		----Crocheted
	---其他纺织材料制:								---Of other textile materials:
6303.1991	----针织的	14	130		16	17	千克		----Knitted
6303.1992	----钩编的	14	130		16	17	千克		----Crocheted
	-其他:								-Other:
6303.9100	--棉制	14	90		16	17	千克		--Of cotton
6303 9100.10	棉制非针织网眼窗帘（包括帷帘、帐幔、帘帷及床帷）	14	90		16	17	千克		Curtains（including drapes）and interior blinds; curtain or bed valances, of cotton, openwork, not knitted
6303 9100.90	棉制非针织非钩编窗帘(包括帷帘、帐幔、帘帷及床帷）	14	90		16	17	千克		Curtains（including drapes）and interior blinds; curtain or bed valances, of cotton, openwork, not knitted or crocheted
6303.9200	--合成纤维制	16	130		16	17	千克		--Of synthetic fibres

税则号列 Tariff Item	商品名称及备注	进口税率 最惠	进口税率 普通	进口税率 暂定	出口退税	增值税率	计量单位	监管条件	Article Description
6303 9200.10	合纤百叶窗、卷帘和窗幔(非针织非钩编)	16	130		16	17	千克		Curtains (including drapes) and interior blinds; curtain or bed valances, of synthetic fibres, not knitted or crocheted
6303 9200.90	其他合纤制非针织非钩编窗帘等(包括帷帘、帐幔、帘帷及床帷)	16	130		16	17	千克		Curtains (including drapes) and interior blinds; curtain or bed valances, of synthetic fibres, not knitted or crocheted
6303.9900	--其他纺织材料制	14	100		16	17	千克		--Of other textile materials
6303 9900.10	毛制非针织非钩编窗帘(包括帷帘、帐幔、帘帷及床帷)	14	100		16	17	千克		Curtains (including drapes) and interior blinds; curtain or bed valances, not knitted or crocheted, of wool or fine animal hair
6303 9900.20	人造纤维制非针织非钩编窗帘(包括帷帘、帐幔、帘帷及床帷)	14	100		16	17	千克		Curtains (including drapes) and interior blinds; curtain or bed valances, not knitted or crocheted, of artificials fibres
6303 9900.31	丝制非针织非钩编窗帘(包括帷帘、帐幔、帘帷及床帷,含丝85%及以上)	14	100		16	17	千克		Curtains (including drapes) and interior blinds; curtain or bed valances, of silk, not knitted or crocheted, containing 85% or more by weight of silk
6303 9900.39	丝制非针织非钩编窗帘(含帷帘、帐幔、帘帷及床帷,含丝85%以下)	14	100		16	17	千克		Curtains (including drapes) and interior blinds; curtain or bed valances, of silk, not knitted or crocheted, containing less than 85% by weight of silk
6303 9900.40	其他纺织材料无纺织物制窗帘(包括帷帘、帐幔、帘帷及床帷)	14	100		16	17	千克		Curtains (including drapes) and interior blinds; curtain or bed valances, of non-woven fabrics of other textile materials
6303 9900.50	亚麻或苎麻制非针织非钩编窗帘(包括帷帘、帐幔、帘帷及床帷)	14	100		16	17	千克		Curtains (including drapes) and interior blinds; curtain or bed valances, not knitted or crocheted, of flax or ramie
6303 9900.60	其他纺织材料制非针织网眼窗帘(包括帷帘、帐幔、帘帷及床帷)	14	100		16	17	千克		Curtains (including drapes) and interior blinds; curtain or bed valances, not knitted, openwork, of other textile materials
6303 9900.90	其他纺织材料制非针织非钩编窗帘(包括帷帘、帐幔、帘帷及床帷)	14	100		16	17	千克		Curtains (including drapes) and interior blinds; curtain or bed valances, not knitted or crocheted, of other textile materials
63.04	**其他装饰用织物制品,但品目94.04的货品除外:**								**Other furnishing articles, excluding those of heading No.94.04:**
	-床罩:								-Bedspreads:
	--针织或钩编的:								--Knitted or crocheted:
	---针织的:								---Knitted:
6304.1121	----手工制	14	100		16	17	件/千克		----Hand-worked
6304 1121.10	棉制手工针织床罩	14	100		16	17	件/千克		Hand-worked knitted bedspreads of cotton
6304 1121.20	化纤制手工针织床罩	14	100		16	17	件/千克		Hand-worked knitted bedspreads, of man-made fibres
6304 1121.90	其他纺织材料制手工针织床罩	14	100		16	17	件/千克		Hand-worked knitted bedspreads of other textile materials
6304.1129	----其他	14	100		16	17	件/千克		----Other
6304 1129.10	棉制非手工针织床罩	14	100		16	17	件/千克		Non-hand-worked knitted bedspreads of cotton
6304 1129.20	化纤制非手工针织床罩	14	100		16	17	件/千克		Non-hand-worked knitted bedspreads of man-made fibres
6304 1129.90	其他纺织材料制非手工针织床罩	14	100		16	17	件/千克		Non-hand-worked knitted bedspreadsof other textile materials
	---钩编的:								---Crocheted:
6304.1131	----手工制	14	100		16	17	件/千克		----Hand-worked
6304 1131.10	棉制手工钩编床罩	14	100		16	17	件/千克		Hand-worked knitted bedspreads of cotton
6304 1131.20	化纤制手工钩编床罩	14	100		16	17	件/千克		Hand-worked knitted bedspreads of man-made fibres
6304 1131.90	其他纺织材料制手工钩编床罩	14	100		16	17	件/千克		Hand-worked knitted bedspreads, knitted, hand-worked, of other textile materials
6304.1139	----其他	14	100		16	17	件/千克		----Other
6304 1139.10	棉制非手工钩编床罩	14	100		16	17	件/千克		Non-hand-worked knitted bedspreads of cotton
6304 1139.20	化纤制非手工钩编床罩	14	100		16	17	件/千克		Non-hand-worked knitted bedspreads of man-made fibres

税则号列 Tariff Item	商品名称及备注	进口税率 最惠	普通	暂定	出口退税	增值税率	计量单位	监管条件	Article Description
6304 1139.90	其他纺织材料制非手工钩编床罩	14	100		16	17	件/千克		Non-hand-worked knitted bedspreads of other textile materials
	--其他:								--Other:
6304.1910	---丝及绢丝制	14	130		16	17	件/千克		---Of silk or silk waste
6304 1910.10	丝及绢丝制非针织非钩编床罩（含丝 85%及以上）	14	130		16	17	件/千克		Bedspreads of silk or silk waste, containing 85% or more by weight of silk , not knitted or crocheted
6304 1910.90	丝及绢丝制非针织非钩编床罩（含丝 85%以下）	14	130		16	17	件/千克		Bedspreads of silk or silk waste, containing less than 85% by weight of silk , not knitted or crocheted
	---棉或麻制:								---Of cotton or bast fibres:
6304.1921	----刺绣的	14	90		16	17	件/千克		----Embroidered
6304 1921.10	亚麻或苎麻制刺绣床罩(指非针织非钩编)	14	90		16	17	件/千克		Embroidered bedspreads of flax or ramie, not knitted or crocheted
6304 1921.20	其他麻制非针织非钩编刺绣床罩	14	90		16	17	件/千克		Embroidered bedspreads of other bast fibres, not knitted or crocheted
6304 1921.90	棉制非针织非钩编刺绣床罩	14	90		16	17	件/千克		Embroidered bedspreads of cotton, not knitted or crocheted
6304.1929	----其他	14	90		16	17	件/千克		----Other
6304 1929.10	亚麻或苎麻制非针织非钩编床罩	14	90		16	17	件/千克		Bedspreads of flax or ramie, not knitted or crocheted
6304 1929.91	其他麻制其他非针织非钩编床罩	14	90		16	17	件/千克		Bedspreads of other bast fibres, not knitted or crocheted,
6304 1929.99	棉制其他非针织非钩编床罩	14	90		16	17	件/千克		Bedspreads of cotton, not knitted or crocheted
	---化学纤维制:								---Of man-made fibres:
6304.1931	----刺绣的	16	130		16	17	件/千克		----Embroidered
6304.1939	----其他	16	130		16	17	件/千克		----Other
	---其他纺织材料制:								---Of other textile materials:
6304.1991	----刺绣的	14	100		16	17	件/千克		----Embroidered
6304 1991.10	毛制非针织非钩编刺绣床罩(羊毛或动物细毛制)	14	100		16	17	件/千克		Embroidered bedspreads of wool or fine animal hair, not knitted or crocheted
6304 1991.90	其他纺织材料制非针织刺绣床罩（含非钩编的）	14	100		16	17	件/千克		Embroidered bedspreads of other textile materials, not knitted or crocheted
6304.1999	----其他	14	100		16	17	件/千克		----Other
6304 1999.10	毛制其他非针织非钩编床罩(羊毛或动物细毛制)	14	100		16	17	件/千克		Embroidered bedspreads of wool or fine animal hair, not knitted or crocheted
6304 1999.90	其他材料制非针织非钩编其他床罩	14	100		16	17	件/千克		Embroidered bedspreads of other textile materials, not knitted or crocheted
	-其他:								-Other:
	--针织或钩编的:								--Knitted or crocheted:
	---针织的:								---Knitted:
6304.9121	----手工制	14	100		16	17	千克		----Hand-worked
6304 9121.10	棉制手工针织的其他装饰制品	14	100		16	17	千克		Other hand-worked knitted furnishing articles
6304 9121.20	毛制手工针织的其他装饰制品（羊毛或动物细毛制）	14	100		16	17	千克		Other hand-worked knitted furnishing articles
6304 9121.31	丝制手工针织的其他装饰制品（含丝 85%及以上）	14	100		16	17	千克		Other hand-worked knitted furnishing articles, containing 85% or more by weight of silk
6304 9121.39	丝制手工针织的其他装饰制品（含丝 85%以下）	14	100		16	17	千克		Other hand-worked knitted furnishing articles, containing 85% or more by weight of silk
6304 9121.40	化纤制手工针织的其他装饰制品	14	100		16	17	千克		Other hand-worked knitted furnishing articles of man-made fibres
6304 9121.90	其他纺材制手工针织其他装饰制品	14	100		16	17	千克		Other hand-worked knitted furnishing articles, of other textile materials
6304.9129	----其他	14	100		16	17	千克		----Other
6304 9129.10	棉制非手工针织的其他装饰制品	14	100		16	17	千克		Other non-hand-worked knitted furnishing articles of cotton
6304 9129.20	毛制非手工针织的其他装饰制品（羊毛或动物细毛制）	14	100		16	17	千克		Other non-hand-worked furnishing articles of wool or fine animal hair
6304 9129.31	丝制非手工针织的其他装饰制品（含丝 85%及以上）	14	100		16	17	千克		Other non-hand-worked knitted furnishing articles, containing 85% or more by weight of silk

税则号列 Tariff Item	商品名称及备注	进口税率 最惠	普通	暂定	出口退税	增值税率	计量单位	监管条件	Article Description
6304 9129.39	丝制非手工针织的其他装饰制品（含丝85%以下）	14	100		16	17	千克		Other non-hand-worked knitted furnishing articles, containing less than 85% by weight of silk
6304 9129.40	化纤制非手工针织其他装饰制品	14	100		16	17	千克		Other non-hand-worked knitted furnishing articles of man-made fibres
6304 9129.90	其他纺材制非手工针织其他装饰品	14	100		16	17	千克		Other non-hand-worked knitted furnishing articles of other textile materials
	---钩编的:								---Crocheted:
6304.9131	----手工制	14	100		16	17	千克		----Hand-worked
6304 9131.10	棉制手工钩编的其他装饰制品	14	100		16	17	千克		Other hand-worked crocheted furnishing articles of cotton
6304 9131.20	毛制手工钩编的其他装饰制品（羊毛或动物细毛制）	14	100		16	17	千克		Other hand-worked crocheted furnishing articles of wool or fine animal hair
6304 9131.31	丝制手工钩编的其他装饰制品（含丝85%及以上）	14	100		16	17	千克		Other hand-worked crocheted furnishing articles, containing 85% or more by weight of silk
6304 9131.39	丝制手工钩编的其他装饰制品（含丝85%以下）	14	100		16	17	千克		Other hand-worked crocheted furnishing articles of silk , containing less than 85% by weight of silk
6304 9131.40	化纤制手工钩编的其他装饰制品	14	100		16	17	千克		Other hand-worked crocheted furnishing articles of man-made fibres
6304 9131.90	其他制手工钩编的其他材料装饰制品	14	100		16	17	千克		Other hand-worked crocheted furnishing articles of other textile materials
6304.9139	----其他	14	100		16	17	千克		----Other
6304 9139.10	棉制非手工钩编的其他装饰制品	14	100		16	17	千克		Other non hand-worked crocheted furnishing articles of cotton
6304 9139.20	毛制非手工钩编的其他装饰制品（羊毛或动物细毛制）	14	100		16	17	千克		Other non hand-worked crocheted furnishing articles of woo1 or fine animal hair
6304 9139.31	丝制非手工钩编的其他装饰制品（含丝85%及以上）	14	100		16	17	千克		Other non hand-worked crocheted furnishing articles of silk containing 85% or more by weight of silk
6304 9139.39	丝制非手工钩编的其他装饰制品（含丝85%以下）	14	100		16	17	千克		Other non hand-worked crocheted furnishing articles of silk, containing less than 85% by weight of silk
6304 9139.40	化纤制非手工钩编其他装饰制品	14	100		16	17	千克		Other non hand-worked crocheted furnishing articles of man-made fibres
6304 9139.90	其他纺材制非手工钩编其他装饰品	14	100		16	17	千克		Other non hand-worked crocheted furnishing articles of other textile materials
	--非针织或非钩编的，棉制:								--Not knitted or crocheted, of cotton:
6304.9210	---刺绣的	14	90		16	17	千克		---Embroidered
6304.9290	---其他	14	90		16	17	千克		---Other
	—非针织或非钩编的，合成纤维制:								--Not knitted or crocheted, of synthetic fibres:
6304.9310	---刺绣的	16	130		16	17	千克		---Embroidered
6304.9390	---其他	16	130		16	17	千克		---Other
	--非针织或非钩编的，其他纺织材料制:								--Not knitted or crocheted, of other textile materials:
6304.9910	---丝及绢丝制	14	130		16	17	千克		---Of silk or silk waste
6304 9910.10	丝制非针织非钩编的装饰制品（含绢丝制品，含丝85%及以上）	14	130		16	17	千克		Other furnishing articles of silk, not knitted or crocheted, containing 85% or more by weight of silk or silk waste
6304 9910.90	丝制非针织非钩编的装饰制品（含绢丝制品，含丝85%以下）	14	130		16	17	千克		Other furnishing articles of silk, not knitted or crocheted, containing less than 85% by weight of silk or silk waste
	---麻制:								---Of bast fibres:
6304.9921	----刺绣的	14	90		16	17	千克		----Embroidered
6304 9921.10	亚麻或苎麻非针织其他刺绣装饰品（含非钩编制品）	14	90		16	17	千克		Other embroidered furnishing articles of flax or ramie, not knitted or crocheted
6304 9921.90	其他麻制非针织其他刺绣装饰品（包括非钩编的）	14	90		16	17	千克		Other embroidered furnishing articles of other bast fibres, not knitted or crocheted
6304.9929	----其他	14	90		16	17	千克		----Other
6304 9929.10	亚麻或苎麻制其他非针织的装饰品（含非钩编制品）	14	90		16	17	千克		Other furnishing articles of flax or ramie, not knitted or crocheted

税则号列 Tariff Item	商品名称及备注	进口税率			出口退税	增值税率	计量单位	监管条件	Article Description
		最惠	普通	暂定					
6304 9929.90	其他麻制其他非针织的装饰制品（含非钩编制品）	14	90		16	17	千克		Other furnishing articles of other bast fibres not knitted or crocheted,
6304.9990	---其他	14	100		16	17	千克		---Other
6304 9990.10	毛制非针织非钩编装饰制品(羊毛或动物细毛制)	14	100		16	17	千克		Other furnishing articles of wool or fine animal hair, not knitted or crocheted
6304 9990.20	人造纤维制非针织非钩编装饰品	14	100		16	17	千克		Other furnishing articles of man-made fibres, not knitted or crocheted
6304 9990.90	其他材料制非针织非钩编装饰品	14	100		16	17	千克		Other furnishing articles of other textile materials, not knitted or crocheted
63.05	**货物包装用袋：**								**Sacks and bags, of a kind used for the packing of goods:**
6305.1000	-黄麻或品目53.03的其他韧皮纺织纤维制	10	40		16	17	条/千克		-Of jute or of other textile bast fibres of heading No.53.03
6305 1000.10	黄麻制旧的货物包装袋(含品目53.03的其他韧皮纤维制)	10	40		16	17	条/千克		Send-hand sacks and bags, of a kind used for the packing of goods, of jute or of other textile bast fibres of heading No. 53.03
6305 1000.90	黄麻制其他货物包装袋(含品目53.03的其他韧皮纤维制)	10	40		16	17	条/千克		Other sacks and bags, used for the packing of goods, of jute or of other textile bast fibres of heading No.53.03
6305.2000	-棉制	16	90		16	17	条/千克		-Of cotton
	-化学纤维材料制:								-Of man-made textile materials:
6305.3200	--散装货物储运软袋	16	100		16	17	条/千克		--Flexible intermediate bulk containers
6305 3200.11	聚乙烯或聚丙烯制软袋(针织或钩编的，用扁条及类似材料制成，散装货物周转用)	16	100		16	17	条/千克		Flexible intermediate bulk containers of polyethylene or polypropylene strip or the like, used for bulk goods turnover, knitted or crocheted
6305 3200.19	聚乙烯或聚丙烯制软袋(非针织或钩编的，扁条及类似材料制成，散装货物周转用)	16	100		16	17	条/千克		Flexible intermediate bulk containers of polyethylene or polypropylene strip or the like, used for bulk goods turnover, not knitted or crocheted
6305 3200.90	化纤制的散装货物周转软袋	16	100		16	17	条/千克		Flexible intermediate bulk containers of manmade fibres, used for bulk goods turnover
6305.3300	--其他,聚乙烯、聚丙烯扁条或类似材料制	16	100		16	17	条/千克		--Other, of polyethylene or polypropylene strip or the like
6305 3300.10	聚乙烯或聚丙烯制其他货物包装袋(针织或钩编的，用扁条及类似材料制成)	16	100		16	17	条/千克		Other sacks and bags for the packing of goods, of polyethylene or polypropylene strip or the like, knitted or crocheted
6305 3300.90	聚乙烯或聚丙烯制其他货物包装袋(非针织或钩编的，用扁条及类似材料制成)	16	100		16	17	条/千克		Other sacks and bags for the packing of goods, of polyethylene or polypropylene strip or the like, not knitted or crocheted
6305.3900	--其他	16	100		16	17	条/千克		--Other
6305.9000	-其他纺织材料制	14	90		16	17	条/千克		-Of other textile materials
6305 9000.11	亚麻制旧货物包装袋(针织或钩编的)	14	90		16	17	条/千克		Send-hand sacks and bags for the packing of goods of flax, knitted or crocheted
6305 9000.19	其他亚麻制旧货物包装袋	14	90		16	17	条/千克		Send-hand sacks and bags for the packing of goods of flax, not knitted or crocheted
6305 9000.90	其他纺织材料制其他货物包装袋	14	90		16	17	条/千克		Other sacks and bags for the packing of goods, of other textile materials
63.06	**油苫布、天蓬及遮阳蓬；帐蓬；风帆；野营用品：**								**Tarpaulins, awnings and sunblinds; tents; sails for boats, sailboards or landcraft; camping goods:**
	-油苫布、天蓬及遮阳蓬:								-Tarpaulins, awnings and sunblinds:
6306.1200	--合成纤维制	16	130		16	17	件/千克		--Of synthetic fibres
	--其他纺织材料制:								--Of other textile materials:
6306.1910	---麻制	14	80		16	17	件/千克		---Of bast fibres
6306.1920	---棉制	14	80		16	17	件/千克		---Of cotton
6306.1990	---其他	14	100		16	17	件/千克		---Other
6306 1990.10	人造纤维制油苫布、天蓬及遮阳蓬	14	100		16	17	件/千克		Tarpaulins, awnings and sunblinds, of man-made fibres
6306 1990.90	其他材料制油苫布、天蓬及遮阳蓬	14	100		16	17	件/千克		Tarpaulins, awnings and sunblinds, of other textile materials

税则号列 Tariff Item	商品名称及备注	进口税率 最惠	普通	暂定	出口退税	增值税率	计量单位	监管条件	Article Description
	-帐篷:								-Tents:
6306.2200	--合成纤维制	16	130		16	17	件/千克		--Of synthetic fibres
6306 2200.10	合纤制移动帐篷	16	130		16	17	件/千克		Moveable tents, of synthetic fibres
6306 2200.90	合纤制帐篷	16	130		15	17	件/千克		Tents of synthetic fibres
	--其他纺织材料制:								--Of other textile materials:
6306.2910	---棉制	14	80		15	17	件/千克		---Of cotton
6306.2990	---其他	14	100		16	17	件/千克		---Other
	-风帆:								-Sails:
6306.3010	---合成纤维制	16	130		16	17	件/千克		---Of synthetic fibres
6306.3090	---其他纺织材料制	14	100		16	17	件/千克		---Of other textile materials
	-充气褥垫:								-Pneumatic mattresses:
6306.4010	---棉制	14	80		16	17	件/千克		---Of cotton
6306.4020	---化学纤维制	16	130		16	17	件/千克		---Of man-made fibres
6306.4090	---其他纺织材料制	14	100		16	17	件/千克		---Other
	-其他:								-Other:
	--其他纺织材料制:								--Of other textile materials:
6306.9010	---棉制	14	80		16	17	件/千克		---Of cotton
6306.9020	---麻制	14	80		16	17	件/千克		---Of bast fibres
6306.9030	---化学纤维制	16	130		16	17	件/千克		---Of man-made fibres
6306.9090	---其他	14	100		16	17	件/千克		---Other
63.07	**其他制成品，包括服装裁剪样:**								**Other made up articles, including dress patterns:**
6307.1000	-擦地布、擦碗布、抹布及类似擦拭用布	14	130		16	17	千克		-Floor-cloths, dish-cloths, dusters and similar cleaning cloths
6307.2000	-救生衣及安全带	14	70		16	17	千克/件		-Life-jackets and life-belts
6307.9000	-其他	14	100		16	17	千克		-Other
6307 9000.11	棉制标签、服饰辫线及流苏(含紧身胸衣、鞋及类似品的系带)	14	100		16	17	千克		Tags , clothing braid string and fringes, including laces of corsets, shoelaces and similar articles, of cotton
6307 9000.19	其他制标签、服饰辫线及流苏(含紧身胸衣、鞋及类似品的系带)	14	100		16	17	千克		Tags , clothing braid string and fringes, including laces of corsets, shoelaces and similar articles, of other textile materials
6307 9000.20	棉制起绒或簇绒织物制毛巾	14	100		16	17	千克		Towel, pile fabrics, tufting, of cotton
6307 9000.30	棉制枕壳	14	100		16	17	千克		Pillow shell, of cotton
6307 9000.40	棉制被壳、羽绒被壳、盖被壳(含类似品，含棉85%以下)	14	100		16	17	千克		Quilt shell, feather quilt shell or comforter shell, of cotton, containing less than 85% of cotton
6307 9000.51	棉制手术用巾及其他毛巾	14	100		16	17	千克		Towels for surgery operation and other towel, of cotton
6307 9000.59	化学纤维制未列名毛巾	14	100		16	17	千克		Towels of man-made fibres, not specified
6307 9000.61	以棉做面的冷藏包	14	100		16	17	千克		Refrigerating bag with cover of cotton
6307 9000.62	以化纤纺织材料做面的冷藏包	14	100		16	17	千克		Refrigerating bag with cover of man-made textile materials
6307 9000.69	其他纺织材料做面的冷藏包	14	100		16	17	千克		Refrigerating bag with cover of other textile materials
6307 9000.90	纺织材料制未列名制品	14	100		16	17	千克		Other made up articles, not specified, of other textile materials
	第二分章　成套物品								**II. SETS**
63.08	**由机织物及纱线构成的零售包装成套物品，不论是否带附件，用以制作小地毯、装饰毯、绣花台布、餐巾或类似的纺织物品:**								**Sets consisting of woven fabric and yarn, whether or not with accessories, for making up into rugs, tapestries, embroidered table cloths or serviettes, or similar textile articles, put up in packings for retail sale:**
6308.0000	由机织物及纱线构成的零售包装成套物品，不论是否带附件，用以制作小地毯、装饰毯、绣花台布、餐巾或类似的纺织物品	14	130		16	17	千克		Sets consisting of woven fabric and yarn, whether or not with accessories, for making up into rugs, tapestries, embroidered table cloths or serviettes, or similar textile articles, put up in packings for retail sale
6308 0000.10	机织物及纱线制零售包装成套物品(内含羊毛纱的)	14	130		16	17	千克		Sets consisting of woven fabric and yarn, containing woolen yarn, put up for retail sale

税则号列 Tariff Item	商品名称及备注	进口税率			出口退税	增值税率	计量单位	监管条件	Article Description
		最惠	普通	暂定					
6308 0000.20	机织物及纱线制零售包装成套物品(由普通棉机织物及棉绗缝被褥织物与纱线构成的)	14	130		16	17	千克		Sets consisting of woven fabric, quilt mattress fabrics and yarn, of cotton, put up for retail sale
6308 0000.30	机织物及纱线制零售包装成套物品(由合成纤维普通机织物及绗缝被褥织物与纱线构成)	14	130		16	17	千克		Sets consisting of woven fabric, quilt mattress fabrics and yarn, of synthetic fibres, put up in packings for retail sale
6308 0000.90	其他机织物及纱线构成的成套物品(零售包装的)	14	130		16	17	千克		Other sets consisting of woven fabric and yarn, put up for retail sale
	第三分章　旧衣着及旧纺织品；碎织物：								**Ⅲ. WORN CLOTHING AND WORN TEXTILE ARTICLES; RAGS:**
63.09	**旧衣物：**								**Worn clothing and other worn articles:**
6309.0000	旧衣物	14	130			17	千克	9	Worn clothing and other worn articles
63.10	**新或旧的破、碎织物，线、绳、索、缆的废、碎料以及线、绳、索、缆或纺织材料的破旧制品：**								**Used or new rags, scrap twine, cordage, rope and cables and worn out articles of twine, cordage, rope or cables, of textile materials:**
6310.1000	-经分拣的	14	50		16	17	千克		-Sorted
6310 1000.10	新的或未使用过的纺织材料制经分拣的碎织物等(新的或未使用过的，包括废线、绳、索、缆及其制品)	14	50		16	17	千克	AP	Sorted new or not used rags, including scrap twine, cordage, rope and cables and worn out articles of twine, of textile materials
6310 1000.90	其他纺织材料制经分拣的碎织物等(包括废线、绳、索、缆及其制品)	14	50		16	17	千克	9	Sorted rags, including scrap twine, cordage, rope and cables and worn out articles of twine, of other textile materials
6310.9000	-其他	14	50		16	17	千克		-Other
6310 9000.10	新的或未使用过的纺织材料制其他碎织物等(新的或未使用过的，包括废线、绳、索、缆及其制品)	14	50		16	17	千克	AP	New or not used rags, including scrap twine, cordage, rope and cables and worn out articles of twine, of textile materials
6310 9000.90	其他纺织材料制碎织物等(包括废线、绳、索、缆及其制品)	14	50		16	17	千克	9	Other rags, including scrap twine, cordage, rope and cables and worn out articles of twine, of textile materials

第十二类
鞋、帽、伞、杖、鞭及其零件；已加工的羽毛及其制品；人造花；人发制品

SECTION XII
FOOTWEAR, HEADGEAR, UMBRELLAS, SUN UMBRELLAS, WALKING - STICKS, SEAT - STICKS, WHIPS, RIDING - CROPS AND PARTS THEREOF; PREPARED FEATHERS AND ARTICLES MADE THEREWITH; ARTIFICIAL FLOWERS; ARTICLES OF HUMAN HAIR

第六十四章
鞋靴、护腿和类似品及其零件

Chapter 64
Footwear, gaiters and the like; parts of such articles

注释：

一、本章不包括：

（一）易损材料（例如，纸、塑料薄膜）制的无外绱鞋底的一次性鞋靴罩或套，这些产品应按其构成材料归类；

（二）纺织材料制的鞋靴，没有用粘、缝或其他方法将外底固定或安装在鞋面上的（第十一类）；

（三）品目63.09的旧鞋靴；

（四）石棉制品（品目68.12）；

（五）矫形鞋靴或其他矫形器具及其零件（品目90.21）；或

（六）玩具鞋及装有冰刀或轮子的滑冰鞋；护胫或类似的运动防护服装（第九十五章）。

二、品目64.06所称“零件”，不包括鞋钉、护鞋铁掌、鞋眼、鞋钩、鞋扣、饰物、编带、鞋带、绒球或其他装饰带（应分别归入相应品目）及品目96.06的钮扣或其他货品。

三、本章所称：

（一）“橡胶”及“塑料”，包括能用肉眼辨出其外表有一层橡胶或塑料的机织物或其他纺织产品；运用本款时，橡胶或塑料仅引起颜色变化的不计在内；以及

（二）“皮革”，是指品目 41.07 及 41.12 至 41.14 的货品。

四、除本章注释三另有规定的以外：

（一）鞋面的材料应以占表面面积最大的那种材料为准，计算表面面积可不考虑附件及加固件，例如，护踝、裹边、饰物、扣子、拉襻、鞋眼或类似附属件。

（二）外底的主要材料应以与地面接触最广的那种材料为准，计算接触面时可不考虑鞋底钉、铁掌或类似附属件。

子目注释：

子目 6402.12、6402.19、6403.12、6403.19 及 6404.11 所称“运动鞋靴”，仅适用于：

一、带有或可装鞋底钉、止滑柱、夹钳、马蹄掌或类似品的体育专用鞋靴。

Chapter Notes:

1. This Chapter does not cover:

(a) Disposable foot or shoe coverings of flimsy material (for example, paper, sheeting of plastics) without applied soles. These products are classified according to their constituent material;

(b) Footwear of textile material, without an outer sole glued, sewn or otherwise affixed or applied to the upper (Section XI);

(c) Worn footwear of heading 63.09;

(d) Articles of asbestos (heading 68.12);

(e) Orthopaedic footwear or other orthopaedic appliances, or parts thereof (heading 90.21); or

(f) Toy footwear or skating boots with ice or roller skates attached; shin-guards or similar protective sportswear (Chapter 95).

2. For the purposes of heading 64.06, the term “parts” does not include pegs, protectors, eyelets, hooks, buckles, ornaments, braid, laces, pompons or other trimmings (which are to be classified in their appropriate headings) or buttons or other goods of heading 96.06.

3. For the purposes of this Chapter:

(a) The terms “rubber” and “plastics” include woven fabrics or other textile products with an external layer of rubber or plastics being visible to the naked eye; for the purpose of this provision, no account should be taken of any resulting change of colour; and

(b) The term “leather” refers to the goods of headings 41.07 and 41.12 to 41.14.

4. Subject to Note 3 to this Chapter:

(a) The material of the upper shall be taken to be the constituent material having the greatest external surface area, no account being taken of accessories or reinforcements such as ankle patches, edging, ornamentation, buckles, tabs, eyelet stays or similar attachments;

(b) The constituent material of the outer sole shall be taken to be the material having the greatest surface area in contact with the ground, no account being taken of accessories or reinforcements such as spikes, bars, nails, protectors or similar attachments.

Subheading Notes:

For the purposes of subheadings 6402.12, 6402.19, 6403.12, 6403.19 and 6404.11, the expression “sports footwear” applies only to:

1. Footwear which is designed for a sporting activity and has, or has provision for the attachment of, spikes, sprigs, stops, clips, bars or the like;

二、滑冰靴，滑雪靴及越野滑雪用鞋靴、滑雪板靴、角力靴、拳击靴及赛车鞋。

2. Skating boots, ski-boots and cross-country ski footwear, snowboard boots, wrestling boots, boxing boots and cycling shoes.

税则号列 Tariff Item	商品名称及备注	进口税率			出口退税	增值税率	计量单位	监管条件	Article Description
		最惠	普通	暂定					
64.01	**橡胶或塑料制外底及鞋面的防水鞋靴，其鞋面不是用缝、铆、钉、旋、塞或类似方法固定在鞋底上的：**								**Waterproof footwear with outer soles and uppers of rubber or of plastics, the uppers of which are neither fixed to the sole nor assembled by stitching, riveting, nailing, screwing, plugging or similar processes:**
	-装有金属防护鞋头的鞋靴:								-Footwear incorporating a protective metal toe-cap:
6401.1010	---橡胶制鞋面的	24	100		15	17	千克/双		---With uppers of rubber
6401.1090	---塑料制鞋面的	24	100		15	17	千克/双		---With uppers of plastics
	-其他鞋靴:								--Other footwear:
	--中、短筒靴(过踝但未到膝):								--Covering the ankle but not covering the knee:
6401.9210	---橡胶制鞋面的	24	100		15	17	千克/双		---With uppers of rubber
6401.9290	---塑料制鞋面的	24	100		15	17	千克/双		---With uppers of plastics
6401.9900	--其他	24	100		15	17	千克/双		--Other
64.02	**橡胶或塑料制外底及鞋面的其他鞋靴：**								**Other footwear with outer soles and uppers of rubber or plastics:**
	-运动鞋靴:								-Sports footwear:
6402.1200	--滑雪靴、越野滑雪鞋靴及滑雪板靴	10	100			17	千克/双		--Ski-boots, cross-country ski footwear and snowboard boots
6402 1200.10	含濒危动物毛皮橡胶/塑料底及面滑雪靴(包括越野滑雪鞋靴及滑雪板靴)	10	100			17	千克/双	EF	Skiing boots with outer soles and uppers of rubber or plastics, containing skin and hair of endangered animals, including cross-country ski footwear and snowboard boots
6402 1200.90	其他橡胶/塑料底及面滑雪靴(包括越野滑雪鞋靴及滑雪板靴)	10	100		15	17	千克/双		Ski-boots with outer soles and uppers of rubber or plastics, including cross-country ski footwear and snowboard boots
6402.1900	--其他	24	100			17	千克/双		--Other
6402 1900.10	含濒危动物毛皮其他运动鞋靴(橡胶、塑料制底及面)	24	100			17	千克/双	EF	Other sports footwear with outer soles and uppers of rubber or plastics containing skin and hair of endangered animals
6402 1900.90	橡胶、塑料制底及面的其他运动鞋靴	24	100		15	17	千克/双		Other sport footwear, with outer soles and uppers of rubber or plastics
6402.2000	-用栓塞方法将鞋面条带装配在鞋底上的鞋	24	100		15	17	千克/双		-Footwear with upper straps or thongs assembled to the sole by means of plugs
	-其他鞋靴:								-Other footwear:
6402.9100	--短筒靴(过踝)	24	100		15	17	千克/双		--Covering the ankle
	--其他:								--Other:
6402.9910	---橡胶制鞋面的	24	100		15	17	千克/双		---With uppers of rubber
	---塑料制鞋面的:								---With uppers of plastics:
6402.9921	----其他以机织物或其他纺织材料作衬底的	24	100		15	17	千克/双		----On a base of woven fabric or other textile marterial
6402.9929	----其他	24	100		15	17	千克/双		----Other
64.03	**橡胶、塑料、皮革或再生皮革制外底，皮革制鞋面的鞋靴：**								**Footwear with outer soles of rubber, plastics, leather or composition leather and uppers of leather:**
	-运动鞋靴:								-Sports footwear:
6403.1200	--滑雪靴、越野滑雪鞋靴及滑雪板靴	24	100		15	17	千克/双		--Ski-boots, cross-country ski footwear and snowboard boots
6403 1200.10	野生动物皮革制鞋面的滑雪靴	24	100		15	17	千克/双	EF	Ski-boots, with uppers of leather of wild animals
6403 1200.90	其他皮革制鞋面的滑雪靴(包括橡胶、塑料、皮革制外底和越野滑雪鞋靴及板靴)	24	100		15	17	千克/双		Ski-boots, cross-country ski footwear and snowboard boots with uppers of other leather and outer soles of rubber, plastics, leather or composition leather
6403.1900	--其他	15	100		15	17	千克/双		--Other
6403 1900.10	野生动物皮革制鞋面其他运动鞋靴	15	100		15	17	千克/双	EF	Other sports footwear with uppers of leather of wild animals

税则号列 Tariff Item	商品名称及备注	进口税率 最惠	普通	暂定	出口退税	增值税率	计量单位	监管条件	Article Description
6403 1900.90	皮革制鞋面的其他运动鞋靴(橡胶、塑料、皮革或再生皮革制外底)	15	100		15	17	千克/双		Other sports footwear with uppers of leather and outer soles of rubber, plastics, leather or composition leather
6403.2000	-皮革制外底，由交叉于脚背并绕大脚趾的皮革条带构成鞋面的鞋	24	100		15	17	千克/双		-Footwear with outer soles of leather, and uppers which consist of leather straps across the instep and around the big toe
6403 2000.10	野生动物皮革条带为鞋面的皮底鞋	24	100		15	17	千克/双	EF	Footwear with outer soles of leather and with uppers of leather straps of wild animals
6403 2000.90	其他皮革条带为鞋面的皮底鞋（皮革条带交叉于脚背并绕大脚趾的）	24	100		15	17	千克/双		Footwear with outer soles of leather and with uppers which consist of other leather straps across the instep and around the big toe
6403.4000	-装有金属防护鞋头的其他鞋靴	24	100		15	17	千克/双		-Other footwear, incorporating a protective metal toe-cap
6403 4000.10	其他含野生动物皮革面鞋靴(装有金属护鞋头的)	24	100		15	17	千克/双	FE	Other footwear with uppers of leather of wild animals(incorporating a protective metal toe-cap)
6403 4000.90	装有金属护鞋头的其他皮革面鞋靴(橡胶、塑料、皮革或再生皮革制外底)	24	100		15	17	千克/双		Other footwear with uppers of leather, incorporating a protective metal toe-cap (with outer soles of rubber, plastics, leather or composition leather)
	-皮革制外底的其他鞋靴:								-Other footwear with outer soles of leather:
	--短筒靴（过踝）:								--Covering the ankle:
	---过脚踝但低于小腿的短筒靴，按内底长度分类:								---Covering the ankle but not covering the calf,by length of inner soles:
6403.5111	----小于 24 厘米的	10	100		15	17	千克/双		----Less than 24cm
6403 5111.10	野生动物皮革制外底皮革面过脚踝但低于小腿的短筒靴(内底长度小于 24 厘米，运动用靴除外)	10	100		15	17	千克/双	FE	Other short boots with outer soler of leather and uppers of leather of wild animals,covering the ankle but lower than crus, inner sole length less than 24cm (other than sports footwear)
6403 5111.90	皮革制外底皮革面过脚踝但低于小腿的短筒靴(内底长度小于 24 厘米，运动用靴除外)	10	100		15	17	千克/双		Short boots with outer soler of leather and uppers of leather,covering the ankle but lower than crus, inner sole length less than 24cm (other than sports footwear)
6403.5119	----其他	10	100		15	17	千克/双		----Other
6403 5119.10	其他野生动物皮革制外底皮革面过脚踝但低于小腿的短筒靴（运动用靴除外）	10	100		15	17	千克/双	EF	Short boots with outer soler of leather, of wild animals, covering the ankle but lower than crus, uppers of leather(other than sports footwear)
6403 5119.90	其他皮革制外底皮革面过脚踝但低于小腿的短筒靴(运动用靴除外)	10	100		15	17	千克/双		Short boots with outer soler of other leather, covering the ankle but lower than crus, uppers of leather (other than sports footwear)
	---其他，按内底长度分类:								---Other,by length of inner soles:
6403.5191	----小于 24 厘米的	10	100		15	17	千克/双		----Less than 24cm
6403 5191.10	野生动物皮革制外底皮革面短筒靴（内底长度小于 24 厘米，运动用靴除外）	10	100		15	17	千克/双	EF	Short boots with outer soles of leather and uppers of leather of wild animals, of inner soles length less than 24cm (other than sports footwear)
6403 5191.90	皮革制外底的皮革面短筒靴(过踝)（内底长度小于 24 厘米，运动用靴除外）	10	100		15	17	千克/双		Short boots with outer soles of leather and uppers of leather,covering the ankle, of inner soles length less than 24cm (other than sports footwear)
6403.5199	----其他	10	100		15	17	千克/双		----Other
6403 5199.10	野生动物皮革制外底皮革面短筒靴（运动用靴除外）	10	100		15	17	千克/双	FE	Short boots with outer solers of leather and uppers of leather, of wild animals (other than sports footwear)
6403 5199.90	皮革制外底的皮革面短筒靴(过踝) （运动用靴除外）	10	100		15	17	千克/双		Short boots with outer soles of leather and uppers of leather (other than sports footwear)
6403.5900	—其他	10	100		15	17	千克/双		--Other
6403 5900.10	野生动物皮革制外底的皮革面其他鞋（包括靴，运动用鞋靴除外）	10	100		15	17	千克/双	EF	Other footwear with outer soles of leather and uppers of leather, of wild animals, including boots, other than sports footwear
6403 5900.90	皮革制外底的皮革面其他鞋靴（运动用鞋靴除外）	10	100		15	17	千克/双		Other footwear with outer soles of leather and uppers of leather, other than sports footwear

税则号列 Tariff Item	商品名称及备注	进口税率 最惠	普通	暂定	出口退税	增值税率	计量单位	监管条件	Article Description
	-其他鞋靴: --短筒靴（过踝）: ---过脚踝但低于小腿的短筒靴，按内底长度分类:								-Other footwear: --Covering the ankle: ---Covering the ankle but not covering the calf,by length of inner soles:
6403.9111	----小于24厘米的	10	100		15	17	千克/双		----Less than 24cm
6403 9111.10	其他野生动物皮革制面过脚踝但低于小腿的短筒靴(内底＜24厘米，橡胶、塑料、再生皮革制外底，运动用靴除外)	10	100		15	17	千克/双	EF	Short boots with uppers of leather of wild animal, covering the ankle but lower than calf,outer soles of rubber or plastic or composition leather, of inner soles length less than 24cm, other than sports footwear
6403 9111.90	其他皮革制面过脚踝但低于小腿的短筒靴(内底＜24 厘米，橡胶、塑料、再生皮革制外底，运动用靴除外)	10	100		15	17	千克/双		Short boots with uppers of other leather, covering the ankle but lower than calf, outer soles of rubber or plastic or composition leather, of inner soles length less than 24cm, other than sports footwear
6403.9119	----其他	10	100		15	17	千克/双		----Other
6403 9119.10	其他野生动物皮革制面过脚踝但低于小腿的短筒靴(橡胶、塑料、再生皮革制外底，运动用靴除外)	10	100		15	17	千克/双	EF	Short boots with uppers of leather of other wild animals covering the ankle but lower than calf, outer soles of rubber or plastic or composition leather, of inner soles length less than 24cm, other than sports footwear
6403 9119.90	其他皮革制面过脚踝但低于小腿的短筒靴(橡胶、塑料、再生皮革制外底，运动用靴除外)	10	100		15	17	千克/双		Short boots with uppers of other leather, covering the ankle but lower than calf, outer soles of rubber or plastic or composition leather, other than sports footwear
	---其他，按内底长度分类:								---Other, by length of inner soles:
6403.9191	----小于24厘米的	10	100		15	17	千克/双		----Less than 24cm
6403 9191.10	其他野生皮革制面的短筒靴(过踝)(内底＜24厘米，橡胶、塑料、再生皮革制外底，运动用靴除外)	10	100		15	17	千克/双	EF	Short boots with uppers of leather of other wild animals covering the ankle, outer soles of rubber or plastic or composition leather, of inner soles length less than 24cm, other than sports footwear
6403 9191.90	其他皮革制面的短筒靴(过踝)(内底＜24厘米，橡胶、塑料、再生皮革制外底，运动用靴除外)	10	100		15	17	千克/双		Short boots with uppers of other leather,covering the ankle but lower than calf, outer soles of rubber or plastic or composition leather, of inner soles length less than 24cm, other than sports footwear
6403.9199	----其他	10	100		15	17	千克/双		----Other
6403 9199.10	其他野生皮革制面的短筒靴(过踝)(橡胶、塑料、再生皮革制外底，运动用靴除外)	10	100		15	17	千克/双	EF	Short boots with uppers of leather of other wild animals, covering the ankle, outer soles of rubber or plastic or composition leather, other than sports footwear
6403 9199.90	其他皮革制面的短筒靴(过踝)(橡胶、塑料、再生皮革制外底，运动用靴除外)	10	100		15	17	千克/双		Short boots with uppers of other leather,covering the ankle, outer soles of rubber or plastic or composition leather, other than sports footwear
6403.9900	--其他	10	100		15	17	千克/双		--Other
6403 9900.10	野生动物皮革制面的其他鞋靴(橡胶、塑料、再生皮革制外底，运动用鞋靴除外)	10	100		15	17	千克/双	EF	Other footwear with uppers of leather of wild animals,outer soles of rubber or plastic or composition leather, other than sports footwear
6403 9900.90	其他皮革制面的其他鞋靴(橡胶、塑料、再生皮革制外底，运动用鞋靴除外)	10	100		15	17	千克/双		Other footwear with uppers of other leather,outer soles of rubber or plastic or composition leather, other than sports footwear
64.04	**橡胶、塑料、皮革或再生皮革制外底，用纺织材料制鞋面的鞋靴:**								**Footwear with outer soles of rubber, plastics, leather or composition leather and uppers of textile materials:**
	-橡胶或塑料制外底的鞋靴:								-Footwear with outer soles of rubber or plastics:
6404.1100	--运动鞋靴；网球鞋、篮球鞋、体操鞋、训练鞋及类似鞋	24	100		15	17	千克/双		--Sports footwear, tennis shoes, basketball shoes, gym shoes, training shoes and the like
6404.1900	--其他	24	100		15	17	千克/双		--Other
6404.2000	-皮革或再生皮革制外底的鞋靴	24	100		15	17	千克/双		-Footwear with outer soles of leather or composition leather

税则号列 Tariff Item	商品名称及备注	进口税率 最惠	普通	暂定	出口退税	增值税率	计量单位	监管条件	Article Description
64.05	**其他鞋靴:**								**Other footwear:**
	-皮革或再生皮革制鞋面的:								-With uppers of leather or composition leather:
6405.1010	---橡胶、塑料、皮革及再生皮革制外底的	24	100		15	17	千克/双		---With outer soles of rubber, plastics, leather or composition leather
6405.1090	---其他材料制外底的	24	100		15	17	千克/双		---Other
6405 1090.10	野生动物皮革制面的其他鞋靴（外底用橡胶、塑料、皮革及再生皮革以外材料制成）	24	100		15	17	千克/双	EF	Other footwear with uppers of leather of wild animals, outer soles of materials other than rubber, plastics ,leather or composition leather
6405 1090.90	其他皮革或再生皮革制面的其他鞋靴(外底用橡胶,塑料,皮革及再生皮革以外材料制成)	24	100		15	17	千克/双		Other footwear with uppers of leather leather or composition leather, outer soles of materials other than rubber, plastics,leather or composition leather
6405.2000	-纺织材料制鞋面的	22	100		15	17	千克/双		-With uppers of textile materials
6405 2000.10	羊毛毡呢制内底及鞋面的鞋靴（外底用橡胶、塑料、皮革或再生皮革制以外材料制成）	22	100		15	17	千克/双		Footwear with innner soles and uppers of wool felt, outer soles of materials other than rubber, plastics, leather or composition leather
6405 2000.90	纺织材料制鞋面的其他鞋靴(外底用橡胶、塑料、皮革或再生皮革制以外材料制成）	22	100		15	17	千克/双		Other footwear with uppers of textile materials, outer soles of materials other than rubber, plastics, leather or composition leather
	-其他:								-Other:
6405.9010	---橡胶、塑料、皮革及再生皮革制外底的	15	100		15	17	千克/双		---With outer soles of rubber,plastics,leather or composition leather
6405.9090	---其他材料制外底的	15	100		15	17	千克/双		---Other
64.06	**鞋靴零件（包括鞋面，不论是否带有除外底以外的其他鞋底）；活动式鞋内底、跟垫及类似品；护腿、裹腿和类似品及其零件:**								**Parts of footwear（including uppers whether or not attached to soles other than outer soles）；removable in-soles, heel cushions and similar articles; gaiters, leggings and similar articles, and parts thereof:**
6406.1000	-鞋面及其零件，但硬衬除外	15	90		15	17	千克		-Uppers and parts thereof, other than stiffeners
6406 1000.10	含野生动物皮的鞋面及其零件	15	90		15	17	千克	FE	Uppers and parts thereof, containing leather of wild animals
6406 1000.90	其他鞋面及其零件(不包括硬衬及毡呢制品）	15	90		15	17	千克		Other uppers and parts thereof, excluding stiffeners and felt articles
	-橡胶或塑料制的外底及鞋跟:								-Outer soles and heels, of rubber or plastics:
6406.2010	---橡胶制的	15	90		15	17	千克		---Of rubber
6406.2020	---塑料制的	15	90		15	17	千克		---Of plastics
	-其他:								-Other:
6406.9010	---木制	15	90		15	17	千克	A	--Of wood
	---其他材料制:								---Of other materials:
6406.9091	----活动式鞋内底、跟垫及类似品	15	90		15	17	千克		----Removable in-soles, heel cushions and similar articles
6406.9092	----护腿、裹腿和类似品及其零件	15	90		15	17	千克		----Gaiters, leggings and similar articles, and parts thereof
6406.9099	----其他材料制其他鞋靴零件	15	90		15	17	千克		----Other parts of footwear of other materials

第六十五章 帽类及其零件

Chapter 65 Headgear and parts thereof

注释：

一、本章不包括：

（一）品目63.09的旧帽类；

（二）石棉制帽类（品目68.12）；或

（三）第九十五章的玩偶帽、其他玩具帽或狂欢节用品。

二、品目 65.02 不包括缝制的帽坯，但仅将条带缝成螺旋形的除外。

Chapter Notes:

1. This Chapter does not cover:

（a）Worn headgear of heading 63.09;

（b）Asbestos headgear（heading 68.12）; or

（c）"Dolls" hats, other toy hats or carnival articles of Chapter 95.

2. Heading 65.02 does not cover hat-shapes made by sewing, other than those obtained simply by sewing strips in spirals.

税则号列 Tariff Item	商品名称及备注	进口税率			出口退税	增值税率	计量单位	监管条件	Article Description
		最惠	普通	暂定					
65.01	**毡呢制的帽坯、帽身及帽兜，未楦制成形，也未加帽边；毡呢制的圆帽片及制帽用的毡呢筒(包括裁开的毡呢筒)：**								**Hat-forms, hat bodies and hoods of felt, neither blocked to shape nor with made brims; plateaux and manchons（including slit manchons）, of felt:**
6501.0000	毡呢制的帽坯、帽身及帽兜，未楦制成形，也未加帽边；毡呢制的圆帽片及制帽用的毡呢筒(包括裁开的毡呢筒)	22	100		15	17	千克		Hat-forms, hat bodies and hoods of felt, neither blocked to shape nor with made brims; plateaux and manchons（including slit manchons）, of felt
65.02	**编结的帽坯或用任何材料的条带拼制而成的帽坯，未楦制成形，也未加帽边、衬里或装饰物：**								**Hat-shapes, plaited or made by assembling strips of any material, neither blocked to shape, nor with made brims, nor lined, nor trimmed:**
6502.0000	编结的帽坯或用任何材料的条带拼制而成的帽坯，未楦制成形，也未加帽边、衬里或装饰物	20	100		15	17	千克		Hat-shapes, plaited or made by assembling strips of any material, neither blocked to shape, nor with made brims, nor lined, nor trimmed
65.04	**编结帽或用任何材料的条带拼制而成的帽类，不论有无衬里或装饰物：**								**Hats and other headgear, plaited or made by assembling strips of any material, whether or not lined or trimmed:**
6504.0000	编结帽或用任何材料的条带拼制而成的帽类，不论有无衬里或装饰物	20	130		15	17	个/千克		Hats and other headgear, plaited or made by assembling strips of any material, whether or not lined or trimmed
65.05	**针织或钩编的帽类，用成匹的花边、毡呢或其他纺织物（条带除外）制成的帽类，不论有无衬里或装饰物；任何材料制的发网，不论有无衬里或装饰物：**								**Hats and other headgear, knitted or crocheted, or made up from lace, felt or other textile fabric, in the piece（not in strips）, whether or not lined or trimmed; hair-nets of any material, whether or not lined or trimmed:**
6505.0010	---发网	10	130		15	17	个/千克		---Hair-nets
6505.0020	---钩编的帽类	20	130		15	17	个/千克		---Hats and other headgear, knitted or crocheted
	---其他								---Other
6505.0091	----用税目 65.01 的帽身、帽兜或圆帽片制成的毡呢帽类，不论有无衬里或装饰物	22	130		15	17	个/千克		---Felt hats and other felt headgear, made from the hat bodies, hoods or plateaux of heading No.65.01, whether or not lined or trimmed
6505.0099	----其他	20	130		15	17	个/千克		----Other
65.06	**其他帽类，不论有无衬里或装饰物：**								**Other headgear, whether or not lined or trimmed:**
6506.1000	-安全帽	10	100		15	17	个/千克		-Safety headgear
6506 1000.10	防护罩(带有能够滤除生物因子滤器的面罩)	10	100		15	17	个/千克	3	Protective mask (with filter, which can filtered biological factors)
6506 1000.90	其他安全帽(不论有无衬里或饰物)	10	100		15	17	个/千克		Other safety headgear, whether or not lined or trimmed
	-其他:								-Other:
6506.9100	--橡胶或塑料制	10	100		15	17	个/千克		--Of rubber or of plastics
	--其他材料制:								-Of other materials:
6506.9910	---皮革制	10	130		15	17	个/千克		---Of leather

税则号列 Tariff Item	商品名称及备注	进口税率			出口退税	增值税率	计量单位	监管条件	Article Description
		最惠	普通	暂定					
6506 9910.10	野生动物皮革制帽类	10	130		15	17	个/千克	EF	Other headgear, of leather of wild animals
6506 9910.90	其他皮革制帽类	10	130		15	17	个/千克		Other headgear, of leather of other animals
6506.9920	---毛皮制	10	130		15	17	个/千克		---Of furskin
6506 9920.10	野生动物毛皮制的帽类(无论有无衬里或饰物)	10	130		15	17	个/千克	EF	Headgear, of leather of wild animals, whether or not lined or trimmed
6506 9920.90	其他毛皮制的帽类(无论有无衬里或饰物)	10	130		15	17	个/千克		Headgear, of leather of other animals, whether or not lined or trimmed
6506.9990	---其他	24	100		15	17	个/千克		---Other
65.07	**帽圈、帽衬、帽套、帽帮、帽骨架、帽舌及帽颏带:**								**Head-bands, linings, covers, hat foundations, hat frames, peaks and chinstraps, for headgear:**
6507.0000	帽圈、帽衬、帽套、帽帮、帽骨架、帽舌及帽颏带	24	100		15	17	千克		Head-bands, linings, covers, hat foundations, hat frames, peaks and chinstraps, for headgear
6507 0000.10	含野生动物成分的帽类附件(指帽圈、衬、套、帮、骨架、舌及颏带)	24	100		15	17	千克	FE	Headwear accessories, including headbands, linings, covers, hat foundations, hat frames, peaks and chinstraps,containing materials of wild animals
6507 0000.90	其他帽类附件(指帽圈、衬、套、帮、骨架、舌及颏带)	24	100		15	17	千克		Other headwear accessories, head-bands, linings, covers,hat foundations, hat frames, peaks and chinstraps

第六十六章
雨伞、阳伞、手杖、鞭子、马鞭及其零件

Chapter 66
Umbrellas, sun umbrellas, walking-sticks, seat-sticks, whips, riding-crops and parts thereof

注释：

一、本章不包括：

（一）丈量用杖及类似品（品目 90.17）

（二）火器手杖、刀剑手杖、灌铅手杖及类似品（第九十三章）；或

（三）第九十五章的货品（例如，玩具雨伞、玩具阳伞）。

二、品目 66.03 不包括纺织材料制的零件、附件及装饰品或者任何材料制的罩套、流苏、鞭梢、伞套及类似品。此类货品即使与品目 66.01 或 66.02 的物品一同报验，只要未装配在一起，则不应视为上述品目所列物品的组成零件，而应分别归入各有关品目。

Chapter Notes:

1. This Chapter does not cover:

（a）Measure walking-sticks or the like（heading 90.17）;

（b）Firearm-sticks, sword-sticks, loaded walking-sticks or the like（Chapter 93）; or

（c）Goods of Chapter95（for example, toy umbrellas, toy sun umbrellas）.

2. Heading 66.03 does not cover parts, trimmings or accessories of textile material, or covers, tassels, thongs, umbrella cases or the like, of any material. Such goods presented with, but not fitted to, articles of heading 66.01or 66.02 are to be classified separately and not to be treated as forming part of those articles.

税则号列 Tariff Item	商品名称及备注	进口税率			出口退税	增值税率	计量单位	监管条件	Article Description
		最惠	普通	暂定					
66.01	**雨伞及阳伞（包括手杖伞、庭园用伞及类似伞）：**								**Umbrellas and sun umbrellas（including walking-stick umbrellas, garden umbrellas and similar umbrellas）:**
6601.1000	-庭园用伞及类似伞	14	130		15	17	千克/把		-Garden or similar umbrellas
	-其他:								-Other:
6601.9100	--折叠伞	10	130		15	17	千克/把		--Having a telescopic shaft
6601.9900	--其他	10	130		15	17	千克/把		--Other
66.02	**手杖、带座手杖、鞭子、马鞭及类似品：**								**Walking-sticks, seat-sticks, whips, riding-crops and the like:**
6602.0000	手杖、带座手杖、鞭子、马鞭及类似品	10	130		15	17	千克/把		Walking-sticks, seat-sticks, whips, riding-crops and the like
6602 0000.11	含野生动物成分的手杖、带座手杖（包括马鞭、鞭子及类似品）	10	130		15	17	千克/把	EF	Walking-sticks, seat-sticks, whips, riding-crops and the like, containing composition of wild animals
6602 0000.19	动植物材料制手杖、鞭子及类似品（包括带座手杖）	10	130		15	17	千克/把		Walking-sticks, seat-sticks, whips, riding-crops and the like, of vegetable or animal materials
6602 0000.90	其他手杖、带座手杖、鞭子及类似品	10	130		15	17	千克/把		Other walking-sticks, seat-sticks, whips, riding-crops and the like
66.03	**品目66.01或66.02所列物品的零件及装饰品：**								**Parts, trimmings and accessories of articles of heading No.66.01 or 66.02:**
6603.2000	-伞骨，包括装在伞柄上的伞骨	14	130		15	17	千克		-Umbrella frames, including frames mounted on shafts（sticks）
6603.9000	-其他	14	130		15	17	千克		-Other
6603 9000.10	含野生动物成分的伞、手杖的零件及装饰品(包括鞭子的其他零件及饰品)	14	130		15	17	千克	EF	Parts, trimmings and accessories of umbrella, walking-sticks, whips, containing composition of wild animals
6603 9000.90	伞、手杖及鞭子的其他零件及饰品（罩套、流苏、鞭梢及纺织材料制品除外）	14	130		15	17	千克		Other parts, trimmings and accessories of umbrella, walking-sticks, whips, other than covers, tassels, lash and other articles of textile material

第六十七章 已加工羽毛、羽绒及其制品；人造花；人发制品

Chapter 67 Prepared feathers and down and articles made of feathers or of down; artificial flowers; articles of human hair

注释：

一、本章不包括：

（一）人发制滤布（品目 59.11）；

（二）花边、刺绣品或其他纺织物制成的花卉图案（第十一类）；

（三）鞋靴（第六十四章）；

（四）帽类及发网（第六十五章）；

（五）玩具、运动用品或狂欢节用品（第九十五章）；或

（六）羽毛掸帚、粉扑及人发制的筛子（第九十六章）。

二、品目 67.01 不包括：

（一）羽毛或羽绒仅在其中作为填充料的物品（例如，品目 94.04 的寝具）；

（二）羽毛或羽绒仅作为饰物或填充料的衣服或衣着附件；或

（三）品目 67.02 的人造花、叶及其部分品，以及它们的制成品。

三、品目 67.C2 不包括：

（一）玻璃制品（第七十章）；或

（二）用陶器、石料、金属、木料或其他材料经模铸、锻造、雕刻、冲压或其他方法整件制成形的人造花、叶或果实；用捆扎、胶粘及类似方法以外的其他方法将部分品组合而成的上述制品。

Chapter Notes:

1. Th s Chapter does not cover:

(a) Straining cloth of human hair (heading 59.11);

(b) Floral motifs of lace, of embroidery or other textile fabric (Section XI);

(c) Footwear (Chapter 64);

(d) Headgear or hair-nets (Chapter 65);

(e) Toys, sports requisites or carnival articles (Chapter 95); or

(f) Feather dusters, powder-puffs or hair sieves (Chapter 96).

2. Heading 67.01 does not cover:

(a) Articles in which feathers or down constitute only filling or padding (for example, bedding of heading 94.04);

(b) Articles of apparel or clothing accessories in which feathers or down constitute no more than mere trimming or padding; or

(c) Artificial flowers or foliage or parts thereof or made up articles of heading 67.02.

3. Heading 67.02 does not cover:

(a) Articles of glass (Chapter 70); or

(b) Artificial flowers, foliage or fruit of pottery, stone, metal, wood or other materials, obtained in one piece by moulding, forging, carving, stamping or other process, or consisting of parts assembled otherwise than by binding, gluing, fitting into one another or similar methods.

税则号列 Tariff Item	商品名称及备注	进口税率			出口退税	增值税率	计量单位	监管条件	Article Description
		最惠	普通	暂定					
67.01	**带羽毛或羽绒的鸟皮及鸟体其他部分、羽毛、部分羽毛、羽绒及其制品(品目 05.05 的货品和经加工的羽管及羽轴除外)：**								**Skins and other parts of birds with their feathers or down, feathers, parts of feathers, down and articles thereof (other than goods of heading No.05.05 and worked quills and scapes):**
6701.0000	带羽毛或羽绒的鸟皮及鸟体其他部分、羽毛、部分羽毛、羽绒及其制品(品目 05.05 的货品和经加工的羽管及羽轴除外)	20	130		15	17	千克		Skins and other parts of birds with their feathers or down, feathers, parts of feathers, down and articles thereof (other than goods of heading No. 05.05 and worked quills and scapes)
6701 0000.10	已加工野禽羽毛、羽绒及其制品	20	130		15	17	千克	AFEB	Worked feathers, down and articles thereof, of wildbirds
6701 0000.90	其他已加工羽毛、羽绒及其制品(品目 05.05 的货品及经加工的羽管及羽轴除外)	20	130		15	17	千克	AB	Other worked feathers, down and articles thereof (other than goods of heading No.05.05 and worked quills and scapes)
67.02	**人造花、叶、果实及其零件；用人造花、叶或果实制成的物品：**								**Artificial flowers, foliage and fruit and parts thereof; articles made of artificial flowers, foliage or fruit:**
6702.1000	-塑料制	20	130		15	17	千克		-Of plastics
	-其他材料制：								-Of other materials:
6702.9010	---羽毛制	20	130		15	17	千克		---Of feathers or down
6702 9010.10	野禽羽毛制花、叶、果实及其制品	20	130		15	17	千克	AFEB	Flowers, foliage and fruit and articles thereof, of feathers or down of wild birds

税则号列 Tariff Item	商品名称及备注	进口税率			出口退税	增值税率	计量单位	监管条件	Article Description
		最惠	普通	暂定					
6702 9010.90	其他羽毛制花、叶、果实及其制品(包括花、叶、果实的零件)	20	130		15	17	千克	AB	Flowers, foliage and fruit and parts thereof; of other feathers or down, including flowers, foliage and fruit and articles thereof
6702.9020	---丝及绢丝制	24	130		15	17	千克		---Of silk or silk waste
6702.9030	---化学纤维制	24	130		15	17	千克		---Of man-made fibres
6702.9090	---其他	20	130		15	17	千克		---Other
67.03	**经梳理、稀疏、脱色或其他方法加工的人发;作假发及类似品用的羊毛、其他动物毛或其他纺织材料:**								**Human hair, dressed, thinned, bleached or otherwise worked; wool or other animal hair or other textile materials, prepared for use in making wigs or the like:**
6703.0000	经梳理、稀疏、脱色或其他方法加工的人发;作假发及类似品用的羊毛、其他动物毛或其他纺织材料	20	100		15	17	千克		Human hair, dressed, thinned, bleached or otherwise worked; wool or other animal hair or other textile materials, prepared for use in making wigs or the like
67.04	**人发、动物毛或纺织材料制的假发、假胡须、假眉毛、假睫毛及类似品;其他品目未列名的人发制品:**								**Wigs, false beards, eyebrows and eyelashes, switches and the like, of human or animal hair or of textile materials; articles of human hair not elsewhere specified or included:**
	-合成纤维纺织材料制:								-Of synthetic textile materials:
6704.1100	--整头假发	25	130		15	17	千克		-Complete wigs
6704.1900	--其他	25	130		15	17	千克		--Other
6704.2000	-人发制	15	130		15	17	千克		-Of human hair
6704.9000	-其他材料制	25	130		15	17	千克		-Of other materials

第十三类
石料、石膏、水泥、石棉、云母及类似材料的制品；陶瓷产品；玻璃及其制品

SECTION XIII
ARTICLES OF STONE, PLASTER, CEMENT, ASBESTOS, MICA OR SIMILAR MATERIALS; CERAMIC PRODUCTS; GLASS AND GLASSWARE

第六十八章
石料、石膏、水泥、石棉、云母及类似材料的制品

Chapter 68
Articles of stone, plaster, cement, asbestos, mica or similar materials

注释：

一、本章不包括：

（一）第二十五章的货品；

（二）品目 48.10 或 48.11 的经涂布、浸渍或覆盖的纸及纸板（例如，用云母粉或石墨涂布的纸及纸板、沥青纸及纸板）；

（三）第五十六章或第五十九章的经涂布、浸渍或包覆的纺织物（例如，用云母粉、沥青涂布或包覆的织物）；

（四）第七十一章的物品；

（五）第八十二章的工具及其零件；

（六）品目 84.42 的印刷用石板；

（七）绝缘子（品目 85.46）或绝缘材料制的零件（品目 85.47）；

（八）牙科用磨锉（品目 90.18）；

（九）第九十一章的物品（例如，钟及钟壳）；

（十）第九十四章的物品（例如，家具、灯具及照明装置、活动房屋）；

（十一）第九十五章的物品（例如，玩具、游戏品及运动用品）；

（十二）用第九十六章注释二（二）所述材料制成的品目 96.02 的物品或品目 96.06 的物品（例如，钮扣）、品目 96.09 的物品（例如石笔）或品目 96.10 的物品（例如，绘画石板）；或

（十三）第九十七章的物品（例如艺术品）。

二、品目 68.02 所称“已加工的碑石或建筑用石”，不仅适用于已加工的品目 25.15、25.16 的各种石料，也适用于所有经类似加工的其他天然石料（例如，石英岩、燧石、白云石及冻石），但不适用于板岩。

Chapter Notes:

1. This Chapter does not cover:

(a) Goods of Chapter 25;

(b) Coated, impregnated or covered paper and paperboard of heading 48.10 or 48.11 (for example, paper and paperboard coated with mica powder or graphite, bituminised or asphalted paper and paperboard);

(c) Coated, impregnated or covered textile fabric of Chapter 56 or 59 (for example, fabric coated or covered with mica powder, bituminised or asphalted fabric);

(d) Articles of Chapter 71;

(e) Tools or parts of tools, of Chapter 82;

(f) Lithographic stones of heading 84.42;

(g) Electrical insulators (heading 85.46) or fittings of insulating material of heading 85.47;

(h) Dental burrs (heading 90.18);

(ij) Articles of Chapter91 (for example, clocks and clock cases);

(k) Articles of Chapter 94 (for example, furniture, lamps and lighting fittings, prefabricated buildings);

(l) Articles of Chapter 95 (for example, toys, games and sports requisites);

(m) Articles of heading 96.02, if made of materials specified in Note 2 (b) to Chapter 96, or of heading 96.06 (for example, buttons), 96.09 (for example, slate pencils) or 96.10 (for example, drawing slates); or

(n) Articles of Chapter 97 (for example, works of art).

2. In heading 68.02, the expression "worked monumental or building stone" applies not only to the varieties of stone referred to in heading 25.15 or 25.16, but also to all other natural stone (for example, quartzite, flint, dolomite and steatite) similarly worked; it does not, however, apply to slate.

税则号列 Tariff Item	商品名称及备注	进口税率 最惠	普通	暂定	出口退税	增值税率	计量单位	监管条件	Article Description
68.01	天然石料（不包括板岩）制的长方砌石、路缘石、扁平石：								**Setts, curbstones and flagstones, of natural stone (except slate):**
6801.0000	天然石料（不包括板岩）制的长方砌石、路缘石、扁平石	12	70			17	千克		Setts, curbstones and flagstones, of natural stone (except slate)
68.02	已加工的碑石或建筑用石（不包括板岩）及其制品，但品目 68.01 的货品除外；天然石料（包括板岩）制的镶嵌石（马赛克）及类似品，不论是否有衬背；天然石料（包括板岩）制的人工染色石粒、石片及石粉：								**Worked monumental or building stone (except slate) and articles thereof, other than goods of heading No.68.01; mosaic cubes and the like, of natural stone (including slate), whether or not on a backing; artificially coloured granules, chippings and powder, of natural stone (including slate):**

税则号列 Tariff Item	商品名称及备注	进口税率 最惠	普通	暂定	出口退税	增值税率	计量单位	监管条件	Article Description
	-砖、瓦、方块及类似品，不论是否为矩形（包括正方形），其最大表面积以可置入边长小于7厘米的方格为限；人工染色的石粒、石片及石粉：								-Tiles, cubes and similar articles, whether or not rectangular（including square）, the largest surface area of which is capable of being enclosed in a square the side of which is less than 7cm; artificially coloured granules, chippings and powder:
6802.1010	---大理石	24	90			17	千克		---Marble
6802.1090	---其他	20	90			17	千克		---Other
	-简单切削或锯开并具有一个平面的其他碑石或建筑用石及其制品：								-Other monumental or building stone and articles thereof, simply cut or sawn, with a flat or even surface:
	--大理石、石灰华及蜡石：								--Marble, travertine and alabaster:
6802.2110	---大理石	10	90			17	千克		---Marble
6802.2120	---石灰华	24	90		9	17	千克		---Travertine
6802.2190	---其他	24	90			17	千克		---Other
6802.2300	--花岗岩	10	90			17	千克	A	--Granite
	--其他石：								--Other stone:
6802.2910	---其他石灰石	24	90			17	千克		---Other calcareous stone
6802.2990	---其他	15	90			17	千克		---Other
	-其他：								-Other:
	--大理石、石灰华及蜡石：								--Marble, travertine and alabaster:
6802.9110	---石刻	24	90		13	17	千克		---Carvings
6802.9190	---其他	10	90		9	17	千克		---Other
	--其他石灰石：								--Other calcareous stone:
6802.9210	---石刻	24	90		13	17	千克		---Carvings
6802.9290	---其他	10	90		9	17	千克		---Other
	--花岗岩：								--Granite:
	---石刻：								---Carvings:
6802.9311	----墓碑石	24	90		13	17	千克	A	----Gravestone
6802.9319	----其他	24	90		13	17	千克	A	----Other
6802.9390	---其他	10	90		9	17	千克	A	---Other
	--其他石：								--Other stone:
6802.9910	---石制	24	90		13	17	千克		---Carvings
6802.9990	---其他	24	90		9	17	千克		---Other
68.03	**已加工的板岩及板岩或粘聚板岩的制品：**								**Worked slate and articles of slate or of agglomerated slate:**
6803.0010	---板岩制	20	80		5	17	千克		---Of slate
6803.0090	---其他	20	80		5	17	千克		---Other
68.04	**未装支架的石磨、石碾、砂轮和类似品及其零件，用于研磨、磨刃、抛光、整形或切割，以及手用磨石、手用抛光石及其零件，用天然石料、粘聚的天然磨料、人造磨料或陶瓷制成，不论是否装有由其他材料制成的零件：**								**Millstones, grindstones, grinding wheels and the like, without frameworks, for grinding, sharpening, polishing, trueing or cutting, hand sharpening or polishing stones, and parts thereof, of natural stone, of agglomerated natural or artificial abrasives, or of ceramics, with or without parts of other materials:**
6804.1000	-碾磨或磨浆用石磨、石碾	8	40		5	17	千克		-Millstones and grindstones for milling, grinding or pulping
	-其它石磨、石碾、砂轮及类似品：								-Other millstones, grindstones, grinding wheels and the like:
6804.2100	--粘聚合成或天然金刚石制	8	17		5	17	千克		--Of agglomerated synthetic or natural diamond
	--其他粘聚磨料或陶瓷制：								--Of other agglomerated abrasives or of ceramics:
6804.2210	---砂轮	8	17		5	17	千克		---Grinding wheels
6804.2290	---其他	8	40		5	17	千克		---Other
	--天然石料制：								--Of natural stone:
6804.2310	---砂轮	8	17		5	17	千克		---Grinding wheels
6804.2390	---其他	8	40		5	17	千克		---Other
	-手用磨石及手用抛光石：								-Hand sharpening or polishing stones:
6804.3010	---琢磨油石	8	17		5	17	千克		---Oilstones

税则号列 Tariff Item	商品名称及备注	进口税率 最惠	进口税率 普通	进口税率 暂定	出口退税	增值税率	计量单位	监管条件	Article Description
6804.3090	---其他	8	40		5	17	千克		---Other
68.05	**砂布、砂纸及以其他材料为底的类似品，不论是否裁切、缝合或用其他方法加工成形：**								**Natural or artificial abrasive powder or grain, on a base of textile material, of paper, of paperboard or of other materials, whether or not cut to shape or sewn or otherwise made up:**
6805.1000	-砂布	8	40		5	17	千克		-On a base of woven textile fabric only
6805.2000	-砂纸	8	40		5	17	千克		-On a base of paper or paperboard only
6805.3000	-其他	8	40		5	17	千克		-On a base of other materials
68.06	**矿渣棉、岩石棉及类似的矿质棉；页状蛭石、膨胀黏土、泡沫矿渣及类似的膨胀矿物材料；具有隔热、隔音或吸音性能的矿物材料的混合物及制品，但品目68.11、68.12 或第六十九章的货品除外：**								**Slag wool, rock wool and similar mineral wools; exfoliated vermiculite, expanded clays, foamed slag and similar expanded mineral materials; mixtures and articles of heatinsulating, soundinsulating or soundabsorbing mineral materials, other than those of heading No.68.11 or 68.12 or of Chapter 69:**
	-矿渣棉、岩石棉及类似的矿质棉（包括其相互混合物），块状、成片或成卷								-Slag wool, rock wool and similar mineral wools （including intermixtures thereof）, in bulk, sheets or rolls
6806.1010	---硅酸铝纤维及其制品	10.5	40		5	17	千克		--- Alumino-silicate fibre and arlicles of its products alumino-silicate fibre
6806.1090	---其他	10.5	40		5	17	千克		---Other
6806 1090.01[暂]	其他矿物纤维，渣球含量小于5%	10.5	40	5	5	17	千克		Other mineral fiber, slag content of less than 5%
6806 1090.90	其他矿渣棉，岩石棉及类似矿质棉（包括相互混合物，块状、成片或成卷）	10.5	40		5	17	千克		The other slag wool, rock wool and similar mineral wools (including intermixtures thereof)
6806.2000	-页状硅石、膨胀粘土、泡沫矿渣及类似的膨胀矿物材料（包括其相互混合物）	10.5	40			17	千克		-Exfoliated vermiculite, expanded clays,foamed slag and similar expanded mineral materials（including intermixtures thereof）
6806.9000	-其他	10	50			17	千克		-Other
68.07	**沥青或类似原料（例如，石油沥青或煤焦油沥青）的制品：**								**Articles of asphalt or of similar material（for example, petroleum bitumen or coal tar pitch）:**
6807.1000	-成卷	12	50			17	千克		-In rolls
6807 1000.01[暂]	聚酯-铜复合胎基改性沥青根阻防水卷材	12	50	1		17	千克		Waterproofing materials In rolls, by modifying asphalt based on Polyester – Cu composite
6807 1000.90	成卷的沥青或类似原料的制品（如石油沥青或煤焦油沥青）	12	50			17	千克		Articles of asphalt or of similar material in rolls（for example, petroleum bitumen or coal tar pitch）
6807.9000	-其他	12	50			17	千克		-Other
68.08	**镶板、平板、瓦、砖及类似品，用水泥、石膏及其他矿物粘合材料粘合植物纤维、稻草、刨花、木片屑、木粉、锯末或木废料制成：**								**Panels, boards, tiles, blocks and similar articles of vegetable fibre, of strsw or of shavings, chips, particles, sawdust or other waste, of wood, agglomerated with cement, plaster or other mineral binders:**
6808.0000	镶板、平板、瓦、砖及类似品，用水泥、石膏及其他矿物粘合材料粘合植物纤维、稻草、刨花、木片屑、木粉、锯末或木废料制成	10.5	40		5	17	千克		Panels, boards, tiles, blocks and similar articles of vegetable fibre, of straw or of shavings, chips, particles, sawdust or other waste, of wood, agglomerated with cement, plaster or other mineral binders
68.09	**石膏制品及以石膏为基本成分的混合材料制品：**								**Articles of plaster or of compositions based on plaster:**
	-未经装饰的板、片、砖、瓦及类似品：								-Boards, sheets, panels, tiles and similar articles, not ornamented:
6809.1100	--仅用纸、纸板贴面或加强的	28	100		5	17	千克		--Faced or reinforced with paper or paper board only
6809.1900	--其他	25	100		5	17	千克		--Other
6809.9000	-其他制品	25	100		5	17	千克		-Other articles
68.10	**水泥、混凝土或人造石制品，不**								**Articles of cement, of concrete or of artificial**

税则号列 Tariff Item	商品名称及备注	进口税率 最惠	进口税率 普通	进口税率 暂定	出口退税	增值税率	计量单位	监管条件	Article Description
	论是否加强:								stone, whether or not reinforced:
	-砖、瓦、扁平石及类似品:								-Tiles, flagstones, bricks and similar articles:
6810.1100	--建筑用砖及石砌块	10.5	40		5	17	千克		--Building blocks and bricks
	--其他:								--Other:
6810.1910	---人造石制	10.5	70		5	17	千克		---Of artificial stone
6810.1990	---其他	10.5	70		5	17	千克		---Other
	-其他制品:								-Other articles:
	--建筑或土木工程用的预制结构件:								--Prefabricated structural components for building or civil engineering:
6810.9110	---钢筋混凝土和预应力混凝土管、杆、板、桩等	10.5	40		5	17	千克		---Reinforced concrete and prestressed concrete tubes, pipes, rods, plates, piles and similar articles
6810.9190	---其他	10.5	40		5	17	千克		---Other
	--其他:								--Other:
6810.9910	---铁道用水泥枕	8	14		5	17	千克		---Railway sleepers of concrete
6810.9990	---其他	10.5	70		5	17	千克		---Other
68.11	**石棉水泥、纤维素水泥或类似材料的制品:**								**Articles of asbestos-cement, of cellulose fibre-cement or the like:**
	-含石棉的:								---Containing asbestos:
6811.4010	---瓦楞板	5	40		5	17	千克		---Corrugated sheets
6811.4020	---其他片、板、砖、瓦及类似制品	10.5	40		5	17	千克		---Other sheets, panels, tiles and similar articles
6811.4030	---管子及管子附件	8	40		5	17	千克		----Tubes, pipes and tube or pipe fittings
6811.4090	---其他制品	8.4	40		5	17	千克		---Other articles
	-不含石棉的:								-Not containing asbestos:
6811.8100	--瓦楞板	5	40		5	17	千克		--Corrugated sheets
6811.8200	--其他片、板、砖、瓦及类似制品	10.5	40		5	17	千克		--Other sheets, panels, tiles and similar articles
	--其他制品:								--Other articles:
6811.8910	---管子及管子附件	8	40		5	17	千克		---Tubes, pipes and tube or pipe fittings
6811.8990	---其他	8.4	40		5	17	千克		---Other
68.12	**已加工的石棉纤维；以石棉为基本成分或以石棉和碳酸镁为基本成分的混合物；上述混合物或石棉的制品（例如，纱线、机织物、服装、帽类、鞋靴、衬垫），不论是否加强，但品目 68.11 或 68.13 的货品除外:**								**Fabricated asbestos fibres; mixtures with a basis of asbestos or with a basis of asbestos and magnesium carbonate; articles of such mixtures or of asbestos（for example, thread, woven fabric, clothing, headgear, footwear, gaskets）, whether or not reinforced, other than goods of heading No.68.11 or 68.13:**
6812.8000	-青石棉的	10.5	40		5	17	千克		-Of crocidolite
	-其他:								-Other:
6812.9100	--服装、衣着附件、帽类及鞋靴	10.5	40		5	17	千克		--Clothing, clothing accessories, footwear and headgear
6812.9200	--纸、麻丝板及毡子	10.5	40		5	17	千克		--Paper, millboard and felt
6812.9300	--成片或成卷的压缩石棉纤维接合材料	10.5	40		5	17	千克		--Compressed asbestos fibre jointing, in sheets or rolls
6812.9900	--其他	10	40		5	17	千克		--Other
68.13	**以石棉、其他矿物质或纤维素为基本成分的未装配磨擦材料及其制品（例如，片、卷、带、盘、圈、垫及扇形），适于作制动器、离合器及类似品，不论是否与织物或其他材料结合而成:**								**Friction material and articles thereof （for example, sheets, rolls, strips, segments, discs, washers, pads）, not mounted, for brakes, for clutches or the like, with a basis of asbestos, of other mineral substances or of cellulose, whether or not combined with textile or other materials:**
	-含石棉的:								-Containing asbestos:
6813.2010	---闸衬、闸垫	10	40		5	17	千克		--Brake linings and pads
6813.2090	---其他	12	40		5	17	千克		---Other
	-不含石棉的:								-Not containing asbestos:
6813.8100	--闸衬、闸垫	10	40		5	17	千克		--Brake linings and pads
6813.8900	--其他	12	40		5	17	千克		--Other
68.14	**已加工的云母及其制品，包括粘聚或复制的云母，不论是否附于纸、纸板或其他材料上:**								**Worked mica and articles of mica, including agglomerated or reconstituted mica, whether or not on a support of paper, paperboard or other**

税则号列 Tariff Item	商品名称及备注	进口税率 最惠	进口税率 普通	进口税率 暂定	出口退税	增值税率	计量单位	监管条件	Article Description
									meterials:
6814.1000	-粘聚或复制云母制的板、片、带，不论是否附于其他材料上	10.5	35		5	17	千克		-Plates, sheets and strips of agglomerated or reconstituted mica, whether or not on a support
6814.9000	-其他	10.5	35		5	17	千克		-Other
68.15	**其他品目未列名的石制品及其他矿物制品（包括碳纤维及其制品和泥煤制品）：**								**Articles of stone or of other mineral substances （including carbon fibres, articles of carbon fibres and articles of peat）, not elsewhere specified or included:**
6815.1000	-非电器用的石墨或其他碳精制品	15	70			17	千克	3	-Non-electrical articles of graphite or other carbon
6815.2000	-泥煤制品	15	70			17	千克		-Articles of peat
	-其他制品:								-Other articles:
6815.9100	--含有菱镁矿、白云石或铬铁矿的	15	70			17	千克		--Containing magnesite, dolomite or chromite
	--其他:								--Other:
6815.9920	---碳纤维	17.5	70		5	17	千克		---Carbon fibres
6815 9920.10	两用物项管制的碳纤维（比模量≥12.7×10^6 m，或比抗拉强度≥23.5×10^4 m）	17.5	70		5	17	千克	3	Carbon fibers under the control of dual-use items (specific modulus≥12.7×10 ^{6} m or tensile strength ≥23.5×10 ^{4} m)
6815 9920.90	其他碳纤维	17.5	70		5	17	千克		Other carbon fibers
	---碳纤维制品:								---Articles of carbon fibres:
6815.9931	----碳布	17.5	70		5	17	千克		---Carbon fabric
6815.9932	----碳纤维预浸料	17.5	70		5	17	千克		----Prepreg material of carbon fibres
6815 9932.10	两用物项管制的碳纤维预浸料（制品）	17.5	70		5	17	千克	3	Prepreg material of carbon fibres under dual-use items control (products)
6815 9932.90	其他碳纤维预浸料（制品）	17.5	70		5	17	千克		Other prepreg material of carbon fibres (products)
6815.9939	----其他	17.5	70		5	17	千克		----Other
6815 9939.91[暂]	碳含量>90%碳纤维纱线	17.5	70	15	5	17	千克		Carbon fiberes yarn, cantaining more than 90%by weight of carbon
6815 9939.99	其他碳纤维制品	17.5	70		5	17	千克		Other carbon fibres articles
6815.9940	---玄武岩纤维及其制品	17.5	70			17	千克		--- Basalt fiber and articles there-of
6815.9990	---其他	17.5	70			17	千克		---Other

第六十九章 陶 瓷 产 品

Chapter 69 Ceramic products

注释：

一、本章仅适用于成形后经过烧制的陶瓷产品。品目69.04至69.14仅适用于不能归入品目69.01至69.03的产品。

二、本章不包括：

（一）品目28.44的产品；

（二）品目68.04的物品；

（三）第七十一章的物品（例如，仿首饰）；

（四）品目81.13的金属陶瓷；

（五）第八十二章的物品；

（六）绝缘子（品目85.46）或绝缘材料制的零件（品目85.47）；

（七）假牙（品目90.21）；

（八）第九十一章的物品（例如，钟及钟壳）；

（九）第九十四章的物品（例如，家具、灯具及照明装置、活动房屋）；

（十）第九十五章的物品（例如，玩具、游戏品及运动用品）；

（十一）品目96.06的物品（例如，钮扣）或品目96.14的物品（例如，烟斗）；或

（十二）第九十七章的物品（例如，艺术品）。

Chapter Notes:

1. This Chapter applies only to ceramic products which have been fired after shaping. Headings 69.04 to 69.14 apply only to such products other than those classifiable in headings 69.01 to 69.03.

2. This Chapter does not cover:

(a) Products of heading 28.44;

(b) Articles of heading 68.04;

(c) Articles of Chapter 71 (for example, imitation jewellery);

(d) Cermets of heading 81.13;

(e) Articles of Chapter 82;

(f) Electrical insulators (heading 85.46) or fittings of insulating material of heading 85.47;

(g) Artificial teeth (heading 90.21);

(h) Articles of Chapter 91 (for example, clocks and clock cases);

(ij) Articles of Chapter 94 (for example, furniture, lamps and lighting fittings, prefabricated buildings);

(k) Articles of Chapter 95 (for example, toys, games and sports requisites);

(l) Articles of heading 96.06 (for example, buttons) or of heading 96.14 (for example, smoking pipes); or

(m) Articles of Chapter 97 (for example, works of art).

税则号列 Tariff Item	商品名称及备注	进口税率			出口退税	增值税率	计量单位	监管条件	Article Description
		最惠	普通	暂定					
	第一分章 硅化石粉或类似硅土及耐火材料制品								Ⅰ. GOODS OF SILICEOUS FOSSIL MEALS OR OF SIMILAR SILICEOUS EARTHS, AND REFRACTORY GOODS
69.01	硅质化石粉（例如各种硅藻土）或类似硅土制的砖、块、瓦及其他陶瓷制品：								**Bricks, blocks, tiles and other ceramic goods of siliceous fossil meals (for example, kieseiguhr, tripolite or diatimite) or of similar siliceous earths:**
6901.0000	硅质化石粉（例如各种硅藻土）或类似硅土制的砖、块、瓦及其他陶瓷制品	8	50			17	千克		Bricks, blocks, tiles and other ceramic goods of siliceous fossil meals (for example, kieselguhr, tripolite or diatomite) or of similar siliceous earths
69.02	耐火砖、块、瓦及类似耐火陶瓷建材制品，但硅质化石粉及类似硅土制的除外：								**Refractory bricks, blocks, tiles and similar refractory ceramic constructional goods, other than those of siliceous fossil meals or similar siliceous earths:**
6902.1000	-单独或同时含有按重量计超过50%的镁、钙或铬（分别以氧化镁、氧化钙及三氧化二铬的含量计）	8	30			17	千克		-Containing by weight, singly or together, more than 50% of the elements Mg, Ca or Cr, expressed as MgO, CaO or Cr_2O_3
6902.2000	-含有按重量计超过50%的三氧化二铝、二氧化硅或其混合物或化合物	8	30			17	千克		-Containing by weight more than 50% of alumina (Al_2O_3), of silica (SiO_2) or of a mixture or compound of these products
6902.9000	-其他	8	30			17	千克		-Othe
69.03	其他耐火陶瓷制品（例如、甑、坩埚、马弗罩、喷管、栓塞、支架、烤钵、管子、护套及棒条），但硅质化石粉及类似硅土制的除外：								**Other refractory, ceramic goods (for example, retorts, crucibles, muffles, nozzles, plugs, supports, cupels, tubes, pipes, sheaths and rods), other than those of siliceous fossil meals or of similar siliceous earthes:**
6903.1000	-含有按重量计超过50%的石墨、其他碳或其混合物	8	20			17	千克		-Containing by weight more than 50% of graphite or other carbon or of a mixture of these products

税则号列 Tariff Item	商品名称及备注	进口税率			出口退税	增值税率	计量单位	监管条件	Article Description
		最惠	普通	暂定					
6903.2000	-含有按重量计超过 50%的三氧化二铝或三氧化二铝和二氧化硅的混合物或化合物	8	20			17	千克		-Containing by weight more than 50% of alumina（AL_2O_3）or of a mixture of compound of alumina and of silica （SiO_2）
6903.9000	-其他	8	20		9	17	千克		-Other
	第二分章 其他陶瓷产品								**Ⅱ. OTHER CERAMIC PRODUCTS**
69.04	陶瓷制建筑用砖、铺地砖、支撑或填充用砖及类似品：								**Ceramic building bricks, flooring blocks, support or filler tiles and the like:**
6904.1000	-建筑用砖	15	90		9	17	千克/千块		-Building bricks
6904.9000[暂]	-其他	24.5	90	15	9	17	千克		-Other
69.05	屋顶瓦、烟囱罩、通风帽、烟囱衬壁、建筑装饰及其他建筑用陶瓷制品：								**Roofing tiles, chimney-pots, cowls,chimney liners, architectural ornaments and other ceramic constructional goods:**
6905.1000[暂]	-屋顶瓦	24.5	90	15	9	17	千克		-Roofing tiles
6905.9000[暂]	-其他	24.5	90	15	9	17	千克		-Other
69.06	陶瓷套管、导管、槽管及管子附件：								**Ceramic pipes, conduits, guttering and pipe fittings:**
6906.0000[暂]	陶瓷套管、导管、槽管及管子附件	15	90	10	9	17	千克		Ceramic pipes, conduits, guttering and pipe fittings
69.07	未上釉的陶瓷贴面砖、铺面砖，包括炉面砖及墙面砖；未上釉的陶瓷镶嵌砖（马赛克）及类似品，不论是否有衬背：								**Unglazed ceramic flags and paving,hearth or wall tiles; unglazed ceramic mosaic cubes and the like, whether or not on a backing:**
6907.1000[暂]	-砖、瓦、块及类似品，不论是否矩形，其最大表面积以可置入边长小于 7 厘米的方格为限	24.5	90	12	9	17	千克/平方米		-Tiles, cubes and similar articles,whether or not rectangular,the largest surface area of which is capable of being enclosed in a square the side of which is less than 7cm
6907 1000.10[暂]	瓷砖、陶瓷等产品，未打磨上釉陶瓷（表面最宽＜7cm）	24.5	90	12	9	17	千克/平方米		Ceramic tile, ceramics products,unglazed or unpolished,（the widest side of surface square＜7cm）
6907 1000.90[暂]	未上釉的小陶瓷砖、瓦、块及类似品（小指最大表面积可置入边长＜7cm 的方格为限）	24.5	90	12	9	17	千克/平方米		Unglazed small ceramic tiles,cubes and similar articles(the largest surface area of which is capable of being enclosed in a square, side＜7cm
6907.9000[暂]	-其他	12	90	8	9	17	千克/平方米		-Other
69.08	上釉的陶瓷贴面砖、铺面砖，包括炉面砖及墙面砖；上釉的陶瓷镶嵌砖（马赛克）及类似品，不论是否有衬背：								**Glazed ceramic flags and paving,hearth or wall tiles; glazed ceramic mosaic cubes and the like, whether or not on a backing:**
6908.1000	-砖、瓦、块及类似品，不论是否矩形，其最大表面积以可置入边长小于 7 厘米的方格为限	12	100		9	17	千克/平方米		-Tiles, cubes and similar articles, whether or not rectangular, the largest surface area of which is capable of being enclosed in a square the side of which is less than 7cm
6908.9000	-其他	12	100		9	17	千克/平方米		-Other
69.09	实验室、化学或其他专门技术用途的陶瓷器；农业用陶瓷槽、缸及类似容器；通常供运输及盛装货物用的陶瓷罐、坛及类似品：								**Ceramic wares for laboratory, chemical or other technical uses; ceramic troughs, tubs and similar receptacles of a kind used in agriculture; ceramic pots, jars and similar articles of a kind used for the conveyance or packing of goods:**
	-实验室、化学或其他专门技术用途的陶瓷器：								-Ceramic wares for laboratory, chemical or other technical uses:
6909.1100	-瓷制	8	30		13	17	千克		--Of porcelain or china
6909.1200	-摩氏硬度为 9 或以上的物品	8	30		13	17	千克		--Articles having a hardness equivalent to 9 or more on the Mohs scale
6909.1900	--其他	8	30		13	17	千克		--Other
6909.9000[暂]	-其他	21	90	15	9	17	千克		-Other

税则号列 Tariff Item	商品名称及备注	进口税率			出口退税	增值税率	计量单位	监管条件	Article Description
		最惠	普通	暂定					
69.10	陶瓷洗涤槽、脸盆、脸盆座、浴缸、坐浴盆，抽水马桶、水箱、小便池及类似的固定卫生设备：								**Ceramic sinks, wash basins, wash basin pedestals, baths, bidets, water closet pans, flushing cisterns, urinals and similar sanitary fixtures:**
6910.1000	-瓷制	10	100		9	17	千克/件		-Of porcelain or china
6910.9000	-其他	10	100		9	17	千克/件	A	-Other
69.11	瓷餐具、厨房器具及其他家用或盥洗用瓷器：								**Tableware, kitchenware, other household articles and toilet articles, of porcelain or china:**
	-餐具及厨房器具:								-Tableware and kitchenware：
	---餐具:								---Tableware:
6911.1011[暂]	----骨瓷	12	100	8	13	17	千克	AB	----Bone China
6911.1019[暂]	----其他	12	100	8	13	17	千克	AB	----Other
	---厨房器具:								---Kitchenware:
6911.1021[暂]	----刀具	15	100	10	13	17	千克	AB	----Knives and the like
6911.1029[暂]	----其他	15	100	10	13	17	千克	AB	----Other
6911.9000	-其他	24.5	100		13	17	千克		-Other
69.12	陶餐具、厨房器具及其他家用或盥洗用陶器：								**Ceramic tableware，kitchenware，other household articles and toilet articles, other than of procelain or china:**
6912.0010[暂]	---餐具	15	100	10	13	17	千克	AB	---Tableware
6912.0090[暂]	---其他	15	100	10	13	17	千克	AB	---Other
69.13	塑像及其他装饰用陶瓷制品:								**Statuettes and other ornamental ceramic articles:**
6913.1000	-瓷制	15	100		13	17	千克		-Of porcelain or china
6913.9000	-其他	15	100		13	17	千克		-Other
69.14	其他陶瓷制品:								**Other ceramic articles:**
6914.1000	-瓷制	24.5	100		9	17	千克		-Of porcelain or china
6914.9000	-其他	10	100		9	17	千克		-Other

第七十章
玻璃及其制品

注释：

一、本章不包括：

（一）品目 32.07 的货品（例如，珐琅和釉料、搪瓷玻璃料及其他玻璃粉、粒或粉片）；

（二）第七十一章的物品（例如，仿首饰）；

（三）品目 85.44 的光缆、品目 85.46 的绝缘子或品目 85.47 所列绝缘材料制的零件；

（四）光导纤维、经光学加工的光学元件、注射用针管、假眼、温度计、气压计、液体比重计或第九十章的其他物品；

（五）有永久固定电光源的灯具及照明装置、灯箱标志或铭牌和类似品及其零件（品目 94.05）；

（六）玩具、游戏品、运动用品、圣诞树装饰品及第九十五章的其他物品（供玩偶或第九十五章其他物品用的无机械装置的玻璃假眼除外）；或

（七）钮扣、保温瓶、香水喷雾器和类似的喷雾器及第九十六章的其他物品。

二、对于品目 70.03、70.04 及 70.05：

（一）玻璃在退火前的各种处理都不视为“已加工”；

（二）玻璃切割成一定形状并不影响其作为板片归类；

（三）所称“吸收、反射或非反射层”，是指极薄的金属或化合物（例如，金属氧化物）镀层，该镀层可以吸收红外线等光线或可以提高玻璃的反射性能，同时仍然使玻璃具有一定程度的透明性或半透明性；或者该镀层可以防止光线在玻璃表面的反射。

三、品目 70.06 所述产品，不论是否具有制成品的特性仍归入该品目。

四、品目 70.19 所称“玻璃棉”，是指：

（一）按重量计二氧化硅的含量在 60%及以上的矿质棉；

（二）按重量计二氧化硅的含量在 60%以下，但碱性氧化物（氧化钾或氧化钠）的含量在 5%以上或氧化硼的含量在 2%以上的矿质棉。

不符合上述规定的矿质棉归入品目 68.06。

五、本目录所称“玻璃”，包括熔融石英及其他熔融硅石。

子目注释：

子目 7013.22、7013.33、7013.41 及 7013.91 所称“铅晶质玻璃”，仅指按重量计氧化铅含量不低于 24%的玻璃。

Chapter 70
Glass and glassware

Chapter Notes:

1. This Chapter does not cover:

（a）Goods of heading 32.07（for example, vitrifiable enamels and glazes, glass frit, other glass in the form of powder, granules or flakes）;

（b）Articles of Chapter 71（for example, imitation jewellery）;

（c）Optical fibre cables of heading 85.44, electrical insulators（heading 85.46）or fittings of insulating material of heading 85.47;

（d）Optical fibres, optically worked optical elements, hypodermic syringes, artificial eyes, thermometers, barometers, hydrometers or other articles of Chapter 90;

（e）Lamps or lighting fittings, illuminated signs, illuminated name-plates or the like, having a permanently fixed light source, or parts thereof of heading 94.05;

（f）Toys, games, sports requisites, Christmas tree ornaments or other articles of Chapter 95（excluding glass eyes without mechanisms for dolls or for other articles of Chapter 95）;or

（g）Buttons, fitted vacuum flasks, scent or similar sprays or other articles of Chapter 96.

2. For the purposes of headings 70.03, 70.04 and 70.05:

（a）Glass is not regarded as "worked"by reason of any process it has undergone before annealing;

（b）Cutting to shape does not affect the classification of glass in sheets;

（c）The expression "absorbent, reflecting or non-reflecting layer" means a microscopically thin coating of metal or of a chemical compound（for example, metal oxide）which absorbs, for example, infra-red light or improves the reflecting qualities of the glass while still allowing it to retain a degree of transparency or translucency; or which prevents light from being reflected on the surface of the glass.

3. The products referred to in heading 70.06 remain classified in that heading whether or not they have the character of articles.

4. For the purposes of heading 70.19, the expression "glass wool" means:

（a）Mineral wools with a silica（SiO_2）content not less than 60% by weight;

（b）Mineral wools with a silica（SiO_2）content less than 60% but with an alkaline oxide（K_2O or Na_2O）content exceeding 5% by weight or a boric oxide（B_2O_3）content exceeding 2% by weight.

Mineral wools which do not comply with the above specifications fall in heading 68.06.

5. Throughout the Nomenclature, the expression "glass" includes fused quartz and other fused silica.

Subheading Note:

For the purposes of subheadings 7013.22, 7013.33, 7013.41 and 7013.91, the expression "lead crystal" means only glass having a minimum lead monoxide（PbO）content by weight of 24%.

税则号列 Tariff Item	商品名称及备注	进口税率 最惠	普通	暂定	出口退税	增值税率	计量单位	监管条件	Article Description
70.01	**碎玻璃及废玻璃；玻璃块料：**								**Cullet and other waste and scrap of glass; glass in the mass:**
7001.0000	碎玻璃及废玻璃；玻璃块料	12	50			17	千克		Cullet and other waste and scrap of glass;glass in the mass
7001 0000.10	废碎玻璃	12	50			17	千克	9	Cullet and other waste and scrap of glass
7001 0000.90	玻璃块料	12	50			17	千克		Glass in the mass
70.02	**未加工的玻璃球、棒及管（品目 70.18 的微型玻璃球除外）：**								**Glass in balls (other than microspheres of heading No.70.18), roads or tubes,unworked:**
7002.1000	-玻璃球	12	50			17	千克		-Balls
	-玻璃棒:								-Rods:
7002.2010	---光导纤维预制棒	6	50		13	17	千克		---Preformed bars for drawing optical fibre
7002.2090	---其他	12	50			17	千克		---Other
	-玻璃管:								-Tubes:
	—熔融石英或其他熔融硅石制:								--Of fused quartz or other fused silica:
7002.3110[暂]	---光导纤维用波导级石英玻璃管	5	17	1	13	17	千克		---Waveguide quartz tubes for optical fibres use
7002.3190	---其他	14	50			17	千克		---Other
7002.3200	--温度在 0℃至 300℃时线膨胀系数不超过 5×10^{-6}/开尔文的其他玻璃制	12	50		13	17	千克		--Of other glass having a linear coefficient of expansion not exceeding 5×10^{-6} per Kelvin within a temperature range of 0℃ to 300℃
7002.3900	--其他	12	50		13	17	千克		--Other
7002 3900.01[暂]	光通信用微光组件的玻璃毛细管、定位管（外径小于 3mm）	12	50	3	13	17	千克		Glass capillaries or positioning tube of micro-optical assemblies for optical communications（external diameter＜3mm）
7002 3900.90	未列名、未加工的玻璃管	12	50		13	17	千克		Glass tubes, not specified, unworked
70.03	**铸制或轧制玻璃板、片或型材及异型材，不论是否有吸收、反射或非反射层，但未经其他加工：**								**Cast glass and rolled glass, in sheets or profiles, whether or not having an absorbent, reflecting or non-reflecting layer, but not otherwise worked:**
	-非夹丝玻璃板、片:								-Non-wired sheets:
7003.1200	--整块着色、不透明、镶色或具有吸收、反射或非反射层的	15	50			17	千克/平方米		--Coloured throughout the mass（body tinted）, opacified, flashed or having an absorbent, reflecting or non-reflecting layer
7003.1900	--其他	17.5	50			17	千克/平方米		--Other
7003 1900.01[暂]	液晶或有机发光二极管（OLED）显示屏用原板玻璃，包括保护屏用含碱玻璃(铸、轧制的非夹丝玻璃板、片，未着色，透明及不具吸收层的，未经其他加工)	17.5	50	3	5	17	千克/平方米		Rough glass plate and OLED used for LCD (not colored, transparent and not having an absorbent layer, not otherwise worked)
7003 1900.90	铸、轧制的其他非夹丝玻璃板、片（未着色、透明及不具吸收层的，未经其他加工）	17.5	50			17	千克/平方米		Cast and rolled other non-wired glass, in sheets (not colored, transparent and not having an absorbent layer, not otherwise worked)
7003.2000	-夹丝玻璃板、片	15	50			17	千克/平方米		-Wired sheets
7003.3000	-型材及异型材	15	50			17	千克/平方米		-Profiles
70.04	**拉制或吹制玻璃板、片，不论是否有吸收、反射或非反射层，但未经其他加工：**								**Drawn glass and blown glass, in sheets, whether or not having an absorbent, reflecting or non-reflecting layer, but not otherwise worked:**
7004.2000	-整块着色、不透明、镶色或具有吸收、反射或非反射层的	17.5	50			17	千克/平方米		-Glass, coloured throughout the mass （body tinted）, opacified, flashed or having an absorbent, reflecting or non-reflecting layer
7004.9000	-其他玻璃	17.5	50			17	千克/平方米		-Other glass
7004 9000.01[暂]	光学平板玻璃，厚度 0.7mm 以下（未着色、透明及不具吸收层的，未经其他加工）	17.5	50	9		17	千克/平方米		Optial plate glass, thickness<0.7mm（not coloured, transparent and not having an absorbent layer, not otherwise worked）

税则号列 Tariff Item	商品名称及备注	进口税率 最惠	普通	暂定	出口退税	增值税率	计量单位	监管条件	Article Description
7004 9000.90	拉、吹制的其他玻璃板、片（未着色、透明及不具吸收层的，未经其他加工）	17.5	50			17	千克/平方米		Drawn glass and blown glass, in sheets（not coloured, transparent and not having an absorbent layer, not otherwise worked）
70.05	**浮法玻璃板、片及表面研磨或抛光玻璃板、片，不论是否有吸收、反射或非反射层，但未经其他加工：**								**Float glass and surface ground or polished glass, in sheets, whether or not having an absorbent, reflecting or non-reflecting layer, but not otherwise worked:**
7005.1000	-具有吸收、反射或非反射层的非夹丝玻璃	15	50			17	千克/平方米		-Non-wired glass, having an absorbent, reflecting or non-reflecting layer
	-其他非夹丝玻璃:								-Other non-wired glass:
7005.2100	--整块着色、不透明、镶色或仅表面研磨的	15	50			17	千克/平方米		--Coloured throughout the mass（body tinted）, opacified, flashed or merely surface ground
7005.2900	--其他	15	50			17	千克/平方米		--Other
7005 2900.02 [暂]	液晶或有机发光二极管（OLED）显示屏用原板玻璃，包括保护屏用含碱玻璃（非夹丝浮法玻璃板、片）	15	50	3	5	17	千克/平方米		Lidquid crystal or organic luminous diode (OLED) original plate galss used for display (Non-wired float glass and piece
7005 2900.90	其他非夹丝浮法玻璃板、片	15	50			17	千克/平方米		Other non-wired float glass, in sheets
7005.3000	-夹丝玻璃	17.5	50			17	千克/平方米		-Wired glass
70.06	**经弯曲、磨边、镂刻、钻孔、涂珐琅或其他加工的品目 70.03、70.04 或 70.05 的玻璃，但未用其他材料镶框或装配:**								**Glass of heading No.70.03, 70.04 or 70.05, bent, edge-worked, engraved, drilled, enamelled or otherwise worked, but not framed or fitted with other materials:**
7006.0000	经弯曲、磨边、镂刻、钻孔、涂珐琅或其他加工的品目 70.03, 70.04 或 70.05 的玻璃，但未用其他材料镶框或装配	15	50		13	17	千克		Glass of heading No.70.03, 70.04 or 70.05, bent, edge-worked, engraved, drilled, enamelled or otherwise worked, but not framed or fitted with other materials
7006 0000.01 [暂]	液晶玻璃基板，6 代（1850mm×1500mm）以上，不含 6 代（经弯曲、磨边、镂刻、钻孔、涂珐琅等加工，未镶框或装配）	15	50	4	13	17	千克		Liquid crystal plate glass,of square 1850mm×1500mm,bent,edge-worked,engraved,drilled,enameled or otherwise worked,but not framed or fitted
7006 0000.02 [暂]	液晶玻璃基板，6 代（1850mm×1500mm）及以下（经弯曲、磨边、镂刻、钻孔、涂珐琅等加工，未镶框或装配）	15	50	6	13	17	千克		Liquid crystal plate glass,of square 1850mm×1500mm or less,bent,edge-worked,engraved,drilled, enameled or otherwise worked,but not framed or fitted
7006 0000.90	经其他加工编号 70.03～70.05 的玻璃（经弯曲、磨边、镂刻、钻孔、涂珐琅等加工，未镶框或装配）	15	50		13	17	千克		Glass of heading No. 70.03 to 70.05, bent, edge-worked, engraved, drilled, enamelled or otherwise worked, but not framed or fitted
70.07	**钢化或层压玻璃制的安全玻璃:**								**Safety glass,consisting of toughened (tempered) or laminated glass:**
	-钢化安全玻璃:								-Toughened（tempered）safety glass:
	--规格及形状适于安装在车辆、航空器、航天器及船舶上:								--Of size and shape suitable for incorporation in vehicles, aircraft, spacecraft or vessels:
7007.1110	---航空器、航天器及船舶用	2	11		13	17	千克		---For aircraft, spacecraft or vessels
7007 1110.01 [暂]	空载重量≥25 吨飞机的挡风玻璃	2	11	1	13	17	千克		Toughened（tempered）safety glass, for wind shield of aircraft, anunladen weight≥25 ton
7007 1110.90	航空航天器及船舶用钢化安全玻璃（其他规格及形状适于安装在航空航天器及船上的）	2	11		13	17	千克		Toughened（tempered）safety glass, of other size and shape suitable for incor poration in spacecraft or vessels
7007.1190	---其他	10	50		13	17	千克	A	---Other
7007.1900	--其他	14	50		13	17	千克/平方米		--Other
7007 1900.01 [暂]	低铁钢化太阳能电池组件封装	14	50	12	13	17	千克/		Low-ferrous toughened safety glass, specially for

税则号列 Tariff Item	商品名称及备注	进口税率 最惠	普通	暂定	出口退税	增值税率	计量单位	监管条件	Article Description
	专用玻璃（指最大含铁量0.02%Fe_2O_3，厚度为2.5mm～3.5mm的玻璃）						平方米		sealing of solar cell and components, （maximum ferrous content: 0.02% Fe_2O_3, thickness: 2.5mm to 3.5mm）
7007 1900.90	其他钢化安全玻璃	14	50		13	17	千克/平方米		Other safety glass, consisting of toughened （tempered）
	-层压安全玻璃:								-Laminated safety glass:
	--规格及形状适于安装在车辆、航空器、航天器及船舶上:								--Of size and shape suitable for incorporation in vehicles, aircraft, spacecraft or vessels:
7007.2110	---航空器、航天器及船舶用	2	11		13	17	千克		---For aircraft, spacecraft or vessels
7007.2190	---其他	20	50		13	17	千克	A	---Other
7007.2900	--其他	14	50		13	17	千克/平方米		--Other
70.08	多层隔温、隔音玻璃组件:								**Multiple-walled insulating units of glass:**
7008.0010	---中空或真空隔温、隔音玻璃	14	50		13	17	千克		---Sealed or vacuum insulating glass
7008.0090	---其他	14	50		13	17	千克		---Other
70.09	玻璃镜（包括后视镜），不论是否镶框:								**Glass mirrors, whether or not framed, including rear-view mirrors:**
7009.1000	-车辆后视镜	10	100		13	17	千克		-Rear-view mirrors for vehicles
	-其他:								-Other:
7009.9100	--未镶框	21	70		13	17	千克		--Unframed
7009 9100.01 暂	槽式太阳能抛物面反射镜	21	70	10	13	17	千克		Trough solar power parabolic mirror
7009 9100.90	其他未镶框玻璃镜(包括后视镜)	21	70		13	17	千克		Other unframed glass mirror (including rearview mirror)
7009.9200	--已镶框	12	100		13	17	千克		--Framed
70.10	玻璃制的坛、瓶、缸、罐、安瓿及其他容器，用于运输或盛装货物；玻璃制保藏罐；玻璃塞、盖及类似的封口器:								**Carboys, bottles, flasks, jars, pots, phials, ampoules and other containers, of glass, of a kind used for the conveyance or packing of goods; preserving jars of glass; stoppers, lids and other chosures, of glass:**
7010.1000	-安瓿	14	50		13	17	千克		-Ampoules
7010.2000	-塞、盖及类似的封口器	14	50		13	17	千克		-Stoppers, lids and other closures
	-其他:								-Other:
7010.9010	---超过1升	14	50		13	17	千克		---Exceeding 1L
7010.9020	---超过0.33升，但不超过1升	14	50		13	17	千克		---Exceeding 0.33L but not exceeding 1L
7010.9030	---超过0.15升，但不超过0.33升	14	50		13	17	千克		---Exceeding 0.15L but not exceeding 0.33L
7010.9090	---不超过0.15升	14	50		13	17	千克		---Not exceeding 0.15L
70.11	制灯泡、阴极射线管及类似品用的未封口玻璃外壳(包括玻璃泡及管）及其玻璃零件，但未装有配件:								**Glass envelopes（including bulbs and tubes）, open, and glass parts thereof, without fittings, for electric lamps, cathode-ray tubes or the like:**
7011.1000	-电灯用	21	80			17	千克		-For electric lighting
	-阴极射线管用:								-For cathode-ray tubes:
7011.2010	---显像管玻壳及其零件	10	35		13	17	千克	6	---Glass envelopes for kinescope and glass parts thereof
7011.2090	---其他	10	35		5	17	千克		---Other
7011 2090.01 暂	显示管玻壳及其零件（包括零件，但未装有配件）	10	35	6	5	17	千克	6	Glass envelopes for kinescope and parts thereof （including parts thereof, without fittings）
7011 2090.90	其他阴极射线管用的未封口玻壳（包括零件，但未装有配件）	10	35		5	17	千克	6	Glass envelopes for cathode-ray tubes, open, including glass parts thereof,but without fittings
	-其他:								-Other
7011.9010	---电子管用（阴极射线管用的除外）	8	35		5	17	千克		---For electronic tubes and valves（other than cathode-ray tubes）
7011.9090	---其他	21	80			17	千克		---Other:
70.13	玻璃器，供餐桌、厨房、盥洗室、								**Glassware of a kind used for table,kitchen, toilet,**

税则号列 Tariff Item	商品名称及备注	进口税率 最惠	进口税率 普通	进口税率 暂定	出口退税	增值税率	计量单位	监管条件	Article Description
	办公室、室内装饰或类似用途（品目70.10或70.18的货品除外）：								office, indoor decoration or similar purposes （other than that of heading No.70.10 or 70.18）:
7013.1000	-玻璃陶瓷制	24.5	100		13	17	千克		-Of glass-ceramics
	-高脚杯，但玻璃陶瓷制的除外:								-Stemware drinking glasses, other than of glass-ceramics:
7013.2200[暂]	--铅晶质玻璃制	24.5	100	15	13	17	千克		--Of lead crystal
7013.2800	--其他	8	100		13	17	千克	A	--Other
	-其他杯子，但玻璃陶瓷制的除外:								-Other drinking glasses, other than of glass ceramics:
7013.3300[暂]	--铅晶质玻璃制	24.5	100	15	13	17	千克		--Of lead crystal
7013.3700	--其他	8	100		13	17	千克	A	--Other
	-餐桌或厨房用玻璃器皿（不包括杯子），但玻璃陶瓷制的除外:								-Glassware of a kind used for table（other than drinking glasses）or kitchen purposes, other than of glass-ceramics ：
7013.4100[暂]	--铅晶质玻璃制	24.5	100	15	13	17	千克	A	--Of lead crystal
7013.4200	--温度在0℃至300℃时线膨胀系数不超过 5×10^{-6}/开尔文的其他玻璃制	10	100		13	17	千克	A	-Of glass having a linear coefficient of expansion not exceeding 5×10^{-6} per Kelvin within a temperature range of 0℃ to 300℃
7013.4900	--其他	10	100		13	17	千克	A	--Other
	-其他玻璃器:								-Other glassware:
7013.9100	--铅晶质玻璃制	10	100		13	17	千克		--Of lead crystal
7013.9900	--其他	10	100		13	17	千克		--Other
70.14	未经光学加工的信号玻璃器及玻璃制光学元件（品目 70.15的货品除外）：								**Signalling glassware and optical elements of glass（other than those of heading No.70.15）, not optically worked:**
7014.0010	---光学仪器用光学元件毛坯	10	40		13	17	千克		---Blanks of optical elements, for optical instruments
7014.0090	---其他	17.5	80		13	17	千克		---Other
7014 0090.01[暂]	滤波玻璃（带有抗红外和防反射薄膜的）	17.5	80	9	13	17	千克		Light-filtering glass（with film of anti-infrared-ray and counterrudiation protection）
7014 0090.90	其他未经光学加工的信号玻璃器（包括玻璃制光学元件，品目70.15的物品除外）	17.5	80		13	17	千克		Other signaling glasswareincluding glass optical elements, other than those of heading No. 70.15), not optically worked
70.15	钟表玻璃及类似玻璃、视力矫正或非视力矫正眼镜用玻璃，呈弧面、弯曲、凹形或类似形状但未经光学加工的；制造上述玻璃用的凹面圆形及扇形玻璃:								**Clock or watch glasses and similar glasses, glasses for non-corrective or corrective spectacles, curved, bent, hollowed or the like, not optically worked; hollow glass spheres and their segments, for the manufacture of such glasses:**
	-视力矫正眼镜用玻璃:								-Glasses for corrective spectacles:
7015.1010[暂]	---变色镜片坯件	21	80	15	13	17	千克		---Blanks for photochromic spectacles
7015.1090[暂]	---其他	17.5	70	10	13	17	千克		---Other
	-其他:								-Other:
7015.9010	---钟表玻璃	17.5	70			17	千克		---Clock and watch glasses
7015.9020[暂]	---平光变色镜片坯件	18	80	10	13	17	千克		---Blanks for plane photochromic spectacles
7015.9090	---其他	12	80			17	千克		---Other
70.16	建筑用压制或模制的铺面用玻璃块、砖、片、瓦及其他制品，不论是否夹丝；供镶嵌或类似装饰用的玻璃马赛克及其他小件玻璃品，不论是否有衬背；花饰铅条窗玻璃及类似品；多孔或泡沫玻璃块、板、片及类似品:								**Paving blocks, slabs, bricks, squares, tiles and other articles of pressed or moulded glass, whether or not wired, of a kind used for building or construction purposes; glass cubes and other glass smallwares, whether or not on a backing, for mosaics or similar decorative purposes; leaded lights and the like; multicellular or foam glass in blocks, panels, plates, shells or similar forms:**
7016.1000	-供镶嵌或类似装饰用的玻璃马赛克及其他小件玻璃品，不论是	22	100		13	17	千克		-Glass cubes and other glass smallwares, whether or not on a backing, for mosaics or similar decorative

税则号列 Tariff Item	商品名称及备注	进口税率 最惠	普通	暂定	出口退税	增值税率	计量单位	监管条件	Article Description
	否有衬背								purposes
	-其他:								-Other:
7016.9010	---花饰铅条窗玻璃及类似品	24	90		13	17	千克		---Leaded lights and the like
7016.9090	---其他	18	90		13	17	千克		---Other
70.17	**实验室、卫生及配药用的玻璃器，不论有无刻度或标量:**								**Laboratory, hygienic or pharmaceutical glassware, whether or not graduated or calibrated:**
7017.1000	-熔融石英或其他熔融硅石制	0	30		13	17	千克		-Of fused quartz or other fused silica
7017.2000	-温度在0℃至300℃时线膨胀系数不超过5×10^{-6}/开尔文的其他玻璃制	8	30		13	17	千克		-Of other glass having a linear coefficient of expansion not exceeding 5×10^{-6} per Kelvin within a temperature range of 0℃ to 300℃
7017.9000	-其他	8	30		13	17	千克		-Other
70.18	**玻璃珠、仿珍珠、仿宝石或仿半宝石和类似小件玻璃品及其制品，但仿首饰除外；玻璃假眼，但医用假眼除外；灯工方法制作的玻璃塑像及其他玻璃装饰品，但仿首饰除外；直径不超过1毫米的微型玻璃球:**								**Glass beads, imitation pearls, imitation precious or semi-precious stones and similar glass smallwares, and articles thereof other than imitation jewellery; glass eyes other than prosthetic articles; statuettes and other ornaments of lampworked glass, other than imitation jewellery; glass microspheres not exceeding 1mm in diameter:**
7018.1000	-玻璃珠、仿珍珠、仿宝石或仿半宝石及类似小件玻璃品	10	100		13	17	千克		-Glass beads, imitation pearls, imitation precious or semi-precious stones and similar glass smallwares
7018.2000	-直径不超过1毫米的微型玻璃球	20	100		13	17	千克		-Glass microspheres not exceeding 1mm in diameter
7018 2000.01[暂]	熔融球形二氧化硅微粉，直径≤100um	20	100	5.5	13	17	千克		Fused spherical silicon powder, diameter≤100um
7018 2000.90	其他直径≤1毫米的玻璃珠	20	100		13	17	千克		Other glass microspheres, diameter≤1mm
7018.9000[暂]	-其他	20	100	10	13	17	千克		-Other
70.19	**玻璃纤维（包括玻璃棉）及其制品（例如，玻璃纤维纱线及其织物）:**								**Glass fibres（including glass wool）and articles thereof（for example, yarn, woven fabrics）:**
	-梳条、粗纱、纱线及短切纤维:								-Slivers, rovings, yarn and chopped strands:
7019.1100	--长度不超过50毫米的短切纤维	12	50		5	17	千克		--Chopped strands, of a length of not more than 50mm
7019 1100.10	两用物项管制的长度不超过50mm的短切玻璃纤维(比模量≥3.18×10^{6}m,以及比抗拉强度≥7.62×10^{4}m)	12	50		5	17	千克	3	Chopped glass strands under the dual-use items control, of a length of not more than 50mm (specific modulus≥ 3.18×10^{6}m, the tensile strength≥7.62×10^{4}m)
7019 1100.90	其他长度不超过50mm的短切玻璃纤维	12	50		5	17	千克		Other chopped glass strands, of a length of not more than 50mm
7019.1200	--粗纱	12	50		5	17	千克		--Rovings
7019 1200.20	两用物项管制的玻璃纤维粗纱(比模量≥3.18×10^{6} m,以及比抗拉强度≥7.62×10^{4} m)	12	50		5	17	千克	3	Glass fiber rovings under dual-use items control (specific modulus≥3.18×10^{6}m, the tensile strength ≥7.62×10^{4} m)
7019 1200.90	其他玻璃纤维粗纱	12	50		5	17	千克		Other glass fibres rovings
7019.1900	--其他	10	50		5	17	千克		--Other
7019 1900.11	间苯二酚甲醛胶浸渍的玻璃纤维纱(用于生产非导电玻璃纤维长丝粗纱机织轮胎帘子布的)	10	50		5	17	千克		Glass fibers yarn impregnated with resorcinol-formaldehyde glue, used for manufacturing woven tyre cord fabrics of nonconductive fiber glass roving)
7019 1900.12	玻璃纤维或纤丝材料(其“比模量”为3.18×10^{6}米或更大和“比抗拉强度”为7.62×10^{4}米或更大的玻璃纤维或纤丝材料)	10	50		5	17	千克	3	Glass fiber or filaments (Glass fiber or filaments of specific modulus≥ 3.18×10^{6}m or more , the tensile strength of ≥7.62×10^{4} m or more)
7019 1900.19	其他玻璃纱线（包括长度超过50mm的短切纤维）	10	50		5	17	千克		Other glass yarn, including chopped fiber of a length exceeding 50mm

税则号列 Tariff Item	商品名称及备注	进口税率			出口退税	增值税率	计量单位	监管条件	Article Description
		最惠	普通	暂定					
7019 1900.90	其他玻璃纤维（含长度超过50mm的短切纤维）	10	50		5	17	千克		Other glass fibres,including chopped fiber of a length exceeding 50mm）
	-薄片（巴厘纱）、纤维网、席、垫、板及类似无纺产品:								-Thin sheets（voiles）, webs, mats, mattresses, boards and similar nonwoven products:
7019.3100	--席	5	40		5	17	千克		--Mats
7019.3200	--薄片（巴厘纱）	14	40		5	17	千克		--Thin sheets（voiles）
	--其他:								--Other:
7019.3910	---垫	10.5	40		5	17	千克		---Mattresses
7019.3990	---其他	10.5	40		5	17	千克		---Other
7019.4000	-粗纱机织物	12	40		5	17	千克		-Woven fabrics of rovings
	-其他机织物:								-Other woven fabrics:
7019.5100	--宽度不超过30厘米的	12	40		5	17	千克		--Of a width not exceeding 30cm
7019 5100.10	两用物项管制的宽度≤15mm的玻璃纤维机织物	12	40		5	17	千克	3	Glass fiber woven fabrics under dualuse items control, of a width not exceeding 15mm
7019 5100.90	其他宽度≤30cm的玻璃纤维机织物	12	40		5	17	千克		Other glass fiber woven fabrics, of a width not exceeding 30cm
7019.5200	--宽度超过30厘米的长丝平纹织物，每平方米重量不超过250克，单根纱线细度不超过136特克斯	12	40		5	17	千克		--Of a width exceeding 30cm, plain weave, weighing less than 250g/m², of filaments measuring per single yarn not more than 136 tex
7019 5200.01 暂	覆铜板用玻璃纤维长丝平纹布，开纤或每平方米重≤180g(宽度＞30cm，单根纱线细度≤136特)	12	40	10	5	17	千克		Glass fiber filament plain weave for CCL, splitting or weighing less than 180g (of a width exceeding 30cm, of filaments measuring per single yarn not more than 136 tex)
7019 5200.90	其他平方米重≤250g玻璃长丝平纹布（宽度超过30cm，单根纱线细度不超过136特）	12	40		5	17	千克		Glass fiber filament plain weave, of a width exceeding 30cm, weighing less than 250g/m², of filaments measuring per single yarn not more than 136 tex
7019.5900	--其他	12	40		5	17	千克		--Other
	-其他:								-Other:
7019.9010	---玻璃棉及其制品	7	40		5	17	千克		---Glass wool and articles thereof
	---玻璃纤维布浸胶制品:								---Impregnated glass fabrics:
7019.9021	----每平方米重量小于450克	7	40		5/13	17	千克		----Weighing less than 450 g/m2
7019.9029	----其他	7	40		5	17	千克		----Other
7019.9090	---其他	7	40		13	17	千克		---Other
70.20	其他玻璃制品:								**Other articles of glass:**
	---工业用:								---For technical use:
7020.0011 暂	----导电玻璃	10.5	40	7	13	17	千克		----Conductivity glass
7020.0012	----绝缘子用玻璃伞盘	10.5	40			17	千克		----Glass umbrella for insulator
7020.0013	----熔融石英或其他熔融硅石制	10.5	40			17	千克		---- Of fused quartz or other fused silica
7020 0013.01	半导体晶片生产用石英反应管及夹持器(熔融石英或其他熔融硅石制）(用于插入熔化和氧化炉内)	0	40			17	千克	s	Quartz reaction tube and holder for manufacturing semiconductor wafer, (fused quartz or fused silica) (used for inserting melting and oxidizing furnace)
7020 0013.90	熔融石英或其他熔融硅石制工业用其他玻璃制品(导电玻璃及绝缘子用玻璃伞盘除外)	10.5	40			17	千克		Other glass products made of fused quartz or other fused silica for industrial use (other than conductive glass or insulator glass shells) (conductive glass and glass umbrella for insulator)
7020.0019	----其他		40			17	千克		----Other
7020 0019.01	半导体晶片生产用石英反应管及夹持器(用于插入熔化和氧化炉内）	0	40			17	千克	s	Quartz reactor tubes and grippers for manufacturing semiconductor chips, used for inserting the furnace for melting and oxidation
7020 0019.02 暂	等离子模块生产用高应变点玻璃（应变点在550摄氏度及以上）	10.5	40	5	5	17	千克		High strain point glass for manufacturing plasma module（strain point at 550℃ or more）

税则号列 Tariff Item	商品名称及备注	进口税率			出口退税	增值税率	计量单位	监管条件	Article Description
		最惠	普通	暂定					
7020 0019.90	其他工业用玻璃制品	10.5	40			17	千克		Articles of glass for other technical use
	---其他:								---Other:
7020.0091	----保温瓶或其他保温容器用的玻璃胆	21	100		13	17	千克/个	A	----Glass inners for vacuum flasks or for other vacuum vessels
7020.0099	----其他	15	100			17	千克		----Other
7020 0099.01[暂]	石英玻璃,平整度小于等于1微米	15	100	4		17	千克		Quartz glass, degree of plainness less than 1 micron
7020 0099.90	其他非工业用玻璃制品	15	100			17	千克		Other articles of glass not for technical use

第十四类 天然或养殖珍珠、宝石或半宝石、贵金属、包贵金属及其制品；仿首饰；硬币

SECTION XIV NATURAL OR CULTURED PEARLS, PRECIOUS OR SEMI-PRECIOUS STONES. PRECIOUS METALS, METALS CLAD WITH PRECIOUS METAL, AND ARTICLES THEREOF; IMITATION JEWELLERY; COIN

第七十一章 天然或养殖珍珠、宝石或半宝石、贵金属、包贵金属及其制品；仿首饰；硬币

Chapter 71 Natural or cultured pearls, precious or semi-precious stones, precious metals, metals clad with precious metal, and articles thereof; imitation jewellery; coin

注释：

一、除第六类注释一（一）及下列各款另有规定的以外，凡制品的全部或部分由下列物品构成，均应归入本章：

（一）天然或养殖珍珠、宝石或半宝石（天然、合成或再造）；或

（二）贵金属或包贵金属。

二、（一）品目71.13、71.14及71.15不包括带有贵金属或包贵金属制的小零件或小装饰品（例如，交织字母、套、箍、套环）的制品，上述注释一（二）也不适用于这类制品[①]；

（二）品目71.16不包括含有贵金属或包贵金属（仅作为小零件或小装饰品的除外）的制品。

三、本章不包括：

（一）贵金属汞齐及胶态贵金属（品目28.43）；

（二）第三十章的外科用无菌缝合材料、牙科填料或其他货品；

（三）第三十二章的货品（例如，光瓷釉）；

（四）载体催化剂（品目38.15）；

（五）第四十二章注释三（二）所述的品目42.02或42.03的物品；

（六）品目43.03或43.04的物品；

（七）第十一类的货品（纺织原料及纺织制品）；

（八）第六十四章或第六十五章的鞋靴、帽类及其他物品；

（九）第六十六章的伞、手杖及其他物品；

（十）品目68.04或68.05及第八十二章含有宝石或半宝石（天然或合成）粉末的研磨材料制品；第八十二章装有宝石或半宝石（天然、合成或再造）工作部件的器具；第十六类的机器、机械器具、电气设备及其零件。然而，完全以宝石或半宝石（天然、合成或再造）制成的物品及其零件，除未安装的唱针用已加工蓝宝石或钻石外（品目85.22），其余仍应归入本章；

Chapter Notes:

1. Subject to Note 1（a）to Section Ⅵ and except as provided below, all articles consisting wholly or partly:

（a）Of natural or cultured pearls or of precious or semi-precious stones（natural, synthetic or reconstructed）; or

（b）Of precious metal or of metal clad with precious metal, are to be classified in this Chapter.

2.（a）Headings 71.13, 71.14 and 71.15 do not cover articles in which precious metal or metal clad with precious metal is present as minor constituents only, such as minor fittings or minor ornamentation（for example, monograms, ferrules and rims）, and Note1（b）of the foregoing Note does not apply to such articles[①];

（b）Heading 71.16 does not cover articles containing precious metal or metal clad with precious metal（other than as minor constituents）.

3. This Chapter does not cover:

（a）Amalgams of precious metal, or colloidal precious metal（heading 28.43）;

（b）Sterile surgical suture materials, dental fillings or other goods of Chapter 30;

（c）Goods of Chapter 32（for example, lustres）;

（d）Supported catalysts（heading 38.15）;

（e）Articles of heading 42.02 or 42.03 referred to in Note 3（b）to Chapter42;

（f）Articles of heading 43.03 or 43.04;

（g）Goods of Section Ⅺ（textiles and textile articles）;

（h）Footwear, headgear or other articles of Chapter 64 or 65;

（i）Umbrellas, walking-sticks or other articles of Chapter 66;

（j）Abrasive goods of heading 68.04 or 68.05 or Chapter 82, containing dust or powder of precious or semi-precious stones（natural or synthetic）; articles of Chapter 82 with a working part of precious or semi-precious stones（natural, synthetic or reconstructed）; machinery, mechanical appliances or electrical goods, or parts thereof, of Section XVI. However, articles and parts thereof, wholly of precious or semi-precious stones（natural, synthetic or reconstructed）remain classified in this Chapter, except unmounted worked sapphires and diamonds for styli（heading 85.22）;

（十一）第九十章、第九十一章或第九十二章的物品（科学仪器、钟表及乐器）；
（十二）武器及其零件（第九十三章）；
（十三）第九十五章注释二所述物品；
（十四）根据第九十六章注释四应归入该章的物品；或
（十五）雕塑品原件（品目 97.03）、收藏品（品目 97.05）或超过 100 年的古物（品目 97.06）、但天然或养殖珍珠、宝石及半宝石除外。

（k）Articles of Chapter 90, 91 or 92 （scientific instruments, clocks and watches, musical instruments）;
（l） Arms or parts thereof（Chapter 93）;
（m）Articles covered by Note 2 to Chapter 95;
（n）Articles classified in Chapter 96 by virtue of Note 4 to that Chapter; or
（o）Original sculptures or statuary（heading 97.03）, collectors' pieces （heading 97.05）or antiques of an age exceeding one hundred years（heading 97.06）, other than natural or cultured pearls or precious or semi-precious stones.

四、（一）所称"贵金属"，是指银、金及铂；
（二）所称"铂"，是指铂、铱、锇、钯、铑及钌；
（三）所称"宝石或半宝石"，不包括第九十六章注释二（二）所述任何物质。

4. （a）The expression "precious metal" means silver, gold and platinum;
（b）The expression "platinum" means platinum, iridium, osmium, palladium, rhodium and ruthenium;
（c）The expression "precious or semi-precious stones" does not include any of the substances specified in Note 2（b）to Chapter 96.

五、含有贵金属的合金（包括烧结及化合的），只要其中任何一种贵金属的含量达到合金重量的 2%，即应视为本章的贵金属合金。贵金属合金应按下列规则归类：
（一）按重量计含铂量在 2%及以上的合金，应视为铂合金；
（二）按重量计含金量在 2%及以上，但不含铂或按重量计含铂量在 2%以下的合金，应视为金合金；
（三）按重量计含银量在 2%及以上的其他合金，应视为银合金。

5. For the purposes of this Chapter, any alloy（including a sintered mixture and an inter-metallic compound）containing precious metal is to be treated as an alloy of precious metal if any one precious metal constitutes as much as 2%, by weight, of the alloy. Alloys of precious metal are to be classified according to the following rules:
（a）An alloy containing 2% or more, by weight, of platinum is to be treated as an alloy of platinum;
（b）An alloy containing 2% or more, by weight, of gold but no platinum, or less than 2%, by weight, of platinum, is to be treated as an alloy of gold;
（c）Other alloys containing 2% or more, by weight, of silver are to be treated as alloys of silver.

六、除条文另有规定的以外，本税则所称贵金属应包括上述注释五所规定的贵金属合金，但不包括包贵金属或表面镀以贵金属的贱金属及非金属。

6. Except where the context otherwise requires, any reference in the Nomenclature to precious metal or to any particular precious metal includes a reference to alloys treated as alloys of precious metal or of the particular metal in accordance with the rules in Note 5 above, but not to metal clad with precious metal or to base metal or non-metals plated with precious metal.

七、本税则所称"包贵金属"，是指以贱金属为底料，在其一面或多面用焊接、熔接、热轧或类似机械方法覆盖一层贵金属的材料。除条文另有规定的以外，也包括镶嵌贵金属的贱金属。

7. Throughout the Nomenclature the expression "metal clad with precious metal" means material made with a base of metal upon one or more surfaces of which there is affixed by soldering, brazing, welding, hot-rolling or similar mechanical means a covering of precious metal. Except where the context otherwise requires, the expression also covers base metal inlaid with precious metal.

八、除第六类注释一（一）另有规定的以外，凡符合品目 71.12 规定的货品，应归入该品目而不归入本目录的其他品目。

8. Subject to Note 1（a）to Section Ⅵ, goods answering to a description in heading 71.12 are to be classified in that heading and in no other heading of the Nomenclature.

九、品目 71.13 所称"首饰"，是指：
（一）个人用小饰物（例如，戒指、手镯、项圈、饰针、耳环、表链、表链饰物、垂饰、领带别针、袖扣、饰扣、宗教性或其他勋章及徽章）；以及
（二）通常放置在衣袋、手提包或佩戴在身上的个人用品（例如，雪茄盒或烟盒、鼻烟盒、口香糖盒或药丸盒、粉盒、链袋、念珠）。

这些物品可以和下列物品组合或镶嵌：例如，天

9. For the purposes of heading 71.13, the expression "articles of jewellery" means:
（a）Any small objects of personal adornment（for example, rings, bracelets, necklaces, brooches, ear-rings, watch-chains, fobs,pendants, tie-pins, cuff-links, dress-studs, religious or other medals and insignia）; and
（b）Articles of personal use of a kind normally carried in the pocket, in the handbag or on the person（for example, cigar or cigarette cases, snuff boxes, cachou or pill boxes, powderboxes, chain purses or prayer beads）.

These articlea, may be combined or set, for example, with natural or

然或养殖珍珠、宝石或半宝石、合成或再造的宝石或半宝石、玳瑁壳、珍珠母、兽牙、天然或再生琥珀、黑玉或珊瑚。

十、品目 71.14 所称“金银器”，包括装饰品、餐具、梳妆用具、吸烟用具及类似的家庭、办公室或宗教用的其他物品。

十一、品目 71.17 所称“仿首饰”，是指不含天然或养殖珍珠、宝石或半宝石（天然、合成或再造）及贵金属或包贵金属（仅作为镀层或小零件、小装饰品的除外）的上述注释九（一）所述的首饰（不包括品目 96.06 的钮扣及其他物品或品目 96.15 的梳子、发夹及类似品）。

子目注释：

一、子目 7106.10、7108.11、7110.11、7110.21、7110.31 及 7110.41 所称“粉末”，是指按重量计 90%及以上可从网眼孔径为 0.5 毫米的筛子通过的产品；

二、子目 7110.11 及 7110.19 所称“铂”，可不受本章注释四（二）的规定约束，不包括铱、锇、钯、铑及钌；

三、对于品目 71.10 项下的子目所列合金的归类，按其所含铂、钯、铑、铱、锇或钌中重量最大的一种金属归类。

①在本章注释中划有黑线的条文属选择性规定。

cultured pearls, precious or semi-precious stones, synthetic or reconstructed precious or semi-precious stones, tortoise shell, mother-of-pearl, ivory, natural or reconstituted amber, jet or coral.

10.For the purposes of heading 71.14, the expression “articles of goldsmiths' or silversmiths' wares” includes such articles as ornaments, tableware, toilet-ware, smokers' requisites and other articles of household, office or religious use.

11.For the purposes of heading 71.17, the expression “imitation jewellery” means articles of jewellery within the meaning of Note 9 (a) above（but not including buttons or other articles of heading 96.06, or dress-combs, hair-slides or the like, or hairpins, of heading 96.15）, not incorporating natural or cultured pearls, precious or semi-precious stones（natural, synthetic or reconstructed）nor（except as plating or as minor constituents）precious metal or metal clad with precious metal.

Subheading Notes:

1. For the purposes of subheadings 7106.10, 7108.11, 7110.11, 7110.21, 7110.31 and 7110.41, the expressions “powder” and “in powder form” mean products of which 90% or more by weight passes through a sieve having a mesh aperture of 0.5mm.
2. Notwithstanding the provisions of Chapter Note 4（b）, for the purposes of subheadings 7110.11 and 7110.19, the expression“platinum” does not include iridium, osmium, palladium,rhodium or ruthenium.
3. For the classification of alloys in the subheadings of heading71.10, each alloy is to be classified with that metal, platinum, palladium, rhodium, iridium, osmium or ruthenium which predominates by weight over each other of these metals.

①The underlined portion of this Note constitutes an optional text.

税则号列 Tariff Item	商品名称及备注	进口税率			出口退税	增值税率	计量单位	监管条件	Article Description
		最惠	普通	暂定					
	第一分章 天然或养殖珍珠、宝石或半宝石								**I. NATURAL OR CULTURED PEARLS AND PRECIOUS OR SEM-IPRECIOUS STONES**
71.01	天然或养殖珍珠，不论是否加工或分级，但未成串或镶嵌；天然或养殖珍珠，为便于运输而暂穿成串：								**Pearls, natural or cultured, whether or not worked or graded but not strung, mounted or set; ungraded pearls,natural or cultured, temporarily strung for convenience of transport:**
	-天然珍珠:								-Natural pearls:
	---未分级:								---Ungraded:
7101.1011[暂]	----黑珍珠	21	100	0	5	17	克	AB	----Tahitian pearls
7101.1019	----其他	21	100		5	17	克	AB	----Other
	---其他:								---Other:
7101.1091[暂]	----黑珍珠	21	130	0	5	17	克	AB	----Tahitian pearls
7101.1099	----其他	21	130		5	17	克	AB	----Other
	-养殖珍珠:								-Cultured pearls:
	--未加工:								--Unworked:
7101.2110	---未分级	21	100		5	17	千克		---Ungraded
7101 2110.01[暂]	未分级、未加工的养殖黑珍珠（未制成制品）	21	100	0	5	17	千克	AB	Cultured Tahitan pearls, ungraded and unworked (semi-manufactured)
7101 2110.90	其他未分级、未加工的养殖珍珠（未制成制品）	21	100		5	17	千克	AB	Other cultured pearls, uagraded and unworked, semi-manufactured
7101.2190	---其他	21	130		5	17	千克		---Other
7101 2190.01[暂]	其他未加工的养殖黑珍珠(未制成制品)	21	130	0	5	17	千克	AB	Other cultured Tahitan pearls, unworked (semimanufactured)
7101 2190.90	其他未加工的养殖珍珠(未制成制品)	21	130		5	17	千克	AB	Other cultured pearls , unkowrked (semimanufactured)
	--已加工:								--Worked:

税则号列 Tariff Item	商品名称及备注	进口税率 最惠	普通	暂定	出口退税	增值税率	计量单位	监管条件	Article Description
7101.2210	---未分级	21	100		5	17	千克		---Ungraded
7101 2210.01[暂]	未分级、已加工的养殖黑珍珠（未制成制品）	21	100	0	5	17	千克		Culture Tahitan pearls, ungraded,worked (semimanufactured)
7101 2210.90	其他未分级、已加工的养殖珍珠（未制成制品）	21	100		5	17	千克		Other cultured pearls, ungraded, worked (semimanufactured)
7101.2290	---其他	21	130		5	17	千克		---Other
7101 2290.01[暂]	其他已加工的养殖黑珍珠(未制成制品)	21	130	0	5	17	千克		Other cultured Tahitan pearls, worked (semimanufactured)
7101 2290.90	其他已加工的养殖珍珠(未制成制品)	21	130		5	17	千克		Other cultured pearls,worked (semi-manufactured)
71.02	钻石，不论是否加工，但未镶嵌:								**Diamonds, whether or not worked, but not mounted or set:**
7102.1000	-未分级	3	14			17	克拉	D	-Unsorted
	-工业用:								-Industrial:
7102.2100	--未加工或经简单锯开、劈开或粗磨	0	14		5	17	克拉	D	--Unworked or simply sawn, cleaved or bruted
7102.2900	--其他	0	14		5	17	克拉		--Other
	-非工业用:								-Non-industrial:
7102.3100	--未加工或经简单锯开、劈开或粗磨	3	14			17	克拉	D	--Unworked or simply sawn, cleaved or bruted
7102.3900	--其他	8	35			17	克拉		--Other
71.03	宝石（钻石除外）或半宝石，不论是否加工或分级，但未成串或镶嵌，未分级的宝石(钻石除外)或半宝石，为便于运输而暂穿成串:								**Precious stones（other than diamonds）and semi-precious stones,whether or not worked or graded but not strung, mounted or set; ungraded precious stones(other than diamonds) and semi-precious stones, temporarily strung for convenience of transport:**
7103.1000	-未加工或经简单锯开或粗制成形	3	14		5	17	千克		-Unworked or simply sawn or roughly shaped
	-经其他加工:								-Otherwise worked:
7103.9100	--红宝石、蓝宝石、祖母绿	8	35		5	17	克拉		--Rubies, sapphires and emeralds
	--其他:								--Other:
7103.9910	---翡翠	8	35		5	17	克拉		---Jadeite
7103.9920	---水晶	8	35		5	17	克拉		---Crystal
7103.9930	---碧玺	8	35		5	17	克拉		---Tourmaline
7103.9940	---软玉	8	35		5	17	克拉		---Nephrite
7103.9990	---其他	8	35		5	17	克拉		---Other
71.04	合成或再造的宝石或半宝石，不论是否加工或分级，但未成串或镶嵌的;未分级的合成或再造的宝石或半宝石，为便于运输而暂穿成串:								**Synthetic or reconstructed precious or semiprecious stones, whether or not worked or graded but not strung, mounted or set; ungraded synthetic or reconstructed precious or semi-precious stones, temporarily strung for convenience of transport:**
7104.1000	-压电石英	6	14		5	17	克		-Piezo-electric quartz
	-其他，未加工或经简单锯开或粗制成形:								-Other, unworked or simply sawn or roughly shaped:
7104.2010	---钻石	0	14			17	克		---Diamonds
7104.2090	---其他	0	14		5	17	克		---Other
	-其他:								-Other:
	---工业用:								---For technical use:
7104.9011	----钻石	6	14		5	17	克		----Diamonds
7104.9012	----蓝宝石	6	14		5	17	克		----Sapphires
7104 9012.01[暂]	蓝宝石衬底(由人造刚玉加工而成）(厚度<0.5mm)	6	14	1	5	17	克		Sapphire substrate (processed from aloxite),of a thickness less than 0.5mm
7104 9012.90	其他工业用蓝宝石(合成或再造宝石、半宝石)	6	14		5	17	克		Other sapphire substrate used on industry (synthetic or reconstructed precious or semi-precious stones)
7104.9019	----其他	6	14		5	17	克		----Other

税则号列 Tariff Item	商品名称及备注	进口税率 最惠	普通	暂定	出口退税	增值税率	计量单位	监管条件	Article Description
	---其他:								---Other:
7104.9091	----钻石	8	35			17	克		----Diamonds
7104.9099	----其他	8	35		5	17	克		----Other
71.05	**天然或合成的宝石或半宝石的粉末:**								**Dust and powder of natural or synthetic precious or semi-precious stones:**
	-钻石的:								-Of diamonds:
7105.1010	---天然的	0	17			17	克拉		---Natural
7105.1020	---人工合成的	0	17		5	17	克拉		---Synthetic
7105.9000	-其他	0	17		5	17	克		-Other
	第二分章 贵金属及包贵金属								**Ⅱ. PRECIOUS METALS AND METALS CLAD WITH PRECIOUS METAL**
71.06	**银（包括镀金、镀铂的银），未锻造、半制成或粉末状:**								**Silver（including silver plated with gold or platinum）, unwrought or in semimanufactured forms, or in powder form:**
	-银粉:								-Powder:
	---非片状粉末:								---Not Flake:
7106.1011	----平均粒径小于3微米	0	0			17	克	A	----Average diameter less than 3μm
7106.1019	----其他	0	0			17	克	A	----Other
	---片状粉末:								---Flake:
7106.1021	----平均粒径小于10微米	0	0			17	克	4xy	----Average diameter less than 10μm
7106.1029	----其他	0	0			17	克	4xy	----Other
	-其他:								-Other:
	--未锻造:								--Unwrought:
7106.9110	---纯度达99.99%及以上	0	0			17	克	4xy	---Of a purity of 99.99% or more
7106.9190	---其他	0	0			17	克	4xy	---Other
	--半制成:								--Semi-manufactured:
7106.9210	---纯度达99.99%及以上	0	50			17	克	4xy	---Of a purity of 99.99% or more
7106.9290	---其他	0	50			17	克	4xy	---Other
71.07	**以贱金属为底的包银材料:**								**Base metals clad with silver, not further worked than semi-manufactured:**
7107.0000	以贱金属为底的包银材料	10.5	50		5	17	千克		Base metals clad with silver, not further worked than semi-manufactured
71.08	**金（包括镀铂的金），未锻造、半制成或粉末状:**								**Gold（including gold plated with platinum）unwrought or in semi-manufactured forms, or in powder form:**
	-非货币用:								-Non-monetary:
7108.1100	--金粉	0	0			0	克	J	--Powder
7108.1200	--其他未锻造形状	0	0			0	克	J	--Other unwrought forms
7108.1300	--其他半制成形状	0	50			0	克	J	--Other semi-manufactured forms
7108.2000	-货币用	0	0			0	克	J	-Monetary
71.09	**以贱金属或银为底的包金材料:**								**Base metals or silver, clad with gold, not further worked than semi-manufactured:**
7109.0000	以贱金属或银为底的包金材料	10.5	50		5	17	克		Base metals or silver, clad with gold, not further worked than semi-manufactured
71.10	**铂，未锻造、半制成或粉末状:**								**Platinum, unwrought or in semi-manufactured forms, or in powder form:**
	-铂:								-Platinum:
7110.1100	--未锻造或粉末状	0	0			0	克	8x	--Unwrought or in powder form
	--其他:								--Other:
7110.1910	---板、片	0	0			0	克	8x	---Plates and sheets
7110.1990	---其他	3	11			0	克	4xy	---Other
	-钯:								-Palladium:
7110.2100	--未锻造或粉末状	0	10			17	克	4xy	--Unwrought or in powder form
	--其他:								--Other:
7110.2910	---板、片	0	0			17	克	4xy	---Plates and sheets
7110.2990	---其他	3	11			17	克	4xy	---Other
	-铑:								-Rhodium:

税则号列 Tariff Item	商品名称及备注	进口税率 最惠	进口税率 普通	进口税率 暂定	出口退税	增值税率	计量单位	监管条件	Article Description
7110.3100	--未锻造或粉末状	0	0			17	克	4xy	--Unwrought or in powder form
	--其他:								--Other:
7110.3910	---板、片	0	0			17	克	4xy	---Plates and sheets
7110.3990	---其他	3	11			17	克	4xy	---Other
	-铱、锇及钌:								-Iridium, osmium and ruthenium:
7110.4100	--未锻造或粉末状	0	0			17	克	4xy	--Unwrought or in powder form
	--其他:								--Other:
7110.4910	---板、片	0	0			17	克	4xy	---Plates and sheets
7110.4990	---其他	3	11			17	克	4xy	---Other
71.11	**以贱金属、银或金为底的包铂材料:**								**Base metals, silver or gold, clad with platinum, not further worked than semi-manufactured:**
7111.0000	以贱金属、银或金为底的包铂材料	3	11		0/5	17	克	4xy	Base metals, silver or gold, clad with platinum, not further worked than semi-manufactured
71.12	**贵金属或包贵金属的废碎料;含有贵金属或贵金属化合物的其他废碎料,主要用于回收贵金属:**								**Waste and scrap of precious metal or of metal clad with precious metal; other waste and scrap containing precious metal or precious metal compounds, of a kind used principally for the recovery of precious metal:**
	-含有贵金属或金属化合物的灰:								-Ash containing precious metal or precious metal compounds:
7112.3010	---含有银或银化合物的	8	50		5	17	克	9	---Of silver or silver compounds
7112.3090	---其他	6	50			17	克	9	---Other
	-其他:								-Other:
	--金及包金的废碎料,但含有其他贵金属的除外:								--Of gold, including metal clad with gold but excluding sweepings containing other precious metals:
7112.9110	---金及包金的废碎料	0	0			17	克		---Of gold or gold compounds
7112 9110.10	金的废碎料	0	0			17	克	AJP	Waste and scrap of gold
7112 9110.90	包金的废碎料(但含有其他贵金属的除外)	0	0			17	克	AP	Waste and scrap of gold compounds, but excluding sweepings containing other precious metals:
7112.9120	---含有金或金化合物的废碎料	6	35			17	克	9	---Waste and scrap with gold or gold compounds
	--铂及包铂的废碎料,但含有其他贵金属的除外:								--Of platinum, including metal clad with platinum but excluding sweepings containing other precious metals:
7112.9210	---铂及包铂的废碎料	0	0			17	克	4APxy	---Of platinum
7112.9220	---含有铂或铂化合物的废碎料	6	35			17	克		---Wasted and scrap with platinum
7112 9220.01[暂]	铂含量在3%以上的其他含有铂或铂化合物的废碎料(但含有其他贵金属除外,主要用于回收铂)	6	35	0		17	克	4xy	Other waste and scraps containing 3% or more of platinum, but excluding sweepings containg other precious metals, used for recycling platinum
7112 9220.90	其他含有铂及铂化合物的废碎料(但含有其他贵金属除外,主要用于回收铂)	6	35			17	克	4xy	Other waste and scraps containing platinum, but excluding sweepings containg other precious metals, used for recycling platinum
	--其他:								--Other:
7112.9910	---含有银或银化合物的废碎料	8	35		5	17	克	9	---Waste and scrap with silver or silver compounds
7112.9920	---含有其他贵金属或贵金属化合物的废碎料	6	35			17	克	9	---Waste and scrap with other precious metals
7112.9990	---其他	0	50			17	克		---Other
	第三分章 珠宝首饰、金银器及其他制品								**Ⅲ. JEWELLERY, GOLDSMITHS' AND SILVERSMITHS' WARES AND OTHER ARTICLES**
71.13	**贵金属或包贵金属制的首饰及其零件:**								**Articles of jewellery and parts thereof, of precious metal or of metal clad with precious metal:**
	-贵金属制,不论是否包、镀贵金属:								-Of precious metal whether or not plated or clad with precious metal:
	--银制,不论是否包、镀其他贵金属:								--Of silver, whether or not plated or clad with other precious metal:
7113.1110	---镶嵌钻石的	20	130			17	克		---Diamond mounted or set
7113.1190	---其他	20	130			17	克		---Other

税则号列 Tariff Item	商品名称及备注	进口税率 最惠	普通	暂定	出口退税	增值税率	计量单位	监管条件	Article Description
7113 1190.10	镶嵌濒危物种制品的银首饰及零件(不论是否包、镀其他贵金属)	20	130			17	克	FE	Silver jewellery and parts thereof, inlaid with articles of endangered species (whether or not plated or clad with other precious metal)
7113 1190.90	其他银首饰及其零件(不论是否包、镀其他贵金属)	20	130		5	17	克		Other silver jewellery and parts thereof, whether or not plated or clad with other precious metal
	--其他贵金属制，不论是否包、镀贵金属:								--Of other precious metal, whether or not plated or clad with predious metal:
	---黄金制:								---Of gold:
7113.1911	----镶嵌钻石的	20	130			17	克	J	----Diamond mounted
7113.1919	----其他	20	130			17	克		----Other
7113 1919.10	镶嵌濒危物种制品的金首饰及零件(不论是否包、镀其他贵金属)	20	130			17	克	FEJ	Gold jewellery and parts thereof, inlaid with articles of endangered species (whether or not plated or clad with other precious metal)
7113 1919.90	其他黄金制首饰及其零件(不论是否包、镀其他贵金属)	20	130			17	克	J	Other gold jewellery and parts thereof (whether or not plated or clad with other precious metal)
	---铂制:								---Of platinum:
7113.1921	----镶嵌钻石的	35	130			17	克		----Diamond mounted
7113.1929	----其他	35	130			17	克		----Other
7113 1929.10	镶嵌濒危物种制品的铂金首饰及零件(不论是否包、镀其他贵金属)	35	130			17	克	EF	Platnum and parts thereof, inlaid with articles of endangered species (whether or not plated or clad with other precious metal)
7113 1929.90	其他铂金制首饰及其零件(不论是否包、镀其他贵金属)	35	130			17	克		Other platnum and parts thereof, whether or not plated or clad with other precious metal
7113.1991	----镶嵌钻石的	35	130			17	克		----Diamond mounted or set
7113.1999	----其他	35	130			17	克		----Other
7113 1999.10	镶嵌濒危物种制品其他贵金属首饰(不论是否包、镀其他贵金属)	35	130			17	克	FE	Jewellery and parts thereof, of precious metal, inlaid with articles of endangered species (whether or not plated or clad with other precious metal)
7113 1999.90	其他贵金属制首饰及其零件(不论是否包、镀其他贵金属)	35	130			17	克		Other jewellery and parts thereof, of precious metal (whether or not plated or clad with other precious metal)
	-以贱金属为底的包贵金属制:								-Of base metal clad with precious metal:
7113.2010	---镶嵌钻石的	35	130			17	克		---Diamond mounted or set
7113.2090	---其他	35	130			17	克		---Other
7113 2090.10	镶嵌濒危物种制品以贱金属为底的包贵金属制首饰(包括零件)	35	130			17	克	FE	Jewellery and parts thereof, of base Metal, inlaid with articles of endangered Species
7113 2090.90	其他以贱金属为底的包贵金属制首饰(包括零件)	35	130		5	17	克		Other jewellery and parts thereof, of base metal clad with precious metal
71.14	**贵金属或包贵金属制的金银器及其零件:**								**Articles of goldsmiths' or silversmiths'wares and parts thereof, of precious metal or of metal clad with precious metal:**
	-贵金属制，不论是否包、镀贵金属:								-Of precious metal whether or not plated or clad with precious metal:
7114.1100	--银制，不论是否包、镀其他贵金属	35	100			17	克		--Of silver, whether or not plated or clad with other precious metal
7114 1100.10	镶嵌濒危物种制品的银器及零件(不论是否包、镀贵金属)	35	100			17	克	FE	Silversmiths' wares and parts thereof,inlaid with articles of endangered species (whether or not plated or clad with precious metal)
7114 1100.90	其他银器及零件(不论是否包、镀贵金属)	35	100		5	17	克		Other silversmiths' wares and parts thereof (whether or not plated or clad with precious metal)
7114.1900	--其他贵金属制，不论是否包、镀贵金属	35	100			17	克		--Of other precious metal, whether or not plated or clad with precious metal
7114 1900.10	镶嵌濒危物种制品的金银器及零件(不论是否包、镀贵金属)	35	100			17	克	FE	Goldsmiths' or silversmiths' wares and parts thereof, inlaid with articles of endangered species (whether or

税则号列 Tariff Item	商品名称及备注	进口税率 最惠	普通	暂定	出口退税	增值税率	计量单位	监管条件	Article Description
									not plated or clad with precious metal）
7114 1900.90	其他贵金属制金银器及零件(不论是否包、镀贵金属）	35	100			17	克		Other goldsmiths' or silversmiths' wares and parts thereof, of precious metal (whether or not plated or clad with other precious metal)
7114.2000	-以贱金属为底的包贵金属制	35	100			17	克		-Of base metal clad with precious metal
7114 2000.10	以贱金属为底的包贵金属制金银器（镶嵌濒危物种制品，包括零件）	35	100			17	克	FE	Goldsmiths' or silversmiths' wares and parts thereof, of base metal clad with precious metal（inlaid with articles of endangered species）
7114 2000.90	其他贱金属为底包贵金属制金银器（包括零件）	35	100		0/5	17	克		Goldsmiths' or silversmiths' wares of other base metal clad with precious metal (and parts thereof)
71.15	**贵金属或包贵金属的其他制品:**								**Other articles of precious metal or of metal clad with precious metal:**
7115.1000	-金属丝布或格栅形状的铂催化剂	3	11			17	克	4xy	-Catalysts in the form of wire cloth or grill, of platinum
	-其他:								-Other:
7115.9010[暂]	---工业或实验室用	3	11	0		17	克		---For technical or laboratory use
7115 9010.10[暂]	银制工业、实验室用制品	3	11	0	5	17	克		Articles of silver used for industrial or laboratory
7115 9010.20[暂]	金制工业、实验室用制品	3	11	0		17	克	J	Articles of gold used for industrial or laboratory
7115 9010.90[暂]	其他工业、实验室用贵或包贵金制品	3	11	0	0/5	17	克		Articles of precious metal or of metal clad with precious metal, used for other industrial or laboratory
7115.9090	---其他	35	100		0/5	17	克		---Other
71.16	**用天然或养殖珍珠、宝石或半宝石（天然、合成或再造）制成的物品:**								**Articles of natural or cultured pearls,precious or semi-precious stones（natural, synthetic or reconstructed）:**
7116.1000	-天然或养殖珍珠制	35	130		5	17	千克		-Of natural or cultured pearls
7116.2000	-宝石或半宝石（天然、合成或再造）制	35	130		0/5	17	千克		-Of precious or semi-precious stones （natural, synthetic or reconstructed）
71.17	**仿首饰:**								**Imitation jewellery:**
	-贱金属制，不论是否镀贵金属:								-Of base metal, whether or not plated with precious metal:
7117.1100	--袖扣、饰扣	35	130		9	17	千克	A	--Cuff-links and studs
7117.1900	--其他	17	130		9	17	千克	A	--Other
7117.9000	-其他	35	130		9	17	千克	A	-Other
71.18	**硬币:**								**Coin:**
7118.1000	-非法定货币的硬币（金币除外）	0	0		5	17	千克		-Coin（other than gold coin）, not being legal tender
7118.9000	-其他	0	0			17	千克		-Other

第十五类
贱金属及其制品

SECTION XV
BASE METALS AND ARTICLES OF BASE METAL

注释：

一、本类不包括：

（一）以金属粉末为基本成分的调制油漆、油墨或其他产品（品目32.07至32.10、32.12、32.13或32.15）；

（二）铈铁或其他引火合金（品目36.06）；

（三）品目65.06或65.07的帽类及其零件；

（四）品目66.03的伞骨及其他物品；

（五）第七十一章的货品（例如，贵金属合金、以贱金属为底的包贵金属、仿首饰）；

（六）第十六类的物品（机器、机械器具及电气设备）；

（七）已装配的铁道或电车道轨道（品目86.08）或第十七类的其他物品（车辆、船舶、航空器）；

（八）第十八类的仪器及器具，包括钟表发条；

（九）做弹药用的铅弹（品目93.06）或第十九类的其他物品（武器、弹药）；

（十）第九十四章的物品（例如，家具、弹簧床垫、灯具及照明装置、发光标志、活动房屋）；

（十一）第九十五章的物品（例如，玩具、游戏品及运动用品）；

（十二）手用筛子、纽扣、钢笔、铅笔套、钢笔尖或第九十六章的其他物品（杂项制品）；或

（十三）第九十七章的物品（例如，艺术品）。

二、本税则所称“通用零件”，是指：

（一）品目73.07、73.12、73.15、73.17或73.18的物品及其他贱金属制的类似品；

（二）贱金属制的弹簧及弹簧片，但钟表发条（品目91.14）除外；以及

（三）品目83.01、83.02、83.08、83.10的物品及品目83.06的贱金属制的框架及镜子。

第七十三章至第七十六章（品目73.15除外）及第七十八章至第八十二章所列货品的零件，不包括上述的通用零件。

除上段及第八十三章注释一另有规定的以外，第七十二章至第七十六章及第七十八章至第八十一章不包括第八十二章、第八十三章的物品。

三、本目录所称“贱金属”是指：铁及钢、铜、镍、铝、铅、锌、锡、钨、钼、钽、镁、钴、铋、镉、钛、锆、锑、锰、铍、铬、锗、钒、镓、铪、铟、铌（钶）、铼及铊。

Section Notes:

1. This Section does not cover:

(a) Prepared paints, inks or other products with a basis of metallic flakes or powder (headings 32.07 to 32.10, 32.12, 32.13 or 32.15);

(b) Ferro-cerium or other pyrophoric alloys (heading 36.06);

(c) Headgear or parts thereof of heading 65.06 or 65.07;

(d) Umbrella frames or other articles of heading 66.03;

(e) Goods of Chapter 71 (for example, precious metal alloys, base metal clad with precious metal, imitation jewellery);

(f) Articles of Section XVI (machinery, mechanical appliances and electrical goods);

(g) Assembled railway or tramway track (heading 86.08) or other articles of Section XVII (vehicles, ships and boats, aircraft);

(h) Instruments or apparatus of Section XVIII, including clock or watch springs;

(ij) Lead shot prepared for ammunition (heading 93.06) or other articles of Section XIX (arms and ammunition);

(k) Articles of Chapter 94 (for example, furniture, mattress supports, lamps and lighting fittings, illuminated signs, prefabricated buildings);

(l) Articles of Chapter 95 (for example, toys, games, sports requisites);

(m) Hand sieves, buttons, pens, pencil-holders, pen nibs or other articles of Chapter 96 (miscellaneous manufactured articles); or

(n) Articles of Chapter 97 (for example, works of art).

2. Throughout the Nomenclature, the expression “parts of general use” means:

(a) Articles of heading 73.07, 73.12, 73.15, 73.17 or 73.18 and similar articles of other base metals;

(b) Springs and leaves for springs, of base metal, other than clock or watch springs (heading 91.14); and

(c) Articles of headings 83.01, 83.02, 83.08, 83.10 and frames and mirrors, of base metal, of heading 83.06.

In Chapters 73 to 76 and 78 to 82 (but not in heading 73.15) references to parts of goods do not include references to parts of general use as defined above.

Subject to the preceding paragraph and to Note 1 to Chapter 83, the articles of Chapter 82 or 83 are excluded from Chapters 72 to 76 and 78 to 81.

3. Throughout the Nomenclature, the expression “base metals” means: iron and steel, copper, nickel, aluminium, lead, zinc, tin, tungsten (wolfram), molybdenum, tantalum, magnesium, cobalt, bismuth, cadmium, titanium, zirconium, antimony, manganese, beryllium, chromium, germanium,

vanadium, gallium, hafnium,indium, niobium（columbium）, rhenium and thallium.

四、本税则所称“金属陶瓷”，是指金属与陶瓷成分以极细微粒不均匀结合而成的产品。“金属陶瓷”包括硬质合金（金属碳化物与金属烧结而成）。

4. Throughout the Nomenclature, the term “cermets” means products containing a microscopic heterogeneous combination of a metallic component and a ceramic component. The term “cermets” includes sintered metal carbides（metal carbides sintered with a metal）.

五、合金的归类规则（第七十二章、第七十四章所规定的铁合金及母合金除外）：

（一）贱金属的合金按其所含重量最大的金属归类；

（二）由本类的贱金属和非本类的元素构成的合金，如果所含贱金属的总重量等于或超过所含其他元素的总重量，应作为本类贱金属合金归类；

（三）本类所称“合金”，包括金属粉末的烧结混合物、熔化而得的不均匀紧密混合物（金属陶瓷除外）及金属间化合物。

5. Classification of alloys（other than ferro-alloys and master alloys as defined in Chapters 72 and 74）:

（a）An alloy of base metals is to be classified as an alloy of the metal which predominates by weight over each of the other metals;

（b）An alloy composed of base metals of this Section and of elements not falling within this Section is to be treated as an alloy of base metals of this Section if the total weight of such metals equals or exceeds the total weight of the other elements present;

（c）In this Section the term “alloys” includes sintered mixtures of metal powders, heterogeneous intimate mixtures obtained by melting（other than cermets）and intermetallic compounds.

六、除条文另有规定的以外，本税则所称的贱金属包括贱金属合金，这类合金应按上述注释五的规则进行归类。

6. Unless the context otherwise requires, any reference in the Nomenclature to a base metal includes a reference to alloys which, by virtue of Note 5 above, are to be classified as alloys of that metal.

七、复合材料制品的归类规则：

除各品目另有规定的以外，贱金属制品（包括根据“归类总规则”作为贱金属制品的混合材料制品）如果含有两种或两种以上贱金属的，按其所含重量最大的贱金属的制品归类。

为此：

（一）钢、铁或不同种类的钢铁，均视为一种金属；

（二）按照注释五的规定作为某一种金属归类的合金，应视为一种金属；以及

（三）品目81.13的金属陶瓷，应视为一种贱金属。

7. Classification of composite articles:

Except where the headings otherwise require, articles of base metal（including articles of mixed materials treated as articles of base metal under the Interpretative Rules）containing two or more base metals are to be treated as articles of the base metal predominating by weight over each of the other metals.

For this purpose:

（a）Iron and steel, or different kinds of iron or steel, are regarded as one and the same metal;

（b）An alloy is regarded as being entirely composed of that metal as an alloy of which, by virtue of Note 5, it is classified; and

（c）A cermet of heading 81.13 is regarded as a single base metal.

八、本类所用有关名词解释如下：

（一）废碎料

在金属生产或机械加工中产生的废料及碎屑以及因破裂、切断、磨损及其他原因而明显不能作为原物使用的金属货品。

（二）粉末

按重量计90%及以上可从网眼孔径为1毫米的筛子通过的产品。

8. In this Section, the following expressions have the meanings hereby assigned to them:

（a）Waste and scrap

Metal waste and scrap from the manufacture of mechanical working of metals, and metal goods definitely not usable as such because of breakage, cutting-up, wear or other reasons.

（b）Powders

Products of which 90% or more by weight passes through a sieve having a mesh aperture of 1mm.

第七十二章 钢 铁

Chapter 72 Iron and steel

注释：

一、本章所述有关名词解释如下[本条注释（四）、（五）、（六）适用于本目录其他各章]：

Chapter Notes:

1. In this Chapter and, in the case of Notes（d）,（e）and（f）throughout the Nomenclature, the following expressions have the meanings hereby assigned to them:

（一）生铁

无实用可锻性的铁碳合金，按重量计含碳量在 2%以上并可含有一种或几种下列含量范围的其他元素：

铬不超过 10%；

锰不超过 6%；

磷不超过 3%；

硅不超过 8%；

其他元素合计不超过 10%。

（二）镜铁

按重量计含锰量在 6%以上，但不超过 30%的铁碳合金，其他方面符合上述（一）款所列标准。

（三）铁合金

锭、块、团或类似初级形状、连续铸造而形成的各种形状及颗粒、粉末状的合金，不论是否烧结，通常用于其他合金生产过程中的添加剂或在黑色金属冶炼中作除氧剂、脱硫剂及类似用途，一般无实用可锻性，按重量计铁元素含量在 4%及以上并含有下列一种或几种元素：

铬超过 10%；

锰超过 30%；

磷超过 3%；

硅超过 8%；

除碳以外的其他元素，合计超过 10%，但最高含铜量不得超过 10%。

（四）钢

除品目 72.03 以外的黑色金属材料（某些铸造而成的种类除外），具有实用可锻性，按重量计含碳量在 2%及以下，但铬钢可具有较高的含碳量。

（五）不锈钢

按重量计含碳量在 1.2%及以下，含铬量在 10.5%及以上的合金钢，不论是否含有其他元素。

（六）其他合金钢

不符合以上不锈钢定义的钢，含有一种或几种按重量计符合下列含量比例的元素：

铝 0.3%及以上；

硼 0.0008%及以上；

铬 0.3%及以上；

钴 0.3%及以上；

铜 0.4%及以上；

铅 0.4%及以上；

锰 1.65%及以上；

钼 0.08%及以上；

镍 0.3%及以上；

铌 0.06%及以上；

硅 0.6%及以上；

钛 0.05%及以上；

钨 0.3%及以上；

(a) Pig iron

Iron-carbon alloys not usefully malleable, containing more than2% by weight of carbon and which may contain by weight one or more other elements within the following limits:

not more than 10% of chromium;

not more than 6% of manganese;

not more than 3% of phosphorus;

not more than 8% of silicon;

a total of not more than 10% of other elements.

(b) Spiegeleisen

Iron-carbon alloys containing by weight more than 6% but not more than 30% of manganese and otherwise conforming to the specification at (a) above.

(c) Ferro-alloys

Alloys in ingots, blocks, lumps or similar primary forms, in forms obtained by continuous casting and also in granular or powder forms, whether or not agglomerated, commonly used as an additive in the manufacture of other alloys or as de-oxidants, de-sulphurising agents or for similar uses in ferrous metallurgy and generally not usefully malleable, containing by weight 4% or more of the element iron and one or more of the following:

more than 10% of chromium;

more than 30% of manganese;

more than 3% of phosphorus;

more than 8% of silicon;

a total of more than 10% of other elements, excluding carbon, subject to a maximum content of 10% in the case of copper.

(d) Steel

Ferrous materials other than those of heading 72.03 which (with the exception of certain types produced in the form of castings) are usefully malleable and which contain by weight 2% or less of carbon. However, chromium steels may contain higher proportions of carbon.

(e) Stainless steel

Alloy steels containing, by weight, 1.2% or less of carbon and 10.5% or more of chromium, with or without other elements.

(f) Other alloy steel

Steels not complying with the definition of stainless steel and containing by weight one or more of the following elements in the proportion shown:

0.3% or more of aluminium;

0.0008% or more of boron;

0.3% or more of chromium;

0.3% or more of cobalt;

0.4% or more of copper;

0.4% or more of lead;

1.65% or more of manganese;

0.08% or more of molybdenum;

0.3% or more of nickel;

0.06% or more of niobium;

0.6% or more of silicon;

0.05% or more of titanium;

0.3% or more of tungsten (wolfram);

0.1% or more of vanadium;

钒 0.1%及以上；
锆 0.05%及以上；
其他元素（硫、磷、碳及氮除外）单项含量在 0.1%及以上。

（七）供再熔的碎料钢铁锭

粗铸成形无缩孔或冒口的锭块产品，表面有明显瑕疵，化学成分不同于生铁、镜铁及铁合金。

（八）颗粒

按重量计不到 90%可从网眼孔径为 1 毫米的筛子通过，而 90%及以上可从网眼孔径为 5 毫米的筛子通过的产品。

（九）半制成品

连续铸造的实心产品，不论是否初步热轧；其他实心产品，除经初步热轧或锻造粗制成形以外未经进一步加工，包括角材、型材及异型材的坯件。

本类产品不包括成卷的产品。

（十）平板轧材

截面为矩形（正方形除外）并且不符合以上第（九）款所述定义的下列形状实心轧制产品：

1. 层叠的卷材；或
2. 平直形状，其厚度如果在 4.75 毫米以下，则宽度至少是厚度的十倍；其厚度如果在 4.75 毫米及以上，其宽度应超过 150 毫米，并且至少应为厚度的两倍。

平板轧材包括直接轧制而成并有凸起式样（例如，凹槽、肋条形、格槽、珠粒、菱形）的产品以及穿孔、抛光或制成瓦楞形的产品，但不具有其他品目所列制品或产品的特征。

各种规格的平板轧材（矩形或正方形除外），但不具有其他品目所列制品或产品的特征，都应作为宽度为 600 毫米及以上的产品归类。

（十一）不规则盘绕的热轧条、杆

经热轧不规则盘绕的实心产品，其截面为圆形、扇形、椭圆形、矩形（包括正方形）、三角形或其他外凸多边形（包括“扁圆形”及“变形矩形”，即相对两边为孤拱形，另外两边为等长平行直线形）。这类产品可带有在轧制过程中产生的凹痕、凸缘、槽沟或其他变形（钢筋）。

（十二）其他条、杆

不符合上述（九）、（十）、（十一）款或“丝”定义的实心产品，其全长截面均为圆形、扇形、椭圆形、矩形（包括正方形）三角形或其他外凸多边形（包括“扁圆形”及“变形矩形”，即相对两边为弧拱形，另外两边为等长平行直线形）。这些产品可以：

1. 带有在轧制过程中产生的凹痕、凸

0.05% or more of zirconium;
0.1% or more of other elements（except sulphur, phosphorus, carbon and nitrogen）, taken separately.

（g）Remelting scrap ingots of iron or steel

Products roughly cast in the form of ingots without feeder-heads or hot tops, or of pigs, having obvious surface faults and not complying with the chemical composition of pig iron, spiegeleisen or ferro-alloys.

（h）Granules

Products of which less than 90% by weight passes through a sieve with a mesh aperture of 1mm and of which 90% or more by weight passes through a sieve with a mesh aperture of 5mm.

（i）Semi-finished products

Continuous cast products of solid section, whether or not subjected to primary hot-rolling; and other products of solid section,which have not been further worked than subjected to primary hot-rolling or roughly shaped by forging, including blanks for angles, shapes or sections.

These products are not presented in coils.

（j）Flat-rolled products

Rolled products of solid rectangular（other than square）cross-section, which do not conform to the definition at（i）above in the form of:

（i）Coils of successively superimposed layers; or

（ii）Straight lenghths, which if of a thickness less than 4. 75 mm are of a width measuring at least ten times the thickness or if of a thickness of 4.75mm or more are of a width which exceeds 150mm and measures at least twice the thickness.

Flat-rolled products include those with patterns in relief derived directly from rolling（for example, grooves, ribs, chequers, tears, buttons,lozenges）and those which have been perforated, corrugated or polished, provided that they do not thereby assume the character of articles or products of other headings.

Flat-rolled products of a shape other than rectangular or square, of any size, are to be classified as products of a width of 600mm or more, provided that they do not assume the character of articles or products of other headings.

（k）Bars and rods, hot-rolled, in irregularly wound coils Hot-rolled products in irregularly wound coils, which have a solid cross-section in the shape of circles, segments of circles, ovals, rectangles（including squares）, triangles or other convex polygons（including “flattened circles” and “modified rectangles”, of which two opposite sides are convex arcs, the other two sides being straight, of equal length and parallel）. These products may have indentations, ribs, grooves or other deformations produced during the rolling process（reinforcing bars and rods）.

（l）Other bars and rods

Products which do not conform to any of the definitions at （i）,（j）or （k）above or to the definition of wire, which have a uniform solid cross-section along their whole length in the shape of circles, segments of circles, ovals, rectangles （including squares）, triangles or other convex polygons（including “flattened circles” and “modified rectangles”, of which two opposite sides are convex arcs, the other two sides being straight, of equal length and parallel）. These products may:

缘、槽沟或其他变形（钢筋）；

2. 轧制后扭曲的。

（十三）角材、型材及异型材

不符合上述（九）、（十）、（十一）、（十二）款或“丝”定义，但其全长截面均为同样形状的实心产品。

第七十二章不包括品目 73.01 或 73.02 的产品。

（十四）丝

不符合平板轧材定义但全长截面均为同样形状的盘卷冷成形实心产品。

（十五）空心钻钢

适合钻探用的各种截面的空心条、杆，其最大外形尺寸超过15毫米但不超过52毫米，最大内孔尺寸不超过最大外形尺寸的二分之一。不符合本定义的钢铁空心条、杆应归入品目73.04。

二、用一种黑色金属包覆不同种类的黑色金属，应按其中重量最大的材料归类。

三、用电解沉积法、压铸法或烧结法所得的钢铁产品，应按其形状、成分及外观归入本章类似热轧产品的相应品目。

子目注释：

一、本章所用有关名词解释如下

（一）合金生铁

按重量计含有一种或几种下列比例的元素的生铁：

铬 0.2%以上；

铜 0.3%以上；

镍 0.3%以上；

0.1%以上的任何下列元素：铝、钼、钛、钨、钒。

（二）非合金易切削钢

按重量计含有一种或几种下列比例的元素的非合金钢：

硫 0.08%及以上；

铅 0.1%及以上；

硒 0.05%以上；

碲 0.01%以上；

铋 0.05%以上。

（三）硅电钢

按重量计含硅量至少为 0.6%但不超过6%，含碳量不超过 0.08%的合金钢。这类钢还可含有按重量计不超过 1%的铝，但所含其他元素的比例并不使其具有其他合金钢的特性。

（四）高速钢

不论是否含有其他元素，但至少含有按重量计合计含量在 7%及以上的钼、钨、钒中两种元素的合金钢，按重量计其含

（i）Have indentations, ribs, grooves or other deformations produced during the rolling process（reinforcing bars and rods）;

（ii）Be twisted after rolling.

（m）Angles, shapes and sections

Products having a uniform solid cross-section along their whole length which do not conform to any of the definitions at （i）,（j）,（k）or（l）above or to the definition of wire.

Chapter 72 does not include products of heading 73.01 or 73.02.

（n）Wire

Cold-formed products in coils, of any uniform solid cross-section along their whole length, which do not conform to the definition of flat-rolled products.

（o）Hollow drill bars and rods

Hollow bars and rods of any cross-section, suitable for drills,of which the greatest external dimension of the cross-section exceeds 15mm but does not exceed 52mm, and of which the greatest internal dimension does not exceed one half of the greatest external dimension. Hollow bars and rods of iron or steel not conforming to this definition are to be classified in heading 73.04.

2. Ferrous metals clad with another ferrous metal are to be classified as products of the ferrous metal predominating by weight.

3. Iron or steel products obtained by electrolytic deposition, by pressure casting or by sintering are to be classified, according to their form, their composition and their appearance, in the headings of this Chapter appropriate to similar hot-rolled products.

Subheading Notes:

1. In this Chapter the following expressions have the meanings hereby assigned to them:

（a）Alloy pig iron

Pig iron containing, by weight, one or more of the following elements in the specified proportions:

more than 0.2% of chromium;

more than 0.3% of copper;

more than 0.3% of nickel;

more than 0.1% of any of the following elements:

aluminium, molybdenum, titanium, tungsten（wolfram）, vanadium.

（b）Non-alloy free-cutting steel

Non-alloy steel containing, by weight, one or more of the following elements in the specified proportions:

0.08% or more of sulphur;

0.1% or more of lead;

more than 0.05% of selenium;

more than 0.01% of tellurium;

more than 0.05% of bismuth.

（c）Silicon-electrical steel

Alloy steels containing by weight at least 0.6% but not more than 6% of silicon and not more than 0.08% of carbon. They may also contain by weight not more than 1% of aluminium but no other element in a proportion that would give the steel the characteristics of another alloy steel.

（d）High speed steel

Alloy steels containing, with or without other elements,at least two of the three elements molybdenum, tungsten and vanadium with a combined content by weight of 7% or more, 0.6% or more of carbon and 3% to 6%

碳量在 0.6%及以上，含铬量在 3%-6%。

（五）硅锰钢

按重量计同时含有下列元素的合金钢：

碳不超过 0.7%：

锰 0.5%及以上，但不超过 1.9%；以及

硅 0.6%及以上，但不超过 2.3%；但所含其他元素的比例并不使其具有其他合金钢的特性。

二、品目 72.02 项下的子目所列铁合金，归类：

对于只有一种元素超出本章注释一（三）规定的最低百分比的铁合金，应作为二元合金归入相应的子目。以此类推，如果有两种或三种合金元素超出了最低百分比的，则可分别作为三元或四元合金。

在运用本规定时，本章注释一（三）所述的未列名的“其他元素”，按重量计单项含量必须超过 10%。

of chromium.

（e）Silicon-manganese steel

Alloy steels containing by weight:

not more than 0.7% of carbon;

0.5% or more but not more than 1.9% of manganese;and

0.6% or more but not more than 2.3% of silicon, but no other element in a proportion that would give the steel the characteristics of another alloy steel.

2. For the classification of ferro-alloys in the subheadings of heading 72.02 the following rule should be observed:

A ferro-alloy is considered as binary and classified under the relevant subheading（if it exists）if only one of the alloy elements exceeds the minimum percentage laid down in Chapter Note 1（c）; by analogy, it is considered respectively as ternary or quaternary if two or three alloy elements exceed the minimum percentage.

For the application of this rule the unspecified “other elements” referred to in Chapter Note 1（c）must each exceed 10% by weight.

税则号列 Tariff Item	商品名称及备注	进口税率 最惠	普通	暂定	出口退税	增值税率	计量单位	监管条件	Article Description
	第一分章 原料；粒状及粉状产品								Ⅰ. PRIMARY MATERIALS; PRODUCTS IN GRANULAR OR POWDER FORM
72.01	生铁及镜铁，锭、块或其他初级形状：								**Pig iron and spiegeleisen in ingots,blocks or other primary forms:**
7201.1000	-非合金生铁，按重量计含磷量在 0.5%及以下	1	8			17	千克		-Non-alloy pig iron containing by weight 0.5% or less of phosphorus
7201.2000	-非合金生铁，按重量计含磷量在 0.5%以上	1	8			17	千克		-Non-alloy pig iron containing by weight more than 0.5% of phosphorus
7201.5000	-合金生铁；镜铁	1	8			17	千克		-Alloy pig iron; spiegeleisen
7201 5000.10	合金生铁	1	8			17	千克		Alloy pig iron
7201 5000.90	镜铁	1	8			17	千克		Spiegeleisen
72.02	铁合金：								**Ferro-alloys:**
	-锰铁：								-Ferro-manganese:
7202.1100	--按重量计含碳量在 2%以上	2	11			17	千克	4xy	--Containing by weight more than 2% of carbon
7202.1900	--其他	2	11			17	千克	4xy	--Other
	-硅铁：								-Ferro-silicon:
7202.2100	--按重量计含硅量在 55%以上	2	11			17	千克		--Containing by weight more than 55% of silicon
7202 2100.10	硅铁，含硅量大于 55%，小于 90%	2	11			17	千克	4Axy	Ferro-silicon,containing by weight more than 55% and less than 90% of silicon
7202 2100.90	硅铁，含硅量大于 90%	2	11			17	千克	4xy	Ferro-silicon,containing by weight more than 90% of silicon
7202.2900	--其他	2	11			17	千克		--Other
7202 2900.10	硅铁，含硅量大于等于 30%且不超过 55%	2	11			17	千克	4Axy	Ferro-silicon,containing by weight more than 30% and not exceeding 90% of silicon
7202 2900.90	硅铁，含硅量小于 30%	2	11			17	千克	4xy	Ferro-silicon,containing by weight less than 30% of silicon
7202.3000	-硅锰铁	2	11			17	千克	4xy	-Ferro-silicon-manganese
	-铬铁：								-Ferro-chromium:
7202.4100[暂]	--按重量计含碳量在 4%以上	2	8	1		17	千克	4xy	--Containing by weight more than 4% of carbon
7202.4900[暂]	--其他	2	8	1		17	千克	4xy	--Other
7202.5000	-硅铬铁	2	11			17	千克	4xy	-Ferro-silicon-chromium
7202.6000[暂]	-镍铁	2	11	1		17	千克	4xy	-Ferro-nickel
7202.7000[暂]	-钼铁	2	11	1		17	千克	4xy	-Ferro-molybdenum
	-钨铁及硅钨铁：								-Ferro-tungsten and ferro-silicon-tungsten:
7202.8010[暂]	---钨铁	2	11	1		17	千克	4xy	---Ferro-tungsten
7202.8020	---硅钨铁	2	11			17	千克	4xy	---Ferro-silicon-tungsten
	-其他：								-Other:

税则号列 Tariff Item	商品名称及备注	进口税率			出口退税	增值税率	计量单位	监管条件	Article Description
		最惠	普通	暂定					
7202.9100[暂]	--钛铁及硅钛铁	2	11	1		17	千克	4xy	--Ferro-titanium and ferro-silicon-titanium
	--钒铁:								--Ferro-vanadium:
7202.9210	---按重量计含钒量在75%及以上	9	30			17	千克	4xy	---Containing by weight more than 75% of vanadium
7202.9290	---其他	9	30			17	千克	4xy	---Other
7202.9300[暂]	--铌铁	2	11	1		17	千克		--Ferro-niobium
7202 9300.10[暂]	铁钽铌合金（钽含量＜10%）	2	11	1		17	千克	4xy	Ferro-tantalum-niobium alloy, containing by weight less than 10% of tantalum
7202 9300.90[暂]	其他铌铁	2	11	1		17	千克	4xy	Other ferro-niobium
	--其他:								--Other:
	---钕铁硼合金:								---Nd-Fe-B alloy:
7202.9911	----速凝永磁片	2	11			17	千克	4xy	----Rapidly solidified permanent magnetic sheet
7202.9912	----磁粉	2	11			17	千克	4xy	----Magnetic powder
7202.9919	----其他	2	11			17	千克	4xy	----Other
	---其他:								---Other:
7202.9991	----按重量计稀土元素总含量在10%以上的	2	11			17	千克		----Containing by weight more than 10% of rare-earth
7202 9991.10	按重量计中重稀土总含量≥30%的铁合金(按重量计稀土元素总含量在10%以上)	2	11			17	千克	4xy	containing by weight more than 30% of rare earth elements(containing by weight more than 10% of rare earth elements)
7202 9991.91	稀土硅铁合金(按重量计稀土元素总含量在10%以上)	2	11			17	千克	4xy	Tombarthite ferrosilicon alloy,(containing by weight more than 10% of rare earth elements)
7202 9991.99	其他按重量计稀土元素总含量在10%以上的铁合金	2	11			17	千克	4xy	Other containing by weight more than 10% of rare earth elements
7202.9999	----其他	2	11			17	千克	4xy	----Other
72.03	**直接从铁矿还原所得的铁产品及其他海绵铁产品，块、团、团粒及类似形状；按重量计纯度在99.94%及以上的铁，块、团、团粒及类似形状：**								**Ferrous products obtained by direct reduction of iron ore and other spongy ferrous products, in lumps, pellets or similar forms; iron having a minimum purity by weight of 99.94%, in lumps, pellets or similar forms:**
7203.1000	-直接从铁矿还原所得的铁产品	2	8			17	千克		-Ferrous products obtained by direct reduction of iron ore
7203 1000.01[暂]	热压铁块	2	8	0		17	千克		Ferrous products in lumps, hot pressed
7203 1000.90	直接从铁矿还原的铁产品（铁团、铁粒及类似形状）	2	8			17	千克		Ferrous products obtained by direct reduction of iron ore (in lumps, pellets or similar forms)
7203.9000	-其他	2	8			17	千克		-Other
72.04	**钢铁废碎料；供再熔的碎料钢铁锭：**								**Ferrous waste and scrap; remelting scrap ingots of iron steel:**
7204.1000[暂]	-铸铁废碎料	2	8	0		17	千克	AP	-Waste and scrap of cast iron
	-合金钢废碎料:								-Waste and scrap of alloy steel:
7204.2100	--不锈钢废碎料	0	8			17	千克	AP	--Of stainless steel
7204.2900	--其他	0	8			17	千克	AP	--Other
7204.3000[暂]	-镀锡钢铁废碎料	2	8	0		17	千克	AP	-Waste and scrap of tinned iron or steel
	-其他废碎料:								-Other waste and scrap:
7204.4100[暂]	--车、刨、铣、磨、锯、锉、剪、冲加工过程中产生的废料，不论是否成捆	2	8	0		17	千克	AP	--Turnings, shavings, chips, milling waste, sawdust, filings, trimmings and stampings, whether or not in bundles
7204.4900	--其他	0	8			17	千克		--Other
7204 4900.10	废汽车压件	0	8			17	千克	AP	Compressed auto body
7204 4900.20	以回收钢铁为主的废五金电器	0	8			17	千克	AP	Waste hardware and electric appliance mainly for recycling steel and iron
7204 4900.90	未列名钢铁废碎料	0	8			17	千克	AP	Ferrous waste and scrap, not elsewhere specified or included
7204.5000	-供再熔的碎料钢铁锭	0	8			17	千克	AP	-Remelting scrap ingots
72.05	**生铁、镜铁及钢铁的颗粒和粉末：**								**Granules and powders, of pig iron, spiegeleisen, iron or steel:**
7205.1000	-颗粒	2	30			17	千克		-Granules
7205 1000.01	棱角钢砂(不带球弧面的棱角形颗粒数量大于80%)	2	30			17	千克		Angular steel grit with non ball-shaped angular granules >80%

税则号列 Tariff Item	商品名称及备注	进口税率			出口退税	增值税率	计量单位	监管条件	Article Description
		最惠	普通	暂定					
7205 1000.02	铸钢丸和铸钢砂(筛网孔径在0.3-2.8mm的铸钢丸和铸钢砂)	2	30			17	千克		Steel shot and Cast Steel Grit (0.3mm≤diameter of Screen hole≤2.8mm
7205 1000.90	其他生铁、镜铁及钢铁颗粒	2	30			17	千克		Other granuless of pig iron, spiegeleisen, iron or steel
	-粉末:								-Powders:
7205.2100	--合金钢的	2	17			17	千克		--Of alloy steel
7205.2900	--其他	2	17			17	千克		--Other
7205 2900.01	生铁、镜铁及其他钢铁粉末(平均粒径＜10μm的超细铁粉的除外)	2	17			17	千克		Pig iron,spiegeleisen and other iron or steel powder (other than ultrafine iron powder with average particle diameter ＜10μm)
7205 2900.90	生铁、镜铁及其他钢铁粉末(平均粒径＜10μm的超细铁粉)	2	17			17	千克		Pig iron, spiegeleisen and other steel powder (ultrafine iron powder with average particle diameter＜10μm)
	第二分章 铁及非合金钢								**Ⅱ. IRON AND NON-ALLOY STEEL**
72.06	**铁及非合金钢,锭状或其他初级形状(品目72.03的铁除外):**								**Iron and non-alloy steel in ingots or other primary forms(excluding iron of heading No.72.03):**
7206.1000	-锭状	2	11			17	千克		-Ingots
7206.9000	-其他	2	11			17	千克		-Other
72.07	**铁及非合金钢的半制成品:**								**Semi-finished products of iron or non-alloy steel:**
	-按重量计含碳量在0.25%以下:								-Containing by weight less than 0.25% of carbon:
7207.1100	--矩形(包括正方形)截面,宽度小于厚度的两倍	2	11			17	千克		--Of rectangular(including square)cross-section, the width measuring less than twice the thickness
7207.1200	--其他矩形(正方形除外)截面的	2	11			17	千克		--Other, of rectangular(other than square) crosssection
7207.1900	--其他	2	11			17	千克		--Other
7207.2000	-按重量计含碳量在0.25%及以上	2	11			17	千克		-Containing by weight 0.25% or more of carbon
72.08	**宽度在600毫米及以上的铁或非合金钢平板轧材,经热轧,但未经包覆、镀层或涂层:**								**Flat-rolled products of iron or non-alloy steel of a width of 600 mm or more, hot-rolled, not clad, plated or coated:**
7208.1000	-除热轧外未经进一步加工的卷材,已轧压花纹	5	14			17	千克	A	-In coils, not further worked than hot-rolled, with patterns in relief
	-其他经酸洗的卷材,除热轧外未经进一步加工:								-Other, in coils, not further worked than hot-rolled, pickled:
7208.2500	--厚度在4.75毫米及以上	5	14			17	千克	A	--Of a thickness of 4.75mm or more
	--厚度在3毫米及以上,但小于4.75毫米:								--Of a thickness of 3mm or more but less than 4.75mm:
7208.2610	---屈服强度大于355牛顿/平方毫米	5	14			17	千克	A	---Of a yield strength exceeding 355N/mm^2
7208.2690	---其他	5	14			17	千克	A	---Other
	--厚度小于3毫米:								--Of a thickness of 1ess than 3mm:
7208.2710	---厚度小于1.5毫米	5	14			17	千克	A	---Of a thickness of less than 1.5mm
7208.2790	---其他	5	14			17	千克	A	---Other
	-其他卷材,除热轧外未经进一步加工:								-Other, in coils, not further worked than hot-rolled:
7208.3600	--厚度超过10毫米	6	14			17	千克	A	--Of a thickness exceeding 10mm
7208.3700	--厚度在4.75毫米及以上,但不超过10毫米	5	14			17	千克	A	--Of a thickness of 4.75mm or more but not exceeding 10mm
	--厚度在3毫米及以上,但小于4.75毫米:								--Of a thickness of 3mm or more but less than 4.75mm:
7208.3810	---屈服强度大于355牛顿/平方毫米	5	14			17	千克	A	---Of a yield strength exceeding 355N/mm^2
7208.3890	---其他	5	14			17	千克	A	---Other
	--厚度小于3毫米:								--Of a thickness of less than 3mm:
7208.3910	---厚度小于1.5毫米	3	14			17	千克	A	---Of a thickness of less than 1.5mm
7208.3990	---其他	3	14			17	千克	A	---Other
7208.4000	-已轧压花纹的非卷材,除热轧外未经进一步加工	6	17			17	千克	A	-Not in coils, not further worked than hot-rolled, with patterns in relief
	-其他非卷材,除热轧外未经进								-Other, not in coils, not further worked than hot-rolled:

税则号列 Tariff Item	商品名称及备注	进口税率 最惠	普通	暂定	出口退税	增值税率	计量单位	监管条件	Article Description
	一步加工:								
	--厚度超过10毫米:								--Of a thickness exceeding 10mm:
7208.5110	---厚度超过50毫米	6	17			17	千克	A	---Of a thinkness exceeding 50mm
7208.5120	---厚度在20毫米以上,但不超过50毫米	6	17			17	千克	A	---Of a thickness exceeding 20mm but not exceeding 50mm
7208.5190	---其他	6	17			17	千克	A	---Other
7208.5200	--厚度在4.75毫米及以上，但不超过10毫米	6	17			17	千克	A	--Of a thickness of 4.75 mm or more but not exceeding 10 mm
	--厚度在3毫米及以上,但小于4.75毫米:								--Of a thickness of 3mm or more but less than 4.75 mm：
7208.5310	---屈服强度大于355牛顿/平方毫米	6	17			17	千克	A	---Of a yield strength exceeding 355N/ mm^2
7208.5390	---其他	6	17			17	千克	A	---Other
	--厚度小于3毫米:								--Of a thickness of less than 3mm：
7208.5410	---厚度小于1.5毫米	6	17			17	千克	A	---Of a thickness of less than l.5mm
7208.5490	---其他	6	17			17	千克	A	---Other
7208.9000	-其他	6	17			17	千克	A	-Other
72.09	**宽度在600毫米及以上的铁或非合金钢平板轧材，经冷轧，但未经包覆、镀层或涂层:**								**Flat-rolled products of iron or non-alloy steel, of a width of 600mm or more, cold-rolled（cold-reduced）, not clad, plated or coated:**
	-卷材，除冷轧外未经进一步加工:								-In coils, not further worked than cold-rolled（cold-reduced）:
	--厚度在3毫米及以上:								--Of a thickness of 3mm or more:
7209.1510	---屈服强度大于355牛顿/平方毫米	6	17			17	千克	A	---Of a yield strength exceeding 355N/mm^2
7209.1590	---其他	6	17		13	17	千克	A	---Other
	--厚度超过1毫米，但小于3毫米:								--Of a thickness exceeding 1 mm but less than 3mm:
7209.1610	---屈服强度大于275牛顿/平方毫米	6	17		13	17	千克	A	---Of a yield strength exceeding 275N/mm^2
7209.1690	---其他	6	17		13	17	千克	A	---Other
	--厚度在0.5毫米及以上,但不超过1毫米:								--Of a thickness of 0.5mm or more but not exceeding 1mm:
7209.1710	---屈服强度大于275牛顿/平方毫米	3	17		13	17	千克	A	---Of a yield strength exceeding 275N/ mm^2
7209.1790	---其他	3	17		13	17	千克	A	---Other
	--厚度小于0.5毫米:								--Of a thickness of less than 0.5mm:
7209.1810	---厚度小于0.3毫米	6	17		13	17	千克	A	---Of a thickness less than 0.3mm
7209.1890	---其他	6	17		13	17	千克	A	---Other
	-非卷材，除冷轧外未经进一步加工:								-Not in coils, not further worked than cold-rolled（cold-reduced）:
7209.2500	--厚度在3毫米及以上	6	17		13	17	千克	A	--Of a thickness of 3mm or more
7209.2600	--厚度超过1毫米，但小于3毫米	6	17		13	17	千克	A	--Of a thickness exceeding 1 mm but less than 3mm
7209.2700	--厚度在0.5毫米及以上,但不超过1毫米	6	17		13	17	千克	A	--Of a thickness of 0.5mm or more but not exceeding 1 mm
7209.2800	--厚度小于0.5毫米	6	17		13	17	千克	A	--Of a thickness of less than 0.5mm
7209.9000	-其他	6	17		13	17	千克	A	-Other
72.10	**宽度在600毫米及以上的铁或非合金钢平板轧材，经包覆、镀层或涂层:**								**Flat-rolled products of iron or non-alloy steel, of a width of 600mm or more, clad, plated or coated:**
	-镀或涂锡的:								-Plated or coated with tin:
7210.1100	--厚度在0.5毫米及以上	10	20		13	17	千克	A	--Of a thickness of 0.5mm or more
7210.1200	--厚度小于0.5毫米	5	20		13	17	千克	A	--Of a thickness of less than 0.5mm
7210.2000	-镀或涂铅的，包括镀铅锡钢板	4	20		13	17	千克		-Plated or coated with lead, including terneplate
7210.3000	-电镀锌的	8	20		13	17	千克	A	-Electrolytically plated or coated with zinc
	-用其他方法镀或涂锌的:								-Otherwise plated or coated with zinc:

税则号列 Tariff Item	商品名称及备注	进口税率 最惠	普通	暂定	出口退税	增值税率	计量单位	监管条件	Article Description
7210.4100	--瓦楞形	8	20		13	17	千克	A	--Corrugated
7210.4900	--其他	4	20		13	17	千克	A	--Other
7210.5000	-镀或涂氧化铬或铬及氧化铬的	8	20		13	17	千克		-Plated or coated with chromium oxides or with chromium and chromium oxides
	-镀或涂铝的:								-Plated or coated with aluminium:
7210.6100	--镀或涂铝锌合金的	8	20		13	17	千克		--Plated or coated with aluminium-zinc alloys
7210.6900	--其他	8	20		13	17	千克		--Other
	-涂漆或涂塑的								-Painted, varnished or coated with plastics
7210.7010	---厚度小于1.5毫米	4	20		13	17	千克		--- Of a thickness of less than 1.5mm
7210.7090	---其他	4	20		13	17	千克		---Other
7210.9000	-其他	8	20		13	17	千克		-Other
72.11	**宽度小于600毫米的铁或非合金钢平板轧材，但未经包覆、镀层或涂层:**								**Flat-rolled products of iron or non-alloy steel, of a width of less than 600 mm, not clad, plated or coated:**
	-除热轧外未经进一步加工:								-Not further worked than hot-rolled:
7211.1300	--经四面轧制或在闭合匣内轧制的非卷材，宽度超过150毫米，厚度不小于4毫米，未轧压花纹	6	30			17	千克	A	--Rolled on four faces or in a closed box pass, of a width exceeding 150mm and a thickness of not less than 4mm, not in coils and without patterns in relief
7211.1400	--其他，厚度在4.75毫米及以上	6	30			17	千克	A	--Other, of a thickness of 4.75mm or more
7211.1900	--其他	6	30			17	千克	A	--Other
	-除冷轧外未经进一步加工:								-Not further worked than cold-rolled（cold- reduced）:
7211.2300	--按重量计含碳量低于0.25%	6	30			17	千克	A	--Containing by weight less than 0.25% of carbon
7211.2900	--其他	6	30			17	千克	A	--Other
7211.9000	-其他	6	30			17	千克	A	-Other
72.12	**宽度小于600毫米的铁或非合金钢平板轧材，经包覆、镀层或涂层:**								**Flat-rolled products of iron or non-alloy steel, of a width of less than 600mm, clad, plated or coated:**
7212.1000	-镀或涂锡的	5	20			17	千克	A	-Plated or coated with tin
7212.2000	-电镀锌的	8	20			17	千克	A	-Electrolytically plated or coated with zinc
7212.3000	-用其他方法镀或涂锌的	8	20			17	千克	A	-Otherwise plated or coated with zinc
7212.4000	-涂漆或涂塑的	4	20			17	千克		-Painted, varnished or coated with plastics
7212.5000	-镀或涂其他材料的	8	20			17	千克		-Otherwise plated or coated
7212.6000	-经包覆的	8	20			17	千克		-Clad
72.13	**不规则盘卷的铁及非合金钢的热轧条、杆:**								**Bars and rods, hot-rolled, in irregulurly wound coils, of iron or non-alloy steel:**
7213.1000	-带有轧制过程中产生的凹痕、凸缘、槽沟及其他变形的	3	20			17	千克	A	-Containing indentations, ribs, grooves or other deformations produced during the rolling process
7213.2000	-其他，易切削钢制	3	20			17	千克	A	-Other, of free-cutting steel
	-其他:								-Other:
7213.9100	--直径小于14毫米圆形截面的	5	20			17	千克	A	--Of circular cross-section measuring less than 14mm in diameter
7213.9900	--其他	5	20			17	千克	A	--Other
72.14	**铁或非合金钢的其他条、杆，除锻造、热轧、热拉拔或热挤压外未经进一步加工，包括轧制后扭曲的:**								**Other bars and rods of iron or non-alloy steel, not further worked than forged, hot-rolled, hot-drawn or hot-extruded, but including those twisted after rolling:**
7214.1000	-锻造的	7	10		9	17	千克	A	-Forged
7214.2000	-带有轧制过程中产生的凹痕、凸缘、槽沟或其他变形以及轧制后扭曲的	3	20			17	千克	A	-Containing indentations, ribs, grooves or other deformations produced during the rolling process or twisted after rolling
7214.3000	-其他，易切削钢制	7	20			17	千克	A	-Other, of free-cutting steel
	-其他:								-Other:
7214.9100	--矩形（正方形除外）截面的	3	20			17	千克	A	--Of rectangular cross section（other than square）
7214.9900	--其他	3	20			17	千克	A	--Other
72.15	**铁及非合金钢的其他条、杆:**								**Other bars and rods of iron or non-alloy steel:**

税则号列 Tariff Item	商品名称及备注	进口税率			出口退税	增值税率	计量单位	监管条件	Article Description
		最惠	普通	暂定					
7215.1000	-易切削钢制，除冷成形或冷加工外未经进一步加工	7	20			17	千克	A	-Of free-cutting steel, not further worked than cold-formed or cold-finished
7215.5000	-其他，除冷成形或冷加工外未经进一步加工	7	20			17	千克	A	-Other, not further worked than cold-formed or cold-finished
7215.9000	-其他	3	20			17	千克	A	-Other
72.16	**铁或非合金钢的角材、型材及异型材：**								**Angles, shapes and sections of iron or non-alloy steel:**
	-槽钢、工字钢及H型钢，除热轧、热拉拔或热挤压外未经进一步加工，截面高度低于80毫米：								-U, I or H sections, not further worked than hot-rolled, hot-drawn or extruded, of a height of less than 80mm:
7216.1010	---H型钢	3	14			17	千克	A	---H sections
7216.1020	---工字钢	3	14			17	千克	A	---I sections
7216.1090	---其他	3	14			17	千克	A	---Other
	-角钢及丁字钢，除热轧、热拉拔或热挤压外未经进一步加工，截面高度低于80毫米：								-L or T sections, not further worked than hot-rolled, hot-drawn or extruded, of a height of less than 80mm:
7216.2100	--角钢	6	17			17	千克	A	--L sections
7216.2200	--丁字钢	6	14			17	千克	A	--T sections
	-槽钢、工字钢及H型钢，除热轧、热拉拔或热挤压外未经进一步加工，截面高度在80毫米及以上：								-U, I or H sections, not further worked than hot-rolled, hot-drawn or extruded of a height of 80mm or more:
7216.3100	--槽钢	6	14			17	千克	A	--U sections
	--工字钢：								--I sections:
7216.3210	---截面高度在200毫米以上	6	14			17	千克	A	---Of a height exceeding 200mm
7216.3290	---其他	6	14			17	千克	A	---Other
	--H型钢：								--H sections:
	---截面高度在200毫米以上：								---Of a height exceeding 200mm:
7216.3311	----截面高度在800毫米以上	6	14			17	千克	A	----Of a height exceeding 800mm
7216.3319	----其他	6	14			17	千克	A	----Other
7216.3390	---其他	6	14			17	千克	A	---Other
	-角钢及丁字钢，除热轧、热拉拔或热挤压外未经进一步加工，截面高度在80毫米及以上：								-L or T sections, not further worked than hot-rolled, hot-drawn or extruded, of a height of 80mm or more:
7216.4010	---角钢	3	17			17	千克	A	---L sections
7216.4020	---丁字钢	3	14			17	千克	A	---T sections
	-其他角材、型材及异型材，除热轧、热拉拔或热挤压外未经进一步加工：								-Other angles, shapes and sections, not further worked than hot-rolled, hot-drawn or extruded:
7216.5010	---乙字钢	6	14			17	千克	A	---Z sections
7216.5020	---球扁钢	3	20			17	千克	A	--- Bulb-flat steel
7216.5090	---其他	3	20			17	千克	A	---Other
	-角材、型材及异型材，除冷成形或冷加工外未经进一步加工：								-Angles, shapes and sections, not further worked than cold-formed or cold-finished:
7216.6100	--平板轧材制的	3	20			17	千克	A	--Obtained from flat-rolled products
7216.6900	--其他	3	20			17	千克	A	--Other
	-其他：								-Other:
7216.9100	--平板轧材经冷成形或冷加工制的	3	20			17	千克	A	--Cold-formed or cold-finished from flatrolled products
7216.9900	--其他	3	20			17	千克	A	--Other
72.17	**铁丝或非合金钢丝：**								**Wire of iron or non-alloy steel:**
7217.1000	-未经镀或涂层，不论是否抛光	8	40			17	千克		-Not plated or coated, whether or not polished
7217.2000	-镀或涂锌的	8	40		9	17	千克		-Plated or coated with zinc
	-镀或涂其他贱金属的：								-Plated or coated with other base metals:
7217.3010	---镀或涂铜的	8	40		9	17	千克		---Plated or coated with copper
7217.3090	---其他	8	40		9	17	千克		---Other

税则号列 Tariff Item	商品名称及备注	进口税率 最惠	普通	暂定	出口退税	增值税率	计量单位	监管条件	Article Description
7217.9000	-其他	8	40			17	千克		-Other
	第三分章 不锈钢								Ⅲ. STAINLESS STEEL
72.18	**不锈钢，锭状或其他初级形状；不锈钢半制成品：**								**Stainless steel in ingots or other primary forms; semi-finished products of stainless steel:**
7218.1000	-锭状及其他初级形状	2	11			17	千克		-Ingots and other primary forms
	-其他：								-Other:
7218.9100	--矩形（正方形除外）截面的	2	11			17	千克		--Of rectangular（other than square）crosssection
7218.9900	--其他	2	11			17	千克		--Other
72.19	**不锈钢平板轧材，宽度在600毫米及以上：**								**Flat-rolled products of stainless steel, of a width of 600mm or more:**
	-除热轧外未经进一步加工的卷材：								-Not further worked than hot-rolled, in coils:
7219.1100	--厚度超过10毫米	4	14		13	17	千克	A	--Of a thickness exceeding 10mm
7219.1200	--厚度在4.75毫米及以上，但不超过10毫米	4	14		13	17	千克	A	--Of a thickness of 4.75mm or more but not exceeding 10mm
	--厚度在3毫米及以上,但小于4.75毫米：								--Of a thickness of 3mm or more but less than 4.75mm:
	---未经酸洗的：								---Not acid pickled:
7219.1312	----按重量计含锰量在5.5%及以上的铬锰系不锈钢	4	14			17	千克	A	----Containing more than 5.5% by weight of manganese of Ferro-chromium-manganese steel
7219.1319	----其他	4	14		13	17	千克	A	----Other
	---经酸洗的：								---Acid pickled:
7219.1322	----按重量计含锰量在5.5%及以上的铬锰系不锈钢	4	14			17	千克	A	----Containing more than 5.5% by weight of manganese of Ferro-chromium-manganese steel
7219.1329	----其他	4	14		13	17	千克	A	----Other
	--厚度小于3毫米：								--Of a thickness of less than 3 mm:
	---未经酸洗的：								---Not acid pickled:
7219.1412	----按重量计含锰量在5.5%及以上的铬锰系不锈钢	4	14			17	千克	A	----Containing more than 5.5% by weight of manganese of Ferro-chromium-manganese steel
7219.1419	----其他	4	14		13	17	千克	A	----Other
	---经酸洗的：								---Acid pickled:
7219.1422	----按重量计含锰量在5.5%及以上的铬锰系不锈钢	4	14			17	千克	A	----Containing more than 5.5% by weight of manganese of Ferro-chromium-manganese steel
7219.1429	----其他	4	14		13	17	千克	A	----Other
	-除热轧外未经进一步加工的非卷材：								-Not further worked than hot-rolled, not in coils:
7219.2100	--厚度超过10毫米	10	40		13	17	千克	A	--Of a thickness exceeding 10mm
7219.2200	--厚度在4.75毫米及以上，但不超过10毫米	10	40		13	17	千克	A	--Of a thickness of 4.75mm or more but not exceeding 10mm
7219.2300	--厚度在3毫米及以上,但小于4.75毫米	10	40		13	17	千克	A	--Of a thickness of 3mm or more but less than 4.75mm
	--厚度小于3毫米：								--Of a thickness of less than 3mm:
7219.2410	---厚度超过1毫米但小于3毫米	10	40		13	17	千克	A	---Of a thickness exceeding 1mm but less than 3mm
7219.2420	---厚度在0.5毫米及以上，但不超过1毫米	10	40		13	17	千克	A	---Of a thickness of 0.5mm or more but not exceeding 1mm
7219.2430	---厚度小于0.5毫米	10	40		13	17	千克	A	---Of a thickness of less than 0.5mm
	-除冷轧外未经进一步加工：								-Not further worked than cold-rolled（cold- reduced）:
7219.3100	--厚度在4.75毫米及以上	10	40		13	17	千克	A	--Of a thickness of 4.75mm or more
7219.3200	--厚度在3毫米及以上,但小于4.75毫米	10	40		13	17	千克	A	--Of a thickness of 3mm or more but less than 4.75mm
	--厚度超过1mm，但小于3mm								--Of a thickness exceeding1mm but less than 3mm
7219.3310	---按重量计含锰量在5.5%及以上的铬锰系不锈钢	10	40		13	17	千克	A	---Of chromium-manganese stainless steel, containing by weight 5.5% of manganese or more
7219.3390	---其他	10	40		13	17	千克	A	---Other
7219.3400	--厚度在0.5毫米及以上，但不超过1毫米	10	40		13	17	千克	A	--Of a thickness of 0.5mm or more but not exceeding 1mm

税则号列 Tariff Item	商品名称及备注	进口税率 最惠	普通	暂定	出口退税	增值税率	计量单位	监管条件	Article Description
7219.3500	--厚度小于0.5毫米	10	40		13	17	千克	A	--Of a thickness of less than 0.5 mm
7219.9000	-其他	10	40		13	17	千克	A	-Other
72.20	**不锈钢平板轧材，宽度小于600毫米：**								**Flat-rolled products stainless steel, of a width of less than 600mm:**
	-除热轧外未经进一步加工：								-Not further worked than hot-rolled:
7220.1100	--厚度在4.75毫米及以上	10	20		9	17	千克	A	--Of a thickness of 4.75mm or more
7220.1200	--厚度小于4.75毫米	10	20		9	17	千克	A	--Of a thickness of less than 4.75mm
	-除冷轧外未经进一步加工：								-Not further worked than cold-rolled （cold-reduced）:
7220.2020	---厚度在0.35毫米及以下	10	20		9	17	千克	A	---Of a thickness of 0.35mm or less
7220.2030	---厚度在0.35毫米以上但小于3毫米	10	20		9	17	千克	A	---Of a thickness of more than 0.35mm but less than 3mm
7220.2040	---厚度在3毫米及以上	10	20		9	17	千克	A	---Other
7220.9000	-其他	10	20		9	17	千克	A	-Other
72.21	**不规则盘卷的不锈钢热轧条、杆：**								**Bars and rods, hot-rolled, in irregularly wound coils, of stainless steel:**
7221.0000	不规则盘卷的不锈钢热轧条、杆	10	20		13	17	千克	A	Bars and rods, hot-rolled, in irregularly wound coils, of stainless steel
72.22	**不锈钢其他条、杆；不锈钢角材、型材及异型材：**								**Other bars and rods of stainless steel; angles, shapes and sections of stainless steel:**
	-条、杆，除热轧、热拉拔或热挤压外未经进一步加工：								-Bars and rods, not further worked than hot-rolled, hot-drawn or extruded:
7222.1100	--圆形截面的	10	40		5	17	千克	A	--Of circular cross-section
7222.1900	--其他	10	40		5	17	千克	A	--Other
7222.2000	-条、杆，除冷成形或冷加工外未经进一步加工	10	40		5	17	千克		-Bars and rods, not further worked than cold- formed or cold-finished
7222.3000	-其他条、杆	10	40		5	17	千克		-Other bars and rods
7222.4000	-角材、型材及异型材	10	17		5	17	千克	A	-Angles, shapes and sections
72.23	**不锈钢丝：**								**Wire of stainless steel:**
7223.0000	不锈钢丝	10	20		5	17	千克		Wire of stainless steel
	第四分章 其他合金钢；合金钢或非合金钢制的空心钻钢								**Ⅳ. OTHER ALLOY STEEL; HOLLOW DRILL BARS AND RODS, OF ALLOY OR NON-ALLOY STEEL**
72.24	**其他合金钢，锭状或其他初级形状；其他合金钢制的半制成品：**								**Other alloy steel in ingots or other primary forms; semi-finished products of other alloy steel:**
7224.1000	-锭状及其他初级形状	2	11			17	千克		-Ingots and other primary forms
	-其他：								-Other:
7224.9010	---单件重量在10吨及以上的粗铸锻件坯	2	11			17	千克		---Raw casting forging stocks, individual piece weight of 10t or more
7224.9090	---其他	2	11			17	千克		---Other
72.25	**其他合金钢平板轧材，宽度在600毫米及以上：**								**Flat-rolled products of other alloy steel, of a width of 600mm or more:**
	-硅电钢制：								-Of silicon-electrical steel:
7225.1100	--取向性硅电钢	3	20		13	17	千克	A7	--Grain-oriented
7225.1900	--其他	6	20		13	17	千克	A	--Other
7225.3000	-其他卷材，除热轧外未经进一步加工	3	14		9	17	千克	A	-Other, not further worked than hot-rolled, in coils
	-其他非卷材，除热轧外未经进一步加工：								-Other, not further worked than hot-rolled, not in coils:
7225.4010	---工具钢	3	17		13	17	千克	A	---Of tool steels
	---其他：								---Other:
7225.4091	----含硼合金钢	3	17		13	17	千克	A	----Of boron-containing alloy steel
7225.4099	----其他	3	17		13	17	千克	A	----Other
7225.5000	-其他，除冷轧外未经进一步加工	3	17		13	17	千克	A	-Other, not further worked than cold-rolled （cold-reduced）
	-其他：								-Other:
7225.9100	--电镀或涂锌的	7	17		9	17	千克	A	--Electrolytically plated or coated with zinc
7225.9200	--用其他方法镀或涂锌的	7	17		9	17	千克	A	--Otherwise plated or coated with zinc
	--其他：								--Other:

税则号列 Tariff Item	商品名称及备注	进口税率 最惠	进口税率 普通	进口税率 暂定	出口退税	增值税率	计量单位	监管条件	Article Description
7225.9910	---高速钢制	3	17		9	17	千克	A	---Of high speed steel
7225.9990	---其他	7	17		9	17	千克	A	---Other
72.26	**其他合金钢平板轧材，宽度小于600毫米:**								**Flat-rolled products of other alloy steel, of a width of less than 600mm:**
	-硅电钢制:								-Of silicon-electrical steel:
7226.1100	--取向性硅电钢	3	20		13	17	千克	A	--Grain-oriented
7226.1900	--其他	3	20		13	17	千克	A	--Other
7226.2000	-高速钢制	3	20		9	17	千克	A	-Of high speed steel
	-其他:								-Other:
	-除热轧外未经进一步加工:								-Not further worked than hot-rolled:
7226.9110	---工具钢	3	20		9	17	千克	A	---Of tool steels
	---其他:								---Other:
7226.9191	----含硼合金钢	3	20		9	17	千克	A	----Of boron-containing alloy steel
7226.9199	----其他	3	20		9	17	千克	A	----Other
7226.9200	--除冷轧外未经进一步加工	3	20		9	17	千克	A	--Not further worked than cold-rolled（cold- reduced）
	--其他:								--Other:
7226.9910	---电镀锌的	7	20		9	17	千克	A	---Electrolytically plated or coated with zinc
7226.9920	---用其他方法镀或涂锌的	7	20		9	17	千克	A	---Otherwise plated or coated with zinc
7226.9990	---其他	7	20		9	17	千克		---Other
7226 9990.01 暂	铁镍合金带材(生产集成电路框架用)（宽度＜600mm）	7	20	4	9	17	千克	A	Flat-rolled products of Fe-Ni alloy steel, of a width of less than 600mm, used for manufacturing the frame for electronic integrated circuits）
7226 9990.90	其他合金板材（宽度＜600mm）	7	20		9	17	千克	A	Flat-rolled products of other alloy steel, of a width of less than 600mm
72.27	**不规则盘卷的其他合金钢热轧条、杆:**								**Bars and rods, hot-rolled, in irregularly wound coils, of other alloy steel:**
7227.1000	-高速钢制	3	20		9	17	千克	A	-Of high speed steel
7227.2000	-硅锰钢制	6	20		9	17	千克	A	-Of silicon-manganese steel
	-其他:								-Other:
7227.9010	---含硼合金钢制	3	20		9	17	千克	A	---Of boron-containing alloy steel
7227.9090	---其他	3	20		9	17	千克	A	---Other
72.28	**其他合金钢条、杆；其他合金钢角材、型材及异型材；合金钢或非合金钢制的空心钻钢:**								**Other bars and rods of other alloy steel; angles, shapes and sections, of other alloy steel; hollow drill bars and rods, of alloy or non-alloy steel:**
7228.1000	-高速钢条、杆	3	20		13	17	千克	A	-Bars and rods, of high speed steel
7228.2000	-硅锰钢条、杆	6	20			17	千克	A	-Bars and rods, of silicon-manganese steel
	-其他条、杆，除热轧、热拉拔或热挤压外未经进一步加工								-Other bars and rods, not further worked than hot-rolled, hot-drawn or extruded
7228.3010	---含硼合金钢制	3	20		13	17	千克	A	---Of boron-containing alloy steel
7228.3090	---其他	3	20		13	17	千克	A	---Other
7228.4000	-其他条、杆，除锻造外未经进一步加工	3	20		13	17	千克	A	-Other bars and rods, not further worked than forged
7228.5000	-其他条、杆，除冷成形或冷加工外未经进一步加工	3	20		13	17	千克	A	-Other bars and rods, not further worked than cold-formed of cold-finished
7228.6000	-其他条、杆	3	20		9	17	千克	A	-Other bars and rods
	-角材、型材及异型材:								-Angles, shapes and sections:
7228.7010	---履带板型钢	6	17		9	17	千克	A	---Shapes of crawler tread
7228.7090	---其他	6	17		9	17	千克	A	---Other
7228.8000	-空心钻钢	7	35		13	17	千克	A	-Hollow drill bars and rods
72.29	**其他合金钢丝:**								**Wire of other alloy steel:**
7229.2000	-硅锰钢制	7	20			17	千克		-Of silicon-manganese steel
	-其他:								-Other:
7229.9010	---高速钢制	3	20		13	17	千克		---Of high speed steel
7229.9090	---其他	7	20		9	17	千克		---Other

第七十三章 钢铁制品

Chapter 73 Articles of iron or steel

注释：

一、本章所称"铸铁"，适用于经铸造而得的产品，按重量计其铁元素含量超过其他元素单项含量并与第七十二章注释一（四）所述的钢的化学成分不同。

二、本章所称"丝"，是指热或冷成形的任何截面形状的产品，但其截面尺寸均不超过16毫米。

Chapter Notes:

1. In this Chapter the expression "cast iron" applies to products obtained by casting in which iron predominates by weight over each of the other elements and which do not comply with the chemical composition of steel as defined in Note 1（d）to Chapter 72.
2. In this Chapter the word "wire" means hot or cold-formed products of any cross-sectional shape, of which no cross-sectional dimension exceeds 16mm.

税则号列 Tariff Item	商品名称及备注	进口税率 最惠	普通	暂定	出口退税	增值税率	计量单位	监管条件	Article Description
73.01	钢铁板桩，不论是否钻孔、打眼或组装；焊接的钢铁角材、型材及异型材：								**Sheet piling of iron or steel, whether or not drilled, punched or made from assembled elements; welded angles, shapes and sections, of iron or steel:**
7301.1000	-钢铁板桩	7	20		9	17	千克		-Sheet piling
7301.2000	-角材、型材及异型材	7	30		9	17	千克		-Angles, shapes and sections
73.02	铁道及电车道铺轨用钢铁材料（钢轨、护轨、齿轨、道岔尖轨、辙叉、尖轨拉杆及其他叉道段体、轨枕、鱼尾板、轨座、轨座楔、钢轨垫板、钢轨夹、底板、固定板及其他专门用于连接或加固路轨的材料）：								**Railway or tramway track construction material of iron or steel, the following:rails, check-rails and rack rails, switch blades, crossing frogs, point rods and other crossing pieces, sleepers（cross-ties）, fishplates, chairs, chair wedges,sole plates（base plates）, rail clips,bedplates, ties and other material specialized for jointing or fixing rails:**
7302.1000	-钢轨	6	14		9	17	千克	A	-Rails
7302.3000	-道岔尖轨、辙叉、尖轨拉杆及其他岔道段体	8	17		9	17	千克	A	-Switch blades, crossing frogs, point rods and other crossing pieces
7302.4000	-鱼尾板及钢轨垫板	7	17		9	17	千克	A	-Fish-plates and sole plates
	-其他：								-Other:
7302.9010	---轨枕	6	14		9	17	千克	A	---Sleepers（cross-ties）
7302.9090	---其他	7	17		9	17	千克	A	---Other
73.03	铸铁管及空心异型材：								**Tubes, pipes and hollow profiles, of cast iron:**
7303.0010	---内径在500毫米及以上的圆形截面管	4	40		9	17	千克		---Tubes and pipes of circular cross-section, of the internal diameter of 500mm or more
7303.0090	---其他	4	40		9	17	千克		---Other
73.04	无缝钢铁管及空心异型材（铸铁的除外）：								**Tubes, pipes and hollow profiles, seamless, of iron（other than cast iron）or steel:**
	-石油或天然气管道管：								-Line pipe of a kind used for oil or gas pipelines:
	--不锈钢制：								--Of stainless steel:
7304.1110	---外径大于等于215.9毫米，但不超过406.4毫米	5	17		13	17	千克	A	---Having an outside diameter of 215.9mm or more but not exceeding 406.4mm
7304.1120	---外径超过114.3毫米，但小于215.9毫米	5	17		13	17	千克	A	---Having an outside diameter exceeding 114.3mm but less than 215.9mm
7304.1130	---外径不超过114.3毫米	5	17		13	17	千克	A	---Having an outside diament not exceeding 114.3mm
7304.1190	---其他	5	17		13	17	千克	A	---Other
	--其他：								--Other:
7304.1910	---外径大于等于215.9毫米，但不超过406.4毫米	5	17		13	17	千克	A	---Having an outside diameter of 215.9mm or more but not exceeding 406.4mm
7304.1920	---外径超过114.3毫米，但小于215.9毫米	5	17		13	17	千克	A	---Having an outside diameter exceeding 114.3mm but less than 215.9mm
7304.1930	---外径不超过114.3毫米	5	17		13	17	千克	A	---Having an outside diameter not exceeding 114.3mm
7304.1990	---其他	5	17		13	17	千克	A	---Other
	-钻探石油及天然气用的套管、								-Casing, tubing and drill pipe, of a kind used in drilling

税则号列 Tariff Item	商品名称及备注	进口税率 最惠	进口税率 普通	进口税率 暂定	出口退税	增值税率	计量单位	监管条件	Article Description
	导管及钻管:								for oil or gas:
	--不锈钢制钻管:								--Drill pipe of stainless steel:
7304.2210	---外径不超过168.3毫米	4	17		13	17	千克	A	---Having an outside diameter not exceeding 168.3mm
7304.2290	---其他	4	17		13	17	千克	A	---Other
	--其他钻管:								--Other drill pipe:
7304.2310	---外径不超过168.3毫米	4	17		13	17	千克	A	---Having an outside diameter not exceeding 168.3mm
7304.2390	---其他	4	17		13	17	千克	A	---Other
7304.2400	--其他不锈钢管	4	17		13	17	千克	A	--Other, of stainless steel
	--其他:								--Other:
7304.2910	---屈服强度小于552兆帕的	4	17		13	17	千克	A	--- Yield strength less than 552 MPa
7304.2920	---屈服强度大于等于552兆帕,但小于758兆帕的	4	17		13	17	千克	A	---Yield strength greater than or equal to 552 MPa, but less than 758 MPa
7304.2930	---屈服强度大于等于758兆帕的	4	17		13	17	千克	A	--- Yield strength greater than or equal to 758 MPa
	-铁或非合金钢的其他圆形截面管:								-Other, of circular cross-section, of iron or non-alloysteel:
	--冷拔或冷轧的:								--Cold-drawn or cold-rolled（cold-reduced）:
7304.3110	---锅炉管	4	17		9	17	千克	A	---Boiler tubes and pipes
7304.3120	---地质钻管、套管	8	17		9	17	千克	A	---Geological casing and drill pipes
7304.3190	---其他	4	17		9	17	千克	A	---Other
	--其他:								--Other:
7304.3910	---锅炉管	4	17		9	17	千克	A	---Boiler tubes and pipes
7304.3920	---地质钻管、套管	5	17		9	17	千克	A	---Geological casing and drill pipes
7304.3990	---其他	4	17		9	17	千克	A	---Other
	-不锈钢的其他圆形截面管:								-Other, of circular cross-section, of stainless steel:
	--冷拔或冷轧的:								--Cold-drawn or cold-rolled（cold-reduced）:
7304.4110	---锅炉管	10	17		9	17	千克		---Boiler tubes and pipes
7304 4110.01	冷轧的不锈钢制无缝锅炉管(抗拉强度大于等于550Mpa 屈服强度大于200Mpa)	10	17		9	17	千克	A	The cold-rolled stainless, seamless steel boiler tubes (tensile strength greater than or equal to 550Mpa, yield strength greater than 200Mpa)
7304 4110.90	其他冷轧的不锈钢制无缝锅炉管(冷拔或冷轧的,包括内螺纹)	10	17		9	17	千克	A	Other cold-rolled stainless, seamless steel boiler pipe (cold drawn or cold rolled, including internal thread)
7304.4190	---其他	10	40		13	17	千克	A	---Other
	--其他:								--Other:
7304.4910	---锅炉管	10	17		13	17	千克		---Boiler tubes and pipes
7304 4910.01	非冷轧(拔)不锈钢制无缝锅炉管(抗拉强度大于等于550Mpa 屈服强度大于200Mpa)	10	17		13	17	千克	A	Non-cold-rolled (drawn) stainless, seamless steel boiler tube (tensile strength greater than or equal to 550Mpa, yield strength greater than 200Mpa)
7304 4910.90	其他非冷轧(拔)不锈钢制无缝锅炉管(包括内螺纹)	10	17		13	17	千克	A	Other non-rolled (drawn) stainless, seamless steel boiler tubes (including internal thread)
7304.4990	---其他	10	40		9	17	千克	A	---Other
	-其他合金钢的其他圆形截面管:								-Other, of circular cross-section, of other alloy steel:
	--冷拔或冷轧的:								--Cold-drawn or cold-rolled（cold-reduced）:
7304.5110	---锅炉管	4	17		9	17	千克		---Boiler tubes and pipes
7304 5110.01	高温承压用合金钢无缝钢管(抗拉强度≧620MPa、屈服强度≧440MPa)(锅炉管外径≧127mm,化学成分(wt%)0.07≦C≦0.13、8.5≦Cr≦9.5、0.3≦Mo≦0.6、1.5≦W≦2.0,冷拔或冷轧,不论是否经进一步加工,包括内螺纹)	4	17		9	17	千克	A	Alloysteel seamless steel pipe for High temperature pressure, tensile strength ≧620MPa, yield strength ≧440MPa, outside diameter≧127mm,chemical（wt%）0.07≦C≦0.13、8.5≦Cr≦9.5、0.3≦Mo≦0.6、1.5≦W≦2.0, cold-drawn or cold- rolled, whether or not further processing, including internal thread
7304 5110.90	冷轧的其他合金钢无缝锅炉管(冷拔或冷轧的,包括内螺纹)	4	17		9	17	千克	A	Other boiler tubes and pipes, of other alloy steel, cold-drawn or cold- rolled
7304.5120	---地质钻管、套管	4	17		9	17	千克	A	---Geological casing and drill pipes
7304.5190	---其他	4	17		9	17	千克		---Other
7304 5190.01	高温承压用合金钢无缝钢管(抗	4	17		9	17	千克	A	Alloysteel seamless steel pipe for High temperature

税则号列 Tariff Item	商品名称及备注	进口税率 最惠	进口税率 普通	进口税率 暂定	出口退税	增值税率	计量单位	监管条件	Article Description
	拉强度≧620MPa、屈服强度≧440MPa)(外径≧127mm，化学成分（wt%）0.07≦C≦0.13、8.5≦Cr≦9.5、0.3≦Mo≦0.6、1.5≦W≦2.0，冷拔或冷轧，不论是否经进一步加工)								pressure, tensile strength ≧620MPa, yield strength ≧440MPa, outside diameter≧127mm,chemical（wt%）0.07≦C≦0.13、8.5≦Cr≦9.5、0.3≦Mo≦0.6、1.5≦W≦2.0, cold-drawn or cold- rolled, whether or not further processing
7304 5190.90	冷轧的其他合金钢制其他无缝管(冷拔或冷轧的)	4	17		9	17	千克	A	Other boiler tubes and pipes, of other alloy steel, cold-drawn or cold- rolled
	--其他:								--Other:
7304.5910	---锅炉管	4	17		9	17	千克		---Boiler tubes and pipes
7304 5910.01	高温承压用合金钢无缝钢管(抗拉强度≧620MPa、屈服强度≧440MPa)(锅炉管外径≧127mm，化学成分(wt%)0.07≦C≦0.13、8.5≦Cr≦9.5、0.3≦Mo≦0.6、1.5≦W≦2.0，非冷拔或冷轧，不论是否经进一步加工)	4	17		9	17	千克	A	Alloysteel seamless steel pipe for High temperature pressure, tensile strength ≧620MPa, yield strength ≧440MPa, outside diameter≧127mm,chemical（wt%）0.07≦C≦0.13、8.5≦Cr≦9.5、0.3≦Mo≦0.6、1.5≦W≦2.0, non cold-drawn or non cold-rolled, whether or not further processing, including internal thread
7304 5910.90	非冷轧其他合金钢无缝锅炉管(非冷拔或冷轧的)	4	17		9	17	千克	A	Other boiler tubes and pipes, of other alloy steel, non cold-drawn or non cold- rolled
7304.5920	---地质钻管、套管	4	17		9	17	千克	A	---Geological casing and drill pipes
7304.5990	---其他	4	17		9	17	千克		---Other
7304 5990.01	高温承压用合金钢无缝钢管(抗拉强度≧620MPa、屈服强度≧440MPa)(外径≧127mm，化学成分（wt%）0.07≦C≦0.13、8.5≦Cr≦9.5、0.3≦Mo≦0.6、1.5≦W≦2.0，非冷拔或冷轧，不论是否经进一步加工)	4	17		9	17	千克	A	Alloysteel seamless steel pipe for High temperature pressure, tensile strength ≧620MPa, yield strength ≧440MPa, outside diameter≧127mm,chemical（wt%）0.07≦C≦0.13、8.5≦Cr≦9.5、0.3≦Mo≦0.6、1.5≦W≦2.0, non cold-drawn or non cold-rolled, whether or not further processing, including internal thread
7304 5990.90	非冷轧其他合金钢制无缝圆形截面管(非冷拔或冷轧的)	4	17		9	17	千克	A	Other boiler tubes and pipes, of circular cross-section, of other alloy steel, non cold-drawn or non cold- rolled
7304.9000	-其他	4	17		9	17	千克	A	-Other
73.05	**其他圆形截面钢铁管(例如，焊、铆及用类似方法接合的管)，外径超过406.4毫米:**								**Other tubes and pipes（for example,welded, riveted or similarly closed）,having circular crosssections, the external diameter of which exceeds 406.4mm, of iron or steel:**
	-石油或天然气管道管:								-Line pipe of a kind used for oil or gas pipelines:
7305.1100	--纵向埋弧焊接的	7	17		13	17	千克	A	--Longitudinally submerged arc welded
7305.1200	--其他纵向焊接的	3	17		13	17	千克	A	--Other, longitudinally welded
7305.1900	--其他	7	17		13	17	千克	A	--Other
7305.2000	-钻探石油或天然气用套管	7	17		13	17	千克	A	-Casing of a kind used in drilling for oil or gas
	-其他焊接的:								-Other, welded:
7305.3100	--纵向焊接的	6	30		9	17	千克	A	--Longitudinally welded
7305.3900	--其他	6	30		9	17	千克	A	--Other
7305.9000	-其他	6	30		9	17	千克	A	-Other
73.06	**其他钢铁管及空心异型材(例如，辊缝、焊、铆及类似方法接合的)：**								**Other tubes, pipes and hollow profiles （for example, open seam or welded, riveted or similarly closed）, of iron or steel:**
	-石油及天然气管道管:								-Line pipe of a kind used for oil or gas pipelines:
7306.1100	--不锈钢焊缝管	7	17		13	17	千克	A	--Welded, of stainless steel
7306.1900	--其他	7	17		13	17	千克	A	--Other
	-钻探石油及天然气用的套管及导管:								-Casing and tubing of a kind used in drilling for oil or gas:
7306.2100	--不锈钢焊缝管	3	17		13	17	千克	A	--Welded, of stainless steel
7306.2900	--其他	3	17		13	17	千克	A	--Other
	-铁或非合金钢的其他圆形截面								-Other,welded,of circular cross-section,of iron or

税则号列 Tariff Item	商品名称及备注	进口税率 最惠	普通	暂定	出口退税	增值税率	计量单位	监管条件	Article Description
	焊缝管:								non-alloy steel:
	---外径不超过10毫米的:								---Having an outeside diameter not exceeding 10mm:
7306.3011	----壁厚在0.7毫米及以下	3	30		13	17	千克		----Having a wall thickness of 0.7mm or less
7306.3019	----其他	3	30		9	17	千克		----Other
7306.3090	---其他	3	30		9	17	千克		---Other
7306.4000	-不锈钢的其他圆形截面焊缝管	6	30		9	17	千克		-Other, welded, of circular cross-section,of stainless steel
7306.5000	-其他合金钢的圆形截面焊缝管	3	30		9	17	千克		-Other, welded, of circular cross-section,of other alloy steel
	-非圆形截面的其他焊缝管:								-Other, welded, of non-circular cross-section:
7306.6100	--矩形或正方形截面的	3	30		9	17	千克		--Of square or rectangular cross-section
7306.6900	--其他非圆形截面的	3	30		9	17	千克		--Of other non-circular cross-section
7306.9000	-其他	6	30		9	17	千克		-Other
7306 9000.10	多壁式管道(直接与化学品接触表面由特殊耐腐蚀材料制成)	6	30		9	17	千克	3A	Multiple-wall pipes (directly contact the chemicals and its surface produced by special erosion-proof materials)
7306 9000.90	未列名其他钢铁管及空心异型材	6	30		9	17	千克	A	Other tubes, pipes and hollow profiles,not elsewhere specified or included
73.07	钢铁管子附件(例如，接头、肘管、管套)：								**Tube or pipe fittings (for example, couplings, elbows, sleeves), of iron or steel:**
	-铸件:								-Cast fittings:
7307.1100	--无可锻性铸铁制	5	20		9	17	千克		--Of non-malleable cast iron
7307.1900	--其他	8	20		9	17	千克		--Other
	-其他，不锈钢制:								-Other, of stainless steel:
7307.2100	--法兰	8.4	20		9	17	千克		--Flanges
7307.2200	--螺纹肘管、弯管及管套	8.4	20		9	17	千克		--Threaded elbows, bends and sleeves
7307.2300	--对焊件	8.4	20		9	17	千克		--Butt welding fittings
7307.2900	--其他	8.4	20		9	17	千克		--Other
	-其他:								-Other:
7307.9100	--法兰	7	20		9	17	千克		--Flanges
7307.9200	--螺纹肘管、弯管及管套	4	20		9	17	千克		--Threaded elbows, bends and sleeves
7307.9300	--对焊件	7	20		9	17	千克		--Butt welding fittings
7307.9900	--其他	4	20		9	17	千克		--Other
73.08	钢铁结构体(品目94.06的活动房屋除外)及其部件(例如，桥梁及桥梁体段、闸门、塔楼、格构杆、屋顶、屋顶框架、门窗及其框架、门槛、百叶窗、栏杆、支柱及立柱);上述结构体用的已加工钢铁板、杆、角材、型材、异型材、管子及类似品:								**Structures (excluding prefabricated buildings of heading No. 94.06) and parts of structures (for example, bridges and bridge-sections, lock-gates, towers, lattice masts, roofs, roofing frameworks, doors and windows and their frames and thresholds for doors, shutters, balustrades, pillars and columns), of iron or steel; plates, rods, angles, shapes, sections, tubes and the like, prepared for use in structures, of iron or steel:**
7308.1000	-桥梁及桥梁体段	8	30		9	17	千克		-Bridges and bridge-sections
7308.2000	-塔楼及格构杆	8.4	30		9	17	千克		-Towers and lattice masts
7308.3000	-门窗及其框架、门槛	10	50		9	17	千克		-Doors, windows and their frames and thresholds for doors
7308.4000	-脚手架、模板或坑道支撑用的支柱及类似设备	8.4	30		9	17	千克		-Equipment for scaffolding, shuttering,propping or pit-propping
7308.9000	-其他	4	30		9	17	千克		-Other
73.09	盛装物料用的钢铁囤、柜、罐、桶及类似容器(装压缩气体或液化气体的除外)，容积超过300升，不论是否衬里或隔热，但无机械或热力装置:								**Reservoirs, tanks, vats and similar containers for any material (other than compressed or liquefied gas), of iron or steel, of a capacity exceeding 300L, whether or not lined or heat-insulated, but not fitted with mechanical or thermal equipment:**

税则号列 Tariff Item	商品名称及备注	进口税率 最惠	普通	暂定	出口退税	增值税率	计量单位	监管条件	Article Description
7309.0000	盛装物料用的钢铁囤、柜、罐、桶及类似容器(装压缩气体或液化气体的除外)，容积超过300升，不论是否衬里或隔热，但无机械或热力装置	10.5	35		5	17	千克		Reservoirs, tanks, vats and similar containers for any material (other than compressed or liquefied gas), of iron or steel, of a capacity exceeding 300L, whether or not lined or heat-insulated,but not fitted with mechanical or thermal equipment
73.10	**盛装物料用的钢铁柜、桶、罐、听、盒及类似容器(装压缩气体或液化气体的除外)，容积不超过 300 升，不论是否衬里或隔热，但无机械或热力装置：**								**Tanks, casks, drums, cans, boxes and similar containers, for any material (other than compressed or liquefied gas), of iron or steel, of a capacity not exceeding 300L, whether or not lined or heat-insulated, but not fitted with mechanical or thermal equipment:**
7310.1000	-容积在50升及以上	10.5	40		5	17	千克		-Of a capacity of 50L or more
7310 1000.10	100L<总容积≤300L 的容器(与所处理或盛放的化学品接触表面由特殊耐腐蚀材料制成)	10.5	40		5	17	千克	3	Containers, of a capacity more than 100L, but not exceeding 300L, its surface in contact with chemicals treated or contained is made of special erosion-resistant materials
7310 1000.90	50L≤容积≤300L 的其他钢铁制盛物容器(钢铁柜、桶、罐、听及类似容器)	10.5	40		5	17	千克		Other containers, of iron or steel, of a capacity 50L or more, but not exceeding 300L (tanks, casks, drums, cans, boxes and similar containers)
	-容积在50升以下:								-Of a capacity of less than 50L:
	--焊边或卷边接合的罐:								--Cans which are to be closed by soldering or crimping:
7310.2110	---易拉罐及罐体	17.5	70		5	17	千克		---Tear tab ends and bodies
7310.2190	---其他	17.5	70		5	17	千克		---Other
	--其他:								--Other:
7310.2910	---易拉罐及罐体	17.5	70		9	17	千克	A	---Cans and tanks
7310.2990	---其他	17.5	70		9	17	千克	A	---Other
73.11	**装压缩气体或液化气体用的钢铁容器:**								**Containers for compressed or liquefied gas, of iron or steel:**
7311.0010	---零售包装用	17.5	70		5	17	千克	6A	---For retail packing
7311.0090	---其他	8	17		13	17	千克	6A	---Other
73.12	**非绝缘的钢铁绞股线、绳、缆、编带、吊索及类似品:**								**Stranded wire, ropes, cables, plaited bands, slings and the like, of iron or steel, not electrically insulated:**
7312.1000	-绞股线、绳、缆	4	20		5	17	千克	A	-Stranded wire, ropes and cables
7312.9000	-其他	4	20		5	17	千克		-Other
73.13	**带刺钢铁丝；围篱用的钢铁绞带或单股扁丝(不论是否带刺)及松绞的双股丝:**								**Barbed wire of iron or steel; twisted hoop or single flat wire, barbed or not, and loosely twisted double wire, of a kind used for fencing, of iron or steel:**
7313.0000	带刺钢铁丝;围篱用的钢铁绞带或单股扁丝(不论是否带刺)及松绞的双股丝	7	70		5	17	千克		Barbed wire of iron or steel; twisted hoop or single flat wire, barbed or not, and loosely twisted double wire, of a kind used for fencing, of iron or steel
73.14	**钢铁丝制的布(包括环形带)、网、篱、格栅；网眼钢铁板:**								**Cloth (including endless bands), grill, netting and fencing, of iron or steel wire; expanded metal of iron or steel:**
	-机织品:								-Woven cloth:
7314.1200	--不锈钢制的机器用环形带	12	20		5	17	千克		--Endless bands for machinery, of stainless steel
7314.1400	--不锈钢制的其他机织品	12	20		5	17	千克		--Other woven cloth, of stainless steel
7314.1900	--其他	7	20		5	17	千克		--Other
7314.2000	-交点焊接的网、篱及格栅，其丝的最大截面尺寸在3毫米及以上，网眼尺寸在100平方厘米及以上	7	70		5	17	千克		-Grill, netting and fencing, welded at the intersection, of wire with a maximum cross-sectional dimension of 3mm or more and having a mesh size of $100cm^2$ or more
	-其他交点焊接的网、篱及格栅:								-Other grill, netting and fencing, welded at the intersection:
7314.3100	--镀或涂锌的	7	70		5	17	千克		--Plated or coated with zinc
7314.3900	--其他	7	70		5	17	千克		--Other
	-其他网、篱及格栅:								-Other grill, netting and fencing:

税则号列 Tariff Item	商品名称及备注	进口税率 最惠	普通	暂定	出口退税	增值税率	计量单位	监管条件	Article Description
7314.4100	--镀或涂锌的	8	20		5	17	千克		--Plated or coated with zinc
7314.4200	--涂塑的	8	20		5	17	千克		--Coated with plastics
7314.4900	--其他	8	20		5	17	千克		--Other
7314.5000	-网眼钢铁板	8	70		5	17	千克		-Expanded metal
73.15	**钢铁链及其零件:**								**Chain and parts thereof, of iron or steel:**
	-铰接链及其零件:								-Articulated link chain and parts thereof:
	--滚子链:								--Roller chain:
7315.1110	---自行车用	12	80		9	17	千克		---For bicycles
7315.1120	---摩托车用	12	80		5	17	千克		---For motorcycles
7315.1190	---其他	12	80		13	17	千克		---Other
7315.1200	--其他链	12	80		5	17	千克		--Other chain
7315.1900	--零件	12	80		5	17	千克		--Parts
7315.2000	-防滑链	12	80		5	17	千克		-Skid chain
	-其他链:								-Other chain:
7315.8100	--日字环节链	12	80		13	17	千克		--Stud-link
7315.8200	--其他焊接链	12	80		13	17	千克		--Other ,welded link
7315.8900	--其他	12	80		13	17	千克		--Other
7315.9000	-其他零件	10	80		5	17	千克		-Other parts
73.16	**钢铁锚、多爪锚及其零件:**								**Anchors, grapnels and parts thereof,of iron or steel:**
7316.0000	钢铁锚、多爪锚及其零件	10	40		9	17	千克		Anchors, grapnels and parts thereof, of iron or steel
73.17	**钢铁制的钉、平头钉、图钉、波纹钉、U形钉(品目 83.05 的货品除外)及类似品，不论钉头是否用其他材料制成,但不包括铜头钉:**								**Nails, tacks, drawing pins, corrugated nails, staples（other than those of heading No. 83.05）and similar articles, of iron or steel, whether or not with heads of other material, but excluding such articles with heads of copper:**
7317.0000	钢铁制的钉、平头钉、图钉、波纹钉、U形钉（品目 83.05 的货品除外）及类似品，不论钉头是否用其他材料制成,但不包括铜头钉	10	80		5	17	千克		Nails, tacks, drawing pins, corrugated nails, staples（other than those of heading No.83.05）and similar articles, of iron or steel, whether or not with heads of other material, but excluding such articles with heads of copper
73.18	**钢铁制的螺钉、螺栓、螺母、方头螺钉、钩头螺钉、铆钉、销、开尾销、垫圈（包括弹簧垫圈）及类似品:**								**Screws, bolts, nuts, coach screws, screw hooks, rivets, cotters, cotterpins, washers（including spring washers）and similar articles, of iron of steel:**
	-螺纹制品:								-Threaded articles:
7318.1100	--方头螺钉	10	80		5	17	千克		--Coach screws
7318.1200	--其他木螺钉	10	80		5	17	千克		--Other wood screws
7318 1200.01	非用于民用航空器维护和修理的其他木螺钉	10	80		5	17	千克		Other wood screws, not used for the maintenance and repair of Civil Aircraft
7318 1200.90	其他木螺钉	10	80		5	17	千克		Other wood screws
7318.1300	--钩头螺钉及环头螺钉	10	80		5	17	千克		--Screw hooks and screw rings
7318.1400	--自攻螺钉	10	80		5	17	千克		--Self-tapping screws
7318 1400.01	非用于民用航空器维护和修理的自攻螺钉	10	80		5	17	千克		Self-tapping screws, not used for the maintenance and repair of Civil Aircraft
7318 1400.90	其他自攻螺钉	10	80		5	17	千克		Other self-tapping screws
	--其他螺钉及螺栓,不论是否带有螺母或垫圈								--Other screws and bolts, whether or not with their nuts or washers
7318.1510	---抗拉强度在800兆帕及以上的	8	80		5	17	千克		Tensile strength≥800 MPa,
7318 1510.01	抗拉强度≥800 兆帕， 杆径＞6mm 的其他螺钉及螺栓(不论是否带有螺母或垫圈,非用于民用航空器维护和修理的)	8	80		5	17	千克		Other bolt and screw with tensile strength≥800 MPa stem diameter＞6mm, (whether or not with their nuts or washers, not used for the maintenance and repair of Civil Aircraft)
7318 1510.90	其他抗拉强度≥800 兆帕的螺钉及螺栓(不论是否带有螺母或垫圈)	8	80		5	17	千克		Other bolt and screw with tensile strength ≥800 MPa, (whether or not with their nuts or washers)
7318.1590	---其他	8	80		5	17	千克		----Other
7318 1590.01	杆径＞6mm 的其他螺钉及螺栓	8	80		5	17	千克		Other bolt and screw with stem diameter ＞6mm,

税则号列 Tariff Item	商品名称及备注	进口税率 最惠	普通	暂定	出口退税	增值税率	计量单位	监管条件	Article Description
	(不论是否带有螺母或垫圈，非用于民用航空器维护和修理的)								(whether or not with their nuts or washers, not used for the maintenance and repair of Civil Aircraft)
7318 1590.90	其他螺钉及螺栓(不论是否带有螺母或垫圈)	8	80		5	17	千克		Other bolt and screw(whether or not with their nuts or washers)
7318.1600	--螺母	8	80		5	17	千克		--Nuts
7318.1900	--其他	5	80		5	17	千克		--Other
	-无螺纹制品:								-Non-threaded articles:
7318.2100	--弹簧垫圈及其他防松垫圈	10	80		5	17	千克		--Spring washers and other lock washers
7318 2100.01	弹簧垫圈及其他防松垫圈(非用于民用航空器维护和修理的)	10	80		5	17	千克		Spring washers and other lock washers (not used for the maintenance and repair of Civil Aircraft)
7318 2100.90	其他弹簧垫圈及其他防松垫圈	10	80		5	17	千克		Other spring washers and other lock washers
7318.2200	--其他垫圈	10	80		5	17	千克		--Other washers
7318 2200.01	其他垫圈(非用于民用航空器维护和修理的)	10	80		5	17	千克		Other washers(not used for the maintenance and repair of Civil Aircraft)
7318 2200.90	其他垫圈	10	80		5	17	千克		Other washers
7318.2300	--铆钉	10	80		5	17	千克		--Rivets
7318.2400	--销及开尾销	10	80		5	17	千克		--Cotters and cotter-pins
7318.2900	--其他	10	80		5	17	千克		--Other
73.19	**钢铁制的手工缝针、编织针、引针、钩针、刺绣穿孔锥及类似制品；其他品目未列名的钢铁制安全别针及其他别针:**								**Sewing needles, knitting needles, bod-kins, crochet hooks, embroidery stilettos and similar articles, for use in the hand, of iron or steel; safety pins and other pins of iron or steel, not elsewhere specified or included:**
	-安全别针及其他别针:								-Safety pins and other pins:
7319.4010	---安全别针	10	90		5	17	千克		---Safety pins
7319.4090	---其他	10	90		5	17	千克		---Other
7319.9000	-其他	10	80		5	17	千克		-Other
73.20	**钢铁制弹簧及弹簧片:**								**Springs and leaves for springs, of iron or steel:**
	-片簧及簧片:								-Leaf-springs and leaves thereof:
7320.1010	---铁道车辆用	6	14		5	17	千克		---For railway locomotives and rollingstock
7320.1020	---汽车用	10	14		5	17	千克		---For motor vehicles
7320.1090	---其他	10	50		5	17	千克		---Other
	-螺旋弹簧:								-Helical springs:
7320.2010	---铁道车辆用	6	14		5	17	千克		---For railway locomotives and rollingstock
7320.2090	---其他	10	50		5	17	千克		---Other
	-其他:								-Other:
7320.9010	---铁道车辆用	6	14		5	17	千克		---For railway locomotives and rollingstock
7320.9090	---其他	12	50		5	17	千克		---Other
73.21	**非电热的钢铁制家用炉、灶（包括附有集中供暖用的热水锅的炉）、烤肉架、烤炉、煤气灶、加热板和类似非电热的家用器具及其零件:**								**Stoves, ranges, grates, cookers（including those with subsidiary boilers for central heating）, barbecues, braziers, gas-rings, plate warmers and similar non-electric domestic appliances, and parts thereof, of iron or steel:**
	-炊事器具及加热板:								-Cooking appliances and plate warmers:
7321.1100	--使用气体燃料或可使用气体燃料及其他燃料的	15	80		9	17	千克/个	6	--For gas fuel or for both gas and other fuels
	--使用液体燃料的:								--For liquid fuel:
7321.1210	---煤油炉	21	80		5	17	千克/个		---Kerosene cooking stoves
7321.1290	---其他	21	80		9	17	千克/个		---Other
7321.1900	--其他，包括使用固体燃料的	21	80		9	17	千克/个		--Other, including appliances for solid fuel
	-其他器具:								-Other appliances:
7321.8100	--使用气体燃料或可使用气体燃料及其他燃料的	23	80		5	17	千克/个	6	--For gas fuel or for both gas and other fuels
7321.8200	--使用液体燃料的	21	80		5	17	千克/个		--For liquid fuel
7321.8900	--其他，包括使用固体燃料的	21	80		9	17	千克/个		--Other, including appliances for solid fuel
7321.9000	-零件	12	80		9	17	千克		-Parts
73.22	**非电热的钢铁制集中供暖用散**								**Radiators for central heating, not electrically**

税则号列 Tariff Item	商品名称及备注	进口税率 最惠	进口税率 普通	进口税率 暂定	出口退税	增值税率	计量单位	监管条件	Article Description
	热器及其零件；非电热的钢铁制空气加热器、暖气分布器（包括可分布新鲜空气或调节空气的）及其零件，装有电动风扇或鼓风机：								**heated, and parts thereof,of iron or steel; air heaters and hot air distributors（including distributors which can also distribute fresh or conditioned air）, not electrically heated, incorporating a motor-dirven fan or blower, and parts thereof, of iron or steel:**
	-散热器及其零件:								-Radiators and parts thereof:
7322.1100	--铸铁制	21	80		5	17	千克		--Of cast iron
7322.1900	--其他	21	80		5	17	千克		--Other
7322.9000	-其他	20	80		5	17	千克		-Other
73.23	**餐桌、厨房或其他家用钢铁器具及其零件；钢铁丝绒；钢铁制擦锅器、洗刷擦光用的块垫、手套及类似品：**								**Table, kitchen or other household articles and parts thereof, of iron or steel; iron or steel wool; pot scourers and scouring or polishing pads, gloves and the like, of iron or steel:**
7323.1000	-钢铁丝绒；擦锅器及洗刷擦光用的块垫、手套及类似品	14	80		5	17	千克	A	-Iron or steel wool; pot scourers and scouring or polishing pads, gloves and the like
	-其他:								-Other:
7323.9100[暂]	--铸铁制，未搪瓷	20	80	10	9	17	千克	A	--Of cast iron, not enamelled
7323.9200[暂]	--铸铁制，已搪瓷	20	100	10	9	17	千克	AB	--Of cast iron, enamelled
7323.9300	--不锈钢制	12	80		9	17	千克	AB	--Of stainless steel
	--钢铁（铸铁除外）制，已搪瓷:								--Of iron（other than cast iron）or steel, enamelled:
7323.9410[暂]	---面盆	20	100	10	9	17	千克	AB	---Basin
7323.9420[暂]	---烧锅	20	100	10	9	17	千克	AB	---Casserole
7323.9490	---其他	20	100		9	17	千克	AB	---Other
7323.9900	--其他	20	80		9	17	千克	A	--Other
73.24	**钢铁制卫生器具及其零件：**								**Sanitary ware and parts thereof, of iron or steel:**
7324.1000[暂]	-不锈钢制洗涤槽及脸盆	18	80	10	9	17	千克		-Sinks and wash basins, of stainless steel
	-浴缸:								-Baths:
7324.2100	--铸铁制，不论是否搪瓷	10	100		9	17	千克		--Of cast iron, whether or not enamelled
7324.2900[暂]	--其他	30	100	15	9	17	千克		--Other
7324.9000[暂]	-其他，包括零件	25	100	15	9	17	千克		-Other, including parts
73.25	**其他钢铁铸造制品：**								**Other cast articles of iron or steel:**
	-无可锻性铸铁制:								-Of non-malleable cast iron:
7325.1010	---工业用	7	40		5	17	千克		---For technical use
7325.1090	---其他	20	90		5	17	千克		---Other
	-其他:								-Other:
7325.9100	--研磨机用的研磨球及类似品	10.5	40		5	17	千克		--Grinding balls and similar articles for mills
	--其他:								--Other:
7325.9910	---工业用	10.5	40		5	17	千克		---For technical use
7325.9990	---其他	20	90		5	17	千克		---Other
73.26	**其他钢铁制品：**								**Other articles of iron or steel:**
	-经锻造或冲压，但未经进一步加工:								-Forged or stamped, but not further worked:
7326.1100	--研磨机用的研磨球及类似品	10.5	40		5	17	千克		--Grinding balls and similar articles for mills
	--其他:								--Other:
7326.1910	---工业用	10.5	40		5	17	千克		---For technical use
7326.1990	---其他	20	90		5	17	千克		---Other
	-钢铁丝制品:								-Articles of iron or steel wire:
7326.2010	---工业用	10	40		5	17	千克		---For technical use
7326.2090	---其他	18	90		9	17	千克		---Other
	-其他:								-Other:
	---工业用:								---For technical use:
7326.9011	----钢铁纤维及其制品	10.5	40		5	17	千克		----Steel fibres and articles thereof
7326.9019	----其他	10.5	40		5	17	千克		----Other
7326.9090	---其他	8	90		9	17	千克		---Other

第七十四章 铜及其制品

注释：

本章所用有关名词解释如下：

一、精炼铜

按重量计含铜量至少为99.85%的金属；或

按重量计含铜量至少为97.5%，但其他各种元素的含量不超过下表中规定的限量的金属：

其他元素表

元素		所含重量百分比
Ag	银	0.25
As	砷	0.5
Cd	镉	1.3
Cr	铬	1.4
Mg	镁	0.8
Pb	铅	1.5
S	硫	0.7
Sn	锡	0.8
Te	碲	0.8
Zn	锌	1
Zr	锆	0.3
其他元素①，每种		0.3

①其他元素，例如，铝、铍、钴、铁、锰、镍、硅。

二、铜合金

除未精炼铜以外的金属物质，按重量计含铜量大于其他元素单项含量，但：

（一）按重量计至少有一种其他元素的含量超过上表中规定的限量；或

（二）按重量计其他元素的总含量超过2.5%。

三、铜母合金

含有其他元素，但按重量计含铜量超过10%的合金，该合金无实用可锻性，通常用作生产其他合金的添加剂或用作冶炼有色金属的脱氧剂、脱硫剂及类似用途。但按重量计含磷量超过15%的磷化铜归入品目28.48。

四、条、杆

轧、挤、拔或锻制的实心产品，非成卷的，其全长截面均为圆形、椭圆形、矩形（包括正方形）、等边三角形或规则外凸多边形（包括相对两边为弧拱形，另外两边为等长平行直线的“扁圆形”及“变形矩形”）。对于矩形（包括正方形）、三角形或多边形截面的产品，其全长边角可经磨圆。矩形（包括“变形矩形”）截面的产品，其厚度应大于宽度的1/10。所述条、杆也包括同样形状及尺寸的铸造或烧结产品。该产品在铸造或烧结后再经加工（简单剪修或去氧化皮的除外），但不具有其他品

Chapter 74 Copper and articles thereof

Chapter Notes:

In this Chapter the following expressions have the meanings hereby assigned to them:

1. Refined copper

Metal containing at least 99.85% by weight of copper; or

metal containing at least 97.5% by weight of copper, provided that the content by weight of any other element does not exceed the limit specified in the following table:

TABLE-Other elements

Element		Limiting content % by weight
Ag	Silver	0.25
As	Arsenic	0.5
Cd	Cadmium	1.3
Cr	Chromium	1.4
Mg	Magnesium	0.8
Pb	Lead	1.5
S	Sulphur	0.7
Sn	Tin	0.8
Te	Tellurium	0.8
Zn	Zinc	1
Zr	Zirconium	0.3
Other elements①, each		0.3

①Other elements are, for example, Al, Be, Co, Fe, Mn, Ni, Si.

2. Copper alloys

Metallic substances other than unrefined copper in which copper predominates by weight over each of the other elements, provided that:

(a) the content by weight of at least one of the other elements is greater than the limit specified in the foregoing table; or

(b) the total content by weight of such other elements exceeds 2.5%.

3. Master alloys

Alloys containing with other elements more than 10% by weight of copper, not usefully malleable and commonly used as an additive in the manufacture of other alloys or as de-oxidants, de-sulphurising agents or for similar uses in the metallurgy of non-ferrous metals. However, copper phosphide (phosphor copper) containing more than 15% by weight of phosphorus falls in heading 28.48.

4. Bars and rods

Rolled, extruded, drawn or forged products, not in coils, which have a uniform solid cross-section along their whole length in the shape of circles, ovals, rectangles (including squares), equilateral triangles or regular convex polygons (including "flattened circles" and "modified rectangles", of which two opposite sides are convex arcs, the other two sides being straight, of equal length and parallel). Products, with a rectangular (including square), triangular or polygonal cross-section may have corners rounded along their whole length. The thickness of such products which have a rectangular (including "modified rectangular") cross-section exceeds one-tenth of the width. The expression also covers cast or sintered products, of the same forms and dimensions, which have been subsequently worked after

目所列制品或产品的特征。

线锭及坯段,已具锥形尾端或经其他简单加工以便送入机器制成盘条或管子等的,仍应作为未锻轧铜归入品目 74.03。

五、型材及异型材

轧、挤、拔、锻制的产品或其他成型产品,不论是否成卷,其全长截面相同,但与条、杆、丝、板、片、带、箔、管的定义不相符合。同时也包括同样形状的铸造或烧结产品。该产品在铸造或烧结后再经加工(简单剪修或去氧化皮的除外),但不具有其他品目所列制品或产品的特征。

六、丝

盘卷的轧、挤或拔制实心产品,其全长截面均为圆形、椭圆形、矩形(包括正方形)、等边三角形或规则外凸多边形(包括相对两边为弧拱形,另外两边为等长平行直线的"扁圆形"及"变形矩形")。对于矩形(包括正方形)、三角形或多边形截面的产品,其全长边角可经磨圆。矩形(包括"变形矩形")截面的产品,其厚度应大于宽度的 1/10。

七、板、片、带、箔

成卷或非成卷的平面产品(品目 74.03 的未锻轧产品除外),截面均为厚度相同的实心矩形(不包括正方形),不论边角是否磨圆(包括相对两边为弧拱形,另外两边为等长平行直线的"变形矩形"),并且符合以下规格:

(一) 矩形(包括正方形)的,厚度不超过宽度的 1/10;

(二)矩形或正方形以外形状的,任何尺寸,但不具有其他品目所列制品或产品的特征。

品目 74.09 及 74.10 还适用于具有花样(例如,凹槽、肋条形、格槽、珠粒及菱形)的板、片、带、箔以及穿孔、抛光、涂层或制成瓦楞形的这类产品,但不具有其他品目所列制品或产品的特征。

八、管

全长截面及管壁厚度相同并只有一个闭合空间的空心产品,成卷或非成卷的,其截面为圆形、椭圆形、矩形(包括正方形)、等边三角形或规则外凸多边形。对于截面为矩形(包括正方形)、等边三角形或规则外凸多边形的产品,不论全长边角是否磨圆,只要其内外截面为同一圆心并为同样形状及同一轴向,也可视为管子。上述截面的管子可经抛光、涂层、弯曲、攻丝、钻孔、缩腰、胀口、成锥形或装法兰、颈圈或套环。

production (otherwise than by simple trimming or de-scaling), provided that they have not thereby assumed the character of articles or products of other headings.

Wire-bars and billets with their ends tapered or otherwise worked simply to facilitate their entry into machines for converting them into, for example, drawing stock (wire-rod) or tubes, are however to be taken to be unwrought copper of heading 74.03.

5. Profiles

Rolled, extruded, drawn, forged or formed products, coiled or not, of a uniform cross-section along their whole length, which do not conform to any of the definitions of bars, rods, wire, plates, sheets, strip, foil, tubes or pipes. The expression also covers cast or sintered products, of the same forms, which have been subsequently worked after production (otherwise than by simple trimming or de-scaling), provided that they have not thereby assumed the character of articles or products of other headings.

6. Wire

Rolled, extruded or drawn products, in coils, which have a uniform solid cross-section along their whole length in the shape of circles, ovals, rectangles (including squares), equilateral triangles or regular convex polygons (including "flattened circles" and "modified rectangles", of which two opposite sides are convex arcs, the other two sides being straight, of equal length and parallel). Products with a rectangular (including square), triangular or polygonal cross-section may have corners rounded along their whole length. The thickness of such products which have a rectangular (including "modified rectangular") cross-section exceeds one-tenth of the width.

7. Plates, sheets, strip and foil

Flat-surfaced products (other than the unwrought products of heading 74.03), coiled or not, of soild rectangular (other than square) cross-section with or without rounded corners (including "modified rectangles" of which two opposite sides are convex arcs, the other two sides being straight, of equal length and parallel) of a uniform thickness, which are:

(a) Of rectangular (including square) shape with a thickness not exceeding one-tenth of the width;

(b) Of a shape other than rectangular or square, of any size, provided that they do not assume the character of articles or products of other headings.

Headings 74.09 and 74.10 apply, inter alia, to plates, sheets, strip and foil with patterns (for example, grooves, ribs, chequers, tears, buttons, lozenges) and to such products which have been perforated, corrugated, polished or coated, provided that they do not thereby assume the character of articles or products of other headings.

8. Tubes and pipes

Hollow products, coiled or not, which have a uniform cross-section with only one enclosed void along their whole length in the shape of circles, ovals, rectangles (including squares), equilateral triangles or regular convex polygons, and which have a uniform wall thickness. Products with a rectangular (including square), equilateral triangular or regular convex polygonal cross-section, which may have corners rounded along their whole length, are also to be taken to be tubes and pipes provided the inner and outer cross-sections are concentric and have the same form and orientation. Tubes and pipes of the foregoing cross-sections may be polished, coated, bent, threaded, drilled, waisted, expanded, cone-shaped or fitted with flanges, collars or rings.

子目注释：

本章所用有关名词解释如下：

一、铜锌合金（黄铜）

铜与锌的合金，不论是否含有其他元素。含有其他元素时：

（一）按重量计含锌量应大于其他各种元素的单项含量；

（二）按重量计含镍量应低于5%[参见铜镍锌合金（德银）]；以及

（三）按重量计含锡量应低于 3%[参见铜锡合金（青铜）]。

二、铜锡合金（青铜）

铜与锡的合金，不论是否含有其他元素。含有其他元素时，按重量计含锡量应大于其他各种元素的单项含量。当按重量计含锡量在3%及以上时，锌的含量可大于锡的含量，但必须小于10%。

三、铜镍锌合金（德银）

铜、镍、锌的合金，不论是否含有其他元素，按重量计含镍量在 5%及以上[参见铜锌合金（黄铜）]。

四、铜镍合金

铜与镍的合金，不论是否含有其他元素，但按重量计含锌量不得大于 1%。含有其他元素时，按重量计含镍量应大于其他各种元素的单项含量。

Subheading Note:

In this Chapter the following expressions have the meanings hereby assigned to them:

1. Copper-zinc base alloys（brasses）

Alloys of copper and zinc, with or without other elements. When other elements are present:

（a）zinc predominates by weight over each of such other elements;

（b）any nickel content by weight is less than 5%[see copper-nickel-zinc alloys（nickel silvers）]; and

（c）any tin content by weight is less than 3%[see copper-tin alloys（bronzes）].

2. Copper-tin base alloys（bronzes）

Alloys of copper and tin, with or without other elements. When other elements are present, tin predominates by weight over each of such other elements, except that when the tin content is 3% or more the zinc content by weight may exceed that of tin but must be less than 10%.

3. Copper-nickel-zinc base alloys（nickel silvers）.

Alloys of copper, nickel and zinc, with or without other elements. The nickel content is 5% or more by weight [see copper-zinc alloys（brasses）].

4. Copper-nickel base alloys

Alloys of copper and nickel, with or without other elements but in any case containing by weight not more than 1% of zinc. When other elements are present, nickel predominates by weight over each of such other elements.

税则号列 Tariff Item	商品名称及备注	进口税率 最惠	普通	暂定	出口退税	增值税率	计量单位	监管条件	Article Description
74.01	铜锍；沉积铜（泥铜）：								**Copper mattes；cement copper（precipitated copper）：**
7401.0000	铜锍；沉积铜（泥铜）	2	11			17	千克		Copper mattes; cement copper（precipitated copper）
7401 0000.10	沉积铜(泥铜)	2	11			17	千克	9A	Cement copper (precipitated copper)
7401 0000.90 [暂]	铜锍	2	11	0		17	千克		Copper mattes
74.02	**未精炼铜；电解精炼用的铜阳极：**								**Unrefined copper; copper anodes for electrolytic refining:**
7402.0000 [暂]	未精炼铜;电解精炼用的铜阳极	2	11	0			千克		Unrefined copper; copper anodes for electrolytic refining
7402 0000.01 [暂]	未精炼铜、电解精炼用铜阳极(含黄金价值部分)	2	11	0		0	千克		Unrefined copper; copper anodes for electrolytic refining, containing gold
7402 0000.90 [暂]	未精炼铜、电解精炼用铜阳极(非黄金价值部分)	2	11	0		17	千克		Unrefined copper; copper anodes for electrolytic refining, without gold
74.03	**未锻轧的精炼铜及铜合金：**								**Refined copper and copper alloys, unwrought:**
	-精炼铜:								-Refined copper:
	--阴极及阴极型材:								--Cathodes and sections of cathodes:
	---阴极:								---Cathodes:
7403.1111 [暂]	----按重量计铜含量超过99.9935%的	2	11	0		17	千克		----Containing at least 99.9935% by weight of copper
7403 1111.01 [暂]	高纯阴极铜（99.9999％＞铜含量＞99.9935％）(未锻轧的)	2	11	0		17	千克		Purity copper cathode, containing less than 99.9999% and at least 99.9935% by weight of copper,unwrought
7403 1111.90 [暂]	高纯阴极铜（铜含量≥99.9999％）(未锻轧的)	2	11	0		17	千克		Purity copper cathode containing more than 99.9999% by weight of copper,unwrought
7403.1119 [暂]	----其他	2	11	0		17	千克		----Other
7403.1190 [暂]	---阴极型材	2	11	0		17	千克		---Sections of cathodes
7403.1200 [暂]	--线锭	2	11	0		17	千克		--Wire-bars
7403.1300 [暂]	--坯段	2	11	0		17	千克		--Billets
7403.1900 [暂]	--其他	2	11	0		17	千克		--Other

税则号列 Tariff Item	商品名称及备注	进口税率 最惠	普通	暂定	出口退税	增值税率	计量单位	监管条件	Article Description
	-铜合金:								-Copper alloys:
7403.2100	--铜锌合金(黄铜)	1	14			17	千克		--Copper-zinc base alloys (brass)
7403.2200	--铜锡合金(青铜)	1	17			17	千克		--Copper-tin base alloys (bronze)
7403.2900	--其他铜合金(品目74.05的铜母合金除外)	1	17			17	千克		--Other copper alloys other than master alloys of heading No. 74.05
74.04	**铜废碎料:**								**Copper waste and scrap:**
7404.0000[暂]	铜废碎料	1.5	11	0		17	千克		Copper waste and scrap
7404 0000.10[暂]	以回收铜为主的废电机等(包括废电机、电线、电缆、五金电器)	1.5	11	0		17	千克	AP	Waste electric machines mainly for recyclinging copper, including waste wires, cables, hardware and electric appliance
7404 0000.90[暂]	其他铜废碎料	1.5	11	0		17	千克	AP	Other copper waste and scrap
74.05	**铜母合金:**								**Master alloys of copper:**
7405.0000	铜母合金	4	17			17	千克		Master alloys of copper
74.06	**铜粉及片状粉末:**								**Copper powders and flakes:**
	-非片状粉末:								-Powders of non-lamellar structure:
7406.1010	---精炼铜制	3	14			17	千克		---Of refined copper
7406.1020	---铜镍合金(白铜)或铜镍锌合金(德银)制	6	40			17	千克		---Of copper-nickel base alloys (cupronickel) or copper-nickel-zinc base alloys (nickel silver)
7406.1030	---铜锌合金(黄铜)制	6	30			17	千克		---Of copper-zinc base alloys (brass)
7406.1040	---铜锡合金(青铜)制	6	30			17	千克		---Of copper-tin base alloys (bronze)
7406.1090	---其他铜合金制	6	30			17	千克		---Other
	-片状粉末:								-Powders of lamellar structure; flakes:
7406.2010	---精炼铜制	4	14			17	千克		---Of refined copper
7406.2020	---铜镍合金(白铜)或铜镍锌合金(德银)制	6	40			17	千克		---Of copper-nickel base alloys (cupronickel) or copper-nickel-zinc base alloys (nickel silver)
7406.2090	---其他铜合金制	6	30			17	千克		---Other
74.07	**铜条、杆、型材及异型材:**								**Copper bars, rods and profiles:**
	-精炼铜制:								-Of refined copper:
7407.1010	---铬锆铜制	4	14			17	千克		---Of chromium ziroconium copper
7407.1090	---其他	4	14			17	千克		---Other
	-铜合金制:								-Of copper alloys:
	--铜锌合金(黄铜):								--Of copper-zinc base alloys (brass):
	---铜条、杆:								---Copper bars and rods:
7407.2111	——直线度不大于0.5毫米/米	7	20			17	千克		----Straightness≤0.5mm/m
7407.2119	----其他	7	20			17	千克		----Other
7407.2190	---其他	7	20			17	千克		---Other
7407.2900	--其他	7	20			17	千克		--Other
74.08	**铜丝:**								**Copper wire:**
	-精炼铜制:								-Of refined copper:
7408.1100	--最大截面尺寸超过6毫米	4	14			17	千克		--Of which the maximum cross-sectional dimension exceeds 6mm
7408.1900	--其他	4	14			17	千克		--Other
7408 1900.01[暂]	其他含氧量<5PPM的精炼铜丝(截面尺寸≤6mm)	4	14	2		17	千克		Other refining copper wire with oxygen content <5PPM (sectional dimension≤6mm)
7408 1900.90	其他截面尺寸≤6mm的精炼铜丝	4	14			17	千克		Other refining copper wire with sectional dimension≤6mm
	-铜合金制:								-Of copper alloys:
7408.2100	--铜锌合金(黄铜)	7	20			17	千克		--Of copper-zinc base alloys (brass)
	--铜镍合金(白铜)或铜镍锌合金(德银):								--Of copper-nickel base alloys (cupronickel) or copper-nickel-zinc base alloys (nickel silver)
7408.2210	---铜镍锌铅合金(加铅德银)丝	8	40			17	千克		—Of copper-nickel-zinc-lead base alloys (leaded nickel silver)
7408.2290	---其他	8	40			17	千克		---Other
7408.2900	--其他	7	20			17	千克		--Other
74.09	**铜板、片及带,厚度超过0.15毫米:**								**Copper plates, sheets and strip, of a thickness exceeding 0.15mm:**
	-精炼铜制:								-Of refined copper:
	--盘卷的:								--In coils:

税则号列 Tariff Item	商品名称及备注	进口税率 最惠	普通	暂定	出口退税	增值税率	计量单位	监管条件	Article Description
7409.1110	---含氧量不超过10PPM的	4	14		9	17	千克		---Containing oxygen not exceeding 10 PPM
7409.1190	---其他	4	14		9	17	千克		---Other
7409.1900	--其他	4	14		9	17	千克		--Other
	-铜锌合金（黄铜）制:								-Of copper-zinc base alloys（brass）:
7409.2100	--盘卷的	7	20		9	17	千克		--In coils
7409.2900	--其他	7	20		9	17	千克		--Other
	-铜锡合金（青铜）制:								-Of copper-tin base alloys（bronze）:
7409.3100	--盘卷的	7	20		9	17	千克		--In coils
7409.3900	--其他	7	20		9	17	千克		--Other
7409.4000	-铜镍合金（白铜）或铜镍锌合金（德银）制	7	40		9	17	千克		-Of copper-nickel base alloys（cupronickel）or copper-nickel-zinc base alloys（nickel silver）
7409.9000	-其他铜合金制	7	20		9	17	千克		-Of other copper alloys
74.10	**铜箔（不论是否印花或用纸、纸板、塑料或类似材料衬背），厚度（衬背除外）不超过0.15毫米:**								**Copper foil（whether or not printed or backed with paper, paperboard, plastics or similar backing materials）of a thickness（excluding any backing）not exceeding 0.15mm:**
	-无衬背:								-Not backed:
7410.1100	--精炼铜制	4	14		13	17	千克		--Of refined copper
7410 1100.01 暂	覆铜板及印刷线路板用铜箔(厚度≤0.15毫米)	4	14	3	13	17	千克		Copper foil for copper-clad plate and printed- wiring board, of a thickness not exceeding 0.15mm
7410 1100.90	其他无衬背的精炼铜箔(厚度≤0.15毫米)	4	14		13	17	千克		Other copper foil of refined copper, not backed, of a thickness not exceeding 0.15mm
	--铜合金制:								--Of copper alloys:
7410.1210	---铜镍合金（白铜）或铜镍锌合金（德银）	7	40		13	17	千克		---Of copper-nickel base alloys（cupronickel）or copper-nickel-zinc base alloys（nickel silver）
7410.1290	---其他	7	20		13	17	千克		---Other
	-有衬背:								-Backed:
	--精炼铜制:								--Of refined copper:
7410.2110	---印制电路用覆铜板	4	14		17	17	千克		---Copper-clad board used to print circuit
7410.2190	---其他	4	14		13	17	千克		---Other
	--铜合金制:								--Of copper alloys:
7410.2210	---铜镍合金（白铜）或铜镍锌合金（德银）	7	40		13	17	千克		---Of copper-nickel base alloys（cupronickel）or copper-nickel-zinc base alloys（nickel silver）
7410.2290	---其他	7	20		13	17	千克		---Other
74.11	**铜管:**								**Copper tubes and pipes:**
	-精炼铜制:								-Of refined copper:
	---外径不超过25毫米的:								---Having an outside diameter not exceeding 25mm:
7411.1011	----带有螺纹或翅片的	4	14		13	17	千克		----Threaded or with fins
7411.1019	----其他	4	14		13	17	千克		----Other
7411 1019.01 暂	其他含氧量＜5PPM,外径≤25mm的精炼铜管	4	14	2	13	17	千克		Other pipes of refined copper, an outside diameter not exceeding 25mm, containing H2O less than 5PPM
7411 1019.90	外径≤25mm的其他精炼铜管	4	14		13	17	千克		Other pipes of refined copper, an outside diameter not exceeding 25mm
7411.1020	---外径超过70毫米的	4	14		13	17	千克		---Having an outside diameter exceeding 70mm
7411.1090	---其他	4	14		13	17	千克		---Other
	-铜合金制:								-Of copper alloys:
	--铜锌合金（黄铜）:								--Of copper-zinc base alloys（brass）:
7411.2110	---盘卷的	7	20		13	17	千克		---In coils
7411.2190	---其他	7	20		13	17	千克		---Other
7411.2200	--铜镍合金（白铜）或铜镍锌合金（德银）	7	40		13	17	千克		--Of copper-nickel base alloys（cupronickel）or copper-nickel-zinc base alloys（nickel silver）
7411.2900	--其他	7	20		13	17	千克		--Other
74.12	**铜制管子附件(例如，接头、肘管、管套）:**								**Copper tube or pipe fittings（for example, couplings, elbows, sleeves）:**
7412.1000	-精炼铜制	4	14			17	千克		-Of refined copper
	-铜合金制:								-Of copper alloys:
7412.2010	---铜镍合金（白铜）或铜镍锌	7	40			17	千克		---Of copper-nickel base alloys（cupronickel）or

税则号列 Tariff Item	商品名称及备注	进口税率 最惠	普通	暂定	出口退税	增值税率	计量单位	监管条件	Article Description
	合金（德银）								copper-nickel-zinc base alloys（nickel silver）
7412.2090	---其他	7	20			17	千克		---Other
74.13	**非绝缘的铜丝绞股线、缆、编带及类似品：**								**Stranded wire, cables, plaited bands and the like, of copper, not electrically insulated:**
7413.0000	非绝缘的铜丝绞股线、缆、编带及类似品	5	14			17	千克	A	Stranded wire, cables, plaited bands and the like, of copper, not electrically insulated
74.15	**铜制或钢铁制带铜头的钉、平头钉、图钉、U形钉（品目83.05的货品除外）及类似品；铜制螺钉、螺栓、螺母、钩头螺钉、铆钉、销、开尾销、垫圈（包括弹簧垫圈）及类似品：**								**Nails, tacks, drawing pins, staples（other than those of heading No. 83.05）and similar articles, of copper or of iron or steel with heads of copper; screws, bolts, nuts, screw hooks, rivets, cotters, cotter-pins, washers（including spring washers）and similar articles, of copper:**
7415.1000	-钉、平头钉、图钉U形钉及类似品	8	80			17	千克		-Nails and tacks, drawing pins, staples and similar articles
	-其他无螺纹制品：								-Other articles, not threaded:
7415.2100	--垫圈（包括弹簧垫圈）	10	80			17	千克		--Washers（including spring washers）
7415.2900	--其他	10	80			17	千克		--Other
	-其他螺纹制品：								-Other threaded articles:
	--螺钉；螺栓及螺母：								--Screws; bolts and nuts:
7415.3310	---木螺钉	8	80			17	千克		---Screws for wood
7415.3390	---其他	8	80			17	千克		---Other
7415.3900	--其他	10	80			17	千克		--Other
74.18	**餐桌、厨房或其他家用铜制器具及其零件；铜制刷锅器、洗刷擦光用的块垫、手套及类似品；铜制卫生器具及其零件：**								**Table, kitchen or other household articles and parts thereof, of copper; potscourers and scouring or polishing pads, gloves and the like, of copper; sanitary ware and parts thereof, of copper:**
	-餐桌、厨房或其他家用器具及其零件；擦锅器及洗刷擦光用的块垫、手套及类似品：								-Table, kitchen or other household articles and parts thereof; pot scourers and scouring or polishing pads, gloves and the like:
7418.1010	--擦锅器及洗刷、擦光用的块垫、手套及类似品	18	80		9	17	千克	A	--Pot scourers and scouring or polishing pads, gloves and the like
7418.1020	---非电热的铜制家用烹饪器具及其零件	20	80		9	17	千克	A	---Cooking apparatus of a kind used for domestic purposes, non-electric, and parts thereof, of copper
7418.1090[暂]	---其他	18	80	10	9	17	千克	A	---Other
7418.2000[暂]	-卫生器具及其零件	18	80	10	9	17	千克		-Sanitary ware and parts thereof
74.19	**其他铜制品：**								**Other articles of copper:**
7419.1000	-链条及其零件	14	80			17	千克		-Chain and parts thereof
	-其他：								-Other:
	--铸造、模压、冲压或锻造，但未经进一步加工的：								--Cast, moulded, stamped or forged, but not further worked:
7419.9110	---工业用	10	40			17	千克		---For technical use
7419.9190	---其他	20	80		5	17	千克		---Other
	--其他：								--Other:
7419.9920	---铜弹簧	10	40		5	17	千克		---Copper springs
7419.9930	---铜丝制的布（包括环形带）	7	20		5	17	千克		---Cloth（including endless hands），of copper wire
7419.9940	---铜丝制的网、格栅、网眼铜板	8	20		5	17	千克		---Grill and netting, of copper wire; expanded metal, of copper
7419.9950	---非电热的铜制家用供暖器具及其零件	20	80		5	17	千克		---Heating apparatus of a kind used for domestic purposes, non-electric, and parts thereof, of copper
	---其他：								---Other:
7419.9991	----工业用	10	40			17	千克		----For technical use
7419.9999	----其他	20	80		5	17	千克		----Other

第七十五章 镍及其制品

Chapter 75 Nickel and articles thereof

注释：

本章所用有关名词解释如下

一、条、杆

轧、挤、拔或锻制的实心产品，非成卷的，其全长截面均为圆形、椭圆形、矩形（包括正方形）、等边三角形或规则外凸多边形（包括相对两边为弧拱形，另外两边为等长平行直线的“扁圆形”及“变形矩形”）。对于矩形（包括正方形）、三角形或多边形截面的产品，其全长边角可经磨圆。矩形（包括“变形矩形”）截面的产品，其厚度应大于宽度的1/10。所述条、杆也包括同样形状及尺寸的铸造或烧结产品。该产品在铸造或烧结后再经加工（简单剪修或去氧化皮的除外），但不具有其他品目所列制品或产品的特征。

二、型材及异型材

轧、挤、拔、锻制的产品或其他成型产品，不论是否成卷，其全长截面相同，但与条、杆、丝、板、片、带、箔、管的定义不相符合。同时也包括同样形状的铸造或烧结产品。该产品在铸造或烧结后再经加工（简单剪修或去氧化皮的除外），但不具有其他品目所列制品或产品的特征。

三、丝

盘卷的轧、挤或拔制实心产品，其全长截面均为圆形、椭圆形、矩形（包括正方形）、等边三角形或规则外凸多边形（包括相对两边为弧拱形，另外两边为等长平行直线的“扁圆形”及“变形矩形”）。对于矩形（包括正方形）、三角形或多边形截面的产品，其全长边角可经磨圆。矩形（包括“变形矩形”）截面的产品，其厚度应大于宽度的1/10。

四、板、片、带、箔

成卷或非成卷的平面产品（品目75.02的未锻轧产品除外），截面均为厚度相同的实心矩形（不包括正方形），不论边角是否磨圆（包括相对两边为弧拱形，另外两边为等长平行直线的“变形矩形”），并且符合以下规格：

（一）矩形（包括正方形）的，厚度不超过宽度的1/10；

（二）矩形或正方形以外形状的，任何尺寸，但不具有其他品目所列制品或产品的特征。

品目75.06还适用于具有花样（例如，凹槽、肋条形、格槽、珠粒及菱形）的板、片、带、箔、

Chapter Notes:

In this Chapter the following expressions have the meanings hereby assigned to them:

1. Bars and rods

Rolled, extruded, drawn or forged products, not in coils, which have a uniform soild cross-section along their whole length in the shape of circles, ovals, rectangles (including squares), equilateral triangles or regular convex polygons (including “flattened circles” and “modified rectangles”, of which two opposite sides are convex arcs, the other two sides being straight, of equal length and parallel). Products with a rectangular (including square), triangular or polygonal cross-section may have corners rounded along their whole length. The thickness of such products which have a rectangular (including “modified rectangular”) cross-section exceeds one-tenth of the width. The expression also covers cast or sintered products, of the same forms and dimensions, which have been subsequently worked after production (otherwise than by simple trimming or de-scaling), provided that they have not thereby assumed the character of articles or products of other headings.

2. Profiles

Rolled, extruded, drawn, forged or formed products, coiled or not, of a uniform cross-section along their whole length, which do not conform to any of the definitions of bars, rods, wire, plates, sheets, strip, foil, tubes or pipes. The expression also covers cast or sintered products, of the same forms, which have been subsequently worked after production (otherwise than by simple trimming or de-scaling), provided that they have not thereby assumed the character of articles or products of other headings.

3. Wire

Rolled, extruded or drawn products, in coils, which have a uniform soild cross-section along their whole length in the shape of circles, ovals, rectangles (including squares), equilateral triangles or regular convex polygons (including “flattened circles” and “modified rectangles”, of which two opposite sides are convex arcs, the other two sides being straight, of equal length and parallel). Products with a rectangular (including square), triangular or polygonal cross-section may have corners rounded along their whole length. The thickness of such products which have a rectangular (including “modified rectangular”) cross-section exceeds one-tenth of the width.

4. Plates, sheets, strip and foil

Flat-surfaced products (other than the unwrought products of heading 75.02), coiled or not, of soild rectangular (other than square) cross-section with or without rounded corners (including“modified rectangles” of which two opposite sides are convex arcs, the other two sides being straight, of equal length and parallel) of a uniform thickness, which are:

(a) Of rectanglular (including square) shape with a thickness not exceeding one-tenth of the width;

(b) Of a shape other than rectangular or square, of any size, provided that they do not assume the character of articles or products of other headings.

Heading 75.06 applies, inter alia, to plates, sheets, strip and foil with

以及穿孔、抛光、涂层或制成瓦楞形的这类产品，但不具有其他品目所列制品或产品的特征。

五、管

全长截面及管壁厚度相同并只有一个闭合空间的空心产品，成卷或非成卷的，其截面为圆形、椭圆形、矩形（包括正方形）、等边三角形或规则外凸多边形。对于截面为矩形（包括正方形）、等边三角形或规则外凸多边形的产品，不论全长边角是否磨圆，只要其内外截面为同一圆心并为同样形状及同一轴向，也可视为管子。上述截面的管子可经抛光、涂层、弯曲、攻丝、钻孔、缩腰、胀口、成锥形或装法兰、颈圈或套环。

patterns (for example, grooves, ribs, chequers, tears, buttons, lozenges) and to such products which have been perforated, corrugated, polished or coated, provided that they do not thereby assume the character of articles or products of other headings.

5. Tubes and pipes

Hollow products, coiled or not, which have a uniform cross-section with only one enclosed void along their whole length in the shape of circles, ovals, rectangles (including squares), equilateral triangles or regular convex polygons, and which have a uniform wall thickness. Products with a rectangular (including square), equilateral triangular, or regular convex polygonal cross-section, which may have corners rounded along their whole length, are also to be considered as tubes and pipes provided the inner and outer cross-sections are concentric and have the same form and orientation Tubes and pipes of the foregoing cross-sections may be polished, coated, bent, threaded, drilled, waisted, expanded, cone-shaped or fitted with flanges, collars or rings.

子目注释：

一、本章所用有关名词解释如下

（一）非合金镍

按重量计镍及钴的含量至少为99%的金属，但：

1. 按重量计含钴量不超过1.5%；以及
2. 按重量计其他各种元素的含量不超过下表中规定的限量：

其他元素表

元　　素	所含重量百分比
Fe　铁	0.5
O　氧	0.4
其他元素，每种	0.3

（二）镍合金

按重量计含镍量大于其他元素单项含量的金属物质，但：

1. 按重量计含钴量超过1.5%；
2. 按重量计至少有一种其他元素的含量超过上表中规定的限量；或
3. 除镍及钴以外，按重量计其他元素的总含量超过1%。

二、子目7508.10所称“丝”，不受本章注释三的限制，仅适用于截面尺寸不超过6毫米的任何截面形状的产品，不论是否盘卷。

Subheading Notes:

1. In this Chapter the following expressions have the meanings hereby assigned to them:

(a) Nickel, not alloyed

Metal containing by weight at least 99% of nickel plus cobalt, provided that:

(i) the cobalt content by weight does not exceed 1.5%;and

(ii) the content by weight of any other element does not exceed the limit specified in the following table:

TABLE-Other elements

Element	Limiting content% by weight
Fe　Iron	0.5
O　Oxygen	0.4
Other elements, each	0.3

(b) Nickel alloys

Metallic substances in which nickel predominates by weight over each of the other elements provided that:

(i) the content by weight of cobalt exceeds 1.5%;

(ii) the content by weight of at least one of the other elements is greater than the limit specified in the foregoing table; or

(iii) the total content by weight of elements other than nickel plus cobalt exceeds 1%.

2. Notwithstanding the provisions of Chapter Note 3, for the purposes of subheading 7508.10 the term “wire” applies only to products, whether or not in coils, of any cross-sectional shape, of which no cross-sectional dimension exceeds 6mm.

税则号列 Tariff Item	商品名称及备注	进口税率 最惠	普通	暂定	出口退税	增值税率	计量单位	监管条件	Article Description
75.01	镍锍、氧化镍烧结物及镍冶炼的其他中间产品：								**Nickel mattes, nickel oxide sinters and other intermediate products of nickel metallurgy:**
7501.1000 暂	-镍锍	3	11	0		17	千克	4xy	-Nickel mattes
	-氧化镍烧结物及镍冶炼的其他中间产品：								-Nickel oxide sinters and other intermediate products of nickel metallurgy:
7501.2010 暂	---镍湿法冶炼中间品	3	11	0		17	千克	4xy	---Intermediate products of nickel metallurgy by wet process

税则号列 Tariff Item	商品名称及备注	进口税率			出口退税	增值税率	计量单位	监管条件	Article Description
		最惠	普通	暂定					
7501.2090[暂]	---其他	3	11	0		17	千克	4xy	---Other
75.02	**未锻轧镍:**								**Unwrought nickel:**
	-非合金镍:								-Nickel, not alloyed:
7502.1010[暂]	---按重量计镍、钴总量在99.99%及以上的,但钴含量不超过0.005%	3	11	1		17	千克	4xy	---Containing 99.99% or more by total weight of nickel and cobalt, but containing cobalt not exceeding 0.005%
7502.1090[暂]	---其他	3	11	1		17	千克	4xy	---Other
7502.2000	-镍合金	3	11			17	千克	4xy	-Nickel, alloys
75.03	**镍废碎料:**								**Nickel waste and scrap:**
7503.0000[暂]	镍废碎料	1.5	11	1		17	千克	4APxy	Nickel waste and scrap
75.04	**镍粉及片状粉末:**								**Nickel powders and flakes:**
7504.0010	---非合金镍粉及片状粉末	4	17			17	千克	3	---Nickel powders and flakes, not alloyed
7504.0020	---合金镍粉及片状粉末	4	17			17	千克		---Nickel powders and flakes, alloys
75.05	**镍条、杆、型材及异型材或丝:**								**Nickel bars, rods, profiles and wire:**
	-条、杆、型材及异型材:								-Bars， rods and profiles:
7505.1100	--非合金镍制	6	14		5	17	千克		--Of nickel, not alloyed
7505.1200	--镍合金制	6	14		13	17	千克		--Of nickel alloys
	-丝:								-Wire:
7505.2100	--非合金镍制	6	17		5	17	千克		--Of nickel, not alloyed
7505.2200	--镍合金制	6	17		13	17	千克		--Of nickel alloys
75.06	**镍板、片、带、箔:**								**Nickel plates, sheets, strip and foil:**
7506.1000	-非合金镍制	6	14		5	17	千克		-Of nickel, not alloyed
7506.2000	-镍合金制	6	14			17	千克		-Of nickel alloys
75.07	**镍管及管子附件(例如，接头、肘管、管套）：**								**Nickel tubes, pipes and tube or pipe fittings（for example, couplings, elbows,sleeves）:**
	-镍管:								-Tubes and pipes:
7507.1100	--非合金镍制	6	17			17	千克		--Of nickel, not alloyed
7507.1200	--镍合金制	6	17		13	17	千克		--Of nickel alloys
7507.2000	-管子附件	6	17			17	千克		-Tube or pipe fittings
75.08	**其他镍制品:**								**Other articles of nickel:**
	-镍丝布、网及格栅:								-Cloth, grill and netting, of nickel wire:
7508.1010	---镍丝布	6	20			17	千克		---Wire cloth
7508.1080	---其他工业用镍制品	6	40			17	千克		---Other articles of nickel, for technical use
7508.1090	---其他	6	70			17	千克		---Other
	-其他:								-Other:
7508.9010	---电镀用镍阳极	4	14			17	千克		---Electroplating anodes
7508.9080	---其他工业用镍制品	6	40			17	千克		---Other articles of nickel, for technical use
7508.9090	---其他	6	70			17	千克		---Other

第七十六章 铝及其制品

Chapter 76 Aluminium and articles thereof

注释：

本章所用有关名词解释如下：

一、条、杆

轧、挤、拔或锻制的实心产品，非成卷的，其全长截面均为圆形、椭圆形、矩形（包括正方形）、等边三角形或规则外凸多边形（包括相对两边为弧拱形，另外两边为等长平行直线的"扁圆形"及"变形矩形"）。对于矩形（包括正方形）、三角形或多边形截面的产品，其全长边角可经磨圆。矩形（包括"变形矩形"）截面的产品，其厚度应大于宽度的1/10。所述条、杆也包括同样形状及尺寸的铸造或烧结产品。该产品在铸造或烧结后再经加工（简单剪修或去氧化皮的除外），但不具有其他品目所列制品或产品的特征。

二、型材及异型材

轧、挤、拔、锻制的产品或其他成型产品，不论是否成卷，其全长截面相同，但与条、杆、丝、板、片、带、箔、管的定义不相符合。同时也包括同样形状的铸造或烧结产品。该产品在铸造或烧结后再经加工（简单剪修或去氧化皮的除外），但不具有其他品目所列制品或产品的特征。

三、丝

盘卷的轧、挤或拔制实心产品，其全长截面均为圆形、椭圆形、矩形（包括正方形）、等边三角形或规则外凸多边形（包括相对两边为弧拱形，另外两边为等长平行直线的"扁圆形"及"变形矩形"）。对于矩形（包括正方形）、三角形或多边形截面的产品，其全长边角可经磨圆。矩形（包括"变形矩形"）截面的产品，其厚度应大于宽度的1/10。

四、板、片、带、箔

成卷或非成卷的平面产品（品目76.01的未锻轧产品除外），截面均为厚度相同的实心矩形（不包括正方形），不论边角是否磨圆（包括相对两边为弧拱形，另外两边为等长平行直线的"变形矩形"），并且符合以下规格：

（一）矩形（包括正方形）的，厚度不超过宽度的1/10；

（二）矩形或正方形以外形状的，任何尺寸，但不具有其他品目所列制品或产品的特征。

品目76.06和76.07还适用于具有花样（例如，凹槽、肋条形、格槽、珠粒及菱形）的板、片、

Chapter Notes:

In this Chapter the following expressions have the meanings hereby assigned to them:

1. Bars and rods

Rolled, extruded, drawn or forged products, not in coils, which have a uniform solid cross-section along their whole length in the shape of circles, ovals, rectangles (including squares), equilateral triangles or regular convex polygons (including "flattened circles" and "modified rectangles", of which two opposite sides are convex arcs, the other two sides being straight, of equal length and parallel). Products with a rectangular (including square), triangular or polygonal crosssection may have corners rounded along their whole length. The thickness of such products which have a rectangular (including "modified rectangular") cross-section exceeds one-tenth of the width. The expression also covers cast or sintered products, of the same forms and dimensions, which have been subsequently worked after production (otherwise than by simple trimming or de-scaling), provided that they have not thereby assumed the character of articles or products of other headings.

2. Profiles

Rolled, extruded, drawn, forged or formed products, coiled or not, of a uniform cross-section along their whole length, which do not conform to any of the definitions of bars, rods, wire, plates, sheets, strip, foil, tubes or pipes. The expression also covers cast or sintered products, of the same forms, which have been subsequently worked after production (otherwise than by simple trimming or de-scaling), provided that they have not thereby assumed the character of articles or products of other headings.

3. Wire

Rolled, extruded or drawn products, in coils, which have a uniform solid cross-section along their whole length in the shape of circles, ovals, rectangles (including squares), equilateral triangles or regular convex polygons (including "flattened circles" and "modified rectangles", of which two opposite sides are convex arcs, the other two sides being straight, of equal length and parallel). Products with a rectangular (including square), triangular or polygonal cross-section may have corners rounded along their whole length. The thickness of such products which have a rectangular (including "modified rectangular") cross-section exceeds one-tenth of the width.

4. Plates, sheets, strip and foil

Flat-surfaced products (other than the unwrought products of heading 76.01), coiled or not, of solid rectangular (other than square) cross-section with or without rounded corners (including "modified rectangles" of which two opposite sides are convex arcs, the other two sides being straight, of equal length and parallel)of a uniform thickness, which are:

(a) Of rectangular (including square) shape with a thickness not exceeding one-tenth of the width;

(b) Of a shape other than rectangular or square, of any size,provided that they do not assume the character of articles or products of other headings.

Headings 76.06 and 76.07 apply, inter alia, to plates, sheets, strip and

带、箔以及穿孔、抛光、涂层或制成瓦楞形的这类产品，但不具有其他品目所列制品或产品的特征。

五、管

全长截面及管壁厚度相同并只有一个闭合空间的空心产品，成卷或非成卷的，其截面为圆形、椭圆形、矩形（包括正方形）、等边三角形或规则外凸多边形。对于截面为矩形（包括正方形）、等边三角形或规则外凸多边形的产品，不论全长边角是否磨圆，只要其内外截面为同一圆心并为同样形状及同一轴向，也可视为管子。上述截面的管子可经抛光、涂层、弯曲、攻丝、钻孔、缩腰、胀口、成锥形或装法兰、颈圈或套环。

子目注释：

一、本章所用有关名词解释如下：

（一）非合金铝

按重量计含铝量至少为 99%的金属，但其他各种元素的含量不超过下表中规定的限量：

其他元素表

元　素	所含重量百分比
Fe+Si（铁+硅） 其他元素（1），每种	1 0.1（2）

(1)其他元素，例如，铬、铜、镁、锰、镍、锌。
(2)含铜成分可大于 0.1%，但不得大于 0.2%，且铬和锰的含量均不得超过 0.05%。

（二）铝合金

按重量计含铝量大于其他元素单项含量的金属物质，但：

1. 按重量计至少有一种其他元素或铁加硅的含量大于上表中规定的限量；或

2. 按重量计其他元素的总含量超过 1%

二、子目 7616.91 所称"丝"，不受本章注释三的限制，仅适用于截面尺寸不超过 6 毫米的任何截面形状的产品，不论是否盘卷。

foil with patterns（for example, grooves, ribs, chequers, tears,buttons, lozenges）and to such products which have been perforated, corrugat-ed, polished or coated, provided that they do not thereby assume the character of articles or products of other headings.

5. Tubes and pipes

Hollow products, coiled or not, which have a uniform cross-section with only one enclosed void along their whole length in the shape of circles, ovals, rectangles（including squares）, equilateral triangles or regular convex polygons, and which have a uniform wall thickness. Products with a rectangular（including square）, equilateral triangular or regular convex polygonal cross-section, which may have corners rounded along their whole length, are also to be considered as tubes and pipes provided the inner and outer cross-sections are concentric and have the same form and orientation. Tubes and pipes of the foregoing cross-sections may be polished, coated, bent, threaded, drilled, waisted, expanded, cone-shaped or fitted with flanges, collars or rings.

Subheading Notes:

1. In this Chapter the following expressions have the meanings hereby assigned to them:

（a）Aluminum, not alloyed

Metal containing by weight at least 99% of aluminium,provided that the content by weight of any other element does not exceed the limit specified in the following table:

TABLE - Other elements

Element	Limiting content%by weight
Fe+Si（iron plus silicon） Other elements（1）, each	1 0.1（2）

（1）Other elements are, for example, Cr, Cu, Mg, Mn,Ni, Zn.
（2）Copper is permitted in a proportion greater than 0.1% but not more than 0.2%, provided that neither the chromium nor manganese content exceeds 0.05 %.

（b）Aluminum alloys

Metallic substances in which aluminium predominates by weight over each of the other elements, provided that:

（i）The content by weight of at least one of the other elements or of iron plus silicon taken together is greater than the limit specified in the foregoing table; or

（ii）The total content by weight of such other elements exceeds 1%.

2. Notwithstanding the provisions of Chapter Note 3, for the purposes of subheading 7616.91 the term "wire" applies only to products,whether or not in coils, of any cross-sectional shape, of which no cross-sectional dimension exceeds 6 mm.

税则号列 Tariff Item	商品名称及备注	进口税率			出口退税	增值税率	计量单位	监管条件	Article Description
		最惠	普通	暂定					
76.01	**未锻轧铝:**								**Unwrought aluminum:**
	-非合金铝:								-Aluminium, not alloyed:
7601.1010	---按重量计含铝量在99.95%及以上	5	14			17	千克		---Containing by weight 99.95% or more of aluminium
7601.1090[暂]	---其他（电解铝）	5	14	0		17	千克		---Other（electrolytic aluminium）
7601.2000	-铝合金	7	14			17	千克		-Aluminium alloys
76.02	**铝废碎料:**								**Aluminium waste and scrap:**
7602.0000[暂]	铝废碎料	1.5	14	0		17	千克		Aluminium waste and scrap
7602 0000.10[暂]	以回收铝为主的废电线等(包括废电线、电缆、五金电器)	1.5	14	0		17	千克	AP	Waste electric machines mainly for recyclinging aluminium, including waste wires, cables, hardware and electric appliance
7602 0000.90[暂]	其他铝废碎料	1.5	14	0		17	千克	AP	Aluminium waste and scrap
76.03	**铝粉及片状粉末:**								**Aluminium powders and flakes:**
7603.1000	-非片状粉末	6	30			17	千克		-Powders of non-lamellar structure
7603 1000.10	颗粒＜500微米的微细球形铝粉（颗粒均匀，铝含量≥97%）	6	30			17	千克	3A	Microspherical aluminium powder, granularity below 500μm, containing 97% or more by weight of aluminium
7603 1000.90	其他非片状铝粉	6	30			17	千克	AB	Other powders of non-lamellar structure, of aluminium
7603.2000	-片状铝粉末	7	30			17	千克		-Powders of lamellar structure; flakes
76.04	**铝条、杆、型材及异型材:**								**Aluminium bars, rods and profiles:**
	-非合金铝制:								-Of aluminium, not alloyed:
7604.1010	---铝条、杆	5	30			17	千克		---Bars and rods
7604.1090	---其他	5	30			17	千克		---Other
	-铝合金制:								--Of aluminium alloys:
7604.2100	--空心异型材	5	30		13	17	千克	A	--Hollow profiles
	--其他:								--Other:
7604.2910	---铝合金条、杆	5	30			17	千克		---Bars and rods
7604 2910.11	柱形实心体铝合金[在293K(20摄氏度)时的极限抗拉强度能达到460兆帕（0.46×10^9牛顿/平方米)或更大(截面周长≥210毫米）]	5	30			17	千克	3A	Solid aluminum alloy in column-shaped [tensile strength reaches at least 460 mega-P (0.46* 10^9Newton/m^2) at 293K (20 degree centigrade), perimeter of section is greater or equal to 210mm]
7604 2910.19	柱形实心体铝合金[在293K(20摄氏度)时的极限抗拉强度能达到460兆帕（0.46×10^9牛顿/平方米)或更大(截面周长＜210毫米）]	5	30			17	千克	3A	Solid aluminum alloy in column-shaped [tensile strength reaches at least 460 mega-P(0.46* 10^9Newton/ m^2) at 293K (20 degree centigrade) perimeter of section is less than 210mm]
7604 2910.91	其他铝合金制条、杆(截面周长≥210毫米)	5	30			17	千克	A	Other bars,rods and profiles,of aluminium alloys(perimeter of section is greater or equal to 210mm)
7604 2910.99	其他铝合金制条、杆(截面周长＜210毫米)	5	30			17	千克	A	Other bars,rods and profiles,of aluminium alloys(perimeter of section is less than 210mm)
7604.2990	---其他	5	30		13	17	千克	A	---Other
76.05	**铝丝:**								**Aluminium wire:**
	-非合金铝制:								-Of aluminium, not alloyed:
7605.1100	--最大截面尺寸超过7毫米	8	17			17	千克		--Of which the maximum cross-sectional dimension exceeding 7 mm
7605.1900	--其他	8	17			17	千克		--Other
	-铝合金制:								-Of aluminium alloys:
7605.2100	--最大截面尺寸超过7毫米	8	17			17	千克		--Of which the maximum cross-sectional dimension exceeding 7 mm
7605.2900	--其他	8	17			17	千克		--Other
76.06	**铝板、片及带，厚度超过0.2毫米:**								**Aluminium plates, sheets and strip, of a thickness exceeding 0.2 mm:**
	-矩形（包括正方形）:								-Rectangular（including square）:
	--非合金铝制:								--Of aluminium, not alloyed:

税则号列 Tariff Item	商品名称及备注	进口税率 最惠	普通	暂定	出口退税	增值税率	计量单位	监管条件	Article Description
	---厚度在0.30毫米及以上,但不超过0.36毫米:								---Of a thickness of 0.30 mm or more but not exceeding 0.36 mm:
7606.1121	----铝塑复合的	6	50		13	17	千克	A	----Aluminium-plastic composite
7606.1129 暂	----其他	6	50	4	13	17	千克	A	----Other
	---其他:								---Other:
7606.1191	----铝塑复合的	6	30		13	17	千克	A	----Aluminium-plastic composite
7606.1199	----其他	6	30		13	17	千克	A	----Other
	--铝合金制:								--Of aluminium alloys:
7606.1220	---厚度小于0.28毫米	6	30		13	17	千克	A	---Of a thickness less than 0.28mm
7606.1230	---厚度在0.28毫米及以上,但不超过0.35毫米	6	30		13	17	千克	A	---Of a thickness of 0.28mm or more but not exceeding 0.35mm
	---厚度在0.35毫米以上,但不超过4毫米:								---Of a thickness more than 0.35mm but not exceeding 4mm:
7606.1251	----铝塑复合的	6	50		13	17	千克	A	----Aluminium-plastic composite
7606.1259	----其他	6	50		13	17	千克	A	----Other
7606.1290	---其他	6	50		13	17	千克	A	---Other
	-其他:								-Other:
7606.9100	--非合金铝制	6	30		13	17	千克		--Of aluminium, not alloyed
7606.9200	--铝合金制	10	30		13	17	千克	A	--Of aluminium alloys
76.07	**铝箔(不论是否印花或用纸、纸板、塑料或类似材料衬背),厚度(衬背除外)不超过0.2毫米:**								**Aluminium foil (whether or not printed or backed with paper, paperboard, plastics or similar backing materials) of a thickness (excluding any backing) not exceeding 0.2 mm:**
	-无衬背:								-Not backed:
	--轧制后未经进一步加工的:								--Rolled but not further worked:
7607.1110	---厚度不超过0.007毫米	6	35		15	17	千克		---Of a thickness not exceeding 0.007mm
7607.1120	---厚度大于0.007毫米,但不超过0.01毫米	6	35		15	17	千克		---Of a thickness exceeding 0.007mm but not exceeding 0.01mm
7607.1190	---其他	6	35		15	17	千克		---Other
7607.1900	--其他	6	35		15	17	千克		--Other
7607 1900.01 暂	化成箔(厚度≤0.2毫米)	6	35	3	15	17	千克		Formed foils (thickness not exceeding 0.2 mm)
7607 1900.90	其他无衬背铝箔(厚度≤0.2毫米)	6	35		15	17	千克		Other aluminum foils, not backed (thickness not exceeding 0.2 mm)
7607.2000	-有衬背	6	35		15	17	千克		-Backed
76.08	**铝管:**								**Aluminium tubes and pipes:**
7608.1000	-非合金铝制	8	30		13	17	千克		-Of aluminium, not alloyed
	-铝合金制:								-Of aluminium alloys:
7608.2010	---外径不超过10厘米的	8	30		13	17	千克		---Having an outside diameter not exceeding 10cm
7608 2010.10	外径≤10厘米的管状铝合金[在293K(20摄氏度)时的极限抗拉强度能达到460兆帕(0.46×109牛顿/平方米)或更大]	8	30		13	17	千克	3A	Tubes and pipes of aluminum alloy, of an outside diameter not exceeding 10cm,tensile strength reaches 460 mega-P (0.46*10^9Newton/ m^2) or more at 293K (20 degree centigrade), of an outside diameter more than 10cm
7608 2010.90	外径≤10厘米的其他合金制铝管	8	30		13	17	千克	A	Tubes and pipes of other aluminum alloy, of an outside diameter not exceeding 10cm
	---其他:								---Other:
7608.2091	----壁厚不超过25毫米	8	30		13	17	千克		----Having a wall thickness not exceeding 25mm
7608 2091.10	外径>10厘米,壁厚度≤25毫米的管状铝合金[在293K(20摄氏度)时的极限抗拉强度能达到460兆帕(0.46×10^9牛顿/平方米)或更大]	8	30		13	17	千克	3A	Tubes and pipes of aluminum alloy, of an outside diameter more than 10cm, and of an wall thickness not exceeding 25mm,tensile strength reaches 460 mega-P (0.46*10^9Newton/ m^2) or more at 293K (20 degree centigrade), of an outside diameter more than 10cm
7608 2091.90	外径>10厘米,壁厚度≤25毫米的其他合金制铝管	8	30		13	17	千克	A	Tubes and pipes of other aluminum alloy, of an outside diameter more than 10cm, of an wall thickness not exceeding 25mm
7608.2099	----其他	8	30		13	17	千克		----Other

税则号列 Tariff Item	商品名称及备注	进口税率 最惠	普通	暂定	出口退税	增值税率	计量单位	监管条件	Article Description
7608 2099.10	外径＞10厘米，其他管状铝合金[在293K(20摄氏度)时的极限抗拉强度能达到460兆帕(0.46×109牛顿/平方米)或更大]	8	30		13	17	千克	3A	Tubes and pipes of other aluminum alloy, tensile strength reaches 460 mega-P (0.46*10^{9}Newton/ m^2) or more at 293K (20 degree centigrade), of an outside diameter more than 10cm
7608 2099.90	外径＞10厘米，其他合金制铝管	8	30		13	17	千克	A	Tubes and pipes of other aluminium alloys, of an outside diameter more than 10cm
76.09	**铝制管子附件(例如，接头、肘管、管套)：**								**Aluminium tube or pipe fittings（for example, couplings, elbows, sleeves）:**
7609.0000	铝制管子附件(例如，接头、肘管、管套)	8	35		13	17	千克		Aluminium tube or pipe fittings（for example, couplings, elbows, sleeves）
76.10	**铝制结构体(品目94.06的活动房屋除外)及其部件(例如，桥梁及桥梁体段、塔、格构杆、屋顶、屋顶框架、门窗及其框架、门槛、栏杆、支柱及立柱)；上述结构体用的已加工铝板、杆、型材、异型材、管子及类似品：**								**Aluminium structures（excluding prefabricated buildings of heading No. 94.06）and parts of structures（for example,bridges and bridge-sections, towers, lattice masts, roofs, roofing frameworks, doors and windows and their frames and thresholds for doors, balustrades, pillars and columns）; aluminium plates, rods profiles, tubes and the like, prepared for use in structures:**
7610.1000	-门窗及其框架、门槛	25	80		13	17	千克		-Doors, windows and their frames and thresholds for doors
7610.9000	-其他	6	50		13	17	千克		-Other
76.11	**盛装物料用的铝制囤、柜、罐、桶及类似容器(装压缩气体或液化气体的除外)，容积超过300升，不论是否衬里或隔热，但无机械或热力装置：**								**Aluminium reservoirs, tanks, vats and similar containers, for any material（other than compressed or liquefied gas）, of a capacity exceeding 300L, whether or not lined or heat-insulated, but not fitted with mechanical or thermal equipment:**
7611.0000	盛装物料用的铝制囤、柜、罐、桶及类似容器(装压缩气体或液化气体的除外)，容积超过300升，不论是否衬里或隔热，但无机械或热力装置	12	35		13	17	千克		Aluminium reservoirs, tanks, vats and similar containers, for any material（other than compressed or liquefied gas）, of a capacity exceeding 300L, whether or not lined or heat-insulated, but not fitted with mechanical or thermal equipment
76.12	**盛装物料用的铝制桶、罐、听、盒及类似容器，包括软管容器及硬管容器(装压缩气体或液化气体的除外)，容积不超过300升，不论是否衬里或隔热，但无机械或热力装置：**								**Aluminium casks, drums, cans, boxes and similar containers（including rigid or collapsible tubular containers）, for any material（other than compressed or liquefied gas）, of a capacity not exceeding 300L, whether or not lined or heat-insulated, but not fitted with mechanical or thermal equipment:**
7612.1000	-软管容器	12	50		13	17	千克		-Collapsible tubular containers
	-其他：								-Other:
7612.9010	---易拉罐及罐体	30	100		13	17	千克	A	---Tear tab ends and bodies thereof
7612.9090	---其他	12	70		13	17	千克		---Other
76.13	**装压缩气体或液化气体用的铝制容器：**								**Aluminium containers for compressed or liquefied gas:**
7613.0010	---零售包装用	12	70		13	17	千克		---For retail packing
7613.0090	---其他	6	17		13	17	千克	6	---Other
76.14	**非绝缘的铝制绞股线、缆、编带及类似品：**								**Stranded wire, cables, plaited bands and the like, of aluminium, not electrically insulated:**
7614.1000	-带钢芯的	6	20		13	17	千克	A	-With steel core
7614.9000	-其他	6	20		13	17	千克		-Other
76.15	**餐桌、厨房或其他家用铝制器具及其零件；铝制擦锅器、洗刷擦光用的块垫、手套及类似品；铝制卫生器具及其零件：**								**Table, kitchen or other household articles and parts thereof, of aluminium; pot scourers and scouring or polishing pads, gloves and the like, of aluminum; sanitary ware and parts thereof, of aluminium:**

税则号列 Tariff Item	商品名称及备注	进口税率			出口退税	增值税率	计量单位	监管条件	Article Description
		最惠	普通	暂定					
	-餐桌、厨房或其他家用器具及其零件;擦锅器及洗刷擦光用的块垫、手套及类似品:								-Table, kitchen or other household articles and parts thereof; pot scourers and scouring or polishing pads, gloves and the like:
7615.1010	--擦锅器、洗刷、擦光用的块垫、手套及类似品	18	90		13	17	千克	A	--Pot scourers and scouring or polishing pads, gloves and the like
7615.1090[暂]	--其他	15	90	10	13	17	千克		--Other
7615 1090.10[暂]	铝制高压锅	15	90	10	13	17	千克	AB	Pressure cooker, of aluminum
7615 1090.90[暂]	其他餐桌、厨房等家用铝制器具及其零件	15	90	10	13	17	千克	A	Table, kitchen or other household articles and parts thereof, of aluminum
7615.2000	-卫生器具及其零件	18	90		13	17	千克		-Sanitary ware and parts thereof
76.16	**其他铝制品:**								**Other articles of aluminium:**
7616.1000	-钉、平头钉、U形钉(品目83.05的货品除外)、螺钉、螺栓、螺母、钩头螺钉、铆钉、销、开尾销、垫圈及类似品	10	40		13	17	千克		-Nails, tacks, staples（other than those of heading No. 83.05）, screws, bolts, nuts, screw hooks, rivets, cotters, cotter-pins, washers and similar articles
	-其他:								-Other:
7616.9100	--铝丝制的布、网、篱及格栅	10	40		13	17	千克		--Cloth, grill, netting and fencing, of aluminium wire
	--其他:								--Other:
7616.9910	---工业用	10	40		13	17	千克		---For technical use
7616 9910.10	高度小于直径的柱形实心体铝合金[在293K(20摄氏度)时的权限抗拉强度能达到460兆帕(0.46×10^9牛顿/平方米)或更大]	10	40		13	17	千克	3	Solid aluminum alloy in column-shaped, tensile strength reaches 460 mega-P (0.46*10^9Newton/ m^2) or more at 293K (20 degree centigrade), of an height less than diameter
7616 9910.90	其他工业用铝制品(不包括铝丝布、网、格栅及栅栏)	10	40		13	17	千克		Other articles of aluminium, for technical use, excluding cloth, grill, netting and fencing, of aluminium wire
7616.9990	---其他	15	80		13	17	千克		---Other

第七十八章
铅及其制品

注释：

本章所用有关名词解释如下：

一、条、杆

轧、挤、拔或锻制的实心产品，非成卷的，其全长截面均为圆形、椭圆形、矩形（包括正方形）、等边三角形或规则外凸多边形（包括相对两边为弧拱形，另外两边为等长平行直线的"扁圆形"及"变形矩形"）。对于矩形（包括正方形）、三角形或多边形截面的产品，其全长边角可经磨圆。矩形（包括"变形矩形"）截面的产品，其厚度应大于宽度的 1/10。所述条、杆也包括同样形状及尺寸的铸造或烧结产品。该产品在铸造或烧结后再经加工（简单剪修或去氧化皮的除外），但不具有其他品目所列制品或产品的特征。

二、型材及异型材

轧、挤、拔、锻制的产品或其他成型产品，不论是否成卷，其全长截面相同，但与条、杆、丝、板、片、带、箔、管的定义不相符合。同时也包括同样形状的铸造或烧结产品。该产品在铸造或烧结后再经加工（简单剪修或去氧化皮的除外），但不具有其他品目所列制品或产品的特征。

三、丝

盘卷的轧、挤或拔制实心产品，其全长截面均为圆形、椭圆形、矩形（包括正方形）、等边三角形或规则外凸多边形（包括相对两边为弧拱形，另外两边为等长平行直线的"扁圆形"及"变形矩形"）。对于矩形（包括正方形）、三角形或多边形截面的产品，其全长边角可经磨圆。矩形（包括"变形矩形"）截面的产品，其厚度应大于宽度的 1/10。

四、板、片、带、箔

成卷或非成卷的平面产品（品目 78.01 的未锻轧产品除外），截面均为厚度相同的实心矩形（不包括正方形），不论边角是否磨圆（包括相对两边为孤拱形，另外两边为等长平行直线的"变形矩形"），并且符合以下规格：

（一）矩形（包括正方形）的，厚度不超过宽度的 1/10；

（二）矩形或正方形以外形状的，任何尺寸，但不具有其他品目所列制品或产品的特征。

品目 78.04 还适用于具有花样（例如，凹槽、

Chapter 78
Lead and articles thereof

Chapter Notes:

In this chapter the following expressions have the meanings hereby assigned to them:

1. Bars and rods

Rolled, extruded, drawn or forged products, not in coils, which have a uniform solid cross-section along their whole length in the shape of circles, ovals, rectangles (including squares), equilateral triangles or regular convex polygons (including "flattened circles" and "modified rectangles", of which two opposite sides are convex arcs, the other two sides being straight, of equal length and parallel). Products with a rectangular (including square), triangular or polygonal cross-section may have corners rounded along their whole length. The thickness of such products which have a rectangular (including "modified rectangular") cross-section exceeds one-tenth of the width. The expression also covers cast or sintered products, of the same forms and dimensions, which have been subsequently worked after production (otherwise than by simple trimming or de-scaling), provided that they have not thereby assumed the character of articles or products of other headings.

2. Profiles

Rolled, extruded, drawn, forged or formed products, coiled or not, of a uniform cross-section along their whole length, which do not conform to any of the definitions of bars, rods, wire, plates, sheets, strip, foil, tubes or pipes. The expression also covers cast or sintered products, of the same forms, which have been subsequently worked after production (otherwise than by simple trimming or de-scaling), provided that they have not thereby assumed the character of articles or products of other headings.

3. Wire

Rolled, extruded or drawn products, in coils, which have a uniform solid cross-section along their whole length in the shape of circles, ovals, rectangles (including squares), equilateral triangles or regular convex polygons (including "flattened circles" and "modified rectangles", of which two opposite sides are convex arcs, the other two sides being straight, of equal length and parallel). Products with a rectangular (including square), triangular or polygonal cross-section may have corners rounded along their whole length. The thickness of such products which have a rectangular (including "modified rectangular") cross-section exceeds one-tenth of the width.

4. Plates, sheets, strip and foil

Flat-surfaced products (other than the unwrought products of heading 78.01), coiled or not, of solid rectangular (other than square) cross-section with or without rounded corners (including "modified rectangles" of which two opposite sides are convex arcs, the other two sides being straight, of equal length and parallel) of a uniform thickness, which are:

(a) Of rectangular (including square) shape with a thickness not exceeding one-tenth of the width;

(b) Of a shape other than rectangular or square, of any size, provided that they do not assume the character of articles or products of other headings.

Heading 78.04 applies, inter alia, to plates, sheets, strip and foil with patterns (for example, grooves, ribs, chequers, tears, buttons, lozenges) and to such products which have been perforated, corrugated, polished

肋条形、格槽、珠粒及菱形）的板、片、带、箔以及穿孔、抛光、涂层或制成瓦楞形的这类产品，但不具有其他品目所列制品或产品的特征。

五、管

全长截面及管壁厚度相同并只有一个闭合空间的实心产品，成卷或非成卷的，其截面为圆形、椭圆形、矩形（包括正方形）、等边三角形或规则外凸多边形。对于截面为矩形（包括正方形）、等边三角形或规则外凸多边形的产品，不论全长边角是否磨圆，只要其内外截面为同一圆心并为同样形状及同一轴向，也可视为管子。上述截面的管子可经抛光、涂层、弯曲、攻丝、钻孔、缩腰、胀口、成锥形或装法兰、颈圈或套环。

子目注释：

本章所称“精炼铅”，是指：

按重量计含铅量至少为 99.9%的金属，但其他各种元素的含量不超过下表中规定的限量：

其他元素表

元　素	所含重量百分比
Ag 银	0.02
As 砷	0.005
Bi 铋	0.05
Ca 钙	0.002
Cd 镉	0.002
Cu 铜	0.08
Fe 铁	0.002
S 硫	0.002
Sb 锑	0.005
Sn 锡	0.005
Zn 锌	0.002
其他（例如碲），每种	0.001

or coated, provided that they do not thereby assume the character of articles or products of other headings.

5. Tubes and pipes

Hollow products, coiled or not, which have a uniform cross-section with only one enclosed void along their whole length in the shape of circles, ovals, rectangles (including squares), equilateral triangles or regular convex polygons, and which have a uniform wall thickness. Products with a rectangular (including square), equilateral triangular or regular convex polygonal cross-section, which may have corners rounded along their whole length, are also to be considered as tubes and pipes provided the inner and outer cross-sections are concentric and have the same form and orientation. Tubes and pipes of the foregoing cross-sections may be polished, coated, bent, threaded, drilled, waisted, expanded, cone-shaped or fitted with flanges, collars or rings.

Subheading Note:

In this Chapter the expression “refined lead” means:

Metal containing by weight at least 99.9% of lead, provided that the content by weight of any other element does not exceed the limit specified in the following table:

TABLE-Other elements

Element	Limiting content%by weight
Ag Silver	0.02
As Arsenic	0.005
Bi Bismuth	0.05
Ca Calcium	0.002
Cd Cadmium	0.002
Cu Copper	0.08
Fe Iron	0.002
S Sulphur	0.002
Sb Antimony	0.005
Sn Tin	0.005
Zn Zinc	0.002
Other(for example Te),each	0.001

税则号列 Tariff Item	商品名称及备注	进口税率 最惠	普通	暂定	出口退税	增值税率	计量单位	监管条件	Article Description
78.01	**未锻轧铅：**								**Unwrought lead:**
7801.1000	-精炼铅	3	20			17	千克		-Refined lead
	-其他：								-Other:
7801.9100	--按重量计所含其他元素是以锑为主的	3	20			17	千克		--Containing by weight antimony as the principal other element
7801.9900	--其他	3	20			17	千克		--Other
78.02	**铅废碎料：**								**Lead waste and scrap:**
7802.0000	铅废碎料	1.5	10			17	千克	9	Lead waste and scrap
78.04	**铅板、片、带、箔；铅粉及片状粉末：**								**Lead plates, sheets, strip and foil; lead powders and flakes:**
	-板、片、带、箔：								-Plates, sheets, strip and foil:
7804.1100	--片、带及厚度（衬背除外）不超过 0.2 毫米的箔	6	30		5	17	千克		--Sheets, strip and foil of a thickness (excluding any backing)not exceeding 0.2 mm
7804.1900	--其他	6	30			17	千克		--Other
7804.2000	-粉末及片状粉末	6	35			17	千克		-Powders and flakes
78.06	**其他铅制品：**								**Other articles of lead:**
7806.0010	---铅条、杆、型材及异型材或丝	6	30			17	千克		---Lead bars, rods, profiles and wire
7806.0090	---其他	6	40			17	千克		---Other

第七十九章 锌及其制品

注释：

本章所用名词解释如下：

一、条、杆

轧、挤、拔或锻制的实心产品，非成卷的，其全长截面均为圆形、椭圆形、矩形（包括正方形）、等边三角形或规则外凸多边形（包括相对两边孤拱形，另外两边为等长平行直线的“扁圆形”及“变形矩形”）。对于矩形（包括正方形）、三角形或多边形截面的产品，其全长边角可经磨圆。矩形（包括“变形矩形”）截面的产品，其厚度应大于宽度的 1/10。所述条、杆也包括同样形状及尺寸的铸造或烧结产品。该产品在铸造烧结后再经加工（简单剪修或去氧化皮的除外），但不具有其他品目所列制品或产品的特征。

二、型材及异型材

轧、挤、拔、锻制的产品或其他成型产品，不论是否成卷，其全长截面相同，但与条、杆、丝、板、片、带、箔、管的定义不相符合。同时也包括同样形状的铸造或烧结产品。该产品在铸造或烧结后再经加工（简单剪修或去氧化皮的除外），但不具有其他品目所列制品或产品的特征。

三、丝

盘卷的轧、挤或拔制实心产品，其全长截面均为圆形、椭圆形、矩形（包括正方形）、等边三角形或规则外凸多边形（包括相对两边为弧拱形，另外两边为等长平行直线的“扁圆形”及“变形矩形”）。对于矩形（包括正方形）、三角形或多边形截面的产品，其全长边角可经磨圆。矩形（包括“变形矩形”）截面的产品，其厚度应大于宽度的 1/10。

四、板、片、带、箔

成卷或非成卷的平面产品（品目 79.01 的未锻轧产品除外），截面均为厚度相同的实心矩形（不包括正方形），不论边角是否磨圆（包括相对两边为弧拱形，另外两边为等长平行直线的“变形矩形”），并且符合以下规格：

（一）矩形（包括正方形）的，厚度不超过宽度的 1/10；

（二）矩形或正方形以外形状的，任何尺寸，但不具有其他品目所列制品或产品的特征。

品目 79.05 还适用于具有花样（例如，凹槽、肋条形、格槽、珠粒及菱形）的板、片、带、

Chapter 79 Zinc and articles thereof

Chapter Notes:

In this Chapter the following expressions have the meanings hereby assigned to them:

1. Bar and rods

Rolled, extruded, drawn or forged products, not in coils, which have a uniform solid cross-section along their whole length in the shape of circles, ovals, rectangles（including squares）, equilateral triangles or regular convex polygons（including “flattened circles” and “modified rectangles”, of which two opposite sides are convex arcs, the other two sides being straight, of equal length and parallel). Products with a rectangular（including square）, triangular or polygonal cross-section may have corners rounded along their whole length. The thickness of such products which have a rectangular（including “modified rectangular”） cross-section exceeds one-tenth of the width. The expression also covers cast or sintered products, of the same forms and dimensions, which have been subsequently worked after production（otherwise than by simple trimming or descaling）, provided that they have not thereby assumed the character of articles or products of other headings.

2. Profiles

Rolled, extruded, drawn, forged or formed products, coiled or not,of a uniform cross-section along their whole length, which do not conform to any of the definitions of bars, rods, wire, plates, sheets, strip, foil, tubes or pipes. The expression also covers cast or sintered products, of the same forms, which have been subsequently worked after production（otherwise than by simple trimming or de-scaling）, provided that they have not thereby assumed the character of articles or products of other headings.

3. Wire

Rolled, extruded or drawn products, in coils, which have a uniform solid cross-section along their whole length in the shape of circles, ovals, rectangles（including squares）, equilateral triangles or regular convex polygons（including “flattened circles” and “modified rectangles”, of which two opposite sides are convex arcs, the other two sides being straight, of equal length and parallel）. Products with a rectangular（including square）, triangular or polygonal cross-section may have corners rounded along their whole length. The thickness of such products which have a rectangular（including “modified rectangular”）cross-section exceeds one-tenth of the width.

4. Plates, sheets, strip and foil

Flat-surfaced products（other than the unwrought products of heading 79.01）, coiled or not, of solid rectangular（other than square）cross-section with or without rounded corners （includeing “modified rectangles” of which two opposite sides are convex arcs, the other two sides being straight, of equal length and parallel）of a uniform thickness, which are:

（a）Of rectangular（including square）shape with a thickness not exceeding one-tenth of the width;

（b）Of a shape other than rectangular or square, of any size, provided that they do not assume the character of articles or products of other headings.

Heading 79.05 applies, inter alia, to plates, sheets, strip and foil with

箔以及穿孔、抛光、涂层或制成瓦楞形的这类产品，但不具有其他品目所列制品或产品的特征。

五、管

全长截面及管壁厚度相同并只有一个闭合空间的空心产品，成卷或非成卷的，其截面为圆形、椭圆形、矩形（包括正方形）、等边三角形或规则外凸多边形。对于截面为矩形（包括正方形）、等边三角形或规则外凸多边形的产品，不论全长边角是否磨圆，只要其内外截面为同一圆心并为同样形状及同一轴向，也可视为管子。上述截面的管子可经抛光、涂层、弯曲、攻丝、钻孔、缩腰、胀口、成锥形或装法兰、颈圈或套环。

patterns (for example, grooves, ribs, chequers, tears, buttons, lozenges) and to such products which have been perforated, corrugated, polished or coated, provided that they do not thereby assume the character of articles or products of other headings.

5.Tubes and pipes

Hollow products, coiled or not, which have a uniform cross-section with only one enclosed void along their whole length in the shape of circles, ovals, rectangles (including squares), equilateral triangles or regular convex polygons, and which have a uniform wall thickness. Products with a rectangular (including square), equilateral triangular or regular convex polygonal cross-section, which may have corners rounded along their whole length, are also to be considered as tubes and pipes provided the inner and outer cross-sections are concentric and have the same form and orientation. Tubes and pipes of the foregoing cross-sections may be polished, coated, bent, threaded,drilled, waisted, expanded, cone-shaped or fitted with flanges,collars or rings.

子目注释：

本章所用有关名词解释如下：

一、非合金锌

按重量计含锌量至少为97.5%的金属。

二、锌合金

按重量计含锌量大于其他元素单项含量的金属物质，但按重量计其他元素的总含量超过2.5%。

三、锌末

冷凝锌雾所得的锌末。该产品由球形微粒组成，比锌粉更为精细，按重量计至少80%的微粒可以通过孔径为63微米的筛子，而且必须含有按重量计至少为85%的金属锌。

Subheading Notes:

In this Chapter the following expressions have the meanings hereby assigned to them:

1. Zinc, not alloyed

Metal containing by weight at least 97.5% of zinc.

2. Zinc alloys

Metallic substances in which zinc predominates by weight over each of the other elements, provided that the total content by weight of such other elements exceeds 2.5%.

3. Zinc dust

Dust obtained by condensation of zinc vapour, consisting of spherical particles which are finer than zinc powders. At least 80% by weight of the particles pass through a sieve with 63 micrometers (microns) mesh. It must contain at least 85%by weight of metallic zinc.

税则号列 Tariff Item	商品名称及备注	进口税率			出口退税	增值税率	计量单位	监管条件	Article Description
		最惠	普通	暂定					
79.01	**未锻轧锌：**								**Unwrought zinc:**
	-非合金锌：								-Zinc, not alloyed:
	--按重量计含锌量在99.99%及以上：								--Containing by weight 99.99% or more of zinc:
7901.1110[暂]	---按重量计含锌量在99.995%及以上	3	20	1		17	千克		---Containing by weight 99.995% or more of zinc
7901.1190[暂]	---其他	3	20	1		17	千克		---Other
7901.1200[暂]	--按重量计含锌量低于99.99%	3	20	1		17	千克		--Containing by weight less than 99.99% of zinc
7901.2000[暂]	-锌合金	3	20	1		17	千克		-Zinc alloys
79.02	**锌废碎料：**								**Zinc waste and scrap:**
7902.0000[暂]	锌废碎料	1.5	20	1		17	千克	AP	Zinc waste and scrap
79.03	**锌末、锌粉及片状粉末：**								**Zinc dust, powders and flakes:**
7903.1000	-锌末	6	20			17	千克	A	-Zinc dust
7903.9000	-其他	6	20			17	千克		-Other
7903 9000.10	颗粒＜500微米的锌及其合金（含量≥97%，不论球形、椭球体、雾化、片状、研碎金属燃料）	6	20			17	千克	3A	Zinc and its alloys, granularity＜500μm (containing by weight 97% or more of zinc, whether spheroid, ellipsoid, atomized, flake formed, crush metal fuel)
7903 9000.90	其他锌粉及片状粉末	6	20			17	千克	AB	Other zinc powders and flakes
79.04	**锌条、杆、型材及异型材或丝：**								**Zinc bars, rods, profiles and wire:**
7904.0000	锌条、杆、型材及异型材或丝	6	30			17	千克		Zinc bars, rods, profiles and wire
79.05	**锌板、片、带、箔：**								**Zinc plates, sheets, strip and foil:**
7905.0000	锌板、片、带、箔	6	30			17	千克		Zinc plates, sheets, strip and foil
79.07	**其他锌制品：**								**Other articles of zinc:**

税则号列 Tariff Item	商品名称及备注	进口税率			出口退税	增值税率	计量单位	监管条件	Article Description
		最惠	普通	暂定					
7907.0020	---锌管及锌制管子附件(例如,接头、肘管、管套)	6	30			17	千克		---Zinc tubes,pipes and tube or pipe fittings (for example couplings, elbows, sleeves)
7907.0030	---电池壳体坯料(锌饼)	6	40			17	千克		---Cellpacking blanks (zinc biscuits)
7907.0090	---其他	6	40			17	千克		---Other

第八十章
锡及其制品

注释：

本章所用有关名词解释如下：

一、条、杆

轧、挤、拔或锻制的实心产品，非成卷的，其全长截面均为圆形、椭圆形、矩形（包括正方形）、等边三角形或规则外凸多边形（包括相对两边为弧拱形，另外两边为等长平行直线的"扁圆形"及"变形矩形"）。对于矩形（包括正方形）、三角形或多边形截面的产品，其全长边角可经磨圆。矩形（包括"变形矩形"）截面的产品，其厚度应大于宽度的1/10。所述条、杆也包括同样形状及尺寸的铸造或烧结产品。该产品在铸造或烧结后再经加工（简单剪修或去氧化皮的除外），但不具有其他品目所列制品或产品的特征。

二、型材及异型材

轧、挤、拔、锻制的产品或其他成型产品，不论是否成卷，其全长截面相同，但与条、杆、丝、板、片、带、箔、管的定义不相符合。同时也包括同样形状的铸造或烧结产品。该产品在铸造或烧结后再经加工（简单剪修或去氧化皮前除外），但不具有其他品目所列制品或产品的特征。

三、丝

盘卷的轧、挤或拔制实心产品，其全长截面均为圆形、椭圆形、矩形（包括正方形）、等边三角形或规则外凸多边形（包括相对两边为弧拱形，另外两边为等长平行直线的"扁圆形"及"变形矩形"）。对于矩形（包括正方形）、三角形或多边形截面的产品，其全长边角可经磨圆。矩形（包括"变形矩形"）截面的产品，其厚度应大于宽度的1/10。

四、板、片、带、箔

成卷或非成卷的平面产品（品目80.01的未锻轧产品除外），截面均为厚度相同的实心矩形（不包括正方形），不论边角是否磨圆（包括相对两边为弧拱形,另外两边为等长平行直线的变形矩形"），并且符合以下规格：

（一）矩形（包括正方形）的，厚度不超过宽度的1/10；

（二）矩形或正方形以外形状的,任何尺寸,但不具有其他品目所列制品或产品的特征。

五、管

全长截面及管壁厚度相同并只有一个闭合空间的空心产品,成卷或非成卷的,其截面为圆形、椭

Chapter 80
Tin and articles thereof

Chapter Notes:

In this Chapter the following expressions have the meanings hereby assigned to them:

1. Bars and rods

Rolled, extruded, drawn or forged products, not in coils, which have a uniform solid cross-section along their whole length in the shape of circles, ovals, rectangles (including squares), equilateral triangles or regular convex polygons (including "flattened circles" and "modified rectangles", of which two opposite sides are convex arcs, the other two sides being straight, of equal length and parallel). Products with a rectangular (including square), triangular or polygonal cross-section may have corners rounded along their whole length. The thickness of such products which have a rectangular (including "modified rectangular") cross-section exceeds one-tenth of the width The expression also covers cast or sintered products, of the same forms and dimensions, which have been subsequently worked after production (otherwise than by simple trimming or de-scaling), provided that they have not thereby assumed the character of articles or products of other headings.

2. Profiles

Rolled, extruded, drawn, forged or formed products, coiled or not, of a uniform cross-section along their whole length, which do not conform to any of the definitions of bars, rods, wire, plates, sheets, strip, foil, tubes or pipes. The expression also covers cast or sintered products, of the same forms, which have been subsequently worked after production (otherwise than by simple trimming or de-scaling), provided that they have not thereby assumed the character of articles or products of other headings.

3. Wire

Rolled, extruded or drawn products, in coils, which have a uniform solid cross-section along their whole length in the shape of circles, ovals, rectangles (including squares), equilateral triangles or regular convex polygons (including "flattened circles" and "modified rectangles", of which two opposite sides are convex arcs, the other two sides being straight, of equal length and parallel). Products with a rectangular (including square), triangular or polygonal cross-section may have corners rounded along their whole length. The thickness of such products which have a rectangular (including "modified rectangular") cross-section exceeds one-tenth of the width.

4. Plates, sheets, strip and foil

Flat-surfaced products (other than the unwrought products of heading 80.01), coiled or not, of solid rectangular (other than square) cross-section with or without rounded corners (includeing "modified rectangles" of which two opposite sides are convex arcs, the other two sides being straight, of equal length and parallel) of a uniform thickness, which are:

(a) Of rectangular (including square) shape with a thickness not exceeding one-tenth of the width;

(b) Of a shape other than rectangular or square, of any size, provided that they do not assume the character of articles or products of other headings.

5. Tubes and pipes

Hollow products, coiled or not, which have a uniform cross-section with only one enclosed void along their whole length in the shape of circles, ovals,

圆形、矩形（包括正方形）、等边三角形或规则外凸多边形。对于截面为矩形（包括正方形）、等边三角形或规则外凸多边形的产品，不论全长边角是否磨圆，只要其内外截面为同一圆心并为同样形状及同一轴向，也可视为管子。上述截面的管子可经抛光、涂层、弯曲、攻丝、钻孔、缩腰、胀口、成锥形或装法兰、颈圈或套环。

rectangles（including squares）, equilateral triangles or regular convex polygons, and which have a uniform wall thickness. Products with a rectangular （including square）, equilateral triangular or regular convex polygonal cross-section, which may have corners rounded along their whole length, are also to be considered as tubes and pipes provided the inner and outer cross-sections are concentric and have the same form and orientation. Tubes and pipes of the foregoing cross-sections may be polished, coated, bent, threaded,drilled, waisted, expanded, cone-shaped or fitted with flanges, collars or rings.

子目注释：

本章所用有关名词解释如下：

一、非合金锡

按重量计含锡量至少为 99%的金属，但含铋量或含铜量不超过下表中规定的限量：

其他元素表

元　素	所含重量百分比
Bi　铋	0.1
Cu　铜	0.4

二、锡合金

按重量计含锡量大于其他元素单项含量的金属物质，但：

（一）按重量计其他元素的总含量超过 1%；或

（二）按重量计含铋量或含铜量应等于或大于上表中规定的限量。

Subheading Notes:

In this Chapter the following expressions have the meanings hereby assigned to them:

1. Tin, not alloyed

Metal containing by weight at least 99% of tin, provided that the content by weight of any bismuth or copper is less than the limit specified in the following table:

TABLE—Other elements

Element	Limiting content%by weight
Bi　　Bismuth	0.1
Cu　　Copper	0.4

2. Tin alloys

Metallic substances in which tin predominates by weight over each of the other elements, provided that:

（a）The total content by weight of such other elements exceeds 1%; or

（b）The content by weight of either bismuth or copper is equal to or greater than the limit specified in the foregoing table.

税则号列 Tariff Item	商品名称及备注	进口税率 最惠	普通	暂定	出口退税	增值税率	计量单位	监管条件	Article Description
80.01	**未锻轧锡：**								**Unwrought tin:**
8001.1000	-非合金锡	3	20			17	千克	4xy	-Tin, not alloyed
	-锡合金：								-Tin alloys:
8001.2010	---锡基巴毕脱合金	3	20			17	千克	4xy	---Babbitt metal
	---焊锡：								---Solder:
8001.2021	----按重量计含铅量在 0.1%以下的	3	30			17	千克	4xy	----Containing by weight less than 0.1% of lead
8001.2029	----其他	3	30			17	千克	4xy	----Other
8001.2090	---其他	3	30			17	千克	4xy	---Other
80.02	**锡废碎料：**								**Tin waste and scrap:**
8002.0000	锡废碎料	1.5	30			17	千克	4APxy	Tin waste and scrap
80.03	**锡条、杆、型材及异型材或丝：**								**Tin bars, rods, profiles and wire:**
8003.0000	锡条、杆、型材及异型材或丝	8	40			17	千克	4xy	Tin bars, rods, profiles and wire
80.07	**其他锡制品：**								**Other articles of tin:**
8007.0020	---锡板、片及带，厚度超过 0.2 毫米	8	40			17	千克	4xy	---Tin plates, sheets and strip, of a thickness exceeding 0.2mm
8007.0030	---锡箔（不论是否印花或用纸、纸板、塑料或类似材料衬背），厚度（衬背除外）不超过 0.2 毫米；锡粉及片状粉末	8	40		5	17	千克		---Tin foil（whether or not printed or backed with paper, paperboard, plastics or similar backing materials）, of a thickness（excluding any backing）not exceeding 0.2mm; tin powders and flakes
8007.0040	---锡管及管子附件（例如，接头、肘管、管套）	8	45			17	千克	4xy	---Tin tubes, pipes and tube or pipe fittings（for example, couplings, elbows,sleeves）
8007.0090	---其他	8	80			17	千克		---Other

第八十一章
其他贱金属、金属陶瓷及其制品

Chapter 81
Other base metals; cermets; articles thereof

子目注释：

第七十四章注释中有关"条、杆"、"型材及异型材"、"丝"及"板、片、带、箔"的规定也适用于本章。

Subheading Note:

Notes to Chapter 74, defining "bars and rods", "profiles", "wire",and "plates, sheets, strip and foil" applies, mutatis mutandis, to this Chapter.

税则号列 Tariff Item	商品名称及备注	进口税率			出口退税	增值税率	计量单位	监管条件	Article Description
		最惠	普通	暂定					
81.01	钨及其制品，包括废碎料：								Tungsten（wolfram）and articles thereof, including waste and scrap:
8101.1000	-粉末	6	20			17	千克		-Powders
8101 1000.10	颗粒＜500微米的钨及其合金（含量≥97%，不论球形、椭球体、雾化、片状、研碎金属燃料）	6	20			17	千克	3	Tungsten and its alloys, granularity＜500μm,（containing by weight 97% or more of tungsten, whether spheroid, ellipsoid, atomized, flake formed, crush metal fuel）
8101 1000.90	其他钨粉末	6	20			17	千克	4xy	Other tungsten powders
	-其他:								-Other:
8101.9400	--未锻轧钨，包括简单烧结而成的条、杆	3	20			17	千克	4xy	--Unwrought tungsten, including bars and rods obtained simply by sintering
8101.9600	-丝	8	20		5	17	千克		--Wire
8101.9700 暂	--废碎料	3	20	1		17	千克	4APxy	--Waste and scrap
	--其他:								--Other:
8101.9910	---条、杆，但简单烧结而成的除外；型材及异型材，板、片、带、箔	5	30			17	千克		---Bars and rods, other than those obtained simply by sintering, profiles, plates, sheets, strip and foil
8101.9990	---其他	8	70			17	千克		---Other
81.02	钼及其制品，包括废碎料：								Molybdenum and articles thereof, including waste and scrap:
8102.1000	-粉末	6	20			17	千克	4xy	-Powders
	-其他:								-Other:
8102.9400	--未锻轧钼，包括简单烧结而成的条、杆	3	20			17	千克	4xy	--Unwrought molybdenum, including bars and rods obtained simply by sintering
8102.9500	--条、杆，但简单烧结而成的除外；型材及异型材、板、片、带、箔	8	30			17	千克		--Bars and rods, other than those obtained simply by sintering, profiles, plates, sheets, strip and foil
8102.9600	--丝	8	20		5	17	千克		--Wire
8102.9700	--废碎料	3	20			17	千克	49xy	--Waste and scrap
8102.9900	--其他	8	70			17	千克	4xy	--Other
81.03	钽及其制品，包括废碎料：								Tantalum and articles thereof, including waste and scrap:
	-未锻轧钽，包括简单烧结而成的条、杆、粉末：								-Unwrought tantalum, including bars and rods obtained simply by sintering; powders:
	---钽粉:								---Powders:
8103.2011	----松装密度小于2.2g/cm³的	6	14		13	17	千克	4xy	----Loose density less than 2.2g／cm³
8103.2019	----其他	6	14			17	千克	4xy	----Other
8103.2090	---其他	6	14			17	千克	4xy	---Other
8103.3000 暂	-废碎料	6	14	0		17	千克	4APxy	-Waste and scrap
	-其他:								-Other:
	---钽丝:								---Wire of tantalum:
8103.9011	----直径小于0.5毫米	8	30		13	17	千克	4xy	----Less than 0.5mm in diameter
8103.9019	----其他	8	30		9	17	千克	4xy	----Other
8103.9090	---其他	8	30			17	千克		---Other
8103 9090.10	钽坩埚（容积在50毫升至2升之间，钽纯度≥98%）	8	30			17	千克	3	Tantalum crucible, of a volume between 50ml and 2L, purity≥98%
8103 9090.90	其他锻轧钽及其制品	8	30		9	17	千克	4xy	Other wrought tantalum and articles thereof

税则号列 Tariff Item	商品名称及备注	进口税率			出口退税	增值税率	计量单位	监管条件	Article Description
		最惠	普通	暂定					
81.04	镁及其制品，包括废碎料：								**Magnesium and articles thereof, including waste and scrap:**
	-未锻轧镁:								-Unwrought magnesium:
8104.1100	--按重量计含镁量至少为99.8%	6	20			17	千克		--Containing at least 99.8% by weight of magnesium
8104.1900	--其他	6	20			17	千克		--Other
8104.2000	-废碎料	1.5	20			17	千克	AP	-Waste and scrap
8104.3000	-锉屑、车屑及颗粒，已按规格分级的；粉末	8	30			17	千克		-Raspings, turnings and granules, graded according to size; powders
8104 3000.10	颗粒＜500微米的镁及其合金（含量≥97%，不论球形、椭球体、雾化、片状、研碎金属燃料）	8	30			17	千克	3	Magnesium and its alloys, granularity＜500μm（containing 97％or more by weight of magnesium, whether spheroid, ellipsoid, atomized, flake formed, crush metal fuel）
8104 3000.90	其他已分级的镁锉屑、车屑、颗粒；粉末	8	30			17	千克		Other magnesium raspings, turnings and granules, graded according to size; powders
	-其他:								-Other:
8104.9010	---锻轧镁	8	30			17	千克		---Wrought magnesium
8104.9020	---镁制品	8.4	70			17	千克		---Magnesium articles
8104 9020.10	镁金属基复合材料(包括各种结构件和制品、各种预成形件，其中增强材料的比拉伸强度大于 7.62×10^4 米和比模量大于 3.18×10^6 米)	8.4	70		5	17	千克	3	Masnesium composite materials（including all sorts of structural parts and articles and Pre-formed parts, tensile strength reinforced materials＞7.62×10^4m and specific modulus bigger than 3.18×10^7m）
8104 9020.90	其他镁制品	8.4	70			17	千克		Other masnesium articles
81.05	钴锍及其他冶炼钴时所得的中间产品；钴及其制品，包括废碎料：								**Cobalt mattes and other intermediate products of cobalt metallurgy; cobalt and articles thereof, including waste and scrap:**
	-钴锍及其他冶炼钴时所得的中间产品；未锻轧钴；粉末:								-Cobalt mattes and other intermediate products of cobalt metallurgy; unwrought cobalt; powders:
8105.2010 暂	---钴湿法冶炼中间品	4	14	0		17	千克	4xy	---Intermediate products of cobalt metallurgy by wet process
8105.2020	---未锻轧钴	4	14			17	千克	4xy	---Unwrought cobalt
8105.2090	---其他	4	14			17	千克		---Other
8105 2090.01 暂	钴锍及其他冶炼钴时所得中间产品	4	14	0		17	千克	4xy	Cobalt mattes and other intermediate products of cobalt metallurgy
8105 2090.10	钴≥99.5%的超细钴粉（费氏粒度0.8～1.5微米，松装密度0.4～0.8克/立方厘米）	4	14			17	千克		Supper-fine cobalt powders, containing 99.5% or more of cobalt（Fischer granularinty 0.8-1.5μm, fill density 0.4-0.89/cm^3）
8105 2090.90	其他钴锍、粉末	4	14			17	千克	4xy	Other cobalt mattes; powders
8105.3000	-废碎料	4	14			17	千克	49xy	-Waste and scrap
8105.9000	-其他	8	30			17	千克	4xy	-Other
81.06	铋及其制品，包括废碎料：								**Bismuth and articles thereof, including waste and scrap:**
8106.0010	---未锻轧铋；废碎料；粉末	3	20			17	千克		---Unwrought bismuth; waste and scrap; powders
8106 0010.11 暂	高纯度未锻轧的铋（纯度≥99.99%，含银量低于十万分之一）	3	20	1		17	千克	3	Hight-pure unwrought bismuth , purity≥99.99%, containing 1.0X10^{-6}or less by weight of silver
8106 0010.19	高纯度未锻轧的铋废料、粉末（纯度≥99.99%,含银量低于十万分之一）	3	20			17	千克	3	Highly–pure unwroght bismuth , waste and scrap, purity≥99.99%, containing 1.0X10^{-6}or less by weight of silver
8106 0010.91 暂	其他未锻轧铋	3	20	1		17	千克	4xy	Other unwrought bismuth
8106 0010.92	其他未锻轧铋废碎料	3	20			17	千克	4APxy	Other unwrought bismuth waste and scrap
8106 0010.99	其他未锻轧铋粉末	3	20			17	千克	4xy	Other unwrought bismuth powders
8106.0090	---其他	8	30			17	千克		---Other
8106 0090.10	高纯度铋及铋制品（纯度≥99.99%，含银量低于十万分之一）	8	30		5	17	千克	3	Highly-pure Unwrought bismuth and articles thereof, purity≧99.99%, containing 1.0X10^{-6}or less by weight of silver
8106 0090.90	其他铋及铋制品	8	30			17	千克	4xy	Other bismuth and articles thereof

税则号列 Tariff Item	商品名称及备注	进口税率 最惠	普通	暂定	出口退税	增值税率	计量单位	监管条件	Article Description
81.07	镉及其制品，包括废碎料：								**Cadmium and articles thereof, including waste and scrap:**
8107.2000	-未锻轧镉；粉末	3	14			17	千克		-Unwrought cadmium; powder
8107.3000	-废碎料	3	14			17	千克	9	-Waste and scrap
8107.9000	-其他	8	30			17	千克		-Other
81.08	钛及其制品，包括废碎料：								**Titanium and articles thereof, including waste and scrap:**
	-未锻轧钛；粉末：								-Unwrought titanium; powder:
	---未锻轧钛：								---Unwrought titanium:
8108.2021	----海绵钛	3	14			17	千克	4xy	----Sponge titanium
8108.2029	----其他	3	14			17	千克		----Other
8108 2029.10	颗粒＜500微米的钛及其合金（含量≥97%，不论球形、椭球体、雾化、片状、研碎金属燃料）	3	14			17	千克	A	Titanium and alloys, granularity＜500 μm（containing 97% or more by weight of titanium, whether spheroid, ellipsoid, atomized, flake formed, ground metallic fuels）
8108 2029.90	其他未锻轧钛	3	14			17	千克	4xy	Other unwrought titanium; powders
8108.2030	---粉末	3	14			17	千克	4Axy	---Powders
8108.3000	-废碎料	3	14			17	千克	4APxy	-Waste and scrap
	-其他：								-Other:
8108.9010	---条、杆、型材及异型材	8	30		13	17	千克		---Bars, rods, shapes and sections
8108 9010.10	钛合金，实心圆柱体，包括锻件（20℃下极限抗拉强度≥900兆帕，外径超过75毫米）	8	30		13	17	千克	3	Titanium alloys, solid cylinder, including castings（ultimate tensile strength≥900MPa at 20℃, of an outer diameter exceeding 75 mm）
8108 9010.20	钛金属基复合材料的条、杆、型材及异型材（其中增强材料的比拉伸强度大于7.62×10^6米和比模量大于3.18×10^7米）	8	30		13	17	千克	3	Bars, rods, shaps and sections, made of composite material of titanium metal （the degree of strength of intensity material is more than 7.62×10^6 m, and specific modulus is bigger than 3.18×10^7m）
8108 9010.90	其他钛条、杆、型材及异型材	8	30		13	17	千克		Other bars, rods, shapes and sections, of titanium
8108.9020	---丝	8	30		13	17	千克		---Wire
	---板、片、带、箔：								---Plates, sheets, strap, foil:
8108.9031[暂]	----厚度不超过0.8毫米	8	30	4	13	17	千克		----Of a thickness not more than 0.8mm
8108.9032[暂]	----厚度超过0.8毫米	8	30	4	13	17	千克		----Of a thickness more than 0.8mm
8108 9032.10[暂]	钛金属基复合材料的板、片、带、箔（其中增强材料的比拉伸强度大于7.62×10^4米和比模量大于3.18×10^7米，厚度大于0.8毫米）	8	30	4	13	17	千克	3	Plates, sheets, strip and foil, made of titanium metal（tensile strength of reinforced material is more than 7.62×10^4m, specific modulis is bigger than 3.18×10^7 m, of a thickness exceeding 0.8mm）
8108 9032.90[暂]	其他厚度＞0.8毫米钛板、片、带、箔	8	30	4	13	17	千克		Other plates, sheets, strap, foil, of titanium of a thickness exceeding 0.8mm
8108.9040	---管	8	30		13	17	千克		---Tubes or pipes
8108 9040.10	钛合金管（20℃下极限抗拉强度≥900兆帕，外径＞75毫米）	8	30		13	17	千克	3	Tubes or pipes of titanium alloys,（ultimate tensile strength≥900MPa at 20℃, of an outer diameter exceeding 75mm）
8108 9040.90	其他钛管	8	30		13	17	千克		Other titanium tubes or pipes
8108.9090	---其他	8	30		13	17	千克		---Other
81.09	锆及其制品，包括废碎料：								**Zirconium and articles thereof, including waste and scrap:**
8109.2000	-未锻轧锆；粉末	3	20			17	千克		-Unwrought zirconium; powders
8109 2000.10	颗粒＜500微米的锆及其合金（含量≥97%，不论球形、椭球体、雾化、片状、研碎金属燃料）	3	20			17	千克	A	Zirconium and alloys, granularity < 500μm（containing 97% or more of Zirconium, whether spheroid, ellipsoid, atomized, flake formed, crush metal fuels）
8109 2000.90	其他未锻轧锆；粉末	3	20			17	千克	3A	Other unwrought zirconium; powders
8109.3000	-废碎料	3	20			17	千克	3AP	-Waste and scrap
8109.9000	-其他	8	30			17	千克		-Other
8109 9000.10	锆管（铪与锆重量比低于1：500的锆金属和合金的管或组件）	8	30		5	17	千克	3	Tubes or pipes of zirconium and its alloys（ratio of weight of hafnium and zirconium is less than 1:500）
8109 9000.90	其他锻轧锆及锆制品	8	30			17	千克	3	Other wrought zirconium and articles thereof
81.10	锑及其制品，包括废碎料：								**Antimony and articles thereof, including waste**

税则号列 Tariff Item	商品名称及备注	进口税率 最惠	进口税率 普通	进口税率 暂定	出口退税	增值税率	计量单位	监管条件	Article Description
									and scrap:
	-未锻轧锑；粉末：								-Unwrought antimony; powders:
8110.1010[暂]	---未锻轧锑	3	30	1		17	千克	4xy	----Unwrought antimony
8110.1020	---粉末	3	30			17	千克	4Axy	---Powders
8110.2000	-废碎料	3	30			17	千克	49xy	-Antimony waste and scrap
8110.9000	-其他	8	40			17	千克	4xy	-Other
81.11	**锰及其制品，包括废碎料：**								**Manganese and articles thereof, including waste and scrap:**
8111.0010	---未锻轧锰；废碎料；粉末	3	20			17	千克		---Unwrought manganese; waste and scrap; powders
8111 0010.10	锰废碎料	3	20			17	千克	49xy	Manganese waste and scraps
8111 0010.90	未锻轧锰；粉末	3	20			17	千克	4Axy	Unwrought manganese, powders
8111.0090	---其他	8	30			17	千克	4xy	---Other
81.12	**铍、铬、锗、钒、镓、铪、铟、铼、铌、铊及其制品，包括废碎料：**								**Beryllium, chromium, germanium, vanadium, gallium, hafnium, indium,niobium(columbium), rhenium and thallium, and articles of these metals, including waste and scrap:**
	-铍：								-Beryllium:
8112.1200	--未锻轧铍；粉末	3	30			17	千克	3A	--Unwrought; powders
8112.1300	--废碎料	3	30			17	千克	39	--Waste and scrap
8112.1900	--其他	8	30			17	千克	3	--Other
	-铬：								-Chromium:
8112.2100	--未锻轧铬；粉末	3	20			17	千克	4xy	--Unwrought; powders
8112.2200	--废碎料	3	20			17	千克	49xy	--Waste and scrap
8112.2900	--其他	3	20			17	千克	4xy	--Other
	-铊：								-Thallium:
8112.5100	--未锻轧铊；粉末	3	20			17	千克	AB	--Unwrought; powders
8112.5200	--废碎料	3	20			17	千克	9	--Waste and scrap
8112.5900	--其他	8	30			17	千克		--Other
	-其他：								-Other:
	--未锻轧；废碎料；粉末：								--Unwrought; waste and scrap; powders:
8112.9210	---锗	3	20			17	千克		---Germanium
8112 9210.10	未锻轧锗废碎料	3	20			17	千克	4APxy	Unwrought germanium waste and scraps
8112 9210.90	未锻轧的锗；锗粉末	3	20			17	千克	4xy	Unwrought germanium; powders
8112.9220	---钒	3	20			17	千克		---Vanadium
8112 9220.01[暂]	未锻轧、废碎料或粉末状的钒氮合金	3	20	0		17	千克	4xy	Unwrought, waste and scrap; powders , of vanadium and nitrogen alloys
8112 9220.10	未锻轧的钒废碎料	3	20			17	千克	4APxy	Unwrought vanadium waste and scrap
8112 9220.90	未锻轧的钒；钒粉末	3	20			17	千克	4xy	Unwrought vanadium and its powders
8112.9230	---铟	3	20			17	千克		---Indium
8112 9230.01	未锻轧的铟	3	20			17	千克	4xy	---Unwrought indium
8112 9230.02	铟粉末	3	20			17	千克	4xy	Indium powders
8112 9230.90	未锻轧铟废碎料	3	20			17	千克	49xy	Unwrought indium waste and scrap
8112.9240[暂]	---铌	3	20	1		17	千克		---Niobium
8112 9240.10[暂]	铌废碎料	3	20	1		17	千克	4APxy	Unwrought niobium waste and scrap
8112 9240.90[暂]	未锻轧的铌；铌粉末	3	20	1		17	千克	4xy	Unwrought niobium and its powders
8112.9290	---其他	3	20			17	千克		---Other
8112 9290.11	未锻轧的铪废碎料	3	20			17	千克	3AP	Unwrought hafnium waste and scrap
8112 9290.19	未锻轧的铪；粉末	3	20			17	千克	3A	Unwrought hafnium and its powders
8112 9290.91	未锻轧的镓、铼废碎料	3	20			17	千克	4APxy	Unrolled gallium, rhenium waste and scraps
8112 9290.99	未锻轧的镓、铼；粉末	3	20			17	千克	4Axy	Unrolled gallium and rhenium and its powders
	--其他：								--Other:
8112.9910	---锗	3	20		5	17	千克	4xy	---Germanium
8112.9920	---钒	3	20			17	千克		---Vanadium
8112 9920.01[暂]	其他钒氮合金	3	20	0		17	千克	4xy	Other vanadium and nitrogen alloys
8112 9920.90	其他钒及其制品	3	20			17	千克	4xy	Other vanadium and articles thereof
8112.9930	---铟	8	20			17	千克	4xy	---Indium
8112.9940	---铌	8	20			17	千克	4xy	---Niobium

税则号列 Tariff Item	商品名称及备注	进口税率			出口退税	增值税率	计量单位	监管条件	Article Description
		最惠	普通	暂定					
8112.9990	---其他	8	30			17	千克		---Other
8112 9990.10	锻轧的铪及其制品	8	30			17	千克	3	Wrought hafnium, and articles thereof
8112 9990.90	锻轧的镓、铼及其制品	8	30			17	千克	4xy	Other wrought gallium and rhenium and articles thereof
81.13	金属陶瓷及其制品，包括废碎料:								**Cermets and articles thereof, including waste and scrap:**
8113.0010	---颗粒;粉末	8.4	30			17	千克		---Granules; powders
8113 0010.10	颗粒或粉末状碳化钨废碎料	8.4	30			17	千克	AP	Waste and scrap tungsten carbide in granular or powder
8113 0010.90	颗粒或粉末状其他金属陶瓷及其制品	8.4	30			17	千克		Other metal ceramics and related products
8113.0090	---其他	8.4	30			17	千克		---Other
8113 0090.10	其他碳化钨废碎料,颗粒或粉末除外	8.4	30			17	千克	AP	Other waste and scrap of tungsten carbide, other than granules or powder
8113 0090.90	其他金属陶瓷及其制品,颗粒或粉末除外(包括废料)	8.4	30			17	千克		Other metal ceramics and related products, including waste, other than other than granules or powder

第八十二章 贱金属工具、器具、利口器、餐匙、餐叉及其零件

Chapter 82 Tools, implements, cutlery, spoons and forks, of base metal; parts thereof of base metal

注释：

一、除喷灯、轻便锻炉、带支架的砂轮、修指甲和修脚用器具及品目 82.09 的货品外，本章仅包括带有用下列材料制成的刀片、工作刃、工作面或其他工作部件的物品：

（一）贱金属；

（二）硬质合金或金属陶瓷；

（三）装于贱金属、硬质合金或金属陶瓷底座上的宝石或半宝石（天然、合成或再造）；或

（四）附于贱金属底座上的磨料，当附上磨料后，所具有的切齿、沟、槽或类似结构仍保持其特性及功能。

二、本章所列物品的贱金属零件，应与该制品归入同一品目，但具体列名的零件及手工工具的工具夹具（品目 84.66）除外。第十五类注释二所述的通用零件，均不归入本章。

电动剃须刀及电动毛发推剪的刀头、刀片应归入品目 85.10。

三、由品目 82.11 的一把或多把刀具与品目 82.15 至少数量相同的物品构成的成套货品应归入品目 82.15。

Chapter Notes:

1. Apart from blow lamps, portable forges, grinding wheels with frameworks, manicure or pedicure sets, and goods of heading 82. 09, this Chapter covers only articles with a blade, working edge, working surface or other working part of:

(a) Base metal;

(b) Metal carbides or cermets;

(c) Precious or semi-precious stones (natural, synthetic or reconstructed) on a support of base metal, metal carbide or cermet; or

(d) Abrasive materials on a support of base metal, provided that the articles have cutting teeth, flutes, grooves or the like, of base metal, which retain their identity and function after the application of the abrasive.

2. Parts of base metal of the articles of this Chapter are to be classified with the articles of which they are parts, except parts separately specified as such and tool-holders for hand tools (heading 84.66). However, parts of general use as defined in Note 2 to Section XV are in all cases excluded from this Chapter.

Heads, blades and cutting plates for electric shavers and electric hair clippers are to be classified in heading 85.10.

3. Sets consisting of one or more knives of heading 82.11 and at least an equal number of articles of heading 82.15 are to be classified in heading 82.15.

税则号列 Tariff Item	商品名称及备注	进口税率 最惠	普通	暂定	出口退税	增值税率	计量单位	监管条件	Article Description
82.01	锹、铲、镐、锄、叉及耙；斧子、钩刀及类似砍伐工具；各种修枝用剪刀；镰刀、秣刀、树篱剪、伐木楔子及其他农业、园艺或林业用手工工具：								**Hand tools, the following: spades, shovels, mattocks, picks, hoes, forks and rakes; axes, bill hooks and similar hewing tools; secateurs and prundrs of any kind; scythes, hay knives, hedge shears, timber wedges and other tools of a kind used in agriculture, horticulture or forestry:**
8201.1000	-锹及铲	8	50		5	13	千克/把		-Spades and shovels
8201 1000.10	含植物性材料的锹及铲	8	50		5	13	千克/把	AB	Spades and shovels with vegetable materials
8201 1000.90	其他锹及铲	8	50		5	13	千克/把		Other spades and shovels
8201.3000	-镐、锄及耙	8	50		5	13	千克/把		-Mattocks, picks, hoes and rakes
8201 3000.10	含植物性材料的镐、锄、耙	8	50		5	13	千克/把	AB	Mattocks, picks, hoes and rakes with vegetable materials
8201 3000.90	其他镐、锄、耙	8	50		5	13	千克/把		Other Mattocks, picks, hoes and rakes
8201.4000	-斧子、钩刀及类似砍伐工具	8	50		5	13	千克/把		-Axes, bill hooks and similar hewing tools
8201 4000.10	含植物性材料的砍伐工具（包括斧子、钩刀及类似砍伐工具）	8	50		5	13	千克/把	AB	Axes, bill hooks and similar hewing tools with vegetable materials
8201 4000.90	其他斧子、钩刀及类似砍伐工具	8	50		5	13	千克/把		Other axes, bill hooks and similar hewing tools
8201.5000	-修枝剪及类似的单手操作剪刀（包括家禽剪）	8	50		5	13	千克/把		-Secateurs and similar one-handed pruners and shears (including poultry shears)
8201 5000.10	含植物性材料的单手操作农用剪（包括家禽剪）	8	50		5	13	千克/把	AB	Secateurs and similar one-handed pruners and shears (including poultry shears), with vegetable materials, for agricultural use

税则号列 Tariff Item	商品名称及备注	进口税率 最惠	普通	暂定	出口退税	增值税率	计量单位	监管条件	Article Description
8201 5000.90	其他修枝剪等单手操作农用剪(包括家禽剪)	8	50		5	13	千克/把		Other Secateurs and similar one-handed pruners and shears（including poultry shears）for agricultural use
8201.6000	-树篱剪、双手修枝剪及类似的双手操作剪刀	8	50			13	千克/把		-Hedge shears, two-handed pruning shears and similar two-handed shears
8201 6000.10	含植物性材料的双手操作农用剪	8	50		5	13	千克/把	AB	Two-handed shears, with vegetable materials, for agricultural use
8201 6000.90	其他修枝等双手操作农用剪	8	50		9	13	千克/把		Other hedge shears, two-handed pruning shears and similar two-handed shears, for agricultural use
	-用于农业、园艺或林业的其他手工工具								-Other hand tools of a kind used in agriculture, horticulture or forestry
8201.9010	---叉	8	50		5	13	千克/把		---Forks
8201 9010.10	含植物性材料的农业、园艺、林业用叉	8	50		5	13	千克/把	AB	Forks,with vegetable materials, for agricultural use
8201 9010.90	其他农业、园艺、林业用叉	8	50		5	13	千克/把		Other Forks used in agriculture, horticulture or forestry
8201.9090	---其他	8	50		5	13	千克/把		---Other
8201 9090.10	含植物性材料的农业、园艺、林业用手工工具	8	50		5	13	千克/把	AB	Hand tools of a kind used in agriculture, horticulture or forestry, with vegetable materials
8201 9090.90	其他农业、园艺、林业用手工工具	8	50		5/9	13	千克/把		Other hand tools of a kind used in agriculture, horticulture or forestry
82.02	**手工锯；各种锯的锯片（包括切条、切槽或无齿锯片）：**								**Hand saws; blades for saws of all kinds（including slitting, slotting or toothless saw blades）:**
8202.1000	-手工锯	8.4	50		9	17	千克/把		-Hand saws
	-带锯片:								-Band saw blades:
8202.2010	---双金属带锯条	8	20		9	17	千克		---Double metal band saw blade
8202.2090	---其他	8	20		9	17	千克		---Other
	-圆锯片（包括切条或切槽锯片）:								-Circular saw blades（including slitting or slotting saw blades）:
8202.3100	--带有钢制工作部件	8	20		9	17	千克		--With working part of steel
	--其他,包括部件：								--Other, including parts:
8202.3910	---带有天然或合成金刚石、立方氮化硼制的工作部件	8	20		9	17	千克		With working part of natural or synthetic diamonds or cubic boron nitride
8202.3990	---其他	8	20		9	17	千克		---Other
8202.4000	-链锯片	8	20		9	17	千克		-Chain saw blades
	-其他锯片:								-Other saw blades:
	--直锯片，加工金属用:								--Straight saw blades, for working metal:
8202.9110	---机械锯用	8	20		9	17	千克		---For sawing machines
8202.9190	---其他	8	50		9	17	千克		---Other
	--其他:								--Other:
8202.9910	---机械锯用	8.4	20		9	17	千克		---For sawing machines
8202.9990	---其他	10.5	50		9	17	千克		---Other
82.03	**钢锉、木锉、钳子（包括剪钳）、镊子、白铁剪、切管器、螺栓切头器、打孔冲子及类似手工工具：**								**Files, rasps, pliers（including cutting pliers）, pincers, tweezers, metal cutting shears, pipe-cutters, bolt croppers, perforating punches and similar hand tools:**
8203.1000	-钢锉、木锉及类似工具	10.5	50		9	17	千克/把		-Files, rasps and similar tools
8203.2000	-钳子（包括剪钳）、镊子及类似工具	10.5	50		9	17	千克/把		-Pliers（including cutting pliers）, pincers, tweezers and similar tools
8203.3000	-白铁剪及类似工具	10.5	50		9	17	千克/把		-Metal cutting shears and similar tools
8203.4000	-切管器、螺栓切头器、打孔冲子及类似工具	10.5	50		9	17	千克/把		-Pipe-cutters, bolt croppers, perforating punches and similar tools
82.04	**手动扳手及扳钳（包括转矩扳手，但不包括丝锥扳手）；可互换的扳手套筒，不论是否带手柄：**								**Hand-operated spanners and wrenches（including torque meter wrenches but not including tap wrenches）; interchangeable spanner sockets, with or without handles:**
	-手动扳手及扳钳:								-Hand-operated spanners and wrenches:

税则号列 Tariff Item	商品名称及备注	进口税率 最惠	普通	暂定	出口退税	增值税率	计量单位	监管条件	Article Description
8204.1100	--固定的	10.5	50		9	17	千克/把		--Non-adjustable
8204.1200	--可调的	10	50		9	17	千克/把		--Adjustable
8204.2000	-可互换的扳手套筒，不论是否带手柄	10	50		9	17	千克/套		-Interchangeable spanner sockets, with or without handles
82.05	**其他品目未列名的手工工具(包括玻璃刀)；喷灯；台钳、夹钳及类似品，但作为机床附件或零件的除外；砧；轻便锻炉；带支架的手摇或脚踏砂轮：**								**Hand tools（including glaziers' diamonds）, not elsewhere specified or included; blow lamps; vices, clamps and the like, other than accessories for and parts of, machine tools; anvils; portable forges; hand or pedal operated grinding wheels with frame-works:**
8205.1000	-钻孔或攻丝工具	10	50		9	17	千克/个		-Drilling, threading or tapping tools
8205.2000	-锤子	10	50		9	17	千克/个		-Hammers and sledge hammers
8205.3000	-木工用刨子、凿子及类似切削工具	10.5	50		9	17	千克/个		-Planes, chisels, gouges and similar cutting tools for working wood
8205.4000	-螺丝刀	10.5	50		9	17	千克/个		-Screwdrivers
	-其他手工工具(包括玻璃刀)：								-Other hand tools（including glaziers' diamonds）:
8205.5100	--家用工具	10.5	50		9	17	千克/个		--Household tools
8205.5900	--其他	10	50		9	17	千克/个		--Other
8205.6000	-喷灯	10	50		9	17	千克/个		-Blow lamps
8205.7000	-台钳、夹钳及类似品	10.5	50		9	17	千克/个		-Vices, clamps and the like
8205.9000	-其他，包括由本税目项下两个或多个子目所列物品组成的成套货品	10.5	50		9	17	千克		-Other, including sets of articles of two or more Subheadings of this heading
82.06	**由品目82.02至82.05中两个或多个品目所列工具组成的零售包装成套货品：**								**Tools of two or more of the headings No.82.02 to 82.05, put up in sets for retail sale:**
8206.0000	由品目82.02至82.05中两个或多个品目所列工具组成的零售包装成套货品	10.5	50		9	17	千克		Tools of two or more of the headings No.82.02 to 82.05, put up in sets for retail sale
82.07	**手工工具（不论是否有动力装置）及机床（例如，锻压、冲压、攻丝、钻孔、镗孔、铰孔及铣削、车削或上螺丝用的机器）的可互换工具，包括金属拉拔或挤压用模以及凿岩或钻探工具：**								**Interchangeable tools for hand tools, whether or not power-operated, or for machine-tools（for example, for pressing, stamping, punching, tapping, threading, drilling, boring, broaching, milling, turning or screw driving）, including dies for drawing or extruding metal, and rock drilling or earth boring tools:**
	-凿岩或钻探工具：								-Rock drilling or earth boring tools:
8207.1300	--带金属陶瓷制的工作部件	8	20		13	17	千克		--With working part of cermets
	--其他，包括部件：								--Other，including parts：
8207.1910	---带有天然或合成金钢石、立方氮化硼制的工作部件	8	20		13	17	千克		---With working part of natural or synthetic diamonds or cubic boron nitride
8207.1990	---其他	8	20		13	17	千克		---Other
	-金属拉拔或挤压用模：								-Dies for drawing or extruding metal:
8207.2010	---带有天然或合成金刚石、立方氮化硼制的工作部件	8	20		13	17	千克/套		---With working part of natural or synthetic diamonds or cubic boron nitride
8207.2090	---其他	8	20		13	17	千克/套		---Other
8207.3000	-锻压或冲压工具	8	20		13	17	千克		-Tools for pressing, stamping or punching
8207 3000.01[暂]	加工小轿车车身冲压件用的4种关键模具(侧围外板、翼子板、拼接整体侧围内板、拼焊整体侧围加强板用模具)	8	20	4	13	17	千克		Four key mold stamping, used for body stamping and press parts for processing automobile (mold for side outer plate, fender, splicing whole side inner plate, welding whole side inner strength plate)
8207 3000.02[暂]	加工小轿车车身冲压件用的4种特种模具(σb≥980N/mm² 的冷冲压、热成型、内高压成型和铝板用模具)	8	20	4	13	17	千克		Four special mold used for body stamping and press parts for processing automobile (mold of σb≥980N/mm², used for cold stamping, thermoforming, high-pressure molding, aluminum plate)
8207 3000.90	其他锻压或冲压工具	8	20		13	17	千克		Other tools for pressing, stamping or punching
8207.4000	-攻丝工具	8	20		13	17	千克/件		-Tools for tapping or threading

税则号列 Tariff Item	商品名称及备注	进口税率 最惠	进口税率 普通	进口税率 暂定	出口退税	增值税率	计量单位	监管条件	Article Description
	-钻孔工具，但凿岩及钻探用的除外:								-Tools for drilling, other than for rock drilling:
8207.5010	---带有天然或合成金刚石、立方氮化硼制的工作部件	8	20		13	17	千克/件		---With working part of natural or synthetic diamonds or cubic boron nitride
8207.5090	---其他	8	20		13	17	千克/件		---Other
	-镗孔或铰孔工具:								-Tools for boring or broaching:
8207.6010	---带有天然或合成金刚石、立方氮化硼制的工作部件	8	20		13	17	千克/件		---With working part of natural or synthetic diamonds or cubic boronnitride
8207.6090	---其他	8	20		13	17	千克/件		---Other
	-铣削工具								-Tools for milling
8207.7010	---带有天然或合成金刚石、立方氮化硼制的工作部件	8	20		13	17	千克/件		---With working part of natural or synthetic diamonds or cubic boronnitride
8207.7090	---其他	8	20		13	17	千克/件		---Other
	-车削工具:								-Tools for turning
8207.8010	---带有天然或合成金刚石、立方氮化硼制的工作部件	8	20		13	17	千克/件		---With working part of natural or synthetic diamonds or cubic boronnitride
8207.8090	---其他	8	20		13	17	千克/件		---Other
	-其他可互换工具:								-Other interchangeable tools：
8207.9010	---带有天然或合成金刚石、立方氮化硼制的工作部件	8	20		13	17	千克/件		---With working part of natural or synthetic diamonds or cubic boron nitride
8207.9090	---其他	8	20		13	17	千克/件		---Other
82.08	**机器或机械器具的刀及刀片:**								**Knives and cutting blades, for machines or for mechanical appliances:**
	-金属加工用:								-For metal working:
	---硬质合金制的:								---Of metal carbides:
8208.1011	----经镀或涂层的	8	20		13	17	千克		----Plated or coated
8208.1019	----其他	8	20		13	17	千克		----Other
8208.1090	---其他	8	20		5	17	千克		---Other
8208.2000	-木器材加工用	8	20		5	17	千克		-For wood working
8208.3000	-厨房器具或食品加工机器用	8	20		5	17	千克	A	-For kitchen appliances or for machines used by the food industry
8208.4000	-农业、园艺或林业机器用	8	20		5	13	千克		-For agricultural, horticultural or forestry machines
8208.9000	-其他	8	20		5	17	千克		-Other
82.09	**未装配的工具用金属陶瓷板、杆、刀头及类似品:**								**Plates, sticks, tips and the like for tools, unmounted, of cermets:**
8209.0010	---板	8	20		9	17	千克		---Plates
	---条、杆：								---Bars, sticks:
8209.0021	----晶粒度小于0.8微米的	8	20		9	17	千克		----Grain size＜0.8um
8209.0029	----其他	8	20		9	17	千克		----Other
8209.0030	---刀头	8	20		9	17	千克		---Tips
8209.0090	---其他	8	20		9	17	千克		---Other
82.10	**用于加工或调制食品或饮料的手动机械器具，重量不超过10千克:**								**Hand-operated mechanical appliances, weighing 10 kg or less, used in the preparation, conditioning or serving of food or drink:**
8210.0000	用于加工或调制食品或饮料的手动机械器具，重量不超过10千克	18	80		5	17	千克	A	Hand-operated mechanical appliances, weighing 10 kg or less, used in the preparation, conditioning or serving of food or drink
82.11	**有刃口的刀及其刀片，不论是否有锯齿（包括整枝刀），但品目82.08的刀除外:**								**Knives with cutting blades, serrated or not （including pruning knives）, other than knives of heading No.82.08, and blades therefor:**
8211.1000[暂]	-成套货品	18	80	10	9	17	千克/套		-Sets of assorted articles
	-其他:								-Other:
8211.9100[暂]	--刃面固定的餐刀	18	80	10	9	17	千克/把	AB	--Table knives having fixed blades
8211.9200	--刃面固定的其他刀	12	80		9	17	千克/把		--Other knives having fixed blades
8211.9300[暂]	--刃面不固定的刀	18	80	10	9	17	千克/把		--Knives having other than fixed blades
8211.9400	--刀片	14	80		9	17	千克		--Blades
8211.9500	--贱金属制的刀柄	12	80		5	17	千克		--Handles of base metal

税则号列 Tariff Item	商品名称及备注	进口税率			出口退税	增值税率	计量单位	监管条件	Article Description
		最惠	普通	暂定					
82.12	**剃刀及其刀片(包括未分开的刀片条)：**								**Razors and razor blades（including razor blade blanks in strips）:**
8212.1000	-剃刀	12	80		9	17	千克/把		-Razors
8212.2000	-安全刀片，包括未分开的刀片条	14	80		9	17	千克/片		-Safety razor blades, including razor blade blanks in strips
8212.9000	-其他零件	12	80		9	17	千克		-Other parts
82.13	**剪刀、裁缝剪刀及类似品、剪刀片:**								**Scissors, tailors' shears and similar shears, and blades therefor:**
8213.0000	剪刀、裁缝剪刀及类似品、剪刀片	12	80		9	17	千克		Scissors, tailors'shears and similar shears,and blades therefor
82.14	**其他利口器（例如，理发推剪、屠刀、砍骨刀、切肉刀、切菜刀、裁纸刀）;修指甲及修脚用具(包括指甲锉)：**								**Other articles of cutlery（for example, hair clippers, butchers' or kitchen cleavers, choppers and mincing knives, paper knives）; manicure or pedicure sets and instruments（including nail files）:**
8214.1000	-裁纸刀、开信刀、改错刀、铅笔刀及其刀片	12	80		5	17	千克		-Paper knives, letter openers, erasing knives, pencil sharpeners and blades therefor
8214.2000	-修指甲及修脚用具(包括指甲锉)	18	90		9	17	千克		-Manicure or pedicure sets and instruments（including nail files）
8214.9000	-其他	18	80		9	17	千克		-Other
8214 9000.10	切菜刀等厨房用利口器	18	80		9	17	千克	A	Kitchen cleavers, chopping or mincing knives and other articles of cutlery
8214 9000.90	理发推子等其他利口器	18	80		9	17	千克		Hair clippers and other articles of cutlery
82.15	**餐匙、餐叉、长柄勺、漏勺、糕点夹、鱼刀、黄油刀、糖块夹及类似的厨房或餐桌用具:**								**Spoons, forks, ladles, skimmers, cakeservers, fish-knives, butter-knives, sugar tongs and similar kitchen or tableware:**
8215.1000	-成套货品，至少其中一件物品是镀贵金属的	18	80		5	17	千克	A	-Sets of assorted articles containing at least one article plated with precious metal
8215.2000	-其他成套货品	18	80		9	17	千克	A	-Other sets of assorted articles
	-其他:								-Other:
8215.9100	--镀贵金属的	18	80		5	17	千克	A	--Plated with precious metal
8215.9900 [暂]	--其他	18	80	10	9	17	千克	A	--Other

第八十三章
贱金属杂项制品

Chapter 83
Miscellaneous articles of base metal

注释：

一、在本章，贱金属零件应与制品一同归类。但品目73.12、73.15、73.17、73.18及73.20的钢铁制品或其他贱金属（第七十四章至第七十六章及第七十八章至第八十一章）制的类似物品不应视为本章制品的零件。

二、品目83.02所称“脚轮”，是指直径（对于有胎的，连胎计算在内，下同）不超过75毫米的或直径虽超过75毫米，但所装轮或胎的宽度必须小于30毫米的脚轮。

Chapter Notes:

1. For the purposes of this chapter, parts of base metal are to be classified with their parent articles. However, articles of iron or steel of heading 73.12, 73.15, 73.17, 73.18, or 73.20, or similar articles of other base metal (Chapters 74 to 76 and 78 to 81) are not to be taken as parts of articles of this Chapter.

2. For the purposes of heading 83.02, the word “castors” means those having a diameter (including, where appropriate, tyres) not exceeding 75 mm, or those having a diameter (including, where appropriate, tyres) exceeding 75 mm, provided that the width of the wheel or tyre fitted thereto is less than 30 mm.

税则号列 Tariff Item	商品名称及备注	进口税率 最惠	普通	暂定	出口退税	增值税率	计量单位	监管条件	Article Description
83.01	贱金属制的锁（钥匙锁、数码锁及电动锁）；贱金属制带锁的扣环及扣环框架；上述锁的贱金属制钥匙：								**Padlocks and locks (key, combination or electrically operated), of base metal; clasps and frames with clasps, incorporating locks, of base metal; keys for any of the foregoing articles, of base metal:**
8301.1000	-挂锁	14	80		9	17	千克/把		-Padlocks
	-机动车用锁：								-Locks of a kind used for motor vehicles:
8301.2010	---中央控制门锁	10	80		13	17	千克/套		---Central control door lock
8301.2090	---其他	10	80		9	17	千克/套		---Other
8301.3000	-家具用锁	14	80		9	17	千克/个		-Locks of a kind used for furniture
8301.4000	-其他锁	14	80		9	17	千克/个		-Other locks
8301.5000	-带锁的扣环及扣环框架	14	80		9	17	千克		-Clasps and frames with clasps, incorporating locks
8301.6000	-锁零件	12	80		9	17	千克		-Parts of locks
8301.7000	-钥匙	10	80		9	17	千克		-Keys presented separately
83.02	用于家具、门窗、楼梯、百叶窗、车厢、鞍具、衣箱、盒子及类似品的贱金属附件及架座；贱金属制帽架、帽钩、托架及类似品；用贱金属做支架的小脚轮；贱金属制的自动闭门器：								**Base metal mountings, fittings and similar articles suitable for furniture, doors, staircases, windows, blinds, coachwork, saddlery, trunks, chests, caskets, or the like; base metal hatracks, hat-pegs, brackets and similar fixtures; castors with mountings of base metal; automatic door closers of base metal:**
8302.1000	-铰链（折叶）	10	80		5	17	千克		-Hinges
8302.2000	-小脚轮	12	80		9	17	千克		-Castors
8302.3000	-机动车辆用的其他附件及架座	10	80		5	17	千克		-Other mountings, fittings and similar articles suitable for motor vehicles
	-其他附件及架座：								-Other mountings, fittings and similar articles:
8302.4100	--建筑用	14	80		5	17	千克		--Suitable for buildings
8302.4200	--其他，家具用	12	80		5	17	千克		--Other, suitable for furniture
8302.4900	--其他	12	80		5	17	千克		--Other
8302.5000	-帽架、帽钩、托架及类似品	14	80		9	17	千克		-Hat-racks, hat-pegs, brackets and similar fixtures
8302.6000	-自动闭门器	12	80		5	17	千克/个		-Automatic door closets
83.03	装甲或加强的贱金属制保险箱、保险柜及保险库的门和带锁保险储存橱、钱箱、契约箱及类似品：								**Armoured or reinforced safes, strongboxes and doors and safe deposit lockers for strong-rooms, cash or deed boxes and the like, of base metal:**
8303.0000	装甲或加强的贱金属制保险箱、保险柜及保险库的门和带锁保险储存橱、钱箱、契约箱及类似品	14	50		5	17	千克/个		Armoured or reinforced safes, strong boxes and doors and safe deposit lockers for strong-rooms, cash or deed boxes and the like, of base metal

税则号列 Tariff Item	商品名称及备注	进口税率 最惠	普通	暂定	出口退税	增值税率	计量单位	监管条件	Article Description
83.04	**贱金属制的档案柜、卡片索引柜、文件盘、文件篮、笔盘、公章架及类似的办公用具，但品目94.03的办公室家具除外：**								**Filing cabinets, card-index cabinets, paper trays, paper rests, pen trays, office-stamp stands and similar office or desk equipment, of base metal, other than office furniture of heading No.94.03:**
8304.0000	贱金属制的档案柜、卡片索引柜、文件盘、文件篮、笔盘、公章架及类似的办公用具，但品目94.03的办公室家具除外	10.5	80		5	17	千克		Filing cabinets, card-index cabinets, paper trays, paper rests, pen trays, office-stamp stands and similar office or desk equipment, of base metal, other than office furniture of heading No.94.03
83.05	**活页夹、卷宗夹的贱金属附件，贱金属制的信夹、信角、文件夹、索引标签及类似的办公用品；贱金属制的成条订书钉（例如，供办公室、室内装饰或包装用）：**								**Fittings for loose-leaf binders or files, letter clips, letter corners, paper clips, indexing tags and similar office articles, of base metal; staples in strips（for example, for offices, upholstery, packaging）, of base metal:**
8305.1000	-活页夹或宗卷夹的附件	10.5	80		5	17	千克		-Fittings for loose-leaf binders of files
8305.2000	-成条订书钉	10.5	80		5	17	千克		-Staples in strips
8305.9000	-其他，包括零件	10.5	80		5	17	千克		-Other, including parts
83.06	**非电动的贱金属铃、钟、锣及类似品；贱金属雕塑像及其他装饰品；贱金属相框或画框及类似框架；贱金属镜子：**								**Bells, gongs and the like, non-electric, of base metal; statuettes and other ornaments, of base metal; photograph, picture or similar frames, of base metal; mirrors of base metal:**
8306.1000	-铃、钟、锣及类似品	8	80		5	17	千克		-Bells, gongs and the like
	-雕塑像及其他装饰品：								-Statuettes and other ornaments:
8306.2100	--镀贵金属的	8	100		5	17	千克		--Plated with precious metal
	--其他：								--Other:
8306.2910	---景泰蓝的	8	100		9	17	千克		---Cloisonne
8306.2990	---其他	8	100		13	17	千克		---Other
8306.3000	-相框、画框及类似框架；镜子	8	100		5	17	千克		-Photograph, picture or similar frames; mirrors
83.07	**贱金属软管，不论是否有附件：**								**Flexible tubing of base metal, with or without fittings:**
8307.1000	-钢铁制	8.4	35		5	17	千克		-Of iron or steel
8307.9000	-其他贱金属制	8.4	35		5	17	千克		-Of other base metal
83.08	**贱金属制的扣、钩、环、眼及类似品，用于衣着、鞋靴、天篷、提包、旅行用品或其他制成品；贱金属制的管形铆钉及开口铆钉；贱金属制的珠子及亮晶片：**								**Clasps, frames with clasps, buckles, buckle-clasps, hooks, eyes, eyelets and the like, of base metal, of a kind used for clothing, footwear, awnings, handbags, travel goods or other made up articles; tubular or bifurcated rivets, of base metal; beads and spangles, of base metal:**
8308.1000	-钩、环及眼	10.5	80		9	17	千克		-Hooks, eyes and eyelets
8308.2000	-管形铆钉及开口铆钉	10.5	80		5	17	千克		-Tubular or bifurcated rivets
8308.9000	-其他，包括零件	10.5	80		5	17	千克		-Other， including parts
83.09	**贱金属制的塞子、盖子（包括冠形瓶塞、螺口盖及倒水塞）、瓶帽、螺口塞、塞子帽、封志及其他包装用附件：**								**Stoppers, caps and lids（including crown corks, screw caps and pouring stoppers）, capsules for bottles, threaded bungs, bung covers, seals and other packing accessories, of base metal:**
8309.1000	-冠形瓶塞	18	90		5	17	千克		-Crown corks
8309.9000	-其他	12	80		5	17	千克		-Other
83.10	**贱金属制的标志牌、铭牌、地名牌及类似品、号码、字母及类似标志，但品目94.05的货品除外：**								**Sign-plates, name-plates, address plates and similar plates, numbers, letters and other symbols, of base metal, excluding those of heading No.94.05:**
8310.0000	贱金属制的标志牌、铭牌、地名牌及类似品、号码、字母及类似标志，但品目94.05的货品除外	18	80		5	17	千克		Sign-plates, name-plates, address-plates and similar plates, numbers, letters and other symbols, of base metal, excluding those of heading No.94.05

税则号列 Tariff Item	商品名称及备注	进口税率			出口退税	增值税率	计量单位	监管条件	Article Description
		最惠	普通	暂定					
83.11	**贱金属或硬质合金制的丝、条、管、板、电极及类似品，以焊剂涂面或以焊剂为芯，用于焊接或沉积金属、硬质合金；贱金属粉粘聚而成的丝或条，供金属喷镀用：**								**Wire, rods, tubes, plates, electrodes and similar products, of base metal or of metal carbides, coated or cored with flux material, of a kind used for soldering, brazing, welding or deposition of metal or of metal carbides; wire and rods, of agglomerated base-metal powder, used for metal spraying:**
8311.1000	-以焊剂涂面的贱金属制电极，电弧焊用	8	30		13	17	千克		-Coated electrodes of base metal, for electric arcwelding
8311.2000	-以焊剂为芯的贱金属制焊丝，电弧焊用	8	30		13	17	千克		-Cored wire of base metal, for electric arcwelding
8311.3000	-以焊剂涂面或以焊剂为芯的贱金属条或丝，钎焊或气焊用	8	30		13	17	千克		-Coated rods and cored wire, of base metal, for soldering, brazing or welding by flame
8311.9000	-其他	8	30		13	17	千克		-Other

第十六类 机器、机械器具、电气设备及其零件；录音机及放声机、电视图像、声音的录制和重放设备及其零件、附件

SECTION XVI MACHINERY AND MECHANICAL APPLIANCES; ELECTRICAL EQUIPMENT; PARTS THEREOF; SOUND RECORDERS AND REPRODUCERS,TELEVISION IMAGE AND SOUND RECORDERS AND REPRODUCERS, AND PARTS AND ACCESSORIES OF SUCH ARTICLES

注释：

一、本类不包括：

（一）第三十九章的塑料或品目 40.10 的硫化橡胶制的传动带、输送带；除硬质橡胶以外的硫化橡胶制的机器、机械器具、电气器具或其他专门技术用途的物品（品目 40.16）；

（二）机器、机械器具或其他专门技术用途的皮革、再生皮革（品目 42.05）或毛皮（品目 43.03）的制品；

（三）各种材料（例如，第三十九章、第四十章、第四十四章、第四十八章及第十五类的材料）制的筒管、卷轴、纡子、锥形筒管、芯子、线轴及类似品；

（四）提花机及类似机器用的穿孔卡片（例如，归入第三十九章、第四十八章或第十五类的）；

（五）纺织材料制的传动带、输送带及其带料（品目 59.10）或专门技术用途的其他纺织材料制品（品目 59.11）；

（六）品目 71.02 至 71.04 的宝石或半宝石（天然、合成或再造）或品目 71.16 的完全以宝石或半宝石制成的物品，但已加工未装配的唱针用蓝宝石和钻石除外（品目 85.22）；

（七）第十五类注释二所规定的贱金属制通用零件（第十五类）及塑料制的类似品（第三十九章）；

（八）钻管（品目 73.04）；

（九）金属丝、带制的环形带（第十五类）；

（十）第八十二章或第八十三章的物品；

（十一）第十七类的物品；

（十二）第九十章的物品；

（十三）第九十一章的钟、表及其他物品；

（十四）品目 82.07 的可互换工具及作为机器零件的刷子（品目 96.03）；类似的可互换工具应按其构成工作部件的材料归类（例如，归入第四十章、第四十二章、第四十三章、第四十五章、第五十九章或品目 68.04、69.09）；

（十五）第九十五章的物品；或

（十六）打字机色带或类似色带，不论是否带轴或装盒（应按其材料属性归类；如已上油或经其他方法处理能着色的，应归入品目 96.12）。

Section Notes:

1. This Section does not cover:

（a）Transmission or conveyor belts or belting, of plastics of Chapter 39, or of vulcanised rubber（heading 40.10）, or other articles of a kind used in machinery or mechanical or electrical appliances or for other technical uses, of vulcanised rubber other than hard rubber（heading 40.16）;

（b）Articles of leather or of composition leather（heading 42.04）or of furskin（heading 43.03）, of a kind used in machinery or mechanical appliances or for other technical uses;

（c）Bobbins, spools, cops, cones, cores, reels or similar supports, of any material（for example, Chapter 39, 40, 44 or 48 or Section XV）;

（d）Perforated cards for Jacquard or similar machines（for example, Chapter 39 or 48 or SectionXV）;

（e）Transmission or conveyor belts or belting of textile material（heading 59.10）or other articles of textile material for technical uses（heading 59.11）;

（f）Precious or semi-precious stones（natural, synthetic or reconstruct -ed）of headings 71.02 to 71.04, or articles wholly of such stones of heading 71.16, except unmounted worked sapphires and diamonds for styli（heading 85.22）;

（g）Parts of general use, as defined in Note 2 to SectionXV,of base metal（SectionXV）, or similar goods of plastics（Chapter 39）;

（h）Drill pipe（heading 73.04）;

（ij）Endless belts of metal wire or strip（SectionXV）;

（k）Articles of Chapter 82 or 83;

（l）Articles of Section XVII;

（m）Articles of Chapter 90;

（n）Clocks, watches or other articles of Chapter 91;

（o）Interchangeable tools of heading 82.07 or brushes of a kind used as parts of machines（heading 96.03）; similar interchangeable tools are to be classified according to the constituent material of their working part（for example, in Chapter 40, 42, 43, 45 or 59 or heading 68.04 or 69.09）;

（p）Articles of Chapter 95; or

（q）Typewriter or similar ribbons, whether or not on spools or in cartridg -es（classified according to their constituent material,or in heading 96.12 if inked or otherwise prepared for giving impressions）.

二、除本类注释一、第八十四章注释一及第八十五章注释一另有规定的以外，机器零件（不属于品目 84.84、85.44、85.45、85.46 或 85.47 所列物品的零件）应按下列规定归类：

（一）凡在第八十四章、第八十五章的品目（品目 84.09、84.31、84.48、84.66、84.73、84.87、85.03、85.22、85.29、85.38 及 85.48 除外）列名的货品，均应归入该两章的相应品目；

（二）专用于或主要用于某一种机器或同一品目的多种机器（包括品目 84.79 或 85.43 的机器）的其他零件，应与该种机器一并归类，或酌情归入品目 84.09、84.31、84.48、84.66、84.73、85.03、85.22、85.29 或 85.38。但能同时主要用于品目 85.17 和 85.25 至 85.28 所列机器的零件，应归入品目 85.17；

（三）所有其他零件应酌情归入品目 84.09、84.31、84.48、84.66、84.73、85.03、85.22、85.29 或 85.38，如不能归入上述品目，则应归入品目 84.87 或 85.48。

三、由两部及两部以上机器装配在一起形成的组合式机器，或具有两种及两种以上互补或交替功能的机器，除条文另有规定的以外，应按具有主要功能的机器归类。

四、由不同独立部件（不论是否分开或由管道、传动装置、电缆或其他装置连接）组成的机器（包括机组），如果组合后明显具有一种第八十四章或第八十五章某个税号所列功能，则全部机器应按其功能归入有关品目。

五、上述各注释所称"机器"，是指第八十四章或第八十五章各品目所列的各种机器、设备、装置及器具。

第八十四章
核反应堆、锅炉、机器、机械器具及其零件

注释：

一、本章不包括：

（一）第六十八章的石磨、石碾及其他物品；

（二）陶瓷材料制的机器或器具（例如，泵）及供任何材料制的机器或器具用的陶瓷零件（第六十九章）；

（三）实验室用玻璃器（品目 70.17）；玻璃制的机器、器具或其他专门技术用途的物品及其零件（品目 70.19 或 70．20）；

（四）品目 73.21 或 73.22 的物品或其他贱金属制的类似物品（第七十四章至第七十六章或第七十八章至第八十一章）；

（五）品目 85.08 的真空吸尘器；

2. Subject to Note 1 to this Section, Note 1 to Chapter 84 and Note 1 to Chapter 85, parts of machines (not being parts of the articles of heading 84.84, 85.44, 85.45, 85.46 or 85.47) are to be classified according to the following rules:

(a) Parts which are goods included in any of the headings of Chapter 84 or 85 (other than headings 84.09, 84.31, 84.48, 84.66, 84.73, 84.87, 85.03, 85.22, 85.29, 85.38 and 85.48) are in all cases to be classified in their respective headings;

(b) Other parts, if suitable for use solely or principally with a particular kind of machine, or with a number of machines of the same heading (including a machine of heading 84.79 or 85.43) are to be classified with the machines of that kind or in heading 84.09, 84.31, 84.48, 84.66, 84.73, 85.03, 85.22, 85.29 or 85.38 as appropriate. However, parts which are equally suitable for use principally with the goods of headings 85.17 and 85.25 to 85.28 are to be classified in heading 85.17;

(c) All other parts are to be classified in heading 84.09, 84.31, 84.48, 84.66, 84.73, 85.03, 85.22, 85.29 or 85.38 as appropriate or, failing that, in heading 84.87 or 85.48.

3. Unless the context otherwise requires, composite machines consisting of two or more machines fitted together to form a whole and other machines designed for the purpose of performing two or more complementary or alternative functions are to be classified as if consisting only of that component or as being that machine which performs the principal function.

4. Where a machine (including a combination of machines) consists of individual components (whether separate or interconnected by piping, by transmission devices, by electric cables or by other devices) intended to contribute together to a clearly defined function covered by one of the headings in Chapter 84 or Chapter 85, then the whole falls to be classified in the heading appropriate to that function.

5. For the purposes of these Notes, the expression "machine" means any machine, machinery, plant, equipment, apparatus or appliance cited in the headings of Chapter 84 or 85.

Chapter 84
Nuclear reactors, boilers, machinery and mechanical appliances; parts thereof

Chapter Notes:

1. This Chapter does not cover:

(a) Millstones, grindstones or other articles of Chapter 68;

(b) Machinery or appliances (for example, pumps) of ceramic material and ceramic parts of machinery or appliances of any material (Chapter 69);

(c) Laboratory glassware (heading 70.17); machinery, appliances or other articles for technical uses or parts thereof, of glass (heading 70.19 or 70.20);

(d) Articles of heading 73.21 or 73.22 or similar articles of other base metals (Chapters 74 to 76 or 78 to 81);

(e) Vacuum cleaners of heading 85.08;

（六）品目 85.09 的家用电动器具；品目 85.25 的数字照相机；或

（七）非机动的手工操作地板清扫器（品目 96.03）。

二、除第十六类注释三及本章注释九另有规定以外，如果某种机器或器具既符合品目 84.01 至 84.24 中一个或几个品目的规定，或符合品目 84.86 的规定，又符合品目 84.25 至 84.80 中一个或几个品目的规定，则应酌情归入品目 84.01 至 84.24 中的相应品目或品目 84.86，而不归入品目 84.25 至 84.80 中的有关品目。

但品目 84.19 不包括：

（一）催芽装置、孵卵器或育雏器（品目 84.36）；

（二）谷物调湿机（品目 84.37）；

（三）萃取糖汁的浸提装置（品目 84.38）；

（四）纱线、织物及纺织制品的热处理机器（品目 84.51）；或

（五）温度变化（即使必不可少）仅作为辅助功能的机器设备。

品目 84.22 不包括：

（一）缝合袋子或类似品用的缝纫机（品目 84.52）；或

（二）品目 84.72 的办公室用机器。

品目 84.24 不包括：

（一）喷墨印刷（打印）机器（品目 84.43），或

（二）水射流切割机（品目 84.56）

三、如果用于加工各种材料的某种机床既符合品目 84.56 的规定，又符合品目 84.57、84.58、84.59、84.60、84.61、84.64 或 84.65 的规定，则应归入品目 84.56。

四、品目 84.57 仅适用于可以完成下列不同形式机械操作的金属加工机床，但车床（包括车削中心）除外：

（一）按照机械加工程序从刀具库中自动更换刀具（加工中心）；

（二）同时或顺序地自动使用不同的动力头对固定不动的工件进行加工（单工位组合机床）；或

（三）自动将工件送向不同的动力头（多工位组合机床）。

五、（一）品目 84.71 所称“自动数据处理设备”，是指具有以下功能的机器：

1. 存储处理程序及执行程序直接需要的起码的数据；
2. 按照用户的要求随意编辑程序；
3. 按照用户指令进行算术计算；以及
4. 在运行过程中，可不需人为干预而通过逻辑判断，执行一个处理程序，这个处理程序可改变计算机指令的执行。

（二）自动数据处理设备可以是一套由若干单独部件所组成的系统。

(f) Electro-mechanical domestic appliance of heading 85.09;digital cameras of heading 85.25; or

(g) Hand-operated mechanical floor sweepers, not motorised (heading 96.03).

2. Subject to the operation of Note 3 to Section XVI and subject to Note 9 to this chapter, a machine or appliance which answers to a description in one or more of the headings 84.01 to 84.24, or heading84.86 and at the same time to a description in one or other of the headings 84.25 to 84.80 is to be classified under the appropriate heading of the former group or under heading 84.86, as the case may be, and not the latter group.

Heading 84.19 does not, however, cover:

(a) Germination plant, incubators or brooder (heading 84.36);

(b) Grain dampening machines (heading 84.37);

(c) Diffusing apparatus for sugar juice extraction (heading84.38);

(d) Machinery for the heat-treatment of textile yarns, fabrics or made up textile articles (heading 84.51); or

(e) Machinery or plant, designed for a mechanical operation, in which a change of temperature, even if necessary, is subsidiary.

Heading 84.22 does not cover:

(a) Sewing machines for closing bags or similar containers (heading 84.52); or

(b) Office machinery of heading 84.72.

Heading 84.24 does not cover:

(a) Ink-jet printing machines (heading 84.43); or

(b) Water-jet cutting machines (heading 84.56).

3. A machine-tool for working any material which answers to a description in heading 84.56 and at the same time to a description in heading 84.57, 84.58, 84.59, 84.60, 84.61, 84.64 or 84.65 is to be classified in heading 84.56.

4. Heading 84.57 applies only to machine-tools for working metal,other than lathes (including turning centers), which can carry out different types of machining operations either:

(a)by automatic tool change from a magazine or the like in conformity with a machining programme (machining centres);

(b) by the automatic use, simultaneously or sequentially, of different unit heads working on a fixed position workpiece (unit construction machines, single station); or

(c) by the automatic transfer of the workpiece to different unit heads (multi-station transfer machines).

5. (a) For the purposes of heading 84.71, the expression "automatic data processing machines" means machines capable of:

(i) Storing the processing program or programs and at least the data immediately necessary for the execution of the program;

(ii) Being freely programmed in accordance with the requirements of the user;

(iii) Performing arithmetical computations specified by the user; and

(iv) Executing, without human intervertion, a processing program which requires them to modify their execution,by logical decision during the processing run.

(b) Automatic data processing machines may be in the form of systems consisting of a variable number of separate units.

（三）除本条注释（四）及（五）另有规定的以外，一个部件如果符合下列所有规定，即可视为自动数据处理系统的一部分：

1. 专用于或主要用于自动数据处理系统；
2. 可以直接或通过一个或几个其他部件同中央处理器相联接；以及
3. 能够以本系统所使用的方式（代码或信号）接收或传送数据。

自动数据处理设备的部件如果单独报验，应归入品目 84.71。

但是，键盘、X-Y 坐标输入装置及盘（片）式存储部件，只要符合上述注释（三）2 及（三）3 所列的规定，应一律作为品目 84.71 的部件归类。

（四）品目 84.71 不包括单独报验的下述设备，即使它们符合上述注释五（三）的所有规定：

1. 打印机、复印机、传真机，不论是否组合式；
2. 发送或接收声音、图像或其他数据的设备，包括有线或无线网络（例如，局域网或广域网）通信设备；
3. 扬声器及传声器（麦克风）；
4. 电视摄像机、数字照相机及视频摄录一体机；
5. 监视器及投影机，未装有电视接收装置。

（五）装有自动数据处理设备或与自动数据处理设备连接使用，但却从事数据处理以外的某项专门功能的机器，应按其功能归入相应的品目，对于无法按功能归类的，应归入未列名品目。

六、品目 84.82 还包括最大直径及最小直径与标称直径相差均不超过 1% 或 0.05 毫米（以相差数值较小的为准）的抛光钢珠，其他钢珠归入品目 73.26。

七、具有一种以上用途的机器在归类时，其主要用途可作为唯一的用途对待。

除本章注释二、第十六类注释三另有规定的以外，凡任何品目都未列明其主要用途的机器，以及没有哪一种用途是主要用途的机器，均应归入品目 84.79。品目 84.79 还包括将金属丝、纺织纱线或其他各种材料以及它们的混合材料制成绳、缆的机器（例如，捻股机、绞扭机、制缆机）。

八、品目 84.70 所称"袖珍式"，仅适用于外形尺寸不超过 170 毫米×100 毫米×45 毫米的机器。

九、（一）第八十五章注释八（一）及（二）同样适用于本条注释及品目 84.86 中所称的"半导体器件"及"集成电路"。但本条注释及品目 84.86 所称"半导体器件"，也包括光敏半导体器件及发光二极管。

(c) Subject to paragraphs (d) and (e) below, a unit is to be regarded as being part of an automatic data processing system if it meets all of the following conditions:

(i) It is of a kind solely or principally used in an automatic data processing system;

(ii) It is connectable to the central processing unit either directly or through one or more other units; and

(iii) It is able to accept or deliver data in a form (codes or signals) which can be used by the system.

Separately presented units of an automatic data processing machine are to be classified in heading 84.71.

However, keyboards, X-Y co-ordinate input devices and disk storage units which satisfy the conditions of paragraphs (c) (ii) and (c) (iii) above, are in all cases to be classified as units of heading 84.71.

(d) Heading 84.71 dose not cover the following when presented separately, even if they meet all of the conditions set forth in Note 5 (c) above:

(i) Printers, copying machines, facsimile machines, whether or not combined;

(ii) Apparatus for the transmission or reception of voice,images or other data, including apparatus for communication in a wired or wireless network (such as a local or wide area network);

(iii) Loudspeakers and microphones;

(iv) Television cameras, digital cameras and video camera recorders;

(v) Monitors and projectors, not incorporating television reception apparatus.

(e) Machines incorporating or working in conjunction with an automatic data processing machine and performing a specific function other than data processing are to be classified in the headings appropriate to their respective functions or,failing that, in residual headings.

6. Heading 84.82 applies, inter alia, to polished steel balls, the maximum and minimum diameters of which do not differ from the nominal diameter by more than 1% or by more than 0.05 mm, whichever is less. Other steel balls are to be classified in heading 73.26.

7. A machine which is used for more than one purpose is, for the purposes of classification, to be treated as if its principal purpose were its sole purpose.

Subject to Note 2 to this Chapter and Note 3 to Section XVI, a machine the principal purpose of which is not described in any heading or for which no one purpose is the principal purpose is, unless the context otherwise requires, to be classified in heading 84.79. Heading 84.79 also covers machines for making rope or cable (for example, stranding, twisting or cabling machines) from metal wire, textile yarn or any other material or from a combination of such materials.

8. For the purposes of heading 84.70, the term "pocket-size" applies only to machines the dimensions of which do not exceed 170mm×100mm×45 mm.

9. (a) Notes 8 (a) and 8 (b) of Chapter 85 also apply with respect to the expressions "semiconductor devices and electronic integrated circuit", respectively, as used in this Note and in heading 84.86. However, for the purposes of this Note and of heading 84.86, the expression, semiconductor devices also covers photosensitive semiconductor devices and light emitting diodes.

（二）本条注释及品目 84.86 所称“平板显示器的制造”，包括将各层基片制造成一层平板，但不包括玻璃的制造或将印刷电路板或其他电子元件装配在平板上。所称“平板显示”不包括阴极射线管技术。

（三）品目 84.86 也包括专用于或主要用于下列用途的机器及装置：

1. 制造或修补掩膜版及刻线；
2. 组装半导体器件或集成电路；
3. 升降、搬运、装卸单晶柱、圆片、半导体器件、集成电路及平板显示器。

（四）除第十六类注释一及第八十四章注释一另有规定的以外，符合品目 84.86 规定的设备及装置，应归入该品目而不归入本目录的其他品目。

(b) For the purposes of this Note and of heading 84.86, the expression “manufacture of flat panel displays” covers the fabrication of substrates into a flat panel. It does not cover the manufacture of glass or the assembly of printed circuit boards or other electronic components onto the flat panel. The expression “flat panel display” does not cover cathode-ray tube technology.

(c) Heading 84.86 also includes machines and apparatus solely or principally of a kind used for:

(i) the manufacture or repair of masks and reticles;
(ii) assembling semiconductor devices or electronic integrated circuits;
(iii) lifting, handling, loading or unloading of boules, wafers, semicondutor devices, electronic integrated circuits and flat panel displays.

(d) Subject to Note 1 to Section ⅩⅥ and Note 1 to Chapter 84, machines and apparatus answering to the description in heading 84.86 are to be classified in that heading and in no other heading of the Nomenclature.

子目注释：

一、子目 8471.49 所称“系统”，是指各部件符合第八十四章注释五（三）所列条件，并且至少由一个中央处理部件、一个输入部件（例如，键盘或扫描器）及一个输出部件（例如，视频显示器或打印机）组成的自动数据处理设备。

二、子目 8482.40 仅包括滚柱直径相同，最大不超过5毫米，且长度至少是直径三倍的圆滚柱轴承，滚柱的两端可以磨圆。

Subheading Notes:

1. For the purposes of subheading 8471.49, the term “systems” means automatic data processing machines whose units satisfy the conditions laid down in Note 5 (c) to Chapter 84 and which comprise at least a central processing unit, one input unit (for example, a keyboard or a scanner), and one output unit (for example, a visual display unit or a printer).
2. Subheading 8482.40 applies only to bearings with cylindrical rollers of a uniform diameter not exceeding 5mm and having a length which is at least three times the diameter. The ends of the rollers may be rounded.

税则号列 Tariff Item	商品名称及备注	进口税率 最惠	进口税率 普通	进口税率 暂定	出口退税	增值税率	计量单位	监管条件	Article Description
84.01	**核反应堆；核反应堆的未辐照燃料元件（释热元件）；同位素分离机器及装置：**								**Nuclear reactors; fuel elements (cartridges), non-irradiated, for nuclear reactors; machinery and apparatus for isotopic separation:**
8401.1000	-核反应堆	2	8		17	17	千克	3	-Nuclear reactors
8401.2000	-同位素分离机器、装置及其零件	1	8		17	17	个/千克	3	-Machinery and apparatus for isotopic separation, and parts thereof
	-未辐照燃料元件(释热元件):								-Fuel elements (cartridges), non-irradiated:
8401.3010	---未辐照燃料元件	2	8		17	17	千克		---Fuel elements, non-irradiated
8401.3090	---未辐照燃料元件的零件	1	8		17	17	千克		---Parts for fuel elements non-irradiated
	-核反应堆零件:								-Parts of nuclear reactors:
8401.4010	---未辐照相关组件	1	8		17	17	千克		---Non-irradiated Associated Assembly
8401.4020	---堆内构件	1	8		17	17	千克	3	---Reactor internals
8401.4090	---其他	1	8		17	17	千克		---Other
8401 4090.10	核反应堆压力容器(包括其顶板)(专门设计或制造来用于容纳核反应堆的堆芯)	1	8		17	17	千克	3	Pressure vessels for nuclear reactors (including the top slabs) (specially designed or produced to hold the reactor core of the nuclear reactors)
8401 4090.20	核反应堆控制棒和设备(专用于核反应堆裂变控制棒、支承结构或悬吊结构等)	1	8		17	17	千克	3	Control rods and devices for nuclear reactors (control rods, supporting structures or suspended structures used exclusively for nuclear fission)
8401 4090.30	核反应堆压力管(专用于容纳核燃料元件和一次冷却剂的，压力＞5.1 兆帕)	1	8		17	17	千克	3	Pressure pipes for nuclear reactors (used exclusively for holding nuclear fuel elements and primary coolant, pressure＞5.1mpa)
8401 4090.90	其他核反应堆零件	1	8		17	17	千克		Other parts for nuclear reactors

税则号列 Tariff Item	商品名称及备注	进口税率 最惠	普通	暂定	出口退税	增值税率	计量单位	监管条件	Article Description
84.02	蒸汽锅炉(能产生低压水蒸汽的集中供暖用的热水锅炉除外);过热水锅炉:								**Steam or other vapour generating boilers (other than central heating hot water boilers capable also of producting low pressure steam); super-heated water boilers:**
	-蒸汽锅炉:								-Steam or other vapour generating boilers:
	--蒸发量超过45吨/时的水管锅炉:								--Watertube boilers with a steam production exceeding 45t per hour:
8402.1110	---蒸发量在900吨/时及以上的发电用锅炉	3	11		17	17	台/千克	6A	---Boilers for generating electricity with a steam production 900t or more per hour
8402.1190	---其他	14	35		17	17	台/千克	6A	---Other
8402.1200	--蒸发量不超过45吨/时的水管锅炉	5	35		17	17	台/千克		--Watertube boilers with a steam production not exceeding 45t per hour
8402 1200.10	纸浆厂废料锅炉(蒸发≤45吨/时蒸汽水管锅炉)	5	35		17	17	台/千克	6A	Waste material boilers from pulp mills (steam water tube boilers with their evaporation of ≤45 tons/hour)
8402 1200.90	其他蒸发量未超45吨/时水管锅炉	5	35		17	17	台/千克	6A	Other water tube boilers with their evaporation of ≤45 tons/hour)
8402.1900	--其他蒸汽锅炉,包括混合式锅炉	5	35		17	17	台/千克	6A	--Other vapour generating boilers, including hybrid boilers
8402.2000	-过热水锅炉	16	35		17	17	台/千克	6A	-Super-heated water boilers
8402.9000	-零件	2	11		17	17	千克		-Parts
84.03	集中供暖用的热水锅炉,但品目84.02的货品除外:								**Central heating boilers other than those of heading No.84.02:**
	-锅炉:								-Boilers:
8403.1010	---家用型	10	80		17	17	台/千克	6A	---Household type
8403.1090	---其他	10	80		17	17	台/千克	6A	---Other
8403.9000	-零件	6	80		17	17	千克		-Parts
84.04	品目84.02或84.03所列锅炉的辅助设备(例如,节热器、过热器、除灰器、气体回收器);水蒸汽或其他蒸汽动力装置的冷凝器:								**Auxiliary plant for use with boilers of heading No.84.02 or 84.03 (for example, economizers, super-heaters, soot removers, gas recoverers); condensers for steam or other vapour power units:**
	-税号84.02或84.03所列锅炉的辅助设备:								-Auxiliary plant for use with boilers of heading No.84.02 or 84.03:
8404.1010	---税号84.02所列锅炉的辅助设备	7	35		17	17	千克	6A	---For use with boilers of heading No.84.02
8404.1020	---税号84.03所列锅炉的辅助设备	10	80		17	17	千克	6A	---For use with boilers of heading No.84.03
8404.2000	-水蒸汽或其他蒸汽动力装置的冷凝器	14	35		17	17	千克	6A	-Condensers for steam or other vapour power units
	-零件:								-Parts:
8404.9010	---子目号8404.1020所列设备的零件	10	80		17	17	千克		---Of the auxiliary plant of subheading No.8404.1020
8404.9090	---其他	7	35		17	17	千克		---Other
84.05	煤气发生器,不论有无净化器;乙炔发生器及类似水解气体发生器,不论有无净化器:								**Producer gas or water gas generators, with or without their purifiers; acetylene gas generators and similar water process gas generators, with or without their purifiers:**
8405.1000	-煤气发生器,不论有无净化器;乙炔发生器及类似的水解气体发生器,不论有无净化器	14	30		17	17	千克	A	-Producer gas or water gas generators, with or without their purifiers; acetylene gas generators and similar water process gas generators, with or without their purifiers
8405.9000	-零件	8	30		17	17	千克		-Parts
84.06	汽轮机:								**Steam turbines and other vapour turbines:**
8406.1000	-船舶动力用汽轮机	5	35		17	17	台/千瓦		-Turbines for marine propulsion
	-其他汽轮机:								-Other turbines:
	--输出功率超过40兆瓦的:								--Of an output exceeding 40MW:
8406.8110	---输出功率不超过100兆瓦的	5	35		17	17	台/千瓦		---Of an output not exceeding 100 MW

税则号列 Tariff Item	商品名称及备注	进口税率 最惠	普通	暂定	出口退税	增值税率	计量单位	监管条件	Article Description
8406.8120	---输出功率超过 100 兆瓦,但不超过 350 兆瓦的	5	35		17	17	台/千瓦		---Of an output exceeding 100MW but not exceeding 350MW
8406.8130	---输出功率超过 350 兆瓦的	6	11		17	17	台/千瓦		---Of an output exceeding 350MW
8406.8200	--输出功率不超过 40 兆瓦的	5	35		17	17	台/千瓦	O	--Of an output not exceeding 40MW
8406.9000	-零件	2	11		17	17	千克		-Parts
84.07	**点燃往复式或旋转式活塞内燃发动机:**								**Spark-ignition reciprocating or rotary internal combustion piston engines:**
	-航空器发动机:								-Aircraft engines:
8407.1010 暂	---输出功率不超过 298 千瓦	2	11	1	17	17	台/千瓦	6	---Of an output not exceeding 298kW
8407.1020 暂	---输出功率超过 298 千瓦	2	11	1	15	17	台/千瓦	6	---Of an output exceeding 298kW
	-船舶发动机:								-Marine propulsion engines:
8407.2100	--舷外发动机	8	35		17	17	台/千瓦	6	--Outboard motors
8407.2900	--其他	8	20		17	17	台/千瓦	6	--Other
	-用于第八十七章所列车辆的往复式活塞发动机:								-Reciprocating piston engines of a kind used for the propulsion of vehicles of Chapter 87:
8407.3100	--气缸容量(排气量)不超过 50 毫升	10	35		15	17	台/千瓦	y4xA6	--Of a cylinder capacity not exceeding 50cc
8407.3200	--气缸容量(排气量)超过 50 毫升,但不超过 250 毫升	10	35		15	17	台/千瓦	y4xA6	--Of a cylinder capacity exceeding 50cc but not exceeding 250cc
8407.3300	--气缸容量(排气量)超过 250 毫升,但不超过 1000 毫升	10	70		15	17	台/千瓦	AO6	--Of a cylinder capacity exceeding 250cc but not exceeding 1000cc
	--气缸容量(排气量)超过 1000 毫升:								--Of a cylinder capacity exceeding 1000 cc:
8407.3410	---气缸容量(排气量)超过 1000 毫升,但不超过 3000 毫升	10	70		17	17	台/千瓦	A6O	---Of a cylinder capacity exceeding 1000cc but not exceeding 3000cc
8407.3420	---气缸容量(排气量)超过 3000 毫升	10	35		17	17	台/千瓦		---Of a cylinder capacity exceeding 3000cc
8407 3420.10	排气量≥5.9 升的天然气发动机(第八十七章所列车辆用的点燃往复式活塞发动机)	10	35		17	17	台/千瓦	A6O	Natural gas engines with displacement≥5.9L (spark-ignition reciprocating piston engines for the vehicles listed in Chapter 87)
8407 3420.90	其他排气量>3000 毫升车用往复式活塞引擎(第八十七章所列车辆用的点燃往复式活塞发动机)	10	35		17	17	台/千瓦	A6O	Other vehicle-use reciprocating piston engines with displacement>3000cc (spark-ignition reciprocating piston engines for the vehicles listed in Chapter 87)
	-其他发动机:								-Other engines:
8407.9010	---沼气发动机	12	35		17	17	台/千瓦	6	---Firedamp engines
8407.9090	---其他	18	35		17	17	台/千瓦		---Other
8407 9090.03 暂	立式输出轴汽油发动机(非第八十七章所列车辆用其他往复式活塞发动机)	18	35	9	17	17	台/千瓦	6	Vertical output axis gasoline engines (other reciprocating piston engines for the vehicles not listed in Chapter 87)
8407 9090.10	转速<3600r/min 汽油发动机(发电机用)	18	35		17	17	台/千瓦	O6	Gasoline engines with rotational speed<3600r/min (for generators)
8407 9090.20	转速<4650r/min 汽油发动机(品目 8426、8428-8430 所列机械用)	18	35		17	17	台/千瓦	O6	Gasoline engines with rotational speed<4650 r/min (for machinery listed in Heading 84.26, 84.28-84.30)
8407 9090.30	转速<4650r/min 汽油发动机(品目 8427 所列机械用)	18	35		17	17	台/千瓦	O6	Gasoline engines with rotational speed<4650 r/min (for machinery listed in Heading 84.27)
8407 9090.90	其他往复或旋转式活塞内燃引擎(非第八十七章所列车辆用其他点燃往复式或旋转式活塞发动机)	18	35		17	17	台/千瓦	6	Other reciprocating or rotary internal combustion piston engines (other spark-ignition reciprocating or rotary piston engines for the vehicles not listed in Chapter 87)
84.08	**压燃式活塞内燃发动机(柴油或半柴油发动机):**								**Compression-ignition internal combustion piston engines (diesel or semidiesel engines):**
8408.1000	-船舶发动机	5	11		17	17	台/千瓦	O6	-Marine propulsion engines
	-用于第八十七章所列车辆的发动机:								-Engines of a kind used for the propulsion of vehicles of Chapter 87:

税则号列 Tariff Item	商品名称及备注	进口税率			出口退税	增值税率	计量单位	监管条件	Article Description
		最惠	普通	暂定					
8408.2010	---输出功率在 132.39 千瓦（180 马力）及以上	9	14		17	17	台/千瓦		---Of an output of 132.39kW（180hp） or more
8408 2010.01[暂]	输出功率在441千瓦(600马力)及以上的柴油发动机	9	14	4	17	17	台/千瓦	O6	Diesel engineswith output power≥441kW (600hp)
8408 2010.10	功率≥132.39 千瓦拖拉机用柴油机	9	14		17	13	台/千瓦	6	Diesel engines for tractors with output power≥132.39kw
8408 2010.90	功率≥132.39 千瓦其他用柴油机[指八十七章车辆用压燃式活塞内燃发动机（132.39 千瓦=180 马力）]	9	14		17	17	台/千瓦	O6	Diesel engines for other uses with output power≥132.39kw (refers to compression-ignition internal combustion piston engines for the vehicles listed in Chapter 87（132.39kw=180hp）)
8408.2090	---其他	25	35				台/千瓦		---Other
8408 2090.01[暂]	升功率≥40kw 的额定功率＜132.39kw的轿车用柴油发动机	25	35	10	17	17	台/千瓦	6O	Diesel engines for cars with rated power<150kw (power per liter≥40kw）
8408 2090.10	功率＜132.39 千瓦拖拉机用柴油机	25	35		13/17	13	台/千瓦	6	Diesel engines for tractors with output power＜132.39kw
8408 2090.90	功率<132.39 千瓦其他用柴油机(指第八十七章车辆用压燃式活塞内燃发动机)	25	35		15	17	台/千瓦	6O	Diesel engines for other uses with outpout power<132.39kw (refers to compression-ignition internal combustion piston engines for the vehicles listed in Chapter 87)
	-其他发动机:								-Other engines:
8408.9010	---机车发动机	6	11		17	17	台/千瓦	O6	---Locomotive engines
	---其他:								---Other:
8408.9091	----输出功率不超过 14 千瓦	5	35		13	13	台/千瓦		----Of an output not exceeding 14kW
8408 9091.11	功率≤14 千瓦农业用单缸柴油机[非八十七章车辆用压燃式活塞内燃发动机（14 千瓦=19.05 马力）]	5	35		13	13	台/千瓦	6	Single cyclinder diesel engines for agriculatural use with output power≤14kw (compression-ignition internal combustion piston engines for the vehicles not listed in Chapter 87（14kw=19.05hp）)
8408 9091.19	功率≤14 千瓦农业用柴油发动机[非八十七章车辆用压燃式活塞内燃发动机（14 千瓦=19.05 马力）]	5	35		13	13	台/千瓦	6	Diesel engines for agriculatural use with output power≤14kw (compression-ignition internal combustion piston engines for the vehicles not listed in Chapter 87（14kw=19.05hp）)
8408 9091.91	功率≤14 千瓦其他用单缸柴油机[非八十七章车辆用压燃式活塞内燃发动机（14 千瓦=19.05 马力）]	5	35		13	17	台/千瓦	6	Single cyclinder diesel engines for other uses with output power≤14kw (compression-ignition internal combustion piston engines for the vehicles not listed in Chapter 87（14kw=19.05hp）)
8408 9091.99	功率≤14 千瓦其他用柴油发动机[非八十七章车辆用压燃式活塞内燃发动机（14 千瓦=19.05 马力）]	5	35		13	17	台/千瓦	6	Diesel engines for other uses with output power≤14kw (compression-ignition internal combustion piston engines for the vehicles not listed in Chapter 87（14kw=19.05hp）)
8408.9092	----输出功率超过 14 千瓦，但小于 132.39 千瓦（180 马力）	8.4	35				台/千瓦		----Of an output exceeding 14kW but not exceeding 132.39kW（180hp）
8408 9092.10	转速＜4650 转/分柴油发动机,14千瓦<功率＜132.39 千瓦（品目 84.26～84.30 所列工程机械用）	8.4	35		17	17	台/千瓦	6O	Diesel engines, rotational speed＜4650r/min, 14kW<power＜132.39kW (for engineering machinery listed in Heading No. 8426～8430)
8408 9092.20	14 千瓦<功率<132.39 千瓦的农业用柴油机[非八十七章车辆用压燃式活塞内燃发动机（1 千瓦=1.36 马力）]	8.4	35		13/17	13	台/千瓦	6	Diesel engines for agricultural use, 14kw<power <132.39kw (compression-ignition internal combustion piston engines for the vehicles not listed in Chapter 87（1kw=1.36hp）)
8408 9092.90	14 千瓦<功率<132.39 千瓦的其他用柴油机[非八十七章车辆用压燃式活塞内燃发动机（1 千瓦=1.36 马力）]	8.4	35		17	17	台/千瓦	6	Diesel engines for other uses, 14kW<power <132.39kW (compression-ignition internal combustion piston engines for the vehicles not listed in Chapter 87（1kw=1.36hp）)
8408.9093	----输出功率在 132.39 千瓦（180 马力）及以上	5	14		17		台/千瓦		----Of an output of 132.39kW（180hp） or more
8408 9093.10	功率≥132.39 千瓦的农业用柴油机[非八十七章用压燃式活塞	5	14		17	13	台/千瓦	6	Diesel engines for agricultural use with power≥132.39kw (compression-ignition internal

税则号列 Tariff Item	商品名称及备注	进口税率 最惠	进口税率 普通	进口税率 暂定	出口退税	增值税率	计量单位	监管条件	Article Description
	内燃发动机（132.39 千瓦=180 马力）]								combustion piston engines for the vehicles not listed in Chapter 87（132.93Kw=180hp）)
8408 9093.90	功率≥132.39 千瓦其他用柴油发动机[非八十七章用压燃式活塞内燃发动机（132.39 千瓦=180 马力）]	5	14		17	17	台/千瓦	6O	Diesel engines for other uses with power≥132.39kw (compression-ignition internal combustion piston engines for the vehicles not listed in Chapter 87（132.93Kw=180hp）)
84.09	专用于或主要用于品目 84.07 或 84.08 所列发动机的零件:								**Parts suitable for use solely or principally with the engines of heading No.84.07 or 84.08:**
8409.1000	-航空器发动机用	2	11		17	17	千克		-For aircraft engines
	-其他:								-Other:
	--专用于或主要用于点燃式活塞内燃发动机的:								--Suitable for use solely or principally with spark-ignition internal combustion piston engines:
8409.9110	---船舶发动机用	6	17		17	17	千克		---For marine propulsion engines
	---其他:								---Other:
8409.9191	----电控燃油喷射装置	5	35		17	17	千克/套	O	----Electric fuel injection devices
8409.9199	----其他	5	35		15/17	17	千克		----Other
8409 9199.20	废气再循环(EGR)装置（专用或主要用于内燃发动机）	5	35		15/17	17	千克		EGR (Exhaust Gas Recycle) apparatuses (suitable for use solely or principally with internal combustion engines)
8409 9199.30	连杆(专用或主要用于内燃发动机)	5	35		15/17	17	千克		Connecting rods (suitable for use solely or principally with internal combustion engines)
8409 9199.40	喷嘴(专用或主要用于内燃发动机)	5	35		15/17	17	千克		Nozzles (suitable for use solely or principally with internal combustion engines)
8409 9199.50	气门摇臂(专用或主要用于内燃发动机)	5	35		15/17	17	千克		Valve rocker arms (suitable for use solely or principally with internal combustion engines)
8409 9199.90	其他点燃式活塞内燃发动机用零件	5	35		15/17	17	千克		Other parts of spark-ignition internal combustion piston engines
	--其他:								--Other:
8409.9910	---船舶发动机用	5	11		17	17	千克		---For marine propulsion engines
8409.9920	---机车发动机用	2	11		17	17	千克		---For locomotive engines
	---其他:								---Other:
8409.9991	----输出功率在 132.39 千瓦(180 马力)及以上的发动机用	2	11		17	17	千克		----For engines with an output of 132.39 kW（180hp）or more
8409.9999	----其他	8.4	35		17	17	千克		----Other
8409 9999.01 暂	电控柴油喷射装置（指品目 84.08 所列的其他发动机用）	8.4	35	5	17	17	千克	O	Electronically controlled diesel injection systems (other engines listed in Heading No. 84.08)
8409 9999.90	其他发动机的专用零件(指品目 84.07 或 84.08 所列的其他发动机)	8.4	35		17	17	千克		Special parts for other engines (other engines listed in Heading No. 84.07 and 84.08)
84.10	水轮机、水轮及其调节器:								**Hydraulic turbines, water wheels, and regulators therefor:**
	-水轮机及水轮:								-Hydraulic turbines and water wheels:
8410.1100	--功率不超过 1000 千瓦	10	35		17	17	台		--Of a power not exceeding 1000kW
8410.1200	--功率超过 1000 千瓦，但不超过 10000 千瓦	10	35		17	17	台		--Of a power exceeding 1000kW but not exceeding 10000kW
	--功率超过 10000 千瓦:								--Of a power exceeding 10000kW:
8410.1310	---功率超过 30000 千瓦的冲击式水轮机及水轮	10	35		17	17	台		---Impulse hydraulic turbines and water wheels of a power exceeding 30000kW
8410.1320	---功率超过 35000 千瓦的贯流式水轮机及水轮	10	35		17	17	台		---Radial hydraulic turbines and water wheels of a power exceeding 35000kW
8410.1330	---功率超过 200000 千瓦的水泵式水轮机及水轮	10	35		17	17	台		---Pumping hydraulic turbines and water wheels of a power exceeding 200000kW
8410.1390	---其他	10	35		17	17	台		---Other
	-零件，包括调节器:								-Parts, including regulators:
8410.9010	---调节器	6	35		17	17	千克/套		---Regulators
8410.9090	---其他	6	35		17	17	千克		---Other
84.11	涡轮喷气发动机，涡轮螺桨发动								**Turbo-jets, turbo-propellers and other gas**

税则号列 Tariff Item	商品名称及备注	进口税率 最惠	进口税率 普通	进口税率 暂定	出口退税	增值税率	计量单位	监管条件	Article Description
	机及其他燃气轮机:								**turbines:**
	-涡轮喷气发动机:								-Turbo-jets:
	--推力不超过25千牛顿:								--Of a thrust not exceeding 25KN:
8411.1110	---涡轮风扇发动机	1	11		17	17	台	3	---Turbofan engines
8411.1190	---其他	1	11		17	17	台		---Other
	--推力超过25千牛顿:								--Of a thrust exceeding 25KN:
8411.1210	---涡轮风扇发动机	1	11		17	17	台	3	---Turbofan engines
8411.1290	---其他	1	11		17	17	台		---Other
8411 1290.10	小型燃烧率高轻型涡轮喷气发动机（推力≥90千牛顿的涡轮喷气发动机）	1	11		17	17	台	3	Small light turbo-jets with high combustion efficiency (turbo-jets with propulsive force≥90KN)
8411 1290.90	其他涡轮喷气发动机(推力超过25千牛顿)	1	11		17	17	台		Other turbo-jets (propulsive force≥25KN)
	-涡轮螺桨发动机:								-Turbo-propellers:
8411.2100	--功率不超过1100千瓦	2	11		17	17	台/千瓦		--Of a power not exceeding 1100kW
	--功率超过1100千瓦:								--Of a power exceeding 1100kW:
8411.2210	---功率超过1100千瓦,但不超过2238千瓦	2	11		17	17	台/千瓦		---Of a power exceeding 1100kW but not exceeding 2238kW
8411.2220	---功率超过2238千瓦,但不超过3730千瓦	2	11		17	17	台/千瓦		---Of a power exceeding 2238kW but not exceeding 3730kW
8411.2230	---功率超过3730千瓦	2	11		17	17	台/千瓦		---Of a power exceeding 3730kW
	-其他燃气轮机:								-Other gas turbines:
8411.8100	--功率不超过5000千瓦	15	35		17	17	台/千瓦		--Of a power not exceeding 5000kW
8411 8100.01 暂	涡轮轴航空发动机（功率≤5000kw）	15	35	1	17	17	台/千瓦		Turbine shaft aircraft engine, of a power exceeding 5000kW
8411 8100.90	功率≤5000kw的其他燃气轮机	15	35		17	17	台/千瓦		Other gas turbine with Power≤5000kw
8411.8200	--功率超过5000千瓦	3	35		17	17	台/千瓦	O	--Of a power exceeding 5000kW
	-零件:								-Parts:
8411.9100	--涡轮喷气发动机或涡轮螺桨发动机用	1	11		17	17	千克		--Of turbo-jets or turbo-propellers
	--其他:								--Other:
8411.9910	---涡轮轴发动机用	5	35		17	17	千克		---Of turboshaft engines
8411 9910.01 暂	涡轮轴航空发动机用零件	5	35	0	17	17	千克		Parts of turboshaft aeroengines
8411 9910.90	其他涡轮轴发动机用零件	5	35		17	17	千克		Other parts of turboshaft engines
8411.9990	---其他	5	35		17	17	千克		---Other
84.12	其他发动机及动力装置:								**Other engines and motors:**
	-喷气发动机，但涡轮喷气发动机除外:								-Jet engines other than turbo-jets:
8412.1010	---航空器及航天器用	3	11		17	17	台		---For aircraft or spacecraft
8412 1010.10	冲压喷气发动机(包括超燃冲压喷气发动机)	3	11		17	17	台	3	Ramjet engines (including scramjet engines)
8412 1010.20	脉冲喷气发动机	3	11		17	17	台	3	Pulse jet engines
8412 1010.30	组合循环发动机	3	11		17	17	台	3	Combined cycle engines
8412 1010.90	其他航空、航天器用喷气发动机（涡轮喷气发动机除外）	3	11		17	17	台		Other jet engines for aviation and aerospace vehicles (excluding turbo-jets engines)
8412.1090	---其他	10	35		17	17	台		---Other
	-液压动力装置:								-Hydraulic power engines and motors:
8412.2100	--直线作用(液压缸)的	12	35		17	17	台		--Linear acting（cylinders）
	--其他:								--Other:
8412.2910	---液压马达	10	35		17	17	台		---Hydraulic motors
8412.2990	---其他	14	35		17	17	台		---Other
8412 2990.01 暂	抓桩器（抱桩器）	14	35	7	17	17	台	O	Grab pile device (pile gripper)
8412 2990.90	其他液压动力装置	14	35		17	17	台	O	Other hydraulic power engines and motors
	-气压动力装置:								-Pneumatic power engines and motors:
8412.3100	--直线作用(气压缸)的	14	35		17	17	台		--Linear acting（cylinders）
8412 3100.01 暂	三坐标测量机用平衡气缸	14	35	7	17	17	台		Pneumatic cylinders for three dimensional measuring machines

税则号列 Tariff Item	商品名称及备注	进口税率 最惠	普通	暂定	出口退税	增值税率	计量单位	监管条件	Article Description
8412 3100.90	其他直线作用的气压动力装置(气压缸)	14	35		17	17	台		Other line-straightening pneumatic motors (pneumatic cyclinders)
8412.3900	--其他	14	35		17	17	台	O	--Other
8412.8000	-其他	10	35		17	17	台		-Other
8412 8000.10	液体火箭发动机(推力≥90千牛顿可贮存推进剂的)	10	35		17	17	台	3	Liquid-propellant rocket engines (propulsive force≥90KN, and being able to store propellants)
8412 8000.20	固体火箭发动机(总冲≥1100千牛顿秒的)	10	35		17	17	台	3	Solid-propellant rocket engines (total impulse≥1100KN per second)
8412 8000.90	其他发动机及动力装置	10	35		17	17	台		Other engines and motors
	-零件:								-Parts:
8412.9010	---子目号8412.1010所列机器的零件	2	11		17	17	千克		---For machines of subheading No.8412.1010
8412 9010.10	燃烧调节装置(冲压或脉冲喷气发动机的)	2	11		17	17	千克	3	Combustion regulating systems (for ramject engines or pulse jet engines)
8412 9010.20	火箭发动机的壳体	2	11		17	17	千克	3	Shells of rocket engines
8412 9010.90	航空、航天器用喷气发动机的零件(涡轮喷气发动机的零件,品目84129010.10除外)	2	11		17	17	千克		Parts of jet engines for aviation and aerospace vehicles (excluding the parts of turbo-jets and 84129010.10)
8412.9090	---其他	8	35		17	17	千克		---Other
84.13	**液体泵,不论是否装有计量装置;液体提升机:**								**Pumps for liquids, whether or not fitted with a measuring device; liquid elevators:**
	-装有或可装计量装置的泵:								-Pumps fitted or designed to be fitted with a measuring device:
8413.1100 暂	--分装燃料或润滑油的泵,用于加油站或车库	10	30	6	15	17	台		--Pumps for dispensing fuel or lubricants, of the type used in filling-stations or in garages
8413.1900 暂	--其他	10	30	6	15	17	台		--Other
8413.2000	-手泵,但子目号8413.11或8413.19的货品除外	10	30		15	17	台		-Hand pumps, other than those of subheading No.8413.11 or 8413.19
	-活塞式内燃发动机用的燃油泵、润滑油泵或冷却剂泵:								-Fuel, lubricating or cooling medium pumps for internal combustion piston engines:
	---燃油泵:								---Fuel pumps:
8413.3021	----输出功率在132.39千瓦(180马力)及以上的发动机用燃油泵	3	30		15	17	台		----Fuel pumps for engines of an output of 132.39kW (180hp) or more
8413.3029	----其他	3	30		15	17	台		----Other
8413.3030	---润滑油泵	3	30		15	17	台		---Lubricating oil pumps
8413.3090	---其他	3	30		15	17	台		---Other
8413.4000	-混凝土泵	8	30		15	17	台		-Concrete pumps
	-其他往复式排液泵:								-Other reciprocating positive displacement pumps:
8413.5010 暂	---气动式	10	40	6			台		---Pneumatic
8413 5010.10 暂	农业用气动往复式排液泵	10	40	6	13	13	台		Pneumatic reciprocating positive displacement pumps for agricultural use
8413 5010.20 暂	气动式耐腐蚀波纹或隔膜泵(流量>0.6m³/h,接触表面由特殊耐腐蚀材料制成)	10	40	6	15	17	台	3	Pneumatic corrosion-resistent bellows or diaphragm pumps (flow rate>0.6m³/h, with contact surface being made of special corrosion-resistent materials)
8413 5010.90 暂	其他非农业用气动往复式排液泵	10	40	6	15	17	台		Other pneumatic reciprocating positive displacement pumps for non-agricultural use
8413.5020 暂	---电动式	10	40	6			台		---Electric
8413 5020.10 暂	农业用电动往复式排液泵	10	40	6	13	13	台		Electric reciprocating positive displacement pumps for agricultural use
8413 5020.20 暂	电动式耐腐蚀波纹或隔膜泵(流量>0.6m³/h,接触表面由特殊耐腐蚀材料制成)	10	40	6	15	17	台	3	Electric corrosion-resistent bellows or diaphragm pumps(flow rate>0.6m³/h, with contact surface being made of special corrosion-resistent materials)
8413 5020.30 暂	电动往复式排液多重密封泵(两用物项管制)	10	40	6	15	17	台	3	Reciprocating highly-sealed positive displacement pumps (sensisitve articles control)
8413 5020.90 暂	其他非农业用电动往复式排液泵	10	40	6	15	17	台		Other electric reciprocating positive displacement pumps for non-agricultural use

税则号列 Tariff Item	商品名称及备注	进口税率 最惠	进口税率 普通	进口税率 暂定	出口退税	增值税率	计量单位	监管条件	Article Description
	---液压式:								---Hydraulic:
8413.5031[暂]	----柱塞泵	10	40	6			台		----Plunger pumps
8413 5031.01[暂]	农业用柱塞泵	10	40	6	13	13	台		Plunger pumps for agricultural use
8413 5031.90[暂]	其他非农业用柱塞泵	10	40	6	15	17	台		Other plunger pumps for non-agricultural use
8413.5039[暂]	----其他	10	40	6			台		----Other
8413 5039.01[暂]	其他农业用液压往复式排液泵	10	40	6	13	13	台		Other hydraulic reciprocating positive displacement pumps for agricultural use
8413 5039.20[暂]	液压式耐腐蚀波纹或隔膜泵(流量＞0.6 立方米/小时,接触表面由特殊耐腐蚀材料制成)	10	40	6	15	17	台	3	Hydraulic corrosion-resistent bellows or diaphragm pumps(flow rate＞0.6m³/h, with contact surface being made of special corrosion-resistent materials)
8413 5039.90[暂]	其他非农业用液压往复式排液泵	10	40	6	15	17	台		Other hydraulic reciprocating positive displacement pumps for non-agricultural use
8413.5090[暂]	---其他	10	40	6			台		---Other
8413 5090.10[暂]	其他农用往复式排液泵	10	40	6	13	13	台		Other reciprocating positive displacement pumps for agricultural use
8413 5090.20[暂]	其他耐腐蚀波纹或隔膜泵(流量＞0.6 立方米/小时,接触表面由特殊耐腐蚀材料制成)	10	40	6	15	17	台	3	Other corrosion-resistent bellows or diaphragm pumps(flow rate＞0.6m³/h, with contact surface being made of special corrosion-resistent materials)
8413 5090.90[暂]	其他非农业用往复式排液泵	10	40	6	15	17	台		Other reciprocating positive displacement pumps for non-agricultural use
	-其他回转式排液泵:								-Other rotary positive displacement pumps:
	---齿轮泵:								---Gear pumps:
8413.6021[暂]	----电动式	10	40	6			台		----Electric
8413 6021.01[暂]	农业用电动齿轮泵(回转式排液泵)	10	40	6	13	13	台		Other reciprocating positive displacement pumps for non-agricultural use
8413 6021.10[暂]	电动齿轮多重密封泵(非农业用回转式排液泵)	10	40	6	15	17	台	3	Electric highly-sealed gear pumps (rotary positive displacement pumps for non-agricultural use)
8413 6021.90[暂]	其他非农业用电动齿轮泵(回转式排液泵,多重密封泵除外)	10	40	6	15	17	台		Other electric gear pumps for non-agricultural use (excluding rotary positive displacement pumps and highly-sealed pumps)
8413.6022	----液压式	10	40				台		----Hydraulic
8413 6022.01[暂]	农业用回转式液压油泵(输入转速＞2000 转/分,输入功率＞190 千瓦,最大流量＞2×280 升/分钟)	10	40	3	13	13	台		Rotary hydraulic oil pump for agricultural use (input speed＞2000r/min, input power＞190kw, maximum flow rate＞2×280L/min)
8413 6022.02[暂]	非农业用回转式液压油泵(输入转速＞2000 转/分,输入功率＞190 千瓦,最大流量＞2×280 升/分钟)	10	40	3	15	17	台		Rotary hydraulic oil pump for non-agricultural use (input speed＞2000r/min, input power＞190kw, maximum flow rate＞2×280L/min)
8413 6022.10[暂]	其他农业用液压齿轮泵(回转式排液泵)	10	40	6	13	13	台		Other hydraulic gear pumps for agricultural use (rotary positive displacement pumps)
8413 6022.20[暂]	液压齿轮多重密封泵(非农业用回转式排液泵)	10	40	6	15	17	台	3	Hydraulic highly-sealed pumps (rotary positive displacement pumps for non-agricultural use)
8413 6022.90[暂]	其他非农业用液压齿轮泵(回转式排液泵,多重密封泵除外)	10	40	6	15	17	台		Other hydraulic gear pumps for non-agricultural use (excluding rotary positive displacement pumps and highly-sealed pumps)
8413.6029[暂]	----其他	10	40	6			台		----Other
8413 6029.01[暂]	其他农业用齿轮泵(回转式排液泵)	10	40	6	13	13	台		Other gear pumps for agricultural use (rotary positive displacement pumps)
8413 6029.90[暂]	其他非农业用齿轮泵(回转式排液泵)	10	40	6	15	17	台		Other gear pumps for non-agricultural use (rotary positive displacement pumps)
	---叶片泵:								---Vane pumps:
8413.6031[暂]	----电动式	10	40	6			台		---Electric
8413 6031.01[暂]	农业用电动叶片泵(回转式排液	10	40	6	13	13	台		Electric blade pumps for agricultural use (rotary

税则号列 Tariff Item	商品名称及备注	进口税率 最惠	普通	暂定	出口退税	增值税率	计量单位	监管条件	Article Description
	泵）								positive displacement pumps)
8413 6031.10 暂	电动叶片多重密封泵(非农业用回转式排液泵）	10	40	6	15	17	台	3	Electric blade highly-sealed pumps (rotary positive displacement pumps for non-agricultural use)
8413 6031.90 暂	其他非农业用电动叶片泵(回转式排液泵，多重密封泵除外）	10	40	6	15	17	台		Other electric blade pumps for non-agricultural use (excluding rotary positive displacement pumps and highly-sealed pumps)
8413.6032 暂	----液压式	10	40	6			台		----Hydraulic
8413 6032.01 暂	农业用液压叶片泵(回转式排液泵）	10	40	6	13	13	台		Hydraulic blade pumps for agricultural use (rotary positive displacement pumps)
8413 6032.10 暂	液压叶片多重密封泵(非农业用回转式排液泵）	10	40	6	15	17	台	3	Hydraulic blade highly-sealed pumps (rotary positive displacement pumps for non-agricultural use)
8413 6032.90 暂	其他非农业用液压叶片泵(回转式排液泵，多重密封泵除外）	10	40	6	15	17	台		Other hydraulic blade pumps for non-agricultural use (excluding rotary positive displacement pumps and highly-sealed pumps)
8413.6039 暂	----其他	10	40	6			台		----Other
8413 6039.01 暂	其他农业用叶片泵(回转式排液泵）	10	40	6	13	13	台		Other blade pumps for agricultural use (rotary positive displacement pumps)
8413 6039.90 暂	其他非农业用叶片泵(回转式排液泵）	10	40	6	15	17	台		Other blade pumps for non-agricultural use (rotary positive displacement pumps)
8413.6040 暂	---螺杆泵	10	40	6			台		---Helicoidal pumps (screw pumps)
8413 6040.01 暂	农业用螺杆泵（回转式排液泵）	10	40	6	13	13	台		Helicoidal pumps for agricultural use (rotary positive displacement pumps)
8413 6040.10 暂	螺杆多重密封泵(非农业用回转式排液泵）	10	40	6	15	17	台	3	Helicoidal highly-sealed pumps (rotary positive displacement pumps for non-agricultural use)
8413 6040.90 暂	其他非农业用螺杆泵(回转式排液泵，多重密封泵除外）	10	40	6	15	17	台		Other helicoidal pumps for non-agricultural use (excluding rotary positive displacement pumps and highly-sealed pumps)
8413.6050 暂	---径向柱塞泵	10	40	6			台		---Radial plunger pumps
8413 6050.01 暂	农业用径向柱塞泵(回转式排液泵）	10	40	6	13	13	台		Radial plunger pumps for agricultural use (rotary positive displacement pumps)
8413 6050.90 暂	其他非农业用径向柱塞泵(回转式排液泵）	10	40	6	15	17	台		Other radial plunger pumps for non-agricultural use (rotary positive displacement pumps)
8413.6060 暂	---轴向柱塞泵	10	40	6			台		---Axial plunger pumps
8413 6060.01 暂	农业用轴向柱塞泵(回转式排液泵）	10	40	6	13	13	台		Axial plunger pumps for agricultural use (rotary positive displacement pumps)
8413 6060.90 暂	其他非农业用轴向柱塞泵(回转式排液泵）	10	40	6	15	17	台		Other axial plunger pumps for non-agricultural use (rotary positive displacement pumps)
8413.6090 暂	---其他	10	40	6			台		---Other
8413 6090.10 暂	农业用其他回转式排液泵	10	40	6	13	13	台		Other rotary positive displacement pumps for agricultural use
8413 6090.90 暂	其他回转式排液泵	10	40	6	15	17	台		Other rotary positive displacement pumps
	-其他离心泵:								-Other centrifugal pumps:
8413.7010	---转速在10000转/分及以上	8	40				台		---Rotational speed no less than 10000r/min
8413 7010.10	农业用其他离心泵（转速在10000转/分及以上）	8	40		13	13	台		Other centrifugal pumps for agricultural use (rotational speed≥10000r/min)
8413 7010.20	液体推进剂用泵（转速≥10000转/分,出口压力≥7000千帕的）	8	40		15	17	台	3	Liquid-propellant pumps (rotational speed≥10000r/min, outlet pressure≥7000Kpa)
8413 7010.30	离心泵多重密封泵（两用物项管制）	8	40		15	17	台	3	Highly-sealed centrifugal pumps (sensitive articles control)
8413 7010.90	其他非农用离心泵（转速在10000转/分及以上）	8	40		15	17	台		Other centrifugal pumps for non-agricultural use (rotational speed≥10000r/min)
	---其他:								---Other:
8413.7091 暂	----电动潜油泵及潜水电泵	10	40	8			台		----Electric submersible oil pumps and electric submersible pumps
8413 7091.10 暂	农业用电动潜油泵及潜水电泵（转速在10000转/分以下）	10	40	8	13	13	台		Electric submersible oil pumps and submersible pumps for agricultural use(rotational speed＜10000r/min)

税则号列 Tariff Item	商品名称及备注	进口税率 最惠	进口税率 普通	进口税率 暂定	出口退税	增值税率	计量单位	监管条件	Article Description
8413 7091.90 暂	其他非农业用电动潜油泵及潜水电泵（转速在10000转/分以下）	10	40	8	15	17	台		Other electric submersible oil pumps and submersible pumps for non-agricultural use (rotational speed＜10000r/min)
8413.7099	----其他	8	40				台		----Other
8413 7099.10	其他农业用离心泵（转速在10000转/分以下）	8	40		13	13	台		Other centrifugal pumps for agricultural use (rotational speed＜10000r/min)
8413 7099.20	一次冷却剂泵（全密封驱动泵，有惯性质量系统的泵，及鉴定为NC-1泵等）	8	40		15	17	台	3	Primary coolant pumps (completely-sealed driven pumps, pumps with inertia mass system and NC-1 pumps, etc.)
8413 7099.30	转速小于10000转/分的离心式屏蔽泵（流量大于0.6立方米/小时，接触表面由特殊耐腐蚀材料制成）	8	40		15	17	台	3	Canned centrifugal pumps with rotational speed＜10000r/min (flow rate＞0.6m³/h, with contact surface being made of special corrosion-resistent materials)
8413 7099.40	转速小于10000转/分的离心式磁力泵（流量大于0.6立方米/小时，接触表面由特殊耐腐蚀材料制成）	8	40		15	17	台	3	Magnetically-driven centrifugal pumps with rotational speed＜10000r/min (flow rate＞0.6m³/h, with contact surface being made of special corrosion-resistent materials)
8413 7099.50	液体推进剂用泵（8000转/分＜转速＜10000转/分，出口压力≥7000千帕的）	8	40		15	17	台	3	Liquid-propellant pumps (8000r/min＜rotational speed＜10000r/min, outlet pressure≥7000Kpa)
8413 7099.60	其他离心泵多重密封泵(两用物项管制)	8	40		15	17	台	3O	Other centrifugal pumps and highly-sealed pumps (sensitative articles control)
8413 7099.90	其他非农业用离心泵（转速在10000转/分以下）	8	40		15	17	台		Other centrifugal pumps for non-agricultural use (rotational speed＜10000r/min)
	-其他泵；液体提升机:								-Other pumps; liquid elevators:
8413.8100	--泵	8	40				台		--Pumps
8413 8100.10	农业用其他液体泵	8	40		13	13	台		Other liquid pumps for agricultural use
8413 8100.20	生产重水用多级泵(专门为利用氨-氢交换法生产重水而设计或制造的多级泵)	8	40		15	17	台	3	Multistage pumps for producing heavy water (multistage pumps specially designed or made to produce heavy water by utilizing the ammonia-hydrogen transformation method)
8413 8100.90	其他非农用液体泵	8	40		15	17	台		Other liquid pumps for non-agricultural use
8413.8200	--液体提升机	8	30		15	17	台		--Liquid elevators
	-零件:								-Parts:
8413.9100	--泵用	5	30		15	17	千克		--Of pumps
8413.9200 暂	--液体提升机用	6	30	4	15	17	千克		--Of liquid elevators
84.14	**空气泵或真空泵、空气及其他气体压缩机、风机、风扇；装有风扇的通风罩或循环气罩，不论是否装有过滤器:**								**Air or vacuum pumps, air or other gas compressors and fans; ventilating or recycling hoods incorporating a fan, whether or not fitted with filters:**
8414.1000 暂	-真空泵	8	30	5	15	17	台		-Vacuum pumps
8414 1000.10 暂	耐腐蚀真空泵(流量大于5立方米/小时，接触表面由特殊耐腐蚀材料制成)	8	30	5	15	17	台	3	Corrosion-resistent vaccum pumps (flow rate＞5m³/h, with contact surface being made of special corrosion-resistent materials)
8414 1000.20 暂	真空泵（抽气口≥38厘米，速度≥15立方米/秒，产生小于10^{-4}托极限真空度）	8	30	5	15	17	台	3	Vaccum pumps (aspirating hole≥38cm, speed≥15kl/s, capacity＜10^{-4}absolute vaccum degree）
8414 1000.30 暂	能在含UF_6气氛中使用的真空泵（用铝、镍或含镍高于60%的合金制成或为衬里的）	8	30	5	15	17	台	3	Vaccum pumps that can be used in UF_6 atmosphere（made of aluminium, nickel or alloys with the content of nickel being more than 60% or used as a lining）
8414 1000.40 暂	专门设计或制造的抽气能力≥5立方米/分的真空泵（专用于同位素气体扩散浓缩）	8	30	5	15	17	台	3	Specially-designed or specially-made vaccum pumps with exhaust capacity≥5m³/min (used exclusively for diffusion and concentration of isotopic gases
8414 1000.50 暂	能在含UF_6气氛中使用的真空泵（耐UF_6腐蚀的，也可用氟碳密封和特殊工作流体）	8	30	5	15	17	台	3	Vaccum pumps that can be used in UF_6 atmosphere（UF_6-resistent pumps can be sealed with fluorocarbon or special working fluid）
8414 1000.90 暂	其他真空泵	8	30	5	15	17	台		Other vaccum pumps
8414.2000	-手动或脚踏式空气泵	8	30		15	17	台/千克		-Hand-or foot-operated pumps

税则号列 Tariff Item	商品名称及备注	进口税率 最惠	普通	暂定	出口退税	增值税率	计量单位	监管条件	Article Description
	-用于制冷设备的压缩机:								-Compressors of a kind used in refrigerating equipment:
	---电动机驱动的压缩机:								---Driven by a motor:
8414.3011	----冷藏箱或冷冻箱用,电动机额定功率不超过0.4千瓦	8	80		17	17	台		----For refrigerators or freezers, of a motor power not exceeding 0.4kW
8414 3011.01[暂]	功率≤0.4千瓦的冷藏、冷冻箱用无级变速压缩机	8	80	3	17	17	台	AB	Infinitely variable speed compressors for refrigerators or freezers with power≤0.4kW
8414 3011.90	其他小型电驱动冷藏或冷冻箱用压缩机(小型指电动机额定功率≤0.4千瓦)	8	80		17	17	台	AB	Other small electrically-driven compressors for refrigerators or freezers (the term "small" means: the rated power of the electric motor ≤0.4kW)
8414.3012	----其他电驱动冷藏或冷冻箱用压缩机(指电动机额定功率>0.4kw,但≤5kw)	10	80		17	17	台	AB	----For refrigerators or freezers, of a motor power exceeding 0.4kW but not exceeding 5kW
8414.3013	----空气调节器用,电动机额定功率超过0.4千瓦,但不超过5千瓦	10	80		17	17	台		----For air conditioning machines, of a motor power exceeding 0.4kW but not exceeding 5kW
8414 3013.01[暂]	0.4千瓦<功率≤5千瓦的空气调节器用无级变速压缩机	10	80	3	17	17	台	A	Infinitely variable speed compressors for air conditioners, 0.4kW<power≤5kW
8414 3013.02[暂]	0.4千瓦<功率≤5千瓦的空气调节器用定速压缩机	10	80	6	17	17	台	A	Fixed speed compressors for air conditioners, 0.4kW<power≤5kW
8414 3013.90	其他小型电动机驱动空调器用压缩机(指电动机额定功率>0.4千瓦,但≤5千瓦的)	10	80		17	17	台	A	Other small motor-driven compressors for air conditioners (0.4kW<the rated power of the electric motor≤5kW)
8414.3014	----空气调节器用,电动机额定功率超过5千瓦	10	80		17	17	台		----For air conditioning machines, of a motor power exceeding 5kW
8414 3014.01[暂]	功率>5千瓦的空气调节器用无级变速压缩机	10	80	3	17	17	台	AB	Infinitely variable speed compressors for air conditioners with power>5kW
8414 3014.02[暂]	功率>5千瓦的空气调节器用定速压缩机	10	80	6	17	17	台	AB	Fixed speed compressors for air conditioners with power>5kW
8414 3014.90	其他大型电动机驱动空调器用压缩机(大型指电动机额定功率超过5千瓦的)	10	80		17	17	台	AB	Other large motor-driven compressors for air conditioners (the term "large" means: the rated power of the electric motor>5kW)
8414.3015	----冷冻或冷藏设备用,电动机额定功率超过5千瓦	10	30		17	17	台		----For refrigerators or freezers, of a motor power exceeding 5kW
8414 3015.01[暂]	电动机额定功率>5千瓦的电动机驱动的无级变速压缩机(冷冻或冷藏设备用)	10	30	4	17	17	台	AB	Motor-driven infinitely variable speed compressors with the rated power of the electric motor>5kW (for freezing and refrigerating equipments)
8414 3015.02[暂]	电动机额定功率>5千瓦的电动机驱动定速压缩机(冷冻或冷藏设备用)	10	30	6	17	17	台	AB	Motor-driven fixed speed compressors with the rated power of the electric motor>5kW (for freezing and refrigerating equipments)
8414 3015.90	其他大型电动机驱动冷冻或冷藏设备用压缩机(大型指电动机额定功率超过5千瓦的)	10	30		17	17	台	AB	Other large motor-driven compressors for freezing or refrigerating equipments (the term "large" means: the rated power of the electric motor>5kW)
8414.3019	----其他	10	30		17	17	台		----Other
8414 3019.01[暂]	其他制冷设备用无级变速压缩机	10	30	4	17	17	台	A	Other infinitely variable speed compressors for refrigeration equipments
8414 3019.02[暂]	其他制冷设备用定速压缩机	10	30	6	17	17	台	A	Other fixed speed compressors for refrigeration equipments
8414 3019.90	电动机驱动其他用于制冷设备的压缩机	10	30		17	17	台	A	Other motor-driven compressors for refrigeration equipments
8414.3090	---非电动机驱动的压缩机	9	80		17	17	台		---Driven by a non-motor
8414 3090.10	汽车空调压缩机	9	80		17	17	台		Compressors for auto air conditioners
8414 3090.90	非电机驱动其他制冷设备用压缩机	9	80		17	17	台		Other non-motor-driven compressors for refrigeration equipments
8414.4000	-装在拖车底盘上的空气压缩机	8	30		17	17	台		-Air compressors mounted on a wheeled chassis for towing
	-风机、风扇:								-Fans:
	--台扇、落地扇、壁扇、换气扇								--Table, floor, wall, window, ceiling or roof fans, with a

税则号列 Tariff Item	商品名称及备注	进口税率 最惠	进口税率 普通	进口税率 暂定	出口退税	增值税率	计量单位	监管条件	Article Description
	或吊扇，包括风机，本身装有一个输出功率不超过 125 瓦的电动机:								self-contained electric motor of an output not exceeding 125W:
8414.5110	---吊扇	20	130		15	17	台	A	---Ceiling or roof fans
8414.5120	---换气扇	20	130		15	17	台	A	---Window fans
8414.5130	---具有旋转导风轮的风扇	12	130		15	17	台		---Repeating front louver fan
	---其他:								---Other:
8414.5191	----台扇	10	130		15	17	台	A	----Table fans
8414.5192	----落地扇	10	130		15	17	台	A	----Floor fans
8414.5193	----壁扇	10	130		15	17	台	A	----Wall fans
8414.5199	----其他	10	130		15	17	台		----Other
	--其他:								--Other:
8414.5910	---吊扇	8	30		15	17	台	A	---Ceiling or roof fans
8414.5920	---换气扇	8	30		15	17	台	A	---Window fans
8414.5930	---离心通风机	10	30		17	17	台		---Centrifugal ventilation fans
8414.5990	---其他	8	30			17	台		---Other
8414 5990.10	罗茨式鼓风机	8	30		17	17	台	A	Roots blower
8414 5990.20	吸气＞1 立方米/分的耐 UF_6 腐蚀的鼓风机(轴向离心式或正排量鼓风机，压力比在 2:1 和 6:1 之间)	8	30		15	17	台	3A	UF_6-resistent blowers with air breathing＞$1m^3$/min (axial centrifugal or positive displacement blowers, with pressure ratio standing between 2:1 and 6:1)
8414 5990.30	吸气≥2 立方米/分的耐 UF_6 腐蚀的鼓风机(轴向离心式或正排量鼓风机，压力比在 1.2:1 和 6:1 之间)	8	30		15	17	台	3A	UF_6-resistent blowers with air breathing＞$2m^3$/min (axial centrifugal or positive displacement blowers, with pressure ratio between 1.2:1 and 6:1)
8414 5990.40	吸气≥56 立方米/秒的鼓风机(用于循环硫化氢气体的单级、低压头离心式鼓风机)	8	30		15	17	台	3A	Blowers with air breathing≥$56m^3$/s (one-stage, low-pressure centrifugal blowers used for cycling hydrogen sulphide gas)
8414 5990.50	电子产品散热用轴流风扇	8	30		17	17	台	A	Axial-flow fans for heat elimination of electronic products
8414 5990.91	其他台扇、落地扇、壁扇(电动机输出功率超过 125 瓦的)	8	30		15	17	台	A	Other desk fans, floor-standing fans and wall-mounted fans (the output power of the electric motor＞125w)
8414 5990.99	其他风机、风扇	8	30		15	17	台	A	Other fans
	-罩的平面最大边长不超过 120 厘米的通风罩或循环气罩:								-Hoods having a maximum horizontal side not exceeding 120cm:
8414.6010[暂]	---抽油烟机	10	130	6	15	17	台		---Range hoods
8414.6090	---其他	10	130		15	17	台		---Other
8414 6090.11	生物安全柜(符合世界卫生组织规定的生物安全水平三级标准，罩的最大边长≤120 厘米)	10	130		15	17	台	3	Biosafety cabinets (being up to Biosafety Level 3 prescribed by the World Health Organization, the maximum side length of the hood≤120cm)
8414 6090.12	活动(柔软的)隔离装置;手套箱(具有与三级生物安全柜类似标准，罩的最大边长≤120 厘米)	10	130		15	17	台	3	Movable (soft) partitions; glove boxes (with the similar standard of Biosafety Level 3 cabinets, the maximum side length of the hood≤120cm)
8414 6090.13	层流罩(柜)(垂直流密闭通风柜，具有三级生物安全柜类似标准，罩的最大边长≤120 厘米)	10	130		15	17	台	3	Laminar hoods (cabinets) (vertifcal flow sealed fume hoods, with the similar standard of Biosafety Level 3 cabinets, the maximum side length of the hood≤120cm)
8414 6090.14	吸收塔(两用物项管制，罩的最大边长≤120 厘米)	10	130		15	17	台	3	Absorption tower (control of sentitive items, the maximum side length of the hood≤120cm)
8414 6090.15	带有风扇的高效空气粒子过滤单元的封闭洁净设备〔高效空气粒子过滤单元(HEPA)，罩的最大边长≤120 厘米〕	10	130		15	17	台	3	HEPA closed cleaning equipments with a fan (HEPA: high efficiency particulate air filter, the maximum side length of the hood≤120cm)
8414 6090.16	厌氧微生物柜(具有与三级生物安全柜类似标准，罩的最大边长≤120 厘米)	10	130		15	17	台	3	Anaerobic microorganism cabinet (with the similar standard of Biosafety Level 3 cabinets, the maximum side length of the hood≤120cm)
8414 6090.90	其他≤120 厘米的通风罩或循	10	130		15	17	台		Other ventilating or recycling hoods with the side

税则号列 Tariff Item	商品名称及备注	进口税率 最惠	普通	暂定	出口退税	增值税率	计量单位	监管条件	Article Description
	环气罩(指罩的平面最大边长不超过120厘米,装有风扇的)								length≤120cm (meaning the maximum side length≤120cm, fitted with a fan)
	-其他:								-Other :
8414.8010	---燃气轮机用的自由活塞式发生器	8	50		15	17	台		---Free piston generators for gas turbines
8414.8020	---二氧化碳压缩机	7	30		15	17	台		---CO_2 compressors
8414.8030	---发动机用增压器	7	30		15	17	台		---Superchargers for engines
8414 8030.01[暂]	乘用车机械增压器	7	30	5	15	17	台		Mechanical supercharger for passenger cars
8414 8030.90	发动机用增压器	7	30		15	17	台		Superchargers for engines
8414.8090	---其他	7	30			17	台		---Other
8414 8090.10	吸气>1立方米/分的耐UF_6腐蚀的压缩机(轴向离心式或正排量压缩机,压力比在2:1和6:1之间)	7	30		17	17	台	3	UF_6-resistent compressors with air breathing>1m^3/min (axial centrifugal or positive displacement compressors, with pressure ratio standing between 2:1 and 6:1)
8414 8090.20	MLIS用UF_6/载气压缩机(能在UF_6环境中长期操作UF_6/载气混合气压缩机)	7	30		17	17	台	3	UF_6/carrier gas compressors for MLIS (UF_6/carrier gas, mixed gases compressors can be operated in UF_6 environment on a long-term basis)
8414 8090.30	吸气≥56立方米/秒的压缩机(用于循环硫化氢气体的单级、低压头离心式压缩机)	7	30		17	17	台	3	Compressors with air breathing≥56m^3/s (one-stage, low-pressure centrifugal compressors used for cycling hydrogen sulphide gas))
8414 8090.40	吸气≥2立方米/分的耐UF_6腐蚀压缩机(轴向离心式或正排量压缩机,压力比在1.2:1和6:1之间)	7	30		17	17	台	3	UF_6-resistent compressors with air breathing≥2m^3/min (axial centrifugal or positive displacement compressors, with pressure ratio standing between 1.2:1 and 6:1)
8414 8090.51	其他生物安全柜(符合世界卫生组织规定的生物安全水平三级标准)	7	30		17	17	台	3	Other biosafety cabinets (being up to Biosafety Level 3 prescribed by the World Health Organization)
8414 8090.52	其他活动(柔软的)隔离装置与其他手套箱(具有与三级生物安全柜类似标准)	7	30		17	17	台	3	Other movable (soft) partitions and glove boxes (with the similar standard of Biosafety Level 3 cabinets)
8414 8090.53	其他层流罩(柜)(垂直流密闭通风柜,具有与三级生物安全柜类似标准)	7	30		17	17	台	3	Other laminar hoods (cabinets) (vertifcal flow sealed fume hoods, with the similar standard of Biosafety Level 3 cabinets)
8414 8090.54	其他吸收塔(两用物项管制)	7	30		17	17	台	3	Other absorption towers (control of sensitive items)
8414 8090.55	其他带有风扇的高效空气粒子过滤单元的封闭洁净设备[高效空气粒子过滤单元(HEPA)]	7	30		17	17	台	3	Other HEPA closed cleaning equipments with a fan (HEPA: high efficiency particulate air filter)
8414 8090.56	其他厌氧微生物柜(具有与三级生物安全柜类似标准)	7	30		15	17	台	3	Other Anaerobic microorganism cabinet (with the similar standard of Biosafety Level 3 cabinets)
8414 8090.90	其他空气泵、气体压缩机及通风罩(通风罩指装有风扇的通风罩或循环气罩,平面边长>120厘米)	7	30		17	17	台		Other air pumps, air compressors and ventilating hoods (hood refers to the ventilating or recycling hoods fitted with a fan, the plane side length>120cm)
	-零件:								-Parts:
	---子目号8414.3011至8414.3014及8414.3090所列机器的零件:								---Of the machines of subheadings No.8414. 3011 to 8414.3014 and 8414.3090:
8414.9011[暂]	----压缩机进、排气阀片	8	80	5	15	17	千克		----In take valve leaf or discharge valve leaf
8414.9019[暂]	----其他	8	80	5	15	17	千克		----Other
8414.9020[暂]	---子目8414.5110至8414.5199及8414.6000所列机器的零件	12	130	6	15	17	千克		---Of the machines of subheadings No.8414. 5110 to 8414.5199 or 8414.6000
8414.9090[暂]	---其他	7	30	4	15	17	千克		---Other
8414 9090.10[暂]	分子泵(气体离心机的静态部件,专门设计或制造的内部有已加工或挤压的螺纹槽和已加工的腔的泵体。)	7	30	4	15	17	千克	3	Molecular pumps (static components of gas centrifuge, specially designed, processed or pressed thread grooves and processing cavities of pump

税则号列 Tariff Item	商品名称及备注	进口税率			出口退税	增值税率	计量单位	监管条件	Article Description
		最惠	普通	暂定					
8414 9090.90[暂]	品目 84.14 其他未列名零件	7	30	4	15	17	千克		Other parts not specified or included in heading No. 8414
84.15	**空气调节器，装有电扇及调温、调湿装置，包括不能单独调湿的空调器：**								**Air conditioning machines, comprising a motor-driven fan and elements for changing the temperature and humidity, including those machines in which the humidity cannot be separately regulated:**
	-窗式或壁式，独立的或分体的：								-Window or wall types, self-contained or “split-system”:
8415.1010	---独立式	15	130		17	17	台	A	---Self-contained
	---分体式：								---Split-systerm:
8415.1021	----制冷量不超过 4000 大卡/时	15	130		17	17	台	A	----Of a refrigerating effect not exceeding 4000 Cal per hour
8415.1022	----制冷量超过 4000 大卡/时	15	90		17	17	台		----Of a refrigerating effect exceeding 4000 Cal per hour
8415 1022.01	4000 大卡/时＜制冷量≤12046 大卡/时（14000W）分体式空调，窗式或壁式（装有电扇及调温、调湿装置，包括不能单独调湿的空调器）	15	90		17	17	台	A	Split-system, window or wall types air-conditioner, 4000 cal/per hour＜refrigerating effect≤ 12046 cal/per hour (14000W) (comprising a motor-driven fan and elements for changing the temperature and humidity, including those machines in which the humidity cannot be separately regulated)
8415 1022.90	其他制冷量＞12046 大卡/时（14000W）分体式空调，窗式或壁式（装有电扇及调温、调湿装置，包括不能单独调湿的空调器）	15	90		17	17	台	A	Split-system, window or wall types air-conditioner, refrigerating effect＞12046 cal/per hour (14000W) (comprising a motor-driven fan and elements for changing the temperature and humidity, including those machines in which the humidity cannot be separately regulated)
8415.2000[暂]	-机动车辆上供人使用的	20	110	10	17	17	台	A	-Of a kind used for persons, in motor vehicles
	-其他：								-Other:
	--装有制冷装置及一个冷热循环换向阀的（可逆式热泵）：								--Incorporating a refrigerating unit and a valve for reversal of the cooling/heat cycle（reversible heat pumps）:
8415.8110	---制冷量不超过 4000 大卡/时	15	130		17	17	台	A	---Of a refrigerating effect not exceeding 4000 Cal per hour
8415.8120[暂]	---制冷量超过 4000 大卡/时	20	90	12	17	17	台		---Of a refrigerating effect exceeding 4000 Cal per hour
8415 8120.01[暂]	4000 大卡/时＜制冷量≤12046 大卡/时（14000W）热泵式空调器（装有制冷装置及一个冷热循环换向阀的）	20	90	12	17	17	台	AB	Heat pump air conditioner, 4000cal/per hour< refrigerating effect≤ 12046 cal per hour（14000W）(incorporating a refrigerating unit and a valve for reversal of the cooling/heat cycle)
8415 8120.90[暂]	其他制冷量＞12046 大卡/时（14000W）热泵式空调器（装有制冷装置及一个冷热循环换向阀的）	20	90	12	17	17	台	AB	Other heat pump air conditioner, refrigerating effect> 12046 cal per hour（14000W）(incorporating a refrigerating unit and a valve for reversal of the cooling/heat cycle)
	--其他，装有制冷装置的：								--Other, incorporating a refrigerating unit:
8415.8210	---制冷量不超过 4000 大卡/时	15	130		17	17	台	A	---Of a refrigerating effect not exceeding 4000 Cal per hour
8415.8220[暂]	---制冷量超过 4000 大卡/时	20	90	12	17	17	台		---Of a refrigerating effect exceeding 4000 Cal per hour
8415 8220.01[暂]	4000 大卡＜制冷量≤12046 大卡/时（14000W）的其他空调（仅装有制冷装置，而无冷热循环装置的）	20	90	12	17	17	台	AB	Other air conditioners, 4000 Cal per/hour<refrigerating effect ≤12046 Cal per/hour(14000W) (incorporating a refrigerating unit and without thermal cycling device)
8415 8220.90[暂]	其他制冷量＞12046 大卡/时（14000W）的其他空调（仅装有制冷装置，而无冷热循环装置的）	20	90	12	17	17	台	AB	Other air conditioners, refrigerating effect>12046 Cal per/hour (14000W) (incorporating a refrigerating unit and without thermal cycling device)
8415.8300	--未装有制冷装置的	10	90		17	17	台	A	--Not incorporating a refrigerating unit

税则号列 Tariff Item	商品名称及备注	进口税率 最惠	普通	暂定	出口退税	增值税率	计量单位	监管条件	Article Description
	-零件:								-Parts:
8415.9010[暂]	---子目号 8415.1010、8415.1021、8415.8110、8415.8210 所列设备的零件	10	130	6	15	17	千克		---Of the machines of subheadings No.8415.1010, 8415.1021, 8415.8110 and 8415.8210
8415.9090[暂]	---其他	10	90	6	15	17	千克		---Other
84.16	**使用液体燃料、粉状固体燃料或气体燃料的炉用燃烧器;机械加煤机,包括其机械炉篦、机械出灰器及类似装置:**								**Furnace burners for liquid fuel, for pulverized solid fuel or for gas; mechanical stokers, including their mechanical grates, mechanical ash dischargers and similar appliances:**
8416.1000	-使用液体燃料的炉用燃烧器	10	35		15	17	千克	6	-Furnace burners for liquid fuel
	-其他炉用燃烧器,包括复式燃烧器:								-Other furnace burners, including combination burners:
	---气体的:								---For gas:
8416.2011	----使用天然气的	10.5	35		15	17	千克		----Of using natural gas
8416 2011.01[暂]	溴化锂空调用天然气燃烧机	10.5	35	5	15	17	千克	6	Natural gas burners for lithium bromide air conditioners
8416 2011.90	其他使用天然气的炉用燃烧器	10.5	35		15	17	千克	6	Other natural gas furnace burners
8416.2019	----其他	10.5	35		15	17	千克	6	----Other
8416.2090	---其他	10.5	35		15	17	千克		---Other
8416 2090.01[暂]	溴化锂空调用复式燃烧机	10.5	35	5	15	17	千克	6	Combination burners for lithium bromide air conditioners
8416 2090.90	其他使用粉状固体燃料炉用燃烧器(包括其他复式燃烧器)	10.5	35		15	17	千克	6	Other furnace burners for pulverized solid fuel (including other combination burners)
8416.3000	-机械加煤机,包括其机械炉篦、机械出灰器及类似装置	8.4	35		15	17	千克	6	-Mechanical stokers, including their mechanical grates, mechanical ash dischargers and similar appliances
8416.9000	-零件	6	35		15	17	千克		-Parts
84.17	**非电热的工业或实验室用炉及烘箱,包括焚烧炉:**								**Industrial or laboratory furnaces and ovens, including incinerators, non-electric:**
8417.1000	-矿砂、黄铁矿或金属的焙烧、熔化或其他热处理用炉及烘箱	10	35		15	17	台	6OA	-Furnaces and ovens for the roasting, melting or other heat treatment of ores,pyrites or of metals
8417.2000	-面包房用烤炉及烘箱,包括做饼干用的	10	35		15	17	台	A	-Bakery ovens, including biscuit ovens
	-其他:								-Other:
8417.8010	---炼焦炉	10	35		15	17	台	6A	---Coke ovens
8417.8020	---放射性废物焚烧炉	5	35		15	17	台	6A	---Burn furnaces for radioactive waste
8417.8030	---水泥回转窑	10	35		15	17	台	AO	---Cement rotary kilns
8417.8040	---石灰石分解炉	10	35		15	17	台	A	---Limestone decomposition furnace
8417.8050	---垃圾焚烧炉	10	35		15	17	台/千克	6AO	--- Refuse incinerator
8417.8090	---其他	10	35		15	17	台		---Other
8417 8090.10	平均温度>1000℃的耐腐蚀焚烧炉(为销毁管制化学品或化学弹药用)	10	35		15	17	台	36AO	Corrosion-resistent incinerators with an average temperature>1000℃ (to destroy controlled chemicals or chemical ammunition)
8417 8090.90	其他非电热的工业用炉及烘箱(包括实验室用炉、烘箱和焚烧炉)	10	35		15	17	台	6OA	Other non-electric industrial furnances and ovens (including laboratory furnaces, ovens and incinerators)
	-零件:								-Parts:
8417.9010	---海绵铁回转窑用	7	35		15	17	千克		---For sponge iron rotary kiln
8417.9020	---炼焦炉用	7	35		15	17	千克		---For coke ovens
8417.9090	---其他	7	35		15	17	千克		---Other
84.18	**电气或非电气的冷藏箱、冷冻箱及其他制冷设备;热泵,但品目84.15的空气调节器除外:**								**Refrigerators, freezers and other refrigerating or freezing equipment, electric or other; heat pumps other than air conditioning machines of heading No.84.15:**
	-冷藏-冷冻组合机,各自装有单独外门的:								-Combined refrigerator-freezers, fitted with separate external doors:
8418.1010	---容积超过500升	10	100		17	17	台/千克	AB	---Of a capacity exceeding 500L
8418.1020	---容积超过200升,但不超过	15	130		17	17	台/千克	A	---Of a capacity exceeding 200L, not exceeding 500L

税则号列 Tariff Item	商品名称及备注	进口税率 最惠	普通	暂定	出口退税	增值税率	计量单位	监管条件	Article Description
	500升								
8418.1030	---容积不超过200升	15	130		17	17	台/千克	A	---Of a capacity not exceeding 200L
	-家用型冷藏箱:								-Refrigerators, household type:
	--压缩式:								--Compression-type:
8418.2110	---容积超过150升	10	130		17	17	台/千克	A	---Of a capacity exceeding 150L
8418.2120	---容积超过50升，但不超过150升	10	130		17	17	台/千克	A	---Of a capacity exceeding 50L, not exceeding 150L
8418.2130	---容积不超过50升	10	130		17	17	台/千克	A	---Of a capacity not exceeding 50L
	--其他:								--Other:
8418.2910	---半导体制冷式	30	130		17	17	台/千克	A	---Semiconductor freezing type
8418.2920	---电气吸收式	15	130		17	17	台/千克	A	---Absorption-type, electrical
8418.2990	---其他	30	130		17	17	台/千克	A	---Other
	-柜式冷冻箱，容积不超过800升:								-Freezers of the chest type, not exceeding 800L capacity:
8418.3010	---制冷温度在-40℃及以下	9	50		17	17	台/千克	A	---Of a refrigerating temperature of -40℃ or lower
	---制冷温度在-40℃以上:								---Of a refrigerating temperature higher than -40℃:
8418.3021	----容积超过500升	23	100		17	17	台/千克	AB	----Of a capacity exceeding 500L
8418.3029	----其他	30	130		17	17	台/千克	A	----Other
	-立式冷冻箱，容积不超过900升:								-Freezers of the upright type, not exceeding 900L capacity:
8418.4010	---制冷温度在-40℃及以下	9	50		17	17	台/千克	A	---Of a refrigerating temperature of -40℃ or lower
	---制冷温度在-40℃以上:								---Of a refrigerating temperature higher than -40℃:
8418.4021	----容积超过500升	15	100		17	17	台/千克	AB	----Of a capacity exceeding 500L
8418.4029	----其他	30	130		17	17	台/千克	A	----Other
8418.5000	-装有冷藏或冷冻装置的其他设备（柜、箱、展示台、陈列箱及类似品）用于存储及展示	10	100		17	17	台/千克	AB	-Other furniture（chests, cabinets, display counters, show-cases and the like）for storage and display, incorporating refrigerating or freezing equipment
	-其他制冷设备；热泵:								-Other refrigerating or freezing equipment; heat pumps:
	--热泵，品目84.15的空气调节器除外:								--Heat pumps other than air conditioning machines of heading No.84.15:
8418.6120	---压缩式	10	90		17	17	台/千克		---Compression-type
8418 6120.10	压缩式制冷机组的热泵(介质为氢、氦的可冷却到≤23K且排热>150瓦)	10	90		17	17	台/千克	3	Heat pumps for compression-type refrigerating units (cooled to≤23K, and heat elimination＞150W, with hydrogen and helium as their media)
8418 6120.90	其他压缩式热泵，品目84.15的空气调节器除外	10	90		17	17	台/千克		Other compression type heat pumps, excluding air conditioning machines of heading No. 8415
8418.6190	---其他	15	130		17	17	台/千克		---Other
	--其他:								--Other:
8418.6920	---制冷机组	10	90		17	17	台/千克		---Refrigerating units
8418 6920.10	其他压缩式制冷设备(介质为氢或氦，可冷却到≤23K且排热>150瓦)	10	90		17	17	台/千克	3	Other compression type refrigeration equipments (cooled to≤23K, and heat elimination＞150W, with hydrogen and helium as their media)
8418 6920.90	其他制冷机组	10	90		17	17	台/千克		Other refrigerating units
8418.6990	---其他	10	130		17	17	台/千克		---Other
8418 6990.10	带制冷装置的发酵罐(不发散气溶胶，且容积大于20升)	10	130		17	17	台/千克	3	Fermenters with refrigeration appliances (non-divergent aerosol, volume＞20L)
8418 6990.20	制冰机、冰激凌机	10	130		17	17	台/千克	AB	Ice makers and ice cream machines
8418 6990.90	其他制冷设备	10	130		17	17	台/千克		Other refrigeration equipments
	-零件:								-Parts:
8418.9100	--冷藏或冷冻设备专用的特制家具	18	130		15	17	千克		--Furniture designed to receive refrigerating or freezing equipment
	--其他:								--Other:
8418.9910 暂	---制冷机组及热泵用	10	90	6	17	17	千克		---Of refrigerating units and heat pumps
	---其他:								---Other:
8418.9991 暂	----制冷温度-40℃及以下的冷冻设备用	9.5	50	6	15	17	千克		----Of freezing equipment of a refrigerating temperature of -40℃ or lower

税则号列 Tariff Item	商品名称及备注	进口税率 最惠	普通	暂定	出口退税	增值税率	计量单位	监管条件	Article Description
8418.9992[暂]	----制冷温度-40℃以上，但容积超过 500 升的冷藏或冷冻设备用	10	100	6	15	17	千克		----Of refrigerating or freezing equipment of a refrigerating temperature higher than -40ºC and a capacity exceeding 500L
8418.9999[暂]	----其他	10	130	6	15	17	千克		----Other
8418 9999.10[暂]	耐腐蚀冷凝器(20 平方米＞换热面积＞0.15 平方米)	10	130	6	15	17	千克	3	Corrosion-resistent condensers (0.15 sq m＜heat transfer area＜20 sq m)
8418 9999.90[暂]	品目 84.18 其他制冷设备用零件	10	130	6	15	17	千克		Other parts for refrigeration equipments of heading No. 8418
84.19	**利用温度变化处理材料的机器、装置及类似的实验室设备，例如，加热、烹煮、烘炒、蒸馏、精馏、消毒、灭菌、汽蒸、干燥、蒸发、气化、冷凝、冷却的机器设备，不论是否电热的（不包括品目 85.14 的炉，烘箱及其他设备），但家用的除外；非电热的快速热水器或贮备式热水器：**								**Machinery, plant or laboratory equipment, whether or not electrically heated（excluding furnaces, ovens and other equipment of heading No. 85. 14）, for the treatment of materials by a process involving a change of temperature such as heating, cooking, roasting, distilling, rectifying, sterilizing, pasteurizing, steaming, drying, evaporating, vaporizing, condensing or cooling, other than machinery or plant of a kind used for domestic purposes;instantaneous or storage water heaters, non-electric:**
	-非电热的快速热水器或贮备式热水器:								-Instantaneous or storage water heaters, non- electric:
8419.1100	--燃气快速热水器	35	100		15	17	台	A	--Instantaneous gas water heaters
	--其他:								--Other
8419.1910	---太阳能热水器	35	100		17	17	台	A	---Solar water heaters
8419.1990	---其他	35	100		17	17	台	A	---Other
8419.2000	-医用或实验室用消毒器具	4	30		15	17	台	A	-Medical, surgical or laboratory sterilizers
	-干燥器:								-Dryers：
8419.3100	--农产品干燥用	8	30		13	13	台	A	--For agricultural products
8419.3200	--木材、纸浆、纸或纸板干燥用	9	30		15	17	台	A	--For wood, paper pulp, paper or paperboard
	--其他:								--Other:
8419.3910	---微空气流动陶瓷坯件干燥器	9	30		15	17	台	A	---Breeze pottery blanks dryers
8419.3990	---其他	9	30		15	17	台		---Other
8419 3990.01[暂]	生产奶粉用干燥器	9	30	4	15	17	台	A	Dryers for producing milk powder
8419 3990.02[暂]	污泥涡轮干燥机	9	30	4	15	17	台	A	Ludge turbo dryer
8419 3990.10	冻干设备(10 千克≤24 小时凝冰量≤1000 千克，并可蒸汽消毒)	9	30		15	17	台	3A	Freeze-drying equipment (10kg≤24 hour ice-freezing quantity≤1000kg, can be evaporated and sterilized)
8419 3990.20	烟丝烘干机	9	30		15	17	台	AO	Tobacco dryer
8419 3990.30	干燥箱(具有与三级生物安全柜类似标准)	9	30		15	17	台	3A	Drying cabinet(with the similar standard of Biosafety Level 3 cabinets)
8419 3990.90	其他用途的干燥器	9	30		15	17	台	A	Dryers for other purposes
	-蒸馏或精馏设备:								-Distilling or rectifying plant:
8419.4010	---提净塔	10	30		15	17	台	A	---Stripping towers
8419.4020	---精馏塔	10	30		15	17	台	A	---Rectifying towers
8419.4090	---其他	10	30		15	17	台		---Other
8419 4090.10	氢－低温蒸馏塔(温度≤-238℃，压力为 0.5～5 兆帕，内径≥1 米等条件)	10	30		15	17	台	3AO	Hydrogen low temperature distilling towers (temperature ≤ -238 ℃, pressure of 0.5 to 5 MPa, inner diameter ≥ 1)
8419 4090.20	耐腐蚀蒸馏塔（内径＞0.1 米，接触表面由特殊耐腐蚀材料制成）	10	30		15	17	台	3AO	Corrosion-resistent distillation towers (inner diameter ＞0.1m, with contact surface made of special corrosion-resistent materials)
8419 4090.90	其他蒸馏或精馏设备	10	30		15	17	台	AO	Other distilling or rectifying plant
8419.5000	-热交换装置	10	30		15	17	台		-Heat exchange units
8419 5000.10	热交换器(专用于核反应堆的一次冷却剂回路的)	10	30		15	17	台	3O	Heat exchangers (used exclusively for nuclear reactor primary coolant loop)
8419 5000.20	蒸汽发生器(专用于核反应堆内生成的热量输送到进水以产生蒸汽的)	10	30		15	17	台	3	Steam generators (used exclusively to transmit the heat generated within nuclear reactors to the inlet to produce vapor)

税则号列 Tariff Item	商品名称及备注	进口税率			出口退税	增值税率	计量单位	监管条件	Article Description
		最惠	普通	暂定					
8419 5000.30	冷却UF_6的热交换器（在压差为100千帕下渗透压力变化率小于10帕/小时）	10	30		15	17	台	3A	Heat exchangers for cooling UF_6（osmotic pressure change rate＜10pa/h under the differential pressure of less than 100kPa）
8419 5000.40	冷却气体用热交换器（用耐UF_6腐蚀材料制成或加以保护的）	10	30		15	17	台	3AO	Heat exchangers for cooling gases (made of or protected by UF_6–resistent materials)
8419 5000.50	耐腐蚀热交换器（0.15平方米＜换热面积＜20平方米）	10	30		15	17	台	3AO	Corrosion-resistent heat exchangers（0.15 sq m＜heat transfer area＜20 sq m）
8419 5000.90	其他热交换装置	10	30		15	17	台	A	Other heat exchange units
	-液化空气或其他气体的机器:								-Machinery for liquefying air or other gases:
	---制氧机:								---Oxygen producers:
8419.6011	----制氧量在15000立方米/小时及以上	12	30		17	17	台	A	---Oxygen preparation volume no less than 15000m^3/h
8419.6019	----其他	13	30		17	17	台	A	----Other
8419.6090	---其他	10	30		15	17	台		---Other
8419 6090.10	液化器（将来自级联的UF_6气体压缩并冷凝成液态UF_6）	10	30		15	17	台	3AO	Liquefiers (compress and condense cascaded UF_6 gases into liquid)
8419 6090.90	其他液化空气或其他气体用的机器	10	30		15	17	台	AO	Other machinery for liquefying air or other gases
	-其他机器设备:								-Other machinery, plant and equipment:
8419.8100[暂]	--加工热饮料或烹调、加热食品用	10	30	6	15	17	台	A	--For making hot drinks of for cooking or heating food
	--其他:								--Other:
8419.8910	---加氢反应器	0	30		15	17	台	A	---Hydroformer vessels
8419.8990	---其他	0	30		15	17	台		---Other
8419 8990.10	带加热装置的发酵罐(不发散气溶胶，且容积大于20升）	0	30		15	17	台	3AO	Fermenters fitted with heat devices (non-divergent aerosol, volume＞20L)
8419 8990.21	凝华器(或冷阱)(从扩散级联中取出UF_6并可再蒸发转移）	0	30		15	17	台	3AO	Sublimators (or cold traps) (extract UF6 from diffusion cascade and transfer it by evaporation
8419 8990.22	低温制冷设备（能承受－120℃或更低的温度）	0	30		15	17	台	3A	Low-temperature refrigeration equipment (with the capacity to stand －120℃ or lower)
8419 8990.23	UF_6冷阱（能承受－20℃或更低的温度）	0	30		15	17	台	3AO	UF_6 cold traps (with the capacity to stand－120℃ or lower)
8419 8990.90	其他利用温度变化处理材料的机器（包括类似的实验室设备）	0	30		15	17	台	A	Other machines for the treatment of materials by a process involving a change of temperature (including similar laboratory equipments)
	-零件:								-Parts:
8419.9010	---热水器用	0	100		17	17	千克		---Of water heaters
8419.9090	---其他	4	30		15	17	千克		---Other
84.20	**研光机或其他滚压机器及其滚筒，但加工金属或玻璃用的除外:**								**Calendering or other rolling machines, other than for metals or glass, and cylinders therefor:**
8420.1000	-研光机或其他滚压机器	8.4	30		15	17	台		-Calendering or other rolling machines
8420 1000.01[暂]	织物轧光机	8.4	30	6	15	17	台		Fabric calenders
8420 1000.90	其他研光机或滚压机器(加工金属或玻璃用的除外）	8.4	30		15	17	台		Other calenders or rolling machines (excluding those for processing metals and glass)
	-零件:								-Parts:
8420.9100	--滚筒	8	30		15	17	个/千克		--Cylinders
8420.9900	--其他	8	30		15	17	千克		--Other
84.21	**离心机，包括离心干燥机；液体或气体的过滤、净化机器及装置:**								**Centrifuges, including centrifugal dryers; filtering or purifying machinery and apparatus, for liquids or gases:**
	-离心机，包括离心干燥机:								-Centrifuges, including centrifugal dryers:
8421.1100	--奶油分离器	8.4	30		15	17	台	A	--Cream separators
	--干衣机:								--Clothes-dryers:
8421.1210	----干衣量不超过10千克	17.5	70		15	17	台		---Of a dry linen capacity not exceeding 10kg
8421.1290	----其他	8	30		15	17	台		---Other
	--其他:								--Other:
8421.1910[暂]	---脱水机	10	30	6	15	17	台		---Dewaterers

税则号列 Tariff Item	商品名称及备注	进口税率 最惠	进口税率 普通	进口税率 暂定	出口退税	增值税率	计量单位	监管条件	Article Description
8421.1920	---固液分离机	10	30		15	17	台		---Solid-liquor separators
8421.1990	---其他	10	30		15	17	台		---Other
8421 1990.20	液-液离心接触器（为化学交换过程的铀浓缩而专门设计或制造的）	10	30		15	17	台	3	Centrifugal liquid-liquid separators (specially designed or made for uranium enrichment in the chemical exchange process
8421 1990.30	离心分离器,包括倾析器（不发散气溶胶、可对致病性微生物进行连续分离的）	10	30		15	17	台	3	Centrifugal separators, including decanters (non-divergent aerosol which can continuously separate pathogenic microorganisms)
8421 1990.90	其他离心机及离心干燥机	10	30		15	17	台		Other centrifugal machines and centrifugal dryers
	-液体的过滤、净化机器及装置:								-Filtering or purifying machinery and apparatus for liquids:
	--过滤或净化水用:								--For filtering or purifying water:
8421.2110 暂	---家用型	25	63	12	15	17	台/千克	AB	---Of the household type
	---其他:								---Other:
8421.2191	----船舶压载水处理设备	5	50		15	17	台/千克		----Ship ballast water treatment equipments
8421.2199	----其他	5	50		15	17	台/千克		----Other
8421 2199.01 暂	喷灌设备用叠式净水过滤器	5	50	0	15	17	台/千克		Stacked water purification filter used for spray irrigation equipment
8421 2199.02 暂	船舶压载水处理设备用过滤器	5	50	2	15	17	台/千克		Filters for ship ballast water treatment equipments
8421 2199.90	其他非家用型过滤或净化水的装置	5	50		15	17	台/千克		Other non-residential filtration or water purification devices
8421.2200	--过滤或净化饮料(水除外)用	12	40		15	17	台	A	--For filtering or purifying beverages other than water
8421.2300	--内燃发动机的滤油器	10	40		15	17	个		--Oil or petrol-filters for internal combustion engines
	--其他:								--Other:
8421.2910	---压滤机	5	40		15	17	个	O	---Press filters
8421.2990	---其他	5	40		15	17			---Other
8421 2990.40	液体截流过滤设备(可连续分离致病性微生物、毒素和细胞培养物)	5	40		15	17	个	3	Liquid closure filtration equipment (which can continuously separate pathogenic microorganisms, toxins and cell culture)
8421 2990.90	其他液体的过滤、净化机器及装置	5	40		15	17	个		Other filtering, purifying machines and apparatuses liquids
	-气体的过滤、净化机器及装置:								-Filtering or purifying machinery and apparatus for gases:
8421.3100	--内燃发动机的进气过滤器	10	40		15	17	个		--Intake air filters for internal combustion engines
	--其他:								--Other:
8421.3910 暂	---家用型	15	100	8	15	17	个		---Of the household type
	---工业用除尘器:								---Dust collectors for industry uses:
8421.3921	----静电除尘器	5	40		15	17	个		----Electrostatic
8421.3922	----袋式除尘器	5	40		15	17	个		----Baghoused
8421.3923	----旋风式除尘器	5	40		15	17	个		----Cyclone
8421.3924	----电袋复合除尘器	5	40		15	17	个/千克		----Electrostatic Fabric Filter
8421.3929	----其他	5	40		15	17	个		----Other
8421.3930	---内燃发动机排气过滤及净化装置	5	40		15	17	个		---Exhaust air filtering or purifying apparatus for internal combustion engines
8421 3930.01 暂	摩托车发动机排气过滤及净化装置	5	40	3	15	17	个		Other filtering and purifying apparatuses for motorcycle engines
8421 3930.90	其他内燃发动机排气过滤及净化装置	5	40		15	17	个		Other filtering and purifying apparatuses for internal combustion engines
8421.3940	---烟气脱硫装置	5	40		15	17	个		---Flue gas desulfurization apparatus
8421.3950	---烟气脱硝装置	5	40		15	17	个		---Flue gas denitration apparatus
8421.3990	---其他	5	40		15	17	个		---Other
	-零件:								-Parts:
	--离心机用，包括离心干燥机用:								--Of centrifuges, including centrifugaldryers:
8421.9110	---干衣量不超过 10 千克的干衣机用	0	70		15	17	千克		---Of clothes-dryers of a dry linen capacity not exceeding 10kg
8421.9190	---其他	0	30		15	17	千克		---Other

税则号列 Tariff Item	商品名称及备注	进口税率 最惠	普通	暂定	出口退税	增值税率	计量单位	监管条件	Article Description
8421 9190.11	离心机壳/收集器(容纳气体离心机的转筒组件的耐 UF_6 部件)	0	30		15	17	千克	3	Centrifugal chassis/collectors (UF_6-resistent components that hold air centrifugal machines)
8421 9190.12	收集器(由内径不同的同心管组成用于供取 UF_6 气体的管件)	0	30		15	17	千克	3	Collectors (pipes that consist of concentric tubes with different inner diameters for supplying and extracting UF_6 gases)
8421 9190.13	气体扩散膜(由耐 UF_6 材料制成的多细孔过滤薄膜)	0	30		15	17	千克	3	Air diffusion membrances (multiple-pore filter membrances made of UF_6–resistent materials)
8421 9190.14	扩散室(含一个进气管两个出气管的容纳气体扩散膜的密闭式容器)	0	30		15	17	千克	3	Diffusion rooms (airtight containers with one inlet and two outlets intake for holding air diffusion membrances)
8421 9190.90	其他离心机用零件	0	30		15	17	千克		Other parts for centrifugal machines
	--其他:								--Other:
8421.9910 暂	---家用型过滤、净化装置用	10	100	6	15	17	千克		---Of household-type filtering or purifying machines
8421.9990	---其他	5	40		15	17	千克		---Other
84.22	洗碟机;瓶子及其他容器的洗涤或干燥机器;瓶、罐、箱、袋或其他容器装填、封口、密封、贴标签的机器;瓶、罐、管、筒或类似容器的包封机器;其他包装或打包机器(包括热缩包装机器);饮料充气机:								**Dish washing machines; machinery for cleaning or drying bottles or other containers; machinery for filling, closing, sealing or labelling bottles, cans, boxes, bags or other containers; machinery for capsuling booties,jars, tubes and similar containers other packing or wrapping machinery (including heat-shrink wrapping machinery); machinery for aerating beverages:**
	-洗碟机:								-Dish washing machines:
8422.1100 暂	--家用型	10	90	6	15	17	台/千克		--Of the household type
8422.1900	--其他	14	90		15	17	台/千克		--Other
8422.2000	-瓶子或其他容器的洗涤或干燥机器	10	35		15	17	台		-Machinery for cleaning or drying bottles or other containers
	-瓶、罐、箱、袋或其他容器装填、封口、密封、贴标签的机器;瓶、罐、管、筒或类似容器的包封机器;饮料充气机:								-Machinery for filling, closing, sealing, or labelling bottles, cans, boxes, bags or other containers; machinery for capsuling bottles, jars, tubes and similar containers; machinery for aerating beverages:
8422.3010	---饮料及液体食品灌装设备	12	45		15	17	台		---Bottling or canning machinery for beverages or liquid food
8422 3010.01 暂	乳品加工用自动化灌装设备	12	45	6	15	17	台	OA	Automated bottling or canning machinery for dairy processing
8422 3010.90	其他饮料及液体食品灌装设备	12	45		15	17	台	OA	Other bottling or canning machinery for beverages and liquid food
	---水泥包装机:								---Machinery for packing cement:
8422.3021	----全自动灌包机	12	45		15	17	台		----Automatic filling and sacking machines
8422.3029	----其他	12	45		15	17	台		----Other
8422.3030	---其他包装机	10	35		15	17	台		---Other packing machines
8422 3030.01 暂	全自动无菌灌装生产线用包装机(加工速度≥20000只/小时)	10	35	6	15	17	台	OA	Packaging machines for automatic aseptic filling lines (processing speed ≥ 20000 pcs / hour)
8422 3030.90	其他包装机	10	35		15	17	台	OA	Other packaging machines
8422.3090	---其他	10	35		15	17	台		---Other
8422 3090.01 暂	全自动无菌灌装生产线用贴吸管机(加工速度≥22000只/小时)	10	35	6	15	17	台	A	Posted straw machines for fully automatic aseptic filling lines (processing speed ≥ 22000 pcs / hour)
8422 3090.10	充装设备(两用物项管制)	10	35		15	17	台	3A	Filling equipments (control of sensitive items)
8422 3090.90	饮料充气机及其他包封机	10	35		15	17	台	A	Inflatable beverage machines and other encapsulation machines
8422.4000	-其他包装或打包机器(包括热缩包装机器)	10	35		13/15	17	台		-Other packing or wrapping machinery (including heat-shrink wrapping machinery)
	-零件:								-Parts:
8422.9010 暂	---洗碟机用	10.5	90	6	15	17	千克		---Of dish washing machines
8422.9020	---饮料及液体食品灌装设备用	8.5	45		15	17	千克	A	---Of bottling or canning machinery for beverages or liquid food
8422.9090	---其他	8.5	35		15	17	千克		---Other
84.23	衡器(感量为50毫克或更精密								**Weighing machinery (excluding balances of a**

税则号列 Tariff Item	商品名称及备注	进口税率 最惠	普通	暂定	出口退税	增值税率	计量单位	监管条件	Article Description
	的天平除外），包括计数或检验用的衡器；衡器用的各种砝码、秤砣：								sensitivity of 50mg or better）, including weight operated counting or checking machines; weighing machine weights of all kinds:
8423.1000	-体重计，包括婴儿秤；家用秤	10.5	80		15	17	台		-Personal weighing machines, including baby scales; household scales
	-输送带上连续称货的秤:								-Scales for continuous weighing of goods on conveyors:
8423.2010	---电子皮带秤	10	80		15	17	台		---Electronic belt weighing machines
8423.2090	---其他	10	80		15	17	台		---Other
	-恒定秤、物料定量装袋或装容器用的秤，包括库秤:								-Constant weight scales and scales for discharging a predetermined weight of material into a bag or container, including hopper scales:
8423.3010	---定量包装秤	10.5	80		15	17	台		---Rationed packing scales
8423.3020	---定量分选秤	10.5	80		15	17	台		---Rationed sorting scales
8423.3030	---配料秤	10.5	80		15	17	台		---Proporating scales
8423.3090	---其他	10.5	80		15	17	台		---Other
	-其他衡器:								-Other weighing machinery:
	--最大称量不超过30千克:								--Having a maximum weighing capacity not exceeding 30kg:
8423.8110	---计价秤	10.5	80		15	17	台		---Account balances
8423.8120	---弹簧秤	10.5	80		15	17	台		---Spring balances
8423.8190	---其他	10.5	80		15	17	台		---Other
	--最大称量超过30千克，但不超过5000千克:								--Having a maximum weighing capacity exceeding 30kg but not exceeding 5000kg:
8423.8210	---地中衡	10.5	80		15	17	台		---Weighbridges
8423.8290	---其他	10.5	80		15	17	台		---Other
	--其他:								--Other:
8423.8910	---地中衡	10	80		15	17	台		---Weighbridges
8423.8920	---轨道衡	10	80		15	17	台		---Track scales
8423.8930	---吊秤	10	80		15	17	台		---Hanging scales
8423.8990	---其他	10	80		15	17	台		---Other
8423.9000	-衡器用的各种砝码、秤砣；衡器的零件	10	80		15	17	千克		-Weighing machine weights of all kinds; parts of weighing machinery
84.24	液体或粉末的喷射、散布或喷雾的机械器具（不论是否手工操作）；灭火器，不论是否装药；喷枪及类似器具；喷汽机、喷砂机及类似的喷射机器:								**Mechanical appliances（whether or not hand-operated）for projecting, dispersing or spraying liquids or powders; fire extinguishers, whether or not charged; spray guns and similar appliances; steam or sand blasting machines and similar jet projecting machines:**
8424.1000	-灭火器，不论是否装药	8.4	70		15	17	个	A	-Fire extinguishers, whether or not charged
8424.2000	-喷枪及类似器具	8.4	40		15	17	个		-Spray guns and similar appliances
8424.3000	-喷汽机、喷砂机及类似喷射机器	8.4	40		15	17	台		-Steam or sand blasting machines and similar jet projecting machines
	-其他器具:								-Other appliances:
8424.8100	--农业或园艺用	8	30		13	13	台		--Agricultural or horticultural
	--其他:								--Other:
8424.8910	---家用型	0	80		15	17	台/千克		---Of the household type
8424.8920	---喷涂机器人	0	80		15	17	台/千克		---Spraypainting robot
	---其他:								---Other:
8424.8991	----船用洗舱机	0	30		15	17	台		----Marine cabinet washer
8424.8999	----其他	0	30		15	17	台		----Other
8424 8999.10	分离喷嘴（由狭缝状、曲率半径极小的弯曲通道组成，内有分离楔尖）	0	30		15	17	台	3	Separated nozzles (consisting of slit-like curved channels of a very small curvature radius, with a separated wedge tip inside)
8424 8999.90	其他用途的喷射、喷雾机械器具	0	30		15	17	台		Projecting or spraying mechanical appliances for other purposes
	-零件:								-Parts:

税则号列 Tariff Item	商品名称及备注	进口税率			出口退税	增值税率	计量单位	监管条件	Article Description
		最惠	普通	暂定					
8424.9010	---子目号8424.1000所列器具的零件	0	70		15	17	千克		---Of the apparatus of subheading No.8424.1000
8424.9020	---子目号8424.8910所列器具的零件	0	80		15	17	千克		---Of the apparatus of subheading No.8424. 8910
8424.9090	---其他	0	30		15	17	千克		---Other
84.25	**滑车及提升机,但倒卸式提升机除外;卷扬机及绞盘;千斤顶:**								**Pulley tackle and hoists other than skip hoists; winches and capstans; jacks:**
	-滑车及提升机,但倒卸式提升机及提升车辆用的提升机除外:								-Pulley tackle and hoists other than skip hoists or hoists of a kind used for raising vehicles:
8425.1100	--电动的	6	30		17	17	台		--Powered by electric motor
8425.1900	--其他	5	30		17	17	台		--Other
	-卷扬机;绞盘:								-Winches; capstans:
	--电动的:								--Powered by electric motor:
8425.3110	---矿井口卷扬装置;专为井下使用设计的卷扬机	10	30		17	17	台		---Pit-head winding gear; winches specially designed for use underground
8425.3190	---其他	5	30		17	17	台		---Other
	--其他:								--Other:
8425.3910	---矿井口卷扬装置;专为井下使用设计的卷扬机	10	30		17	17	台		---Pit-head winding gear; winches specially designed for use underground
8425.3990	---其他	5	30		17	17	台		---Other
	-千斤顶;提升车辆用的提升机:								-Jacks; hoists of a kind used for raising vehicles:
8425.4100	--车库中使用的固定千斤顶系统	3	30		17	17	台		--Built-in jacking systems of a type used in garages
	--其他液压千斤顶及提升机:								--Other jacks and hoists, hydraulic:
8425.4210	---液压千斤顶	3	30		17	17	台		---Hydraulic jacks
8425.4290	---其他	5	30		17	17	台		---Other
	--其他:								--Other:
8425.4910	---其他千斤顶	5	30		17	17	台		---Other jacks
8425.4990	---其他	10	30		17	17	台		---Other
84.26	**船用桅杆式起重机;起重机,包括缆式起重机;移动式吊运架、跨运车及装有起重机的工作车:**								**Ships derricks; cranes, including cable cranes; mobile lifting frames, straddle carriers and works trucks fitted with a crane:**
	-高架移动式起重机、桁架桥式起重机、龙门起重机、桥式起重机、移动式吊运架及跨运车:								-Overhead travelling cranes, transporter cranes, gantry cranes, bridge cranes, mobile lifting frames and straddle carriers:
	--固定支架的高架移动式起重机:								--Overhead travelling cranes on fixed support:
8426.1120	---通用桥式起重机	8	30		17	17	台		---Bridge cranes, all-purpose
8426.1190	---其他	8	30		17	17	台		---Other
8426.1200	--带胶轮移动式吊运架及跨运车	6	30		17	17	台		--Mobile lifting frames on tyres and straddle carriers
	--其他:								--Other:
8426.1910	---装船机	5	30		17	17	台		---Ship loading cranes
	---卸船机:								---Ship unloading cranes:
8426.1921	----抓斗式	5	30		17	17	台		----Grab ship unloading cranes
8426.1929	----其他	5	30		17	17	台	O	----Other
8426.1930	---龙门式起重机	10	30		17	17	台	O	---Gantry cranes
	---装卸桥:								---Loading and unloading bridges:
8426.1941	----门式装卸桥	10	30		17	17	台		----Frame loading and unloading bridges
8426.1942	----集装箱装卸桥	10	30		17	17	台	O	----Container loading and unloading bridges
8426.1943	----其他动臂式装卸桥	10	30		17	17	台		----Derrick loading and unloading bridges
8426.1949	----其他	10	30		17	17	台		----Other
8426.1990	---其他	10	30		17	17	台		---Other
8426.2000	-塔式起重机	10	30		17	17	台	O	-Tower cranes
8426.3000	-门座式起重机及座式旋臂起重机	6	30		17	17	台	O	-Portal or pedestal jib cranes
	-其他自推进机械:								-Other machinery, self-propelled:
	--带胶轮的:								--On tyres:

税则号列 Tariff Item	商品名称及备注	进口税率 最惠	进口税率 普通	进口税率 暂定	出口退税	增值税率	计量单位	监管条件	Article Description
8426.4110	---轮胎式起重机	5	30		17	17	台	O	---Wheel-mounted cranes
8426.4190	---其他	5	30		17	17	台		---Other
	--其他:								--Other:
8426.4910	---履带式起重机	8	30		17	17	台	O	---Crawler cranes
8426.4990	---其他	13	30		17	17	台		---Other
	-其他机械:								-Other machinery:
8426.9100	--供装于公路车辆的	10	30		17	17	台		--Designed for mounting on road vehicles
8426.9900	--其他	6	30		17	17	台		--Other
84.27	**叉车;其他装有升降或搬运装置的工作车:**								**Fork-lift trucks; other works trucks fitted with lifting or handling equipment:**
	-电动机推进的机动车:								-Self-propelled trucks powered by an electric motor:
8427.1010	---有轨巷道堆垛机	9	30		17	17	台	A	---Track alleyway stackers
8427.1020	---无轨巷道堆垛机	9	30		17	17	台	A	---Trackless alleyway stackers
8427.1090	---其他	9	30		17	17	台	A	---Other
	-其他机动叉车:								-Other self-propelled trucks:
8427.2010	---集装箱叉车	9	30		17	17	台	A	---Fork-lift trucks cranes
8427.2090	---其他	9	30		17	17	台	A	---Other
8427.9000	-其他车	9	30		17	17	台	A	-Other trucks
84.28	**其他升降、搬运、装卸机械（例如，升降机、自动梯、输送机、缆车）:**								**Other lifting, handling, loading or unloading machinery（for example, lifts, escalators, conveyors, teleferics）:**
	-升降机及倒卸式起重机:								-Lifts and skip hoists:
8428.1010	---载客电梯	8	30		17	17	台		---Designed for the transport of persons
8428 1010.01[暂]	无障碍升降机	8	30	4	17	17	台	A	Accessibility-free lifts
8428 1010.90	其他载客电梯	8	30		17	17	台	A	Other passenger elevators
8428.1090	---其他	6	30		17	17	台	A	---Other
8428.2000	-气压升降机及输送机	5	30		17	17	台		-Pneumatic elevators and conveyors
	-其他用于连续运送货物或材料的升降机及输送机:								--Other continuous-action elevators and conveyors, for goods or materials:
8428.3100	--地下专用的	5	30		17	17	台		--Specially designed for underground use
8428.3200	--其他,斗式	5	30		17	17	台		--Other, bucket type
8428.3300	--其他,带式	5	30		17	17	台		--Other, belt type
	--其他:								--Other:
8428.3910	---链式	5	30		17	17	台		---Chain type
8428.3920	---辊式	5	30		17	17	台		---Roller type
8428.3990	---其他	5	30		17	17	台		---Other
8428.4000	-自动梯及自动人行道	5	30		17	17	台	A	-Escalators and moving walkways
	-缆车、座式升降机、滑雪拉索、索道用牵引装置:								-Teleferics, chair-lifts, ski-draglines; traction mechanisms for funiculars:
8428.6010	---货运架空索道	8	30		17	17	台		---Cargo aerial cableways
	---客运架空索道:								---Passanger aerial cableways:
8428.6021	----单线循环式	8	30		17	17	台		----Monocable endless
8428.6029	----其他	8	30		17	17	台		----Other
8428.6090	---其他	8	30		17	17	台		---Other
	-其他机械:								-Other machinery:
8428.9010	---矿车推动机、铁道机车或货车的转车台、货车倾卸装置及类似的铁道货车搬运装置	10	30		17	17	台		---Mine wagon pushers, locmotive or wagon traversers, wagon tippers and similar railway wagon handing equipment
8428.9020	---机械式停车设备	5	30		17	17	台		---Machincal parking equipment
	---其他装载机械:								---Other loading or unloading machinery:
8428.9031	----堆取料机械	5	30		17	17	台		----Stacker-reclaimers
8428.9039	----其他	5	30		17	17	台		---Other
8428.9040	---搬运机器人	5	30		17	17	台		---Transfer robot
8428.9090	---其他	5	30		17	17	台		---Other
8428 9090.10	放化分离作业和热室用遥控机械手(能贯穿 0.6 米以上热室壁	5	30		17	17	台	3	Remote control robots for radiochemical separation operations and hot cells (able to run through hot walls

税则号列 Tariff Item	商品名称及备注	进口税率 最惠	普通	暂定	出口退税	增值税率	计量单位	监管条件	Article Description
	或壁厚为0.6米以上热室顶)								or tops of above 0.6m)
8428 9090.20	核反应堆燃料装卸机(用于在核反应堆中插入或取出燃料的操作设备)	5	30		17	17	台	3	Loading and unloading machines for fuel of nuclear reactors (used to insert or remove the fuel from nuclear reactors)
8428 9090.90	其他升降、搬运、装卸机械	5	30		17	17	台		Other lifting, carrying, loading and unloading mechanical appliances
84.29	**机动推土机、侧铲推土机、筑路机、平地机、铲运机、机械铲、挖掘机、机铲装载机、捣固机械及压路机:**								**Self-propelled bulldozers, angledozers, graders, levellers, scrapers, me-chanical shovels, excavators, shovel loaders, tamping machines and road rollers:**
	-推土机及侧铲推土机:								-Bulldozers and angledozers:
	--履带式:								--Track laying:
8429.1110	---发动机输出功率超过235.36千瓦(320马力)的	7	17		17	17	台	OA	---With an engine of an output exceeding 235.36KW (320hp)
8429.1190	---其他	7	30		17	17	台	AO	---Other
	--其他:								--Other:
8429.1910	---发动机输出功率超过235.36千瓦(320马力)的	7	17		17	17	台	A	---With an engine of an output exceeding 235.36KW (320hp)
8429.1990	---其他	7	30		17	17	台	A	---Other
	-筑路机及平地机:								-Graders and levellers:
8429.2010	---发动机输出功率超过235.36千瓦(320马力)的	5	17		13/17	17	台	A	---With an engine of an output exceeding 235.36KW (320hp)
8429.2090	---其他	5	30		13/17	17	台	OA	---Other:
	-铲运机:								-Scrapers:
8429.3010	---斗容量超过10立方米的	3	17		17	17	台	A	---Having a capacity of shovel exceeding 10m³
8429.3090	---其他	5	30		17	17	台	A	---Other
	-捣固机械及压路机:								-Tamping machines and road rollers:
	---机动压路机:								---Self-propelled road rollers:
8429.4011	----机重18吨及以上的振动式压路机	7	20		17	17	台	OA	----Vibration type, of a deadweight of 18t or more
8429.4019	----其他	8	40		17	17	台	OA	----Other
8429.4090	---其他	6	30		17	17	台	OA	---Other
	-机械铲、挖掘机及机铲装载机:								-Mechanical shovels, excavators and shovel loaders:
8429.5100	--前铲装载机	5	30		17	17	台	A	--Front-end shovel loaders
	--上部结构可旋转360度的机械:								--Machinery with a 360° revolving superstructure:
	---挖掘机:								---Excavators:
8429.5211	----轮胎式	8	30		17	17	台	OA	----Tyre-mounted
8429.5212	----履带式	8	30		17	17	台	OA	----Track-mounted
8429.5219	----其他	8	30		17	17	台	OA	----Other
8429.5290	---其他	8	30		17	17	台	OA	---Other
8429.5900	--其他	8	30		17	17	台	OA	--Other
84.30	**泥土、矿物或矿石的运送、平整、铲运、挖掘、捣固、压实、开采或钻探机械;打桩机及拔桩机;扫雪机及吹雪机:**								**Other moving, grading, levelling, scraping, excavating, tamping, compacting, extracting or boring machinery, for earth, minerals or ores; piledrivers and pile-extractors; snow-ploughs and snow-blowers:**
8430.1000	-打桩机及拔桩机	10	30		17	17	台		-Pile-drivers and pile-extractors
8430.2000	-扫雪机及吹雪机	10	30		17	17	台		-Snow-ploughs and snow-blowers
	-采(截)煤机、凿岩机及隧道掘进机:								-Coal or rock cutters and tunnelling machinery:
	--自推进的:								--Self-propelled:
8430.3110	---采(截)煤机	10	30		17	17	台/千克	O	---Coal cutters or coal-winning machine
8430.3120	---凿岩机	10	30		17	17	台/千克	O	---Rock cutters
8430.3130	---隧道掘进机	10	30		17	17	台/千克	O	---Tunnelling machinery
8430.3900	--其他	6	30		17	17	台		--Other
	-其他钻探或凿井机械:								-Other boring or sinking machinery:
	--自推进的:								--Self-propelled:

税则号列 Tariff Item	商品名称及备注	进口税率 最惠	普通	暂定	出口退税	增值税率	计量单位	监管条件	Article Description
	---石油及天然气钻探机:								---Oil and natural gas drilling machinery:
8430.4111	----钻探深度在6000米及以上的	5	11		17	17	台		---Of drilling depth of 6000m or more
8430.4119	----其他	5	17		17	17	台		----Other
	---其他钻探机:								---Other drilling machinery:
8430.4121	----钻探深度在6000米及以上的	5	11		17	17	台		----Of drilling depth of 6000m or more
8430.4122	----钻探深度在6000米以下的履带式自推进钻机	5	17		17	17	台		----Crawler boring machinery of drilling depth not exceeding 6000 m
8430.4129	----钻探深度在6000米以下的其他钻探机	5	17		17	17	台		----Other boring machinery of drilling depth exceeding 6000 m
8430.4190	---其他	5	30		17	17	台		---Other
8430.4900	--其他	5	30		17	17	台		--Other
	-其他自推进机械:								-Other machinery, self-propelled:
8430.5010	---其他采油机械	3	17		17	17	台		---For oil production
8430.5020	---矿用电铲	7	30		17	17	台		---Mining power shovels
	---采矿钻机:								---Mining drills:
8430.5031	----牙轮直径380毫米及以上	5	30		17	17	台		----Gear wheel diameter more than 380mm
8430.5039	----其他	5	30		17	17	台		----Other
8430.5090	---其他	5	30		17	17	台		---Other
	-其他非自推进机械:								-Other machinery, not self-propelled:
8430.6100	--捣固或压实机械	6	30		17	17	台		--Tamping or compacting machinery
	--其他:								--Other:
	---工程钻机:								---Engineering drills:
8430.6911	----钻筒直径3米及以上	6	30		17	17	台		----Boring casing diameter more than 3m
8430.6919	----其他	6	30		17	17	台		----Other
8430.6920	---铲运机	6	30		17	17	台		---Scrapers
8430.6990	---其他	6	30		17	17	台		---Other
84.31	**专用于或主要用于品目84.25至84.30所列机械的零件:**								**Parts suitable for use solely or principally with the machinery of headings No.84.25 to 84.30:**
8431.1000	-税号84.25所列机械的零件	3	30		15	17	千克		-Of machinery of heading No.84.25
	-税号84.27所列机械的零件:								-Of machinery of heading No.84.27:
8431.2010	---装有差速器的驱动桥及其零件,不论是否装有其他传送部件	6	30		15	17	千克/个		--- Equipped with differential drive axle and its parts, whether or not equipped with other transmission parts
8431.2090[暂]	---其他	6	30	3	15	17	千克		---Other
	-税号84.28所列机械的零件:								-Of machinery of heading No.84.28:
8431.3100	--升降机、倒卸式起重机或自动梯的零件	3	30		15	17	千克		--Of lifts, skip hoists or escalators
8431 3100.01[暂]	无障碍升降机的零件	3	30	1	15	17	千克		Parts of accessibility-free lifts
8431 3100.90	其他升降机、倒卸式起重机零件（包括自动梯零件）	3	30		15	17	千克		Parts of other lifters and inverted unloading cranes (including parts of escalators)
8431.3900	--其他	5	30		15	17	千克		--Other
	-税号84.26、84.29、或84.30所列机械的零件:								-Of machinery of heading No.84.26, 84.29 or 84.30:
8431.4100	--戽斗、铲斗、抓斗及夹斗	6	17		15	17	千克/个		--Buckets, shovels, grabs and grips
8431.4200	--推土机或侧铲推土机用铲	6	17		15	17	千克/个		--Bulldozer or angledozer blades
	--子目8430.41或8430.49所列钻探或凿井机械的零件:								--Parts of boring or sinking machinery of subheading No.8430.41 or 8430.49:
8431.4310	---石油或天然气钻探机用	4	11		15	17	千克		---Of oil and natural gas drilling machinery
8431.4320	---其他钻探机用	4	11		15	17	千克		---Of other drilling machinery
8431.4390	---其他	5	17		15	17	千克		---Of sinking machinery
	--其他:								--Other:
8431.4920	---装有差速器的驱动桥及其零件,不论是否装有其他传送部件	5	17		15	17	千克/个		--- Equipped with differential drive axle and its parts, whether or not equipped with other transmission parts
	---其他:								---Other:
8431.4991	---矿用电铲用	5	17		15	17	千克		---For mining power shovels
8431.4999	---其他	5	17		15	17	千克		---Other

税则号列 Tariff Item	商品名称及备注	进口税率 最惠	普通	暂定	出口退税	增值税率	计量单位	监管条件	Article Description
84.32	**农业、园艺及林业用整地或耕作机械；草坪及运动场地滚压机：**								**Agricultural, horticultural or forestry machinery for soil preparation or cultivation; lawn or sports-ground rollers:**
8432.1000	-犁	5	30		13	13	台/千克		-Ploughs
	-耙、松土机、中耕机、除草机及耕耘机：								-Harrows, scarifiers, cultivators, weeders and hoes:
8432.2100	--圆盘耙	5	30		13	13	台/千克		--Disc harrows
8432.2900	--其他	4	30		13	13	台/千克		--Other
	-播种机、种植机及移植机								-Seeders, planters and transplanters:
	---播种机:								---Seeders:
8432.3011	----谷物播种机	4	30		13	13	台		----Seeders for grain
8432.3019	----其他	4	30		13	13	台		----Other
	---种植机:								---Planters:
8432.3021	----马铃薯种植机	4	30		13	13	台		----Planters for potato
8432.3029	----其他	4	30		13	13	台		----Other
	---移植机(栽植机)：								---Transplanters:
8432.3031	----水稻插秧机	4	30		13	13	台		----Transplanters for rice
8432.3039	----其他	4	30		13	13	台		----Other
8432.4000	-施肥机	4	30		13	13	台		--Manure spreaders and fertilizer distributors
	-其他机械:								-Other machinery:
8432.8010	---草坪及运动场地滚压机	7	40		15	17	台		---Lawn or sports-ground rollers
8432.8090	---其他	4	30		13/15	13	台		---Other
8432.9000	-零件	4	17		15	17	千克		-Parts
84.33	**收割机、脱粒机，包括草料打包机；割草机；蛋类、水果或其他农产品的清洁、分选、分级机器，但品目84.37的机器除外：**								**Harvesting or threshing machinery, including straw or fodder balers; grass or hay mowers; machines for cleaning, sorting or grading eggs, fruit or other agricultural produce, other than machinery of heading No.84.37:**
	-草坪、公园或运动场地用的割草机:								-Mowers for lawns, parks or sports grounds:
8433.1100	--机动的，切割装置在同一水平面上旋转的	6	30		15	13	台		--Powered, with the cutting device rotating in a horizontal plane
8433.1900	--其他	6	30		15	17	台		--Other
8433.2000	-其他割草机，包括牵引装置用的刀具杆	4	30		13	13	台		-Other mowers, including cutter bars for tractor mounting
8433.3000	-其他干草切割、翻晒机器	5	30		13	13	台		-Other haymaking machinery
8433.4000	-草料打包机，包括收集打包机	5	30		13	13	台		-Straw or fodder balers, including pickup balers
	-其他收割机；脱粒机:								-Other harvesting machinery; threshing machinery:
8433.5100	--联合收割机	8	17		13	13	台		--Combine harvester-threshers
8433 5100.01[暂]	功率≥160马力的联合收割机	8	17	5	13	13	台		Combine harvester-threshers with power≥160hp
8433 5100.90	功率＜160马力的联合收割机	8	17		13	13	台		Combine harvester-threshers with power＜160hp
8433.5200	--其他脱粒机	8	30		13	13	台		--Other threshing machinery
8433.5300	--根茎或块茎收获机	8	30		13	13	台		--Root or tuber harvesting machines
8433 5300.01[暂]	功率≥160马力的土豆、甜菜收获机	8	30	4	13	13	台		Potato, beet harvesters with power≥160hp
8433 5300.90	其他根茎或块茎收获机	8	30		13	13	台		Other root or tuber harvesting machines
	--其他:								--Other:
8433.5910	---甘蔗收获机	8	30		13	13	台		---Sugarcane harvesters
8433 5910.01[暂]	功率≥160马力的甘蔗收获机	8	30	4	13	13	台		Sugarcane harvesters with power≥160hp
8433 5910.90	其他甘蔗收获机	8	30		13	13	台		Other sugarcane harvesters
8433.5920[暂]	---棉花采摘机	8	30	5	13	13	台		---Cotton picker
8433.5990	---其他	8	30		13	13	台		---Other
8433 5990.01[暂]	自走式青储饲料收获机	8	30	5	13	13	台		Self-propelled forage harvesters
8433 5990.02[暂]	茶叶采摘机	8	30	4	13	13	台		Tea pickers
8433 5990.90	其他收割机及脱粒机	8	30		13	13	台		Other harvesters and threshers
8433.6000	-蛋类、水果或其他农产品的清洁、分选、分级机器	5	30		13	13	台		-Machines for cleaning, sorting or grading eggs, fruit or other agricultural produce

税则号列 Tariff Item	商品名称及备注	进口税率 最惠	进口税率 普通	进口税率 暂定	出口退税	增值税率	计量单位	监管条件	Article Description
	-零件:								-Parts:
8433.9010	---联合收割机用	5	11		15	17	千克		---Of combine harvester-threshers
8433.9090	---其他	3	17		15	17	千克		---Other
84.34	**挤奶机及乳品加工机器:**								**Milking machines and dairy machinery:**
8434.1000	-挤奶机	10	20		13	13	台		-Milking machines
8434.2000[暂]	-乳品加工机器	6	30	2	15	17	台	A	-Dairy machinery
8434.9000	-零件	5	17		15	17	千克	A	-Parts
84.35	**制酒、制果汁或制类似饮料用的压榨机、轧碎机及类似机器:**								**Presses, crushers and similar machinery used in the manufacture of wine, cider, fruit juices or similar beverages:**
8435.1000	-机器	10	30		15	17	台	A	-Machinery
8435.9000	-零件	6	30		15	17	千克	A	-Parts
84.36	**农业、园艺、林业、家禽饲养业或养蜂业用的其他机器,包括装有机械或热力装置的催芽设备;家禽孵卵器及育雏器:**								**Other agricultural, horticultural, forestry, poultry-keeping or bee-keeping machinery, including germination plant fitted with mechanical or thermal equipment; poultry incubators and brooders:**
8436.1000	-动物饲料配制机	7	30		13	13	台		-Machinery for preparing animal feeding stuffs
	-家禽饲养用的机器;家禽孵卵器及育雏器:								-Poultry-keeping machinery; poultry incubators and brooders:
8436.2100	--家禽孵卵器及育雏器	5	30		13	13	台		--Poultry incubators and brooders
8436.2900	--其他	10	30		13	13	台		--Other
8436.8000	-其他机器	10	30		13/15		台		-Other machinery
8436 8000.01[暂]	青储饲料切割上料机	10	30	3	13/15	13	台		Forage cutting feeders
8436 8000.02[暂]	自走式饲料搅拌投喂车	10	30	5	13/15	13	台		Self-propelled feed mixing feeding car
8436 8000.90	农业、林业、园艺等用的其他机器(包括装有机械或热力装置的催芽设备)	10	30		13/15	13	台		Other machines for agricultural, forestry, and horticultural use (including germination equipments fitted with mechanical or thermal devices)
	-零件:								-Parts:
8436.9100	--家禽饲养用机器的零件或家禽孵卵器及育雏器的零件	6	17		15	17	千克		--Of poultry-keeping machinery or poultry incubators and brooders
8436.9900	--其他	6	17		15	17	千克		--Other
84.37	**种子、谷物或干豆的清洁、分选或分级机器;谷物磨粉业加工机器或谷物、干豆加工机器,但农业用机器除外:**								**Machines for cleaning, sorting or grading seed, grain or dried leguminous vegetables; machinery used in the milling industry or for the working of cereals or dried leguminous vegetables, other than farm-type machinery:**
	-种子、谷物或干豆的清洁、分选或分级机器:								-Machines for cleaning, sorting or grading seed, grain or dried leguminous vegetables:
8437.1010	---光学色差颗粒选别机(色选机)	10	30		13	13	台		---Color sorters
8437.1090	---其他	10	30		13	13	台		---Other
8437.8000	-其他机器	10	30		13	17	台	A	-Other machinery
8437.9000	-零件	6	30		15	17	千克		-Parts
84.38	**本章其他品目未列名的食品、饮料工业用的生产或加工机器,但提取、加工动物油脂或植物固定油脂的机器除外:**								**Machinery, not specified or included elsewhere in this chapter, for the industrial preparation or manufacture of food or drink, other than machinery for the extraction or preparation of animal or fixed vegetable fats or oils:**
8438.1000	-糕点加工机器及生产通心粉、面条或类似产品的机器	7	30		15	17	台		-Bakery machinery and machinery for the manufacture of macaroni, spaghetti or similar products
8438 1000.10	糕点生产线	7	30		15	17	台	A	Production lines for bakery
8438 1000.90	通心粉,面条的生产加工机器(包括类似产品的加工机)	7	30		15	17	台	A	Machines for producing and processing macaroni and noodles (including processing machines of similar products)

税则号列 Tariff Item	商品名称及备注	进口税率 最惠	普通	暂定	出口退税	增值税率	计量单位	监管条件	Article Description
8438.2000	-生产糖果、可可粉、巧克力的机器	8	30		15	17	台	A	-Machinery for the manufacture of confectionery, cocoa or chocolate
8438.3000	-制糖机器	10	30		15	17	台	A	-Machinery for sugar manufacture
8438.4000	-酿酒机器	7	30		15	17	台	A	-Brewery machinery
8438.5000	-肉类或家禽加工机器	7	30		15	17	台/千克	A	-Machinery for the preparation of meat or poultry
8438.6000	-水果、坚果或蔬菜加工机器	10	30		15	17	台/千克	A	-Machinery for the preparation of fruits, nuts or vegetables
8438.8000	-其他机器	8.5	30		15	17	台/千克	A	-Other machinery
8438.9000	-零件	5	30		15	17	千克	A	-Parts
84.39	**纤维素纸浆、纸及纸板的制造或整理机器:**								**Machinery for making pulp of fibrous cellulosic material or for making or finishing paper or paperboard:**
8439.1000	-制造纤维素纸浆的机器	8.4	30		15	17	台	O	-Machinery for making pulp of fibrous cellulosic material
8439.2000	-纸或纸板的抄造机器	8.4	30		15	17	台	O	-Machinery for making paper or paper board
8439.3000	-纸或纸板的整理机器	8.4	30		15	17	台	O	-Machinery for finishing paper or paper board
	-零件:								-Parts:
8439.9100	--制造纤维素纸浆的机器	6	30		15	17	千克		--Of machinery for making pulp of fibrous cellulosic material
8439.9900	--其他	6	30		15	17	千克		--Other
84.40	**书本装订机器，包括锁线订书机:**								**Book-binding machinery, including booksewing machines:**
	-机器:								-Machinery:
8440.1010	---锁线装订机	10	35		15	17	台		---Sewing bookbinders
8440.1020	---胶订机	12	35		15	17	台		---Glueing bookbinders
8440.1090	---其他	12	35		15	17	台		---Other
8440.9000	-零件	8	35		15	17	千克		-Parts
84.41	**其他制造纸浆制品、纸制品或纸板制品的机器，包括各种切纸机:**								**Other machinery for making up paper pulp, paper or paperboard, including cutting machines of all kinds:**
8441.1000	-切纸机	12	50		15	17	台		-Cutting machines
8441.2000	-制造包、袋或信封的机器	12	30		15	17	台		-Machines for making bags, sacks or envelopes
	-制造箱、盒、管、桶或类似容器的机器，但模制成型机器除外:								-Machines for making cartons, boxes, cases, tubes, drums or similar containers, other than by moulding:
8441.3010	---制造纸塑铝复合罐的生产设备	13.5	30		15	17	台		---Machines for paper, plastic and aluminium composite can manufacture
8441.3090	---其他	13.5	30		15	17	台		---Other
8441.4000	-纸浆、纸或纸板制品模制成型机器	12	30		15	17	台	O	-Machines for moulding articles in paper pulp, paper or paperboard
	-其他机器:								-Other machinery:
8441.8010	---制造纸塑铝软包装的生产设备	12	30		15	17	台		---Machines for paper plastic and aluminium flexible packaging manufature
8441.8090	---其他	12	30		15	17	台	O	---Other
	-零件:								-Parts:
8441.9010	---切纸机用	8	50		15	17	千克		---Of cutting machines
8441 9010.01 暂	切纸机用弧形辊	8	50	4	15	17	千克		Curved roll for cutting machines
8441 9010.02 暂	切纸机用横切刀单元	8	50	3	15	17	千克		Cutting machines with cross-cutting knives unit
8441 9010.90	其他切纸机零件	8	50		15	17	千克		Other parts of cutting machines
8441.9090	---其他	8.4	30		15	17	千克		---Othe
84.42	**制版用的机器、器具及设备（品目 84.56 至 84. 65 的机床除外）；印刷用版（片）、滚筒及其他印刷部件；制成供印刷用（例如，刨平、压纹或抛光）的板（片）、滚筒及石板:**								**Machinery,apparatus and equipment （other than the machine-tools of headings No.84.56 to 84.65）, for preparing or making plates, cylinders or other printing components; plates, cylinders and other printing components; plates, cylinders and lithographic stones, prepared for printing purposes（for example, planed, grained or**

税则号列 Tariff Item	商品名称及备注	进口税率 最惠	进口税率 普通	进口税率 暂定	出口退税	增值税率	计量单位	监管条件	Article Description
									polished）:
	-机器、器具及设备:								-Machinery, apparatus and equipment:
8442.3010	---铸字机	9	35		15	17	台		---Type casters
	---制版机器、器具及设备:								---Other machinery, apparatus and equipment for typesetting:
8442.3021 暂	----计算机直接制版设备	9	35	5	15	17	台		----Machines for preparing CTP plates
8442.3029	----其他	9	35		15	17	台		----Other
8442.3090	---其他	9	35		15	17	台		---Other
8442.4000	-上述机器、器具及设备的零件	7	20		15	17	千克		-Parts of the foregoing machinery, apparatus or equipment
8442 4000.01 暂	计算机直接制版机器用零件	7	20	0	15	17	千克		Parts of machines for preparing CTP plates of computer
8442 4000.90	其他铸字、排字、制版机器的零件	7	20		15	17	千克		Parts of other typecasting, typesetting and platemaking machines
8442.5000	-印刷用版（片）、滚筒及其他印刷部件;制成供印刷用(例如,刨平、压纹或抛光)的板(片)、滚筒及石板	7	35		15	17	千克		-Plates, cylinders and other printing components; plates, cylinders and lithographic stones, prepared for printing purposes（for example, planed, grained or polished）
84.43	**用品目84.42的印刷用版(片)、滚筒及其他印刷部件进行印刷的机器;其他打印机、复印机及传真机,不论是否组合式;上述机器的零件及附件:**								**Printing machinery used for printing by means of plates cylinders and other printing components of heading No. 84.42; other printers, copying machines and facsimile machines, whether or not combined; parts and accessories thereof:**
	-用税号 84.42 的印刷用版（片）、滚筒及其他印刷部件进行印刷的机器:								-Printing machinery used for printing by means of plates, cylinders and other printing components of heading No.84.42:
8443.1100	--卷取进料式胶印机	10	35		15	17	台		--Offset printing machinery, reel-fed
8443.1200	--办公室用片取进料式胶印机（以未折叠计,片尺寸一边长不超过22厘米，另一边长不超过36厘米）	12	35		15	17	台		--Offset printing machinery, sheet-fed, office type（using sheets with one side not exceeding 22cm and the other side not exceeding 36cm in the unfolded state）
	--其他胶印机:								--Other offset printing machinery:
	---平张纸进料式:								---Sheet fed:
8443.1311	----单色机	10	35		15	17	台		----Single color
8443.1312	----双色机	10	35		15	17	台		----Two colors
8443.1313	----四色机	10	35		15	17	台		----Four colors
8443 1313.01 暂	四色平张纸胶印机(对开单张单面印刷速度≥17000张/小时)	10	35	7	15	17	台		Four-color sheet-fed offset printing machinery (speed ≥ 16000 pcs / h)
8443 1313.02 暂	四色平张纸胶印机(对开单张双面印刷速度≥13000张/小时)	10	35	7	15	17	台		Four color Sheet-fed offset printing machinery (Single folio double sides printing speed≥13000 pcs/ hr)
8443 1313.03 暂	四色平张纸胶印机(全张或超全张单张单面印刷速度≥13000张/小时)	10	35	7	15	17	台		Four color Sheet-fed offset printing machinery (Sheetwise or full-sheet one piece single side printing speed≥13000 pcs/ hr)
8443 1313.90	其他四色平张纸胶印机(用品目84.42 项下商品进行印刷的机器)	10	35		15	17	台		Other four-color sheet-fed offset printing presses machinery (machines using the commodities of the heading No. 8442 for printing)
8443.1319	----其他	10	35		15	17	台		----Other
8443 1319.01 暂	五色及以上平张纸胶印机(对开单张单面印刷速度≥17000 张/小时)	10	35	7	15	17	台		Five (or higher) -color sheet-fed offset printing machinery (one piece single side printing speed ≥ 17000 pcs / h)
8443 1319.02 暂	五色及以上平张纸胶印机(对开单张双面印刷速度≥13000 张/小时)	10	35	7	15	17	台		Five color or more Sheet-fed offset press (Single folio double sides printing speed≥13000pcs/ hr)
8443 1319.03 暂	五色及以上平张纸胶印机(全张或超全张单张单面)印刷速度≥13000张/小时)	10	35	7	15	17	台		Five color or more Sheet-fed offset press (Sheetwise or full-sheet one piece single side printing speed≥13000 pcs/ hr)
8443 1319.90	其他平张纸进料式胶印机(用品	10	35		15	17	台		Other sheet-feed offset printing presses (machines

税则号列 Tariff Item	商品名称及备注	进口税率 最惠	进口税率 普通	进口税率 暂定	出口退税	增值税率	计量单位	监管条件	Article Description
	目 84.42 项下商品进行印刷的机器）								using the commodities of heading No. 84.42 for printing)
8443.1390	---其他	10	35		15	17	台		---Other
8443.1400	--卷取进料式凸版印刷机，但不包括苯胺印刷机	12	35		15	17	台		--Letterpress printing machinery, reel fed, excluding flexographic printing
8443.1500	--除卷取进料式以外的凸版印刷机，但不包括苯胺印刷机	12	35		15	17	台		--Letterpress printing machinery, other than reel fed, excluding flexographic printing
8443.1600	--苯胺印刷机	10	35		15	17	台		--Flexographic printing machinery
8443 1600.01[暂]	苯胺印刷机，线速度≥350 米/分钟，幅宽≥800 毫米（柔性版印刷机，用品目 8442 项下商品进行印刷的机器）	10	35	3	15	17	台		Flexographic printing machinery, linear speed≥ 300m /min， breadth ≥800mm（flexographic printing machines using the commodities of heading No. 84.42 for printing）
8443 1600.02[暂]	机组式柔性版印刷机，线速度≥160 米/分钟，250 毫米≤幅宽＜800 毫米（具有烫印或全息或丝网印刷功能单元的）	10	35	5	15	17	台		Unit-type Flexographic Press，Linear velocity≥160m /min，250mm≤width＜800mm (Supporting Thermoprinting、holographic printing or screen printing
8443 1600.90	其他苯胺印刷机（柔性版印刷机，用品目 84.42 项下商品进行印刷的机器）	10	35		15	17	台		Other flexographic printing machinery（flexographic printing machines using the commodities of heading No. 8442 for printing）
8443.1700	--凹版印刷机	18	35		15	17	台		--Gravure printing machinery
8443 1700.01[暂]	凹版印刷机，印刷速度≥350 米/分钟（用品目 84.42 项下商品进行印刷的机器）	18	35	9	15	17	台		Gravure printing machinery, linear speed≥350m/min，breadth≥800mm（machines using the commodities of heading No. 84.42 for printing）
8443 1700.90	其他凹版印刷机（用品目 84.42 项下商品进行印刷的机器）	18	35		15	17	台		Other gravure printing machinery（machines using the commodities of heading No. 84.42 for printing）
	--其他:								--Other:
	---网式印刷机:								---Screen printing machinery:
8443.1921	----圆网印刷机	10	35		15	17	台		----Cylinder screen press
8443 1921.01[暂]	纺织用圆网印花机	10	35	6	15	17	台	O	Cylinder screen printing machinery for Textile
8443 1921.90	其他圆网印刷机（用品目 84.42 项下商品进行印刷的机器）	10	35		15	17	台	O	Other cylinder screen printing machinery（machines using the goods of heading No. 84.42 for printing）
8443.1922	----平网印刷机	10	35		15	17	台		----Platen screen press
8443 1922.01[暂]	纺织用平网印花机	10	35	6	15	17	台	O	Pflat screen printing machines for Textile
8443 1922.10	用于光盘生产的盘面印刷机（用品目 84.42 项下商品进行印刷的机器）	10	35		15	17	台	6	Disk presses for producing compact disks（machines using the goods of heading No. 8442 for printing）
8443 1922.90	其他平网印刷机（用品目 84.42 项下商品进行印刷的机器）	10	35		15	17	台	O	Other Pflat screen presses（machines using the goods of heading No. 8442 for printing）
8443.1929	----其他	10	35		15	17	台	O	----Other
8443.1980	---其他	8	35		15	17	台	O	---Other
	-其他印刷（打印）机、复印机及传真机，不论是否组合式:								-Other printers, copying machines and facsimile machines, whether or not combined:
	--具有打印、复印或传真中两种及以上功能的机器，可与自动数据处理设备或网络连接:								--Machines which perform two or more of the functions of printing,copying or facsimile transmission, capable of connecting to an automatic data processing machine or to a network:
8443.3110[暂]	---静电感光式	10	70	3	17	17	台		---Electrostatic photosensitive-type
8443 3110.10[暂]	静电感光式多功能一体加密传真机（可与自动数据处理设备或网络连接）	10	70	3	17	17	台	M	Static light-sensitive multi-functional encryption faxes (can be connected to auto data processing equipments or network)
8443 3110.90[暂]	其他静电感光式多功能一体机（可与自动数据处理设备或网络连接）	10	70	3	17	17	台		Other static light-sensitive multi-functional faxes (can be connected to auto data processing equipments or network)
8443.3190	---其他	0	17		17	17	台		---Other
8443 3190.10	其他具有打印和复印两种功能的机器（可与自动数据处理设备或网络连接）	0	17		17	17	台	A	Other machines with both printing and copying functions (can be connected to auto data processing equipment or network)

税则号列 Tariff Item	商品名称及备注	进口税率			出口退税	增值税率	计量单位	监管条件	Article Description
		最惠	普通	暂定					
8443 3190.20	其他多功能一体加密传真机(兼有打印、复印中一种及以上功能的机器)	0	17		17	17	台	AM	Other multi-functional encryption facsimile machines (machines with at least one of the two functions: printing or copying)
8443 3190.90	其他具有打印、复印或传真中两种及以上功能的机器(具有打印和复印两种功能的机器除外,可与自动数据处理设备或网络连接)	0	17		17	17	台	A	Other machines with at least one of the three functions: printing, copying or faxing (excluding machines with two functions: printing and copying, able to be connected to auto data processing equipment or network)
	--其他,可与自动数据处理设备或网络连接:								-Other, capable of connecting to an automatic data processing machine or to a network:
	---专用于品目 84.71 所列设备的打印机:								---Printers, of a kind solely used in the machines of heading No. 84.71:
8443.3211	----针式打印机	0	14		17	17	台	A	----Stylus printers
8443.3212	----激光打印机	0	14		17	17	台	A	----Laser printers
8443.3213	----喷墨打印机	0	14		17	17	台	A	----Ink-jet printers
8443.3214	----热敏打印机	0	14		17	17	台	A	----Thermal printers
8443.3219	----其他	0	14		17	17	台	A	----Other
	---数字式印刷设备:								---Digital printing machines:
8443.3221	----喷墨印刷机	8	30		17	17	台		----Ink-jet printing machines
8443 3221.01 暂	幅宽>60 厘米的喷墨印刷设备(可与自动数据处理设备或网络连接)	8	30	3	17	17	台		Ink-jet printing equipments with breadth>60cm (can be connected to auto data processing equipment or network)
8443 3221.02 暂	297mm<幅宽≤360mm 的喷墨印刷设备(可与自动数据处理设备或网络连接)	8	30	5	17	17	台		297mm <width≤360mm inkjet printing equipment (with automatic data processing equipment or network connection)
8443 3221.90	其他数字式喷墨印刷机(可与自动数据处理设备或网络连接)	8	30		17	17	台		Other digital ink-jet presses with breadth>60cm (can be connected to auto data processing equipment or network)
8443.3222	----静电照相印刷机(激光印刷机)	8	35		15	17	台		----Electrostatic photographic printing machines（laser printing machines）
8443 3222.01 暂	幅宽≥32.9 厘米的静电照相印刷设备(激光印刷机)(可与自动数据处理设备或网络连接)	8	35	3	15	17	台		Electrostatic photo-printing machines with breadth> 60cm (laser printing machines) (can be connected to auto data processing equipment or network)
8443 3222.90	其他数字式静电照相印刷机(激光印刷机)(可与自动数据处理设备或网络连接)	8	35		15	17	台		Other digital electrostatic photo-printing machines (laser printing machines) (can be connected to auto data processing equipment or network)
8443.3229	----其他	8	30		15	17	台		----Other
8443.3290	---其他	0	17		15	17	台		---Other
8443 3290.10	其他加密传真机(可与自动数据处理设备或网络连接)	0	17		15	17	台	AM	Other encryption facsimile machine (can be connected to auto data processing equipment or network)
8443 3290.90	其他印刷(打印)机、复印机、传真机和电传打字机(可与自动数据处理设备或网络连接)	0	17		15	17	台	A	Other presses (printers), copying machine, facsimile machine and teleprinters(can be connected to auto data processing equipment or network)
	--其他:								--Other:
	---静电感光复印设备:								---Electrostatic photo-copying apparatus:
8443.3911	----将原件直接复印的(直接法)	0	70		15	17	台		----Operting by reproducing the original image directly onto the copy（direct process）
8443.3912	----将原件通过中间体转印的(间接法)	10	70		15	17	台		----Operting by reproducing the original image via an intermediate onto the copy（indirect process）
	---其他感光复印设备:								---Other photocopying apparatus:
8443.3921	----带有光学系统的	0	70		15	17	台		----Incorporating an optical system
8443.3922	----接触式的	20	70		15	17	台		----Of the contact type
8443.3923	----热敏复印设备	20	70		15	17	台		----Thermo-copying apparatus
8443.3924	----热升华复印设备	20	70		15	17	台		----Thermo-sublime copying apparatus
	---数字式印刷设备:								---Digital printing machines:
8443.3931	----喷墨印刷机	8	30		15	17	台		----Ink-jet printing machines
8443.3932	----静电照相印刷机(激光印刷	8	35		15	17	台		----Electrostatic photographic printing machines（laser

税则号列 Tariff Item	商品名称及备注	进口税率 最惠	进口税率 普通	进口税率 暂定	出口退税	增值税率	计量单位	监管条件	Article Description
	机)								printing machines)
8443.3939	----其他	8	30		15	17	台		----Other
8443.3990	---其他	0	30		15	17	台		---Other
	-零件及附件:								-Parts and accessories:
	--用于品目 84.42 的印刷用版(片)、滚筒及其他印刷部件进行印刷的机器零件及附件:								--Parts and accessories of printing machinery used for printing by means of plates, cylinders and other printing components of heading No. 84.42:
	---印刷用辅助机器:								---Machines for uses ancillary to printing:
8443.9111	----卷筒料给料机	12	35		15				----Web feeder
8443 9111.01[暂]	卷筒料自动给料机，给料线速度≥12米/秒	12	35	4	15	17	千克/台	O	Automatic web feeder, Feeding linear velocity≥12m/s
8443 9111.90	其他卷筒料给料机	12	35		15	17	千克/台	O	Other web feeder
8443.9119[暂]	----其他	12	35	6	15	17	千克/台	O	----Other
8443.9190	---其他	6	20		15	17	千克/个		---Other
8443 9190.01[暂]	胶印机用墨量遥控装置(包括墨色控制装置，墨量调节装置、墨斗体等组成部分)	6	20	0	15	17	千克/个	O	Remote controllers for controlling the use of ink by offset printers (including ink color control devices, ink amount regulation devices, and ink fountain containers, etc.)
8443 9190.90[暂]	其他用品目 84.42 项下商品进行印刷的机器零件与附件	6	20	3	15	17	千克/个		Parts and accessories of other machines using the goods of heading No. 8442 for printing
	--其他:								--Other:
8443.9910	---数字印刷设备用辅助机器	12	35		15	17	千克/台	O	---Machines for uses ancillary to digital printing machines
	---数字印刷设备的零件:								---Parts of digital printing machines:
8443.9921	----热敏打印头	6	20		15	17	千克/个		----Thermal print heads
8443.9929	----其他	6	20		15	17	千克		----Other
8443 9929.01[暂]	压电式喷墨头(非用品目 84.42 项下商品进行印刷的机器零件)	6	20	3	15	17	千克		Piezoelectric ink gun (printing machine parts not in the heading No.84.42)
8443 9929.90	其他数字印刷设备的零件(非用品目 84.42 项下商品进行印刷的机器零件)	6	20		15	17	千克		Parts of other types of digital print machines (printing machine parts not in the heading No.84.42))
8443.9990	---其他	0	35		15	17	千克		---Other
8443 9990.10	其他印刷(打印)机、复印机及传真机的感光鼓和含感光鼓的碳粉盒	0	35		15	17	千克		Photosensitive drums and toner cartridges of other presses (printers), copying machines and facsimile machines
8443 9990.90	其他印刷(打印)机、复印机及传真机的零件和附件	0	35		15	17	千克		Parts and accessories of other presses (printers), copying machines and facsimile machines
84.44	**化学纺织纤维挤压、拉伸、变形或切割机器:**								**Machines for extruding, drawing, texturing or cutting man-made textile materials:**
8444.0010	---合成纤维长丝纺丝机	10	30		17	17	台		---Synthetic filaments spinning jets
8444.0020	---合成纤维短纤纺丝机	10	30		17	17	台		---Synthetic staple fibres spinning jets
8444.0030	---人造纤维纺丝机	10	30		17	17	台		---Artificial fibres spinning jets
8444.0040	---化学纤维变形机	10	30		17	17	台		---Man-made filaments crimping machinery
8444.0050	---化学纤维切断机	10	30		17	17	台		---Man-made filaments cutting machinery
8444.0090	---其他	10	30		17	17	台		---Other
84.45	**纺织纤维的预处理机器；纺纱机、并线机、加捻机及其他生产纺织纱线的机器；摇纱机、络纱机(包括卷纬机)及处理品目 84.46 或 84.47 所列机器用的纺织纱线的机器:**								**Machines for preparing textile fibres; spinning, doubling or twisting machines and other machinery for producing textile yarns; textile reeling or winding (including weft-winding) machines and machines for preparing textile yarns for use on the machines of heading No.84.46 or 84.47:**
	-纺织纤维的预处理机器:								-Machines for preparing textile fibres:
	--梳理机:								--Carding machines:
	---棉纤维型:								---For cotton type fibres:
8445.1111	----清梳联合机	10	30		17	17	台	AO	----Blowing-carding Machinery

税则号列 Tariff Item	商品名称及备注	进口税率 最惠	普通	暂定	出口退税	增值税率	计量单位	监管条件	Article Description
8445.1112	----自动抓棉机	10	30		17	17	台	AO	----Bale Plucker
8445.1113	----梳棉机	10	30		17	17	台	A	----Card or Carding Machine
8445.1119	----其他	10	30		17	17	台	AO	----Other
8445.1120	---毛纤维型	10	30		17	17	台	AO	---For wool type fibres
8445.1190	---其他	10	30		17	17	台		---Other
8445 1190.01 暂	宽幅非织造布梳理机(工作幅宽＞3.5 米，工作速度＞120 米/分钟)	10	30	6	17	17	台	A	Wide non-woven carding machines (working width＞3.5 m, working speed ＞ 120 m / min)
8445 1190.90	其他纺织纤维梳理机	10	30		17	17	台	A	Other textile fiber carding machines
	--精梳机:								---Combing Machines:
8445.1210	---棉精梳机	10	30		17	17	台	A	---Cotton Comber
8445.1220	---毛精梳机	10	30		17	17	台	AO	---Worsted Comber
8445.1290	---其他	10	30		17	17	台	A	---Other
	--拉伸机或粗纱机:								--Drawing or roving machines:
8445.1310	---拉伸机	10	30		17	17	台	A	---Drawing machines
	---粗纱机:								---Roving machines:
8445.1321	----棉纺粗纱机	10	30		17	17	台	A	----Cotton Roving Frames
8445.1322	----毛纺粗纱机	10	30		17	17	台	A	----Worsted Roving Machines
8445.1329	----其他	10	30		17	17	台	A	----Other
8445.1900	--其他	10	30		17	17	台	A	--Other
	-纺纱机:								-Textile spinning machines:
	---自由端纺纱机:								---Open-end spinner:
8445.2031	----转杯纺纱机	10	30		17	17	台		----Rotor Spinning Machine
8445 2031.01 暂	全自动转杯纺纱机	10	30	5	17	17	台	AO	Automatic rotor spinning machine
8445 2031.90	其他自由端转杯纺纱机	10	30		17	17	台	AO	Other free end rotor spinning machine
8445.2032	----喷气纺纱机	10	30		17	17	台	A	----Jet spinner
8445.2039	----其他	10	30		17	17	台	A	----Other
	---环锭细纱机:								---Ring spinning frames:
8445.2041	----棉细纱机	10.5	40		17	17	台	AO	----Cotton Ring Spinning Frame
8445.2042	----毛细纱机	10	40		17	17	台	A	----Worsted Ring Spinning Frame
8445.2049	----其他	10	40		17	17	台	A	----Other
8445.2090	---其他	10	30		17	17	台	A	---Other
8445.3000	-并线机或加捻机	10	30		17	17	台	A	-Textile doubling or twisting machines
	-络纱机（包括卷纬机）或摇纱机:								-Textile winding（including weft-winding） or reeling machines:
8445.4010 暂	---自动络筒机	10	30	6	17	17	台	AO	---Automatic bobbin winders
8445.4090	---其他	10	30		17	17	台	A	---Other
	-其他:								-Other:
8445.9010	---整经机	10	30		17	17	台	A	---Warping machines
8445.9020	---浆纱机	10	30		17	17	台	A	---Sizing machines
8445.9090	---其他	10	30		17	17	台	OA	---Other
84.46	**织机:**								**Weaving machines（looms）:**
8446.1000	-所织织物宽度不超过 30 厘米的织机	8	30		17	17	台	A	-For weaving fabrics of a width not exceeding 30cm
	-所织织物宽度超过 30 厘米的梭织机:								-For weaving fabrics of width exceeding 30cm, shuttle type:
	--动力织机:								--Power looms:
8446.2110	---地毯织机	12	35		17	17	台	A	---For making carpets or rugs
8446.2190	---其他	10	30		17	17	台	A	---Other
8446.2900	--其他	10	30		17	17	台	A	--Other
	-所织织物宽度超过 30 厘米的无梭织机:								-For weaving fabrics of with exceeding 30cm, shuttleless type:
8446.3020	---剑杆织机	8	30		17	17	台	AO	---Rapier looms
8446.3030	---片梭织机	8	30		17	17	台	AO	---Carrier looms
8446.3040	---喷水织机	8	30		17	17	台	OA	---Water jet looms
8446.3050 暂	---喷气织机	8	30	0	17	17	台	AO	---Air jet looms
8446.3090	---其他	8	30		17	17	台	OA	---Other

税则号列 Tariff Item	商品名称及备注	进口税率 最惠	普通	暂定	出口退税	增值税率	计量单位	监管条件	Article Description
84.47	针织机、缝编机及制粗松螺旋花线、网眼薄纱、花边、刺绣品、装饰带、编织带或网的机器及簇绒机：								**Knitting machines, stitch-bonding machines and machines for making gimped yarn, tulle lace, embroidery, trimmings, braid or net and machines for tufting:**
	-圆型针织机:								-Circular knitting machines:
8447.1100	--圆筒直径不超过165毫米	8	30		17	17	台	A	-With cylinder diameter not exceeding 165mm
8447.1200	--圆筒直径超过165毫米	8	30		17	17	台	A	--With cylinder diameter exceeding 165 mm
	-平型针织机；缝编机:								-Flat knitting machines; stitch-bonding machines:
	---经编机:								---Warp knitting machines:
8447.2011	----特里科经编机	8	30		17	17	台	A	----Tricot machines
8447.2012	----拉舍尔经编机	8	30		17	17	台	A	----Rashel machines
8447.2019	----其他	8	30		17	17	台	A	----Other
8447.2020	---平型纬编机	8	30		17	17	台	A	---Flat weft knitting machines
8447.2030	---缝编机	8	30		17	17	台	A	---Stitch-bonding machines
	-其他:								-Other:
	---簇绒机:								---Tufting machines:
8447.9011	----地毯织机	7	35		17	17	台	A	----For making carpets or rugs
8447.9019	----其他	8	30		17	17	台	A	----Other
8447.9020	---绣花机	8	30		17	17	台	A	---Embroidery machines
8447.9090	---其他	10	30		17	17	台	A	---Other
84.48	品目84.44、84.45、84.46或84.47所列机器的辅助机器（例如，多臂机、提花机、自停装置及换梭装置）；专用于或主要用于品目84.44、84.45、84.46或84.47所列机器的零件、附件（例如，锭子、锭壳、钢丝针布、梳、喷丝头、梭子、综丝、综框、针织机用针）：								**Auxiliary machinery for use with machines of heading No.84.44, 84.45, 84.46 or 84.47（for example, dobbies, Jacquards, automatic stop motions, shuttle changing mechanisms）; parts and accessories suitable for use solely or principally with the machines of this heading or of heading No.84.44, 84.45, 84.46 or 84.47（for example, spindles and spindle flyers, card clothing, combs, extruding nipples, shuttles, healds and heald-frames, hosiery needles）:**
	-税号84.44、84.45、84.46或84.47所列机器的辅助机器:								-Auxiliary machinery for machines of heading No.84.44, 84.45, 84.46 or 84.47:
8448.1100	--多臂机或提花机及其所用的卡片缩小、复制、穿孔或汇编机器	8	20		17	17	千克		--Dobbies and Jacquards; card reducing, copying, punching or assembling machines for use there with
8448 1100.01[暂]	多臂机或提花机（转速指标500转/分以上）	8	20	4	17	17	千克		Dobbies or Jacquards (speed indicator 500 r / min or above)
8448 1100.90	多臂机或提花机所用卡片缩小、复制、穿孔或汇编机器（包括其所用的卡片缩小、复制、穿孔或汇编机器）	8	20		17	17	千克		Card reducing, copying, punching or assembling machines used by dobbies or Jacquards (including the use of card reducing, copying, punching or assembling machines)
8448.1900	--其他	8	20		17	17	千克		--Other
	-税号84.44所列机器及其辅助机器的零件、附件:								-Parts and accessories of machines of heading No.84.44 or of their auxiliary machinery:
8448.2020	---喷丝头或喷丝板	6	14		17	17	个/千克		---Extruding nipples or spinnerets
8448.2090	---其他	6	17		17	17	千克		---Other
	-税号84.45所列机器及其辅助机器的零件、附件:								-Parts and accessories of machines of heading No.84.45 or of their auxiliary machinery:
8448.3100	--钢丝针布	6	17		17	17	千克		--Card clothing
8448.3200	--纺织纤维预处理机器的零件、附件，但钢丝针布除外	6	17		17	17	千克		--Of machines for preparing textile fibres, other than card clothing
	--锭子、锭壳、纺丝环、钢丝圈:								--Spindles, spindle flyers, spinning rings and ring travellers:
8448.3310	---络筒锭	6	17		17	17	个/千克		---Winding spindle
8448.3390	---其他	6	17		17	17	千克		---Other
	--其他:								--Other:
8448.3910	---气流杯	6	14		17	17	个/千克		---Open-end rotors

税则号列 Tariff Item	商品名称及备注	进口税率			出口退税	增值税率	计量单位	监管条件	Article Description
		最惠	普通	暂定					
8448.3920 暂	---电子清纱器	6	17	3	17	17	个/千克		---Electronic yarn clearers
8448.3930 暂	---空气捻接器	6	17	3	17	17	个/千克		---Air twisting devices
8448.3940 暂	---环锭细纱机紧密纺装置	6	17	0	17	17	个/千克		----Compact set of ring spinring farmes
8448.3990 暂	---其他	6	17	3	17	17	千克		---Other
	-织机及其辅助机器的零件、附件:								-Parts and accessories of weaving machines（looms）or of their auxiliary machinery:
8448.4200	--织机用筘、综丝及综框	6	50		17	17	千克		--Reeds for looms, healds and heald-frames
	--其他:								--Other:
8448.4910	---接、投梭箱	6	17		17	17	个/千克		---Catching and throwing shuttle boxes
8448.4920 暂	---引纬、送经装置	6	17	3	17	17	个/千克		---Weft insertion and let-off motions
8448.4930	---梭子	6	50		17	17	个/千克		---Shuttles
8448.4990 暂	---其他	6	17	3	17	17	千克		---Other
	-税号84.47所列机器及其辅助机器的零件、附件:								-Parts and accessories of machines of heading No.84.47 or of their auxiliary machinery:
	--沉降片、织针及其他成圈机件:								--Sinkers, needles and other articles used in forming stitches:
8448.5120	---针织机用28号以下的弹簧针、钩针及复合针	6	50		17	17	千克		---Barbered needles, crotchet hooks and complex needles for knitting machines, smaler than gauge No.28
8448.5190	---其他	6	17		17	17	千克		---Other
8448.5900 暂	--其他	6	17	3	17	17	千克		--Other
84.49	**成匹、成形的毡呢或无纺织物制造或整理机器,包括制毡呢帽机器;帽模:**								**Machinery for the manufacture or finishing of felt or nonwovens in the piece or in shapes, including machinery for making felt hats; blocks for making hats:**
8449.0010	---针刺机	8	30		17	17	台/千克		---Machinery for stitch
8449 0010.01 暂	高速针刺机,针刺频率＞2000次/分钟	8	30	6	17	17	台/千克		High-speed stitch machinery, stroke frequency ＞ 2000 times / min
8449 0010.90	其他针刺机	8	30		17	17	台/千克		Other machinery for stitch
8449.0020	---水刺设备	8	30		17	17	台/千克		---Spunlaced Equipment
8449 0020.01 暂	高速宽幅水刺设备(工作幅宽＞3.5米,工作速度＞250米/分钟,水刺压力≥400帕)	8	30	6	17	17	台/千克		High-Speed wide spunlace equipments (working width ＞3.5 m, working speed＞250 m / min, spun-laced pressure ≥ 400 Pa)
8449 0020.90	其他水刺设备	8	30		17	17	台/千克		Other spun-laced equipments
8449.0090	---其他	8	30		17	17	千克		---Other
84.50	**家用型或洗衣房用洗衣机,包括洗涤干燥两用机:**								**Household or laundry-type washing machines, including machines which both wash and dry:**
	-干衣量不超过10千克的洗衣机:								-Machines, each of a dry linen capacity not exceeding 10kg:
	--全自动的:								--Fully-automatic machines:
8450.1110	---波轮式	10	130		17	17	台	A	---Of the continuously rotating impeller
8450.1120	---滚筒式	10	130		17	17	台	A	---Of the drum type
8450.1190	---其他	10	130		17	17	台	A	---Other
8450.1200	--其他机器,装有离心甩干机	30	130		17	17	台	A	--Other machines, with built-in centrifugal drier
8450.1900	--其他	30	130		17	17	台	A	--Other
	-干衣量超过10千克的洗衣机:								-Machines, each of a dry linen capacity exceeding 10kg:
	---全自动的:								---Fully-automatic machines:
8450.2011	----波轮式	10	80		17	17	台		----Of the continuously rotating impeller
8450.2012	----滚筒式	10	80		17	17	台		----Of the drum type
8450.2019	----其他	10	80		17	17	台		----Other
8450.2090	---其他	10	80		17	17	台		---Other
	-零件:								-Parts:
8450.9010	---干衣量不超过10千克的洗衣机用	5	130		15	17	千克		---Of the machines of subheadings No.8450.1110 to 8450.1900
8450.9090 暂	---其他	16	80	5	15	17	千克		---Other
84.51	**纱线、织物及纺织制品的洗涤、**								**Machinery（other than machines of heaing**

税则号列 Tariff Item	商品名称及备注	进口税率 最惠	普通	暂定	出口退税	增值税率	计量单位	监管条件	Article Description
	清洁、绞拧、干燥、熨烫、挤压（包括熔压）、漂白、染色、上浆、整理、涂布或浸渍机器（品目 84.50 的机器除外）；列诺伦（亚麻油地毡）及类似铺地制品的布基或其他底布的浆料涂布机器；纺织物的卷绕、退绕、折叠、剪切或剪齿边机器：								**No.84.50）for washing, cleaning, wringing, drying, ironing, pressing （including fusing presses）, bleaching, dyeing, dressing, finishing, coating or impregnating textile yarns, fabrics or made up textile articles and machines for applying the paste to the base fabric or other support used in the manufacture of floor coverings such as linoleum; machines for reeling, unreeling, folding, cutting or pinking textile fabrics:**
8451.1000	-干洗机	21	80		15	17	台		--Dry-cleaning machines
	-干燥机:								-Drying machines:
8451.2100	--干衣量不超过 10 千克	15	80		15	17	台		--Each of a dry linen capacity not exceeding 10kg
8451.2900	--其他	8	30		15	17	台		--Other
8451.3000	-熨烫机及挤压机(包括熔压机)	8	30		15	17	台		-Ironing machines and presses（including fusing presses）
8451.4000	-洗涤、漂白或染色机器	8.4	20		15	17	台		-Washing, bleaching or dyeing machines
8451.5000	-纺织物的卷绕、退绕、折叠、剪切或剪齿边机器	8	20		15	17	台		-Machines for reeling, unreeling, folding, cutting or pinking textile fabrics
8451.8000	-其他机器	12	30		15	17	台		-Other machinery
8451 8000.01[暂]	服装定型焙烘炉、服装液氨整理机、预缩机、罐蒸机	12	30	10	15	17	台		Clothing stereotyped baking furnaces, clothes ammonia finishing machines, pre-shrinking machines; pot steaming machine
8451 8000.02[暂]	剪绒、洗缩联合机；剪毛联合机；柔软整理机	12	30	10	15	17	台		Shearing, washing-shrinking combined machines; shearing combined machines; softening machines
8451 8000.03[暂]	定型机、精炼机、丝光机、磨毛机	12	30	10	15	17	台		Shaping machines; refining machines; mercerization machines; sanding machines
8451 8000.04[暂]	涂层机	12	30	8	15	17	台		Coating machine
8451 8000.90	品目 84.51 未列名的其他机器	12	30		15	17	台		Other machines not specified or included in heading No 84.51
8451.9000	-零件	8	20		15	17	千克		-Parts
84.52	缝纫机，但品目 84.40 的锁线订书机除外；缝纫机专用的特制家具、底座及罩盖；缝纫机针：								**Sewing machines, other than book-sewing machines of heading No.84.40; furniture, bases and covers specially designed for sewing machines; sewing machine needles:**
	-家用型缝纫机:								-Sewing machines of household type:
8452.1010	---多功能家用缝纫机	21	80		17	17	台		---Multifuncitonal sewing machines of household type
	---其他:								---Other:
8452.1091	----手动式	21	80		17	17	台		----Hand operated
8452.1099	----其他	21	80		17	17	台		----Other
	-其他缝纫机:								-Other sewing machines:
	--自动的:								--Automatic units:
8452.2110	---平缝机	12	40		17	17	台		---Flatseam
8452.2120	---包缝机	12	40		17	17	台		---Overlock machine
8452.2130	---绷缝机	12	40		17	17	台		---Interlock machine
8452.2190	---其他	12	40		17	17	台		---Other
8452.2900	--其他	12	40		17	17	台		--Other
8452.3000	-缝纫机针	14	100		15	17	千克		-Sewing machine needles
	-缝纫机专用的特制家具、底座和罩盖及其零件；缝纫机的其他零件:								-Furniture,bases and covers for sewing machines and parts thereof; other parts of sewing machines :
	---家用型缝纫机用:								---Of sewing machines of the household type:
8452.9011	----旋梭	14	80		15	17	千克		----Rotating shuttles
8452.9019	----其他	14	80		15	17	千克		----Other
	---其他:								---Other:
8452.9091	----旋梭	14	80		15	17	千克		----Rotating shuttles
8452.9092	----缝纫机专用的特制家具、底座和罩盖及其零件	14	100		15	17	千克		----Furniture,bases and covers for sewing machines and parts thereof

税则号列 Tariff Item	商品名称及备注	进口税率 最惠	普通	暂定	出口退税	增值税率	计量单位	监管条件	Article Description
8452.9099	----其他	14	80		15	17	千克		----Other
84.53	**生皮、皮革的处理、鞣制或加工机器，鞋靴、毛皮及其他皮革制品的制作或修理机器，但缝纫机除外：**								**Machinery for preparing, tanning or working hides, skins or leather or for making or repairing footwear or other articles of hides, skins or leather, other than sewing machines:**
8453.1000	-生皮、皮革的处理、鞣制或加工机器	8.4	30		15	17	台		-Machinery for preparing, tanning or working hides, skins or leather
8453.2000	-鞋靴制作或修理机器	8.4	30		15	17	台		-Machinery for making or repairing footwear
8453.8000	-其他机器	8.4	30		15	17	台		-Other machinery
8453.9000	-零件	8	30		15	17	千克		-Parts
84.54	**金属冶炼及铸造用的转炉、浇包、锭模及铸造机：**								**Converters, ladles, ingot moulds and casting machines, of a kind used in metallurgy or in metal foundries:**
8454.1000	-转炉	8.4	35		17	17	台		-Converters
	-锭模及浇包：								-Ingot moulds and ladles:
8454.2010	---炉外精炼设备	8.4	35		17	17	台		---Fining equipments, outside of converters
8454 2010.10	VOD炉(真空脱气炉)	8.4	35		17	17	台	O	VOD furnaces (vacuum degassing furnaces)
8454 2010.90	其他炉外精炼设备	8.4	35		17	17	台	O	Other fining equipments, outside of converters
8454.2090	---其他	8.4	35		17	17	台		---Other
	-铸造机：								-Casting machines:
8454.3010	---冷室压铸机	12	35		17	17	台	O	---Cold chamber die-casting machines
	---钢坯连铸机：								---Ingot continuous casting machines:
8454.3021	----方坯连铸机	10	35		17	17	台		----Ingot block
8454.3022	----板坯连铸机	12	35		17	17	台	O	----Ingot slab
8454.3029	----其他	12	35		17	17	台	O	----Other
8454.3090	---其他	12	35		17	17	台		---Other
	-零件：								-Parts:
8454.9010	---炉外精炼设备用	8	20		17	17	千克		---For the fining equipments outside of converters
	---钢坯连铸机用：								---For ingot continuous casting machines:
8454.9021	----结晶器	8	20		17	17	千克		----Crystallizers
8454.9022	----振动装置	8	20		17	17	千克		----Vibrating devices
8454.9029	----其他	8	20		17	17	千克		----Other
8454.9090	---其他	8	20		17	17	千克		---Other
84.55	**金属轧机及其轧辊：**								**Metal-rolling mills and rolls therefor:**
	-轧管机：								-Tube mills:
8455.1010	---热轧管机	12	35		17	17	台		---Tube mills, for hot-rolled
8455.1020	---冷轧管机	12	35		17	17	台	O	---Tube mills for cold-rolled
8455.1030	---定减径轧管机	12	35		17	17	台	O	---Fixed and reduced tube mills
8455.1090	---其他	12	35		17	17	台	O	---Other
	-其他轧机：								-Other rolling mills:
	--热轧机或冷热联合轧机：								--Hot or combination hot and cold:
8455.2110	---板材热轧机	15	35		17	17	台	O	---Sheet mills, hot-rolled
8455.2120	---型钢轧机	15	35		17	17	台	O	---Rolled-steel section mills
8455.2130	---线材轧机	15	35		17	17	台	O	---Wire mills
8455.2190	---其他	15	35		17	17	台	O	---Other
	--冷轧机：								--Cold:
8455.2210	---板材冷轧机	10	35		17	17	台	O	---Sheet mills
8455.2290	---其他	15	35		17	17	台		---Other
8455 2290.10	铝箔粗轧机	15	35		17	17	台		Aluminum foil roughing mills
8455 2290.90	其他金属冷轧机	15	35		17	17	台		Other metal cold rolling mills
8455.3000	-轧机用轧辊	8.4	20		17	17	个		-Rolls for rolling mills
8455.9000	-其他零件	8	20		17	17	千克		-Other parts
84.56	**用激光、其他光、光子束、超声波、放电、电化学法、电子束、离子束或等离子弧处理各种材料的加工机床；水射流切割机：**								**Machine-tools for working any material by removal of material, by laser or other light or photon beam, ultrasonic, electro-discharge, electro-chemical, electron beam, ionic-beam or plasma arc**

税则号列 Tariff Item	商品名称及备注	进口税率 最惠	进口税率 普通	进口税率 暂定	出口退税	增值税率	计量单位	监管条件	Article Description
									processes; water-jet cutting machines:
8456.1000	-用激光、其他光或光子束处理的	0	30		17	17	台		-Operated by laser or other light or photon beam processes
8456 1000.10	辐照元件激光切割机(切割燃料包壳以使辐照核材料能熔解,含遥控设备)	0	30		17	17	台	3AO	Irradiated-component laser cutting machines (cutting the fuel claddings to make the irradiated nuclear materials to melt down, with a remote control)
8456 1000.90	其他用激光或其他光或光子束处理的机床	0	30		17	17	台	AO	Other machine tools using laser or other light or photon beam
8456.2000	-用超声波处理的	10	30		17	17	台	A	-Operated by ultrasonic processes
	-用放电处理的:								-Operated by electro-discharge processes:
8456.3010	---数控的	9.7	30		17	17	台		---Numerically controlled
8456 3010.10	数控放电加工机床(两轴或多轴成形控制的无线型放电加工机床)	9.7	30		17	17	台	3AO	Numerically controlled machine tools operated by electro-discharge processes (wireless-type electro-discharge machine tools controlled by 2-axis or multi-axis contours)
8456 3010.90	其他数控的放电处理加工机床	9.7	30		17	17	台	AO	Other numerically controlled machine tools operated by electro-discharge processes
8456.3090	---其他	10	30		17	17	台		---Other
8456 3090.10	非数控放电加工机床(两轴或多轴成形控制的无线型放电加工机床)	10	30		17	17	台	3A	Non- numerically controlled machine tools operated by electro-discharge processes (wireless-type electro-discharge machine tools controlled by 2-axis or multi-axis contours)
8456 3090.90	其他非数控的放电处理加工机床	10	30		17	17	台	A	Other non- numerically controlled machine tools operated by electro-discharge processes
	-其他:								-Other:
8456.9010	---等离子切割机	0	30		17	17	台	AO	---Cutting machines of plasma arc
8456.9020	---水射流切割机	0	30		15	17	台	A	---water-jet cutting machines
8456.9090	---其他	0	30		17	17	台	AO	---Other
84.57	**加工金属的加工中心、单工位组合机床及多工位组合机床:**								**Machining centres, unit construction machines （single station） and multistation transfer machines, for working metal:**
	-加工中心:								-Machining centres:
8457.1010	---立式	9.7	20		17	17	台	AO	---Vertical
8457.1020	---卧式	9.7	20		17	17	台	AO	---Horizontal
8457.1030	---龙门式	9.7	20		17	17	台	AO	---Plano
	---其他:								---Other:
8457.1091	----铣车复合	9.7	20		17	17	台	AO	----mill-turn centres
8457.1099	----其他	9.7	20		17	17	台	AO	----Other
8457.2000	-单工位组合机床	8	20		17	17	台	OA	-Unit construction machines （single station）
8457.3000	-多工位组合机床	5	20		17	17	台	AO	-Multi-station transfer machines
84.58	**切削金属的车床（包括车削中心）:**								**Lathes （including turning centres） for removing metal:**
	-卧式车床:								-Horizontal lathes:
8458.1100	--数控的	9.7	20		17	17	台		--Numerically controlled
8458 1100.10	两用物项管制的切削金属的卧式数控车床(包括车削中心)	9.7	20		17	17	台	3AO	Numerically controlled horizontal lathes for removing metal (including turning centers) under sensitive items control
8458 1100.90	其他切削金属的卧式数控车床(包括车削中心)	9.7	20		17	17	台	AO	Other numerically controlled horizontal lathes for removing metal (including turning centers)
8458.1900	--其他	12	50		17	17	台	A	--Other
	-其他车床:								-Other lathes:
	--数控的:								--Numerically controlled:
8458.9110	---立式	5	20		17	17	台		---Vertical
8458 9110.10	两用物项管制的切削金属立式数控车床(包括车削中心)	5	20		17	17	台/千克	3AO	Numerically controlled vertical lathes for removing metal (including turning centers) under sensitive items control

税则号列 Tariff Item	商品名称及备注	进口税率 最惠	普通	暂定	出口退税	增值税率	计量单位	监管条件	Article Description
8458 9110.90	其他切削金属的立式数控车床(包括车削中心)	5	20		17	17	台/千克	AO	Other numerically controlled vertical lathes for removing metal (including turning centers)
8458.9120	---其他	5	20		17	17	台/千克		---Other
8458 9120.10	其他两用物项管制的切削金属数控车床(包括车削中心)	5	20		17	17	台/千克	3AO	Other Numerically controlled lathes for removing metal including turning centers under sensitive items control
8458 9120.90	其他切削金属的数控车床(包括车削中心)	5	20		17	17	台/千克	AO	Other numerically controlled lathes for removing metal (including turning centers)
8458.9900	--其他	12	50		17	17	台	A	--Other
84.59	**切削金属的钻床、镗床、铣床、攻丝机床(包括直线移动式动力头钻床),但品目84.58的车床(包括车削中心)除外:**								**Machine-tools (including way-type unit head machines) for drilling, boring, milling, threading or tapping by removing metal, other than lathes (including turning centres) of heading No.84.58:**
8459.1000	-直线移动式动力头钻床	15	50		17	17	台	A	-Way-type unit head machines
	-其他钻床:								-Other drilling machines:
8459.2100	--数控的	9.7	20		17	17	台	AO	--Numerically controlled
8459.2900	--其他	15	50		17	17	台	A	--Other
	-其他镗铣机床:								-Other boring-milling machines:
8459.3100	--数控的	9.7	20		17	17	台	OA	--Numerically controlled
8459.3900	--其他	10	50		17	17	台	A	--Other
	-其他镗床:								-Other boring machines:
8459.4010	---数控的	9.7	20		17	17	台	OA	---Numerically controlled
8459.4090	---其他	15	50		17	17	台	A	---Other
	-升降台式铣床:								-Milling machines, knee-type:
8459.5100	--数控的	9.7	20		17	17	台	OA	--Numerically controlled
8459.5900	--其他	15	50		17	17	台	A	--Other
	-其他铣床:								-Other milling machines:
	--数控的:								--Numerically controlled:
8459.6110	---龙门铣床	5	20		17	17	台	OA	---Planomilling machines
8459.6190	---其他	5	20		17	17	台	OA	---Other
	--其他:								--Other:
8459.6910	---龙门铣床	12	50		17	17	台	A	---Planomilling machines
8459.6990	---其他	12	50		17	17	台	A	---Other
8459.7000	-其他攻丝机床	12	50		17	17	台	A	-Other threading or tapping machines
84.60	**用磨石、磨料或抛光材料对金属或金属陶瓷进行去毛刺、刃磨、磨削、珩磨、研磨、抛光或其他精加工机床,但品目84.61的切齿机、齿轮磨床或齿轮精加工机床除外:**								**Machine-tools for deburring, sharpenling, grinding, honing, lapping, polishing or otherwise finishing metal or cermets by means of grinding stones, abrasives or polishing products, other than gear cutting, gear grinding or gear finishing machines of heading No.84.61:**
	-平面磨床,在任一坐标的定位精度至少是0.01毫米:								-Flat-surface grinding machines, in which the positioning in any one axis can be set up to an accuracy of at least 0.01mm:
8460.1100	--数控的	9.7	20		17	17	台	OA	--Numerically controlled
8460.1900	--其他	15	50		17	17	台		--Other
	-其他磨床,在任一坐标的定位精度至少是0.01毫米:								-Other grinding machines, in which the positioning in any one axis can be set up to an accuracy of at least 0.01mm:
	--数控的:								--Numerically controlled:
	---外圆磨床:								---Cylindrical grinding machines:
8460.2111	----曲轴磨床	9.7	20		17	17	台	OA	----Crank shaft grinding machines
8460.2119	----其他	9.7	20		17	17	台	OA	----Other
8460.2120	---内圆磨床	9.7	20		17	17	台	OA	---Internal grinding machines
8460.2190	---其他	9.7	20		17	17	台	OA	---Other
	--其他:								--Other:
8460.2910	---外圆磨床	15	50		17	17	台	A	---Cylindrical grinding machines
8460.2920	---内圆磨床	15	50		17	17	台	A	---Internal grinding machines

税则号列 Tariff Item	商品名称及备注	进口税率 最惠	进口税率 普通	进口税率 暂定	出口退税	增值税率	计量单位	监管条件	Article Description
8460.2930	---轧辊磨床	13	50		17	17	台		---Grinding machines of roll
8460.2990	---其他	13	50		17	17	台	A	---Other
	-刃磨（工具或刀具）机床:								-Sharpening（tool or cutter grinding）machines:
8460.3100	--数控的	9.7	20		17	17	台	A	--Numerically controlled
8460.3900	--其他	15	50		17	17	台	A	--Other
	-珩磨或研磨机床:								-Honing or lapping machines:
8460.4010	---珩磨	13	50		17	17	台	A	---Honing
8460.4020	---研磨	13	50		17	17	台	A	---Lapping
	-其他:								-Other:
8460.9010	---砂轮机	15	50		17	17	台		---Grinding wheel machines
8460.9020	---抛光机床	15	50		17	17	台	A	---Polishing machines
8460.9090	---其他	15	50		17	17	台	A	---Other
84.61	**切削金属或金属陶瓷的刨床、牛头刨床、插床、拉床、切齿机、齿轮磨床或齿轮精加工机床、锯床、切断机及其他品目未列名的切削机床:**								**Machine-tools for planing, shaping, slotting, broaching, gear cutting, gear grinding or gear finishing, sawing, cutting-off and other machine-tools working by removing metal or cermets, not elsewhere specified or included:**
	-牛头刨床或插床:								-Shaping or slotting machines:
8461.2010	---牛头刨床	15	50		17	17	台		---Shaping machines
8461.2020	---插床	15	50		17	17	台		---Slotting machines
8461.3000	-拉床	12	50		17	17	台		-Broaching machines
	-切齿机、齿轮磨床或齿轮精加工机床:								-Gear cutting, gear grinding or gear finishing machines:
	---数控的:								---Numerically controlled:
8461.4011	----齿轮磨床	9.7	20		17	17	台	OA	----Gear grinding machines
8461.4019	----其他	9.7	20		17	17	台	OA	----Other
8461.4090	---其他	15	50		17	17	台	A	---Other
8461.5000	-锯床或切断机	12	50		17	17	台		-Sawing or cutting-off machines
8461 5000.10	辐照元件刀具切割机[切割燃料包壳以使辐照核材料能熔解(含遥控设备)]	12	50		17	17	台	3	Irradiated-component cutting machine tools (cutting the fuel claddings to make the irradiated nuclear materials to melt down, with a remote control)
8461 5000.90	其他锯床或切断机	12	50		17	17	台		Other sawing or cutting-off machines
	-其他:								-Other:
	---刨床:								---Planing machines:
8461.9011	----龙门刨床	15	50		17	17	台		----Double-column（open-side）planing machines
8461.9019	----其他	15	50		17	17	台		----Other
8461.9090	---其他	12	50		17	17	台		---Other
84.62	**加工金属的锻造（包括模锻）或冲压机床；加工金属的弯曲、折叠、矫直、矫平、剪切、冲孔或开槽机床；其他加工金属或硬质合金的压力机:**								**Machine-tools（including presses）for working metal by forging, hammering or die-stamping; machine-tools（including presses）for working metal by bending, folding, straightening, flattening, shearing, punching or notching; presses for working metal or metal carbides, not specified above:**
	-锻造（包括模锻）或冲压机床及锻锤:								-Forging or die-stamping machines（including presses）and hammers:
8462.1010	---数控的	9.7	20		17	17	台	O	---Numerically controlled
8462.1090	---其他	12	50		17	17	台		---Other
	-弯曲、折叠、矫直或矫平机床								-Bending, folding, straightening or flattening machines（including presses）:
	--数控的:								--Numerically controlled:
8462.2110	---矫直机	9.7	20		17	17	台		---Straightening machines
8462.2190	---其他	9.7	20		17	17	台	O	---Other
	--其他:								--Other:
8462.2910	---矫直机	10	50		17	17	台		---Straightening machines
8462.2990	---其他	10	50		17	17	台		---Other
	-剪切机床,但冲剪两用机除外:								-Shearing machines（including presses）, other than

税则号列 Tariff Item	商品名称及备注	进口税率 最惠	普通	暂定	出口退税	增值税率	计量单位	监管条件	Article Description
									combined punching and shearing machines:
	--数控的:								--Numerically controlled:
8462.3110	---板带纵剪机	7	20		17	17	台	O	---Shearing lengthwise
8462.3120	---板带横剪机	7	20		17	17	台	O	---Shearing transverse
8462.3190	---其他	7	20		17	17	台	O	---Other
	--其他:								--Other:
8462.3910	---板带纵剪机	10	50		17	17	台		---Shearing lengthwise
8462.3920	---板带横剪机	10	50		17	17	台		---Shearing transverse
8462.3990	---其他	10	50		17	17	台		---Other
	-冲孔或开槽机床，包括冲剪两用机:								-Punching or notching machines（including presses）, including combined punching and shearing machines:
	--数控的:								--Numerically controlled:
	---冲床:								---Punch press:
8462.4111	----自动模式数控步冲压力机	9.7	20		17	17	台		----CNC automatic tool change punch press
8462.4119	----其他	9.7	20		17	17	台	O	----Other
8462.4190	---其他	9.7	20		17	17	台		---Other
8462.4900	--其他	10	50		17	17	台		--Other
	-其他:								-Other:
	--液压压力机:								--Hydraulic presses:
8462.9110	---金属型材挤压机	10	50		17	17	台	O	---Metal section squeezing machine
8462.9190	---其他	10	50		17	17	台		---Other
	--其他:								--Other:
8462.9910	---机械压力机	10	50		17	17	台	O	---Mechanical presses
8462.9990	---其他	10	50		17	17	台		---Other
84.63	**金属或金属陶瓷的其他非切削加工机床:**								**Other machine-tools for working metal or cermets, without removing material:**
	-杆、管、型材、异型材、丝及类似品的拉拔机:								-Draw-benches for bars, tubes, profiles, wire or the like:
	---冷拔管机:								---Cold-drawing tube benches:
8463.1011	----拉拔力为300吨及以下	10	50		17	17	台		----With 300t or less
8463.1019	----其他	10	50		17	17	台		----Other
8463.1020	---拔丝机	10	50		17	17	台		---Wiredrawing machines
8463.1090	---其他	10	50		17	17	台		---Other
8463.2000	-螺纹滚轧机	15	50		17	17	台		-Thread rolling machines
8463.3000	-金属丝加工机	10	50		17	17	台		-Machines for working wire
8463.9000	-其他	10	50		17	17	台		-Other
8463 9000.10	滚压成形机床(数控，装3个以上压辊)	10	50		17	17	台	3	Roll forming machine tools (numerically controlled, fitted with three or more sticks)
8463 9000.20	具有滚压功能的旋压成形机床(数控，装3个以上压辊)	10	50		17	17	台	3	Spin forming machine tools with roll forming functions (numerically controlled, fitted with three or more sticks)
8463 9000.90	其他非切削加工机床(是指加工金属或金属陶瓷的)	10	50		17	17	台		Other machine-tools for working metal or cermets, without removing material
84.64	**石料、陶瓷、混凝土、石棉水泥或类似矿物材料的加工机床、玻璃冷加工机床:**								**Machine-tools for working stone, ceramics, concrete, asbestos-cement or like mineral materials or for cold working glass:**
	-锯床:								-Sawing machines:
8464.1010	---圆盘锯	0	30		17	17	台		---Of disk saw
8464.1020	---钢丝锯	0	30		17	17	台		--Of scroll saw
8464.1090	---其他	0	30		17	17	台		---Other
	-研磨或抛光机床:								-Grinding or polishing machines:
8464.2010	---玻璃研磨或抛光机床	0	30		17	17	台		---Machines for grinding or polishing glass or glassware
8464.2090	---其他	0	30		17	17	台		---Other
	-其他:								-Other:
	---玻璃的其他冷加工机床:								---Other machines for coldworking glass or glassware:
8464.9011	----切割机	0	30		17	17	台		---Cutting-off machines

税则号列 Tariff Item	商品名称及备注	进口税率 最惠	进口税率 普通	进口税率 暂定	出口退税	增值税率	计量单位	监管条件	Article Description
8464.9012	----刻花机	0	30		17	17	台		----Carving machines
8464.9019	----其他	0	30		17	17	台		---Other
8464.9090	---其他	0	30		17	17	台		---Other
84.65	**木材、软木、骨、硬质橡胶、硬质塑料或类似硬质材料的加工机床（包括用打钉或打U形钉、胶黏或其他方法组合前述材料的机器）:**								**Machine-tools（induding machines for nailing, stapling, glueing or otherwise assembling）for working wood, cork, bone, hard rubber, hard plastics or similar hard materials:**
8465.1000	-不需更换工具即可进行不同机械加工的机器	10	30		17	17	台		-Machines which can carry out different types of machining operations without tool change between such operations
	-其他:								-Other:
8465.9100	--锯床	10	30		17	17	台		--Sawing machines
8465.9200	--刨、铣或切削成形机器	10	30		17	17	台		--Planing, milling or moulding（by cutting）machines
8465.9300	--研磨、砂磨或抛光机器	10	30		17	17	台		--Grinding, sanding or polishing machines
8465.9400	--弯曲或装配机器	10	30		17	17	台		--Bending or assembling machines
8465.9500	--钻孔或凿榫机器	10	30		17	17	台		--Drilling or mortising machines
8465.9600	--剖开、切片或刮削机器	10	30		17	17	台		--Splitting, slicing or paring machines
8465.9900	--其他	10	30		17	17	台		--Other
84.66	**专用于或主要用于品目 84.56 至 84.65 所列机器的零件、附件，包括工件或工具的夹具、自启板牙切头、分度头及其他专用于机床的附件；各种手提工具的工具夹具:**								**Parts and accessories suitable for use solely or principally with the machines of headings No.84.56 to 84.65, including work or tool holders, self-opening dieheads, dividing heads and other special attachments for machine-tools; tool holders for any type of tool for working in the hand:**
8466.1000	-工具夹具及自启板牙切头	7	17		15	17	千克		-Tool holders and self-opening dieheads
8466.2000	-工件夹具	7	17		15	17	千克		-Work holders
8466.3000	-分度头及其他专用于机床的附件	7	17		15	17	千克		-Dividing heads and other special attachments for machine-tools
	-其他:								-Other:
8466.9100	--税号 84.64 所列机器用	0	17		15	17	千克		--For machines of heading No.84.64
8466.9200	--税号 84.65 所列机器用	6	17		15	17	千克		--For machines of heading No.84.65
	--税号 84.56 至 84.61 所列机器用:								--For machines of headings No.84.56 to 84.61:
8466.9310	---刀库及自动换刀装置	0	17		15	17	千克		---Tool magazine and tool change device
8466.9390	---其他	0	17		15	17	千克		---Other
8466.9400	--税号 84.62 或 84.63 所列机器用	6	17		15	17	千克		--For machines of heading No.84.62 or 84.63
8466 9400.10	滚压成形机床用芯轴(转筒成形用的芯轴，内径在75毫米至400毫米之间)	6	17		15	17	千克	3	Mandrels for roll forming machine tools (the inner diameter of the mandrels for rolling formability is between 75mm and 400mm)
8466 9400.20	有滚压功能的旋压成形机用芯轴(转筒成形用的芯轴，内径在75毫米至400毫米之间)	6	17		15	17	千克	3	Mandrels for spin forming machine tools with roll forming functions (the inner diameter of the mandrels for rolling formability is between 75mm and 400mm)
8466 9400.90	品目 84.62～84.63 机器用其他零件	6	17		15	17	千克		Other parts for the machines in heading No. 84.62~No.84.63
84.67	**手提式风动或液压工具及本身装有电动或非电动动力装置的手提式工具:**								**Tools for working in the hand, pneumatic and hydraulic and with self-contained electric or non-electric motor:**
	-风动的:								-Pneumatic:
8467.1100	--旋转式（包括旋转冲击式的）	8	30		15	17	台		--Rotary type（including combined rotarypercussion）
8467.1900	--其他	8	30		15	17	台		--Other
	-本身装有电动动力装置的:								-With self-contained electric motor:
8467.2100	--各种钻	10	30		15	17	台	A	--Drills of all kinds
	--锯:								--Saws:
8467.2210	---链锯	10	30		15	17	台	A	---Chain saws

税则号列 Tariff Item	商品名称及备注	进口税率			出口退税	增值税率	计量单位	监管条件	Article Description
		最惠	普通	暂定					
8467.2290	---其他	10	30		15	17	台	A	---Other
	--其他:								--Other:
8467.2910	---砂磨工具（包括磨光机、砂光机、砂轮机等）	10	30		15	17	台	A	---Grinding tools（including burnisher, belt sander, wheel-sander）
8467.2920	---电刨	10	30		15	17	台	A	---Planings
8467.2990	---其他	10	30		15	17	台	A	---Other
	-其他工具:								-Other tools:
8467.8100	--链锯	8	30		15	17	台		--Chain saws
8467.8900	--其他	8	30		15	17	台		--Other
	-零件:								-Parts:
	--链锯用:								--Of chain saws:
8467.9110	---电动的	6	30		15	17	千克		---With self-contained electric motor
8467.9190	---其他	6	30		15	17	千克		---Other
8467.9200	--风动工具用	6	30		15	17	千克		--Of pneumatic tools
	--其他:								--Other:
8467.9910	---电动工具用	10	30		15	17	千克		---With self-contained electric motor
8467.9990	---其他	6	30		15	17	千克		---Other
84.68	**焊接机器及装置，不论是否兼有切割功能，但品目85.15的货品除外；气体加温表面回火机器及装置:**								**Machinery and apparatus for soldering, brazing or welding, whether or not capable of cutting, other than those of heading No.85.15; gas-operated surface tempering machines and appliances:**
8468.1000	-手提喷焊器	12	30		15	17	台		-Hand-held blow pipes
8468.2000	-其他气体焊接或表面回火机器及装置	12	30		15	17	台		-Other gas-operated machinery and apparatus
8468 2000.10	自动焊接机[将端塞焊接于燃料细棒（或棒）的自动焊接机]	12	30		15	17	台	3	Automatic welding machines （that weld the end plug on the thin fuel rods）
8468 2000.90	其他气体焊接或表面回火机器及装置	12	30		15	17	台		Other gas-operated surface tempering machinery and apparatus
8468.8000	-其他机器及装置	12	30		15	17	台		--Other machinery and apparatus
8468.9000[暂]	-零件	7	30	3	15	17	千克		-Parts
84.69	**打字机，但品目84.43的打印机除外；文字处理机:**								**Typewriters other than printers of heading No.84.43; word-processing machines:**
	---自动打字机及文字处理机:								---Automatic typewriters and word-processing machines:
8469.0011	----文字处理机	0	40		15	17	台		----Word-processing machines
8469.0012	----自动打字机	12	40		15	17	台		----Automatic typewriters
8469.0020	---其他电动打字机	12	40		15	17	台		----Other typewriters, electric
8469.0030	---其他非电动打字机	12	40		15	17	台		---Other typewriters, non-electric
84.70	**计算机器及具有计算功能的袖珍式数据记录、重现及显示机器；装有计算装置的会计计算机、邮资盖戳机、售票机及类似机器；现金出纳机:**								**Calculating machines and pocketsize data recording, reproducing and displaying machines with calculating functions; accounting machines, postage-franking machines, ticket-is-suing machines and similar machines, incorporating a calculating device; cash registers:**
8470.1000	-不需外接电源的电子计算器及具有计算功能的袖珍式数据记录、重现及显示机器	0	80		15	17	台		-Electronic calculators capable of operation without an external source of electric power and pocket-size data recording, reproducing and displaying machines with calculating functions
	-其他电子计算器:								-Other electronic calculating machines:
8470.2100	--装有打印装置的	0	80		15	17	台		--Incorporating a printing device
8470.2900	--其他	0	80		15	17	台		--Other
8470.3000	-其他计算机器	0	40		15	17	台		-Other calculating machines
	-现金出纳机:								-Cash registers:
8470.5010	---销售点终端出纳机	0	40		15	17	台		---Terminal registers for market
8470.5090	---其他	0	40		15	17	台		---Other
8470.9000	-其他	0	40		15	17	台		-Other
84.71	**自动数据处理设备及其部件；其**								**Automatic data processing machines and units**

税则号列 Tariff Item	商品名称及备注	进口税率			出口退税	增值税率	计量单位	监管条件	Article Description
		最惠	普通	暂定					
	他品目未列名的磁性或光学阅读机、将数据以代码形式转录到数据记录媒体的机器及处理这些数据的机器：								**thereof; magnetic or optical readers, machines for transcribing, data onto data media in coded form and machines for processing such data, not elsewhere specified or included:**
	-重量不超过 10 千克的便携式自动数据处理设备，至少由一个中央处理部件、一个键盘及一个显示器组成：								-Portable automatic data processing machines, weighing not more than 10kg, consisting of at least a central processing unit, a keyboard and a display:
8471.3010	---平板电脑	0	70		17	17	台	A	----Tablet computer
8471.3090	---其他	0	70		17	17	台	A	---Other
	-其他自动数据处理设备：								-Other automatic data processing machines:
	--同一机壳内至少有一个中央处理部件及一个输入和输出部件，不论是否组合式：								--Comprising in the same housing at least a central processing unit and an input and output unit, whether or not combined:
8471.4110	---巨型机、大型机及中型机	0	14		17	17	台	3	---Mainframes
8471.4120	---小型机	0	14		17	17	台	3	---Mini-computers
8471.4140	---微型机	0	70		17	17	台	A	---Microprocessings
8471.4190	---其他	0	70		17	17	台		---Other
	--其他，以系统形式进口或出口的：								--Other, presented in the form of systems:
8471.4910	---巨型机、大型机及中型机	0	29		17	17	台	3	---Mainframes
8471.4920	---小型机	0	29		17	17	台	3	---Mini-computers
8471.4940	---微型机	0	70		17	17	台		---Microprocessings
	---其他：								---Other:
8471.4991	----分散型工业过程控制设备	0	70		17	17	台		----Processing machines for the distributed control system
8471.4999	----其他	0	70		17	17	台		----Other
	-子目号 8471.41 或 8471.49 所列以外的处理部件，不论是否在同一机壳内有一个或两个下列部件：存储部件、输入部件、输出部件：								-Processing units other than those of subheading 8471.41 or 8471.49, whether or not containing in the same housing one or two of the following types of unit: storage units, input units, output units:
8471.5010	---巨型机、大型机及中型机的	0	14		17	17	台	3	---Mainframes
8471.5020	---小型机的	0	14		17	17	台	3	---Mini-computers
8471.5040	---微型机的	0	70		17	17	台		---Microprocessings
8471 5040.01	含显示器和主机的微型机（不论是否在同一机壳内有一或两个存储，输入或输出部件）	0	70		17	17	台		Microprocessings including monitor and host (whether or not containing in the same housing one or two of the following types of unit: storage, input, output units)
8471 5040.90	其他的微型机的处理部件（不论是否在同一机壳内有一或两个存储，输入或输出部件）	0	70		17	17	台		Other processing parts of Microprocessings (whether or not containing in the same housing one or two of the following types of unit: storage, input or output units)
8471.5090	---其他	0	70		17	17	台		---Other
	-输入或输出部件，不论是否在同一机壳内有存储部件：								-Input or output units, whether or not containing storage units in the same housing:
8471.6040	---巨型机、大型机、中型机及小型机用终端	0	14		17	17	台		---Terminating machines for the huge computers, mainframes and minicomputers
8471.6050	---扫描仪	0	14		17	17	台		---Scanner
8471.6060	---数字化仪	0	14		17	17	台		---Digitizer
	---键盘、鼠标器：								---Keyboards, mouses:
8471.6071	----键盘	0	40		17	17	个		----Keyboards
8471.6072	----鼠标器	0	40		17	17	个		----Mouses
8471.6090	---其他	0	14		17	17	台		---Other
	-存储部件：								-Storage units:
8471.7010	---硬盘驱动器	0	14		17	17	台		---Rigid disk drivers
8471.7020	---软盘驱动器	0	14		17	17	台		---Floppy disk drivers

税则号列 Tariff Item	商品名称及备注	进口税率 最惠	普通	暂定	出口退税	增值税率	计量单位	监管条件	Article Description
8471.7030	---光盘驱动器	0	14		17	17	台		---CD drivers
8471 7030.10	具有刻录功能的光盘驱动器(自动数据处理设备的光盘驱动器)	0	14		17	17	台		CD- drives with writing function (CD- drives for automatic data processing equipments)
8471 7030.90	其他光盘驱动器(自动数据处理设备的光盘驱动器)	0	14		17	17	台		Other CD- drives (CD- drives for automatic data processing equipments)
8471.7090	---其他	0	14		17	17	台		---Other
8471.8000	-自动数据处理设备的其他部件	0	40		17	17	台		-Other units of automatic data processing machines
8471.9000	-其他	0	40		17	17	台		-Other
8471 9000.10	专用于复制的光盘刻录机(也称光盘复读机)	0	40		17	17	台		CD-burner used exclusively for copying (also called CD repeaters)
8471 9000.90	未列名的磁性或光学阅读器(包括将数据以代码形式转录的机器及处理这些数据的机器)	0	40		17	17	台		Magnetic or optical readers not elsewhere specified or included (including the machines for transcribing data in coded form and machines for processing such data)
84.72	**其他办公室用机器(例如,胶版复印机、油印机、地址印写机、自动付钞机、硬币分类、计数及包装机、削铅笔机、打洞机或订书机):**								**Other office machines(for example, hectograph or stencil duplicating machines, addressing machines, automatic banknote dispensers, coinsorting machines, coincounting or wrapping machines, pencil-sharpening machines, perforating or stapling machines):**
8472.1000	-胶版复印机、油印机	14	40		15	17	台		-Duplicating machines
	-信件分类或折叠机或信件装封机、信件开封或闭封机、粘贴或盖销邮票机:								-Machines for sorting or folding mail or for inserting mail in envelopes or bands, machines for opening, closing or sealing mail and machines for affixing or cancelling postage stamps:
8472.3010	---邮政信件分拣及封装设备	10	40		15	17	台		---Machines for sorting or banding mail
8472.3090	---其他	14	40		15	17	台		---Other
	-其他:								-Other:
8472.9010	---自动柜员机	0	40		15	17	台		---Automated teller
	---装订用机器:								---Stapling machines:
8472.9021	----打洞机	0	40		15	17	台		---Perforator
8472.9022	----订书机	0	40		15	17	台		----Stapler
8472.9029	----其他	0	40		15	17	台		----Other
8472.9030	---碎纸机	0	40		15	17	台		---Paper shrudders
8472.9040	---地址印写机及地址铭牌压印机	14	40		15	17	台		---Addressing machines and address plate embossing machines
8472.9090	---其他	0	40		15	17	台		---Other
84.73	**专用于或主要用于品目 84.69 至 84.72 所列机器的零件、附件(罩套、提箱及类似品除外):**								**Parts and accessories(other than covers, carrying cases and the like) suitable for use solely or principally with machines of headings No.84.69 to 84.72:**
8473.1000	-税号 84.69 所列机器的零件、附件	8	35		15	17	千克		-Parts and accessories of the machines of heading No.84.69
	-税号 84.70 所列机器的零件、附件:								-Parts and accessories of the machines of heading No.84.70:
8473.2100	--子目号 8470.10、8470.21 或 8470.29 所列电子计算器的零件、附件	0	50		15	17	千克		--Of the electronic calculating machines of subheading No.8470.10, 8470.21 or 8470.29
8473.2900	--其他	0	35		15	17	千克		--Other
	-税号 84.71 所列机器的零件、附件:								-Parts and accessories of the machines of heading No.84.71:
8473.3010	---子目号 8471.4110、8471.4120、8471.4910、8471.4920、8471.5010、8471.5020、8471.6090、8471.7010、8471.7020、8471.7030及8471.7090所列机	0	14		17	17	千克		---Of the machines of subheading No.8471.4110, 8471.4120, 8471.4910, 8471.4920, 8471.5010, 8471.5020, 8471.6090, 8471.7010, 8471.7020, 8471.7030 and 8471.7090

税则号列 Tariff Item	商品名称及备注	进口税率 最惠	进口税率 普通	进口税率 暂定	出口退税	增值税率	计量单位	监管条件	Article Description
	器及装置的零件、附件								
8473.3090	---其他	0	40		17	17	千克		---Other
	-税号 84.72 所列机器的零件、附件:								-Parts and accessories of the machines of heading No.84.72:
8473.4010 [暂]	---自动柜员机用出钞器	10.5	35	1	15	17	千克		---Banknote dispenser of automated teller
8473.4090	---其他	10.5	35		15	17	千克		---Other
8473 4090.01 [暂]	钞票清分机零附件	10.5	35	3	15	17	千克		Parts and accessories of banknote sorters
8473 4090.90	其他办公室用机器零附件	10.5	35		15	17	千克		Parts and accessories of other office machine
8473.5000	-同样适用于品目 84.69 至 84.72 中两个或两个以上品目所列机器的零件、附件	0	35		15	17	千克		-Parts and accessories equally suitable for use with machines of two or more of the headings No.84.69 to 84.72
84.74	**泥土、石料、矿石或其他固体(包括粉状、浆状)矿物质的分类、筛选、分离、洗涤、破碎、磨粉、混合或搅拌机器;固体矿物燃料、陶瓷坯泥、未硬化水泥、石膏材料或其他粉状、浆状矿产品的黏聚或成形机器;铸造用砂模的成形机器:**								**Machinery for sorting, screening, separating, washing, crushing, grinding, mixing or kneading earth, stone, ores or other mineral substances, in solid (including powder or paste) form; machinery for agglomerating, shaping or moulding solid mineral fuels, ceramic paste, unhardened cements, plastering materials or other mineral products in powder or paste form; machines for forming foundry moulds of sand:**
8474.1000	-分类、筛选、分离或洗涤机器	5	30		15	17	台		-Sorting, screening, separating or washing machines
	-破碎或磨粉机器:								-Crushing or grinding machines:
8474.2010	---齿辊式	5	30		15	17	台		---Toothing roller type
8474.2020	---球磨式	5	30		15	17	台		---Em-Peters type
8474.2090	---其他	5	30		15	17	台		---Other
	-混合或搅拌机器:								-Mixing or kneading machines:
8474.3100	--混凝土或砂浆混合机器	7	30		17	17	台		--Concrete or mortar mixers
8474.3200	--矿物与沥青的混合机器	7	30		17	17	台		--Machines for mixing mineral substances with bitumen
8474.3900	--其他	5	30		17	17	台		--Other
	-其他机器:								-Other machinery:
8474.8010	---辊压成型机	5	30		17	17	台		---Rolling forming machines
8474.8020	---模压成型机	5	30		17	17	台		---Moulding forming machines
8474.8090	---其他	5	30		17	17	台		---Other
8474 8090.10	纸面角线石膏板搅拌成型机	5	30		17	17	台		Mixing forming machines for paper angle line gypsum board
8474 8090.90	品目 84.74 未列名的其他机器(如矿产品的粘聚或成型机器及铸造用砂模的成型机器)	5	30		17	17	台		Other machines not specified or included in heading No. 8474 (Such as machinery for agglomerating, shaping or moulding mineral products; machines for forming foundry moulds of sand)
8474.9000	-零件	5	30		15	17	千克		-Parts
84.75	**白炽灯泡、灯管、放电灯管、电子管、闪光灯泡及类似品的封装机器;玻璃或玻璃制品的制造或热加工机器:**								**Machines for assembling electric or electronic lamps, tubes or valves or flashbulbs, in glass envelopes; machines for manufacturing or hot working glass or glassware:**
8475.1000	-白炽灯泡、灯管、放电灯管、电子管、闪光灯泡及类似品的封装机器	8	30		15	17	台		-Machines for assembling electric or electronic lamps, tubes or valves or flashbulbs, in glass envelopes
	-玻璃或玻璃制品的制造或热加工机器:								-Machines for manufacturing or hot working glass or glassware:
8475.2100	--制造光导纤维及其预制棒的机器	10	30		15	17	台		--Machines for making optical fibres and preforms thereof
	--其他:								--Other:
	---玻璃的热加工设备:								---Equipments for hot working glass or glasswares:
8475.2911	----连续式玻璃热弯炉	10	30		15	17	台		----Continuous hot bending furnaces
8475.2912	----玻璃纤维拉丝机(光纤拉丝机除外)	10	30		15	17	台		----Fiber glass winder (excluding Opticalfiber winder)

税则号列 Tariff Item	商品名称及备注	进口税率			出口退税	增值税率	计量单位	监管条件	Article Description
		最惠	普通	暂定					
8475.2919	----其他	10	30		15	17	台		----Other
8475.2990	---其他	10	30		15	17	台		---Other
8475.9000	-零件	8	30		15	17	千克		-Parts
84.76	**自动售货机（例如，出售邮票、香烟、食品或饮料的机器），包括钱币兑换机：**								**Automatic goods-vending machines（for example, postage stamp, cigarette, food or beverage machines）, including money-changing machines:**
	-饮料自动销售机:								-Automatic beverage-vending machines:
8476.2100	--装有加热或制冷装置的	14	50		15	17	台	A	--Incorporating heating or refrigerating devices
8476.2900	--其他	15	50		15	17	台	A	--Other
	-其他机器:								-Other machines:
8476.8100	--装有加热或制冷装置的	14	50		15	17	台		--Incorporating heating or refrigerating devices
8476.8900	--其他	15	50		15	17	台		--Other
8476.9000	-零件	10	50		15	17	千克		-Parts
84.77	**本章其他品目未列名的橡胶或塑料及其产品的加工机器：**								**Machinery for working rubber or plastics or for the manufacture of products from these materials, not specified or included elsewhere in this Chapter:**
	-注射机:								-Injection-moulding machines:
8477.1010	---注塑机	0	45		15	17	台		---For working plastics
8477 1010.10	用于光盘生产的精密注塑机(加工塑料的)	0	45		15	17	台	6O	Precision injection molding machines for producing compact disks (processing plastics)
8477 1010.90	其他注塑机	0	45		15	17	台		Other injection molding machines
8477.1090	---其他	0	30		15	17	台		---Other
	-挤出机:								-Extruders:
8477.2010	---塑料造粒机	5	30		15	17	台		---Plastic pelletizers
8477.2090	---其他	5	30		15	17	台		---Other
	-吹塑机:								-Blow moulding machines:
8477.3010	---挤出吹塑机	5	30		15	17	台		---Extrusion blow moulding machines
8477.3020	---注射吹塑机	5	30		15	17	台		---Injection blow moulding machines
8477.3090	---其他	5	30		15	17	台		---Other
	-真空模塑机器及其他热成型机器:								-Vacuum moulding machines and other thermoforming machines:
8477.4010	---塑料中空成型机	5	30		15	17	台		---Plastics brideg-die-forming machines
8477.4020	---塑料压延成型机	5	30		15	17	台		---Plastics calender-forming machines
8477.4090	---其他	5	30		15	17	台		---Other
	-其他模塑或成型机器:								-Other machinery for moulding or otherwise forming:
8477.5100	--用于充气轮胎模塑或翻新的机器及内胎模塑或用其他方法成型的机器	5	30		15	17	台		--For moulding or retreading pneumatic tyres or for moulding or otherwise forming inner tubes
	--其他:								--Other:
8477.5910	---三维打印机（3D打印机）	5	30		15	17	台		---3D Printer
8477.5990	---其他	5	30		15	17	台		---Other
8477.8000	-其他机器	5	30		15	17	台		-Other machinery
8477.9000	-零件	0	30		15	17	千克		-Parts
84.78	**本章其他品目未列名的烟草加工及制作机器：**								**Machinery for preparing or making up tobacco, not specified or included elsewhere in this Chapter:**
8478.1000	-机器	5	30		15	17	台	O	-Machinery
8478.9000 暂	-零件	10	30	5	15	17	千克	O	-Parts
84.79	**本章其他品目未列名的具有独立功能的机器及机械器具：**								**Machines and mechanical appliances having individual functions, not specified or included elsewhere in this chapter:**
	--公共工程用机器:								--Machinery for public works, building or the like:
	---摊铺机								---Spreading machines:
8479.1021	----沥青混凝土摊铺机	8	30		17	17	台	O	----Machines for spreading bituminous concrete
8479.1022	----稳定土摊铺机	8	30		17	17	台		----Stabilizer spreading machines
8479.1029	----其他	8	30		17	17	台	O	----Other

税则号列 Tariff Item	商品名称及备注	进口税率 最惠	进口税率 普通	进口税率 暂定	出口退税	增值税率	计量单位	监管条件	Article Description
8479.1090	---其他	8	30		17	17	台		---Other
8479.2000	-提取、加工动物油脂或植物固定油脂的机器	10	30		15	17	台	A	-Machinery for the extraction or preparation of animal or fixed vegetable fats or oils
8479.3000	-木碎料板或木纤维板的挤压机及其他木材或软木处理机	10	30		15	17	台		-Presses for the manufacture of particle board or fibre building board of wood or other ligneous materials and other machinery for treating wood or cork
8479.4000[暂]	-绳或缆的制造机器	7	30	5	15	17	台		-Rope or cable-making machines
	-未列名工业机器人:								-Industrial robots, not elsewhere specified or included:
8479.5010	---多功能工业机器人	0	20		17	17	台		---Industrial robots for multiple uses
8479.5090	---其他	0	30		17	17	台		---Other
8479 5090.10	机器人,末端操纵装置[能处理高能炸药或能抗大于 5×10^4 戈瑞(硅)辐射的]	0	30		17	17	台	3	Robots, end-control devices (capable of handling high- energy explosives or resisting radiation of more than 5×10^4 Gy (Si))
8479 5090.90	其他工业机器人(多功能工业机器人除外)	0	30		17	17	台		Other industrial robots (other than Industrial robots for multiple uses)
8479.6000	-蒸发式空气冷却器	10	30		15	17	台	A	-Evaporative air coolers
	-旅客登机(船)桥:								-Passenger boarding bridges:
8479.7100	--用于机场的	0	30		15	17	台	A	--Of a kind used in airports
8479.7900	--其他	0	30		15	17	台	A	--Other
	-其他机器及机械器具:								-Other machines and mechanical appliances:
	--处理金属的机械,包括线圈绕线机:								--For treating metal, including electric wire coil-winders:
8479.8110	---绕线机	9.5	30		15	17	台		---Filament winding machines
8479.8190	---其他	9.5	30		15	17	台		---Other
8479.8200	--混合、搅拌、轧碎、研磨、筛选、均化或乳化机器	7	30		15	17	台		--Mixing, kneading, crushing, grinding, screening, sifting, homogenizing, emulsifying or stirring machines
8479 8200.10	两用物项管制搅拌器(耐腐蚀热交换器、搅拌器用,带搅拌的发酵罐)	7	30		15	17	台	3	Blenders under sensitive items control (for corrosion-resistant heat exchangers and mixers, fermentors with stirring function)
8479 8200.90	其他混合、搅拌、轧碎、研磨机器(包括筛选、均化、乳化机器)	7	30		15	17	台		Other mixing, stirring, rolling, grinding machines (including screening, homogenizing, emulsifying machines)
	--其他:								--Other:
8479.8910	---船舶用舵机及陀螺稳定器	0	14		15	17	台		---Steering and rudder equipment or gyroscopic stabilizers for ships
8479.8920	---空气增湿器及减湿器	0	70		15	17	台		---Air humidifiers or dehumidifiers
8479.8940	---邮政用包裹、印刷品分拣设备	0	30		15	17	台	A	---Bundle and printed matter sorting machines used in post offices
8479.8950	---放射性废物压实机	0	30		15	17	台		---Presses for radioactive waste material
	---在印刷电路电路板上装配元器件的机器:								---Machines for assemblying elements on printed circuit boards:
8479.8961	----自动插件机	0	30		15	17	台	A	----Automatic plug-in machines
8479.8962	----自动贴片机	0	30		15	17	台	A	----Automatic coreslice adhering machines
8479.8969	----其他	0	30		15	17	台	A	----Other
	---其他:								----Other:
8479.8992	----自动化立体仓储设备	0	30		15	17	台	A	----Three-dimensional automatic warehouse equipment
8479.8999	----其他	0	30		15	17	台		----Other
8479 8999.10	用于光盘生产的金属母盘生产设备(具有独立功能的)	0	30		15	17	台	6AO	Metal master disk equipments for producing compact disks (with individual functions)
8479 8999.20	用于光盘生产的黏合机(具有独立功能的)	0	30		15	17	台	6AO	Bonders for producing compact disks (with with individual functions)
8479 8999.30	用于光盘生产的真空金属溅镀机(具有独立功能的)	0	30		15	17	台	6AO	Vacuum metal sputtering machines for producing compact disks (with individual functions)
8479 8999.40	保护胶涂覆机及染料层旋涂机(光盘生产用,具有独立功能的)	0	30		15	17	台	6AO	Protective rubber-coated and dye-layer spin-coating machines (for producing compact disks, with individual functions)

税则号列 Tariff Item	商品名称及备注	进口税率 最惠	普通	暂定	出口退税	增值税率	计量单位	监管条件	Article Description
8479 8999.51	等静压压力机(两用物项管制机器及机械器具)	0	30		15	17	台	3A	Isostatic pressing machine (machines and mechanical appliances under control of sensitve items)
8479 8999.52	生物反应器(两用物项管制机器及机械器具)	0	30		15	17	台	3A	Bioreactor(machines and mechanical appliances under control of sensitve items)
8479 8999.53	恒化器(两用物项管制机器及机械器具)	0	30		15	17	台	3A	Chemostat(machines and mechanical appliances under control of sensitve items)
8479 8999.54	连续灌流系统(两用物项管制机器及机械器具)	0	30		15	17	台	3A	Continuous perfusion system(machines and mechanical appliances under sensitve items control)
8479 8999.55	三坐标或多坐标联动和程控的纤维缠绕机(两用物项管制机器及机械器具)	0	30		15	17	台	3A	Three-coordinate or multi-coordinate linkage and program control filament winding machine(machines and appliances under sensitve items control
8479 8999.59	其他两用物项管制机器及机械器具	0	30		15	17	台	3A	Other machines and mechanical appliances under sensitve items control
8479 8999.60	绕线机（能卷绕直径在 75 毫米至 400 毫米、长度为 600 毫米或更长的）	0	30		15	17	台	3A	Winding machines (capable of winding the diameters of 75mm to 400mm, or the length of 600mm or more)
8479 8999.90	本章其他未列名机器及机械器具（具有独立功能的）	0	30		15	17	台	A	Machines and mechanical appliances having individual functions, not specified or included elsewhere in this Chapte
	-零件:								-Parts:
8479.9010	---船舶用舵机及陀螺稳定器用	0	14		15	17	千克		---Of the machines of subheading No.8479.8910
8479.9020	---空气增湿器及减湿器用	0	70		15	17	千克		---Of the machines of subheading No.8479.8920
8479.9090	---其他	0	20		15	17	千克		---Other
8479 9090.10	绕线机的精密芯轴(专用于税号 84798990.60 绕线机的精密芯轴)	0	20		15	17	千克	3	Precision mandrels for winding machines (exclusively used for No. 84798990.60 winding machines)
8479 9090.90	品目 84.79 所列机器的其他零件	0	20		15	17	千克		Other parts for the machines of heading No. 84.79
84.80	**金属铸造用型箱；型模底板；阳模；金属用型模（锭模除外）、硬质合金、玻璃、矿物材料、橡胶或塑料用型模：**								**Moulding boxes for metal foundry; mould bases; moulding patterns; moulds for metal（other than ingot moulds）, metal carbides, glass, mineral materials, rubber or plastics:**
8480.1000	-金属铸造用型箱	10	20		15	17	千克		-Moulding boxes for metal foundry
8480.2000	-型模底板	8	20		15	17	千克		-Mould bases
8480.3000	-阳模	10	20		15	17	千克		-Moulding patterns
	-金属、硬质合金用型模:								-Moulds for metal or metal carbides:
	--注模或压模：								--Injection or compression types
8480.4110	---压铸模	8	20		15	17	千克		---Pressure-casting moulds
8480.4120	---粉末冶金用压膜	8	20		15	17	千克		---Moulds for powder metallurgy
8480.4190	---其他	8	20		15	17	千克		---Other
8480.4900	--其他	8	20		15	17	千克		--Other
8480.5000	-玻璃用型模	8.4	20		15	17	套/千克		-Moulds for glass
8480.6000	-矿物材料用型模	8.4	20		15	17	套/千克		-Moulds for mineral materials
	-塑料或橡胶用型模:								-Moulds for rubber or plastics:
	--注模或压模:								--Injection or compression types:
8480.7110	---硫化轮胎用囊式型模	0	20		15	17	套/千克		---"Bladder" moulds for vulcanising tyres
8480.7190	---其他	0	20		15	17	套/千克		---Other
8480 7190.10	用于光盘生产的专用模具(注模或压模)	0	20		15	17	套/千克	6O	Special moulds used for producing compact disks (injection or compression types)
8480 7190.90	其他塑料或橡胶用注模或压模	0	20		15	17	套/千克		Injection or compression types for other plastic or rubber
8480.7900	--其他	5	20		15	17	套/千克		--Other
8480 7900.10	农用双壁波纹管生产线用其他模具	5	20		15	17	套/千克		Other molds for production lines of agricultural double-wall corrugated pipe
8480 7900.90	塑料或橡胶用其他型模	5	20		15	17	套/千克		Other molds for producing plastics or rubber
84.81	**用于管道、锅炉、罐、桶或类似品的龙头、旋塞、阀门及类似装**								**Taps, cocks, valves and similar appliances for pipes, boilershells, tanks, vats or the like,**

税则号列 Tariff Item	商品名称及备注	进口税率 最惠	普通	暂定	出口退税	增值税率	计量单位	监管条件	Article Description
	置，包括减压阀及恒温控制阀:								**including pressure-reducing valves and thermostatically controlled valves:**
8481.1000	-减压阀	5	30		15	17	套/千克		-Pressure-reducing valves
8481 1000.01[暂]	喷灌设备用减压阀（用于管道、锅炉、罐、桶或类似品的）	5	30	2	15	17	套/千克		Pressure reducing valves for irrigation appliance (for pipes, boilershells, tanks, vats or the like)
8481 1000.90	其他减压阀（用于管道、锅炉、罐、桶或类似品的）	5	30		15	17	套/千克		Other pressure reducing valves (for pipes, boiler-shells, tanks, vats or the like)
	-油压或气压传动阀:								-Valves for oleohydraulic or pneumatic transmissions:
8481.2010	---油压的	5	30		15	17	套/千克		---For oleohydraulic transmissions
8481.2020	---气压的	5	30		15	17	套/千克		---For pneumatic transmissions
8481.3000[暂]	-止回阀	5	30	3	15	17	套/千克		-Check（nonreturn）valves
8481.4000	-安全阀或溢流阀	5	30		15	17	套/千克		-Safety or relief valves
	-其他器具:								-Other appliances:
	---换向阀:								---Directional control valves:
8481.8021	----电磁式	7	30		15	17	套/千克		----Electromagnetic
8481 8021.10	两用物项管制的电磁式换向阀	7	30		15	17	套/千克	3	Electromagnetic directional control valve under control of sensitive items
8481 8021.90	其他电磁式换向阀(用于管道、锅炉、罐、桶或类似品的)	7	30		15	17	套/千克		Other electromagnetic directional control valve for pipes, boiler, shells vats or the like
8481.8029	----其他	7	30		15	17	套/千克		----Other
8481 8029.10	两用物项管制的其他换向阀	7	30		15	17	套/千克	3	Other directional control valve under sensitive items control
8481 8029.90	其他换向阀(用于管道、锅炉、罐、桶或类似品的)	7	30		15	17	套/千克		Other directional control valve for pipes, boiler, shells vats or the like
	---流量阀								---Flow control valves:
8481.8031	----电子膨胀阀	7	30		15	17	套/千克		----Electronic expansion valves
8481 8031.10	两用物项管制的电子膨胀流量阀	7	30		15	17	套/千克	3	Electronic expansion flow valve under sensitive items control
8481 8031.90	其他电子膨胀流量阀(用于管道、锅炉、罐、桶或类似品的)	7	30		15	17	套/千克		Other electronic expansion flow valve for pipes, boiler, shells vats or the like
8481.8039	----其他	7	30		15	17	套/千克		----Other
8481 8039.10	两用物项管制的其他流量阀	7	30		15	17	套/千克	3	Other flow valve under sensitive items control
8481 8039.90	其他流量阀(用于管道、锅炉、罐、桶或类似品的)	7	30		15	17	套/千克		Other flow valve for pipes, boiler, shells vats or the like
8481.8040[暂]	---其他阀门	7	30	3	15	17	套/千克		---Other valves
8481 8040.10[暂]	两用物项管制的其他阀门	7	30	3	15	17	套/千克	3	Other valves under sensitive items control
8481 8040.90[暂]	其他阀门(用于管道、锅炉、罐、桶或类似品的)	7	30	3	15	17	套/千克		Other valves (for pipes, boilers, tanks, barrels or the like)
8481.8090	---其他	5	50		15	17	套/千克		---Other
	-零件:								---Parts:
8481.9010[暂]	---阀门用	8	30	4	15	17	千克		---Of valves
8481.9090	---其他	8	50		15	17	千克		---Other
84.82	**滚动轴承:**								**Ball or roller bearings:**
	-滚珠轴承:								-Ball bearings
8482.1010	---调心球轴承	8	20		15	17	套		---Self-aliging ball bearing
8482.1020	---深沟球轴承	8	20		15	17	套		---Deep groove ball bearing
8482.1030	---角接触轴承	8	20		15	17	套		---Angular contact ball bearing
8482.1040	---推力球轴承	8	20		15	17	套		---Thrust ball bearing
8482.1090	---其他	8	20		15	17	套		---Other
8482.2000	-锥形滚子轴承，包括锥形滚子组件	8	20		15	17	套		-Tapered roller bearings, including cone and tapered roller assemblies
8482.3000[暂]	-鼓形滚子轴承	8	20	6	15	17	套		-Spherical roller bearings
8482.4000[暂]	-滚针轴承	8	20	6	15	17	套		-Needle roller bearings
8482.5000	-其他圆柱形滚子轴承:	8	20		15	17	套		-Other cylindrical roller bearings
8482 5000.01[暂]	三环偏心滚动轴承	8	20	4	15	17	套		Three row cylindrical roller bearings
8482 5000.90	其他圆柱形滚子轴承	8	20		15	17	套		Other cylindrical roller bearings
8482.8000	-其他，包括球、柱混合轴承	8	20		15	17	套		-Other, including combined ball/roller bearings
	-零件:								-Parts:

税则号列 Tariff Item	商品名称及备注	进口税率 最惠	普通	暂定	出口退税	增值税率	计量单位	监管条件	Article Description
8482.9100 暂	--滚珠、滚针及滚柱	8	20	6	15	17	千克		--Balls, needles and rollers
8482.9900 暂	--其他	6	20	3	15	17	千克		--Other
84.83	**传动轴（包括凸轮轴及曲柄轴）及曲柄；轴承座及滑动轴承；齿轮及齿轮传动装置；滚珠或滚子螺杆传动装置；齿轮箱及其他变速装置，包括扭矩变换器；飞轮及滑轮，包括滑轮组；离合器及联轴器（包括万向节）：**								**Transmission shafts（including cam shafts and crank shafts）and cranks;bearing housings and plain shaft bearings; gears and gearing ball or roller screws; gear boxes and other speed changers, including torque converters; flywheels and pulleys, including pulley blocks; clutches and shaft couplings （including universal joints）:**
	-传动轴(包括凸轮轴及曲柄轴)及曲柄:								-Transmission shafts（including cam shafts and crank shafts）and cranks:
	---船舶用传动轴								---Transmission shafts for ships
8483.1011	----柴油机曲轴	6	14		17	17	个		----Crank shafts of diesel engine
8483.1019	----其他	6	14		17	17	个		----Other
8483.1090	---其他	6	30		17	17	个		---Other
8483.2000	-装有滚珠或滚子轴承的轴承座	6	30		15	17	个		-Bearing housings, incorporating ball or roller bearings
8483.3000 暂	-未装有滚珠或滚子轴承的轴承座；滑动轴承	6	30	3	15	17	个		-Bearing housings, not incorporating ball or roller bearings; plain shaft bearings
8483 3000.10 暂	磁悬浮轴承（轴承组合件，由悬浮在充满阻尼介质的环形磁铁组成）	6	30	3	15	17	个	3	Magnetic bearing (bearing assembly, consisting of the ring magnets suspended in damping medium)
8483 3000.20 暂	轴承/阻尼器（安装在阻尼器上的具有枢轴/盖的轴承）	6	30	3	15	17	个	3	Bearings / dampers (installed on the bearing with a pivot / bearing cover on the damper)
8483 3000.90 暂	其他未装有滚珠或滚子轴承的轴承座；其他滑动轴承	6	30	3	15	17	个		Other bearing housings, not incorporating ball or roller bearings; other plain shaft bearings
	-齿轮及齿轮传动装置，但单独进口或出口的带齿的轮、链轮及其他传动元件除外；滚珠或滚子螺杆传动装置；齿轮箱及其他变速装置，包括扭矩变换器:								-Gears and gearing, other than toothed wheels, chain sprockets and other transmission elements presented separately; ball or roller screws; gear boxes and other speed changers, including torque converters:
8483.4010	---滚子螺杆传动装置	8	30		15	17	个		---Roller Screws
8483.4020	---行星齿轮减速器	8	30		15	17	个		---Planet decelerators
8483 4020.01 暂	磨煤机用行星齿轮减速器(由螺旋伞齿轮加行星齿轮二级立式减速机构组成,转盘外圆直径为1300～2400毫米)	8	30	2	15	17	个		Planet decelerators for coal-grinding machines (consisting of a spiral bevel gear and a two-stage vertical planetary gear reducing structure, rotary cylindrical diameter is 1,300 ~ 2,400mm)
8483 4020.90	其他行星齿轮减速器	8	30		15	17	个		Other planet decelerators
8483.4090	---其他	8	30		17	17	个		---Other
8483.5000	-飞轮及滑轮，包括滑轮组	8	30		15	17	个		-Flywheels and pulleys, including pulley blocks
8483.6000	-离合器及联轴器(包括万向节)	8	30		17	17	个		-Clutches and shaft couplings（including universal joints）
8483 6000.01 暂	压力机用组合式湿式离合/制动器（离合扭矩为60KNM～300KNM，制动扭矩为30KNM～100KNM）	8	30	4	17	17	个		Combined wet clutches/brakes for presses (clutch torque is 60-300KNM, and brake torque 30-100KNM)
8483 6000.90	离合器及联轴器（包括万向节）	8	30		17	17	个		Clutches and shaft couplings (including universal joints）
8483.9000	-单独报验的带齿的轮、链轮及其他传动元件；零件	8	30		17	17	千克		-Toothed wheels, chain sprockets and other transmission elements presented separately; parts
84.84	**密封垫或类似接合衬垫，用金属片与其他材料制成或用双层或多层金属片制成；成套或各种不同材料的密封垫或类似接合衬垫，装于袋、套或类似包装内；机械密封件:**								**Gaskets and similar joints of metal sheeting combined with other material or of two or more layers of metal; sets or assortments of gaskets and similar joints, dissimilar in composition, put up in pouches, envelopes or similar packings; mechanical seals:**
8484.1000 暂	-密封垫或类似接合衬垫，用金属片与其他材料制成或用双层及多	8	30	5	17	17	千克		-Gaskets and similar joints of metal sheeting combined with other material or of two or more layers

税则号列 Tariff Item	商品名称及备注	进口税率			出口退税	增值税率	计量单位	监管条件	Article Description
		最惠	普通	暂定					
	层金属片制成								of metal
8484.2000[暂]	-机械密封件	8	30	5		17	千克		-Mechanical seals
8484 2000.10[暂]	耐 UF_6 腐蚀的转动轴封（专门设计的真空密封装置，缓冲气体泄漏率 1000cm³/min）	8	30	5	17	17	千克	3	UF_6-resistant rotary shaft gaskets (specially designed vacuum airtight devices, the buffer gas leakage rate 1,000cm³/min)
8484 2000.20[暂]	转动轴封（专门设计的带有密封式进气口和出气口的转动轴封）	8	30	5	17	17	千克	3	Rotary shaft gaskets (specially designed shaft gaskets with an airtight inlet and outlet)
8484 2000.30[暂]	MLIS 用转动轴封（专门设计的带密封进气口和出气口的转动轴封）	8	30	5	15	17	千克	3	Rotary shaft gaskets for MLIS (specially designed shaft gaskets with an airtight inlet and outlet)
8484 2000.90[暂]	其他机械密封件	8	30	5	15	17	千克		Other mechanical seals
8484.9000[暂]	-其他	8	30	5	15	17	千克		-Other
84.86	**专用于或主要用于制造半导体单晶柱或晶圆、半导体器件、集成电路或平板显示器的机器及装置；本章注释九（三）规定的机器及装置；零件及附件：**								**Machines and apparatus of a kind used solely or principally for the manufacture of semiconductor boules or wafers, semiconductor devices, electronic integrated circuits or flat panel displays; machines and apparatus specified in note 9（c）to this chapter;parts and accessories:**
	-制造单晶柱或圆片用的机器及装置:								-Machines and apparatus for the manufacture of boules or wafers:
8486.1010	---利用温度变化处理单晶硅的机器及装置	0	30		17	17	台		---Machines and apparatus for the treatment of monocrystalline sillicon by a process involving a change of temperature
8486.1020	---研磨设备	0	30		17	17	台		---Grinding machines
8486.1030	---切割设备	0	30		17	17	台		---Sawing machines
8486.1040	---化学机械抛光设备（CMP）	0	30		17	17	台		---Chemical mechanical polishers（CMP）
8486.1090	---其他	0	30		17	17	台		---Other
	-制造半导体器件或集成电路用的机器及装置:								-Machines and apparatus for the manufacture of semiconductor devices or of electronic integrated circuis:
8486.2010	---氧化、扩散、退火及其他热处理设备	0	30		17	17	台		---Oxidation, diffusion, annealing and other heat treatment equipment
	---薄膜沉积设备:								---Film deposition equipment:
8486.2021	----化学气相沉积装置（CVD）	0	30		17	17	台		----Chemical Vapour Deposition（CVD）equipment
8486.2022	----物理气相沉积装置（PVD）	0	30		17	17	台		----Physical Vapour Deposition（PVD）equipment
8486.2029	----其他	0	30		17	17	台		----Other
	---将电路图投影或绘制到感光半导体材料上的装置:								---Apparatus for the projection or drawing of circuit patterns on sensitized semiconductor materials:
8486.2031	----分步重复光刻机（步进光刻机）	0	100		17	17	台		----Step and repeat aligners
8486.2039	----其他	0	100		17	17	台		----Other
	---刻蚀及剥离设备:								---Etching and stripping equipment:
8486.2041	----等离子体干法刻蚀机	0	30		17	17	台		----Dry plasma etching
8486.2049	----其他	0	30		17	17	台		----Other
8486.2050	---离子注入机	0	11		17	17	台		---Ion implanters
8486.2090	---其他	0	30		17	17	台		---Other
	-制造平板显示器用的机器及装置:								-Machines and apparatus for the manufacture of flat panel displays:
8486.3010	---扩散、氧化、退火及其他热处理设备	0	30		17	17	台		---Oxidation, diffusion, annealing and other heat treatment equipment
	---薄膜沉积设备:								---Film deposition equipment:
8486.3021	----化学气相沉积设备（CVD）	0	30		17	17	台		----Chemical Vapour Deposition（CVD）equipment
8486.3022	----物理气相沉积设备（PVD）	0	30		17	17	台		----Physical Vapour Deposition （PVD）equipment
8486.3029	----其他	0	30		17	17	台		----Other
	---将电路图投影或绘制到感光半导体材料上的装置:								---Apparatus for the projection or drawing of circuit patterns on sensitized semiconductor materials:

税则号列 Tariff Item	商品名称及备注	进口税率 最惠	普通	暂定	出口退税	增值税率	计量单位	监管条件	Article Description
8486.3031	----分布重复光刻机	0	100		17	17	台		----Step and repeat aligners
8486.3039	----其他	0	100		17	17	台		----Other
	---湿法蚀刻、显影、剥离、清洗装置:								---Apparatus for wet etching, developing, stripping or cleaning:
8486.3041 暂	----超声波清洗装置	10	30	5	17	17	台		----Ultrasonic apparatus for cleaning
8486.3049	----其他	0	30		17	17	台		---Other
8486.3090	---其他	0	30		17	17	台		----Other
	-本章注释九（三）规定的机器及装置:								-Machines and apparatus specified in Note 9（c）to this Chapter:
8486.4010	---主要用于或专用于制作和修复掩膜版(mask)或投影掩膜版(reticle)的装置	0	70		17	17	台		---Apparatus solely or principally of a kind used for the manufacture or repair of masks and reticles
	---主要用于或专用于装配与封装半导体器件或集成电路的设备:								---Machines solely or principally of a kind used for assembling or encapsulating semiconductor devices or electronic integrated circuits:
8486.4021	----塑封机	5	30		17	17	台		----Plastics encapsulating machines
8486.4022	----引线键合装置	8	30		17	17	台		----Wire bonders
8486 4022.01 暂	全自动铝丝焊接机(主要用于或专用于装配与封装半导体器件和集成电路的设备)	8	30	6	17	17	台		Automatic welders for aluminum wire (solely or principally used for assembling and encapsulating semiconductor devices and integrated circuit devices)
8486 4022.90	其他引线键合装置(主要用于或专用于装配与封装半导体器件和集成电路的设备)	8	30		17	17	台		Other wire bonding device (solely or principally used for assembling and encapsulating semiconductor devices and integrated circuit devices)
8486.4029	----其他	0	17		17	17	台		----Other
	---主要用于或专用于升降、装卸、搬运单晶柱、晶圆、半导体器件、集成电路或平板显示器的装置:								---Apparatus solely or principally of a kind used for lifting, handling, loading or unloading of boules, wafers, semiconductor devices, electronic integrated circuits and flat panel displays:
8486.4031	----集成电路工厂专用的自动搬运机器人	0	20		17	17	台		----Automated material handling machines solely or principally of a kind used in the electronic integrated circuits factories
8486.4039	----其他	5	30		17	17	台		----Other
	-零件及附件:								-Parts and accessories:
8486.9010	---升降、搬运、装卸机器用(自动搬运设备用除外)	5	30		17	17	千克		---Of machines for lifting, handling, loading or unloading（other than automated material handling machines ）
8486.9020	---引线键合装置用	6	30		17	17	千克		---Of wire bonders
	---其他:								---Other:
8486.9091	----带背板的溅射靶材组件	0	17		17	17	千克		----Componets of sputtering target material with backing
8486.9099	----其他	0	17		17	17	千克		----Other
84.87	**本章其他品目未列名的机器零件,不具有电气接插件、绝缘体、线圈、触点或其他电气器材特征的:**								**Machinery parts, not containing electrical connectors insulators, coils, contacts or other electrical features, not specified or included elsewhere in this Chapter:**
8487.1000	-船用推进器及桨叶	6	14		17	17	千克		-Ships' or boats' propellers and blades therefor
8487.9000	-其他	8	30		15	17	千克		-Other

第八十五章
电机、电气设备及其零件；录音机及放声机、电视图像、声音的录制和重放设备及其零件、附件

注释：

一、本章不包括：

（一）电暖的毯子、褥子、足套及类似品，电暖的衣服、靴、鞋、耳套或其他供人穿戴的电暖物品；

（二）品目 70.11 的玻璃制品；

（三）品目 84.86 的机器及装置；

（四）用于医疗、外科、牙科或兽医的真空设备（品目 90.18）；或

（五）第九十四章的电热家具。

二、品目 85.01 至 85.04 不适用于品目 85.11、85.12、85.40、85.41 或 85.42 的货品。

但金属槽汞弧整流器仍归入品目 85.04。

三、品目 85.09 仅包括通常供家用的下列电动器具：

（一）任何重量的地板打蜡机、食品研磨机及食品搅拌器，水果或蔬菜的榨汁器；

（二）重量不超过 20 千克的其他机器。

但该品目不适用于风机、风扇或装有风扇的通风罩及循环气罩（不论是否装有过滤器）（品目 84.14）、离心干衣机（品目 84.21）、洗碟机（品目 84.22）、家用洗衣机（品目 84.50）、滚筒式或其他形式的熨烫机器（品目 84.20 或 84.51）、缝纫机（品目 84.52）、电剪子（品目 84.67）或电热器具（品目 85.16）。

四、品目 85.23 所称：

（一）“固态、非易失性存储器件”（例如，“闪存卡”或“电子闪存卡”）是指带有接口的存储器件，其在同一壳体内包含一个或多个闪存（FLASH E^2PROM），以集成电路的形式装配在一块印刷电路板上。它们可以包括一个集成电路形式的控制器及多个分立无源元件，例如，电容器及电阻器；

（二）所称“智能卡”是指装有一个或多个集成电路[微处理器、随机存取存储器（RAM）或只读存储器（ROM）]芯片的卡。这些卡可带有触点、磁条或嵌入式天线，但不包含任何其他有源或无源电路元件。

五、品目 85.34 所称“印刷电路”，是指采用各种印制方法（例如，压印、覆镀、腐蚀）或采用“膜电路”工艺，将导线、接点或其他印制元件（例如，电感器、电阻器、电容器）按预定的图形单

Chapter 85
Electrical machinery and equipment and parts thereof; sound recorders and reproducers, television image and sound recorders and reproducers,and parts and accessories of such articles

Chapter Notes:

1. This Chapter does not cover:

(a) Electrically warmed blankets, bed pads, foot-muffs or the like; electrically warmed clothing, footwear or ear pads or other electrically warmed articles worn on or about the person;

(b) Articles of glass of heading 70.11;

(c) Machines and apparatus of heading 84.86;

(c) Vacuum apparatus of a kind used in medical, surgical, dental or veterinary sciences (heading 90.18); or

(e) Electrically heated furniture of Chapter 94.

2. Headings 85.01 to 85.04 do not apply to goods described in heading 85.11, 85.12, 85.40, 85.41 or 85.42.

However, metal tank mercury arc rectifiers remain classified in heading 85.04.

3. Heading 85.09 covers only the following electro-mechanical machines of the kind commonly used for domestic purposes:

(a) Floor polishers, food grinders and mixers, and fruit or vegetable juice extractors, of any weight;

(b) Other machines provided the weight of such machines does not exceed 20kg.

The heading does not, however, apply to fans or ventilating or recycling hoods incorporating a fan, whether or not fitted with filters (heading 84.14), centrifugal clothes-dryers (heading 84.21), dish washing machines (heading 84.22), household washing machines (heading 84.50), roller or other ironing machines (heading 84.20 or 84.51), sewing machines (heading84.52), electric scissors (heading 84.67) or to electrothermic appliances (heading 85.16).

4. For the purposes of heading 85.23:

(a) "Solid-state non-volatile storage devices" (for example, "flash memory cards" or "flash electronic storage cards") are storage devices with a connecting socket, comprising in the same housing one or more flash memories (for example, FLASH E^2PROM) in the form of integrated circuits mounted on a printed circuit board. They may include a controller in the form of an integrated circuit and discrete passive components, such as capacitors and resistors;

(b) The term "smart cards" means cards which have embedded in them one or more electronic integrated circuits[a microprocessor, random access memory (RAM) or read-only memory (ROM)]in the form of chips. These cards may contain contacts, a magnetic stripe or an embedded antenna but do not contain any other active or passive circuit elements.

5. For the purposes of heading 85.34 "printed circuits" are circuits obtained by forming on an insulating base, by any printing process (for example, embossing, plating-up, etching) or by the "film circuit" technique, conductor elements, contacts or other printed components (for example, inductances,

独或互相连接地印制在绝缘基片上的电路，但能够产生、整流、调制或放大电信号的元件（例如，半导体元件）除外。

所称“印刷电路”，不包括装有非印制元件的电路，也不包括单个的分立式电阻器、电容器及电感器。但印刷电路可配有非经印刷的连接元件。用同样工艺制得的无源元件及有源元件组成的薄膜电路或厚膜电路应归入品目 85.42。

六、品目 85.36 所称“光导纤维、光导纤维束或光缆用连接器”，是指在有线数字通讯设备中，简单机械地把光纤端部相连成一线的连接器。它们不具备诸如对信号进行放大、再生或修正等其他功能。

七、品目 85.37 不包括电视接收机或其他电气设备用的无绳红外遥控器（品目 85.43）。

八、品目 85.41 及 85.42 所称：

（一）“二极管、晶体管及类似的半导体器件”，是指那些依靠外加电场引起电阻率的变化而进行工作的半导体器件。

（二）“集成电路”，是指：

1．单片集成电路，即电路元件（二极管、晶体管、电阻器、电容器、电感器等）主要整体制作在一片半导体材料或化合物半导体材料（例如，掺杂硅、砷化镓、硅锗或磷化铟）基片的表面，并不可分割地连接在一起的电路；

2．混合集成电路，即通过薄膜或厚膜工艺制得的无源元件（电阻器、电容器、电感器等）和通过半导体工艺制得的有源元件（二极管、晶体管、单片集成电路等）用互连或连接线实际上不可分割地组合在同一绝缘基片（玻璃、陶瓷等）上的电路。这种电路也可包括分立元件；

3．多芯片集成电路是由两个或多个单片集成电路实际上不可分割地组合在一片或多片绝缘基片上构成的电路，不论是否带有引线框架，但不带有其他有源或无源的电路元件。

本注释所述物品在归类时，即使本税则其他品目涉及上述物品，尤其是物品的功能，仍应优先考虑归入品目 85.41 及 85.42，但涉及品目 85.23 的情况除外。

九、品目 85.48 所称“废原电池、废原电池组及废蓄电池”，是指因破损、拆解、耗尽或其他原因而不能再使用，也不能再充电的电池。

子目注释：

子目 8527.12 仅包括有内置放大器但无内置扬声器

resistors, capacitors) alone or interconnected according to a preestablished pattern, other than elements which can produce, rectify, modulate or amplify an electrical signal（for example, semiconductor elements）.

The expression “printed circuits” does not cover circuits combined with elements other than those obtained during the printing process, nor does it cover individual, discrete resistors, capacitors or inductances.Printed circuits may,however be fitted with non-printed connecting elements.

Thin-or-thick-film circuits comprising passive and active elements obtained during the same technological process are to be classified in heading 85.42.

6. For the purpose of heading 85.36, “connectors for optical fibres,optical fibre bundles or cables” means connectors that simply mechanically align optical fibres end to end in a digital line system. They perform no other function, such as the amplification, regeneration or modification of a signal.

7. Heading 85.37 dose not include cordless infrared devices for the remote control of television receivers or other electrical equipment（heading 85.43）.

8. For the purposes of headings 85.41 and 85.42:

（a）“Diodes，transistors and similar semiconductor devices” are semiconductor devices the operation of which depends on variations in resistivity on the application of an electric field;

（b）“Electronic integrated circuits” are:

（ i ）Monolithic integrated circuits in which the circuit elements（diodes, transistors, resistors, capacitors,inductances, etc.）are created in the mass（essentially）and on the surface of a semiconductor or compound semiconductor material（for example, doped silicon, gallium arsenide, silicon germanium, indium phosphide）and are inseparably associated;

（ii）Hybrid integrated circuits in which passive elements（resistors, capacitors, inductances, etc.）, obtained by thin-or-thick-film technology, and active elements（diodes, transistors, monolithic integrated circuits, etc.）, obtained by semiconductor technology, are combined to all intents and purposes indivisibly, by interconnections or interconnecting cables, on a single insulating substrate（glass, ceramic, etc.）. These circuits may also include discrete components;

（iii）Multichip integrated circuits consisting of two or more interconnected monolithic integrated circuits combined to all intents and purposes indivisibly, whether or not on one or more insulating substrates, with or without leadframes, but with no other active or passive circuit elements.

For the classification of the articles defined in this Note, headings 85.41 and 85.42 shall take precedence over any other heading in the Nomenclature,except in the case of heading 85.23, which might cover them by reference to, in particular, their function.

9. For the purposes of heading 85.48, “spent primary cells, spent primary batteries and spent electric accumulators” are those which are neither usable as such because of breakage, cutting-up,wear or other reasons, nor capable of being recharged.

Subheading Notes:

Subheadings 8527.12 covers only cassette-players with built-in amplifier,

的盒式磁带放声机，它不需外接电源即能工作，且外型尺寸不超过170毫米×100毫米×45毫米。

without built-in loudspeaker, capable of operating without an external source of electric power and the dimensions of which do not exceed 170mm×100mm×45mm.

税则号列 Tariff Item	商品名称及备注	进口税率			出口退税	增值税率	计量单位	监管条件	Article Description
		最惠	普通	暂定					
85.01	电动机及发电机(不包括发电机组)：								**Electric motors and generators（excluding generating sets）:**
	-输出功率不超过37.5瓦的电动机:								-Motors of an output not exceeding 37.5W:
8501.1010	---玩具用	24.5	80		17	17	台		---For use in toys
	---其他:								---Other:
8501.1091	----微电机,机座尺寸在20毫米及以上，但不超过39毫米	9	70		17	17	台		----Micromotors with a housing size of 20mm or more but not exceeding 39mm
8501 1091.01[暂]	激光视盘机机芯精密微型电机(1瓦≤功率≤18瓦，20mm≤直径≤30mm)	9	70	5	17	17	台		Precision micromotors for the movement of laser disc players (20mm≤diameter≤30mm;1w≤power≤18w)
8501 1091.02[暂]	摄像机、摄录一体机用精密微型电机(0.5 瓦≤功率≤10 瓦，20mm≤直径≤39mm)	9	70	5	17	17	台		Precision micromotors for cameras or video camera recorders(20mm≤diameter≤39mm;0.5w≤power≤10w)
8501 1091.90	其他机座最大尺寸在20-39毫米微电机（输出功率不超过37.5瓦）	9	70		17	17	台		Other kinds of micromotors with frames sized between 20mm and 39mm (power output: no more than 37.5W)
8501.1099	----其他	9	35		17	17	台		----Other
8501 1099.01[暂]	功率≤0.5 瓦非用于激光视盘机机芯的微型电机(圆柱形直径≤6毫米，高≤25毫米；扁圆型直径≤15毫米，厚度≤5毫米)	9	35	5	17	17	台		Micromotors not for the movement of laser disc players (power: ≤0.5W,cylindrical diameter: ≤6mm; height:≤25mm; oblate diameter: ≤15mm; thickness: ≤5mm)
8501 1099.02[暂]	激光视盘机机芯用精密微型电机(0.5瓦≤功率≤2瓦，5mm≤直径<20mm)	9	35	5	17	17	台		Precision micro-motor for the movement of camera, camcorder, laser disc player movement with (0.5 watts ≤ power ≤ 2 watts, 5mm ≤ diameter <20mm)
8501 1099.03[暂]	摄像机、摄录一体机用精密微型电机(0.5瓦≤功率≤10瓦,5mm≤直径<20mm 或 39mm<直径≤40mm)	9	35	5	17	17	台		Precision micro-motor for the movement of camera, camcorder, laser disc player movement with (0.5 watts ≤ power ≤ 10 watts, 39mm ≤ diameter <40mm)
8501 1099.90	其他微电机（输出功率不超过37.5瓦）	9	35		17	17	台		Other kinds of micro motors' (power output: no more than 37.5W)
8501.2000	-交直流两用电动机，输出功率超过37.5瓦	12	35		17	17	台		-Universal AC/DC motors of an output exceeding 37.5 W
	-其他直流电动机；直流发电机:								-Other DC motors; DC generators:
8501.3100	--输出功率不超过750瓦	12	35		17	17	台		--Of an output not exceeding 750W
8501.3200	--输出功率超过750瓦,但不超过75千瓦	10	35		17	17	台		--Of an output exceeding 750W but not exceeding 75kW
8501.3300	--输出功率超过75千瓦，但不超过375千瓦	5	35		17	17	台		--Of an output exceeding 75kW but not exceeding 375kW
8501.3400	--输出功率超过375千瓦	12	35		17	17	台		--Of an output exceeding 375kW
8501.4000	-其他单相交流电动机	12	35		17	17	台		-Other AC motors, single-phase
	-其他多相交流电动机:								-Other AC motors, multi-phase:
8501.5100	--输出功率不超过750瓦	5	35		17	17	台		--Of an output not exceeding 750W
8501 5100.10	发电机（功率≥40瓦特，频率600-2000赫兹，谐波畸变低于10%等）	5	35		17	17	台	3	Generator (power: ≥40W; frequency: 600-2000HZ; harmonic distortion rate: <10%, etc.)
8501 5100.90	其他输出功率≤750瓦多相交流电动机	5	35		17	17	台		Others' power output≤750W; multi-phase AC motors
8501.5200	--输出功率超过750瓦,但不超过75千瓦	10	35		17	17	台		--Of an output exceeding 750W but not exceeding 75KW
8501.5300	--输出功率超过75千瓦	12	35		17	17	台		--Of an output exceeding 75KW
8501 5300.01[暂]	高速电力机车交流异步牵引电	12	35	3	17	17	台		Asynchronous AC traction motor for electric express

税则号列 Tariff Item	商品名称及备注	进口税率 最惠	进口税率 普通	进口税率 暂定	出口退税	增值税率	计量单位	监管条件	Article Description
	动机[用于(200千米/小时)电力机车]								locomotive (for electric locomotives with the speed of 200KM/h)
8501 5300.90	其他功率>75千瓦多相交流电动机	12	35		17	17	台		Others' power:>75KW; multi-phase AC motors
	-交流发电机:								-AC generators (alternators):
8501.6100	--输出功率不超过75千伏安	5	30		17	17	台/千瓦		--Of an output not exceeding 75KVA
8501.6200	--输出功率超过75千伏安,但不超过375千伏安	12	30		17	17	台/千瓦		--Of an output exceeding 75KVA but not exceeding 375KVA
8501.6300	--输出功率超过375千伏安,但不超过750千伏安	12	30		17	17	台/千瓦		---Of an output exceeding 375KVA but not exceeding 750KVA
	--输出功率超过750千伏安:								--Of an output exceeding 750KVA:
8501.6410	---输出功率超过750千伏安,但不超过350兆伏安	10	30		17	17	台/千瓦	O	---Of an output exceeding 750KVA but not exceeding 350MVA
8501.6420	---输出功率超过350兆伏安,但不超过665兆伏安	5.8	14		17	17	台/千瓦	O	---Of an output exceeding 350MVA but not exceeding 665MVA
8501.6430	---输出功率超过665兆伏安	6	11		17	17	台/千瓦	O	---Of an output exceeding 665MVA
85.02	**发电机组及旋转式变流机:**								**Electric generating sets and rotary converters:**
	-装有压燃式活塞内燃发动机(柴油或半柴油发动机)的发电机组:								-Generating sets with compression-ignition internal combustion piston engines (diesel or semi-diesel engines):
8502.1100	--输出功率不超过75千伏安	10	45		17	17	台/千瓦		--Of an output not exceeding 75KVA
8502.1200	--输出功率超过75千伏安,但不超过375千伏安	10	45		17	17	台/千瓦	O	--Of an output exceeding 75KVA but not exceeding 375KVA
	--输出功率超过375千伏安:								--Of an output exceeding 375KVA:
8502.1310	---输出功率超过375千伏安,但不超过2兆伏安	10	45		17	17	台/千瓦	O	---Of an output exceeding 375KVA but not exceeding 2MVA
8502.1320	---输出功率超过2兆伏安	10	30		17	17	台/千瓦	O	---Of an output exceeding 2MVA
8502.2000	-装有点燃式活塞内燃发动机的发电机组	10	45		17	17	台/千瓦		-Generating sets with spark-ignition internal combustion piston engines
	-其他发电机组:								-Other generating sets:
8502.3100	--风力驱动的	8	30		17	17	台/千瓦		--Wind-powered
8502.3900	--其他	10	30		17	17	台/千瓦		--Other
8502.4000	-旋转式变流机	10	30		17	17	台		-Electric rotary converters
85.03	**专用于或主要用于品目85.01或85.02所列机器的零件:**								**Parts suitable for use solely or principally with the machines of heading No.85.01 or 85.02:**
8503.0010	---子目号8501.1010及8501.1091所列电动机用	12	70		17	17	千克		---Of the motors of subheading No.8501.1010 or 8501.1091
8503.0020	---子目号8501.6420及8501.6430所列发电机用	3	11		17	17	千克		---Of the generators of subheading No.8501.6420 or 8501.6430
8503.0030[暂]	---子目号8502.3100所列发电机组用	3	30	1	17	17	千克		---Of the generating sets of subheading No.8502.3100
8503.0090	---其他	8	30		17	17	千克		---Other
8503 0090.10	电动机定子(用于真空中频率600~2000赫兹、功率50~1000伏安条件下)	8	30		17	17	千克	3	Motor stator (used when the frequency is between 600-2000Hz and power between 50-1000VA in vacuum)
8503 0090.90	其他电动机、发电机(组)零件	8	30		17	17	千克		Other kinds of motors and motor (set) parts
85.04	**变压器、静止式变流器(例如,整流器)及电感器:**								**Electrical transformers, static converters (for example, rectifiers) and inductors:**
	-放电灯或放电管用镇流器:								-Ballasts for discharge lamps or tubes:
8504.1010	---电子镇流器	10	35		17	17	个		---Electronic ballats
8504.1090	---其他	10	35		17	17	个		---Other
	-液体介质变压器:								-Liquid dielectric transformers:
8504.2100	--额定容量不超过650千伏安	10.5	50		17	17	个		--Having a power handling capacity not exceeding 650KVA
8504.2200	--额定容量超过650千伏安,但不超过10兆伏安	12.6	50		17	17	个		--Having a power handling capacity exceeding 650KVA but not exceeding 10MVA

税则号列 Tariff Item	商品名称及备注	进口税率 最惠	普通	暂定	出口退税	增值税率	计量单位	监管条件	Article Description
	--额定容量超过10兆伏安:								--Having a power handling capacity exceeding 10MVA:
	---额定容量超过10兆伏安,但小于400兆伏安:								---Having a power handling capacity exceeding 10MVA but less than 400MVA:
8504.2311	----额定容量超过10兆伏安,但小于220兆伏安	10	50		17	17	个		----Having a power handling capacity exceeding 10MVA but less than 220 MVA
8504.2312	----额定容量在220兆伏安及以上,但小于330兆伏安	10	50		17	17	个		----Having a power handling capacity exceeding 220MVA but less than 330MVA
8504.2313	----额定容量在330兆伏安及以上,但小于400兆伏安	10	50		17	17	个		----Having a power handling capacity exceeding 330MVA but less than 400 MVA
	---额定容量在400兆伏安及以上:								---Having a power handling capacity of 400MVA or more:
8504.2321	----额定容量在400兆伏安及以上,但小于500兆伏安	6	11		17	17	个		----Having a power handling capacity exceeding 400MVA but less than 500MVA
8504.2329	----其他	6	11		17	17	个		----Other
	-其他变压器:								-Other transformers:
	--额定容量不超过1千伏安:								--Having a power handling capacity not exceeding 1KVA:
8504.3110	---互感器	5	50		17	17	个		---Mutual inductor
8504.3190	---其他	5	50		17	17	个		---Other
	--额定容量超过1千伏安,但不超过16千伏安:								--Having a power handling capacity exceeding 1KVA but not exceeding 16KVA:
8504.3210	---互感器	5	50		17	17	个		---Mutual inductor
8504.3290	---其他	5	50		17	17	个		---Other
	--额定容量超过16千伏安,但不超过500千伏安:								--Having a power handling capacity exceeding 16KVA but not exceeding 500KVA:
8504.3310	---互感器	5	50		17	17	个/千克		---Transformer
8504.3390	---其他	5	50		17	17	个/千克		---Other
	--额定容量超过500千伏安:								--Having a power handling capacity exceeding 500KVA:
8504.3410	---互感器	14	50		17	17	个/千克		---Transformer
8504.3490	---其他	14	50		17	17	个/千克		---Other
	-静止式变流器:								-Static converters:
	---稳压电源:								---Voltage-stabilized suppliers:
8504.4013	----品目84.71所列机器用	0	40		17	17	个	A	----Of the machines of heading No.84.71
8504.4014 暂	----其他直流稳压电源,功率小于1千瓦,精度低于万分之一	7	80	3	17	17	个		----Other DC voltage-stabilized suppliers,of a power of less than 1KW and an accuracy of not better than 0.0001
8504.4015	----其他交流稳压电源,功率小于10千瓦,精度低于千分之一	0	80		17	17	个		----Other AC voltage-stabilized suppliers,of a power of less than 10KW and an accuracy of not better than 0.001
8504.4019	----其他	0	50		17	17	个		----Other
8504 4019.10	同位素电磁分离器离子源磁体电源(高功率直流型)	0	50		17	17	个	3	Magnet power for the ion source of electromagnetic isotope separator (high power DC)
8504 4019.20	直流高功率电源(能8小时连续产生100伏,500安电流,稳定度优于0.1%)	0	50		17	17	个	3	High power DC power supply (be able to generate the 100V, 500A electric current for 8 hours consecutively with its stability higher than 0.1%)
8504 4019.30	高压直流电源(能8小时连续产生20千伏,1安电流,稳定度优于0.2%)	0	50		17	17	个	3	High voltage DC power supply (able to generate the 20kV, 1A electric current for 8 hours consecutively with its stability higher than 0.2%)
8504 4019.40	同位素电磁分离器离子源高压电源	0	50		17	17	个	3	High voltage power supply for the ion source of electromagnetic isotope separator
8504 4019.90	其他稳压电源	0	50		17	17	个		Other kinds of regulated power supplies
8504.4020	---不间断供电电源	10	50		17	17	台		---Uninterrupted power suppliers
8504.4030	---逆变器	10	30		17	17	个		---Inverter
8504 4030.01 暂	电动汽车用逆变器模块(功率密度≥8千瓦/升)	10	30	6	17	17	个		Electric vehicle inverter module (power density ≥ 8 kW / liter)

税则号列 Tariff Item	商品名称及备注	进口税率 最惠	进口税率 普通	进口税率 暂定	出口退税	增值税率	计量单位	监管条件	Article Description
8504 4030.10	两用物项管制的逆变器(功率≥40瓦特,频率600至2000赫兹,谐波畸变低于10%等)	10	30		17	17	个	3	Inverter under control of dual-use items(power ≥ 40 watt, Frequency: 600-2000 Hz, Harmonic distortion less than 10%)
8504 4030.90	其他逆变器	10	30		17	17	个		Other inverter
	---其他:								---Other:
8504.4091 暂	----具有变流功能的半导体模块		30	3	17	17	个		----Semiconductor modules with converting function
8504 4091.01 暂	具有变流功能的半导体模块(自动数据处理设备机器及组件、电讯设备用的)	0	30	3	17	17	个	s	Semi-conductor modules with converting function (for automatic data-processing machines and units as well as telecommunication equipments)
8504 4091.09 暂	其他具有变流功能的半导体模块	10	30	3	17	17	个		Other kinds of semi-conductors with converting function
8504.4099	----其他		30		17	17	个		----Other
8504 4099.01	静止式变流器(自动数据处理设备机器及组件、电讯设备用)	0	30		17	17	个	s	Static converters (for automatic data-processing machines and units as well as telecommunication equipments)
8504 4099.02	ITA产品用的印刷电路组件(包括外接组件,如符合PCMCIA标准的卡)	0	30		17	17	个	s	Printed circuit assembly for ITA products (including external assembly, such as the cards in line with the PCMCIA standard)
8504 4099.03 暂	高速电力机车的牵引变流器[用于(200千米/小时)电力机车]	10	30	3	17	17	个		Traction converter for electric express locomotives (for electric locomotives with the speed of 200KM/h)
8504 4099.04 暂	汽车冲压线用压力机变频调速装置	10	30	5	17	17	个		Press frequency and speed control devices for automobile press line
8504 4099.05 暂	电动汽车用电机控制器	10	30	6	17	17	个		Motor controller of electric vehicle
8504 4099.30	频率变换器(专用85030090.10电动机定子的频率变换器)	10	30		17	17	个	3	Frequency converters under sensitive items control (those only using 85030090.10 motor stators)
8504 4099.40	两用物项管制的频率变换器(功率≥40瓦特,频率600至2000赫兹,谐波畸变低于10%等)	10	30		17	17	个	3	Frequency converters (power: ≥40W, frequency: 600-2000HZ, harmonic distortion rate: <10%)
8504 4099.50	电源(真空或受控环境感应炉用电源,额定输出功率≥5千瓦)	10	30		17	17	个	3	Power supply (for vacuum or controlled atmosphere induction furnaces; rated power output: ≥5KW)
8504 4099.60	模块式电脉冲发生器(在15毫秒内输出电流>100安,密封在防尘罩内,温宽范围大)	10	30		17	17	个	3	Modular electric pulse generator (output current＞101A in 16ms; sealed in dust-proof cover; with a wide temperature range)
8504 4099.90	其他未列名静止式变流器	10	30		17	17	个		Other kinds of static converters
8504.5000	-其他电感器	0	35		17	17	个		-Other inductors
	-零件:								-Parts:
	---变压器用:								---Of transformers:
8504.9011	----子目号8504.2321,8504.2329所列变压器用	5	11		17	17	千克		----Of the transformers of subheading No.8504.2321, 8504.2329
8504.9019	----其他	8	50		17	17	千克		----Other
8504.9020	---稳压电源及不间断供电电源用	8	50		17	17	千克		---Of voltage-stabilized suppliers and uninterrupted power suppliers
8504.9090	---其他	8	30		17	17	千克		---Other
85.05	**电磁铁;永磁铁及磁化后准备制永磁铁的物品;电磁铁或永磁铁卡盘、夹具及类似的工件夹具;电磁联轴节、离合器及制动器;电磁起重吸盘:**								**Electro-magnets; permanent magnets and articles intended to become permanent magnets after magnetization;electro-magnetic or permanent magnet chucks, clamps and similar holding devices; electro-magnetic couplings,clutches and brakes; electro-magnetic lifting heads:**
	-永磁铁及磁化后准备制永磁铁的物品:								-Permanent magnets and articles intended to become permanent magnets after magnetization:
	--金属的:								--Of metal:
8505.1110	---稀土的	7	20		17	17	千克		---Rare-earth
8505.1190	---其他	7	20		17	17	千克		---Other
8505.1900	--其他	7	20		17	17	千克		--Other
8505 1900.10	磁极块(直径大于2米,用在同位素电磁分离器内)	7	20		17	17	千克	3	Magnet pole pieces (diameter: ＞2m; used for electromagnetic isotope separator)

税则号列 Tariff Item	商品名称及备注	进口税率			出口退税	增值税率	计量单位	监管条件	Article Description
		最惠	普通	暂定					
8505 1900.90	其他非金属的永磁铁及永磁体	7	20		17	17	千克		Other non-metal permanent magnet and articles
8505.2000	-电磁联轴节、离合器及制动器	8	20		17	17	千克		-Electro-magnetic couplings, clutches and brakes
	-其他，包括零件:								-Other, including parts:
8505.9010	---电磁起重吸盘	8	20		17	17	个/千克		---Electro-magnetic lifting heads
8505.9090	---其他	8	20		17	17	个/千克		---Other
8505 9090.10	超导螺线电磁体（产生超过2个泰斯拉磁场，长径比≥2，内径≥300毫米等）	8	20		17	17	个/千克	3	Superconducting spiral electromagnets (generating more than two Tesla magnetic fields; L/D ratio: ≥2; ID≥300mm, etc.)
8505 9090.90	其他电磁夹具等及品目85.05的零件	8	20		17	17	个/千克		Other kinds of magnetic holding devices and spare parts belonging to the 85.05 item
85.06	**原电池及原电池组:**								**Primary cells and primary batteries:**
	-二氧化锰的:								-Manganese dioxide:
	---碱性锌锰的:								---Alkaline zinc-manganese dioxide:
8506.1011	----扣式	20	80		0/15	17	个	A	----Button shape
8506.1012	----圆柱型	20	80		0/15	17	个	A	----Cylindrical shape
8506.1019	----其他	20	80		15	17	个	A	----Other
8506.1090	---其他	20	80		15	17	个	A	---Other
8506.3000	-氧化汞的	14	40			17	个	A	-Mercuric oxide
8506.4000	-氧化银的	14	40		15	17	个	A	-Silver oxide
8506.5000	-锂的	14	40		15	17	个	A	-Lithium
8506.6000	-锌空气的	14	40		15	17	个	A	-Air-zinc
8506.8000	-其他原电池及原电池组	14	40		15	17	个	A	-Other primary cells and primary batteries
	-零件:								-Parts:
8506.9010	---子目号8506.1000所列电池用	14	80		15	17	千克	A	---Of the cells of subheading No.8506.1000
8506.9090	---其他	10	40		15	17	千克	A	---Other
85.07	**蓄电池，包括隔板，不论是否矩形（包括正方形）:**								**Electric accumulators, including separators therefor, whether or not rectangular（including square）:**
8507.1000	-铅酸蓄电池，用于启动活塞式发动机	10	90			17	个	AB	-Lead-acid, of a kind used for starting piston engines
8507.2000	-其他铅酸蓄电池	10	90			17	个	A	-Other lead-acid accumulators
8507.3000	-镍镉蓄电池	10	40			17	个	A	-Nickel-cadmium
8507.4000	-镍铁蓄电池	12	40		15	17	个	A	-Nickel-iron
8507.5000	-镍氢蓄电池	12	40		15	17	个		-Nickel-metal hydride
8507 5000.01 [暂]	电动汽车用镍氢蓄电池单体(容量≥6Ah，比功率≥1000w/kg)	12	40	8	15	17	个	A	Nickel-metal hydride monomer for electric vehicle (capacity ≥6AH, specific power ≥ 1000W/kg)
8507 5000.02 [暂]	电动汽车用镍氢蓄电池系统(包含蓄电池模块、容器、盖、冷却系统、管理系统等，比功率≥700W/kg)	12	40	10	15	17	个	A	Nickel-metal hydride system of electric vehicles (including battery module, container, cover, cooling system, management system, the specific power ≥ 700W/kg)
8507 5000.90	其他镍氢蓄电池	12	40		15	17	个	A	Other nickel-metal hydride
8507.6000	-锂离子蓄电池	12	40		17	17	个		-Lithium-ion
8507 6000.01 [暂]	电动汽车或插电式混合动力汽车用锂离子蓄电池单体(容量≥10Ah，比能量≥110Wh/kg)	12	40	6	17	17	个	A	Lithium ion battery monomer for electric vehicle (capacity ≥ 10Ah, specific power ≥ 110Wh/kg)
8507 6000.02 [暂]	电动汽车或插电式混合动力汽车用锂离子蓄电池系统(包含蓄电池模块、容器、盖、冷却系统、管理系统等,比能量≥80Wh/kg)	12	40	8	17	17	个	A	Lithium ion battery monomer system for electric vehicle (including battery module, container, cover, cooling system, management system, the specific energy ≥ 80Wh/kg)
8507 6000.90	其他锂离子蓄电池	12	40		17	17	个	A	Other lithium-ion battery
	-其他蓄电池:								-Other accumulators:
8507.8030	---全钒液流电池	12	40		15	17	个/千克	A	--- Vanadium redox flow battery
8507.8090	---其他	12	40		15	17	个/千克	AB	---Other
	-零件:								-Parts:
8507.9010	---铅酸蓄电池用	10	90			17	千克		---Of lead-acid accumulators
8507 9010.01 [暂]	铅酸蓄电池电极	10	90	5		17	千克	A	Electrodes of lead-acid accumulators
8507 9010.90	其他铅酸蓄电池零件	10	90			17	千克	A	Other Parts of lead-acid accumulators

税则号列 Tariff Item	商品名称及备注	进口税率 最惠	进口税率 普通	进口税率 暂定	出口退税	增值税率	计量单位	监管条件	Article Description
8507.9090[暂]	---其他	8	40	5	15	17	千克	A	---Other
85.08	**真空吸尘器:**								**Vacuum cleaners:**
	-电动的:								-With self-contained electric motor:
8508.1100	--功率不超过1500瓦，且带有容积不超过20升的集尘袋或其他集尘容器	10	130		17	17	台/千克	A	--Of a power not exceeding 1500W and having a dust bag or other receptacle capacity not exceeding 20L
8508.1900	--其他	0	30		17	17	台/千克	A	--Other
8508.6000	-其他真空吸尘器	0	30		17	17	台/千克	A	-Other vacuum cleaners
	-零件:								-Parts:
8508.7010	---子目8508.1100所列吸尘器用	12	100		17	17	千克		---Of the cleaners of subheading No.8508.1100
8508.7090	---其他	0	20		17	17	千克		---Other
85.09	**家用电动器具，品目85.08的真空吸尘器除外:**								**Electro-mechanical domestic appliances, with selfcontained electric motor, other than vacuum cleaners of heading 85.08:**
	-食品研磨机及搅拌器；水果或蔬菜的榨汁机:								-Food grinders and mixers; fruit or vegetable juice extractors:
8509.4010[暂]	---水果或蔬菜的榨汁机	10	100	6	17	17	台/千克	AB	---Fruit or vegetable juice extractors
8509.4090[暂]	---其他	10	100	6	17	17	台/千克	AB	---Other
	-其他器具:								----Other appliances:
8509.8010	---地板打蜡机	30	100		17	17	台/千克		---Floor polishers
8509.8020	---厨房废物处理器	20	100		17	17	台/千克		---Kitchen waste disposers
8509.8090[暂]	---其他	30	100	15	17	17	台/千克	A	---Other
8509.9000[暂]	-零件	12	100	6	17	17	千克		-Parts
85.10	**电动剃须刀、电动毛发推剪及电动脱毛器:**								**Shavers, hair clippers and hair-removing appliances, with self-contained electric motor:**
8510.1000[暂]	-剃须刀	30	100	15	17	17	个		-Shavers
8510.2000	-毛发推剪	30	100		17	17	个		-Hair clippers
8510.3000	-脱毛器	20	100		17	17	个		-Hair-removing appliances
8510.9000[暂]	-零件	24.5	100	12	17	17	千克		-Parts
85.11	**点燃式或压燃式内燃发动机用的电点火及电起动装置（例如，点火磁电机、永磁直流发电机、点火线圈、火花塞、电热塞及起动电机）；附属于上述内燃发动机的发电机（例如，直流发电机、交流发电机）及断流器**								**Electrical ignition or starting equipment of a kind used for spark-ignition or compression-ignition internal combustion engines（for example, ignition magnetos, magnetodynamos, ignition coils, sparking plugs and glow plugs, starter motors）; generators （for example, dynamos, alternators） and cutouts of a kind used in conjunction with such engines:**
8511.1000	-火花塞	10	30		17	17	个		-Sparking plugs
	-点火磁电机；永磁直流发电机；磁飞轮:								-Ignition magnetos; magneto-dynamos; magnetic flywheels:
8511.2010	---机车、航空器及船舶用	5	11		17	17	个		---For locomotives, aircraft or ships
8511.2090	---其他	10	30		17	17	个		---Other
	--分电器；点火线圈:								--Distributors; ignition coils:
8511.3010	---机车、航空器及船舶用	5	11		17	17	个		---For locomotives, aircraft or ships
8511.3090	---其他	8.4	30		17	17	个		---Other
	-启动电机及两用启动发电机:								-Starter motors and dual purpose starter generators:
8511.4010	---机车、航空器及船舶用	5	11		17	17	个		---For locomotives, aircraft or ships
	---其他:								---Other:
8511.4091	----输出功率在132.39千瓦（180马力）及以上的发动机用启动电机	8.4	30		17	17	个		----Starter motors for engines of an output of 132.39KW（180hp） or more
8511.4099	----其他	8.4	30		17	17	个		----Other
	-其他发电机:								-Other generators:
8511.5010	---机车、航空器及船舶用	5	11		17	17	个		---For locomotives, aircraft or ships
8511.5090	---其他	8.4	30		17	17	个		---Other
8511.8000	-其他装置	8.4	30		17	17	个		-Other equipment
	-零件:								-Parts:
8511.9010	---本品目所列供机车、航空器	4.5	11		17	17	千克		---Of the equipment of heading No.85.11 used for

税则号列 Tariff Item	商品名称及备注	进口税率 最惠	进口税率 普通	进口税率 暂定	出口退税	增值税率	计量单位	监管条件	Article Description
	及船舶用各种装置的零件								locomotives, aircraft or ships
8511.9090	---其他	5	30		17	17	千克		---Other
85.12	**自行车或机动车辆用的电气照明或信号装置(品目85.39的物品除外)、风挡刮水器、除霜器及去雾器:**								**Electrical lighting or signalling equipment (excluding articles of heading No.85.39), windscreen wipers, defrosters and demisters, of a kind used for cycles or motor vehicles:**
8512.1000	-自行车用照明或视觉信号装置	10.5	45		17	17	个		-Lighting or visual signalling equipment of a kind used on bicycles
	-其他照明或视觉信号装置:								-Other lighting or visual signalling equipment:
8512.2010	---机动车辆用照明装置	10	45		17	17	个		---Lighting equipment of a kind used for motor vehicles
8512.2090	---其他	10	45		17	17	个		---Other
	-音响信号装置:								-Sound signalling equipment:
	---机动车辆用:								---For motor vehicles:
8512.3011	----喇叭、蜂鸣器	10	45		17	17	个		----Loudspeaker, buzzers
8512.3012	----防盗报警器	10	40		17	17	个		----Burglar alarm
8512.3019	----其他	10	45		17	17	个		----Other
8512.3090	---其他	10	45		17	17	个		---Other
8512.4000	-风挡刮水器、除霜器及去雾器	10	45		17	17	个		-Windscreen wipers, defrosters and demisters
8512.9000	-零件	8	45		17	17	千克		-Parts
85.13	**自供能源(例如，使用干电池、蓄电池、永磁发电机)的手提式电灯,但品目85.12的照明装置除外:**								**Portable electric lamps designed to function by their own source of energy (for example, dry batteries, accumulators, magnetos), other than lighting equipment of heading No.85.12:**
	-灯:								-Lamps:
8513.1010	---手电筒	15	100		17	17	个		---Portable electric torches designed to function by dry batteries
8513.1090	---其他	17.5	70		17	17	个		---Other
	-零件:								-Parts:
8513.9010	---手电筒用	14	100		17	17	千克		---Of the torches of subheading No.8513.1010
8513.9090	---其他	14	70		17	17	千克		---Other
85.14	**工业或实验室用电炉及电烘箱(包括通过感应的或电介质的);工业或实验室用其他通过感应或介质损耗对材料进行热处理的设备**								**Industrial or laboratory electric furnaces and ovens (including those functioning by induction or dielectric loss); other industrial or laboratory equipment for the heat treatment of materials by induction or dielectric loss:**
	-电阻加热的炉及烘箱:								-Resistance heated furnaces and ovens:
8514.1010	---可控气氛热处理炉	0	30		17	17	台		---Furnaces for heat treatment, atmosphere controllabie
8514.1090	---其他	0	30		17	17	台		---Other
8514.2000	-通过感应或介质损耗工作的炉及烘箱	0	30		17	17	台		-Furnaces and ovens functioning by induction or dielectric loss
8514 2000.10	真空感应炉或受控环境感应炉(工作温度＞850℃，感应线圈直径≤600毫米,功率≥5千瓦)	0	30		17	17	台	3	Vacuum or controlled atmosphere induction furnaces (working temperature:＞850℃; induction coil diameter: ≤600mm; power: ≥5KW)
8514 2000.90	其他感应或介质损耗工作炉及烘箱(包括实验室用)	0	30		17	17	台		Other induction furnaces or dielectric losing furnaces and ovens (including those for laboratory use)
8514.3000	-其他炉及烘箱	0	30		17	17	台		-Other furnaces and ovens
8514 3000.20	电弧重熔炉和铸造用炉(容量1100～20000cm³,使用自耗电极,工作温度1700℃以上)	0	30		17	17	台	3	Arc remelting furnace and casting furnace (capacity: 1100cm³-20000cm³; using consutrode; working temperature: below 1700℃)
8514 3000.30	电子束熔化炉(功率≥50千瓦,能在＞1200℃的熔化温度工作)	0	30		17	17	台	3	Electron beam melting furnace (power: ≥50KW; able to work above the melting temperature of 1200℃)
8514 3000.40	等离子体雾化和熔化炉(功率≥50千瓦，能在＞1200℃的熔化温度工作)	0	30		17	17	台	3	Plasm atomization furnaces and melting furnaces (power: ≥50KW; able to work above the melting temperature of 1200℃)
8514 3000.90	工业用其他电炉及电烘箱(包括实验室用)	0	30		17	17	台		Other electric furnaces and ovens for industrial use (including those for laboratory use)

税则号列 Tariff Item	商品名称及备注	进口税率 最惠	普通	暂定	出口退税	增值税率	计量单位	监管条件	Article Description
8514.4000	-其他通过感应或介质损耗对材料进行热处理的设备	10	30		17	17	台		-Other equipment for the heat treatment of materials by induction or dielectric loss
8514 4000.01 暂	焊缝中频退火装置	10	30	7	17	17	台		Frequency weld annealers
8514 4000.90	其他感应或介质损耗的加热设备（包括实验室用）	10	30		17	17	台		Other kinds of induction furnaces or dielectric losing heating devices (including those for laboratory use)
	-零件:								-Parts:
8514.9010	---炼钢电炉用	8	30		17	17	千克		---Of steel making electric furnaces
8514.9090	---其他	0	30		17	17	千克		---Other
85.15	**电气（包括电热气体）、激光、其他光、光子束、超声波、电子束、磁脉冲或等离子弧焊接机器及装置，不论是否兼有切割功能；用于热喷金属或金属陶瓷的电气机器及装置**								**Electric（including electrically heated gas）, laser or other light or photon beam, ultrasonic, electron beam, magnetic pulse or plasma are soldering, brazing or welding machines and apparatus, whether or not capable of cutting; electric machines and apparatus for hot spraying of metals or cermets:**
	-钎焊机器及装置:								-Brazing or soldering machines and apparatus:
8515.1100	--烙铁及焊枪	10	30		17	17	个		--Soldering irons and guns
8515.1900	--其他	10	30		17	17	台		--Other
	-电阻焊接机器及装置:								-Machines and apparatus for resistance welding of metals:
	--全自动或半自动的:								--Fully or partly automatic:
8515.2120	---机器人	10	30		17	17	台		---Robot
8515 2120.01 暂	汽车生产线电阻焊接机器人	10	30	5	17	17	台	AO	Welding robot of electric resistance on automobile production line
8515 2120.90	其它电阻焊接机器人	10	30		17	17	台	AO	Robot for resistance welding of metals:
	---其他:								---Other:
8515.2191	----直缝焊管机	10	30		17	17	台		---Aligning tube welding machines
8515.2199	-----其他	10	30		17	17	台	AO	----Other
8515.2900	--其他	10	30		17	17	台	A	--Other
	-电弧（包括等离子弧）焊接机器及装置:								-Machines and apparatus for（including plasma are）welding of metals:
	--全自动或半自动的:								--Fully or partly automatic:
8515.3120	---机器人	10	30		17	17	台	AO	---Robot
	---其他:								---Other
8515.3191	----螺旋焊管机	10	30		17	17	台		---Spiralling tube welding machines
8515.3199	-----其他	10	30		17	17	台	AO	----Other
8515.3900	--其他	10	30		17	17	台	A	--Other
	-其他机器及装置:								-Other machines and apparatus:
8515.8010	---激光焊接机器人	8	30		17	17	台		---Laser welding robot
8515 8010.01 暂	汽车生产线激光焊接机器人	8	30	5	17	17	台		Laser welding robot on automobile production line
8515 8010.90	其他激光焊接机器人	8	30		17	17	台		Other Laser welding robot
8515.8090	---其他	8	30		17	17	台		---Other
8515 8090.10	电子束、激光自动焊接机(将端塞焊接于燃料细棒（或棒）的自动焊接机)	8	30		17	17	台	3	Automatic electron beam Laser weldingmachine (automatic welding machine for welding end plug onto fuelpins or rods
8515 8090.90	其他焊接机器及装置	8	30		17	17	台		Other machines and apparatus of welding
8515.9000 暂	-零件	6	30	3	17	17	千克		-Parts
85.16	**电热的快速热水器、储存式热水器、浸入式液体加热器；电气空间加热器及土壤加热器；电热的理发器具（例如，电吹风机、电卷发器、电热发钳）及干手器；电熨斗；其他家用电热器具；加热电阻器，但品目 8545 的货品除外**								**Electric instantaneous or storage water heaters and immersion heaters; electric space heating apparatus and soil heating apparatus; electro-thermichair-dressing apparatus（for example, hair dryers, hair curlers, curling tong heaters）and hand dryers; electric smoothing irons; other electro-thermic appliances of a kind used for domestic purposes; electric heating resistors,other than those of heading No.85.45:**

税则号列 Tariff Item	商品名称及备注	进口税率 最惠	进口税率 普通	进口税率 暂定	出口退税	增值税率	计量单位	监管条件	Article Description
	-电热的快速热水器、储存式热水器、浸入式液体加热器:								-Electric instantaneous or storage waterheaters and immersion heaters:
8516.1010	---储存式电热水器	10	100		17	17	个	A	---Electric storage waterheaters
8516.1020	---即热式电热水器	10	100		17	17	个	A	---Electric instantaneous waterheaters
8516.1090	---其他	10	100		17	17	个	A	---Other
	-电气空间加热器及土壤加热器:								-Electric space heating apparatus and electric soil heating apparatus:
8516.2100	--储存式散热器	35	100		17	17	个		--Storage heating radiators
	--其他:								--Other:
8516.2910	---土壤加热器	10	40		17	17	个		---Electric soil heating apparatus
8516.2920	---辐射式空间加热器	10	100		17	17	个		---Radiant space heating apparatus
	---对流式空间加热器:								---Convection space heating apparatus:
8516.2931	----风扇式	10	100		17	17	个		----Fan type
8516.2932	----充液式	10	100		17	17	个		----Oil-filled type
8516.2939	----其他	10	100		17	17	个		----Other
8516.2990	---其他	10	100		17	17	个		---Other
	-电热的理发器具及干手器:								-Electro-thermic hair-dressing or hand-drying apparatus:
8516.3100	--吹风机	10	100		17	17	个	A	--Hair dryers
8516.3200	--其他理发器具	35	100		17	17	个	A	--Other hair-dressing apparatus
8516.3300	--干手器	35	100		17	17	个	A	--Hand-drying apparatus
8516.4000 暂	-电熨斗	35	100	17	17	17	个	A	-Electric smoothing irons
8516.5000 暂	-微波炉	15	130	8	17	17	个	AB	-Microwave ovens
	-其他炉；电锅、电热板、加热环、烧烤炉及烘烤器:								-Other ovens; cookers, cooking plates, boiling rings, grillers and roasters:
8516.6010	---电磁炉	15	130		17	17	个	A	---Electromagnetic ovens
8516.6030 暂	---电饭锅	15	130	8	17	17	个	AB	---Electric rice cookers
8516.6040	---电炒锅	15	130		17	17	个	AB	---Electric frying pans
8516.6050 暂	---电烤箱	15	130	8	17	17	个	AB	---Roaster oven
8516.6090 暂	---其他	15	130	8	17	17	个	AB	---Other
	-其他电热器具:								-Other electro-thermic appliances:
	--咖啡壶或茶壶:								--Coffee or tea makers:
8516.7110 暂	---滴液式咖啡机	32	130	16	17	17	个	AB	---Drip coffee makers
8516.7120 暂	---蒸馏渗滤式咖啡机	32	130	16	17	17	个	AB	---Steam espresso makers
8516.7130 暂	---泵压式咖啡机	32	130	16	17	17	个	AB	---Pump espresso makers
8516.7190 暂	---其他	32	130	16	17	17	个	AB	---Other
	--烤面包器:								--Toasters:
8516.7210	---家用自动面包机	32	130		17	17	个	AB	---Household automoted bread makers
8516.7220	---片式烤面包机(多士炉)	32	130		17	17	个	AB	---Slice pop-up toasters
8516.7290	---其他	32	130		17	17	个	AB	---Other
	--其他:								--Other:
8516.7910	---电热饮水机	32	100		17	17	台	AB	---Electro-thermic water dispensers
8516.7990 暂	---其他	32	100	16	17	17	个	A	---Other
8516.8000	-加热电阻器	10	40		17	17	个		-Electric heating resistors
	-零件:								-Parts:
8516.9010	---土壤加热器及加热电阻器用	8	40		17	17	千克		---Of apparatus of subheading No.8516.2910 or 8516.8000
8516.9090 暂	---其他	12	100	8	17	17	千克		---Other
85.17	**电话机，包括用于蜂窝网络或其他无线网络的电话机、其他发送或接收声音、图象或其他数据用的设备，包括有线或无线网络（例如，局域网或广播网）的通信设备，品目 8443、8525、8527 或 8528 的发送或接收设备除外**								**Telephone sets, including telephones for cellular networks or for other wireless networks; other apparatus for the transmission or reception of voice, images or other data, including apparatus for communication in a wired or wireless network （such as a local or wide area network）, other than transmission or reception apparatus of heading No. 84.43 , 85.25, 85.27 , 85.28:**
	-电话机，包括蜂窝网络或其他无线网络用电话机:								-Telephone sets, including telephones for cellular networks or for other wireless networks:

税则号列 Tariff Item	商品名称及备注	进口税率 最惠	进口税率 普通	进口税率 暂定	出口退税	增值税率	计量单位	监管条件	Article Description
8517.1100	--无绳电话机	0	30		17	17	台		--Line telephone sets with cordless handsets
8517 1100.10	无绳加密电话机	0	30		17	17	台	AM	Encrypted cordless phone
8517 1100.90	其他无绳电话机	0	30		17	17	台	A	Other kinds of cordless phone
	--用于蜂窝网络或其他无线网络的电话机:								--Telephones for cellular networks or for other wireless networks:
8517.1210	---手持（包括车载）式无线电话机	0	20		17	17	台		---Wireless telephone handsets (including installed in the vehicle)
8517 1210.11	GSM 数字式手持无线电话整套散件	0	20		17	17	台	AO	Full set of parts of GSM handheld digital cordless phone
8517 1210.19	其他 GSM 数字式手持无线电话机	0	20		17	17	台	AO	Other kinds of parts of GSM handheld digital cordless phone
8517 1210.21	CDMA 数字式手持无线电话整套散件	0	20		17	17	台	AO	Full set of parts of CDMA handheld digital cordless phone
8517 1210.29	其他 CDMA 数字式手持无线电话机	0	20		17	17	台	AO	Other kinds of parts of CDMA handheld digital cordless phone
8517 1210.90	其他手持式无线电话机(包括车载式无线电话机)	0	20		17	17	台	AO	Other kinds of cordless phone (including car cordless phones)
8517.1220	---对讲机	0	17		17	17	台		---Walkie-talkie
8517.1290	---其他	0	14		17	17	台	O	---Other
8517.1800	--其他	0	30		17	17	台		--Other
8517 1800.10	其他加密电话机	0	30		17	17	台	AM	Other kinds of encrypted phones
8517 1800.90	其他电话机	0	30		17	17	台	A	Other kinds of phones
	-其他发送或接收声音、图像或其他数据用的设备,包括有线或无线网络(例如,局域网或广域网)的通信设备:								-Other apparatus for transmission or reception of voice,images or other data, including apparatus for communication in a wired or wireless network (such as a local or wide area network):
	--基站:								--Base stations:
8517.6110	---移动通信基站	0	14		17	17	台		---Mobile communication base stations
8517 6110.10	GSM 式移动通信基地站	0	14		17	17	台	O	GSM mobile communication base station
8517 6110.20	CDMA 式移动通信基地站	0	14		17	17	台	O	CDMA mobile communication base station
8517 6110.30	TACS 式移动通信基地站	0	14		17	17	台		TACS mobile communication base station
8517 6110.90	其他移动通信基地站	0	14		17	17	台	O	Other kinds of mobile communication base station
8517.6190	---其他	0	14		17	17	台	O	---Other
	--接收、转换并且发送或再生声音、图像或其他数据用的设备,包括交换及路由设备:								--Machines for the reception, conversion and transmission or regeneration of voice, images or other data, including switching and routing apparatus:
	---数字式程控电话或电报交换机:								---Digital program-controlled telephonic or telegraphic switching apparatus:
8517.6211	----局用电话交换机;长途电话交换机;电报交换机	0	17		17	17	台		----Public telephonic switching apparatus;toll telephonic switching apparatus ;telegraphic switching apparatus
8517.6212	----移动通信交换机	0	40		17	17	台	O	----Mobile communication switching system
8517.6219	----其他电话交换机	0	40		17	17	台	A	----Other telephonic switching apparatus
	---光通讯设备:								---Optical communication equipments:
8517.6221	----光端机及脉冲编码调制设备(PCM)	0	17		17	17	台	O	----Optical line terminal equipments and pulse code modulation equipments
8517.6222	----波分复用光传输设备	0	30		17	17	台	O	----Optical transmission equipments for wave-division multiplexing
8517.6229	----其他	0	30		17	17	台		----Other
8517 6229.10	光通讯加密路由器	0	30		17	17	台	AMO	Encrypted optical communication routers
8517 6229.90	其他光通讯设备	0	30		17	17	台	OA	Other kinds of optical communication equipments
	---其他有线数字通信设备:								---Other telecommunication apparatus for digital line system:
8517.6231	----通信网络时钟同步设备	0	30		17	17	台		----Communication network synchronizing equipments
8517.6232	----以太网络交换机	0	30		17	17	台		----Ethernet exchangers
8517 6232.10	非光通讯加密以太网络交换机	0	30		17	17	台	M	Encrypted ethernet switches for non-optical communication

税则号列 Tariff Item	商品名称及备注	进口税率 最惠	普通	暂定	出口退税	增值税率	计量单位	监管条件	Article Description
8517 6232.90	其他非光通讯以太网络交换机	0	30		17	17	台		Other kinds of ethernet switches for non-optical communication
8517.6233	----IP 电话信号转换设备	0	30		17	17	台	A	----IP telephone signal converters
8517.6234	----调制解调器	0	30		17	17	台	A	----Modem
8517.6235	----集线器	0	40		17	17	台	A	----Hubs
8517.6236	----路由器	0	40		17	17	台		----Routers
8517 6236.10	非光通讯加密路由器	0	40		17	17	台	M	Encrypted routers for non-optical communication
8517 6236.90	其他路由器	0	40		17	17	台		Other kinds of routers
8517.6237	----有线网络接口卡	0	30		17	17	台		----Wired network interface cards
8517.6239	----其他	0	30		17	17	台	O	----Other
	---其他:								---Other：
8517.6292	----无线网络接口卡	0	14		17	17	台		----Wireless network interface cards
8517.6293	----无线接入固定台	0	14		17	17	台		----Fixed wireless access station
8517.6294	----无线耳机	0	14		17	17	个		----Wireless headphones
8517.6299	----其他	0	14		17	17	台		----Other
	--其他:								--Other:
8517.6910	---其他无线设备		14		17	17	台		---Other equipments in a wireless network
8517 6910.01	用于呼叫、提示和寻呼的便携式接收器	0	14		17	17	台	As	Portable receptors for calling, promoting and paging
8517 6910.90	其他无线通信设备	9	14		17	17	台	AO	Other kinds of wireless telecommunication equipments
8517.6990	---其他有线设备	0	30		17	17	台		---Other equipments in a wired network
	-零件:								-Parts:
8517.7010	---数字式程控电话或电报交换机用	0	14		17	17	千克		---Of digital program-controlled telephonic or telegraphic switching apparatus
8517.7020	---光端机及脉冲编码调制设备（PCM）用	0	14		17	17	千克		---Of optical line terminal equipments and pulse code modulation equipments
8517.7030	---手持式无线电话机用（天线除外）	0	17		17	17	千克		---Of wireless telephones hand-sets（Other than aerials）
8517.7040	---对讲机用（天线除外）	8	20		17	17	千克		---Of walkie-talkie（Other than aerials）
8517.7060	---光通信设备的激光收发模块	0	30		17	17	千克		---Laser transmitting and receiving unit of optical communication equipments
8517.7070	---税号 85.17 所列设备用天线及其零件		20		17	17	千克		---Aerials and parts thereof of heading 85.17
8517 7070.01	无线电话电报装置的天线	0	20		17	17	千克	s	Aerials for wireless phones and telegraphs
8517 7070.90	品目 85.17 所列设备用其他天线及其零件	2	20		17	17	千克		Other aerials and parts for the equipments listed in the 85.17 item
8517.7090	---其他	0	20		17	17	千克		---Other
85.18	**传声器（麦克风）及其座架；扬声器，不论是否装成音箱；耳机、耳塞，不论是否装有传声器，由传声器及一个或多个扬声器组成的组合机；音频扩大器；电气扩音机组**								**Microphones and stands therefore ; loudspeakers, whether or not mounted in their enclosures; headphones earphones, whether or not combined with a microphone, and sets consisting of a microphone and one or more loudspeakers; audio-frequency electric amplifiers;electric sound amplifier sets:**
8518.1000	-传声器（麦克风）及其座架		40		17	17	个		-Microphones and stands therefore
8518 1000.01	电讯用频率在 300～3400 赫兹麦克风（直径不超过 10 毫米，高不超过 3 毫米）	0	40		17	17	个	s	Microphones used for telecommunication with the frequency between 300 and 3400 Hz(with a diameter ≤10mm and height≤3mm)
8518 1000.90[暂]	其他传声器(麦克风)及其座架	10	40	6	17	17	个		Other kinds of microphone and its seat frames
	-扬声器，不论是否装成音箱:								-Loudspeakers, whether or not mounted in their enclosures:
8518.2100[暂]	--单喇叭音箱	10	40	6	17	17	个	A	--Single loudspeakers, mounted in their enclosures
8518.2200[暂]	--多喇叭音箱	10	40	6	17	17	个	A	--Multiple loudspeakers, mounted in the same enclosure
8518.2900	--其他	0	40		17	17	个		--Other
8518.3000	-耳机、耳塞机，不论是否装有传声器，以及由传声器及一个或多个扬声器组成的组合机	0	40		17	17	个		-Headphones and earphones, whether or not combined with a microphone, and sets consisting of a microphone and one or more loudspeakers

税则号列 Tariff Item	商品名称及备注	进口税率 最惠	进口税率 普通	进口税率 暂定	出口退税	增值税率	计量单位	监管条件	Article Description
8518.4000	-音频扩大器		40		17	17	台		-Audio-frequency electric amplifiers
8518 4000.01	电器扩音器(列入ITA的有线电话重复器用的)	0	40		17	17	台	s	Loud-speakers for electrical appliances (for the cable phone repeaters in the ITA list)
8518 4000.90	其他音频扩大器	12	40		17	17	台	A	Other kinds of sound amplifiers
8518.5000	-电气扩音机组	10	40		17	17	套		-Electric sound amplifier sets
8518.9000	-零件		40		17	17	千克		-Parts
8518 9000.01	税号 85184000.01 所列货品的零件(列入ITA的有线电话重复器用的)	0	40		17	17	千克	s	Parts for goods of heading 85184000.01 item (for the cable phone repeaters in the ITA list)
8518 9000.90	品目 85.18 所列货品的其他零件	10.5	40		17	17	千克		Other parts listed in the 85.18 item
85.19	**声音录制或重放设备,未装有声音录制装置:**								**Sound recording or reproducing apparatus:**
8519.2000	-用硬币、钞票、银行卡、代币或其他支付方式使其工作的设备	20	80		17	17	台		-Apparatus operated by coins, banknotes,bank cards, tokens or by other means of payment
8519 2000.10	以特定支付方式使其工作的激光唱机(用硬币、钞票、银行卡、代币或其他支付方式使其工作)	20	80		17	17	台	A	Laser disc players operated through specific means of payment (coins, banknotes, bank cards, tokens or other means of payment)
8519 2000.90	其他以特定支付方式使其工作的声音录制或重放设备(用硬币、钞票、银行卡、代币或其他支付方式使其工作)	20	80		17	17	台		Sound recording or replaying devices perated through specific means of payment (coins, banknotes, bank cards, tokens or other means of payment)
8519.3000	-转盘(唱机唱盘)	30	130		17	17	台		-Turntables (record-decks)
8519.5000	-电话应答机	0	80		17	17	台		-Telephone answering machines
	-其他设备:								-Other apparatus:
	--使用磁性、光学或半导体媒体的:								--Using magnetic, optical or semiconductor media:
	---使用磁性媒体的:								---Using magnetic media:
8519.8111	----未装有声音录制装置的盒式磁带型声音重放装置,编辑节目用放声机除外	17	130		17	17	台	A	----Cassette-type sound reproducing apparatus, not incorporating a sound recording device,other than transcribing machines
8519.8112	----装有声音重放装置的盒式磁带型录音机	30	130		17	17	台	A	----Cassette-type recorders incorporating sound reproducing apparatus
8519.8119	----其他	20	80		17	17	台	6A	----Other
	---使用光学媒体的:								---Using optical media:
8519.8121	----激光唱机,未装有声音录制装置	30	80		17	17	台	A	----Compact dise players, not incorporating a sound recording device
8519.8129	----其他	20	80		17	17	台		----Other
8519 8129.10	具有录音功能的激光唱机	20	80		17	17	台	6A	Laser disc players with recording function
8519 8129.90	其他使用光学媒体的声音录制或重放设备	20	80		17	17	台	A	Other sound recording or replaying devices using optical medias
	---使用半导体媒体的:								---Using semiconductor media:
8519.8131[暂]	----装有声音重放装置的闪速存储器型声音录制设备	20	80	12	17	17	台	6A	----Flash memory type recorders, incorporating sound reproducing apparatus
8519.8139[暂]	----其他	20	80	12	17	17	台	6A	----Other
	--其他:								--Other:
8519.8910	---不带录制装置的其他唱机,不论是否带有扬声器	30	130		17	17	台	A	---Other record-players, not incorporating a sound recording device, with or without loudspeakers
8519.8990[暂]	---其他声音录制或重放设备	20	80	12	17	17	台	6A	---Other sound recording or reproducing apparatus
85.21	**视频信号录制或重放设备,不论是否装有高频调谐器:**								**Video recording or reproducing apparatus, whether or not incorporating a video tuner:**
	-磁带型:								-Magnetic tape-type:
	---录像机:								---Video tape recorders:

税则号列 Tariff Item	商品名称及备注	进口税率			出口退税	增值税率	计量单位	监管条件	Article Description
		最惠	普通	暂定					
8521.1011 暂	----广播级	(1)	(2)	(3)	17	17	台	A	----Broadcast quality
8521.1019	----其他	(1)	(2)		17	17	台	A	----Other
8521.1020	---放像机	(1)	(2)		17	17	台	A	---Video tape reproducers
	-其他:								-Other:
	---激光视盘机:								---Laser video compact disk player:
8521.9011	----视频高密光盘（VCD）播放机	20	130		17	17	台		----Video Compact Disc player
8521 9011.10	具有录制功能的视频高密光盘(VCD)播放机（不论是否装有高频调谐放大器）	20	130		17	17	台	A	Recordable VCD players (whether or not incorporated with a high-frequency tuned amplifier)
8521 9011.90	其他视频高密光盘(VCD)播放机（不论是否装有高频调谐放大器）	20	130		17	17	台	A	Other VCD players (whether or not incorporated with a high-frequency tuned amplifier)
8521.9012	----数字化视频光盘（DVD）播放机	20	130		17	17	台		----Digital Video Disc player
8521 9012.10	具有录制功能的数字化视频光盘(DVD)播放机（不论是否装有高频调谐放大器）	20	130		17	17	台	A	Recordable DVD players (whether or not incorporated with a high-frequency tuned amplifier)
8521 9012.90	其他数字化视频光盘(DVD)播放机(不论是否装有高频调谐放大器）	20	130		17	17	台	A	Other DVD players (whether or not incorporated with a high-frequency tuned amplifier)
8521.9019	----其他	20	130		17	17	台		----Other
8521 9019.10	具有录制功能的其他激光视盘播放机(不论是否装有高频调谐放大器）	20	130		17	17	台	A	Other recordable laser disc players (whether or not incorporated with a high-frequency tuned amplifier)
8521 9019.90	其他激光视盘播放机(不论是否装有高频调谐放大器）	20	130		17	17	台	A	Other laser disc players (whether or not incorporated with a high-frequency tuned amplifier)
8521.9090	---其他	20	130		17	17	台		---Other
8521 9090.01 暂	光盘型广播级录像机	20	130	(4)	17	17	台	6A	Disc-type broadcast-quality video recorders
8521 9090.10	用于光盘生产的金属母盘生产设备(不论是否装有高频调谐放大器）	20	130		17	17	台	6AO	Metal master disc production equipments (whether or not incorporated with a high-frequency tuned amplifier)
8521 9090.90	其他视频信号录制或重放设备（不论是否装有高频调谐放大器）	20	130		17	17	台	6A	Other video recording or replaying devices (whether or not incorporated with a high-frequency tuned amplifier)
85.22	**专用于或主要用于品目 8519 至 8521 所列设备的零件、附件**								**Parts and accessories suitable for use solely or principally with the apparatus of heading 85.19 or 85.21:**
8522.1000	-拾音头	35	130		17	17	个/千克		-Pick-up cartridges
	-其他:								-Other:
8522.9010	---转盘或唱机用	25	130		17	17	千克		---Of turntables（record decks）or record-players
	---盒式磁带录音机或放声机用:								---Of cassette magnetic tape recorders or reproducers:
8522.9021	----走带机构(机芯)，不论是否装有磁头	25	100		17	17	千克		----Transport mechanisms, whether or not incorporating a magnetic head
8522.9022	----磁头	25	100		17	17	个/千克		----Magnetic heads
8522.9023	----磁头零件	20	100		17	17	千克		----Parts of magnetic heads
8522.9029 暂	----其他	30	100	15	17	17	千克		----Other
	---视频信号录制或重放设备用:								---Of video recording or reproducing apparatus:
8522.9031	----激光视盘机的机芯	30	100		17	17	千克		----Movements for laser video compact disk player
8522 9031.02 暂	车载导航仪视频播放机机芯	30	100	17	17	17	千克		Movements for video player with antomobile navigator
8522 9031.90	其他激光视盘机的机芯	30	100		17	17	千克		Other movements for laser video compact disk player
8522.9039	----其他	30	100		17	17	千克		----Other
8522 9039.02 暂	激光视盘机激光收发装置用零件	30	100	8	17	17	千克		Parts for laser receiver-transmitter of laser video compact disk player

（1）完税价格不高于2000美元/台：30%；完税价格高于2000美元/台：3%，加3283元
（2）完税价格不高于2000美元/台：130%；完税价格高于2000美元/台：6%，加20600元
（3）完税价格不超过5000美元/台：15%；完税价格高于5000美元/台：3%，加3648元
（4）完税价格不超过7000美元/台：15%；完税价格高于7000美元/台：5%，加4256元

税则号列 Tariff Item	商品名称及备注	进口税率			出口退税	增值税率	计量单位	监管条件	Article Description
		最惠	普通	暂定					
8522.9039.09[暂]	其他视频信号录制或重放设备的零件	30	100	15	17	17	千克		Parts for other kinds of viedo signal recording or reproducing devices
	---其他:								---Other:
8522.9091[暂]	----车载音频转播器或发射器	20	80	10	17	17	台/千克		----Tone converters or transmission apparatus of a kind used for vehicles
8522.9099[暂]	----其他	20	80	10	17	17	千克		----Other
85.23	**录制声音或其他信息用的圆盘、磁带、固态非易失性数据存储器件、“智能卡”及其他媒体，不论是否已录制，包括供复制圆盘用的母片及母带，但不包括第三十七章的产品**								**Discs, tapes, solid-state non-volatile storage devices, smart cards and other media for the recording of sound or of other phenomena, whether or not recorded, including matrices and masters for the production of discs,but excluding products of chapter 37:**
	-磁性媒体:								-Magnetic media:
	--磁条卡:								--Cards incorporating a magnetic stripe:
8523.2110	---未录制	17.5	70		17	17	个/千克		---Unrecorded
8523.2120	---已录制	15	130		13/17	13	个/千克		---Recorded
	--其他:								--Other:
	---磁盘:								---Magnetic discs:
8523.2911	----未录制	0	14		17	17	个/千克		----Unrecorded
8523.2919	----其他	0	14		13/17	13	个/千克		----Other
	---磁带:								---Magnetic tapes:
8523.2921	----未录制的宽度不超过 4 毫米的磁带	0	130		17	17	盘/千克	A	----Of a width not exceeding 4mm,unrecorded
8523.2922	----未录制的宽度超过 4 毫米，但不超过 6.5 毫米的磁带	0	130		17	17	盘/千克		----Of a width exceeding 4mm but not exceeding 6.5mm,unrecorded
8523.2923	----未录制的宽度超过 6.5 毫米的磁带	0	20		17	17	盘/千克		----Of a width exceeding 6.5mm,unrecorded
8523.2928[暂]	----重放声音或图像信息的磁带	10	130	6	13/17	13	盘/千克	Z	----For reproducing sound or image phenomena
8523.2929	----已录制的其他磁带	0	14		13/17	17	盘/千克	Z	----Other recorded magnetic tapes
8523.2990	---其他	0	14		13/17	17	盘/千克	Z	---Other
	-光学媒体:								-Optical media:
8523.4100	--未录制	0	14		17	17	张/千克		--Unrecorded
	--其他:								--Other:
8523.4910[暂]	---仅用于重放声音信息的	10	130	6	13/17	13	张/千克	Z	---For reproducing sound only
8523.4920	---用于重放声音、图像以外信息的，品目 84.71 所列机器用	0	14		13/17	13	张/千克		---For reproducing phenomena other than sound or image for the machines of heading No.84.71
8523.4990	---其他	0	14		13/17	17	张/千克	Z	---Other
	-半导体媒体:								-Semiconductor media:
	--固态非易失性存储器件(闪速存储器):								--Solid-state non-volatile storage devices（flash memorizer）:
8523.5110	---未录制	0	70		17	17	个/千克		---Unrecorded
8523.5120	---已录制	0	14		13/17	13	个/千克		---Recorded
	--“智能卡”:								--“Smart cards”
8523.5210	---未录制	0	21		17	13	个/千克		----Unrecorded
8523.5290	---其他	0	21		13/17	13	个/千克		----Other
	--其他:								----Other:
8523.5910	---未录制	0	70		17	17	个/千克		---Unrecorded
8523.5920	---已录制	0	14		13/17	13	个/千克		---Recorded
	-其他:								-Other:
	---唱片:								---Gramophone records:
8523.8011	----已录制	15	130		13/17	13	张/千克	Z	----Recorded
8523.8019	----其他	0	70		13/17	17	张/千克		----Other
	---税号 84.71 所列机器用:								---For the machines of heading No.84.71
8523.8021	----未录制	0	14		17	17	张/千克		----Unrecorded
8523.8029	----其他	0	14		13/17	17	张/千克		----Other
	---其他:								---Other

税则号列 Tariff Item	商品名称及备注	进口税率 最惠	普通	暂定	出口退税	增值税率	计量单位	监管条件	Article Description
8523.8091	----未录制	0	14		17	13	张/千克		----Unrecorded
8523.8099	----其他	0	14		13/17	13	张/千克	Z	----Other
85.25	**无线电广播、电视发送设备，不论是否装有接收装置或声音的录制、重放装置；电视摄像机、数字照相机及视频摄录一体机：**								**Transmission apparatus for radio broadcasting or television, whether or not incorporating reception apparatus or sound recording or reproducing apparatus; television cameras, digital cameras and video camera recorders:**
8525.5000	-发送设备	0	30		17	17	台	O	-Transmission apparatus
	-装有接收装置的发送设备:								-Transmission apparatus incorporating reception apparatus:
8525.6010	---卫星地面站设备	0	14		17	17	台	O	---Satellite earth station
8525.6090	---其他	0	30		17	17	台	O	---Other
	-电视摄像机、数字照相机及视频摄录一体机:								-Television cameras, digital cameras and video camera recorders:
	---电视摄像机:								---Telvision cameras:
8525.8011	----特种用途的	10	17		17	17	台		----For special purposes
8525 8011.10	抗辐射电视摄像机[能抗 5×10^4 戈瑞(硅)以上辐射而又不会降低使用质量]	10	17		17	17	台	3A	Radiation-resistant telecamera (able to resist radiations above 5×10^4 Gy while not reducing the service quality)
8525 8011.90	其他特种用途电视摄像机	10	17		17	17	台	A	Other telecameras for special purposes
8525.8012	----非特种用途的广播机	(1)	(2)		17	17	台	A	----Broadcast quality,not for special purposes
8525.8013	----非特种用途的其他类型	(1)	(2)		17	17	台		----Other,not for special purposes
8525 8013.01[暂]	手机用摄像组件（由镜头+CCD/CMOS+数字信号处理电路三部分构成）	(1)	(2)	4	17	17	台		Camera components for cellphones (including lens, CCD/CMOS and digital signal processing electric circuit)
8525 8013.02[暂]	高清摄像头(必须满足以下三个条件：1、镜头元件必须使用5层及以上玻璃镜头；2、使用USB 2.0 及以上高速接口；3、硬件传感器像素达到130万及以上)	(1)	(2)	10	17	17	台		High definition cameras (the following three requirements must be fulfilled: 1. 5 layers glass lens; 2. USB2. 0 High Speed Interface；3、Hardware Sensor: 130 Mega pixel and above)
8525 8013.90	其他非特种用途电视摄像机及其他摄像组件(其他摄像组件由非广播级镜头+CCD/CMOS+数字信号处理电路构成)	(1)	(2)		17	17	台		Other telecameras not for special purposes and other camera components (the latter is composed of non-broadcast-quality lens CCD/CMOS and digital signal processing electric circuit)
	---数字照相机:								---Digital cameras:
8525.8021	----特种用途的	0	17		17	17	台		----For special purposes
8525.8022	----非特种用途的单镜头反光型	0	(2)		17	17	台		--Single lens reflex, not for special purposes
8525.8025	----非特种用途的，其他可换镜头的	0	(2)		17	17	台		----Other changeable lens, not for special purposes
8525.8029	----非特种用途的其他类型	0	(2)		17	17	台		----Other , not for special purposes
	---视频摄录一体机:								---Video camera recorders:
8525.8031	----特种用途的	0	17		17	17	台	A	----For special purposes
8525.8032	----非特种用途的广播机	0	(2)		17	17	台	A	----Broadcast quality, not for special purposes
8525.8033	----非特种用途的家用型	0	130		17	17	台	A	----Household-type, not for special purposes
8525.8039	----非特种用途的其他类型	0	(2)		17	17	台	A	----Other, not for special purposes
85.26	**雷达设备、无线电导航设备及无线电遥控设备：**								**Radar apparatus, radio navigational aid apparatus and radio remote control apparatus:**
	-雷达设备:								-Radar apparatus:
8526.1010	---导航用	2	8		17	17	台		---For navigational aid
8526 1010.10	用于导弹、火箭等的导航雷达设备（用于弹道导弹、运载火箭、探空火箭等的目标探测）	2	8		17	17	台	3	Navigational radar equipments for missiles and rockets (for ballistic missiles, carrier rockets and sounding rockets, etc. to detect targets)
8526 1010.90	其他导航用雷达设备	2	8		17	17	台	O	Other navigational radar equipments
8526.1090	---其他	5	14		17	17	台		---Other

（1）完税价格不高于5000美元/台：35%；完税价格高于5000美元/台：3%，加9728元

（2）完税价格不高于5000美元/台：130%；完税价格高于5000美元/台：6%，加51500元

税则号列 Tariff Item	商品名称及备注	进口税率 最惠	普通	暂定	出口退税	增值税率	计量单位	监管条件	Article Description
8526 1090.01 [暂]	飞机机载雷达（包括气象雷达、地形雷达和空中交通管制应答系统）	5	14	1	17	17	台		Airborne radars (including meteorological radars, terrain following radars and air traffic control response system)
8526 1090.02 [暂]	雷达生命探测仪	5	14	2	17	17	台	O	Radar life detecting instrument
8526 1090.11	用于导弹、火箭等的机载雷达设备（用于弹道导弹、运载火箭、探空火箭等的目标探测）	5	14		17	17	台	3	Airborne radars for missiles and rockets (for ballistic missiles, carrier rockets and sounding rockets, etc. to detect targets)
8526 1090.91	用于导弹、火箭等的其他雷达设备（用于弹道导弹、运载火箭、探空火箭等的目标探测）	5	14		17	17	台	3	Other radars for missiles and rockets (ballistic missiles, carrier rockets and sounding rockets, etc. to detect targets)
8526 1090.99	其他雷达设备	5	14		17	17	台	O	Other radar
	-其他:								-Other:
	--无线电导航设备:								--Radio navigational aid apparatus:
8526.9110	---机动车辆用	2	8		17	17	台		---For motor vehicles
8526.9190	---其他	2	8		17	17	台		---Other
8526 9190.10	制导装置(使300千米射程导弹达到≤10千米圆公算偏差)	2	8		17	17	台	3O	Guidance devices (making the circular error probable of 300km-range missiles≤10km)
8526 9190.90	其他无线电导航设备	2	8		17	17	台	O	Other radio navigation devices
8526.9200	--无线电遥控设备	5	14		17	17	台	O	--Radio remote control apparatus
85.27	**无线电广播接收设备，不论是否与声音的录制、重放装置或时钟组合在同一机壳内:**								**Reception apparatus for radio-broadcasting, whether or not combined, in the same housing, with sound recording or reproducing apparatus or a clock:**
	-不需外接电源的无线电收音机:								-Radio-broadcast receivers capable of operating without an external source of power:
8527.1200	--袖珍盒式磁带收放机	20	130		17	17	台		--Pocket-size radio cassette-players
8527.1300	--其他收录(放)音组合机	15	130		17	17	台		--Other apparatus combined with sound recording or reproducing apparatus
8527.1900	--其他	15	130		17	17	台		--Other
	-需外接电源的汽车用无线电收音机:								-Radio-broadcast receivers not capable of operating without an external source of power, of a kind used in motor vehicles:
8527.2100 [暂]	--收录(放)音组合机	15	130	8	17	17	台		--Combined with sound recording or reproducing apparatus
8527.2900 [暂]	--其他	15	130	8	17	17	台		--Other
	-其他:								-Other:
8527.9100 [暂]	--收录(放)音组合机	15	130	8	17	17	台	A	--Combined with sound recording or reproducing apparatus
8527.9200	--带时钟的收音机	15	130		17	17	台		--Not combined with sound recording or reproducing apparatus but combined with a clock
8527.9900 [暂]	--其他	27	130	8	17	17	台	A	--Other
85.28	**监视器及投影机，未装电视接收装置；电视接收装置，不论是否装有无线电收音装置或声音、图像的录制或重放装置:**								**Monitors and projectors, not incorporating television reception apparatus; reception apparatus for television, whether or not incorporating radio-broadcast receivers or sound or video recording or reproducing apparatus:**
	-阴极射线管监视器:								-Cathode-ray tube monitors:
8528.4100	--专用于或主要用于品目84.71的自动数据处理系统的	0	40		17	17	台	6A	--Of a kind solely or principally used in an automatic data processing system of heading 84.71
	--其他:								--Other:
8528.4910	---彩色的	30	130		17	17	台	6A	---Colour
8528.4990	---单色的	19	100		17	17	台	6A	---Monochrome
	-其他监视器:								-Other monitors:
	--专用于或主要用于品目84.71的自动数据处理系统的:								--Of a kind solely or principally used in an automatic data processing system of heading 84.71:
8528.5110	---液晶的	0	40		17	17	台	A	---Of LCD

税则号列 Tariff Item	商品名称及备注	进口税率 最惠	进口税率 普通	进口税率 暂定	出口退税	增值税率	计量单位	监管条件	Article Description
8528.5190	---其他	0	40		17	17	台	A	---Other
	--其他:								--Other:
8528.5910	---彩色的	30	130		17	17	台		---Colour
8528 5910.01[暂]	专用于车载导航仪的液晶监视器	30	130	15	17	17	台	6A	LCD Monitors, specially used for Vehicle Navigator
8528 5910.90	其他彩色的监视器	30	130		17	17	台	6A	Other color monitor
8528.5990	---单色的	19	100		17	17	台	6A	---Monochrome
	-投影机:								-Projectors:
8528.6100	--专用于或主要用于品目 84.71 的自动数据处理系统的	0	14		17	17	台		--Of a kind solely or principally used in an automatic data processing system of heading 84.71
8528 6100.10	专用或主要用于品目 84.71 商品的彩色投影机	0	14		17	17	台	A	Color video projectors solely or principally used for goods of heading NO. 84.71
8528 6100.90	其他专用或主要用于品目 84.71 商品的投影机	0	14		17	17	台	A	Other projectors solely or principally used for goods of heading No.84.71
	--其他:								--Other:
8528.6910	---彩色的	30	130		17	17	台	6A	---Colour
8528.6990	---单色的	15	100		17	17	台	A	---Monochrome
	-电视接收装置，不论是否装有无线电收音装置或声音、图像的录制或重放装置:								-Reception apparatus for television ,whether or not incorporating radio-broadcast receivers or sound or video recording or reproducing apparatus:
	--在设计上不带有视频显示器或屏幕的:								--Not designed to incorporate a video display or screen:
8528.7110	---彩色卫星电视接收机	30	130		17	17	台	AO	---Colour satellite television receivers
8528.7180	---其他彩色的	30	130		17	17	台	A	---Other, colour
8528.7190	---单色的	15	100		17	17	台	A	---Monochrome
	--其他，彩色的:								--Other, colour:
	---阴极射线显像管的:								---Of CRT:
8528.7211	----模拟电视接收机	30	130		17	17	台	6A	----Analogue
8528.7212	----数字电视接收机	30	130		17	17	台	6A	----Digital
8528.7219	----其他	30	130		17	17	台	6A	----Other
	---液晶显示器的:								---Of LCD:
8528.7221	----模拟电视接收机	30	130		17	17	台	A	----Analogue
8528.7222	----数字电视接收机	30	130		17	17	台	A	----Digital
8528.7229	----其他	30	130		17	17	台	A	----Other
	---等离子显示器的:								---Of plasma:
8528.7231	----模拟电视接收机	30	130		17	17	台	A	----Analogue
8528.7232	----数字电视接收机	30	130		17	17	台	A	----Digital
8528.7239	----其他	30	130		17	17	台	A	----Other
	---其他:								---Other:
8528.7291	----模拟电视接收机	30	130		17	17	台	A	----Analogue
8528.7292	----数字电视接收机	30	130		17	17	台	A	----Digital
8528.7299	----其他	30	130		17	17	台	A	----Other
8528.7300	--其他，单色的	15	100		17	17	台	6A	--Other, monochrome
85.29	**专用于或主要用于品目 85.25 至 85.28 所列装置或设备的零件:**								**Parts suitable for use solely or principally with the apparatus of headings No.85.25 to 85.28:**
	-各种天线或天线反射器及其零件:								-Aerials and aerial reflectors of all kinds;parts suitable for use therewith:
8529.1010	---雷达设备及无线电导航设备用	1.5	8		17	17	千克		---For radar apparatus and radio navigational aid apparatus
8529.1020	---无线电收音机及其组合机、电视接收机用	0	90		17	17	千克		---For radio-broadcast receivers and their combinations, television receivers
8529.1090	---其他	2	20		17	17	千克/个		---Other
8529 1090.21	卫星电视接收用天线	2	20		17	17	千克/个	O	Satellite TV antenna
8529 1090.29	其他无线广播电视用天线(品目 85.25 至 85.28 所列其他装置或设备的，包括天线反射器)	2	20		17	17	千克/个	O	Other radio broadcasting & television (suitable for apparatus of heading No. 85.25-85.28, including aerials reflectors)
8529 1090.90	其他无线电设备天线及其零件	2	20		17	17	千克/个		Other radio antennas and parts (suitable for apparatus

税则号列 Tariff Item	商品名称及备注	进口税率			出口退税	增值税率	计量单位	监管条件	Article Description
		最惠	普通	暂定					
	（品目85.25至85.28所列其他装置或设备的，包括天线反射器）								of heading No. 85.25-85.28, including antenna reflector)
	-其他:								-Other:
8529.9010	---电视发送、差转设备及卫星电视地面接收转播设备用	0	30		17	17	千克/个		---Of television transmission or translation apparatus, satellite television ground receiving and relaying apparatus
8529 9010.11	卫星电视接收用解码器	0	30		17	17	千克/个	O	Satellite TV decorder
8529 9010.12	卫星电视接收用收视卡	0	30		17	17	千克/个	O	Access cards for receiving satellite television
8529 9010.13	卫星电视接收用器件板卡	0	30		17	17	千克/个	O	CRD card for receiving satellite television
8529 9010.14	卫星电视接收用专用零件	0	30		17	17	千克/个	O	Parts exclusively for receiving statellite TV signals
8529 9010.90	其他电视发送、差转等设备零件（包括其他卫星电视地面接收转播设备零件）	0	30		17	17	千克/个		Other parts for TV transmission or transposing devices (including other parts of ground receiving and relaying equipments for satellite television)
	---电视摄像机、其他视频摄录一体机、数字照相机用:								---Of television cameras, other video camera recorders and digital cameras:
8529.9041	----特种用途的	8	17		17	17	千克		----Of special purposes
8529.9042	----非特种用途的取像模块	12	100		17	17	千克		----Camera modules without special purposes
8529 9042.01 暂	摄录一体机、数码相机用取像模块	12	100	2	17	17	千克		Image pick-up modules for camcorder, digital cameras
8529 9042.02 暂	手机、平板电脑用取像模块	12	100	4	17	17	千克		Image pick-up module for cellphones, tablet computer
8529 9042.90	其他非特种用途的取像模块	12	100		17	17	千克		Other image pick-up modules not for special purpose
8529.9049 暂	----其他	12	100	2	17	17	千克		----Other
8529.9050	---雷达设备及无线电导航设备用	1.5	8		17	17	千克		---Of radar apparatus and radio navigational aid apparatus
8529.9060 暂	---无线电收音机及其组合机用	15	130	7	17	17	千克		---Of radio-broadcast receivers and their combinations
	---电视接收机用（高频调谐器除外）:								---Of television receivers（Other than H.F. tuners）:
8529.9081 暂	----彩色电视接收机用(等离子显像组件及其零件、有机发光二极管显示屏除外)(高频调谐器除外)	15	80	6	17	17	千克		----Of colour television receivers（Other than plasma display modules or parts thereof, organic light emitting diode display）
8529.9082 暂	----等离子显像组件及其零件	15	80	5	17	17	千克		----Plasma display modules and part thereof
8529.9083 暂	----有机发光二极管显示屏	15	50	5	17	17	千克/个		----Organic light emitting diode display
8529.9089	----其他	0	50		17	17	千克		----Other
8529.9090	---其他	0	57		17	17	千克/个		---Other
8529 9090.11	卫星电视接收用高频调谐器	0	57		17	17	千克/个	O	High-frequency tuners for satellite television
8529 9090.19	其他高频调谐器	0	57		17	17	千克/个		Other High-frequency tuners
8529 9090.90	品目85.25至85.28所列设备其他零件	0	57		17	17	千克/个		Other parts of heading No. 85.25-85.28
85.30	**铁道、电车道、道路或内河航道、停车场、港口或机场用的电气信号、安全或交通管理设备（品目86.08的货品除外）:**								**Electrical signaling, safety or traffic control equipment for railways, tramways, roads, inland waterways, parking facilities, port installations or airfields（other than those of heading No.86.08）:**
8530.1000	-铁道或电车道用的设备	10	20		17	17	个	O	-Equipment for railways or tramways
8530.8000	-其他设备	8	20		17	17	个	O	-Other equipment
8530.9000	-零件	8	20		17	17	千克		-Parts
85.31	**电气音响或视觉信号装置（例如，电铃、电笛、显示板、防盗或防火报警器），但品目85.12或85.30的货品除外:**								**Electric sound or visual signaling apparatus（for example, bells, sirens, indicator panels, burglar or fire alarms）, other than those of heading No.85. 12 or 85.30:**
8531.1000	-防盗或防火报警器及类似装置	10	40		17	17	个	A	-Burglar or fire alarms and similar apparatus
8531.2000	-装有液晶装置(LCD)或发光二极管（LED）的显示板	0	70		17	17	个		-Indicator panels incorporating liquid crystal devices（LCD）or light emitting diodes（LED）
	-其他装置:								-Other apparatus:
8531.8010	---蜂鸣器	15	70		17	17	个		---Buzzers
8531 8010.01 暂	音量不超过110分贝的小型蜂	15	70	7.5	17	17	个		Small-sized buzzers with volumn not more than 110db

税则号列 Tariff Item	商品名称及备注	进口税率 最惠	进口税率 普通	进口税率 暂定	出口退税	增值税率	计量单位	监管条件	Article Description
	鸣器								
8531 8010.90	其他蜂鸣器	15	70		17	17	个		Other buzzers
8531.8090	---其他	10	70		17	17	个		---Other
	-零件:								-Parts:
8531.9010	---防盗或防火报警器及类似装置用	0	40		17	17	千克	A	---Of burglar or fire alarms and similar apparatus
8531.9090	---其他	0	70		17	17	千克		---Other
85.32	**固定、可变或可调（微调）电容器：**								**Electrical capacitors, fixed, variable or adjustable（pre-set）：**
8532.1000	-固定电容器，用于50/60赫兹电路，其额定无功功率不低于0.5千瓦（电力电容器）	0	20		17	17	千克/千个		-Fixed capacitors designed for use in 50/60 Hz circuits and having a reactive power handling capacity of not less than 0.5kVar（power capacitors）
	-其他固定电容器:								-Other fixed capacitors:
	--钽电容器:								--Tantalum:
8532.2110	---片式	0	35		17	17	千克/千个		---Laminate
8532.2190	---其他	0	35		17	17	千克/千个		---Other
	--铝电解电容器:								--Aluminium electrolytic:
8532.2210	---片式	0	35		17	17	千克/千个		---Laminate
8532.2290	---其他	0	35		17	17	千克/千个		---Other
8532.2300	--单层瓷介电容器	0	35		17	17	千克/千个		--Ceramic dielectric, single layer
	--多层瓷介电容器:								--Ceramic dielectric, multilayer:
8532.2410	---片式	0	35		17	17	千克/千个		---Laminate
8532.2490	---其他	0	35		17	17	千克/千个		---Other
	--纸介质或塑料介质电容器:								--Dielectric of paper or plastics:
8532.2510	---片式	0	35		17	17	千克/千个		---Laminate
8532.2590	---其他	0	35		17	17	千克/千个		---Other
8532.2900	--其他	0	35		17	17	千克/千个		--Other
8532.3000	-可变或可调(微调)电容器	0	35		17	17	千克/千个		-Variable or adjustable（pre-set）capacitors
	-零件:								-Parts:
8532.9010	---子目号8532.1000所列电容器用	0	20		17	17	千克		---Of the capacitors of subheading No. 8532.1000
8532.9090	---其他	0	35		17	17	千克		---Other
85.33	**电阻器(包括变阻器及电位器)，但加热电阻器除外:**								**Electrical resistors（including rheostats and potentiometers），other than heating resistors:**
8533.1000	-固定碳质电阻器，合成或薄膜式	0	50		17	17	千克/千个		-Fixed carbon resistors, composition or film types
	-其他固定电阻器:								-Other fixed resistors：
	--额定功率不超过20瓦:								--For a power handling capacity not exceeding 20W:
8533.2110	---片式	0	50		17	17	千克/千个		---Laminate
8533.2190	---其他	0	50		17	17	千克/千个		---Other
8533.2900	--其他	0	50		17	17	千克/千个		--Other
	-线绕可变电阻器，包括变阻器及电位器:								-Wirewound variable resistors, including rheostats and potentiometers:

税则号列 Tariff Item	商品名称及备注	进口税率 最惠	进口税率 普通	进口税率 暂定	出口退税	增值税率	计量单位	监管条件	Article Description
8533.3100	--额定功率不超过20瓦	0	50		17	17	千克/千个		--For a power handling capacity not exceeding 20W
8533.3900	--其他	0	50		17	17	千克/千个		--Other
8533.4000	-其他可变电阻器，包括变阻器及电位器	0	50		17	17	千克/千个		-Other variable resistors, including rheostats and potentiometers
8533.9000	-零件	0	50		17	17	千克		-Parts
85.34	**印刷电路：**								**Printed circuits:**
8534.0010	---4层以上的	0	35		17	17	块/千克		---Of more than 4 layers
8534.0090	---其他	0	50		17	17	块/千克		---Other
85.35	**电路的开关、保护或连接用的电气装置（例如，开关、熔断器、避雷器、电压限幅器、电涌抑制器、插头及其他连接器、接线盒），用于电压超过1000伏的线路：**								**Electrical apparatus for switching or protecting electrical circuits, or for making connections to or in electrical circuits（for example, switches, fuses, lightning arresters,voltage limiters,surge suppressors, plugs and other connectors, junction boxes）, for a voltage exceeding 1000 V:**
8535.1000	-熔断器	14	50		17	17	个/千克	A	-Fuses
	-自动断路器：								-Automatic circuit breakers:
8535.2100	--用于电压低于72.5千伏的线路	14	50		17	17	个/千克	A	--For a voltage of less than 72.5kV
	--其他：								--Other:
8535.2910	---用于电压在72.5千伏及以上，但不高于220千伏的线路	10	50		17	17	个/千克		---For a voltage of 72.5kV or more, but not exceeding 220kV
8535.2920	---用于电压高于220千伏，但不高于750千伏的线路	10	50		17	17	个/千克		---For a voltage exceeding 220 kV, but not exceeding 750kV
8535.2990	---其他(用于电压＞750千伏的)	10	50		17	17	个/千克		---Other(for voltage＞750kv)
	-隔离开关及断续开关：								-Isolating switches and makeand-break switches:
8535.3010	---用于电压在72.5千伏及以上，但不高于220千伏的线路	10	50		17	17	个/千克		---For a voltage of 72.5kV or more, but not exceeding 220kV
8535.3020	---用于电压高于220千伏，但不高于750千伏的线路	10	50		17	17	个/千克		---For a voltage exceeding 220 kV, but not exceeding 750kV
8535.3090	---其他	10	50		17	17	个/千克	A	---Other
8535.4000	-避雷器、电压限幅器及电涌抑制器	18	50		17	17	个/千克		-Lightning arresters, voltage limiters and surge suppressors
8535.9000	-其他	10	50		17	17	千克		-Other
8535 9000.10	触发式火花隙(阳极延迟时间≤15毫秒，阳极峰值额定电流≥500A)	10	50		17	17	千克	3	Triggered spark gap (anode delay time ≤ 15ms, Anode peak rated current ≥ 500A)
8535 9000.20	具有快速开关功能的模件或组件（阳极峰值电压≥2KV；电流≥500A;接通时间为1微秒或更短）	10	50		17	17	千克	3	Modules or assemblies with swift ON/OFF switch (anode peak voltage ≥ 201V; current≥501A; switch time≤on 1ms or less)
8535 9000.90	其他电压>1000V电路开关等电气装置	10	50		17	17	千克		Other electric apparatuses such as circuit switches with its voltage>1000V
85.36	**电路的开关、保护或连接用的电气装置（例如，开关、继电器、熔断器、电涌抑制器、插头、插座、灯座及其他连接器、接线盒），用于电压不超过1000伏的线路；光导纤维、光导纤维束或光缆用连接器**								**Electrical apparatus for switching or protecting electrical circuits, or for making connections to or in electrical circuits（for example, switches, relays, fuses, surge suppressors, plugs, sockets, lamp-holders and other connectors, junction boxes）, for a voltage not exceeding 1000 volts; connectors for optical fibres, optical fibre bundles or cables:**
8536.1000	-熔断器	10	50		17	17	个/千克	A	-Fuses
8536.2000	-自动断路器	9	50		17	17	个/千克	A	-Automatic circuit breakers
8536.3000	-其他电路保护装置	9	50		17	17	个/千克	A	-Other apparatus for protecting electrical circuits
	-继电器：								-Relays:
	--用于电压不超过60伏的线路：								--For a voltage not exceeding 60V:
8536.4110	---用于电压不超过36伏的线路	10	50		17	17	个/千克		---For a voltage not exceeding 36V
8536.4190	---其他	10	50		17	17	个/千克	A	---Other

税则号列 Tariff Item	商品名称及备注	进口税率 最惠	普通	暂定	出口退税	增值税率	计量单位	监管条件	Article Description
8536.4900	--其他	10	50		17	17	个/千克	A	--Other
8536.5000	-其他开关	0	50		17	17	个/千克	A	-Other switches
	-灯座、插头及插座:								-Lamp-holders, plugs and sockets:
8536.6100	--灯座	10	50		17	17	个/千克		--Lamp-holders
8536.6900	--其他	0	50		17	17	个/千克		--Other
8536.7000	-光导纤维、光导纤维束或光缆用连接器	8	30		17	17	千克		-Connectors for optical fibres, optical fibre bundles or cables
	-其他装置:								-Other apparatus:
	---接插件:								---Connector:
8536.9011	----工作电压不超过36伏的	0	50		17	17	千克	A	----For a voltage not exceeding 36V
8536.9019	----其他	0	50		17	17	千克	A	----Other
8536.9090	---其他	0	50		17	17	千克	A	---Other
85.37	**用于电气控制或电力分配的盘、板、台、柜及其他基座，装有两个或多个品目8535或8536所列的装置，包括装有第九十章所列的仪器或装置，以及数控装置，但品目8517的交换机除外**								**Boards, panels, consoles, desks, cabinets and other bases, equipped with two or more apparatus of heading No.85.35 or 85.36, for electric control or the distribution of electricity, including those incorporating instruments or apparatus of Chapter 90, and numerical control apparatus, other than switching apparatus of heading No.85.17:**
	-用于电压不超过1000伏的线路:								-For a voltage not exceeding 1000V:
	---数控装置:								---Numerical control panels:
8537.1011	----可编程序控制器	5	14		17	17	个/千克		----Programmable logic controller（PLC）
8537 1011.01[暂]	机床用可编程序控制器（PLC）	5	14	3	17	17	个/千克		Programmable logic controllers for machine tools
8537 1011.10	调节和编程控制器（84798999.60绕线机用）	5	14		17	17	个/千克	3	Conditioning and Programming controllers for winding machines of subheading No.84798999.60
8537 1011.90	其他可编程控制器(用于电压不超过1000伏的线路)	5	14		17	17	个/千克		Other programmable logic controllers (for the circuit with its voltage no more than 1000V)
8537.1019	----其他	5	14		17	17	个/千克		----Other
8537 1019.01[暂]	机床用其他数控单元(包括单独进口的CNC操作单元)	5	14	3	17	17	个/千克		Other digital control units for machine tools(including seperately import CNC operating unit)
8537 1019.90	其他非机床用数控装置(用于电压不超过1000伏的线路)	5	14		17	17	个/千克		Digital control appratuses not for machine tools (for the circuit with its voltage no more than 1000V)
8537.1090	---其他	8.4	50		17	17	个/千克		---Other
8537 1090.01[暂]	电梯用控制柜及控制柜专用印刷电路板（电压不超过1000伏的线路）	8.4	50	4	17	17	个/千克		Control cabinet for elevators (electric cabinet) and printed circuit boards for control cabinets ((for the circuit with its voltage no more than 1000V)
8537 1090.21	控制器〔用于机器人或末端操纵装置（详见核两用清单）〕	8.4	50		17	17	个/千克	3	Controllers (for robots or end effectors, see the dual-use nuclear goods list for details)
8537 1090.22	数字控制器（专用于税号84798990.71电动式振动试验系统）	8.4	50		17	17	个/千克	3	Digital controllers (exclusively for electrodynamic vibration test systems of subheading No. 84798990.71)
8537 1090.90	其他电力控制或分配的装置(电压不超过1000伏的线路)	8.4	50		17	17	个/千克	A	Other power control or distribution devices ((for the circuit with its voltage no more than 1000V)
	-用于电压超过1000伏的线路:								-For a voltage exceeding 1000V:
8537.2010	---全封闭组合式高压开关装置,用于电压在500千伏及以上的线路	8.4	30		17	17	台/千克		---Gas insulated switch gear, for a voltage of 500kV or more
8537.2090	---其他	8.4	50		17	17	千克		---Other
85.38	**专用于或主要用于品目85.35、85.36或85.37所列装置的零件:**								**Parts suitable for use solely or principally with the apparatus of heading No.85.35, 85.36 or 85.37:**
	-品目85.37所列货品用的盘、板、台、柜及其他基座，但未装有关装置:								-Boards, panels, consoles, desks, cabinets and other bases for the goods of heading No.85.37, not equipped with their apparatus:
8538.1010	---品目8537.2010所列货品用	8.4	50		17	17	千克		---For the goods of heading No.8537.2010
8538.1090	---其他	7	50		17	17	千克		---Other
8538.9000	-其他	7	50		17	17	千克		-Other

税则号列 Tariff Item	商品名称及备注	进口税率 最惠	进口税率 普通	进口税率 暂定	出口退税	增值税率	计量单位	监管条件	Article Description
85.39	白炽灯泡、放电灯管，包括封闭式聚光灯及紫外线灯管或红外线灯泡；弧光灯：								**Electric filament or discharge lamps,including sealed beam lamp units and ultra-violet or infra-red lamps; arclamps:**
8539.1000	-封闭式聚光灯	10	45		17	17	只		-Sealed beam lamp units
	-其他白炽灯泡，但不包括紫外线灯管或红外线灯泡:								-Other filament lamps, excluding ultraviolet or infra-red lamps:
	--卤钨灯:								--Tungsten halogen:
8539.2110	---科研、医疗专用	8	20		17	17	只		---For scientific or medical uses only
8539.2120	---火车、航空器及船舶用	8	20		17	17	只		---For locomotives and rolling stock, aircraft or ships
8539.2130	---机动车辆用	10	45		17	17	只		---For motor vehicles
8539.2190	---其他	10.5	70		17	17	只		---Other
	--其他灯，功率不超过200瓦，但额定电压超过100伏:								--Other, of a power not exceeding 200W and for a voltage exceeding 100V:
8539.2210	---科研、医疗专用	10.5	20		17	17	只		---For scientific or medical uses only
8539.2290	---其他	5	70		17	17	只		---Other
	--其他:								--Other:
8539.2910	---科研、医疗专用	5	20		17	17	只		---For scientific or medical uses only
8539.2920	---火车、航空器及船舶用	10.5	20		17	17	只		---For locomotives and rolling-stock, aircraft or ships
8539.2930	---机动车辆用	5	45		17	17	只		---For motor vehicles
	---其他:								---Other:
8539.2991	----12伏及以下的	12	70		17	17	只		----Of a voltage 12V or less
8539.2999	----其他	12	70		17	17	只		----Other
	-放电灯管，但紫外线灯管除外:								-Discharge lamps, other than ultra-violet lamps:
	--热阴极荧光灯:								--Fluorescent, hot cathode:
8539.3110	---科研、医疗专用	8	20		17	17	只		---For scientific or medical uses only
8539.3120	---火车、航空器及船舶用	8	20		17	17	只		---For locomotives and rolling-stock, aircraft or ships
	---其他:								---Other：
8539.3191	----紧凑型	8	70		17	17	只		----Compact type
8539.3199	----其他	8	70		17	17	只		----Other
	--汞或钠蒸汽灯；金属卤化物灯:								--Mercury or sodium vapour lamps; metal halide lamps:
8539.3230	---钠蒸气灯	8	20		17	17	只		---Sodium vapour lamps
8539.3240	---汞蒸气灯	8	20		17	17	只		---Mercury vapour lamps
8539 3240.01[暂]	彩色投影机用的照明光源(汞蒸汽灯)	8	20	3	17	17	只		Lighting (ercury vapor lamps) used for Color LCD projector
8539 3240.90	其他汞蒸汽灯	8	20		17	17	只		Other mercury vapor lamps
8539.3290	---其他	8	70		17	17	只		---Other
	--其他:								--Other:
8539.3910	---科研、医疗专用	8	20		17	17	只		---For scientific or medical uses only
8539.3920	---火车、航空器及船舶用	8	20		17	17	只		---For locomotives and rolling-stock, aircraft or ships
8539.3990	---其他	8	70		17	17	只		---Other
8539 3990.01[暂]	液晶显示器背光模组用冷阴极灯管	8	70	3	17	17	只		Cold cathode florescent lamps for LCD Backlight Modules
8539 3990.90	其他用途的其他放电灯管	8	70		17	17	只		Other discharge lamps for other purposes
	-紫外线灯管或红外线灯泡；弧光灯:								-Ultra-violet or infra-red lamps; arc-lamps:
8539.4100	--弧光灯	8	20		17	17	只		--Arc-lamps
8539.4900	--其他	8	20		17	17	只		--Other
8539.9000	-零件	8	20		17	17	千克		-Parts
85.40	热电子管、冷阴极管或光阴极管（例如，真空管或充气管、汞弧整流管、阴极射线管、电视摄像管）：								**Thermionic, cold cathode or photocathode valves and tubes（for example, vacuum or vapour or gas filled valves and tubes, mercury arc rectifying valves and tubes, cathode-ray tubes,television camera tubes）:**
	-阴极射线电视显像管，包括视频监视器用阴极射线管:								-Cathode-ray television picture tubes, including video monitor cathode-ray tubes:
8540.1100	--彩色的	12	40		17	17	只	6A	--Colour

税则号列 Tariff Item	商品名称及备注	进口税率 最惠	普通	暂定	出口退税	增值税率	计量单位	监管条件	Article Description
8540.1200	--单色的	15	40		17	17	只	6A	--Monochrome
	-电视摄像管；变像管及图像增强管；其他光阴极管：								-Television camera tubes; image converters and intensifiers; other photocathode tubes:
8540.2010	---电视摄像管	12	35		17	17	只		---Television camera tubes
8540.2090	---其他	8	17		17	17	只		---Other
8540 2090.10	电子条纹相机的条纹显像管(专用于税号 90065900.40 的条纹显像管)	8	17		17	17	只	3	Streak kinescopes for electronic streak cameras (exclusively for Streak kinescopes of subheading No. 84798990.71)
8540 2090.90	其他电视摄像管;其他变像管及图像增强管；其他光阴极管	8	17		17	17	只		Other television camera tubes; other image converter and image intensifier; other photocathode tubes
	-单色的数据/图形显示管;彩色的数据/图形显示管，屏幕荧光点间距小于 0.4 毫米：								-Data/graphic display tubes, monochrome; data/graphic displaytubes, colour, with a phosphor dot screen pitch smaller than 0.4mm:
8540.4010	---彩色的数据/图形显示管,屏幕荧光点间距小于 0.4 毫米	8	17		17	17	只	6	---Data/graphic diaplaytubes, colour, with a phosphor dot smaller than 0.4mm
8540.4020	---单色的数据/图形显示管	8	17		17	17	只	6	---Data/graphic display tubes, monochrome
	-其他阴极射线管：								-Other cathode-ray tubes:
8540.6010	---雷达显示管	6	14		17	17	只		---Radar display tubes
8540.6090	---其他	8	17		17	17	只	6	---Other
	-微波管（例如，磁控管、速调管、行波管、返波管），但不包括栅控管：								-Microwave tubes（for example, magnetrons, klystrons, traveling wave tubes, carcinotrons）, excluding gridcontrolled tubes:
8540.7100	--磁控管	8	17		17	17	只		--Magnetrons
	--其他:								--Other:
8540.7910	---速调管	8	17		17	17	只		---Klystrons
8540.7990	---其他	8	17		17	17	只		---Other
	-其他管:								-Other valves and tubes:
8540.8100	--接收管或放大管	8	17		17	17	只		--Receiver or amplifier valves and tubes
8540.8900	--其他	8	17		17	17	只		--Other
8540 8900.10	光电倍增管(光电阴极面积大于 20 平方厘米，并且阳极脉冲上升时间小于 1 纳秒)	8	17		17	17	只	3	Photomultiplier(photo cathode area of more than 20 square centimeters, and anode pulse rise time less than 1 ns)
8540 8900.90	其他电子管(包括光阴极管或汞弧整流管)	8	17		17	17	只		Other electron tubes(photocathode tubes or emission mercury arc rectifier)
	-零件:								-Parts:
	--阴极射线管用:								--Of cathode-ray tubes:
8540.9110 暂	---电视显像管用	6	40	3	17	17	千克		---Of television picture tubes
8540.9120	---雷达显示管用	5	14		17	17	千克		---Of radar display tubes
8540.9190 暂	---其他	8	17	4	17	17	千克		---Other
	--其他:								--Other:
8540.9910	---电视摄像管用	8	35		17	17	千克		---Of television camera tubes
8540.9990	---其他	8	17		17	17	千克		---Other
85.41	**二极管、晶体管及类似的半导体器件；光敏半导体器件，包括不论是否装在组件内或组装成块的光电池；发光二极管；已装配的压电晶体**								**Diodes, transistors and similar semiconductor devices; photosensitive semiconductor devices, including photovoltaic cells whether or not assembled in modules or made up into panels; light emitting diodes; mounted piezoelectric crystals:**
8541.1000	-二极管，但光敏二极管或发光二极管除外	0	30		17	17	个/千克		-Diodes, other than photosensitive or light emitting diodes
	-晶体管，但光敏晶体管除外:								-Transistors, other than photosensitive transistors:
8541.2100	--耗散功率小于 1 瓦的	0	30		17	17	个/千克		--With a dissipation rate of less than 1W
8541.2900	--其他	0	30		17	17	个/千克		--Other
8541.3000	-半导体开关元件、两端交流开关元件及三端双向可控硅开关元件，但光敏器件除外	0	30		17	17	个/千克		-Thyristors, diacs and triacs, other than photosensitive devices
	-光敏半导体器件，包括不论是								-Photosensitive semiconductor devices,including

税则号列 Tariff Item	商品名称及备注	进口税率 最惠	普通	暂定	出口退税	增值税率	计量单位	监管条件	Article Description
	否装在组件内或组装成块的光电池；发光二极管：								photovoltaic cells whether or not assembled in modules or made up into panels; light emitting diodes:
8541.4010	---发光二极管	0	30		17	17	个/千克		---Light emitting diodes
8541.4020	---太阳能电池	0	30		17	17	个/千克		---Solar cells
8541.4090	---其他	0	30		17	17	个/千克		---Other
8541.5000	-其他半导体器件	0	30		17	17	个/千克		-Other semiconductor devices
8541.6000	-已装配的压电晶体	0	30		17	17	个/千克		-Mounted piezo-electric crystals
8541.9000	-零件	0	30		17	17	千克		-Parts
85.42	**集成电路：**								**Electronic integrated circuits:**
	-集成电路：								-Electronic integrated circuits:
8542.3100	--处理器及控制器，不论是否带有存储器、转换器、逻辑电路、放大器、时钟及时序电路或其他电路	0	24		17	17	个/千克		--Processors and controllers, whether or not combined with memories converters, logic circuits, amplifiers, clock and timing circuits or other circuits
8542.3200	--存储器	0	24		17	17	个/千克		--Memories
8542.3300	--放大器	0	24		17	17	个/千克		--Amplifiers
8542.3900	--其他	0	24		17	17	个/千克		--Other
8542.9000	-零件	0	30		17	17	千克		-Parts
85.43	**本章其他品目未列名的具有独立功能的电气设备及装置：**								**Electrical machines and apparatus, having individual functions, not specified or included elsewhere in this Chapter:**
8543.1000	-粒子加速器：	5	11		17	17	台		-Particle accelerators:
8543 1000.10	脉冲电子加速器（峰值能量为500千电子伏或更高）	5	11		17	17	台	3	Pulsed electron accelerators (with the peak energy of or above 500 KEV)
8543 1000.20	中子发生器系统，包括中子管（真空下，利用静电加速来诱发氚—氘核反应）	5	11		17	17	台	3	Neutron generator systems, including neutron tubes (evoking tritium-deuterium reaction through electrostatic acceleration in vacuum)
8543 1000.90	其他粒子加速器	5	11		17	17	台		Other particle accelerators
	-信号发生器：								-Signal generators:
8543.2010	---输出信号频率在1500兆赫兹以下的通用信号发生器	15	80		17	17	台		---Universal signal generators, with a frequency range of less than 1500MHz
8543.2090	---其他	8	20		17	17	台		---Other
8543 2090.10	高速脉冲发生器（脉冲上升时间小于500ps）	8	20		17	17	台	3	High-speed pulse generators (pulse rise time less than 500ps)
8543 2090.90	其他输出信号频率≥1500兆赫的通用信号发生器	8	20		17	17	台		Other versatile signal generators with the output signal frequency ≥1500Mhz
8543.3000	-电镀、电解或电泳设备及装置	0	35		17	17	台		-Machines and apparatus for electroplating, electrolysis or electrophoresis
8543 3000.10	电化学还原槽；锂汞齐电解槽（电化学还原槽为化学交换过程的铀浓缩设计的）	0	35		17	17	台	3	Electrochemical reduction cells; electrolytic cell for lithium-amalgam (with the former designed for uranium enrichment in chemical exchange processes)
8543 3000.20	产氟电解槽（每小时产250克以上）	0	35		17	17	台	3	Fluorine-generating electrolytic cells (above 250g of fluorine per hour)
8543 3000.90	其他电镀、电解或电泳设备及装置	0	35		17	17	台		Other electroplating, electrolyzing or electrophoresis equipments and appratuses
	-其他设备及装置：								-Other machines and apparatus:
8543.7091	----金属、矿藏探测器	0	17		17	17	台		----Metal or mine detectors
8543.7092	----高、中频放大器	0	17		17	17	台		----High or intermediate frequency amplifiers
8543.7093	----电篱网激发器	10	35		17	17	台		----Electric fence energizers
8543.7099	----其他	0	35		17	17	台		----Other
8543 7099.10	飞行数据记录器、报告器	0	35		17	17	台		Flight data recorders and reporters
8543 7099.20	无线广播电视用激励器（具有独立功能）	0	35		17	17	台	O	Exciters for wireless television broadcasting (with independent function)
8543 7099.30	模/数转换器（能设计或改进成军用，或设计成抗辐射的）	0	35		17	17	台	3	Analog-to-digital converters (can be designed or improved for military use or designed to be radiation-resistant)

税则号列 Tariff Item	商品名称及备注	进口税率			出口退税	增值税率	计量单位	监管条件	Article Description
		最惠	普通	暂定					
8543 7099.40	质谱仪用的离子源(原子质量单位≥230，分辨率＞2/230)	0	35		17	17	台	3	Ion source for mass spectrometers (atomic mass unit≥230; resolution＞2/230)
8543 7099.50	密码机、密码卡(不包括数字电视智能卡、蓝牙模块、用于知识产权保护的加密狗)	0	35		17	17	台	M	Cipher machines, crypto cards (excluding digital TV card, Bluetooth module, softdog for intellectual property protection)
8543 7099.90	其他未列名的具有独立功能的电气设备及装置	0	35		17	17	台		Other independently functional electric equipments and apparatus, not specified or included elsewhere
	-零件:								-Parts:
8543.9010	---粒子加速器用	0	11		17	17	千克		---Of particle accelerators
	---信号发生器用:								---Of signal generators:
8543.9021	----输出信号频率在1500兆赫兹以下的通用信号发生器用	0	80		17	17	千克		----Of the generators of subheading No.8543.2010
8543.9029	----其他	0	20		17	17	千克		----Other
8543.9030	---金属、矿藏探测器用	0	17		17	17	千克		---Of metal or mine detectors
8543.9040	---高、中频放大器用	0	17		17	17	千克		---Of high or intermediate frequency amplifiers
8543.9090	---其他	0	35		17	17	千克		---Other
85.44	**绝缘(包括漆包或阳极化处理)电线、电缆(包括同轴电缆)及其他绝缘电导体，不论是否有接头；由每根被覆光纤组成的光缆，不论是否与电导体装配或装有接头**								**Insulated (including enamelled or anodized) wire, cable (including co-axial cable) and other insulated electric conductors, whether or not fitted with connectors; optical fibre cables, made up of individually sheathed fibres, whether or not assembled with electric conductors or fitted with connectors:**
	-绕组电线:								-Winding wire:
8544.1100[暂]	--铜制	10	70	6	17	17	千克	A	--Of copper
8544.1900	--其他	20	70		17	17	千克	A	--Other
8544.2000	-同轴电缆及其他同轴电导体	10	20		17	17	千克	A	-Co-axial cable and other co-axial electric conductors
	-车辆、航空器、船舶用点火布线组及其他布线组:								-Ignition wiring sets and other wiring sets of a kind used in vehicles, aircraft or ships:
8544.3020	---机动车辆用	10	20		17	17	千克		---For motor vehicles
8544 3020.01[暂]	车辆用电控柴油机的线束	10	20	5	17	17	千克	A	Wiring harness for electronic diesel engines of vehicles
8544 3020.90	机动车辆用其他点火布线组及其他布线组	10	20		17	17	千克	A	Other ignition wiring sets and other wiring sets for motor vehicles
8544.3090	---其他	5	70		17	17	千克	A	---Other
	-其他电导体，额定电压不超过1000伏:								-Other electric conductors, for a voltage not exceeding 1000V:
	--有接头:								--Fitted with connectors:
	---额定电压不超过80伏:								---For a voltage not exceeding 80V:
8544.4211	----电缆	0	20		17	17	千克	A	----Electric cable
8544.4219	----其他	0	70		17	17	千克	A	----Other
	---额定电压超过80伏，但不超过1000伏:								---For a voltage exceeding 80V but not exceeding 1000V:
8544.4221	----电缆	0	20		17	17	千克	A	----Electric cable
8544.4229	----其他	0	70		17	17	千克	A	----Other
	--其他:								--Other:
	---额定电压不超过80伏:								---For a voltage not exceeding 80V:
8544.4911	----电缆	0	20		17	17	千克	A	----Electric cable
8544.4919	----其他	0	70		17	17	千克	A	----Other
	---额定电压超过80伏，但不超过1000伏:								---For a voltage exceeding 80V but not exceeding 1000V:
8544.4921	----电缆	6	20		17	17	千克	A	----Electric cable
8544.4929	----其他	12	70		17	17	千克	A	----Other
	-其他电导体，额定电压超过1000伏:								-Other electric conductors, for a voltage exceeding 1000V:
	---电缆:								---Electric cable:

税则号列 Tariff Item	商品名称及备注	进口税率			出口退税	增值税率	计量单位	监管条件	Article Description
		最惠	普通	暂定					
8544.6012	----额定电压不超过35千伏	10	50		17	17	千克	A	----For a voltage not exceeding 35kV
8544.6013	----额定电压超过35千伏，但不超过110千伏	8.4	20		17	17	千克	A	----For a voltage exceeding 35kV but not exceeding 110kV
8544.6014	----额定电压超过110千伏，但不超过220千伏	8.4	20		17	17	千克	A	----For a voltage exceeding 110kV but not exceeding 220kV
8544.6019	----其他	8.4	20		17	17	千克	A	----Other
8544.6090	---其他	21	70		17	17	千克	A	---Other
8544 6090.01[暂]	额定电压≥500千伏的气体绝缘金属封闭输电线	21	70	10	17	17	千克	A	Gas insulation metal close transmission wire with Rated voltage ≥500 kv
8544 6090.90	额定电压>1千伏的其他电导体	21	70		17	17	千克	A	Other electric conductor with a rated voltage>1kv
8544.7000	-光缆	0	20		17	17	千克	A	-Optical fibre cables
85.45	**碳电极、碳刷、灯碳棒、电池碳棒及电气设备用的其他石墨或碳精制品，不论是否带金属：**								**Carbon electrodes, carbon brushes, lamp carbons, battery carbons and other articles of graphite or other carbon, with or without metal, of a kind used for electrical purposes:**
	-碳电极：								-Electrodes:
8545.1100	--炉用	8	35			17	千克	3	--Of a kind used for furnaces
8545.1900	--其他	10.5	35			17	千克	3	--Other
8545.2000	-碳刷	10.5	35		17	17	千克		-Brushes
8545.9000	-其他	10.5	35		17	17	千克	3	-Other
85.46	**各种材料制的绝缘子：**								**Electrical insulators of any material:**
8546.1000	-玻璃制	10.5	35		17	17	千克		-Of glass
	-陶瓷制：								-Of ceramics:
8546.2010	---输变电线路绝缘瓷套管	6	35		17	17	千克		---Power transmission and converting ceramic bushings
8546.2090	---其他	12	35		17	17	千克		---Other
8546 2090.01[暂]	输变电架空线路用长棒形瓷绝缘子瓷件（单支长度为1～2米，实芯）	12	35	3	17	17	千克		Ceramic parts of long-rod ceramic insulators for electric transmission and transformation overhead lines (length of a single rod: 1-2m; solid)
8546 2090.90	其他陶瓷制绝缘子（包括非输变电线路绝缘瓷套管）	12	35		17	17	千克		Other ceramics electrical insulators (including non-power transmission and converting ceramic bushings)
8546.9000	-其他	10	35		17	17	千克		-Other
85.47	**电气机器、器具或设备用的绝缘零件，除了为装配需要而在模制时装入的小金属零件（例如螺纹孔）以外，全部用绝缘材料制成，但品目8546的绝缘子除外；内衬绝缘材料的贱金属制线路导管及其接头**								**Insulating fittings for electrical machines, appliances or equipment, being fittings wholly of insulating material apart from any minor components of metal（for example, threaded sockets）incorporated during moulding solely for purposes of assembly, other than insulators of heading No.85.46; electrical conduit tubing and joints therefor, of base metal lined with insulating material:**
8547.1000	-陶瓷制绝缘零件	8	35		17	17	千克		-Insulating fittings of ceramics
8547.2000	-塑料制绝缘零件	8	35		17	17	千克		-Insulating fittings of plastics
	-其他：								-Other:
8547.9010	---内衬绝缘材料的贱金属制线路导管及其接头	10	50		17	17	千克		---Electrical conduit tubing and joints therefor, of base metal lined with insulating material
8547.9090	---其他	8	35		17	17	千克		---Other
85.48	**原电池、原电池组及蓄电池的废碎料；废原电池、废原电池组及废蓄电池；机器或设备的本章其他品目未列名的电气零件**								**Waste and scrap of primary cells, primary batteries and electric accumulators; spent primary cells, spent primary batteries and spent electric accumulators; electrical parts of machinery or apparatus, not specified or included elsewhere in this Chapter:**
8548.1000	-原电池、原电池组及蓄电池的废碎料；废原电池、废原电池组及废蓄电池	8	36		17	17	千克	9	-Waste and scrap of primary cells, primary batteries and electric accumulators; spent primary cells, spent primary batteries and spent electric accumulators
8548.9000	-其他	12	40			17	千克		-Other

税则号列 Tariff Item	商品名称及备注	进口税率			出口退税	增值税率	计量单位	监管条件	Article Description
		最惠	普通	暂定					
8548 9000.01[暂]	电磁干扰滤波器	12	40	3	17	17	千克		Electromagnetic interference filters
8548 9000.02[暂]	非电磁干扰滤波器	12	40	6	17	17	千克		Non Electromagnetic interference filters
8548 9000.10	可调脉冲单模染料振荡器(平均输出功率＞1瓦，重复率＞1千赫兹，脉宽＜100纳秒可见光范围)	12	40		17	17	千克	3	Tunable pulsed single-mode dye oscillators (average output power＞1w; repetition rate＞1khz; pulse width＜100ns of Wavelength range of visible light)
85489000.20	可调脉冲染料激光放大器和振荡器(不包括单模振荡器)(平均输出功率＞30瓦，重复率＞1千赫兹，脉宽＜100纳秒可见光范围)	12	40		17	17	千克	3	Tunable pulsed laser dye amplifiers and oscillators (average output power＞30w;repetition rate＞1khz; pulse width＜100ns of Wavelength range of visible light, excluding single-mode oscillators)
8548 9000.90	第八十五章其他税号未列名的电气零件	12	40		15	17	千克		Other electrical parts, not specified or included elsewhere in Chapter 85

第十七类 车辆、航空器、船舶及有关运输设备

SECTION XVII VEHICLES, AIRCRAFT, VESSELS AND ASSOCIATED TRANSPORT EQUIPMENT

注释：

一、本类不包括品目 95.03 或 95.08 的物品以及品目 95.06 的长雪橇、平底雪橇及类似品。

二、本类所称“零件”及“零件、附件”，不适用于下列货品，不论其是否确定为供本类货品使用：

（一）各种材料制的接头、垫圈或类似品（按其构成材料归类或归入品目 84.84）或硫化橡胶（硬质橡胶除外）的其他制品（品目 40.16）；

（二）第十五类注释二所规定的贱金属制通用零件（第十五类）或塑料制的类似品（第三十九章）；

（三）第八十二章的物品（工具）；

（四）品目 83.06 的物品；

（五）品目 84.01 至 84.79 的机器或装置及其零件；品目 84.81 或 84.82 的物品及品目 84.83 的物品（这些物品是构成发动机或其他动力装置所必需的）；

（六）电机或电气设备（第八十五章）；

（七）第九十章的物品；

（八）第九十一章的物品；

（九）武器（第九十三章）；

（十）品目 94.05 的灯具或照明装置；或

（十一）作为车辆零件的刷子（品目 96.03）。

三、第八十六章至第八十八章所称“零件”或“附件”，不适用于那些非专用于或非主要用于这几章所列物品的零件、附件。同时符合这几章内两个或两个以上品目规定的零件、附件，应按其主要用途归入相应的品目。

四、在本类中：

（一）既可在道路上，又可在轨道上行驶的特殊构造的车辆，应归入第八十七章的相应品目；

（二）水陆两用的机动车辆，应归入第八十七章的相应品目；

（三）可兼作地面车辆使用的特殊构造的航空器，应归入第八十八章的相应品目。

五、气垫运输工具应按本类最相似的运输工具归类，其规定如下：

（一）在导轨上运行的（气垫火车），归入第八十六章；

（二）在陆地行驶或水陆两用的，归入第八十七章；

（三）在水上航行的，不论能否在海滩或浮码头登陆及能否在冰上行驶，一律归入第八十九章。

Section Notes:

1. This Section does not cover articles of heading 95.03 or 95.08, or bobsleighs, toboggans or the like of heading 95.06.

2. The expressions “parts” and “parts and accessories” do not apply to the following articles, whether or not they are identifiable as for the goods of this Section:

（a）Joints, washers or the like of any material（classified according to their constituent material or in heading 84.84）or other articles of vulcanised rubber other than hard rubber（heading 40.16）;

（b）Parts of general use, as defined in Note 2 to Section XV, of base metal（Section XV ）, or similar goods of plastics（Chapter 39）;

（c）Articles of Chapter 82（tools）;

（d）Articles of heading 83.06;

（e）Machines or apparatus of headings 84.01 to 84.79, or parts thereof; articles of heading 84.81 or 84.82 or, provided they constitute integral parts of engines or motors, articles of heading 84.83;

（f）Electrical machinery or equipment（Chapter 85）;

（g）Articles of Chapter 90;

（h）Articles of Chapter 91;

（ij）Arms（Chapter 93）;

（k）Lamps or lighting fittings of heading 94.05; or

（l）Brushes of a kind used as parts of vehicles（heading 96.03）.

3. References in Chapters 86 to 88 to “parts” or “accessories” do not apply to parts or accessories which are not suitable for use solely or principally with the articles of those Chapters. A part or accessory which answers to a description in two or more of the headings of those Chapters is to be classified under that heading which corresponds to the principal use of that part or accessory.

4. For the purposes of this Section:

（a）Vehicles specially constructed to travel on both road and rail are classified under the appropriate heading of Chapter 87;

（b）Amphibious motor vehicles are classified under the appropriate heading of Chapter 87;

（c）Aircraft specially constructed so that they can also be used as road vehicles are classified under the appropriate heading of Chapter 88.

5. Air-cushion vehicles are to be classified within this Section with the vehicles to which they are most akin as follows:

（a）In Chapter 86 if designed to travel on a guide-track（hovertrains）;

（b）In Chapter 87 if designed to travel over land or over both land and water;

（c）In Chapter 89 if designed to travel over water, whether or not able to land on beaches or landingstages or also able to travel over ice.

气垫运输工具的零件、附件，应按照上述规定，与最相类似的运输工具的零件、附件一并归类。气垫火车的导轨固定装置及附件应与铁道轨道固定装置及附件一并归类。气垫火车运行系统的信号、安全或交通管理设备应与铁路的信号、安全或交通管理设备一并归类。

Parts ar d accessories of air-cushion vehicles are to be classified in the same way as :hose of vehicles of the heading in which the air-cushion vehicles are classified under the above provisions.

Hovertrain track fixtures and fittings are to be classified as railway track fixtures and fittings, and signalling, safety or traffic control equipment for hovertrain transport systems as signalling, safety or traffic control equipment for railways.

第八十六章
铁道及电车道机车、车辆及其零件；铁道及电车道轨道固定装置及其零件、附件；各种机械（包括电动机械）交通信号设备

Chapter 86
Railway or trainway locomotives, rolling-stock and parts thereof; railway or trainway track fixtures and fittings and parts thereof; mechanical (including electro-mechanical) traffic signalling equipment of all kinds

注释：

一、本章不包括：

（一）木制或混凝土制的铁道或电车道轨枕及气垫火车用的混凝土导轨（品目 44.06 或 68.10）；

（二）品目 73.02 的铁道及电车道铺轨用钢铁材料；或

（三）品目 85.30 的电气信号、安全或交通管理设备。

二、品目 86.07 主要适用于：

（一）轴、轮、行走机构、金属轮箍、轮圈、毂及轮子的其他零件；

（二）车架、底架、转向架；

（三）轴箱；制动装置；

（四）车辆缓冲器；钩或其他联结器及车厢走廊联结装置；

（五）车身。

三、除上述注释一另有规定的以外，品目 86.08 包括：

（一）已装配的轨道、转车台、站台缓冲器、量载规；

（二）铁道及电车道、道路、内河航道、停车场、港口或机场用的臂板信号机、机械信号盘、平交道口控制器、信号及道岔控制器及其他机械（包括电动机械）信号、安全或交通管理设备，不论是否装有电力照明装置。

Chapter Notes:

1. This Chapter does not cover:

(a) Railway or trainway sleepers of wood or of concrete, or concrete guide-track sections for hovertrain (heading 44.06 or 68.10);

(b) Railway or tramway track construction material of iron or steel of heading73.02; or

(c) Electrical signalling, safety of traffic control equipment of heading 85.30.

2. Heading 86.07 applies, inter alia, to:

(a) Axles, wheels, wheel sets (running gear), metal tyres, hoops and hubs and other parts of wheels;

(b) Frames, underframes, bogies and bissel-bogies;

(c) Axle boxes; brake gear;

(d) Buffers for rolling-stock; hooks and other coupling gear and corridor connections;

(e) Coachwork.

3. Subject to the provisions of Note 1 above, heading 86.08 applies, nteralia, to:

(a) Assembled track, turntables, platform buffers, loading gauges;

(b) Semaphores, mechanical signal discs, level crossing control gear, signal and point controls, and other mechanical (including electro-mechanical) signalling, safety or traffic control equipment, whether or not fitted for electric lighting, for railways, trainways, roads, inland waterways, parking facilities, port installations or airfields.

税则号列 Tariff Item	商品名称及备注	进口税率 最惠	进口税率 普通	进口税率 暂定	出口退税	增值税率	计量单位	监管条件	Article Description
86.01	铁道电力机车，由外部电力或蓄电池驱动：								**Rail locomotives powered from an external source of electricity or by electric accumulators:**
	-由外部电力驱动：								-Powered from an external source of electricity:
	---直流电机驱动的：								---Drived by DC motors:
8601.1011	----微型机控制的	3	11		17	17	辆		----Controlled by microprocessings
8601.1019	----其他	3	11		17	17	辆		----Other
8601.1020	---交流电机驱动的	3	11		17	17	辆	O	---Drived by AC motors
8601.1090	---其他	3	11		17	17	辆	O	---Other

税则号列 Tariff Item	商品名称及备注	进口税率			出口退税	增值税率	计量单位	监管条件	Article Description
		最惠	普通	暂定					
8601.2000	-由蓄电池驱动	3	11		17	17	辆		-Powered by electric accumulators
86.02	其他铁道机车；机车煤水车：								**Other rail locomotives; locomotive tenders:**
	-柴油电力机车：								-Diesel-electric locomotives:
8602.1010	---微型机控制的	3	11		17	17	辆		---Controled by microprocessings
8602.1090	---其他	3	11		17	17	辆		---Other
8602.9000	-其他	3	11		17	17	辆		-Other
86.03	铁道及电车道用的机动客车、货车、敞车，但品目86.04的货品除外：								**Self-propelled railway or trainway coaches, vans and trucks, other than those of heading No.86.04:**
8603.1000	-由外部电力驱动	3	11		17	17	辆	O	-Powered from an external source of electricity
8603.9000	-其他	3	11		17	17	辆		-Other
86.04	铁道及电车道用的维修或服务车，不论是否机动（例如，工场车、起重机车、道碴捣固车、轨道校正车、检验车及查道车）：								**Railway or trainway maintenance or service vehicles, whether or not selfpropelled（for example, workshops, cranes, ballast tampers, trackliners,testing coaches and track inspection vehicles）:**
	---检验车及查道车：								---Testing coaches and track inspection vehicles
8604.0011	----隧道限界检查车	3	14		17	17	辆		----Inspection vehicles for tunnel clearance
8604.0012	----钢轨在线打磨列车	3	14		17	17	辆		----Sanding vehicles for on-line rails
8604.0019	----其他	5	14		17	17	辆	O	----Other
	---其他：								---Other:
8604.0091	----电气化接触网架线机(轨行式)	5	20		17	17	辆		----Installing vehicles for suspension of contact wire（running on rails）
8604.0099	----其他	7	20		17	17	辆		----Other
86.05	铁道及电车道用的非机动客车；行李车、邮政车和其他铁道及电车道用的非机动特殊用途车辆（品目86.04的货品除外）：								**Railway or tramway passenger coaches,not self-propelled; luggage vans, post office coaches and other special purpose railway or trainway coaches, not selfpropelled（excluding those of heading No. 86.04）:**
8605.0010	---铁道客车	5	14		17	17	辆		---Railway passenger coaches
8605.0090	---其他	5	14		17	17	辆		---Other
86.06	铁道及电车道用的非机动有篷及无篷货车：								**Railway or trainway goods vans and wagons, not self-propelled:**
8606.1000	-油罐货车及类似车	5	14		17	17	辆		-Tank wagons and the like
8606.3000	-自卸货车，但子目8606.1000的货品除外	5	14		17	17	辆		-Self-discharging wans and wagons, other than those of subheading No.8606.1000
	-其他：								-Other:
8606.9100	--带篷及封闭的	5	14		17	17	辆		--Covered and closed
8606.9200	--敞篷的，厢壁固定且高度超过60厘米	5	14		17	17	辆		--Open, with non-removable sides of a height exceeding 60 cm
8606.9900	--其他	5	14		17	17	辆		--Other
86.07	铁道及电车道机车或其他车辆的零件：								**Parts of railway or trainway locomotives or rolling-stock:**
	-转向架、轴、轮及其零件：								-Bogies, bissel-bogies, axles and wheels,and parts thereof:
8607.1100	--驾驶转向架	3	11		15	17	套/千克		--Driving bogies and bissel-bogies
8607.1200	--其他转向架	3	11		15	17	套/千克		--Other bogies and bissel-bogies
	--其他，包括零件：								--Other, including parts:
8607.1910	---轴	3	11		17	17	根/千克	A	---Axles
8607.1990	---其他	3	11		17	17	千克	A	---Other
	-制动装置及其零件：								-Brakes and parts thereof:
8607.2100	--空气制动器及其零件：	3	11		17	17	千克		--Air brakes and parts thereof
8607.2900	--其他	3	11		17	17	千克		--Other
8607.3000	-钩、其他联结器、缓冲器及其零件	3	11		17	17	千克		-Hooks and other coupling devices, buffers, and parts there of
	-其他：								-Other:
8607.9100	--机车用	3	11		17	17	千克		--Of locomotives

税则号列 Tariff Item	商品名称及备注	进口税率			出口退税	增值税率	计量单位	监管条件	Article Description
		最惠	普通	暂定					
8607.9900	--其他	3	11		17	17	千克		--Other
86.08	铁道及电车道轨道固定装置及附件；供铁道、电车道、道路、内河航道、停车场、港口或机场用的机械(包括电动机械)信号、安全或交通管理设备；上述货品的零件：								**Railway or trainway track fixtures and fittings; mechanical (including electro-mechanical) signalling, safety or traffic control equipment for railways, trainways, roads, inland waterways, parking facilities, port installations or airfields; parts of the foregoing:**
8608.0010	---轨道自动计轴设备	3	20		17	17	千克/台		---Rail automatic axle counting equipments
8608.0090	---其他	4	20		17	17	千克		---Other
86.09	集装箱（包括运输液体的集装箱），经特殊设计、装备适用于各种运输方式：								**Containers (including containers for the transport of fluids) specially designed and equipped for carriage by one or more modes of transport:**
	---20英尺的：								---Of 20 feet:
8609.0011	----保温式	10.5	35		15	17	个	AB	----Insulated
8609.0012	----罐式	10.5	35		15	17	个	AB	----Tank type
8609.0019	----其他	10.5	35		15	17	个	AB	----Other
	---40英尺的：								---Of 40 feet:
8609.0021	----保温式	10.5	35		15	17	个	AB	----Insulated
8609.0022	----罐式	10.5	35		15	17	个	AB	----Tank type
8609.0029	----其他	10.5	35		15	17	个	AB	----Other
8609.0030	---45、48、53英尺的	10.5	35		15	17	个	AB	---Of 45, 48, 53 feet
8609.0090	---其他	10.5	35		15	17	个	AB	-Other

第八十七章
车辆及其零件、附件，但铁道及电车道车辆除外

Chapter 87
Vehicles other than railway or trainway rolling-stock, and parts and accessories thereof

注释：

一、本章不包括仅可在钢轨上运行的铁道及电车道车辆。

二、本章所称“牵引车、拖拉机”，是指主要为牵引或推动其他车辆、器具或重物的车辆。除了上述主要用途以外，不论其是否还具有装运工具、种子、肥料或其他货品的辅助装置。

用于安装在品目 87.01 的牵引车或拖拉机上，作为可替换设备的机器或作业工具，即使与牵引车或拖拉机一同报验，不论其是否已安装在车（机）上，仍应归入其各自相应的品目。

三、装有驾驶室的机动车辆底盘，应归入品目 87.02 至 87.04，而不归入品目 87.06。

四、品目 87.12 包括所有儿童两轮车，其他儿童脚踏车归入品目 95.03。

Chapter Notes:

1. This Chapter does not cover railway or trainway rolling-stock designed solely for running on rails.
2. For the purposes of this Chapter, “tractors” means vehicles constructed essentially for hauling or pushing another vehicle, appliance or load, whether or not they contain subsidiary provision for the transport, in connection with the main use of the tractor, of tools, seeds, fertilisers or other goods.

   Machines and working tools designed for fitting to tractors of heading 87.01 as interchangeable equipment remain classified in their respective headings even if presented with the tractor, and whether or not mounted on it.
3. Motor chassis fitted with cabs fall in headings 87.02 to 87.04, and not in heading 87.06.
4. Heading 87.12 includes all children’s bicycles. Other children’s cycles fall in heading 95.03.

税则号列 Tariff Item	商品名称及备注	进口税率 最惠	普通	暂定	出口退税	增值税率	计量单位	监管条件	Article Description
87.01	牵引车、拖拉机（品目 87.09 的牵引车除外）：								**Tractors（other than tractors of heading No. 87.09）：**
8701.1000	-手扶拖拉机	9	20		13	13	辆	6	-Pedestrian controlled tractors
8701.2000	-半挂车用的公路牵引车	6	20		17	17	辆	46AOxy	-Road tractors for semi-trailers
8701.3000	-履带式牵引车、拖拉机	6	20		13/17		辆		-Track-laying tractors
8701 3000.10	履带式拖拉机	6	20		13/17	13	辆	6A	Track-laying tractors
8701 3000.90	履带式牵引车	6	20		13/17	17	辆	6A	Other track-laying tractors
	-其他:								-Other:
	---拖拉机:								---Tractors:
8701.9011	----轮式	8	20		13/17	13	辆		----Wheeled
8701 9011.01 [暂]	功率大于150马力的轮式拖拉机	8	20	5	13/17	13	辆	6A	Wheeled tractors, power greater than 150 hp
8701 9011.90	其他轮式拖拉机	8	20		13/17	13	辆	6A	Other wheeled tractors
8701.9019	----其他	8	20		13/17	13	辆		----Other
8701 9019.01 [暂]	其他功率大于 150 马力的拖拉机	8	20	5	13/17	13	辆	6A	Other tractor, power greater than 150 hp
8701 9019.90	其他拖拉机	8	20		13/17	13	辆	6A	Other tractor
8701.9090	---其他	8	20		13/17	17	辆	6A	---Other
87.02	客运机动车辆，10座及以上（包括驾驶座）：								**Motor vehicles for the transport of ten or more persons, including the driver:**
	-装有压燃式活塞内燃发动机(柴油或半柴油发动机)的车辆:								-With compression-ignition internal combustion piston engine（diesel or semidiesel）:
8702.1020	---机坪客车	4	90		17	17	辆	6ABO	---Buses for transport passengers at airport
	---其他:								---Other:
8702.1091	----30座及以上(大型客车)	25	90		17	17	辆	46ABOxy	----With 30 seats or more
8702.1092	----20座及以上，但不超过29座	25	230		17	17	辆		----With 20 seats or more, but not exceeding 29 seats
8702 1092.01	20≤座≤23 装有压燃式活塞内燃发动机的客车	25	230		17	17	辆	46ABOxy	Passenger buses, 20-23 seats, with compressionignition internal combustion piston engine
8702 1092.90	24≤座≤29 装有压燃式活塞内燃发动机的客车	25	230		17	17	辆	46ABOxy	Passenger buses, 24-29 seats, with compressionignition internal combustion piston engine
8702.1093	----10座及以上，但不超过19座	25	230		17	17	辆	46ABOxy	----With 10 seats or more, but not exceeding 19 seats
	-其他:								-Other:
8702.9010	---30座及以上(大型客车)	25	90		17	17	辆	46ABOxy	---With 30 seats or more

税则号列 Tariff Item	商品名称及备注	进口税率 最惠	普通	暂定	出口退税	增值税率	计量单位	监管条件	Article Description
8702.9020	---20座及以上，但不超过29座	25	230		17	17	辆		---With 20 seats or more,but not exceeding 29 seats
8702 9020.01	20≤座≤23 装有非压燃式活塞内燃发动机的客车	25	230		17	17	辆	46ABOxy	Passenger buses, with non compression-ignition internal combustion piston engine, 20-23 seats
8702 9020.90	24≤座≤29 装有非压燃式活塞内燃发动机的客车	25	230		17	17	辆	46ABOxy	Passenger buses, with non compression-ignition internal combustion piston engine, 24-29 seats
8702.9030	---10座及以上，但不超过19座	25	230		17	17	辆	46ABOxy	---With 10 seats or more, but not exceeding 19 seats
87.03	**主要用于载人的机动车辆(品目87.02的货品除外)，包括旅行小客车及赛车：**								**Motor cars and other motor vehicles principally designed for the transport of persons（other than those of heading No. 87.02）, including station wagons and racing cars:**
	-雪地行走专用车；高尔夫球车及类似车辆:								-Vehicles specially designed for travelling on snow; golf cars and similar vehicles:
	---高尔夫球车及类似车辆:								---Golf cars and similar vehicles:
8703.1011	----全地形车	25	150		15	17	辆	46Bxy	----All terrain vehicles
8703.1019	----其他	25	150		15	17	辆	6	----Other
8703.1090	---其他	25	150		15	17	辆	6	---Other
	-装有点燃往复式活塞内燃发动机的其他车辆:								-Other vehicles, with spark-ignition internal combustion reciprocating piston engine:
	--气缸容量（排气量）不超过1000毫升:								--Of a cylinder capacity not exceeding 1000cc:
8703.2130	---小轿车	25	230		17	17	辆		---Saloon cars
8703 2130.01	排气量≤1 升的装有点燃往复式活塞内燃发动机的小轿车	25	230		17	17	辆	46ABOxy	Saloon cars of cylinder capacity not exceeding 1L with spark-ignition internal combustion reciprocating piston engine
8703 2130.90	排气量≤1 升的装有点燃往复式活塞内燃发动机小轿车的成套散件	25	230		17	17	辆	46BOxy	Complete parts of Saloon cars of cylinder capacity not exceeding 1L, with spark-ignition internal combustion reciprocating piston engine
8703.2140	---越野车（4轮驱动）	25	230		17	17	辆		---Cross-country cars（4WD）
8703 2140.01	排量≤1 升的带点燃往复式活塞内燃发动机的越野车（4轮驱动）	25	230		17	17	辆	46ABOxy	Cross-country cars（4WD）of cylinder capacity not exceeding 1L, with spark-ignition internal combustion reciprocating piston engine
8703 2140.90	排量≤1 升的带点燃往复式活塞内燃发动机的越野车（4轮驱动）的成套散件	25	230		17	17	辆	46ABOxy	Complete parts of cylinder capacity not exceeding 1L, with spark-ignition internal combustion reciprocating piston engine
8703.2150	---9座及以下的小客车	25	230		17	17	辆		---Station wagons（with 9 seats or less）
8703 2150.01	排量≤1 升的带点燃往复式活塞内燃发动机的小客车（9座及以下）	25	230		17	17	辆	46ABOxy	Station wagons of cylinder capacity not exceeding 1L with spark-ignition internal combustion reciprocating piston engine, 9 seats or less
8703 2150.90	排量≤1 升的带点燃往复式活塞内燃发动机的小客车的成套散件（9座及以下）	25	230		17	17	辆	46ABOxy	Complete parts of station wagons of cylinder capacity not exceeding 1L, with spark-ignition internal combustion reciprocating piston engine
8703.2190	---其他	25	230		17	17	辆		---Other
8703 2190.01	排量≤1 升的带点燃往复式活塞内燃发动机的其他车辆	25	230		17	17	辆	46ABOxy	Others vehicles of cylinder capacity not exceeding 1L with spark-ignition internal combustion reciprocating piston engine
8703 2190.90	排量≤1 升的带点燃往复式活塞为燃发动机的其他车辆的成套散件	25	230		17	17	辆	46ABOxy	Complete parts of Others vehicles of cylinder capacity not exceeding 1L with spark-ignition internal combustion reciprocating piston engine
	--气缸容量（排气量）超过1000毫升，但不超过1500毫升:								--Of a cylinder capacity exceeding 1000cc but not exceeding 1500cc:
8703.2230	---小轿车	25	230		17	17	辆		----Saloon cars
8703 2230.01	1升＜排量≤1.5 升带点燃往复式活塞内燃发动机小轿车	25	230		17	17	辆	46ABOxy	Saloon cars of a cylinder capacity from 1L to 1.5L, with spark-ignition internal combustion reciprocating piston engine
8703 2230.90	1升＜排量≤1.5 升带点燃往复式活塞内燃发动机的小轿车的成套散件	25	230		17	17	辆	46ABOxy	Complete parts of saloon cars of a cylinder capacity from 1L to 1.5L, with spark-ignition internal combustion reciprocating piston engine

税则号列 Tariff Item	商品名称及备注	进口税率 最惠	进口税率 普通	进口税率 暂定	出口退税	增值税率	计量单位	监管条件	Article Description
8703.2240	---越野车（4轮驱动）	25	230		17	17	辆		---Cross-country cars（4WD）
8703 2240.01	1升＜排量≤1.5升带点燃往复活塞内燃发动机四轮驱动越野车	25	230		17	17	辆	46ABOxy	Cross-country cars（4WD）of a cylinder capacity from 1L to 1.5L,, with spark- ignition internal combustion reciprocating piston engine
8703 2240.90	1升＜排量≤1.5升带点燃往复活塞内燃发动机四轮驱动越野车的成套散件	25	230		17	17	辆	46ABOxy	Complete parts of cross-country cars of a cylinder capacity from 1L to 1.5L,, with spark-ignition internal combustion reciprocating piston engine
8703.2250	---9座及以下的小客车	25	230		17	17	辆		---Station wagons（with 9 seats or less）
8703 2250.01	1升＜排量≤1.5升带点燃往复式活塞内燃发动机小客车（9座及以下）	25	230		17	17	辆	46ABOxy	Station wagons, 9 seats or less, of a cylinder capacity from 1L to 1.5L, with spark-ignition internal combustion reciprocating piston engine
8703 2250.90	1升＜排量≤1.5升的带点燃往复式活塞内燃发动机小客车的成套散件（9座及以下）	25	230		17	17	辆	46ABOxy	Complete parts, of a cylinder capacity from 1L to 1.5L, with spark-ignition internal combustion reciprocating piston engine
8703.2290	---其他	25	230		17	17	辆		---Other
8703 2290.01	1升＜排量≤1.5升带点燃往复式活塞内燃发动机的其他车	25	230		17	17	辆	46ABOxy	Other vehicles of a cylinder capacity from 1L to 1.5L, with spark-ignition internal combustion reciprocating piston engine
8703 2290.90	1升＜排量≤1.5升带点燃往复式活塞内燃发动机的其他车的成套散件	25	230		17	17	辆	46ABOxy	Complete parts, of a cylinder capacity from 1L to 1.5L, with spark-ignition internal combustion reciprocating piston engine
	--气缸容量（排气量）超过1500毫升，但不超过3000毫升:								--Of a cylinder capacity exceeding 1500cc but not exceeding 3000cc:
	---气缸容量（排气量）超过1500毫升，但不超过2000毫升:								---Of a cylinder capacity exceeding 1500cc but not exceeding 2000cc:
8703.2341	----小轿车	25	230		17	17	辆		----Saloon cars
8703 2341.01	1.5升＜排量≤2升装点燃往复式活塞内燃发动机的小轿车	25	230		17	17	辆	46ABOxy	Saloon cars of a cylinder capacity from 1.5L to 2L, with spark-ignition internal combustion reciprocating piston engine
8703 2341.90	1.5升＜排量≤2升装点燃往复式活塞内燃发动机的小轿车的成套散件	25	230		17	17	辆	46ABOxy	Complete parts of saloon cars of a cylinder capacity from 1.5L to 2L, with spark-ignition internal combustion reciprocating piston engine
8703.2342	----越野车（4轮驱动）	25	230		17	17	辆		----Cross-country cars（4WD）
8703 2342.01	1.5升＜排量≤2升装点燃往复式活塞内燃发动机的越野车（4轮驱动）	25	230		17	17	辆	46ABOxy	Cross-country cars（4WD）of a cylinder capacity from 1.5L to 2L, with spark- ignition internal combustion reciprocating piston engine
8703 2342.90	1.5升＜排量≤2升装点燃往复式活塞内燃发动机的越野车的成套散件（4轮驱动）	25	230		17	17	辆	46ABOxy	Complete parts of cross-country cars of a cylinder capacity from 1.5L to 2L, with spark-ignition internal combustion reciprocating piston engine
8703.2343	----9座及以下的小客车	25	230		17	17	辆		----Station wagons（with 9 seats or less）
8703 2343.01	1.5升＜排量≤2升装点燃往复式活塞内燃发动机的小客车（9座及以下的）	25	230		17	17	辆	46ABOxy	Station wagons, 9 seats or less, of a cylinder capacity from 1.5L to 2L, with spark-ignition internal combustion reciprocating piston engine
8703 2343.90	1.5升＜排量≤2升装点燃往复式活塞内燃发动机的小客车的成套散件（9座及以下的）	25	230		17	17	辆	46ABOxy	Complete parts, of a cylinder capacity from 1.5L to 2L, with spark-ignition internal combustion reciprocating piston engine
8703.2349	----其他	25	230		17	17	辆		----Other
8703 2349.01	1.5升＜排量≤2升装点燃往复式活塞内燃发动机的其他载人车辆	25	230		17	17	辆	46ABOxy	Other vehicles of a cylinder capacity from 1.5L to 2L, with spark-ignition internal combustion reciprocating piston engine
8703 2349.90	1.5升＜排量≤2升装点燃往复式活塞内燃发动机的其他载人车辆的成套散件	25	230		17	17	辆	46ABOxy	Complete parts, of a cylinder capacity from1.5L to 2L, with spark-ignition internal combustion reciprocating piston engine
	—气缸容量（排气量）超过2000毫升，但不超过2500毫升:								---Of a cylinder capacity exceeding 2000cc but not exceeding 2500cc:
8703.2351	----小轿车	25	230		17	17	辆		----Saloon cars

税则号列 Tariff Item	商品名称及备注	进口税率 最惠	普通	暂定	出口退税	增值税率	计量单位	监管条件	Article Description
8703 2351.01	2 升＜排量≤2.5 升装点燃往复式活塞内燃发动机的小轿车	25	230		17	17	辆	46ABOxy	Saloon cars of a cylinder capacity from 2L to 2.5L, with spark-ignition internal combustion reciprocating piston engine
8703 2351.90	2 升＜排量≤2.5 升装点燃往复式活塞内燃发动机的小轿车的成套散件	25	230		17	17	辆	46ABOxy	Complete parts of saloon cars of a cylinder capacity from 2L to 2.5L, with spark-ignition internal combustion reciprocating piston engine
8703.2352	----越野车（4 轮驱动）	25	230		17	17	辆		----Cross-country cars（4WD）
8703 2352.01	2 升＜排量≤2.5 升装点燃往复式活塞内燃发动机的越野车（4 轮驱动）	25	230		17	17	辆	46ABOxy	Cross-country cars（4WD）of a cylinder capacity from 2L to 2.5L, with spark- ignition internal combustion reciprocating piston engine
8703 2352.90	2 升＜排量≤2.5 升装点燃往复式活塞内燃发动机的越野车的成套散件（4 轮驱动）	25	230		17	17	辆	46ABOxy	Complete parts of cross-country cars of a cylinder capacity from 2L to 2.5L, with spark-ignition internal combustion reciprocating piston engine
8703.2353	----9 座及以下的小客车	25	230		17	17	辆		----Station wagons（with 9 seats or less）
8703 2353.01	2 升＜排量≤2.5 升装点燃往复式活塞内燃发动机的小客车（9 座及以下的）	25	230		17	17	辆	46ABOxy	Station wagons, 9 seats or less, of a cylinder capacity from 2L to 2.5L, with spark-ignition internal combustion reciprocating piston engine
8703 2353.90	2 升＜排量≤2.5 升装点燃往复式活塞内燃发动机的小客车的成套散件（9 座及以下的）	25	230		17	17	辆	46ABOxy	Complete parts, of a cylinder capacity from 2L to 2.5L, with spark-ignition internal combustion reciprocating piston engine
8703.2359	----其他	25	230		17	17	辆		----Other
8703 2359.01	2 升＜排量≤2.5 升装点燃往复式活塞内燃发动机的其他载人车辆	25	230		17	17	辆	46ABOxy	Other vehicles of a cylinder capacity from 2L to 2.5L, with spark-ignition internal combustion reciprocating piston engine
8703 2359.90	2 升＜排量≤2.5 升装点燃往复式活塞内燃发动机的其他载人车辆的成套散件	25	230		17	17	辆	46ABOxy	Complete parts, of a cylinder capacity from 2L to 2.5L, with spark-ignition internal combustion reciprocating piston engine
	---气缸容量（排气量）超过 2500 毫升，但不超过 3000 毫升:								---Of a cylinder capacity exceeding 2500cc but not exceeding 3000cc:
8703.2361	----小轿车	25	270		17	17	辆		----Saloon cars
8703 2361.01	2.5 升＜排量≤3 升装点燃往复式活塞内燃发动机的小轿车	25	270		17	17	辆	46AOxy	Saloon cars of a cylinder capacity from 2.5L to 3L, with spark-ignition internal combustion reciprocating piston engine
8703 2361.90	2.5 升＜排量≤3 升装点燃往复式活塞内燃发动机的小轿车的成套散件	25	270		17	17	辆	46Oxy	Complete parts of saloon cars of a cylinder capacity from 2.5L to 3L, with spark-ignition internal combustion reciprocating piston engine
8703.2362	----越野车（4 轮驱动）	25	270		17	17	辆		----Cross-country cars（4WD）
8703 2362.01	2.5 升＜排量≤3 升装点燃往复式活塞内燃发动机的越野车（4 轮驱动）	25	270		17	17	辆	46AOxy	Cross-country cars（4WD）of a cylinder capacity from 2.5L to 3L, with spark- ignition internal combustion reciprocating piston engine
8703 2362.90	2.5 升＜排量≤3 升装点燃往复式活塞内燃发动机的越野车的成套散件（4 轮驱动）	25	270		17	17	辆	46Oxy	Complete parts of cross-country cars of a cylinder capacity from 2.5L to 3L, with spark-ignition internal combustion reciprocating piston engine
8703.2363	----9 座及以下的小客车	25	270		17	17	辆		----Station wagons（with 9 seats or less）
8703 2363.01	2.5 升＜排量≤3 升装点燃往复式活塞内燃发动机的小客车（9 座及以下的）	25	270		17	17	辆	46AOxy	Station wagons, 9 seats or less, of a cylinder capacity from 2.5L to 3L, with spark-ignition internal combustion reciprocating piston engine
8703 2363.90	2.5 升＜排量≤3 升装点燃往复式活塞内燃发动机的小客车的成套散件（9 座及以下的）	25	270		17	17	辆	46Oxy	Complete parts, of a cylinder capacity from 2.5L to 3L, with spark-ignition internal combustion reciprocating piston engine
8703.2369	----其他	25	270		17	17	辆		----Other
8703 2369.01	2.5 升＜排量≤3 升装点燃往复式活塞内燃发动机的其他载人车辆（不包括非 4 轮驱动越野车）	25	270		17	17	辆	46AOxy	Other vehicles of a cylinder capacity from 2.5L to 3L, with spark-ignition internal combustion reciprocating piston engine(excluding non-4WD cross-country cars)
8703 2369.02	2.5 升＜排量≤3 升装点燃往复式活塞内燃发动机的非 4 轮驱动越野车	25	270		17	17	辆	46AOxy	Cross-country cars （non-4WD）of a cylinder capacity from 2.5L to 3L, with spark-ignition internal combustion reciprocating piston engine

税则号列 Tariff Item	商品名称及备注	进口税率 最惠	普通	暂定	出口 退税	增值 税率	计量 单位	监管 条件	Article Description
8703 2369.91	2.5升<排量≤3升装点燃往复式活塞内燃发动机的非4轮驱动越野车的成套散件	25	270		17	17	辆	46Oxy	Complete parts of cross-country cars（non-4WD）of a cylinder capacity from 2.5L to 3L, with spark-ignition internal combustion reciprocating piston engine
8703 2369.99	2.5升<排量≤3升装点燃往复式活塞内燃发动机的其他载人车辆的成套散件(不包括非4轮驱动越野车的成套散件)	25	270		17	17	辆	46Oxy	Complete parts of vehicles of a cylinder capacity from 2.5L to 3L, with spark-ignition internal combustion reciprocating piston engine(excluding non-4WD cross-country cars)
	--气缸容量（排气量）超过3000毫升:								--of a cylinder capacity exceeding 3000cc:
	--气缸容量(排气量)超过3000毫升，但不超过4000毫升:								---Of a cylinder capacity exceeding 3000cc, but not exceeding 4000cc:
8703.2411	----小轿车	25	270		17	17	辆		----Saloon cars
8703 2411.01	3升<排量≤4升装点燃往复式活塞内燃发动机小轿车	25	270		17	17	辆	46ABOxy	Saloon cars of a cylinder capacity from 3L to 4L, with spark-ignition internal combustion reciprocating piston engine
8703 2411.90	3升<排量≤4升装点燃往复式活塞内燃发动机小轿车的成套散件	25	270		17	17	辆	46ABOxy	Complete parts of saloon cars of a cylinder capacity from 3L to 4L, with spark-ignition internal combustion reciprocating piston engine
8703.2412	----越野车（4轮驱动）	25	270		17	17	辆		----Cross-country cars（4WD）
8703 2412.01	3升<排量≤4升装点燃往复式活塞内燃发动机越野车（4轮驱动）	25	270		17	17	辆	46ABOxy	Cross-country cars（4WD）of a cylinder capacity from 3L to 4L, with spark- ignition internal combustion reciprocating piston engine
8703 2412.90	3升<排量≤4升装点燃往复式活塞内燃发动机越野车的成套散件（4轮驱动）	25	270		17	17	辆	46BOxy	Complete parts of cross-country cars of a cylinder capacity from 3L to 4L, with spark-ignition internal combustion reciprocating piston engine
8703.2413	----9座及以下的小客车	25	270		17	17	辆		----Station wagons（with 9 seats or less）
8703 2413.01	3升<排量≤4升装点燃往复式活塞内燃发动机的小客车（9座及以下）	25	270		17	17	辆	46ABOxy	Station wagons, 9 seats or less, of a cylinder capacity from 3L to 4L, with spark-ignition internal combustion reciprocating piston engine
8703 2413.90	3升<排量≤4升装点燃往复式活塞内燃发动机的小客车的成套散件（9座及以下）	25	270		17	17	辆	46ABOxy	Complete parts, of a cylinder capacity from 3L to 4L, with spark-ignition internal combustion reciprocating piston engine
8703.2419	----其他	25	270		17	17	辆		----Other
8703 2419.01	3升<排量≤4升装点燃往复式活塞内燃发动机的其他载人车辆(不包括非4轮驱动越野车)	25	270		17	17	辆	46ABOxy	Other vehicles of a cylinder capacity from 3L to 4L, with spark-ignition internal combustion reciprocating piston engine (excluding non-4WD cross-country cars)
8703 2419.02	3升<排量≤4升装点燃往复式活塞内燃发动机的非4轮驱动越野车	25	270		17	17	辆	46ABOxy	Cross-country cars （non-4WD）of a cylinder capacity from 3L to 4L, with spark-ignition internal combustion reciprocating piston engine
8703 2419.91	3升<排量≤4升装点燃往复式活塞内燃发动机的非4轮驱动越野车成套散件	25	270		17	17	辆	46ABOxy	Complete parts of cross-country cars （non-4WD） of a cylinder capacity from 3L to 4L, with spark-ignition internal combustion reciprocating piston engine
8703 2419.99	3升<排量≤4升装点燃往复式活塞内燃发动机的其他载人车辆的成套散件(不包括非4轮驱动越野车成套散件)	25	270		17	17	辆	46ABOxy	Complete parts of vehicles of a cylinder capacity from 3L to 4L, with spark-ignition internal combustion reciprocating piston engine(excluding non-4WD cross-country cars)
	---气缸容量（排气量）超过4000毫升:								---Of a cylinder capacity exceeding 4000cc:
8703.2421	----小轿车	25	270		17	17	辆		----Saloon cars
8703 2421.01	排量>4升装点燃往复式活塞内燃发动机的小轿车	25	270		17	17	辆	46ABOxy	Saloon cars of a cylinder capacity exceeding 4L, with spark-ignition internal combustion reciprocating piston engine
8703 2421.90	排量>4升装点燃往复式活塞内燃发动机的小轿车的成套散件	25	270		17	17	辆	46ABOxy	Complete parts of saloon cars of a cylinder capacity exceeding 4L, with spark-ignition internal combustion reciprocating piston engine
8703.2422	----越野车（4轮驱动）	25	270		17	17	辆		----Cross-country cars（4WD）

税则号列 Tariff Item	商品名称及备注	进口税率 最惠	进口税率 普通	进口税率 暂定	出口退税	增值税率	计量单位	监管条件	Article Description
8703 2422.01	排量＞4 升装点燃往复式活塞内燃发动机的越野车（4 轮驱动）	25	270		17	17	辆	46ABOxy	Cross-country cars（4WD）of a cylinder capacity exceeding 4L, with spark- ignition internal combustion reciprocating piston engine
8703 2422.90	排量＞4 升装点燃往复式活塞内燃发动机的越野车的成套散件（4 轮驱动）	25	270		17	17	辆	46BOxy	Complete parts of cross-country cars of a cylinder capacity exceeding 4L, with spark-ignition internal combustion reciprocating piston engine
8703.2423	----9 座及以下的小客车	25	270		17	17	辆		----Station wagons（with 9 seats or less）
8703 2423.01	排量＞4 升装点燃往复式活塞内燃发动机的小客车（9 座及以下）	25	270		17	17	辆	46ABOxy	Station wagons, 9 seats or less, of a cylinder capacity exceeding 4L, with spark-ignition internal combustion reciprocating piston engine
8703 2423.90	排量＞4 升装点燃往复式活塞内燃发动机的小客车的成套散件（9 座及以下）	25	270		17	17	辆	46ABOxy	Complete parts, of a cylinder capacity exceeding 4L, with spark-ignition internal combustion reciprocating piston engine
8703.2429	----其他	25	270		17	17	辆		----Other
8703 2429.01	排量＞4 升装点燃往复式活塞内燃发动机的其他载人车辆(不包括非 4 轮驱动越野车)	25	270		17	17	辆	46ABOxy	Other vehicles of a cylinder capacity exceeding 4L, with spark-ignition internal combustion reciprocating piston engine (excluding non-4WD cross-country cars)
8703 2429.02	排量＞4 升装点燃往复式活塞内燃发动机的非 4 轮驱动越野车	25	270		17	17	辆	46ABOxy	Cross-country cars （non-4WD）of a cylinder capacity exceeding 4L, with spark-ignition internal combustion reciprocating piston engine
8703 2429.91	排量＞4 升装点燃往复式活塞内燃发动机的非 4 轮驱动越野车的成套散件	25	270		17	17	辆	46ABOxy	Complete parts of cross-country cars （non-4WD） of a cylinder capacity exceeding 4L, with spark-ignition internal combustion reciprocating piston engine
8703 2429.99	排量＞4 升装点燃往复式活塞内燃发动机的其他载人车辆的成套散件(不包括非 4 轮驱动越野车成套散件)	25	270		17	17	辆	46ABOxy	Complete parts of other vehicles of a cylinder capacity exceeding 4L, with spark-ignition internal combustion reciprocating piston engine(excluding non-4WD cross-country cars)
	-装有压燃式活塞内燃发动机（柴油或半柴油发动机）的其他车辆:								-Other vehicles, with compression-ignition internal combustion piston engine （diesel or semi-diesel）:
	--气缸容量（排气量）不超过 1500 毫升:								--Of a cylinder capacity not exceeding 1500cc:
	--气缸容量（排气量）不超过 1000 毫升:								--Of a cylinder capacity not exceeding 1000cc:
8703.3111	----小轿车	25	230		17	17	辆		----Saloon cars
8703 3111.01	排量≤1 升装压燃往复式活塞内燃发动机小轿车	25	230		17	17	辆	46ABOxy	Saloon cars of a cylinder capacity not exceeding 1L, with compression-ignition internal combustion reciprocating piston engine
8703 3111.90	排量≤1 升装压燃往复式活塞内燃发动机小轿车的成套散件	25	230		17	17	辆	46ABOxy	Complete parts of a cylinder capacity not exceeding 1L, with compression-ignition internal combustion reciprocating piston engine
8703.3119	----其他	25	230		17	17	辆		----Other
8703 3119.01	排量≤1 升装压燃往复式活塞内燃发动机的其他载人车辆	25	230		17	17	辆	46ABOxy	Other cars of a cylinder capacity not exceeding 1L, with compression-ignition internal combustion reciprocating piston engine
8703 3119.90	排量≤1 升装压燃往复式活塞内燃发动机的其他载人车辆的成套散件	25	230		17	17	辆	46ABOxy	Complete parts of a cylinder capacity not exceeding 1L, with compression-ignition internal combustion reciprocating piston engine
	--气缸容量(排气量)超过 1000 毫升，但不超过 1500 毫升:								--Of a cylinder capacity exceeding 1,000cc but not exceeding 1,500cc:
8703.3121	----小轿车	25	230		17	17	辆		----Saloon cars
8703 3121.01	1 升＜排量≤1.5 升装压燃往复式活塞内燃发动机的小轿车	25	230		17	17	辆	46ABOxy	Saloon cars of a cylinder capacity from 1L to 1.5L, with compression-ignition internal combustion reciprocating piston engine
8703 3121.90	1 升＜排量≤1.5 升装压燃往复式活塞内燃发动机的小轿车的成套散件	25	230		17	17	辆	46ABOxy	Complete parts of a cylinder capacity from1L to 1.5 L, with compression-ignition internal combustion reciprocating piston engine
8703.3122	----越野车（4 轮驱动）	25	230		17	17	辆		---Cross-country cars（4WD）

税则号列 Tariff Item	商品名称及备注	进口税率			出口退税	增值税率	计量单位	监管条件	Article Description
		最惠	普通	暂定					
8703 3122.01	1升＜排量≤1.5升装压燃式活塞内燃发动机的越野车（4轮驱动）	25	230		17	17	辆	46ABOxy	Cross-country cars（4WD）of a cylinder capacity from 1L to 1.5L, with compression-ignition internal combustion reciprocating piston engine
8703 3122.90	1升＜排量≤1.5升装压燃式活塞内燃发动机的越野车的成套散件（4轮驱动）	25	230		17	17	辆	46ABOxy	Complete parts of a cylinder capacity from1L to 1.5 L, with compression-ignition internal combustion reciprocating piston engine
8703.3123	----9座及以下的小客车	25	230		17	17	辆		---Station wagons（with 9 seats or less）
8703 3123.01	1升＜排量≤1.5升装压燃往复式活塞内燃发动机的小客车（9座及以下的）	25	230		17	17	辆	46ABOxy	Station wagons (9 seats or less), of a cylinder capacity from 1L to 1.5L,with compression-ignition internal combustion reciprocating piston engine
8703 3123.90	1升＜排量≤1.5升装压燃往复式活塞内燃发动机的小客车的成套散件（9座及以下的）	25	230		17	17	辆	46ABOxy	Complete parts of a cylinder capacity from1L to 1.5 L, with compression-ignition internal combustion reciprocating piston engine
8703.3129	----其他	25	230		17	17	辆		----Other
8703 3129.01	1升＜排量≤1.5升装压燃往复式活塞内燃发动机的其他载人车辆	25	230		17	17	辆	46ABOxy	Other of a cylinder capacity from 1L to 1.5L, with compression-ignition internal combustion reciprocating piston engine
8703 3129.90	1升＜排量≤1.5升装压燃往复式活塞内燃发动机的其他载人车辆的成套散件	25	230		17	17	辆	46ABOxy	Complete parts of a cylinder capacity from 1L to 1.5 L, with compression-ignition internal combustion reciprocating piston engine
	--气缸容量（排气量）超过1500毫升，但不超过2500毫升:								---Of a cylinder capacity exceeding 1500 cc, but not exceeding 2500cc:
	---气缸容量（排气量）超过1500毫升，但不超过2000毫升:								---Of a cylinder capacity exceeding 1500 cc, but not exceeding 2000cc:
8703.3211	----小轿车	25	230		17	17	辆		----Saloon cars
8703 3211.01	1.5＜排量≤2升装压燃往复式活塞内燃发动机的小轿车	25	230		17	17	辆	46ABOxy	Saloon cars of a cylinder capacity from 1.5L to 2L, with compression-ignition internal combustion reciprocating piston engine
8703 3211.90	1.5＜排量≤2升装压燃往复式活塞内燃发动机的小轿车的成套散件	25	230		17	17	辆	46ABOxy	Complete parts of a cylinder capacity from 1.5L to 2L, with compression-ignition internal combustion reciprocating piston engine
8703.3212	----越野车（4轮驱动）	25	230		17	17	辆		---Cross-country cars（4WD）
8703 3212.01	1.5＜排量≤2升装压燃往复式活塞内燃发动机的越野车（4轮驱动）	25	230		17	17	辆	46ABOxy	Cross-country cars（4WD）of a cylinder capacity from 1.5L to 2L, with compression-ignition internal combustion reciprocating piston engine
8703 3212.90	1.5＜排量≤2升装压燃往复式活塞内燃发动机的越野车的成套散件（4轮驱动）	25	230		17	17	辆	46ABOxy	Complete parts of a cylinder capacity from 1.5L to 2L, with compression-ignition internal combustion reciprocating piston engine
8703.3213	----9座及以下的小客车	25	230		17	17	辆		---Station wagons（with 9 seats or less）
8703 3213.01	1.5＜排量≤2升装压燃往复式活塞内燃发动机的小客车（9座及以下）	25	230		17	17	辆	46ABOxy	Station wagons (9 seats or less), of a cylinder capacity from 1.5L to 2L,with compression-ignition internal combustion reciprocating piston engine
8703 3213.90	1.5＜排量≤2升装压燃往复式活塞内燃发动机的小客车的成套散件（9座及以下）	25	230		17	17	辆	46ABOxy	Complete parts of a cylinder capacity from 1.5L to 2L, with compression-ignition internal combustion reciprocating piston engine
8703.3219	----其他	25	230		17	17	辆		----Other
8703 3219.01	1.5＜排量≤2升装压燃往复式活塞内燃发动机的其他载人车辆	25	230		17	17	辆	46ABOxy	Other of a cylinder capacity from 1.5L to 2L, with compression-ignition internal combustion reciprocating piston engine
8703 3219.90	1.5＜排量≤2升装压燃往复式活塞内燃发动机的其他载人车辆的成套散件	25	230		17	17	辆	46ABOxy	Complete parts of a cylinder capacity from 1.5L to 2L, with compression-ignition internal combustion reciprocating piston engine
	---气缸容量（排气量）超过2000毫升，但不超过2500毫升:								---Of a cylinder capacity exceeding 2000 cc, but not exceeding 2500cc:
8703.3221	----小轿车	25	230		17	17	辆		----Saloon cars
8703 3221.01	2＜排量≤2.5升装压燃往复式	25	230		17	17	辆	46ABOxy	Saloon cars of a cylinder capacity from 2L to 2.5L,

税则号列 Tariff Item	商品名称及备注	进口税率 最惠	普通	暂定	出口退税	增值税率	计量单位	监管条件	Article Description
	活塞内燃发动机的小轿车								with compression-ignition internal combustion reciprocating piston engine
8703 3221.90	2＜排量≤2.5 升装压燃往复式活塞内燃发动机的小轿车的成套散件	25	230		17	17	辆	46ABOxy	Complete parts of a cylinder capacity from 2L to 2.5L with compression-ignition internal combustion reciprocating piston engine
8703.3222	----越野车（4轮驱动）	25	230		17	17	辆		---Cross-country cars（4WD）
8703 3222.01	2＜排量≤2.5 升装压燃往复式活塞内燃发动机的越野车（4轮驱动）	25	230		17	17	辆	46ABOxy	Cross-country cars（4WD）of a cylinder capacity from 2L to 2.5L, with compression-ignition internal combustion reciprocating piston engine
8703 3222.90	2＜排量≤2.5 升装压燃往复式活塞内燃发动机的越野车的成套散件（4轮驱动）	25	230		17	17	辆	46ABOxy	Complete parts of a cylinder capacity from 2L to 2.5L, with compression-ignition internal combustion reciprocating piston engine
8703.3223	----9座及以下的小客车	25	230		17	17	辆		---Station wagons（with 9 seats or less）
8703 3223.01	2＜排量≤2.5 升装压燃往复式活塞内燃发动机的小客车（9座及以下）	25	230		17	17	辆	46ABOxy	Station wagons (9 seats or less), of a cylinder capacity from 2L to 2.5L,with compression-ignition internal combustion reciprocating piston engine
8703 3223.90	2＜排量≤2.5 升装压燃往复式活塞内燃发动机的小客车的成套散件（9座及以下）	25	230		17	17	辆	46ABOxy	Complete parts of a cylinder capacity from 2L to 2.5L, with compression-ignition internal combustion reciprocating piston engine
8703.3229	----其他	25	230		17	17	辆		----Other
8703 3229.01	2＜排量≤2.5 升装压燃往复式活塞内燃发动机的其他载人车辆	25	230		17	17	辆	46ABOxy	Other of a cylinder capacity from 2L to 2.5L, with compression-ignition internal combustion reciprocating piston engine
8703 3229.90	2＜排量≤2.5 升装压燃往复式活塞内燃发动机的其他载人车辆的成套散件	25	230		17	17	辆	46ABOxy	Complete parts of a cylinder capacity from 2L to 2.5L, with compression-ignition internal combustion reciprocating piston engine
	--气缸容量（排气量）超过2500毫升:								---Of a cylinder capacity exceeding 2500 cc:
	--气缸容量（排气量）超过2500毫升，但不超过3000毫升:								---Of a cylinder capacity exceeding 2500 cc, but not exceeding 3000cc:
8703.3311	----小轿车	25	270		17	17	辆		----Saloon cars
8703 3311.01	2.5＜排量≤3 升装压燃往复式活塞内燃发动机的小轿车	25	270		17	17	辆	46ABOxy	Saloon cars of a cylinder capacity from 2.5L to 3L, with compression-ignition internal combustion reciprocating piston engine
8703 3311.90	2.5＜排量≤3 升装压燃往复式活塞内燃发动机的小轿车的成套散件	25	270		17	17	辆	46ABOxy	Complete parts of a cylinder capacity from 2.5L to 3L,with compression-ignition internal combustion reciprocating piston engine
8703.3312	----越野车（4轮驱动）	25	270		17	17	辆		---Cross-country cars（4WD）
8703 3312.01	2.5＜排量≤3 升装压燃往复式活塞内燃发动机的越野车（4轮驱动）	25	270		17	17	辆	46ABOxy	Cross-country cars（4WD）of a cylinder capacity from 2.5L to 3L, with compression-ignition internal combustion reciprocating piston engine
8703 3312.90	2.5＜排量≤3 升装压燃往复式活塞内燃发动机的越野车的成套散件（4轮驱动）	25	270		17	17	辆	46ABOxy	Complete parts of a cylinder capacity from 2.5L to 3L, with compression-ignition internal combustion reciprocating piston engine
8703 3313	----9座及以下的小客车	25	270		17	17	辆		---Station wagons（with 9 seats or less）
8703 3313.01	2.5＜排量≤3 升装压燃往复式活塞内燃发动机的小客车（9座及以下）	25	270		17	17	辆	46ABOxy	Station wagons (9 seats or less), of a cylinder capacity from 2.5L to 3L,with compression-ignition internal combustion reciprocating piston engine
8703 3313.90	2.5＜排量≤3 升装压燃往复式活塞内燃发动机的小客车的成套散件（9座及以下）	25	270		17	17	辆	46ABOxy	Complete parts of a cylinder capacity from 2.5L to 3L,with compression-ignition internal combustion reciprocating piston engine（with 9 seats or less）
8703.3319	----其他	25	270		17	17	辆		----Other
8703 3319.01	2.5＜排量≤3 升装压燃往复式活塞内燃发动机的其他载人车辆(不包括非4轮驱动越野车)	25	270		17	17	辆	46ABOxy	Other vehicles of a cylinder capacity from 2.5L to 3L,with compression-ignition internal combustion reciprocating piston engine (excluding non-4WD cross-country cars)
8703 3319.02	2.5＜排量≤3 升装压燃往复式	25	270		17	17	辆	46ABOxy	Cross-country cars （non-4WD）of a cylinder capacity

税则号列 Tariff Item	商品名称及备注	进口税率 最惠	普通	暂定	出口退税	增值税率	计量单位	监管条件	Article Description
	活塞内燃发动机的非 4 轮驱动越野车								from 2.5L to 3L, with compression-ignition internal combustion reciprocating piston engine
8703 3319.91	2.5＜排量≤3 升装压燃往复式活塞内燃发动机的非 4 轮驱动越野车成套散件	25	270		17	17	辆	46ABOxy	Complete parts of Cross-country cars （non-4WD） of a cylinder capacity from 2.5L to 3L, with compression- ignition internal combustion reciprocating piston engine
8703 3319.99	2.5＜排量≤3 升装压燃往复式活塞内燃发动机的其他载人车辆的成套散件(不包括非 4 轮驱动越野车成套散件)	25	270		17	17	辆	46ABOxy	Complete parts of other vehicles of a cylinder capacity from 2.5L to 3L,with compression-ignition internal combustion reciprocating piston engine(excluding non-4WD cross-country cars)
	---气缸容量（排气量）超过 3000 毫升，但不超过 4000 毫升:								---Of a cylinder capacity exceeding 3000 cc, but not exceeding 4000cc:
8703.3321	----小轿车	25	270		17	17	辆		----Saloon cars
8703 3321.01	3＜排量≤4 升装压燃往复式活塞内燃发动机的小轿车	25	270		17	17	辆	46ABOxy	Saloon cars of a cylinder capacity from 3L to 4L, with compression-ignition internal combustion reciprocating piston engine
8703 3321.90	3＜排量≤4 升装压燃往复式活塞内燃发动机的小轿车的成套散件	25	270		17	17	辆	46ABOxy	Complete parts of a cylinder capacity from 3L to 4L,with compression-ignition internal combustion reciprocating piston engine
8703.3322	----越野车（4 轮驱动）	25	270		17	17	辆		---Cross-country cars（4WD）
8703 3322.01	3＜排量≤4 升装压燃往复式活塞内燃发动机的越野车（4 轮驱动）	25	270		17	17	辆	46ABOxy	Cross-country cars（4WD）of a cylinder capacity from 3L to 4L, with compression-ignition internal combustion reciprocating piston engine
8703 3322.90	3＜排量≤4 升装压燃往复式活塞内燃发动机的越野车的成套散件（4 轮驱动）	25	270		17	17	辆	46ABOxy	Complete parts of a cylinder capacity from 3L to 4L, with compression-ignition internal combustion reciprocating piston engine
8703 3323	----9 座及以下的小客车	25	270		17	17	辆		---Station wagons（with 9 seats or less）
8703 3323.01	3＜排量≤4 升装压燃往复式活塞内燃发动机的小客车（9 座及以下）	25	270		17	17	辆	46ABOxy	Station wagons (9 seats or less), of a cylinder capacity from 3L to 4L,with compression-ignition internal combustion reciprocating piston engine
8703 3323.90	3＜排量≤4 升装压燃往复式活塞内燃发动机的小客车的成套散件（9 座及以下）	25	270		17	17	辆	46ABOxy	Complete parts of a cylinder capacity from 3L to 4L,with compression-ignition internal combustion reciprocating piston engine
8703.3329	----其他	25	270		17	17	辆		----Other
8703 3329.01	3＜排量≤4 升装压燃往复式活塞内燃发动机的其他载人车辆(不包括非 4 轮驱动越野车)	25	270		17	17	辆	46ABOxy	Other of a cylinder capacity from 3L to 4L,with compression-ignition internal combustion reciprocating piston engine (excluding non-4WD cross-country cars)
8703 3329.02	3＜排量≤4 升装压燃往复式活塞内燃发动机的非 4 轮驱动越野车	25	270		17	17	辆	46ABOxy	Cross-country cars （non-4WD）of a cylinder capacity from 3L to 4L, with compression-ignition internal combustion reciprocating piston engine
8703 3329.91	3＜排量≤4 升装压燃往复式活塞内燃发动机的非 4 轮驱动越野车成套散件	25	270		17	17	辆	46ABOxy	Complete parts of Cross-country cars （non-4WD） of a cylinder capacity from 3L to 4L, with compression-ignition internal combustion reciprocating piston engine
8703 3329.99	3＜排量≤4 升装压燃往复式活塞内燃发动机的其他载人车辆的成套散件(不包括非 4 轮驱动越野车成套散件)	25	270		17	17	辆	46ABOxy	Complete parts of other vehicles of a cylinder capacity from 3L to 4L,with compression-ignition internal combustion reciprocating piston engine (excluding non-4WD cross-country cars)
	---气缸容量（排气量）超过 4000 毫升:								---Of a cylinder capacity exceeding 4000 cc:
8703.3361	----小轿车	25	270		17	17	辆		----Saloon cars
8703 3361.01	排量＞4 升装压燃往复式活塞内燃发动机的小轿车	25	270		17	17	辆	46ABOxy	Saloon cars of a cylinder capacity exceeding 4L, with compression-ignition internal combustion reciprocating piston engine
8703 3361.90	排量＞4 升装压燃往复式活塞内燃发动机的小轿车的成套散件	25	270		17	17	辆	46ABOxy	Complete parts of a cylinder capacity exceeding 4L,with compression-ignition internal combustion reciprocating piston engine
8703.3362	----越野车（4 轮驱动）	25	270		17	17	辆		---Cross-country cars（4WD）

税则号列 Tariff Item	商品名称及备注	进口税率 最惠	普通	暂定	出口退税	增值税率	计量单位	监管条件	Article Description
8703 3362.01	排量＞4 升装压燃往复式活塞内燃发动机的越野车（4 轮驱动）	25	270		17	17	辆	46ABOxy	Cross-country cars（4WD）of a cylinder capacity exceeding 4L, with compression-ignition internal combustion reciprocating piston engine
8703 3362.90	排量＞4 升装压燃往复式活塞内燃发动机的越野车的成套散件（4 轮驱动）	25	270		17	17	辆	46ABOxy	Complete parts of a cylinder capacity exceeding 4L, with compression-ignition internal combustion reciprocating piston engine
8703.3363	----9 座及以下的小客车	25	270		17	17	辆		---Station wagons（with 9 seats or less）
8703 3363.01	排量＞4 升装压燃往复式活塞内燃发动机的小客车（9 座及以下）	25	270		17	17	辆	46ABOxy	Station wagons (9 seats or less), of a cylinder capacity exceeding 4L,with compression-ignition internal combustion reciprocating piston engine
8703 3363.90	排量＞4 升装压燃往复式活塞内燃发动机的小客车的成套散件（9 座及以下）	25	270		17	17	辆	46ABOxy	Complete parts of a cylinder capacity exceeding 4L,with compression-ignition internal combustion reciprocating piston engine
8703.3369	----其他	25	270		17	17	辆		----Other
8703 3369.01	排量＞4 升装压燃往复式活塞内燃发动机的其他载人车辆(不包括非 4 轮驱动越野车)	25	270		17	17	辆	46ABOxy	Other passenger vehicles of a cylinder capacity exceeding 4L,with compression-ignition internal combustion recipro cating piston engine (excluding non-4WD cross-country cars)
8703 3369.02	排量＞4 升装压燃往复式活塞内燃发动机非 4 轮驱动越野车	25	270		17	17	辆	46ABOxy	Cross-country cars （non-4WD）of a cylinder capacity exceeding 4L, with compression-ignition internal combustion reciprocating piston engine
8703 3369.91	排量＞4 升装压燃往复式活塞内燃发动机非 4 轮驱动越野车的成套散件	25	270		17	17	辆	46ABOxy	Complete parts of Cross-country cars （non-4WD） of a cylinder capacity exceeding 4L, with compressionignition internal combustion reciprocating piston engine
8703 3369.99	排量＞4 升装压燃往复式活塞内燃发动机其他载人车辆的成套散件(不包括非 4 轮驱动越野车成套散件)	25	270		17	17	辆	46ABOxy	Complete parts of other vehicles of a cylinder capacity exceeding 4L,with compression-ignition internal combustion reciprocating piston engine (excluding non-4WD cross-country cars)
8703.9000	-其他	25	270		17	17	辆		-Other
8703 9000.01	其他型排气量≤1 升的其他载人车辆	25	270		17	17	辆	46ABOxy	Other passenger vehicles, of a cylinder capacity not exceeding 1L, with other engine
8703 9000.02	其他型 1.5 升＜排气量≤2 升的其他载人车辆	25	270		17	17	辆	46ABOxy	Other passenger vehicles, of a cylinder capacity from 1.5L to 2L, with other engine
8703 9000.03	其他型 2 升＜排气量≤2.5 升的其他载人车辆	25	270		17	17	辆	46ABOxy	Other passenger vehicles, of a cylinder capacity from 2L to 2.5L, with other engine
8703 9000.04	其他型 2.5 升＜排气量≤3 升的其他载人车辆（不包括编号 8703900014 所述小轿车和越野车）	25	270		17	17	辆	46ABOxy	Other passenger vehicles, of a cylinder capacity from 2.5L to 3L, with other engine(excluding item 87039000.14 saloon cars and cross-country cars)
8703 9000.05	其他型 3 升＜排气量≤4 升的其他载人车辆（不包括编号 8703900015 所述小轿车和越野车）	25	270		17	17	辆	46ABOxy	Other passenger vehicles, of a cylinder capacity from 3L to 4.L, with other engine(excluding item87039000. 15 saloon cars and cross-country cars)
8703 9000.06	其他型排气量＞4 升的其他载人车辆(不包括编号 8703900016 所述小轿车和越野车)	25	270		17	17	辆	46ABOxy	Other passenger vehicles, of a cylinder capacity exceeding 4L, with other engine(excluding item87039000. 16 saloon cars and cross-country cars)
8703 9000.07	其他型 1 升＜排气量≤1.5 升的其他载人车辆	25	270		17	17	辆	46ABOxy	Other passenger vehicles, of a cylinder capacity from 1 L to 1.5L, with other engine
8703 9000.10	电动汽车和其他无法区分排气量的载人车辆	25	270		17	17	辆	6ABO	Electronic vehicles and other passenger vehicles which can not distingguished cylinder capacity
8703 9000.14	其他型 2.5 升＜排气量≤3 升的小轿车、越野车	25	270		17	17	辆	46ABOxy	Other Saloon cars and cross-country cars, of a cylinder capacity from 2.5L to 3L, with other engine
8703 9000.15	其他型 3 升＜排气量≤4 升的小轿车、越野车	25	270		17	17	辆	46ABOxy	Other Saloon cars and cross-country cars, of a cylinder capacity from3L to 4L, with other engine
8703 9000.16	其他型排气量＞4 升的小轿车、	25	270		17	17	辆	46ABOxy	Other Saloon cars and cross-country cars, of a

税则号列 Tariff Item	商品名称及备注	进口税率 最惠	进口税率 普通	进口税率 暂定	出口退税	增值税率	计量单位	监管条件	Article Description
	越野车								cylinder capacity exceeding 4L, with other engine
8703 9000.91	其他型排气量＞2.5 升的小轿车、越野车的成套散件	25	270		17	17	辆	6ABO	Other complete parts of Saloon cars and cross-country cars of a cylinder capacity exceeding 2.5L
8703 9000.99	其他型载人车辆的成套散件	25	270		17	17	辆	6ABO	Other complete parts of passenger vehicles
87.04	**货运机动车辆：**								**Motor vehicles for the transport of goods:**
	-非公路用自卸车：								-Dumpers designed for off-highway use:
8704.1030	---电动轮货运自卸车	6	20		17	17	辆	OAB6	---Electromobile dumpers for the transport of goods
8704.1090	---其他	6	20		17	17	辆	ABO6	---Other
	-装有压燃式活塞内燃发动机（柴油或半柴油发动机）的其他货车：								-Other, with compression-ignition internal combustion piston engine（diesel or semidiesesl）:
8704.2100	--车辆总重量不超过5吨	25	70		17	17	辆	46ABOxy	--G.v.w. not exceeding 5 tons
	--车辆总重量超过5吨，但不超过20吨：								--G.v.w. exceeding 5 tons but not exceeding 20 tons:
8704.2230	---车辆总重量超过5吨，但小于14吨	20	70		17	17	辆	46ABOxy	---G.v.w. exceeding 5 tons but not exceeding 14 tons
8704.2240	---车辆总重量在14吨及以上，但不超过20吨	20	40		17	17	辆	46ABOxy	---G.v.w. of 14 tons or more but not exceeding 20 tons
8704.2300	--车辆总重量超过20吨	15	40		17	17	辆		--G.v.w. exceeding 20 tons
8704 2300.01[暂]	固井水泥车、压裂车、混砂车底盘（车辆总重量＞35 吨，装驾驶室）	15	40	10	17	17	辆	46ABOxy	Chassis for cementing vehicle,fracturing truck and blender truck , g. v. w exceeding 35 tons, with cabs
8704 2300.02[暂]	起重≥55 吨的汽车起重机用底盘（装有压燃式活塞内燃发动机）	15	40	8	17	17	辆	46ABOxy	Chassis for crane lorries, lifting capacity exceeding 55 tons, with compression-ignition internal combustion piston engine
8704 2300.03[暂]	车辆总重量≥31 吨的清障车专用底盘	15	40	10	17	17	辆	46ABOxy	Chassis for wrecker truck, g. v. w exceeding 35 tons
8704 2300.90	柴油型的其他超重型货车（装有压燃式活塞内燃发动机，超重型指车辆总重量＞20吨）	15	40		17	17	辆	46ABOxy	Other heavy truck , with compression-ignition internal combustion piston engine（diesel）, g. v. w exceeding 20 tons
	-装有点燃式活塞内燃发动机的其他货车：								-Other, with spark-ignition internal combustion piston engine:
8704.3100	--车辆总重量不超过5吨	25	70		17	17	辆	46ABOxy	--G.v.w. not exceeding 5 tons
	--车辆总重量超过5吨：								--G.v.w. exceeding 5 tons:
8704.3230	---车辆总重量超过5吨，但不超过8吨	20	70		17	17	辆	46ABOxy	---G.v.w. exceeding 5 tons, but not exceeding 8 tons.
8704.3240	---车辆总重量超过8吨	20	70		17	17	辆	46ABOxy	---G.v.w. exceeding 8 tons
8704.9000	-其他	25	70		17	17	辆	46ABOxy	-Other
87.05	**特殊用途的机动车辆（例如，抢修车、起重车、救火车、混凝土搅拌车、道路清洁车、喷洒车、流动工场车及流动放射线检查车），但主要用于载人或运货的车辆除外**								**Special purpose motor vehicles, other than those principally designed for the transport of persons or goods（for example, breakdown lorries, crane lorries, fire fighting vehicles, concrete mixer lorries, road sweeper lorries,spraying lorries, mobile workshops, mobile radiological units）:**
	-起重车：								-Crane lorries:
	---全路面起重车：								---All-road crane lorries:
8705.1021	----最大起重重量不超过50吨	15	30		17	17	辆	6AO	----Of maxium lifting capacity not more than 50 tons
8705.1022	----最大起重重量超过50吨，但不超过100吨	10	30		17	17	辆	6AO	----Of a maxium lifting capacity exceeding 50 tons but not exceeding 100 tons
8705.1023	----最大起重重量超过100吨	10	30		17	17	辆	6AO	----Of a maxium lifting capacity exceeding 100 tons
	---其他：								---Other:
8705.1091	----最大起重重量不超过50吨	15	30		17	17	辆	6AO	----Of maxium lifting capacity not more than 50 tons
8705.1092	----最大起重重量超过50吨，但不超过100吨	10	30		17	17	辆	6AO	----Of a maxium lifting capacity exceeding 50 tons but not exceeding 100 tons
8705.1093	----最大起重重量超过100吨	10	30		17	17	辆	6AO	----Of a maxium lifting capacity exceeding 100 tons
8705.2000	-钻探车	12	17		17	17	辆	6AO	-Mobile drilling derricks
	-救火车：								-Fire fighting vehicles:

税则号列 Tariff Item	商品名称及备注	进口税率 最惠	普通	暂定	出口退税	增值税率	计量单位	监管条件	Article Description
8705.3010	---装有云梯的救火车	3	8		17	17	辆	AB6O	---Mounted with scaling ladder
8705.3090	---其他	3	8		17	17	辆	AB6O	---Other
8705.4000	-混凝土搅拌车	15	35		17	17	辆	AB6O	-Concrete mixer lorries
	-其他:								-Other:
8705.9010	---无线电通信车	9	35		17	17	辆	AB6O	---Radio communication vans
8705.9020	---放射线检查车	9	14		17	17	辆	6AO	---Mobile radiological units
8705.9030	---环境监测车	12	20		17	17	辆	6AO	---Mobile environmental monitoring units
8705.9040	---医疗车	12	30		17	17	辆	6AO	---Mobile clinics
	---电源车:								---Mobile electric generator sets:
8705.9051	----航空电源车(频率为400赫兹)	12	30		17	17	辆	O6	----Airplane charging vehicles（frequency 400Hz ）
8705.9059	----其他	12	30		17	17	辆	6AO	----Other
8705.9060	---飞机加油车、调温车、除冰车	12	35		17	17	辆	OAB6	---Mobile vehicles for aircraft refuelling, air-conditioning or deicing
8705.9070	---道路(包括跑道)扫雪车	12	35		17	17	辆	OAB6	---Snow sweep vehicles for cleansing streets or airfield runways
8705.9080	---石油测井车、压裂车、混沙车	12	35		17	17	辆	OAB6	---Petroleum well logging trucks, fracturing unit trucks and mixing sand trucks
	---其他								---Other
8705.9091	----混凝土泵车	12	35		17	17	辆/千克	AB6O	----Concrete pump truck
8705.9099	----其他	12	35		17	17	辆/千克		----Other
8705 9099.01[暂]	跑道除冰车	12	35	10	17	17	辆/千克	AB6O	Runway deicing vehicle
8705 9099.30	用于导弹、火箭等的车辆(为弹道导弹、运载火箭等运输、装卸和发射而设计的)	12	35		17	17	辆/千克	36AB	Vehicles for missiles or rockets（specially designed for transportation, loading, unloading and firing of ballistic missiles or carrier rockets）
8705 9099.90	其他特殊用途的机动车辆(主要用于载人或运货的车辆除外)	12	35		17	17	辆/千克	AB6O	Other special purpose motor vehicles, other than vehicles mainly used for the transport of persons or goods
87.06	**装有发动机的机动车辆底盘，品目87.01至87.05所列车辆用:**								**Chassis fitted with engines, for the motor vehicles of headings No. 87.01 to 87.05:**
8706.0010	---非公路用自卸车底盘	8	14		17	17	台	6	---For the vehicles of subheading No. 8704.1030 or 8704.1090
	---货车底盘:								---For the vehicles of subheadings No.8704.2100 to 8704.9000:
8706.0021	----车辆总重量在14吨及以上的	10	30		17	17	台	46AOxy	----For vehicles g.v.w of 14 tons or more
8706.0022	----车辆总重量在14吨以下的	10	45		17	17	台	46AOxy	----For vehicles g.v.w less than 14 tons
8706.0030	---大型客车底盘	20	70		17	17	台	46Oxy	---For passenger motor vehicles with 30 seats or more
8706.0040	---汽车起重机底盘	20	100		17	17	台	6AO	---For crane lorries
8706.0090	---其他	10	100		17	17	台	46AOxy	---Other
87.07	**机动车辆的车身(包括驾驶室)，品目87.01至87.05所列车辆用:**								**Bodies（including cabs）, for the motor vehicles of headings No. 87.01 to 87.05:**
8707.1000	-品目87.03所列车辆用	10	100		17	17	台	6O	-For the vehicles of heading No. 87.03
	-其他:								-Other:
8707.9010	---品目8702.1092、8702.1093、8702.9020及8702.9030所列车辆用	10	70		17	17	台	6O	---For the vehicles of subheadings No. 8702.1092,8702.1093,8702.9020 or 8702.9030
8707.9090	---其他	10	70		17	17	台	6O	---Other
87.08	**机动车辆的零件、附件，品目87.01至87.05所列车辆用:**								**Parts and accessories of the motor vehicles of headings No. 87.01 to 87.05:**
8708.1000	-缓冲器(保险杠)及其零件	10	100		17	17	千克	6	-Bumpers and parts thereof
	-车身(包括驾驶室)的其他零件、附件:								-Other parts and accessories of bodies （including cabs）:
8708.2100	--座椅安全带	10	100		17	17	千克	6A	--Safety seat belts
	--其他:								--Other:
8708.2930	---车窗玻璃升降器	10	100		15	17	千克	6	---Windowpane raiser

税则号列 Tariff Item	商品名称及备注	进口税率 最惠	进口税率 普通	进口税率 暂定	出口退税	增值税率	计量单位	监管条件	Article Description
	---天窗:								---Sunroofs:
8708.2941	----电动的	10	100		17	17	千克/套	6	----Electric
8708.2942	----手动的	10	100		17	17	千克/套	6	----Head-operated
	---其他车身覆盖件:								---Other covered parts of bodies:
8708.2951	----侧围	10	100		17	17	千克	6	----Side appearance of bodies
8708.2952	----车门	10	100		17	17	千克/个	6	----Doors
8708.2953	----发动机罩盖	10	100		17	17	千克	6	----Bonnets
8708.2954	----前围	10	100		17	17	千克	6	----Frontal appearance of bodies
8708.2955	----行李箱盖(或背门)	10	100		17	17	千克	6	----Rear compartment covers（or rear door）
8708.2956	----后围	10	100		17	17	千克	6	----Rear appearance of bodies
8708.2957	----翼子板(或叶子板)	10	100		17	17	千克	6	----Running-boards
8708.2959	----其他	10	100		17	17	千克	6	----Other
8708.2990	---其他	10	100		17	17	千克	6	---Other
	-制动器、助力制动器及其零件:								-Brakes and servo-brakes;parts thereof:
8708.3010	---装在蹄片上的制动摩擦片	10	100		17	17	千克	6	---Mounted brake linings
	---防抱死制动系统（ABS）:								---Anti-slid brake system:
8708.3021	----品目 87.01、8704.1030 及 8704.1090 所列车辆用	6	11		17	17	千克	6	----Of the vehicles of heading No. 87.01 and subheadings 8704.1030 and 8704.1090
8708.3029	----其他	10	100		17	17	千克	6	----Other
	---其他:								---Other:
8708.3091	----品目 87.01 所列车辆用	6	14		17	17	千克	6	----Of the vehicles of heading No. 87.01
8708.3092	----子目号 8702.1091 及 8702.9010 所列车辆用	10	70		17	17	千克	6	----Of the vehicles of subheadings No. 8702.1091 and 8702.9010
8708.3093	----子目号 8704.1030 及 8704.1090 所列车辆用	6	11		17	17	千克	6	----Of the vehicles of subheadings No. 8704.1030 and 8704.1090
8708.3094	----子目号 8704.2100、8704.2230、8704.3100 及 8704.3230 所列车辆用	10	45		17	17	千克	6	----Of the vehicles of subheadings No. 8704.2100, 8704.2230, 8704.3100 and 8704.3230
8708.3095	----子目号 8704.2240、8704.2300 及 8704.3240 所列车辆用	10	30		17	17	千克	6	----Of the vehicles of subheadings No. 8704.2240, 8704.2300 and 8704.3240
8708.3096	----品目 87.05 所列车辆用	10	100		17	17	千克	6	----Of the vehicles of heading No. 87.05
8708.3099	----其他车辆用	10	100		17	17	千克/个		----Other
8708 3099.10	其他机动车辆用制动器(包括助力制动器)	10	100		17	17	千克/个	6O	Brakes and servobrake of other vehicles
8708 3099.90	其他机动车辆用制动器(包括助力制动器)的零件	10	100		17	17	千克/个	6	Parts of brakes and servo-brakes for other vehicle
	-变速箱及其零件:								-Gear boxes and parts thereof:
8708.4010	---品目 87.01 所列车辆用	6	14		17	17	个/千克	6	---Of the vehicles of heading No. 87.01
8708.4020	---子目号 8702.1091 及 8702.9010 所列车辆用	10	70		17	17	个/千克	6	---Of the vehicles of subheadings No. 8702.1091 and 8702.9010
8708.4030	---子目号 8704.1030 及 8704.1090 所列车辆用	6	11		17	17	个/千克		---Of the vehicles of subheadings No. 8704.1030 and 8704.1090
8708 4030.01[暂]	扭矩>1500 牛米非公路自卸车用变速箱	6	11	3	17	17	个/千克	6	Gear boxes for off-highway dumpers use, of a troque less than 1500 mm
8708 4030.90	其他非公路自卸车用变速箱及其零件	6	11		17	17	个/千克	6	Other gear boxes and parts off-highway dumpers use
8708.4040	---子目号 8704.2100、8704.2230、8704.3100 及 8704.3230 所列车辆用	10	45		17	17	个/千克	6	---Of the vehicles of subheadings No. 8704.2100, 8704.2230, 8704.3100 and 8704.3230
8708.4050	---子目号 8704.2240、8704.2300 及 8704.3240 所列车辆用	10	30		17	17	个/千克	6	---Of the vehicles of subheading No. 8704.2240, 8704.2300 and 8704.3240
8708.4060	---品目 87.05 所列车辆用	10	100		17	17	个/千克	6	---Of the vehicles of heading No. 87.05
	---其他:								---Other:
8708.4091	----小轿车用自动换挡变速箱及其零件	10	100		17	17	个/千克		----Automatic gearshift for saloon cars and parts thereof

税则号列 Tariff Item	商品名称及备注	进口税率 最惠	普通	暂定	出口退税	增值税率	计量单位	监管条件	Article Description
8708 4091.01[暂]	小轿车用自动换挡变速箱（6挡及6挡以上）	10	100	6.5	17	17	个/千克	60	Automatic gearshift for saloon cars, (with six gears or more)
8708 4091.04[暂]	小轿车用自动换挡变速箱的零件（6挡及6挡以上）	10	100	6.5	17	17	个/千克	6	Other parts with automatic shift transmission for saloon cars (with six gears or more)
8708 4091.91	其他小轿车用自动换挡变速箱	10	100		17	17	个/千克	60	Automatic gearshift for other saloon cars
8708 4091.99	其他小轿车用自动换挡变速箱的零件	10	100		17	17	个/千克	6	Parts of automatic gearshift for other saloon cars
8708.4099	----其他	10	100		17	17	个/千克		----Other
8708 4099.10	其他未列名机动车辆用变速箱	10	100		17	17	个/千克	60	Gear boxes for other vehicle use, not elsewhere specified or included
8708 4099.90	其他未列名机动车辆用变速箱的零件	10	100		17	17	个/千克	6	Parts of gear boxes for other vehicle use, not elsewhere specified or included
	-装有差速器的驱动桥及其零件，不论是否装有其他传动部件；非驱动桥及其零件:								-Drive-axles with differential, whether or not provided with other transmission components, and non-driving axles; parts thereof:
	---装有差速器的驱动桥及其零件，不论是否装有其他传动部件:								---Drive-axles with differential and parts thereof, whether or not provided with other transmission components:
8708.5071	----品目87.01所列车辆用	6	14		17	17	个/千克	6	----Of the vehicles of heading No. 87.01
8708.5072	----子目号8702.1091及8702.9010所列车辆用	10	70		17	17	个/千克		----Of the vehicles of subheadings No. 8702.1091 and 8702.9010
8708 5072.01[暂]	轴荷≥10吨的中后驱动桥的零件	10	70	8	17	17	个/千克	6	Middle and rear drive-axles and parts thereof, axle load exceeding 10 tons
8708 5072.91	其他大型客车用驱动桥(装有差速器的,不论是否装有其他传动件)	10	70		17	17	个/千克	60	Drive-axles for large bus, with differential, whether or not provided with other transmission components
8708 5072.99	其他大型客车用驱动桥的零件（装有差速器的,不论是否装有其他传动件）	10	70		17	17	个/千克	6	Drive-axles and parts thereof for large bus, with differential, whether or not provided with other transmission components
8708.5073	----子目号8704.1030及8704.1090所列车辆用	6	11		17	17	个/千克	6	----Of the vehicles of subheadings No. 8704.1030 and 8704.1090
8708.5074	----子目号8704.2100、8704.2230、8704.3100及8704.3230所列车辆用	10	45		17	17	个/千克		----Of the vehicles of subheadings No. 8704.2100, 8704.2230, 8704.3100 and 8704.3230
8708 5074.10	柴油、汽油型轻型货车用驱动桥（税号8704.2100、8704.2230、8704.3100、8704.3230所列总重量≤14吨车辆用，装差速器）	10	45		17	17	个/千克	60	Drive-axles for diesel or gasoline light vehicles, used for the vehicles weighing less than 14t of subheading No. 8704.2100, 8704.2230, 8704.3100 or 8704.3230, with differential
8708 5074.90	柴油、汽油型轻型货车用驱动桥的零件（税号8704.2100、8704.2230、8704.3100、8704.3230所列总重量≤14吨车辆用，装差速器）	10	45		17	17	个/千克	6	Parts of drive-axles for diesel or gasoline light vehicles, used for the vehicles weighing less than 14t of subheading No. 8704. 2100, 8704.2230, 8704.3100 or 8704.3230,with differential
8708.5075	----子目号8704.2240、8704.2300及8704.3240所列车辆用	10	30		17	17	个/千克		----Of the vehicles of subheadings No. 8704.2240, 8704.2300 and 8704.3240
8708 5075.10	其他柴油、汽油型重型货车用驱动桥（指税号8704.2240、8704.2300及8704.3240所列车辆用）	10	30		17	17	个/千克	60	Drive-axles for other diesel or gasoline heavy vehicles, used for the vehicles of subheading No. 8704.2240, 8704.2300 or 8704.3240
8708 5075.90	其他柴油、汽油型重型货车用驱动桥的零件（指税号8704.2240、8704.2300及8704.3240所列车辆用）	10	30		17	17	个/千克	6	Parts of drive-axles for diesel or gasoline heavy vehicles, used for the vehicles vehicles of subheading No. 8704.2240, 8704.2300 or 8704.3240
8708.5076	----品目87.05所列车辆用	10	100		17	17	个/千克		----Of the vehicles of heading No. 87.05
8708 5076.10	特种车用驱动桥（指品目87.05所列车辆用，装有差速器，不论	10	100		17	17	个/千克	60	Drive-axles with differential for special vehicles, whether or not provided with other transmission

税则号列 Tariff Item	商品名称及备注	进口税率 最惠	普通	暂定	出口退税	增值税率	计量单位	监管条件	Article Description
	是否装有其他传动件）								components (the vehicles of heading No. 87.05)
8708 5076.90	特种车用驱动桥的零件（指品目87.05所列车辆用，装有差速器，不论是否装有其他传动件）	10	100		17	17	个/千克	6	Parts of drive-axles with differential for special vehicles, whether or not provided with other transmission components (the vehicles of heading No. 87.05)
8708.5079	----其他	10	100		17	17	个/千克		----Other
8708 5079.10	未列名机动车辆用驱动桥(装有差速器的,不论是否装有其他传动件）	10	100		17	17	个/千克	6O	Drive-axles with differential for vehicles, not elsewhere specified or included, whether or not provided with other transmission components
8708 5079.90	未列名机动车辆用驱动桥的零件(装有差速器的，不论是否装有其他传动件）	10	100		17	17	个/千克	6	Parts of drive-axles with differential for vehicles, not elsewhere specified or included, whether or not provided with other transmission components
	---非驱动桥及其零件:								---Non-driving axles and parts thereof:
8708.5081	----品目 87.01 所列车辆用	6	14		17	17	千克	6	----Of the vehicles of heading No. 87.01
8708.5082	---- 子目号 8702.1091 及 8702.9010 所列车辆用	15	70		17	17	千克	6	----Of the vehicles of subheadings No. 8702.1091 and 8702.9010
8708.5083	---- 子目号 8704.1030 及 8704.1090 所列车辆用	6	11		17	17	千克	6	----Of the vehicles of subheadings No. 8704.1030 and 8704.1090
8708.5084	----- 子目号 8704.2100、8704.2230、8704.3100 及 8704.3230 所列车辆用	10	45		17	17	千克	6	----Of the vehicles of subheadings No. 8704.2100, 8704.2230, 8704.3100 and 8704.3230
8708.5085	---- 子目号 8704.2240、8704.2300及8704.3240所列车辆用	10	30		17	17	千克	6	----Of the vehicles of subheadings No. 8704.2240, 8704.2300 and 8704.3240
8708.5086	----品目 87.05 所列车辆用	10	100		17	17	千克	6	----Of the vehicles of heading No. 87.05
8708.5089	----其他	10	100		17	17	千克/个		----Other
8708 5089.10	未列名机动车辆用非驱动桥	10	100		17	17	千克/个	6O	Non-driving axles for vehicles, not elsewhere specified or included
8708 5089.90	未列名机动车辆用非驱动桥的零件	10	100		17	17	千克/个	6	Parts of non-driving axles for vehicles,not elsewhere specified or included
	-车轮及其零件、附件:								-Road wheels and parts and accessories thereof:
8708.7010	---子目号87.01所列车辆用	6	14		17	17	千克	6	---Of the vehicles of heading No. 87.01
8708.7020	--- 子目号 8702.1091 及 8702.9010 所列车辆用	10	70		17	17	千克	6	---Of the vehicles of subheadings No. 8702.1091 and 8702.9010
8708.7030	--- 子目号 8704.1030 及 8704.1090 所列车辆用	6	11		17	17	千克	6	---Of the vehicles of subheadings No. 8704.1030 and 8704.1090
8708.7040	--- 子目号 8704.2100、8704.2230、8704.3100 及 8704.3230 所列车辆用	10	45		17	17	千克	6	---Of the vehicles of subheadings No. 8704.2100, 8704.2230, 8704.3100 and 8704.3230
8708.7050	--- 子目号 8704.2240、8704.2300及8704.3240所列车辆用	10	30		17	17	千克	6	---Of the vehicles of subheadings No. 8704.2240, 8704.2300 and 8704.3240
8708.7060	---品目 87.05 所列车辆用	10	100		17	17	千克	6	---Of the vehicles of heading No. 87.05
	---其他:								---Other:
8708.7091	----铝合金制的	10	100		17	17	千克	6	----Of Aluminum alloy
8708.7099	----其他	10	100		17	17	千克	6	----Other
	-悬挂系统及其零件（包括减震器）:								-Suspension systems and parts thereof （including shock-absorbers）:
8708.8010	---品目 87.03 所列车辆用	10	100		17	17	千克	6	---Of the vehicles of heading No. 87.03
8708.8090	---其他	10	100		17	17	千克	6	---Other
	-其他零件、附件:								-Other parts and accessories:
	--散热器及其零件:								--Radiators and parts thereof:
8708.9110	---水箱散热器	10	100		17	17	个/千克	6	---Water tank radiators
8708.9120	---机油冷却器	10	100		17	17	个/千克	6	---Oil coolers
8708.9190	---其他	10	100		17	17	个/千克	6	---Other
8708.9200	--消声器(消音器)、排气管及其	10	100		17	17	千克	6	--Silencers（mufflers）and exhaust pipes; parts thereof

税则号列 Tariff Item	商品名称及备注	进口税率			出口退税	增值税率	计量单位	监管条件	Article Description
		最惠	普通	暂定					
	零件								
	--离合器及其零件:								--Clutches and parts thereof:
8708.9310	---品目87.01所列车辆用	6	14		17	17	千克	6	---Of the vehicles of heading No. 87.01
8708.9320	---子目号8702.1091及8702.9010所列车辆用	10	70		17	17	千克	6	---Of the vehicles of subheadings No. 8702.1091 and 8702.9010
8708.9330	---子目号8704.1030及8704.1090所列车辆用	6	11		17	17	千克	6	---Of the vehicles of subheadings No. 8704.1030 and 8704.1090
8708.9340	---子目号8704.2100、8704.2230、8704.3100及8704.3230所列车辆用	10	45		17	17	千克	6	---Of the vehicles of subheadings No. 8704.2100, 8704.2230, 8704.3100 and 8704.3230
8708.9350	---子目号8704.2240、8704.2300及8704.3240所列车辆用	10	30		17	17	千克	6	---Of the vehicles of subheadings No. 8704.2240, 8704.2300 and 8704.3240
8708.9360	---品目87.05所列车辆用	10	100		17	17	千克	6	---Of the vehicles of heading No. 87.05
8708.9390	---其他	10	100		17	17	千克	6	---Other
	--转向盘、转向柱、转向器及其零件:								--Steering wheels, steering columns and steering boxes; parts thereof:
8708.9410	---品目87.01所列车辆用	6	14		17	17	千克	6	---Of the vehicles of heading No. 87.01
8708.9420	---子目号8702.1091及8702.9010所列车辆用	10	70		17	17	千克		---Of the vehicles of subheadings No. 8702.1091 and 8702.9010
8708 9420.01[暂]	座位≥30的客车用转向器零件	10	70	8	17	17	千克	6	Parts of steering boxes for the buses with 30 seats or more
8708 9420.90	大型客车用其他转向盘、转向柱及其零件（包括转向器）	10	70		17	17	千克	6	Steering wheels, columns and boxes for big buses; parts thereof
8708.9430	---子目号8704.1030及8704.1090所列车辆用	6	11		17	17	千克	6	---Of the vehicles of subheadings No. 8704.1030 and 8704.1090
8708.9440	---子目号8704.2100、8704.2230、8704.3100及8704.3230所列车辆用	10	45		17	17	千克	6	---Of the vehicles of subheadings No. 8704.2100, 8704.2230, 8704.3100 and 8704.3230
8708.9450	---子目号8704.2240、8704.2300及8704.3240所列车辆用	10	30		17	17	千克		---Of the vehicles of subheadings No.8704.2240, 8704.2300 and 8704.3240
8708 9450.01[暂]	总重≥14吨的柴油型货车转向器的零件	10	30	8	17	17	千克	6	Redirector components of diesel oil trucks whose weight≥14 tons
8708 9450.90	其他重型货车用转向盘、转向柱、转向器及其零件（指税号8704.2240、8704.2300及8704.3240所列车辆用）	10	30		17	17	千克	6	Steering wheels, steering columns, and steering boxes of the vehicles of subheading No. 8704.2240, 8704.2300 or 8704.3240
8708.9460	---品目87.05所列车辆用转向器	10	100		17	17	千克	6	---Of the vehicles of heading No.87.05
8708.9490	---其他	10	100		17	17	千克		---Other
8708 9490.01[暂]	采用电动转向系统的转向盘、转向柱、转向器及其零件	10	100	8	17	17	千克	6	Steering wheels, columns and boxes; parts thereof, of electric power steering system
8708 9490.90	其他未列名机动车辆用转向盘、转向柱及其零件（包括转向器）	10	100		17	17	千克	6	Other steering wheels, columns and boxes; parts thereof, not elsewhere specified or included
8708.9500	--带充气系统的安全气囊及其零件	10	100		17	17	千克	6	--Safety airbags with inflater system; parts thereof
	--其他:								--Other:
8708.9910	---税号87.01所列车辆用	6	14		17	17	千克	6	---Of the vehicles of heading No. 87.01
	---子目号8702.1091及8702.9010所列车辆用:								---Of the vehicles of subheadings No. 8702.1091 and 8702.9010:
8708.9921	----车架	25	70		17	17	千克	6	----Frames
8708.9929	----其他	25	70		17	17	千克	6	----Other
	---子目号8704.1030及8704.1090所列车辆用:								---Of the vehicles of subheadings No. 8704.1030 and 8704.1090:
8708.9931	----车架	6	11		17	17	千克	6	----Frames
8708.9939[暂]	----其他	6	11	3	17	17	千克	6	----Other

税则号列 Tariff Item	商品名称及备注	进口税率 最惠	 普通	 暂定	出口 退税	增值 税率	计量 单位	监管 条件	Article Description
	---子目号8704.2100、8704.2230、8704.3100及8704.3230所列车辆用:								---Of the vehicles of subheadings No. 8704.2100, 8704.2230, 8704.3100 and 8704.3230:
8708.9941	----车架	25	45		17	17	千克	6	----Frames
8708.9949	----其他	25	45		17	17	千克	6	----Other
	---子目号8704.2240、8704.2300及8704.3240所列车辆用:								---Of the vehicles of subheadings No. 8704.2240, 8704.2300 and 8704.3240:
8708.9951	----车架	10	30		17	17	千克	6	----Frames
8708.9959	----其他	10	30		17	17	千克	6	----Other
8708.9960	---税号87.05所列车辆用	15	100		17	17	千克	6	---Of the vehicles of heading No. 87.05
	---其他:								---Other:
8708.9991	----车架	10	100		17	17	千克/个	6O	----Frames
8708.9992	----传动轴	10	100		17	17	千克	6	----Transmission shafts
8708.9999	----其他	10	100		17	17	千克		----Other
8708 9999.01[暂]	混合动力汽车动力传动装置(由发电机、电动机和动力分配装置组成,品目87.01至87.04所列车辆用)	10	100	6	17	17	千克	6	Transmission device of vehicles with engines using electricity and gasoline,(made of generator, electromotor and power allocation device, of the vehicles of subheading No. from 87.01 to 87.04)
8708 9999.90	机动车辆用未列名零件、附件(品目87.01至87.04所列车辆用)	10	100		17	17	千克	6	Parts and accessories of motor vehicles, not elsewhere specified or included (of the vehicles of subheading No. from 87.01 to 87.04)
87.09	**短距离运输货物的机动车辆,未装有提升或搬运设备,用于工厂、仓库、码头或机场;火车站台上用的牵引车;上述车辆的零件**								**Works trucks, self-propelled, not fitted with lifting or handling equipment, of the type used in factories, warehouses, dock areas or airports for short distance transport of goods; tractors of the type used on railway station platforms; parts of the foregoing vehicles:**
	-车辆:								-Vehicles:
	--电动的:								--Electrical:
8709.1110	---牵引车	10	30		15	17	辆	6	---Tractors
8709.1190	---其他	10	30		15	17	辆	6	---Other
	--其他:								--Other:
8709.1910	---牵引车	10.5	30		15	17	辆	6	---Tractors
8709.1990	---其他	10.5	30		15	17	辆	6	---Other
8709.9000	-零件	8.4	17		15	17	千克	6	-Parts
87.10	**坦克及其他机动装甲战斗车辆,不论是否装有武器;上述车辆的零件:**								**Tanks and other armoured fighting vehicles, motorized, whether or not fitted with weapons, and parts of such vehicles:**
8710.0010	---整车	15	100			17	辆	6	---Assembled
8710.0090	---零件	15	100			17	千克	6	---Parts and accessories
87.11	**摩托车(包括机器脚踏两用车)及装有辅助发动机的脚踏车,不论有无边车;边车:**								**Motorcycles(including mopeds) and cycles fitted with an auxiliary motor, with or without side-cars; side-cars:**
8711.1000	-装有往复式活塞内燃发动机,气缸容量(排气量)不超过50毫升	45	150		15	17	辆		-With reciprocating internal combustion piston engine of a cylinder capacity not exceeding 50cc
8711 1000.10	微马力摩托车及脚踏两用车(装有往复式活塞发动机,微马力指排气量=50毫升)	45	150		15	17	辆	y4xAB6	Motorcycles and mopeds, with reciprocating internal combustion piston engine, of a cylinder capacity equal to 50cc
8711 1000.90	微马力摩托车及脚踏两用车(装有往复式活塞发动机,微马力指排气量<50毫升)	45	150		15	17	辆	6AB	Motorcycles and mopeds, with reciprocating internal combustion piston engine, of a cylinder capacity not exceeding 50cc
	-装有往复式活塞内燃发动机,气缸容量(排气量)超过50毫升,但不超过250毫升:								-With reciprocating internal combustion piston engine of a cylinder capacity exceeding 50cc but not exceeding 250cc:
8711.2010	---气缸容量超过50毫升,但不	45	150		15	17	辆	y4xAB6	---Of a cylinder capacity exceeding 50cc but not

税则号列 Tariff Item	商品名称及备注	进口税率 最惠	普通	暂定	出口退税	增值税率	计量单位	监管条件	Article Description
	超过100毫升								exceeding 100cc
8711.2020	---气缸容量超过100毫升，但不超过125毫升	45	150		15	17	辆	y4xAB6	---Of a cylinder capacity exceeding 100 cc but not exceeding 125cc
8711.2030	---气缸容量超过125毫升，但不超过150毫升	45	150		15	17	辆	y4xAB6	---Of a cylinder capacity exceeding 125 cc but not exceeding 150cc
8711.2040	---气缸容量超过150毫升，但不超过200毫升	45	150		15	17	辆	y4xAB6	---Of a cylinder capacity exceeding 150 cc but not exceeding 200cc
8711.2050	---气缸容量超过200毫升，但不超过250毫升	45	150		15	17	辆	y4xAB6	---Of a cylinder capacity exceeding 200 cc but not exceeding 250cc
	-装有往复式活塞内燃发动机，气缸容量（排气量）超过250毫升，但不超过500毫升:								-With reciprocating internal combustion piston engine of a cylinder capacity exceeding 250cc but not exceeding 500cc:
8711.3010	---气缸容量超过250毫升，但不超过400毫升	45	150		15	17	辆	46ABxy	---Of a cylinder capacity exceeding 250cc but not exceeding 400cc
8711.3020	---气缸容量超过400毫升，但不超过500毫升	45	150		15	17	辆	46ABxy	---Of a cylinder capacity exceeding 400cc but not exceeding 500cc
8711.4000	-装有往复式活塞内燃发动机，气缸容量（排气量）超过500毫升，但不超过800毫升	40	150		15	17	辆	46ABxy	-With reciprocating internal combustion piston engine of a cylinder capacity exceeding 500cc but not exceeding 800cc
8711.5000	-装有往复式活塞内燃发动机，气缸容量（排气量）超过800毫升	30	150		15	17	辆	46ABxy	-With reciprocating internal combustion piston engine of a cylinder capacity exceeding 800cc
	-其他:								-Other:
8711.9010	---电动及电动助力的	45	150		15	17	辆		---Electric or with electrical assistant
8711 9010.10	电动自行车	45	150		15	17	辆	6A	Electric bicycle
8711 9010.90	其他电动及电动助力的摩托车及边车（包括机器脚踏两用车、脚踏车）	45	150		15	17	辆	6A	Other electric and electric auxiliary motorcycles and side-cars, including mopeds and bicycle
8711.9090	---其他	45	150		15	17	辆		---Other
8711 9090.01	排量≤250毫升摩托车及脚踏两用车	45	150		15	17	辆	6AB	Motorcycles and mopedes, of a cylinder capacity not exceeding 250m
8711 9090.02	排量>250毫升摩托车及脚踏两用车	45	150		15	17	辆	6AB	Motorcycles and mopedes, of a cylinder capacity exceeding 250m
8711 9090.09	其他无法区分排气量的摩托车及脚踏两用车	45	150		15	17	辆	6AB	Motorcycles and mopedes, a cylinder capacity of its engine can not be distinguished
8711 9090.90	装有其他辅助发动机的脚踏车及边车	45	150		15	17	辆	6A	Mopeds and side-cars, fitted with an auxiliary motor
87.12	**自行车及其他非机动脚踏车（包括运货三轮脚踏车）:**								**Bicycles and other cycles（including delivery tricycles）, not motorized:**
8712.0020	---竞赛型自行车	13	130		15	17	辆	6	---Racing bicycle
8712.0030	---山地自行车	13	130		15	17	辆	6	---Mountain bicycle
	---越野自行车:								---Cross-country bicycles:
8712.0041	----16、18及20英寸	13	130		15	17	辆	6	----16", 18", or 20"
8712.0049	----其他	13	130		15	17	辆	6	----Other
	---其他自行车:								---Other bicycles:
8712.0081	----16英寸及以下	13	130		15	17	辆		----Not larger than 16"
8712 0081.10	12~16英寸的未列名自行车	13	130		15	17	辆	6	Bicycles, 12-16 inches, not elsewhere specified
8712 0081.90	11英寸及以下的未列名自行车	13	130		15	17	辆	6	Bicycles, 11 inches or less, not elsewhere specified
8712.0089	----其他	13	130		15	17	辆	6	----Other
8712.0090	---其他	23	130		15	17	辆	6	---Other
87.13	**残疾人用车，不论是否机动或其他机械驱动:**								**Carriages for disabled persons, whether or not motorized or otherwise mechanically propelled:**
8713.1000	-非机械驱动	6	20		15	0	辆	6	-Not mechanically propelled
8713.9000	-其他	4	20		15	0	辆	6	-Other
87.14	**零件、附件，品目87.11至87.13所列车辆用:**								**Parts and accessoris of vehicles of headings No. 87.11 to 87.13:**
8714.1000	-摩托车（包括机器脚踏两用车）用	30	100		15	17	千克		-Of motorcycles（including mopeds）

税则号列 Tariff Item	商品名称及备注	进口税率			出口退税	增值税率	计量单位	监管条件	Article Description
		最惠	普通	暂定					
8714 1000.01[暂]	星型轮及碟刹件	30	100	10	15	17	千克	6	Star wheel and disk brake parts
8714 1000.10	摩托车架	30	100		15	17	千克	46xy	Motorcycle bracket
8714 1000.90	摩托车其他零件、附件(包括机动脚踏两用车的零件、附件)	30	100		15	17	千克	6	Other parts and accessoris of motorcycles(including parts and accessories of mopeds)
8714.2000	-残疾人车辆用	5	17		15	17	千克	6	-Of carriages for disabled persons
	-其他:								-Other:
8714.9100	--车架、轮叉及其零件	12	80		15	17	千克	6	--Frames and forks, and parts thereof
	--轮圈及辐条:								--Wheel rims and spokes:
8714.9210	---轮圈	12	80		15	17	千克	6	---Wheel rims
8714.9290	---辐条	12	80		15	17	千克	6	---Spokes
	--轮毂(倒轮制动毂及毂闸除外);飞轮、链轮:								--Hubs, other than coaster braking hubs and hub brakes, and freewheel, sprocket wheels
8714.9310	---轮毂	12	80		15	17	千克	6	---Hubs
8714.9320	---飞轮	12	80		15	17	千克	6	---Free wheel
8714.9390	---其他	12	80		15	17	千克	6	---Other
8714.9400	--制动器(包括倒轮制动毂及毂闸)及其零件	12	80		15	17	千克	6	--Brakes, including coaster braking hubs and hub brakes, and parts thereof
8714.9500	--鞍座	12	80		15	17	千克/个	6	--Saddles
	--脚蹬、曲柄链轮及其零件:								--Pedals and crank-gear, and parts thereof:
8714.9610	---脚蹬及其零件	12	80		15	17	千克	6	--Pedals and parts thereof
8714.9620	---曲柄链轮及其零件	12	80		15	17	千克	6	---Crank-gear and parts thereof
8714.9900	--其他	12	80		15	17	千克	6	--Other
87.15	**婴孩车及其零件:**								**Baby carriages and parts thereof:**
8715.0000	婴孩车及其零件	20	80		15	17	千克	6AB	Baby carriages and parts thereof
87.16	**挂车及半挂车或其他非机械驱动车辆及其零件:**								**Trailers and semi-trailers; other vehicles, not mechanically propelled; parts thereof:**
8716.1000	-供居住或野营用厢式挂车及半挂车	10	35		15	17	辆	6	-Trailers and semi-trailers of the caravan type, for housing or camping
8716.2000	-农用自装或自卸式挂车及半挂车	10	35		13/15	17	辆	6	-Self-loading or self-unloading trailers and semi-trailers for agricultural purposes
	-其他货运挂车及半挂车:								-Other trailers and semi-trailers for the transport of goods:
	--罐式挂车及半挂车:								--Tanker trailers and tanker semi-trailers:
8716.3110	---油罐挂车及半挂车	10	20		15	17	辆	6A	---Oil tanker trailers and semi-trailers
8716.3190	---其他	10	35		15	17	辆	6A	---Other
	--其他:								--Other:
8716.3910	---货柜挂车及半挂车	10	20		15	17	辆	6A	---Van trailers and semi-trailers
8716.3990	---其他	10	35		15	17	辆	6A	---Other
8716.4000	-其他挂车及半挂车	10	35		15	17	辆	6A	-Other trailers and semi-trailers
8716.8000	-其他车辆	10	80		15	17	辆	6	-Other vehicles
8716.9000	-零件	10	35		15	17	千克	6	-Parts

第八十八章
航空器、航天器及其零件

Chapter 88
Aircraft, spacecraft, and parts thereof

子目注释：

子目 8802.11 至 8802.40 所称“空载重量”，是指航空器在正常飞行状态下，除去机组人员、燃料及非永久性安装设备后的重量。

Subheading Note:

For the purposes of subheadings 8802.11 to 8802.40, the expression "unladen weight" means the weight of the machine in normal flying order, excluding the weight of the crew and of fuel and equipment other than permanently fitted items of equipment

税则号列 Tariff Item	商品名称及备注	进口税率 最惠	普通	暂定	出口退税	增值税率	计量单位	监管条件	Article Description
88.01	气球及飞艇；滑翔机、悬挂滑翔机及其他无动力航空器：								**Balloons and dirigibles; gliders, hang gliders and other non-powered aircraft:**
8801.0010	---滑翔机及悬挂滑翔机	3	11		17	17	架		---Gliders and hang gliders
8801.0090	---其他	3	11		17	17	架		---Other
88.02	其他航空器（例如，直升机、飞机）；航天器(包括卫星)及其运载工具、亚轨道运载工具：								**Other aircraft（for example, helicopters, aeroplanes）; spacecraft（including satellites）and suborbital and spacecraft launch vehicles:**
	-直升机：								-Helicopters:
8802.1100	--空载重量不超过 2000 千克	2	11		17	17	架	O	--Of an unladen weight not exceeding 2000kg
	--空载重量超过 2000 千克：								--Of an unladen weight exceeding 2000 kg:
8802.1210	---空载重量超过 2000 千克，但不超过 7000 千克	2	11		17	17	架	O	---Of an unladen weight exceeding 2000 kg but not exceeding 7000 kg
8802.1220	---空载重量超过 7000 千克	2	11		17	17	架	O	---Of an unladen weight exceeding 7000 kg
8802.2000	-飞机及其他航空器，空载重量不超过 2000 千克	5	11		17	17	架		-Aeroplanes and other aircraft, of an unladen weight not exceeding 2000 kg
8802 2000.10	无人驾驶航空飞行器(空载重量＜ 2 吨）	5	11		17	17	架	30	Pilotless aircraft（of an unladen weight less than 2000 kg）
8802 2000.90	其他小型飞机及其他航空器(小型指空载重量≤2 吨）	5	11		17	17	架		Other small planes and other aircrafts（of an unladen weight not exceeding 2000 kg）
8802.3000	-飞机及其他航空器，空载重量超过 2000 千克，但不超过 15000 千克	4	11		17	17	架	O	-Aeroplanes and other aircraft, of an unladen weight exceeding 2000 kg but not exceeding 15000 kg
	-飞机及其他航空器，空载重量超过 15000 千克：								-Aeroplanes and other aircraft, of an unladen weight exceeding 15000 kg:
8802.4010	---空载重量超过 15000 千克，但不超过 45000 千克	5	11		17	17	架	O	---Of an unladen weight exceeding 15000 kg but not exceeding 45000 kg
8802.4020	---空载重量超过 45000 千克	1	11		17	17	架	O	---Of an unladen weight exceeding 45000 kg
8802.6000	-航天器(包括卫星)及其运载工具、亚轨道运载工具	2	11		17	17	架		-Spacecraft（including satellites）and suborbital and spacecraft launch vehicles
88.03	品目 88.01 或 88.02 所列货品的零件：								**Parts of goods of heading No. 88.01 or88.02:**
8803.1000	-推进器、水平旋翼及其零件	1	11		17	17	千克		-Propellers and rotors and parts thereof
8803.2000	-起落架及其零件	1	11		17	17	千克		-Under-carriages and parts thereof
8803.3000	-飞机及直升机的其他零件	1	11		17	17	千克		-Other parts of aeroplanes or helicopters
8803.9000	-其他	0	11		17	17	千克		-Other
8803 9000.10	两用物项管制的火箭及其零部件	0	11		17	17	千克	3	Missile and its parts & accessories under sensitive item control
8803 9000.90	其他未列名的航空器、航天器零件(指品目 88.01 或 88.02 所列货品用的）	0	11		17	17	千克		Parts of other aircraft, spacecraft, not elsewhere specified or included（parts of goods of heading No. 88.01 or 88.02）
88.04	降落伞(包括可操纵降落伞及滑翔伞）、旋翼降落伞及其零件、附件：								**Parachutes（including dirigible parachutes and paragliders）and rotoehutes; parts thereof and accessories thereto:**
8804.0000	降落伞(包括可操纵降落伞及滑翔伞）、旋翼降落伞及其零件、附件	2	11		17	17	千克		Parachutes（including dirigible parachutes and paragliders）and rotochutes; parts thereof and accessories thereto

税则号列 Tariff Item	商品名称及备注	进口税率			出口退税	增值税率	计量单位	监管条件	Article Description
		最惠	普通	暂定					
88.05	**航空器的发射装置、甲板停机装置或类似装置和地面飞行训练器及其零件:**								**Aircraft launching gear; deck-arrestor or similar gear; ground flying trainers; parts of the foregoing articles:**
8805.1000	-航空器的发射装置及其零件;甲板停机装置或类似装置及其零件	1.5	11		17	17	千克		-Aircraft launching gear and parts thereof; deck-arrestor or similar gear and parts thereof
	-地面飞行训练器及其零件:								-Ground flying trainers and parts thereof
8805.2100	--空战模拟器及其零件	1.5	11		17	17	千克		--Air combat simulators and parts thereof
8805.2900	--其他	1.5	11		17	17	千克	O	--Other

第八十九章
船舶及浮动结构体

Chapter 89
Ships, boats and floating structures

注释：

已装配、未装配或已拆卸的船体、未完工或不完整的船舶以及未装配或已拆卸的完整船舶，如果不具有某种船舶的基本特征，应归入品目 89.06。

Chapter Notes:

A hull, an unfinished or incomplete vessel, assembled, unassembled or disassembled, or a complete vessel unassembled or disassembled, is to be classified in heading 89.06 if it does not have the essential character of a vessel of a particular kind.

税则号列 Tariff Item	商品名称及备注	进口税率			出口退税	增值税率	计量单位	监管条件	Article Description
		最惠	普通	暂定					
89.01	巡航船、游览船、渡船、货船、驳船及其类似的客运或货运船舶：								**Cruise ships, excursion boats, ferryboats, cargo ships, barges and similar vessels for the transport of persons or goods:**
	-巡航船、游览船及主要用于客运的类似船舶；各式渡船：								-Cruise ships, excursion boats and similar vessels principally designed for the transport of persons; ferryboats of all kinds:
8901.1010	---机动船舶	5	14		17	17	艘		---Motor vessels
8901 1010.10	高速客船(包括主要用于客运的类似船舶)	5	14		17	17	艘	O	Hi-speed passenger vessels (including similar vessels principally designed for the transport of persons)
8901 1010.90	其他机动巡航船游览船及各式渡船(包括主要用于客运的类似船舶)	5	14		17	17	艘	O	Other motor cruise ships, motor excursion boats and motor ferry-boats of all kinds (including similar vessels principally designed for the transport of persons)
8901.1090	---非机动船舶	8	30		17	17	艘		---Other
	-液货船：								-Tankers:
	---成品油船：								---Finished oil tankers:
8901.2011	----载重量不超过10万吨	9	14		17	17	艘	O	----Loading not exceeding 100000t
8901.2012	----载重量超过10万吨，但不超过30万吨	9	14		17	17	艘		----Loading exceeding 100000t, but not exceeding 300000t
8901.2013	----载重量超过30万吨	6	14		17	17	艘		----Loading exceeding 300000t
	---原油船：								---Crude oil tankers:
8901.2021	----载重量不超过15万吨	9	14		17	17	艘	O	----Loading not exceeding 150000t
8901.2022	----载重量超过15万吨，但不超过30万吨	9	14		17	17	艘		----Loading exceeding 150000t, but not exceeding 300000t
8901.2023	----载重量超过30万吨	6	14		17	17	艘		----Loading exceeding 300000t
	---液化石油气船：								---Liquified petroleum gas carriers:
8901.2031	----容积在20000立方米及以下	9	14		17	17	艘	O	----Volume with 20000m^3 or less
8901.2032	----容积在20000立方米以上	6	14		17	17	艘		----Volume more than 20000m^3
	---液化天然气船：								---Liquified natural gas carriers:
8901.2041	----容积在20000立方米及以下	9	14		17	17	艘		----Volume with 20000m^3 or less
8901.2042	----容积在20000立方米以上	6	14		17	17	艘		----Volume more than 20000m^3
8901.2090	---其他	9	14		17	17	艘	O	---Other
8901.3000	-冷藏船，但子目号8901.20的船舶除外	9	14		17	17	艘		-Refrigerated vessels, other than those of subheading No. 8901.20
	-其他货运船舶及其他客货兼运船舶：								-Other vessels for the transport of goods and other vessels for the transport of both persons and goods:
	---机动集装箱船：								---Motor container vessels:
8901.9021	----可载标准集装箱在6000箱及以下	9	14		17	17	艘	O	----Capable loading standard containers with 6000 or less
8901.9022	----可载标准集装箱在6000箱以上	6	14		17	17	艘		----Capable loading standard containers more than 6000
	---机动滚装船：								---Motor Ro-Ro carriers:
8901.9031	----载重量在2万吨及以下	9	14		17	17	艘	O	----Loading with 20000t or less
8901.9032	----载重量在2万吨以上	6	14		17	17	艘		----Loading more than 20000t
	---机动散货船：								---Motor bulk carriers:
8901.9041	----载重量不超过15万吨	9	14		17	17	艘	O	----Loading not exceeding 150000t

税则号列 Tariff Item	商品名称及备注	进口税率			出口退税	增值税率	计量单位	监管条件	Article Description
		最惠	普通	暂定					
8901.9042	----载重量超过15万吨，但不超过30万吨	9	14		17	17	艘		----Loading exceeding 150000t, not exceeding 300000t
8901.9043	----载重量超过30万吨	9	14		17	17	艘		----Loading exceeding 300000t
8901.9050	---机动多用途船	9	14		17	17	艘	O	---Multi-purposes motor vessels
8901.9080	---其他机动船舶	9	14		17	17	艘	O	---Other motor vessels
8901.9090	---其他非机动船舶	8	30		15/17	17	艘	O	---Other non-motor vessels
89.02	**捕鱼船；加工船及其他加工保藏鱼类产品的船舶：**								**Fishing vessels; factory ships and other vessels for processing or preserving fishery products:**
8902.0010	---机动船舶	7	14		17	17	艘	O	---Motor vessels
8902.0090	---非机动船舶	8	30		13/17	17	艘		---Other
89.03	**娱乐或运动用快艇及其他船舶；划艇及轻舟：**								**Yachts and other vessels for pleasure or sports; rowing boats and canoes:**
8903.1000	-充气的	10	30		15	17	艘		-Inflatable
	-其他：								-Other:
8903.9100	--帆船，不论是否装有辅助发动机	8	30		15	17	艘		--Sailboats, with or without auxiliary motor
8903 9100.01	8米＜长度＜90米的机动帆船	8	30		15	17	艘		Motor sailboats, length: 8m-90m
8903 9100.90	其他帆船（不论是否装有辅助发动机）	8	30		15	17	艘		Other sailboats, with or without auxiliary motor
8903.9200	--汽艇，但装有舷外发动机的除外	10.5	30		15	17	艘		--Motorboats, other than outboard motorboats
8903 9200.01	8米＜长度＜90米的汽艇（装有舷外发动机的除外）	10.5	30		15	17	艘		Motor boats, length: 8m-90m, other than outboard motorboats
8903 9200.90	其他汽艇（装有舷外发动机的除外）	10.5	30		15	17	艘		Other motorboats, other than outboard motorboats
8903.9900	--其他	10	30		15	17	艘		--Other
8903 9900.01	8米＜长度＜90米的娱乐或运动用其他机动船舶或快艇	10	30		15	17	艘		Yachts and other vessels for pleasure or sports, length: 8m-90m
8903 9900.90	娱乐或运动用其他船舶或快艇（包括划艇及轻舟）	10	30		15	17	艘		Other yachts and other vessels for pleasure or sports; rowing boats and canoes
89.04	**拖轮及顶推船：**								**Tugs and pusher craft:**
8904.0000	拖轮及顶推船	9	14		17	17	艘	O	Tugs and pusher craft
89.05	**灯船、消防船、挖泥船、起重船及其他不以航行为主要功能的船舶；浮船坞；浮动或潜水式钻探或生产平台：**								**Light-vessels, fire-floats, dredgers, floating cranes, and other vessels the navigability of which is subsidiary to their main function; floating docks; floating or submersible drilling or production platforms:**
8905.1000	-挖泥船	3	11		17	17	艘	O	-Dredgers
8905.2000	-浮动或潜水式钻探或生产平台	6	11		17	17	座	O	-Floating or submersible drilling or production platforms
	-其他：								-Other:
8905.9010	---浮船坞	8	30		17	17	个	O	---Floating docks
8905.9090	---其他	3	11		17	17	个	O	---Other
89.06	**其他船舶，包括军舰及救生船，但划艇除外：**								**Other vessels, including warships and lifeboats other than rowing boats:**
8906.1000	-军舰	5	14		17	17	艘		-Warships
	-其他：								-Other:
8906.9010	---机动船舶	5	14		17	17	艘		---Motor vessels
8906.9020	---非机动船舶	8	30			17	艘		---Not-motorized vessels
8906.9030	---未制成或不完整的船舶，包括船舶分段	8	30			17	艘		---Unfinished or incomplete vessels, including segments of vessels
89.07	**其他浮动结构体（例如，筏、柜、潜水箱、浮码头、浮筒及航标）：**								**Other floating structures(for example, rafts, tanks, cofferdams, landingstages, buoys and beacons）:**
8907.1000	-充气筏	8	30		15	17	艘		-Inflatable rafts
8907.9000	-其他	8	30		15	17	个		-Other
8907 9000.10	含植物性材料的浮动结构体（例如，筏、柜、潜水箱、浮筒及航	8	30		15	17	个		Floating structures containing vegetable materials（for example rafts, tanks, cofferdams, buoys and

税则号列 Tariff Item	商品名称及备注	进口税率			出口退税	增值税率	计量单位	监管条件	Article Description
		最惠	普通	暂定					
	标）								beacons）
8907 9000.90	其他浮动结构体（例如，筏、柜、潜水箱、浮筒及航标）	8	30		15	17	个		Other floating structures（for example, rafts, tanks, coffer-dams, buoys and beacons）
89.08	**供拆卸的船舶及其他浮动结构体：**								**Vessels and other floating structures for breaking up:**
8908.0000	供拆卸的船舶及其他浮动结构体	3	11		15	17	艘/千克	ABP	Vessels and other floating structures for breaking up

第十八类
光学、照相、电影、计量、检验、医疗或外科用仪器及设备、精密仪器及设备；钟表；乐器；上述物品的零件、附件

SECTION XVIII
OPTICAL, PHOTOGRAPHIC, CINEMATOGRAPHIC, MEASURING, CHECKING, PRECISION, MEDICAL OR SURGICAL INSTRUMENTS AND APPARATUS; CLOCKS AND WATCHES; MUSICAL INSTRUMENTS; PARTS AND ACCESSORIES THEREOF

第九十章
光学、照相、电影、计量、检验、医疗或外科用仪器及设备、精密仪器及设备；上述物品的零件、附件

Chapter 90
Optical, photographic, cinematographic, measuring, checking, precision, medical or surgical instruments and apparatus; parts and accessories thereof

注释：

一、本章不包括：

（一）机器、设备或其他专门技术用途的硫化橡胶（硬质橡胶除外）制品（品目 40.16）、皮革或再生皮革制品（品目 42.05）或纺织材料制品（品目 59.11）；

（二）纺织材料制的承托带及其他承托物品，其承托器官的作用仅依靠自身的弹性（例如，孕妇用的承托带，用于胸部、腹部、关节或肌肉的承托绷带）（第十一类）；

（三）品目 69.03 的耐火材料制品；品目 69.09 的实验室、化学或其他专门技术用途的陶瓷器；

（四）品目 70.09 的未经光学加工的玻璃镜及品目83.06或第七十一章的非光学元件的贱金属或贵金属制的镜子；

（五）品目 70.07、70.08、70.11、70.14、70.15 或 70.17 的货品；

（六）第十五类注释二所规定的贱金属制通用零件（第十五类）或塑料制的类似品（第三十九章）；

（七）品目 84.13 的装有计量装置的泵；计数和检验用的衡器或单独报验的天平砝码（品目 84.23）；升降、起重及搬运机械（品目 84.25 至 84.28）；纸张或纸板的各种切割机器（品目 84.41）；品目 84.66 的用于机床上调整工件或工具的附件，包括具有读度用的光学装置的附件（例如，“光学”分度头），但其本身主要是光学仪器的除外（例如，校直望远镜）；计算机器（品目 84.70）；品目 84.81 的阀门及其他装置；品目 84.86 的机器及装置（包括将电路图投影或绘制到感光半导体材料上的装置）；

（八）自行车或机动车辆用探照灯或聚光灯（品

Chapter Notes:

1. This Chapter does not cover:

（a）Articles of a kind used in machines, appliances or for other technical uses, of vulcanised rubber other than hard rubber （heading 40.16）, of leather or of composition leather （heading 42.05）or of textile material（heading 59.11）;

（b）Supporting belts or other support articles of textile material,whose intended effect on the organ to be supprted or held derives solely from their elasticity（for example, maternity belts, thoracic support bandages, abdominal support bandages, supports for joints or muscles）（Section XI）;

（c）Refractory goods of heading 69.03; ceramic wares for laboratory, chemical or other technical uses, of heading 69.09;

（d）Glass mirrors, not optically worked, of heading 70.09, or mirrors of base metal or of precious metal, not being optical elements（heading 83.06 or Chapter 71）;

（e）Goods of heading 70.07, 70.08, 70.11, 70.14, 70.15 or 70.17;

（f）Parts of general use, as defined in Note 2 to SectionXV, of base metal（SectionXV）or similar goods of plastics（Chapter39）;

（g）Pumps incorporating measuring devices, of heading 84.13; weight-operated counting or checking machinery, or separately presented weights for balances（heading 84.23）; lifting or handling machinery（headings 84.25 to 84.28）; paper or paperboard cutting machines of all kinds（heading 84.41）; fittings for adjusting work or tools on machine-tools, of heading 84.66, including fittings with optical devices for reading the scale（for example, “optical” dividing heads）but not those which are in themselves essentially optical instruments（for example, alignment telescopes）; calculating machines（heading 84.70）; valves or other appliances of heading 84.81; machines and apparatus（induding apparatus for the projection or drawing of circuit patterns on sensitised semiconductor materials）of heading 84.86

（h）Searchlights or spotlights of a kind used for cycles or motor vehicles

目85.12）；品目85.13的手提式电灯；电影录音机、还音机及转录机（品目85.19）；拾音头或录音头（品目85.22）；电视摄像机、数字照相机及视频摄录一体机（品目85.25）；雷达设备、无线电导航设备或无线电遥控设备（品目85.26）；光导纤维、光导纤维束或光缆用连接器（品目85.36）；品目85.37的数字控制装置；品目85.39的封闭式聚光灯；品目85.44的光缆；

（九）品目94.05的探照灯及聚光灯；

（十）第九十五章的物品；

（十一）容量的计量器具（按其构成的材料归类）；或

（十二）卷轴、线轴及类似芯子（按其构成材料归类，例如，归入品目39.23或第十五类）。

二、除上述注释一另有规定的以外，本章各品目所列机器、设备、仪器或器具的零件、附件，应按下列规定归类：

（一）凡零件、附件本身已构成本章或第八十四章、第八十五章或第九十一章各品目（品目84.87、85.48或90.33除外）所包括的货品，应一律归入其相应的品目；

（二）其他零件、附件，如果专用于或主要用于某种或同一品目项下的多种机器、仪器或器具（包括品目90.10、90.13或90.31的机器、仪器或器具），应归入相应机器、仪器或器具的品目；

（三）所有其他零件、附件均应归入品目90.33。

三、第十六类注释三及四的规定也适用于本章。

四、品目90.05不包括武器用望远镜瞄准具、潜艇或坦克上的潜望镜式望远镜及本章或第十六类的机器、设备、仪器或器具用的望远镜；这类望远镜瞄准具及望远镜应归入品目90.13。

五、计量或检验用的光学仪器、器具或机器，如果既可归入品目90.13，又可归入品目90.31，则应归入品目90.31。

六、品目90.21所称"矫形器具"，是指下列用途的器具：

预防或矫正躯体畸变；或

生病、手术或受伤后人体部位的支撑或固定。

矫形器具包括用于矫正畸形的鞋及特种鞋垫，但需符合下列任一条件：

（一）定制的；

（二）成批生产的，单独报验、且不成双的、设计为左右两脚同样适用。

七、品目90.32仅适用于：

（一）液体或气体的流量、液位、压力或其他变化量的自动控制仪器及装置或温度自动控制装置，不论其是否依靠要被自动控制的因素所发生的不同的电现象来进行工

(heading 85.12); portable electric lamps of heading 85.13; cinematographic sound recording, reproducing or re-recording apparatus (heading 85.19); sound-heads (heading 85.22); television cameras, digital cameras and video camera recorders (heading 85.25) radar apparatus, radio navigational aid apparatus or radio remote control apparatus (heading 85. 26); connectors for optical fibres, optical fibre bundles or cables (heading 85.36); numerical control apparatus of heading 85.37; sealed beam lamp units of heading 85.39; optical fibre cables of heading 85.44:

(ij) Searchlights or spotlights of heading 94.05;

(k) Articles of Chapter 95;

(l) Capacity measures, which are to be classified according to their constituent material; or

(m) Spools, reels or similar supports (which are to be classified according to their constituent material, for example, in heading 39.23 or SectionXV).

2. Subject to Note 1 above, parts and accessories for machines, apparatus, instruments or articles of this Chapter are to be classified according to the following rules:

(a) Parts and accessories which are goods included in any of the headings of this Chapter or of Chapter 84, 85 or 91 (other than heading 84.87, 85.48 or 90.33) are in all cases to be classified in their respective headings;

(b) Other parts and accessories, if suitable for use solely or principally with a particular kind of machine, instrument or apparatus, or with a number of machines, instruments or apparatus of the same heading (including a machine, instrument or apparatus of heading 90.10, 90.13 or 90.31) are to be classified with the machines, instruments or apparatus of that kind;

(c) All other parts and accessories are to be classified in heading90.33.

3. The provisions of Note 3 and 4 to Section XVI apply also to this Chapter.

4. Heading 90.05 does not apply to telescopic sights for fitting to arms, periscopic telescopes for fitting to submarines or tanks, or to telescopes for machines, appliances, instruments or apparatus of this Chapter or SectionXVI; such telescopic sights and telescopes are to be classified in heading 90.13.

5. Measuring or checking optical instruments, appliances or machines which, but for this Note, could be classified both in heading 90.13 and in heading 90.31 are to be classified in heading 90.31.

6. For the purpose of heading 90.21, the expression "orthopaedic appliances" means appliances for:

Preventing or correcting bodily deformities; or

Supporting or holding parts of the body following an illness, operation or injury.

Orthopaedic appliances include footwear and special insoles designed to correct orthopaedic conditions, provided that they are either

(1) made to measure; or

(2) mass-produced presented singly and not in pairs and designed to fit either foot equally.

7. Heading 90.32 applies only to:

(a) Instruments and apparatus for automatically controlling the flow, level, pressure or other variables of liquids or gases, or for automatically controlling temperature, whether or not their operation depends on an

作的，它们将要被自控的因素调到并保持在一设定值上，通过持续或定期测量实际值来保持稳定，修正任何偏差；以及

（二）电量自动调节器及自动控制非电量的仪器或装置，依靠要被控制的因素所发生的不同的电现象进行工作的，它们将要被控制的因素调到并保持在一设定值上，通过持续或定期测量实际值来保持稳定，修正任何偏差。

electrical phenomenon which varies according to the factor to be automatically controlled; which are designed to bring this factor to, and maintain it at a desired value, stabilized against disturbances, by constantly or periodically measuring its actual value; and

（b）Automatic regulators of electrical quantities, and instruments or apparatus for automatically controlling non-electrical quantities the operation of which depends on an electrical phenomenon varying according to the factor to be controlled, which are designed to bring this factor to, and maintain it at a desired value, stabilized against disturbances,by constantly or periodically measuring its actual value.

税则号列 Tariff Item	商品名称及备注	进口税率			出口退税	增值税率	计量单位	监管条件	Article Description
		最惠	普通	暂定					
90.01	**光导纤维及光导纤维束；光缆，但品目 8544 的货品除外；偏振材料制的片及板；未装配的各种材料制透镜（包括隐形眼镜片）、棱镜、反射镜及其他光学元件，但未经光学加工的玻璃制上述元件除外**								**Optical fibres and optical fibre bundles; optical fibre cables, other than those of heading No. 85.44; sheets and plates of polarizing material; lenses （including contact lenses）, prisms, mirrors and other optical elements, of any material, unmounted, other than such elements of glass not optically worked:**
9001.1000	-光导纤维、光导纤维束及光缆	5	20		15	17	千克		-Optical fibres, optical fibre bundles and cables
9001 1000.01	非色散位移单模光纤(G.652,包括 G652A、G652B、G652C、G652D 等)	5	20		15	17	千克		Non-dispersive displacement single-mode optical fibers （G.652 including G652A、G652B、G652C、G652D）
9001 1000.09	其他光导纤维（但品目 85.44 的货品除外）	5	20		15	17	千克		Other optical fibers (other than the goods of heading No.85.44)
9001 1000.90	光导纤维束及光缆（但品目 85.44 的货品除外）	5	20		15	17	千克		Optical fiber bundles and cables (other than the goods of heading No.85.44)
9001.2000	-偏振材料制的片及板	8	20		15	17	千克		-Sheets and plates of polarizing material
9001 2000.02[暂]	液晶投影仪用偏光板	8	20	6	15	17	千克		Polarizer for LCD Projectors
9001 2000.03[暂]	数字电影放映机用偏光板	8	20	6	15	17	千克		Polarizers of digital cinema projectors
9001 2000.90	其他偏振材料制的片及板	8	20		15	17	千克		Sheets and plates made of other polarizing materials
9001.3000[暂]	-隐形眼镜片	10	70	6	15	17	片		-Contact lenses
	-玻璃制眼镜片：								-Spectacle lenses of glass:
9001.4010[暂]	---变色镜片	20	90	15	15	17	片		---Photochromic
	---其他：								---Other:
9001.4091	----太阳镜片	20	90		15	17	片		----For sunglasses
9001.4099	----其他	20	70		15	17	片		----Other
	-其他材料制眼镜片：								-Spectacle lenses of other materials:
9001.5010[暂]	---变色镜片	20	90	15	15	17	片		---Photochromic
	---其他：								---Other:
9001.5091	----太阳镜片	20	90		15	17	片		----For sunglasses
9001.5099[暂]	----其他	20	70	12	15	17	片		----Other
	-其他：								-Other:
9001.9010	---彩色滤光片	8	20		15	17	千克		---Color filters
9001.9090	---其他	8	20		15	17	千克		---Other
9001 9090.01[暂]	光通信用微光组件的光学元件（包括波长 800～1700 纳米薄膜滤光片，自聚焦透镜，法拉第旋转片）	8	20	0	15	17	千克		Low-light optical components for optical communication (nano film with wavelength standing between 800nm and 1700nm, self-focusing lens, faraday rotation tablets)
9001 9090.02[暂]	微型镜片(激光视盘机激光收发装置用）	8	20	3	15	17	千克		Micro-lens (laser transceiver devices of video CD players)
9001 9090.03[暂]	非涅耳透镜投影屏(屏幕对角线≥80 英寸，投射比≤0.26，增益比≥0.8，镜头间距≤100 微米)	8	20	6	15	17	千克		Fresnel-projection screens (screens diagonal≥80inches,project ratio≤0.26 ,plus ratio≥0.8,lens spacing ≤100um)
9001 9090.04[暂]	液晶显示屏背光模组的光学元件（包括导光板、反射板、扩散	8	20	2	15	17	千克		Optical components of LCD backlight modules (including light guide plates, reflection plates,

税则号列 Tariff Item	商品名称及备注	进口税率 最惠	进口税率 普通	进口税率 暂定	出口退税	增值税率	计量单位	监管条件	Article Description
	片、增亮片）								diffusion sheets, and brightening sheets)
9001 9090.05[暂]	液晶投影仪用偏光元件	8	20	6	15	17	千克		Polariser for LED projector
9001 9090.06[暂]	数字电影放映机用偏光元件	8	20	6	15	17	千克		Polariser for digital cinematographic projector
9001 9090.90	品目 90.01 未列名的其他光学元件（未经光学加工的玻璃制元件除外）	8	20		15	17	千克		Other optical components not specified or included in heading No.90.01 (other than not optically processed glass-made components)
90.02	**已装配的各种材料制透镜、棱镜、反射镜及其他光学元件，作为仪器或装置的零件、配件，但未经光学加工的玻璃制上述元件除外：**								**Lenses, prisms, mirrors and other optical elements, of any material, mounted, being parts of or fittings for instruments or apparatus, other than such elements of glass not optically worked:**
	-物镜：								-Objective lenses:
	--照相机、投影仪、照片放大机及缩片机用：								–For cameras, projectors or photographic enlargers or reducers:
9002.1110	---子目号 9006.1010 至 9006.3000 所列照相机用	8	14		15	17	千克/个		---For the photographic cameras of subheadings No.9006.1010 to 9006.3000
9002.1120	---缩微阅读机用	8	14		15	17	千克/个		---For microfilm, microfiche or other microform readers
	---其他照相机用：								---For other cameras:
9002.1131[暂]	----单反相机镜头	15	80	4	15	17	千克/个		---Lens for single lens reflex cameras
9002.1139[暂]	----其他	15	80	4	15	17	千克/个		----Other
9002.1190	---其他	15	80		15	17	千克/个		---Other
9002 1190.01[暂]	彩色投影机和数字光处理器的镜头及镜头组件	15	80	4	15	17	千克/个		Lenses and lens components of color LCD projectors and digital light processor
9002 1190.90	其他照相机，投影仪等用物镜（包括照片放大机用物镜）	15	80		15	17	千克/个		Other objective lenses for cameras and projectors (including objective lenses for photographic enlargers)
	--其他：								--Other:
9002.1910	---摄影机或放映机用	15	40		15	17	千克/个		---For cinematographic cameras or projectors
9002.1990	---其他	15	50		15	17	千克/个		---Other
9002 1990.01[暂]	摄像机、摄录一体机的镜头	15	50	4	15	17	千克/个		Lens of video camera, camcorder
9002 1990.02[暂]	手机、平板电脑用物镜（800 万像素及以上）	15	50	10	15	17	千克/个		Objective lenses for cellphones and tablt computer (with resolution not less than 8 million pixels)
9002 1990.90	品目 90.02 未列名的其他物镜	15	50		15	17	千克/个		Other objective lenses not specified or included in Heading No.90.02
	-滤色镜：								-Filters:
9002.2010	---照相机用	15	80		15	17	千克/个		---For cameras
9002.2090	---其他	15	40		15	17	千克/个		---Other
	-其他：								-Other:
9002.9010	---照相机用	15	80		15	17	千克		---For cameras
9002 9010.01[暂]	照相机用带屈光度调节装置的目镜（但物镜，滤色镜除外）	15	80	10	15	17	千克		Camera eyepiece with diopter adjustment device (other than the objective lens, filters)
9002 9010.90	其他照相机用未列名光学元件（但物镜，滤色镜除外）	15	80		15	17	千克		Other cameras optical elements not elsewhere specified or included (other than objective lens, color filter, except)
9002.9090	---其他	15	40		15	17	千克		---Other
9002 9090.01[暂]	其他带屈光度调节装置的目镜	15	40	10	15	17	千克		Other eyepiece with diopter adjustment device
9002 9090.02[暂]	掩模版	15	40	10	15	17	千克		Mask
9002 9090.10	抗辐射镜头（能抗 5×10^4 戈瑞（硅）以上辐射而又不会降低使用质量）	15	40		15	17	千克	3	Anti-radiation lens（capable of resisting the radiation of 5×10^4 Gy (Si) or more without sacrificing the quality of service）
9002 9090.90	其他光学仪器用未列名光学元件（但物镜，滤色镜除外）	15	40		15	17	千克		Optical components for other optical instruments not elsewhere specified or included (other than objective lenses and filters)
90.03	**眼镜架及其零件：**								**Frames and mountings for spectacles, goggles or the like, and parts thereof:**
	-眼镜架：								-Frames and mountings:
9003.1100[暂]	--塑料制	18	70	12	15	17	千克/副		--Of plastics
	--其他材料制：								--Of other materials:

税则号列 Tariff Item	商品名称及备注	进口税率			出口退税	增值税率	计量单位	监管条件	Article Description
		最惠	普通	暂定					
9003.1910[暂]	---金属材料制	10	70	6	15	17	千克/副		---Of metal materials
9003.1920	---天然材料制	10	70			17	千克/副		---Of natural materials
9003 1920.10	濒危动植物产品制眼镜架	10	70			17	千克/副	FE	Spectacle frames made of endangered animals and plants
9003 1920.90	其他天然材料制眼镜架	10	70		15	17	千克/副		Spectacle frames made of other natural materials
9003.1990	---其他	10	70		15	17	千克/副		---Other
9003.9000[暂]	-零件	10	70	6	15	17	千克		-Parts
90.04	矫正视力、保护眼睛或其他用途的眼镜、挡风镜及类似品:								**Spectacles, goggles and the like, corrective, protective or other:**
9004.1000[暂]	-太阳镜	20	100	12	15	17	千克/副		-Sunglasses
	-其他:								-Other:
9004.9010[暂]	---变色镜	16	100	10	15	17	千克/副		---Photochromic spectacles
9004.9090[暂]	---其他	20	90	12	15	17	千克/副		---Other
90.05	双筒望远镜、单筒望远镜、其他光学望远镜及其座架;其他天文仪器及其座架,但不包括射电天文仪器:								**Binoculars, monoculars, other optical telescopes, and mountings therefor; other astronomical instruments and mountings therefor, but not including instruments for radio-astronomy:**
9005.1000	-双筒望远镜	15	50		15	17	个		-Binoculars
	-其他仪器:								-Other instruments:
9005.8010	---天文望远镜及其他天文仪器	3	8		17	17	台		---Astronomical telescopes and other astronomical instruments
9005.8090	---其他	12	50		15	17	台		---Other
	-零件、附件(包括座架):								-Parts and accessories (including mountings):
9005.9010	---天文望远镜及其他天文仪器用	2	8		15	17	千克		---Of instruments of subheading No. 9005.8010
9005.9090	---其他	8	30		15	17	千克		---Other
90.06	照相机(电影摄影机除外);照相闪光灯装置及闪光灯泡,但品目85.39的放电灯泡除外:								**Photographic (other than cinematographic) cameras; photographic flashlight apparatus and flashbulbs, other than discharge lamps of heading No.85.39:**
	-制版照相机:								-Cameras of a kind used for preparing printing plates or cylinders:
9006.1010	---电子分色机	12	20		15	17	台		---Electronic colour scanners
9006.1090	---其他	10	20		15	17	台	A	---Other
9006.3000	-水下、航空测量或体内器官检查用的特种照相机;法庭或犯罪学用的比较照相机	9	17		15	17	台		-Cameras specially designed for under-water use, for aerial survey or for medical or surgical examination of internal organs; comparison cameras for forensic or criminological purposes
9006.4000	--一次成像照相机	5	70		15	17	台		-Instant print cameras
	-其他照相机:								-Other cameras:
9006.5100	--通过镜头取景[单镜头反光式(SLR)],使用胶片宽度不超过35毫米	25	100		15	17	架		--With a through-the-lens viewfinder (single lens reflex(SLR)), for roll film of a width not exceeding 35 mm
	--其他,使用胶片宽度小于35毫米:								--Other, for roll film of a width less than 35 mm:
9006.5210	---缩微照相机,使用缩微胶卷、胶片或其他缩微品的	9	17		15	17	架		---Cameras of a kind used for recording documents on microfilm, microfiche or other microforms
9006.5290	---其他	25	100		15	17	架		---Other
9006.5300	--其他,使用胶片宽度为35mm	20	100		15	17	架		--Other, for roll film of a width of 35mm
	--其他:								--Other:
9006.5910	---激光照相排版设备	9	35		15	17	台	A	---Laser photo typesetting equipments
9006.5990	---其他	25	100		15	17	架		---Other
9006 5990.10	分幅相机(记录速率超过225000帧/秒)	25	100		15	17	架	3A	Framing camera (with a recording rate of more than 225,000 frames per second)
9006 5990.20	电子(或电子快门)分幅相机(帧曝光时间为51纳秒或更短)	25	100		15	17	架	3A	Electronic (or electronically shuttered) framing cameras (frame exposure time ≤51 nanoseconds)
9006 5990.30	条纹相机(书写速度>0.5毫米/微秒)	25	100		15	17	架	3A	Streak cameras (with a writing speed of more than 0.5mm per microsecond)

税则号列 Tariff Item	商品名称及备注	进口税率 最惠	普通	暂定	出口退税	增值税率	计量单位	监管条件	Article Description
9006 5990.40	电子条纹相机(时间分辨率≤51纳秒)	25	100		15	17	架	3A	Electronic streak cameras (time resolution ≤51 nanoseconds)
9006 5990.90	使用胶片宽度>35 毫米的其他照相机	25	100		15	17	架		Other cameras using the films of more than 35mm in width
	-照相闪光灯装置及闪光灯泡:								-Photographic flashlight apparatus and flashbulbs:
9006.6100	--放电式(电子式)闪光灯装置	18	80		15	17	个		--Discharge lamp（electronic）flashlight apparatus
9006 6100.01[暂]	照相手机用闪光灯组件	18	80	4	15	17	个		Flashlight assembly of photographic mobilephone
9006 6100 02[暂]	照相机外置式电子闪光灯(闪光指数 GN≥30,具有无线闪光功能,支持自动变焦)	18	80	15	15	17	个		External electronic flashlight apparatus for cameras (GN≥30,with wireless flashing function,support automatic
9006 6100.90	其他放电式(电子式)闪光灯装置	18	80		15	17	个		Other discharge lamp (electronic) flashlight apparatus
	--其他:								--Other:
9006.6910	---闪光灯泡	18	80		15	17	个		---Flashbulbs
9006.6990	---其他	18	80		15	17	个		---Other
	-零件、附件:								-Parts and accessories:
	--照相机用:								--For cameras:
9006.9110	--- 子目号 9006.1010 至 9006.3000 所列相机用	8	17		15	17	千克		---For cameras of subheadings No.9006.1010 to 9006.3000
9006.9120	----一次成像照相机用	5	100		15	17	千克		---For instant print cameras
	---其他:								---Other:
9006.9191[暂]	----自动调焦组件	10	100	6	15	17	千克/套		----Automatic focal setting units
9006.9192[暂]	----快门组件	10	100	6	15	17	千克/套		----Shutter units
9006.9199[暂]	----其他	10	100	6	15	17	千克		----Other
9006.9900	--其他	12	80		15	17	千克		--Other
90.07	**电影摄影机、放映机,不论是否带有声音的录制或重放装置:**								**Cinematographic cameras and projectors, whether or not incorporating sound recording or reproducing apparatus:**
	-摄影机:								-Cameras:
9007.1010	---高速摄影机	14	40		15	17	台		---High speed cameras
9007.1090	---其他	14	40		15	17	台		---Other
	-放映机:								-Projectors:
9007.2010	---数字式	14	40		15	17	台		---Digital
9007 2010.01[暂]	2K 及以上分辨率的硬盘式数字电影放映机	14	40	8	15	17	台		Hard disk digit film projector with a resolution ratio of 2K or above
9007 2010.90	其他数字式放映机	14	40		15	17	台		Other digital projectors
9007.2090	---其他	14	40		15	17	台		---Other
	-零件、附件:								-Parts and accessories:
9007.9100[暂]	--摄影机用	8.4	40	5	15	17	千克		--For cameras
9007.9200[暂]	--放映机用	8.4	40	5	15	17	千克		--For projectors
90.08	**影像投影仪,但电影用除外;照片(电影片除外)放大机及缩片机:**								**Image projectors, other than cinematographic; photographic（other than cinematographic）enlargers and reducers:**
	-投影仪、放大机及缩片机:								-Projectors, enlargers and reducers
9008.5010	---幻灯机	14	40		15	17	台		---Slide projectors
9008.5020	---缩微胶卷、缩微胶片或其他缩微品的阅读机,不论是否可以进行复制	10	17		15	17	台		---Microfilm, microfiche or other microform readers, whether or not capable of producing copies
	---其他影像投影仪:								---Other image projectors:
9008.5031	----正射投影仪	18	40		15	17	台		----Orthographical projectors
9008.5039	----其他	18	40		15	17	台		----Other
9008.5040	---照片(电影片除外)放大机及缩片机	20	80		15	17	台		---Photographic（other than cinematographic）enlargers and reducers
	-零件、附件:								-Parts and accessories:
9008.9010	---缩微阅读机用	8	17		15	17	千克		---Of microfilm, microfiche or other microform readers
9008.9020	---照片放大机及缩片机用	14	80		15	17	千克		---Of photographic enlargers and reducers
9008.9090	---其他	14	40		15	17	千克		---Other
90.10	**本章其他品目未列名的照相(包**								**Apparatus and equipment for photographic**

税则号列 Tariff Item	商品名称及备注	进口税率 最惠	普通	暂定	出口退税	增值税率	计量单位	监管条件	Article Description
	括电影）洗印用装置及设备；负片显示器；银幕及其他投影屏幕：								**(including cinematographic) laboratories, not specified or included elsewhere in this Chapter; negatoscopes; projection screens:**
	-照相（包括电影）胶卷或成卷感光纸的自动显影装置及设备或将已冲洗胶卷自动曝光到成卷感光纸上的装置及设备：								-Apparatus and equipment for automatically developing photographic (including cinematographic) film or paper in rolls or for automatically exposing developed film to rolls of photographic paper:
9010.1010	---电影用	14	40		15	17	台		---Of a kind used in cinematographic film
9010.1020	---特种照相用	8.4	20		15	17	台		---Of a kind used in special photographic film or paper
	---其他：								---Other:
9010.1091	----彩色胶卷用	25	100		15	17	台		----For the colour photographic film in rolls
9010.1099	----其他	15	100		15	17	台		----Other
	-照相（包括电影）洗印用其他装置及设备；负片显示器：								-Other apparatus and equipment for photographic (including cinematographic) laboratories; negatoscope:
9010.5010	---负片显示器	14	50		15	17	台		---Negatoscopes
	---其他：								---Other:
9010.5021	----电影用	14	40		15	17	台		----Of a kind used in cinematographic film
9010.5022	----特种照相用	8.4	20		15	17	台		----Of a kind used in special photographic film or paper
9010.5029	----其他	17	100		15	17	台		----Other
9010.6000	-银幕及其他投影屏幕	14	50		15	17	个		-Projection screens
	-零件、附件：								-Parts and accessories:
9010.9010	---电影用	0	40		15	17	千克		---Of a kind used in cinematographic film
9010.9020	---特种照相用	0	20		15	17	千克		---Of a kind used in special photographic film or paper
9010.9090	---其他	0	100		15	17	千克		---Other
90.11	**复式光学显微镜，包括用于缩微照相、显微电影摄影及显微投影的：**								**Compound optical microscopes, including those for photomicrography, cinephotomicrography or microprojection:**
9011.1000	-立体显微镜	0	14		17	17	台		-Stereoscopic microscopes
9011.2000	-显微照相、显微电影摄影及显微投影用的其他显微镜	0	14		15	17	台		-Other microscopes, for photomicro graphy, cinephotomicrography or microprojection
9011.8000	-其他显微镜	7	14		15	17	台		-Other microscopes
9011 8000.01 暂	高倍测量显微镜，放大倍数≥1000倍，分辨率≤0.08微米	7	14	3	15	17	台		High-power measuring microscope, magnification ≥ 1000 times, the resolution of ≤ 0.08 microns
9011 8000.90	其他显微镜	7	14		15	17	台		Other microscopes
9011.9000	-零件、附件	0	14		15	17	千克		-Parts and accessories
90.12	**显微镜，但光学显微镜除外；衍射设备：**								**Microscopes other than optical microscopes; diffraction apparatus:**
9012.1000	-显微镜，但光学显微镜除外；衍射设备	0	14		15	17	台		-Microscopes other than optical microscopes; and diffraction apparatus
9012.9000	-零件、附件	0	14		15	17	千克		-Parts and accessories
90.13	**其他品目未列名的液晶装置；激光器，但激光二极管除外；本章其他品目未列名的光学仪器及器具：**								**Liquid crystal devices not constituting articles provided for more specifically in other headings; lasers, other than laser diodes; other optical appliances and instruments, not specified or included elsewhere in this Chapter:**
9013.1000	-武器用望远镜瞄准具；潜望镜式望远镜；作为本章或第十六类的机器、设备、仪器或器具部件的望远镜	8	14		15	17	个		-Telescopic sights for fitting to arms; periscopes; telescopes designed to form parts of machines, appliances, instruments or apparatus of this Chapter or Section XVI
9013.2000	-激光器，但激光二极管除外	6	11		17	17	个		-Lasers, other than laser diodes
9013 2000.01 暂	2.5GB/S及以上SDH、波分复用光传输设备980纳米、1480纳米的泵浦激光器	6	11	3	17	17	个		Pump lasers of optical transmission equipments of 980nm~1480nm for SDH and WDM of 2.5GB / S and above
9013 2000.02 暂	激光切割机用气体激光发生器，切割功率≥2千瓦	6	11	3	17	17	个		Gas laser generators for laser cutting machines, cutting power ≥ 2kW

税则号列 Tariff Item	商品名称及备注	进口税率 最惠	普通	暂定	出口退税	增值税率	计量单位	监管条件	Article Description
9013 2000.20	AVLIS、MLIS 和 CRISLA 激光系统	6	11		17	17	个	3	Laser systems such as AVLIS, MLIS and CRISLA
9013 2000.30	氩离子激光器(平均输出功率≥40 瓦特、工作波长 400 纳米～515 纳米)	6	11		17	17	个	3	Argon ion lasers (average output power ≥ 40 watts, operating wavelength standing between 400nm and 515nm)
9013 2000.40	紫翠玉激光器(宽带≤0.005 纳米，重复率＞125 赫兹，功率＞30 瓦等)	6	11		17	17	个	3	Alexandrite lasers (broadband≤0.005nm, repetition rate＞125HZ, power＞30W, etc.)
9013 2000.50	脉冲二氧化碳激光器(重复率＞250 赫兹，功率＞500 瓦，脉冲宽度＜200 纳秒等)	6	11		17	17	个	3	Pulsed carbon dioxide lasers (repetition rate＞250HZ, power＞500W, pulse width＜200 ns, etc.)
9013 2000.60	脉冲受激准分子激光器(XeF、XeCl、KrF 型，重复率＞250 赫兹，功率＞500 瓦等)	6	11		17	17	个	3	Pulsed excimer lasers (XeF, XeCl, KrF type, repetition rate＞250HZ, power＞500W, etc.)
9013 2000.70	铜蒸汽激光器(平均输出功率≥40 瓦特、工作波长 500 纳米～600 纳米)	6	11		17	17	个	3	Copper vapor lasers (average output power ≥ 40W, operating wavelength standing between 500nm and 600nm)
9013 2000.80	掺钕激光器(非玻璃激光器)(两用物项管制商品)	6	11		17	17	个	3	Neodymium-doped laser (non-glass laser)
9013 2000.90	其他激光器(但激光二极管除外)	6	11		17	17	个		Other lasers (excluding laser diodes)
	-其他装置、仪器及器具:								-Other devices, appliances and instruments:
9013.8010	---放大镜	12	50		15	17	个		---Hand magnifying glasses
9013.8020	---光学门眼	12	50		15	17	个		---"Door eyes"
9013.8030	---液晶显示板	5	50		17	17	个/千克		---Liquid crystal display panel
9013 8030.10	10.1 英寸及以下的液晶显示板	5	50		17	17	个/千克		Liquid crystal display panel (size≤10.1 inches)
9013 8030.20	10.1 英寸＜尺寸≤32 英寸的液晶显示板	5	50		17	17	个/千克		Liquid crystal display panel (10.1 inches ＜size≤32 inches)
9013 8030.90	其他液晶显示板	5	50		17	17	个/千克		Other liquid crystal display panel
9013.8090	---其他	5	17		15	17	个		---Other
	-零件、附件:								-Parts and accessories:
9013.9010	---子目 9013.1000 及 9013.2000 所列货品用	6	11		17	17	千克		---For goods of subheadings No. 9013.1000 and 9013.2000
9013.9020	---子目录 9013.8030 所列货品用	8	17		17	17	千克		---For goods of subheading 9013.8030
9013.9090	---其他	8	17		17	17	千克		---Other
90.14	**定向罗盘；其他导航仪器及装置:**								**Direction finding compasses; other navigational instruments and appliances:**
9014.1000	-定向罗盘	2	8		17	17	个		-Direction finding compasses
	-航空或航天导航仪器及装置(罗盘除外):								-Instruments and appliances for aeronautical or space navigation（other than compasses）:
9014.2010[暂]	---自动驾驶仪	2	8	1	17	17	个		---Automatic pilots
9014 2010.10[暂]	无人航空飞行器的自动驾驶仪	2	8	1	17	17	个	3	Automatic pilots for unmanned aerial vehicles (UAV)
9014 2010.90[暂]	其他自动驾驶仪	2	8	1	17	17	个		Other automatic pilots
9014.2090	---其他	2	8		17	17	个		---Other
9014 2090.11[暂]	航空惯性导航仪	2	8	1	17	17	个	3	Aeronautical inertial navigational instruments
9014 2090.12	其他航天惯性导航仪(天文陀螺盘及其他利用天体或卫星进行导航的装置)	2	8		17	17	个	3	Other air inertial navigational instruments (gyroastro compasses and other devices which derive position or orientation by means of automatically tracking celestrial bodies or satellites)
9014 2090.13	陀螺稳定平台	2	8		17	17	个	3	Gyroscope-stabilized platforms
9014 2090.15	陀螺仪(额定漂移率小于 0.5 度/小时的陀螺仪)	2	8		17	17	个	3	Gyros (gyros with a rated drift rate stability of less than 0.5 degree per hour)
9014 2090.16	专门设计的导航信息处理机(用于弹道导弹、运载火箭、探空火箭等的目标探测)	2	8		17	17	个	3	Specially-designed navigation information processors (used by ballistic missiles, launch vehicles, and sounding rockets for target detection)
9014 2090.17	地形等高线绘制设备(用于弹道导弹、运载火箭、探空火箭等的目标探测)	2	8		17	17	个	3	Terrain contour mapping equipments (used by ballistic missiles, launch vehicles, and sounding rockets for target detection)

税则号列 Tariff Item	商品名称及备注	进口税率 最惠	普通	暂定	出口退税	增值税率	计量单位	监管条件	Article Description
9014 2090.18	场景绘图及相关设备(用于弹道导弹、运载火箭、探空火箭等的目标探测)	2	8		17	17	个	3	Scene mapping and correlation equipments (used by ballistic missiles, launch vehicles, and sounding rockets for target detection)
9014 2090.90	其他航空或航天导航仪器及装置(但罗盘除外)	2	8		17	17	个		Other aeronautical and astronautical navigational instruments and appliances (excluding compasses)
9014.8000	-其他仪器及装置	2	8		17	17	个		-Other instruments and appliances
9014 8000.10	比例误差小于0.25%的加速度表	2	8		17	17	个	3	Accelerometers, proportion error less than 0.25%
9014 8000.20	高度表(用于弹道导弹、运载火箭、探空火箭等的目标探测)	2	8		17	17	个	3	Altimeters (used by ballistic missiles, launch vehicles, and sounding rockets for target detection)
9014 8000.90	其他导航仪器及装置	2	8		17	17	个		Other navigational instruments and appliances
	-零件、附件:								-Parts and accessories:
9014.9010[暂]	---自动驾驶仪用	1.5	8	1	17	17	千克		---For automatic pilots
9014.9090	---其他	1.5	8		17	17	千克		---Other
90.15	**大地测量(包括摄影测量)、水道测量、海洋、水文、气象或地球物理用仪器及装置,不包括罗盘;测距仪:**								**Surveying (including photogrammetrical surveying), hydrographic, oceanographic, hydrological, meteorological or geophysical instruments and appliances, excluding compasses; rangefinders:**
9015.1000	-测距仪	9	14		17	17	台		-Rangefinders
9015.2000	-经纬仪及视距仪	9	14		17	17	台		-Theodolites and tachymeters (tacheometers)
9015.3000	-水平仪	9	14		17	17	台		-Levels
9015.4000	-摄影测量用仪器及装置	9	14		17	17	千克		-Photogrammetrical surveying instruments and appliances
9015.8000	-其他仪器及装置	5	14		17	17	台		-Other instruments and appliances
9015 8000.10	机载或舰载重力仪(精度为1毫伽或更好、稳态记录时间至多为2分钟的)	5	14		17	17	台	3	Airborne or ship-borne gravitmeters (with an accuracy of 1 mgal or higher, steady-state recording time ≤2 minutes)
9015 8000.20	机载或舰载重力梯度仪(精度为1毫伽或更好、稳态记录时间至多为2分钟的)	5	14		17	17	台	3	Airborne or ship-borne gravity gradiometers (with an accuracy of 1 mgal or higher, steady-state recording time ≤2 minutes)
9015 8000.90	其他测量仪器及装置	5	14		17	17	台		Other measuring instruments and devices
9015.9000	-零件、附件	5	14		17	17	千克		-Parts and accessories
9015 9000.10	机、舰载重力仪和重力梯度仪部件	5	14		17	17	千克	3	Parts and components of airborne or ship-borne gravitmeters and gradiometers
9015 9000.90	其他大地测量仪及装置的零、附件	5	14		17	17	千克		Parts and components of other surveying instruments and devices
90.16	**感量为50毫克或更精密的天平,不论是否带有砝码:**								**Balances of a sensitivity of 50mg or better, with or without weights:**
9016.0010	---感量为0.1毫克或更精密的天平	9	14		17	17	台/千克		---Of a sensitivity of 0.1mg or better
9016.0090	---其他	10.5	30		17	17	台/千克		---Other
90.17	**绘图、划线或数学计算仪器及器具(例如,绘图机、比例缩放仪、分度规、绘图工具、计算尺及盘式计算器);本章其他品目未列名的手用测量长度的器具(例如,量尺、量带、千分尺及卡尺):**								**Drawing, marking-out or mathematical calculating instruments (for example,drafting machines, pantographs protractors, drawing sets, slide rules, disc calculators); instruments for measuring length, for use in the hand (for example, measuring rods and tapes, micrometers, callipers), not specified or included elsewhere in this Chapter:**
9017.1000	-绘图台及绘图机,不论是否自动	8	20		15	17	台		-Drafting tables and machines, whether or not automatic
9017.2000	-其他绘图、划线或数学计算器具	0	70		15	17	个		-Other drawing, marking-out or mathematical calculating instruments
9017.3000	-千分尺、卡尺及量规	8	20		15	17	个		-Micrometers, callipers and gauges
9017.8000	-其他仪器及器具	8	20		15	17	个		-Other instruments
9017.9000	-零件、附件	0	20		15	17	千克		-Parts and accessories
90.18	**医疗、外科、牙科或兽医用仪器**								**Instruments and appliances used in medical,**

税则号列 Tariff Item	商品名称及备注	进口税率 最惠	普通	暂定	出口退税	增值税率	计量单位	监管条件	Article Description
	及器具，包括闪烁扫描装置、其他电气医疗装置及视力检查仪器:								surgical, dental or veterinary sciences, including scintigraphic apparatus, other electro-medical apparatus and sight-testing instruments:
	-电气诊断装置（包括功能检查或生理参数检查用装置）:								-Electro-diagnostic apparatus（including apparatus for functional exploratory examination or for checking physiological parameters）:
9018.1100	--心电图记录仪	5	17		17	17	台/千克		--Electro-cardiographs
	--超声波扫描装置:								--Ultrasonic scanning apparatus:
9018.1210	---B型超声波诊断仪	7	35		17	17	台/千克	6OA	---B-ultrasonic diagnostic equipment
	---其他:								---Other:
9018.1291	----彩色超声波诊断仪	5	17		17	17	台/千克	6OA	----Chromoscope ultrasonic diagnostic equipment
9018.1299	----其他	5	17		17	17	台/千克	6A	----Other
	--核磁共振成像装置：								--Magnetic resonance imaging apparatus:
9018.1310	---成套装置	4	17		17	17	套/千克	6OA	---Complete equipments
9018.1390	---零件	4	17		17	17	个/千克	6OA	---Parts
9018.1400	--闪烁摄影装置	5	17		17	17	台/千克	6A	--Scintigraphic apparatus
	--其他:								--Other:
9018.1930	---病员监护仪	4	17		17	17	台/千克	6A	---Patient monitors
	---听力诊断装置:								---Hearing diagnostic apparatus:
9018.1941	----听力计	4	17		17	17	台/千克	6A	----Andiometers
9018.1949	----其他	4	17		17	17	台/千克	6A	----Other
9018.1990	---其他	4	17		17	17	台/千克	6A	---Other
9018.2000	-紫外线及红外线装置	4	17		17	17	台/千克	6A	-Ultra-violet or infra-red ray apparatus
	-注射器、针、导管、插管及类似品:								-Syringes, needles, catheters, cannulae and the like:
9018.3100	--注射器，不论是否装有针头	8	50		17	17	个/千克	6A	--Syringes, with or without needles
	--管状金属针头及缝合用针:								--Tubular metal needles and needles for sutures:
9018.3210	---管状金属针头	8	50		17	17	千克	6A	---Tubular metal needles
9018.3220	---缝合用针	4	17		17	17	千克	6A	---Needles for sutures
9018.3900	--其他	4	17		17	17	个/千克	6A	--Other
	-牙科用其他仪器及器具:								-Other instruments and appliances, used in dental sciences:
9018.4100	--牙钻机，不论是否与其他牙科设备组装在同一底座上	4	17		17	17	台/千克	6A	--Dental drill engines, whether or not combined on a single base with other dental equipment
	--其他:								--Other:
9018.4910	---装有牙科设备的牙科用椅	4	17		17	17	台/千克	6A	---Dentists' chairs incorporating dental equipment
9018.4990	---其他	4	17		17	17	台/千克	6A	---Other
9018.5000	-眼科用其他仪器及器具	4	17		17	17	千克	6A	-Other ophthalmic instruments and appliances
	-其他仪器及器具:								-Other instruments and appliances:
9018.9010	---听诊器	4	17		17	17	个/千克	6	---Stethoscopes
9018.9020	---血压测量仪器及器具	4	17		17	17	个/千克	6A	---Sphygmomanometers and appliances
9018.9030	---内窥镜	4	17		17	17	台/千克	6A	---Endoscopes
9018.9040	---肾脏透析设备(人工肾)	4	17		17	17	台/千克	6A	---Artificial kidney（dialysis）apparatus
9018.9050	---透热疗法设备	4	17		17	17	台/千克	6A	---Diathermy apparatus
9018.9060	---输血设备	4	17		17	17	台/千克	6A	---Blood transfusion apparatus
9018.9070	---麻醉设备	4	17		17	17	台/千克	6A	---Anaesthetic apparatus and instruments
9018.9080 暂	---宫内节育器	4	17	0		0	个/千克	6A	---Intrauterine contraceptive device
9018.9090	---其他	4	17		17	17	台/千克	6A	---Other
90.19	机械疗法器具；按摩器具；心理功能测验装置；臭氧治疗器；氧气治疗器、喷雾治疗器、人工呼吸器及其他治疗用呼吸器具:								**Mechano-therapy appliances; massage apparatus; psychological aptitudetesting apparatus; ozone therapy, oxygen therapy, aerosol therapy, artificial respiration or other therapeutic respiration apparatus:**
	-机械疗法器具；按摩器具；心理功能测验装置:								-Mechano-therapy appliances; massage apparatus; psychological aptitudetesting apparatus:

税则号列 Tariff Item	商品名称及备注	进口税率 最惠	进口税率 普通	进口税率 暂定	出口退税	增值税率	计量单位	监管条件	Article Description
9019.1010	---按摩器具	15	40		17	17	台/千克	A	---Massage apparatus
9019.1090	---其他	4	30		17	17	台/千克		---Other
9019.2000	-臭氧治疗器、氧气治疗器、喷雾治疗器、人工呼吸器及其他治疗用呼吸器具	4	17		17	17	台/千克		-Ozone therapy, oxygen therapy, aerosol therapy, artificial respiration or other therapeutic respiration apparatus
90.20	**其他呼吸器具及防毒面具，但不包括既无机械零件又无可互换过滤器的防护面具：**								**Other breathing appliances and gas masks, excluding protective masks having neither mechanical parts nor replaceable filters:**
9020.0000[暂]	其他呼吸器具及防毒面具，但不包括既无机械零件又无可互换过滤器的防护面具	8	30	4	17	17	千克		Other breathing appliances and gas masks, excluding protective masks having neither mechanical parts nor replaceable filters
90.21	**矫形器具，包括支具、外科手术带、疝气带；夹板及其他骨折用具；人造的人体部分；助听器及为弥补生理缺陷或残疾而穿戴、携带或植入人体内的其他器具：**								**Orthopaedic appliances, including crutches, surgical belts and trusses; splints and other fracture appliances; artificial parts of the body; hearing aids and other appliances which are worn or carried, or implanted in the body, to compensate for a defect or disability:**
9021.1000	-矫形或骨折用器具	4	17		15	17	千克		-Orthopaedic or fracture appliances
	-假牙及牙齿固定件：								-Artificial teeth and dental fittings:
9021.2100	--假牙	4	17		15	17	千克		--Artificial teeth
9021.2900	--其他	4	17		15	17	千克		--Other
	-其他人造的人体部分：								-Other artificial parts of the body:
9021.3100	--人造关节	4	17		15	17	千克/套		--Artificial joints
9021.3900	--其他	4	17		15	17	千克		--Other
9021.4000	-助听器，不包括零件、附件	4	17		15	17	个		-Hearing aids, excluding parts and accessories
9021.5000[暂]	-心脏起搏器，不包括零件、附件	4	17	2	15	17	个	A	-Pacemakers for stimulating heart muscles, excluding parts and accessories
	-其他：								-Other:
	---支架：								---Stents:
9021.9011[暂]	----血管支架	4	17	2	15	17	千克/个		----Stents in blood vessel
9021.9019[暂]	----其他	4	17	2	15	17	千克/个		----Other
9021.9090	---其他	4	17		15	17	千克		---Other
9021 9090.01[暂]	人工耳蜗植入装置	4	17	0	15	17	千克		Cochlear implant devices
9021 9090.90	其他弥补生理缺陷，残疾用器具等(包括穿戴、携带或植入人体的器具及零件)	4	17		15	17	千克		Other appliances for redeeming physical defects and disabilities (including the apparatuses and parts for wearing and carrying or those implanted in the body)
90.22	**X射线或α射线、β射线、γ射线的应用设备，不论是否用于医疗、外科、牙科或兽医，包括射线照相及射线治疗设备，X射线管及其他X射线发生器、高压发生器、控制板及控制台、荧光屏、检查或治疗用的桌 、椅及类似品**								**Apparatus based on the use of X-rays or of alpha, beta or gamma radiations, whether or not for medical, surgical, dental or veterinary uses, including radiography or radiotherapy apparatus, X-ray tubes and other X-ray generators, high tension generators, control panels and desks, screens, examination or treatment tables, chairs and the like:**
	-X射线的应用设备，不论是否用于医疗、外科、牙科或兽医，包括射线照相或射线治疗设备：								-Apparatus based on the use of X-rays, whether or not for medical, surgical, dental or veterinary uses, including radiography or radiotherapy apparatus:
9022.1200	--X射线断层检查仪	4	11		17	17	台	6OA	--Computed tomography apparatus
9022.1300	--其他，牙科用	4	11		17	17	台	6OA	--Other, for dental uses
9022.1400	--其他，医疗、外科或兽医用	4	11		17	17	台		--Other, for medical, surgical or veterinary uses
9022 1400.10	医用直线加速器	4	11		17	17	台	6OA	Medical linear accelerators
9022 1400.90	其他医疗或兽医用X射线应用设备	4	11		17	17	台	6OA	Other medical or veterinary X-ray applications
	--其他：								--For other uses:
9022.1910	---低剂量X射线安全检查设备	4	11		15	17	台		---Low dosage X-ray security inspecting equipment
9022 1910.01	采用X光机技术或X射线加速器技术的X射线安全检查设备(能	4	11		15	17	台	6A	x-ray security inspection equipments adopting the technology of x-ray apparatuses or x-ray accelerators

税则号列 Tariff Item	商品名称及备注	进口税率 最惠	进口税率 普通	进口税率 暂定	出口退税	增值税率	计量单位	监管条件	Article Description
	量大于100千电子伏,不包括采用X射线交替双能加速器技术的第二代X射线安全检查设备)								(with energy higher than 100 kilo electron volt, excluding the second generation security inspection equipments adopting the technology of alternating dual-energy x-ray accelerators)
9022 1910.90	其他低剂量X射线安全检查设备	4	11		15	17	台	6A	other types of low dose X-ray security inspection equipments
9022.1920	---X射线无损探伤检测仪	4	11		17	17	台	6A	x-ray nondestructive inspection apparatus
9022.1990	---其他	4	11		17	17	台		---Other
9022 1990.10	X射线全自动燃料芯块检查台(专门设计或制造用于检验燃料芯块的最终尺寸和表面缺陷)	4	11		17	17	台	36A	X-ray fully-automatic fuel pellet inspection stations (specially designed or manufactured to examine the final dimensions and surface defects of the fuel pellets)
9022 1990.90	其他X射线应用设备	4	11		17	17	台	6A	Other X-ray applications
	-α射线、β射线、γ射线的应用设备,不论是否用于医疗、外科、牙科或兽医,包括射线照相或射线治疗设备:								-Apparatus based on the use of alpha, beta or gamma radiations, whether or not for medical, surgical, dental or veterinary uses, including radiography or radiotherapy apparatus:
9022.2100	--医疗、外科、牙科或兽医用	4	11		17	17	台	6A	--For medical, surgical, dental or veterinary uses
	--其他:								--For other uses:
9022.2910	---γ射线无损探伤检测仪	6	11		15	17	台	6A	---Gamma ray nondestructive inspection apparatus
9022.2990	---其他	6	11		15	17	台		---Other
9022 2990.10	γ射线全自动燃料芯块检查台(专门设计或制造用于检验燃料芯块的最终尺寸和表面缺陷)	6	11		15	17	台	36A	γ-ray automatic fuel pellet inspection stand (specially designed or manufactured for inspecting the final size and surface blemish of fuel pellets)
9022 2990.90	其他非医疗用α、β、γ射线设备	6	11		15	17	台	6A	Other types of α-ray, β-ray and γ-ray equipments for non-medical use
9022.3000	-X射线管	2	11		15	17	个	6A	-X-ray tubes
	-其他,包括零件、附件:								-Other, including parts and accessories:
9022.9010	---X射线影像增强器	6	11		15	17	个/千克	6OA	---X-ray intensifiers
9022.9090	---其他	6	11		15	17	个/千克		---Other
9022 9090.01[暂]	射线发生器的零部件	6	11	1	15	17	个/千克	6	Parts and components of ray generators
9022 9090.20	闪光X射线发生器(峰值能量≥500千电子伏)	6	11		15	17	个/千克	36O	Flash X-ray generators (peak energy≥500 keV)
9022 9090.30	X射线断层检查仪专用探测器	6	11		15	17	个/千克	6O	Special probes for X-ray tomography instruments
9022 9090.90	品目90.22所列其他设备及零件(包括高压发生器、控制板及控制台、荧光屏等)	6	11		15	17	个/千克	6	Other equipments and spare parts listed in heading No.90.22 (including high-voltage generators, control panels and consoles, and screens, etc.)
90.23	**专供示范(例如,教学或展览)而无其他用途的仪器、装置及模型:**								**Instruments, apparatus and models, designed for demonstrational purposes (for example, in education or exhibitions), unsuitable for other uses:**
9023.0000	专供示范(例如,教学或展览)而无其他用途的仪器、装置及模型	7	20		15	17	千克		Instruments, apparatus and models, designed for demonstrational purposes (for example, in education or exhibitions), unsuitable for other uses
90.24	**各种材料(例如,金属、木材、纺织材料、纸张、塑料)的硬度、强度、压缩性、弹性或其他机械性能的试验机器及器具:**								**Machines and appliances for testing the hardness, strength, compressibility, elasticity or other mechanical properties of materials (for example, metals, wood, textiles, paper, plastics):**
	-金属材料的试验用机器及器具:								-Machines and appliances for testing metals:
9024.1010	---电子万能试验机	7	20		15	17	台		---Electric multitesting machines
9024.1020	---硬度计	7	20		15	17	台		---Machines and applinances for testing hardness
9024.1090	---其他	7	20		15	17	台		---Other
9024.8000	-其他机器及器具	5	20		15	17	台		-Other machines and appliances
9024.9000	-零件、附件	6	20		15	17	千克		-Parts and accessories
90.25	**记录式或非记录式的液体比重计及类似的浮子式仪器、温度计、高温计、气压计、湿度计、干湿**								**Hydrometers and similar floating instruments, thermometers and pyrometers, barometers, hygrometers and psychrometers, recording or not,**

税则号列 Tariff Item	商品名称及备注	进口税率 最惠	普通	暂定	出口退税	增值税率	计量单位	监管条件	Article Description
	球湿度计及其组合装置:								and any combination of these instruments:
	-温度计及高温计，未与其他仪器组合:								-Thermometers and pyrometers, not combined with other instruments:
9025.1100	--液体温度计,可直接读数	4	40		15	17	个		--Liquid-filled, for direct reading
	--其他:								--Other:
9025.1910	---工业用	8.4	20		15	17	个		---For technical use
9025.1990	---其他	8.4	80		15	17	个		---Other
9025 1990.01 暂	红外线人体测温仪	8.4	80	4	15	17	个		Infrared body thermometer
9025 1990.90	非液体的其他温度计、高温计	8.4	80		15	17	个		Other non-fluid thermometer and pyrometer
9025.8000	-其他仪器	11	30		15	17	个		-Other instruments
9025.9000	-零件、附件	8	20		15	17	千克		-Parts and accessories
9025 9000.01 暂	红外线测温仪传感器元件	8	20	3	15	17	千克		Sensor element of infrared thermometer
9025 9000.90	其他比重计、温度计等类似仪器的零件	8	20		15	17	千克		Parts of other densimeter and thermometer or the like
90.26	**液体或气体的流量、液位、压力或其他变化量的测量或检验仪器及装置（例如，流量计、液位计、压力表、热量计），但不包括品目9014、9015、9028或9032的仪器及装置**								**Instruments and apparatus for measuring or checking the flow, level, pressure or other variables of liquids or gases （for example, flow meters, level gauges, manometers, heat meters）, excluding instruments and apparatus of heading No.90.14, 90.15, 90.28 or 90.32:**
9026.1000	-测量、检验液体流量或液位的仪器及装置	0	17		17	17	个		-For measuring or checking the flow or level of liquids
	-测量、检验压力的仪器及装置:								-For measuring or checking pressure:
9026.2010	---压力/差压变送器	0	17		15	17	个		---Pressure/differential pressure transmitters
9026 2010.10	锰铜压力计（压力超过10GPa）	0	17		15	17	个	3	Manganin pressure gauges (pressure≥100 kPa)
9026 2010.90	其他压力、差压变送器	0	17		15	17	个		Other pressure, differential pressure transmitters
9026.2090	---其他	0	17		15	17	个		---Other
9026 2090.10	压力传感器(两用物项管制商品)	0	17		15	17	个	3	Pressure sensor
9026 2090.90	其他测量、检验压力的仪器及装置	0	17		15	17	个		Instruments or apparatus for measuring or checking pressure
	-其他仪器及装置:								-Other instruments or apparatus:
9026.8010	---测量气体流量的仪器及装置	0	17		15	17	个/千克		--- Instruments and apparatus of measuring gas flow
9026.8090	---其他	0	17		15	17	个/千克		---Other
9026.9000	-零件、附件	0	17		15	17	千克		-Parts and accessories
90.27	**理化分析仪器及装置（例如，偏振仪、折光仪、分光仪、气体或烟雾分析仪）;测量或检验粘性、多孔性、膨胀性、表面张力及类似性能的仪器及装置;测量或检验热量、声量或光量的仪器及装置（包括曝光表）;检镜切片机**								**Instruments and apparatus for physical or chemical analysis（for example,polarimeters, refractometers, spectrometers, gas or smoke analysis apparatus）; instruments and apparatus for measuring or checking viscosity, porosity, expansion, surface tension or the like; instruments and apparatus for measuring or checking quantities of heat, sound or light （including exposure meters）; microtomes:**
9027.1000	-气体或烟雾分析仪	7	17		15	17	台		-Gas or smoke analysis apparatus
9027 1000.10	用于连续操作的气体检测器[可用于出口管制的化学品或有机化合物（含有磷、硫、氟或氯，其浓度低于0.3mg/m³）的检测，或为检测受抑制的胆碱酯酶的活性而设计]	7	17		15	17	台	3	Gas detectors for continuous operations (used to detect the chemicals with export control or organic compounds (containing phosphorus, sulfur, fluorine or chlorine, with the concentration lower than 0.3mg/m³), or detect the activity of inhibited cholinesterase)
9027 1000.90	其他气体或烟雾分析仪	7	17		15	17	台		Other gas or smoke analysis apparatus
	-色谱仪和电泳仪:								-Chromatographs and electrophoresis instruments:
	---色谱仪:								---Chromatographs instruments:
9027.2011	----气相色谱仪	0	17		17	17	台		----Gas chromatographs instruments
9027.2012	----液相色谱仪	0	17		17	17	台		----Liquid chromatographs instruments
9027.2019	----其他	0	17		17	17	台		----Other
9027.2020	---电泳仪	0	17		17	17	台		---Electrophoresis instruments

税则号列 Tariff Item	商品名称及备注	进口税率 最惠	普通	暂定	出口退税	增值税率	计量单位	监管条件	Article Description
9027.3000	-使用光学射线（紫外线、可见光、红外线）的分光仪、分光光度计及摄谱仪	0	17		17	17	台		-Spectrometers, spectrophotometers and spectrographs using optical radiations （UV, visible, IR）
9027.5000	-使用光学射线（紫外线、可见光、红外线）的其他仪器及装置	0	17		15	17	台		-Other instruments and apparatus using optical radiations（UV, visible, IR）
	-其他仪器及装置:								-Other instruments and apparatus:
	---质谱仪:								--Mass spectrograph:
9027.8011	----集成电路生产用氦质谱检漏台	0	17		15	17	台		---Integrated circuit belium spectra leak detectors
9027.8012	----质谱联用仪	0	17		15	17	台		----Mass spectrometers combined with other instruments
9027.8019	----其他	0	17		15	17	台		----Other
9027 8019.10	UF_6质谱仪/离子源（能从UF_6气流中在线取得供料、产品或尾料样品谱仪）	0	17		15	17	台	3	UF_6 mass spectrometers/ion sources (capable of obtaining feed, products or tailing sample spectrometers from UF_6 air streams)
9027 8019.20	测大于 230 质量单位离子质谱仪（分辨率高于 2/230）	0	17		15	17	台	3	Measuring ion mass spectrometers of more than 230 mass units (resolution: higher than 2/230)
9027 8019.90	其他质谱仪	0	17		15	17	台		Other mass spectrometers
	---其他:								---Other:
9027.8091	----曝光表	14	70		15	17	个		----Exposure meters
9027.8099	----其他	0	17		15	17	台		----Other
9027.9000	-检镜切片机;零件、附件	0	17		15	17	千克		-Microtomes; parts and accessories
90.28	**生产或供应气体、液体及电力用的计量仪表，包括它们的校准仪表:**								**Gas, liquid or electricity supply or production meters, including calibrating meters thereof:**
	-气量计:								-Gas meters:
9028.1010	---煤气表	10	30		15	17	个		---Coal gas meters
9028.1090	---其他	10	30		15	17	个		---Other
	-液量计:								-Liquid meters:
9028.2010	---水表	10	30		15	17	个		---Water meters
9028.2090	---其他	10	30		15	17	个		---Other
	-电量计:								-Electricity meters:
	---电度表:								---Watt-hour meter:
9028.3011	----单相感应式	10	30		15	17	个		----Single-phase induction types
9028.3012	----三相感应式	10	30		15	17	个		----Three-phase induction types
9028.3013	----单相电子式(静止式)	10	30		15	17	个		----Single-phase electronic types(Static)
9028.3014	----三相电子式(静止式)	10	30		15	17	个		----Three-phase electronic types(Static)
9028.3019	----其他	10	30		15	17	个		----Other
9028.3090	---其他	10	30		15	17	个		---Other
	-零件、附件:								-Parts and accessories:
9028.9010	---工业用	8.4	30		15	17	千克		---For technical use
9028.9090	---其他	8.4	50		15	17	千克		---Other
90.29	**转数计、产量计数器、车费计、里程计、步数计及类似仪表；速度计及转速表，品目 90.14 及 90.15 的仪表除外；频闪观测仪:**								**Revolution counters, production counters, taximeters, mileometers, pedometers and the like; speed indicators and tachometers, other than those of headings No. 90.14 and 90.15; stroboscopes:**
	-转数计、产量计数器、车费计、里程计、步数计及类似仪表:								-Revolution counters, production counters, taximeters, mileometers, pedometers and the like:
9029.1010	---转数计	15	50		15	17	个		---Revolution counters
9029.1020	---车费计、里程计	15	35		15	17	个		---Taximeters and mileometers
9029.1090	---其他	15	35		15	17	个		---Other
	-速度计及转速表，频闪观测仪:								-Speed indicators and tachometers; stroboscopes:
9029.2010	---车辆用速度计	10	35		15	17	个		---Speed indicators for motor vehicles
9029.2090	---其他	10	35		15	17	个		---Other
9029.9000	-零件、附件	6	35		15	17	千克		-Parts and accessories

税则号列 Tariff Item	商品名称及备注	进口税率			出口退税	增值税率	计量单位	监管条件	Article Description
		最惠	普通	暂定					
90.30	**示波器、频谱分析仪及其他用于电量测量或检验的仪器和装置，但不包括品目 90.28 的各钟仪表；α 射线、β 射线、γ 射线、X 射线、宇宙射线或其他离子射线的测量或检验仪器及装置：**								**Oscilloscopes, spectrum analysers and other instruments and apparatus for measuring or checking electrical quantities, excluding meters of heading No. 90. 28; instruments and apparatus for measuring or detecting alpha, beta, gamma, X-ray, cosmic or other ionizing radiations:**
9030.1000	-离子射线的测量或检验仪器及装置	5	20		17	17	台		-Instruments and apparatus for measuring or detecting ionizing radiations
	-示波器:								-Oscilloscopes and oscillographs:
9030.2010	---测试频率在 300 兆赫兹以下的通用示波器	8	80		15	17	台		---For general use, of test frequency less than 300 MHz
9030.2090	---其他	5	20		15	17	台		---Other
	-检测电压、电流、电阻或功率的其他仪器及装置:								-Other instruments and apparatus, for measuring or checking voltage, current, resistance or power:
	--万用表，不带记录装置:								--Multimeters without a recording device:
9030.3110	---量程在五位半及以下的数字万用表	15	130		15	17	台		---Digital, of measuring range of 5.5 or less
9030.3190	---其他	5	20		15	17	台		---Other
9030.3200	--万用表,带记录装置	8	20		15	17	台		--Multimeters, with a recording device
	--其他，不带记录装置:								--Other, without a recording device:
9030.3310	---量程在五位半及以下的数字电流表、电压表	15	130		15	17	台		---Digital ammeters or voltmeters, of measuring range of 5.5 or less
9030.3320	---电阻测试仪	14	80		15	17	台		---Resistance measuring instruments
9030.3390	---其他	9	20		15	17	台		---Other
9030.3900	--其他,带记录装置	8	20		15	17	台		--Other, with a recording device
	-通讯专用的其他仪器及装置（例如，串音测试器、增益测量仪、失真度表、噪声计）:								-Other instruments and apparatus, specially designed for telecommunications （for example, cross-talk meters, gain measuring instruments, distortion factor meters, psophometers）:
9030.4010	---测试频率在 12.4 千兆赫兹以下的数字式频率计	0	80		17	17	台		---Digital frequency meters, of test frequency less than 12.4 GHz
9030.4090	---其他	0	20		17	17	台		---Other
	-其他仪器及装置:								-Other instruments and apparatus:
9030.8200	--测试或检验半导体晶片或器件用	0	20		15	17	台		--For measuring or checking semiconductor wafers or devices
	--其他，带记录装置:								--Other, with a recording device:
9030.8410	---电感及电容测试仪	10	80		17	17	台		---For measuring inductances or capacitances
9030.8490	---其他	8	20		17	17	台		---Other
	--其他:								--Other:
9030.8910	---电感及电容测试仪	14	80		15	17	台		---For measuring inductances or capacitances
9030.8990	---其他	8	20		15	17	台		---Other
9030 8990.10	中子探测和测量仪表(专用于测定核反应堆堆芯内中子通量的)	8	20		15	17	台	3	Neutron detection and measuring instruments (used exclusively to measure the neutron flux of the reactor cores)
9030 8990.90	其他电量的测量或检验仪器及装置（未装有记录装置的）	8	20		15	17	台		Other instruments and devices for measuring or testing electricity (not fitted with recording devices)
9030.9000	-零件、附件		17		15	17	千克		-Parts and accessories
9030 9000.01	检测半导体晶片及器件的仪器零件（包括附件）	0	17		15	17	千克	s	Parts of the instruments for measuring semiconductor wafers and devices (including accessories)
9030 9000.02	ITA 产品用的印刷电路组件(包括外接组件，如符合 PCMCIA 标准的卡）	0	17		15	17	千克	s	Printed circuit components for ITA products (including external components, such as the cards in compliance with the PCMCIA standard)
9030 9000.90	品目 90.30 所属货品的零件及附件	7	17		15	17	千克		Parts and accessories of the goods of heading No.90.30
90.31	**本章其他品目未列名的测量或**								**Measuring or checking instruments, appliances**

税则号列 Tariff Item	商品名称及备注	进口税率 最惠	普通	暂定	出口退税	增值税率	计量单位	监管条件	Article Description
	检验仪器、器具及机器；轮廓投影仪：								and machines, not specified or included elsewhere in this Chapter; profile projectors:
9031.1000	-机械零件平衡试验机	7	17		15	17	台		-Machines for balancing mechanical parts
9031 1000.10	陀螺动态平衡测试仪	7	17		15	17	台	3	Testers for gyro dynamic balance
9031 1000.90	其他机械零件平衡试验机	7	17		15	17	台		Other machines for balancing mechanical parts
9031.2000	-试验台	7	17		15	17	台		-Test benches
9031 2000.10	陀螺/马达运转试验台	7	17		15	17	台	3	Gyro run-in/motor test benches
9031 2000.20	加速度表测试台	7	17		15	17	台	3	Accelerometer test benches
9031 2000.30	试车台（能试推力＞90 千牛顿火箭发动机的或同时测量三个推力分量的）	7	17		15	17	台	3	Test benches (which have the capacity to handle solid or liquid propellant rocket motors of more than 90 kN of thrust, or which are capable of simultaneously measuring the three axial thrust components)
9031 2000.40	惯性平台测试台(测试平台包括高精度离心机和转台）	7	17		15	17	台	3	Test benches for inertial platform (including high-accuracy centrifuges and rotating benches)
9031 2000.90	其他试验台	7	17		15	17	台		Other test benches
	-其他光学仪器及器具:								-Other optical instruments and appliances:
9031.4100	--制造半导体器件时检验半导体晶片、器件或检测光掩模或光栅用	0	17		15	17	台		--For inspecting semiconductor wafers or devices or for inspecting photomasks or reticles used in manufacturing semiconductor devices
	--其他:								--Other:
9031.4910	---轮廓投影仪	10	20		15	17	台		---Profile projectors
9031.4920	---光栅测量装置	0	17		15	17	台		Optical grating measuring devices
9031.4990	---其他	0	17		15	17	台		---Other
9031 4990.10	光盘质量在线检测仪及离线检测仪	0	17		15	17	台	6O	CD quality online and offline detectors
9031 4990.90	其他光学测量或检验仪器和器具（第九十章其他税号未列名的）	0	17		15	17	台		Other optical measuring or testing instruments and apparatuses (not specified or included elsewhere in Chapter 90)
	-其他仪器、器具及机器:								-Other instruments, appliances and machines:
9031.8010	---光纤通信及光纤性能测试仪	5	17		17	17	台		---Optical telecommunication and optical fibre performance testing instruments
9031.8020	---坐标测量仪	5	17		17	17	台		---Coordinate measuring machine
	---无损探伤检测仪器(射线探伤仪除外):								---Apparatus for examinations,without damaging structure(other than apparatus for radiological examinations):
9031.8031	----超声波探伤检测仪	5	17		17	17	台		----Apparatus for ultrasonic examinations
9031.8032	----磁粉探伤检测仪	5	17		17	17	台		----Apparatus for magnetic examinations
9031.8033[暂]	----涡流探伤检测仪	5	17	3	17	17	台		----Apparatus for eddy examinations
9031.8039	----其他	5	17		17	17	台		----Other
9031.8090	---其他	5	17		17	17	台		---Other
9031 8090.01[暂]	跑道摩擦系数测试仪	5	17	3	17	17	台		Runway friction coefficient testers
9031 8090.02[暂]	音频生命探测仪	5	17	2	17	17	台		Audio life-detection instrument
9031 8090 03[暂]	音视频生命探测仪	5	17	2	17	17	台		Audio-video life-detection instrument
9031 8090.10	惯性测量单元测试仪	5	17		17	17	台	3	Inertial measurement unit testers
9031 8090.20	陀螺调谐测试仪	5	17		17	17	台	3	Gyro tuning testers
9031 8090.90	其他测量、检验仪器、器具及机器(指第九十章其他税号未列名的）	5	17		17	17	台		Other measuring and testing equipments, apparatuses and machines (not specified or included elsewhere in Chapter 90)
9031.9000	-零件、附件	0	17		15	17	千克		-Parts and accessories
9031 9000.20	惯性测量单元稳定元件加工夹具	0	17		15	17	千克	3	Inertial Measurement Unit (IMU) stable element handling fixture
9031 9000.30	惯性平台平衡夹具	0	17		15	17	千克	3	Inertial Measurement Unit (IMU) platform balance fixture
9031 9000.90	品目 90.31 的仪器及器具的其他零件(第九十章其他税号未列名的）	0	17		15	17	千克		Other parts of the instruments and appliances of heading No.90.31 (not specified or included elsewhere in Chapter 90)

税则号列 Tariff Item	商品名称及备注	进口税率 最惠	进口税率 普通	进口税率 暂定	出口退税	增值税率	计量单位	监管条件	Article Description
90.32	自动调节或控制仪器及装置:								**Automatic regulating or controlling instruments and apparatus:**
9032.1000	-恒温器	7	17		15	17	台		-Thermostats
9032.2000	-恒压器	7	17		15	17	台		-Manostats
	-其他仪器及装置:								-Other instruments and apparatus:
9032.8100	--液压或气压的	7	17		17	17	台		--Hydraulic or pneumatic
	--其他:								--Other:
	---列车自动控制系统(ATC)车载设备:								---Devices of Automatic Train Control System (ATC), installed on trains:
9032.8911	----列车自动防护系统(ATP)车载设备	7	17		17	17	台		----Devices of Automatic Train Protection System (ATP), installed on trains
9032.8912	----列车自动运行系统(ATO)车载设备	7	17		17	17	台		----Devices of Automatic Train Operation System (ATO), installed on trains
9032.8919	----其他	7	17		17	17	台		----Other
9032.8990	---其他	7	17		17	17	台		---Other
9032 8990.01[暂]	三坐标测量机用自动控制柜	7	17	3	17	17	台		Automatic control cabinets for Coordinate Measuring Machine (CMM)
9032 8990.02[暂]	飞机自动驾驶系统(包括自动驾驶、电子控制飞行、自动故障分析、警告系统配平系统及推力监控设备及其相关仪表)	7	17	1	17	17	台		Aircraft autopilot system (including autopilot system, electronic flight control system, automatic trouble analysis system, warning system, trimming system, thrust monitoring devices and its related meters)
9032 8990.03[暂]	机床用成套数控伺服装置(包括CNC操作单元,带有配套的伺服放大器和伺服电机)	7	17	3	17	17	台		Numerical control servo set for machine tools (including CNC operation units, with matched servo amplifiers and servo motors)
9032 8990.04[暂]	风力发电设备用控制器	7	17	4	17	17	台		Controllers for wind power equipments
9032 8990.06[暂]	电喷点火程序控制单元(自动控制、调节装置)	7	17	3	17	17	台		Control unit for electrojet ignition procedure(automatic controlling and regulating devices)
9032 8990.07[暂]	印刷机用成套数控伺服传动装置(包括运动控制器或可编程序自动控制器、人机界面单元,带有配套的伺服驱动器和伺服电机)	7	17	3	17	17	台		A complete set of digital servo drives for printing machine (including motion controller or programmable automatic controller, human-machine interface unit, with servo drivers and servo motors)
9032 8990.20	组合喷气发动机的燃烧调节装置(自动控制、调节装置)	7	17		17	17	台	3	Combustion regulating devices for combined jet engines (automatic controlling and regulating devices)
9032 8990.90	其他自动调节或控制仪器及装置	7	17		17	17	台		Other automatic regulating and controlling apparatuses and devices
9032.9000	-零件、附件	5	17		17	17	千克		-Parts and accessories
9032 9000.01[暂]	飞机自动驾驶系统的零件(包括自动驾驶、电子控制飞行、自动故障分析、警告系统配平系统及推力监控设备及其相关仪表的零件)	5	17	1	17	17	千克		Parts of aircraft autopilot system(including parts, of autopilot, electronically controlled, automatic fault analysis, the flight warning system, balancing the system, thrust monitoring equipment)
9032 9000.90	其他自动调节或控制仪器零件、附件	5	17		17	17	千克		Other parts and accessories of automatic regulating or controlling instruments
90.33	**第九十章所列机器、器具、仪器或装置用的本章其他品目未列名的零件、附件:**								**Parts and accessories（not specified or included elsewhere in this Chapter）for machines, appliances, instruments or apparatus of Chapter 90:**
9033.0000	第九十章所列机器、器具、仪器或装置用的本章其他品目未列名的零件、附件	6	17		17	17	千克		Parts and accessories（not specified or included elsewhere in this Chapter）for machines, appliances, instruments or apparatus of Chapter 90

第九十一章
钟表及其零件

注释：

一、本章不包括：

（一）钟表玻璃及钟锤（按其构成材料归类）；

（二）表链（根据不同情况，归入品目 71.13 或 71.17）；

（三）第十五类注释二所规定的贱金属制通用零件（第十五类）、塑料制的类似品（第三十九章）及贵金属或包贵金属制的类似品（一般归入品目 71.15）；但钟、表发条则应作为钟、表的零件归类（品目 91.14）；

（四）轴承滚珠（根据不同情况，归入品目 73.26 或 84.82）；

（五）品目 84.12 的物品，不需擒纵器可以工作的；

（六）滚珠轴承（品目 84.82）；或

（七）第八十五章的物品，本身未组装在或未与其他零件组装在钟、表机芯内，也未组装成专用于或主要用于钟、表机芯零件的（第八十五章）。

二、品目 91.01 仅包括表壳完全以贵金属或包贵金属制的表，以及用贵金属或包贵金属与品目 71.01 至 71.04 的天然、养殖珍珠或宝石、半宝石（天然、合成或再造）合制的表。用贱金属上镶嵌贵金属制成表壳的表应归入品目 91.02。

三、本章所称"表芯"，是指由摆轮及游丝、石英晶体或其他能确定时间间隔的装置来进行调节的机构，并带有显示器或可装机械指示器的系统。表芯的厚度不超过 12 毫米，长、宽或直径不超过 50 毫米。

四、除注释一另有规定的以外，钟、表的机芯及其他零件，既适用于钟或表，又适用于其他物品（例如，精密仪器）的，均应归入本章。

Chapter 91
Clocks and watches and parts thereof

Chapter Notes:

1. This Chapter does not cover:

(a) Clock or watch glasses or weights (classified according to their constituent material);

(b) Watch chains (heading71.13 or 71.17, as the case may be);

(c) Parts of general use defined in Note 2 to Section XV, of base metal (Section XV), or similar goods of plastics(Chapter 39)or of precious metal or metal clad with precious metal (generally heading 71.15); clock or watch springs are, however, to be classified as clock or watch parts (heading 91.14);

(d) Bearing balls (heading 73.26 or 84.82, as the case may be);

(e) Articles of heading 84.12 constructed to work without an escapement;

(f) Ball bearings (heading 84.82); or

(g) Articles of Chapter 85, not yet assembled together or with other components into watch or clock movements or into articles suitable for use solely or principally as parts of such movements(Chapter 85).

2. Heading 91.01 covers only watches with case wholly of precious metal or of metal clad with precious metal, or of the same materials combined with natural or cultured pearls, or precious or semi-precious stones (natural, synthetic or reconstructed) of headings 71.01 to 71.04. Watches with case of base metal inlaid with precious metal fall in heading 91.02.

3. For the purposes of this Chapter, the expression "watch movements" means devices regulated by a balance-wheel and hairspring, quartz crystal or any other system capable of determining intervals of time, with a display or a system to which a mechanical display can be incorporated. Such watch movements shall not exceed 12mm in thickness and 50mm in width, length or diameter.

4. Except as provided in Note 1, movements and other parts suitable for use both in clocks or watches and in other articles (for example, precision instruments) are to be classified in this Chapter.

税则号列 Tariff Item	商品名称及备注	进口税率 最惠	普通	暂定	出口退税	增值税率	计量单位	监管条件	Article Description
91.01	手表、怀表及其他表，包括秒表，表壳用贵金属或包贵金属制成的：								**Wrist-watches, pocket-watches and other watches, including stop-watches, with case of precious metal or of metal clad with precious metal:**
	-电力驱动的手表，不论是否附有秒表装置：								-Wrist-watches, electrically operated whether or not incorporating a stop-watch facility:
9101.1100	--仅有机械指示器的	11	100		13	17	只		--With mechanical display only
	--其他：								---Other:
9101.1910	---仅有光电显示器的	16	100		13	17	只		---With optoelectronic display only
9101.1990	---其他	15	100		13	17	只		---Other
	-其他手表，不论是否附有秒表装置：								-Other wrist-watches, whether or not incorporating a stop-watch facility:
9101.2100	--自动上弦的	11	80			17	只		--Automatic winding
9101 2100.10	含濒危动物皮自动上弦贵金属机械手表（表壳用贵金属或包贵金属制成的）	11	80			17	只	EF	Mechanical wrist watches of precious metal, automatic winding, with endangered animal skin (with case of precious metal or of metal clad with precious metal)

税则号列 Tariff Item	商品名称及备注	进口税率 最惠	普通	暂定	出口退税	增值税率	计量单位	监管条件	Article Description
9101 2100.90	其他自动上弦贵金属机械手表（表壳用贵金属或包贵金属制成的）	11	80		13	17	只		Other mechanical wrist watches of precious metal, automatic winding（with case of precious metal or of metal clad with precious metal）
9101.2900	--其他	15	80			17	只		--Other
9101 2900.10	含濒危动物皮非自动上弦贵金属机械手表(表壳用贵金属或包贵金属制成的)	15	80			17	只	EF	Mechanical wrist watches of precious metal, non-automatic winding, with endangered animal skin（with case of precious metal or of metal clad with precious metal）
9101 2900.90	其他非自动上弦贵金属机械手表(表壳用贵金属或包贵金属制成的)	15	80		13	17	只		Other mechanical wrist watches of precious metal, non-automatic winding（with case of precious metal or of metal clad with precious metal）
	-其他:								-Other:
9101.9100	--电力驱动的	15	100		13	17	只		--Electrically operated
9101.9900	--其他	20	80		13	17	只		--Other
91.02	**手表、怀表及其他表，包括秒表，但品目 91.01 的货品除外：**								**Wrist-watches, pocket-watches and other watches, including stop-watches, other than those of heading No. 91. 01:**
	-电力驱动的手表，不论是否附有秒表装置:								-Wrist-watches, electrically operated, whether or not incorporating a stop-watch facility:
9102.1100	--仅有机械指示器的	12.5	100		13	17	只		--With mechanical display only
9102.1200	--仅有光电显示器的	23	100		13	17	只		--With optoelectronic display only
9102.1900	--其他	15	100		13	17	只		--Other
	-其他手表，不论是否装有秒表装置:								-Other wrist-watches, whether or not incorporating a stop-watch facility:
9102.2100	--自动上弦的	11	80			17	只		--Automatic winding
9102 2100.10	含濒危动物皮其他自动上弦的机械手表(用贵金属或包贵金属制壳的除外)	11	80			17	只	EF	Other mechanical wrist watches, automatic winding, with endangered animal skin（other than with case of precious metal or of metal clad with precious metal）
9102 2100.90	其他自动上弦的机械手表(用贵金属或包贵金属制壳的除外)	11	80		13	17	只		Other mechanical wrist watches, automatic winding（other than with case of precious metal or of metal clad with precious metal）
9102.2900	--其他	15	80			17	只		--Other
9102 2900.10	含濒危动物皮其他非自动上弦机械手表(用贵金属或包贵金属制壳的除外)	15	80			17	只	EF	Mechanical wrist watches, non automatic winding, with endangered animal skin（other than with case of precious metal or of metal clad with precious metal）
9102 2900.90	其他非自动上弦的机械手表(用贵金属或包贵金属制壳的除外)	15	80		13	17	只		Other mechanical wrist watches, non-automatic winding（other than with case of precious metal or of metal clad with precious metal）
	--其他:								--Other:
9102.9100	--电力驱动的	15	100		13	17	只		--Electrically operated
9102.9900	--其他	20	80		13	17	只		--Other
91.03	**以表芯装成的钟，但不包括品目 91.04 的钟：**								**Clocks with watch movements excluding clocks of heading No.91.04:**
9103.1000	-电力驱动的	23	100		13	17	只		-Electrically operated
9103.9000	-其他	20	100		13	17	只		-Other
91.04	**仪表板钟及车辆、航空器、航天器或船舶用的类似钟：**								**Instrument panel clocks and clocks of a similar type for vehicles, aircraft,spacecraft or vessels:**
9104.0000	仪表板钟及车辆、航空器、航天器或船舶用的类似钟	10	100		13	17	只		Instrument panel clocks and clocks of a similar type for vehicles, aircraft, spacecraft or vessels
91.05	**其他钟：**								**Other clocks:**
	-闹钟:								-Alarm clocks:
9105.1100	--电力驱动的	23	100		13	17	只		--Electrically operated
9105.1900	--其他	20	100		13	17	只		--Other
	-挂钟:								Wall clocks:
9105.2100	--电力驱动的	23	100		13	17	只		--Electrically operated
9105.2900	--其他	20	100		13	17	只		--Other
	-其他:								-Other:

税则号列 Tariff Item	商品名称及备注	进口税率 最惠	普通	暂定	出口退税	增值税率	计量单位	监管条件	Article Description
	--电力驱动的:								--Electrically operated:
9105.9110	---天文钟	3	8		13	17	只		---Astronomical chronometer
9105.9190	---其他	23	100		13	17	只		---Other
9105.9900	--其他	16	100		13	17	只		--Other
91.06	**时间记录器以及测量、记录或指示时间间隔的装置，装有钟、表机芯或同步电动机的（例如，考勤钟、时刻记录器）:**								**Time of day recording apparatus and apparatus for measuring, recording or otherwise indicating intervals of time, with clock or watch movement or with synchronous motor（for example, time-registers, time-recorders）:**
9106.1000	-考勤钟、时刻记录器	16	50		13	17	只		-Time-registers; time-recorders
9106.9000	-其他	16	50		13	17	只		-Other
91.07	**装有钟、表机芯或同步电动机的定时开关:**								**Time switches with clock or watch movement or with synchronous motor:**
9107.0000	装有钟、表机芯或同步电动机的定时开关	12	50		13	17	个		Time switches with clock or watch movement or with synchronous motor
91.08	**已组装的完整表芯:**								**Watch movements, complete and assembled:**
	-电力驱动的:								-Electrically operated:
9108.1100[暂]	--仅有机械指示器或有可装机械指示器的装置的	16	80	10	13	17	只		--With mechanical display only or with a device to which a mechanical display can be incorporated
9108.1200	--仅有光电显示器的	16	80		13	17	只		--With optoelectronic display only
9108.1900	--其他	16	80		13	17	只		--Other
9108.2000	-自动上弦的	16	80		13	17	只		-Automatic winding
	-其他:								-Other:
9108.9010	---表面尺寸在33.8毫米及以下	16	80		13	17	只		---Measuring 33.8 mm or less
9108.9090	---其他	16	80		13	17	只		---Other
91.09	**已组装的完整钟芯:**								**Clock movements, complete and assembled:**
9109.1000	-电力驱动的	16	100		13	17	只		-Electrically operated
9109.9000	-其他	16	100		13	17	只		-Other
91.10	**未组装或部分组装的完整钟、表机芯（机芯套装件）；已组装的不完整钟、表机芯；未组装的不完整钟、表机芯:**								**Complete watch or clock movements, unassembled or partly assembled（movement sets）; incomplete watch or clock movements, assembled; rough watch or clock movements:**
	-表的:								-Of watches:
9110.1100	--未组装或部分组装的完整表机芯（机芯套装件）	16	80		13	17	只		--Complete movements, unassembled or partly assembled（movement sets）
9110.1200	--已组装的不完整表机芯	16	70		13	17	千克		--Incomplete movements, assembled
9110.1900	--未组装的不完整表机芯	16	70		13	17	千克		--Rough movements
	-其他:								-Other:
9110.9010	---未组装或部分组装的完整机芯	16	100		13	17	千克/只		---Complete movements, unassembled or partly assembled
9110.9090	---其他	16	80		13	17	千克		---Other
91.11	**表壳及其零件:**								**Watch cases and parts thereof:**
9111.1000	-贵金属表壳或包贵金属表壳	14	80			17	只		-Cases of precious metal or of metal clad with precious metal
9111 1000.10	按重量计含金量在80%及以上的黄金表壳	14	80			17	只	J	Watch cases of gold, containing 80% or more by weight of gold
9111 1000.90	其他贵金属或包贵金属制的表壳	14	80		0/13	17	只		Other watchcases of precious metal or of metal clad with precious metal
9111.2000	-贱金属表壳，不论是否镀金或镀银	14	80		13	17	只		-Cases of base metal, whether or not gold-plated or silver-plated
9111.8000	-其他表壳	14	80		13	17	只		-Other cases
9111.9000	-零件	14	80		0/13	17	千克		-Parts
91.12	**钟壳和本章所列其他货品的类似外壳及其零件:**								**Clock cases and cases of a similar type for other goods of this Chapter, and parts thereof:**
9112.2000	-壳	14	80		13	17	只		-Cases
9112.9000	-零件	12	80		13	17	千克		-Parts

税则号列 Tariff Item	商品名称及备注	进口税率			出口退税	增值税率	计量单位	监管条件	Article Description
		最惠	普通	暂定					
91.13	**表带及其零件：**								**Watch straps, watch bands and watch bracelets, and parts thereof:**
9113.1000	-贵金属或包贵金属制	20	130			17	千克		-Of precious metal or of metal clad with precious metal
9113 1000.10	按重量计含金量在 80%及以上的黄金表带	20	130			17	千克	J	Gold watch straps, containing 80% or more by weight of gold
9113 1000.90	其他贵金属或包贵金属制的表带及零件	20	130		0/13	17	千克		Watch bands and parts thereof, of precious metal or of metal clad with precious metal
9113.2000	-贱金属制，不论是否镀金或镀银	14	100		13	17	千克		-Of base metal,whether or not gold-plated or silver-plated
9113.9000	-其他	14	100			17	千克		-Other
9113 9000.10	濒危动物皮制的表带及其零件	14	100			17	千克	FE	Watch straps and bands, and parts thereof, of endangered animal skin
9113 9000.90	其他非金属制的表带及其零件	14	100		13	17	千克		Other non-metal watch straps, watch bands and watch bracelets, and parts thereof
91.14	**钟、表的其他零件：**								**Other clock or watch parts:**
9114.1000	-发条，包括游丝	14	50		13	17	千克		-Springs, including hair-springs
9114.3000	-钟面或表面	14	50		13	17	千克		-Dials
9114.4000	-夹板及横担(过桥)	14	50		13	17	千克		-Plates and bridges
	-其他：								-Other:
9114.9010	---宝石轴承	14	50		13	17	千克		---Jewel bearings
9114.9090	---其他	14	70		13	17	千克		---Other

第九十二章
乐器及其零件、附件

Chapter 92
Musical instruments; parts and accessories of such articles

注释：

一、本章不包括：

（一）第十五类注释二所规定的贱金属制通用零件（第十五类）或塑料制的类似品（第三十九章）；

（二）第八十五章或第九十章的传声器、扩大器、扬声器、耳机、开关、频闪观测仪及其他附属仪器、器具或设备，虽用于本章物品但未与该物品组成一体或安装在同一机壳内；

（三）玩具乐器或器具（品目95.03）；

（四）清洁乐器用的刷子（品目96.03）；或

（五）收藏品或古物（品目97.05或97.06）。

二、用于演奏品目92.02、92.06所列乐器的弓、槌及类似品，如果与该乐器一同报验，数量合理，用途明确，应归入有关乐器的相应品目。

品目92.09的卡片、盘或卷，即使与乐器一同报验，也不视为该乐器的组成部分，而应作为单独报验的物品对待。

Chapter Notes:

1. This Chapter does not cover:

（a）Parts of general use, as defined in Note 2 to SectionXV, of base metal（SectionXV）, or similar goods of plastics（Chapter 39）;

（b）Microphones, amplifiers, loud-speakers, headphones, switches, stroboscopes or other accessory instruments, apparatus or equipment of Chapter 85 or 90, for use with but not incorporated in or housed in the same cabinet as instruments of this chapter;

（c）Toy instruments or apparatus（heading 95.03）;

（d）Brushes for cleaning musical instruments（heading No96.03）; or

（e）Collectors' pieces or antiques（heading 97.05 or 97.06）.

2. Bows and sticks and similar devices used in playing the musical instruments of headings 92.02 and 92.06 presented with such instruments in numbers normal thereto and clearly intended for use therewith, are to be classified in the same heading as the relative instruments.

Cards, discs and rolls of heading 92.09 presented with an instrument are to be treated as separate articles and not as forming a part of such instrument.

税则号列 Tariff Item	商品名称及备注	进口税率 最惠	进口税率 普通	进口税率 暂定	出口退税	增值税率	计量单位	监管条件	Article Description
92.01	钢琴，包括自动钢琴、拨弦古钢琴及其他键盘弦乐器：								**Pianos, including automatic pianos; harpsichords and other keyboard stringed instruments:**
9201.1000	-竖式钢琴	17.5	70		13	17	台		-Upright pianos
9201.2000	-大钢琴	17.5	70		13	17	台		-Grand pianos
9201 2000.01[暂]	完税价格≥5万美元的大钢琴	17.5	70	1	13	17	台		Grand pianos, duty-payed value ≥$ 50000 each
9201 2000.90	其他大钢琴	17.5	70		13	17	台		Other grand pianos
9201.9000	-其他	17.5	70		13	17	台		-Other
92.02	其他弦乐器（例如，吉他、小提琴、竖琴）：								**Other string musical instruments（for example, guitars, violins, harps）:**
9202.1000	-弓弦乐器	17.5	70			17	只		-Played with a bow
9202 1000.11[暂]	完税价格≥1.5万美元的含濒危动物皮及濒危木的弓弦乐器	17.5	70	1		17	只	FE	Musical instruments played with a bow, duty-payed value≥$15000 each, with skin or wood of endangered animals
9202 1000.19	其他含濒危动物皮及濒危木的弓弦乐器	17.5	70			17	只	FE	Other musical instruments played with a bow, with skin or wood of endangered animals
9202 1000.91[暂]	完税价格≥1.5万美元的不含野生动物皮弓弦乐器	17.5	70	1	13	17	只		Musical instruments played with a bow,duty-payed value≥$15000 each, without skin of endangered animals
9202 1000.99	其他弓弦乐器	17.5	70		13	17	只		Others played with a bow
9202.9000	-其他	17.5	70			17	只		-Other
9202 9000.10	含濒危物种成分的其他弦乐器	17.5	70			17	只	FE	Other string musical instruments, with parts of endang-ered species
9202 9000.90	其他弦乐器	17.5	70		13	17	只		Other string musical instruments
92.05	管乐器（例如，键盘管风琴、手风琴、单簧管、小号、风笛），但游艺场风琴及手摇风琴除外：								**Wind musical instruments（for example, keyboard pipe organs, accordions, clarinets, trumpets, bag pipes）, other than fairground organs and mechanical street organs:**
9205.1000	-铜管乐器	17.5	70		13	17	只		-Brass-wind instruments
9205 1000.01[暂]	完税价格≥2000美元的铜管乐	17.5	70	1	13	17	只		Brass-wind musical instruments, duty-payed value

税则号列 Tariff Item	商品名称及备注	进口税率 最惠	普通	暂定	出口退税	增值税率	计量单位	监管条件	Article Description
	器								≥$2000 each
9205 1000.90	其他铜管乐器	17.5	70		13	17	只		Other brass-wind musical instruments
	-其他:								-Other:
9205.9010	---键盘管风琴、簧风琴及类似的游离金属簧片键盘乐器	20	80		13	17	只		---Keyboard pipe organs; harmoniums and similar keyboard instruments with free metal reeds
9205.9020	---手风琴及类似乐器	21	80		13	17	只		---Accordions and similar instruments
9205.9030	---口琴	21	80		13	17	只		---Mouth organs
9205.9090	---其他	17.5	70		13	17	只		---Other
9205 9090.01 暂	完税价格≥1 万美元的其他管乐器(但游艺场风琴及手摇风琴除外)	17.5	70	1	13	17	只		Other wind musical instruments, duty-payed value ≥$10000 each (excluding accordions and similar instruments of amusement park)
9205 9090.90	其他管乐器(但游艺场风琴及手摇风琴除外)	17.5	70		13	17	只		Other wind musical instruments(excluding accordions and similar instruments of amusement park)
92.06	**打击乐器(例如，鼓、木琴、铙、钹、响板、响葫芦):**								**Percussion musical instruments（for example, drums, xylophones, cymbals, castanets, maracas）:**
9206.0000	打击乐器(例如，鼓、木琴、铙、钹、响板、响葫芦)	17.5	70			17	只		Percussion musical instruments（for example, drums,xylophones,cymbals,castanets,maracas）
9206 0000.10	含濒危动物皮及濒危木的打击乐器(例如,鼓、木琴、钹、响板)	17.5	70			17	只	AEF	Percussion musical instruments, for example, drums, xylophones, cymbals, castanets,maracas, with the leather or wood of endangered animals
9206 0000.90	其他打击乐器(例如，鼓、木琴、钹、响板)	17.5	70		13	17	只		Other percussion musical instruments, for example, drums, xylophones, cymbals, castanets, maracas
92.07	**通过电产生或扩大声音的乐器(例如，电风琴、电吉他、电手风琴):**								**Musical instruments, the sound of which is produced or must be amplified electrically（for example, organs, guitars, accordions）:**
9207.1000 暂	-键盘乐器,但手风琴除外	30	100	15	13	17	只		-Keyboard instruments, other than accordions
9207.9000	-其他	30	100		13	17	个		-Other
92.08	**百音盒、游艺场风琴、手摇风琴、机械鸣禽、乐锯及本章其他品目未列名的其他乐器;各种媒诱音响器、哨子、号角、口吹音响信号器:**								**Musical boxes, fairground organs, mechanical street organs, mechanical singing birds, musical saws and other musical instruments not falling within any other heading of this Chapter; decoy calls of all kinds; whistles, call horns and other mouth-blown sound signalling instruments:**
9208.1000	-百音盒	22	80		13	17	个		-Musical boxes
9208.9000	-其他	22	80		13	17	个		-Other
92.09	**乐器的零件(例如百音盒的机械装置)、附件(例如，机械乐器用的卡片、盘及带卷)，节拍器、音叉及各种定音管:**								**Parts (for example, mechanisms for musical boxes) and accessories(for example, cards, discs and rolls for mechanical instruments）of musical instruments; metronomes, tuning forks and pitch pipes of all kinds:**
9209.3000	-乐器用的弦	17.5	70		13	17	千克		-Musical instrument strings
	-其他:								-Other:
9209.9100	--钢琴的零件、附件	17.5	70		13	17	千克		--Parts and accessories for pianos
9209.9200	--品目 92.02 所列乐器的零件、附件	17.5	70		13	17	千克		--Parts and accessories for the musical instruments of heading No. 92.02
9209.9400 暂	--品目 92.07 所列乐器的零件、附件	17.5	70	10	13	17	千克		--Parts and accessories for the musical instruments of heading No. 92.07
	--其他:								--Other:
9209.9910	---节拍器、音叉及定音管	17.5	70		13	17	千克		---Metronomes, tuning forks and pitch pipes
9209.9920	---百音盒的机械装置	17.5	70		13	17	千克		---Mechanisms for musical boxes
9209.9990	---其他	17.5	70		13	17	千克		---Other

第十九类 武器、弹药及其零件、附件

SECTION XIX ARMS AND AMMUNITION; PARTS AND ACCESSORIES THEREOF

第九十三章 武器、弹药及其零件、附件

Chapter 93 Arms and ammunition; parts and accessories thereof

注释：

一、本章不包括：

（一）第三十六章的货品（例如，火帽、雷管、信号弹）；

（二）第十五类注释二所规定的贱金属制通用零件（第十五类）或塑料制的类似品（第三十九章）；

（三）装甲战斗车辆（品目87.10）；

（四）武器用的望远镜瞄准具及其他光学装置（第九十章），但安装在武器上或与武器一同报验以备安装在该武器上的除外；

（五）弓、箭、钝头击剑或玩具（第九十五章）；或

（六）收藏品及古物（品目97.05或97.06）。

二、品目93.06所称“零件”，不包括税目85.26的无线电设备及雷达设备。

Chapter Notes:

1. This Chapter does not cover:

(a) Goods of Chapter 36 (for example, percussion caps, detonators, signalling flares);

(b) Parts of general use, as defined in Note 2 to Section XV, of base metal (Section XV), or similar goods of plastics (Chapter 39);

(c) Armoured fighting vehicles (heading 87.10);

(d) Telescopic sights and other optical devices suitable for use with arms, unless mounted on a firearm or presented with the firearm on which they are designed to be mounted (Chapter 90);

(e) Bows, arrows, fencing foils or toys (Chapter 95); or

(f) Collectors' pieces or antiques (heading 97.05 or 97.06).

2. In heading 93.06, the reference to "parts thereof" does not include radio or radar apparatus of heading 85.26.

税则号列 Tariff Item	商品名称及备注	进口税率 最惠	进口税率 普通	进口税率 暂定	出口退税	增值税率	计量单位	监管条件	Article Description
93.01	军用武器，但左轮手枪、其他手枪及品目93.07的兵器除外：								**Military weapons, other than revolvers, pistols and the arms of heading No. 93.07:**
	-火炮武器（例如，榴弹炮及迫击炮）：								-Artillery weapons (for example, guns, howitzers and mortars):
9301.1010	--自推进的	13	80			17	座		--Self-propelled
9301.1090	--其他	13	80			17	座		--Other
9301.2000	-火箭发射装置；火焰喷射器；手榴弹发射器；鱼雷发射管及类似发射装置	13	80			17	个		-Rocket launchers; flame-throwers; grenade launchers; torpedo tubes and similar projectors
9301.9000	-其他	13	80			17	支		-Other
93.02	**左轮手枪及其他手枪，但品目93.03或93.04的货品除外：**								**Revolvers and pistols, other than those of heading No. 93.03 or 93.04:**
9302.0000	左轮手枪及其他手枪，但品目93.03或93.04的货品除外	13	80			17	支		Revolvers and pistols, other than those of heading No. 93.03 or 93.04
93.03	**靠爆炸药发射的其他火器及类似装置（例如，运动用猎枪及步枪、前装枪、维利式信号枪及其他专为发射信号弹的装置、发射空包弹的左轮手枪和其他手枪、弩枪式无痛捕杀器、抛缆枪）：**								**Other firearms and similar devices which operate by the firing of an explosive charge (for example, sporting shotguns and rifles, muzzle-loading firearms, Very pistols and other devices designed to project only signal flares, pistols and revolvers for firing blank ammunition, captive-bolt humane killers, line throwing guns):**
9303.1000	-前装枪	13	80		13	17	支		-Muzzle-loading firearms
9303.2000	-其他运动、狩猎或打靶用猎枪，包括组合式滑膛来复枪	13	80		13	17	支		-Other sporting, hunting or target shooting shotguns, including combination shotgun rifles
9303.3000	-其他运动、狩猎或打靶用步枪	13	80		13	17	支		-Other sporting, hunting or target shooting rifles
9303.9000	-其他	13	80		13	17	支		-Other
93.04	**其他武器（例如，弹簧枪、气枪、气手枪、警棍），但不包括品目93.07的货品：**								**Other arms (for example, spring, air or gas guns and pistols, truncheons), excluding those of heading No. 93.07:**

税则号列 Tariff Item	商品名称及备注	进口税率 最惠	普通	暂定	出口退税	增值税率	计量单位	监管条件	Article Description
9304.0000	其他武器(例如，弹簧枪、气枪、气手枪、警棍)，但不包括品目93.07的货品	13	80		13	17	支		Other arms（for example, spring, air or gas guns and pistols, truncheons）, excluding those of heading No. 93.07:
93.05	**品目93.01至93.04所列物品的零件、附件:**								**Parts and accessories of articles of headings No.93.01 to 93.04:**
9305.1000	-左轮手枪或其他手枪用	13	80		0/13	17	千克		-Of revolvers or pistols
9305.2000	-品目93.03的猎枪或步枪用	13	80		0/13	17	千克		-Of shotguns or rifles of heading 93.03
	-其他:								--Other:
9305.9100	--品目93.01的军用武器用	13	80			17	千克		--Of military weapons of heading No. 93.01
9305.9900	--其他	13	80		0/13	17	千克		-Other:
93.06	**炸弹、手榴弹、鱼雷、地雷、水雷、导弹及类似武器及其零件;子弹,其他弹药和射弹及其零件,包括弹丸及弹垫:**								**Bombs, grenades, torpedoes, mines, missiles, and similar munitions of war and parts thereof; cartridges and other ammunition and projectiles and parts thereof, including shot and cartridge wads:**
	-猎枪子弹及其零件;气枪弹丸:								-Shotgun cartridges and parts thereof; air gun pellets:
9306.2100	--猎枪子弹	13	80		13	17	千克		--Cartridges
9306.2900	--其他	13	80		13	17	千克		--Other
	-其他子弹及其零件:								-Other cartridges and parts thereof:
9306.3080	---铆接机或类似工具用及弩枪式无痛捕杀器用子弹及其零件	13	80		0/13	17	千克		---Cartridges for riveting or similar tools or for captive-bolt humane killers and parts thereof
9306.3090	---其他	13	80		0/13	17	千克		---Other
9306.9000	-其他	13	80			17	千克		-Other
9306 9000.10	两用物项管制的导弹及其零件(能把500千克以上有效载荷投掷到300千米以上的)	13	80			17	千克	3	Missiles and parts thereof under control of sensitive item（capable of throwing payload over 500kg to 300km above）
9306 9000.20	运载火箭(能把500千克以上有效载荷投掷到300千米以上的)	13	80			17	千克	3	Carrier rockets (capable of throwing payload over 500kg to 300 km above)
9306 9000.30	探空火箭 (能把500千克以上有效载荷投掷到 300 千米以上的)	13	80			17	千克	3	Sounding rockets（capable of throwing payload over 500kg to 300 km above）
9306 9000.40	巡航导弹(能把500千克以上有效载荷投掷到300千米以上的)	13	80			17	千克	3	Cruise missiles（capable of throwing payload over 500kg to 300 km above）
9306 9000.90	其他弹药和射弹及其零件(包括炸弹、手榴弹、鱼雷、地雷、水雷、导弹等)	13	80		0/13	17	千克		Other ammunition and projectiles and parts thereof（including bombs, grenades, torpedoes, mines, missiles, etc.）
93.07	**剑、短弯刀、刺刀、长矛和类似的武器及其零件;刀鞘、剑鞘:**								**Swords, cutlasses, bayonets, lances and similar arms and parts thereof; scabbards and sheaths therefor:**
	剑、短弯刀、刺刀、长矛和类似的武器及其零件;刀鞘、剑鞘:								Swords, cutlasses, bayonets, lances and similar arms and parts thereof; scabbards and sheaths therefor:
9307.0010	---军用	13	80			17	千克/件		---For military use
9307 0010.10	军用刀鞘、剑鞘,濒危动物制	13	80			17	千克/件	FE	Military scabbard, sheaths, made of endangered animals
9307 0010.90	其他军用剑,刀,长矛和类似的武器及其零件(包括刀鞘、剑鞘)	13	80			17	千克/件		Other military sword, knife, spear and similar arms and parts thereof (including scabbard, sheaths)
9307.0090	---其他	13	80			17	千克/件		---Other
9307 0090.10	其他濒危动物制的刀鞘、剑鞘	13	80			17	千克/件	FE	Other scabbard, sheaths made of endangered animals made
9307 0090.90	其他剑、刀、长矛和类似的武器及其零件(包括刀鞘、剑鞘)	13	80			17	千克/件		Other swords, cutlasses, lances and similar arms and parts thereof, including scabbards and sheaths

第二十类
杂　项　制　品

SECTION XX
MISCELLANEOUS MANUFACTURED ARTICLES

第九十四章
家具；寝具、褥垫、弹簧床垫、软坐垫及类似的填充制品；未列名灯具及照明装置；发光标志、发光铭牌及类似品；活动房屋

Chapter 94
Furniture; bedding, mattresses, mattress supports, cushions and similar stuffed furnishings; lamps and lighting fittings, not elsewhere specified or included; illuminated signs, illuminated name-plates and the like; prefabricated buildings

注释：

一、本章不包括：

（一）第三十九章、第四十章或第六十三章的充气或充水的褥垫、枕头及坐垫；

（二）落地镜[例如，品目 70.09 的试衣镜（旋转镜）]；

（三）第七十一章的物品；

（四）第十五类注释二所规定的贱金属制通用零件（第十五类）、塑料制的类似品（第三十九章）或品目 83.03 的保险箱；

（五）冷藏或冷冻设备专用的特制家具（品目 84.18）；缝纫机专用的特制家具（品目 84.52）；

（六）第八十五章的灯具及照明装置；

（七）品目 85.18、85.19、85.21 或品目 85.25 至 85.28 所列装置专用的特制家具（应分别归入品目 85.18、85.22 或 85.29）；

（八）品目 87.14 的物品；

（九）装有品目 90.18 所列牙科用器具或漱口盂的牙科用椅（品目 90.18）；

（十）第九十一章的物品（例如，钟及钟壳）；或

（十一）玩具家具、玩具灯或玩具照明装置（品目 95.03）、台球桌或其他供游戏用的特制家具（品目 95.04）、魔术用的特制家具或中国灯笼及类似的装饰品（电气彩灯串除外）（品目 95.05）。

二、品目 94.01 至 94.03 的物品（零件除外），只适用于落地式的物品。

对下列物品，即使是悬挂的、固定在墙壁上的或叠摞的，仍归入上述各品目：

（一）碗橱、书柜、其他架式家具（包括与将其固定于墙上的支撑物一同报验的单层搁架）及组合家具；

（二）坐具及床。

三、（一）品目 94.01 至 94.03 所列货品的零件，不包括玻璃（包括镜子）、大理石或其他石料

Chapter Notes:

1. This Chapter does not cover:

（a）Pneumatic or water mattresses, pillows or cushions, of Chapter 39, 40 or 63;

（b）Mirrors designed for placing on the floor or ground[for example,cheval-glasses（swing-mirrors）]of heading 70.09;

（c）Articles of Chapter 71;

（c）Parts of general use as defined in Note 2 to Section XV,of base metal（SectionXV）, or similar goods of plastics（Chapter 39）,or safes of heading 83.03;

（e）Furniture specially designed as parts of refrigerating or freezing equipment of heading 84.18; furniture specially designed for sewing machines（heading 84.52）;

（f）Lamps or lighting fittings of Chapter 85;

（g）Furniture specially designed as parts of apparatus of heading 85.18（heading 85.18）, of headings 85.19 or 85.21（heading 85.22）or of headings 85.25 to 85.28（heading 85.29）;

（h）Articles of heading 87.14;

（ij）Dentists' chairs incorporating dental appliances of heading 90.18 or dentists' spittoons（heading 90.18）;

（k）Articles of Chapter 91（for example, clocks and clock cases）; or

（l）Toy furniture or toy lamps or lighting fittings（heading 95.03）,billiard tables or other furniture specially constructed for games （heading 95.04）, furniture for conjuring tricks or decorations （other than electric garlands）such as Chinese lanterns（heading 95.05）.

2. The articles（other than parts）referred to in headings 94.01 to 94.03 are to be classified in those headings only if they are designed for placing on the floor or ground.

The following are, however, to be classified in the above-mentioned headings even if they are designed to be hung, to be fixed to the wall or to stand one on the other:

（a）Cupboards, bookcases, other shelved furniture（including single shelves presented with supports for fixing them to the wall ）and unit furniture;

（b）Seats and beds.

3. （a）In headings 94.01 to 94.03 references to parts of goods do not include references to sheets or slabs（whether or not cut to shape but not

以及第六十八章及第六十九章所列任何其他材料的片、块（不论是否切割成形，但未与其他零件组装）。

（二）品目 94.04 的货品，如果单独报验，不能作为品目 94.01、94.02 或 94.03 所列货品的零件归类。

四、品目 94.06 所称“活动房屋”，是指在工厂制成成品或制成部件并一同报验，供以后在有关地点上组装的房屋，例如，工地用房、办公室、学校、店铺、工作棚、车房或类似的建筑物。

combined with other parts）of glass（including mirrors）, marble or other stone or of any other material referred to in Chapter 68 or 69.

（b） Goods described in heading 94.04, presented separately, are not to be classified in heading 94.01, 94.02 or 94.03 as parts of goods.

4. For the purpose of heading94.06, the expression “prefabricated buildings” means buildings which are finished in the factory or put up as elements, presented together, to be assembled on site, such as housing or worksite accommodation, offices, schools, shops, sheds, garages or similar buildings.

税则号列 Tariff Item	商品名称及备注	进口税率			出口退税	增值税率	计量单位	监管条件	Article Description
		最惠	普通	暂定					
94.01	**坐具（包括能作床用的两用椅，但品目 94.02 的货品除外）及其零件：**								**Seats（other than those of heading No. 94. 02, whether or not convertible into beds）, and parts thereof:**
9401.1000	-飞机用坐具	0	100		15	17	个/千克		-Seats of a kind used for aircraft
	-机动车辆用坐具:								-Seats of a kind used for motor vehicles:
9401.2010	---皮革或再生皮革面的	10	100		15	17	个/千克		---With outer surface of leather or composition leather
9401.2090	---其他	10	100		15	17	个/千克		---Other
9401.3000	-可调高度的转动坐具	0	100		15	17	个/千克		-Swivel seats with variable height adjustment
	-能做床用的两用椅，但庭园坐具或野营设备除外:								-Seats other than garden seats or camping equipment, convertible into beds:
9401.4010	---皮革或再生皮革面的	0	100		15	17	个/千克		---With outer surface of leather or composition leather
9401.4090	---其他	0	100		15	17	个/千克		---Other
	-藤、柳条、竹及类似材料制的坐具:								-Seats of cane, osier, bamboo or similar materials:
9401.5100	--竹制或藤制的	0	100		15	17	个/千克	AB	--Of bamboo or rattan
9401.5900	--其他	0	100		15	17	个/千克	AB	--Other
	-木框架的其他坐具:								-Other seats, with wooden frames:
	--装软垫的:								--Upholstered:
9401.6110	---皮革或再生皮革面的	0	100		15	17	个/千克	AB	---With outer surface of leather or composition leather
9401.6190	---其他	0	100		15	17	个/千克	AB	---Other
9401.6900	--其他	0	100			17	个/千克		--Other
9401 6900.10	其他濒危木框架的坐具	0	100			17	个/千克	ABEF	Seats, with other endangered wood frames
9401 6900.90	其他木框架的坐具(不包括编号94011000-94015000 的坐具)	0	100		15	17	个/千克	AB	Seats, with other wood frames(other than those of heading 94011000-94015000)
	-金属框架的其他坐具:								-Other seats, with metal frames:
	--装软垫的:								--Upholstered:
9401.7110	---皮革或再生皮革面的	0	100		15	17	个/千克		---With outer surface of leather or composition leather
9401.7190	---其他	0	100		15	17	个/千克		---Other
9401.7900	--其他	0	100		15	17	个/千克		--Other
	-其他坐具:								--Other seats:
9401.8010	---石制的	0	100		15	17	个/千克		---Of stone
9401.8090	---其他	0	100			17	个/千克		---Other
9401 8090.10	其他濒危木制坐具	0	100			17	个/千克	EF	Seats, of other endangered wood
9401 8090.90	其他坐具	0	100		15	17	个/千克		Other seats
	-零件:								-Parts:
	---机动车辆用:								--Of the motor vehicles:
9401.9011	----座椅调角器	10	100		15	17	套/千克		----Seat angle regulating devices
9401.9019	----其他	0	100		15	17	千克		----Other
9401.9090	---其他	0	100		15	17	千克		---Other
94.02	**医疗、外科、牙科或兽医用家具（例如，手术台、检查台、带机械装置的病床、牙科用椅）；有旋转、倾斜、升降装置的理发用椅及类似椅；上述物品的零件：**								**Medical, surgical, dental or veterinary furniture（for example, operating tables, examination tables, hospital beds with mechanical fittings, dentists' chairs）; barbers' chairs and similar chairs, having rotating as well as both reclining and elevating movements; parts of the foregoing articles:**

税则号列 Tariff Item	商品名称及备注	进口税率			出口退税	增值税率	计量单位	监管条件	Article Description
		最惠	普通	暂定					
	-牙科、理发及类似用途的椅及其零件:								-Dentists', barbers' or similar chairs and parts thereof:
9402.1010	---理发用椅及其零件	0	100		15	17	个/千克		---Barbers' chairs and parts thereof
9402.1090	---其他	0	30		15	17	个/千克		---Other
9402.9000	-其他	0	30		15	17	件/千克		-Other
94.03	**其他家具及零件:**								**Other furniture and parts thereof:**
9403.1000	-办公室用金属家具	0	100		15	17	件/千克		-Metal furniture of a kind used in offices
9403.2000	-其他金属家具	0	100		15	17	件/千克		-Other metal furniture
9403.3000	-办公室用木家具	0	100			17	件/千克		-Wooden furniture of a kind used in offices
9403 3000.10	濒危木制办公室用木家具	0	100			17	件/千克	ABFE	Furniture of endangered wood, used in offices
9403 3000.90	其他办公室用木家具	0	100		15	17	件/千克	AB	Other wooden furniture, used in offices
9403.4000	-厨房用木家具	0	100			17	件/千克		-Wooden furniture of a kind used in the kitchen
9403 4000.10	濒危木制厨房用木家具	0	100			17	件/千克	ABFE	Furniture of endangered wood, used in the kitchen
9403 4000.90	其他厨房用木家具	0	100		15	17	件/千克	AB	Wooden furniture, used in the kitchen
	-卧室用木家具:								-Wooden furniture of a kind used in the bedroom:
9403.5010	---红木制	0	100			17	件/千克		---Of rose wood
9403 5010.10	卧室用濒危红木制家具	0	100			17	件/千克	ABFE	Furniture of endangered rose wood, used in the bedroom
9403 5010.90	其他卧室用红木制家具	0	100		15	17	件/千克	AB	Other furniture of rose wood, used in the bedroom
	---其他:								---Other:
9403.5091	----天然漆(大漆)漆木家具	0	100		15	17	件/千克	AB	----Of lacquered wood
9403.5099	----其他	0	100			17	件/千克		----Other
9403 5099.10	卧室用其他濒危木家具	0	100			17	件/千克	ABFE	Furniture of endangered wood, used in bedroom
9403 5099.90	卧室用其他木家具	0	100		15	17	件/千克	AB	Furniture of other wood, used in bedroom
	-其他木家具:								-Other wooden furniture:
9403.6010	---红木制	0	100			17	件/千克		---Of rose wood
9403 6010.10	濒危红木制其他家具(非卧室用)	0	100			17	件/千克	ABFE	Other furniture of endangered rose wood (not used in the bedroom)
9403 6010.90	其他红木制家具(非卧室用)	0	100		15	17	件/千克	AB	Other furniture of rose wood(not used in bedroom)
	---其他:								---Other:
9403.6091	----天然漆(大漆)漆木家具	0	100		15	17	件/千克	AB	----Of lacquered wood
9403.6099	----其他	0	100			17	件/千克		----Other
9403 6099.10	濒危木制其他家具(非卧室用)	0	100			17	件/千克	ABFE	Other furniture of endangered wood(not use in the bedroom)
9403 6099.90	其他木家具(非卧室用)	0	100		15	17	件/千克	AB	Other furniture of wood (not used in the bedroom)
9403.7000	-塑料家具	0	100		15	17	件/千克		-Furniture of plastics
	-其他材料制的家具，包括藤、柳条、竹或类似材料制的:								-Furniture of other materials, including cane, osier, bamboo or similar materials:
9403.8100	--竹制或藤制的	0	100		15	17	件/千克	AB	--Of bamboo or rattan
	--其他:								--Other:
9403.8910	---柳条及类似材料制的	0	100		15	17	件/千克	AB	---Of osier or similar materials
9403.8920	---石制的	0	100		15	17	件/千克		---Of stone
9403.8990	---其他	0	100		15	17	件/千克		---Other
9403.9000	-零件	0	100		15	17	千克		-Parts
9403 9000.10	飞机内厨房家具零件	0	100		15	17	千克		Parts of furnitures, used in kitchens of airplanes
9403 9000.90	其他品目94.03所列物品的零件	0	100		15	17	千克		Parts of the articles of heading No. 94.03
94.04	**弹簧床垫；寝具及类似用品，装有弹簧、内部用任何材料填充、衬垫或用海绵橡胶、泡沫塑料制成，不论是否包面(例如，褥垫、棉被、羽绒被、靠垫、座垫及枕头)：**								**Mattress supports; articles of bedding and similar furniture (for example, mattresses, quilts, eiderdowns, cushions, pouffes and pillows) fitted with springs or stuffed or internally fitted with any material or of cellular rubber or plastics, whether or not covered:**
9404.1000[暂]	-弹簧床垫	20	100	10	15	17	个/千克		-Mattress supports
	-褥垫:								-Mattresses:
9404.2100[暂]	--海绵橡胶或泡沫塑料制，不论是否包面	20	100	10	15	17	个/千克		--Of cellular rubber or plastics, whether or not covered
9404 2100.10[暂]	蔺草包面的垫子(单件面积大于1平方米，无论是否包边)	20	100	10	15	17	个/千克	4ABxy	Mattresses covered with rush (area of one piece exceeding lm^2, whether or not edged)

税则号列 Tariff Item	商品名称及备注	进口税率 最惠	普通	暂定	出口退税	增值税率	计量单位	监管条件	Article Description
9404 2100.90[暂]	海绵橡胶或泡沫塑料制褥垫(不论是否包面)	20	100	10	15	17	个/千克		Mattresses fitted with cellular rubber or plastics (whether or not covered)
9404.2900[暂]	--其他材料制	20	100	10	16	17	个/千克		--Of other materials
	-睡袋:								-Sleeping bags:
9404.3010[暂]	---羽毛或羽绒填充的	20	130	10		17	个/千克		---Stuffed with feathers or down
9404 3010.10[暂]	濒危野禽羽毛或羽绒填充的睡袋	20	130	10		17	个/千克	FE	Sleeping bags stuffed with feathers or down of endangered wild birds
9404 3010.90[暂]	其他羽毛或羽绒填充的睡袋	20	130	10	16	17	个/千克		Sleeping bags stuffed with other feathers or down
9404.3090[暂]	---其他	20	100	10	16	17	个/千克		---Other
	-其他:								-Other:
9404.9010[暂]	---羽毛或羽绒填充的	20	130	10		17	千克		---Stuffed with feathers or down
9404 9010.10[暂]	濒危野禽羽绒或羽毛填充其他寝具(含类似品)	20	130	10		17	千克	EF	Articles of bedding and similar furnishing, stuffed with feathers or down of endangered wild birds
9404 9010.90[暂]	其他羽绒或羽毛填充的其他寝具(含类似品)	20	130	10	16	17	千克		Articles of bedding and similar furnishing, stuffed with other feathers or down
9404.9020[暂]	---兽毛填充的	20	130	10		17	千克		---Stuffed with animal hair
9404 9020.10[暂]	濒危兽毛填充的寝具(用野生兽毛填充的，含盖被及类似品)	20	130	10		17	千克	EF	Articles of bedding, stuffed with endangered animal hair and wild animal hair (including quilts and similar furnishing)
9404 9020.90[暂]	其他兽毛填充的其他寝具(含类似品)	20	130	10	16	17	千克		Articles of bedding and similar furnishing, stuffed with other animal hair
9404.9030[暂]	---丝棉填充的	20	130	10	16	17	千克		---Stuffed with silk wadding
9404.9040[暂]	---化纤棉填充的	20	130	10	16	17	千克		---Stuffed with man-made fibres
9404.9090[暂]	---其他	20	130	10	16	17	千克		---Other
94.05	其他品目未列名的灯具及照明装置，包括探照灯、聚光灯及其零件；装有固定光源的发光标志、发光名牌及类似品，以及其他品目未列名的这些货品的零件：								**Lamps and lighting fittings including searchlights and spotlights and parts thereof, not elsewhere specified or included; illuminated signs, illuminated name-plates and the like, having a permanently fixed light source, and parts thereof not elsewhere specified or included:**
9405.1000	-枝形吊灯及天花板或墙壁上的其他电气照明装置，但不包括公共露天场所或街道上的电器照明装置	10	80		13	17	个/千克		-Chandeliers and other electric ceiling or wall lighting fittings, excluding those of a kind used for lighting public open spaces or thorough-fares
9405.2000	-电气的台灯、床头灯或落地灯	20	80		13	17	台/千克		-Electric table, desk, bedside or floorstanding lamps
9405 2000.10	含濒危物种成分的电气台灯、床头灯、落地灯	20	80		13	17	台/千克	EF	Electric table, desk, bedside or floorstanding lamps containing endangered plants
9405 2000.90	其他电气台灯、床头灯、落地灯	20	80		13	17	台/千克		Other electric table, desk, bedside or floorstanding lamps
9405.3000	-圣诞树用的成套灯具	16	100		13	17	套/千克		-Lighting sets of a kind used for Christmas trees
	-其他电灯及照明装置:								-Other electric lamps and lighting fittings:
9405.4010	---探照灯	17.5	70		13	17	台/千克		---Searchlights
9405.4020	---聚光灯	17.5	70		13	17	台/千克	A	---Spotlights
9405.4090	---其他	10	80		13	17	千克	A	---Other
9405.5000	-非电气的灯具及照明装置	20	80		13	17	千克		-Non-electrical lamps and lighting fittings
9405.6000	-发光标志、发光铭牌及类似品	20	80		13	17	千克		-Illuminated signs, illuminated nameplates and the like
	-零件:								-Parts:
9405.9100	--玻璃制	20	70		13	17	千克		--Of glass
9405.9200	--塑料制	20	70		13	17	千克		--Of plastics
9405.9900	--其他	20	70		13	17	千克		--Other
94.06	活动房屋:								**Prefabricated buildings:**
9406.0000	活动房屋	10	70		13	17	千克		Prefabricated buildings
9406 0000.10	用动植物材料制作的活动房屋	10	70		13	17	千克	AB	Prefabricated buildings of materials of animal or vegetable
9406 0000.20	带有风扇的高效空气粒子过滤单元(HEPA)的封闭洁净室	10	70		13	17	千克	3	Sealed clean room with fan, for filtering unit of high efficiency particulate air (HEPA)
9406 0000.90	其他活动房屋	10	70		13	17	千克		Other prefabricated buildings

第九十五章
玩具、游戏品、运动用品及其零件、附件

注释：

一、本章不包括：

（一）蜡烛（品目34.06）；

（二）品目36.04的烟花、爆竹或其他烟火制品；

（三）已切成一定长度但未制成钓鱼线的纱线、单丝、绳、肠线及类似品（第三十九章、品目42.06或第十一类）；

（四）品目42.02、43.03或43.04的运动用袋或其他容器；

（五）第六十一章或第六十二章的纺织品制的运动服或化妆舞会服装；

（六）第六十三章的纺织品制的旗帜及帆板或滑行车用帆；

（七）第六十四章的运动鞋靴（装有冰刀或滑轮的溜冰鞋除外）或第六十五章的运动用帽；

（八）手杖、鞭子、马鞭或类似品（品目66.02）及其零件（品目66.03）；

（九）品目70.18的未装配的玩偶或其他玩具用的玻璃假眼；

（十）第十五类注释二所规定的贱金属制通用零件（第十五类）或塑料制的类似货品（第三十九章）；

（十一）品目83.06的铃、钟、锣及类似品；

（十二）液体泵（品目84.13）、液体或气体的过滤、净化机器及装置（品目84.21）、电动机（品目85.01）、变压器（品目85.04）；录制声音或其他信息用的圆盘、磁带、固态非易失性数据存储器件、‘智能卡’及其他媒体，不论是否已录制（品目85.23）；无线电遥控设备（品目85.26）或无绳红外线遥控器件（品目85.43）；

（十三）第十七类的运动用车辆（长雪橇、平底雪橇及类似品除外）；

（十四）儿童两轮车（品目87.12）；

（十五）运动用船艇，例如，轻舟、赛艇（第八十九章）及其桨、橹和类似品（木制的归入第四十四章）；

（十六）运动及户外游戏用的眼镜、护目镜及类似品（品目90.04）；

（十七）媄诱音响器及哨子（品目92.08）；

（十八）第九十三章的武器及其他物品；

（十九）各种电气彩灯串（品目94.05）；

（二十）球拍线、帐篷或类似的野营用品、分指手套、连指手套及露指手套（按其构成材料归类）；或

（二十一）餐具、厨房用具、盥洗用品、地毯及

Chapter 95
Toys, games and sports requisites; parts and accessories thereof

Chapter Notes:

1. This Chapter does not cover:

(a) Candles (heading 34.06);

(b) Fireworks or other pyrotechnic articles of heading 36.04;

(c) Yarns, monofilament, cords or gut or the like for fishing, cut to length but not made up into fishing lines, of Chapter 39, heading 42.06 or Section XI;

(d) Sports bags or other containers of heading 42.02, 43.03 or 43.04;

(e) Sports clothing or fancy dress, of textiles, of Chapter 61 or 62;

(f) Textile flags or bunting, or sails for boats, sailboards or land craft, of Chapter 63;

(g) Sports footwear (other than skating boots with ice or roller skates attached) of Chapter 64, or sports headgear of Chapter 65;

(h) Walking-sticks, whips, riding-crops or the like (heading 66.02), or parts thereof (heading 66.03);

(j) Unmounted glass eyes for dolls or other toys, of heading 70.18;

(k) Parts of general use, as defined in Note 2 to Section XV, of base metal (Section XV), or similar goods of plastics (Chapter 39);

(l) Bells, gongs or the like of heading 83.06;

(m) Pumps for liquids (heading 84.13), filtering or purifying machinery and apparatus for liquids or gases (heading 84.21), electric motors (heading 85.01), electric transformers (heading 85.04), discs, tapes, solid-state non-volatile storage devices, " smart cards " and other media for the recording of sound or of other phenomena, whether or not recorded (heading 85.23), radio remote control apparatus (heading 85.26) or cordless infrared remote control devices(heading 85.43);

(n) Sports vehicles (other than bobsleighs, toboggans and the like) of Section XVII;

(o) Children's bicycles (heading 87.12);

(p) Sports craft such as canoes and skiffs (Chapter 89), or their means of propulsion (Chapter 44 for such articles made of wood);

(q) Spectacles, goggles or the like, for sports or outdoor games (heading 90.04);

(r) Decoy calls or whistles (heading 92.08);

(s) Arms or other articles of Chapter 93;

(t) Electric garlands of all kinds (heading 94.05);

(u) Racket strings, tents or other camping goods, or gloves, mittens and mitts (classified according to their constituent material); or

(v) Tableware, kitchenware, toilet articles, carpets and other textile floor coverings, apparel, bed linen, table linen, toilet linen, kitchen linen

纺织材料制的其他铺地制品、服装、床上、餐桌、盥洗及厨房用的织物制品及具有实用功能的类似货品(按其构成材料归类)。

and similar articles having a utilitarian function (classified according to their constituent material).

二、本章包括天然或养殖珍珠、宝石或半宝石(天然、合成或再造)、贵金属或包贵金属只作为小零件的物品。

2. This Chapter includes articles in which natural or cultured pearls,precious or semi-precious stones (natural, synthetic or reconstructed), precious metal or metal clad with precious metal constitute only minor constituents.

三、除上述注释一另有规定的以外，凡专用于或主要用于本章各品目所列物品的零件、附件，应与有关物品一并归类。

3. Subject to Note 1 above, parts and accessories which are suitable for use solely or principally with articles of this Chapter are to be classified with those articles.

四、除上述注释一另有规定的以外，品目 95.03 主要适用于该品目所列物品与一项或多项其他货品组合而成的物品，只要这些物品为零售包装，且组合后具有玩具的基本特征。这些组合物品不能视为归类总规定三（二）所指的成套货品，如果单独报验，应归入其它品目。

4. Subject to the provision of Note 1 above, heading 95.03 applies, inter alia, to articles of this heading combined with one or more items, which cannot be considered as sets under the terms of General Interpretative Rule 3 (b), and which, if presented separately, would be classified in other headings, provided the articles are put up together for retail sale and the combinations have the essential character of toys.

五、品目 95.03 不包括因其设计、形状或构成材料可确认为专供动物使用的物品，例如，“宠物玩具”（归入其适当品目）。

5. Heading 95.03 does not cover articles which, on account of their design, shape or constituent material, are identifiable as intended exclusively for animals, for example, “pet toys” (classification in their own appropriate heading).

子目注释：

一、子目 9504.50 包括：

（一） 在电视机、监视器或其他外部屏幕或表面上重放图像的视频游戏控制器；或

（二） 自带显示屏的视频游戏设备，不论是否便携式。

本子目不包括用硬币、钞票、银行卡、代币或任何其他支付方式使其工作的视频游戏控制器或设备（子目 9504.30）。

Subheading Notes:

1. Subheading 9504.50 covers :

(a) Video game consoles from which the image is reproduced on a television receiver, a monitor or other external screen or surface; or

(b) Video game machines having a selfcontained video screen, whether or not portable.

This subheading does not cover video game consoles or machines operated by coins, banknotes, bank cards, tokens or by any other means of payment (subheading 9504.30).

税则号列 Tariff Item	商品名称及备注	进口税率			出口退税	增值税率	计量单位	监管条件	Article Description
		最惠	普通	暂定					
95.03	**三轮车、踏板车、踏板汽车和类似的带轮玩具；玩偶车；玩偶；其他玩具；缩小（按比例缩小）的模型及类似的娱乐用模型，不论是否活动；各种智力玩具：**								**Tricycles, scooters, pedal cars and similar wheeled toys; dolls' carriages; dolls; other toys; reduced-size (“scale”) models and similar recreational models, working or not; puzzles of all kinds:**
9503.0010	---三轮车、踏板车、踏板汽车和类似的带轮玩具；玩偶车	0	80		15	17	千克	B	---Tricycles, scooters, pedal cars and similar wheeled toys; dolls' carriages
	---玩偶，不论是否着装；玩具动物：								---Dolls, whether or not dressed; Toy representing animals or non-human creatures:
9503.0021	----动物	0	80		15	17	个/千克	AB	----Animals
9503.0029	----其他	0	80		15	17	个/千克	AB	----Other
	---缩小（按比例缩小）的全套模型组件，不论是否活动：								---Reduced-size (“scale”) model assembly kits, whether or not working models:
9503.0031	----电动火车	0	80		15	17	千克	AB	----Electric trains
9503.0039	----其他	0	80		15	17	套/千克	AB	----Other
9503.0040	---其他建筑套件及建筑玩具	0	80		15	17	套/千克	AB	---Other construction sets and constructional toys
9503.0050	---玩具乐器	0	80		15	17	千克	AB	---Toy musical instruments and apparatus
9503.0060	---智力玩具	0	80		15	17	套/千克	AB	---Puzzles
	---其他玩具：								---Other toys:
9503.0081	----组装成套或全套的	0	80		15	17	套/千克	AB	----Put up in sets or outfits
9503.0082	----其他带动力装置的玩具及模型	0	80		15	17	个/千克	AB	----Other toys and models, incorporating a motor
9503.0089	----其他	0	80		15	17	个/千克	AB	----Other
9503.0090	---零件、附件	0	80		15	17	千克	AB	---Parts and accessories

税则号列 Tariff Item	商品名称及备注	进口税率			出口退税	增值税率	计量单位	监管条件	Article Description
		最惠	普通	暂定					
95.04	**视频游戏控制器及设备、游艺场所、桌上或室内游戏用品，包括弹球机、台球、娱乐专用桌及保龄球自动球道设备**								**Video game consoles and machines, articles for funfair, table or parlour games, including pintables, billiards, special tables for casino games and automatic bowling alley equipment:**
9504.2000	-各种台球用品及附件	0	80			17	千克		-Articles and accessories for billiards of all kinds
9504 2000.10	濒危木制的台球用品及附件	0	80			17	千克	EF	Articles and accessories for billiards of endangered wood
9504 2000.90	其他台球用品及附件	0	80		13	17	千克		Other articles and accessories for billiards
	-用硬币、钞票、银行卡、代币或其他支付方式使其工作的其他游戏用品，但保龄球自动球道设备除外:								-Other games, operated by coins, banknotes , bank cards, tokens or by any other means of payment, other than automatic bowling alley equipment:
9504.3010	---电子游戏机	0	130		13	17	台/千克	6O	---Video games
9504.3090	---其他	0	80		13	17	台/千克	6O	---Other
9504.4000	-扑克牌	0	80		13	17	副		-Playing cards
	-视频游戏控制器及设备，但子目 9504.30 的货品除外:								-Video game consoles and machines, other than those of subheading9504.30 :
	---与电视接收机配套使用的:								---Of a kind used with a television receiver:
9504.5011	----零件	0	130		15	17	个/千克	6O	----Parts
9504.5019	----其他	0	130		15	17	台/千克	6O	----Other
	---其他:								---Other:
9504.5091	----零件	0	130		13	17	个/千克	6O	----Parts
9504.5099	----其他	0	130		13	17	台/千克	6O	----Other
	-其他:								-Other:
9504.9010	---其他电子游戏机	0	130		13	17	台/千克	6O	---Other video games
	---保龄球自动球道设备及器具:								---Automatic bowling alley equipments and appliances:
9504.9021	----保龄球自动分瓶机	0	80		13	17	台/千克		----Automatic bowling pin distributing machines
9504.9022	----保龄球	0	80		13	17	个		----Bowling balls
9504.9023	----保龄球瓶	0	80		13	17	个		----Bowling pins
9504.9029	----其他	0	80		13	17	台/千克		----Other
9504.9030	---口国象棋、国际象棋、跳棋等棋类用品	0	80		13	17	副/千克		---Chess and other board games, including Chinese chess, international chess Chinese cherkers and draughts
9504.9040	---麻将及类似桌上游戏用品	0	80		13	17	副/千克		---Mahjong and similar table games
9504.9090	---其他	0	80		13	17	台/千克		---Other
95.05	**节日(包括狂欢节)用品或其他娱乐用品，包括魔术道具及嬉戏品:**								**Festive, carnival or other entertainment articles, including conjuring tricks and novelty jokes:**
9505.1000	-圣诞节用品	0	100		13	17	千克		-Articles for Christmas festivities
9505 1000.10	含动植物性材料的圣诞用品(不包括成套圣诞节灯具)	0	100		13	17	千克	AB	Articles for Christmas festivities containing animals or vegetable materials (other than complete sets of Christmas lights)
9505 1000.90	其他圣诞节用品(不包括成套圣诞节灯具)	0	100		13	17	千克		Other articles for Christmas festivities (other than complete sets of Christmas lights)
9505.9000	-其他	0	100		13	17	千克	B	-Other
95.06	**一般的体育活动、体操、竞技及其他运动(包括乒乓球运动)或户外游戏用的本章其他品目未列名用品及设备;游泳池或戏水池:**								**Articles and equipment for general physical exercise, gymnastics, athletics, other sports （including table-tennis） or outdoor games, not specified or included elsewhere in this Chapter; swimming pools and paddling pools:**
	-滑雪屐及其他滑雪用具:								-Snow-skis and other snow-ski equipment:
9506.1100	--滑雪屐	14	50		13	17	双		--Skis
9506.1200	--滑雪屐扣件(滑雪屐带)	14	50		13	17	千克		--Ski-fastenings（ski-bindings）
9506.1900	--其他	14	50		13	17	千克		--Other
	-滑水板、冲浪板、帆板及其他水上运动用具:								-Water-skis, surf-boards, sailboards and other water-sport equipment:

税则号列 Tariff Item	商品名称及备注	进口税率 最惠	普通	暂定	出口退税	增值税率	计量单位	监管条件	Article Description
9506.2100	--帆板	12	50		13	17	个/千克		-Sailboards
9506.2900	--其他	14	50		13	17	个/千克		--Other
	-高尔夫球棍及其他高尔夫球用具:								-Golf clubs and other golf equipment:
9506.3100	--棍，全套	14	50		13	17	根		--Clubs, complete
9506.3200	--球	12	50		13	17	个		--Balls
9506.3900	--其他	14	50		13	17	千克		--Other
	-乒乓球运动用品及器械:								-Articles and equipment for table-tennis:
9506.4010	---乒乓球	12	50		13	17	百个/千克		---Table-tennis balls
9506.4090 暂	---其他	14	50	7	13	17	千克		---Other
	-网球拍、羽毛球拍或类似的球拍，不论是否装弦:								-Tennis, badminton or similar rackets, whether or not strung:
9506.5100	--草地网球拍，不论是否装弦	14	50		13	17	支		-Lawn-tennis rackets, whether or not strung
9506.5900	--其他	14	50		13	17	支		--Other
	-球，但高尔夫球及乒乓球除外:								-Balls, other than golf balls and table-tennis balls:
9506.6100	--草地网球	12	50		13	17	个		--Lawn-tennis balls
	--可充气的球:								--Inflatable:
9506.6210 暂	---篮球、足球、排球	12	50	6	13	17	个		---Basketballs, footballs or volleyballs
9506.6290	---其他	12	50		13	17	个		---Other
9506.6900	--其他	12	50		13	17	个		--Other
	-溜冰鞋及旱冰鞋，包括装有冰刀的溜冰靴:								-Ice skates and roller skates, including skating boots with skates attached:
9506.7010	---溜冰鞋	14	50		13	17	双/千克		---Ice skates
9506.7020	---旱冰鞋	14	50		13	17	双/千克		---Roller skates
	-其他:								-Other:
	---一般的体育活动、体操或竞技用品及设备:								-Articles and equipment for general physical exercise, gymnastics or athletics:
	---健身及康复器械:								---Equipment for exercise and recovery:
9506.9111 暂	----跑步机	12	50	6	13	17	台/千克		----Running machine
9506.9119 暂	----其他	12	50	6	13	17	千克		----Other
9506.9120 暂	---滑板	12	50	6	13	17	个/千克		---Skateboards
9506.9190 暂	---其他	12	50	6	13	17	千克		---Other
9506.9900	--其他	12	50		13	17	个/千克		--Other
95.07	钓鱼竿、钓鱼钩及其他钓鱼用品；捞鱼网、捕蝶网及类似网；囮子“鸟”(品目92.08或97.05的货品除外)以及类似的狩猎用品:								**Fishing rods, fish-hooks and other linefishing tackle; fish landing nets, butterfly nets and similar nets; decoy “birds” (other than those of heading No. 92.08 or 97.05) and similar hunting or shooting requisites:**
9507.1000	-钓鱼竿	21	80		13	17	副/千克		-Fishing rods
9507 1000.10	用植物性材料制作的钓鱼竿	21	80		13	17	副/千克	AB	Fishing rods of vegetable materials
9507 1000.90	其他钓鱼竿	21	80		13	17	副/千克		Other fishing rods
9507.2000	-钓鱼钩，不论有无系钓丝	21	80		13	17	千克		-Fish-hooks, whether or not snelled
9507.3000	-钓线轮	21	80		13	17	个/千克		-Fishing reels
9507.9000	-其他	21	80		13	17	千克		-Other
95.08	旋转木马、秋千、射击用靶及其他游乐场的娱乐设备；流动马戏团及流动动物园；流动剧团:								**Roundabouts, swings, shooting galleries and other fairground amusements; travelling circuses and travelling menageries; travelling theatres:**
9508.1000	-流动马戏团及流动动物园	15	100			17	千克		-Travelling circuses and travelling menageries
9508 1000.10	有濒危动物的流动马戏团(包括流动动物园)	15	100			17	千克	FEAB	Traveling circuses with endangered animals (including traveling menageries)
9508 1000.90	其他流动马戏团及流动动物园	15	100		13	17	千克	AB	Other travelling circuses and traveling menageries
9508.9000	-其他	15	100		13	17	千克	AB	-Other

第九十六章
杂 项 制 品

注释：

一、本章不包括：

（一）化妆盥洗用笔（第三十三章）；

（二）第六十六章的制品（例如，伞或手杖的零件）；

（三）仿首饰（品目 71.17）；

（四）第十五类注释二所规定的贱金属制通用零件（第十五类）或塑料制的类似品（第三十九章）；

（五）第八十二章的利口器及其他物品，其柄或其他零件是雕刻或模塑材料制的；但品目 96.01 或 96.02 适用于单独报验的上述物品的柄或其他零件；

（六）第九十章的物品，例如，眼镜架（品目 90.03）、数学绘图笔（品目 90.17）、各种牙科、医疗、外科或兽医专用刷子（品目 90.18）；

（七）第九十一章的物品（例如，钟壳或表壳）；

（八）乐器及其零件、附件（第九十二章）；

（九）第九十三章的物品（武器及其零件）；

（十）第九十四章的物品（例如，家具、灯具及照明装置）；

（十一）第九十五章的物品（玩具、游戏品、运动用品）；或

（十二）艺术品、收藏品及古物（第九十七章）。

二、品目 96.02 所称“植物质或矿物质雕刻材料”，是指：

（一）用于雕刻的硬种子、硬果核、硬果壳、坚果及类似植物材料（例如，象牙果及棕榈子）；

（二）琥珀、海泡石、粘聚琥珀、粘聚海泡石、黑玉及其矿物代用品。

三、品目 96.03 所称“制帚、制刷用成束、成簇的材料”，仅指未装配的成束、成簇的兽毛、植物纤维或其他材料。这些成束、成簇的材料无需分开即可安装在帚、刷之上，或只需经过简单加工（例如，将顶端修剪成形）即可安装的。

四、除品目 96.01 至 96.06 或 96.15 的货品以外，本章的物品还包括全部或部分用贵金属、包贵金属、天然或养殖珍珠、宝石或半宝石（天然、合成或再造）制成的物品。而且，品目 96.01 至 96.06 及 96.15 包括天然或养殖珍珠、宝石或半宝石（天然、合成或再造）、贵金属或包贵金属只作为小零件的物品。

Chapter 96
Miscellaneous manufactured articles

Chapter Notes:

1. This Chapter does not cover:

（a）Pencils for cosmetic or toilet uses（Chapter 33）;

（b）Articles of Chapter 66（for example, parts of umbrellas or walking-sticks）;

（c）Imitation jewellery（heading 71.17）;

（d）Parts of general use, as defined in Note 2 to SectionXV, of base metal（SectionXV）, or similar goods of plastics（Chapter 39）;

（e）Cutlery or other articles of Chapter 82 with handles or other parts of carving or moulding materials; heading 96.01 or 96.02 applies, however, to separately presented handles or other parts of such articles;

（f）Articles of Chapter 90, (for example, spectacle flames（heading90.03）, mathematical drawing pens（heading 90.17）, brushes of a kind odeling ed for use in dentistry or for medical, surgical or veterinary purposes（heading 90.18）);

（g）Articles of Chapter 91（for example, clock or watch cases）;

（h）Musical instruments or parts or accessories thereof（Chapter 92）;

（ij）Articles of Chapter 93（arms and parts thereof）;

（k）Articles of Chapter 94（for example, furniture, lamps and lighting fittings）;

（l）Articles of Chapter 95（toys, games, sports requisites）; or

（m）Works of art, collectors' pieces or antiques（Chapter 97）.

2. In heading 96.02 the expression“vegetable or mineral carving material” means:

（a）Hard seeds, pips, hulls and nuts and similar vegetable materials of a kind used for carving（for example, corozo and dom）;

（b）Amber, meerschaum, agglomerated amber and agglomerated meerschaum, jet and mineral substitutes for jet.

3. In heading 96.03 the expression “prepared knots and tufts for broom or brush making” applies only to unmounted knots and tufts of animal hair, vegetable fiber or other material, which are ready for incorporation without division in brooms or brushes, or which require only such further minor processes as trimming to shape at the top, to render them ready for such incorporation.

4. Articles of this Chapter, other than those of headings 96.01 to 96.06 or 96.15, remain classified in the Chapter whether or not composed wholly or partly of precious metal or metal clad with precious metal, of natural or cultured pearls, or precious or semi-precious stones （natural, synthetic or reconstructed）. However, headings 96.01 to 96.06 and 96.15 include articles in which natural or cultured pearls,precious or semi-precious stones（natural, synthetic or reconstructed）, precious metal or metal clad with precious metal constitute only minor constituents.

税则号列 Tariff Item	商品名称及备注	进口税率 最惠	普通	暂定	出口退税	增值税率	计量单位	监管条件	Article Description
96.01	已加工的兽牙、骨、玳瑁壳、角、鹿角、珊瑚、珍珠母及其他动物质雕刻材料及其制品（包括塑模制品）：								**Worked ivory, bone, tortoiseshell, horn, antlers, coral, mother-of-pearl and other animal carving material and articles of these materials（including articles obtained by moulding）:**
9601.1000	-已加工的兽牙及其制品	20	100			17	千克		-Worked ivory and articles of ivory
9601 1000.10	已加工的濒危兽牙及其制品	20	100			17	千克	AFEB	Worked ivory and articles of ivory, of endangered animals
9601 1000.90	其他已加工的兽牙及其制品	20	100		13	17	千克	AB	Other worked ivory and articles of ivory,of animals
9601.9000	-其他	20	100			17	千克		-Other
9601 9000.10	其他已加工濒危动物质雕刻料（包括其制品）	20	100			17	千克	AFEB	Other worked carving material and articles of these materials of endangered animals
9601 9000.90	其他已加工动物质雕刻料及其制品	20	100		13	17	千克	AB	Other worked animal carving material, and articles of these materials
96.02	已加工的植物质或矿物质雕刻材料及其制品；蜡、硬脂、天然树胶、天然树脂或塑型膏制成的模塑或雕刻制品以及其他品目未列名的模塑或雕刻制品；已加工的未硬化明胶（品目35.03的明胶除外）及未硬化明胶制品：								**Worked vegetable or mineral carving material and articles of these materials; moulded or carved articles of wax, of stearin, of natural gums or natural resins or of odeling pastes, and other moulded or carved articles, not elsewhere specified or included; worked, unhardened gelatin（except gelatin of heading No. 35.03）and articles of unhardened gelatin:**
9602.0010	---装药用胶囊	10.5	40		13	17	千克		---Pharmaceutical capsules
9602.0090	---其他	25	100		13	17	千克	AB	---Other
96.03	帚、刷（包括作为机器、器具、车辆零件的刷）、非机动的手工操作地板清扫器、拖把及毛掸；供制帚、刷用的成束或成簇的材料；油漆块垫及滚筒；橡皮扫帚（橡皮辊除外）：								**Brooms, brushes（including brushes constituting parts of machines, appliances or vehicles）, hand-operated mechanical floor sweepers, not motorized, mops and feather dusters; prepared knots and tufts for broom or brush making; paint pads and rollers; squeegees（other than roller squeegees）:**
9603.1000	-用枝条或其他植物材料捆扎而成的帚及刷，不论是否有把	25	100		13	17	把	AB	-Brooms and brushes, consisting of twigs or other vegetable materials bound together, with or without handles
	-牙刷、剃须刷、发刷、指甲刷、睫毛刷及其他人体化妆用刷，包括作为器具零件的上述刷：								-Tooth brushes, shaving brushes, hair brushes, nail brushes, eyelash brushes and other toilet brushes for use on the person, including such brushes constituting parts of appliances:
9603.2100 暂	--牙刷，包括齿板刷	25	100	10	13	17	把		--Tooth brushes, including ventalplate brushes
9603.2900	--其他	15	100		13	17	支		--Other
9603 2900.10	野生动物毛制剃须刷，发刷（包括睫毛刷等人体化妆刷）	15	100		13	17	支	FE	Shaving brushes, hair brushes, of wild animal hair（including eyelash brushes and other toilet brushes for use on the person）
9603 2900.90	剃须刷，发刷，睫毛刷等人体化妆刷（包括作为器具零件的子目9603.29所属的刷）	15	100		13	17	支		Shaving brushes, hair brushes and eyelash brushes and other toilet brushes for use on the person（including parts of appliances of subheading No. 9603.29）
	-画笔、毛笔及化妆用的类似笔：								-Artists' brushes, writing brushes and similar brushes for the application of cosmetics:
9603.3010	---画笔	25	100			17	支		---Artists' brushes
9603 3010.10	濒危动物毛制的画笔	25	100			17	支	FE	Artists' brushes, made of endangered animal hair
9603 3010.90	其他画笔	25	100		13	17	支		Other artists' brushes
9603.3020	---毛笔	20	100			17	支		---Writing brushes
9603 3020.10	濒危动物毛制的毛笔	20	100			17	支	FE	Writing brushes, of endangered animal hair
9603 3020.90	其他毛笔	20	100		13	17	支		Other writing brushes
9603.3090	---其他	25	100			17	支		---Other
9603 3090.10	濒危动物毛制化妆用的类似笔	25	100			17	支	FE	Toilet brushes and similar brushes, of endangered

税则号列 Tariff Item	商品名称及备注	进口税率 最惠	普通	暂定	出口退税	增值税率	计量单位	监管条件	Article Description
									animal hair
9603 3090.90	其他化妆用的类似笔	25	100		13	17	支		Other toilet brushes and similar brushes
	-油漆刷、涂料刷、清漆刷及类似的刷（子目号 9603.30 的货品除外）；油漆块垫及滚筒:								-Paint, distemper, varnish or similar brushes（other than brushes of subheading No. 9603.30）; paint pads and rollers:
	---漆刷及类似刷:								---Paint,distemper,varnish or similar brushes:
9603.4011	----猪鬃制	20	100		13	17	把		---Of pigs',hogs' or boars' bristle
9603.4019	----其他	23	100		13	17	把		----Other
9603.4020	---油漆块垫及滚筒	23	100		13	17	个		---Paint pads and rollers
	-作为机器、器具、车辆零件的刷:								-Other brushes constituting parts of machines, appliances or vehicles:
	---金属丝刷:								---Brushes of metal wire:
9603.5011	----作为机器、器具零件的刷	14	50		13	17	个		----Constituting parts of machines or appliances
9603.5019	----其他	14	100		13	17	个		----Other
	---其他:								---Other:
9603.5091	----作为机器、器具零件的刷	14	50			17	个		----Constituting parts of machines or appliances
9603 5091.10	濒危动物毛制作为机器零件其他刷（包括器具零件的其他刷）	14	50			17	个	FE	Other brushes constituting parts of machines and appliances, of endangered animal hair
9603 5091.90	其他作为机器、器具零件的其他刷	14	50		13	17	个		Other brushes constituting parts of machines or appliances
9603.5099	----其他	14	100			17	个		----Other
9603 5099.10	濒危动物毛制作为车辆零件其他刷	14	100			17	个	FE	Other brushes constituting parts of vehicles, of endangered animal hair
9603 5099.90	其他作为车辆零件的其他刷	14	100		13	17	个		Other brushes constituting parts of vehicles
	-其他:								-Other:
9603.9010	---羽毛掸	21	130			17	个		---Feather dusters
9603 9010.10	濒危野禽羽毛掸	21	130			17	个	AFEB	Feather dusters of feathers of endangered wild birds
9603 9010.90	其他羽毛掸	21	130		13	17	个	AB	Other feather dusters
9603.9090	---其他	15	100			17	个		---Other
9603 9090.10	濒危动物毛、鬃、尾制其他帚，刷（包括拖把及其他毛掸）	15	100			17	个	AFEB	Brooms, brushes, mops and feather dusters of endangered animal hair, bristles or tails
9603 9090.20	其他动植物材料制帚、刷、拖把等(包括动植物材料制非机动的手工操作地板清扫器、毛掸)	15	100		13	17	个	AB	Brooms, brushes, mops, of other animal or vegetable materials, including hand-operated mechanical floor sweepers and feather dusters, not motorized
9603 9090.90	其他材料制帚、刷、拖把及毛掸（包括其他材料制非机动的手工操作地板清扫器等）	15	100		13	17	个		Brooms, brushes, mops and feather dusters, of other materials, including hand-operated mechanical floor sweepers, not motorized,
96.04	**手用粗筛、细筛:**								**Hand sieves and hand riddles:**
9604.0000	手用粗筛、细筛	21	100		13	17	个	AB	Hand sieves and hand riddles
96.05	**个人梳妆、缝纫或清洁鞋靴、衣服用的成套旅行用具:**								**Travel sets for personal toilet, sewing or shoe or clothes cleaning:**
9605.0000	个人梳妆、缝纫或清洁鞋靴、衣服用的成套旅行用具	15	100		13	17	套		Travel sets for personal toilet, sewing or shoe or clothes cleaning
96.06	**钮扣、揿扣、钮扣芯及钮扣和揿扣的其他零件；钮扣坯:**								**Buttons, press-fasteners, snap-fasteners and press-studs, button moulds and other parts of these articles; button blanks:**
9606.1000	-揿扣及其零件	21	100		13	17	千克		-Press-fasteners, snap-fasteners and press-studs and parts thereof
	-钮扣:								-Buttons:
9606.2100	--塑料制，未用纺织材料包裹	21	100		13	17	千克		--Of plastics, not covered with textile material
9606.2200	--贱金属制，未用纺织材料包裹	15	100		13	17	千克		--Of base metal, not covered with textile material
9606.2900	--其他	15	100			17	千克		--Other
9606 2900.10	含濒危动物成分的其他钮扣	15	100			17	千克	FE	Other buttons containing component of endangered animal
9606 2900.90	其他钮扣	15	100		13	17	千克		Other buttons
9606.3000	-钮扣芯及钮扣的其他零件；钮扣坯	15	100		13	17	千克		-Button moulds and other parts of buttons; button blanks

税则号列 Tariff Item	商品名称及备注	进口税率 最惠	进口税率 普通	进口税率 暂定	出口退税	增值税率	计量单位	监管条件	Article Description
96.07	**拉链及其零件:**								**Slide fasteners and parts thereof:**
	-拉链:								-Slide fasteners:
9607.1100	--装有贱金属制咪牙齿的	21	130		13	17	米/千克		--Fitted with chain scoops of base metal
9607.1900	--其他	21	130		13	17	米/千克		--Other
9607.2000	-零件	21	130		13	17	千克		-Parts
96.08	**圆珠笔;毡尖和其他渗水式笔尖笔及唛头笔;自来水笔、铁笔型自来水笔及其他钢笔;蜡纸铁笔;活动铅笔;钢笔杆、铅笔套及类似的笔套;上述物品的零件(包括帽、夹),但品目96.09的货品除外:**								**Ball point pens; felt tipped and other porous-tipped pens and markers; fountain pens, stylograph pens and other pens; duplicating stylos; propelling or sliding pencils; pen-holders, pencil-holders and similar holders; parts (including caps and clips) of the foregoing articles, other than those of heading No.96.09:**
9608.1000	-圆珠笔	15	80		13	17	支		-Ball point pens
9608.2000	-毡尖和其他渗水式笔尖笔及唛头笔	21	80		13	17	支		-Felt tipped and other porous-tipped pens and markers
	-自来水笔、铁笔型自来水笔及其他钢笔:								-Fountain pens, stylograph pens and other pens:
9608.3010	--墨汁画笔	21	80		13	17	支		--Indian ink drawing pens
9608.3020	---自来水笔	21	80		13	17	支		---Fountain pens
9608.3090	---其他	21	80		13	17	支		---Other
9608.4000	-活动铅笔	21	80		13	17	支		-Propelling or sliding pencils
9608.5000	-由上述两个或多个子目所列物品组成的成套货品	21	80		13	17	套		-Sets of articles from two or more of the foregoing subheadings
9608.6000	-圆珠笔芯,由圆珠笔头和墨芯构成	21	80		13	17	支		-Refills for ball point pens, comprising the ball point and ink-reservoir
	-其他:								-Other:
9608.9100	--钢笔头及笔尖粒	12	70		13	17	支		--Pen nibs and nib points
	--其他:								--Other:
9608.9910	---机器、仪器用笔	17.5	40		13	17	支/千克		---Of a kind used on machines or instruments
9608.9920	---蜡纸铁笔;钢笔杆、铅笔杆及类似的笔杆	21	80		13	17	支/千克		---Duplicating stylos; pen-holders, pencil-holders and similar holders
9608.9990	---其他	21	80		13	17	千克		---Other
96.09	**铅笔(品目96.08的铅笔除外)、颜色铅笔、铅笔芯、蜡笔、图画碳笔、书写或绘画用粉笔及裁缝划粉:**								**Pencils(other than pencils of heading No. 96.08), crayons, pencil leads, pastels, drawing charcoals, writing or drawing chalks and tailors' chalks:**
	-铅笔及颜色铅笔:								Pencils and crayons, with leads encased in a rigid sheath:
9609.1010	---铅笔	21	80		13	17	千克/百支		---Pencils
9609.1020	---颜色铅笔	21	80		13	17	千克		---Crayons
9609.2000	-铅笔芯,黑的或其他颜色的	21	80		13	17	千克		-Pencil leads, black or coloured
9609.9000	-其他	15	80		13	17	千克		-Other
96.10	**具有书写或绘画面的石板、黑板及类似板,不论是否镶框:**								**Slates and boards, with writing or drawing surfaces, whether or not framed:**
9610.0000	具有书写或绘画面的石板、黑板及类似板,不论是否镶框	15	80		13	17	千克		Slates and boards, with writing or drawing surfaces, whether or not framed
96.11	**手用日期戳、封缄戳、品目戳及类似印戳(包括标签压印器);手工操作的排字盘及带有排字盘的手印器:**								**Date, sealing or numbering stamps, and the like (including devices for printing or embossing labels),designed for operating in the hand; hand-operated composing sticks and hand printing sets incorporating such composing sticks:**
9611.0000	手用日期戳、封缄戳、品目戳及类似印戳(包括标签压印器);手工操作的排字盘及带有排字盘的手印器	21	80			17	千克		Date, sealing or numbering stamps, and the like (including devices for printing or embossing labels),designed for operating in the hand; hand-operated composing sticks and hand printing sets

税则号列 Tariff Item	商品名称及备注	进口税率 最惠	普通	暂定	出口退税	增值税率	计量单位	监管条件	Article Description
									incorporating such composing sticks
9611 0000.10	含濒危动物成分的手用日期戳（包括封缄戳及类似印戳）	21	80			17	千克	FE	Date, sealing, and the like, designed for operating in the hand, containing component of endangered animal
9611 0000.90	手用日期戳、封缄戳及类似印戳（包括编号戳、标签压印器；手工排字盘及带有字盘的手印器）	21	80		13	17	千克		Date, sealing or numbering stamps, and the like (including devices for printing or embossing labels, designed for operating in the hand; hand-operated composing sticks and hand printing sets incorporating such composing sticks)
96.12	**打字机色带或类似色带，已上油或经其他方法处理能着色的，不论是否装轴或装盒；印台，不论是否已加印油或带盒子：**								**Typewriter or similar ribbons, inked or otherwise prepared for giving impressions, whether or not on spools or in cartridges; ink-pads, whether or not inked, with or without boxes:**
9612.1000	-色带	10.5	35		13	17	个/千克		-Inked ribbons
9612.2000	-印台	25	100		13	17	个		-Ink-pads
96.13	**香烟打火机和其他打火器（不论是机械的，还是电气的）及其零件，但打火石及打火机芯除外：**								**Cigarette lighters and other lighters, whether or not mechanical or electrical, and parts thereof other than flints and wicks:**
9613.1000	-袖珍气体打火机，一次性的	25	130		13	17	个	B	-Pocket lighters, gas fuelled, non refillable
9613.2000	-袖珍气体打火机，可充气的	25	130		13	17	个	B	-Pocket lighters, gas fuelled, refillable
9613.8000	-其他打火器	25	130		13	17	个	B	-Other lighters
9613.9000	-零件	25	130		13	17	千克		-Parts
96.14	**烟斗（包括烟斗头）和烟嘴及其零件：**								**Smoking pipes (including pipe bowls) and cigar or cigarette holders, and parts thereof:**
9614.0010	---烟斗及烟斗头	25	130			17	个/千克		---Pipes and pipe bowls
9614 0010.10	含濒危动物成分的烟斗及烟斗头（仅指野生哺乳类牙齿制产品）	25	130			17	个/千克	ABEF	Smoking pipes and pipe bowls, containing component of endangered animal（only referring to articles of ivory of wild mammals）
9614 0010.20	用植物性材料制作的烟斗及烟斗头	25	130		13	17	个/千克	AB	Smoking pipes and pipe bowls, of vegetable materials
9614 0010.90	其他烟斗及烟斗头	25	130		13	17	个/千克		Other smoking pipes and pipe bowls
9614.0090	---其他	25	130			17	千克		---Other
9614 0090.10	含濒危野生动物成分的烟嘴及其零件（仅指野生哺乳类牙齿制产品）	25	130			17	千克	FE	Cigar or cigarette holders, and parts thereof, containing component of wild animal（only referring to articles of ivory of wild mammals）
9614 0090.90	其他烟嘴及其零件	25	130		13	17	千克		Other cigar or cigarette holders, and parts thereof
96.15	**梳子、发夹及类似品；发卡、卷发夹、卷发器或类似品及其零件，但品目85.16的货品除外：**								**Combs, hair-slides and the like; hair-pins, curling pins, curling grips, haircurlers and the like, other than those of heading No. 85.16, and parts thereof:**
	-梳子、发夹及类似品：								-Combs, hair-slides and the like:
9615.1100	--硬质橡胶或塑料制	18	130		13	17	千克		--Of hard rubber or plastics
9615.1900	--其他	18	130			17	千克		--Other
9615 1900.10	含濒危动物成分的其他材料制梳子（包括角质发夹等，金属、塑料及家畜来源的产品除外）	18	130			17	千克	FE	Combs of other materials containing component with endangered animal（including hair-slides of horn, other than articles of metal, plastic or materials of domestic animal）
9615 1900.20	用其他动植物材料制的梳子（包括角质发夹等，金属、塑料及家畜来源的产品除外）	18	130		13	17	千克		Combs of other animal and vegetable materials (including hair-slides of horns, other than articles of metal, plastic or materials of domestic animal)
9615 1900.90	其他材料制梳子、角质发夹等（包括类似品，但橡胶、塑料制的除外）	18	130		13	17	千克		Combs, hair-slides of horns and the like, of other materials（other than articles of rubber or plastics materials）
9615.9000	-其他	18	130		13	17	千克		-Other
96.16	**香水喷雾器或类似的化妆用喷雾器及其座架、喷头；粉扑及粉拓，施敷脂粉或化妆品用：**								**Scent sprays and similar toilet sprays, and mounts and heads thereof; powder puffs and pads for the application of cosmetics or toilet preparations:**
9616.1000	-香水喷雾器或类似的化妆用喷	18	130		13	17	千克		-Scent sprays and similar toilet sprays, and mounts

税则号列 Tariff Item	商品名称及备注	进口税率 最惠	普通	暂定	出口退税	增值税率	计量单位	监管条件	Article Description
	雾器及其座架、喷头								and heads thereof
9616.2000	-粉扑及粉拍，施敷脂粉或化妆品用	18	130		13	17	千克		-Powder puffs and pads for the application of cosmetics or toilet preparations
96.17	**带壳的保温瓶和其他真空容器及其零件，但玻璃瓶胆除外：**								**Vacuum flasks and other vacuum vessels, complete with cases; parts thereof other than glass inners:**
	---保温瓶:								--Vacuum flasks:
9617.0011	----玻璃内胆制	24	130		13	17	个/千克		----Of glass internal liner
9617.0019	----其他	24	130		13	17	个/千克		----Other
9617.0090	---其他	18	130		13	17	千克		---Other
96.18	**裁缝用人体模型及其他人体活动模型；橱窗装饰用自动模型及其他活动陈列品：**								**Tailors' dummies and other lay figures; automata and other animated displays used for shop window dressing:**
9618.0000	裁缝用人体模型及其他人体活动模型；橱窗装饰用自动模型及其他活动陈列品	21	80		13	17	千克		Tailors' dummies and other lay figures; automata and other animated displays used for shop window dressing
9618 0000.10	用植物性材料制作的人体模型	21	80		13	17	千克	AB	Tailors' dummies and other lay figures, of vegetable materials
9618 0000.90	裁缝用其他人体模型(包括橱窗装饰用的自动模型及其他活动陈列品)	21	80		13	17	千克		Other tailors' dummies and lay figures（including automatons and other animated displays used for shop window dressing）
96.19	**任何材料制的卫生巾（护垫）及止血塞、婴儿尿布及尿布衬里和类似品：**								**Sanitary towels(pads) and tampons, napkins and napkin liners for babies and similar articles, of any material:**
9619.0010	---尿裤及尿布	7.5	80		13	17	千克	A	---Diaper and napkins
9619.0020	---卫生巾（护垫）及止血塞	10	80		13	17	千克	A	---Sanitary towels(pads) and tampons
9619.0090	---其他	14	80		13	17	千克	A	---Other

第二十一类 艺术品、收藏品及古物

SECTION XXI WORKS OF ART, COLLECTORS' PIECES AND ANTIQUES

第九十七章 艺术品、收藏品及古物

Chapter 97 Works of art, collectors' pieces and antiques

注释：

一、本章不包括：

（一）品目 49.07 的未经使用的邮票、印花税票、邮政信笺（印有邮票的纸品）及类似的票证；

（二）作舞台、摄影的布景及类似用途的已绘制画布（品目 59.07），但可归入品目 97.06 的除外；或

（三）天然或养殖珍珠、宝石或半宝石（品目 71.01 至 71.03）。

二、品目 97.02 所称"雕版画、印制画、石印画的原本"，是指以艺术家完全手工制作的单块或数块印版直接印制出来的黑白或彩色原本，不论艺术家使用何种方法或材料，但不包括使用机器或照相制版方法制作的。

三、品目 97.03 不适用于成批生产的复制品及具有商业性质的传统手工艺品，即使这些物品是艺术家设计或创造的。

四、（一）除上述注释一至三另有规定的以外，可归入本章各品目的物品，均应归入本章的相应品目而不归入本章的其他品目

（二）品目 97.06 不适用于可以归入本章其他各品目的物品。

五、已装框的油画、粉画及其他绘画、版画、拼贴画及类似装饰板，如果框架的种类及价值与作品相称，应与作品一并归类。如果框架的种类及价值 与作品不相称，应分别归类。

Chapter Notes:

1. This Chapter does not cover:

(a) Unused postage or revenue stamps, postal stationery (stamped paper) or the like, of heading 49.07;

(b) Theatrical scenery, studio back-cloths or the like, of painted canvas (heading 59.07) except if they may be classified in heading 97.06; or

(c) Pearls, natural or cultured, or precious or semi-precious stones (headings 71.01 to 71.03).

2. For the purposes of heading 97.02, the expression "original engravings, prints and lithographs" means impressions produced directly, in black and white or in colour, of one or of several plates wholly executed by hand by the artist, irrespective of the process or of the material employed by him, but not including any mechanical or photomechanical process.

3. Heading 97.03 does not apply to mass-produced reproductions or works of conventional craftsmanship of a commercial character, even if these articles are designed or created by artists.

4. (a) Subject to Notes 1 to 3 above, articles of this Chapter are to be classified in this Chapter and not in any other Chapter of the Nomenclature;

(b) Heading 97.06 does not apply to articles of the preceding headings of this Chapter.

5. Frames around paintings, drawings, pastels, collages or similar decorative plaques, engravings, prints or lithographs are to be classified with those articles, provided they are of a kind and of a value normal to those articles. Frames which are not of a kind or of a value normal to the articles referred to in this Note are to be classified separately.

税则号列 Tariff Item	商品名称及备注	进口税率			出口退税	增值税率	计量单位	监管条件	Article Description
		最惠	普通	暂定					
97.01	油画、粉画及其他手绘画，但带有手工绘制及手工描饰的制品或品目 49.06 的图纸除外；拼贴画及类似装饰板：								**Paintings, drawings and pastels, executed entirely by hand, other than drawings of heading No. 49.06 and other than hand-painted or hand-decorated manufactured articles; collages and similar decorative plaques:**
	-油画、粉画及其他手绘画：								-Paintings, drawings and pastels:
	---原件：								---The originals:
9701.1011[暂]	----唐卡	12	50	6		17	幅		----Thangka
9701.1019[暂]	----其他	12	50	6		17	幅		----Other
9701.1020	---复制品	14	50			17	幅		---Reproductions
9701.9000	-其他	14	50			17	千克		-Other
9701 9000.10	含濒危动物成分的拼贴画(包括类似装饰板，指一切源自濒危动物的产品)	14	50			17	千克	ABFE	Collages and similar decorative plaques with component of endangered animal (referring to articles from all kinds of endangered animals)
9701 9000.20	用其他动植物材料制作的拼贴画(包括类似装饰板，指一切源	14	50			17	千克	AB	Collages and similar decorative plaques of other animal or vegetable materials (referring to articles

税则号列 Tariff Item	商品名称及备注	进口税率 最惠	普通	暂定	出口退税	增值税率	计量单位	监管条件	Article Description
	自野生动物的产品）								from all kinds of wild animals）
9701 9000.90	其他拼贴画及类似装饰板	14	50			17	千克		Other collages and similar decorative plaques
97.02	**雕版画、印制画、石印画的原本:**								**Original engravings, prints and lithographs:**
9702.0000 [暂]	雕版画、印制画、石印画的原本	12	50	6		17	幅		Original engravings, prints and lithographs
97.03	**各种材料制的雕塑品原件:**								**Original sculptures and statuary, in any material:**
9703.0000 [暂]	各种材料制的雕塑品原件	12	50	6		17	幅		Original sculptures and statuary, in any material
9703 0000.10 [暂]	濒危动植物材料制的雕塑品原件（指一切源自濒危动植物的产品）	12	50	6		17	幅	FE	Original sculptures and statuary, in endangered animal and vegetable material（referring to articles from endangered animal and vegetable）
9703 0000.90 [暂]	其他各种材料制的雕塑品原件	12	50	6		17	幅		Original sculptures and statuary in other materials
97.04	**使用过或未使用过的邮票、印花税票、邮戳印记、首日封、邮政信笺（印有邮票的纸品）及类似品，但品目 49.07 的货品除外:**								**Postage or revenue stamps, stamp-post-marks, first-day covers, postal stationery（stamped paper）, and the like, used or unused other than those of heading No. 49.07:**
9704.0010	---邮票	8	50			17	千克		---Postage
9704.0090	---其他	14	50			17	千克		---Other
97.05	**具有动物学、植物学、矿物学、解剖学、历史学、考古学、古生物学、人种学或钱币学意义的收集品及珍藏品:**								**Collections and collectors' pieces of zoological, botanical,mineralogical,anatomical, historical, archaeological, palaeontological, ethnographic or numismatic interest:**
9705.0000	具有动物学、植物学、矿物学、解剖学、历史学、考古学、古生物学、人种学或钱币学意义的收集品及珍藏品	0	0			17	千克		Collections and collectors' pieces of zoological, botanical, mineralogical, anatomical, historical, archaeolohical, palaeontological, ethnographic or numismatic interest
9705 0000.10	含濒危动植物的收藏品（具有动植物学意义的）	0	0			17	千克	ABFE	Collections and collectors' pieces containing endangered animal or vegetable（with zoological, botanical interest）
9705 0000.90	具有动、植、矿物学意义的收藏品（还包括具有解剖、历史、考古、古生物学意义的收藏品）	0	0			17	千克	AB	Collections and collectors' pieces of zoological, botanical, mineralogical, anatomical, historical, archaeological, palaeontological, ethnographic or numismatic interest
97.06	**超过一百年的古物:**								**Antiques of an age exceeding one hundred years:**
9706.0000	超过一百年的古物	0	0			17	千克		Antiques of an age exceeding 100 years
9706 0000.10	超过一百年的濒危野生动植古物（具收藏或文史价值的）	0	0			17	千克	ABFE	Antiques of an age exceeding 100 years of endangered wild animal or vegetable（having literary or historical collection value）
9706 0000.90	其他超过一百年的古物	0	0			17	千克		Other antiques of an age exceeding100 years

第二十二类
特殊交易品及未分类商品

SECTION XII
TRADING PRODUCTS SPECIAL AND NOT OTHERWISE CLASSIFIED

第九十八章
特殊交易品及未分类商品

Chapter 98
Trading products Special and otherwise classified

税则号列 Tariff Item	商品名称及备注	进口税率			出口退税	增值税率	计量单位	监管条件	Article Description
		最惠	普通	暂定					
98.01	未分类商品：								**Commodities not classified:**
9801.0010	人民币2000元及以下的非税、非证进口商品	0	0			0	千克		Import commodities of RMB 2000 and the following, non-tariff, non-imports certificate
9801.0090	其他未分类商品	0	0		13	0	千克		Other commodities not classified
9801.3000	流通中的货币现钞(包括纸币及硬币)	0	0			0	千克	T	Currency notes in circulation (including paper money and coins)
98.03	计算机软件(仅用于出口，不包括与产品固化或集成为一体的软件)：								**Computer software, only for export, other than software of curing or integrated with the product as a whole software**
9803.0010	系统软件	0	0			0	套		System software
9803.0020	支撑软件	0	0			0	套		Support software
9803.0030	应用软件	0	0			0	套		Application software
9803.0090	其他软件	0	0			0	套		Other software

出口商品关税、暂定税率和特别关税税率表
Interim Duty Rate and Special Duty Rate on Export Goods

EX[①]	税则号列	商品名称（简称）	出口税率(%)	2014年暂定税率(%)
	03019210	鳗鱼苗	20	
	05061000	经酸处理的骨胶原及骨	40	
	05069011	含牛羊成分的骨粉及骨废料	40	
	05069019	其他骨粉及骨废料	40	
ex	05069090	其他骨及角柱(已脱胶骨、角柱除外)	40	
ex	05069090	已脱胶骨、角柱	40	0
	25041010	鳞片状天然石墨		20
	25041099	其它粉末状天然石墨		20
	25049000	其他天然石墨		20
	25085000	红柱石,蓝晶石及硅线石，不论是否煅烧		10
	25086000	富铝红柱石		10
	25101010	未碾磨磷灰石		35
	25101090	未碾磨天然磷酸钙、天然磷酸铝钙及磷酸盐白垩，磷灰石除外		35
	25102010	已碾磨磷灰石		35
	25102090	已碾磨天然磷酸钙、天然磷酸铝钙及磷酸盐白垩，磷灰石除外		35
	25111000	天然硫酸钡(重晶石)		10
	25112000	天然碳酸钡(毒重石)，不论是否煅烧		10
	25191000	天然碳酸镁（菱镁矿）		5
	25199010	熔凝镁氧矿		10
	25199020	烧结镁氧矿（重烧镁）		10
	25199030	碱烧镁（轻烧镁）		5
	25199099	非纯氧化镁		5
	25261020	未破碎及未研粉的滑石,不论是否粗加修整或切割成矩形板块		10
ex	25262020	已破碎或已研粉的天然滑石(体积百分比90%及以上的产品粒度小于等于18微米的滑石粉除外)		10
ex	25262020	体积百分比90%及以上的产品粒度小于等于18微米的滑石粉		5
	25301010	未膨胀的绿泥石		10
	25309020	稀土金属矿		15
ex	25309099	其他氧化镁含量在70%(含70%)以上的矿产品		5
	26011110	平均粒径小于0.8毫米的未煅烧铁矿砂及其精矿；但焙烧黄铁矿除外		10
	26011120	平均粒径不小于0.8毫米，但不大于6.3毫米的未煅烧铁矿砂及其精矿；但焙烧黄铁矿除外		10
	26011190	平均粒径大于6.3毫米的未烧结铁矿砂及其精矿，但焙烧黄铁矿除外		10
	26011200	已烧结铁矿砂及其精矿		10
	26012000	焙烧黄铁矿		10
	26030000	铜矿砂及其精矿		10
	26040000	镍矿砂及其精矿		15
	26050000	钴矿砂及其精矿		15
	26070000	铅矿砂及其精矿	30	
ex	26080000	锌矿砂及其精矿（氧化锌含量大于80%的灰色饲料氧化锌除外）	30	
ex	26080000	灰色饲料氧化锌（氧化锌ZnO含量大于80%）	30	0
	26090000	锡矿砂及其精矿	50	20
	26100000	铬矿砂及其精矿		15
	26110000	钨矿砂及其精矿	20	
	26121000	铀矿砂及其精矿		10
	26122000	钍矿砂及其精矿		10
	26131000	已焙烧钼矿砂及其精矿		15
	26139000	其他钼矿砂及其精矿		15
	26140000	钛矿砂及其精矿		10
	26151000	锆矿砂及其精矿		10
	26159010	水合钽铌原料（钽铌富集物）	30	

EX[①]	税则号列	商品名称（简称）	出口税率(%)	2014年暂定税率(%)
	26159090	其他铌钽矿砂及其精矿	30	
	26161000	银矿砂及其精矿		10
	26169000	其他贵金属矿砂及其精矿		10
	26171010	生锑（锑精矿，选矿产品）	20	
	26171090	其他锑矿砂及其精矿		10
	26179010	朱砂(辰砂)		10
	26179090	其他矿砂及其精矿		10
	26180010	冶炼钢铁产生的锰渣		10
	26180090	冶炼钢铁产生的其他粒状熔渣(熔渣砂)		10
	26190000	冶炼钢铁产生的熔渣、浮渣、氧化皮及其他废料		10
	26202100	含铅汽油的淤渣及含铅抗震化合物的淤渣		10
	26202900	其他主要含铅的矿灰及残渣		10
	26203000	主要含铜的矿灰及残渣		10
	26206000	含砷、汞、铊及其混合物，用于提取或生产砷、汞、铊及其化合物的矿灰及残渣		10
	26209100	含锑、铍、镉、铬及其混合物的矿灰及残渣		10
	26209910	主要含钨的矿灰及残渣		10
	26209990	含其他金属及化合物的矿灰及残渣		10
	27011100	未制成型的无烟煤，不论是否粉化		10
	27011210	未制成型的炼焦烟煤，不论是否粉化		10
	27011290	未制成型的其他烟煤，不论是否粉化		10
	27011900	未制成型的其他煤，不论是否粉化		10
	27012000	煤砖、煤球及类似用煤制固体燃料		10
	27021000	褐煤		10
	27022000	制成型的褐煤		10
	27030000	泥煤(包括肥料用泥煤) 不论是否成型		10
ex	27060000	从煤、褐煤、或泥煤蒸馏所得的焦油及矿物焦油，不论是否脱水或部分蒸馏，包括再造焦油（含蒽油≥50%及沥青≥40%的“炭黑油”除外）		15
	27071000	粗苯		10
	27090000	石油原油及从沥青矿物提取的原油		5
	28047010	黄磷(白磷)	20	
	28047090	其他磷	20	10
	28053011	钕		25
	28053012	镝		25
	28053013	铽		25
	28053014	镧		25
	28053015	铈		25
	28053016	镨		25
	28053017	钇		25
	28053019	其他未相互混合或熔合的稀土金属、钪及钇		25
	28053021	已相互混合或熔合的稀土金属、钪及钇，电池级		25
	28053029	其他已相互混合或熔合的稀土金属、钪及钇		25
	28092019	磷酸		300元/吨
	28111100	氢氟酸（氟化氢）		10
	28141000	氨		180元/吨
	28142000	氨水		60元/吨
	28220090	其他钴的氧化物及氢氧化物；商品氧化钴		10
	28253010	五氧化二钒		5
ex	28256000	锗的氧化物		5
	28257000	钼的氧化物及氢氧化物		5
	28259011	钨酸		5
	28259012	三氧化钨		5
	28259019	其他钨的氧化物和氢氧化物		5
	28261290	其他氟化铝		5
	28261910	铵的氟化物		
	28261920	钠的氟化物		5
	28261990	其他氟化物		5

EX①	税则号列	商品名称（简称）	出口税率(%)	2014年暂定税率(%)
ex	28269090	氟钽酸钾	30	
	28271010	肥料用氯化铵		5
	28331100	硫酸钠		5
	28342110	肥料用硝酸钾		5
	28417010	钼酸铵		5
	28417090	其他钼酸盐		5
	28418010	仲钨酸铵		5
	28418020	钨酸钠		5
	28418030	钨酸钙		5
	28418040	偏钨酸铵		5
	28418090	其他钨酸盐		5
	28461010	氧化铈		15
	28461020	氢氧化铈		15
	28461030	碳酸铈		15
	28461090	铈的其他化合物		15
	28469011	氧化钇		25
	28469012	氧化镧		15
	28469013	氧化钕		15
	28469014	氧化铕		25
	28469015	氧化镝		25
	28469016	氧化铽		25
	28469017	氧化镨		25
ex	28469019	其他氧化稀土（灯用红粉除外）		15
	28469021	氯化铽		25
	28469022	氯化镝		25
	28469023	氯化镧		25
	28469024	氯化钕		15
	28469025	氯化镨		15
	28469026	氯化钇		15
	28469028	混合氯化稀土		15
	28469029	未混合氯化稀土		15
	28469031	氟化铽		15
	28469032	氟化镝		15
	28469033	氟化镧		15
	28469034	氟化钕		15
	28469035	氟化镨		15
	28469036	氟化钇		15
	28469039	其他氟化稀土		15
	28469041	碳酸镧		15
	28469042	碳酸铽		25
	28469043	碳酸镝		25
	28469044	碳酸钕		15
	28469045	碳酸镨		15
	28469046	碳酸钇		15
	28469048	混合碳酸稀土		15
	28469049	未混合碳酸稀土		15
	28469091	镧的其他化合物		25
	28469092	钕的其他化合物		25
	28469093	铽的其他化合物		25
	28469094	镝的其他化合物		25
	28469095	镨的其他化合物		25
ex	28469096	钇的其他化合物（LED用荧光粉除外）		25
ex	28469099	稀土金属、钇、钪的其他化合物（LED用荧光粉除外）		25
	28499020	碳化钨		5
	29022000	苯	40	0
	31021000	尿素②		淡季（7-10月）：40元/吨

EX①	税则号列	商品名称（简称）	出口税率(%)	2014 年暂定税率(%)
				旺季(1-6 月，11、12 月)：15%，加上 40 元/吨
	31024000	硝酸铵与碳酸钙或其他无肥效无机物的混合物		
	31025000	硝酸钠		
	31026000	硝酸钙和硝酸铵的复盐及混合物		
	31028000	尿素及硝酸铵混合物的水溶液或氨水溶液		
	31029010	氰氨化钙		
	31029090	其他矿物氮肥及化学氮肥，包括上述子目未列名的混合物		淡季（7-10 月）：40 元/吨 旺季(1-6 月，11、12 月)：15%，加上 40 元/吨
	31031010	重过磷酸钙		5
	31031090	其他过磷酸钙		5
	31039000	其他矿物磷肥或化学磷肥		5
	31042090	其他氯化钾		600 元/吨
	31043000	硫酸钾		600 元/吨
	31049010	光卤石、钾盐及其他天然粗钾盐		30
	31049090	其他矿物钾肥及化学钾肥		30
	31051000	制成片状及类似形状或每包毛重不超过 10 公斤的 31 章各货品		淡季（5 月 16 日-10 月 15 日）：50 元/吨; 旺季(1 月 1 日-5 月 15 日，10 月 16 日-12 月 31 日)：15%，加上 50 元/吨;
	31052000	三元复合肥		30
	31053000	磷酸氢二铵②		淡季（5 月 16 日-10 月 15 日）：50 元/吨; 旺季(1 月 1 日-5 月 15 日，10 月 16 日-12 月 31 日)：15%，加上 50 元/吨;
	31054000	磷酸二氢铵及磷酸二氢铵与磷酸氢二铵的混合物②		淡季（5 月 16 日-10 月 15 日）：50 元/吨; 旺季(1 月 1 日-5 月 15 日，10 月 16 日-12 月 31 日)：15%，加上 50 元/吨;
	31055100	含有硝酸盐及磷酸盐的肥料		5
	31055900	其他含氮磷两种肥效元素的矿物肥料或化学肥料		淡季（5 月 16 日-10 月 15 日）：50 元/吨; 旺季(1 月 1 日-5 月 15 日，10 月 16 日-12 月 31 日)：15%，加上 50 元/吨;
	31056000	含磷钾两种元素的肥料		5
	31059000	其他肥料		淡季（5 月 16 日-10 月 15 日）：50 元/吨; 旺季(1 月 1 日-5 月 15 日，10 月 16 日-12 月 31 日)：15%，加上 50 元/吨;
	38249091	含滑石 50%以上的混合物		10
	41039011	经退鞣处理的山羊板皮	20	
	41039019	山羊板皮，经退鞣处理的除外	20	
	44012100	针叶木木片或木粒		15
	44012200	非针叶木木片或木粒		15
	44091010	针叶木地板条（块）		10
	44092910	其他非针叶木地板条		10
	44190031	木制一次性筷子		10
	44219021	木制圆签、圆棒、冰果棒、压舌片及类似一次性制品		10
	47010000	机械木浆		10
	47020000	化学木浆，溶解级		10

EX①	税则号列	商品名称（简称）	出口税率(%)	2014年暂定税率(%)
	47031100	未漂白针叶木碱木浆或硫酸盐木浆		10
	47031900	未漂白非针叶木碱木浆或硫酸盐木浆		10
	47032100	漂白针叶木碱木浆或硫酸盐木浆		10
	47032900	漂白非针叶木碱木浆或硫酸盐木浆		10
	47041100	未漂白的针叶木亚硫酸盐木浆		10
	47041900	未漂白的非针叶木亚硫酸盐木浆		10
	47042100	漂白的针叶木亚硫酸盐木浆		10
	47042900	漂白的非针叶木亚硫酸盐木浆		10
	47050000	半化学木浆		10
	47062000	从回收纸或纸板提取的纤维浆		10
	47063000	竹浆		10
	47069100	其他纤维状纤维素机械浆		10
	47069200	其他纤维状纤维素化学浆		10
	47069300	其他纤维状纤维素半化学浆		10
	72011000	非合金生铁，含磷量小于或等于 0.5%	20	25
	72012000	非合金生铁，含磷量大于 0.5%	20	25
	72015000	合金生铁	20	25
	72021100	锰铁，含碳量>2%	20	
	72021900	锰铁，含碳量≤2%	20	
	72022100	硅铁，含硅量>55%	25	
	72022900	硅铁，含硅量≤55%	25	
	72023000	硅锰铁	20	
	72024100	铬铁，含碳量>4%	40	20
	72024900	铬铁，含碳量≤4%	40	20
	72025000	硅铬铁		20
	72026000	镍铁		20
	72027000	钼铁		20
	72028010	钨铁		20
	72028020	硅钨铁		20
	72029100	钛铁及硅钛铁		20
	72029290	其他钒铁		20
	72029300	铌铁		20
	72029911	钕铁硼速凝永磁片		20
	72029919	其他钕铁硼合金		20
	72029991	按重量计含稀土元素 10%以上的铁合金		25
	72029999	其他铁合金		20
	72031000	直接从铁矿还原的铁产品		25
	72039000	其他铁，海绵铁，产品纯度＞99.94%		25
	72041000	铸铁废碎料	40	
	72042100	不锈钢废碎料	40	
	72042900	其他合金钢废碎料	40	
	72043000	镀锡钢铁废碎料	40	
	72044100	机械加工中产生的废料	40	
	72044900	其他钢铁废碎料	40	
	72045000	供再熔的碎料钢铁锭	40	
ex	72051000	生铁、镜铁及钢铁颗粒（不带球弧面的棱角形颗粒数量大于 80%的棱角钢砂、筛网孔径在 0.3-2.8mm 的铸钢丸和铸钢砂除外）		25
ex	72052900	生铁、镜铁及其他钢铁粉末（平均粒径小于 10μm 的超细铁粉除外）		25
	72061000	铁及非合金钢锭		25
	72069000	其他初级形状的铁及非合金钢		25
	72071100	宽度＜厚度两倍的矩形截面钢坯，C<0.25%		25
	72071200	其他矩形截面钢坯，C，0.25%		25
	72071900	其他含碳量＜0.25%的钢坯		25
	72072000	含碳量≥0.25%的钢坯		25
	72131000	带有轧制花纹的热轧盘条		15
	72132000	其他易切削钢制热轧盘条		15
	72139100	直径＜14mm 圆截面的其他热轧盘条		15

EX①	税则号列	商品名称（简称）	出口税率(%)	2014年暂定税率(%)
	72139900	其他热轧盘条		15
	72142000	热加工带有轧制花纹的条、杆		15
	72143000	热加工易切削钢的条、杆		15
	72149100	热加工其他矩形截面的条杆		15
	72149900	热加工其他条、杆		15
	72151000	冷加工其他易切削钢制条、杆		15
	72155000	冷加工或冷成形的其他条、杆		15
	72159000	铁及非合金钢的其他条、杆		15
	72181000	不锈钢锭及其他初级形状产品		15
	72189100	矩形截面的不锈钢半制成品		15
	72189900	其他不锈钢半制成品		15
	72191312	厚度在3毫米及以上,但小于4.75毫米的未经酸洗的按重量计含锰量在5.5%及以上的铬锰系不锈钢卷板		10
	72191322	厚度在3毫米及以上，但小于4.75毫米的经酸洗的按重量计含锰量在5.5%及以上的铬锰系不锈钢卷板		10
	72191412	厚度小于3毫米的未经酸洗的按重量计含锰量在5.5%及以上的铬锰系不锈钢卷板		10
	72191422	厚度小于3毫米的经酸洗的按重量计含锰量在5.5%及以上的铬锰系不锈钢卷板		10
	72241000	合金钢锭及其他初级形状合金钢		15
	72249010	单重≥10吨的粗铸锻件坯		15
	72249090	其他合金钢坯		15
	74010000	铜锍、沉积铜（泥铜）		15
	74020000	未精炼铜，电解精炼用的铜阳极	30	15
ex	74031111	高纯阴极铜（铜含量不低于99.9999%）	30	0
ex	74031111	高纯阴极铜（铜含量高于99.9935%，但低于99.9999%）	30	5
	74031119	其他阴极精炼铜	30	10
	74031190	其他精炼铜的阴极型材	30	10
	74031200	精炼铜的线锭	30	10
	74031300	精炼铜的坯段	30	10
	74031900	其他未锻轧的精炼铜	30	10
	74032100	未锻轧的铜锌合金(黄铜)	30	5
	74032200	未锻轧的铜锡合金(青铜)	30	5
	74032900	未锻轧的其他铜合金	30	5
	74040000	铜废碎料	30	15
	74050000	铜母合金		10
	74071010	铬锆铜制条、杆及型材及异型材	30	0
	74071090	其他精炼铜制条、杆及型材及异型材	30	0
	74072111	直线度不大于0.5毫米/米铜锌合金条、杆	30	0
	74072119	其他铜锌合金条、杆	30	0
	74072190	其他铜锌合金型材及异型材	30	0
	74072900	其他铜合金条杆、型材及异型材	30	0
	74081100	最大截面尺寸＞6mm的精炼铜丝	30	0
	74081900	其它精炼铜丝	30	0
	74082100	铜锌合金丝	30	0
	74082210	铜镍锌铅合金（加铅德银）丝	30	0
	74082290	其他白铜或德银丝	30	0
	74082900	其他铜合金丝	30	0
	74091110	含氧量不超过10PPM的成卷的精炼铜板、片、带	30	0
	74091190	其他成卷的精炼铜板、片、带	30	0
	74091900	其他精炼铜板、片、带	30	0
	74092100	成卷的铜锌合金板、片、带	30	0
	74092900	其他铜锌合金板、片、带	30	0
	74093100	成卷的铜锡合金板、片、带	30	0
	74093900	其他铜锡合金板、片、带	30	0
	74094000	铜镍合金或铜镍锌合金板、片、带	30	0
	74099000	其他铜合金板、片、带	30	0

EX[1]	税则号列	商品名称（简称）	出口税率(%)	2014 年暂定税率(%)
	75021010	高纯镍（镍含量大于 99.99%，钴含量不大于 0.005%)，	40	5
	75021090	未锻轧的非合金镍	40	15
	75022000	未锻轧镍合金	40	15
	75030000	镍废碎料		10
	75089010	电镀用镍阳极	40	15
	76011010	按重量计含铝量在 99.95%及以上的非合金铝	30	0
	76011090	按重量计含铝量在 99.95%以下的非合金铝	30	15
	76012000	未锻轧铝合金	30	15
	76020000	铝废碎料	30	15
	76041010	非合金铝条、杆	20	15
	76041090	非合金铝型材及异型材	20	0
	76042100	铝合金制空心异型材	20	0
ex	76042910	截面周长大于等于 210 毫米的铝合金制条、杆	20	15
ex	76042910	截面周长小于 210 毫米的铝合金条杆	20	5
	76042990	铝合金制其他型材及异型材	20	0
	76051100	最大截面尺寸超过 7mm 的非合金铝丝	20	0
	76051900	其他非合金铝丝	20	0
	76052100	最大截面尺寸超过 7mm 的铝合金丝	20	0
	76052900	其他铝合金丝	20	0
	76061121	厚度在 0.3mm 及以上，但不超过 0.36mm 的非合金铝与塑料复合的矩形铝板片带	20	0
	76061129	厚度在 0.3mm 及以上，但不超过 0.36mm 的其他非合金铝制矩形铝板片带	20	0
	76061191	非合金铝与塑料复合的矩形的其他板、片及带	20	0
	76061199	非合金铝制矩形的其他板、片及带	20	0
	76061220	厚度小于 0.28mm 的铝合金制矩形铝板片带	20	0
	76061230	厚度在 0.28mm 及以上，但不超过 0.35mm 的铝合金制矩形铝板片带	20	0
	76061251	厚度在 0.35mm 以上,但不超过 4mm 的铝合金与塑料复合的矩形铝板片带	20	0
	76061259	厚度在 0.35mm 以上,但不超过 4mm 的其他铝合金制矩形铝板片带	20	0
	76061290	厚度>4mm 的铝合金制矩形铝板片带	20	0
	76069100	非合金铝制非矩形的板、片及带	20	0
	76069200	铝合金制非矩形的板、片及带	20	0
	78011000	未锻轧精炼铅		10
	78020000	铅废碎料		10
	79011110	按重量计含锌量在 99.995%及以上的未锻轧锌	20	0
	79011190	99.99 ≤ 含锌量<99.995%的未锻轧锌	20	5
	79011200	含锌量 < 99.99%的未锻轧锌	20	15
	79012000	未锻轧锌合金	20	0
	80011000	非合金锡		10
	80020000	锡废碎料		10
	81011000	钨粉		5
	81019400	未锻轧钨		5
	81019700	钨废碎料		15
	81021000	钼粉		5
	81029400	未锻轧钼		5
	81029700	钼废碎料		15
	81033000	钽废碎料		10
	81101010	未锻轧锑	20	5
	81101020	锑粉末	20	
	81102000	锑废碎料	20	
	81122100	未锻轧铬、铬粉末		15
	81122200	铬废碎料		15
	81129230	未锻轧铟；铟废碎料；铟粉末		2

注① “ex”表示应税商品范围以“商品名称”描述为准,其余以税号为准。

② 出口价格包括货物的货价、货物运至中华人民共和国境内输出地点装载前的运输及其相关费用、保险费,但是其中包含的出口关税税额，应当予以扣除。有关税率计算结果四舍五入保留 3 位小数;

③ 表中有特别出口税率的商品，出口的适用税率为：暂定税率+特别出口税率。

附表一

2014年进口商品消费税税率表
Consumption Tax on Import Goods 2014

商品编码	商品名称	进口从价消费税税率（%）	进口从量消费税税率/低
2106902000	制造饮料用的复合酒精制品	50	
2203000000	麦芽酿造的啤酒		进口完税价格≥0.3745美元/升的麦芽酿造啤酒，税率为0.253元/升 进口完税价格<0.3745美元/升的麦芽酿造啤酒，税率为0.2227元/升
2204100000	葡萄汽酒	10	
2204210000	小包装的鲜葡萄酿造的酒（小包装指装入两升及以下容器的）	10	
2204290000	其他包装鲜葡萄酿造的酒（其他包装指装入两升以上容器的）	10	
2204300000	其他酿酒葡萄汁(品目2009以外的)	10	
2205100000	小包装的味美思酒及类似酒（两升及以下容器包装，加植物或香料的用鲜葡萄酿造的酒）	10	
2205900000	其他包装的味美思酒及类似酒（两升以上容器包装，加植物或香料的用鲜葡萄酿造的酒）	10	
2206001000	黄酒（以稻米、黍米、玉米、小米、小麦等为主要原料，经进一步加工制成）		0.2495元/升
2206009000	其他发酵饮料（未列名的发酵饮料混合物及发酵饮料与无酒精饮料的混合物）	10	
2207100000	酒精浓度在80%及以上的未改性乙醇	5	
2207200010	任何浓度的改性乙醇	5	
2207200090	任何浓度的其他酒精	5	
2208200000	蒸馏葡萄酒制得的烈性酒	20	0.912元/升
2208300000	威士忌酒	20	0.912元/升
2208400000	朗姆酒及蒸馏已发酵甘蔗产品制得的其他烈性酒	20	0.912元/升
2208500000	杜松子酒	20	0.912元/升
2208600000	伏特加酒	20	0.912元/升
2208700000	利口酒及柯迪尔酒	20	0.912元/升
2208901010	濒危龙舌兰酒	20	0.912元/升
2208901090	其他龙舌兰酒	20	0.912元/升
2208902000	白酒	20	0.912元/升
2208909001	酒精浓度在80%以下的未改性乙醇	5	
2208909021	含濒危野生动植物成分的薯类蒸馏酒	20	0.912元/升
2208909029	其他薯类蒸馏酒	20	0.912元/升
2208909091	含濒危野生动植物成分的其他蒸馏酒及酒精饮料	20	0.912元/升
2208909099	其他蒸馏酒及酒精饮料	20	0.912元/升
2402100000	烟草制的雪茄烟	36	
2402200000	烟草制的卷烟		每标准条进口完税价格≥50元人民币，45%+150元/标准箱 每标准条进口完税价格<50元人民币，30%+150元/标准箱
2402900001	烟草代用品制的卷烟		每标准条进口完税价格≥50元人民币，45%+150元/标准箱 每标准条进口完税价格<50元人民币，30%+150元/标准箱
2402900009	烟草代用品制的雪茄烟	36	
2403110000	供吸用的本章子目注释所述的水烟料（不论是否含有任何比例的烟草代用品）	30	
2403190000	其他供吸用的烟草（不论是否含有任何比例的烟草代用品）	30	
2403910010	再造烟草	30	

商品编码	商品名称	进口从价消费税税率（%）	进口从量消费税税率/低
2403910090	均化烟草	30	
2403990090	其他烟草及烟草代用品的制品	30	
2710121001	车用汽油及航空汽油，不含生物柴油(铅含量每升不超过0.013克)		1元/升
2710121002	车用汽油及航空汽油，不含生物柴油（铅含量每升超过0.013克）		1.4元/升
2710122000	石脑油，不含生物柴油		1元/升
2710123000	橡胶溶剂油、油漆溶剂油、抽提溶剂油，不含生物柴油		1元/升
2710192200	5～7号燃料油，不含生物柴油		0.8元/升
2710192310	车用、普通柴油，不含生物柴油		0.8元/升
2710192390	其他柴油，不含生物柴油		0.8元/升
2710192910	蜡油：不含生物柴油（350℃以下馏出物体积百分比小于20%，550℃以下馏出物体积百分比大于80%）		0.8元/升
2710192990	其他燃料油，不含生物柴油		0.8元/升
2710199100	润滑油，不含生物柴油		1 /升
2710199200	润滑脂，不含生物柴油		1 /升
2710199300	润滑油基础油，不含生物柴油		1 /升
2710199900	其他重油；其他重油制品，不含生物柴油(包括按重量计含油≥70%的制品)		0.8元/升
3302109001	生产食品、饮料用混合香料及制品(含以香料为基本成分的混合物，按容量计酒精浓度>0.5%)	5	
3303000000	香水及花露水	30	
3304100010	含濒危植物成分唇用化妆品	30	
3304100090	其他唇用化妆品	30	
3304200010	含濒危植物成分眼用化妆品	30	
3304200090	其他眼用化妆品	30	
3304300000	指（趾）甲化妆品	30	
3304910090	粉，不论是否压紧	30	
3304990091	其他含濒危植物成分美容品或化妆品	30	
3304990099	其他美容品或化妆品	30	
3604100000	烟花，爆竹	15	
4011100090	机动小客车用新充气非子午线轮胎(橡胶轮胎，包括旅行小客车及赛车用)	3	
4011200019	断面宽度≥30英寸的客或货车用新的非子午线充气橡胶轮胎	3	
4011200099	客或货车用新的其他非子午线充气橡胶轮胎	3	
4011400000	摩托车用新的充气橡胶轮胎	3	
4011610019	断面宽度≥24 英寸人字形非子午线轮胎（新充气橡胶轮胎，含胎面类似人字形的，农林车辆机械用）	3	
4011610099	其他人字形胎面非子午线轮胎(新充气橡胶轮胎，含胎面类似人字形的，农林车辆机械用)	3	
4011620019	断面宽度≥24 英寸人字形非子午线轮胎（建筑业、工业用，辋圈≤61厘米，新充气橡胶胎，含类似人字形）	3	
4011620099	其他人字形胎面非子午线轮胎(建筑业、工业用，辋圈≤61厘米，新充气橡胶胎，含类似人字形)	3	
4011630019	断面宽度≥24英寸人字形非子午线轮胎(建筑业、工业用，辋圈>61厘米，新充气橡胶胎，含类人字形)	3	
4011630099	其他人字形胎面非子午线轮胎(建筑业、工业用，辋圈>61 厘米，新充气橡胶胎，含类似人字形)	3	
4011690019	断面宽度≥30英寸人字形非子午线轮胎(其他用途，新充气橡胶轮胎，含胎面类似人字形的)	3	
4011690099	其他人字形胎面非子午线轮胎（其他用途，新充气橡胶轮胎，含胎面类似人字形的）	3	
4011920019	其他断面宽度≥24英寸非子午线轮胎(新充气橡胶轮胎，非人字形胎面，农林车辆机械用)	3	
4011920099	其他新的充气橡胶非子午线轮胎(新充气橡胶轮胎，非人字形胎面，农林车辆机械用)	3	
4011930019	其他断面宽度≥24英寸非子午线轮胎(建筑业、工业用，辋圈≤61厘米，新充气橡胶胎，非人字形胎面)	3	
4011930099	其他新的充气橡胶非子午线轮胎（建筑业、工业用，辋圈≤61 厘米，新充气橡胶胎，非人字形胎面)	3	
4011940019	其他断面宽度≥24 英寸非子午线轮胎(建筑业，工业用，辋圈>61厘米，新充气橡胶胎，非人字形胎面)	3	
4011940099	其他新的充气橡胶非子午线轮胎(建筑业，工业用，辋圈>61厘米，	3	

商品编码	商品名称	进口从价消费税税率（%）	进口从量消费税税率/低
	新充气橡胶胎，非人字形胎面）		
4011990019	其他断面宽度≥30英寸非子午线轮胎（其他用途，新充气橡胶轮胎，非人字形胎面）	3	
4011990099	其他新的充气橡胶非子午线轮胎（其他用途，新充气橡胶轮胎，非人字形胎面）	3	
4012201090	汽车用旧的充气橡胶非子午线轮胎	3	
4012209090	其他用旧的充气橡胶非子午线轮胎	3	
4012902090	汽车用实心或半实心非子午线轮胎（还包括可互换橡胶胎面及橡胶轮胎衬带）	3	
4012909090	其他用实心或半实心非子午线轮胎（还包括可互换橡胶胎面及橡胶轮胎衬带）	3	
4013100000	汽车用橡胶内胎[机动小客车（包括旅行小客车及赛车）、客运车或货运车用]	3	
4013909000	其他用橡胶内胎	3	
4409101010	一边或面制成连续形状的濒危针叶木制地板条、块（包括未装拼的拼花地板用板条及缘板）	5	
4409101090	一边或面制成连续形状的其他针叶木地板条、块（包括未装拼的拼花地板用板条及缘板）	5	
4409291010	一边或面制成连续形状的拉敏木地板条、块（包括未装拼的拉敏木拼花地板用板条及缘板）	5	
4409291020	一边或面制成连续形状的桃花心木地板条、块（包括未装拼的桃花心木拼花地板用板条及缘板）	5	
4409291030	一边或面制成连续形状的其他濒危木地板条、块（包括未装拼的其他濒危木拼花地板用板条及缘板）	5	
4409291090	一边或面制成连续形状的其他非针叶木地板条、块（包括未装拼的其他非针叶木拼花地板用板条及缘板）	5	
4419003100	木制一次性筷子	5	
7101101100	未分级的天然黑珍珠（不论是否加工，但未制成制品）	10	
7101101900	其他未分级的天然珍珠（不论是否加工，但未制成制品）	10	
7101109100	其他天然黑珍珠（不论是否加工，但未制成制品）	10	
7101109900	其他天然珍珠（不论是否加工，但未制成制品）	10	
7101211001	未分级、未加工的养殖黑珍珠（未制成制品）	10	
7101211090	其他未分级、未加工的养殖珍珠（未制成制品）	10	
7101219001	其他未加工的养殖黑珍珠（未制成制品）	10	
7101219090	其他未加工的养殖珍珠（未制成制品）	10	
7101221001	未分级、已加工的养殖黑珍珠（未制成制品）	10	
7101221090	其他未分级、已加工的养殖珍珠（未制成制品）	10	
7101229001	其他已加工的养殖黑珍珠（未制成制品）	10	
7101229090	其他已加工的养殖珍珠（未制成制品）	10	
7103100000	未加工宝石或半宝石（经简单锯开或粗制成形，未成串或镶嵌）	10	
7103910000	经其他加工的红宝石、蓝宝石、祖母绿（未成串或镶嵌）	10	
7103991000	经其他加工的翡翠（未成串或镶嵌）	10	
7103992000	经其他加工的水晶（未成串或镶嵌）	10	
7103993000	经其他加工的碧玺（未成串或镶嵌）	10	
7103994000	经其他加工的软玉（未成串或镶嵌）	10	
7103999000	经其他加工的其他宝石或半宝石（未成串或镶嵌）	10	
7104209000	未加工合成或再造其他宝石或半宝石（经简单锯开或粗制成形，未成串或镶嵌）	10	
7104901201	蓝宝石衬底（由人造刚玉加工而成）（厚度<0.5毫米）	10	
7104901290	其他工业用蓝宝石（合成或再造宝石、半宝石）	10	
7104901900	其他工业用合成或再造宝石、半宝石	10	
7104909900	其他非工业用合成宝石或半宝石（未成串或镶嵌）	10	
7105900000	其他天然或合成宝石或半宝石粉末	10	
7113209010	镶嵌濒危物种制品以贱金属为底的包贵金属制首饰（包括零件）	10	
7113209090	其他以贱金属为底的包贵金属制首饰（包括零件）	10	
7116100000	天然或养殖珍珠制品	10	
7116200000	宝石或半宝石制品（包括天然、合成或再造的）	10	
8702109201	20座≤座位≤23座装有压燃式活塞内燃发动机的客车	5	
8702109300	10座≤座位≤19座装有压燃式活塞内燃发动机的客车	5	
8702902001	20座≤座位≤23座装有非压燃式活塞内燃发动机的客车	5	
8702903000	10座≤座位≤19座装有非压燃式活塞内燃发动机的客车	5	

商品编码	商品名称	进口从价消费税税率（%）	进口从量消费税税率/低
8703213001	排量≤1 升的装有点燃往复式活塞内燃发动机的小轿车	1	
8703214001	排量≤1 升的带点燃往复式活塞内燃发动机的越野车（四轮驱动）	1	
8703215001	排量≤1 升的带点燃往复式活塞内燃发动机的小客车（9 座及以下）	1	
8703219001	排量≤1 升的带点燃往复式活塞内燃发动机的其他车辆	1	
8703223001	1 升<排量≤1.5 升带点燃往复式活塞内燃发动机小轿车	3	
8703224001	1 升<排量≤1.5 升带点燃往复式活塞内燃发动机四轮驱动越野车	3	
8703225001	1 升<排量≤1.5 升带点燃往复式活塞内燃发动机小客车（9 座及以下）	3	
8703229001	1 升<排量≤1.5 升带点燃往复式活塞内燃发动机其他车	3	
8703234101	1.5 升<排量≤2 升装点燃往复式活塞内燃发动机小轿车	5	
8703234201	1.5 升<排量≤2 升装点燃往复式活塞内燃发动机越野车（四轮驱动）	5	
8703234301	1.5 升<排量≤2 升装点燃往复式活塞内燃发动机小客车（9 座及以下的）	5	
8703234901	1.5 升<排量≤2 升装点燃往复式活塞内燃发动机的其他载人车辆	5	
8703235101	2 升<排量≤2.5 升装点燃往复式活塞内燃发动机小轿车	9	
8703235201	2 升<排量≤2.5 升装点燃往复式活塞内燃发动机越野车（四轮驱动）	9	
8703235301	2 升<排量≤2.5 升装点燃往复式活塞内燃发动机小客车（9 座及以下的）	9	
8703235901	2 升<排量≤2.5 升装点燃往复式活塞内燃发动机的其他载人车辆	9	
8703236101	2.5 升<排量≤3 升装点燃往复式活塞内燃发动机小轿车	12	
8703236201	2.5 升<排量≤3 升装点燃往复式活塞内燃发动机越野车（四轮驱动）	12	
8703236301	2.5 升<排量≤3 升装点燃往复式活塞内燃发动机小客车（9 座及以下的）	12	
8703236901	2.5 升<排量≤3 升装点燃往复式活塞内燃发动机的其他载人车辆（不包括非四轮驱动越野车）	12	
8703236902	2.5 升<排量≤3 升装点燃往复式活塞内燃发动机的非四轮驱动越野车	12	
8703241101	3 升<排量≤4 升装点燃往复式活塞内燃发动机小轿车	25	
8703241201	3 升<排量≤4 升装点燃往复式活塞内燃发动机越野车（四轮驱动）	25	
8703241301	3 升<排量≤4 升装点燃往复式活塞内燃发动机的小客车（9 座及以下的）	25	
8703241901	3 升<排量≤4 升装点燃往复式活塞内燃发动机的其他载人车辆(不包括非四轮驱动越野车）	25	
8703241902	3 升<排量≤4 升装点燃往复式活塞内燃发动机的非四轮驱动越野车	25	
8703242101	排气量>4 升装点燃往复式活塞内燃发动机小轿车	40	
8703242201	排气量>4 升装点燃往复式活塞内燃发动机越野车（四轮驱动）	40	
8703242301	排气量>4 升装点燃往复式活塞内燃发动机的小客车（9 座及以下的）	40	
8703242901	排量>4 升装点燃往复式活塞内燃发动机的其他载人车辆（不包括非四轮驱动越野车）	40	
8703242902	排量>4 升装点燃往复式活塞内燃发动机的非四轮驱动越野车	40	
8703311101	排气量≤1 升的装有压燃往复式活塞内燃发动机小轿车	1	
8703311901	排气量≤1 升的装有压燃往复式活塞内燃发动机的其他载人车辆	1	
8703312101	1 升<排气量≤1.5 升装压燃往复式活塞内燃发动机小轿车	3	
8703312201	1 升<排气量≤1.5 升装压燃式活塞内燃发动机越野车（四轮驱动）	3	
8703312301	1 升<排气量≤1.5 升装压燃往复式活塞内燃发动机小客车（9 座及以下的）	3	
8703312901	1 升<排量≤1.5 升装压燃往复式活塞内燃发动机的其他载人车辆	3	
8703321101	1.5 升<排量≤2 升装压燃往复式活塞内燃发动机小轿车	5	
8703321201	1.5 升<排量≤2 升装压燃往复式活塞内燃发动机越野车（四轮驱动）	5	
8703321301	1.5 升<排量≤2 升装压燃往复式活塞内燃发动机小客车（9 座及以下的）	5	
8703321901	1.5 升<排量≤2 升装压燃往复式活塞内燃发动机的其他载人车辆	5	
8703322101	2 升<排量≤2.5 升装压燃往复式活塞内燃发动机小轿车	9	
8703322201	2 升<排量≤2.5 升装压燃往复式活塞内燃发动机越野车（四轮驱动）	9	
8703322301	2 升<排量≤2.5 升装压燃往复式活塞内燃发动机小客车（9 座及以下的）	9	
8703322901	2 升<排量≤2.5 升装压燃往复式活塞内燃发动机的其他载人车辆	9	
8703331101	2.5 升<排量≤3 升装压燃往复式活塞内燃发动机小轿车	12	
8703331201	2.5 升<排量≤3 升装压燃往复式活塞内燃发动机越野车（四轮驱动）	12	
8703331301	2.5 升<排量≤3 升装压燃往复式活塞内燃发动机小客车（9 座及以下的）	12	
8703331901	2.5 升<排量≤3 升装压燃往复式活塞内燃发动机的其他载人车辆（不包括非四轮驱动越野车）	12	

商品编码	商品名称	进口从价消费税税率（%）	进口从量消费税税率/低
8703331902	2.5 升<排量≤3 升装压燃往复式活塞内燃发动机的非四轮驱动越野车	12	
8703332101	3 升<排量≤4 升装压燃往复式活塞内燃发动机小轿车	25	
8703332201	3 升<排量≤4 升装压燃往复式活塞内燃发动机越野车（四轮驱动）	25	
8703332301	3 升<排量≤4 升装压燃往复式活塞内燃发动机小客车（9 座及以下的）	25	
8703332901	3 升<排量≤4 升装压燃往复式活塞内燃发动机的其他载人车辆（不包括非四轮驱动越野车）	25	
8703332902	3 升<排量≤4 升装压燃往复式活塞内燃发动机的非四轮驱动越野车	25	
8703336101	排量>4 升装压燃往复式活塞内燃发动机小轿车	40	
8703336201	排量>4 升装压燃往复式活塞内燃发动机越野车（四轮驱动）	40	
8703336301	排量>4 升装压燃往复式活塞内燃发动机的小客车（9 座及以下的）	40	
8703336901	排量>4 升装压燃往复式活塞内燃发动机的其他载人车辆（不包括非四轮驱动越野车）	40	
8703336902	排量>4 升装压燃往复式活塞内燃发动机的非四轮驱动越野车	40	
8703900001	其他型排气量≤1 升的其他载人车辆	1	
8703900002	其他型 1.5 升<排气量≤2 升的其他载人车辆	5	
8703900003	其他型 2 升<排气量≤2.5 升的其他载人车辆	9	
8703900004	其他型 2.5 升<排气量≤3 升的其他载人车辆（不包括编号 8703900014 所述小轿车和越野车）	12	
8703900005	其他型 3 升<排气量≤4 升的其他载人车辆（不包括编号 8703900015 所述小轿车和越野车）	25	
8703900006	其他型排气量>4 升的其他载人车辆（不包括编号 8703900016 所述小轿车和越野车）	40	
8703900007	其他型 1 升<排气量≤1.5 升的其他载人车辆	3	
8703900014	其他型 2.5 升<排气量≤3 升的小轿车、越野车	12	
8703900015	其他型 3 升<排气量≤4 升的小轿车、越野车	25	
8703900016	其他型排气量>4 升的小轿车、越野车	40	
8711100010	微马力摩托车及脚踏两用车（装有往复式活塞发动机，微马力指排气量=50 毫升）	3	
8711100090	微马力摩托车及脚踏两用车（装有往复式活塞发动机，微马力指排气量<50 毫升）	3	
8711201000	50 毫升<排量≤100 毫升装往复式活塞内燃发动机摩托车及脚踏两用车	3	
8711202000	100 毫升<排量≤125 毫升装往复式活塞内燃发动机摩托车及脚踏两用车	3	
8711203000	125 毫升<排量≤150 毫升装往复式活塞内燃发动机摩托车及脚踏两用车	3	
8711204000	150 毫升<排量≤200 毫升装往复式活塞内燃发动机摩托车及脚踏两用车	3	
8711205000	200 毫升<排量≤250 毫升装往复式活塞内燃发动机摩托车及脚踏两用车	3	
8711301000	250 毫升<排量≤400 毫升装往复式活塞内燃发动机摩托车及脚踏两用车	10	
8711302000	400 毫升<排量≤500 毫升装往复式活塞内燃发动机摩托车及脚踏两用车	10	
8711400000	500 毫升<排量≤800 毫升装往复式活塞内燃发动机摩托车及脚踏两用车	10	
8711500000	排量>800 毫升装往复式活塞内燃发动机摩托车及脚踏两用车	10	
8711909001	排量≤250 毫升摩托车及脚踏两用车	3	
8711909002	排量>250 毫升摩托车及脚踏两用车	10	
8711909009	其他无法区分排气量的摩托车及脚踏两用车	3	
8903910001	8 米<长度<90 米的机动帆船（不论是否装有辅助发动机）	10	
8903920001	8 米<长度<90 米的汽艇（装有舷外发动机的除外）	10	
8903990001	8 米<长度<90 米的娱乐或运动用其他机动船舶或快艇	10	
9101110000	机械指示式的贵金属电子手表（表壳用贵金属或包贵金属制成的）	进口关税完税价格在 10000 元人民币及以上时，税率为 20%	
9101191000	光电显示式的贵金属电子手表（表壳用贵金属或包贵金属制成的）	进口关税完税价格在 10000 元人民币及以上时，税率为 20%	
9101199000	其他贵金属电子手表（表壳用贵金属或包贵金属制成的）	进口关税完税价格在 10000 元人民币及以上时，税率为 20%	

商品编码	商品名称	进口从价消费税税率（%）	进口从量消费税税率/低
9101210010	含濒危动物皮自动上弦贵金属机械手表（表壳用贵金属或包贵金属制成的）	进口关税完税价格在10000元人民币及以上时，税率为20%	
9101210090	其他自动上弦贵金属机械手表（表壳用贵金属或包贵金属制成的）	进口关税完税价格在10000元人民币及以上时，税率为20%	
9101290010	含濒危动物皮非自动上弦贵金属机械手表（表壳用贵金属或包贵金属制成的）	进口关税完税价格在10000元人民币及以上时，税率为20%	
9101290090	其他非自动上弦贵金属机械手表（表壳用贵金属或包贵金属制成的）	进口关税完税价格在10000元人民币及以上时，税率为20%	
9102110000	机械指示式的其他电子手表（贵金属或包贵金属制壳的除外）	进口关税完税价格在10000元人民币及以上时，税率为20%	
9102120000	光电显示式的其他电子手表（贵金属或包贵金属制壳的除外）	进口关税完税价格在10000元人民币及以上时，税率为20%	
9102190000	其他电子手表（贵金属或包贵金属制壳的除外）	进口关税完税价格在10000元人民币及以上时，税率为20%	
9102210010	含濒危动物皮其他自动上弦的机械手表（用贵金属或包贵金属制壳的除外）	进口关税完税价格在10000元人民币及以上时，税率为20%	
9102210090	其他自动上弦的机械手表（用贵金属或包贵金属制壳的除外）	进口关税完税价格在10000元人民币及以上时，税率为20%	
9102290010	含濒危动物皮其他非自动上弦机械手表（用贵金属或包贵金属制壳的除外）	进口关税完税价格在10000元人民币及以上时，税率为20%	
9102290090	其他非自动上弦的机械手表（用贵金属或包贵金属制壳的除外）	进口关税完税价格在10000元人民币及以上时，税率为20%	
9506310000	完整的高尔夫球棍	10	
9506320000	高尔夫球	10	

附表二

非全税目信息技术产品进口税率表
Duty Rate on Specific Information Technology Products

EX[①]	税则号列	商品名称	全税号最惠国税率（%）	EX 项税率（%）
ex	70200013、70200019	用于插入熔化和氧化炉内以制备半导体晶片的石英反应管及夹持器	10.5	0
ex	85044091	自动数据处理设备机器及组件、电讯设备用的具有变流功能的半导体模块	10	0
ex	85044099	自动数据处理设备机器及组件、电讯设备用的其他静止变流器；ITA产品用的印刷电路组件，包括外接组件，如符合PCMCIA标准的卡	10	0
ex	85176910	用于呼叫、提示和寻呼的便携式接收器	9	0
ex	85181000	电讯用麦克风、频率范围在300赫兹到3.4千赫之间，直径不超过10毫米，高度不超过3毫米	10	0
ex	85184000	列入ITA的有线电话重复器用的电器扩音器	12	0
ex	85189000	列入ITA的有线电话重复器用的电器扩音器的零件	10.5	0
ex	85177070	无线电话电报装置的天线	2	0
ex	90309000	用于检测半导体晶片及器件的仪器的零件和附件；ITA产品用的印刷电路组件，包括外接组件，如符合PCMCIA标准的卡	7	0

注①“ex”表示实施暂定税率的商品以“商品名称”描述为准

附表三

计量单位换算表
Conversion Table

面（地）积换算

公制		英美制			
平方米	平方厘米	平方码	平方英尺	平方英寸	平方尺
1	10000	1.1960	10.7639	1550	9
0.0001	1	0.00012	0.00108	0.155	0.0009
0.8361	8361	1	9	1296	7.525
0.0929	929	0.1111	1	144	0.836
0.00065	6.45	0.00077	0.00694	1	0.0058
0.111	1111	0.133	1.196	172.2	1

长度换算

公制		中国市制	英美制		
米	厘米	尺	码	英尺	英寸
1	100	3	1.094	3.2808	39.37
0.01	1	0.03	0.01094	0.03281	0.3937
0.3333	33.33	1	0.3646	1.094	13.123
0.9144	91.44	2.743	1	3	36
0.3048	30.48	0.9144	0.3334	1	12
0.0254	2.54	0.0752	0.0278	0.833	1

1 米=100 厘米=1000 毫米

重量换算（一）

公制	英制	美制	港制
公吨	长吨	短吨	司马担
1	0.9842	1.1023	16.535
1.016	1	1.12	16.8
0.9072	0.8929	1	15
0.05	0.04921	0.0551	0.8267
0.0508	0.05	0.056	0.8402
0.0605	0.0594	0.0667	1

港制 1 司马担=100 司马斤

美制 1 短吨=20 短担(CWT)

公制 1 公吨=10 公担

1 短担=100 磅=45.36 千克

英制 1 长吨=20 英担（CWT）

1 英担=50.8024 千克

公制	中国市制	英美制
千克	斤	磅
1000	2000	2204.6
1016	2032	2242
907	1814	2000
50	100	110.23
50.8	101.6	112
60.48	120.96	133.33
1	2	2.2046
0.5	1	1.1023
0.4536	0.9072	1

重量换算（二）

公制		英美制常衡		英美制金衡或药衡		中国市制
千克	克	磅	哂	磅	哂	两
1	1000	2.2046	35.2736	2.679	31.1507	20
0.001	1	0.0022	0.03527	0.00268	0.0321	0.02
0.4536	453.59	1	16	1.2153	14.5833	9.072
0.02835	28.35	0.0625	1	0.07595	0.9114	0.567
0.3732	373.24	0.82286	13.1657	1	12	7.465
0.0311	31.10	0.06857	1.0971	0.08333	1	0.622
0.05	50	0.1102	1.76368	0.13396	1.6075	1

宝石：1 克拉=0.2 克　　1 金衡=155.5 克拉

容（体）积换算（一）

公制	中国市制	英制	美制
升	升	英加仑	美加仑
1	1	0.22	0.264
4.546	4.546	1	1.201
3.785	3.785	0.833	1

1000 升=1 立方米　1 升=1000 毫升=1000 立方厘米（c.c.）

英制 1 加仑=277.42 立方英寸　　英制 1 加仑=231 立方英寸

容（体）积换算（二）

公制		英美制			中国市制
立方米	立方厘米	立方码	立方英尺	立方英寸	立方尺
1	1000000	1.303	35.3147	61024	27
0.000001	1	0.0000013	0.00004	0.06102	0.000027
0.7636	764555	1	27	46656	20.643
0.02832	28317	0.037	1	1728	0.7646
0.000016	16.387	0.00002	0.00058	1	0.00044
0.037	37037	0.0484	1.308	2260	1

木材体积单位换算

板（Board Foot Measure，BFM）：

指厚一英寸、面积一平方英尺的木材

板材的换算：100 板=2.36 立方米

原木的换算：100 板=5 立方米（近似值）

功率换算

1 千瓦(kW)=1.34 英制马力（hp）=1.36 公制马力（hp）

1 英制马力=0.746 千瓦(kW)

1 公制马力=0.735 千瓦(kW)

$$1\text{ 千伏安（kVA）} = \frac{\text{千瓦(kW)}}{0.80}$$

粮谷重量容积换算

品名	1 公吨折合蒲式耳	1 蒲式耳折合	
		磅	千克
小麦、大豆	36.743	60	27.216
玉米	39.368	56	25.402
大麦（英制）	44.092	50	22.68
大麦（美制）	45.931	48	21.773

1 英制蒲式耳（1.0321 美制蒲式耳）合 36.3677 升。

石（原）油重量、容积换算

国别	1 公吨折合			
	千升	美制桶	英制加仑	美制加仑
美国、印度尼西亚	1.18	7.4	259.1	310.6
伊朗、沙特阿拉伯	1.19	7.49	261.8	314.5
日本	1.11	6.99	244.5	293.3
英国、科威特	1.16	7.31	255.8	306.7
委内瑞拉	1.09	6.84	239.2	287.4

注：世界平均比重的原油通常以 1 公吨=7.35 桶（每桶为 42 美制加仑）或 1174 升计。

常用度量衡英文名称和简写

名称	英文名称	简写	名称	英文名称	简写
克	gram	g.	码	yard	yd.
千克	kilogram	kg.	英尺	foot	ft.
公担	quintal	q.	英寸	inch	in.
公吨	metric ton	m. t.	平方米	square metre	sq. m.
长吨	long ton	l. t.	平方英尺	square foot	sq. ft
短吨	short ton	sh. t.	平方码	square yard	sq. yd
英担	hundredweight	cwt.	立方米	cubic metre	cu. m.
美担	hundredweight	cwt.	立方英尺	cubic toor	cu. ft.
磅	pound	lb.	升	litre	l.
唡（常衡）	ounce	oz.	毫升	Millilitre	ml.
（金衡）	ounce	oz. t	加仑	gallon	gal.
司马担	picul		蒲式耳	bushel	bu.
米	metre	m.	克拉	carat	car.
公里	kilometre	km.	马力	horse power	hp.
厘米	centimetre	cm.	千瓦	kilowatt	kw.
毫米	millimetre	mm.	公吨度	metric ton unit	m. t. u.

附表四

2014 年进口商品从量税及复合税税率表
Specific and Compound Duty Rates on Import Goods 2014

税则号列	商品名称(简称)	普通税率	2014 年最惠国税率
02071200	冻的整只鸡	5.6 元/千克	1.3 元/千克
02071411	冻的带骨鸡块(包括鸡胸脯、鸡大腿等)	4.2 元/千克	0.6 元/千克
02071419	冻的不带骨鸡块(包括鸡胸脯、鸡大腿等)	9.5 元/千克	0.7 元/千克
02071421	冻的鸡翼（不包括翼尖）	8.1 元/千克	0.8 元/千克
02071422	冻的鸡爪	3.2 元/千克	1 元/千克
02071429	冻的其他鸡杂碎（包括鸡翼尖、鸡肝等）	3.2 元/千克	0.5 元/千克
05040021	冷、冻的鸡肫（即鸡胃）	7.7 元/千克	1.3 元/千克
22030000	麦芽酿造的啤酒	7.5 元/升	0
27090000	石油原油（包括从沥青矿物提取的原油）	85 元/吨	0
37023190	未曝光无齿孔彩色窄胶卷（窄胶卷指宽度≤105 毫米，彩色摄影用）	433 元/平方米	56 元/平方米
37023220	照相制版涂卤化银液无齿孔窄胶卷（成卷未曝光感光胶片，窄胶卷指宽度≤105 毫米）	104 元/平方米	4.5 元/平方米
37023290	其他涂卤化银乳液无齿孔窄胶卷（成卷未曝光感光胶片，窄胶卷指宽度≤105 毫米）	202 元/平方米	21 元/平方米
37023920	照相制版用其他无齿孔窄感光胶卷（成卷未曝光感光胶片，窄胶卷指宽度≤105 毫米）	104 元/平方米	12 元/平方米
37023990	其他用无齿孔窄感光胶卷（成卷未曝光感光胶片，窄胶卷指宽度≤105 毫米）	202 元/平方米	24 元/平方米
37024100	未曝光无齿孔宽长彩色胶卷（宽长胶卷指宽度>610 毫米，长度>200 米）	202 元/平方米	7.1 元/平方米
37024221	印刷电路板制造用光致抗蚀干膜（指宽度>610 毫米，长度>200 米）	110 元/平方米	0.6 元/平方米
37024229	照相制版其他未曝光无齿宽长胶卷（宽长指宽度>610 毫米，长度>200 米）	110 元/平方米	1.6 元/平方米
37024292	红色或红外激光胶片	213 元/平方米	2.4 元/平方米
37024299	黑白其他未曝光无齿孔宽长胶卷（宽长胶卷指宽度>610 毫米，长度>200 米）	213 元/平方米	7 元/平方米
37024321	照相制版用激光照排片（宽度>610 毫米，长度≤200 米）	104 元/平方米	10 元/平方米
37024329	其他照相制版用未曝光无齿孔胶卷（指宽度>610 毫米，长度≤200 米）	104 元/平方米	3.7 元/平方米
37024390	彩色或黑白其他用未曝光无齿孔中长胶卷（中长胶卷指宽度>610 毫米，长度≤200 米）	202 元/平方米	17 元/平方米
37024421	照相制版用未曝光激光照排片（宽度大于 105 毫米，小于等于 610 毫米）	115 元/平方米	2.0 元/平方米
37024422	印刷电路板制造用光致抗蚀干膜（宽度大于 105 毫米，小于等于 610 毫米）	115 元/平方米	5 元/平方米
37024429	其他照相制版用无齿孔未曝光胶卷（宽度大于 105 毫米，小于等于 610 毫米）	115 元/平方米	2.9 元/平方米
37024490	彩色或黑白其他用无齿孔未曝光中宽胶卷（中宽胶卷指宽度>105 毫米，但≤610 毫米）	202 元/平方米	27 元/平方米
37025200	彩色摄影用未曝光彩色胶卷 ，宽度≤16 毫米	433 元/平方米	95 元/平方米
37025300	幻灯片用未曝光彩色摄影胶卷（宽度>16 毫米，但≤35 毫米，长度≤30 米）	433 元/平方米	128 元/平方米
37025410	非幻灯片用彩色摄影胶卷（宽度=35 毫米，长度≤2 米）	433 元/平方米	18 元/平方米
37025490	其他非幻灯片用彩色摄影胶卷（宽度>16 毫米，但≤35 毫米，长度≤30 米）	433 元/平方米	24 元/平方米
37025520	未曝光的窄长彩色电影胶卷（窄长胶卷指宽度>16 毫米，但≤35 毫米，长度>30 米）	232 元/平方米	9 元/平方米
37025590	其他未曝光窄长彩色胶卷窄长胶卷指宽度>16 毫米，但≤35 毫米，长度>30 米）	433 元/平方米	27 元/平方米
37025620	未曝光的中宽彩色电影胶卷（中宽胶卷指宽度>35 毫米）	232 元/平方米	13 元/平方米
37025690	其他未曝光的中宽彩色胶卷（中宽胶卷指宽度>35 毫米）	433 元/平方米	74 元/平方米
37029600	未曝光非彩色胶卷(宽度≤35 毫米,长度≤30 米)	210 元/平方米	21 元/平方米
37029700	未曝光非彩色胶卷(宽度≤35 毫米，长度＞30 米)	210 元/平方米	9 元/平方米
37029800	未曝光的非彩色胶卷，宽度＞35 毫米	210 元/平方米	10 元/平方米

税则号列	商品名称(简称)	普通税率	2014年最惠国税率
85211011	广播级磁带录像机	完税价格不高于2000美元/台：130%; 完税价格高于2000美元/台：6%，加20600元	完税价格不高于2000美元/台：30%; 完税价格高于2000美元/台：3%，加3283元
85211019	其他磁带录像机	完税价格不高于2000美元/台：130%; 完税价格高于2000美元/台：6%，加20600元	完税价格不高于2000美元/台：30%; 完税价格高于2000美元/台：3%，加3283元
85211020	磁带放像机	完税价格不高于2000美元/台：130%; 完税价格高于2000美元/台：6%，加20600元	完税价格不高于2000美元/台：30%; 完税价格高于2000美元/台：3%，加3283元
85258012	非特种用途的广播级电视摄像机	完税价格不高于5000美元/台：130%; 完税价格高于5000美元/台：6%，加51500元	完税价格不高于5000美元/台，35%; 完税价格高于5000美元/台：3%，加9728元
85258013	非特种用途的其他电视摄像机	完税价格不高于5000美元/台：130%; 完税价格高于5000美元/台：6%，加51500元	完税价格不高于5000美元/台，35%; 完税价格高于5000美元/台：3%，加9728元
85258022	非特种用途的单镜头反光型数字照相机	完税价格不高于5000美元/台：130%; 完税价格高于5000美元/台：6%，加51500元	0
85258025	非特种用途的其他可换镜头的数字照相机	完税价格不高于5000美元/台：130%; 完税价格高于5000美元/台：6%，加51500元	0
85258029	非特种用途的其他数字照相机	完税价格不高于5000美元/台：130%; 完税价格高于5000美元/台：6%，加51500元	0
85258032	非特种用途的广播级视频摄录一体机	完税价格不高于5000美元/台：130%; 完税价格高于5000美元/台：6%，加51500元	0
85258039	非特种用途的其他视频摄录一体机（家用型摄录一体机除外）	完税价格不高于5000美元/台：130%; 完税价格高于5000美元/台：6%，加51500元	0

附表 5

中华人民共和国进境物品完税价格表
Import Tariff Rates for Entry Goods of the People's Republic of China

税号	品名及规格	单位	完税价格（人民币：元）	税率
01000000	食品、饮料			
01010000	- 食品			
01010100	- - 水产品			
01010110	- - - 干鱼翅	千克	3000	10%
01010120	- - - 干鲍鱼	千克	5000	10%
01010130	- - - 干海参	千克	1500	10%
01010140	- - - 干瑶柱	千克	700	10%
01010150	- - - 干海马、干海龙	千克	1500	10%
01010160	- - - 鱼肚（花胶）	千克	1500	10%
01010190	- - - 其他水产品	千克	另行确定	10%
01010200	- - 燕窝			
01010210	- - - 燕盏	千克	30000	10%
01010220	- - - 燕饼（燕丝、燕条）	千克	15000	10%
01010230	- - - 燕碎	千克	5000	10%
01010290	- - - 其他燕窝制品	千克	另行确定	10%
01010300	- - 冬虫夏草	千克	100000	10%
01010400	- - 参	千克	1500	10%
01010500	- - 鹿茸	千克	2000	10%
01010600	- - 阿胶	千克	250	10%
01010700	- - 奶粉	千克	200	10%
01010800	- - 调味品	千克	200	10%
01019900	- - 其他食品	千克	另行确定	10%
01020000	- 饮料			
01020100	- - 茶叶	千克	200	10%
01020200	- - 咖啡	千克	200	10%
01029900	- - 其他饮料	千克	另行确定	10%
02000000	酒			
02010000	- 啤酒			
02010100	- - 12 度以下（不含 12 度）	瓶（不超过 750 毫升）	5	50%
02010200	- - 12 度至 22 度（不含 22 度）	瓶（不超过 750 毫升）	10	50%
02020000	- 葡萄酒			
02020100	- - 12 度以下（不含 12 度）	瓶（不超过 750 毫升）	100	50%
02020200	- - 12 度至 22 度（不含 22 度）	瓶（不超过 750 毫升）	200	50%
02030000	- 清酒			
02030100	- - 12 度以下（不含 12 度）	瓶（不超过 750 毫升）	30	50%
02030200	- - 12 度至 22 度（不含 22 度）	瓶（不超过 750 毫升）	50	50%
02030300	- - 22 度及以上	瓶（不超过 750 毫升）	80	50%
02040000	- 白兰地	瓶（不超过 750 毫升）	500	50%
02050000	- 威士忌	瓶（不超过 750 毫升）	300	50%
02060000	- 伏特加	瓶（不超过 750 毫升）	100	50%
02070000	- 白酒	瓶（不超过 750 毫升）	300	50%
02080000	- 药酒	瓶（不超过 750 毫升）	200	50%
02990000	- 其他酒	瓶（不超过 750 毫升）	另行确定	50%
03000000	烟草			
03010000	- 卷烟	支	0.5	50%
03020000	- 雪茄烟	支	10	50%
03030000	- 烟丝	克	0.5	50%
03990000	- 其他烟	克、支	另行确定	50%
04000000	纺织品及其制成品			
04010000	- 衣着			
04010100	- - 外衣	件	300	20%
04010200	- - 外裤	条	200	20%
04010300	- - 内衣裤	条/件	100	20%

税号	品名及规格	单位	完税价格（人民币：元）	税率
04010400	－－衬衫/T恤衫	件	200	20%
04019900	－－其他衣着	件	另行确定	20%
04020000	－配饰			
04020100	－－帽子	件	100	20%
04020200	－－丝巾、头巾、围巾	条	100	20%
04020300	－－领带	条	100	20%
04020400	－－腰带	条	100	20%
04020500	－－手套	双	100	20%
04029900	－－其他配饰	件	另行确定	20%
04030000	－家纺用品			
04030100	－－毛毯、被子、床罩、睡袋	床、件	400	20%
04030200	－－枕头、床单、毛巾被、被套	条、件	100	20%
04030300	－－地毯	平方米	200	20%
04030400	－－窗帘	千克	100	20%
04039900	－－其他家纺用品	件	另行确定	20%
04990000	－其他纺织品及其制成品	件	另行确定	20%
05000000	皮革服装及配饰			
05010000	－－皮革服装			
05010100	－－裘皮衣	件	另行确定	10%
05010200	－－皮大衣	件	2000	10%
05010300	－－皮上衣	件	1500	10%
05010400	－－皮背心	件	1000	10%
05010500	－－皮裤	件	1000	10%
05010600	－－皮裙	件	1000	10%
05019900	－－其他皮革服装	件	另行确定	10%
05020000	－皮革配饰			
05020100	－－皮帽	件	200	10%
05020200	－－皮带	条	100	10%
05020300	－－皮手套	双	100	10%
05029900	－－其他皮革配饰	件	另行确定	10%
05990000	－其他皮革制品（箱包和鞋靴除外）	件	另行确定	10%
06000000	箱包和鞋靴			
06010000	－箱包			
06010100	－－箱	个	500	10%
06010200	－－挎包、背包、提包	个	200	10%
06010300	－－钱包、钥匙包	个	100	10%
06019900	－－其他箱包	个	另行确定	10%
06020000	－鞋靴			
06020100	－－皮鞋	双	300	10%
06020200	－－皮靴	双	400	10%
06020300	－－运动鞋	双	200	10%
06029900	－－其他鞋靴	双	另行确定	10%
07000000	表、钟及其配件、附件			
07010000	－表			
07010100	－－高档手表（审定价格在人民币10000元及以上）	块	另行确定	30%
07010200	－－其他表			
07010210	－－－石英表（电子表）	块	200	20%
07010220	－－－机械表	块	500	20%
07010290	－－－其他表	块	另行确定	20%
07020000	－钟			
07020100	－－座钟、挂钟、台钟	个、台	200	20%
07020200	－－落地钟	台	600	20%
07029900	－－其他钟	台	另行确定	20%
07030000	－钟表配件、附件	件	另行确定	20%
08000000	金、银、珠宝及其制品、艺术品、收藏品			
08010000	－金、银及其制品	件	另行确定	10%
08020000	－珠、宝及其制品	件	另行确定	10%
08030000	－艺术品、收藏品	件	另行确定	10%
09000000	化妆品			
09010000	－芳香类化妆品			
09010100	－－香水	瓶	300	50%

税号	品名及规格	单位	完税价格（人民币：元）	税率
09019900	- - 其他芳香类化妆品	件	另行确定	50%
09020000	- 清洁/护理类化妆品			
09020100	- - 洗面奶/洁面霜	支、瓶	100	50%
09020200	- - 眼霜	支、瓶	200	50%
09020300	- - 面霜及乳液	支、瓶	200	50%
09020400	- - 精华液/素	支、瓶	300	50%
09020500	- - 润唇膏	支	20	50%
09020600	- - 面膜	张、瓶	20	50%
09020700	- - 爽肤水	支、瓶	150	50%
09020800	- - 护手霜	支、瓶	50	50%
09020900	- - 防晒霜（露、乳液）	支	150	50%
09029900	- - 其他清洁/护理类化妆品	支	另行确定	50%
09030000	- 美容/修饰类化妆品			
09030100	- - 粉底及粉底液	盒、支	200	50%
09030200	- - 睫毛液（膏）	支、瓶	100	50%
09030300	- - 指甲油	瓶	20	50%
09030400	- - 唇膏	支	150	50%
09039900	- - 其他美容/修饰类化妆品	件	另行确定	50%
09040000	- 特殊功能类化妆品	件	另行确定	50%
10000000	家用医疗、保健及美容器材			
10010000	- 家用医疗器材			
10010100	- - 血糖计	个	500	10%
10010200	- - 血糖试纸	张	5	10%
10010300	- - 红外线耳探热针	个	200	10%
10010400	- - 家用雾化机	台	2000	10%
10010500	- - 血压计	个	500	10%
10019900	- - 其他家用医疗器材	件	另行确定	10%
10020000	- 家用保健器材			
10020100	- - 按摩床	张	10000	10%
10020200	- - 按摩椅	张	5000	10%
10029900	- - 其他家用保健器材	件	另行确定	10%
10030000	- 家用美容器材			
10030100	- - 蒸汽仪	台	200	10%
10030200	- - 喷雾器	台	400	10%
10039900	- - 其他家用美容器材	台	另行确定	10%
11000000	厨卫用具及小家电			
11010000	- 厨房用具			
11010100	- - 餐具/刀具	个、把	20	10%
11010200	- - 炊具	件	100	10%
11010300	- - 灶具	件	1000	10%
11010400	- - 净水器（含过滤芯）	个	500	10%
11010500	- - 净水器过滤芯	个	200	10%
11011100	- - 电饭煲	个	500	20%
11011200	- - 微波炉	台	600	20%
11011300	- - 电磁炉	台	800	20%
11011400	- - 抽油烟机	台	1000	20%
11011500	- - 家用洗碗机	台	1500	20%
11011600	- - 电动榨汁机	台	100	20%
11011700	- - 咖啡机	台	4000	20%
11019900	- - 其他厨房用具			
11019910	- - - 其他厨房非电动用具	件、个	另行确定	10%
11019990	- - - 其他厨房小电器	台	另行确定	20%
11020000	- 卫生用具、洁具			
11020100	- - 卫生间非电动用具	件	另行确定	10%
11021100	- - 卫生间小电器			
11021110	- - - 电热水器	台	1000	20%
11021120	- - - 电吹风机	个	200	20%
11021130	- - - 电动剃须刀	个	200	20%
11021140	- - - 电动牙刷	个	200	20%
11021190	- - - 其他卫生间小电器	台	另行确定	20%
11030000	- 小家电			

税号	品名及规格	单位	完税价格（人民币：元）	税率
11030100	－－电话机			
11030110	－－－普通电话机	台	200	10%
11030120	－－－手持移动电话机	台		
11030121	－－－－键盘式手持移动电话机	台	1000	10%
11030122	－－－－触屏式手持移动电话机	台	另行确定	10%
11030130	－－－电话传真机	台	1000	10%
11030140	－－－可视电话机	台	1000	10%
11030150	－－－电话机配件、附件	件	另行确定	10%
11030190	－－－其他电话机	台	另行确定	10%
11030200	－－游戏机			
11030210	－－－便携式游戏机	台	1000	10%
11030220	－－－游戏机配件、附件			
11030221	－－－－游戏碟、盘、卡	张、个	60	10%
11030222	－－－－游戏机遥控器、控制器	个	200	10%
11030229	－－－－其他游戏机配件、附件	件	另行确定	10%
11030290	－－－其他游戏机	台	另行确定	10%
11030300	－－手动缝纫机、编织机	台	400	10%
11031100	－－便携式复印机	台	1500	20%
11031200	－－电风扇	台	400	20%
11031300	－－电熨斗	台	200	20%
11031400	－－电暖器	台	400	20%
11031500	－－增/除湿机、增除湿一体机	台	1500	20%
11031600	－－空气清新机	台	1000	20%
11031700	－－吸尘器	台	500	20%
11031800	－－地板打蜡机	台	500	20%
11031900	－－电动剪草机	台	2000	20%
11032000	－－电动缝纫机、编织机	台	2000	20%
11032100	－－灯具	台、件	另行确定	20%
11039900	－－其他家庭用具、小家电			
11039910	－－－其他家庭用具	件、个	另行确定	10%
11039990	－－－其他小家电	台	另行确定	20%
12000000	家具			
12010000	－实木家具	件	另行确定	10%
12020000	－皮质家具	件	1000	10%
12030000	－藤、竹质家具	件	600	10%
12990000	－其他家具	件	另行确定	10%
13000000	空调及其配件、附件			
13010000	－空调			
13010100	－－1 匹及以下	台	2000	20%
13010200	－－1 匹以上 2 匹以下（含 2 匹）	台	4000	20%
13010300	－－2 匹以上 3 匹以下（含 3 匹）	台	6000	20%
13010400	－－3 匹以上	台	另行确定	20%
13020000	－空调配件、附件	个	另行确定	20%
13990000	－其他空调	台	另行确定	20%
14000000	电冰箱及其配件、附件			
14010000	－电冰箱、冰柜			
14010100	－－100 公升及以下	台	1000	20%
14010200	－－101～200 公升	台	2000	20%
14010300	－－201～250 公升	台	3000	20%
14010400	－－251～300 公升	台	5000	20%
14010500	－－301～400 公升	台	10000	20%
14010600	－－401～500 公升	台	15000	20%
14010700	－－501 公升及以上	台	另行确定	20%
14020000	－红酒柜			
14020100	－－12 瓶及以下	台	1000	20%
14020200	－－13～18 瓶	台	2000	20%
14020300	－－19～45 瓶	台	3000	20%
14020400	－－46～75 瓶	台	4000	20%
14020500	－－76～120 瓶	台	5000	20%
14020600	－－121 瓶及以上	台	另行确定	20%
14030000	－电冰箱配件、附件	件	另行确定	20%

税号	品名及规格	单位	完税价格（人民币：元）	税率
14990000	－ 其他电冰箱	台	另行确定	20%
15000000	洗衣设备及其配件、附件			
15010000	－ 洗衣机			
15010100	－ － 波轮式	台	1000	20%
15010200	－ － 滚筒式	台	3000	20%
15020000	－ 干衣机/烘干机	台	2000	20%
15030000	－ 洗衣设备配件、附件	件	另行确定	20%
15990000	－ 其他洗衣设备	台	另行确定	20%
16000000	电视机及其配件、附件			
16010000	－ 电视机			
16010100	－ － 22 英寸及以下	台	1000	20%
16010200	－ － 23 英寸至 32 英寸	台	2000	20%
16010300	－ － 33 英寸至 39 英寸	台	4000	20%
16010400	－ － 40 英寸至 42 英寸	台	6000	20%
16010500	－ － 43 英寸至 45 英寸	台	8000	20%
16010600	－ － 46 英寸至 49 英寸	台	10000	20%
16010700	－ － 50 英寸至 54 英寸	台	20000	20%
16010800	－ － 55 英寸至 59 英寸	台	30000	20%
16010900	－ － 60 英寸至 64 英寸	台	35000	20%
16011000	－ － 65 英寸以上	台	另行确定	20%
16020000	－ 电视机配件、附件	件、个	另行确定	20%
16990000	－ 其他电视机	台	另行确定	20%
17000000	摄影（像）设备及其配件、附件			
17010000	－ 照相机			
17010100	－ － 数码照相机			
17010110	－ － － 一体式数码照相机	台	2000	10%
17010120	－ － － 镜头可拆卸式数码照相机			
17010121	－ － － － 可拆卸式数码照相机机身	台	5000	10%
17010122	－ － － － 可拆卸式数码照相机镜头	个	2000	10%
17019900	－ － 其他照相机	台	另行确定	10%
17020000	－ 摄像机			
17020100	－ － 便携式摄录一体机	台	4000	10%
17020200	－ － 电视摄像机	台	另行确定	20%
17030000	－ 摄影（像）设备配件、附件			
17030100	－ － 数码存储卡			
17030110	－ － － 存储容量 8G 及以下	个	50	10%
17030120	－ － － 存储容量 8G 以上	个	200	10%
17030200	－ － 闪光灯	个	500	10%
17030300	－ － 支架	个	300	10%
17030400	－ － 胶卷	个	20	10%
17030500	－ － 数码相框	台	500	10%
17039900	－ － 其他摄影（像）设备配件、附件	件	另行确定	10%
17990000	－ 其他摄影（像）设备	台、件	另行确定	10%
18000000	影音设备及其配件、附件			
18010000	－ 便携式影音设备			
18010100	－ － 录音笔	台	200	20%
18010200	－ － 录音机	台	200	20%
18010300	－ － 收音机	台	200	20%
18010400	－ － MP3 播放器（音频多媒体播放器）	台	100	20%
18010500	－ － MP4 播放器（视频多媒体播放器）	台	500	20%
18019900	－ － 其他便携式影音设备	台	另行确定	20%
18020000	－ 音响设备			
18020100	－ － 电唱机（含便携式激光唱机）	台	500	20%
18020200	－ － 放像机	台	500	20%
18020300	－ － 录像机	台	800	20%
18020400	－ － 激光视盘机（LD、VCD、DVD 等）	台	500	20%
18020500	－ － （单）功能座（功放、调谐、均衡等）	台	1000	20%
18020600	－ － 音箱	个	1000	20%
18020700	－ － 便携式收音、录音、激光唱盘一体机	台	1000	20%
18029900	－ － 其他音响设备	件	另行确定	20%
18030000	－ 影音设备配件、附件			

税号	品名及规格	单位	完税价格（人民币：元）	税率
18030100	－－唱片	张	50	20%
18030200	－－录音带（非教育专用）	盘	10	20%
18030300	－－录像带（非教育专用）	盘	30	20%
18030400	－－激光唱盘（CD）	张	30	20%
18030500	－－激光视盘（LD、VCD、DVD 等）	张	50	20%
18039900	－－其他影音设备配件、附件	个、件	另行确定	20%
18990000	－其他影音设备	个、台	另行确定	20%
19000000	计算机及其外围设备			
19010000	－计算机			
19010100	－－台式个人计算机主机	台	2000	10%
19010200	－－主机、显示器一体机	台	3000	10%
19010300	－－笔记本电脑（含平板电脑、掌上电脑、上网本等）	台		
19010310	－－－键盘式笔记本电脑	台	2000	10%
19010320	－－－触屏式笔记本电脑	台	另行确定	10%
19010400	－－计算机配件			
19010410	－－－主板	块	500	10%
19010420	－－－中央处理器（CPU）	个	500	10%
19010430	－－－内存条			
19010431	－－－－4G 及以下	条	200	10%
19010432	－－－－4G 以上	条	300	10%
19010440	－－－功能卡	块	300	10%
19010490	－－－其他计算机配件	块、个	另行确定	10%
19019900	－－其他计算机	台	另行确定	10%
19020000	－计算机外围设备			
19020100	－－鼠标	个	50	10%
19020200	－－键盘	个	80	10%
19020300	－－音箱	个	50	10%
19020400	－－显示器			
19020410	－－－液晶显示器			
19020411	－－－－19 英寸及以下	台	800	10%
19020412	－－－－19 英寸以上，24 英寸及以下	台	1200	10%
19020413	－－－－24 英寸以上	台	另行确定	10%
19020420	－－－显像管（CRT）显示器			
19020421	－－－－17 英寸及以下	台	300	10%
19020422	－－－－17 英寸以上	台	500	10%
19020490	－－－其他显示器	台	另行确定	10%
19020500	－－打印机			
19020510	－－－激光打印机			
19020511	－－－－黑白激光打印机	台	1000	10%
19020512	－－－－彩色激光打印机	台	3000	10%
19020520	－－－喷墨打印机	台	500	10%
19020530	－－－针式打印机	台	1000	10%
19020540	－－－多功能一体打印机			
19020541	－－－－喷墨多功能一体打印机	台	600	10%
19020542	－－－－激光多功能一体打印机	台	1500	10%
19020590	－－－其他打印机	台	另行确定	10%
19020600	－－扫描仪	台	1000	10%
19020700	－－视频投影仪	台	5000	10%
19020800	－－驱动器			
19020810	－－－CD	台	100	10%
19020820	－－－DVD	台	200	10%
19020890	－－－其他驱动器	台	另行确定	10%
19020900	－－存储器			
19020910	－－－硬盘/移动硬盘			
19020911	－－－－1T 及以下	个	300	10%
19020912	－－－－1T 以上 2T 以下（含 2T）	个	500	10%
19020913	－－－－2T 以上	个	另行确定	10%
19020920	－－－U 盘	个	50	10%
19020990	－－－其他存储器	个、盒	另行确定	10%
19029900	－－其他计算机外围设备	台	另行确定	10%
20000000	书报、刊物及其他各类印刷品		另行确定	10%

税号	品名及规格	单位	完税价格（人民币：元）	税率
21000000	教育专用的电影片、幻灯片、原版录音带、录像带			
21010000	- 幻灯片	片	10	10%
21020000	- 录音带	盘	10	10%
21030000	- 录像带	盘	50	10%
21990000	- 其他教育专用影片、录音、录像带	件	另行确定	10%
22000000	文具用品、玩具			
22010000	- 文具用品			
22010100	- - 电子计算器	个	200	10%
22010200	- - 电子字典/记事簿	个	300	10%
22010300	- - 电子（纸）书	台	800	10%
22010400	- - 笔	支	50	10%
22019900	- - 其他文具用品	件	另行确定	10%
22020000	- 玩具	件	另行确定	10%
23000000	邮票			
23010000	- 中国邮票、小型张、纪念封	张	另行确定	10%
23020000	- 港澳台、外国邮票	张	5	10%
23030000	- 港澳台、外国小型张、纪念封	张	10	10%
24000000	乐器			
24010000	- 钢琴			
24010100	- - 三角钢琴	架	90000	10%
24010200	- - 立式钢琴	架	15000	10%
24010300	- - 电子钢琴	架	5000	10%
24019900	- - 其他钢琴	架	另行确定	10%
24020000	- 电子琴			
24020100	- - 49 键以下	台	800	10%
24020200	- - 49 键及以上	台	3000	10%
24030000	- 萨克斯	把	10000	10%
24040000	- 电子吉他	把	2000	10%
24050000	- 数码小提琴	把	5000	10%
24060000	- 长、短笛	支	5000	10%
24070000	- 单簧管	支	4000	10%
24080000	- 双簧管	支	10000	10%
24090000	- 古筝	架	2000	10%
24990000	- 其他乐器	件	另行确定	10%
25000000	体育用品			
25010000	- 高尔夫球及球具			
25010100	- - 球杆	根	1000	30%
25010200	- - 球	个	20	30%
25019900	- - 其他高尔夫球具	件	另行确定	30%
25020000	- 运动器具			
25020100	- - 网球拍	个	500	10%
25020200	- - 羽毛球拍	个	300	10%
25029900	- - 其他运动器具	件	另行确定	10%
25030000	- 多功能健身器具			
25030100	- - 跑步机	件	2000	10%
25030200	- - 健身车	件	1000	10%
25030300	- - 综合训练器	件	3000	10%
25039900	- - 其他多功能健身器具	件	另行确定	10%
25990000	- 其他体育用品	件	另行确定	10%
26000000	自行车、三轮车、童车及其配件、附件			
26010000	- 自行车	辆	500	20%
26020000	- 三轮车	辆	500	20%
26030000	- 童车	辆	200	20%
26040000	- 自行车、三轮车、童车配件、附件	件	另行确定	20%
27000000	其他物品	件	另行确定	10%

注：对编号 02000000 项下的各类酒，单瓶容量超出 750 毫升的，每满 750 毫升按照 1 瓶计征税赋，超出部分不足 750 毫升的不予计算。

附表六

2014 年进口关税与进口环节代征税（增值税）计税常数表
Table of Import Tariff and Import Tax (Value Added Tax) 2014

关税税率（%）	增值税税率（%）		关税税率（%）	增值税税率（%）		关税税率（%）	增值税税率（%）	
	13	17		13	17		13	17
0	0.1300	0.1700	9.5	0.2374	0.2812	20.0	0.3560	0.4040
1.0	0.1413	0.1817	9.7	0.2396	0.2835	21.0	0.3673	0.4157
1.5	0.1470	0.1876	10.0	0.2430	0.2870	22.0	0.3786	0.4274
2.0	0.1526	0.1934	10.5	0.2487	0.2929	23.0	0.3899	0.4391
3.0	0.1639	0.2051	11.0	0.2543	0.2987	24.0	0.4012	0.4508
4.0	0.1752	0.2168	12.0	0.2656	0.3104	24.5	0.4069	0.4567
4.5	0.1809	0.2227	12.5	0.2713	0.3163	25.0	0.4125	0.4625
5.0	0.1865	0.2285	12.6	0.2724	0.3174	27.0	0.4351	0.4859
5.5	0.1922	0.2344	13.0	0.2769	0.3221	28.0	0.4464	0.4976
5.8	0.1955	0.2379	13.5	0.2826	0.3280	30.0	0.4690	0.5210
6.0	0.1978	0.2402	14.0	0.2882	0.3338	32.0	0.4916	0.5444
6.5	0.2035	0.2461	14.4	0.2927	0.3385	35.0	0.5255	0.5795
7.0	0.2091	0.2519	15.0	0.2995	0.3455	38.0	0.5594	0.6146
7.5	0.2148	0.2578	16.0	0.3108	0.3572	40.0	0.5820	0.6380
8.0	0.2204	0.2636	17.0	0.3221	0.3689	45.0	0.6385	0.6965
8.4	0.2249	0.2683	17.5	0.3278	0.3748	50.0	0.6950	0.7550
8.5	0.2261	0.2695	18.0	0.3334	0.3806	57.0	0.7741	0.8369
9.0	0.2317	0.2753	19.0	0.3447	0.3923	65.0	0.8645	0.9305

注：

常数=进口关税税率+增值税税率+进口关税税率×增值税税率

附表七

关税配额商品进口税率表
Tariff Quota Rate on Import Goods

商品类别	税则号列	普通税率（%）	最惠国税率（%）	关税配额税率（%）	国别关税配额税率（中国-新西兰自贸区）（%）
小麦	10011100	180	65	1	
	10011900	180	65	1	
	10019100	180	65	1	
	10019900	180	65	1	
	11010000	130	65	6	
	11031100	130	65	9	
	11032010	130	65	10	
玉米	10051000	180	20	1	
	10059000	180	65	1	
	11022000	130	40	9	
	11031300	130	65	9	
	11042300	180	65	10	
稻谷和大米	10061011	180	65	1	
	10061019	180	65	1	

	10061091	180	65	1	
	10061099	180	65	1	
	10062010	180	65	1	
	10062090	180	65	1	
	10063010	180	65	1	
	10063090	180	65	1	
	10064010	180	65	1	
	10064090	180	65	1	
	11029011	130	40	9	
	11029019	130	40	9	
	11031921	70	10	9	
	11031929	70	10	9	
糖	17011200	125	50	15	
	17011300	125	50	15	
	17011400	125	50	15	
	17019100	125	50	15	
	17019910	125	50	15	
	17019920	125	50	15	
	17019990	125	50	15	
羊毛	51011100	50	38	1	0
	51011900	50	38	1	0
	51012100	50	38	1	0
	51012900	50	38	1	0
	51013000	50	38	1	0
	51031010	50	38	1	0
毛条	51051000	50	38	3	0
	51052100	50	38	3	0
	51052900	50	38	3	0
棉花	52010000	125	40[注 1]	1	
	52030000	125	40	1	
化肥	31021000	150	50	4[注 2]	
	31052000	150	50	4[注 3]	
	31053000	150	50	4[注 4]	

[注1]：对配额外进口的一定数量棉花，适用滑准税形式暂定关税，具体方式如下：

1. 当进口棉花完税价格高于或等于15.000元/千克时，暂定从量税率为0.570元/千克；

2. 当进口棉花完税价格低于15.000元/千克时，暂定从价税率按下式计算：

$$Ri=9.337/Pi +2.77\%\times Pi -1 \quad (Ri<=40\%)$$

其中：Ri-暂定从价税率，对上式计算结果小数点后第4位四舍五入保留前3位；

Pi-关税完税价格，单位为元/千克。

[注2、3、4]：暂定税率为1%。

附表八

2014 年进口关税与进口环节代征税（消费税及增值税）计税常数表

Table of Import Tariff and Import Tax (Consumption Tax & Value Added Tax) 2014

关税税率（%）	消费税税率（%）											
	1	3	5	9	10	12	15	20	25	30	36	40
0	0.1818	0.2062	0.2316	0.2857	0.3000	0.3295	0.3765	0.4625	0.5600	0.6714	0.8281	0.9500
1.0	0.1936	0.2182	0.2439	0.2986	0.3130	0.3428	0.3902	0.4771	0.5756	0.6881	0.8464	0.9695
1.5	0.1995	0.2243	0.2501	0.3050	0.3195	0.3495	0.3971	0.4844	0.5834	0.6965	0.8555	0.9793

关税税率（%）	消费税税率（%）											
	1	3	5	9	10	12	15	20	25	30	36	40
2.0	0.2055	0.2303	0.2562	0.3114	0.3260	0.3561	0.4040	0.4918	0.5912	0.7049	0.8647	0.9890
3.0	0.2173	0.2424	0.2685	0.3243	0.3390	0.3694	0.4178	0.5064	0.6068	0.7216	0.8830	1.0085
4.0	0.2291	0.2544	0.2808	0.3371	0.3520	0.3827	0.4315	0.5210	0.6224	0.7383	0.9013	1.0280
4.5	0.2350	0.2605	0.2870	0.3436	0.3585	0.3894	0.4384	0.5283	0.6302	0.7466	0.9104	1.0378
5.0	0.2409	0.2665	0.2932	0.3500	0.3650	0.3960	0.4453	0.5356	0.6380	0.7550	0.9195	1.0475
5.5	0.2468	0.2725	0.2993	0.3564	0.3715	0.4027	0.4522	0.5429	0.6458	0.7634	0.9287	1.0573
5.8	0.2504	0.2761	0.3030	0.3603	0.3754	0.4067	0.4563	0.5473	0.6505	0.7684	0.9342	1.0631
6.0	0.2527	0.2786	0.3055	0.3629	0.3780	0.4093	0.4591	0.5503	0.6536	0.7717	0.9378	1.0670
6.5	0.2586	0.2846	0.3116	0.3693	0.3845	0.4160	0.4659	0.5576	0.6614	0.7801	0.9470	1.0768
7.0	0.2645	0.2906	0.3178	0.3757	0.3910	0.4226	0.4728	0.5649	0.6692	0.7884	0.9561	1.0865
7.5	0.2705	0.2966	0.3239	0.3821	0.3975	0.4293	0.4797	0.5722	0.6770	0.7968	0.9652	1.0963
8.0	0.2764	0.3027	0.3301	0.3886	0.4040	0.4359	0.4866	0.5795	0.6848	0.8051	0.9744	1.1060
8.4	0.2811	0.3075	0.3350	0.3937	0.4092	0.4412	0.4921	0.5854	0.6910	0.8118	0.9817	1.1138
8.5	0.2823	0.3087	0.3363	0.3950	0.4105	0.4426	0.4935	0.5868	0.6926	0.8135	0.9835	1.1158
9.0	0.2882	0.3147	0.3424	0.4014	0.4170	0.4492	0.5004	0.5941	0.7004	0.8219	0.9927	1.1255
9.5	0.2941	0.3208	0.3486	0.4079	0.4235	0.4559	0.5072	0.6014	0.7082	0.8302	1.0018	1.1353
9.7	0.2965	0.3232	0.3510	0.4104	0.4261	0.4585	0.5100	0.6044	0.7113	0.8336	1.0055	1.1392
10.0	0.3000	0.3268	0.3547	0.4143	0.4300	0.4625	0.5141	0.6088	0.7160	0.8386	1.0109	1.1450
10.5	0.3059	0.3328	0.3609	0.4207	0.4365	0.4692	0.5210	0.6161	0.7238	0.8469	1.0201	1.1548
11.0	0.3118	0.3389	0.3671	0.4271	0.4430	0.4758	0.5279	0.6234	0.7316	0.8553	1.0292	1.1645
12.0	0.3236	0.3509	0.3794	0.4400	0.4560	0.4891	0.5416	0.6380	0.7472	0.8720	1.0475	1.1840
12.5	0.3295	0.3570	0.3855	0.4464	0.4625	0.4957	0.5485	0.6453	0.7550	0.8804	1.0566	1.1938
12.6	0.3307	0.3582	0.3868	0.4477	0.4638	0.4971	0.5499	0.6468	0.7566	0.8820	1.0585	1.1957
13.0	0.3355	0.3630	0.3917	0.4529	0.4690	0.5024	0.5554	0.6526	0.7628	0.8887	1.0658	1.2035
13.5	0.3414	0.3690	0.3978	0.4593	0.4755	0.5090	0.5623	0.6599	0.7706	0.8971	1.0749	1.2133
14.0	0.3473	0.3751	0.4040	0.4657	0.4820	0.5157	0.5692	0.6673	0.7784	0.9054	1.0841	1.2230
14.4	0.3520	0.3799	0.4089	0.4709	0.4872	0.5210	0.5747	0.6731	0.7846	0.9121	1.0914	1.2308
15.0	0.3591	0.3871	0.4163	0.4786	0.4950	0.5290	0.5829	0.6819	0.7940	0.9221	1.1023	1.2425
16.0	0.3709	0.3992	0.4286	0.4914	0.5080	0.5423	0.5967	0.6965	0.8096	0.9389	1.1206	1.2620
17.0	0.3827	0.4112	0.4409	0.5043	0.5210	0.5556	0.6105	0.7111	0.8252	0.9556	1.1389	1.2815
17.5	0.3886	0.4173	0.4471	0.5107	0.5275	0.5622	0.6174	0.7184	0.8330	0.9639	1.1480	1.2913
18.0	0.3945	0.4233	0.4533	0.5171	0.5340	0.5689	0.6242	0.7258	0.8408	0.9723	1.1572	1.3010
19.0	0.4064	0.4354	0.4656	0.5300	0.5470	0.5822	0.6380	0.7404	0.8564	0.9890	1.1755	1.3205
20.0	0.4182	0.4474	0.4779	0.5429	0.5600	0.5955	0.6518	0.7550	0.8720	1.0057	1.1938	1.3400
21.0	0.4300	0.4595	0.4902	0.5557	0.5730	0.6088	0.6655	0.7696	0.8876	1.0224	1.2120	1.3595
22.0	0.4418	0.4715	0.5025	0.5686	0.5860	0.6220	0.6793	0.7843	0.9032	1.0391	1.2303	1.3790
23.0	0.4536	0.4836	0.5148	0.5814	0.5990	0.6353	0.6931	0.7989	0.9188	1.0559	1.2486	1.3985
24.0	0.4655	0.4957	0.5272	0.5943	0.6120	0.6486	0.7068	0.8135	0.9344	1.0726	1.2669	1.4180
24.5	0.4714	0.5017	0.5333	0.6007	0.6185	0.6553	0.7137	0.8208	0.9422	1.0809	1.2760	1.4278
25.0	0.4773	0.5077	0.5395	0.6071	0.6250	0.6619	0.7206	0.8281	0.9500	1.0893	1.2852	1.4375
27.0	0.5009	0.5319	0.5641	0.6329	0.6510	0.6885	0.7481	0.8574	0.9812	1.1227	1.3217	1.4765
28.0	0.5127	0.5439	0.5764	0.6457	0.6640	0.7018	0.7619	0.8720	0.9968	1.1394	1.3400	1.4960
30.0	0.5364	0.5680	0.6011	0.6714	0.6900	0.7284	0.7894	0.9013	1.0280	1.1729	1.3766	1.5350
32.0	0.5600	0.5922	0.6257	0.6971	0.7160	0.7550	0.8169	0.9305	1.0592	1.2063	1.4131	1.5740
35.0	0.5955	0.6284	0.6626	0.7357	0.7550	0.7949	0.8582	0.9744	1.1060	1.2564	1.4680	1.6325
38.0	0.6309	0.6645	0.6996	0.7743	0.7940	0.8348	0.8995	1.0183	1.1528	1.3066	1.5228	1.6910
40.0	0.6545	0.6887	0.7242	0.8000	0.8200	0.8614	0.9271	1.0475	1.1840	1.3400	1.5594	1.7300
45.0	0.7136	0.7490	0.7858	0.8643	0.8850	0.9278	0.9959	1.1206	1.2620	1.4236	1.6508	1.8275
50.0	0.7727	0.8093	0.8474	0.9286	0.9500	0.9943	1.0647	1.1938	1.3400	1.5071	1.7422	1.9250
57.0	0.8555	0.8937	0.9336	1.0186	1.0410	1.0374	1.1611	1.2961	1.4492	1.6241	1.8702	2.0615
65.0	0.9500	0.9902	1.0321	1.1214	1.1450	1.1938	1.2712	1.4131	1.5740	1.7579	2.0164	2.2175

注：

1. 鉴于应征消费税的进口商品的法定增值税税率均为 17%，故本表省略了增值税税率一栏，但所列常数均已包括增值税在内。
2. 常数计算公式为：
   常数=（进口关税税率+消费税税率+增值税税率+进口关税税率×增值税税率）÷（1-消费税税率）

附表九

2014 年进口商品协定税率表
Conventional Tariff Rates on Import Goods 2014

税则号列	商品名称（简称）	最惠国	东盟										亚太	智利	巴基斯坦	新加坡	新西兰	秘鲁	哥斯达黎加	香港	澳门	台湾
			文	柬	印	老	马	缅	菲	新	泰	越										
01012900	其他马	10	0	0	0	0	0	0	0	0	0	0		1	5		0	5	0			
01013090	其他驴	10	0	0	0	0	0	0	0	0	0	0		1	5		0	5	0			
01019000	骡	10	0	0	0	0	0	0	0	0	0	0		1	5		0	5	0			
01022900	其他家牛	10	0	0	0	0	0	0	0	0	0	0		1	5		0	5	0			
01023900	其他水牛	10	0	0	0	0	0	0	0	0	0	0		1	5		0	5	0			
01029090	其他牛	10	0	0	0	0	0	0	0	0	0	0		1	5		0	5	0			
01039110	重量<10kg 的猪	10	0	0	0	0	0	0	0	0	0	0		0	5		0	0	0			
01039120	重量在 10-50kg 的猪，包括 10kg	10	0	0	0	0	0	0	0	0	0	0		0	5		0	0	0			
01039200	重量≥50kg 的猪	10	0	0	0	0	0	0	0	0	0	0		0	5		0	0	0			
01041090	其他绵羊	10	0	0	0	0	0	0	0	0	0	0		0	5		0	0	0			
01042090	其他山羊	10	0	0	0	0	0	0	0	0	0	0		0	5		0	0	0			
01051190	重量≤185g 的其他鸡	10	0	0	0	0	0	0	0	0	0	0		1	5		0	5	0			
01051290	重量≤185g 的其他火鸡	10	0	0	0	0	0	0	0	0	0	0		1	5		0	5	0			
01051390	重量不超过 185 克的其他鸭	10	0	0	0	0	0	0	0	0	0	0		0	5		0	0	0			
01051490	重量不超过 185 克的其他鹅	10	0	0	0	0	0	0	0	0	0	0		0	5		0	0	0			
01051590	重量不超过 185 克的其他珍珠鸡	10	0	0	0	0	0	0	0	0	0	0		0	5		0	0	0			
01059490	重量>185g 的其他鸡	10	0	0	0	0	0	0	0	0	0	0		0	5		0	0	0			
01059991	重量>185g 的非改良种用鸭	10	0	0	0	0	0	0	0	0	0	0		0	5		0	0	0			
01059992	重量>185g 的非改良种用鹅	10	0	0	0	0	0	0	0	0	0	0		0	5		0	0	0			
01059993	重量>185g 的非改良种用珍珠鸡	10	0	0	0	0	0	0	0	0	0	0		0	5		0	0	0			
01059994	重量>185g 的非改良种用火鸡	10	0	0	0	0	0	0	0	0	0	0		0	5		0	0	0			
01061190	其他灵长目动物	10	0	0	0	0	0	0	0	0	0	0		0	5		0	0	0			
01061211	改良种用鲸、海豚及鼠海豚；海牛及儒艮	10	0	0	0	0	0	0	0	0	0	0		0	5		0	0	0			
01061219	其他鲸、海豚及鼠海豚；海牛及儒艮	10	0	0	0	0	0	0	0	0	0	0		0	5		0	0	0			
01061229	其他海豹、海狮及海象	10	0	0	0	0	0	0	0	0	0	0		1	5		0	5	0			
01061390	其他骆驼及其他骆驼科动物	10	0	0	0	0	0	0	0	0	0	0		1	5		0	5	0			
01061490	其他家兔及野兔	10	0	0	0	0	0	0	0	0	0	0		1	5		0	5	0			
01061990	其他哺乳动物	10	0	0	0	0	0	0	0	0	0	0		1	5		0	5	0			
01062020	食用爬行动物	10	0	0	0	0	0	0	0	0	0	0		0	5		0	0	0			
01062090	其他爬行动物	10	0	0	0	0	0	0	0	0	0	0		0	5		0	0	0			
01063190	其他猛禽	10	0	0	0	0	0	0	0	0	0	0		0	5		0	0	0			
01063290	其他鹦形目鸟	10	0	0	0	0	0	0	0	0	0	0		0	5		0	0	0			
01063390	其他鸵鸟；鸸鹋	10	0	0	0	0	0	0	0	0	0	0		0	5		0	0	0			
01063921	乳鸽	10	0	0	0	0	0	0	0	0	0	0		0	5		0	0	0			
01063923	野鸭	10	0	0	0	0	0	0	0	0	0	0		0	5		0	0	0			
01063929	其他食用鸟	10	0	0	0	0	0	0	0	0	0	0		0	5		0	0	0			
01063990	其他鸟	10	0	0	0	0	0	0	0	0	0	0		0	5		0	0	0			
01064190	其他蜂	10	0	0	0	0	0	0	0	0	0	0	9	1	5		0	5	0			
01064990	其他昆虫	10	0	0	0	0	0	0	0	0	0	0	9	1	5		0	5	0			
01069090	其他动物	10	0	0	0	0	0	0	0	0	0	0	9	1	5		0	5	0			
02011000	整头及半头鲜、冷牛肉	20	0	0	0	0	0	0	0	0	0	0		0			4.4	13.3	14.7			
02012000	鲜、冷的带骨牛肉	12	0	0	0	0	0	0	0	0	0	0		1.2	6		2.7	8.5	8.8			
02013000	鲜、冷的去骨牛肉	12	0	0	0	0	0	0	0	0	0	0		1.2	6		2.7	8.5	8.8			
02021000	冻的整头及半头牛肉	25	0	0	0	0	0	0	0	0	0	0		0			5.6	16.7	5			
02022000	冻的带骨牛肉	12	0	0	0	0	0	0	0	0	0	0		1.2	6		2.7	8.5	2.4			
02023000	冻的去骨牛肉	12	0	0	0	0	0	0	0	0	0	0		1.2	6		2.7	8.5	2.4			
02031110	鲜、冷的整头及半头乳猪肉	20	0	0	0	0	0	0	0	0	0	0		0			0	10	4			
02031190	其他鲜、冷的整头及半头猪肉	20	0	0	0	0	0	0	0	0	0	0		0			0	0	4			
02031200	鲜、冷的带骨猪前腿、后腿及其肉块	20	0	0	0	0	0	0	0	0	0	0		2			0	10	4			
02031900	其他鲜、冷猪肉	20	0	0	0	0	0	0	0	0	0	0		0			0	0	4			
02032110	冻整头及半头乳猪肉	12	0	0	0	0	0	0	0	0	0	0		1.2	6		0	6	2.4			
02032190	其他冻整头及半头猪肉	12	0	0	0	0	0	0	0	0	0	0		1.2	6		0	6	2.4			

税则号列	商品名称（简称）	最惠国	东盟 文	柬	印	老	马	缅	菲	新	泰	越	亚太	智利	巴基斯坦	新加坡	新西兰	秘鲁	哥斯达黎加	香港	澳门	台湾
02032200	冻的带骨猪前腿、后腿及其肉块	12	0	0	0	0	0	0	0	0	0	0		0	6		0	0	2.4			
02032900	其他冻猪肉	12	0	0	0	0	0	0	0	0	0	0		0	6		0	8	2.4			
02041000	鲜或冷的整头及半头羔羊	15	0	0	0	0	0	0	0	0	0	0		0	12		3.3	10	11			
02042100	鲜或冷的整头及半头绵羊肉	23	0	0	0	0	0	0	0	0	0	0		0			5.1	15.3	16.9			
02042200	鲜或冷的带骨绵羊肉	15	0	0	0	0	0	0	0	0	0	0		0	12		3.3	10	11			
02042300	鲜或冷的去骨绵羊肉	15	0	0	0	0	0	0	0	0	0	0		0	12		3.3	8.8	11			
02043000	冻的整头及半头羔羊	15	0	0	0	0	0	0	0	0	0	0		1.5	12		3.3	10.6	11			
02044100	冻的整头及半头绵羊肉	23	0	0	0	0	0	0	0	0	0	0		2.3			5.1	16.2	16.9			
02044200	冻的其他带骨绵羊肉	12	0	0	0	0	0	0	0	0	0	0		1.2	6		2.7	8.5	8.8			
02044300	冻的其他去骨绵羊肉	15	0	0	0	0	0	0	0	0	0	0		1.5	12		3.3	10.6	11			
02045000	鲜、冷、冻的山羊肉	20	0	0	0	0	0	0	0	0	0	0		0			4.4	11.7	14.7			
02050000	鲜、冷、冻的马、驴、骡肉	20	0	0	0	0	0	0	0	0	0	0		0			0	10	4			
02061000	鲜、冷的牛杂碎	12	0	0	0	0	0	0	0	0	0	0		0	6		2.7	7	2.4			
02062100	冻牛舌	12	0	0	0	0	0	0	0	0	0	0		1.2	6		0	6	2.4			
02062200	冻牛肝	12	0	0	0	0	0	0	0	0	0	0		0	6		0	0	2.4			
02062900	其他冻牛杂碎	12	0	0	0	0	0	0	0	0	0	0		1.2	6		0	6	2.4			
02063000	鲜、冷的猪杂碎	20	0	0	0	0	0	0	0	0	0	0		0			0	10	4			
02064100	冻猪肝	20	0	0	0	0	0	0	0	0	0	0		0			0	10	4			
02064900	其他冻猪杂碎	12	0	0	0	0	0	0	0	0	0	0		1.2	6		0	6	2.4			
02068000	鲜、冷的羊、马、驴、骡杂碎	20	0	0	0	0	0	0	0	0	0	0		0			4.4	11.7	4			
02069000	冻的羊、马、驴、骡杂碎	18	0	0	0	0	0	0	0	0	0	0		1.8	14.4		4	12.7	3.6			
02071100	整只，鲜或冷的鸡	20	0	0	0	0	0	0	0	0	0	0		0			0	0	4			
02071200	整只，冻的鸡	20	0		0	0	0	0	0	0	0	0		0.13元/千克			0	10	4			
02071311	鲜或冷的带骨鸡块	20	0	0	0	0	0	0	0	0	0	0		0			0	0	4			
02071319	鲜或冷的其他鸡块	20	0	0	0	0	0	0	0	0	0	0		0			0	0	4			
02071321	鲜或冷的鸡翼（不包括翼尖）	20	0	0	0	0	0	0	0	0	0	0		0			0	0	4			
02071329	鲜或冷的其他鸡杂碎	20	0	0	0	0	0	0	0	0	0	0		0			0	0	4			
02071411	冻的的带骨鸡块	10	0		0	0	0	0	0	0	0	0		0	0.3元/千克		0	0	0			
02071419	冻的其他鸡块	10	0		0	0	0	0	0	0	0	0		0.07元/千克	0.35元/千克		0	5	0			
02071421	冻的鸡翼（不包括翼尖）	10	0		0	0	0	0	0	0	0	0		0	0.4元/千克		0	0	0			
02071422	鲜、冷、冻鸡爪	10	0		0	0	0	0	0	0	0	0		0.1元/千克	0.25元/千克		0	5	0			
02071429	冻的其他鸡杂碎	10	0		0	0	0	0	0	0	0	0		0.05元/千克	0.25元/千克		0	5	0			
02072400	整只，鲜或冷的火鸡	20	0	0	0	0	0	0	0	0	0	0		0			0	0	4			
02072500	整只，冻的火鸡	20	0	0	0	0	0	0	0	0	0	0		2			0	10	4			
02072600	鲜或冷的火鸡块及杂碎	20	0	0	0	0	0	0	0	0	0	0		0			0	0	4			
02072700	冻的火鸡块及杂碎	10	0	0	0	0	0	0	0	0	0	0		1	5		0	5	0			
02074100	鲜或冷的整只鸭	20	0	0	0	0	0	0	0	0	0	0		0			0	10	4			
02074200	冻的整只鸭	20	0	0	0	0	0	0	0	0	0	0		0			0	10	4			
02074300	鲜或冷的鸭肥肝	20	0	0	0	0	0	0	0	0	0	0		0			0	10	4			
02074400	鲜或冷的其他鸭	20	0	0	0	0	0	0	0	0	0	0		0			0	10	4			
02074500	冻的其他鸭	20	0	0	0	0	0	0	0	0	0	0		0			0	10	4			
02075100	鲜或冷的整只鹅	20	0	0	0	0	0	0	0	0	0	0		0			0	10	4			
02075200	冻的整只鹅	20	0	0	0	0	0	0	0	0	0	0		0			0	10	4			
02075300	鲜或冷的鹅肥肝	20	0	0	0	0	0	0	0	0	0	0		0			0	10	4			
02075400	鲜或冷的其他鹅	20	0	0	0	0	0	0	0	0	0	0		0			0	10	4			
02075500	冻的其他鹅	20	0	0	0	0	0	0	0	0	0	0		0			0	10	4			
02076000	鲜、冷、冻珍珠鸡	20	0	0	0	0	0	0	0	0	0	0		0			0	10	4			
02081010	鲜或冷藏的家兔肉或野兔，不包括兔头	20	0	0	0	0	0	0	0	0	0	0		2			0	10	4			
02081020	冻家兔或野兔，不包括兔头	20	0	0	0	0	0	0	0	0	0	0		2			0	10	4			
02081090	鲜、冷、冻的家兔及野兔食用杂碎	20	0	0	0	0	0	0	0	0	0	0		2			0	10	4			
02083000	鲜、冷、冻的灵长目动物的肉及其食用杂碎	23	0	0	0	0	0	0	0	0	0	0		0			0	11.5	4.6			
02084000	鲜、冷、冻鲸、海豚及鼠海豚；鲜、冷、冻海牛及儒艮；鲜、冷、冻海豹、海狮及海象	23	0	0	0	0	0	0	0	0	0	0		0			0	11.5	4.6			

税则号列	商品名称（简称）	最惠国	东盟 文	东盟 柬	东盟 印	东盟 老	东盟 马	东盟 缅	东盟 菲	东盟 新	东盟 泰	东盟 越	亚太	智利	巴基斯坦	新加坡	新西兰	秘鲁	哥斯达黎加	香港	澳门	台湾
02085000	鲜、冷、冻的爬行动物的肉及其食用杂碎	23	0	0	0	0	0	0	0	0	0	0		0			0	11.5	4.6			
02086000	鲜、冷、冻骆驼及其他骆驼科动物	23	0	0	0	0	0	0	0	0	0	0		0			0	11.5	4.6			
02089010	鲜、冷、冻的乳鸽肉及其食用杂碎	20	0	0	0	0	0	0	0	0	0	0		2			0	10	4			
02089090	其他鲜、冷、冻肉及食用杂碎	23	0	0	0	0	0	0	0	0	0	0		0			0	11.5	4.6			
02091000	未炼制猪脂肪	20	0	0	0	0	0	0	0	0	0	0		2			0	10	4			
02099000	未炼制家禽脂肪	20	0	0	0	0	0	0	0	0	0	0		2			0	10	4			
02101110	干、熏、盐制的带骨猪腿	25	0	0	0	0	0	0	0	0	0	0		0			0	0	5			
02101190	干、熏、盐制的带骨猪腿肉块	25	0	0	0	0	0	0	0	0	0	0		0			0	0	5			
02101200	干、熏、盐制的猪腹肉	25	0	0	0	0	0	0	0	0	0	0		0			0	0	5			
02101900	干、熏、盐制的其他猪肉	25	0	0	0	0	0	0	0	0	0	0		2.5			0	12.5	5			
02102000	干、熏、盐制的牛肉	25	0	0	0	0	0	0	0	0	0	0		0			0	12.5	5			
02109100	干、熏、盐制的灵长目动物肉及食用杂碎	25	0	0	0	0	0	0	0	0	0	0		0			0	12.5	5			
02109200	鲸、海豚及鼠海豚的；海牛及儒艮的；海豹、海狮及海象的肉及食用杂碎	25	0	0	0	0	0	0	0	0	0	0		0			0	12.5	5			
02109300	干、熏、盐制的爬行动物肉及食用杂碎	25	0	0	0	0	0	0	0	0	0	0		0			0	12.5	5			
02109900	干、熏、盐制的其他肉及食用杂碎	25	0	0	0	0	0	0	0	0	0	0		2.5			0	12.5	5			
03011100	淡水观赏鱼	17.5	0	0	0	0	0	0	0	0	0	0		0	14		0	0	10.5	0		
03011900	其他观赏鱼	17.5	0	0	0	0	0	0	0	0	0	0		0	14		0	0	10.5	0		
03019190	其他活鳟鱼	10.5	0	0	0	0	0	0	0	0	0	0	8	0	5		0	0	6.3			
03019290	其他活鳗鱼	10	0	0	0	0	0	0	0	0	0	0	6.7	0	5		0	0	6			
03019390	其他鲤科鱼	10.5	0	0	0	0	0	0	0	0	0	0	8	0	5		0	0	6.3			
03019491	大西洋蓝鳍金枪鱼	10.5	0	0	0	0	0	0	0	0	0	0	8	1.1	5		0	0	6.3	0		
03019492	太平洋蓝鳍金枪鱼	10.5	0	0	0	0	0	0	0	0	0	0	8	1.1	5		0	5.3	6.3	0		0
03019590	其他活南方蓝鳍金枪鱼	10.5	0	0	0	0	0	0	0	0	0	0	8	1.1	5		0	0	6.3	0		
03019991	活罗非鱼	10.5	0	0	0	0	0	0	0	0	0	0		1.1	5		0	5.3	6.3	0		
03019992	活鲀	10.5	0	0	0	0	0	0	0	0	0	0	8	1.1	5		0	0	6.3	0		
03019993	其他鲤科鱼	10.5	0	0	0	0	0	0	0	0	0	0	8	0	5		0	0	6.3			
03019999	其他活鱼	10.5	0	0	0	0	0	0	0	0	0	0	8	1.1	5		0	5.3	6.3	0		0
03021100	鲜、冷鳟鱼	12	0	0	0	0	0	0	0	0	0	0		1.2	6		0	6	7.2			
03021300	鲜、冷大麻哈鱼	10	0	0	0	0	0	0	0	0	0	0		1	5		0	5	6			
03021410	鲜、冷大西洋鲑鱼	10	0	0	0	0	0	0	0	0	0	0		1	5		0	5	6			
03021420	鲜、冷多瑙哲罗鱼	10	0	0	0	0	0	0	0	0	0	0		1	5		0	5	6			
03021900	其他鲜、冷鲑鱼	12	0	0	0	0	0	0	0	0	0	0	8	0	5		0	0	7.2			
03022100	鲜、冷庸鲽鱼	12	0	0	0	0	0	0	0	0	0	0	9	0	5		0	0	7.2			
03022200	鲜、冷鲽鱼	12	0	0	0	0	0	0	0	0	0	0	9	0	5		0	0	7.2			
03022300	鲜、冷鳎鱼	12	0	0	0	0	0	0	0	0	0	0	9	0	5		0	0	7.2			
03022400	鲜、冷大菱鲆	12	0	0	0	0	0	0	0	0	0	0	6	1.2	5		0	6	7.2			
03022900	其他鲜、冷比目鱼	12	0	0	0	0	0	0	0	0	0	0	6	1.2	5		0	6	7.2			
03023100	鲜、冷长鳍金枪鱼	12	0	0	0	0	0	0	0	0	0	0	9	1.2	5		0	6	7.2			
03023200	鲜、冷黄鳍金枪鱼	12	0	0	0	0	0	0	0	0	0	0	9	0	5		0	0	7.2	0		
03023300	鲜、冷鲣鱼或狐鲣	12	0	0	0	0	0	0	0	0	0	0	8	0	5		0	0	7.2			
03023400	鲜、冷大眼金枪鱼	12	0	0	0	0	0	0	0	0	0	0		0	6		0	0	7.2			
03023510	鲜、冷大西洋蓝鳍金枪鱼	12	0	0	0	0	0	0	0	0	0	0		0	6		0	0	7.2			
03023520	鲜、冷太平洋蓝鳍金枪鱼	12	0	0	0	0	0	0	0	0	0	0	8	0	5		0	0	7.2			
03023600	鲜、冷南方蓝鳍金枪鱼	12	0	0	0	0	0	0	0	0	0	0		0	6		0	0	7.2			
03023900	其他鲜、冷金枪鱼	12	0	0	0	0	0	0	0	0	0	0	8	0	5		0	0	7.2			
03024100	鲜、冷鲱鱼（大西洋鲱鱼、太平洋鲱鱼）	12	0	0	0	0	0	0	0	0	0	0	8	0	5		0	0	7.2			
03024200	鲜、冷鳀鱼	12	0	0	0	0	0	0	0	0	0	0	8	1.2	5		0	0	7.2	0		0
03024300	鲜、冷沙丁鱼（沙丁鱼、沙瑙鱼属）、小沙丁鱼属、黍鲱或西鲱	12	0	0	0	0	0	0	0	0	0	0	8	0	5		0	0	7.2			
03024400	鲜、冷鲭鱼	12	0	0	0	0	0	0	0	0	0	0	8	0	5		0	0	7.2			
03024500	鲜、冷对称竹荚鱼、新西兰竹荚鱼及竹荚鱼	12	0	0	0	0	0	0	0	0	0	0	8	1.2	5		0	0	7.2	0		0
03024600	鲜、冷军曹鱼	12	0	0	0	0	0	0	0	0	0	0	8	1.2	5		0	0	7.2	0		0
03024700	鲜、冷剑鱼	12	0	0	0	0	0	0	0	0	0	0	8	1.2	5		0	0	7.2	0		
03025100	鳕鱼（大西洋鳕鱼、格陵兰鳕鱼、太平洋鳕鱼）	12	0	0	0	0	0	0	0	0	0	0	8	0	5		0	0	7.2			
03025200	鲜、冷黑线鳕鱼	12	0	0	0	0	0	0	0	0	0	0	8	0	5		0	0	7.2			
03025300	鲜、冷绿青鳕鱼	12	0	0	0	0	0	0	0	0	0	0	8	0	5		0	0	7.2			

税则号列	商品名称（简称）	最惠国	东盟										亚太	智利	巴基斯坦	新加坡	新西兰	秘鲁	哥斯达黎加	香港	澳门	台湾
			文	柬	印	老	马	缅	菲	新	泰	越										
03025400	鲜、冷狗鳕鱼	12	0	0	0	0	0	0	0	0	0	0	8	1.2	5		0	0	7.2	0		0
03025500	鲜、冷狭鳕鱼	12	0	0	0	0	0	0	0	0	0	0	8	1.2	5		0	0	7.2	0		0
03025600	鲜、冷蓝鳕鱼	12	0	0	0	0	0	0	0	0	0	0	8	1.2	5		0	0	7.2	0		0
03025900	鲜、冷其他鳕科鱼	12	0	0	0	0	0	0	0	0	0	0	8	1.2	5		0	0	7.2	0		0
03027100	鲜、冷罗非鱼	12	0	0	0	0	0	0	0	0	0	0		1.2	6		0	6	7.2			
03027200	鲜、冷鲶鱼	12	0	0	0	0	0	0	0	0	0	0	8	1.2	5		0	0	7.2	0		0
03027300	鲜、冷鲤科鱼	12	0	0	0	0	0	0	0	0	0	0	8	1.2	5		0	0	7.2	0		0
03027400	鲜、冷鳗鱼	12	0	0	0	0	0	0	0	0	0	0	8	0	5		0	0	7.2	0		
03027900	鲜、冷尼罗河鲈鱼及黑鱼	12	0	0	0	0	0	0	0	0	0	0	8	1.2	5		0	0	7.2	0		0
03028100	鲜、冷角鲨及其他鲨鱼	12	0	0	0	0	0	0	0	0	0	0	9	1.2	5		0	6	7.2	0		
03028200	鲜、冷魟鱼及鳐鱼	12	0	0	0	0	0	0	0	0	0	0	8	1.2	5		0	0	7.2	0		0
03028300	鲜、冷南极犬牙鱼	12	0	0	0	0	0	0	0	0	0	0	8	1.2	5		0	0	7.2	0		
03028400	鲜、冷尖吻鲈鱼	12	0	0	0	0	0	0	0	0	0	0	8	1.2	5		0	0	7.2	0		0
03028500	鲜、冷菱羊鲷	12	0	0	0	0	0	0	0	0	0	0	8	1.2	5		0	0	7.2	0		0
03028910	鲜、冷带鱼	12	0	0	0	0	0	0	0	0	0	0	8	1.2	8		0	6	7.2	0		
03028920	鲜、冷黄鱼	12	0	0	0	0	0	0	0	0	0	0	8	1.2	5		0	6	7.2	0		
03028930	鲜、冷鲳鱼	12	0	0	0	0	0	0	0	0	0	0	8	1.2	5		0	6	7.2	0		
03028940	鲜、冷鲕	12	0	0	0	0	0	0	0	0	0	0	8	1.2	5		0	6	7.2	0		
03028990	鲜、冷其他鱼	12	0	0	0	0	0	0	0	0	0	0	8	1.2	5		0	0	7.2	0		0
03029000	鲜、冷鱼肝及鱼卵	12	0	0	0	0	0	0	0	0	0	0		0	6		0	0	7.2			
03031100	冻红大麻哈鱼	10	0	0	0	0	0	0	0	0	0	0	6.7	1	5		0	5	6			
03031200	冻其他大麻哈鱼	10	0	0	0	0	0	0	0	0	0	0	6.7	1	5		0	5	6			
03031300	冻大西洋鲑鱼及多瑙哲罗鱼	10	0	0	0	0	0	0	0	0	0	0		1	5		0	5	6			
03031400	冻鳟鱼	12	0	0	0	0	0	0	0	0	0	0		1.2	6		0	6	7.2			
03031900	冻其他鲑科鱼	10	0	0	0	0	0	0	0	0	0	0	6.7	0	5		0	0	6			
03032300	冻罗非鱼	10	0	0	0	0	0	0	0	0	0	0	5	1	5		0	5	6			
03032400	冻鲶鱼	10	0	0	0	0	0	0	0	0	0	0	5	1	5		0	3.8	6	0		0
03032500	冻鲤科鱼	10	0	0	0	0	0	0	0	0	0	0	5	1	5		0	3.8	6	0		0
03032600	冻鳗鱼	12	0	0	0	0	0	0	0	0	0	0	8	1.2	8		0	6	7.2	0		
03032900	冻尼罗河鲈鱼及黑鱼	10	0	0	0	0	0	0	0	0	0	0	5	1	5		0	3.8	6	0		0
03033110	冻格陵兰庸鲽鱼	10	0	0	0	0	0	0	0	0	0	0	6.7	0	5		0	0	6	0		
03033190	冻庸鲽鱼	10	0	0	0	0	0	0	0	0	0	0	6.7	0	5		0	0	6	0		
03033200	冻鲽鱼	12	0	0	0	0	0	0	0	0	0	0	8	0	8		0	0	7.2			
03033300	冻鳎鱼	12	0	0	0	0	0	0	0	0	0	0	8	0	8		0	0	7.2			
03033400	冻大菱鲆	10	0	0	0	0	0	0	0	0	0	0	8	1	8		0	5	6			
03033900	其他冻比目鱼	10	0	0	0	0	0	0	0	0	0	0	8	1	8		0	5	6			
03034100	冻长鳍金枪鱼	12	0	0	0	0	0	0	0	0	0	0	9	0	5		0	0	7.2			
03034200	冻黄鳍金枪鱼	12	0	0	0	0	0	0	0	0	0	0	9	0	5		0	0	7.2			
03034300	冻鲣鱼或狐鲣	12	0	0	0	0	0	0	0	0	0	0	9	0	5		0	0	7.2			
03034400	冻大眼金枪鱼，但鱼肝及鱼卵除外	12	0	0	0	0	0	0	0	0	0	0		0	6		0	0	7.2	0		
03034510	冻大西洋蓝鳍金枪鱼	12	0	0	0	0	0	0	0	0	0	0		0	6		0	0	7.2			
03034520	冻太平洋蓝鳍金枪鱼	12	0	0	0	0	0	0	0	0	0	0	9	1.2	5		0	0	7.2			
03034600	冻南方蓝鳍金枪鱼，但鱼肝及鱼卵除外	12	0	0	0	0	0	0	0	0	0	0		0	6		0	0	7.2			
03034900	其他冻金枪鱼，但鱼肝及鱼卵除外	12	0	0	0	0	0	0	0	0	0	0	9	1.2	5		0	0	7.2			
03035100	冻鲱鱼（大西洋鲱鱼、太平洋鲱鱼），但鱼肝及鱼卵除外	10	0	0	0	0	0	0	0	0	0	0	6.7	0	5		0	0	6			
03035300	冻沙丁鱼、小沙丁鱼属、黍鲱或西鲱	12	0	0	0	0	0	0	0	0	0	0	8	1.2	5		0	6	7.2			
03035400	冻鲭鱼	10	0	0	0	0	0	0	0	0	0	0	6.7	1	6.7		0	3.8	6			
03035500	冻对称竹荚鱼、新西兰竹荚鱼及竹荚鱼	10	0	0	0	0	0	0	0	0	0	0	5	1	5		0	3.8	6	0		0
03035600	冻军曹鱼	10	0	0	0	0	0	0	0	0	0	0	5	1	5		0	3.8	6	0		0
03035700	冻剑鱼	10	0	0	0	0	0	0	0	0	0	0	5	1	5		0	0	6	0		
03036300	鳕鱼（大西洋鳕鱼、格陵兰鳕鱼、太平洋鳕鱼）	10	0	0	0	0	0	0	0	0	0	0	6.7	0	5		0	0	6			
03036400	冻黑线鳕鱼	12	0	0	0	0	0	0	0	0	0	0	8	0	5		0	0	7.2			
03036500	冻绿青鳕鱼	12	0	0	0	0	0	0	0	0	0	0	8	0	5		0	0	7.2			
03036600	冻狗鳕鱼	12	0	0	0	0	0	0	0	0	0	0		1.2	6		0	6	7.2			
03036700	冻狭鳕鱼	10	0	0	0	0	0	0	0	0	0	0	5	1	5		0	3.8	6	0		0
03036800	冻蓝鳕鱼	10	0	0	0	0	0	0	0	0	0	0	5	1	5		0	3.8	6	0		0
03036900	其他冻鳕鱼	10	0	0	0	0	0	0	0	0	0	0	5	1	5		0	3.8	6	0		0
03038100	冻角鲨及其他鲨鱼	12	0	0	0	0	0	0	0	0	0	0	9	1.2	9		0	6	7.2			

税则号列	商品名称（简称）	最惠国	东盟										亚太	智利	巴基斯坦	新加坡	新西兰	秘鲁	哥斯达黎加	香港	澳门	台湾
			文	柬	印	老	马	缅	菲	新	泰	越										
03038200	冻魟鱼及鳐鱼	10	0	0	0	0	0	0	0	0	0	0	5	1	5		0	3.8	6	0		0
03038300	冻南极犬牙鱼	10	0	0	0	0	0	0	0	0	0	0	5	1	5		0	0	6	0		
03038400	冻尖吻鲈鱼	12	0	0	0	0	0	0	0	0	0	0	8	0	5		0	0	7.2	0		
03038910	冻带鱼	10	0	0	0	0	0	0	0	0	0	0	5	1	5		0	5	6	0		
03038920	冻黄鱼	10	0	0	0	0	0	0	0	0	0	0	5	1	5		0	5	6	0		
03038930	冻鲳鱼	10	0	0	0	0	0	0	0	0	0	0	5	1	5		0	5	6	0		
03038990	其他冻鱼	10	0	0	0	0	0	0	0	0	0	0	5	1	5		0	3.8	6	0		0
03039000	冻鱼肝及鱼卵	10	0	0	0	0	0	0	0	0	0	0	9	1	5		0		6			
03043100	鲜、冷罗非鱼片	12	0	0	0	0	0	0	0	0	0	0	9	1.2	5		0	6	2.4	0		
03043200	鲜、冷鲶鱼片	12	0	0	0	0	0	0	0	0	0	0	9	1.2	5		0	6	2.4	0		
03043300	鲜、冷尼罗河鲈鱼片	12	0	0	0	0	0	0	0	0	0	0	9	1.2	5		0	6	2.4	0		
03043900	鲜、冷鲤科鱼、鳗鱼、黑鱼片	12	0	0	0	0	0	0	0	0	0	0	9	1.2	5		0	6	2.4	0		
03044100	鲜、冷大麻哈鱼片	12	0	0	0	0	0	0	0	0	0	0	9	1.2	5		0	6	2.4	0		
03044200	鲜、冷鳟鱼片	12	0	0	0	0	0	0	0	0	0	0	9	1.2	5		0	6	2.4	0		
03044300	鲜、冷比目鱼片	12	0	0	0	0	0	0	0	0	0	0	9	1.2	5		0	6	2.4	0		
03044400	鲜、冷犀鳕科等鳕科鱼片	12	0	0	0	0	0	0	0	0	0	0	9	1.2	5		0	6	2.4	0		
03044500	鲜、冷剑鱼片	12	0	0	0	0	0	0	0	0	0	0	9	1.2	5		0	0	2.4	0		
03044600	鲜、冷南极犬牙鱼片	12	0	0	0	0	0	0	0	0	0	0	9	1.2	5		0	0	2.4	0		
03044900	鲜、冷其他鱼片	12	0	0	0	0	0	0	0	0	0	0	9	1.2	5		0	6	2.4	0		
03045100	鲜、冷罗非鱼等鱼鱼肉	12	0	0	0	0	0	0	0	0	0	0	9	1.2	5		0	6	2.4	0		
03045200	鲜、冷鲑科鱼肉	12	0	0	0	0	0	0	0	0	0	0	9	1.2	5		0	6	2.4	0		
03045300	鲜、冷犀鳕科等鳕科鱼肉	12	0	0	0	0	0	0	0	0	0	0	9	1.2	5		0	6	2.4	0		
03045400	鲜、冷剑鱼肉	12	0	0	0	0	0	0	0	0	0	0	9	1.2	5		0	0	2.4	0		
03045500	鲜、冷南极犬牙鱼肉	12	0	0	0	0	0	0	0	0	0	0	9	1.2	5		0	0	2.4	0		
03045900	鲜、冷其他鱼肉	12	0	0	0	0	0	0	0	0	0	0	9	1.2	5		0	6	2.4	0		
03046100	冻罗非鱼等鱼鱼片	10	0	0	0	0	0	0	0	0	0	0		1	5		0	0	0	0		
03046211	冻斑点叉尾鮰鱼片	10	0	0	0	0	0	0	0	0	0	0		1	5		0	0	0	0		
03046219	冻其他叉尾鮰鱼片	10	0	0	0	0	0	0	0	0	0	0		1	5		0	0	0	0		
03046290	冻其他鲶鱼片	10	0	0	0	0	0	0	0	0	0	0		1	5		0	3.8	0	0		0
03046300	冻尼罗河鲈鱼片	10	0	0	0	0	0	0	0	0	0	0		1	5		0	3.8	0	0		0
03046900	冻鲤科鱼、鳗鱼、黑鱼片	10	0	0	0	0	0	0	0	0	0	0		1	5		0	3.8	0	0		0
03047100	鳕鱼(大西洋鳕鱼、格陵兰鳕鱼、太平洋鳕鱼)	10	0	0	0	0	0	0	0	0	0	0		1	5		0	3.8	0	0		0
03047200	冻黑线鳕鱼片	10	0	0	0	0	0	0	0	0	0	0		1	5		0	3.8	0	0		0
03047300	冻绿青鳕鱼片	10	0	0	0	0	0	0	0	0	0	0		1	5		0	3.8	0	0		0
03047400	冻狗鳕鱼片	10	0	0	0	0	0	0	0	0	0	0		1	5		0	3.8	0	0		0
03047500	冻狭鳕鱼片	10	0	0	0	0	0	0	0	0	0	0		1	5		0	3.8	0	0		0
03047900	冻其他鳕鱼片	10	0	0	0	0	0	0	0	0	0	0		1	5		0	3.8	0	0		0
03048100	冻大麻哈鱼、大西洋鲑鱼及多瑙哲罗鱼片	10	0	0	0	0	0	0	0	0	0	0		1	5		0	3.8	0	0		0
03048200	冻鳟鱼片	10	0	0	0	0	0	0	0	0	0	0		1	5		0	3.8	0	0		0
03048300	冻比目鱼片	10	0	0	0	0	0	0	0	0	0	0		1	5		0	3.8	0	0		0
03048400	冻剑鱼片	10	0	0	0	0	0	0	0	0	0	0		1	5		0	0	0	0		
03048500	冻南极犬牙鱼片	10	0	0	0	0	0	0	0	0	0	0		1	5		0	0	0	0		
03048600	冻鲱鱼片	10	0	0	0	0	0	0	0	0	0	0		1	5		0	3.8	0	0		0
03048700	冻金枪鱼、鲣鱼或狐鲣(鲣)片	10	0	0	0	0	0	0	0	0	0	0		1	5		0	3.8	0			0
03048900	冻其他鱼片	10	0	0	0	0	0	0	0	0	0	0		1	5		0	3.8	0	0		0
03049100	冻的剑鱼肉	10	0	0	0	0	0	0	0	0	0	0		1	5		0	0	0			
03049200	冻的南极犬牙鱼肉	10	0	0	0	0	0	0	0	0	0	0		1	5		0	0	0			
03049300	冻罗非鱼等鱼鱼肉	10	0	0	0	0	0	0	0	0	0	0		1	5		0	0	0			
03049400	冻狭鳕鱼肉	10	0	0	0	0	0	0	0	0	0	0		1	5		0	0	0			
03049500	冻犀鳕科等鳕科鱼肉	10	0	0	0	0	0	0	0	0	0	0		1	5		0	0	0			
03049900	其他冻鱼肉	10	0	0	0	0	0	0	0	0	0	0		1	5		0	0	0			
03051000	供人食用的鱼粉及团粒	10	0	0	0	0	0	0	0	0	0	0		0	5		0	0	0		0	
03052000	干、熏、盐制的鱼肝及鱼卵	10	0	0	0	0	0	0	0	0	0	0		1	5		0		6			
03053100	干、盐腌罗非鱼等鱼鱼片	10	0	0	0	0	0	0	0	0	0	0	7.8	1	5		0	5	0	0	0	
03053200	干、盐腌犀鳕科等鳕科鱼片	10	0	0	0	0	0	0	0	0	0	0	7.8	1	5		0	5	0	0	0	
03053900	干、盐腌其他鱼片	10	0	0	0	0	0	0	0	0	0	0	7.8	1	5		0	5	0	0	0	
03054110	熏大西洋鲑鱼，食用杂碎除外	14	0	0	0	0	0	0	0	0	0	0		0	7		0	0	2.8	0		
03054120	熏鲱鱼，食用杂碎除外	14	0	0	0	0	0	0	0	0	0	0		0	11.2		0	0	2.8			

税则号列	商品名称（简称）	最惠国	东盟 文	东盟 柬	东盟 印	东盟 老	东盟 马	东盟 缅	东盟 菲	东盟 新	东盟 泰	东盟 越	亚太	智利	巴基斯坦	新加坡	新西兰	秘鲁	哥斯达黎加	香港	澳门	台湾
03054200	熏鲱鱼，食用杂碎除外	16	0	0	0	0	0	0	0	0	0	0		0	12.8		0	0	3.2			
03054300	熏鳟鱼，食用杂碎除外	14	0	0	0	0	0	0	0	0	0	0		1.4	11.2		0	7	2.8		0	
03054400	熏罗非鱼等鱼，食用杂碎除外	14	0	0	0	0	0	0	0	0	0	0		1.4	11.2		0	7	2.8		0	
03054900	熏其他鱼，食用杂碎除外	14	0	0	0	0	0	0	0	0	0	0		1.4	11.2		0	7	2.8		0	
03055100	鳕鱼(大西洋鳕鱼、格陵兰鳕鱼、太平洋鳕鱼)	16	0	0	0	0	0	0	0	0	0	0		0	12.8		0	0	3.2		0	
03055910	干海马、干海龙	2	0	0	0	0	0	0	0	0	0	0		0	0		0	0	0			
03055990	干其他鱼，食用杂碎除外	16	0	0	0	0	0	0	0	0	0	0		1.6			0	8	9.6	0	0	
03056100	盐腌及盐渍的鲱鱼，食用杂碎除外	16	0	0	0	0	0	0	0	0	0	0	11.1	0	8		0	0	3.2			
03056200	鳕鱼(大西洋鳕鱼、格陵兰鳕鱼、太平洋鳕鱼)	16	0	0	0	0	0	0	0	0	0	0	12	0	8		0	0	3.2			
03056300	盐腌及盐渍的鳀鱼，食用杂碎除外	16	0	0	0	0	0	0	0	0	0	0	12	1.6	8		0	8	3.2			
03056400	盐腌及盐渍的罗非鱼等鱼，食用杂碎除外	16	0	0	0	0	0	0	0	0	0	0		1.6	12.8		0	8	3.2	0		
03056910	盐腌及盐渍的带鱼，食用杂碎除外	16	0	0	0	0	0	0	0	0	0	0		1.6	12.8		0	8	3.2	0		
03056920	盐腌及盐渍的黄鱼，食用杂碎除外	16	0	0	0	0	0	0	0	0	0	0		1.6	12.8		0	8	3.2	0		
03056930	盐腌及盐渍的鲳鱼，食用杂碎除外	16	0	0	0	0	0	0	0	0	0	0		1.6	12.8		0	8	3.2	0		
03056990	盐腌及盐渍的其他鱼，食用杂碎除外	16	0	0	0	0	0	0	0	0	0	0		1.6	12.8		0	8	3.2	0		
03057100	鲨鱼翅	15	0	0	0	0	0	0	0	0	0	0		1.5			0	7.5	9		0	
03057200	鱼头、鱼尾、鱼鳔	16	0	0	0	0	0	0	0	0	0	0		0	12.8		0	0	3.2			
03057900	其他可食用杂碎	16	0	0	0	0	0	0	0	0	0	0		0	12.8		0	0	3.2			
03061100	岩礁虾和其他龙虾（真龙虾属、龙虾属、岩龙虾属）	10	0	0	0	0	0	0	0	0	0	0		0	5		0	0	0			
03061200	螯龙虾(螯龙虾属)	10	0	0	0	0	0	0	0	0	0	0	7.2	0	5		0	0	0			
03061410	冻梭子蟹	10	0	0	0	0	0	0	0	0	0	0		1	5		0	5	0			
03061490	其他冻蟹	10	0	0	0	0	0	0	0	0	0	0		1	5		0	5	0			
03061500	冻挪威海螯虾	16	0	0	0	0	0	0	0	0	0	0		1.6	12.8		0	8	3.2			
03061611	冻冷水小虾虾仁	8	0	0	0	0	0	0	0	0	0	0	4	0	0		0	0	0	0		
03061612	冻北方长额虾虾仁	5	0	0	0	0	0	0	0	0	0	0	2.5	0	0		0	0	0	0		
03061619	冻其他冷水小虾	5	0	0	0	0	0	0	0	0	0	0	2.5	0	0		0	0	0	0		
03061621	冻冷水对虾虾仁	8	0	0	0	0	0	0	0	0	0	0	4	0	0		0	0	0	0		
03061629	冻其他冷水对虾	5	0	0	0	0	0	0	0	0	0	0	2.5	0	0		0	0	0	0		
03061711	冻小虾虾仁	8	0	0	0	0	0	0	0	0	0	0	4	0	0		0	0	0	0		
03061719	冻其他小虾	5	0	0	0	0	0	0	0	0	0	0	2.5	0	0		0	0	0	0		
03061721	冻对虾虾仁	8	0	0	0	0	0	0	0	0	0	0	4	0	0		0	0	0	0		
03061729	冻其他对虾	5	0	0	0	0	0	0	0	0	0	0	2.5	0	0		0	0	0	0		
03061911	冻淡水小龙虾仁	16	0	0	0	0	0	0	0	0	0	0		0	12.8		0	0	3.2			
03061919	冻带壳淡水小龙虾	16	0	0	0	0	0	0	0	0	0	0		0	12.8		0	0	3.2			
03061990	其他冻甲壳动物	16	0	0	0	0	0	0	0	0	0	0		1.6	12.8		0	8	3.2			
03062190	其他岩礁虾和其他龙虾（真龙虾属、龙虾属、岩龙虾属）	15	0	0	0	0	0	0	0	0	0	0		0			0	0	3	0		
03062290	其他螯龙虾（螯龙虾属）	15	0	0	0	0	0	0	0	0	0	0		0	12		0	0	3	0		
03062491	未冻的中华绒毛蟹(大闸蟹)	14	0	0	0	0	0	0	0	0	0	0		1.4	7		0	0	2.8			
03062492	未冻的梭子蟹	14	0	0	0	0	0	0	0	0	0	0		1.4	11.2		0	7	2.8	0		
03062499	未冻的其他蟹	14	0	0	0	0	0	0	0	0	0	0		1.4			0	7	2.8	0		
03062590	未冻的其他挪威海螯虾	14	0	0	0	0	0	0	0	0	0	0		1.4	11.2		0	0	2.8	0		
03062620	鲜、冷冷水对虾	15	0	0	0	0	0	0	0	0	0	0		0	12		0	0	3	0		
03062690	未冻的其他冷水小虾及对虾	12	0	0	0	0	0	0	0	0	0	0		0	6		0	0	2.4	0		
03062720	鲜、冷对虾	15	0	0	0	0	0	0	0	0	0	0		0	12		0	0	3	0		
03062790	未冻的其他小虾及对虾	12	0	0	0	0	0	0	0	0	0	0		0	6		0	0	2.4	0		
03062990	其他带壳或去壳的未冻的甲壳动物	14	0	0	0	0	0	0	0	0	0	0		1.4	11.2		0	0	2.8	0		
03071190	活、鲜或冷的其他牡蛎（蚝）	14	0	0	0	0	0	0	0	0	0	0		1.4	11.2		0	7	2.8	0		
03071900	冻、干、盐腌或盐渍的牡蛎（蚝）	14	0	0	0	0	0	0	0	0	0	0		1.4	11.2		0	7	2.8	0		
03072190	其他活、鲜、冷扇贝	14	0	0	0	0	0	0	0	0	0	0		1.4	11.2		0	7	2.8	0		
03072900	其他冻、干、盐腌或盐渍的扇贝	14	0	0	0	0	0	0	0	0	0	0		1.4	11.2		0	5.2	2.8			
03073190	其他活、鲜、冷贻贝	14	0	0	0	0	0	0	0	0	0	0		0	11.2		0	0	2.8	0		
03073900	其他冻、干、盐制的贻贝	14	0	0	0	0	0	0	0	0	0	0	9.8	1.4	7		0	7	2.8			
03074190	其他活、鲜或冷墨鱼及鱿鱼	12	0	0	0	0	0	0	0	0	0	0		1.2	6		0	6	2.4	0		
03074900	其他冻、干、盐制的墨鱼及鱿鱼	12	0	0	0	0	0	0	0	0	0	0	10	1.2	10		0	6	2.4	0	0	
03075100	活、鲜、冷章鱼	17	0	0	0	0	0	0	0	0	0	0		1.7	13.6		0	8.5	3.4	0		
03075900	其他冻、干、盐制的章鱼	17	0	0	0	0	0	0	0	0	0	0		1.7	13.6		0	8.5	3.4	0	0	

税则号列	商品名称（简称）	最惠国	东盟										亚太	智利	巴基斯坦	新加坡	新西兰	秘鲁	哥斯达黎加	香港	澳门	台湾
			文	柬	印	老	马	缅	菲	新	泰	越										
03076090	其他蜗牛及螺，海螺除外	14	0	0	0	0	0	0	0	0	0	0		0	11.2		0	0	2.8			
03077191	活、鲜或冷的蛤	14	0	0	0	0	0	0	0	0	0	0		1.4	11.2		0	0	2.8	0		
03077199	活、鲜或冷的乌蛤及舟贝	14	0	0	0	0	0	0	0	0	0	0		1.4	11.2		0	7	2.8	0		
03077910	冻、干、盐腌或盐渍的蛤	10	0	0	0	0	0	0	0	0	0	0		1			0		0			
03077990	冻、干、盐腌或盐渍的乌蛤及舟贝	10	0	0	0	0	0	0	0	0	0	0		1			0	5	0		0	
03078190	活、鲜或冷的其他鲍鱼	14	0	0	0	0	0	0	0	0	0	0		1.4	11.2		0	7	2.8	0		
03078900	冻、干、盐腌或盐渍的鲍鱼	10	0	0	0	0	0	0	0	0	0	0		1	5		0		0	0	0	
03079190	活、鲜或冷的其他软体动物	14	0	0	0	0	0	0	0	0	0	0		1.4	11.2		0	7	2.8	0		
03079900	冻、干、盐腌或盐渍的软体动物	10	0	0	0	0	0	0	0	0	0	0		1			0	5	0		0	
03081190	活、鲜或冷的其他海参	14	0	0	0	0	0	0	0	0	0	0		1.4	11.2		0	7	2.8	0		
03081900	冻、干、盐腌或盐渍的海参	10	0	0	0	0	0	0	0	0	0	0		1			0	5	0			
03082190	活、鲜或冷的其他海胆	14	0	0	0	0	0	0	0	0	0	0		1.4	11.2		0	7	2.8	0		
03082900	冻、干、盐腌或盐渍的海胆	10	0	0	0	0	0	0	0	0	0	0		1			0	5	0		0	
03083019	活、鲜或冷的其他海蜇	14	0	0	0	0	0	0	0	0	0	0		1.4	11.2		0	7	2.8	0		
03083090	冻、干、盐腌或盐渍的海蜇	10	0	0	0	0	0	0	0	0	0	0		1			0	5	0		0	
03089012	活、鲜或冷的其他沙蚕	14	0	0	0	0	0	0	0	0	0	0		1.4	11.2		0	7	2.8	0		
03089019	活、鲜或冷的其他水生无脊椎动物	14	0	0	0	0	0	0	0	0	0	0		1.4	11.2		0	7	2.8	0		
03089090	冻、干、盐腌或盐渍的其他水生无脊椎动物	10	0	0	0	0	0	0	0	0	0	0		1			0	5	0		0	
04011000	脂肪含量未超1%未浓缩及未加糖的乳及奶油	15	0	0	0	0	0	0	0	0	0	0		1.5	12		0	7.5	11		0	
04012000	脂肪含量在1-6%未浓缩及未加糖的乳及奶油	15	0	0	0	0	0	0	0	0	0	0		1.5	12		4.5	7.5	11	0	0	
04014000	按重量计脂肪含量超过 6%，但不超过10%的未浓缩及未加糖或其他甜物质的乳及奶油	15	0	0	0	0	0	0	0	0	0	0		1.5	12		4.5	7.5	11		0	
04015000	按重量计脂肪含量超过10%的未浓缩及未加糖或其他甜物质的乳及奶油	15	0	0	0	0	0	0	0	0	0	0		1.5	12		4.5	7.5	11		0	
04021000	脂肪含量≤1.5%固状乳及奶油	10	0	0	0	0	0	0	0	0	0	0	7	1	5		4.2	7.1	7.3	0	0	
04022100	脂肪量>1.5%未加糖固状乳及奶油	10	0	0	0	0	0	0	0	0	0	0	7	1	7		4.2	7.1	7.3	0	0	
04022900	脂肪量>1.5%的加糖固状乳及奶油	10	0	0	0	0	0	0	0	0	0	0		1	5		4.2	7.1	7.3	0	0	
04029100	浓缩但未加糖的非固状乳及奶油	10	0	0	0	0	0	0	0	0	0	0		1	5		4.2	5	7.3	0	0	
04029900	浓缩并已加糖的非固状乳及奶油	10	0	0	0	0	0	0	0	0	0	0		1	5		0	7.1	7.3			
04031000	酸乳	10	0	0	0	0	0	0	0	0	0	0		1	5		0	5	7.3	0	0	
04039000	酪乳及其他发酵或酸化的乳及奶油	20	0	0	0	0	0	0	0	0	0	0		2			0	10	14.7	0	0	
04041000	乳清及改性乳清	6	0	0	0	0	0	0	0	0	0	0		0	5		0	0	4.4			
04049000	其他编号未列名的含天然乳的产品	20	0	0	0	0	0	0	0	0	0	0		0			0	10	14.7			
04051000	黄油	10	0	0	0	0	0	0	0	0	0	0		1	5		3	5	7.3			
04052000	乳酱	10	0	0	0	0	0	0	0	0	0	0	8.1	0	5		0	0	7.3		0	
04059000	其他从乳中提取的脂和油	10	0	0	0	0	0	0	0	0	0	0		0	5		3	5	7.3			
04061000	鲜乳酪(未熟化或未固化的)	12	0	0	0	0	0	0	0	0	0	0		1.2	6		3.6	6	8.8	0	0	
04062000	各种磨碎或粉化的乳酪	12	0	0	0	0	0	0	0	0	0	0		0	6		0	8	8.8	0		
04063000	经加工的乳酪，但磨碎或粉化的除外	12	0	0	0	0	0	0	0	0	0	0		0	6		3.6	8	8.8			
04064000	蓝纹乳酪和娄地青霉生产的带有纹理的其他乳酪	15	0	0	0	0	0	0	0	0	0	0		0	12		0	7.5	11			
04069000	其他乳酪	12	0	0	0	0	0	0	0	0	0	0		0	6		3.6	6	8.8			
04072100	鲜鸡蛋	20	0	0	0	0	0	0	0	0	0	0		0			0	10	4			
04072900	其他鲜禽蛋	20	0	0	0	0	0	0	0	0	0	0		0			0	10	4			
04079010	咸蛋	20	0	0	0	0	0	0	0	0	0	0		0			0	0	4			
04079020	皮蛋	20	0	0	0	0	0	0	0	0	0	0		0			0	0	4			
04079090	其他蛋	20	0	0	0	0	0	0	0	0	0	0		0			0	0	4			
04081100	干蛋黄	20	0	0	0	0	0	0	0	0	0	0		0			0	10	4			
04081900	其他蛋黄	20	0	0	0	0	0	0	0	0	0	0		0			0	10	4			
04089100	干的其他去壳禽蛋	20	0	0	0	0	0	0	0	0	0	0		2			0	10	4			
04089900	其他去壳禽蛋	20	0	0	0	0	0	0	0	0	0	0		0			0	10	4	0		
04090000	天然蜂蜜	15	0	0	0	0	0	0	0	0	0	0		1.5	12		0	7.5	3			
04100010	燕窝	25	0	0	0	0	0	0	0	0	0	0		0			0	12.5	5	0	0	
04100041	鲜蜂王浆	15	0	0	0	0	0	0	0	0	0	0		0	12		0	7.5	3			
04100042	鲜蜂王浆粉	15	0	0	0	0	0	0	0	0	0	0		0	12		0	7.5	3			
04100043	蜂花粉	20	0	0	0	0	0	0	0	0	0	0		0			0	10	4			
04100049	其他蜂产品	20	0	0	0	0	0	0	0	0	0	0		0			0	10	4			

税则号列	商品名称（简称）	最惠国	东盟 文	柬	印	老	马	缅	菲	新	泰	越	亚太	智利	巴基斯坦	新加坡	新西兰	秘鲁	哥斯达黎加	香港	澳门	台湾
04100090	其他编号未列名的食用动物产品	20	0	0	0	0	0	0	0	0	0	0		0			0	10	4			0
05010000	未经加工的人发；废人发	15	0	0	0	0	0	0	0	0	0	0		0	12		0	7.5	3			
05021010	猪鬃	20	0	0	0	0	0	0	0	0	0	0		0			0	10	4			
05021020	猪毛	20	0	0	0	0	0	0	0	0	0	0		0			0	10	4			
05021030	猪鬃或猪毛的废料	20	0	0	0	0	0	0	0	0	0	0		0			0	10	4			
05029011	山羊毛	20	0	0	0	0	0	0	0	0	0	0		0			0	10	4			
05029012	黄鼠狼尾毛	20	0	0	0	0	0	0	0	0	0	0		0			0	10	4			
05029019	獾毛及其他制刷用兽毛	20	0	0	0	0	0	0	0	0	0	0		0			0	10	4			
05029020	獾毛及其他制刷用兽毛的废料	20	0	0	0	0	0	0	0	0	0	0		0			0	10	4			
05040011	整个或切块的盐渍猪肠衣（猪大肠头除外）	20	0	0	0	0	0	0	0	0	0	0	10	2	10		0	10	4			
05040012	整个或切块的盐渍绵羊肠衣	18	0	0	0	0	0	0	0	0	0	0	9	1.8	9		0	9	3.6			
05040013	整个或切块的盐渍山羊肠衣	18	0	0	0	0	0	0	0	0	0	0	9	1.8	9		0	9	3.6			
05040014	整个或切块的盐渍猪大肠头	20	0	0	0	0	0	0	0	0	0	0	10	2	10		0	10	4			
05040019	整个或切块的其他动物肠衣	18	0	0	0	0	0	0	0	0	0	0	9	1.8	9		0	9	3.6			
05040021	冷和冻的鸡肫	20	0	0	0		0	0	0	0	0	0	0.65元/千克	0.13元/千克	0.65元/千克		0	10	4			
05040029	鲜、冷、冻、干、盐制的其他动物胃	20	0	0	0	0	0	0	0	0	0	0	10	2	10		0	10	4			
05040090	鲜、冷、冻、干、盐制的其他动物肠、膀胱、胃	20	0	0	0	0	0	0	0	0	0	0	10	2	10		0	10	4			
05051000	填充用羽毛；羽绒	10	0	0	0	0	0	0	0	0	0	0	7.5	0	5		0	0	0			
05059010	羽毛或不完整羽毛的粉末及废料	10	0	0	0	0	0	0	0	0	0	0		0	5		0	0	0			
05059090	其他羽毛，羽绒，带有羽毛，羽绒，的鸟皮及鸟体其他部分	10	0	0	0	0	0	0	0	0	0	0		0	5		0	0	0			
05061000	经酸处理的骨胶原及骨	12	0	0	0	0	0	0	0	0	0	0		0	6		0	0	2.4			
05069011	含牛羊成分的骨粉及骨废料	12	0	0	0	0	0	0	0	0	0	0		1.2	6		0	6	2.4			
05069019	骨粉及骨废料	12	0	0	0	0	0	0	0	0	0	0		1.2	6		0	6	2.4			
05069090	其他骨及角柱	12	0	0	0	0	0	0	0	0	0	0		1.2	6		0	6	7.2		0	
05071000	兽牙；兽牙粉末及废料	10	0	0	0	0	0	0	0	0	0	0		0	5		0	0	0			
05079010	羚羊角及其粉末和废料	3	0	0	0	0	0	0	0	0	0	0		0	0		0	0	0			
05079020	鹿茸及其粉末	11	0	0	0	0	0	0	0	0	0	0		0	5		0	0	2.2			
05079090	龟壳、鲸须、鲸须毛、鹿角及其他角	10	0	0	0	0	0	0	0	0	0	0		0	5		0	0	0			
05080010	珊瑚及水产品壳、骨的粉末及废料	12	0	0	0	0	0	0	0	0	0	0		1.2			0	6	2.4	0		
05080090	珊瑚及介、贝、棘皮动物的壳、骨	12	0	0	0	0	0	0	0	0	0	0		1.2	6		0	6	2.4	0		
05100010	黄药	3	0	0	0	0	0	0	0	0	0	0		0	0		0	0	0			
05100020	龙涎香、海狸香、灵猫香	7	0	0	0	0	0	0	0	0	0	0		0	5		0	0	0			
05100030	麝香	7	0	0	0	0	0	0	0	0	0	0		0	5		0	0	0			
05100040	斑蝥	7	0	0	0	0	0	0	0	0	0	0		0	5		0	0	0			
05100090	胆汁，配药用腺体及其他动物产品	6	0	0	0	0	0	0	0	0	0	0		0	5		0	0	0			
05119111	受精鱼卵	12	0	0	0	0	0	0	0	0	0	0		1.2	6		0	0	2.4			
05119119	其他鱼产品	12	0	0	0	0	0	0	0	0	0	0		1.2			0	6	2.4			
05119190	其他未列名水产品；第三章的死动物	12	0	0	0	0	0	0	0	0	0	0		1.2	6		0	6	2.4			
05119940	马毛及废马毛，不论是否制成有或无衬垫的毛片	15	0	0	0	0	0	0	0	0	0	0		0	12		0	7.5	3			
05119990	其他编号未列名的动物产品；不适合供人食用的第一章的死动物	12	0	0	0	0	0	0	0	0	0	0		0	6		0	6	2.4			
06011010	休眠的番红花球茎	4	0	0	0	0	0	0	0	0	0	0	2	0	0		0	0	0			
06011029	其他百合球茎	5	0	0	0	0	0	0	0	0	0	0	2.5	0	0		0	0	0			
06011099	其它休眠的鳞茎、块茎、块根等	5	0	0	0	0	0	0	0	0	0	0	2.5	0	0		0	0	0			
06012000	生长或开花的鳞茎等及菊苣植物	15	0	0	0	0	0	0	0	0	0	0	7.5	1.5	7.5		0	7.5	3			
06022090	其他食用水果及坚果树及灌木	10	0	0	0	0	0	0	0	0	0	0	5	1	5		0	5	0			
06023090	其他杜鹃	15	0	0	0	0	0	0	0	0	0	0		0	12		0	7.5	3			
06024090	其他玫瑰	15	0	0	0	0	0	0	0	0	0	0		0	12		0	7.5	3			
06029092	兰花	10	0	0	0	0	0	0	0	0	0	0		1	5		0	5	0			
06029093	菊花	10	0	0	0	0	0	0	0	0	0	0		1	5		0	5	0			
06029094	百合	10	0	0	0	0	0	0	0	0	0	0		1	5		0	5	0			
06029095	康乃馨	10	0	0	0	0	0	0	0	0	0	0		1	5		0	5	0			
06029099	其他非种用活植物	10	0	0	0	0	0	0	0	0	0	0	5	1	5		0	5	0			
06031100	鲜玫瑰	10	0	0	0	0	0	0	0	0	0	0	5	1	5		0	0	0			
06031200	鲜康乃馨	10	0	0	0	0	0	0	0	0	0	0	5	1	5		0	0	0			
06031300	鲜兰花	10	0	0	0	0	0	0	0	0	0	0	5	1	5		0	0	0			0

税则号列	商品名称（简称）	最惠国	东盟										亚太	智利	巴基斯坦	新加坡	新西兰	秘鲁	哥斯达黎加	香港	澳门	台湾
			文	柬	印	老	马	缅	菲	新	泰	越										
06031400	鲜菊花	10	0	0	0	0	0	0	0	0	0	0	5	1	5		0	0	0			
06031500	鲜百合花	10	0	0	0	0	0	0	0	0	0	0	5	1	5		0	0	0			
06031900	其他鲜花	10	0	0	0	0	0	0	0	0	0	0	5	1	5		0	0	0			
06039000	干的及经过染色等加工的插花及花蕾	23	0	0	0	0	0	0	0	0	0	0	11.5	0	11.5		0	11.5	4.6	0		
06042010	鲜苔藓及地衣	23	0	0	0	0	0	0	0	0	0	0		2.3			0	11.5	4.6			
06042090	鲜植物枝、叶等	10	0	0	0	0	0	0	0	0	0	0		1	5		0	5	0			
06049010	其他苔藓及地衣	23	0	0	0	0	0	0	0	0	0	0		2.3			0	11.5	4.6			
06049090	其他植物枝、叶等	10	0	0	0	0	0	0	0	0	0	0		0	5		0	0	0	0		
07011000	种用马铃薯	13	0	0	0	0	0	0	0	0	0	0		0	6.5		0	0	2.6			
07019000	其他鲜或冷的马铃薯	13	0	0	0	0	0	0	0	0	0	0	9	0	5		0	0	2.6			
07020000	鲜或冷藏的番茄	13	0	0	0	0	0	0	0	0	0	0		0	6.5		0	0	2.6			
07031010	鲜或冷的洋葱	13	0	0	0	0	0	0	0	0	0	0	6.5	0	5		0	0	2.6			
07031020	鲜或冷的青葱	13	0	0	0	0	0	0	0	0	0	0	6.5	0	5		0	0	2.6			
07032010	鲜或冷藏的大蒜头	13	0	0	0	0	0	0	0	0	0	0	6.5	0	0		0	0	2.6			
07032020	鲜或冷藏的大蒜蒜台及蒜苗(青蒜)	13	0	0	0	0	0	0	0	0	0	0	6.5	0	0		0	0	2.6			
07032090	其他鲜或冷藏的大蒜	13	0	0	0	0	0	0	0	0	0	0	6.5	0	0		0	0	2.6			
07039010	鲜或冷的韭葱	13	0	0	0	0	0	0	0	0	0	0		0	6.5		0	0	2.6			
07039020	鲜或冷的大葱	13	0	0	0	0	0	0	0	0	0	0		0	6.5		0	0	2.6			
07039090	鲜或冷的其他葱属蔬菜	13	0	0	0	0	0	0	0	0	0	0		0	6.5		0	0	2.6			
07041000	鲜或冷的菜花及硬花甘蓝	10	0	0	0	0	0	0	0	0	0	0		0	5		0	0	0			
07042000	鲜或冷的抱子甘蓝	13	0	0	0	0	0	0	0	0	0	0		0	6.5		0	0	2.6			
07049010	卷心菜	13	0	0	0	0	0	0	0	0	0	0		0	6.5		0	0	2.6			
07049020	西兰花	13	0	0	0	0	0	0	0	0	0	0		0	6.5		0	0	2.6			
07049090	鲜或冷的其他食用芥菜类蔬菜	13	0	0	0	0	0	0	0	0	0	0		0	6.5		0	0	2.6			
07051100	鲜或冷的结球莴苣(包心生菜)	10	0	0	0	0	0	0	0	0	0	0		0	0		0	0	0			
07051900	鲜或冷的其他莴苣	10	0	0	0	0	0	0	0	0	0	0		0	0		0	0	0			
07052100	鲜或冷的维特罗夫菊苣	13	0	0	0	0	0	0	0	0	0	0		0	0		0	0	2.6			
07052900	鲜或冷的其他菊苣	13	0	0	0	0	0	0	0	0	0	0		0	0		0	0	2.6			
07061000	鲜或冷的胡萝卜及萝卜	13	0	0	0	0	0	0	0	0	0	0		0	6.5		0	0	2.6			
07069000	鲜或冷的小萝卜及类似食用根茎	13	0	0	0	0	0	0	0	0	0	0		0	6.5		0	0	2.6			
07070000	鲜或冷的黄瓜及小黄瓜	13	0	0	0	0	0	0	0	0	0	0	6.5	0	5		0	0	2.6			
07081000	鲜或冷的豌豆	13	0	0	0	0	0	0	0	0	0	0	6.5	0	0		0	0	2.6			
07082000	鲜或冷的豇豆及菜豆	13	0	0	0	0	0	0	0	0	0	0	6.5	0	0		0	0	2.6			
07089000	鲜或冷的其他豆类蔬菜	13	0	0	0	0	0	0	0	0	0	0	6.5	0	0		0	0	2.6			
07092000	鲜或冷的芦笋	13	0	0	0	0	0	0	0	0	0	0	6.5	0	0		0	0	2.6			
07093000	鲜或冷的茄子	13	0	0	0	0	0	0	0	0	0	0	6.5	0	0		0	0	2.6			
07094000	鲜或冷的芹菜，但块根芹除外	10	0	0	0	0	0	0	0	0	0	0		0	0		0	0	0			
07095100	鲜或冷的其他伞菌属蘑菇	13	0	0	0	0	0	0	0	0	0	0		0	0		0	0	2.6			
07095910	鲜或冷的松茸	13	0	0	0	0	0	0	0	0	0	0		0	0		0	0	2.6			
07095920	鲜或冷的香菇	13	0	0	0	0	0	0	0	0	0	0		0	0		0	0	2.6			
07095930	鲜或冷的金针菇	13	0	0	0	0	0	0	0	0	0	0		0	0		0	0	2.6			0
07095940	鲜或冷的草菇	13	0	0	0	0	0	0	0	0	0	0		0	0		0	0	2.6			
07095950	鲜或冷的口蘑	13	0	0	0	0	0	0	0	0	0	0		0	0		0	0	2.6			
07095960	鲜或冷的块菌	13	0	0	0	0	0	0	0	0	0	0		0	0		0	0	2.6			
07095990	鲜或冷的其他蘑菇	13	0	0	0	0	0	0	0	0	0	0		0	0		0	0	2.6			
07096000	鲜或冷的辣椒，包括甜椒	13	0	0	0	0	0	0	0	0	0	0	6.5	0	0		0	0	2.6			
07097000	鲜或冷的菠菜	13	0	0	0	0	0	0	0	0	0	0		0	0		0	0	2.6	0		
07099100	鲜或冷藏的洋蓟	13	0	0	0	0	0	0	0	0	0	0		0	0		0	0	2.6	0		
07099200	鲜或冷藏的油橄榄	13	0	0	0	0	0	0	0	0	0	0		0	0		0	0	2.6	0		
07099300	鲜或冷藏的南瓜、笋瓜及瓠瓜	13	0	0	0	0	0	0	0	0	0	0		0	0		0	0	2.6	0		
07099910	鲜或冷藏的竹笋	13	0	0	0	0	0	0	0	0	0	0		0	0		0	0	2.6			
07099990	鲜或冷藏的其他蔬菜	13	0	0	0	0	0	0	0	0	0	0		0	0		0	0	2.6	0		
07101000	冷冻马铃薯	13	0	0	0	0	0	0	0	0	0	0		0	6.5		0	0	2.6			
07102100	冷冻豌豆	13	0	0	0	0	0	0	0	0	0	0		0	6.5		0	0	2.6			
07102210	红小豆（赤豆）	13	0	0	0	0	0	0	0	0	0	0		0	6.5		0	0	2.6			
07102290	其他冷冻豇豆及菜豆	13	0	0	0	0	0	0	0	0	0	0		0	6.5		0	0	2.6			
07102900	冷冻其他豆类蔬菜	13	0	0	0	0	0	0	0	0	0	0		0	6.5		0	0	2.6			
07103000	冷冻菠菜	13	0	0	0	0	0	0	0	0	0	0		0	6.5		0	0	2.6			
07104000	冷冻甜玉米	10	0	0	0	0	0	0	0	0	0	0		0	5		0	0	0			
07108010	冷冻松茸	13	0	0	0	0	0	0	0	0	0	0		0	6.5		0	0	2.6			

税则号列	商品名称（简称）	最惠国	东盟										亚太	智利	巴基斯坦	新加坡	新西兰	秘鲁	哥斯达黎加	香港	澳门	台湾
			文	柬	印	老	马	缅	菲	新	泰	越										
07108020	冻其他蒜台及蒜苗(青蒜)	13	0	0	0	0	0	0	0	0	0	0		0	6.5		0	0	2.6			
07108030	冻蒜头	13	0	0	0	0	0	0	0	0	0	0		0	6.5		0	0	2.6			
07108040	冻牛肝菌	13	0	0	0	0	0	0	0	0	0	0		0	6.5		0	0	2.6			
07108090	冷冻未列名蔬菜	13	0	0	0	0	0	0	0	0	0	0		0	6.5		0	0	2.6			
07109000	冷冻什锦蔬菜	10	0	0	0	0	0	0	0	0	0	0		0	5		0	0	0			
07112000	暂时保藏的油橄榄	13	0	0	0	0	0	0	0	0	0	0		0	0		0	0	2.6			
07114000	暂时保藏的黄瓜及小黄瓜	13	0	0	0	0	0	0	0	0	0	0		0	0		0	0	2.6			
07115112	盐水小白蘑菇	13	0	0	0	0	0	0	0	0	0	0		0	0		0	0	2.6			
07115119	盐水的其他伞菌属蘑菇	13	0	0	0	0	0	0	0	0	0	0		0	0		0	0	2.6			
07115190	其他伞菌属蘑菇	13	0	0	0	0	0	0	0	0	0	0		0	0		0	0	2.6			
07115911	盐水松茸	13	0	0	0	0	0	0	0	0	0	0		0	0		0	0	2.6			
07115919	盐水其他蘑菇及菌块	13	0	0	0	0	0	0	0	0	0	0		0	0		0	0	2.6			
07115990	暂时保藏的其他蘑菇及菌块	13	0	0	0	0	0	0	0	0	0	0		0	0		0	0	2.6			
07119031	盐水竹笋	13	0	0	0	0	0	0	0	0	0	0	6.5	0	0		0	0	2.6			
07119034	盐水大蒜	13	0	0	0	0	0	0	0	0	0	0	6.5	0	0		0	0	2.6			
07119039	盐水其他蔬菜；什锦蔬菜	13	0	0	0	0	0	0	0	0	0	0	6.5	0	0		0	0	2.6			
07119090	暂时保藏的其他蔬菜；什锦蔬菜	13	0	0	0	0	0	0	0	0	0	0	6.5	0	0		0	0	2.6			
07122000	干制洋葱	13	0	0	0	0	0	0	0	0	0	0		0	6.5		0	0	2.6			
07123100	干伞菌属蘑菇	13	0	0	0	0	0	0	0	0	0	0	9	0	5		0	0	2.6			
07123200	干木耳	13	0	0	0	0	0	0	0	0	0	0		0	6.5		0	0	2.6			
07123300	干银耳	13	0	0	0	0	0	0	0	0	0	0		0	6.5		0	0	2.6			
07123910	干香菇	13	0	0	0	0	0	0	0	0	0	0	9	0	5		0	0	2.6			
07123920	干金针菇	13	0	0	0	0	0	0	0	0	0	0	9	0	5		0	0	2.6			
07123930	干草菇	13	0	0	0	0	0	0	0	0	0	0	9	0	5		0	0	2.6			
07123940	干口蘑	13	0	0	0	0	0	0	0	0	0	0	9	0	5		0	0	2.6			
07123950	干牛肝菌	13	0	0	0	0	0	0	0	0	0	0	9	0	5		0	0	2.6			
07123990	其他干制蘑菇及块菌	13	0	0	0	0	0	0	0	0	0	0	9	0	9		0	0	2.6			
07129010	笋干丝	13	0	0	0	0	0	0	0	0	0	0		0	6.5		0	0	2.6			
07129020	紫萁(薇菜干)	13	0	0	0	0	0	0	0	0	0	0		0	6.5		0	0	2.6			
07129030	干金针菜(黄花菜)	13	0	0	0	0	0	0	0	0	0	0		0	6.5		0	0	2.6			
07129040	蕨菜干	13	0	0	0	0	0	0	0	0	0	0		0	6.5		0	0	2.6			
07129050	干制的大蒜	13	0	0	0	0	0	0	0	0	0	0		0	6.5		0	0	2.6			
07129060	干甜椒	13	0	0	0	0	0	0	0	0	0	0		0	6.5		0	0	2.6			
07129091	干制的辣根	13	0	0	0	0	0	0	0	0	0	0		0	6.5		0	0	2.6			
07129099	干制的其他蔬菜及什锦蔬菜	13	0	0	0	0	0	0	0	0	0	0		0	6.5		0	0	2.6			
07131090	其他干豌豆	5	0	0	0	0	0	0	0	0	0	0		0	0		0	0	0			
07132090	其他干鹰嘴豆	7	0	0	0	0	0	0	0	0	0	0		0	5		0	0	0			
07133190	其他干绿豆	3	0	0	0	0	0	0	0	0	0	0	1.5	0	0		0	0	0			
07133290	其他红小豆（赤豆）	3	0	0	0	0	0	0	0	0	0	0		0	0		0	0	0			
07133390	其他干芸豆	7.5	0	0	0	0	0	0	0	0	0	0		0	5		0	0	0			
07133400	干巴姆巴拉豆	7	0	0	0	0	0	0	0	0	0	0	3.5	0	0		0	0	0			
07133500	干牛豆	7	0	0	0	0	0	0	0	0	0	0	3.5	0	0		0	0	0			
07133900	干豇豆及菜豆	7	0	0	0	0	0	0	0	0	0	0	3.5	0	0		0	0	0			
07134090	其他干扁豆	7	0	0	0	0	0	0	0	0	0	0		0	5		0	0	0			
07135090	其他干蚕豆	7	0	0	0	0	0	0	0	0	0	0		0	5		0	0	0			
07136090	其他干木豆	7	0	0	0	0	0	0	0	0	0	0		0	5		0	0	0			
07139090	其它干豆	7	0	0	0	0	0	0	0	0	0	0		0	5		0	0	0			
07141010	鲜木薯	10	0	0	0	0	0	0	0	0	0	0		0	5		0	0	0			
07141020	干木薯	5	0	0	0	0	0	0	0	0	0	0		0	0		0	0	0			
07141030	冷或冻的木薯	10	0	0	0	0	0	0	0	0	0	0		0	5		0	0	0			
07142019	其他鲜甘薯	13	0	0	0	0	0	0	0	0	0	0	6.5	0	5		0	0	2.6			
07142020	干甘薯	13	0	0	0	0	0	0	0	0	0	0	6.5	0	5		0	0	2.6			
07142030	冷或冻的甘薯	13	0	0	0	0	0	0	0	0	0	0	6.5	0	5		0	0	2.6			
07143000	山药	13	0	0	0	0	0	0	0	0	0	0	6.5	0	5		0	0	2.6			
07144000	芋头	13	0	0	0	0	0	0	0	0	0	0	6.5	0	5		0	0	2.6			
07145000	箭叶黄体芋	13	0	0	0	0	0	0	0	0	0	0	6.5	0	5		0	0	2.6			
07149010	鲜、干或冷、冻的荸荠	13	0	0	0	0	0	0	0	0	0	0	6.5	0	5		0	0	2.6			
07149029	其他藕	13	0	0	0	0	0	0	0	0	0	0	6.5	0	5		0	0	2.6			
07149090	含有高淀粉或菊粉的其他类似根茎	13	0	0	0	0	0	0	0	0	0	0	6.5	0	5		0	0	2.6			
08011100	干的椰子	12	0	0	0	0	0	0	0	0	0	0	6	0	5		0	0	8.8		0	

税则号列	商品名称（简称）	最惠国	东盟										亚太	智利	巴基斯坦	新加坡	新西兰	秘鲁	哥斯达黎加	香港	澳门	台湾
			文	柬	印	老	马	缅	菲	新	泰	越										
08011200	未去内壳的鲜椰子	12	0	0	0	0	0	0	0	0	0	0	6	0	5		0	0	8.8			
08011990	其他鲜椰子	12	0	0	0	0	0	0	0	0	0	0	6	0	5		0	0	8.8			
08012100	鲜或干的未去壳巴西果	10	0	0	0	0	0	0	0	0	0	0		0	5		0	0	7.3		0	
08012200	鲜或干的去壳巴西果	10	0	0	0	0	0	0	0	0	0	0		0	5		0	0	7.3		0	
08013100	鲜或干的未去壳腰果	20	0	0	0	0	0	0	0	0	0	0		0			0	10	14.7		0	
08013200	鲜或干的去壳腰果	10	0	0	0	0	0	0	0	0	0	0		0	5		0	0	7.3		0	
08021100	未去壳扁桃仁	24	0	0	0	0	0	0	0	0	0	0		2.4			0	12	17.6		0	
08021200	其他扁桃仁	10	0	0	0	0	0	0	0	0	0	0		1	5		0	5	7.3		0	
08022100	鲜或干的未去壳榛子	25	0	0	0	0	0	0	0	0	0	0		2.5			0	12.5	18.3		0	
08022200	鲜或干的去壳榛子	10	0	0	0	0	0	0	0	0	0	0		0	5		0	0	7.3		0	
08023100	鲜或干的未去壳核桃	25	0	0	0	0	0	0	0	0	0	0		2.5			0	12.5	18.3		0	
08023200	鲜或干的去壳核桃	20	0	0	0	0	0	0	0	0	0	0		2			0	10	14.7		0	
08024110	未去壳板栗	25	0	0	0	0	0	0	0	0	0	0		2.5			0	12.5	18.3		0	
08024190	未去壳其他栗子	25	0	0	0	0	0	0	0	0	0	0		2.5			0	12.5	18.3		0	
08024210	去壳板栗	25	0	0	0	0	0	0	0	0	0	0		2.5			0	12.5	18.3		0	
08024290	去壳其他栗子	25	0	0	0	0	0	0	0	0	0	0		2.5			0	12.5	18.3		0	
08025100	未去壳阿月浑子果	10	0	0	0	0	0	0	0	0	0	0		0	5		0	0	7.3		0	
08025200	去壳阿月浑子果	10	0	0	0	0	0	0	0	0	0	0		0	5		0	0	7.3		0	
08026190	未去壳其他马卡达姆坚果	24	0	0	0	0	0	0	0	0	0	0		0			0	12	17.6		0	
08026200	去壳马卡达姆坚果	24	0	0	0	0	0	0	0	0	0	0		0			0	12	17.6		0	
08027000	可乐果	24	0	0	0	0	0	0	0	0	0	0		0			0	12	17.6		0	
08028000	槟榔果	10	0	0	0	0	0	0	0	0	0	0	5	0	5		0	0	7.3		0	
08029020	鲜或干的白果	25	0	0	0	0	0	0	0	0	0	0		0			0	12.5	18.3		0	
08029030	鲜或干的松子仁	25	0	0	0	0	0	0	0	0	0	0		0			0	12.5	18.3		0	
08029090	其他鲜或干坚果	24	0	0	0	0	0	0	0	0	0	0		0			0	12	17.6		0	
08031000	鲜或干的芭蕉	10	0	0	0	0	0	0	0	0	0	0	6.9	1	5		0	5	7.3		0	0
08039000	鲜或干的其他香蕉	10	0	0	0	0	0	0	0	0	0	0	6.9	1	5		0	5	7.3		0	0
08041000	鲜或干的椰枣	15	0	0	0	0	0	0	0	0	0	0		0	0		0	7.5	11		0	
08042000	鲜或干的无花果	30	0	0	0	0	0	0	0	0	0	0		3	0		0	15	22		0	
08043000	鲜或干菠萝	12	0	0	0	0	0	0	0	0	0	0	7.9	0	0		0	0	8.8	0	0	
08044000	鲜或干鳄梨	25	0	0	0	0	0	0	0	0	0	0	12.5	2.5	0		0	0	18.3		0	
08045010	鲜或干番石榴	15	0	0	0	0	0	0	0	0	0	0	7.5	0	0		0	7.5	11		0	
08045020	鲜或干芒果	15	0	0	0	0	0	0	0	0	0	0	10.6	0	0		0	0	11		0	
08045030	鲜或干山竹果	15	0	0	0	0	0	0	0	0	0	0	7.5	0	0		0	0	11		0	
08051000	鲜或干橙	11	0	0	0	0	0	0	0	0	0	0		1.1	0		2.4	4.1	8.1		0	0
08052010	鲜或干蕉柑	12	0	0	0	0	0	0	0	0	0	0		1.2	0		2.7	6	8.8		0	
08052020	阔叶柑橘	12	0	0	0	0	0	0	0	0	0	0		1.2	0		2.7	6	8.8		0	
08052090	其他鲜或干的柑桔及杂交柑桔	12	0	0	0	0	0	0	0	0	0	0		1.2	0		2.7	4.5	8.8		0	
08054000	鲜或干的葡萄柚,包括柚	12	0	0	0	0	0	0	0	0	0	0		1.2	0		0	6	8.8	0	0	
08055000	鲜或干的柠檬及酸橙	11	0	0	0	0	0	0	0	0	0	0	5.5	1.1	0		2.4	4.1	8.1		0	0
08059000	其他鲜或干的柑桔属水果	30	0	0	0	0	0	0	0	0	0	0	15	0	0		0	0	22		0	
08061000	鲜葡萄	13	0	0	0	0	0	0	0	0	0	0		1.3	6.5		0	1.3	2.6			
08062000	葡萄干	10	0	0	0	0	0	0	0	0	0	0		1	5		0	5	0		0	
08071100	鲜西瓜	25	0	0	0	0	0	0	0	0	0	0	12.5	0	12.5		0	12.5	5			
08071910	鲜哈密瓜	12	0	0	0	0	0	0	0	0	0	0	6	0	5		0	0	2.4			0
08071920	鲜罗马甜瓜及加勒比甜瓜	12	0	0	0	0	0	0	0	0	0	0	6	1.2	5		0	6	2.4			
08071990	其他鲜甜瓜	12	0	0	0	0	0	0	0	0	0	0	6	1.2	5		0	6	7.2			
08072000	鲜木瓜	25	0	0	0	0	0	0	0	0	0	0		0			0	12.5	5			
08081000	鲜苹果	10	0	0	0	0	0	0	0	0	0	0		1	5		0	5	0			
08083010	鲜鸭梨及雪梨	12	0	0	0	0	0	0	0	0	0	0	10	1.2	5		0	6	2.4			
08083020	鲜香梨	12	0	0	0	0	0	0	0	0	0	0	10	1.2	5		0	6	2.4			
08083090	其他鲜梨	10	0	0	0	0	0	0	0	0	0	0		1	5		0	5	0			
08084000	鲜榅桲	16	0	0	0	0	0	0	0	0	0	0		1.6	12.8		0	8	3.2			
08091000	鲜杏	25	0	0	0	0	0	0	0	0	0	0		2.5			0	12.5	5			
08092100	鲜欧洲酸樱桃	10	0	0	0	0	0	0	0	0	0	0		0	5		0	5	0			
08092900	其他鲜樱桃	10	0	0	0	0	0	0	0	0	0	0		0	5		0	5	0			
08093000	鲜桃,包括鲜油桃	10	0	0	0	0	0	0	0	0	0	0		0	5		0	5	0			
08094000	鲜梅及李	10	0	0	0	0	0	0	0	0	0	0		0	5		0	5	0			
08101000	鲜草莓	14	0	0	0	0	0	0	0	0	0	0		1.4			0	0	3.1			
08102000	鲜的木莓、黑莓、桑椹及罗甘莓	25	0	0	0	0	0	0	0	0	0	0		2.5			0	12.5	5			

税则号列	商品名称（简称）	最惠国	东盟										亚太	智利	巴基斯坦	新加坡	新西兰	秘鲁	哥斯达黎加	香港	澳门	台湾
			文	柬	印	老	马	缅	菲	新	泰	越										
08103000	鲜黑、白或红的穗醋栗（加仑子）及醋栗	25	0	0	0	0	0	0	0	0	0	0		2.5			0	12.5	5			
08104000	鲜蔓越桔及越桔	30	0	0	0	0	0	0	0	0	0	0		3			0	0	6			
08105000	鲜猕猴桃	20	0	0	0	0	0	0	0	0	0	0	16.5	2	16		4.4	10	4			
08106000	鲜榴莲	20	0	0	0	0	0	0	0	0	0	0		0			0	10	4			
08107000	鲜柿子	20	0	0	0	0	0	0	0	0	0	0	16.4	2	16		0	0	4	0		
08109010	鲜荔枝	30	0	0	0	0	0	0	0	0	0	0	20	0	20		0	15	6			
08109030	鲜龙眼	12	0	0	0	0	0	0	0	0	0	0		0	6		0	0	2.4			
08109040	鲜红毛丹	20	0	0	0	0	0	0	0	0	0	0		0			0	10	4			
08109050	鲜蕃荔枝	20	0	0	0	0	0	0	0	0	0	0		0			0	0	4			
08109060	鲜杨桃	20	0	0	0	0	0	0	0	0	0	0		0			0	0	4			
08109070	莲雾	20	0	0	0	0	0	0	0	0	0	0	16.4	0	16		0	10	4			
08109080	火龙果	20	0	0	0	0	0	0	0	0	0	0	16.4	0	16		0	10	4			0
08109090	其他鲜果	20	0	0	0	0	0	0	0	0	0	0	16.4	2	16		0	0	4	0		
08111000	冷冻草莓	30	0	0	0	0	0	0	0	0	0	0		3			0	15	6			
08112000	冷冻其他浆果	30	0	0	0	0	0	0	0	0	0	0		3			0	15	6			
08119010	未去壳的冷冻栗子	30	0	0	0	0	0	0	0	0	0	0		0			0	15	6			
08119090	其他冷冻水果及坚果	30	0	0	0	0	0	0	0	0	0	0		3			0	15	6			
08121000	暂时保藏的樱桃	30	0	0	0	0	0	0	0	0	0	0		3			0	15	6			
08129000	暂时保藏的其他水果及坚果	25	0	0	0	0	0	0	0	0	0	0		2.5			0	12.5	5			
08131000	杏干	25	0	0	0	0	0	0	0	0	0	0		0			0	12.5	5		0	
08132000	梅干及李干	25	0	0	0	0	0	0	0	0	0	0		2.5			0	12.5	5		0	
08133000	苹果干	25	0	0	0	0	0	0	0	0	0	0		2.5			0	12.5	5		0	
08134010	龙眼干、肉	20	0	0	0	0	0	0	0	0	0	0		0			0	10	4		0	
08134020	柿饼	25	0	0	0	0	0	0	0	0	0	0		0			0	12.5	5		0	
08134030	干红枣	25	0	0	0	0	0	0	0	0	0	0		0			0	12.5	5		0	
08134040	荔枝干	25	0	0	0	0	0	0	0	0	0	0		0			0	12.5	5		0	
08134090	其他干果	25	0	0	0	0	0	0	0	0	0	0		2.5			0	12.5	5		0	
08135000	本章的什锦坚果或干果	18	0	0	0	0	0	0	0	0	0	0		0	14.4		0	9	3.6		0	
08140000	柑桔属水果或甜瓜的果皮	25	0	0	0	0	0	0	0	0	0	0		2.5			0	12.5	5		0	
09011100	未浸除咖啡碱的未焙炒咖啡	8												0			0		4.8			
09011200	已浸除咖啡碱的未焙炒咖啡	8												0			0					
09012100	未浸除咖啡碱的已焙炒咖啡	15												1.5			0		9	0	0	
09012200	已浸除咖啡碱的已焙炒咖啡	15	0	0	0	0	0	0	0	0	0	0		1.5	12		0				0	
09019010	咖啡豆荚及咖啡豆皮	10	0	0	0	0	0	0	0	0	0	0		0	5	0	0	0	0			
09019020	含咖啡的咖啡代用品	30	0	0	0	0	0	0	0	0	0	0		0		0	0				0	
09021010	每件净重≤3kg的花茶	15	0	0	0	0	0	0	0	0	0	0	7.5	0	7.5	0	0	7.5	3		0	
09021090	每件净重≤3kg的其他绿茶	15	0	0	0	0	0	0	0	0	0	0	7.5	0	7.5	0	0	7.5	3		0	0
09022010	每件净重>3kg的花茶	15	0	0	0	0	0	0	0	0	0	0	7.5	0	7.5	0	0	7.5	3		0	
09022090	每件净重>3kg的其他绿茶	15	0	0	0	0	0	0	0	0	0	0	7.5	0	7.5	0	0	7.5	3		0	0
09023010	每件净重≤3kg的乌龙茶	15	0	0	0	0	0	0	0	0	0	0	7.5	0	7.5	0	0	7.5	3	0	0	0
09023020	每件净重≤3kg的普洱茶	15	0	0	0	0	0	0	0	0	0	0	7.5	0	7.5	0	0	7.5	3	0	0	
09023090	每件净重≤3kg 的其他发酵、半发酵红茶	15	0	0	0	0	0	0	0	0	0	0	7.5	0	7.5	0	0	7.5	3	0	0	0
09024010	每件净重>3kg的乌龙茶	15	0	0	0	0	0	0	0	0	0	0	7.5	0	7.5	0	0	7.5	3	0	0	0
09024020	每件净重>3kg的普洱茶	15	0	0	0	0	0	0	0	0	0	0	7.5	0	7.5	0	0	7.5	3	0	0	
09024090	每件净重>3kg 的其他红茶(已发酵)及半发酵茶	15	0	0	0	0	0	0	0	0	0	0	7.5	0	7.5	0	0	7.5	3	0	0	0
09030000	马黛茶	10	0	0	0	0	0	0	0	0	0	0		0	5	0	0	0	0			
09041100	未磨胡椒	20												0			0	10	4			
09041200	已磨胡椒	20											10	0	10		0	10	4	0		
09042100	未磨干辣椒	20	0	0	0	0	0	0	0	0	0	0	10	0	10	0	0	0	4	0		
09042200	已磨辣椒	20	0	0	0	0	0	0	0	0	0	0	10	0	10	0	0	0	4	0		
09051000	未磨香子兰豆	15	0	0	0	0	0	0	0	0	0	0		0	12	0	0	7.5	3			
09052000	已磨香子兰豆	15	0	0	0	0	0	0	0	0	0	0		0	12	0	0	7.5	3			
09061100	未磨锡兰肉桂	5	0	0	0	0	0	0	0	0	0	0		0	0		0	0	0			
09061900	其他未磨的肉桂及肉桂花	5	0	0	0	0	0	0	0	0	0	0		0	0		0	0	0			
09062000	已磨肉桂及肉桂花	15	0	0	0	0	0	0	0	0	0	0		0	12	0	0	7.5	3	0		
09071000	未磨丁香	3	0	0	0	0	0	0	0	0	0	0		0	0		0	0	0			
09072000	已磨丁香	3	0	0	0	0	0	0	0	0	0	0		0	0		0	0	0			

税则号列	商品名称（简称）	最惠国	东盟										亚太	智利	巴基斯坦	新加坡	新西兰	秘鲁	哥斯达黎加	香港	澳门	台湾
			文	柬	印	老	马	缅	菲	新	泰	越										
09081100	未磨肉豆蔻	8	0	0	0	0	0	0	0	0	0	0		0	5		0	0	0			
09081200	已磨肉豆蔻	8	0	0	0	0	0	0	0	0	0	0		0	5		0	0	0			
09082100	未磨肉豆蔻衣	8	0	0	0	0	0	0	0	0	0	0		0	5		0	0	0			
09082200	已磨肉豆蔻衣	8	0	0	0	0	0	0	0	0	0	0		0	5		0	0	0			
09083100	未磨豆蔻	3	0	0	0	0	0	0	0	0	0	0		0	0		0	0	0			
09083200	已磨豆蔻	3	0	0	0	0	0	0	0	0	0	0		0	0		0	0	0			
09092100	未磨芫荽子	15	0	0	0	0	0	0	0	0	0	0		0	12	0	0	7.5	3			
09092200	已磨芫荽子	15	0	0	0	0	0	0	0	0	0	0		0	12	0	0	7.5	3			
09093100	未磨枯茗子	15	0	0	0	0	0	0	0	0	0	0	7.5	0	7.5	0	0	7.5	3			
09093200	已磨枯茗子	15	0	0	0	0	0	0	0	0	0	0	7.5	0	7.5	0	0	7.5	3			
09096110	未磨八角茴香	20	0	0	0	0	0	0	0	0	0	0		0		0	0	10	4			
09096190	未磨其他茴香	15	0	0	0	0	0	0	0	0	0	0		0	12	0	0	7.5	3			
09096210	已磨八角茴香	20	0	0	0	0	0	0	0	0	0	0		0		0	0	10	4			
09096290	已磨其他茴香	15	0	0	0	0	0	0	0	0	0	0		0	12	0	0	7.5	3			
09101100	未磨姜	15	0	0	0	0	0	0	0	0	0	0	7.5	0	7.5	0	0	7.5	3			
09101200	已磨姜	15	0	0	0	0	0	0	0	0	0	0	7.5	0	7.5	0	0	7.5	3			
09102000	番红花	2	0	0	0	0	0	0	0	0	0	0		0	0		0	0	0			
09103000	姜黄	15	0	0	0	0	0	0	0	0	0	0	7.5	0	7.5	0	0	7.5	3	0		
09109100	混合调味香料	15	0	0	0	0	0	0	0	0	0	0	7.5	0	7.5	0	0	7.5	3	0	0	
09109900	其他调味香料	15	0	0	0	0	0	0	0	0	0	0		0	12	0	0	7.5	3	0		
10011100	种用硬粒小麦	65	20	20	20	20	20	20	20	20	20	20										
10011900	其他硬粒小麦	65	20	20	20	20	20	20	20	20	20	20										
10019100	种用其他小麦及混合麦	65	20	20	20	20	20	20	20	20	20	20										
10019900	其他小麦及混合麦	65	20	20	20	20	20	20	20	20	20	20										
10029000	其他黑麦	3	0	0	0	0	0	0	0	0	0	0		0	0		0	0	0			
10039000	其他大麦	3	0	0	0	0	0	0	0	0	0	0	0	0	0		0	0	0			
10049000	其他燕麦	2	0	0	0	0	0	0	0	0	0	0		0	0		0	0	0			
10061019	种用稻谷	65	20	20	20	20	20	20	20	20	20	20										
10061099	其他稻谷	65	20	20	20	20	20	20	20	20	20	20										
10062090	其他糙米	65	20	20	20	20	20	20	20	20	20	20										
10063090	其他精米	65	20	20	20	20	20	20	20	20	20	20										
10064010	籼米碎米	65	20	20	20	20	20	20	20	20	20	20										
10064090	其他碎米	65	20	20	20	20	20	20	20	20	20	20										
10079000	其他高粱	2	0	0	0	0	0	0	0	0	0	0		0	0		0	0	0			
10081000	荞麦	2	0	0	0	0	0	0	0	0	0	0		0	0		0	0	0			
10082100	种用谷子	2	0	0	0	0	0	0	0	0	0	0		0	0		0	0	0			
10082900	其他谷子	2	0	0	0	0	0	0	0	0	0	0		0	0		0	0	0			
10083000	加那利草子	2	0	0	0	0	0	0	0	0	0	0		0	0		0	0	0			
10084090	其他直长马唐	3	0	0	0	0	0	0	0	0	0	0		0	0		0	0	0			
10085090	其他昆诺阿藜	3	0	0	0	0	0	0	0	0	0	0		0	0		0	0	0			
10086090	其他黑小麦	3	0	0	0	0	0	0	0	0	0	0		0	0		0	0	0			
10089090	其他谷物	3	0	0	0	0	0	0	0	0	0	0		0	0		0	0	0			
11029019	其他大米细粉	40	20	20	20	20	20	20	20	20	20	20										
11029090	其他谷物细粉	5	0	0	0	0	0	0	0	0	0	0		0	0		0	0	0			
11031910	燕麦粗粒及粗粉	5	0	0	0	0	0	0	0	0	0	0		0	0		0	0	0			
11031990	其他谷物粗粒及粗粉	5	0	0	0	0	0	0	0	0	0	0		0	0		0	0	0			
11032090	其他谷物团粒	20	0	0	0	0	0	0	0	0	0	0		0		0	0	10	4			
11041200	滚压或制片的燕麦	20	0	0	0	0	0	0	0	0	0	0		2		0	0	10	4			
11041910	滚压或制片的大麦	20	0	0	0	0	0	0	0	0	0	0		0		0	0	10	4			
11041990	滚压或制片的其他谷物	20	0	0	0	0	0	0	0	0	0	0		0		0	0	10	4			
11042200	经其他加工的燕麦	20	0	0	0	0	0	0	0	0	0	0		2		0	0	10	4			
11042910	经其他加工的大麦	65	0	0	0	0	0	0	0	0	0	0		0		0	0	32.5	13			
11042990	经其他加工的其他谷物	20	0	0	0	0	0	0	0	0	0	0		0		0	0	10	4			
11043000	整粒或经加工的谷物胚芽	20	0	0	0	0	0	0	0	0	0	0		0		0	0	10	4			
11051000	马铃薯细粉、粗粉及粉末	15	0	0	0	0	0	0	0	0	0	0		0	12	0	0	0	3			
11052000	马铃薯粉片、颗粒及团粒	15	0	0	0	0	0	0	0	0	0	0		1.5	12	0	0	7.5	3			
11061000	干豆细粉、粗粉及粉末	10	0	0	0	0	0	0	0	0	0	0		0		0	0	0	0			
11062000	用品目 0714 的西谷茎髓、植物根茎、块茎制成的细粉、粗粉、粉末	20	0	0	0	0	0	0	0	0	0	0		0		0	0	0	4			
11063000	水果及坚果的细粉、粗粉及粉末	20	0	0	0	0	0	0	0	0	0	0	10	2	10	0	0	10	4			

税则号列	商品名称（简称）	最惠国	东盟										亚太	智利	巴基斯坦	新加坡	新西兰	秘鲁	哥斯达黎加	香港	澳门	台湾
			文	柬	印	老	马	缅	菲	新	泰	越										
11071000	未焙制麦芽	10	0	0	0	0	0	0	0	0	0	0		1	5	0	0	5	0			
11072000	已焙制麦芽	10	0	0	0	0	0	0	0	0	0	0		1	5	0	0	5	0			
11081100	小麦淀粉	20	0	0	0	0	0	0	0	0	0	0		0		0	0	10	4			
11081200	玉米淀粉	20	0	0	0	0	0	0	0	0	0	0		0		0	0	0	4			
11081300	马铃薯淀粉	15	0	0	0	0	0	0	0	0	0	0		0	12	0	0	7.5	3			
11081400	木薯淀粉	10	0	0	0	0	0	0	0	0	0	0		0	5	0	0	0	0			
11081900	其他淀粉	20	0	0	0	0	0	0	0	0	0	0		0		0	0	10	4			
11082000	菊粉	20	0	0	0	0	0	0	0	0	0	0		0		0	0	10	4			
11090000	面筋，不论是否干制	18	0	0	0	0	0	0	0	0	0	0		0	14.4	0	0	9	3.6			
12019010	黄大豆	3	0	0	0	0	0	0	0	0	0	0	0	0.3	0		0	0	0			
12019020	黑大豆	3	0	0	0	0	0	0	0	0	0	0	0	0	0		0	0	0			
12019030	青大豆	3	0	0	0	0	0	0	0	0	0	0	0	0	0		0	0	0			
12019090	其他大豆	3	0	0	0	0	0	0	0	0	0	0	0	0	0		0	0	0			
12024100	去壳花生	15	0	0	0	0	0	0	0	0	0	0		0	12	0	0	7.5	3			
12024200	未去壳花生	15	0	0	0	0	0	0	0	0	0	0		0	12	0	0	7.5	3			
12030000	干椰子肉	15	0	0	0	0	0	0	0	0	0	0	7.5	0	7.5	0	0	7.5	3			
12040000	亚麻子	15	0	0	0	0	0	0	0	0	0	0		0	12	0	0	7.5	3			
12051090	其他低芥子酸油菜子	9	0	0	0	0	0	0	0	0	0	0	0	0.9	0		0	0	0			
12059090	其他油菜子	9	0	0	0	0	0	0	0	0	0	0	0	0.9	0		0	0	0			
12060090	其他葵花籽	15	0	0	0	0	0	0	0	0	0	0		1.5	12	0	0	7.5	3			
12071090	其他棕榈果及棕榈仁	10	0	0	0	0	0	0	0	0	0	0		0	5	0	0	0	0			
12072900	其他棉子	15	0	0	0	0	0	0	0	0	0	0		0	12	0	0	7.5	3			
12073090	其他蓖麻子	15	0	0	0	0	0	0	0	0	0	0		0		0	0	7.5	3			
12074090	其他芝麻	10	0	0	0	0	0	0	0	0	0	0	9	0	9	0	0	0	0			
12075090	其他芥子	15	0	0	0	0	0	0	0	0	0	0		0	12	0	0	7.5	3			
12076090	其他红花子	20	0	0	0	0	0	0	0	0	0	0		0		0	0	10	4			
12077091	黑瓜子	20	0	0	0	0	0	0	0	0	0	0		0		0	0	10	4			
12077092	红瓜子	20	0	0	0	0	0	0	0	0	0	0		0		0	0	10	4			
12077099	其他瓜子	30	0	0	0	0	0	0	0	0	0	0		0			0	15	6			
12079100	罂粟子	20	0	0	0	0	0	0	0	0	0	0		0		0	0	10	4			
12079991	牛油树果	20	0	0	0	0	0	0	0	0	0	0		2		0	0	10	4			
12079999	其他含油子仁及果实	10	0	0	0	0	0	0	0	0	0	0		1	5	0	0	5	0			
12081000	大豆粉	9	0	0	0	0	0	0	0	0	0	0		0	5		0	0	0			
12089000	其他含油子仁或果实的细粉及粗粉	15	0	0	0	0	0	0	0	0	0	0		0	12	0	0	7.5	3	0		
12101000	未研磨也未制成团粒的啤酒花	20	0	0	0	0	0	0	0	0	0	0		0		0	0	10	4			
12102000	已研磨或制成团粒的啤酒花；蛇麻腺	10	0	0	0	0	0	0	0	0	0	0		0	5	0	0	0	0			
12112010	鲜或干的西洋参	7.5	0	0	0	0	0	0	0	0	0	0		0	5	0	0	0	0	0	0	
12112020	鲜或干的野山参(西洋参除外)	20	0	0	0	0	0	0	0	0	0	0	16.4	0	16	0	0	10	4			
12112091	其他鲜人参	20	0	0	0	0	0	0	0	0	0	0		0		0	0	10	4	0		
12112099	其他干人参	20	0	0	0	0	0	0	0	0	0	0		0		0	0	10	4	0		
12113000	古柯叶	9	0	0	0	0	0	0	0	0	0	0		0	5		0	0	0			
12114000	罂粟杆	9	0	0	0	0	0	0	0	0	0	0		0	5		0	0	0			
12119011	鲜或干的当归	6	0	0	0	0	0	0	0	0	0	0	3	0	0		0	0	0			
12119012	三七（田七）	6	0	0	0	0	0	0	0	0	0	0	3	0	0		0	0	0			
12119013	鲜或干的党参	6	0	0	0	0	0	0	0	0	0	0	3	0	0		0	0	0			
12119014	鲜或干的黄连	6	0	0	0	0	0	0	0	0	0	0	3	0	0		0	0	0			
12119015	鲜或干的菊花	6	0	0	0	0	0	0	0	0	0	0	3	0	0		0	0	0			
12119016	鲜或干的冬虫夏草	6	0	0	0	0	0	0	0	0	0	0	3	0	0		0	0	0		0	
12119017	鲜或干的贝母	6	0	0	0	0	0	0	0	0	0	0	3	0	0		0	0	0			
12119018	鲜或干的川芎	6	0	0	0	0	0	0	0	0	0	0	3	0	0		0	0	0			
12119019	鲜或干的半夏	6	0	0	0	0	0	0	0	0	0	0	3	0	0		0	0	0			
12119021	鲜或干的白芍	6	0	0	0	0	0	0	0	0	0	0	3	0	0		0	0	0			
12119022	鲜或干的天麻	6	0	0	0	0	0	0	0	0	0	0	3	0	0		0	0	0			
12119023	鲜或干的黄芪	6	0	0	0	0	0	0	0	0	0	0	3	0	0		0	0	0			
12119024	鲜或干的大黄、籽黄	6	0	0	0	0	0	0	0	0	0	0	3	0	0		0	0	0			
12119025	鲜或干的白术	6	0	0	0	0	0	0	0	0	0	0	3	0	0		0	0	0			
12119026	鲜或干的地黄	6	0	0	0	0	0	0	0	0	0	0	3	0	0		0	0	0			
12119027	鲜或干的槐米	6	0	0	0	0	0	0	0	0	0	0	3	0	0		0	0	0			
12119028	鲜或干的杜仲	6	0	0	0	0	0	0	0	0	0	0	3	0	0		0	0	0			
12119029	鲜或干的茯苓	6	0	0	0	0	0	0	0	0	0	0	3	0	0		0	0	0			

税则号列	商品名称（简称）	最惠国	东盟										亚太	智利	巴基斯坦	新加坡	新西兰	秘鲁	哥斯达黎加	香港	澳门	台湾
			文	柬	印	老	马	缅	菲	新	泰	越										
12119031	鲜或干的枸杞	6	0	0	0	0	0	0	0	0	0	0	3	0	0		0	0	0			
12119032	鲜或干的大海子	6	0	0	0	0	0	0	0	0	0	0	3	0	0		0	0	0			
12119033	鲜或干的沉香	3	0	0	0	0	0	0	0	0	0	0	1.5	0	0		0	0	0			
12119034	鲜或干的沙参	6	0	0	0	0	0	0	0	0	0	0	3	0	0		0	0	0			
12119035	鲜或干的青蒿	6	0	0	0	0	0	0	0	0	0	0		0	5		0	0	0			
12119036	鲜或干的甘草	6	0	0	0	0	0	0	0	0	0	0		0	5		0	0	0			
12119037	鲜或干的黄芩	6	0	0	0	0	0	0	0	0	0	0	3	0	0		0	0	0			
12119038	椴树(欧椴)花及叶	6	0	0	0	0	0	0	0	0	0	0	3	0	0		0	0	0			
12119039	其他主要用作药料的鲜或干的植物	6	0	0	0	0	0	0	0	0	0	0	3	0	0		0	0	0			
12119050	主要用作香料的植物	8	0	0	0	0	0	0	0	0	0	0	4	0	0		0	0	0			
12119091	鲜或干的鱼藤根、除虫菊	3	0	0	0	0	0	0	0	0	0	0	1.5	0	0		0	0	0			
12119099	其他鲜或干的杀虫、杀菌用植物	9	0	0	0	0	0	0	0	0	0	0	4.5	0	4.5		0	0	0			
12122110	适合供人食用的海带	20	0	0	0	0	0	0	0	0	0	0	10	2	10	0	0	10	4			
12122120	适合供人食用的发菜	20	0	0	0	0	0	0	0	0	0	0	10	2	10	0	0	10	4			
12122131	适合供人食用的干裙带菜	15	0	0	0	0	0	0	0	0	0	0	7.5	1.5	7.5	0	0	8.8	3			
12122132	适合供人食用的鲜裙带菜	15	0	0	0	0	0	0	0	0	0	0	7.5	1.5	7.5	0	0	8.8	3			
12122139	适合供人食用的其他裙带菜	15	0	0	0	0	0	0	0	0	0	0	7.5	1.5	7.5	0	0	8.8	3			
12122141	适合供人食用的干紫菜	15	0	0	0	0	0	0	0	0	0	0	7.5	1.5	7.5	0	0	8.8	3			
12122142	适合供人食用的鲜紫菜	15	0	0	0	0	0	0	0	0	0	0	7.5	1.5	7.5	0	0	8.8	3			
12122149	适合供人食用的其他紫菜	15	0	0	0	0	0	0	0	0	0	0	7.5	1.5	7.5	0	0	8.8	3			
12122161	适合供人食用的干麒麟菜	15	0	0	0	0	0	0	0	0	0	0	7.5	1.5	7.5		0	8.8	3			
12122169	适合供人食用的其他麒麟菜	15	0	0	0	0	0	0	0	0	0	0	7.5	1.5	7.5		0	8.8	3			
12122171	适合供人食用的干江蓠	15	0	0	0	0	0	0	0	0	0	0	7.5	1.5	7.5		0	8.8	3			
12122179	适合供人食用的其他江蓠	15	0	0	0	0	0	0	0	0	0	0	7.5	1.5	7.5		0	8.8	3			
12122190	其他适合供人食用的海草及其他藻类	15	0	0	0	0	0	0	0	0	0	0	7.5	1.5	7.5	0	0	8.8	3			
12122900	其他海草及藻类	15	0	0	0	0	0	0	0	0	0	0	7.5	1.5	7.5	0	0	8.8	3			
12129100	鲜、冷、冻或干的甜菜	20	0	0	0	0	0	0	0	0	0	0		0		0	0	10	4			
12129200	刺槐豆	20	0	0	0	0	0	0	0	0	0	0	10	0	10	0	0	10	4			
12129300	甘蔗	20	0	0	0	0	0	0	0	0	0	0		0			0	10	4			
12129400	菊苣根	20	0	0	0	0	0	0	0	0	0	0		0			0	15	6			
12129911	主要供人食用的苦杏仁	20	0	0	0	0	0	0	0	0	0	0		2		0	0	10	4			
12129912	主要供人食用的甜杏仁	20	0	0	0	0	0	0	0	0	0	0		2		0	0	10	4	0		
12129919	主要供人食用的桃(包括油桃)、梅或李的核及核仁	20	0	0	0	0	0	0	0	0	0	0		2		0	0	10	4			
12129993	鲜、冷、冻或干的白瓜子	20	0	0	0	0	0	0	0	0	0	0		0		0	0	10	4			
12129994	鲜、冷、冻或干的莲子	20	0	0	0	0	0	0	0	0	0	0		0		0	0	10	4			
12129996	甜叶菊叶	30	0	0	0	0	0	0	0	0	0	0		0		0	0	15	6			
12129999	鲜、冷、冻或干的其他主要供人食用的其他税号未列明的果核、果仁及植物产品	30	0	0	0	0	0	0	0	0	0	0		0		0	0	15	6			
12130010	未经处理的稻草的茎、杆	12	0	0	0	0	0	0	0	0	0	0		0	6	0	0	0	2.4			
12130090	其他未经处理的谷类植物茎、杆及谷壳	12	0	0	0	0	0	0	0	0	0	0		0	6	0	0	0	2.4			
12141000	紫苜蓿粗粉及团粒	5	0	0	0	0	0	0	0	0	0	0		0	0		0	0	0			
12149000	芜菁甘蓝、饲料甜菜等其他植物饲料	9	0	0	0	0	0	0	0	0	0	0		0	5		0	0	0			
13012000	阿拉伯胶	15	0	0	0	0	0	0	0	0	0	0		0	0	0	0	0	3			
13019010	胶黄耆树胶	15	0	0	0	0	0	0	0	0	0	0		0	0	0	0	0	3			
13019020	乳香、没药及血竭	3	0	0	0	0	0	0	0	0	0	0		0	0		0	0	0			
13019030	阿魏	3	0	0	0	0	0	0	0	0	0	0		0	0		0	0	0			
13019040	松脂	15	0	0	0	0	0	0	0	0	0	0		0	0	0	0	0	3			
13019090	其他天然树胶、树脂	15	0	0	0	0	0	0	0	0	0	0		0	0	0	0	0	3			
13021200	甘草液汁及浸膏	6	0	0	0	0	0	0	0	0	0	0		0	5		0	0	0			
13021300	啤酒花液汁及浸膏	10	0	0	0	0	0	0	0	0	0	0		0	5	0	0	0	0			
13021910	生漆	20	0	0	0	0	0	0	0	0	0	0		2		0	0	10	4			
13021920	印楝素	3	0	0	0	0	0	0	0	0	0	0		0	0		0	0	0			
13021930	除虫菊或含鱼藤酮植物根茎的液汁及浸膏	3	0	0	0	0	0	0	0	0	0	0		0	0		0	0	0			
13021940	银杏的液汁及浸膏	20	0	0	0	0	0	0	0	0	0	0	15	2	15	0	0	10	4			
13021990	其他植物液汁及浸膏	20	0	0	0	0	0	0	0	0	0	0	15	2	15	0	0	10	4			
13022000	果胶、果胶酸盐及果胶酸酯	20	0	0	0	0	0	0	0	0	0	0		0		0	0	10	4			
13023100	琼脂	10	0	0	0	0	0	0	0	0	0	0		1	5	0	0	5	0			
13023200	刺槐豆、刺槐豆子或瓜尔豆制得的胶	15	0	0	0	0	0	0	0	0	0	0	10	1.5	0	0	0	7.5	3			

税则号列	商品名称（简称）	最惠国	东盟 文	东盟 柬	东盟 印	东盟 老	东盟 马	东盟 缅	东盟 菲	东盟 新	东盟 泰	东盟 越	亚太	智利	巴基斯坦	新加坡	新西兰	秘鲁	哥斯达黎加	香港	澳门	台湾
	液及增稠剂																					
13023911	卡拉胶	15	0	0	0	0	0	0	0	0	0	0		1.5	12	0	0	7.5	3			
13023912	褐藻胶	15	0	0	0	0	0	0	0	0	0	0		1.5	12	0	0	7.5	3			
13023919	其他海草及藻类制品	15	0	0	0	0	0	0	0	0	0	0		1.5	12	0	0	10.6	3			
13023990	其他植物胶液及增稠剂	15	0	0	0	0	0	0	0	0	0	0		1.5	12	0	0	8.8	3			
14011000	竹	10	0	0	0	0	0	0	0	0	0	0		0	5	0	0	0	0			
14012000	藤	10	0	0	0	0	0	0	0	0	0	0		0	5	0	0	0	0			
14019010	谷类植物的茎秆(麦秸除外)	10	0	0	0	0	0	0	0	0	0	0		1	5	0	0	5	0			
14019020	芦苇	10	0	0	0	0	0	0	0	0	0	0		0	5	0	0	0	0			
14019031	蔺草	10	0	0	0	0	0	0	0	0	0	0		0	5	0	0	0	0			
14019039	灯芯草属的其他主要作编结用的植物材料	10	0	0	0	0	0	0	0	0	0	0		0	5	0	0	0	0			
14019090	未列名主要用作编结用的植物材料	10	0	0	0	0	0	0	0	0	0	0		1	5	0	0	5	0			
14042000	棉短绒	4	0	0	0	0	0	0	0	0	0	0		0	0		0	0	0			
14049010	主要供染料或鞣料用的植物原料	5	0	0	0	0	0	0	0	0	0	0	4.3	0	0		0	2.9	0			
14049090	其他植物产品	15	0	0	0	0	0	0	0	0	0	0		0		0	0	0	3			
15011000	猪油	10	0	0	0	0	0	0	0	0	0	0		0		0	0	0	0	0	0	
15012000	其他猪脂肪	10	0	0	0	0	0	0	0	0	0	0		0		0	0	0	0	0	0	
15019000	家禽脂肪	10	0	0	0	0	0	0	0	0	0	0		0		0	0	0	0	0	0	
15021000	牛、羊油脂	8	0	0	0	0	0	0	0	0	0	0	0	0	0		0	0	0		0	
15029000	其他牛、羊脂肪	8	0	0	0	0	0	0	0	0	0	0	0	0	0		0	0	0		0	
15030000	未经制作的猪油硬脂、油硬脂等	10	0	0	0	0	0	0	0	0	0	0		0		0	0	0	0		0	
15041000	鱼肝油及其分离品	12	0	0	0	0	0	0	0	0	0	0		0		0	0	0	2.4		0	
15042000	其他鱼油、脂及其分离品	12	0	0	0	0	0	0	0	0	0	0		1.2		0	0	4.5	2.4		0	
15043000	海生哺乳动物的油、脂及其分离品	14.4	0	0	0	0	0	0	0	0	0	0		0		0	0	0	2.9		0	
15050000	羊毛脂及羊毛脂肪物质	20	0	0	0	0	0	0	0	0	0	0		2		0	0	10	4			
15060000	其他动物油、脂及其分离品	20	0	0	0	0	0	0	0	0	0	0		0		0	0	10	4		0	
15081000	初榨花生油的分离品	10	0	0	0	0	0	0	0	0	0	0				0						
15089000	精制的花生油及其分离品	10	0	0	0	0	0	0	0	0	0	0				0						
15091000	初榨油橄榄油及其分离品	10	0	0	0	0	0	0	0	0	0	0		1		0	0	5	0		0	
15099000	精制的油橄榄油及其分离品	10	0	0	0	0	0	0	0	0	0	0		1		0	0	0	0	0	0	
15100000	其他橄榄油及其分离品	10	0	0	0	0	0	0	0	0	0	0		1		0	0	0	0		0	
15121100	初榨葵花油或红花油的分离品	9	0	0	0	0	0	0	0	0	0	0									0	
15121900	精制的葵花油或红花油及其分离品	9	0	0	0	0	0	0	0	0	0	0									0	
15122100	初榨棉子油的分离品	10	0	0	0	0	0	0	0	0	0	0				0					0	
15122900	精制的棉子油及其分离品	10	0	0	0	0	0	0	0	0	0	0				0					0	
15131100	初榨椰子油分离品	9	0	0	0	0	0	0	0	0	0	0	4.5	0	4.5		0	0	0		0	
15131900	椰子油及其分离品	9	0	0	0	0	0	0	0	0	0	0	4.5	0	4.5		0	0	0		0	
15132100	初榨棕榈仁油或巴巴苏棕榈果油及其分离品	9	0	0	0	0	0	0	0	0	0	0		0			0	0	0		0	
15132900	精制的棕榈仁油或巴巴苏棕榈果油及其分离品	9	0	0	0	0	0	0	0	0	0	0		0			0	0	0		0	
15151100	初榨亚麻子油及其分离品	15	0	0	0	0	0	0	0	0	0	0		0		0	0	7.5	3		0	
15151900	精制的亚麻子油及其分离品	15	0	0	0	0	0	0	0	0	0	0		0		0	0	7.5	3		0	
15152100	初榨玉米油的分离品	10	0	0	0	0	0	0	0	0	0	0				0					0	
15152900	精制的玉米油及其分离品	10	0	0	0	0	0	0	0	0	0	0				0					0	
15153000	蓖麻油及其分离品	10	0	0	0	0	0	0	0	0	0	0		0		0	0	0	0		0	
15155000	芝麻油及其分离品	12	0	0	0	0	0	0	0	0	0	0		0		0	0	0	2.4		0	
15159010	希蒙得木油及其分离品	20	0	0	0	0	0	0	0	0	0	0		2		0	0		4		0	
15159020	印楝油及其分离品	20	0	0	0	0	0	0	0	0	0	0		2		0	0		4		0	
15159030	桐油及其分离品	20	0	0	0	0	0	0	0	0	0	0		0		0	0		4		0	
15159090	其他固定植物油、脂及其分离品	20	0	0	0	0	0	0	0	0	0	0		2		0	0		4		0	
15161000	氢化、酯化或反油酸化动物油、脂及其分离品，但未进一步加工的	5	0		0		0	0	0	0	0	0		0			0	0	0		0	
15162000	氢化、酯化或反油酸化植物油、脂及其分离品,但未进一步加工的	25	0	0	0	0	0	0	0	0	0	0		2.5			0	12.5	5		0	
15171000	人造黄油,非液态	30	0	0	0	0	0	0	0	0	0	0		3		0	0		6		0	
15179010	起酥油	25	0	0	0	0	0	0	0	0	0	0		0			0	12.5	5	0	0	
15179090	混合制成的食用油脂或制品	25	0	0	0	0	0	0	0	0	0	0		0			0	12.5	5	0	0	
15180000	化学改性的动、植物油、脂及其制品；其他税号未列名的非食用油、脂或制品	10	0	0	0	0	0	0	0	0	0	0		1		0	0	5	0		0	

税则号列	商品名称（简称）	最惠国	东盟										亚太	智利	巴基斯坦	新加坡	新西兰	秘鲁	哥斯达黎加	香港	澳门	台湾
			文	柬	印	老	马	缅	菲	新	泰	越										
15200000	粗甘油,甘油水及甘油碱液	20	0	0	0	0	0	0	0	0	0	0		0		0	0	10	4	0	0	
15211000	植物蜡	20	0	0	0	0	0	0	0	0	0	0		0		0	0	10	4			
15219010	蜂蜡	20	0	0	0	0	0	0	0	0	0	0		0		0	0	10	4			
15219090	其他虫蜡及鲸蜡	20	0	0	0	0	0	0	0	0	0	0		0		0	0	10	4			
15220000	油鞣回收脂;加工处理油脂及动、植物蜡所剩残渣	20	0	0	0	0	0	0	0	0	0	0		0		0	0	10	4			
16010010	用天然肠衣做外包装的香肠及类似产品	15	0	0	0	0	0	0	0	0	0	0		1.5	12	0	0	7.5	3	0	0	
16010020	其他香肠及类似产品	15	0	0	0	0	0	0	0	0	0	0		1.5	12	0	0	7.5	3	0	0	
16010030	用香肠制成的食品	15	0	0	0	0	0	0	0	0	0	0		1.5	12	0	0	7.5	3		0	
16021000	肉或食用杂碎的均化食品	15	0	0	0	0	0	0	0	0	0	0		0	12	0	0	7.5	3			
16022000	制作或保藏的动物肝	15	0	0	0	0	0	0	0	0	0	0		0	12	0	0	7.5	3	0		
16023100	制作或保藏的火鸡肉及杂碎	15	0	0	0	0	0	0	0	0	0	0		0	12	0	0	7.5	3			
16023210	鸡罐头	15	0	0	0	0	0	0	0	0	0	0		1.5	12	0	0	7.5	3		0	
16023291	鸡胸肉	15	0	0	0	0	0	0	0	0	0	0		0	12	0	0	7.5	3	0		
16023292	鸡腿肉	15	0	0	0	0	0	0	0	0	0	0		1.5	12	0	0	7.5	3	0		
16023299	其他鸡肉	15	0	0	0	0	0	0	0	0	0	0		1.5	12	0	0	7.5	3	0	0	
16023910	其他品目 0105 所列家禽肉及杂碎的罐头	15	0	0	0	0	0	0	0	0	0	0		0	12	0	0	7.5	3		0	
16023991	鸭肉	15	0	0	0	0	0	0	0	0	0	0		0	12	0	0	7.5	3	0		
16023999	经制作或保藏的其他品目 0105 所列家禽肉及杂碎	15	0	0	0	0	0	0	0	0	0	0		0	12	0	0	7.5	3		0	
16024100	制作或保藏的猪后腿及其肉块	15	0	0	0	0	0	0	0	0	0	0		0	12	0	0	7.5	3		0	
16024200	制作或保藏的猪前腿及其肉块	15	0	0	0	0	0	0	0	0	0	0		0	12	0	0	7.5	3		0	
16024910	其他猪肉及杂碎的罐头	15	0	0	0	0	0	0	0	0	0	0		1.5	12	0	0	7.5	3		0	
16024990	制作或保藏的其他猪肉、杂碎及血	15	0	0	0	0	0	0	0	0	0	0		1.5	12	0	0	7.5	3	0	0	
16025010	牛肉及牛杂碎罐头	12	0	0	0	0	0	0	0	0	0	0		1.2	6	0	0	6	2.4		0	
16025090	其他制作或保藏的牛肉、杂碎及血	12	0	0	0	0	0	0	0	0	0	0		1.2	6	0	0	6	2.4	0	0	
16029010	其他肉及杂碎罐头	15	0	0	0	0	0	0	0	0	0	0		0	12	0	0	7.5	3		0	
16029090	经制作或保藏的其他肉、杂碎及血	15	0	0	0	0	0	0	0	0	0	0		0	12	0	0	7.5	3		0	
16030000	肉及水产品的精、汁	23	0	0	0	0	0	0	0	0	0	0		0		0	0	11.5	4.6	0		
16041110	制作或保藏的大西洋鲑鱼，整条或切块，但未绞碎	12	0	0	0	0	0	0	0	0	0	0		1.2	6	0	0		2.4	0		
16041190	制作或保藏的其他鲑鱼，整条或切块，但未绞碎	12	0	0	0	0	0	0	0	0	0	0		1.2	6	0	0		2.4			
16041200	制作或保藏的鲱鱼，整条或切块，但未绞碎	12	0	0	0	0	0	0	0	0	0	0		0	6	0	0	0	2.4			
16041300	制作或保藏的沙丁鱼、小沙丁鱼属、黍鲱或西鲱	5	0	0	0	0	0	0	0	0	0	0		0.5	0		0	1.9	0		0	
16041400	制作或保藏的金枪鱼、鲣鱼及狐鲣	5	0	0	0	0	0	0	0	0	0	0		0.5	0		0	0	0	0		
16041500	制作或保藏的鲭鱼，整条或切块，但未绞碎	12	0	0	0	0	0	0	0	0	0	0		1.2	6	0	0	4.5	2.4			
16041600	制作保藏的 Anchovies(醍鱼)，整条或切块，但未绞碎	12	0	0	0	0	0	0	0	0	0	0		1.2	6	0	0	4.5	2.4			
16041700	制作或保藏的鳗鱼	12	0	0	0	0	0	0	0	0	0	0	9.9	1.2	5	0	0		2.4	0		
16041920	制作或保藏的罗非鱼，整条或切块，但未绞碎	12	0	0	0	0	0	0	0	0	0	0		1.2	6	0	0		2.4	0		
16041931	制作或保藏的斑点叉尾鮰鱼	12	0	0	0	0	0	0	0	0	0	0	9.9	1.2	5	0	0		2.4	0		
16041939	制作或保藏的其他叉尾鮰鱼	12	0	0	0	0	0	0	0	0	0	0	9.9	1.2	5	0	0		2.4	0		
16041990	制作或保藏的其他鱼，整条或切块，但未绞碎	12	0	0	0	0	0	0	0	0	0	0	9.9	1.2	5	0	0		2.4	0	0	
16042011	鱼翅罐头	12	0	0	0	0	0	0	0	0	0	0	9.9	1.2	5	0	0	6	2.4	0	0	
16042019	其他制作或保藏的鱼罐头	12	0	0	0	0	0	0	0	0	0	0	9.9	1.2	5	0	0	6	2.4	0	0	
16042091	鱼翅	12	0	0	0	0	0	0	0	0	0	0	9.9	1.2	5	0	0	6	2.4	0	0	
16042099	其他制作或保藏的鱼	12	0	0	0	0	0	0	0	0	0	0	9.9	1.2	5	0	0	6	2.4	0	0	
16043100	鲟鱼子酱	12	0	0	0	0	0	0	0	0	0	0		0	6	0	0	0	2.4			
16043200	鲟鱼子酱代用品	12	0	0	0	0	0	0	0	0	0	0		0	6	0	0	0	2.4			
16051000	制作或保藏的蟹	5	0		0		0	0	0	0	0	0		0.5	0		0	0	0	0		
16052100	制作或保藏的非密封包装小虾及对虾	5	0	0	0	0	0	0	0	0	0	0		0.5	0		0	0	0	0		
16052900	制作或保藏的其他小虾及对虾	5	0	0	0	0	0	0	0	0	0	0		0.5	0		0	0	0	0		
16053000	制作或保藏的龙虾	5	0		0		0	0	0	0	0	0		0	0		0	0	0	0		
16054011	制作或保藏的淡水小龙虾仁	5	0		0		0	0	0	0	0	0		0	0		0	0	0			

税则号列	商品名称（简称）	最惠国	东盟										亚太	智利	巴基斯坦	新加坡	新西兰	秘鲁	哥斯达黎加	香港	澳门	台湾
			文	柬	印	老	马	缅	菲	新	泰	越										
16054019	制作或保藏的带壳淡水小龙虾	5	0		0		0	0	0	0	0	0		0	0		0	0	0			
16054090	制作或保藏的其他甲壳动物	5	0		0		0	0	0	0	0	0		0	0		0	0	0		0	
16055100	制作或保藏的牡蛎	5	0		0		0	0	0	0	0	0	3.9	0.5	0		0	1.9	0	0	0	
16055200	制作或保藏的扇贝	5	0		0		0	0	0	0	0	0	3.9	0.5	0		0	1.9	0	0	0	
16055300	制作或保藏的贻贝	5	0		0		0	0	0	0	0	0	3.9	0.5	0		0	1.9	0	0	0	
16055400	制作或保藏的墨鱼及鱿鱼	5	0		0		0	0	0	0	0	0	3.9	0.5	0		0	1.9	0	0	0	
16055500	制作或保藏的章鱼	5	0		0		0	0	0	0	0	0	3.9	0.5	0		0	1.9	0	0	0	
16055610	制作或保藏的蛤	5	0		0		0	0	0	0	0	0	3.9	0.5	0		0		0	0		
16055620	制作或保藏的鸟蛤及舟贝	5	0		0		0	0	0	0	0	0	3.9	0.5	0		0	1.9	0	0	0	
16055700	制作或保藏的鲍鱼	5	0		0		0	0	0	0	0	0	3.9	0.5	0		0	1.9	0	0	0	
16055800	制作或保藏的蜗牛及螺	5	0		0		0	0	0	0	0	0	3.9	0.5	0		0	1.9	0	0	0	
16055900	制作或保藏的其他软体动物	5	0		0		0	0	0	0	0	0	3.9	0.5	0		0	1.9	0	0	0	
16056100	制作或保藏的海参	5	0		0		0	0	0	0	0	0	3.9	0.5	0		0	1.9	0	0	0	
16056200	制作或保藏的海胆	5	0		0		0	0	0	0	0	0	3.9	0.5	0		0	1.9	0	0	0	
16056300	制作或保藏的海蜇	15	0	0	0	0	0	0	0	0	0	0		1.5	12	0	0		3	0		
16056900	制作或保藏的其他水生无脊椎动物	5	0		0		0	0	0	0	0	0	3.9	0.5	0		0	1.9	0	0	0	
17021100	无水乳糖，按重量计含量＞99%	10	0	0	0	0	0	0	0	0	0	0		0	5	0	0	0	0		0	
17021900	其他乳糖及乳糖浆	10	0	0	0	0	0	0	0	0	0	0		0	5	0	0	0	0		0	
17022000	槭糖及槭糖浆	30	0	0	0	0	0	0	0	0	0	0		0		0	0	15	6		0	
17023000	低果糖含量的葡萄糖及糖浆	30	0	0	0	0	0	0	0	0	0	0		0		0	0	15	6		0	
17024000	中果糖含量的葡萄糖及糖浆	30	0	0	0	0	0	0	0	0	0	0		0		0	0	15	6		0	
17025000	化学纯果糖	30	0	0	0	0	0	0	0	0	0	0		0		0	0	15	6		0	
17026000	其他果糖及糖浆	30	0	0	0	0	0	0	0	0	0	0		0		0	0	15	6		0	
17029000	其他固体糖；人造蜜；焦糖	30	0	0	0	0	0	0	0	0	0	0		3		0	0	21.2	6	0	0	
17031000	甘蔗糖蜜	8	0	0	0	0	0	0	0	0	0	0		0	5		0	0	0			
17039000	其他糖蜜	8	0	0	0	0	0	0	0	0	0	0		0	5		0	0	0			
17041000	口香糖，不论是否裹糖	12	0	0	0	0	0	0	0	0	0	0	9.5	1.2	5	0	0	8.5	2.4	0		
17049000	其他不含可可的糖食	10	0	0	0	0	0	0	0	0	0	0	8.2	1	8.2	0	0	5	0	0	0	
18010000	生或焙炒的整颗或破碎的可可豆	8	0	0	0	0	0	0	0	0	0	0		0	5		0	0	0			
18020000	可可荚、壳、皮及废料	10	0	0	0	0	0	0	0	0	0	0		0	5	0	0	0	0			
18031000	未脱脂可可膏	10	0	0	0	0	0	0	0	0	0	0		0	5		0	0	0			
18032000	全脱脂或部分脱脂的可可膏	10	0	0	0	0	0	0	0	0	0	0		0	5		0	0	0			
18040000	可可油，可可脂	22	0	0	0	0	0	0	0	0	0	0		0			0	11	4.4			
18050000	未加糖或其他甜物质的可可粉	15	0	0	0	0	0	0	0	0	0	0		0	12		0	7.5	3			
18061000	含糖或其他甜物质的可可粉	10	0	0	0	0	0	0	0	0	0	0		1	5		0	5	0			
18062000	每件净重＞2kg的含可可食品	10	0	0	0	0	0	0	0	0	0	0	7.7	1	5	0	0	5	0	0	0	
18063100	其他夹心块状或条状的含可可食品	8	0	0	0	0	0	0	0	0	0	0	6.4	0	5		0	0	0	0	0	
18063200	其他不夹心块状或条状含可可食品	10	0	0	0	0	0	0	0	0	0	0	7.7	1	5	0	0	5	0	0	0	
18069000	其他巧克力及含可可的食品	8	0	0	0	0	0	0	0	0	0	0	6.4	0	5		0	0	0	0	0	
19011010	配方奶粉	15	0	0	0	0	0	0	0	0	0	0		1.5	12	0	0	7.5	3		0	
19011090	其他供婴幼儿食用的零售包装食品	15	0	0	0	0	0	0	0	0	0	0		1.5	12	0	0	7.5	3		0	
19012000	供焙烘面包糕点用的调制品及面团	25	0	0	0	0	0	0	0	0	0	0		2.5		0	0	12.5	5	0	0	
19019000	其他麦精制的其他税号未列名食品	10	0	0	0	0	0	0	0	0	0	0		1	5	0	0	5	0	0	0	
19021100	未包馅或未制作的含蛋生面食	15	0	0	0	0	0	0	0	0	0	0		1.5	12	0	0	7.5	3	0	0	
19021900	其他未包馅或未制作的生面食	15	0	0	0	0	0	0	0	0	0	0		1.5	12	0	0	7.5	3	0	0	
19022000	包馅面食	15	0	0	0	0	0	0	0	0	0	0		1.5	12	0	0	7.5	3	0	0	
19023010	米粉二	15	0	0	0	0	0	0	0	0	0	0		0	12	0	0	7.5	3		0	
19023020	粉丝	15	0	0	0	0	0	0	0	0	0	0		0	12	0	0	7.5	3		0	
19023030	即食或快熟面条	15	0	0	0	0	0	0	0	0	0	0	13.1	0	7.5	0	0	7.5	3	0	0	
19023090	其他面食	15	0	0	0	0	0	0	0	0	0	0	13.1	1.5	7.5	0	0	7.5	3	0	0	
19024000	古斯古斯面食	25	0	0	0	0	0	0	0	0	0	0		0		0	0	12.5	5		0	
19030000	珍粉及淀粉制成的珍粉代用品	15	0	0	0	0	0	0	0	0	0	0		0	12	0	0	7.5	3		0	
19041000	谷物或谷物产品经膨化或烘炒制的食品	25	0	0	0	0	0	0	0	0	0	0		2.5		0	0	12.5	5		0	
19042000	未烘炒谷物片制成的食品	30	0	0	0	0	0	0	0	0	0	0		0		0	0	20	6			
19043000	碾碎的干小麦	30	0	0	0	0	0	0	0	0	0	0		0		0	0	20	6		0	
19049000	其他谷物制品	30	0	0	0	0	0	0	0	0	0	0		0		0	0	17.5	6	0	0	
19051000	黑麦脆面包片	20	0	0	0	0	0	0	0	0	0	0		0		0	0	10	4		0	
19052000	姜饼及类似品	20	0	0	0	0	0	0	0	0	0	0		0		0	0	10	4		0	
19053100	甜饼干	15	0	0	0	0	0	0	0	0	0	0	12.4	1.5	12.4	0	0	7.5	3	0	0	
19053200	华夫饼干及圣餐饼	15	0	0	0	0	0	0	0	0	0	0	12.4	1.5	7.5	0	0	7.5	3	0	0	

税则号列	商品名称（简称）	最惠国	东盟 文	柬	印	老	马	缅	菲	新	泰	越	亚太	智利	巴基斯坦	新加坡	新西兰	秘鲁	哥斯达黎加	香港	澳门	台湾
19054000	面包干、吐司及类似的烤面包	20	0	0	0	0	0	0	0	0	0	0		0		0	0	10	4		0	
19059000	其他面包、糕点、饼干及其焙烘糕饼	20	0	0	0	0	0	0	0	0	0	0	17.1	2	16	0	0	10	4	0	0	
20011000	用醋或醋酸制作的黄瓜及小黄瓜	25	0	0	0	0	0	0	0	0	0	0		0		0	0	12.5	5			
20019010	用醋制作的大蒜	25	0	0	0	0	0	0	0	0	0	0		0		0	0	12.5	5			
20019090	用醋制作的其他果、菜及食用植物	25	0	0	0	0	0	0	0	0	0	0		2.5		0	0	12.5	5		0	
20021010	非用醋制作的整个或切片番茄罐头	19	0	0	0	0	0	0	0	0	0	0		1.9		0	0	9.5	3.8		0	
20021090	非用醋制作的其他整个或切片番茄	25	0	0	0	0	0	0	0	0	0	0		2.5		0	0	12.5	5			
20029011	重量不超过5kg的番茄酱罐头	20	0	0	0	0	0	0	0	0	0	0		0		0	0	0	4		0	
20029019	重量大于5kg的番茄酱罐头	20	0	0	0	0	0	0	0	0	0	0		0		0	0	0	4		0	
20029090	非用醋制作的绞碎番茄	18	0	0	0	0	0	0	0	0	0	0		0	14.4	0	0	0	3.6		0	
20031011	伞菌属小白蘑菇罐头	25	0	0	0	0	0	0	0	0	0	0		2.5		0	0	12.5	5		0	
20031019	其他非用醋制作的伞菌属蘑菇罐头	25	0	0	0	0	0	0	0	0	0	0		2.5		0	0	12.5	5		0	
20031090	非用醋制作的其他伞菌属蘑菇	25	0	0	0	0	0	0	0	0	0	0		2.5		0	0	12.5	5		0	
20039010	其他蘑菇及块菌罐头	25	0	0	0	0	0	0	0	0	0	0		0		0	0	12.5	5		0	
20039090	其他蘑菇及块菌	25	0	0	0	0	0	0	0	0	0	0		0		0	0	12.5	5		0	
20041000	非用醋制作的冷冻马铃薯	13	0	0	0	0	0	0	0	0	0	0		1.3	6.5	0	0	6.5	2.6			
20049000	非用醋制作的其他冷冻蔬菜	25	0	0	0	0	0	0	0	0	0	0		2.5		0	0	12.5	5			
20051000	非用醋制作的未冷冻均化蔬菜	25	0	0	0	0	0	0	0	0	0	0		0		0	0	12.5	5			
20052000	非用醋制作的未冷冻马铃薯	15	0	0	0	0	0	0	0	0	0	0		1.5	12	0	0	7.5	3	0		
20054000	非用醋制作的未冷冻豌豆	25	0	0	0	0	0	0	0	0	0	0		0		0	0	12.5	5			
20055111	非用醋或醋酸制作或保藏的未冷冻的赤豆馅罐头	25	0	0	0	0	0	0	0	0	0	0		0		0	0	12.5	5	0	0	
20055119	非用醋或醋酸制作或保藏的未冷冻的其他脱荚豇豆及菜豆罐头	25	0	0	0	0	0	0	0	0	0	0		0		0	0	12.5	5	0	0	
20055191	非用醋或醋酸制作或保藏的未冷冻的赤豆馅，不包括罐头	25	0	0	0	0	0	0	0	0	0	0		0		0	0	12.5	5			
20055199	非用醋或醋酸制作或保藏的未冷冻的其他脱荚豇豆及菜豆	25	0	0	0	0	0	0	0	0	0	0		0		0	0	12.5	5	0		
20055910	非用醋制作的其他豇豆及菜豆罐头	25	0	0	0	0	0	0	0	0	0	0		0		0	0	12.5	5		0	
20055990	非用醋制作的其他豇豆及菜豆	25	0	0	0	0	0	0	0	0	0	0		0		0	0	12.5	5			
20056010	非用醋制作的芦笋罐头	25	0	0	0	0	0	0	0	0	0	0		0		0	0	12.5	5		0	
20056090	非用醋制作的其他芦笋	25	0	0	0	0	0	0	0	0	0	0		0		0	0	12.5	5			
20057000	非用醋制作的未冷冻油橄榄	10	0	0	0	0	0	0	0	0	0	0		1	5	0	0	5	0			
20058000	非用醋制作的未冷冻甜玉米	10	0	0	0	0	0	0	0	0	0	0		0	5	0	0	0	0			
20059110	非用醋制作或保藏的竹笋罐头	25	0	0	0	0	0	0	0	0	0	0		2.5		0	0	12.5	5		0	
20059190	非用醋制作或保藏的未冷冻的其他竹笋	25	0	0	0	0	0	0	0	0	0	0		2.5		0	0	12.5	5			
20059920	蚕豆罐头	25	0	0	0	0	0	0	0	0	0	0		2.5		0	0	12.5	5		0	
20059940	榨菜	25	0	0	0	0	0	0	0	0	0	0		0		0	0	12.5	5			
20059950	咸蕨菜	25	0	0	0	0	0	0	0	0	0	0		0		0	0	12.5	5			
20059960	咸荞头	25	0	0	0	0	0	0	0	0	0	0		0		0	0	12.5	5			
20059991	其他蔬菜及什锦蔬菜罐头	25	0	0	0	0	0	0	0	0	0	0		2.5		0	0	0	5		0	
20059999	非用醋制作的其他蔬菜及什锦蔬菜	25	0	0	0	0	0	0	0	0	0	0		2.5		0	0	0	5			
20060010	蜜枣	30	0	0	0	0	0	0	0	0	0	0		0		0	0	15	6	0		
20060020	糖渍制橄榄	30	0	0	0	0	0	0	0	0	0	0		3		0	0	21.2	6	0		
20060090	其他糖渍蔬菜、水果、坚果、果皮	30	0	0	0	0	0	0	0	0	0	0		3		0	0	21.2	6	0	0	
20071000	烹煮制成的果子均化食品	30	0	0	0	0	0	0	0	0	0	0		3		0	0	21.2	6			
20079100	烹煮制成的柑桔属水果	30	0	0	0	0	0	0	0	0	0	0		0		0	0	15	6		0	
20079910	烹煮制成的其他果酱、果冻罐头	5	0	0	0	0	0	0	0	0	0	0		0.5	0		0	2.5	1		0	
20079990	烹煮制成的其他果酱、果冻	5	0	0	0	0	0	0	0	0	0	0		0.5	0		0	2.5	3.7		0	
20081110	花生米罐头	30	0	0	0	0	0	0	0	0	0	0		0		0	0		6	0	0	
20081120	烘焙花生	30	0	0	0	0	0	0	0	0	0	0		0		0	0		6	0	0	
20081130	花生酱	30	0	0	0	0	0	0	0	0	0	0		0		0	0		6			
20081190	其他非用醋制作的花生	30	0	0	0	0	0	0	0	0	0	0		0		0	0		6	0	0	
20081910	核桃仁罐头	20	0	0	0	0	0	0	0	0	0	0	10	2	10	0	0	10	4	0	0	
20081920	其他果仁罐头	13	0	0	0	0	0	0	0	0	0	0	6.5	1.3	5	0	0	6.5	2.6	0	0	
20081991	栗仁	10	0	0	0	0	0	0	0	0	0	0	5	1	5	0	0	5	0	0	0	
20081992	用其他方法制作或保藏的芝麻	10	0	0	0	0	0	0	0	0	0	0	5	1	5	0	0	0	0	0	0	
20081999	其他坚果及子仁	10	0	0	0	0	0	0	0	0	0	0	5	1	5	0	0	5	0	0	0	
20082010	菠萝罐头	15												0			0	7.5	11		0	
20082090	非用醋制作的其他菠萝	15												0			0	7.5	11			
20083010	柑桔属水果罐头	20	0	0	0	0	0	0	0	0	0	0		0		0	0	0	14.7		0	

税则号列	商品名称（简称）	最惠国	东盟										亚太	智利	巴基斯坦	新加坡	新西兰	秘鲁	哥斯达黎加	香港	澳门	台湾
			文	柬	印	老	马	缅	菲	新	泰	越										
20083090	非用醋制作的其他柑桔属水果	20	0	0	0	0	0	0	0	0	0	0		0		0	0	0	0	0		
20084010	梨罐头	20	0	0	0	0	0	0	0	0	0	0		2		0	0	10	4		0	
20084090	非用醋制作的其他梨	20	0	0	0	0	0	0	0	0	0	0		2		0	0	10	4			
20085000	非用醋制作的杏	20	0	0	0	0	0	0	0	0	0	0		2		0	0	10	4			
20086010	用其他方法制作或保藏的樱桃罐头	20	0	0	0	0	0	0	0	0	0	0		2		0	0	10	4			
20086090	用其他方法制作或保藏的其他樱桃	20	0	0	0	0	0	0	0	0	0	0		2		0	0	10	4			
20087010	桃罐头	10	0	0	0	0	0	0	0	0	0	0		0	5	0	0	5	0		0	
20087090	非用醋制作的其他桃	20	0	0	0	0	0	0	0	0	0	0		2		0	0	10	4	0		
20088000	非用醋制作的草莓	15	0	0	0	0	0	0	0	0	0	0		1.5	12	0	0	7.5	3			
20089100	非用醋制作的棕榈芯	5	0	0	0	0	0	0	0	0	0	0		0	0		0	0	0			
20089300	用其他方法制作或保藏的蔓越橘	15	0	0	0	0	0	0	0	0	0	0		1.5	12	0	0	7.5	3	0	0	
20089700	用其他方法制作或保藏的什锦果实	10	0	0	0	0	0	0	0	0	0	0		1	5	0	0	5	0		0	
20089910	荔枝罐头	20	0	0	0	0	0	0	0	0	0	0		0		0	0	10	4	0	0	
20089920	龙眼罐头	15												0			0	7.5	3	0	0	
20089931	调味紫菜	15	0	0	0	0	0	0	0	0	0	0		0		0	0	7.5	3	0	0	
20089932	盐渍海带	15	0	0	0	0	0	0	0	0	0	0		1.5	12		0	7.5	3	0	0	
20089933	盐渍裙带菜	15	0	0	0	0	0	0	0	0	0	0		1.5	12		0	7.5	3	0	0	
20089939	其他海草及藻类制品	15	0	0	0	0	0	0	0	0	0	0		1.5	12		0	7.5	3	0	0	
20089940	清水荸荠（马蹄）罐头	25	0	0	0	0	0	0	0	0	0	0		2.5		0	0	12.5	5		0	
20089990	未列名制作或保藏的水果、坚果	15	0	0	0	0	0	0	0	0	0	0		1.5	12	0	0	7.5	3	0	0	
20091100	冷冻的橙汁	7.5	0	0	0	0	0	0	0	0	0	0		0	5		1.7	3.8	0	0	0	
20091200	非冷冻的，白利糖度值不超过20的橙汁	30	0	0	0	0	0	0	0	0	0	0		3		0	6.7	15		0	0	
20091900	其他橙汁	30	0	0	0	0	0	0	0	0	0	0		0		0	6.7	15			0	
20092100	白利糖度值不超过20的葡萄柚(包括柚)汁	15	0	0	0	0	0	0	0	0	0	0		0	12	0	0	0	3	0	0	
20092900	其他葡萄柚(包括柚)汁	15	0	0	0	0	0	0	0	0	0	0		0	12	0	0	0	3		0	
20093110	白利糖度不超过20的柠檬汁	18	0	0	0	0	0	0	0	0	0	0	16.8	1.8	14.4	0	0	9	3.6	0	0	
20093190	其他未混合的白利糖度值不超过20的桔汁属水果汁	18	0	0	0	0	0	0	0	0	0	0	16.8	1.8	14.4	0	0	9	3.6	0	0	
20093910	白利糖度超过20的柠檬汁	18	0	0	0	0	0	0	0	0	0	0	16.8	0	14.4	0	0	0	3.6		0	
20093990	其他未混合的柑桔属水果汁，白利糖度值不超过20	18	0	0	0	0	0	0	0	0	0	0	16.8	0	14.4	0	0	0	3.6		0	
20094100	白利糖度值不超过20的菠萝汁	10												0			0	0	2	0	0	
20094900	其他菠萝汁	10												0			0	0	2		0	
20095000	番茄汁	30	0	0	0	0	0	0	0	0	0	0		0		0	0	15	6		0	
20096100	白利糖度值不超过30的的葡萄汁,包括酿酒葡萄汁	20	0	0	0	0	0	0	0	0	0	0		2		0	0	11.7	4	0	0	
20096900	葡萄汁,包括酿酒葡萄汁	20	0	0	0	0	0	0	0	0	0	0		2		0	0	11.7	4		0	
20097100	白利糖度值不超过20的苹果汁	20	0	0	0	0	0	0	0	0	0	0		0		0	0	0	4	0	0	
20097900	其他苹果汁	20	0	0	0	0	0	0	0	0	0	0		2		0	0	10	4		0	
20098100	蔓越橘汁	20	0	0	0	0	0	0	0	0	0	0	10	2	10	0	0	10	4	0	0	
20098912	芒果汁	20	0	0	0	0	0	0	0	0	0	0	17.4	2	16	0	0	10	4	0	0	
20098913	西番莲果汁	20	0	0	0	0	0	0	0	0	0	0	17.4	2	16	0	0	10	4	0	0	
20098914	番石榴果汁	20	0	0	0	0	0	0	0	0	0	0	17.4	2	16	0	0	10	4	0	0	
20098915	梨汁	20	0	0	0	0	0	0	0	0	0	0	10	2	10	0	0	10	4	0	0	
20098919	其他未混合的水果汁	20	0	0	0	0	0	0	0	0	0	0	10	2	10	0	0	10	4	0	0	
20098920	其他未混合蔬菜汁	20	0	0	0	0	0	0	0	0	0	0	10	2	10	0	0	10	4	0	0	
20099010	混合水果汁	20	0	0	0	0	0	0	0	0	0	0	17.4	0	16	0	0	0	4	0	0	
20099090	混合蔬菜汁、水果与蔬菜的混合汁	20	0	0	0	0	0	0	0	0	0	0		0		0	0	0	4	0	0	
21011100	咖啡浓缩精汁	17	0	0	0	0	0	0	0	0	0	0		1.7	13.6	0	0		3.4	0	0	
21011200	以咖啡浓缩精汁或咖啡为基本成分的制品	30	0	0	0	0	0	0	0	0	0	0		3		0	0		6	0		
21012000	茶、马黛茶浓缩精汁及其制品	32	0	0	0	0	0	0	0	0	0	0	16	3.2	16	0	0	16	6.4	0	0	
21013000	烘焙咖啡代用品及其浓缩精汁	32	0	0	0	0	0	0	0	0	0	0		3.2		0	0		6.4			
21021000	活性酵母	25	0	0	0	0	0	0	0	0	0	0		2.5		0	0	12.5	5	0	0	
21022000	非活性酵母；已死的其他单细胞微生物	25	0	0	0	0	0	0	0	0	0	0		2.5		0	0	12.5	5		0	
21023000	发酵粉	25	0	0	0	0	0	0	0	0	0	0		0		0	0	12.5	5		0	
21031000	酱油	28	0	0	0	0	0	0	0	0	0	0		0		0	0	14	5.6	0	0	
21032000	番茄沙司及其他番茄调味汁	15	0	0	0	0	0	0	0	0	0	0		1.5	12	0	0	7.5	3	0	0	
21033000	芥子粉及其调味品	15	0	0	0	0	0	0	0	0	0	0		0	12	0	0	7.5	3		0	
21039010	味精	21	0	0	0	0	0	0	0	0	0	0	18.2	0	18.2	0	0	10.5	4.2	0	0	

税则号列	商品名称（简称）	最惠国	东盟										亚太	智利	巴基斯坦	新加坡	新西兰	秘鲁	哥斯达黎加	香港	澳门	台湾
			文	柬	印	老	马	缅	菲	新	泰	越										
21039020	别特油（Aromatic bitters）	21	0	0	0	0	0	0	0	0	0	0		2.1		0	0	14.8	4.2	0	0	
21039090	其他调味品	21	0	0	0	0	0	0	0	0	0	0	18.4	2.1	18.4	0	0	12.3	4.2	0	0	
21041000	汤料及其制品	15	0	0	0	0	0	0	0	0	0	0		1.5	12	0	0	7.5	3	0	0	
21042000	均化混合食品	32	0	0	0	0	0	0	0	0	0	0		3.2		0	0	16	6.4		0	
21050000	冰淇淋及其他冰制食品不论是否含可可	19	0	0	0	0	0	0	0	0	0	0		1.9		0	0	9.5	3.8	0	0	
21061000	浓缩蛋白质及人造蛋白物质	10	0	0	0	0	0	0	0	0	0	0		1	5	0	0	5	0		0	
21069010	制造碳酸饮料的浓缩物	35	0	0	0	0	0	0	0	0	0	0		3.5		0	0	17.5	7	0	0	
21069020	制造饮料用的复合酒精制品	20	0	0	0	0	0	0	0	0	0	0		2		0	0	10	4	0	0	
21069030	蜂王浆制剂	3	0	0	0	0	0	0	0	0	0	0		0	0		0	0	0	0	0	
21069040	椰子汁	10						0					9	1	9		0	5	0	0	0	
21069050	海豹油胶囊	20	0	0	0	0	0	0	0	0	0	0	18.4	2	18.4	0	0	10	4	0	0	
21069090	其他税号未列名的食品	20	0	0	0	0	0	0	0	0	0	0	18.4	2	18.4	0	0	10	4	0	0	
22011010	未加糖及未加味的矿泉水	20	0	0	0	0	0	0	0	0	0	0		0		0	0	10	4	0	0	
22011020	未加糖及未加味的汽水	20	0	0	0	0	0	0	0	0	0	0		0		0	0	10	4		0	
22019010	天然水	10	0	0	0	0	0	0	0	0	0	0		0	5	0	0	0	0	0	0	
22019090	其他水、冰及雪	10	0	0	0	0	0	0	0	0	0	0		0	5	0	0	0	0	0		
22021000	加味、加糖或其他甜物质的水	20	0	0	0	0	0	0	0	0	0	0		2		0	0	10	4	0	0	
22029000	其他无酒精饮料	35	0	0	0	0	0	0	0	0	0	0	29.5	3.5	29.5	0	0	17.5	7	0	0	
22041000	葡萄汽酒	14	0	0	0	0	0	0	0	0	0	0		1.4	11.2	0	0	7	2.8			
22042100	小包装的鲜葡萄酿造的酒	14	0	0	0	0	0	0	0	0	0	0		1.4	11.2	0	0	9.3	2.8	0		
22042900	其他包装的鲜葡萄酿造的酒	20	0	0	0	0	0	0	0	0	0	0		2		0	0	13.3	4			
22043000	其他酿酒葡萄汁	30	0	0	0	0	0	0	0	0	0	0		3		0	0	17.5	6			
22051000	小包装的味美思酒及类似酒	65	0	0	0	0	0	0	0	0	0	0		6.5		0	0	37.9	13			
22059000	其他包装的味美思酒及类似酒	65	0	0	0	0	0	0	0	0	0	0		0		0	0	37.9	13			
22060010	黄酒	40	0	0	0	0	0	0	0	0	0	0		0		0	0	22.2	8	0	0	
22060090	其他发酵饮料	40	0	0	0	0	0	0	0	0	0	0		0		0	0	22.2	8	0	0	
22071000	浓度≥80%的未改性乙醇	40	0	0	0	0	0	0	0	0	0	0		0	0	0	0	20	8		0	
22072000	任何浓度的改性乙醇及其他酒精	30	0	0	0	0	0	0	0	0	0	0		3	0	0	0	0	6			
22082000	蒸馏葡萄酒制得的烈性酒	10	0	0	0	0	0	0	0	0	0	0		1	5	0	0	5	0			
22083000	威士忌酒	10	0	0	0	0	0	0	0	0	0	0		1	5	0	0	5	0			
22084000	朗姆酒及蒸馏已发酵甘蔗产品制得的其他烈性酒	10	0	0	0	0	0	0	0	0	0	0		0	5	0	0	0	0			
22085000	杜松子酒	10	0	0	0	0	0	0	0	0	0	0		0	5	0	0	0	0			
22086000	伏特加酒	10	0	0	0	0	0	0	0	0	0	0	8.8	0	5	0	0	0	0			
22087000	利口酒及柯迪尔酒	10	0	0	0	0	0	0	0	0	0	0	8.8	1	5	0	0	5	0			
22089010	龙舌兰酒	10	0	0	0	0	0	0	0	0	0	0	8.8	0	5	0	0	0	0			
22089020	白酒	10	0	0	0	0	0	0	0	0	0	0	8.8	1	5	0	0	5	0		0	
22089090	其他蒸馏酒及酒精饮料	10	0	0	0	0	0	0	0	0	0	0	8.8	1	5	0	0	5	0		0	
22090000	醋及醋酸制得的醋代用品	20	0	0	0	0	0	0	0	0	0	0		2		0	0	10	4	0	0	
23011011	含牛羊成分的肉骨粉	2	0	0	0	0	0	0	0	0	0	0		0	0		0	0	0			
23011019	其他动物的肉骨粉	2	0	0	0	0	0	0	0	0	0	0		0	0		0	0	0			
23011020	油渣	5	0	0	0	0	0	0	0	0	0	0		0	0		0	0	0	0		
23011090	其他不适于供人食用的肉渣粉	5	0	0	0	0	0	0	0	0	0	0		0	0		0	0	0			
23012010	饲料用鱼粉	2	0	0	0	0	0	0	0	0	0	0	0	0.2	0		0	0.2	1.2	0		
23012090	其他不适于供人食用的水产品渣粉	5	0	0	0	0	0	0	0	0	0	0	0	0.5	0		0	1.9	0	0		
23021000	玉米糠、麸及其他残渣	5	0	0	0	0	0	0	0	0	0	0		0	0		0	0	0			
23023000	小麦糠、麸及其他残渣	3	0	0	0	0	0	0	0	0	0	0		0	0		0	0	0			
23024000	其他谷物糠、麸及其他残渣	5	0	0	0	0	0	0	0	0	0	0		0	0		0	0	0			
23025000	豆类植物糠、麸及其他残渣	5	0	0	0	0	0	0	0	0	0	0		0	0		0	0	0	0		
23031000	制造淀粉过程中的残渣及类似品	5	0	0	0	0	0	0	0	0	0	0		0	0		0	0	0			
23032000	甜菜渣、甘蔗渣及制糖过程中的其他残渣	5	0	0	0	0	0	0	0	0	0	0		0	0		0	0	0			
23033000	酿造及蒸馏过程中的糟粕及残渣	5	0	0	0	0	0	0	0	0	0	0		0	0		0	0	0			
23040010	提炼豆油所得的油渣饼(豆饼)	5	0	0	0	0	0	0	0	0	0	0	0	0.5	0		0	0	0			
23040090	提炼豆油所得的其他固体残渣	5	0	0	0	0	0	0	0	0	0	0	0	0	0		0	0	0			
23050000	花生饼及类似油渣	5	0	0	0	0	0	0	0	0	0	0		0	0		0	0	0			
23061000	棉子油渣饼及固体残渣	5	0	0	0	0	0	0	0	0	0	0		0	0		0	0	0			
23062000	亚麻子油渣饼及固体残渣	5	0	0	0	0	0	0	0	0	0	0		0	0		0	0	0			
23063000	葵花子油渣饼及固体残渣	5	0	0	0	0	0	0	0	0	0	0		0	0		0	0	0			
23064100	低芥子酸的油菜子油渣饼及固体残渣	5	0	0	0	0	0	0	0	0	0	0		0	0		0	0	0			

税则号列	商品名称（简称）	最惠国	东盟										亚太	智利	巴基斯坦	新加坡	新西兰	秘鲁	哥斯达黎加	香港	澳门	台湾
			文	柬	印	老	马	缅	菲	新	泰	越										
23064900	油菜子油渣饼及固体残渣	5	0	0	0	0	0	0	0	0	0	0		0	0		0	0	0			
23065000	椰子或干椰肉油渣饼及固体残渣	5	0	0	0	0	0	0	0	0	0	0	2.5	0	0		0	0	0			
23066000	油棕果或油棕仁油渣饼及固体残渣	5	0	0	0	0	0	0	0	0	0	0		0	0		0	0	0			
23069000	其他油渣饼及固体残渣	5	0	0	0	0	0	0	0	0	0	0		0	0		0	0	0			
23070000	葡萄酒渣、粗酒石	5	0	0	0	0	0	0	0	0	0	0		0	0		0	0	0			
23080000	动物饲料用其他植物产品	5	0	0	0	0	0	0	0	0	0	0		0	0		0	0	0			
23091010	零售包装的狗食或猫食罐头	15	0	0	0	0	0	0	0	0	0	0		1.5	12	0	0	7.5	3	0	0	
23091090	零售包装的其他狗食或猫食	15	0	0	0	0	0	0	0	0	0	0		1.5	12	0	0	7.5	3	0	0	
23099010	制成的饲料添加剂	5	0	0	0	0	0	0	0	0	0	0	2.5	0.5	0		0	2.5	0	0		
23099090	其他配制的动物饲料	6.5	0	0	0	0	0	0	0	0	0	0	3.3	0.7	0		0	3.2	0	0	0	
24011010	未去梗的烤烟	10											9.4	1	9.4		0					
24011090	其他未去梗的烟草	10												1			0					
24012010	部分或全部去梗的烤烟	10												1			0					
24012090	部分或全部去梗的其他烟草	10												1			0					
24013000	烟草废料	10												1			0	5				
24021000	烟草制的雪茄烟	25												2.5			0					
24022000	烟草制的卷烟	25												2.5			0					
24029000	烟草代用品制的雪茄烟及卷烟	25												2.5			0					
24031100	本章子目注释所述的水烟料	57											50	5.7	50		0					
24031900	其他供吸用的烟草	57											50	5.7	50		0					
24039100	“均化”或“再造”烟草	57												5.7			0					
24039900	其他烟草及烟草代用品的制品；烟草精汁	57												5.7			0					
25010020	纯氯化钠	3	0	0	0	0	0	0	0	0	0	0		0	0		0	0	0			
25020000	未焙烧的黄铁矿	3	0	0	0	0	0	0	0	0	0	0		0	0		0	0	0			
25030000	硫磺，但升华硫磺、沉淀硫磺及胶态硫磺除外	3	0	0	0	0	0	0	0	0	0	0		0	0		0	0	0			
25041010	鳞片状天然石墨	3	0	0	0	0	0	0	0	0	0	0		0	0		0	0	0			
25041091	球化石墨	3	0	0	0	0	0	0	0	0	0	0		0	0		0	0	0			
25041099	其他粉末状天然石墨	3	0	0	0	0	0	0	0	0	0	0		0	0		0	0	0			
25049000	其他天然石墨	3	0	0	0	0	0	0	0	0	0	0		0	0		0	0	0			
25051000	硅砂及石英砂，不论是否着色	3	0	0	0	0	0	0	0	0	0	0		0	0		0	0	0			
25059000	其他天然砂，不论是否着色	3	0	0	0	0	0	0	0	0	0	0		0	0		0	0	0			
25061000	石英	3	0	0	0	0	0	0	0	0	0	0		0	0		0	0	0			
25062000	石英岩，不论是否切割成矩形板、块	3	0	0	0	0	0	0	0	0	0	0		0	0		0	0	0			
25070010	不论是否煅烧的高岭土	3	0	0	0	0	0	0	0	0	0	0		0	0		0	0	0			
25070090	不论是否煅烧的类似土	3	0	0	0	0	0	0	0	0	0	0		0	0		0	0	0			
25081000	膨润土，不论是否煅烧	3	0	0	0	0	0	0	0	0	0	0		0	0		0	0	0			
25083000	耐火粘土，不论是否煅烧	3	0	0	0	0	0	0	0	0	0	0		0	0		0	0	0			
25084000	其他粘土，不论是否煅烧	3	0	0	0	0	0	0	0	0	0	0		0	0		0	0	0			
25085000	红柱石.蓝晶石及硅线石，不论是否煅烧	3	0	0	0	0	0	0	0	0	0	0		0	0		0	0	0			
25086000	富铝红柱石	3	0	0	0	0	0	0	0	0	0	0		0	0		0	0	0			
25087000	火泥及第纳斯土	3	0	0	0	0	0	0	0	0	0	0		0	0		0	0	0			
25090000	白垩	3	0	0	0	0	0	0	0	0	0	0		0	0		0	0	0			
25101010	未碾磨磷灰石	3	0	0	0	0	0	0	0	0	0	0		0	0		0	0	0			
25101090	未碾磨天然磷酸钙、天然磷酸铝钙及磷酸盐白垩，磷灰石除外	3	0	0	0	0	0	0	0	0	0	0		0	0		0	0	0			
25102010	已碾磨磷灰石	3	0	0	0	0	0	0	0	0	0	0		0	0		0	0	0			
25102090	已碾磨天然磷酸钙、天然磷酸铝钙及磷酸盐白垩，磷灰石除外	3	0	0	0	0	0	0	0	0	0	0		0	0		0	0	0			
25111000	天然硫酸钡(重晶石)	3	0	0	0	0	0	0	0	0	0	0		0	0		0	0	0			
25112000	天然碳酸钡(毒重石)，不论是否煅烧	3	0	0	0	0	0	0	0	0	0	0		0	0		0	0	0			
25120010	硅藻土	3	0	0	0	0	0	0	0	0	0	0		0	0		0	0	0			
25120090	其他硅质化石粗粉及类似的硅质土	3	0	0	0	0	0	0	0	0	0	0		0	0		0	0	0			
25131000	浮石	3	0	0	0	0	0	0	0	0	0	0		0	0		0	0	0			
25132000	刚玉岩、天然刚玉砂、天然石榴石及其他天然磨料	3	0	0	0	0	0	0	0	0	0	0		0	0		0	0	0			
25140000	板岩，不论是否粗加修整或切割成矩形板块	3	0	0	0	0	0	0	0	0	0	0		0	0		0	0	0			
25151100	原状或粗加修整大理石及石灰华	4	0	0	0	0	0	0	0	0	0	0		0	0		0	0	0			
25151200	矩形大理石及石灰华	4	0	0	0	0	0	0	0	0	0	0		0	0		0	0	0			

税则号列	商品名称（简称）	最惠国	东盟										亚太	智利	巴基斯坦	新加坡	新西兰	秘鲁	哥斯达黎加	香港	澳门	台湾
			文	柬	印	老	马	缅	菲	新	泰	越										
25152000	其他石灰质碑用或建筑用石；蜡石，不论是否粗加修整或切割成矩形板块	3	0	0	0	0	0	0	0	0	0	0		0	0		0	0	0			
25161100	原状或粗加修整的花岗岩	4	0	0	0	0	0	0	0	0	0	0	2	0	0		0	0	0			
25161200	矩形或正方形的花岗岩	4	0	0	0	0	0	0	0	0	0	0	2	0	0		0	0	0			
25162000	砂岩，不论是否粗加修整或切割成矩形板块	3	0	0	0	0	0	0	0	0	0	0	2.1	0	0		0	0	0			
25169000	其他碑用或建筑用石，不论是否粗加修整或切割成矩形板块	3	0	0	0	0	0	0	0	0	0	0	2.1	0	0		0	0	0			
25171000	通常做混凝土粒料、铺路、铁道路基或其他路基用的卵石、砾石及碎石，圆石子及燧石，不论是否热处理	4	0	0	0	0	0	0	0	0	0	0		0	0		0	0	0			
25172000	矿渣、浮渣及类似的工业残渣	3	0	0	0	0	0	0	0	0	0	0		0	0		0	0	0			
25173000	沥青碎石	3	0	0	0	0	0	0	0	0	0	0		0	0		0	0	0			
25174100	大理石碎粒、碎屑及粉末，不论是否热处理	3	0	0	0	0	0	0	0	0	0	0		0	0		0	0	0			
25174900	税目 2515 及 2616 所列各种石料的碎粒、碎屑及粉末，大理石的除外，不论是否热处理	3	0	0	0	0	0	0	0	0	0	0		0	0		0	0	0			
25181000	未煅烧或烧结的白云石，不论是否粗加修整或切割成矩形板块	3	0	0	0	0	0	0	0	0	0	0		0	0		0	0	0			
25182000	已煅烧或烧结的白云石，不论是否粗加修整或切割成矩形板块	3	0	0	0	0	0	0	0	0	0	0		0	0		0	0	0			
25183000	夯混白云石	3	0	0	0	0	0	0	0	0	0	0		0	0		0	0	0			
25191000	天然碳酸镁（菱镁矿）	3	0	0	0	0	0	0	0	0	0	0		0	0		0	0	0			
25199010	熔凝镁氧矿	3	0	0	0	0	0	0	0	0	0	0		0	0		0	0	0			
25199020	烧结镁氧矿（重烧镁）	3	0	0	0	0	0	0	0	0	0	0		0	0		0	0	0			
25199030	碱烧镁（轻烧镁）	3	0	0	0	0	0	0	0	0	0	0		0	0		0	0	0			
25199091	化学纯氧化镁	3	0	0	0	0	0	0	0	0	0	0		0	0		0	0	0			
25199099	非纯氧化镁	3	0	0	0	0	0	0	0	0	0	0		0	0		0	0	0			
25201000	生石膏；硬石膏	5	0	0	0	0	0	0	0	0	0	0		0	0		0	0	0	0		
25202010	牙科用熟石膏，不论是否着色及带有少量促凝剂或缓凝剂	5	0	0	0	0	0	0	0	0	0	0		0.5	0		0	0	0			
25202090	其他熟石膏，不论是否着色及带有少量促凝剂或缓凝剂	5	0	0	0	0	0	0	0	0	0	0		0.5	0		0	0	0			
25210000	石灰石助熔剂；通常用于制造石灰或水泥的石灰石及其他钙质石	5	0	0	0	0	0	0	0	0	0	0		0	0		0	0	0	0		
25221000	生石灰	5	0	0	0	0	0	0	0	0	0	0		0.5	0		0	0	0			
25222000	熟石灰	5	0	0	0	0	0	0	0	0	0	0		0	0		0	0	0			
25223000	水硬石灰	5	0	0	0	0	0	0	0	0	0	0		0	0		0	0	0			
25231000	水泥熟料，不论是否着色	8	0	0	0	0	0	0	0	0	0	0		0	5		0	0	0	0		0
25232100	白水泥，不论是否人工着色	6	0	0	0	0	0	0	0	0	0	0	4.5	0	0		0	0	0			0
25232900	其他硅酸盐水泥，不论是否着色	8	0	0	0	0	0	0	0	0	0	0	6	0	5		0	0	0	0	0	0
25233000	矾土水泥，不论是否着色	6	0	0	0	0	0	0	0	0	0	0		0	5		0	0	0			
25239000	其他水凝水泥，不论是否着色	8	0	0	0	0	0	0	0	0	0	0		0	5		0	0	0			
25241000	青石棉	5	0	0	0	0	0	0	0	0	0	0		0	0		0	0	0			
25249010	其他长纤维石棉	5	0	0	0	0	0	0	0	0	0	0		0	0		0	0	0			
25249090	其他石棉	5	0	0	0	0	0	0	0	0	0	0		0	0		0	0	0			
25251000	原状云母及劈开的云母片	5	0	0	0	0	0	0	0	0	0	0		0	0		0	0	0			
25252000	云母粉	5	0	0	0	0	0	0	0	0	0	0		0	0		0	0	0			
25253000	云母废料	5	0	0	0	0	0	0	0	0	0	0		0	0		0	0	0			
25261010	未破碎及未研粉的天然冻石，不论是否粗加修整或切割成矩形板块	3	0	0	0	0	0	0	0	0	0	0		0	0		0	0	0			
25261020	未破碎及未研粉的滑石，不论是否粗加修整或切割成矩形板块	3	0	0	0	0	0	0	0	0	0	0		0	0		0	0	0			
25262010	已破碎或已研粉的天然冻石	3	0	0	0	0	0	0	0	0	0	0		0	0		0	0	0			
25262020	已破碎或已研粉的天然滑石	3	0	0	0	0	0	0	0	0	0	0		0	0		0	0	0			
25280010	天然硼砂及其精矿，不论是否煅烧	3	0	0	0	0	0	0	0	0	0	0		0	0		0	0	0			
25280090	硼酸盐（硼砂除外），不论是否煅烧；天然粗硼酸，含硼酸干重不超 85%	5	0	0	0	0	0	0	0	0	0	0		0.5	0		0	2.5	0			
25291000	长石	3	0	0	0	0	0	0	0	0	0	0		0	0		0	0	0			
25292100	按重量计氟化钙含量≤97%的萤石	3	0	0	0	0	0	0	0	0	0	0		0	0		0	0	0			

税则号列	商品名称（简称）	最惠国	东盟 文	柬	印	老	马	缅	菲	新	泰	越	亚太	智利	巴基斯坦	新加坡	新西兰	秘鲁	哥斯达黎加	香港	澳门	台湾
25292200	按重量计氟化钙含量＞97%的萤石	3	0	0	0	0	0	0	0	0	0	0		0	0		0	0	0			
25293000	白榴石；霞石及霞石正长岩	5	0	0	0	0	0	0	0	0	0	0		0	0		0	0	0			
25301010	未膨胀的绿泥石	5	0	0	0	0	0	0	0	0	0	0		0	0		0	0	0			
25301020	未膨胀的蛭石及珍珠岩	5	0	0	0	0	0	0	0	0	0	0		0	0		0	0	0			
25302000	硫镁矾矿及泻盐矿(天然硫酸镁)	3	0	0	0	0	0	0	0	0	0	0		0	0		0	0	0			
25309010	矿物性药材	3	0	0	0	0	0	0	0	0	0	0		0	0		0	0	0			
25309091	硅灰石	3	0	0	0	0	0	0	0	0	0	0		0	0		0	0	0			
25309099	其他矿产品	3	0	0	0	0	0	0	0	0	0	0		0	0		0	0	0			
26179010	朱砂(辰砂)	3	0	0	0	0	0	0	0	0	0	0		0	0		0	0	0			
26180010	冶炼钢铁产生的锰渣	4	0	0	0	0	0	0	0	0	0	0		0.4	0		0	0	0			
26180090	冶炼钢铁产生的其他粒状熔渣(熔渣砂)	4	0	0	0	0	0	0	0	0	0	0		0.4	0		0	0	0			
26190000	冶炼钢铁产生的熔渣、浮渣、氧化皮及其他废料	4	0	0	0	0	0	0	0	0	0	0		0.4	0		0	0	0			
26201100	含硬锌的矿灰及残渣	4	0	0	0	0	0	0	0	0	0	0		0.4	0		0	0	0			
26201900	含其他锌的矿灰及残渣	4	0	0	0	0	0	0	0	0	0	0		0.4	0		0	0	0			
26202100	含铅汽油的淤渣及含铅抗震化合物的淤渣	4	0	0	0	0	0	0	0	0	0	0		0	0		0	0	0			
26202900	其他主要含铅的矿灰及残渣	4	0	0	0	0	0	0	0	0	0	0		0	0		0	0	0			
26203000	主要含铜的矿灰及残渣	4	0	0	0	0	0	0	0	0	0	0		0.4	0		0	0	0			
26204000	主要含铝的矿灰及残渣	4	0	0	0	0	0	0	0	0	0	0		0	0		0	0	0			
26206000	含砷、汞、铊及其混合物，用于提取或生产砷、汞、铊及其化合物的矿灰及残渣	4	0	0	0	0	0	0	0	0	0	0		0	0		0	0	0			
26209100	含锑、铍、镉、铬及其混合物的矿灰及残渣	4	0	0	0	0	0	0	0	0	0	0		0	0		0	0	0			
26209910	主要含钨的矿灰及残渣	4	0	0	0	0	0	0	0	0	0	0		0.4	0		0	0	0			
26209990	含其他金属及化合物的矿灰及残渣	4	0	0	0	0	0	0	0	0	0	0		0.4	0		0	0	0			
26211000	焚化城市垃圾所产生的灰、渣	4	0	0	0	0	0	0	0	0	0	0		0	0		0	0	0			
26219000	其他矿渣及矿灰	4	0	0	0	0	0	0	0	0	0	0		0.4	0		0	0	0	0		
27011100	未制成型的无烟煤，不论是否粉化	3	0	0	0	0	0	0	0	0	0	0		0	0		0	0	0			
27011210	未制成型的炼焦烟煤，不论是否粉化	3	0	0	0	0	0	0	0	0	0	0		0	0		0	0	0			
27011290	未制成型的其他烟煤，不论是否粉化	6	0	0	0	0	0	0	0	0	0	0		0	5		0	0	0			
27011900	未制成型的其他煤，不论是否粉化	5	0	0	0	0	0	0	0	0	0	0	3.5	0	0		0	0	0			
27012000	煤砖、煤球及类似用煤制固体燃料	5	0	0	0	0	0	0	0	0	0	0		0	0		0	0	0			
27021000	褐煤	3	0	0	0	0	0	0	0	0	0	0		0	0		0	0	0			
27022000	制成型的褐煤	3	0	0	0	0	0	0	0	0	0	0		0	0		0	0	0			
27030000	泥煤(包括肥料用泥煤) 不论是否成型	5	0	0	0	0	0	0	0	0	0	0		0	0		0	0	0			
27040010	煤制焦炭及半焦炭不论是否成型	5	0	0	0	0	0	0	0	0	0	0	2.5	0.5	0		0	0	0			
27040090	甑炭	5	0	0	0	0	0	0	0	0	0	0	2.5	0.5	0		0	0	0			
27050000	煤气、水煤气、炉煤气及类似气体，石油气及其他烃类气除外	5	0	0	0	0	0	0	0	0	0	0		0	0		0	0	0			
27060000	从煤、褐煤、或泥煤蒸馏所得的焦油及矿物焦油，不论是否脱水或部分蒸馏，包括再造焦油	6	0	0	0	0	0	0	0	0	0	0		0	5		0	0	0			
27071000	粗苯	6	0	0	0	0	0	0	0	0	0	0		0	5		0	0	0			
27072000	粗甲苯	6	0	0	0	0	0	0	0	0	0	0		0	5		0	0	0			
27073000	粗二甲苯	6	0	0	0	0	0	0	0	0	0	0		0	5		0	0	0			
27074000	萘	7	0	0	0	0	0	0	0	0	0	0	6	0	5		0	0	0			
27075000	其他芳烃混合物，温度在 250℃时蒸馏出的芳烃含量以体积计(包括损耗)在 65%及以上(以美国标准实验法 D86 为准)	7	0	0	0	0	0	0	0	0	0	0		0	5		0	0	0			
27079100	杂酚油	7	0	0	0	0	0	0	0	0	0	0		0	5		0	0	0			
27079910	酚	7	0	0	0	0	0	0	0	0	0	0		0	5		0	0	0			
27079990	蒸馏煤焦油所得的其他产品；芳族成分重量超过非芳族成分的类似产品	7	0	0	0	0	0	0	0	0	0	0		0	5		0	0	0			
27081000	从煤焦油或其他矿物焦油所得的沥青	7	0	0	0	0	0	0	0	0	0	0		0.7	5		0	0	0			
27082000	从煤焦油或其他矿物焦油所得的沥青焦	6	0	0	0	0	0	0	0	0	0	0		0	5		0	0	0			
27101210	车用汽油及航空汽油	5	0	0	0	0	0	0	0	0	0	0		0.5	0	0	0		0			
27101220	石脑油	6	0	0	0	0	0	0	0	0	0	0	5.4	0.6	0	0	0		0			

税则号列	商品名称（简称）	最惠国	东盟										亚太	智利	巴基斯坦	新加坡	新西兰	秘鲁	哥斯达黎加	香港	澳门	台湾
			文	柬	印	老	马	缅	菲	新	泰	越										
27101230	橡胶溶剂油、油漆溶剂油、抽提溶剂油	6												0.6			0		0			
27101291	壬烯	9												0.9			0		0			
27101299	其他轻油馏分产品	9												0.9			0		0			
27101911	航空煤油	9	0	0	0	0	0	0	0	0	0	0		0.9	5	0	0	0	0			0
27101912	灯用煤油	9												0.9			0	4.5	0			
27101919	其他煤油馏分产品	6	0	0	0	0	0	0	0	0	0	0		0.6	5	0	0	0	0			0
27101922	5-7 号燃料油	6	0	0	0	0	0	0	0	0	0	0		0.6	5	0	0	0	0			
27101923	柴油	6												0.6			0	3	0			
27101929	其他柴油及其他燃料油	6	0	0	0	0	0	0	0	0	0	0		0.6	5	0	0	3	0		0	
27101991	润滑油	6	0	0	0	0	0	0	0	0	0	0	5.4	0.6	0		0	0	0	0	0	
27101992	润滑脂	6	0	0	0	0	0	0	0	0	0	0	5.4	0.6	0		0	0	0			
27101993	润滑油基础油	6	0	0	0	0	0	0	0	0	0	0		0.6	5		0	0	0			0
27101994	液体石蜡和重质液体石蜡	6	0	0	0	0	0	0	0	0	0	0	5.4	0.6	0		0	0	0			0
27101999	其他重油及重油制品	6	0	0	0	0	0	0	0	0	0	0		0.6	5		0	0	0	0		
27102000	石油及从沥青矿物提取的油类以及以上述油为基本成分（按重量计不低于70%）的其他税目未列名制品，含有生物柴油，但废油除外	6	0	0	0	0	0	0	0	0	0	0		0.6	0	0	0		0			0
27109100	含多氯联苯(PCBs)、多氯三联苯(PCTs)或多溴联苯(PBBs)的废油	6	0	0	0	0	0	0	0	0	0	0		0	5		0	0	1.2			
27109900	其他废油	6	0	0	0	0	0	0	0	0	0	0		0	5		0	0	1.2			
27111200	液化丙烷	5	0	0	0	0	0	0	0	0	0	0	3.5	0.5	0		0	0	0			
27111310	直接灌注香烟打火机及类似打火器用，其包装容器的容积超过 300 立方厘米的液化丁烷	11	0	0	0	0	0	0	0	0	0	0		1.1	5	0	0	0	2.2			
27111390	其他液化丁烷	5	0	0	0	0	0	0	0	0	0	0		0.5	0		0	2.5	0			
27111400	液化的乙烯、丙烯、丁烯及丁二烯	5	0	0	0	0	0	0	0	0	0	0		0	0		0	0	0			
27111910	直接灌注香烟打火机及类似打火器用，其包装容器的容积超过 300 立方厘米的其他液化燃料	10	0	0	0	0	0	0	0	0	0	0	7	1	5		0	0	0			
27111990	其他液化石油气及烃类气	3	0	0	0	0	0	0	0	0	0	0	2.1	0	0		0	1.5	0			
27112900	其他气态石油气及烃类气	6	0	0	0	0	0	0	0	0	0	0		0	5		0	0	0			
27121000	凡士林	8	0	0	0	0	0	0	0	0	0	0		0.8	5		0	0	0			
27122000	石蜡，不论是否着色，按重量计含油小于 0.75%	8	0	0	0	0	0	0	0	0	0	0		0	5		0	0	0			
27129010	微晶石蜡，不论是否着色	8	0	0	0	0	0	0	0	0	0	0		0	5		0	0	0			
27129090	其他矿物蜡及用合成或其他方法制得的类似产品，不论是否着色	8	0	0	0	0	0	0	0	0	0	0		0	5		0	0	0			
27131110	硫的重量百分比小于 3%的未煅烧石油焦	3	0	0	0	0	0	0	0	0	0	0		0	0		0	0	0			
27131190	未煅烧石油焦	3	0	0	0	0	0	0	0	0	0	0		0	0		0	0	0			
27131210	硫的重量百分比小于 0.8%的已煅烧石油焦	3	0	0	0	0	0	0	0	0	0	0		0	0		0	0	0			
27131290	已煅烧石油焦	3	0	0	0	0	0	0	0	0	0	0		0	0		0	0	0			
27132000	石油沥青	8	0	0	0	0	0	0	0	0	0	0	5.6	0	5		0	0	0			
27139000	其他石油或从沥青矿物提取油类的残渣	6	0	0	0	0	0	0	0	0	0	0		0	5		0	0	0			
27141000	沥青页岩、油页岩及焦油砂	6	0	0	0	0	0	0	0	0	0	0		0	5		0	0	0			
27149010	天然沥青（地沥青）	8	0	0	0	0	0	0	0	0	0	0		0	5		0	0	0			
27149090	沥青岩	3	0	0	0	0	0	0	0	0	0	0		0	0		0	0	0			
27150000	以天然沥青（地沥青）、石油沥青、矿物焦油或矿物焦油沥青为基本成分的沥青混合物	8	0	0	0	0	0	0	0	0	0	0		0.8	5		0	0	0		0	
28011000	氯	5.5	0	0	0	0	0	0	0	0	0	0		0.6	5		0	0	0			
28012000	碘	5.5	0	0	0	0	0	0	0	0	0	0			5		0		0			
28013010	氟	5.5	0	0	0	0	0	0	0	0	0	0		0	0		0	0	0			
28013020	溴	5.5	0	0	0	0	0	0	0	0	0	0		0	0		0	0	0			
28020000	升华、沉淀、胶态硫磺	5.5	0	0	0	0	0	0	0	0	0	0		0	0		0	0	0			
28030000	碳（碳黑及其他税号未列名的其他形状的碳）	5.5	0	0	0	0	0	0	0	0	0	0	4.4	0	0		0	0	0	0		0
28041000	氢	5.5	0	0	0	0	0	0	0	0	0	0		0	0		0	0	0	0		
28042100	氩	5.5	0	0	0	0	0	0	0	0	0	0		0.6	5		0	0	0	0		

税则号列	商品名称（简称）	最惠国	东盟										亚太	智利	巴基斯坦	新加坡	新西兰	秘鲁	哥斯达黎加	香港	澳门	台湾
			文	柬	印	老	马	缅	菲	新	泰	越										
28042900	其他稀有气体	5.5	0	0	0	0	0	0	0	0	0	0		0	5		0	0	0	0		
28043000	氮	5.5	0	0	0	0	0	0	0	0	0	0		0	5		0	0	0	0		
28044000	氧	5.5	0	0	0	0	0	0	0	0	0	0		0.6	5		0	0	0	0		
28045000	硼、碲	5.5	0	0	0	0	0	0	0	0	0	0		0	0		0	0	0			
28046117	电子工业用直径≥30cm单晶硅棒	4	0	0	0	0	0	0	0	0	0	0		0	0		0	0	0			
28046119	电子工业用7.5≤直径<30cm单晶硅棒	4	0	0	0	0	0	0	0	0	0	0		0	0		0	0	0			
28046120	电子工业用直径<7.5cm单晶硅棒	4	0	0	0	0	0	0	0	0	0	0		0	0		0	0	0			
28046190	其他含硅量≥99.99%的硅	4	0	0	0	0	0	0	0	0	0	0		0	0		0	0	0			
28046900	其他含硅量<99.99%的硅	4	0	0	0	0	0	0	0	0	0	0		0	0		0	0	0			
28047010	黄磷(白磷)	5.5	0	0	0	0	0	0	0	0	0	0		0	0		0	0	0			
28047090	其他磷	5.5	0	0	0	0	0	0	0	0	0	0		0	0		0	0	0			
28048000	砷	5.5	0	0	0	0	0	0	0	0	0	0		0	0		0	0	0			
28049010	经掺杂用于电子工业的硒晶体棒	4	0	0	0	0	0	0	0	0	0	0		0.4	0		0	2	0			
28049090	其他硒	5.5	0	0	0	0	0	0	0	0	0	0		0.6	0		0	4.1	0			
28051100	钠	5.5	0	0	0	0	0	0	0	0	0	0		0	0		0	0	0			
28051200	钙	5.5	0	0	0	0	0	0	0	0	0	0		0	0		0	0	0			
28051900	其他碱金属及碱土金属	5.5	0	0	0	0	0	0	0	0	0	0		0	0		0	0	0			
28053011	钕	5.5	0	0	0	0	0	0	0	0	0	0		0	0		0	0	0			
28053012	镝	5.5	0	0	0	0	0	0	0	0	0	0		0	0		0	0	0			
28053013	铽	5.5	0	0	0	0	0	0	0	0	0	0		0	0		0	0	0			
28053014	镧	5.5	0	0	0	0	0	0	0	0	0	0		0	0		0	0	0			
28053015	铈	5.5	0	0	0	0	0	0	0	0	0	0		0	0		0	0	0			
28053016	镨	5.5	0	0	0	0	0	0	0	0	0	0		0	0		0	0	0			
28053017	钇	5.5	0	0	0	0	0	0	0	0	0	0		0	0		0	0	0			
28053019	其他未相互混合或熔合的稀土金属、钪及钇	5.5	0	0	0	0	0	0	0	0	0	0		0	0		0	0	0			
28053021	已相互混合或熔合的稀土金属、钪及钇，电池级	5.5	0	0	0	0	0	0	0	0	0	0		0	0		0	0	0			
28053029	其他已相互混合或熔合的稀土金属、钪及钇	5.5	0	0	0	0	0	0	0	0	0	0		0	0		0	0	0			
28054000	汞	5.5	0	0	0	0	0	0	0	0	0	0		0.6	0		0	0	0			
28061000	氯化氢(盐酸)	5.5	0	0	0	0	0	0	0	0	0	0		0.6	5		0	0	0			
28062000	氯磺酸	5.5	0	0	0	0	0	0	0	0	0	0		0	0		0	0	0			
28070000	硫酸、发烟硫酸	5.5	0	0	0	0	0	0	0	0	0	0		0.6	5		0	0	0			
28080000	硝酸及磺硝酸	5.5	0	0	0	0	0	0	0	0	0	0		0.6	5		0	0	0			
28091000	五氧化二磷	1	0	0	0	0	0	0	0	0	0	0		0	0		0	0	0			
28092011	食品级磷酸	1	0	0	0	0	0	0	0	0	0	0		0	0		0	0	0			
28092019	其他磷酸及偏磷酸、焦磷酸	1	0	0	0	0	0	0	0	0	0	0		0	0		0	0	0			
28092090	其他多磷酸	5.5	0	0	0	0	0	0	0	0	0	0		0	5		0	0	0			
28100010	硼的氧化物	5.5	0	0	0	0	0	0	0	0	0	0		0.6	0		0	2.8	0			
28100020	硼酸	5.5	0	0	0	0	0	0	0	0	0	0		0.6	0		0	2.8	0			
28111100	氟化氢(氢氟酸)	5.5	0	0	0	0	0	0	0	0	0	0		0	0		0	0	0			
28111910	氢氰酸	5.5	0	0	0	0	0	0	0	0	0	0		0.6	0		0	0	0			
28111920	硒化氢	5.5	0	0	0	0	0	0	0	0	0	0		0.6	5		0	0	0			
28111990	其他无机酸	5.5	0	0	0	0	0	0	0	0	0	0		0.6	5		0	0	0			
28112100	二氧化碳	5.5	0	0	0	0	0	0	0	0	0	0		0	5		0	0	0	0		
28112210	硅胶	5.5	0	0	0	0	0	0	0	0	0	0		0	5		0	0	0		0	
28112290	其他二氧化硅	5.5	0	0	0	0	0	0	0	0	0	0		0	5		0	0	0		0	
28112900	其他非金属无机氧化物	5.5	0	0	0	0	0	0	0	0	0	0		0.6	5		0	0	0	0		
28121010	氯化亚砜	5.5	0	0	0	0	0	0	0	0	0	0		0.6	5		0	0	0			
28121020	氧氯化磷(磷酰氯;三氯氧磷)	5.5	0	0	0	0	0	0	0	0	0	0		0.6	5		0	0	0			
28121030	碳酰二氯(光气)	5.5	0	0	0	0	0	0	0	0	0	0		0.6	0		0	0	0			
28121041	一氯化硫(氯化硫)	5.5	0	0	0	0	0	0	0	0	0	0		0.6	0		0	0	0			
28121042	二氯化硫	5.5	0	0	0	0	0	0	0	0	0	0		0.6	0		0	0	0			
28121043	三氯化磷	5.5	0	0	0	0	0	0	0	0	0	0		0.6	0		0	0	0			
28121044	三氯化砷	5.5	0	0	0	0	0	0	0	0	0	0		0.6	0		0	0	0			
28121045	五氯化磷	5.5	0	0	0	0	0	0	0	0	0	0		0.6	0		0	0	0			
28121049	其他非金属氯化物	5.5	0	0	0	0	0	0	0	0	0	0		0.6	5		0	0	0			
28121090	其他非金属氯化物及氯氧化物	5.5	0	0	0	0	0	0	0	0	0	0		0.6	0		0	0	0			
28129011	三氟化氮	5.5	0	0	0	0	0	0	0	0	0	0		0	0		0	0	0			

税则号列	商品名称（简称）	最惠国	东盟										亚太	智利	巴基斯坦	新加坡	新西兰	秘鲁	哥斯达黎加	香港	澳门	台湾
			文	柬	印	老	马	缅	菲	新	泰	越										
28129019	其他氟化物及氟氧化物	5.5	0	0	0	0	0	0	0	0	0	0		0	0		0	0	0			
28129090	其他非金属卤化物及卤氧化物	5.5	0	0	0	0	0	0	0	0	0	0		0	0		0	0	0			
28131000	二硫化碳	5.5	0	0	0	0	0	0	0	0	0	0		0	0		0	0	0	0		
28139000	其他非金属硫化物,商品三硫化二磷	5.5	0	0	0	0	0	0	0	0	0	0		0	0		0	0	0			
28141000	氨	5.5	0	0	0	0	0	0	0	0	0	0		0.6	0		0	0	0			
28142000	氨水	5.5	0	0	0	0	0	0	0	0	0	0		0	0		0	0	0			
28151100	固体氢氧化钠	10											7	0	7		0	0	0			
28151200	氢氧化钠水溶液及液体烧碱	8											5.6	0	5.6		0	0	0			
28152000	氢氧化钾(苛性钾)	5.5	0	0	0	0	0	0	0	0	0	0		0	5		0	0	0			
28153000	过氧化钠及过氧化钾	5.5	0	0	0	0	0	0	0	0	0	0		0	0		0	0	0			
28161000	氢氧化镁及过氧化镁	5.5	0	0	0	0	0	0	0	0	0	0		0	5		0	0	0			
28164000	锶或钡的氧化物、氢氧化物及过氧化物	5.5	0	0	0	0	0	0	0	0	0	0		0	5		0	0	0			
28170010	氧化锌	5.5	0	0	0	0	0	0	0	0	0	0		0	0		0	2.1	0			
28170090	过氧化锌	5.5	0	0	0	0	0	0	0	0	0	0		0	0		0	2.8	0			
28181010	棕刚玉	5.5	0	0	0	0	0	0	0	0	0	0		0	0		0	0	0			
28181090	其他人造刚玉，不论是否已有化学定义	5.5	0	0	0	0	0	0	0	0	0	0		0	0		0	0	0			
28182000	氧化铝，但人造刚玉除外	8	0	0	0	0	0	0	0	0	0	0		0	5	0	0	0	0			
28183000	氢氧化铝	5.5	0	0	0	0	0	0	0	0	0	0		0	0		0	0	0			
28191000	三氧化铬	5.5	0	0	0	0	0	0	0	0	0	0		0	0		0	0	0			
28199000	其他铬的氧化物及氢氧化物	5.5	0	0	0	0	0	0	0	0	0	0		0	0		0	0	0			
28201000	二氧化锰	5.5	0	0	0	0	0	0	0	0	0	0		0	0		0	0	0			
28209000	其他锰的氧化物	5.5	0	0	0	0	0	0	0	0	0	0		0	0		0	0	0			
28211000	铁的氧化物及氢氧化物	5.5	0	0	0	0	0	0	0	0	0	0		0	0		0	0	0			
28212000	土色料	5.5	0	0	0	0	0	0	0	0	0	0		0	0		0	0	0			
28220010	四氧化三钴	5.5	0	0	0	0	0	0	0	0	0	0		0	0		0	0	0			
28220090	其他钴的氧化物及氢氧化物；商品氧化钴	5.5	0	0	0	0	0	0	0	0	0	0		0	0		0	0				
28230000	钛的氧化物	5.5	0	0	0	0	0	0	0	0	0	0		0	0		0	0	0			
28241000	一氧化铅(铅黄、黄丹)	5.5	0	0	0	0	0	0	0	0	0	0		0.6	0		0	0	0			
28249010	铅丹及铅橙	5.5	0	0	0	0	0	0	0	0	0	0		0.6	0		0	0	0			
28249090	其他铅的氧化物	5.5	0	0	0	0	0	0	0	0	0	0		0	0		0	0	0			
28251010	水合肼	5.5	0	0	0	0	0	0	0	0	0	0		0	0		0	0	0			
28251020	硫酸羟胺	5.5	0	0	0	0	0	0	0	0	0	0		0	5		0	0	0			
28251090	其他肼、胲及其无机盐	5.5	0	0	0	0	0	0	0	0	0	0		0	5		0	0	0			
28252010	氢氧化锂	5.5	0	0	0	0	0	0	0	0	0	0		0	0		0	0	0			
28252090	锂的氧化物	5.5	0	0	0	0	0	0	0	0	0	0		0	0		0	0	0			
28253010	五氧化二钒	5.5	0	0	0	0	0	0	0	0	0	0		0	0		0	0	0			
28253090	其他钒的氧化物及氢氧化物	5.5	0	0	0	0	0	0	0	0	0	0		0	0		0	0	0			
28254000	镍的氧化物及氢氧化物	5.5	0	0	0	0	0	0	0	0	0	0		0	0		0	0	0			
28255000	铜的氧化物及氢氧化物	5.5	0	0	0	0	0	0	0	0	0	0		0.6	0		0	0	0			
28256000	锗的氧化物及二氧化锆	5.5	0	0	0	0	0	0	0	0	0	0		0	0		0	0	0			
28257000	钼的氧化物及氢氧化物	5.5	0	0	0	0	0	0	0	0	0	0		0.6	0		0		0			
28258000	锑的氧化物	5.5	0	0	0	0	0	0	0	0	0	0		0	0		0	0	0			
28259011	钨酸	5.5	0	0	0	0	0	0	0	0	0	0		0	0		0	0	0			
28259012	三氧化钨	5.5	0	0	0	0	0	0	0	0	0	0		0	0		0	0	0			
28259019	其他钨的氧化物及氢氧化物	5.5	0	0	0	0	0	0	0	0	0	0		0	0		0	0	0			
28259021	三氧化二铋	5.5	0	0	0	0	0	0	0	0	0	0		0	0		0	0	0			
28259029	其他铋的氧化物及氢氧化物	5.5	0	0	0	0	0	0	0	0	0	0		0	0		0	0	0			
28259031	二氧化锡	5.5	0	0	0	0	0	0	0	0	0	0		0	0		0	0	0			
28259039	其他锡的氧化物及氢氧化物	5.5	0	0	0	0	0	0	0	0	0	0		0	0		0	0	0			
28259041	一氧化铌	5.5	0	0	0	0	0	0	0	0	0	0		0	0		0	0	0			
28259049	其他铌的氧化物及氢氧化物	5.5	0	0	0	0	0	0	0	0	0	0		0	0		0	0	0			
28259090	其他无机碱；其他金属的氧化物及氢氧化物及过氧化物	5.5	0	0	0	0	0	0	0	0	0	0		0	0		0	0				
28261210	无水氟化铝	5.5	0	0	0	0	0	0	0	0	0	0		0	0		0	0	0			
28261290	其他氟化铝	5.5	0	0	0	0	0	0	0	0	0	0		0	0		0	0	0			
28261910	铵的氟化物	5.5	0	0	0	0	0	0	0	0	0	0		0	0		0	0	0			
28261920	钠的氟化物	5.5	0	0	0	0	0	0	0	0	0	0		0	0		0	0	0			
28261990	其他氟化物	5.5	0	0	0	0	0	0	0	0	0	0		0	5		0	0	0			
28263000	六氟铝酸钠(人造冰晶石)	5.5	0	0	0	0	0	0	0	0	0	0		0	0		0	0	0			

税则号列	商品名称（简称）	最惠国	东盟										亚太	智利	巴基斯坦	新加坡	新西兰	秘鲁	哥斯达黎加	香港	澳门	台湾
			文	柬	印	老	马	缅	菲	新	泰	越										
28269010	氟硅酸盐	5.5	0	0	0	0	0	0	0	0	0	0		0	5		0	0	0	0		
28269090	氟铝酸盐及其他氟络盐	5.5	0	0	0	0	0	0	0	0	0	0		0	5		0	0	0			
28271010	肥料用氯化铵	4	0	0	0	0	0	0	0	0	0	0		0	0		0	0	0			
28271090	非肥料用氯化铵	5.5	0	0	0	0	0	0	0	0	0	0		0	5		0	0	0			
28272000	氯化钙	5.5	0	0	0	0	0	0	0	0	0	0		0	5		0	0	0			
28273100	氯化镁	5.5	0	0	0	0	0	0	0	0	0	0		0	5		0	0	0			
28273200	氯化铝	5.5	0	0	0	0	0	0	0	0	0	0		0	5		0	0	0			
28273500	氯化镍	5.5	0	0	0	0	0	0	0	0	0	0		0	5		0	0	0			
28273910	氯化锂	5.5	0	0	0	0	0	0	0	0	0	0	4.4	0.6	0		0		0			
28273920	氯化钡	5.5	0	0	0	0	0	0	0	0	0	0	4.4	0.6	0		0		0			
28273930	氯化钴	5.5	0	0	0	0	0	0	0	0	0	0	4.4	0.6	0		0	0	0			
28273990	其他未列名氯化物	5.5	0	0	0	0	0	0	0	0	0	0	4.4	0.6	0		0		0			
28274100	铜的氯氧化物及氢氧基氯化物	5.5	0	0	0	0	0	0	0	0	0	0		0.6	0		0	2.8	0			
28274910	锆的氯氧化物及氢氧基氯化物	5.5	0	0	0	0	0	0	0	0	0	0		0	5		0	0	0			
28274990	其他氯氧化物及氢氧基氯化物	5.5	0	0	0	0	0	0	0	0	0	0		0	5		0	0	0			
28275100	溴化钠及溴化钾	5.5	0	0	0	0	0	0	0	0	0	0		0	0		0	0	0			
28275900	其他溴化物及溴氧化物	5.5	0	0	0	0	0	0	0	0	0	0		0	5		0	0	0			
28276000	碘化物及碘氧化物	5.5	0	0	0	0	0	0	0	0	0	0		0.6	5		0		0			
28281000	商品次氯酸钙及其他钙的次氯酸盐	12	0	0	0	0	0	0	0	0	0	0	8.4	0	5	0	0	0	2.4			
28289000	次氯酸盐；亚氯酸盐及次溴酸盐	5.5	0	0	0	0	0	0	0	0	0	0		0	5		0	0	0			
28291100	氯酸钠	12	0	0	0	0	0	0	0	0	0	0		0	6	0	0	0	2.4			
28291910	氯酸钾(洋硝)	5.5	0	0	0	0	0	0	0	0	0	0		0	0		0	0	0			
28291990	其他氯酸盐	5.5	0	0	0	0	0	0	0	0	0	0		0	0		0	0	0			
28299000	高氯酸盐；溴酸盐及过溴酸盐；碘酸盐及高碘酸盐	5.5	0	0	0	0	0	0	0	0	0	0		0.6	5		0	0	0			
28301010	硫化钠	5.5	0	0	0	0	0	0	0	0	0	0		0.6	5		0	0	0			
28301090	其他钠的硫化物	5.5	0	0	0	0	0	0	0	0	0	0		0.6	0		0	0	0			
28309020	硫化锑	5.5	0	0	0	0	0	0	0	0	0	0		0	0		0	0	0			
28309030	硫化钴	5.5	0	0	0	0	0	0	0	0	0	0		0	0		0	0	0			
28309090	其他硫化物、多硫化物	5.5	0	0	0	0	0	0	0	0	0	0		0	5		0	0	0			
28311010	钠的连二硫酸盐	5.5	0	0	0	0	0	0	0	0	0	0		0	5		0	0	0			
28311020	钠的次硫酸盐	5.5	0	0	0	0	0	0	0	0	0	0		0	5		0	0	0			
28319000	其他连二亚硫酸盐及次硫酸盐	5.5	0	0	0	0	0	0	0	0	0	0		0	5		0	0	0			
28321000	钠的亚硫酸盐	5.5	0	0	0	0	0	0	0	0	0	0		0.6	5		0	0	0			
28322000	其他亚硫酸盐	5.5	0	0	0	0	0	0	0	0	0	0		0	0		0	0	0			
28323000	硫代硫酸盐	5.5	0	0	0	0	0	0	0	0	0	0		0	5		0	0	0			
28331100	硫酸钠	5.5	0	0	0	0	0	0	0	0	0	0		0.6	5		0	0	0			
28331900	钠的其他硫酸盐	5.5	0	0	0	0	0	0	0	0	0	0		0	5		0	0	0			
28332100	硫酸镁	5.5	0	0	0	0	0	0	0	0	0	0		0.6	5		0	0	0			
28332200	硫酸铝	5.5	0	0	0	0	0	0	0	0	0	0		0.6	5		0	0	0			
28332400	镍的硫酸盐	5.5	0	0	0	0	0	0	0	0	0	0		0	5		0	0	0			
28332500	铜的硫酸盐	5.5	0	0	0	0	0	0	0	0	0	0		0.6	5		0	0	0			
28332700	硫酸钡	5.5	0	0	0	0	0	0	0	0	0	0		0	5		0	0	0			
28332910	硫酸亚铁	5.5	0	0	0	0	0	0	0	0	0	0		0	5		0	0	0			
28332920	铬的硫酸盐	5.5	0	0	0	0	0	0	0	0	0	0		0	0		0	0	0			
28332930	硫酸锌	5.5	0	0	0	0	0	0	0	0	0	0		0	5		0	0	0			
28332990	其他硫酸盐	5.5	0	0	0	0	0	0	0	0	0	0		0	5		0	0	0			
28333010	钾铝矾	5.5	0	0	0	0	0	0	0	0	0	0		0	0		0	0	0			
28333090	其他矾	5.5	0	0	0	0	0	0	0	0	0	0		0	0		0	0	0			
28334000	过硫酸盐	5.5	0	0	0	0	0	0	0	0	0	0		0	5		0	0	0			
28341000	亚硝酸盐	5.5	0	0	0	0	0	0	0	0	0	0		0	5		0	0	0			
28342110	肥料用硝酸钾	4	0	0	0	0	0	0	0	0	0	0		0.4	0		0	0	0			
28342190	非肥料用硝酸钾	5.5	0	0	0	0	0	0	0	0	0	0		0.6	5		0	0	0			
28342910	硝酸钴	5.5	0	0	0	0	0	0	0	0	0	0		0	0		0	0	0			
28342990	其他硝酸盐	5.5	0	0	0	0	0	0	0	0	0	0		0	5		0	0	0			
28351000	次磷酸盐及亚磷酸盐	5.5	0	0	0	0	0	0	0	0	0	0		0	5		0	0	0			
28352200	磷酸一钠及磷酸二钠	5.5	0	0	0	0	0	0	0	0	0	0		0	5		0	0	0			
28352400	钾的磷酸盐	5.5	0	0	0	0	0	0	0	0	0	0		0	5		0	0	0			
28352510	饲料级的正磷酸氢钙（磷酸二钙）	5.5	0	0	0	0	0	0	0	0	0	0		0	5		0	0	0			
28352520	食品级的正磷酸氢钙（磷酸二钙）	5.5	0	0	0	0	0	0	0	0	0	0		0	5		0	0	0			

税则号列	商品名称（简称）	最惠国	东盟										亚太	智利	巴基斯坦	新加坡	新西兰	秘鲁	哥斯达黎加	香港	澳门	台湾
			文	柬	印	老	马	缅	菲	新	泰	越										
28352590	其他正磷酸氢钙（磷酸二钙）	5.5	0	0	0	0	0	0	0	0	0	0		0	5		0	0	0			
28352600	其他磷酸钙	5.5	0	0	0	0	0	0	0	0	0	0		0	5		0	0	0			
28352910	磷酸三钠	5.5	0	0	0	0	0	0	0	0	0	0		0	5		0	0	0			
28352990	其他磷酸盐	5.5	0	0	0	0	0	0	0	0	0	0		0	5		0	0	0			
28353110	食品级的三磷酸钠（三聚磷酸钠）	5.5	0	0	0	0	0	0	0	0	0	0		0	5		0	0	0			
28353190	其他三磷酸钠（三聚磷酸钠）	5.5	0	0	0	0	0	0	0	0	0	0		0	5		0	0	0			
28353911	食品级的六偏磷酸钠	5.5	0	0	0	0	0	0	0	0	0	0		0	5		0	0	0			
28353919	其他六偏磷酸钠	5.5	0	0	0	0	0	0	0	0	0	0		0	5		0	0	0			
28353990	其他多磷酸盐	5.5	0	0	0	0	0	0	0	0	0	0		0	5		0	0	0			
28362000	碳酸钠(纯碱)	5.5	0	0	0	0	0	0	0	0	0	0		0	5		0	0	0			
28363000	碳酸氢钠(小苏打)	5.5	0	0	0	0	0	0	0	0	0	0		0	5		0	0	0			
28364000	钾的碳酸盐	5.5	0	0	0	0	0	0	0	0	0	0		0	5		0	0	0			
28365000	碳酸钙	5.5	0	0	0	0	0	0	0	0	0	0		0	5		0	0	0			
28366000	碳酸钡	5.5	0	0	0	0	0	0	0	0	0	0		0	5		0	0	0			
28369100	锂的碳酸盐	5.5	0	0	0	0	0	0	0	0	0	0		0.6	5		0		0			
28369200	锶的碳酸盐	5.5	0	0	0	0	0	0	0	0	0	0		0	5		0	0	0			
28369910	碳酸镁	5.5	0	0	0	0	0	0	0	0	0	0		0.6	5		0	0	0			
28369930	碳酸钴	5.5	0	0	0	0	0	0	0	0	0	0		0.6	5		0	0	0			
28369940	商品碳酸铵及其他铵的碳酸盐	5.5	0	0	0	0	0	0	0	0	0	0		0	0		0	0	0			
28369950	碳酸锆	5.5	0	0	0	0	0	0	0	0	0	0		0	5		0	0	0			
28369990	其他碳酸盐；过碳酸盐	5.5	0	0	0	0	0	0	0	0	0	0		0	5		0	0	0		0	
28371110	氰化钠	5.5	0	0	0	0	0	0	0	0	0	0		0.6	0		0	0	0			
28371120	氧氰化钠	5.5	0	0	0	0	0	0	0	0	0	0	5	0.6	0		0	0	0			
28371910	氰化钾	5.5	0	0	0	0	0	0	0	0	0	0		0	0		0	0	0			
28371990	其他氰化物及氧氰化物	5.5	0	0	0	0	0	0	0	0	0	0		0	0		0	0	0			
28372000	氰络合物	5.5	0	0	0	0	0	0	0	0	0	0		0	0		0	0	0			
28391100	偏硅酸钠	5.5	0	0	0	0	0	0	0	0	0	0		0	5		0	0	0			
28391910	硅酸钠	5.5	0	0	0	0	0	0	0	0	0	0		0	5		0	0	0			
28391990	其他钠的硅酸盐；商品硅酸钠	5.5	0	0	0	0	0	0	0	0	0	0		0	5		0	0	0			
28399000	其他硅酸盐；商品碱金属硅酸盐	5.5	0	0	0	0	0	0	0	0	0	0		0	5		0	0	0			
28401100	无水四硼酸钠	5.5	0	0	0	0	0	0	0	0	0	0		0	0		0	0	0			
28401900	其他四硼酸钠	5.5	0	0	0	0	0	0	0	0	0	0		0.6	0		0	0	0			
28402000	其他硼酸盐	5.5	0	0	0	0	0	0	0	0	0	0		0	0		0	0	0			
28403000	过硼酸盐	5.5	0	0	0	0	0	0	0	0	0	0		0	0		0	0	0			
28413000	重铬酸钠	5.5	0	0	0	0	0	0	0	0	0	0		0	0		0	0	0			
28415000	其他铬酸盐及重铬酸盐；过铬酸盐	5.5	0	0	0	0	0	0	0	0	0	0		0	5		0	0	0			
28416100	高锰酸钾	5.5	0	0	0	0	0	0	0	0	0	0		0	5		0	0	0			
28416910	锰酸锂	5.5	0	0	0	0	0	0	0	0	0	0		0	0		0	0	0			
28416990	其他亚锰酸盐、锰酸盐及高锰酸盐	5.5	0	0	0	0	0	0	0	0	0	0		0	0		0	0	0			
28417010	钼酸铵	5.5	0	0	0	0	0	0	0	0	0	0		0.6	5		0	0	0			
28417090	其他钼酸盐	5.5	0	0	0	0	0	0	0	0	0	0		0.6	5		0	0	0			
28418010	仲钨酸铵	5.5	0	0	0	0	0	0	0	0	0	0		0	0		0	0	0			
28418020	钨酸钠	5.5	0	0	0	0	0	0	0	0	0	0		0	0		0	0	0			
28418030	钨酸钙	5.5	0	0	0	0	0	0	0	0	0	0		0	0		0	0	0			
28418040	偏钨酸铵	5.5	0	0	0	0	0	0	0	0	0	0		0	0		0	0	0			
28418090	其他钨酸盐	5.5	0	0	0	0	0	0	0	0	0	0		0	0		0	0	0			
28419000	其他金属酸盐及过金属酸盐	5.5	0	0	0	0	0	0	0	0	0	0		0	5		0	0	0			
28421000	硅酸复盐及硅酸络盐（包括不论是否已有化学定义的硅铝酸盐）	5.5	0	0	0	0	0	0	0	0	0	0		0	5		0	0	0	0		
28429011	硫氰酸钠	5.5	0	0	0	0	0	0	0	0	0	0		0	5		0	0	0			
28429019	其他雷酸盐、氰酸盐及硫氰酸盐	5.5	0	0	0	0	0	0	0	0	0	0		0	5		0	0	0			
28429020	碲化镉	5.5	0	0	0	0	0	0	0	0	0	0		0	5		0	0	0			
28429030	锂镍钴锰氧化物	5.5	0	0	0	0	0	0	0	0	0	0		0	5		0	0	0			
28429040	磷酸铁锂	5.5	0	0	0	0	0	0	0	0	0	0		0	5		0	0	0			
28429050	硒酸盐及亚硒酸盐	5.5	0	0	0	0	0	0	0	0	0	0		0	5		0	0	0			
28429090	其他无机酸盐及过氧酸盐，叠氮化物除外	5.5	0	0	0	0	0	0	0	0	0	0		0	5		0	0	0			
28431000	胶态贵金属	5.5	0	0	0	0	0	0	0	0	0	0		0	0		0	0	0			
28432100	硝酸银	5.5	0	0	0	0	0	0	0	0	0	0		0	0		0	0	0	0		
28432900	其他银化合物，不论是否已有化学定义	5.5	0	0	0	0	0	0	0	0	0	0		0	0		0	0	0	0		

税则号列	商品名称（简称）	最惠国	东盟										亚太	智利	巴基斯坦	新加坡	新西兰	秘鲁	哥斯达黎加	香港	澳门	台湾
			文	柬	印	老	马	缅	菲	新	泰	越										
28433000	金化合物，不论是否已有化学定义	5.5	0	0	0	0	0	0	0	0	0	0		0	0		0	0	0	0		
28439000	其他贵金属化合物，不论是否已有化学定义；贵金属汞齐	5.5	0	0	0	0	0	0	0	0	0	0		0.6	5		0	0	0	0		
28441000	天然铀及其化合物（包括其合金，分散体，陶瓷产品及混合物）	5.5	0	0	0	0	0	0	0	0	0	0		0	0		0	0	0			
28442000	U235浓缩铀、钚及它们的化合物（包括其合金，分散体，陶瓷产品及混合物）	5.5	0	0	0	0	0	0	0	0	0	0		0	0		0	0	0			
28443000	U235贫化铀、钍及它们的化合物（包括其合金，分散体，陶瓷产品及混合物）	5.5	0	0	0	0	0	0	0	0	0	0		0	0		0	0	0			
28444010	镭及镭盐（包括其合金，分散体，陶瓷产品及混合物）	4	0	0	0	0	0	0	0	0	0	0		0	0		0	0	0			
28444020	放射性钴及放射性钴盐(包括其合金，分散体，陶瓷产品及混合物)	4	0	0	0	0	0	0	0	0	0	0		0	0		0	0	0			
28444090	其他放射性元素同位素及其化合物（包括其合金，分散体，陶瓷产品及混合物）；放射性残渣	5.5	0	0	0	0	0	0	0	0	0	0		0	0		0	0	0			
28445000	核反应堆已耗尽的燃料元件	5.5	0	0	0	0	0	0	0	0	0	0		0	0		0	0	0			
28451000	重水(氧化氘)	5.5	0	0	0	0	0	0	0	0	0	0		0	0		0	0	0			
28459000	其他同位素及其化合物,不论是否已有化学定义	5.5	0	0	0	0	0	0	0	0	0	0		0	0		0	0	0			
28461010	氧化铈	5.5	0	0	0	0	0	0	0	0	0	0	3.9	0	0		0	0	0			
28461020	氢氧化铈	5.5	0	0	0	0	0	0	0	0	0	0	3.9	0	0		0	0	0			
28461030	碳酸铈	5.5	0	0	0	0	0	0	0	0	0	0	3.9	0	0		0	0	0			
28461090	铈的其他化合物	5.5	0	0	0	0	0	0	0	0	0	0	3.9	0	0		0	0	0			
28469011	氧化钇	5.5	0	0	0	0	0	0	0	0	0	0		0	0		0	0	0			
28469012	氧化镧	5.5	0	0	0	0	0	0	0	0	0	0		0	0		0	0	0			
28469013	氧化钕	5.5	0	0	0	0	0	0	0	0	0	0		0	0		0	0	0			
28469014	氧化铕	5.5	0	0	0	0	0	0	0	0	0	0		0	0		0	0	0			
28469015	氧化镝	5.5	0	0	0	0	0	0	0	0	0	0		0	0		0	0	0			
28469016	氧化铽	5.5	0	0	0	0	0	0	0	0	0	0		0	0		0	0	0			
28469017	氧化镨	5.5	0	0	0	0	0	0	0	0	0	0		0	0		0	0	0			
28469019	其他氧化稀土	5.5	0	0	0	0	0	0	0	0	0	0		0	0		0	0	0			
28469021	氯化铽	5.5	0	0	0	0	0	0	0	0	0	0		0	0		0	0	0			
28469022	氯化镝	5.5	0	0	0	0	0	0	0	0	0	0		0	0		0	0	0			
28469023	氯化镧	5.5	0	0	0	0	0	0	0	0	0	0		0	0		0	0	0			
28469024	氯化钕	5.5	0	0	0	0	0	0	0	0	0	0		0	0		0	0	0			
28469025	氯化镨	5.5	0	0	0	0	0	0	0	0	0	0		0	0		0	0	0			
28469026	氯化钇	5.5	0	0	0	0	0	0	0	0	0	0		0	0		0	0	0			
28469028	混合氯化稀土	5.5	0	0	0	0	0	0	0	0	0	0		0	0		0	0	0			
28469029	未混合氯化稀土	5.5	0	0	0	0	0	0	0	0	0	0		0	0		0	0	0			
28469031	氟化铽	5.5	0	0	0	0	0	0	0	0	0	0		0	0		0	0	0			
28469032	氟化镝	5.5	0	0	0	0	0	0	0	0	0	0		0	0		0	0	0			
28469033	氟化镧	5.5	0	0	0	0	0	0	0	0	0	0		0	0		0	0	0			
28469034	氟化钕	5.5	0	0	0	0	0	0	0	0	0	0		0	0		0	0	0			
28469035	氟化镨	5.5	0	0	0	0	0	0	0	0	0	0		0	0		0	0	0			
28469036	氟化钇	5.5	0	0	0	0	0	0	0	0	0	0		0	0		0	0	0			
28469039	其他氟化稀土	5.5	0	0	0	0	0	0	0	0	0	0		0	0		0	0	0			
28469041	碳酸镧	5.5	0	0	0	0	0	0	0	0	0	0		0	0		0	0	0			
28469042	碳酸铽	5.5	0	0	0	0	0	0	0	0	0	0		0	0		0	0	0			
28469043	碳酸镝	5.5	0	0	0	0	0	0	0	0	0	0		0	0		0	0	0			
28469044	碳酸钕	5.5	0	0	0	0	0	0	0	0	0	0		0	0		0	0	0			
28469045	碳酸镨	5.5	0	0	0	0	0	0	0	0	0	0		0	0		0	0	0			
28469046	碳酸钇	5.5	0	0	0	0	0	0	0	0	0	0		0	0		0	0	0			
28469048	混合碳酸稀土	5.5	0	0	0	0	0	0	0	0	0	0		0	0		0	0	0			
28469049	未混合碳酸稀土	5.5	0	0	0	0	0	0	0	0	0	0		0	0		0	0	0			
28469091	镧的其他化合物	5.5	0	0	0	0	0	0	0	0	0	0		0	0		0	0	0			
28469092	钕的其他化合物	5.5	0	0	0	0	0	0	0	0	0	0		0	0		0	0	0			
28469093	铽的其他化合物	5.5	0	0	0	0	0	0	0	0	0	0		0	0		0	0	0			
28469094	镝的其他化合物	5.5	0	0	0	0	0	0	0	0	0	0		0	0		0	0	0			
28469095	镨的其他化合物	5.5	0	0	0	0	0	0	0	0	0	0		0	0		0	0	0			
28469096	钇的其他化合物	5.5	0	0	0	0	0	0	0	0	0	0		0	0		0	0	0			

税则号列	商品名称（简称）	最惠国	东盟										亚太	智利	巴基斯坦	新加坡	新西兰	秘鲁	哥斯达黎加	香港	澳门	台湾
			文	柬	印	老	马	缅	菲	新	泰	越										
28469099	稀土金属、钇、钪的其他化合物	5.5	0	0	0	0	0	0	0	0	0	0		0	0		0	0	0			
28470000	过氧化氢（不论是否用尿素固化）	5.5	0	0	0	0	0	0	0	0	0	0		0	5		0	0	0			
28480000	磷化物，不论是否已有化学定义，，但不包括磷铁	5.5	0	0	0	0	0	0	0	0	0	0		0.6	0		0	0	0			
28491000	碳化钙，不论是否已有化学定义，	5.5	0	0	0	0	0	0	0	0	0	0		0	0		0	0	0			
28492000	碳化硅，不论是否已有化学定义，	5.5	0	0	0	0	0	0	0	0	0	0		0	5		0	0	0			
28499010	碳化硼，不论是否已有化学定义，	5.5	0	0	0	0	0	0	0	0	0	0		0	0		0	0	0			
28499020	碳化钨，不论是否已有化学定义，	5.5	0	0	0	0	0	0	0	0	0	0		0	0		0	0	0			
28499090	其他碳化物，不论是否已有化学定义，	5.5	0	0	0	0	0	0	0	0	0	0		0	0		0	0	0			
28500011	氮化锰	5.5	0	0	0	0	0	0	0	0	0	0	3.9	0	0		0	0	0	0		
28500019	其他氮化物	5.5	0	0	0	0	0	0	0	0	0	0	3.9	0	0		0	0	0	0		
28500090	氢化物、迭氮化物、硅化物及硼化物，不论是否已有化学定义，但可归入税号 28.49 的碳化物除外：	5.5	0	0	0	0	0	0	0	0	0	0	3.9	0	0		0	0	0	0		
28521000	汞的有机或无机化合物，汞齐除外	5.5	0	0	0	0	0	0	0	0	0	0		0	0		0	0	0	0		
28529000	无化学定义的汞化合物	5.5	0	0	0	0	0	0	0	0	0	0		0	5		0	0	0			
28530010	饮用蒸馏水	5.5	0	0	0	0	0	0	0	0	0	0		0.6	0		0	0	0	0	0	
28530020	氯化氰	5.5	0	0	0	0	0	0	0	0	0	0		0.6	0		0	0	0			
28530030	镍钴锰氢氧化物	6.5	0	0	0	0	0	0	0	0	0	0		0.7	5		0	0	0	0	0	
28530090	其他无机化合物、液态空气、压缩空气，汞齐，但贵金属汞齐除外	5.5	0	0	0	0	0	0	0	0	0	0		0.6	5		0	0	0	0	0	
29011000	饱和无环烃	2	0	0	0	0	0	0	0	0	0	0		0	0		0	0	0	0		
29012100	乙烯	2	0	0	0	0	0	0	0	0	0	0		0	0		0	0	0			
29012200	丙烯	2	0	0	0	0	0	0	0	0	0	0		0	0		0	0	0			0
29012310	1-丁烯	2	0	0	0	0	0	0	0	0	0	0		0	0		0	0	0			
29012320	2-丁烯	2	0	0	0	0	0	0	0	0	0	0		0	0		0	0	0			
29012330	2-甲基丙稀	2	0	0	0	0	0	0	0	0	0	0		0	0		0	0	0			
29012410	1,3-丁二烯	2	0	0	0	0	0	0	0	0	0	0		0	0		0	0	0			0
29012420	异戊二烯	2	0	0	0	0	0	0	0	0	0	0		0	0		0	0	0			0
29012910	异戊烯	2	0	0	0	0	0	0	0	0	0	0		0	0		0	0	0			
29012920	乙炔	2	0	0	0	0	0	0	0	0	0	0		0	0		0	0	0			
29012990	其他不饱和无环烃	2	0	0	0	0	0	0	0	0	0	0		0	0		0	0	0			
29021100	环己烷	2	0	0	0	0	0	0	0	0	0	0		0	0		0	0	0			
29021910	蒎烯	2	0	0	0	0	0	0	0	0	0	0		0	0		0	0	0			
29021920	---4-烷基-4′-烷基双环己烷	2	0	0	0	0	0	0	0	0	0	0		0	0		0	0	0			
29021990	其他环烷烃、环烯及环萜烯	2	0	0	0	0	0	0	0	0	0	0		0	0		0	0	0			
29022000	苯	2	0	0	0	0	0	0	0	0	0	0		0	0		0	0	0			
29023000	甲苯	2	0	0	0	0	0	0	0	0	0	0		0	0		0	0	0			
29024100	邻二甲苯	2	0	0	0	0	0	0	0	0	0	0		0	0		0	0	0			0
29024200	间二甲苯	2	0	0	0	0	0	0	0	0	0	0		0	0		0	0	0			0
29024300	对二甲苯	2	0	0	0	0	0	0	0	0	0	0		0	0		0	0	0			0
29024400	混合二甲苯异构体	2	0	0	0	0	0	0	0	0	0	0		0	0		0	0	0			0
29025000	苯乙烯	2											1.4	0	0		0	0	0			
29026000	乙苯	2	0	0	0	0	0	0	0	0	0	0		0	0		0	0	0			
29027000	异丙基苯	2	0	0	0	0	0	0	0	0	0	0		0	0		0	0	0			
29029010	四氢萘	2	0	0	0	0	0	0	0	0	0	0		0	0		0	0	0			
29029020	精萘	2	0	0	0	0	0	0	0	0	0	0		0	0		0	0	0			
29029030	十二烷基苯	2	0	0	0	0	0	0	0	0	0	0		0	0		0	0	0			0
29029040	4-(4′-烷基环己基)环己基乙烯	2	0	0	0	0	0	0	0	0	0	0		0	0		0	0	0			
29029090	其他芳香烃	2	0	0	0	0	0	0	0	0	0	0		0	0		0	0	0			
29031100	一氯甲烷及氯乙烷	5.5	0	0	0	0	0	0	0	0	0	0		0	0		0	0	0			
29031200	二氯甲烷	8	0	0	0	0	0	0	0	0	0	0		0	5		0	0	0	0		
29031300	氯仿(三氯甲烷)	10	0	0	0	0	0	0	0	0	0	0	9	0	5		0	0	0			0
29031400	四氯化碳	8	0	0	0	0	0	0	0	0	0	0		0	5		0	0	0			
29031500	1,2-二氯乙烷（ISO）	5.5												0			0		0			
29031910	1,1,1-三氯乙烷(甲基氯仿)	8	0	0	0	0	0	0	0	0	0	0		0	5		0	0	0			
29031990	其他无环烃的饱和氯化衍生物	5.5	0	0	0	0	0	0	0	0	0	0		0	5		0	0	0			
29032100	氯乙烯	5.5	0	0	0	0	0	0	0	0	0	0	3.9	0	0		0	0	0			0
29032200	三氯乙烯	8	0	0	0	0	0	0	0	0	0	0		0	5		0	0	0			
29032300	四氯乙烯	5.5	0	0	0	0	0	0	0	0	0	0		0	0		0	0	0			
29032910	3-氯-1-丙稀（氯丙稀）	5.5	0	0	0	0	0	0	0	0	0	0		0	0		0	0	0			

税则号列	商品名称（简称）	最惠国	东盟 文	柬	印	老	马	缅	菲	新	泰	越	亚太	智利	巴基斯坦	新加坡	新西兰	秘鲁	哥斯达黎加	香港	澳门	台湾
29032990	其他无环烃的不饱和氯化衍生物	5.5	0	0	0	0	0	0	0	0	0	0		0	0		0	0	0			
29033100	1，2－二溴乙烷（ISO）	5.5	0	0	0	0	0	0	0	0	0	0		0	5		0	0	0	0		
29033910	全氟异丁烯(八氟异丁烯)	5.5	0	0	0	0	0	0	0	0	0	0		0	0		0	0	0			
29033990	其他无环烃的氟化、溴化或碘化衍生物	5.5	0	0	0	0	0	0	0	0	0	0		0	5		0	0	0	0		
29037100	一氯二氟甲烷	5.5	0	0	0	0	0	0	0	0	0	0		0	5		0	0	0			
29037200	二氯三氟乙烷	5.5	0	0	0	0	0	0	0	0	0	0		0	5		0	0	0			
29037300	二氯一氟乙烷	5.5	0	0	0	0	0	0	0	0	0	0		0	5		0	0	0			
29037400	一氯二氟乙烷	5.5	0	0	0	0	0	0	0	0	0	0		0	5		0	0	0			
29037500	二氯五氟丙烷	5.5	0	0	0	0	0	0	0	0	0	0		0	5		0	0	0			
29037600	溴氯二氟甲烷、溴三氟甲烷及二溴四氟乙烷	5.5	0	0	0	0	0	0	0	0	0	0		0	0		0	0	0			
29037710	三氯氟甲烷	5.5	0	0	0	0	0	0	0	0	0	0		0	5		0	0	0			
29037720	其他仅含氟和氯的甲烷、乙烷及丙烷的全卤化物	5.5	0	0	0	0	0	0	0	0	0	0		0	0		0	0	0			
29037790	其他仅含氟氯的无环烃全卤化衍生物	5.5	0	0	0	0	0	0	0	0	0	0		0	5		0	0	0			
29037800	其他无环烃全卤化衍生物	5.5	0	0	0	0	0	0	0	0	0	0		0	0		0	0	0			
29037910	其他仅含氟和氯的甲烷、乙烷及丙烷的卤化衍生物	5.5	0	0	0	0	0	0	0	0	0	0		0	5		0	0	0			
29037990	其他含有两种或两种以上不同卤素的无环烃卤化衍生物	5.5	0	0	0	0	0	0	0	0	0	0		0	0		0	0	0			
29038100	1,2,3,4,5,6-六氯环己烷[六六六（ISO）],包括林丹（ISO，INN）	5.5	0	0	0	0	0	0	0	0	0	0		0	0		0	0	0			
29038200	艾氏剂（ISO）、氯丹（ISO）及七氯（ISO）	5.5	0	0	0	0	0	0	0	0	0	0		0	0		0	0	0			
29038900	其他环烷烃或环烯烃等卤化衍生物	5.5	0	0	0	0	0	0	0	0	0	0		0	0		0	0	0			
29039110	邻二氯苯	5.5	0	0	0	0	0	0	0	0	0	0		0	0		0	0	0			
29039190	氯苯及对二氯苯	5.5	0	0	0	0	0	0	0	0	0	0		0	5		0	0	0			
29039200	六氯苯（ISO）及滴滴涕（ISO，INN）	5.5	0	0	0	0	0	0	0	0	0	0		0	0		0	0	0			
29039910	对氯甲苯	5.5	0	0	0	0	0	0	0	0	0	0		0	0		0	0	0			
29039920	3,4-二氯三氟甲苯	5.5	0	0	0	0	0	0	0	0	0	0		0	0		0	0	0			
29039930	4-(4′-烷基苯基)-1-(4′-烷基苯基)-2-氟苯	5.5	0	0	0	0	0	0	0	0	0	0		0	5		0	0	0			
29039990	其他芳烃卤化衍生物	5.5	0	0	0	0	0	0	0	0	0	0		0	5		0	0	0			
29041000	仅含磺基的衍生物及其盐和乙酯	5.5	0	0	0	0	0	0	0	0	0	0		0	5		0	0	0	0		
29042010	硝基苯	5.5	0	0	0	0	0	0	0	0	0	0		0.6	0		0	0	0			
29042020	硝基甲苯	5.5	0	0	0	0	0	0	0	0	0	0		0.6	0		0	0	0			
29042030	二硝基甲苯	5.5	0	0	0	0	0	0	0	0	0	0		0.6	0		0	0	0			
29042040	三硝基甲苯(TNT)	5.5	0	0	0	0	0	0	0	0	0	0		0.6	0		0	0	0			
29042090	其他仅含硝基或亚硝基衍生物	5.5	0	0	0	0	0	0	0	0	0	0		0.6	5		0	0	0			
29049011	邻硝基氯化苯	5.5	0	0	0	0	0	0	0	0	0	0		0	0		0	0	0			
29049012	间硝基氯化苯	5.5	0	0	0	0	0	0	0	0	0	0		0	0		0	0	0			
29049013	对硝基氯化苯	5.5	0	0	0	0	0	0	0	0	0	0		0	0		0	0	0			
29049020	二硝基氯化苯	5.5	0	0	0	0	0	0	0	0	0	0		0	0		0	0	0			
29049030	三氯硝基甲烷(氯化苦;硝基氯仿)	5.5	0	0	0	0	0	0	0	0	0	0		0	0		0	0	0			
29049090	其他烃的磺化、硝化、亚硝化衍生物，不论是否卤化	5.5	0	0	0	0	0	0	0	0	0	0		0	5		0	0	0			
29051100	甲醇	5.5	0	0	0	0	0	0	0	0	0	0		0.6	0		0		0	0		
29051210	丙醇	5.5	0	0	0	0	0	0	0	0	0	0		0.6	0		0	0	0			
29051220	异丙醇	5.5	0	0	0	0	0	0	0	0	0	0		0.6	0		0	0	0			0
29051300	正丁醇	5.5	0	0	0	0	0	0	0	0	0	0		0	0		0	0	0			0
29051410	异丁醇	5.5	0	0	0	0	0	0	0	0	0	0		0	0		0	0	0			0
29051420	仲丁醇	5.5	0	0	0	0	0	0	0	0	0	0		0	0		0	0	0			
29051430	叔丁醇	5.5	0	0	0	0	0	0	0	0	0	0		0	0		0	0	0			
29051610	正辛醇	5.5	0	0	0	0	0	0	0	0	0	0		0	5		0		0			
29051690	其他辛醇	5.5	0	0	0	0	0	0	0	0	0	0		0	5		0		0			
29051700	十二醇、十六醇及十八醇	7	0	0	0	0	0	0	0	0	0	0		0	5		0	0	0			
29051910	3,3-二甲基丁-2-醇(频哪基醇)	5.5	0	0	0	0	0	0	0	0	0	0		0.6	0		0	0	0			
29051990	其他饱和一元醇	5.5	0	0	0	0	0	0	0	0	0	0		0	5		0	0	0			
29052210	香叶醇、 橙花醇	5.5	0	0	0	0	0	0	0	0	0	0		0	0		0	0	0			
29052220	香茅醇	5.5	0	0	0	0	0	0	0	0	0	0		0	5		0	0	0			
29052230	芳樟醇	5.5	0	0	0	0	0	0	0	0	0	0		0	5		0	0	0			

税则号列	商品名称（简称）	最惠国	东盟										亚太	智利	巴基斯坦	新加坡	新西兰	秘鲁	哥斯达黎加	香港	澳门	台湾
			文	柬	印	老	马	缅	菲	新	泰	越										
29052290	其他无环萜烯醇	5.5	0	0	0	0	0	0	0	0	0	0		0	5		0	0	0			
29052900	其他不饱和一元醇(无环萜烯醇除外)	5.5	0	0	0	0	0	0	0	0	0	0		0	5		0	0	0			
29053100	1,2-乙二醇	5.5												0			0		0			
29053200	丙二醇	5.5	0	0	0	0	0	0	0	0	0	0		0	5		0	0	0			
29053910	2,5-二甲基己二醇	4	0	0	0	0	0	0	0	0	0	0		0	0		0	0	0			
29053990	其他二元醇	5.5	0	0	0	0	0	0	0	0	0	0		0	5		0	0	0			
29054100	三羟甲基丙烷	5.5	0	0	0	0	0	0	0	0	0	0		0	0		0	0	0			
29054200	季戊四醇	5.5	0	0	0	0	0	0	0	0	0	0		0.6	5		0	0	0			
29054300	甘露糖醇	8	0	0	0	0	0	0	0	0	0	0		0	5		0	0	0			
29054400	山梨醇	14	0	0	0	0	0	0	0	0	0	0		0	11.2	0	0	0	2.8			
29054500	丙三醇(甘油)	14	0	0	0	0	0	0	0	0	0	0	11.2	0	7	0	0	0	2.8		0	
29054910	木糖醇	5.5	0	0	0	0	0	0	0	0	0	0		0	5		0	0	0			
29054990	其他多元醇	5.5	0	0	0	0	0	0	0	0	0	0		0	5		0	0	0			
29055100	乙氯维诺	5.5	0	0	0	0	0	0	0	0	0	0		0	0		0	0	0			
29055900	无环醇的卤化、磺化、硝化、或亚硝化的衍生物(乙氯维诺除外)	5.5	0	0	0	0	0	0	0	0	0	0		0	5		0	0	0			
29061100	薄荷醇	5	0	0	0	0	0	0	0	0	0	0		0	0		0	0	0			
29061200	环己醇、甲基环己醇、二甲基环己醇	5.5	0	0	0	0	0	0	0	0	0	0		0	5		0	0	0			
29061310	固醇	5.5	0	0	0	0	0	0	0	0	0	0		0	0		0	0	0			
29061320	肌醇	5.5	0	0	0	0	0	0	0	0	0	0		0	5		0	0	0			
29061910	萜品醇	5.5	0	0	0	0	0	0	0	0	0	0		0.6	5		0	0	0			
29061990	其他环烷醇、环烯醇及环萜烯醇	5.5	0	0	0	0	0	0	0	0	0	0		0	5		0	0	0			
29062100	苄醇	5	0	0	0	0	0	0	0	0	0	0		0	0		0	0	0			
29062910	2-苯基乙醇	5.5	0	0	0	0	0	0	0	0	0	0		0	5		0	0	0			
29062990	其他芳香醇及它们的衍生物	5.5	0	0	0	0	0	0	0	0	0	0		0	5		0	0	0			
29071110	苯酚	5.5	0	0	0	0	0	0	0	0	0	0		0	0		0	0	0			
29071190	苯酚的盐	5.5	0	0	0	0	0	0	0	0	0	0		0	0		0	0	0			
29071211	间甲酚	5.5	0	0	0	0	0	0	0	0	0	0		0	0		0	0	0			
29071212	邻甲酚	5.5	0	0	0	0	0	0	0	0	0	0		0	0		0	0	0			
29071219	其他甲酚（对甲酚）	5.5	0	0	0	0	0	0	0	0	0	0		0	5		0	0	0			
29071290	甲酚的盐	5.5	0	0	0	0	0	0	0	0	0	0		0	0		0	0	0			
29071310	壬基酚	5.5	0	0	0	0	0	0	0	0	0	0		0	0		0	0	0			
29071390	辛基酚及其异构体的盐和壬基酚盐	5.5	0	0	0	0	0	0	0	0	0	0		0	0		0	0	0			
29071510	β-萘酚(2-萘酚)	5.5	0	0	0	0	0	0	0	0	0	0		0	0		0	0	0			
29071590	其他萘酚及其盐	5.5	0	0	0	0	0	0	0	0	0	0		0	5		0	0	0			
29071910	邻仲丁基酚、邻异丙基酚	4	0	0	0	0	0	0	0	0	0	0		0	0		0	0	0			
29071990	其他一元酚	5.5	0	0	0	0	0	0	0	0	0	0		0	5		0	0	0			
29072100	间苯二酚及其盐	5.5	0	0	0	0	0	0	0	0	0	0		0	5		0	0	0			
29072210	对苯二酚	5.5	0	0	0	0	0	0	0	0	0	0		0	5		0	0	0			
29072290	对苯二酚的盐	5.5	0	0	0	0	0	0	0	0	0	0		0	0		0	0	0			
29072300	4,4′-异亚丙基联苯酚（双酚A）及其盐	5.5	0	0	0	0	0	0	0	0	0	0		0	5		0	0	0			
29072910	邻苯二酚	4	0	0	0	0	0	0	0	0	0	0		0	0		0	0	0			
29072990	其他多元酚；酚醇	5.5	0	0	0	0	0	0	0	0	0	0		0	5		0	0	0			
29081100	五氯苯酚（ISO）	5.5	0	0	0	0	0	0	0	0	0	0		0	5		0	0	0			
29081910	对氯苯酚	4	0	0	0	0	0	0	0	0	0	0		0	0		0	0	0			
29081990	其他仅含卤素取代基的酚及酚醇衍生物及其盐	5.5	0	0	0	0	0	0	0	0	0	0		0	5		0	0	0			
29089100	地乐酚（ISO）及其盐	5.5	0	0	0	0	0	0	0	0	0	0		0	5		0	0	0			
29089200	4,6—二硝基邻甲酚〔二硝酚（ISO）〕及其盐	5.5	0	0	0	0	0	0	0	0	0	0		0	5		0	0	0			
29089910	对硝基酚、对硝基酚钠	5.5	0	0	0	0	0	0	0	0	0	0		0	0		0	0	0			
29089990	其他酚及酚醇的卤化、磺化、硝化、或亚硝化的等衍生物	5.5	0	0	0	0	0	0	0	0	0	0		0	5		0	0	0			
29091100	乙醚	5.5	0	0	0	0	0	0	0	0	0	0		0	0		0	0	0			
29091910	甲醚	5.5	0	0	0	0	0	0	0	0	0	0		0	5		0		0			
29091990	其他无环醚及其卤化、磺化、硝化或亚硝化衍生物:	5.5	0	0	0	0	0	0	0	0	0	0		0	5		0		0			
29092000	环烷醚、环烯醚或环萜烯醚及其卤化、磺化、硝化或亚硝化衍生物	5.5	0	0	0	0	0	0	0	0	0	0		0	0		0	0	0			
29093010	---1-烷氧基-4-（4-乙烯基环己基）-2，3-二氟苯	5.5	0	0	0	0	0	0	0	0	0	0		0	5		0	0	0			

税则号列	商品名称（简称）	最惠国	东盟										亚太	智利	巴基斯坦	新加坡	新西兰	秘鲁	哥斯达黎加	香港	澳门	台湾
			文	柬	印	老	马	缅	菲	新	泰	越										
29093090	其他芳香醚及其卤化、磺化、硝化或亚硝化衍生物	5.5	0	0	0	0	0	0	0	0	0	0		0	5		0	0	0			
29094100	2,2′-氧联二乙醇(二甘醇)	5.5	0	0	0	0	0	0	0	0	0	0		0	0		0		0			0
29094300	乙二醇或二甘醇的单丁醚	5.5	0	0	0	0	0	0	0	0	0	0		0	5		0	0	0		0	0
29094400	乙二醇或二甘醇的其他单烷基醚	5.5	0	0	0	0	0	0	0	0	0	0		0	5		0	0	0			
29094910	间苯氧基苄醇	4	0	0	0	0	0	0	0	0	0	0		0.4	0		0	0	0			
29094990	其他醚醇及其卤化、磺化、硝化、或亚硝化的衍生物	5.5	0	0	0	0	0	0	0	0	0	0		0.6	5		0	0	0			
29095000	醚酚、醚醇酚及其卤化、磺化、硝化、或亚硝化的衍生物	5.5	0	0	0	0	0	0	0	0	0	0		0	5		0	0	0			
29096000	过氧化醇、过氧化醚、过氧化酮及其卤化、磺化、硝化、或亚硝化的衍生物	5.5	0	0	0	0	0	0	0	0	0	0		0.6	5		0	0	0			
29101000	环氧乙烷(氧化乙烯)	5.5	0	0	0	0	0	0	0	0	0	0		0	0		0	0	0			
29102000	甲基环氧乙烷(氧化丙烯)	5.5	0	0	0	0	0	0	0	0	0	0		0	0		0	0	0			
29103000	1-氯-2,3-环氧丙烷(表氯醇)	5.5	0	0	0	0	0	0	0	0	0	0		0	5		0	0	0			0
29104000	狄氏剂（ISO，INN）	5.5	0	0	0	0	0	0	0	0	0	0		0	5		0	0	0			
29109000	三节环环氧化物，环氧醇(酚、醚)及其卤化、磺化、硝化、或亚硝化的衍生物	5.5	0	0	0	0	0	0	0	0	0	0		0	5		0	0	0		0	
29110000	缩醛、半缩醛，不论是否含有其它含氧基，及其卤化、磺化、硝化、或亚硝化的衍生物	5.5	0	0	0	0	0	0	0	0	0	0		0	5		0	0	0			
29121100	甲醛	5.5	0	0	0	0	0	0	0	0	0	0		0.6	0		0	0	0			
29121200	乙醛	5.5	0	0	0	0	0	0	0	0	0	0		0	0		0	0	0			
29121900	其他无环醛（不含其他含氧基）	5.5	0	0	0	0	0	0	0	0	0	0		0	5		0	0	0			
29122100	苯甲醛	5.5	0	0	0	0	0	0	0	0	0	0		0	5		0	0	0			
29122910	铃兰醛(对叔丁基-α-甲基-氧化肉桂醛)	5.5	0	0	0	0	0	0	0	0	0	0		0	5		0	0	0			
29122990	其他环醛（不含其他含氧基）	5.5	0	0	0	0	0	0	0	0	0	0		0	5		0	0	0			
29124100	香草醛(3-甲氧基-4-羟基苯甲醛)	5.5	0	0	0	0	0	0	0	0	0	0		0	5		0	0	0			
29124200	乙基香草醛	5.5	0	0	0	0	0	0	0	0	0	0		0	5		0	0	0			
29124910	醛醇	5.5	0	0	0	0	0	0	0	0	0	0		0	5		0	0	0			
29124990	其他醛醚、醛酚、其他含氧基的醛	5.5	0	0	0	0	0	0	0	0	0	0		0	5		0	0	0			
29125000	环聚醛	5.5	0	0	0	0	0	0	0	0	0	0		0	0		0	0	0			
29126000	多聚甲醛	5.5	0	0	0	0	0	0	0	0	0	0		0	5		0	0	0			
29130000	税目2912所列产品的卤化、磺化、硝化、或亚硝化的衍生物	5.5	0	0	0	0	0	0	0	0	0	0		0	5		0	0	0			
29141100	丙酮	5.5	0	0	0	0	0	0	0	0	0	0		0	0		0	0	0			
29141200	丁酮	5.5	0	0	0	0	0	0	0	0	0	0		0.6	0		0	0	0		0	
29141300	4-甲基-2-戊酮	5.5	0	0	0	0	0	0	0	0	0	0		0	0		0	0	0			
29141900	其他不含其他含氧基的无环酮	5.5	0	0	0	0	0	0	0	0	0	0		0	5		0	0	0			
29142200	环己酮及甲基环己酮	5.5	0	0	0	0	0	0	0	0	0	0		0	0		0	0	0			
29142300	芷香酮及甲基芷香酮	5.5	0	0	0	0	0	0	0	0	0	0		0	0		0	0	0			
29142910	樟脑	5.5	0	0	0	0	0	0	0	0	0	0		0	5		0	0	0			
29142990	其他不含含氧基环烷酮、环烯酮或环萜烯酮	5.5	0	0	0	0	0	0	0	0	0	0		0	5		0	0	0			
29143100	苯丙酮(苯基丙-2-酮)	5.5	0	0	0	0	0	0	0	0	0	0		0	0		0	0	0			
29143910	苯乙酮	4	0	0	0	0	0	0	0	0	0	0		0	0		0	0	0			
29143990	其他不含其他含氧基的芳香酮	5.5	0	0	0	0	0	0	0	0	0	0		0	5		0	0	0			
29144000	酮醇及酮醛	5.5	0	0	0	0	0	0	0	0	0	0		0	5		0	0	0			
29145011	覆盆子酮	5.5	0	0	0	0	0	0	0	0	0	0		0	0		0	0	0			
29145019	其他酮酚	5.5	0	0	0	0	0	0	0	0	0	0		0	5		0	0	0			
29145020	2-羟基-4-甲氧基二苯甲酮	5.5	0	0	0	0	0	0	0	0	0	0		0	5		0	0	0			
29145090	酮酚及含其他含氧基酮	5.5	0	0	0	0	0	0	0	0	0	0		0	5		0	0	0			
29146100	蒽醌	5.5	0	0	0	0	0	0	0	0	0	0		0	5		0	0	0			
29146910	辅酶Q10	5.5	0	0	0	0	0	0	0	0	0	0		0	0		0	0	0			
29146990	其他醌，不论是否含有其他含氧基，及其卤化、磺化、硝化或亚硝化衍生物	5.5	0	0	0	0	0	0	0	0	0	0		0	0		0	0	0			
29147000	其他酮及醌的卤化、磺化、硝化、或亚硝化的衍生物	5.5	0	0	0	0	0	0	0	0	0	0		0	5		0	0	0			
29151100	甲酸	5.5	0	0	0	0	0	0	0	0	0	0		0	5		0	0	0			
29151200	甲酸盐	5.5	0	0	0	0	0	0	0	0	0	0		0.6	5		0	0	0			

税则号列	商品名称（简称）	最惠国	东盟										亚太	智利	巴基斯坦	新加坡	新西兰	秘鲁	哥斯达黎加	香港	澳门	台湾
			文	柬	印	老	马	缅	菲	新	泰	越										
29151300	甲酸酯	5.5	0	0	0	0	0	0	0	0	0	0		0	5		0	0	0			
29152111	食品级冰乙酸	5.5	0	0	0	0	0	0	0	0	0	0		0	5		0	0	0			0
29152119	其他冰乙酸(冰醋酸)	5.5	0	0	0	0	0	0	0	0	0	0		0	5		0	0	0			0
29152190	其他乙酸	5.5	0	0	0	0	0	0	0	0	0	0		0	5		0	0	0			
29152400	乙酸酐	5.5	0	0	0	0	0	0	0	0	0	0		0	0		0	0	0			
29152910	乙酸钠	5.5	0	0	0	0	0	0	0	0	0	0		0	5		0	0	0			
29152990	其他乙酸盐	5.5	0	0	0	0	0	0	0	0	0	0		0	5		0	0	0			
29153100	乙酸乙酯	5.5	0	0	0	0	0	0	0	0	0	0		0	5		0	0	0			
29153200	乙酸乙烯酯	5.5	0	0	0	0	0	0	0	0	0	0		0	5		0	0	0			0
29153300	乙酸正丁酯	5.5	0	0	0	0	0	0	0	0	0	0		0	0		0	0	0			
29153600	地乐酚（ISO）乙酸酯	5.5	0	0	0	0	0	0	0	0	0	0		0.6	5		0	0	0			
29153900	其他乙酸酯	5.5	0	0	0	0	0	0	0	0	0	0		0	5		0	0	0			
29154000	一、二、三氯代乙酸及其盐和酯	5.5	0	0	0	0	0	0	0	0	0	0		0	5		0	0	0			
29155010	丙酸	5.5	0	0	0	0	0	0	0	0	0	0		0	5		0	0	0			
29155090	丙酸盐和酯	5.5	0	0	0	0	0	0	0	0	0	0		0	5		0	0	0			
29156000	丁酸、戊酸及其盐和酯	5.5	0	0	0	0	0	0	0	0	0	0		0	5		0	0	0			
29157010	硬脂酸	7	0	0	0	0	0	0	0	0	0	0		0.7	5		0	0	0			
29157090	棕榈酸及其盐和酯、硬脂酸盐、酯	5.5	0	0	0	0	0	0	0	0	0	0		0.6	5		0	0	0			
29159000	其他饱和无环一元羧酸及其酸酐	5.5	0	0	0	0	0	0	0	0	0	0		0	5		0	0	0		0	
29161100	丙烯酸及其盐	6.5	0	0	0	0	0	0	0	0	0	0		0			0	0	0			
29161210	丙烯酸甲酯	6.5	0	0	0	0	0	0	0	0	0	0		0	5	0	0	0	0			
29161220	丙烯酸乙酯	6.5	0	0	0	0	0	0	0	0	0	0		0	5	0	0	0	0			
29161230	丙烯酸丁酯	6.5	0	0	0	0	0	0	0	0	0	0		0	5	0	0	0	0			
29161240	丙烯酸异辛酯	6.5	0	0	0	0	0	0	0	0	0	0		0	5	0	0	0	0			
29161290	其他丙烯酸酯	6.5	0	0	0	0	0	0	0	0	0	0		0	5	0	0	0	0			
29161300	甲基丙烯酸及其盐	6.5	0	0	0	0	0	0	0	0	0	0		0	5		0	0	0			0
29161400	甲基丙烯酸酯	6.5	0	0	0	0	0	0	0	0	0	0		0	5		0	0	0			0
29161500	油酸、亚油酸或亚麻酸及其盐和酯	6.5	0	0	0	0	0	0	0	0	0	0		0	5		0	0	0	0		
29161600	乐杀螨（ISO）	6.5	0	0	0	0	0	0	0	0	0	0		0	5		0	0	0			
29161900	其他不饱和无环一元羧酸（包括其酸酐，酰卤化物，过氧化物和过氧酸及它们的衍生物）	6.5	0	0	0	0	0	0	0	0	0	0		0	5		0	0	0			
29162010	DV 菊酸甲酯、二溴菊酸	4	0	0	0	0	0	0	0	0	0	0		0	0		0	0	0			
29162090	其他(环烷、环烯、环萜烯)一元羧酸（包括其酸酐，酰卤化物，过氧化物和过氧酸及它们的衍生物）	6.5	0	0	0	0	0	0	0	0	0	0		0	5		0	0	0			
29163100	苯甲酸及其盐和酯	6.5	0	0	0	0	0	0	0	0	0	0		0	5		0	0	0			
29163200	过氧化苯甲酰及苯甲酰氯	6.5	0	0	0	0	0	0	0	0	0	0		0	5		0	0	0			
29163400	苯乙酸及其盐	6.5	0	0	0	0	0	0	0	0	0	0		0	5		0	0	0			
29163910	邻甲基苯甲酸	6.5	0	0	0	0	0	0	0	0	0	0		0	5		0	0	0			
29163920	布洛芬	6.5	0	0	0	0	0	0	0	0	0	0		0	5		0	0	0			
29163990	其他芳香一元羧酸（包括其酸酐，酰卤化物，过氧化物和过氧酸及它们的衍生物）	6.5	0	0	0	0	0	0	0	0	0	0		0	5		0	0	0			
29171110	草酸	6.5	0	0	0	0	0	0	0	0	0	0		0	5		0	0	0			
29171120	草酸钴	9	0	0	0	0	0	0	0	0	0	0		0	5		0	0	0			
29171190	其他草酸盐和酯	6.5	0	0	0	0	0	0	0	0	0	0		0	5		0	0	0			
29171200	己二酸及其盐和酯	6.5	0	0	0	0	0	0	0	0	0	0		0	5		0	0	0			
29171310	癸二酸及其盐和酯	6.5	0	0	0	0	0	0	0	0	0	0		0	5		0	0	0			
29171390	壬二酸及其盐和酯	6.5	0	0	0	0	0	0	0	0	0	0		0	5		0	0	0			
29171400	马来酐	6.5	0	0	0	0	0	0	0	0	0	0		0	5		0	0	0			
29171900	其他无环多元羧酸（包括其酸酐，酰卤化物，过氧化物和过氧酸及它们的衍生物）	6.5	0	0	0	0	0	0	0	0	0	0		0	5		0	0	0		0	
29172010	四氢苯酐	4	0	0	0	0	0	0	0	0	0	0		0	0		0	0	0			
29172090	其他(环烷、环烯、环萜烯)多元羧酸（包括其酸酐，酰卤化物，过氧化物和过氧酸及它们的衍生物）	6.5	0	0	0	0	0	0	0	0	0	0		0	5		0	0	0			
29173200	邻苯二甲酸二辛酯	6.5	0	0	0	0	0	0	0	0	0	0		0.7	5		0	0	0			0
29173300	邻苯二甲酸二壬酯,邻苯二甲酸二癸酯	6.5	0	0	0	0	0	0	0	0	0	0		0.7	5		0	0	0			0
29173410	邻苯二甲酸二丁酯	6.5	0	0	0	0	0	0	0	0	0	0		0.7	5		0	0	0			

税则号列	商品名称（简称）	最惠国	东盟										亚太	智利	巴基斯坦	新加坡	新西兰	秘鲁	哥斯达黎加	香港	澳门	台湾
			文	柬	印	老	马	缅	菲	新	泰	越										
29173490	其他邻苯二甲酸酯	6.5	0	0	0	0	0	0	0	0	0	0		0.7	5		0	0	0			0
29173500	邻苯二甲酸酐(苯酐)	6.5	0	0	0	0	0	0	0	0	0	0		0.7	5		0	0	0			
29173611	精对苯二甲酸	6.5	0	0	0	0	0	0	0	0	0	0	6	0	6	0	0		0			
29173619	其他对苯二甲酸	6.5	0	0	0	0	0	0	0	0	0	0	6	0	6	0	0	0	0			
29173690	对苯二甲酸盐	6.5	0	0	0	0	0	0	0	0	0	0		0	5		0	0	0			
29173700	对苯二甲酸二甲酯	6.5	0	0	0	0	0	0	0	0	0	0		0	5		0	0	0			
29173910	间苯二甲酸	6.5	0	0	0	0	0	0	0	0	0	0		0.7	5		0	0	0			
29173990	其他芳香多元羧酸（包括其酸酐，酰卤化物，过氧化物和过氧酸及它们的衍生物）	6.5	0	0	0	0	0	0	0	0	0	0		0.7	5		0	0	0			
29181100	乳酸及其盐和酯	6.5	0	0	0	0	0	0	0	0	0	0		0	5		0	0	0			
29181200	酒石酸	6.5	0	0	0	0	0	0	0	0	0	0		0.7	5		0	0	0			
29181300	酒石酸盐及酒石酸酯	6.5	0	0	0	0	0	0	0	0	0	0		0.7	5		0	0	0			
29181400	柠檬酸	6.5	0	0	0	0	0	0	0	0	0	0		0.7	5		0	0	0			
29181500	柠檬酸盐及柠檬酸酯	6.5	0	0	0	0	0	0	0	0	0	0		0	5		0	0	0			
29181600	葡糖酸及其盐和酯	6.5	0	0	0	0	0	0	0	0	0	0		0	5		0	0	0			
29181800	乙酯杀螨醇（ISO）	6.5	0	0	0	0	0	0	0	0	0	0		0	5		0	0	0			
29181910	2,2-二苯基-2-羟基乙酸	6.5	0	0	0	0	0	0	0	0	0	0		0	5		0	0	0			
29181990	其他含醇基但不含其他含氧基的羧酸（包括其酸酐，酰卤化物，过氧化物和过氧酸及它们的衍生物）	6.5	0	0	0	0	0	0	0	0	0	0		0	5		0	0	0			
29182110	水杨酸、水杨酸钠	6.5	0	0	0	0	0	0	0	0	0	0		0	5		0	0	0			
29182190	其他水杨酸盐	6.5	0	0	0	0	0	0	0	0	0	0		0	5		0	0	0			
29182210	邻乙酰水杨酸(阿斯匹林)	6	0	0	0	0	0	0	0	0	0	0		0	5		0	0	0			
29182290	邻乙酰水杨酸盐和酯	6.5	0	0	0	0	0	0	0	0	0	0		0	5		0	0	0			
29182300	水杨酸其他酯及其盐	6.5	0	0	0	0	0	0	0	0	0	0		0	5		0	0	0			
29182900	其他含酚基但不含其他含氧基羧酸及其酸酐（酰卤化物，过氧化物和过氧酸及它们的衍生物）	6.5	0	0	0	0	0	0	0	0	0	0		0.7	5		0	0	0		0	
29183000	含醛基或酮基不含其他含氧基羧酸及其酸酐（酰卤化物，过氧化物和过氧酸及它们的衍生物）	6.5	0	0	0	0	0	0	0	0	0	0		0	5		0	0	0			
29189100	2，4，5－涕（ISO）（2，4，5－三氯苯氧基乙酸）及其盐或酯	6.5	0	0	0	0	0	0	0	0	0	0		0	5		0	0	0			
29189900	其他含其他附加含氧基羧酸及其酸酐（酰卤化物，过氧化物和过氧酸及它们的衍生物）	6.5	0	0	0	0	0	0	0	0	0	0		0	5		0	0	0			
29191000	三（2，3－二溴丙基）磷酸酯	6.5	0	0	0	0	0	0	0	0	0	0		0	5		0	0	0			
29199000	其他磷酸酯及其盐(包括乳磷酸盐)，及它们的卤化、磺化、硝化、或亚硝化的衍生物	6.5	0	0	0	0	0	0	0	0	0	0		0	5		0	0	0			
29201100	对硫磷（ISO）及甲基对硫磷（ISO）	6.5	0	0	0	0	0	0	0	0	0	0		0	5		0	0	0			
29201900	其他硫代磷酸酯及其盐，及它们的卤化、磺化、硝化、或亚硝化的衍生物	6.5	0	0	0	0	0	0	0	0	0	0		0	5		0	0	0			
29209011	亚磷酸三甲酯	6.5	0	0	0	0	0	0	0	0	0	0		0.7	5		0	0	0			
29209012	亚磷酸三乙酯	6.5	0	0	0	0	0	0	0	0	0	0		0.7	5		0	0	0			
29209013	亚磷酸二甲酯	6.5	0	0	0	0	0	0	0	0	0	0		0.7	5		0	0	0			
29209014	亚磷酸二乙酯	6.5	0	0	0	0	0	0	0	0	0	0		0.7	5		0	0	0			
29209019	其他亚磷酸酯	6.5	0	0	0	0	0	0	0	0	0	0		0.7	5		0	0	0			
29209090	其他无机酸酯（不包括卤化氢的酯）及其盐，及它们的卤化、磺化、硝化、或亚硝化的衍生物	6.5	0	0	0	0	0	0	0	0	0	0		0.7	5		0	0	0			
29211100	甲胺、二甲胺或三甲胺及其盐	6.5	0	0	0	0	0	0	0	0	0	0		0	5		0	0	0			
29211910	二正丙胺	4	0	0	0	0	0	0	0	0	0	0		0	0		0	0	0			
29211920	异丙胺	6.5	0	0	0	0	0	0	0	0	0	0		0	5		0	0	0			
29211930	N,N-二(2-氯乙基)乙胺	6.5	0	0	0	0	0	0	0	0	0	0		0	5		0	0	0			
29211940	N,N-二(2-氯乙基)甲胺	6.5	0	0	0	0	0	0	0	0	0	0		0	5		0	0	0			
29211950	三(2-氯乙基)胺	6.5	0	0	0	0	0	0	0	0	0	0		0	5		0	0	0			
29211960	二烷氨基乙基-2-氯及其质子化盐	6.5	0	0	0	0	0	0	0	0	0	0		0	5		0	0	0			
29211990	其他无环单胺及其衍生物，及它们的盐	6.5	0	0	0	0	0	0	0	0	0	0		0	5		0	0	0			
29212110	乙二胺	6.5	0	0	0	0	0	0	0	0	0	0		0	5		0	0	0			

税则号列	商品名称（简称）	最惠国	东盟										亚太	智利	巴基斯坦	新加坡	新西兰	秘鲁	哥斯达黎加	香港	澳门	台湾
			文	柬	印	老	马	缅	菲	新	泰	越										
29212190	乙二胺盐	6.5	0	0	0	0	0	0	0	0	0	0		0	5		0	0	0			
29212210	己二酸己二胺盐(尼龙-66盐)	6.5	0	0	0	0	0	0	0	0	0	0		0	5		0	0	0			
29212290	六亚甲基二胺及其他盐	6.5	0	0	0	0	0	0	0	0	0	0		0	5		0	0	0			
29212900	其他无环多胺及其衍生物，及它们的盐	6.5	0	0	0	0	0	0	0	0	0	0		0	5		0	0	0			
29213000	环(烷、烯、萜烯)单胺或多胺及衍生物，及它们的盐	6.5	0	0	0	0	0	0	0	0	0	0		0	5		0	0	0			
29214110	苯胺	6.5	0	0	0	0	0	0	0	0	0	0		0	5		0	0	0			
29214190	苯胺盐	6.5	0	0	0	0	0	0	0	0	0	0		0	5		0	0	0			
29214200	苯胺衍生物及其盐	6.5	0	0	0	0	0	0	0	0	0	0		0	5		0	0	0			
29214300	甲苯胺及其衍生物，及它们的盐	6.5	0	0	0	0	0	0	0	0	0	0		0	5		0	0	0			
29214400	二苯胺及其衍生物，及它们的盐	6.5	0	0	0	0	0	0	0	0	0	0		0	5		0	0	0			
29214500	1-萘胺、2-萘胺及其衍生物及盐	6.5	0	0	0	0	0	0	0	0	0	0		0	5		0	0	0			
29214600	安非他明、苄非他明、右苯丙胺、乙非他明、芬坎法明、利非他明、左苯丙胺、美芬雷司、芬特明以及它们的盐	6.5	0	0	0	0	0	0	0	0	0	0		0	5		0	0	0			
29214910	对异丙基苯胺	4	0	0	0	0	0	0	0	0	0	0		0	0		0	0	0			
29214920	二甲基苯胺	6.5	0	0	0	0	0	0	0	0	0	0		0	5		0	0	0			
29214930	2,6-甲基乙基苯胺	4	0	0	0	0	0	0	0	0	0	0		0	0		0	0	0			
29214940	2,6-二乙基苯胺	6.5	0	0	0	0	0	0	0	0	0	0		0	5		0	0	0			
29214990	其他芳香单胺及衍生物及它们的盐	6.5	0	0	0	0	0	0	0	0	0	0		0	5		0	0	0			
29215110	邻苯二胺	4	0	0	0	0	0	0	0	0	0	0		0	0		0	0	0			
29215190	间-、对-苯二胺、二氨基甲苯及其衍生物及它们的盐	6.5	0	0	0	0	0	0	0	0	0	0		0	5		0	0	0			
29215900	其他芳香多胺及衍生物及它们的盐	6.5	0	0	0	0	0	0	0	0	0	0		0	5		0	0	0			
29221100	单乙醇胺及其盐	6.5	0	0	0	0	0	0	0	0	0	0		0	5		0	0	0			
29221200	二乙醇胺及其盐	6.5	0	0	0	0	0	0	0	0	0	0		0	5		0	0	0			
29221310	三乙醇胺	6.5	0	0	0	0	0	0	0	0	0	0		0	5		0	0	0			
29221320	三乙醇胺盐	6.5	0	0	0	0	0	0	0	0	0	0		0	5		0	0	0			
29221400	右丙氧吩及其盐	6.5	0	0	0	0	0	0	0	0	0	0		0	5		0	0	0			
29221910	乙胺丁醇	6.5	0	0	0	0	0	0	0	0	0	0		0	5		0	0	0			
29221921	二甲氨基乙醇及其质子化盐	6.5	0	0	0	0	0	0	0	0	0	0		0	5		0	0	0			
29221922	二乙氨基乙醇及其质子化盐	6.5	0	0	0	0	0	0	0	0	0	0		0	5		0	0	0			
29221929	其他二烷氨基乙-2-醇及其质子化	6.5	0	0	0	0	0	0	0	0	0	0		0	5		0	0	0			
29221930	乙基二乙醇胺	6.5	0	0	0	0	0	0	0	0	0	0		0	5		0	0	0			
29221940	甲基二乙醇胺	6.5	0	0	0	0	0	0	0	0	0	0		0	5		0	0	0			
29221950	本芴醇	6.5	0	0	0	0	0	0	0	0	0	0		0	5		0	0	0			
29221990	其他氨基醇及其醚、酯和它们的盐(但含有一种以上含氧基的除外)	6.5	0	0	0	0	0	0	0	0	0	0		0	5		0	0	0			
29222100	氨基羟基萘磺酸及其盐	6.5	0	0	0	0	0	0	0	0	0	0		0	5		0	0	0			
29222910	茴香胺、二茴香胺、氨基苯乙醚及其盐	6.5	0	0	0	0	0	0	0	0	0	0		0	5		0	0	0			
29222990	其他氨基(萘酚、酚)及醚、酯、盐(但含有一种以上含氧基的除外)	6.5	0	0	0	0	0	0	0	0	0	0		0	5		0	0	0			
29223100	安非拉酮、美沙酮和去甲美沙酮以及它们的盐	6.5	0	0	0	0	0	0	0	0	0	0		0	5		0	0	0			
29223910	4-甲基甲卡西酮	6.5	0	0	0	0	0	0	0	0	0	0		0	5		0	0	0			
29223990	其他氨基醛、氨基酮、氨基醌及其盐(但含有一种以上含氧基的除外)	6.5	0	0	0	0	0	0	0	0	0	0		0	5		0	0	0			
29224110	赖氨酸	5	0	0	0	0	0	0	0	0	0	0		0	0		0	0	0			
29224190	赖氨酸酯和赖氨酸盐	6	0	0	0	0	0	0	0	0	0	0		0	5		0	0	0			
29224210	谷氨酸	10	0	0	0	0	0	0	0	0	0	0	8.6	0	5	0	0	0	0			
29224220	谷氨酸钠	10	0	0	0	0	0	0	0	0	0	0		0	5	0	0	0	0	0		
29224290	其他谷氨酸盐	6.5	0	0	0	0	0	0	0	0	0	0		0	5		0	0	0			
29224310	邻氨基苯甲酸(氨茴酸)	6.5	0	0	0	0	0	0	0	0	0	0		0	5		0	0	0			
29224390	邻氨基苯甲酸(氨茴酸)盐	6.5	0	0	0	0	0	0	0	0	0	0		0	5		0	0	0			
29224400	替利定及其盐	6.5	0	0	0	0	0	0	0	0	0	0		0	5		0	0	0			
29224911	氨甲环酸	6.5	0	0	0	0	0	0	0	0	0	0		0	5		0	0	0			
29224919	其他氨基酸	6.5	0	0	0	0	0	0	0	0	0	0		0	5		0	0	0			
29224991	普鲁卡因	6	0	0	0	0	0	0	0	0	0	0		0	5		0	0	0			
29224999	其他氨基酸及其酯及它们的盐(但含有一种以上含氧基的除外)	6.5	0	0	0	0	0	0	0	0	0	0		0	5		0	0	0			
29225010	对羟基苯甘氨酸及其邓甲盐	6.5	0	0	0	0	0	0	0	0	0	0		0	5		0	0	0			

税则号列	商品名称（简称）	最惠国	东盟										亚太	智利	巴基斯坦	新加坡	新西兰	秘鲁	哥斯达黎加	香港	澳门	台湾
			文	柬	印	老	马	缅	菲	新	泰	越										
29225020	莱克多巴胺和盐酸莱克多巴胺	6.5	0	0	0	0	0	0	0	0	0	0		0	5		0	0	0			
29225090	其他氨基醇酚、氨基酸酚及其他含氧基氨基化合物	6.5	0	0	0	0	0	0	0	0	0	0		0	5		0	0	0			
29231000	胆碱及其盐	6.5	0	0	0	0	0	0	0	0	0	0		0	5		0	0	0			
29232000	卵磷脂及其他磷氨基类脂	6.5	0	0	0	0	0	0	0	0	0	0		0	5		0	0	0			
29239000	其他季铵盐及季铵碱	6.5	0	0	0	0	0	0	0	0	0	0		0	5		0	0	0			
29241100	甲丙氨酯	6.5	0	0	0	0	0	0	0	0	0	0		0	5		0	0	0			
29241200	氟乙酰胺（ISO）、久效磷（ISO）及磷胺（ISO）	6.5	0	0	0	0	0	0	0	0	0	0		0.7	5		0	0	0			
29241910	二甲基甲酰胺	6.5	0	0	0	0	0	0	0	0	0	0		0.7	5		0	0	0	0		0
29241990	其他无环酰胺及其衍生物以及他们的盐	6.5	0	0	0	0	0	0	0	0	0	0		0.7	5		0	0	0			
29242100	酰脲及其衍生物，及它们的盐	6.5	0	0	0	0	0	0	0	0	0	0		0	5		0	0	0			
29242300	2-乙酰氨基苯甲酸（N-乙酰邻氨基苯甲酸）及其盐	6.5	0	0	0	0	0	0	0	0	0	0		0	5		0	0	0			
29242400	炔己蚁胺	6.5	0	0	0	0	0	0	0	0	0	0		0	5		0	0	0			
29242910	对乙酰氨基苯乙醚(非那西丁)	6	0	0	0	0	0	0	0	0	0	0		0.6	5		0	0	0			
29242920	对乙酰氨基酚(扑热息痛)	6	0	0	0	0	0	0	0	0	0	0		0.6	5		0	0	0			
29242930	阿斯巴甜	6.5	0	0	0	0	0	0	0	0	0	0		0.7	5		0	0	0		0	
29242990	其他环酰胺（包括环氨基甲酸酯）	6.5	0	0	0	0	0	0	0	0	0	0		0.7	5		0	0	0		0	
29251100	糖精及其盐	9	0	0	0	0	0	0	0	0	0	0		0.9	5		0	0	0			
29251200	格鲁米特	6.5	0	0	0	0	0	0	0	0	0	0		0	5		0	0	0			
29251900	其他酰亚胺及其衍生物、盐	6.5	0	0	0	0	0	0	0	0	0	0		0	5		0	0	0			
29252100	杀虫脒	6.5	0	0	0	0	0	0	0	0	0	0		0	5		0	0	0			
29252900	其他亚胺及其衍生物以及它们的盐	6.5	0	0	0	0	0	0	0	0	0	0		0	5		0	0	0			
29261000	丙烯腈	6.5												0			0	0	0			
29262000	1-氰基胍(双氰胺)	6.5	0	0	0	0	0	0	0	0	0	0		0	5		0	0	0			
29263000	芬普雷司及其盐；美沙酮中间体（4-氰基-2-二甲氨基-4,4-二苯基丁烷）	6.5	0	0	0	0	0	0	0	0	0	0		0	5		0	0	0			
29269010	对氯氰苄	4	0	0	0	0	0	0	0	0	0	0		0.4	0		0	0	0			
29269020	间苯二甲腈	6.5	0	0	0	0	0	0	0	0	0	0		0.7	5		0	0	0			
29269090	其他腈基化合物	6.5	0	0	0	0	0	0	0	0	0	0		0.7	5		0	0	0	0		
29270000	重氮化合物、偶氮化合物及氧化偶氮化合物	6.5	0	0	0	0	0	0	0	0	0	0		0	5		0	0	0		0	
29280000	肼(联氨)及胲(羟胺)的有机衍生物	6.5	0	0	0	0	0	0	0	0	0	0		0	5		0	0	0			
29291010	2,4和2,6甲苯二异氰酸酯混合物(甲苯二异氰酸酯TDI)	6.5	0	0	0	0	0	0	0	0	0	0		0	5		0	0	0			0
29291020	二甲苯二异氰酸酯（TODI）	6.5	0	0	0	0	0	0	0	0	0	0		0	5		0	0	0			
29291030	二苯基甲烷二异氰酸酯(纯MDI)	6.5	0	0	0	0	0	0	0	0	0	0		0	5		0	0	0			
29291040	六亚甲基二异氰酸酯	6.5	0	0	0	0	0	0	0	0	0	0		0	5		0	0	0			
29291090	其他异氰酸酯	6.5	0	0	0	0	0	0	0	0	0	0		0	5		0	0	0			
29299010	环已基氨基磺酸钠(甜蜜素)	9	0	0	0	0	0	0	0	0	0	0		0	5		0	0	0			
29299020	二烷(甲、乙、正丙或异丙)氨基膦酰二卤	6.5	0	0	0	0	0	0	0	0	0	0		0	5		0	0	0			
29299030	二烷氨基膦酸二烷酯	6.5	0	0	0	0	0	0	0	0	0	0		0	5		0	0	0			
29299040	乙酰甲胺磷	6.5	0	0	0	0	0	0	0	0	0	0		0	5		0	0	0			
29299090	其他含氮基化合物	6.5	0	0	0	0	0	0	0	0	0	0		0	5		0	0	0			
29302000	其他硫代氨基甲酸盐(或酯)	6.5	0	0	0	0	0	0	0	0	0	0		0.7	5		0	0	0			
29303000	（一硫化、二硫化、三硫化）二烃氨基硫羰	6.5	0	0	0	0	0	0	0	0	0	0		0	5		0	0	0			
29304000	甲硫氨酸(蛋氨酸)	6.5	0	0	0	0	0	0	0	0	0	0		0	5		0	0	0			
29305000	敌菌丹（ISO）及甲胺磷（ISO）	6.5	0	0	0	0	0	0	0	0	0	0		0.7	5		0	0	0			
29309010	双巯丙氨酸(胱氨酸)	6.5	0	0	0	0	0	0	0	0	0	0		0.7	5		0	0	0			
29309020	二硫代碳酸酯(或盐)[黄原酸酯（或盐）]	6.5	0	0	0	0	0	0	0	0	0	0		0.7	5		0	0	0			
29309090	其他有机硫化合物	6.5	0	0	0	0	0	0	0	0	0	0		0.7	5		0	0	0	0		
29311000	四甲基铅及四乙基铅	6.5	0	0	0	0	0	0	0	0	0	0		0.7	5		0	0	0			
29312000	三丁基锡化合物	6.5	0	0	0	0	0	0	0	0	0	0		0.7	5		0	0	0			
29319011	双甘膦	6.5	0	0	0	0	0	0	0	0	0	0		0.7	5		0	0	0			
29319019	其他含有磷原子的有机-无机化合物	6.5	0	0	0	0	0	0	0	0	0	0		0.7	5		0	0	0			
29319090	其他有机-无机化合物	6.5	0	0	0	0	0	0	0	0	0	0		0.7	5		0	0	0			
29321100	四氢呋喃	6	0	0	0	0	0	0	0	0	0	0		0	5		0	0	0	0		0

税则号列	商品名称（简称）	最惠国	东盟										亚太	智利	巴基斯坦	新加坡	新西兰	秘鲁	哥斯达黎加	香港	澳门	台湾
			文	柬	印	老	马	缅	菲	新	泰	越										
29321200	2-糠醛	6	0	0	0	0	0	0	0	0	0	0		0	5		0	0	0			
29321300	糠醇及四氢糠醇	6	0	0	0	0	0	0	0	0	0	0		0	5		0	0	0			
29321900	其他结构上有非稠合呋喃环化合物（不论是否氢化）	6.5	0	0	0	0	0	0	0	0	0	0		0	5		0	0	0			
29322010	香豆素、甲基香豆素及乙基香豆素	6.5	0	0	0	0	0	0	0	0	0	0		0	5		0	0	0			
29322090	其他内酯	6.5	0	0	0	0	0	0	0	0	0	0		0	5		0	0	0			
29329100	4-丙烯基-1,2-亚甲二氧基苯	6.5	0	0	0	0	0	0	0	0	0	0		0	5		0	0	0			
29329200	1-(1,3-苯并二恶茂-5-基)丙-2-酮	6.5	0	0	0	0	0	0	0	0	0	0		0	5		0	0	0			
29329300	3,4-亚甲二氧基苯甲醛(胡椒醛)	6.5	0	0	0	0	0	0	0	0	0	0		0	5		0	0	0			
29329400	4-烯丙基-1,2-亚甲二氧基苯（黄樟脑）	6.5	0	0	0	0	0	0	0	0	0	0		0	5		0	0	0			
29329500	四氢大麻酚（所有异构体）	6.5	0	0	0	0	0	0	0	0	0	0		0	5		0	0	0			
29329910	7-羟基苯并呋喃(呋喃酚)	4	0	0	0	0	0	0	0	0	0	0		0	0		0	0	0			
29329920	联苯双酯	6.5	0	0	0	0	0	0	0	0	0	0		0	5		0	0	0			
29329930	蒿甲醚	6.5	0	0	0	0	0	0	0	0	0	0		0	5		0	0	0			
29329990	其他仅含氧杂原子的杂环化合物	6.5	0	0	0	0	0	0	0	0	0	0		0	5		0	0	0			
29331100	二甲基苯基吡唑酮（安替比林）及其衍生物	6.5	0	0	0	0	0	0	0	0	0	0	6	0	5		0	0	0			
29331920	安乃近	6	0	0	0	0	0	0	0	0	0	0		0	5		0	0	0			
29331990	其他结构上有非稠合吡唑环化合物（不论是否氢化）	6.5	0	0	0	0	0	0	0	0	0	0		0	5		0	0	0			
29332100	乙内酰脲及其衍生物	6.5	0	0	0	0	0	0	0	0	0	0		0	5		0	0	0			
29332900	其他结构上有非稠合咪唑环化合物（不论是否氢化）	6.5	0	0	0	0	0	0	0	0	0	0		0	5		0	0	0			
29333100	吡啶及其盐	6	0	0	0	0	0	0	0	0	0	0		0	5		0	0	0			0
29333210	哌啶(六氢吡啶)	4	0	0	0	0	0	0	0	0	0	0		0	0		0	0	0			
29333220	哌啶(六氢吡啶)盐	6.5	0	0	0	0	0	0	0	0	0	0		0	5		0	0	0			
29333300	阿芬太尼、阿尼利定、氰苯双哌酰胺、溴西泮、地芬诺新、地芬诺酯、地匹哌酮、芬太尼、凯托米酮、哌醋甲酯、喷他左辛、哌替啶、哌替啶中间体A、苯环利定、苯哌利定、哌苯甲醇、哌氰米特、丙吡兰和三甲利定以及它们的盐	6.5	0	0	0	0	0	0	0	0	0	0		0	5		0	0	0			
29333910	二苯乙醇酸-3-奎宁环脂	6.5	0	0	0	0	0	0	0	0	0	0		0	5		0	0	0			
29333920	奎宁环-3-醇	6.5	0	0	0	0	0	0	0	0	0	0		0	5		0	0	0			
29333990	其他结构上有非稠合吡啶环化合物（不论是否氢化）	6.5	0	0	0	0	0	0	0	0	0	0		0	5		0	0	0			
29334100	左非诺及其盐	6.5	0	0	0	0	0	0	0	0	0	0		0	5		0	0	0			
29334910	环丙氟哌酸	6.5	0	0	0	0	0	0	0	0	0	0	6	0	5		0	0	0			
29334990	其他含喹啉或异喹啉环系的化合物（但未经进一步稠合）	6.5	0	0	0	0	0	0	0	0	0	0		0	5		0	0	0			
29335200	丙二酰脲（巴比土酸）及其盐	6.5	0	0	0	0	0	0	0	0	0	0		0	5		0	0	0			
29335300	阿洛巴比妥、异戊巴比妥、巴比妥、布他比妥、正丁巴比妥、环己巴比妥、甲苯巴比妥、戊巴比妥、苯巴比妥、仲丁巴比妥、司可巴比妥和乙烯比妥以及他们的盐	6.5	0	0	0	0	0	0	0	0	0	0		0	5		0	0	0			
29335400	其他丙二酰脲的衍生物以及他们的盐	6.5	0	0	0	0	0	0	0	0	0	0		0	5		0	0	0			
29335500	氯普唑仑、甲氯喹酮等以及他们的盐	6.5	0	0	0	0	0	0	0	0	0	0		0	5		0	0	0			
29335910	胞嘧啶	6.5	0	0	0	0	0	0	0	0	0	0	4.6	0	0		0	0	0			
29335990	其他结构上有嘧啶环或哌嗪环的化合物（不论是否氢化）	6.5	0	0	0	0	0	0	0	0	0	0	4.6	0	0		0	0	0			
29336100	三聚氰胺(蜜胺)	6.5	0	0	0	0	0	0	0	0	0	0		0	5		0	0	0			
29336910	三聚氰氯	6	0	0	0	0	0	0	0	0	0	0		0	5		0	0	0		0	
29336921	二氯异氰脲酸	6.5	0	0	0	0	0	0	0	0	0	0		0	5		0	0	0		0	
29336922	三氯异氰脲酸	6.5	0	0	0	0	0	0	0	0	0	0		0	5		0	0	0		0	
29336929	其他异氰脲酸氯化衍生物	6.5	0	0	0	0	0	0	0	0	0	0		0	5		0	0	0		0	
29336990	其他结构上含非稠合三嗪环化合物（不论是否氢化）	6.5	0	0	0	0	0	0	0	0	0	0		0	5		0	0	0		0	
29337100	6-己内酰胺	9												0			0		0			
29337200	氯巴占和甲乙哌酮	9	0	0	0	0	0	0	0	0	0	0		0	5		0	0	0			
29337900	其他内酰胺	9	0	0	0	0	0	0	0	0	0	0		0	5		0	0	0			

税则号列	商品名称（简称）	最惠国	东盟										亚太	智利	巴基斯坦	新加坡	新西兰	秘鲁	哥斯达黎加	香港	澳门	台湾
			文	柬	印	老	马	缅	菲	新	泰	越										
29339100	阿普唑仑、卡马西泮等以及它们的盐	6.5	0	0	0	0	0	0	0	0	0	0		0	5		0	0	0			
29339900	其他仅含氮杂原子的杂环化合物	6.5	0	0	0	0	0	0	0	0	0	0		0.7	5		0	0	0			
29341000	结构上含有非稠合噻唑环的化合物（不论是否氢化）	6.5	0	0	0	0	0	0	0	0	0	0		0	5		0	0	0			
29342000	含一个苯并噻唑环系的化合物（但未经进一步稠合，不论是否氢化）	6.5	0	0	0	0	0	0	0	0	0	0		0	5		0	0	0			
29343000	含一个吩噻嗪环系的化合物（但未经进一步稠合，不论是否氢化）	6.5	0	0	0	0	0	0	0	0	0	0		0	5		0	0	0			
29349100	阿米雷司、溴替唑仑、氯噻西泮等以及他们的盐	6.5	0	0	0	0	0	0	0	0	0	0		0	5		0	0	0			
29349910	磺内酯及磺内酰胺	6.5	0	0	0	0	0	0	0	0	0	0		0.7	5		0	0	0			
29349920	呋喃唑酮	6	0	0	0	0	0	0	0	0	0	0		0.6	5		0	0	0			
29349930	核酸及其盐	6.5	0	0	0	0	0	0	0	0	0	0		0.7	5		0	0	0			
29349940	奈韦拉平、依发韦仑、利托那韦及它们的盐	6.5	0	0	0	0	0	0	0	0	0	0		0.7	5		0	0	0			
29349950	克拉维酸及其盐	6.5	0	0	0	0	0	0	0	0	0	0		0.7	5		0	0	0			
29349960	7-苯乙酰氨基-3-氯甲基-4-头孢烷酸对甲氧基苄酯、7-氨基头孢烷酸、7-氨基脱乙酰氧基头孢烷酸	6	0	0	0	0	0	0	0	0	0	0	5	0.6	0		0	0	0			
29349990	其他杂环化合物	6.5	0	0	0	0	0	0	0	0	0	0		0.7	5		0	0	0			
29350010	磺胺嘧啶	6.5	0	0	0	0	0	0	0	0	0	0		0	5		0	0	0			
29350020	磺胺双甲基嘧啶	6.5	0	0	0	0	0	0	0	0	0	0		0	5		0	0	0			
29350030	磺胺甲恶唑	6.5	0	0	0	0	0	0	0	0	0	0		0	5		0	0	0			
29350090	其他磺(酰)胺	6.5	0	0	0	0	0	0	0	0	0	0		0	5		0	0	0			
29362100	未混合的维生素A及其衍生物	4	0	0	0	0	0	0	0	0	0	0		0	0		0	0	0		0	
29362200	未混合的维生素B1及其衍生物	4	0	0	0	0	0	0	0	0	0	0		0	0		0	0	0		0	
29362300	未混合的维生素B2及其衍生物	4	0	0	0	0	0	0	0	0	0	0		0	0		0	0	0		0	
29362400	未混合的D或DL-泛酸及其衍生物	4	0	0	0	0	0	0	0	0	0	0		0	0		0	0	0		0	
29362500	未混合的维生素B6及其衍生物	4	0	0	0	0	0	0	0	0	0	0		0	0		0	0	0		0	
29362600	未混合的维生素B12及其衍生物	4	0	0	0	0	0	0	0	0	0	0		0	0		0	0	0		0	
29362700	未混合的维生素C及其衍生物	4	0	0	0	0	0	0	0	0	0	0		0.4	0		0	0	0		0	
29362800	未混合的维生素E及其衍生物	4	0	0	0	0	0	0	0	0	0	0		0	0		0	0	0		0	
29362900	其他未混合的维生素及其衍生物	4	0	0	0	0	0	0	0	0	0	0		0	0		0	0	0		0	
29369000	维生素原、混合维生素及其衍生物	4	0	0	0	0	0	0	0	0	0	0		0.4	0		0	0	0		0	
29371100	生长激素及其衍生物和类似结构物	4	0	0	0	0	0	0	0	0	0	0		0	0		0	0	0			
29371210	重组人胰岛素及其盐	4	0	0	0	0	0	0	0	0	0	0		0	0		0	0	0			
29371290	其他胰岛素及其盐	4	0	0	0	0	0	0	0	0	0	0		0	0		0	0	0			
29371900	其他多肽激素、蛋白激素、糖蛋白激素及其衍生物和类似结构物	4	0	0	0	0	0	0	0	0	0	0		0	0		0	0	0			
29372100	可的松、氢化可的松及脱氢可的松及脱氢皮质（甾）醇	4	0	0	0	0	0	0	0	0	0	0		0	0		0	0	0			
29372210	地塞米松	4	0	0	0	0	0	0	0	0	0	0		0	0		0	0	0			
29372290	其他皮质（甾）激素的卤化衍生物	4	0	0	0	0	0	0	0	0	0	0		0	0		0	0	0			
29372311	孕马结合雌激素	4	0	0	0	0	0	0	0	0	0	0		0	0		0	0	0			
29372319	其他动物源的雌（甾）激素和孕激素	4	0	0	0	0	0	0	0	0	0	0		0	0		0	0	0			
29372390	其他皮质甾类激素的卤化衍生物	4	0	0	0	0	0	0	0	0	0	0		0	0		0	0	0			
29372900	其他甾族激素及其衍生物和类似结构物	4	0	0	0	0	0	0	0	0	0	0		0	0		0	0	0			
29375000	前列腺素、血栓烷和白细胞三烯及其衍生物和结构类似物	4	0	0	0	0	0	0	0	0	0	0		0	0		0	0	0			
29379000	其他天然或合成再制的激素及其衍生物和结构类似物，包括主要用作激素的改性链多肽	4	0	0	0	0	0	0	0	0	0	0		0	0		0	0	0			
29381000	芸香苷及其衍生物	6.5	0	0	0	0	0	0	0	0	0	0		0	5		0	0	0			
29389010	齐多夫定、拉米夫定、司他夫定、地达诺新及它们的盐	6.5	0	0	0	0	0	0	0	0	0	0		0	5		0	0	0			
29389090	其他天然或合成再制的苷及其盐、醚、酯和其他衍生物	6.5	0	0	0	0	0	0	0	0	0	0		0	5		0	0	0			
29391100	罂粟杆浓缩物、丁丙诺啡、可待因等以及他们的盐	4	0	0	0	0	0	0	0	0	0	0		0	0		0	0	0			
29391900	其他鸦片碱及其衍生物，及它们的盐	4	0	0	0	0	0	0	0	0	0	0		0	0		0	0	0			
29392000	其他金鸡纳生物碱及其衍生物，及它	4	0	0	0	0	0	0	0	0	0	0		0	0		0	0	0			

税则号列	商品名称（简称）	最惠国	东盟 文	东盟 柬	东盟 印	东盟 老	东盟 马	东盟 缅	东盟 菲	东盟 新	东盟 泰	东盟 越	亚太	智利	巴基斯坦	新加坡	新西兰	秘鲁	哥斯达黎加	香港	澳门	台湾
	们的盐																					
29393000	咖啡因及其盐	4	0	0	0	0	0	0	0	0	0	0		0	0		0	0	0			
29394100	麻黄碱及其盐	4	0	0	0	0	0	0	0	0	0	0		0	0		0	0	0			
29394200	假麻黄碱及其盐	4	0	0	0	0	0	0	0	0	0	0		0	0		0	0	0			
29394300	d－去甲麻黄碱（INN)及其盐	4	0	0	0	0	0	0	0	0	0	0		0	0		0	0	0			
29394400	去甲麻黄碱及其盐	4	0	0	0	0	0	0	0	0	0	0		0	0		0	0	0			
29394900	其他麻黄碱类及其盐	4	0	0	0	0	0	0	0	0	0	0		0	0		0	0	0			
29395100	芬乙茶碱（INN）及其盐	4	0	0	0	0	0	0	0	0	0	0		0	0		0	0	0			
29395900	其他茶碱和氨茶碱及其衍生物，及它们的盐	4	0	0	0	0	0	0	0	0	0	0		0	0		0	0	0			
29396100	麦角新碱及其盐	4	0	0	0	0	0	0	0	0	0	0		0	0		0	0	0			
29396200	麦角胺及其盐	4	0	0	0	0	0	0	0	0	0	0		0	0		0	0	0			
29396300	麦角酸及其盐	4	0	0	0	0	0	0	0	0	0	0		0	0		0	0	0			
29396900	其他麦角生物碱及其衍生物，及它们的盐	4	0	0	0	0	0	0	0	0	0	0		0	0		0	0	0			
29399110	可卡因及其盐	4	0	0	0	0	0	0	0	0	0	0		0	0		0	0	0			
29399190	芽子碱、左甲苯丙胺、去氧麻黄碱、去氧麻黄碱外消旋体，它们的盐、酯及其他衍生物；可卡因的酯及其他衍生物	4	0	0	0	0	0	0	0	0	0	0		0	0		0	0	0			
29399910	烟碱及其盐	4	0	0	0	0	0	0	0	0	0	0		0	0		0	0	0			
29399920	番木鳖碱(士的年)及其盐	4	0	0	0	0	0	0	0	0	0	0		0	0		0	0	0			
29399990	其他天然或合成再制的生物碱及其盐、醚、酯和其他衍生物	4	0	0	0	0	0	0	0	0	0	0		0	0		0	0	0			
29400000	化学纯糖,但蔗糖、乳糖、麦芽糖、葡萄糖及果糖除外；糖醚、糖酯及其盐，但不包括税目 29.37、29.38、29.39的产品	6	0	0	0	0	0	0	0	0	0	0		0	5		0	0	0			
29411011	氨苄青霉素	6	0	0	0	0	0	0	0	0	0	0	5	0	0		0	0	0			
29411012	氨苄青霉素三水酸	6	0	0	0	0	0	0	0	0	0	0	5	0	0		0	0	0			
29411019	其他氨苄青霉素盐	6	0	0	0	0	0	0	0	0	0	0	5	0	0		0	0	0			
29411091	羟氨苄青霉素	4	0	0	0	0	0	0	0	0	0	0		0	0		0	0	0			
29411092	羟氨苄青霉素三水酸	4	0	0	0	0	0	0	0	0	0	0		0	0		0	0	0			
29411093	6 氨基青霉烷酸(6APA)	4	0	0	0	0	0	0	0	0	0	0		0	0		0	0	0			
29411094	青霉素 V	4	0	0	0	0	0	0	0	0	0	0		0	0		0	0	0			
29411095	磺苄青霉素	4	0	0	0	0	0	0	0	0	0	0		0	0		0	0	0			
29411096	邻氯青霉素	4	0	0	0	0	0	0	0	0	0	0		0	0		0	0	0			
29411099	其他青霉素及其衍生物，及它们的盐	4	0	0	0	0	0	0	0	0	0	0		0	0		0	0	0			
29412000	链霉素及其衍生物，及它们的盐	4	0	0	0	0	0	0	0	0	0	0		0	0		0	0	0			
29413011	四环素	4	0	0	0	0	0	0	0	0	0	0		0	0		0	0	0		0	
29413012	四环素盐	4	0	0	0	0	0	0	0	0	0	0		0	0		0	0	0		0	
29413020	四环素衍生物及其盐	4	0	0	0	0	0	0	0	0	0	0		0	0		0	0	0		0	
29414000	氯霉素及其衍生物，及它们的盐	4	0	0	0	0	0	0	0	0	0	0		0	0		0	0	0			
29415000	红霉素及其衍生物，及它们的盐	4	0	0	0	0	0	0	0	0	0	0		0	0		0	0	0		0	
29419010	庆大霉素及其衍生物，及它们的盐	4	0	0	0	0	0	0	0	0	0	0		0.4	0		0	0	0			
29419020	卡那霉素及其衍生物，及它们的盐	4	0	0	0	0	0	0	0	0	0	0		0.4	0		0	0	0			
29419030	利福平及其衍生物，及它们的盐	4	0	0	0	0	0	0	0	0	0	0		0.4	0		0	0	0			
29419040	林可霉素及其衍生物，及它们的盐	4	0	0	0	0	0	0	0	0	0	0		0.4	0		0	0	0			
29419052	头孢氨苄及其盐	6	0	0	0	0	0	0	0	0	0	0	5	0.6	0		0	0	0			
29419053	头孢唑啉及其盐	6	0	0	0	0	0	0	0	0	0	0	5	0.6	0		0	0	0			
29419054	头孢拉啶及其盐	6	0	0	0	0	0	0	0	0	0	0	5	0.6	0		0	0	0			
29419055	头孢三嗪(头孢曲松)及其盐	6	0	0	0	0	0	0	0	0	0	0	5	0.6	0		0	0	0			
29419056	头孢哌酮及其盐	6	0	0	0	0	0	0	0	0	0	0	5	0.6	0		0	0	0			
29419057	头孢噻肟及其盐	6	0	0	0	0	0	0	0	0	0	0	5	0.6	0		0	0	0			
29419058	头孢克罗及其盐	6	0	0	0	0	0	0	0	0	0	0	5	0.6	0		0	0	0			
29419059	其他头孢菌素及其衍生物以及它们的盐	6	0	0	0	0	0	0	0	0	0	0	5	0.6	0		0	0	0			
29419060	麦迪霉素及其衍生物，及它们的盐	6	0	0	0	0	0	0	0	0	0	0	4.2	0.6	0		0	0	0			
29419070	乙酰螺旋霉素及其衍生物，及它们的盐	4	0	0	0	0	0	0	0	0	0	0		0.4	0		0	0	0			
29419090	其他抗菌素	6	0	0	0	0	0	0	0	0	0	0	5	0.6	0		0	0	0			
29420000	其他有机化合物	6.5	0	0	0	0	0	0	0	0	0	0		0	5		0	0	0			
30012000	腺体、其他器官及其分泌物提取物	3	0	0	0	0	0	0	0	0	0	0		0	0		0	0	0			

税则号列	商品名称（简称）	最惠国	东盟 文	东盟 柬	东盟 印	东盟 老	东盟 马	东盟 缅	东盟 菲	东盟 新	东盟 泰	东盟 越	亚太	智利	巴基斯坦	新加坡	新西兰	秘鲁	哥斯达黎加	香港	澳门	台湾
30019010	肝素及其盐	3	0	0	0	0	0	0	0	0	0	0		0	0		0	0	0			
30019090	其他未列名的人体或动物制品(供治疗或预防疾病用)	3	0	0	0	0	0	0	0	0	0	0		0	0		0	0	0			
30021000	抗血清、其他血份及免疫制品(不论是否修饰通过生物工艺加工制得)	3	0	0	0	0	0	0	0	0	0	0		0	0		0	0	0			
30022000	人用疫苗	3	0	0	0	0	0	0	0	0	0	0		0	0		0	0	0			
30023000	兽用疫苗	3	0	0	0	0	0	0	0	0	0	0		0	0		0	0	0			
30029010	石房蛤毒素	3	0	0	0	0	0	0	0	0	0	0		0	0		0	0	0			
30029020	蓖麻毒素	3	0	0	0	0	0	0	0	0	0	0		0	0		0	0	0			
30029030	细菌及病毒	3	0	0	0	0	0	0	0	0	0	0		0	0		0	0	0			
30029040	遗传物质和基因修饰生物体	3	0	0	0	0	0	0	0	0	0	0		0	0		0	0	0			
30029090	人血；治病、防病或诊断用动物血制品；其他毒素、培养微生物（不包括酵母）及类似产品	3	0	0	0	0	0	0	0	0	0	0		0	0		0	0	0	0		
30031011	含有氨苄青霉素的混合药品（两种或两种以上成分混合而成的，治病或防病用，未配定剂量或非零售包装）	6	0	0	0	0	0	0	0	0	0	0	4.5	0	0		0	0	0			
30031012	含有羟氨苄青霉素的混合药品（两种或两种以上成分混合而成的，治病或防病用未配定剂量或非零售包装）	6	0	0	0	0	0	0	0	0	0	0	4.5	0	0		0	0	0			
30031013	含有青霉素 V 的混合药品（两种或两种以上成分混合而成的，治病或防病用未配定剂量或非零售包装）	6	0	0	0	0	0	0	0	0	0	0	4.5	0	0		0	0	0			
30031019	含有其他青霉素及具有青霉烷酸结构的青霉素衍生物的混合药品（两种或两种以上成分混合而成的，治病或防病用未配定剂量或非零售包装）	6	0	0	0	0	0	0	0	0	0	0	4.5	0	0		0	0	0			
30031090	含有含有链霉素的混合药品（两种或两种以上成分混合而成的，治病或防病用未配定剂量或非零售包装）	6	0	0	0	0	0	0	0	0	0	0	4.5	0	0		0	0	0			
30032011	含有头孢噻肟的混合药品（两种或两种以上成分混合而成的，治病或防病用未配定剂量或非零售包装）	6	0	0	0	0	0	0	0	0	0	0	5.4	0	0		0	0	0			
30032012	含有头孢他啶的混合药品（两种或两种以上成分混合而成的，治病或防病用未配定剂量或非零售包装）	6	0	0	0	0	0	0	0	0	0	0	5.4	0	0		0	0	0			
30032013	含有头孢西丁的混合药品（两种或两种以上成分混合而成的，治病或防病用未配定剂量或非零售包装）	6	0	0	0	0	0	0	0	0	0	0	5.4	0	0		0	0	0			
30032014	含有头孢替唑的混合药品（两种或两种以上成分混合而成的，治病或防病用未配定剂量或非零售包装）	6	0	0	0	0	0	0	0	0	0	0	5.4	0	0		0	0	0			
30032015	含有头孢克罗的混合药品（两种或两种以上成分混合而成的，治病或防病用未配定剂量或非零售包装）	6	0	0	0	0	0	0	0	0	0	0	5.4	0	0		0	0	0			
30032016	含有头孢呋辛的混合药品（两种或两种以上成分混合而成的，治病或防病用未配定剂量或非零售包装）	6	0	0	0	0	0	0	0	0	0	0	5.4	0	0		0	0	0			
30032017	含有头孢三嗪(头孢曲松）的混合药品（两种或两种以上成分混合而成的，治病或防病用未配定剂量或非零售包装）	6	0	0	0	0	0	0	0	0	0	0	5.4	0	0		0	0	0			
30032018	含有头孢哌酮的混合药品（两种或两种以上成分混合而成的，治病或防病用未配定剂量或非零售包装）	6	0	0	0	0	0	0	0	0	0	0	5.4	0	0		0	0	0			
30032019	含有其他头孢菌素的混合药品（两种或两种以上成分混合而成的，治病或防病用未配定剂量或非零售包装）	6	0	0	0	0	0	0	0	0	0	0	5.4	0	0		0	0	0			
30032090	其他含有其他抗菌素的混合药品（两种或两种以上成分混合而成的，治病或防病用未配定剂量或非零售包装）	6	0	0	0	0	0	0	0	0	0	0	4.2	0	0		0	0	0			
30033100	含有胰岛素但不含抗菌素的混合药品	5	0	0	0	0	0	0	0	0	0	0	3.5	0	0		0	0	0			

税则号列	商品名称（简称）	最惠国	东盟										亚太	智利	巴基斯坦	新加坡	新西兰	秘鲁	哥斯达黎加	香港	澳门	台湾
			文	柬	印	老	马	缅	菲	新	泰	越										
	（两种或两种以上成分混合而成的，治病或防病用未配定剂量或非零售包装）																					
30033900	含激素（胰岛素除外）或税目 29.37 其他产品，但不含抗菌素的混合药品（两种或两种以上成分混合而成的，治病或防病用未配定剂量或非零售包装）	6	0	0	0	0	0	0	0	0	0	0	4.2	0	0		0	0	0			
30034010	含奎宁或其盐，但不含抗菌素及税目 2937 的产品的混合药品（两种或两种以上成分混合而成的，治病或防病用未配定剂量或非零售包装）	5	0	0	0	0	0	0	0	0	0	0		0	0		0	0	0			
30034090	含生物碱及其衍生物（ 奎宁或其盐除外），但不含抗菌素及税目 2937 的激素或其他产品的混合药品（两种或两种以上成分混合而成的，治病或防病用未配定剂量或非零售包装）	5	0	0	0	0	0	0	0	0	0	0		0	0		0	0	0			
30039010	含磺胺类的混合药品（两种或两种以上成分混合而成的，治病或防病用未配定剂量或非零售包装）	6	0	0	0	0	0	0	0	0	0	0	4.2	0.6	0		0	0	0		0	
30039020	含有青蒿素及其衍生物药品	5	0	0	0	0	0	0	0	0	0	0		0.5	0		0	0	0		0	
30039090	含其他成份混合药品（两种或两种以上成分混合而成的，治病或防病用未配定剂量或非零售包装）	5	0	0	0	0	0	0	0	0	0	0		0.5	0		0	0	0		0	
30041011	氨苄青霉素制剂（混合，治病或防病用，已配定剂量或制成零售包装）	6	0	0	0	0	0	0	0	0	0	0	4.5	0.6	0		0	0	0	0	0	
30041012	羟氨苄青霉素制剂（两种或两种以上成分混合而成的，治病或防病用，已配定剂量或制成零售包装）	6	0	0	0	0	0	0	0	0	0	0	4.5	0.6	0		0	0	0	0	0	
30041013	青霉素 V 制剂（两种或两种以上成分混合而成的，治病或防病用，已配定剂量或制成零售包装）	6	0	0	0	0	0	0	0	0	0	0	4.5	0.6	0		0	0	0	0	0	
30041019	其他青霉素制剂（混合或非混合，治病或防病用，已配定剂量或制成零售包装）	6	0	0	0	0	0	0	0	0	0	0	4.5	0.6	0		0	0	0	0	0	
30041090	含有其他青霉素及具有青霉烷酸结构的青霉素衍生物或链霉素及其衍生物的药品（混合或非混合，治病或防病用，已配定剂量或制成零售包装）	6	0	0	0	0	0	0	0	0	0	0	4.5	0.6	0		0	0	0	0	0	
30042011	头孢塞肟制剂（混合或非混合，治病或防病用已配定剂量或制成零售包装）	6	0	0	0	0	0	0	0	0	0	0	5	0.6	0		0	0	0	0		
30042012	头孢他啶制剂（混合或非混合，治病或防病用，已配定剂量或制成零售包装）	6	0	0	0	0	0	0	0	0	0	0	5	0.6	0		0	0	0	0		
30042013	头孢西丁制剂（混合或非混合，治病或防病用，已配定剂量或制成零售包装）	6	0	0	0	0	0	0	0	0	0	0	5	0.6	0		0	0	0	0		
30042014	头孢替唑制剂（混合或非混合，治病或防病用，已配定剂量或制成零售包装）	6	0	0	0	0	0	0	0	0	0	0	5	0.6	0		0	0	0	0		
30042015	头孢克罗制剂（混合或非混合，治病或防病用，已配定剂量或制成零售包装）	6	0	0	0	0	0	0	0	0	0	0	5	0.6	0		0	0	0	0		
30042016	头孢呋辛制剂（混合或非混合，治病或防病用，已配定剂量或制成零售包装）	6	0	0	0	0	0	0	0	0	0	0	5	0.6	0		0	0	0	0		
30042017	头孢三嗪（头孢曲松）制剂（混合或非混合，治病或防病用，已配定剂量或制成零售包装）	6	0	0	0	0	0	0	0	0	0	0	5	0.6	0		0	0	0	0		
30042018	头孢哌酮制剂（混合或非混合，治病或防病用，已配定剂量或制成零售包装）	6	0	0	0	0	0	0	0	0	0	0	5	0.6	0		0	0	0	0		
30042019	含有其他头孢菌素制剂（混合或非混合，治病或防病用，已配定剂量或制成零售包装）	6	0	0	0	0	0	0	0	0	0	0	5	0.6	0		0	0	0	0		
30042090	含有其他抗菌素的药品（混合或非混合，治病或防病用，已配定剂量或制成零售包装）	6	0	0	0	0	0	0	0	0	0	0	4.2	0.6	0		0	0	0	0	0	
30043110	含有重组人胰岛素但不含抗菌素的药品（混合或非混合，治病或防病用已	5	0	0	0	0	0	0	0	0	0	0	3.5	0.5	0		0	0	0			

税则号列	商品名称（简称）	最惠国	东盟										亚太	智利	巴基斯坦	新加坡	新西兰	秘鲁	哥斯达黎加	香港	澳门	台湾
			文	柬	印	老	马	缅	菲	新	泰	越										
	配定剂量或零售包装）																					
30043190	含有其他胰岛素但不含抗菌素的药品（混合或非混合，治病或防病用已配定剂量或零售包装）	5	0	0	0	0	0	0	0	0	0	0	3.5	0.5	0		0	0	0			
30043200	含肾上腺皮混合或非混合质激素但不含抗菌素的药品（，治病或防病用已配定剂量或零售包装）	5	0	0	0	0	0	0	0	0	0	0	3.5	0.5	0		0	0	0	0		
30043900	含有税目 29.37 其他产品但不含抗菌素的药品（混合或非混合，治病或防病用已配定剂量或零售包装）	5	0	0	0	0	0	0	0	0	0	0	3.5	0.5	0		0	0	0	0		
30044010	含有奎宁或其盐，但不含抗菌素及税目 29.37 的产品的药品（混合或非混合，治病或防病用已配定剂量或零售包装）	5	0	0	0	0	0	0	0	0	0	0	4	0.5	0		0	0	0	0		
30044090	含有其他生物碱及其衍生物，但不含抗菌素及税目 29.37 的产品的药品（混合或非混合，治病或防病用已配定剂量或零售包装）	5	0	0	0	0	0	0	0	0	0	0		0.5	0		0	0	0	0		
30045000	含有维生素或税目 29.36 其他产品的其他药品（混合或非混合，治病或防病用已配定剂量或零售包装）	6	0	0	0	0	0	0	0	0	0	0	5	0.6	0		0	0	0		0	
30049010	含有磺胺类的药品（两种或两种以上成分混合而成的，治病或防病用已配定剂量或零售包装）	6	0	0	0	0	0	0	0	0	0	0	4.2	0.6	0		0	0	0	0	0	
30049020	含联苯双酯的药品（混合或非混合，治病或防病用已配定剂量或零售包装）	4	0	0	0	0	0	0	0	0	0	0	2.8	0.4	0		0	0	0		0	
30049051	中药酒（混合或非混合，治病或防病用已配定剂量或零售包装）	3	0	0	0	0	0	0	0	0	0	0	2	0	0		0	0	0	0	0	
30049052	片仔癀（混合或非混合，治病或防病用已配定剂量或零售包装）	3	0	0	0	0	0	0	0	0	0	0	2	0	0		0	0	0	0	0	
30049053	白药（混合或非混合，治病或防病用已配定剂量或零售包装）	3	0	0	0	0	0	0	0	0	0	0	2	0	0		0	0	0	0	0	
30049054	清凉油（混合或非混合，治病或防病用已配定剂量或零售包装）	3	0	0	0	0	0	0	0	0	0	0	2	0	0		0	0	0	0	0	
30049055	安宫牛黄丸	3	0	0	0	0	0	0	0	0	0	0	2	0	0		0	0	0	0	0	
30049059	其他中式成药（混合或非混合，治病或防病用已配定剂量或零售包装）	3	0	0	0	0	0	0	0	0	0	0	2	0	0		0	0	0	0	0	
30049060	含有青蒿素及其衍生物的中成药	4	0	0	0	0	0	0	0	0	0	0		0.4	0		0	0	0	0	0	
30049090	其他药品（混合或非混合，治病或防病用已配定剂量或零售包装）	4	0	0	0	0	0	0	0	0	0	0	2.8	0.4	0		0	0	0	0	0	
30051010	橡皮膏（经药物浸涂或制定零售包装供医疗、外科、牙科或兽医用）	5	0	0	0	0	0	0	0	0	0	0		0.5	0		0	0	0		0	
30051090	其他胶粘敷料及有胶粘涂层的物品（经药物浸涂或制定零售包装供医疗、外科、牙科或兽医用）	5	0	0	0	0	0	0	0	0	0	0		0.5	0		0	0	0		0	
30059010	药棉、纱布、绷带（经药物浸涂或制定零售包装供医疗、外科、牙科或兽医用）	5	0	0	0	0	0	0	0	0	0	0	3	0.5	0		0	0	0	0		
30059090	其他医用软填料及类似物品（经药物浸涂或制定零售包装供医疗、外科、牙科或兽医用）	5	0	0	0	0	0	0	0	0	0	0		0.5	0		0	0	0	0	0	
30061000	无菌外科肠线；无菌昆布、无菌粘合胶布、无菌吸收性止血材料、外科或牙科用无菌抗粘连阻隔材料及类似无菌材料	5	0	0	0	0	0	0	0	0	0	0		0	0		0	0	0	0	0	
30062000	血型试剂	3	0	0	0	0	0	0	0	0	0	0		0	0		0	0	0			
30063000	X 光检查造影剂；诊断试剂	4	0	0	0	0	0	0	0	0	0	0		0	0		0	0	0			
30064000	牙科粘固剂及其他牙科填料（包括骨骼粘固剂）	5	0	0	0	0	0	0	0	0	0	0		0	0		0	0	0			
30065000	急救药箱、药包	5	0	0	0	0	0	0	0	0	0	0		0	0		0	0	0			
30067000	专用于人类或作兽药用的凝胶制品，作为外科手术或体检时躯体部位的润	6.5	0	0	0	0	0	0	0	0	0	0		0	5		0	0	0	0		

税则号列	商品名称（简称）	最惠国	东盟										亚太	智利	巴基斯坦	新加坡	新西兰	秘鲁	哥斯达黎加	香港	澳门	台湾
			文	柬	印	老	马	缅	菲	新	泰	越										
	滑剂，或者作为躯体和医疗器械之间的偶合剂																					
30069100	可确定用于造口术用具	10	0	0	0	0	0	0	0	0	0	0	9.2	1	9.2	0	0	0	0	0	0	
30069200	废药物	5	0	0	0	0	0	0	0	0	0	0		0	0		0	0	0			
31010011	未经化学处理的鸟粪	3	0	0	0	0	0	0	0	0	0	0		0	0		0	0	0			
31010019	未经化学处理的其他动植物肥料	6.5	0	0	0	0	0	0	0	0	0	0		0.7	5		0	0	0		0	
31010090	动植物产品经混合或化学处理的制成的肥料	4	0	0	0	0	0	0	0	0	0	0		0.4	0		0	0	0			
31021000	尿素（不论是否水溶液）	50											40		40					0		
31022100	硫酸铵	4	0	0	0	0	0	0	0	0	0	0		0	0		0	0	0			
31022900	硫酸铵和硝酸铵的复盐及混合物	4	0	0	0	0	0	0	0	0	0	0		0	0		0	0	0			
31023000	硝酸铵（不论是否水溶液）	4	0	0	0	0	0	0	0	0	0	0		0.4	0		0	0	0			
31024000	硝酸铵与碳酸钙或其他无肥效无机物的混合物	4	0	0	0	0	0	0	0	0	0	0		0	0		0	0	0			
31025000	硝酸钠	4	0	0	0	0	0	0	0	0	0	0		0.4	0		0	0	0			
31026000	硝酸钙和硝酸铵的复盐及混合物	4	0	0	0	0	0	0	0	0	0	0		0.4	0		0	0	0			
31028000	尿素及硝酸铵混合物的水溶液或氨水溶液	4	0	0	0	0	0	0	0	0	0	0		0	0		0	0	0			
31029010	氰氨化钙	4	0	0	0	0	0	0	0	0	0	0		0	0		0	0	0			
31029090	其他矿物氮肥及化学氮肥，包括上述子目未列名的混合物	4	0	0	0	0	0	0	0	0	0	0		0.4	0		0	0	0			
31031010	重过磷酸钙	4	0	0	0	0	0	0	0	0	0	0		0	0		0	0	0			
31031090	其他过磷酸钙	4	0	0	0	0	0	0	0	0	0	0		0	0		0	0	0			
31039000	其他矿物磷肥或化学磷肥	4	0	0	0	0	0	0	0	0	0	0		0	0		0	0	0			
31042020	纯氯化钾	3	0	0	0	0	0	0	0	0	0	0		0	0		0	0	0			
31042090	其他氯化钾	3	0	0	0	0	0	0	0	0	0	0		0	0		0	0	0			
31043000	硫酸钾	3	0	0	0	0	0	0	0	0	0	0		0	0		0	0	0			
31049010	光卤石、钾盐及其他天然粗钾盐	3	0	0	0	0	0	0	0	0	0	0		0	0		0	0	0			
31049090	其他矿物钾肥及化学钾肥	3	0	0	0	0	0	0	0	0	0	0		0	0		0	0	0			
31051000	制成片状及类似形状或每包毛重不超过10公斤的31章各货品	4	0	0	0	0	0	0	0	0	0	0		0.4	0		0	0	0	0		
31054000	磷酸二氢铵及磷酸二氢铵与磷酸氢二铵的混合物	4	0	0	0	0	0	0	0	0	0	0		0	0		0	0	0			
31055100	含有硝酸盐及磷酸盐的肥料	4	0	0	0	0	0	0	0	0	0	0		0.4	0		0	0	0			
31055900	其他含氮、磷两种肥效元素的矿物肥料或化学肥料	4	0	0	0	0	0	0	0	0	0	0		0	0		0	0	0			
31056000	含磷、钾两种元素的肥料	4	0	0	0	0	0	0	0	0	0	0		0	0		0	0	0			
31059000	其他肥料	4	0	0	0	0	0	0	0	0	0	0		0.4	0		0	0	0	0		
32011000	坚木浸膏	5	0	0	0	0	0	0	0	0	0	0		0	0		0	0	0			
32012000	荆树皮浸膏	6.5	0	0	0	0	0	0	0	0	0	0		0	5		0	0	0			
32019010	其他植物鞣料浸膏	6.5	0	0	0	0	0	0	0	0	0	0		0	5		0	0	0			
32019090	鞣酸及其盐、醚、酯和其他衍生物	6.5	0	0	0	0	0	0	0	0	0	0		0	5		0	0	0			
32021000	有机合成鞣料	6.5	0	0	0	0	0	0	0	0	0	0		0	5		0	0	0	0		
32029000	无机鞣料；鞣料制剂等，不论是否含有天然鞣料；预鞣用酶制剂	6.5	0	0	0	0	0	0	0	0	0	0		0	5		0	0	0	0	0	
32030011	天然靛蓝及以其为基本成分的制品，包括染料浸膏（不论是否已有化学定义）	6.5	0	0	0	0	0	0	0	0	0	0		0.7	5		0	4.9	0			
32030019	其他植物质着色料及以其为基本成分的制品包括染料浸膏（不论是否已有化学定义）；32章注释三所述的以植物质着色料为基本成分的制品	6.5	0	0	0	0	0	0	0	0	0	0		0.7	5		0	4.9	0		0	
32030020	动物质着色料及以其为基本成分的制品包括染料浸膏（不论是否已有化学定义，但动物炭黑除外）；32章注释三所述的以动物质着色料为基本成分的制品	6.5	0	0	0	0	0	0	0	0	0	0		0.7	5		0	4.9	0			
32041100	分散染料及以其为基本成分的制品（不论是否已有化学定义）	6.5	0	0	0	0	0	0	0	0	0	0	5.8	0	0		0	0	0			
32041200	酸性染料（不论是否预金属络合）及以其为基本成分的制品（不论是否已有化学定义）；媒染染料及以其为基本成	6.5	0	0	0	0	0	0	0	0	0	0	5.8	0	0		0	0	0	0		0

税则号列	商品名称（简称）	最惠国	东盟										亚太	智利	巴基斯坦	新加坡	新西兰	秘鲁	哥斯达黎加	香港	澳门	台湾
			文	柬	印	老	马	缅	菲	新	泰	越										
	分的制品(不论是否已有化学定义)																					
32041300	碱性染料及以其为基本成分的制品(不论是否已有化学定义)	6.5	0	0	0	0	0	0	0	0	0	0	6	0	0		0	0	0			
32041400	直接染料及以其为基本成分的制品(不论是否已有化学定义)	6.5	0	0	0	0	0	0	0	0	0	0	6	0	0		0	0	0			0
32041510	合成靛蓝(还原靛蓝)（不论是否已有化学定义)	6.5	0	0	0	0	0	0	0	0	0	0	6	0	0		0	0	0			
32041590	其他瓮染料（包括颜料用的）及以其为基本成分的制品(不论是否已有化学定义)	6.5	0	0	0	0	0	0	0	0	0	0	6	0	0		0	0	0			
32041600	活性染料及以其为基本成分的制品(不论是否已有化学定义)	6.5	0	0	0	0	0	0	0	0	0	0	5.8	0	0		0	0	0	0		0
32041700	颜料及以其为基本成分的制品(不论是否已有化学定义)	6.5	0	0	0	0	0	0	0	0	0	0	4.6	0.7	0		0	0	0	0		0
32041911	硫化黑(硫化青)及以其为基本成分的制品(不论是否已有化学定义)	6.5	0	0	0	0	0	0	0	0	0	0	6	0	0		0	0	0			
32041919	其他硫化染料及以其为基本成分的制品(不论是否已有化学定义)	6.5	0	0	0	0	0	0	0	0	0	0	6	0	0		0	0	0			
32041990	由子目号 3204.11 至 3204.19 中两个或多个子目所列着色料组成的混合物，(不论是否已有化学定义)	6.5	0	0	0	0	0	0	0	0	0	0	6	0	0		0	0	0			0
32042000	用作萤光增白剂的有机合成产品(不论是否已有化学定义)	6.5	0	0	0	0	0	0	0	0	0	0	6	0	0		0	0	0	0		0
32049010	生物染色剂及染料指示剂(不论是否已有化学定义)	6.5	0	0	0	0	0	0	0	0	0	0	6	0	0		0	0	0			
32049090	其他用作发光体的有机合成产品(不论是否已有化学定义)	6.5	0	0	0	0	0	0	0	0	0	0	6	0	0		0	0	0			
32050000	色淀及 32 章注释三所述的以色淀为基本成分的制品	6.5	0	0	0	0	0	0	0	0	0	0		0	5		0	0	0			
32061110	钛白粉	6.5	0	0	0	0	0	0	0	0	0	0		0	5		0	0	0			0
32061190	干量计二氧化钛≥80%的颜料及制品，钛白粉除外	6.5	0	0	0	0	0	0	0	0	0	0		0	5		0	0	0			
32061900	二氧化钛为基料的颜料及制品，干量计二氧化钛＜80%	10	0	0	0	0	0	0	0	0	0	0		0	5	0	0	0	0	0		0
32062000	铬化合物为基本成分的颜料及制品	6.5	0	0	0	0	0	0	0	0	0	0		0	5		0	0	0			
32064100	群青及以其为基本成分的制品	6.5	0	0	0	0	0	0	0	0	0	0		0	5		0	0	0			
32064210	锌钡白	6.5	0	0	0	0	0	0	0	0	0	0		0	5		0	0	0			
32064290	其他以硫化锌为基本成份的颜料和制品	6.5	0	0	0	0	0	0	0	0	0	0		0	5		0	0	0			
32064911	以钒酸铋为基本成分的颜料及制品	6.5	0	0	0	0	0	0	0	0	0	0	3.3	0	0		0	0	0	0		0
32064919	其他以铋化合物为基本成分的颜料及制品	6.5	0	0	0	0	0	0	0	0	0	0	3.3	0	0		0	0	0	0		0
32064990	其他着色料及其他制品	6.5	0	0	0	0	0	0	0	0	0	0	3.3	0	0		0	0	0	0		0
32065000	用作发光体的无机产品，不论是否已有化学定义	6.5	0	0	0	0	0	0	0	0	0	0	5.9	0	5		0	0	0			
32071000	调制颜料、遮光剂、着色剂及类似制品(用于陶瓷、搪瓷及玻璃工业)	5	0	0	0	0	0	0	0	0	0	0		0.5	0		0	0	0			
32072000	珐琅和釉料、釉底料及类似制品(用于陶瓷、搪瓷及玻璃工业)	5	0	0	0	0	0	0	0	0	0	0		0.5	0		0	0	0			
32073000	光瓷釉及类似制品(用于陶瓷、搪瓷及玻璃工业)	5	0	0	0	0	0	0	0	0	0	0		0	0		0	0	0			
32074000	呈粉、粒状搪瓷玻璃料及其他玻璃	5	0	0	0	0	0	0	0	0	0	0		0.5	0		0	0	0			
32081000	分散或溶于非水介质的聚酯油漆及清漆等	10	0	0	0	0	0	0	0	0	0	0	9	1	5	0	0	5	0	0	0	0
32082010	分散或溶于非水介质的丙烯酸聚合物油漆及清漆	10	0	0	0	0	0	0	0	0	0	0	9	1	5	0	0	5	0			0
32082020	分散或溶于非水介质的乙烯聚合物油漆及清漆	10	0	0	0	0	0	0	0	0	0	0	9	1	5		0	5	0			
32089010	分散或溶于非水介质的聚胺酯类油漆及清漆	10	0	0	0	0	0	0	0	0	0	0	9	1	5	0	0	5	0			
32089090	分散或溶于非水介质其他油漆、清漆溶液	10	0	0	0	0	0	0	0	0	0	0	9	1	5	0	0	5	0	0	0	0
32091000	分散或溶于水介质的丙烯酸聚合物或	10	0	0	0	0	0	0	0	0	0	0	9	1	5	0	0	5	0		0	

税则号列	商品名称（简称）	最惠国	东盟										亚太	智利	巴基斯坦	新加坡	新西兰	秘鲁	哥斯达黎加	香港	澳门	台湾
			文	柬	印	老	马	缅	菲	新	泰	越										
	乙烯聚合物油漆及清漆																					
32099010	以环氧树脂为基本成分的溶于水介质其他聚合物油漆及清漆	10	0	0	0	0	0	0	0	0	0	0		1	5	0	0	0	0			0
32099020	以氟树脂为基本成分的溶于水介质其他聚合物油漆及清漆	10	0	0	0	0	0	0	0	0	0	0		1	5	0	0	0	0			
32099090	溶于水介质其他聚合物油漆及清漆	10	0	0	0	0	0	0	0	0	0	0		1	5	0	0	0	0	0		0
32100000	其他油漆及清漆(包括瓷漆\大漆及水浆涂料)；皮革用水性颜料	10	0	0	0	0	0	0	0	0	0	0	9	1	5	0	0	5	0	0	0	0
32110000	配制的催干剂	10	0	0	0	0	0	0	0	0	0	0		0	5	0	0	0	0			
32121000	压印箔	15	0	0	0	0	0	0	0	0	0	0		1.5	12	0	0	7.5	3			
32129000	制漆用颜料（分散于非水介质中呈液状或浆状的）及零售形状或零售包装的染料、色料	10	0	0	0	0	0	0	0	0	0	0		0	5	0	0	0	0			
32131000	成套的颜料(艺术家、学生和广告美工用的)	10	0	0	0	0	0	0	0	0	0	0		1	5		0	5	0			
32139000	非成套颜料、调色料及类似品（艺术家、学生和广告美工用的,片状、管装、罐装、瓶装、扁盒装等类似形状或包装的）	10	0	0	0	0	0	0	0	0	0	0	9	0	5		0	0	0			
32141010	半导体器件封装材料	9	0	0	0	0	0	0	0	0	0	0		0.9	5		0	0	0			
32141090	其他安装玻璃用油灰、接缝用油灰、树脂胶泥、嵌缝胶及其他类似胶粘剂；漆工用填料	9	0	0	0	0	0	0	0	0	0	0		0.9	5		0	0	0			
32149000	非耐火涂面制剂，涂门面、内墙、地板、天花板等用	9	0	0	0	0	0	0	0	0	0	0		0.9	5		0	0	0	0		
32151100	黑色印刷油墨(不论是否固体或浓缩)	6.5	0	0	0	0	0	0	0	0	0	0	4.6	0.7	0		0	0	0	0	0	
32151900	其他印刷油墨(不论是否固体或浓缩)，黑色印刷油墨除外	6.5	0	0	0	0	0	0	0	0	0	0	4.6	0.7	0		0	0	0	0	0	0
32159010	书写墨水(不论是否固体或浓缩)	6.5	0	0	0	0	0	0	0	0	0	0		0	5		0	0	0	0	0	
32159020	水性喷墨墨水	10	0	0	0	0	0	0	0	0	0	0		0	5	0	0	0	0	0	0	
32159090	绘图墨水及其他墨类(不论是否固体或浓缩)	10	0	0	0	0	0	0	0	0	0	0		0	5	0	0	0	0	0	0	
33011200	橙油（包括浸膏及净油）	20	0	0	0	0	0	0	0	0	0	0		0		0	0	10	4		0	
33011300	柠檬油（包括浸膏及净油）	20	0	0	0	0	0	0	0	0	0	0		0		0	0	0	4		0	
33011910	白柠檬油(酸橙油)（包括浸膏及净油）	20	0	0	0	0	0	0	0	0	0	0		0		0	0	0	4		0	
33011990	其他柑桔属果实的精油（包括浸膏及净油）	20	0	0	0	0	0	0	0	0	0	0		0		0	0	0	4		0	
33012400	胡椒薄荷油（包括浸膏及净油）	20	0	0	0	0	0	0	0	0	0	0		0		0	0	10	4		0	
33012500	其他薄荷油（包括浸膏及净油）	15	0	0	0	0	0	0	0	0	0	0	14	0	12	0	0	7.5	3		0	
33012910	樟脑油（包括浸膏及净油）	20	0	0	0	0	0	0	0	0	0	0		0		0	0	10	4		0	
33012920	香茅油（包括浸膏及净油）	15	0	0	0	0	0	0	0	0	0	0		0	12	0	0	7.5	3		0	
33012930	茴香油（包括浸膏及净油）	20	0	0	0	0	0	0	0	0	0	0		0		0	0	10	4		0	
33012940	桂油（包括浸膏及净油）	20	0	0	0	0	0	0	0	0	0	0		0		0	0	10	4		0	
33012950	山苍子油（包括浸膏及净油）	20	0	0	0	0	0	0	0	0	0	0		0		0	0	10	4		0	
33012960	桉叶油（包括浸膏及净油）	20	0	0	0	0	0	0	0	0	0	0		0		0	0	10	4		0	
33012991	老鹳草油(香叶油)（包括浸膏及净油）	20	0	0	0	0	0	0	0	0	0	0		0		0	0	10	4		0	
33012999	其他非柑桔属果实的精油（包括浸膏及净油）	15	0	0	0	0	0	0	0	0	0	0		0	12	0	0	0	3		0	
33013010	鸢尾凝脂	20	0	0	0	0	0	0	0	0	0	0		0		0	0	10	4		0	
33013090	其他香膏	20	0	0	0	0	0	0	0	0	0	0		0		0	0	10	4		0	
33019010	提取的油树脂	20	0	0	0	0	0	0	0	0	0	0	18	0	18	0	0	0	4		0	
33019020	柑桔属果实的精油脱萜所得的萜烯副产品	20	0	0	0	0	0	0	0	0	0	0	18	0	18	0	0	0	4		0	
33019090	用花香吸取法或浸渍法制定的含浓缩精油的脂肪、固定油、蜡及类似品；精油脱萜所得的萜烯副产品（柑桔属果实的除外）；精油水溶液及水馏液	20	0	0	0	0	0	0	0	0	0	0	18	0	18	0	0	0	4		0	
33021010	生产饮料用的混合香料以及以香料为基本成分的制品，按容量计酒精浓度≤0.5%	15	0	0	0	0	0	0	0	0	0	0	12.8	1.5	7.5	0	0	7.5	3		0	
33021090	其他食品或饮料工业用混合香料以及以香料为基本成分的制品	15	0	0	0	0	0	0	0	0	0	0		1.5	12	0	0	7.5	3		0	

税则号列	商品名称（简称）	最惠国	东盟										亚太	智利	巴基斯坦	新加坡	新西兰	秘鲁	哥斯达黎加	香港	澳门	台湾
			文	柬	印	老	马	缅	菲	新	泰	越										
33029000	其他工业用混合香料及以香料为基本成分的混合物和制品	10	0	0	0	0	0	0	0	0	0	0		1	5	0	0	5	0	0	0	
33030000	香水及花露水	10	0	0	0	0	0	0	0	0	0	0	8.2	1	5	0	0	0	0	0	0	
33041000	唇用化妆品	10	0	0	0	0	0	0	0	0	0	0		1	5	0	0	0	0	0	0	
33042000	眼用化妆品	10	0	0	0	0	0	0	0	0	0	0		1	5	0	0	0	0	0	0	
33043000	指(趾)甲化妆品	15	0	0	0	0	0	0	0	0	0	0		1.5	12	0	0	7.5	3	0	0	
33049100	香粉，不论是否压紧	10	0	0	0	0	0	0	0	0	0	0		1	5	0	0	0	0		0	
33049900	其他美容品或化妆品及护肤品	6.5	0	0	0	0	0	0	0	0	0	0		0.7	5.2	0	0	0	0	0	0	
33051000	洗发剂(香波)	6.5	0	0	0	0	0	0	0	0	0	0	5.4	0.7	5	0	0	0	0	0	0	
33052000	烫发剂	15	0	0	0	0	0	0	0	0	0	0		0	12	0	0	7.5	3		0	
33053000	定型剂	15	0	0	0	0	0	0	0	0	0	0		1.5	12	0	0	7.5	3		0	
33059000	其他护发品	10	0	0	0	0	0	0	0	0	0	0	8.5	1	5	0	0	0	0	0	0	
33061010	牙膏	10	0	0	0	0	0	0	0	0	0	0	7	1	5	0	0	0	0	0	0	
33061090	其他洁齿品	10	0	0	0	0	0	0	0	0	0	0	7	1	5	0	0	0	0			
33062000	牙线	10	0	0	0	0	0	0	0	0	0	0	9.2	1	5		0	0	0			
33069000	其他口腔及牙齿清洁剂	10	0	0	0	0	0	0	0	0	0	0		1	5	0	0	0	0	0	0	
33071000	剃须用制剂	10	0	0	0	0	0	0	0	0	0	0	7	1	5	0	0	0	0			
33072000	人体除臭剂及止汗剂	10	0	0	0	0	0	0	0	0	0	0	7	1	5	0	0	0	0		0	
33073000	香浴盐及其他沐浴用制剂	10	0	0	0	0	0	0	0	0	0	0	8.5	1	5	0	0	0	0	0	0	
33074100	神香及其他通过燃烧散发香气制品	10	0	0	0	0	0	0	0	0	0	0		0	5	0	0	0	0	0		
33074900	室内除臭制品	10	0	0	0	0	0	0	0	0	0	0		1	5	0	0	0	0	0		
33079000	脱毛剂、其他编号未列名的芳香料制品及化妆盥洗品	9	0	0	0	0	0	0	0	0	0	0	6.3	0	5		0	0	0		0	
34011100	盥洗用肥皂及有机表面活性产品，条状、块状或模制形状的，以及用肥皂或洗涤剂浸渍、涂面或包覆的纸、絮胎、毡呢及无纺织物	10	0	0	0	0	0	0	0	0	0	0	8.3	1	8.3	0	0	0	0	0	0	
34011910	洗衣皂	10	0	0	0	0	0	0	0	0	0	0		0	5	0	0	0	0		0	
34011990	其他用肥皂及有机表面活性产品，条状、块状或模制形状的，以及用肥皂或洗涤剂浸渍、涂面或包覆的纸、絮胎、毡呢及无纺织物	15	0	0	0	0	0	0	0	0	0	0		0	12		0	7.5	3			
34012000	其他形状的肥皂	15	0	0	0	0	0	0	0	0	0	0	12.4	1.5	7.5		0	7.5	3	0	0	
34013000	洁肤用的有机表面活性产品及制品，液状或膏状并制成零售包装的，不论是否含有肥皂	10	0	0	0	0	0	0	0	0	0	0		1	5	0	0	0	0		0	
34021100	阴离子型有机表面活性剂	6.5	0	0	0	0	0	0	0	0	0	0	6	0.7	5		0	0	0	0	0	
34021200	阳离子型有机表面活性剂	6.5	0	0	0	0	0	0	0	0	0	0	6	0	5		0	0	0	0	0	
34021300	非离子型有机表面活性剂	6.5	0	0	0	0	0	0	0	0	0	0	5.9	0.7	5		0	0	0	0	0	0
34021900	其他有机表面活性剂	6.5	0	0	0	0	0	0	0	0	0	0	6	0.7	5		0	0	0		0	
34022010	零售包装的合成洗涤粉	10	0	0	0	0	0	0	0	0	0	0	8.5	1	5	0	0	0	0		0	
34022090	零售包装有机表面活性剂制品（合成洗涤粉除外）	10	0	0	0	0	0	0	0	0	0	0	8.5	1	5	0	0	0	0	0	0	
34029000	非零售包装有机表面活性剂制品、洗涤剂及清洁剂	9	0	0	0	0	0	0	0	0	0	0	7.8	0.9	5	0	0	0	1.8	0	0	
34031100	用于纺织材料、皮革、毛皮或其他材料油脂处理的制剂（含有石油或从沥青矿物提取的油类且按重量计＜70%）	10	0	0	0	0	0	0	0	0	0	0	9.5	0	5	0	0	0	0	0		
34031900	润滑剂（含有石油或从沥青矿物提取的油类且按重量计＜70%）	10	0	0	0	0	0	0	0	0	0	0		1	5	0	0	0	0	0		
34039100	用于纺织、皮革、毛皮或其他材料油脂处理的制剂（不含有石油或从沥青矿物提取的油类）	10	0	0	0	0	0	0	0	0	0	0		1	5	0	0	5	0	0		
34039900	润滑剂（不含有石油或从沥青矿物提取的油类）	10	0	0	0	0	0	0	0	0	0	0		1	5	0	0	5	0		0	
34042000	聚乙二醇蜡	10	0	0	0	0	0	0	0	0	0	0		0	5		0	0	0			
34049000	其他人造蜡及调制蜡	10	0	0	0	0	0	0	0	0	0	0		0	5		0	5	0			
34051000	鞋靴或皮革用的上光剂及类似制品	10	0	0	0	0	0	0	0	0	0	0		1	5	0	0	5	0	0		
34052000	保养木制品的上光剂及类似制品	10	0	0	0	0	0	0	0	0	0	0		1	5	0	0	5	0	0		
34053000	车身用的上光剂及类似制品	10	0	0	0	0	0	0	0	0	0	0		1	5	0	0	5	0			
34054000	擦洗膏、去污粉及类似制品	10	0	0	0	0	0	0	0	0	0	0		0	5		0	0	0			

税则号列	商品名称（简称）	最惠国	东盟										亚太	智利	巴基斯坦	新加坡	新西兰	秘鲁	哥斯达黎加	香港	澳门	台湾
			文	柬	印	老	马	缅	菲	新	泰	越										
34059000	玻璃或金属用的光洁剂	10	0	0	0	0	0	0	0	0	0	0	8.5	1	5	0	0	5	0	0		
34060000	各种蜡烛及类似品	10	0	0	0	0	0	0	0	0	0	0		1	5	0	0	0	0		0	
34070010	牙科用蜡及造型膏	6.5	0	0	0	0	0	0	0	0	0	0		0	5		0	0	0			
34070020	以熟石膏为成分的牙科用其他制品	6.5	0	0	0	0	0	0	0	0	0	0		0	5		0	0	0			
34070090	塑型用膏	10	0	0	0	0	0	0	0	0	0	0		0	5		0	0	0			
35011000	酪蛋白	10	0	0	0	0	0	0	0	0	0	0		0	5	0	0	0	0			
35019000	酪蛋白衍生物；酪蛋白胶	10	0	0	0	0	0	0	0	0	0	0		1	5		0	5	0			
35021100	干的卵清蛋白	10	0	0	0	0	0	0	0	0	0	0		0	5		0	0	0			
35021900	其他卵清蛋白	10	0	0	0	0	0	0	0	0	0	0		0	5		0	0	0			
35022000	乳白蛋白，包括两种或两种以上的乳清蛋白浓缩物	10	0	0	0	0	0	0	0	0	0	0		0	5		0	0	0			
35029000	其他白蛋白及白蛋白盐及其衍生物	10	0	0	0	0	0	0	0	0	0	0		1	5		0	5	0	0		
35030010	明胶及其衍生物	12	0	0	0	0	0	0	0	0	0	0		0	6	0	0	0	2.4			
35030090	鱼胶；其他动物胶	12	0	0	0	0	0	0	0	0	0	0		0	6	0	0	0	2.4			
35040010	蛋白胨	3	0	0	0	0	0	0	0	0	0	0		0	0		0	0	0		0	
35040090	其他税号未列名蛋白质及其衍生物，皮粉	8	0	0	0	0	0	0	0	0	0	0		0	5		0	0	0		0	
35051000	糊精及其他改性淀粉	12	0	0	0	0	0	0	0	0	0	0		1.2	6	0	0	6	2.4	0	0	
35052000	以淀粉、糊精或其他改性淀粉为基本成分的胶	20	0	0	0	0	0	0	0	0	0	0		0		0	0	10	4			
35061000	适于作胶或粘合剂的产品，零售包装每件净重≤1kg	10	0	0	0	0	0	0	0	0	0	0	9.2	1	5	0	0	5	0	0		0
35069110	以聚酰胺为基本成份的粘合剂	10	0	0	0	0	0	0	0	0	0	0	7	1	5	0	0	5	0	0	0	0
35069120	以环氧树脂为基本成分的粘合剂	10	0	0	0	0	0	0	0	0	0	0	7	1	5	0	0	5	0	0	0	0
35069190	以其他橡胶或塑料为基本成分的粘合剂	10	0	0	0	0	0	0	0	0	0	0	7	1	5	0	0	5	0	0	0	0
35069900	其他调制胶、粘合剂	10	0	0	0	0	0	0	0	0	0	0	8.6	1	5	0	0	5	0	0	0	0
35071000	粗制凝乳酶及其浓缩物	6	0	0	0	0	0	0	0	0	0	0		0	5		0	0	0			
35079010	碱性蛋白酶	6	0	0	0	0	0	0	0	0	0	0		0.6	5		0	0	0			
35079020	碱性脂肪酶	6	0	0	0	0	0	0	0	0	0	0		0.6	5		0	0	0			
35079090	其他酶及未列名的酶制品	6	0	0	0	0	0	0	0	0	0	0		0.6	5		0	0	0		0	
36010000	发射药	9	0	0	0	0	0	0	0	0	0	0		0	5		0	0	0			
36020010	硝铵炸药，但发射药除外	9	0	0	0	0	0	0	0	0	0	0		0.9	5		0	0	0			
36020090	其他配制炸药，但发射药除外	9	0	0	0	0	0	0	0	0	0	0		0.9	5		0	0	0			
36030000	安全导火索、导爆索；火帽或雷管；引爆器；电雷管	9	0	0	0	0	0	0	0	0	0	0		0.9	5		0	0	0			
36041000	烟花、爆竹	6	0	0	0	0	0	0	0	0	0	0		0	5		0	0	0			
36049000	信号弹、降雨火箭、浓雾信号弹及其他烟火制品	6	0	0	0	0	0	0	0	0	0	0		0	5		0	0	0			
36050000	火柴，但税目 3604 的烟火制品除外	6	0	0	0	0	0	0	0	0	0	0		0.6	5		0	0	0			
36061000	灌注打火机等用的液体或液化气体燃料，其包装容器的容积≤300cm3	10	0	0	0	0	0	0	0	0	0	0		0	5		0	0	0	0		
36069011	已切成形可直接使用的铈铁及其他引火合金	9	0	0	0	0	0	0	0	0	0	0		0	5		0	0	0			
36069019	未切成形不可直接使用的铈铁及其他引火合金	9	0	0	0	0	0	0	0	0	0	0		0	5		0	0	0			
36069090	其他易燃材料制品	9	0	0	0	0	0	0	0	0	0	0		0	5		0	0	0			
37011000	未曝光的 X 光感光硬片及平面软片，用纸、纸板及纺织物以外任何材料制成	20												2			0	10	4			
37012000	未曝光的一次成像感光平片，用纸、纸板及纺织物以外任何材料制成	5	0	0	0	0	0	0	0	0	0	0		0	0		0	0	0			
37013021	激光照排片（任何一边超过 255mm），用纸、纸板及纺织物以外任何材料制成	10												0			0	0	0		0	
37013022	PS 版（预涂感光版）（任何一边超过 255mm），用纸、纸板及纺织物以外任何材料制成	10												0			0	0	0		0	
37013024	CTP 版	10	0		0		0	0	0	0	0	0		0	5		0	0	0		0	
37013025	柔性印刷版	10												0			0	0	0		0	
37013029	其他未曝光照相制版用感光硬片及软片（任何一边超过 255mm），用纸、纸板及纺织物以外任何材料制成	10												0			0	0	0		0	
37013090	未曝光其他用途的感光硬片及软片（任何一边超过 255mm），用纸、纸板	20	0	0	0	0	0	0	0	0	0	0		0		0	0	10	4			

税则号列	商品名称（简称）	最惠国	东盟										亚太	智利	巴基斯坦	新加坡	新西兰	秘鲁	哥斯达黎加	香港	澳门	台湾
			文	柬	印	老	马	缅	菲	新	泰	越										
	及纺织物以外任何材料制成																					
37019100	彩色摄影用未曝光彩色硬片及平面软片，用纸、纸板及纺织物以外任何材料制成，任何一边≤ 255mm	22	0	0	0	0	0	0	0	0	0	0		0		0	0	11	4.4			
37019920	照相制版用其他未曝光软片及硬片，用纸、纸板及纺织物以外任何材料制成，任何一边≤ 255mm	10	0	0	0	0	0	0	0	0	0	0		1	5		0	5	0			
37019990	其他用未曝光软片及硬片，用纸、纸板及纺织物以外任何材料制成，任何一边≤ 255mm	25	0	0	0	0	0	0	0	0	0	0		2.5		0	0	12.5	5			
37021000	成卷的未曝光的 X 光感光胶片，用纸、纸板及纺织物以外任何材料制成	10												0			0	0	0			
37023110	彩色摄影用未曝光一次成像感光卷片，宽度≤105 mm，用纸、纸板及纺织物以外任何材料制成	5	0	0	0	0	0	0	0	0	0	0		0	0		0	0	0			
37023190	彩色摄影用未曝光无齿孔彩色胶卷，宽度≤105 mm，用纸、纸板及纺织物以外任何材料制成	40	0	0	0	0	0	0	0	0	0	0		0		0	0	20	8			
37023210	照相制版用未曝光涂卤化银液无齿孔一次成像感光卷片，宽度≤105 mm，用纸、纸板及纺织物以外任何材料制成	5	0	0	0	0	0	0	0	0	0	0		0	0		0	0	0			
37023220	照相制版用未曝光涂卤化银液无齿孔胶卷，宽度≤105 mm，用纸、纸板及纺织物以外任何材料制成	10	0		0		0	0	0	0	0	0		0	2.25元/平方米		0	0	0			
37023290	其他未曝光涂乳液无齿孔胶卷，宽度≤105 mm，用纸、纸板及纺织物以外任何材料制成	22	0		0		0	0	0	0	0	0		0		0	0	11	4.4			
37023920	照相制版用未曝光未涂卤化银无齿孔感光胶卷，宽度≤105 mm，用纸、纸板及纺织物以外任何材料制成	10	0		0		0	0	0	0	0	0		0	6元/平方米		0	0	0			
37023990	其他未曝光未涂卤化银无齿孔感光胶卷，宽度≤105 m，用纸、纸板及纺织物以外任何材料制成	22	0		0		0	0	0	0	0	0		0		0	0	11	4.4			
37024100	彩色摄影用未曝光无齿孔彩色胶卷，宽度＞610 mm，长度＞200m，用纸、纸板及纺织物以外任何材料制成	16												0			0	8	3.2			
37024221	印刷电路板制造用未曝光光致抗蚀干膜，宽度＞610 mm，长度＞200m，用纸、纸板及纺织物以外任何材料制成	10	0		0		0	0	0	0	0	0		0	0.3元/平方米	0	0	0	0			
37024229	照相制版用其他未曝光无齿孔胶卷，宽度＞610 mm，长度＞200m，用纸、纸板及纺织物以外任何材料制成	10	0		0		0	0	0	0	0	0		0	0.8元/平方米		0	0	0			
37024292	红色或红外激光胶片	16	0		0		0	0	0	0	0	0		0		0	0	8	3.2			
37024299	其他未曝光无齿孔宽长胶卷	16	0		0		0	0	0	0	0	0		0		0	0	8	3.2			
37024321	照相制版用未曝光无齿孔激光照排片，宽度＞610 mm，长度≤200m，用纸、纸板及纺织物以外任何材料制成	10	0		0		0	0	0	0	0	0		0	0.9元/平方米		0	0	0			
37024329	其他照相制版用未曝光无齿孔胶卷，宽度＞610 mm，长度≤200m，用纸、纸板及纺织物以外任何材料制成	10	0		0		0	0	0	0	0	0		0	1.85元/平方米		0	0	0			
37024390	其他用未曝光无齿孔胶卷，宽度 610 mm，长度≤200m，用纸、纸板及纺织物以外任何材料制成	20	0		0		0	0	0	0	0	0		0		0	0	10	4			
37024421	照相制版用无齿孔未曝光激光照排片，105mm＜宽度≤610mm，用纸、纸板及纺织物以外任何材料制成	10	0		0		0	0	0	0	0	0		0	1.0元/平方米		0	0	0			
37024422	印刷电路板制造用未曝光光致抗蚀干膜，105mm＜宽度≤610mm，用纸、纸板及纺织物以外任何材料制成	10	0		0		0	0	0	0	0	0		0	0.45元/平方米		0	0	0			
37024429	其他照相制版用无齿孔未曝光胶卷，105mm＜宽度≤610mm，用纸、纸板及纺织物以外任何材料制成	10	0		0		0	0	0	0	0	0		0	1.45元/平方米		0	0	0			

税则号列	商品名称（简称）	最惠国	东盟										亚太	智利	巴基斯坦	新加坡	新西兰	秘鲁	哥斯达黎加	香港	澳门	台湾
			文	柬	印	老	马	缅	菲	新	泰	越										
37024490	其他用无齿孔未曝光胶卷，105mm＜宽度≤610mm，用纸、纸板及纺织物以外任何材料制成	20	0		0		0	0	0	0	0	0		0		0	0	10	4			
37025200	彩色摄影用未曝光彩色胶卷 ，宽度≤16 mm	47	0		0		0	0	0	0	0	0		0		0	0	23.5	9.4			
37025300	幻灯片用未曝光彩色摄影胶卷，16 mm＜宽度≤35 mm，长度＜30m，用纸、纸板及纺织物以外任何材料制成	47	0		0		0	0	0	0	0	0		0		0	0	23.5	9.4	0		
37025410	非幻灯片用未曝光彩色胶卷，宽度35mm，长度≤2 m，用纸、纸板及纺织物以外任何材料制成	18												0			0	9	3.6	0		
37025490	非幻灯片用彩色摄影用未曝光彩色胶卷，16 mm＜宽度＜35 mm，2 m＜长度≤30m，用纸、纸板及纺织物以外任何材料制成	18												0			0	9	3.6	0		
37025520	未曝光的彩色电影胶片，16mm＜ 宽度≤35mm， 长度＞30m，用纸、纸板及纺织物以外任何材料制成	26	6.92元/平方米	6.92元/平方米	6.92元/平方米	6.92元/平方米	6.92元/平方米	6.92元/平方米	6.92元/平方米	6.92元/平方米	6.92元/平方米	6.92元/平方米		0.9元/平方米			0	13	5.2			
37025590	未曝光彩色摄影用胶卷，16mm＜ 宽度≤35mm，长度＞30m，用纸、纸板及纺织物以外任何材料制成，电影胶片除外	40	13.5元/平方米	13.5元/平方米	13.5元/平方米	13.5元/平方米	13.5元/平方米	13.5元/平方米	13.5元/平方米	13.5元/平方米	13.5元/平方米	13.5元/平米		2.7元/平方米			0		8			
37025620	未曝光的彩色电影胶片，宽度＞35mm，用纸、纸板及纺织物以外任何材料制成	24	0		0		0	0	0	0	0	0		0		0	0	12	4.8			
37025690	未曝光的彩色摄影用胶卷，宽度＞35mm，用纸、纸板及纺织物以外任何材料制成，电影胶片除外	40	0	0	0	0	0	0	0	0	0	0		0		0	0	20	8			
37029600	未曝光非彩色胶卷，宽度≤35mm，长度≤30m，用纸、纸板及纺织物以外任何材料制成	20												0			0	10	4			
37029700	未曝光的非彩色胶卷， 宽度≤35mm，长度＞30m，用纸、纸板及纺织物以外任何材料制成	18												0.9元/平方米	9元/平方米		0	9	3.6			
37029800	未曝光的非彩色胶卷，宽度＞35mm，用纸、纸板及纺织物以外任何材料制成	18	0		0		0	0	0	0	0	0		0	8元/平方米	0	0	9	3.6			
37031010	成卷未曝光的感光纸及纸板，宽度＞610mm	18												1.8			0	9	3.6			
37031090	成卷未曝光的感光布，宽度＞610mm	18												1.8			0	9	3.6			
37032010	未曝光的彩色摄影用感光纸及纸板，非成卷或宽度≤610mm	35	20	20	20	20	20	20	20	20	20	20		0			0		7	0		
37032090	未曝光的彩色摄影用感光布，非成卷或宽度≤610mm	18												0			0	9	3.6	0		
37039010	未曝光的非彩色摄影用感光纸及纸板，非成卷或宽度≤610mm	35	20	20	20	20	20	20	20	20	20	20		3.5			0		7			
37039090	未曝光的非彩色摄影用感光布，非成卷或宽度≤610mm	18												1.8			0	9	3.6			
37040010	已曝光未冲洗的电影胶片	6.5	0	0	0	0	0	0	0	0	0	0		0	5		0	0	0			
37040090	已曝光未冲洗的摄影硬片、软片、纸、纸板及纺织物，电影胶片除外	18	0	0	0	0	0	0	0	0	0	0		0	14.4	0	0	9	3.6			
37051000	已曝光已冲洗供复制胶版用摄影硬片及软片	18	0	0	0	0	0	0	0	0	0	0		1.8	14.4	0	0	9	3.6			
37059029	已曝光已冲洗的缩微胶片，书籍、报刊用除外	4	0	0	0	0	0	0	0	0	0	0		0	0		0	0	0			
37059090	已曝光已冲洗的其他摄影硬片及软片	18	0	0	0	0	0	0	0	0	0	0		0	14.4	0	0	9	3.6			
37061090	已曝光已冲洗的电影胶片， 宽度≥35mm，不论是否配有声道或仅有声道，教学专用除外	5	0	0	0	0	0	0	0	0	0	0		0.5	0		0	0	0	0		
37069090	已曝光已冲洗的电影胶片， 宽度＜35mm，不论是否配有声道或仅有声道，教学专用除外	4	0	0	0	0	0	0	0	0	0	0		0	0		0	0	0	0		
37071000	摄影用感光乳液	8	0	0	0	0	0	0	0	0	0	0		0	5		0	0	0		0	
37079010	冲洗胶卷及相片用化学制剂或摄影用未混合品（定量包装或零售包装可立即使用的）	16	0	0	0	0	0	0	0	0	0	0		1.6	12.8	0	0	8	3.2	0		

税则号列	商品名称（简称）	最惠国	东盟										亚太	智利	巴基斯坦	新加坡	新西兰	秘鲁	哥斯达黎加	香港	澳门	台湾
			文	柬	印	老	马	缅	菲	新	泰	越										
37079020	复印机用化学制剂或摄影用未混合品（定量包装或零售包装可立即使用的）	10	0	0	0	0	0	0	0	0	0	0		1	5	0	0	5	0	0	0	
37079090	其他摄影用化学制剂或摄影用未混合品（定量包装或零售包装可立即使用的）	8	0	0	0	0	0	0	0	0	0	0		0.8	5		0	0	0	0	0	
38011000	人造石墨	6.5	0	0	0	0	0	0	0	0	0	0		0	5		0	0	0	0		
38012000	胶态或半胶态石墨	6.5	0	0	0	0	0	0	0	0	0	0		0	5		0	0	0			
38013000	电极用碳糊及炉衬用的类似糊	6.5	0	0	0	0	0	0	0	0	0	0		0	5		0	0	0			
38019010	表面处理的球化石墨	6.5	0	0	0	0	0	0	0	0	0	0		0	5		0	0	0			
38019090	其他石墨	6.5	0	0	0	0	0	0	0	0	0	0		0	5		0	0	0			
38021010	木质活性碳	6.5	0	0	0	0	0	0	0	0	0	0	5.5	0	5		0	0	0			
38021090	其他活性碳	6.5	0	0	0	0	0	0	0	0	0	0	5.5	0	5		0	0	0			
38029000	活性天然矿产品；动物炭黑（包括废动物炭黑）	10	0	0	0	0	0	0	0	0	0	0		1	5	0	0	5	0			
38030000	妥尔油，不论是否精炼	6.5	0	0	0	0	0	0	0	0	0	0		0	5		0	0	0			
38040000	木浆残余碱液，不论是否浓缩、脱糖或经化学处理，包括木素磺酸盐，但不包括税目38.03的妥尔油	6.5	0	0	0	0	0	0	0	0	0	0		0	5		0	0	0			
38051000	脂松节油、木松节油和硫酸松节油	6.5	0	0	0	0	0	0	0	0	0	0		0	5		0	0	0			
38059010	以α萜品醇为基本成分的松油，用蒸馏或其他方法从针叶木制得	6.5	0	0	0	0	0	0	0	0	0	0		0.7	5		0	0	0			
38059090	粗制二聚戊烯；亚硫酸盐松节油及其他粗制对异丙基苯甲烷；其他萜烯油，用蒸馏或其他方法从针叶木制得	6.5	0	0	0	0	0	0	0	0	0	0		0	5		0	0	0			
38061010	松香	10	0	0	0	0	0	0	0	0	0	0		0	5	0	0	0	0		0	
38061020	树脂酸	10	0	0	0	0	0	0	0	0	0	0		0	5		0	0	0		0	
38062010	松香盐及树脂酸盐	6.5	0	0	0	0	0	0	0	0	0	0		0	5		0	0	0		0	
38062090	松香或树脂酸衍生物的盐，但松香加合物的盐除外	6.5	0	0	0	0	0	0	0	0	0	0		0	5		0	0	0		0	
38063000	酯胶	6.5	0	0	0	0	0	0	0	0	0	0		0	5		0	0	0		0	
38069000	其他松香和树脂酸的衍生物；松香精及松香油；再熔胶	6.5	0	0	0	0	0	0	0	0	0	0		0	5		0	0	0		0	
38070000	木焦油；精制木焦油；木杂酚油；粗木精；植物沥青；以松香、树脂酸或植物沥青为基本成分的啤酒桶沥青及类似制品	6.5	0	0	0	0	0	0	0	0	0	0		0	5		0	0	0			
38085010	零售包装的本章注释一规定货物	9	0	0	0	0	0	0	0	0	0	0		0.9	5		0	0	0	0		
38085090	非零售包装的本章注释一规定货物	5	0	0	0	0	0	0	0	0	0	0		0.5			0	0	0	0		
38089111	蚊香	10	0	0	0	0	0	0	0	0	0	0	0	1	0		0	0	0		0	
38089112	生物杀虫剂	10	0	0	0	0	0	0	0	0	0	0	7	1	5		0	0	0	0	0	
38089119	零售包装杀虫剂	10	0	0	0	0	0	0	0	0	0	0	7	1	5		0	0	0	0	0	
38089190	非零售包装杀虫剂	6	0	0	0	0	0	0	0	0	0	0	4.2	0.6	0		0	0	0	0	0	
38089210	零售包装的杀菌剂	9	0	0	0	0	0	0	0	0	0	0		0.9	5		0	0	0	0		
38089290	非零售包装的杀菌剂	6	0	0	0	0	0	0	0	0	0	0		0.6	5		0	0	0			
38089311	零售包装的除草剂	9	0	0	0	0	0	0	0	0	0	0		0.9	5		0	0	0			
38089319	非零售包装的除草剂	5	0	0	0	0	0	0	0	0	0	0	4.5	0.5	0		0	0	0			
38089391	零售包装抗萌剂及植物生长调节剂	9	0	0	0	0	0	0	0	0	0	0	8.3	0.9	5		0	0	0			
38089399	非零售抗萌剂及植物生长调节剂	6	0	0	0	0	0	0	0	0	0	0	5.5	0.6	5		0	0	0			
38089400	消毒剂	9	0	0	0	0	0	0	0	0	0	0		0.9	5		0	0	0	0		
38089910	零售包装的杀鼠剂及其他类似产品	9	0	0	0	0	0	0	0	0	0	0		0.9	5		0	0	0	0		
38089990	非零售包装的杀鼠剂及其他类似产品	9	0	0	0	0	0	0	0	0	0	0		0.9	5		0	0	0		0	
38091000	以淀粉物质为基本成分，纺织、造纸、制革及类似工业用的其他税号未列名的整理剂、染料加速着色或固色助剂及其他产品和制剂	10	0	0	0	0	0	0	0	0	0	0		0	0	0	0	0				
38099100	纺织工业及类似工业用其他税号未列名整理剂、染料加速着色剂或固色助剂及其他产品和制剂	6.5	0	0	0	0	0	0	0	0	0	0	6	0	0		0	0	0	0		
38099200	造纸工业用其他税号未列名整理剂、染料加速着色剂或固色助剂及其他产品和制剂	6.5	0	0	0	0	0	0	0	0	0	0		0.7	0		0	0	0	0		
38099300	制革工业用其他税号未列名整理剂、	6.5	0	0	0	0	0	0	0	0	0	0		0.7	0		0	0	0	0		

税则号列	商品名称（简称）	最惠国	东盟										亚太	智利	巴基斯坦	新加坡	新西兰	秘鲁	哥斯达黎加	香港	澳门	台湾
			文	柬	印	老	马	缅	菲	新	泰	越										
	染料加速着色剂或固色助剂及其他产品和制剂																					
38101000	金属表面酸洗剂；金属及其他材料制成的焊粉或焊膏	6.5	0	0	0	0	0	0	0	0	0	0	6	0.7	5		0	0	0	0	0	
38109000	焊接用的焊剂及其他辅助剂；作焊条芯子或焊条涂料用的制品	6.5	0	0	0	0	0	0	0	0	0	0		0	5		0	0	0			
38111100	以铅化合物为基本成分的抗震剂，用于矿物油或与矿物油同样用途的其他液体	6.5	0	0	0	0	0	0	0	0	0	0		0	5		0	0	0			
38111900	抗震剂（以铅化合物为基本成分的除外），用于矿物油或与矿物油同样用途的其他液体	6.5	0	0	0	0	0	0	0	0	0	0		0	5		0	0	0			
38112100	含有石油或从沥青矿物提取的油类的润滑油添加剂	6.5	0	0	0	0	0	0	0	0	0	0		0.7	5		0	0	0			
38112900	不含石油或从沥青矿物提取的油类的润滑油添加剂	6.5	0	0	0	0	0	0	0	0	0	0	5.5	0	5		0	0	0		0	
38119000	抗氧剂、防胶剂、粘度改良剂、防腐剂配制添加剂，用于矿物油或与矿物油同样用途的其他液体	6.5	0	0	0	0	0	0	0	0	0	0		0	5		0	0	0	0	0	
38121000	配制的橡胶促进剂	6	0	0	0	0	0	0	0	0	0	0		0	5		0	0	0			
38122000	橡胶或塑料用复合增塑剂	6.5	0	0	0	0	0	0	0	0	0	0		0.7	5		0	0	0			
38123010	橡胶的防老剂	6	0	0	0	0	0	0	0	0	0	0		0.6	5		0	0	0	0		
38123090	其他橡胶、塑料用抗氧剂及其他稳定剂	6.5	0	0	0	0	0	0	0	0	0	0	4.6	0.7	0		0	0	0	0		
38130010	灭火器的装配药	6.5	0	0	0	0	0	0	0	0	0	0		0	5		0	0	0			
38130020	已装药的灭火弹	10	0	0	0	0	0	0	0	0	0	0		0	5		0	0	0			
38140000	其他税号未列名的有机复合溶剂及稀释剂；除漆剂	10	0	0	0	0	0	0	0	0	0	0	9	1	5	0	0	5	0	0	0	
38151100	以镍及其化合物为活性物的载体催化剂	6.5	0	0	0	0	0	0	0	0	0	0		0.7	5		0	0	0			
38151200	以贵金属及其化合物为活性物的载体催化剂	6.5	0	0	0	0	0	0	0	0	0	0		0	5		0	0	0	0		
38151900	其他载体催化剂	6.5	0	0	0	0	0	0	0	0	0	0	4.6	0.7	0		0	0	0			
38159000	其他未列名的反应引发剂、促进剂	6.5	0	0	0	0	0	0	0	0	0	0	6	0.7	5		0	0	0		0	
38160000	耐火水泥、灰泥、混凝土及类似耐火材料，但税目 38.01 的产品除外	6.5	0	0	0	0	0	0	0	0	0	0		0.7	5		0	0	0			
38170000	混合烷基苯及混合烷基萘，但税目 27.07 及 29.02 的产品除外	6.5	0	0	0	0	0	0	0	0	0	0		0	5		0	0	0			0
38190000	闸用液压油及其他液压传动用液体，不含石油或从沥青矿物提取的油类，或者按重量计石油或从沥青矿物提取的油类含量低于 70%	6.5	0	0	0	0	0	0	0	0	0	0		0	5		0	0	0		0	
38200000	防冻剂及解冻剂	10	0	0	0	0	0	0	0	0	0	0		0	5	0	0	0	0		0	
38210000	制成的微生物培养基	3	0	0	0	0	0	0	0	0	0	0		0	0		0	0	0	0		
38220010	附于衬背上的诊断或实验用试剂，但税目 32.02, 32.06 的货品除外	4	0	0	0	0	0	0	0	0	0	0		0.4	0		0	0	0	0		
38220090	无论是否附于衬背上的诊断或实验用配制试剂，但税目 32.02, 32.06 的货品除外	5	0	0	0	0	0	0	0	0	0	0		0.5	0		0	0	0	0		
38231100	硬脂酸	16	0	0	0	0	0	0	0	0	0	0		1.6	12.8		0	8	3.2			
38231200	油酸	16	0	0	0	0	0	0	0	0	0	0		0	12.8	0	0	8	3.2	0		
38231300	妥尔油脂肪酸	16	0	0	0	0	0	0	0	0	0	0		0	12.8	0	0	8	3.2			
38231900	其他工业用单羧脂肪酸；精炼所得的酸性油	16	0	0	0	0	0	0	0	0	0	0		0	12.8	0	0	8	3.2	0	0	
38237000	工业用脂肪醇	13	0	0	0	0	0	0	0	0	0	0		0	6.5	0	0	0	2.6			
38241000	铸模及铸芯用粘合剂	6.5	0	0	0	0	0	0	0	0	0	0		0	5		0	0	0			
38243000	自身混合或与金属粘合剂混合的未烧结金属碳化物	6.5	0	0	0	0	0	0	0	0	0	0		0	5		0	0	0			
38244010	高效减水剂	6.5	0	0	0	0	0	0	0	0	0	0		0.7	5		0	0	0	0		
38244090	其他水泥、灰泥及混凝土用添加剂	6.5	0	0	0	0	0	0	0	0	0	0		0.7	5		0	0	0	0		
38245000	非耐火的灰泥及混凝土	6.5	0	0	0	0	0	0	0	0	0	0		0.7	5		0	0	0	0	0	
38246000	子目号 2905.44 以外的山梨醇	14	0	0	0	0	0	0	0	0	0	0		0	11.2	0	0	0	2.8			
38247100	含全氯氟烃的，不论是否含氢氯氟烃、全氟烃或氢氟烃的含有甲烷、乙烷、	6.5	0	0	0	0	0	0	0	0	0	0		0	5		0	0	0	0	0	

税则号列	商品名称（简称）	最惠国	东盟										亚太	智利	巴基斯坦	新加坡	新西兰	秘鲁	哥斯达黎加	香港	澳门	台湾
			文	柬	印	老	马	缅	菲	新	泰	越										
	丙烷卤化衍生物混合物																					
38247200	含溴氯二氟甲烷、溴三氟甲烷或二溴四氟乙烷的含有甲烷、乙烷、丙烷卤化衍生物混合物	6.5	0	0	0	0	0	0	0	0	0	0		0	5		0	0	0			
38247300	含氢溴氟烃的含有甲烷、乙烷、丙烷卤化衍生物混合物	6.5	0	0	0	0	0	0	0	0	0	0		0	5		0	0	0	0	0	
38247400	含氢氯氟烃的，不论是否含全氟烃或氢氟烃，但不含全氯氟烃的含有甲烷、乙烷、丙烷卤化衍生物混合物	6.5	0	0	0	0	0	0	0	0	0	0		0	5		0	0	0	0	0	
38247500	含四氯化碳的含有甲烷、乙烷、丙烷卤化衍生物混合物	6.5	0	0	0	0	0	0	0	0	0	0	6	0.7	5		0	0	0	0	0	
38247600	含 1，1，1－三氯乙烷（甲基氯仿）的含有甲烷、乙烷、丙烷卤化衍生物混合物	6.5	0	0	0	0	0	0	0	0	0	0	6	0.7	5		0	0	0	0	0	
38247700	含溴化甲烷（甲基溴）或溴氯甲烷的含有甲烷、乙烷、丙烷卤化衍生物混合物	6.5	0	0	0	0	0	0	0	0	0	0		0	5		0	0	0	0	0	
38247800	含全氟烃或氢氟烃的，但不含全氯氟烃或氢氯氟烃的含有甲烷、乙烷、丙烷卤化衍生物混合物	6.5	0	0	0	0	0	0	0	0	0	0	6	0.7	5		0	0	0	0	0	
38247900	其他含有甲烷、乙烷、丙烷卤化衍生物的混合物	6.5	0	0	0	0	0	0	0	0	0	0		0	5		0	0	0	0	0	
38248100	含环氧乙烷的混合物及制品	6.5	0	0	0	0	0	0	0	0	0	0	6	0.7	5		0	0	0	0	0	
38248200	含多氯联苯、多氯三联苯或多溴联苯的混合物及制品	6.5	0	0	0	0	0	0	0	0	0	0	6	0.7	5		0	0	0	0	0	
38248300	含三（2，3－二溴丙基）磷酸酯的混合物及制品	6.5	0	0	0	0	0	0	0	0	0	0	6	0.7	5		0	0	0	0	0	
38249010	杂醇油	6.5	0	0	0	0	0	0	0	0	0	0	5.5	0.7	5		0	0	0			
38249020	除墨剂、蜡纸改正液及类似品	9	0	0	0	0	0	0	0	0	0	0	8.3	0.9	5	0	0	0	0			
38249030	增炭剂	6.5	0	0	0	0	0	0	0	0	0	0		0.7	5		0	0	0			
38249091	含滑石 50%以上的混合物	6.5	0	0	0	0	0	0	0	0	0	0	6	0	5		0	0	0	0	0	
38249092	按重量计含氧化镁 70%以上的混合物	6.5	0	0	0	0	0	0	0	0	0	0	6	0	5		0	0	0	0	0	
38249093	表层包覆钴化合物的氢氧化镍（掺杂炭）	6.5	0	0	0	0	0	0	0	0	0	0	6	0	5		0	0	0	0	0	
38249099	其他税目未列名的化学工业及其相关工业的化学产品及配制品	6.5	0	0	0	0	0	0	0	0	0	0	6	0	5		0	0	0	0	0	
38251000	城市垃圾	6.5	0	0	0	0	0	0	0	0	0	0		0	5		0	0	0			
38252000	下水道淤泥	6.5	0	0	0	0	0	0	0	0	0	0		0	5		0	0	0			
38253000	医疗废物	6.5	0	0	0	0	0	0	0	0	0	0		0	5		0	0	0			
38254100	含卤化物的废有机溶剂	6.5	0	0	0	0	0	0	0	0	0	0		0	5		0	0	0			
38254900	其他废有机溶剂	6.5	0	0	0	0	0	0	0	0	0	0		0	5		0	0	0			
38255000	废的金属酸洗液、液压油、制动油及防冻液	6.5	0	0	0	0	0	0	0	0	0	0		0	5	0	0	0	0			
38256100	主要含有机成分的化工及相关工业废物	6.5	0	0	0	0	0	0	0	0	0	0		0.7	5		0	0	0			
38256900	其他税目未列名的化工及相关工业废物	6.5	0	0	0	0	0	0	0	0	0	0		0	5		0	0	0			
38259000	其他税目未列名的化学工业及相关工业的副产品	6.5	0	0	0	0	0	0	0	0	0	0		0	5		0	0	0	0		
38260000	生物柴油及其混合物，不含或含有按重量计低于 70%的石油或从沥青矿物提取的油类	6.5	0	0	0	0	0	0	0	0	0	0	6	0	5		0	0	0	0	0	
39011000	初级形状比重＜0.94 的聚乙烯	6.5											6	0.7	6		0		0	0	0	
39012000	初级形状比重⩾0.94 的聚乙烯	6.5											6	0.7	6		0		0	0	0	
39013000	初级形状乙烯-乙酸乙烯酯共聚物	6.5	0	0	0	0	0	0	0	0	0	0	6	0.7	5		0	0	0	0		
39019010	初级形状的乙烯丙烯共聚物（乙丙橡胶，乙烯单体单元的含量大于丙烯单体单元）	6.5	0	0	0	0	0	0	0	0	0	0		0	5	0	0	0	0			
39019020	线型低密度聚乙烯	6.5	0	0	0	0	0	0	0	0	0	0		0	5	0	0		0			
39019090	其他初级形状的乙烯聚合物	6.5	0	0	0	0	0	0	0	0	0	0	6.3	0	5	0	0	0	0	0	0	
39021000	初级形状的聚丙烯	6.5	0	0	0	0	0	0	0	0	0	0		0.7	5	0	0		0	0	0	
39022000	初级形状的聚异丁烯	6.5	0	0	0	0	0	0	0	0	0	0		0	5		0		0			
39023010	初级形状的乙烯丙烯共聚物（乙丙橡胶丙烯单体单元的含量大于乙烯单体单元））	6.5	0	0	0	0	0	0	0	0	0	0	6	0.7	5	0	0	0	0	0		0

税则号列	商品名称（简称）	最惠国	东盟										亚太	智利	巴基斯坦	新加坡	新西兰	秘鲁	哥斯达黎加	香港	澳门	台湾
			文	柬	印	老	马	缅	菲	新	泰	越										
39023090	初级形状的其他丙烯共聚物	6.5	0	0	0	0	0	0	0	0	0	0	6	0.7	5	0	0	0	0	0		
39029000	其他初级形状的烯烃聚合物	6.5	0	0	0	0	0	0	0	0	0	0		0	5	0	0	0	0			0
39031100	初级形状的可发性聚苯乙烯	6.5	0	0	0	0	0	0	0	0	0	0	6	0.7	5	0	0	0	0			
39031910	初级形状的改性非可发性聚苯乙烯	6.5	0	0	0	0	0	0	0	0	0	0	6	0	5	0	0	0	0	0		
39031990	初级形状的其他聚苯乙烯	6.5	0	0	0	0	0	0	0	0	0	0	6	0	5	0	0	0	0	0		
39032000	初级形状苯乙烯-丙烯腈共聚物	12	0	0	0	0	0	0	0	0	0	0		0	6	0	0	0	2.4			0
39033010	初级形状的改性丙烯腈-丁二烯-苯乙烯共聚物	6.5	0	0	0	0	0	0	0	0	0	0	6	0	5	0	0	0	0	0	0	
39033090	其它丙烯腈-丁二烯-苯乙烯共聚物	6.5	0	0	0	0	0	0	0	0	0	0	6	0	5	0	0	0	0	0	0	
39039000	初级形状的其他苯乙烯聚合物	6.5	0	0	0	0	0	0	0	0	0	0	6	0.7	5	0	0	0	0	0		0
39041010	聚氯乙烯糊树脂	6.5	0	0	0	0	0	0	0	0	0	0	6	0.7	6	0	0	0	0			
39041090	其他初级形状的纯聚氯乙烯	6.5	0	0	0	0	0	0	0	0	0	0	6	0.7	6	0	0	0	0			
39042100	初级形状未塑化的聚氯乙烯	6.5	0	0	0	0	0	0	0	0	0	0		0	5	0	0	0	0	0		
39042200	初级形状已塑化的聚氯乙烯	6.5	0	0	0	0	0	0	0	0	0	0		0.7		0	0	0	0	0		
39043000	氯乙烯-乙酸乙烯酯共聚物	9	0	0	0	0	0	0	0	0	0	0	8.6	0	5		0	0	0			
39044000	初级形状的其他氯乙烯共聚物	12	0	0	0	0	0	0	0	0	0	0	11.4	0	6	0	0	6	2.4			
39045000	初级形状的偏二氯乙烯聚合物	6.5	0	0	0	0	0	0	0	0	0	0		0	5		0	0	0			
39046100	初级形状的聚四氟乙烯	10	0	0	0	0	0	0	0	0	0	0		0	5	0	0	0	0			
39046900	初级形状的其他氟聚合物	6.5	0	0	0	0	0	0	0	0	0	0		0	5		0	0	0			
39049000	初级形状的其他卤化烯烃聚合物	10	0	0	0	0	0	0	0	0	0	0		0	5		0	0	0			
39051200	聚乙酸乙烯酯的水分散体	10	0	0	0	0	0	0	0	0	0	0		1		0	0	5	0			
39051900	其他初级形状聚乙酸乙烯酯	10	0	0	0	0	0	0	0	0	0	0		0	5		0	0	0			
39052100	乙酸乙烯酯共聚物的水分散体	10	0	0	0	0	0	0	0	0	0	0		0	5	0	0	0	0			0
39052900	其他初级形状的乙酸乙烯酯共聚物	10	0	0	0	0	0	0	0	0	0	0		0	5	0	0	0	0			
39053000	初级形状的聚乙烯醇（不论是否含有未水解的乙酸酯基）	14	0	0	0	0	0	0	0	0	0	0		0	11.2	0	0	0	2.8			0
39059100	其他乙烯酯或乙烯基的共聚物	10	0	0	0	0	0	0	0	0	0	0		0	5		0	0	0			
39059900	其他乙烯酯或乙烯基的聚合物	10	0	0	0	0	0	0	0	0	0	0		1			0	5	0	0		
39061000	初级形状的聚甲基丙烯酸甲酯	6.5	0	0	0	0	0	0	0	0	0	0	6	0	5		0	0	0			0
39069010	聚丙稀酰胺	6.5	0	0	0	0	0	0	0	0	0	0	6	0.7	5		0	0	0	0		0
39069090	其他初级形状的丙烯酸聚合物	6.5	0	0	0	0	0	0	0	0	0	0	6	0.7	5		0	0	0	0		0
39071010	初级形状的聚甲醛	6.5	0	0	0	0	0	0	0	0	0	0	6	0	5	0	0	0	0	0		0
39071090	其他初级形状的聚缩醛	6.5	0	0	0	0	0	0	0	0	0	0	6	0	5	0	0	0	0	0		
39072010	聚四亚甲基醚二醇	6.5	0	0	0	0	0	0	0	0	0	0	6	0	5	0	0	0	0			0
39072090	其他初级形状的聚醚	6.5	0	0	0	0	0	0	0	0	0	0	6	0	5	0	0	0	0			
39073000	初级形状的环氧树脂	6.5	0	0	0	0	0	0	0	0	0	0	6	0.7	5	0	0	0	0	0		0
39074000	初级形状的聚碳酸酯	6.5	0	0	0	0	0	0	0	0	0	0	6.1	0	5		0	0	0	0		0
39075000	初级形状的醇酸树脂	10	0	0	0	0	0	0	0	0	0	0	9.5	1	5	0	0	5	0			0
39076011	高粘度聚对苯二甲酸乙二酯切片	6.5												0			0	0	0			
39076019	其他聚对苯二甲酸乙二酯切片	6.5												0			0	0	0		0	
39076090	其他初级形状聚对苯二甲酸乙二酯	6.5	0	0	0	0	0	0	0	0	0	0		0			0	0	0		0	
39077000	聚乳酸	6.5	0	0	0	0	0	0	0	0	0	0	6.2	0.7	5		0	0	0	0	0	
39079100	初级形状的不饱和聚酯	6.5	0	0	0	0	0	0	0	0	0	0		0.7	5	0	0	0	0			0
39079910	聚对苯二甲酸丁二酯	6.5	0	0	0	0	0	0	0	0	0	0	6.2	0.7	5		0	0	0	0	0	
39079991	聚对苯二甲酸-己二醇-丁二醇酯	6.5	0	0	0	0	0	0	0	0	0	0	6.2	0.7	5		0	0	0	0	0	0
39079999	其他聚酯	6.5	0	0	0	0	0	0	0	0	0	0	6.2	0.7	5		0	0	0	0	0	0
39081011	聚酰胺-6,6 切片	6.5	0	0	0	0	0	0	0	0	0	0		0	5	0	0	0	0	0		
39081012	聚酰胺-6 切片	6.5	0	0	0	0	0	0	0	0	0	0		0	5	0	0	0	0	0		
39081019	初级形状聚酰胺切片	6.5	0	0	0	0	0	0	0	0	0	0		0	5	0	0	0	0	0		
39081090	其他初级形状的聚酰胺	6.5	0	0	0	0	0	0	0	0	0	0		0	5		0	0	0	0		
39089000	初级形状的其他聚酰胺	10	0	0	0	0	0	0	0	0	0	0		0	5	0	0	0	0			
39091000	初级形状的尿素树脂及硫尿树脂	6.5	0	0	0	0	0	0	0	0	0	0	6.1	0.7	5		0	0	0			0
39092000	初级形状的蜜胺树脂	6.5	0	0	0	0	0	0	0	0	0	0	6.1	0	5		0	0	0			0
39093010	聚合 MDI	6.5	0	0	0	0	0	0	0	0	0	0	6	0.7	5	0	0	0	0	0		
39093090	其他初级形状的其他氨基树脂	6.5	0	0	0	0	0	0	0	0	0	0		0.7	5	0	0	0	0			0
39094000	初级形状的酚醛树脂	6.5	0	0	0	0	0	0	0	0	0	0	6.1	0.7	5		0	0	0			0
39095000	初级形状的聚亚氨酯	6.5	0	0	0	0	0	0	0	0	0	0	6	0.7	5	0	0	0	0	0	0	0
39100000	初级形状的聚硅氧烷	6.5	0	0	0	0	0	0	0	0	0	0	6.1	0	5		0	0	0	0		0
39111000	初级形状的石油树脂、苯并呋喃-茚树脂、多萜树脂	6.5	0	0	0	0	0	0	0	0	0	0	6.1	0	5		0	0	0			0

税则号列	商品名称（简称）	最惠国	东盟										亚太	智利	巴基斯坦	新加坡	新西兰	秘鲁	哥斯达黎加	香港	澳门	台湾
			文	柬	印	老	马	缅	菲	新	泰	越										
39119000	其他初级形状的多硫化物、聚砜及39章注释3所规定的其他税号未列名新产品	6.5	0	0	0	0	0	0	0	0	0	0		0	5		0	0	0			
39121100	初级形状的未塑化醋酸纤维素	6.5	0	0	0	0	0	0	0	0	0	0		0	5		0	0	0			
39121200	初级形状的已塑化醋酸纤维素	6.5	0	0	0	0	0	0	0	0	0	0		0	5		0	0	0			
39122000	初级形状的硝酸纤维素	6.5	0	0	0	0	0	0	0	0	0	0		0	5		0	0	0			
39123100	初级形状的羧甲基纤维素及其盐	6.5	0	0	0	0	0	0	0	0	0	0		0	5		0	0	0			
39123900	初级形状的其他纤维素醚	6.5	0	0	0	0	0	0	0	0	0	0		0.7	5		0	0	0			
39129000	初级形状的其他未列名的纤维素(包括化学衍生物)	6.5	0	0	0	0	0	0	0	0	0	0		0	5		0	0	0	0		
39131000	初级形状的藻酸及盐和酯	10	0	0	0	0	0	0	0	0	0	0		1	5	0	0		0			
39139000	初级形状的其他未列名天然聚合物（包括改性天然聚合物）	6.5	0	0	0	0	0	0	0	0	0	0		0	5		0	0	0			
39140000	初级形状的离子交换剂	6.5	0	0	0	0	0	0	0	0	0	0		0	5		0	0	0			
39151000	乙烯聚合物的废碎料及下脚料	6.5	0	0	0	0	0	0	0	0	0	0		0.7	5	0	0	0	0	0	0	
39152000	苯乙烯聚合物的废碎料及下脚料	6.5	0	0	0	0	0	0	0	0	0	0		0.7	5	0	0	0	0	0	0	
39153000	氯乙烯聚合物的废碎料及下脚料	6.5	0	0	0	0	0	0	0	0	0	0		0	5	0	0	0	0	0	0	
39159010	聚对苯二甲酸乙二酯的塑料废碎料及下脚料	6.5	0	0	0	0	0	0	0	0	0	0		0.7	5	0	0	0	1.3	0	0	
39159090	其他塑料的废碎料及下脚料	6.5	0	0	0	0	0	0	0	0	0	0		0.7	5	0	0	0	1.3	0	0	
39161000	乙烯聚合物制单丝、条、杆及型材	10	0	0	0	0	0	0	0	0	0	0		1	5	0	0	5	0			
39162010	聚氯乙烯异型材	10	0	0	0	0	0	0	0	0	0	0	7	1	5		0	0	0			
39162090	氯乙烯聚合物制单丝、条、杆及型材	10	0	0	0	0	0	0	0	0	0	0	7	1	5		0	0	0			
39169010	聚酰胺制的单丝、条、杆及型材	10	0	0	0	0	0	0	0	0	0	0		0	5	0	0	0	0	0		
39169090	其他塑料制单丝、条、杆及型材	10	0	0	0	0	0	0	0	0	0	0		0	5	0	0	0	0			
39171000	硬化蛋白或纤维素材料制人造肠衣	10	0	0	0	0	0	0	0	0	0	0		1	5		0	0	0			
39172100	乙烯聚合物制的硬管	10	0	0	0	0	0	0	0	0	0	0		1	5	0	0	5	0			
39172200	丙烯聚合物制的硬管	10	0	0	0	0	0	0	0	0	0	0		0	5		0	0	0			
39172300	氯乙烯聚合物制的硬管	10	0	0	0	0	0	0	0	0	0	0		1	5	0	0	5	0	0		
39172900	其他塑料制的硬管	10	0	0	0	0	0	0	0	0	0	0		0	5	0	0	0	0			
39173100	塑料制的软管	10	0	0	0	0	0	0	0	0	0	0	7	1	5	0	0	0	0	0		
39173200	其他未装有附件的塑料制管子	6.5	0	0	0	0	0	0	0	0	0	0	4.6	0.7	0		0	0	0			
39173300	其他装有附件的塑料管子	6.5	0	0	0	0	0	0	0	0	0	0	4.6	0.7	0		0	0	0			
39173900	塑料制的其他管子	6.5	0	0	0	0	0	0	0	0	0	0	4.5	0.7	4.5	0	0	0	0			
39174000	塑料制的管子附件	10	0	0	0	0	0	0	0	0	0	0	7	1	5	0	0	5	0			
39181010	氯乙烯聚合物制糊墙品	10	0	0	0	0	0	0	0	0	0	0		1	5		0	5	0			
39181090	氯乙烯聚合物制的铺地制品	10	0	0	0	0	0	0	0	0	0	0		1	5		0	5	0			
39189010	其他塑料制的糊墙品	10	0	0	0	0	0	0	0	0	0	0		0	5		0	0	0	0		
39189090	其他塑料制的铺地制品	10	0	0	0	0	0	0	0	0	0	0		0	5		0	0	0	0		
39191010	丙烯酸树脂为基本成份的成卷胶粘板片条等，宽度≤20cm	6.5	0	0	0	0	0	0	0	0	0	0		0.7	5		0	0	0			
39191091	宽度≤20cm成卷的胶囊型反光膜	6.5	0	0	0	0	0	0	0	0	0	0		0.7	5		0	0	0			
39191099	其他材料制的，宽度≤20cm的其他成卷塑料胶粘板片等	6.5	0	0	0	0	0	0	0	0	0	0		0.7	5		0	0	0			0
39199010	其他胶囊型反光膜	6.5	0	0	0	0	0	0	0	0	0	0	4.6	0.7	0		0	0	0	0		
39199090	其他自粘塑料板、片、膜等材料	6.5	0	0	0	0	0	0	0	0	0	0	4.6	0.7	0		0	0	0	0		0
39201010	乙烯聚合物制电池隔膜	6.5	0	0	0	0	0	0	0	0	0	0	4.6	0.7	0		0	0	0	0		
39201090	其他乙烯聚合物制板、片、带	6.5	0	0	0	0	0	0	0	0	0	0	4.6	0.7	0		0	0	0	0	0	0
39202010	丙烯聚合物制电池隔膜	6.5	0	0	0	0	0	0	0	0	0	0		0.7	5		0	0	0	0		
39202090	其他丙烯聚合物制板、片、带	6.5	0	0	0	0	0	0	0	0	0	0		0.7	5		0	0	0	0	0	0
39203000	非泡沫聚苯乙烯板、片、膜、箔及扁条	6.5	0	0	0	0	0	0	0	0	0	0	4.6	0.7	0		0	0	0	0		0
39204300	按重量计增塑剂含量不小于6%的聚氯乙烯板、片、膜、箔及扁条	6.5	0	0	0	0	0	0	0	0	0	0	4.5	0	4.5	0	0	0	0	0		0
39204900	按重量计增塑剂含量小于6%的聚氯乙烯板、片、膜、箔及扁条	6.5	0	0	0	0	0	0	0	0	0	0	4.5	0.7	4.5		0	0	0	0	0	0
39205100	聚甲基丙烯酸甲酯板片膜箔及扁条	6.5	0	0	0	0	0	0	0	0	0	0	4.6	0	0		0	0	0			0
39205900	其他丙烯酸聚合物板片膜箔及扁条	6.5	0	0	0	0	0	0	0	0	0	0		0	5		0	0	0			
39206100	聚碳酸酯制板、片、膜、箔及扁条	6.5	0	0	0	0	0	0	0	0	0	0	4.6	0.7	0		0	0	0			0
39206200	聚对苯二甲酸乙二酯板片膜箔扁条	6.5	0	0	0	0	0	0	0	0	0	0	4.6	0	0		0	0	0	0	0	0
39206300	不饱和聚酯板、片、膜、箔及扁条	10	0	0	0	0	0	0	0	0	0	0		0	5		0	0	0			
39206900	其他聚酯板、片、膜、箔及扁条	10	0	0	0	0	0	0	0	0	0	0	9	1	5	0	0	5	0			0
39207100	再生纤维素制板、片、膜、箔及扁条	6.5	0	0	0	0	0	0	0	0	0	0		0	5		0	0	0			

税则号列	商品名称（简称）	最惠国	东盟										亚太	智利	巴基斯坦	新加坡	新西兰	秘鲁	哥斯达黎加	香港	澳门	台湾
			文	柬	印	老	马	缅	菲	新	泰	越										
39207300	醋酸纤维素制板、片、膜、箔及扁条	6.5	0	0	0	0	0	0	0	0	0	0		0	5		0	0	0	0		
39207900	纤维素衍生物制板、片、膜箔及扁条	10	0	0	0	0	0	0	0	0	0	0		0	5		0	0	0			
39209100	聚乙烯醇缩丁醛板、片、膜、箔及扁条	6.5	0	0	0	0	0	0	0	0	0	0		0	5		0	0	0			
39209200	聚酰胺板、片、膜、箔及扁条	10	0	0	0	0	0	0	0	0	0	0		0	5	0	0	0	0			
39209300	氨基树脂板、片、膜、箔及扁条	6.5	0	0	0	0	0	0	0	0	0	0		0	5		0	0	0			
39209400	酚醛树脂板、片、膜、箔及扁条	10	0	0	0	0	0	0	0	0	0	0	7	0	5	0	0	0	0			
39209910	聚四氟乙烯制的非泡沫塑料板片	6.5	0	0	0	0	0	0	0	0	0	0		0	5		0	0	0			
39209990	其他塑料制的非泡沫塑料板片	6.5	0	0	0	0	0	0	0	0	0	0		0	5		0	0	0	0		0
39211100	泡沫聚苯乙烯板、片、带、箔及扁条	10	0	0	0	0	0	0	0	0	0	0	9	0	5		0	0	0			
39211210	泡沫聚氯乙烯人造革及合成革	9	0	0	0	0	0	0	0	0	0	0		0.9	5	0	0	0	0	0		0
39211290	泡沫聚氯乙烯板、片、带、箔及扁条	6.5	0	0	0	0	0	0	0	0	0	0		0.7	5		0	0	0	0		
39211310	泡沫聚氨酯制人造革及合成革	9	0	0	0	0	0	0	0	0	0	0	6.3	0.9	5	0	0	0	0	0		0
39211390	泡沫聚氨酯板、片、带、箔及扁条	6.5	0	0	0	0	0	0	0	0	0	0	4.6	0.7	0		0	0	0	0		
39211400	泡沫再生纤维素板、片、膜、箔及扁条	10	0	0	0	0	0	0	0	0	0	0		0	5		0	0	0			
39211910	其他泡沫塑料制人造革及合成革	9	0	0	0	0	0	0	0	0	0	0	6.3	0	5		0	0	0			
39211990	其他泡沫塑料板、片、膜、箔及扁条	6.5	0	0	0	0	0	0	0	0	0	0	4.6	0	0		0	0	0			0
39219020	嵌有玻璃纤维的聚乙烯板、片	6.5	0	0	0	0	0	0	0	0	0	0	4.6	0.7	0		0	0	0	0		
39219030	聚异丁烯为基本成分的附有人造毛毡的板、片、卷材	6.5	0	0	0	0	0	0	0	0	0	0	4.6	0.7	0		0	0	0	0		
39219090	未列名塑料板、片、膜、箔及扁条	6.5	0	0	0	0	0	0	0	0	0	0	4.6	0.7	0		0	0	0	0		0
39221000	塑料浴缸、淋浴盘及盥洗盆	10	0	0	0	0	0	0	0	0	0	0		0	5		0	0	0		0	
39222000	塑料马桶坐圈及盖	10	0	0	0	0	0	0	0	0	0	0		1	5		0	5	0		0	
39229000	塑料便盆、抽水箱等类似卫生洁具	10	0	0	0	0	0	0	0	0	0	0		1	5		0	0	0			
39231000	塑料制盒、箱及类似品	10	0	0	0	0	0	0	0	0	0	0	7	1	5	0	0	5	0	0	0	0
39232100	乙烯聚合物制袋及包	10	0	0	0	0	0	0	0	0	0	0		1	5	0	0	5	0	0	0	
39232900	其他塑料制的袋及包	10	0	0	0	0	0	0	0	0	0	0		1	5	0	0	5	0	0	0	
39233000	塑料制坛、瓶及类似品	6.5	0	0	0	0	0	0	0	0	0	0		0.7	5	0	0		0	0		
39234000	塑料制卷轴、纡子、筒管及类似品	10	0	0	0	0	0	0	0	0	0	0	7	0	5	0	0	0	0			
39235000	塑料制塞子、盖子及类似品	10	0	0	0	0	0	0	0	0	0	0		1	5	0	0	5	0	0		0
39239000	供运输或包装货物用其他塑料制品	10	0	0	0	0	0	0	0	0	0	0	7	1	5	0	0	5	0	0	0	0
39241000	塑料制餐具及厨房用具	10	0	0	0	0	0	0	0	0	0	0		1	5	0	0	5	0	0	0	
39249000	塑料制其他家庭用具及卫生或盥洗用具	10	0	0	0	0	0	0	0	0	0	0		1	5	0	0	5	0	0	0	
39251000	塑料制囤、柜、罐、桶及类似容器	10	0	0	0	0	0	0	0	0	0	0		1	5		0	5	0			
39252000	塑料制门、窗及其框架、门槛	10	0	0	0	0	0	0	0	0	0	0	7	1	5		0	5	0			
39253000	塑料制窗板、百叶窗及类似制品	10	0	0	0	0	0	0	0	0	0	0		0	5		0	0	0			
39259000	其他未列名的建筑用塑料制品	10	0	0	0	0	0	0	0	0	0	0		1	5		0	5	0	0		
39261000	办公室或学校用塑料制品	10	0	0	0	0	0	0	0	0	0	0		1	5	0	0	0	0			
39262011	聚氯乙稀制手套（包括分指手套、连指手套及露指手套）	10	0	0	0	0	0	0	0	0	0	0		1		0	0	0	0	0		
39262019	其他手套（包括分指手套、连指手套及露指手套）	10	0	0	0	0	0	0	0	0	0	0		1		0	0	0	0	0		
39262090	其他塑料制衣服及衣着附件	10	0	0	0	0	0	0	0	0	0	0		1		0	0	0	0	0		
39263000	塑料制家具、车厢及类似品的附件	10	0	0	0	0	0	0	0	0	0	0		1	5	0	0	5	0			
39264000	塑料制小雕塑品及其他装饰品	10	0	0	0	0	0	0	0	0	0	0	8.3	0	5		0	0	0			
39269010	塑料制机器及仪器用零件	10	0	0	0	0	0	0	0	0	0	0	9	1	5	0	0	5	0	0	0	0
39269090	其他塑料制品	10	0	0	0	0	0	0	0	0	0	0	9.2	1	9.2	0	0	5	0	0	0	0
40011000	天然胶乳	20												0			0		4			
40012100	天然橡胶烟胶片	20											17	0	17		0		4			
40012200	技术分类天然橡胶(TSNR)	20												0			0		4			
40012900	其他初级形状的天然橡胶	20											17	0	17		0		4			
40013000	巴拉塔胶、古塔波胶、银胶菊胶、糖胶树胶及类似的天然树胶	20	0	0	0	0	0	0	0	0	0	0		0		0	0	10	4			
40021110	羧基丁苯橡胶胶乳	7.5	0	0	0	0	0	0	0	0	0	0		0	5		0	0	0	0		
40021190	丁苯橡胶胶乳	7.5	0	0	0	0	0	0	0	0	0	0		0	5		0	0	0	0		
40021911	初级形状未经任何加工的丁苯橡胶	7.5	0	0	0	0	0	0	0	0	0	0		0	5		0	0	0	0		
40021912	初级形状的充油丁苯橡胶	7.5	0	0	0	0	0	0	0	0	0	0		0	5		0	0	0	0		
40021913	初级形状的热塑丁苯橡胶	7.5	0	0	0	0	0	0	0	0	0	0		0	5		0	0	0	0		
40021914	初级形状的充油热塑丁苯橡胶	7.5	0	0	0	0	0	0	0	0	0	0		0	5		0	0	0	0		
40021919	初级形状的其他丁苯橡胶及羧基丁苯橡胶	7.5												0			0	0	0	0		
40021990	丁苯橡胶及羧基丁苯橡胶板、片、带	7.5	0	0	0	0	0	0	0	0	0	0	7.1	0	5		0	0	0	0		

税则号列	商品名称（简称）	最惠国	东盟										亚太	智利	巴基斯坦	新加坡	新西兰	秘鲁	哥斯达黎加	香港	澳门	台湾
			文	柬	印	老	马	缅	菲	新	泰	越										
40022010	初级形状的丁二烯橡胶	7.5	0	0	0	0	0	0	0	0	0	0		0	5		0	0	0			
40022090	丁二烯橡胶板、片、带	7.5	0	0	0	0	0	0	0	0	0	0	7	0	5		0	0	0			
40023110	初级形状的异丁烯-异戊二烯橡胶	6	0	0	0	0	0	0	0	0	0	0	5.6	0	5		0	0	0			
40023190	异丁烯-异戊二烯橡胶板、片、带	7.5	0	0	0	0	0	0	0	0	0	0	7.1	0	5		0	0	0			
40023910	初级形状的其他卤代丁基橡胶	7.5	0	0	0	0	0	0	0	0	0	0		0	5		0	0	0			
40023990	卤代丁基橡胶板、片、带	7.5	0	0	0	0	0	0	0	0	0	0	7.1	0	5		0	0	0			
40024100	氯丁二烯橡胶胶乳	7.5	0	0	0	0	0	0	0	0	0	0	7.1	0	5		0	0	0			
40024910	初级形状的氯丁二烯橡胶	7.5	0	0	0	0	0	0	0	0	0	0		0	5		0	0	0			
40024990	氯丁二烯橡胶板、片、带	7.5	0	0	0	0	0	0	0	0	0	0	7.1	0	5		0	0	0			
40025100	丁腈橡胶胶乳	7.5	0	0	0	0	0	0	0	0	0	0	7.1	0	5		0	0	0			
40025910	初级形状的丁腈橡胶	7.5	0	0	0	0	0	0	0	0	0	0		0	5		0	0	0			
40025990	丁腈橡胶板、片、带	7.5	0	0	0	0	0	0	0	0	0	0		0	5		0	0	0			
40026010	初级形状的异戊二烯橡胶	3	0	0	0	0	0	0	0	0	0	0		0	0		0	0	0			
40026090	异戊二烯橡胶板、片、带	5	0	0	0	0	0	0	0	0	0	0	4.5	0	0		0	0	0			
40027010	初级形状的乙丙非共轭二烯橡胶	7.5	0	0	0	0	0	0	0	0	0	0		0	5		0	0	0			
40027090	乙丙非共轭二烯橡胶板、片、带	7.5	0	0	0	0	0	0	0	0	0	0	7.1	0	5		0	0	0			
40028000	天然橡胶与合成橡胶的混合物	7.5	0	0	0	0	0	0	0	0	0	0		0	5		0	0	0			
40029100	其他未列名的合成橡胶胶乳	7.5	0	0	0	0	0	0	0	0	0	0		0	5		0	0	0			
40029911	其他初级形状的合成橡胶	7.5	0	0	0	0	0	0	0	0	0	0		0	5		0	0	0	0		0
40029919	其他合成橡胶板、片、带	7.5	0	0	0	0	0	0	0	0	0	0		0	5		0	0	0	0		
40029990	从油类提取的油膏	4	0	0	0	0	0	0	0	0	0	0		0	0		0	0	0			
40030000	初级形状或板、片、带状再生橡胶	8	0	0	0	0	0	0	0	0	0	0		0	5		0	0	0	0		
40040000	橡胶(硬质橡胶除外)废碎料及下脚料及其粉、粒	8	0	0	0	0	0	0	0	0	0	0	7.6	0	5		0	0	0			
40051000	与碳黑等混合的未硫化复合橡胶	8	0	0	0	0	0	0	0	0	0	0		0	5		0	0	0		0	
40052000	未硫化的复合橡胶溶液及分散体	8	0	0	0	0	0	0	0	0	0	0		0	5		0	0	0			
40059100	其他未硫化的复合橡胶板、片、带	8	0	0	0	0	0	0	0	0	0	0		0	5		0	0	0			
40059900	其他未硫化的初级形状复合橡胶	8	0	0	0	0	0	0	0	0	0	0		0	5		0	0	0	0		
40061000	未硫化轮胎翻新用胎面补料胎条	8	0	0	0	0	0	0	0	0	0	0		0	5		0	0	0			
40069010	未硫化橡胶的杆、管或型材及异型材	8	0	0	0	0	0	0	0	0	0	0		0	5		0	0	0			
40069020	未硫化橡胶制品	14	0	0	0	0	0	0	0	0	0	0		0	11.2	0	0	0	2.8			
40070000	硫化橡胶线及绳	14	0	0	0	0	0	0	0	0	0	0		0	11.2	0	0	0	2.8	0		
40081100	海绵硫化橡胶制的板、片及带	8	0	0	0	0	0	0	0	0	0	0		0	5		0	0	0			
40081900	海绵硫化橡胶制型材、异型材及杆	8	0	0	0	0	0	0	0	0	0	0		0	5		0	0	0			
40082100	非海绵硫化橡胶制板、片及带	8	0	0	0	0	0	0	0	0	0	0		0	5		0	0	0			
40082900	非海绵硫化橡胶型材、异型材及杆	8	0	0	0	0	0	0	0	0	0	0		0	5		0	0	0			
40091100	未加强或未与其他材料合制硫化橡胶管，未装有附件	10.5	0	0	0	0	0	0	0	0	0	0		0	5	0	0	0	2.1			
40091200	未加强或未与其他材料合制硫化橡胶管，装有附件	10	0	0	0	0	0	0	0	0	0	0		0	5		0	0	0			
40092100	用金属加强或只与金属合制的硫化橡胶管，未装有附件	10.5	0	0	0	0	0	0	0	0	0	0		1.1	5	0	0	5.3	2.1			
40092200	用金属加强或只与金属合制的硫化橡胶管，装有附件	10	0	0	0	0	0	0	0	0	0	0		0	5	0	0	0	0			
40093100	用纺织材料加强或只与纺织材料合制硫化橡胶管，未装有附件	10.5	0	0	0	0	0	0	0	0	0	0		1.1	5	0	0	5.3	2.1			
40093200	用纺织材料加强或只与纺织材料合制硫化橡胶管，装有附件	10	0	0	0	0	0	0	0	0	0	0		0	5		0	0	0			
40094100	用其他材料加强或与其他材料合制硫化橡胶管，未装有附件	10.5	0	0	0	0	0	0	0	0	0	0		1.1	5	0	0	5.3	2.1			
40094200	用其他材料加强或与其他材料合制硫化橡胶管，装有附件	10	0	0	0	0	0	0	0	0	0	0		1	5	0	0	5	0			
40101100	金属加强的硫化橡胶输送带及带料	10	0	0	0	0	0	0	0	0	0	0		1	5		0	5	0			
40101200	纺织材料加强的硫化橡胶输送带及带料	10	0	0	0	0	0	0	0	0	0	0		1	5		0	5	0			
40101900	其他硫化橡胶制的输送带及带料	10	0	0	0	0	0	0	0	0	0	0		0	5		0	5	0			
40103100	梯形截面的环形传动带（三角带），V形肋状的，外周长超过60厘米，但不超过180厘米	8	0	0	0	0	0	0	0	0	0	0		0	5		0	0	0			
40103200	梯形截面的环形传动带（三角带），V形肋状的除外，外周长超过60厘米，但不超过180厘米	8	0	0	0	0	0	0	0	0	0	0		0	5		0	0	0			

税则号列	商品名称（简称）	最惠国	东盟										亚太	智利	巴基斯坦	新加坡	新西兰	秘鲁	哥斯达黎加	香港	澳门	台湾
			文	柬	印	老	马	缅	菲	新	泰	越										
40103300	180CM＜外周长≤240CM 的三角带，V形肋状的	8	0	0	0	0	0	0	0	0	0	0		0	5		0	0	0			
40103400	180CM＜外周长≤240CM 的三角带，V形肋状的除外	8	0	0	0	0	0	0	0	0	0	0		0	5		0	0	0			
40103500	60CM＜外周长≤150CM 的环形同步带	10	0	0	0	0	0	0	0	0	0	0		0	5	0	0	0	0			
40103600	150CM＜外周长≤198CM 的环形同步带	10	0	0	0	0	0	0	0	0	0	0		0	5		0	0	0			
40103900	其他硫化橡胶制的传动带及带料	8	0	0	0	0	0	0	0	0	0	0	7.6	0	5		0	0	0			
40111000	机动小客车用新的充气橡胶轮胎	10	0	0	0	0	0	0	0	0	0	0	9.4	1	5	0	0		0			0
40112000	客或货运车用新的充气橡胶轮胎	10	0	0	0	0	0	0	0	0	0	0	9.4	1	5	0	0	5	0			0
40113000	航空器用新的充气橡胶轮胎	1	0	0	0	0	0	0	0	0	0	0		0	0		0	0	0			
40114000	摩托车用新的充气橡胶轮胎	15	0	0	0	0	0	0	0	0	0	0		0	12	0	0	7.5	3			0
40115000	自行车用新的充气橡胶轮胎	20	0	0	0	0	0	0	0	0	0	0		0		0	0	10	4			0
40116100	农业或林业车辆及机器用人字形胎面或类似胎面的新充气橡胶轮胎	17.5	0	0	0	0	0	0	0	0	0	0		0	14	0	0	8.8	3.5			0
40116200	辋圈尺寸不超过 61CM 的建筑或工业搬运车辆及机器用人字形胎面或类似胎面的新充气橡胶轮胎	17.5	0	0	0	0	0	0	0	0	0	0		1.8	14	0	0	8.8	3.5			
40116300	辋圈>61CM 建筑或工业搬运车辆及机器用人字形胎面或类似胎面的新充气橡胶轮胎	17.5	0	0	0	0	0	0	0	0	0	0		1.8	14	0	0	8.8	3.5			
40116900	其他人字形胎面或类似胎面的新充气橡胶轮胎	17.5	0	0	0	0	0	0	0	0	0	0		1.8	14	0	0	8.8	3.5			0
40119200	农业或林业车辆及机器用非人字形胎面或类似胎面的新充气橡胶轮胎	25	0	0	0	0	0	0	0	0	0	0		0		0	0		5			0
40119300	辋圈尺寸不超过 61CM 的建筑或工业搬运车辆及机器用非人字形胎面或类似胎面的新充气橡胶轮胎	25	0	0	0	0	0	0	0	0	0	0		0		0	0		5			
40119400	辋圈>61CM 建筑或工业搬运车辆及机器用非人字形胎面或类似胎面的新充气橡胶轮胎	25	0	0	0	0	0	0	0	0	0	0		2.5		0	0		5			
40119900	其他新的充气橡胶轮胎	25	0	0	0	0	0	0	0	0	0	0		2.5		0	0		5			
40121100	机动小客车（包括旅行小客车及赛车）用翻新轮胎	20	0	0	0	0	0	0	0	0	0	0		0		0	0	10	4			
40121200	机动大客车或货运机动车用翻新轮胎	20	0	0	0	0	0	0	0	0	0	0		0		0	0	10	4	0		
40121300	航空器用翻新轮胎	20	0	0	0	0	0	0	0	0	0	0		0		0	0	10	4	0		
40121900	其他翻新轮胎	20	0	0	0	0	0	0	0	0	0	0		0		0	0	10	4			
40122010	汽车用旧的充气橡胶轮胎	25	0	0	0	0	0	0	0	0	0	0		0		0	0		5	0		
40122090	其他用途旧的充气橡胶轮胎	25	0	0	0	0	0	0	0	0	0	0		0		0	0		5	0		
40129010	航空器用实心或半实心橡胶轮胎	3	0	0	0	0	0	0	0	0	0	0		0	0		0	0	0			
40129020	汽车用实心或半实心橡胶轮胎	22	0	0	0	0	0	0	0	0	0	0		0		0	0	11	4.4			
40129090	其他用实心或半实心橡胶轮胎	22	0	0	0	0	0	0	0	0	0	0		0		0	0	11	4.4			
40131000	汽车用橡胶内胎	15	0	0	0	0	0	0	0	0	0	0	13	0	7.5	0	0	7.5	3			
40132000	自行车用橡胶内胎	15	0	0	0	0	0	0	0	0	0	0		0	12	0	0	7.5	3			
40139010	航空器用橡胶内胎	3	0	0	0	0	0	0	0	0	0	0		0	0		0	0	0			
40139090	其他用橡胶内胎	15	0	0	0	0	0	0	0	0	0	0		0	12	0	0	7.5	3			
40149000	硫化橡胶制其他卫生及医疗用品	17.5	0	0	0	0	0	0	0	0	0	0		0	14	0	0	8.8	3.5		0	
40151100	硫化橡胶制外科用手套	8	0	0	0	0	0	0	0	0	0	0		0	5		0	0	0			
40151900	硫化橡胶制其他手套	18	0	0	0	0	0	0	0	0	0	0		0		0	0	9	3.6			
40159010	医疗用硫化橡胶衣着用品及附件	8	0	0	0	0	0	0	0	0	0	0		0	5		0	0	0			
40159090	其他硫化橡胶制衣着用品及附件	15	0	0	0	0	0	0	0	0	0	0		0		0	0	7.5	3			
40161010	硫化海绵橡胶制机器及仪器用零件	8	0	0	0	0	0	0	0	0	0	0		0	5		0	0	0			
40161090	硫化海绵橡胶制其他制品	15	0	0	0	0	0	0	0	0	0	0		0	12	0	0	7.5	3			
40169100	硫化橡胶制铺地制品及门垫	18	0	0	0	0	0	0	0	0	0	0		1.8		0	0	9	3.6	0		
40169200	硫化橡胶制橡皮擦	18	0	0	0	0	0	0	0	0	0	0		0			0	9	3.6			
40169310	硫化橡胶制机器、仪器用垫片、垫圈及其他密封垫	8	0	0	0	0	0	0	0	0	0	0		0	5		0	0	0	0		
40169390	硫化橡胶制其他用垫片、垫圈、及其他密封垫	15	0	0	0	0	0	0	0	0	0	0		0		0	0	7.5	3	0		
40169400	硫化橡胶制船舶或码头的碰垫	18	0	0	0	0	0	0	0	0	0	0		0		0	0	9	3.6			
40169500	硫化橡胶制其他可充气制品	18	0	0	0	0	0	0	0	0	0	0		0		0	0	9	3.6		0	
40169910	硫化橡胶制机器及仪器用其他零件	8	0	0	0	0	0	0	0	0	0	0	7.6	0	5		0	0	0		0	
40169990	其他未列名硫化橡胶制品	10	0	0	0	0	0	0	0	0	0	0	9.5	1	5	0	0	5	0		0	

税则号列	商品名称（简称）	最惠国	东盟										亚太	智利	巴基斯坦	新加坡	新西兰	秘鲁	哥斯达黎加	香港	澳门	台湾
			文	柬	印	老	马	缅	菲	新	泰	越										
40170010	各种形状的硬质橡胶(包括废碎料)	8	0	0	0	0	0	0	0	0	0	0		0	5		0	0	0		0	
40170020	硬质橡胶制品	15	0	0	0	0	0	0	0	0	0	0		0	12	0	0	7.5	3		0	
41012011	规定重量范围内的未剖层整张生牛皮，经逆鞣处理的	8	0	0	0	0	0	0	0	0	0	0	6	0	5		0	0	0	0		
41012019	规定重量范围内的未剖层整张生牛皮，经逆鞣处理的除外	5	0	0	0	0	0	0	0	0	0	0		0	0		0	0	0	0		
41012020	规定重量范围内的未剖层整张生马皮	5	0	0	0	0	0	0	0	0	0	0		0	0		0	0	3	0		
41015011	经逆鞣处理的重量＞16 公斤的整张生牛皮	8.4	0	0	0	0	0	0	0	0	0	0	7	0	5		0	0	0			
41015019	重量＞16 公斤的整张生牛皮，经逆鞣处理的除外	5	0	0	0	0	0	0	0	0	0	0		0	0		0	0	0			
41015020	重量＞16 公斤的整张生马皮	5	0	0	0	0	0	0	0	0	0	0		0	0		0	0	3			
41019011	其他（包括整张或半张的背皮及腹皮）经逆鞣处理的生牛皮	8.4	0	0	0	0	0	0	0	0	0	0	7	0	5		0	0	0			
41019019	其他（包括整张或半张的背皮及腹皮）生牛皮，经逆鞣处理的除外	5	0	0	0	0	0	0	0	0	0	0		0	0		0	0	0			
41019020	其他（包括整张或半张的背皮及腹皮）生马皮	5	0	0	0	0	0	0	0	0	0	0		0	0		0	0	3			
41021000	带毛的绵羊或羔羊生皮	7	0	0	0	0	0	0	0	0	0	0		0.7	5		0		4.2			
41022110	浸酸的不带毛绵羊或羔羊生皮，经逆鞣处理的	14	0	0	0	0	0	0	0	0	0	0		0	11.2	0	3.1		8.4			
41022190	浸酸的不带毛绵羊或羔羊生皮，经逆鞣处理的除外	9	0	0	0	0	0	0	0	0	0	0	8	0	5		0	0	5.4			
41022910	其他不带毛的绵羊或羔羊生皮，经逆鞣处理的	14	0	0	0	0	0	0	0	0	0	0		0	7	0	0	0	8.4			
41022990	其他不带毛的绵羊或羔羊生皮，经逆鞣处理的除外	7	0	0	0	0	0	0	0	0	0	0	6	0	5		0	0	4.2			
41032000	爬行动物的生皮	9	0	0	0	0	0	0	0	0	0	0		0	5		0	0	5.4			
41033000	生猪皮	9	0	0	0	0	0	0	0	0	0	0		0	5		0	0	5.4			
41039011	经逆鞣处理的山羊板皮	14	0	0	0	0	0	0	0	0	0	0		0	7	0	0	0	8.4			
41039019	山羊板皮，经逆鞣处理的除外	9	0	0	0	0	0	0	0	0	0	0		0	5		0	0	5.4			
41039021	经逆鞣处理的其他山羊或小山羊皮	14	0	0	0	0	0	0	0	0	0	0		0	7	0	0	0	8.4			
41039029	其他山羊或小山羊皮，经逆鞣处理的除外	9	0	0	0	0	0	0	0	0	0	0		0	5		0	0	5.4			
41039090	其他生皮	9	0	0	0	0	0	0	0	0	0	0		0	5		0	0	5.4	0		
41041111	全粒面未剖层或粒面剖层蓝湿牛皮	7	0	0	0	0	0	0	0	0	0	0	3.5	0	0		0	0	4.2			
41041119	其他全粒面未剖层或粒面剖层湿牛皮革	8	0	0	0	0	0	0	0	0	0	0	4	0	0		0	0	4.8	0		
41041120	全粒面未剖层或粒面剖层马皮革	5	0	0	0	0	0	0	0	0	0	0	2.5	0	0		0	0	3	0		
41041911	其他蓝湿牛皮	6	0	0	0	0	0	0	0	0	0	0	3	0	3		0	0	4.2			
41041919	其他湿牛皮革	7	0	0	0	0	0	0	0	0	0	0	3.5	0	0		0	0	4.2	0		
41041920	其他湿马皮革	7	0	0	0	0	0	0	0	0	0	0	3.5	0	0		0	0	4.2	0		
41044100	全粒面未剖层或粒面剖层干革（坯革）	5	0	0	0	0	0	0	0	0	0	0	3.5	0	0		0	0	3	0		
41044910	其他机器带用干革（坯革）	5	0	0	0	0	0	0	0	0	0	0	3.5	0	0		0	0	3			
41044990	其他干革（坯革）	7	0	0	0	0	0	0	0	0	0	0	4.9	0	4.9		0	0	4.2	0		
41051010	蓝湿绵羊或羔羊皮	14	0	0	0	0	0	0	0	0	0	0	7	0	5	0	3.1		8.4			
41051090	其他他绵羊或羔羊湿皮革	10	0	0	0	0	0	0	0	0	0	0	5	0	5		0	0	6			
41053000	绵羊或羔羊干革（坯革）	8	0	0	0	0	0	0	0	0	0	0	5.6	0	5.6		0	0	4.8			
41062100	山羊或小山羊皮湿革	14	0	0	0	0	0	0	0	0	0	0	12	0	12	0	0	0	8.4			
41062200	山羊或小山羊皮干革（坯革）	14	0	0	0	0	0	0	0	0	0	0	9.8	0	9.8	0	3.1		8.4			
41063110	蓝湿猪皮	14	0	0	0	0	0	0	0	0	0	0		0	11.2	0	0	0	8.4			
41063190	其他猪皮湿革	14	0	0	0	0	0	0	0	0	0	0		0	7	0	0	0	8.4			
41063200	猪皮干革（坯革）	14	0	0	0	0	0	0	0	0	0	0		0	11.2	0	0	0	8.4			
41064000	爬行动物皮革	14	0	0	0	0	0	0	0	0	0	0		0	7	0	0	0	8.4			
41069100	其他未列名动物皮湿革（包括蓝湿皮革）	14	0	0	0	0	0	0	0	0	0	0		0	11.2	0	0	0	8.4			
41069200	其他未列名动物皮干革（坯革）	14	0	0	0	0	0	0	0	0	0	0		0	11.2	0	0	0	8.4			
41071110	已鞣全粒面未剖层整张牛皮革	8	0	0	0	0	0	0	0	0	0	0		0			0		4.8	0		
41071120	已鞣全粒面未剖层整张马皮革	5	0	0	0	0	0	0	0	0	0	0		0	0		0	0	3	0		
41071210	已鞣粒面剖层整张牛皮革	8	0	0	0	0	0	0	0	0	0	0		0			0		4.8	0		
41071220	已鞣粒面剖层整张马皮革	5	0	0	0	0	0	0	0	0	0	0		0	0		0	0	3	0		
41071910	已鞣机器带用整张牛马皮革	5	0	0	0	0	0	0	0	0	0	0		0	0		0	0	3			
41071990	其他已鞣整张牛马皮革	7	0	0	0	0	0	0	0	0	0	0		0			0		4.2	0		

税则号列	商品名称（简称）	最惠国	东盟										亚太	智利	巴基斯坦	新加坡	新西兰	秘鲁	哥斯达黎加	香港	澳门	台湾
			文	柬	印	老	马	缅	菲	新	泰	越										
41079100	已鞣全粒面未剖层非整张牛马皮革	5	0	0	0	0	0	0	0	0	0	0		0	0		0	0	3			
41079200	已鞣粒面剖层非整张牛马皮革	5	0	0	0	0	0	0	0	0	0	0		0			0	0	3			
41079910	已鞣机器带用非整张牛马皮革	5	0	0	0	0	0	0	0	0	0	0		0	0		0	0	3			
41079990	其他已鞣非整张牛马皮革	7	0	0	0	0	0	0	0	0	0	0		0			0	0	4.2	0		
41120000	已鞣进一步加工的不带毛绵羊或羔羊皮革	8	0	0	0	0	0	0	0	0	0	0	5.6	0	5.6		0	0	4.8	0		
41131000	已鞣进一步加工的不带毛山羊或小山羊皮革	14	0	0	0	0	0	0	0	0	0	0	9.8	0	9.8	0	3.1		8.4	0		
41132000	已鞣进一步加工的不带毛猪皮革	14	0	0	0	0	0	0	0	0	0	0		0		0	0	0	8.4	0		
41133000	已鞣进一步加工的不带毛爬行动物皮革	14	0	0	0	0	0	0	0	0	0	0		0	11.2	0	0	0	8.4			
41139000	其他已鞣进一步加工的不带毛动物皮革	14	0	0	0	0	0	0	0	0	0	0		0		0	0	0	8.4			
41141000	油鞣皮革	14	0	0	0	0	0	0	0	0	0	0		1.4		0	0	7	8.4			
41142000	漆皮及层压漆皮；镀金属皮革	10	0	0	0	0	0	0	0	0	0	0	9	1	9	0	0		6			
41151000	以皮革或皮革纤维为基本成分的再生皮革，成块、成张或成条，不论是否成卷	14	0	0	0	0	0	0	0	0	0	0		0		0	0		8.4			
41152000	皮革或再生皮革边角料；皮革粉末	14	0	0	0	0	0	0	0	0	0	0		0		0	0	0	8.4			
42010000	各种材料制成的鞍具及挽具，适合各种动物用	20	0	0	0	0	0	0	0	0	0	0	12	0	10	0	0	10	4		0	
42021110	以皮革、再生皮革作面的衣箱	15	0	0	0	0	0	0	0	0	0	0		0	12	0	0	7.5	3			
42021190	以皮革、再生皮革作面的箱包	10	0	0	0	0	0	0	0	0	0	0		0	5		0	0	0			
42021210	以塑料或纺织材料作面的衣箱	20	0	0	0	0	0	0	0	0	0	0	17	0	16	0	0	10	4			0
42021290	塑料或纺织材料作面的其他箱包	20	0	0	0	0	0	0	0	0	0	0	17	0	16	0	0	10	4		0	0
42021900	其他材料制箱包	20	0	0	0	0	0	0	0	0	0	0		0		0	0	10	4			0
42022100	以皮革、再生皮革作面的手提包	10	0	0	0	0	0	0	0	0	0	0	6.9	1	5		0	5	0	0	0	
42022200	以塑料片或纺织材料作面的手提包	10	0	0	0	0	0	0	0	0	0	0	8.2	1	5	0	0	5	0		0	0
42022900	以钢纸或纸板作面的手提包	20	0	0	0	0	0	0	0	0	0	0	14	0	14	0	0	10	4		0	
42023100	以皮革、再生皮革作面的钱包等物品	10	0	0	0	0	0	0	0	0	0	0	6.9	0	5		0	0	0		0	
42023200	以塑料或纺织品作面的钱包等物品	20	0	0	0	0	0	0	0	0	0	0	14	0	14	0	0	10	4		0	
42023900	以钢纸或纸板作面的钱包等物品	20	0	0	0	0	0	0	0	0	0	0	14	0	14	0	0	10	4			
42029100	皮革、再生皮革作面的其他容器	10	0	0	0	0	0	0	0	0	0	0	8.5	0	5		0	0	0		0	
42029200	以塑料或纺织材料作面的其他容器	10	0	0	0	0	0	0	0	0	0	0	8.5	1	5	0	0	5	0		0	
42029900	以钢纸或纸板作面的其他容器	20	0	0	0	0	0	0	0	0	0	0		0		0	0	10	4		0	
42031000	皮革或再生皮革制的衣服	10	0	0	0	0	0	0	0	0	0	0		1	0		0	5	0	0	0	
42032100	皮革或再生皮革制专供运动用手套	20	0	0	0	0	0	0	0	0	0	0	14	0	0	0	0	10	4	0	0	
42032910	皮革或再生皮革制的劳保手套	20	0	0	0	0	0	0	0	0	0	0		2	0	0	0	10	4	0	0	
42032990	皮革或再生皮革制的其他手套	20	0	0	0	0	0	0	0	0	0	0		2	0	0	0	10	4	0	0	
42033010	皮革或再生皮革制腰带	10	0	0	0	0	0	0	0	0	0	0		1	0		0	5	0	0	0	
42033020	皮革或再生皮革制的腰带及子弹带	10	0	0	0	0	0	0	0	0	0	0		1	0		0	5	0	0		
42034000	皮革或再生皮革制的其他衣着附件	20	0	0	0	0	0	0	0	0	0	0		0	0	0	0	10	4	0	0	
42050010	皮革或再生皮革制坐具套	12	0	0	0	0	0	0	0	0	0	0		0	6	0	0	0	2.4	0		
42050020	机器、机械器具或其他专门技术用途的皮革或再生皮革制品	8	0	0	0	0	0	0	0	0	0	0		0	5		0	0	0			
42050090	皮革或再生皮革的其他制品	12	0	0	0	0	0	0	0	0	0	0		0	6	0	0	6	2.4	0		
42060000	肠线、肠膜、膀胱或筋腱制品	20	0	0	0	0	0	0	0	0	0	0		0		0	0	10	4			
43011000	整张生水貂皮	15	0	0	0	0	0	0	0	0	0	0		0	12	0	0	7.5	3	0		
43013000	阿斯特拉罕等羔羊的整张生毛皮，不论是否带头、尾或爪	20	0	0	0	0	0	0	0	0	0	0		0		0	0	10	4	0		
43016000	整张生狐皮	20	0	0	0	0	0	0	0	0	0	0		0		0	0	10	4	0		
43018010	整张生兔皮	20	0	0	0	0	0	0	0	0	0	0		0		0	0	10	4	0		
43018090	整张的其他生毛皮	20	0	0	0	0	0	0	0	0	0	0		0		0	0	10	4	0		
43019010	黄鼠狼尾	20	0	0	0	0	0	0	0	0	0	0		0		0	0	10	4	0		
43019090	适合加工皮货用的其他未鞣头、尾、爪	20	0	0	0	0	0	0	0	0	0	0		0		0	0	10	4	0		
43021100	已鞣未缝制的整张水貂皮	12	0	0	0	0	0	0	0	0	0	0		0	6	0	0	0	2.4	0		
43021910	已鞣未缝制的贵重毛皮（貂皮、狐皮、水獭及旱獭等）	10	0	0	0	0	0	0	0	0	0	0		0	5		0	0	0	0		
43021920	已鞣未缝制的整张兔皮	10	0	0	0	0	0	0	0	0	0	0		0	5		0	0	0	0		
43021930	已鞣未缝制阿斯特拉罕等羔羊皮，不论是否带头、尾或爪	20	0	0	0	0	0	0	0	0	0	0		0		0	0	10	4	0		
43021990	已鞣未缝制的其他毛皮	10	0	0	0	0	0	0	0	0	0	0		0			0	0	0	0		
43022000	已鞣未缝制的头、尾、爪及其他块片	20	0	0	0	0	0	0	0	0	0	0		0		0	0	10	4	0		

税则号列	商品名称（简称）	最惠国	东盟										亚太	智利	巴基斯坦	新加坡	新西兰	秘鲁	哥斯达黎加	香港	澳门	台湾
			文	柬	印	老	马	缅	菲	新	泰	越										
43023010	已鞣已缝制的贵重毛皮及其块、片	20	0	0	0	0	0	0	0	0	0	0		0		0	0	10	4	0		
43023090	已鞣已缝制的其他整张毛皮及块片	20	0	0	0	0	0	0	0	0	0	0		0		0	0	10	4	0		
43031010	毛皮衣服	23	0	0	0	0	0	0	0	0	0	0		2.3		0	0	11.5	4.6	0		
43031020	毛皮衣着附件	18	0	0	0	0	0	0	0	0	0	0		1.8		0	0	9	3.6	0		
43039000	毛皮制其他物品	18	0	0	0	0	0	0	0	0	0	0		0	14.4	0	0	0	3.6	0		
43040010	人造毛皮	18	0	0	0	0	0	0	0	0	0	0		0		0	0	9	3.6	0		
43040020	人造毛皮制品	18	0	0	0	0	0	0	0	0	0	0		0	14.4	0	0	9	3.6	0		
44021000	竹炭	10.5	0	0	0	0	0	0	0	0	0	0		0	5	0	0	0	2.1			
44029000	木炭	10.5	0	0	0	0	0	0	0	0	0	0		0	5	0	0	0	2.1			
44041000	针叶木的箍木、木劈条、木桩、木棒及类似品，木片条	8	0	0	0	0	0	0	0	0	0	0		0.8	5	0	0	0	0			
44042000	非针叶木箍木、木劈条、木桩、木棒及类似品，木片条	8	0	0	0	0	0	0	0	0	0	0		0.8	5	0	0	0	0			
44050000	木丝及木粉	8	0	0	0	0	0	0	0	0	0	0		0.8	5	0	0	0	0			
44081011	用胶合板等多层板制的饰面用针叶木薄板，不论是否刨平、砂光或指榫结合	8												0			0	0	0			
44081019	饰面用针叶木薄板，不论是否刨平、砂光或指榫结合，用胶合板等多层板制的除外	4	0	0	0	0	0	0	0	0	0	0		0.4	0	0	0	0	0			
44081020	制胶合板用针叶木薄板，不论是否刨平、砂光或指榫结合	4	0	0	0	0	0	0	0	0	0	0		0.4	0	0	0	0	0			
44081090	其他针叶木薄板材，不论是否刨平、砂光或指榫结合	4	0	0	0	0	0	0	0	0	0	0		0.4	0	0	0	0	0			
44083111	用胶合板等多层板制的深红色红柳桉木、浅红色红柳桉木及巴梼红柳桉木制的饰面用薄板，不论是否刨平、砂光或指榫结合	10												0			0	0	0			
44083119	深红色红柳桉木、浅红色红柳桉木及巴梼红柳桉木制的饰面用薄板，不论是否刨平、砂光或指榫结合，用胶合板等多层板制的除外	4	0	0	0	0	0	0	0	0	0	0		0	0	0	0	0	0			
44083120	深红色红柳桉木、浅红色红柳桉木及巴梼红柳桉木制的胶合板用薄板，不论是否刨平、砂光或指榫结合	4	0	0	0	0	0	0	0	0	0	0		0	0	0	0	0	0			
44083190	深红色红柳桉木、浅红色红柳桉木及巴梼红柳桉木制的其他薄板，不论是否刨平、砂光或指榫结合	4	0	0	0	0	0	0	0	0	0	0		0	0	0	0	0	0			
44083911	用胶合板等多层板制的其他列名的热带木制的饰面用薄板，不论是否刨平、砂光或指榫结合	10												0			0	0	0			
44083919	其他列名的热带木制的饰面用薄板，不论是否刨平、砂光或指榫结合，用胶合板等多层板制的除外	4	0	0	0	0	0	0	0	0	0	0		0	0	0	0	0	0			
44083920	其他列名热带木制的胶合板用薄板，不论是否刨平、砂光或指榫结合	4	0	0	0	0	0	0	0	0	0	0		0	0	0	0	0	0			
44083990	其他列名的热带木制的其他薄板材，不论是否刨平、砂光或指榫结合	4	0	0	0	0	0	0	0	0	0	0		0	0	0	0	0	0			
44089011	用胶合板等多层板制的其他木制饰面用薄板，不论是否刨平、砂光或指榫结合	4												0.4			0	0	0			
44089012	温带非针叶木制饰面用单板	3	0	0	0	0	0	0	0	0	0	0		0	0	0	0	0	0			
44089013	竹制饰面用单板	4												0.4			0	0	0			
44089019	其他木制饰面用薄板，不论是否刨平、砂光或指榫结合，用胶合板等多层板制的除外	3	0	0	0	0	0	0	0	0	0	0		0	0	0	0	0	0			
44089021	其他温带非针叶木制胶合板用单板	3	0	0	0	0	0	0	0	0	0	0		0	0	0	0	0	0			
44089029	其他木制胶合板用单板	3	0	0	0	0	0	0	0	0	0	0		0	0	0	0	0	0			
44089091	其他温带非针叶木制木材	3	0	0	0	0	0	0	0	0	0	0		0	0	0	0	0	0			
44089099	其他木材	3	0	0	0	0	0	0	0	0	0	0		0	0	0	0	0	0			
44091010	针叶木地板条（块）	7.5	0	0	0	0	0	0	0	0	0	0		0.8	5	0	0	0	0			
44091090	一边或面制成连续形状的针叶木材，不论是否刨平、砂光或指榫结合	7.5	0	0	0	0	0	0	0	0	0	0		0.8	5	0	0	0	0			
44092110	竹制地板条	4	0	0	0	0	0	0	0	0	0	0		0.4	0	0	0	0	0			

税则号列	商品名称（简称）	最惠国	东盟										亚太	智利	巴基斯坦	新加坡	新西兰	秘鲁	哥斯达黎加	香港	澳门	台湾
			文	柬	印	老	马	缅	菲	新	泰	越										
44092190	一边或面制成连续形状的竹材，不论是否刨平、砂光或指榫结合	4	0	0	0	0	0	0	0	0	0	0		0.4	0	0	0	0	0			
44092910	其他非针叶木地板条	4	0	0	0	0	0	0	0	0	0	0		0.4	0	0	0	0	0			
44092990	一边或面制成连续形状的其他非针叶木材，不论是否刨平、砂光或指榫结合	4	0	0	0	0	0	0	0	0	0	0		0.4	0	0	0	0	0			
44111221	辐射松制的厚度不超过 5 毫米的中密度木纤维板，密度超过每立方厘米 0.5 克，但未超过每立方厘米 0.8 克	4															0					
44111321	辐射松制的厚度超过 5 毫米但未超过 9 毫米的中密度木纤维板，密度超过每立方厘米 0.5 克，但未超过每立方厘米 0.8 克	4															0					
44111421	辐射松制的厚度超过 9 毫米的中密度木纤维板，密度超过每立方厘米 0.5 克，但未超过每立方厘米 0.8 克	4															0					
44119310	辐射松制的其他木纤维板，密度超过每立方厘米 0.5 克，但未超过每立方厘米 0.8 克	4															0					
44121011	至少有一表层为热带木的竹胶合板	12												0			0	0	2.4			
44121020	竹面多层板	10													5		0	0	0			
44121099	其他竹面多层板	4	0	0	0	0	0	0	0	0	0	0		0	0	0	0	0	0			
44123100	其他至少有一表层为热带木薄板制的胶合板	12												0			0	0	0			
44123900	其他仅由薄木板制胶合板	4	0	0	0	0	0	0	0	0	0	0		0.4	0	0	0	0	0			
44129410	木块芯胶合板，侧板条芯胶合板及板条芯胶合板，至少有一表层是非针叶木	10													5							
44129499	其他木块芯胶合板，侧板条芯胶合板及板条芯胶合板	4	0	0	0	0	0	0	0	0	0	0		0	0	0	0	0	0			
44129910	至少有一表层是非针叶木的其他木面多层板	10													5							
44129999	其他木面多层板	4	0	0	0	0	0	0	0	0	0	0		0	0	0	0	0	0			
44130000	强化木	6	0	0	0	0	0	0	0	0	0	0		0.6	5	0	0	0	0			
44140010	辐射松制的画框、相框、镜框及类似品	20															0					
44151000	木箱及类似的包装容器；电缆卷筒	7.5	0	0	0	0	0	0	0	0	0	0		0.8	5	0	0	0	0			
44152010	辐射松制的木托板、箱形托盘及其他装载用木板；辐射松制制的托盘护框	7.5															0					
44160010	辐射松制的大桶、琵琶桶、盆和其他辐射松制箍桶及其零件，包括桶板	16															0					
44170010	辐射松制的工具、工具支架、工具柄、扫帚及刷子的身及柄；辐射松制鞋靴楦及楦头	16															0					
44181010	辐射松制的窗、法兰西式（落地）窗及其框架	4															0					
44181090	其他木制的窗、法兰西式（落地）窗及其框架	4																			0	
44182000	木门及其框架和门槛	4	0	0	0	0	0	0	0	0	0	0		0.4	0	0	0	0	0		0	
44184000	水泥构件的木模板	4	0	0	0	0	0	0	0	0	0	0		0	0		0	0	0			
44185000	木瓦及盖屋板	7.5	0	0	0	0	0	0	0	0	0	0		0	5		0	0	0			
44186000	柱和梁	4	0	0	0	0	0	0	0	0	0	0		0.4	0	0	0	0	0			
44187100	已拼装的马赛克地板	4	0	0	0	0	0	0	0	0	0	0		0.4	0	0	0	0	0			
44187210	竹制已拼装的多层地板	4	0	0	0	0	0	0	0	0	0	0		0.4	0	0	0	0	0			
44187290	其他已拼装的多层地板	4	0	0	0	0	0	0	0	0	0	0		0.4	0	0	0	0	0			
44187910	竹制已拼装的地板	4	0	0	0	0	0	0	0	0	0	0		0.4	0	0	0	0	0			
44187990	其他已拼装的地板	4	0	0	0	0	0	0	0	0	0	0		0.4	0	0	0	0	0			
44189010	竹制建筑用制品	4	0	0	0	0	0	0	0	0	0	0		0.4	0	0	0	0	0			
44189090	其他建筑用木工制品	4	0	0	0	0	0	0	0	0	0	0		0.4	0	0	0	0	0			
45011000	未加工或简单加工的天然软木	6	0	0	0	0	0	0	0	0	0	0		0	5		0	0	0			
45020000	除去表皮或粗切成方形或成块、板、片或条状的天然软木	8	0	0	0	0	0	0	0	0	0	0		0	5		0	0	0			
45031000	天然软木塞子	8	0	0	0	0	0	0	0	0	0	0		0.8	5		0	0	0			
45039000	其他天然软木制品	10.5	0	0	0	0	0	0	0	0	0	0		0	5	0	0	0	2.1			

税则号列	商品名称（简称）	最惠国	东盟 文	东盟 柬	东盟 印	东盟 老	东盟 马	东盟 缅	东盟 菲	东盟 新	东盟 泰	东盟 越	亚太	智利	巴基斯坦	新加坡	新西兰	秘鲁	哥斯达黎加	香港	澳门	台湾
45041000	块、板、片及条状压制软木；任何形状的砖、瓦；实心圆柱体，包括原片	8.4	0	0	0	0	0	0	0	0	0	0		0	5		0	0	0			
46012100	竹制的席子、席料、帘子	9	0	0	0	0	0	0	0	0	0	0		0	5		0	0	0		0	
46012200	藤制的席子、席料及帘子	9	0	0	0	0	0	0	0	0	0	0		0	5		0	0	0		0	
46012911	蔺草制的席子、席料及帘子	9	0	0	0	0	0	0	0	0	0	0		0	5		0	0	0		0	
46012919	其他草制的席子、席料及帘子	9	0	0	0	0	0	0	0	0	0	0		0	5		0	0	0			
46012921	苇帘	9	0	0	0	0	0	0	0	0	0	0		0	5		0	0	0			
46012929	芦苇制的席子、席料	9	0	0	0	0	0	0	0	0	0	0		0	5		0	0	0			
46012990	其他植物材料制席子、席料及帘子	9	0	0	0	0	0	0	0	0	0	0		0	5		0	0	0			
46019210	竹缏条及类似产品，不论是否缝合成宽条	9	0	0	0	0	0	0	0	0	0	0		0	5		0	0	0		0	
46019290	其他竹编结产品	9	0	0	0	0	0	0	0	0	0	0		0	5		0	0	0		0	
46019310	藤缏条及类似产品，不论是否缝合成宽条	9	0	0	0	0	0	0	0	0	0	0		0	5		0	0	0		0	
46019390	其他藤编结产品	9	0	0	0	0	0	0	0	0	0	0		0	5		0		0		0	
46019411	稻草制的鞭条（绳）	10	0	0	0	0	0	0	0	0	0	0		0	5		0	0	0			
46019419	稻草制的其他编结材料产品	10	0	0	0	0	0	0	0	0	0	0		0	5		0	0	0			
46019491	其他植物编结材料的缏条及类似产品，不论是否缝合成宽条	9	0	0	0	0	0	0	0	0	0	0		0	5		0	0	0			
46019499	其他植物编结材料产品	9	0	0	0	0	0	0	0	0	0	0		0	5		0	0	0			
46019910	其他非植物编结材料的缏条及类似产品，不论是否缝合成宽条	9	0	0	0	0	0	0	0	0	0	0		0	5		0	0	0			
46019990	其他非植物编结材料产品	9	0	0	0	0	0	0	0	0	0	0		0	5		0	0	0			
46021100	竹编制的篮筐及其他制品	9	0	0	0	0	0	0	0	0	0	0		0	5		0	0	0			
46021200	藤编制的篮筐及其他制品	9	0	0	0	0	0	0	0	0	0	0		0	5		0		0			
46021910	草编制的篮筐及其他制品	9	0	0	0	0	0	0	0	0	0	0		0	5		0	0	0			
46021920	玉米皮编制的篮筐及其他制品	9	0	0	0	0	0	0	0	0	0	0		0	5		0	0	0			
46021930	柳条编制的篮筐及其他制品	9	0	0	0	0	0	0	0	0	0	0		0	5		0	0	0			
46021990	其他植物材料编制篮筐及其他制品	9	0	0	0	0	0	0	0	0	0	0		0	5		0		0			
46029000	其他编结材料制品及其他制品	9	0	0	0	0	0	0	0	0	0	0	8	0	5		0	0	0		0	
48022010	照相原纸	7.5																		0		
48022090	光敏、热敏、电敏纸，纸板的原纸、板	7.5																		0		
48024000	墙壁纸原纸	7.5																		0		
48025400	书写、印刷等用未涂布薄纸及纸板，不含用机械方法制得的纤维或所含前述纤维不超过全部纤维重量的10%	7.5																		0		
48025500	其他书写印刷等用未涂中厚纸(板)，不含用机械方法制得的纤维或所含前述纤维不超过全部纤维重量的10%，成卷	5																		0		
48025600	书写、印刷等用未涂布中厚纸及纸板，不含用机械方法制得的纤维或所含前述纤维不超过全部纤维重量的10%，成张，一边≤435mm，另一边≤297mm	5																		0		
48025700	其他书写印刷等用未涂中厚纸(板)，不含用机械方法制得的纤维或所含前述纤维不超过全部纤维重量的10%，其他成张	5																		0		
48025800	书写、印刷等用未涂布厚纸及纸板，不含用机械方法制得的纤维或所含前述纤维不超过全部纤维重量的10%	5																		0		
48026190	其他书写、印刷等用未涂布纸及纸板，所含用机械方法制得的纤维超过全部纤维重量的10%，成卷的其他纸	5																		0		
48026200	其他书写、印刷等用未涂布纸及纸板，所含用机械方法制得的纤维超过全部纤维重量的10%，成张的，一边≤435mm、另一边≤297mm（以未折叠计）	5																		0		
48026990	其他书写、印刷等用未涂布纸及纸板，所含用机械方法制得的纤维超过全部纤维重量的10%，成张的其他纸	5																		0		
48051100	半化学的瓦楞纸(瓦楞原纸)	7.5																		0		

税则号列	商品名称（简称）	最惠国	东盟										亚太	智利	巴基斯坦	新加坡	新西兰	秘鲁	哥斯达黎加	香港	澳门	台湾
			文	柬	印	老	马	缅	菲	新	泰	越										
48051200	草浆瓦楞原纸	7.5																		0		
48051900	其他瓦楞原纸	7.5																		0		
48052400	薄强韧箱纸板	7.5																		0		
48052500	厚强韧箱纸板	7.5																		0		
48059110	每平方米重量在150克及以下的电解电容器原纸	7.5																		0		
48059190	每平方米重量在150克及以下的薄纸及纸板	7.5																		0		
48059300	其他未经涂布厚纸及纸板	7.5																		0		
48101300	涂无机物书写(印刷)纸(板)，不含用机械方法制得的纤维或所含前述纤维不超过全部纤维重量的10%，成卷的	5																		0		
48101400	涂无机物书写(印刷)纸(板)，不含用机械方法制得的纤维或所含前述纤维不超过全部纤维重量的10%，成张的，一边≤435mm，另一边≤297mm（以未折叠计）	5																		0		
48101900	其他涂无机物书写(印刷)纸(板)，不含用机械方法制得的纤维或所含前述纤维不超过全部纤维重量的10%，成张的	5																		0		
48102900	其他涂无机物的书写、印刷纸及纸板，所含用机械方法制得的纤维超过全部纤维重量的10%	5																		0		
48103100	涂无机物的薄漂白牛皮纸及纸板，书写、印刷或类似用途的除外	5																		0	0	
48103200	涂无机物的厚漂白牛皮纸及纸板，书写、印刷或类似用途的除外	5																		0	0	
48103900	涂无机物的其他牛皮纸及纸板，书写、印刷或类似用途的除外	5																		0	0	
48109200	其他涂无机物的多层纸及纸板	5																		0	0	
48109900	其他涂无机物的纸及纸板	7.5																		0	0	
48111000	焦油纸及纸板、沥青纸及纸板	7.5																		0	0	
48114100	自粘的胶粘纸及纸板	7.5																		0	0	
48114900	其他胶粘纸及纸板	7.5																		0	0	
48115110	漂白的彩色相纸用双面涂塑厚纸	7.5																		0	0	
48115190	漂白的其他涂、浸、盖厚纸及纸板	7.5																		0	0	
48115910	绝缘纸及纸板	7.5																		0	0	
48115991	镀铝的用塑料涂布、浸渍的其他纸及纸板	7.5																		0	0	
48115999	其他用塑料涂布、浸渍的其他纸及纸板	7.5																		0	0	
48116010	用蜡或油等涂布的绝缘纸及纸板	7.5																		0	0	
48116090	用蜡或油等涂布的其他纸及纸板	7.5																		0	0	
48119000	其他经涂布、浸渍、覆盖的纸及纸板	7.5																		0	0	
48185000	纸制衣服及衣着附件	7.5	0	0	0	0	0	0	0	0	0	0		0	5		0	0	0			
48191000	瓦楞纸或纸板制的箱、盒、匣	5																		0	0	
48192000	非瓦楞纸或纸板制可折叠箱、盒、匣	5																		0	0	
48193000	底宽≥40cm的纸袋	7.5	0	0	0	0	0	0	0	0	0	0		0.8	5	0	0	0	0			
48204000	多联商业表格纸、页间夹有复写纸的本	7.5	0	0	0	0	0	0	0	0	0	0		0	5		0	0	0			
48211000	纸或纸板印制的各种标签	7.5																		0	0	
48236100	竹浆纸、纸板制的盘、碟、盆、杯及类似品	7.5	0	0	0	0	0	0	0	0	0	0		0.8	5		0	0	0			
48236910	非木植物浆制	7.5	0	0	0	0	0	0	0	0	0	0		0.8	5		0	0	0			
48236990	其他纸或纸板制的盘、碟、盆、杯及类似品	7.5	0	0	0	0	0	0	0	0	0	0		0.8	5		0	0	0			
48239020	神纸及类似用品	7.5	0	0	0	0	0	0	0	0	0	0		0.8	5		0	0	0			
48239030	纸扇	7.5	0	0	0	0	0	0	0	0	0	0		0.8	5		0	0	0			
48239090	其他纸及纸制品	7.5																		0	0	
49111090	其他商业广告品及类似印刷品	7.5																		0		
49119910	纸质的其他印刷品	7.5																		0		
49119990	其他印刷品	7.5																		0		

税则号列	商品名称（简称）	最惠国	东盟										亚太	智利	巴基斯坦	新加坡	新西兰	秘鲁	哥斯达黎加	香港	澳门	台湾
			文	柬	印	老	马	缅	菲	新	泰	越										
50010010	适于缫丝的桑蚕茧	6	0	0	0	0	0	0	0	0	0	0		0	5		0	0	0			
50010090	适于缫丝的其他蚕茧	6	0	0	0	0	0	0	0	0	0	0		0	5		0	0	0			
50020011	厂丝	9	0	0	0	0	0	0	0	0	0	0		0	5		0	0	0			
50020012	土丝	9	0	0	0	0	0	0	0	0	0	0		0	5		0	0	0			
50020013	双宫丝	9	0	0	0	0	0	0	0	0	0	0		0	5		0	0	0			
50020019	其他未加捻桑蚕丝	9	0	0	0	0	0	0	0	0	0	0		0	5		0	0	0			
50020020	未加捻柞蚕丝	9	0	0	0	0	0	0	0	0	0	0		0	5		0	0	0			
50020090	未加捻其他生丝	9	0	0	0	0	0	0	0	0	0	0		0	5		0	0	0			
50030011	下茧、茧衣、长吐、滞头	9	0	0	0	0	0	0	0	0	0	0		0	5		0	0	0			
50030012	回收纤维	9	0	0	0	0	0	0	0	0	0	0		0	5		0	0	0			
50030019	其他	9	0	0	0	0	0	0	0	0	0	0		0	5		0	0	0			
50030091	绵球	9	0	0	0	0	0	0	0	0	0	0		0	5		0	0	0			
50030099	其他	9	0	0	0	0	0	0	0	0	0	0		0	5		0	0	0			
50040000	非供零售用丝纱线	6	0	0	0	0	0	0	0	0	0	0		0	5		0	0	0		0	
50050010	非供零售用绸丝纱线	6	0	0	0	0	0	0	0	0	0	0		0	5		0	0	0		0	
50050090	非供零售用其他绢纺纱线	6	0	0	0	0	0	0	0	0	0	0		0	5		0	0	0		0	
50060000	零售用丝纱线、绢纺纱线；蚕胶丝	6	0	0	0	0	0	0	0	0	0	0		0	5		0	0	0		0	
50071010	未漂白或漂白的绸丝机织物	10	0	0	0	0	0	0	0	0	0	0		0	5		0	0	0			
50071090	其他绸丝机织物	10	0	0	0	0	0	0	0	0	0	0		0	5		0	0	0			
50072011	未漂白或漂白的纯桑蚕丝机织物	10	0	0	0	0	0	0	0	0	0	0	9	0	5		0	0	0			
50072019	其他纯桑蚕丝机织物	10	0	0	0	0	0	0	0	0	0	0	9	0	5		0	0	0	0		
50072021	未漂白或漂白的纯柞蚕丝机织物	10	0	0	0	0	0	0	0	0	0	0	9	0	5		0	0	0			
50072029	其他纯柞蚕丝机织物	10	0	0	0	0	0	0	0	0	0	0	9	0	5		0	0	0			
50072031	未漂白或漂白的纯绢丝机织物	10	0	0	0	0	0	0	0	0	0	0	9	0	5		0	0	0			
50072039	其他纯绢丝机织物	10	0	0	0	0	0	0	0	0	0	0	9	0	5		0	0	0			
50072090	其他纯丝机织物	10	0	0	0	0	0	0	0	0	0	0	9	0	5		0	0	0			
50079010	未漂白或漂白其他丝机织物	10	0	0	0	0	0	0	0	0	0	0	8.5	0	5		0	0	0			
50079090	其他丝机织物	10	0	0	0	0	0	0	0	0	0	0	8.5	0	5		0	5	0			
51011100	未梳的含脂剪羊毛	38	20	20	20	20	20	20	20	20	20	20										
51011900	未梳的其他含脂羊毛	38	20	20	20	20	20	20	20	20	20	20										
51012100	未梳的脱脂剪羊毛(未碳化)	38	20	20	20	20	20	20	20	20	20	20										
51012900	未梳的其他脱脂羊毛(未碳化)	38	20	20	20	20	20	20	20	20	20	20										
51013000	未梳碳化羊毛	38	20	20	20	20	20	20	20	20	20	20									0	
51021100	未梳喀什米尔山羊毛	9	0	0	0	0	0	0	0	0	0	0		0	5		0	0	0			
51021910	未梳兔毛	9	0	0	0	0	0	0	0	0	0	0		0	5		0	0	0			
51021920	未梳其他山羊绒	9	0	0	0	0	0	0	0	0	0	0		0	5		0	0	0			
51021930	未梳骆驼毛、骆驼绒	9	0	0	0	0	0	0	0	0	0	0		0	5		0	0	0			
51021990	未梳的其他动物细毛	9	0	0	0	0	0	0	0	0	0	0		0	5		0	0	0			
51022000	未梳的动物粗毛	9	0	0	0	0	0	0	0	0	0	0		0	5		0	0	0			
51031010	羊毛落毛	38	20	20	20	20	20	20	20	20	20	20										
51031090	其他动物细毛落毛	9	0	0	0	0	0	0	0	0	0	0		0	5		0	0	0			
51032010	羊毛废料	13.5	0	0	0	0	0	0	0	0	0	0		1.4	6.8	0	0	6.8	2.7			
51032090	其他动物细毛废料	9	0	0	0	0	0	0	0	0	0	0		0	5		0	0	0			
51033000	动物粗毛废料	9	0	0	0	0	0	0	0	0	0	0		0	5		0	0	0			
51040010	羊毛回收纤维	15	0	0	0	0	0	0	0	0	0	0		0	12	0	0	7.5	3			
51040090	其他动物细毛或粗毛的回收纤维	5	0	0	0	0	0	0	0	0	0	0		0	0		0	0	0			
51053100	已梳喀什米尔山羊毛	5	0	0	0	0	0	0	0	0	0	0		0	0		0	0	0			
51053910	已梳兔毛	5	0	0	0	0	0	0	0	0	0	0		0	0		0		0			
51053921	已梳无毛山羊绒	5	0	0	0	0	0	0	0	0	0	0		0	0		0		0			
51053929	其他已梳山羊绒	5	0	0	0	0	0	0	0	0	0	0		0	0		0		0			
51053990	其他已梳动物细毛	5	0	0	0	0	0	0	0	0	0	0		0	0		0		0			
51054000	已梳动物粗毛	5	0	0	0	0	0	0	0	0	0	0		0	0		0		0			
51061000	非供零售用粗梳纯羊毛纱线	5	0	0	0	0	0	0	0	0	0	0		0	0		0	0	0	0	0	
51062000	非供零售用粗梳混纺羊毛纱线	5	0	0	0	0	0	0	0	0	0	0		0	0		0	0	0	0	0	
51071000	非供零售用精梳纯羊毛纱线	5	0	0	0	0	0	0	0	0	0	0	2.5	0	0		0	0	0	0	0	
51072000	非供零售用精梳混纺羊毛纱线	5	0	0	0	0	0	0	0	0	0	0		0	0		0	0	0		0	
51081011	按重量计山羊绒的含量在85%及以上的非供零售用的粗梳纱线	5	0	0	0	0	0	0	0	0	0	0	4.3	0	0		0	0	0		0	
51081019	按重量计其他动物细毛含量在35%及以上的非供零售用的粗梳纱线	5	0	0	0	0	0	0	0	0	0	0	4.3	0	0		0	0	0		0	

税则号列	商品名称（简称）	最惠国	东盟										亚太	智利	巴基斯坦	新加坡	新西兰	秘鲁	哥斯达黎加	香港	澳门	台湾
			文	柬	印	老	马	缅	菲	新	泰	越										
51081090	按重量计动物细毛含量在85%以下的非供零售用的粗梳纱线	5	0	0	0	0	0	0	0	0	0	0	4.3	0	0		0	0	0		0	
51082011	按重量计山羊绒含量在85%及以上的非供零售用的精梳纱线	5	0	0	0	0	0	0	0	0	0	0		0	0		0		0		0	
51082019	按重量计其他动物细毛含量在85%及以上的非供零售用的精梳纱线	5	0	0	0	0	0	0	0	0	0	0		0	0		0		0		0	
51082090	按重量计动物细毛含量在85%以下的非供零售用的精梳纱线	5	0	0	0	0	0	0	0	0	0	0		0	0		0		0		0	
51091011	按重量计山羊绒含量在85%及以上的供零售用的纱线	6	0	0	0	0	0	0	0	0	0	0		0	5		0	0	0			
51091019	按重量计其他动物细毛含量在85%及以上的供零售用的纱线	6	0	0	0	0	0	0	0	0	0	0		0	5		0	0	0		0	
51091090	按重量计羊毛含量在85%及以上的供零售用的纱线	6	0	0	0	0	0	0	0	0	0	0		0	5		0	0	0		0	
51099011	供零售用的其他山羊绒纱线	6	0	0	0	0	0	0	0	0	0	0		0	5		0		0		0	
51099019	供零售用的其他动物细毛纱线	6	0	0	0	0	0	0	0	0	0	0		0	5		0		0		0	
51099090	供零售用的羊毛纱线	6	0	0	0	0	0	0	0	0	0	0		0	5		0		0		0	
51100000	动物粗毛或马毛的纱线	6	0	0	0	0	0	0	0	0	0	0		0	5		0	0	0		0	
51111111	按重量计山羊绒含量在85%及以上，每平方米重量不超过300克的山羊绒机织物	10	0	0	0	0	0	0	0	0	0	0	8.5	0	5	0	0	0	0			
51111119	按重量计其他动物细毛含量在85%及以上，每平方米重量不超过300克的其他动物细毛机织物	10	0	0	0	0	0	0	0	0	0	0	8.5	0	5	0	0	0	0			
51111190	按重量计羊毛含量在85%及以上，每平方米重量不超过300克的羊毛机织物	10	0	0	0	0	0	0	0	0	0	0	8.5	0	5	0	0	5	0		0	
51111911	按重量计山羊绒含量在85%及以上，每平方米重量超过300克的山羊绒的机织物	10	0	0	0	0	0	0	0	0	0	0	8.5	0	5	0	0	0	0			
51111919	按重量计其他动物细毛含量在85%及以上，每平方米超过300克的其他动物细毛机织物	10	0	0	0	0	0	0	0	0	0	0	8.5	0	5	0	0	0	0			
51111990	按重量计羊毛含量在85%及以上，每平方米超过300克的羊毛机织物	10	0	0	0	0	0	0	0	0	0	0	8.5	0	5	0	0	5	0			
51112000	与化纤长丝混纺粗梳毛布	10	0	0	0	0	0	0	0	0	0	0		0	5	0	0	0	0			
51113000	与化纤短纤混纺粗梳毛布	10	0	0	0	0	0	0	0	0	0	0	8.5	0	5	0	0	0	0			
51119000	与其他纤维混纺的粗梳毛布	10	0	0	0	0	0	0	0	0	0	0		0	5	0	0	0	0			
51121100	重量≤200g/平米精梳全毛布	10	0	0	0	0	0	0	0	0	0	0	5	0	5	0	0	5	0	0	0	
51121900	重量＞200g/平米精梳全毛布	10	0	0	0	0	0	0	0	0	0	0	5	0	5	0	0	5	0	0	0	
51122000	与化纤长丝混纺精梳毛布	10	0	0	0	0	0	0	0	0	0	0		0	5	0	0	0	0		0	
51123000	与化纤短纤混纺精梳毛布	10	0	0	0	0	0	0	0	0	0	0		0	5	0	0	0	0		0	
51129000	与其他纤维混纺精梳毛布	10	0	0	0	0	0	0	0	0	0	0		0	5	0	0	5	0		0	
51130000	动物粗毛或马毛机织物	10	0	0	0	0	0	0	0	0	0	0		0	5	0	0	0	0		0	
52010000	未梳的棉花	40	20	20	20	20	20	20	20	20	20	20										
52021000	废棉纱线	10	0	0	0	0	0	0	0	0	0	0		0		0	0	5	0			
52029100	棉的回收纤维	10	0	0	0	0	0	0	0	0	0	0		0		0	0	0	0	0		
52029900	其他废棉	10	0	0	0	0	0	0	0	0	0	0		0		0	0		0			
52041100	非供零售用全棉缝纫线	5	0	0	0	0	0	0	0	0	0	0		0			0	0	0		0	
52041900	非供零售用其他棉缝纫线	5	0	0	0	0	0	0	0	0	0	0		0			0	0	0		0	
52042000	零售用棉制缝纫线	5	0	0	0	0	0	0	0	0	0	0		0			0	0	0		0	
52051100	非零售粗梳粗支纯棉单纱	5	0	0	0	0	0	0	0	0	0	0	3.5	0	3.5		0	0	0	0	0	0
52051200	非零售粗梳中支纯棉单纱	5	0	0	0	0	0	0	0	0	0	0	3.5	0	3.5		0	0	0	0		0
52051300	非零售粗梳细支纯棉单纱	5	0	0	0	0	0	0	0	0	0	0	3.5	0	3.5		0	0	0	0		
52051400	非零售粗梳较细支纯棉单纱	5	0	0	0	0	0	0	0	0	0	0	3.5	0	3.5		0	0	0	0		
52051500	非零售粗梳特细支纯棉单纱	5	0	0	0	0	0	0	0	0	0	0	3.5	0	3.5		0	0	0			
52052100	非零售精梳粗支纯棉单纱	5	0	0	0	0	0	0	0	0	0	0	3.5	0	3.5		0	0	0	0		
52052200	非零售精梳中支纯棉单纱	5	0	0	0	0	0	0	0	0	0	0	3.5	0	3.5		0	0	0	0		
52052300	非零售精梳细支纯棉单纱	5	0	0	0	0	0	0	0	0	0	0	3.5	0	3.5		0	0	0	0		
52052400	非零售精梳较细支纯棉单纱	5	0	0	0	0	0	0	0	0	0	0	3.5	0	3.5		0	0	0	0		
52052600	非零售精梳较特细支纯棉单纱	5	0	0	0	0	0	0	0	0	0	0		0			0	0	0	0		
52052700	非零售精梳特细支纯棉单纱	5	0	0	0	0	0	0	0	0	0	0		0			0	0	0	0		

税则号列	商品名称（简称）	最惠国	东盟										亚太	智利	巴基斯坦	新加坡	新西兰	秘鲁	哥斯达黎加	香港	澳门	台湾
			文	柬	印	老	马	缅	菲	新	泰	越										
52052800	非零售精梳超细支纯棉单纱	5	0	0	0	0	0	0	0	0	0	0		0			0	0	0	0		
52053100	非零售粗梳粗支纯棉多股纱	5	0	0	0	0	0	0	0	0	0	0	4.5	0	4.5		0		0	0	0	
52053200	非零售粗梳中支纯棉多股纱	5	0	0	0	0	0	0	0	0	0	0	3.5	0	3.5		0	0	0	0	0	
52053300	非零售粗梳细支纯棉多股纱	5	0	0	0	0	0	0	0	0	0	0		0			0	0	0	0	0	
52053400	非零售粗梳较细支纯棉多股纱	5	0	0	0	0	0	0	0	0	0	0		0			0	0	0	0	0	
52053500	非零售粗梳特细支纯棉多股纱	5	0	0	0	0	0	0	0	0	0	0		0			0	0	0		0	
52054100	非零售精梳粗支纯棉多股纱	5	0	0	0	0	0	0	0	0	0	0	4.5	0	4.5		0		0	0	0	
52054200	非零售精梳中支纯棉多股纱	5											3.5	0	3.5		0	0	0	0	0	
52054300	非零售精梳细支纯棉多股纱	5	0	0	0	0	0	0	0	0	0	0		0			0		0	0	0	
52054400	非零售精梳较细支纯棉多股纱	5	0	0	0	0	0	0	0	0	0	0		0			0	0	0	0	0	
52054600	非零售精梳较特细支纯棉多股纱	5	0	0	0	0	0	0	0	0	0	0	4.5	0	4.5		0	0	0	0	0	
52054700	非零售精梳特细支纯棉多股纱	5	0	0	0	0	0	0	0	0	0	0	4.5	0	4.5		0	0	0	0	0	
52054800	非零售精梳超细支纯棉多股纱	5	0	0	0	0	0	0	0	0	0	0	4.5	0	4.5		0	0	0	0	0	
52061100	非零售粗梳粗支混纺棉单纱	5	0	0	0	0	0	0	0	0	0	0	3.5	0	3.5		0		0	0	0	
52061200	非零售粗梳中支混纺棉单纱	5	0	0	0	0	0	0	0	0	0	0	3.5	0	3.5		0	0	0	0	0	0
52061300	非零售粗梳细支混纺棉单纱	5	0	0	0	0	0	0	0	0	0	0		0			0	0	0	0	0	
52061400	非零售粗梳较细支混纺棉单纱	5	0	0	0	0	0	0	0	0	0	0		0			0	0	0	0	0	
52061500	非零售粗梳特细支混纺棉单纱	5	0	0	0	0	0	0	0	0	0	0	3.5	0	3.5		0	0	0	0	0	
52062100	非零售精梳粗支混纺棉单纱	5	0	0	0	0	0	0	0	0	0	0	4.5	0	4.5		0	0	0	0	0	
52062200	非零售精梳中支混纺棉单纱	5	0	0	0	0	0	0	0	0	0	0		0			0	0	0	0	0	0
52062300	非零售精梳细支混纺棉单纱	5	0	0	0	0	0	0	0	0	0	0		0			0	0	0	0	0	
52062400	非零售精梳较细支混纺棉单纱	5	0	0	0	0	0	0	0	0	0	0		0			0	0	0	0	0	0
52062500	非零售精梳特细支混纺棉单纱	5	0	0	0	0	0	0	0	0	0	0		0			0	0	0	0	0	
52063100	非零售粗梳粗支混纺棉多股纱	5	0	0	0	0	0	0	0	0	0	0		0			0	0	0	0	0	
52063200	非零售粗梳中支混纺棉多股纱	5	0	0	0	0	0	0	0	0	0	0		0			0	0	0	0	0	
52063300	非零售粗梳细支混纺棉多股纱	5	0	0	0	0	0	0	0	0	0	0		0			0	0	0	0	0	
52063400	非零售粗梳较细混纺棉多股纱	5	0	0	0	0	0	0	0	0	0	0		0			0	0	0	0	0	
52063500	非零售粗梳特细混纺棉多股纱	5	0	0	0	0	0	0	0	0	0	0		0			0	0	0	0	0	
52064100	非零售精梳粗支混纺棉多股纱	5	0	0	0	0	0	0	0	0	0	0		0			0	0	0	0	0	
52064200	非零售精梳中支混纺棉多股纱	5	0	0	0	0	0	0	0	0	0	0		0			0	0	0	0	0	
52064300	非零售精梳细支混纺棉多股纱	5	0	0	0	0	0	0	0	0	0	0		0			0	0	0	0	0	
52064400	非零售精梳较细混纺棉多股纱	5	0	0	0	0	0	0	0	0	0	0		0			0	0	0	0	0	
52064500	非零售精梳特细混纺棉多股纱	5	0	0	0	0	0	0	0	0	0	0		0			0	0	0	0	0	
52071000	供零售用纯棉纱线	6	0	0	0	0	0	0	0	0	0	0	5	0	5		0	0	0		0	
52079000	供零售用混纺棉纱线	6	0	0	0	0	0	0	0	0	0	0		0	5		0	0	0		0	
52081100	未漂白轻质全棉平纹布	10	0	0	0	0	0	0	0	0	0	0		0	0		0	0	0	0		
52081200	未漂白较轻质全棉平纹布	10	0	0	0	0	0	0	0	0	0	0		0	0	0	0	0	0	0		
52081300	未漂白轻质全棉三、四线斜纹布	10	0	0	0	0	0	0	0	0	0	0	8.5	0	0		0	0	0	0		
52081900	未漂白轻质其他全棉机织物	10	0	0	0	0	0	0	0	0	0	0		0	0	0	0	0	0	0		
52082100	漂白的轻质全棉平纹布	10	0	0	0	0	0	0	0	0	0	0		0	0		0	0	0	0		
52082200	漂白的较轻质全棉平纹布	10	0	0	0	0	0	0	0	0	0	0		0	0	0	0	0	0	0		
52082300	漂白的轻质全棉三、四线斜纹布	12	0	0	0	0	0	0	0	0	0	0		0	0	0	0	0	2.4	0		
52082900	漂白的轻质其他全棉机织物	10	0	0	0	0	0	0	0	0	0	0		0	0		0	0	0	0		
52083100	染色的轻质全棉平纹布	10	0	0	0	0	0	0	0	0	0	0		0	0		0	0	0	0		0
52083200	染色的较轻质全棉平纹布	10	0	0	0	0	0	0	0	0	0	0	8.5	0	0	0	0	0	0	0		0
52083300	染色的轻质全棉三、四线斜纹布	10	0	0	0	0	0	0	0	0	0	0	8.5	0	0		0	0	0	0		
52083900	染色的轻质其他全棉机织物	10	0	0	0	0	0	0	0	0	0	0	8.5	0	0	0	0	0	0	0		0
52084100	色织的轻质全棉平纹布	10	0	0	0	0	0	0	0	0	0	0		0	0	0	0	0	0	0		
52084200	色织的较轻质全棉平纹布	10	0	0	0	0	0	0	0	0	0	0	7	0	0	0	0	0	0	0		0
52084300	色织的轻质全棉三、四线斜纹布	10	0	0	0	0	0	0	0	0	0	0		0	0		0	0	0	0		
52084900	色织的轻质其他全棉机织物	10	0	0	0	0	0	0	0	0	0	0	9	0	0	0	0	0	0	0		
52085100	印花的轻全棉平纹布	10	0	0	0	0	0	0	0	0	0	0		0	0		0	0	0	0		
52085200	印花的较轻全棉平纹布	10	0	0	0	0	0	0	0	0	0	0	8.5	0	0	0	0	0	0	0		
52085910	印花的轻质全棉三、四线斜纹布	10	0	0	0	0	0	0	0	0	0	0		0	0		0	0	0	0		
52085990	印花的轻质其他全棉机织物	10	0	0	0	0	0	0	0	0	0	0	8.5	0	0		0	0	0			0
52091100	未漂白重质全棉平纹布	10												0	0		0		0	0		
52091200	未漂白重质全棉三、四线斜纹布	10	0	0	0	0	0	0	0	0	0	0	7	0	0	0	0	0	0	0		
52091900	未漂白重质其他全棉机织物	10	0	0	0	0	0	0	0	0	0	0		0	0	0	0	0	0	0		
52092100	漂白的重质全棉平纹布	12	0	0	0	0	0	0	0	0	0	0		0	0	0	0	0	2.4	0		
52092200	漂白的重质全棉三、四线斜纹布	12	0	0	0	0	0	0	0	0	0	0		0	0	0	0	0	2.4	0		

税则号列	商品名称（简称）	最惠国	东盟										亚太	智利	巴基斯坦	新加坡	新西兰	秘鲁	哥斯达黎加	香港	澳门	台湾
			文	柬	印	老	马	缅	菲	新	泰	越										
52092900	漂白的重质其他全棉机织物	12	0	0	0	0	0	0	0	0	0	0		0	0	0	0	0	2.4	0		
52093100	染色的重质全棉平纹布	10	0	0	0	0	0	0	0	0	0	0	8.5	0	0	0	0	0	0	0		0
52093200	染色的重质全棉三、四线斜纹布	10	0	0	0	0	0	0	0	0	0	0	8.5	0	0	0	0	0	0	0		0
52093900	染色的重质其他全棉机织物	10	0	0	0	0	0	0	0	0	0	0	8.5	0	0	0	0	0	0	0		0
52094100	色织的重质全棉平纹布	10	0	0	0	0	0	0	0	0	0	0		0	0	0	0	0	0	0		0
52094200	色织的重质全棉粗斜纹布(劳动布)	10	0	0	0	0	0	0	0	0	0	0	8.5	0	0	0	0	0	0	0	0	0
52094300	其他三线或四线斜纹机织物，包括双面斜纹机织物	10	0	0	0	0	0	0	0	0	0	0	9.3	0	0		0	0	0	0		
52094900	色织的重质其他全棉机织物	10	0	0	0	0	0	0	0	0	0	0		0	0	0	0	0	0	0		
52095100	印花的重质全棉平纹布	10	0	0	0	0	0	0	0	0	0	0	9.3	0	0	0	0	0	0	0		
52095200	印花的重质全棉三、四线斜纹布	10	0	0	0	0	0	0	0	0	0	0		0	0		0	0	0	0		
52095900	印花的重质其他全棉机织物	10	0	0	0	0	0	0	0	0	0	0	8.5	0	0		0	0	0	0		
52101100	与化纤混纺未漂白轻质平纹棉布	12	0	0	0	0	0	0	0	0	0	0	10.2	0	0	0	0	0	2.4	0		
52101910	化纤混纺未漂白轻质3、4线斜纹棉布	12	0	0	0	0	0	0	0	0	0	0		0	0	0	0	0	2.4	0		
52101990	与化纤混纺未漂白轻质其他棉布	12	0	0	0	0	0	0	0	0	0	0		0	0	0	0	0	2.4	0		
52102100	与化纤混纺漂白的轻质平纹棉布	14	0	0	0	0	0	0	0	0	0	0		0	0	0	0	0	2.8	0		
52102910	化纤混纺漂白的轻质三线或线斜纹棉布	14	0	0	0	0	0	0	0	0	0	0		0	0	0	0	0	2.8	0		
52102990	与化纤混纺漂白的轻质其他棉布	14	0	0	0	0	0	0	0	0	0	0		0	0	0	0	0	2.8			
52103100	与化纤混纺染色的轻质平纹棉布	10	0	0	0	0	0	0	0	0	0	0	8.5	0	0	0	0	0	0	0		0
52103200	化纤混纺染色的轻质三线或四线斜纹棉布	10	0	0	0	0	0	0	0	0	0	0	8.5	0	0	0	0	0	0	0		
52103900	与化纤混纺染色的轻质其他棉布	10	0	0	0	0	0	0	0	0	0	0	8.5	0	0	0	0	5	0	0		0
52104100	与化纤混纺色织的轻质平纹棉布	10	0	0	0	0	0	0	0	0	0	0		0	0	0	0	0	0	0		0
52104910	化纤混纺色织的轻质三线或四线斜纹棉布	10	0	0	0	0	0	0	0	0	0	0		0	0	0	0	0	0	0		
52104990	与化纤混纺色织的轻质其他棉布	10	0	0	0	0	0	0	0	0	0	0		0	0	0	0	0	0	0		0
52105100	与化纤混纺印花的轻质平纹棉布	10	0	0	0	0	0	0	0	0	0	0		0	0		0	0	0			
52105910	化纤混纺印花的轻质三线或四线斜纹棉布	10	0	0	0	0	0	0	0	0	0	0		0	0		0	0	0			
52105990	与化纤混纺印花的轻质其他棉布	10	0	0	0	0	0	0	0	0	0	0		0	0		0	0	0			
52111100	与化纤混纺未漂白重质平纹棉布	12	0	0	0	0	0	0	0	0	0	0		0	0	0	0	0	2.4	0		
52111200	化纤混纺未漂白重质三线或四线斜纹棉布	12	0	0	0	0	0	0	0	0	0	0		0	0	0	0	0	2.4	0		
52111900	与化纤混纺未漂白重质其他棉布	12	0	0	0	0	0	0	0	0	0	0		0	0	0	0	0	2.4	0		
52112000	与化纤混纺漂白的重质其他棉布	14	0	0	0	0	0	0	0	0	0	0		0	0	0	0	0	2.8	0		
52113100	与化纤混纺染色的重质平纹棉布	10	0	0	0	0	0	0	0	0	0	0	8.5	0	0	0	0	0	0	0		
52113200	化纤混纺染色的重质三线或四线斜纹棉布	10	0	0	0	0	0	0	0	0	0	0	8.5	0	0	0	0	0	0	0		
52113900	与化纤混纺染色的重质其他棉布	10	0	0	0	0	0	0	0	0	0	0	8.5	0	0	0	0	5	0	0		0
52114100	与化纤混纺色织的重质平纹棉布	10	0	0	0	0	0	0	0	0	0	0		0	0		0	0	0	0		
52114200	与化纤混纺色织的重质粗斜纹棉布	10	0	0	0	0	0	0	0	0	0	0		0	0	0	0	0	0	0		
52114300	其他三线或四线斜纹机织物，包括双面斜纹机织物	10	0	0	0	0	0	0	0	0	0	0		0	0		0	0	0	0		
52114900	与化纤混纺色织的重质其他棉布	10	0	0	0	0	0	0	0	0	0	0		0	0	0	0	0	0			
52115100	与化纤混纺印花的重质平纹棉布	10	0	0	0	0	0	0	0	0	0	0		0	0		0	0	0			
52115200	化纤混纺印花的重质三线或四线斜纹棉布	10	0	0	0	0	0	0	0	0	0	0		0	0		0	0	0			
52115900	与化纤混纺印花的重质其他棉布	10	0	0	0	0	0	0	0	0	0	0	8.5	0	0		0	0	0			
52121100	未漂白的其他混纺轻质棉布	12	0	0	0	0	0	0	0	0	0	0		0	0	0	0	0	2.4	0		
52121200	漂白的其他混纺轻质棉布	14	0	0	0	0	0	0	0	0	0	0		0	0	0	0	0	2.8	0		
52121300	染色的其他混纺轻质棉布	10	0	0	0	0	0	0	0	0	0	0		0	0		0	0	0	0		
52121400	色织的其他混纺轻质棉布	10	0	0	0	0	0	0	0	0	0	0		0	0		0	0	0			
52121500	印花的其他混纺轻质棉布	10	0	0	0	0	0	0	0	0	0	0		0	0		0	0	0			
52122100	未漂白的其他混纺重质棉布	12	0	0	0	0	0	0	0	0	0	0		0	0	0	0	0	2.4	0		
52122200	漂白的其他混纺重质棉布	14	0	0	0	0	0	0	0	0	0	0		0	0	0	0	0	2.8	0		
52122300	染色的其他混纺重质棉布	10	0	0	0	0	0	0	0	0	0	0		0	0		0	0	0	0		
52122400	色织的其他混纺重质棉布	10	0	0	0	0	0	0	0	0	0	0		0	0		0	0	0			
52122500	印花的其他混纺重质棉布	10	0	0	0	0	0	0	0	0	0	0		0	0		0	0	0			
53011000	生的或沤制的亚麻	6	0	0	0	0	0	0	0	0	0	0		0	5		0	0	0			
53012100	破开或打成的亚麻	6	0	0	0	0	0	0	0	0	0	0		0	5		0	0	0			
53012900	栉梳或经其他加工未纺制的亚麻	6	0	0	0	0	0	0	0	0	0	0		0	5		0	0	0			

税则号列	商品名称（简称）	最惠国	东盟										亚太	智利	巴基斯坦	新加坡	新西兰	秘鲁	哥斯达黎加	香港	澳门	台湾
			文	柬	印	老	马	缅	菲	新	泰	越										
53013000	亚麻短纤及废麻	6	0	0	0	0	0	0	0	0	0	0		0	5		0	0	0			
53021000	生的或沤制的大麻	6	0	0	0	0	0	0	0	0	0	0		0	5		0	0	0			
53029000	经加工、未纺的大麻、大麻短纤及废麻	6	0	0	0	0	0	0	0	0	0	0		0	5		0	0	0			
53031000	生或沤制黄麻，其他纺织用韧皮纤维	5	0	0	0	0	0	0	0	0	0	0		0	0		0	0	0			
53039000	经加工、未纺的黄麻及其他纺织用韧皮纤维	5	0	0	0	0	0	0	0	0	0	0		0	0		0	0	0			
53050011	生的苎麻	5	0	0	0	0	0	0	0	0	0	0		0	0		0	0	0			
53050012	经加工、未纺制的苎麻	5	0	0	0	0	0	0	0	0	0	0		0	0		0	0	0			
53050013	苎麻的短纤及废麻	5	0	0	0	0	0	0	0	0	0	0		0	0		0	0	0			
53050019	其他苎麻	5	0	0	0	0	0	0	0	0	0	0		0	0		0	0	0			
53050020	经加工、未纺制的蕉麻及蕉麻废料	3	0	0	0	0	0	0	0	0	0	0		0	0		0	0	0			
53050091	经加工、未纺的西沙尔麻及其他龙舌兰类纤维	5	0	0	0	0	0	0	0	0	0	0		0	0		0	0	0			
53050092	加工、未纺的椰壳纤维及椰壳纤维废料	5	0	0	0	0	0	0	0	0	0	0	4	0	0		0	0	0			
53050099	经加工的其他未列名纺织用植物纤维及其废麻	5	0	0	0	0	0	0	0	0	0	0		0	0		0	0	0			
53061000	亚麻单纱	6	0	0	0	0	0	0	0	0	0	0		0	5		0	0	0	0	0	
53062000	亚麻多股纱线或缆线	10	0	0	0	0	0	0	0	0	0	0		0	5		0	0	0	0	0	
53071000	黄麻及其他纺织用韧皮纤维单纱	6	0	0	0	0	0	0	0	0	0	0		0	5		0	0	0		0	
53072000	黄麻及其他纺织用韧皮纤维多股纱或缆线	6	0	0	0	0	0	0	0	0	0	0		0	5		0	0	0		0	
53081000	椰壳纤维纱线	6	0	0	0	0	0	0	0	0	0	0		0	5		0	0	0		0	
53082000	大麻纱线	6	0	0	0	0	0	0	0	0	0	0		0	5		0	0	0		0	
53089011	未漂白或漂白的全苎麻纱线	6	0	0	0	0	0	0	0	0	0	0		0	5		0	0	0		0	
53089012	全苎麻色纱线	6	0	0	0	0	0	0	0	0	0	0		0	5		0	0	0		0	
53089013	未漂白或漂白的混纺苎麻纱线	6	0	0	0	0	0	0	0	0	0	0		0	5		0	0	0		0	
53089014	混纺苎麻色纱线	6	0	0	0	0	0	0	0	0	0	0		0	5		0	0	0		0	
53089091	纸纱线	6	0	0	0	0	0	0	0	0	0	0		0	5		0	0	0		0	
53089099	其他植物纺织纤维纱线	6	0	0	0	0	0	0	0	0	0	0		0	5		0	0	0		0	
53091110	未漂白全亚麻机织物	10	0	0	0	0	0	0	0	0	0	0		0	0		0	0	0			
53091120	漂白的全亚麻机织物	10	0	0	0	0	0	0	0	0	0	0		0	0		0	0	0			
53091900	其他全亚麻机织物	10	0	0	0	0	0	0	0	0	0	0	9.3	0	0		0	0	0	0		
53092110	未漂白的混纺亚麻机织物	10	0	0	0	0	0	0	0	0	0	0		0	0		0	0	0		0	
53092120	漂白的混纺亚麻机织物	10	0	0	0	0	0	0	0	0	0	0		0	0		0	0	0		0	
53092900	其他混纺亚麻机织物	10	0	0	0	0	0	0	0	0	0	0	8.5	0	0		0	0	0	0	0	
53101000	未漂白黄麻或其他韧皮纤维织物	10	0	0	0	0	0	0	0	0	0	0		0	5		0	0	0			
53109000	其他黄麻机织物或韧皮鲜为纤维织物	10	0	0	0	0	0	0	0	0	0	0		0	5		0	0	0			
53110012	未漂白全苎麻机织物	10	0	0	0	0	0	0	0	0	0	0		0	5		0	0	0		0	
53110013	其他全苎麻机织物	12	0	0	0	0	0	0	0	0	0	0		0	6	0	0	0	2.4		0	
53110014	未漂白混纺苎麻机织物	10	0	0	0	0	0	0	0	0	0	0		0	5		0	0	0			
53110015	其他混纺苎麻机织物	12	0	0	0	0	0	0	0	0	0	0		0	6	0	0	0	2.4		0	
53110020	纸纱线机织物	10	0	0	0	0	0	0	0	0	0	0		0	5		0	0	0			
53110030	大麻的机织物	10	0	0	0	0	0	0	0	0	0	0	9.3	0	5		0	0	0			
53110090	其他纺织用植物纤维机织物	10	0	0	0	0	0	0	0	0	0	0	9.3	0	5		0	0	0			
54011010	非供零售用合成纤维长丝缝纫线	5	0	0	0	0	0	0	0	0	0	0		0	0		0	0	0	0	0	0
54011020	供零售用合成纤维长丝缝纫线	5	0	0	0	0	0	0	0	0	0	0		0	0		0	0	0			
54012010	非供零售用人纤长丝缝纫线	5	0	0	0	0	0	0	0	0	0	0		0	0		0	0	0			
54012020	供零售用人纤长丝缝纫线	5	0	0	0	0	0	0	0	0	0	0		0	0		0	0	0			
54021110	非零售用聚间苯二甲酰间苯二胺纺制的长丝高强力纱	5	0	0	0	0	0	0	0	0	0	0		0	0		0	0	0		0	
54021120	非零售用聚对苯二甲酰对苯二胺纺制的长丝高强力纱	5	0	0	0	0	0	0	0	0	0	0		0	0		0	0	0		0	
54021190	非零售用其他芳香族聚酰胺纺制的长丝高强力纱	5	0	0	0	0	0	0	0	0	0	0		0	0		0	0	0		0	
54021910	非零售用聚酰胺-6纺制的长丝高强力纱	5	0	0	0	0	0	0	0	0	0	0		0	0		0	0	0		0	
54021920	非零售用聚酰胺-66 纺制的长丝高强力纱	5	0	0	0	0	0	0	0	0	0	0		0	0		0	0	0		0	
54021990	非零售用其他尼龙长丝高强纱	5	0	0	0	0	0	0	0	0	0	0		0	0		0	0	0		0	
54022000	非零售聚酯长丝高强力纱	5	0	0	0	0	0	0	0	0	0	0		0	0		0	0	0		0	0
54023111	非零售用聚酰胺-6纺制的细弹力丝	5	0	0	0	0	0	0	0	0	0	0		0	0		0	0	0	0	0	
54023112	非零售用聚酰胺-66纺制的细弹力丝	5	0	0	0	0	0	0	0	0	0	0		0	0		0	0	0	0	0	

税则号列	商品名称（简称）	最惠国	东盟										亚太	智利	巴基斯坦	新加坡	新西兰	秘鲁	哥斯达黎加	香港	澳门	台湾
			文	柬	印	老	马	缅	菲	新	泰	越										
54023113	非零售用芳香族聚酰胺纺制的细弹力丝	5	0	0	0	0	0	0	0	0	0	0		0	0		0	0	0	0	0	
54023119	非零售其他细尼龙弹力丝	5	0	0	0	0	0	0	0	0	0	0		0	0		0	0	0	0	0	
54023190	非零售其他细尼龙变形纱线	5	0	0	0	0	0	0	0	0	0	0		0	0		0	0	0	0	0	
54023211	非零售用聚酰胺-6 纺制的粗弹力丝	5	0	0	0	0	0	0	0	0	0	0		0	0		0	0	0	0	0	
54023212	非零售用聚酰胺-66 纺制的粗弹力丝	5	0	0	0	0	0	0	0	0	0	0		0	0		0	0	0	0	0	
54023213	非零售用芳香族聚酰胺纺制的粗弹力丝	5	0	0	0	0	0	0	0	0	0	0		0	0		0	0	0	0	0	
54023219	非零售其他粗尼龙弹力丝	5	0	0	0	0	0	0	0	0	0	0		0	0		0	0	0	0	0	
54023290	非零售其他粗尼龙变形纱线	5	0	0	0	0	0	0	0	0	0	0	4.5	0	0		0	0	0	0	0	
54023310	非零售聚酯弹力丝	5	0		0		0	0	0	0	0	0		0	0		0	0	0		0	0
54023390	非零售其他聚酯变形纱线	5												0	0		0	0	0		0	
54023400	非零售用聚丙烯变形纱线	5	0	0	0	0	0	0	0	0	0	0		0	0		0	0	0		0	
54023900	非零售其他合成纤维长丝变形纱线	5	0	0	0	0	0	0	0	0	0	0		0	0		0	0	0		0	
54024410	弹性氨纶纱线，未加捻或捻度每米不超过 50 转	5	0	0	0	0	0	0	0	0	0	0		0	0		0	0	0		0	
54024490	其他弹性纱线，未加捻或捻度每米不超过 50 转	5	0	0	0	0	0	0	0	0	0	0	4.7	0	0		0	0	0	0	0	
54024510	聚酰胺-6 纺制的其他单纱，未加捻或捻度每米不超过 50 转	5	0	0	0	0	0	0	0	0	0	0	4.7	0	0		0	0	0		0	
54024520	聚酰胺-6，6 纺制的其他单纱，未加捻或捻度每米不超过 50 转	5	0	0	0	0	0	0	0	0	0	0	4.7	0	0		0	0	0		0	
54024530	芳香族聚酰胺纺制的其他单纱，未加捻或捻度每米不超过 50 转	5	0	0	0	0	0	0	0	0	0	0	4.7	0	0		0	0	0		0	
54024590	其他尼龙或聚酰胺纱线纺制的，未加捻或捻度每米不超过 50 转的单纱	5	0	0	0	0	0	0	0	0	0	0	4.7	0	0		0	0	0		0	
54024600	其他部分定向聚酯纱线，未加捻或捻度每米不超过 50 转	5												0	0		0	0	0		0	
54024700	其他聚酯纱线，未加捻或捻度每米不超过 50 转	5											4.7	0	0		0	0	0		0	
54024800	其他聚丙烯纱线，未加捻或捻度每米不超过 50 转	5	0	0	0	0	0	0	0	0	0	0		0	0		0	0	0		0	
54024910	断裂强度大于等于 22cN/dtex，且初始模量大于等于 750cN/dtex 的聚乙烯纱线	5	0	0	0	0	0	0	0	0	0	0		0	0		0	0	0		0	
54024990	其他纱线，未加捻或捻度每米不超过 50 转	5	0	0	0	0	0	0	0	0	0	0		0	0		0	0	0		0	
54025110	非零售用聚酰胺-6 纺制的加捻单纱	5												0	0		0	0	0		0	
54025120	非零售用聚酰胺-66 纺制的加捻单纱	5	0	0	0	0	0	0	0	0	0	0		0	0		0	0	0		0	
54025130	非零售用芳香族聚酰胺纺制的加捻单纱	5	0	0	0	0	0	0	0	0	0	0		0	0		0	0	0		0	
54025190	非零售用其他尼龙加捻单纱	5	0	0	0	0	0	0	0	0	0	0		0	0		0	0	0		0	
54025200	非零售加捻的其他聚酯加捻单纱	5											4.3	0	0		0	0	0		0	
54025910	非零售用聚丙烯加捻单纱	5	0	0	0	0	0	0	0	0	0	0		0	0		0	0	0		0	
54025920	断裂强度大于等于 22cN/dtex，且初始模量大于等于 750cN/dtex 的聚乙烯纱线	5	0	0	0	0	0	0	0	0	0	0		0	0		0	0	0		0	
54025990	非零售加捻的其他合成纤维长丝单纱	5	0	0	0	0	0	0	0	0	0	0		0	0		0	0	0		0	
54026110	非零售用聚己内酰胺（尼龙-6）制多股纱线	5	0	0	0	0	0	0	0	0	0	0		0	0		0	0	0		0	
54026120	非零售用聚酰胺-66 制多股纱线	5	0	0	0	0	0	0	0	0	0	0		0	0		0	0	0		0	
54026130	非零售用芳香族聚酰胺制多股纱线	5	0	0	0	0	0	0	0	0	0	0		0	0		0	0	0		0	
54026190	非零售用其他尼龙制多股纱线	5	0	0	0	0	0	0	0	0	0	0		0	0		0	0	0		0	
54026200	非零售聚酯多股纱线	5	0	0	0	0	0	0	0	0	0	0		0	0		0	0	0		0	0
54026910	非零售用聚丙烯多股纱线	5	0	0	0	0	0	0	0	0	0	0		0	0		0	0	0		0	
54026920	非零售用氨纶多股纱线	5	0	0	0	0	0	0	0	0	0	0		0	0		0	0	0		0	
54026990	非零售其他合成纤维长丝多股纱线	5	0	0	0	0	0	0	0	0	0	0		0	0		0	0	0		0	
54031000	非零售粘胶纤维高强力纱	5	0	0	0	0	0	0	0	0	0	0		0	0		0	0	0		0	
54033110	竹制非零售未捻的粘胶纤维单纱	5	0	0	0	0	0	0	0	0	0	0		0	0		0	0	0		0	
54033190	其他非零售未捻的粘胶纤维单纱	5	0	0	0	0	0	0	0	0	0	0		0	0		0	0	0		0	
54033210	竹制非零售加捻的粘胶纤维单纱	5	0	0	0	0	0	0	0	0	0	0		0	0		0	0	0		0	
54033290	其他非零售加捻的粘胶纤维单纱	5	0	0	0	0	0	0	0	0	0	0		0	0		0	0	0		0	
54033310	非零售二醋酸纤维单纱	5	0	0	0	0	0	0	0	0	0	0		0	0		0	0	0		0	
54033390	非零售其他醋酸纤维单纱	5	0	0	0	0	0	0	0	0	0	0		0	0		0	0	0		0	

税则号列	商品名称（简称）	最惠国	东盟										亚太	智利	巴基斯坦	新加坡	新西兰	秘鲁	哥斯达黎加	香港	澳门	台湾
			文	柬	印	老	马	缅	菲	新	泰	越										
54033900	非零售其他人造纤维长丝单纱	5	0	0	0	0	0	0	0	0	0	0		0	0		0	0	0		0	
54034100	非零售粘胶长丝多股纱线或缆线	5	0	0	0	0	0	0	0	0	0	0		0	0		0	0	0		0	
54034200	非零售醋酸长丝多股纱线或缆线	5	0	0	0	0	0	0	0	0	0	0		0	0		0	0	0		0	
54034900	非零售其他人造纤维长丝多股纱或缆线	5	0	0	0	0	0	0	0	0	0	0		0	0		0	0	0		0	
54041100	细度≥67分特、≤1mm的弹性单丝	5	0		0		0	0	0	0	0	0		0	0		0	0	0	0		
54041200	细度≥67分特、≤1mm的的聚丙烯单丝	5	0		0		0	0	0	0	0	0		0	0		0	0	0	0		
54041900	细度≥67分特、≤1mm的其他合成纤维单丝	5	0		0		0	0	0	0	0	0		0	0		0	0	0	0		
54049000	其他宽≤5mm合成纺织材料制扁条及类似品	5	0		0		0	0	0	0	0	0		0	0		0	0	0		0	
54050000	细度≥67分特、≤1mm人造纤维单丝；宽≤5mm扁条及类似品	5	0	0	0	0	0	0	0	0	0	0		0	0		0	0	0		0	
54060010	供零售用合成纤维长丝纱线	5	0	0	0	0	0	0	0	0	0	0		0	0		0	0	0		0	
54060020	供零售用人造纤维长丝纱线	5	0	0	0	0	0	0	0	0	0	0		0	0		0	0	0		0	
54071010	尼龙或其他聚酰胺高强力纱制机织物	10	0	0	0	0	0	0	0	0	0	0		0	0	0	0	0	0	0		0
54071020	聚酯高强力纱制机织物	10	0	0	0	0	0	0	0	0	0	0		0	0	0	0	0	0			0
54072000	合成纤维扁条及类似品的机织物	10	0	0	0	0	0	0	0	0	0	0		0	0	0	0	0	0			
54073000	多层平行纱线相互层迭并粘合机织物	10	0	0	0	0	0	0	0	0	0	0		0	0	0	0	0	0			
54074100	未漂白或漂白的纯尼龙布	10	0	0	0	0	0	0	0	0	0	0		0	0	0	0	0	0	0		0
54074200	染色的纯尼龙布	10	0	0	0	0	0	0	0	0	0	0	9.5	0	0	0	0	0	0	0	0	0
54074300	色织的纯尼龙布	10	0	0	0	0	0	0	0	0	0	0	7	0	0	0	0	0	0	0		0
54074400	印花的纯尼龙布	10	0	0	0	0	0	0	0	0	0	0		0	0	0	0	0	0			
54075100	未漂白或漂白纯聚酯变形长丝布	10	0	0	0	0	0	0	0	0	0	0	7	0	0	0	0	0	0			0
54075200	染色的纯聚酯变形长丝布	10	0	0	0	0	0	0	0	0	0	0	9.5	0	0	0	0	0	0	0		0
54075300	色织的纯聚酯变形长丝布	10	0	0	0	0	0	0	0	0	0	0		0	0	0	0	0	0			0
54075400	印花的纯聚酯变形长丝布	10	0	0	0	0	0	0	0	0	0	0		0	0	0	0	0	0			0
54076100	其他纯聚酯非变形长丝布	10	0	0	0	0	0	0	0	0	0	0	9.5	0	0	0	0	0	0	0	0	0
54076900	其他纯聚酯长丝布	10	0	0	0	0	0	0	0	0	0	0	9.5	0	0	0	0	0	0			0
54077100	未漂白或漂白其他纯合成纤维长丝布	10	0	0	0	0	0	0	0	0	0	0	8.8	0	0	0	0	0	0	0		0
54077200	染色的其他纯合成纤维长丝布	10	0	0	0	0	0	0	0	0	0	0	9.5	0	0	0	0	0	0	0		0
54077300	色织的其他纯合成纤维长丝布	10	0	0	0	0	0	0	0	0	0	0		0	0	0	0	0	0			
54077400	印花的其他纯合成纤维长丝布	10	0	0	0	0	0	0	0	0	0	0	9.5	0	0	0	0	0	0			
54078100	未漂或漂白的与棉混纺合成纤维长丝布	10	0	0	0	0	0	0	0	0	0	0		0	0	0	0	0	0	0		
54078200	染色的与棉混纺合成纤维长丝布	10	0	0	0	0	0	0	0	0	0	0		0	0	0	0	0	0	0		0
54078300	色织的与棉混纺合成纤维长丝布	10	0	0	0	0	0	0	0	0	0	0		0	0	0	0	0	0			0
54078400	印花的与棉混纺合成纤维长丝布	10	0	0	0	0	0	0	0	0	0	0		0	0	0	0	0	0			
54079100	未漂或漂白的其他混纺合成纤维长丝布	10	0	0	0	0	0	0	0	0	0	0		0	0	0	0	0	0	0		
54079200	染色的其他混纺合成纤维长丝布	10	0	0	0	0	0	0	0	0	0	0		0	0	0	0	0	0	0		0
54079300	色织的其他混纺合成纤维长丝布	10	0	0	0	0	0	0	0	0	0	0		0	0	0	0	0	0			0
54079400	印花的其他混纺合成纤维长丝布	10	0	0	0	0	0	0	0	0	0	0		0	0	0	0	0	0			
54081000	粘胶长丝高强力纱的机织物	10	0	0	0	0	0	0	0	0	0	0		0	0	0	0	0	0			
54082110	粘胶长丝制未漂白或漂白的机织物	12	0	0	0	0	0	0	0	0	0	0		0	0	0	0	0	2.4			
54082120	醋酸长丝制未漂白或漂白的机织物	12	0	0	0	0	0	0	0	0	0	0		0	0	0	0	0	2.4			
54082190	其他人造长丝制未漂白或漂白的机织物	12	0	0	0	0	0	0	0	0	0	0		0	0	0	0	0	2.4			
54082210	纯粘胶长丝制染色机织物	10	0	0	0	0	0	0	0	0	0	0		0	0	0	0	0	0	0		
54082220	纯醋酸长丝制染色机织物	10	0	0	0	0	0	0	0	0	0	0		0	0	0	0	0	0	0		0
54082290	纯其他人造长丝制染色机织物	10	0	0	0	0	0	0	0	0	0	0		0	0	0	0	0	0	0		0
54082310	纯粘胶长丝制色织机织物	10	0	0	0	0	0	0	0	0	0	0		0	0	0	0	0	0			
54082320	纯醋酸长丝制色织机织物	10	0	0	0	0	0	0	0	0	0	0		0	0	0	0	0	0			
54082390	纯其他人造长丝制色织机织物	10	0	0	0	0	0	0	0	0	0	0		0	0	0	0	0	0			0
54082410	纯粘胶长丝制印花机织物	10	0	0	0	0	0	0	0	0	0	0		0	0	0	0	0	0	0		
54082420	纯醋酸长丝制印花机织物	10	0	0	0	0	0	0	0	0	0	0		0	0	0	0	0	0	0		
54082490	纯其他人造长丝制印花机织物	10	0	0	0	0	0	0	0	0	0	0		0	0	0	0	0	0	0		
54083100	未漂白或漂白人造纤维长丝混纺布	10	0	0	0	0	0	0	0	0	0	0		0	0	0	0	0	0			
54083200	染色的人纤长丝混纺布	10	0	0	0	0	0	0	0	0	0	0	9.5	0	0	0	0	0	0			0
54083300	色织的人纤长丝混纺布	10	0	0	0	0	0	0	0	0	0	0		0	0	0	0	0	0			
54083400	印花的人纤长丝混纺布	10	0	0	0	0	0	0	0	0	0	0		0	0	0	0	0	0			
55011000	尼龙或其他聚酰胺长丝丝束	5	0	0	0	0	0	0	0	0	0	0		0	0		0	0	0			
55012000	聚酯长丝丝束	5												0	0		0	0	0			
55013000	聚丙烯腈长丝丝束	5											4.5	0	0		0		0			

税则号列	商品名称（简称）	最惠国	东盟										亚太	智利	巴基斯坦	新加坡	新西兰	秘鲁	哥斯达黎加	香港	澳门	台湾
			文	柬	印	老	马	缅	菲	新	泰	越										
55014000	聚丙烯长丝丝束	5	0	0	0	0	0	0	0	0	0	0		0	0		0	0	0	0		
55019000	其他合成纤维长丝丝束	5	0	0	0	0	0	0	0	0	0	0		0	0		0	0	0	0		
55020010	二醋酸纤维丝束	3	0	0	0	0	0	0	0	0	0	0	2.1	0	0		0	0	0			
55020090	其他人造纤维长丝丝束	5	0	0	0	0	0	0	0	0	0	0	3.5	0	0		0	0	0			
55031110	未梳的聚间苯二甲酰间苯二胺纺制的合成纤维短纤	5	0	0	0	0	0	0	0	0	0	0		0	0		0	0	0			
55031120	未梳的聚对苯二甲酰对苯二胺纺制的合成纤维短纤	5	0	0	0	0	0	0	0	0	0	0		0	0		0	0	0			
55031190	未梳的其他芳香聚酰胺纺制的合成纤维短纤	5	0	0	0	0	0	0	0	0	0	0		0	0		0	0	0			
55031900	未梳的尼龙或其他聚酰胺合成纤维短纤	5	0	0	0	0	0	0	0	0	0	0		0	0		0	0	0			
55032000	未梳的聚酯合成纤维短纤	5											4.5	0	0		0	0	0			
55033000	未梳的聚丙烯腈合成纤维短纤	5											4.5	0	0		0	0	0			
55034000	未梳的聚丙烯合成纤维短纤	5	0	0	0	0	0	0	0	0	0	0		0	0		0	0	0			
55039010	聚苯硫醚制未梳的纤维短纤	5	0	0	0	0	0	0	0	0	0	0		0	0		0	0	0			0
55039090	未梳的其他合成纤维短纤	5	0	0	0	0	0	0	0	0	0	0		0	0		0	0	0			0
55041010	竹制未梳的粘胶纤维短纤	5	0	0	0	0	0	0	0	0	0	0		0	0		0	0	0			
55041021	木制未梳的阻燃的粘胶纤维短纤	5	0	0	0	0	0	0	0	0	0	0		0	0		0	0	0			
55041029	其他木制未梳的粘胶纤维短纤	5	0	0	0	0	0	0	0	0	0	0		0	0		0	0	0			
55041090	其他未梳的粘胶纤维短纤	5	0	0	0	0	0	0	0	0	0	0		0	0		0	0	0			
55049000	未梳的其他人造纤维短纤	5	0	0	0	0	0	0	0	0	0	0		0	0		0	0	0			0
55051000	合成纤维废料	5	0	0	0	0	0	0	0	0	0	0		0	0		0	0	0			
55052000	人造纤维废料	5	0	0	0	0	0	0	0	0	0	0		0	0		0	0	0	0		
55061011	已梳的聚间苯二甲酰间苯二胺纤维短纤	5	0	0	0	0	0	0	0	0	0	0		0	0		0	0	0			
55061012	已梳的聚对苯二甲酰对苯二胺纤维短纤	5	0	0	0	0	0	0	0	0	0	0		0	0		0	0	0			
55061019	已梳的其他芳香族聚酰胺纤维短纤	5	0	0	0	0	0	0	0	0	0	0		0	0		0	0	0			
55061090	已梳的尼龙或其他聚酰胺纤维短纤	5	0	0	0	0	0	0	0	0	0	0		0	0		0	0	0			
55062000	已梳的聚酯纤维短纤	5											4.5	0	4.5		0	0	0			
55063000	已梳的聚丙烯腈及其变性纤维短纤	5											4.5	0	4.5		0	0	0			
55069010	聚苯硫醚制已梳的纤维短纤	5	0	0	0	0	0	0	0	0	0	0		0	0		0	0	0			
55069090	已梳的其他合成纤维短纤	5	0	0	0	0	0	0	0	0	0	0		0	0		0	0	0			
55070000	已梳的人造纤维短纤	5	0	0	0	0	0	0	0	0	0	0		0	0		0	0	0			
55081000	合成纤维短纤纺制的缝纫线	5	0		0		0	0	0	0	0	0	4.5	0	0		0	0	0	0	0	
55082000	人造纤维短纤纺制的缝纫线	5	0	0	0	0	0	0	0	0	0	0		0	0		0	0	0			
55091100	非零售纯尼龙短纤单纱	5	0	0	0	0	0	0	0	0	0	0		0	0		0	0	0	0	0	
55091200	非零售纯尼龙短纤多股纱线	5	0	0	0	0	0	0	0	0	0	0		0	0		0	0	0	0	0	
55092100	非零售纯聚酯短纤单纱	5	0		0		0	0	0	0	0	0		0	0		0	0	0	0	0	
55092200	非零售纯聚酯短纤多股纱线	5	0		0		0	0	0	0	0	0		0	0		0	0	0	0	0	
55093100	非零售纯聚丙烯腈短纤单纱	5	0		0		0	0	0	0	0	0		0	0		0	0	0	0	0	
55093200	非零售纯聚丙烯腈短纤多股纱线	5	0		0		0	0	0	0	0	0	4.8	0	0		0	0	0	0	0	0
55094100	非零售纯其他合成纤维短纤单纱	5	0		0		0	0	0	0	0	0		0	0		0	0	0	0	0	
55094200	非零售纯其他合成纤维短纤多股纱线	5	0		0		0	0	0	0	0	0		0	0		0	0	0	0	0	
55095100	非零售与人造纤维短纤混纺聚酯短纤纱	5	0		0		0	0	0	0	0	0		0	0		0	0	0	0	0	
55095200	非零售与毛混纺聚酯短纤纱线	5	0		0		0	0	0	0	0	0		0	0		0	0	0	0	0	
55095300	非零售与棉混纺聚酯短纤纱线	5	0		0		0	0	0	0	0	0	3.5	0	0		0	0	0	0	0	0
55095900	非零售其他混纺聚酯短纤纱线	5	0		0		0	0	0	0	0	0		0	0		0	0	0	0	0	
55096100	非零售与毛混纺腈纶短纤纱线	5	0		0		0	0	0	0	0	0		0	0		0	0	0	0	0	
55096200	非零售与棉混纺腈纶短纤纱线	5	0		0		0	0	0	0	0	0	4.8	0	0		0	0	0	0	0	
55096900	非零售与其他混纺腈纶短纤纱线	5	0		0		0	0	0	0	0	0		0	0		0	0	0	0	0	
55099100	非零售与毛混纺其他合成纤维短纤纱线	5	0		0		0	0	0	0	0	0		0	0		0	0	0	0	0	
55099200	非零售与棉混纺其他合成纤维短纤纱线	5	0		0		0	0	0	0	0	0		0	0		0	0	0	0	0	0
55099900	非零售与其他混纺合成纤维短纤纱线	5	0		0		0	0	0	0	0	0		0	0		0	0	0	0	0	
55101100	非零售纯人造纤维短纤单纱	5	0	0	0	0	0	0	0	0	0	0	4.5	0	0		0	0	0	0	0	0
55101200	非零售纯人造纤维短纤多股纱线	5	0	0	0	0	0	0	0	0	0	0		0	0		0	0	0	0	0	0
55102000	非零售与毛混纺人造纤维短纤纱线	5	0	0	0	0	0	0	0	0	0	0		0	0		0	0	0	0	0	
55103000	非零售与棉混纺人造纤维短纤纱线	5	0	0	0	0	0	0	0	0	0	0	3.5	0	0		0	0	0	0	0	0
55109000	非零售与其他混纺人造纤维短纤纱线	5	0	0	0	0	0	0	0	0	0	0	4.5	0	0		0	0	0	0	0	
55111000	零售用纯合成纤维短纤纱线	5	0		0		0	0	0	0	0	0		0	0		0	0	0			
55112000	零售用混纺合成纤维短纤纱线	5	0		0		0	0	0	0	0	0		0	0		0	0	0			
55113000	零售用人造纤维短纤纱线	5	0	0	0	0	0	0	0	0	0	0		0	0		0	0	0			

税则号列	商品名称（简称）	最惠国	东盟										亚太	智利	巴基斯坦	新加坡	新西兰	秘鲁	哥斯达黎加	香港	澳门	台湾
			文	柬	印	老	马	缅	菲	新	泰	越										
55121100	未漂或漂白的纯聚酯布	15	0	0	0	0	0	0	0	0	0	0	10.5	0	0	0	0	7.5	3			0
55121900	其他纯聚酯布	10	0	0	0	0	0	0	0	0	0	0		0	0	0	0	5	0	0		0
55122100	未漂或漂白的纯腈纶布	13	0	0	0	0	0	0	0	0	0	0		0	0	0	0	0	2.6			
55122900	其他纯腈纶布	10	0	0	0	0	0	0	0	0	0	0	9.3	0	0	0	0	0	0			
55129100	未漂或漂白的纯其他合成纤维布	18	0	0	0	0	0	0	0	0	0	0		0	0	0	0	9	3.6			
55129900	其他纯合成纤维布	10	0	0	0	0	0	0	0	0	0	0		0	0	0	0	0	0	0	0	0
55131110	与棉混纺未漂白的轻质聚酯平纹布	16	0	0	0	0	0	0	0	0	0	0		0	0	0	0	8	3.2	0		
55131120	与棉混纺漂白的轻质聚酯平纹布	15	0	0	0	0	0	0	0	0	0	0		0	0	0	0	7.5	3	0		
55131210	与棉混纺未漂白的轻质聚酯斜纹布	16	0	0	0	0	0	0	0	0	0	0		0	0	0	0	8	3.2	0		
55131220	与棉混纺漂白的轻质聚酯斜纹布	18	0	0	0	0	0	0	0	0	0	0		0	0	0	0	9	3.6	0		
55131310	与棉混纺未漂白的其他轻质聚酯布	16	0	0	0	0	0	0	0	0	0	0		0	0	0	0	8	3.2			
55131320	与棉混纺漂白的其他轻质聚酯布	18	0	0	0	0	0	0	0	0	0	0		0	0	0	0	9	3.6			
55131900	与棉混纺未漂白或漂白的轻质其他合成纤维布	18	0	0	0	0	0	0	0	0	0	0		0	0	0	0	9	3.6			
55132100	与棉混纺染色的轻质聚酯平纹布	10	0	0	0	0	0	0	0	0	0	0	9.1	0	0	0	0	0	0	0	0	0
55132310	与棉混纺染色的轻质聚酯斜纹布	10	0	0	0	0	0	0	0	0	0	0		0	0	0	0	0	0	0		
55132390	与棉混纺染色的其他轻质聚酯布	10	0	0	0	0	0	0	0	0	0	0		0	0	0	0	0	0			
55132900	与棉混纺染色的轻质其他合成纤维布	10	0	0	0	0	0	0	0	0	0	0		0	0	0	0	0	0			
55133100	与棉混纺色织的轻质聚酯平纹布	10	0	0	0	0	0	0	0	0	0	0		0	0	0	0	0	0	0		
55133910	与棉混纺色织的轻质聚酯斜纹布	10	0	0	0	0	0	0	0	0	0	0	8.8	0	0	0	0	0	0	0		
55133920	与棉混纺色织的其他轻质聚酯布	10	0	0	0	0	0	0	0	0	0	0		0	0	0	0	0	0	0		
55133990	与棉混纺色织的轻质其他合成纤维布	10	0	0	0	0	0	0	0	0	0	0		0	0	0	0	0	0			
55134100	与棉混纺印花的轻质聚酯平纹布	10	0	0	0	0	0	0	0	0	0	0		0	0	0	0	0	0			
55134910	与棉混纺印花的轻质聚酯斜纹布	10	0	0	0	0	0	0	0	0	0	0		0	0	0	0	0	0			
55134920	与棉混纺印花的其他轻质聚酯布	10	0	0	0	0	0	0	0	0	0	0		0	0	0	0	0	0			
55134990	与棉混纺印花的轻质其他合成纤维布	10	0	0	0	0	0	0	0	0	0	0		0	0	0	0	0	0			
55141110	与棉混纺未漂白的重质聚酯平纹布	16	0	0	0	0	0	0	0	0	0	0	14.4	0	0	0	0	8	3.2			
55141120	与棉混纺漂白的重质聚酯平纹布	18	0	0	0	0	0	0	0	0	0	0		0	0	0	0	9	3.6			
55141210	与棉混纺未漂白的重质聚酯斜纹布	16	0	0	0	0	0	0	0	0	0	0		0	0	0	0	8	3.2	0		
55141220	与棉混纺漂白的重质聚酯斜纹布	18	0	0	0	0	0	0	0	0	0	0		0	0	0	0	9	3.6	0		
55141911	与棉混纺未漂白的重质其他聚酯布	16	0	0	0	0	0	0	0	0	0	0		0	0	0	0	8	3.2			
55141912	与棉混纺漂白的重质其他聚酯布	18	0	0	0	0	0	0	0	0	0	0		0	0	0	0	9	3.6			
55141990	与棉混纺未漂白或漂白的重质其他合成纤维布	16	0	0	0	0	0	0	0	0	0	0	15.2	0	0	0	0	8	3.2			
55142100	与棉混纺染色的重质聚酯平纹布	10	0	0	0	0	0	0	0	0	0	0		0	0	0	0	0	0	0		
55142200	与棉混纺染色的重质聚酯斜纹布	10	0	0	0	0	0	0	0	0	0	0		0	0	0	0	0	0	0		
55142300	与棉混纺染色的其他重质聚酯布	10	0	0	0	0	0	0	0	0	0	0		0	0	0	0	0	0			
55142900	与棉混纺染色的重质其他合成维纤布	10	0	0	0	0	0	0	0	0	0	0		0	0	0	0	0	0			
55143010	与棉混纺色织的重质聚酯平纹布	10	0	0	0	0	0	0	0	0	0	0		0	0	0	0	0	0	0		
55143020	与棉混纺色织的重质聚酯斜纹布	10	0	0	0	0	0	0	0	0	0	0		0	0	0	0	0	0	0		
55143030	与棉混纺色织的其他重质聚酯布	10	0	0	0	0	0	0	0	0	0	0		0	0	0	0	0	0			
55143090	与棉混纺色织的重质其他合成纤维布	10	0	0	0	0	0	0	0	0	0	0		0	0	0	0	0	0			
55144100	与棉混纺印花的重质聚酯平纹布	10	0	0	0	0	0	0	0	0	0	0		0	0	0	0	0	0			
55144200	与棉混纺印花的重质聚酯斜纹布	10	0	0	0	0	0	0	0	0	0	0		0	0	0	0	0	0			
55144300	与棉混纺印花的其他重质聚酯布	10	0	0	0	0	0	0	0	0	0	0		0	0	0	0	0	0			
55144900	与棉混纺印花的重质其他合成纤维布	10	0	0	0	0	0	0	0	0	0	0		0	0	0	0	0	0			
55151100	与粘胶纤维短纤混纺的聚酯布	10	0	0	0	0	0	0	0	0	0	0	8.8	0	0	0	0	0	0			0
55151200	与化纤长丝混纺的聚酯布	10	0	0	0	0	0	0	0	0	0	0	9	0	0	0	0	0	0			0
55151300	与毛混纺的聚酯布	10	0	0	0	0	0	0	0	0	0	0		0	0	0	0	0	0			
55151900	与其他纤维混纺的聚酯布	10	0	0	0	0	0	0	0	0	0	0	9	0	0	0	0	0	0			
55152100	与化纤长丝混纺的腈纶布	10	0	0	0	0	0	0	0	0	0	0		0	0	0	0	0	0			
55152200	与毛混纺的腈纶布	12	0	0	0	0	0	0	0	0	0	0		0	0	0	0	0	2.4			
55152900	与其他纤维混纺的腈纶布	10	0	0	0	0	0	0	0	0	0	0		0	0	0	0	0	0			
55159100	与化纤长丝混纺的其他合成纤维短纤布	10	0	0	0	0	0	0	0	0	0	0		0	0	0	0	0	0			
55159900	与其他纤维混纺的其他合成纤维短纤布	10	0	0	0	0	0	0	0	0	0	0	9	0	0	0	0	0	0			
55161100	未漂白或漂白的纯人造纤维短纤布	12	0	0	0	0	0	0	0	0	0	0		0	0	0	0	0	2.4	0		
55161200	染色的纯人造纤维短纤布	10	0	0	0	0	0	0	0	0	0	0		0	0	0	0	0	0	0		0
55161300	色织的纯人造纤维短纤布	10	0	0	0	0	0	0	0	0	0	0		0	0	0	0	0	0	0		
55161400	印花的纯人造纤维短纤布	10	0	0	0	0	0	0	0	0	0	0		0	0	0	0	0	0	0		
55162100	与化纤长丝混纺未漂白或漂白的人造	12	0	0	0	0	0	0	0	0	0	0		0	0	0	0	0	2.4	0		

税则号列	商品名称（简称）	最惠国	东盟										亚太	智利	巴基斯坦	新加坡	新西兰	秘鲁	哥斯达黎加	香港	澳门	台湾
			文	柬	印	老	马	缅	菲	新	泰	越										
	纤维布																					
55162200	与化纤长丝混纺的染色人造纤维布	10	0	0	0	0	0	0	0	0	0	0	9.5	0	0	0	0	0	0	0		0
55162300	与化纤长丝混纺的色织人造纤维布	10	0	0	0	0	0	0	0	0	0	0		0	0	0	0	0	0	0		
55162400	与化纤长丝混纺的印花人造纤维布	10	0	0	0	0	0	0	0	0	0	0		0	0	0	0	0	0	0		
55163100	与毛混纺的未漂或漂白人造纤维布	12	0	0	0	0	0	0	0	0	0	0		0	0	0	0	0	2.4	0		
55163200	与毛混纺的染色人造纤维布	10	0	0	0	0	0	0	0	0	0	0		0	0	0	0	0	0	0		
55163300	与毛混纺的色织人造纤维布	10	0	0	0	0	0	0	0	0	0	0		0	0	0	0	0	0	0		
55163400	与毛混纺的印花人造纤维布	10	0	0	0	0	0	0	0	0	0	0		0	0	0	0	0	0	0		
55164100	与棉混纺的未漂或漂白人造纤维布	12	0	0	0	0	0	0	0	0	0	0		0	0	0	0	0	2.4	0		
55164200	与棉混纺的染色人造纤维布	12	0	0	0	0	0	0	0	0	0	0		0	0	0	0	0	2.4	0		
55164300	与棉混纺的色织人造纤维布	10	0	0	0	0	0	0	0	0	0	0		0	0	0	0	0	0	0		
55164400	与棉混纺的印花人造纤维布	10	0	0	0	0	0	0	0	0	0	0		0	0	0	0	0	0	0		
55169100	与其他纤维混纺未漂白或漂白的人造纤维布	12	0	0	0	0	0	0	0	0	0	0		0	0	0	0	0	2.4	0		
55169200	与其他纤维混纺的染色人造纤维布	10	0	0	0	0	0	0	0	0	0	0		0	0	0	0	0	0	0		
55169300	与其他纤维混纺的色织人造纤维布	10	0	0	0	0	0	0	0	0	0	0		0	0	0	0	0	0	0		
55169400	与其他纤维混纺的印花人造纤维布	10	0	0	0	0	0	0	0	0	0	0	9.4	0	0	0	0	0	0	0		
56012100	棉制的絮胎及其他絮胎制品	10	0	0	0	0	0	0	0	0	0	0		0	5	0	0	0	0		0	
56012210	化学纤维制的卷烟滤嘴	12	0	0	0	0	0	0	0	0	0	0		0	6	0	0	0	2.4			
56012290	化学纤维制的絮胎及其他絮胎制品	12	0	0	0	0	0	0	0	0	0	0		0		0	0	0	2.4			0
56012900	其他材料制絮胎及其他絮胎制品	10	0	0	0	0	0	0	0	0	0	0		0	5	0	0	0	0			
56013000	纺织纤维屑、纤维粉末及球结	10	0	0	0	0	0	0	0	0	0	0		0	5	0	0	0	0			
56021000	针刺机制毡呢及纤维缝编织物	10	0	0	0	0	0	0	0	0	0	0		0	5	0	0	0	0			
56022100	未浸、涂的毛制其他毡呢	10	0	0	0	0	0	0	0	0	0	0		0	5	0	0	0	0			
56022900	未浸、涂的其他纺织材料制其他毡呢	10	0	0	0	0	0	0	0	0	0	0		0	5	0	0	0	0			
56029000	经浸、涂、包覆或层压的其他毡呢	10	0	0	0	0	0	0	0	0	0	0		0	5	0	0	0	0			
56031110	每平米≤25g经浸渍化纤长丝无纺织物	10	0	0	0	0	0	0	0	0	0	0	8.5	0	0	0	0	0	0			0
56031190	每平米≤25g的其他化纤长丝无纺织物	10	0	0	0	0	0	0	0	0	0	0	8.5	0	0	0	0	0	0			
56031210	25g ＜每平米≤70g 浸渍化纤长丝无纺织物	10	0	0	0	0	0	0	0	0	0	0	8.5	0	0	0	0	0	0	0	0	
56031290	25g ＜每平米≤70g 其他化纤长丝无纺织物	10	0	0	0	0	0	0	0	0	0	0		0	0	0	0	0	0	0	0	0
56031310	70g＜每平米≤150g 浸渍化纤长丝无纺织物	10	0	0	0	0	0	0	0	0	0	0	8.5	0	0	0	0	0	0		0	0
56031390	70g ＜每平米≤150g 其他化纤长丝无纺织物	10	0	0	0	0	0	0	0	0	0	0		0	0	0	0	0	0		0	0
56031410	每平米＞150g经浸渍化纤长丝无纺织物	10	0	0	0	0	0	0	0	0	0	0	8.5	0	0	0	0	0	0			0
56031490	每平米＞150g的其他化纤长丝无纺织物	10	0	0	0	0	0	0	0	0	0	0	7	0	0	0	0	0	0			0
56039110	每平米≤25g经浸渍其他无纺织物	10	0	0	0	0	0	0	0	0	0	0	8.5	0	0	0	0	0	0			
56039190	每平米≤25g的其他无纺织物	10	0	0	0	0	0	0	0	0	0	0	8.5	0	0	0	0	0	0			
56039210	25g＜每平米≤70g浸渍其他无纺织物	10	0	0	0	0	0	0	0	0	0	0	8.5	0	0	0	0	0	0	0	0	
56039290	25g ＜每平米≤70g 其他无纺织物	10	0	0	0	0	0	0	0	0	0	0	9.3	0	0		0	0	0	0	0	0
56039310	70g ＜每平米≤150g浸渍其他无纺织物	10	0	0	0	0	0	0	0	0	0	0	8.5	0	0	0	0	0	0	0	0	
56039390	70g ＜每平米≤150g的其他无纺织物	10	0	0	0	0	0	0	0	0	0	0	9.3	0	0	0	0	0	0	0	0	0
56039410	每平米＞150g经浸渍其他无纺织物	10	0	0	0	0	0	0	0	0	0	0	8.5	0	0	0	0	0	0	0		0
56039490	每平米＞150g的其他无纺织物	10	0	0	0	0	0	0	0	0	0	0	9.3	0	0	0	0	0	0	0		0
56041000	用纺织材料包覆的橡胶线及绳	5	0		0		0	0	0	0	0	0		0	0		0	0	0		0	
56049000	用橡、塑浸渍涂布的其他纺织纱线	5	0		0		0	0	0	0	0	0		0	0		0	0	0		0	
56050000	含金属纱线	5	0		0		0	0	0	0	0	0		0	0		0	0	0		0	
56060000	绳绒线及粗松螺旋花线	5	0		0		0	0	0	0	0	0		0	0		0	0	0		0	
56072100	剑麻或其他龙舌兰纤维制包扎用绳	5	0	0	0	0	0	0	0	0	0	0		0	0		0	0	0		0	
56072900	剑麻或龙舌兰纤维制其他线绳索缆	5	0	0	0	0	0	0	0	0	0	0		0	0		0	0	0		0	
56074100	聚乙烯或聚丙烯制包扎用绳	5	0		0		0	0	0	0	0	0		0	0		0	0	0		0	
56074900	聚乙烯或聚丙烯制线、绳、索、缆	5	0		0		0	0	0	0	0	0		0	0		0	0	0		0	
56075000	其他合纤制线、绳、索、缆	5	0		0		0	0	0	0	0	0		0	0		0	0	0		0	0
56079010	蕉麻或硬质纤维制线、绳、索、缆	5	0	0	0	0	0	0	0	0	0	0		0	0		0	0	0		0	
56079090	其他纺织材料制线、绳、索、缆	5	0		0		0	0	0	0	0	0		0	0		0	0	0		0	
56081100	化纤材料制成的渔网	10	0	0	0	0	0	0	0	0	0	0		0	5		0	5	0			
56081900	化纤材料制成的其他网	12	0	0	0	0	0	0	0	0	0	0		0	6	0	0	0	2.4			0
56089000	其他纤维制成的渔网及其他网	10	0	0	0	0	0	0	0	0	0	0		0	5		0	0	0	0		
56090000	用纱线、扁条、绳、索、缆制其他物品	10	0	0	0	0	0	0	0	0	0	0		0	5		0	0	0			

税则号列	商品名称（简称）	最惠国	东盟										亚太	智利	巴基斯坦	新加坡	新西兰	秘鲁	哥斯达黎加	香港	澳门	台湾
			文	柬	印	老	马	缅	菲	新	泰	越										
57011000	羊毛结织栽绒地毯及其他铺地制品	14	0	0	0	0	0	0	0	0	0	0		0		0	0	0	2.8			
57019010	化纤结织栽绒地毯及其他铺地制品	16	0	0	0	0	0	0	0	0	0	0		0	12.8	0	0	8	3.2			
57019020	丝制结织栽绒地毯及铺地制品	14	0	0	0	0	0	0	0	0	0	0		0	7	0	0	0	2.8			
57019090	其他材料结织栽绒地毯及铺地制品	14	0	0	0	0	0	0	0	0	0	0		0	7	0	0	0	2.8			
57021000	“开来姆”等手织地毯	14	0	0	0	0	0	0	0	0	0	0		0	0	0	0	0	2.8			
57022000	椰壳纤维制的铺地制品	14	0	0	0	0	0	0	0	0	0	0		0	0	0	0	0	2.8			
57023100	未制成的毛制起绒地毯及铺地制品	10	0	0	0	0	0	0	0	0	0	0		0	0	0	0	0	0			
57023200	未制成的化纤起绒地毯及铺地制品	16	0	0	0	0	0	0	0	0	0	0		0	0	0	0	8	3.2			
57023900	未制成其他纺织材料起绒铺地制品	14	0	0	0	0	0	0	0	0	0	0		0	0	0	0	0	2.8			
57024100	制成的毛制起绒地毯及铺地制品	10	0	0	0	0	0	0	0	0	0	0		0	0	0	0	0	0			
57024200	制成的化纤起绒地毯及铺地制品	10	0	0	0	0	0	0	0	0	0	0		0	0	0	0	0	0			
57024900	制成的其他纺织材料起绒铺地制品	14	0	0	0	0	0	0	0	0	0	0	9.3	0	0	0	0	0	2.8			
57025010	未制成毛制非起绒地毯及铺地制品	14	0	0	0	0	0	0	0	0	0	0		0	0	0	0	0	2.8			
57025020	未制成化纤非起绒地毯及铺地制品	16	0	0	0	0	0	0	0	0	0	0		0	0	0	0	8	3.2			
57025090	未制成其他纺织材料非起绒地毯及铺地制品	14	0	0	0	0	0	0	0	0	0	0		0	0	0	0	0	2.8			
57029100	制成的毛制非起绒地毯及铺地制品	14	0	0	0	0	0	0	0	0	0	0		0	0	0	0	0	2.8			
57029200	制成的化纤非起绒地毯及铺地制品	16	0	0	0	0	0	0	0	0	0	0		0	0	0	0	8	3.2			
57029900	制成的其他纺织材料非起绒地毯及铺地制品	14	0	0	0	0	0	0	0	0	0	0		0	0	0	0	0	2.8			
57031000	毛制簇绒地毯及其他簇绒铺地制品	14	0	0	0	0	0	0	0	0	0	0		0		0	0	0	2.8			
57032000	尼龙簇绒地毯及其他簇绒铺地制品	10	0	0	0	0	0	0	0	0	0	0		0	5	0	0	0	0			
57033000	化纤簇绒地毯及其他簇绒铺地制品	10	0	0	0	0	0	0	0	0	0	0		0		0	0	0	0			
57039000	其他纺织材料簇绒地毯及其他簇绒铺地制品	14	0	0	0	0	0	0	0	0	0	0		0	11.2	0	0	0	2.8			
57041000	小块毡呢地毯及其他毡呢铺地制品	14	0	0	0	0	0	0	0	0	0	0		0	7	0	0	0	2.8			
57049000	大块毡呢地毯及其他毡呢铺地制品	10	0	0	0	0	0	0	0	0	0	0		0	5	0	0	0	0			
57050010	毛制其他地毯及其他铺地制品	14	0	0	0	0	0	0	0	0	0	0		0	11.2	0	0	0	2.8			
57050020	化纤制其他地毯及其他铺地制品	10	0	0	0	0	0	0	0	0	0	0		0	5	0	0	0	0			
57050090	其他纺织材料制其他地毯及铺地制品	14	0	0	0	0	0	0	0	0	0	0		0	11.2	0	0	0	2.8			
58011000	毛制起绒机织物及绳绒织物	10	0	0	0	0	0	0	0	0	0	0		0	0	0	0	0	0			
58012100	不割绒的棉制纬起绒织物	12	0	0	0	0	0	0	0	0	0	0		0	0	0	0	0	2.4			
58012200	割绒的棉制灯芯绒	10	0	0	0	0	0	0	0	0	0	0		0	0		0	0	0	0		0
58012300	其他棉制纬起绒织物	10	0	0	0	0	0	0	0	0	0	0		0	0		0	0	0			
58012600	棉制绳绒织物	10	0	0	0	0	0	0	0	0	0	0		0	0		0	0	0			
58012710	棉制的不割绒的经起绒织物（棱纹绸）	10	0	0	0	0	0	0	0	0	0	0		0	0		0	0	0			
58012720	棉制的割绒的经起绒织物	10	0	0	0	0	0	0	0	0	0	0		0	0		0	0	0	0		
58013100	不割绒的化纤制纬起绒织物	10	0	0	0	0	0	0	0	0	0	0		0	0	0	0	0	0			
58013200	割绒的化纤制灯芯绒	10	0	0	0	0	0	0	0	0	0	0		0	0	0	0	0	0			
58013300	其他化纤纬起绒织物	10	0	0	0	0	0	0	0	0	0	0		0	0	0	0	0	0			0
58013600	化纤绳绒织物	10	0	0	0	0	0	0	0	0	0	0		0	0	0	0	0	0			
58013710	化学纤维制的不割绒的经起绒织物（棱纹绸）	10	0	0	0	0	0	0	0	0	0	0		0	0	0	0	0	0			
58013720	化学纤维制的割绒的经起绒织物	10	0	0	0	0	0	0	0	0	0	0		0	0	0	0	0	0			
58019010	丝及绢丝制起绒机织物及绳绒织物	10	0	0	0	0	0	0	0	0	0	0		0	0	0	0	0	0			
58019090	其他材料制起绒机织物及绳绒织物	10	0	0	0	0	0	0	0	0	0	0		0	0	0	0	0	0			
58021100	未漂白棉毛巾织物及类似毛圈机织物	12	0	0	0	0	0	0	0	0	0	0		0	0	0	0	0	2.4		0	
58021900	其他棉毛巾织物及类似毛圈机织物	10	0	0	0	0	0	0	0	0	0	0		0	0		0	0	0		0	
58022010	丝及绢丝毛巾织物及类似毛圈机织物	12	0	0	0	0	0	0	0	0	0	0		0	0	0	0	0	2.4		0	
58022020	羊毛等毛巾织物及类似毛圈机织物	12	0	0	0	0	0	0	0	0	0	0		0	0	0	0	0	2.4		0	
58022030	化纤毛巾织物及类似毛圈机织物	14	0	0	0	0	0	0	0	0	0	0		0	0	0	0	0	2.8		0	
58022090	其他纺织材料毛巾织物及类似毛圈织物	12	0	0	0	0	0	0	0	0	0	0		0	0	0	0	0	2.4		0	
58023010	丝及绢丝制簇绒织物	10	0	0	0	0	0	0	0	0	0	0		0	0	0	0	0	0			
58023020	羊毛或动物细毛制簇绒织物	10	0	0	0	0	0	0	0	0	0	0		0	0	0	0	0	0			
58023030	棉或麻制簇绒织物	10	0	0	0	0	0	0	0	0	0	0		0	0		0	0	0			
58023040	化学纤维制簇绒织物	10	0	0	0	0	0	0	0	0	0	0		0	0	0	0	5	0			
58023090	其他纺织材料制簇绒织物	10	0	0	0	0	0	0	0	0	0	0		0	0	0	0	0	0			
58030010	棉制纱罗	10	0	0	0	0	0	0	0	0	0	0		0	5		0	0	0			
58030020	丝及绢丝制纱罗	10	0	0	0	0	0	0	0	0	0	0		0	5	0	0	0	0			
58030030	化学纤维制纱罗	10	0	0	0	0	0	0	0	0	0	0		0	5	0	0	0	0			
58030090	其他纺织材料制纱罗	10	0	0	0	0	0	0	0	0	0	0		0	5	0	0	0	0			

税则号列	商品名称（简称）	最惠国	东盟										亚太	智利	巴基斯坦	新加坡	新西兰	秘鲁	哥斯达黎加	香港	澳门	台湾
			文	柬	印	老	马	缅	菲	新	泰	越										
58041010	丝及绢丝网眼薄纱及其他网眼织物	10	0	0	0	0	0	0	0	0	0	0	7	0	5	0	0	0	0			
58041020	棉制网眼薄纱及其他网眼织物	10	0	0	0	0	0	0	0	0	0	0	7	0	5		0	0	0			
58041030	化纤制网眼薄纱及其他网眼织物	12	0	0	0	0	0	0	0	0	0	0	8.4	0	5	0	0	0	2.4			0
58041090	其他纺织材料网眼薄纱及其他网眼织物	10	0	0	0	0	0	0	0	0	0	0	7	0	5	0	0	0	0			0
58042100	化纤机制花边	10	0	0	0	0	0	0	0	0	0	0		0	5	0	0	0	0	0	0	0
58042910	丝及绢丝机制花边	10	0	0	0	0	0	0	0	0	0	0		0	5	0	0	0	0			
58042920	棉机制花边	10	0	0	0	0	0	0	0	0	0	0		0	5		0	0	0			
58042990	其他纺织材料制机制花边	10	0	0	0	0	0	0	0	0	0	0		0	5	0	0	0	0			
58043000	手工制花边	10	0	0	0	0	0	0	0	0	0	0		0	5	0	0	0	0			
58050010	手工针绣嵌花装饰毯	12	0	0	0	0	0	0	0	0	0	0		0	6	0	0	0	2.4			
58050090	“哥白林”等手织装饰毯	12	0	0	0	0	0	0	0	0	0	0		0	6	0	0	0	2.4			
58061010	棉或麻狭幅起绒机织物及绳绒织物	10	0	0	0	0	0	0	0	0	0	0		0	5		0	0	0			
58061090	其他材料狭幅起绒织物及绳绒织物	10	0	0	0	0	0	0	0	0	0	0	9.1	0	5	0	0	0	0			0
58062000	含弹性纱线≥5%的狭幅织物	10	0	0	0	0	0	0	0	0	0	0		0	5	0	0	0	0	0	0	0
58063100	棉制其他狭幅机织物	10	0	0	0	0	0	0	0	0	0	0		0	5		0	0	0			
58063200	化纤制其他狭幅机织物	10	0	0	0	0	0	0	0	0	0	0	7	0	5	0	0	0	0		0	0
58063910	丝及绢丝制其他狭幅机织物	10	0	0	0	0	0	0	0	0	0	0		0	5	0	0	0	0			
58063920	毛制其他狭幅机织物	10	0	0	0	0	0	0	0	0	0	0		0	5	0	0	0	0			
58063990	其他材料制其他狭幅机织物	10	0	0	0	0	0	0	0	0	0	0		0	5	0	0	0	0			
58064010	棉或麻粘合有经纱无纬纱狭幅织物	10	0	0	0	0	0	0	0	0	0	0		0	5		0	0	0			
58064090	其他材料粘合有经纱无纬纱狭幅织物	10	0	0	0	0	0	0	0	0	0	0		0	5	0	0	0	0			
58071000	机织非绣制纺织材料标签、徽章等	10	0	0	0	0	0	0	0	0	0	0	8.5	0	8.5	0	0	5	0	0	0	0
58079000	非机织非绣制纺织材料标签徽章等	10	0	0	0	0	0	0	0	0	0	0		0	5	0	0	0	0			
58081000	成匹的编带	10	0	0	0	0	0	0	0	0	0	0		0		0	0	0	0		0	
58089000	非绣制成匹装饰带、流苏、绒球	10	0	0	0	0	0	0	0	0	0	0		0	5	0	0	0	0		0	
58090010	与棉混制金属线布及含金属纱线布	10	0	0	0	0	0	0	0	0	0	0		0	5	0	0	0	0			
58090020	与化纤混制金属线布及含金属纱布	10	0	0	0	0	0	0	0	0	0	0		0	5	0	0	0	0			
58090090	其他金属线布及含金属纱线布	10	0	0	0	0	0	0	0	0	0	0		0	5	0	0	0	0			
58101000	不见底布的刺绣品	10	0	0	0	0	0	0	0	0	0	0		0	5	0	0	0	0			
58109100	棉制见底布的刺绣品	10	0	0	0	0	0	0	0	0	0	0		0		0	0	5	0			
58109200	化学纤维制见底布刺绣品	10	0	0	0	0	0	0	0	0	0	0		0	5	0	0	0	0			0
58109900	其他纺织材料制见底布刺绣品	10	0	0	0	0	0	0	0	0	0	0		0	5	0	0	0	0			
58110010	丝及绢丝制绗缝被褥状纺织品	10	0	0	0	0	0	0	0	0	0	0		0	0	0	0	0	0			
58110020	羊毛或动物细毛制绗缝被褥状纺织品	10	0	0	0	0	0	0	0	0	0	0		0	0	0	0	0	0			
58110030	棉制绗缝被褥状纺织品	10	0	0	0	0	0	0	0	0	0	0		0	0		0	0	0			
58110040	化学纤维制绗缝被褥状纺织品	12	0	0	0	0	0	0	0	0	0	0		0	0	0	0	0	2.4			
58110090	其他纺织材料制绗缝被褥状纺织品	10	0	0	0	0	0	0	0	0	0	0		0	0	0	0	0	0			
59011010	用胶或淀粉涂布的棉或麻纺织物	10	0	0	0	0	0	0	0	0	0	0		0	5	0	0	0	0			
59011020	用胶或淀粉涂布的化纤纺织物	10	0	0	0	0	0	0	0	0	0	0		0	5	0	0	0	0			
59011090	用胶或淀粉涂布的其他纤维纺织物	10	0	0	0	0	0	0	0	0	0	0		0	5	0	0	0	0			
59019010	制成的油画布	10	0	0	0	0	0	0	0	0	0	0		0	5		0	0	0			
59019091	棉或麻制描图布、帽里硬衬布等	10	0	0	0	0	0	0	0	0	0	0		0	5		0	0	0			
59019092	化纤制描图布、帽里硬衬布等	10	0	0	0	0	0	0	0	0	0	0		0	5		0	0	0			
59019099	其他纺织纤维制描图布、帽里硬衬布等	10	0	0	0	0	0	0	0	0	0	0		0	5		0	0	0			
59021010	聚酰胺-6（尼龙-6）制的帘子布	10	0	0	0	0	0	0	0	0	0	0	9	0	5	0	0	0	0			
59021020	聚酰胺-6，6（尼龙-6，6）制的帘子布	10	0	0	0	0	0	0	0	0	0	0	9	0	5	0	0	0	0			
59021090	其他尼龙等高强力纱制的帘子布	10	0	0	0	0	0	0	0	0	0	0	9	0	5	0	0	0	0			
59022000	聚酯高强力纱制的帘子布	10	0	0	0	0	0	0	0	0	0	0	9	0	5	0	0	0	0			
59029000	粘胶纤维高强力纱制帘子布	10	0	0	0	0	0	0	0	0	0	0		0	5		0	0	0			
59031010	用聚氯乙烯浸、涂的绝缘布或带	10	0	0	0	0	0	0	0	0	0	0	8.5	0	5		0	0	0			
59031020	用聚氯乙烯浸、涂的人造革	10	0	0	0	0	0	0	0	0	0	0	8.5	0	5	0	0	0	0	0		0
59031090	用聚氯乙烯浸、涂的其他纺织物	10	0	0	0	0	0	0	0	0	0	0	8.5	0	5	0	0	0	0	0		0
59032010	用聚氨基甲酸酯浸、涂的绝缘布或带	10	0	0	0	0	0	0	0	0	0	0	8.5	0	5		0	0	0			
59032020	用聚氨基甲酸酯浸、涂的人造革	10	0	0	0	0	0	0	0	0	0	0	8.5	0	5	0	0	0	0			0
59032090	用聚氨基甲酸酯浸、涂的其他纺织物	10	0	0	0	0	0	0	0	0	0	0	8.5	0	8.5	0	0	0	0	0		0
59039010	用其他塑料浸、涂的绝缘布或带	10	0	0	0	0	0	0	0	0	0	0	8.5	0	5		0	0	0			
59039020	用其他塑料浸、涂的人造革	10	0	0	0	0	0	0	0	0	0	0	8.5	0	5	0	0	0	0			0
59039090	用其他塑料浸、涂的其他纺织物	10	0	0	0	0	0	0	0	0	0	0	8.5	0	8.5	0	0	0	0	0		0
59041000	列诺伦(亚麻油地毡)	14	0	0	0	0	0	0	0	0	0	0		0	11.2	0	0	0	2.8			
59049000	以织物为底涂布的铺地品	14	0	0	0	0	0	0	0	0	0	0		0	7	0	0	0	2.8			

税则号列	商品名称（简称）	最惠国	东盟										亚太	智利	巴基斯坦	新加坡	新西兰	秘鲁	哥斯达黎加	香港	澳门	台湾
			文	柬	印	老	马	缅	菲	新	泰	越										
59050000	糊墙织物	10	0	0	0	0	0	0	0	0	0	0		0	5	0	0	0	0			
59061010	用橡胶处理宽≤20cm纺织绝缘胶粘带	10	0	0	0	0	0	0	0	0	0	0		0	5		0	0	0			
59061090	用橡胶处理宽≤20cm其他纺丝胶粘带	10	0	0	0	0	0	0	0	0	0	0		0	5	0	0	0	0			
59069100	用橡胶处理的针织或钩编的纺织物	10	0	0	0	0	0	0	0	0	0	0		0	5	0	0	0	0			0
59069910	用橡胶处理宽其他绝缘布或带	10	0	0	0	0	0	0	0	0	0	0		0	5		0	0	0			
59069990	用橡胶处理的其他纺织物	10	0	0	0	0	0	0	0	0	0	0		0	5	0	0	0	0			0
59070010	用其他材料浸、涂的绝缘布或带	10	0	0	0	0	0	0	0	0	0	0	8.5	0	5		0	0	0			
59070020	用其他材料浸、涂的已绘制画布	10	0	0	0	0	0	0	0	0	0	0	8.5	0	5		0	0	0			
59070090	用其他材料浸、涂的其他纺织物	10	0	0	0	0	0	0	0	0	0	0	8.5	0	5	0	0	0	0			
59080000	纺织材料制灯芯、炉芯等和煤气灯纱筒及纱罩	10	0	0	0	0	0	0	0	0	0	0		0	5		0	0	0			
59090000	纺织材料制水龙软管及类似管子	8	0	0	0	0	0	0	0	0	0	0		0	5		0	0	0		0	
59100000	纺织材料制的传动带或输送带及带料	8	0	0	0	0	0	0	0	0	0	0		0	5		0	0	0			0
59111010	包覆纺锤用浸胶的起绒狭幅织物	8	0	0	0	0	0	0	0	0	0	0	7.2	0	5		0	0	0			
59111090	其他涂胶等针布及专门技术用途的纺织物起绒狭幅织物	8	0	0	0	0	0	0	0	0	0	0		0	5		0	0	0			
59112000	筛布	8	0	0	0	0	0	0	0	0	0	0		0	5		0	0	0			
59113100	造纸等机器用轻的环状或有联接装置的布或毡呢	8	0	0	0	0	0	0	0	0	0	0		0	5		0	0	0			
59113200	造纸等机器用重的环状或有联接装置的布或毡呢	8	0	0	0	0	0	0	0	0	0	0		0	5		0	0	0			
59114000	用于榨油机器或类似机器的滤布	8	0	0	0	0	0	0	0	0	0	0		0	5		0	0	0			
59119000	其他专门技术用途纺织产品及制品	8	0	0	0	0	0	0	0	0	0	0		0	5		0	0	0			
60011000	针织或钩编的长毛绒织物	10	0	0	0	0	0	0	0	0	0	0	8.5	0	0	0	0	0	0			
60012100	棉制针织或钩编的毛圈绒头织物	10	0	0	0	0	0	0	0	0	0	0	8.5	0	0		0	0	0			
60012200	化纤制针织或钩编毛圈绒头织物	10	0	0	0	0	0	0	0	0	0	0	8.5	0	0	0	0	0	0			
60012900	其他材料制针织或钩编毛圈绒头布	12	0	0	0	0	0	0	0	0	0	0		0	0	0	0	0	2.4			
60019100	棉制针织或钩编起绒织物	10	0	0	0	0	0	0	0	0	0	0	7	0	0		0	0	0			
60019200	化纤制针织或钩编起绒织物	10	0	0	0	0	0	0	0	0	0	0	8.5	0	0	0	0	0	0	0	0	0
60019900	其他纤维制针织或钩编起绒织物	12	0	0	0	0	0	0	0	0	0	0		0	0	0	0	0	2.4			
60024010	宽≤30cm，弹性纱线≥5%棉针织、钩编织物	10	0	0	0	0	0	0	0	0	0	0	8.5	0	0		0	0	0			
60024020	宽≤30cm，弹性纱线≥5%丝及绢丝制针织、钩编织物	10	0	0	0	0	0	0	0	0	0	0	8.5	0	0	0	0	0	0			
60024030	宽≤30cm，弹性纱线≥5%合成纤维制针织、钩编织物	10	0	0	0	0	0	0	0	0	0	0		0	0	0	0	0	0			
60024040	宽≤30cm，弹性纱线≥5%人造纤维制针织、钩编织物	10	0	0	0	0	0	0	0	0	0	0		0	0	0	0	0	0			
60024090	宽≤30cm，弹性纱线≥5%其他纺织材料针织、钩编织物	10	0	0	0	0	0	0	0	0	0	0	7	0	0	0	0	0	0			
60029010	宽≤30cm含橡胶线的棉针织、钩编织物	10	0	0	0	0	0	0	0	0	0	0	8.5	0	0		0	0	0			
60029020	宽≤30cm 含橡胶线的丝及绢丝制针织、钩编织物	10	0	0	0	0	0	0	0	0	0	0	8.5	0	0	0	0	0	0			
60029030	宽≤30cm 含橡胶线的合成纤维制针织、钩编织物	10	0	0	0	0	0	0	0	0	0	0	5	0	0	0	0	0	0			
60029040	宽≤30cm 含橡胶线的人造纤维制针织、钩编织物	10	0	0	0	0	0	0	0	0	0	0	5	0	0	0	0	0	0			
60029090	宽≤30cm含橡胶线的其他纺织材料针织、钩编织物	10	0	0	0	0	0	0	0	0	0	0	8.5	0	0	0	0	0	0			
60031000	宽≤30cm羊毛或动物细毛制的针织、钩编织物	10	0	0	0	0	0	0	0	0	0	0		0	0	0	0	0	0			
60032000	宽≤30cm其他棉制的针织、钩编织物	10	0	0	0	0	0	0	0	0	0	0		0	0		0	0	0			
60033000	宽≤30cm合成纤维制的针织、钩编织物	10	0	0	0	0	0	0	0	0	0	0	9.4	0	0	0	0	0	0			
60034000	宽≤30cm人造纤维制的针织、钩编织物	10	0	0	0	0	0	0	0	0	0	0	9.4	0	0	0	0	0	0			
60039000	宽≤30cm其他针织、钩编织物	10	0	0	0	0	0	0	0	0	0	0		0	0	0	0	0	0			
60041010	宽＞30cm，弹性纱线≥5%棉针织、钩编织物	10	0	0	0	0	0	0	0	0	0	0	7	0	0	0	0	0	0	0		
60041020	宽＞30cm，弹性纱线≥5%丝及绢丝制针织、钩编织物	10	0	0	0	0	0	0	0	0	0	0	8.5	0	0	0	0	0	0			
60041030	宽＞30cm，弹性纱线≥5%合成纤维制针织、钩编织物	10	0	0	0	0	0	0	0	0	0	0		0	0	0	0	0	0	0	0	0

税则号列	商品名称（简称）	最惠国	东盟										亚太	智利	巴基斯坦	新加坡	新西兰	秘鲁	哥斯达黎加	香港	澳门	台湾
			文	柬	印	老	马	缅	菲	新	泰	越										
60041040	宽＞30cm，弹性纱线≥5%人造纤维制针织、钩编织物	10	0	0	0	0	0	0	0	0	0	0		0	0	0	0	0	0	0	0	
60041090	宽＞30cm，弹性纱线≥5%其他纺织材料针织、钩编织物	10	0	0	0	0	0	0	0	0	0	0	8.5	0	0	0	0	0	0	0	0	0
60049010	宽＞30cm含橡胶线的棉针织、钩编织物	10	0	0	0	0	0	0	0	0	0	0	8.5	0	0		0	0	0	0		
60049020	宽＞30cm 含橡胶线的丝及绢丝制针织、钩编织物	10	0	0	0	0	0	0	0	0	0	0	8.5	0	0	0	0	0	0			
60049030	宽＞30cm 含橡胶线的合成纤维制针织、钩编织物	10	0	0	0	0	0	0	0	0	0	0		0	0	0	0	0	0	0	0	0
60049040	宽＞30cm 含橡胶线的人造纤维制针织、钩编织物	10	0	0	0	0	0	0	0	0	0	0		0	0	0	0	0	0	0	0	
60049090	宽＞30cm含橡胶线的其他纺织材料针织、钩编织物	10	0	0	0	0	0	0	0	0	0	0	7	0	0	0	0	0	0	0	0	0
60052100	未漂白或漂白棉制的其他经编织物	10	0	0	0	0	0	0	0	0	0	0		0	0		0	0	0	0		
60052200	染色棉制的其他经编织物	10	0	0	0	0	0	0	0	0	0	0		0	0		0	0	0	0		
60052300	色织棉制的其他经编织物	10	0	0	0	0	0	0	0	0	0	0		0	0		0	0	0	0		
60052400	印花棉制的其他经编织物	10	0	0	0	0	0	0	0	0	0	0		0	0		0	0	0	0		
60053100	未漂白或漂白合成纤维制的其他经编织物	10	0	0	0	0	0	0	0	0	0	0	8.5	0	0	0	0	0	0			0
60053200	染色合成纤维制的其他经编织物	10	0	0	0	0	0	0	0	0	0	0	8.5	0	0	0	0	0	0			0
60053300	色织合成纤维制的其他经编织物	10	0	0	0	0	0	0	0	0	0	0	8.5	0	0	0	0	0	0			
60053400	印花合成纤维制的其他经编织物	10	0	0	0	0	0	0	0	0	0	0	8.5	0	0	0	0	0	0			
60054100	未漂白或漂白人造纤维制的其他经编织物	10	0	0	0	0	0	0	0	0	0	0	8.5	0	0	0	0	0	0			
60054200	染色人造纤维制的其他经编织物	10	0	0	0	0	0	0	0	0	0	0	8.5	0	0	0	0	0	0			
60054300	色织人造纤维制的其他经编织物	10	0	0	0	0	0	0	0	0	0	0	8.5	0	0	0	0	0	0			
60054400	印花人造纤维制的其他经编织物	10	0	0	0	0	0	0	0	0	0	0	8.5	0	0	0	0	0	0			
60059010	羊毛或动物细毛制的其他经编织物	12	0	0	0	0	0	0	0	0	0	0		0	0	0	0	0	2.4			
60059090	其他纺织材料经编织物	12	0	0	0	0	0	0	0	0	0	0		0	0	0	0	0	2.4			
60061000	羊毛或动物细毛制的其他针织、钩编织物	12	0	0	0	0	0	0	0	0	0	0		0	0	0	0	0	2.4			
60062100	未漂白或漂白棉制的其他针织、钩编织物	10	0	0	0	0	0	0	0	0	0	0	7	0	0		0	0	0	0	0	
60062200	染色棉制的其他针织、钩编织物	10	0	0	0	0	0	0	0	0	0	0	8.5	0	0	0	0	0	0	0	0	
60062300	色织棉制的其他针织、钩编织物	10	0	0	0	0	0	0	0	0	0	0	7	0	0	0	0	0	0	0	0	
60062400	印花棉制的其他针织、钩编织物	10	0	0	0	0	0	0	0	0	0	0	8.5	0	0		0	0	0	0	0	0
60063100	未漂白或漂白合成纤维制的其他针织、钩编织物	10	0	0	0	0	0	0	0	0	0	0	8.5	0	0	0	0	0	0	0	0	0
60063200	染色合成纤维制的其他针织、钩编织物	10	0	0	0	0	0	0	0	0	0	0	8.5	0	0	0	0	0	0	0	0	0
60063300	色织合成纤维制的其他针织、钩编织物	10	0	0	0	0	0	0	0	0	0	0	8.5	0	0	0	0	0	0	0	0	0
60063400	印花合成纤维制的其他针织、钩编织物	10	0	0	0	0	0	0	0	0	0	0	8.5	0	0	0	0	0	0	0	0	0
60064100	未漂白或漂白人造纤维制的其他针织、钩编织物	10	0	0	0	0	0	0	0	0	0	0	8.5	0	0	0	0	0	0	0	0	
60064200	染色人造纤维制的其他针织、钩编织物	10	0	0	0	0	0	0	0	0	0	0	8.5	0	0	0	0	0	0	0	0	0
60064300	色织人造纤维制的其他针织、钩编织物	10	0	0	0	0	0	0	0	0	0	0	8.5	0	0	0	0	0	0	0	0	
60064400	印花人造纤维制的其他针织、钩编织物	10	0	0	0	0	0	0	0	0	0	0	8.5	0	0	0	0	0	0	0	0	
60069000	未列名针织、钩编织物	12	0	0	0	0	0	0	0	0	0	0	10.2	0	0	0	0	0	2.4			
61012000	棉制针织或钩编男式大衣、防风衣	17.5	0	0	0	0	0	0	0	0	0	0	14	0	14	0	0	8.8	3.5	0	0	
61013000	化纤制针织或钩编男式大衣等	17.5	0	0	0	0	0	0	0	0	0	0	12.3	0	8.8	0	0	8.8	3.5	0	0	
61019010	毛制针织或钩编男式大衣、防风衣	25	0	0	0	0	0	0	0	0	0	0	18	0	18	0	0	12.5	5	0	0	
61019090	其他纺织材料制针织或钩编男式大衣、防风衣	17.5	0	0	0	0	0	0	0	0	0	0	12.3	0	8.8	0	0	8.8	3.5	0	0	
61021000	毛制针织或钩编女式大衣、防风衣	25	0	0	0	0	0	0	0	0	0	0	18	0	18	0	0	12.5	5	0	0	
61022000	棉制针织或钩编女式大衣、防风衣	17.5	0	0	0	0	0	0	0	0	0	0	14	0	14	0	0		3.5	0	0	
61023000	化纤制针织或钩编女式大衣等	17.5	0	0	0	0	0	0	0	0	0	0	12.3	0	8.8	0	0	8.8	3.5	0	0	
61029000	其他纺织材料制针织或钩编女式大衣、防风衣	20	0	0	0	0	0	0	0	0	0	0	13.8	0	10	0	0	10	4	0	0	
61031010	毛制针织或钩编男式西服套装	25	0	0	0	0	0	0	0	0	0	0	18	0	18	0	0	12.5	5	0	0	
61031020	合纤制针织或钩编男西服套装	25	0	0	0	0	0	0	0	0	0	0	18	0	18	0	0	12.5	5	0	0	
61031090	其他纺织材料制针织或钩编男式西服套装	17.5	0	0	0	0	0	0	0	0	0	0	12.3	0	8.8	0	0	8.8	3.5	0	0	

税则号列	商品名称（简称）	最惠国	东盟										亚太	智利	巴基斯坦	新加坡	新西兰	秘鲁	哥斯达黎加	香港	澳门	台湾
			文	柬	印	老	马	缅	菲	新	泰	越										
61032200	棉制针织或钩编男式便服套装	20	0	0	0	0	0	0	0	0	0	0	14.8	0	14.8	0	0	10	4	0	0	
61032300	合纤制针织或钩编男便服套装	25	0	0	0	0	0	0	0	0	0	0	18	0	18	0	0	12.5	5	0	0	
61032910	毛制针织或钩编男式便服套装	25	0	0	0	0	0	0	0	0	0	0	18	0	18	0	0	12.5	5	0	0	
61032990	其他纺织材料制针织或钩编男式便服套装	25	0	0	0	0	0	0	0	0	0	0	18	0	18	0	0	12.5	5		0	
61033100	毛制针织或钩编男式上衣	16	0	0	0	0	0	0	0	0	0	0	11.7	0	8	0	0	8	3.2	0	0	
61033200	棉制针织或钩编男式上衣	16	0	0	0	0	0	0	0	0	0	0	12	0	8	0	0	8	3.2	0	0	
61033300	合纤制针织或钩编男式上衣	19	0	0	0	0	0	0	0	0	0	0	13.6	0	9.5	0	0	9.5	3.8	0	0	
61033900	其他纺织材料制针织或钩编男式上衣	16	0	0	0	0	0	0	0	0	0	0	11.7	0	8	0	0	8	3.2	0	0	
61034100	毛制针织或钩编男长裤、工装裤等	16	0	0	0	0	0	0	0	0	0	0	11.7	0	8	0	0	8	3.2	0	0	
61034200	棉制针织或钩编男长裤、工装裤等	16	0	0	0	0	0	0	0	0	0	0	13.6	0	8	0	0	8	3.2	0	0	
61034300	合纤制针织或钩编男长裤等	17.5	0	0	0	0	0	0	0	0	0	0	12.3	0	8.8	0	0	8.8	3.5	0	0	
61034900	其他纺织材料制针织或钩编男长裤等	16	0	0	0	0	0	0	0	0	0	0	11.7	0	8	0	0	8	3.2	0	0	
61041300	合纤制针织或钩编女西服套装	25	0	0	0	0	0	0	0	0	0	0	18	0	18	0	0	12.5	5	0	0	
61041910	毛制针织或钩编女式西服套装	17.5	0	0	0	0	0	0	0	0	0	0	12.3	0	8.8	0	0	8.8	3.5	0	0	
61041920	棉制针织或钩编女式西服套装	17.5	0	0	0	0	0	0	0	0	0	0	14	0	14	0	0	8.8	3.5	0	0	
61041990	其他纺织材料制针织或钩编女式西服套装	17.5	0	0	0	0	0	0	0	0	0	0	12.3	0	8.8	0	0	8.8	3.5	0	0	
61042200	棉制针织或钩编女式便服套装	17.5	0	0	0	0	0	0	0	0	0	0	14	0	14	0	0	8.8	3.5	0	0	
61042300	合纤制针织或钩编女便服套装	25	0	0	0	0	0	0	0	0	0	0	18	0	18	0	0	12.5	5	0	0	
61042910	毛制针织或钩编女式便服套装	17.5	0	0	0	0	0	0	0	0	0	0	12.3	0	8.8	0	0	8.8	3.5	0	0	
61042990	其他纺织材料制针织或钩编女式便服套装	15	0	0	0	0	0	0	0	0	0	0	10.4	0	7.5	0	0	7.5	3	0	0	
61043100	毛制针织女式上衣	16	0	0	0	0	0	0	0	0	0	0	11.7	0	8	0	0	8	3.2	0	0	
61043200	棉制针织女式上衣	16	0	0	0	0	0	0	0	0	0	0	13.6	0	13.6	0	0	8	3.2	0	0	
61043300	合纤制针织女上衣	19	0	0	0	0	0	0	0	0	0	0	13.6	0	9.5	0	0	9.5	3.8	0	0	
61043900	其他纺织材料制针织女上衣	16	0	0	0	0	0	0	0	0	0	0	11.7	0	8	0	0	8	3.2	0	0	
61044100	毛制针织或钩编连衣裙	16	0	0	0	0	0	0	0	0	0	0	11.7	0	8	0	0	8	3.2	0	0	
61044200	棉制针织或钩编连衣裙	16	0	0	0	0	0	0	0	0	0	0	13.6	0	8	0	0	8	3.2	0	0	
61044300	合纤制针织或钩编连衣裙	17.5	0	0	0	0	0	0	0	0	0	0	12.3	0	8.8	0	0	8.8	3.5	0	0	
61044400	人纤制针织或钩编连衣裙	16	0	0	0	0	0	0	0	0	0	0	11.7	0	8	0	0	8	3.2	0	0	
61044900	其他纺织材料制针织或钩编连衣裙	16	0	0	0	0	0	0	0	0	0	0	11.7	0	8	0	0	8	3.2	0	0	
61045100	毛制针织或钩编裙子及裙裤	14	0	0	0	0	0	0	0	0	0	0	10.8	0	7	0	0	0	2.8	0	0	
61045200	棉制针织裙子及裙裤	14	0	0	0	0	0	0	0	0	0	0	10.3	0	7	0	0	0	2.8	0	0	
61045300	合纤制针织或钩编裙子及裙裤	16	0	0	0	0	0	0	0	0	0	0	11.7	0	8	0	0	8	3.2	0	0	
61045900	其他纺织材料制针织或钩编裙子及裙裤	14	0	0	0	0	0	0	0	0	0	0	10.8	0	7	0	0	0	2.8	0	0	
61046100	毛制针织或钩编女长裤、工装裤等	16	0	0	0	0	0	0	0	0	0	0	11.7	0	8	0	0	8	3.2	0	0	
61046200	棉制针织或钩编女长裤、工装裤等	16	0	0	0	0	0	0	0	0	0	0	13.6	0	8	0	0	8	3.2	0	0	
61046300	合纤制针织或钩编女长裤等	17.5	0	0	0	0	0	0	0	0	0	0	12.3	0	8.8	0	0	8.8	3.5	0	0	
61046900	其他纺织材料制针织或钩编女长裤等	16	0	0	0	0	0	0	0	0	0	0	12	0	8	0	0	8	3.2	0	0	
61051000	棉制针织或钩编男衬衫	16	0	0	0	0	0	0	0	0	0	0	13.6	0	13.6	0	0		3.2	0	0	0
61052000	化纤制针织或钩编男衬衫	17.5	0	0	0	0	0	0	0	0	0	0	12.3	0	8.8	0	0	8.8	3.5	0	0	
61059000	其他纺织材料制针织或钩编男衬衫	16	0	0	0	0	0	0	0	0	0	0	11.7	0	8	0	0	8	3.2	0	0	
61061000	棉制针织或钩编女衬衫	16	0	0	0	0	0	0	0	0	0	0	13.6	0	8	0	0	8	3.2	0	0	
61062000	化纤制针织或钩编女衬衫	17.5	0	0	0	0	0	0	0	0	0	0	12.3	0	8.8	0	0	8.8	3.5	0	0	
61069000	其他纺织材料制针织或钩编女衬衫	16	0	0	0	0	0	0	0	0	0	0	11.7	0	8	0	0	8	3.2	0	0	0
61071100	棉制针织或钩编男内裤及三角裤	14	0	0	0	0	0	0	0	0	0	0		0	11.2	0	0	7	2.8	0	0	
61071200	化纤制针织或钩编男内裤及三角裤	16	0	0	0	0	0	0	0	0	0	0	10.9	0	8	0	0	8	3.2	0	0	
61071910	丝及绢丝制针织或钩编男内裤及三角裤	14	0	0	0	0	0	0	0	0	0	0	9.3	0	7	0	0	0	2.8	0	0	
61071990	其他纺织材料制针织或钩编男内裤及三角裤	14	0	0	0	0	0	0	0	0	0	0	9.3	0	7	0	0	0	2.8	0	0	
61072100	棉制针织或钩编男长睡衣及睡衣裤	14	0	0	0	0	0	0	0	0	0	0		0	11.2	0	0		2.8	0	0	
61072200	化纤制针织或钩编男睡衣裤	16	0	0	0	0	0	0	0	0	0	0	10.9	0	8	0	0	8	3.2	0	0	
61072910	丝及绢丝制针织或钩编男长睡衣及睡衣裤	14	0	0	0	0	0	0	0	0	0	0	9.3	0	7	0	0	0	2.8	0		
61072990	其他纺织材料制针织或钩编男长睡衣及睡衣裤	14	0	0	0	0	0	0	0	0	0	0	9.3	0	7	0	0	0	2.8	0		
61079100	棉制针织或钩编男浴衣、晨衣	14	0	0	0	0	0	0	0	0	0	0		0	7	0	0	0	2.8	0		
61079910	化纤制针织或钩编男浴衣、晨衣	16	0	0	0	0	0	0	0	0	0	0	10.9	0	8	0	0	8	3.2	0		
61079990	其他纺织材料制针织或钩编男浴衣、晨衣	14	0	0	0	0	0	0	0	0	0	0	9.3	0	7	0	0	0	2.8			

税则号列	商品名称（简称）	最惠国	东盟										亚太	智利	巴基斯坦	新加坡	新西兰	秘鲁	哥斯达黎加	香港	澳门	台湾
			文	柬	印	老	马	缅	菲	新	泰	越										
61081100	化纤制针织或钩编长衬裙及衬裙	16	0	0	0	0	0	0	0	0	0	0	10.9	0	8	0	0	8	3.2	0		
61081910	棉制针织或钩编女式长衬裙及衬裙	14	0	0	0	0	0	0	0	0	0	0		0	7	0	0	0	2.8	0		
61081920	丝及绢丝制针织或钩编女式长衬裙及衬裙	14	0	0	0	0	0	0	0	0	0	0		0	7	0	0	0	2.8	0		
61081990	其他纺织材料制针织或钩编女式长衬裙及衬裙	14	0	0	0	0	0	0	0	0	0	0	9.3	0	7	0	0	0	2.8	0		
61082100	棉制针织或钩编女三角裤及短衬裤	14	0	0	0	0	0	0	0	0	0	0		0	11.2	0	0	0	2.8	0	0	
61082200	化纤制针织或钩编女三角裤及短衬裤	16	0	0	0	0	0	0	0	0	0	0	10.9	0	8	0	0	8	3.2	0	0	
61082910	丝及绢丝制针织或钩编女三角裤及短衬裤	14	0	0	0	0	0	0	0	0	0	0	9.3	0	7	0	0	0	2.8	0	0	
61082990	其他纺织材料制针织或钩编女三角裤及短衬裤	14	0	0	0	0	0	0	0	0	0	0	9.3	0	7	0	0	0	2.8	0	0	
61083100	棉制针织或钩编女睡衣及睡衣裤	14	0	0	0	0	0	0	0	0	0	0		0	11.2	0	0	7	2.8	0	0	
61083200	化纤制针织或钩编女睡衣及睡衣裤	16	0	0	0	0	0	0	0	0	0	0	10.9	0	8	0	0	8	3.2	0	0	
61083910	丝及绢丝制针织或钩编女睡衣及睡衣裤	14	0	0	0	0	0	0	0	0	0	0	9.3	0	7	0	0	0	2.8	0		
61083990	其他纺织材料制针织或钩编女睡衣及睡衣裤	14	0	0	0	0	0	0	0	0	0	0	9.3	0	7	0	0	0	2.8	0		
61089100	棉制针织或钩编女浴衣、晨衣	14	0	0	0	0	0	0	0	0	0	0		0	11.2	0	0	7	2.8	0	0	
61089200	化纤制针织或钩编女浴衣、晨衣	16	0	0	0	0	0	0	0	0	0	0	10.9	0	8	0	0	8	3.2	0	0	
61089900	其他纺织材料制针织或钩编女浴衣、晨衣	14	0	0	0	0	0	0	0	0	0	0	9.3	0	7	0	0	0	2.8	0	0	
61091000	棉制针织或钩编T恤衫、汗衫等	14	0	0	0	0	0	0	0	0	0	0	9.4	0	9.4	0	0	7	2.8	0	0	
61099010	丝及绢丝制针织或钩编T恤衫、汗衫等	14	0	0	0	0	0	0	0	0	0	0	9.3	0	7	0	0	0	2.8	0	0	
61099090	其他纺织材料制针织或钩编T恤衫、汗衫等	14	0	0	0	0	0	0	0	0	0	0	9.3	0	9.3	0	0	7	2.8	0	0	
61101100	羊毛制针织或钩编套头衫等	14	0	0	0	0	0	0	0	0	0	0	9.3	0	0	0	0	7	2.8	0	0	0
61101200	喀什米尔山羊细毛制针织或钩编套头衫等	14	0	0	0	0	0	0	0	0	0	0	9.3	0	0	0	0	0	2.8	0	0	
61101910	其他山羊细毛制针织或钩编套头衫等	14	0	0	0	0	0	0	0	0	0	0	9.3	0	0	0	0	0	2.8	0	0	
61101920	兔毛制针织或钩编套头衫等	14	0	0	0	0	0	0	0	0	0	0	9.3	0	0	0	0	0	2.8	0	0	
61101990	其他毛制针织或钩编套头衫等	14	0	0	0	0	0	0	0	0	0	0	9.3	0	0	0	0	7	2.8	0	0	
61102000	棉制针织或钩编套头衫等	14	0	0	0	0	0	0	0	0	0	0	11	0	0	0	0	7	2.8	0	0	0
61103000	化纤制针织或钩编套头衫等	16	0	0	0	0	0	0	0	0	0	0	10.9	0	0	0	0	8	3.2	0	0	0
61109010	丝及绢丝制针织或钩编套头衫等	14	0	0	0	0	0	0	0	0	0	0	9.3	0	0	0	0	0	2.8	0	0	
61109090	其他纺织材料制针织或钩编套头衫等	14	0	0	0	0	0	0	0	0	0	0	9.3	0	0	0	0	7	2.8	0	0	
61112000	棉制针织或钩编婴儿服装及附件	14	0	0	0	0	0	0	0	0	0	0		0	11.2	0	0	0	2.8	0	0	
61113000	合纤制针织婴儿服装及附件	16	0	0	0	0	0	0	0	0	0	0	10.9	0	8	0	0	8	3.2	0	0	
61119010	毛制针织或钩编婴儿服装及附件	14	0	0	0	0	0	0	0	0	0	0	9.3	0	7	0	0	0	2.8	0	0	
61119090	其他纺织材料制针织或钩编婴儿服装及附件	14	0	0	0	0	0	0	0	0	0	0	9.3	0	7	0	0	7	2.8	0	0	
61121100	棉制针织或钩编运动服	16	0	0	0	0	0	0	0	0	0	0	13.6	0	8	0	0	8	3.2	0	0	
61121200	合纤制针织或钩编运动服	17.5	0	0	0	0	0	0	0	0	0	0	12.3	0	8.8	0	0	8.8	3.5	0	0	
61121900	其他纺织材料制针织或钩编运动服	16	0	0	0	0	0	0	0	0	0	0	11.7	0	8	0	0	8	3.2	0	0	
61122010	棉制针织或钩编滑雪服	16	0	0	0	0	0	0	0	0	0	0	13.6	0	8	0	0	8	3.2			
61122090	其他纺织材料制针织或钩编滑雪服	19	0	0	0	0	0	0	0	0	0	0	13.6	0	9.5	0	0	9.5	3.8			
61123100	合纤制针织或钩编男式游泳服	17.5	0	0	0	0	0	0	0	0	0	0	12.3	0	8.8	0	0	8.8	3.5	0		
61123900	其他纺织材料制针织或钩编男式游泳服	16	0	0	0	0	0	0	0	0	0	0	11.7	0	8	0	0	8	3.2	0		
61124100	合纤制针织或钩编女式游泳服	17.5	0	0	0	0	0	0	0	0	0	0	12.3	0	8.8	0	0	8.8	3.5	0		0
61124900	其他纺织材料制针织或钩编女式游泳服	16	0	0	0	0	0	0	0	0	0	0	11.7	0	8	0	0	8	3.2	0		
61130000	涂层经处理针织或钩编织物制服装	16	0	0	0	0	0	0	0	0	0	0	11.7	0	8	0	0	8	3.2	0	0	
61142000	棉制针织或钩编的其他服装	16	0	0	0	0	0	0	0	0	0	0		0	12.8	0	0		3.2	0	0	
61143000	化纤制针织或钩编的其他服装	17.5	0	0	0	0	0	0	0	0	0	0		0	14	0	0	8.8	3.5	0	0	
61149010	毛制针织或钩编的其他服装	16	0	0	0	0	0	0	0	0	0	0		0	12.8	0	0	8	3.2	0		
61149090	其他纺织材料制针织或钩编的其他服装	16	0	0	0	0	0	0	0	0	0	0		0	12.8	0	0	8	3.2	0		
61151000	渐紧压袜类连裤袜	16	0	0	0	0	0	0	0	0	0	0	9.3	0	8	0	0	8	3.2	0		
61152100	单丝<67 分特合纤制连裤袜等	16	0	0	0	0	0	0	0	0	0	0	14.4	0	12.8	0	0	8	3.2	0	0	
61152200	单丝≥67 分特合纤制连裤袜等	16	0	0	0	0	0	0	0	0	0	0	10.9	0	8	0	0	8	3.2		0	0
61152910	棉制针织或钩编连裤袜及紧身裤袜	14	0	0	0	0	0	0	0	0	0	0		0	11.2	0	0	0	2.8		0	
61152990	其他纺织材料制针织连裤袜及紧身裤袜	14	0	0	0	0	0	0	0	0	0	0	9.3	0	7	0	0	0	2.8		0	0
61153000	单丝<67 分特制针织或钩编女统袜	14	0	0	0	0	0	0	0	0	0	0	9.3	0	7	0	0	0	2.8			
61159400	毛制针织或钩编短袜及其他袜类	14	0	0	0	0	0	0	0	0	0	0		0	11.2	0	0	0	2.8	0		

税则号列	商品名称（简称）	最惠国	东盟										亚太	智利	巴基斯坦	新加坡	新西兰	秘鲁	哥斯达黎加	香港	澳门	台湾
			文	柬	印	老	马	缅	菲	新	泰	越										
61159500	棉制针织或钩编短袜及其他袜类	14	0	0	0	0	0	0	0	0	0	0		0	11.2	0	0	7	2.8	0		
61159600	合纤制针织或钩编短袜及其他袜类	16	0	0	0	0	0	0	0	0	0	0	10.9	0	8	0	0	8	3.2	0		
61159900	其他纺织材料制针织或钩编短袜及其他袜类	14	0	0	0	0	0	0	0	0	0	0	9.3	0	7	0	0	0	2.8	0		0
61161000	塑料或橡胶浸渍的针织或钩织手套	14	0	0	0	0	0	0	0	0	0	0		0		0	0	0	2.8	0		
61169100	毛制其他针织或钩编手套	14	0	0	0	0	0	0	0	0	0	0		0	7	0	0	0	2.8	0		
61169200	棉制其他针织或钩编手套	14	0	0	0	0	0	0	0	0	0	0		0		0	0	0	2.8	0	0	
61169300	合纤制其他针织或钩编手套	16	0	0	0	0	0	0	0	0	0	0	10.9	0	8	0	0	8	3.2	0	0	
61169900	其他纺织材料制针织或钩编手套	14	0	0	0	0	0	0	0	0	0	0	9.3	0	9.3	0	0	7	2.8	0		
61171011	山羊绒制披巾、头巾、围巾、披纱、面纱及类似品	14	0	0	0	0	0	0	0	0	0	0	9.3	0	0	0	0	7	2.8	0		
61171019	其他动物细毛制披巾、头巾、围巾、披纱、面纱及类似品	14	0	0	0	0	0	0	0	0	0	0	9.3	0	0	0	0	7	2.8	0		
61171020	羊毛制披巾、头巾、围巾、披纱、面纱及类似品	14	0	0	0	0	0	0	0	0	0	0	9.3	0	0	0	0	7	2.8	0		
61171090	其他制的披巾、头巾、围巾、披纱、面纱及类似品	14	0	0	0	0	0	0	0	0	0	0	9.3	0	0	0	0	7	2.8	0		
61178010	针织或钩编领带及领结	14	0	0	0	0	0	0	0	0	0	0	9.3	0	0	0	0	0	2.8	0		0
61178090	针织或钩编其他衣着附件	14	0	0	0	0	0	0	0	0	0	0	9.3	0	0	0	0	7	2.8	0		0
61179000	其他针织或钩编衣着零件	14	0	0	0	0	0	0	0	0	0	0	7	0	0	0	0	0	2.8	0	0	0
62011100	毛制男式大衣、斗篷及类似品	16	0	0	0	0	0	0	0	0	0	0	11.7	0	8	0	0	8	3.2	0	0	
62011210	棉制男式羽绒服	16	0	0	0	0	0	0	0	0	0	0		0	12.8	0	0	8	3.2	0	0	
62011290	棉制男式大衣、斗篷及类似品	16	0	0	0	0	0	0	0	0	0	0		0	12.8	0	0	8	3.2	0	0	
62011310	化纤制男式羽绒服	17.5	0	0	0	0	0	0	0	0	0	0	12.3	0	8.8	0	0	8.8	3.5	0	0	
62011390	化纤制男式大衣、斗篷及类似品	17.5	0	0	0	0	0	0	0	0	0	0	12.3	0	8.8	0	0	8.8	3.5	0	0	
62011900	其他纺织材料制男式大衣、斗篷及类似品	16	0	0	0	0	0	0	0	0	0	0	11.7	0	8	0	0	8	3.2	0	0	
62019100	毛制男式带风帽防寒短上衣、防风衣	16	0	0	0	0	0	0	0	0	0	0	11.7	0	8	0	0	8	3.2	0	0	
62019210	棉制男式其他羽绒服	16	0	0	0	0	0	0	0	0	0	0		0	12.8	0	0	8	3.2	0	0	
62019290	棉制男式带风帽防寒短上衣、防风衣	16	0	0	0	0	0	0	0	0	0	0		0	12.8	0	0	8	3.2	0	0	
62019310	化纤制男式其他羽绒服	17.5	0	0	0	0	0	0	0	0	0	0	12.3	0	8.8	0	0	8.8	3.5	0	0	
62019390	化纤制男式防寒短上衣、防风衣	17.5	0	0	0	0	0	0	0	0	0	0	12.3	0	8.8	0	0	8.8	3.5	0	0	
62019900	其他纺织材料制男式防寒短上衣、防风衣	16	0	0	0	0	0	0	0	0	0	0	11.7	0	8	0	0	8	3.2	0	0	
62021100	毛制女式大衣、斗篷及类似品等	16	0	0	0	0	0	0	0	0	0	0	11.7	0	8	0	0	8	3.2	0	0	
62021210	棉制女式羽绒服	16	0	0	0	0	0	0	0	0	0	0		0	12.8	0	0	8	3.2	0	0	
62021290	棉制女式大衣、斗篷及类似品等	16	0	0	0	0	0	0	0	0	0	0		0	12.8	0	0	8	3.2	0	0	
62021310	化纤制女式羽绒服	19	0	0	0	0	0	0	0	0	0	0	13.6	0	9.5	0	0	9.5	3.8	0	0	
62021390	化纤制女式大衣、斗篷及类似品	19	0	0	0	0	0	0	0	0	0	0	13.6	0	9.5	0	0	9.5	3.8	0	0	
62021900	其他纺织材料制女式大衣、斗篷及类似品	16	0	0	0	0	0	0	0	0	0	0	11.7	0	8	0	0	8	3.2	0	0	
62029100	毛制女式带风帽防寒短上衣、防风衣	16	0	0	0	0	0	0	0	0	0	0	11.7	0	8	0	0	8	3.2	0	0	
62029210	棉制女式其他羽绒服	16	0	0	0	0	0	0	0	0	0	0		0	12.8	0	0	8	3.2	0	0	
62029290	棉制女式带风帽防寒短上衣、防风衣	16	0	0	0	0	0	0	0	0	0	0		0	12.8	0	0	8	3.2	0	0	
62029310	化纤制女式其他羽绒服	17.5	0	0	0	0	0	0	0	0	0	0	12.3	0	8.8	0	0	8.8	3.5	0	0	
62029390	化纤制女式防风衣等	17.5	0	0	0	0	0	0	0	0	0	0	12.3	0	8.8	0	0	8.8	3.5	0	0	
62029900	其他纺织材料制防风衣、防风短上衣等	16	0	0	0	0	0	0	0	0	0	0	11.7	0	8	0	0	8	3.2	0	0	
62031100	毛制男式西服套装	17.5	0	0	0	0	0	0	0	0	0	0	12.3	0	8.8	0	0	8.8	3.5	0	0	
62031200	合纤制男式西服套装	17.5	0	0	0	0	0	0	0	0	0	0	12.3	0	8.8	0	0	8.8	3.5	0	0	
62031910	丝及绢丝制男式西服套装	17.5	0	0	0	0	0	0	0	0	0	0	12.3	0	8.8	0	0	8.8	3.5	0	0	
62031990	其他纺织材料制男式西服套装	17.5	0	0	0	0	0	0	0	0	0	0	12.3	0	8.8	0	0	8.8	3.5	0	0	
62032200	棉制男式便服套装	17.5	0	0	0	0	0	0	0	0	0	0		0	14	0	0	8.8	3.5	0	0	
62032300	合纤制男式便服套装	17.5	0	0	0	0	0	0	0	0	0	0	12.3	0	8.8	0	0	8.8	3.5	0	0	
62032910	丝及绢丝制男式便服套装	17.5	0	0	0	0	0	0	0	0	0	0	12.3	0	8.8	0	0	8.8	3.5		0	
62032920	毛制男式便服套装	17.5	0	0	0	0	0	0	0	0	0	0	12.3	0	8.8	0	0	8.8	3.5	0	0	
62032990	其他纺织材料制男式便服套装	17.5	0	0	0	0	0	0	0	0	0	0	12.3	0	8.8	0	0	8.8	3.5	0	0	
62033100	毛制男式上衣	16	0	0	0	0	0	0	0	0	0	0	11.7	0	8	0	0	8	3.2	0	0	
62033200	棉制男式上衣	16	0	0	0	0	0	0	0	0	0	0	14.4	0	12.8	0	0	8	3.2	0	0	
62033300	合纤制男式上衣	17.5	0	0	0	0	0	0	0	0	0	0	12.3	0	8.8	0	0	8.8	3.5	0	0	
62033910	丝及绢丝制男式上衣	16	0	0	0	0	0	0	0	0	0	0	11.7	0	8	0	0	8	3.2	0	0	
62033990	其他纺织材料制男式上衣	16	0	0	0	0	0	0	0	0	0	0	11.7	0	8	0	0	8	3.2	0	0	

税则号列	商品名称（简称）	最惠国	东盟										亚太	智利	巴基斯坦	新加坡	新西兰	秘鲁	哥斯达黎加	香港	澳门	台湾
			文	柬	印	老	马	缅	菲	新	泰	越										
62034100	毛制男式长裤、工装裤等	16	0	0	0	0	0	0	0	0	0	0	11.7	0	8	0	0	8	3.2	0	0	
62034210	棉制男式阿拉伯裤	16	0	0	0	0	0	0	0	0	0	0	12.9	0	8	0	0	8	3.2	0	0	
62034290	棉制男式长裤、工装裤等	16	0	0	0	0	0	0	0	0	0	0	12.9	0	8	0	0	8	3.2	0	0	
62034310	合成纤维制男式阿拉伯裤	17.5	0	0	0	0	0	0	0	0	0	0	13.1	0	8.8	0	0	8.8	3.5	0	0	
62034390	合纤制男式长裤、工装裤等	17.5	0	0	0	0	0	0	0	0	0	0	13.1	0	8.8	0	0	8.8	3.5	0	0	
62034910	其他纺织材料制男式阿拉伯裤	16	0	0	0	0	0	0	0	0	0	0	11.7	0	8	0	0	8	3.2	0	0	
62034990	其他纺织材料制男童裤、工装裤	16	0	0	0	0	0	0	0	0	0	0	11.7	0	8	0	0	8	3.2	0	0	
62041100	毛制女式西服套装	17.5	0	0	0	0	0	0	0	0	0	0	12.3	0	8.8	0	0	8.8	3.5	0	0	
62041200	棉制女式西服套装	17.5	0	0	0	0	0	0	0	0	0	0		0	14	0	0	8.8	3.5	0	0	
62041300	合纤制女式西服套装	17.5	0	0	0	0	0	0	0	0	0	0	12.3	0	8.8	0	0	8.8	3.5	0	0	
62041910	丝及绢丝制女式西服套装	17.5	0	0	0	0	0	0	0	0	0	0	12.3	0	8.8	0	0	8.8	3.5	0	0	
62041990	其他纺织材料制女式西服套装	17.5	0	0	0	0	0	0	0	0	0	0	12.3	0	8.8	0	0	8.8	3.5	0	0	
62042100	毛制女式便服套装	17.5	0	0	0	0	0	0	0	0	0	0	12.3	0	8.8	0	0	8.8	3.5	0	0	
62042200	棉制女式便服套装	17.5	0	0	0	0	0	0	0	0	0	0		0	14	0	0	8.8	3.5	0	0	
62042300	合纤制女式便服套装	20	0	0	0	0	0	0	0	0	0	0	13.8	0	10	0	0	10	4	0	0	
62042910	丝及绢丝制女式便服套装	20	0	0	0	0	0	0	0	0	0	0	13.8	0	10	0	0	10	4		0	
62042990	其他纺织材料制女式便服套装	14	0	0	0	0	0	0	0	0	0	0	9.9	0	7	0	0	0	2.8	0	0	
62043100	毛制女式上衣	16	0	0	0	0	0	0	0	0	0	0	11.7	0	8	0	0	8	3.2	0	0	
62043200	棉制女式上衣	16	0	0	0	0	0	0	0	0	0	0		0	12.8	0	0	8	3.2	0	0	
62043300	合纤制女式上衣	17.5	0	0	0	0	0	0	0	0	0	0	12.3	0	8.8	0	0	8.8	3.5	0	0	
62043910	丝及绢丝制女式上衣	16	0	0	0	0	0	0	0	0	0	0	11.7	0	8	0	0	8	3.2	0	0	
62043990	其他纺织材料制女式上衣	16	0	0	0	0	0	0	0	0	0	0	11.7	0	8	0	0	8	3.2	0	0	
62044100	毛制连衣裙	16	0	0	0	0	0	0	0	0	0	0	11.7	0	8	0	0	8	3.2	0	0	
62044200	棉制连衣裙	16	0	0	0	0	0	0	0	0	0	0		0	12.8	0	0	8	3.2	0	0	
62044300	合纤制女式连衣裙	17.5	0	0	0	0	0	0	0	0	0	0	12.3	0	8.8	0	0	8.8	3.5	0	0	
62044400	人纤制女式连衣裙	16	0	0	0	0	0	0	0	0	0	0	11.7	0	8	0	0	8	3.2	0	0	
62044910	丝及绢丝制连衣裙	16	0	0	0	0	0	0	0	0	0	0	11.7	0	8	0	0	8	3.2	0	0	
62044990	其他纺织材料制连衣裙	16	0	0	0	0	0	0	0	0	0	0	11.7	0	8	0	0	8	3.2	0	0	
62045100	毛制裙子及裙裤	14	0	0	0	0	0	0	0	0	0	0	9.3	0	7	0	0	0	2.8	0	0	
62045200	棉制裙子及裙裤	14	0	0	0	0	0	0	0	0	0	0		0	11.2	0	0	0	2.8	0	0	
62045300	合纤制裙子及裙裤	16	0	0	0	0	0	0	0	0	0	0	11.7	0	8	0	0	8	3.2	0	0	
62045910	丝及绢丝制裙子及裙裤	14	0	0	0	0	0	0	0	0	0	0	9.3	0	7	0	0	0	2.8	0	0	
62045990	其他纺织材料制裙子及裙裤	14	0	0	0	0	0	0	0	0	0	0	9.3	0	7	0	0	7	2.8	0	0	
62046100	毛制女式长裤、工装裤等	16	0	0	0	0	0	0	0	0	0	0	11.7	0	8	0	0	8	3.2	0	0	
62046200	棉制女式长裤、工装裤等	16	0	0	0	0	0	0	0	0	0	0	14.4	0	12.8	0	0	8	3.2	0	0	
62046300	合纤制女式长裤、工装裤等	17.5	0	0	0	0	0	0	0	0	0	0	12.3	0	8.8	0	0	8.8	3.5	0	0	
62046900	其他纺织材料制女式长裤、工装裤等	16	0	0	0	0	0	0	0	0	0	0	12	0	8	0	0	8	3.2	0	0	
62052000	棉制男衬衫	16	0	0	0	0	0	0	0	0	0	0	8	0	8	0	0	8	3.2	0	0	
62053000	化纤制男衬衫	16	0	0	0	0	0	0	0	0	0	0	11.7	0	8	0	0	8	3.2	0	0	
62059010	丝及绢丝制男衬衫	16	0	0	0	0	0	0	0	0	0	0	11.7	0	8	0	0	8	3.2	0	0	
62059020	毛制男衬衫	16	0	0	0	0	0	0	0	0	0	0	11.7	0	8	0	0	8	3.2	0	0	
62059090	其他纺织材料制男衬衫	16	0	0	0	0	0	0	0	0	0	0	11.7	0	8	0	0	8	3.2	0	0	
62061000	丝及绢丝制女式衬衫	16	0	0	0	0	0	0	0	0	0	0	11.7	0	8	0	0	8	3.2	0	0	
62062000	毛制女衬衫	16	0	0	0	0	0	0	0	0	0	0	11.7	0	8	0	0	8	3.2	0	0	
62063000	棉制女衬衫	16	0	0	0	0	0	0	0	0	0	0	13.6	0	8	0	0	8	3.2	0	0	
62064000	化纤制女衬衫	17.5	0	0	0	0	0	0	0	0	0	0	12.3	0	8.8	0	0	8.8	3.5	0	0	
62069000	其他纺织材料制女衬衫	16	0	0	0	0	0	0	0	0	0	0	11.7	0	8	0	0	8	3.2	0	0	
62071100	棉制男式内裤及三角裤	14	0	0	0	0	0	0	0	0	0	0	10.3	0	7	0	0	7	2.8	0	0	
62071910	丝制男式内裤及三角裤	14	0	0	0	0	0	0	0	0	0	0		0	7	0	0	0	2.8	0	0	
62071920	化纤制男式内裤及三角裤	16	0	0	0	0	0	0	0	0	0	0		0	12.8	0	0	8	3.2	0	0	
62071990	其他纺织材料制男式内裤及三角裤	14	0	0	0	0	0	0	0	0	0	0		0	7	0	0	0	2.8	0	0	
62072100	棉制男式长睡衣及睡衣裤	14	0	0	0	0	0	0	0	0	0	0		0	11.2	0	0	0	2.8	0	0	
62072200	化纤制男式长睡衣及睡衣裤	16	0	0	0	0	0	0	0	0	0	0		0	12.8	0	0	8	3.2	0	0	
62072910	丝及绢丝制男式长睡衣及睡衣裤	14	0	0	0	0	0	0	0	0	0	0		0	7	0	0	0	2.8			
62072990	其他纺织材料制男式长睡衣及睡衣裤	14	0	0	0	0	0	0	0	0	0	0		0	7	0	0	0	2.8			
62079100	棉制男式浴衣、晨衣及类似品	14	0	0	0	0	0	0	0	0	0	0		0	11.2	0	0	0	2.8	0	0	
62079910	丝及绢丝制男浴衣、晨衣及类似品	14	0	0	0	0	0	0	0	0	0	0	12.6	0	7	0	0	0	2.8	0	0	
62079920	化纤制男浴衣、晨衣及类似品	16	0	0	0	0	0	0	0	0	0	0		0	12.8	0	0	8	3.2	0	0	
62079990	其他纺织材料制男浴衣、晨衣及类似品	14	0	0	0	0	0	0	0	0	0	0	12.6	0	7	0	0	0	2.8	0	0	
62081100	化纤制长衬裙及衬裙	16	0	0	0	0	0	0	0	0	0	0		0	12.8	0	0	8	3.2	0		

税则号列	商品名称（简称）	最惠国	东盟										亚太	智利	巴基斯坦	新加坡	新西兰	秘鲁	哥斯达黎加	香港	澳门	台湾
			文	柬	印	老	马	缅	菲	新	泰	越										
62081910	丝及绢丝制长衬裙及衬裙	14	0	0	0	0	0	0	0	0	0	0		0	7	0	0	0	2.8	0		
62081920	棉制长衬裙及衬裙	14	0	0	0	0	0	0	0	0	0	0		0	7	0	0	0	2.8	0		
62081990	其他纺织材料制长衬裙及衬裙	14	0	0	0	0	0	0	0	0	0	0		0	7	0	0	0	2.8	0		
62082100	棉制女式睡衣及睡衣裤	14	0	0	0	0	0	0	0	0	0	0	10.3	0	7	0	0	0	2.8	0	0	
62082200	化纤制女式睡衣及睡衣裤	16	0	0	0	0	0	0	0	0	0	0		0	12.8	0	0	8	3.2	0	0	
62082910	丝及绢丝制女式睡衣及睡衣裤	14	0	0	0	0	0	0	0	0	0	0		0	7	0	0	0	2.8	0		
62082990	其他纺织材料制女式睡衣及睡衣裤	14	0	0	0	0	0	0	0	0	0	0		0	7	0	0	0	2.8	0		
62089100	棉制女式背心.内衣.浴衣及类似品	14	0	0	0	0	0	0	0	0	0	0		0	11.2	0	0	7	2.8	0	0	
62089200	化纤制女式背心、内衣及类似品	16	0	0	0	0	0	0	0	0	0	0		0	12.8	0	0	8	3.2	0	0	0
62089910	丝制女式背心、内衣及类似品	14	0	0	0	0	0	0	0	0	0	0	12.6	0	7	0	0	0	2.8	0	0	
62089990	其他纺织材料制女式背心、内衣及类似	14	0	0	0	0	0	0	0	0	0	0	12.6	0	7	0	0	0	2.8	0	0	
62092000	棉制婴儿服装及衣着附件	14	0	0	0	0	0	0	0	0	0	0		0	7	0	0	0	2.8	0	0	
62093000	合纤制婴儿服装及衣着附件	16	0	0	0	0	0	0	0	0	0	0		0	12.8	0	0	8	3.2	0	0	
62099010	毛制婴儿服装及衣着附件	14	0	0	0	0	0	0	0	0	0	0		0	7	0	0	0	2.8	0	0	
62099090	其他纺织材料制婴儿服装及衣着附件	14	0	0	0	0	0	0	0	0	0	0		0	7	0	0	0	2.8	0	0	
62101010	毛制毡呢或无纺织物服装	16	0	0	0	0	0	0	0	0	0	0	11.7	0	8	0	0	8	3.2	0	0	
62101020	棉或麻制毡呢或无纺织物服装	16	0	0	0	0	0	0	0	0	0	0		0	12.8	0	0	8	3.2	0	0	
62101030	化纤制毡呢或无纺织物服装	17.5	0	0	0	0	0	0	0	0	0	0	12.3	0	8.8	0	0	8.8	3.5	0	0	
62101090	其他纺织材料制毡呢或无纺织物服装	16	0	0	0	0	0	0	0	0	0	0		0	12.8	0	0	8	3.2	0	0	
62102000	用塑料、橡胶等处理的织物制男大衣等	16	0	0	0	0	0	0	0	0	0	0	11.7	0	8	0	0	8	3.2	0	0	
62103000	用塑料、橡胶等处理的织物制女大衣等	16	0	0	0	0	0	0	0	0	0	0	11.7	0	8	0	0	8	3.2	0	0	
62104000	用塑料、橡胶等处理的织物制的其他男式服装	16	0	0	0	0	0	0	0	0	0	0	11.7	0	8	0	0	8	3.2	0	0	
62105000	用塑料、橡胶等处理的织物制的其他女式服装	16	0	0	0	0	0	0	0	0	0	0	11.7	0	8	0	0	8	3.2	0	0	
62111100	男式游泳服	16	0	0	0	0	0	0	0	0	0	0	11.7	0	8	0	0	8	3.2	0	0	
62111200	女式游泳服	16	0	0	0	0	0	0	0	0	0	0	11.7	0	8	0	0	8	3.2	0		
62112010	棉制滑雪服	16	0	0	0	0	0	0	0	0	0	0		0	12.8	0	0	8	3.2	0		
62112090	其他纺织材料制滑雪服	19	0	0	0	0	0	0	0	0	0	0	13.6	0	9.5	0	0	9.5	3.8	0		
62113210	棉制男式阿拉伯袍	16	0	0	0	0	0	0	0	0	0	0		0	12.8	0	0	8	3.2	0		
62113220	棉制男式运动服	16	0	0	0	0	0	0	0	0	0	0		0		0	0	8	3.2	0	0	
62113290	棉制其他男式服装	16	0	0	0	0	0	0	0	0	0	0		0		0	0	8	3.2	0	0	
62113310	化纤制男式阿拉伯袍	17.5	0	0	0	0	0	0	0	0	0	0	12.3	0	8.8	0	0	8.8	3.5	0		
62113320	化纤制男式运动服	18	0	0	0	0	0	0	0	0	0	0	12.3	0	12.3	0	0	9	3.6	0	0	
62113390	化纤制其他男式服装	17.5	0	0	0	0	0	0	0	0	0	0	12.3	0	12.3	0	0	8.8	3.5	0	0	
62113910	丝及绢丝制男式运动服及其他服装	16	0	0	0	0	0	0	0	0	0	0	11.7	0	8	0	0	8	3.2	0	0	
62113920	毛制男式运动服及其他服装	16	0	0	0	0	0	0	0	0	0	0	11.7	0	8	0	0	8	3.2	0	0	
62113990	其他纺织材料制男式运动服及其他服装	16	0	0	0	0	0	0	0	0	0	0	11.7	0	8	0	0	8	3.2	0	0	
62114210	棉制女式运动服	16	0	0	0	0	0	0	0	0	0	0		0	12.8	0	0	8	3.2	0	0	
62114290	棉制其他女式服装	16	0	0	0	0	0	0	0	0	0	0		0	12.8	0	0	8	3.2	0	0	
62114310	化纤制女式运动服	17.5	0	0	0	0	0	0	0	0	0	0	12.3	0	8.8	0	0	8.8	3.5	0	0	
62114390	化纤制其他女式服装	17.5	0	0	0	0	0	0	0	0	0	0	12.3	0	8.8	0	0	8.8	3.5	0	0	
62114910	丝及绢丝制女式运动服及其他服装	16	0	0	0	0	0	0	0	0	0	0	11.7	0	8	0	0	8	3.2	0	0	
62114990	其他纺织材料制女式运动服及其他服装	16	0	0	0	0	0	0	0	0	0	0	11.7	0	8	0	0	8	3.2	0	0	
62121010	化纤制胸罩	16	0	0	0	0	0	0	0	0	0	0	14.4	0	12.8	0	0	8	3.2	0	0	0
62121090	其他纺织材料制胸罩	14	0	0	0	0	0	0	0	0	0	0	12.6	0	7	0	0	0	2.8	0	0	0
62122010	化纤制束腰带及腹带	16	0	0	0	0	0	0	0	0	0	0		0	12.8	0	0	8	3.2	0	0	0
62122090	其他纺织材料制束腰带及腹带	14	0	0	0	0	0	0	0	0	0	0		0	11.2	0	0	0	2.8	0	0	0
62123010	化纤制紧身胸衣	16	0	0	0	0	0	0	0	0	0	0		0	12.8	0	0	8	3.2	0	0	
62123090	其他纺织材料制紧身胸衣	14	0	0	0	0	0	0	0	0	0	0		0	7	0	0	0	2.8	0	0	
62129010	化纤制吊裤带、吊袜带等	16	0	0	0	0	0	0	0	0	0	0	14.4	0	12.8	0	0	8	3.2	0	0	0
62129090	其他纺织材料制吊裤带、吊袜带等	14	0	0	0	0	0	0	0	0	0	0	12.6	0	7	0	0	0	2.8	0	0	0
62132010	棉制刺绣手帕	14	0	0	0	0	0	0	0	0	0	0		0	7	0	0	0	2.8	0		
62132090	其他棉制手帕	14	0	0	0	0	0	0	0	0	0	0		0	11.2	0	0	0	2.8	0		
62139020	其他纺织材料制刺绣手帕	14	0	0	0	0	0	0	0	0	0	0		0	7	0	0	0	2.8			
62139090	其他纺织材料制手帕	14	0	0	0	0	0	0	0	0	0	0		0	7	0	0	0	2.8	0		
62141000	丝制披巾、头巾、围巾及类似品	14	0	0	0	0	0	0	0	0	0	0		0	11.2	0	0	0	2.8	0		
62142010	羊毛制披巾、领巾、围巾、披纱、面纱及类似品	14	0	0	0	0	0	0	0	0	0	0		0	11.2	0	0	7	2.8	0		
62142020	山羊绒制披巾、领巾、围巾、披纱、面纱及类似品	14	0	0	0	0	0	0	0	0	0	0		0	11.2	0	0	7	2.8	0		

税则号列	商品名称（简称）	最惠国	东盟										亚太	智利	巴基斯坦	新加坡	新西兰	秘鲁	哥斯达黎加	香港	澳门	台湾
			文	柬	印	老	马	缅	菲	新	泰	越										
62142090	其他动物细毛制披巾、领巾、围巾、披纱、面纱及类似品	14	0	0	0	0	0	0	0	0	0	0		0	11.2	0	0	7	2.8	0		
62143000	合纤制披巾、头巾及类似品	16	0	0	0	0	0	0	0	0	0	0		0	12.8	0	0	8	3.2	0		
62144000	人纤制披巾、头巾及类似品	14	0	0	0	0	0	0	0	0	0	0		0	11.2	0	0	0	2.8	0		
62149000	其他纺织材料制披巾、头巾及类似品	14	0	0	0	0	0	0	0	0	0	0		0	11.2	0	0	0	2.8	0		
62151000	丝及绢丝制领带及领结	14	0	0	0	0	0	0	0	0	0	0		0	11.2	0	0	0	2.8	0		
62152000	化纤制领带及领结	16	0	0	0	0	0	0	0	0	0	0	14.4	0	12.8	0	0	8	3.2	0		
62159000	其他纺织材料制领带及领结	14	0	0	0	0	0	0	0	0	0	0		0	7	0	0	0	2.8	0		
62160000	非针织非钩编手套	14	0	0	0	0	0	0	0	0	0	0		0		0	0	0	2.8	0	0	
62171010	非针织非钩编袜子及袜套	14	0	0	0	0	0	0	0	0	0	0	12.2	0	7	0	0	0	2.8			0
62171020	非针织非钩编和服腰带	14	0	0	0	0	0	0	0	0	0	0	12.2	0	7	0	0	0	2.8	0		0
62171090	非针织非钩编服装或衣着附件	14	0	0	0	0	0	0	0	0	0	0	12.2	0	12.2	0	0	0	2.8	0		0
62179000	非针织非钩编服装或衣着零件	14	0	0	0	0	0	0	0	0	0	0	12.6	0	12.6	0	0	0	2.8	0	0	0
63011000	电暖毯	16	0	0	0	0	0	0	0	0	0	0		0	12.8	0	0	8	3.2			
63012000	毛制毯子及旅行毯	16	0	0	0	0	0	0	0	0	0	0		0	12.8	0	0	8	3.2		0	
63013000	棉制毯子及旅行毯	16	0	0	0	0	0	0	0	0	0	0		0	12.8	0	0	8	3.2		0	
63014000	合纤制毯子及旅行毯	17.5	0	0	0	0	0	0	0	0	0	0		0	14	0	0	8.8	3.5		0	
63019000	其他纺织材料制毯子及旅行毯	16	0	0	0	0	0	0	0	0	0	0		0	12.8	0	0	8	3.2		0	0
63021010	棉制针织或钩编的床上用织物制品	14	0	0	0	0	0	0	0	0	0	0		0	0	0	0	0	2.8			
63021090	其他纺织材料制针织或钩编的床上用织物制品	14	0	0	0	0	0	0	0	0	0	0		0	0	0	0	0	2.8			
63022110	棉制印花床单	14	0	0	0	0	0	0	0	0	0	0		0	0	0	0	0	2.8			
63022190	棉制印花床上用织物制品	14	0	0	0	0	0	0	0	0	0	0		0	0	0	0	0	2.8			
63022210	化纤制印花床单	16	0	0	0	0	0	0	0	0	0	0		0	0	0	0	8	3.2			
63022290	化纤制印花床上用织物制品	16	0	0	0	0	0	0	0	0	0	0		0	0	0	0	8	3.2			
63022910	丝及绢丝制印花床上用织物制品	14	0	0	0	0	0	0	0	0	0	0		0	0	0	0	0	2.8			
63022920	麻制印花床上用织物制品	14	0	0	0	0	0	0	0	0	0	0		0	0	0	0	0	2.8			
63022990	其他纺织材料制印花床上用织物制品	14	0	0	0	0	0	0	0	0	0	0		0	0	0	0	0	2.8			
63023110	棉制刺绣其他床上用织物制品	14	0	0	0	0	0	0	0	0	0	0		0	0	0	0	0	2.8			
63023191	棉制其他床单	14	0	0	0	0	0	0	0	0	0	0		0	0	0	0	0	2.8			
63023192	棉制其他毛巾被	14	0	0	0	0	0	0	0	0	0	0		0	0	0	0	0	2.8			
63023199	棉制其他床上用织物制品	14	0	0	0	0	0	0	0	0	0	0		0	0	0	0	0	2.8			
63023210	化纤制刺绣其他床上用织物制品	16	0	0	0	0	0	0	0	0	0	0		0	0	0	0	8	3.2			
63023290	化纤制其他床上用织物制品	16	0	0	0	0	0	0	0	0	0	0		0	0	0	0	8	3.2			
63023910	丝及绢丝制其他床上用织物制品	14	0	0	0	0	0	0	0	0	0	0		0	0	0	0	0	2.8			
63023921	麻制刺绣的其他床上用织物制品	14	0	0	0	0	0	0	0	0	0	0		0	0	0	0	0	2.8			
63023929	麻制其他床上用织物制品	14	0	0	0	0	0	0	0	0	0	0		0	0	0	0	0	2.8			
63023991	其他纺织材料制刺绣床上用织物制品	14	0	0	0	0	0	0	0	0	0	0		0	0	0	0	0	2.8			
63023999	其他纺织材料制其他床上用织物制品	14	0	0	0	0	0	0	0	0	0	0		0	0	0	0	0	2.8			
63024010	手工针织或钩编的餐桌用织物制品	14	0	0	0	0	0	0	0	0	0	0		0	0	0	0	0	2.8			
63024090	其他针织或钩编的餐桌用织物制品	14	0	0	0	0	0	0	0	0	0	0		0	0	0	0	0	2.8			
63025110	棉制刺绣其他餐桌用织物制品	14	0	0	0	0	0	0	0	0	0	0		0	0	0	0	0	2.8	0		
63025190	棉制其他餐桌用织物制品	14	0	0	0	0	0	0	0	0	0	0		0	0	0	0	0	2.8	0	0	
63025310	化纤制刺绣其他餐桌织物制品	14	0	0	0	0	0	0	0	0	0	0		0	0	0	0	0	2.8			
63025390	化纤制其他餐桌用织物制品	16	0	0	0	0	0	0	0	0	0	0		0	0	0	0	8	3.2			
63025911	亚麻制刺绣其他餐桌用织物制品	14	0	0	0	0	0	0	0	0	0	0		0	0	0	0	0	2.8			
63025919	亚麻制其他餐桌用织物制品	14	0	0	0	0	0	0	0	0	0	0		0	0	0	0	0	2.8			
63025990	其他纺织材料制餐桌用织物制品	14	0	0	0	0	0	0	0	0	0	0		0	0	0	0	0	2.8			
63026010	棉制浴巾	14	0	0	0	0	0	0	0	0	0	0		0	0	0	0	0	2.8			0
63026090	棉制盥洗及厨房用毛巾织物	14	0	0	0	0	0	0	0	0	0	0		0	0	0	0	0	2.8			0
63029100	棉制其他盥洗及厨房织物制品	14	0	0	0	0	0	0	0	0	0	0		0	0	0	0	0	2.8			
63029300	化纤制其他盥洗及厨房织物制品	16	0	0	0	0	0	0	0	0	0	0		0	0	0	0	8	3.2	0		
63029910	亚麻制其他盥洗及厨房织物制品	14	0	0	0	0	0	0	0	0	0	0		0	0	0	0	0	2.8			
63029990	其他材料制其他盥洗及厨房织物	14	0	0	0	0	0	0	0	0	0	0		0	0	0	0	0	2.8			
63031210	合纤制针织的窗帘等	16	0	0	0	0	0	0	0	0	0	0		0	0	0	0	8	3.2			
63031220	合纤制钩编的窗帘等	16	0	0	0	0	0	0	0	0	0	0		0	0	0	0	8	3.2			
63031931	棉制针织的窗帘等	14	0	0	0	0	0	0	0	0	0	0		0	0	0	0	0	2.8			
63031932	棉制钩编的窗帘等	14	0	0	0	0	0	0	0	0	0	0		0	0	0	0	0	2.8			
63031991	其他纺织材料制针织的窗帘等	14	0	0	0	0	0	0	0	0	0	0		0	0	0	0	0	2.8			
63031992	其他纺织材料制钩编的窗帘等	14	0	0	0	0	0	0	0	0	0	0		0	0	0	0	0	2.8			

税则号列	商品名称（简称）	最惠国	东盟										亚太	智利	巴基斯坦	新加坡	新西兰	秘鲁	哥斯达黎加	香港	澳门	台湾
			文	柬	印	老	马	缅	菲	新	泰	越										
63039100	棉制非针织非钩编窗帘等	14	0	0	0	0	0	0	0	0	0	0		0	0	0	0	0	2.8			
63039200	合纤制非针织非钩编窗帘等	16	0	0	0	0	0	0	0	0	0	0		0	0	0	0	8	3.2	0		
63039900	其他纺织材料制非针织非钩编窗帘等	14	0	0	0	0	0	0	0	0	0	0		0	0	0	0	0	2.8			
63041121	手工针织床罩	14	0	0	0	0	0	0	0	0	0	0		0	7	0	0	0	2.8		0	
63041129	非手工针织床罩	14	0	0	0	0	0	0	0	0	0	0		0	7	0	0	0	2.8		0	
63041131	手工钩编床罩	14	0	0	0	0	0	0	0	0	0	0		0	7	0	0	0	2.8			
63041139	非手工钩编床罩	14	0	0	0	0	0	0	0	0	0	0		0	7	0	0	0	2.8			
63041910	丝及绢丝制非针织非钩编床罩	14	0	0	0	0	0	0	0	0	0	0		0	7	0	0	0	2.8			
63041921	棉或麻制非针织非钩编刺绣床罩	14	0	0	0	0	0	0	0	0	0	0		0	7	0	0	0	2.8			
63041929	棉或麻制其他非针织非钩编床罩	14	0	0	0	0	0	0	0	0	0	0		0		0	0	0	2.8			
63041931	化纤制非针织非钩编刺绣床罩	16	0	0	0	0	0	0	0	0	0	0		0	12.8	0	0	8	3.2			
63041939	化纤制其他非针织非钩编床罩	16	0	0	0	0	0	0	0	0	0	0		0	12.8	0	0	8	3.2			
63041991	其他纺织材料制非针织、非钩编刺绣床罩	14	0	0	0	0	0	0	0	0	0	0		0	7	0	0	0	2.8			
63041999	其他材料制其他非针织非钩编床罩	14	0	0	0	0	0	0	0	0	0	0		0	7	0	0	0	2.8			
63049121	手工针织的其他装饰制品	14	0	0	0	0	0	0	0	0	0	0		0	7	0	0	0	2.8			
63049129	非手工针织的其他装饰制品	14	0	0	0	0	0	0	0	0	0	0		0	7	0	0	0	2.8		0	
63049131	手工钩编的其他装饰制品	14	0	0	0	0	0	0	0	0	0	0		0	11.2	0	0	0	2.8			
63049139	非手工钩编的其他装饰制品	14	0	0	0	0	0	0	0	0	0	0		0	7	0	0	0	2.8			
63049210	棉制非针织、非钩编的其他刺绣装饰制品	14	0	0	0	0	0	0	0	0	0	0		0	7	0	0	0	2.8			
63049290	棉制非针织或钩编的其他装饰制品	14	0	0	0	0	0	0	0	0	0	0		0	11.2	0	0	0	2.8			
63049310	合纤制非针织、非钩编其他刺绣装饰制品	16	0	0	0	0	0	0	0	0	0	0		0	12.8	0	0	8	3.2			
63049390	合纤制其他非针织、非钩编装饰制品	16	0	0	0	0	0	0	0	0	0	0		0	12.8	0	0	8	3.2			
63049910	丝制非针织非钩编的装饰制品	14	0	0	0	0	0	0	0	0	0	0		0	7	0	0	0	2.8			
63049921	麻制非针织、非钩编的其他刺绣装饰制品	14	0	0	0	0	0	0	0	0	0	0		0	7	0	0	0	2.8			
63049929	麻制其他非针织非钩编的装饰制品	14	0	0	0	0	0	0	0	0	0	0		0	7	0	0	0	2.8			
63049990	其他纺织材料制非针织非钩编装饰制品	14	0	0	0	0	0	0	0	0	0	0		0	7	0	0	0	2.8			
63051000	黄麻或其他韧皮纤维制货物包装袋	10	0	0	0	0	0	0	0	0	0	0		0	5		0	0	0			
63052000	棉制货物包装袋	16	0	0	0	0	0	0	0	0	0	0		0	12.8	0	0	8	3.2			
63053200	化纤制的散装货物储运软袋	16	0	0	0	0	0	0	0	0	0	0		0	12.8	0	0	8	3.2			
63053300	聚乙烯或聚丙烯扁条制其他货物包装袋	16	0	0	0	0	0	0	0	0	0	0	13.6	0	8	0	0	8	3.2			
63053900	其他化纤制货物包装袋	16	0	0	0	0	0	0	0	0	0	0		0	12.8	0	0	8	3.2			
63059000	其他纺织材料制货物包装袋	14	0	0	0	0	0	0	0	0	0	0		0	11.2	0	0	0	2.8			
63061200	合纤制油苫布、天篷及遮阳篷	16	0	0	0	0	0	0	0	0	0	0		0	0	0	0	8	3.2			
63061910	麻制油苫布、天篷及遮阳篷	14	0	0	0	0	0	0	0	0	0	0		0	0	0	0	0	2.8			
63061920	棉制油苫布、天篷及遮阳篷	14	0	0	0	0	0	0	0	0	0	0		0	0	0	0	0	2.8			
63061990	其他纺织材料制油苫布、天篷及遮阳篷	14	0	0	0	0	0	0	0	0	0	0		0	0	0	0	0	2.8			
63062200	合纤制帐篷	16	0	0	0	0	0	0	0	0	0	0		0	0	0	0	8	3.2			
63062910	棉制帐篷	14	0	0	0	0	0	0	0	0	0	0		0	0	0	0	0	2.8			
63062990	其他纺织材料制帐篷	14	0	0	0	0	0	0	0	0	0	0		0	0	0	0	0	2.8			
63063010	合纤制风帆	16	0	0	0	0	0	0	0	0	0	0		0	0	0	0	8	3.2	0		
63063090	其他纺织材料制风帆	14	0	0	0	0	0	0	0	0	0	0		0	0	0	0	0	2.8			
63064010	棉制充气褥垫	14	0	0	0	0	0	0	0	0	0	0		0	0	0	0	0	2.8			
63064020	化纤制充气褥垫	16	0	0	0	0	0	0	0	0	0	0		0	0	0	0	8	3.2			
63064090	其他纺织材料制充气褥垫	14	0	0	0	0	0	0	0	0	0	0		0	0	0	0	0	2.8			
63069010	棉制其他野营用品	14	0	0	0	0	0	0	0	0	0	0		0	0	0	0	0	2.8			
63069020	麻制其他野营用品	14	0	0	0	0	0	0	0	0	0	0		0	0	0	0	0	2.8			
63069030	化学纤维制其他野营用品	16	0	0	0	0	0	0	0	0	0	0		0	0	0	0	8	3.2			
63069090	其他野营用品	14	0	0	0	0	0	0	0	0	0	0		0	0	0	0	0	2.8			
63071000	擦地布、擦碗布等	14	0	0	0	0	0	0	0	0	0	0	11.9	0	7	0	0	0	2.8			0
63072000	救生衣及安全带	14	0	0	0	0	0	0	0	0	0	0		0	11.2	0	0	0	2.8			
63079000	其他纺织材料制成品	14	0	0	0	0	0	0	0	0	0	0		0	11.2	0	0	0	2.8	0	0	
63080000	零售包装成套物品	14	0	0	0	0	0	0	0	0	0	0		0	7	0	0	0	2.8			
63090000	旧衣物	14	0	0	0	0	0	0	0	0	0	0		0	7	0	0	0	2.8			
63101000	经分拣的纺织材料制碎织物等	14	0	0	0	0	0	0	0	0	0	0		0	11.2	0	0	0	2.8			
63109000	纺织材料制其他碎织物等	14	0	0	0	0	0	0	0	0	0	0		0		0	0	0	2.8			
64011010	橡胶制鞋面的装金属护头的塑料、橡胶制防水鞋靴	24	0	0	0	0	0	0	0	0	0	0	12	0	12	0	0	12	4.8			

税则号列	商品名称（简称）	最惠国	东盟										亚太	智利	巴基斯坦	新加坡	新西兰	秘鲁	哥斯达黎加	香港	澳门	台湾
			文	柬	印	老	马	缅	菲	新	泰	越										
64011090	塑料制鞋面的装金属护头的塑料、橡胶制防水鞋靴	24	0	0	0	0	0	0	0	0	0	0	12	0	12	0	0	12	4.8			
64019210	橡胶制鞋面的橡胶、塑料底及面的中、短统防水靴	24	0	0	0	0	0	0	0	0	0	0	12	0	12	0	0	12	4.8			
64019290	塑料制鞋面的橡胶、塑料底及面的中、短统防水靴	24	0	0	0	0	0	0	0	0	0	0	12	0	12	0	0	12	4.8			
64019900	其他橡胶、塑料制外底及鞋面防水靴	24	0	0	0	0	0	0	0	0	0	0	12	0	12	0	0	12	4.8			
64021200	橡胶、塑料底及面的滑雪靴	10	0	0	0	0	0	0	0	0	0	0	5	0	5		0	0	0			
64021900	橡胶、塑料制底及面的其他运动靴	24	0	0	0	0	0	0	0	0	0	0	12	0	12	0	0	12	4.8			
64022000	橡胶、塑料的将鞋面条带栓塞在鞋底上的鞋	24	0	0	0	0	0	0	0	0	0	0	12	0	12	0	0	12	4.8			
64029100	其他橡胶、塑料短统靴(过踝)	24	0	0	0	0	0	0	0	0	0	0	12	0	12	0	0	12	4.8		0	
64029910	橡胶制鞋面的其他橡胶、塑料鞋靴	24	0	0	0	0	0	0	0	0	0	0	12	0	12	0	0	12	4.8		0	
64029921	以机织物或其他纺织材料作衬底的	24	0	0	0	0	0	0	0	0	0	0	12	0	12	0	0	12	4.8		0	
64029929	塑料制鞋面的其他橡胶、塑料鞋靴	24	0	0	0	0	0	0	0	0	0	0	12	0	12	0	0	12	4.8		0	
64031200	皮革制鞋面的滑雪靴	24	0	0	0	0	0	0	0	0	0	0		0		0	0	12	4.8			
64031900	皮革制鞋面的其他运动鞋靴	15	0	0	0	0	0	0	0	0	0	0		0	12	0	0	7.5	3		0	
64032000	皮革条带为鞋面的皮底鞋	24	0	0	0	0	0	0	0	0	0	0		0		0	0	12	4.8		0	
64034000	装有金属护鞋头的其他皮革面鞋靴	24	0	0	0	0	0	0	0	0	0	0		0		0	0	12	4.8			
64035111	低于小腿的内底长度＜24cm的皮革制外底皮革面的短统靴(过踝)	10	0	0	0	0	0	0	0	0	0	0		0	5		0	0	0		0	
64035119	低于小腿的内底长度≥24cm的皮革制外底皮革面的短统靴(过踝)	10	0	0	0	0	0	0	0	0	0	0		0	5		0	0	0			
64035191	其他内底长度＜24cm的皮革制外底的皮革面短统靴（过踝）	10	0	0	0	0	0	0	0	0	0	0		0	5		0	0	0			
64035199	其他内底长度≥24cm的皮革制外底皮革面短统靴（过踝）	10	0	0	0	0	0	0	0	0	0	0		0	5		0	0	0			
64035900	皮革制外底的皮革面其他鞋靴	10	0	0	0	0	0	0	0	0	0	0		0	5		0	5	0		0	
64039111	其他低于小腿的内底长度＜24cm的皮革面的短统靴(过踝)	10	0	0	0	0	0	0	0	0	0	0		0	5	0	0	0	0		0	
64039119	其他低于小腿的内底长度≥24cm的皮革面的短统靴(过踝)	10	0	0	0	0	0	0	0	0	0	0		0	5	0	0	0	0		0	
64039191	其他内底长度＜24cm的皮革面短统靴（过踝）	10	0	0	0	0	0	0	0	0	0	0		0	5	0	0	0	0		0	
64039199	其他内底长度≥24cm的皮革面短统靴（过踝）	10	0	0	0	0	0	0	0	0	0	0		0	5	0	0	0	0		0	
64039900	皮革制面的其他鞋靴	10	0	0	0	0	0	0	0	0	0	0	8.5	0	5	0	0	0	0		0	
64041100	纺织材料制鞋面的运动鞋靴	24	0	0	0	0	0	0	0	0	0	0	12	0	12	0	0	12	4.8		0	
64041900	纺织材料制鞋面胶底的其他鞋靴	24	0	0	0	0	0	0	0	0	0	0	12	0	12	0	0	12	4.8		0	
64042000	纺织材料制鞋面皮革底的鞋靴	24	0	0	0	0	0	0	0	0	0	0	12	0	12	0	0	12	4.8			
64051010	橡胶、塑料、皮革及再生皮革制外底的皮革或再生皮革制面的其他鞋靴	24	0	0	0	0	0	0	0	0	0	0	12	0	12	0	0	12	4.8			
64051090	其他材料制外底的皮革或再生皮革制面的其他鞋靴	24	0	0	0	0	0	0	0	0	0	0	12	0	12	0	0	12	4.8			
64052000	纺织材料制面的其他鞋靴	22	0	0	0	0	0	0	0	0	0	0	11	0	11	0	0	11	4.4			
64059010	橡胶、塑料、皮革及再生皮革制外底的其他材料制面的鞋靴	15	0	0	0	0	0	0	0	0	0	0	10.5	0	7.5	0	0	7.5	3			
64059090	其他材料制外底的其他材料制面的鞋靴	15	0	0	0	0	0	0	0	0	0	0	10.5	0	7.5	0	0	7.5	3			
64061000	鞋面及其零件，硬衬除外	15	0	0	0	0	0	0	0	0	0	0	13.2	0	7.5	0	0	7.5	3			0
64062010	橡胶制的外底及鞋跟	15	0	0	0	0	0	0	0	0	0	0		0	12	0	0	7.5	3			0
64062020	塑料制的外底及鞋跟	15	0	0	0	0	0	0	0	0	0	0		0	12	0	0	7.5	3			
64069010	木制鞋靴零件,活动式鞋内底等	15	0	0	0	0	0	0	0	0	0	0	10.5	0	7.5	0	0	7.5	3			
64069091	活动式鞋内底、跟垫及类似品	15	0	0	0	0	0	0	0	0	0	0	10.5	0	7.5	0	0	7.5	3	0	0	0
64069092	护腿、裹腿和类似品及其零件	15	0	0	0	0	0	0	0	0	0	0	10.5	0	7.5	0	0	7.5	3	0	0	0
64069099	其他鞋靴零件（包括鞋面，不论是否带有除外底以外的其他鞋底）;活动式鞋内底、跟垫及类似品;护腿、裹腿和类似品及其零件	15	0	0	0	0	0	0	0	0	0	0	10.5	0	7.5	0	0	7.5	3	0	0	0
65010000	毡呢制帽坯及圆帽片	22	0	0	0	0	0	0	0	0	0	0		0		0	0	11	4.4			
65020000	编结或用条带拼制的帽坯	20	0	0	0	0	0	0	0	0	0	0		0		0	0	10	4			
65040000	编结或用条带拼制成的帽类	20	0	0	0	0	0	0	0	0	0	0		0		0	0	10	4			

税则号列	商品名称（简称）	最惠国	东盟										亚太	智利	巴基斯坦	新加坡	新西兰	秘鲁	哥斯达黎加	香港	澳门	台湾
			文	柬	印	老	马	缅	菲	新	泰	越										
65050010	发网	10	0	0	0	0	0	0	0	0	0	0		0	5		0	0	0			
65050020	钩编的帽类	20	0	0	0	0	0	0	0	0	0	0	19	2	19	0	0	10	4			
65050091	成品毡呢帽类	22	0	0	0	0	0	0	0	0	0	0		0		0	0	11	4.4			
65050099	针织或成匹织物制成的帽类	20	0	0	0	0	0	0	0	0	0	0	19	2	19	0	0	10	4		0	
65061000	安全帽	10	0	0	0	0	0	0	0	0	0	0		0	5		0	0	0			
65069100	橡胶或塑料制帽类	10	0	0	0	0	0	0	0	0	0	0		1	5		0	0	0			
65069910	皮革制帽类	10	0	0	0	0	0	0	0	0	0	0		1	5		0	0	0			
65069920	毛皮制帽类	10	0	0	0	0	0	0	0	0	0	0		0	5		0	0	0	0		
65069990	其他材料制的未列名帽类	24	0	0	0	0	0	0	0	0	0	0		2.4		0	0	12	4.8			
65070000	帽类附件	24	0	0	0	0	0	0	0	0	0	0		0		0	0	12	4.8		0	
66011000	庭园用伞及类似品	14	0	0	0	0	0	0	0	0	0	0		0	7	0	0	0	2.8			
66019100	折叠伞	10	0	0	0	0	0	0	0	0	0	0		0	5		0	0	0			
66019900	其他伞	10	0	0	0	0	0	0	0	0	0	0		0	5		0	0	0			
66020000	手杖、带座手杖、鞭子及类似品	10	0	0	0	0	0	0	0	0	0	0		0	5		0	0	0			
66032000	伞骨	14	0	0	0	0	0	0	0	0	0	0		0	11.2	0	0	0	2.8			
66039000	伞、手杖及鞭子的其他零件及饰品	14	0	0	0	0	0	0	0	0	0	0		0	11.2	0	0	0	2.8			
67010000	已加工羽毛、羽绒及其制品	20	0	0	0	0	0	0	0	0	0	0		0		0	0	10	4		0	
67021000	塑料制花、叶、果实及其制品	20	0	0	0	0	0	0	0	0	0	0		0		0	0	10	4			
67029010	羽毛制花、叶、果实及其制品	20	0	0	0	0	0	0	0	0	0	0		0		0	0	10	4			
67029020	丝或绢丝制花、叶、果实及其制品	24	0	0	0	0	0	0	0	0	0	0		0		0	0	12	4.8			
67029030	化学纤维制花、叶、果实及其制品	24	0	0	0	0	0	0	0	0	0	0		0		0	0	12	4.8			
67029090	其他材料制花、叶、果实及其制品	20	0	0	0	0	0	0	0	0	0	0		0		0	0	10	4			
67030000	经梳理、稀疏等方法加工的人发及假发材料	20	0	0	0	0	0	0	0	0	0	0	18	0	18	0	0	10	4			
67041100	合成纺织材料制整头假发	25	0	0	0	0	0	0	0	0	0	0		0		0	0	12.5	5			
67041900	合成纺织材料制其他假发、须等	25	0	0	0	0	0	0	0	0	0	0		0		0	0	12.5	5		0	
67042000	人发制假发、须、眉及类似品	15	0	0	0	0	0	0	0	0	0	0		0	12	0	0	7.5	3		0	
67049000	其他材料制假发、须眉及类似品	25	0	0	0	0	0	0	0	0	0	0		0		0	0	12.5	5		0	
68010000	长方砌石、路缘石、扁平石	12	0	0	0	0	0	0	0	0	0	0		0	6	0	0	0	2.4		0	
68021010	大理石制砖、瓦、方块及类似品	24	0	0	0	0	0	0	0	0	0	0	19.2	0	0	0	0	0	4.8	0	0	
68021090	其他石料制砖瓦、方块及类似品	20	0	0	0	0	0	0	0	0	0	0	16	0	0	0	0	0	4	0	0	
68022110	具有一个平面的大理石及制品	10	0	0	0	0	0	0	0	0	0	0		0	0		0	0	0		0	
68022120	石灰华	24	0	0	0	0	0	0	0	0	0	0		0	0	0	0	0	4.8		0	
68022190	具有一个平面石灰华及蜡石及制品	24	0	0	0	0	0	0	0	0	0	0		0	0	0	0	0	4.8			
68022300	具有一个平面的花岗岩及制品	10	0	0	0	0	0	0	0	0	0	0	9.2	0	0		0	0	0		0	
68022910	具有一个平面的其他石灰石及制品	24	0	0	0	0	0	0	0	0	0	0		0	0	0	0	12	4.8		0	
68022990	具有一个平面的其他石及制品	15	0	0	0	0	0	0	0	0	0	0		0	0	0	0	7.5	3		0	
68029110	大理石、石灰华及蜡石制石刻	24	0	0	0	0	0	0	0	0	0	0		0	0	0	0	0	4.8		0	
68029190	其他大理石、石灰华及蜡石及制品	10	0	0	0	0	0	0	0	0	0	0		0	0		0	0	0	0	0	
68029210	其他石灰石制石刻	24	0	0	0	0	0	0	0	0	0	0		0	0	0	0	12	4.8		0	
68029290	其他加工形式石灰石制品	10	0	0	0	0	0	0	0	0	0	0		0	0		0	5	0	0	0	
68029311	花岗岩制墓碑石	24	0	0	0	0	0	0	0	0	0	0		0	0	0	0	12	4.8		0	
68029319	其他花岗岩制石刻	24	0	0	0	0	0	0	0	0	0	0		0	0	0	0	12	4.8	0	0	
68029390	其他加工形式花岗岩制品	10	0	0	0	0	0	0	0	0	0	0	9.2	0	0		0	0	0		0	
68029910	其他石制成的石刻	24	0	0	0	0	0	0	0	0	0	0		2.4	0	0	0	0	4.8		0	
68029990	其他石及制品	24	0	0	0	0	0	0	0	0	0	0		2.4	0	0	0	0	4.8	0	0	
68030010	板岩制品	20	0	0	0	0	0	0	0	0	0	0		0		0	0	10	4		0	
68030090	已加工板岩及板岩或粘聚板岩制品	20	0	0	0	0	0	0	0	0	0	0		0		0	0	10	4			
68041000	碾磨或磨浆用石磨、石碾	8	0	0	0	0	0	0	0	0	0	0		0	5		0	0	0			
68042100	金刚石制石磨、石碾及砂轮	8	0	0	0	0	0	0	0	0	0	0		0	5		0	0	0	0		
68042210	其他砂轮	8	0	0	0	0	0	0	0	0	0	0		0	5		0	0	0	0		
68042290	其他石磨、石碾及类似品	8	0	0	0	0	0	0	0	0	0	0		0	5		0	0	0	0		
68042310	天然石料制的砂轮	8	0	0	0	0	0	0	0	0	0	0		0	5		0	0	0			
68042390	天然石料制其他石磨、石碾等	8	0	0	0	0	0	0	0	0	0	0		0	5		0	0	0			
68043010	手用琢磨油石	8	0	0	0	0	0	0	0	0	0	0	6.4	0	5		0	0	0			
68043090	手用其他磨石及抛光石	8	0	0	0	0	0	0	0	0	0	0	6.4	0	5		0	0	0			
68051000	砂布	8	0	0	0	0	0	0	0	0	0	0		0.8	5		0	0	0			
68052000	砂纸	8	0	0	0	0	0	0	0	0	0	0		0.8	5		0	0	0			
68053000	其他材料为底的天然或人造研磨料	8	0	0	0	0	0	0	0	0	0	0		0	5		0	0	0			
68061010	硅酸铝纤维及其制品	10.5	0	0	0	0	0	0	0	0	0	0		0	5	0	0	0	2.1			

税则号列	商品名称（简称）	最惠国	东盟										亚太	智利	巴基斯坦	新加坡	新西兰	秘鲁	哥斯达黎加	香港	澳门	台湾
			文	柬	印	老	马	缅	菲	新	泰	越										
68061090	其他矿渣棉、岩石棉及类似的矿质棉（包括其相互混合物），块状、成片或成卷	10.5	0	0	0	0	0	0	0	0	0	0		0	5	0	0	0	2.1			
68062000	页状硅石、膨胀粘土、泡沫矿渣	10.5	0	0	0	0	0	0	0	0	0	0		0	5	0	0	0	2.1			
68069000	其他矿物材料的混合物及制品	10	0	0	0	0	0	0	0	0	0	0		0	5		0	0	0			
68071000	成卷的沥青或类似原料的制品	12	0	0	0	0	0	0	0	0	0	0		0	6	0	0	0	2.4			
68079000	其他形状的沥青或类似原料的制品	12	0	0	0	0	0	0	0	0	0	0	9.6	0	5	0	0	0	2.4			
68080000	镶板、平板、瓦、砖及类似品	10.5	0	0	0	0	0	0	0	0	0	0		0	5	0	0	0	2.1			
68091100	纸贴面未饰的石膏板、片、砖、瓦及类似品	28	0	0	0	0	0	0	0	0	0	0		2.8		0	0	14	5.6			
68091900	以其他材料贴面加强的未饰石膏板	25	0	0	0	0	0	0	0	0	0	0		0		0	0	12.5	5		0	
68099000	其他石膏制品	25	0	0	0	0	0	0	0	0	0	0		0		0	0	12.5	5			
68101100	水泥制建筑用砖及石砌块	10.5	0	0	0	0	0	0	0	0	0	0	8.4	0	5	0	0	0	2.1	0		
68101910	人造石制砖、瓦、扁平石及类似品	10.5	0	0	0	0	0	0	0	0	0	0	8.4	1.1	5	0	0	0	2.1		0	
68101990	水泥制其他砖、瓦、扁平石	10.5	0	0	0	0	0	0	0	0	0	0	8.4	1.1	5	0	0	0	2.1			
68109110	钢筋混凝土和预应力混凝土管、杆、板、桩等	10.5	0	0	0	0	0	0	0	0	0	0		0	5	0	0	0	2.1	0		
68109190	其他水泥制建筑或土木工程用预制构件	10.5	0	0	0	0	0	0	0	0	0	0		0	5	0	0	0	2.1	0	0	
68109910	铁道用水泥枕	8	0	0	0	0	0	0	0	0	0	0		0	5		0	0	0			
68109990	水泥、混凝土或人造石制其他制品	10.5	0	0	0	0	0	0	0	0	0	0		0	5	0	0	0	2.1			
68114010	含石棉的瓦楞板	5	0	0	0	0	0	0	0	0	0	0		0	0		0	0	0			
68114020	含石棉的片、板、砖、瓦及类似品	10.5	0	0	0	0	0	0	0	0	0	0		1.1	5	0	0	0	2.1			
68114030	含石棉的管子及管子配件	8	0	0	0	0	0	0	0	0	0	0		0	5		0	0	0			
68114090	含石棉的其他制品	8.4	0	0	0	0	0	0	0	0	0	0		0	5		0	0	0			
68118100	不含石棉的瓦楞板	5	0	0	0	0	0	0	0	0	0	0		0	0		0	0	0			
68118200	不含石棉的片、板、砖、瓦及类似品	10.5	0	0	0	0	0	0	0	0	0	0		1.1	5	0	0	0	2.1			
68118910	不含石棉的管子及管子配件	8	0	0	0	0	0	0	0	0	0	0		0	5		0	0	0			
68118990	不含石棉的其他制品	8.4	0	0	0	0	0	0	0	0	0	0		0	5		0	0	0			
68128000	青石棉或青石棉混合物制品	10.5	0	0	0	0	0	0	0	0	0	0		0	5	0	0	0	2.1			
68129100	其他石棉或石棉混合物制的服装	10.5	0	0	0	0	0	0	0	0	0	0		0	5	0	0	0	2.1			
68129200	其他石棉或石棉混合物制的纸、麻丝板	10.5	0	0	0	0	0	0	0	0	0	0		0	5	0	0	0	2.1			
68129300	其他成片成卷的压缩石棉纤维接合材料	10.5	0	0	0	0	0	0	0	0	0	0		0	5	0	0	0	2.1			
68129900	其他石棉或石棉混合物制品	10	0	0	0	0	0	0	0	0	0	0		0	5		0	0	0			
68132010	含石棉的闸衬、闸垫	10	0	0	0	0	0	0	0	0	0	0		1	5		0	0	0			
68132090	含石棉的磨擦料及其他用于制动等用途制品	12	0	0	0	0	0	0	0	0	0	0		1.2	6	0	0	0	2.4			
68138100	不含石棉的闸衬、闸垫	10	0	0	0	0	0	0	0	0	0	0		1	5		0	0	0			
68138900	不含石棉的磨擦料及其他用于制动等用途制品	12	0	0	0	0	0	0	0	0	0	0		1.2	6	0	0	0	2.4			
68141000	粘聚或复制云母制的板、片、带	10.5	0	0	0	0	0	0	0	0	0	0		0	5	0	0	0	2.1			
68149000	其他已加工的云母及其制品	10.5	0	0	0	0	0	0	0	0	0	0		0	5	0	0	0	2.1			
68151000	非电器用的石墨或其他碳精制品	15	0	0	0	0	0	0	0	0	0	0		0	12	0	0	7.5	3			
68152000	泥煤制品	15	0	0	0	0	0	0	0	0	0	0		0	12	0	0	7.5	3			
68159100	含菱镁矿、白云石或铬铁矿的制品	15	0	0	0	0	0	0	0	0	0	0		0	12	0	0	7.5	3			
68159920	碳纤维	17.5	0	0	0	0	0	0	0	0	0	0		1.8		0	0	8.8	3.5			
68159931	碳布	17.5	0	0	0	0	0	0	0	0	0	0		1.8		0	0	8.8	3.5			
68159932	碳纤维预浸料	17.5	0	0	0	0	0	0	0	0	0	0		1.8		0	0	8.8	3.5			
68159939	其他碳纤维制品	17.5	0	0	0	0	0	0	0	0	0	0		1.8		0	0	8.8	3.5			
68159940	玄武岩纤维及其制品	17.5	0	0	0	0	0	0	0	0	0	0		1.8		0	0	8.8	3.5			
68159990	其他未列名石制品及矿物制品	17.5	0	0	0	0	0	0	0	0	0	0		1.8		0	0	8.8	3.5			
69010000	硅质化石粉或类似硅土制的砖、瓦	8	0	0	0	0	0	0	0	0	0	0	6.4	0	5		0	0	0			
69021000	含＞50%镁、钙、铬耐火砖及类似品	8	0	0	0	0	0	0	0	0	0	0		0.8	5		0	0	0			
69022000	含＞50%氧化铝、硅耐火砖及类似品	8	0	0	0	0	0	0	0	0	0	0		0.8	5		0	0	0			
69029000	其他耐火砖及耐火陶瓷建材制品	8	0	0	0	0	0	0	0	0	0	0		0	5		0	0	0			
69031000	含＞50%石墨其他耐火陶瓷制品	8	0	0	0	0	0	0	0	0	0	0		0	5		0	0	0			
69032000	含＞50%氧化铝其他耐火陶瓷制品	8	0	0	0	0	0	0	0	0	0	0		0.8	5		0	0	0			
69039000	其他耐火陶瓷制品	8	0	0	0	0	0	0	0	0	0	0		0.8	5		0	0	0			
69041000	陶瓷制建筑用砖	15	0	0	0	0	0	0	0	0	0	0		0	12	0	0	7.5	3			
69049000	陶瓷制铺地砖、支撑或填充用砖	24.5	0	0	0	0	0	0	0	0	0	0		0		0	0	12.3	4.9			
69051000	陶瓷制屋顶瓦	24.5	0	0	0	0	0	0	0	0	0	0		0		0	0	12.3	4.9			
69059000	其他建筑用陶瓷制品	24.5	0	0	0	0	0	0	0	0	0	0		0		0	0	12.3	4.9			

税则号列	商品名称（简称）	最惠国	东盟										亚太	智利	巴基斯坦	新加坡	新西兰	秘鲁	哥斯达黎加	香港	澳门	台湾
			文	柬	印	老	马	缅	菲	新	泰	越										
69060000	陶瓷套管、导管、槽管及管子配件	15	0	0	0	0	0	0	0	0	0	0		0	12	0	0	7.5	3			
69071000	未上釉的小陶瓷砖、瓦、块及类似品	24.5	0	0	0	0	0	0	0	0	0	0		0		0	0	12.3	4.9			
69079000	未上釉的大陶瓷砖、瓦、块及类似品	12	0	0	0	0	0	0	0	0	0	0		0	6	0	0	0	2.4			
69081000	上釉的小陶瓷砖、瓦、块及类似品	12	0	0	0	0	0	0	0	0	0	0	10.4	0	5	0	0	0	2.4			
69089000	上釉的大陶瓷砖、瓦、块及类似品	12	0	0	0	0	0	0	0	0	0	0		0	6	0	0	0	2.4			
69091100	实验室、化学或其他技术用瓷器	8	0	0	0	0	0	0	0	0	0	0		0	5		0	0	0			
69091200	莫氏硬度≥9的技术用陶瓷器	8	0	0	0	0	0	0	0	0	0	0		0	5		0	0	0			
69091900	其他实验室、化学用陶瓷器	8	0	0	0	0	0	0	0	0	0	0		0.8	5		0	0	0			
69099000	农业用、运输或盛装货物用陶瓷容器	21	0	0	0	0	0	0	0	0	0	0		0		0	0	10.5	4.2			
69101000	瓷制脸盆、浴缸及类似卫生器具	10	0	0	0	0	0	0	0	0	0	0	9	0	5	0	0	0	0			
69109000	陶制脸盆、浴缸及类似卫生器具	10	0	0	0	0	0	0	0	0	0	0		1	5	0	0	0	0			
69111011	骨瓷餐具	12	0	0	0	0	0	0	0	0	0	0	10	1.2	5	0	0	0	2.4			
69111019	其他餐具	12	0	0	0	0	0	0	0	0	0	0	10	1.2	5	0	0	0	2.4			
69111021	刀具	15	0	0	0	0	0	0	0	0	0	0	12.5	1.5	7.5	0	0	7.5	3			
69111029	其他厨房器具	15	0	0	0	0	0	0	0	0	0	0	12.5	1.5	7.5	0	0	7.5	3			
69119000	其他家用或盥洗用瓷器	24.5	0	0	0	0	0	0	0	0	0	0	20	0	20	0	0	12.3	4.9			
69120010	陶餐具	15	0	0	0	0	0	0	0	0	0	0		1.5	12	0	0	7.5	3			
69120090	陶制厨房器具	15	0	0	0	0	0	0	0	0	0	0		1.5	12	0	0	7.5	3			
69131000	瓷塑像及其他装饰用瓷制品	15	0	0	0	0	0	0	0	0	0	0		0	12	0	0	7.5	3			
69139000	陶塑像及其他装饰用陶制品	15	0	0	0	0	0	0	0	0	0	0		1.5	12	0	0	7.5	3			
69141000	其他瓷制品	24.5	0	0	0	0	0	0	0	0	0	0		0		0	0	12.3	4.9			
69149000	其他陶制品	10	0	0	0	0	0	0	0	0	0	0		0	5	0	0	0	0			
70010000	废碎玻璃及玻璃块料	12	0	0	0	0	0	0	0	0	0	0		0	6	0	0	0	2.4			
70021000	未加工的玻璃球	12	0	0	0	0	0	0	0	0	0	0		0	6	0	0	0	2.4			
70022010	光导纤维预制棒	6	0	0	0	0	0	0	0	0	0	0		0	5		0	0	0			
70022090	其他未加工的玻璃棒	12	0	0	0	0	0	0	0	0	0	0		0	6	0	0	0	2.4			
70023110	光导纤维用波导级石英玻璃管	5	0	0	0	0	0	0	0	0	0	0		0	0		0	0	0			
70023190	熔融石英或熔融硅石制其他玻璃管	14	0	0	0	0	0	0	0	0	0	0		0	11.2	0	0	0	2.8			
70023200	其他未加工的玻璃管	12	0	0	0	0	0	0	0	0	0	0		0	6	0	0	0	2.4			
70023900	未列名、未加工的玻璃管	12	0	0	0	0	0	0	0	0	0	0		0	6	0	0	0	2.4			
70031200	铸、轧制着色的非夹丝玻璃板、片	15	0	0	0	0	0	0	0	0	0	0		0	12	0	0	7.5	3			
70031900	铸、轧制的其他非夹丝玻璃板、片	17.5	0	0	0	0	0	0	0	0	0	0		0	14	0	0	8.8	3.5			0
70032000	铸、轧制的夹丝玻璃板、片	15	0	0	0	0	0	0	0	0	0	0		0	12	0	0	7.5	3			
70033000	铸、轧制的玻璃型材及异型材	15	0	0	0	0	0	0	0	0	0	0		0	12	0	0	7.5	3			
70042000	拉、吹制的着色玻璃板、片	17.5	0	0	0	0	0	0	0	0	0	0		0	14	0	0	8.8	3.5			
70049000	拉、吹制的其他玻璃板、片	17.5	0	0	0	0	0	0	0	0	0	0		0	14	0	0	8.8	3.5			
70051000	有吸收层非夹丝浮法或抛光玻璃板	15	0	0	0	0	0	0	0	0	0	0		0	12	0	0	7.5	3			
70052100	其他着色非夹丝浮法玻璃板、片	15	0	0	0	0	0	0	0	0	0	0		1.5	12	0	0	7.5	3			
70052900	其他非夹丝浮法玻璃板、片	15	0	0	0	0	0	0	0	0	0	0		1.5	12	0	0	7.5	3			
70053000	夹丝浮法玻璃板、片	17.5	0	0	0	0	0	0	0	0	0	0		0	14	0	0	8.8	3.5			
70060000	经其他加工税号70.03-70.05的玻璃	15	0	0	0	0	0	0	0	0	0	0		0	12	0	0	7.5	3			0
70071110	航空航天器及船舶用钢化安全玻璃	2	0	0	0	0	0	0	0	0	0	0		0	0		0	0	0	0		
70071190	车辆用钢化安全玻璃	10	0	0	0	0	0	0	0	0	0	0		0	5		0	0	0	0		
70071900	其他钢化安全玻璃	14	0	0	0	0	0	0	0	0	0	0		1.4	11.2	0	0	0	2.8			
70072110	航空航天器及船舶用层压安全玻璃	2	0	0	0	0	0	0	0	0	0	0		0	0		0	0	0			
70072190	车辆用层压安全玻璃	20	0	0	0	0	0	0	0	0	0	0		2		0	0	10	4			
70072900	其他层压安全玻璃	14	0	0	0	0	0	0	0	0	0	0		1.4	11.2	0	0	0	2.8			
70080010	中空或真空隔温、隔音玻璃	14	0	0	0	0	0	0	0	0	0	0		0	11.2	0	0	0	2.8			
70080090	其他多层隔温、隔音玻璃组件	14	0	0	0	0	0	0	0	0	0	0		0	11.2	0	0	0	2.8		0	
70091000	车辆后视镜	10	0	0	0	0	0	0	0	0	0	0		1	5	0	0	0	0			0
70099100	其他未镶框玻璃镜(包括后视镜)	21	0	0	0	0	0	0	0	0	0	0		2.1		0	0	10.5	4.2			
70099200	其他镶框玻璃镜(包括后视镜)	12	0	0	0	0	0	0	0	0	0	0	10.8	1.2	5	0	0	0	2.4			
70101000	玻璃安瓿	14	0	0	0	0	0	0	0	0	0	0		1.4	11.2	0	0	0	2.8			
70102000	玻璃制的塞、盖及类似封口器	14	0	0	0	0	0	0	0	0	0	0		0	11.2	0	0	0	2.8			
70109010	装运货物或保藏用的玻璃大容器	14	0	0	0	0	0	0	0	0	0	0		1.4	11.2	0	0	0	2.8			
70109020	装运货物或保藏用的玻璃中容器	14	0	0	0	0	0	0	0	0	0	0		1.4	11.2	0	0	0	2.8			
70109030	装运货物或保藏用的玻璃小容器	14	0	0	0	0	0	0	0	0	0	0		1.4	11.2	0	0	0	2.8			
70109090	装运货物或保藏用的玻璃特小容器	14	0	0	0	0	0	0	0	0	0	0		1.4	11.2	0	0	0	2.8			
70111000	电灯用未封口玻璃外壳及玻璃零件	21	0	0	0	0	0	0	0	0	0	0		0		0	0	10.5	4.2			
70112010	显象管玻壳及其零件	10	0	0	0	0	0	0	0	0	0	0	7	0	5		0	0	0			

税则号列	商品名称（简称）	最惠国	东盟										亚太	智利	巴基斯坦	新加坡	新西兰	秘鲁	哥斯达黎加	香港	澳门	台湾
			文	柬	印	老	马	缅	菲	新	泰	越										
70112090	阴极射线管用玻壳及零件	10	0	0	0	0	0	0	0	0	0	0	7	0	5		0	0	0			
70119010	电子管未封口玻璃外壳及玻璃零件	8	0	0	0	0	0	0	0	0	0	0		0	5		0	0	0			
70119090	其他类似品用未封口玻璃外壳零件	21	0	0	0	0	0	0	0	0	0	0		0		0	0	10.5	4.2			
70131000	玻璃陶瓷制玻璃器皿	24.5	0	0	0	0	0	0	0	0	0	0		0		0	0	12.3	4.9			
70132200	铅晶质高脚杯	24.5	0	0	0	0	0	0	0	0	0	0		0		0	0	12.3	4.9			
70132800	其他高脚杯	8	0	0	0	0	0	0	0	0	0	0		0	5	0	0	0	0			
70133300	其他铅晶质玻璃杯	24.5	0	0	0	0	0	0	0	0	0	0		0		0	0	12.3	4.9			
70133700	其他玻璃杯	8	0	0	0	0	0	0	0	0	0	0		0	5	0	0	0	0			
70134100	铅晶质玻璃制餐桌、厨房用器皿	24.5	0	0	0	0	0	0	0	0	0	0		0		0	0	12.3	4.9			
70134200	低膨胀系数玻璃制餐桌厨房用器皿	10	0	0	0	0	0	0	0	0	0	0		0	5	0	0	0	0			
70134900	其他玻璃制餐桌、厨房用器皿	10	0	0	0	0	0	0	0	0	0	0		0	5	0	0	0	0			
70139100	其他铅晶质玻璃器皿	10	0	0	0	0	0	0	0	0	0	0		0	5	0	0	0	0			
70139900	其他玻璃器皿	10	0	0	0	0	0	0	0	0	0	0		1	5	0	0	0	0			
70140010	光学仪器用光学元件毛坯	10	0	0	0	0	0	0	0	0	0	0		0	5	0	0	0	0		0	
70140090	其他未经光学加工的信号玻璃器	17.5	0	0	0	0	0	0	0	0	0	0		0	14	0	0	8.8	3.5			
70151010	视力矫正眼镜用变色镜片坯件	21	0	0	0	0	0	0	0	0	0	0		0		0	0	10.5	4.2			
70151090	其他视力矫正眼镜用镜片坯件	17.5	0	0	0	0	0	0	0	0	0	0		0	14	0	0	8.8	3.5			
70159010	钟表玻璃	17.5	0	0	0	0	0	0	0	0	0	0		0	14	0	0	8.8	3.5			
70159020	平光变色镜片坯件	18	0	0	0	0	0	0	0	0	0	0		0	14.4	0	0	9	3.6			
70159090	税号 7015 的其他未经光学加工玻璃	12	0	0	0	0	0	0	0	0	0	0		0	6	0	0	0	2.4			
70161000	供镶嵌或装饰用玻璃马赛克	22	0	0	0	0	0	0	0	0	0	0		0		0	0	11	4.4			
70169010	花饰铅条窗玻璃及类似品	24	0	0	0	0	0	0	0	0	0	0		0		0	0	12	4.8			
70169090	建筑用压制或模制铺面玻璃块、砖	18	0	0	0	0	0	0	0	0	0	0		0		0	0	9	3.6			
70172000	其他玻璃制实验室等用玻璃器	8	0	0	0	0	0	0	0	0	0	0		0	5		0	0	0			
70179000	其他实验室、卫生及配药用玻璃器	8	0	0	0	0	0	0	0	0	0	0		0	5		0	0	0			
70181000	玻璃珠、仿珍珠及类似小件玻璃品	10	0	0	0	0	0	0	0	0	0	0		0	5	0	0	0	0			
70182000	直径≤1mm 的玻璃珠	20	0	0	0	0	0	0	0	0	0	0		0		0	0	10	4			
70189000	玻璃假眼；灯工方法制的玻璃塑像及玻璃饰品	20	0	0	0	0	0	0	0	0	0	0		0		0	0	10	4			
70191100	长度≤50mm 的短切玻璃纤维	12	0	0	0	0	0	0	0	0	0	0		0	6	0	0	0	2.4			0
70191200	玻璃纤维粗纱	12	0	0	0	0	0	0	0	0	0	0		0	6	0	0	0	2.4			
70191900	玻璃纤维、梳条、纱线	10	0	0	0	0	0	0	0	0	0	0		0	5		0	0	0		0	0
70193100	玻璃纤维(包括玻璃棉)制的席	5	0	0	0	0	0	0	0	0	0	0		0	0		0	0	0			
70193200	玻璃纤维(包括玻璃棉)制的薄片	14	0	0	0	0	0	0	0	0	0	0		0	11.2	0	0	0	2.8			
70193910	垫	10.5	0	0	0	0	0	0	0	0	0	0		1.1	5	0	0	0	2.1			0
70193990	玻璃纤维（包括玻璃棉）及其制品	10.5	0	0	0	0	0	0	0	0	0	0		1.1	5	0	0	0	2.1			0
70194000	玻璃纤维粗纱机织物	12	0	0	0	0	0	0	0	0	0	0		0	6	0	0	0	2.4			
70195100	宽度≤30mm 的玻璃纤维机织物	12	0	0	0	0	0	0	0	0	0	0		0	6	0	0	0	2.4	0		
70195200	每平米≤250g 的玻璃长丝平纹织物	12	0	0	0	0	0	0	0	0	0	0		0	6	0	0	0	2.4	0	0	
70195900	其他玻璃纤维机织物	12	0	0	0	0	0	0	0	0	0	0	8.4	0	5	0	0	0	2.4	0	0	
70199010	玻璃棉及其制品	7	0	0	0	0	0	0	0	0	0	0		0.7	5		0	0	0		0	
70199021	每平方米重量小于450克的玻璃纤维布浸胶制品	7	0	0	0	0	0	0	0	0	0	0		0.7	5		0	0	0		0	
70199029	其他玻璃纤维布浸胶制品	7	0	0	0	0	0	0	0	0	0	0		0.7	5		0	0	0		0	
70199090	其他玻璃纤维及其制品	7	0	0	0	0	0	0	0	0	0	0		0.7	5		0	0	0		0	
70200011	导电玻璃	10.5	0	0	0	0	0	0	0	0	0	0		1.1	5	0	0	0	2.1	0		
70200012	绝缘子用玻璃伞盘	10.5	0	0	0	0	0	0	0	0	0	0	9.5	1.1	5	0	0	0	2.1			
70200013	熔融石英或其他熔融硅石制	10.5	0	0	0	0	0	0	0	0	0	0	8.9	1.1	5	0	0	0	2.1			
70200019	其他工业用玻璃制品	10.5	0	0	0	0	0	0	0	0	0	0	8.9	1.1	5	0	0	0	2.1			
70200091	保温瓶或其他保温器用玻璃胆	21	0	0	0	0	0	0	0	0	0	0		0		0	0	10.5	4.2	0		
70200099	其他非工业用玻璃制品	15	0	0	0	0	0	0	0	0	0	0	12.8	1.5	7.5	0	0	7.5	3	0		
71011011	未分级的天然黑珍珠	21	0	0	0	0	0	0	0	0	0	0		0		0	0	10.5	4.2			
71011019	其他未分级的天然珍珠	21	0	0	0	0	0	0	0	0	0	0		0		0	0	10.5	4.2			
71011091	其他天然黑珍珠	21	0	0	0	0	0	0	0	0	0	0		0		0	0	10.5	4.2			
71011099	其他天然珍珠	21	0	0	0	0	0	0	0	0	0	0		0		0	0	10.5	4.2			
71012110	未分级、未加工的养殖珍珠	21	0	0	0	0	0	0	0	0	0	0		0		0	0	10.5	4.2			
71012190	其他未加工的养殖珍珠	21	0	0	0	0	0	0	0	0	0	0		0		0	0	10.5	4.2			
71012210	未分级、已加工的养殖珍珠	21	0	0	0	0	0	0	0	0	0	0		0		0	0	10.5	4.2			
71012290	其他已加工的养殖珍珠	21	0	0	0	0	0	0	0	0	0	0		0		0	0	10.5	4.2			
71021000	未分级钻石	3	0	0	0	0	0	0	0	0	0	0		0	0		0	0	0			

税则号列	商品名称（简称）	最惠国	东盟										亚太	智利	巴基斯坦	新加坡	新西兰	秘鲁	哥斯达黎加	香港	澳门	台湾
			文	柬	印	老	马	缅	菲	新	泰	越										
71023100	未加工或简单加工非工业用钻石	3	0	0	0	0	0	0	0	0	0	0		0	0		0	0	0	0		
71023900	其他非工业用钻石	8	0	0	0	0	0	0	0	0	0	0	0	0	0		0	0	0			
71031000	未加工宝石或半宝石	3	0	0	0	0	0	0	0	0	0	0	2.8	0	0		0	0	0			
71039100	经其他加工的红宝石、蓝宝石、祖母绿	8	0	0	0	0	0	0	0	0	0	0	4	0	0		0	0	0			
71039910	经其他加工的翡翠	8	0	0	0	0	0	0	0	0	0	0	4	0	0		0	0	0			
71039920	水晶	8	0	0	0	0	0	0	0	0	0	0	4	0	0		0	0	0			
71039930	碧玺	8	0	0	0	0	0	0	0	0	0	0	4	0	0		0	0	0			
71039940	软玉	8	0	0	0	0	0	0	0	0	0	0	4	0	0		0	0	0			
71039990	经其他加工的其他宝石或半宝石	8	0	0	0	0	0	0	0	0	0	0	4	0	0		0	0	0			
71041000	压电石英	6	0	0	0	0	0	0	0	0	0	0		0	5		0	0	0			
71042090	未加工合成或再造其他宝石或半宝石	0																		0		
71049011	其他工业用合成或再造的钻石	6	0	0	0	0	0	0	0	0	0	0		0	5		0	0	0			
71049012	工业用蓝宝石	6	0	0	0	0	0	0	0	0	0	0		0	5		0	0	0	0		
71049019	其他工业用合成或再造的其他宝石或半宝石	6	0	0	0	0	0	0	0	0	0	0		0	5		0	0	0			
71049091	其他非工业用合成钻石	8	0	0	0	0	0	0	0	0	0	0		0	5		0	0	0			
71049099	其他非工业用合成其他宝石或半宝石	8	0	0	0	0	0	0	0	0	0	0		0	5		0	0	0			
71070000	以贱金属为底的包银材料	10.5	0	0	0	0	0	0	0	0	0	0		0	5	0	0	0	2.1			
71090000	以贱金属或银为底的包金材料	10.5	0	0	0	0	0	0	0	0	0	0		0	5	0	0	0	2.1			
71101990	其他半制成铂	3	0	0	0	0	0	0	0	0	0	0		0	0		0	0	0	0		
71102990	其他半制成钯	3	0	0	0	0	0	0	0	0	0	0		0	0		0	0	0	0		
71103990	其他半制成铑	3	0	0	0	0	0	0	0	0	0	0		0	0		0	0	0			
71104990	其他半制成铱、锇、钌	3	0	0	0	0	0	0	0	0	0	0		0	0		0	0	0			
71110000	以贱金属、银或金为底的包铂材料	3	0	0	0	0	0	0	0	0	0	0		0	0		0	0	0			
71123010	含银或银化合物的灰	8	0	0	0	0	0	0	0	0	0	0		0	5		0	0	0			
71123090	其他含贵金属或贵金属化合物的灰	6	0	0	0	0	0	0	0	0	0	0		0	5		0	0	0			
71129120	其他含金或金化合物的废碎料	6	0	0	0	0	0	0	0	0	0	0		0	5		0	0	0			
71129220	其他含铂或铂化合物的废碎料	6	0	0	0	0	0	0	0	0	0	0		0.6	5		0	0	0			
71129910	含银及银化合物的废碎料	8	0	0	0	0	0	0	0	0	0	0		0.8	5		0	0	0			
71129920	含有其他贵金属或贵金属化合物的废碎料	6	0	0	0	0	0	0	0	0	0	0		0.6	5		0	0	0			
71131110	镶嵌钻石的银首饰及其零件	20	0	0	0	0	0	0	0	0	0	0	16.5	2	16	0	0	10	4	0	0	
71131190	其他银首饰及其零件	20	0	0	0	0	0	0	0	0	0	0	16.5	2	16	0	0	10	4	0	0	
71131911	镶嵌钻石的黄金制首饰及其零件	20	0	0	0	0	0	0	0	0	0	0	14	2	14	0	0	10	4	0	0	
71131919	其他黄金制首饰及其零件	20	0	0	0	0	0	0	0	0	0	0	16	2	16	0	0	10	4	0	0	
71131921	镶嵌钻石的铂制首饰及其零件	35	0	0	0	0	0	0	0	0	0	0	28	3.5	28	0	0	17.5	7	0	0	
71131929	其他铂制首饰及其零件	35	0	0	0	0	0	0	0	0	0	0	28	3.5	28	0	0	17.5	7	0	0	
71131991	镶嵌钻石的其他贵金属制首饰及其零件	35	0	0	0	0	0	0	0	0	0	0	28	3.5	28	0	0	17.5	7	0	0	
71131999	其他贵金属制首饰及其零件	35	0	0	0	0	0	0	0	0	0	0	28	3.5	28	0	0	17.5	7	0	0	
71132010	镶嵌钻石的以贱金属为底的包贵金属制首饰	35	0	0	0	0	0	0	0	0	0	0	30	0	30	0	0	17.5	7	0	0	
71132090	其他以贱金属为底的包贵金属制首饰	35	0	0	0	0	0	0	0	0	0	0	30	0	30	0	0	17.5	7	0	0	
71141100	银器及零件	35	0	0	0	0	0	0	0	0	0	0		0		0	0	0	7	0	0	
71141900	其他贵金属制金银器及零件	35	0	0	0	0	0	0	0	0	0	0		0		0	0	17.5	7	0	0	
71142000	以贱金属为底的包贵金属制金银器	35	0	0	0	0	0	0	0	0	0	0		0		0	0	17.5	7	0	0	
71151000	金属丝布或格栅状的铂催化剂	3	0	0	0	0	0	0	0	0	0	0		0	0		0	0	0	0		
71159010	工业或实验室用贵或包贵金属制品	3	0	0	0	0	0	0	0	0	0	0		0	0		0	0	0	0	0	
71159090	其他用途的贵或包贵金属制品	35	0	0	0	0	0	0	0	0	0	0		0		0	0	17.5	7	0	0	
71161000	天然或养殖珍珠制品	35	0	0	0	0	0	0	0	0	0	0		0		0	0	17.5	7	0	0	
71162000	宝石或半宝石制品	35	0	0	0	0	0	0	0	0	0	0		3.5		0	0	17.5	7	0	0	
71171100	贱金属制袖扣、饰扣	35	0	0	0	0	0	0	0	0	0	0		0		0	0	17.5	7	0	0	
71171900	其他贱金属制仿首饰	17	0	0	0	0	0	0	0	0	0	0	15.3	1.7	13.6	0	0	8.5	3.4	0	0	
71179000	未列名材料制仿首饰	35	0	0	0	0	0	0	0	0	0	0	30	3.5	30	0	0	17.5	7	0	0	
72011000	非合金生铁，含磷量≤0.5%	1	0	0	0	0	0	0	0	0	0	0		0	0		0	0	0			
72012000	非合金生铁，含磷量>0.5%	1	0	0	0	0	0	0	0	0	0	0		0	0		0	0	0			
72015000	合金生铁、镜铁	1	0	0	0	0	0	0	0	0	0	0		0	0		0	0	0			
72021100	锰铁，含碳量≥2%	2	0	0	0	0	0	0	0	0	0	0		0	0		0	0	0			
72021900	锰铁，含碳量≤2%	2	0	0	0	0	0	0	0	0	0	0		0	0		0	0	0			
72022100	硅铁，含硅量≥55%	2	0	0	0	0	0	0	0	0	0	0		0	0		0	0	0			
72022900	硅铁，含硅量≤55%	2	0	0	0	0	0	0	0	0	0	0		0	0		0	0	0			

税则号列	商品名称（简称）	最惠国	东盟										亚太	智利	巴基斯坦	新加坡	新西兰	秘鲁	哥斯达黎加	香港	澳门	台湾
			文	柬	印	老	马	缅	菲	新	泰	越										
72023000	硅锰铁	2	0	0	0	0	0	0	0	0	0	0		0	0		0	0	0			
72024100	铬铁,含碳量≥4%	2	0	0	0	0	0	0	0	0	0	0		0	0		0	0	0			
72024900	铬铁,含碳量≤4%	2	0	0	0	0	0	0	0	0	0	0		0	0		0	0	0			
72025000	硅铬铁	2	0	0	0	0	0	0	0	0	0	0		0	0		0	0	0			
72026000	镍铁	2	0	0	0	0	0	0	0	0	0	0		0	0		0	0	0			
72027000	钼铁	2	0	0	0	0	0	0	0	0	0	0		0	0		0	0	0			
72028010	钨铁	2	0	0	0	0	0	0	0	0	0	0		0	0		0	0	0			
72028020	硅钨铁	2	0	0	0	0	0	0	0	0	0	0		0	0		0	0	0			
72029100	钛铁及硅钛铁	2	0	0	0	0	0	0	0	0	0	0		0	0		0	0	0			
72029210	按重量计含钒量在75%及以上的钒铁	9	0	0	0	0	0	0	0	0	0	0		0	5		0	0	0			
72029290	其他钒铁	9	0	0	0	0	0	0	0	0	0	0		0	5		0	0	0			
72029300	铌铁	2	0	0	0	0	0	0	0	0	0	0		0	0		0	0	0			
72029911	钕铁硼速凝永磁片	2	0	0	0	0	0	0	0	0	0	0		0	0		0	0	0			
72029912	钕铁硼磁粉	2	0	0	0	0	0	0	0	0	0	0		0	0		0	0	0			
72029919	其他钕铁硼合金	2	0	0	0	0	0	0	0	0	0	0		0	0		0	0	0			
72029991	按重量计稀土元素总含量在10%以上的其他铁合金	2	0	0	0	0	0	0	0	0	0	0		0	0		0	0	0			
72029999	其他铁合金	2	0	0	0	0	0	0	0	0	0	0		0	0		0	0	0			
72031000	直接从铁矿还原的铁产品	2	0	0	0	0	0	0	0	0	0	0		0	0		0	0	0			
72039000	其他海绵铁,产品纯度＞99.94%	2	0	0	0	0	0	0	0	0	0	0		0	0		0	0	0			
72041000	铸铁废碎料	2	0	0	0	0	0	0	0	0	0	0		0	0		0	0	0			
72043000	镀锡钢铁废碎料	2	0	0	0	0	0	0	0	0	0	0		0	0		0	0	0			
72044100	机械加工中产生的废料	2	0	0	0	0	0	0	0	0	0	0		0	0		0	0	0			
72051000	生铁、镜铁及钢铁颗粒	2	0	0	0	0	0	0	0	0	0	0		0	0		0	0	0			
72052100	合金钢粉末	2	0	0	0	0	0	0	0	0	0	0		0	0		0	0	0			
72052900	生铁、镜铁及其他钢铁粉末	2	0	0	0	0	0	0	0	0	0	0		0	0		0	0	0			
72061000	铁及非合金钢锭	2	0	0	0	0	0	0	0	0	0	0		0	0		0	0	0			
72069000	其他初级形状的铁及非合金钢	2	0	0	0	0	0	0	0	0	0	0		0	0		0	0	0			
72071100	宽度＜厚度两倍的矩形截面钢坯,C<0.25%	2	0	0	0	0	0	0	0	0	0	0		0	0		0	0	0			
72071200	其他矩形截面钢坯,C,0.25%	2	0	0	0	0	0	0	0	0	0	0		0	0		0	0	0			
72071900	其他含碳量＜0.25%的钢坯	2	0	0	0	0	0	0	0	0	0	0		0	0		0	0	0			
72072000	含碳量≥0.25%的钢坯	2	0	0	0	0	0	0	0	0	0	0		0	0		0	0	0			
72081000	轧压花纹的热轧卷材	5	0	0	0	0	0	0	0	0	0	0		0	0		0	0	0			
72082500	厚度≥4.75mm其他经酸洗的热轧卷材	5	0	0	0	0	0	0	0	0	0	0		0	0		0	0	0			
72082610	屈服强度大于355牛顿/平方毫米，3mm≤厚度＜4.75mm其他经酸洗热轧卷材	5	0	0	0	0	0	0	0	0	0	0		0	0		0	0	0			
72082690	其他3mm≤厚度＜4.75mm其他经酸洗热轧卷材	5	0	0	0	0	0	0	0	0	0	0		0	0		0	0	0			
72082710	厚度＜1.5mm的其他经酸洗的热轧卷材	5	0	0	0	0	0	0	0	0	0	0		0	0		0	0	0			
72082790	其他厚度＜3mm的其他经酸洗的热轧卷材	5	0	0	0	0	0	0	0	0	0	0		0	0		0	0	0			0
72083600	厚度＞10mm的其他热轧卷材	6	0	0	0	0	0	0	0	0	0	0		0	5		0	0	0			
72083700	4.75mm≤厚度≤10mm的其他热轧卷材	5	0	0	0	0	0	0	0	0	0	0		0	0		0	0	0			
72083810	屈服强度大于355牛顿/平方毫米，3mm≤厚度＜4.75mm的其他卷材	5	0	0	0	0	0	0	0	0	0	0		0	0		0	0	0			
72083890	其他3mm≤厚度＜4.75mm的其他卷材	5	0	0	0	0	0	0	0	0	0	0		0	0		0	0	0			0
72083910	厚度＜1.5mm的其他热轧卷材	3	0	0	0	0	0	0	0	0	0	0		0	0		0	0	0			
72083990	其他厚度＜3mm的其他热轧卷材	3	0	0	0	0	0	0	0	0	0	0		0	0		0	0	0			0
72084000	轧有凸起花纹的热轧非卷材	6	0	0	0	0	0	0	0	0	0	0		0	5		0	0	0			
72085110	厚度＞50mm的其他热轧非卷材	6	0	0	0	0	0	0	0	0	0	0		0.6	5		0	0	0			
72085120	厚度＞20mm，但不超过50毫米的其他热轧非卷材	6	0	0	0	0	0	0	0	0	0	0		0.6	5		0	0	0			
72085190	其他厚度＞10mm的其他热轧非卷材	6	0	0	0	0	0	0	0	0	0	0		0.6	5		0	0	0			
72085200	4.75mm≤厚度≤10mm的热轧非卷材	6	0	0	0	0	0	0	0	0	0	0		0	5		0	0	0			
72085310	屈服强度大于355牛顿/平方毫米，3mm≤厚度＜4.75mm的热轧非卷材	6	0	0	0	0	0	0	0	0	0	0	5.1	0	0		0	0	0			
72085390	其他3mm≤厚度＜4.75mm的热轧非卷材	6	0	0	0	0	0	0	0	0	0	0	5.1	0	0		0	0	0			
72085410	厚度＜1.5mm的热轧非卷材	6	0	0	0	0	0	0	0	0	0	0	5.1	0	0		0	0	0			
72085490	其他厚度＜3mm的热轧非卷材	6	0	0	0	0	0	0	0	0	0	0	5.1	0	0		0	0	0			
72089000	其他热轧铁或非合金钢宽平板轧材	6	0	0	0	0	0	0	0	0	0	0		0	5		0	0	0			

税则号列	商品名称（简称）	最惠国	东盟										亚太	智利	巴基斯坦	新加坡	新西兰	秘鲁	哥斯达黎加	香港	澳门	台湾
			文	柬	印	老	马	缅	菲	新	泰	越										
72091510	屈服强度大于355牛顿/平方毫米，厚度≥3mm的冷轧卷材	6	0	0	0	0	0	0	0	0	0	0		0	5		0	0	0			
72091590	其他厚度≥3mm的冷轧卷材	6	0	0	0	0	0	0	0	0	0	0		0	5		0	0	0			
72091610	屈服强度大于275牛顿/平方毫米，1mm＜厚度＜3mm的冷轧卷材	6	0	0	0	0	0	0	0	0	0	0	4.2	0.6	0		0	0	0			
72091690	其他1mm＜厚度＜3mm的冷轧卷材	6	0	0	0	0	0	0	0	0	0	0	4.2	0.6	0		0	0	0			0
72091710	屈服强度大于275牛顿/平方毫米：0.5mm≤厚度≤1mm的冷轧卷材	3	0	0	0	0	0	0	0	0	0	0	2.1	0	0		0	0	0			
72091790	其他0.5mm≤厚度≤1mm的冷轧卷材	3	0	0	0	0	0	0	0	0	0	0	2.1	0	0		0	0	0			0
72091810	厚度＜0.3mm的冷轧卷材	6	0	0	0	0	0	0	0	0	0	0	4.2	0.6	0		0	0	0			
72091890	其他厚度＜0.5mm的冷轧卷材	6	0	0	0	0	0	0	0	0	0	0	4.2	0.6	0		0	0	0			0
72092500	厚度≥3mm的冷轧非卷材	6	0	0	0	0	0	0	0	0	0	0		0	5		0	0	0			
72092600	1mm＜厚度＜3mm的冷轧非卷材	6	0	0	0	0	0	0	0	0	0	0		0	5		0	0	0			
72092700	0.5mm≤厚度≤1mm的冷轧非卷材	6	0	0	0	0	0	0	0	0	0	0	4.2	0	0		0	0	0			
72092800	厚度＜0.5mm的冷轧非卷材	6	0	0	0	0	0	0	0	0	0	0		0	5		0	0	0			
72099000	其他冷轧铁或非合金钢宽平板轧材	6	0	0	0	0	0	0	0	0	0	0	4.2	0	0		0	0	0			
72101100	镀锡的铁或非合金钢厚宽平板轧材	10	0	0	0	0	0	0	0	0	0	0		0	5	0	0	0	0			
72101200	镀锡的铁或非合金钢薄宽平板轧材	5	0	0	0	0	0	0	0	0	0	0		0.5	0		0	0	0			
72102000	镀铅的铁或非合金钢宽平板轧材	4	0	0	0	0	0	0	0	0	0	0		0	0		0	0	0			
72103000	电镀锌的铁或非合金钢宽板材	8	0	0	0	0	0	0	0	0	0	0		0	5		0	0	0			0
72104100	镀锌的瓦楞形铁或非合金钢宽板材	8	0	0	0	0	0	0	0	0	0	0		0	5		0	0	0			
72104900	镀锌的其他形铁或非合金钢宽板材	4	0	0	0	0	0	0	0	0	0	0		0	0		0	0	0			0
72105000	镀氧化铬的铁或非合金钢宽板材	8	0	0	0	0	0	0	0	0	0	0		0	5		0	0	0			
72106100	镀或涂铝锌合金的铁宽平板轧材	8	0	0	0	0	0	0	0	0	0	0		0.8	5		0	0	0			
72106900	其他镀或涂铝的铁宽平板轧材	8	0	0	0	0	0	0	0	0	0	0		0	5		0	0	0			
72107010	厚度小于1.5毫米涂漆或涂塑的宽度在600毫米及以上的铁或非合金钢平板轧材，经包覆、镀层或涂层	4	0	0	0	0	0	0	0	0	0	0		0.4	0		0	0	0	0		
72107090	其他涂漆或涂塑的宽度在600毫米及以上的铁或非合金钢平板轧材，经包覆、镀层或涂层	4	0	0	0	0	0	0	0	0	0	0		0.4	0		0	0	0	0		
72109000	涂镀其他材料铁或非合金钢宽板材	8	0	0	0	0	0	0	0	0	0	0		0	5		0	0	0			
72111300	未轧花纹的四面轧制的热轧非卷材	6	0	0	0	0	0	0	0	0	0	0		0	5		0	0	0			
72111400	厚度≥4.75mm的其他热轧板材	6	0	0	0	0	0	0	0	0	0	0		0	5		0	0	0			
72111900	其他热轧铁或非合金钢窄板材	6	0	0	0	0	0	0	0	0	0	0		0	5		0	0	0			
72112300	冷轧含炭量＜0.25%的板材	6	0	0	0	0	0	0	0	0	0	0		0	5		0	0	0			
72112900	冷轧其他铁或非合金钢窄板材	6	0	0	0	0	0	0	0	0	0	0		0	5		0	0	0			
72119000	冷轧的铁或非合金钢其他窄板材	6	0	0	0	0	0	0	0	0	0	0		0.6	5		0	0	0			
72121000	镀或涂锡的铁或非合金钢窄板材	5	0	0	0	0	0	0	0	0	0	0		0	0		0	0	0			
72122000	电镀锌的铁或非合金钢窄板材	8	0	0	0	0	0	0	0	0	0	0		0	5		0	0	0			
72123000	其他镀或涂锌的铁窄板材	8	0	0	0	0	0	0	0	0	0	0		0.8	5		0	0	0			
72124000	涂漆或涂塑的铁或非合金钢窄板材	4	0	0	0	0	0	0	0	0	0	0		0.4	0		0	0	0	0		
72125000	涂镀其他材料铁或非合金钢窄板材	8	0	0	0	0	0	0	0	0	0	0		0	5		0	0	0			
72126000	经包覆的铁或非合金钢窄板材	8	0	0	0	0	0	0	0	0	0	0		0	5		0	0	0			
72131000	带有轧制花纹的热轧盘条	3	0	0	0	0	0	0	0	0	0	0		0	0		0	0	0			
72132000	其他易切削钢制热轧盘条	3	0	0	0	0	0	0	0	0	0	0		0	0		0	0	0			
72139100	直径＜14mm圆截面的其他热轧盘条	5	0	0	0	0	0	0	0	0	0	0	4.3	0.5	0		0	0	0			
72139900	其他热轧盘条	5	0	0	0	0	0	0	0	0	0	0		0	0		0	0	0			
72141000	锻造的铁或非合金钢条、杆	7	0	0	0	0	0	0	0	0	0	0		0.7	5		0	0	0			
72142000	热加工带有轧制花纹的条、杆	3	0	0	0	0	0	0	0	0	0	0	0	0	0		0	0	0	0		
72143000	热加工易切削钢的条、杆	7	0	0	0	0	0	0	0	0	0	0		0	5		0	0	0			
72149100	热加工其他矩形截面的条杆	3	0	0	0	0	0	0	0	0	0	0		0	0		0	0	0			
72149900	热加工其他条、杆	3	0	0	0	0	0	0	0	0	0	0		0	0		0	0	0			
72151000	冷加工其他易切削钢制条、杆	7	0	0	0	0	0	0	0	0	0	0		0	5		0	0	0			
72155000	冷加工或冷成形的其他条、杆	7	0	0	0	0	0	0	0	0	0	0		0	5		0	0	0			
72159000	铁及非合金钢的其他条、杆	3	0	0	0	0	0	0	0	0	0	0		0	0		0	0	0			
72161010	截面高度＜80mm的H型钢	3	0	0	0	0	0	0	0	0	0	0		0	0		0	0	0			
72161020	截面高度低于80毫米的工字钢	3	0	0	0	0	0	0	0	0	0	0		0	0		0	0	0			
72161090	截面高度＜80mmU型钢	3	0	0	0	0	0	0	0	0	0	0		0	0		0	0	0			
72162100	热加工截面高度＜80mm角钢	6	0	0	0	0	0	0	0	0	0	0		0.6	5		0	0	0			
72162200	热加工截面高度＜80mm丁字钢	6	0	0	0	0	0	0	0	0	0	0		0	5		0	0	0			

税则号列	商品名称（简称）	最惠国	东盟 文	柬	印	老	马	缅	菲	新	泰	越	亚太	智利	巴基斯坦	新加坡	新西兰	秘鲁	哥斯达黎加	香港	澳门	台湾
72163100	热加工截面高度≥80mm槽型钢	6	0	0	0	0	0	0	0	0	0	0		0.6	5		0	0	0			
72163210	截面高度在200毫米以上的工字钢	6	0	0	0	0	0	0	0	0	0	0		0	5		0	0	0			
72163290	热加工截面高度≥80mm工字型钢	6	0	0	0	0	0	0	0	0	0	0		0	5		0	0	0			
72163311	截面高度在800毫米以上的H型缸	6	0	0	0	0	0	0	0	0	0	0		0	5		0	0	0			
72163319	截面高度≥200mmH型钢	6	0	0	0	0	0	0	0	0	0	0		0	5		0	0	0			
72163390	其他截面高度≥80mmH型钢	6	0	0	0	0	0	0	0	0	0	0		0	5		0	0	0			
72164010	热加工截面高度≥80mm角钢	3	0	0	0	0	0	0	0	0	0	0		0	0		0	0	0			
72164020	热加工截面高度≥80mm丁字钢	3	0	0	0	0	0	0	0	0	0	0		0	0		0	0	0			
72165010	热加工乙字钢	6	0	0	0	0	0	0	0	0	0	0		0	5		0	0	0			
72165020	热加工球扁钢	3	0	0	0	0	0	0	0	0	0	0		0	0		0	0	0			
72165090	热加工其他角材、型材及异型材	3	0	0	0	0	0	0	0	0	0	0		0	0		0	0	0			
72166100	冷加工板材制的角材、型材及异型材	3	0	0	0	0	0	0	0	0	0	0		0	0		0	0	0			
72166900	冷加工其他角材、型材及异型材	3	0	0	0	0	0	0	0	0	0	0		0	0		0	0	0			
72169100	冷加工其他板材制角材、型材及异型材	3	0	0	0	0	0	0	0	0	0	0		0	0		0	0	0			
72169900	其他角材、型材及异型材	3	0	0	0	0	0	0	0	0	0	0		0	0		0	0	0			
72171000	未镀或涂层的铁或非合金钢丝	8	0	0	0	0	0	0	0	0	0	0		0.8	5		0	0	0			0
72172000	镀或涂锌的铁或非合金钢丝	8	0	0	0	0	0	0	0	0	0	0		0.8	5		0	0	0			
72173010	镀或涂铜的铁丝和非合金钢丝	8	0	0	0	0	0	0	0	0	0	0	6.4	0.8	5		0	0	0			
72173090	镀或涂其他贱金属的铁丝和非合金钢丝	8	0	0	0	0	0	0	0	0	0	0	6.4	0.8	5		0	0	0			
72179000	其他铁丝或非合金钢丝	8	0	0	0	0	0	0	0	0	0	0		0	5		0	0	0	0		
72181000	不锈钢锭及其他初级形状产品	2	0	0	0	0	0	0	0	0	0	0		0	0		0	0	0			
72189100	矩形截面的不锈钢半制成品	2	0	0	0	0	0	0	0	0	0	0		0	0		0	0	0			
72189900	其他不锈钢半制成品	2	0	0	0	0	0	0	0	0	0	0		0	0		0	0	0			
72191100	厚度＞10mm热轧不锈钢卷板	4	0	0	0	0	0	0	0	0	0	0		0	0		0	0	0			
72191200	4.75mm≤厚度≤10mm热轧不锈钢卷板	4	0	0	0	0	0	0	0	0	0	0		0	0		0	0	0			0
72191312	按重量计含锰量在5.5%及以上的未经酸洗3mm≤厚度＜4.75mm铬锰系不锈钢	4	0	0	0	0	0	0	0	0	0	0		0	0		0	0	0			
72191319	厚度在3毫米及以上，但小于4.75毫米的未经酸洗的其他不锈钢卷板	4	0	0	0	0	0	0	0	0	0	0		0	0		0	0	0			0
72191322	按重量计含锰量在5.5%及以上的经酸洗3mm≤厚度＜4.75mm铬锰系不锈钢	4	0	0	0	0	0	0	0	0	0	0		0	0		0	0	0			
72191329	厚度在3毫米及以上，但小于4.75毫米的经酸洗的其他不锈钢卷板	4	0	0	0	0	0	0	0	0	0	0		0	0		0	0	0			0
72191412	按重量计含锰量在5.5%及以上的未经酸洗厚度＜3mm的铬锰系不锈钢	4	0	0	0	0	0	0	0	0	0	0		0	0		0	0	0			
72191419	厚度在3毫米以下的未经酸洗的其他不锈钢卷板	4	0	0	0	0	0	0	0	0	0	0		0	0		0	0	0			
72191422	按重量计含锰量在5.5%及以上的经酸洗厚度＜3mm的铬锰系不锈钢	4	0	0	0	0	0	0	0	0	0	0		0	0		0	0	0			
72191429	厚度在3毫米以下的经酸洗的其他不锈钢卷板	4	0	0	0	0	0	0	0	0	0	0		0	0		0	0	0			
72192100	厚度＞10mm热轧不锈钢平板	10	0	0	0	0	0	0	0	0	0	0	9.3	0	5	0	0	0	0	0		
72192200	4.75mm≤厚度≤10mm热轧不锈钢平板	10	0	0	0	0	0	0	0	0	0	0	9.3	1	5	0	0	5	0	0		
72192300	3mm≤厚度＜4.75mm热轧不锈钢平板	10	0	0	0	0	0	0	0	0	0	0	9.3	0	5	0	0	0	0			0
72192410	1mm＜厚度＜3mm热轧不锈钢平板	10	0	0	0	0	0	0	0	0	0	0	9.3	0	5	0	0	0	0			0
72192420	0.5mm≤厚度≤1mm热轧不锈钢平板	10	0	0	0	0	0	0	0	0	0	0	9.3	0	5	0	0	0	0			
72192430	厚度＜0.5mm热轧不锈钢平板	10	0	0	0	0	0	0	0	0	0	0	9.3	0	5	0	0	0	0			
72193100	厚度≥4.75mm冷轧不锈钢板	10	0	0	0	0	0	0	0	0	0	0		1	5	0	0	5	0			0
72193200	3mm≤厚度＜4.75mm冷轧不锈钢板材	10	0	0	0	0	0	0	0	0	0	0		1	5	0	0	5	0			0
72193310	1mm＜厚度＜3mm冷轧按重量计含锰量在5.5%及以上的铬锰系不锈钢板材	10	0	0	0	0	0	0	0	0	0	0		1	5	0	0	5	0	0		0
72193390	其他1mm＜厚度＜3mm冷轧不锈钢板材	10	0	0	0	0	0	0	0	0	0	0		1	5	0	0	5	0	0		0
72193400	0.5mm≤厚度≤1mm冷轧不锈钢板材	10	0	0	0	0	0	0	0	0	0	0		1	5	0	0	5	0	0		0
72193500	厚度＜0.5mm冷轧不锈钢板材	10	0	0	0	0	0	0	0	0	0	0		1	5	0	0	5	0	0		0
72199000	其他不锈钢冷轧板材	10	0	0	0	0	0	0	0	0	0	0		0	5	0	0	0	0			0
72201100	热轧不锈钢带材厚度≥4.75mm	10	0	0	0	0	0	0	0	0	0	0		0	5	0	0	0	0	0		
72201200	热轧不锈钢带材厚度＜4.75mm	10	0	0	0	0	0	0	0	0	0	0		0	5	0	0	0	0			
72202020	厚度在0.35毫米及以下的冷轧不锈钢带材	10	0	0	0	0	0	0	0	0	0	0		0	5	0	0	0	0			
72202030	厚度在0.35毫米以上但小于3毫米的冷轧不锈钢带材	10	0	0	0	0	0	0	0	0	0	0		0	5	0	0	0	0			

税则号列	商品名称（简称）	最惠国	东盟										亚太	智利	巴基斯坦	新加坡	新西兰	秘鲁	哥斯达黎加	香港	澳门	台湾
			文	柬	印	老	马	缅	菲	新	泰	越										
72202040	厚度在3毫米及以上的冷轧不锈钢带材	10	0	0	0	0	0	0	0	0	0	0		0	5	0	0	0	0			
72209000	其他不锈钢带材	10	0	0	0	0	0	0	0	0	0	0		0	5	0	0	0	0			0
72210000	不锈钢热轧条、杆	10	0	0	0	0	0	0	0	0	0	0	8	0	5	0	0	0	0			
72221100	热加工的圆形截面不锈钢条、杆	10	0	0	0	0	0	0	0	0	0	0	9	0	5	0	0	0	0			
72221900	热加工其他截面形状不锈钢条杆	10	0	0	0	0	0	0	0	0	0	0	9	0	5	0	0	0	0			
72222000	冷成形或冷加工的不锈钢条、杆	10	0	0	0	0	0	0	0	0	0	0		0	5	0	0	0	0			
72223000	其他不锈钢条、杆	10	0	0	0	0	0	0	0	0	0	0	8.9	0	5	0	0	0	0			
72224000	不锈钢角材、型材及异型材	10	0	0	0	0	0	0	0	0	0	0		0	5	0	0	0	0			
72230000	不锈钢丝	10	0	0	0	0	0	0	0	0	0	0		1	5	0	0	0	0	0		
72241000	其他合金钢锭及其他初级形状	2	0	0	0	0	0	0	0	0	0	0		0	0		0	0	0			
72249010	单重≥10吨的粗铸锻件坯	2	0	0	0	0	0	0	0	0	0	0		0	0		0	0	0			
72249090	其他合金钢坯	2	0	0	0	0	0	0	0	0	0	0		0	0		0	0	0			
72251100	取向性硅电钢宽板	3	0	0	0	0	0	0	0	0	0	0	2.1	0	0		0	0	0			
72251900	其他硅电钢宽板	6	0	0	0	0	0	0	0	0	0	0		0	5		0	0	0			0
72253000	宽度≥600mm热轧其他合金钢卷材	3	0	0	0	0	0	0	0	0	0	0		0	0		0	0	0			
72254010	工具钢	3	0	0	0	0	0	0	0	0	0	0		0	0		0	0	0			
72254091	含硼合金钢	3	0	0	0	0	0	0	0	0	0	0		0	0		0	0	0			
72254099	其他非卷材,除热轧外未经进一步加工	3	0	0	0	0	0	0	0	0	0	0		0	0		0	0	0			
72255000	宽度≥600mm冷轧其他合金钢板材	3	0	0	0	0	0	0	0	0	0	0		0	0		0	0	0			
72259100	电镀锌的其他合金钢宽平板轧材	7	0	0	0	0	0	0	0	0	0	0		0	5		0	0	0			
72259200	其他镀或涂锌的其他合金钢宽板材	7	0	0	0	0	0	0	0	0	0	0		0	5		0	0	0			
72259910	宽度≥600mm的高速钢平板轧材	3	0	0	0	0	0	0	0	0	0	0		0	0		0	0	0			
72259990	宽度≥600mm的其他合金钢平板轧材	7	0	0	0	0	0	0	0	0	0	0		0	5		0	0	0			
72261100	取向性硅电钢窄板	3	0	0	0	0	0	0	0	0	0	0		0	0		0	0	0			
72261900	其他硅电钢窄板	3	0	0	0	0	0	0	0	0	0	0		0	0		0	0	0			
72262000	宽度＜500mm的高速钢平板轧材	3	0	0	0	0	0	0	0	0	0	0		0	0		0	0	0			
72269110	工具钢	3	0	0	0	0	0	0	0	0	0	0		0	0		0	0	0			
72269191	含硼合金钢	3	0	0	0	0	0	0	0	0	0	0		0	0		0	0	0			
72269199	其他除热轧外未经进一步加工的合金钢平板轧材，宽度小于600毫米	3	0	0	0	0	0	0	0	0	0	0		0	0		0	0	0			
72269200	宽度＜600mm冷轧其他合金钢板材	3	0	0	0	0	0	0	0	0	0	0		0	0		0	0	0			
72269910	电镀锌的其他合金钢窄平板轧材	7	0	0	0	0	0	0	0	0	0	0		0	5		0	0	0			
72269920	其他镀或涂锌的其他合金钢窄板材	7	0	0	0	0	0	0	0	0	0	0		0	5		0	0	0			
72269990	宽度＜600mm的其他合金板材	7	0	0	0	0	0	0	0	0	0	0		0	5		0	0	0			
72271000	高速钢的热轧盘条	3	0	0	0	0	0	0	0	0	0	0		0	0		0	0	0			
72272000	硅锰钢的热轧盘条	6	0	0	0	0	0	0	0	0	0	0		0	5		0	0	0			
72279010	含硼合金钢制不规则盘卷的其他合金钢热轧条、杆	3	0	0	0	0	0	0	0	0	0	0		0	0		0	0	0			
72279090	其他不规则盘卷的其他合金钢热轧条、杆	3	0	0	0	0	0	0	0	0	0	0		0	0		0	0	0			
72281000	其他高速钢的条、杆	3	0	0	0	0	0	0	0	0	0	0		0	0		0	0	0			
72282000	其他硅锰钢的条、杆	6	0	0	0	0	0	0	0	0	0	0		0	5		0	0	0			
72283010	含硼合金钢制其他条、杆，除热轧、热拉拔或热挤压外未经进一步加工	3	0	0	0	0	0	0	0	0	0	0		0	0		0	0	0			
72283090	其他条、杆，除热轧、热拉拔或热挤压外未经进一步加工	3	0	0	0	0	0	0	0	0	0	0		0	0		0	0	0			
72284000	其他合金钢锻造条、杆	3	0	0	0	0	0	0	0	0	0	0		0	0		0	0	0			
72285000	其他合金钢冷成形或冷加工条、杆	3	0	0	0	0	0	0	0	0	0	0		0	0		0	0	0			
72286000	其他合金钢条、杆	3	0	0	0	0	0	0	0	0	0	0		0	0		0	0	0			
72287010	履带板型钢	6	0	0	0	0	0	0	0	0	0	0		0.6	5		0	0	0			
72287090	其他合金钢角材、型材及异型材	6	0	0	0	0	0	0	0	0	0	0		0.6	5		0	0	0			
72288000	其他合金钢空心钻钢	7	0	0	0	0	0	0	0	0	0	0		0.7	5		0	0	0			
72292000	硅锰钢丝	7	0	0	0	0	0	0	0	0	0	0		0	5		0	0	0			
72299010	高速钢丝	3	0	0	0	0	0	0	0	0	0	0		0	0		0	0	0			
72299090	其他合金钢丝	7	0	0	0	0	0	0	0	0	0	0		0.7	5		0	0	0			
73011000	钢铁板桩	7	0	0	0	0	0	0	0	0	0	0	6.3	0	5		0	0	0			
73012000	焊接的钢铁角材、型材及异型材	7	0	0	0	0	0	0	0	0	0	0		0	5		0	0	0			
73021000	钢轨	6	0	0	0	0	0	0	0	0	0	0		0	5		0	0	0			
73023000	道岔尖轨、辙叉、尖轨拉杆	8	0	0	0	0	0	0	0	0	0	0		0	5		0	0	0			
73024000	钢铁制鱼尾板、钢轨垫板	7	0	0	0	0	0	0	0	0	0	0		0	5		0	0	0			
73029010	钢铁轨枕	6	0	0	0	0	0	0	0	0	0	0	5.1	0	0		0	0	0			

税则号列	商品名称（简称）	最惠国	东盟 文	东盟 柬	东盟 印	东盟 老	东盟 马	东盟 缅	东盟 菲	东盟 新	东盟 泰	东盟 越	亚太	智利	巴基斯坦	新加坡	新西兰	秘鲁	哥斯达黎加	香港	澳门	台湾
73029090	其他铁道电车道铺轨用钢铁材料	7	0	0	0	0	0	0	0	0	0	0	6	0	5		0	0	0			
73030010	内径＞500mm的铸铁圆型截面管	4	0	0	0	0	0	0	0	0	0	0		0	0		0	0	0			
73030090	其他铸铁管及空心异型材	4	0	0	0	0	0	0	0	0	0	0		0	0		0	0	0			
73041110	外径大于等于215.9毫米，但不超过406.4毫米的不锈钢制石油或天然气套管	5	0	0	0	0	0	0	0	0	0	0		0	0		0	0	0			
73041120	外径大于114.3毫米，但小于215.9毫米的不锈钢制石油或天然气套管	5	0	0	0	0	0	0	0	0	0	0		0	0		0	0	0			
73041130	外径不超过114.3毫米的不锈钢制石油或天然气套管	5	0	0	0	0	0	0	0	0	0	0		0	0		0	0	0			
73041190	其他不锈钢制石油或天然气套管	5	0	0	0	0	0	0	0	0	0	0		0	0		0	0	0			
73041910	外径大于等于215.9毫米，但不超过406.4毫米的非不锈钢制石油或天然气套管	5	0	0	0	0	0	0	0	0	0	0		0	0		0	0	0			
73041920	外径大于114.3毫米，但小于215.9毫米的非不锈钢制石油或天然气套管	5	0	0	0	0	0	0	0	0	0	0		0	0		0	0	0			
73041930	外径不超过114.3毫米的非不锈钢制石油或天然气套管	5	0	0	0	0	0	0	0	0	0	0		0	0		0	0	0			
73041990	其他非不锈钢制石油或天然气套管	5	0	0	0	0	0	0	0	0	0	0		0	0		0	0	0			
73042210	外径不超过168.3毫米的不锈钢制钻管	4	0	0	0	0	0	0	0	0	0	0		0.4	0		0	0	0			
73042290	其他不锈钢制钻管	4	0	0	0	0	0	0	0	0	0	0		0.4	0		0	0	0			
73042310	外径不超过168.3毫米的非不锈钢制钻管	4	0	0	0	0	0	0	0	0	0	0		0.4	0		0	0	0			
73042390	其他非不锈钢制钻管	4	0	0	0	0	0	0	0	0	0	0		0.4	0		0	0	0			
73042400	其他不锈钢制钻探石油用天然气套管、导管	4	0	0	0	0	0	0	0	0	0	0	2	0	0		0	0	0			
73042910	屈服强度小于552兆帕的钻探石油及天然气用的套管、导管及钻管	4	0	0	0	0	0	0	0	0	0	0	2	0	0		0	0	0			
73042920	屈服强度大于等于552兆帕，但小于758兆帕的钻探石油及天然气用的套管、导管及钻管	4	0	0	0	0	0	0	0	0	0	0	2	0	0		0	0	0			
73042930	屈服强度大于等于758兆帕的钻探石油及天然气用的套管、导管及钻管	4	0	0	0	0	0	0	0	0	0	0	2	0	0		0	0	0			
73043110	冷轧的钢铁制无缝锅炉管	4	0	0	0	0	0	0	0	0	0	0		0.4	0		0	0	0			
73043120	冷轧的铁制无缝地质钻管、套管	8	0	0	0	0	0	0	0	0	0	0		0.8	5		0	0	0			
73043190	其他冷轧的铁制无缝圆形截面管	4	0	0	0	0	0	0	0	0	0	0		0.4	0		0	0	0			
73043910	非冷轧的铁制无缝锅炉管	4	0	0	0	0	0	0	0	0	0	0		0	0		0	0	0	0		
73043920	非冷轧的铁制无缝地质钻管套管	5	0	0	0	0	0	0	0	0	0	0		0	0		0	0	0	0		
73043990	非冷轧的铁制其他无缝管	4	0	0	0	0	0	0	0	0	0	0		0	0		0	0	0	0		
73044110	冷轧的不锈钢制无缝锅炉管	10	0	0	0	0	0	0	0	0	0	0		0	5	0	0	0	0			
73044190	冷轧的不锈钢制的其他无缝管	10	0	0	0	0	0	0	0	0	0	0		0	5	0	0	0	0			
73044910	非冷轧的不锈钢制无缝锅炉管	10	0	0	0	0	0	0	0	0	0	0		0	5	0	0	0	0			
73044990	非冷轧的不锈钢制其他无缝管	10	0	0	0	0	0	0	0	0	0	0		0	5	0	0	0	0			
73045110	冷轧的其他合金钢无缝锅炉管	4	0	0	0	0	0	0	0	0	0	0		0	0		0	0	0			
73045120	冷轧的其他合金钢无缝地质钻套管	4	0	0	0	0	0	0	0	0	0	0		0	0		0	0	0			
73045190	冷轧的其他合金钢制其他无缝管	4	0	0	0	0	0	0	0	0	0	0		0	0		0	0	0			
73045910	非冷轧其他合金钢无缝锅炉管	4	0	0	0	0	0	0	0	0	0	0		0.4	0		0	0	0			
73045920	非冷轧其他合金钢无缝地质钻套管	4	0	0	0	0	0	0	0	0	0	0		0.4	0		0	0	0			
73045990	非冷轧其他合金钢制无缝圆形截面	4	0	0	0	0	0	0	0	0	0	0		0.4	0		0	0	0			
73049000	未列名无缝钢铁管及空心异型材	4	0	0	0	0	0	0	0	0	0	0		0	0		0	0	0			
73051100	纵向埋弧焊接石油、天然气粗钢管	7	0	0	0	0	0	0	0	0	0	0		0.7	5		0	0	0			
73051200	其他纵向焊接石油、天然气粗钢管	3	0	0	0	0	0	0	0	0	0	0		0	0		0	0	0			
73051900	其他石油、天然气粗钢管	7	0	0	0	0	0	0	0	0	0	0		0	5		0	0	0			
73052000	其他钻探石油、天然气用粗套管	7	0	0	0	0	0	0	0	0	0	0		0	5		0	0	0			
73053100	纵向焊接的其他粗钢铁管	6	0	0	0	0	0	0	0	0	0	0		0.6	5		0	0	0			
73053900	其他方法焊接其他粗钢铁管	6	0	0	0	0	0	0	0	0	0	0		0.6	5		0	0	0			
73059000	未列名圆形截面粗钢铁管	6	0	0	0	0	0	0	0	0	0	0		0	5		0	0	0			
73061100	不锈钢焊缝石油、天然气管道管	7	0	0	0	0	0	0	0	0	0	0		0	5		0	0	0			
73061900	其他石油、天然气管道管	7	0	0	0	0	0	0	0	0	0	0		0	5		0	0	0			
73062100	不锈钢焊缝钻探石油天然气用套、导管	3	0	0	0	0	0	0	0	0	0	0		0	0		0	0	0			
73062900	其他钻探石油天然气用套、导管	3	0	0	0	0	0	0	0	0	0	0		0	0		0	0	0			

税则号列	商品名称（简称）	最惠国	东盟										亚太	智利	巴基斯坦	新加坡	新西兰	秘鲁	哥斯达黎加	香港	澳门	台湾
			文	柬	印	老	马	缅	菲	新	泰	越										
73063011	壁厚在0.7毫米及以下的外径不超过10毫米的其他铁或非合金刚圆形截面焊缝管	3	0	0	0	0	0	0	0	0	0	0		0	0		0	0	0			
73063019	壁厚在0.7毫米以上外径不超过10毫米的其他铁或非合金刚圆形截面焊缝管	3	0	0	0	0	0	0	0	0	0	0		0	0		0	0	0			
73063090	外径超过10毫米的其他铁或非合金刚圆形截面焊缝管	3	0	0	0	0	0	0	0	0	0	0		0	0		0	0	0			
73064000	不锈钢其他圆形截面细焊缝管	6	0	0	0	0	0	0	0	0	0	0		0	5		0	0	0			
73065000	其他合金钢的圆形截面细焊缝管	3	0	0	0	0	0	0	0	0	0	0		0	0		0	0	0			
73066100	矩形或正方形截面的其他焊缝管	3	0	0	0	0	0	0	0	0	0	0		0	0		0	0	0			
73066900	其他非圆形截面的其他焊缝管	3	0	0	0	0	0	0	0	0	0	0		0	0		0	0	0			
73069000	未列名其他钢铁管及空心异型材	6	0	0	0	0	0	0	0	0	0	0		0.6	5		0	0	0			
73071100	无可锻性铸铁制管子附件	5	0	0	0	0	0	0	0	0	0	0		0	0		0	0	0			
73071900	可锻性铸铁及铸钢管子附件	8	0	0	0	0	0	0	0	0	0	0		0.8	5		0	0	0			
73072100	不锈钢制法兰	8.4	0	0	0	0	0	0	0	0	0	0	6.7	0	5		0	0	0			
73072200	不锈钢制螺纹肘管、弯管、管套	8.4	0	0	0	0	0	0	0	0	0	0		0	5		0	0	0	0		
73072300	不锈钢制对焊件	8.4	0	0	0	0	0	0	0	0	0	0		0	5		0	0	0			
73072900	不锈钢制其他管子附件	8.4	0	0	0	0	0	0	0	0	0	0		0.8	5		0	0	0	0		
73079100	未列名钢铁制法兰	7	0	0	0	0	0	0	0	0	0	0		0	5		0	0	0			
73079200	未列名钢铁制螺纹肘管、弯管、管套	4	0	0	0	0	0	0	0	0	0	0		0	0		0	0	0			
73079300	未列名钢铁制对焊件	7	0	0	0	0	0	0	0	0	0	0		0	5		0	0	0			
73079900	未列名钢铁制其他管子附件	4	0	0	0	0	0	0	0	0	0	0		0.4	0		0	0	0			
73081000	钢铁制桥梁及桥梁体段	8	0	0	0	0	0	0	0	0	0	0		0.8	0		0	0	0			
73082000	钢铁制塔楼及格构杆	8.4	0	0	0	0	0	0	0	0	0	0		0.8	0		0	0	0			
73083000	钢铁制门窗及其框架、门槛	10	0	0	0	0	0	0	0	0	0	0		0	0	0	0	0	0	0	0	
73084000	钢铁制脚手架模板坑凳用支柱及类	8.4	0	0	0	0	0	0	0	0	0	0		0.8	0		0	0	0			
73089000	其他钢铁结构体及部件	4	0	0	0	0	0	0	0	0	0	0		0.4	0		0	0	0	0		
73090000	容积＞300L钢铁制盛物容器	10.5	0	0	0	0	0	0	0	0	0	0		1.1	5	0	0	5.3	2.1			
73101000	容积50-300L钢铁制盛物容器	10.5	0	0	0	0	0	0	0	0	0	0		1.1	5	0	0	5.3	2.1	0		
73102110	易拉罐及罐体	17.5	0	0	0	0	0	0	0	0	0	0		1.8	14	0	0	8.8	3.5	0		
73102190	其他容积在50升以下焊边或卷边接合的罐	17.5	0	0	0	0	0	0	0	0	0	0		1.8	14	0	0	8.8	3.5	0		
73102910	易拉罐及罐体	17.5	0	0	0	0	0	0	0	0	0	0		1.8	14	0	0	8.8	3.5	0		
73102990	其他盛装物料用的钢铁柜、桶、罐、听、盒及类似容器（装压缩气体或液化气体的除外），容积不超过300升，不论是否衬里或隔热，但无机械或热力装置	17.5	0	0	0	0	0	0	0	0	0	0		1.8	14	0	0	8.8	3.5	0		
73110010	装压缩或液化气的钢铁容器	17.5	0	0	0	0	0	0	0	0	0	0		1.8	14	0	0	8.8	3.5	0		
73110090	其他装压缩或液化气的容器	8	0	0	0	0	0	0	0	0	0	0		0.8	5		0	0	0	0		
73121000	非绝缘的钢铁绞股线、绳、缆	4	0	0	0	0	0	0	0	0	0	0		0.4	0		0	0	0			
73129000	非绝缘钢铁编带、吊索及类似品	4	0	0	0	0	0	0	0	0	0	0		0	0		0	0	0			
73130000	带刺钢铁丝、围篱用钢铁绞带	7	0	0	0	0	0	0	0	0	0	0	6.3	0.7	5		0	0	0			
73141200	不锈钢制的机器用环形带	12	0	0	0	0	0	0	0	0	0	0		0	6	0	0	0	2.4			
73141400	不锈钢制的机织品	12	0	0	0	0	0	0	0	0	0	0		0	6	0	0	0	2.4			
73141900	其他钢铁丝制机织品	7	0	0	0	0	0	0	0	0	0	0		0	3.5		0	0	0			
73142000	交点焊接的粗钢铁丝网、篱及格栅	7	0	0	0	0	0	0	0	0	0	0		0	5		0	0	0	0		
73143100	交点焊接的镀或涂锌细钢铁丝网	7	0	0	0	0	0	0	0	0	0	0		0	5		0	0	0	0		
73143900	交点焊接的其他细钢铁丝网、篱	7	0	0	0	0	0	0	0	0	0	0		0	5		0	0	0	0		
73144100	其他镀锌的钢铁丝网、篱及格栅	8	0	0	0	0	0	0	0	0	0	0	6	0.8	5		0	0	0			
73144200	其他涂塑的钢铁丝网、篱及格栅	8	0	0	0	0	0	0	0	0	0	0		0	5		0	0	0			
73144900	其他钢铁丝网、篱及格栅	8	0	0	0	0	0	0	0	0	0	0		0.8	5		0	0	0			
73145000	网眼钢铁板	8	0	0	0	0	0	0	0	0	0	0		0	5		0	0	0	0		
73151110	自行车滚子链	12	0	0	0	0	0	0	0	0	0	0		0	6	0	0	0	2.4	0		
73151120	摩托车滚子链	12	0	0	0	0	0	0	0	0	0	0		0	6	0	0	0	2.4	0		
73151190	其他滚子链	12	0	0	0	0	0	0	0	0	0	0		0	6	0	0	0	2.4	0		
73151200	其他铰接链	12	0	0	0	0	0	0	0	0	0	0		0	6	0	0	0	2.4			
73151900	铰接链零件	12	0	0	0	0	0	0	0	0	0	0		0	6	0	0	0	2.4			
73152000	防滑链	12	0	0	0	0	0	0	0	0	0	0		0	6	0	0	0	2.4			
73158100	日字环节链	12	0	0	0	0	0	0	0	0	0	0		0	6	0	0	0	2.4			
73158200	其他焊接链	12	0	0	0	0	0	0	0	0	0	0		0	6	0	0	0	2.4			

税则号列	商品名称（简称）	最惠国	东盟										亚太	智利	巴基斯坦	新加坡	新西兰	秘鲁	哥斯达黎加	香港	澳门	台湾
			文	柬	印	老	马	缅	菲	新	泰	越										
73158900	未列名链	12	0	0	0	0	0	0	0	0	0	0		1.2	6	0	0	6	2.4			
73159000	非铰接链零件	10	0	0	0	0	0	0	0	0	0	0		0	5		0	0	0			
73160000	钢铁锚、多爪锚及其零件	10	0	0	0	0	0	0	0	0	0	0		0	5		0	0	0			
73170000	铁钉、图钉、平头钉及类似品	10	0	0	0	0	0	0	0	0	0	0		1	5		0	5	0			
73181100	方头螺钉	10	0	0	0	0	0	0	0	0	0	0		1	5		0	5	0			
73181200	其他木螺钉	10	0	0	0	0	0	0	0	0	0	0		1	5		0	5	0			
73181300	钩头螺钉及环头螺钉	10	0	0	0	0	0	0	0	0	0	0		0	5		0	0	0			
73181400	自攻螺钉	10	0	0	0	0	0	0	0	0	0	0		1	5	0	0	5	0			
73181510	抗拉强度在800兆帕及以上的螺钉及螺栓，不论是否带有螺母或垫圈	8	0	0	0	0	0	0	0	0	0	0	4	0.8	0		0	0	0	0		
73181590	其他螺钉及螺栓	8	0	0	0	0	0	0	0	0	0	0	4	0.8	0		0	0	0	0		
73181600	螺母	8	0	0	0	0	0	0	0	0	0	0		0.8	5		0	0	0			
73181900	未列名螺纹制品	5	0	0	0	0	0	0	0	0	0	0		0	0		0	0	0			
73182100	弹簧垫圈及其他防松垫圈	10	0	0	0	0	0	0	0	0	0	0		0	5	0	0	0	0	0		
73182200	其他垫圈	10	0	0	0	0	0	0	0	0	0	0		0	5	0	0	5	0			
73182300	铆钉	10	0	0	0	0	0	0	0	0	0	0		0	5	0	0	0	0	0		
73182400	销及开尾销	10	0	0	0	0	0	0	0	0	0	0		0	5	0	0	0	0			
73182900	其他无螺纹紧固件	10	0	0	0	0	0	0	0	0	0	0		1	5	0	0	0	0			
73194010	安全别针	10	0	0	0	0	0	0	0	0	0	0		0	5		0	0	0		0	
73194090	其他别针	10	0	0	0	0	0	0	0	0	0	0		0	5		0	0	0			
73199000	未列名钢铁制针及类似品	10	0	0	0	0	0	0	0	0	0	0		0	5		0	5	0			
73201010	铁道车辆用片簧及簧片	6	0	0	0	0	0	0	0	0	0	0		0	5		0	0	0			
73201020	汽车用片簧及弹簧	10	0	0	0	0	0	0	0	0	0	0		0	5		0	0	0			
73201090	其他片簧及簧片	10	0	0	0	0	0	0	0	0	0	0		0	5	0	0	0	0			
73202010	铁道车辆用螺旋弹簧	6	0	0	0	0	0	0	0	0	0	0		0.6	5		0	0	0			
73202090	其他螺旋弹簧	10	0	0	0	0	0	0	0	0	0	0	8.5	1	5	0	0	0	0			
73209010	铁道车辆用其他弹簧	6	0	0	0	0	0	0	0	0	0	0		0	5		0	0	0			
73209090	其他弹簧	12	0	0	0	0	0	0	0	0	0	0		0	6	0	0	0	2.4			
73211100	可使用气体燃料的家用炉灶	15	0	0	0	0	0	0	0	0	0	0		1.5	12	0	0	7.5	3			
73211210	煤油炉	21	0	0	0	0	0	0	0	0	0	0		0		0	0	10.5	4.2			
73211290	其他使用液体燃料的家用炉灶	21	0	0	0	0	0	0	0	0	0	0		0		0	0	10.5	4.2			
73211900	其他炊事用具及加热板	21	0	0	0	0	0	0	0	0	0	0		0		0	0	10.5	4.2			
73218100	可使用气体燃料的其他家用器具	23	0	0	0	0	0	0	0	0	0	0	13.8	0	11.5	0	0	11.5	4.6			
73218200	使用液体燃料的其他家用器具	21	0	0	0	0	0	0	0	0	0	0		2.1		0	0	10.5	4.2			
73218900	其他非电热家用器具	21	0	0	0	0	0	0	0	0	0	0		2.1		0	0	10.5	4.2			
73219000	非电热家用器具零件	12	0	0	0	0	0	0	0	0	0	0	9.6	1.2	5	0	0	6	2.4			
73221100	非电热铸铁制集中供暖用散热器	21	0	0	0	0	0	0	0	0	0	0		0		0	0	10.5	4.2			
73221900	非电热钢制集中供暖用散热器	21	0	0	0	0	0	0	0	0	0	0		0		0	0	10.5	4.2			
73229000	非电热空气加热器、暖气分布器	20	0	0	0	0	0	0	0	0	0	0		2		0	0	10	4			
73231000	钢铁丝绒、擦锅器、洗擦用块垫等	14	0	0	0	0	0	0	0	0	0	0		1.4	11.2	0	0	7	2.8			
73239100	餐桌、厨房等家用铸铁制器具	20	0	0	0	0	0	0	0	0	0	0		0		0	0	10	4			
73239200	餐桌、厨房等家用铸铁制搪瓷器	20	0	0	0	0	0	0	0	0	0	0		0		0	0	10	4			
73239300	餐桌、厨房等家用不锈钢器具	12	0	0	0	0	0	0	0	0	0	0	8.4	1.2	5	0	0	0	2.4	0	0	
73239410	钢铁制搪瓷面盆	20	0	0	0	0	0	0	0	0	0	0		2		0	0	10	4			
73239420	钢铁制搪瓷烧锅	20	0	0	0	0	0	0	0	0	0	0		2		0	0	10	4			
73239490	其他餐桌、厨房等家用钢铁制搪瓷器	20	0	0	0	0	0	0	0	0	0	0		2		0	0	10	4			
73239900	其他餐桌、厨房等用钢铁器具	20	0	0	0	0	0	0	0	0	0	0		2		0	0	10	4			
73241000	不锈钢制洗涤槽及脸盆	18	0	0	0	0	0	0	0	0	0	0		0		0	0	9	3.6	0		
73242100	铸铁制浴缸	10	0	0	0	0	0	0	0	0	0	0		1	5	0	0	5	0			
73242900	其他钢铁制浴缸	30	0	0	0	0	0	0	0	0	0	0		0		0	0	15	6			
73249000	其他钢铁制卫生器具及零件	25	0	0	0	0	0	0	0	0	0	0		2.5		0	0	12.5	5			
73251010	工业用无可锻性制品	7	0	0	0	0	0	0	0	0	0	0		0	5		0	0	0			
73251090	其他无可锻性铸铁制品	20	0	0	0	0	0	0	0	0	0	0		0		0	0	10	4			
73259100	可锻性铸铁及铸钢研磨机的研磨球	10.5	0	0	0	0	0	0	0	0	0	0		1.1	5	0	0	5.2	2.1			
73259910	工业用未列名可锻性铸铁制品	10.5	0	0	0	0	0	0	0	0	0	0	8.9	1.1	5	0	0	5.2	2.1			
73259990	非工业用未列名可锻性铸铁制品	20	0	0	0	0	0	0	0	0	0	0	12	2	10	0	0	10	4			
73261100	钢铁制研磨机用研磨球及类似品	10.5	0	0	0	0	0	0	0	0	0	0		1.1	5	0	0	5.2	2.1			
73261910	工业用未列名钢铁制品	10.5	0	0	0	0	0	0	0	0	0	0		1.1	5	0	0	5.2	2.1			
73261990	非工业用未列名钢铁制品	20	0	0	0	0	0	0	0	0	0	0		2		0	0	10	4			
73262010	工业用钢铁丝制品	10	0	0	0	0	0	0	0	0	0	0	5	0	5		0	0	0			

税则号列	商品名称（简称）	最惠国	东盟										亚太	智利	巴基斯坦	新加坡	新西兰	秘鲁	哥斯达黎加	香港	澳门	台湾
			文	柬	印	老	马	缅	菲	新	泰	越										
73262090	非工业用钢铁丝制品	18	0	0	0	0	0	0	0	0	0	0	12.6	0	9	0	0	9	3.6			
73269011	钢铁纤维及其制品	10.5	0	0	0	0	0	0	0	0	0	0	8.9	1.1	5	0	0	5.2	2.1	0		
73269019	其他工业用钢铁制品	10.5	0	0	0	0	0	0	0	0	0	0	8.9	1.1	5	0	0	5.2	2.1	0		
73269090	其他非工业用钢铁制品	8	0	0	0	0	0	0	0	0	0	0	6.8	0.8	5	0	0	0	0	0		
74010000	铜锍、沉积铜(泥铜)	2	0	0	0	0	0	0	0	0	0	0		0	0		0	0	0			
74020000	未精炼铜、电解精炼用铜阳极	2	0	0	0	0	0	0	0	0	0	0		0	0		0		0			
74031111	按重量计铜含量超过99.9935%的阴极精炼铜	2	0	0	0	0	0	0	0	0	0	0		0	0		0	0	0			
74031119	其他阴极精炼铜	2	0	0	0	0	0	0	0	0	0	0		0	0		0	0	0			
74031190	精炼铜阴极型材	2	0	0	0	0	0	0	0	0	0	0		0	0		0	0	0			
74031200	精炼铜的线锭	2	0	0	0	0	0	0	0	0	0	0		0	0		0	0	0			
74031300	精炼铜的坯段	2	0	0	0	0	0	0	0	0	0	0		0	0		0	0	0			
74031900	其他未锻轧的精炼铜	2	0	0	0	0	0	0	0	0	0	0		0	0		0	0	0			
74032100	未锻轧的铜锌合金(黄铜)	1	0	0	0	0	0	0	0	0	0	0		0	0		0	0	0		0	
74032200	未锻轧的铜锡合金(青铜)	1	0	0	0	0	0	0	0	0	0	0		0	0		0	0	0			
74032900	未锻轧的其他铜合金	1	0	0	0	0	0	0	0	0	0	0		0	0		0	0	0			
74040000	铜废碎料	1.5	0	0	0	0	0	0	0	0	0	0		0	0		0		0	0		
74050000	铜母合金	4	0	0	0	0	0	0	0	0	0	0		0.4	0		0	0	0	0		
74061010	精炼铜制非片状粉末	3	0	0	0	0	0	0	0	0	0	0		0	0		0	0	0			
74061020	白铜或德银制非片状粉末	6	0	0	0	0	0	0	0	0	0	0		0.6	5		0	0	0			
74061030	铜锌合金(黄铜)制非片状铜粉粉末	6	0	0	0	0	0	0	0	0	0	0		0.6	5		0	0	0			
74061040	铜锡合金(青铜)制非片状铜粉粉末	6	0	0	0	0	0	0	0	0	0	0		0.6	5		0	0	0			
74061090	其他铜合金制非片状粉末	6	0	0	0	0	0	0	0	0	0	0		0.6	5		0	0	0			
74062010	精炼铜制片状粉末	4	0	0	0	0	0	0	0	0	0	0		0.4	0		0	0	0			
74062020	白铜或德银制片状粉末	6	0	0	0	0	0	0	0	0	0	0		0.6	5		0	0	0			
74062090	其他铜合金制片状粉末	6	0	0	0	0	0	0	0	0	0	0		0.6	5		0	0	0			
74071010	铬锆铜制条、杆及型材及异型材	4	0	0	0	0	0	0	0	0	0	0		0.4	0		0	0	0			0
74071090	其他精炼铜条、杆及型材及异型材	4	0	0	0	0	0	0	0	0	0	0		0.4	0		0	0	0			0
74072111	直线度不大于0.5毫米/米铜锌合金条、杆	7	0	0	0	0	0	0	0	0	0	0		0.7	5		0	0	0		0	0
74072119	其他铜锌合金条、杆	7	0	0	0	0	0	0	0	0	0	0		0.7	5		0	0	0		0	0
74072190	其他黄铜条、杆及型材及异型材	7	0	0	0	0	0	0	0	0	0	0		0.7	5		0	0	0		0	0
74072900	其他铜合金条杆、型材及异型材	7	0	0	0	0	0	0	0	0	0	0		0	5		0	0	0			0
74081100	最大截面尺寸＞6mm的精炼铜丝	4	0	0	0	0	0	0	0	0	0	0	2.8	0.4	0		0	2	0			0
74081900	截面尺寸≤6mm的精炼铜丝	4	0	0	0	0	0	0	0	0	0	0	3.4	0.4	0		0	0	0	0		0
74082100	黄铜丝	7	0	0	0	0	0	0	0	0	0	0		0.7	5		0	0	0			0
74082210	铜镍锌铅合金(加铅德银)丝	8	0	0	0	0	0	0	0	0	0	0		0	5		0	0	0			
74082290	其他白铜丝或德银(铜镍锌合金)丝	8	0	0	0	0	0	0	0	0	0	0		0	5		0	0	0			
74082900	其他铜合金丝	7	0	0	0	0	0	0	0	0	0	0		0	5		0	0	0			
74091110	含氧量不超过10PPM，厚度超过0.15mm的盘卷精炼铜板、片、带	4	0	0	0	0	0	0	0	0	0	0		0.4	0		0	0	0			
74091190	厚度超过0.15mm的其他盘卷精炼铜板、片、带	4	0	0	0	0	0	0	0	0	0	0		0.4	0		0	0	0			
74091900	其他精炼铜板、片、带	4	0	0	0	0	0	0	0	0	0	0		0.4	0		0	0	0			0
74092100	成卷的黄铜板、片、带	7	0	0	0	0	0	0	0	0	0	0		0.7	5		0	0	0	0		0
74092900	其他黄铜板、片、带	7	0	0	0	0	0	0	0	0	0	0		0.7	5		0	0	0	0		0
74093100	成卷的青铜板、片、带	7	0	0	0	0	0	0	0	0	0	0		0	5		0	0	0			0
74093900	其他青铜板、片、带	7	0	0	0	0	0	0	0	0	0	0		0	5		0	0	0			0
74094000	白铜或德银制板、片、带	7	0	0	0	0	0	0	0	0	0	0		0.7	5		0	0	0			0
74099000	其他铜合金板、片、带	7	0	0	0	0	0	0	0	0	0	0		0	5		0	0	0	0		0
74101100	无衬背的精炼铜箔	4	0	0	0	0	0	0	0	0	0	0	2.8	0.4	0		0	0	0	0		0
74101210	无衬背的白铜或德银铜箔	7	0	0	0	0	0	0	0	0	0	0		0	5		0	0	0			0
74101290	无衬背的其他铜合金箔	7	0	0	0	0	0	0	0	0	0	0		0	5		0	0	0			0
74102110	印刷电路用覆铜板	4	0	0	0	0	0	0	0	0	0	0	3.4	0	0		0	0	0	0	0	0
74102190	有衬背的其他精炼铜箔	4	0	0	0	0	0	0	0	0	0	0	3.4	0	0		0	0	0	0	0	0
74102210	有衬背的白铜或德银铜箔	7	0	0	0	0	0	0	0	0	0	0		0	5		0	0	0			
74102290	有衬背的其他铜合金箔	7	0	0	0	0	0	0	0	0	0	0		0	5		0	0	0			
74111011	外径小于等于25mm的带有内（外）螺纹或翅片的精炼铜管	4	0	0	0	0	0	0	0	0	0	0	2.8	0.4	0		0	0	0			
74111019	外径小于等于25mm的其他精炼铜管	4	0	0	0	0	0	0	0	0	0	0	2.8	0.4	0		0	0	0			
74111020	外径超过70mm的精炼铜管	4	0	0	0	0	0	0	0	0	0	0	2.8	0.4	0		0	0	0			

税则号列	商品名称（简称）	最惠国	东盟										亚太	智利	巴基斯坦	新加坡	新西兰	秘鲁	哥斯达黎加	香港	澳门	台湾
			文	柬	印	老	马	缅	菲	新	泰	越										
74111090	其他精炼铜管	4	0	0	0	0	0	0	0	0	0	0	2.8	0.4	0		0	0	0			
74112110	盘卷黄铜管	7	0	0	0	0	0	0	0	0	0	0		0.7	5		0	0	0	0		
74112190	铜锌合金(黄铜)管	7	0	0	0	0	0	0	0	0	0	0		0.7	5		0	0	0	0		
74112200	白铜或德银管	7	0	0	0	0	0	0	0	0	0	0		0	5		0	0	0			
74112900	其他铜合金管	7	0	0	0	0	0	0	0	0	0	0		0	5		0	0	0			
74121000	精炼铜管子附件	4	0	0	0	0	0	0	0	0	0	0		0	0		0	0	0			
74122010	白铜或德银管子配件	7	0	0	0	0	0	0	0	0	0	0	6	0.7	5		0	0	0			
74122090	其他铜合金管子配件	7	0	0	0	0	0	0	0	0	0	0	6	0.7	5		0	0	0			
74130000	非绝缘的铜丝绞股线、缆、编带等	5	0	0	0	0	0	0	0	0	0	0		0.5	0		0	0	0			
74151000	铜钉、平头钉、图钉U型钉及类似品	8	0	0	0	0	0	0	0	0	0	0		0	5		0	0	0			
74152100	铜垫圈(包括弹簧垫圈)	10	0	0	0	0	0	0	0	0	0	0		0	5	0	0	0	0	0		
74152900	铜制其他无螺纹制品	10	0	0	0	0	0	0	0	0	0	0		0	5	0	0	0	0	0		
74153310	铜制木螺钉	8	0	0	0	0	0	0	0	0	0	0		0.8	5		0	0	0	0		
74153390	铜制其他螺钉螺栓螺母	8	0	0	0	0	0	0	0	0	0	0		0.8	5		0	0	0	0		
74153900	其他铜制螺纹制品	10	0	0	0	0	0	0	0	0	0	0		0	5		0	0	0	0		
74181010	擦锅器及洗刷擦光用的块垫、手套	18	0	0	0	0	0	0	0	0	0	0		1.8	14.4	0	0	9	3.6			
74181020	非电热的铜制家用烹饪、供暖器具	20	0	0	0	0	0	0	0	0	0	0		2		0	0	10	4			
74181090	餐桌厨房等家用铜制器具及其零件	18	0	0	0	0	0	0	0	0	0	0		0	14.4	0	0	9	3.6			
74182000	铜制卫生器具及其零件	18	0	0	0	0	0	0	0	0	0	0		0		0	0	9	3.6			
74191000	铜链条及其零件	14	0	0	0	0	0	0	0	0	0	0		0	11.2	0	0	0	2.8	0		
74199110	工业用铸造、模压、冲压其他铜制品	10	0	0	0	0	0	0	0	0	0	0		0	5	0	0	0	0			
74199190	非工业用铸造、模压、冲压铜制品	20	0	0	0	0	0	0	0	0	0	0		0		0	0	10	4			
74199920	铜弹簧	10	0	0	0	0	0	0	0	0	0	0		0	5		0	0	0			
74199930	铜丝制的布（包括环形带）	7	0	0	0	0	0	0	0	0	0	0		0	5.6		0	0	0			
74199940	铜丝制的网、格栅、网眼和铜板	8	0	0	0	0	0	0	0	0	0	0		0	6.4		0	0	0			
74199950	非电热的铜制家用供暖器及其零件	20	0	0	0	0	0	0	0	0	0	0		2		0	0	10	4			
74199991	工业用其他铜制品	10	0	0	0	0	0	0	0	0	0	0	8.5	1	5	0	0	0	0			
74199999	非工业用其他铜制品	20	0	0	0	0	0	0	0	0	0	0	17	2	16	0	0	10	4			
75011000	镍锍	3	0	0	0	0	0	0	0	0	0	0		0	0		0	0	0			
75012010	镍湿法冶炼中间品	3	0	0	0	0	0	0	0	0	0	0		0	0		0	0	0			
75012090	氧化镍烧结物、镍的其他中间产品	3	0	0	0	0	0	0	0	0	0	0		0	0		0	0	0			
75021010	按重量计镍、钴总量在99.99％及以上的，但钴含量不超过0.005％的非合金镍	3	0	0	0	0	0	0	0	0	0	0		0	0		0	0	0			
75021090	其他非合金镍	3	0	0	0	0	0	0	0	0	0	0		0	0		0	0	0			
75022000	未锻轧镍合金	3	0	0	0	0	0	0	0	0	0	0		0	0		0	0	0			
75030000	镍废碎料	1.5	0	0	0	0	0	0	0	0	0	0		0	0		0	0	0			
75040010	非合金镍粉及片状粉末	4	0	0	0	0	0	0	0	0	0	0		0	0		0	0	0			
75040020	合金镍粉及片状粉末	4	0	0	0	0	0	0	0	0	0	0		0	0		0	0	0			
75051100	纯镍条、杆、型材及异型材	6	0	0	0	0	0	0	0	0	0	0		0	5		0	0	0			
75051200	合金镍条、杆、型材及异型材	6	0	0	0	0	0	0	0	0	0	0		0	5		0	0	0			
75052100	纯镍丝	6	0	0	0	0	0	0	0	0	0	0		0	5		0	0	0			
75052200	镍合金丝	6	0	0	0	0	0	0	0	0	0	0		0	5		0	0	0			
75061000	纯镍板、片、带、箔	6	0	0	0	0	0	0	0	0	0	0		0	5		0	0	0			
75062000	镍合金板、片、带、箔	6	0	0	0	0	0	0	0	0	0	0		0	5		0	0	0	0		
75071100	纯镍管	6	0	0	0	0	0	0	0	0	0	0		0	5		0	0	0			
75071200	镍合金管	6	0	0	0	0	0	0	0	0	0	0		0	5		0	0	0			
75072000	镍及镍合金管子附件	6	0	0	0	0	0	0	0	0	0	0		0	5		0	0	0			
75081010	镍丝制的布	6	0	0	0	0	0	0	0	0	0	0		0	5		0	0	0			
75081080	工业用镍丝制的网及格栅	6	0	0	0	0	0	0	0	0	0	0		0	5		0	0	0			
75081090	其他镍丝制的网及格栅	6	0	0	0	0	0	0	0	0	0	0		0	5		0	0	0			
75089010	电镀用镍阳极	4	0	0	0	0	0	0	0	0	0	0		0	0		0	0	0			
75089080	其他工业用镍制品	6	0	0	0	0	0	0	0	0	0	0		0	5		0	0	0			
75089090	其他非工业用镍制品	6	0	0	0	0	0	0	0	0	0	0		0	5		0	0	0			
76011010	按重量计含铝量在99.95%及以上的未煅轧非铝合金	5	0	0	0	0	0	0	0	0	0	0		0	0		0	0	0	0		
76011090	其他非煅轧非铝合金	5	0	0	0	0	0	0	0	0	0	0		0	0		0	0	0	0		
76012000	未锻轧铝合金	7	0	0	0	0	0	0	0	0	0	0	6	0	5		0	0	0		0	
76020000	铝废碎料	1.5	0	0	0	0	0	0	0	0	0	0		0	0		0		0	0		
76031000	非片状铝粉	6	0	0	0	0	0	0	0	0	0	0		0.6	5		0	0	0			
76032000	片状铝粉末	7	0	0	0	0	0	0	0	0	0	0		0	5		0	0	0			

税则号列	商品名称（简称）	最惠国	东盟 文	柬	印	老	马	缅	菲	新	泰	越	亚太	智利	巴基斯坦	新加坡	新西兰	秘鲁	哥斯达黎加	香港	澳门	台湾
76041010	非合金铝条、杆	5	0	0	0	0	0	0	0	0	0	0		0.5	0		0	0	0			
76041090	非合金铝型材及异形材	5	0	0	0	0	0	0	0	0	0	0		0.5	0		0	0	0			
76042100	铝合金制空心异型材	5	0	0	0	0	0	0	0	0	0	0		0	0		0	0	0			
76042910	铝合金条、杆	5	0	0	0	0	0	0	0	0	0	0	3.5	0	0		0	0	0			
76042990	铝合金型材及异形材	5	0	0	0	0	0	0	0	0	0	0	3.5	0	0		0	0	0			
76051100	纯铝制的粗丝	8	0	0	0	0	0	0	0	0	0	0		0.8	5		0	0	0			
76051900	纯铝制的细丝	8	0	0	0	0	0	0	0	0	0	0	6.8	0	5		0	0	0	0		
76052100	铝合金制的粗丝	8	0	0	0	0	0	0	0	0	0	0		0	5		0	0	0			
76052900	铝合金制的细丝	8	0	0	0	0	0	0	0	0	0	0		0	5		0	0	0			
76061121	0.3mm≦厚度<0.36mm的非合金铝与塑料复合的矩形板片带	6	0	0	0	0	0	0	0	0	0	0	4.2	0	0		0	0	0			
76061129	其他0.3mm≦厚度<0.36mm的非合金铝制矩形铝板片带	6	0	0	0	0	0	0	0	0	0	0	4.2	0	0		0	0	0			
76061191	其他非合金铝与塑料复合的矩形板片带	6	0	0	0	0	0	0	0	0	0	0	4.2	0	0		0	0	0	0		0
76061199	纯铝制矩形的其他板、片及带	6	0	0	0	0	0	0	0	0	0	0	4.2	0	0		0	0	0	0		0
76061220	厚度<0.28mm的铝合金制矩形铝板片带	6	0	0	0	0	0	0	0	0	0	0	4.2	0	0		0	0	0	0		0
76061230	0.28mm≦厚度≤0.35mm的铝合金制矩形铝板片带	6	0	0	0	0	0	0	0	0	0	0	4.2	0	0		0	0	0	0		0
76061251	0.35mm<厚度≤0.4mm的铝合金与塑料复合的矩形板片带	6	0	0	0	0	0	0	0	0	0	0	4.2	0	0		0	0	0	0		
76061259	其他0.35mm<厚度≤0.4mm的铝合金制矩形铝板片带	6	0	0	0	0	0	0	0	0	0	0	4.2	0	0		0	0	0	0		
76061290	厚度>0.4mm的铝合金制矩形铝板片带	6	0	0	0	0	0	0	0	0	0	0	4.2	0	0		0	0	0	0		
76069100	纯铝制非矩形的板、片及带	6	0	0	0	0	0	0	0	0	0	0		0	5		0	0	0	0		0
76069200	铝合金制非矩形的板、片及带	10	0	0	0	0	0	0	0	0	0	0		0	5	0	0	0	0	0		0
76071110	厚度不超过0.007毫米的无衬背铝箔	6	0	0	0	0	0	0	0	0	0	0	5.7	0.6	5		0	0	0			
76071120	厚度大于0.007毫米，但不超过0.01毫米的无衬背铝箔	6	0	0	0	0	0	0	0	0	0	0	5.7	0.6	5		0	0	0			
76071190	轧制后未进一步加工的无衬背铝箔	6	0	0	0	0	0	0	0	0	0	0	5.7	0.6	5		0	0	0			0
76071900	其他无衬背铝箔	6	0	0	0	0	0	0	0	0	0	0	5.1	0.6	5		0	0	0			0
76072000	有衬背铝箔	6	0	0	0	0	0	0	0	0	0	0		0.6	5		0	0	0	0		0
76081000	纯铝管	8	0	0	0	0	0	0	0	0	0	0		0.8	5		0	0	0			
76082010	外径不超过10厘米的铝合金管	8	0	0	0	0	0	0	0	0	0	0		0.8	5		0	0	0			
76082091	外径超过10厘米壁厚不超过25毫米铝合金管	8	0	0	0	0	0	0	0	0	0	0		0.8	5		0	0	0			
76082099	其他铝合金管	8	0	0	0	0	0	0	0	0	0	0		0.8	5		0	0	0			
76090000	铝制管子附件	8	0	0	0	0	0	0	0	0	0	0		0	5		0	0	0			
76101000	铝制门窗及其框架、门槛	25	0	0	0	0	0	0	0	0	0	0		0		0	0	12.5	5		0	
76109000	其他铝制结构体及其部件	6	0	0	0	0	0	0	0	0	0	0		0.6	5		0	0	0			
76110000	容积＞300L的铝制囤、罐等容器	12	0	0	0	0	0	0	0	0	0	0		0	6	0	0	0	2.4			
76121000	铝制软管容器	12	0	0	0	0	0	0	0	0	0	0		1.2	6	0	0	6	2.4			
76129010	铝制易拉罐及罐体	30	0	0	0	0	0	0	0	0	0	0		3		0	0	15	6			
76129090	容积≤300L的铝制囤、罐等容器	12	0	0	0	0	0	0	0	0	0	0		1.2	6	0	0	6	2.4			
76130010	零售包装装压缩、液化气体铝容器	12	0	0	0	0	0	0	0	0	0	0		0	6	0	0	0	2.4			
76130090	非零售装装压缩、液化气体铝容器	6	0	0	0	0	0	0	0	0	0	0		0	5		0	0	0			
76141000	带钢芯的铝制绞股线、缆、编带	6	0	0	0	0	0	0	0	0	0	0		0	5		0	0	0			
76149000	不带钢芯的铝制绞股线、缆、编带	6	0	0	0	0	0	0	0	0	0	0		0	5		0	0	0			
76151010	擦锅器及洗刷擦光用的块垫、手套	18	0	0	0	0	0	0	0	0	0	0		0	14.4	0	0	9	3.6			
76151090	餐桌厨房等家用铝制器具及其零件	15	0	0	0	0	0	0	0	0	0	0		1.5	12	0	0	7.5	3			
76152000	铝制卫生器具及其零件	18	0	0	0	0	0	0	0	0	0	0		1.8	14.4	0	0	9	3.6			
76161000	铝钉、螺钉、螺母、垫圈等紧固件	10	0	0	0	0	0	0	0	0	0	0	8.5	0	5	0	0	0	0	0		
76169100	铝丝制的布、网、篱及格栅	10	0	0	0	0	0	0	0	0	0	0		0		0	0	0	0			
76169910	其他工业用铝制品	10	0	0	0	0	0	0	0	0	0	0	8.5	1	5	0	0	5	0			
76169990	其他非工业用铝制品	15	0	0	0	0	0	0	0	0	0	0	12.8	1.5	7.5	0	0	7.5	3			
78011000	未锻轧精炼铅	3	0	0	0	0	0	0	0	0	0	0		0	0		0	0	0			
78019100	未锻轧铅锑合金	3	0	0	0	0	0	0	0	0	0	0		0	0		0	0	0			
78019900	未锻轧的其他铅合金	3	0	0	0	0	0	0	0	0	0	0		0	0		0	0	0			
78020000	铅废碎料	1.5	0	0	0	0	0	0	0	0	0	0		0	0		0	0	0			
78041100	铅片、带及厚度≤0.2mm的箔	6	0	0	0	0	0	0	0	0	0	0		0	5		0	0	0			
78041900	铅及铅合金板、厚度＞0.2mm的箔	6	0	0	0	0	0	0	0	0	0	0		0	5		0	0	0			
78042000	铅及铅合金粉末、片状粉末	6	0	0	0	0	0	0	0	0	0	0		0	5		0	0	0			

税则号列	商品名称（简称）	最惠国	东盟										亚太	智利	巴基斯坦	新加坡	新西兰	秘鲁	哥斯达黎加	香港	澳门	台湾
			文	柬	印	老	马	缅	菲	新	泰	越										
78060010	铅及铅合金条、杆、丝、型材	6	0	0	0	0	0	0	0	0	0	0		0	5		0	0	0			
78060090	其他铅制品	6	0	0	0	0	0	0	0	0	0	0		0	5		0	0	0			
79011110	按重量计含锌量在99.995%及以上的未煅轧锌	3	0	0	0	0	0	0	0	0	0	0		0	0		0	0	0			
79011190	含锌量不小于99.99%，并小于99.995%的未煅轧锌	3	0	0	0	0	0	0	0	0	0	0		0	0		0	0	0			
79011200	含锌量＜99.99%的未锻轧锌	3	0	0	0	0	0	0	0	0	0	0		0	0		0	0	0			
79012000	未锻轧锌合金	3	0	0	0	0	0	0	0	0	0	0		0	0		0	0	0	0		
79020000	锌废碎料	1.5	0	0	0	0	0	0	0	0	0	0		0	0		0	0	0			
79031000	锌末	6	0	0	0	0	0	0	0	0	0	0		0	5		0	0	0			
79039000	锌粉及片状粉末	6	0	0	0	0	0	0	0	0	0	0		0	5		0	0	0			
79040000	锌及锌合金条、杆、型材、丝	6	0	0	0	0	0	0	0	0	0	0		0	5		0	0	0			
79050000	锌板、片、带、箔	6	0	0	0	0	0	0	0	0	0	0		0.6	5		0	0	0			
79070020	锌管及锌制管子附件	6	0	0	0	0	0	0	0	0	0	0		0	5		0	0	0			
79070030	电池壳体坯料（锌饼）	6	0	0	0	0	0	0	0	0	0	0		0	5		0	4.5	0			
79070090	其他非工业用锌制品	6	0	0	0	0	0	0	0	0	0	0		0	5		0	0	0			
80011000	未锻轧非合金锡	3	0	0	0	0	0	0	0	0	0	0		0	0		0	0	0	0		
80012010	锡基巴毕脱合金	3	0	0	0	0	0	0	0	0	0	0		0	0		0	0	0	0		
80012021	按重量计含铅量在0.1%以下的焊锡	3	0	0	0	0	0	0	0	0	0	0		0	0		0	0	0	0	0	
80012029	其他焊锡	3	0	0	0	0	0	0	0	0	0	0		0	0		0	0	0	0	0	
80012090	其他锡合金	3	0	0	0	0	0	0	0	0	0	0		0	0		0	0	0	0		
80020000	锡废碎料	1.5	0	0	0	0	0	0	0	0	0	0		0	0		0	0	0	0		
80030000	锡及锡合金条、杆、型材、丝	8	0	0	0	0	0	0	0	0	0	0		0	5		0	0	0	0		
80070020	锡及锡合金板、片及带，厚度＞0.2mm	8	0	0	0	0	0	0	0	0	0	0		0	5		0	0	0			
80070030	锡箔、锡粉及片状粉末	8	0	0	0	0	0	0	0	0	0	0		0	5		0	0	0			
80070040	锡及锡合金管、管子附件	8	0	0	0	0	0	0	0	0	0	0		0	5		0	0	0			
80070090	其他锡制品	8	0	0	0	0	0	0	0	0	0	0		0	6.4		0	0	0	0		
81011000	钨粉	6	0	0	0	0	0	0	0	0	0	0		0	5		0	0	0			
81019400	未锻轧钨	3	0	0	0	0	0	0	0	0	0	0		0	0		0	0	0			
81019600	钨丝	8	0	0	0	0	0	0	0	0	0	0		0	5		0	0	0			
81019700	钨废碎料	3	0	0	0	0	0	0	0	0	0	0		0	0		0	0	0			
81019910	锻轧钨条、杆、型材；废碎料	5	0	0	0	0	0	0	0	0	0	0		0	0		0	0	0			
81019990	其他钨制品	8	0	0	0	0	0	0	0	0	0	0		0	5		0	0	0			
81021000	钼粉	6	0	0	0	0	0	0	0	0	0	0		0	5		0	0	0			
81029400	未锻轧钼、钼废碎料	3	0	0	0	0	0	0	0	0	0	0		0	0		0	0	0			
81029500	锻轧钼条杆、型材、板片带箔	8	0	0	0	0	0	0	0	0	0	0		0	5		0	0	0			
81029600	钼丝	8	0	0	0	0	0	0	0	0	0	0		0	5		0	0	0			
81029700	钼废碎料	3	0	0	0	0	0	0	0	0	0	0		0	0		0	0	0			
81029900	钼制品	8	0	0	0	0	0	0	0	0	0	0		0	5		0	0	0			
81032011	松装密度小于2.2g/cm3的钽粉	6	0	0	0	0	0	0	0	0	0	0		0	5		0	0	0			
81032019	松装密度大于等于2.2g/cm3的钽粉	6	0	0	0	0	0	0	0	0	0	0		0	5		0	0	0			
81032090	未锻轧钽	6	0	0	0	0	0	0	0	0	0	0		0	5		0	0	0			
81033000	钽废碎料	6	0	0	0	0	0	0	0	0	0	0		0	5		0	0	0			
81039011	直径＜0.5mm的钽丝	8	0	0	0	0	0	0	0	0	0	0		0	5		0	0	0			
81039019	直径⩾0.5mm的钽丝	8	0	0	0	0	0	0	0	0	0	0		0	5		0	0	0			
81039090	其他锻轧钽及其制品	8	0	0	0	0	0	0	0	0	0	0		0	5		0	0	0			
81041100	含镁量⩾99.8%的未锻轧镁	6	0	0	0	0	0	0	0	0	0	0	4.2	0	0		0	0	0			
81041900	其他未锻轧的镁及镁合金	6	0	0	0	0	0	0	0	0	0	0		0	5		0	0	0			
81042000	镁废碎料	1.5	0	0	0	0	0	0	0	0	0	0		0	0		0	0	0			
81043000	已分级的镁锉屑、车屑、颗粒；粉末	8	0	0	0	0	0	0	0	0	0	0		0	5		0	0	0			
81049010	锻轧镁	8	0	0	0	0	0	0	0	0	0	0		0	5		0	0	0			
81049020	镁制品	8.4	0	0	0	0	0	0	0	0	0	0		0	5		0	0	0			
81052010	钴湿法冶炼中间品	4	0	0	0	0	0	0	0	0	0	0		0	0		0	0	0			
81052020	未锻轧钴	4	0	0	0	0	0	0	0	0	0	0		0	0		0	0	0			
81052090	钴锍及其他钴冶炼时所得的中间产品、粉末	4	0	0	0	0	0	0	0	0	0	0		0	0		0	0	0			
81053000	钴锍废碎料	4	0	0	0	0	0	0	0	0	0	0		0	0		0	0	0			
81059000	其他钴及制品	8	0	0	0	0	0	0	0	0	0	0		0.8	5		0	0	0			
81060010	未锻轧铋、废碎料、粉末	3	0	0	0	0	0	0	0	0	0	0		0	0		0	0	0			
81060090	其他铋及铋制品	8	0	0	0	0	0	0	0	0	0	0		0	5		0	0	0			

税则号列	商品名称（简称）	最惠国	东盟										亚太	智利	巴基斯坦	新加坡	新西兰	秘鲁	哥斯达黎加	香港	澳门	台湾
			文	柬	印	老	马	缅	菲	新	泰	越										
81072000	未锻轧镉、粉末	3	0	0	0	0	0	0	0	0	0	0		0	0		0		0			
81073000	镉废碎料	3	0	0	0	0	0	0	0	0	0	0		0	0		0	0	0			
81079000	其他镉及镉制品	8	0	0	0	0	0	0	0	0	0	0		0	5		0	0	0			
81082021	海绵钛	3	0	0	0	0	0	0	0	0	0	0		0	0		0	0	0			
81082029	其他未锻轧钛	3	0	0	0	0	0	0	0	0	0	0		0	0		0	0	0			
81082030	钛粉末	3	0	0	0	0	0	0	0	0	0	0		0	0		0	0	0			
81083000	钛废碎料	3	0	0	0	0	0	0	0	0	0	0		0	0		0	0	0			
81089010	钛条、杆、型材及异型材	8	0	0	0	0	0	0	0	0	0	0		0	5		0	0	0			
81089020	钛丝	8	0	0	0	0	0	0	0	0	0	0		0	5		0	0	0			
81089031	厚度≤0.8mm钛板、片、带、箔	8	0	0	0	0	0	0	0	0	0	0		0	5		0	0	0			
81089032	厚度＞0.8mm钛板、片、带、箔	8	0	0	0	0	0	0	0	0	0	0		0	5		0	0	0			
81089040	钛管	8	0	0	0	0	0	0	0	0	0	0		0	5		0	0	0			
81089090	其他钛及钛制品	8	0	0	0	0	0	0	0	0	0	0		0	5		0	0	0			
81092000	未锻轧锆、粉末	3	0	0	0	0	0	0	0	0	0	0		0	0		0	0	0			
81093000	锆废碎料	3	0	0	0	0	0	0	0	0	0	0		0	0		0	0	0			
81099000	锻轧锆及锆制品	8	0	0	0	0	0	0	0	0	0	0		0	5		0	0	0			
81101010	未锻轧锑	3	0	0	0	0	0	0	0	0	0	0		0	0		0	0	0			
81101020	锑粉末	3	0	0	0	0	0	0	0	0	0	0		0	0		0	0	0			
81102000	锑废碎料	3	0	0	0	0	0	0	0	0	0	0		0	0		0	0	0			
81109000	其他锑及锑制品	8	0	0	0	0	0	0	0	0	0	0		0	5		0	0	0			
81110010	未锻轧锰；锰废碎料；粉末	3	0	0	0	0	0	0	0	0	0	0		0	0		0	0	0			
81110090	其他锰及制品	8	0	0	0	0	0	0	0	0	0	0		0	5		0	0	0			
81121200	未锻轧铍、粉末	3	0	0	0	0	0	0	0	0	0	0		0	0		0	0	0			
81121300	铍废碎料	3	0	0	0	0	0	0	0	0	0	0		0	0		0	0	0			
81121900	其他铍及其制品	8	0	0	0	0	0	0	0	0	0	0		0	5		0	0	0			
81122100	未锻轧铬、粉末	3	0	0	0	0	0	0	0	0	0	0		0	0		0	0	0			
81122200	铬废碎料	3	0	0	0	0	0	0	0	0	0	0		0	0		0	0	0			
81122900	其他铬制品	3	0	0	0	0	0	0	0	0	0	0		0	0		0	0	0			
81125100	未锻轧铊、粉末	3	0	0	0	0	0	0	0	0	0	0		0	0		0	0	0			
81125200	铊废碎料	3	0	0	0	0	0	0	0	0	0	0		0	0		0	0	0			
81125900	其他铊制品	8	0	0	0	0	0	0	0	0	0	0		0	5		0	0	0			
81129210	未锻轧锗	3	0	0	0	0	0	0	0	0	0	0		0	0		0	0	0			
81129220	未锻轧钒	3	0	0	0	0	0	0	0	0	0	0		0	0		0	0	0			
81129230	未锻轧铟、铟废碎料、粉末	3	0	0	0	0	0	0	0	0	0	0		0	0		0	0	0			
81129240	未锻轧铌、铌废碎料、粉末	3	0	0	0	0	0	0	0	0	0	0		0	0		0	0	0			
81129290	未锻轧的未列名贱金属及其制品	3	0	0	0	0	0	0	0	0	0	0		0	0		0	0	0			
81129910	锗及其制品	3	0	0	0	0	0	0	0	0	0	0		0	0		0	0	0			
81129920	钒及其制品	3	0	0	0	0	0	0	0	0	0	0		0	0		0	0	0			
81129930	锻扎铟及其制品	8	0	0	0	0	0	0	0	0	0	0		0.8	5		0	0	0			
81129940	锻扎铌及其制品	8	0	0	0	0	0	0	0	0	0	0		0.8	5		0	0	0			
81129990	锻轧的未列名贱金属及其制品	8	0	0	0	0	0	0	0	0	0	0		0.8	0		0	0	0			
81130010	金属陶瓷颗粒、粉末	8.4	0	0	0	0	0	0	0	0	0	0		0	5		0	0	0			0
81130090	其他金属陶瓷及其制品，包括废碎料	8.4	0	0	0	0	0	0	0	0	0	0		0	5		0	0	0			0
82011000	锹及铲	8	0	0	0	0	0	0	0	0	0	0		0	5		0	0	0			
82013000	镐、锄、耙	8	0	0	0	0	0	0	0	0	0	0		0	5		0	0	0			
82014000	斧子、钩刀及类似砍伐工具	8	0	0	0	0	0	0	0	0	0	0		0	5		0	0	0			
82015000	修枝剪等单手操作农用剪	8	0	0	0	0	0	0	0	0	0	0		0	5		0	0	0			
82016000	修枝等双手操作农用剪	8	0	0	0	0	0	0	0	0	0	0		0	5		0	0	0			
82019010	农用叉	8	0	0	0	0	0	0	0	0	0	0		0	5		0	0	0			
82019090	其他农业、园艺、林业用手工工具	8	0	0	0	0	0	0	0	0	0	0		0	5		0	0	0			
82021000	手工锯	8.4	0	0	0	0	0	0	0	0	0	0		0	5		0	0	0			
82022010	双金属带锯条	8	0	0	0	0	0	0	0	0	0	0		0	5		0	0	0			
82022090	其他带锯片手工锯	8	0	0	0	0	0	0	0	0	0	0		0	5		0	0	0			
82023100	带有钢制工作部件的圆锯片	8	0	0	0	0	0	0	0	0	0	0		0	5		0	0	0			
82023910	带有天然或合成金刚石、立方氮化硼制工作部件的圆锯片	8	0	0	0	0	0	0	0	0	0	0		0	5		0	0	0	0		
82023990	其他圆锯片，包括部件	8	0	0	0	0	0	0	0	0	0	0		0	5		0	0	0	0		
82024000	链锯片	8	0	0	0	0	0	0	0	0	0	0		0	5		0	0	0			
82029110	加工金属用的机械锯的直锯片	8	0	0	0	0	0	0	0	0	0	0	7	0	5		0	0	0			
82029190	加工金属用的非机械锯的直锯片	8	0	0	0	0	0	0	0	0	0	0		0	5		0	0	0			

税则号列	商品名称（简称）	最惠国	东盟										亚太	智利	巴基斯坦	新加坡	新西兰	秘鲁	哥斯达黎加	香港	澳门	台湾
			文	柬	印	老	马	缅	菲	新	泰	越										
82029910	机械锯用的其他锯片	8.4	0	0	0	0	0	0	0	0	0	0		0	5		0	0	0			
82029990	非机械锯用的其他锯片	10.5	0	0	0	0	0	0	0	0	0	0		0	5	0	0	0	2.1			
82031000	钢锉、木锉及类似工具	10.5	0	0	0	0	0	0	0	0	0	0		0	5	0	0	0	2.1			
82032000	钳子、镊子及类似工具	10.5	0	0	0	0	0	0	0	0	0	0		0		0	0	0	2.1		0	0
82033000	白铁剪及类似工具	10.5	0	0	0	0	0	0	0	0	0	0		0	5	0	0	0	2.1			
82034000	切管器、螺栓切头器、打孔冲子等	10.5	0	0	0	0	0	0	0	0	0	0		0	5	0	0	0	2.1			
82041100	固定式的手动扳手及板钳	10.5	0	0	0	0	0	0	0	0	0	0		0	5	0	0	0	2.1			
82041200	可调式的手动扳手及板钳	10	0	0	0	0	0	0	0	0	0	0		0	5		0	0	0			0
82042000	可互换的扳手套筒	10	0	0	0	0	0	0	0	0	0	0		0	5		0	0	0			
82051000	手工钻孔或攻丝工具	10	0	0	0	0	0	0	0	0	0	0		0	5		0	0	0			
82052000	手工锤子	10	0	0	0	0	0	0	0	0	0	0		0	5		0	0	0			0
82053000	木工用刨子、凿子及类似切削工具	10.5	0	0	0	0	0	0	0	0	0	0		0	5	0	0	0	2.1			
82054000	手工螺丝刀	10.5	0	0	0	0	0	0	0	0	0	0		0	5	0	0	0	2.1			0
82055100	其他家用手工工具	10.5	0	0	0	0	0	0	0	0	0	0		1.1	5	0	0	0	2.1			
82055900	其他手工工具	10	0	0	0	0	0	0	0	0	0	0	8.5	0	5		0	0	0			0
82056000	喷灯	10	0	0	0	0	0	0	0	0	0	0		0	5		0	0	0			
82057000	台钳、夹钳及类似品	10.5	0	0	0	0	0	0	0	0	0	0		0	5	0	0	0	2.1			
82059000	成套手工工具	10.5	0	0	0	0	0	0	0	0	0	0		0	5	0	0	0	2.1			
82060000	成套工具组成的零售包装货品	10.5	0	0	0	0	0	0	0	0	0	0		1.1	5	0	0	0	2.1			
82071300	带金属陶瓷工作部件的凿岩工具	8	0	0	0	0	0	0	0	0	0	0		0.8	5		0	0	0			
82071910	带超硬材料部件的凿岩或钻探工具	8	0	0	0	0	0	0	0	0	0	0		0.8	5		0	0	0			
82071990	带其他材料工作部件的凿岩工具	8	0	0	0	0	0	0	0	0	0	0		0.8	5		0	0	0			
82072010	带超硬部件的金属拉拔或挤压用模	8	0	0	0	0	0	0	0	0	0	0		0	5		0	0	0			0
82072090	其他金属拉拔或挤压用模	8	0	0	0	0	0	0	0	0	0	0		0	5		0	0	0			0
82073000	锻压或冲压工具	8	0	0	0	0	0	0	0	0	0	0	6.8	0.8	5		0	0	0	0		0
82074000	攻丝工具	8	0	0	0	0	0	0	0	0	0	0		0	5		0	0	0			0
82075010	带超硬材料部件的钻孔工具	8	0	0	0	0	0	0	0	0	0	0		0.8	5		0	0	0	0		0
82075090	带其他材料工作部件的钻孔工具	8	0	0	0	0	0	0	0	0	0	0		0.8	5		0	0	0	0		0
82076010	带超硬材料部件的镗孔或铰孔工具	8	0	0	0	0	0	0	0	0	0	0		0	5		0	0	0			0
82076090	其他镗孔或铰孔工具	8	0	0	0	0	0	0	0	0	0	0		0	5		0	0	0			
82077010	带有天然或合成金刚石、立方氮化硼制的工作部件的铣削工具	8	0	0	0	0	0	0	0	0	0	0		0.8	5		0	0	0	0		0
82077090	其他铣削工具	8	0	0	0	0	0	0	0	0	0	0		0.8	5		0	0	0	0		0
82078010	带有天然或合成金刚石、立方氮化硼制的车削工具	8	0	0	0	0	0	0	0	0	0	0	6.8	0	5		0	0	0			0
82078090	其他车削工具	8	0	0	0	0	0	0	0	0	0	0	6.8	0	5		0	0	0			0
82079010	带超硬材料部件的其他可互换工具	8	0	0	0	0	0	0	0	0	0	0	6.8	0	5		0	0	0	0		0
82079090	其他可互换工具	8	0	0	0	0	0	0	0	0	0	0	6.8	0	5		0	0	0	0		0
82081011	经镀或涂层的硬质合金制的金工机械用刀及刀片	8	0	0	0	0	0	0	0	0	0	0		0	5		0	0	0	0		
82081019	其他硬质合金制的金工机械用刀及刀片	8	0	0	0	0	0	0	0	0	0	0		0	5		0	0	0	0		
82081090	其他金工机械用刀及刀片	8	0	0	0	0	0	0	0	0	0	0		0	5		0	0	0	0		
82082000	木工机械用刀及刀片	8	0	0	0	0	0	0	0	0	0	0		0	5		0	0	0			0
82083000	厨房或食品加工机器用刀及刀片	8	0	0	0	0	0	0	0	0	0	0		0	5		0	0	0			
82084000	农、林业机器用刀及刀片	8	0	0	0	0	0	0	0	0	0	0		0	5		0	0	0			0
82089000	其他机器或机械器具用刀及刀片	8	0	0	0	0	0	0	0	0	0	0	7.2	0	5		0	0	0			0
82090010	未装配的工具用金属陶瓷板	8	0	0	0	0	0	0	0	0	0	0	7.2	0	5		0	0	0			
82090021	晶粒度小于0.8微米的金属陶瓷条、杆	8	0	0	0	0	0	0	0	0	0	0	7.2	0	5		0	0	0			
82090029	其他未装配的工具用金属陶瓷条、杆	8	0	0	0	0	0	0	0	0	0	0	7.2	0	5		0	0	0			
82090030	未装配的工具用金属陶瓷刀头	8	0	0	0	0	0	0	0	0	0	0	7.2	0	5		0	0	0			
82090090	其他未装配的工具用金属陶瓷类似品	8	0	0	0	0	0	0	0	0	0	0	7.2	0	5		0	0	0			
82100000	加工调制食品、饮料用手动机械	18	0	0	0	0	0	0	0	0	0	0	16.2	1.8	14.4	0	0	9	3.6		0	
82111000	以刀为主的成套货品	18	0	0	0	0	0	0	0	0	0	0		0	0	0	0	9	3.6			
82119100	刃面固定的餐刀	18	0	0	0	0	0	0	0	0	0	0		0	0	0	0	9	3.6			
82119200	刃面固定的其他刀	12	0	0	0	0	0	0	0	0	0	0		0	0	0	0	0	2.4			
82119300	可换刃面刀	18	0	0	0	0	0	0	0	0	0	0		0	0	0	0	9	3.6			
82119400	税号82.11所列刀的刀片	14	0	0	0	0	0	0	0	0	0	0		0	0	0	0	0	2.8			
82119500	贱金属制的刀柄	12	0	0	0	0	0	0	0	0	0	0		0	0	0	0	0	2.4			
82121000	剃刀	12	0	0	0	0	0	0	0	0	0	0		0	0	0	0	0	2.4			
82122000	安全剃刀片	14	0	0	0	0	0	0	0	0	0	0		1.4	0	0	0	0	2.8			

税则号列	商品名称（简称）	最惠国	东盟										亚太	智利	巴基斯坦	新加坡	新西兰	秘鲁	哥斯达黎加	香港	澳门	台湾
			文	柬	印	老	马	缅	菲	新	泰	越										
82129000	剃刀零件	12	0	0	0	0	0	0	0	0	0	0		0	0	0	0	0	2.4			
82130000	剪刀、裁缝剪刀及类似品、剪刀片	12	0	0	0	0	0	0	0	0	0	0	10.8	0	0	0	0	0	2.4			
82141000	裁纸刀、信刀、铅笔刀及刀片	12	0	0	0	0	0	0	0	0	0	0	10.8	0	5	0	0	0	2.4			
82142000	修指甲及修脚用具(包括指甲锉)	18	0	0	0	0	0	0	0	0	0	0	16.2	1.8	16.2	0	0	9	3.6			
82149000	理发推子、切菜刀等其他利口器	18	0	0	0	0	0	0	0	0	0	0		0		0	0	9	3.6			
82151000	成套含镀贵金属制厨房或餐桌用具	18	0	0	0	0	0	0	0	0	0	0		1.8	0	0	0	9	3.6			
82152000	成套的其他厨房或餐桌用具	18	0	0	0	0	0	0	0	0	0	0		0	0	0	0	9	3.6			
82159100	非成套镀贵金属制厨房或餐桌用具	18	0	0	0	0	0	0	0	0	0	0		0	0	0	0	9	3.6			
82159900	其他非成套的厨房或餐桌用具	18	0	0	0	0	0	0	0	0	0	0		1.8	0	0	0	9	3.6	0		
83011000	挂锁	14	0	0	0	0	0	0	0	0	0	0		0	11.2	0	0	0	2.8			
83012010	机动车用中央控制门锁	10												0			0	0	0			
83012090	其他机动车用锁	10												0			0	0	0			
83013000	家具用锁	14	0	0	0	0	0	0	0	0	0	0		0	11.2	0	0	0	2.8			
83014000	其他锁	14	0	0	0	0	0	0	0	0	0	0		1.4	11.2	0	0	0	2.8			
83015000	带锁的扣环及扣环框架	14	0	0	0	0	0	0	0	0	0	0		0	11.2	0	0	0	2.8	0		
83016000	锁零件	12	0	0	0	0	0	0	0	0	0	0		0	6	0	0	0	2.4			
83017000	钥匙	10	0	0	0	0	0	0	0	0	0	0		0	5		0	0	0			
83021000	铰链(折叶)	10	0	0	0	0	0	0	0	0	0	0		1	5		0	0	0	0		
83022000	用贱金属支架的小脚轮	12	0	0	0	0	0	0	0	0	0	0		1.2	6	0	0	0	2.4			
83023000	机动车辆用贱金属附件及架座	10	0	0	0	0	0	0	0	0	0	0		0	5		0	0	0			
83024100	建筑用贱金属配件及架座	14	0	0	0	0	0	0	0	0	0	0		0	11.2	0	0	0	2.8			
83024200	家具用贱金属配件及架座	12	0	0	0	0	0	0	0	0	0	0		1.2	6	0	0	0	2.4			
83024900	其他用贱金属配件及架座	12	0	0	0	0	0	0	0	0	0	0		0	6	0	0	0	2.4			
83025000	帽架、帽钩、托架及类似品	14	0	0	0	0	0	0	0	0	0	0		1.4	11.2	0	0	0	2.8			
83026000	自动闭门器	12	0	0	0	0	0	0	0	0	0	0		0	6	0	0	0	2.4			
83030000	保险箱、柜、保险库的门	14	0	0	0	0	0	0	0	0	0	0		1.4	11.2	0	0	0	2.8			
83040000	贱金属档案柜、文件箱等办公用具	10.5	0	0	0	0	0	0	0	0	0	0		0	5	0	0	0	2.1	0		
83051000	活页夹或宗卷夹的附件	10.5	0	0	0	0	0	0	0	0	0	0		1.1	5	0	0	0	2.1			
83052000	成条钉书钉	10.5	0	0	0	0	0	0	0	0	0	0		0	5	0	0	0	2.1			
83059000	信夹、信角、文件夹等办公用品	10.5	0	0	0	0	0	0	0	0	0	0		0	5	0	0	0	2.1	0		
83061000	非电动铃、钟、锣及其类似品	8	0	0	0	0	0	0	0	0	0	0		0	5		0	0	0			
83062100	镀贵金属的雕塑像及其他装饰品	8	0	0	0	0	0	0	0	0	0	0		0	5		0	0	0			
83062910	景泰兰雕塑像及其他装饰品	8	0	0	0	0	0	0	0	0	0	0		0.8	5		0	0	0			
83062990	其他雕塑像及其他装饰品	8	0	0	0	0	0	0	0	0	0	0		0.8	5	0	0	0	0			
83063000	相框、画框及类似框架、镜子	8	0	0	0	0	0	0	0	0	0	0		0	5		0	0	0			
83071000	钢铁制软管、可有配件	8.4	0	0	0	0	0	0	0	0	0	0		0	5		0	0	0			
83079000	其他贱金属软管,可有配件	8.4	0	0	0	0	0	0	0	0	0	0		0	5		0	0	0	0		
83081000	贱金属制钩、环及眼	10.5	0	0	0	0	0	0	0	0	0	0		0	5	0	0	0	2.1	0		
83082000	贱金属制管形铆钉及开口铆钉	10.5	0	0	0	0	0	0	0	0	0	0		0	5	0	0	0	2.1	0		
83089000	贱金属制珠子及亮晶片	10.5	0	0	0	0	0	0	0	0	0	0		0	5	0	0	0	2.1	0		
83091000	贱金属制冠形瓶塞	18	0	0	0	0	0	0	0	0	0	0		0	14.4	0	0	0	3.6	0		
83099000	盖子瓶帽螺口塞封志等包装用配件	12	0	0	0	0	0	0	0	0	0	0		1.2	6	0	0	0	2.4	0		
83100000	标志牌、铭牌、号码、字母等标志	18	0	0	0	0	0	0	0	0	0	0		0		0	0	9	3.6			
83111000	焊剂涂面的贱金属电极、电弧焊用	8	0	0	0	0	0	0	0	0	0	0		0.8	5		0	0	0	0		
83112000	以焊剂为芯的贱金属制焊丝	8	0	0	0	0	0	0	0	0	0	0		0	5		0	0	0	0		
83113000	以焊剂涂面或作芯的贱金属条或丝	8	0	0	0	0	0	0	0	0	0	0		0.8	5		0	0	0	0		
83119000	贱金属粘聚成的丝或条	8	0	0	0	0	0	0	0	0	0	0	5.6	0.8	5		0	0	0	0		
84011000	核反应堆	2	0	0	0	0	0	0	0	0	0	0		0	0		0	0	0			
84012000	同位素分离机器、装置及其零件	1	0	0	0	0	0	0	0	0	0	0		0	0		0	0	0			
84013010	未辐照燃料元件(释热元件)	2	0	0	0	0	0	0	0	0	0	0		0	0		0	0	0			
84013090	未辐照燃料元件的零件	1	0	0	0	0	0	0	0	0	0	0		0	0		0	0	0			
84014010	未辐照相关组件	1	0	0	0	0	0	0	0	0	0	0		0	0		0	0	0			
84014020	堆内构件	1	0	0	0	0	0	0	0	0	0	0		0	0		0	0	0			
84014090	其他核反应堆零件	1	0	0	0	0	0	0	0	0	0	0		0	0		0	0	0			
84021110	蒸发量≥900t/hr发电锅炉	3	0	0	0	0	0	0	0	0	0	0	2.5	0	0		0	0	0			
84021190	蒸发量>45t/hr,<900t/hr发电锅炉	14	0	0	0	0	0	0	0	0	0	0	13.3	1.4	7	0	0	0	2.8			
84021200	蒸发量≤45t/hr水管锅炉	5	0	0	0	0	0	0	0	0	0	0	3.9	0	0		0	0	0			
84021900	其他蒸汽锅炉	5	0	0	0	0	0	0	0	0	0	0		0	0		0	0	0			
84022000	过热水锅炉	16	0	0	0	0	0	0	0	0	0	0		0	12.8	0	0	8	3.2			
84029000	蒸汽锅炉及过热水锅炉的零件	2	0	0	0	0	0	0	0	0	0	0		0	0		0	0	0			

税则号列	商品名称（简称）	最惠国	东盟										亚太	智利	巴基斯坦	新加坡	新西兰	秘鲁	哥斯达黎加	香港	澳门	台湾
			文	柬	印	老	马	缅	菲	新	泰	越										
84031010	家用型集中供暖用热水锅炉	10	0	0	0	0	0	0	0	0	0	0	9.5	0	5		0	0	0			
84031090	其他集中供暖用的热水锅炉	10	0	0	0	0	0	0	0	0	0	0	9.5	0	5		0	0	0			
84039000	集中供暖用热水锅炉的零件	6	0	0	0	0	0	0	0	0	0	0		0	5		0	0	0			
84041010	蒸汽锅炉、过热水锅炉的辅助设备	7	0	0	0	0	0	0	0	0	0	0	3.5	0	0		0	0	0			
84041020	集中供暖用热水锅炉的辅助设备	10	0	0	0	0	0	0	0	0	0	0	5	0	5		0	0	0			
84042000	水及其他蒸汽动力装置的冷凝器	14	0	0	0	0	0	0	0	0	0	0		0	11.2	0	0	0	2.8			
84049010	集中供暖热水锅炉辅助设备的零件	10	0	0	0	0	0	0	0	0	0	0	0	0	0		0	0	0			
84049090	其他辅助设备用零件	7	0	0	0	0	0	0	0	0	0	0	0	0	0		0	0	0			
84051000	煤气、乙炔及类似水解气体发生器	14	0	0	0	0	0	0	0	0	0	0		1.4	11.2	0	0	0	2.8			
84059000	煤气、乙炔等气体发生器的零件	8	0	0	0	0	0	0	0	0	0	0		0	5		0	0	0			
84061000	船舶动力用汽轮机	5	0	0	0	0	0	0	0	0	0	0		0	0		0	0	0			
84068110	40MW＜输出功率≤100MW的汽轮机	5	0	0	0	0	0	0	0	0	0	0		0	0		0	0	0			
84068120	100MW＜输出功率≤350MW的汽轮机	5	0	0	0	0	0	0	0	0	0	0		0	0		0	0	0			
84068130	输出功率＞350MW的汽轮机	6	0	0	0	0	0	0	0	0	0	0		0	5		0	0	0			
84068200	输出功率≤40MW的汽轮机	5	0	0	0	0	0	0	0	0	0	0		0	0		0	0	0			
84069000	汽轮机用的零件	2	0	0	0	0	0	0	0	0	0	0		0	0		0	0	0			
84071010	输出功率≤298kw航空器点燃式发动机	2	0	0	0	0	0	0	0	0	0	0		0	0		0	0	0			
84071020	输出功率＞298kw航空器点燃式发动机	2	0	0	0	0	0	0	0	0	0	0		0	0		0	0	0			
84072100	船舶用舷外点燃式发动机	8	0	0	0	0	0	0	0	0	0	0		0	5		0	0	0			
84072900	船舶用其他未列名点燃式发动机	8	0	0	0	0	0	0	0	0	0	0		0	5		0	0	0			
84073100	排气量≤50cc往复式活塞发动机	10	0	0	0	0	0	0	0	0	0	0		0	5		0	0	0			
84073200	排气量50-250cc往复式活塞发动机	10	0	0	0	0	0	0	0	0	0	0		0	5		0	0	0			
84073300	排气量250-1000cc往复式活塞发动机	10	0	0	0	0	0	0	0	0	0	0		0	8	0	0	0	0	0		
84073410	排气量1000-3000cc往复式活塞发动机	10											7	0	7		0		0	0		
84073420	排气量＞3000cc往复式活塞发动机	10											7	0	7		0		0	0		
84079010	沼气发动机	12	0	0	0	0	0	0	0	0	0	0		0	6	0	0	0	2.4			
84079090	其他点燃往复或旋转式内燃发动机	18	0	0	0	0	0	0	0	0	0	0		0		0	0	9	3.6			
84081000	船舶用压燃式内燃发动机	5	0	0	0	0	0	0	0	0	0	0	2.5	0.5	0	0	0	0	0			
84082010	输出功率≥132.39kw车用柴油发动机	9											6.3	0.9	6.3		0	0	0	0		
84082090	输出功率＜132.39kw车用柴油发动机	25	20	20	20	20	20	20	20	20	20	20	17.5	2.5	17.5		0		5			
84089010	机车用柴油发动机	6	0	0	0	0	0	0	0	0	0	0	5.4	0.6	0		0	0	0			
84089091	功率≤14kw其他用柴油发动机	5	0	0	0	0	0	0	0	0	0	0	4.5	0.5	0		0	0	0			
84089092	14kw＜功率＜132.39kw其他柴油发动机	8.4	0	0	0	0	0	0	0	0	0	0	7.6	0.8	5		0	0	0			
84089093	功率≥132.39kw其他用柴油发动机	5	0	0	0	0	0	0	0	0	0	0	4.5	0.5	0		0	0	0			
84091000	航空器发动机用零件	2	0	0	0	0	0	0	0	0	0	0		0	0		0	0	0			
84099110	船舶用点燃式发动机专用零件	6	0	0	0	0	0	0	0	0	0	0	4.2	0	0		0	0	0			
84099191	电控燃油喷射装置	5	0	0	0	0	0	0	0	0	0	0	3.5	0	0	0	0	0	0			
84099199	其他点燃式活塞内燃发动机用零件	5	0	0	0	0	0	0	0	0	0	0	3.5	0	0	0	0	0	0			
84099910	其他船舶发动机专用零件	5	0	0	0	0	0	0	0	0	0	0	4.5	0.5	0	0	0	0	0			
84099920	其他机车发动机专用零件	2	0	0	0	0	0	0	0	0	0	0	1.5	0	0		0	0	0			
84099991	功率≥132.39kw发动机的专用零件	2	0	0	0	0	0	0	0	0	0	0	1.5	0	0		0	0	0			
84099999	其他未列名发动机的专用零件	8.4	0	0	0	0	0	0	0	0	0	0	8	0.8	5	0	0	0	0			
84101100	功率≤1000kw的水轮机及水轮	10	0	0	0	0	0	0	0	0	0	0		0	5		0	0	0			
84101200	功率1千kw-1万kw的水轮机及水轮	10	0	0	0	0	0	0	0	0	0	0		0	5	0	0	0	0			
84101310	功率＞3万kw的冲击式水轮机及水轮	10	0	0	0	0	0	0	0	0	0	0		0	5	0	0	0	0			
84101320	功率＞3.5万kw的贯流水轮机及水轮	10	0	0	0	0	0	0	0	0	0	0		0	5	0	0	0	0			
84101330	功率＞20万kw的水泵式水轮机及水轮	10	0	0	0	0	0	0	0	0	0	0		0	5		0	0	0			
84101390	其他功率＞1万kw的水轮机及水轮	10	0	0	0	0	0	0	0	0	0	0		0	5		0	0	0			
84109010	水轮机及水轮的调节器	6	0	0	0	0	0	0	0	0	0	0		0	5		0	0	0			
84109090	水轮机及水轮的其他零件	6	0	0	0	0	0	0	0	0	0	0		0	5		0	0	0			
84111110	推力≤25千牛顿的涡轮风扇发动机	1	0	0	0	0	0	0	0	0	0	0		0	0		0	0	0			
84111190	推力≤25千牛顿的其他的涡轮喷气发动机	1	0	0	0	0	0	0	0	0	0	0		0	0		0	0	0			
84111210	推力＞25千牛顿的涡轮风扇发动机	1	0	0	0	0	0	0	0	0	0	0	0	0	0		0	0	0			
84111290	推力＞25千牛顿的其他涡轮喷气发动机	1	0	0	0	0	0	0	0	0	0	0	0.5	0	0		0	0	0			
84112100	功率≤1100kw的涡轮螺桨发动机	2	0	0	0	0	0	0	0	0	0	0		0	0		0	0	0			
84112210	功率1100-2238kw涡轮螺桨发动机	2	0	0	0	0	0	0	0	0	0	0		0	0		0	0	0			
84112220	功率2238-3730kw涡轮螺桨发动机	2	0	0	0	0	0	0	0	0	0	0		0	0		0	0	0			
84112230	功率＞3730kw涡轮螺桨发动机	2	0	0	0	0	0	0	0	0	0	0		0	0		0	0	0			
84118100	功率≤5000kw的其他燃气轮机	15	0	0	0	0	0	0	0	0	0	0		1.5	12	0	0	7.5	3			

税则号列	商品名称（简称）	最惠国	东盟										亚太	智利	巴基斯坦	新加坡	新西兰	秘鲁	哥斯达黎加	香港	澳门	台湾
			文	柬	印	老	马	缅	菲	新	泰	越										
84118200	功率＞5000kw的其他燃气轮机	3	0	0	0	0	0	0	0	0	0	0		0	0		0	0	0			
84119100	涡轮喷气或涡轮螺桨发动机用零件	1	0	0	0	0	0	0	0	0	0	0		0	0		0	0	0			
84119910	涡轮轴发动机用零件	5	0	0	0	0	0	0	0	0	0	0		0.5	0		0	0	0			
84119990	其他燃气轮机用零件	5	0	0	0	0	0	0	0	0	0	0		0.5	0		0	0	0			
84121010	航空、航天器用喷气发动机	3	0	0	0	0	0	0	0	0	0	0		0	0		0	0	0			
84121090	非航空、航天器用喷气发动机	10	0	0	0	0	0	0	0	0	0	0		0	5		0	0	0			
84122100	直线作用的液压动力装置(液压缸)	12	0	0	0	0	0	0	0	0	0	0		1.2	6	0	0	6	2.4	0		0
84122910	液压马达	10	0	0	0	0	0	0	0	0	0	0		1	5	0	0	0	0			
84122990	其他液压动力装置	14	0	0	0	0	0	0	0	0	0	0		1.4	11.2	0	0	0	2.8			
84123100	直线作用的气压动力装置(气压缸)	14	0	0	0	0	0	0	0	0	0	0	13.3	0	7	0	0	0	2.8			0
84123900	其他气压动力装置	14	0	0	0	0	0	0	0	0	0	0		0	11.2	0	0	0	2.8			
84128000	其他发动机及动力装置	10	0	0	0	0	0	0	0	0	0	0		0	5		0	0	0			
84129010	航空、航天器用喷气发动机的零件	2	0	0	0	0	0	0	0	0	0	0		0	0		0	0	0			
84129090	其他发动机及动力装置的零件	8	0	0	0	0	0	0	0	0	0	0		0	5		0	0	0			
84131100	分装燃料或润滑油的泵	10	0	0	0	0	0	0	0	0	0	0		0	5	0	0	0	0			
84131900	其他装有或可装计量装置的泵	10	0	0	0	0	0	0	0	0	0	0		0	5	0	0	0	0			
84132000	手泵	10	0	0	0	0	0	0	0	0	0	0		0	5	0	0	0	0			
84133021	输出功率在132.39千瓦（180马力）及以上的发动机用燃油泵	3	0	0	0	0	0	0	0	0	0	0	2.5	0	0		0	0	0			
84133029	其他燃油泵	3	0	0	0	0	0	0	0	0	0	0		0	0		0	0	0			
84133030	润滑油泵	3	0	0	0	0	0	0	0	0	0	0		0	0		0	0	0			
84133090	其他燃油泵、润滑油泵或冷却剂泵	3	0	0	0	0	0	0	0	0	0	0	2.5	0	0		0	0	0			
84134000	混凝土泵	8	0	0	0	0	0	0	0	0	0	0		0.8	5		0	0	0	0		
84135010	气动式往复式排液泵	10	0	0	0	0	0	0	0	0	0	0		0	5	0	0	0	0			
84135020	电动式往复式排液泵	10	0	0	0	0	0	0	0	0	0	0		0	5	0	0	0	0	0		
84135031	往复式柱塞泵	10	0	0	0	0	0	0	0	0	0	0		1	5	0	0	0	0			
84135039	其他液压式往复泵	10	0	0	0	0	0	0	0	0	0	0		1	5	0	0	0	0			
84135090	其他往复式排液泵	10	0	0	0	0	0	0	0	0	0	0		1	5	0	0	5	0			
84136021	电动式齿轮回转泵	10	0	0	0	0	0	0	0	0	0	0		0	5	0	0	0	0			
84136022	液压式齿轮回转泵	10	0	0	0	0	0	0	0	0	0	0		0	5		0	0	0			
84136029	其他齿轮回转泵	10	0	0	0	0	0	0	0	0	0	0		0	5		0	0	0			
84136031	电动式叶片回转泵	10	0	0	0	0	0	0	0	0	0	0		0	5		0	0	0			
84136032	液压式叶片回转泵	10	0	0	0	0	0	0	0	0	0	0		0	5		0	0	0			
84136039	其他叶片回转泵	10	0	0	0	0	0	0	0	0	0	0		0	5		0	0	0			
84136040	螺杆回转泵	10	0	0	0	0	0	0	0	0	0	0		0	5		0	0	0			
84136050	径向柱塞泵	10	0	0	0	0	0	0	0	0	0	0		0	5		0	0	0			
84136060	轴向柱塞泵	10	0	0	0	0	0	0	0	0	0	0		0	5		0	0	0			
84136090	其他回转式排液泵	10	0	0	0	0	0	0	0	0	0	0		0	5	0	0	0	0			
84137010	转速≥10000转/分离心泵	8	0	0	0	0	0	0	0	0	0	0	7.6	0	5		0	0	0			
84137091	电动潜油泵及潜水电泵	10	0	0	0	0	0	0	0	0	0	0		0	5	0	0	0	0			
84137099	其他离心泵	8	0	0	0	0	0	0	0	0	0	0	7.6	0	5		0	0	0	0		
84138100	其他液体泵	8	0	0	0	0	0	0	0	0	0	0	4	0	0		0	0	0			0
84138200	液体提升机	8	0	0	0	0	0	0	0	0	0	0		0	5		0	0	0			
84139100	液体泵用零件	5	0	0	0	0	0	0	0	0	0	0	2.5	0	0		0	0	0	0		0
84139200	液体提升机用零件	6	0	0	0	0	0	0	0	0	0	0		0	5		0	0	0			
84141000	真空泵	8	0	0	0	0	0	0	0	0	0	0		0	5		0	0	0			0
84142000	手动或脚踏式空气泵	8	0	0	0	0	0	0	0	0	0	0		0	5		0	0	0			
84143011	功率≤0.4kw的冷藏、冷冻箱用压缩机	8	0	0	0	0	0	0	0	0	0	0	5.9	0.8	5	0	0	0	0	0		
84143012	功率0.4-5kw的冷藏、冷冻箱用压缩机	10	0	0	0	0	0	0	0	0	0	0	8.5	1	5	0	0	5	0	0		
84143013	功率0.4-5kw的空气调节器用压缩机	10	0	0	0	0	0	0	0	0	0	0	8.5	1	5	0	0	5	0	0		0
84143014	功率＞5kw的空气调节器用压缩机	10	0	0	0	0	0	0	0	0	0	0	8.5	1	5	0	0	5	0	0		0
84143015	冷冻或冷藏设备用，电动机额定功率超过5千瓦的电动机驱动压缩机	10	0	0	0	0	0	0	0	0	0	0	9.2	1	5		0	5	0	0		
84143019	其他制冷设备用压缩机	10	0	0	0	0	0	0	0	0	0	0	9	1	5	0	0	5	0	0		
84143090	非电机驱动的压缩机	9	0	0	0	0	0	0	0	0	0	0	8.1	0.9	5	0	0	0	0	0		
84144000	装在拖车底盘上的空气压缩机	8	0	0	0	0	0	0	0	0	0	0		0.8	5		0	0	0	0		
84145110	功率≤125瓦的吊扇	20	0	0	0	0	0	0	0	0	0	0		0		0	0	10	4			
84145120	功率≤125瓦的换气扇	20	0	0	0	0	0	0	0	0	0	0		0		0	0	10	4			0
84145130	功率≤125瓦，有旋转导风轮的风扇	12	0	0	0	0	0	0	0	0	0	0		0	6	0	0	0	2.4			
84145191	功率≤125瓦的台扇	10	0	0	0	0	0	0	0	0	0	0		0	5		0	0	0			

税则号列	商品名称（简称）	最惠国	东盟										亚太	智利	巴基斯坦	新加坡	新西兰	秘鲁	哥斯达黎加	香港	澳门	台湾
			文	柬	印	老	马	缅	菲	新	泰	越										
84145192	功率≤125瓦的落地扇	10	0	0	0	0	0	0	0	0	0	0		0	5		0	0	0			
84145193	功率≤125瓦的壁扇	10	0	0	0	0	0	0	0	0	0	0		0	5		0	0	0			
84145199	功率≤125瓦其他风扇、风机	10	0	0	0	0	0	0	0	0	0	0		0	5	0	0	0	0			0
84145910	其他吊扇	8	0	0	0	0	0	0	0	0	0	0	7.2	0.8	5		0	0	0			
84145920	其他换气扇	8	0	0	0	0	0	0	0	0	0	0	7.2	0.8	5		0	0	0			
84145930	离心通风机	10	0	0	0	0	0	0	0	0	0	0	9.5	1	5	0	0	5	0			
84145990	其他扇，风机	8	0	0	0	0	0	0	0	0	0	0	7.2	0.8	5		0	0	0			0
84146010	抽油烟机	10	0	0	0	0	0	0	0	0	0	0		0	5		0	0	0			
84146090	罩最大边长≤120cm的通风罩或循环气罩	10	0	0	0	0	0	0	0	0	0	0		0	5	0	0	0	0			
84148010	燃气轮机用的自由活塞式发生器	8	0	0	0	0	0	0	0	0	0	0	5.6	0.8	5		0	0	0			
84148020	二氧化碳压缩机	7	0	0	0	0	0	0	0	0	0	0	4.9	0.7	0		0	0	0			
84148030	发动机用增压器	7	0	0	0	0	0	0	0	0	0	0	4.9	0	0		0		0			
84148090	其他气体压缩机及通风罩或循环气罩	7	0	0	0	0	0	0	0	0	0	0	4.9	0	0		0	0	0	0		0
84149011	用于制冷设备的压缩机进、排气阀片	8	0	0	0	0	0	0	0	0	0	0	7.2	0.8	5		0	0	0			
84149019	其他用于制冷设备的压缩机零件	8	0	0	0	0	0	0	0	0	0	0	7.2	0.8	5		0	0	0			0
84149020	风机、风扇、通风罩及循环气罩零件	12	0	0	0	0	0	0	0	0	0	0	11.4	1.2	6	0	0	6	2.4			0
84149090	税号84.14其他所列机器零件	7	0	0	0	0	0	0	0	0	0	0	6.5	0.7	5		0	0	0	0		0
84151010	独立窗式或壁式空气调节器	15	0	0	0	0	0	0	0	0	0	0	13.5	0	7.5	0	0	7.5	3			
84151021	分体式制冷量制冷量≤4千大卡/时窗式或壁式空气调节器	15	0	0	0	0	0	0	0	0	0	0	13.5	0	7.5	0	0	7.5	3			
84151022	分体式制冷量制冷量＞4千大卡/时窗式或壁式空气调节器	15	0	0	0	0	0	0	0	0	0	0	13.5	0	7.5	0	0	7.5	3			
84152000	机动车辆上供人使用的空气调节器	20												2			0		4	0		
84158110	制冷量≤4千大卡/时热泵式空调器	15	0	0	0	0	0	0	0	0	0	0		0	12	0	0	7.5	3			
84158120	制冷量＞4千大卡/时热泵式空调器	20	0	0	0	0	0	0	0	0	0	0		0		0	0	10	4			
84158210	制冷量≤4千大卡/时的其他空调器	15	0	0	0	0	0	0	0	0	0	0		0	12	0	0	7.5	3			
84158220	制冷量＞4千大卡/时的其他空调器	20	0	0	0	0	0	0	0	0	0	0		0		0	0	10	4			
84158300	未装有制冷装置的空调器	10	0	0	0	0	0	0	0	0	0	0		0	5	0	0	0	0			
84159010	制冷量≤4千大卡/时等空调的零件	10	0	0	0	0	0	0	0	0	0	0	8	0	5	0	0	0	0	0		
84159090	制冷量＞4千大卡/时等空调的零件	10	0	0	0	0	0	0	0	0	0	0	8	0	5	0	0	0	0	0		0
84161000	使用液体燃料的炉用燃烧器	10	0	0	0	0	0	0	0	0	0	0	9.5	1	5	0	0	0	0			
84162011	使用天然气的燃烧器	10.5	0	0	0	0	0	0	0	0	0	0		0	5	0	0	0	2.1			
84162019	其他使用气体燃料的炉用燃烧器	10.5	0	0	0	0	0	0	0	0	0	0		0	5	0	0	0	2.1			
84162090	使用粉状固体燃料的炉用燃烧器	10.5	0	0	0	0	0	0	0	0	0	0		0	5	0	0	0	2.1			
84163000	机械加煤机及类似装置	8.4	0	0	0	0	0	0	0	0	0	0		0	5		0	0	0			
84169000	炉用燃烧器、机械加煤机等的零件	6	0	0	0	0	0	0	0	0	0	0		0	5		0	0	0			
84171000	矿砂、金属的热处理用炉及烤箱	10	0	0	0	0	0	0	0	0	0	0		0	5	0	0	0	0			
84172000	面包房用烤炉及烘箱等	10	0	0	0	0	0	0	0	0	0	0		0	5		0	0	0			
84178010	炼焦炉	10	0	0	0	0	0	0	0	0	0	0		0	5		0	0	0			
84178020	放射性废物焚烧炉	5	0	0	0	0	0	0	0	0	0	0		0	0		0	0	0			
84178030	水泥回转窑	10	0	0	0	0	0	0	0	0	0	0		0	5	0	0	0	0			
84178040	石灰石分解炉	10	0	0	0	0	0	0	0	0	0	0		0	5		0	0	0			
84178050	垃圾焚烧炉	10	0	0	0	0	0	0	0	0	0	0		0	5	0	0	0	0			0
84178090	其他非电热的工业用炉及烘箱	10	0	0	0	0	0	0	0	0	0	0		0	5	0	0	0	0			0
84179010	海绵铁回转窑的零件	7	0	0	0	0	0	0	0	0	0	0		0	5		0	0	0			
84179020	炼焦炉的零件	7	0	0	0	0	0	0	0	0	0	0		0	5		0	0	0			
84179090	其他非电热工业用炉及烘箱的零件	7	0	0	0	0	0	0	0	0	0	0		0	5		0	0	0			
84181010	容积＞500L冷藏-冷冻组合机	10	0	0	0	0	0	0	0	0	0	0		1	5	0	0	5	0			
84181020	200L＜容积≤500L冷藏冷冻组合机	15	0	0	0	0	0	0	0	0	0	0		1.5	12	0	0	7.5	3			
84181030	容积≤200L冷藏-冷冻组合机	15	0	0	0	0	0	0	0	0	0	0		1.5	12	0	0	7.5	3			
84182110	容积＞150L压缩式家用型冷藏箱	10	0	0	0	0	0	0	0	0	0	0		1	5	0	0	0	0			
84182120	50L＜容积≤150L压缩式家用型冷藏箱	10	0	0	0	0	0	0	0	0	0	0	9	1	5	0	0	0	0			
84182130	容积≤50L压缩式家用型冷藏箱	10	0	0	0	0	0	0	0	0	0	0	9	1	5	0	0	0	0			
84182910	半导体制冷式家用型冷藏箱	30	0	0	0	0	0	0	0	0	0	0		0		0	0	15	6			
84182920	电气吸收式家用型冷藏箱	15	0	0	0	0	0	0	0	0	0	0		0	12	0	0	7.5	3			
84182990	其他家用型冷藏箱	30	0	0	0	0	0	0	0	0	0	0		0		0	0	15	6			
84183010	制冷温度≤-40℃，容积≤800L柜式冷冻箱	9	0	0	0	0	0	0	0	0	0	0		0	5		0	0	0		0	
84183021	制冷温度＞-40℃，容积500-800L柜式冷冻箱	23	0	0	0	0	0	0	0	0	0	0		0		0	0	11.5	4.6		0	

税则号列	商品名称（简称）	最惠国	东盟										亚太	智利	巴基斯坦	新加坡	新西兰	秘鲁	哥斯达黎加	香港	澳门	台湾
			文	柬	印	老	马	缅	菲	新	泰	越										
84183029	制冷温度＞-40℃，容积≤500L柜式冷冻箱	30	0	0	0	0	0	0	0	0	0	0		0		0	0	15	6		0	
84184010	制冷温度≤-40℃，容积≤900L立式冷冻箱	9	0	0	0	0	0	0	0	0	0	0		0	5		0	0	0		0	
84184021	制冷温度＞-40℃，容积500-900L立式冷冻箱	15	0	0	0	0	0	0	0	0	0	0		0	12	0	0	7.5	3		0	
84184029	制冷温度＞-40℃，容积≤500L立式冷冻箱	30	0	0	0	0	0	0	0	0	0	0		0		0	0	15	6		0	
84185000	其他装有冷藏或冷冻装置的柜、箱、展示台	10	0	0	0	0	0	0	0	0	0	0		1	5	0	0	5	0	0	0	
84186120	压缩式热泵，税目8415的空气调节器除外	10	0	0	0	0	0	0	0	0	0	0	7	0	5	0	0	0	0			
84186190	其他热泵，税目8415的空气调节器除外	15	0	0	0	0	0	0	0	0	0	0	7	1.5	7	0	0	7.5	3		0	
84186920	其他制冷机组	10	0	0	0	0	0	0	0	0	0	0	7	0	5	0	0	0	0		0	
84186990	其他制冷设备	10	0	0	0	0	0	0	0	0	0	0	7	0	5	0	0	5	0		0	
84189100	冷藏或冷冻设备用特制家具零件	18	0	0	0	0	0	0	0	0	0	0	17.1	0	14.4	0	0	9	3.6			
84189910	制冷机组及热泵用零件	10	0	0	0	0	0	0	0	0	0	0		1	5	0	0	5	0			
84189991	制冷温度≤-40℃冷冻设备零件	9.5	0	0	0	0	0	0	0	0	0	0		1	5		0	0	0		0	
84189992	制冷温度＞-40℃，容积＞500L冷藏设备零件	10	0	0	0	0	0	0	0	0	0	0		1	5		0	5	0		0	
84189999	税号84.18其他制冷设备用零件	10	0	0	0	0	0	0	0	0	0	0		1	5	0	0	5	0		0	
84191100	燃气快速热水器	35	0	0	0	0	0	0	0	0	0	0		3.5		0	0	17.5	7			
84191910	太阳能热水器	35	0	0	0	0	0	0	0	0	0	0		0		0	0	17.5	7			0
84191990	其他非电热的快速或贮备式热水器	35	0	0	0	0	0	0	0	0	0	0		0		0	0	17.5	7			0
84192000	医用或实验室用消毒器具	4	0	0	0	0	0	0	0	0	0	0		0.4	0		0	0	0			
84193100	农产品干燥器	8	0	0	0	0	0	0	0	0	0	0		0	5		0	0	0			
84193200	木材、纸浆、纸或纸板用干燥器	9	0	0	0	0	0	0	0	0	0	0		0.9	5		0	0	0			0
84193910	微空气流动陶瓷坯件干燥器	9	0	0	0	0	0	0	0	0	0	0	4.5	0.9	4.5		0	0	0			
84193990	其他用途的干燥器	9	0	0	0	0	0	0	0	0	0	0	4.5	0.9	4.5		0	0	0			0
84194010	提净塔	10	0	0	0	0	0	0	0	0	0	0		0	5	0	0	0	0			
84194020	精馏塔	10	0	0	0	0	0	0	0	0	0	0		0	5	0	0	0	0			
84194090	其他蒸馏或精馏设备	10	0	0	0	0	0	0	0	0	0	0		0	5	0	0	0	0			
84195000	热交换装置	10	0	0	0	0	0	0	0	0	0	0	9.5	1	5	0	0	5	0	0		0
84196011	制氧量≥15000立方米/小时制氧机	12	0	0	0	0	0	0	0	0	0	0		0	6	0	0	0	2.4	0		
84196019	制氧量＜15000立方米/小时制氧机	13	0	0	0	0	0	0	0	0	0	0		0	6.5	0	0	0	2.6	0		
84196090	其他液化空气或其他气体的机器	10	0	0	0	0	0	0	0	0	0	0		0	5	0	0	0	0	0		
84198100	加工热饮料、烹调、加热食品的机器	10	0	0	0	0	0	0	0	0	0	0		1	5	0	0	5	0			
84199090	税号84.19的其他机器设备用零件	4	0	0	0	0	0	0	0	0	0	0		0.4	0		0	0	0	0		0
84201000	砑光机或其他滚压机器	8.4	0	0	0	0	0	0	0	0	0	0		0.8	5		0	0	0			0
84209100	砑光机或其他滚压机器的滚筒	8	0	0	0	0	0	0	0	0	0	0		0	5		0	0	0			
84209900	砑光机或其他滚压机的未列名零件	8	0	0	0	0	0	0	0	0	0	0		0	5		0	0	0			
84211100	奶油分离器	8.4	0	0	0	0	0	0	0	0	0	0		0	5		0	0	0			
84211210	干衣量≤10kg的离心干衣机	17.5	0	0	0	0	0	0	0	0	0	0		1.8	14	0	0	8.8	3.5			
84211290	干衣量＞10kg的离心干衣机	8	0	0	0	0	0	0	0	0	0	0		0.8	5		0	0	0			
84211910	脱水机	10	0	0	0	0	0	0	0	0	0	0		1	5		0	0	0			
84211920	固液分离机	10	0	0	0	0	0	0	0	0	0	0		1	5	0	0	0	0			
84211990	其他离心机	10	0	0	0	0	0	0	0	0	0	0		1	5	0	0	0	0			
84212110	家用型过滤或净化水的机器及装置	25	0	0	0	0	0	0	0	0	0	0	17.5	2.5	17.5	0	0	12.5	5	0	0	
84212191	船舶压载水处理设备	5	0	0	0	0	0	0	0	0	0	0	3.5	0.5	0		0	0	0	0	0	0
84212199	其他过滤或净化水的装置	5	0	0	0	0	0	0	0	0	0	0	3.5	0.5	0		0	0	0	0	0	0
84212200	过滤或净化饮料的机器及装置	12	0	0	0	0	0	0	0	0	0	0		0	6	0	0	0	2.4		0	
84212300	内燃发动机的燃油过滤器	10	0	0	0	0	0	0	0	0	0	0		1	5	0	0	5	0	0		
84212910	其他压滤机	5	0	0	0	0	0	0	0	0	0	0	3.5	0.5	0		0	0	0	0		
84212990	其他液体的过滤、净化机器及装置	5	0	0	0	0	0	0	0	0	0	0	3.5	0.5	0		0	0	0	0		0
84213100	内燃发动机的进气过滤器	10	0	0	0	0	0	0	0	0	0	0		1	5		0	5	0	0		
84213910	家用型气体过滤、净化机器及装置	15	0	0	0	0	0	0	0	0	0	0	10.5	1.5	7.5	0	0	7.5	3	0		0
84213921	工业用静电除尘器	5	0	0	0	0	0	0	0	0	0	0	3.5	0.5	0		0	0	0	0		0
84213922	工业用袋式除尘器	5	0	0	0	0	0	0	0	0	0	0	3.5	0.5	0		0	0	0	0		
84213923	工业用旋风式除尘器	5	0	0	0	0	0	0	0	0	0	0	3.5	0.5	0		0	0	0	0		0
84213924	电袋复合除尘器	5	0	0	0	0	0	0	0	0	0	0	3.5	0.5	0		0	0	0	0		0
84213929	工业用其他除尘器	5	0	0	0	0	0	0	0	0	0	0	3.5	0.5	0		0	0	0	0		0

税则号列	商品名称（简称）	最惠国	东盟										亚太	智利	巴基斯坦	新加坡	新西兰	秘鲁	哥斯达黎加	香港	澳门	台湾
			文	柬	印	老	马	缅	菲	新	泰	越										
84213930	内燃发动机排气过滤及净化装置	5	0	0	0	0	0	0	0	0	0	0	3.5	0.5	0		0	0	0	0		
84213940	烟气脱硫装置	5	0	0	0	0	0	0	0	0	0	0	3.5	0.5	0		0	0	0	0		0
84213950	烟气脱硝装置	5	0	0	0	0	0	0	0	0	0	0	3.5	0.5	0		0	0	0	0		0
84213990	其他气体的过滤、净化机器及装置	5	0	0	0	0	0	0	0	0	0	0	3.5	0.5	0		0	0	0	0		0
84219910	家用型过滤、净化装置用零件	10	0	0	0	0	0	0	0	0	0	0	9	1	5	0	0	5	0	0		
84219990	其他过滤、净化装置用零件	5	0	0	0	0	0	0	0	0	0	0	4.5	0.5	0		0	0	0	0		0
84221100	家用型洗碟机	10	0	0	0	0	0	0	0	0	0	0		0	5		0	0	0			
84221900	非家用型洗碟机	14	0	0	0	0	0	0	0	0	0	0		0	11.2	0	0	0	2.8			
84222000	瓶子及其他容器的洗涤或干燥机器	10	0	0	0	0	0	0	0	0	0	0		1	5	0	0	5	0		0	
84223010	饮料及液体食品罐装设备	12	0	0	0	0	0	0	0	0	0	0	8.4	1.2	5	0	0	0	2.4	0		
84223021	水泥全自动灌包机	12	0	0	0	0	0	0	0	0	0	0	8.4	1.2	5	0	0	6	2.4	0		
84223029	其他水泥包装机	12	0	0	0	0	0	0	0	0	0	0	8.4	1.2	5	0	0	6	2.4	0		
84223030	其他包装机	10	0	0	0	0	0	0	0	0	0	0	7	1	5	0	0	5	0	0		
84223090	其他装填密封等包封机器	10	0	0	0	0	0	0	0	0	0	0	7	1	5	0	0	5	0	0		
84224000	其他包装或打包机器	10	0	0	0	0	0	0	0	0	0	0	9.5	1	5	0	0	5	0	0		
84229010	洗碟机用零件	10.5	0	0	0	0	0	0	0	0	0	0		1.1	5	0	0	5.2	2.1			
84229020	饮料及液体食品灌装设备用零件	8.5	0	0	0	0	0	0	0	0	0	0		0.9	5		0	0	0			
84229090	税号84.22其他未列名机器零件	8.5	0	0	0	0	0	0	0	0	0	0		0.9	5		0	0	0	0		
84231000	体重计、婴儿秤及家用秤	10.5	0	0	0	0	0	0	0	0	0	0		0	5	0	0	0	2.1		0	
84232010	电子皮带秤	10	0	0	0	0	0	0	0	0	0	0		0	5		0	0	0			
84232090	其他输送带上连续称货的秤	10	0	0	0	0	0	0	0	0	0	0		0	5		0	0	0			
84233010	定量包装秤	10.5	0	0	0	0	0	0	0	0	0	0		0	5	0	0	0	2.1			
84233020	定量分选秤	10.5	0	0	0	0	0	0	0	0	0	0		0	5	0	0	0	2.1			
84233030	配料秤	10.5	0	0	0	0	0	0	0	0	0	0		0	5	0	0	0	2.1			
84233090	其他恒定秤、物料定量装袋或容器用秤	10.5	0	0	0	0	0	0	0	0	0	0		0	5	0	0	0	2.1			
84238110	最大称量≤30kg的计价秤	10.5	0	0	0	0	0	0	0	0	0	0		0	5	0	0	0	2.1			
84238120	最大称量≤30kg的弹簧秤	10.5	0	0	0	0	0	0	0	0	0	0		0	5	0	0	0	2.1			
84238190	最大称量≤30kg的其他衡器	10.5	0	0	0	0	0	0	0	0	0	0		0	5	0	0	0	2.1			
84238210	最大称量30-5000kg的地中衡	10.5	0	0	0	0	0	0	0	0	0	0		0	5	0	0	0	2.1			
84238290	最大称量30-5000kg的其他衡器	10.5	0	0	0	0	0	0	0	0	0	0		0	5	0	0	0	2.1			
84238910	其他地中衡	10	0	0	0	0	0	0	0	0	0	0		1	5		0	5	0			
84238920	其他轨道衡	10	0	0	0	0	0	0	0	0	0	0		1	5		0	5	0			
84238930	其他吊秤	10	0	0	0	0	0	0	0	0	0	0		1	5		0	5	0			
84238990	其他衡器	10	0	0	0	0	0	0	0	0	0	0		1	5		0	5	0			
84239000	衡器用的各种砝码、秤砣及其零件	10	0	0	0	0	0	0	0	0	0	0		0	5	0	0	0	0			
84241000	灭火器	8.4	0	0	0	0	0	0	0	0	0	0		0	5		0	0	0			
84242000	喷枪及类似器具	8.4	0	0	0	0	0	0	0	0	0	0	8	0	5		0	0	0			
84243000	喷汽机、喷砂机及类似喷射机	8.4	0	0	0	0	0	0	0	0	0	0		0	5		0	0	0			0
84248100	农业或园艺用喷射、喷雾机械器具	8	0	0	0	0	0	0	0	0	0	0	7.6	0.8	5		0	0	0	0		
84251100	电动滑车及提升机	6	0	0	0	0	0	0	0	0	0	0		0	5		0	0	0			
84251900	非电动滑车及提升机	5	0	0	0	0	0	0	0	0	0	0		0.5	0		0	0	0			
84253110	矿井口电动卷扬装置；专为井下使用设计的电动卷扬机	10	0	0	0	0	0	0	0	0	0	0		0	5		0	0	0			
84253190	其他电动卷扬机及绞盘	5	0	0	0	0	0	0	0	0	0	0		0.5	0		0	0	0			
84253910	其他矿井口卷扬装置；其他专为井下使用设计的卷扬机	10	0	0	0	0	0	0	0	0	0	0		0	5		0	0	0			
84253990	其他非电动卷扬机及绞盘	5	0	0	0	0	0	0	0	0	0	0		0.5	0		0	0	0	0		
84254100	车库中使用的固定千斤顶系统	3	0	0	0	0	0	0	0	0	0	0	2.5	0	0		0	0	0			
84254210	其他液压千斤顶	3	0	0	0	0	0	0	0	0	0	0		0	0		0	0	0			
84254290	提升车辆用液压提升机	5	0	0	0	0	0	0	0	0	0	0		0.5	0		0	0	0			
84254910	其他千斤顶	5	0	0	0	0	0	0	0	0	0	0		0.5	0		0	0	0			
84254990	其他提升车辆用提升机	10	0	0	0	0	0	0	0	0	0	0		1	5		0	5	0			
84261120	通用桥式起重机	8	0	0	0	0	0	0	0	0	0	0		0.8	5		0	0	0			
84261190	其他固定支架的高架移动式起重机	8	0	0	0	0	0	0	0	0	0	0		0.8	5		0	0	0			
84261200	胶轮移动式吊运架及跨运车	6	0	0	0	0	0	0	0	0	0	0		0	5		0	0	0			
84261910	装船机	5	0	0	0	0	0	0	0	0	0	0	2.5	0	0		0	0	0			
84261921	抓斗式卸船机	5	0	0	0	0	0	0	0	0	0	0	3.5	0	0		0	0	0			
84261929	其他卸船机	5	0	0	0	0	0	0	0	0	0	0	3.5	0	0		0	0	0			
84261930	龙门式起重机	10	0	0	0	0	0	0	0	0	0	0	7	0	5		0	0	0			
84261941	门式装卸桥	10	0	0	0	0	0	0	0	0	0	0	7	0	5		0	0	0			

税则号列	商品名称（简称）	最惠国	东盟 文	东盟 柬	东盟 印	东盟 老	东盟 马	东盟 缅	东盟 菲	东盟 新	东盟 泰	东盟 越	亚太	智利	巴基斯坦	新加坡	新西兰	秘鲁	哥斯达黎加	香港	澳门	台湾
84261942	集装箱装卸桥	10	0	0	0	0	0	0	0	0	0	0	7	0	5		0	0	0			
84261943	其他动臂式装卸桥	10	0	0	0	0	0	0	0	0	0	0	7	0	5		0	0	0			
84261949	其他装卸桥	10	0	0	0	0	0	0	0	0	0	0	7	0	5		0	0	0			
84261990	其他高架移动式起重机等	10	0	0	0	0	0	0	0	0	0	0	7	0	5	0	0	0	0			
84262000	塔式起重机	10	0	0	0	0	0	0	0	0	0	0		0	5		0	0	0			
84263000	门座式起重机及座式旋臂起重机	6	0	0	0	0	0	0	0	0	0	0		0	5		0	0	0			
84264110	轮胎式起重机	5	0	0	0	0	0	0	0	0	0	0		0.5	0		0	0	0			
84264190	其他带胶轮的自推进起重机	5	0	0	0	0	0	0	0	0	0	0		0.5	0		0	0	0			
84264910	履带式起重机	8	0	0	0	0	0	0	0	0	0	0		0.8	5		0	0	0	0		
84264990	其他不带胶轮的自推进起重机	13	0	0	0	0	0	0	0	0	0	0		1.3	6.5	0	0	6.5	2.6	0		
84269100	供装于公路车辆的其他起重机	10	0	0	0	0	0	0	0	0	0	0		0	5		0	0	0			
84269900	其他起重设备	6	0	0	0	0	0	0	0	0	0	0		0.6	5		0	0	0			
84271010	有轨巷道堆垛机	9	0	0	0	0	0	0	0	0	0	0		0.9	5		0	0	0			
84271020	无轨巷道堆垛机	9	0	0	0	0	0	0	0	0	0	0		0.9	5		0	0	0			
84271090	其他电动机推进的叉车及可升降工作车	9	0	0	0	0	0	0	0	0	0	0		0.9	5		0	0	0			
84272010	集装箱叉车	9	0	0	0	0	0	0	0	0	0	0	8.6	0	5		0	0	0			
84272090	其他机动叉车及有类似装置工作车	9	0	0	0	0	0	0	0	0	0	0	8.6	0	5		0	0	0			
84279000	其他叉车及可升降的工作车	9	0	0	0	0	0	0	0	0	0	0		0	5		0	0	0			
84281010	载客电梯	8	0	0	0	0	0	0	0	0	0	0	5.6	0	5	0	0	0	0	0	0	
84281090	其他升降机及倒卸式起重机	6	0	0	0	0	0	0	0	0	0	0	4.2	0	0		0	0	0	0	0	0
84282000	气压升降机及输送机	5	0	0	0	0	0	0	0	0	0	0		0.5	0		0	0	0			
84283100	地下连续运货或材料升降、输送机	5	0	0	0	0	0	0	0	0	0	0		0	0		0	0	0			
84283200	其他斗式连续运货升降、输送机	5	0	0	0	0	0	0	0	0	0	0		0	0		0	0	0	0		
84283300	其他带式连续运货升降、输送机	5	0	0	0	0	0	0	0	0	0	0	4.3	0.5	0		0	0	0	0		0
84283910	链式连续运送货物的升降机及输送机	5	0	0	0	0	0	0	0	0	0	0	3.5	0.5	0		0	0	0	0		0
84283920	辊式连续运送货物的升降机及输送机	5	0	0	0	0	0	0	0	0	0	0	3.5	0.5	0		0	0	0	0		0
84283990	其他未列名连续运货升降、输送机	5	0	0	0	0	0	0	0	0	0	0	3.5	0.5	0		0	0	0	0		0
84284000	自动梯及自动人行道	5	0	0	0	0	0	0	0	0	0	0		0	0		0	0	0			
84286010	货运架空索道	8	0	0	0	0	0	0	0	0	0	0		0	5		0	0	0			
84286021	单线循环式客运架空索道	8	0	0	0	0	0	0	0	0	0	0		0	5		0	0	0			
84286029	其他客运架空索道	8	0	0	0	0	0	0	0	0	0	0		0	5		0	0	0			
84286090	其他缆车、座式升降机用牵引装置	8	0	0	0	0	0	0	0	0	0	0		0	5		0	0	0			
84289010	矿车推动机、铁道机车等的转车台	10	0	0	0	0	0	0	0	0	0	0		0	5		0	0	0			
84289020	机械式停车设备	5	0	0	0	0	0	0	0	0	0	0		0.5	0		0	0	0	0		
84289031	堆取料机械	5	0	0	0	0	0	0	0	0	0	0		0.5	0		0	0	0	0		0
84289039	其他装卸机械	5	0	0	0	0	0	0	0	0	0	0		0.5	0		0	0	0	0		0
84289040	搬运机器人	5	0	0	0	0	0	0	0	0	0	0		0.5	0		0	0	0	0		0
84289090	其他升降、搬运、装卸机械	5	0	0	0	0	0	0	0	0	0	0		0.5	0		0	0	0	0		0
84291110	功率＞235.36kw的履带式推土机	7	0	0	0	0	0	0	0	0	0	0		0.7	5		0	0	0			
84291190	功率≤235.36kw的履带式推土机	7	0	0	0	0	0	0	0	0	0	0		0.7	5		0	0	0			
84291910	功率＞235.36kw的其他推土机	7	0	0	0	0	0	0	0	0	0	0		0	5		0	0	0			
84291990	功率≤235.36kw的其他推土机	7	0	0	0	0	0	0	0	0	0	0		0	5		0	0	0			
84292010	功率＞235.36kw的筑路机及平地机	5	0	0	0	0	0	0	0	0	0	0		0.5	0		0	0	0			
84292090	其他筑路机及平地机	5	0	0	0	0	0	0	0	0	0	0		0.5	0		0	0	0			
84293010	斗容量＞10立方米的铲运机	3	0	0	0	0	0	0	0	0	0	0		0	0		0	0	0			
84293090	斗容量≤10立方米的铲运机	5	0	0	0	0	0	0	0	0	0	0		0	0		0	0	0			
84294011	机重≥18吨的震动式压路机	7	0	0	0	0	0	0	0	0	0	0		0.7	5		0	0	0			
84294019	其他机动压路机	8	0	0	0	0	0	0	0	0	0	0		0.8	5		0	0	0			
84294090	其他未列名捣固机械及压路机	6	0	0	0	0	0	0	0	0	0	0		0.6	5		0	0	0			
84295100	前铲装载机	5	0	0	0	0	0	0	0	0	0	0		0.5	0		0	0	0			
84295211	轮胎式挖掘机	8	0	0	0	0	0	0	0	0	0	0	7.2	0.8	5		0	0	0			
84295212	履带式挖掘机	8	0	0	0	0	0	0	0	0	0	0		0.8	5		0	0	0	0		
84295219	其他挖掘机	8	0	0	0	0	0	0	0	0	0	0	7.2	0.8	5		0	0	0			
84295290	其他上部结构可转360度的挖掘机类似机械	8	0	0	0	0	0	0	0	0	0	0	7.2	0.8	5		0	0	0			
84295900	其他机械铲、挖掘机及机铲装载机	8	0	0	0	0	0	0	0	0	0	0		0.8	5		0	0	0			
84301000	打桩机及拔桩机	10	0	0	0	0	0	0	0	0	0	0		0	5		0	0	0			
84302000	扫雪机及吹雪机	10	0	0	0	0	0	0	0	0	0	0		0	5		0	0	0			
84303110	采（截）煤机	10	0	0	0	0	0	0	0	0	0	0		1	5	0	0	5	0			
84303120	凿岩机	10	0	0	0	0	0	0	0	0	0	0		1	5	0	0	5	0			

税则号列	商品名称（简称）	最惠国	东盟										亚太	智利	巴基斯坦	新加坡	新西兰	秘鲁	哥斯达黎加	香港	澳门	台湾
			文	柬	印	老	马	缅	菲	新	泰	越										
84303130	隧道掘进机	10	0	0	0	0	0	0	0	0	0	0		1	5	0	0	5	0			
84303900	其他非自推进截煤机、采石机及掘进机	6	0	0	0	0	0	0	0	0	0	0		0	5		0	0	0			
84304111	钻探深度≥6000米的自推进石油钻探机	5	0	0	0	0	0	0	0	0	0	0		0.5	0		0	0	0	0		
84304119	其他自推进石油及天然气钻探机	5	0	0	0	0	0	0	0	0	0	0		0.5	0		0	0	0	0		
84304121	钻探深度≥6000米的其他钻探机	5	0	0	0	0	0	0	0	0	0	0		0.5	0		0	0	0	0		
84304122	钻探深度＜6000米履带式自推进钻机	5	0	0	0	0	0	0	0	0	0	0		0.5	0		0	0	0	0		
84304129	钻探深度＜6000米的其他自推进钻机	5	0	0	0	0	0	0	0	0	0	0		0.5	0		0	0	0	0		
84304190	其他自推进的凿井机械	5	0	0	0	0	0	0	0	0	0	0		0.5	0		0	0	0	0		
84304900	非自推进的钻探或凿井机械	5	0	0	0	0	0	0	0	0	0	0		0.5	0		0	0	0			
84305010	其他自推进采油机械	3	0	0	0	0	0	0	0	0	0	0		0	0		0	0	0			
84305020	矿用电铲	7	0	0	0	0	0	0	0	0	0	0		0.7	5		0	0	0			
84305031	牙轮直径≥380mm的采矿牙轮钻机	5	0	0	0	0	0	0	0	0	0	0		0.5	0		0	0	0			
84305039	牙轮直径＜380mm的采矿牙轮钻机	5	0	0	0	0	0	0	0	0	0	0		0.5	0		0	0	0			
84305090	其他自推进未列名机械	5	0	0	0	0	0	0	0	0	0	0		0.5	0		0	0	0			
84306100	非自推进捣固或压实机械	6	0	0	0	0	0	0	0	0	0	0		0	5		0	0	0			
84306911	钻筒直径＞3m的工程钻机	6	0	0	0	0	0	0	0	0	0	0		0	5		0	0	0			
84306919	钻筒直径≤3m的工程钻机	6	0	0	0	0	0	0	0	0	0	0		0	5		0	0	0			
84306920	非自推进铲运机	6	0	0	0	0	0	0	0	0	0	0		0	5		0	0	0			
84306990	其他非自推进未列名机械	6	0	0	0	0	0	0	0	0	0	0		0	5		0	0	0			
84311000	滑车、绞盘、千斤顶等机械用零件	3	0	0	0	0	0	0	0	0	0	0		0	0		0	0	0			
84312010	税号84.27所列机械的装有差速器的驱动桥及其零件，不论是否装有其他传动部件	6	0	0	0	0	0	0	0	0	0	0	5.4	0	0		0	0	0			
84312090	其他税号84.27所列机械的零件	6	0	0	0	0	0	0	0	0	0	0	5.4	0	0		0	0	0			
84313100	升降机、倒卸式起重机或自动梯的零件	3	0	0	0	0	0	0	0	0	0	0		0	0		0	0	0			
84313900	税号84.28所列其他机械的零件	5	0	0	0	0	0	0	0	0	0	0	2.5	0.5	0		0	0	0	0		
84314100	戽斗、铲斗、抓斗及夹斗	6	0	0	0	0	0	0	0	0	0	0	5.4	0.6	0		0	0	0			
84314200	推土机或侧铲推土机用铲	6	0	0	0	0	0	0	0	0	0	0		0	5		0	0	0			
84314310	石油或天然气钻探机用零件	4	0	0	0	0	0	0	0	0	0	0	2.8	0.4	0		0	0	0	0		
84314320	其他钻探机用零件	4	0	0	0	0	0	0	0	0	0	0	2.8	0.4	0		0	0	0	0		
84314390	其他凿井机用零件	5	0	0	0	0	0	0	0	0	0	0	3.5	0.5	0		0	0	0	0		
84314920	税号84.26、84.29、或84.30所列机械的装有差速器的驱动桥及其零件，不论是否装有其他传动部件	5	0	0	0	0	0	0	0	0	0	0	4.5	0.5	0		0	0	0	0		
84314991	矿用电铲用零件	5	0	0	0	0	0	0	0	0	0	0	4.5	0.5	0		0	0	0	0		
84314999	其他税号84.26、84.29、或84.30所列机械的零件	5	0	0	0	0	0	0	0	0	0	0	4.5	0.5	0		0	0	0	0		
84321000	犁	5	0	0	0	0	0	0	0	0	0	0		0	0		0	0	0			
84322100	圆盘耙	5	0	0	0	0	0	0	0	0	0	0		0	0		0	0	0			
84322900	其他耙、松土机等耕作机械	4	0	0	0	0	0	0	0	0	0	0		0	0		0	0	0			
84323011	谷物播种机	4	0	0	0	0	0	0	0	0	0	0	3.5	0	0		0	0	0			
84323019	其他播种机	4	0	0	0	0	0	0	0	0	0	0	3.5	0	0		0	0	0			
84323021	马铃薯种植机	4	0	0	0	0	0	0	0	0	0	0	3.5	0	0		0	0	0			
84323029	其他种植机	4	0	0	0	0	0	0	0	0	0	0	3.5	0	0		0	0	0			
84323031	水稻插秧机	4	0	0	0	0	0	0	0	0	0	0	3.5	0	0		0	0	0			
84323039	其他移植机(栽植机)	4	0	0	0	0	0	0	0	0	0	0	3.5	0	0		0	0	0			
84324000	施肥机	4	0	0	0	0	0	0	0	0	0	0		0	0		0	0	0			
84328010	草坪及运动场地滚压机	7	0	0	0	0	0	0	0	0	0	0		0	5		0	0	0			
84328090	其他未列名整地或耕作机械	4	0	0	0	0	0	0	0	0	0	0		0	0		0	0	0			
84329000	整地或耕作机械、滚压机零件	4	0	0	0	0	0	0	0	0	0	0		0.4	0		0	0	0			
84331100	机动旋转式割草机	6	0	0	0	0	0	0	0	0	0	0		0	5		0	0	0			
84331900	草坪、公园等用其他割草机	6	0	0	0	0	0	0	0	0	0	0		0	5		0	0	0			
84332000	其他割草机	4	0	0	0	0	0	0	0	0	0	0		0	0		0	0	0			
84333000	其他干草切割、翻晒机器	5	0	0	0	0	0	0	0	0	0	0		0	0		0	0	0			
84334000	草料打包机	5	0	0	0	0	0	0	0	0	0	0		0	0		0	0	0			
84335100	联合收割机	8	0	0	0	0	0	0	0	0	0	0	7.6	0	5		0	0	0			
84335200	其他脱粒机	8	0	0	0	0	0	0	0	0	0	0		0	5		0	0	0			
84335300	根茎或块茎收获机	8	0	0	0	0	0	0	0	0	0	0		0	5		0	0	0			
84335910	甘蔗收获机	8	0	0	0	0	0	0	0	0	0	0		0.8	5		0	0	0			
84335920	棉花采摘机	8	0	0	0	0	0	0	0	0	0	0		0.8	5		0	0	0			
84335990	其他收割机	8	0	0	0	0	0	0	0	0	0	0		0.8	5		0	0	0			

税则号列	商品名称（简称）	最惠国	东盟										亚太	智利	巴基斯坦	新加坡	新西兰	秘鲁	哥斯达黎加	香港	澳门	台湾
			文	柬	印	老	马	缅	菲	新	泰	越										
84336000	蛋类、水果等清洁、分选、分级机	5	0	0	0	0	0	0	0	0	0	0		0.5	0		0	0	0			
84339010	联合收割机用零件	5	0	0	0	0	0	0	0	0	0	0		0	0		0	0	0			
84339090	税号84.33所列其他机械零件	3	0	0	0	0	0	0	0	0	0	0		0	0		0	0	0			
84341000	挤奶机	10	0	0	0	0	0	0	0	0	0	0		0	5		2.2		0			
84342000	乳品加工机器	6	0	0	0	0	0	0	0	0	0	0		0.6	5		0	0	0			
84349000	挤奶机及乳品加工机器用零件	5	0	0	0	0	0	0	0	0	0	0		0.5	0		0	0	0			
84351000	制酒、果汁等的压榨、轧碎机	10	0	0	0	0	0	0	0	0	0	0		1	5		0	0	0		0	
84359000	制酒、果汁等压榨、轧碎机零件	6	0	0	0	0	0	0	0	0	0	0		0	5		0	0	0			
84361000	动物饲料配制机	7	0	0	0	0	0	0	0	0	0	0		0	5		0	0	0			
84362100	家禽孵卵器及育雏器	5	0	0	0	0	0	0	0	0	0	0		0	0		0	0	0			
84362900	家禽饲养用机器	10	0	0	0	0	0	0	0	0	0	0		1	5		0	0	0			
84368000	农、林业、园艺等用的其他机器	10	0	0	0	0	0	0	0	0	0	0		0	5		0	0	0			
84369100	家禽饲养机、孵卵器及育雏器零件	6	0	0	0	0	0	0	0	0	0	0		0	5		0	0	0			
84369900	税号84.36所列其他机器的零件	6	0	0	0	0	0	0	0	0	0	0		0	5		0	0	0			
84371010	光学色差颗粒选别机（色选机）	10	0	0	0	0	0	0	0	0	0	0		0	5		0	0	0			
84371090	其他种子、谷物或干豆的清洁、分选或分级机	10	0	0	0	0	0	0	0	0	0	0		0	5		0	0	0			
84378000	谷物磨粉业加工机器	10	0	0	0	0	0	0	0	0	0	0	8.5	0	5		0	0	0			
84379000	税号84.37所列机械的零件	6	0	0	0	0	0	0	0	0	0	0		0	5		0	0	0			
84381000	糕点、通心粉、面条的生产加工机器	7	0	0	0	0	0	0	0	0	0	0		0.7	5		0	0	0			
84382000	生产糖果、可可粉、巧克力的机器	8	0	0	0	0	0	0	0	0	0	0		0.8	5		0	0	0			
84383000	制糖机器	10	0	0	0	0	0	0	0	0	0	0		0	5		0	0	0			
84384000	酿酒机器	7	0	0	0	0	0	0	0	0	0	0		0	5		0	0	0			
84385000	肉类或家禽加工机器	7	0	0	0	0	0	0	0	0	0	0		0.7	5		0	0	0			
84386000	水果、坚果或蔬菜加工机器	10	0	0	0	0	0	0	0	0	0	0		1	5	0	0	5	0			
84388000	84章其他未列名食品等加工机器	8.5	0	0	0	0	0	0	0	0	0	0	8.1	0.9	5		0	0	0			0
84389000	食品、饮料工业用机器的零件	5	0	0	0	0	0	0	0	0	0	0		0.5	0		0	0	0			
84391000	制造纤维素纸浆的机器	8.4	0	0	0	0	0	0	0	0	0	0		0.8	5		0	0	0			
84392000	纸或纸板的抄造机器	8.4	0	0	0	0	0	0	0	0	0	0		0	5		0	0	0			0
84393000	纸或纸板的整理机器	8.4	0	0	0	0	0	0	0	0	0	0		0	5		0	0	0			0
84399100	制造纤维素纸浆的机器零件	6	0	0	0	0	0	0	0	0	0	0		0.6	5		0	0	0			
84399900	制造或整理纸及纸板的机器零件	6	0	0	0	0	0	0	0	0	0	0	3	0.6	0		0	0	0			
84401010	锁线装订机	10	0	0	0	0	0	0	0	0	0	0		0	5		0	0	0			
84401020	胶订机	12	0	0	0	0	0	0	0	0	0	0		0	6	0	0	0	2.4			
84401090	其他书本装订机器	12	0	0	0	0	0	0	0	0	0	0		0	6	0	0	0	2.4			
84409000	书本装订机器的零件	8	0	0	0	0	0	0	0	0	0	0		0	5		0	0	0			
84411000	切纸机	12	0	0	0	0	0	0	0	0	0	0		1.2	6	0	0	0	2.4			0
84412000	制造包、袋或信封的机器	12	0	0	0	0	0	0	0	0	0	0	11.4	1.2	6	0	0	6	2.4			
84413010	纸塑铝复合罐生产设备	13.5	0	0	0	0	0	0	0	0	0	0	12.8	1.4	6.8	0	0	6.8	2.7			
84413090	其他制造箱、盒、桶及类似容器的机器	13.5	0	0	0	0	0	0	0	0	0	0	12.8	1.4	6.8	0	0	6.8	2.7			
84414000	纸浆、纸或纸板制品模制成型机器	12	0	0	0	0	0	0	0	0	0	0		0	6	0	0	0	2.4			
84418010	制造纸塑铝软包装的生产设备	12	0	0	0	0	0	0	0	0	0	0	11.4	1.2	6	0	0	0	2.4			
84418090	其他制造纸浆制品、纸制品的机器	12	0	0	0	0	0	0	0	0	0	0	11.4	1.2	6	0	0	0	2.4			0
84419010	切纸机零件	8	0	0	0	0	0	0	0	0	0	0		0.8	5		0	0	0			
84419090	其他制造纸浆、纸制品的机器零件	8.4	0	0	0	0	0	0	0	0	0	0		0.8	5		0	0	0			
84423010	铸字机	9	0	0	0	0	0	0	0	0	0	0		0	5		0	0	0			
84423021	计算机直接制版设备	9	0	0	0	0	0	0	0	0	0	0		0	5		0	0	0			
84423029	去制版机器、器具及设备	9	0	0	0	0	0	0	0	0	0	0		0	5		0	0	0			
84423090	其他铸字、制版用机器、器具及设备	9	0	0	0	0	0	0	0	0	0	0		0	5		0	0	0			
84424000	铸字、排字、制版机器的零件	7	0	0	0	0	0	0	0	0	0	0		0	5		0	0	0			
84425000	活字、印刷用版、片及其他部件	7	0	0	0	0	0	0	0	0	0	0		0	5		0	0	0	0		
84431100	卷取进料式胶印机	10	0	0	0	0	0	0	0	0	0	0	7	1	5		0	5	0			
84431200	办公室用片取进料式胶印机	12	0	0	0	0	0	0	0	0	0	0		0	6	0	0	0	2.4			
84431311	平张纸进料式单色胶印机	10	0	0	0	0	0	0	0	0	0	0	7	1	5		0	0	0			
84431312	平张纸进料式双色胶印机	10	0	0	0	0	0	0	0	0	0	0	7	1	5		0	0	0			
84431313	平张纸进料式四色胶印机	10	0	0	0	0	0	0	0	0	0	0	7	1	5		0	0	0			
84431319	平张纸进料式其他胶印机	10	0	0	0	0	0	0	0	0	0	0	7	1	5		0	0	0			
84431390	其他胶印机	10	0	0	0	0	0	0	0	0	0	0	7	1	5		0	0	0			
84431400	卷取进料式凸版印刷机	12	0	0	0	0	0	0	0	0	0	0		0	6	0	0	0	2.4	0		
84431500	其他凸版印刷机	12	0	0	0	0	0	0	0	0	0	0		1.2	6	0	0	0	2.4			

税则号列	商品名称（简称）	最惠国	东盟										亚太	智利	巴基斯坦	新加坡	新西兰	秘鲁	哥斯达黎加	香港	澳门	台湾
			文	柬	印	老	马	缅	菲	新	泰	越										
84431600	苯胺印刷机	10	0	0	0	0	0	0	0	0	0	0		1	5		0	0	0			
84431700	照像凹版印刷机	18	0	0	0	0	0	0	0	0	0	0	16.2	0	14.4	0	0	9	3.6			
84431921	圆网印刷机	10	0	0	0	0	0	0	0	0	0	0	9	0	5		0	0	0			
84431922	平网印刷机	10	0	0	0	0	0	0	0	0	0	0	9	0	5		0	0	0			0
84431929	其他网式印刷机	10	0	0	0	0	0	0	0	0	0	0	9	0	5	0	0	0	0			0
84431980	其它印刷机	8	0	0	0	0	0	0	0	0	0	0	7.2	0	5		0	0	0	0		0
84433110	静电感光式多功能机	10	0	0	0	0	0	0	0	0	0	0		1	5	0	0	0	0			
84433221	可以网络连接的喷墨印刷机	8	0	0	0	0	0	0	0	0	0	0		0	5	0	0	0	0			
84433222	可以网络连接的静电照相印刷机(激光印刷机)	8	0	0	0	0	0	0	0	0	0	0	7.2	0	5		0	0	0			
84433229	可以网络连接的其他数字印刷设备	8	0	0	0	0	0	0	0	0	0	0	7.2	0	5		0	0	0			
84433912	间接法静电感光复印设备	10	0	0	0	0	0	0	0	0	0	0		1	5	0	0	0	0			
84433922	接触式感光复印设备	20	0	0	0	0	0	0	0	0	0	0		0		0	0	10	4			
84433923	热敏复印设备	20	0	0	0	0	0	0	0	0	0	0		0		0	0	10	4			
84433924	热升华复印设备	20	0	0	0	0	0	0	0	0	0	0		0		0	0	10	4			
84433931	其他独立的喷墨印刷机	8	0	0	0	0	0	0	0	0	0	0		0	5	0	0	0	0			
84433932	其他独立的静电照相印刷机(激光印刷机)	8	0	0	0	0	0	0	0	0	0	0	7.2	0	5		0	0	0			
84433939	其他独立的数字印刷设备	8	0	0	0	0	0	0	0	0	0	0	7.2	0	5	0	0	0	0			
84439111	卷筒料给料机	12	0	0	0	0	0	0	0	0	0	0		1.2	6	0	0	0	2.4			
84439119	其他传统印刷机用辅助机器	12	0	0	0	0	0	0	0	0	0	0		1.2	6	0	0	0	2.4			
84439190	传统印刷机用零件及附件	6	0	0	0	0	0	0	0	0	0	0		0	5		0	0	0			
84439910	数字印刷设备用辅助机器	12	0	0	0	0	0	0	0	0	0	0		1.2	6	0	0	0	2.4			
84439921	热敏打印头	6	0	0	0	0	0	0	0	0	0	0		0	5		0	0	0			
84439929	数字印刷设备的其他零件	6	0	0	0	0	0	0	0	0	0	0		0	5		0	0	0			
84440010	合成纤维长丝纺丝机	10	0	0	0	0	0	0	0	0	0	0	7	0	5		0	0	0			0
84440020	合成纤维短丝纺丝机	10	0	0	0	0	0	0	0	0	0	0	7	0	5		0	0	0			
84440030	人造纤维纺丝机	10	0	0	0	0	0	0	0	0	0	0	7	0	5		0	0	0			
84440040	化学纤维变形机	10	0	0	0	0	0	0	0	0	0	0	7	0	5		0	0	0			
84440050	化学纤维切断机	10	0	0	0	0	0	0	0	0	0	0	7	0	5		0	0	0			
84440090	其他化学纤维挤压、拉伸、变形或切割机器	10	0	0	0	0	0	0	0	0	0	0	7	0	5		0	0	0			
84451111	棉纤维清梳联合机	10	0	0	0	0	0	0	0	0	0	0	9	0	5		0	0	0			
84451112	棉纤维自动抓棉机	10	0	0	0	0	0	0	0	0	0	0	9	0	5		0	0	0			
84451113	棉纤维梳棉机	10	0	0	0	0	0	0	0	0	0	0	9	0	5		0	0	0			
84451119	其他棉纤维梳理机	10	0	0	0	0	0	0	0	0	0	0	9	0	5		0	0	0			
84451120	毛纤维梳理机	10	0	0	0	0	0	0	0	0	0	0	9	0	5		0	0	0			
84451190	其他纺织纤维梳理机	10	0	0	0	0	0	0	0	0	0	0	9	0	5		0	0	0			
84451210	棉纺织纤维精梳机	10	0	0	0	0	0	0	0	0	0	0		0	5		0	0	0			
84451220	毛纺织纤维精梳机	10	0	0	0	0	0	0	0	0	0	0		0	5		0	0	0			
84451290	其他纺织纤维精梳机	10	0	0	0	0	0	0	0	0	0	0		0	5		0	0	0			
84451310	拉伸机	10	0	0	0	0	0	0	0	0	0	0		0	5		0	0	0			
84451321	棉纺粗纱机	10	0	0	0	0	0	0	0	0	0	0		0	5		0	0	0			
84451322	毛纺粗纱机	10	0	0	0	0	0	0	0	0	0	0		0	5		0	0	0			
84451329	其他粗纱机	10	0	0	0	0	0	0	0	0	0	0		0	5		0	0	0			
84451900	纺织纤维的其他预处理机器	10	0	0	0	0	0	0	0	0	0	0	9	1	5		0	5	0			
84452031	转杯纺纱机	10	0	0	0	0	0	0	0	0	0	0	9	0	5		0	0	0			
84452032	喷气纺纱机	10	0	0	0	0	0	0	0	0	0	0		0	5		0	0	0			
84452039	其他自由端纺纱机	10	0	0	0	0	0	0	0	0	0	0		0	5		0	0	0			
84452041	棉环锭细纱机	10.5	0	0	0	0	0	0	0	0	0	0	9.5	0	5	0	0	0	2.1			
84452042	毛环锭细纱机	10	0	0	0	0	0	0	0	0	0	0		0	5		0	0	0			
84452049	其他环锭细纱机	10	0	0	0	0	0	0	0	0	0	0		0	5		0	0	0			
84452090	其他纺纱机	10	0	0	0	0	0	0	0	0	0	0	9	0	5		0	0	0			
84453000	并线机或加捻机	10	0	0	0	0	0	0	0	0	0	0	9	0	5		0	0	0			
84454010	自动络筒机	10	0	0	0	0	0	0	0	0	0	0	9	1	5		0	5	0			
84454090	其他络纱机(包括卷纬机)或摇纱机	10	0	0	0	0	0	0	0	0	0	0	9	1	5		0	5	0			
84459010	整经机	10	0	0	0	0	0	0	0	0	0	0	9	1	5		0	0	0			
84459020	浆纱机	10	0	0	0	0	0	0	0	0	0	0	9	1	5		0	0	0			
84459090	其他生产及处理纺织纱线的机器	10	0	0	0	0	0	0	0	0	0	0	9	1	5		0	0	0			
84461000	所织织物宽度≤30cm的织机	8	0	0	0	0	0	0	0	0	0	0	7.2	0	5		0	0	0			

税则号列	商品名称（简称）	最惠国	东盟										亚太	智利	巴基斯坦	新加坡	新西兰	秘鲁	哥斯达黎加	香港	澳门	台湾
			文	柬	印	老	马	缅	菲	新	泰	越										
84462110	所织织物宽度＞30cm的梭织动力地毯织机	12	0	0	0	0	0	0	0	0	0	0	10.8	1.2	5	0	0	6	2.4			
84462190	所织织物宽度＞30cm的其他梭织动力织机	10	0	0	0	0	0	0	0	0	0	0	9	1	5	0	0	5	0			
84462900	所织织物宽度＞30cm的梭织非动力织机	10	0	0	0	0	0	0	0	0	0	0		1	5		0	5	0			
84463020	所织织物宽度＞30cm的剑杆织机	8	0	0	0	0	0	0	0	0	0	0	6.8	0.8	5		0	0	0			
84463030	所织织物宽度＞30cm的片梭织机	8	0	0	0	0	0	0	0	0	0	0	5.6	0.8	5		0	0	0			
84463040	所织织物宽度＞30cm的喷水织机	8	0	0	0	0	0	0	0	0	0	0	6.8	0.8	5		0	0	0			0
84463050	所织织物宽度＞30cm的喷气织机	8	0	0	0	0	0	0	0	0	0	0	6.8	0.8	5		0	0	0			
84463090	所织织物宽度＞30cm的其他无梭织机	8	0	0	0	0	0	0	0	0	0	0	6.8	0.8	5		0	0	0			
84471100	圆筒直径≤165mm的圆型针织机	8	0	0	0	0	0	0	0	0	0	0	7	0	5		0	0	0			0
84471200	圆筒直径＞165mm的圆型针织机	8	0	0	0	0	0	0	0	0	0	0		0	5		0	0	0			0
84472011	特里科经编机	8	0	0	0	0	0	0	0	0	0	0	6.8	0	5		0	0	0			
84472012	拉舍尔经编机	8	0	0	0	0	0	0	0	0	0	0	6.8	0	5		0	0	0			
84472019	其他经编机	8	0	0	0	0	0	0	0	0	0	0	6.8	0	5		0	0	0			
84472020	平型纬编机	8	0	0	0	0	0	0	0	0	0	0	6.8	0	5		0	0	0			0
84472030	缝编机	8	0	0	0	0	0	0	0	0	0	0	6.8	0	5		0	0	0			
84479011	地毯织机	7	0	0	0	0	0	0	0	0	0	0	4.9	0	0		0	0	0			
84479019	其他簇绒机	8	0	0	0	0	0	0	0	0	0	0	5.6	0	5		0	0	0			
84479020	绣花机	8	0	0	0	0	0	0	0	0	0	0	6.8	0	5		0	0	0			
84479090	税号84.47其他未列名机器	10	0	0	0	0	0	0	0	0	0	0	5	0	5		0	0	0			
84481100	多臂机或提花机	8	0	0	0	0	0	0	0	0	0	0		0	5		0	0	0			
84481900	税号84.44至84.47所列的其他辅助机器	8	0	0	0	0	0	0	0	0	0	0		0	5		0	0	0			
84482020	喷丝头或喷丝板	6	0	0	0	0	0	0	0	0	0	0		0	5		0	0	0			
84482090	纤维挤压机及其辅助机器的其他零附件	6	0	0	0	0	0	0	0	0	0	0		0	5		0	0	0			
84483100	钢丝针布	6	0	0	0	0	0	0	0	0	0	0		0	5		0	0	0			
84483200	纺织纤维预处理机器的其他零附件	6	0	0	0	0	0	0	0	0	0	0		0	5		0	0	0			
84483310	络筒锭	6	0	0	0	0	0	0	0	0	0	0		0	5		0	0	0			
84483390	其他锭子、锭壳、纺丝环、钢丝圈	6	0	0	0	0	0	0	0	0	0	0		0	5		0	0	0			
84483910	气流杯	6	0	0	0	0	0	0	0	0	0	0		0	5		0	0	0			
84483920	电子清纱器	6	0	0	0	0	0	0	0	0	0	0		0	5		0	0	0			
84483930	空气捻接器	6	0	0	0	0	0	0	0	0	0	0		0	5		0	0	0			
84483940	环锭细纱机紧密纺装置	6	0	0	0	0	0	0	0	0	0	0		0	5		0	0	0			
84483990	税号84.45所机器的其他零附件	6	0	0	0	0	0	0	0	0	0	0		0	5		0	0	0			
84484200	织机用筘、综丝及综框	6	0	0	0	0	0	0	0	0	0	0		0	5		0	0	0			
84484910	接、投梭箱	6	0	0	0	0	0	0	0	0	0	0		0	5		0	0	0			
84484920	引纬、送经装置	6	0	0	0	0	0	0	0	0	0	0		0	5		0	0	0			
84484930	梭子	6	0	0	0	0	0	0	0	0	0	0		0	5		0	0	0			
84484990	织机及其辅助机器用其他零附件	6	0	0	0	0	0	0	0	0	0	0		0	5		0	0	0			
84485120	针织机用28号以下的弹簧针、钩针及复合针	6	0	0	0	0	0	0	0	0	0	0		0	5		0	0	0			
84485190	沉降片、其他织针及成圈机件	6	0	0	0	0	0	0	0	0	0	0		0	5		0	0	0			
84485900	税号84.47机器用的其他零附件	6	0	0	0	0	0	0	0	0	0	0		0	5		0	0	0	0		0
84490010	针刺机	8	0	0	0	0	0	0	0	0	0	0		0	5		0	0	0			
84490020	水刺设备	8	0	0	0	0	0	0	0	0	0	0		0	5		0	0	0			
84490090	其他毡呢或无纺织物制造或整理机器；帽模	8	0	0	0	0	0	0	0	0	0	0		0	5		0	0	0			
84501110	干衣量≤10kg的波轮式全自动洗衣机	10	0	0	0	0	0	0	0	0	0	0	8.7	1	5	0	0	0	0			
84501120	干衣量≤10kg的滚筒式全自动洗衣机	10	0	0	0	0	0	0	0	0	0	0	8.7	1	5	0	0	0	0			
84501190	干衣量≤10kg的其他全自动洗衣机	10	0	0	0	0	0	0	0	0	0	0	8.7	1	5	0	0	0	0			
84501200	装有离心甩干机的非全自动洗衣机	30	0	0	0	0	0	0	0	0	0	0	24.9	0	24.9	0	0	15	6			
84501900	干衣量≤10kg的其他洗衣机	30	0	0	0	0	0	0	0	0	0	0		0		0	0	15	6			
84502011	波轮式洗衣机	10	0	0	0	0	0	0	0	0	0	0		0	5		0	0	0			
84502012	滚筒式洗衣机	10	0	0	0	0	0	0	0	0	0	0		0	5		0	0	0			
84502019	其他全自动洗衣机	10	0	0	0	0	0	0	0	0	0	0		0	5		0	0	0			
84502090	其他干衣量超过10公斤的洗衣机	10	0	0	0	0	0	0	0	0	0	0		0	5		0	0	0			
84509010	干衣量≤10kg的洗衣机零件	5	0	0	0	0	0	0	0	0	0	0	4.2	0	0		0	0	0			
84509090	干衣量＞10kg的洗衣机零件	16	0	0	0	0	0	0	0	0	0	0	14.4	0	12.8	0	0	8	3.2			
84511000	干洗机	21	0	0	0	0	0	0	0	0	0	0	16	0	16	0	0	10.5	4.2			
84512100	干衣量≤10kg的干燥机	15	0	0	0	0	0	0	0	0	0	0	13.5	1.5	7.5	0	0	7.5	3			
84512900	干衣量＞10kg的干燥机	8	0	0	0	0	0	0	0	0	0	0	7.2	0	5		0	0	0			

税则号列	商品名称（简称）	最惠国	东盟										亚太	智利	巴基斯坦	新加坡	新西兰	秘鲁	哥斯达黎加	香港	澳门	台湾
			文	柬	印	老	马	缅	菲	新	泰	越										
84513000	熨烫机及挤压机(包括熔压机)	8	0	0	0	0	0	0	0	0	0	0	7.2	0	5	0	0	0	0			
84514000	洗涤、漂白或染色机器	8.4	0	0	0	0	0	0	0	0	0	0	7	0	5		0	0	0	0	0	0
84515000	纺织物卷绕、退绕、折叠、剪切或剪齿边机器	8	0	0	0	0	0	0	0	0	0	0	7.2	0.8	5		0	0	0			0
84518000	税号84.51所列其他未列名的机器	12	0	0	0	0	0	0	0	0	0	0	10.8	1.2	5	0	0	6	2.4	0		0
84519000	税号84.51所列机器的零件	8	0	0	0	0	0	0	0	0	0	0	7.2	0	5		0	0	0			
84521010	多功能家用缝纫机	21	0	0	0	0	0	0	0	0	0	0	17	2.1	16.8	0	0	10.5	4.2			
84521091	手动式家用型缝纫机	21	0	0	0	0	0	0	0	0	0	0	17	2.1	16.8	0	0	10.5	4.2			
84521099	其他家用型缝纫机	21	0	0	0	0	0	0	0	0	0	0	17	2.1	16.8	0	0	10.5	4.2			
84522110	非家用自动平缝机	12	0	0	0	0	0	0	0	0	0	0	10.7	1.2	5	0	0	0	2.4			
84522120	非家用自动包缝机	12	0	0	0	0	0	0	0	0	0	0	10.7	1.2	5	0	0	0	2.4			0
84522130	非家用自动绷缝机	12	0	0	0	0	0	0	0	0	0	0	10.7	1.2	5	0	0	0	2.4			0
84522190	其他非家用自动缝纫机	12	0	0	0	0	0	0	0	0	0	0	10.7	1.2	5	0	0	0	2.4			0
84522900	其他非家用非自动缝纫机	12	0	0	0	0	0	0	0	0	0	0	10.8	1.2	5	0	0	0	2.4	0		
84523000	缝纫机针	14	0	0	0	0	0	0	0	0	0	0	12.6	0	7	0	0	0	2.8			
84529011	家用型缝纫机用旋梭	14	0	0	0	0	0	0	0	0	0	0	9.8	1.4	7	0	0	0	2.8			
84529019	家用型缝纫机用其他零件	14	0	0	0	0	0	0	0	0	0	0	9.8	1.4	7	0	0	0	2.8			
84529091	其他缝纫机用旋梭	14	0	0	0	0	0	0	0	0	0	0	9.8	1.4	7	0	0	0	2.8			
84529092	其他缝纫机专用的特制家具、底座和罩盖及其零件	14	0	0	0	0	0	0	0	0	0	0		0	11.2	0	0	0	2.8			
84529099	其他缝纫机用其他零件	14	0	0	0	0	0	0	0	0	0	0	9.8	1.4	7	0	0	0	2.8			0
84531000	生皮、皮革的处理、鞣制或加工机器	8.4	0	0	0	0	0	0	0	0	0	0	8	0.8	5		0	0	0			
84532000	鞋靴制作或修理机器	8.4	0	0	0	0	0	0	0	0	0	0	8	0	5		0	0	0			
84538000	毛皮及其他皮革的制作或修理机器	8.4	0	0	0	0	0	0	0	0	0	0		0	5		0	0	0			
84539000	税号84.53所列机器的零件	8	0	0	0	0	0	0	0	0	0	0		0	5		0	0	0			
84541000	金属冶炼及铸造用转炉	8.4	0	0	0	0	0	0	0	0	0	0		0	5		0	0	0			
84542010	炉外精炼设备	8.4	0	0	0	0	0	0	0	0	0	0		0	5		0	0	0			
84542090	其他金属冶炼及铸造用锭模及浇包	8.4	0	0	0	0	0	0	0	0	0	0		0	5		0	0	0			
84543010	冷室压铸机	12	0	0	0	0	0	0	0	0	0	0	11.4	0	6	0	0	0	2.4			
84543021	方坯连铸机	10	0	0	0	0	0	0	0	0	0	0	9.5	0	5		0	0	0			
84543022	板坯连铸机	12	0	0	0	0	0	0	0	0	0	0	11.4	0	6	0	0	0	2.4			
84543029	其他钢坯连铸机	12	0	0	0	0	0	0	0	0	0	0	11.4	0	6	0	0	0	2.4			
84543090	其他金属冶炼及铸造用铸造机	12	0	0	0	0	0	0	0	0	0	0	11.4	0	6	0	0	0	2.4			
84549010	炉外精炼设备用零件	8	0	0	0	0	0	0	0	0	0	0		0.8	5		0	0	0			
84549021	结晶器	8	0	0	0	0	0	0	0	0	0	0		0.8	5		0	0	0			
84549022	振动装置	8	0	0	0	0	0	0	0	0	0	0		0.8	5		0	0	0			
84549029	其他钢坯连铸机用零件	8	0	0	0	0	0	0	0	0	0	0		0.8	5		0	0	0			
84549090	其他冶炼等用转炉及铸造机的零件	8	0	0	0	0	0	0	0	0	0	0		0.8	5		0	0	0			
84551010	热轧管机	12	0	0	0	0	0	0	0	0	0	0	8.4	0	5	0	0	0	2.4			
84551020	冷轧管机	12	0	0	0	0	0	0	0	0	0	0	8.4	0	5	0	0	0	2.4			
84551030	定、减径轧管机	12	0	0	0	0	0	0	0	0	0	0	8.4	0	5	0	0	0	2.4			
84551090	其他金属轧管机	12	0	0	0	0	0	0	0	0	0	0	8.4	0	5	0	0	0	2.4			
84552110	板材热轧机	15	0	0	0	0	0	0	0	0	0	0	10.5	1.5	7.5	0	0	7.5	3			
84552120	型钢轧机	15	0	0	0	0	0	0	0	0	0	0	10.5	1.5	7.5	0	0	7.5	3			
84552130	线材轧机	15	0	0	0	0	0	0	0	0	0	0	10.5	1.5	7.5	0	0	7.5	3			
84552190	其他金属热轧或冷热联合轧机	15	0	0	0	0	0	0	0	0	0	0	10.5	1.5	7.5	0	0	7.5	3			
84552210	板材冷轧机	10	0	0	0	0	0	0	0	0	0	0		0	5		0	0	0			
84552290	其他金属冷轧机	15	0	0	0	0	0	0	0	0	0	0		0	12	0	0	7.5	3			
84553000	金属轧机用轧辊	8.4	0	0	0	0	0	0	0	0	0	0		0	5		0	0	0			
84559000	金属轧机的其他零件	8	0	0	0	0	0	0	0	0	0	0	4	0	0		0	0	0			
84562000	用超声波处理各种材料的加工机床	10	0	0	0	0	0	0	0	0	0	0		0	5	0	0	0	0			
84563010	数控的用放电处理各种材料的加工机床	9.7	0	0	0	0	0	0	0	0	0	0		0	5		0	0	0			
84563090	非数控的用放电处理各种材料的加工机床	10	0	0	0	0	0	0	0	0	0	0		0	5	0	0	0	0			
84571010	立式加工中心	9.7	0	0	0	0	0	0	0	0	0	0	6.8	0	5		0	0	0			
84571020	卧式加工中心	9.7	0	0	0	0	0	0	0	0	0	0	8.8	0	5		0	0	0			
84571030	龙门式加工中心	9.7	0	0	0	0	0	0	0	0	0	0	6.8	0	5		0	0	0			
84571091	铣车复合	9.7	0	0	0	0	0	0	0	0	0	0	6.8	0	5		0	0	0			
84571099	其他加工中心	9.7	0	0	0	0	0	0	0	0	0	0	6.8	0	5		0	0	0			
84572000	加工金属的单工位组合机床	8	0	0	0	0	0	0	0	0	0	0		0	5		0	0	0			

税则号列	商品名称（简称）	最惠国	东盟										亚太	智利	巴基斯坦	新加坡	新西兰	秘鲁	哥斯达黎加	香港	澳门	台湾
			文	柬	印	老	马	缅	菲	新	泰	越										
84573000	加工金属的多工位组合机床	5	0	0	0	0	0	0	0	0	0	0		0.5	0		0	0	0			
84581100	切削金属的数控卧式车床	9.7	0	0	0	0	0	0	0	0	0	0		0	5		0	0	0	0		0
84581900	切削金属的非数控卧式车床	12	0	0	0	0	0	0	0	0	0	0		0	6	0	0	0	2.4	0		
84589110	立式数控机床	5	0	0	0	0	0	0	0	0	0	0		0	0		0	0	0			0
84589120	其他数控机床	5	0	0	0	0	0	0	0	0	0	0		0	0		0	0	0			0
84589900	切削金属的其他车床	12	0	0	0	0	0	0	0	0	0	0		0	6	0	0	0	2.4			
84591000	切削金属的直线移动式动力头钻床	15	0	0	0	0	0	0	0	0	0	0		0	12	0	0	7.5	3			
84592100	切削金属的数控钻床	9.7	0	0	0	0	0	0	0	0	0	0		0	5		0	0	0			0
84592900	切削金属的其他钻床	15	0	0	0	0	0	0	0	0	0	0		0	12	0	0	7.5	3			
84593100	切削金属的数控镗铣机床	9.7	0	0	0	0	0	0	0	0	0	0		0	5		0	0	0			
84593900	切削金属的其他镗铣机床	10	0	0	0	0	0	0	0	0	0	0		0	5		0	0	0			
84594010	切削金属的数控镗床	9.7	0	0	0	0	0	0	0	0	0	0		0	5		0	0	0			
84594090	切削金属的其他镗床	15	0	0	0	0	0	0	0	0	0	0		0	12	0	0	7.5	3			
84595100	切削金属的升降台式数控铣床	9.7	0	0	0	0	0	0	0	0	0	0		0	5		0	0	0			
84595900	切削金属的其他升降台式铣床	15	0	0	0	0	0	0	0	0	0	0		0	12	0	0	7.5	3			
84596110	切削金属的数控龙门铣床	5	0	0	0	0	0	0	0	0	0	0		0	0		0	0	0			
84596190	切削金属的其他数控铣床	5	0	0	0	0	0	0	0	0	0	0		0	0		0	0	0			
84596910	切削金属的非数控龙门铣床	12	0	0	0	0	0	0	0	0	0	0	10	0	5	0	0	0	2.4			
84596990	切削金属的其他铣床	12	0	0	0	0	0	0	0	0	0	0	11	0	6	0	0	0	2.4			
84597000	切削金属的其他攻丝机床	12	0	0	0	0	0	0	0	0	0	0		0	6	0	0	0	2.4			
84601100	数控平面磨床	9.7	0	0	0	0	0	0	0	0	0	0		0	5		0	0	0			0
84601900	其他平面磨床	15	0	0	0	0	0	0	0	0	0	0		0	12	0	0	7.5	3			
84602111	曲轴磨床	9.7	0	0	0	0	0	0	0	0	0	0		0	5		0	0	0			
84602119	其他外圆磨床	9.7	0	0	0	0	0	0	0	0	0	0		0	5		0	0	0			
84602120	数控内圆磨床	9.7	0	0	0	0	0	0	0	0	0	0		0	5		0	0	0			
84602190	其他数控磨床	9.7	0	0	0	0	0	0	0	0	0	0		0	5		0	0	0			
84602910	其他外圆磨床	15	0	0	0	0	0	0	0	0	0	0		0	12	0	0	7.5	3			
84602920	其他内圆磨床	15	0	0	0	0	0	0	0	0	0	0		0	12	0	0	7.5	3			
84602930	非数控轧辊磨床	13	0	0	0	0	0	0	0	0	0	0		0	6.5	0	0	0	2.6			
84602990	其他磨床	13	0	0	0	0	0	0	0	0	0	0		0	6.5	0	0	0	2.6			
84603100	数控刃磨（工具或刀具）机床	9.7	0	0	0	0	0	0	0	0	0	0		0	5		0	0	0			
84603900	其他刃磨（工具或刀具）机床	15	0	0	0	0	0	0	0	0	0	0		0	12	0	0	7.5	3	0		
84604010	珩磨机床	13	0	0	0	0	0	0	0	0	0	0		0	6.5	0	0	0	2.6			
84604020	研磨机床	13	0	0	0	0	0	0	0	0	0	0		0	6.5	0	0	0	2.6			0
84609010	砂轮机	15	0	0	0	0	0	0	0	0	0	0		1.5	12	0	0	7.5	3			0
84609020	抛光机床	15	0	0	0	0	0	0	0	0	0	0		1.5	12	0	0	7.5	3			0
84609090	其他磨削等精加工机床	15	0	0	0	0	0	0	0	0	0	0		1.5	12	0	0	7.5	3			
84612010	牛头刨床	15	0	0	0	0	0	0	0	0	0	0		0	12	0	0	7.5	3			
84612020	插床	15	0	0	0	0	0	0	0	0	0	0		0	12	0	0	7.5	3			0
84613000	拉床	12	0	0	0	0	0	0	0	0	0	0		0	6	0	0	0	2.4			0
84614011	齿轮磨床	9.7	0	0	0	0	0	0	0	0	0	0		0	5		0	0	0			
84614019	其他数控的切齿机、齿轮磨床或齿轮精加工机床	9.7	0	0	0	0	0	0	0	0	0	0		0	5		0	0	0			
84614090	非数控切齿机、齿轮磨床齿轮精加工机床	15	0	0	0	0	0	0	0	0	0	0		0	12	0	0	7.5	3			
84615000	锯床或切断机	12	0	0	0	0	0	0	0	0	0	0		0	6	0	0	0	2.4			0
84619011	龙门刨床	15	0	0	0	0	0	0	0	0	0	0		0	12	0	0	7.5	3			0
84619019	其他刨床	15	0	0	0	0	0	0	0	0	0	0		0	12	0	0	7.5	3			0
84619090	税号84.61的未列名机床	12	0	0	0	0	0	0	0	0	0	0		0	6	0	0	0	2.4			
84621010	数控锻造或冲压机床及锻锤	9.7	0	0	0	0	0	0	0	0	0	0	6.8	1	5		0	0	0			0
84621090	非数控锻造或冲压机床及锻锤	12	0	0	0	0	0	0	0	0	0	0	8.4	1.2	5	0	0	6	2.4			0
84622110	数控矫直机	9.7	0	0	0	0	0	0	0	0	0	0		0	5		0	0	0			
84622190	数控的其他弯曲、折迭、矫直或矫平机床	9.7	0	0	0	0	0	0	0	0	0	0		0	5		0	0	0			
84622910	非数控矫直机	10	0	0	0	0	0	0	0	0	0	0		1	5		0	5	0			
84622990	非数控的其他弯曲、折迭、矫直或矫平机床	10	0	0	0	0	0	0	0	0	0	0		1	5	0	0	5	0			
84623110	数控的板带纵剪机	7	0	0	0	0	0	0	0	0	0	0		0	5		0	0	0			
84623120	数控的板带横剪机	7	0	0	0	0	0	0	0	0	0	0		0	5		0	0	0			
84623190	数控的其他剪切机床	7	0	0	0	0	0	0	0	0	0	0		0	5		0	0	0			
84623910	非数控板带纵剪机	10	0	0	0	0	0	0	0	0	0	0	9.5	0	5		0	0	0			

税则号列	商品名称（简称）	最惠国	东盟 文	东盟 柬	东盟 印	东盟 老	东盟 马	东盟 缅	东盟 菲	东盟 新	东盟 泰	东盟 越	亚太	智利	巴基斯坦	新加坡	新西兰	秘鲁	哥斯达黎加	香港	澳门	台湾
84623920	非数控板带横剪机	10	0	0	0	0	0	0	0	0	0	0	9.5	0	5		0	0	0			
84623990	其他剪切机床	10	0	0	0	0	0	0	0	0	0	0	9.5	0	5		0	0	0			
84624111	自动换模式数控步冲压力机	9.7	0	0	0	0	0	0	0	0	0	0		0	5		0	0	0			
84624119	其他数控冲床	9.7	0	0	0	0	0	0	0	0	0	0		0	5		0	0	0			
84624190	其他数控冲孔、开槽机、冲剪两用机	9.7	0	0	0	0	0	0	0	0	0	0		0	5		0	0	0			
84624900	非数控冲孔、开槽机、冲剪两用机	10	0	0	0	0	0	0	0	0	0	0		0	5	0	0	0	0			0
84629110	金属型材挤压机	10	0	0	0	0	0	0	0	0	0	0	9.2	1	5		0	0	0			
84629190	其他液压压力机	10	0	0	0	0	0	0	0	0	0	0	9.2	1	5	0	0	0	0			
84629910	其他机械压力机	10	0	0	0	0	0	0	0	0	0	0	9.5	1	5	0	0	0	0			0
84629990	税号84.62的未列名机床	10	0	0	0	0	0	0	0	0	0	0	9.5	1	5	0	0	0	0			
84631011	拉拔力为300吨及以下的冷拔管机	10	0	0	0	0	0	0	0	0	0	0		0	5		0	0	0			
84631019	其他冷拔管机	10	0	0	0	0	0	0	0	0	0	0		0	5	0	0	0	0			0
84631020	拔丝机	10	0	0	0	0	0	0	0	0	0	0		0	5		0	0	0			
84631090	其他金属杆、管、型材及类似品的拉拔机	10	0	0	0	0	0	0	0	0	0	0		0	5		0	0	0			
84632000	金属或金属陶瓷的螺纹滚轧机	15	0	0	0	0	0	0	0	0	0	0		0	12	0	0	7.5	3			
84633000	金属丝加工机	10	0	0	0	0	0	0	0	0	0	0		0	5		0	0	0			
84639000	其他非切削加工机床	10	0	0	0	0	0	0	0	0	0	0		1	5		0	5	0			
84651000	不需变换工具即可进行加工的机床	10	0	0	0	0	0	0	0	0	0	0		1	5	0	0	5	0	0		
84659100	加工木材等材料的锯床	10	0	0	0	0	0	0	0	0	0	0		1	5		0	5	0	0		
84659200	加工木材等材料的刨、铣或切削机器	10	0	0	0	0	0	0	0	0	0	0		0	5	0	0	0	0	0		
84659300	加工木材等材料的研磨或抛光机器	10	0	0	0	0	0	0	0	0	0	0		0	5		0	0	0	0		
84659400	加工木材等材料的弯曲或装配机器	10	0	0	0	0	0	0	0	0	0	0		0	5	0	0	0	0			
84659500	加工木材等材料的钻孔或凿榫机器	10	0	0	0	0	0	0	0	0	0	0		0	5	0	0	0	0	0		
84659600	加工木材等材料的剖、切或刮削机器	10	0	0	0	0	0	0	0	0	0	0		0	5	0	0	0	0			
84659900	加工木材等材料的其他机床	10	0	0	0	0	0	0	0	0	0	0		1	5	0	0	5	0	0		
84661000	工具夹具及自启板牙切头	7	0	0	0	0	0	0	0	0	0	0		0	5		0	0	0			
84662000	工件夹具	7	0	0	0	0	0	0	0	0	0	0	4.9	0	0		0	0	0			0
84663000	分度头及其他专用于机床的附件	7	0	0	0	0	0	0	0	0	0	0		0	5		0	0	0			
84669200	税号84.65所列机器用的零附件	6	0	0	0	0	0	0	0	0	0	0		0	5		0	0	0	0		
84669400	税号84.62-84.63机器用其他零附件	6	0	0	0	0	0	0	0	0	0	0		0.6	5		0	0	0			0
84671100	旋转式手提风动工具	8	0	0	0	0	0	0	0	0	0	0		0	5		0	0	0			
84671900	其他手提式风动工具	8	0	0	0	0	0	0	0	0	0	0		0	5		0	0	0			
84672100	电动钻	10	0	0	0	0	0	0	0	0	0	0	9	1	5	0	0	5	0	0		
84672210	电动链锯	10	0	0	0	0	0	0	0	0	0	0	9	1	5		0	5	0	0		
84672290	其他电动锯	10	0	0	0	0	0	0	0	0	0	0	9	1	5	0	0	5	0	0		
84672910	电动砂磨工具	10	0	0	0	0	0	0	0	0	0	0	8	1	5	0	0	5	0	0		
84672920	电刨	10	0	0	0	0	0	0	0	0	0	0	8	1	5		0	5	0	0		
84672990	其他电动工具	10	0	0	0	0	0	0	0	0	0	0	8	1	5	0	0	5	0	0		
84678100	手提式液压或其他动力链锯	8	0	0	0	0	0	0	0	0	0	0		0	5		0	0	0			
84678900	其他手提式液压或其他动力工具	8	0	0	0	0	0	0	0	0	0	0		0	5		0	0	0			
84679110	电动链锯用零件	6	0	0	0	0	0	0	0	0	0	0	4.8	0	0		0	0	0	0		
84679190	其他链锯用零件	6	0	0	0	0	0	0	0	0	0	0		0	5		0	0	0			
84679200	风动工具零件	6	0	0	0	0	0	0	0	0	0	0		0	5		0	0	0			
84679910	其他手提式电动工具用零件	10	0	0	0	0	0	0	0	0	0	0	9	0	5	0	0	0	0	0		
84679990	其他手提式工具用零件	6	0	0	0	0	0	0	0	0	0	0		0	5		0	0	0			
84681000	手提喷焊器	12	0	0	0	0	0	0	0	0	0	0		0	6	0	0	0	2.4			
84682000	其他气体焊或表面回火机器及装置	12	0	0	0	0	0	0	0	0	0	0		0	6	0	0	0	2.4			
84688000	其他焊接机器及装置	12	0	0	0	0	0	0	0	0	0	0		0	6	0	0	0	2.4			
84689000	焊接机器用零件	7	0	0	0	0	0	0	0	0	0	0		0	5		0	0	0			
84690012	自动打字机	12	0	0	0	0	0	0	0	0	0	0		0	6	0	0	0	2.4			
84690020	其他电动打字机	12	0	0	0	0	0	0	0	0	0	0	10.8	0	5	0	0	0	2.4			
84690030	其他非电动打字机	12	0	0	0	0	0	0	0	0	0	0		0	6	0	0	0	2.4			
84721000	胶版复印机、油印机	14	0	0	0	0	0	0	0	0	0	0		0	11.2	0	0	0	2.8			
84723010	邮政信件分拣及封装设备	10	0	0	0	0	0	0	0	0	0	0		0	5		0	0	0			
84723090	其他信件分类、折迭、信封装封机等机器	14	0	0	0	0	0	0	0	0	0	0		0	7	0	0	0	2.8			
84729040	地址印写机及地址铭牌压印机	14	0	0	0	0	0	0	0	0	0	0		0	11.2	0	0	0	2.8			
84731000	打字机、文字处理机的零附件	8	0	0	0	0	0	0	0	0	0	0		0	5		0	0	0			
84734010	自动柜员机用出钞器	10.5	0	0	0	0	0	0	0	0	0	0		0	5	0	0	0	2.1			

税则号列	商品名称（简称）	最惠国	东盟										亚太	智利	巴基斯坦	新加坡	新西兰	秘鲁	哥斯达黎加	香港	澳门	台湾
			文	柬	印	老	马	缅	菲	新	泰	越										
84734090	税号84.72所列其他办公室用机器零附件	10.5	0	0	0	0	0	0	0	0	0	0		0	5	0	0	0	2.1			
84741000	固体矿物的分类、筛选、分离或洗涤机器	5	0	0	0	0	0	0	0	0	0	0		0.5	0		0	0	0			
84742010	齿辊式破碎及磨粉机器	5	0	0	0	0	0	0	0	0	0	0		0.5	0		0	0	0			
84742020	球磨式破碎及磨粉机器	5	0	0	0	0	0	0	0	0	0	0		0.5	0		0	0	0			
84742090	其他破碎及磨粉机器	5	0	0	0	0	0	0	0	0	0	0		0.5	0		0	0	0			
84743100	混凝土或砂浆混合机器	7	0	0	0	0	0	0	0	0	0	0		0	5		0	0	0			
84743200	矿物与沥青的混合机器	7	0	0	0	0	0	0	0	0	0	0		0.7	5		0	0	0			
84743900	其他混合或搅拌机器	5	0	0	0	0	0	0	0	0	0	0		0.5	0		0	0	0			
84748010	固体矿物的辊压成型机	5	0	0	0	0	0	0	0	0	0	0	4.5	0.5	0		0	0	0			
84748020	模压成型机	5	0	0	0	0	0	0	0	0	0	0	4.5	0.5	0		0	0	0			
84748090	税号8474所列的其他机器	5	0	0	0	0	0	0	0	0	0	0	4.5	0.5	0		0	0	0			
84749000	税号8474所列机器的零件	5	0	0	0	0	0	0	0	0	0	0		0.5	0		0	0	0			
84751000	白炽灯泡、灯管等的封装机	8	0	0	0	0	0	0	0	0	0	0		0.8	5		0	0	0			
84752100	制造光导纤维及其预制棒的机器	10	0	0	0	0	0	0	0	0	0	0		0	5	0	0	0	0			
84752911	连续式玻璃热弯炉	10	0	0	0	0	0	0	0	0	0	0		0	5		0	0	0			
84752912	玻璃纤维拉丝机（光纤拉丝机除外）	10	0	0	0	0	0	0	0	0	0	0		0	5		0	0	0			
84752919	其他玻璃热加工设备	10	0	0	0	0	0	0	0	0	0	0		0	5	0	0	0	0			
84752990	其他玻璃及其制品的制造或热加工机器	10	0	0	0	0	0	0	0	0	0	0		0	5		0	0	0			
84759000	税号84.75所列机器的零件	8	0	0	0	0	0	0	0	0	0	0		0.8	5		0	0	0			
84762100	装有加热或制冷装置的饮料自动销售机	14	0	0	0	0	0	0	0	0	0	0		1.4	11.2	0	0	0	2.8			
84762900	其他饮料自动销售机	15	0	0	0	0	0	0	0	0	0	0		0	12	0	0	7.5	3			
84768100	装有加热或制冷装置的自动售货机	14	0	0	0	0	0	0	0	0	0	0		0	7	0	0	0	2.8			
84768900	其他自动售货机	15	0	0	0	0	0	0	0	0	0	0		1.5	12	0	0	7.5	3			
84769000	税号8476所列机器的零件	10	0	0	0	0	0	0	0	0	0	0		0	5		0	0	0			
84772010	塑料造粒机	5	0	0	0	0	0	0	0	0	0	0	4.5	0	0		0	0	0	0		0
84772090	其他加工橡胶或塑料的挤出机	5	0	0	0	0	0	0	0	0	0	0	4.5	0	0		0	0	0	0		0
84773010	挤出吹塑机	5	0	0	0	0	0	0	0	0	0	0		0.5	0		0	0	0	0		
84773020	注射吹塑机	5	0	0	0	0	0	0	0	0	0	0		0.5	0		0	0	0	0		
84773090	其他吹塑机	5	0	0	0	0	0	0	0	0	0	0		0.5	0		0	0	0	0		
84774010	塑料中空成型机	5	0	0	0	0	0	0	0	0	0	0	4.5	0	0		0	0	0			0
84774020	塑料压延成型机	5	0	0	0	0	0	0	0	0	0	0	4.5	0	0		0	0	0			0
84774090	其他真空模塑及热成型机器	5	0	0	0	0	0	0	0	0	0	0	4.5	0	0		0	0	0			0
84775100	用于充气轮胎或内胎模塑或翻新的机器	5	0	0	0	0	0	0	0	0	0	0		0.5	0		0	0	0			
84775910	三维打印机（3D打印机）	5	0	0	0	0	0	0	0	0	0	0	3.5	0	0		0	0	0	0		0
84775990	其他模塑或成型机器	5	0	0	0	0	0	0	0	0	0	0	3.5	0	0		0	0	0	0		0
84778000	其他橡胶或塑料加工机器	5	0	0	0	0	0	0	0	0	0	0	4.5	0	0		0	0	0	0		0
84781000	其他未列名的烟草加工及制作机器	5	0	0	0	0	0	0	0	0	0	0	2.5	0	0		0	0	0			
84789000	烟草加工及制作机器用的零件	10	0	0	0	0	0	0	0	0	0	0		0	5		0	0	0			
84791021	沥青混凝土摊铺机	8	0	0	0	0	0	0	0	0	0	0	5.6	0.8	5		0	0	0			
84791022	稳定土摊铺机	8	0	0	0	0	0	0	0	0	0	0	5.6	0.8	5		0	0	0			
84791029	其他摊铺机	8	0	0	0	0	0	0	0	0	0	0	5.6	0.8	5		0	0	0			
84791090	其他公共工程用的机器	8	0	0	0	0	0	0	0	0	0	0	5.6	0.8	5		0	0	0			
84792000	提取加工动物或植物油脂的机器	10	0	0	0	0	0	0	0	0	0	0		1	5	0	0	0	0			
84793000	木碎料板或木纤维板的挤压机	10	0	0	0	0	0	0	0	0	0	0		0	5		0	0	0			
84794000	绳或缆的制造机器	7	0	0	0	0	0	0	0	0	0	0		0	5		0	0	0			
84796000	蒸发式空气冷却器	10	0	0	0	0	0	0	0	0	0	0	9	0	5		0	0	0			
84798110	绕线机	9.5	0	0	0	0	0	0	0	0	0	0	9	1	5		0	0	0	0		0
84798190	其他处理金属的机械	9.5	0	0	0	0	0	0	0	0	0	0	9	1	5		0	0	0	0		0
84798200	其他混合、研磨、筛选、均化等机器	7	0	0	0	0	0	0	0	0	0	0	4.9	0	0		0	0	0			0
84801000	金属铸造用型箱	10	0	0	0	0	0	0	0	0	0	0		0	5		0	0	0			
84802000	型模底板	8	0	0	0	0	0	0	0	0	0	0		0	5		0	0	0			
84803000	阳模	10	0	0	0	0	0	0	0	0	0	0		0	5	0	0	0	0			
84804110	压铸模	8	0	0	0	0	0	0	0	0	0	0	5.6	0	5		0	0	0	0		0
84804120	粉末冶金用压模	8	0	0	0	0	0	0	0	0	0	0	5.6	0	5		0	0	0	0		0
84804190	其他金属、硬质合金用注模或压模	8	0	0	0	0	0	0	0	0	0	0	5.6	0	5		0	0	0	0		0
84804900	金属、硬质合金用其他型模	8	0	0	0	0	0	0	0	0	0	0	5.6	0	5		0	0	0			
84805000	玻璃用型模	8.4	0	0	0	0	0	0	0	0	0	0		0	5		0	0	0			
84806000	矿物材料用型模	8.4	0	0	0	0	0	0	0	0	0	0		0.8	5		0	0	0			

税则号列	商品名称（简称）	最惠国	东盟										亚太	智利	巴基斯坦	新加坡	新西兰	秘鲁	哥斯达黎加	香港	澳门	台湾
			文	柬	印	老	马	缅	菲	新	泰	越										
84807900	塑料或橡胶用其他型模	5	0	0	0	0	0	0	0	0	0	0	3.5	0	0		0	0	0	0		0
84811000	减压阀	5	0	0	0	0	0	0	0	0	0	0		0.5	0		0	0	0			
84812010	油压传动阀	5	0	0	0	0	0	0	0	0	0	0		0.5	0		0	0	0			0
84812020	气压传动阀	5	0	0	0	0	0	0	0	0	0	0		0.5	0		0	0	0			
84813000	止回阀	5	0	0	0	0	0	0	0	0	0	0		0.5	0		0	0	0			0
84814000	安全阀或溢流阀	5	0	0	0	0	0	0	0	0	0	0		0.5	0		0	0	0			0
84818021	电磁换向阀	7	0	0	0	0	0	0	0	0	0	0	4.9	0.7	0		0	0	0	0		0
84818029	其他换向阀	7	0	0	0	0	0	0	0	0	0	0	4.9	0.7	0		0	0	0	0		0
84818031	电子膨胀阀	7	0	0	0	0	0	0	0	0	0	0	4.9	0.7	0		0	0	0	0		0
84818039	其他流量阀	7	0	0	0	0	0	0	0	0	0	0	4.9	0.7	0		0	0	0	0		0
84818040	其他阀门	7	0	0	0	0	0	0	0	0	0	0	4.9	0.7	0		0	0	0	0		0
84818090	未列名龙头、旋塞及类似装置	5	0	0	0	0	0	0	0	0	0	0		0.5	0		0	0	0	0		
84819010	阀门用零件	8	0	0	0	0	0	0	0	0	0	0		0.8	5		0	0	0			0
84819090	龙头、旋塞及类似装置的零件	8	0	0	0	0	0	0	0	0	0	0		0.8	5		0	0	0			0
84821010	调心球轴承	8	0	0	0	0	0	0	0	0	0	0	7.6	0.8	5	0	0	0	0	0		
84821020	深沟球轴承	8	0	0	0	0	0	0	0	0	0	0	7.6	0.8	5	0	0	0	0	0		
84821030	角接触轴承	8	0	0	0	0	0	0	0	0	0	0	7.6	0.8	5	0	0	0	0	0		
84821040	推力球轴承	8	0	0	0	0	0	0	0	0	0	0	7.6	0.8	5	0	0	0	0	0		
84821090	其他滚珠轴承	8	0	0	0	0	0	0	0	0	0	0	7.6	0.8	5	0	0	0	0	0		
84822000	锥形滚子轴承	8	0	0	0	0	0	0	0	0	0	0		0	5		0	0	0			
84823000	鼓形滚子轴承	8	0	0	0	0	0	0	0	0	0	0		0	5		0	0	0			
84824000	滚针轴承	8	0	0	0	0	0	0	0	0	0	0		0	5		0	0	0			0
84825000	其他圆柱形滚子轴承	8	0	0	0	0	0	0	0	0	0	0		0	5	0	0	0	0			
84828000	其他滚动轴承及球、柱混合轴承	8	0	0	0	0	0	0	0	0	0	0	5.6	0.8	5		0	0	0			
84829100	滚珠、滚针及滚柱	8	0	0	0	0	0	0	0	0	0	0		0	5		0	0	0			
84829900	滚动轴承的其他零件	6	0	0	0	0	0	0	0	0	0	0		0	5		0	0	0			0
84831011	船舶用柴油机曲轴	6	0	0	0	0	0	0	0	0	0	0	5.1	0.6	5		0	0	0	0	0	
84831019	其他船舶用传动轴	6	0	0	0	0	0	0	0	0	0	0	5.1	0.6	5		0	0	0	0	0	
84831090	其他传动轴及曲柄	6	0	0	0	0	0	0	0	0	0	0	5.4	0.6	5		0	0	0	0	0	
84832000	装有滚珠或滚子轴承的轴承座	6	0	0	0	0	0	0	0	0	0	0		0	5		0	0	0		0	
84833000	未装滚珠或滚子轴承的轴承座	6	0	0	0	0	0	0	0	0	0	0		0.6	5		0	0	0		0	
84834010	滚子螺杆传动装置	8	0	0	0	0	0	0	0	0	0	0	5.6	0.8	5		0	0	0	0	0	0
84834020	行星齿轮减速器	8	0	0	0	0	0	0	0	0	0	0	5.6	0.8	5		0	0	0	0	0	
84834090	其他齿轮及齿轮传动装置	8	0	0	0	0	0	0	0	0	0	0	5.6	0.8	5		0	0	0	0	0	0
84835000	飞轮、滑轮及滑轮组	8	0	0	0	0	0	0	0	0	0	0		0	5		0	0	0		0	
84836000	离合器及联轴器(包括万向节)	8	0	0	0	0	0	0	0	0	0	0		0	5		0	0	0		0	
84839000	单独报验的带齿的轮及其他传动元件；零件	8	0	0	0	0	0	0	0	0	0	0		0.8	5		0	0	0	0	0	0
84841000	金属片密封垫或类似接合衬垫	8	0	0	0	0	0	0	0	0	0	0		0	5		0	0	0			0
84842000	机械密封件	8	0	0	0	0	0	0	0	0	0	0		0	5		0	0	0			
84849000	其他材料制密封垫及类似接合衬垫	8	0	0	0	0	0	0	0	0	0	0		0	5		0	0	0			
84863041	制造平板显示器用的超声波清洗装置	10	0	0	0	0	0	0	0	0	0	0		0	5	0	0	0	0			
84864021	专用于装配与封装半导体器件或集成电路的塑封机	5	0	0	0	0	0	0	0	0	0	0	4.5	0	0		0	0	0			
84864022	专用于装配与封装半导体器件或集成电路的引线键合设备	8	0	0	0	0	0	0	0	0	0	0	7.6	0	5		0	0	0	0		
84864039	其他集成电路或液晶显示屏工厂专用升降、装卸、搬运装置	5	0	0	0	0	0	0	0	0	0	0	3.5	0.5	0		0	0	0			
84869010	升降、搬运、装卸机器用零件及附件(自动搬运设备用除外)	5	0	0	0	0	0	0	0	0	0	0	2.5	0.5	0		0	0	0			
84869020	引线键合装置用零件及附件	6	0	0	0	0	0	0	0	0	0	0	5.7	0	5		0	0	0			
84871000	船用推进器及桨叶	6	0	0	0	0	0	0	0	0	0	0		0	5		0	0	0			
84879000	本章其他税号未列名机器零件	8	0	0	0	0	0	0	0	0	0	0		0.8	5		0	0	0	0		0
85011010	输出功率≤37.5W玩具电动机	24.5	0	0	0	0	0	0	0	0	0	0	23.3	0	23.3	0	0	12.3	4.9	0		0
85011091	机座20mm≤直径＜39mm微电机	9	0	0	0	0	0	0	0	0	0	0	8.6	0	5	0	0	0	0	0		
85011099	其他输出功率≤37.5W微电机	9	0	0	0	0	0	0	0	0	0	0	8.6	0	5	0	0	0	0	0		0
85012000	输出功率＞37.5W交直流两用电动机	12	0	0	0	0	0	0	0	0	0	0		1.2	6	0	0	6	2.4			
85013100	输出功率≤750瓦直流电动机、发电机	12	0	0	0	0	0	0	0	0	0	0	11	0	6	0	0	0	2.4	0	0	0
85013200	750W＜输出功率≤75KW直流电动机、发电机	10	0	0	0	0	0	0	0	0	0	0		0	5	0	0	0	0			
85013300	75KW＜输出功率≤375KW直流电动机、	5	0	0	0	0	0	0	0	0	0	0		0.5	0		0	0	0			

税则号列	商品名称（简称）	最惠国	东盟										亚太	智利	巴基斯坦	新加坡	新西兰	秘鲁	哥斯达黎加	香港	澳门	台湾
			文	柬	印	老	马	缅	菲	新	泰	越										
	发电机																					
85013400	输出功率＞375KW直流电动机、发电机	12	0	0	0	0	0	0	0	0	0	0		1.2	6	0	0	0	2.4			
85014000	单相交流电动机	12	0	0	0	0	0	0	0	0	0	0		1.2	6	0	0	6	2.4			
85015100	输出功率≤750W多相交流电动机	5	0	0	0	0	0	0	0	0	0	0		0	0		0	0	0			
85015200	输出功率＞750W≤75KW多相交流电动机	10	0	0	0	0	0	0	0	0	0	0		0	5	0	0	0	0			
85015300	输出功率＞75KW多相交流电动机	12	0	0	0	0	0	0	0	0	0	0	11.4	0	6	0	0	0	2.4			
85016100	输出功率≤75KVA交流发电机	5	0	0	0	0	0	0	0	0	0	0		0.5	0		0	0	0			
85016200	75KVA＜输出功率≤375KVA交流发电机	12	0	0	0	0	0	0	0	0	0	0		1.2	6	0	0	6	2.4			
85016300	375KVA＜输出功率≤750KVA交流发电机	12	0	0	0	0	0	0	0	0	0	0		1.2	6	0	0	6	2.4			
85016410	750KVA＜输出功率＜350MVA交流发电机	10	0	0	0	0	0	0	0	0	0	0		1	5	0	0	5	0			
85016420	350KVA≤输出功率＜665MVA交流发电机	5.8	0	0	0	0	0	0	0	0	0	0		0.6	5		0	0	0			
85016430	输出功率≥665MVA交流发电机	6	0	0	0	0	0	0	0	0	0	0		0.6	5		0	0	0			
85021100	输出功率≤75KVA柴油发电机组	10	0	0	0	0	0	0	0	0	0	0		0	5	0	0	0	0	0		
85021200	75KVA＜输出功率≤375KVA柴油发电机组	10	0	0	0	0	0	0	0	0	0	0		1	5	0	0	5	0	0		
85021310	375KVA＜输出功率≤2MVA柴油发电机组	10	0	0	0	0	0	0	0	0	0	0	7	0	5	0	0	0	0	0		
85021320	输出功率＞2MVA柴油发电机组	10	0	0	0	0	0	0	0	0	0	0	7	0	5	0	0	0	0	0		
85022000	装有点燃式活塞发动机的发电机组	10	0	0	0	0	0	0	0	0	0	0		0	5	0	0	0	0			
85023100	风力驱动的发电机组	8	0	0	0	0	0	0	0	0	0	0		0	5		0	0	0			
85023900	其他发电机组	10	0	0	0	0	0	0	0	0	0	0		0	5		0	0	0			
85024000	旋转式变流机	10	0	0	0	0	0	0	0	0	0	0		0	5		0	0	0			
85030010	玩具用电动机微电机零件	12	0	0	0	0	0	0	0	0	0	0	11.4	1.2	6	0	0	6	2.4	0		0
85030020	输出功率＞350MVA交流发电机零件	3	0	0	0	0	0	0	0	0	0	0	2.5	0	0		0	0	0	0		
85030030	风力驱动发电机组的零件	3	0	0	0	0	0	0	0	0	0	0	2.5	0	0		0	0	0	0		
85030090	其他电动机、发电机(组)零件	8	0	0	0	0	0	0	0	0	0	0	7.6	0.8	5		0	0	0	0		0
85041010	电子镇流器	10	0	0	0	0	0	0	0	0	0	0		1	5	0	0	5	0		0	
85041090	其他放电灯或放电管用镇流器	10	0	0	0	0	0	0	0	0	0	0		1	5		0	5	0		0	
85042100	额定容量≤650KVA的液体介质变压器	10.5	0	0	0	0	0	0	0	0	0	0		1.1	5	0	0	5.3	2.1			
85042200	650KVA＜额定容量≤10MVA的液体介质变压器	12.6	0	0	0	0	0	0	0	0	0	0		1.3	6.3	0	0	6.3	2.5			
85042311	10MVA＜额定容量≤220MVA的液体变压器	10	0	0	0	0	0	0	0	0	0	0	7	0	5		0	0	0			
85042312	200MVA≤额定容量＜330MVA的液体变压器	10	0	0	0	0	0	0	0	0	0	0	7	0	5		0	0	0			
85042313	330MVA≤额定容量＜400MVA的液体变压器	10	0	0	0	0	0	0	0	0	0	0	7	0	5		0	0	0			
85042321	400MVA≤液体变压器额定容量＜500MVA	6	0	0	0	0	0	0	0	0	0	0	4.2	0	0		0	0	0			
85042329	其他额定容量≥500MVA的液体变压器	6	0	0	0	0	0	0	0	0	0	0	4.2	0	0		0	0	0			
85043110	额定容量≤1KVA的互感器	5	0	0	0	0	0	0	0	0	0	0	4.3	0	0		0	0	0		0	0
85043190	额定容量≤1KVA的其他变压器	5	0	0	0	0	0	0	0	0	0	0	4.3	0	0	0	0	0	0	0	0	0
85043210	1KVA＜额定容量≤16KVA的互感器	5	0	0	0	0	0	0	0	0	0	0		0	0		0	0	0		0	
85043290	1KVA＜额定容量≤16KVA的其他变压器	5	0	0	0	0	0	0	0	0	0	0		0	0		0	0	0		0	
85043310	额定容量超过16千伏安，但不超过500千伏安的互感器	5	0	0	0	0	0	0	0	0	0	0		0.5	0		0	0	0		0	
85043390	其他额定容量超过16千伏安，但不超过500千伏安的变压器、静止式变流器（例如整流器）及电感器	5	0	0	0	0	0	0	0	0	0	0		0.5	0		0	0	0		0	
85043410	额定容量超过500千伏的安互感器	14	0	0	0	0	0	0	0	0	0	0		0	11.2	0	0	0	2.8		0	
85043490	其他额定容量超过500千伏安的变压器、静止式变流器（例如整流器）及电感器	14	0	0	0	0	0	0	0	0	0	0		0	11.2	0	0	0	2.8		0	
85044014	功率＜1KW高精度直流稳压电源	7	0	0	0	0	0	0	0	0	0	0	5.6	0.7	5		0	0	0			
85044020	不间断供电电源(UPS)	10	0	0	0	0	0	0	0	0	0	0	8.5	0	5	0	0	0	0	0		
85044030	逆变器	10	0	0	0	0	0	0	0	0	0	0		1	5	0	0	5	0	0	0	
85044091	具有变流功能的半导体模块	10	0	0	0	0	0	0	0	0	0	0		1	5	0	0	5	0	0	0	
85044099	其他未列名静止式变流器	10	0	0	0	0	0	0	0	0	0	0		1	5	0	0	5	0	0	0	
85049011	额定容量＞400KVA液体介质变压器零件	5	0	0	0	0	0	0	0	0	0	0	4.5	0	0		0	0	0	0		
85049019	其他变压器零件	8	0	0	0	0	0	0	0	0	0	0	4.5	0	4.5		0	0	0	0		0
85049020	稳压电源及不间断供电电源零件	8	0	0	0	0	0	0	0	0	0	0	5.6	0	5		0	0	0	0	0	0
85049090	其他静止式变流器及电感器零件	8	0	0	0	0	0	0	0	0	0	0	5.6	0	5		0	0	0	0	0	0

税则号列	商品名称（简称）	最惠国	东盟										亚太	智利	巴基斯坦	新加坡	新西兰	秘鲁	哥斯达黎加	香港	澳门	台湾
			文	柬	印	老	马	缅	菲	新	泰	越										
85051110	稀土的永磁铁及磁化后准备制永磁铁的物品	7	0	0	0	0	0	0	0	0	0	0		0	5		0	0	0			0
85051190	其他金属的永磁体	7	0	0	0	0	0	0	0	0	0	0		0	5		0	0	0	0		0
85051900	非金属永磁体	7	0	0	0	0	0	0	0	0	0	0	6.7	0	5		0	0	0	0		
85052000	电磁联轴节、离合器及制动器	8	0	0	0	0	0	0	0	0	0	0	7.6	0	5		0	0	0			
85059010	电磁起重吸盘	8	0	0	0	0	0	0	0	0	0	0		0	5		0	0	0			
85059090	电磁夹具等及税号85.02的零件	8	0	0	0	0	0	0	0	0	0	0	7.6	0	5		0	0	0			
85061011	扣式碱性锌锰电池	20	0	0	0	0	0	0	0	0	0	0		0		0	0	10	4	0		
85061012	圆柱型碱性锌锰电池	20	0	0	0	0	0	0	0	0	0	0		0		0	0	10	4	0		
85061019	其他碱性锌锰电池	20	0	0	0	0	0	0	0	0	0	0		0		0	0	10	4	0		
85061090	二氧化锰的原电池及原电池组	20	0	0	0	0	0	0	0	0	0	0		0		0	0	10	4	0		
85063000	氧化汞的原电池及原电池组	14	0	0	0	0	0	0	0	0	0	0		0	11.2	0	0	0	2.8			
85064000	氧化银的原电池及原电池组	14	0	0	0	0	0	0	0	0	0	0		0	11.2	0	0	0	2.8			
85065000	锂的原电池及原电池组	14	0	0	0	0	0	0	0	0	0	0		0	11.2	0	0	0	2.8			
85066000	锌空气的原电池及原电池组	14	0	0	0	0	0	0	0	0	0	0		0	11.2	0	0	0	2.8			
85068000	其他原电池及原电池组	14	0	0	0	0	0	0	0	0	0	0		0	11.2	0	0	0	2.8	0		
85069010	二氧化锰原电池或原电池组的零件	14	0	0	0	0	0	0	0	0	0	0		0	11.2	0	0	0	2.8			
85069090	其他原电池组或原电池组的零件	10	0	0	0	0	0	0	0	0	0	0		0	5	0	0	0	0			
85071000	起动活塞式发动机用铅酸蓄电池	10	0	0	0	0	0	0	0	0	0	0	6.9	1	5	0	0	5	0		0	
85072000	其他铅酸蓄电池	10	0	0	0	0	0	0	0	0	0	0	6.9	0	5	0	0	0	0		0	
85073000	镍镉蓄电池	10	0	0	0	0	0	0	0	0	0	0	8	0	5	0	0	0	0	0		
85074000	镍铁蓄电池	12	0	0	0	0	0	0	0	0	0	0	9.6	0	5	0	0	0	2.4			
85075000	镍氢蓄电池	12	0	0	0	0	0	0	0	0	0	0	9.6	0	5	0	0	0	2.4	0		
85076000	锂离子蓄电池	12	0	0	0	0	0	0	0	0	0	0	9.6	0	5	0	0	0	2.4	0		0
85078030	全钒液流电池	12	0	0	0	0	0	0	0	0	0	0	9	0	5	0	0	0	2.4	0		
85078090	其他蓄电池	12	0	0	0	0	0	0	0	0	0	0	9	0	5	0	0	0	2.4	0		
85079010	铅酸蓄电池零件	10	0	0	0	0	0	0	0	0	0	0		0	5		0	0	0	0		
85079090	其他蓄电池零件	8	0	0	0	0	0	0	0	0	0	0		0	5		0	0	0	0		
85081100	功率不超过1500瓦，且带有容积不超过20升的电动真空吸尘器	10	0	0	0	0	0	0	0	0	0	0	8.2	0	5	0	0	0	0	0		0
85087010	税号8508.1100所列电动真空吸尘器用零件	12	0	0	0	0	0	0	0	0	0	0		0	6	0	0	0	2.4	0		
85094010	水果或蔬菜榨汁机	10	0	0	0	0	0	0	0	0	0	0		0	5	0	0	0	0		0	
85094090	食品研磨机及搅拌器或果、菜榨汁器	10	0	0	0	0	0	0	0	0	0	0		0	5	0	0	0	0			0
85098010	地板打蜡机	30	0	0	0	0	0	0	0	0	0	0		3		0	0	15	6			
85098020	厨房废物处理器	20	0	0	0	0	0	0	0	0	0	0		0		0	0	10	4			
85098090	其他家用电动器具	30	0	0	0	0	0	0	0	0	0	0		3		0	0	15	6			
85099000	家用电动器具的零件	12	0	0	0	0	0	0	0	0	0	0		0	6	0	0	0	2.4	0		
85101000	电动剃须刀	30	0	0	0	0	0	0	0	0	0	0		0		0	0	15	6			
85102000	电动毛发推剪	30	0	0	0	0	0	0	0	0	0	0		0		0	0	15	6	0		
85103000	电动脱毛器	20	0	0	0	0	0	0	0	0	0	0		0		0	0	10	4		0	
85109000	税号85.10所列货品的零件	24.5	0	0	0	0	0	0	0	0	0	0		0		0	0	12.2	4.9			
85111000	火花塞	10	0	0	0	0	0	0	0	0	0	0		0	5	0	0	5	0			
85112010	车、船、飞机等用点火磁电机、永磁直流发电机、磁飞轮	5	0	0	0	0	0	0	0	0	0	0		0	0		0	0	0			
85112090	其他点火磁电机、磁飞轮	10	0	0	0	0	0	0	0	0	0	0		0	5		0	0	0			
85113010	分电器及点火线圈	5	0	0	0	0	0	0	0	0	0	0		0	0		0	0	0			
85113090	其他用途用分电器、点火线圈	8.4	0	0	0	0	0	0	0	0	0	0		0	5		0	0	0			
85114010	机车等用起动电机及两用起动发电机	5	0	0	0	0	0	0	0	0	0	0		0	0		0	0	0			
85114091	输出功率≥132.39千瓦启动电机	8.4	0	0	0	0	0	0	0	0	0	0		0	5		0	0	0			
85114099	其他用途的启动电机	8.4	0	0	0	0	0	0	0	0	0	0		0	5		0	0	0			
85115010	其他机车、航空器、船舶用发电机	5	0	0	0	0	0	0	0	0	0	0		0.5	0		0	0	0			
85115090	其他附属于内燃发动机的发电机	8.4	0	0	0	0	0	0	0	0	0	0		0.8	5		0	0	0			
85118000	发动机用电点火、起动的其他装置	8.4	0	0	0	0	0	0	0	0	0	0		0.8	5		0	0	0			
85119010	机车、船、航空器用电点火、起动装置零件	4.5	0	0	0	0	0	0	0	0	0	0		0	0		0	0	0			
85119090	其他用电点火、电起动装置的零件	5	0	0	0	0	0	0	0	0	0	0		0	0		0	0	0			
85121000	自行车用照明或视觉信号装置	10.5	0	0	0	0	0	0	0	0	0	0		0	5	0	0	0	2.1			
85122010	机动车辆用照明装置	10												0			0	0	0			0
85122090	其他机动车用照明或视觉信号装置	10												0			0	0	0			
85123011	机动车辆用喇叭、蜂鸣器	10											8.5	0	8.5		0	0	0			

税则号列	商品名称（简称）	最惠国	东盟										亚太	智利	巴基斯坦	新加坡	新西兰	秘鲁	哥斯达黎加	香港	澳门	台湾
			文	柬	印	老	马	缅	菲	新	泰	越										
85123012	防盗报警器	10	0	0	0	0	0	0	0	0	0	0	9	1	5		0	0	0			
85123019	其他机动车辆用音响信号装置	10											8.5	0	8.5		0	0	0			
85123090	其他车辆用音响信号装置	10											8.5	0	8.5		0	0	0			
85124000	车辆风档刮水器、除霜器及去雾器	10												0			0	0	0			
85129000	税号85.12所列装置的零件	8	0	0	0	0	0	0	0	0	0	0		0	5		0	0	0			0
85131010	手电筒	15	0	0	0	0	0	0	0	0	0	0	13.2	1.5	7.5	0	0	7.5	3		0	
85131090	其他自供能源手提式电灯	17.5	0	0	0	0	0	0	0	0	0	0		1.8	14	0	0	8.8	3.5		0	
85139010	手电筒零件	14	0	0	0	0	0	0	0	0	0	0		0	11.2	0	0	0	2.8	0	0	
85139090	其他自供能源手提式电灯零件	14	0	0	0	0	0	0	0	0	0	0		0	11.2	0	0	0	2.8	0	0	
85144000	其他通过感应或介质损耗工作的的加热设备	10	0	0	0	0	0	0	0	0	0	0		0	5	0	0	0	0			
85149010	炼钢电炉用零件	8	0	0	0	0	0	0	0	0	0	0		0	5		0	0	0			
85149090	工业用电阻加热炉及烘箱等零件	0																				
85151100	钎焊机器及装置用烙铁及焊枪	10	0	0	0	0	0	0	0	0	0	0		0	5	0	0	0	0			
85151900	其他钎焊机器及装置	10	0	0	0	0	0	0	0	0	0	0		0	5	0	0	0	0			
85152120	机器人	10	0	0	0	0	0	0	0	0	0	0		1	5	0	0	0	0	0		
85152191	直缝焊管机	10	0	0	0	0	0	0	0	0	0	0		1	5		0	0	0	0		
85152199	其他全自动或半自动电阻焊接机器及装置	10	0	0	0	0	0	0	0	0	0	0		1	5	0	0	0	0	0		
85152900	其他电阻焊接机器及装置	10	0	0	0	0	0	0	0	0	0	0	9.5	0	5	0	0	0	0			
85153120	机器人	10												1			0	0	0			
85153191	螺旋焊管机	10	0	0	0	0	0	0	0	0	0	0		1	5		0	0	0			
85153199	其他全自动或半自动的电弧（包括等离子弧）焊接机器及装	10												1			0	0	0			
85153900	其他电弧焊接机器及装置	10	0	0	0	0	0	0	0	0	0	0		1	5		0	0	0			
85158010	激光焊接机器人	8	0	0	0	0	0	0	0	0	0	0	7.6	0	5		0	0	0	0		0
85158090	其他机器及装置	8	0	0	0	0	0	0	0	0	0	0	7.6	0	5		0	0	0	0		0
85159000	电气等焊接机器及装置零件	6	0	0	0	0	0	0	0	0	0	0	5.7	0	5		0	0	0	0		
85161010	储存式电热水器	10	0	0	0	0	0	0	0	0	0	0		1	5	0	0	0	0			
85161020	即热式电热水器	10	0	0	0	0	0	0	0	0	0	0		1	5	0	0	0	0			
85161090	其他电热的快速热水器、浸入式液体加热器	10	0	0	0	0	0	0	0	0	0	0		1	5	0	0	0	0			
85162100	电气储存式散热器	35	0	0	0	0	0	0	0	0	0	0		0		0	0	17.5	7		0	0
85162910	电气土壤加热器	10	0	0	0	0	0	0	0	0	0	0		1	5		0	0	0	0	0	
85162920	辐射式空间加热器	10	0	0	0	0	0	0	0	0	0	0		1	5	0	0	0	0	0	0	
85162931	风扇式对流式空间加热器	10	0	0	0	0	0	0	0	0	0	0		1	5	0	0	0	0	0	0	
85162932	充液式对流式空间加热器	10	0	0	0	0	0	0	0	0	0	0		1	5	0	0	0	0	0	0	
85162939	其他对流式空间加热器	10	0	0	0	0	0	0	0	0	0	0		1	5	0	0	0	0	0	0	
85162990	电气空间加热器	10	0	0	0	0	0	0	0	0	0	0		1	5	0	0	0	0	0	0	
85163100	电吹风机	10	0	0	0	0	0	0	0	0	0	0		0	5	0	0	0	0		0	
85163200	其他电热理发器具	35	0	0	0	0	0	0	0	0	0	0		0		0	0	17.5	7		0	
85163300	电热干手器	35	0	0	0	0	0	0	0	0	0	0		0		0	0	17.5	7		0	
85164000	电熨斗	35	0	0	0	0	0	0	0	0	0	0		0		0	0	17.5	7		0	0
85165000	微波炉	15	0	0	0	0	0	0	0	0	0	0	13.5	0	7.5	0	0	7.5	3			
85166010	电磁炉	15	0	0	0	0	0	0	0	0	0	0		0	12	0	0	7.5	3		0	
85166030	电饭锅	15	0	0	0	0	0	0	0	0	0	0		0	12	0	0	7.5	3		0	0
85166040	电炒锅	15	0	0	0	0	0	0	0	0	0	0		0	12	0	0	7.5	3		0	
85166050	电烤箱	15	0	0	0	0	0	0	0	0	0	0		0	12		0	7.5	3		0	0
85166090	其他电热炉	15	0	0	0	0	0	0	0	0	0	0		0	12	0	0	7.5	3		0	
85167110	滴液式咖啡机	32	0	0	0	0	0	0	0	0	0	0		0		0	0	16	6.4		0	
85167120	蒸馏渗滤式咖啡机	32	0	0	0	0	0	0	0	0	0	0		0		0	0	16	6.4		0	
85167130	泵压式咖啡机	32	0	0	0	0	0	0	0	0	0	0		0		0	0	16	6.4		0	
85167190	其他电热咖啡机或茶壶	32	0	0	0	0	0	0	0	0	0	0		0		0	0	16	6.4		0	
85167210	家用自动面包机	32	0	0	0	0	0	0	0	0	0	0		0		0	0	16	6.4		0	0
85167220	片式烤面包机（多士炉）	32	0	0	0	0	0	0	0	0	0	0		0		0	0	16	6.4		0	
85167290	电热烤面包器	32	0	0	0	0	0	0	0	0	0	0		0		0	0	16	6.4		0	
85167910	电热饮水机	32	0	0	0	0	0	0	0	0	0	0		0		0	0	16	6.4		0	
85167990	其他电热器具	32	0	0	0	0	0	0	0	0	0	0		0		0	0	16	6.4	0	0	
85168000	加热电阻器	10	0	0	0	0	0	0	0	0	0	0		0	5	0	0	0	0			
85169010	土壤加热器及加热电阻器零件	8	0	0	0	0	0	0	0	0	0	0		0	5		0	0	0	0		
85169090	税号85.16所列货品的其他零件	12	0	0	0	0	0	0	0	0	0	0		0	6	0	0	0	2.4	0		

税则号列	商品名称（简称）	最惠国	东盟										亚太	智利	巴基斯坦	新加坡	新西兰	秘鲁	哥斯达黎加	香港	澳门	台湾
			文	柬	印	老	马	缅	菲	新	泰	越										
85176910	其他无线设备	9	0	0	0	0	0	0	0	0	0	0		0	0		0	0	0			
85177040	对讲机用（天线除外）	8	0	0	0	0	0	0	0	0	0	0	5.6	0.8	5		0	0	0	0		
85177070	税号8517所列设备用天线及其零件	2	0	0	0	0	0	0	0	0	0	0		0	0		0	0	0			
85181000	传声器(麦克风)及其座架	10	0	0	0	0	0	0	0	0	0	0		0	5	0	0	0	0	0		0
85182100	单喇叭音箱	10	0	0	0	0	0	0	0	0	0	0		1	5	0	0	0	0	0		
85182200	多喇叭音箱	10	0	0	0	0	0	0	0	0	0	0		1	5	0	0	5	0	0		
85184000	音频扩大器	12	0	0	0	0	0	0	0	0	0	0		1.2	6	0	0	6	2.4	0		0
85185000	电气扩音机组	10	0	0	0	0	0	0	0	0	0	0		0	5	0	0	0	0			
85189000	税号85.18所列货品的零件	10.5	0	0	0	0	0	0	0	0	0	0		0	5	0	0	0	2.1	0		0
85192000	用硬币、钞票、银行卡、代币使其工作的声音录放设备	20	0	0	0	0	0	0	0	0	0	0	16.4	0	16.4	0	0	10	4			
85193000	转盘（唱机唱盘）	30	0	0	0	0	0	0	0	0	0	0		0		0	0	15	6			
85195000	电话应答机	0																				
85198111	不带录音功能的盒式磁带型声音重放装置，编辑节目用放声机除外	17	0	0	0	0	0	0	0	0	0	0		0	13.6	0	0	8.5	3.4			
85198112	装有声音重放装置的盒式磁带型录音机	30	0	0	0	0	0	0	0	0	0	0		0		0	0	15	6			
85198119	其他使用磁性媒体的声音录放机	20	0	0	0	0	0	0	0	0	0	0	16.4	0	16.4	0	0	10	4			
85198121	不带录音功能的激光唱机	30	0	0	0	0	0	0	0	0	0	0	26	0	26	0	0	15	6			
85198129	使用光学媒体的其他声音录放装置	20	0	0	0	0	0	0	0	0	0	0	16.4	0	16	0	0	10	4			
85198131	闪速存储器型声音录放机	20	0	0	0	0	0	0	0	0	0	0		2		0	0	10	4			
85198139	使用半导体媒体的其他声音录放装置	20	0	0	0	0	0	0	0	0	0	0	16.4	0	16.4	0	0	10	4			
85198910	不带录制装置的其他唱机，不论是否带有扬声器	30	0	0	0	0	0	0	0	0	0	0		0		0	0	15	6			
85198990	其他声音录制或重放设备	20	0	0	0	0	0	0	0	0	0	0	16.4	0	16	0	0	10	4			
85211011	广播级录像机	30	0	0	0	0	0	0	0	0	0	0	(1)	0	(1)	0	0	15	6			
85211019	其他磁带录像机	30	0	0	0	0	0	0	0	0	0	0	(2)	0	(2)	0	0	15	6			
85211020	磁带放像机	30	0	0	0	0	0	0	0	0	0	0	(3)	0	(3)	0	0	15	6			
85219011	视频高密光盘机VCD	20	0	0	0	0	0	0	0	0	0	0	16	0	16	0	0	10	4			
85219012	数字化视频光盘机DVD	20	0	0	0	0	0	0	0	0	0	0	16	0	16	0	0	10	4			
85219019	其他激光视盘放像机	20	0	0	0	0	0	0	0	0	0	0	16	0	16	0	0	10	4			
85219090	其他视频信号录制或重放设备	20	0	0	0	0	0	0	0	0	0	0	16	2	16	0	0	10	4	0		
85221000	拾音头	35	0	0	0	0	0	0	0	0	0	0		0		0	0	17.5	7	0		
85229010	转盘或唱机用零附件	25	0	0	0	0	0	0	0	0	0	0	20	0	20	0	0	12.5	5	0		
85229021	录音机走带机构(机芯)	25	0	0	0	0	0	0	0	0	0	0	22.5	0	22.5	0	0	12.5	5	0		
85229022	磁头	25	0	0	0	0	0	0	0	0	0	0	22.5	0	22.5	0	0	12.5	5	0		
85229023	磁头零件	20	0	0	0	0	0	0	0	0	0	0	18	0	18	0	0	10	4	0		
85229029	盒式磁带录音机或放声机其他零件	30	0	0	0	0	0	0	0	0	0	0	27	0	27	0	0	15	6	0		
85229031	激光视盘机的机芯	30	0	0	0	0	0	0	0	0	0	0	21	0	21	0	0	15	6	0		
85229039	其他视频信号录放设备的零件附件	30	0	0	0	0	0	0	0	0	0	0	21	0	21	0	0	15	6	0		
85229091	车载音频转播器或发射器	20	0	0	0	0	0	0	0	0	0	0	16	0	16	0	0	10	4	0		
85229099	声音录制或重放设备用其他零件	20	0	0	0	0	0	0	0	0	0	0	16	0	16	0	0	10	4	0		
85232110	未录制的磁条卡	17.5	0	0	0	0	0	0	0	0	0	0		0	14	0	0	8.8	3.5	0	0	
85232120	已录制的磁条卡	15	0	0	0	0	0	0	0	0	0	0		0	12	0	0	7.5	3	0	0	
85232928	用于重放声音或图像信息的磁带	10	0	0	0	0	0	0	0	0	0	0		1	5	0	0	0	0	0		
85234910	仅用于重放声音信息的光学媒体	10	0	0	0	0	0	0	0	0	0	0		1	5		0	0	0	0	0	
85238011	已录制的唱片	15	0	0	0	0	0	0	0	0	0	0		0	12	0	0	7.5	3		0	
85258011	特种用途电视摄像机	10	0	0	0	0	0	0	0	0	0	0	9	0	5	0	0	0	0			
85258012	非特种用途的广播级电视摄像机	35	0	0	0	0	0	0	0	0	0	0	(4)	0	(4)	0	0	17.5	7			
85258013	非特种用途的其他电视摄像机	35	0	0	0	0	0	0	0	0	0	0	(4)	0	(4)	0	0	17.5	7	0	0	0
85261010	导航用雷达设备	2	0	0	0	0	0	0	0	0	0	0		0	0		0	0	0			
85261090	其他雷达设备	5	0	0	0	0	0	0	0	0	0	0		0	0		0	0	0			
85269110	机动车辆用	2	0	0	0	0	0	0	0	0	0	0		0	0		0	0	0			
85269190	其他无线电导航设备	2	0	0	0	0	0	0	0	0	0	0		0	0		0	0	0			
85269200	无线电遥控设备	5	0	0	0	0	0	0	0	0	0	0		0	0		0	0	0			
85271200	不需外接电源袖珍盒式磁带收放机	20	0	0	0	0	0	0	0	0	0	0		0		0	0	10	4			
85271300	不需外接电源收录(放)音组合机	15	0	0	0	0	0	0	0	0	0	0		0	12	0	0	7.5	3			
85271900	不需外接电源无线电收音机	15	0	0	0	0	0	0	0	0	0	0		0	12	0	0	7.5	3			
85272100	需外接电源汽车收录(放)音组合机	15	0	0	0	0	0	0	0	0	0	0		0	12	0	0	7.5	3			
85272900	需外接电源汽车用无线电收音机	15	0	0	0	0	0	0	0	0	0	0		0	12	0	0	7.5	3			
85279100	其他收录(放)音组合机	15	0	0	0	0	0	0	0	0	0	0		0	12	0	0	7.5	3			

税则号列	商品名称（简称）	最惠国	东盟										亚太	智利	巴基斯坦	新加坡	新西兰	秘鲁	哥斯达黎加	香港	澳门	台湾
			文	柬	印	老	马	缅	菲	新	泰	越										
85279200	带时钟的收音机	15	0	0	0	0	0	0	0	0	0	0		0	12	0	0	7.5	3			
85279900	其他收音机	27	0	0	0	0	0	0	0	0	0	0		0		0	0	13.5	5.4			
85284910	其他彩色阴极射线管监视器	30	0	0	0	0	0	0	0	0	0	0	26	3	26	0	0	15	6		0	
85284990	单色的阴极射线管监视器	19	0	0	0	0	0	0	0	0	0	0	15.2	1.9	15.2	0	0	9.5	3.8		0	
85285910	其他彩色监视器	30	0	0	0	0	0	0	0	0	0	0	26	3	26	0	0	15			0	
85285990	单色的其他监视器	19	0	0	0	0	0	0	0	0	0	0	15.2	1.9	15.2	0	0	9.5	3.8	0	0	
85286910	其他彩色投影机	30	0	0	0	0	0	0	0	0	0	0	25.5	3	25.5	0	0	15	6	0	0	
85286990	单色的其他投影机	15	0	0	0	0	0	0	0	0	0	0		1.5	12	0	0	7.5	3		0	
85287110	不带显示屏的彩色卫星电视接收机	30											24	3	24		0		6			
85287180	不带显示屏的其他彩色电视接收机	30	0	0	0	0	0	0	0	0	0	0	21	3	21	0	0		6			
85287190	单色的不带视频显示器的电视接收机	15	0	0	0	0	0	0	0	0	0	0		1.5	12	0	0	7.5	3		0	
85287211	其他彩色模拟电视接收机，带阴极射线显像管的	30											21	3	21		0		6			
85287212	其他彩色数字电视接收机，带阴极射线显像管的	30											21	3	21		0		6			
85287219	其他彩色电视接收机，带阴极射线显像管的	30											21	3	21		0		6			
85287221	其他彩色模拟电视接收机，带液晶显示器的	30	20	20	20	20	20	20	20	20	20	20	21	3	21		0				0	
85287222	其他彩色数字电视接收机，带液晶显示器的	30	20	20	20	20	20	20	20	20	20	20	21	3	21		0					
85287229	其他彩色电视接收机，带液晶显示器的	30	20	20	20	20	20	20	20	20	20	20	21	3	21		0				0	
85287231	其他彩色模拟电视接收机，带等离子显示器的	30	20	20	20	20	20	20	20	20	20	20	21	3	21		0				0	
85287232	其他彩色数字电视接收机，带等离子显示器的	30	20	20	20	20	20	20	20	20	20	20	21	3	21		0					
85287239	其他彩色电视接收机，带等离子显示器的	30	20	20	20	20	20	20	20	20	20	20	21	3	21		0				0	
85287291	其他彩色模拟电视接收机	30	12	20	20	20	20	20	12	12	20	20	21	3	21		0	15	6			
85287292	其他彩色数字电视接收机	30	12	20	20	20	20	20	12	12	20	20	21	3	21		0					
85287299	其他彩色电视接收机	30	12	20	20	20	20	20	12	12	20	20	21	3	21		0		6			
85287300	其他单色的电视接收装置	15	0	0	0	0	0	0	0	0	0	0		1.5	12	0	0	7.5	3		0	
85291010	雷达及无线电导航设备天线及零件	1.5	0	0	0	0	0	0	0	0	0	0		0	0		0	0	0	0		
85291090	其他无线电设备天线及其零件	2	0	0	0	0	0	0	0	0	0	0		0	0		0	0	0			
85299041	特种用途电视摄像机、静像视频摄像机及其他视频摄录一体机，数字相机零件	8	0	0	0	0	0	0	0	0	0	0	6.8	0.8	5		0	0	0	0		
85299042	非特种用途的取像模块	12	0	0	0	0	0	0	0	0	0	0	10.8	1.2	5	0	0	6	2.4	0		0
85299049	其他电视摄像机、静像视频摄像机及其他视频摄录一体机、数字相机零件	12	0	0	0	0	0	0	0	0	0	0	10.8	1.2	5	0	0	0	2.4	0		0
85299050	雷达及无线电导航设备零件	1.5	0	0	0	0	0	0	0	0	0	0	1.4	0	0		0	0	0			
85299060	收音机及其组合机的其他零件	15	0	0	0	0	0	0	0	0	0	0	12	1.5	7.5	0	0	7.5	3	0		
85299081	彩色电视接收机用（等离子显像组件及其零件、有机发光二极管显示屏除外）	15	0	0	0	0	0	0	0	0	0	0	12	0	7.5	0	0	7.5				
85299082	等离子显像组件及其零件	15	0	0	0	0	0	0	0	0	0	0	12	0	7.5		0					
85299083	有机发光二极管显示屏	15	0	0	0	0	0	0	0	0	0	0	12	0	7.5	0	0	7.5				
85301000	铁道或电车道用电气信号等设备	10	0	0	0	0	0	0	0	0	0	0		0	5		0	0	0			
85308000	其他用电气信号、安全、交通设备	8	0	0	0	0	0	0	0	0	0	0		0.8	5		0	0	0			
85309000	税号85.30所列设备的零件	8	0	0	0	0	0	0	0	0	0	0		0	5		0	0	0			
85311000	防盗或防火报警器及类似装置	10	0	0	0	0	0	0	0	0	0	0		0	5	0	0	0	0	0		
85318010	蜂鸣器	15	0	0	0	0	0	0	0	0	0	0		0	12	0	0	7.5	3	0		
85318090	其他电气音响或视觉信号装置	10	0	0	0	0	0	0	0	0	0	0		0	5	0	0	0	0	0		
85351000	电路熔断器(电压＞1000V)	14	0	0	0	0	0	0	0	0	0	0		0	11.2	0	0	0	2.8			
85352100	电压＜72.5KV自动断路器	14	0	0	0	0	0	0	0	0	0	0		0	11.2	0	0	0	2.8			
85352910	用于电压在72.5千伏及以上，但不高于220千伏的线路的自动断路器	10	0	0	0	0	0	0	0	0	0	0		0	5		0	0	0			
85352920	用于电压高于220千伏，但不高于750千伏的线路的自动断路器	10	0	0	0	0	0	0	0	0	0	0		0	5		0	0	0			
85352990	其他电压≥72.5KV自动断路器	10	0	0	0	0	0	0	0	0	0	0		0	5		0	0	0			
85353010	用于电压在72.5千伏及以上，但不高于220千伏的线路的隔离开关及断续	10	0	0	0	0	0	0	0	0	0	0		0	5		0	0	0			

税则号列	商品名称（简称）	最惠国	东盟										亚太	智利	巴基斯坦	新加坡	新西兰	秘鲁	哥斯达黎加	香港	澳门	台湾
			文	柬	印	老	马	缅	菲	新	泰	越										
	开关																					
85353020	用于电压高于220千伏，但不高于750千伏的线路的隔离开关及断续开关	10	0	0	0	0	0	0	0	0	0	0		0	5		0	0	0			
85353090	其他隔离开关及断续开关	10	0	0	0	0	0	0	0	0	0	0		0	5		0	0	0			
85354000	避雷器、电压限幅器及电涌抑制器	18	0	0	0	0	0	0	0	0	0	0		0		0	0	9	3.6	0		
85359000	其他＞1000V电路开关等电气装置	10	0	0	0	0	0	0	0	0	0	0	9.5	1	5	0	0	5	0	0		
85361000	熔断器(电压≤1000V)	10	0	0	0	0	0	0	0	0	0	0		0	5	0	0	0	0	0		0
85362000	电压≤1000V自动断路器	9	0	0	0	0	0	0	0	0	0	0		0	5		0	0	0	0		
85363000	电压≤1000V其他电路保护装置	9	0	0	0	0	0	0	0	0	0	0		0	5		0	0	0	0		
85364110	用于电压不超过36伏线路的继电器	10	0	0	0	0	0	0	0	0	0	0		0	5	0	0	0	0			
85364190	用于电压超过36伏，但不超过60伏线路的继电器	10	0	0	0	0	0	0	0	0	0	0		0	5	0	0	0	0			
85364900	电压>60V的继电器	10	0	0	0	0	0	0	0	0	0	0		1	5	0	0	5	0	0		
85366100	电压≤1000V的灯座	10	0	0	0	0	0	0	0	0	0	0		0	5	0	0	0	0			
85367000	光导纤维、光导纤维束或光缆用连接器	8	0	0	0	0	0	0	0	0	0	0		0.8	5		0	0	0	0	0	
85371011	可编程序控制器	5	0	0	0	0	0	0	0	0	0	0	2.5	0.5	0		0	0	0	0		0
85371019	其他数控装置	5	0	0	0	0	0	0	0	0	0	0	2.5	0.5	0		0	0	0	0		0
85371090	其他电力控制或分配的装置	8.4	0	0	0	0	0	0	0	0	0	0	4.2	0.8	0		0	0	0	0	0	
85372010	电压≥500KV高压开关装置	8.4	0	0	0	0	0	0	0	0	0	0	4.2	0.8	0		0	0	0			
85372090	其他电力控制或分配装置	8.4	0	0	0	0	0	0	0	0	0	0	4.2	0.8	0		0	0	0	0		
85381010	子目号8537.2010所列装置的零件	8.4	0	0	0	0	0	0	0	0	0	0	4.2	0.8	0		0	0	0			
85381090	税号85.37货品用的其他盘、板等	7	0	0	0	0	0	0	0	0	0	0	3.5	0.7	0		0	0	0			
85389000	税号85.35、85.36或85.37装置的零件	7	0	0	0	0	0	0	0	0	0	0		0.7	5		0	0	0	0		0
85391000	封闭式聚光灯	10	0	0	0	0	0	0	0	0	0	0		0	5		0	0	0			
85392110	科研、医疗专用卤钨灯	8	0	0	0	0	0	0	0	0	0	0		0.8	5		0	0	0			
85392120	火车、航空器及船舶用卤钨灯	8	0	0	0	0	0	0	0	0	0	0		0.8	5		0	0	0			
85392130	机动车辆用卤钨灯	10	0	0	0	0	0	0	0	0	0	0		1	5		0	0	0			
85392190	其他卤钨灯	10.5	0	0	0	0	0	0	0	0	0	0		1.1		0	0	0	2.1			
85392210	科研、医疗用功率≤200W白炽灯泡	10.5	0	0	0	0	0	0	0	0	0	0		1.1	5	0	0	0	2.1			
85392290	其他用功率≤200W白炽灯泡	5	0	0	0	0	0	0	0	0	0	0		0.5	0		0	0	0			
85392910	科研、医疗专用其他白炽灯泡	5	0	0	0	0	0	0	0	0	0	0		0.5	0		0	0	0			
85392920	火车、航空及船舶用其他白炽灯泡	10.5	0	0	0	0	0	0	0	0	0	0		1.1	5	0	0	0	2.1			
85392930	机动车辆用其他白炽灯泡	5	0	0	0	0	0	0	0	0	0	0		0.5	0		0	0	0			
85392991	电压≤12V未列名的白炽灯泡	12	0	0	0	0	0	0	0	0	0	0		1.2	6	0	0	0	2.4	0		
85392999	其他未列名的白炽灯泡	12	0	0	0	0	0	0	0	0	0	0		1.2	6	0	0	0	2.4			
85393110	科研、医疗专用热阴极荧光灯	8	0	0	0	0	0	0	0	0	0	0		0.8	5		0	0	0			
85393120	火车、航空器、船舶用热阴极荧光灯	8	0	0	0	0	0	0	0	0	0	0		0.8	5		0	0	0			
85393191	紧凑型荧光灯	8	0	0	0	0	0	0	0	0	0	0		0.8	5		0	0	0			
85393199	其他热阴极荧光灯	8	0	0	0	0	0	0	0	0	0	0		0.8	5		0	0	0			
85393230	钠蒸气灯	8	0	0	0	0	0	0	0	0	0	0		0	5		0	0	0			
85393240	汞蒸气灯	8	0	0	0	0	0	0	0	0	0	0		0	5		0	0	0			
85393290	金属卤化物灯	8	0	0	0	0	0	0	0	0	0	0		0	5		0	0	0			
85393910	科研、医疗专用其他放电灯	8	0	0	0	0	0	0	0	0	0	0		0	5		0	0	0			
85393920	火车、航空器、船舶用其他放电灯	8	0	0	0	0	0	0	0	0	0	0		0	5		0	0	0			
85393990	其他用途的其他放电灯管	8	0	0	0	0	0	0	0	0	0	0		0	5		0	0	0		0	0
85394100	弧光灯	8	0	0	0	0	0	0	0	0	0	0		0	5		0	0	0			
85394900	紫外线或红外线灯	8	0	0	0	0	0	0	0	0	0	0		0	5		0	0	0			
85399000	税号85.39所列货品的零件	8	0	0	0	0	0	0	0	0	0	0		0	5		0	0	0			0
85401100	彩色阴极射线电视显像管	12	0	0	0	0	0	0	0	0	0	0		0	6	0	0	0	2.4			
85401200	黑白或单色阴极射线电视显像管	15	0	0	0	0	0	0	0	0	0	0		0	12	0	0	7.5	3			
85402010	电视摄像管	12	0	0	0	0	0	0	0	0	0	0		0	6	0	0	0	2.4			
85402090	变像管、图像增强管及光阴极管	8	0	0	0	0	0	0	0	0	0	0		0	5		0	0	0			
85404010	彩色的数据/图形显示管，屏幕荧光点间距小于0.4毫米	8	0	0	0	0	0	0	0	0	0	0		0	5		0	0	0	0		
85404020	单色的数据/图形显示管	8	0	0	0	0	0	0	0	0	0	0		0	5		0	0	0			
85406010	雷达显示管	6	0	0	0	0	0	0	0	0	0	0		0	5		0	0	0			
85406090	其他阴极射线管	8	0	0	0	0	0	0	0	0	0	0		0	5		0	0	0			
85407100	磁控管	8	0	0	0	0	0	0	0	0	0	0		0	5		0	0	0			
85407910	调速管	8	0	0	0	0	0	0	0	0	0	0		0	5		0	0	0			
85407990	其他微波管	8	0	0	0	0	0	0	0	0	0	0		0	5		0	0	0			

税则号列	商品名称（简称）	最惠国	东盟										亚太	智利	巴基斯坦	新加坡	新西兰	秘鲁	哥斯达黎加	香港	澳门	台湾
			文	柬	印	老	马	缅	菲	新	泰	越										
85408100	接收管或放大管	8	0	0	0	0	0	0	0	0	0	0		0	5		0	0	0			
85408900	其他电子管	8	0	0	0	0	0	0	0	0	0	0		0	5		0	0	0			0
85409110	电视显像管零件	6	0	0	0	0	0	0	0	0	0	0		0	5		0	0	0			
85409120	雷达显示管零件	5	0	0	0	0	0	0	0	0	0	0		0	0		0	0	0			
85409190	其他阴极射线管零件	8	0	0	0	0	0	0	0	0	0	0		0	5		0	0	0			
85409910	电视摄像管零件	8	0	0	0	0	0	0	0	0	0	0		0	5		0	0	0			
85409990	其他热电子管、冷阴极管零件	8	0	0	0	0	0	0	0	0	0	0		0	5		0	0	0			
85431000	其他粒子加速器	5	0	0	0	0	0	0	0	0	0	0		0	0		0	0	0			
85432010	输出信号频率＜1500MHZ的通用信号发生器	15	0	0	0	0	0	0	0	0	0	0		1.5	12	0	0	7.5	3			0
85432090	输出信号频率≥1500MHZ的通用信号发生器	8	0	0	0	0	0	0	0	0	0	0		0.8	5		0	0	0			0
85437093	电篱网激发器	10	0	0	0	0	0	0	0	0	0	0		0	5	0	0	0	0			
85441100	铜制绕组电线	10	0	0	0	0	0	0	0	0	0	0	7	0	5	0	0	0	0	0	0	0
85441900	其他绕组电线	20	0	0	0	0	0	0	0	0	0	0		0		0	0	10	4			
85442000	同轴电缆及其他同轴电导体	10	0	0	0	0	0	0	0	0	0	0	9	1	5	0	0	5	0			0
85443020	机动车辆用点火布线组及其他布线组	10												0			0	0	0			
85443090	车辆用点火布线组	5												0			0	0	0			
85444921	1000V≥耐压＞80V无接头电缆	6	0	0	0	0	0	0	0	0	0	0	4.2	0.6	0		0	0	0	0		
85444929	1000V≥耐压＞80V无接头电导体	12	0	0	0	0	0	0	0	0	0	0	8.4	1.2	5	0	0	0	2.4	0	0	0
85446012	额定电压不超过35千伏的电缆	10	0	0	0	0	0	0	0	0	0	0	8.9	1	5	0	0	0	0	0		
85446013	额定电压超过35千伏，但不超过110千伏的电缆	8.4	0	0	0	0	0	0	0	0	0	0	8	0.8	5		0	0	0	0		
85446014	额定电压超过110千伏，但不超过220千伏的电缆	8.4	0	0	0	0	0	0	0	0	0	0	8	0.8	5		0	0	0	0		
85446019	其他额定电压超过1000伏的电缆	8.4	0	0	0	0	0	0	0	0	0	0	8	0.8	5		0	0	0	0		
85446090	耐压＞1KV的其他电导体	21	0	0	0	0	0	0	0	0	0	0	20	2.1	20	0	0	10.5	4.2	0		
85451100	炉用碳电极	8	0	0	0	0	0	0	0	0	0	0		0	5		0	0	0			
85451900	其他碳电极	10.5	0	0	0	0	0	0	0	0	0	0		0	5	0	0	0	2.1			
85452000	碳刷	10.5	0	0	0	0	0	0	0	0	0	0		1.1	5	0	0	0	2.1			
85459000	灯碳棒、电池碳棒及其他石墨制品	10.5	0	0	0	0	0	0	0	0	0	0		0	5	0	0	0	2.1			
85461000	玻璃制绝缘子	10.5	0	0	0	0	0	0	0	0	0	0		0	5	0	0	0	2.1			
85462010	输变电线路绝缘瓷套管	6	0	0	0	0	0	0	0	0	0	0		0.6	5		0	0	0			
85462090	其他陶瓷制绝缘子	12	0	0	0	0	0	0	0	0	0	0		1.2	6	0	0	6	2.4			
85469000	其他材料制绝缘子	10	0	0	0	0	0	0	0	0	0	0		0	5	0	0	0	0			
85471000	陶瓷制绝缘零件	8	0	0	0	0	0	0	0	0	0	0		0	5		0	0	0			
85472000	塑料制绝缘零件	8	0	0	0	0	0	0	0	0	0	0		0	5		0	0	0	0		
85479010	内衬绝缘材料的贱金属导管及其接头	10	0	0	0	0	0	0	0	0	0	0		0	5	0	0	0	0			
85479090	其他材料制绝缘配件	8	0	0	0	0	0	0	0	0	0	0		0	5		0	0	0			
85481000	电池废碎料及废电池	8	0	0	0	0	0	0	0	0	0	0		0.8	5		0	0	0			
85489000	85章其他未列名的电气零件	12	0	0	0	0	0	0	0	0	0	0		0	6	0	0	0	2.4			
86011011	微机控制的外部直流电动铁道机车	3	0	0	0	0	0	0	0	0	0	0		0	0		0	0	0			
86011019	由外部直流电驱动的其他铁道机车	3	0	0	0	0	0	0	0	0	0	0		0	0		0	0	0			
86011020	由外部交流电驱动的铁道机车	3	0	0	0	0	0	0	0	0	0	0		0	0		0	0	0			
86011090	由其他外部电力驱动的铁道机车	3	0	0	0	0	0	0	0	0	0	0		0	0		0	0	0			
86012000	由蓄电池驱动的铁道电力机车	3	0	0	0	0	0	0	0	0	0	0		0	0		0	0	0			
86021010	微机控制的柴油电力铁道机车	3	0	0	0	0	0	0	0	0	0	0		0	0		0	0	0			
86021090	其他柴油电力铁道机车	3	0	0	0	0	0	0	0	0	0	0		0	0		0	0	0			
86029000	其他铁道机车及机车煤水车	3	0	0	0	0	0	0	0	0	0	0		0	0		0	0	0			
86031000	由外电力驱动铁道及电车道用机动客车、货车、敞车	3	0	0	0	0	0	0	0	0	0	0		0	0		0	0	0			
86039000	其他铁道及电车道用机动客车、货车、敞车	3	0	0	0	0	0	0	0	0	0	0		0	0		0	0	0			
86040011	隧道限界检查车	3	0	0	0	0	0	0	0	0	0	0		0	0		0	0	0			
86040012	钢轨在线打磨列车	3	0	0	0	0	0	0	0	0	0	0		0	0		0	0	0			
86040019	铁道及电车道用其他检验车及查道车	5	0	0	0	0	0	0	0	0	0	0		0.5	0		0	0	0			
86040091	电气化接触网架线机(轨行式)	5	0	0	0	0	0	0	0	0	0	0		0.5	0		0	0	0			
86040099	铁道及电车道用其他维修或服务车	7	0	0	0	0	0	0	0	0	0	0		0.7	5		0	0	0			
86050010	铁道及电车道用非机动客车	5	0	0	0	0	0	0	0	0	0	0		0	0		0	0	0			
86050090	铁道及电车道用其他非机动客车	5	0	0	0	0	0	0	0	0	0	0		0	0		0	0	0			
86061000	铁道及电车道用非机动油罐货车及类	5	0	0	0	0	0	0	0	0	0	0		0	0		0	0	0			

税则号列	商品名称（简称）	最惠国	东盟										亚太	智利	巴基斯坦	新加坡	新西兰	秘鲁	哥斯达黎加	香港	澳门	台湾
			文	柬	印	老	马	缅	菲	新	泰	越										
	似车																					
86063000	铁道及电车道用非机动自卸货车	5	0	0	0	0	0	0	0	0	0	0		0	0		0	0	0			
86069100	铁道及电车道用非机动带篷及封闭货车	5	0	0	0	0	0	0	0	0	0	0		0	0		0	0	0			
86069200	铁道及电车道用非机动厢高＞60cm敞篷货车	5	0	0	0	0	0	0	0	0	0	0		0	0		0	0	0			
86069900	税号86.06所列其他未列名非机动车	5	0	0	0	0	0	0	0	0	0	0		0	0		0	0	0			
86071100	铁道及电车道机车的驾驶转向架	3	0	0	0	0	0	0	0	0	0	0		0	0		0	0	0			
86071200	铁道及电车道机车非驾驶转向架	3	0	0	0	0	0	0	0	0	0	0		0	0		0	0	0			
86071910	铁道及电车道机车用车轴	3	0	0	0	0	0	0	0	0	0	0		0	0		0	0	0			
86071990	转向轮及其零件	3	0	0	0	0	0	0	0	0	0	0		0	0		0	0	0			
86072100	铁道及电车道机车用空气制动器及其零件	3	0	0	0	0	0	0	0	0	0	0		0	0		0	0	0			
86072900	铁道及电车道机车用非空气制动器	3	0	0	0	0	0	0	0	0	0	0		0	0		0	0	0			
86073000	铁道及电车道机车用钩、联结器、缓冲器及其零件	3	0	0	0	0	0	0	0	0	0	0		0	0		0	0	0			
86079100	铁道及电车道机车用其他零件	3	0	0	0	0	0	0	0	0	0	0		0	0		0	0	0			
86079900	铁道及电车道非机车用其他零件	3	0	0	0	0	0	0	0	0	0	0		0	0		0	0	0			
86080010	轨道自动计轴设备	3	0	0	0	0	0	0	0	0	0	0		0	0		0	0	0			
86080090	铁道及电车道轨道固定装置及附件	4	0	0	0	0	0	0	0	0	0	0		0	0		0	0	0			
86090011	20英尺保温式集装箱	10.5	0	0	0	0	0	0	0	0	0	0		1.1	5	0	0	0	2.1			
86090012	20英尺罐式集装箱	10.5	0	0	0	0	0	0	0	0	0	0		1.1	5	0	0	0	2.1			
86090019	20英尺其他集装箱	10.5	0	0	0	0	0	0	0	0	0	0		1.1	5	0	0	0	2.1			
86090021	40英尺保温式集装箱	10.5	0	0	0	0	0	0	0	0	0	0		1.1	5	0	0	0	2.1			
86090022	40英尺罐式集装箱	10.5	0	0	0	0	0	0	0	0	0	0		1.1	5	0	0	0	2.1			
86090029	40英尺其他集装箱	10.5	0	0	0	0	0	0	0	0	0	0		1.1	5	0	0	0	2.1			
86090030	45、48、53英尺的集装箱	10.5	0	0	0	0	0	0	0	0	0	0		1.1	5	0	0	0	2.1			
86090090	其他集装箱	10.5	0	0	0	0	0	0	0	0	0	0		1.1	5	0	0	0	2.1			
87011000	手扶拖拉机	9	0	0	0	0	0	0	0	0	0	0		0	5		0	0	0			
87012000	半挂车用的公路牵引车	6												0			0		0			
87013000	履带式牵引车、拖拉机	6	0	0	0	0	0	0	0	0	0	0		0	5		0	0	0			
87019011	轮式拖拉机	8	0	0	0	0	0	0	0	0	0	0		0	5		0	0	0			
87019019	其他拖拉机	8	0	0	0	0	0	0	0	0	0	0		0	5		0	0	0			
87019090	其他牵引车	8	0	0	0	0	0	0	0	0	0	0		0	5		0	0	0			
87021020	机坪客车	4	0	0	0	0	0	0	0	0	0	0		0	0		0	0	0			
87021091	≥30座大型客车(柴油型)	25												0			0		5			
87021092	≥20座，但≤29座的客车	25												0			0		5			
87021093	≥10座，但≤19座的客车	25												0			0		5			
87029010	≥30座大型客车(非柴油型)	25	20	20	20	20	20	20	20	20	20	20		0			0		5			
87029020	≥20座，但≤29座的客车(非柴油型)	25	20	20	20	20	20	20	20	20	20	20		0			0		5			
87029030	≥10座，但≤19座的客车(非柴油型)	25	20	20	20	20	20	20	20	20	20	20		0			0	12.5	5			
87031011	全地形车	25	0	0	0	0	0	0	0	0	0	0		0		0	0	12.5	5			
87031019	其他高尔夫球车及类似车辆	25	0	0	0	0	0	0	0	0	0	0		0		0	0	12.5	5			
87031090	雪地行走专用车	25	0	0	0	0	0	0	0	0	0	0		0		0	0	12.5	5			
87032130	排气量≤1000ml的小轿车	25											22.5	0	22.5		0		5			
87032140	排气量≤1000ml的越野车（4轮驱动）	25											22.5	0	22.5		0		5			
87032150	排气量≤1000ml的≤9座的小客车	25											22.5	0	22.5		0		5			
87032190	排气量≤1000ml的其他车辆	25											22.5	0	22.5		0		5			
87032230	1L＜排气量≤1.5L的小轿车	25											22.5	0	22.5		0		5			
87032240	1L＜排气量≤1.5L的越野车	25											22.5	0	22.5		0		5			
87032250	1L＜排气量≤1.5L，≤9座的小客车	25											22.5	0	22.5		0		5			
87032290	1L＜排气量≤1.5L的其他车辆	25											22.5	0	22.5		0		5			
87032341	1.5L＜排气量≤2L的小轿车	25											22.5	0	22.5		0		5			
87032342	1.5L＜排气量≤2L的越野车	25											22.5	0	22.5		0		5			
87032343	1.5L＜排气量≤2L，≤9座的小客车	25											22.5	0	22.5		0		5			
87032349	1.5L＜排气量≤2L的其他车辆	25											22.5	0	22.5		0		5			
87032351	2L＜排气量≤2.5L的小轿车	25											22.5	0	22.5		0		5			
87032352	2L＜排气量≤2.5L的越野车	25											22.5	0	22.5		0		5			
87032353	2L＜排气量≤2.5L，≤9座的小客车	25											22.5	0	22.5		0		5			
87032359	2L＜排气量≤2.5L的其他车辆	25											22.5	0	22.5		0		5			
87032361	2.5L＜排气量≤3L的小轿车	25											22.5	0	22.5		0		5			

税则号列	商品名称（简称）	最惠国	东盟										亚太	智利	巴基斯坦	新加坡	新西兰	秘鲁	哥斯达黎加	香港	澳门	台湾
			文	柬	印	老	马	缅	菲	新	泰	越										
87032362	2.5L＜排气量≤3L的越野车	25	0	0	0	0	0	0	0	0	0	0	22.5	0	22.5	0	0		5			
87032363	2.5L＜排气量≤3L，≤9座的小客车	25	0	0	0	0	0	0	0	0	0	0	22.5	0	22.5	0	0		5			
87032369	2.5L＜排气量≤3L的其他车辆	25	0	0	0	0	0	0	0	0	0	0	22.5	0	22.5	0	0		5			
87032411	3L＜排气量≤4L的小轿车	25											22.5	0	22.5		0		5			
87032412	3L＜排气量≤4L的越野车	25											22.5	0	22.5		0		5			
87032413	3L＜排气量≤4L，≤9座的小客车	25											22.5	0	22.5		0		5			
87032419	3L＜排气量≤4L的其他车辆	25											22.5	0	22.5		0		5			
87032421	排气量>4L的小轿车	25											22.5	0	22.5		0		5			
87032422	排气量>4L的越野车	25											22.5	0	22.5		0		5			
87032423	排气量>4L，≤9座的小客车	25											22.5	0	22.5		0		5			
87032429	排气量>4L的其他车辆	25											22.5	0	22.5		0		5			
87033111	排气量≤1L的柴油型小轿车	25												0			0		5			
87033119	排气量≤1L的柴油型其他车辆	25	0	0	0	0	0	0	0	0	0	0		0		0	0	12.5	5			
87033121	1L＜排气量≤1.5L的柴油型小轿车	25												0			0		5			
87033122	1L＜排气量≤1.5L的柴油型越野车	25												0			0		5			
87033123	1L＜排气量≤1.5L，≤9座的柴油型小客车	25												0			0		5			
87033129	1L＜排气量≤1.5L的柴油型其他车辆	25	0	0	0	0	0	0	0	0	0	0		0		0	0	12.5	5			
87033211	1.5L＜排气量≤2L的柴油型小轿车	25											22.5	0	22.5		0		5			
87033212	1.5L＜排气量≤2L的柴油型越野车	25											22.5	0	22.5		0		5			
87033213	1.5L＜排气量≤2L，≤9座的柴油型小客车	25											22.5	0	22.5		0		5			
87033219	1.5L＜排气量≤2L的柴油型其他车辆	25											22.5	0	22.5		0		5			
87033221	2L＜排气量≤2.5L的柴油型小轿车	25											22.5	0	22.5		0		5			
87033222	2L＜排气量≤2.5L的柴油型越野车	25											22.5	0	22.5		0		5			
87033223	2L＜排气量≤2.5L，≤9座的柴油型小客车	25											22.5	0	22.5		0		5			
87033229	2L＜排气量≤2.5L的柴油型其他车辆	25											22.5	0	22.5		0		5			
87033311	2.5L＜排气量≤3L的柴油型小轿车	25	0	0	0	0	0	0	0	0	0	0	22.5	0	22.5	0	0		5			
87033312	2.5L＜排气量≤3L的柴油型越野车	25	0	0	0	0	0	0	0	0	0	0	22.5	0	22.5	0	0		5			
87033313	2.5L＜排气量≤3L，≤9座的柴油型小客车	25	0	0	0	0	0	0	0	0	0	0	22.5	0	22.5	0	0		5			
87033319	2.5L＜排气量≤3L的柴油型其他车辆	25	0	0	0	0	0	0	0	0	0	0	22.5	0	22.5	0	0		5			
87033321	3L＜排气量≤4L的柴油型小轿车	25	0	0	0	0	0	0	0	0	0	0	22.5	0	22.5	0	0		5			
87033322	3L＜排气量≤4L的柴油型越野车	25	0	0	0	0	0	0	0	0	0	0	22.5	0	22.5	0	0		5			
87033323	3L＜排气量≤4L，≤9座的柴油型小客车	25	0	0	0	0	0	0	0	0	0	0	22.5	0	22.5	0	0		5			
87033329	3L＜排气量≤4L的柴油型其他车辆	25	0	0	0	0	0	0	0	0	0	0	22.5	0	22.5	0	0		5			
87033361	排气量>4L的柴油型小轿车	25	0	0	0	0	0	0	0	0	0	0	22.5	0	22.5	0	0		5			
87033362	排气量>4L的柴油型越野车	25	0	0	0	0	0	0	0	0	0	0	22.5	0	22.5	0	0		5			
87033363	排气量>4L，≤9座的柴油型小客车	25	0	0	0	0	0	0	0	0	0	0	22.5	0	22.5	0	0		5			
87033369	排气量>4L的柴油型其他车辆	25	0	0	0	0	0	0	0	0	0	0	22.5	0	22.5	0	0		5			
87039000	装有压燃式内燃发动机的其他载人机动车辆	25	0	0	0	0	0	0	0	0	0	0	22.5	0	22.5	0	0	12.5	5			
87041030	非公路用电动轮货运自卸车	6	0	0	0	0	0	0	0	0	0	0		0	5		0	0	0			
87041090	其他非公路用货运自卸车	6	0	0	0	0	0	0	0	0	0	0		0	5		0	0	0			
87042100	柴油型其他小型货车	25												0			0		5			
87042230	柴油型其他中型货车	20											18	0	18		0	10	4			
87042240	柴油型其他重型货车	20											18	0	18		0	10	4			
87042300	柴油型的其他超重型货车	15												0			0		3			
87043100	汽油型≤5吨的其他货车	25	20	20	20	20	20	20	20	20	20	20		2.5			0		5			
87043230	5吨＜汽油型≤8吨的其他货车	20												0			0	10	4			
87043240	汽油型＞8吨的其他货车	20												0			0	10	4			
87049000	装有其他发动机的货车	25	0	0	0	0	0	0	0	0	0	0		0		0	0	12.5	5			
87051021	最大起重重量≤50吨的全路面汽车起重车	15	0	0	0	0	0	0	0	0	0	0		0	12	0	0	7.5	3			
87051022	50吨＜最大起重重量≤100吨的全路面汽车起重车	10	0	0	0	0	0	0	0	0	0	0		0	5	0	0	0	0			
87051023	最大起重重量＞100吨的全路面汽车起重车	10	0	0	0	0	0	0	0	0	0	0		0	5	0	0	0	0			
87051091	最大起重重量≤50吨的其他汽车起重车	15	0	0	0	0	0	0	0	0	0	0		0	12	0	0	7.5	3			
87051092	50吨＜最大起重重量≤100吨的其他	10	0	0	0	0	0	0	0	0	0	0		0	5	0	0	0	0			

税则号列	商品名称（简称）	最惠国	东盟										亚太	智利	巴基斯坦	新加坡	新西兰	秘鲁	哥斯达黎加	香港	澳门	台湾
			文	柬	印	老	马	缅	菲	新	泰	越										
	汽车起重车																					
87051093	最大起重重量＞100吨的其他汽车起重车	10	0	0	0	0	0	0	0	0	0	0		0	5	0	0	0	0			
87052000	机动钻探车	12	0	0	0	0	0	0	0	0	0	0		0	6	0	0	0	2.4			
87053010	装有云梯的救火车	3	0	0	0	0	0	0	0	0	0	0		0	0		0	0	0			
87053090	其他机动救火车	3	0	0	0	0	0	0	0	0	0	0		0	0		0	0	0			
87054000	机动混凝土搅拌车	15	0	0	0	0	0	0	0	0	0	0	13.5	0	7.5	0	0	7.5	3			
87059010	无线电通信车	9	0	0	0	0	0	0	0	0	0	0	8.1	0	5	0	0	0	0			
87059020	机动放射线检查车	9	0	0	0	0	0	0	0	0	0	0	8.1	0	5		0	0	0			
87059030	机动环境监测车	12	0	0	0	0	0	0	0	0	0	0	10.8	0	5	0	0	0	2.4			
87059040	机动医疗车	12	0	0	0	0	0	0	0	0	0	0	10.8	0	5	0	0	0	2.4			
87059051	航空电源车(频率为400赫兹)	12	0	0	0	0	0	0	0	0	0	0	10.8	0	5	0	0	0	2.4			
87059059	其他机动电源车	12	0	0	0	0	0	0	0	0	0	0	10.8	0	5	0	0	0	2.4			
87059060	飞机加油车、调温车、除冰车	12	0	0	0	0	0	0	0	0	0	0	10.8	0	5	0	0	0	2.4			
87059070	道路(包括跑道)扫雪车	12	0	0	0	0	0	0	0	0	0	0	10.8	0	5	0	0	0	2.4			
87059080	石油测井车、压裂车、混沙车	12	0	0	0	0	0	0	0	0	0	0	10.8	0	5	0	0	0	2.4			
87059091	混凝土泵车	12	0	0	0	0	0	0	0	0	0	0	10.8	0	5	0	0	0	2.4			
87059099	其他特殊用途的机动车辆	12	0	0	0	0	0	0	0	0	0	0	10.8	0	5	0	0	0	2.4			
87060010	非公路用货运自卸车底盘	8	0	0	0	0	0	0	0	0	0	0		0	5		0	0	0			
87060021	车辆总重量≥14吨的货车底盘	10												0			0		0			
87060022	车辆总重量＜14吨的货车底盘	10												0			0	0	0			
87060030	大型客车底盘	20	0	0	0	0	0	0	0	0	0	0		0		0	0		4			
87060040	汽车起重机底盘	20	0	0	0	0	0	0	0	0	0	0		0		0	0	10	4			
87060090	其他机动车辆底盘	10	0	0	0	0	0	0	0	0	0	0		0		0	0	0	0			
87071000	税号87.03所列车辆用车身(含驾驶室)	10	0	0	0	0	0	0	0	0	0	0		0		0	0	0	0			
87079010	税号8702.1092、.1093、.9020及.9030所列车辆用车身	10	0	0	0	0	0	0	0	0	0	0	9	0	5	0	0	0	0			
87079090	其他车辆用车身(含驾驶室)	10	0	0	0	0	0	0	0	0	0	0	9	0	5	0	0	0	0			
87081000	缓冲器(保险杠)及其零件	10	0	0	0	0	0	0	0	0	0	0	9.6	0	5	0	0	0	0			0
87082100	座椅安全带	10	0	0	0	0	0	0	0	0	0	0		0	5	0	0	0	0		0	
87082930	车窗玻璃升降器	10											9	0	9		0	0	0	0		0
87082941	汽车电动天窗	10	0	0	0	0	0	0	0	0	0	0	9	0	5	0	0	0	0	0		0
87082942	汽车手动天窗	10	0	0	0	0	0	0	0	0	0	0	9	0	5	0	0	0	0	0		0
87082951	侧围	10	0	0	0	0	0	0	0	0	0	0	9	0	5	0	0	0	0			0
87082952	车门	10	0	0	0	0	0	0	0	0	0	0	9	0	5	0	0	0	0			0
87082953	发动机罩盖	10	0	0	0	0	0	0	0	0	0	0	9	0	5	0	0	0	0			0
87082954	前围	10	0	0	0	0	0	0	0	0	0	0	9	0	5	0	0	0	0			0
87082955	行李箱盖（或背门）	10	0	0	0	0	0	0	0	0	0	0	9	0	5	0	0	0	0			0
87082956	后围	10	0	0	0	0	0	0	0	0	0	0	9	0	5	0	0	0	0			0
87082957	翼子板（或叶子板）	10	0	0	0	0	0	0	0	0	0	0	9	0	5	0	0	0	0			0
87082959	车身的其他覆盖件	10	0	0	0	0	0	0	0	0	0	0	9	0	5	0	0	0	0			0
87082990	车身的未列名零部件	10	0	0	0	0	0	0	0	0	0	0	9	0	5	0	0	0	0			0
87083010	装在蹄片上的制动摩擦片	10	0	0	0	0	0	0	0	0	0	0		0	5	0	0	5	0			
87083021	牵引车、拖拉机、非公路自卸车用防抱死制动系统（ABS）	6	0	0	0	0	0	0	0	0	0	0	5.4	0	0		0	0	0			
87083029	其他车辆用防抱死制动系统（ABS）	10											9	0	9		0	0	0			
87083091	牵引车、拖拉机用制动器及其零件	6	0	0	0	0	0	0	0	0	0	0	5.4	0	0		0	0	0			
87083092	大型客车用制动器及其零件	10											9	0	9		0	0	0			
87083093	非公路自卸车用制动器及其零件	6	0	0	0	0	0	0	0	0	0	0	5.4	0	0		0	0	0			
87083094	柴、汽油轻型货车用制动器及零件	10											9	0	9		0	0	0			
87083095	柴油型重型货车用制动器及其零件	10	0	0	0	0	0	0	0	0	0	0	9	0	5	0	0	0	0			
87083096	特种车用制动器及其零件	10	0	0	0	0	0	0	0	0	0	0	9	0	5	0	0	0	0			
87083099	其他未列名机动车辆用制动器及零件	10											9	0	9		0	0	0			
87084010	牵引车、拖拉机用变速箱及零件	6	0	0	0	0	0	0	0	0	0	0		0	5		0	0	0			0
87084020	大型客车用变速箱及零件	10												0			0		0			0
87084030	非公路自卸车用变速箱及零件	6	0	0	0	0	0	0	0	0	0	0		0	5		0		0			0
87084040	柴、汽油轻型货车用变速箱及零件	10												0			0		0			0
87084050	其他柴油型重型货车用变速箱及零件	10												0			0		0			0
87084060	特种车用变速箱及零件	10	0	0	0	0	0	0	0	0	0	0		0	5	0	0	0	0			0
87084091	自动换档变速箱及零件	10												0			0		0			

税则号列	商品名称（简称）	最惠国	东盟										亚太	智利	巴基斯坦	新加坡	新西兰	秘鲁	哥斯达黎加	香港	澳门	台湾
			文	柬	印	老	马	缅	菲	新	泰	越										
87084099	未列名机动车辆用变速箱及零件	10	0	0	0	0	0	0	0	0	0	0		0		0	0		0			0
87085071	牵引车、拖拉机用驱动桥及零件	6	0	0	0	0	0	0	0	0	0	0	5.4	0	0		0	0	0			
87085072	其他大型客车用驱动桥及零件	10											9	0	9		0	0	0			
87085073	非公路自卸车用驱动桥及零件	6	0	0	0	0	0	0	0	0	0	0	5.4	0	0		0	0	0			
87085074	柴、汽油型轻型货车用驱动桥及零件	10											9	0	9		0	0	0			
87085075	其他柴油型重型货车用驱动桥及零件	10											9	0	9		0	0	0			
87085076	特种车用驱动桥及零件	10	0	0	0	0	0	0	0	0	0	0	9	0	5	0	0	0	0			
87085079	未列名机动车辆用驱动桥及零件	10											9	0	9		0	0	0			
87085081	牵引车、拖拉机用非驱动桥及零件	6	0	0	0	0	0	0	0	0	0	0		0	5		0	0	0			
87085082	座位≥30客车用非驱动桥及零件	15	0	0	0	0	0	0	0	0	0	0		0	9.7	0	0	7.5	3			
87085083	非公路自卸车用非驱动桥及零件	6	0	0	0	0	0	0	0	0	0	0		0	5		0	0	0			
87085084	柴、汽油轻货车用非驱动桥及零件	10	0	0	0	0	0	0	0	0	0	0		0	5	0	0	0	0			
87085085	柴油重型货车用非驱动桥及零件	10	0	0	0	0	0	0	0	0	0	0		0	5	0	0	0	0			
87085086	特种车用非驱动桥及其零件	10	0	0	0	0	0	0	0	0	0	0		0	5	0	0	0	0			
87085089	未列名机动车辆用非驱动桥及零件	10	0	0	0	0	0	0	0	0	0	0		0	5	0	0	0	0			
87087010	牵引车及拖拉机用车轮及其零附件	6	0	0	0	0	0	0	0	0	0	0		0	5		0	0	0			0
87087020	大型客车用车轮及其零附件	10	0	0	0	0	0	0	0	0	0	0		0	5	0	0	0	0			0
87087030	非公路货运自卸车用车轮及其零件	6	0	0	0	0	0	0	0	0	0	0		0	5		0	0	0			0
87087040	中小型货车用车轮及其零件	10	0	0	0	0	0	0	0	0	0	0		0	5	0	0	0	0			0
87087050	大型货车用车轮及其零件	10	0	0	0	0	0	0	0	0	0	0		0	5	0	0	0	0			0
87087060	特种车用车轮及其零件	10	0	0	0	0	0	0	0	0	0	0		0	5	0	0	0	0			0
87087091	铝合金制的车轮及其零件、附件	10	0	0	0	0	0	0	0	0	0	0		0	5	0	0	0	0			0
87087099	其他车轮及其零件、附件	10	0	0	0	0	0	0	0	0	0	0		0	5	0	0	0	0			0
87088010	税号87.03所列车辆用的悬挂减震器及零件	10	0	0	0	0	0	0	0	0	0	0	9	0	5	0	0	0	0			
87088090	机动车辆用的其他悬挂减震器及零件	10	0	0	0	0	0	0	0	0	0	0	9	0	5	0	0	0	0			
87089110	水箱散热器	10	0	0	0	0	0	0	0	0	0	0		0	5	0	0	0	0			
87089120	机油冷却器	10	0	0	0	0	0	0	0	0	0	0		0	5	0	0	0	0			
87089190	其他散热器及其零件	10	0	0	0	0	0	0	0	0	0	0		0	5	0	0	0	0			
87089200	机动车辆的消声器及排气管及零件	10	0	0	0	0	0	0	0	0	0	0		0	5	0	0	0	0			
87089310	牵引车、拖拉机用离合器及其零件	6	0	0	0	0	0	0	0	0	0	0		0	5		0	0	0			
87089320	座位≥30客车用离合器及其零件	10	0	0	0	0	0	0	0	0	0	0		0	5	0	0	0	0			
87089330	非公路自卸车用离合器及其零件	6	0	0	0	0	0	0	0	0	0	0		0	5		0	0	0			
87089340	柴、汽油轻型货车用离合器及零件	10	0	0	0	0	0	0	0	0	0	0		0	5	0	0	0	0			
87089350	总重≥14吨柴油货车离合器及零件	10	0	0	0	0	0	0	0	0	0	0		0	5	0	0	0	0			
87089360	特种车用的离合器及其零件	10	0	0	0	0	0	0	0	0	0	0		0	5	0	0	0	0			
87089390	未列名机动车辆用离合器及其零件	10	0	0	0	0	0	0	0	0	0	0		0	5	0	0	0	0			
87089410	牵引车、拖拉机用转向盘、转向柱及转向器及零件	6	0	0	0	0	0	0	0	0	0	0		0	5		0	0	0			
87089420	大型客车用转向盘、转向柱及转向器及零件	10	0	0	0	0	0	0	0	0	0	0		0	5	0	0	0	0			
87089430	非公路自卸车用转向盘、转向柱及转向器及零件	6	0	0	0	0	0	0	0	0	0	0		0	5		0	0	0			
87089440	柴、汽油轻货车用转向盘、转向柱及转向器及零件	10	0	0	0	0	0	0	0	0	0	0		0	5	0	0	0	0			
87089450	柴油型重型货车用转向盘、转向柱及转向器及零件	10	0	0	0	0	0	0	0	0	0	0		0	5	0	0	0	0			
87089460	特种车用转向盘、转向柱及转向器及零件	10	0	0	0	0	0	0	0	0	0	0		0	5	0	0	0	0			
87089490	未列名机动车辆用转向盘、转向柱及转向器及零件	10	0	0	0	0	0	0	0	0	0	0		0	5	0	0	0	0			
87089500	机动车辆的安全气囊装置	10											9	0	9		0		0	0		
87089910	牵引车及拖拉机用其他零附件	6	0	0	0	0	0	0	0	0	0	0		0	5		0	0	0			
87089921	税号8702.1091及8702.9010所列车辆用车架	25	0	0	0	0	0	0	0	0	0	0		0		0	0	12.5	5			
87089929	大型客车用其他零附件	25	0	0	0	0	0	0	0	0	0	0		0		0	0	12.5	5			
87089931	税号8704.1030及8704.1090所列车辆用车架	6	0	0	0	0	0	0	0	0	0	0		0	5		0	0	0			
87089939	非公路货运自卸车用其他零附件	6	0	0	0	0	0	0	0	0	0	0		0	5		0	0	0			
87089941	税号8704.2100、8704.2230、8704.3100及8704.3230所列车辆用车架	25	0	0	0	0	0	0	0	0	0	0		0		0	0	12.5	5			

税则号列	商品名称（简称）	最惠国	东盟										亚太	智利	巴基斯坦	新加坡	新西兰	秘鲁	哥斯达黎加	香港	澳门	台湾
			文	柬	印	老	马	缅	菲	新	泰	越										
87089949	中小型货车用其他零附件	25	0	0	0	0	0	0	0	0	0	0		0		0	0	12.5	5			
87089951	税号8704.2240、8704.2300及8704.3240所列车辆用车架	10	0	0	0	0	0	0	0	0	0	0		0	5	0	0	0	0			
87089959	总重≥14吨货车用其他零附件	10	0	0	0	0	0	0	0	0	0	0		0	5	0	0	0	0			
87089960	特种车用其他零附件	15	0	0	0	0	0	0	0	0	0	0		0	12	0	0	7.5	3			
87089991	其他税号所列车辆用车架	10	0	0	0	0	0	0	0	0	0	0		0	5	0	0	0	0			0
87089992	汽车传动轴	10	0	0	0	0	0	0	0	0	0	0		0	5	0	0	0	0			0
87089999	机动车辆用未列名零附件	10	0	0	0	0	0	0	0	0	0	0		0	5	0	0	0	0			0
87091110	短距离运输货物电动牵引车	10	0	0	0	0	0	0	0	0	0	0		0	5	0	0	0	0			
87091190	其他电动短矩离运货车	10	0	0	0	0	0	0	0	0	0	0		0	5	0	0	0	0			
87091910	短距离运输货物其他牵引车	10.5	0	0	0	0	0	0	0	0	0	0		0	5	0	0	0	2.1			
87091990	其他非电动短矩离运货车	10.5	0	0	0	0	0	0	0	0	0	0		0	5	0	0	0	2.1			
87099000	短距离运货车、站台牵引车用零件	8.4	0	0	0	0	0	0	0	0	0	0		0	5		0	0	0			
87100010	坦克及其他机动装甲战斗车辆	15	0	0	0	0	0	0	0	0	0	0		0	12	0	0	7.5	3			
87100090	坦克及其他机动装甲战斗车辆零件	15	0	0	0	0	0	0	0	0	0	0		0	12	0	0	7.5	3			
87111000	汽油型微马力摩托车及脚踏两用车	45	0	0	0	0	0	0	0	0	0	0		0		0	0	22.5	9			
87112010	装有往复式活塞发动机，气缸容量超过50毫升，但不超过100毫升的汽油型小马力摩托车及脚踏两用车	45	0	0	0	0	0	0	0	0	0	0		0		0	0	22.5	9			
87112020	装有往复式活塞发动机，气缸容量超过100毫升，但不超过125毫升的汽油型小马力摩托车及脚踏两用车	45	0	0	0	0	0	0	0	0	0	0		0		0	0	22.5	9			
87112030	装有往复式活塞发动机，气缸容量超过125毫升，但不超过150毫升的汽油型小马力摩托车及脚踏两用车	45	0	0	0	0	0	0	0	0	0	0		0		0	0	22.5	9			
87112040	装有往复式活塞发动机，气缸容量超过150毫升，但不超过200毫升的汽油型小马力摩托车及脚踏两用车	45	0	0	0	0	0	0	0	0	0	0		0		0	0		9			
87112050	装有往复式活塞发动机，气缸容量超过200毫升，但不超过250毫升的汽油型小马力摩托车及脚踏两用车	45	0	0	0	0	0	0	0	0	0	0		0		0	0		9			
87113010	汽油型中小马力摩托车及脚踏两用车	45	0	0	0	0	0	0	0	0	0	0	32.8	0	32.8	0	0		9			
87113020	汽油型中大马力摩托车及脚踏两用车	45	0	0	0	0	0	0	0	0	0	0	32.8	0	32.8	0	0		9			
87114000	汽油型大马力摩托车及脚踏两用车	40	0	0	0	0	0	0	0	0	0	0		0		0	0		8			
87115000	汽油型超大马力摩托车及类似车	30	0	0	0	0	0	0	0	0	0	0		0		0	0		6			
87119010	电动的或电动助力的摩托车（包括机器脚踏两用车）	45	0	0	0	0	0	0	0	0	0	0		0		0	0		9			
87119090	装有其他发动机的摩托车及边车	45	0	0	0	0	0	0	0	0	0	0		0		0	0		9			
87120020	竞赛型自行车	13	0	0	0	0	0	0	0	0	0	0	9.1	0	5	0	0	0	2.6			0
87120030	山地自行车	13	0	0	0	0	0	0	0	0	0	0	9.1	0	5	0	0	0	2.6			0
87120041	16、18、20英寸自行车	13	0	0	0	0	0	0	0	0	0	0	9.1	0	5	0	0	0	2.6			0
87120049	其他越野自行车	13	0	0	0	0	0	0	0	0	0	0	9.1	0	5	0	0	0	2.6			0
87120081	≤16英寸的未列名自行车	13	0	0	0	0	0	0	0	0	0	0	9.1	0	5	0	0	0	2.6		0	0
87120089	其他未列名自行车	13	0	0	0	0	0	0	0	0	0	0	9.1	0	5	0	0	0	2.6		0	0
87120090	其他非机动脚踏车	23	0	0	0	0	0	0	0	0	0	0	16.1	0	16.1	0	0	11.5	4.6		0	0
87131000	非机械驱动的残疾人用车	6	0	0	0	0	0	0	0	0	0	0		0	5		0	0	0			
87139000	其他机动残疾人用车	4	0	0	0	0	0	0	0	0	0	0		0	0		0	0	0			
87141000	摩托车及机动脚踏两用车用零附件	30	0	0	0	0	0	0	0	0	0	0		0		0	0	15	6			
87142000	残疾人车辆用零附件	5	0	0	0	0	0	0	0	0	0	0		0	0		0	0	0			
87149100	非机动脚踏车车架、轮叉及其零件	12	0	0	0	0	0	0	0	0	0	0		0	6	0	0	0	2.4			0
87149210	轮圈	12	0	0	0	0	0	0	0	0	0	0		0	6	0	0	0	2.4			0
87149290	辐条	12	0	0	0	0	0	0	0	0	0	0		0	6	0	0	0	2.4			0
87149310	非机动脚踏车的轮毂	12	0	0	0	0	0	0	0	0	0	0		0	6	0	0	0	2.4			0
87149320	飞轮	12	0	0	0	0	0	0	0	0	0	0		0	6	0	0	0	2.4			0
87149390	其他非机动脚踏车的飞轮	12	0	0	0	0	0	0	0	0	0	0		0	6	0	0	0	2.4			0
87149400	非机动脚踏车的制动器及其零件	12	0	0	0	0	0	0	0	0	0	0		0	6	0	0	0	2.4			0
87149500	非机动脚踏车的鞍座	12	0	0	0	0	0	0	0	0	0	0		0	6	0	0	0	2.4			0
87149610	非机动脚踏车脚蹬及其零件	12	0	0	0	0	0	0	0	0	0	0		0	6	0	0	0	2.4			0
87149620	非机动脚踏车曲柄、链轮及其零件	12	0	0	0	0	0	0	0	0	0	0		0	6	0	0	0	2.4			0
87149900	非机动脚踏车的其他零附件	12	0	0	0	0	0	0	0	0	0	0	8.4	0	5	0	0	0	2.4			0
87150000	婴孩车及其零件	20	0	0	0	0	0	0	0	0	0	0		0		0	0	10	4		0	

税则号列	商品名称（简称）	最惠国	东盟										亚太	智利	巴基斯坦	新加坡	新西兰	秘鲁	哥斯达黎加	香港	澳门	台湾
			文	柬	印	老	马	缅	菲	新	泰	越										
87161000	供居住或野营用厢式挂车及半挂车	10	0	0	0	0	0	0	0	0	0	0		0	5	0	0	0	0			
87162000	农用自装或自卸式挂车及半挂车	10	0	0	0	0	0	0	0	0	0	0		0	5		0	0	0			
87163110	油罐挂车及半挂车	10	0	0	0	0	0	0	0	0	0	0		0	5	0	0	0	0			
87163190	其他罐式挂车及半挂车	10	0	0	0	0	0	0	0	0	0	0		0	5		0	0	0			
87163910	货柜挂车及半挂车	10	0	0	0	0	0	0	0	0	0	0		0	5		0	0	0			
87163990	其他货运挂车及半挂车	10	0	0	0	0	0	0	0	0	0	0		0	5		0	0	0			
87164000	其他未列名挂车及半挂车	10	0	0	0	0	0	0	0	0	0	0		0	5		0	0	0			
87168000	其他未列名非机械驱动车辆	10	0	0	0	0	0	0	0	0	0	0		0	5	0	0	0	0		0	
87169000	挂车、半挂车及非机动车用零件	10	0	0	0	0	0	0	0	0	0	0		0	5	0	0	0	0			
88010010	滑翔机及悬挂滑翔机	3	0	0	0	0	0	0	0	0	0	0		0	0		0	0	0			
88010090	汽球、飞艇及其他无动力航空器	3	0	0	0	0	0	0	0	0	0	0		0	0		0	0	0			
88021100	空载重量≤2吨的直升机	2	0	0	0	0	0	0	0	0	0	0		0	0		0	0	0			
88021210	2吨＜空载重量≤7吨的直升机	2	0	0	0	0	0	0	0	0	0	0		0	0		0	0	0			
88021220	空载重量＞7吨的直升机	2	0	0	0	0	0	0	0	0	0	0		0	0		0	0	0			
88022000	小型飞机及其他航空器	5	0	0	0	0	0	0	0	0	0	0		0.5	0		0	0	0			
88023000	中型飞机及其他航空器	4	0	0	0	0	0	0	0	0	0	0		0.4	0		0	0	0			
88024010	大型飞机及其他航空器	5	0	0	0	0	0	0	0	0	0	0	3.5	0	0		0	0	0			
88024020	特大型飞机及其他航空器	1	0	0	0	0	0	0	0	0	0	0	0.7	0	0		0	0	0			
88026000	航天器(包括卫星)及其运载工具	2	0	0	0	0	0	0	0	0	0	0		0	0		0	0	0			
88031000	飞机等用推进器、水平旋翼及零件	1	0	0	0	0	0	0	0	0	0	0		0	0		0	0	0			
88032000	飞机等用起落架及其零件	1	0	0	0	0	0	0	0	0	0	0		0	0		0	0	0			
88033000	飞机及直升机的其他零件	1	0	0	0	0	0	0	0	0	0	0		0	0		0	0	0			
88040000	降落伞及其零附件	2	0	0	0	0	0	0	0	0	0	0		0	0		0	0	0			
88051000	航空器的发射装置及其零件等	1.5	0	0	0	0	0	0	0	0	0	0		0	0		0	0	0			
88052100	空战模拟器及其零件	1.5	0	0	0	0	0	0	0	0	0	0		0	0		0	0	0			
88052900	其他地面飞行训练器及其零件	1.5	0	0	0	0	0	0	0	0	0	0		0	0		0	0	0			
89011010	机动巡航船、游览船及各式渡船	5	0	0	0	0	0	0	0	0	0	0		0.5	0	0	0	0	0	0		
89011090	非机动巡航船、游览船及各式渡船	8	0	0	0	0	0	0	0	0	0	0		0.8	5		0	0	0			
89012011	载重≤10万吨的成品油船	9												0			0	0	0			
89012012	10万吨＜载重≤30万吨的成品油船	9												0			0	0	0			
89012013	载重＞30万吨的成品油船	6												0			0	0	0			
89012021	载重≤15万吨的原油船	9												0			0	0	0			
89012022	15万吨＜载重≤30万吨的原油船	9												0			0	0	0			
89012023	载重＞30万吨的原油船	6												0			0	0	0			
89012031	容积≤20000立方米的液化石油气船	9												0			0	0	0			
89012032	容积＞20000立方米的液化石油气船	6												0			0	0	0			
89012041	容积≤20000立方米的液化天然气船	9												0			0	0	0			
89012042	容积＞20000立方米的液化天然气船	6												0			0	0	0			
89012090	其他液货船	9												0			0	0	0			
89013000	冷藏船	9	0	0	0	0	0	0	0	0	0	0		0	5	0	0	0	0			
89019021	可载标准集装箱≤6000箱的机动集装箱船	9												0.9			0	0	0			
89019022	可载标准集装箱＞6000箱的机动集装箱船	6												0.6			0	0	0			
89019031	载重≤2万吨的机动滚装船	9												0.9			0	0	0			
89019032	载重＞2万吨的机动滚装船	6												0.6			0	0	0			
89019041	载重≤15万吨的机动散货船	9												0.9			0	0	0			
89019042	15万吨＜载重≤30万吨的机动散货船	9												0.9			0	0	0			
89019043	载重＞30万吨的机动散货船	9												0.9			0	0	0			
89019050	机动多用途船	9												0.9			0	0	0			
89019080	其他机动货运船舶	9	0	0	0	0	0	0	0	0	0	0		0.9	5	0	0	0	0			
89019090	非机动货运船舶及客货兼运船舶	8	0	0	0	0	0	0	0	0	0	0		0.8	5	0	0	0	0			
89020010	机动捕鱼船	7	0	0	0	0	0	0	0	0	0	0		0.7	5	0	0	0	0			
89020090	非机动捕鱼船	8	0	0	0	0	0	0	0	0	0	0		0.8	5		0	0	0			
89031000	充气的娱乐或运动用快艇	10	0	0	0	0	0	0	0	0	0	0		0	5		0	0	0			
89039100	帆船	8	0	0	0	0	0	0	0	0	0	0		0.8	5		0	0	0			
89039200	汽艇	10.5	0	0	0	0	0	0	0	0	0	0		1.1	5	0	0	5.2	2.1	0		
89039900	娱乐或运动用其他船舶或快艇	10	0	0	0	0	0	0	0	0	0	0		1	5		0	0	0			
89040000	拖轮及顶推船	9	0	0	0	0	0	0	0	0	0	0		0.9	5	0	0	0	0			
89051000	挖泥船	3	0	0	0	0	0	0	0	0	0	0		0	0		0	0	0			

税则号列	商品名称（简称）	最惠国	东盟										亚太	智利	巴基斯坦	新加坡	新西兰	秘鲁	哥斯达黎加	香港	澳门	台湾
			文	柬	印	老	马	缅	菲	新	泰	越										
89052000	浮动或潜水式钻探或生产平台	6	0	0	0	0	0	0	0	0	0	0		0	5		0	0	0			
89059010	浮船坞	8												0.8			0	0	0			
89059090	其他不以航行为主要功能的船舶	3	0	0	0	0	0	0	0	0	0	0		0	0		0	0	0			
89061000	军舰	5	0	0	0	0	0	0	0	0	0	0		0	0		0	0	0			
89069010	其他未列名的机动船舶	5	0	0	0	0	0	0	0	0	0	0		0.5	0		0	0	0			
89069020	非机动船舶	8	0	0	0	0	0	0	0	0	0	0		0.8	5		0	0	0			
89069030	未制成或不完整的船舶，包括船舶分段	8	0	0	0	0	0	0	0	0	0	0		0.8	5		0	0	0			
89071000	充气筏	8	0	0	0	0	0	0	0	0	0	0		0	5		0	0	0			
89079000	其他浮动结构体	8	0	0	0	0	0	0	0	0	0	0		0.8	5		0	0	0			
89080000	供拆卸的船舶及其他浮动结构体	3	0	0	0	0	0	0	0	0	0	0		0	0		0	0	0			
90011000	光导纤维束及光缆	5	0	0	0	0	0	0	0	0	0	0	4.5	0	0		0	0	0	0		
90012000	偏振材料制的片及板	8	0	0	0	0	0	0	0	0	0	0	7.6	0	5		0	0	0	0		
90013000	隐形眼镜片	10	0	0	0	0	0	0	0	0	0	0		0	5	0	0	0	0	0		
90014010	玻璃制变色镜片	20	0	0	0	0	0	0	0	0	0	0		0		0	0	10	4	0		
90014091	玻璃制太阳镜片	20	0	0	0	0	0	0	0	0	0	0		0		0	0	10	4	0		
90014099	玻璃制其他眼镜片	20	0	0	0	0	0	0	0	0	0	0		0		0	0	10	4	0		
90015010	非玻璃材料制变色镜片	20	0	0	0	0	0	0	0	0	0	0		0		0	0	10	4	0		
90015091	非玻璃材料制太阳镜片	20	0	0	0	0	0	0	0	0	0	0		0		0	0	10	4	0		
90015099	非玻璃材料制其他眼镜片	20	0	0	0	0	0	0	0	0	0	0		0		0	0	10	4	0		
90019010	彩色滤光片	8	0	0	0	0	0	0	0	0	0	0	7.6	0	5		0	0	0	0		
90019090	其他光学元件	8	0	0	0	0	0	0	0	0	0	0	7.6	0	5		0	0	0	0		
90021110	特殊用途照相机用物镜	8	0	0	0	0	0	0	0	0	0	0		0	5		0	0	0			
90021120	缩微阅读机用物镜	8	0	0	0	0	0	0	0	0	0	0		0	5		0	0	0			
90021131	单反相机镜头	15	0	0	0	0	0	0	0	0	0	0		0	12	0	0	7.5	3			
90021139	其他照相机用镜头	15	0	0	0	0	0	0	0	0	0	0		0	12	0	0	7.5	3			
90021190	其他照相机、投影仪等用物镜	15	0	0	0	0	0	0	0	0	0	0		0	12	0	0	7.5	3			0
90021910	摄影机或放映机用物镜	15	0	0	0	0	0	0	0	0	0	0		0	12	0	0	7.5	3			
90021990	税号90.02未列名的其他物镜	15	0	0	0	0	0	0	0	0	0	0		0	12	0	0	7.5	3	0		0
90022010	照相机用滤色镜	15	0	0	0	0	0	0	0	0	0	0	14.3	0	12	0	0	7.5	3			
90022090	其他光学仪器或装置滤色镜	15	0	0	0	0	0	0	0	0	0	0	14.3	0	12	0	0	7.5	3			
90029010	照相机用未列名光学元件	15	0	0	0	0	0	0	0	0	0	0		1.5	12	0	0	7.5	3	0		0
90029090	其他光学仪器用未列名光学元件	15	0	0	0	0	0	0	0	0	0	0		1.5	12	0	0	7.5	3	0		0
90031100	塑料制眼镜架	18	0	0	0	0	0	0	0	0	0	0		0		0	0	9	3.6	0	0	
90031910	金属材料制眼镜架	10	0	0	0	0	0	0	0	0	0	0		1	5		0	0	0	0	0	
90031920	天然材料制眼镜架	10	0	0	0	0	0	0	0	0	0	0		1	5		0	0	0	0	0	
90031990	其他眼镜架	10	0	0	0	0	0	0	0	0	0	0		1	5		0	0	0	0	0	
90039000	眼镜架零件	10	0	0	0	0	0	0	0	0	0	0		0	5		0	0	0	0		
90041000	太阳镜	20	0	0	0	0	0	0	0	0	0	0		2		0	0	10	4	0	0	
90049010	变色镜	16	0	0	0	0	0	0	0	0	0	0		0	12.8	0	0	8	3.2	0	0	
90049090	其他眼镜	20	0	0	0	0	0	0	0	0	0	0		0		0	0	10	4	0	0	
90051000	双筒望远镜	15	0	0	0	0	0	0	0	0	0	0		0	12	0	0	7.5	3			
90058010	天文望远镜及其他天文仪器	3	0	0	0	0	0	0	0	0	0	0		0	0		0	0	0			
90058090	其他光学望远镜	12	0	0	0	0	0	0	0	0	0	0		0	6	0	0	0	2.4			
90059010	天文望远镜及其他天文仪器用零件	2	0	0	0	0	0	0	0	0	0	0		0	0		0	0	0			
90059090	其他望远镜零附件	8	0	0	0	0	0	0	0	0	0	0		0	5		0	0	0			
90061010	电子分色机	12	0	0	0	0	0	0	0	0	0	0		0	6	0	0	0	2.4			
90061090	其他制版照相机	10	0	0	0	0	0	0	0	0	0	0		0	5		0	0	0			
90063000	特种用途的照相机	9	0	0	0	0	0	0	0	0	0	0		0	5		0	0	0			
90064000	一次成相照相机	5	0	0	0	0	0	0	0	0	0	0		0	0		0	0	0			
90065100	通过镜头取景的照相机	25	0	0	0	0	0	0	0	0	0	0		0		0	0		5			
90065210	缩微照相机	9	0	0	0	0	0	0	0	0	0	0		0	5		0	0	0			
90065290	使用胶片宽＜35mm的其他照相机	25	0	0	0	0	0	0	0	0	0	0		0		0	0		5			
90065300	其他照相机	20	0	0	0	0	0	0	0	0	0	0		2		0	0	10	4			
90065910	激光照排设备	9	0	0	0	0	0	0	0	0	0	0		0	5	0	0	0	0			
90065990	其他照相机	25	0	0	0	0	0	0	0	0	0	0		0		0	0		5			
90066100	放电式(电子式)闪光灯装置	18	0	0	0	0	0	0	0	0	0	0		0		0	0	9	3.6			
90066910	闪光灯泡、方形闪光灯及类似品	18	0	0	0	0	0	0	0	0	0	0		0	14.4	0	0	9	3.6			
90066990	其他照相闪光灯装置	18	0	0	0	0	0	0	0	0	0	0		0	14.4	0	0	9	3.6			
90069110	特种用途照相机的零附件	8	0	0	0	0	0	0	0	0	0	0	5.6	0	5		0	0	0	0		
90069120	一次成像照相机的零附件	5	0	0	0	0	0	0	0	0	0	0	3.5	0	0		0	0	0	0		

税则号列	商品名称（简称）	最惠国	东盟 文	柬	印	老	马	缅	菲	新	泰	越	亚太	智利	巴基斯坦	新加坡	新西兰	秘鲁	哥斯达黎加	香港	澳门	台湾
90069191	照相机自动调焦组件	10	0	0	0	0	0	0	0	0	0	0	7	0	5	0	0	0	0	0		
90069192	其他照相机的快门组件	10	0	0	0	0	0	0	0	0	0	0	7	0	5	0	0	0	0	0		
90069199	其他照相机的其他零附件	10	0	0	0	0	0	0	0	0	0	0	7	0	5	0	0	0	0	0		
90069900	照相闪光灯装置及闪光灯泡的零件	12	0	0	0	0	0	0	0	0	0	0		0	6	0	0	0	2.4			
90071010	高速摄影机	14	0	0	0	0	0	0	0	0	0	0		1.4	7	0	0	0	2.8			
90071090	其他摄影机	14	0	0	0	0	0	0	0	0	0	0		0	11.2	0	0	0	2.8			
90072010	数字式放映机	14	0	0	0	0	0	0	0	0	0	0		0	11.2	0	0	0	2.8	0		
90072090	放映机	14	0	0	0	0	0	0	0	0	0	0		0	11.2	0	0	0	2.8			
90079100	电影摄影机用零附件	8.4	0	0	0	0	0	0	0	0	0	0		0	5		0	0	0			
90079200	电影放映机用零附件	8.4	0	0	0	0	0	0	0	0	0	0		0	5		0	0	0			
90085010	幻灯机	14	0	0	0	0	0	0	0	0	0	0		0	7	0	0	0	2.8			
90085020	缩微胶卷、缩微胶片或其他缩微品的阅读机，不论是否可以进行复制	10	0	0	0	0	0	0	0	0	0	0		0	5		0	0	0			
90085031	正射投影仪	18	0	0	0	0	0	0	0	0	0	0		0		0	0	9	3.6			
90085039	其他影像投影仪	18	0	0	0	0	0	0	0	0	0	0		1.8		0	0	9	3.6			
90085040	照片（电影片除外）放大机及缩片机	20	0	0	0	0	0	0	0	0	0	0		0		0	0	10	4			
90089010	缩微阅读机的零附件	8	0	0	0	0	0	0	0	0	0	0		0	5		0	0	0			
90089020	照片放大机及缩片机的零附件	14	0	0	0	0	0	0	0	0	0	0		0	7	0	0	0	2.8			
90089090	其他影像投影仪的零附件	14	0	0	0	0	0	0	0	0	0	0		0	11.2	0	0	0	2.8			
90101010	电影用胶卷的自动显影装置及设备	14	0	0	0	0	0	0	0	0	0	0		1.4	7	0	0	0	2.8	0		
90101020	特种照相胶卷自动显影装置及设备	8.4	0	0	0	0	0	0	0	0	0	0		0.8	5		0	0	0	0		
90101091	彩色胶卷用自动显影及设备	25	0	0	0	0	0	0	0	0	0	0		2.5		0	0	12.5	5	0		
90101099	其他胶卷的自动显影装置及设备	15	0	0	0	0	0	0	0	0	0	0		1.5	12	0	0	7.5	3	0		
90105010	负片显示器	14	0	0	0	0	0	0	0	0	0	0		0	7	0	0	0	2.8			
90105021	电影用的洗印装置	14	0	0	0	0	0	0	0	0	0	0		0	11.2	0	0	0	2.8			
90105022	特种照相用的洗印装置	8.4	0	0	0	0	0	0	0	0	0	0		0	5		0	0	0			
90105029	其他照相用的洗印装置	17	0	0	0	0	0	0	0	0	0	0		0	13.6	0	0	8.5	3.4			
90106000	银幕及其他投影屏幕	14	0	0	0	0	0	0	0	0	0	0		0	11.2	0	0	0	2.8			
90118000	其他显微镜	7	0	0	0	0	0	0	0	0	0	0		0	5		0	0	0			
90131000	武器用望远镜瞄准具及其他望远镜	8	0	0	0	0	0	0	0	0	0	0		0	5		0	0	0			
90132000	激光器	6	0	0	0	0	0	0	0	0	0	0		0	5		0	0	0		0	
90138010	放大镜	12	0	0	0	0	0	0	0	0	0	0	8.4	0	5	0	0	0	2.4	0	0	
90138020	光学门眼	12	0	0	0	0	0	0	0	0	0	0	8.4	0	5	0	0	0	2.4			
90138030	液晶显示板	5	0	0	0	0	0	0	0	0	0	0		0	0		0			0	0	
90138090	其他液晶装置及光学仪器	5	0	0	0	0	0	0	0	0	0	0		0	0		0	0	0	0	0	
90139010	激光器、望远镜等装置的零附件	6	0	0	0	0	0	0	0	0	0	0		0	5		0	0	0	0	0	
90139020	子目录9013.8030所列货品用零附件	8	0	0	0	0	0	0	0	0	0	0		0	5		0	0	0	0	0	
90139090	税号90.13所列其他货品的零附件	8	0	0	0	0	0	0	0	0	0	0		0	5		0	0	0	0	0	
90141000	定向罗盘	2	0	0	0	0	0	0	0	0	0	0		0	0		0	0	0			
90142010	自动驾驶仪	2	0	0	0	0	0	0	0	0	0	0		0	0		0	0	0			
90142090	其他航空或航天导航仪器及装置(罗盘除外)	2	0	0	0	0	0	0	0	0	0	0		0	0		0	0	0			
90148000	其他导航仪器及装置	2	0	0	0	0	0	0	0	0	0	0		0	0		0	0	0			
90149010	自动驾驶仪用零件、附件	1.5	0	0	0	0	0	0	0	0	0	0		0	0		0	0	0			
90149090	其他导航仪器及设备用零件、附件	1.5	0	0	0	0	0	0	0	0	0	0		0	0		0	0	0			
90151000	测距仪	9	0	0	0	0	0	0	0	0	0	0		0	5		0	0	0			
90152000	经纬仪及视距仪	9	0	0	0	0	0	0	0	0	0	0		0	5		0	0	0			
90153000	水平仪	9	0	0	0	0	0	0	0	0	0	0		0	5		0	0	0			
90154000	摄影测量用仪器及装置	9	0	0	0	0	0	0	0	0	0	0		0	5		0	0	0			
90158000	其他大地测量仪器及装置	5	0	0	0	0	0	0	0	0	0	0	3.5	0.5	0		0	0	0			
90159000	大地测量仪器及装置的零附件	5	0	0	0	0	0	0	0	0	0	0		0	0		0	0	0			
90160010	感量为0.1mg或更精密的天平	9	0	0	0	0	0	0	0	0	0	0		0	5		0	0	0			
90160090	0.1mg＜感量≤50mg的天平	10.5	0	0	0	0	0	0	0	0	0	0		0	5	0	0	0	2.1			
90171000	绘图台及绘图机，不论是否自动	8	0	0	0	0	0	0	0	0	0	0		0	5		0	0	0			
90173000	千分尺、卡尺及量规	8	0	0	0	0	0	0	0	0	0	0		0	5		0	0	0			
90178000	其他手用测量长度的器具	8	0	0	0	0	0	0	0	0	0	0		0	5		0	0	0			
90181100	心电图记录仪	5	0	0	0	0	0	0	0	0	0	0		0	0		0	0	0			
90181210	B型超声波诊断仪	7	0	0	0	0	0	0	0	0	0	0	6	0	0		0	0	0			
90181291	彩色超声波诊断仪	5	0	0	0	0	0	0	0	0	0	0	4.5	0	0		0	0	0			
90181299	其他超声扫描装置	5	0	0	0	0	0	0	0	0	0	0	4.5	0	0		0	0	0			

税则号列	商品名称（简称）	最惠国	东盟										亚太	智利	巴基斯坦	新加坡	新西兰	秘鲁	哥斯达黎加	香港	澳门	台湾
			文	柬	印	老	马	缅	菲	新	泰	越										
90181310	核磁共振成像成套装置	4	0	0	0	0	0	0	0	0	0	0		0	0		0	0	0	0		
90181390	其他核磁共振成象装置	4	0	0	0	0	0	0	0	0	0	0		0	0		0	0	0	0		
90181400	闪烁摄影装置	5	0	0	0	0	0	0	0	0	0	0		0	0		0	0	0			
90181930	病员监护仪	4	0	0	0	0	0	0	0	0	0	0	3.5	0	0		0	0	0			
90181941	听力计	4	0	0	0	0	0	0	0	0	0	0	3.5	0	0		0	0	0			
90181949	其他听力诊断装置	4	0	0	0	0	0	0	0	0	0	0	3.5	0	0		0	0	0			
90181990	其他电气诊断装置	4	0	0	0	0	0	0	0	0	0	0	3.5	0	0		0	0	0			
90182000	紫外线及红外线装置	4	0	0	0	0	0	0	0	0	0	0		0	0		0	0	0			
90183100	注射器	8	0	0	0	0	0	0	0	0	0	0	7.6	0.8	0		0	0	0			
90183210	管状金属针头	8	0	0	0	0	0	0	0	0	0	0	7	0	0		0	0	0			
90183220	缝合用针	4	0	0	0	0	0	0	0	0	0	0	3.5	0	0		0	0	0			
90183900	导管、插管及类似品	4	0	0	0	0	0	0	0	0	0	0		0.4	0		0	0	0			
90184100	牙钻机	4	0	0	0	0	0	0	0	0	0	0		0	0		0	0	0			
90184910	装有牙科设备的牙科用椅	4	0	0	0	0	0	0	0	0	0	0		0.4	0		0	0	0			
90184990	牙科用其他仪器及器具	4	0	0	0	0	0	0	0	0	0	0		0.4	0		0	0	0			
90185000	眼科用其他仪器及器具	4	0	0	0	0	0	0	0	0	0	0	3.5	0.4	0		0	0	0			
90189010	听诊器	4	0	0	0	0	0	0	0	0	0	0	3.5	0.4	0		0	0	0	0		
90189020	血压测量仪器及器具	4	0	0	0	0	0	0	0	0	0	0	3.5	0.4	0		0	0	0	0		
90189030	内窥镜	4	0	0	0	0	0	0	0	0	0	0	3.5	0.4	0		0	0	0	0		
90189040	肾脏透析设备(人工肾)	4	0	0	0	0	0	0	0	0	0	0	3.5	0.4	0		0	0	0	0		
90189050	透热疗法设备	4	0	0	0	0	0	0	0	0	0	0	3.5	0.4	0		0	0	0	0		
90189060	输血设备	4	0	0	0	0	0	0	0	0	0	0	3.5	0.4	0		0	0	0	0		
90189070	麻醉设备	4	0	0	0	0	0	0	0	0	0	0	3.5	0.4	0		0	0	0	0		
90189080	宫内节育器	4	0	0	0	0	0	0	0	0	0	0	2	0.4	0		0	0	0	0		
90189090	税号90.18中未列名的医疗仪器	4	0	0	0	0	0	0	0	0	0	0	3.5	0.4	0		0	0	0	0	0	
90191010	按摩器具	15	0	0	0	0	0	0	0	0	0	0		1.5	12	0	0	7.5	3	0		
90191090	机械疗法器具、心理功能测验装置	4	0	0	0	0	0	0	0	0	0	0		0.4	0		0	0	0	0		
90192000	臭氧治疗器、氧气治疗器等器具	4	0	0	0	0	0	0	0	0	0	0		0	0		0	0	0		0	
90200000	其他呼吸器具及防毒面具	8	0	0	0	0	0	0	0	0	0	0		0.8	5		0	0	0	0	0	
90211000	矫形或骨折用器具	4	0	0	0	0	0	0	0	0	0	0		0.4	0		0	0	0			
90212100	假牙	4	0	0	0	0	0	0	0	0	0	0		0	0		0	0	0	0		
90212900	牙齿固定件	4	0	0	0	0	0	0	0	0	0	0		0	0		0	0	0			
90213100	人造关节	4	0	0	0	0	0	0	0	0	0	0		0	0		0	0	0			0
90213900	其他人造的人体部分	4	0	0	0	0	0	0	0	0	0	0		0.4	0		0	0	0			
90214000	助听器，不包括零附件	4	0	0	0	0	0	0	0	0	0	0		0	0		0	0	0			
90215000	心脏起搏器，不包括零附件	4	0	0	0	0	0	0	0	0	0	0		0	0		0	0	0			
90219011	血管支架	4	0	0	0	0	0	0	0	0	0	0		0.4	0		0	0	0			
90219019	其他支架	4	0	0	0	0	0	0	0	0	0	0		0.4	0		0	0	0			
90219090	其他税号90.21中未列名的矫形器具	4	0	0	0	0	0	0	0	0	0	0		0.4	0		0	0	0			
90221200	X射线断层检查仪	4	0	0	0	0	0	0	0	0	0	0	2.8	0	0		0	0	0			
90221300	其他牙科用x射线应用设备	4	0	0	0	0	0	0	0	0	0	0		0	0		0	0	0			
90221400	其他医疗或兽医用x射线应用设备	4	0	0	0	0	0	0	0	0	0	0		0	0		0	0	0			
90221910	低剂量x射线安全检查设备	4	0	0	0	0	0	0	0	0	0	0		0	0		0	0	0			
90221920	X射线无损探伤检测仪	4	0	0	0	0	0	0	0	0	0	0		0	0		0	0	0	0		
90221990	其他非医疗用X射线设备	4	0	0	0	0	0	0	0	0	0	0		0	0		0	0	0	0		
90222100	医疗用α、β、γ射线设备	4	0	0	0	0	0	0	0	0	0	0		0	0		0	0	0			
90222910	γ射线无损探伤检测仪	6	0	0	0	0	0	0	0	0	0	0		0	5		0	0	0			
90222990	其他非医疗用α、β、γ射线设备	6	0	0	0	0	0	0	0	0	0	0		0	5		0	0	0			
90223000	X射线管	2	0	0	0	0	0	0	0	0	0	0		0	0		0	0	0			
90229010	X射线影像增强器	6	0	0	0	0	0	0	0	0	0	0		0.6	5		0	0	0			
90229090	税号90.22所列其他设备及零件	6	0	0	0	0	0	0	0	0	0	0		0.6	5		0	0	0			
90230000	专供示范的仪器、装置及模型	7	0	0	0	0	0	0	0	0	0	0		0	5		0	0	0			
90241010	电子万能试验机	7	0	0	0	0	0	0	0	0	0	0	6.5	0	5		0	0	0			
90241020	硬度计	7	0	0	0	0	0	0	0	0	0	0	6.5	0	5		0	0	0			
90241090	其他金属材料的试验用机器及器具	7	0	0	0	0	0	0	0	0	0	0	6.5	0	5		0	0	0			
90248000	非金属材料的试验用机器及器具	5	0	0	0	0	0	0	0	0	0	0		0	0		0	0	0			
90249000	各种材料的试验用机器零附件	6	0	0	0	0	0	0	0	0	0	0		0	5		0	0	0			
90251100	可直接读数的液体温度计	4	0	0	0	0	0	0	0	0	0	0		0	0		0	0	0		0	
90251910	非液体的工业用温度计及高温计	8.4	0	0	0	0	0	0	0	0	0	0	8	0.8	5		0	0	0			
90251990	非液体的其他温度计、高温计	8.4	0	0	0	0	0	0	0	0	0	0	8	0.8	5		0	0	0		0	

税则号列	商品名称（简称）	最惠国	东盟 文	东盟 柬	东盟 印	东盟 老	东盟 马	东盟 缅	东盟 菲	东盟 新	东盟 泰	东盟 越	亚太	智利	巴基斯坦	新加坡	新西兰	秘鲁	哥斯达黎加	香港	澳门	台湾
90258000	其他温度汁、比重计、湿度计等仪器	11	0	0	0	0	0	0	0	0	0	0		1.1	5	0	0	5.5	2.2			
90259000	比重计、温度计等类似仪器的零件	8	0	0	0	0	0	0	0	0	0	0	7.6	0.8	5		0	0	0			
90271000	气体或烟雾分析仪	7	0	0	0	0	0	0	0	0	0	0		0.7	5		0	0	0	0		
90278091	曝光表	14	0	0	0	0	0	0	0	0	0	0		0	11.2	0	0	0	2.8			
90281010	煤气表	10	0	0	0	0	0	0	0	0	0	0		0	5		0	0	0			
90281090	其他气量计	10	0	0	0	0	0	0	0	0	0	0		0	5	0	0	0	0			
90282010	水表	10	0	0	0	0	0	0	0	0	0	0		1	5	0	0	0	0			
90282090	其他液量计	10	0	0	0	0	0	0	0	0	0	0		1	5	0	0	5	0			
90283011	单相感应式电度表	10	0	0	0	0	0	0	0	0	0	0		1	5		0	0	0	0		
90283012	三相感应式电度表	10	0	0	0	0	0	0	0	0	0	0		1	5		0	0	0	0		
90283013	单相电子式(静止式)电度表	10	0	0	0	0	0	0	0	0	0	0		1	5		0	0	0	0		
90283014	三相电子式(静止式)电度表	10	0	0	0	0	0	0	0	0	0	0		1	5		0	0	0	0		
90283019	其他电度表	10	0	0	0	0	0	0	0	0	0	0		1	5		0	0	0	0		
90283090	其他电量计	10	0	0	0	0	0	0	0	0	0	0		1	5	0	0	0	0	0		
90289010	工业用计量仪表零附件	8.4	0	0	0	0	0	0	0	0	0	0		0.8	5		0	0	0			
90289090	非工业用计量仪表零附件	8.4	0	0	0	0	0	0	0	0	0	0		0.8	5		0	0	0			
90291010	转数计	15	0	0	0	0	0	0	0	0	0	0		0	12	0	0	7.5	3			
90291020	车费计、里程计	15	0	0	0	0	0	0	0	0	0	0		0	12	0	0	7.5	3			
90291090	产量计数器、步数计及类似仪表	15	0	0	0	0	0	0	0	0	0	0		0	12	0	0	7.5	3			
90292010	车辆用速度计	10	0	0	0	0	0	0	0	0	0	0		0	5		0	0	0			
90292090	其他速度计及转速表、频闪观测仪	10	0	0	0	0	0	0	0	0	0	0		0	5		0	0	0			
90299000	转数计、车费计及类似仪表零件	6	0	0	0	0	0	0	0	0	0	0		0	5		0	0	0			
90301000	离子射线的测量或检验仪器及装置	5	0	0	0	0	0	0	0	0	0	0		0	0		0	0	0			
90302010	测试频率＜300兆赫的通用示波器	8	0	0	0	0	0	0	0	0	0	0		0	5	0	0	0	0			
90302090	其他阴极射线示波器	5	0	0	0	0	0	0	0	0	0	0		0	0		0	0	0			
90303110	量程≤五位半的数字万用表，不带记录装置	15	0	0	0	0	0	0	0	0	0	0		0	12	0	0	7.5	3		0	
90303190	其他不带记录装置的万用表	5	0	0	0	0	0	0	0	0	0	0		0	0		0	0	0			
90303200	带记录装置的万用表	8	0	0	0	0	0	0	0	0	0	0		0	5		0	0	0			
90303310	量程≤五位半的数字电流表、电压表，不带记录装置	15	0	0	0	0	0	0	0	0	0	0		1.5	12	0	0	7.5	3	0		
90303320	不带记录装置的电阻测试仪	14	0	0	0	0	0	0	0	0	0	0		1.4	11.2	0	0	0	2.8	0		
90303390	检测电压、电流及功率的其他仪器，不带记录装置	9	0	0	0	0	0	0	0	0	0	0		0.9	5		0	0	0	0		
90303900	检测电压、电流、电阻或功率的其他仪器，带记录装置	8	0	0	0	0	0	0	0	0	0	0		0	5		0	0	0			
90308410	电感及电容测试仪	10	0	0	0	0	0	0	0	0	0	0		0	5	0	0	0	0			
90308490	其他电量的测量或检验仪器及装置	8	0	0	0	0	0	0	0	0	0	0		0	5		0	0	0			
90308910	其他电感及电容测试仪	14	0	0	0	0	0	0	0	0	0	0		1.4	11.2	0	0	0	2.8			
90308990	其他电量的测量或检验仪器及装置	8	0	0	0	0	0	0	0	0	0	0		0.8	5		0	0	0			
90309000	税号90.30所属货品的零件及附件	7	0	0	0	0	0	0	0	0	0	0		0	5		0	0	0	0		
90311000	机械零件平衡试验机	7	0	0	0	0	0	0	0	0	0	0	6.5	0	5		0	0	0			
90312000	试验台	7	0	0	0	0	0	0	0	0	0	0		0	5		0	0	0			
90314910	轮廓投影仪	10	0	0	0	0	0	0	0	0	0	0		0	5		0	0	0			
90318010	光纤通信及光纤性能测试仪	5	0	0	0	0	0	0	0	0	0	0	4	0.5	0		0	0	0	0		
90318020	坐标测量仪	5	0	0	0	0	0	0	0	0	0	0		0.5	0		0	0	0	0		
90318031	超声波探伤检测仪	5	0	0	0	0	0	0	0	0	0	0	4	0.5	0		0	0	0	0		
90318032	磁粉探伤检测仪	5	0	0	0	0	0	0	0	0	0	0	4	0.5	0		0	0	0	0		
90318033	涡流探伤检测仪	5	0	0	0	0	0	0	0	0	0	0	4	0.5	0		0	0	0	0		
90318039	其他无损探伤检测仪器(射线探伤仪除外)	5	0	0	0	0	0	0	0	0	0	0	4	0.5	0		0	0	0	0		
90318090	未列名测量、检验仪器器具及机器	5	0	0	0	0	0	0	0	0	0	0	4	0.5	0		0	0	0	0		0
90321000	恒温器	7	0	0	0	0	0	0	0	0	0	0		0	5		0	0	0	0		
90322000	恒压器	7	0	0	0	0	0	0	0	0	0	0		0	5		0	0	0	0		
90328100	液压或气压的其他仪器及装置	7	0	0	0	0	0	0	0	0	0	0	6.5	0	5		0	0	0	0		
90328911	列车自动防护系统(ATP)车载设备	7	0	0	0	0	0	0	0	0	0	0		0.7	5		0	0	0	0		
90328912	列车自动运行系统(ATO)车载设备	7	0	0	0	0	0	0	0	0	0	0		0.7	5		0	0	0	0		
90328919	其他列车自动控制系统（ATC）车载设备	7	0	0	0	0	0	0	0	0	0	0		0.7	5		0	0	0	0		
90328990	非液压或气压的其他自动调节或控制仪器及装置	7	0	0	0	0	0	0	0	0	0	0		0.7	5		0	0	0	0		
90329000	自动调节或控制仪器零附件	5	0	0	0	0	0	0	0	0	0	0		0	0		0	0	0			

税则号列	商品名称（简称）	最惠国	东盟										亚太	智利	巴基斯坦	新加坡	新西兰	秘鲁	哥斯达黎加	香港	澳门	台湾
			文	柬	印	老	马	缅	菲	新	泰	越										
90330000	90章未列名零附件	6	0	0	0	0	0	0	0	0	0	0		0	5		0	0	0			
91011100	机械指示式的贵金属电子手表	11	0	0	0	0	0	0	0	0	0	0	9.9	0	5	0	0	0	2.2			
91011910	光电显示式的贵金属电子手表	16	0	0	0	0	0	0	0	0	0	0		0	12.8	0	0	8	3.2			
91011990	其他贵金属电子手表	15	0	0	0	0	0	0	0	0	0	0		0	12	0	0	7.5	3			
91012100	自动上弦的贵金属机械手表	11	0	0	0	0	0	0	0	0	0	0		0	5	0	0	0	2.2			
91012900	非自动上弦贵金属机械手表	15	0	0	0	0	0	0	0	0	0	0		0	12	0	0	7.5	3			
91019100	贵金属电子怀表及其他电子表	15	0	0	0	0	0	0	0	0	0	0		0	12	0	0	7.5	3			
91019900	贵金属机械怀表及其他机械表	20	0	0	0	0	0	0	0	0	0	0		0		0	0	10	4			
91021100	机械指示式的其他电子手表	12.5	0	0	0	0	0	0	0	0	0	0	11.1	1.3	6.2	0	0	0	2.5	0	0	
91021200	光电显示式的其他电子手表	23	0	0	0	0	0	0	0	0	0	0		0		0	0	11.5	4.6	0	0	
91021900	其他电子手表	15	0	0	0	0	0	0	0	0	0	0		0	12	0	0	7.5	3			
91022100	其他自动上弦的机械手表	11	0	0	0	0	0	0	0	0	0	0		1.1	5	0	0	0	2.2	0		
91022900	其他非自动上弦的机械手表	15	0	0	0	0	0	0	0	0	0	0		0	12	0	0	7.5	3	0		
91029100	电力驱动的电子怀表及其他电子表	15	0	0	0	0	0	0	0	0	0	0		0	12	0	0	7.5	3			
91029900	其他机械怀表、秒表及其他表	20	0	0	0	0	0	0	0	0	0	0		0		0	0	10	4			
91031000	以表芯装成的电子钟	23	0	0	0	0	0	0	0	0	0	0		0		0	0	11.5	4.6	0	0	
91039000	以表芯装成的机械钟	20	0	0	0	0	0	0	0	0	0	0		0		0	0	10	4			
91040000	仪表板钟及车辆船舶等用的类似钟	10	0	0	0	0	0	0	0	0	0	0		0	5		0	0	0			
91051100	电子闹钟	23	0	0	0	0	0	0	0	0	0	0		0		0	0	11.5	4.6	0	0	
91051900	机械闹钟	20	0	0	0	0	0	0	0	0	0	0		0		0	0	10	4			
91052100	电子挂钟	23	0	0	0	0	0	0	0	0	0	0		2.3		0	0	11.5	4.6			
91052900	机械挂钟	20	0	0	0	0	0	0	0	0	0	0		0		0	0	10	4			
91059110	电子天文钟	3	0	0	0	0	0	0	0	0	0	0		0	0		0	0	0			
91059190	其他电子钟	23	0	0	0	0	0	0	0	0	0	0		0		0	0	11.5	4.6			
91059900	其他机械钟	16	0	0	0	0	0	0	0	0	0	0		0	12.8	0	0	8	3.2			
91061000	考勤钟、时刻记录器	16	0	0	0	0	0	0	0	0	0	0		0	12.8	0	0	8	3.2			
91069000	其他时间记录器及其他类似装置	16	0	0	0	0	0	0	0	0	0	0		1.6	12.8	0	0	8	3.2			
91070000	定时开关	12	0	0	0	0	0	0	0	0	0	0		0	6	0	0	0	2.4			
91081100	已组装的机械指示式完整电子表芯	16	0	0	0	0	0	0	0	0	0	0		0	12.8	0	0	8	3.2	0	0	
91081200	已组装的光电显示式完整电子表芯	16	0	0	0	0	0	0	0	0	0	0		0	12.8	0	0	8	3.2	0	0	
91081900	其他已组装的完整电子表芯	16	0	0	0	0	0	0	0	0	0	0	12	0	8	0	0	8	3.2	0	0	
91082000	已组装的自动上弦完整表芯	16	0	0	0	0	0	0	0	0	0	0		0	12.8	0	0	8	3.2			
91089010	已组装表面≤33.8mm机械完整表芯	16	0	0	0	0	0	0	0	0	0	0		0	12.8	0	0	8	3.2			
91089090	其他已组装完整机械表芯	16	0	0	0	0	0	0	0	0	0	0		0	12.8	0	0	8	3.2	0	0	
91091000	已组装的完整电子钟芯	16	0	0	0	0	0	0	0	0	0	0		0	12.8	0	0	8	3.2			
91099000	已组装的完整机械钟芯	16	0	0	0	0	0	0	0	0	0	0		0	12.8	0	0	8	3.2			
91101100	未组装的完整表机芯	16	0	0	0	0	0	0	0	0	0	0		0	12.8	0	0	8	3.2			
91101200	已组装的不完整表机芯	16	0	0	0	0	0	0	0	0	0	0		0	12.8	0	0	8	3.2			
91101900	未组装的不完整表机芯	16	0	0	0	0	0	0	0	0	0	0		0	12.8	0	0	8	3.2			
91109010	未组装的完整的钟机芯	16	0	0	0	0	0	0	0	0	0	0		0	12.8	0	0	8	3.2			
91109090	不完整的钟机芯	16	0	0	0	0	0	0	0	0	0	0		0	12.8	0	0	8	3.2			
91111000	贵金属或包贵金属制的表壳	14	0	0	0	0	0	0	0	0	0	0		0	11.2	0	0	0	2.8			
91112000	贱金属制的表壳	14	0	0	0	0	0	0	0	0	0	0	10	0	7	0	0	0	2.8	0	0	
91118000	非金属制的表壳	14	0	0	0	0	0	0	0	0	0	0		0	11.2	0	0	0	2.8			
91119000	表壳的零件	14	0	0	0	0	0	0	0	0	0	0		0	11.2	0	0	0	2.8			
91122000	钟壳	14	0	0	0	0	0	0	0	0	0	0		0	11.2	0	0	0	2.8			
91129000	钟壳零件	12	0	0	0	0	0	0	0	0	0	0		0	6	0	0	0	2.4			
91131000	贵金属或包贵金属制的表带及零件	20	0	0	0	0	0	0	0	0	0	0		0		0	0	10	4			
91132000	贱金属制的表带及其零件	14	0	0	0	0	0	0	0	0	0	0		0	11.2	0	0	0	2.8	0	0	
91139000	非金属制的表带及其零件	14	0	0	0	0	0	0	0	0	0	0		0	11.2	0	0	0	2.8	0		
91141000	钟、表的发条	14	0	0	0	0	0	0	0	0	0	0		0	7	0	0	0	2.8			
91143000	钟面或表面	14	0	0	0	0	0	0	0	0	0	0		0	11.2	0	0	0	2.8			
91144000	钟、表的夹板及横担(过桥)	14	0	0	0	0	0	0	0	0	0	0		0	11.2	0	0	0	2.8			
91149010	钟、表的宝石轴承	14	0	0	0	0	0	0	0	0	0	0		0	7	0	0	0	2.8			
91149090	钟、表的其他零件	14	0	0	0	0	0	0	0	0	0	0		0	11.2	0	0	0	2.8	0	0	
92011000	竖式钢琴	17.5	0	0	0	0	0	0	0	0	0	0		0	14	0	0	8.8	3.5		0	
92012000	大钢琴	17.5	0	0	0	0	0	0	0	0	0	0		0	14	0	0	8.8	3.5			
92019000	其他钢琴	17.5	0	0	0	0	0	0	0	0	0	0		0	14	0	0	8.8	3.5			
92021000	弓弦乐器	17.5	0	0	0	0	0	0	0	0	0	0		0	14	0	0	8.8	3.5			
92029000	其他弦乐器	17.5	0	0	0	0	0	0	0	0	0	0		0	14	0	0	8.8	3.5			

税则号列	商品名称（简称）	最惠国	东盟										亚太	智利	巴基斯坦	新加坡	新西兰	秘鲁	哥斯达黎加	香港	澳门	台湾
			文	柬	印	老	马	缅	菲	新	泰	越										
92051000	铜管乐器	17.5	0	0	0	0	0	0	0	0	0	0		0	14	0	0	8.8	3.5			
92059010	键盘管风琴、簧风琴及类似乐器	20	0	0	0	0	0	0	0	0	0	0		0		0	0	10	4			
92059020	手风琴及类似乐器	21	0	0	0	0	0	0	0	0	0	0		0		0	0	10.5	4.2			
92059030	口琴	21	0	0	0	0	0	0	0	0	0	0		0		0	0	10.5	4.2			
92059090	其他管乐器，但游艺场风琴和手摇风琴除外	17.5	0	0	0	0	0	0	0	0	0	0		1.8	14	0	0	8.8	3.5			
92060000	打击乐器	17.5	0	0	0	0	0	0	0	0	0	0		0	14	0	0	0	3.5			
92071000	通过电产生或扩大声音的键盘乐器	30	0	0	0	0	0	0	0	0	0	0		0		0	0	15	6			
92079000	其他通过电产生或扩大声音的乐器	30	0	0	0	0	0	0	0	0	0	0		0		0	0	15	6			
92081000	百音盒	22	0	0	0	0	0	0	0	0	0	0		0		0	0	11	4.4			
92089000	92章未列名的其他乐器	22	0	0	0	0	0	0	0	0	0	0		0		0	0	11	4.4			
92093000	乐器用的弦	17.5	0	0	0	0	0	0	0	0	0	0		0	14	0	0	8.8	3.5			
92099100	钢琴的零附件	17.5	0	0	0	0	0	0	0	0	0	0		0	14	0	0	8.8	3.5			
92099200	编号9202所列乐器的零附件	17.5	0	0	0	0	0	0	0	0	0	0		0	14	0	0	8.8	3.5			
92099400	编号9207所列乐器的零附件	17.5	0	0	0	0	0	0	0	0	0	0		0	14	0	0	8.8	3.5			
92099910	节拍器、音叉及定音管	17.5	0	0	0	0	0	0	0	0	0	0		0	14	0	0	8.8	3.5			
92099920	百音盒的机械装置	17.5	0	0	0	0	0	0	0	0	0	0		0	14	0	0	8.8	3.5			
92099990	本章其他编号未列名的乐器零件	17.5	0	0	0	0	0	0	0	0	0	0		0	14	0	0	8.8	3.5			
93011010	自动推进的火炮武器	13	0	0	0	0	0	0	0	0	0	0		0	6.5	0	0	0	2.6			
93011090	其他火炮武器	13	0	0	0	0	0	0	0	0	0	0		1.3	6.5	0	0	0	2.6			
93012000	火箭发射装置、火焰喷射器等	13	0	0	0	0	0	0	0	0	0	0		0	6.5	0	0	0	2.6			
93019000	其他军用武器	13	0	0	0	0	0	0	0	0	0	0		1.3	6.5	0	0	0	2.6			
93020000	左轮手枪及其他手枪	13	0	0	0	0	0	0	0	0	0	0		0	6.5	0	0	0	2.6			
93031000	前装枪	13	0	0	0	0	0	0	0	0	0	0		0	6.5	0	0	0	2.6			
93032000	其他运动、狩猎或打靶用滑膛枪	13	0	0	0	0	0	0	0	0	0	0		0	6.5	0	0	0	2.6			
93033000	其他运动、狩猎或打靶用步枪	13	0	0	0	0	0	0	0	0	0	0		0	6.5	0	0	0	2.6			
93039000	其他火器及类似装置	13	0	0	0	0	0	0	0	0	0	0		0	6.5	0	0	0	2.6			
93040000	其他武器(如弹簧枪、气枪、警棍等)	13	0	0	0	0	0	0	0	0	0	0		0	6.5	0	0	0	2.6			
93051000	左轮手枪或其他手枪的零件及附件	13	0	0	0	0	0	0	0	0	0	0		0	6.5	0	0	0	2.6			
93052000	猎枪或步枪用零件及附件	13	0	0	0	0	0	0	0	0	0	0		0	6.5	0	0	0	2.6			
93059100	军用武器的零附件	13	0	0	0	0	0	0	0	0	0	0		0	6.5	0	0	0	2.6			
93059900	其他武器的零附件	13	0	0	0	0	0	0	0	0	0	0		0	6.5	0	0	0	2.6			
93062100	猎枪弹	13	0	0	0	0	0	0	0	0	0	0		0	6.5	0	0	0	2.6			
93062900	猎枪弹的零件及气枪弹丸	13	0	0	0	0	0	0	0	0	0	0		0	6.5	0	0	0	2.6			
93063080	接机或类似工具用子弹及其零件	13	0	0	0	0	0	0	0	0	0	0		0	6.5	0	0	0	2.6			
93063090	其他子弹及其零件	13	0	0	0	0	0	0	0	0	0	0		0	6.5	0	0	0	2.6			
93069000	其他弹药和射弹及其零件	13	0	0	0	0	0	0	0	0	0	0		1.3	6.5	0	0	0	2.6			
93070010	军用剑、短弯刀、刺刀、长矛和类似的武器及其零件；军用刀鞘、剑鞘	13	0	0	0	0	0	0	0	0	0	0		0	6.5	0	0	0	2.6			
93070090	其他剑、短弯刀、刺刀、长矛和类似的武器及其零件；其他刀鞘、剑鞘	13	0	0	0	0	0	0	0	0	0	0		0	6.5	0	0	0	2.6			
94012010	皮革或再生皮革面的机动车辆用坐具	10												0			0	0	0		0	
94012090	机动车辆用坐具	10												0			0	0	0		0	
94019011	机动车辆的座椅调角器	10												1			0	5	0	0		
94041000	弹簧床垫	20	0	0	0	0	0	0	0	0	0	0		2		0	0	10	4			
94042100	海绵橡胶或泡沫塑料制褥垫	20	0	0	0	0	0	0	0	0	0	0		0		0	0	10	4	0	0	
94042900	其他材料制褥垫	20	0	0	0	0	0	0	0	0	0	0	14	2	14	0	0	10	4	0	0	
94043010	羽毛或羽绒填充的睡袋	20	0	0	0	0	0	0	0	0	0	0		0		0	0	10	4		0	
94043090	其他睡袋	20	0	0	0	0	0	0	0	0	0	0		0		0	0	10	4		0	
94049010	羽绒或羽毛填充的寝具及类似品	20	0	0	0	0	0	0	0	0	0	0		2		0	0	10	4	0	0	
94049020	兽毛填充的寝具及类似品	20	0	0	0	0	0	0	0	0	0	0		2		0	0	10	4	0	0	
94049030	丝棉填充的寝具及类似品	20	0	0	0	0	0	0	0	0	0	0		2		0	0	10	4	0	0	
94049040	化纤棉填充的寝具及类似品	20	0	0	0	0	0	0	0	0	0	0		2		0	0	10	4	0	0	
94049090	其他材料制的寝具及类似品	20	0	0	0	0	0	0	0	0	0	0		2		0	0	10	4	0	0	
94051000	枝形吊灯	10	0	0	0	0	0	0	0	0	0	0		1	5		0	0	0			
94052000	电气台灯、床头灯、落地灯	20	0	0	0	0	0	0	0	0	0	0		2		0	0	10	4			
94053000	圣诞树用的成套灯具	16	0	0	0	0	0	0	0	0	0	0		0	12.8	0	0	8	3.2			
94054010	探照灯	17.5	0	0	0	0	0	0	0	0	0	0		1.8	14	0	0	8.8	3.5		0	
94054020	聚光灯	17.5	0	0	0	0	0	0	0	0	0	0		1.8	14	0	0	8.8	3.5		0	
94054090	其他电灯及照明装置	10	0	0	0	0	0	0	0	0	0	0		1	5	0	0	0	0	0	0	

税则号列	商品名称（简称）	最惠国	东盟										亚太	智利	巴基斯坦	新加坡	新西兰	秘鲁	哥斯达黎加	香港	澳门	台湾
			文	柬	印	老	马	缅	菲	新	泰	越										
94055000	非电气灯具及照明装置	20	0	0	0	0	0	0	0	0	0	0		0		0	0	10	4			
94056000	发光标志、发光铭牌及类似品	20	0	0	0	0	0	0	0	0	0	0		0		0	0	10	4	0		
94059100	税号94.05所列物品的玻璃制零件	20	0	0	0	0	0	0	0	0	0	0		0		0	0	10	4			
94059200	税号94.05所列物品的塑料制零件	20	0	0	0	0	0	0	0	0	0	0		0		0	0	10	4		0	
94059900	税号94.05所列物品其他材料制零件	20	0	0	0	0	0	0	0	0	0	0		2		0	0	10	4		0	
94060000	活动房屋	10	0	0	0	0	0	0	0	0	0	0	7	1	5	0	0	5	0		0	
95061100	滑雪屐	14	0	0	0	0	0	0	0	0	0	0		0	0	0	0	0	2.8			
95061200	滑雪屐扣件(滑雪屐带)	14	0	0	0	0	0	0	0	0	0	0		0	0	0	0	0	2.8			
95061900	其他滑雪用具	14	0	0	0	0	0	0	0	0	0	0		0	0	0	0	0	2.8			
95062100	帆板	12	0	0	0	0	0	0	0	0	0	0		0	0	0	0	0	2.4			
95062900	其他水上运动用具	14	0	0	0	0	0	0	0	0	0	0		0	0	0	0	0	2.8	0		
95063100	完整的高尔夫球棍	14	0	0	0	0	0	0	0	0	0	0		0	0	0	0	0	2.8			
95063200	高尔夫球	12	0	0	0	0	0	0	0	0	0	0		0	0	0	0	0	2.4			
95063900	其他高尔夫球用具	14	0	0	0	0	0	0	0	0	0	0		0	0	0	0	0	2.8			0
95064010	乒乓球	12	0	0	0	0	0	0	0	0	0	0		1.2	0	0	0	0	2.4			
95064090	其他乒乓球运动用品及器械	14	0	0	0	0	0	0	0	0	0	0		1.4	0	0	0	0	2.8			
95065100	草地网球拍	14	0	0	0	0	0	0	0	0	0	0		0	0	0	0	0	2.8			
95065900	其他网球拍、羽毛球拍或类似球拍	14	0	0	0	0	0	0	0	0	0	0		0	0	0	0	0	2.8			
95066100	草地网球	12	0	0	0	0	0	0	0	0	0	0		0	0	0	0	0	2.4			
95066210	篮球、足球、排球	12	0	0	0	0	0	0	0	0	0	0		1.2	0	0	0	0	2.4			
95066290	其他可充气的球	12	0	0	0	0	0	0	0	0	0	0		1.2	0	0	0	0	2.4			
95066900	其他球	12	0	0	0	0	0	0	0	0	0	0		0	0	0	0	0	2.4			
95067010	溜冰鞋	14	0	0	0	0	0	0	0	0	0	0	12	0	0	0	0	0	2.8			
95067020	旱冰鞋	14	0	0	0	0	0	0	0	0	0	0	12	0	0	0	0	0	2.8			
95069111	跑步机	12	0	0	0	0	0	0	0	0	0	0		1.2	0	0	0	0	2.4	0		0
95069119	其他健身及康复器械	12	0	0	0	0	0	0	0	0	0	0		1.2	0	0	0	0	2.4	0		0
95069120	滑板	12	0	0	0	0	0	0	0	0	0	0		1.2	0	0	0	0	2.4	0		
95069190	一般的体育活动、体操或竞技用品	12	0	0	0	0	0	0	0	0	0	0		1.2	0	0	0	0	2.4	0	0	
95069900	其他未列名的95章用品及设备	12	0	0	0	0	0	0	0	0	0	0		1.2	0	0	0	0	2.4	0	0	
95071000	钓鱼竿	21	0	0	0	0	0	0	0	0	0	0		0		0	0	10.5	4.2			
95072000	钓鱼钩	21	0	0	0	0	0	0	0	0	0	0		2.1		0	0	10.5	4.2			
95073000	钓线轮	21	0	0	0	0	0	0	0	0	0	0		0		0	0	10.5	4.2			
95079000	其他钓鱼用品	21	0	0	0	0	0	0	0	0	0	0	18.9	0	18.9	0	0	10.5	4.2			
95081000	流动马戏团及流动动物园	15	0	0	0	0	0	0	0	0	0	0		0	12	0	0	7.5	3			
95089000	其他旋转木马、秋千等游乐场娱乐设备	15	0	0	0	0	0	0	0	0	0	0		1.5	12	0	0	7.5	3			
96011000	已加工的兽牙及其制品	20	0	0	0	0	0	0	0	0	0	0		0		0	0	10	4			
96019000	其他已加工动物质雕刻料及其制品	20	0	0	0	0	0	0	0	0	0	0		0		0	0	10	4			
96020010	装药用胶囊	10.5	0	0	0	0	0	0	0	0	0	0		0	5	0	0	0	2.1			
96020090	已加工植物或矿物质雕刻料及制品	25	0	0	0	0	0	0	0	0	0	0		0		0	0	12.5	5			
96031000	用枝条或其他植物材料捆扎成的帚	25	0	0	0	0	0	0	0	0	0	0		0		0	0	12.5	5		0	
96032100	牙刷，包括齿板刷	25	0	0	0	0	0	0	0	0	0	0		0		0	0	12.5	5	0	0	
96032900	剃须刷、发刷、睫毛刷等人体化妆用刷	15	0	0	0	0	0	0	0	0	0	0	13.5	1.5	7.5	0	0	7.5	3		0	
96033010	画笔	25	0	0	0	0	0	0	0	0	0	0	15	2.5	15	0	0	12.5	5			
96033020	毛笔	20	0	0	0	0	0	0	0	0	0	0	18	2	18	0	0	10	4			
96033090	化妆用的类似笔	25	0	0	0	0	0	0	0	0	0	0	22.5	2.5	22.5	0	0	12.5	5			
96034011	猪鬃制漆刷及类似刷	20	0	0	0	0	0	0	0	0	0	0		0		0	0	10	4			
96034019	其他材料制漆刷及类似刷	23	0	0	0	0	0	0	0	0	0	0		0		0	0	11.5	4.6			
96034020	油漆块垫及滚筒	23	0	0	0	0	0	0	0	0	0	0		0		0	0	11.5	4.6			
96035011	作为机器、器具零件的金属丝刷	14	0	0	0	0	0	0	0	0	0	0		1.4	11.2	0	0	0	2.8			
96035019	作为车辆零件的金属丝刷	14	0	0	0	0	0	0	0	0	0	0		1.4	7	0	0	0	2.8			
96035091	作为机器、器具零件的其他刷	14	0	0	0	0	0	0	0	0	0	0		1.4	11.2	0	0	0	2.8			
96035099	作为车辆零件的其他刷	14	0	0	0	0	0	0	0	0	0	0		1.4	7	0	0	0	2.8			
96039010	羽毛掸	21	0	0	0	0	0	0	0	0	0	0	18.9	2.1	18.9	0	0	10.5	4.2			
96039090	其他帚、刷、拖把及其他毛掸	15	0	0	0	0	0	0	0	0	0	0		1.5		0	0	7.5	3			
96040000	手用粗筛、细筛	21	0	0	0	0	0	0	0	0	0	0		0		0	0	10.5	4.2			
96050000	个人梳妆、缝纫等用成套旅行用品	15	0	0	0	0	0	0	0	0	0	0		0	12	0	0	7.5	3			
96061000	揿扣及其零件	21	0	0	0	0	0	0	0	0	0	0		0		0	0	10.5	4.2			
96062100	塑料制钮扣，未用纺织材料包裹	21	0	0	0	0	0	0	0	0	0	0		0		0	0	10.5	4.2			0
96062200	贱金属制，未用纺织材料包裹的纽扣	15	0	0	0	0	0	0	0	0	0	0		0	12	0	0	7.5	3	0	0	0
96062900	其他钮扣	15	0	0	0	0	0	0	0	0	0	0		0	12	0	0	7.5	3	0		

税则号列	商品名称（简称）	最惠国	东盟										亚太	智利	巴基斯坦	新加坡	新西兰	秘鲁	哥斯达黎加	香港	澳门	台湾
			文	柬	印	老	马	缅	菲	新	泰	越										
96063000	钮扣芯及钮扣的其他零件	15	0	0	0	0	0	0	0	0	0	0		0	12	0	0	7.5	3	0		
96071100	装有贱金属齿的拉链	21	0	0	0	0	0	0	0	0	0	0		0		0	0	10.5	4.2	0	0	
96071900	其他拉链	21	0	0	0	0	0	0	0	0	0	0	14.7	0	14.7	0	0	10.5	4.2	0	0	
96072000	拉链零件	21	0	0	0	0	0	0	0	0	0	0		0		0	0	10.5	4.2			
96081000	圆珠笔	15	0	0	0	0	0	0	0	0	0	0	13.5	1.5	7.5	0	0	7.5	3			
96082000	毡尖和其他渗水式笔尖笔及唛头笔	21	0	0	0	0	0	0	0	0	0	0		0		0	0	10.5	4.2			
96083010	墨汁画笔	21	0	0	0	0	0	0	0	0	0	0		0		0	0	10.5	4.2			
96083020	自来水笔	21	0	0	0	0	0	0	0	0	0	0		0		0	0	10.5	4.2			
96083090	其他钢笔	21	0	0	0	0	0	0	0	0	0	0		0		0	0	10.5	4.2			
96084000	活动铅笔	21	0	0	0	0	0	0	0	0	0	0		0		0	0	10.5	4.2			
96085000	含有≥两种笔的成套货品	21	0	0	0	0	0	0	0	0	0	0		0		0	0	10.5	4.2			
96086000	圆珠笔芯	21	0	0	0	0	0	0	0	0	0	0		0		0	0	10.5	4.2	0	0	
96089100	钢笔头及笔尖粒	12	0	0	0	0	0	0	0	0	0	0		0	6	0	0	0	2.4	0	0	
96089910	机器、仪器用笔	17.5	0	0	0	0	0	0	0	0	0	0		0	14	0	0	8.8	3.5	0		
96089920	蜡纸铁笔、钢笔杆、铅笔杆等	21	0	0	0	0	0	0	0	0	0	0		0		0	0	10.5	4.2	0	0	
96089990	其他笔零件	21	0	0	0	0	0	0	0	0	0	0		0		0	0	10.5	4.2	0	0	
96091010	铅笔	21	0	0	0	0	0	0	0	0	0	0		2.1		0	0	10.5	4.2			
96091020	颜色铅笔	21	0	0	0	0	0	0	0	0	0	0		2.1		0	0	10.5	4.2			
96092000	铅笔芯，黑的或其他颜色的	21	0	0	0	0	0	0	0	0	0	0		2.1		0	0	10.5	4.2			
96099000	蜡笔、图画碳笔、书写或绘画用粉笔	15	0	0	0	0	0	0	0	0	0	0		1.5	12	0	0	7.5	3			
96100000	具有书写或绘画面的石板、黑板	15	0	0	0	0	0	0	0	0	0	0		0	12	0	0	7.5	3			
96110000	手用日期戳、封缄戳、编号戳及类似印戳	21	0	0	0	0	0	0	0	0	0	0		2.1		0	0	10.5	4.2			
96121000	打字机色带或类似色带	10.5	0	0	0	0	0	0	0	0	0	0		0	5	0	0	0	2.1		0	
96122000	印台	25	0	0	0	0	0	0	0	0	0	0		0		0	0	12.5	5			
96131000	一次性袖珍气体打火机	25	0	0	0	0	0	0	0	0	0	0		2.5		0	0	12.5	5			
96132000	可充气袖珍气体打火机	25	0	0	0	0	0	0	0	0	0	0		0		0	0	12.5	5			
96138000	其他打火器	25	0	0	0	0	0	0	0	0	0	0		0		0	0	12.5	5			
96139000	打火机及打火器零件	25	0	0	0	0	0	0	0	0	0	0		0		0	0	12.5	5			
96140010	烟斗及烟斗头	25	0	0	0	0	0	0	0	0	0	0		0		0	0	12.5	5			
96140090	烟嘴及其零件	25	0	0	0	0	0	0	0	0	0	0		0		0	0	12.5	5			
96151100	硬质橡胶或塑料制梳子、发夹及类似品	18	0	0	0	0	0	0	0	0	0	0	16.2	1.8	14.4	0	0	9	3.6			
96151900	其他材料制梳子、发夹及类似品	18	0	0	0	0	0	0	0	0	0	0		0		0	0	9	3.6			
96159000	其他发夹、卷发器等及其零件	18	0	0	0	0	0	0	0	0	0	0	16.2	0	14.4	0	0	9	3.6			
96161000	香水喷雾器或类似的化妆用喷雾器	18	0	0	0	0	0	0	0	0	0	0	16.2	1.8	14.4	0	0	9	3.6			
96162000	施敷脂粉或化妆品用粉扑及粉拍	18	0	0	0	0	0	0	0	0	0	0	16.2	0	14.4	0	0	9	3.6			
96170011	玻璃内胆制保温瓶	24	0	0	0	0	0	0	0	0	0	0		0		0	0	12	4.8	0		
96170019	其他保温瓶	24	0	0	0	0	0	0	0	0	0	0		0		0	0	12	4.8	0		
96170090	其他真空容器及零件	18	0	0	0	0	0	0	0	0	0	0		0		0	0	9	3.6	0		
96180000	裁缝用人体模型及其他人体模型	21	0	0	0	0	0	0	0	0	0	0		0		0	0	10.5	4.2			
96190010	尿布及尿裤	7.5	0	0	0	0	0	0	0	0	0	0		0			0	0	1.5	0	0	0
96190020	卫生巾（护垫）及止血塞	10	0	0	0	0	0	0	0	0	0	0		0	7.5		0	0	0	0	0	0
96190090	任何材料制的卫生巾或尿布的类似品	14	0	0	0	0	0	0	0	0	0	0	9.3	0	7.5	0	0	7	2.8	0	0	0
97011011	唐卡	12	0	0	0	0	0	0	0	0	0	0		1.2	6	0	0	6	2.4			
97011019	其他手绘油画、粉画及其他画	12	0	0	0	0	0	0	0	0	0	0		1.2	6	0	0	6	2.4			
97011020	手绘油画、粉画及其他画的复制品	14	0	0	0	0	0	0	0	0	0	0		1.4	11.2	0	0	0	2.8			
97019000	拼贴画及类似装饰板	14	0	0	0	0	0	0	0	0	0	0		0	11.2	0	0	0	2.8			
97020000	雕版画、印制画、石印画的原本	12	0	0	0	0	0	0	0	0	0	0		0	6	0	0	6	2.4			
97030000	各种材料制的雕塑品原件	12	0	0	0	0	0	0	0	0	0	0		0	6	0	0	0	2.4			
97040010	使用或未使用的邮票	8	0	0	0	0	0	0	0	0	0	0		0	5		0	0	0	0	0	
97040090	其他使用或未使用的印花税票及类似票证	14	0	0	0	0	0	0	0	0	0	0		0	7	0	0	0	2.8	0	0	

注：

（1）完税价格不高于 2000 美元/台：15%；完税价格高于 2000 美元/台：3%，加 1581 元

（2）完税价格不高于 2000 美元/台：24.5%；完税价格高于 2000 美元/台：3%，加 2614 元

（3）完税价格不高于 2000 美元/台：18%；完税价格高于 2000 美元/台：3%，加 1824 元

（4）完税价格不高于 5000 美元/台：29.8%；完税价格高于 5000 美元/台：3%，加 8147 元

附表十

2014 年进口商品特惠税目税率表
Special Preferential Tariff Rates on Import Goods 2014

税则号列	商品名称（简称）	最惠税率	亚太2国	东盟			最不发达35国	最不发达4国
				缅	老	柬		
01012100	改良种用马	0					0	0
01012900	其他马	10					0	0
01013010	改良种用驴	0					0	0
01013090	其他驴	10					0	0
01019000	骡	10					0	0
01022100	改良种用家牛	0					0	0
01022900	其他家牛	10		0	0	0	0	0
01023100	改良种用水牛	0					0	0
01023900	其他水牛	10		0	0	0	0	0
01029010	改良种用其他牛	0					0	0
01029090	其他牛	10		0	0	0	0	0
01031000	改良种用猪	0					0	0
01039110	重量＜10kg 的猪	10		0		0	0	0
01039120	重量在 10-50kg 的猪，包括 10kg	10		0		0	0	0
01039200	重量≥50kg 的猪	10		0	0	0	0	0
01041010	改良种用的绵羊	0					0	0
01041090	其他绵羊	10					0	0
01042010	改良种用的山羊	0					0	0
01042090	其他山羊	10					0	0
01051110	重量≤185g 的改良种用鸡	0					0	0
01051190	重量≤185g 的其他鸡	10		0	0		0	0
01051210	重量≤185g 的改良种用火鸡	0					0	0
01051290	重量≤185g 的其他火鸡	10					0	0
01051310	重量不超过 185 克的改良种用鸭	0					0	0
01051390	重量不超过 185 克的其他鸭	10			0		0	0
01051410	重量不超过 185 克的改良种用鹅	0					0	0
01051490	重量不超过 185 克的其他鹅	10			0		0	0
01051510	重量不超过 185 克的改良种用珍珠鸡	0					0	0
01051590	重量不超过 185 克的其他珍珠鸡	10			0		0	0
01059410	重量＞185g 的改良种用鸡	0					0	0
01059490	重量＞185g 的其他鸡	10					0	0
01059910	重量＞185g 的其他改良种用家禽	0					0	0
01059991	重量＞185g 的非改良种用鸭	10					0	0
01059992	重量＞185g 的非改良种用鹅	10					0	0
01059993	重量＞185g 的非改良种用珍珠鸡	10					0	0
01059994	重量＞185g 的非改良种用火鸡	10					0	0
01061110	改良种用灵长目动物	0					0	0
01061190	其他灵长目动物	10					0	0
01061211	改良种用鲸、海豚及鼠海豚；海牛及儒艮	10					0	0
01061219	其他鲸、海豚及鼠海豚；海牛及儒艮	10					0	0
01061221	改良种用海豹、海狮及海象	0					0	0
01061229	其他海豹、海狮及海象	10					0	0

注：① 亚太 2 国：孟加拉人民共和国、老挝人民民主共和国

② 最不发达 35 国：埃塞俄比亚联邦民主共和国、安哥拉共和国、贝宁共和国、布隆迪共和国、多哥共和国、厄立特里亚国、刚果民主共和国、吉布提共和国、几内亚共和国、几内亚比绍共和国、科摩罗联盟、莱索托王国、利比里亚共和国、卢旺达共和国、马达加斯加共和国、马拉维共和国、马里共和国、莫桑比克共和国、尼日尔共和国、塞拉利昂共和国、苏丹共和国、坦桑尼亚联合共和国、乌干达共和国、赞比亚共和国、乍得共和国、中非共和国、阿富汗伊斯兰共和国、东帝汶民主共和国、柬埔寨王国、缅甸联邦共和国、尼泊尔联邦民主共和国、也门共和国、萨摩亚独立国、瓦努阿图共和国、塞内加尔共和国。（共 35 国）

③赤道几内亚共和国、毛里塔尼亚伊斯兰共和国、索马里联邦共和国、孟加拉人民共和国（共4国）

税则号列	商品名称（简称）	最惠税率	亚太2国	东盟			最不发达35国	最不发达4国
				缅	老	柬		
01061310	改良种用骆驼及其他骆驼科动物	0					0	0
01061390	其他骆驼及其他骆驼科动物	10					0	0
01061410	改良种用家兔及野兔	0					0	0
01061490	其他家兔及野兔	10					0	0
01061910	改良种用哺乳动物	0					0	0
01061990	其他哺乳动物	10					0	0
01062011	改良种用鳄鱼苗	0					0	0
01062019	其他改良种用爬行动物	0					0	0
01062020	食用爬行动物	10		0			0	0
01062090	其他爬行动物	10					0	0
01063110	改良种用猛禽	0					0	0
01063190	其他猛禽	10					0	0
01063210	改良种用鹦形目鸟	0					0	0
01063290	其他鹦形目鸟	10					0	0
01063310	改良种用鸵鸟；鸸鹋	0					0	0
01063390	其他鸵鸟；鸸鹋	10					0	0
01063910	其他改良种用鸟	0					0	0
01063921	乳鸽	10		0			0	0
01063923	野鸭	10		0			0	0
01063929	其他食用鸟	10		0			0	0
01063990	其他鸟	10					0	0
01064110	改良种用蜂	0					0	0
01064190	其他蜂	10					0	0
01064910	改良种用其他昆虫	0					0	0
01064990	其他昆虫	10					0	0
01069011	改良种用蛙苗	0					0	0
01069019	其他改良种用动物	0					0	0
01069090	其他动物	10					0	0
02011000	整头及半头鲜、冷牛肉	20			0	0	0	0
02012000	鲜、冷的带骨牛肉	12			0	0	0	0
02013000	鲜、冷的去骨牛肉	12				0	0	0
02021000	冻的整头及半头牛肉	25			0	0	0	0
02022000	冻的带骨牛肉	12			0	0	0	0
02023000	冻的去骨牛肉	12				0	0	0
02031110	鲜、冷的整头及半头乳猪肉	20			0	0	0	0
02031190	其他鲜、冷的整头及半头猪肉	20			0	0	0	0
02031200	鲜、冷的带骨猪前腿、后腿及其肉块	20			0	0	0	0
02031900	其他鲜、冷猪肉	20			0	0	0	0
02032110	冻整头及半头乳猪肉	12			0	0	0	0
02032190	其他冻整头及半头猪肉	12			0	0	0	0
02032200	冻的带骨猪前腿、后腿及其肉块	12			0	0	0	0
02032900	其他冻猪肉	12				0	0	0
02041000	鲜或冷的整头及半头羔羊	15					0	
02042100	鲜或冷的整头及半头绵羊肉	23					0	
02042200	鲜或冷的带骨绵羊肉	15					0	
02042300	鲜或冷的去骨绵羊肉	15					0	
02043000	冻的整头及半头羔羊	15					0	
02044100	冻的整头及半头绵羊肉	23					0	
02044200	冻的其他带骨绵羊肉	12					0	
02044300	冻的其他去骨绵羊肉	15					0	
02045000	鲜、冷、冻的山羊肉	20					0	
02050000	鲜、冷、冻的马、驴、骡肉	20					0	
02061000	鲜、冷的牛杂碎	12			0	0	0	0
02062100	冻牛舌	12			0	0	0	0
02062200	冻牛肝	12			0	0	0	0
02062900	其他冻牛杂碎	12			0	0	0	0
02063000	鲜、冷的猪杂碎	20		0	0	0	0	0
02064100	冻猪肝	20			0	0	0	0

税则号列	商品名称（简称）	最惠税率	亚太2国	东盟 缅	东盟 老	东盟 柬	最不发达35国	最不发达4国
02064900	其他冻猪杂碎	12			0	0	0	0
02068000	鲜、冷的羊、马、驴、骡杂碎	20				0	0	0
02069000	冻的羊、马、驴、骡杂碎	18				0	0	0
02071100	整只，鲜或冷的鸡	20		0	0	0	0	0
02071200	整只，冻的鸡	20		0	0	0	0	0
02071311	鲜或冷的带骨鸡块	20		0	0	0	0	0
02071319	鲜或冷的其他鸡块	20		0	0	0	0	0
02071321	鲜或冷的鸡翼（不包括翼尖）	20		0	0	0	0	0
02071329	鲜或冷的其他鸡杂碎	20		0	0	0	0	0
02071411	冻的的带骨鸡块	10		0	0	0	0	0
02071419	冻的其他鸡块	10		0	0	0	0	0
02071421	冻的鸡翼（不包括翼尖）	10		0	0	0	0	0
02071422	鲜、冷、冻鸡爪	10		0	0	0	0	0
02071429	冻的其他鸡杂碎	10		0	0	0	0	0
02072400	整只，鲜或冷的火鸡	20			0		0	0
02072500	整只，冻的火鸡	20			0		0	0
02072600	鲜或冷的火鸡块及杂碎	20			0		0	0
02072700	冻的火鸡块及杂碎	10			0		0	0
02074100	鲜或冷的整只鸭	20		0	0	0	0	0
02074200	冻的整只鸭	20		0	0	0	0	0
02074300	鲜或冷的鸭肥肝	20			0	0	0	0
02074400	鲜或冷的其他鸭	20		0	0	0	0	0
02074500	冻的其他鸭	20		0	0	0	0	0
02075100	鲜或冷的整只鹅	20		0	0	0	0	0
02075200	冻的整只鹅	20		0	0	0	0	0
02075300	鲜或冷的鹅肥肝	20			0	0	0	0
02075400	鲜或冷的其他鹅	20		0	0	0	0	0
02075500	冻的其他鹅	20		0	0	0	0	0
02076000	鲜、冷、冻珍珠鸡	20			0	0	0	0
02081010	鲜或冷藏的家兔肉或野兔，不包括兔头	20					0	
02081020	冻家兔或野兔，不包括兔头	20					0	
02081090	鲜、冷、冻的家兔及野兔食用杂碎	20					0	
02083000	鲜、冷、冻的灵长目动物的肉及其食用杂碎	23					0	
02084000	鲜、冷、冻鲸、海豚及鼠海豚；鲜、冷、冻海牛及儒艮；鲜、冷、冻海豹、海狮及海象	23					0	
02085000	鲜、冷、冻的爬行动物的肉及其食用杂碎	23					0	
02086000	鲜、冷、冻骆驼及其他骆驼科动物	23					0	
02089010	鲜、冷、冻的乳鸽肉及其食用杂碎	20					0	
02089090	其他鲜、冷、冻肉及食用杂碎	23					0	
02091000	未炼制猪脂肪	20					0	
02099000	未炼制家禽脂肪	20					0	
02101110	干、熏、盐制的带骨猪腿	25			0	0	0	0
02101190	干、熏、盐制的带骨猪腿肉块	25			0	0	0	0
02101200	干、熏、盐制的猪腹肉	25			0	0	0	0
02101900	干、熏、盐制的其他猪肉	25		0		0	0	0
02102000	干、熏、盐制的牛肉	25			0	0	0	0
02109100	干、熏、盐制的灵长目动物肉及食用杂碎	25			0	0	0	0
02109200	鲸、海豚及鼠海豚的；海牛及儒艮的；海豹、海狮及海象的肉及食用杂碎	25			0	0	0	0
02109300	干、熏、盐制的爬行动物肉及食用杂碎	25			0	0	0	0
02109900	干、熏、盐制的其他肉及食用杂碎	25			0	0	0	0
03011100	淡水观赏鱼	17.5					0	0
03011900	其他观赏鱼	17.5					0	0
03019110	鳟鱼苗	0					0	0
03019190	其他活鳟鱼	10.5					0	0
03019210	鳗鱼苗	0					0	0
03019290	其他活鳗鱼	10		0		0	0	0
03019310	鲤科鱼鱼苗	0					0	0
03019390	其他鲤科鱼	10.5		0		0	0	0
03019410	大西洋及太平洋蓝鳍金枪鱼鱼苗	0					0	0

税则号列	商品名称（简称）	最惠税率	亚太2国	东盟			最不发达35国	最不发达4国
				缅	老	柬		
03019491	大西洋蓝鳍金枪鱼	10.5		0		0	0	0
03019492	太平洋蓝鳍金枪鱼	10.5		0		0	0	0
03019510	南方蓝鳍金枪鱼鱼苗	0					0	0
03019590	其他活南方蓝鳍金枪鱼	10.5		0		0	0	0
03019911	鲈鱼鱼苗	0					0	0
03019912	鲟鱼鱼苗	0					0	0
03019919	其他鱼苗	0					0	0
03019991	活罗非鱼	10.5		0		0	0	0
03019992	活鲀	10.5		0		0	0	0
03019993	其他鲤科鱼	10.5		0		0	0	0
03019999	其他活鱼	10.5		0		0	0	0
03021100	鲜、冷鳟鱼	12					0	0
03021300	鲜、冷大麻哈鱼	10					0	0
03021410	鲜、冷大西洋鲑鱼	10					0	0
03021420	鲜、冷多瑙哲罗鱼	10					0	0
03021900	其他鲜、冷鲑鱼	12					0	0
03022100	鲜、冷庸鲽鱼	12					0	0
03022200	鲜、冷鲽鱼	12					0	0
03022300	鲜、冷鳎鱼	12					0	0
03022400	鲜、冷大菱鲆	12				0	0	0
03022900	其他鲜、冷比目鱼	12				0	0	0
03023100	鲜、冷长鳍金枪鱼	12				0	0	0
03023200	鲜、冷黄鳍金枪鱼	12					0	0
03023300	鲜、冷鲣鱼或狐鲣	12					0	0
03023400	鲜、冷大眼金枪鱼	12		0		0	0	0
03023510	鲜、冷大西洋蓝鳍金枪鱼	12		0		0	0	0
03023520	鲜、冷太平洋蓝鳍金枪鱼	12		0		0	0	0
03023600	鲜、冷南方蓝鳍金枪鱼	12		0		0	0	0
03023900	其他鲜、冷金枪鱼	12		0		0	0	0
03024100	鲜、冷鲱鱼（大西洋鲱鱼、太平洋鲱鱼）	12					0	0
03024200	鲜、冷鳀鱼	12		0		0	0	0
03024300	鲜、冷沙丁鱼（沙丁鱼、沙瑙鱼属）、小沙丁鱼属、黍鲱或西鲱	12					0	0
03024400	鲜、冷鲭鱼	12					0	0
03024500	鲜、冷对称竹荚鱼、新西兰竹荚鱼及竹荚鱼	12		0		0	0	0
03024600	鲜、冷军曹鱼	12		0		0	0	0
03024700	鲜、冷剑鱼	12					0	0
03025100	鳕鱼(大西洋鳕鱼、格陵兰鳕鱼、太平洋鳕鱼)	12					0	0
03025200	鲜、冷黑线鳕鱼	12					0	0
03025300	鲜、冷绿青鳕鱼	12					0	0
03025400	鲜、冷狗鳕鱼	12		0		0	0	0
03025500	鲜、冷狭鳕鱼	12		0		0	0	0
03025600	鲜、冷蓝鳕鱼	12		0		0	0	0
03025900	鲜、冷其他鳕科鱼	12		0		0	0	0
03027100	鲜、冷罗非鱼	12		0		0	0	0
03027200	鲜、冷鲶鱼	12		0		0	0	0
03027300	鲜、冷鲤科鱼	12		0		0	0	0
03027400	鲜、冷鳗鱼	12		0			0	0
03027900	鲜、冷尼罗河鲈鱼及黑鱼	12		0		0	0	0
03028100	鲜、冷角鲨及其他鲨鱼	12					0	0
03028200	鲜、冷魟鱼及鳐鱼	12		0		0	0	0
03028300	鲜、冷南极犬牙鱼	12		0		0	0	0
03028400	鲜、冷尖吻鲈鱼	12		0		0	0	0
03028500	鲜、冷菱羊鲷	12		0		0	0	0
03028910	鲜、冷带鱼	12					0	0
03028920	鲜、冷黄鱼	12					0	0
03028930	鲜、冷鲳鱼	12					0	0
03028940	鲜、冷鲀	12		0		0	0	0
03028990	鲜、冷其他鱼	12		0		0	0	0

税则号列	商品名称（简称）	最惠税率	亚太2国	东盟			最不发达35国	最不发达4国
				缅	老	柬		
03029000	鲜、冷鱼肝及鱼卵	12				0	0	0
03031100	冻红大麻哈鱼	10				0	0	0
03031200	冻其他大麻哈鱼	10				0	0	0
03031300	冻大西洋鲑鱼及多瑙哲罗鱼	10					0	0
03031400	冻鳟鱼	12					0	0
03031900	冻其他鲑科鱼	10					0	0
03032300	冻罗非鱼	10	0	0		0	0	0
03032400	冻鲶鱼	10	0	0		0	0	0
03032500	冻鲤科鱼	10	0	0		0	0	0
03032600	冻鳗鱼	12					0	0
03032900	冻尼罗河鲈鱼及黑鱼	10	0	0		0	0	0
03033110	冻格陵兰庸鲽鱼	10					0	0
03033190	冻庸鲽鱼	10					0	0
03033200	冻鲽鱼	12					0	0
03033300	冻鳎鱼	12					0	0
03033400	冻大菱鲆	10					0	0
03033900	其他冻比目鱼	10					0	0
03034100	冻长鳍金枪鱼	12					0	0
03034200	冻黄鳍金枪鱼	12					0	0
03034300	冻鲣鱼或狐鲣	12					0	0
03034400	冻大眼金枪鱼，但鱼肝及鱼卵除外	12		0		0	0	0
03034510	冻大西洋蓝鳍金枪鱼	12		0		0	0	0
03034520	冻太平洋蓝鳍金枪鱼	12		0		0	0	0
03034600	冻南方蓝鳍金枪鱼，但鱼肝及鱼卵除外	12		0		0	0	0
03034900	其他冻金枪鱼，但鱼肝及鱼卵除外	12		0		0	0	0
03035100	冻鲱鱼(大西洋鲱鱼、太平洋鲱鱼)，但鱼肝及鱼卵除外	10					0	0
03035300	冻沙丁鱼、小沙丁鱼属、黍鲱或西鲱	12					0	0
03035400	冻鲭鱼	10					0	0
03035500	冻对称竹荚鱼、新西兰竹荚鱼及竹荚鱼	10	0	0		0	0	0
03035600	冻军曹鱼	10	0	0		0	0	0
03035700	冻剑鱼	10	0				0	0
03036300	鳕鱼(大西洋鳕鱼、格陵兰鳕鱼、太平洋鳕鱼)	10					0	0
03036400	冻黑线鳕鱼	12					0	0
03036500	冻绿青鳕鱼	12					0	0
03036600	冻狗鳕鱼	12					0	0
03036700	冻狭鳕鱼	10	0	0		0	0	0
03036800	冻蓝鳕鱼	10	0	0		0	0	0
03036900	其他冻鳕鱼	10	0	0		0	0	0
03038100	冻角鲨及其他鲨鱼	12					0	0
03038200	冻魟鱼及鳐鱼	10	0	0		0	0	0
03038300	冻南极犬牙鱼	10	0	0		0	0	0
03038400	冻尖吻鲈鱼	12					0	0
03038910	冻带鱼	10	0	0		0	0	0
03038920	冻黄鱼	10	0	0		0	0	0
03038930	冻鲳鱼	10	0	0		0	0	0
03038990	其他冻鱼	10	0	0		0	0	0
03039000	冻鱼肝及鱼卵	10					0	0
03043100	鲜、冷罗非鱼片	12		0			0	0
03043200	鲜、冷鲶鱼片	12		0			0	0
03043300	鲜、冷尼罗河鲈鱼片	12		0			0	0
03043900	鲜、冷鲤科鱼、鳗鱼、黑鱼片	12		0			0	0
03044100	鲜、冷大麻哈鱼片	12		0			0	0
03044200	鲜、冷鳟鱼片	12		0			0	0
03044300	鲜、冷比目鱼片	12		0			0	0
03044400	鲜、冷犀鳕科等鳕科鱼片	12		0			0	0
03044500	鲜、冷剑鱼片	12		0			0	0
03044600	鲜、冷南极犬牙鱼片	12		0			0	0
03044900	鲜、冷其他鱼片	12		0			0	0

税则号列	商品名称（简称）	最惠税率	亚太2国	东盟			最不发达35国	最不发达4国
				缅	老	柬		
03045100	鲜、冷罗非鱼等鱼鱼肉	12		0			0	0
03045200	鲜、冷鲑科鱼肉	12		0			0	0
03045300	鲜、冷犀鳕科等鳕科鱼肉	12		0			0	0
03045400	鲜、冷剑鱼肉	12		0			0	0
03045500	鲜、冷南极犬牙鱼肉	12		0			0	0
03045900	鲜、冷其他鱼肉	12		0			0	0
03046100	冻罗非鱼等鱼鱼片	10		0		0	0	0
03046211	冻斑点叉尾鮰鱼片	10					0	0
03046219	冻其他叉尾鮰鱼片	10					0	0
03046290	冻其他鲶鱼片	10		0		0	0	0
03046300	冻尼罗河鲈鱼片	10		0		0	0	0
03046900	冻鲤科鱼、鳗鱼、黑鱼片	10		0		0	0	0
03047100	鳕鱼(大西洋鳕鱼、格陵兰鳕鱼、太平洋鳕鱼)	10		0		0	0	0
03047200	冻黑线鳕鱼片	10		0		0	0	0
03047300	冻绿青鳕鱼片	10		0		0	0	0
03047400	冻狗鳕鱼片	10		0		0	0	0
03047500	冻狭鳕鱼片	10		0		0	0	0
03047900	冻其他鳕鱼片	10		0		0	0	0
03048100	冻大麻哈鱼、大西洋鲑鱼及多瑙哲罗鱼片	10		0		0	0	0
03048200	冻鳟鱼片	10		0		0	0	0
03048300	冻比目鱼片	10		0		0	0	0
03048400	冻剑鱼片	10		0		0	0	0
03048500	冻南极犬牙鱼片	10		0		0	0	0
03048600	冻鲱鱼片	10		0		0	0	0
03048700	冻金枪鱼、鲣鱼或狐鲣(鲣)片	10		0		0	0	0
03048900	冻其他鱼片	10		0		0	0	0
03049100	冻的剑鱼肉	10	0	0			0	0
03049200	冻的南极犬牙鱼肉	10	0	0			0	0
03049300	冻罗非鱼等鱼鱼肉	10	0	0			0	0
03049400	冻狭鳕鱼肉	10	0	0			0	0
03049500	冻犀鳕科等鳕科鱼肉	10	0	0			0	0
03049900	其他冻鱼肉	10	0	0			0	0
03051000	供人食用的鱼粉及团粒	10					0	0
03052000	干、熏、盐制的鱼肝及鱼卵	10					0	0
03053100	干、盐腌罗非鱼等鱼鱼片	10	0	0			0	0
03053200	干、盐腌犀鳕科等鳕科鱼片	10	0	0			0	0
03053900	干、盐腌其他鱼片	10	0	0			0	0
03054110	熏大西洋鲑鱼，食用杂碎除外	14					0	
03054120	熏鲱鱼，食用杂碎除外	14					0	
03054200	熏鲱鱼，食用杂碎除外	16					0	
03054300	熏鳟鱼，食用杂碎除外	14	0	0			0	0
03054400	熏罗非鱼等鱼，食用杂碎除外	14	0	0			0	0
03054900	熏其他鱼，食用杂碎除外	14	0	0			0	0
03055100	鳕鱼(大西洋鳕鱼、格陵兰鳕鱼、太平洋鳕鱼)	16					0	
03055910	干海马、干海龙	2	0	0		0	0	0
03055990	干其他鱼，食用杂碎除外	16	0	0			0	0
03056100	盐腌及盐渍的鲱鱼，食用杂碎除外	16					0	
03056200	鳕鱼(大西洋鳕鱼、格陵兰鳕鱼、太平洋鳕鱼)	16					0	0
03056300	盐腌及盐渍的鳀鱼，食用杂碎除外	16					0	
03056400	盐腌及盐渍的罗非鱼等鱼，食用杂碎除外	16	0	0			0	0
03056910	盐腌及盐渍的带鱼，食用杂碎除外	16	0	0			0	0
03056920	盐腌及盐渍的黄鱼，食用杂碎除外	16	0	0			0	0
03056930	盐腌及盐渍的鲳鱼，食用杂碎除外	16	0	0			0	0
03056990	盐腌及盐渍的其他鱼，食用杂碎除外	16	0	0			0	0
03057100	鲨鱼翅	15	0	0		0	0	0
03057200	鱼头、鱼尾、鱼鳔	16					0	
03057900	其他可食用杂碎	16					0	
03061100	岩礁虾和其他龙虾（真龙虾属、龙虾属、岩龙虾属）	10		0		0	0	0

税则号列	商品名称（简称）	最惠税率	亚太2国	东盟			最不发达35国	最不发达4国
				缅	老	柬		
03061200	螯龙虾(螯龙虾属)	10				0	0	0
03061410	冻梭子蟹	10	0	0		0	0	0
03061490	其他冻蟹	10	0	0		0	0	0
03061500	冻挪威海螯虾	16				0	0	0
03061611	冻冷水小虾虾仁	8		0		0	0	0
03061612	冻北方长额虾虾仁	5		0		0	0	0
03061619	冻其他冷水小虾	5		0		0	0	0
03061621	冻冷水对虾虾仁	8		0		0	0	0
03061629	冻其他冷水对虾	5		0		0	0	0
03061711	冻小虾虾仁	8		0		0	0	0
03061719	冻其他小虾	5		0		0	0	0
03061721	冻对虾虾仁	8		0		0	0	0
03061729	冻其他对虾	5		0		0	0	0
03061911	冻淡水小龙虾仁	16				0	0	0
03061919	冻带壳淡水小龙虾	16				0	0	0
03061990	其他冻甲壳动物	16				0	0	0
03062110	岩礁虾和其他龙虾（真龙虾属、龙虾属、岩龙虾属）种苗	0					0	0
03062190	其他岩礁虾和其他龙虾（真龙虾属、龙虾属、岩龙虾属）	15		0		0	0	0
03062210	螯龙虾（螯龙虾属）种苗	0					0	0
03062290	其他螯龙虾（螯龙虾属）	15		0		0	0	0
03062410	蟹种苗	0					0	0
03062491	未冻的中华绒毛蟹(大闸蟹)	14				0	0	0
03062492	未冻的梭子蟹	14				0	0	0
03062499	未冻的其他蟹	14				0	0	0
03062510	未冻的挪威海螯虾种苗	0					0	0
03062590	未冻的其他挪威海螯虾	14		0		0	0	0
03062610	未冻的冷水小虾及对虾种苗	0					0	0
03062620	鲜、冷冷水对虾	15		0		0	0	0
03062690	未冻的其他冷水小虾及对虾	12		0		0	0	0
03062710	未冻的其他小虾及对虾种苗	0					0	0
03062720	鲜、冷对虾	15		0		0	0	0
03062790	未冻的其他小虾及对虾	12		0		0	0	0
03062910	其他食用甲壳动物种苗	0					0	0
03062990	其他带壳或去壳的未冻的甲壳动物	14		0		0	0	0
03071110	活、鲜或冷的牡蛎（蚝）种苗	0					0	0
03071190	活、鲜或冷的其他牡蛎（蚝）	14		0			0	0
03071900	冻、干、盐腌或盐渍的牡蛎（蚝）	14		0			0	0
03072110	扇贝(包括海扇)种苗	0					0	0
03072190	其他活、鲜、冷扇贝	14		0			0	0
03072900	其他冻、干、盐腌或盐渍的扇贝	14		0			0	0
03073110	贻贝种苗	0					0	0
03073190	其他活、鲜、冷贻贝	14		0		0	0	0
03073900	其他冻、干、盐制的贻贝	14		0		0	0	0
03074110	墨鱼及鱿鱼种苗	0					0	0
03074190	其他活、鲜或冷墨鱼及鱿鱼	12		0		0	0	0
03074900	其他冻、干、盐制的墨鱼及鱿鱼	12		0		0	0	0
03075100	活、鲜、冷章鱼	17					0	
03075900	其他冻、干、盐制的章鱼	17					0	0
03076010	蜗牛及螺的种苗，海螺种苗除外	0					0	0
03076090	其他蜗牛及螺，海螺除外	14				0	0	0
03077110	活、鲜或冷的蛤、鸟蛤及舟贝种苗	0					0	0
03077191	活、鲜或冷的蛤	14					0	
03077199	活、鲜或冷的鸟蛤及舟贝	14		0		0	0	0
03077910	冻、干、盐腌或盐渍的蛤	10					0	0
03077990	冻、干、盐腌或盐渍的鸟蛤及舟贝	10		0		0	0	0
03078110	活、鲜或冷的鲍鱼种苗	0					0	0
03078190	活、鲜或冷的其他鲍鱼	14		0		0	0	0
03078900	冻、干、盐腌或盐渍的鲍鱼	10		0		0	0	0

税则号列	商品名称（简称）	最惠税率	亚太2国	东盟			最不发达35国	最不发达4国
				缅	老	柬		
03079110	活、鲜或冷的其他软体动物种苗	0					0	0
03079190	活、鲜或冷的其他软体动物	14		0		0	0	0
03079900	冻、干、盐腌或盐渍的软体动物	10		0		0	0	0
03081110	活、鲜或冷的海参种苗	0					0	0
03081190	活、鲜或冷的其他海参	14		0		0	0	0
03081900	冻、干、盐腌或盐渍的海参	10		0		0	0	0
03082110	活、鲜或冷的海胆种苗	0					0	0
03082190	活、鲜或冷的其他海胆	14		0		0	0	0
03082900	冻、干、盐腌或盐渍的海胆	10		0		0	0	0
03083011	活、鲜或冷的海蜇种苗	0					0	0
03083019	活、鲜或冷的其他海蜇	14		0		0	0	0
03083090	冻、干、盐腌或盐渍的海蜇	10		0		0	0	0
03089011	活、鲜或冷的其他水生无脊椎动物种苗	0					0	0
03089012	活、鲜或冷的其他沙蚕	14		0		0	0	0
03089019	活、鲜或冷的其他水生无脊椎动物	14		0		0	0	0
03089090	冻、干、盐腌或盐渍的其他水生无脊椎动物	10		0		0	0	0
04011000	脂肪含量未超1%未浓缩及未加糖的乳及奶油	15					0	0
04012000	脂肪含量在1-6%未浓缩及未加糖的乳及奶油	15					0	0
04014000	按重量计脂肪含量超过6%，但不超过10%的未浓缩及未加糖或其他甜物质的乳及奶油	15					0	0
04015000	按重量计脂肪含量超过10%的未浓缩及未加糖或其他甜物质的乳及奶油	15					0	0
04021000	脂肪含量≤1.5%固状乳及奶油	10					0	0
04022100	脂肪量>1.5%未加糖固状乳及奶油	10					0	0
04022900	脂肪量>1.5%的加糖固状乳及奶油	10					0	0
04029100	浓缩但未加糖的非固状乳及奶油	10					0	0
04029900	浓缩并已加糖的非固状乳及奶油	10					0	0
04031000	酸乳	10					0	0
04039000	酪乳及其他发酵或酸化的乳及奶油	20					0	
04041000	乳清及改性乳清	6					0	
04049000	其他编号未列名的含天然乳的产品	20					0	
04051000	黄油	10					0	0
04052000	乳酱	10					0	0
04059000	其他从乳中提取的脂和油	10					0	0
04061000	鲜乳酪(未熟化或未固化的)	12					0	0
04063000	经加工的乳酪，但磨碎或粉化的除外	12					0	
04064000	蓝纹乳酪和娄地青霉生产的带有纹理的其他乳酪	15					0	
04069000	其他乳酪	12					0	0
04071100	种用鸡蛋	0					0	0
04071900	种用其他禽蛋	0					0	0
04072100	鲜鸡蛋	20		0		0	0	0
04072900	其他鲜禽蛋	20		0		0	0	0
04079010	咸蛋	20		0			0	0
04079020	皮蛋	20					0	
04079090	其他蛋	20					0	
04081100	干蛋黄	20					0	
04081900	其他蛋黄	20					0	
04089100	干的其他去壳禽蛋	20					0	
04089900	其他去壳禽蛋	20					0	
04090000	天然蜂蜜	15			0	0	0	0
04100010	燕窝	25		0		0	0	0
04100041	鲜蜂王浆	15					0	
04100042	鲜蜂王浆粉	15					0	
04100043	蜂花粉	20					0	
04100049	其他蜂产品	20					0	
04100090	其他编号未列名的食用动物产品	20		0			0	0
05010000	未经加工的人发；废人发	15					0	
05021010	猪鬃	20					0	
05021020	猪毛	20					0	
05021030	猪鬃或猪毛的废料	20					0	

税则号列	商品名称（简称）	最惠税率	亚太2国	东盟			最不发达35国	最不发达4国
				缅	老	柬		
05029011	山羊毛	20					0	
05029012	黄鼠狼尾毛	20					0	
05029019	獾毛及其他制刷用兽毛	20					0	
05029020	獾毛及其他制刷用兽毛的废料	20					0	
05040011	整个或切块的盐渍猪肠衣(猪大肠头除外)	20					0	
05040012	整个或切块的盐渍绵羊肠衣	18					0	
05040013	整个或切块的盐渍山羊肠衣	18					0	
05040014	整个或切块的盐渍猪大肠头	20					0	
05040019	整个或切块的其他动物肠衣	18					0	
05040021	冷和冻的鸡肫	20					0	
05040029	鲜、冷、冻、干、盐制的其他动物胃	20					0	0
05040090	鲜、冷、冻、干、盐制的其他动物肠、膀胱、胃	20					0	
05051000	填充用羽毛;羽绒	10					0	0
05059010	羽毛或不完整羽毛的粉末及废料	10					0	0
05059090	其他羽毛,羽绒,带有羽毛,羽绒,的鸟皮及鸟体其他部分	10					0	0
05061000	经酸处理的骨胶原及骨	12			0		0	0
05069011	含牛羊成分的骨粉及骨废料	12			0		0	0
05069019	骨粉及骨废料	12			0		0	0
05069090	其他骨及角柱	12			0		0	0
05071000	兽牙;兽牙粉末及废料	10					0	0
05079010	羚羊角及其粉末和废料	3					0	0
05079020	鹿茸及其粉末	11					0	0
05079090	龟壳、鲸须、鲸须毛、鹿角及其他角	10					0	0
05080010	珊瑚及水产品壳、骨的粉末及废料	12					0	0
05080090	珊瑚及介、贝、棘皮动物的壳、骨	12					0	0
05100010	黄药	3					0	0
05100020	龙涎香、海狸香、灵猫香	7					0	
05100030	麝香	7					0	
05100040	斑蝥	7					0	0
05100090	胆汁,配药用腺体及其他动物产品	6					0	0
05111000	牛的精液	0					0	0
05119111	受精鱼卵	12					0	0
05119119	其他鱼产品	12					0	0
05119190	其他未列名水产品；第三章的死动物	12					0	0
05119910	动物精液(牛的精液除外)	0					0	0
05119920	动物胚胎	0					0	0
05119930	蚕种	0					0	0
05119940	马毛及废马毛,不论是否制成有或无衬垫的毛片	15					0	
05119990	其他编号未列名的动物产品；不适合供人食用的第一章的死动物	12					0	0
06011010	休眠的番红花球茎	4			0		0	0
06011021	种用百合球茎	0					0	0
06011029	其他百合球茎	5			0		0	0
06011091	种用休眠的鳞茎、块茎、块根等	0					0	0
06011099	其它休眠的鳞茎、块茎、块根等	5			0		0	0
06012000	生长或开花的鳞茎等及菊苣植物	15					0	
06021000	无根插枝及接穗	0					0	0
06022010	食用水果及坚果树的种用苗木	0					0	0
06022090	其他食用水果及坚果树及灌木	10					0	0
06023010	种用杜鹃	0					0	0
06023090	其他杜鹃	15					0	
06024010	种用玫瑰	0					0	0
06024090	其他玫瑰	15					0	
06029010	蘑菇菌丝	0					0	0
06029091	其他种用苗木	0					0	0
06029092	兰花	10					0	0
06029093	菊花	10					0	0
06029094	百合	10					0	0
06029095	康乃馨	10					0	0

税则号列	商品名称（简称）	最惠税率	亚太2国	东盟			最不发达35国	最不发达4国
				缅	老	柬		
06029099	其他非种用活植物	10					0	0
06031100	鲜玫瑰	10			0		0	0
06031200	鲜康乃馨	10			0		0	0
06031300	鲜兰花	10			0		0	0
06031400	鲜菊花	10			0		0	0
06031500	鲜百合花	10			0		0	0
06031900	其他鲜花	10			0		0	0
06039000	干的及经过染色等加工的插花及花蕾	23			0		0	0
06042010	鲜苔藓及地衣	23					0	
06042090	鲜植物枝、叶等	10					0	0
06049010	其他苔藓及地衣	23					0	
06049090	其他植物枝、叶等	10					0	0
07011000	种用马铃薯	13					0	0
07019000	其他鲜或冷的马铃薯	13				0	0	0
07020000	鲜或冷藏的番茄	13					0	0
07031010	鲜或冷的洋葱	13		0		0	0	0
07031020	鲜或冷的青葱	13		0		0	0	0
07032010	鲜或冷藏的大蒜头	13					0	
07032020	鲜或冷藏的大蒜蒜台及蒜苗(青蒜)	13					0	
07032090	其他鲜或冷藏的大蒜	13					0	
07039010	鲜或冷的韭葱	13				0	0	0
07039020	鲜或冷的大葱	13				0	0	0
07039090	鲜或冷的其他葱属蔬菜	13				0	0	0
07041000	鲜或冷的菜花及硬花甘蓝	10					0	0
07042000	鲜或冷的抱子甘蓝	13					0	
07049010	卷心菜	13			0		0	0
07049020	西兰花	13			0		0	0
07049090	鲜或冷的其他食用芥菜类蔬菜	13			0		0	0
07051100	鲜或冷的结球莴苣(包心生菜)	10					0	0
07051900	鲜或冷的其他莴苣	10					0	0
07052100	鲜或冷的维特罗夫菊苣	13					0	
07052900	鲜或冷的其他菊苣	13					0	
07061000	鲜或冷的胡萝卜及萝卜	13					0	
07069000	鲜或冷的小萝卜及类似食用根茎	13					0	
07070000	鲜或冷的黄瓜及小黄瓜	13				0	0	0
07081000	鲜或冷的豌豆	13				0	0	0
07082000	鲜或冷的豇豆及菜豆	13			0	0	0	0
07089000	鲜或冷的其他豆类蔬菜	13				0	0	0
07092000	鲜或冷的芦笋	13					0	0
07093000	鲜或冷的茄子	13					0	0
07094000	鲜或冷的芹菜，但块根芹除外	10					0	0
07095100	鲜或冷的其他伞菌属蘑菇	13				0	0	0
07095910	鲜或冷的松茸	13				0	0	0
07095920	鲜或冷的香菇	13				0	0	0
07095930	鲜或冷的金针菇	13				0	0	0
07095940	鲜或冷的草菇	13				0	0	0
07095950	鲜或冷的口蘑	13				0	0	0
07095960	鲜或冷的块菌	13					0	
07095990	鲜或冷的其他蘑菇	13				0	0	0
07096000	鲜或冷的辣椒，包括甜椒	13				0	0	0
07097000	鲜或冷的菠菜	13					0	0
07099100	鲜或冷藏的洋蓟	13				0	0	0
07099200	鲜或冷藏的油橄榄	13				0	0	0
07099300	鲜或冷藏的南瓜、笋瓜及瓠瓜	13				0	0	0
07099910	鲜或冷藏的竹笋	13			0	0	0	0
07099990	鲜或冷藏的其他蔬菜	13				0	0	0
07101000	冷冻马铃薯	13					0	
07102100	冷冻豌豆	13					0	

税则号列	商品名称（简称）	最惠税率	亚太2国	东盟			最不发达35国	最不发达4国
				缅	老	柬		
07102210	红小豆（赤豆）	13				0	0	0
07102290	其他冷冻豇豆及菜豆	13				0	0	0
07102900	冷冻其他豆类蔬菜	13				0	0	0
07103000	冷冻菠菜	13					0	
07104000	冷冻甜玉米	10					0	0
07108010	冷冻松茸	13				0	0	0
07108020	冻其他蒜台及蒜苗(青蒜)	13				0	0	0
07108030	冻蒜头	13				0	0	0
07108040	冻牛肝菌	13				0	0	0
07108090	冷冻未列名蔬菜	13				0	0	0
07109000	冷冻什锦蔬菜	10				0	0	0
07112000	暂时保藏的油橄榄	13					0	
07114000	暂时保藏的黄瓜及小黄瓜	13					0	
07115112	盐水小白蘑菇	13					0	
07115119	盐水的其他伞菌属蘑菇	13					0	
07115190	其他伞菌属蘑菇	13					0	
07115911	盐水松茸	13					0	
07115919	盐水其他蘑菇及菌块	13					0	
07115990	暂时保藏的其他蘑菇及菌块	13					0	
07119031	盐水竹笋	13					0	
07119034	盐水大蒜	13					0	
07119039	盐水其他蔬菜；什锦蔬菜	13					0	
07119090	暂时保藏的其他蔬菜；什锦蔬菜	13					0	
07122000	干制洋葱	13					0	0
07123100	干伞菌属蘑菇	13					0	0
07123200	干木耳	13					0	
07123300	干银耳	13					0	
07123910	干香菇	13					0	
07123920	干金针菇	13					0	
07123930	干草菇	13					0	
07123940	干口蘑	13					0	
07123950	干牛肝菌	13					0	
07123990	其他干制蘑菇及块菌	13					0	
07129010	笋干丝	13					0	0
07129020	紫萁(薇菜干)	13					0	
07129030	干金针菜(黄花菜)	13					0	
07129040	蕨菜干	13					0	
07129050	干制的大蒜	13					0	
07129060	干甜椒	13					0	
07129091	干制的辣根	13					0	0
07129099	干制的其他蔬菜及什锦蔬菜	13					0	0
07131010	种用豌豆	0					0	0
07131090	其他干豌豆	5					0	0
07132010	种用鹰嘴豆	0					0	0
07132090	其他干鹰嘴豆	7					0	0
07133110	种用绿豆	0					0	0
07133190	其他干绿豆	3		0		0	0	0
07133210	种用红小豆（赤豆）	0					0	0
07133290	其他红小豆（赤豆）	3				0	0	0
07133310	种用芸豆	0					0	0
07133390	其他干芸豆	7.5				0	0	0
07133400	干巴姆巴拉豆	7				0	0	0
07133500	干牛豆	7				0	0	0
07133900	干豇豆及菜豆	7				0	0	0
07134010	种用扁豆	0					0	0
07134090	其他干扁豆	7					0	0
07135010	种用蚕豆	0					0	0
07135090	其他干蚕豆	7					0	0

税则号列	商品名称（简称）	最惠税率	亚太2国	东盟			最不发达35国	最不发达4国
				缅	老	柬		
07136010	种用干木豆	0					0	0
07136090	其他干木豆	7					0	0
07139010	种用干豆	0					0	0
07139090	其它干豆	7					0	0
07141010	鲜木薯	10			0	0	0	0
07141020	干木薯	5			0	0	0	0
07141030	冷或冻的木薯	10			0	0	0	0
07142011	种用鲜甘薯	0			0	0	0	0
07142019	其他鲜甘薯	13			0	0	0	0
07142020	干甘薯	13			0	0	0	0
07142030	冷或冻的甘薯	13			0	0	0	0
07143000	山药	13			0	0	0	0
07144000	芋头	13					0	
07145000	箭叶黄体芋	13			0	0	0	0
07149010	鲜、干或冷、冻的荸荠	13			0	0	0	0
07149021	种用藕	0					0	0
07149029	其他藕	13			0	0	0	0
07149090	含有高淀粉或菊粉的其他类似根茎	13			0	0	0	0
08011100	干的椰子	12				0	0	0
08011200	未去内壳的鲜椰子	12				0	0	0
08011910	种用椰子	0					0	0
08011990	其他鲜椰子	12				0	0	0
08012100	鲜或干的未去壳巴西果	10					0	0
08012200	鲜或干的去壳巴西果	10					0	0
08013100	鲜或干的未去壳腰果	20				0	0	0
08013200	鲜或干的去壳腰果	10		0		0	0	0
08021100	未去壳扁桃仁	24					0	
08021200	其他扁桃仁	10					0	0
08022100	鲜或干的未去壳榛子	25					0	
08022200	鲜或干的去壳榛子	10					0	0
08023100	鲜或干的未去壳核桃	25					0	
08023200	鲜或干的去壳核桃	20					0	
08024110	未去壳板栗	25					0	
08024190	未去壳其他栗子	25					0	
08024210	去壳板栗	25					0	
08024290	去壳其他栗子	25					0	
08025100	未去壳阿月浑子果	10					0	
08025200	去壳阿月浑子果	10					0	
08026110	未去壳种用马卡达姆坚果	0					0	0
08026190	未去壳其他马卡达姆坚果	24					0	
08026200	去壳马卡达姆坚果	24					0	
08027000	可乐果	24					0	
08028000	槟榔果	10					0	0
08029020	鲜或干的白果	25					0	
08029030	鲜或干的松子仁	25					0	
08029090	其他鲜或干坚果	24					0	
08031000	鲜或干的芭蕉	10			0	0	0	0
08039000	鲜或干的其他香蕉	10			0	0	0	0
08041000	鲜或干的椰枣	15					0	
08042000	鲜或干的无花果	30					0	
08043000	鲜或干菠萝	12				0	0	0
08044000	鲜或干鳄梨	25				0	0	0
08045010	鲜或干番石榴	15					0	
08045020	鲜或干芒果	15					0	0
08045030	鲜或干山竹果	15					0	
08051000	鲜或干橙	11					0	0
08052010	鲜或干蕉柑	12					0	
08052020	阔叶柑橘	12					0	

税则号列	商品名称（简称）	最惠税率	亚太2国	东盟			最不发达35国	最不发达4国
				缅	老	柬		
08052090	其他鲜或干的柑桔及杂交柑桔	12					0	
08054000	鲜或干的葡萄柚，包括柚	12					0	0
08055000	鲜或干的柠檬及酸橙	11					0	0
08059000	其他鲜或干的柑桔属水果	30					0	
08061000	鲜葡萄	13					0	
08062000	葡萄干	10					0	
08071910	鲜哈密瓜	12					0	0
08071920	鲜罗马甜瓜及加勒比甜瓜	12					0	0
08071990	其他鲜甜瓜	12					0	0
08072000	鲜木瓜	25				0	0	0
08081000	鲜苹果	10					0	0
08083010	鲜鸭梨及雪梨	12					0	
08083020	鲜香梨	12					0	
08083090	其他鲜梨	10					0	
08084000	鲜榅桲	16					0	
08091000	鲜杏	25					0	
08092100	鲜欧洲酸樱桃	10					0	0
08092900	其他鲜樱桃	10					0	0
08093000	鲜桃，包括鲜油桃	10					0	0
08094000	鲜梅及李	10					0	
08101000	鲜草莓	14					0	0
08102000	鲜的木莓、黑莓、桑椹及罗甘莓	25					0	
08103000	鲜黑、白或红的穗醋栗（加仑子）及醋栗	25					0	
08105000	鲜猕猴桃	20					0	
08106000	鲜榴莲	20				0	0	0
08107000	鲜柿子	20					0	
08109010	鲜荔枝	30					0	
08109030	鲜龙眼	12				0	0	0
08109040	鲜红毛丹	20					0	
08109050	鲜蕃荔枝	20					0	
08109060	鲜杨桃	20					0	
08109070	莲雾	20					0	
08109080	火龙果	20					0	
08109090	其他鲜果	20					0	
08111000	冷冻草莓	30					0	
08112000	冷冻其他浆果	30					0	
08119010	未去壳的冷冻栗子	30					0	
08129000	暂时保藏的其他水果及坚果	25					0	
08131000	杏干	25					0	
08132000	梅干及李干	25					0	
08133000	苹果干	25					0	
08134010	龙眼干、肉	20				0	0	0
08134020	柿饼	25				0	0	0
08134030	干红枣	25				0	0	0
08134040	荔枝干	25				0	0	0
08134090	其他干果	25				0	0	0
08135000	本章的什锦坚果或干果	18					0	
08140000	柑桔属水果或甜瓜的果皮	25					0	
09011100	未浸除咖啡碱的未焙炒咖啡	8			0	0	0	0
09011200	已浸除咖啡碱的未焙炒咖啡	8			0	0	0	0
09012100	未浸除咖啡碱的已焙炒咖啡	15			0	0	0	0
09012200	已浸除咖啡碱的已焙炒咖啡	15			0	0	0	0
09019010	咖啡豆荚及咖啡豆皮	10			0	0	0	0
09019020	含咖啡的咖啡代用品	30			0	0	0	0
09021010	每件净重≤3kg 的花茶	15					0	
09021090	每件净重≤3kg 的其他绿茶	15					0	0
09022010	每件净重>3kg 的花茶	15					0	
09022090	每件净重>3kg 的其他绿茶	15					0	0

税则号列	商品名称（简称）	最惠税率	亚太2国	东盟			最不发达35国	最不发达4国
				缅	老	柬		
09023010	每件净重≤3kg 的乌龙茶	15					0	
09023020	每件净重≤3kg 的普洱茶	15					0	
09023090	每件净重≤3kg 的其他发酵、半发酵红茶	15					0	0
09024010	每件净重＞3kg 的乌龙茶	15		0	0	0	0	0
09024020	每件净重＞3kg 的普洱茶	15		0	0	0	0	0
09024090	每件净重＞3kg 的其他红茶(已发酵)及半发酵茶	15		0	0	0	0	0
09030000	马黛茶	10					0	0
09041100	未磨胡椒	20					0	
09041200	已磨胡椒	20					0	
09042100	未磨干辣椒	20					0	
09042200	已磨辣椒	20					0	
09051000	未磨香子兰豆	15					0	0
09052000	已磨香子兰豆	15					0	0
09061100	未磨锡兰肉桂	5					0	0
09061900	其他未磨的肉桂及肉桂花	5					0	0
09062000	已磨肉桂及肉桂花	15					0	
09071000	未磨丁香	3				0	0	0
09072000	已磨丁香	3				0	0	0
09081100	未磨肉豆蔻	8			0	0	0	0
09081200	已磨肉豆蔻	8			0	0	0	0
09082100	未磨肉豆蔻衣	8			0	0	0	0
09082200	已磨肉豆蔻衣	8			0	0	0	0
09083100	未磨豆蔻	3			0	0	0	0
09083200	已磨豆蔻	3			0	0	0	0
09092100	未磨芫荽子	15					0	
09092200	已磨芫荽子	15					0	
09093100	未磨枯茗子	15					0	
09093200	已磨枯茗子	15					0	
09096110	未磨八角茴香	20					0	
09096190	未磨其他茴香	15					0	
09096210	已磨八角茴香	20					0	
09096290	已磨其他茴香	15					0	
09101100	未磨姜	15			0	0	0	0
09101200	已磨姜	15			0	0	0	0
09102000	番红花	2					0	0
09103000	姜黄	15				0	0	0
09109100	混合调味香料	15					0	0
09109900	其他调味香料	15					0	0
10021000	种用黑麦	0					0	0
10029000	其他黑麦	3					0	0
10031000	种用大麦	0					0	0
10039000	其他大麦	3					0	0
10041000	种用燕麦	0					0	0
10049000	其他燕麦	2					0	0
10071000	种用高粱	0					0	0
10079000	其他高粱	2					0	
10081000	荞麦	2					0	0
10082100	种用谷子	2			0		0	0
10082900	其他谷子	2			0		0	0
10083000	加那利草子	2			0		0	0
10084010	种用直长马唐	0					0	0
10084090	其他直长马唐	3			0		0	0
10085010	种用昆诺阿藜	0					0	0
10085090	其他昆诺阿藜	3			0		0	0
10086010	种用黑小麦	0					0	0
10086090	其他黑小麦	3			0		0	0
10089010	其他种用谷物	0					0	0
10089090	其他谷物	3			0		0	0

税则号列	商品名称（简称）	最惠税率	亚太2国	东盟			最不发达35国	最不发达4国
				缅	老	柬		
11029090	其他谷物细粉	5				0	0	0
11031910	燕麦粗粒及粗粉	5					0	0
11031990	其他谷物粗粒及粗粉	5				0	0	0
11032090	其他谷物团粒	20					0	
11041200	滚压或制片的燕麦	20					0	
11041910	滚压或制片的大麦	20					0	
11041990	滚压或制片的其他谷物	20					0	
11042200	经其他加工的燕麦	20					0	
11042910	经其他加工的大麦	65					0	
11042990	经其他加工的其他谷物	20					0	
11043000	整粒或经加工的谷物胚芽	20					0	
11051000	马铃薯细粉、粗粉及粉末	15					0	
11052000	马铃薯粉片、颗粒及团粒	15					0	
11061000	干豆细粉、粗粉及粉末	10				0	0	0
11062000	用品目 0714 的西谷茎髓、植物根茎、块茎制成的细粉、粗粉、粉末	20		0	0	0	0	0
11063000	水果及坚果的细粉、粗粉及粉末	20					0	
11071000	未焙制麦芽	10					0	
11072000	已焙制麦芽	10					0	
11081100	小麦淀粉	20					0	
11081200	玉米淀粉	20					0	
11081300	马铃薯淀粉	15					0	
11081400	木薯淀粉	10					0	0
11081900	其他淀粉	20					0	
11082000	菊粉	20					0	
11090000	面筋，不论是否干制	18					0	
12011000	种用大豆	0					0	0
12019010	黄大豆	3			0	0	0	0
12019020	黑大豆	3			0	0	0	0
12019030	青大豆	3			0	0	0	0
12019090	其他大豆	3					0	0
12023000	种用花生	0					0	0
12024100	去壳花生	15			0		0	0
12024200	未去壳花生	15			0		0	0
12030000	干椰子肉	15				0	0	0
12040000	亚麻子	15					0	
12051010	种用的低芥子酸油菜子	0					0	0
12051090	其他低芥子酸油菜子	9					0	
12059010	其他种用油菜子	0					0	0
12059090	其他油菜子	9					0	
12060010	种用葵花籽	0					0	0
12060090	其他葵花籽	15					0	
12071010	种用棕榈果及棕榈仁	0					0	0
12071090	其他棕榈果及棕榈仁	10				0	0	0
12072100	种用棉子	0					0	0
12072900	其他棉子	15					0	
12073010	种用蓖麻子	0					0	0
12073090	其他蓖麻子	15		0	0	0	0	0
12074010	种用芝麻	0					0	0
12074090	其他芝麻	10		0	0	0	0	0
12075010	种用芥子	0					0	0
12075090	其他芥子	15					0	
12076010	种用红花子	0					0	0
12076090	其他红花子	20					0	
12077010	种用甜瓜子	0					0	0
12077091	黑瓜子	20					0	
12077092	红瓜子	20					0	
12077099	其他瓜子	30					0	0
12079100	罂粟子	20					0	

税则号列	商品名称（简称）	最惠税率	亚太2国	东盟			最不发达35国	最不发达4国
				缅	老	柬		
12079910	其他种用含油子仁及果实	0					0	0
12079991	牛油树果	20		0			0	0
12079999	其他含油子仁及果实	10		0	0	0	0	0
12081000	大豆粉	9				0	0	0
12089000	其他含油子仁或果实的细粉及粗粉	15				0	0	0
12091000	糖甜菜子	0					0	0
12092100	紫苜蓿子	0					0	0
12092200	三叶草子	0					0	0
12092300	羊茅子	0					0	0
12092400	草地早熟禾子	0					0	0
12092500	黑麦草种子	0					0	0
12092910	甜菜籽，糖甜菜子除外	0					0	0
12092990	其他饲料植物种子	0					0	0
12093000	草本花卉植物种子	0					0	0
12099100	蔬菜种子	0					0	0
12099900	其他种植用的种子、果实及孢子	0					0	0
12101000	未研磨也未制成团粒的啤酒花	20					0	
12102000	已研磨或制成团粒的啤酒花；蛇麻腺	10					0	0
12112010	鲜或干的西洋参	7.5					0	0
12112020	鲜或干的野山参(西洋参除外)	20					0	
12112091	其他鲜人参	20					0	
12112099	其他干人参	20					0	
12113000	古柯叶	9				0	0	0
12114000	罂粟杆	9				0	0	0
12119011	鲜或干的当归	6				0	0	0
12119012	三七（田七）	6				0	0	0
12119013	鲜或干的党参	6					0	0
12119014	鲜或干的黄连	6					0	0
12119015	鲜或干的菊花	6				0	0	0
12119016	鲜或干的冬虫夏草	6				0	0	0
12119017	鲜或干的贝母	6				0	0	0
12119018	鲜或干的川芎	6				0	0	0
12119019	鲜或干的半夏	6				0	0	0
12119021	鲜或干的白芍	6				0	0	0
12119022	鲜或干的天麻	6				0	0	0
12119023	鲜或干的黄芪	6				0	0	0
12119024	鲜或干的大黄、籽黄	6				0	0	0
12119025	鲜或干的白术	6				0	0	0
12119026	鲜或干的地黄	6				0	0	0
12119027	鲜或干的槐米	6				0	0	0
12119028	鲜或干的杜仲	6				0	0	0
12119029	鲜或干的茯苓	6		0	0	0	0	0
12119031	鲜或干的枸杞	6				0	0	0
12119032	鲜或干的大海子	6				0	0	0
12119033	鲜或干的沉香	3				0	0	0
12119034	鲜或干的沙参	6				0	0	0
12119035	鲜或干的青蒿	6				0	0	0
12119036	鲜或干的甘草	6					0	0
12119037	鲜或干的黄芩	6		0	0	0	0	0
12119038	椴树(欧椴)花及叶	6		0	0	0	0	0
12119039	其他主要用作药料的鲜或干的植物	6		0	0	0	0	0
12119050	主要用作香料的植物	8				0	0	0
12119091	鲜或干的鱼藤根、除虫菊	3				0	0	0
12119099	其他鲜或干的杀虫、杀菌用植物	9				0	0	0
12122110	适合供人食用的海带	20					0	
12122120	适合供人食用的发菜	20					0	
12122131	适合供人食用的干裙带菜	15					0	
12122132	适合供人食用的鲜裙带菜	15					0	

税则号列	商品名称（简称）	最惠税率	亚太2国	东盟			最不发达35国	最不发达4国
				缅	老	柬		
12122139	适合供人食用的其他裙带菜	15					0	
12122141	适合供人食用的干紫菜	15					0	
12122142	适合供人食用的鲜紫菜	15					0	
12122149	适合供人食用的其他紫菜	15					0	
12122161	适合供人食用的干麒麟菜	15					0	0
12122169	适合供人食用的其他麒麟菜	15					0	
12122171	适合供人食用的干江蓠	15					0	
12122179	适合供人食用的其他江蓠	15					0	
12122190	其他适合供人食用的海草及其他藻类	15					0	0
12122900	其他海草及藻类	15					0	0
12129100	鲜、冷、冻或干的甜菜	20					0	
12129200	刺槐豆	20					0	
12129300	甘蔗	20		0	0	0	0	0
12129400	菊苣根	20					0	0
12129911	主要供人食用的苦杏仁	20					0	
12129912	主要供人食用的甜杏仁	20					0	
12129919	主要供人食用的桃(包括油桃)、梅或李的核及核仁	20					0	
12129993	鲜、冷、冻或干的白瓜子	20					0	
12129994	鲜、冷、冻或干的莲子	20					0	
12129996	甜叶菊叶	30					0	0
12129999	鲜、冷、冻或干的其他主要供人食用的其他税号未列明的果核、果仁及植物产品	30					0	0
12130010	未经处理的稻草的茎、杆	12				0	0	0
12130090	其他未经处理的谷类植物茎、杆及谷壳	12				0	0	0
12141000	紫苜蓿粗粉及团粒	5				0	0	0
12149000	芜菁甘蓝、饲料甜菜等其他植物饲料	9				0	0	0
13012000	阿拉伯胶	15					0	0
13019010	胶黄耆树胶	15					0	
13019020	乳香、没药及血竭	3					0	0
13019030	阿魏	3					0	0
13019040	松脂	15					0	0
13019090	其他天然树胶、树脂	15					0	0
13021100	鸦片液汁及浸膏	0					0	0
13021200	甘草液汁及浸膏	6					0	0
13021300	啤酒花液汁及浸膏	10					0	0
13021910	生漆	20					0	
13021920	印楝素	3					0	0
13021930	除虫菊或含鱼藤酮植物根茎的液汁及浸膏	3					0	0
13021940	银杏的液汁及浸膏	20					0	
13021990	其他植物液汁及浸膏	20					0	
13022000	果胶、果胶酸盐及果胶酸酯	20					0	
13023100	琼脂	10					0	0
13023200	刺槐豆、刺槐豆子或瓜尔豆制得的胶液及增稠剂	15					0	
13023911	卡拉胶	15					0	
13023912	褐藻胶	15					0	
13023919	其他海草及藻类制品	15					0	
13023990	其他植物胶液及增稠剂	15					0	
14011000	竹	10			0	0	0	0
14012000	藤	10			0	0	0	0
14019010	谷类植物的茎秆(麦秸除外)	10				0	0	0
14019020	芦苇	10				0	0	0
14019031	蔺草	10				0	0	0
14019039	灯芯草属的其他主要作编结用的植物材料	10				0	0	0
14019090	未列名主要用作编结用的植物材料	10				0	0	0
14042000	棉短绒	4					0	0
14049010	主要供染料或鞣料用的植物原料	5					0	0
14049090	其他植物产品	15					0	0
15011000	猪油	10					0	0
15012000	其他猪脂肪	10					0	0

税则号列	商品名称（简称）	最惠税率	亚太2国	东盟			最不发达35国	最不发达4国
				缅	老	柬		
15019000	家禽脂肪	10					0	0
15021000	牛、羊油脂	8					0	0
15029000	其他牛、羊脂肪	8					0	0
15030000	未经制作的猪油硬脂、油硬脂等	10					0	0
15041000	鱼肝油及其分离品	12					0	
15042000	其他鱼油、脂及其分离品	12					0	
15043000	海生哺乳动物的油、脂及其分离品	14.4					0	
15050000	羊毛脂及羊毛脂肪物质	20					0	
15060000	其他动物油、脂及其分离品	20					0	
15091000	初榨油橄榄油及其分离品	10					0	
15099000	精制的油橄榄油及其分离品	10					0	
15100000	其他橄榄油及其分离品	10					0	
15131100	初榨椰子油分离品	9					0	
15131900	椰子油及其分离品	9					0	0
15132100	初榨棕榈仁油或巴巴苏棕榈果油及其分离品	9					0	
15132900	精制的棕榈仁油或巴巴苏棕榈果油及其分离品	9					0	
15151100	初榨亚麻子油及其分离品	15					0	
15151900	精制的亚麻子油及其分离品	15					0	
15152100	初榨玉米油的分离品	10			0	0	0	0
15152900	精制的玉米油及其分离品	10			0	0	0	0
15153000	蓖麻油及其分离品	10			0	0	0	0
15155000	芝麻油及其分离品	12			0	0	0	0
15159010	希蒙得木油及其分离品	20				0	0	0
15159020	印楝油及其分离品	20					0	
15159030	桐油及其分离品	20				0	0	0
15159090	其他固定植物油、脂及其分离品	20		0	0	0	0	0
15161000	氢化、酯化或反油酸化动物油、脂及其分离品，但未进一步加工的	5					0	0
15162000	氢化、酯化或反油酸化植物油、脂及其分离品,但未进一步加工的	25					0	
15179010	起酥油	25					0	
15179090	混合制成的食用油脂或制品	25					0	
15180000	化学改性的动、植物油、脂及其制品；其他税号未列名的非食用油、脂或制品	10					0	0
15200000	粗甘油,甘油水及甘油碱液	20					0	
15211000	植物蜡	20					0	
15219010	蜂蜡	20					0	
15219090	其他虫蜡及鲸蜡	20					0	
15220000	油鞣回收脂;加工处理油脂及动、植物蜡所剩残渣	20					0	
16010010	用天然肠衣做外包装的香肠及类似产品	15					0	
16010020	其他香肠及类似产品	15					0	
16010030	用香肠制成的食品	15					0	
16021000	肉或食用杂碎的均化食品	15					0	
16022000	制作或保藏的动物肝	15					0	
16023100	制作或保藏的火鸡肉及杂碎	15					0	
16023210	鸡罐头	15					0	
16023291	鸡胸肉	15					0	
16023292	鸡腿肉	15					0	
16023299	其他鸡肉	15					0	
16023910	其他品目 0105 所列家禽肉及杂碎的罐头	15					0	
16023991	鸭肉	15					0	
16023999	经制作或保藏的其他品目 0105 所列家禽肉及杂碎	15					0	
16024100	制作或保藏的猪后腿及其肉块	15					0	
16024200	制作或保藏的猪前腿及其肉块	15					0	
16024910	其他猪肉及杂碎的罐头	15					0	
16024990	制作或保藏的其他猪肉、杂碎及血	15					0	
16025010	牛肉及牛杂碎罐头	12					0	
16025090	其他制作或保藏的牛肉、杂碎及血	12					0	
16029010	其他肉及杂碎罐头	15					0	
16029090	经制作或保藏的其他肉、杂碎及血	15					0	
16030000	肉及水产品的精、汁	23					0	

税则号列	商品名称（简称）	最惠税率	亚太2国	东盟			最不发达35国	最不发达4国
				缅	老	柬		
16041110	制作或保藏的大西洋鲑鱼，整条或切块，但未绞碎	12					0	
16041190	制作或保藏的其他鲑鱼，整条或切块，但未绞碎	12					0	
16041200	制作或保藏的鲱鱼，整条或切块，但未绞碎	12					0	
16041300	制作或保藏的沙丁鱼、小沙丁鱼属、黍鲱或西鲱	5				0	0	0
16041400	制作或保藏的金枪鱼、鲣鱼及狐鲣	5				0	0	0
16041500	制作或保藏的鲭鱼，整条或切块，但未绞碎	12					0	
16041600	制作保藏的Anchovies(鳀鱼)，整条或切块，但未绞碎	12					0	
16041700	制作或保藏的鳗鱼	12					0	0
16041920	制作或保藏的罗非鱼，整条或切块，但未绞碎	12					0	
16041931	制作或保藏的斑点叉尾鮰鱼	12					0	0
16041939	制作或保藏的其他叉尾鮰鱼	12					0	0
16041990	制作或保藏的其他鱼，整条或切块，但未绞碎	12					0	0
16042011	鱼翅罐头	12					0	
16042019	其他制作或保藏的鱼罐头	12					0	
16042091	鱼翅	12					0	
16042099	其他制作或保藏的鱼	12					0	
16043100	鲟鱼子酱	12					0	
16043200	鲟鱼子酱代用品	12					0	
16051000	制作或保藏的蟹	5					0	0
16052100	制作或保藏的非密封包装小虾及对虾	5				0	0	0
16052900	制作或保藏的其他小虾及对虾	5				0	0	0
16053000	制作或保藏的龙虾	5				0	0	0
16054011	制作或保藏的淡水小龙虾仁	5				0	0	0
16054019	制作或保藏的带壳淡水小龙虾	5				0	0	0
16054090	制作或保藏的其他甲壳动物	5				0	0	0
16055100	制作或保藏的牡蛎	5					0	0
16055200	制作或保藏的扇贝	5					0	0
16055300	制作或保藏的贻贝	5					0	0
16055400	制作或保藏的墨鱼及鱿鱼	5					0	0
16055500	制作或保藏的章鱼	5					0	0
16055610	制作或保藏的蛤	5					0	0
16055620	制作或保藏的鸟蛤及舟贝	5					0	0
16055700	制作或保藏的鲍鱼	5					0	0
16055800	制作或保藏的蜗牛及螺	5					0	0
16055900	制作或保藏的其他软体动物	5					0	0
16056100	制作或保藏的海参	5					0	0
16056200	制作或保藏的海胆	5					0	0
16056300	制作或保藏的海蜇	15					0	0
16056900	制作或保藏的其他水生无脊椎动物	5					0	0
17021100	无水乳糖，按重量计含量＞99%	10					0	0
17021900	其他乳糖及乳糖浆	10					0	0
17029000	其他固体糖；人造蜜；焦糖	30					0	0
17031000	甘蔗糖蜜	8					0	0
17039000	其他糖蜜	8					0	0
17041000	口香糖，不论是否裹糖	12					0	0
17049000	其他不含可可的糖食	10					0	0
18010000	生或焙炒的整颗或破碎的可可豆	8					0	0
18020000	可可荚、壳、皮及废料	10					0	0
18031000	未脱脂可可膏	10					0	
18032000	全脱脂或部分脱脂的可可膏	10					0	
18040000	可可油，可可脂	22					0	0
18050000	未加糖或其他甜物质的可可粉	15					0	
18061000	含糖或其他甜物质的可可粉	10					0	
18062000	每件净重＞2kg的含可可食品	10					0	
18063100	其他夹心块状或条状的含可可食品	8					0	0
18063200	其他不夹心块状或条状含可可食品	10					0	
18069000	其他巧克力及含可可的食品	8					0	0
19011010	配方奶粉	15					0	

税则号列	商品名称（简称）	最惠税率	亚太2国	东盟			最不发达35国	最不发达4国
				缅	老	柬		
19011090	其他供婴幼儿食用的零售包装食品	15					0	
19012000	供焙烘面包糕点用的调制品及面团	25					0	
19019000	其他麦精制的其他税号未列名食品	10					0	
19021100	未包馅或未制作的含蛋生面食	15					0	0
19021900	其他未包馅或未制作的生面食	15					0	0
19022000	包馅面食	15					0	0
19023010	米粉干	15					0	
19023020	粉丝	15					0	
19023030	即食或快熟面条	15					0	0
19023090	其他面食	15					0	
19024000	古斯古斯面食	25					0	
19030000	珍粉及淀粉制成的珍粉代用品	15					0	0
19041000	谷物或谷物产品经膨化或烘炒制的食品	25					0	
19051000	黑麦脆面包片	20					0	
19052000	姜饼及类似品	20					0	
19053100	甜饼干	15	7.5				0	0
19053200	华夫饼干及圣餐饼	15	7.5				0	0
19054000	面包干、吐司及类似的烤面包	20					0	
19059000	其他面包、糕点、饼干及其焙烘糕饼	20	10				0	
20011000	用醋或醋酸制作的黄瓜及小黄瓜	25					0	
20019010	用醋制作的大蒜	25	12.5				0	
20019090	用醋制作的其他果、菜及食用植物	25	12.5				0	
20021010	非用醋制作的整个或切片番茄罐头	19					0	
20021090	非用醋制作的其他整个或切片番茄	25					0	
20029011	重量不超过5kg的番茄酱罐头	20					0	
20029019	重量大于5kg的番茄酱罐头	20					0	
20029090	非用醋制作的绞碎番茄	18					0	
20031011	伞菌属小白蘑菇罐头	25					0	
20031019	其他非用醋制作的伞菌属蘑菇罐头	25					0	
20031090	非用醋制作的其他伞菌属蘑菇	25					0	
20039010	其他蘑菇及块菌罐头	25					0	
20039090	其他蘑菇及块菌	25					0	
20041000	非用醋制作的冷冻马铃薯	13					0	0
20049000	非用醋制作的其他冷冻蔬菜	25					0	
20051000	非用醋制作的未冷冻均化蔬菜	25					0	
20052000	非用醋制作的未冷冻马铃薯	15					0	
20054000	非用醋制作的未冷冻豌豆	25					0	
20055111	非用醋或醋酸制作或保藏的未冷冻的赤豆馅罐头	25					0	
20055119	非用醋或醋酸制作或保藏的未冷冻的其他脱荚豇豆及菜豆罐头	25					0	
20055191	非用醋或醋酸制作或保藏的未冷冻的赤豆馅，不包括罐头	25					0	
20055199	非用醋或醋酸制作或保藏的未冷冻的其他脱荚豇豆及菜豆	25					0	
20055910	非用醋制作的其他豇豆及菜豆罐头	25					0	
20055990	非用醋制作的其他豇豆及菜豆	25					0	
20056010	非用醋制作的芦笋罐头	25					0	
20056090	非用醋制作的其他芦笋	25					0	
20057000	非用醋制作的未冷冻油橄榄	10					0	
20058000	非用醋制作的未冷冻甜玉米	10					0	
20059110	非用醋制作或保藏的竹笋罐头	25					0	
20059190	非用醋制作或保藏的未冷冻的其他竹笋	25					0	
20059920	蚕豆罐头	25					0	
20059940	榨菜	25					0	
20059950	咸蕨菜	25					0	
20059960	咸荞头	25					0	
20059991	其他蔬菜及什锦蔬菜罐头	25					0	
20059999	非用醋制作的其他蔬菜及什锦蔬菜	25					0	
20060010	蜜枣	30		0			0	0
20060020	糖渍制橄榄	30		0			0	0
20060090	其他糖渍蔬菜、水果、坚果、果皮	30		0			0	0

税则号列	商品名称（简称）	最惠税率	亚太2国	东盟 缅	东盟 老	东盟 柬	最不发达35国	最不发达4国
20079100	烹煮制成的柑桔属水果	30		0			0	0
20079910	烹煮制成的其他果酱、果冻罐头	5	2.5				0	0
20079990	烹煮制成的其他果酱、果冻	5	2.5				0	0
20081120	烘焙花生	30				0	0	0
20081910	核桃仁罐头	20			0	0	0	0
20081920	其他果仁罐头	13			0	0	0	0
20081991	栗仁	10			0	0	0	0
20081992	用其他方法制作或保藏的芝麻	10					0	
20081999	其他坚果及子仁	10			0	0	0	0
20082010	菠萝罐头	15			0		0	0
20082090	非用醋制作的其他菠萝	15			0		0	0
20083010	柑桔属水果罐头	20			0		0	0
20083090	非用醋制作的其他柑桔属水果	20			0		0	0
20084010	梨罐头	20			0		0	0
20084090	非用醋制作的其他梨	20			0		0	0
20085000	非用醋制作的杏	20					0	
20086010	用其他方法制作或保藏的樱桃罐头	20					0	
20086090	用其他方法制作或保藏的其他樱桃	20					0	
20087010	桃罐头	10			0		0	0
20087090	非用醋制作的其他桃	20			0		0	0
20088000	非用醋制作的草莓	15					0	
20089100	非用醋制作的棕榈芯	5				0	0	0
20089300	用其他方法制作或保藏的蔓越橘	15				0	0	0
20089700	用其他方法制作或保藏的什锦果实	10				0	0	0
20089910	荔枝罐头	20					0	
20089920	龙眼罐头	15				0	0	0
20089931	调味紫菜	15				0	0	0
20089932	盐渍海带	15				0	0	0
20089933	盐渍裙带菜	15				0	0	0
20089939	其他海草及藻类制品	15				0	0	0
20089940	清水荸荠（马蹄）罐头	25					0	
20089990	未列名制作或保藏的水果、坚果	15				0	0	0
20091100	冷冻的橙汁	7.5			0	0	0	0
20091200	非冷冻的，白利糖度值不超过20的橙汁	30			0	0	0	0
20091900	其他橙汁	30			0	0	0	0
20092100	白利糖度值不超过20的葡萄柚(包括柚)汁	15			0		0	0
20092900	其他葡萄柚(包括柚)汁	15			0		0	0
20093110	白利糖度不超过20的柠檬汁	18	9			0	0	0
20093190	其他未混合的白利糖度值不超过20的桔汁属水果汁	18	9			0	0	0
20093910	白利糖度超过20的柠檬汁	18	9			0	0	0
20093990	其他未混合的柑桔属水果汁，白利糖度值不超过20	18	9			0	0	0
20094100	白利糖度值不超过20的菠萝汁	10			0	0	0	0
20094900	其他菠萝汁	10			0	0	0	0
20095000	番茄汁	30	15		0		0	0
20096100	白利糖度值不超过30的的葡萄汁,包括酿酒葡萄汁	20					0	
20096900	葡萄汁,包括酿酒葡萄汁	20					0	
20097100	白利糖度值不超过20的苹果汁	20					0	
20097900	其他苹果汁	20					0	
20098100	蔓越橘汁	20		0	0		0	0
20098912	芒果汁	20		0	0		0	0
20098913	西番莲果汁	20		0	0		0	0
20098914	番石榴果汁	20		0	0		0	0
20098915	梨汁	20		0	0		0	0
20098919	其他未混合的水果汁	20		0	0		0	0
20098920	其他未混合蔬菜汁	20		0			0	0
20099010	混合水果汁	20	10		0	0	0	0
20099090	混合蔬菜汁、水果与蔬菜的混合汁	20	10		0	0	0	0
21011100	咖啡浓缩精汁	17					0	0

税则号列	商品名称（简称）	最惠税率	亚太2国	东盟			最不发达35国	最不发达4国
				缅	老	柬		
21012000	茶、马黛茶浓缩精汁及其制品	32					0	
21013000	烘焙咖啡代用品及其浓缩精汁	32					0	
21021000	活性酵母	25					0	
21022000	非活性酵母；已死的其他单细胞微生物	25					0	
21023000	发酵粉	25					0	
21031000	酱油	28				0	0	0
21032000	番茄沙司及其他番茄调味汁	15				0	0	0
21033000	芥子粉及其调味品	15				0	0	0
21039010	味精	21					0	
21039020	别特油（Aromatic bitters）	21					0	
21039090	其他调味品	21					0	0
21041000	汤料及其制品	15					0	
21042000	均化混合食品	32					0	
21050000	冰淇淋及其他冰制食品不论是否含可可	19					0	
21061000	浓缩蛋白质及人造蛋白物质	10					0	
21069010	制造碳酸饮料的浓缩物	35					0	
21069020	制造饮料用的复合酒精制品	20					0	
21069030	蜂王浆制剂	3			0		0	0
21069040	椰子汁	10		0	0		0	0
21069050	海豹油胶囊	20					0	
21069090	其他税号未列名的食品	20					0	
22011010	未加糖及未加味的矿泉水	20					0	0
22011020	未加糖及未加味的汽水	20					0	0
22019010	天然水	10					0	
22019090	其他水、冰及雪	10					0	
22021000	加味、加糖或其他甜物质的水	20					0	
22029000	其他无酒精饮料	35					0	0
22030000	麦芽酿造的啤酒	0					0	0
22041000	葡萄汽酒	14					0	
22042100	小包装的鲜葡萄酿造的酒	14					0	
22042900	其他包装的鲜葡萄酿造的酒	20					0	
22060010	黄酒	40					0	
22060090	其他发酵饮料	40					0	
22071000	浓度≥80%的未改性乙醇	40					0	
22072000	任何浓度的改性乙醇及其他酒精	30					0	
22082000	蒸馏葡萄酒制得的烈性酒	10					0	0
22083000	威士忌酒	10					0	0
22084000	朗姆酒及蒸馏已发酵甘蔗产品制得的其他烈性酒	10					0	0
22085000	杜松子酒	10					0	0
22086000	伏特加酒	10					0	0
22087000	利口酒及柯迪尔酒	10					0	0
22089010	龙舌兰酒	10					0	
22089020	白酒	10					0	0
22089090	其他蒸馏酒及酒精饮料	10					0	0
22090000	醋及醋酸制得的醋代用品	20					0	
23011011	含牛羊成分的肉骨粉	2					0	0
23011019	其他动物的肉骨粉	2					0	0
23011020	油渣	5					0	0
23011090	其他不适于供人食用的肉渣粉	5					0	0
23012010	饲料用鱼粉	2					0	0
23012090	其他不适于供人食用的水产品渣粉	5					0	0
23021000	玉米糠、麸及其他残渣	5					0	0
23023000	小麦糠、麸及其他残渣	3					0	0
23024000	其他谷物糠、麸及其他残渣	5					0	0
23025000	豆类植物糠、麸及其他残渣	5					0	0
23031000	制造淀粉过程中的残渣及类似品	5					0	0
23032000	甜菜渣、甘蔗渣及制糖过程中的其他残渣	5					0	0
23033000	酿造及蒸馏过程中的糟粕及残渣	5					0	0

税则号列	商品名称（简称）	最惠税率	亚太2国	东盟			最不发达35国	最不发达4国
				缅	老	柬		
23040010	提炼豆油所得的油渣饼(豆饼)	5					0	0
23040090	提炼豆油所得的其他固体残渣	5					0	0
23050000	花生饼及类似油渣	5					0	0
23061000	棉子油渣饼及固体残渣	5					0	0
23062000	亚麻子油渣饼及固体残渣	5			0		0	0
23063000	葵花子油渣饼及固体残渣	5					0	0
23064100	低芥子酸的油菜子油渣饼及固体残渣	5					0	
23064900	油菜子油渣饼及固体残渣	5					0	
23065000	椰子或干椰肉油渣饼及固体残渣	5				0	0	0
23066000	油棕果或油棕仁油渣饼及固体残渣	5				0	0	0
23069000	其他油渣饼及固体残渣	5			0		0	0
23070000	葡萄酒渣、粗酒石	5					0	0
23080000	动物饲料用其他植物产品	5					0	
23091010	零售包装的狗食或猫食罐头	15					0	
23091090	零售包装的其他狗食或猫食	15					0	
23099010	制成的饲料添加剂	5					0	0
23099090	其他配制的动物饲料	6.5					0	0
24013000	烟草废料	10					0	0
25010011	食用盐	0					0	0
25010019	其他盐	0					0	0
25010020	纯氯化钠	3			0		0	0
25010030	海水	0					0	0
25020000	未焙烧的黄铁矿	3					0	0
25030000	硫磺，但升华硫磺、沉淀硫磺及胶态硫磺除外	3					0	
25041010	鳞片状天然石墨	3					0	0
25041091	球化石墨	3					0	0
25041099	其他粉末状天然石墨	3					0	0
25049000	其他天然石墨	3					0	0
25051000	硅砂及石英砂，不论是否着色	3					0	0
25059000	其他天然砂，不论是否着色	3					0	0
25061000	石英	3					0	0
25062000	石英岩，不论是否切割成矩形板、块	3					0	0
25070010	不论是否煅烧的高岭土	3					0	0
25070090	不论是否煅烧的类似土	3					0	0
25081000	膨润土，不论是否煅烧	3					0	0
25083000	耐火粘土，不论是否煅烧	3					0	0
25084000	其他粘土，不论是否煅烧	3					0	0
25085000	红柱石，蓝晶石及硅线石，不论是否煅烧	3					0	0
25086000	富铝红柱石	3					0	0
25087000	火泥及第纳斯土	3					0	0
25090000	白垩	3					0	0
25101010	未碾磨磷灰石	3					0	0
25101090	未碾磨天然磷酸钙、天然磷酸铝钙及磷酸盐白垩，磷灰石除外	3					0	0
25102010	已碾磨磷灰石	3					0	0
25102090	已碾磨天然磷酸钙、天然磷酸铝钙及磷酸盐白垩，磷灰石除外	3					0	0
25111000	天然硫酸钡(重晶石)	3					0	
25112000	天然碳酸钡(毒重石)，不论是否煅烧	3					0	
25120010	硅藻土	3					0	0
25120090	其他硅质化石粗粉及类似的硅质土	3					0	0
25131000	浮石	3					0	0
25132000	刚玉岩、天然刚玉砂、天然石榴石及其他天然磨料	3					0	0
25140000	板岩，不论是否粗加修整或切割成矩形板块	3					0	0
25151100	原状或粗加修整大理石及石灰华	4					0	0
25151200	矩形大理石及石灰华	4					0	0
25152000	其他石灰质碑用或建筑用石；蜡石，不论是否粗加修整或切割成矩形板块	3					0	0
25161100	原状或粗加修整的花岗岩	4					0	0
25161200	矩形或正方形的花岗岩	4					0	0
25162000	砂岩，不论是否粗加修整或切割成矩形板块	3					0	0

税则号列	商品名称（简称）	最惠税率	亚太2国	东盟			最不发达35国	最不发达4国
				缅	老	柬		
25169000	其他碑用或建筑用石，不论是否粗加修整或切割成矩形板块	3					0	0
25171000	通常做混凝土粒料、铺路、铁道路基或其他路基用的卵石、砾石及碎石，圆石子及燧石，不论是否热处理	4					0	0
25172000	矿渣、浮渣及类似的工业残渣	3					0	0
25173000	沥青碎石	3					0	0
25174100	大理石碎粒、碎屑及粉末，不论是否热处理	3					0	0
25174900	税目2515及2616所列各种石料的碎粒、碎屑及粉末，大理石的除外，不论是否热处理	3					0	0
25181000	未煅烧或烧结的白云石，不论是否粗加修整或切割成矩形板块	3					0	0
25182000	已煅烧或烧结的白云石，不论是否粗加修整或切割成矩形板块	3					0	0
25183000	夯混白云石	3					0	0
25191000	天然碳酸镁（菱镁矿）	3					0	0
25199010	熔凝镁氧矿	3					0	0
25199020	烧结镁氧矿（重烧镁）	3					0	0
25199030	碱烧镁（轻烧镁）	3					0	0
25199091	化学纯氧化镁	3					0	0
25199099	非纯氧化镁	3					0	0
25201000	生石膏；硬石膏	5			0		0	0
25202010	牙科用熟石膏，不论是否着色及带有少量促凝剂或缓凝剂	5			0		0	0
25202090	其他熟石膏，不论是否着色及带有少量促凝剂或缓凝剂	5			0		0	0
25210000	石灰石助熔剂；通常用于制造石灰或水泥的石灰石及其他钙质石	5					0	0
25221000	生石灰	5					0	0
25222000	熟石灰	5					0	0
25223000	水硬石灰	5					0	0
25231000	水泥熟料，不论是否着色	8					0	0
25232100	白水泥，不论是否人工着色	6					0	0
25232900	其他硅酸盐水泥，不论是否着色	8					0	0
25233000	矾土水泥，不论是否着色	6					0	0
25239000	其他水凝水泥，不论是否着色	8					0	0
25241000	青石棉	5					0	
25249010	其他长纤维石棉	5					0	
25249090	其他石棉	5					0	
25251000	原状云母及劈开的云母片	5					0	0
25252000	云母粉	5					0	0
25253000	云母废料	5					0	0
25261010	未破碎及未研粉的天然冻石，不论是否粗加修整或切割成矩形板块	3					0	0
25261020	未破碎及未研粉的滑石，不论是否粗加修整或切割成矩形板块	3					0	0
25262010	已破碎或已研粉的天然冻石	3					0	0
25262020	已破碎或已研粉的天然滑石	3					0	0
25280010	天然硼砂及其精矿，不论是否煅烧	3					0	0
25280090	硼酸盐（硼砂除外），不论是否煅烧；天然粗硼酸，含硼酸干重不超85%	5					0	0
25291000	长石	3					0	0
25292100	按重量计氟化钙含量≤97%的萤石	3					0	0
25292200	按重量计氟化钙含量>97%的萤石	3					0	0
25293000	白榴石；霞石及霞石正长岩	5					0	0
25301010	未膨胀的绿泥石	5					0	0
25301020	未膨胀的蛭石及珍珠岩	5					0	0
25302000	硫镁矾矿及泻盐矿（天然硫酸镁）	3					0	0
25309010	矿物性药材	3					0	0
25309020	稀土金属矿	0					0	0
25309091	硅灰石	3					0	0
25309099	其他矿产品	3					0	0
26011110	平均粒径小于0.8毫米的未煅烧铁矿砂及其精矿；但焙烧黄铁矿除外	0					0	0
26011120	平均粒径不小于0.8毫米，但不大于6.3毫米的未煅烧铁矿砂及其精矿；但焙烧黄铁矿除外	0					0	0
26011190	平均粒径大于6.3毫米的未烧结铁矿砂及其精矿，但焙烧黄铁矿除外	0					0	0
26011200	已烧结铁矿砂及其精矿	0					0	0
26012000	焙烧黄铁矿	0					0	0
26020000	锰矿砂及其精矿，包括以干重计含锰量在20%及以上的锰铁砂及其精矿	0					0	0

税则号列	商品名称（简称）	最惠税率	亚太2国	东盟			最不发达35国	最不发达4国
				缅	老	柬		
26030000	铜矿砂及其精矿	0					0	0
26040000	镍矿砂及其精矿	0					0	0
26050000	钴矿砂及其精矿	0					0	0
26060000	铝矿砂及其精矿	0					0	0
26070000	铅矿砂及其精矿	0					0	0
26080000	锌矿砂及其精矿	0					0	0
26090000	锡矿砂及其精矿	0					0	0
26100000	铬矿砂及其精矿	0					0	0
26110000	钨矿砂及其精矿	0					0	0
26121000	铀矿砂及其精矿	0					0	0
26122000	钍矿砂及其精矿	0					0	0
26131000	已焙烧钼矿砂及其精矿	0					0	0
26139000	其他钼矿砂及其精矿	0					0	0
26140000	钛矿砂及其精矿	0					0	0
26151000	锆矿砂及其精矿	0					0	0
26159010	水合钽铌原料（钽铌富集物）	0					0	0
26159090	其他铌钽钒矿砂及其精矿	0					0	0
26161000	银矿砂及其精矿	0					0	0
26169000	其他贵金属矿砂及其精矿	0					0	0
26171010	生锑（锑精矿，选矿产品）	0					0	0
26171090	其他锑矿砂及其精矿	0					0	0
26179010	朱砂(辰砂)	3					0	0
26179090	其他矿砂及其精矿	0					0	0
26180010	冶炼钢铁产生的锰渣	4					0	
26180090	冶炼钢铁产生的其他粒状熔渣(熔渣砂)	4					0	
26190000	冶炼钢铁产生的熔渣、浮渣、氧化皮及其他废料	4					0	
26201100	含硬锌的矿灰及残渣	4					0	0
26201900	含其他锌的矿灰及残渣	4					0	0
26202100	含铅汽油的淤渣及含铅抗震化合物的淤渣	4					0	0
26202900	其他主要含铅的矿灰及残渣	4					0	0
26203000	主要含铜的矿灰及残渣	4					0	0
26204000	主要含铝的矿灰及残渣	4					0	0
26206000	含砷、汞、铊及其混合物，用于提取或生产砷、汞、铊及其化合物的矿灰及残渣	4					0	0
26209100	含锑、铍、镉、铬及其混合物的矿灰及残渣	4					0	0
26209910	主要含钨的矿灰及残渣	4					0	0
26209990	含其他金属及化合物的矿灰及残渣	4					0	0
26211000	焚化城市垃圾所产生的灰、渣	4					0	0
26219000	其他矿渣及矿灰	4					0	0
27011100	未制成型的无烟煤，不论是否粉化	3			0		0	0
27011210	未制成型的炼焦烟煤，不论是否粉化	3			0		0	0
27011290	未制成型的其他烟煤，不论是否粉化	6			0		0	0
27011900	未制成型的其他煤，不论是否粉化	5			0		0	0
27012000	煤砖、煤球及类似用煤制固体燃料	5			0		0	0
27021000	褐煤	3					0	0
27022000	制成型的褐煤	3					0	0
27030000	泥煤(包括肥料用泥煤) 不论是否成型	5					0	
27040010	煤制焦炭及半焦炭不论是否成型	5					0	
27040090	甑炭	5					0	
27050000	煤气、水煤气、炉煤气及类似气体，石油气及其他烃类气除外	5					0	
27060000	从煤、褐煤、或泥煤蒸馏所得的焦油及矿物焦油，不论是否脱水或部分蒸馏，包括再造焦油	6					0	
27071000	粗苯	6					0	0
27072000	粗甲苯	6					0	0
27073000	粗二甲苯	6					0	0
27074000	萘	7					0	0
27075000	其他芳烃混合物，温度在250℃时蒸馏出的芳烃含量以体积计（包括损耗）在65%及以上（以美国标准实验法D86 为准）	7					0	0
27079100	杂酚油	7					0	0

税则号列	商品名称（简称）	最惠税率	亚太2国	东盟			最不发达35国	最不发达4国
				缅	老	柬		
27079910	酚	7					0	0
27079990	蒸馏煤焦油所得的其他产品；芳族成分重量超过非芳族成分的类似产品	7					0	0
27081000	从煤焦油或其他矿物焦油所得的沥青	7					0	
27082000	从煤焦油或其他矿物焦油所得的沥青焦	6					0	
27090000	石油原油及从沥青矿物提取的原油	0					0	0
27101210	车用汽油及航空汽油	5					0	
27101220	石脑油	6					0	
27101911	航空煤油	9					0	
27101919	其他煤油馏分产品	6					0	
27101922	5-7号燃料油	6					0	
27101991	润滑油	6					0	0
27101992	润滑脂	6					0	
27101993	润滑油基础油	6					0	
27101994	液体石蜡和重质液体石蜡	6					0	
27101999	其他重油及重油制品	6					0	
27102000	石油及从沥青矿物提取的油类以及以上述油为基本成分(按重量计不低于70%)的其他税目未列名制品，含有生物柴油，但废油除外	6					0	
27109100	含多氯联苯(PCBs)、多氯三联苯(PCTs)或多溴联苯(PBBs)的废油	6					0	
27109900	其他废油	6					0	
27111100	液化天然气	0					0	0
27111200	液化丙烷	5					0	
27111310	直接灌注香烟打火机及类似打火器用，其包装容器的容积超过300立方厘米的液化丁烷	11					0	
27111400	液化的乙烯、丙烯、丁烯及丁二烯	5					0	
27111910	直接灌注香烟打火机及类似打火器用，其包装容器的容积超过300立方厘米的其他液化燃料	10					0	
27112100	气态天然气	0					0	0
27112900	其他气态石油气及烃类气	6					0	
27121000	凡士林	8					0	0
27122000	石蜡，不论是否着色，按重量计含油小于0.75%	8					0	0
27129010	微晶石蜡，不论是否着色	8					0	0
27129090	其他矿物蜡及用合成或其他方法制得的类似产品，不论是否着色	8					0	0
27131110	硫的重量百分比小于3%的未煅烧石油焦	3					0	0
27131190	未煅烧石油焦	3					0	0
27131210	硫的重量百分比小于0.8%的已煅烧石油焦	3					0	0
27131290	已煅烧石油焦	3					0	0
27132000	石油沥青	8					0	0
27139000	其他石油或从沥青矿物提取油类的残渣	6					0	0
27141000	沥青页岩、油页岩及焦油砂	6					0	0
27149010	天然沥青(地沥青)	8					0	0
27149020	乳化沥青	0					0	0
27149090	沥青岩	3					0	0
27150000	以天然沥青（地沥青）、石油沥青、矿物焦油或矿物焦油沥青为基本成分的沥青混合物	8					0	0
27160000	电力	0					0	0
28011000	氯	5.5					0	
28012000	碘	5.5					0	
28013010	氟	5.5					0	
28013020	溴	5.5					0	
28020000	升华、沉淀、胶态硫磺	5.5					0	
28030000	碳（碳黑及其他税号未列名的其他形状的碳）	5.5					0	0
28041000	氢	5.5					0	0
28042100	氩	5.5					0	0
28042900	其他稀有气体	5.5					0	0
28043000	氮	5.5					0	0
28044000	氧	5.5					0	0
28045000	硼、碲	5.5					0	0
28046117	电子工业用直径≥30cm单晶硅棒	4					0	0
28046119	电子工业用7.5≤直径<30cm单晶硅棒	4					0	0

税则号列	商品名称（简称）	最惠税率	亚太2国	东盟			最不发达35国	最不发达4国
				缅	老	柬		
28046120	电子工业用直径＜7.5cm单晶硅棒	4					0	0
28046190	其他含硅量≥99.99%的硅	4					0	0
28046900	其他含硅量＜99.99%的硅	4					0	0
28047010	黄磷(白磷)	5.5					0	0
28047090	其他磷	5.5					0	0
28048000	砷	5.5					0	0
28049010	经掺杂用于电子工业的硒晶体棒	4					0	0
28049090	其他硒	5.5					0	
28051100	钠	5.5					0	
28051200	钙	5.5					0	
28051900	其他碱金属及碱土金属	5.5					0	
28053011	钕	5.5					0	
28053012	镝	5.5					0	
28053013	铽	5.5					0	
28053014	镧	5.5					0	
28053015	铈	5.5					0	
28053016	镨	5.5					0	
28053017	钇	5.5					0	
28053019	其他未相互混合或熔合的稀土金属、钪及钇	5.5					0	
28053021	已相互混合或熔合的稀土金属、钪及钇，电池级	5.5					0	
28053029	其他已相互混合或熔合的稀土金属、钪及钇	5.5					0	
28054000	汞	5.5					0	
28061000	氯化氢(盐酸)	5.5					0	
28062000	氯磺酸	5.5					0	
28070000	硫酸、发烟硫酸	5.5					0	
28080000	硝酸及磺硝酸	5.5					0	
28091000	五氧化二磷	1					0	
28092011	食品级磷酸	1					0	
28092019	其他磷酸及偏磷酸、焦磷酸	1					0	
28092090	其他多磷酸	5.5					0	
28100010	硼的氧化物	5.5					0	
28100020	硼酸	5.5					0	
28111100	氟化氢(氢氟酸)	5.5					0	0
28111910	氢氰酸	5.5					0	0
28111920	硒化氢	5.5					0	0
28111990	其他无机酸	5.5					0	0
28112100	二氧化碳	5.5					0	0
28112210	硅胶	5.5					0	0
28112290	其他二氧化硅	5.5					0	0
28112900	其他非金属无机氧化物	5.5					0	0
28121010	氯化亚砜	5.5					0	
28121020	氧氯化磷(磷酰氯;三氯氧磷)	5.5					0	
28121030	碳酰二氯(光气)	5.5					0	
28121041	一氯化硫(氯化硫)	5.5					0	
28121042	二氯化硫	5.5					0	
28121043	三氯化磷	5.5					0	
28121044	三氯化砷	5.5					0	
28121045	五氯化磷	5.5					0	
28121049	其他非金属氯化物	5.5					0	
28121090	其他非金属氯化物及氯氧化物	5.5					0	
28129011	三氟化氮	5.5					0	
28129019	其他氟化物及氟氧化物	5.5					0	
28129090	其他非金属卤化物及卤氧化物	5.5					0	
28131000	二硫化碳	5.5					0	
28139000	其他非金属硫化物,商品三硫化二磷	5.5					0	
28141000	氨	5.5					0	0
28142000	氨水	5.5					0	0
28151100	固体氢氧化钠	10					0	0

税则号列	商品名称（简称）	最惠税率	亚太2国	东盟			最不发达35国	最不发达4国
				缅	老	柬		
28151200	氢氧化钠水溶液及液体烧碱	8					0	0
28152000	氢氧化钾(苛性钾)	5.5					0	0
28153000	过氧化钠及过氧化钾	5.5					0	0
28161000	氢氧化镁及过氧化镁	5.5					0	
28164000	锶或钡的氧化物、氢氧化物及过氧化物	5.5					0	
28170010	氧化锌	5.5					0	0
28170090	过氧化锌	5.5					0	0
28181010	棕刚玉	5.5					0	0
28181090	其他人造刚玉，不论是否已有化学定义	5.5					0	0
28182000	氧化铝，但人造刚玉除外	8					0	0
28183000	氢氧化铝	5.5					0	0
28191000	三氧化铬	5.5					0	0
28199000	其他铬的氧化物及氢氧化物	5.5					0	0
28201000	二氧化锰	5.5					0	0
28209000	其他锰的氧化物	5.5					0	0
28211000	铁的氧化物及氢氧化物	5.5					0	0
28212000	土色料	5.5					0	0
28220010	四氧化三钴	5.5					0	
28220090	其他钴的氧化物及氢氧化物；商品氧化钴	5.5					0	
28230000	钛的氧化物	5.5					0	
28241000	一氧化铅(铅黄、黄丹)	5.5					0	
28249010	铅丹及铅橙	5.5					0	
28249090	其他铅的氧化物	5.5					0	
28251010	水合肼	5.5					0	0
28251020	硫酸羟胺	5.5					0	0
28251090	其他肼、胲及其无机盐	5.5					0	0
28252010	氢氧化锂	5.5					0	0
28252090	锂的氧化物	5.5					0	0
28253010	五氧化二钒	5.5					0	0
28253090	其他钒的氧化物及氢氧化物	5.5					0	0
28254000	镍的氧化物及氢氧化物	5.5					0	0
28255000	铜的氧化物及氢氧化物	5.5					0	0
28256000	锗的氧化物及二氧化锆	5.5					0	0
28257000	钼的氧化物及氢氧化物	5.5					0	0
28258000	锑的氧化物	5.5					0	0
28259011	钨酸	5.5					0	0
28259012	三氧化钨	5.5					0	0
28259019	其他钨的氧化物及氢氧化物	5.5					0	0
28259021	三氧化二铋	5.5					0	0
28259029	其他铋的氧化物及氢氧化物	5.5					0	0
28259031	二氧化锡	5.5					0	0
28259039	其他锡的氧化物及氢氧化物	5.5					0	0
28259041	一氧化铌	5.5					0	0
28259049	其他铌的氧化物及氢氧化物	5.5					0	0
28259090	其他无机碱；其他金属的氧化物及氢氧化物及过氧化物	5.5					0	0
28261210	无水氟化铝	5.5					0	0
28261290	其他氟化铝	5.5					0	0
28261910	铵的氟化物	5.5					0	0
28261920	钠的氟化物	5.5					0	0
28261990	其他氟化物	5.5					0	0
28263000	六氟铝酸钠(人造冰晶石)	5.5					0	0
28269010	氟硅酸盐	5.5					0	0
28269090	氟铝酸盐及其他氟络盐	5.5					0	0
28271010	肥料用氯化铵	4					0	0
28271090	非肥料用氯化铵	5.5					0	0
28272000	氯化钙	5.5					0	0
28273100	氯化镁	5.5					0	0
28273200	氯化铝	5.5					0	0

税则号列	商品名称（简称）	最惠税率	亚太2国	东盟			最不发达35国	最不发达4国
				缅	老	柬		
28273500	氯化镍	5.5					0	0
28273910	氯化锂	5.5					0	0
28273920	氯化钡	5.5					0	0
28273930	氯化钴	5.5					0	0
28273990	其他未列名氯化物	5.5					0	0
28274100	铜的氯氧化物及氢氧基氯化物	5.5					0	0
28274910	锆的氯氧化物及氢氧基氯化物	5.5					0	0
28274990	其他氯氧化物及氢氧基氯化物	5.5					0	0
28275100	溴化钠及溴化钾	5.5					0	0
28275900	其他溴化物及溴氧化物	5.5					0	0
28276000	碘化物及碘氧化物	5.5					0	0
28281000	商品次氯酸钙及其他钙的次氯酸盐	12					0	
28289000	次氯酸盐；亚氯酸盐及次溴酸盐	5.5					0	
28291100	氯酸钠	12					0	
28291910	氯酸钾(洋硝)	5.5					0	
28291990	其他氯酸盐	5.5					0	
28299000	高氯酸盐；溴酸盐及过溴酸盐；碘酸盐及高碘酸盐	5.5					0	
28301010	硫化钠	5.5					0	0
28301090	其他钠的硫化物	5.5					0	0
28309020	硫化锑	5.5					0	0
28309030	硫化钴	5.5					0	0
28309090	其他硫化物、多硫化物	5.5					0	0
28311010	钠的连二硫酸盐	5.5					0	
28311020	钠的次硫酸盐	5.5					0	
28319000	其他连二亚硫酸盐及次硫酸盐	5.5					0	
28321000	钠的亚硫酸盐	5.5					0	
28322000	其他亚硫酸盐	5.5					0	
28323000	硫代硫酸盐	5.5					0	
28331100	硫酸钠	5.5					0	
28331900	钠的其他硫酸盐	5.5					0	
28332100	硫酸镁	5.5					0	0
28332200	硫酸铝	5.5					0	0
28332400	镍的硫酸盐	5.5					0	0
28332500	铜的硫酸盐	5.5					0	0
28332700	硫酸钡	5.5					0	0
28332910	硫酸亚铁	5.5					0	0
28332920	铬的硫酸盐	5.5					0	0
28332930	硫酸锌	5.5					0	0
28332990	其他硫酸盐	5.5					0	0
28333010	钾铝矾	5.5					0	0
28333090	其他矾	5.5					0	0
28334000	过硫酸盐	5.5					0	0
28341000	亚硝酸盐	5.5					0	0
28342110	肥料用硝酸钾	4					0	0
28342190	非肥料用硝酸钾	5.5					0	0
28342910	硝酸钴	5.5					0	0
28342990	其他硝酸盐	5.5					0	0
28351000	次磷酸盐及亚磷酸盐	5.5					0	0
28352200	磷酸一钠及磷酸二钠	5.5					0	0
28352400	钾的磷酸盐	5.5					0	0
28352510	饲料级的正磷酸氢钙（磷酸二钙）	5.5					0	0
28352520	食品级的正磷酸氢钙（磷酸二钙）	5.5					0	0
28352590	其他正磷酸氢钙（磷酸二钙）	5.5					0	0
28352600	其他磷酸钙	5.5					0	0
28352910	磷酸三钠	5.5					0	0
28352990	其他磷酸盐	5.5					0	0
28353110	食品级的三磷酸钠（三聚磷酸钠）	5.5					0	0
28353190	其他三磷酸钠（三聚磷酸钠）	5.5					0	0

税则号列	商品名称（简称）	最惠税率	亚太2国	东盟			最不发达35国	最不发达4国
				缅	老	柬		
28353911	食品级的六偏磷酸钠	5.5					0	0
28353919	其他六偏磷酸钠	5.5					0	0
28353990	其他多磷酸盐	5.5					0	0
28362000	碳酸钠(纯碱)	5.5					0	0
28363000	碳酸氢钠(小苏打)	5.5					0	0
28364000	钾的碳酸盐	5.5					0	0
28365000	碳酸钙	5.5					0	0
28366000	碳酸钡	5.5					0	0
28369100	锂的碳酸盐	5.5					0	0
28369200	锶的碳酸盐	5.5					0	0
28369910	碳酸镁	5.5					0	0
28369930	碳酸钴	5.5					0	0
28369940	商品碳酸铵及其他铵的碳酸盐	5.5					0	0
28369950	碳酸锆	5.5					0	0
28369990	其他碳酸盐；过碳酸盐	5.5					0	0
28371110	氰化钠	5.5					0	
28371120	氧氰化钠	5.5					0	
28371910	氰化钾	5.5					0	
28371990	其他氰化物及氧氰化物	5.5					0	
28372000	氰络合物	5.5					0	
28391100	偏硅酸钠	5.5					0	
28391910	硅酸钠	5.5					0	
28391990	其他钠的硅酸盐；商品硅酸钠	5.5					0	
28399000	其他硅酸盐；商品碱金属硅酸盐	5.5					0	
28401100	无水四硼酸钠	5.5					0	
28401900	其他四硼酸钠	5.5					0	
28402000	其他硼酸盐	5.5					0	
28403000	过硼酸盐	5.5					0	
28413000	重铬酸钠	5.5					0	0
28415000	其他铬酸盐及重铬酸盐；过铬酸盐	5.5					0	0
28416100	高锰酸钾	5.5					0	0
28416910	锰酸锂	5.5					0	0
28416990	其他亚锰酸盐、锰酸盐及高锰酸盐	5.5					0	0
28417010	钼酸铵	5.5					0	0
28417090	其他钼酸盐	5.5					0	0
28418010	仲钨酸铵	5.5					0	0
28418020	钨酸钠	5.5					0	0
28418030	钨酸钙	5.5					0	0
28418040	偏钨酸铵	5.5					0	0
28418090	其他钨酸盐	5.5					0	0
28419000	其他金属酸盐及过金属酸盐	5.5					0	0
28421000	硅酸复盐及硅酸络盐（包括不论是否已有化学定义的硅铝酸盐）	5.5					0	
28429011	硫氰酸钠	5.5					0	
28429019	其他雷酸盐、氰酸盐及硫氰酸盐	5.5					0	
28429020	碲化镉	5.5					0	
28429030	锂镍钴锰氧化物	5.5					0	
28429040	磷酸铁锂	5.5					0	
28429050	硒酸盐及亚硒酸盐	5.5					0	
28429090	其他无机酸盐及过氧酸盐，叠氮化物除外	5.5					0	
28431000	胶态贵金属	5.5					0	
28432100	硝酸银	5.5					0	
28432900	其他银化合物，不论是否已有化学定义	5.5					0	
28433000	金化合物，不论是否已有化学定义	5.5					0	
28439000	其他贵金属化合物，不论是否已有化学定义；贵金属汞齐	5.5					0	
28441000	天然铀及其化合物（包括其合金，分散体，陶瓷产品及混合物）	5.5					0	0
28442000	U235浓缩铀、钚及它们的化合物（包括其合金，分散体，陶瓷产品及混合物）	5.5					0	0
28443000	U235贫化铀、钍及它们的化合物（包括其合金，分散体，陶瓷产品及混合物）	5.5					0	0
28444010	镭及镭盐（包括其合金，分散体，陶瓷产品及混合物）	4					0	0

税则号列	商品名称（简称）	最惠税率	亚太2国	东盟 缅	东盟 老	东盟 柬	最不发达35国	最不发达4国
28444020	放射性钴及放射性钴盐（包括其合金，分散体，陶瓷产品及混合物）	4					0	0
28444090	其他放射性元素同位素及其化合物（包括其合金，分散体，陶瓷产品及混合物）；放射性残渣	5.5					0	0
28445000	核反应堆已耗尽的燃料元件	5.5					0	
28451000	重水(氧化氘)	5.5					0	
28459000	其他同位素及其化合物,不论是否已有化学定义	5.5					0	
28461010	氧化铈	5.5					0	
28461020	氢氧化铈	5.5					0	
28461030	碳酸铈	5.5					0	
28461090	铈的其他化合物	5.5					0	
28469011	氧化钇	5.5					0	
28469012	氧化镧	5.5					0	
28469013	氧化钕	5.5					0	
28469014	氧化铕	5.5					0	
28469015	氧化镝	5.5					0	
28469016	氧化铽	5.5					0	
28469017	氧化镨	5.5					0	
28469019	其他氧化稀土	5.5					0	
28469021	氯化铽	5.5					0	
28469022	氯化镝	5.5					0	
28469023	氯化镧	5.5					0	
28469024	氯化钕	5.5					0	
28469025	氯化镨	4					0	
28469026	氯化钇	5.5					0	
28469028	混合氯化稀土	5.5					0	
28469029	未混合氯化稀土	5.5					0	
28469031	氟化铽	5.5					0	
28469032	氟化镝	5.5					0	
28469033	氟化镧	5.5					0	
28469034	氟化钕	5.5					0	
28469035	氟化镨	5.5					0	
28469036	氟化钇	5.5					0	
28469039	其他氟化稀土	5.5					0	
28469041	碳酸镧	5.5					0	
28469042	碳酸铽	5.5					0	
28469043	碳酸镝	5.5					0	
28469044	碳酸钕	5.5					0	
28469045	碳酸镨	5.5					0	
28469046	碳酸钇	5.5					0	
28469048	混合碳酸稀土	5.5					0	
28469049	未混合碳酸稀土	5.5					0	
28469091	镧的其他化合物	5.5					0	
28469092	钕的其他化合物	5.5					0	
28469093	铽的其他化合物	5.5					0	
28469094	镝的其他化合物	5.5					0	
28469095	镨的其他化合物	5.5					0	
28469096	钇的其他化合物	5.5					0	
28469099	稀土金属、钇、钪的其他化合物	5.5					0	
28470000	过氧化氢（不论是否用尿素固化）	5.5					0	
28480000	磷化物，不论是否已有化学定义，，但不包括磷铁	5.5					0	
28491000	碳化钙，不论是否已有化学定义，	5.5					0	
28492000	碳化硅，不论是否已有化学定义，	5.5					0	
28499010	碳化硼，不论是否已有化学定义，	5.5					0	
28499020	碳化钨，不论是否已有化学定义，	5.5					0	
28499090	其他碳化物，不论是否已有化学定义，	5.5					0	
28500011	氮化锰	5.5					0	
28500019	其他氮化物	5.5					0	
28500090	氢化物、迭氮化物、硅化物及硼化物，不论是否已有化学定义，但可归入税号 28.49 的碳化物除外:	5.5					0	

税则号列	商品名称（简称）	最惠税率	亚太2国	东盟			最不发达35国	最不发达4国
				缅	老	柬		
28521000	汞的有机或无机化合物，汞齐除外	5.5					0	
28529000	无化学定义的汞化合物	5.5					0	0
28530010	饮用蒸馏水	5.5					0	
28530020	氯化氰	5.5					0	
28530030	镍钴锰氢氧化物	6.5					0	
28530090	其他无机化合物、液态空气、压缩空气，汞齐，但贵金属汞齐除外	5.5					0	
29011000	饱和无环烃	2					0	
29012100	乙烯	2					0	
29012200	丙烯	2					0	
29012310	1-丁烯	2					0	
29012320	2-丁烯	2					0	
29012330	2-甲基丙稀	2					0	
29012410	1,3-丁二烯	2					0	
29012420	异戊二烯	2					0	
29012910	异戊烯	2					0	
29012920	乙炔	2					0	
29012990	其他不饱和无环烃	2					0	
29021100	环己烷	2					0	
29021910	蒎烯	2					0	
29021920	---4-烷基-4′-烷基双环己烷	2					0	
29021990	其他环烷烃、环烯及环萜烯	2					0	
29022000	苯	2					0	
29023000	甲苯	2					0	
29024100	邻二甲苯	2					0	
29024200	间二甲苯	2					0	
29024300	对二甲苯	2					0	
29024400	混合二甲苯异构体	2					0	
29026000	乙苯	2					0	
29027000	异丙基苯	2					0	
29029010	四氢萘	2					0	
29029020	精萘	2					0	
29029030	十二烷基苯	2					0	
29029040	4-(4′-烷基环己基)环己基乙烯	2					0	
29029090	其他芳香烃	2					0	
29031100	一氯甲烷及氯乙烷	5.5					0	
29031200	二氯甲烷	8					0	
29031300	氯仿(三氯甲烷)	10					0	
29031400	四氯化碳	8					0	
29031910	1,1,1-三氯乙烷(甲基氯仿)	8					0	
29031990	其他无环烃的饱和氯化衍生物	5.5					0	
29032100	氯乙烯	5.5					0	
29032200	三氯乙烯	8					0	
29032300	四氯乙烯	5.5					0	
29032910	3-氯-1-丙稀（氯丙稀）	5.5					0	
29032990	其他无环烃的不饱和氯化衍生物	5.5					0	
29033100	1，2－二溴乙烷（ISO）	5.5					0	
29033910	全氟异丁烯(八氟异丁烯)	5.5					0	
29033990	其他无环烃的氟化、溴化或碘化衍生物	5.5					0	
29037100	一氯二氟甲烷	5.5					0	
29037200	二氯三氟乙烷	5.5					0	
29037300	二氯一氟乙烷	5.5					0	
29037400	一氯二氟乙烷	5.5					0	
29037500	二氯五氟丙烷	5.5					0	
29037600	溴氯二氟甲烷、溴三氟甲烷及二溴四氟乙烷	5.5					0	
29037710	三氯氟甲烷	5.5					0	
29037720	其他仅含氟和氯的甲烷、乙烷及丙烷的全卤化物	5.5					0	
29037790	其他仅含氟氯的无环烃全卤化衍生物	5.5					0	
29037800	其他无环烃全卤化衍生物	5.5					0	

税则号列	商品名称（简称）	最惠税率	亚太2国	东盟			最不发达35国	最不发达4国
				缅	老	柬		
29037910	其他仅含氟和氯的甲烷、乙烷及丙烷的卤化衍生物	5.5					0	
29037990	其他含有两种或两种以上不同卤素的无环烃卤化衍生物	5.5					0	
29038100	1,2,3,4,5,6-六氯环己烷[六六六（ISO）],包括林丹（ISO，INN）	5.5					0	
29038200	艾氏剂（ISO）、氯丹（ISO）及七氯（ISO）	5.5					0	
29038900	其他环烷烃或环烯烃等卤化衍生物	5.5					0	
29039110	邻二氯苯	5.5					0	
29039190	氯苯及对二氯苯	5.5					0	
29039200	六氯苯（ISO）及滴滴涕（ISO，INN）	5.5					0	
29039910	对氯甲苯	5.5					0	
29039920	3,4-二氯三氟甲苯	5.5					0	
29039930	4-(4′-烷基苯基)-1-(4′-烷基苯基)-2-氟苯	5.5					0	
29039990	其他芳烃卤化衍生物	5.5					0	
29041000	仅含磺基的衍生物及其盐和乙酯	5.5					0	
29042010	硝基苯	5.5					0	
29042020	硝基甲苯	5.5					0	
29042030	二硝基甲苯	5.5					0	
29042040	三硝基甲苯(TNT)	5.5					0	
29042090	其他仅含硝基或亚硝基衍生物	5.5					0	
29049011	邻硝基氯化苯	5.5					0	
29049012	间硝基氯化苯	5.5					0	
29049013	对硝基氯化苯	5.5					0	
29049020	二硝基氯化苯	5.5					0	
29049030	三氯硝基甲烷(氯化苦;硝基氯仿)	5.5					0	
29049090	其他烃的磺化、硝化、亚硝化衍生物,不论是否卤化	5.5					0	
29051210	丙醇	5.5					0	
29051220	异丙醇	5.5					0	
29051300	正丁醇	5.5					0	
29051410	异丁醇	5.5					0	
29051420	仲丁醇	5.5					0	
29051430	叔丁醇	5.5					0	
29051700	十二醇、十六醇及十八醇	7					0	
29051910	3,3-二甲基丁-2- 醇(频哪基醇)	5.5					0	
29051990	其他饱和一元醇	5.5					0	
29052210	香叶醇、 橙花醇	5.5					0	
29052220	香茅醇	5.5					0	
29052230	芳樟醇	5.5					0	
29052290	其他无环萜烯醇	5.5					0	
29052900	其他不饱和一元醇(无环萜烯醇除外)	5.5					0	
29053200	丙二醇	5.5					0	
29053910	2,5-二甲基己二醇	4					0	
29053990	其他二元醇	5.5					0	
29054100	三羟甲基丙烷	5.5					0	
29054200	季戊四醇	5.5					0	
29054300	甘露糖醇	8					0	0
29054400	山梨醇	14					0	
29054500	丙三醇(甘油)	14					0	
29054910	木糖醇	5.5					0	
29054990	其他多元醇	5.5					0	
29055100	乙氯维诺	5.5					0	
29055900	无环醇的卤化、磺化、硝化、或亚硝化的衍生物(乙氯维诺除外)	5.5					0	
29061100	薄荷醇	5					0	
29061200	环己醇、甲基环己醇、二甲基环己醇	5.5					0	
29061310	固醇	5.5					0	
29061320	肌醇	5.5					0	
29061910	萜品醇	5.5					0	
29061990	其他环烷醇、环烯醇及环萜烯醇	5.5					0	
29062100	苄醇	5					0	
29062910	2-苯基乙醇	5.5					0	

税则号列	商品名称（简称）	最惠税率	亚太2国	东盟			最不发达35国	最不发达4国
				缅	老	柬		
29062990	其他芳香醇及它们的衍生物	5.5					0	
29071110	苯酚	5.5					0	0
29071190	苯酚的盐	5.5					0	0
29071211	间甲酚	5.5					0	0
29071212	邻甲酚	5.5					0	0
29071219	其他甲酚（对甲酚）	5.5					0	0
29071290	甲酚的盐	5.5					0	0
29071310	壬基酚	5.5					0	0
29071390	辛基酚及其异构体的盐和壬基酚盐	5.5					0	0
29071510	β-萘酚(2-萘酚)	5.5					0	0
29071590	其他萘酚及其盐	5.5					0	0
29071910	邻仲丁基酚、邻异丙基酚	4					0	0
29071990	其他一元酚	5.5					0	0
29072100	间苯二酚及其盐	5.5					0	0
29072210	对苯二酚	5.5					0	0
29072290	对苯二酚的盐	5.5					0	0
29072300	4,4′-异亚丙基联苯酚（双酚A）及其盐	5.5					0	0
29072910	邻苯二酚	4					0	0
29072990	其他多元酚；酚醇	5.5					0	0
29081100	五氯苯酚（ISO）	5.5					0	
29081910	对氯苯酚	4					0	
29081990	其他仅含卤素取代基的酚及酚醇衍生物及其盐	5.5					0	
29089100	地乐酚（ISO）及其盐	5.5					0	
29089200	4,6—二硝基邻甲酚〔二硝酚（ISO）〕及其盐	5.5					0	
29089910	对硝基酚、对硝基酚钠	5.5					0	
29089990	其他酚及酚醇的卤化、磺化、硝化、或亚硝化的等衍生物	5.5					0	
29091100	乙醚	5.5					0	0
29092000	环烷醚、环烯醚或环萜烯醚及其卤化、磺化、硝化或亚硝化衍生物	5.5					0	0
29093010	---1-烷氧基-4-（4-乙烯基环己基）-2，3-二氟苯	5.5					0	0
29093090	其他芳香醚及其卤化、磺化、硝化或亚硝化衍生物	5.5					0	0
29094300	乙二醇或二甘醇的单丁醚	5.5					0	0
29094400	乙二醇或二甘醇的其他单烷基醚	5.5					0	0
29094910	间苯氧基苄醇	4					0	0
29094990	其他醚醇及其卤化、磺化、硝化、或亚硝化的衍生物	5.5					0	0
29095000	醚酚、醚醇酚及其卤化、磺化、硝化、或亚硝化的衍生物	5.5					0	0
29096000	过氧化醇、过氧化醚、过氧化酮及其卤化、磺化、硝化、或亚硝化的衍生物	5.5					0	0
29101000	环氧乙烷(氧化乙烯)	5.5					0	
29102000	甲基环氧乙烷(氧化丙烯)	5.5					0	
29103000	1-氯-2,3-环氧丙烷(表氯醇)	5.5					0	
29104000	狄氏剂（ISO，INN）	5.5					0	
29109000	三节环环氧化物，环氧醇(酚、醚)及其卤化、磺化、硝化、或亚硝化的衍生物	5.5					0	
29110000	缩醛、半缩醛，不论是否含有其它含氧基，及其卤化、磺化、硝化、或亚硝化的衍生物	5.5					0	
29121100	甲醛	5.5					0	
29121200	乙醛	5.5					0	
29121900	其他无环醛（不含其他含氧基）	5.5					0	
29122100	苯甲醛	5.5					0	
29122910	铃兰醛(对叔丁基-α-甲基-氧化肉桂醛)	5.5					0	
29122990	其他环醛（不含其他含氧基）	5.5					0	
29124100	香草醛(3-甲氧基-4-羟基苯甲醛)	5.5					0	
29124200	乙基香草醛	5.5					0	
29124910	醛醇	5.5					0	
29124990	其他醛醚、醛酚、其他含氧基的醛	5.5					0	
29125000	环聚醛	5.5					0	
29126000	多聚甲醛	5.5					0	
29130000	税目2912所列产品的卤化、磺化、硝化、或亚硝化的衍生物	5.5					0	
29141100	丙酮	5.5					0	
29141200	丁酮	5.5					0	

税则号列	商品名称（简称）	最惠税率	亚太2国	东盟			最不发达35国	最不发达4国
				缅	老	柬		
29141300	4-甲基-2-戊酮	5.5					0	
29141900	其他不含其他含氧基的无环酮	5.5					0	
29142200	环己酮及甲基环己酮	5.5					0	
29142300	芷香酮及甲基芷香酮	5.5					0	
29142910	樟脑	5.5					0	
29142990	其他不含含氧基环烷酮、环烯酮或环萜烯酮	5.5					0	
29143100	苯丙酮(苯基丙-2-酮)	5.5					0	
29143910	苯乙酮	4					0	
29143990	其他不含其他含氧基的芳香酮	5.5					0	
29144000	酮醇及酮醛	5.5					0	
29145011	覆盆子酮	5.5					0	
29145019	其他酮酚	5.5					0	
29145020	2-羟基-4-甲氧基二苯甲酮	5.5					0	
29145090	酮酚及含其他含氧基酮	5.5					0	
29146100	蒽醌	5.5					0	
29146910	辅酶Q10	5.5					0	
29146990	其他醌，不论是否含有其他含氧基，及其卤化、磺化、硝化或亚硝化衍生物	5.5					0	
29147000	其他酮及醌的卤化、磺化、硝化、或亚硝化的衍生物	5.5					0	
29151100	甲酸	5.5					0	0
29151200	甲酸盐	5.5					0	0
29151300	甲酸酯	5.5					0	0
29152111	食品级冰乙酸	5.5					0	0
29152119	其他冰乙酸(冰醋酸)	5.5					0	0
29152190	其他乙酸	5.5					0	0
29152400	乙酸酐	5.5					0	0
29152910	乙酸钠	5.5					0	0
29152990	其他乙酸盐	5.5					0	0
29153100	乙酸乙酯	5.5					0	0
29153200	乙酸乙烯酯	5.5					0	0
29153300	乙酸正丁酯	5.5					0	0
29153600	地乐酚（ISO）乙酸酯	5.5					0	0
29153900	其他乙酸酯	5.5					0	0
29154000	一、二、三氯代乙酸及其盐和酯	5.5					0	0
29155010	丙酸	5.5					0	0
29155090	丙酸盐和酯	5.5					0	0
29156000	丁酸、戊酸及其盐和酯	5.5					0	0
29157010	硬脂酸	7					0	0
29157090	棕榈酸及其盐和酯、硬脂酸盐、酯	5.5					0	0
29159000	其他饱和无环一元羧酸及其酸酐	5.5					0	0
29161100	丙烯酸及其盐	6.5					0	
29161210	丙烯酸甲酯	6.5					0	
29161220	丙烯酸乙酯	6.5					0	
29161230	丙烯酸丁酯	6.5					0	
29161240	丙烯酸异辛酯	6.5					0	
29161290	其他丙烯酸酯	6.5					0	
29161300	甲基丙烯酸及其盐	6.5					0	
29161400	甲基丙烯酸酯	6.5					0	
29161500	油酸、亚油酸或亚麻酸及其盐和酯	6.5					0	
29161600	乐杀螨（ISO）	6.5					0	
29161900	其他不饱和无环一元羧酸（包括其酸酐，酰卤化物，过氧化物和过氧酸及它们的衍生物）	6.5					0	
29162010	DV菊酸甲酯、二溴菊酸	4					0	
29162090	其他(环烷、环烯、环萜烯)一元羧酸（包括其酸酐，酰卤化物，过氧化物和过氧酸及它们的衍生物）	6.5					0	
29163100	苯甲酸及其盐和酯	6.5					0	
29163200	过氧化苯甲酰及苯甲酰氯	6.5					0	
29163400	苯乙酸及其盐	6.5					0	
29163910	邻甲基苯甲酸	6.5					0	
29163920	布洛芬	6.5					0	

税则号列	商品名称（简称）	最惠税率	亚太2国	东盟 缅	东盟 老	东盟 柬	最不发达35国	最不发达4国
29163990	其他芳香一元羧酸（包括其酸酐，酰卤化物，过氧化物和过氧酸及它们的衍生物）	6.5					0	
29171110	草酸	6.5					0	
29171120	草酸钴	9					0	
29171190	其他草酸盐和酯	6.5					0	
29171200	己二酸及其盐和酯	6.5					0	
29171310	癸二酸及其盐和酯	6.5					0	
29171390	壬二酸及其盐和酯	6.5					0	
29171400	马来酐	6.5					0	
29171900	其他无环多元羧酸（包括其酸酐，酰卤化物，过氧化物和过氧酸及它们的衍生物）	6.5					0	
29172010	四氢苯酐	4					0	
29172090	其他(环烷、环烯、环萜烯)多元羧酸（包括其酸酐，酰卤化物，过氧化物和过氧酸及它们的衍生物）	6.5					0	
29173200	邻苯二甲酸二辛酯	6.5					0	
29173300	邻苯二甲酸二壬酯,邻苯二甲酸二癸酯	6.5					0	
29173410	邻苯二甲酸二丁酯	6.5					0	
29173490	其他邻苯二甲酸酯	6.5					0	
29173500	邻苯二甲酸酐(苯酐)	6.5					0	
29173611	精对苯二甲酸	6.5					0	
29173619	其他对苯二甲酸	6.5					0	
29173690	对苯二甲酸盐	6.5					0	
29173700	对苯二甲酸二甲酯	6.5					0	
29173910	间苯二甲酸	6.5					0	
29173990	其他芳香多元羧酸（包括其酸酐，酰卤化物，过氧化物和过氧酸及它们的衍生物）	6.5					0	
29181100	乳酸及其盐和酯	6.5					0	
29181200	酒石酸	6.5					0	
29181300	酒石酸盐及酒石酸酯	6.5					0	
29181400	柠檬酸	6.5					0	
29181500	柠檬酸盐及柠檬酸酯	6.5					0	
29181600	葡糖酸及其盐和酯	6.5					0	
29181800	乙酯杀螨醇（ISO）	6.5					0	
29181910	2,2-二苯基-2-羟基乙酸	6.5					0	
29181990	其他含醇基但不含其他含氧基的羧酸（包括其酸酐，酰卤化物，过氧化物和过氧酸及它们的衍生物）	6.5					0	
29182110	水杨酸、水杨酸钠	6.5					0	
29182190	其他水杨酸盐	6.5					0	
29182210	邻乙酰水杨酸(阿斯匹林)	6					0	
29182290	邻乙酰水杨酸盐和酯	6.5					0	
29182300	水杨酸其他酯及其盐	6.5					0	
29182900	其他含酚基但不含其他含氧基羧酸及其酸酐（酰卤化物，过氧化物和过氧酸及它们的衍生物）	6.5					0	
29183000	含醛基或酮基不含其他含氧基羧酸及其酸酐（酰卤化物，过氧化物和过氧酸及它们的衍生物）	6.5					0	
29189100	2，4，5-涕（ISO）（2，4，5-三氯苯氧基乙酸）及其盐或酯	6.5					0	
29189900	其他含其他附加含氧基羧酸及其酸酐（酰卤化物，过氧化物和过氧酸及它们的衍生物）	6.5					0	
29191000	三（2，3-二溴丙基）磷酸酯	6.5					0	
29199000	其他磷酸酯及其盐(包括乳磷酸盐)，及它们的卤化、磺化、硝化、或亚硝化的衍生物	6.5					0	
29201100	对硫磷（ISO）及甲基对硫磷（ISO）	6.5					0	
29201900	其他硫代磷酸酯及其盐，及它们的卤化、磺化、硝化、或亚硝化的衍生物	6.5					0	
29209011	亚磷酸三甲酯	6.5					0	
29209012	亚磷酸三乙酯	6.5					0	
29209013	亚磷酸二甲酯	6.5					0	
29209014	亚磷酸二乙酯	6.5					0	
29209019	其他亚磷酸酯	6.5					0	
29209090	其他无机酸酯（不包括卤化氢的酯）及其盐，及它们的卤化、磺化、硝化、或亚硝化的衍生物	6.5					0	

税则号列	商品名称（简称）	最惠税率	亚太2国	东盟 缅	东盟 老	东盟 柬	最不发达35国	最不发达4国
29211100	甲胺、二甲胺或三甲胺及其盐	6.5					0	
29211910	二正丙胺	4					0	
29211920	异丙胺	6.5					0	
29211930	N,N-二(2-氯乙基)乙胺	6.5					0	
29211940	N,N-二(2-氯乙基)甲胺	6.5					0	
29211950	三(2-氯乙基)胺	6.5					0	
29211960	二烷氨基乙基-2-氯及其质子化盐	6.5					0	
29211990	其他无环单胺及其衍生物，及它们的盐	6.5					0	
29212110	乙二胺	6.5					0	
29212190	乙二胺盐	6.5					0	
29212210	己二酸己二胺盐(尼龙-66盐)	6.5					0	
29212290	六亚甲基二胺及其他盐	6.5					0	
29212900	其他无环多胺及其衍生物，及它们的盐	6.5					0	
29213000	环(烷、烯、萜烯)单胺或多胺及衍生物，及它们的盐	6.5					0	
29214110	苯胺	6.5					0	
29214190	苯胺盐	6.5					0	
29214200	苯胺衍生物及其盐	6.5					0	
29214300	甲苯胺及其衍生物，及它们的盐	6.5					0	
29214400	二苯胺及其衍生物，及它们的盐	6.5					0	
29214500	1-萘胺、2-萘胺及其衍生物及盐	6.5					0	
29214600	安非他明、苄非他明、右苯丙胺、乙非他明、芬坎法明、利非他明、左苯丙胺、美芬雷司、芬特明以及它们的盐	6.5					0	
29214910	对异丙基苯胺	4					0	
29214920	二甲基苯胺	6.5					0	
29214930	2,6-甲基乙基苯胺	4					0	
29214940	2,6-二乙基苯胺	6.5					0	
29214990	其他芳香单胺及衍生物及它们的盐	6.5					0	
29215110	邻苯二胺	4					0	
29215190	间-、对-苯二胺、二氨基甲苯及其衍生物及它们的盐	6.5					0	
29215900	其他芳香多胺及衍生物及它们的盐	6.5					0	
29221100	单乙醇胺及其盐	6.5					0	
29221200	二乙醇胺及其盐	6.5					0	
29221310	三乙醇胺	6.5					0	
29221320	三乙醇胺盐	6.5					0	
29221400	右丙氧吩及其盐	6.5					0	
29221910	乙胺丁醇	6.5					0	
29221921	二甲氨基乙醇及其质子化盐	6.5					0	
29221922	二乙氨基乙醇及其质子化盐	6.5					0	
29221929	其他二烷氨基乙-2-醇及其质子化	6.5					0	
29221930	乙基二乙醇胺	6.5					0	
29221940	甲基二乙醇胺	6.5					0	
29221950	本芴醇	6.5					0	
29221990	其他氨基醇及其醚、酯和它们的盐（但含有一种以上含氧基的除外）	6.5					0	
29222100	氨基羟基萘磺酸及其盐	6.5					0	
29222910	茴香胺、二茴香胺、氨基苯乙醚及其盐	6.5					0	
29222990	其他氨基(萘酚、酚)及醚、酯、盐（但含有一种以上含氧基的除外）	6.5					0	
29223100	安非拉酮、美沙酮和去甲美沙酮以及它们的盐	6.5					0	
29223910	4-甲基甲卡西酮	6.5					0	
29223990	其他氨基醛、氨基酮、氨基醌及其盐（但含有一种以上含氧基的除外）	6.5					0	
29224110	赖氨酸	5					0	
29224190	赖氨酸酯和赖氨酸盐	6					0	
29224210	谷氨酸	10					0	
29224220	谷氨酸钠	10					0	
29224290	其他谷氨酸盐	6.5					0	
29224310	邻氨基苯甲酸(氨茴酸)	6.5					0	
29224390	邻氨基苯甲酸(氨茴酸)盐	6.5					0	
29224400	替利定及其盐	6.5					0	
29224911	氨甲环酸	6.5					0	
29224919	其他氨基酸	6.5					0	

税则号列	商品名称（简称）	最惠税率	亚太2国	东盟 缅	老	柬	最不发达35国	最不发达4国
29224991	普鲁卡因	6					0	
29224999	其他氨基酸及其酯及它们的盐（但含有一种以上含氧基的除外）	6.5					0	
29225010	对羟基苯甘氨酸及其邓甲盐	6.5					0	
29225020	莱克多巴胺和盐酸莱克多巴胺	6.5					0	
29225090	其他氨基醇酚、氨基酸酚及其他含氧基氨基化合物	6.5					0	
29231000	胆碱及其盐	6.5					0	
29232000	卵磷脂及其他磷氨基类脂	6.5					0	
29239000	其他季铵盐及季铵碱	6.5					0	
29241100	甲丙氨酯	6.5					0	
29241200	氯乙酰胺（ISO）、久效磷（ISO）及磷胺（ISO）	6.5					0	
29241910	二甲基甲酰胺	6.5					0	
29241990	其他无环酰胺及其衍生物以及他们的盐	6.5					0	
29242100	酰脲及其衍生物，及它们的盐	6.5					0	
29242300	2-乙酰氨基苯甲酸（N-乙酰邻氨基苯甲酸）及其盐	6.5					0	
29242400	炔己蚁胺	6.5					0	
29242910	对乙酰氨基苯乙醚(非那西丁)	6					0	
29242920	对乙酰氨基酚(扑热息痛)	6					0	
29242930	阿斯巴甜	6.5					0	
29242990	其他环酰胺（包括环氨基甲酸酯）	6.5					0	
29251100	糖精及其盐	9					0	
29251200	格鲁米特	6.5					0	
29251900	其他酰亚胺及其衍生物、盐	6.5					0	
29252100	杀虫脒	6.5					0	
29252900	其他亚胺及其衍生物以及它们的盐	6.5					0	
29261000	丙烯腈	6.5					0	
29262000	1-氰基胍(双氰胺)	6.5					0	
29263000	芬普雷司及其盐；美沙酮中间体（4-氰基-2-二甲氨基-4,4-二苯基丁烷）	6.5					0	
29269010	对氯氰苄	4					0	
29269020	间苯二甲腈	6.5					0	
29269090	其他腈基化合物	6.5					0	
29270000	重氮化合物、偶氮化合物及氧化偶氮化合物	6.5					0	
29280000	肼(联氨)及胲(羟胺)的有机衍生物	6.5					0	
29291010	2，4和2，6甲苯二异氰酸酯混合物(甲苯二异氰酸酯TDI)	6.5					0	
29291020	二甲苯二异氰酸酯（TODI）	6.5					0	
29291030	二苯基甲烷二异氰酸酯(纯MDI)	6.5					0	
29291040	六亚甲基二异氰酸酯	6.5					0	
29291090	其他异氰酸酯	6.5					0	
29299010	环已基氨基磺酸钠(甜蜜素)	9					0	
29299020	二烷(甲、乙、正丙或异丙)氨基膦酰二卤	6.5					0	
29299030	二烷氨基膦酸二烷酯	6.5					0	
29299040	乙酰甲胺磷	6.5					0	
29299090	其他含氮基化合物	6.5					0	
29302000	其他硫代氨基甲酸盐(或酯)	6.5					0	
29303000	（一硫化、二硫化、三硫化）二烃氨基硫羰	6.5					0	
29304000	甲硫氨酸(蛋氨酸)	6.5					0	
29305000	敌菌丹（ISO）及甲胺磷（ISO）	6.5					0	
29309010	双巯丙氨酸(胱氨酸)	6.5					0	
29309020	二硫代碳酸酯(或盐)[黄原酸酯（或盐）]	6.5					0	
29309090	其他有机硫化合物	6.5					0	
29311000	四甲基铅及四乙基铅	6.5					0	
29312000	三丁基锡化合物	6.5					0	
29319011	双甘膦	6.5					0	
29319019	其他含有磷原子的有机-无机化合物	6.5					0	
29319090	其他有机-无机化合物	6.5					0	
29321100	四氢呋喃	6					0	
29321200	2-糠醛	6					0	
29321300	糠醇及四氢糠醇	6					0	
29321900	其他结构上有非稠合呋喃环化合物（不论是否氢化）	6.5					0	

税则号列	商品名称（简称）	最惠税率	亚太2国	东盟 缅	老	柬	最不发达35国	最不发达4国
29322010	香豆素、甲基香豆素及乙基香豆素	6.5					0	
29322090	其他内酯	6.5					0	
29329100	4-丙烯基-1,2-亚甲二氧基苯	6.5					0	
29329200	1-(1,3-苯并二恶茂-5-基)丙-2-酮	6.5					0	
29329300	3,4-亚甲二氧基苯甲醛(胡椒醛)	6.5					0	
29329400	4-烯丙基-1,2-亚甲二氧基苯（黄樟脑）	6.5					0	
29329500	四氢大麻酚（所有异构体）	6.5					0	
29329910	7-羟基苯并呋喃(呋喃酚)	4					0	
29329920	联苯双酯	6.5					0	
29329930	蒿甲醚	6.5					0	
29329990	其他仅含氧杂原子的杂环化合物	6.5					0	
29331100	二甲基苯基吡唑酮（安替比林）及其衍生物	6.5					0	
29331920	安乃近	6					0	
29331990	其他结构上有非稠合吡唑环化合物（不论是否氢化）	6.5					0	
29332100	乙内酰脲及其衍生物	6.5					0	
29332900	其他结构上有非稠合咪唑环化合物（不论是否氢化）	6.5					0	
29333100	吡啶及其盐	6					0	
29333210	哌啶(六氢吡啶)	4					0	
29333220	哌啶(六氢吡啶)盐	6.5					0	
29333300	阿芬太尼、阿尼利定、氰苯双哌酰胺、溴西泮、地芬诺新、地芬诺酯、地匹哌酮、芬太尼、凯托米酮、哌醋甲酯、喷他左辛、哌替啶、哌替啶中间体A、苯环利定、苯哌利定、哌苯甲醇、哌氰米特、丙吡兰和三甲利定以及它们的盐	6.5					0	
29333910	二苯乙醇酸-3-奎宁环脂	6.5					0	
29333920	奎宁环-3-醇	6.5					0	
29333990	其他结构上有非稠合吡啶环化合物（不论是否氢化）	6.5					0	
29334100	左非诺及其盐	6.5					0	
29334910	环丙氟哌酸	6.5					0	
29334990	其他含喹琳或异喹啉环系的化合物（但未经进一步稠合）	6.5					0	
29335200	丙二酰脲（巴比土酸）及其盐	6.5					0	
29335300	阿洛巴比妥、异戊巴比妥、巴比妥、布他比妥、正丁巴比妥、环己巴比妥、甲苯巴比妥、戊巴比妥、苯巴比妥、仲丁巴比妥、司可巴比妥和乙烯比妥以及他们的盐	6.5					0	
29335400	其他丙二酰脲的衍生物以及他们的盐	6.5					0	
29335500	氯普唑仑、甲氯喹酮等以及他们的盐	6.5					0	
29335910	胞嘧啶	6.5					0	
29335990	其他结构上有嘧啶环或哌嗪环的化合物（不论是否氢化）	6.5					0	
29336100	三聚氰胺(蜜胺)	6.5					0	
29336910	三聚氰氯	6					0	
29336921	二氯异氰脲酸	6.5					0	
29336922	三氯异氰脲酸	6.5					0	
29336929	其他异氰脲酸氯化衍生物	6.5					0	
29336990	其他结构上含非稠合三嗪环化合物（不论是否氢化）	6.5					0	
29337200	氯巴占和甲乙哌酮	9					0	
29337900	其他内酰胺	9					0	
29339100	阿普唑仑、卡马西泮等以及它们的盐	6.5					0	
29339900	其他仅含氮杂原子的杂环化合物	6.5					0	
29341000	结构上含有非稠合噻唑环的化合物（不论是否氢化）	6.5					0	
29342000	含一个苯并噻唑环系的化合物（但未经进一步稠合，不论是否氢化）	6.5					0	
29343000	含一个吩噻嗪环系的化合物（但未经进一步稠合，不论是否氢化）	6.5					0	
29349100	阿米雷司、溴替唑仑、氯噻西泮等以及他们的盐	6.5					0	
29349910	磺内酯及磺内酰胺	6.5					0	
29349920	呋喃唑酮	6					0	
29349930	核酸及其盐	6.5					0	
29349940	奈韦拉平、依发韦仑、利托那韦及它们的盐	6.5					0	
29349950	克拉维酸及其盐	6.5					0	
29349960	7-苯乙酰氨基-3-氯甲基-4-头孢烷酸对甲氧基苄酯、7-氨基头孢烷酸、7-氨基脱乙酰氧基头孢烷酸	6					0	
29349990	其他杂环化合物	6.5					0	

税则号列	商品名称（简称）	最惠税率	亚太2国	东盟			最不发达35国	最不发达4国
				缅	老	柬		
29350010	磺胺嘧啶	6.5					0	
29350020	磺胺双甲基嘧啶	6.5					0	
29350030	磺胺甲恶唑	6.5					0	
29350090	其他磺(酰)胺	6.5					0	
29362100	未混合的维生素 A 及其衍生物	4					0	0
29362200	未混合的维生素 B1 及其衍生物	4					0	0
29362300	未混合的维生素 B2 及其衍生物	4					0	0
29362400	未混合的 D 或 DL-泛酸及其衍生物	4					0	0
29362500	未混合的维生素 B6 及其衍生物	4					0	0
29362600	未混合的维生素 B12 及其衍生物	4					0	0
29362700	未混合的维生素 C 及其衍生物	4					0	0
29362800	未混合的维生素 E 及其衍生物	4					0	0
29362900	其他未混合的维生素及其衍生物	4					0	0
29369000	维生素原、混合维生素及其衍生物	4					0	0
29371100	生长激素及其衍生物和类似结构物	4					0	
29371210	重组人胰岛素及其盐	4					0	
29371290	其他胰岛素及其盐	4					0	
29371900	其他多肽激素、蛋白激素、糖蛋白激素及其衍生物和类似结构物	4					0	
29372100	可的松、氢化可的松及脱氢可的松及脱氢皮质（甾）醇	4					0	
29372210	地塞米松	4					0	
29372290	其他皮质（甾）激素的卤化衍生物	4					0	
29372311	孕马结合雌激素	4					0	
29372319	其他动物源的雌（甾）激素和孕激素	4					0	
29372390	其他皮质甾类激素的卤化衍生物	4					0	
29372900	其他甾族激素及其衍生物和类似结构物	4					0	
29375000	前列腺素、血栓烷和白细胞三烯及其衍生物和结构类似物	4					0	
29379000	其他天然或合成再制的激素及其衍生物和结构类似物，包括主要用作激素的改性链多肽	4					0	
29381000	芸香苷及其衍生物	6.5					0	
29389010	齐多夫定、拉米夫定、司他夫定、地达诺新及它们的盐	6.5					0	
29389090	其他天然或合成再制的苷及其盐、醚、酯和其他衍生物	6.5					0	
29391100	罂粟秆浓缩物、丁丙诺啡、可待因等以及他们的盐	4					0	0
29391900	其他鸦片碱及其衍生物，及它们的盐	4					0	0
29392000	其他金鸡纳生物碱及其衍生物，及它们的盐	4					0	0
29393000	咖啡因及其盐	4					0	0
29394100	麻黄碱及其盐	4					0	0
29394200	假麻黄碱及其盐	4					0	0
29394300	d－去甲麻黄碱（INN)及其盐	4					0	0
29394400	去甲麻黄碱及其盐	4					0	0
29394900	其他麻黄碱类及其盐	4					0	0
29395100	芬乙茶碱（INN）及其盐	4					0	0
29395900	其他茶碱和氨茶碱及其衍生物，及它们的盐	4					0	0
29396100	麦角新碱及其盐	4					0	0
29396200	麦角胺及其盐	4					0	0
29396300	麦角酸及其盐	4					0	0
29396900	其他麦角生物碱及其衍生物，及它们的盐	4					0	0
29399110	可卡因及其盐	4					0	0
29399190	芽子碱、左甲苯丙胺、去氧麻黄碱、去氧麻黄碱外消旋体，它们的盐、酯及其他衍生物；可卡因的酯及其他衍生物	4					0	0
29399910	烟碱及其盐	4					0	0
29399920	番木鳖碱(士的年)及其盐	4					0	0
29399990	其他天然或合成再制的生物碱及其盐、醚、酯和其他衍生物	4					0	0
29400000	化学纯糖,但蔗糖、乳糖、麦芽糖、葡萄糖及果糖除外；糖醚、糖酯及其盐，但不包括税目 29.37、29.38、29.39 的产品	6					0	0
29411011	氨苄青霉素	6					0	0
29411012	氨苄青霉素三水酸	6					0	0
29411019	其他氨苄青霉素盐	6					0	0
29411091	羟氨苄青霉素	4					0	0
29411092	羟氨苄青霉素三水酸	4					0	0

税则号列	商品名称（简称）	最惠税率	亚太2国	东盟			最不发达35国	最不发达4国
				缅	老	柬		
29411093	6氨基青霉烷酸(6APA)	4					0	0
29411094	青霉素V	4					0	0
29411095	磺苄青霉素	4					0	0
29411096	邻氯青霉素	4					0	0
29411099	其他青霉素及其衍生物，及它们的盐	4					0	0
29412000	链霉素及其衍生物，及它们的盐	4					0	0
29413011	四环素	4					0	0
29413012	四环素盐	4					0	0
29413020	四环素衍生物及其盐	4					0	0
29414000	氯霉素及其衍生物，及它们的盐	4					0	0
29415000	红霉素及其衍生物，及它们的盐	4					0	0
29419010	庆大霉素及其衍生物，及它们的盐	4					0	0
29419020	卡那霉素及其衍生物，及它们的盐	4					0	0
29419030	利福平及其衍生物，及它们的盐	4					0	0
29419040	林可霉素及其衍生物，及它们的盐	4					0	0
29419052	头孢氨苄及其盐	6					0	0
29419053	头孢唑啉及其盐	6					0	0
29419054	头孢拉啶及其盐	6					0	0
29419055	头孢三嗪(头孢曲松)及其盐	6					0	0
29419056	头孢哌酮及其盐	6					0	0
29419057	头孢噻肟及其盐	6					0	0
29419058	头孢克罗及其盐	6					0	0
29419059	其他头孢菌素及其衍生物以及它们的盐	6					0	0
29419060	麦迪霉素及其衍生物，及它们的盐	6					0	0
29419070	乙酰螺旋霉素及其衍生物，及它们的盐	4					0	0
29419090	其他抗菌素	6					0	0
29420000	其他有机化合物	6.5					0	0
30012000	腺体、其他器官及其分泌物提取物	3					0	
30019010	肝素及其盐	3					0	
30019090	其他未列名的人体或动物制品(供治疗或预防疾病用)	3					0	
30021000	抗血清、其他血份及免疫制品(不论是否修饰通过生物工艺加工制得)	3					0	0
30022000	人用疫苗	3					0	0
30023000	兽用疫苗	3					0	0
30029010	石房蛤毒素	3					0	0
30029020	蓖麻毒素	3					0	0
30029030	细菌及病毒	3					0	0
30029040	遗传物质和基因修饰生物体	3					0	0
30029090	人血；治病、防病或诊断用动物血制品；其他毒素、培养微生物（不包括酵母）及类似产品	3					0	0
30031011	含有氨苄青霉素的混合药品（两种或两种以上成分混合而成的，治病或防病用，未配定剂量或非零售包装）	6					0	0
30031012	含有羟氨苄青霉素的混合药品（两种或两种以上成分混合而成的，治病或防病用未配定剂量或非零售包装）	6					0	0
30031013	含有青霉素V的混合药品（两种或两种以上成分混合而成的，治病或防病用未配定剂量或非零售包装）	6					0	0
30031019	含有其他青霉素及具有青霉烷酸结构的青霉素衍生物的混合药品（两种或两种以上成分混合而成的，治病或防病用未配定剂量或非零售包装）	6					0	0
30031090	含有含有链霉素的混合药品（两种或两种以上成分混合而成的，治病或防病用未配定剂量或非零售包装）	6					0	0
30032011	含有头孢噻肟的混合药品（两种或两种以上成分混合而成的，治病或防病用未配定剂量或非零售包装）	6					0	0
30032012	含有头孢他啶的混合药品（两种或两种以上成分混合而成的，治病或防病用未配定剂量或非零售包装）	6					0	0
30032013	含有头孢西丁的混合药品（两种或两种以上成分混合而成的，治病或防病用未配定剂量或非零售包装）	6					0	0
30032014	含有头孢替唑的混合药品（两种或两种以上成分混合而成的，治病或防病用未配定剂量或非零售包装）	6					0	0
30032015	含有头孢克罗的混合药品（两种或两种以上成分混合而成的，治病或防病用未配定剂量或非零售包装）	6					0	0
30032016	含有头孢呋辛的混合药品（两种或两种以上成分混合而成的，治病或防病用	6					0	0

税则号列	商品名称（简称）	最惠税率	亚太2国	东盟			最不发达35国	最不发达4国
				缅	老	柬		
	未配定剂量或非零售包装）							
30032017	含有头孢三嗪（头孢曲松）的混合药品（两种或两种以上成分混合而成的，治病或防病用未配定剂量或非零售包装）	6					0	0
30032018	含有头孢哌酮的混合药品（两种或两种以上成分混合而成的，治病或防病用未配定剂量或非零售包装）	6					0	0
30032019	含有其他头孢菌素的混合药品（两种或两种以上成分混合而成的，治病或防病用未配定剂量或非零售包装）	6					0	0
30032090	其他含有其他抗菌素的混合药品（两种或两种以上成分混合而成的，治病或防病用未配定剂量或非零售包装）	6					0	0
30033100	含有胰岛素但不含抗菌素的混合药品（两种或两种以上成分混合而成的，治病或防病用未配定剂量或非零售包装）	5					0	0
30033900	含激素（胰岛素除外）或税目29.37其他产品，但不含抗菌素的混合药品（两种或两种以上成分混合而成的，治病或防病用未配定剂量或非零售包装）	6					0	0
30034010	含奎宁或其盐，但不含抗菌素及税目2937的产品的混合药品（两种或两种以上成分混合而成的，治病或防病用未配定剂量或非零售包装）	5					0	0
30034090	含生物碱及其衍生物（奎宁或其盐除外），但不含抗菌素及税目2937的激素或其他产品的混合药品（两种或两种以上成分混合而成的，治病或防病用未配定剂量或非零售包装）	5					0	0
30039010	含磺胺类的混合药品（两种或两种以上成分混合而成的，治病或防病用未配定剂量或非零售包装）	6					0	0
30039020	含有青蒿素及其衍生物药品	5					0	0
30039090	含其他成份混合药品（两种或两种以上成分混合而成的，治病或防病用未配定剂量或非零售包装）	5					0	0
30041011	氨苄青霉素制剂（混合，治病或防病用，已配定剂量或制成零售包装）	6					0	0
30041012	羟氨苄青霉素制剂（两种或两种以上成分混合而成的，治病或防病用，已配定剂量或制成零售包装）	6					0	0
30041013	青霉素V制剂（两种或两种以上成分混合而成的，治病或防病用，已配定剂量或制成零售包装）	6					0	0
30041019	其他青霉素制剂（混合或非混合，治病或防病用，已配定剂量或制成零售包装）	6					0	0
30041090	含有其他青霉素及具有青霉烷酸结构的青霉素衍生物或链霉素及其衍生物的药品（混合或非混合，治病或防病用，已配定剂量或制成零售包装）	6					0	0
30042011	头孢噻肟制剂（混合或非混合，治病或防病用已配定剂量或制成零售包装）	6					0	0
30042012	头孢他啶制剂（混合或非混合，治病或防病用，已配定剂量或制成零售包装）	6					0	0
30042013	头孢西丁制剂（混合或非混合，治病或防病用，已配定剂量或制成零售包装）	6					0	0
30042014	头孢替唑制剂（混合或非混合，治病或防病用，已配定剂量或制成零售包装）	6					0	0
30042015	头孢克罗制剂（混合或非混合，治病或防病用，已配定剂量或制成零售包装）	6					0	0
30042016	头孢呋辛制剂（混合或非混合，治病或防病用，已配定剂量或制成零售包装）	6					0	0
30042017	头孢三嗪（头孢曲松）制剂（混合或非混合，治病或防病用，已配定剂量或制成零售包装）	6					0	0
30042018	头孢哌酮制剂（混合或非混合，治病或防病用，已配定剂量或制成零售包装）	6					0	0
30042019	含有其他头孢菌素制剂（混合或非混合，治病或防病用，已配定剂量或制成零售包装）	6					0	0
30042090	含有其他抗菌素的药品（混合或非混合，治病或防病用，已配定剂量或制成零售包装）	6					0	0
30043110	含有重组人胰岛素但不含抗菌素的药品（混合或非混合，治病或防病用已配定剂量或零售包装）	5					0	0
30043190	含有其他胰岛素但不含抗菌素的药品（混合或非混合，治病或防病用已配定剂量或零售包装）	5					0	0
30043200	含肾上腺皮混合或非混合质激素但不含抗菌素的药品（，治病或防病用已配定剂量或零售包装）	5					0	0
30043900	含有税目29.37其他产品但不含抗菌素的药品（混合或非混合，治病或防病用已配定剂量或零售包装）	5					0	0
30044010	含有奎宁或其盐，但不含抗菌素及税目29.37的产品的药品（混合或非混合，治病或防病用已配定剂量或零售包装）	5					0	0
30044090	含有其他生物碱及其衍生物，但不含抗菌素及税目29.37的产品的药品（混合或非混合，治病或防病用已配定剂量或零售包装）	5					0	0
30045000	含有维生素或税目29.36其他产品的其他药品（混合或非混合，治病或防病用已配定剂量或零售包装）	6					0	0
30049010	含有磺胺类的药品（两种或两种以上成分混合而成的，治病或防病用已配定剂量或零售包装）	6					0	0
30049020	含联苯双酯的药品（混合或非混合，治病或防病用已配定剂量或零售包装）	4					0	0
30049051	中药酒（混合或非混合，治病或防病用已配定剂量或零售包装）	3					0	0

税则号列	商品名称（简称）	最惠税率	亚太2国	东盟			最不发达35国	最不发达4国
				缅	老	柬		
30049052	片仔癀（混合或非混合，治病或防病用已配定剂量或零售包装）	3					0	0
30049053	白药（混合或非混合，治病或防病用已配定剂量或零售包装）	3					0	0
30049054	清凉油（混合或非混合，治病或防病用已配定剂量或零售包装）	3					0	0
30049055	安宫牛黄丸	3					0	0
30049059	其他中式成药（混合或非混合，治病或防病用已配定剂量或零售包装）	3					0	0
30049060	含有青蒿素及其衍生物的中成药	4					0	0
30049090	其他药品（混合或非混合，治病或防病用已配定剂量或零售包装）	4					0	
30051010	橡皮膏（经药物浸涂或制定零售包装供医疗、外科、牙科或兽医用）	5					0	0
30051090	其他胶粘敷料及有胶粘涂层的物品（经药物浸涂或制定零售包装供医疗、外科、牙科或兽医用）	5					0	0
30059010	药棉、纱布、绷带（经药物浸涂或制定零售包装供医疗、外科、牙科或兽医用）	5					0	0
30059090	其他医用软填料及类似物品（经药物浸涂或制定零售包装供医疗、外科、牙科或兽医用）	5					0	0
30061000	无菌外科肠线；无菌昆布、无菌粘合胶布、无菌吸收性止血材料、外科或牙科用无菌抗粘连阻隔材料及类似无菌材料	5					0	0
30062000	血型试剂	3					0	0
30063000	X光检查造影剂；诊断试剂	4					0	0
30064000	牙科粘固剂及其他牙科填料（包括骨骼粘固剂）	5					0	0
30065000	急救药箱、药包	5					0	0
30066010	以激素等为基本成分的化学避孕药	0					0	0
30066090	其他化学避孕药物	0					0	0
30067000	专用于人类或作兽药用的凝胶制品，作为外科手术或体检时躯体部位的润滑剂，或者作为躯体和医疗器械之间的偶合剂	6.5					0	0
30069100	可确定用于造口术用具	10					0	0
30069200	废药物	5					0	0
31010011	未经化学处理的鸟粪	3					0	0
31010019	未经化学处理的其他动植物肥料	6.5					0	0
31010090	动植物产品经混合或化学处理的制成的肥料	4					0	0
31022100	硫酸铵	4					0	
31022900	硫酸铵和硝酸铵的复盐及混合物	4					0	
31023000	硝酸铵（不论是否水溶液）	4					0	
31024000	硝酸铵与碳酸钙或其他无肥效无机物的混合物	4					0	
31025000	硝酸钠	4					0	
31026000	硝酸钙和硝酸铵的复盐及混合物	4					0	
31028000	尿素及硝酸铵混合物的水溶液或氨水溶液	4					0	
31029010	氰氨化钙	4					0	
31029090	其他矿物氮肥及化学氮肥，包括上述子目未列名的混合物	4					0	
31031010	重过磷酸钙	4					0	
31031090	其他过磷酸钙	4					0	
31039000	其他矿物磷肥或化学磷肥	4					0	
31042020	纯氯化钾	3					0	
31042090	其他氯化钾	3					0	
31043000	硫酸钾	3					0	
31049010	光卤石、钾盐及其他天然粗钾盐	3					0	
31049090	其他矿物钾肥及化学钾肥	3					0	
31051000	制成片状及类似形状或每包毛重不超过10公斤的31章各货品	4					0	
31054000	磷酸二氢铵及磷酸二氢铵与磷酸氢二铵的混合物	4					0	
31055100	含有硝酸盐及磷酸盐的肥料	4					0	
31055900	其他含氮、磷两种肥效元素的矿物肥料或化学肥料	4					0	
31056000	含磷、钾两种元素的肥料	4					0	
31059000	其他肥料	4					0	
32011000	坚木浸膏	5					0	
32012000	荆树皮浸膏	6.5					0	
32019010	其他植物鞣料浸膏	6.5					0	
32019090	鞣酸及其盐、醚、酯和其他衍生物	6.5					0	
32021000	有机合成鞣料	6.5					0	
32029000	无机鞣料；鞣料制剂等，不论是否含有天然鞣料；预鞣用酶制剂	6.5					0	
32030011	天然靛蓝及以其为基本成分的制品，包括染料浸膏（不论是否已有化学定义）	6.5					0	0

税则号列	商品名称（简称）	最惠税率	亚太2国	东盟			最不发达35国	最不发达4国
				缅	老	柬		
32030019	其他植物质着色料及以其为基本成分的制品包括染料浸膏(不论是否已有化学定义)；32章注释三所述的以植物质着色料为基本成分的制品	6.5					0	0
32030020	动物质着色料及以其为基本成分的制品包括染料浸膏(不论是否已有化学定义，但动物炭黑除外)； 32章注释三所述的以动物质着色料为基本成分的制品	6.5					0	0
32041100	分散染料及以其为基本成分的制品(不论是否已有化学定义)	6.5					0	0
32041200	酸性染料(不论是否预金属络合)及以其为基本成分的制品(不论是否已有化学定义)；媒染染料及以其为基本成分的制品(不论是否已有化学定义)	6.5					0	0
32041300	碱性染料及以其为基本成分的制品(不论是否已有化学定义)	6.5					0	0
32041400	直接染料及以其为基本成分的制品(不论是否已有化学定义)	6.5					0	0
32041510	合成靛蓝(还原靛蓝)(不论是否已有化学定义)	6.5					0	0
32041590	其他瓮染料（包括颜料用的）及以其为基本成分的制品(不论是否已有化学定义)	6.5					0	0
32041600	活性染料及以其为基本成分的制品(不论是否已有化学定义)	6.5					0	0
32041700	颜料及以其为基本成分的制品(不论是否已有化学定义)	6.5					0	0
32041911	硫化黑(硫化青)及以其为基本成分的制品(不论是否已有化学定义)	6.5					0	0
32041919	其他硫化染料及以其为基本成分的制品(不论是否已有化学定义)	6.5					0	0
32041990	由子目号3204.11至3204.19中两个或多个子目所列着色料组成的混合物，(不论是否已有化学定义)	6.5					0	0
32042000	用作萤光增白剂的有机合成产品(不论是否已有化学定义)	6.5					0	0
32049010	生物染色剂及染料指示剂(不论是否已有化学定义)	6.5					0	0
32049090	其他用作发光体的有机合成产品(不论是否已有化学定义)	6.5					0	0
32050000	色淀及32章注释三所述的以色淀为基本成分的制品	6.5					0	0
32061110	钛白粉	6.5					0	0
32061190	干量计二氧化钛≥80%的颜料及制品，钛白粉除外	6.5					0	0
32061900	二氧化钛为基料的颜料及制品，干量计二氧化钛＜80%	10					0	0
32062000	铬化合物为基本成分的颜料及制品	6.5					0	0
32064100	群青及以其为基本成分的制品	6.5					0	0
32064210	锌钡白	6.5					0	0
32064290	其他以硫化锌为基本成份的颜料和制品	6.5					0	0
32064911	以钒酸铋为基本成分的颜料及制品	6.5					0	0
32064919	其他以铋化合物为基本成分的颜料及制品	6.5					0	0
32064990	其他着色料及其他制品	6.5					0	0
32065000	用作发光体的无机产品，不论是否已有化学定义	6.5					0	0
32071000	调制颜料、遮光剂、着色剂及类似制品(用于陶瓷、搪瓷及玻璃工业)	5					0	0
32072000	珐琅和釉料、釉底料及类似制品(用于陶瓷、搪瓷及玻璃工业)	5					0	0
32073000	光瓷釉及类似制品(用于陶瓷、搪瓷及玻璃工业)	5					0	0
32074000	呈粉、粒状搪瓷玻璃料及其他玻璃	5					0	0
32081000	分散或溶于非水介质的聚酯油漆及清漆等	10					0	0
32082010	分散或溶于非水介质的丙烯酸聚合物油漆及清漆	10					0	
32082020	分散或溶于非水介质的乙烯聚合物油漆及清漆	10					0	
32089010	分散或溶于非水介质的聚胺酯类油漆及清漆	10					0	
32089090	分散或溶于非水介质其他油漆、清漆溶液	10					0	
32091000	分散或溶于水介质的丙烯酸聚合物或乙烯聚合物油漆及清漆	10					0	0
32099010	以环氧树脂为基本成分的溶于水介质其他聚合物油漆及清漆	10					0	
32099020	以氟树脂为基本成分的溶于水介质其他聚合物油漆及清漆	10					0	
32099090	溶于水介质其他聚合物油漆及清漆	10					0	
32100000	其他油漆及清漆(包括瓷漆\大漆及水浆涂料)；皮革用水性颜料	10					0	0
32110000	配制的催干剂	10					0	
32121000	压印箔	15					0	
32129000	制漆用颜料（分散于非水介质中呈液状或浆状的）及零售形状或零售包装的染料、色料	10					0	
32131000	成套的颜料(艺术家、学生和广告美工用的)	10					0	
32139000	非成套颜料、调色料及类似品（艺术家、学生和广告美工用的，片状、管装、罐装、瓶装、扁盒装等类似形状或包装的）	10					0	0
32141010	半导体器件封装材料	9					0	0
32141090	其他安装玻璃用油灰、接缝用油灰、树脂胶泥、嵌缝胶及其他类似胶粘剂；漆工用填料	9					0	0
32149000	非耐火涂面制剂，涂门面、内墙、地板、天花板等用	9					0	0
32151100	黑色印刷油墨(不论是否固体或浓缩)	6.5					0	0

税则号列	商品名称（简称）	最惠税率	亚太2国	东盟			最不发达35国	最不发达4国
				缅	老	柬		
32151900	其他印刷油墨(不论是否固体或浓缩)，黑色印刷油墨除外	6.5					0	0
32159010	书写墨水(不论是否固体或浓缩)	6.5					0	0
32159020	水性喷墨墨水	10					0	0
32159090	绘图墨水及其他墨类(不论是否固体或浓缩)	10					0	0
33011200	橙油（包括浸膏及净油）	20					0	
33011300	柠檬油（包括浸膏及净油）	20					0	0
33011910	白柠檬油(酸橙油)（包括浸膏及净油）	20					0	
33011990	其他柑桔属果实的精油（包括浸膏及净油）	20					0	
33012400	胡椒薄荷油（包括浸膏及净油）	20					0	
33012500	其他薄荷油（包括浸膏及净油）	15					0	0
33012910	樟脑油（包括浸膏及净油）	20					0	
33012920	香茅油（包括浸膏及净油）	15					0	0
33012930	茴香油（包括浸膏及净油）	20					0	
33012940	桂油（包括浸膏及净油）	20					0	
33012950	山苍子油（包括浸膏及净油）	20					0	
33012960	桉叶油（包括浸膏及净油）	20					0	
33012991	老鹳草油(香叶油)（包括浸膏及净油）	20					0	
33012999	其他非柑桔属果实的精油（包括浸膏及净油）	15					0	0
33013010	鸢尾凝脂	20					0	
33013090	其他香膏	20					0	
33019010	提取的油树脂	20					0	
33019020	柑桔属果实的精油脱萜所得的萜烯副产品	20					0	
33019090	用花香吸取法或浸渍法制定的含浓缩精油的脂肪、固定油、蜡及类似品；精油脱萜所得的萜烯副产品（柑桔属果实的除外）；精油水溶液及水馏液	20					0	0
33021010	生产饮料用的混合香料以及以香料为基本成分的制品，按容量计酒精浓度≤0.5%	15					0	
33021090	其他食品或饮料工业用混合香料以及以香料为基本成分的制品	15					0	0
33029000	其他工业用混合香料及以香料为基本成分的混合物和制品	10					0	0
33030000	香水及花露水	10					0	0
33041000	唇用化妆品	10					0	
33042000	眼用化妆品	10					0	
33043000	指(趾)甲化妆品	15					0	
33049100	香粉，不论是否压紧	10					0	
33049900	其他美容品或化妆品及护肤品	6.5					0	
33051000	洗发剂(香波)	6.5					0	0
33052000	烫发剂	15					0	
33053000	定型剂	15					0	
33059000	其他护发品	10					0	0
33061010	牙膏	10					0	0
33061090	其他洁齿品	10					0	
33062000	牙线	10					0	
33069000	其他口腔及牙齿清洁剂	10					0	
33071000	剃须用制剂	10					0	
33072000	人体除臭剂及止汗剂	10					0	
33073000	香浴盐及其他沐浴用制剂	10					0	
33074100	神香及其他通过燃烧散发香气制品	10					0	0
33074900	室内除臭制品	10					0	0
33079000	脱毛剂、其他编号未列名的芳香料制品及化妆盥洗品	9					0	0
34011100	盥洗用肥皂及有机表面活性产品，条状、块状或模制形状的，以及用肥皂或洗涤剂浸渍、涂面或包覆的纸、絮胎、毡呢及无纺织物	10	0				0	0
34011910	洗衣皂	10					0	0
34011990	其他用肥皂及有机表面活性产品，条状、块状或模制形状的，以及用肥皂或洗涤剂浸渍、涂面或包覆的纸、絮胎、毡呢及无纺织物	15					0	
34012000	其他形状的肥皂	15	0				0	0
34013000	洁肤用的有机表面活性产品及制品，液状或膏状并制成零售包装的，不论是否含有肥皂	10					0	0
34021100	阴离子型有机表面活性剂	6.5					0	0
34021200	阳离子型有机表面活性剂	6.5					0	0
34021300	非离子型有机表面活性剂	6.5					0	0

税则号列	商品名称（简称）	最惠税率	亚太2国	东盟			最不发达35国	最不发达4国
				缅	老	柬		
34021900	其他有机表面活性剂	6.5					0	0
34022010	零售包装的合成洗涤粉	10					0	
34022090	零售包装有机表面活性剂制品（合成洗涤粉除外）	10					0	
34029000	非零售包装有机表面活性剂制品、洗涤剂及清洁剂	9					0	0
34031100	用于纺织材料、皮革、毛皮或其他材料油脂处理的制剂（含有石油或从沥青矿物提取的油类且按重量计＜70%）	10					0	
34031900	润滑剂（含有石油或从沥青矿物提取的油类且按重量计＜70%）	10					0	0
34039100	用于纺织、皮革、毛皮或其他材料油脂处理的制剂（不含有石油或从沥青矿物提取的油类）	10					0	
34039900	润滑剂（不含有石油或从沥青矿物提取的油类）	10					0	
34042000	聚乙二醇蜡	10					0	
34049000	其他人造蜡及调制蜡	10					0	0
34051000	鞋靴或皮革用的上光剂及类似制品	10					0	
34052000	保养木制品的上光剂及类似制品	10					0	
34053000	车身用的上光剂及类似制品	10					0	
34054000	擦洗膏、去污粉及类似制品	10					0	
34059000	玻璃或金属用的光洁剂	10					0	
34060000	各种蜡烛及类似品	10					0	
34070010	牙科用蜡及造型膏	6.5					0	0
34070020	以熟石膏为成分的牙科用其他制品	6.5					0	0
34070090	塑型用膏	10					0	
35011000	酪蛋白	10					0	
35019000	酪蛋白衍生物；酪蛋白胶	10					0	
35021100	干的卵清蛋白	10					0	
35021900	其他卵清蛋白	10					0	
35022000	乳白蛋白，包括两种或两种以上的乳清蛋白浓缩物	10					0	
35029000	其他白蛋白及白蛋白盐及其衍生物	10					0	
35030010	明胶及其衍生物	12					0	
35030090	鱼胶；其他动物胶	12					0	
35040010	蛋白胨	3					0	0
35040090	其他税号未列名蛋白质及其衍生物，皮粉	8					0	0
35051000	糊精及其他改性淀粉	12					0	
35052000	以淀粉、糊精或其他改性淀粉为基本成分的胶	20					0	
35061000	适于作胶或粘合剂的产品，零售包装每件净重≤1kg	10					0	0
35069110	以聚酰胺为基本成份的粘合剂	10					0	0
35069120	以环氧树脂为基本成分的粘合剂	10					0	0
35069190	以其他橡胶或塑料为基本成分的粘合剂	10					0	0
35069900	其他调制胶、粘合剂	10					0	0
35071000	粗制凝乳酶及其浓缩物	6					0	0
35079010	碱性蛋白酶	6					0	0
35079020	碱性脂肪酶	6					0	0
35079090	其他酶及未列名的酶制品	6					0	0
36010000	发射药	9					0	
36020010	硝铵炸药，但发射药除外	9					0	
36020090	其他配制炸药，但发射药除外	9					0	
36030000	安全导火索、导爆索；火帽或雷管；引爆器；电雷管	9					0	0
36041000	烟花、爆竹	6					0	
36049000	信号弹、降雨火箭、浓雾信号弹及其他烟火制品	6					0	
36050000	火柴，但税目 3604 的烟火制品除外	6					0	0
36061000	灌注打火机等用的液体或液化气体燃料，其包装容器的容积≤300cm3	10					0	
36069011	已切成形可直接使用的铈铁及其他引火合金	9					0	0
36069019	未切成形不可直接使用的铈铁及其他引火合金	9					0	0
36069090	其他易燃材料制品	9					0	0
37011000	未曝光的 X 光感光硬片及平面软片，用纸、纸板及纺织物以外任何材料制成	20					0	
37012000	未曝光的一次成像感光平片，用纸、纸板及纺织物以外任何材料制成	5					0	0
37013021	激光照排片（任何一边超过 255mm），用纸、纸板及纺织物以外任何材料制成	10					0	
37013022	PS 版（预涂感光版）（任何一边超过 255mm），用纸、纸板及纺织物以外任何材料制成	10					0	
37013024	CTP 版	10					0	

税则号列	商品名称（简称）	最惠税率	亚太2国	东盟			最不发达35国	最不发达4国
				缅	老	柬		
37013025	柔性印刷版	10					0	
37013029	其他未曝光照相制版用感光硬片及软片(任何一边超过255mm)，用纸、纸板及纺织物以外任何材料制成	10					0	
37013090	未曝光其他用途的感光硬片及软片(任何一边超过255mm)，用纸、纸板及纺织物以外任何材料制成	20					0	
37019100	彩色摄影用未曝光彩色硬片及平面软片，用纸、纸板及纺织物以外任何材料制成，任何一边≤ 255mm	22					0	
37019920	照相制版用其他未曝光软片及硬片，用纸、纸板及纺织物以外任何材料制成，任何一边≤ 255mm	10					0	
37019990	其他用未曝光软片及硬片，用纸、纸板及纺织物以外任何材料制成，任何一边≤ 255mm	25					0	
37021000	成卷的未曝光的X光感光胶片，用纸、纸板及纺织物以外任何材料制成	10					0	
37023110	彩色摄影用未曝光一次成像感光卷片，宽度≤105 mm，用纸、纸板及纺织物以外任何材料制成	5					0	0
37023190	彩色摄影用未曝光无齿孔彩色胶卷，宽度≤105 mm，用纸、纸板及纺织物以外任何材料制成	40					0	
37023210	照相制版用未曝光涂卤化银液无齿孔一次成像感光卷片，宽度≤105 mm，用纸、纸板及纺织物以外任何材料制成	5					0	0
37023220	照相制版用未曝光涂卤化银液无齿孔胶卷，宽度≤105 mm，用纸、纸板及纺织物以外任何材料制成	10					0	
37023290	其他未曝光涂乳液无齿孔胶卷，宽度≤105 mm，用纸、纸板及纺织物以外任何材料制成	22					0	
37023920	照相制版用未曝光未涂卤化银无齿孔感光胶卷，宽度≤105 mm，用纸、纸板及纺织物以外任何材料制成	10					0	
37023990	其他未曝光未涂卤化银无齿孔感光胶卷，宽度≤105 m，用纸、纸板及纺织物以外任何材料制成	22					0	
37024100	彩色摄影用未曝光无齿孔彩色胶卷，宽度＞610 mm，长度＞200m，用纸、纸板及纺织物以外任何材料制成	16					0	
37024221	印刷电路板制造用未曝光光致抗蚀干膜，宽度＞610 mm，长度＞200m，用纸、纸板及纺织物以外任何材料制成	10					0	
37024229	照相制版用其他未曝光无齿孔胶卷，宽度＞610 mm，长度＞200m，用纸、纸板及纺织物以外任何材料制成	10					0	
37024292	红色或红外激光胶片	16					0	
37024299	其他未曝光无齿孔宽长胶卷	16					0	
37024321	照相制版用未曝光无齿孔激光照排片，宽度＞610 mm，长度≤200m，用纸、纸板及纺织物以外任何材料制成	10					0	
37024329	其他照相制版用未曝光无齿孔胶卷，宽度＞610 mm，长度≤200m，用纸、纸板及纺织物以外任何材料制成	10					0	
37024390	其他用未曝光无齿孔胶卷，宽度610 mm，长度≤200m，用纸、纸板及纺织物以外任何材料制成	20					0	
37024421	照相制版用无齿孔未曝光激光照排片，105mm＜宽度≤610mm，用纸、纸板及纺织物以外任何材料制成	10					0	
37024422	印刷电路板制造用未曝光光致抗蚀干膜，105mm＜宽度≤610mm，用纸、纸板及纺织物以外任何材料制成	10					0	
37024429	其他照相制版用无齿孔未曝光胶卷，105mm＜宽度≤610mm，用纸、纸板及纺织物以外任何材料制成	10					0	
37024490	其他用无齿孔未曝光胶卷，105mm＜宽度≤610mm，用纸、纸板及纺织物以外任何材料制成	20					0	
37025200	彩色摄影用未曝光彩色胶卷，宽度≤16 mm	47					0	
37025300	幻灯片用未曝光彩色摄影胶卷，16 mm＜宽度≤35 mm，长度＜30m，用纸、纸板及纺织物以外任何材料制成	47					0	
37025410	非幻灯片用未曝光彩色胶卷，宽度35mm，长度≤2 m，用纸、纸板及纺织物以外任何材料制成	18					0	
37025490	非幻灯片用彩色摄影用未曝光彩色胶卷，16 mm＜宽度＜35 mm，2 m＜长度≤30m，用纸、纸板及纺织物以外任何材料制成	18					0	
37025520	未曝光的彩色电影胶片，16mm＜ 宽度≤35mm，长度＞30m，用纸、纸板及纺织物以外任何材料制成	26					0	
37025620	未曝光的彩色电影胶片，宽度＞35mm，用纸、纸板及纺织物以外任何材料制成	24					0	
37025690	未曝光的彩色摄影用胶卷，宽度＞35mm，用纸、纸板及纺织物以外任何材料制成，电影胶片除外	40					0	
37029600	未曝光非彩色胶卷，宽度≤35mm，长度≤30m，用纸、纸板及纺织物以外任何材料制成	20					0	

税则号列	商品名称（简称）	最惠税率	亚太2国	东盟			最不发达35国	最不发达4国
				缅	老	柬		
37029700	未曝光的非彩色胶卷， 宽度≤35mm，长度>30m，用纸、纸板及纺织物以外任何材料制成	18					0	
37029800	未曝光的非彩色胶卷，宽度>35mm，用纸、纸板及纺织物以外任何材料制成	18					0	
37031010	成卷未曝光的感光纸及纸板，宽度>610mm	18					0	
37031090	成卷未曝光的感光布，宽度>610mm	18					0	
37032090	未曝光的彩色摄影用感光布，非成卷或宽度≤610mm	18					0	
37039090	未曝光的非彩色摄影用感光布，非成卷或宽度≤610mm	18					0	
37040010	已曝光未冲洗的电影胶片	6.5					0	
37040090	已曝光未冲洗的摄影硬片、软片、纸、纸板及纺织物，电影胶片除外	18					0	
37051000	已曝光已冲洗供复制胶版用摄影硬片及软片	18					0	
37059010	已曝光已冲洗的教学专用幻灯片	0					0	0
37059021	书籍、报刊用的已曝光已冲洗的缩微胶片	0					0	0
37059029	已曝光已冲洗的缩微胶片，书籍、报刊用除外	4					0	
37059090	已曝光已冲洗的其他摄影硬片及软片	18					0	
37061010	已曝光已冲洗的教学专用电影胶片，宽度≥35mm，不论是否配有声道或仅有声道	0					0	0
37061090	已曝光已冲洗的电影胶片，宽度≥35mm，不论是否配有声道或仅有声道，教学专用除外	5					0	0
37069010	已曝光已冲洗的教学专用电影胶片，宽度<35mm，不论是否配有声道或仅有声道	0					0	0
37069090	已曝光已冲洗的电影胶片，宽度<35mm，不论是否配有声道或仅有声道，教学专用除外	4					0	0
37071000	摄影用感光乳液	8					0	0
37079010	冲洗胶卷及相片用化学制剂或摄影用未混合品（定量包装或零售包装可立即使用的）	16					0	
37079020	复印机用化学制剂或摄影用未混合品（定量包装或零售包装可立即使用的）	10					0	0
37079090	其他摄影用化学制剂或摄影用未混合品（定量包装或零售包装可立即使用的）	8					0	0
38011000	人造石墨	6.5					0	0
38012000	胶态或半胶态石墨	6.5					0	0
38013000	电极用碳糊及炉衬用的类似糊	6.5					0	0
38019010	表面处理的球化石墨	6.5					0	0
38019090	其他石墨	6.5					0	0
38021010	木质活性碳	6.5					0	
38021090	其他活性碳	6.5					0	
38029000	活性天然矿产品；动物炭黑（包括废动物炭黑）	10					0	
38030000	妥尔油，不论是否精炼	6.5					0	0
38040000	木浆残余碱液，不论是否浓缩、脱糖或经化学处理，包括木素磺酸盐，但不包括税目38.03的妥尔油	6.5					0	
38051000	脂松节油、木松节油和硫酸松节油	6.5					0	0
38059010	以α萜品醇为基本成分的松油，用蒸馏或其他方法从针叶木制得	6.5					0	0
38059090	粗制二聚戊烯；亚硫酸盐松节油及其他粗制对异丙基苯甲烷；其他萜烯油，用蒸馏或其他方法从针叶木制得	6.5					0	0
38061010	松香	10					0	
38061020	树脂酸	10					0	
38062010	松香盐及树脂酸盐	6.5					0	
38062090	松香或树脂酸衍生物的盐，但松香加合物的盐除外	6.5					0	
38063000	酯胶	6.5					0	
38069000	其他松香和树脂酸的衍生物；松香精及松香油；再熔胶	6.5					0	
38070000	木焦油；精制木焦油；木杂酚油；粗木精；植物沥青；以松香、树脂酸或植物沥青为基本成分的啤酒桶沥青及类似制品	6.5					0	
38085010	零售包装的本章注释一规定货物	9					0	0
38085090	非零售包装的本章注释一规定货物	5					0	0
38089111	蚊香	10					0	0
38089112	生物杀虫剂	10					0	0
38089119	零售包装杀虫剂	10					0	0
38089190	非零售包装杀虫剂	6					0	0
38089210	零售包装的杀菌剂	9					0	0
38089290	非零售包装的杀菌剂	6					0	0
38089311	零售包装的除草剂	9					0	0

税则号列	商品名称（简称）	最惠税率	亚太2国	东盟			最不发达35国	最不发达4国
				缅	老	柬		
38089319	非零售包装的除草剂	5					0	0
38089391	零售包装抗萌剂及植物生长调节剂	9					0	0
38089399	非零售抗萌剂及植物生长调节剂	6					0	0
38089400	消毒剂	9					0	0
38089910	零售包装的杀鼠剂及其他类似产品	9					0	0
38089990	非零售包装的杀鼠剂及其他类似产品	9					0	0
38091000	以淀粉物质为基本成分，纺织、造纸、制革及类似工业用的其他税号未列名的整理剂、染料加速着色或固色助剂及其他产品和制剂	10					0	0
38099100	纺织工业及类似工业用其他税号未列名整理剂、染料加速着色剂或固色助剂及其他产品和制剂	6.5					0	0
38099200	造纸工业用其他税号未列名整理剂、染料加速着色剂或固色助剂及其他产品和制剂	6.5					0	0
38099300	制革工业用其他税号未列名整理剂、染料加速着色剂或固色助剂及其他产品和制剂	6.5					0	0
38101000	金属表面酸洗剂；金属及其他材料制成的焊粉或焊膏	6.5					0	0
38109000	焊接用的焊剂及其他辅助剂；作焊条芯子或焊条涂料用的制品	6.5					0	0
38111100	以铅化合物为基本成分的抗震剂，用于矿物油或与矿物油同样用途的其他液体	6.5					0	
38111900	抗震剂（以铅化合物为基本成分的除外），用于矿物油或与矿物油同样用途的其他液体	6.5					0	
38112100	含有石油或从沥青矿物提取的油类的润滑油添加剂	6.5					0	
38112900	不含石油或从沥青矿物提取的油类的润滑油添加剂	6.5					0	
38119000	抗氧剂、防胶剂、粘度改良剂、防腐剂配制添加剂，用于矿物油或与矿物油同样用途的其他液体	6.5					0	
38121000	配制的橡胶促进剂	6					0	0
38122000	橡胶或塑料用复合增塑剂	6.5					0	0
38123010	橡胶的防老剂	6					0	0
38123090	其他橡胶、塑料用抗氧剂及其他稳定剂	6.5					0	0
38130010	灭火器的装配药	6.5					0	0
38130020	已装药的灭火弹	10					0	0
38140000	其他税号未列名的有机复合溶剂及稀释剂；除漆剂	10					0	0
38151100	以镍及其化合物为活性物的载体催化剂	6.5					0	0
38151200	以贵金属及其化合物为活性物的载体催化剂	6.5					0	0
38151900	其他载体催化剂	6.5					0	0
38159000	其他未列名的反应引发剂、促进剂	6.5					0	0
38160000	耐火水泥、灰泥、混凝土及类似耐火材料，但税目 38.01 的产品除外	6.5					0	
38170000	混合烷基苯及混合烷基萘，但税目 27.07 及 29.02 的产品除外	6.5					0	0
38180011	7.5 cm≤直径≤15.24 cm的单晶硅切片	0					0	0
38180019	经掺杂用于电子工业的，已切成圆片、薄片或类似形状，直径>15.24cm的单晶硅片	0					0	0
38180090	经掺杂用于电子工业的化学元素，，已切成圆片、薄片或类似形状，单晶硅片除外；经掺杂用于电子工业的化合物	0					0	0
38190000	闸用液压油及其他液压传动用液体，不含石油或从沥青矿物提取的油类，或者按重量计石油或从沥青矿物提取的油类含量低于 70%	6.5					0	
38200000	防冻剂及解冻剂	10					0	0
38210000	制成的微生物培养基	3					0	
38220010	附于衬背上的诊断或实验用试剂，但税目 32.02，32.06 的货品除外	4					0	0
38220090	无论是否附于衬背上的诊断或实验用配制试剂，但税目 32.02，32.06 的货品除外	5					0	0
38231100	硬脂酸	16					0	
38231200	油酸	16					0	
38231300	妥尔油脂肪酸	16					0	
38231900	其他工业用单羧脂肪酸；精炼所得的酸性油	16					0	
38237000	工业用脂肪醇	13					0	
38241000	铸模及铸芯用粘合剂	6.5					0	0
38243000	自身混合或与金属粘合剂混合的未烧结金属碳化物	6.5					0	0
38244010	高效减水剂	6.5					0	0
38244090	其他水泥、灰泥及混凝土用添加剂	6.5					0	0
38245000	非耐火的灰泥及混凝土	6.5					0	0
38246000	子目号 2905.44 以外的山梨醇	14					0	

税则号列	商品名称（简称）	最惠税率	亚太2国	东盟			最不发达35国	最不发达4国
				缅	老	柬		
38247100	含全氯氟烃的，不论是否含氢氯氟烃、全氟烃或氢氟烃的含有甲烷、乙烷、丙烷卤化衍生物混合物	6.5					0	0
38247200	含溴氯二氟甲烷、溴三氟甲烷或二溴四氟乙烷的含有甲烷、乙烷、丙烷卤化衍生物混合物	6.5					0	0
38247300	含氢溴氟烃的含有甲烷、乙烷、丙烷卤化衍生物混合物	6.5					0	0
38247400	含氢氯氟烃的，不论是否含全氟烃或氢氟烃，但不含全氯氟烃的含有甲烷、乙烷、丙烷卤化衍生物混合物	6.5					0	0
38247500	含四氯化碳的含有甲烷、乙烷、丙烷卤化衍生物混合物	6.5					0	0
38247600	含1，1，1－三氯乙烷（甲基氯仿）的含有甲烷、乙烷、丙烷卤化衍生物混合物	6.5					0	0
38247700	含溴化甲烷（甲基溴）或溴氯甲烷的含有甲烷、乙烷、丙烷卤化衍生物混合物	6.5					0	0
38247800	含全氟烃或氢氟烃的，但不含全氯氟烃或氢氯氟烃的含有甲烷、乙烷、丙烷卤化衍生物混合物	6.5					0	0
38247900	其他含有甲烷、乙烷、丙烷卤化衍生物的混合物	6.5					0	0
38248100	含环氧乙烷的混合物及制品	6.5					0	0
38248200	含多氯联苯、多氯三联苯或多溴联苯的混合物及制品	6.5					0	0
38248300	含三（2，3－二溴丙基）磷酸酯的混合物及制品	6.5					0	0
38249010	杂醇油	6.5					0	0
38249020	除墨剂、蜡纸改正液及类似品	9					0	0
38249030	增炭剂	6.5					0	0
38249091	含滑石50%以上的混合物	6.5					0	0
38249092	按重量计含氧化镁70%以上的混合物	6.5					0	0
38249093	表层包覆钴化合物的氢氧化镍（掺杂炭）	6.5					0	0
38249099	其他税目未列名的化学工业及其相关工业的化学产品及配制品	6.5					0	0
38251000	城市垃圾	6.5					0	
38252000	下水道淤泥	6.5					0	
38253000	医疗废物	6.5					0	
38254100	含卤化物的废有机溶剂	6.5					0	
38254900	其他废有机溶剂	6.5					0	
38255000	废的金属酸洗液、液压油、制动油及防冻液	6.5					0	
38256100	主要含有机成分的化工及相关工业废物	6.5					0	
38256900	其他税目未列名的化工及相关工业废物	6.5					0	
38259000	其他税目未列名的化学工业及相关工业的副产品	6.5					0	
38260000	生物柴油及其混合物，不含或含有按重量计低于70%的石油或从沥青矿物提取的油类	6.5					0	0
39013000	初级形状乙烯-乙酸乙烯酯共聚物	6.5					0	
39019010	初级形状的乙烯丙烯共聚物(乙丙橡胶，乙烯单体单元的含量大于丙烯单体单元)	6.5					0	
39019020	线型低密度聚乙烯	6.5					0	0
39019090	其他初级形状的乙烯聚合物	6.5					0	
39022000	初级形状的聚异丁烯	6.5					0	0
39023010	初级形状的乙烯丙烯共聚物(乙丙橡胶丙烯单体单元的含量大于乙烯单体单元))	6.5					0	0
39023090	初级形状的其他丙烯共聚物	6.5					0	0
39029000	其他初级形状的烯烃聚合物	6.5					0	0
39031100	初级形状的可发性聚苯乙烯	6.5					0	0
39031910	初级形状的改性非可发性聚苯乙烯	6.5					0	0
39031990	初级形状的其他聚苯乙烯	6.5					0	0
39032000	初级形状苯乙烯-丙烯腈共聚物	12					0	
39033010	初级形状的改性丙烯腈-丁二烯-苯乙烯共聚物	6.5					0	0
39033090	其它丙烯腈-丁二烯-苯乙烯共聚物	6.5					0	0
39039000	初级形状的其他苯乙烯聚合物	6.5					0	0
39041010	聚氯乙烯糊树脂	6.5					0	0
39041090	其他初级形状的纯聚氯乙烯	6.5					0	0
39042100	初级形状未塑化的聚氯乙烯	6.5					0	0
39042200	初级形状已塑化的聚氯乙烯	6.5					0	0
39043000	氯乙烯-乙酸乙烯酯共聚物	9					0	0
39044000	初级形状的其他氯乙烯共聚物	12					0	
39045000	初级形状的偏二氯乙烯聚合物	6.5					0	0

税则号列	商品名称（简称）	最惠税率	亚太2国	东盟			最不发达35国	最不发达4国
				缅	老	柬		
39046100	初级形状的聚四氟乙烯	10					0	0
39046900	初级形状的其他氟聚合物	6.5					0	0
39049000	初级形状的其他卤化烯烃聚合物	10					0	0
39051200	聚乙酸乙烯酯的水分散体	10					0	
39051900	其他初级形状聚乙酸乙烯酯	10					0	
39052100	乙酸乙烯酯共聚物的水分散体	10					0	
39052900	其他初级形状的乙酸乙烯酯共聚物	10					0	
39053000	初级形状的聚乙烯醇（不论是否含有未水解的乙酸酯基）	14					0	
39059100	其他乙烯酯或乙烯基的共聚物	10					0	
39059900	其他乙烯酯或乙烯基的聚合物	10					0	
39061000	初级形状的聚甲基丙烯酸甲酯	6.5					0	0
39069010	聚丙稀酰胺	6.5					0	0
39069090	其他初级形状的丙烯酸聚合物	6.5					0	0
39071010	初级形状的聚甲醛	6.5					0	0
39071090	其他初级形状的聚缩醛	6.5					0	0
39072010	聚四亚甲基醚二醇	6.5					0	0
39072090	其他初级形状的聚醚	6.5					0	0
39073000	初级形状的环氧树脂	6.5					0	0
39074000	初级形状的聚碳酸酯	6.5					0	0
39075000	初级形状的醇酸树脂	10					0	0
39076011	高粘度聚对苯二甲酸乙二酯切片	6.5					0	0
39076019	其他聚对苯二甲酸乙二酯切片	6.5					0	0
39076090	其他初级形状聚对苯二甲酸乙二酯	6.5					0	0
39077000	聚乳酸	6.5					0	0
39079100	初级形状的不饱和聚酯	6.5					0	0
39079910	聚对苯二甲酸丁二酯	6.5					0	0
39079991	聚对苯二甲酸-己二醇-丁二醇酯	6.5					0	0
39079999	其他聚酯	6.5					0	0
39081011	聚酰胺-6,6 切片	6.5					0	0
39081012	聚酰胺-6 切片	6.5					0	0
39081019	初级形状聚酰胺切片	6.5					0	0
39081090	其他初级形状的聚酰胺	6.5					0	0
39089000	初级形状的其他聚酰胺	10					0	0
39091000	初级形状的尿素树脂及硫尿树脂	6.5					0	0
39092000	初级形状的蜜胺树脂	6.5					0	0
39093010	聚合 MDI	6.5					0	0
39093090	其他初级形状的其他氨基树脂	6.5					0	0
39094000	初级形状的酚醛树脂	6.5					0	0
39095000	初级形状的聚亚氨酯	6.5					0	0
39100000	初级形状的聚硅氧烷	6.5					0	0
39111000	初级形状的石油树脂、苯并呋喃-茚树脂、多萜树脂	6.5					0	0
39119000	其他初级形状的多硫化物、聚砜及 39 章注释 3 所规定的其他税号未列名新产品	6.5					0	0
39121100	初级形状的未塑化醋酸纤维素	6.5					0	
39121200	初级形状的已塑化醋酸纤维素	6.5					0	
39122000	初级形状的硝酸纤维素	6.5					0	
39123100	初级形状的羧甲基纤维素及其盐	6.5					0	
39123900	初级形状的其他纤维素醚	6.5					0	
39129000	初级形状的其他未列名的纤维素(包括化学衍生物)	6.5					0	
39131000	初级形状的藻酸及盐和酯	10					0	0
39139000	初级形状的其他未列名天然聚合物（包括改性天然聚合物）	6.5					0	0
39140000	初级形状的离子交换剂	6.5					0	0
39151000	乙烯聚合物的废碎料及下脚料	6.5					0	0
39152000	苯乙烯聚合物的废碎料及下脚料	6.5					0	0
39153000	氯乙烯聚合物的废碎料及下脚料	6.5					0	0
39159010	聚对苯二甲酸乙二酯的塑料废碎料及下脚料	6.5					0	0
39159090	其他塑料的废碎料及下脚料	6.5					0	0
39161000	乙烯聚合物制单丝、条、杆及型材	10					0	
39162010	聚氯乙烯异型材	10					0	

税则号列	商品名称（简称）	最惠税率	亚太2国	东盟			最不发达35国	最不发达4国
				缅	老	柬		
39162090	氯乙烯聚合物制单丝、条、杆及型材	10					0	
39169010	聚酰胺制的单丝、条、杆及型材	10					0	
39169090	其他塑料制单丝、条、杆及型材	10					0	
39171000	硬化蛋白或纤维素材料制人造肠衣	10					0	
39172100	乙烯聚合物制的硬管	10					0	0
39172200	丙烯聚合物制的硬管	10					0	0
39172300	氯乙烯聚合物制的硬管	10					0	0
39172900	其他塑料制的硬管	10					0	0
39173100	塑料制的软管	10					0	0
39173200	其他未装有附件的塑料制管子	6.5					0	0
39173300	其他装有附件的塑料管子	6.5					0	0
39173900	塑料制的其他管子	6.5					0	0
39174000	塑料制的管子附件	10					0	0
39181010	氯乙烯聚合物制糊墙品	10					0	
39181090	氯乙烯聚合物制的铺地制品	10					0	
39189010	其他塑料制的糊墙品	10					0	
39189090	其他塑料制的铺地制品	10					0	
39191010	丙烯酸树脂为基本成份的成卷胶粘板片条等，宽度≤20cm	6.5					0	0
39191091	宽度≤20cm成卷的胶囊型反光膜	6.5					0	0
39191099	其他材料制的,宽度≤20cm的其他成卷塑料胶粘板片等	6.5					0	0
39199010	其他胶囊型反光膜	6.5					0	0
39199090	其他自粘塑料板、片、膜等材料	6.5					0	0
39201010	乙烯聚合物制电池隔膜	6.5					0	0
39201090	其他乙烯聚合物制板、片、带	6.5					0	0
39202010	丙烯聚合物制电池隔膜	6.5					0	0
39202090	其他丙烯聚合物制板、片、带	6.5					0	0
39203000	非泡沫聚苯乙烯板、片、膜、箔及扁条	6.5					0	0
39204300	按重量计增塑剂含量不小于6%的聚氯乙烯板、片、膜、箔及扁条	6.5					0	0
39204900	按重量计增塑剂含量小于6%的聚氯乙烯板、片、膜、箔及扁条	6.5					0	0
39205100	聚甲基丙烯酸甲酯板片膜箔及扁条	6.5					0	0
39205900	其他丙烯酸聚合物板片膜箔及扁条	6.5					0	0
39206100	聚碳酸酯制板、片、膜、箔及扁条	6.5					0	0
39206200	聚对苯二甲酸乙二酯板片膜箔扁条	6.5					0	0
39206300	不饱和聚酯板、片、膜、箔及扁条	10					0	0
39206900	其他聚酯板、片、膜、箔及扁条	10					0	0
39207100	再生纤维素制板、片、膜、箔及扁条	6.5					0	0
39207300	醋酸纤维素制板、片、膜、箔及扁条	6.5					0	0
39207900	纤维素衍生物制板、片、膜箔及扁条	10					0	0
39209100	聚乙烯醇缩丁醛板、片、膜、箔及扁条	6.5					0	0
39209200	聚酰胺板、片、膜、箔及扁条	10					0	0
39209300	氨基树脂板、片、膜、箔及扁条	6.5					0	0
39209400	酚醛树脂板、片、膜、箔及扁条	10					0	0
39209910	聚四氟乙烯制的非泡沫塑料板片	6.5					0	0
39209990	其他塑料制的非泡沫塑料板片	6.5					0	0
39211100	泡沫聚苯乙烯板、片、带、箔及扁条	10					0	0
39211210	泡沫聚氯乙烯人造革及合成革	9					0	0
39211290	泡沫聚氯乙烯板、片、带、箔及扁条	6.5					0	0
39211310	泡沫聚氨酯制人造革及合成革	9					0	0
39211390	泡沫聚氨酯板、片、带、箔及扁条	6.5					0	0
39211400	泡沫再生纤维素板、片、膜、箔及扁条	10					0	0
39211910	其他泡沫塑料制人造革及合成革	9					0	0
39211990	其他泡沫塑料板、片、膜、箔及扁条	6.5					0	0
39219020	嵌有玻璃纤维的聚乙烯板、片	6.5					0	0
39219030	聚异丁烯为基本成分的附有人造毛毡的板、片、卷材	6.5					0	0
39219090	未列名塑料板、片、膜、箔及扁条	6.5					0	0
39221000	塑料浴缸、淋浴盘及盥洗盆	10			0		0	0
39222000	塑料马桶坐圈及盖	10			0		0	0
39229000	塑料便盆、抽水箱等类似卫生洁具	10					0	0

税则号列	商品名称（简称）	最惠税率	亚太2国	东盟			最不发达35国	最不发达4国
				缅	老	柬		
39231000	塑料制盒、箱及类似品	10					0	0
39232100	乙烯聚合物制袋及包	10					0	
39232900	其他塑料制的袋及包	10					0	0
39233000	塑料制坛、瓶及类似品	6.5					0	0
39234000	塑料制卷轴、纡子、筒管及类似品	10					0	
39235000	塑料制塞子、盖子及类似品	10					0	0
39239000	供运输或包装货物用其他塑料制品	10					0	
39241000	塑料制餐具及厨房用具	10	0				0	0
39249000	塑料制其他家庭用具及卫生或盥洗用具	10					0	0
39251000	塑料制囤、柜、罐、桶及类似容器	10					0	0
39252000	塑料制门、窗及其框架、门槛	10					0	
39253000	塑料制窗板、百叶窗及类似制品	10					0	
39259000	其他未列名的建筑用塑料制品	10					0	
39261000	办公室或学校用塑料制品	10					0	0
39262011	聚氯乙稀制手套（包括分指手套、连指手套及露指手套）	10					0	
39262019	其他手套（包括分指手套、连指手套及露指手套）	10					0	
39262090	其他塑料制衣服及衣着附件	10					0	0
39263000	塑料制家具、车厢及类似品的附件	10					0	0
39264000	塑料制小雕塑品及其他装饰品	10					0	0
39269010	塑料制机器及仪器用零件	10					0	0
39269090	其他塑料制品	10					0	0
40013000	巴拉塔胶、古塔波胶、银胶菊胶、糖胶树胶及类似的天然树胶	20					0	
40021110	羧基丁苯橡胶胶乳	7.5					0	0
40021190	丁苯橡胶胶乳	7.5					0	0
40021911	初级形状未经任何加工的丁苯橡胶	7.5					0	0
40021912	初级形状的充油丁苯橡胶	7.5					0	0
40021913	初级形状的热塑丁苯橡胶	7.5					0	0
40021914	初级形状的充油热塑丁苯橡胶	7.5					0	0
40021919	初级形状的其他丁苯橡胶及羧基丁苯橡胶	7.5					0	0
40021990	丁苯橡胶及羧基丁苯橡胶板、片、带	7.5					0	0
40022010	初级形状的丁二烯橡胶	7.5					0	0
40022090	丁二烯橡胶板、片、带	7.5					0	0
40023110	初级形状的异丁烯-异戊二烯橡胶	6					0	0
40023190	异丁烯-异戊二烯橡胶板、片、带	7.5					0	0
40023910	初级形状的其他卤代丁基橡胶	7.5					0	0
40023990	卤代丁基橡胶板、片、带	7.5					0	0
40024100	氯丁二烯橡胶胶乳	7.5					0	0
40024910	初级形状的氯丁二烯橡胶	7.5					0	0
40024990	氯丁二烯橡胶板、片、带	7.5					0	0
40025100	丁腈橡胶胶乳	7.5					0	0
40025910	初级形状的丁腈橡胶	7.5					0	0
40025990	丁腈橡胶板、片、带	7.5					0	0
40026010	初级形状的异戊二烯橡胶	3					0	0
40026090	异戊二烯橡胶板、片、带	5					0	0
40027010	初级形状的乙丙非共轭二烯橡胶	7.5					0	0
40027090	乙丙非共轭二烯橡胶板、片、带	7.5					0	0
40028000	天然橡胶与合成橡胶的混合物	7.5					0	0
40029100	其他未列名的合成橡胶胶乳	7.5					0	0
40029911	其他初级形状的合成橡胶	7.5					0	0
40029919	其他合成橡胶板、片、带	7.5					0	0
40029990	从油类提取的油膏	4					0	0
40030000	初级形状或板、片、带状再生橡胶	8					0	0
40040000	橡胶(硬质橡胶除外)废碎料及下脚料及其粉、粒	8					0	
40051000	与碳黑等混合的未硫化复合橡胶	8					0	0
40052000	未硫化的复合橡胶溶液及分散体	8					0	0
40059100	其他未硫化的复合橡胶板、片、带	8					0	0
40059900	其他未硫化的初级形状复合橡胶	8					0	0
40061000	未硫化轮胎翻新用胎面补料胎条	8					0	0

税则号列	商品名称（简称）	最惠税率	亚太2国	东盟			最不发达35国	最不发达4国
				缅	老	柬		
40069010	未硫化橡胶的杆、管或型材及异型材	8					0	0
40069020	未硫化橡胶制品	14					0	
40070000	硫化橡胶线及绳	14					0	
40081100	海绵硫化橡胶制的板、片及带	8					0	0
40081900	海绵硫化橡胶制型材、异型材及杆	8					0	0
40082100	非海绵硫化橡胶制板、片及带	8					0	0
40082900	非海绵硫化橡胶型材、异型材及杆	8					0	0
40091100	未加强或未与其他材料合制硫化橡胶管，未装有附件	10.5					0	
40091200	未加强或未与其他材料合制硫化橡胶管，装有附件	10					0	
40092100	用金属加强或只与金属合制的硫化橡胶管，未装有附件	10.5					0	
40092200	用金属加强或只与金属合制的硫化橡胶管，装有附件	10					0	
40093100	用纺织材料加强或只与纺织材料合制硫化橡胶管，未装有附件	10.5					0	
40093200	用纺织材料加强或只与纺织材料合制硫化橡胶管，装有附件	10					0	
40094100	用其他材料加强或与其他材料合制硫化橡胶管，未装有附件	10.5					0	
40094200	用其他材料加强或与其他材料合制硫化橡胶管，装有附件	10					0	
40101100	金属加强的硫化橡胶输送带及带料	10					0	
40101200	纺织材料加强的硫化橡胶输送带及带料	10					0	
40101900	其他硫化橡胶制的输送带及带料	10					0	
40103100	梯形截面的环形传动带（三角带），V 形肋状的，外周长超过 60 厘米，但不超过 180 厘米	8					0	0
40103200	梯形截面的环形传动带（三角带），V 形肋状的除外，外周长超过 60 厘米，但不超过 180 厘米	8					0	0
40103300	180CM＜外周长≤240CM 的三角带：V 形肋状的	8					0	0
40103400	180CM＜外周长≤240CM 的三角带：V 形肋状的除外	8					0	0
40103500	60CM＜外周长≤150CM 的环形同步带	10					0	
40103600	150CM＜外周长≤198CM 的环形同步带	10					0	
40103900	其他硫化橡胶制的传动带及带料	8					0	0
40111000	机动小客车用新的充气橡胶轮胎	10					0	0
40112000	客或货运车用新的充气橡胶轮胎	10					0	
40113000	航空器用新的充气橡胶轮胎	1					0	0
40114000	摩托车用新的充气橡胶轮胎	15					0	
40115000	自行车用新的充气橡胶轮胎	20					0	
40116100	农业或林业车辆及机器用人字形胎面或类似胎面的新充气橡胶轮胎	17.5					0	
40116200	辋圈尺寸不超过 61CM 的建筑或工业搬运车辆及机器用人字形胎面或类似胎面的新充气橡胶轮胎	17.5					0	
40116300	辋圈>61CM 建筑或工业搬运车辆及机器用人字形胎面或类似胎面的新充气橡胶轮胎	17.5					0	
40116900	其他人字形胎面或类似胎面的新充气橡胶轮胎	17.5					0	
40119200	农业或林业车辆及机器用非人字形胎面或类似胎面的新充气橡胶轮胎	25					0	0
40121100	机动小客车（包括旅行小客车及赛车）用翻新轮胎	20					0	
40121200	机动大客车或货运机动车用翻新轮胎	20					0	
40121300	航空器用翻新轮胎	20					0	
40121900	其他翻新轮胎	20					0	
40129010	航空器用实心或半实心橡胶轮胎	3					0	
40129020	汽车用实心或半实心橡胶轮胎	22					0	
40129090	其他用实心或半实心橡胶轮胎	22					0	
40131000	汽车用橡胶内胎	15					0	
40132000	自行车用橡胶内胎	15					0	
40139010	航空器用橡胶内胎	3					0	0
40139090	其他用橡胶内胎	15					0	
40141000	硫化橡胶制避孕套	0					0	0
40149000	硫化橡胶制其他卫生及医疗用品	17.5					0	
40151100	硫化橡胶制外科用手套	8					0	0
40151900	硫化橡胶制其他手套	18					0	0
40159010	医疗用硫化橡胶衣着用品及附件	8					0	0
40159090	其他硫化橡胶制衣着用品及附件	15					0	
40161010	硫化海绵橡胶制机器及仪器用零件	8					0	0
40161090	硫化海绵橡胶制其他制品	15					0	
40169100	硫化橡胶制铺地制品及门垫	18					0	

税则号列	商品名称（简称）	最惠税率	亚太2国	东盟			最不发达35国	最不发达4国
				缅	老	柬		
40169200	硫化橡胶制橡皮擦	18					0	
40169310	硫化橡胶制机器、仪器用垫片、垫圈及其他密封垫	8					0	0
40169390	硫化橡胶制其他用垫片、垫圈、及其他密封垫	15					0	0
40169400	硫化橡胶制船舶或码头的碰垫	18					0	
40169500	硫化橡胶制其他可充气制品	18					0	
40169910	硫化橡胶制机器及仪器用其他零件	8					0	0
40169990	其他未列名硫化橡胶制品	10					0	0
40170010	各种形状的硬质橡胶(包括废碎料)	8					0	
40170020	硬质橡胶制品	15					0	
41012011	规定重量范围内的未剖层整张生牛皮，经逆鞣处理的	8					0	0
41012019	规定重量范围内的未剖层整张生牛皮，经逆鞣处理的除外	5			0	0	0	0
41012020	规定重量范围内的未剖层整张生马皮	5			0	0	0	0
41015011	经逆鞣处理的重量＞16公斤的整张生牛皮	8.4					0	0
41015019	重量＞16公斤的整张生牛皮，经逆鞣处理的除外	5			0	0	0	0
41015020	重量＞16公斤的整张生马皮	5			0	0	0	0
41019011	其他（包括整张或半张的背皮及腹皮）经逆鞣处理的生牛皮	8.4					0	0
41019019	其他（包括整张或半张的背皮及腹皮）生牛皮，经逆鞣处理的除外	5			0	0	0	0
41019020	其他（包括整张或半张的背皮及腹皮）生马皮	5			0	0	0	0
41021000	带毛的绵羊或羔羊生皮	7					0	0
41022110	浸酸的不带毛绵羊或羔羊生皮，经逆鞣处理的	14					0	
41022190	浸酸的不带毛绵羊或羔羊生皮，经逆鞣处理的除外	9					0	0
41022910	其他不带毛的绵羊或羔羊生皮，经逆鞣处理的	14					0	
41022990	其他不带毛的绵羊或羔羊生皮，经逆鞣处理的除外	7					0	0
41032000	爬行动物的生皮	9					0	0
41033000	生猪皮	9		0			0	0
41039011	经逆鞣处理的山羊板皮	14					0	
41039019	山羊板皮，经逆鞣处理的除外	9					0	0
41039021	经逆鞣处理的其他山羊或小山羊皮	14					0	
41039029	其他山羊或小山羊皮，经逆鞣处理的除外	9					0	0
41039090	其他生皮	9		0			0	0
41041111	全粒面未剖层或粒面剖层蓝湿牛皮	7	1.4				0	0
41041119	其他全粒面未剖层或粒面剖层湿牛皮革	8	2				0	0
41041120	全粒面未剖层或粒面剖层马皮革	5	2				0	0
41041911	其他蓝湿牛皮	6	1.4				0	0
41041919	其他湿牛皮革	7	1.8				0	0
41041920	其他湿马皮革	7	2.1				0	0
41044100	全粒面未剖层或粒面剖层干革（坯革）	5	2				0	0
41044910	其他机器带用干革（坯革）	5	0				0	0
41044990	其他干革（坯革）	7	2.1				0	0
41051010	蓝湿绵羊或羔羊皮	14	2.1				0	0
41051090	其他他绵羊或羔羊湿皮革	10	2				0	0
41053000	绵羊或羔羊干革（坯革）	8	4.8				0	0
41062100	山羊或小山羊皮湿革	14	2.1				0	0
41062200	山羊或小山羊皮干革（坯革）	14	8.4				0	0
41063110	蓝湿猪皮	14	4.2				0	
41063190	其他猪皮湿革	14	4.2				0	
41063200	猪皮干革（坯革）	14	4.2				0	
41064000	爬行动物皮革	14	0				0	0
41069100	其他未列名动物皮湿革（包括蓝湿皮革）	14	0				0	0
41069200	其他未列名动物皮干革（坯革）	14	0				0	0
41071120	已鞣全粒面未剖层整张马皮革	5					0	0
41071220	已鞣粒面剖层整张马皮革	5					0	0
41071910	已鞣机器带用整张牛马皮革	5					0	0
41079100	已鞣全粒面未剖层非整张牛马皮革	5					0	0
41079200	已鞣粒面剖层非整张牛马皮革	5					0	0
41079910	已鞣机器带用非整张牛马皮革	5					0	0
41079990	其他已鞣非整张牛马皮革	7					0	0
41120000	已鞣进一步加工的不带毛绵羊或羔羊皮革	8					0	0

税则号列	商品名称（简称）	最惠税率	亚太2国	东盟			最不发达35国	最不发达4国
				缅	老	柬		
41131000	已鞣进一步加工的不带毛山羊或小山羊皮革	14					0	0
41132000	已鞣进一步加工的不带毛猪皮革	14					0	
41133000	已鞣进一步加工的不带毛爬行动物皮革	14					0	0
41139000	其他已鞣进一步加工的不带毛动物皮革	14					0	0
41141000	油鞣皮革	14					0	
41152000	皮革或再生皮革边角料；皮革粉末	14	4.2				0	
42010000	各种材料制成的鞍具及挽具，适合各种动物用	20	8				0	0
42021110	以皮革、再生皮革作面的衣箱	15	8.3				0	
42021190	以皮革、再生皮革作面的箱包	10	8				0	0
42021210	以塑料或纺织材料作面的衣箱	20					0	
42021290	塑料或纺织材料作面的其他箱包	20					0	0
42021900	其他材料制箱包	20	8				0	0
42022100	以皮革、再生皮革作面的手提包	10					0	0
42022200	以塑料片或纺织材料作面的手提包	10					0	0
42022900	以钢纸或纸板作面的手提包	20	8				0	
42023100	以皮革、再生皮革作面的钱包等物品	10					0	0
42023200	以塑料或纺织品作面的钱包等物品	20					0	0
42023900	以钢纸或纸板作面的钱包等物品	20	8				0	
42029100	皮革、再生皮革作面的其他容器	10					0	0
42029200	以塑料或纺织材料作面的其他容器	10					0	0
42029900	以钢纸或纸板作面的其他容器	20					0	
42031000	皮革或再生皮革制的衣服	10	8				0	0
42032100	皮革或再生皮革制专供运动用手套	20					0	
42032910	皮革或再生皮革制的劳保手套	20	8				0	
42032990	皮革或再生皮革制的其他手套	20	8				0	
42033010	皮革或再生皮革制腰带	10	8				0	0
42033020	皮革或再生皮革制的腰带及子弹带	10	8				0	0
42034000	皮革或再生皮革制的其他衣着附件	20	8				0	
42050010	皮革或再生皮革制坐具套	12	7.8				0	0
42050020	机器、机械器具或其他专门技术用途的皮革或再生皮革制品	8					0	0
42050090	皮革或再生皮革的其他制品	12	7.8				0	0
42060000	肠线、肠膜、膀胱或筋腱制品	20					0	
43011000	整张生水貂皮	15					0	
43013000	阿斯特拉罕等羔羊的整张生毛皮，不论是否带头、尾或爪	20					0	
43016000	整张生狐皮	20					0	
43018010	整张生兔皮	20					0	
43018090	整张的其他生毛皮	20					0	
43019010	黄鼠狼尾	20					0	
43019090	适合加工皮货用的其他未鞣头、尾、爪	20					0	
43021100	已鞣未缝制的整张水貂皮	12					0	
43021910	已鞣未缝制的贵重毛皮（貂皮、狐皮、水獭及旱獭等）	10					0	
43021920	已鞣未缝制的整张兔皮	10					0	0
43021930	已鞣未缝制阿斯特拉罕等羔羊皮，不论是否带头、尾或爪	20					0	0
43021990	已鞣未缝制的其他毛皮	10					0	0
43022000	已鞣未缝制的头、尾、爪及其他块片	20					0	
43023010	已鞣已缝制的贵重毛皮及其块、片	20					0	
43023090	已鞣已缝制的其他整张毛皮及块片	20					0	
43031010	毛皮衣服	23	10.4				0	
43031020	毛皮衣着附件	18	9.9				0	
43039000	毛皮制其他物品	18	9.9				0	
43040010	人造毛皮	18	10.8				0	
43040020	人造毛皮制品	18	10.8				0	
44011000	薪柴	0					0	0
44012100	针叶木木片或木粒	0					0	0
44012200	非针叶木木片或木粒	0					0	0
44013100	木屑棒	0					0	0
44013900	其他锯末、木废料及碎片，不论是否粘结成原木段、块、片或类似形状	0					0	0
44021000	竹炭	10.5					0	

税则号列	商品名称（简称）	最惠税率	亚太2国	东盟			最不发达35国	最不发达4国
				缅	老	柬		
44029000	木炭	10.5					0	
44031000	用油漆、着色剂、防腐剂等处理的原木	0					0	0
44032010	红松和樟子松	0					0	0
44032020	白松（云杉和冷杉）	0					0	0
44032030	辐射松	0					0	0
44032040	落叶松	0					0	0
44032050	花旗松	0					0	0
44032090	其他针叶木	0					0	0
44034100	深红色红柳桉木、浅红色红柳桉木及巴栲红柳桉木原木	0					0	0
44034910	柚木原木	0					0	0
44034920	奥克曼（奥克榄）原木	0					0	0
44034930	龙脑香木原木	0					0	0
44034940	山樟（香木）原木	0					0	0
44034950	印加木（波罗格）原木	0					0	0
44034960	大干巴豆（门格里斯或康派斯）原木	0					0	0
44034970	异翅香木原木	0					0	0
44034990	其他方法处理的其他热带原木	0					0	0
44039100	栎木原木	0					0	0
44039200	山毛榉木原木	0					0	0
44039910	楠木原木	0					0	0
44039920	樟木原木	0					0	0
44039930	红木原木	0					0	0
44039940	泡桐木原木	0					0	0
44039950	水曲柳原木	0					0	0
44039960	北美硬阔叶木原木（包括樱桃木、黑胡桃木、枫木）	0					0	0
44039980	其他未列名的温带非针叶原木	0					0	0
44039990	其他未列名非针叶原木	0					0	0
44041000	针叶木的箍木、木劈条、木桩、木棒及类似品，木片条	8					0	
44042000	非针叶木箍木、木劈条、木桩、木棒及类似品，木片条	8					0	
44050000	木丝及木粉	8					0	0
44061000	未浸渍的铁道及电车道枕木	0					0	0
44069000	已浸渍的铁道及电车道枕木	0					0	0
44071010	红松和樟子松厚板材	0					0	0
44071020	白松（云杉和冷杉）厚板材	0					0	0
44071030	辐射松厚板材	0					0	0
44071040	花旗松厚板材	0					0	0
44071090	其他针叶木厚板材	0					0	0
44072100	桃花心木板材，经纵锯、纵切、刨切，不论是否刨平、砂光或指榫结合，厚度超过6mm	0					0	0
44072200	维罗蔻、细孔绿心樟、轻木板材，经纵锯、纵切、刨切，不论是否刨平、砂光或指榫结合，厚度超过6mm	0					0	0
44072500	深红色红柳桉木、浅红色红柳桉木及巴栲红柳桉木板材，经纵锯、纵切、刨切，不论是否刨平、砂光或指榫结合，厚度超过6mm	0					0	0
44072600	白柳桉木、白色红柳桉木、白色柳桉木、黄色红柳桉木及阿兰木，经纵锯、纵切、刨切，不论是否刨平、砂光或指榫结合，厚度超过6mm	0					0	0
44072700	卡雅楝木板材，经纵锯、纵切、刨切，不论是否刨平、砂光或指榫结合，厚度超过6mm	0					0	0
44072800	绿柄桑木板材，经纵锯、纵切、刨切，不论是否刨平、砂光或指榫结合，厚度超过6mm	0					0	0
44072910	柚木板材，经纵锯、纵切、刨切，不论是否刨平、砂光或指榫结合，厚度超过6mm	0					0	0
44072920	非洲桃花心木板材	0					0	0
44072930	波罗格板材	0					0	0
44072990	其他列名的热带木板材，经纵锯、纵切、刨切，不论是否刨平、砂光或指榫结合，厚度超过6mm	0					0	0
44079100	栎木板材，经纵锯、纵切、刨切，不论是否刨平、砂光或指榫结合，厚度超过6mm	0					0	0
44079200	山毛榉木板材，经纵锯、纵切、刨切，不论是否刨平、砂光或指榫结合，厚度超过6mm	0					0	0
44079300	枫木厚板材	0					0	0

税则号列	商品名称（简称）	最惠税率	亚太2国	东盟 缅	东盟 老	东盟 柬	最不发达35国	最不发达4国
44079400	樱桃木厚板材	0					0	0
44079500	白蜡木厚板材	0					0	0
44079910	樟木、楠木、红木板材，经纵锯、纵切、刨切，不论是否刨平、砂光或指榫结合，厚度超过 6mm	0					0	0
44079920	泡桐木板材，经纵锯、纵切、刨切，不论是否刨平、砂光或指榫结合，厚度超过 6mm	0					0	0
44079930	北美硬阔叶木（含樱桃木、枫木、黑胡桃木）厚板材	0					0	0
44079980	其他温带非针叶木厚板材	0					0	0
44079990	其他木板材，经纵锯、纵切、刨切，不论是否刨平、砂光或指榫结合，厚度超过 6mm	0					0	0
44081019	饰面用针叶木薄板，不论是否刨平、砂光或指榫结合，用胶合板等多层板制的除外	4					0	
44081020	制胶合板用针叶木薄板，不论是否刨平、砂光或指榫结合	4					0	
44081090	其他针叶木薄板材，不论是否刨平、砂光或指榫结合	4					0	
44083119	深红色红柳桉木、浅红色红柳桉木及巴栲红柳桉木制的饰面用薄板，不论是否刨平、砂光或指榫结合，用胶合板等多层板制的除外	4					0	
44083120	深红色红柳桉木、浅红色红柳桉木及巴栲红柳桉木制的胶合板用薄板，不论是否刨平、砂光或指榫结合	4					0	
44083190	深红色红柳桉木、浅红色红柳桉木及巴栲红柳桉木制的其他薄板，不论是否刨平、砂光或指榫结合	4					0	
44083919	其他列名的热带木制的饰面用薄板，不论是否刨平、砂光或指榫结合，用胶合板等多层板制的除外	4					0	
44083920	其他列名热带木制的胶合板用薄板，不论是否刨平、砂光或指榫结合	4					0	
44083990	其他列名的热带木制的其他薄板材，不论是否刨平、砂光或指榫结合	4					0	
44089012	温带非针叶木制饰面用单板	3					0	
44089019	其他木制饰面用薄板，不论是否刨平、砂光或指榫结合，用胶合板等多层板制的除外	3					0	
44089021	其他温带非针叶木制胶合板用单板	3					0	
44089029	其他木制胶合板用单板	3					0	
44089091	其他温带非针叶木制木材	3					0	
44089099	其他木材	3					0	
44091010	针叶木地板条（块）	7.5					0	0
44091090	一边或面制成连续形状的针叶木材，不论是否刨平、砂光或指榫结合	7.5					0	0
44092110	竹制地板条	4					0	0
44092190	一边或面制成连续形状的竹材，不论是否刨平、砂光或指榫结合	4					0	0
44092910	其他非针叶木地板条	4					0	0
44092990	一边或面制成连续形状的其他非针叶木材，不论是否刨平、砂光或指榫结合	4					0	
44121099	其他竹面多层板	4					0	0
44123900	其他仅由薄木板制胶合板	4					0	0
44129499	其他木块芯胶合板，侧板条芯胶合板及板条芯胶合板	4					0	0
44129999	其他木面多层板	4					0	
44130000	强化木	6					0	0
44151000	木箱及类似的包装容器；电缆卷筒	7.5					0	0
44182000	木门及其框架和门槛	4					0	0
44184000	水泥构件的木模板	4					0	0
44185000	木瓦及盖屋板	7.5					0	0
44186000	柱和梁	4					0	0
44187100	已拼装的马赛克地板	4					0	0
44187210	竹制已拼装的多层地板	4					0	
44187290	其他已拼装的多层地板	4					0	
44187910	竹制已拼装的地板	4					0	
44187990	其他已拼装的地板	4					0	
44189010	竹制建筑用制品	4					0	0
44189090	其他建筑用木工制品	4					0	0
44190031	木制一次性筷子	0					0	0
44190032	竹制一次性筷子	0					0	0
44190091	竹制其他餐具及厨房用具	0					0	0
44190099	其他木制餐具及厨房用具	0					0	0
44201011	木刻	0					0	0
44201012	竹刻	0					0	0

税则号列	商品名称（简称）	最惠税率	亚太2国	东盟			最不发达35国	最不发达4国
				缅	老	柬		
44201020	木扇	0					0	0
44201090	其他木制小雕像及其他装饰品	0					0	0
44209010	镶嵌木	0					0	0
44209090	木盒子及类似品;非落地式木家具	0					0	0
44211000	木衣架	0					0	0
44219010	木卷轴、纡子、筒管、线轴及类似品	0					0	0
44219021	木制园签、园棒、冰果棒、压舌片及类似一次性制品	0					0	0
44219022	竹制园签、园棒、冰果棒、压舌片及类似一次性制品	0					0	0
44219090	其他未列名的木制品	0					0	0
45011000	未加工或简单加工的天然软木	6					0	
45019010	软木废料	0					0	0
45019020	软木废料及碎、粒、粉状的软木	0					0	0
45020000	除去表皮或粗切成方形或成块、板、片或条状的天然软木	8					0	0
45031000	天然软木塞子	8					0	0
45039000	其他天然软木制品	10.5					0	0
45041000	块、板、片及条状压制软木；任何形状的砖、瓦；实心圆柱体，包括原片	8.4					0	0
45049000	其他压制软木及其制品	0					0	0
46012100	竹制的席子、席料、帘子	9			0		0	0
46012200	藤制的席子、席料及帘子	9			0		0	0
46012911	蔺草制的席子、席料及帘子	9			0		0	0
46012919	其他草制的席子、席料及帘子	9			0		0	0
46012921	苇帘	9			0		0	0
46012929	芦苇制的席子、席料	9			0		0	0
46012990	其他植物材料制席子、席料及帘子	9			0		0	0
46019210	竹缏条及类似产品，不论是否缝合成宽条	9			0		0	0
46019290	其他竹编结产品	9					0	0
46019310	藤缏条及类似产品，不论是否缝合成宽条	9			0		0	0
46019411	稻草制的鞭条（绳）	10					0	
46019419	稻草制的其他编结材料产品	10					0	
46019491	其他植物编结材料的缏条及类似产品，不论是否缝合成宽条	9			0		0	0
46019499	其他植物编结材料产品	9					0	0
46019910	其他非植物编结材料的缏条及类似产品，不论是否缝合成宽条	9			0		0	0
46019990	其他非植物编结材料产品	9					0	
46021100	竹编制的篮筐及其他制品	9				0	0	0
46021200	藤编制的篮筐及其他制品	9				0	0	0
46021910	草编制的篮筐及其他制品	9				0	0	0
46021920	玉米皮编制的篮筐及其他制品	9				0	0	0
46021930	柳条编制的篮筐及其他制品	9				0	0	0
46021990	其他植物材料编制篮筐及其他制品	9				0	0	0
46029000	其他编结材料制品及其他制品	9				0	0	0
47010000	机械木浆	0					0	0
47020000	化学木浆，溶解级	0					0	0
47031100	未漂白针叶木碱木浆或硫酸盐木浆	0					0	0
47031900	未漂白非针叶木碱木浆或硫酸盐木浆	0					0	0
47032100	漂白针叶木碱木浆或硫酸盐木浆	0					0	0
47032900	漂白非针叶木碱木浆或硫酸盐木浆	0					0	0
47041100	未漂白的针叶木亚硫酸盐木浆	0					0	0
47041900	未漂白的非针叶木亚硫酸盐木浆	0					0	0
47042100	漂白的针叶木亚硫酸盐木浆	0					0	0
47042900	漂白的非针叶木亚硫酸盐木浆	0					0	0
47050000	半化学木浆	0					0	0
47061000	棉短绒纸浆	0					0	0
47062000	从回收纸或纸板提取的纤维浆	0					0	0
47063000	竹浆	0					0	0
47069100	其他纤维状纤维素机械浆	0					0	0
47069200	其他纤维状纤维素化学浆	0					0	0
47069300	用机械和化学联合法制得的浆	0					0	0
47071000	未漂白牛皮、瓦楞纸或纸板废碎品	0					0	0

税则号列	商品名称（简称）	最惠税率	亚太2国	东盟			最不发达35国	最不发达4国
				缅	老	柬		
47072000	漂白化学木浆制的未经本体染色纸和纸板废碎品	0					0	0
47073000	机械木浆制的纸或纸板的废碎品	0					0	0
47079000	其他回收纸或纸板	0					0	0
48185000	纸制衣服及衣着附件	7.5					0	0
48193000	底宽≥40cm的纸袋	7.5					0	0
48204000	多联商业表格纸、页间夹有复写纸的本	7.5					0	0
48236100	竹浆纸、纸板制的盘、碟、盆、杯及类似品	7.5					0	0
48236910	非木植物浆制	7.5					0	0
48236990	其他纸或纸板制的盘、碟、盆、杯及类似品	7.5					0	0
48239020	神纸及类似用品	7.5					0	0
48239030	纸扇	7.5					0	0
49011000	单张的书籍、小册子及类似印刷品	0					0	0
49019100	字典、百科全书	0					0	0
49019900	其他书籍、小册子及类似的印刷品	0					0	0
49021000	每周至少出版四次的报纸、杂志	0					0	0
49029000	其他报纸、杂志及期刊	0					0	0
49030000	儿童图画书、绘画或涂色书	0					0	0
49040000	乐谱原稿或印本	0					0	0
49051000	地球仪、天体仪	0					0	0
49059100	成册的各种印刷的地图及类似图表	0					0	0
49059900	其他各种印刷的地图及类似图表	0					0	0
49060000	设计图纸原稿或手稿及其复制件	0					0	0
49070010	指运国流通新发行未使用的邮票	7.5					0	
49070020	钞票	0					0	0
49070030	证券凭证	0					0	0
49070090	指运国流通新发行未使用的印花税票及类似票证；印有邮票或印花税票的纸品；空白支票	7.5					0	
49081000	釉转印贴花纸	7.5					0	
49089000	其他转印贴花纸	7.5					0	
49090010	印刷或有图画的明信片	7.5					0	
49090090	其他致贺或通告卡片	7.5					0	
49100000	印刷的各种日历，包括日历芯	7.5					0	0
49111010	无商业价值的广告品及类似印刷品	0					0	0
49111090	其他商业广告品及类似印刷品	7.5					0	
49119100	印刷的图片、设计图样及照片	7.5					0	
49119910	纸质的其他印刷品	7.5					0	
49119990	其他印刷品	7.5					0	
50010010	适于缫丝的桑蚕茧	6					0	0
50010090	适于缫丝的其他蚕茧	6					0	0
50020011	厂丝	9					0	0
50020012	土丝	9					0	0
50020013	双宫丝	9					0	0
50020019	其他未加捻桑蚕丝	9					0	0
50020020	未加捻柞蚕丝	9					0	0
50020090	未加捻其他生丝	9					0	0
50030011	下茧、茧衣、长吐、滞头	9					0	0
50030012	回收纤维	9					0	0
50030019	其他	9					0	0
50030091	绵球	9					0	0
50030099	其他	9					0	0
50040000	非供零售用丝纱线	6					0	0
50050010	非供零售用䌷丝纱线	6					0	0
50050090	非供零售用其他绢纺纱线	6					0	0
50060000	零售用丝纱线、绢纺纱线；蚕胶丝	6					0	0
50071010	未漂白或漂白的䌷丝机织物	10			0		0	0
50071090	其他䌷丝机织物	10			0		0	0
50072011	未漂白或漂白的纯桑蚕丝机织物	10			0		0	0
50072019	其他纯桑蚕丝机织物	10			0		0	0
50072021	未漂白或漂白的纯柞蚕丝机织物	10			0		0	0

税则号列	商品名称（简称）	最惠税率	亚太2国	东盟			最不发达35国	最不发达4国
				缅	老	柬		
50072029	其他纯柞蚕丝机织物	10			0		0	0
50072031	未漂白或漂白的纯绢丝机织物	10			0		0	0
50072039	其他纯绢丝机织物	10			0		0	0
50072090	其他纯丝机织物	10			0		0	0
50079010	未漂白或漂白其他丝机织物	10			0		0	0
50079090	其他丝机织物	10			0		0	0
51021100	未梳喀什米尔山羊毛	9					0	0
51021910	未梳兔毛	9					0	0
51021920	未梳其他山羊绒	9					0	0
51021930	未梳骆驼毛、骆驼绒	9					0	0
51021990	未梳的其他动物细毛	9					0	
51022000	未梳的动物粗毛	9					0	0
51031090	其他动物细毛落毛	9					0	0
51032010	羊毛废料	13.5					0	
51032090	其他动物细毛废料	9					0	
51033000	动物粗毛废料	9					0	0
51040010	羊毛回收纤维	15					0	
51040090	其他动物细毛或粗毛的回收纤维	5					0	0
51053100	已梳喀什米尔山羊毛	5					0	0
51053910	已梳兔毛	5					0	0
51053921	已梳无毛山羊绒	5					0	0
51053929	其他已梳山羊绒	5					0	0
51053990	其他已梳动物细毛	5					0	
51054000	已梳动物粗毛	5					0	0
51061000	非供零售用粗梳纯羊毛纱线	5					0	0
51062000	非供零售用粗梳混纺羊毛纱线	5					0	0
51071000	非供零售用精梳纯羊毛纱线	5					0	0
51072000	非供零售用精梳混纺羊毛纱线	5					0	0
51081011	按重量计山羊绒的含量在85%及以上的非供零售用的粗梳纱线	5					0	0
51081019	按重量计其他动物细毛含量在85%及以上的非供零售用的粗梳纱线	5					0	0
51081090	按重量计动物细毛含量在85%以下的非供零售用的粗梳纱线	5					0	0
51082011	按重量计山羊绒含量在85%及以上的非供零售用的精梳纱线	5					0	0
51082019	按重量计其他动物细毛含量在85%及以上的非供零售用的精梳纱线	5					0	0
51082090	按重量计动物细毛含量在85%以下的非供零售用的精梳纱线	5					0	0
51091011	按重量计山羊绒含量在85%及以上的供零售用的纱线	6					0	0
51091019	按重量计其他动物细毛含量在85%及以上的供零售用的纱线	6					0	0
51091090	按重量计羊毛含量在85%及以上的供零售用的纱线	6					0	0
51099011	供零售用的其他山羊绒纱线	6					0	0
51099019	供零售用的其他动物细毛纱线	6					0	0
51099090	供零售用的羊毛纱线	6					0	0
51100000	动物粗毛或马毛的纱线	6					0	0
51111111	按重量计山羊绒含量在85%及以上，每平方米重量不超过300克的山羊绒机织物	10					0	
51111119	按重量计其他动物细毛含量在85%及以上，每平方米重量不超过300克的其他动物细毛机织物	10					0	
51111190	按重量计羊毛含量在85%及以上，每平方米重量不超过300克的羊毛机织物	10					0	
51111911	按重量计山羊绒含量在85%及以上，每平方米重量超过300克的山羊绒的机织物	10					0	
51111919	按重量计其他动物细毛含量在85%及以上，每平方米超过300克的其他动物细毛机织物	10					0	
51111990	按重量计羊毛含量在85%及以上，每平方米超过300克的羊毛机织物	10					0	
51112000	与化纤长丝混纺粗梳毛布	10					0	
51113000	与化纤短纤混纺粗梳毛布	10					0	
51119000	与其他纤维混纺的粗梳毛布	10					0	
51121100	重量≤200g/平米精梳全毛布	10					0	0
51121900	重量＞200g/平米精梳全毛布	10		0	0	0	0	0
51122000	与化纤长丝混纺精梳毛布	10					0	0
51123000	与化纤短纤混纺精梳毛布	10					0	0
51129000	与其他纤维混纺精梳毛布	10					0	0

税则号列	商品名称（简称）	最惠税率	亚太2国	东盟			最不发达35国	最不发达4国
				缅	老	柬		
51130000	动物粗毛或马毛机织物	10					0	0
52021000	废棉纱线	10					0	
52029100	棉的回收纤维	10					0	0
52041100	非供零售用全棉缝纫线	5			0		0	0
52041900	非供零售用其他棉缝纫线	5					0	0
52042000	零售用棉制缝纫线	5			0		0	0
52051100	非零售粗梳粗支纯棉单纱	5		0	0	0	0	0
52051200	非零售粗梳中支纯棉单纱	5		0	0	0	0	0
52051300	非零售粗梳细支纯棉单纱	5					0	0
52051400	非零售粗梳较细支纯棉单纱	5		0	0		0	0
52051500	非零售粗梳特细支纯棉单纱	5					0	0
52052100	非零售精梳粗支纯棉单纱	5		0			0	0
52052200	非零售精梳中支纯棉单纱	5					0	0
52052300	非零售精梳细支纯棉单纱	5					0	0
52052400	非零售精梳较细支纯棉单纱	5		0	0		0	0
52052600	非零售精梳较特细支纯棉单纱	5					0	0
52052700	非零售精梳特细支纯棉单纱	5					0	0
52052800	非零售精梳超细支纯棉单纱	5					0	0
52053200	非零售粗梳中支纯棉多股纱	5					0	0
52053300	非零售粗梳细支纯棉多股纱	5					0	0
52053400	非零售粗梳较细支纯棉多股纱	5					0	0
52053500	非零售粗梳特细支纯棉多股纱	5					0	0
52054100	非零售精梳粗支纯棉多股纱	5					0	
52054200	非零售精梳中支纯棉多股纱	5					0	0
52054300	非零售精梳细支纯棉多股纱	5					0	0
52054400	非零售精梳较细支纯棉多股纱	5					0	0
52054600	非零售精梳较特细支纯棉多股纱	5					0	0
52054700	非零售精梳特细支纯棉多股纱	5					0	0
52054800	非零售精梳超细支纯棉多股纱	5					0	0
52061200	非零售粗梳中支混纺棉单纱	5					0	
52061300	非零售粗梳细支混纺棉单纱	5					0	0
52061400	非零售粗梳较细支混纺棉单纱	5					0	0
52061500	非零售粗梳特细支混纺棉单纱	5					0	0
52062100	非零售精梳粗支混纺棉单纱	5					0	
52062200	非零售精梳中支混纺棉单纱	5					0	
52062300	非零售精梳细支混纺棉单纱	5					0	0
52062400	非零售精梳较细支混纺棉单纱	5					0	0
52062500	非零售精梳特细支混纺棉单纱	5					0	0
52063100	非零售粗梳粗支混纺棉多股纱	5					0	
52063200	非零售粗梳中支混纺棉多股纱	5					0	
52063300	非零售粗梳细支混纺棉多股纱	5					0	0
52063400	非零售粗梳较细混纺棉多股纱	5					0	0
52063500	非零售粗梳特细混纺棉多股纱	5					0	0
52064100	非零售精梳粗支混纺棉多股纱	5					0	
52064200	非零售精梳中支混纺棉多股纱	5					0	
52064300	非零售精梳细支混纺棉多股纱	5					0	0
52064400	非零售精梳较细混纺棉多股纱	5					0	0
52064500	非零售精梳特细混纺棉多股纱	5					0	0
52071000	供零售用纯棉纱线	6					0	
52079000	供零售用混纺棉纱线	6					0	0
52081100	未漂白轻质全棉平纹布	10					0	
52081200	未漂白较轻质全棉平纹布	10					0	
52081300	未漂白轻质全棉三、四线斜纹布	10					0	
52081900	未漂白轻质其他全棉机织物	10					0	
52082100	漂白的轻质全棉平纹布	10					0	
52082200	漂白的较轻质全棉平纹布	10		0	0	0	0	0
52082300	漂白的轻质全棉三、四线斜纹布	12					0	
52082900	漂白的轻质其他全棉机织物	10					0	

税则号列	商品名称（简称）	最惠税率	亚太2国	东盟			最不发达35国	最不发达4国
				缅	老	柬		
52083100	染色的轻质全棉平纹布	10					0	0
52083200	染色的较轻质全棉平纹布	10					0	0
52083300	染色的轻质全棉三、四线斜纹布	10		0	0	0	0	0
52083900	染色的轻质其他全棉机织物	10					0	0
52084100	色织的轻质全棉平纹布	10					0	
52084200	色织的较轻质全棉平纹布	10					0	0
52084300	色织的轻质全棉三、四线斜纹布	10					0	
52084900	色织的轻质其他全棉机织物	10		0	0	0	0	0
52085100	印花的轻全棉平纹布	10					0	0
52085200	印花的较轻全棉平纹布	10					0	0
52085910	印花的轻质全棉三、四线斜纹布	10					0	
52085990	印花的轻质其他全棉机织物	10					0	
52091100	未漂白重质全棉平纹布	10					0	0
52091200	未漂白重质全棉三、四线斜纹布	10					0	
52091900	未漂白重质其他全棉机织物	10					0	0
52092100	漂白的重质全棉平纹布	12					0	0
52092200	漂白的重质全棉三、四线斜纹布	12					0	
52092900	漂白的重质其他全棉机织物	12					0	
52093100	染色的重质全棉平纹布	10		0	0	0	0	0
52093200	染色的重质全棉三、四线斜纹布	10		0	0	0	0	0
52093900	染色的重质其他全棉机织物	10		0	0	0	0	0
52094100	色织的重质全棉平纹布	10					0	
52094200	色织的重质全棉粗斜纹布(劳动布)	10		0	0	0	0	0
52094300	其他三线或四线斜纹机织物，包括双面斜纹机织物	10					0	
52094900	色织的重质其他全棉机织物	10					0	
52095100	印花的重质全棉平纹布	10					0	0
52095200	印花的重质全棉三、四线斜纹布	10					0	
52095900	印花的重质其他全棉机织物	10					0	0
52101100	与化纤混纺未漂白轻质平纹棉布	12					0	0
52101910	化纤混纺未漂白轻质 3、4 线斜纹棉布	12					0	
52101990	与化纤混纺未漂白轻质其他棉布	12					0	0
52102100	与化纤混纺漂白的轻质平纹棉布	14					0	0
52102910	化纤混纺漂白的轻质三线或线斜纹棉布	14					0	
52102990	与化纤混纺漂白的轻质其他棉布	14					0	
52103100	与化纤混纺染色的轻质平纹棉布	10					0	0
52103200	化纤混纺染色的轻质三线或四线斜纹棉布	10					0	
52103900	与化纤混纺染色的轻质其他棉布	10					0	
52104100	与化纤混纺色织的轻质平纹棉布	10					0	
52104910	化纤混纺色织的轻质三线或四线斜纹棉布	10					0	
52104990	与化纤混纺色织的轻质其他棉布	10					0	0
52105100	与化纤混纺印花的轻质平纹棉布	10					0	0
52105910	化纤混纺印花的轻质三线或四线斜纹棉布	10					0	
52105990	与化纤混纺印花的轻质其他棉布	10					0	0
52111100	与化纤混纺未漂白重质平纹棉布	12					0	0
52111200	化纤混纺未漂白重质三线或四线斜纹棉布	12					0	0
52111900	与化纤混纺未漂白重质其他棉布	12					0	0
52112000	与化纤混纺漂白的重质其他棉布	14					0	
52113100	与化纤混纺染色的重质平纹棉布	10					0	0
52113200	化纤混纺染色的重质三线或四线斜纹棉布	10					0	
52113900	与化纤混纺染色的重质其他棉布	10					0	0
52114100	与化纤混纺色织的重质平纹棉布	10					0	
52114200	与化纤混纺色织的重质粗斜纹棉布	10					0	
52114300	其他三线或四线斜纹机织物，包括双面斜纹机织物	10					0	
52114900	与化纤混纺色织的重质其他棉布	10					0	
52115100	与化纤混纺印花的重质平纹棉布	10					0	
52115200	化纤混纺印花的重质三线或四线斜纹棉布	10					0	
52115900	与化纤混纺印花的重质其他棉布	10					0	
52121100	未漂白的其他混纺轻质棉布	12					0	0

税则号列	商品名称（简称）	最惠税率	亚太2国	东盟			最不发达35国	最不发达4国
				缅	老	柬		
52121200	漂白的其他混纺轻质棉布	14					0	
52121300	染色的其他混纺轻质棉布	10					0	
52121400	色织的其他混纺轻质棉布	10					0	
52121500	印花的其他混纺轻质棉布	10					0	
52122100	未漂白的其他混纺重质棉布	12					0	0
52122200	漂白的其他混纺重质棉布	14					0	
52122300	染色的其他混纺重质棉布	10					0	
52122400	色织的其他混纺重质棉布	10					0	
52122500	印花的其他混纺重质棉布	10					0	0
53011000	生的或沤制的亚麻	6					0	0
53012100	破开或打成的亚麻	6					0	0
53012900	栉梳或经其他加工未纺制的亚麻	6					0	0
53013000	亚麻短纤及废麻	6					0	0
53021000	生的或沤制的大麻	6					0	0
53029000	经加工、未纺的大麻、大麻短纤及废麻	6					0	0
53031000	生或沤制黄麻,其他纺织用韧皮纤维	5	0	0	0	0	0	0
53039000	经加工、未纺的黄麻及其他纺织用韧皮纤维	5		0	0	0	0	0
53050011	生的苎麻	5					0	0
53050012	经加工、未纺制的苎麻	5					0	0
53050013	苎麻的短纤及废麻	5					0	0
53050019	其他苎麻	5					0	0
53050020	经加工、未纺制的蕉麻及蕉麻废料	3					0	0
53050091	经加工、未纺的西沙尔麻及其他龙舌兰类纤维	5					0	0
53050092	加工、未纺的椰壳纤维及椰壳纤维废料	5		0	0	0	0	0
53050099	经加工的其他未列名纺织用植物纤维及其废麻	5					0	0
53061000	亚麻单纱	6					0	0
53062000	亚麻多股纱线或缆线	10					0	0
53071000	黄麻及其他纺织用韧皮纤维单纱	6	3			0	0	0
53072000	黄麻及其他纺织用韧皮纤维多股纱或缆线	6	3			0	0	0
53081000	椰壳纤维纱线	6					0	0
53082000	大麻纱线	6					0	0
53089011	未漂白或漂白的全苎麻纱线	6					0	0
53089012	全苎麻色纱线	6					0	0
53089013	未漂白或漂白的混纺苎麻纱线	6					0	0
53089014	混纺苎麻色纱线	6					0	0
53089091	纸纱线	6					0	0
53089099	其他植物纺织纤维纱线	6					0	0
53091110	未漂白全亚麻机织物	10					0	0
53091120	漂白的全亚麻机织物	10					0	0
53091900	其他全亚麻机织物	10					0	0
53092110	未漂白的混纺亚麻机织物	10					0	0
53092120	漂白的混纺亚麻机织物	10					0	0
53092900	其他混纺亚麻机织物	10					0	0
53101000	未漂白黄麻或其他韧皮纤维织物	10	5			0	0	0
53109000	其他黄麻机织物或韧皮鲜为纤维织物	10	5			0	0	0
53110012	未漂白全苎麻机织物	10					0	0
53110013	其他全苎麻机织物	12					0	0
53110014	未漂白混纺苎麻机织物	10					0	0
53110015	其他混纺苎麻机织物	12					0	
53110020	纸纱线机织物	10					0	0
53110030	大麻的机织物	10					0	0
53110090	其他纺织用植物纤维机织物	10					0	0
54011010	非供零售用合成纤维长丝缝纫线	5					0	0
54011020	供零售用合成纤维长丝缝纫线	5					0	0
54012010	非供零售用人纤长丝缝纫线	5					0	0
54012020	供零售用人纤长丝缝纫线	5					0	0
54021110	非零售用聚间苯二甲酰间苯二胺纺制的长丝高强力纱	5					0	0
54021120	非零售用聚对苯二甲酰对苯二胺纺制的长丝高强力纱	5					0	0

税则号列	商品名称（简称）	最惠税率	亚太2国	东盟 缅	东盟 老	东盟 柬	最不发达35国	最不发达4国
54021190	非零售用其他芳香族聚酰胺纺制的长丝高强力纱	5					0	0
54021910	非零售用聚酰胺-6纺制的长丝高强力纱	5					0	0
54021920	非零售用聚酰胺-66纺制的长丝高强力纱	5					0	0
54021990	非零售用其他尼龙长丝高强纱	5					0	0
54022000	非零售聚酯长丝高强力纱	5					0	0
54023111	非零售用聚酰胺-6纺制的细弹力丝	5					0	0
54023112	非零售用聚酰胺-66纺制的细弹力丝	5					0	0
54023113	非零售用芳香族聚酰胺纺制的细弹力丝	5					0	0
54023119	非零售其他细尼龙弹力丝	5					0	0
54023190	非零售其他细尼龙变形纱线	5					0	0
54023211	非零售用聚酰胺-6纺制的粗弹力丝	5					0	0
54023212	非零售用聚酰胺-66纺制的粗弹力丝	5					0	0
54023213	非零售用芳香族聚酰胺纺制的粗弹力丝	5					0	0
54023219	非零售其他粗尼龙弹力丝	5					0	0
54023290	非零售其他粗尼龙变形纱线	5					0	0
54023310	非零售聚酯弹力丝	5					0	0
54023390	非零售其他聚酯变形纱线	5					0	0
54023400	非零售用聚丙烯变形纱线	5					0	0
54023900	非零售其他合成纤维长丝变形纱线	5					0	0
54024410	弹性氨纶纱线，未加捻或捻度每米不超过50转	5					0	0
54024490	其他弹性纱线，未加捻或捻度每米不超过50转	5					0	0
54024510	聚酰胺-6纺制的其他单纱，未加捻或捻度每米不超过50转	5					0	0
54024520	聚酰胺-6，6纺制的其他单纱，未加捻或捻度每米不超过50转	5					0	0
54024530	芳香族聚酰胺纺制的其他单纱，未加捻或捻度每米不超过50转	5					0	0
54024590	其他尼龙或聚酰胺纱线纺制的，未加捻或捻度每米不超过50转的单纱	5					0	0
54024600	其他部分定向聚酯纱线，未加捻或捻度每米不超过50转	5					0	0
54024700	其他聚酯纱线，未加捻或捻度每米不超过50转	5					0	0
54024800	其他聚丙烯纱线，未加捻或捻度每米不超过50转	5					0	0
54024910	断裂强度大于等于22cN/dtex,且初始模量大于等于750cN/dtex的聚乙烯纱线	5					0	0
54024990	其他纱线，未加捻或捻度每米不超过50转	5					0	0
54025110	非零售用聚酰胺-6纺制的加捻单纱	5					0	0
54025120	非零售用聚酰胺-66纺制的加捻单纱	5					0	0
54025130	非零售用芳香族聚酰胺纺制的加捻单纱	5					0	0
54025190	非零售用其他尼龙加捻单纱	5					0	0
54025200	非零售加捻的其他聚酯加捻单纱	5					0	0
54025910	非零售用聚丙烯加捻单纱	5					0	0
54025920	断裂强度大于等于22cN/dtex,且初始模量大于等于750cN/dtex的聚乙烯纱线	5					0	0
54025990	非零售加捻的其他合成纤维长丝单纱	5					0	0
54026110	非零售用聚己内酰胺(尼龙-6)制多股纱线	5					0	0
54026120	非零售用聚酰胺-66制多股纱线	5					0	0
54026130	非零售用芳香族聚酰胺制多股纱线	5					0	0
54026190	非零售用其他尼龙制多股纱线	5					0	0
54026200	非零售聚酯多股纱线	5					0	0
54026910	非零售用聚丙烯多股纱线	5					0	0
54026920	非零售用氨纶多股纱线	5					0	0
54026990	非零售其他合成纤维长丝多股纱线	5					0	0
54031000	非零售粘胶纤维高强力纱	5					0	0
54033110	竹制非零售未捻的粘胶纤维单纱	5					0	0
54033190	其他非零售未捻的粘胶纤维单纱	5					0	0
54033210	竹制非零售加捻的粘胶纤维单纱	5					0	0
54033290	其他非零售加捻的粘胶纤维单纱	5					0	0
54033310	非零售二醋酸纤维单纱	5					0	0
54033390	非零售其他醋酸纤维单纱	5					0	0
54033900	非零售其他人造纤维长丝单纱	5					0	0
54034100	非零售粘胶长丝多股纱线或缆线	5					0	0
54034200	非零售醋酸长丝多股纱线或缆线	5					0	0
54034900	非零售其他人造纤维长丝多股纱或缆线	5					0	0
54041100	细度≥67分特、≤1mm的弹性单丝	5					0	0

税则号列	商品名称（简称）	最惠税率	亚太2国	东盟			最不发达35国	最不发达4国
				缅	老	柬		
54041200	细度≥67分特、≤1mm的的聚丙烯单丝	5					0	0
54041900	细度≥67分特、≤1mm的其他合成纤维单丝	5					0	0
54049000	其他宽≤5mm合成纺织材料制扁条及类似品	5					0	0
54050000	细度≥67分特、≤1mm人造纤维单丝；宽≤5mm扁条及类似品	5					0	0
54060010	供零售用合成纤维长丝纱线	5					0	0
54060020	供零售用人造纤维长丝纱线	5					0	0
54071010	尼龙或其他聚酰胺高强力纱制机织物	10					0	
54071020	聚酯高强力纱制机织物	10					0	
54072000	合成纤维扁条及类似品的机织物	10					0	
54073000	多层平行纱线相互层迭并粘合机织物	10					0	
54074100	未漂白或漂白的纯尼龙布	10					0	
54074200	染色的纯尼龙布	10		0	0	0	0	0
54074300	色织的纯尼龙布	10					0	
54074400	印花的纯尼龙布	10					0	
54075100	未漂白或漂白纯聚酯变形长丝布	10					0	
54075200	染色的纯聚酯变形长丝布	10		0	0	0	0	0
54075300	色织的纯聚酯变形长丝布	10					0	
54075400	印花的纯聚酯变形长丝布	10					0	
54076100	其他纯聚酯非变形长丝布	10					0	0
54076900	其他纯聚酯长丝布	10					0	0
54077100	未漂白或漂白其他纯合成纤维长丝布	10					0	
54077200	染色的其他纯合成纤维长丝布	10		0	0	0	0	0
54077300	色织的其他纯合成纤维长丝布	10					0	
54077400	印花的其他纯合成纤维长丝布	10					0	
54078100	未漂或漂白的与棉混纺合成纤维长丝布	10					0	
54078200	染色的与棉混纺合成纤维长丝布	10					0	0
54078300	色织的与棉混纺合成纤维长丝布	10					0	
54078400	印花的与棉混纺合成纤维长丝布	10					0	
54079100	未漂或漂白的其他混纺合成纤维长丝布	10					0	
54079200	染色的其他混纺合成纤维长丝布	10		0	0	0	0	0
54079300	色织的其他混纺合成纤维长丝布	10					0	
54079400	印花的其他混纺合成纤维长丝布	10					0	
54081000	粘胶长丝高强力纱的机织物	10					0	
54082110	粘胶长丝制未漂白或漂白的机织物	12					0	
54082120	醋酸长丝制未漂白或漂白的机织物	12					0	
54082190	其他人造长丝制未漂白或漂白的机织物	12					0	
54082210	纯粘胶长丝制染色机织物	10					0	
54082220	纯醋酸长丝制染色机织物	10					0	
54082290	纯其他人造长丝制染色机织物	10					0	
54082310	纯粘胶长丝制色织机织物	10					0	
54082320	纯醋酸长丝制色织机织物	10					0	
54082390	纯其他人造长丝制色织机织物	10					0	
54082410	纯粘胶长丝制印花机织物	10					0	
54082420	纯醋酸长丝制印花机织物	10					0	
54082490	纯其他人造长丝制印花机织物	10					0	
54083100	未漂白或漂白人造纤维长丝混纺布	10					0	
54083200	染色的人纤长丝混纺布	10					0	0
54083300	色织的人纤长丝混纺布	10					0	
54083400	印花的人纤长丝混纺布	10					0	
55011000	尼龙或其他聚酰胺长丝丝束	5					0	0
55012000	聚酯长丝丝束	5					0	0
55013000	聚丙烯腈长丝丝束	5					0	0
55014000	聚丙烯长丝丝束	5					0	0
55019000	其他合成纤维长丝丝束	5					0	0
55020010	二醋酸纤维丝束	3					0	0
55020090	其他人造纤维长丝丝束	5					0	0
55031110	未梳的聚间苯二甲酰间苯二胺纺制的合成纤维短纤	5					0	0
55031120	未梳的聚对苯二甲酰对苯二胺纺制的合成纤维短纤	5					0	0

税则号列	商品名称（简称）	最惠税率	亚太2国	东盟			最不发达35国	最不发达4国
				缅	老	柬		
55031190	未梳的其他芳香聚酰胺纺制的合成纤维短纤	5					0	0
55031900	未梳的尼龙或其他聚酰胺合成纤维短纤	5					0	0
55032000	未梳的聚酯合成纤维短纤	5					0	0
55033000	未梳的聚丙烯腈合成纤维短纤	5					0	0
55034000	未梳的聚丙烯合成纤维短纤	5					0	0
55039010	聚苯硫醚制未梳的纤维短纤	5					0	0
55039090	未梳的其他合成纤维短纤	5					0	0
55041010	竹制未梳的粘胶纤维短纤	5					0	0
55041021	木制未梳的阻燃的粘胶纤维短纤	5					0	0
55041029	其他木制未梳的粘胶纤维短纤	5					0	0
55041090	其他未梳的粘胶纤维短纤	5					0	0
55049000	未梳的其他人造纤维短纤	5					0	0
55051000	合成纤维废料	5					0	0
55052000	人造纤维废料	5					0	0
55061011	已梳的聚间苯二甲酰间苯二胺纤维短纤	5					0	0
55061012	已梳的聚对苯二甲酰对苯二胺纤维短纤	5					0	0
55061019	已梳的其他芳香族聚酰胺纤维短纤	5					0	0
55061090	已梳的尼龙或其他聚酰胺纤维短纤	5					0	0
55062000	已梳的聚酯纤维短纤	5					0	0
55063000	已梳的聚丙烯腈及其变性纤维短纤	5					0	0
55069010	聚苯硫醚制已梳的纤维短纤	5					0	0
55069090	已梳的其他合成纤维短纤	5					0	0
55070000	已梳的人造纤维短纤	5					0	0
55081000	合成纤维短纤纺制的缝纫线	5					0	0
55082000	人造纤维短纤纺制的缝纫线	5					0	0
55091100	非零售纯尼龙短纤单纱	5					0	0
55091200	非零售纯尼龙短纤多股纱线	5					0	0
55092100	非零售纯聚酯短纤单纱	5					0	0
55092200	非零售纯聚酯短纤多股纱线	5					0	0
55093100	非零售纯聚丙烯腈短纤单纱	5					0	0
55093200	非零售纯聚丙烯腈短纤多股纱线	5					0	0
55094100	非零售纯其他合成纤维短纤单纱	5					0	0
55094200	非零售纯其他合成纤维短纤多股纱线	5					0	0
55095100	非零售与人造纤维短纤混纺聚酯短纤纱	5					0	0
55095200	非零售与毛混纺聚酯短纤纱线	5					0	0
55095300	非零售与棉混纺聚酯短纤纱线	5					0	0
55095900	非零售其他混纺聚酯短纤纱线	5					0	0
55096100	非零售与毛混纺腈纶短纤纱线	5					0	0
55096200	非零售与棉混纺腈纶短纤纱线	5					0	0
55096900	非零售与其他混纺腈纶短纤纱线	5					0	0
55099100	非零售与毛混纺其他合成纤维短纤纱线	5					0	0
55099200	非零售与棉混纺其他合成纤维短纤纱线	5					0	0
55099900	非零售与其他混纺合成纤维短纤纱线	5					0	0
55101100	非零售纯人造纤维短纤单纱	5					0	0
55101200	非零售纯人造纤维短纤多股纱线	5					0	0
55102000	非零售与毛混纺人造纤维短纤纱线	5					0	0
55103000	非零售与棉混纺人造纤维短纤纱线	5					0	0
55109000	非零售与其他混纺人造纤维短纤纱线	5					0	0
55111000	零售用纯合成纤维短纤纱线	5					0	0
55112000	零售用混纺合成纤维短纤纱线	5					0	0
55113000	零售用人造纤维短纤纱线	5					0	0
55121100	未漂或漂白的纯聚酯布	15					0	0
55121900	其他纯聚酯布	10					0	0
55122100	未漂或漂白的纯腈纶布	13					0	0
55122900	其他纯腈纶布	10					0	
55129100	未漂或漂白的纯其他合成纤维布	18					0	
55129900	其他纯合成纤维布	10		0	0	0	0	0
55131110	与棉混纺未漂白的轻质聚酯平纹布	16					0	

税则号列	商品名称（简称）	最惠税率	亚太2国	东盟			最不发达35国	最不发达4国
				缅	老	柬		
55131120	与棉混纺漂白的轻质聚酯平纹布	15					0	
55131210	与棉混纺未漂白的轻质聚酯斜纹布	16					0	
55131220	与棉混纺漂白的轻质聚酯斜纹布	18					0	
55131310	与棉混纺未漂白的其他轻质聚酯布	16					0	
55131320	与棉混纺漂白的其他轻质聚酯布	18					0	
55131900	与棉混纺未漂白或漂白的轻质其他合成纤维布	18					0	
55132100	与棉混纺染色的轻质聚酯平纹布	10					0	
55132310	与棉混纺染色的轻质聚酯斜纹布	10					0	
55132390	与棉混纺染色的其他轻质聚酯布	10					0	
55132900	与棉混纺染色的轻质其他合成纤维布	10					0	0
55133100	与棉混纺色织的轻质聚酯平纹布	10					0	
55133910	与棉混纺色织的轻质聚酯斜纹布	10					0	
55133920	与棉混纺色织的其他轻质聚酯布	10					0	
55133990	与棉混纺色织的轻质其他合成纤维布	10					0	
55134100	与棉混纺印花的轻质聚酯平纹布	10		0	0	0	0	0
55134910	与棉混纺印花的轻质聚酯斜纹布	10					0	
55134920	与棉混纺印花的其他轻质聚酯布	10					0	
55134990	与棉混纺印花的轻质其他合成纤维布	10					0	
55141110	与棉混纺未漂白的重质聚酯平纹布	16					0	
55141120	与棉混纺漂白的重质聚酯平纹布	18					0	
55141210	与棉混纺未漂白的重质聚酯斜纹布	16					0	
55141220	与棉混纺漂白的重质聚酯斜纹布	18					0	
55141911	与棉混纺未漂白的重质其他聚酯布	16					0	
55141912	与棉混纺漂白的重质其他聚酯布	18					0	
55141990	与棉混纺未漂白或漂白的重质其他合成纤维布	16					0	
55142100	与棉混纺染色的重质聚酯平纹布	10					0	
55142200	与棉混纺染色的重质聚酯斜纹布	10					0	
55142300	与棉混纺染色的其他重质聚酯布	10		0	0	0	0	0
55142900	与棉混纺染色的重质其他合成维纤布	10					0	0
55143010	与棉混纺色织的重质聚酯平纹布	10					0	
55143020	与棉混纺色织的重质聚酯斜纹布	10					0	
55143030	与棉混纺色织的其他重质聚酯布	10					0	
55143090	与棉混纺色织的重质其他合成纤维布	10					0	
55144100	与棉混纺印花的重质聚酯平纹布	10					0	
55144200	与棉混纺印花的重质聚酯斜纹布	10					0	
55144300	与棉混纺印花的其他重质聚酯布	10					0	
55144900	与棉混纺印花的重质其他合成纤维布	10					0	
55151100	与粘胶纤维短纤混纺的聚酯布	10					0	
55151200	与化纤长丝混纺的聚酯布	10					0	
55151300	与毛混纺的聚酯布	10					0	
55151900	与其他纤维混纺的聚酯布	10					0	
55152100	与化纤长丝混纺的腈纶布	10					0	
55152200	与毛混纺的腈纶布	12					0	0
55152900	与其他纤维混纺的腈纶布	10					0	
55159100	与化纤长丝混纺的其他合成纤维短纤布	10					0	
55159900	与其他纤维混纺的其他合成纤维短纤布	10					0	
55161100	未漂白或漂白的纯人造纤维短纤布	12					0	0
55161200	染色的纯人造纤维短纤布	10					0	
55161300	色织的纯人造纤维短纤布	10					0	
55161400	印花的纯人造纤维短纤布	10					0	
55162100	与化纤长丝混纺未漂白或漂白的人造纤维布	12					0	
55162200	与化纤长丝混纺的染色人造纤维布	10					0	
55162300	与化纤长丝混纺的色织人造纤维布	10					0	
55162400	与化纤长丝混纺的印花人造纤维布	10					0	
55163100	与毛混纺的未漂或漂白人造纤维布	12					0	
55163200	与毛混纺的染色人造纤维布	10					0	
55163300	与毛混纺的色织人造纤维布	10					0	
55163400	与毛混纺的印花人造纤维布	10					0	

税则号列	商品名称（简称）	最惠税率	亚太2国	东盟			最不发达35国	最不发达4国
				缅	老	柬		
55164100	与棉混纺的未漂或漂白人造纤维布	12					0	
55164200	与棉混纺的染色人造纤维布	12					0	
55164300	与棉混纺的色织人造纤维布	10					0	
55164400	与棉混纺的印花人造纤维布	10					0	
55169100	与其他纤维混纺未漂白或漂白的人造纤维布	12					0	
55169200	与其他纤维混纺的染色人造纤维布	10					0	0
55169300	与其他纤维混纺的色织人造纤维布	10					0	
55169400	与其他纤维混纺的印花人造纤维布	10					0	
56012100	棉制的絮胎及其他絮胎制品	10					0	
56012210	化学纤维制的卷烟滤嘴	12					0	
56012290	化学纤维制的絮胎及其他絮胎制品	12					0	0
56012900	其他材料制絮胎及其他絮胎制品	10					0	0
56013000	纺织纤维屑、纤维粉末及球结	10					0	
56021000	针刺机制毡呢及纤维缝编织物	10					0	
56022100	未浸、涂的毛制其他毡呢	10					0	
56022900	未浸、涂的其他纺织材料制其他毡呢	10					0	
56029000	经浸、涂、包覆或层压的其他毡呢	10					0	0
56031110	每平米≤25g经浸渍化纤长丝无纺织物	10		0	0	0	0	0
56031190	每平米≤25g的其他化纤长丝无纺织物	10					0	
56031210	25g <每平米≤70g浸渍化纤长丝无纺织物	10		0	0	0	0	0
56031290	25g <每平米≤70g其他化纤长丝无纺织物	10					0	0
56031310	70g<每平米≤150g浸渍化纤长丝无纺织物	10					0	
56031390	70g <每平米≤150g其他化纤长丝无纺织物	10					0	0
56031410	每平米>150g经浸渍化纤长丝无纺织物	10					0	
56031490	每平米>150g的其他化纤长丝无纺织物	10					0	0
56039110	每平米≤25g经浸渍其他无纺织物	10					0	
56039190	每平米≤25g的其他无纺织物	10					0	
56039210	25g <每平米≤70g浸渍其他无纺织物	10					0	
56039290	25g <每平米≤70g其他无纺织物	10		0	0	0	0	0
56039310	70g <每平米≤150g浸渍其他无纺织物	10					0	
56039390	70g <每平米≤150g的其他无纺织物	10					0	
56039410	每平米>150g经浸渍其他无纺织物	10					0	
56039490	每平米>150g的其他无纺织物	10		0	0	0	0	0
56041000	用纺织材料包覆的橡胶线及绳	5		0	0	0	0	0
56049000	用橡、塑浸渍涂布的其他纺织纱线	5					0	0
56050000	含金属纱线	5					0	0
56060000	绳绒线及粗松螺旋花线	5					0	0
56072100	剑麻或其他龙舌兰纤维制包扎用绳	5					0	0
56072900	剑麻或龙舌兰纤维制其他线绳索缆	5					0	0
56074100	聚乙烯或聚丙烯制包扎用绳	5					0	0
56074900	聚乙烯或聚丙烯制线、绳、索、缆	5					0	0
56075000	其他合纤制线、绳、索、缆	5					0	0
56079010	蕉麻或硬质纤维制线、绳、索、缆	5					0	0
56079090	其他纺织材料制线、绳、索、缆	5	2.5	0	0	0	0	0
56081100	化纤材料制成的渔网	10					0	0
56081900	化纤材料制成的其他网	12					0	
56089000	其他纤维制成的渔网及其他网	10					0	0
56090000	用纱线、扁条、绳、索、缆制其他物品	10	0				0	0
57011000	羊毛结织栽绒地毯及其他铺地制品	14					0	0
57019010	化纤结织栽绒地毯及其他铺地制品	16					0	0
57019020	丝制结织栽绒地毯及铺地制品	14					0	
57019090	其他材料结织栽绒地毯及铺地制品	14					0	
57021000	“开来姆”等手织地毯	14	0				0	0
57022000	椰壳纤维制的铺地制品	14					0	
57023100	未制成的毛制起绒地毯及铺地制品	10					0	0
57023200	未制成的化纤起绒地毯及铺地制品	16					0	
57023900	未制成其他纺织材料起绒铺地制品	14	0				0	0
57024100	制成的毛制起绒地毯及铺地制品	10					0	0

税则号列	商品名称（简称）	最惠税率	亚太2国	东盟			最不发达35国	最不发达4国
				缅	老	柬		
57024200	制成的化纤起绒地毯及铺地制品	10					0	0
57024900	制成的其他纺织材料起绒铺地制品	14					0	
57025010	未制成毛制非起绒地毯及铺地制品	14					0	
57025020	未制成化纤非起绒地毯及铺地制品	16					0	
57025090	未制成其他纺织材料非起绒地毯及铺地制品	14					0	
57029100	制成的毛制非起绒地毯及铺地制品	14					0	
57029200	制成的化纤非起绒地毯及铺地制品	16					0	
57029900	制成的其他纺织材料非起绒地毯及铺地制品	14					0	
57031000	毛制簇绒地毯及其他簇绒铺地制品	14					0	0
57032000	尼龙簇绒地毯及其他簇绒铺地制品	10					0	0
57033000	化纤簇绒地毯及其他簇绒铺地制品	10					0	0
57039000	其他纺织材料簇绒地毯及其他簇绒铺地制品	14	0				0	0
57041000	小块毡呢地毯及其他毡呢铺地制品	14					0	
57049000	大块毡呢地毯及其他毡呢铺地制品	10					0	0
57050010	毛制其他地毯及其他铺地制品	14	0				0	0
57050020	化纤制其他地毯及其他铺地制品	10	0				0	0
57050090	其他纺织材料制其他地毯及铺地制品	14	0				0	0
58011000	毛制起绒机织物及绳绒织物	10					0	0
58012100	不割绒的棉制纬起绒织物	12					0	
58012200	割绒的棉制灯芯绒	10					0	0
58012300	其他棉制纬起绒织物	10					0	0
58012600	棉制绳绒织物	10					0	0
58012710	棉制的不割绒的经起绒织物（棱纹绸）	10					0	0
58012720	棉制的割绒的经起绒织物	10					0	0
58013100	不割绒的化纤制纬起绒织物	10					0	0
58013200	割绒的化纤制灯芯绒	10					0	0
58013300	其他化纤纬起绒织物	10		0	0	0	0	0
58013600	化纤绳绒织物	10					0	0
58013710	化学纤维制的不割绒的经起绒织物（棱纹绸）	10					0	0
58013720	化学纤维制的割绒的经起绒织物	10					0	0
58019010	丝及绢丝制起绒机织物及绳绒织物	10					0	0
58019090	其他材料制起绒机织物及绳绒织物	10					0	0
58021100	未漂白棉毛巾织物及类似毛圈机织物	12	0				0	0
58021900	其他棉毛巾织物及类似毛圈机织物	10					0	0
58022010	丝及绢丝毛巾织物及类似毛圈机织物	12	0				0	0
58022020	羊毛等毛巾织物及类似毛圈机织物	12	0				0	0
58022030	化纤毛巾织物及类似毛圈机织物	14	0				0	0
58022090	其他纺织材料毛巾织物及类似毛圈织物	12	0				0	0
58023010	丝及绢丝制簇绒织物	10					0	0
58023020	羊毛或动物细毛制簇绒织物	10					0	0
58023030	棉或麻制簇绒织物	10					0	0
58023040	化学纤维制簇绒织物	10					0	0
58023090	其他纺织材料制簇绒织物	10					0	0
58030010	棉制纱罗	10					0	0
58030020	丝及绢丝制纱罗	10					0	0
58030030	化学纤维制纱罗	10					0	0
58030090	其他纺织材料制纱罗	10					0	0
58041010	丝及绢丝网眼薄纱及其他网眼织物	10					0	0
58041020	棉制网眼薄纱及其他网眼织物	10					0	0
58041030	化纤制网眼薄纱及其他网眼织物	12		0	0	0	0	0
58041090	其他纺织材料网眼薄纱及其他网眼织物	10					0	0
58042100	化纤机制花边	10					0	0
58042910	丝及绢丝机制花边	10					0	0
58042920	棉机制花边	10		0	0	0	0	0
58042990	其他纺织材料制机制花边	10					0	0
58043000	手工制花边	10					0	0
58050010	手工针绣嵌花装饰毯	12					0	0
58050090	“哥白林”等手织装饰毯	12					0	0

税则号列	商品名称（简称）	最惠税率	亚太2国	东盟			最不发达35国	最不发达4国
				缅	老	柬		
58061010	棉或麻狭幅起绒机织物及绳绒织物	10					0	0
58061090	其他材料狭幅起绒机织物及绳绒织物	10		0	0	0	0	0
58062000	含弹性纱线≥5%的狭幅织物	10		0	0	0	0	0
58063100	棉制其他狭幅机织物	10		0	0	0	0	0
58063200	化纤制其他狭幅机织物	10		0	0	0	0	0
58063910	丝及绢丝制其他狭幅机织物	10					0	0
58063920	毛制其他狭幅机织物	10					0	0
58063990	其他材料制其他狭幅机织物	10					0	0
58064010	棉或麻粘合有经纱无纬纱狭幅织物	10					0	0
58064090	其他材料粘合有经纱无纬纱狭幅织物	10					0	0
58071000	机织非绣制纺织材料标签、徽章等	10		0	0	0	0	0
58079000	非机织非绣制纺织材料标签徽章等	10					0	0
58081000	成匹的编带	10					0	0
58089000	非绣制成匹装饰带、流苏、绒球	10		0	0	0	0	0
58090010	与棉混制金属线布及含金属纱线布	10					0	0
58090020	与化纤混制金属线布及含金属纱布	10					0	0
58090090	其他金属线布及含金属纱线布	10					0	0
58101000	不见底布的刺绣品	10					0	0
58109100	棉制见底布的刺绣品	10					0	0
58109200	化学纤维制见底布刺绣品	10					0	0
58109900	其他纺织材料制见底布刺绣品	10					0	0
58110010	丝及绢丝制絎缝被褥状纺织品	10					0	0
58110020	羊毛或动物细毛制絎缝被褥状纺织品	10					0	0
58110030	棉制絎缝被褥状纺织品	10					0	0
58110040	化学纤维制絎缝被褥状纺织品	12					0	0
58110090	其他纺织材料制絎缝被褥状纺织品	10					0	0
59011010	用胶或淀粉涂布的棉或麻纺织物	10					0	0
59011020	用胶或淀粉涂布的化纤纺织物	10					0	0
59011090	用胶或淀粉涂布的其他纤维纺织物	10					0	0
59019010	制成的油画布	10					0	0
59019091	棉或麻制描图布、帽里硬衬布等	10		0	0	0	0	0
59019092	化纤制描图布、帽里硬衬布等	10					0	0
59019099	其他纺织纤维制描图布、帽里硬衬布等	10					0	0
59021010	聚酰胺-6（尼龙-6）制的帘子布	10					0	0
59021020	聚酰胺-6，6（尼龙-6，6）制的帘子布	10					0	0
59021090	其他尼龙等高强力纱制的帘子布	10					0	0
59022000	聚酯高强力纱制的帘子布	10					0	0
59029000	粘胶纤维高强力纱制帘子布	10					0	0
59031010	用聚氯乙烯浸、涂的绝缘布或带	10					0	0
59031020	用聚氯乙烯浸、涂的人造革	10					0	0
59031090	用聚氯乙烯浸、涂的其他纺织物	10					0	0
59032010	用聚氨基甲酸酯浸、涂的绝缘布或带	10					0	0
59032020	用聚氨基甲酸酯浸、涂的人造革	10					0	0
59032090	用聚氨基甲酸酯浸、涂的其他纺织物	10					0	0
59039010	用其他塑料浸、涂的绝缘布或带	10					0	0
59039020	用其他塑料浸、涂的人造革	10					0	0
59039090	用其他塑料浸、涂的其他纺织物	10		0	0	0	0	0
59041000	列诺伦(亚麻油地毡)	14					0	
59049000	以织物为底涂布的铺地品	14					0	
59050000	糊墙织物	10					0	0
59061010	用橡胶处理宽≤20cm纺织绝缘胶粘带	10					0	0
59061090	用橡胶处理宽≤20cm其他纺丝胶粘带	10					0	0
59069100	用橡胶处理的针织或钩编的纺织物	10					0	0
59069910	用橡胶处理宽其他绝缘布或带	10					0	0
59069990	用橡胶处理的其他纺织物	10					0	0
59070010	用其他材料浸、涂的绝缘布或带	10					0	0
59070020	用其他材料浸、涂的已绘制画布	10					0	0
59070090	用其他材料浸、涂的其他纺织物	10					0	0

税则号列	商品名称（简称）	最惠税率	亚太2国	东盟			最不发达35国	最不发达4国
				缅	老	柬		
59080000	纺织材料制灯芯、炉芯等和煤气灯纱筒及纱罩	10					0	0
59090000	纺织材料制水龙软管及类似管子	8					0	0
59100000	纺织材料制的传动带或输送带及带料	8					0	0
59111010	包覆纺锤用浸胶的起绒狭幅织物	8					0	0
59111090	其他涂胶等针布及专门技术用途的纺织物起绒狭幅织物	8					0	0
59112000	筛布	8					0	0
59113100	造纸等机器用轻的环状或有联接装置的布或毡呢	8					0	0
59113200	造纸等机器用重的环状或有联接装置的布或毡呢	8					0	0
59114000	用于榨油机器或类似机器的滤布	8					0	0
59119000	其他专门技术用途纺织产品及制品	8					0	0
60011000	针织或钩编的长毛绒织物	10					0	0
60012100	棉制针织或钩编的毛圈绒头织物	10					0	0
60012200	化纤制针织或钩编毛圈绒头织物	10					0	0
60012900	其他材料制针织或钩编毛圈绒头布	12					0	
60019100	棉制针织或钩编起绒织物	10					0	0
60019200	化纤制针织或钩编起绒织物	10					0	0
60019900	其他纤维制针织或钩编起绒织物	12					0	
60024010	宽≤30cm，弹性纱线≥5%棉针织、钩编织物	10					0	0
60024020	宽≤30cm，弹性纱线≥5%丝及绢丝制针织、钩编织物	10					0	0
60024030	宽≤30cm，弹性纱线≥5%合成纤维制针织、钩编织物	10					0	0
60024040	宽≤30cm，弹性纱线≥5%人造纤维制针织、钩编织物	10					0	0
60024090	宽≤30cm，弹性纱线≥5%其他纺织材料针织、钩编织物	10					0	0
60029010	宽≤30cm含橡胶线的棉针织、钩编织物	10		0	0	0	0	0
60029020	宽≤30cm含橡胶线的丝及绢丝制针织、钩编织物	10					0	0
60029030	宽≤30cm含橡胶线的合成纤维制针织、钩编织物	10		0	0	0	0	0
60029040	宽≤30cm含橡胶线的人造纤维制针织、钩编织物	10					0	0
60029090	宽≤30cm含橡胶线的其他纺织材料针织、钩编织物	10					0	0
60031000	宽≤30cm羊毛或动物细毛制的针织、钩编织物	10					0	0
60032000	宽≤30cm其他棉制的针织、钩编织物	10					0	0
60033000	宽≤30cm合成纤维制的针织、钩编织物	10					0	0
60034000	宽≤30cm人造纤维制的针织、钩编织物	10					0	0
60039000	宽≤30cm其他针织、钩编织物	10					0	0
60041010	宽>30cm，弹性纱线≥5%棉针织、钩编织物	10		0	0	0	0	0
60041020	宽>30cm，弹性纱线≥5%丝及绢丝制针织、钩编织物	10					0	0
60041030	宽>30cm，弹性纱线≥5%合成纤维制针织、钩编织物	10					0	0
60041040	宽>30cm，弹性纱线≥5%人造纤维制针织、钩编织物	10					0	0
60041090	宽>30cm，弹性纱线≥5%其他纺织材料针织、钩编织物	10					0	0
60049010	宽>30cm含橡胶线的棉针织、钩编织物	10					0	0
60049020	宽>30cm含橡胶线的丝及绢丝制针织、钩编织物	10					0	0
60049030	宽>30cm含橡胶线的合成纤维制针织、钩编织物	10					0	0
60049040	宽>30cm含橡胶线的人造纤维制针织、钩编织物	10					0	0
60049090	宽>30cm含橡胶线的其他纺织材料针织、钩编织物	10					0	0
60052100	未漂白或漂白棉制的其他经编织物	10					0	0
60052200	染色棉制的其他经编织物	10					0	0
60052300	色织棉制的其他经编织物	10					0	0
60052400	印花棉制的其他经编织物	10					0	0
60053100	未漂白或漂白合成纤维制的其他经编织物	10					0	0
60053200	染色合成纤维制的其他经编织物	10		0	0	0	0	0
60053300	色织合成纤维制的其他经编织物	10					0	0
60053400	印花合成纤维制的其他经编织物	10					0	0
60054100	未漂白或漂白人造纤维制的其他经编织物	10					0	0
60054200	染色人造纤维制的其他经编织物	10					0	0
60054300	色织人造纤维制的其他经编织物	10					0	0
60054400	印花人造纤维制的其他经编织物	10					0	0
60059010	羊毛或动物细毛制的其他经编织物	12					0	
60059090	其他纺织材料经编织物	12					0	
60061000	羊毛或动物细毛制的其他针织、钩编织物	12					0	
60062100	未漂白或漂白棉制的其他针织、钩编织物	10					0	0

税则号列	商品名称（简称）	最惠税率	亚太2国	东盟			最不发达35国	最不发达4国
				缅	老	柬		
60062200	染色棉制的其他针织、钩编织物	10		0	0	0	0	0
60062300	色织棉制的其他针织、钩编织物	10		0	0	0	0	0
60062400	印花棉制的其他针织、钩编织物	10					0	0
60063100	未漂白或漂白合成纤维制的其他针织、钩编织物	10					0	0
60063200	染色合成纤维制的其他针织、钩编织物	10					0	0
60063300	色织合成纤维制的其他针织、钩编织物	10					0	0
60063400	印花合成纤维制的其他针织、钩编织物	10					0	0
60064100	未漂白或漂白人造纤维制的其他针织、钩编织物	10					0	0
60064200	染色人造纤维制的其他针织、钩编织物	10					0	0
60064300	色织人造纤维制的其他针织、钩编织物	10					0	0
60064400	印花人造纤维制的其他针织、钩编织物	10					0	0
60069000	未列名针织、钩编织物	12					0	
61012000	棉制针织或钩编男式大衣、防风衣	17.5					0	0
61013000	化纤制针织或钩编男式大衣等	17.5					0	0
61019010	毛制针织或钩编男式大衣、防风衣	25					0	
61019090	其他纺织材料制针织或钩编男式大衣、防风衣	17.5					0	
61021000	毛制针织或钩编女式大衣、防风衣	25					0	
61022000	棉制针织或钩编女式大衣、防风衣	17.5					0	0
61023000	化纤制针织或钩编女式大衣等	17.5					0	0
61029000	其他纺织材料制针织或钩编女式大衣、防风衣	20					0	
61031010	毛制针织或钩编男式西服套装	25					0	
61031020	合纤制针织或钩编男西服套装	25					0	
61031090	其他纺织材料制针织或钩编男式西服套装	17.5			0		0	0
61032200	棉制针织或钩编男式便服套装	20			0		0	0
61032300	合纤制针织或钩编男便服套装	25					0	
61032910	毛制针织或钩编男式便服套装	25					0	
61032990	其他纺织材料制针织或钩编男式便服套装	25			0		0	0
61033100	毛制针织或钩编男式上衣	16					0	
61033200	棉制针织或钩编男式上衣	16		0	0	0	0	0
61033300	合纤制针织或钩编男式上衣	19				0	0	0
61033900	其他纺织材料制针织或钩编男式上衣	16			0	0	0	0
61034100	毛制针织或钩编男长裤、工装裤等	16	0				0	0
61034200	棉制针织或钩编男长裤、工装裤等	16	6.4	0	0	0	0	0
61034300	合纤制针织或钩编男长裤等	17.5	0			0	0	0
61034900	其他纺织材料制针织或钩编男长裤等	16	0		0	0	0	0
61041300	合纤制针织或钩编女西服套装	25					0	
61041910	毛制针织或钩编女式西服套装	17.5					0	0
61041920	棉制针织或钩编女式西服套装	17.5			0		0	0
61041990	其他纺织材料制针织或钩编女式西服套装	17.5			0		0	0
61042200	棉制针织或钩编女式便服套装	17.5			0		0	0
61042300	合纤制针织或钩编女便服套装	25					0	
61042910	毛制针织或钩编女式便服套装	17.5					0	
61042990	其他纺织材料制针织或钩编女式便服套装	15					0	0
61043100	毛制针织女式上衣	16					0	0
61043200	棉制针织女式上衣	16		0	0	0	0	0
61043300	合纤制针织女上衣	19				0	0	0
61043900	其他纺织材料制针织女上衣	16				0	0	0
61044100	毛制针织或钩编连衣裙	16					0	
61044200	棉制针织或钩编连衣裙	16					0	0
61044300	合纤制针织或钩编连衣裙	17.5				0	0	0
61044400	人纤制针织或钩编连衣裙	16				0	0	0
61044900	其他纺织材料制针织或钩编连衣裙	16				0	0	0
61045100	毛制针织或钩编裙子及裙裤	14					0	
61045200	棉制针织裙子及裙裤	14					0	0
61045300	合纤制针织或钩编裙子及裙裤	16				0	0	0
61045900	其他纺织材料制针织或钩编裙子及裙裤	14		0	0	0	0	0
61046100	毛制针织或钩编女长裤、工装裤等	16					0	0
61046200	棉制针织或钩编女长裤、工装裤等	16	6.4				0	0

税则号列	商品名称（简称）	最惠税率	亚太2国	东盟			最不发达35国	最不发达4国
				缅	老	柬		
61046300	合纤制针织或钩编女长裤等	17.5					0	0
61046900	其他纺织材料制针织或钩编女长裤等	16	0				0	0
61051000	棉制针织或钩编男衬衫	16	11.2	0	0	0	0	0
61052000	化纤制针织或钩编男衬衫	17.5	0				0	0
61059000	其他纺织材料制针织或钩编男衬衫	16	0				0	0
61061000	棉制针织或钩编女衬衫	16	6.4	0	0	0	0	0
61062000	化纤制针织或钩编女衬衫	17.5	0				0	0
61069000	其他纺织材料制针织或钩编女衬衫	16	0				0	0
61071100	棉制针织或钩编男内裤及三角裤	14	5.6	0	0	0	0	0
61071200	化纤制针织或钩编男内裤及三角裤	16					0	
61071910	丝及绢丝制针织或钩编男内裤及三角裤	14					0	
61071990	其他纺织材料制针织或钩编男内裤及三角裤	14					0	
61072100	棉制针织或钩编男长睡衣及睡衣裤	14	5.6	0	0	0	0	0
61072200	化纤制针织或钩编男睡衣裤	16	0				0	0
61072910	丝及绢丝制针织或钩编男长睡衣及睡衣裤	14	0				0	0
61072990	其他纺织材料制针织或钩编男长睡衣及睡衣裤	14	0	0	0	0	0	0
61079100	棉制针织或钩编男浴衣、晨衣	14					0	
61079910	化纤制针织或钩编男浴衣、晨衣	16					0	
61079990	其他纺织材料制针织或钩编男浴衣、晨衣	14					0	
61081100	化纤制针织或钩编长衬裙及衬裙	16					0	
61081910	棉制针织或钩编女式长衬裙及衬裙	14					0	0
61081920	丝及绢丝制针织或钩编女式长衬裙及衬裙	14					0	
61081990	其他纺织材料制针织或钩编女式长衬裙及衬裙	14					0	
61082100	棉制针织或钩编女三角裤及短衬裤	14		0	0	0	0	0
61082200	化纤制针织或钩编女三角裤及短衬裤	16					0	0
61082910	丝及绢丝制针织或钩编女三角裤及短衬裤	14					0	
61082990	其他纺织材料制针织或钩编女三角裤及短衬裤	14					0	
61083100	棉制针织或钩编女睡衣及睡衣裤	14	5.6	0	0	0	0	0
61083200	化纤制针织或钩编女睡衣及睡衣裤	16	0				0	0
61083910	丝及绢丝制针织或钩编女睡衣及睡衣裤	14	0				0	0
61083990	其他纺织材料制针织或钩编女睡衣及睡衣裤	14	0				0	0
61089100	棉制针织或钩编女浴衣、晨衣	14		0	0	0	0	0
61089200	化纤制针织或钩编女浴衣、晨衣	16					0	0
61089900	其他纺织材料制针织或钩编女浴衣、晨衣	14					0	
61091000	棉制针织或钩编T恤衫、汗衫等	14		0	0	0	0	0
61099010	丝及绢丝制针织或钩编T恤衫、汗衫等	14	0				0	0
61099090	其他纺织材料制针织或钩编T恤衫、汗衫等	14	0	0	0	0	0	0
61101100	羊毛制针织或钩编套头衫等	14	0	0	0	0	0	0
61101200	喀什米尔山羊细毛制针织或钩编套头衫等	14					0	0
61101910	其他山羊细毛制针织或钩编套头衫等	14					0	0
61101920	兔毛制针织或钩编套头衫等	14					0	
61101990	其他毛制针织或钩编套头衫等	14					0	0
61102000	棉制针织或钩编套头衫等	14	5.6	0	0	0	0	0
61103000	化纤制针织或钩编套头衫等	16	0				0	0
61109010	丝及绢丝制针织或钩编套头衫等	14	0				0	0
61109090	其他纺织材料制针织或钩编套头衫等	14	0				0	0
61112000	棉制针织或钩编婴儿服装及附件	14					0	0
61113000	合纤制针织婴儿服装及附件	16					0	0
61119010	毛制针织或钩编婴儿服装及附件	14					0	0
61119090	其他纺织材料制针织或钩编婴儿服装及附件	14					0	
61121100	棉制针织或钩编运动服	16					0	
61121200	合纤制针织或钩编运动服	17.5					0	0
61121900	其他纺织材料制针织或钩编运动服	16					0	
61122010	棉制针织或钩编滑雪服	16					0	0
61122090	其他纺织材料制针织或钩编滑雪服	19					0	
61123100	合纤制针织或钩编男式游泳服	17.5					0	
61123900	其他纺织材料制针织或钩编男式游泳服	16					0	
61124100	合纤制针织或钩编女式游泳服	17.5					0	

税则号列	商品名称（简称）	最惠税率	亚太2国	东盟			最不发达35国	最不发达4国
				缅	老	柬		
61124900	其他纺织材料制针织或钩编女式游泳服	16					0	
61130000	涂层经处理针织或钩编织物制服装	16	0				0	0
61142000	棉制针织或钩编的其他服装	16	6.4				0	0
61143000	化纤制针织或钩编的其他服装	17.5					0	0
61149010	毛制针织或钩编的其他服装	16					0	
61149090	其他纺织材料制针织或钩编的其他服装	16					0	
61151000	渐紧压袜类连裤袜	16					0	
61152100	单丝＜67 分特合纤制连裤袜等	16					0	
61152200	单丝≥67 分特合纤制连裤袜等	16					0	
61152910	棉制针织或钩编连裤袜及紧身裤袜	14					0	0
61152990	其他纺织材料制针织连裤袜及紧身裤袜	14					0	
61153000	单丝<67 分特制针织或钩编女统袜	14	0				0	0
61159400	毛制针织或钩编短袜及其他袜类	14					0	
61159500	棉制针织或钩编短袜及其他袜类	14					0	0
61159600	合纤制针织或钩编短袜及其他袜类	16					0	0
61159900	其他纺织材料制针织或钩编短袜及其他袜类	14					0	
61161000	塑料或橡胶浸渍的针织或钩织手套	14					0	0
61169100	毛制其他针织或钩编手套	14					0	0
61169200	棉制其他针织或钩编手套	14					0	
61169300	合纤制其他针织或钩编手套	16					0	0
61169900	其他纺织材料制针织或钩编手套	14					0	0
61171011	山羊绒制披巾、头巾、围巾、披纱、面纱及类似品	14					0	0
61171019	其他动物细毛制披巾、头巾、围巾、披纱、面纱及类似品	14					0	0
61171020	羊毛制披巾、头巾、围巾、披纱、面纱及类似品	14					0	0
61171090	其他制的披巾、头巾、围巾、披纱、面纱及类似品	14					0	0
61178010	针织或钩编领带及领结	14					0	0
61178090	针织或钩编其他衣着附件	14					0	0
61179000	其他针织或钩编衣着零件	14					0	0
62011100	毛制男式大衣、斗篷及类似品	16					0	0
62011210	棉制男式羽绒服	16					0	
62011290	棉制男式大衣、斗篷及类似品	16					0	0
62011310	化纤制男式羽绒服	17.5					0	0
62011390	化纤制男式大衣、斗篷及类似品	17.5					0	0
62011900	其他纺织材料制男式大衣、斗篷及类似品	16					0	0
62019100	毛制男式带风帽防寒短上衣、防风衣	16					0	0
62019210	棉制男式其他羽绒服	16					0	0
62019290	棉制男式带风帽防寒短上衣、防风衣	16		0	0	0	0	0
62019310	化纤制男式其他羽绒服	17.5					0	0
62019390	化纤制男式防寒短上衣、防风衣	17.5					0	0
62019900	其他纺织材料制男式防寒短上衣、防风衣	16		0			0	0
62021100	毛制女式大衣、斗篷及类似品等	16					0	0
62021210	棉制女式羽绒服	16					0	
62021290	棉制女式大衣、斗篷及类似品等	16					0	0
62021310	化纤制女式羽绒服	19					0	0
62021390	化纤制女式大衣、斗篷及类似品	19					0	0
62021900	其他纺织材料制女式大衣、斗篷及类似品	16					0	0
62029100	毛制女式带风帽防寒短上衣、防风衣	16					0	
62029210	棉制女式其他羽绒服	16					0	
62029290	棉制女式带风帽防寒短上衣、防风衣	16					0	0
62029310	化纤制女式其他羽绒服	17.5					0	0
62029390	化纤制女式防风衣等	17.5					0	0
62029900	其他纺织材料制防风衣、防风短上衣等	16					0	0
62031100	毛制男式西服套装	17.5					0	0
62031200	合纤制男式西服套装	17.5					0	0
62031910	丝及绢丝制男式西服套装	17.5					0	
62031990	其他纺织材料制男式西服套装	17.5					0	
62032200	棉制男式便服套装	17.5					0	0
62032300	合纤制男式便服套装	17.5					0	0

税则号列	商品名称（简称）	最惠税率	亚太2国	东盟			最不发达35国	最不发达4国
				缅	老	柬		
62032910	丝及绢丝制男式便服套装	17.5					0	
62032920	毛制男式便服套装	17.5					0	
62032990	其他纺织材料制男式便服套装	17.5					0	
62033100	毛制男式上衣	16	9.6	0	0	0	0	0
62033200	棉制男式上衣	16	11.2	0	0	0	0	0
62033300	合纤制男式上衣	17.5					0	0
62033910	丝及绢丝制男式上衣	16	9.6				0	0
62033990	其他纺织材料制男式上衣	16	9.6				0	0
62034100	毛制男式长裤、工装裤等	16	0				0	0
62034210	棉制男式阿拉伯裤	16	11.2				0	
62034290	棉制男式长裤、工装裤等	16	11.2	0	0	0	0	0
62034310	合成纤维制男式阿拉伯裤	17.5					0	
62034390	合纤制男式长裤、工装裤等	17.5					0	0
62034910	其他纺织材料制男式阿拉伯裤	16	0				0	0
62034990	其他纺织材料制男童裤、工装裤	16	0				0	0
62041100	毛制女式西服套装	17.5					0	
62041200	棉制女式西服套装	17.5					0	
62041300	合纤制女式西服套装	17.5					0	
62041910	丝及绢丝制女式西服套装	17.5					0	
62041990	其他纺织材料制女式西服套装	17.5					0	
62042100	毛制女式便服套装	17.5					0	
62042200	棉制女式便服套装	17.5					0	
62042300	合纤制女式便服套装	20					0	
62042910	丝及绢丝制女式便服套装	20					0	
62042990	其他纺织材料制女式便服套装	14					0	
62043100	毛制女式上衣	16					0	0
62043200	棉制女式上衣	16	6.4	0	0	0	0	0
62043300	合纤制女式上衣	17.5	0				0	0
62043910	丝及绢丝制女式上衣	16	0				0	0
62043990	其他纺织材料制女式上衣	16	0				0	0
62044100	毛制连衣裙	16					0	0
62044200	棉制连衣裙	16		0	0	0	0	0
62044300	合纤制女式连衣裙	17.5					0	0
62044400	人纤制女式连衣裙	16					0	0
62044910	丝及绢丝制连衣裙	16					0	0
62044990	其他纺织材料制连衣裙	16					0	0
62045100	毛制裙子及裙裤	14					0	0
62045200	棉制裙子及裙裤	14					0	0
62045300	合纤制裙子及裙裤	16					0	0
62045910	丝及绢丝制裙子及裙裤	14					0	0
62045990	其他纺织材料制裙子及裙裤	14					0	0
62046100	毛制女式长裤、工装裤等	16					0	0
62046200	棉制女式长裤、工装裤等	16	11.2	0	0	0	0	0
62046300	合纤制女式长裤、工装裤等	17.5					0	0
62046900	其他纺织材料制女式长裤、工装裤等	16					0	0
62052000	棉制男衬衫	16	6.4	0	0	0	0	0
62053000	化纤制男衬衫	16	0				0	0
62059010	丝及绢丝制男衬衫	16	0				0	0
62059020	毛制男衬衫	16	0				0	0
62059090	其他纺织材料制男衬衫	16	0				0	0
62061000	丝及绢丝制女式衬衫	16					0	0
62062000	毛制女衬衫	16					0	
62063000	棉制女衬衫	16	6.4	0	0	0	0	0
62064000	化纤制女衬衫	17.5					0	0
62069000	其他纺织材料制女衬衫	16	0				0	0
62071100	棉制男式内裤及三角裤	14					0	0
62071910	丝制男式内裤及三角裤	14					0	
62071920	化纤制男式内裤及三角裤	16					0	

税则号列	商品名称（简称）	最惠税率	亚太2国	东盟			最不发达35国	最不发达4国
				缅	老	柬		
62071990	其他纺织材料制男式内裤及三角裤	14					0	
62072100	棉制男式长睡衣及睡衣裤	14		0	0	0	0	0
62072200	化纤制男式长睡衣及睡衣裤	16					0	
62072910	丝及绢丝制男式长睡衣及睡衣裤	14					0	
62072990	其他纺织材料制男式长睡衣及睡衣裤	14		0	0	0	0	0
62079100	棉制男式浴衣、晨衣及类似品	14					0	0
62079910	丝及绢丝制男浴衣、晨衣及类似品	14					0	
62079920	化纤制男浴衣、晨衣及类似品	16					0	0
62079990	其他纺织材料制男浴衣、晨衣及类似品	14					0	0
62081100	化纤制长衬裙及衬裙	16					0	
62081910	丝及绢丝制长衬裙及衬裙	14					0	
62081920	棉制长衬裙及衬裙	14					0	0
62081990	其他纺织材料制长衬裙及衬裙	14					0	
62082100	棉制女式睡衣及睡衣裤	14		0	0	0	0	0
62082200	化纤制女式睡衣及睡衣裤	16		0	0	0	0	0
62082910	丝及绢丝制女式睡衣及睡衣裤	14					0	
62082990	其他纺织材料制女式睡衣及睡衣裤	14					0	
62089100	棉制女式背心.内衣.浴衣及类似品	14		0	0	0	0	0
62089200	化纤制女式背心、内衣及类似品	16		0	0	0	0	0
62089910	丝制女式背心、内衣及类似品	14					0	
62089990	其他纺织材料制女式背心、内衣及类似	14					0	0
62092000	棉制婴儿服装及衣着附件	14					0	0
62093000	合纤制婴儿服装及衣着附件	16					0	0
62099010	毛制婴儿服装及衣着附件	14					0	
62099090	其他纺织材料制婴儿服装及衣着附件	14					0	
62101010	毛制毡呢或无纺织物服装	16	0				0	0
62101020	棉或麻制毡呢或无纺织物服装	16	6.4				0	
62101030	化纤制毡呢或无纺织物服装	17.5	0				0	0
62101090	其他纺织材料制毡呢或无纺织物服装	16	0				0	0
62102000	用塑料、橡胶等处理的织物制男大衣等	16	0				0	0
62103000	用塑料、橡胶等处理的织物制女大衣等	16					0	0
62104000	用塑料、橡胶等处理的织物制的其他男式服装	16	0				0	0
62105000	用塑料、橡胶等处理的织物制的其他女式服装	16	0				0	0
62111100	男式游泳服	16					0	
62111200	女式游泳服	16					0	0
62112010	棉制滑雪服	16					0	0
62112090	其他纺织材料制滑雪服	19					0	
62113210	棉制男式阿拉伯袍	16					0	
62113220	棉制男式运动服	16					0	0
62113290	棉制其他男式服装	16					0	0
62113310	化纤制男式阿拉伯袍	17.5					0	
62113320	化纤制男式运动服	18					0	0
62113390	化纤制其他男式服装	17.5					0	0
62113910	丝及绢丝制男式运动服及其他服装	16					0	
62113920	毛制男式运动服及其他服装	16					0	
62113990	其他纺织材料制男式运动服及其他服装	16					0	
62114210	棉制女式运动服	16					0	0
62114290	棉制其他女式服装	16					0	0
62114310	化纤制女式运动服	17.5					0	0
62114390	化纤制其他女式服装	17.5					0	0
62114910	丝及绢丝制女式运动服及其他服装	16					0	
62114990	其他纺织材料制女式运动服及其他服装	16					0	0
62121010	化纤制胸罩	16		0	0	0	0	0
62121090	其他纺织材料制胸罩	14					0	0
62122010	化纤制束腰带及腹带	16					0	
62122090	其他纺织材料制束腰带及腹带	14					0	0
62123010	化纤制紧身胸衣	16					0	
62123090	其他纺织材料制紧身胸衣	14					0	0

税则号列	商品名称（简称）	最惠税率	亚太2国	东盟			最不发达35国	最不发达4国
				缅	老	柬		
62129010	化纤制吊裤带、吊袜带等	16					0	
62129090	其他纺织材料制吊裤带、吊袜带等	14					0	
62132010	棉制刺绣手帕	14			0		0	0
62132090	其他棉制手帕	14			0		0	0
62139020	其他纺织材料制刺绣手帕	14			0		0	0
62139090	其他纺织材料制手帕	14			0		0	0
62141000	丝制披巾、头巾、围巾及类似品	14					0	0
62142010	羊毛制披巾、领巾、围巾、披纱、面纱及类似品	14					0	0
62142020	山羊绒制披巾、领巾、围巾、披纱、面纱及类似品	14					0	0
62142090	其他动物细毛制披巾、领巾、围巾、披纱、面纱及类似品	14					0	0
62143000	合纤制披巾、头巾及类似品	16					0	0
62144000	人纤制披巾、头巾及类似品	14					0	0
62149000	其他纺织材料制披巾、头巾及类似品	14					0	0
62151000	丝及绢丝制领带及领结	14					0	0
62152000	化纤制领带及领结	16					0	0
62159000	其他纺织材料制领带及领结	14					0	0
62160000	非针织非钩编手套	14					0	0
62171010	非针织非钩编袜子及袜套	14					0	
62171020	非针织非钩编和服腰带	14					0	0
62171090	非针织非钩编服装或衣着附件	14		0	0	0	0	0
62179000	非针织非钩编服装或衣着零件	14		0	0	0	0	0
63011000	电暖毯	16					0	
63012000	毛制毯子及旅行毯	16					0	0
63013000	棉制毯子及旅行毯	16					0	0
63014000	合纤制毯子及旅行毯	17.5					0	0
63019000	其他纺织材料制毯子及旅行毯	16					0	0
63021010	棉制针织或钩编的床上用织物制品	14					0	0
63021090	其他纺织材料制针织或钩编的床上用织物制品	14					0	
63022110	棉制印花床单	14					0	0
63022190	棉制印花床上用织物制品	14					0	0
63022210	化纤制印花床单	16					0	0
63022290	化纤制印花床上用织物制品	16					0	0
63022910	丝及绢丝制印花床上用织物制品	14					0	
63022920	麻制印花床上用织物制品	14					0	
63022990	其他纺织材料制印花床上用织物制品	14					0	
63023110	棉制刺绣其他床上用织物制品	14					0	0
63023191	棉制其他床单	14					0	0
63023192	棉制其他毛巾被	14					0	
63023199	棉制其他床上用织物制品	14					0	0
63023210	化纤制刺绣其他床上用织物制品	16					0	0
63023290	化纤制其他床上用织物制品	16					0	0
63023910	丝及绢丝制其他床上用织物制品	14					0	
63023921	麻制刺绣的其他床上用织物制品	14					0	
63023929	麻制其他床上用织物制品	14					0	
63023991	其他纺织材料制刺绣床上用织物制品	14					0	
63023999	其他纺织材料制其他床上用织物制品	14					0	0
63024010	手工针织或钩编的餐桌用织物制品	14					0	
63024090	其他针织或钩编的餐桌用织物制品	14					0	0
63025110	棉制刺绣其他餐桌用织物制品	14					0	
63025190	棉制其他餐桌用织物制品	14					0	0
63025310	化纤制刺绣其他餐桌织物制品	14					0	
63025390	化纤制其他餐桌用织物制品	16					0	0
63025911	亚麻制刺绣其他餐桌用织物制品	14					0	
63025919	亚麻制其他餐桌用织物制品	14					0	
63025990	其他纺织材料制餐桌用织物制品	14					0	
63026010	棉制浴巾	14					0	0
63026090	棉制盥洗及厨房用毛巾织物	14					0	0
63029100	棉制其他盥洗及厨房织物制品	14					0	0

税则号列	商品名称（简称）	最惠税率	亚太2国	东盟			最不发达35国	最不发达4国
				缅	老	柬		
63029300	化纤制其他盥洗及厨房织物制品	16					0	
63029910	亚麻制其他盥洗及厨房织物制品	14					0	
63029990	其他材料制其他盥洗及厨房织物	14					0	
63031210	合纤制针织的窗帘等	16					0	
63031220	合纤制钩编的窗帘等	16					0	
63031931	棉制针织的窗帘等	14					0	0
63031932	棉制钩编的窗帘等	14					0	
63031991	其他纺织材料制针织的窗帘等	14					0	
63031992	其他纺织材料制钩编的窗帘等	14					0	
63039100	棉制非针织非钩编窗帘等	14					0	0
63039200	合纤制非针织非钩编窗帘等	16					0	0
63039900	其他纺织材料制非针织非钩编窗帘等	14					0	0
63041121	手工针织床罩	14					0	
63041129	非手工针织床罩	14					0	
63041131	手工钩编床罩	14					0	0
63041139	非手工钩编床罩	14					0	0
63041910	丝及绢丝制非针织非钩编床罩	14					0	
63041921	棉或麻制非针织非钩编刺绣床罩	14					0	
63041929	棉或麻制其他非针织非钩编床罩	14					0	0
63041931	化纤制非针织非钩编刺绣床罩	16					0	
63041939	化纤制其他非针织非钩编床罩	16					0	
63041991	其他纺织材料制非针织、非钩编刺绣床罩	14					0	
63041999	其他材料制其他非针织非钩编床罩	14					0	
63049121	手工针织的其他装饰制品	14					0	0
63049129	非手工针织的其他装饰制品	14					0	0
63049131	手工钩编的其他装饰制品	14					0	
63049139	非手工钩编的其他装饰制品	14					0	
63049210	棉制非针织、非钩编的其他刺绣装饰制品	14					0	
63049290	棉制非针织或钩编的其他装饰制品	14					0	0
63049310	合纤制非针织、非钩编其他刺绣装饰制品	16					0	
63049390	合纤制其他非针织、非钩编装饰制品	16					0	0
63049910	丝制非针织非钩编的装饰制品	14					0	0
63049921	麻制非针织、非钩编的其他刺绣装饰制品	14					0	
63049929	麻制其他非针织非钩编的装饰制品	14					0	
63049990	其他纺织材料制非针织非钩编装饰制品	14					0	0
63051000	黄麻或其他韧皮纤维制货物包装袋	10	0				0	0
63052000	棉制货物包装袋	16					0	0
63053200	化纤制的散装货物储运软袋	16					0	0
63053300	聚乙烯或聚丙烯扁条制其他货物包装袋	16					0	
63053900	其他化纤制货物包装袋	16					0	
63059000	其他纺织材料制货物包装袋	14					0	0
63061200	合纤制油苫布、天篷及遮阳篷	16					0	
63061910	麻制油苫布、天篷及遮阳篷	14					0	
63061920	棉制油苫布、天篷及遮阳篷	14					0	
63061990	其他纺织材料制油苫布、天篷及遮阳篷	14					0	
63062200	合纤制帐篷	16					0	0
63062910	棉制帐篷	14					0	
63062990	其他纺织材料制帐篷	14					0	0
63063010	合纤制风帆	16					0	
63063090	其他纺织材料制风帆	14					0	
63064010	棉制充气褥垫	14					0	
63064020	化纤制充气褥垫	16					0	0
63064090	其他纺织材料制充气褥垫	14					0	
63069010	棉制其他野营用品	14					0	0
63069020	麻制其他野营用品	14					0	
63069030	化学纤维制其他野营用品	16					0	
63069090	其他野营用品	14					0	
63071000	擦地布、擦碗布等	14					0	

税则号列	商品名称（简称）	最惠税率	亚太2国	东盟			最不发达35国	最不发达4国
				缅	老	柬		
63072000	救生衣及安全带	14					0	0
63079000	其他纺织材料制成品	14		0	0	0	0	0
63080000	零售包装成套物品	14					0	
63090000	旧衣物	14					0	
63101000	经分拣的纺织材料制碎织物等	14					0	0
63109000	纺织材料制其他碎织物等	14		0	0	0	0	0
64011010	橡胶制鞋面的装金属护头的塑料、橡胶制防水鞋靴	24					0	
64011090	塑料制鞋面的装金属护头的塑料、橡胶制防水鞋靴	24					0	
64019210	橡胶制鞋面的橡胶、塑料底及面的中、短统防水靴	24					0	
64019290	塑料制鞋面的橡胶、塑料底及面的中、短统防水靴	24					0	
64019900	其他橡胶、塑料制外底及鞋面防水靴	24					0	
64021200	橡胶、塑料底及面的滑雪靴	10					0	0
64021900	橡胶、塑料制底及面的其他运动靴	24					0	
64022000	橡胶、塑料的将鞋面条带栓塞在鞋底上的鞋	24					0	
64029100	其他橡胶、塑料短统靴(过踝)	24					0	
64029910	橡胶制鞋面的其他橡胶、塑料鞋靴	24					0	0
64029921	以机织物或其他纺织材料作衬底的	24					0	0
64029929	塑料制鞋面的其他橡胶、塑料鞋靴	24					0	0
64031200	皮革制鞋面的滑雪靴	24				0	0	0
64031900	皮革制鞋面的其他运动鞋靴	15				0	0	0
64032000	皮革条带为鞋面的皮底鞋	24				0	0	0
64034000	装有金属护鞋头的其他皮革面鞋靴	24				0	0	0
64035111	低于小腿的内底长度＜24cm 的皮革制外底皮革面的短统靴(过踝)	10				0	0	0
64035119	低于小腿的内底长度⩾24cm 的皮革制外底皮革面的短统靴(过踝)	10				0	0	0
64035191	其他内底长度＜24cm 的皮革制外底的皮革面短统靴（过踝）	10				0	0	0
64035199	其他内底长度⩾24cm 的皮革制外底皮革面短统靴（过踝）	10				0	0	0
64035900	皮革制外底的皮革面其他鞋靴	10				0	0	0
64039111	其他低于小腿的内底长度＜24cm 的皮革面的短统靴(过踝)	10				0	0	0
64039119	其他低于小腿的内底长度⩾24cm 的皮革面的短统靴(过踝)	10				0	0	0
64039191	其他内底长度＜24cm 的皮革面短统靴（过踝）	10				0	0	0
64039199	其他内底长度⩾24cm 的皮革面短统靴（过踝）	10				0	0	0
64039900	皮革制面的其他鞋靴	10				0	0	0
64041100	纺织材料制鞋面的运动鞋靴	24					0	
64041900	纺织材料制鞋面胶底的其他鞋靴	24					0	
64042000	纺织材料制鞋面皮革底的鞋靴	24					0	
64051010	橡胶、塑料、皮革及再生皮革制外底的皮革或再生皮革制面的其他鞋靴	24					0	
64051090	其他材料制外底的皮革或再生皮革制面的其他鞋靴	24					0	
64052000	纺织材料制面的其他鞋靴	22					0	
64059010	橡胶、塑料、皮革及再生皮革制外底的其他材料制面的鞋靴	15					0	
64059090	其他材料制外底的其他材料制面的鞋靴	15					0	
64061000	鞋面及其零件，硬衬除外	15					0	
64062010	橡胶制的外底及鞋跟	15					0	0
64062020	塑料制的外底及鞋跟	15					0	0
64069010	木制鞋靴零件,活动式鞋内底等	15					0	
64069091	活动式鞋内底、跟垫及类似品	15					0	
64069092	护腿、裹腿和类似品及其零件	15					0	
64069099	其他鞋靴零件（包括鞋面，不论是否带有除外底以外的其他鞋底）；活动式鞋内底、跟垫及类似品；护腿、裹腿和类似品及其零件	15					0	
65010000	毡呢制帽坯及圆帽片	22					0	
65020000	编结或用条带拼制的帽坯	20					0	
65040000	编结或用条带拼制成的帽类	20					0	
65050010	发网	10					0	0
65050020	钩编的帽类	20					0	0
65050091	成品毡呢帽类	22					0	
65050099	针织或成匹织物制成的帽类	20					0	0
65061000	安全帽	10					0	
65069100	橡胶或塑料制帽类	10					0	
65069910	皮革制帽类	10					0	
65069920	毛皮制帽类	10					0	0

税则号列	商品名称（简称）	最惠税率	亚太2国	东盟			最不发达35国	最不发达4国
				缅	老	柬		
65069990	其他材料制的未列名帽类	24					0	0
65070000	帽类附件	24					0	
66011000	庭园用伞及类似品	14					0	
66019100	折叠伞	10					0	0
66019900	其他伞	10					0	
66020000	手杖、带座手杖、鞭子及类似品	10					0	
66032000	伞骨	14					0	
66039000	伞、手杖及鞭子的其他零件及饰品	14					0	0
67010000	已加工羽毛、羽绒及其制品	20					0	
67021000	塑料制花、叶、果实及其制品	20					0	
67029010	羽毛制花、叶、果实及其制品	20					0	
67029020	丝或绢丝制花、叶、果实及其制品	24					0	
67029030	化学纤维制花、叶、果实及其制品	24					0	
67029090	其他材料制花、叶、果实及其制品	20					0	
67030000	经梳理、稀疏等方法加工的人发及假发材料	20					0	
67041100	合成纺织材料制整头假发	25					0	0
67041900	合成纺织材料制其他假发、须等	25					0	0
67042000	人发制假发、须、眉及类似品	15					0	0
67049000	其他材料制假发、须眉及类似品	25					0	0
68010000	长方砌石、路缘石、扁平石	12					0	
68021010	大理石制砖、瓦、方块及类似品	24					0	0
68021090	其他石料制砖瓦、方块及类似品	20					0	
68022110	具有一个平面的大理石及制品	10					0	0
68022120	石灰华	24					0	
68022190	具有一个平面石灰华及蜡石及制品	24					0	
68022300	具有一个平面的花岗岩及制品	10					0	0
68022910	具有一个平面的其他石灰石及制品	24					0	
68022990	具有一个平面的其他石及制品	15					0	0
68029110	大理石、石灰华及蜡石制石刻	24					0	
68029190	其他大理石、石灰华及蜡石及制品	10					0	0
68029210	其他石灰石制石刻	24					0	
68029290	其他加工形式石灰石制品	10					0	0
68029311	花岗岩制墓碑石	24					0	
68029319	其他花岗岩制石刻	24					0	
68029390	其他加工形式花岗岩制品	10					0	0
68029910	其他石制成的石刻	24					0	
68029990	其他石及制品	24					0	0
68030010	板岩制品	20					0	
68030090	已加工板岩及板岩或粘聚板岩制品	20					0	
68041000	碾磨或磨浆用石磨、石碾	8					0	0
68042100	金刚石制石磨、石碾及砂轮	8					0	0
68042210	其他砂轮	8					0	0
68042290	其他石磨、石碾及类似品	8					0	0
68042310	天然石料制的砂轮	8					0	0
68042390	天然石料制其他石磨、石碾等	8					0	0
68043010	手用琢磨油石	8					0	0
68043090	手用其他磨石及抛光石	8					0	0
68051000	砂布	8					0	0
68052000	砂纸	8					0	0
68053000	其他材料为底的天然或人造研磨料	8					0	0
68061010	硅酸铝纤维及其制品	10.5					0	0
68061090	其他矿渣棉、岩石棉及类似的矿质棉（包括其相互混合物），块状、成片或成卷	10.5					0	0
68062000	页状硅石、膨胀粘土、泡沫矿渣	10.5					0	0
68069000	其他矿物材料的混合物及制品	10					0	0
68071000	成卷的沥青或类似原料的制品	12					0	
68079000	其他形状的沥青或类似原料的制品	12					0	
68080000	镶板、平板、瓦、砖及类似品	10.5					0	
68091100	纸贴面未饰的石膏板、片、砖、瓦及类似品	28					0	

税则号列	商品名称（简称）	最惠税率	亚太2国	东盟			最不发达35国	最不发达4国
				缅	老	柬		
68091900	以其他材料贴面加强的未饰石膏板	25					0	
68099000	其他石膏制品	25					0	
68101100	水泥制建筑用砖及石砌块	10.5					0	0
68101910	人造石制砖、瓦、扁平石及类似品	10.5					0	0
68101990	水泥制其他砖、瓦、扁平石	10.5					0	0
68109110	钢筋混凝土和预应力混凝土管、杆、板、桩等	10.5					0	0
68109190	其他水泥制建筑或土木工程用预制构件	10.5					0	0
68109910	铁道用水泥枕	8					0	0
68109990	水泥、混凝土或人造石制其他制品	10.5					0	0
68114010	含石棉的瓦楞板	5					0	
68114020	含石棉的片、板、砖、瓦及类似品	10.5					0	
68114030	含石棉的管子及管子配件	8					0	
68114090	含石棉的其他制品	8.4					0	
68118100	不含石棉的瓦楞板	5					0	
68118200	不含石棉的片、板、砖、瓦及类似品	10.5					0	
68118910	不含石棉的管子及管子配件	8					0	
68118990	不含石棉的其他制品	8.4					0	
68128000	青石棉或青石棉混合物制品	10.5					0	0
68129100	其他石棉或石棉混合物制的服装	10.5					0	0
68129200	其他石棉或石棉混合物制的纸、麻丝板	10.5					0	0
68129300	其他成片成卷的压缩石棉纤维接合材料	10.5					0	0
68129900	其他石棉或石棉混合物制品	10					0	0
68132010	含石棉的闸衬、闸垫	10					0	0
68132090	含石棉的磨擦料及其他用于制动等用途制品	12					0	
68138100	不含石棉的闸衬、闸垫	10					0	0
68138900	不含石棉的磨擦料及其他用于制动等用途制品	12					0	
68141000	粘聚或复制云母制的板、片、带	10.5					0	0
68149000	其他已加工的云母及其制品	10.5					0	0
68151000	非电器用的石墨或其他碳精制品	15					0	0
68152000	泥煤制品	15					0	
68159100	含菱镁矿、白云石或铬铁矿的制品	15					0	
68159920	碳纤维	17.5					0	0
68159931	碳布	17.5					0	0
68159932	碳纤维预浸料	17.5					0	0
68159939	其他碳纤维制品	17.5					0	0
68159940	玄武岩纤维及其制品	17.5					0	0
68159990	其他未列名石制品及矿物制品	17.5					0	0
69010000	硅质化石粉或类似硅土制的砖、瓦	8					0	
69021000	含＞50%镁、钙、铬耐火砖及类似品	8					0	0
69022000	含＞50%氧化铝、硅耐火砖及类似品	8					0	0
69029000	其他耐火砖及耐火陶瓷建材制品	8					0	0
69031000	含＞50%石墨其他耐火陶瓷制品	8			0		0	0
69032000	含＞50%氧化铝其他耐火陶瓷制品	8			0		0	0
69039000	其他耐火陶瓷制品	8			0		0	0
69041000	陶瓷制建筑用砖	15					0	0
69049000	陶瓷制铺地砖、支撑或填充用砖	24.5					0	
69051000	陶瓷制屋顶瓦	24.5					0	
69059000	其他建筑用陶瓷制品	24.5					0	
69060000	陶瓷套管、导管、槽管及管子配件	15					0	
69071000	未上釉的小陶瓷砖、瓦、块及类似品	24.5					0	
69079000	未上釉的大陶瓷砖、瓦、块及类似品	12					0	
69081000	上釉的小陶瓷砖、瓦、块及类似品	12					0	
69089000	上釉的大陶瓷砖、瓦、块及类似品	12					0	
69091100	实验室、化学或其他技术用瓷器	8					0	0
69091200	莫氏硬度≥9的技术用陶瓷器	8					0	0
69091900	其他实验室、化学用陶瓷器	8					0	0
69099000	农业用、运输或盛装货物用陶瓷容器	21					0	
69101000	瓷制脸盆、浴缸及类似卫生器具	10					0	0

税则号列	商品名称（简称）	最惠税率	亚太2国	东盟			最不发达35国	最不发达4国
				缅	老	柬		
69109000	陶制脸盆、浴缸及类似卫生器具	10					0	0
69111011	骨瓷餐具	12					0	0
69111019	其他餐具	12					0	0
69111021	刀具	15					0	
69111029	其他厨房器具	15					0	
69119000	其他家用或盥洗用瓷器	24.5					0	
69120010	陶餐具	15					0	0
69120090	陶制厨房器具	15					0	
69131000	瓷塑像及其他装饰用瓷制品	15					0	0
69139000	陶塑像及其他装饰用陶制品	15					0	0
69141000	其他瓷制品	24.5					0	
69149000	其他陶制品	10					0	0
70010000	废碎玻璃及玻璃块料	12					0	
70021000	未加工的玻璃球	12					0	
70022010	光导纤维预制棒	6					0	
70022090	其他未加工的玻璃棒	12					0	
70023110	光导纤维用波导级石英玻璃管	5					0	
70023190	熔融石英或熔融硅石制其他玻璃管	14					0	
70023200	其他未加工的玻璃管	12					0	
70023900	未列名、未加工的玻璃管	12					0	
70031200	铸、轧制着色的非夹丝玻璃板、片	15					0	
70031900	铸、轧制的其他非夹丝玻璃板、片	17.5					0	
70032000	铸、轧制的夹丝玻璃板、片	15					0	
70033000	铸、轧制的玻璃型材及异型材	15					0	
70042000	拉、吹制的着色玻璃板、片	17.5					0	0
70049000	拉、吹制的其他玻璃板、片	17.5					0	
70051000	有吸收层非夹丝浮法或抛光玻璃板	15					0	
70052100	其他着色非夹丝浮法玻璃板、片	15					0	
70052900	其他非夹丝浮法玻璃板、片	15					0	
70053000	夹丝浮法玻璃板、片	17.5					0	
70060000	经其他加工税号70.03-70.05的玻璃	15					0	
70071110	航空航天器及船舶用钢化安全玻璃	2					0	0
70071190	车辆用钢化安全玻璃	10					0	0
70071900	其他钢化安全玻璃	14					0	
70072110	航空航天器及船舶用层压安全玻璃	2					0	0
70072190	车辆用层压安全玻璃	20					0	0
70072900	其他层压安全玻璃	14					0	
70080010	中空或真空隔温、隔音玻璃	14					0	
70080090	其他多层隔温、隔音玻璃组件	14					0	
70091000	车辆后视镜	10					0	0
70099100	其他未镶框玻璃镜(包括后视镜)	21					0	
70099200	其他镶框玻璃镜(包括后视镜)	12					0	0
70101000	玻璃安瓿	14					0	
70102000	玻璃制的塞、盖及类似封口器	14					0	
70109010	装运货物或保藏用的玻璃大容器	14					0	
70109020	装运货物或保藏用的玻璃中容器	14					0	
70109030	装运货物或保藏用的玻璃小容器	14					0	
70109090	装运货物或保藏用的玻璃特小容器	14					0	0
70111000	电灯用未封口玻璃外壳及玻璃零件	21					0	
70112010	显象管玻壳及其零件	10					0	
70112090	阴极射线管用玻壳及零件	10					0	
70119010	电子管未封口玻璃外壳及玻璃零件	8					0	
70119090	其他类似品用未封口玻璃外壳零件	21					0	
70131000	玻璃陶瓷制玻璃器皿	24.5					0	0
70132200	铅晶质高脚杯	24.5					0	
70132800	其他高脚杯	8					0	0
70133300	其他铅晶质玻璃杯	24.5					0	
70133700	其他玻璃杯	8					0	0

税则号列	商品名称（简称）	最惠税率	亚太2国	东盟			最不发达35国	最不发达4国
				缅	老	柬		
70134100	铅晶质玻璃制餐桌、厨房用器皿	24.5					0	
70134200	低膨胀系数玻璃制餐桌厨房用器皿	10					0	0
70134900	其他玻璃制餐桌、厨房用器皿	10					0	0
70139100	其他铅晶质玻璃器皿	10					0	0
70139900	其他玻璃器皿	10					0	0
70140010	光学仪器用光学元件毛坯	10					0	0
70140090	其他未经光学加工的信号玻璃器	17.5					0	
70151010	视力矫正眼镜用变色镜片坯件	21					0	
70151090	其他视力矫正眼镜用镜片坯件	17.5					0	
70159010	钟表玻璃	17.5					0	
70159020	平光变色镜片坯件	18					0	
70159090	税号 7015 的其他未经光学加工玻璃	12					0	0
70161000	供镶嵌或装饰用玻璃马赛克	22					0	
70169010	花饰铅条窗玻璃及类似品	24					0	
70169090	建筑用压制或模制铺面玻璃块、砖	18					0	
70171000	实验室、卫生及配药用玻璃器	0					0	0
70172000	其他玻璃制实验室等用玻璃器	8					0	0
70179000	其他实验室、卫生及配药用玻璃器	8					0	0
70181000	玻璃珠、仿珍珠及类似小件玻璃品	10					0	0
70182000	直径≤1mm 的玻璃珠	20					0	
70189000	玻璃假眼；灯工方法制的玻璃塑像及玻璃饰品	20					0	
70191100	长度≤50mm 的短切玻璃纤维	12					0	0
70191200	玻璃纤维粗纱	12					0	0
70191900	玻璃纤维、梳条、纱线	10					0	0
70193100	玻璃纤维(包括玻璃棉)制的席	5					0	0
70193200	玻璃纤维(包括玻璃棉)制的薄片	14					0	
70193910	垫	10.5					0	0
70193990	玻璃纤维（包括玻璃棉）及其制品	10.5					0	0
70194000	玻璃纤维粗纱机织物	12					0	0
70195100	宽度≤30mm 的玻璃纤维机织物	12					0	0
70195200	每平米≤250g 的玻璃长丝平纹织物	12					0	0
70195900	其他玻璃纤维机织物	12					0	0
70199010	玻璃棉及其制品	7					0	0
70199021	每平方米重量小于 450 克的玻璃纤维布浸胶制品	7					0	0
70199029	其他玻璃纤维布浸胶制品	7					0	0
70199090	其他玻璃纤维及其制品	7					0	0
70200011	导电玻璃	10.5					0	0
70200012	绝缘子用玻璃伞盘	10.5					0	0
70200013	熔融石英或其他熔融硅石制	10.5					0	0
70200019	其他工业用玻璃制品	10.5					0	0
70200091	保温瓶或其他保温器用玻璃胆	21					0	
70200099	其他非工业用玻璃制品	15					0	0
71011011	未分级的天然黑珍珠	21					0	
71011019	其他未分级的天然珍珠	21					0	
71011091	其他天然黑珍珠	21					0	
71011099	其他天然珍珠	21					0	
71012110	未分级、未加工的养殖珍珠	21					0	
71012190	其他未加工的养殖珍珠	21					0	
71012210	未分级、已加工的养殖珍珠	21					0	
71012290	其他已加工的养殖珍珠	21					0	
71021000	未分级钻石	3					0	0
71022100	未加工或简单加工的工业用钻石	0					0	0
71022900	其他工业用钻石	0					0	0
71023100	未加工或简单加工非工业用钻石	3					0	0
71023900	其他非工业用钻石	8					0	0
71031000	未加工宝石或半宝石	3			0		0	0
71039100	经其他加工的红宝石、蓝宝石、祖母绿	8			0		0	0
71039910	经其他加工的翡翠	8					0	0

税则号列	商品名称（简称）	最惠税率	亚太2国	东盟			最不发达35国	最不发达4国
				缅	老	柬		
71039920	水晶	8					0	0
71039930	碧玺	8					0	0
71039940	软玉	8					0	0
71039990	经其他加工的其他宝石或半宝石	8					0	0
71041000	压电石英	6					0	0
71042010	未加工合成或再造钻石	0					0	0
71042090	未加工合成或再造其他宝石或半宝石	0					0	0
71049011	其他工业用合成或再造的钻石	6					0	0
71049012	工业用蓝宝石	6					0	0
71049019	其他工业用合成或再造的其他宝石或半宝石	6					0	0
71049091	其他非工业用合成钻石	8					0	0
71049099	其他非工业用合成其他宝石或半宝石	8					0	0
71051010	天然钻石	0					0	0
71051020	人工合成的钻石	0					0	0
71059000	天然或合成宝石或半宝石粉末	0					0	0
71061011	平均粒径小于3微米的非片状银粉	0					0	0
71061019	平均粒径不小于3微米的非片状银粉	0					0	0
71061021	平均粒径小于10微米的片状银粉	0					0	0
71061029	其他银粉	0					0	0
71069110	纯度达99.99%及以上的未锻造银	0					0	0
71069190	其他未锻造银	0					0	0
71069210	纯度达99.99%及以上的半制成银	0					0	0
71069290	其他半制成银	0					0	0
71070000	以贱金属为底的包银材料	10.5			0		0	0
71081100	非货币用金粉	0					0	0
71081200	非货币用未锻造金	0					0	0
71081300	非货币用半制成金	0			0		0	0
71082000	货币用未锻造金(包括镀铂的金)及金粉	0					0	0
71090000	以贱金属或银为底的包金材料	10.5					0	0
71101100	未锻造或粉末状铂	0					0	0
71101910	板、片状铂	0					0	0
71101990	其他半制成铂	3					0	0
71102100	未锻造或粉末状钯	0					0	0
71102910	板、片状钯	0					0	0
71102990	其他半制成钯	3					0	0
71103100	未锻造或粉末状铑	0					0	0
71103910	板、片状铑	0					0	0
71103990	其他半制成铑	3					0	0
71104100	未锻造或粉末状铱、锇、钌	0					0	0
71104910	板、片状铱、锇、钌	0					0	0
71104990	其他半制成铱、锇、钌	3					0	0
71110000	以贱金属、银或金为底的包铂材料	3					0	
71123010	含银或银化合物的灰	8					0	0
71123090	其他含贵金属或贵金属化合物的灰	6					0	0
71129110	金及包金的废碎料	0					0	0
71129120	其他含金或金化合物的废碎料	6					0	0
71129210	铂及包铂的废碎料	0					0	0
71129220	其他含铂或铂化合物的废碎料	6					0	0
71129910	含银及银化合物的废碎料	8					0	0
71129920	含有其他贵金属或贵金属化合物的废碎料	6					0	0
71129990	其他贵金属或包贵金属的废碎料	0					0	0
71131110	镶嵌钻石的银首饰及其零件	20					0	
71131190	其他银首饰及其零件	20					0	0
71131911	镶嵌钻石的黄金制首饰及其零件	20					0	
71131919	其他黄金制首饰及其零件	20					0	
71131921	镶嵌钻石的铂制首饰及其零件	35					0	
71131929	其他铂制首饰及其零件	35					0	0
71131991	镶嵌钻石的其他贵金属制首饰及其零件	35					0	

税则号列	商品名称（简称）	最惠税率	亚太2国	东盟			最不发达35国	最不发达4国
				缅	老	柬		
71131999	其他贵金属制首饰及其零件	35					0	0
71132010	镶嵌钻石的以贱金属为底的包贵金属制首饰	35					0	
71132090	其他以贱金属为底的包贵金属制首饰	35					0	
71141100	银器及零件	35					0	0
71141900	其他贵金属制金银器及零件	35					0	
71142000	以贱金属为底的包贵金属制金银器	35					0	0
71151000	金属丝布或格栅状的铂催化剂	3					0	0
71159010	工业或实验室用贵或包贵金属制品	3					0	0
71159090	其他用途的贵或包贵金属制品	35					0	
71161000	天然或养殖珍珠制品	35					0	
71162000	宝石或半宝石制品	35					0	0
71171100	贱金属制袖扣、饰扣	35					0	
71171900	其他贱金属制仿首饰	17					0	0
71179000	未列名材料制仿首饰	35					0	0
71181000	非法定货币的硬币(金币除外)	0					0	0
71189000	其他硬币	0					0	0
72011000	非合金生铁,含磷量≤0.5%	1					0	0
72012000	非合金生铁,含磷量>0.5%	1					0	0
72015000	合金生铁、镜铁	1					0	0
72021100	锰铁,含碳量≥2%	2					0	0
72021900	锰铁,含碳量≤2%	2					0	0
72022100	硅铁,含硅量≥55%	2					0	0
72022900	硅铁,含硅量≤55%	2					0	0
72023000	硅锰铁	2					0	0
72024100	铬铁,含碳量≥4%	2					0	0
72024900	铬铁,含碳量≤4%	2					0	0
72025000	硅铬铁	2					0	0
72026000	镍铁	2					0	0
72027000	钼铁	2					0	0
72028010	钨铁	2					0	0
72028020	硅钨铁	2					0	0
72029100	钛铁及硅钛铁	2					0	0
72029210	按重量计含钒量在75%及以上的钒铁	9					0	0
72029290	其他钒铁	9					0	0
72029300	铌铁	2					0	0
72029911	钕铁硼速凝永磁片	2					0	0
72029912	钕铁硼磁粉	2					0	0
72029919	其他钕铁硼合金	2					0	0
72029991	按重量计稀土元素总含量在10%以上的其他铁合金	2					0	0
72029999	其他铁合金	2					0	0
72031000	直接从铁矿还原的铁产品	2					0	
72039000	其他海绵铁,产品纯度>99.94%	2					0	
72041000	铸铁废碎料	2					0	0
72042100	不锈钢废碎料	0					0	0
72042900	其他合金钢废碎料	0					0	0
72043000	镀锡钢铁废碎料	2					0	0
72044100	机械加工中产生的废料	2					0	0
72044900	其他钢铁废碎料	0					0	0
72045000	供再熔的碎料钢铁锭	0					0	0
72051000	生铁、镜铁及钢铁颗粒	2					0	0
72052100	合金钢粉末	2					0	0
72052900	生铁、镜铁及其他钢铁粉末	2					0	0
72061000	铁及非合金钢锭	2					0	
72069000	其他初级形状的铁及非合金钢	2					0	
72071100	宽度<厚度两倍的矩形截面钢坯,C<0.25%	2					0	
72071200	其他矩形截面钢坯,C, 0.25%	2					0	
72071900	其他含碳量<0.25%的钢坯	2					0	
72072000	含碳量≥0.25%的钢坯	2					0	

税则号列	商品名称（简称）	最惠税率	亚太2国	东盟			最不发达35国	最不发达4国
				缅	老	柬		
72081000	轧压花纹的热轧卷材	5					0	0
72082500	厚度≥4.75mm 其他经酸洗的热轧卷材	5					0	0
72082610	屈服强度大于 355 牛顿/平方毫米，3mm≤厚度＜4.75mm 其他经酸洗热轧卷材	5					0	0
72082690	其他 3mm≤厚度＜4.75mm 其他经酸洗热轧卷材	5					0	0
72082710	厚度＜1.5mm 的其他经酸洗的热轧卷材	5					0	0
72082790	其他厚度＜3mm 的其他经酸洗的热轧卷材	5					0	0
72083600	厚度＞10mm 的其他热轧卷材	6					0	0
72083700	4.75mm≤厚度≤10mm 的其他热轧卷材	5					0	0
72083810	屈服强度大于 355 牛顿/平方毫米，3mm≤厚度＜4.75mm 的其他卷材	5					0	0
72083890	其他 3mm≤厚度＜4.75mm 的其他卷材	5					0	0
72083910	厚度＜1.5mm 的其他热轧卷材	3					0	0
72083990	其他厚度＜3mm 的其他热轧卷材	3					0	0
72084000	轧有凸起花纹的热轧非卷材	6					0	0
72085110	厚度＞50mm 的其他热轧非卷材	6					0	0
72085120	厚度＞20mm，但不超过 50 毫米的其他热轧非卷材	6					0	0
72085190	其他厚度＞10mm 的其他热轧非卷材	6					0	0
72085200	4.75mm≤厚度≤10mm 的热轧非卷材	6					0	0
72085310	屈服强度大于 355 牛顿/平方毫米，3mm≤厚度＜4.75mm 的热轧非卷材	6					0	0
72085390	其他 3mm≤厚度＜4.75mm 的热轧非卷材	6					0	0
72085410	厚度＜1.5mm 的热轧非卷材	6					0	0
72085490	其他厚度＜3mm 的热轧非卷材	6					0	0
72089000	其他热轧铁或非合金钢宽平板轧材	6					0	0
72091510	屈服强度大于 355 牛顿/平方毫米，厚度≥3mm 的冷轧卷材	6					0	0
72091590	其他厚度≥3mm 的冷轧卷材	6					0	0
72091610	屈服强度大于 275 牛顿/平方毫米，1mm＜厚度＜3mm 的冷轧卷材	6					0	0
72091690	其他 1mm＜厚度＜3mm 的冷轧卷材	6					0	0
72091710	屈服强度大于 275 牛顿/平方毫米，0.5mm≤厚度≤1mm 的冷轧卷材	3					0	0
72091790	其他 0.5mm≤厚度≤1mm 的冷轧卷材	3					0	0
72091810	厚度＜0.3mm 的冷轧卷材	6					0	0
72091890	其他厚度＜0.5mm 的冷轧卷材	6					0	0
72092500	厚度≥3mm 的冷轧非卷材	6					0	0
72092600	1mm＜厚度＜3mm 的冷轧非卷材	6					0	0
72092700	0.5mm≤厚度≤1mm 的冷轧非卷材	6					0	0
72092800	厚度＜0.5mm 的冷轧非卷材	6					0	0
72099000	其他冷轧铁或非合金钢宽平板轧材	6					0	0
72101100	镀锡的铁或非合金钢厚宽平板轧材	10					0	0
72101200	镀锡的铁或非合金钢薄宽平板轧材	5					0	0
72102000	镀铅的铁或非合金钢宽平板轧材	4					0	0
72103000	电镀锌的铁或非合金钢宽板材	8					0	0
72104100	镀锌的瓦楞形铁或非合金钢宽板材	8					0	0
72104900	镀锌的其他形铁或非合金钢宽板材	4					0	0
72105000	镀氧化铬的铁或非合金钢宽板材	8					0	0
72106100	镀或涂铝锌合金的铁宽平板轧材	8					0	0
72106900	其他镀或涂铝的铁宽平板轧材	8					0	0
72107010	厚度小于 1.5 毫米涂漆或涂塑的宽度在 600 毫米及以上的铁或非合金钢平板轧材，经包覆、镀层或涂层	4					0	0
72107090	其他涂漆或涂塑的宽度在 600 毫米及以上的铁或非合金钢平板轧材，经包覆、镀层或涂层	4					0	0
72109000	涂镀其他材料铁或非合金钢宽板材	8					0	0
72111300	未轧花纹的四面轧制的热轧非卷材	6					0	0
72111400	厚度≥4.75mm 的其他热轧板材	6					0	0
72111900	其他热轧铁或非合金钢窄板材	6					0	0
72112300	冷轧含炭量＜0.25%的板材	6					0	0
72112900	冷轧其他铁或非合金钢窄板材	6					0	0
72119000	冷轧的铁或非合金钢其他窄板材	6					0	0
72121000	镀或涂锡的铁或非合金钢窄板材	5					0	0
72122000	电镀锌的铁或非合金钢窄板材	8					0	0
72123000	其他镀或涂锌的铁窄板材	8					0	0
72124000	涂漆或涂塑的铁或非合金钢窄板材	4					0	0

税则号列	商品名称（简称）	最惠税率	亚太2国	东盟			最不发达35国	最不发达4国
				缅	老	柬		
72125000	涂镀其他材料铁或非合金钢窄板材	8					0	0
72126000	经包覆的铁或非合金钢窄板材	8					0	0
72131000	带有轧制花纹的热轧盘条	3					0	0
72132000	其他易切削钢制热轧盘条	3					0	0
72139100	直径＜14mm 圆截面的其他热轧盘条	5					0	0
72139900	其他热轧盘条	5					0	0
72141000	锻造的铁或非合金钢条、杆	7					0	0
72142000	热加工带有轧制花纹的条、杆	3					0	0
72143000	热加工易切削钢的条、杆	7					0	0
72149100	热加工其他矩形截面的条杆	3					0	0
72149900	热加工其他条、杆	3					0	0
72151000	冷加工其他易切削钢制条、杆	7					0	0
72155000	冷加工或冷成形的其他条、杆	7					0	0
72159000	铁及非合金钢的其他条、杆	3					0	0
72161010	截面高度＜80mm 的 H 型钢	3					0	0
72161020	截面高度低于 80 毫米的工字钢	3					0	0
72161090	截面高度＜80mmU 型钢	3					0	0
72162100	热加工截面高度＜80mm 角钢	6					0	0
72162200	热加工截面高度＜80mm 丁字钢	6					0	0
72163100	热加工截面高度≥80mm 槽型钢	6					0	0
72163210	截面高度在 200 毫米以上的工字钢	6					0	0
72163290	热加工截面高度≥80mm 工字型钢	6					0	0
72163311	截面高度在 800 毫米以上的 H 型缸	6					0	0
72163319	截面高度≥200mmH 型钢	6					0	0
72163390	其他截面高度≥80mmH 型钢	6					0	0
72164010	热加工截面高度≥80mm 角钢	3					0	0
72164020	热加工截面高度≥80mm 丁字钢	3					0	0
72165010	热加工乙字钢	6					0	0
72165020	热加工球扁钢	3					0	0
72165090	热加工其他角材、型材及异型材	3					0	0
72166100	冷加工板材制的角材、型材及异型材	3					0	0
72166900	冷加工其他角材、型材及异型材	3					0	0
72169100	冷加工其他板材制角材、型材及异型材	3					0	0
72169900	其他角材、型材及异型材	3					0	0
72171000	未镀或涂层的铁或非合金钢丝	8					0	0
72172000	镀或涂锌的铁或非合金钢丝	8					0	0
72173010	镀或涂铜的铁丝和非合金钢丝	8					0	0
72173090	镀或涂其他贱金属的铁丝和非合金钢丝	8					0	0
72179000	其他铁丝或非合金钢丝	8					0	0
72181000	不锈钢锭及其他初级形状产品	2					0	0
72189100	矩形截面的不锈钢半制成品	2					0	0
72189900	其他不锈钢半制成品	2					0	0
72191100	厚度＞10mm 热轧不锈钢卷板	4					0	0
72191200	4.75mm≤厚度≤10mm 热轧不锈钢卷板	4					0	0
72191312	按重量计含锰量在 5.5%及以上的未经酸洗 3mm≤厚度＜4.75mm 铬锰系不锈钢	4					0	0
72191319	厚度在 3 毫米及以上，但小于 4.75 毫米的未径酸洗的其他不锈钢卷板	4					0	0
72191322	按重量计含锰量在 5.5%及以上的经酸洗 3mm≤厚度＜4.75mm 铬锰系不锈钢	4					0	0
72191329	厚度在 3 毫米及以上，但小于 4.75 毫米的经酸洗的其他不锈钢卷板	4					0	0
72191412	按重量计含锰量在 5.5%及以上的未经酸洗厚度＜3mm 的铬锰系不锈钢	4					0	0
72191419	厚度在 3 毫米以下的未径酸洗的其他不锈钢卷板	4					0	0
72191422	按重量计含锰量在 5.5%及以上的经酸洗厚度＜3mm 的铬锰系不锈钢	4					0	0
72191429	厚度在 3 毫米以下的经酸洗的其他不锈钢卷板	4					0	0
72192100	厚度＞10mm 热轧不锈钢平板	10					0	
72192200	4.75mm≤厚度≤10mm 热轧不锈钢平板	10					0	
72192300	3mm≤厚度＜4.75mm 热轧不锈钢平板	10					0	
72192410	1mm＜厚度＜3mm 热轧不锈钢平板	10					0	
72192420	0.5mm≤厚度≤1mm 热轧不锈钢平板	10					0	
72192430	厚度＜0.5mm 热轧不锈钢平板	10					0	

税则号列	商品名称（简称）	最惠税率	亚太2国	东盟			最不发达35国	最不发达4国
				缅	老	柬		
72193100	厚度≥4.75mm冷轧不锈钢板	10					0	
72193200	3mm≤厚度<4.75mm冷轧不锈钢板材	10					0	
72193310	1mm<厚度<3mm冷轧按重量计含锰量在5.5%及以上的铬锰系不锈钢板材	10					0	
72193390	其他1mm<厚度<3mm冷轧不锈钢板材	10					0	
72193400	0.5mm≤厚度≤1mm冷轧不锈钢板材	10					0	
72193500	厚度<0.5mm冷轧不锈钢板材	10					0	
72199000	其他不锈钢冷轧板材	10					0	
72201100	热轧不锈钢带材厚度≥4.75mm	10					0	
72201200	热轧不锈钢带材厚度<4.75mm	10					0	
72202020	厚度在0.35毫米及以下的冷轧不锈钢带材	10					0	
72202030	厚度在0.35毫米以上但小于3毫米的冷轧不锈钢带材	10					0	
72202040	厚度在3毫米及以上的冷轧不锈钢带材	10					0	
72209000	其他不锈钢带材	10					0	
72210000	不锈钢热轧条、杆	10					0	
72221100	热加工的圆形截面不锈钢条、杆	10					0	
72221900	热加工其他截面形状不锈钢条杆	10					0	
72222000	冷成形或冷加工的不锈钢条、杆	10					0	
72223000	其他不锈钢条、杆	10					0	
72224000	不锈钢角材、型材及异型材	10					0	
72230000	不锈钢丝	10					0	0
72241000	其他合金钢锭及其他初级形状	2					0	0
72249010	单重≥10吨的粗铸锻件坯	2					0	0
72249090	其他合金钢坯	2					0	0
72251100	取向性硅电钢宽板	3					0	0
72251900	其他硅电钢宽板	6					0	0
72253000	宽度≥600mm热轧其他合金钢卷材	3					0	0
72254010	工具钢	3					0	0
72254091	含硼合金钢	3					0	0
72254099	其他非卷材,除热轧外未经进一步加工	3					0	0
72255000	宽度≥600mm冷轧其他合金钢板材	3					0	0
72259100	电镀锌的其他合金钢宽平板轧材	7					0	0
72259200	其他镀或涂锌的其他合金钢宽板材	7					0	0
72259910	宽度≥600mm的高速钢平板轧材	3					0	0
72259990	宽度≥600mm的其他合金钢平板轧材	7					0	0
72261100	取向性硅电钢窄板	3					0	0
72261900	其他硅电钢窄板	3					0	0
72262000	宽度<600mm的高速钢平板轧材	3					0	0
72269110	工具钢	3					0	0
72269191	含硼合金钢	3					0	0
72269199	其他除热轧外未经进一步加工的合金钢平板轧材，宽度小于600毫米	3					0	0
72269200	宽度<600mm冷轧其他合金钢板材	3					0	0
72269910	电镀锌的其他合金钢窄平板轧材	7					0	0
72269920	其他镀或涂锌的其他合金钢窄板材	7					0	0
72269990	宽度<600mm的其他合金板材	7					0	0
72271000	高速钢的热轧盘条	3					0	0
72272000	硅锰钢的热轧盘条	6					0	0
72279010	含硼合金钢制不规则盘卷的其他合金钢热轧条、杆	3					0	0
72279090	其他不规则盘卷的其他合金钢热轧条、杆	3					0	0
72281000	其他高速钢的条、杆	3					0	0
72282000	其他硅锰钢的条、杆	6					0	0
72283010	含硼合金钢制其他条、杆，除热轧、热拉拔或热挤压外未经进一步加工	3					0	0
72283090	其他条、杆，除热轧、热拉拔或热挤压外未经进一步加工	3					0	0
72284000	其他合金钢锻造条、杆	3					0	0
72285000	其他合金钢冷成形或冷加工条、杆	3					0	0
72286000	其他合金钢条、杆	3					0	0
72287010	履带板型钢	6					0	0
72287090	其他合金钢角材、型材及异型材	6					0	0
72288000	其他合金钢空心钻钢	7					0	0

税则号列	商品名称（简称）	最惠税率	亚太2国	东盟 缅	东盟 老	东盟 柬	最不发达35国	最不发达4国
72292000	硅锰钢丝	7					0	
72299010	高速钢丝	3					0	
72299090	其他合金钢丝	7					0	
73011000	钢铁板桩	7					0	0
73012000	焊接的钢铁角材、型材及异型材	7					0	0
73021000	钢轨	6					0	0
73023000	道岔尖轨、辙叉、尖轨拉杆	8					0	0
73024000	钢铁制鱼尾板、钢轨垫板	7					0	0
73029010	钢铁轨枕	6					0	0
73029090	其他铁道电车道铺轨用钢铁材料	7					0	0
73030010	内径＞500mm的铸铁圆型截面管	4					0	0
73030090	其他铸铁管及空心异型材	4					0	0
73041110	外径大于等于215.9毫米，但不超过406.4毫米的不锈钢制石油或天然气套管	5					0	0
73041120	外径大于114.3毫米，但小于215.9毫米的不锈钢制石汩或天然气套管	5					0	0
73041130	外径不超过114.3毫米的不锈钢制石油或天然气套管	5					0	0
73041190	其他不锈钢制石油或天然气套管	5					0	0
73041910	外径大于等于215.9毫米，但不超过406.4毫米的非不锈钢制石油或天然气套管	5					0	0
73041920	外径大于114.3毫米，但小于215.9毫米的非不锈钢制石油或天然气套管	5					0	0
73041930	外径不超过114.3毫米的非不锈钢制石油或天然气套管	5					0	0
73041990	其他非不锈钢制石油或天然气套管	5					0	0
73042210	外径不超过168.3毫米的不锈钢制钻管	4					0	0
73042290	其他不锈钢制钻管	4					0	0
73042310	外径不超过168.3毫米的非不锈钢制钻管	4					0	0
73042390	其他非不锈钢制钻管	4					0	0
73042400	其他不锈钢制钻探石油用天然气套管、导管	4					0	0
73042910	屈服强度小于552兆帕的钻探石油及天然气用的套管、导管及钻管	4					0	0
73042920	屈服强度大于等于552兆帕，但小于758兆帕的钻探石油及天然气用的套管、导管及钻管	4					0	0
73042930	屈服强度大于等于758兆帕的钻探石油及天然气用的套管、导管及钻管	4					0	0
73043110	冷轧的钢铁制无缝锅炉管	4					0	0
73043120	冷轧的铁制无缝地质钻管、套管	8					0	0
73043190	其他冷轧的铁制无缝圆形截面管	4					0	0
73043910	非冷轧的铁制无缝锅炉管	4					0	0
73043920	非冷轧的铁制无缝地质钻管套管	5					0	0
73043990	非冷轧的铁制其他无缝管	4					0	0
73044110	冷轧的不锈钢制无缝锅炉管	10					0	
73044190	冷轧的不锈钢制的其他无缝管	10					0	
73044910	非冷轧的不锈钢制无缝锅炉管	10					0	
73044990	非冷轧的不锈钢制其他无缝管	10					0	
73045110	冷轧的其他合金钢无缝锅炉管	4					0	0
73045120	冷轧的其他合金钢无缝地质钻套管	4					0	0
73045190	冷轧的其他合金钢制其他无缝管	4					0	0
73045910	非冷轧其他合金钢无缝锅炉管	4					0	0
73045920	非冷轧其他合金钢无缝地质钻套管	4					0	0
73045990	非冷轧其他合金钢制无缝圆形截面	4					0	0
73049000	未列名无缝钢铁管及空心异型材	4					0	0
73051100	纵向埋弧焊接石油、天然气粗钢管	7					0	0
73051200	其他纵向焊接石油、天然气粗钢管	3					0	0
73051900	其他石油、天然气粗钢管	7					0	0
73052000	其他钻探石油、天然气用粗套管	7					0	0
73053100	纵向焊接的其他粗钢铁管	6					0	0
73053900	其他方法焊接其他粗钢铁管	6					0	0
73059000	未列名圆形截面粗钢铁管	6					0	0
73061100	不锈钢焊缝石油、天然气管道管	7					0	0
73061900	其他石油、天然气管道管	7					0	0
73062100	不锈钢焊缝钻探石油天然气用套、导管	3					0	0
73062900	其他钻探石油天然气用套、导管	3					0	0

税则号列	商品名称（简称）	最惠税率	亚太2国	东盟			最不发达35国	最不发达4国
				缅	老	柬		
73063011	壁厚在0.7毫米及以下的外径不超过10毫米的其他铁或非合金钢圆形截面焊缝管	3					0	0
73063019	壁厚在0.7毫米以上外径不超过10毫米的其他铁或非合金钢圆形截面焊缝管	3					0	0
73063090	外径超过10毫米的其他铁或非合金钢圆形截面焊缝管	3					0	0
73064000	不锈钢其他圆形截面细焊缝管	6					0	0
73065000	其他合金钢的圆形截面细焊缝管	3					0	0
73066100	矩形或正方形截面的其他焊缝管	3					0	0
73066900	其他非圆形截面的其他焊缝管	3					0	0
73069000	未列名其他钢铁管及空心异型材	6					0	0
73071100	无可锻性铸铁制管子附件	5					0	0
73071900	可锻性铸铁及铸钢管子附件	8					0	0
73072100	不锈钢制法兰	8.4					0	0
73072200	不锈钢制螺纹肘管、弯管、管套	8.4					0	0
73072300	不锈钢制对焊件	8.4					0	0
73072900	不锈钢制其他管子附件	8.4					0	0
73079100	未列名钢铁制法兰	7					0	0
73079200	未列名钢铁制螺纹肘管、弯管、管套	4					0	0
73079300	未列名钢铁制对焊件	7					0	0
73079900	未列名钢铁制其他管子附件	4					0	0
73081000	钢铁制桥梁及桥梁体段	8					0	0
73082000	钢铁制塔楼及格构杆	8.4					0	0
73083000	钢铁制门窗及其框架、门槛	10					0	0
73084000	钢铁制脚手架模板坑凳用支柱及类	8.4					0	0
73089000	其他钢铁结构体及部件	4					0	0
73090000	容积>300L钢铁制盛物容器	10.5					0	0
73101000	容积50-300L钢铁制盛物容器	10.5					0	0
73102110	易拉罐及罐体	17.5					0	
73102190	其他容积在50升以下焊边或卷边接合的罐	17.5					0	
73102910	易拉罐及罐体	17.5					0	0
73102990	其他盛装物料用的钢铁柜、桶、罐、听、盒及类似容器（装压缩气体或液化气体的除外），容积不超过300升，不论是否衬里或隔热，但无机械或热力装置	17.5					0	0
73110010	装压缩或液化气的钢铁容器	17.5					0	
73110090	其他装压缩或液化气的容器	8					0	
73121000	非绝缘的钢铁绞股线、绳、缆	4					0	
73129000	非绝缘钢铁编带、吊索及类似品	4					0	0
73130000	带刺钢铁丝、围篱用钢铁绞带	7					0	0
73141200	不锈钢制的机器用环形带	12					0	0
73141400	不锈钢制的机织品	12					0	0
73141900	其他钢铁丝制机织品	7					0	0
73142000	交点焊接的粗钢铁丝网、篱及格栅	7					0	0
73143100	交点焊接的镀或涂锌细钢铁丝网	7					0	0
73143900	交点焊接的其他细钢铁丝网、篱	7					0	0
73144100	其他镀锌的钢铁丝网、荔及格栅	8					0	0
73144200	其他涂塑的钢铁丝网、篱及格栅	8					0	0
73144900	其他钢铁丝网、篱及格栅	8					0	0
73145000	网眼钢铁板	8					0	0
73151110	自行车滚子链	12					0	
73151120	摩托车滚子链	12					0	
73151190	其他滚子链	12					0	
73151200	其他铰接链	12					0	
73151900	铰接链零件	12					0	
73152000	防滑链	12					0	
73158100	日字环节链	12					0	
73158200	其他焊接链	12					0	0
73158900	未列名链	12					0	
73159000	非铰接链零件	10					0	
73160000	钢铁锚、多爪锚及其零件	10					0	

税则号列	商品名称（简称）	最惠税率	亚太2国	东盟			最不发达35国	最不发达4国
				缅	老	柬		
73170000	铁钉、图钉、平头钉及类似品	10					0	
73181100	方头螺钉	10					0	
73181200	其他木螺钉	10					0	
73181300	钩头螺钉及环头螺钉	10					0	
73181400	自攻螺钉	10					0	
73181510	抗拉强度在800兆帕及以上的螺钉及螺栓，不论是否带有螺母或垫圈	8					0	0
73181590	其他螺钉及螺栓	8					0	0
73181600	螺母	8					0	0
73181900	未列名螺纹制品	5					0	0
73182100	弹簧垫圈及其他防松垫圈	10					0	0
73182200	其他垫圈	10					0	0
73182300	铆钉	10					0	0
73182400	销及开尾销	10					0	0
73182900	其他无螺纹紧固件	10					0	0
73194010	安全别针	10					0	0
73194090	其他别针	10					0	
73199000	未列名钢铁制针及类似品	10					0	0
73201010	铁道车辆用片簧及簧片	6					0	0
73201020	汽车用片簧及弹簧	10					0	0
73201090	其他片簧及簧片	10					0	0
73202010	铁道车辆用螺旋弹簧	6					0	0
73202090	其他螺旋弹簧	10					0	0
73209010	铁道车辆用其他弹簧	6					0	0
73209090	其他弹簧	12					0	0
73211100	可使用气体燃料的家用炉灶	15					0	
73211210	煤油炉	21					0	
73211290	其他使用液体燃料的家用炉灶	21					0	
73211900	其他炊事用具及加热板	21					0	
73218100	可使用气体燃料的其他家用器具	23					0	
73218200	使用液体燃料的其他家用器具	21					0	
73218900	其他非电热家用器具	21					0	
73219000	非电热家用器具零件	12					0	0
73221100	非电热铸铁制集中供暖用散热器	21					0	
73221900	非电热钢制集中供暖用散热器	21					0	
73229000	非电热空气加热器、暖气分布器	20					0	0
73231000	钢铁丝绒、擦锅器、洗擦用块垫等	14					0	
73239100	餐桌、厨房等家用铸铁制器具	20					0	
73239200	餐桌、厨房等家用铸铁制搪瓷器	20					0	
73239300	餐桌、厨房等家用不锈钢器具	12					0	0
73239410	钢铁制搪瓷面盆	20					0	
73239420	钢铁制搪瓷烧锅	20					0	
73239490	其他餐桌、厨房等家用钢铁制搪瓷器	20					0	
73239900	其他餐桌、厨房等用钢铁器具	20					0	
73241000	不锈钢制洗涤槽及脸盆	18					0	0
73242100	铸铁制浴缸	10					0	
73242900	其他钢铁制浴缸	30					0	
73249000	其他钢铁制卫生器具及零件	25					0	
73251010	工业用无可锻性制品	7					0	0
73251090	其他无可锻性铸铁制品	20					0	
73259100	可锻性铸铁及铸钢研磨机的研磨球	10.5					0	
73259910	工业月未列名可锻性铸铁制品	10.5					0	
73259990	非工业用未列名可锻性铸铁制品	20					0	
73261100	钢铁制研磨机用研磨球及类似品	10.5					0	
73261910	工业用未列名钢铁制品	10.5					0	
73261990	非工业用未列名钢铁制品	20					0	
73262010	工业用钢铁丝制品	10					0	
73262090	非工业用钢铁丝制品	18					0	
73269011	钢铁纤维及其制品	10.5					0	0

税则号列	商品名称（简称）	最惠税率	亚太2国	东盟			最不发达35国	最不发达4国
				缅	老	柬		
73269019	其他工业用钢铁制品	10.5					0	0
73269090	其他非工业用钢铁制品	8					0	0
74010000	铜锍、沉积铜(泥铜)	2			0		0	0
74020000	未精炼铜、电解精炼用铜阳极	2					0	0
74031111	按重量计铜含量超过99.9935%的阴极精炼铜	2					0	0
74031119	其他阴极精炼铜	2					0	0
74031190	精炼铜阴极型材	2					0	0
74031200	精炼铜的线锭	2					0	0
74031300	精炼铜的坯段	2					0	0
74031900	其他未锻轧的精炼铜	2					0	0
74032100	未锻轧的铜锌合金(黄铜)	1					0	0
74032200	未锻轧的铜锡合金(青铜)	1					0	0
74032900	未锻轧的其他铜合金	1					0	0
74040000	铜废碎料	1.5			0		0	0
74050000	铜母合金	4					0	
74061010	精炼铜制非片状粉末	3					0	0
74061020	白铜或德银制非片状粉末	6					0	0
74061030	铜锌合金(黄铜)制非片状铜粉粉末	6					0	0
74061040	铜锡合金(青铜)制非片状铜粉粉末	6					0	0
74061090	其他铜合金制非片状粉末	6					0	0
74062010	精炼铜制片状粉末	4					0	0
74062020	白铜或德银制片状粉末	6					0	0
74062090	其他铜合金制片状粉末	6					0	0
74071010	铬锆铜制条、杆及型材及异型材	4					0	0
74071090	其他精炼铜条、杆及型材及异型材	4					0	0
74072111	直线度不大于0.5毫米/米铜锌合金条、杆	7					0	0
74072119	其他铜锌合金条、杆	7					0	0
74072190	其他黄铜条、杆及型材及异型材	7					0	0
74072900	其他铜合金条杆、型材及异型材	7					0	0
74081100	最大截面尺寸＞6mm的精炼铜丝	4					0	0
74081900	截面尺寸≤6mm的精炼铜丝	4					0	0
74082100	黄铜丝	7					0	0
74082210	铜镍锌铅合金(加铅德银)丝	8					0	0
74082290	其他白铜丝或德银(铜镍锌合金)丝	8					0	0
74082900	其他铜合金丝	7					0	0
74091110	含氧量不超过10PPM，厚度超过0.15mm的盘卷精炼铜板、片、带	4					0	0
74091190	厚度超过0.15mm的其他盘卷精炼铜板、片、带	4					0	0
74091900	其他精炼铜板、片、带	4					0	0
74092100	成卷的黄铜板、片、带	7					0	0
74092900	其他黄铜板、片、带	7					0	0
74093100	成卷的青铜板、片、带	7					0	0
74093900	其他青铜板、片、带	7					0	0
74094000	白铜或德银制板、片、带	7					0	0
74099000	其他铜合金板、片、带	7					0	0
74101100	无衬背的精炼铜箔	4					0	
74101210	无衬背的白铜或德银铜箔	7					0	
74101290	无衬背的其他铜合金箔	7					0	
74102110	印刷电路用覆铜板	4					0	
74102190	有衬背的其他精炼铜箔	4					0	
74102210	有衬背的白铜或德银铜箔	7					0	
74102290	有衬背的其他铜合金箔	7					0	
74111011	外径小于等于25mm的带有内（外）螺纹或翅片的精炼铜管	4					0	0
74111019	外径小于等于25mm的其他精炼铜管	4					0	0
74111020	外径超过70mm的精炼铜管	4					0	0
74111090	其他精炼铜管	4					0	0
74112110	盘卷黄铜管	7					0	0
74112190	铜锌合金(黄铜)管	7					0	0
74112200	白铜或德银管	7					0	0

税则号列	商品名称（简称）	最惠税率	亚太2国	东盟			最不发达35国	最不发达4国
				缅	老	柬		
74112900	其他铜合金管	7					0	0
74121000	精炼铜管子附件	4					0	0
74122010	白铜或德银管子配件	7					0	0
74122090	其他铜合金管子配件	7					0	0
74130000	非绝缘的铜丝绞股线、缆、编带等	5					0	0
74151000	铜钉、平头钉、图钉U型钉及类似品	8					0	0
74152100	铜垫圈(包括弹簧垫圈)	10					0	0
74152900	铜制其他无螺纹制品	10					0	0
74153310	铜制木螺钉	8					0	0
74153390	铜制其他螺钉螺栓螺母	8					0	0
74153900	其他铜制螺纹制品	10					0	0
74181010	擦锅器及洗刷擦光用的块垫、手套	18					0	0
74181020	非电热的铜制家用烹饪、供暖器具	20					0	
74181090	餐桌厨房等家用铜制器具及其零件	18					0	0
74182000	铜制卫生器具及其零件	18					0	0
74191000	铜链条及其零件	14					0	
74199110	工业用铸造、模压、冲压其他铜制品	10					0	0
74199190	非工业用铸造、模压、冲压铜制品	20					0	
74199920	铜弹簧	10					0	
74199930	铜丝制的布（包括环形带）	7					0	0
74199940	铜丝制的网、格栅、网眼和铜板	8					0	0
74199950	非电热的铜制家用供暖器及其零件	20					0	
74199991	工业用其他铜制品	10					0	0
74199999	非工业用其他铜制品	20					0	0
75011000	镍锍	3					0	0
75012010	镍湿法冶炼中间品	3					0	0
75012090	氧化镍烧结物、镍的其他中间产品	3					0	0
75021010	按重量计镍、钴总量在99.99%及以上的，但钴含量不超过0.005%的非合金镍	3					0	0
75021090	其他非合金镍	3					0	0
75022000	未锻轧镍合金	3					0	0
75030000	镍废碎料	1.5					0	0
75040010	非合金镍粉及片状粉末	4					0	
75040020	合金镍粉及片状粉末	4					0	
75051100	纯镍条、杆、型材及异型材	6					0	0
75051200	合金镍条、杆、型材及异型材	6					0	0
75052100	纯镍丝	6					0	0
75052200	镍合金丝	6					0	0
75061000	纯镍板、片、带、箔	6					0	
75062000	镍合金板、片、带、箔	6					0	
75071100	纯镍管	6					0	
75071200	镍合金管	6					0	
75072000	镍及镍合金管子附件	6					0	
75081010	镍丝制的布	6					0	
75081080	工业用镍丝制的网及格栅	6					0	
75081090	其他镍丝制的网及格栅	6					0	
75089010	电镀用镍阳极	4					0	
75089080	其他工业用镍制品	6					0	
75089090	其他非工业用镍制品	6					0	
76011010	按重量计含铝量在99.95%及以上的未煅轧非铝合金	5					0	0
76011090	其他非煅轧非铝合金	5					0	0
76012000	未锻轧铝合金	7					0	0
76020000	铝废碎料	1.5					0	0
76031000	非片状铝粉	6					0	0
76032000	片状铝粉末	7					0	0
76041010	非合金铝条、杆	5					0	0
76041090	非合金铝型材及异形材	5					0	0
76042100	铝合金制空心异型材	5					0	0
76042910	铝合金条、杆	5					0	0

税则号列	商品名称（简称）	最惠税率	亚太2国	东盟			最不发达35国	最不发达4国
				缅	老	柬		
76042990	铝合金型材及异形材	5					0	0
76051100	纯铝制的粗丝	8					0	
76051900	纯铝制的细丝	8					0	
76052100	铝合金制的粗丝	8					0	
76052900	铝合金制的细丝	8					0	
76061121	0.3mm≦厚度<0.36mm的非合金铝与塑料复合的矩形板片带	6					0	0
76061129	其他0.3mm≦厚度<0.36mm的非合金铝制矩形铝板片带	6					0	0
76061191	其他非合金铝与塑料复合的矩形板片带	6					0	0
76061199	纯铝制矩形的其他板、片及带	6					0	0
76061220	厚度<0.28mm的铝合金制矩形铝板片带	6					0	0
76061230	0.28mm≦厚度≤0.35mm的铝合金制矩形铝板片带	6					0	0
76061251	0.35mm<厚度≤0.4mm的铝合金与塑料复合的矩形板片带	6					0	0
76061259	其他0.35mm<厚度≤0.4mm的铝合金制矩形铝板片带	6					0	0
76061290	厚度>0.4mm的铝合金制矩形铝板片带	6					0	0
76069100	纯铝制非矩形的板、片及带	6					0	0
76069200	铝合金制非矩形的板、片及带	10					0	0
76071110	厚度不超过0.007毫米的无衬背铝箔	6					0	
76071120	厚度大于0.007毫米，但不超过0.01毫米的无衬背铝箔	6					0	
76071190	轧制后未进一步加工的无衬背铝箔	6					0	
76071900	其他无衬背铝箔	6					0	
76072000	有衬背铝箔	6					0	
76081000	纯铝管	8					0	0
76082010	外径不超过10厘米的铝合金管	8					0	0
76082091	外径超过10厘米壁厚不超过25毫米铝合金管	8					0	0
76082099	其他铝合金管	8					0	0
76090000	铝制管子附件	8					0	0
76101000	铝制门窗及其框架、门槛	25					0	
76109000	其他铝制结构体及其部件	6					0	0
76110000	容积＞300L的铝制囤、罐等容器	12					0	
76121000	铝制软管容器	12					0	0
76129010	铝制易拉罐及罐体	30					0	
76129090	容积≤300L的铝制囤、罐等容器	12					0	0
76130010	零售包装装压缩、液化气体铝容器	12					0	
76130090	非零售装装压缩、液化气体铝容器	6					0	
76141000	带钢芯的铝制绞股线、缆、编带	6					0	0
76149000	不带钢芯的铝制绞股线、缆、编带	6					0	0
76151010	擦锅器及洗刷擦光用的块垫、手套	18					0	0
76151090	餐桌厨房等家用铝制器具及其零件	15					0	0
76152000	铝制卫生器具及其零件	18					0	
76161000	铝钉、螺钉、螺母、垫圈等紧固件	10					0	0
76169100	铝丝制的布、网、篱及格栅	10					0	0
76169910	其他工业用铝制品	10					0	0
76169990	其他非工业用铝制品	15					0	0
78011000	未锻轧精炼铅	3					0	0
78019100	未锻轧铅锑合金	3					0	0
78019900	未锻轧的其他铅合金	3					0	0
78020000	铅废碎料	1.5					0	
78041100	铅片、带及厚度≤0.2mm的箔	6					0	0
78041900	铅及铅合金板、厚度＞0.2mm的箔	6					0	0
78042000	铅及铅合金粉末、片状粉末	6					0	0
78060010	铅及铅合金条、杆、丝、型材	6					0	0
78060090	其他铅制品	6					0	0
79011110	按重量计含锌量在99.995%及以上的未煅轧锌	3					0	0
79011190	含锌量不小于99.99%，并小于99.995%的未煅轧锌	3					0	0
79011200	含锌量＜99.99%的未锻轧锌	3					0	0
79012000	未锻轧锌合金	3					0	0
79020000	锌废碎料	1.5					0	0
79031000	锌末	6					0	0

税则号列	商品名称（简称）	最惠税率	亚太2国	东盟			最不发达35国	最不发达4国
				缅	老	柬		
79039000	锌粉及片状粉末	6					0	0
79040000	锌及锌合金条、杆、型材、丝	6					0	
79050000	锌板、片、带、箔	6					0	0
79070020	锌管及锌制管子附件	6					0	0
79070030	电池壳体坯料（锌饼）	6					0	0
79070090	其他非工业用锌制品	6					0	0
80011000	未锻轧非合金锡	3					0	0
80012010	锡基巴毕脱合金	3					0	0
80012021	按重量计含铅量在0.1%以下的焊锡	3					0	0
80012029	其他焊锡	3					0	0
80012090	其他锡合金	3					0	0
80020000	锡废碎料	1.5					0	
80030000	锡及锡合金条、杆、型材、丝	8					0	0
80070020	锡及锡合金板、片及带,厚度＞0.2mm	8					0	
80070030	锡箔、锡粉及片状粉末	8					0	
80070040	锡及锡合金管、管子附件	8					0	
80070090	其他锡制品	8					0	
81011000	钨粉	6					0	
81019400	未锻轧钨	3					0	
81019600	钨丝	8					0	
81019700	钨废碎料	3					0	
81019910	锻轧钨条、杆、型材；废碎料	5					0	
81019990	其他钨制品	8					0	
81021000	钼粉	6					0	
81029400	未锻轧钼、钼废碎料	3					0	
81029500	锻轧钼条杆、型材、板片带箔	8					0	
81029600	钼丝	8					0	
81029700	钼废碎料	3					0	
81029900	钼制品	8					0	
81032011	松装密度小于2.2g/cm3的钽粉	6					0	
81032019	松装密度大于等于2.2g/cm3的钽粉	6					0	
81032090	未锻轧钽	6					0	
81033000	钽废碎料	6					0	
81039011	直径＜0.5mm的钽丝	8					0	
81039019	直径≥0.5mm的钽丝	8					0	
81039090	其他锻轧钽及其制品	8					0	
81041100	含镁量≥99.8%的未锻轧镁	6					0	
81041900	其他未锻轧的镁及镁合金	6					0	
81042000	镁废碎料	1.5					0	
81043000	已分级的镁锉屑、车屑、颗粒；粉末	8					0	
81049010	锻轧镁	8					0	
81049020	镁制品	8.4					0	
81052010	钴湿法冶炼中间品	4					0	0
81052020	未锻轧钴	4					0	0
81052090	钴锍及其他钴冶炼时所得的中间产品、粉末	4					0	0
81053000	钴锍废碎料	4					0	0
81059000	其他钴及制品	8					0	0
81060010	未锻轧铋、废碎料、粉末	3					0	
81060090	其他铋及铋制品	8					0	
81072000	未锻轧镉、粉末	3					0	
81073000	镉废碎料	3					0	
81079000	其他镉及镉制品	8					0	
81082021	海绵钛	3					0	
81082029	其他未锻轧钛	3					0	
81082030	钛粉末	3					0	
81083000	钛废碎料	3					0	
81089010	钛条、杆、型材及异型材	8					0	
81089020	钛丝	8					0	

税则号列	商品名称（简称）	最惠税率	亚太2国	东盟			最不发达35国	最不发达4国
				缅	老	柬		
81089031	厚度≤0.8mm钛板、片、带、箔	8					0	
81089032	厚度＞0.8mm钛板、片、带、箔	8					0	
81089040	钛管	8					0	
81089090	其他钛及钛制品	8					0	
81092000	未锻轧锆、粉末	3					0	
81093000	锆废碎料	3					0	
81099000	锻轧锆及锆制品	8					0	
81101010	未锻轧锑	3					0	
81101020	锑粉末	3					0	
81102000	锑废碎料	3					0	
81109000	其他锑及锑制品	8					0	
81110010	未锻轧锰;锰废碎料;粉末	3					0	0
81110090	其他锰及制品	8					0	0
81121200	未锻轧铍、粉末	3					0	0
81121300	铍废碎料	3					0	0
81121900	其他铍及其制品	8					0	0
81122100	未锻轧铬、粉末	3					0	0
81122200	铬废碎料	3					0	0
81122900	其他铬制品	3					0	0
81125100	未锻轧铊、粉末	3					0	0
81125200	铊废碎料	3					0	0
81125900	其他铊制品	8					0	0
81129210	未锻轧锗	3					0	0
81129220	未锻轧钒	3					0	0
81129230	未锻轧铟、铟废碎料、粉末	3					0	0
81129240	未锻轧铌、铌废碎料、粉末	3					0	0
81129290	未锻轧的未列名贱金属及其制品	3					0	0
81129910	锗及其制品	3					0	0
81129920	钒及其制品	3					0	0
81129930	锻扎铟及其制品	8					0	0
81129940	锻扎铌及其制品	8					0	0
81129990	锻轧的未列名贱金属及其制品	8					0	0
81130010	金属陶瓷颗粒、粉末	8.4					0	
81130090	其他金属陶瓷及其制品，包括废碎料	8.4					0	
82011000	锹及铲	8					0	0
82013000	镐、锄、耙	8					0	0
82014000	斧子、钩刀及类似砍伐工具	8					0	0
82015000	修枝剪等单手操作农用剪	8					0	0
82016000	修枝等双手操作农用剪	8					0	0
82019010	农用叉	8					0	0
82019090	其他农业、园艺、林业用手工工具	8					0	0
82021000	手工锯	8.4					0	0
82022010	双金属带锯条	8					0	0
82022090	其他带锯片手工锯	8					0	0
82023100	带有钢制工作部件的圆锯片	8					0	0
82023910	带有天然或合成金刚石、立方氮化硼制工作部件的圆锯片	8					0	0
82023990	其他圆锯片,包括部件	8					0	0
82024000	链锯片	8					0	0
82029110	加工金属用的机械锯的直锯片	8					0	0
82029190	加工金属用的非机械锯的直锯片	8					0	0
82029910	机械锯用的其他锯片	8.4					0	0
82029990	非机械锯用的其他锯片	10.5					0	
82031000	钢锉、木锉及类似工具	10.5					0	0
82032000	钳子、镊子及类似工具	10.5					0	
82033000	白铁剪及类似工具	10.5					0	
82034000	切管器、螺栓切头器、打孔冲子等	10.5					0	
82041100	固定式的手动扳手及板钳	10.5					0	0
82041200	可调式的手动扳手及板钳	10					0	0

税则号列	商品名称（简称）	最惠税率	亚太2国	东盟			最不发达35国	最不发达4国
				缅	老	柬		
82042000	可互换的扳手套筒	10					0	
82051000	手工钻孔或攻丝工具	10					0	
82052000	手工锤子	10					0	0
82053000	木工用刨子、凿子及类似切削工具	10.5					0	
82054000	手工螺丝刀	10.5					0	0
82055100	其他家用手工工具	10.5					0	
82055900	其他手工工具	10					0	
82056000	喷灯	10					0	
82057000	台钳、夹钳及类似品	10.5					0	
82059000	成套手工工具	10.5					0	
82060000	成套工具组成的零售包装货品	10.5					0	
82071300	带金属陶瓷工作部件的凿岩工具	8					0	0
82071910	带超硬材料部件的凿岩或钻探工具	8					0	0
82071990	带其他材料工作部件的凿岩工具	8					0	0
82072010	带超硬部件的金属拉拔或挤压用模	8					0	0
82072090	其他金属拉拔或挤压用模	8					0	0
82073000	锻压或冲压工具	8					0	0
82074000	攻丝工具	8					0	0
82075010	带超硬材料部件的钻孔工具	8					0	0
82075090	带其他材料工作部件的钻孔工具	8					0	0
82076010	带超硬材料部件的镗孔或铰孔工具	8					0	0
82076090	其他镗孔或铰孔工具	8					0	0
82077010	带有天然或合成金刚石、立方氮化硼制的工作部件的铣削工具	8					0	0
82077090	其他铣削工具	8					0	0
82078010	带有天然或合成金刚石、立方氮化硼制的车削工具	8					0	0
82078090	其他车削工具	8					0	0
82079010	带超硬材料部件的其他可互换工具	8					0	0
82079090	其他可互换工具	8					0	0
82081011	经镀或涂层的硬质合金制的金工机械用刀及刀片	8					0	
82081019	其他硬质合金制的金工机械用刀及刀片	8					0	
82081090	其他金工机械用刀及刀片	8					0	
82082000	木工机械用刀及刀片	8					0	0
82083000	厨房或食品加工机器用刀及刀片	8					0	0
82084000	农、林业机器用刀及刀片	8					0	
82089000	其他机器或机械器具用刀及刀片	8					0	
82090010	未装配的工具用金属陶瓷板	8					0	0
82090021	晶粒度小于0.8微米的金属陶瓷条、杆	8					0	0
82090029	其他未装配的工具用金属陶瓷条、杆	8					0	0
82090030	未装配的工具用金属陶瓷刀头	8					0	0
82090090	其他未装配的工具用金属陶瓷类似品	8					0	0
82100000	加工调制食品、饮料用手动机械	18					0	
82111000	以刀为主的成套货品	18					0	
82119100	刃面固定的餐刀	18					0	
82119200	刃面固定的其他刀	12					0	0
82119300	可换刃面刀	18					0	
82119400	税号82.11所列刀的刀片	14					0	
82119500	贱金属制的刀柄	12					0	0
82121000	剃刀	12					0	0
82122000	安全剃刀片	14					0	
82129000	剃刀零件	12					0	0
82130000	剪刀、裁缝剪刀及类似品、剪刀片	12					0	0
82141000	裁纸刀、信刀、铅笔刀及刀片	12					0	0
82142000	修指甲及修脚用具(包括指甲锉)	18					0	0
82149000	理发推子、切菜刀等其他利口器	18					0	
82151000	成套含镀贵金属制厨房或餐桌用具	18					0	
82152000	成套的其他厨房或餐桌用具	18					0	
82159100	非成套镀贵金属制厨房或餐桌用具	18					0	
82159900	其他非成套的厨房或餐桌用具	18					0	0

税则号列	商品名称（简称）	最惠税率	亚太2国	东盟			最不发达35国	最不发达4国
				缅	老	柬		
83011000	挂锁	14					0	
83012010	机动车用中央控制门锁	10					0	0
83012090	其他机动车用锁	10					0	0
83013000	家具用锁	14					0	0
83014000	其他锁	14					0	0
83015000	带锁的扣环及扣环框架	14					0	
83016000	锁零件	12					0	0
83017000	钥匙	10					0	0
83021000	铰链(折叶)	10					0	0
83022000	用贱金属支架的小脚轮	12					0	0
83023000	机动车辆用贱金属附件及架座	10					0	0
83024100	建筑用贱金属配件及架座	14					0	
83024200	家具用贱金属配件及架座	12					0	0
83024900	其他用贱金属配件及架座	12					0	0
83025000	帽架、帽钩、托架及类似品	14					0	
83026000	自动闭门器	12					0	0
83030000	保险箱、柜、保险库的门	14					0	
83040000	贱金属档案柜、文件箱等办公用具	10.5					0	0
83051000	活页夹或宗卷夹的附件	10.5					0	0
83052000	成条钉书钉	10.5					0	0
83059000	信夹、信角、文件夹等办公用品	10.5					0	0
83061000	非电动铃、钟、锣及其类似品	8					0	0
83062100	镀贵金属的雕塑像及其他装饰品	8					0	0
83062910	景泰兰雕塑像及其他装饰品	8					0	0
83062990	其他雕塑像及其他装饰品	8					0	0
83063000	相框、画框及类似框架、镜子	8					0	0
83071000	钢铁制软管、可有配件	8.4					0	0
83079000	其他贱金属软管,可有配件	8.4					0	0
83081000	贱金属制钩、环及眼	10.5					0	0
83082000	贱金属制管形铆钉及开口铆钉	10.5					0	0
83089000	贱金属制珠子及亮晶片	10.5					0	0
83091000	贱金属制冠形瓶塞	18					0	
83099000	盖子瓶帽螺口塞封志等包装用配件	12					0	0
83100000	标志牌、铭牌、号码、字母等标志	18					0	
83111000	焊剂涂面的贱金属电极、电弧焊用	8					0	0
83112000	以焊剂为芯的贱金属制焊丝	8					0	0
83113000	以焊剂涂面或作芯的贱金属条或丝	8					0	0
83119000	贱金属粘聚成的丝或条	8					0	0
84011000	核反应堆	2					0	
84012000	同位素分离机器、装置及其零件	1					0	
84013010	未辐照燃料元件(释热元件)	2					0	
84013090	未辐照燃料元件的零件	1					0	
84014010	未辐照相关组件	1					0	
84014020	堆内构件	1					0	
84014090	其他核反应堆零件	1					0	
84021110	蒸发量≥900t/hr 发电锅炉	3					0	
84021190	蒸发量>45t/hr,<900t/hr 发电锅炉	14					0	
84021200	蒸发量≤45t/hr 水管锅炉	5					0	
84021900	其他蒸汽锅炉	5					0	
84022000	过热水锅炉	16					0	
84029000	蒸汽锅炉及过热水锅炉的零件	2					0	
84031010	家用型集中供暖用热水锅炉	10					0	
84031090	其他集中供暖用的热水锅炉	10					0	
84039000	集中供暖用热水锅炉的零件	6					0	
84041010	蒸汽锅炉、过热水锅炉的辅助设备	7					0	
84041020	集中供暖用热水锅炉的辅助设备	10					0	
84042000	水及其他蒸汽动力装置的冷凝器	14					0	
84049010	集中供暖热水锅炉辅助设备的零件	10					0	

税则号列	商品名称（简称）	最惠	亚太	东盟			最不发	最不发
		税率	2 国	缅	老	柬	达 35 国	达 4 国
84049090	其他辅助设备用零件	7					0	
84051000	煤气、乙炔及类似水解气体发生器	14					0	
84059000	煤气、乙炔等气体发生器的零件	8					0	
84061000	船舶动力用汽轮机	5					0	0
84068110	40MW＜输出功率≤100MW 的汽轮机	5					0	0
84068120	100MW＜输出功率≤350MW 的汽轮机	5					0	0
84068130	输出功率＞350MW 的汽轮机	6					0	0
84068200	输出功率≤40MW 的汽轮机	5					0	0
84069000	汽轮机用的零件	2					0	0
84071010	输出功率≤298kw 航空器点燃式发动机	2					0	
84071020	输出功率＞298kw 航空器点燃式发动机	2					0	
84072100	船舶用舷外点燃式发动机	8					0	
84072900	船舶用其他未列名点燃式发动机	8					0	
84073100	排气量≤50cc 往复式活塞发动机	10					0	
84073200	排气量 50-250cc 往复式活塞发动机	10					0	
84073300	排气量 250-1000cc 往复式活塞发动机	10					0	
84079010	沼气发动机	12					0	
84079090	其他点燃往复或旋转式内燃发动机	18					0	
84081000	船舶用压燃式内燃发动机	5					0	
84082010	输出功率≥132.39kw 车用柴油发动机	9					0	
84089010	机车用柴油发动机	6					0	
84089091	功率≤14kw 其他用柴油发动机	5					0	
84089092	14kw＜功率＜132.39kw 其他柴油发动机	8.4					0	
84089093	功率≥132.39kw 其他用柴油发动机	5					0	
84091000	航空器发动机用零件	2					0	0
84099110	船舶用点燃式发动机专用零件	6					0	0
84099191	电控燃油喷射装置	5					0	0
84099199	其他点燃式活塞内燃发动机用零件	5					0	0
84099910	其他船舶发动机专用零件	5					0	0
84099920	其他机车发动机专用零件	2					0	0
84099991	功率≥132.39kw 发动机的专用零件	2					0	0
84099999	其他未列名发动机的专用零件	8.4					0	0
84101100	功率≤1000kw 的水轮机及水轮	10					0	
84101200	功率 1 千 kw-1 万 kw 的水轮机及水轮	10					0	
84101310	功率＞3 万 kw 的冲击式水轮机及水轮	10					0	
84101320	功率＞3.5 万 kw 的贯流水轮机及水轮	10					0	
84101330	功率＞20 万 kw 的水泵式水轮机及水轮	10					0	
84101390	其他功率＞1 万 kw 的水轮机及水轮	10					0	
84109010	水轮机及水轮的调节器	6					0	
84109090	水轮机及水轮的其他零件	6					0	
84111110	推力≤25 千牛顿的涡轮风扇发动机	1					0	0
84111190	推力≤25 千牛顿的其他的涡轮喷气发动机	1					0	0
84111210	推力＞25 千牛顿的涡轮风扇发动机	1					0	0
84111290	推力＞25 千牛顿的其他涡轮喷气发动机	1					0	0
84112100	功率≤1100kw 的涡轮螺桨发动机	2					0	0
84112210	功率 1100-2238kw 涡轮螺桨发动机	2					0	0
84112220	功率 2238-3730kw 涡轮螺桨发动机	2					0	0
84112230	功率＞3730kw 涡轮螺桨发动机	2					0	0
84118100	功率≤5000kw 的其他燃气轮机	15					0	
84118200	功率＞5000kw 的其他燃气轮机	3					0	0
84119100	涡轮喷气或涡轮螺桨发动机用零件	1					0	0
84119910	涡轮轴发动机用零件	5					0	0
84119990	其他燃气轮机用零件	5					0	0
84121010	航空、航天器用喷气发动机	3					0	0
84121090	非航空、航天器用喷气发动机	10					0	
84122100	直线作用的液压动力装置(液压缸)	12					0	
84122910	液压马达	10					0	
84122990	其他液压动力装置	14					0	

税则号列	商品名称（简称）	最惠税率	亚太2国	东盟			最不发达35国	最不发达4国
				缅	老	柬		
84123100	直线作用的气压动力装置(气压缸)	14					0	
84123900	其他气压动力装置	14					0	
84128000	其他发动机及动力装置	10					0	
84129010	航空、航天器用喷气发动机的零件	2					0	0
84129090	其他发动机及动力装置的零件	8					0	0
84131100	分装燃料或润滑油的泵	10					0	0
84131900	其他装有或可装计量装置的泵	10					0	0
84132000	手泵	10					0	0
84133021	输出功率在132.39千瓦（180马力）及以上的发动机用燃油泵	3					0	0
84133029	其他燃油泵	3					0	0
84133030	润滑油泵	3					0	0
84133090	其他燃油泵、润滑油泵或冷却剂泵	3					0	0
84134000	混凝土泵	8					0	0
84135010	气动式往复式排液泵	10					0	0
84135020	电动式往复式排液泵	10					0	0
84135031	往复式柱塞泵	10					0	0
84135039	其他液压式往复泵	10					0	0
84135090	其他往复式排液泵	10					0	0
84136021	电动式齿轮回转泵	10					0	0
84136022	液压式齿轮回转泵	10					0	0
84136029	其他齿轮回转泵	10					0	0
84136031	电动式叶片回转泵	10					0	0
84136032	液压式叶片回转泵	10					0	0
84136039	其他叶片回转泵	10					0	0
84136040	螺杆回转泵	10					0	0
84136050	径向柱塞泵	10					0	0
84136060	轴向柱塞泵	10					0	0
84136090	其他回转式排液泵	10					0	0
84137010	转速≥10000转/分离心泵	8					0	0
84137091	电动潜油泵及潜水电泵	10					0	0
84137099	其他离心泵	8					0	0
84138100	其他液体泵	8					0	0
84138200	液体提升机	8					0	0
84139100	液体泵用零件	5					0	0
84139200	液体提升机用零件	6					0	0
84141000	真空泵	8					0	
84142000	手动或脚踏式空气泵	8					0	
84143011	功率≤0.4kw的冷藏、冷冻箱用压缩机	8					0	0
84143012	功率0.4-5kw的冷藏、冷冻箱用压缩机	10					0	0
84143013	功率0.4-5kw的空气调节器用压缩机	10					0	0
84143014	功率>5kw的空气调节器用压缩机	10					0	0
84143015	冷冻或冷藏设备用，电动机额定功率超过5千瓦的电动机驱动压缩机	10					0	0
84143019	其他制冷设备用压缩机	10					0	0
84143090	非电机驱动的压缩机	9					0	0
84144000	装在拖车底盘上的空气压缩机	8					0	
84145110	功率≤125瓦的吊扇	20			0		0	0
84145120	功率≤125瓦的换气扇	20			0		0	0
84145130	功率≤125瓦，有旋转导风轮的风扇	12			0		0	0
84145191	功率≤125瓦的台扇	10			0		0	0
84145192	功率≤125瓦的落地扇	10			0		0	0
84145193	功率≤125瓦的壁扇	10			0		0	0
84145199	功率≤125瓦其他风扇、风机	10			0		0	0
84145910	其他吊扇	8					0	
84145920	其他换气扇	8					0	
84145930	离心通风机	10					0	
84145990	其他扇，风机	8					0	0
84146010	抽油烟机	10			0		0	0
84146090	罩最大边长≤120cm的通风罩或循环气罩	10			0		0	0

税则号列	商品名称（简称）	最惠税率	亚太2国	东盟			最不发达35国	最不发达4国
				缅	老	柬		
84148010	燃气轮机用的自由活塞式发生器	8					0	
84148020	二氧化碳压缩机	7					0	
84148090	其他气体压缩机及通风罩或循环气罩	7					0	
84149011	用于制冷设备的压缩机进、排气阀片	8			0		0	0
84149019	其他用于制冷设备的压缩机零件	8					0	
84149020	风机、风扇、通风罩及循环气罩零件	12					0	
84149090	税号84.14其他所列机器零件	7					0	
84151010	独立窗式或壁式空气调节器	15					0	
84151021	分体式制冷量制冷量≤4千大卡/时窗式或壁式空气调节器	15					0	
84151022	分体式制冷量制冷量＞4千大卡/时窗式或壁式空气调节器	15					0	
84158110	制冷量≤4千大卡/时热泵式空调器	15					0	
84158120	制冷量＞4千大卡/时热泵式空调器	20					0	
84158210	制冷量≤4千大卡/时的其他空调器	15					0	
84158220	制冷量＞4千大卡/时的其他空调器	20					0	
84158300	未装有制冷装置的空调器	10					0	0
84159010	制冷量≤4千大卡/时等空调的零件	10					0	0
84159090	制冷量＞4千大卡/时等空调的零件	10					0	0
84161000	使用液体燃料的炉用燃烧器	10					0	
84162011	使用天然气的燃烧器	10.5					0	
84162019	其他使用气体燃料的炉用燃烧器	10.5					0	
84162090	使用粉状固体燃料的炉用燃烧器	10.5					0	
84163000	机械加煤机及类似装置	8.4					0	
84169000	炉用燃烧器、机械加煤机等的零件	6					0	
84171000	矿砂、金属的热处理用炉及烤箱	10					0	
84172000	面包房用烤炉及烘箱等	10					0	
84178010	炼焦炉	10					0	
84178020	放射性废物焚烧炉	5					0	
84178030	水泥回转窑	10					0	
84178040	石灰石分解炉	10					0	
84178050	垃圾焚烧炉	10					0	
84178090	其他非电热的工业用炉及烘箱	10					0	
84179010	海绵铁回转窑的零件	7					0	
84179020	炼焦炉的零件	7					0	
84179090	其他非电热工业用炉及烘箱的零件	7					0	
84181010	容积＞500L冷藏-冷冻组合机	10					0	0
84181020	200L＜容积≤500L冷藏冷冻组合机	15					0	
84181030	容积≤200L冷藏-冷冻组合机	15					0	
84182110	容积＞150L压缩式家用型冷藏箱	10					0	0
84182120	50L＜容积≤150L压缩式家用型冷藏箱	10					0	0
84182130	容积≤50L压缩式家用型冷藏箱	10					0	0
84182910	半导体制冷式家用型冷藏箱	30					0	
84182920	电气吸收式家用型冷藏箱	15					0	
84182990	其他家用型冷藏箱	30					0	
84183010	制冷温度≤-40℃，容积≤800L柜式冷冻箱	9					0	0
84183021	制冷温度＞-40℃，容积500-800L柜式冷冻箱	23					0	
84183029	制冷温度＞-40℃，容积≤500L柜式冷冻箱	30					0	
84184010	制冷温度≤-40℃，容积≤900L立式冷冻箱	9					0	0
84184021	制冷温度＞-40℃，容积500-900L立式冷冻箱	15					0	
84184029	制冷温度＞-40℃，容积≤500L立式冷冻箱	30					0	
84185000	其他装有冷藏或冷冻装置的柜、箱、展示台	10					0	0
84186120	压缩式热泵，税目8415的空气调节器除外	10					0	0
84186190	其他热泵，税目8415的空气调节器除外	15					0	
84186920	其他制冷机组	10					0	0
84186990	其他制冷设备	10					0	0
84189100	冷藏或冷冻设备用特制家具零件	18					0	
84189910	制冷机组及热泵用零件	10					0	0
84189991	制冷温度≤-40℃冷冻设备零件	9.5					0	0
84189992	制冷温度＞-40℃，容积＞500L冷藏设备零件	10					0	0

税则号列	商品名称（简称）	最惠税率	亚太2国	东盟			最不发达35国	最不发达4国
				缅	老	柬		
84189999	税号84.18其他制冷设备用零件	10					0	0
84191100	燃气快速热水器	35					0	
84191910	太阳能热水器	35					0	
84191990	其他非电热的快速或贮备式热水器	35					0	
84192000	医用或实验室用消毒器具	4					0	
84193100	农产品干燥器	8			0		0	0
84193200	木材、纸浆、纸或纸板用干燥器	9			0		0	0
84193910	微空气流动陶瓷坯件干燥器	9					0	
84193990	其他用途的干燥器	9					0	
84194010	提净塔	10					0	
84194020	精馏塔	10					0	
84194090	其他蒸馏或精馏设备	10					0	
84195000	热交换装置	10			0		0	0
84196011	制氧量≥15000立方米/小时制氧机	12					0	
84196019	制氧量＜15000立方米/小时制氧机	13					0	
84196090	其他液化空气或其他气体的机器	10					0	
84198100	加工热饮料、烹调、加热食品的机器	10			0		0	0
84198910	加氢反应器	0			0		0	0
84198990	其他利用温度变化处理材料的机器	0			0		0	0
84199010	热水器用零件	0					0	0
84199090	税号84.19的其他机器设备用零件	4					0	
84201000	砑光机或其他滚压机器	8.4					0	0
84209100	砑光机或其他滚压机器的滚筒	8					0	0
84209900	砑光机或其他滚压机的未列名零件	8					0	0
84211100	奶油分离器	8.4					0	
84211210	干衣量≤10kg的离心干衣机	17.5					0	
84211290	干衣量＞10kg的离心干衣机	8					0	
84211910	脱水机	10					0	
84211920	固液分离机	10					0	
84211990	其他离心机	10					0	
84212110	家用型过滤或净化水的机器及装置	25					0	
84212191	船舶压载水处理设备	5					0	
84212199	其他过滤或净化水的装置	5					0	
84212200	过滤或净化饮料的机器及装置	12					0	
84212300	内燃发动机的燃油过滤器	10					0	
84212910	其他压滤机	5					0	
84212990	其他液体的过滤、净化机器及装置	5					0	0
84213100	内燃发动机的进气过滤器	10					0	
84213910	家用型气体过滤、净化机器及装置	15					0	
84213921	工业用静电除尘器	5					0	
84213922	工业用袋式除尘器	5					0	
84213923	工业用旋风式除尘器	5					0	
84213924	电袋复合除尘器	5					0	
84213929	工业用其他除尘器	5					0	
84213930	内燃发动机排气过滤及净化装置	5					0	0
84213940	烟气脱硫装置	5					0	0
84213950	烟气脱硝装置	5					0	0
84213990	其他气体的过滤、净化机器及装置	5					0	0
84219110	干衣量≤10kg离心干衣机零件	0					0	0
84219190	其他离心机用零件	0					0	0
84219910	家用型过滤、净化装置用零件	10					0	
84219990	其他过滤、净化装置用零件	5					0	0
84221100	家用型洗碟机	10					0	0
84221900	非家用型洗碟机	14					0	
84222000	瓶子及其他容器的洗涤或干燥机器	10					0	0
84223010	饮料及液体食品罐装设备	12					0	0
84223021	水泥全自动灌包机	12					0	0
84223029	其他水泥包装机	12					0	0

税则号列	商品名称（简称）	最惠税率	亚太2国	东盟			最不发达35国	最不发达4国
				缅	老	柬		
84223030	其他包装机	10					0	0
84223090	其他装填密封等包封机器	10					0	0
84224000	其他包装或打包机器	10					0	0
84229010	洗碟机用零件	10.5					0	0
84229020	饮料及液体食品灌装设备用零件	8.5					0	0
84229090	税号84.22其他未列名机器零件	8.5					0	0
84231000	体重计、婴儿秤及家用秤	10.5					0	0
84232010	电子皮带秤	10					0	0
84232090	其他输送带上连续称货的秤	10					0	0
84233010	定量包装秤	10.5					0	0
84233020	定量分选秤	10.5					0	0
84233030	配料秤	10.5					0	0
84233090	其他恒定秤、物料定量装袋或容器用秤	10.5					0	0
84238110	最大称量≤30kg的计价秤	10.5					0	0
84238120	最大称量≤30kg的弹簧秤	10.5					0	0
84238190	最大称量≤30kg的其他衡器	10.5					0	0
84238210	最大称量30-5000kg的地中衡	10.5					0	0
84238290	最大称量30-5000kg的其他衡器	10.5					0	0
84238910	其他地中衡	10					0	0
84238920	其他轨道衡	10					0	0
84238930	其他吊秤	10					0	0
84238990	其他衡器	10					0	0
84239000	衡器用的各种砝码、秤砣及其零件	10					0	0
84241000	灭火器	8.4					0	
84242000	喷枪及类似器具	8.4					0	
84243000	喷汽机、喷砂机及类似喷射机	8.4					0	
84248100	农业或园艺用喷射、喷雾机械器具	8					0	
84248910	家用型喷射、喷雾机械器具	0					0	0
84248920	喷涂机器人	0					0	0
84248991	船用洗舱机	0					0	0
84248999	其他液体粉末喷射机械	0					0	0
84249010	灭火器用的零件	0					0	0
84249020	家用型喷射、喷雾器具的零件	0					0	0
84249090	其他喷雾器具及喷气机等用的零件	0					0	0
84251100	电动滑车及提升机	6					0	0
84251900	非电动滑车及提升机	5					0	0
84253110	矿井口电动卷扬装置；专为井下使用设计的电动卷扬机	10					0	0
84253190	其他电动卷扬机及绞盘	5					0	0
84253910	其他矿井口卷扬装置；其他专为井下使用设计的卷扬机	10					0	0
84253990	其他非电动卷扬机及绞盘	5					0	0
84254100	车库中使用的固定千斤顶系统	3					0	0
84254210	其他液压千斤顶	3					0	0
84254290	提升车辆用液压提升机	5					0	0
84254910	其他千斤顶	5					0	0
84254990	其他提升车辆用提升机	10					0	0
84261120	通用桥式起重机	8					0	0
84261190	其他固定支架的高架移动式起重机	8					0	0
84261200	胶轮移动式吊运架及跨运车	6					0	0
84261910	装船机	5					0	0
84261921	抓斗式卸船机	5					0	0
84261929	其他卸船机	5					0	0
84261930	龙门式起重机	10					0	0
84261941	门式装卸桥	10					0	0
84261942	集装箱装卸桥	10					0	0
84261943	其他动臂式装卸桥	10					0	0
84261949	其他装卸桥	10					0	0
84261990	其他高架移动式起重机等	10					0	0
84262000	塔式起重机	10					0	0

税则号列	商品名称（简称）	最惠税率	亚太2国	东盟			最不发达35国	最不发达4国
				缅	老	柬		
84263000	门座式起重机及座式旋臂起重机	6					0	0
84264110	轮胎式起重机	5					0	0
84264190	其他带胶轮的自推进起重机	5					0	0
84264910	履带式起重机	8					0	0
84264990	其他不带胶轮的自推进起重机	13					0	
84269100	供装于公路车辆的其他起重机	10					0	0
84269900	其他起重设备	6					0	0
84271010	有轨巷道堆垛机	9					0	0
84271020	无轨巷道堆垛机	9					0	0
84271090	其他电动机推进的叉车及可升降工作车	9					0	0
84272010	集装箱叉车	9					0	0
84272090	其他机动叉车及有类似装置工作车	9					0	0
84279000	其他叉车及可升降的工作车	9					0	0
84281010	载客电梯	8					0	0
84281090	其他升降机及倒卸式起重机	6					0	0
84282000	气压升降机及输送机	5					0	0
84283100	地下连续运货或材料升降、输送机	5					0	0
84283200	其他斗式连续运货升降、输送机	5					0	0
84283300	其他带式连续运货升降、输送机	5					0	0
84283910	链式连续运送货物的升降机及输送机	5					0	0
84283920	辊式连续运送货物的升降机及输送机	5					0	0
84283990	其他未列名连续运货升降、输送机	5					0	0
84284000	自动梯及自动人行道	5					0	0
84286010	货运架空索道	8					0	0
84286021	单线循环式客运架空索道	8					0	0
84286029	其他客运架空索道	8					0	0
84286090	其他缆车、座式升降机用牵引装置	8					0	0
84289010	矿车推动机、铁道机车等的转车台	10					0	0
84289020	机械式停车设备	5					0	0
84289031	堆取料机械	5					0	0
84289039	其他装卸机械	5					0	0
84289040	搬运机器人	5					0	0
84289090	其他升降、搬运、装卸机械	5					0	0
84291110	功率＞235.36kw的履带式推土机	7					0	0
84291190	功率≤235.36kw的履带式推土机	7					0	0
84291910	功率＞235.36kw的其他推土机	7					0	0
84291990	功率≤235.36kw的其他推土机	7					0	0
84292010	功率＞235.36kw的筑路机及平地机	5					0	0
84292090	其他筑路机及平地机	5					0	0
84293010	斗容量＞10立方米的铲运机	3					0	0
84293090	斗容量≤10立方米的铲运机	5					0	0
84294011	机重≥18吨的震动式压路机	7					0	0
84294019	其他机动压路机	8					0	0
84294090	其他未列名捣固机械及压路机	6					0	0
84295100	前铲装载机	5					0	0
84295211	轮胎式挖掘机	8					0	0
84295212	履带式挖掘机	8					0	0
84295219	其他挖掘机	8					0	0
84295290	其他上部结构可转360度的挖掘机类似机械	8					0	0
84295900	其他机械铲、挖掘机及机铲装载机	8					0	0
84301000	打桩机及拔桩机	10					0	0
84302000	扫雪机及吹雪机	10					0	0
84303110	采（截）煤机	10					0	0
84303120	凿岩机	10					0	0
84303130	隧道掘进机	10					0	0
84303900	其他非自推进截煤机、采石机及掘进机	6					0	0
84304111	钻探深度≥6000米的自推进石油钻探机	5					0	0
84304119	其他自推进石油及天然气钻探机	5					0	0

税则号列	商品名称（简称）	最惠税率	亚太2国	东盟			最不发达35国	最不发达4国
				缅	老	柬		
84304121	钻探深度≥6000米的其他钻探机	5					0	0
84304122	钻探深度<6000米履带式自推进钻机	5					0	0
84304129	钻探深度<6000米的其他自推进钻机	5					0	0
84304190	其他自推进的凿井机械	5					0	0
84304900	非自推进的钻探或凿井机械	5					0	0
84305010	其他自推进采油机械	3					0	0
84305020	矿用电铲	7					0	0
84305031	牙轮直径≥380mm的采矿牙轮钻机	5					0	0
84305039	牙轮直径<380mm的采矿牙轮钻机	5					0	0
84305090	其他自推进未列名机械	5					0	0
84306100	非自推进捣固或压实机械	6					0	0
84306911	钻筒直径>3m的工程钻机	6					0	0
84306919	钻筒直径≤3m的工程钻机	6					0	0
84306920	非自推进铲运机	6					0	0
84306990	其他非自推进未列名机械	6					0	0
84311000	滑车、绞盘、千斤顶等机械用零件	3					0	0
84312010	税号84.27所列机械的装有差速器的驱动桥及其零件，不论是否装有其他传动部件	6					0	0
84312090	其他税号84.27所列机械的零件	6					0	0
84313100	升降机、倒卸式起重机或自动梯的零件	3					0	0
84313900	税号84.28所列其他机械的零件	5					0	0
84314100	戽斗、铲斗、抓斗及夹斗	6					0	0
84314200	推土机或侧铲推土机用铲	6					0	0
84314310	石油或天然气钻探机用零件	4					0	0
84314320	其他钻探机用零件	4					0	0
84314390	其他凿井机用零件	5					0	0
84314920	税号84.26、84.29、或84.30所列机械的装有差速器的驱动桥及其零件，不论是否装有其他传动部件	5					0	0
84314991	矿用电铲用零件	5					0	0
84314999	其他税号84.26、84.29、或84.30所列机械的零件	5					0	0
84321000	犁	5					0	0
84322100	圆盘耙	5					0	0
84322900	其他耙、松土机等耕作机械	4					0	
84323011	谷物播种机	4					0	
84323019	其他播种机	4					0	
84323021	马铃薯种植机	4					0	
84323029	其他种植机	4					0	
84323031	水稻插秧机	4					0	
84323039	其他移植机(栽植机)	4					0	
84324000	施肥机	4					0	
84328010	草坪及运动场地滚压机	7					0	
84328090	其他未列名整地或耕作机械	4					0	
84329000	整地或耕作机械、滚压机零件	4					0	
84331100	机动旋转式割草机	6					0	
84331900	草坪、公园等用其他割草机	6					0	
84332000	其他割草机	4					0	
84333000	其他干草切割、翻晒机器	5					0	
84334000	草料打包机	5					0	
84335100	联合收割机	8					0	
84335200	其他脱粒机	8					0	
84335300	根茎或块茎收获机	8					0	
84335910	甘蔗收获机	8					0	
84335920	棉花采摘机	8					0	
84335990	其他收割机	8					0	
84336000	蛋类、水果等清洁、分选、分级机	5					0	
84339010	联合收割机用零件	5					0	
84339090	税号84.33所列其他机械零件	3					0	0
84341000	挤奶机	10					0	
84342000	乳品加工机器	6					0	

税则号列	商品名称（简称）	最惠税率	亚太2国	东盟			最不发达35国	最不发达4国
				缅	老	柬		
84349000	挤奶机及乳品加工机器用零件	5					0	
84351000	制酒、果汁等的压榨、轧碎机	10					0	
84359000	制酒、果汁等压榨、轧碎机零件	6					0	
84361000	动物饲料配制机	7					0	
84362100	家禽孵卵器及育雏器	5					0	
84362900	家禽饲养用机器	10					0	
84368000	农、林业、园艺等用的其他机器	10					0	
84369100	家禽饲养机、孵卵器及育雏器零件	6					0	
84369900	税号84.36所列其他机器的零件	6					0	
84371010	光学色差颗粒选别机（色选机）	10					0	
84371090	其他种子、谷物或干豆的清洁、分选或分级机	10					0	
84378000	谷物磨粉业加工机器	10					0	
84379000	税号84.37所列机械的零件	6					0	
84381000	糕点、通心粉、面条的生产加工机器	7					0	0
84382000	生产糖果、可可粉、巧克力的机器	8					0	0
84383000	制糖机器	10					0	0
84384000	酿酒机器	7					0	0
84385000	肉类或家禽加工机器	7					0	0
84386000	水果、坚果或蔬菜加工机器	10					0	0
84388000	84章其他未列名食品等加工机器	8.5					0	0
84389000	食品、饮料工业用机器的零件	5					0	0
84391000	制造纤维素纸浆的机器	8.4					0	0
84392000	纸或纸板的抄造机器	8.4					0	0
84393000	纸或纸板的整理机器	8.4					0	0
84399100	制造纤维素纸浆的机器零件	6					0	0
84399900	制造或整理纸及纸板的机器零件	6					0	0
84401010	锁线装订机	10					0	
84401020	胶订机	12					0	
84401090	其他书本装订机器	12					0	
84409000	书本装订机器的零件	8					0	
84411000	切纸机	12					0	0
84412000	制造包、袋或信封的机器	12					0	0
84413010	纸塑铝复合罐生产设备	13.5					0	
84413090	其他制造箱、盒、桶及类似容器的机器	13.5					0	
84414000	纸浆、纸或纸板制品模制成型机器	12					0	0
84418010	制造纸塑铝软包装的生产设备	12					0	0
84418090	其他制造纸浆制品、纸制品的机器	12					0	0
84419010	切纸机零件	8					0	0
84419090	其他制造纸浆、纸制品的机器零件	8.4					0	0
84423010	铸字机	9					0	0
84423021	计算机直接制版设备	9					0	0
84423029	去制版机器、器具及设备	9					0	0
84423090	其他铸字、制版用机器、器具及设备	9					0	0
84424000	铸字、排字、制版机器的零件	7					0	0
84425000	活字、印刷用版、片及其他部件	7					0	0
84431100	卷取进料式胶印机	10					0	0
84431200	办公室用片取进料式胶印机	12					0	0
84431311	平张纸进料式单色胶印机	10					0	0
84431312	平张纸进料式双色胶印机	10					0	0
84431313	平张纸进料式四色胶印机	10					0	0
84431319	平张纸进料式其他胶印机	10					0	0
84431390	其他胶印机	10					0	0
84431400	卷取进料式凸版印刷机	12					0	0
84431500	其他凸版印刷机	12					0	0
84431600	苯胺印刷机	10					0	0
84431700	照像凹版印刷机	18					0	
84431921	圆网印刷机	10					0	0
84431922	平网印刷机	10					0	0

税则号列	商品名称（简称）	最惠税率	亚太2国	东盟			最不发达35国	最不发达4国
				缅	老	柬		
84431929	其他网式印刷机	10					0	0
84431980	其它印刷机	8					0	0
84433110	静电感光式多功能机	10					0	0
84433190	其他多功能机	0					0	0
84433211	针式打印机	0					0	0
84433212	激光打印机	0					0	0
84433213	喷墨打印机	0					0	0
84433214	热敏打印机	0					0	0
84433219	其他打印机	0					0	0
84433221	可以网络连接的喷墨印刷机	8					0	0
84433222	可以网络连接的静电照相印刷机(激光印刷机)	8					0	0
84433229	可以网络连接的其他数字印刷设备	8					0	0
84433290	其他可与网络连接的传真机或打字机	0					0	0
84433911	直接法静电感光复印设备	0					0	0
84433912	间接法静电感光复印设备	10					0	0
84433921	带有光学系统的感光复印设备	0					0	0
84433922	接触式感光复印设备	20					0	
84433923	热敏复印设备	20					0	
84433924	热升华复印设备	20					0	
84433931	其他独立的喷墨印刷机	8					0	0
84433932	其他独立的静电照相印刷机(激光印刷机)	8					0	0
84433939	其他独立的数字印刷设备	8					0	0
84433990	其他独立的电传打字机	0					0	0
84439111	卷筒料给料机	12					0	0
84439119	其他传统印刷机用辅助机器	12					0	0
84439190	传统印刷机用零件及附件	6					0	0
84439910	数字印刷设备用辅助机器	12					0	0
84439921	热敏打印头	6					0	0
84439929	数字印刷设备的其他零件	6					0	0
84439990	其他打印机、复印机、传真机用零件	0					0	0
84440010	合成纤维长丝纺丝机	10					0	
84440020	合成纤维短丝纺丝机	10					0	
84440030	人造纤维纺丝机	10					0	
84440040	化学纤维变形机	10					0	
84440050	化学纤维切断机	10					0	
84440090	其他化学纤维挤压、拉伸、变形或切割机器	10					0	
84451111	棉纤维清梳联合机	10					0	0
84451112	棉纤维自动抓棉机	10					0	0
84451113	棉纤维梳棉机	10					0	0
84451119	其他棉纤维梳理机	10					0	0
84451120	毛纤维梳理机	10					0	0
84451190	其他纺织纤维梳理机	10					0	0
84451210	棉纺织纤维精梳机	10					0	0
84451220	毛纺织纤维精梳机	10					0	0
84451290	其他纺织纤维精梳机	10					0	0
84451310	拉伸机	10					0	0
84451321	棉纺粗纱机	10					0	0
84451322	毛纺粗纱机	10					0	0
84451329	其他粗纱机	10					0	0
84451900	纺织纤维的其他预处理机器	10					0	0
84452031	转杯纺纱机	10					0	0
84452032	喷气纺纱机	10					0	0
84452039	其他自由端纺纱机	10					0	0
84452041	棉环锭细纱机	10.5					0	0
84452042	毛环锭细纱机	10					0	0
84452049	其他环锭细纱机	10					0	0
84452090	其他纺纱机	10					0	0
84453000	并线机或加捻机	10					0	0

税则号列	商品名称（简称）	最惠税率	亚太2国	东盟			最不发达35国	最不发达4国
				缅	老	柬		
84454010	自动络筒机	10					0	0
84454090	其他络纱机(包括卷纬机)或摇纱机	10					0	0
84459010	整经机	10					0	0
84459020	浆纱机	10					0	0
84459090	其他生产及处理纺织纱线的机器	10					0	0
84461000	所织织物宽度≤30cm的织机	8					0	
84462110	所织织物宽度>30cm的梭织动力地毯织机	12					0	
84462190	所织织物宽度>30cm的其他梭织动力织机	10					0	
84462900	所织织物宽度>30cm的梭织非动力织机	10					0	
84463020	所织织物宽度>30cm的剑杆织机	8					0	
84463030	所织织物宽度>30cm的片梭织机	8					0	
84463040	所织织物宽度>30cm的喷水织机	8					0	
84463050	所织织物宽度>30cm的喷气织机	8					0	
84463090	所织织物宽度>30cm的其他无梭织机	8					0	
84471100	圆筒直径≤165mm的圆型针织机	8					0	0
84471200	圆筒直径>165mm的圆型针织机	8					0	0
84472011	特里科经编机	8					0	0
84472012	拉舍尔经编机	8					0	0
84472019	其他经编机	8					0	0
84472020	平型纬编机	8					0	0
84472030	缝编机	8					0	0
84479011	地毯织机	7					0	0
84479019	其他簇绒机	8					0	0
84479020	绣花机	8					0	0
84479090	税号84.47其他未列名机器	10					0	0
84481100	多臂机或提花机	8					0	0
84481900	税号84.44至84.47所列的其他辅助机器	8					0	0
84482020	喷丝头或喷丝板	6					0	0
84482090	纤维挤压机及其辅助机器的其他零附件	6					0	0
84483100	钢丝针布	6					0	0
84483200	纺织纤维预处理机器的其他零附件	6					0	0
84483310	络筒锭	6					0	0
84483390	其他锭子、锭壳、纺丝环、钢丝圈	6					0	0
84483910	气流杯	6					0	0
84483920	电子清纱器	6					0	0
84483930	空气捻接器	6					0	0
84483940	环锭细纱机紧密纺装置	6					0	0
84483990	税号84.45所机器的其他零附件	6					0	0
84484200	织机用筘、综丝及综框	6					0	0
84484910	接、投梭箱	6					0	0
84484920	引纬、送经装置	6					0	0
84484930	梭子	6					0	0
84484990	织机及其辅助机器用其他零附件	6					0	0
84485120	针织机用28号以下的弹簧针、钩针及复合针	6					0	0
84485190	沉降片、其他织针及成圈机件	6					0	0
84485900	税号84.47机器用的其他零附件	6					0	0
84490010	针刺机	8					0	
84490020	水刺设备	8					0	
84490090	其他毡呢或无纺织物制造或整理机器；帽模	8					0	
84501110	干衣量≤10kg的波轮式全自动洗衣机	10					0	0
84501120	干衣量≤10kg的滚筒式全自动洗衣机	10					0	0
84501190	干衣量≤10kg的其他全自动洗衣机	10					0	0
84501200	装有离心甩干机的非全自动洗衣机	30					0	
84501900	干衣量≤10kg的其他洗衣机	30					0	
84502011	波轮式洗衣机	10					0	0
84502012	滚筒式洗衣机	10					0	0
84502019	其他全自动洗衣机	10					0	0
84502090	其他干衣量超过10公斤的洗衣机	10					0	0

税则号列	商品名称（简称）	最惠税率	亚太2国	东盟			最不发达35国	最不发达4国
				缅	老	柬		
84509010	干衣量≤10kg的洗衣机零件	5					0	0
84509090	干衣量＞10kg的洗衣机零件	16					0	
84511000	干洗机	21					0	
84512100	干衣量≤10kg的干燥机	15					0	
84512900	干衣量＞10kg的干燥机	8					0	0
84513000	熨烫机及挤压机(包括熔压机)	8					0	0
84514000	洗涤、漂白或染色机器	8.4					0	0
84515000	纺织物卷绕、退绕、折叠、剪切或剪齿边机器	8					0	0
84518000	税号84.51所列其他未列名的机器	12					0	0
84519000	税号84.51所列机器的零件	8					0	0
84521010	多功能家用缝纫机	21					0	
84521091	手动式家用型缝纫机	21					0	
84521099	其他家用型缝纫机	21					0	
84522110	非家用自动平缝机	12					0	0
84522120	非家用自动包缝机	12					0	0
84522130	非家用自动绷缝机	12					0	0
84522190	其他非家用自动缝纫机	12					0	0
84522900	其他非家用非自动缝纫机	12					0	0
84523000	缝纫机针	14					0	
84529011	家用型缝纫机用旋梭	14					0	
84529019	家用型缝纫机用其他零件	14					0	
84529091	其他缝纫机用旋梭	14					0	0
84529092	其他缝纫机专用的特制家具、底座和罩盖及其零件	14					0	
84529099	其他缝纫机用其他零件	14					0	0
84531000	生皮、皮革的处理、鞣制或加工机器	8.4					0	
84532000	鞋靴制作或修理机器	8.4					0	
84538000	毛皮及其他皮革的制作或修理机器	8.4					0	
84539000	税号84.53所列机器的零件	8					0	
84541000	金属冶炼及铸造用转炉	8.4					0	0
84542010	炉外精炼设备	8.4					0	0
84542090	其他金属冶炼及铸造用锭模及浇包	8.4					0	0
84543010	冷室压铸机	12					0	0
84543021	方坯连铸机	10					0	0
84543022	板坯连铸机	12					0	0
84543029	其他钢坯连铸机	12					0	0
84543090	其他金属冶炼及铸造用铸造机	12					0	0
84549010	炉外精炼设备用零件	8					0	0
84549021	结晶器	8					0	0
84549022	振动装置	8					0	0
84549029	其他钢坯连铸机用零件	8					0	0
84549090	其他冶炼等用转炉及铸造机的零件	8					0	0
84551010	热轧管机	12					0	0
84551020	冷轧管机	12					0	0
84551030	定、减径轧管机	12					0	0
84551090	其他金属轧管机	12					0	0
84552110	板材热轧机	15					0	
84552120	型钢轧机	15					0	
84552130	线材轧机	15					0	
84552190	其他金属热轧或冷热联合轧机	15					0	
84552210	板材冷轧机	10					0	
84552290	其他金属冷轧机	15					0	
84553000	金属轧机用轧辊	8.4					0	0
84559000	金属轧机的其他零件	8					0	0
84561000	用激光等处理各种材料的加工机床	0					0	0
84562000	用超声波处理各种材料的加工机床	10					0	
84563010	数控的用放电处理各种材料的加工机床	9.7					0	
84563090	非数控的用放电处理各种材料的加工机床	10					0	
84569010	等离子切割机	0					0	0

税则号列	商品名称（简称）	最惠税率	亚太2国	东盟			最不发达35国	最不发达4国
				缅	老	柬		
84569020	水射流切割机	0					0	0
84569090	其他用电化学、电子束处理材料的加工机床	0					0	0
84571010	立式加工中心	9.7					0	
84571020	卧式加工中心	9.7					0	
84571030	龙门式加工中心	9.7					0	
84571091	铣车复合	9.7					0	
84571099	其他加工中心	9.7					0	
84572000	加工金属的单工位组合机床	8					0	
84573000	加工金属的多工位组合机床	5					0	
84581100	切削金属的数控卧式车床	9.7					0	0
84581900	切削金属的非数控卧式车床	12					0	0
84589110	立式数控机床	5					0	0
84589120	其他数控机床	5					0	0
84589900	切削金属的其他车床	12					0	0
84591000	切削金属的直线移动式动力头钻床	15					0	
84592100	切削金属的数控钻床	9.7					0	0
84592900	切削金属的其他钻床	15					0	
84593100	切削金属的数控镗铣机床	9.7					0	0
84593900	切削金属的其他镗铣机床	10					0	0
84594010	切削金属的数控镗床	9.7					0	0
84594090	切削金属的其他镗床	15					0	
84595100	切削金属的升降台式数控铣床	9.7					0	0
84595900	切削金属的其他升降台式铣床	15					0	
84596110	切削金属的数控龙门铣床	5					0	0
84596190	切削金属的其他数控铣床	5					0	0
84596910	切削金属的非数控龙门铣床	12					0	0
84596990	切削金属的其他铣床	12					0	0
84597000	切削金属的其他攻丝机床	12					0	0
84601100	数控平面磨床	9.7					0	0
84601900	其他平面磨床	15					0	
84602111	曲轴磨床	9.7					0	0
84602119	其他外圆磨床	9.7					0	0
84602120	数控内圆磨床	9.7					0	0
84602190	其他数控磨床	9.7					0	0
84602910	其他外圆磨床	15					0	
84602920	其他内圆磨床	15					0	
84602930	非数控轧辊磨床	13					0	
84602990	其他磨床	13					0	
84603100	数控刃磨(工具或刀具)机床	9.7					0	0
84603900	其他刃磨(工具或刀具)机床	15					0	
84604010	珩磨机床	13					0	
84604020	研磨机床	13					0	
84609010	砂轮机	15					0	
84609020	抛光机床	15					0	
84609090	其他磨削等精加工机床	15					0	
84612010	牛头刨床	15					0	
84612020	插床	15					0	
84613000	拉床	12					0	
84614011	齿轮磨床	9.7					0	0
84614019	其他数控的切齿机、齿轮磨床或齿轮精加工机床	9.7					0	0
84614090	非数控切齿机、齿轮磨床齿轮精加工机床	15					0	
84615000	锯床或切断机	12					0	
84619011	龙门刨床	15					0	
84619019	其他刨床	15					0	
84619090	税号 84.61 的未列名机床	12					0	
84621010	数控锻造或冲压机床及锻锤	9.7					0	0
84621090	非数控锻造或冲压机床及锻锤	12					0	0
84622110	数控矫直机	9.7					0	0

税则号列	商品名称（简称）	最惠税率	亚太2国	东盟			最不发达35国	最不发达4国
				缅	老	柬		
84622190	数控的其他弯曲、折迭、矫直或矫平机床	9.7					0	0
84622910	非数控矫直机	10					0	0
84622990	非数控的其他弯曲、折迭、矫直或矫平机床	10					0	0
84623110	数控的板带纵剪机	7					0	0
84623120	数控的板带横剪机	7					0	0
84623190	数控的其他剪切机床	7					0	0
84623910	非数控板带纵剪机	10					0	0
84623920	非数控板带横剪机	10					0	0
84623990	其他剪切机床	10					0	0
84624111	自动换模式数控步冲压力机	9.7					0	0
84624119	其他数控冲床	9.7					0	0
84624190	其他数控冲孔、开槽机、冲剪两用机	9.7					0	0
84624900	非数控冲孔、开槽机、冲剪两用机	10					0	0
84629110	金属型材挤压机	10					0	0
84629190	其他液压压力机	10					0	0
84629910	其他机械压力机	10					0	0
84629990	税号84.62的未列名机床	10					0	0
84631011	拉拔力为300吨及以下的冷拔管机	10					0	
84631019	其他冷拔管机	10					0	
84631020	拔丝机	10					0	
84631090	其他金属杆、管、型材及类似品的拉拔机	10					0	
84632000	金属或金属陶瓷的螺纹滚轧机	15					0	
84633000	金属丝加工机	10					0	
84639000	其他非切削加工机床	10					0	
84641010	圆盘锯	0					0	0
84641020	钢丝锯	0					0	0
84641090	其他加工矿物等材料的锯床	0					0	0
84642010	玻璃研磨或抛光机床	0					0	0
84642090	其他加工矿物等材料的研磨或抛光机床	0					0	0
84649011	切割机	0					0	0
84649012	刻花机	0					0	0
84649019	玻璃的其他冷加工机床	0					0	0
84649090	其他税号84.64的未列名机床	0					0	0
84651000	不需变换工具即可进行加工的机床	10					0	
84659100	加工木材等材料的锯床	10					0	
84659200	加工木材等材料的刨、铣或切削机器	10					0	
84659300	加工木材等材料的研磨或抛光机器	10					0	
84659400	加工木材等材料的弯曲或装配机器	10					0	
84659500	加工木材等材料的钻孔或凿榫机器	10					0	
84659600	加工木材等材料的剖、切或刮削机器	10					0	
84659900	加工木材等材料的其他机床	10					0	
84661000	工具夹具及自启板牙切头	7					0	0
84662000	工件夹具	7					0	0
84663000	分度头及其他专用于机床的附件	7					0	0
84669100	税号84.64所列机器用的零附件	0					0	0
84669200	税号84.65所列机器用的零附件	6					0	0
84669310	刀库及自动换刀装置	0					0	0
84669390	税号84.56-84.61机器用其他零附件	0					0	0
84669400	税号84.62-84.63机器用其他零附件	6					0	0
84671100	旋转式手提风动工具	8					0	0
84671900	其他手提式风动工具	8					0	0
84672100	电动钻	10					0	0
84672210	电动链锯	10					0	0
84672290	其他电动锯	10					0	0
84672910	电动砂磨工具	10					0	0
84672920	电刨	10					0	0
84672990	其他电动工具	10					0	0
84678100	手提式液压或其他动力链锯	8					0	0

税则号列	商品名称（简称）	最惠税率	亚太2国	东盟			最不发达35国	最不发达4国
				缅	老	柬		
84678900	其他手提式液压或其他动力工具	8					0	0
84679110	电动链锯用零件	6					0	0
84679190	其他链锯用零件	6					0	0
84679200	风动工具零件	6					0	0
84679910	其他手提式电动工具用零件	10					0	0
84679990	其他手提式工具用零件	6					0	0
84681000	手提喷焊器	12					0	0
84682000	其他气体焊或表面回火机器及装置	12					0	0
84688000	其他焊接机器及装置	12					0	0
84689000	焊接机器用零件	7					0	0
84690011	文字处理机	0					0	0
84690012	自动打字机	12					0	
84690020	其他电动打字机	12					0	
84690030	其他非电动打字机	12					0	
84701000	电子计算器及袖珍式数据录放机器	0					0	0
84702100	装有打印装置的电子计算器	0					0	0
84702900	其他电子计算器	0					0	0
84703000	其他计算机器	0					0	0
84705010	销售点终端出纳机	0					0	0
84705090	其他现金出纳机	0					0	0
84709000	邮资盖戳机、售票机及类似机器	0					0	0
84713010	平板电脑	0					0	0
84713090	其他重量不超过10公斤的便携数字式自动数据处理设备，至少由一个中央处理部件、一个键盘及一个显示器组成自动数据处理设备及其部件	0					0	0
84714110	巨、大、中型计算机	0					0	0
84714120	小型机	0					0	0
84714140	微型机	0					0	0
84714190	其他自动数据处理单体机	0					0	0
84714910	以系统形式进口的巨、大、中型计算机	0					0	0
84714920	以系统形式进口的小型计算机	0					0	0
84714940	以系统形式进口的微型机	0					0	0
84714991	分散型工业过程控制设备	0					0	0
84714999	以系统形式报验的其他计算机	0					0	0
84715010	巨、大、中型机处理部件	0					0	0
84715020	小型机的处理部件	0					0	0
84715040	微型机的处理部件	0					0	0
84715090	8471.41、8471.49以外设备的其他处理部件	0					0	0
84716040	巨、大、中及小型计算机用终端	0					0	0
84716050	扫描仪	0					0	0
84716060	数字化仪	0					0	0
84716071	键盘	0					0	0
84716072	鼠标器	0					0	0
84716090	自动处理设备的其他输入或输出部件	0					0	0
84717010	硬盘驱动器	0					0	0
84717020	软盘驱动器	0					0	0
84717030	光盘驱动器	0					0	0
84717090	自动数据处理设备的其他存储部件	0					0	0
84718000	其他自动数据处理设备的其他部件	0					0	0
84719000	未列名的磁性或光学阅读器及其他数据处理设备	0					0	0
84721000	胶版复印机、油印机	14					0	
84723010	邮政信件分拣及封装设备	10					0	0
84723090	其他信件分类、折迭、信封装封机等机器	14					0	
84729010	自动柜员机	0					0	0
84729021	打洞机	0					0	0
84729022	订书机	0					0	0
84729029	其他装订用机器	0					0	0
84729030	碎纸机	0					0	0
84729040	地址印写机及地址铭牌压印机	14					0	
84729090	其他办公室用机器	0					0	0

税则号列	商品名称（简称）	最惠税率	亚太2国	东盟			最不发达35国	最不发达4国
				缅	老	柬		
84731000	打字机、文字处理机的零附件	8					0	0
84732100	税号84.70所列电子计算器的零附件	0					0	0
84732900	税号84.70所列其他机器的零附件	0					0	0
84733010	数字式大、中、小型计算机零附件	0					0	0
84733090	税号84.71所列计算机的其他零附件	0					0	0
84734010	自动柜员机用出钞器	10.5					0	0
84734090	税号84.72所列其他办公室用机器零附件	10.5					0	0
84735000	税号84.69-84.72中所列机器零附件	0					0	0
84741000	固体矿物的分类、筛选、分离或洗涤机器	5					0	0
84742010	齿辊式破碎及磨粉机器	5					0	0
84742020	球磨式破碎及磨粉机器	5					0	0
84742090	其他破碎及磨粉机器	5					0	0
84743100	混凝土或砂浆混合机器	7					0	0
84743200	矿物与沥青的混合机器	7					0	0
84743900	其他混合或搅拌机器	5					0	0
84748010	固体矿物的辊压成型机	5					0	0
84748020	模压成型机	5					0	0
84748090	税号8474所列的其他机器	5					0	0
84749000	税号8474所列机器的零件	5					0	0
84751000	白炽灯炮、灯管等的封装机	8					0	0
84752100	制造光导纤维及其预制棒的机器	10					0	0
84752911	连续式玻璃热弯炉	10					0	0
84752912	玻璃纤维拉丝机（光纤拉丝机除外）	10					0	0
84752919	其他玻璃热加工设备	10					0	0
84752990	其他玻璃及其制品的制造或热加工机器	10					0	0
84759000	税号84.75所列机器的零件	8					0	0
84762100	装有加热或制冷装置的饮料自动销售机	14					0	
84762900	其他饮料自动销售机	15					0	
84768100	装有加热或制冷装置的自动售货机	14					0	
84768900	其他自动售货机	15					0	
84769000	税号8476所列机器的零件	10					0	0
84771010	注塑机	0					0	0
84771090	其他加工橡胶或塑料的注射机	0					0	0
84772010	塑料造粒机	5					0	0
84772090	其他加工橡胶或塑料的挤出机	5					0	0
84773010	挤出吹塑机	5					0	0
84773020	注射吹塑机	5					0	0
84773090	其他吹塑机	5					0	0
84774010	塑料中空成型机	5					0	0
84774020	塑料压延成型机	5					0	0
84774090	其他真空模塑及热成型机器	5					0	0
84775100	用于充气轮胎或内胎模塑或翻新的机器	5					0	0
84775910	三维打印机（3D打印机）	5					0	0
84775990	其他模塑或成型机器	5					0	0
84778000	其他橡胶或塑料加工机器	5					0	0
84779000	橡胶、塑料等加工机器的零件	0					0	0
84781000	其他未列名的烟草加工及制作机器	5					0	
84789000	烟草加工及制作机器用的零件	10					0	
84791021	沥青混凝土摊铺机	8					0	0
84791022	稳定土摊铺机	8					0	0
84791029	其他摊铺机	8					0	0
84791090	其他公共工程用的机器	8					0	0
84792000	提取加工动物或植物油脂的机器	10					0	0
84793000	木碎料板或木纤维板的挤压机	10					0	0
84794000	绳或缆的制造机器	7					0	0
84795010	多功能工业机器人	0					0	0
84795090	其他工业机器人	0					0	0
84796000	蒸发式空气冷却器	10					0	0

税则号列	商品名称（简称）	最惠税率	亚太2国	东盟 缅	东盟 老	东盟 柬	最不发达35国	最不发达4国
84797100	机场用旅客登机桥	0					0	0
84797900	其他旅客登机（船）桥	0					0	0
84798110	绕线机	9.5					0	0
84798190	其他处理金属的机械	9.5					0	0
84798200	其他混合、研磨、筛选、均化等机器	7					0	0
84798910	船舶用舵机及陀螺稳定器	0					0	0
84798920	空气增湿器及减湿器	0					0	0
84798940	邮政用包裹、印刷品分拣设备	0					0	0
84798950	放射性废物压实机	0					0	0
84798961	自动插件机	0					0	0
84798962	自动贴片机	0					0	0
84798969	印刷电路电路板的其他加工设备	0					0	0
84798992	自动化立体仓储设备	0					0	0
84798999	本章其他税号未列名机器及机械器具	0					0	0
84799010	船舶用舵机及陀螺稳定器零件	0					0	0
84799020	空气增湿器及减湿器零件	0					0	0
84799090	税号84.79所列机器的其他零件	0					0	0
84801000	金属铸造用型箱	10					0	0
84802000	型模底板	8					0	0
84803000	阳模	10					0	0
84804110	压铸模	8					0	0
84804120	粉末冶金用压模	8					0	0
84804190	其他金属、硬质合金用注模或压模	8					0	0
84804900	金属、硬质合金用其他型模	8					0	0
84805000	玻璃用型模	8.4					0	0
84806000	矿物材料用型模	8.4					0	0
84807110	硫化轮胎用囊式型模	0					0	0
84807190	其他塑料或橡胶用注模或压模	0					0	0
84807900	塑料或橡胶用其他型模	5					0	0
84811000	减压阀	5					0	0
84812010	油压传动阀	5					0	0
84812020	气压传动阀	5					0	0
84813000	止回阀	5					0	0
84814000	安全阀或溢流阀	5					0	0
84818021	电磁换向阀	7					0	0
84818029	其他换向阀	7					0	0
84818031	电子膨胀阀	7					0	0
84818039	其他流量阀	7					0	0
84818040	其他阀门	7					0	0
84818090	未列名龙头、旋塞及类似装置	5					0	0
84819010	阀门用零件	8					0	0
84819090	龙头、旋塞及类似装置的零件	8					0	0
84821010	调心球轴承	8					0	0
84821020	深沟球轴承	8					0	0
84821030	角接触轴承	8					0	0
84821040	推力球轴承	8					0	0
84821090	其他滚珠轴承	8					0	0
84822000	锥形滚子轴承	8					0	0
84823000	鼓形滚子轴承	8					0	0
84824000	滚针轴承	8					0	0
84825000	其他圆柱形滚子轴承	8					0	0
84828000	其他滚动轴承及球、柱混合轴承	8					0	0
84829100	滚珠、滚针及滚柱	8					0	0
84829900	滚动轴承的其他零件	6					0	0
84831011	船舶用柴油机曲轴	6					0	0
84831019	其他船舶用传动轴	6					0	0
84831090	其他传动轴及曲柄	6					0	0
84832000	装有滚珠或滚子轴承的轴承座	6					0	0

税则号列	商品名称（简称）	最惠税率	亚太2国	东盟 缅	老	柬	最不发达35国	最不发达4国
84833000	未装滚珠或滚子轴承的轴承座	6					0	0
84834010	滚子螺杆传动装置	8					0	0
84834020	行星齿轮减速器	8					0	0
84834090	其他齿轮及齿轮传动装置	8					0	0
84835000	飞轮、滑轮及滑轮组	8					0	0
84836000	离合器及联轴器(包括万向节)	8					0	0
84839000	单独报验的带齿的轮及其他传动元件；零件	8					0	0
84841000	金属片密封垫或类似接合衬垫	8					0	0
84842000	机械密封件	8					0	0
84849000	其他材料制密封垫及类似接合衬垫	8					0	0
84861010	利用温度变化处理单晶硅的机器及装置	0			0		0	0
84861020	制作单晶硅或晶圆的研磨设备	0					0	0
84861030	制作单晶硅或晶圆的切割设备	0					0	0
84861040	制作单晶硅或晶圆的化学机械抛光设备	0					0	0
84861090	制作单晶硅或晶圆的其他设备	0					0	0
84862010	制造半导体器件或集成电路用的热处理设备	0			0		0	0
84862021	制造半导体器件或集成电路用的化学气相沉积装置	0					0	0
84862022	制造半导体器件或集成电路用的物理气相沉积装置	0					0	0
84862029	制造半导体器件或集成电路用的其他薄膜沉积设备	0					0	0
84862031	制造半导体器件或集成电路用的分步重复光刻机	0					0	0
84862039	制造半导体器件或集成电路用的其他光刻设备	0					0	0
84862041	制造半导体器件或集成电路用的等离子体干法刻蚀机	0					0	0
84862049	制造半导体器件或集成电路用的其他刻蚀及剥离设备	0					0	0
84862050	制造半导体器件或集成电路用的离子注入机	0					0	0
84862090	制造半导体器件或集成电路用的其他机器及装置	0					0	0
84863010	制造平板显示器用的热处理设备	0			0		0	0
84863021	制造平板显示器用的化学气相沉积装置	0					0	0
84863022	制造平板显示器用的物理气相沉积装置	0					0	0
84863029	制造平板显示器用的其他薄膜沉积设备	0					0	0
84863031	制造平板显示器用的分步重复光刻机	0					0	0
84863039	制造平板显示器用的其他光刻设备	0					0	0
84863041	制造平板显示器用的超声波清洗装置	10					0	0
84863049	制造平板显示器用的其他湿法蚀刻、显影、剥离、清洗装置	0					0	0
84863090	制造平板显示器用的其他机器及装置	0					0	0
84864010	专用于制作和修复掩膜版的装置	0					0	0
84864021	专用于装配与封装半导体器件或集成电路的塑封机	5					0	0
84864022	专用于装配与封装半导体器件或集成电路的引线键合设备	8					0	0
84864029	专用于装配与封装半导体器件或集成电路的机器及装置	0					0	0
84864031	集成电路工厂专用的自动搬运机器人	0					0	0
84864039	其他集成电路或液晶显示屏工厂专用升降、装卸、搬运装置	5					0	0
84869010	升降、搬运、装卸机器用零件及附件(自动搬运设备用除外)	5					0	0
84869020	引线键合装置用零件及附件	6					0	0
84869091	带背板的溅射靶材组件	0					0	0
84869099	其他半导体器件、集成电路、液晶显示器生产专用设备的零件及附件	0					0	0
84871000	船用推进器及桨叶	6					0	0
84879000	本章其他税号未列名机器零件	8					0	0
85011010	输出功率≤37.5W玩具电动机	24.5					0	
85011091	机座20mm≤直径＜39mm微电机	9					0	0
85011099	其他输出功率≤37.5W微电机	9					0	0
85012000	输出功率＞37.5W交直流两用电动机	12					0	0
85013100	输出功率≤750瓦直流电动机、发电机	12					0	0
85013200	750W＜输出功率≤75KW直流电动机、发电机	10					0	0
85013300	75KW＜输出功率≤375KW直流电动机、发电机	5					0	0
85013400	输出功率＞375KW直流电动机、发电机	12					0	0
85014000	单相交流电动机	12					0	0
85015100	输出功率≤750W多相交流电动机	5					0	0
85015200	输出功率＞750W≤75KW多相交流电动机	10					0	0
85015300	输出功率＞75KW多相交流电动机	12					0	0

税则号列	商品名称（简称）	最惠税率	亚太2国	东盟			最不发达35国	最不发达4国
				缅	老	柬		
85016100	输出功率≤75KVA 交流发电机	5					0	0
85016200	75KVA＜输出功率≤375KVA 交流发电机	12					0	0
85016300	375KVA＜输出功率≤750KVA 交流发电机	12					0	0
85016410	750KVA＜输出功率＜350MVA 交流发电机	10					0	0
85016420	350KVA≤输出功率＜665MVA 交流发电机	5.8					0	0
85016430	输出功率≥665MVA 交流发电机	6					0	0
85021100	输出功率≤75KVA 柴油发电机组	10					0	0
85021200	75KVA＜输出功率≤375KVA 柴油发电机组	10					0	0
85021310	375KVA＜输出功率≤2MVA 柴油发电机组	10					0	0
85021320	输出功率＞2MVA 柴油发电机组	10					0	0
85022000	装有点燃式活塞发动机的发电机组	10					0	0
85023100	风力驱动的发电机组	8					0	0
85023900	其他发电机组	10					0	0
85024000	旋转式变流机	10					0	0
85030010	玩具用电动机微电机零件	12					0	0
85030020	输出功率＞350MVA 交流发电机零件	3					0	0
85030030	风力驱动发电机组的零件	3					0	0
85030090	其他电动机、发电机(组)零件	8					0	0
85041010	电子镇流器	10					0	0
85041090	其他放电灯或放电管用镇流器	10					0	0
85042100	额定容量≤650KVA 的液体介质变压器	10.5					0	0
85042200	650KVA＜额定容量≤10MVA 的液体介质变压器	12.6					0	0
85042311	10MVA＜额定容量≤220MVA 的液体变压器	10					0	0
85042312	200MVA≤额定容量＜330MVA 的液体变压器	10					0	0
85042313	330MVA≤额定容量＜400MVA 的液体变压器	10					0	0
85042321	400MVA≤液体变压器额定容量＜500MVA	6					0	0
85042329	其他额定容量≥500MVA 的液体变压器	6					0	0
85043110	额定容量≤1KVA 的互感器	5					0	0
85043190	额定容量≤1KVA 的其他变压器	5					0	0
85043210	1KVA＜额定容量≤16KVA 的互感器	5					0	0
85043290	1KVA＜额定容量≤16KVA 的其他变压器	5					0	0
85043310	额定容量超过 16 千伏安，但不超过 500 千伏安的互感器	5					0	0
85043390	其他额定容量超过 16 千伏安，但不超过 500 千伏安的变压器、静止式变流器（例如整流器）及电感器	5					0	0
85043410	额定容量超过 500 千伏的安互感器	14					0	
85043490	其他额定容量超过 500 千伏安的变压器、静止式变流器（例如整流器）及电感器	14					0	
85044013	税号 84.71 所列机器用的稳压电源	0					0	0
85044014	功率＜1KW 高精度直流稳压电源	7					0	0
85044015	功率＜10KW 高精度交流稳压电源	0					0	0
85044019	其他稳压电源	0					0	0
85044020	不间断供电电源(UPS)	10					0	0
85044030	逆变器	10					0	0
85044091	具有变流功能的半导体模块	10					0	0
85044099	其他未列名静止式变流器	10					0	0
85045000	其他电感器	0					0	0
85049011	额定容量＞400KVA 液体介质变压器零件	5					0	0
85049019	其他变压器零件	8					0	0
85049020	稳压电源及不间断供电电源零件	8					0	0
85049090	其他静止式变流器及电感器零件	8					0	0
85051110	稀土的永磁铁及磁化后准备制永磁铁的物品	7					0	0
85051190	其他金属的永磁体	7					0	0
85051900	非金属永磁体	7					0	0
85052000	电磁联轴节、离合器及制动器	8					0	0
85059010	电磁起重吸盘	8					0	0
85059090	电磁夹具等及税号 85.02 的零件	8					0	0
85061011	扣式碱性锌锰电池	20					0	
85061012	圆柱型碱性锌锰电池	20					0	
85061019	其他碱性锌锰电池	20					0	

税则号列	商品名称（简称）	最惠税率	亚太2国	东盟			最不发达35国	最不发达4国
				缅	老	柬		
85061090	二氧化锰的原电池及原电池组	20					0	
85063000	氧化汞的原电池及原电池组	14					0	
85064000	氧化银的原电池及原电池组	14					0	
85065000	锂的原电池及原电池组	14					0	
85066000	锌空气的原电池及原电池组	14					0	
85068000	其他原电池及原电池组	14					0	0
85069010	二氧化锰原电池或原电池组的零件	14					0	
85069090	其他原电池组或原电池组的零件	10					0	
85071000	起动活塞式发动机用铅酸蓄电池	10					0	
85072000	其他铅酸蓄电池	10					0	
85073000	镍镉蓄电池	10					0	
85074000	镍铁蓄电池	12					0	
85075000	镍氢蓄电池	12					0	
85076000	锂离子蓄电池	12					0	
85078030	全钒液流电池	12					0	
85078090	其他蓄电池	12					0	
85079010	铅酸蓄电池零件	10	5				0	
85079090	其他蓄电池零件	8	4				0	0
85081100	功率不超过1500瓦，且带有容积不超过20升的电动真空吸尘器	10					0	0
85081900	其他电动真空吸尘器	0					0	0
85086000	其他真空吸尘器	0					0	0
85087010	税号8508.1100所列电动真空吸尘器用零件	12					0	
85087090	其他真空吸尘器用零件	0					0	0
85094010	水果或蔬菜榨汁机	10					0	
85094090	食品研磨机及搅拌器或果、菜榨汁器	10					0	
85098010	地板打蜡机	30					0	
85098020	厨房废物处理器	20					0	
85098090	其他家用电动器具	30					0	
85099000	家用电动器具的零件	12					0	
85101000	电动剃须刀	30					0	
85102000	电动毛发推剪	30					0	
85103000	电动脱毛器	20					0	
85109000	税号85.10所列货品的零件	24.5					0	
85111000	火花塞	10					0	
85112010	车、船、飞机等用点火磁电机、永磁直流发电机、磁飞轮	5					0	0
85112090	其他点火磁电机、磁飞轮	10					0	0
85113010	分电器及点火线圈	5					0	0
85113090	其他用途用分电器、点火线圈	8.4					0	0
85114010	机车等用起动电机及两用起动发电机	5					0	0
85114091	输出功率≥132.39千瓦启动电机	8.4					0	0
85114099	其他用途的启动电机	8.4					0	0
85115010	其他机车、航空器、船舶用发电机	5					0	0
85115090	其他附属于内燃发动机的发电机	8.4					0	0
85118000	发动机用电点火、起动的其他装置	8.4					0	0
85119010	机车、船、航空器用电点火、起动装置零件	4.5					0	0
85119090	其他用电点火、电起动装置的零件	5					0	0
85121000	自行车用照明或视觉信号装置	10.5					0	0
85122010	机动车辆用照明装置	10					0	0
85122090	其他机动车用照明或视觉信号装置	10					0	0
85123011	机动车辆用喇叭、蜂鸣器	10					0	0
85123012	防盗报警器	10					0	0
85123019	其他机动车辆用音响信号装置	10					0	0
85123090	其他车辆用音响信号装置	10					0	0
85124000	车辆风档刮水器、除霜器及去雾器	10					0	0
85129000	税号85.12所列装置的零件	8					0	0
85131010	手电筒	15					0	0
85131090	其他自供能源手提式电灯	17.5					0	
85139010	手电筒零件	14					0	0

税则号列	商品名称（简称）	最惠税率	亚太2国	东盟			最不发达35国	最不发达4国
				缅	老	柬		
85139090	其他自供能源手提式电灯零件	14					0	
85141010	可控气氛热处理炉	0					0	0
85141090	工业、实验室用其他电阻加热炉及烘箱	0					0	0
85142000	工业、实验室用通过感应或介质损耗工作的炉及烘箱	0					0	0
85143000	工业、实验室用其他电炉及电烘箱	0					0	0
85144000	其他通过感应或介质损耗工作的的加热设备	10					0	0
85149010	炼钢电炉用零件	8					0	0
85149090	工业用电阻加热炉及烘箱等零件	0					0	0
85151100	钎焊机器及装置用烙铁及焊枪	10					0	0
85151900	其他钎焊机器及装置	10					0	0
85152120	机器人	10					0	0
85152191	直缝焊管机	10					0	0
85152199	其他全自动或半自动电阻焊接机器及装置	10					0	0
85152900	其他电阻焊接机器及装置	10					0	0
85153120	机器人	10					0	0
85153191	螺旋焊管机	10					0	0
85153199	其他全自动或半自动的电弧（包括等离子弧）焊接机器及装	10					0	0
85153900	其他电弧焊接机器及装置	10					0	0
85158010	激光焊接机器人	8					0	0
85158090	其他机器及装置	8					0	0
85159000	电气等焊接机器及装置零件	6					0	0
85161010	储存式电热水器	10					0	0
85161020	即热式电热水器	10					0	0
85161090	其他电热的快速热水器、浸入式液体加热器	10					0	0
85162100	电气储存式散热器	35					0	
85162910	电气土壤加热器	10					0	0
85162920	辐射式空间加热器	10					0	0
85162931	风扇式对流式空间加热器	10					0	0
85162932	充液式对流式空间加热器	10					0	0
85162939	其他对流式空间加热器	10					0	0
85162990	电气空间加热器	10					0	0
85163100	电吹风机	10					0	0
85163200	其他电热理发器具	35					0	
85163300	电热干手器	35					0	
85164000	电熨斗	35					0	
85165000	微波炉	15					0	
85166010	电磁炉	15					0	
85166030	电饭锅	15					0	
85166040	电炒锅	15					0	
85166050	电烤箱	15					0	
85166090	其他电热炉	15					0	
85167110	滴液式咖啡机	32					0	
85167120	蒸馏渗滤式咖啡机	32					0	
85167130	泵压式咖啡机	32					0	
85167190	其他电热咖啡机或茶壶	32					0	
85167210	家用自动面包机	32					0	
85167220	片式烤面包机（多士炉）	32					0	
85167290	电热烤面包器	32					0	
85167910	电热饮水机	32					0	
85167990	其他电热器具	32					0	
85168000	加热电阻器	10					0	0
85169010	土壤加热器及加热电阻器零件	8					0	0
85169090	税号85.16所列货品的其他零件	12					0	0
85171100	无绳电话机	0					0	0
85171210	手持（包括车载）式无线电话机	0					0	0
85171220	对讲机	0					0	0
85171290	用于蜂窝网络或无线网络的其他电话机	0					0	0
85171800	其他电话机	0					0	0

税则号列	商品名称（简称）	最惠税率	亚太2国	东盟			最不发达35国	最不发达4国
				缅	老	柬		
85176110	移动通信基站	0					0	0
85176190	其他通信基站	0					0	0
85176211	数字式局用电话交换机；长途电活交换机；电报交换机	0					0	0
85176212	数字式移动通信交换机	0					0	0
85176219	数字式其他电话交换机	0					0	0
85176221	光端机及脉冲编码调制设备	0					0	0
85176222	波分复用光传输设备	0					0	0
85176229	其他光通讯设备	0					0	0
85176231	通信网络时钟同步设备	0					0	0
85176232	以太网络交换机	0					0	0
85176233	IP电话信号交换机	0					0	0
85176234	调制解调器	0					0	0
85176235	集线器	0					0	0
85176236	路由器	0					0	0
85176237	有线网络接口卡	0					0	0
85176239	其他有线数字通信设备	0					0	0
85176292	无线网络接口卡	0					0	0
85176293	无线接入固定台	0					0	0
85176294	无线耳机	0					0	0
85176299	其他接收、转换并且发送或再生声音、图像或数据用的设备	0					0	0
85176910	其他无线设备	9					0	0
85176990	其他有线设备	0					0	0
85177010	数字式程控电话或电报交换机零件	0					0	0
85177020	光端机、脉冲编码调制设备的零件	0					0	0
85177030	手持式无线电话机用（天线除外）	0					0	0
85177040	对讲机用（天线除外）	8					0	0
85177060	光通信设备的激光收发模块	0					0	0
85177070	税号8517所列设备用天线及其零件	2					0	0
85177090	发送或接收声音、图像或数据的设备用其他零件	0					0	0
85181000	传声器(麦克风)及其座架	10					0	0
85182100	单喇叭音箱	10					0	0
85182200	多喇叭音箱	10					0	0
85182900	其他扬声器	0					0	0
85183000	其他耳机、耳塞机	0					0	0
85184000	音频扩大器	12					0	0
85185000	电气扩音机组	10					0	0
85189000	税号85.18所列货品的零件	10.5					0	0
85192000	用硬币、钞票、银行卡、代币使其工作的声音录放设备	20					0	
85193000	转盘（唱机唱盘）	30					0	
85195000	电话应答机	0					0	0
85198111	不带录音功能的盒式磁带型声音重放装置，编辑节目月放声机除外	17					0	
85198112	装有声音重放装置的盒式磁带型录音机	30					0	
85198119	其他使用磁性媒体的声音录放机	20					0	
85198121	不带录音功能的激光唱机	30					0	
85198129	使用光学媒体的其他声音录放装置	20					0	
85198131	闪速存储器型声音录放机	20					0	
85198139	使用半导体媒体的其他声音录放装置	20					0	
85198910	不带录制装置的其他唱机，不论是否带有扬声器	30					0	
85198990	其他声音录制或重放设备	20					0	
85211011	广播级录像机	30					0	
85211019	其他磁带录像机	30					0	
85211020	磁带放像机	30					0	
85219011	视频高密光盘机VCD	20					0	
85219012	数字化视频光盘机DVD	20					0	
85219019	其他激光视盘放像机	20					0	
85219090	其他视频信号录制或重放设备	20					0	
85221000	拾音头	35					0	
85229010	转盘或唱机用零附件	25					0	

税则号列	商品名称（简称）	最惠税率	亚太2国	东盟			最不发达35国	最不发达4国
				缅	老	柬		
85229021	录音机走带机构(机芯)	25					0	
85229022	磁头	25					0	
85229023	磁头零件	20					0	
85229029	盒式磁带录音机或放声机其他零件	30					0	
85229031	激光视盘机的机芯	30					0	
85229039	其他视频信号录放设备的零件附件	30					0	
85229091	车载音频转播器或发射器	20					0	0
85229099	声音录制或重放设备用其他零件	20					0	0
85232110	未录制的磁条卡	17.5					0	
85232120	已录制的磁条卡	15					0	
85232911	未录制磁盘	0					0	0
85232919	已录制磁盘	0					0	0
85232921	宽度≤4mm 的未录制磁带	0					0	0
85232922	宽度＞4mm 且≤6.5mm 的未录制磁带	0					0	0
85232923	宽度＞6.5mm 的未录制磁带	0					0	0
85232928	用于重放声音或图像信息的磁带	10					0	0
85232929	已录制其他信息的磁带	0					0	0
85232990	其他磁性媒体	0					0	0
85234100	未录制的光学媒体	0					0	0
85234910	仅用于重放声音信息的光学媒体	10					0	
85234920	用于重放声音、图像以外信息的，税号 84.71 所列机器用的光学媒体	0					0	0
85234990	其他已录制的光学媒体	0					0	0
85235110	未录制信息的闪速存储器	0					0	0
85235120	已录制信息的闪速存储器	0					0	0
85235210	未录制内容的“智能卡”	0					0	0
85235290	已录制内容的“智能卡”	0					0	0
85235910	未录制信息的其他半导体媒体	0					0	0
85235920	已录制信息的其他半导体媒体	0					0	0
85238011	已录制的唱片	15					0	
85238019	未录制的唱片	0					0	0
85238021	税号 84.71 所列机器用未录制内容的其他媒体	0					0	0
85238029	税号 84.71 所列机器用已录制内容的其他媒体	0					0	0
85238091	其他未录制内容的媒体	0					0	0
85238099	其他已录制内容的媒体	0					0	0
85255000	广播电视发送设备	0					0	0
85256010	卫星地面站设备	0					0	0
85256090	其他装有接收装置的广播电视发送设备	0					0	0
85258011	特种用途电视摄像机	10					0	
85258012	非特种用途的广播级电视摄像机	35					0	
85258013	非特种用途的其他电视摄像机	35					0	
85258021	特种用途的数字照相机	0					0	0
85258022	非特种用途的单反数字照相机	0					0	0
85258025	非特种用途的,其他可换镜头的数字照相机	0					0	0
85258029	非特种用途的其他数字照相机	0					0	0
85258031	特种用途的视频摄录一体机	0					0	0
85258032	非特种用途的广播级视频摄录一体机	0					0	0
85258033	非特种用途的家用视频摄录一体机	0					0	0
85258039	非特种用途的其他视频摄录一体机	0					0	0
85261010	导航用雷达设备	2					0	
85261090	其他雷达设备	5					0	
85269110	机动车辆用	2					0	
85269190	其他无线电导航设备	2					0	
85269200	无线电遥控设备	5					0	
85271200	不需外接电源袖珍盒式磁带收放机	20					0	
85271300	不需外接电源收录(放)音组合机	15					0	
85271900	不需外接电源无线电收音机	15					0	
85272100	需外接电源汽车收录(放)音组合机	15					0	
85272900	需外接电源汽车用无线电收音机	15					0	

税则号列	商品名称（简称）	最惠税率	亚太2国	东盟			最不发达35国	最不发达4国
				缅	老	柬		
85279100	其他收录(放)音组合机	15					0	
85279200	带时钟的收音机	15					0	
85279900	其他收音机	27					0	
85284100	计算机及其他自动数据处理设备用的阴极射线管监视器	0					0	0
85284910	其他彩色阴极射线管监视器	30					0	
85284990	单色的阴极射线管监视器	19					0	
85285110	计算机及其他自动数据处理设备用的液晶显示器	0					0	0
85285190	计算机及其他自动数据处理设备用的其他显示器	0					0	0
85285910	其他彩色监视器	30					0	
85285990	单色的其他监视器	19					0	
85286100	计算机及其他自动数据处理设备用的投影机	0					0	0
85286910	其他彩色投影机	30					0	
85286990	单色的其他投影机	15					0	
85287190	单色的不带视频显示器的电视接收机	15					0	
85287291	其他彩色模拟电视接收机	30					0	
85287300	其他单色的电视接收装置	15					0	
85291010	雷达及无线电导航设备天线及零件	1.5					0	
85291020	收音机、电视机天线及其零件	0					0	0
85291090	其他无线电设备天线及其零件	2					0	
85299010	电视发送、差转等设备零件	0					0	0
85299041	特种用途电视摄像机、静像视频摄像机及其他视频摄录一体机，数字相机零件	8					0	
85299042	非特种用途的取像模块	12					0	
85299049	其他电视摄像机、静像视频摄像机及其他视频摄录一体机、数字相机零件	12					0	
85299050	雷达及无线电导航设备零件	1.5					0	
85299060	收音机及其组合机的其他零件	15					0	0
85299081	彩色电视接收机用(等离子显像组件及其零件、有机发光二极管显示屏除外)	15					0	
85299083	有机发光二极管显示屏	15					0	
85299089	其他电视机零件	0					0	0
85299090	税号85.25至85.28所列设备的零件	0					0	0
85301000	铁道或电车道用电气信号等设备	10					0	
85308000	其他用电气信号、安全、交通设备	8					0	0
85309000	税号85.30所列设备的零件	8					0	0
85311000	防盗或防火报警器及类似装置	10					0	0
85312000	有液晶装置或发光管的显示板	0					0	0
85318010	蜂鸣器	15					0	
85318090	其他电气音响或视觉信号装置	10					0	
85319010	防盗、防火及类似装置用零件	0					0	0
85319090	其他音响或视觉信号装置用零件	0					0	0
85321000	固定电容器(电力电容器)	0					0	0
85322110	片式钽电容器	0					0	0
85322190	其他钽电容器	0					0	0
85322210	片式铝电解电容器	0					0	0
85322290	其他铝电解电容器	0					0	0
85322300	单层瓷介电容器	0					0	0
85322410	片式多层瓷介电容器	0					0	0
85322490	其他多层瓷介电容器	0					0	0
85322510	片式纸介质或塑料介质电容器	0					0	0
85322590	其他纸介质或塑料介质电容器	0					0	0
85322900	其他固定电容器	0					0	0
85323000	其他可变或可调(微调)电容器	0					0	0
85329010	税号8532.1000所列电容器零件	0					0	0
85329090	其他电容器零件	0					0	0
85331000	合成或薄膜式固定碳质电阻器	0					0	0
85332110	额定功率≤20W片式固定电阻器	0					0	0
85332190	额定功率≤20W其他固定电阻器	0					0	0
85332900	其他额定功率>20W固定电阻器	0					0	0
85333100	额定功率≤20W线绕可变电阻器	0					0	0
85333900	额定功率>20W电位器	0					0	0

税则号列	商品名称（简称）	最惠税率	亚太2国	东盟			最不发达35国	最不发达4国
				缅	老	柬		
85334000	其他可变电阻器	0					0	0
85339000	各种电阻器零件	0					0	0
85340010	＞四层的印刷电路	0					0	0
85340090	≤四层的印刷电路	0					0	0
85351000	电路熔断器(电压＞1000V)	14					0	
85352100	电压＜72.5KV 自动断路器	14					0	
85352910	用于电压在72.5千伏及以上，但不高于220千伏的线路的自动断路器	10					0	0
85352920	用于电压高于220千伏，但不高于750千伏的线路的自动断路器	10					0	0
85352990	其他电压≥72.5KV 自动断路器	10					0	0
85353010	用于电压在72.5千伏及以上，但不高于220千伏的线路的隔离开关及断续开关	10					0	0
85353020	用于电压高于220千伏，但不高于750千伏的线路的隔离开关及断续开关	10					0	0
85353090	其他隔离开关及断续开关	10					0	0
85354000	避雷器、电压限幅器及电涌抑制器	18					0	
85359000	其他＞1000V 电路开关等电气装置	10					0	0
85361000	熔断器(电压≤1000V)	10					0	0
85362000	电压≤1000V 自动断路器	9					0	0
85363000	电压≤1000V 其他电路保护装置	9					0	0
85364110	用于电压不超过36伏线路的继电器	10					0	0
85364190	用于电压超过36伏，但不超过60伏线路的继电器	10					0	0
85364900	电压>60V 的继电器	10					0	0
85365000	电压≤1000V 的其他开关	0					0	0
85366100	电压≤1000V 的灯座	10					0	0
85366900	电压≤1000V 的插头及插座	0					0	0
85367000	光导纤维、光导纤维束或光缆用连接器	8					0	0
85369011	工作电压不超过36伏的插接件	0					0	0
85369019	其他插接件	0					0	0
85369090	其他电路的开关、保护或连接用的电气装置	0					0	0
85371011	可编程序控制器	5					0	0
85371019	其他数控装置	5					0	0
85371090	其他电力控制或分配的装置	8.4					0	0
85372010	电压≥500KV 高压开关装置	8.4					0	0
85372090	其他电力控制或分配装置	8.4					0	0
85381010	子目号8537.2010所列装置的零件	8.4					0	0
85381090	税号85.37货品用的其他盘、板等	7					0	0
85389000	税号85.35、85.36或85.37装置的零件	7					0	0
85391000	封闭式聚光灯	10					0	0
85392110	科研、医疗专用卤钨灯	8					0	0
85392120	火车、航空器及船舶用卤钨灯	8					0	0
85392130	机动车辆用卤钨灯	10					0	0
85392190	其他卤钨灯	10.5					0	0
85392210	科研、医疗用功率≤200W 白炽灯泡	10.5					0	0
85392290	其他用功率≤200W 白炽灯泡	5					0	0
85392910	科研、医疗专用其他白炽灯泡	5					0	0
85392920	火车、航空及船舶用其他白炽灯泡	10.5					0	0
85392930	机动车辆用其他白炽灯泡	5					0	0
85392991	电压≤12V 未列名的白炽灯泡	12					0	0
85392999	其他未列名的白炽灯泡	12					0	0
85393110	科研、医疗专用热阴极荧光灯	8					0	0
85393120	火车、航空器、船舶用热阴极荧光灯	8					0	0
85393191	紧凑型荧光灯	8					0	0
85393199	其他热阴极荧光灯	8					0	0
85393230	钠蒸气灯	8					0	0
85393240	汞蒸气灯	8					0	0
85393290	金属卤化物灯	8					0	0
85393910	科研、医疗专用其他放电灯	8					0	0
85393920	火车、航空器、船舶用其他放电灯	8					0	0
85393990	其他用途的其他放电灯管	8					0	0
85394100	弧光灯	8					0	0

税则号列	商品名称（简称）	最惠税率	亚太2国	东盟			最不发达35国	最不发达4国
				缅	老	柬		
85394900	紫外线或红外线灯	8					0	0
85399000	税号85.39所列货品的零件	8					0	0
85401100	彩色阴极射线电视显像管	12					0	
85401200	黑白或单色阴极射线电视显像管	15					0	
85402010	电视摄像管	12					0	
85402090	变像管、图像增强管及光阴极管	8					0	0
85404010	彩色的数据/图形显示管，屏幕荧光点间距小于0.4毫米	8					0	0
85404020	单色的数据/图形显示管	8					0	0
85406010	雷达显示管	6					0	0
85406090	其他阴极射线管	8					0	0
85407100	磁控管	8					0	0
85407910	调速管	8					0	0
85407990	其他微波管	8					0	0
85408100	接收管或放大管	8					0	0
85408900	其他电子管	8					0	0
85409110	电视显像管零件	6					0	0
85409120	雷达显示管零件	5					0	0
85409190	其他阴极射线管零件	8					0	0
85409910	电视摄像管零件	8					0	0
85409990	其他热电子管、冷阴极管零件	8					0	0
85411000	二极管	0					0	0
85412100	耗散功率＜1W的晶体管	0					0	0
85412900	耗散功率⩾1W的晶体管	0					0	0
85413000	半导体及可控硅等开关元件	0					0	0
85414010	发光二极管	0					0	0
85414020	太阳能电池	0					0	0
85414090	其他光敏半导体器件，包括不论是否装在组件内或组装成块的光电池	0					0	0
85415000	其他半导体器件	0					0	0
85416000	已装配的压电晶体	0					0	0
85419000	税号85.41所列货品零件	0					0	0
85423100	集成电路处理器及控制器，不论是否带有存储器、转换器、逻辑电路、放大器、时钟及时序电路或其他电路	0					0	0
85423200	集成电路存储器	0					0	0
85423300	集成电路放大器	0					0	0
85423900	其他集成电路	0					0	0
85429000	集成电路的零件	0					0	0
85431000	其他粒子加速器	5					0	0
85432010	输出信号频率＜1500MHZ的通用信号发生器	15					0	
85432090	输出信号频率⩾1500MHZ的通用信号发生器	8					0	0
85433000	电镀、电介或电泳设备及装置	0					0	0
85437091	金属、矿藏探测器	0					0	0
85437092	高、中频放大器	0					0	0
85437093	电篱网激发器	10					0	0
85437099	未列名的电气设备及装置	0					0	0
85439010	粒子加速器用零件	0					0	0
85439021	输出信号频率＜1500MHZ通用信号发生器零件	0					0	0
85439029	输出信号频率⩾1500MHZ通用信号发生器零件	0					0	0
85439030	金属、矿藏探测器用零件	0					0	0
85439040	高、中频放大器用零件	0					0	0
85439090	85章其他未列名电气设备的零件	0					0	0
85441100	铜制绕组电线	10					0	0
85441900	其他绕组电线	20					0	
85442000	同轴电缆及其他同轴电导体	10					0	0
85443020	机动车辆用点火布线组及其他布线组	10					0	0
85443090	车辆用点火布线组	5					0	0
85444211	耐压⩽80V有接头电缆	0					0	0
85444219	耐压⩽80V有接头电导体	0					0	0
85444221	1000V⩾耐压＞80V有接头电缆	0					0	0
85444229	1000V⩾耐压＞80V有接头电导体	0					0	0

税则号列	商品名称（简称）	最惠税率	亚太2国	东盟			最不发达35国	最不发达4国
				缅	老	柬		
85444911	耐压≤80V 无接头电缆	0					0	0
85444919	耐压≤80V 无接头电导体	0					0	0
85444921	1000V≥耐压＞80V 无接头电缆	6					0	0
85444929	1000V≥耐压＞80V 无接头电导体	12					0	0
85446012	额定电压不超过 35 千伏的电缆	10					0	0
85446013	额定电压超过 35 千伏，但不超过 110 千伏的电缆	8.4					0	0
85446014	额定电压超过 110 千伏，但不超过 220 千伏的电缆	8.4					0	0
85446019	其他额定电压超过 1000 伏的电缆	8.4					0	0
85446090	耐压＞1KV 的其他电导体	21					0	
85447000	光缆	0					0	0
85451100	炉用碳电极	8					0	0
85451900	其他碳电极	10.5					0	0
85452000	碳刷	10.5					0	0
85459000	灯碳棒、电池碳棒及其他石墨制品	10.5					0	0
85461000	玻璃制绝缘子	10.5					0	0
85462010	输变电线路绝缘瓷套管	6					0	0
85462090	其他陶瓷制绝缘子	12					0	0
85469000	其他材料制绝缘子	10					0	0
85471000	陶瓷制绝缘零件	8					0	0
85472000	塑料制绝缘零件	8					0	0
85479010	内衬绝缘材料的贱金属导管及其接头	10					0	0
85479090	其他材料制绝缘配件	8					0	0
85481000	电池废碎料及废电池	8	4				0	
85489000	85 章其他未列名的电气零件	12					0	
86011011	微机控制的外部直流电动铁道机车	3					0	0
86011019	由外部直流电驱动的其他铁道机车	3					0	0
86011020	由外部交流电驱动的铁道机车	3					0	0
86011090	由其他外部电力驱动的铁道机车	3					0	0
86012000	由蓄电池驱动的铁道电力机车	3					0	0
86021010	微机控制的柴油电力铁道机车	3					0	0
86021090	其他柴油电力铁道机车	3					0	0
86029000	其他铁道机车及机车煤水车	3					0	0
86031000	由外电力驱动铁道及电车道用机动客车、货车、敞车	3					0	0
86039000	其他铁道及电车道用机动客车、货车、敞车	3					0	0
86040011	隧道限界检查车	3					0	0
86040012	钢轨在线打磨列车	3					0	0
86040019	铁道及电车道用其他检验车及查道车	5					0	0
86040091	电气化接触网架线机(轨行式)	5					0	0
86040099	铁道及电车道用其他维修或服务车	7					0	0
86050010	铁道及电车道用非机动客车	5					0	0
86050090	铁道及电车道用其他非机动客车	5					0	0
86061000	铁道及电车道用非机动油罐货车及类似车	5					0	0
86063000	铁道及电车道用非机动自卸货车	5					0	0
86069100	铁道及电车道用非机动带篷及封闭货车	5					0	0
86069200	铁道及电车道用非机动厢高＞60cm 敞篷货车	5					0	0
86069900	税号 86.06 所列其他未列名非机动车	5					0	0
86071100	铁道及电车道机车的驾驶转向架	3					0	0
86071200	铁道及电车道机车非驾驶转向架	3					0	0
86071910	铁道及电车道机车用车轴	3					0	0
86071990	转向轮及其零件	3					0	0
86072100	铁道及电车道机车用空气制动器及其零件	3					0	0
86072900	铁道及电车道机车用非空气制动器	3					0	0
86073000	铁道及电车道机车用钩、联结器、缓冲器及其零件	3					0	0
86079100	铁道及电车道机车用其他零件	3					0	0
86079900	铁道及电车道非机车用其他零件	3					0	0
86080010	轨道自动计轴设备	3					0	0
86080090	铁道及电车道轨道固定装置及附件	4					0	0
86090011	20 英尺保温式集装箱	10.5					0	0

税则号列	商品名称（简称）	最惠税率	亚太2国	东盟			最不发达35国	最不发达4国
				缅	老	柬		
86090012	20英尺罐式集装箱	10.5					0	0
86090019	20英尺其他集装箱	10.5					0	0
86090021	40英尺保温式集装箱	10.5					0	0
86090022	40英尺罐式集装箱	10.5					0	0
86090029	40英尺其他集装箱	10.5					0	0
86090030	45、48、53英尺的集装箱	10.5					0	0
86090090	其他集装箱	10.5					0	0
87011000	手扶拖拉机	9					0	
87013000	履带式牵引车、拖拉机	6					0	
87019011	轮式拖拉机	8					0	
87019019	其他拖拉机	8					0	
87019090	其他牵引车	8					0	
87021020	机坪客车	4					0	
87029030	≥10座、但≤19座的客车(非柴油型)	25					0	
87031011	全地形车	25					0	
87031019	其他高尔夫球车及类似车辆	25					0	
87031090	雪地行走专用车	25					0	
87033119	排气量≤1L的柴油型其他车辆	25					0	
87033129	1L＜排气量≤1.5L的柴油型其他车辆	25					0	
87039000	装有压燃式内燃发动机的其他载人机动车辆	25					0	
87041030	非公路用电动轮货运自卸车	6					0	0
87041090	其他非公路用货运自卸车	6					0	0
87042230	柴油型其他中型货车	20					0	
87042240	柴油型其他重型货车	20					0	
87043230	5吨＜汽油型≤8吨的其他货车	20					0	
87043240	汽油型＞8吨的其他货车	20					0	
87049000	装有其他发动机的货车	25					0	
87051021	最大起重重量≤50吨的全路面汽车起重车	15					0	
87051022	50吨＜最大起重重量≤100吨的全路面汽车起重车	10					0	0
87051023	最大起重重量＞100吨的全路面汽车起重车	10					0	0
87051091	最大起重重量≤50吨的其他汽车起重车	15					0	
87051092	50吨＜最大起重重量≤100吨的其他汽车起重车	10					0	0
87051093	最大起重重量＞100吨的其他汽车起重车	10					0	0
87052000	机动钻探车	12					0	0
87053010	装有云梯的救火车	3					0	0
87053090	其他机动救火车	3					0	0
87054000	机动混凝土搅拌车	15					0	
87059010	无线电通信车	9					0	0
87059020	机动放射线检查车	9					0	0
87059030	机动环境监测车	12					0	
87059040	机动医疗车	12					0	
87059051	航空电源车(频率为400赫兹)	12					0	
87059059	其他机动电源车	12					0	
87059060	飞机加油车、调温车、除冰车	12					0	
87059070	道路(包括跑道)扫雪车	12					0	
87059080	石油测井车、压裂车、混沙车	12					0	
87059091	混凝土泵车	12					0	
87059099	其他特殊用途的机动车辆	12					0	
87060010	非公路用货运自卸车底盘	8					0	
87060022	车辆总重量＜14吨的货车底盘	10					0	
87060040	汽车起重机底盘	20					0	
87060090	其他机动车辆底盘	10					0	
87071000	税号87.03所列车辆用车身(含驾驶室)	10					0	
87079010	税号8702.1092、.1093、.9020及.9030所列车辆用车身	10					0	
87079090	其他车辆用车身(含驾驶室)	10					0	
87081000	缓冲器(保险杠)及其零件	10					0	0
87082100	座椅安全带	10					0	0
87082930	车窗玻璃升降器	10					0	0

税则号列	商品名称（简称）	最惠税率	亚太2国	东盟			最不发达35国	最不发达4国
				缅	老	柬		
87082941	汽车电动天窗	10					0	0
87082942	汽车手动天窗	10					0	0
87082951	侧围	10					0	0
87082952	车门	10					0	0
87082953	发动机罩盖	10					0	0
87082954	前围	10					0	0
87082955	行李箱盖（或背门）	10					0	0
87082956	后围	10					0	0
87082957	翼子板（或叶子板）	10					0	0
87082959	车身的其他覆盖件	10					0	0
87082990	车身的未列名零部件	10					0	0
87083010	装在蹄片上的制动摩擦片	10					0	0
87083021	牵引车、拖拉机、非公路自卸车用防抱死制动系统（ABS）	6					0	0
87083029	其他车辆用防抱死制动系统（ABS）	10					0	0
87083091	牵引车、拖拉机用制动器及其零件	6					0	0
87083092	大型客车用制动器及其零件	10					0	0
87083093	非公路自卸车用制动器及其零件	6					0	0
87083094	柴、汽油轻型货车用制动器及零件	10					0	0
87083095	柴油型重型货车用制动器及其零件	10					0	0
87083096	特种车用制动器及其零件	10					0	0
87083099	其他未列名机动车辆用制动器及零件	10					0	0
87084010	牵引车、拖拉机用变速箱及零件	6					0	0
87084060	特种车用变速箱及零件	10					0	0
87085071	牵引车、拖拉机用驱动桥及零件	6					0	0
87085072	其他大型客车用驱动桥及零件	10					0	0
87085073	非公路自卸车用驱动桥及零件	6					0	0
87085074	柴、汽油型轻型货车用驱动桥及零件	10					0	0
87085075	其他柴油型重型货车用驱动桥及零件	10					0	0
87085076	特种车用驱动桥及零件	10					0	0
87085079	未列名机动车辆用驱动桥及零件	10					0	0
87085081	牵引车、拖拉机用非驱动桥及零件	6					0	0
87085082	座位≥30客车用非驱动桥及零件	15					0	
87085083	非公路自卸车用非驱动桥及零件	6					0	0
87085084	柴、汽油轻货车用非驱动桥及零件	10					0	0
87085085	柴油重型货车用非驱动桥及零件	10					0	0
87085086	特种车用非驱动桥及其零件	10					0	0
87085089	未列名机动车辆用非驱动桥及零件	10					0	0
87087010	牵引车及拖拉机用车轮及其零附件	6					0	0
87087020	大型客车用车轮及其零附件	10					0	0
87087030	非公路货运自卸车用车轮及其零件	6					0	0
87087040	中小型货车用车轮及其零件	10					0	0
87087050	大型货车用车轮及其零件	10					0	0
87087060	特种车用车轮及其零件	10					0	0
87087091	铝合金制的车轮及其零件、附件	10					0	0
87087099	其他车轮及其零件、附件	10					0	0
87088010	税号87.03所列车辆用的悬挂减震器及零件	10					0	0
87088090	机动车辆用的其他悬挂减震器及零件	10					0	0
87089110	水箱散热器	10					0	0
87089120	机油冷却器	10					0	0
87089190	其他散热器及其零件	10					0	0
87089200	机动车辆的消声器及排气管及零件	10					0	0
87089310	牵引车、拖拉机用离合器及其零件	6					0	0
87089320	座位≥30客车用离合器及其零件	10					0	0
87089330	非公路自卸车用离合器及其零件	6					0	0
87089340	柴、汽油轻型货车用离合器及零件	10					0	0
87089350	总重≥14吨柴油货车离合器及零件	10					0	0
87089360	特种车用的离合器及其零件	10					0	0
87089390	未列名机动车辆用离合器及其零件	10					0	0

税则号列	商品名称（简称）	最惠税率	亚太2国	东盟			最不发达35国	最不发达4国
				缅	老	柬		
87089410	牵引车、拖拉机用转向盘、转向柱及转向器及零件	6					0	0
87089420	大型客车用转向盘、转向柱及转向器及零件	10					0	0
87089430	非公路自卸车用转向盘、转向柱及转向器及零件	6					0	0
87089440	柴、汽油轻货车用转向盘、转向柱及转向器及零件	10					0	0
87089450	柴油型重型货车用转向盘、转向柱及转向器及零件	10					0	0
87089460	特种车用转向盘、转向柱及转向器及零件	10					0	0
87089490	未列名机动车辆用转向盘、转向柱及转向器及零件	10					0	0
87089910	牵引车及拖拉机用其他零附件	6					0	0
87089921	税号 8702.1091 及 8702.9010 所列车辆用车架	25					0	
87089929	大型客车用其他零附件	25					0	
87089931	税号 8704.1030 及 8704.1090 所列车辆用车架	6					0	0
87089939	非公路货运自卸车用其他零附件	6					0	0
87089941	税号 8704.2100、8704.2230、8704.3100 及 8704.3230 所列车辆用车架	25					0	
87089949	中小型货车用其他零附件	25					0	
87089951	税号 8704.2240、8704.2300 及 8704.3240 所列车辆用车架	10					0	0
87089959	总重≥14 吨货车用其他零附件	10					0	0
87089960	特种车用其他零附件	15					0	
87089991	其他税号所列车辆用车架	10					0	0
87089992	汽车传动轴	10					0	0
87089999	机动车辆用未列名零附件	10					0	0
87091110	短距离运输货物电动牵引车	10					0	0
87091190	其他电动短矩离运货车	10					0	0
87091910	短距离运输货物其他牵引车	10.5					0	0
87091990	其他非电动短矩离运货车	10.5					0	0
87099000	短距离运货车、站台牵引车用零件	8.4					0	0
87100010	坦克及其他机动装甲战斗车辆	15					0	
87100090	坦克及其他机动装甲战斗车辆零件	15					0	
87111000	汽油型微马力摩托车及脚踏两用车	45					0	
87112010	装有往复式活塞发动机，气缸容量超过 50 毫升，但不超过 100 毫升的汽油型小马力摩托车及脚踏两用车	45					0	
87112020	装有往复式活塞发动机，气缸容量超过 100 毫升，但不超过 125 毫升的汽油型小马力摩托车及脚踏两用车	45					0	
87112030	装有往复式活塞发动机，气缸容量超过 125 毫升，但不超过 150 毫升的汽油型小马力摩托车及脚踏两用车	45					0	
87120020	竞赛型自行车	13					0	
87120030	山地自行车	13					0	
87120041	16、18、20 英寸自行车	13					0	0
87120049	其他越野自行车	13					0	
87120081	≤16 英寸的未列名自行车	13					0	
87120089	其他未列名自行车	13					0	
87120090	其他非机动脚踏车	23					0	
87131000	非机械驱动的残疾人用车	6					0	
87139000	其他机动残疾人用车	4					0	
87141000	摩托车及机动脚踏两用车用零附件	30					0	
87142000	残疾人车辆用零附件	5					0	0
87149100	非机动脚踏车车架、轮叉及其零件	12					0	
87149210	轮圈	12					0	
87149290	辐条	12					0	
87149310	非机动脚踏车的轮毂	12					0	
87149320	飞轮	12					0	
87149390	其他非机动脚踏车的飞轮	12					0	
87149400	非机动脚踏车的制动器及其零件	12					0	
87149500	非机动脚踏车的鞍座	12					0	
87149610	非机动脚踏车脚蹬及其零件	12					0	
87149620	非机动脚踏车曲柄、链轮及其零件	12					0	
87149900	非机动脚踏车的其他零附件	12					0	
87150000	婴孩车及其零件	20					0	
87161000	供居住或野营用厢式挂车及半挂车	10					0	
87162000	农用自装或自卸式挂车及半挂车	10					0	

税则号列	商品名称（简称）	最惠税率	亚太2国	东盟			最不发达35国	最不发达4国
				缅	老	柬		
87163110	油罐挂车及半挂车	10					0	
87163190	其他罐式挂车及半挂车	10					0	
87163910	货柜挂车及半挂车	10					0	
87163990	其他货运挂车及半挂车	10					0	
87164000	其他未列名挂车及半挂车	10					0	
87168000	其他未列名非机械驱动车辆	10					0	
87169000	挂车、半挂车及非机动车用零件	10					0	0
88010010	滑翔机及悬挂滑翔机	3					0	0
88010090	汽球、飞艇及其他无动力航空器	3					0	0
88021100	空载重量≤2吨的直升机	2					0	0
88021210	2吨<空载重量≤7吨的直升机	2					0	0
88021220	空载重量>7吨的直升机	2					0	0
88022000	小型飞机及其他航空器	5					0	0
88023000	中型飞机及其他航空器	4					0	0
88024010	大型飞机及其他航空器	5					0	0
88024020	特大型飞机及其他航空器	1					0	0
88026000	航天器(包括卫星)及其运载工具	2					0	0
88031000	飞机等用推进器、水平旋翼及零件	1					0	0
88032000	飞机等用起落架及其零件	1					0	0
88033000	飞机及直升机的其他零件	1					0	
88039000	其他未列名的航空器、航天器零件	0					0	0
88040000	降落伞及其零附件	2					0	0
88051000	航空器的发射装置及其零件等	1.5					0	0
88052100	空战模拟器及其零件	1.5					0	
88052900	其他地面飞行训练器及其零件	1.5					0	0
89011010	机动巡航船、游览船及各式渡船	5					0	
89011090	非机动巡航船、游览船及各式渡船	8					0	
89012011	载重≤10万吨的成品油船	9					0	
89012012	10万吨<载重≤30万吨的成品油船	9					0	
89012013	载重>30万吨的成品油船	6					0	
89012021	载重≤15万吨的原油船	9					0	
89012022	15万吨<载重≤30万吨的原油船	9					0	
89012023	载重>30万吨的原油船	6					0	
89012031	容积≤20000立方米的液化石油气船	9					0	
89012032	容积>20000立方米的液化石油气船	6					0	
89012041	容积≤20000立方米的液化天然气船	9					0	
89012042	容积>20000立方米的液化天然气船	6					0	
89012090	其他液货船	9					0	
89013000	冷藏船	9					0	
89019021	可载标准集装箱≤6000箱的机动集装箱船	9					0	
89019022	可载标准集装箱>6000箱的机动集装箱船	6					0	
89019031	载重≤2万吨的机动滚装船	9					0	
89019032	载重>2万吨的机动滚装船	6					0	
89019041	载重≤15万吨的机动散货船	9					0	
89019042	15万吨<载重≤30万吨的机动散货船	9					0	
89019043	载重>30万吨的机动散货船	9					0	
89019050	机动多用途船	9					0	
89019080	其他机动货运船舶	9					0	
89019090	非机动货运船舶及客货兼运船舶	8					0	
89020010	机动捕鱼船	7					0	
89020090	非机动捕鱼船	8					0	
89031000	充气的娱乐或运动用快艇	10					0	0
89039100	帆船	8					0	0
89039200	汽艇	10.5					0	0
89039900	娱乐或运动用其他船舶或快艇	10					0	0
89040000	拖轮及顶推船	9					0	0
89051000	挖泥船	3					0	0
89052000	浮动或潜水式钻探或生产平台	6					0	0

税则号列	商品名称（简称）	最惠税率	亚太2国	东盟			最不发达35国	最不发达4国
				缅	老	柬		
89059010	浮船坞	8					0	0
89059090	其他不以航行为主要功能的船舶	3					0	0
89061000	军舰	5					0	
89069010	其他未列名的机动船舶	5					0	0
89069020	非机动船舶	8					0	0
89069030	未制成或不完整的船舶，包括船舶分段	8					0	0
89071000	充气筏	8					0	0
89079000	其他浮动结构体	8					0	0
89080000	供拆卸的船舶及其他浮动结构体	3					0	0
90011000	光导纤维束及光缆	5					0	0
90012000	偏振材料制的片及板	8					0	0
90013000	隐形眼镜片	10					0	0
90014010	玻璃制变色镜片	20					0	
90014091	玻璃制太阳镜片	20					0	
90014099	玻璃制其他眼镜片	20					0	
90015010	非玻璃材料制变色镜片	20					0	
90015091	非玻璃材料制太阳镜片	20					0	
90015099	非玻璃材料制其他眼镜片	20					0	
90019010	彩色滤光片	8					0	0
90019090	其他光学元件	8					0	0
90021110	特殊用途照相机用物镜	8					0	0
90021120	缩微阅读机用物镜	8					0	0
90021131	单反相机镜头	15					0	
90021139	其他照相机用镜头	15					0	0
90021190	其他照相机、投影仪等用物镜	15					0	0
90021910	摄影机或放映机用物镜	15					0	
90021990	税号90.02未列名的其他物镜	15					0	0
90022010	照相机用滤色镜	15					0	
90022090	其他光学仪器或装置滤色镜	15					0	
90029010	照相机用未列名光学元件	15					0	
90029090	其他光学仪器用未列名光学元件	15					0	0
90031100	塑料制眼镜架	18					0	
90031910	金属材料制眼镜架	10					0	
90031920	天然材料制眼镜架	10					0	
90031990	其他眼镜架	10					0	
90039000	眼镜架零件	10					0	
90041000	太阳镜	20					0	
90049010	变色镜	16					0	
90049090	其他眼镜	20					0	
90051000	双筒望远镜	15					0	
90058010	天文望远镜及其他天文仪器	3					0	0
90058090	其他光学望远镜	12					0	0
90059010	天文望远镜及其他天文仪器用零件	2					0	0
90059090	其他望远镜零附件	8					0	0
90061010	电子分色机	12					0	0
90061090	其他制版照相机	10					0	0
90063000	特种用途的照相机	9					0	0
90064000	一次成相照相机	5					0	0
90065210	缩微照相机	9					0	0
90065300	其他照相机	20					0	
90065910	激光照排设备	9					0	0
90066100	放电式(电子式)闪光灯装置	18					0	
90066910	闪光灯泡、方形闪光灯及类似品	18					0	
90066990	其他照相闪光灯装置	18					0	
90069110	特种用途照相机的零附件	8	0				0	0
90069120	一次成像照相机的零附件	5	0				0	0
90069191	照相机自动调焦组件	10	0				0	0
90069192	其他照相机的快门组件	10	0				0	0

税则号列	商品名称（简称）	最惠税率	亚太2国	东盟			最不发达35国	最不发达4国
				缅	老	柬		
90069199	其他照相机的其他零附件	10	0				0	0
90069900	照相闪光灯装置及闪光灯泡的零件	12					0	0
90071010	高速摄影机	14					0	
90071090	其他摄影机	14					0	
90072010	数字式放映机	14					0	
90072090	放映机	14					0	
90079100	电影摄影机用零附件	8.4					0	
90079200	电影放映机用零附件	8.4					0	
90085010	幻灯机	14					0	
90085020	缩微胶卷、缩微胶片或其他缩微品的阅读机，不论是否可以进行复制	10					0	
90085031	正射投影仪	18					0	
90085039	其他影像投影仪	18					0	
90085040	照片（电影片除外）放大机及缩片机	20					0	
90089010	缩微阅读机的零附件	8					0	
90089020	照片放大机及缩片机的零附件	14					0	
90089090	其他影像投影仪的零附件	14					0	
90101010	电影用胶卷的自动显影装置及设备	14					0	
90101020	特种照相胶卷自动显影装置及设备	8.4					0	0
90101091	彩色胶卷用自动显影及设备	25					0	
90101099	其他胶卷的自动显影装置及设备	15					0	
90105010	负片显示器	14					0	
90105021	电影用的洗印装置	14					0	
90105022	特种照相用的洗印装置	8.4					0	0
90105029	其他照相用的洗印装置	17					0	
90106000	银幕及其他投影屏幕	14					0	
90109010	电影洗印用洗印装置的零附件	0					0	0
90109020	特种照相洗印用装置的零附件	0					0	0
90109090	其他洗印用装置的零附件	0					0	0
90111000	立体显微镜	0					0	0
90112000	缩微照相等用的其他显微镜	0					0	0
90118000	其他显微镜	7					0	
90119000	复式光学显微镜的零附件	0					0	0
90121000	其他非光学显微镜及衍射设备	0					0	0
90129000	非光学显微镜及衍射设备的零件	0					0	0
90131000	武器用望远镜瞄准具及其他望远镜	8					0	
90132000	激光器	6					0	
90138010	放大镜	12					0	
90138020	光学门眼	12					0	
90138090	其他液晶装置及光学仪器	5					0	
90139010	激光器、望远镜等装置的零附件	6					0	
90139020	子目录9013.8030所列货品用零附件	8					0	
90139090	税号90.13所列其他货品的零附件	8					0	
90141000	定向罗盘	2					0	0
90142010	自动驾驶仪	2					0	0
90142090	其他航空或航天导航仪器及装置(罗盘除外)	2					0	0
90148000	其他导航仪器及装置	2					0	0
90149010	自动驾驶仪用零件、附件	1.5					0	0
90149090	其他导航仪器及设备用零件、附件	1.5					0	
90151000	测距仪	9					0	0
90152000	经纬仪及视距仪	9					0	0
90153000	水平仪	9					0	0
90154000	摄影测量用仪器及装置	9					0	0
90158000	其他大地测量仪器及装置	5					0	0
90159000	大地测量仪器及装置的零附件	5					0	0
90160010	感量为0.1mg或更精密的天平	9					0	0
90160090	0.1mg＜感量≤50mg的天平	10.5					0	0
90171000	绘图台及绘图机，不论是否自动	8					0	0
90172000	其他绘图、划线或数学计算器具	0					0	0

税则号列	商品名称（简称）	最惠税率	亚太2国	东盟			最不发达35国	最不发达4国
				缅	老	柬		
90173000	千分尺、卡尺及量规	8					0	0
90178000	其他手用测量长度的器具	8					0	0
90179000	绘图计算器具等仪器的零附件	0					0	0
90181100	心电图记录仪	5					0	0
90181210	B型超声波诊断仪	7					0	0
90181291	彩色超声波诊断仪	5					0	0
90181299	其他超声扫描装置	5					0	0
90181310	核磁共振成像成套装置	4					0	0
90181390	其他核磁共振成象装置	4					0	0
90181400	闪烁摄影装置	5					0	0
90181930	病员监护仪	4					0	0
90181941	听力计	4					0	0
90181949	其他听力诊断装置	4					0	0
90181990	其他电气诊断装置	4					0	0
90182000	紫外线及红外线装置	4					0	0
90183100	注射器	8					0	0
90183210	管状金属针头	8					0	0
90183220	缝合用针	4					0	0
90183900	导管、插管及类似品	4					0	0
90184100	牙钻机	4					0	0
90184910	装有牙科设备的牙科用椅	4					0	0
90184990	牙科用其他仪器及器具	4					0	0
90185000	眼科用其他仪器及器具	4					0	0
90189010	听诊器	4					0	0
90189020	血压测量仪器及器具	4					0	0
90189030	内窥镜	4					0	0
90189040	肾脏透析设备(人工肾)	4					0	0
90189050	透热疗法设备	4					0	0
90189060	输血设备	4					0	0
90189070	麻醉设备	4					0	0
90189080	宫内节育器	4					0	0
90189090	税号90.18中未列名的医疗仪器	4					0	0
90191010	按摩器具	15					0	
90191090	机械疗法器具、心理功能测验装置	4					0	0
90192000	臭氧治疗器、氧气治疗器等器具	4					0	0
90200000	其他呼吸器具及防毒面具	8					0	0
90211000	矫形或骨折用器具	4					0	0
90212100	假牙	4					0	0
90212900	牙齿固定件	4					0	0
90213100	人造关节	4					0	0
90213900	其他人造的人体部分	4					0	0
90214000	助听器,不包括零附件	4					0	0
90215000	心脏起搏器,不包括零附件	4					0	0
90219011	血管支架	4					0	0
90219019	其他支架	4					0	0
90219090	其他税号90.21中未列名的矫形器具	4					0	0
90221200	X射线断层检查仪	4					0	0
90221300	其他牙科用x射线应用设备	4					0	0
90221400	其他医疗或兽医用x射线应用设备	4					0	0
90221910	低剂量x射线安全检查设备	4					0	0
90221920	X射线无损探伤检测仪	4					0	0
90221990	其他非医疗用X射线设备	4					0	0
90222100	医疗用α、β、γ射线设备	4					0	0
90222910	γ射线无损探伤检测仪	6					0	0
90222990	其他非医疗用α、β、γ射线设备	6					0	0
90223000	X射线管	2					0	0
90229010	X射线影像增强器	6					0	0
90229090	税号90.22所列其他设备及零件	6					0	0

税则号列	商品名称（简称）	最惠税率	亚太2国	东盟			最不发达35国	最不发达4国
				缅	老	柬		
90230000	专供示范的仪器、装置及模型	7					0	0
90241010	电子万能试验机	7					0	0
90241020	硬度计	7					0	0
90241090	其他金属材料的试验用机器及器具	7					0	0
90248000	非金属材料的试验用机器及器具	5					0	0
90249000	各种材料的试验用机器零附件	6					0	0
90251100	可直接读数的液体温度计	4					0	0
90251910	非液体的工业用温度计及高温计	8.4					0	0
90251990	非液体的其他温度计、高温计	8.4					0	0
90258000	其他温度计、比重计、湿度计等仪器	11					0	
90259000	比重计、温度计等类似仪器的零件	8					0	0
90261000	测量、检验液体流量或液位的仪器	0					0	0
90262010	压力/差压变送器	0					0	0
90262090	测量、检验压力的仪器及装置	0					0	0
90268010	测量气体流量的仪器及装置	0					0	0
90268090	测量或检验气体的除流量、压力以外其他变化量的仪器及装置	0					0	0
90269000	液体或气体的测量或检验仪器零件	0					0	0
90271000	气体或烟雾分析仪	7					0	0
90272011	气相色谱仪	0					0	0
90272012	液相色谱仪	0					0	0
90272019	其他色谱仪	0					0	0
90272020	电泳仪	0					0	0
90273000	分光仪、分光光度计及摄谱仪	0					0	0
90275000	使用光学射线的其他仪器及装置	0					0	0
90278011	集成电路生产用氦质谱检漏台	0					0	0
90278012	质谱联用仪	0					0	0
90278019	其他质谱仪	0					0	0
90278091	曝光表	14					0	
90278099	其他理化分析仪器及装置	0					0	0
90279000	检镜切片机；理化分析仪器零件	0					0	0
90281010	煤气表	10					0	
90281090	其他气量计	10					0	
90282010	水表	10					0	
90282090	其他液量计	10					0	
90283011	单相感应式电度表	10					0	
90283012	三相感应式电度表	10					0	
90283013	单相电子式(静止式)电度表	10					0	
90283014	三相电子式(静止式)电度表	10					0	
90283019	其他电度表	10					0	
90283090	其他电量计	10					0	
90289010	工业用计量仪表零附件	8.4					0	0
90289090	非工业用计量仪表零附件	8.4					0	0
90291010	转数计	15					0	
90291020	车费计、里程计	15					0	
90291090	产量计数器、步数计及类似仪表	15					0	
90292010	车辆用速度计	10					0	
90292090	其他速度计及转速表、频闪观测仪	10					0	
90299000	转数计、车费计及类似仪表零件	6					0	0
90301000	离子射线的测量或检验仪器及装置	5					0	0
90302010	测试频率＜300兆赫的通用示波器	8					0	0
90302090	其他阴极射线示波器	5					0	0
90303110	量程≤五位半的数字万用表，不带记录装置	15					0	
90303190	其他不带记录装置的万用表	5					0	0
90303200	带记录装置的万用表	8					0	0
90303310	量程≤五位半的数字电流表、电压表，不带记录装置	15					0	
90303320	不带记录装置的电阻测试仪	14					0	
90303390	检测电压、电流及功率的其他仪器，不带记录装置	9					0	0
90303900	检测电压、电流、电阻或功率的其他仪器，带记录装置	8					0	0

税则号列	商品名称（简称）	最惠税率	亚太2国	东盟			最不发达35国	最不发达4国
				缅	老	柬		
90304010	测试频率＜12.4千兆赫兹数字式频率计	0					0	0
90304090	其他无线电通讯专用仪器及装置	0					0	0
90308200	检测半导体晶片或器件的仪器	0					0	0
90308410	电感及电容测试仪	10					0	
90308490	其他电量的测量或检验仪器及装置	8					0	0
90308910	其他电感及电容测试仪	14					0	
90308990	其他电量的测量或检验仪器及装置	8					0	0
90309000	税号90.30所属货品的零件及附件	7					0	0
90311000	机械零件平衡试验机	7					0	0
90312000	试验台	7					0	0
90314100	制造半导体器件时检验半导体晶片、器件或检验光掩模或光栅用	0					0	0
90314910	轮廓投影仪	10					0	0
90314920	光栅测量装置	0					0	0
90314990	其他光学测量或检验仪器和器具	0					0	0
90318010	光纤通信及光纤性能测试仪	5					0	0
90318020	坐标测量仪	5					0	0
90318031	超声波探伤检测仪	5					0	0
90318032	磁粉探伤检测仪	5					0	0
90318033	涡流探伤检测仪	5					0	0
90318039	其他无损探伤检测仪器(射线探伤仪除外)	5					0	0
90318090	未列名测量、检验仪器器具及机器	5					0	0
90319000	税号90.31的仪器及器具的零件	0					0	0
90321000	恒温器	7					0	0
90322000	恒压器	7					0	0
90328100	液压或气压的其他仪器及装置	7					0	0
90328911	列车自动防护系统(ATP)车载设备	7					0	0
90328912	列车自动运行系统(ATO)车载设备	7					0	0
90328919	其他列车自动控制系统（ATC）车载设备	7					0	0
90328990	非液压或气压的其他自动调节或控制仪器及装置	7					0	0
90329000	自动调节或控制仪器零附件	5					0	0
90330000	90章未列名零附件	6					0	0
91011100	机械指示式的贵金属电子手表	11					0	
91011910	光电显示式的贵金属电子手表	16					0	
91011990	其他贵金属电子手表	15					0	
91012100	自动上弦的贵金属机械手表	11					0	
91012900	非自动上弦贵金属机械手表	15					0	
91019100	贵金属电子怀表及其他电子表	15					0	
91019900	贵金属机械怀表及其他机械表	20					0	
91021100	机械指示式的其他电子手表	12.5					0	
91021200	光电显示式的其他电子手表	23					0	
91021900	其他电子手表	15					0	
91022100	其他自动上弦的机械手表	11					0	
91022900	其他非自动上弦的机械手表	15					0	
91029100	电力驱动的电子怀表及其他电子表	15					0	
91029900	其他机械怀表、秒表及其他表	20					0	
91031000	以表芯装成的电子钟	23					0	
91039000	以表芯装成的机械钟	20					0	
91040000	仪表板钟及车辆船舶等用的类似钟	10					0	
91051100	电子闹钟	23					0	0
91051900	机械闹钟	20					0	
91052100	电子挂钟	23					0	
91052900	机械挂钟	20					0	
91059110	电子天文钟	3					0	0
91059190	其他电子钟	23					0	
91059900	其他机械钟	16					0	
91061000	考勤钟、时刻记录器	16					0	
91069000	其他时间记录器及其他类似装置	16					0	
91070000	定时开关	12					0	

税则号列	商品名称（简称）	最惠税率	亚太2国	东盟			最不发达35国	最不发达4国
				缅	老	柬		
91081100	已组装的机械指示式完整电子表芯	16					0	
91081200	已组装的光电显示式完整电子表芯	16					0	
91081900	其他已组装的完整电子表芯	16					0	
91082000	已组装的自动上弦完整表芯	16					0	
91089010	已组装表面≤33.8mm机械完整表芯	16					0	
91089090	其他已组装完整机械表芯	16					0	
91091000	已组装的完整电子钟芯	16					0	
91099000	已组装的完整机械钟芯	16					0	
91101100	未组装的完整表机芯	16					0	
91101200	已组装的不完整表机芯	16					0	
91101900	未组装的不完整表机芯	16					0	
91109010	未组装的完整的钟机芯	16					0	
91109090	不完整的钟机芯	16					0	
91111000	贵金属或包贵金属制的表壳	14					0	
91112000	贱金属制的表壳	14					0	
91118000	非金属制的表壳	14					0	
91119000	表壳的零件	14					0	
91122000	钟壳	14					0	
91129000	钟壳零件	12					0	
91131000	贵金属或包贵金属制的表带及零件	20					0	
91132000	贱金属制的表带及其零件	14					0	
91139000	非金属制的表带及其零件	14					0	0
91141000	钟、表的发条	14					0	
91143000	钟面或表面	14					0	
91144000	钟、表的夹板及横担(过桥)	14					0	
91149010	钟、表的宝石轴承	14					0	
91149090	钟、表的其他零件	14					0	
92011000	竖式钢琴	17.5					0	
92012000	大钢琴	17.5					0	
92019000	其他钢琴	17.5					0	
92021000	弓弦乐器	17.5					0	0
92029000	其他弦乐器	17.5					0	0
92051000	铜管乐器	17.5					0	0
92059010	键盘管风琴、簧风琴及类似乐器	20					0	
92059020	手风琴及类似乐器	21					0	
92059030	口琴	21					0	
92059090	其他管乐器，但游艺场风琴和手摇风琴除外	17.5					0	
92060000	打击乐器	17.5					0	0
92071000	通过电产生或扩大声音的键盘乐器	30					0	
92079000	其他通过电产生或扩大声音的乐器	30					0	
92081000	百音盒	22					0	
92089000	92章未列名的其他乐器	22					0	
92093000	乐器用的弦	17.5					0	
92099100	钢琴的零附件	17.5					0	
92099200	编号9202所列乐器的零附件	17.5					0	0
92099400	编号9207所列乐器的零附件	17.5					0	
92099910	节拍器、音叉及定音管	17.5					0	
92099920	百音盒的机械装置	17.5					0	
92099990	本章其他编号未列名的乐器零件	17.5					0	0
93011010	自动推进的火炮武器	13					0	
93011090	其他火炮武器	13					0	
93012000	火箭发射装置、火焰喷射器等	13					0	
93019000	其他军用武器	13					0	
93020000	左轮手枪及其他手枪	13					0	
93031000	前装枪	13					0	
93032000	其他运动、狩猎或打靶用滑膛枪	13					0	
93033000	其他运动、狩猎或打靶用步枪	13					0	
93039000	其他火器及类似装置	13					0	

税则号列	商品名称（简称）	最惠税率	亚太2国	东盟			最不发达35国	最不发达4国
				缅	老	柬		
93040000	其他武器(如弹簧枪、气枪、警棍等)	13					0	
93051000	左轮手枪或其他手枪的零件及附件	13					0	
93052000	猎枪或步枪用零件及附件	13					0	
93059100	军用武器的零附件	13					0	
93059900	其他武器的零附件	13					0	
93062100	猎枪弹	13					0	
93062900	猎枪弹的零件及气枪弹丸	13					0	
93063080	接机或类似工具用子弹及其零件	13					0	
93063090	其他子弹及其零件	13					0	
93069000	其他弹药和射弹及其零件	13					0	
93070010	军用剑、短弯刀、刺刀、长矛和类似的武器及其零件;军用刀鞘、剑鞘	13					0	0
93070090	其他剑、短弯刀、刺刀、长矛和类似的武器及其零件;其他刀鞘、剑鞘	13					0	0
94011000	飞机用坐具	0					0	0
94012010	皮革或再生皮革面的机动车辆用坐具	10					0	
94012090	机动车辆用坐具	10					0	
94013000	可调高度的转动坐具	0					0	0
94014010	皮革或再生皮革面的能作床用的两用椅	0					0	0
94014090	能作床用的两用椅	0					0	0
94015100	竹、藤制坐具	0			0		0	0
94015900	柳条及类似材料制的坐具	0			0		0	0
94016110	皮革或再生皮革面的装软垫的木框架其他坐具	0					0	0
94016190	装软垫的木框架的其他坐具	0					0	0
94016900	其他木框架的坐具	0					0	0
94017110	皮革或再生皮革面的装软垫的金属框架其他坐具	0					0	0
94017190	带软垫的金属框架的坐具	0					0	0
94017900	其他金属框架的坐具	0					0	0
94018010	石制坐具	0					0	0
94018090	其他坐具	0					0	0
94019011	机动车辆的座椅调角器	10					0	0
94019019	机动车辆用坐具的其他零件	0					0	0
94019090	其他用途坐具的零件	0					0	0
94021010	理发用椅及其零件	0					0	0
94021090	牙科及类似用途的椅及其零件	0					0	0
94029000	其他医疗、外科或兽医用家具及零件	0					0	0
94031000	办公室用金属家具	0					0	0
94032000	其他金属家具	0					0	0
94033000	办公室用木家具	0			0	0	0	0
94034000	厨房用木家具	0				0	0	0
94035010	卧室用红木制家具	0				0	0	0
94035091	卧室用漆木家具	0				0	0	0
94035099	卧室用其他木家具	0				0	0	0
94036010	其他红木制家具	0				0	0	0
94036091	其他漆木家具	0				0	0	0
94036099	其他木家具	0				0	0	0
94037000	塑料家具	0					0	0
94038100	竹、藤制家具	0				0	0	0
94038910	柳条及类似材料制家具	0				0	0	0
94038920	石制的家具	0					0	0
94038990	其他材料制的家具	0					0	0
94039000	税号94.03所列物品的零件	0					0	0
94041000	弹簧床垫	20					0	
94042100	海绵橡胶或泡沫塑料制褥垫	20					0	0
94042900	其他材料制褥垫	20					0	0
94043010	羽毛或羽绒填充的睡袋	20					0	0
94043090	其他睡袋	20					0	0
94049010	羽绒或羽毛填充的寝具及类似品	20					0	0
94049020	兽毛填充的寝具及类似品	20					0	0
94049030	丝棉填充的寝具及类似品	20					0	0

税则号列	商品名称（简称）	最惠税率	亚太2国	东盟			最不发达35国	最不发达4国
				缅	老	柬		
94049040	化纤棉填充的寝具及类似品	20					0	0
94049090	其他材料制的寝具及类似品	20					0	0
94051000	枝形吊灯	10					0	0
94052000	电气台灯、床头灯、落地灯	20					0	0
94053000	圣诞树用的成套灯具	16					0	0
94054010	探照灯	17.5					0	0
94054020	聚光灯	17.5					0	0
94054090	其他电灯及照明装置	10					0	0
94055000	非电气灯具及照明装置	20					0	
94056000	发光标志、发光铭牌及类似品	20					0	
94059100	税号94.05所列物品的玻璃制零件	20					0	
94059200	税号94.05所列物品的塑料制零件	20					0	
94059900	税号94.05所列物品其他材料制零件	20					0	0
94060000	活动房屋	10					0	0
95030010	供儿童乘骑的带轮玩具及玩偶车	0					0	0
95030021	玩具动物	0					0	0
95030029	其他玩偶	0					0	0
95030031	玩具电动火车	0					0	0
95030039	其他缩小(按比例缩小)的全套模型组件	0					0	0
95030040	其他建筑套件及建筑玩具	0					0	0
95030050	玩具乐器	0					0	0
95030060	智力玩具	0					0	0
95030081	组装成套的其他玩具	0					0	0
95030082	其他带动力装置的玩具及模型	0					0	0
95030089	其他未列名玩具	0					0	0
95030090	玩具的零件	0					0	0
95042000	台球用品及附件	0					0	0
95043010	投币式电子游戏机	0					0	0
95043090	投币式其他游戏用品	0					0	0
95044000	扑克牌	0					0	0
95045011	与电视接收机配套使用的游戏机零件	0					0	0
95045019	其他与电视接收机配套使用的游戏机	0					0	0
95045091	其他游戏机的零件	0					0	0
95045099	其他游戏机	0					0	0
95049010	其他电子游戏机	0					0	0
95049021	保龄球自动分瓶机	0					0	0
95049022	保龄球	0					0	0
95049023	保龄球瓶	0					0	0
95049029	其他保龄球自动球道设备及器具	0					0	0
95049030	中国象棋、国际象棋、跳棋等棋类用品	0					0	0
95049040	麻将及类似桌上游戏用品	0					0	0
95049090	其他游艺场、桌上或室内游戏用品	0					0	0
95051000	圣诞节用品	0					0	0
95059000	其他节日用品或娱乐用品	0					0	0
95061100	滑雪屐	14					0	
95061200	滑雪屐扣件(滑雪屐带)	14					0	
95061900	其他滑雪用具	14					0	
95062100	帆板	12					0	
95062900	其他水上运动用具	14					0	
95063100	完整的高尔夫球棍	14					0	0
95063200	高尔夫球	12					0	
95063900	其他高尔夫球用具	14					0	0
95064010	乒乓球	12					0	
95064090	其他乒乓球运动用品及器械	14					0	
95065100	草地网球拍	14					0	
95065900	其他网球拍、羽毛球拍或类似球拍	14					0	
95066100	草地网球	12					0	
95066210	篮球、足球、排球	12					0	

税则号列	商品名称（简称）	最惠税率	亚太2国	东盟 缅	东盟 老	东盟 柬	最不发达35国	最不发达4国
95066290	其他可充气的球	12					0	
95066900	其他球	12					0	
95067010	溜冰鞋	14					0	
95067020	旱冰鞋	14					0	
95069111	跑步机	12					0	
95069119	其他健身及康复器械	12					0	
95069120	滑板	12					0	
95069190	一般的体育活动、体操或竞技用品	12					0	0
95069900	其他未列名的95章用品及设备	12					0	
95071000	钓鱼竿	21					0	
95072000	钓鱼钩	21					0	0
95073000	钓线轮	21					0	
95079000	其他钓鱼用品	21					0	
95081000	流动马戏团及流动动物园	15					0	
95089000	其他旋转木马、秋千等游乐场娱乐设备	15					0	
96011000	已加工的兽牙及其制品	20					0	
96019000	其他已加工动物质雕刻料及其制品	20					0	0
96020010	装药用胶囊	10.5					0	
96020090	已加工植物或矿物质雕刻料及制品	25					0	0
96031000	用枝条或其他植物材料捆扎成的帚	25					0	
96032100	牙刷，包括齿板刷	25					0	
96032900	剃须刷、发刷、睫毛刷等人体化妆用刷	15					0	0
96033010	画笔	25					0	
96033020	毛笔	20					0	
96033090	化妆用的类似笔	25					0	
96034011	猪鬃制漆刷及类似刷	20					0	
96034019	其他材料制漆刷及类似刷	23					0	
96034020	油漆块垫及滚筒	23					0	
96035011	作为机器、器具零件的金属丝刷	14					0	
96035019	作为车辆零件的金属丝刷	14					0	
96035091	作为机器、器具零件的其他刷	14					0	
96035099	作为车辆零件的其他刷	14					0	
96039010	羽毛掸	21					0	
96039090	其他帚、刷、拖把及其他毛掸	15					0	
96040000	手用粗筛、细筛	21					0	
96050000	个人梳妆、缝纫等用成套旅行用品	15					0	
96061000	揿扣及其零件	21					0	
96062100	塑料制钮扣，未用纺织材料包裹	21					0	0
96062200	贱金属制,未用纺织材料包裹的纽扣	15					0	0
96062900	其他钮扣	15					0	0
96063000	钮扣芯及钮扣的其他零件	15					0	0
96071100	装有贱金属齿的拉链	21					0	0
96071900	其他拉链	21					0	
96072000	拉链零件	21					0	
96081000	圆珠笔	15					0	0
96082000	毡尖和其他渗水式笔尖笔及唛头笔	21					0	
96083010	墨汁画笔	21					0	
96083020	自来水笔	21					0	0
96083090	其他钢笔	21					0	0
96084000	活动铅笔	21					0	
96085000	含有≥两种笔的成套货品	21					0	
96086000	圆珠笔芯	21					0	
96089100	钢笔头及笔尖粒	12					0	
96089910	机器、仪器用笔	17.5					0	
96089920	蜡纸铁笔、钢笔杆、铅笔杆等	21					0	
96089990	其他笔零件	21					0	
96091010	铅笔	21					0	0
96091020	颜色铅笔	21					0	

税则号列	商品名称（简称）	最惠税率	亚太2国	东盟			最不发达35国	最不发达4国
				缅	老	柬		
96092000	铅笔芯，黑的或其他颜色的	21					0	
96099000	蜡笔、图画碳笔、书写或绘画用粉笔	15					0	
96100000	具有书写或绘画面的石板、黑板	15					0	
96110000	手用日期戳、封缄戳、编号戳及类似印戳	21					0	
96121000	打字机色带或类似色带	10.5					0	0
96122000	印台	25					0	
96131000	一次性袖珍气体打火机	25					0	
96132000	可充气袖珍气体打火机	25					0	
96138000	其他打火器	25					0	
96139000	打火机及打火器零件	25					0	
96140010	烟斗及烟斗头	25					0	
96140090	烟嘴及其零件	25					0	
96151100	硬质橡胶或塑料制梳子、发夹及类似品	18					0	0
96151900	其他材料制梳子、发夹及类似品	18					0	0
96159000	其他发夹、卷发器等及其零件	18					0	0
96161000	香水喷雾器或类似的化妆用喷雾器	18					0	
96162000	施敷脂粉或化妆品用粉扑及粉拍	18					0	
96170011	玻璃内胆制保温瓶	24					0	
96170019	其他保温瓶	24					0	
96170090	其他真空容器及零件	18					0	
96180000	裁缝用人体模型及其他人体模型	21					0	
96190010	尿布及尿裤	7.5					0	0
96190020	卫生巾（护垫）及止血塞	10					0	0
96190090	任何材料制的卫生巾或尿布的类似品	14					0	0
97011011	唐卡	12					0	0
97011019	其他手绘油画、粉画及其他画	12					0	0
97011020	手绘油画、粉画及其他画的复制品	14					0	0
97019000	拼贴画及类似装饰板	14					0	0
97020000	雕版画、印制画、石印画的原本	12					0	
97030000	各种材料制的雕塑品原件	12					0	0
97040010	使用或未使用的邮票	8					0	0
97040090	其他使用或未使用的印花税票及类似票证	14					0	
97050000	具有动、植、矿物学意义的收藏品	0					0	0
97060000	超过一百年的古物	0					0	0

中华人民共和国海关进出口货物报关单填制规范

（2008 年第 52 号公告）

为规范进出口货物收发货人的申报行为，统一进出口货物报关单填制要求，保证报关单数据质量，根据《中华人民共和国海关法》及有关法规，制定本规范。

《中华人民共和国海关进（出）口货物报关单》在本规范中采用“报关单”、“进口报关单”、“出口报关单”的提法。

报关单各栏目的填制规范如下：

一、预录入编号

本栏目填报预录入报关单的编号，预录入编号规则由接受申报的海关决定。

二、海关编号

本栏目填报海关接受申报时给予报关单的编号，一份报关单对应一个海关编号。

报关单海关编号为 18 位，其中第 1～4 位为接受申报海关的编号（海关规定的《关区代码表》中相应海关代码），第 5～8 位为海关接受申报的公历年份，第 9 位为进出口标志（“1”为进口，“0”为出口；集中申报清单“I”为进口，“E”为出口），后 9 位为顺序编号。在海关 H883/EDI 通关系统向 H2000 通关系统过渡期间，后 9 位的编号规则同 H883/EDI 通关系统的要求，即 1～2 位为接受申报海关的编号（海关规定的《关区代码表》中相应海关代码的后 2 位），第 3 位为海关接受申报公历年份 4 位数字的最后 1 位，后 6 位为顺序编号。

三、进口口岸/出口口岸

本栏目应根据货物实际进出境的口岸海关，填报海关规定的《关区代码表》中相应口岸海关的名称及代码。特殊情况填报要求如下：

进口转关运输货物应填报货物进境地海关名称及代码，出口转关运输货物应填报货物出境地海关名称及代码。按转关运输方式监管的跨关区深加工结转货物，出口报关单填报转出地海关名称及代码，进口报关单填报转入地海关名称及代码。

在不同海关特殊监管区域或保税监管场所之间调拨、转让的货物，填报对方特殊监管区域或保税监管场所所在的海关名称及代码。

其他无实际进出境的货物，填报接受申报的海关名称及代码。

四、备案号

本栏目填报进出口货物收发货人在海关办理加工贸易合同备案或征、减、免税备案审批等手续时，海关核发的《中华人民共和国海关加工贸易手册》、电子账册及其分册（以下统称《加工贸易手册》）、《进出口货物征免税证明》（以下简称《征免税证明》）或其他备案审批文件的编号。

一份报关单只允许填报一个备案号。具体填报要求如下：

（一）加工贸易项下货物，除少量低值辅料按规定不使用《加工贸易手册》及以后续补税监管方式办理内销征税的外，填报《加工贸易手册》编号。

使用异地直接报关分册和异地深加工结转出口分册在异地口岸报关的，本栏目应填报分册号；本地直接报关分册和本地深加工结转分册限制在本地报关，本栏目应填报总册号。

加工贸易成品凭《征免税证明》转为减免税进口货物的，进口报关单填报《征免税证明》编号，出口报关单填报《加工贸易手册》编号。

对加工贸易设备之间的结转，转入和转出企业分别填制进、出口报关单，在报关单“备案号”栏目填报《加工贸易手册》编号。

（二）涉及征、减、免税备案审批的报关单，填报《征免税证明》编号。

（三）涉及优惠贸易协定项下实行原产地证书联网管理（香港 CEPA、澳门 CEPA，下同）的报关单，填报原产地证书代码“Y”和原产地证书编号。

（四）减免税货物退运出口，填报《减免税进口货物同意退运证明》的编号；减免税货物补税进口，填报《减免税货物补税通知书》的编号；减免税货物结转进口（转入），填报《征免税证明》的编号；相应的结转出口（转出），填报《减免税进口货物结转联系函》的编号。

（五）涉及构成整车特征的汽车零部件的报关单，填报备案的 Q 账册编号。

五、合同协议号

本栏目填报进出口货物合同（包括协议或订单）编号。

六、进口日期/出口日期

进口日期填报运载进口货物的运输工具申报进境的日期。

出口日期指运载出口货物的运输工具办结出境手续的日期，本栏目供海关签发打印报关单证明联用，在申报时免予填报。

无实际进出境的报关单填报海关接受申报的日期。

本栏目为8位数字，顺序为年（4位）、月（2位）、日（2位）。

七、申报日期

申报日期指海关接受进出口货物收发货人、受委托的报关企业申报数据的日期。以电子数据报关单方式申报的，申报日期为海关计算机系统接受申报数据时记录的日期。以纸质报关单方式申报的，申报日期为海关接受纸质报关单并对报关单进行登记处理的日期。

申报日期为8位数字，顺序为年（4位）、月（2位）、日（2位）。本栏目在申报时免予填报。

八、经营单位

本栏目填报在海关注册登记的对外签订并执行进出口贸易合同的中国境内法人、其他组织或个人的名称及海关注册编码。

特殊情况下填制要求如下：

（一）进出口货物合同的签订者和执行者非同一企业的，填报执行合同的企业。

（二）外商投资企业委托进出口企业进口投资设备、物品的，填报外商投资企业，并在标记唛码及备注栏注明“委托某进出口企业进口”。

（三）有代理报关资格的报关企业代理其他进出口企业办理进出口报关手续时，填报委托的进出口企业的名称及海关注册编码。

九、收货单位/发货单位

（一）收货单位填报已知的进口货物在境内的最终消费、使用单位的名称，包括：

1．自行从境外进口货物的单位。

2．委托进出口企业进口货物的单位。

（二）发货单位填报出口货物在境内的生产或销售单位的名称，包括：

1．自行出口货物的单位。

2．委托进出口企业出口货物的单位。

（三）有海关注册编码或加工企业编码的收、发货单位，本栏目应填报其中文名称及编码；没有编码的应填报其中文名称。使用《加工贸易手册》管理的货物，报关单的收、发货单位应与《加工贸易手册》的“经营企业”或“加工企业”一致；减免税货物报关单的收、发货单位应与《征免税证明》的“申请单位”一致。

十、申报单位

自理报关的，本栏目填报进出口企业的名称及海关注册编码；委托代理报关的，本栏目填报经海关批准的报关企业名称及海关注册编码。

本栏目还包括报关单左下方用于填报申报单位有关情况的相关栏目，包括报关员、报关单位地址、邮政编码和电话号码等栏目。

十一、运输方式

运输方式包括实际运输方式和海关规定的特殊运输方式，前者指货物实际进出境的运输方式，按进出境所使用的运输工具分类；后者指货物无实际进出境的运输方式，按货物在境内的流向分类。

本栏目应根据货物实际进出境的运输方式或货物在境内流向的类别，按照海关规定的《运输方式代码表》选择填报相应的运输方式。

（一）特殊情况填报要求如下：

1．非邮件方式进出境的快递货物，按实际运输方式填报；

2．进出境旅客随身携带的货物，按旅客所乘运输工具填报；

3．进口转关运输货物，按载运货物抵达进境地的运输工具填报；出口转关运输货物，按载运货物驶离出境地的运输工具填报；

4．不复运出（入）境而留在境内（外）销售的进出境展览品、留赠转卖物品等，填报“其他运输”（代码9）；

（二）无实际进出境货物在境内流转时填报要求如下：

1．境内非保税区运入保税区货物和保税区退区货物，填报“非保税区”（代码0）；

2．保税区运往境内非保税区货物，填报“保税区”（代码7）；

3．境内存入出口监管仓库和出口监管仓库退仓货物，填报“监管仓库”（代码1）；

4．保税仓库转内销货物，填报“保税仓库”（代码8）；

5．从境内保税物流中心外运入中心或从中心运往境内中心外的货物，填报“物流中心”（代码W）；

6．从境内保税物流园区外运入园区或从园区运往境内园区外的货物，填报“物流园区”（代码X）；

7．从境内保税港区外运入港区（不含直通）或从港区运往境内港区外（不含直通）的货物，填报“保税港区”（代码Y），综合保税区比照保税港区填报；

8．从境内出口加工区、珠澳跨境工业区珠海园区（以下简称珠海园区）外运入加工区、珠海园区或从加工区、珠海园区运往境内区外的货物，区外企业填报“出口加工区”（代码Z），区内企业填报“其他运输”（代码9）；

9．境内运入深港西部通道港方口岸区的货物，填报“边境特殊海关作业区”（代码H）；

10．其他境内流转货物，填报“其他运输”（代码9），包括特殊监管区域内货物之间的流转、调拨货物，特殊监管区域、保税监管场所之间相互流转货物，特殊监管区域外的加工贸易余料结转、深加工结转、内销等货物。

十二、运输工具名称

本栏目填报载运货物进出境的运输工具名称或编号。填报内容应与运输部门向海关申报的舱单（载货清单）所列相应内容一致。具体填报要求如下：

（一）直接在进出境地或采用“属地申报，口岸验放”通关模式办理报关手续的报关单填报要求如下：

1．水路运输：填报船舶编号（来往港澳小型船舶为监管簿编号）或者船舶英文名称。

2．公路运输：填报该跨境运输车辆的国内行驶车牌号，深圳提前报关模式的报关单填报国内行驶车牌号+“/”+“提前报关”。

3．铁路运输：填报车厢编号或交接单号。

4．航空运输：填报航班号。

5．邮件运输：填报邮政包裹单号。

6．其他运输：填报具体运输方式名称，例如：管道、驮畜等。

（二）转关运输货物的报关单填报要求如下：

1．进口

（1）水路运输：直转、提前报关填报“@”+16位转关申报单预录入号（或13位载货清单号）；中转填报进境英文船名。

（2）铁路运输：直转、提前报关填报“@”+16位转关申报单预录入号；中转填报车厢编号。

（3）航空运输：直转、提前报关填报“@”+16位转关申报单预录入号（或13位载货清单号）；中转填报“@”。

（4）公路及其他运输：填报“@”+16位转关申报单预录入号（或13位载货清单号）。

（5）以上各种运输方式使用广东地区载货清单转关的提前报关货物填报“@”+13位载货清单号。

2．出口

（1）水路运输：非中转填报“@”+16位转关申报单预录入号（或13位载货清单号）。如多张报关单需要通过一张转关单转关的，运输工具名称字段填报“@”。

中转货物，境内水路运输填报驳船船名；境内铁路运输填报车名（主管海关4位关别代码+“TRAIN”）；境内公路运输填报车名（主管海关4位关别代码+“TRUCK”）。

（2）铁路运输：填报“@”+16位转关申报单预录入号（或13位载货清单号），如多张报关单需要通过一张转关单转关的，填报“@”。

（3）航空运输：填报“@”+16位转关申报单预录入号（或13位载货清单号），如多张报关单需要通过一张转关单转关的，填报“@”。

（4）其他运输方式：填报“@”+16位转关申报单预录入号（或13位载货清单号）。

（三）采用“集中申报”通关方式办理报关手续的，报关单本栏目填报“集中申报”。

（四）无实际进出境的报关单，本栏目免予填报。

十三、航次号

本栏目填报载运货物进出境的运输工具的航次编号。

具体填报要求如下：

（一）直接在进出境地或采用“属地申报，口岸验放”通关模式办理报关手续的报关单

1．水路运输：填报船舶的航次号。

2．公路运输：填报运输车辆的8位进出境日期[顺序为年（4位）、月（2位）、日（2位），下同]。

3．铁路运输：填报列车的进出境日期。

4．航空运输：免予填报。

5．邮件运输：填报运输工具的进出境日期。

6．其他运输方式：免予填报。

（二）转关运输货物的报关单

1．进口

（1）水路运输：中转转关方式填报“@”+进境干线船舶航次。直转、提前报关免予填报。

（2）公路运输：免予填报。

（3）铁路运输：“@”+8位进境日期。

（4）航空运输：免予填报。

（5）其他运输方式：免予填报。

2．出口

（1）水路运输：非中转货物免予填报。中转货物：境内水路运输填报驳船航次号；境内铁路、公路运输填报6位起运日期[顺序为年（2位）、月（2位）、日（2位）]。

（2）铁路拼车拼箱捆绑出口：免予填报。

（3）航空运输：免予填报。

（4）其他运输方式：免予填报。

（三）无实际进出境的报关单，本栏目免予填报。

十四、提运单号

本栏目填报进出口货物提单或运单的编号。

一份报关单只允许填报一个提单或运单号，一票货物对应多个提单或运单时，应分单填报。

具体填报要求如下：

（一）直接在进出境地或采用“属地申报，口岸验放”通关模式办理报关手续的

1．水路运输：填报进出口提单号。如有分提单的，填报进出口提单号+“*”+分提单号。

2．公路运输：免予填报。

3．铁路运输：填报运单号。

4．航空运输：填报总运单号+“_”+分运单号，无分运单的填报总运单号。

5．邮件运输：填报邮运包裹单号。

（二）转关运输货物的报关单

1．进口

（1）水路运输：直转、中转填报提单号。提前报关免予填报。

（2）铁路运输：直转、中转填报铁路运单号。提前报关免予填报。

（3）航空运输：直转、中转货物填报总运单号+“_”+分运单号。提前报关免予填报。

（4）其他运输方式：免予填报。

（5）以上运输方式进境货物，在广东省内用公路运输转关的，填报车牌号。

2．出口

（1）水路运输：中转货物填报提单号；非中转货物免予填报；广东省内汽车运输提前报关的转关货物，填报承运车辆的车牌号。

（2）其他运输方式：免予填报。广东省内汽车运输提前报关的转关货物，填报承运车辆的车牌号。

（三）采用“集中申报”通关方式办理报关手续的，报关单填报归并的集中申报清单的进出口起止日期[按年（4位）月（2位）日（2位）年（4位）月（2位）日（2位）]。

（四）无实际进出境的，本栏目免予填报。

十五、贸易方式（监管方式）

本栏目应根据实际对外贸易情况按海关规定的《监管方式代码表》选择填报相应的监管方式简称及代码。一份报关单只允许填报一种监管方式。

特殊情况下加工贸易货物监管方式填报要求如下：

（一）进口少量低值辅料（即5000美元以下，78种以内的低值辅料）按规定不使用《加工贸易手册》的，填报“低值辅料”。使用《加工贸易手册》的，按《加工贸易手册》上的监管方式填报。

（二）外商投资企业为加工内销产品而进口的料件，属非保税加工的，填报“一般贸易”。

外商投资企业全部使用国内料件加工的出口成品，填报“一般贸易”。

（三）加工贸易料件结转或深加工结转货物，按批准的监管方式填报。

（四）加工贸易料件转内销货物以及按料件办理进口手续的转内销制成品、残次品、半成品，应填制进口报关单，填报“来料料件内销”或“进料料件内销”；加工贸易成品凭《征免税证明》转为减免税进口货物的，应分别填制进、出口报关单，出口报关单本栏目填报“来料成品减免”或“进料成品减免”，进口报关单本栏目按照实际监管方式填报。

（五）加工贸易出口成品因故退运进口及复运出口的，填报“来料成品退换”或“进料成品退换”；加工贸易进口料件因换料退运出口及复运进口的，填报“来料料件退换”或“进料料件退换”；加工贸易过程中产生的剩余料件、边角料退运出口，以及进口料件因品质、规格等原因退运出口且不再更换同类货物进口的，分别填报“来料料件复出”、“来料边角料复出”、“进料料件复出”、“进料边角料复出”。

（六）备料《加工贸易手册》中的料件结转转入加工出口《加工贸易手册》的，填报“来料加工”或“进料加工”。

（七）保税工厂加工贸易进出口货物，根据《加工贸易手册》填报“来料加工”或“进料加工”。

（八）加工贸易边角料内销和副产品内销，应填制进口报关单，填报“来料边角料内销”或“进料边角料内销”。

（九）加工贸易进口料件不再用于加工成品出口，或生产的半成品（折料）、成品因故不再出口，主动放弃交由海关处理时，应填制进口报关单，填报“料件放弃”或“成品放弃”。

十六、征免性质

本栏目应根据实际情况按海关规定的《征免性质代码表》选择填报相应的征免性质简称及代码，持有海关核发的《征免税证明》的，应按照《征免税证明》中批注的征免性质填报。一份报关单只允许填报一种征免性质。

加工贸易货物报关单应按照海关核发的《加工贸易手册》中批注的征免性质简称及代码填报。特殊情况填报要求如下：

（一）保税工厂经营的加工贸易，根据《加工贸易手册》填报“进料加工”或“来料加工”。

（二）外商投资企业为加工内销产品而进口的料件，属非保税加工的，填报“一般征税”或其他相应征免性质。

（三）加工贸易转内销货物，按实际情况填报（如一般征税、科教用品、其他法定等）。

（四）料件退运出口、成品退运进口货物填报“其他法定”（代码 0299）。

（五）加工贸易结转货物，本栏目免予填报。

十七、征税比例/结汇方式

进口报关单本栏目免予填报。

出口报关单填报结汇方式，按海关规定的《结汇方式代码表》选择填报相应的结汇方式名称或代码。

十八、许可证号

本栏目填报以下许可证的编号：进（出）口许可证、两用物项和技术进（出）口许可证、两用物项和技术出口许可证（定向）、纺织品临时出口许可证、出口许可证（加工贸易）、出口许可证（边境小额贸易）。

一份报关单只允许填报一个许可证号。

十九、起运国（地区）/运抵国（地区）

起运国（地区）填报进口货物起始发出直接运抵我国或者在运输中转国（地）未发生任何商业性交易的情况下运抵我国的国家（地区）。

运抵国（地区）填报出口货物离开我国关境直接运抵或者在运输中转国（地区）未发生任何商业性交易的情况下最后运抵的国家（地区）。

不经过第三国（地区）转运的直接运输进出口货物，以进口货物的装货港所在国（地区）为起运国（地区），以出口货物的指运港所在国（地区）为运抵国（地区）。

经过第三国（地区）转运的进出口货物，如在中转国（地区）发生商业性交易，则以中转国（地区）作为起运/运抵国（地区）。

本栏目应按海关规定的《国别（地区）代码表》选择填报相应的起运国（地区）或运抵国（地区）中文名称及代码。

无实际进出境的，填报“中国”（代码 142）。

二十、装货港/指运港

装货港填报进口货物在运抵我国关境前的最后一个境外装运港。

指运港填报出口货物运往境外的最终目的港；最终目的港不可预知的，按尽可能预知的目的港填报。

本栏目应根据实际情况按海关规定的《港口航线代码表》选择填报相应的港口中文名称及代码。装货港/指运港在《港口航线代码表》中无港口中文名称及代码的，可选择填报相应的国家中文名称或代码。

无实际进出境的，本栏目填报“中国境内”（代码 142）。

二十一、境内目的地 / 境内货源地

境内目的地填报已知的进口货物在国内的消费、使用地或最终运抵地，其中最终运抵地为最终使用单位所在的地区。最终使用单位难以确定的，填报货物进口时预知的最终收货单位所在地。

境内货源地填报出口货物在国内的产地或原始发货地。出口货物产地难以确定的，填报最早发运该出口货物的单位所在地。

本栏目按海关规定的《国内地区代码表》选择填报相应的国内地区名称及代码。

二十二、批准文号

进口报关单中本栏目免予填报。

出口报关单中本栏目填报出口收汇核销单编号。

二十三、成交方式

本栏目应根据进出口货物实际成交价格条款，按海关规定的《成交方式代码表》选择填报相应的成交方式代码。

无实际进出境的报关单，进口填报 CIF，出口填报 FOB。

二十四、运费

本栏目填报进口货物运抵我国境内输入地点起卸前的运输费用，出口货物运至我国境内输出地点装载后的运输费用。进口货物成交价格包含前述运输费用或者出口货物成交价格不包含前述运输费用的，本栏目免予填报。

运费可按运费单价、总价或运费率三种方式之一填报，注明运费标记（运费标记“1”表示运费率，“2”表示每吨货物的运费单价，“3”表示运费总价），并按海关规定的《货币代码表》选择填报相应的币种代码。

运保费合并计算的，填报在本栏目。

二十五、保费

本栏目填报进口货物运抵我国境内输入地点起卸前的保险费用，出口货物运至我国境内输出地点装载后的保险费用。进口货物成交价格包含前述保险费用或者出口货物成交价格不包含前述保险费用的，本栏目免于填报。

保费可按保险费总价或保险费率两种方式之一填报，注明保险费标记（保险费标记“1”表示保险费率，“3”表示保险费总价），并按海关规定的《货币代码表》选择填报相应的币种代码。

运保费合并计算的，本栏目免予填报。

二十六、杂费

本栏目填报成交价格以外的、按照《中华人民共和国进出口关税条例》相关规定应计入完税价格或应从完税价格中扣除的费用。可按杂费总价或杂费率两种方式之一填报，注明杂费标记（杂费标记“1”表示杂费率，“3”表示杂费总价），并按海关规定的《货币代码表》选择填报相应的币种代码。

应计入完税价格的杂费填报为正值或正率，应从完税价格中扣除的杂费填报为负值或负率。

二十七、件数

本栏目填报有外包装的进出口货物的实际件数。特殊情况填报要求如下：

（一）舱单件数为集装箱的，填报集装箱个数。

（二）舱单件数为托盘的，填报托盘数。

本栏目不得填报为零，裸装货物填报为“1”。

二十八、包装种类

本栏目应根据进出口货物的实际外包装种类，按海关规定的《包装种类代码表》选择填报相应的包装种类代码。

二十九、毛重（千克）

本栏目填报进出口货物及其包装材料的重量之和，计量单位为千克，不足一千克的填报为“1”。

三十、净重（千克）

本栏目填报进出口货物的毛重减去外包装材料后的重量，即货物本身的实际重量，计量单位为千克，不足一千克的填报为“1”。

三十一、集装箱号

本栏目填报装载进出口货物（包括拼箱货物）集装箱的箱体信息。一个集装箱填一条记录，分别填报集装箱号（在集装箱箱体上标示的全球唯一编号）、集装箱的规格和集装箱的自重。非集装箱货物填报为“0”。

三十二、随附单证

本栏目根据海关规定的《监管证件代码表》选择填报除本规范第十八条规定的许可证件以外的其他进出口许可证件或监管证件代码及编号。

本栏目分为随附单证代码和随附单证编号两栏，其中代码栏应按海关规定的《监管证件代码表》选择填报相应证件代码；编号栏应填报证件编号。

（一）加工贸易内销征税报关单，随附单证代码栏填写“c”，随附单证编号栏填写海关审核通过的内销征税联系单号。

（二）含预归类商品报关单，随附单证代码项下填写“r”，随附单证编号项下填写XX关预归类书XX号。

（三）优惠贸易协定项下进出口货物

“Y”为原产地证书代码。优惠贸易协定代码选择“01”、“02”、“03”、“04”、“05”、“06”、“07”、“08”、“09”填报：

“01”为“亚太贸易协定”项下的进口货物；

“02”为“中国－东盟自贸区”项下的进口货物；

“03”为“内地与香港紧密经贸关系安排”（香港CEPA）项下的进口货物；

“04”为“内地与澳门紧密经贸关系安排”（澳门CEPA）项下的进口货物；

“05”为“对非洲特惠待遇”项下的进口货物；

“06”为“台湾农产品零关税措施”项下的进口货物；

“07”为“中巴自贸区”项下的进口货物；

“08”为“中智自贸区”项下的进口货物；

“09”为“对也门等国特惠待遇”项下的进口货物。

具体填报要求如下：

1.实行原产地证书联网管理的，随附单证代码栏填写“Y”，随附单证编号栏的“<>”内填写优惠贸易协定代码。例如香港CEPA项下进口商品，应填报为：“Y”和“<03>”。一票进口货物中如涉及多份原产地证书或含有非原产地证书商品，应分单填报。

2．未实行原产地证书联网管理的，随附单证代码栏填写“Y”，随附单证编号栏“<>”内填写优惠贸易协定代码+“:”+需证商品序号。例如《亚太贸易协定》项下进口报关单中第1到第3项和第5项为优惠贸易协定项下商品，应填报为：“<01:1-3,5>”。

优惠贸易协定项下出口货物，本栏目填报原产地证书代码和编号。

三十三、用途／生产厂家

进口货物本栏目填报用途，应根据进口货物的实际用途按海关规定的《用途代码表》选择填报相应的用途代码。

出口货物本栏目填报其境内生产企业。

三十四、标记唛码及备注

本栏目填报要求如下：

（一）标记唛码中除图形以外的文字、数字。

（二）受外商投资企业委托代理其进口投资设备、物品的进出口企业名称。

（三）与本报关单有关联关系的，同时在业务管理规范方面又要求填报的备案号，填报在电子数据报关单中“关联备案”栏。

加工贸易结转货物及凭《征免税证明》转内销货物，其对应的备案号应填报在“关联备案”栏。

减免税货物结转进口（转入），报关单“关联备案”栏应填写本次减免税货物结转所申请的《减免税进口货物结转联系函》的编号。

减免税货物结转出口（转出），报关单“关联备案”栏应填写与其相对应的进口（转入）报关单“备案号”栏中《征免税证明》的编号。

（四）与本报关单有关联关系的，同时在业务管理规范方面又要求填报的报关单号，填报在电子数据报关单中“关联报关单”栏。

加工贸易结转类的报关单，应先办理进口报关，并将进口报关单号填入出口报关单的“关联报关单”栏。

办理进口货物直接退运手续的，除另有规定外，应当先填写出口报关单，再填写进口报关单，并将出口报关单号填入进口报关单的“关联报关单”栏。

减免税货物结转出口（转出），应先办理进口报关，并将进口（转入）报关单号填入出口（转出）报关单的“关联报关单”栏。

（五）办理进口货物直接退运手续的，本栏目填报《准予直接退运决定书》或者《责令直接退运通知书》编号。

（六）申报时其他必须说明的事项填报在本栏目。

三十五、项号

本栏目分两行填报及打印。第一行填报报关单中的商品顺序编号；第二行专用于加工贸易、减免税等已备案、审批的货物，填报和打印该项货物在《加工贸易手册》或《征免税证明》等备案、审批单证中的顺序编号。

优惠贸易协定项下实行原产地证书联网管理的报关单，第一行填报报关单中的商品顺序编号，第二行填报该项商品对应的原产地证书上的商品项号。

加工贸易项下进出口货物的报关单，第一行填报报关单中的商品顺序编号，第二行填报该项商品在《加工贸易手册》中的商品项号，用于核销对应项号下的料件或成品数量。其中第二行特殊情况填报要求如下：

（一）深加工结转货物，分别按照《加工贸易手册》中的进口料件项号和出口成品项号填报。

（二）料件结转货物（包括料件、制成品和半成品折料），出口报关单按照转出《加工贸易手册》中进口料件的项号填报；进口报关单按照转进《加工贸易手册》中进口料件的项号填报。

（三）料件复出货物（包括料件、边角料、来料加工半成品折料），出口报关单按照《加工贸易手册》中进口料件的项号填报；如边角料对应一个以上料件项号时，填报主要料件项号。料件退换货物（包括料件、不包括半成品），进出口报关单按照《加工贸易手册》中进口料件的项号填报。

（四）成品退换货物，退运进境报关单和复运出境报关单按照《加工贸易手册》原出口成品的项号填报。

（五）加工贸易料件转内销货物（以及按料件办理进口手续的转内销制成品、半成品、残次品）应填制进口报关单，填报《加工贸易手册》进口料件的项号；加工贸易边角料、副产品内销，填报《加工贸易手册》中对应的进口料件项号。如边角料或副产品对应一个以上料件项号时，填报主要料件项号。

（六）加工贸易成品凭《征免税证明》转为减免税货物进口的，应先办理进口报关手续。进口报关单填报《征免税证明》中的项号，出口报关单填报《加工贸易手册》原出口成品项号，进、出口报关单货物数量应一致。

（七）加工贸易料件放弃或成品放弃，本栏目应填报《加工贸易手册》中的进口料件或出口成品项号。半成品放弃的应按单耗折回料件，以料件放弃申报，本栏目填报《加工贸易手册》中对应的进口料件项号。

（八）加工贸易副产品退运出口、结转出口或放弃，本栏目应填报《加工贸易手册》中新增的变更副产品的出口项号。

（九）经海关批准实行加工贸易联网监管的企业，按海关联网监管要求，企业需申报报关清单的，应在向海关申报进出口（包括形式进出口）报关单前，向海关申报“清单”。一份报关清单对应一份报关单，报关单上的商品由报关清单归并而得。加工贸易电子账册报关单中项号、品名、规格等栏目的填制规范比照《加工贸易手册》。

三十六、商品编号

本栏目应填报由《中华人民共和国进出口税则》确定的进出口货物的税则号列和《中华人民共和国海关统计商品目录》确定的商品编码，以及符合海关监管要求的附加编号组成的10位商品编号。

三十七、商品名称、规格型号

本栏目分两行填报及打印。第一行填报进出口货物规范的中文商品名称，第二行填报规格型号。

具体填报要求如下：

（一）商品名称及规格型号应据实填报，并与进出口货物收发货人或受委托的报关企业所提交的合同、发票等相关单证相符。

（二）商品名称应当规范，规格型号应当足够详细，以能满足海关归类、审价及许可证件管理要求为准，可参照《中华人民共和国海关进出口商品规范申报目录》中对商品名称、规格型号的要求进行填报。

（三）加工贸易等已备案的货物，填报的内容必须与备案登记中同项号下货物的商品名称一致。

（四）对需要海关签发《货物进口证明书》的车辆，商品名称栏应填报“车辆品牌+排气量（注明 cc）+车型（如越野车、小轿车等）”。进口汽车底盘不填报排气量。车辆品牌应按照《进口机动车辆制造厂名称和车辆品牌中英文对照表》中“签注名称”一栏的要求填报。规格型号栏可填报“汽油型”等。

（五）由同一运输工具同时运抵同一口岸并且属于同一收货人、使用同一提单的多种进口货物，按照商品归类规则应当归入同一商品编号的，应当将有关商品一并归入该商品编号。商品名称填报一并归类后的商品名称；规格型号填报一并归类后商品的规格型号。

（六）加工贸易边角料和副产品内销，边角料复出口，本栏目填报其报验状态的名称和规格型号。

（七）进口货物收货人以一般贸易方式申报进口属于《需要详细列名申报的汽车零部件清单》（海关总署2006年第64号公告）范围内的汽车生产件的，应按以下要求填报：

1. 商品名称填报进口汽车零部件的详细中文商品名称和品牌，中文商品名称与品牌之间用“/”相隔，必要时加注英文商业名称；进口的成套散件或者毛坯件应在品牌后加注“成套散件”、“毛坯”等字样，并与品牌之间用“/”相隔。

2. 规格型号填报汽车零部件的完整编号。在零部件编号前应当加注“S”字样，并与零部件编号之间用“/”相隔，零部件编号之后应当依次加注该零部件适用的汽车品牌和车型。

汽车零部件属于可以适用于多种汽车车型的通用零部件的，零部件编号后应当加注“TY”字样，并用“/”与零部件编号相隔。

与进口汽车零部件规格型号相关的其他需要申报的要素，或者海关规定的其他需要申报的要素，如“功率”、“排气量”等，应当在车型或“TY”之后填报，并用“/”与之相隔。

汽车零部件报验状态是成套散件的，应当在“标记唛码及备注”栏内填报该成套散件装配后的最终完整品的零部件编号。

（八）进口货物收货人以一般贸易方式申报进口属于《需要详细列名申报的汽车零部件清单》（海关总署2006年第64号公告）范围内的汽车维修件的，填报规格型号时，应当在零部件编号前加注“W”，并与零部件编号之间用“/”相隔；进口维修件的品牌与该零部件适用的整车厂牌不一致的，应当在零部件编号前加注“WF”，并与零部件编号之间用“/”相隔。其余申报要求同上条执行。

三十八、数量及单位

本栏目分三行填报及打印。

（一）第一行应按进出口货物的法定第一计量单位填报数量及单位，法定计量单位以《中华人民共和国海关统计商品目录》中的计量单位为准。

（二）凡列明有法定第二计量单位的，应在第二行按照法定第二计量单位填报数量及单位。无法定第二计量单位的，本栏目第二行为空。

（三）成交计量单位及数量应填报并打印在第三行。

（四）法定计量单位为“千克”的数量填报，特殊情况下填报要求如下：

1. 装入可重复使用的包装容器的货物，应按货物扣除包装容器后的重量填报，如罐装同位素、罐装氧气及类似品等。

2. 使用不可分割包装材料和包装容器的货物，按货物的净重填报（即包括内层直接包装的净重重量），如采用供零售包装的罐头、化妆品、药品及类似品等。

3. 按照商业惯例以公量重计价的商品，应按公量重填报，如未脱脂羊毛、羊毛条等。

4. 采用以毛重作为净重计价的货物，可按毛重填报，如粮食、饲料等大宗散装货物。

5. 采用零售包装的酒类、饮料，按照液体部分的重量填报。

（五）成套设备、减免税货物如需分批进口，货物实际进口时，应按照实际报验状态确定数量。

（六）根据《商品名称及编码协调制度》归类规则，零部件按整机或成品归类的，法定计量单位是非重量的，其对应的法定数量填报“0.1”。

（七）具有完整品或制成品基本特征的不完整品、未制成品，根据《商品名称及编码协调制度》归类规则应按完整品归类的，按照构成完整品的实际数量填报。

（八）加工贸易等已备案的货物，成交计量单位必须与《加工贸易手册》中同项号下货物的计量单位一致，加工贸易边角料和副产品内销、边角料复出口，本栏目填报其报验状态的计量单位。

（九）优惠贸易协定项下进出口商品的成交计量单位必须与原产地证书上对应商品的计量单位一致。

（十）法定计量单位为立方米的气体货物，应折算成标准状况（即摄氏零度及1个标准大气压）下的体积进行填报。

三十九、原产国（地区）/最终目的国（地区）

原产国（地区）应依据《中华人民共和国进出口货物原产地条例》、《中华人民共和国海关关于执行〈非优惠原产地规则中实质性改变标准〉的规定》以及海关总署关于各项优惠贸易协定原产地管理规章规定的原产地确定标准填报。同一批进口货物的原产地不同的，应分别填报原产国（地区）。进口货物原产国（地区）无法确定的，填报“国别不详”（代码701）。

最终目的国（地区）填报已知的出口货物的最终实际消费、使用或进一步加工制造国家（地区）。不经过第三国（地区）转运的直接运输货物，以运抵国（地区）为最终目的国（地区）；经过第三国（地区）转运的货物，以最后运往国（地区）为最终目的国（地区）。同一批出口货物的最终目的国（地区）不同的，应分别填报最终目的国（地区）。出口货物不能确定最终目的国（地区）时，以尽可能预知的最后运往国（地区）为最终目的国（地区）。

本栏目应按海关规定的《国别（地区）代码表》选择填报相应的国家（地区）名称及代码。

四十、单价

本栏目填报同一项号下进出口货物实际成交的商品单位价格。无实际成交价格的，本栏目填报单位货值。

四十一、总价

本栏目填报同一项号下进出口货物实际成交的商品总价格。无实际成交价格的，本栏目填报货值。

四十二、币制

本栏目应按海关规定的《货币代码表》选择相应的货币名称及代码填报，如《货币代码表》中无实际成交币种，需将实际成交货币按申报日外汇折算率折算成《货币代码表》列明的货币填报。

四十三、征免

本栏目应按照海关核发的《征免税证明》或有关政策规定，对报关单所列每项商品选择海关规定的《征减免税方式代码表》中相应的征减免税方式填报。

加工贸易货物报关单应根据《加工贸易手册》中备案的征免规定填报；《加工贸易手册》中备案的征免规定为“保金”或“保函”的，应填报“全免”。

四十四、税费征收情况

本栏目供海关批注进（出）口货物税费征收及减免情况。

四十五、录入员

本栏目用于记录预录入操作人员的姓名。

四十六、录入单位

本栏目用于记录预录入单位名称。

四十七、填制日期

本栏目填报申报单位填制报关单的日期。本栏目为8位数字，顺序为年（4位）、月（2位）、日（2位）。

四十八、海关审单批注及放行日期（签章）

本栏目供海关作业时签注。

本规范所述尖括号（〈〉）、逗号（,）、连接符（-）、冒号（:）等标点符号及数字，填报时都必须使用非中文状态下的半角字符。

相关用语的含义：

报关单录入凭单：指申报单位按报关单的格式填写的凭单，用做报关单预录入的依据。该凭单的编号规则由申报单位自行决定。

预录入报关单：指预录入单位按照申报单位填写的报关单凭单录入、打印由申报单位向海关申报，海关尚未接受申报的报关单。

报关单证明联：指海关在核实货物实际进出境后按报关单格式提供的，用做进出口货物收发货人向国税、外汇管理部门办理退税和外汇核销手续的证明文件。

海关通关系统常用代码表及说明

进出口通关申报系统常用代码表

监管方式代码表

监管方式代码	监管方式简称	监管方式全称
0110	一般贸易	一般贸易
0130	易货贸易	易货贸易
0139	旅游购物商品	用于旅游者5万美元以下的出口小批量订货
0200	料件放弃	主动放弃交由海关处理的来料或进料加工料件
0214	来料加工	来料加工装配贸易进口料件及加工出口货物
0245	来料料件内销	来料加工料件转内销
0255	来料深加工	来料深加工结转货物
0258	来料余料结转	来料加工余料结转
0265	来料料件复出	来料加工复运出境的原进口料件
0300	来料料件退换	来料加工料件退换
0314	加工专用油	国营贸易企业代理来料加工企业进口柴油
0320	不作价设备	加工贸易外商提供的不作价进口设备
0345	来料成品减免	来料加工成品凭征免税证明转减免税
0400	成品放弃	主动放弃交由海关处理的来料及进料加工成品
0420	加工贸易设备	加工贸易项下外商提供的进口设备
0444	保区进料成品	按成品征税的保税区进料加工成品转内销货物
0445	保区来料成品	按成品征税的保税区来料加工成品转内销货物
0446	加工设备内销	加工贸易免税进口设备转内销
0456	加工设备结转	加工贸易免税进口设备结转
0466	加工设备退运	加工贸易免税进口设备退运出境
0500	减免设备结转	用于监管年限内减免税设备的结转
0513	补偿贸易	补偿贸易
0544	保区进料料件	按料件征税的保税区进料加工成品转内销货物
0545	保区来料料件	按料件征税的保税区来料加工成品转内销货物
0615	进料对口	进料加工(对口合同)
0642	进料以产顶进	进料加工成品以产顶进
0644	进料料件内销	进料加工料件转内销
0654	进料深加工	进料深加工结转货物
0657	进料余料结转	进料加工余料结转
0664	进料料件复出	进料加工复运出境的原进口料件
0700	进料料件退换	进料加工料件退换
0715	进料非对口	进料加工(非对口合同)
0744	进料成品减免	进料加工成品凭征免税证明转减免税
0815	低值辅料	低值辅料
0844	进料边角料内销	进料加工项下边角料转内销
0845	来料边角料内销	来料加工项下边角料内销
0864	进料边角料复出	进料加工项下边角料复出口
0865	来料边角料复出	来料加工项下边角料复出口
1139	国轮油物料	中国籍运输工具境内添加的保税油料、物料
1200	保税间货物	海关保税场所及保税区域之间往来的货物
1215	保税工厂	保税工厂
1233	保税仓库货物	保税仓库进出境货物
1234	保税区仓储转口	保税区进出境仓储转口货物
1300	修理物品	进出境修理物品
1427	出料加工	出料加工
1500	租赁不满1年	租期不满1年的租赁贸易货物
1523	租赁贸易	租期在1年及以上的租赁贸易货物
1616	寄售代销	寄售、代销贸易
1741	免税品	免税品

监管方式代码	监管方式简称	监管方式全称
1831	外汇商品	免税外汇商品
2025	合资合作设备	合资合作企业作为投资进口设备物品
2225	外资设备物品	外资企业作为投资进口的设备物品
2439	常驻机构公用	外国常驻机构进口办公用品
2600	暂时进出货物	暂时进出口货物
2700	展览品	进出境展览品
2939	陈列样品	驻华商业机构不复运出口的进口陈列样品
3010	货样广告品 A	有经营权单位进出口的货样广告品
3039	货样广告品 B	无经营权单位进出口的货样广告品
3100	无代价抵偿	无代价抵偿进出口货物
3339	其他进出口免费	其他进出口免费提供货物
3410	承包工程进口	对外承包工程进口物资
3422	对外承包出口	对外承包工程出口物资
3511	援助物资	国家和国际组织无偿援助物资
3611	无偿军援	无偿军援
3612	捐赠物资	进出口捐赠物资
3910	军事装备	军事装备
4019	边境小额	边境小额贸易(边民互市贸易除外)
4039	对台小额	对台小额贸易
4139	对台小额商品交易市场	进入对台小额商品交易专用市场的货物
4200	驻外机构运回	我驻外机构运回旧公用物品
4239	驻外机构购进	我驻外机构境外购买运回国的公务用品
4400	来料成品退换	来料加工成品退换
4500	直接退运	直接退运
4539	进口溢误卸	进口溢卸、误卸货物
4561	退运货物	因质量不符、延误交货等原因退运进出境货物
4600	进料成品退换	进料成品退换
5000	料件进出区	料件进出海关特殊监管区域
5010	特殊区域研发货物	海关特殊监管区域与境外之间进出的研发货物
5014	区内来料加工	海关特殊监管区域与境外之间进出的来料加工货物
5015	区内进料加工货物	海关特殊监管区域与境外之间进出的进料加工货物
5033	区内仓储货物	加工区内仓储企业从境外进口的货物
5034	区内物流货物	海关特殊监管区域与境外之间进出的物流货物
5100	成品进出区	成品进出海关特殊监管区域
5200	区内边角调出	用于区内外非实际进出境货物
5300	设备进出区	设备及物资进出海关特殊监管区域
5335	境外设备进区	海关特殊监管区域从境外进口的设备及物资
5361	区内设备退运	海关特殊监管区域设备及物资退运境外
6033	物流中心进出境货物	保税物流中心与境外之间进出仓储货物
9600	内贸货物跨境运输	内贸货物跨境运输
9639	海关处理货物	海关变卖处理的超期未报货物、走私违规货物
9700	后续补税	无原始报关单的后续补税
9739	其他贸易	其他贸易
9800	租赁征税	租赁期 1 年及以上的租赁贸易货物的租金
9839	留赠转卖物品	外交机构转售境内或国际活动留赠放弃特批货物
9900	其他	其他

监管方式代码表说明

进出口货物海关监管方式（以下简称监管方式），即现行进出口货物报关单“监管方式”，是以国际贸易中进出口货物的交易方式为基础，结合海关对进出口货物的征税、统计及监管条件综合设定的海关对进出口货物的管理方式。

由于海关对不同监管方式下进出口货物的监管、征税、统计作业的要求不尽相同，因此为满足海关管理的要求，H2000通关管理系统的监管方式代码采用四位数字结构，其中前二位是按海关监管要求和计算机管理需要划分的分类代码，后二位为海关统计代码。

●一般贸易

一、定义与代码

一般贸易是指我国境内有进出口经营权的企业单边进口或

单边出口的贸易。

本监管方式代码“0110”，简称“一般贸易”。

二、适用范围

(一)本监管方式包括：

1. 以正常交易方式成交的进出口货物。

2. 贷款援助的进出口货物。

3. 外商投资企业进口供加工内销产品的料件。

4. 外商投资企业用国产原材料加工成品出口或采购产品出口。

5. 供应外国籍船舶、飞机等运输工具的国产燃料、物料及零配件。

6. 保税仓库进口供应给中国籍国际航行运输工具使用的燃料、物料等保税货物。

7. 境内企业在境外投资以实物投资带出的设备、物资。

8. 来料养殖、来料种植进出口货物。

(二)本监管方式不适用：

1. 进出口货样广告品，监管方式为“货样广告品 A”(3010)、“货样广告品 B”(3039)。

2. 没有对外贸易经营资格的单位获准临时进出口货物，监管方式为“其他贸易”(9739)。

3. 境外劳务合作项目，对方以实物产品抵偿我劳务人员工资所进口的货物(如钢材、木材、化肥、海产品等)，对外承包工程期间在国外获取及在境外购买的设备、物资等，监管方式为“承包工程进口”(3410)。

●易货贸易

一、定义与代码

易货贸易是指不通过货币媒介而直接用出口货物交换进口货物的贸易。

本监管方式代码 “0130”，简称“易货贸易”。

二、适用范围

本监管方式仅适用于易货贸易经营企业在核准的范围内易货贸易进出口货物。

以下情况不适用本监管方式：

(一)对台小额贸易中签订易货合同的贸易，监管方式为“对台小额”(4039)。

(二)边境小额贸易企业易货贸易进出口货物，监管方式为“边境小额贸易”(4019)。

●旅游购物商品

一、定义与代码

旅游购物商品是指境外旅游者用自带外汇购买的或委托境内企业托运出境 5 万美元以下的旅游商品或小批量订货。

本监管方式代码 “0139”，简称“旅游购物商品”。

二、适用范围

以下情况不适用本监管方式：

(一)出口 5 万美元以上的旅游购物商品。出口旅游商品 5 万美元以上的，有进出口经营权的企业，按“一般贸易”(0110)申报出口；没有进出口经营权的企业，按“其他贸易”(9739)申报出口。

(二)入境旅游者(包括外籍运输工具服务人员)自带出境用外汇购买的旅游纪念品、工艺品、中药材和中成药，由出境地海关旅检部门按照规定限值、限量办理。

●加工贸易料件、成品放弃

一、定义与代码

(一)加工贸易料件放弃是指加工贸易企业来料加工或进料加工进口的料件，不再用于加工成品出口，主动放弃交由海关处理。

本监管方式代码 “0200”，简称“料件放弃”。

(二)加工贸易成品放弃是指加工贸易企业来料加工或进料加工生产的成品因故不再出口，主动放弃交由海关处理。

本监管方式代码 “0400”，简称“成品放弃”。

二、适用范围

(一)料件放弃包括：加工贸易进口料件、剩余料件和边角料。

(二)成品放弃包括：加工贸易进口料件加工的成品、半成品、残次品。

●来料加工

一、定义与代码

来料加工是指进口料件由境外企业提供，经营企业不需要付汇进口，按照境外企业的要求进行加工或者装配，只收取加工费，制成品由境外企业销售的经营活动。

本监管方式代码 “0214”，简称“来料加工”。

二、适用范围

(一)本监管方式包括：

1. 来料加工项下进口的料件和加工出口的成品。

2. 设立保税工厂的加工贸易企业来料加工进口料件和出口成品。

(二)以下情况不适用本监管方式：

1. 国营企业代理来料加工企业进口加工生产用柴油，监管方式为“加工专用油”(0314)。

2. 由特定企业以加工贸易进口原油加工成品油，不返销出境，供应国内市场的，监管方式为“成品油”(0642)。

3. 进口 5000 美元以下的 78 种列名辅料，监管方式为“低值辅料”(0815)。

●加工贸易保税货物深加工结转

一、定义与代码

加工贸易保税货物深加工结转是指来料加工、进料加工经营企业将保税进口料件加工的产品不直接出口，在境内结转给另一个加工贸易企业再加工后复出口。

来料深加工结转货物监管方式代码 “0255”，简称“来料深加工”。

进料深加工结转货物监管方式代码 “0654”，简称“进料深加工”。

二、适用范围

(一)本监管方式适用：

1. 非海关特殊监管区域加工贸易经营企业之间来料、进料深加工货物结转。

2. 非海关特殊监管区域加工贸易经营企业转自海关特殊监管区域加工贸易经营企业加工的货物。

(二)本监管方式不适用：

1. 保税区、保税物流园区等海关特殊监管区域之间结转的货物，监管方式为“保税间货物”(1200)。

2. 出口加工区企业生产的产品结转至其他出口加工区或非海关特殊监管区域加工复出口，加工区企业转出、转入报关单监管方式为“出口加工区成品进出区”(5100)。

3. 经营企业进料加工产品转给享受减免税优惠的企业，监管方式为“进料成品转减免”(0744)。

●加工贸易余料结转

加工贸易余料结转是指加工贸易企业在经营来料加工、进料加工的加工复出口业务过程中剩余的、可以继续用于加工制成品的加工贸易进口料件，结转到同一经营单位、同一加工企业、同样进口料件和同一加工监管方式的另一个加工贸易合同项下继续加工复出口。

来料余料结转监管方式代码“0258”，简称“来料余料结转”。

进料余料结转监管方式代码“0657”，简称“进料余料结转”。

●加工贸易料件复出

一、定义与代码

加工贸易料件复出是指来料加工、进料加工进口的保税料件因品质、规格等原因退运，以及加工过程中产生的剩余料件、边角料、废料退运出境。

来料加工料件复出监管方式代码“0265”，简称“来料料件复出”。

来料加工边角料复出监管方式代码“0865”，简称“来料边角料复出”。

进料加工料件复出监管方式代码“0664”，简称“进料料件复出”。

进料加工边角料复出监管方式代码“0864”，简称“进料边角料复出”。

二、适用范围

(一)加工贸易料件复出适用：

1. 来料加工、进料加工进口的保税料件因品质、规格等原因退运，以及加工过程中产生的剩余料件、边角料、废料退运出境。

2. 经营企业因加工贸易出口产品售后服务需要，申请出口加工贸易手册项下进口的保税料件。

(二)本监管方式不适用：

加工贸易进口料件、剩余料件及边角料、废料复运出境后更换同类货物进口，监管方式为“来料料件退换”(0300)、“进料料件退换”(0700)。

●加工贸易货物退换

一、定义与代码

(一)加工贸易料件退换

加工贸易料件退换是指来料、进料加工进口的保税料件因品质、规格等原因退运出境，更换料件复进口。

来料加工料件退换监管方式代码“0300”，简称“来料料件退换”。

进料加工料件退换监管方式代码“0700”，简称“进料料件退换”。

(二)加工贸易成品退换

加工贸易成品退换是指来料、进料加工出口的成品因品质、规格或其他原因退运进境，经加工、维修或更换同类商品复出口。

来料加工成品退换监管方式代码 “4400”，简称“来料成品退换”。

进料加工成品退换监管方式代码 “4600”，简称“进料成品退换”。

二、适用范围

本监管方式不适用于来料加工、进料加工过程中产生的剩余料件、边角料、废料退运出境，以及进口料件因品质、规格等原因退运出境且不再更换同类货物进境。这几类货物分别适用以下监管方式：来料料件复出(0265)、来料边角料复出(0865)、进料料件复出(0664)、进料边角料复出(0864)。

●加工贸易保税货物转内销

包括以下监管方式：来料料件内销(0245)、来料成品转减免(0345)、进料料件内销(0644)、进料成品转减免(0744)、进料边角料内销(0844)、来料边角料内销(0845)。

一、定义与代码

(一)加工贸易保税料件转内销是指经营企业来料、进料加工过程中产生的剩余料件或用剩余料件生产的制成品、半成品、残次品及受灾保税货物，经批准转为国内销售，不再加工复出口，包括海关事后发现有关企业擅自转内销并准予补办进口手续的货物。

来料加工料件转内销监管方式代码“0245”，简称“来料料件内销”。

进料加工料件转内销监管方式代码”0644”，简称“进料料件内销”。

(二)加工贸易保税货物减免是指来料、进料加工成品在境内销售给凭征免税证明进口货物的企业。

来料加工成品转减免监管方式代码 “0345”，简称“来料成品转减免”。

进料加工成品转减免监管方式代码 “0744”，简称“进料成品转减免”。

(三)加工贸易边角料内销是指经批准在境内销售的来料、进料加工过程中有形损耗产生的、仍有商业价值的边角料，包括来料、进料加工副产品。

来料加工边角料转内销监管方式代码 “0845”，简称“来料边角料内销”。

进料加工边角料转内销监管方式代码 “0844”，简称“进料边角料内销”。

二、适用范围

(一)加工贸易保税货物内销监管方式适用于边角料、剩余料件、残次品、副产品和受灾保税货物。

1. 边角料，是指加工贸易企业经营来料加工、进料加工业务，在海关核定的单耗内、加工过程中产生的、无法再用于加工该合同项下出口制成品的数量合理的废、碎及下脚料件。

2. 剩余料件，是指加工贸易企业在经营业务过程中剩余的、可以继续用于加工制成品的加工贸易进口料件。

3. 残次品，是指加工贸易企业经营来料加工、进料加工业务，在生产过程中产生的有严重缺陷或者达不到出口合同标准，无法复出口的制品(包括完成品和未完成品)。

4. 副产品，是指加工贸易企业经营来料加工、进料加工业务，在加工生产出口合同规定的制成品(即主产品)过程中同时产生的且出口合同未规定应当复出口的一个或者一个以上的其他产品。

5. 受灾保税货物，是指加工贸易企业经营业务过程中，因不可抗力原因或者其他经海关审核认可的正当理由造成灭失、短少、损毁等导致无法复出口的保税进口料件和制品。

（二）以下情况不适用加工贸易保税货物转内销的监管方式：

1. 特定企业以加工贸易的方式进口原油炼制成品油，不返销出境而供应国内市场，监管方式为“成品油”（0642）。

2. 保税区、出口加工区加工贸易转内销货物，监管方式为“保税区进料料件”（0544）、“保税区来料料件”（0545）。

3. 企业擅自内销加工贸易保税货物，按走私或违规处理的。

●加工专用油

加工专用油是指指定国营贸易企业代理来料加工企业进口来料加工生产用柴油。

本监管方式代码 “0314”，简称“加工专用油”。

●加工贸易设备

包括以下监管方式：不作价设备（0320）、加工贸易设备（0420）、加工设备内销（0446）、加工设备结转（0456）、加工设备退运（0466）。

一、定义与代码

（一）外商提供的加工贸易不作价设备是指境外企业与境内企业开展来料、进料加工业务，外商免费向境内加工贸易经营单位提供加工生产所需设备，境内经营单位不需支付外汇、不需用加工费或差价偿还。

外商提供的加工贸易不作价设备监管方式代码为“0320”，简称“不作价设备”。

（二）加工贸易设备是指来料加工、进料加工贸易项下外商作价提供、不扣减企业投资总额的进口设备。

加工贸易设备监管方式代码 “0420”，简称“加工贸易设备”。

（三）加工贸易设备转内销是指在海关监管期内的加工贸易免税进口设备经批准转售给境内非加工贸易企业。

加工贸易设备转内销监管方式代码 “0446”，简称“加工设备内销”。

（四）加工贸易设备结转是指海关监管期内的加工贸易免税进口设备经批准转让给另一加工企业，或从本企业一本《加工贸易手册》结转入另一本《加工贸易手册》。

加工贸易设备结转监管方式代码 “0456”，简称“加工设备结转”。

（五）加工贸易设备退运是指加工贸易免税进口设备退运出境。

加工贸易设备退运监管方式代码 “0466”，简称“加工设备退运”。

二、适用范围

以下情况不适用本监管方式：

（一）暂时进口（期限在半年以内）加工贸易生产所需不作价设备（限模具、单台设备），按暂时进口货物办理。

（二）外商投资企业投资总额内资金进口的设备，监管方式“合资合作设备” （2025）、“外资设备物品”（2225）。

（三）外商投资企业自有资金（投资总额以外）进口设备，监管方式“一般贸易”（0110）。

（四）出口加工区的设备进口、退运及结转，分别适用“境外设备进区”（代码 5335）、“区内设备退运”（代码 5361）和“设备进出区”（代码 5300）。

●监管年限内减免税设备结转

一、定义与代码

监管年限内减免税设备结转是指进口企业在减免税设备监管年限内转让给另一享受减免税待遇的企业。

本监管方式代码“0500”，简称“减免设备结转”。

二、适用范围

本监管方式不适用于加工贸易项下进口设备结转给另一加工贸易企业，监管方式为“加工设备结转”（0456）。

●保税区加工贸易内销货物

保税区进料加工、来料加工的加工成品不复运出境，转为国内使用，按征税方式区分，适用以下监管方式：

一、区内加工企业来料、进料加工全部用境外运入料件加工的制成品销往非保税区，以及来料、进料加工内销制成品所含进口料件的品名、数量、价值难以区分的，按照制成品征税，监管方式为：

（一）按成品征税的保税区来料加工成品转内销货物，监管方式代码”0445”，简称“保区来料成品”。

（二）按成品征税保税区进料加工成品转内销货物，监管方式代码的“0444”，简称“保区进料成品”。

二、区内企业来料、进料加工用含有部分境外运入料件加工的制成品销往非保税区时，对其制成品按照所含进口料件征税，监管方式为：

（一）按料件征税的保税区来料加工成品转内销货物，监管方式代码“0545”，简称“保区来料料件”。

（二）按料件征税的保税区进料加工成品转内销货物，监管方式代码“0544”，简称“保区进料料件”。

●补偿贸易

一、定义与代码

补偿贸易是指由境外厂商提供或者利用国外出口信贷进口生产技术或设备，我方企业（包括外商投资企业）进行生产，以返销其产品的方式分期偿还对方技术、设备价款或贷款本息的交易方式。包括经经贸主管部门批准，使用该企业（包括企业联合体）所生产的其他产品返销给对方，进行间接补偿。

补偿贸易偿还对方技术、设备价款或贷款本息的方式一般有两种：

（一）产品出口先偿还设备价款，还清本息后再出口收汇。

（二）设备价款本息在每批出口货物价款中扣还一部分，直到还清为止。

本监管方式代码“0513”，简称“补偿贸易”。

二、适用范围

本监管方式包括补偿贸易中对方有偿或免费提供的机器设备、模具等。

本监管方式不包括：

（一）直接用国内产品同国外厂商交换设备、料件或成品，以货换货，监管方式为“易货贸易”（0130）。

（二）出口产品收取外汇，监管方式为“一般贸易”（0110）。

（三）在补偿贸易合同中同时订有来料加工合同的，来料加工合同部分，监管方式为“来料加工”（0214）。

●进料加工贸易

一、定义与代码

进料加工贸易，是指进口料件由经营企业付汇进口，制成品由经营企业外销出口的经营活动。

进料加工贸易按照对外签约形式分为“进料加工非对口合同”和“进料加工对口合同”。

进料加工非对口合同是指我方有外贸进出口经营权的企业动用外汇购买进口原料、材料、元器件、零部件、配套件和包装物料(以下简称料件)，加工成品或半成品再返销出口的交易形式。

本监管方式代码“0715”，简称“进料非对口”。

进料加工对口合同是指买卖双方分别签订进出口对口合同，料件进口时，我方先付料件款，加工成品出口时再向对方收取出口成品款项的交易形式，包括动用外汇的对口合同或不同客户的对口的联号合同，以及对开信用证的对口合同。

本监管方式代码“0615”，简称“进料对口”。

境外客户为境内企业加工复出口产品提供进口 5000 美元及以下、数量零星的辅料或包装物料，以及数量合理直接用于服装生产车间的小型易耗性生产工具。

本监管方式代码 “0815”，简称“低值辅料”。

二、适用范围

(一)本监管方式包括：

1.进料加工项下进口料件和加工出口产品。

2.设立保税工厂的加工贸易企业进料加工进口料件和出口成品。

(二)本监管方式不适用出口加工区加工贸易进出口货物，其监管方式为“区内加工货物”(5015)。

●加工贸易成品油以产顶进

加工贸易成品油以产顶进是指特定企业以加工贸易形式进口原油，加工供国内市场的成品油。

本监管方式代码“0642”，简称“成品油”。

●国轮油物料

一、定义与代码

国轮油物料指中国籍国际航行的运输工具在境内添加的保税仓库进口仓储的油料、物料。

本监管方式代码 “1139”，简称“国轮油物料”。

二、适用范围

本监管方式适用于从保税仓库提取，供应航行国际航线的中国籍船舶、民用航空器等运输工具的进口燃料、物料及零配件等。

本监管方式不适用从设在非海关特殊监管区域的保税仓库提取，供应航行国际航线的外国籍船舶、飞机等运输工具的进口燃料、物料，监管方式为“保税仓库货物”(1233)。

●保税区间及保税仓库间货物结转

一、定义与代码

保税区间及保税仓库间货物结转是指保税区、保税物流园区、出口加工区、出口监管仓库、保税仓库、保税物流中心(A、B型)等海关特殊监管区域、保税监管场所间往来的货物。

本监管方式代码“1200”，简称“保税间货物”。

二、适用范围

本监管方式不适用出口加工区间结转货物，不同出口加工区企业结转货物适用“出口加工区成品进出区”(5100)和“料件进出区”(5000)。

●保税仓库进出境仓储、转口货物

一、定义与代码

保税仓库进出境仓储及转口货物，指从境外进口直接存入保税仓库和保税仓库出境的仓储、转口货物，以及出口监管仓库出境的货物。

本监管方式代码 “1233”，简称“保税仓库货物”。

二、适用范围

(一)本监管方式适用于经批准设立的保税仓库进出境和出口监管仓库出境货物。包括从保税仓库提取用于外国籍国际航行运输工具的物料。

(二)下列情况不适用本监管方式：

1.保税仓库、出口监管仓库进口自用的货架、办公用品、管理用具、运输车辆、搬运、起重和包装设备，以及改装用的机器等，监管方式为“一般贸易”(0110)。

2.从保税仓库提取用于本国籍运输工具或用于维修境内设备的仓储货物，按进口申报，监管方式为“一般贸易”(0110)。

3.保税仓库进境货物销往境内，按货物运出保税仓库的实际用途填报相应的监管方式。

4.境内存入出口监管仓库和出口监管仓库退仓货物，分各种监管方式。

5.保税区、保税物流中心进出境仓储、转口货物，监管方式分别为“保税区仓储、转口”(1234)、“物流中心进出境货物”(6033)。

6.保税仓库货物出仓运往境内其他地方转为正式进口的，在仓库主管海关办结出仓报关手续，填制出口报关单，监管方式填写“1200”，进口报关单按实际进口监管方式填报。

7.保税仓库寄售维修零部件申请免税出仓的，进口报关单贸易方式应为“无代价抵偿货物”(代码为“3100”)。

●保税区进出境仓储、转口货物

一、定义与代码

保税区进出境仓储、转口货物是指从境外存入保税区、保税物流园区和从保税区、保税物流园区运出境的仓储、转口货物。

本监管方式代码“1234”，简称“保税区仓储转口”。

二、适用范围

下列情况不适用本监管方式：

(一)保税区、保税物流园区除仓储、转口货物以外的其他进出境货物，按实际监管方式填报。

(二)从境内非海关特殊监管区域、保税监管场所运入保税区、保税物流园区的货物，按实际监管方式填报。

从境内非海关特殊监管区域、保税监管场所运入保锐区、保税物流园区的货物退回境内，按实际监管方式填报。

(三)从保税区、保税物流园区运往境内非海关特殊监管区域、保税监管场所的货物，按实际监管方式填报。

●寄售代销贸易

一、定义与代码

寄售代销贸易是指寄售人把货物运交事先约定的代销人，由代销人按照事先约定或根据寄售代销协议规定的条件，在当地市场代为销售，所得货款扣除代销人的佣金和其他费用后，按协议规定方式将余款付给寄售人的交易形式。寄售人与代销人之间不是买卖关系，而是委托关系，代销人对货物没有所有权。

本监管方式代码“1616”简称“寄售代销”。

二、适用范围

本监管方式包括寄售代销贸易进出口的货物及进口寄售货物的增发部分。

本监管方式不包括：

(一)经营寄售代销业务的企业，接受国外免费提供的样品，监管方式应为“货样广告品B”(3039)。

(二)委托我驻港澳机构代销的鲜活商品，监管方式应为“一般贸易”(0110)。

●进出境修理物品

一、定义与代码

进出境修理物品是指进境或出境维护修理的货物、物品。本监管方式代码“1300”，简称“修理物品”。

二、适用范围

本监管方式适用于各类进出境维修的货物，以及修理货物维修所用的原材料、零部件。

以下情况不适用本监管方式：

(一)按加工贸易保税货物管理的进境维修业务。

(二)加工贸易进口料件和出口成品进出境维修，分别适用来料料件退换(0300)、来料成品退换(4400)、进料料件退换(0700)、进料成品退换(4600)。

●出料加工贸易

一、定义及代码

出料加工贸易是指境内企业将境内原辅料、零部件、元器件或半成品交由境外厂商按我方要求进行加工或装配，成品复运进口，我方支付加工费的交易方式。

本监管方式代码“1427”，简称“出料加工”。

二、适用范围

本监管方式不包括：

(一)运往境外维修的货物，以及石化生产过程中所需催化剂需运至国外添加氢以增加活性后复运进境继续投入生产使用，不改变其物理和化学性质，未产生新的产品，监管方式为“修理物品”(1300)。

(二)出料加工，原则上不改变原出口货物的物理形态。对完全改变原出口货物的物理形态如出口废钢进口钢材，出口废铝进口铝合金板材等，不属出料加工，应按一般贸易货物办理进出口手续。

●租赁贸易

一、定义及代码

租赁贸易是指经营租赁业务的企业与外商签订国际租赁合同项下境内企业租赁进口或出租出口的货物。

租赁期在一年及以上的进出口货物，监管方式代码“1523”，简称“租赁贸易”。

租赁期在一年及以上的进出口货物分期办理征税手续时，每期征税适用监管方式代码“9800”，简称“租赁征税”。

租赁期不满一年的进出口货物，监管方式代码“1500”，简称“租赁不满一年”。

二、适用范围

以下情况不适用本监管方式：

(一)经营租赁业务的企业进口自用的设备、办公用品，监管方式为“一般贸易”(0110)。

(二)加工贸易租赁进口的机器设备，监管方式应为“加工贸易设备”(0420)。

(三)补偿贸易租借进口的货物，监管方式应为“补偿贸易”(0513)。

(四)“租赁贸易”(1523)期满复运出(进)口的货物，监管方式为“退运货物”(4561)，“租赁不满一年”(1500)期满复运出(进)境的货物，监管方式为“租赁不满一年”(1500)。

●免税品

一、定义及代码

免税品是指设在国际机场、港口、车站和过境口岸的免税品商店进口，按有关规定销售给办完出境手续的旅客的免税商品，供外国籍船员和我国远洋船员购买送货上船出售的免税商品，供外交人员购买的免税品，以及在我国际航机、国际班轮上向国际旅客出售的免税商品。

本监管方式代码“1741”，简称“免税品”。

二、适用范围

(一)本监管方式适用于：

1．范围：进出境口岸免税店、运输工具免税店、市内免税店、外交人员免税店和供船免税店等五类免税店进口核定品种的免税品。

2．供应对象：办结出境手续的出境旅客、国际航行运输工具服务人员、外交人员。

(二)本监管方式不适用：

1．境内免税外汇商店销售给为我出国人员、华侨的免税外汇商品，监管方式为“免税外汇商品”(1831)。

2．经营免税品业务的单位进口的供维修使用的零部件、工具、展台、货架，监管方式为“一般贸易”(0110)。

3．免税品退运出境，监管方式为“其他”(9900)。

●免税外汇商品

一、定义及代码

免税外汇商品是指由经批准的经营单位进口，销售专供入境的我国特定出国人员和驻华外交人员的免税外汇商品。

本监管方式代码“1831”，简称“免税外汇商品”。

二、适用范围

(一)本监管方式适用：

1.免税外汇商品供应对象是指我国驻外外交机构人员、留学人员、访问学者、赴境外劳务人员、援外人员和远洋船员。

2.上述人员用结存外汇在境内免税外汇商品店购买限定品种的免税外汇商品。

3.专供外国驻华外交人员免税商品的特定公司进口的免税外汇商品。

(二)本监管方式不适用：

1.设在国际机场、港口、车站和过境口岸的免税品商店所进口的，按有关规定销售给办结出境手续的旅客的免税商品，供外国籍船员和我国远洋船员购买送货上船出售的免税商品，供外交人员购买的免税品，以及在我国际航机、国际班轮上向国际旅客出售的免税商品。监管方式为“免税品”（1741）。

2. 经营免税外汇商品的单位进口供商品维修用的零部件、工具和商场自用的货架、手推车等。监管方式为“一般贸易”（0110）。

3. 因故经批准转内销进口免税外汇商品，监管方式为“一般贸易”（0110）。

4. 免税外汇商品退运出境，监管方式为“退运货物”（4561）。

●外商投资企业作为投资进口的设备、物品

一、定义及代码

外商投资企业作为投资进口的设备、物品是指外商投资企业投资总额内的资金（包括中方投资）进口的机器设备、零部件和其他建厂（场）物料，安装、加固机器所需材料，以及进口本企业自用合理数量的交通工具、生产用车辆、办公用品（设备）（以下简称“设备物品”）。

中外合资、合作企业进口设备、物品，监管方式代码“2025”，简称“合资合作设备”；外商独资企业（以下简称“外资企业”）进口设备、物品，监管方式代码“2225”，简称“外资设备物品”。

二、适用范围

（一）外商投资企业是指中外合资企业、中外合作企业、外商独资企业，包括华侨、港、澳、台同胞投资企业。

（二）设备是指外商投资企业在其投资总额内进口本企业自用的机器设备、零部件和其他物料[指建厂（场）及安装、加固机器所需材料]及生产用车辆。

（三）物品是指外商投资企业进口自用合理数量的办公用品（设备）和交通工具。

（四）下列情况不适用本监管方式：

1. 鼓励类和限制类外商投资企业、外商投资研究开发中心、先进技术型和产品出口型外商投资企业，以及符合中西部省、自治区、直辖市利用外资优势产业和优势项目目录的项目、企业自有资金（投资总额以外，具体是指企业储备基金、发展基金、折旧和税后利润），在原批准的生产经营范围内，对设备进行更新维修，进口国内不能生产或性能不能满足需要的自用设备及其配套的技术、配件、备件，监管方式为“一般贸易”（0110）。

2. 外商投资企业经营来料加工、进料加工、租赁贸易等进口的设备、物品，分别适用“不作价设备”（0320）、“加工贸易设备”（0420）、“租赁不满一年”（1500）、“租赁贸易”（1523）。

3. 外国常驻机构进口自用合理数量的公用物品，监管方式为“常驻机构公用”（2439）。

4. 没有实际进出境，在境内结转的减免税设备，监管方式为“减免设备结转”（0500）。

5. 出口加工区外商投资企业进口设备、物品，监管方式为“出口加工区进口设备”（5035）。

●退运货物

一、定义及代码

退运货物是指原进出口货物因残损、短少、品质不良或者规格不符、延误交货或其他原因退运出、进境的货物。

本监管方式代码“4561”，简称“退运货物”。

二、适用范围

（一）本监管方式适用以下监管方式进出口货物退运出、进境：

代码	名称	代码	名称
0110	一般贸易	3039	货样广告品B
0130	易货贸易	3339	其他进出口免费
0139	旅游购物商品	3410	承包工程进口
1523	租赁贸易	3422	对外承包出口
1616	寄售代销	3511	无偿援助
2025	外商投资企业	3612	捐赠物资
2225	设备物品	4019	边境小额
1831	外汇免税商品	4039	对台小额
3010	货样广告品A	9739	其他贸易

（二）本监管方式不适用：

1. 货物进境后、放行结关前退运的货物，监管方式为“直接退运”（4500）。

2. 加工贸易进出口货物退运，监管方式为“来料料件退换”（0300）、“进料料件退换”（0700）、“来料成品退换”（4400）、“进料成品退换”（4600）。

3. 加工贸易设备退运，监管方式为“加工设备退运”（0466）。

4. “租赁不满一年”（1500）、“免税品”（1741）退运出境，监管方式为“其他”（9900）。

5. 出口加工区进口设备退运出境，监管方式为“区内设备退运”（5361）。

6. 进出口无代价抵偿货物，被更换的原进口货物退运出境，监管方式为“其他”（9900）。

●外国常驻机构进出境公用物品

一、定义及代码

外国常驻机构进出境公用物品是指境外（地区）企业、新闻机构、经贸机构、文化团体及其他境外（地区）法人经我国政府主管部门批准，在境内设立的常驻代表机构为开展公务活动所需进出境的物品。

本监管方式代码”2439”，简称“常驻机构公用”。

二、适用范围

（一）本监管方式包括常驻机构进境自用且数量合理的办公用机器设备、家具、文具、机动车辆等及复运出境的原进境的公用物品。

（二）本监管方式适用于以下机构：

1. 外国企业和其他经济组织常驻机构。

2. 外国民间经济贸易团体常驻机构。

3. 外国常驻新闻机构。

4. 其他外国常驻机构。

5. 华侨、港澳同胞、台湾同胞经营的企业常驻机构。

（三）下列监管业务不适用本监管方式：

1. 外国驻中国使馆、领馆，联合国及其专门机构，以及其他与中国政府签有协议的国际组织驻中国代表机构进出境物品填报“外国使领馆公私用物品进出境申报单”。

2. 外国人员子女学校进出境物品，监管方式为“其他贸易”（9739）。

3. 常驻机构人员进境自用的汽车，监管方式为“其他贸易”（9739）。

4. 外国驻华使、领馆在我国内购运出境的货物，监管方式为“其他”(9900)。

5.暂时进出境的公用物品，监管方式为“暂时进出口”(2600)。

●暂时进出境货物

一、定义及代码

暂时进出境货物是指经海关批准，暂时进出关境并且在规定的期限内复运出境、进境的货物。

本监管方式代码“2600”，简称“暂时进出货物”。

二、适用范围

(一)本监管方式包括：

1.文化、体育交流活动中使用的表演、比赛用品。

2.进行新闻报道或者摄制电影、电视节目使用的仪器、设备及用品。

3.开展科研、教学、医疗活动使用的仪器、设备及用品。

4.在本款第1～3项所列活动中使用的交通工具及特种车辆。

5.货样。

6.慈善活动使用的仪器、设备及用品。

7.供安装、调试、检测、修理设备时使用的仪器及工具。

8.盛装货物的容器。

9.旅游用自驾交通工具及其用品。

10.工程施工中使用的设备、仪器及其用品。

11.海关批准的其他暂时进出境货物。

(二)以下情况不适用本监管方式；

1.进出境展览品，监管方式为“展览品”(2700)。

2.驻华商业机构不复运出口的进口陈列样品，监管方式为“陈列样品”(2939)。

3.对外承包工程出口物资，监管方式为“对外承包出口”(3422)。

4.进出境修理物品，监管方式为“修理物品”(1300)。

5.租赁贸易进出口货物，监管方式为“租期不满一年”(1500)、“租期一年及以上”(1523)。

6.企业使用旧钢瓶容器进口燃料、物料，按进口燃料、物料的监管方式申报，报关单“包装种类”栏目填报“旧钢瓶”。旧钢瓶容器凭“入境货物通关单”验放，复运出境时监管方式填报“其他”(9900)。

7.从境外暂时进境的货物转入保税区、出口加工区等海关特殊监管区域和保税监管场所的，不属于复运出境。

8.用于装载海关监管货物的进出境集装箱。

9.享有外交特权和豁免的外国驻华机构或者人员暂时进出境物品。

●进出境展览品

一、定义及代码

进出境展览品是指外国来华或我国为到国外举办经济、文化、科技等展览或参加博览会而进出口的展览品及展览品有关的宣传品、布置品、招待品、小卖品和其他物品。

本监管方式代码“2700”，简称“展览品”。

二、适用范围

(一)进出境展览品主要包括：

1.在展览会、交易会、会议及类似活动中展示或者使用的货物，包括：

(1)为了示范展览会展出机器或者器具所使用的货物；

(2)设置临时展台的建筑材料及装饰材料；

(3)宣传展示货物的电影片、幻灯片、录像带、录音带、说明书、广告、光盘、显示器材等。

2.上述所列活动中使用的交通工具及特种车辆。

3.其他经海关批准用于展示的进出境货物、物品。

(二)以下情况不适用本监管方式：

1.ATA单证册项下的暂准进出口展览品，持证人免填报关单。

2.不复运出(进)境而留在国内(外)销售的进出境展览品，按实际监管方式填报。

3.在商店或者其他营业场所以销售国外货物为目的而组织的非公共展览会。

●货样、广告品

一、定义及代码

进出口货样是指专供订货参考的进出口货物样品；广告品是指用以宣传有关商品的进出口广告宣传品。

有进出口经营权的企业价购或价售进出口货样广告品，监管方式代码“3010”，简称“货样广告品A”。

没有进出口经营权的企业(单位)进出口及免费提供进出口的货样广告品，监管方式代码“3039”，简称“货样广告品B”。

二、适用范围

上述监管方式除以上定义所述范围外，还包括寄售代销贸易中外商免费提供的货样广告品。

下列情况不适用本监管方式：

(一)暂时进出口的货样、广告品，监管方式为“暂时进出口货物”(2600)。

(二)驻华商业机构不复运出口的进口陈列样品，监管方式应为”陈列样品”(2939)。

●无代价抵偿进出口货物

一、定义及代码

无代价抵偿货物是指进出口货物海关放行后，因残损、短少、品质不良或者规格不符原因，由进出口货物的发货人、承运人或保险公司免费补偿或更换的与原货物相同或者与合同规定相符的货物。

本监管方式代码“3100”，简称“无代价抵偿”。

二、适用范围

下列情况不适用本监管方式：

(一)来料加工、进料加工贸易进口料件和出口成品因残损、短少、品质不良或者规格不符原因，由进出口货物的发货人、承运人或保险公司免费补偿或更换的与原货物相同或者与合同规定相符的货物，分别适用具体列名的料件或成品退换的监管方式。

(二)与无代价抵偿进出口货物相关的原进出口货物退运出、进境，监管方式为“其他”(9900)。

●其他免费提供的进出口货物

一、定义及代码

其他免费提供货物指除已具体列名的礼品、无偿援助和赠送物资、捐赠物资、无代价抵偿进口货物、国外免费提供的货样、广告品等及归入列名监管方式的免费提供货物以外，进出口其他免费提供的货物。

本监管方式代码“3339”，简称“其他进出口免费”。

二、适用范围

(一)本监管方式包括：

1.外商在经贸活动中赠送的物品。

2.外国人捐赠品。

3.驻外中资机构向国内单位赠送的物资。

4.经贸活动中，由外商免费提供的试车材料、消耗性物品等。

(二)下列情况不适用本监管方式：

1.保税仓库中由外商免费提供进口的机械设备、手工工具、运输工具、办公用品等，监管方式为“其他贸易”(9739)。

2. 免税店由外商免费提供进口的货架、柜台、手推车等，监管方式“其他贸易”(9739)。

3.来料加工、进料加工贸易项下外商免费提供的机械设备，监管方式为“不作价设备”(0320)。

4.免费提供进出口的货样广告品，监管方式为“货样广告品B”(3039)。

5.国家和国际组织无偿援助物资，监管方式为“援助物资”(3511)。

6. 捐赠物资，监管方式为“捐赠物资”(3612)。

7. 无代价抵偿进出口货物，监管方式为“无代价抵偿”(3100)。

●对外承包工程进出口物资

一、定义及代码

对外承包工程出口物资是指经商务部批准的有对外承包工程经营权的公司为承包国外建设工程和开展劳务合作等对外合作项目而出口的设备、物资。

承包工程出口物资监管方式代码“3422”，简称“对外承包出口”。

对外承包工程出口物资是指承包工程期间在国外获取的设备、物资，以及境外劳务合作项目对方以实物产品抵偿我劳务人员工资所进口的货物。

监管方式代码“3410”，简称“承包工程进口”。

二、适用范围

(一)本监管方式不包括我劳务人员带出的自用生活物资，监管方式为“其他”(9900)。

(二)援外成套项目出口的货物应根据无偿援助或贷款援助，监管方式代码分别选用“援助物资”(3511)或“一般贸易”(0110)。

(三)边境地区有对外经济技术合作经营权的企业与毗邻国家边境地区开展承包工程和劳务合作项下出口的工程设备、物资(包括在外购买及换回的)运回境内时，监管方式代码“边境小额贸易”(4019)。

(四)承包工程结束后复运进境原从国内运出的承包工程项下的设备、物资，监管方式为“退运货物”(4561)。

●国家或国际组织无偿援助和赠送的物资

一、定义及代码

国家或国际组织无偿援助和赠送的物资是指我国根据两国政府间的协议或临时决定，对外提供无偿援助的物资、捐赠品，或我国政府、组织基于友好关系向对方国家政府、组织赠送的物资，以及我国政府、组织接受国际组织、外国政府、组织无偿援助、捐赠或赠送的物资。

本监管方式代码“3511”，简称“无偿援助”。

二、适用范围

(一)有关名词：

外国政府，是指外国国家的中央政府。

国际组织，是指联合国各专门机构，以及长期与我国有合作关系的其他国际组织。

国际条约，是指依据《中华人民共和国缔结条约程序法》以“中华人民共和国”、“中华人民共和国政府”及“中华人民共和国政府部门”名义同外国缔结协定或协议及参加的国际条约。

(二)以下情况不适用本监管方式：

1.贷款援助的进出口货物(包括我方利用贷款或援助款项自行采购进口的货物)，监管方式为“一般贸易”(0110)。

2.来(出)访的团体和人员相互馈赠的礼品，监管方式为“其他”(9900)。

3.经济贸易往来关系赠送的物资，监管方式为“其他进出口免费提供”(3339)。

4. 随援外物资一并出口或另外发运的批量出口的生活物资，应按照“其他贸易”(9739)报关。

5.以扶贫、慈善、救灾为目的，向我国境内或向境外捐赠的直接用于扶贫、救灾、兴办公益福利事业的物资，监管方式为“捐赠物资”(3612)。

●进出口捐赠物资

一、定义及代码

进出口捐赠物资是指境外捐赠人以扶贫、慈善、救灾为目的，向我国境内捐赠的直接用于扶贫、救灾、兴办公益福利事业的物资，以及境内捐赠人以扶贫、慈善、救灾为目的，向境外捐赠的直接用于扶贫、救灾、兴办公益福利事业的物资。

本监管方式代码“3612”，简称“捐赠物资”。

二、适用范围

(一)本监管方式适用范围：

1. 捐赠人

(1)境外捐赠人，包括华侨，港、澳、台同胞，外籍人，包括法人。

(2)境内捐赠人，包括法人。

2. 扶贫、慈善公益性事业的物资

(1)新的衣服、被褥、鞋帽、帐篷、手套、睡袋、毛毯及其他维持基本生活的必需用品等。

(2)食品类及饮用品(调味品、水产品、水果、饮料、烟酒等除外)。

(3)医疗类，包括直接用于治疗特困患者疾病或贫困地区治疗地方病，以及基本医疗卫生、公共环境卫生所需的基本医疗药品、基本医疗器械、医疗书籍和资料。

(4)直接用于公共图书馆、公共博物馆、各类职业学校、高中、初中、小学、幼儿园教育的教学仪器、器材、图书、资料和一般学习用品。

(5)直接用于环境保护的专用仪器。

(6)经国务院批准的其他直接用于扶贫、慈善事业的物资。

3. 受赠人和使用人

受赠人是指国务院有关部门和各省、自治区、直辖市人民政府，以及从事人道救助和以发展扶贫、慈善事业为宗旨的全国性的社会团体。包括中国红十字会总会、全国妇女联合会、中国残疾人联合会、中华慈善总会、中国初级卫生保健基金会和宋庆龄基金会。

使用人(使用单位)是指捐赠物资的直接使用者或负责分配该捐赠物资的单位或个人。

(二)下列情况不适用本监管方式:

1.国家间、国际组织无偿援助和赠送的物资,监管方式为"援助物资"(3611)。

2.经贸往来中赠送的物品、外国人捐赠品、我驻外(包括驻港、澳)中资机构向国内单位赠送的物资等,监管方式为"其他进出口免费提供货物"(3339)。

●边境小额贸易

一、定义及代码

边境小额贸易指我国沿陆地边境线经国家批准对外开放的边境县(旗)、边境城市辖区内(以下简称边境地区),经批准有边境小额贸易经营权的企业,通过国家指定的陆地边境口岸,与毗邻国家边境地区的企业或其他贸易机构进行的贸易活动。

本监管方式代码"4019",简称"边境小额"。

二、适用范围

(一)本监管方式包括:

1.边境地区有对外经济技术合作经营权的企业与我国毗邻国家边境地区以易货贸易、现汇贸易形式开展的边境小额贸易。

2.边境地区有对外经济技术合作经营权的企业与我国毗邻国家边境地区经济合作(工程承包、劳务输出)项下进出口物资及原出口工程设备、物资(包括在境外购买及换回的)运回境内。

(二)下列情况不适用本监管方式:

1.边民互市贸易(互市进口商品),每人每日价值人民币3000元以下免征进口关税和进口环节税,超出部分照章征税,监管方式为"其他贸易"(9739)。

2.未获准经营边境小额贸易的企业进出口货物。

3.对台湾居民同大陆对台小额贸易公司成交用台湾船只直接运进产自台湾的产品和运出大陆产品到台湾,监管方式为"对台小额"(4039)。

●对台小额

一、定义及代码

对台湾小额贸易是指台湾地区居民与大陆经批准的企业依照有关规定进行的货物交易。

本监管方式代码"4039",简称"对台小额"。

二、适用范围

本监管方式不适用于进入厦门大嶝对台小额商品交易市场的人员带出台湾产品,每人每日价值人民币3000元以下免征进口关税和进口环节税,超出部分照章征税,监管方式为"其他贸易"(9739)。

●对台小额商品交易市场

一、定义及代码

对台小额商品交易市场是经国家批准设立,用于开展对台民间小额商品交易活动,并实行封闭管理的特定区域,以下简称"交易市场"。

本监管方式代码"4139",简称"对台市场"。

二、适用范围

本监管方式仅限于厦门大嶝对台小额商品交易市场。

下列情况不适用本监管方式:

(一)对台湾居民同大陆对台小额贸易公司成交用台湾船只直接运进产自台湾的产品和运出大陆产品到台湾,监管方式为"对台小额"(4039)。

(二)我国沿陆地边境线经国家批准对外开放的边境县(旗)、边境城市辖区内(以下简称边境地区)经批准有边境小额贸易经营权的企业,通过国家指定的陆地边境口岸,与毗邻国家边境地区的企业或其他贸易机构进行的贸易活动,监管方式为"边境小额"(4019)。

●驻外机构运回旧公用物品

一、定义及代码

驻外机构运回旧公用物品是指我驻各国(地区)使、领馆,驻国外、港澳地区的经济、贸易机构,驻国际组织代表处等我驻外机构更新且闲置不用而运回或因机构撤销而运回的物品,包括临时出国展览团、考察团等运回的生产资料和公用物品。

本监管方式代码"4200",简称"驻外机构运回"。

二、适用范围

本监管方式不适用于暂时进出境公用物品。

●直接退运货物

一、定义及代码

直接退运货物是指进口货物收发货人、原运输工具负责人或者其代理人(以下统称当事人)在有关货物进境后、办结海关放行手续前,因海关责令或有正当理由获准退运境外的货物。

本监管方式代码"4500",简称"直接退运货物"。

二、适用范围

(一)在货物进境后、办结海关放行手续前,有下列情形之一的,当事人可以向海关申请办理直接退运手续:

1.因国家贸易管理政策调整,收货人无法提供相关证件的;

2.属于错发、误卸或者溢卸货物,能够提供发货人或者承运人书面证明文书的;

3.收发货人双方协商一致同意退运,能够提供双方同意退运的书面证明文书的;

4.有关贸易发生纠纷,能够提供法院判决书、仲裁机构仲裁决定书或者无争议的有效货物所有权凭证的;

5.货物残损或者国家检验检疫不合格,能够提供国家检验检疫部门根据收货人申请而出具的相关检验证明文书的。

(二)在货物进境后、办结海关放行手续前,有下列情形之一依法应当退运的,由海关责令当事人将进口货物直接退运境外:

1.进口国家禁止进口的货物,经海关依法处理后的;

2.违反国家检验检疫政策法规,经国家检验检疫部门处理并且出具"检验检疫处理通知书"或者其他证明文书后的;

3.未经许可擅自进口属于限制进口的固体废物用做原料,经海关依法处理后的;

4.违反国家有关法律、行政法规,应当责令直接退运的其他情形。

(三)保税区、出口加工区及其他海关特殊监管区域和保税监管场所进口货物的直接退运。

(四)下列情况不适用本监管方式:

1.放行后的进口货物退运出境,监管方式为"退运货物"

(4561)。

2. 进口转关货物在进境地海关放行后，当事人申请办理退运手续的，应当按照一般退运手续办理。

●区内加工货物

区内加工货物指出口加工区内企业经营加工贸易业务从境外进口料件以及加工出口的成品。

本监管方式代码“5015”，简称“区内加工货物”。

●区内仓储货物

区内仓储货物指出口加工区内仓储企业从境外进口供区内企业加工的仓储货物。

本监管方式代码“5033”，简称“区内仓储货物”。

●境外设备进区

境外设备进区指加工区内企业从境外进口用于区内加工生产所需的机器设备和工模具、区内建设所需的基建物资，以及区内企业和行政管理机构自用合理数量的办公用品等。

本监管方式代码“5335”，简称“境外设备进区”。

●区内设备退运

区内设备退运指出口加工区内退运境外的设备。

本监管方式代码“5361”，简称“区内设备退运”。

●加工贸易料件进出出口加工区

加工贸易料件进出出口加工区指出口加工区内加工贸易料件在境内结转、销售，包括从区外购进或加工区内企业经批准销往区外的料件，同一出口加工区或不同出口加工区内的企业之间相互结转(调拨)的料件，深加工结转转入的料件，加工区内企业为区外加工的料件进区，以及上述料件在境内的退运，但不包括退换货物。

本监管方式代码“5000”，简称“料件进出区”。

●加工贸易成品进出出口加工区

加工贸易成品进出出口加工区指出口加工区内加工贸易成品在境内结转、销售，包括销往区外、结转到同一出口加工区或另一出口加工区内的企业，以及加工区内企业为区外加工的成品出区、销往区外的成品因故退运进区，不包括退换货物。

本监管方式代码“5100”，简称“成品进出区”。

●设备进出区

设备进出区指出口加工区内企业设备、物资在境内结转、销售，包括从区外购进设备、物资，设备因故销往区外，设备结转到同一出口加工区或另一出口加工区内的企业，以及上述设备、物资在境内的退运、退换。

本监管方式代码“5300”，简称“设备进出区”。

●出口加工区加工贸易边角料出区

出口加工区加工贸易边角料出区指出口加工区内企业边角料结转到同一加工区或不同加工区的另一企业，或经批准销售到区外。

本监管方式代码“5200”，简称“区内边角调出”。

●物流中心进出境货物

一、定义及代码

保税物流中心进出境仓储货物是指从境外直接存入保税物流中心(A、B 型)和从保税物流中心(A、B 型)运出境的仓储、转口货物。

本监管方式代码“6033”，简称“物流中心进出境货物”。

二、适用范围

(一)保税物流中心(A 型)是指经海关批准，由中国境内企业法人经营，专门从事保税仓储物流业务的海关监管场所。

保税物流中心(A 型)按照服务范围分为公用型物流中心和自用型物流中心。

1. 公用型物流中心是指由专门从事仓储物流业务的中国境内企业法人经营，向社会提供保税仓储物流综合服务的海关监管场所。

2. 自用型物流中心是指中国境内企业法人经营，仅向本企业或者本企业集团内部成员提供保税仓储物流服务的海关监管场所。

(二)保税物流中心(B 型)(以下简称物流中心)是指经海关批准，由中国境内一家企业法人经营、多家企业进入并从事保税仓储物流业务的海关集中监管场所。

(三)下列情况不适用本监管方式：

1. 从境内(海关特殊监管区域除外)运入保税物流中心(A、B 型)货物和从保税物流中心(A、B 型)提取运往境内的货物。

2. 保税物流中心(A、B 型)与保税区、出口加工区、保税物流园区、保税仓库、出口监管仓库及保税物流中心(A、B 型)之间等海关特殊监管区域或保税监管场所之间往来的货物，监管方式填报“保税间货物”(1200)。

3. 保税仓库进出境仓储、转口货物，监管方式为“保税仓库货物”(1233)。

4. 保税区、保税物流园区进出境仓储、转口货物，监管方式为“保税区仓储、转口”(1234)。

●内贸货物跨境运输

一、定义及代码

内贸货物跨境运输是指国内贸易货物由我国关境内一口岸起运，通过境外运至我国关境内另一口岸的业务，以下简称“跨境运输”。

本监管方式代码“9600”，简称“内贸跨境”。

二、适用范围

经海关总署批准的进出境口岸、所经境外口岸、运输方式等实行跨境运输的货物。

●海关处理货物

一、定义及代码

海关处理货物是指由海关提取变卖处理的超期未报关进口货物及误卸、溢卸货物、放弃进口货物，以及走私违规案件查处的货物。

本监管方式代码“9639”，简称“海关处理货物”。

二、适用范围

本监管方式适用以下定义的货物：

(一) 超期未报关货物，是指进口货物的收货人自运输工具申报进境之日起超过 3 个月未向海关申报，由海关提取依法变卖处理的进口货物。

超期未报关货物还包括报税货物，暂时进口货物超过规定的期限 3 个月，未向海关办理复运出境或者其他有关手续，以及过境、转运和通运货物超过规定的期限 3 个月，未运输处境，由海关提取依法变卖处理。

（二）误卸、溢卸货物，是指未列入进境运输工具载货清单、运单申报进境的误卸或者溢卸的货物，运输工具负责人或进口货物收货人未向海关办理退运出境或申报进口手续，由海关提取依法变卖处理的进口货物。

（三）放弃进口货物，是指进口货物的收货人或其所有人声明放弃，由海关提取依法变卖处理的进口货物。

（四）超期未报关进口货物及误卸或者溢卸进口货物属于危险品或者鲜活、易腐、易烂、易失效、易变质、易贬值等不宜长期保存的货物，海关根据实际情况，提前提取依法变卖处理。

（五）进出境物品所有人声明放弃的物品，在海关规定期限内未办理海关手续或者无人认领的物品，以及无法投递又无法退回的进境邮递物品，由海关提取依法变卖处理。

（六）走私违法案件予以没收，由海关依法变卖处理的货物。

●无原始报关单的后续补税

无原始报关单的后续补税是指无法获得原始报关单的后续退补税货物，包括调查、稽查补税及审价、归类等各种原因的后续退补税货物。

本监管方式代码“9700”，简称“后续补税”。

●其他贸易

一、定义及代码

其他贸易是指除本章上述各节列名的监管方式以外，列入海关“其他贸易”统计的进出口货物。

本监管方式代码“9739”，简称“其他贸易”。

二、适用范围

(一)本监管方式适用：

1.我国境内经批准临时进出口货物的机关、团体、学校、企事业单位等进出口货物、物品。

2.外国驻华使、领馆在我国内购买货物出口。

3.外商投资企业外方常驻人员和外国驻华机构的常驻人员，以及持有长期居留证件和来华定居的引进专家等进口自用汽车。

4.进入厦门大嶝对台小额商品交易市场的人员带出台湾产品，每人每日价值人民币 1000 元以下免征进口关税和进口环节税，超出部分照章征税，监管方式为“其他贸易”。

5.外国企业常驻我国办事机构进口不复运出境的陈列用企业产品样品。

6.未列入运输工具进口载货清单、提(运)单，或多于进口载货清单、提(运)单所列数量的货物，运输工具负责人或溢卸货物的收货人申请办理进口溢卸货物。

(二)本监管方式不包括：

1.入境旅客在境内购买 5 万美元以内的旅游商品托运出境，监管方式为“旅游购物商品”(0139)。

2．本国籍运输工具在境内添加进口保税油、物料，监管方式为“国轮油物料”(1139)。

3．外国常驻机构进口办公用品，监管方式为“常驻机构公用”(2439)。

4．驻华商业机构进口不复运出口的陈列样品，监管方式为“陈列样品”(2939)。

5．对台湾小额贸易，监管方式为“对台小额”(4039)。

6．没有进出口经营权的企业或单位进出口货样广告品，监管方式为“货样广告品 B”(3039)。

7，除援助、捐赠以外进出口其他免费提供的货物，监管方式为“其他进山口免费”(3339)。

8．我国驻外机构在境外购买的公务用品、机动车辆运回境内，监管方式为“驻外机构购进。(4239)。

9．海关拍卖处理超期未报货物、走私违规货物，监管方式为“海关处理货物”(9639)。

10．驻华外交机构转售境内非外交机构或个人，国际文体交流活动进口物品获准留赠或放弃，监管方式为“留赠、转卖物品”(9839)。

●留赠、转卖物品

留赠、转卖物品是指外国(地区)驻我国外交机构转售境内非外交机构或国际文体活动留赠、放弃的特批进口物品。

本监管方式代码“9839”，简称“留赠、转卖物品”。

●其他

一、定义及代码

指除已具体列名监管方式以外其他不列入海关统计的进出境货物、物品。

本监管方式代码“9900”，简称“其他”。

二、适用范围

(一)从货运渠道进出境的个人行李物品。

(二)中国驻外国使领馆出口公务或自用物品。

(三)在境内结转的进出口货物：

1．以出顶进货物，指经批准在国内以外汇向有关进出口公司购买出口商品顶替其应进口的同一商品。

2．供应国内外汇免税商店并收取外汇的出口商品。

3．经批准将来料加工、进料加工贸易项下加工的成品转为免税外汇商品。

4．经批准内销征税的进口免税品。

(四)边民互市贸易进出境货物。

(五)我国远洋渔业企业进口自捕水产品。

(六)国有文物收藏单位经国家文物局核准后，接受境外捐赠、归还和从境外追索的文物进口。

国有文物收藏单位系指经国家文物局审核批准从事文物收藏和研究的博物馆(院)、展览馆、研究所(院)等单位。

(七)与无代价抵偿进出口货物相关的原进口货物退运出境或原出口货物退运进境。

(八)我国各银行总行调运进出境的人民币、外币现钞。

征免性质代码表

征免性质代码	征免性质简称	征免性质全称
101	一般征税	一般征税进出口货物
118	整车征税	构成整车特征的汽车零部件纳税
119	零部件征税	不构成整车特征的汽车零部件纳税
201	无偿援助	无偿援助进出口物资
299	其他法定	其他法定减免税进出口货物
301	特定区域	特定区域进口自用物资及出口货物
307	保税区	保税区进口自用物资
399	其他地区	其他执行特殊政策地区出口货物
401	科教用品	大专院校及科研机构进口科教用品
402	示范平台用品	
403	技术改造	企业技术改造进口货物
405	科技开发用品	科学研究、技术开发机构进口科技开发用品
406	重大项目	国家重大项目进口货物
407	动漫用品	动漫开发生产用品
408	重大技术装备	生产重大技术装备进口关键零部件及原材料
409	科技重大专项	科技重大专项进口关键设备、零部件和原材料
412	基础设施	通信、港口、铁路、公路、机场建设进口设备
413	残疾人	残疾人组织和企业进出口货物
417	远洋渔业	远洋渔业自捕水产品
418	国产化	国家定点生产小轿车和摄录机企业进口散件
419	整车特征	构成整车特征的汽车零部件进口
420	远洋船舶	远洋船舶及设备部件
421	内销设备	内销远洋船用设备及关键部件
422	集成电路	集成电路生产企业进口货物
423	新型显示器件	新型显示器件生产企业进口物资
499	ITA 产品	非全税号信息技术产品
501	加工设备	加工贸易外商提供的不作价进口设备
502	来料加工	来料加工装配和补偿贸易进口料件及出口成品
503	进料加工	进料加工贸易进口料件及出口成品
506	边境小额	边境小额贸易进口货物
510	港澳 OPA	港澳在内地加工的纺织品获证出口
601	中外合资	中外合资经营企业进出口货物
602	中外合作	中外合作经营企业进出口货物
603	外资企业	外商独资企业进出口货物
605	勘探开发煤层气	勘探开发煤层气
606	海洋石油	勘探、开发海洋石油进口货物
608	陆上石油	勘探、开发陆上石油进口货物
609	贷款项目	利用贷款进口货物
611	贷款中标	国际金融组织贷款、外国政府贷款中标机电设备零部件
698	公益收藏	国有公益性收藏单位进口藏品
789	鼓励项目	国家鼓励发展的内外资项目进口设备
799	自有资金	外商投资额度外利用自有资金进口设备、备件、配件
801	救灾捐赠	救灾捐赠进口物资
802	扶贫慈善	境外向我境内无偿捐赠用于扶贫慈善的免税进口物资
803	抗艾滋病药物	进口抗艾滋病病毒药物
811	种子种源	进口种子(苗)、种畜(禽)、鱼种(苗)和种用野生动植物种源
818	中央储备粮油	中央储备粮油免征进口环节增值税政策
819	科教图书	进口科研教学用图书资料
888	航材减免	经核准的航空公司进口维修用航空器材
898	国批减免	国务院特准减免税的进出口货物
899	选择征税	选择征税
997	自贸协定	
998	内部暂定	享受内部暂定税率的进出口货物
999	例外减免	例外减免税进出口货物

征免性质代码表说明

征免性质是指海关对进出口货物实施征、减、免税管理的性质类别。

征免性质分为照章征税、法定减免税、特定减免税和临时减免税四部分。其中特定减免税又分为按地区实施的税收政策、按用途实施的税收政策、按贸易性质实施的税收政策、按企业性质和资金来源实施的税收政策等五类。

一份报关单只允许填报一种征免性质，涉及多个征免性质的，应分单填报。

●一般征税进出口货物

一、定义及代码

一般征税进出口货物指海关根据《海关法》、《中华人民共和国进出口关税条例》(国务院令第392号)、《中华人民共和国进出口税则》及其他法律、行政法规、规章的规定征收进出口关税、进口环节税的进出口货物。

本征免性质代码“101”，简称“一般征税”。

二、适用范围

本征免性质限于海关依据法律、行政法规、规章规定的法定税率征收进出口关税、进口环节税的进出口货物，包括按照公开暂定、关税配额、反倾销、反补贴、保障措施等税率、税额征税或补税的进出口货物。

执行 ITA 税率的货物（征免性质代码“499”）不适用本征免性质。

●无偿援助进出口物资

一、定义及代码

无偿援助进出口物资指外国政府、国际组织对我国无偿赠送及我国履行国际条约规定进口的物资，或我国对国外无偿援助或赠送的物资。

本征免性质代码“201”，简称“无偿援助”。

二、适用范围

(一)本征免性质所称外国政府是指外国国家的中央政府；国际组织是指联合国各专门机构，以及长期与我国有合作关系的其他国际组织；国际条约是指依据《中华人民共和国缔结条约程序法》以“中华人民共和国”、“中华人民共和国政府”、“中华人民共和国政府部门”名义同外国缔结协定或协议，以及参加的国际条约。

(二)免税范围

1. 根据中国与外国政府、国际组织间的协定或协议，由外国政府、国际组织直接无偿赠送的物资，或由其提供无偿赠款，由我国受赠单位按照协定或协议规定用途自行采购进口的物资。

2. 外国地方政府或民间组织受外国政府委托无偿赠送的物资。

3. 国际组织成员受国际组织委托无偿赠送的物资。

4. 我国履行国际条约规定免税进口的物资。

(三)外国民间团体、企业、友好人士和华侨、香港居民、以及台湾、澳门同胞及外籍华人无偿向我境内受灾地区捐赠的直接用于救灾的物资(征免性质代码“801”)，境外捐赠人无偿向我国境内捐赠的直接用于扶贫、慈善事业的进口物资(征免性质代码“802”)不适用本征免性质。

●其他法定减免税进出口货物

一、定义及代码

其他法定减免税进出口货物指海关依照《中华人民共和国海关法》、《中华人民共和国进出口关税条例》，对除无偿援助进出口物资外的其他实行法定减免税的进出口货物，以及根据有关规定按非全额货值征税的部分进出口货物。

本征免性质代码“299”，简称“其他法定”。

二、适用范围

本征免性质仅限无代价抵偿货物，货样和广告品，暂时进出境货物，展览会货物，退运货物，残损货物，进出境运输工具装载的途中必需的燃料、物料和饮食用品，我国缔结或者参加的国际条约规定减免税款的货物，因不可抗力因素造成的受灾保税货物等不按“进出口货物征免税证明”管理的减免税货物。

●保税区进口自用物资

一、定义及代码

保税区进口自用物资是指对保税区单独实施征减免税政策的进口自用物资。

本征免性质代码“307”，简称“保税区”。

二、适用范围

本征免性质仅限保税区进口的自用物资，包括区内生产性基础设施建设物资、区内企业自用的生产、管理设备和自用合理数量的办公用品，建设生产厂房、仓储设施所需的物资设备，保税区行政管理机构自用合理数量的管理设备和办公用品等。

保税区内加工贸易进出口货物、仓储货物、转口货物和外商投资企业按照外商投资企业进口税收政策进口的设备等不适用本征免性质。

●其他执行特殊政策地区进出口货物

一、定义及代码

其他执行特殊政策地区进出口货物指除保税区外单独实施特殊税收政策地区进出口的货物。

本征免性质代码“399”，简称“其他地区”。

二、适用范围

(一)本征免性质仅限出口加工区、保税港区、综合保税区、珠澳跨境工业园区等海关特殊监管区进口的基建、生产和管理设备、物资，区内出口货物，以及从境内区外进入上述海关特殊监管区(包括中哈霍尔果斯国际边境合作中心)的基建物资或区内生产企业在国内采购用于生产出口产品的原材料。

(二)本征免性质不适用：

1. 特殊区域内加工贸易进出口货物、仓储货物、转口货物和外商投资企业按照外商投资企业进口税收政策进口的设备等。

2. 保税区进出口货物，征免性质代码“307”。

●科教用品和科技开发用品

一、定义及代码

科教用品指为促进科学研究和教育事业的发展，推动科教兴国战略的实施，科学研究机构和学校以科学研究和教学为目的，在合理数量范围内进口国内不能生产或者性能不能满足需要的科学研究和教学用品。

科技开发用品指为鼓励科学研究和技术开发，促进科技进步，科学研究、技术开发机构在 2010 年 12 月 31 日前，在合理数量范围内进口国内不能生产或者性能不能满足需要的科技开发用品。

本征免性质代码“401”，简称“科教用品”。

二、适用范围

(一)本征免性质所称科研机构和学校是指：

1.国务院部委、直属机构和省、自治区、直辖市、计划单列市所属专门从事科学研究工作的各类科研院所。

2.国家承认学历的实施专科及以上高等学历教育的高等学校。

3.财政部会同国务院有关部门核定的其他科学研究机构和学校。

(二)本征免性质所称科学研究、技术开发机构是指：

1.科技部会同财政部、海关总署和国家税务总局核定的科技体制改革过程中转制为企业和进入企业的主要从事科学研究和技术开发工作的机构。

2.国家发展和改革委员会会同财政部、海关总署和国家税务总局核定的国家工程研究中心。

3.国家发展和改革委员会会同财政部、海关总署、国家税务总局和科技部核定的企业技术中心。

4.科技部会同财政部、海关总署和国家税务总局核定的国家重点实验室和国家工程技术研究中心。

5.财政部会同国务院有关部门核定的其他科学研究、技术开发机构。

(三)具体免税范围限于《免税进口科学研究和教学用品清单》和《免税进口科技开发用品清单》。

(四)转制科研机构进口国家鼓励发展的内外资项目技术和设备(征免性质代码“789”)不适用本征免性质。

●国家重大项目进口货物

一、定义及代码

国家重大项目进口货物指经国务院批准的国家重大建设项目项下进口的设备，以及安装所需材料等。

本征免性质代码“406”，简称“重大项目”。

二、适用范围

(一)本征免性质仅限1996年4月1日前经国务院批准可行性研究报告中列明减免税条款或另有减免税批准文件的重大建设项目。

(二)利用政府贷款、世界银行贷款等外资贷款建设的重大项目(征免性质代码“609”)不适用于本征免性质。

●进口残疾人专用品和专用设备

一、定义及代码

进口残疾人专用品和专用设备指为支持残疾人康复工作、帮助残疾人自立免税进口的残疾人专用品和有关福利机构、康复机构、企业按照国家有关规定免税进口的国内不能生产的残疾人专用设备及专用生产设备。

本征免性质代码“413”，简称“残疾人”。

二、适用范围

(一)本征免性质仅限进口的残疾人专用品和残疾人福利机构、康复机构、企业进口的残疾人专用设备及专用生产设备。

(二)免税货物范围

1.残疾人个人专用品

(1)假肢及其零部件：上肢假肢，包括部分手、前臂、上臂、假手、肘关节；下肢假肢，包括部分足、小腿、大腿、膝关节等。

(2)假眼。

(3)假鼻。

(4)内脏托带：肾托、胃托、疝气带、疝气腰带等。

(5)矫形器：包括脊柱、上肢、下肢、功能性电子刺激器和复合力源矫形器系统等。

(6)矫形鞋：成品矫形鞋、订做的矫形鞋、适配的标准鞋。

(7)非机动助行器：包括单臂操作助行器(手杖、肘拐、前臂支撑拐、腋拐、三脚及多脚拐杖等)、双臂操作助行器(助行架、轮式助行架、助行椅、助行台等)及助行器的附件等。

(8)代步工具(不包括汽车、摩托车)：包括轮椅车(手动、电动、机动)、残疾人专业自行车(如手摇三轮车、串翼自行车、助行自行车手扒推轮椅等)。

(9)辅助器具：移动用辅助器具、翻身用辅助器具(如翻身垫、翻身床单、翻身毯等)、升降用辅助器具(如轮椅爬楼梯装置、升降架等)。

(10)生活自助具：包括残疾人专用服装(如轮椅使用者的连裤服、雨衣、手套，鞋和靴的防滑装置等)，安全防护辅助器具(如用于头部、面部、上肢、下肢及全身的防护装置等)，穿脱衣服的辅助器具，画图和书写辅助器具(如书写板、书写框等)，日常生活用辅助器具(如罐头开启器、防洒碗等)。

(11)专用卫生用品。

(12)视力残疾者用盲杖。

(13)导盲镜。

(14)助视器。

(15)盲人阅读器：电子盲文书写器、手动盲文书写器等。

(16)语言、听力残疾者用的语言训练器：言语训练辅助器具。

(17)智力残疾者用的行为训练器。

(18)生活能力训练用品。

2.残疾人专用设备和专用生产设备

(1)残疾人康复及专用设备：包括床旁监护设备、中心监护设备、生化分析仪和超声诊断仪。

(2)残疾人特殊教育设备和职业教育设备：指对残疾人进行义务教育、学历教育、职业教育所需的各类设备(如聋人助听设备、智力残疾检测设备等)。

(3)残疾人职业能力评估测试设备(如手腕作业检查盘、注意力集中能力测试仪等)。

(4)残疾人专用劳动设备和劳动保护设备(如某种肢残人操作的特殊机床、聋人专用的特殊报警装置等)，以及为残疾人就业设立的福利企业进口的适合残疾人操作的生产设备。

(5)残疾人文体活动专用设备：指残疾人进行文化、娱乐、体育活动和体育竞赛所需的专用设备(如各种运动轮椅、盲人门球等)。

(6)假肢专用生产、装配、检测设备，包括假肢专用铣磨机、假肢专用真空成型机、假肢专用平板加热器和假肢综合检测仪。

(7)听力残疾者用的助听器：包括各类助听器等。

(三)境外捐赠人无偿向我国境内捐赠的直接用于扶贫、慈善事业的进口物资(征免性质代码“802”)不适用本征免性质。

●远洋渔业自捕水产品

一、定义及代码

远洋渔业自捕水产品是指根据国家远洋渔业企业运回自捕水产品的原产地规则，我国远洋渔业企业在公海或按照有关协议规定，在国外海域捕获并运回国内销售的自捕水产品及其加工制品，视同国内产品，免征关税和进口环节税。

本征免性质代码“417”，简称“远洋渔业”。

二、适用范围

本征免性质仅限经农业部批准，获得“农业部远洋渔业企业资格证书”的我国远洋渔业企业。

运回的水产品及其加工制品限于在公海或按照有关协议规定，在国外海域自捕，并符合原产地规则的认定。

●远洋船舶及设备部件

一、定义及代码

远洋船舶及设备部件是指中央关于制定国民经济和社会发展第十一个五年规划期间(以下简称“十一五”期间)，在国内订造、改造远洋渔船进口船用关键设备和部件，进口少量带有入渔配额的二手远洋渔船，以及进口国内不能建造的特种渔船，实施进口税收优惠政策。

本征免性质代码“420”，简称“远洋船舶”。

二、适用范围

(一)本征免性质仅适用于“十一五”期间(2006 年 1 月 1 日至 2010 年 12 月 31 日)经农业部批准的在国内订造、改造远洋渔船所需进口的船用关键设备和部件，国内尚不能建造的特种渔船及少量带有入渔配额的二手远洋渔船。

(二)本征免性质不适用于“十一五”期间为建造内销远洋船所需进口的国内不能生产或性能不能满足要求的关键设备及部件，征免性质代码“421”。

●内销远洋船用设备及关键部件

一、定义及代码

内销远洋船用设备及关键部件是指为建造内销远洋船所需进口的国内不能生产或性能不能满足要求的关键设备及部件。

征免性质代码“421”，简称“内销设备”。

二、适用范围

(一)本征免性质仅适用于“十一五”期间(2006 年 1 月 1 日至 2010 年 12 月 31 日)经国家有关部门共同审定，为建造内销远洋船所需进口的国内不能生产或性能不能满足要求的关键部件及设备。

内销远洋船舶是指中国远洋运输(集团)总公司、中国海运(集团)总公司、中国对外贸易运输(集团)总公司和长江航运(集团)总公司委托中国船舶工业集团公司和中国船舶重工集团公司所属企业(包括造船企业和配套造船企业)建造的远洋船舶。

(二)本征免性质不适用于远洋渔业企业、国内船舶及船用设备制造企业在国内订造、改造远洋渔船所需进口的船用关键设备和部件，征免性质代码“420”。

●集成电路生产企业进口货物

一、定义及代码

集成电路生产企业进口货物是指在中国境内设立的经审核符合条件的集成电路生产企业进口国内无法生产的自用生产性原材料、消耗品、净化室专用建筑材料、配套系统和集成电路生产设备零、配件。

本征免性质代码“422”，简称“集成电路”。

二、适用范围

本征免性质仅适用于集成电路线宽小于 0.8 微米(含)集成电路生产企业进口自用生产性原材料、消耗品，集成电路线宽小于 0.25 微米或投资额超过 80 亿元的集成电路生产企业进口自用生产性原材料、消耗品、净化室专用建筑材料、配套系统和集成电路生产设备零、配件。

●薄膜晶体管液晶显示器件生产企业进口货物

一、定义及代码

薄膜晶体管液晶显示器件生产企业进口货物是指薄膜晶体管液晶显示器件生产企业进口国内不能生产的净化室专用建筑材料、配套系统，以及维修用的生产设备零部件、自用生产性原材料和消耗品。

本征免性质代码“423”，简称“膜晶显”。

二、适用范围

本征免性质仅适用于经国务院有关部门共同审核确定，可享受本税收政策的薄膜晶体管液晶显示器件生产企业(以下简称“膜晶显生产企业”)进口国内不能生产的净化室专用建筑材料、配套系统，以及维修用的生产设备零部件、自用生产性原材料和消耗品。

第一批符合条件的膜晶显生产企业是：北京京东方光电科技有限公司(以下简称京东方)、上海广电 NEC 液晶显示器公司(以下简称上广电)和吉林北方彩晶数码电子有限公司。

●非全税号信息技术产品

一、定义及代码

非全税号信息技术产品是指为执行“信息技术产品协议”，海关核定用途后执行 ITA 税率的部分用于信息技术产品生产的商品。

本征免性质代码“499”，简称。“ITA 产品”。

二、适用范围

本征免性质仅适用于进口《中华人民共和国进出口税则》所列的 ITA 产品。

●加工贸易外商提供的不作价进口设备

一、定义及代码

加工贸易外商提供的不作价进口设备是指与经营企业开展加工贸易(包括来料加工、进料加工)的境外企业，以免费即不需经营企业付汇进口、也不需用加工费或差价偿还方式，向经营企业提供的加工生产所需设备。

本征免性质代码“501”，简称“加工设备”。

二、适用范围

(一)本征免性质仅适用于加工贸易项下境外企业免费提供的不作价进口设备。

(二)本征免性质不适用按暂时进出口货物监管(监管方式“暂时进出口”、代码“2600”)的加工贸易生产所需的不作价设备(限模具、单台设备)，征免性质为“法定减免”(299)。

●来料加工贸易进口料件及出口成品

一、定义及代码

来料加工贸易进口料件及出口成品是指由境外企业提供，经营企业不需要付汇进口的来料加工业务所需全部或部分原辅材料、零部件、元器件和包装物料(以下简称料件)，以及经加工或者装配后复出口的成品。

本征免性质代码“502”，简称“来料加工”。

二、适用范围

(一)本征免性质仅限来料加工项下进口的用于加工复出口成品所需的料件，以及经加工或者装配后复出口的成品。

(二)进口料件或制成品内销的，不适用本征免性质，征免性质为“照章征税”(101)。

●进料加工贸易进口料件及出口成品

一、定义及代码

进料加工贸易进口料件及出口成品是指经营企业付汇进口的进料加工所需的全部或者部分原辅材料、零部件、元器件、包装物料(以下简称料件)，以及经过加工或者装配后复出口的成品。

本征免性质代码“503”，简称“进料加工”。

二、适用范围

(一)本征免性质仅限进料加工项下进口的用于加工复出口成品所需的料件，以及经加工后复出口的成品。

（二）进口料件或制成品内销的，按规定不予保税备案的消耗性物料，不适用本征免性质。征免性质为“照章征税”（101）。

●边境小额贸易进口货物

一、定义及代码

边境小额贸易进口货物是指我国边境地区经批准有小额贸易经营权的企业通过国家指定的陆路边境口岸，进口原产于毗邻国家的货物，包括边境地区开展易货贸易、现汇贸易、互利经济合作（工程承包、劳务输出），以及以除边民互市贸易以外的其他各类边境贸易形式进口的货物。

本征免性质代码“506”，简称“边境小额”。

二、适用范围

（一）本征免性质适用于边境小额贸易企业通过国家指定的陆路边境口岸进口原产于毗邻国家的货物及边境地区外经贸企业与毗邻国家边境地区开展承包工程和劳务合作项下换回的原产于毗邻国家的物资。

（二）本征免性质不适用于边民互市贸易、通过边境口岸进口第三国贸易的商品。

●外商投资企业进出口货物

一、定义及代码

外商投资企业进出口货物指 1997 年 12 月 31 日前按国家规定程序批准设立的国内企业与境外企业在中国境内合资经营的企业、合作经营的企业，以及境外企业在中国境内独资经营的企业在投资总额内进口的设备，以及外商投资企业（不受批准时间限制）生产的出口产品（加工贸易除外）。

中外合资经营企业进出口货物征免性质代码“601”，简称“中外合资”。

中外合作经营企业进出口货物征免性质代码“602”，简称“中外合作”。

外商独资企业进出口货物征免性质代码“603”，简称“外资企业”。

二、适用范围

（一）征免性质“601”、“602”、“603”适用以下经批准设立的外商投资企业、外商投资项目在项目额度或投资总额内进口的自用设备及其按照合同随设备进口的技术及配套件、备件，以及所有外商投资企业生产（加工贸易除外）的出口产品：

1. 1996 年 3 月 31 日前成立的外商投资企业，包括依法批准增资及原外经贸部颁发批准证书的外商投资企业。

2. 1995 年 10 月 1 日至 1996 年 3 月 31 日依照程序经原外经贸部、原国家计委、原国家经贸委备案审核合格并经海关总署关税司转发各海关清单内的外商投资企业。

3. 1995 年 9 月 30 日前地方依法审批报原外经贸部备案的外商投资企业。

4. 1996 年 4 月 1 日至 1997 年 12 月 31 日按国家规定程序批准设立的外商投资项目。

（二）本征免性质不适用：

1. 外商投资企业开展加工贸易进口的不作价设备，征免性质代码“501”。

2. 国家鼓励发展的外资项目项下进口的货物，征免性质代码“789”。

3. 外商投资额度外利用自有资金进口的货物，征免性质代码“799”。

●勘探开发煤层气进口物资

一、定义及代码

勘探开发煤层气进口物资指勘探开发煤层气项目的单位在我国境内进行煤层气勘探开发所需进口的设备、仪器、零附件和专用工具。

本征免性质代码“605”，简称“勘探开发煤层气”。

二、适用范围

勘探开发煤层气所需进口物资的免税政策执行期限为“十一五”期间。

勘探开发煤层气项目的单位为中联煤层气有限责任公司及其他经财政部商海关总署和税务总局审核认定的单位。

具体免税范围限于国内不能生产或国内产品性能不能满足要求，并直接用于勘探开发作业的设备、仪器、零附件和专用工具。上述物资应符合《勘探开发煤层气免税进口物资清单》。

●开采海洋、陆上石油（天然气）进口物资

一、定义及代码

开采海洋、陆上石油（天然气）进口物资指在我国海洋或陆上特定地区进行石油和天然气开采作业所需进口的设备、仪器、零附件和专用工具。

海洋指我国内海、领海、大陆架及其他海洋资源管辖海域，包括浅海滩涂。

陆上特定地区指我国领土内的沙漠、戈壁荒漠和中外合作开采经国家批准的陆上石油、天然气中标区块。

开采海洋石油、天然气进口物资征免性质代码“606”，简称“海洋石油”。

开采陆上石油、天然气进口物资征免性质代码“608”，简称“陆上石油”。

二、适用范围

开采海洋、陆上石油（天然气）所需进口物资的免税政策执行期限为“十一五”期间。

具体免税范围限于国内不能生产或性能不能满足要求，并直接用于开采作业的设备、仪器、零附件、专用工具。上述物资应符合《开采海洋石油（天然气）免税进口物资清单》或《开采陆上特定地区石油（天然气）免税进口物资清单》。

●利用贷款进口货物

一、定义及代码

外国政府贷款和国际金融组织贷款项目进口设备指于 1997 年 12 月 31 日前按国家规定程序批准的利用外国政府贷款和国际金融组织（世界银行、亚洲开发银行、联合国农业发展基金）贷款项目所进口的自用设备，以及按合同随设备进口的技术及数量合理的配套件、备件。

本征免性质代码“609”，简称“贷款项目”。

二、适用范围

（一）本征免性质仅限 1997 年 12 月 31 日前按国家规定程序批准的利用外国政府贷款和国际金融组织贷款项目。

（二）本征免性质不适用：

1. 利用国际金融组织贷款、外国政府贷款生产中标机电设备所需进口的零部件，征免性质代码“611”。

2. 纳入国家鼓励发展内外资项目的利用外国政府贷款和国际金融组织贷款项目，征免性质代码“789”。

●中标机电设备零部件

一、定义及代码

国际金融组织贷款、外国政府贷款中标机电设备零部件指国内中标单位利用国际金融组织贷款、外国政府贷款，为生产中标机电设备而进口国内不能生产或性能不能满足需要的零部件。

本征免性质代码“611”，简称“贷款中标”。

二、适用范围

(一)本征免性质适用于利用国际金融组织贷款、外国政府贷款（世界银行贷款、亚洲开发银行贷款、日本国际协力银行贷款，以及上述组织的赠款)为生产中标机电设备所需进口的零部件。

中标机电设备限于在国际招标中国内企业直接中标、中外联合中标生产的机电设备，以及中标的境外企业、国内企业将中标项目再分包给国内其他企业制造的机电设备，不包括《外商投资项目不予免税的进口商品目录》中所列设备。

(二)本征免性质不适用于1997年12月31日前按国家规定程序批准的利用外国政府贷款和国际金融组织货款项目，征免性质代码“609”。

●国家鼓励发展的内外资项目进口设备

一、定义及代码

国家鼓励发展的内外资项目进口设备指自1998年1月1日起对按国家规定程序审批并出具确认书的国家鼓励发展的国内投资项目和外商投资项目，以及从1999年9月1日起，按国家规定程序审批的外商投资研究开发中心，中西部省、自治区、直辖市利用外资优势产业和优势项目目录的项目，在投资总额内进口的自用设备，以及按合同随设备进口的技术及数量合理的配套件、备件。

本征免性质代码“789”，简称“鼓励项目”。

二、适用范围

(一)本征免性质适用于1998年1月1日后国家鼓励发展的国内投资项目和外商投资项目，以及从1999年9月1日起，按国家规定程序审批的外商投资研究开发中心、中西部省、自治区、直辖市利用外资优势产业和优势项目目录的项目，在投资总额内进口的自用设备，以及按合同随设备进口的技术及数量合理的配套件、备件。

(二)本征免性质不适用：

1．1997年12月31日前批准设立的外商投资企业进口货物，征免性质代码“601”、“602”、“603”。

2．1997年12月31日前按国家规定程序批准的利用外国政府贷款和国际金融组织贷款项目，征免性质代码“609”。

3，外商投资企业投资额度外利用自有资金进口货物，征免性质代码“799”。

●外商投资额度外利用自有资金进口设备、备件、配件

一、定义及代码

外商投资额度外利用自有资金进口设备、备件、配件是指已设立的鼓励类和原限制乙类外商投资企业、外商投资研究开发中心、先进技术型和产品出口型外商投资企业技术改造，在投资总额以外利用自有资金，在原批准的生产经营范围内进口国内不能生产或性能不能满足需要的自用设备及其配套的技术、配件、备件。

本征免性质代码“799”，简称“自有资金”。

二、适用范围

(一)本征免性质适用于已设立的鼓励类和原限制乙类外商投资企业、外商投资研究开发中心、先进技术型和产品出口型外商投资企业(以下简称“五类企业”)技术改造，在投资总额以外利用自有资金，在原批准的生产经营范围内进口国内不能生产或性能不能满足需要的自用设备及其配套的技术、配件、备件。

1．资金来源

“五类企业”投资总额以外的自有资金，具体是指企业储备基金、发展基金、折旧和税后利润。

2．进口商品用途

在原批准的生产经营范围内，对本企业原有设备更新(不包括成套设备和生产线)或维修。

成套设备是指以完成某零、部件或产品生产加工或装配全部过程所有工序所需的全部设备。生产线是指用于完成某种产品一道或多道工序的、有一定节拍要求的、以一定方式连续生产的设备组合。

3．进口商品范围

国内不能生产或性能不能满足需要的设备(即不属于《国内投资项目不予免税的进口商品目录》的商品)，以及与上述设备配套的技术、配件、备件，包括随设备进口或单独进口的。

(二)本征免性质不适用：

1．1997年12月31日前批准设立的外商投资企业进口货物，征免性质代码“601”、“602”、“603”。

2．国家鼓励发展的外资项目项下进口货物，征免性质代码“789”。

●救灾捐赠进口物资

一、定义及代码

救灾捐赠进口物资指外国民间团体、企业、友好人士和华侨，香港居民、以及台湾、澳门同胞及外籍华人无偿向我境内受灾地区捐赠的直接用于救灾的物资。

本征免性质代码“801”，简称“救灾捐赠”。

二、适用范围

（一）本征免性质适用范围

1.外国民间团体、企业、友好人士和华侨、香港居民、以及台湾、澳门同胞及外籍华人无偿向我境内受灾地区捐赠的直接用于救灾的物资。

2.享受救灾捐赠物资进口免税的区域限于新华社对外发布和民政部《中国灾情信息》公布的受灾地区。

●境外向我境内无偿捐赠用于扶贫慈善的免税进口物资

一、定义代码

扶贫、慈善性捐赠物资是指境外捐赠人无偿向我国境内捐赠的直接用于扶贫、慈善事业的进口物资。

本征免性质代码“802”，简称“扶贫慈善”。

二、适用范围

(一)本征免性质适用于境外捐赠人无偿向我国境内捐赠的直接用于扶贫、慈善事业的进口物资。

1.境外捐赠人应为中华人民共和国关境外的自然人、法人或者其他组织。

2．受赠人应为国务院有关部门和各省、自治区、直辖市人民政府，以及从事人道救助和以发展扶贫、慈善事业为宗旨的全国性的社会团体，包括中国红十字会总会、全国妇女联合会、中国残疾人联合会、中华慈善总会、中国初级卫生保健基金会和宋庆龄基金会。

3.使用人应为捐赠物资的直接使用者或负责分配该捐赠物资的单位或个人。

(二)扶贫、慈善公益性事业物资包括：

1．新的衣服、被褥、鞋帽、帐篷、手套、睡袋、毛毯及其他维持基本生活的必需用品等。

2．食品类及饮用品(调味品、水产品、水果、饮料、烟酒等除外)。

3.医疗类包括直接用于治疗特困患者疾病或贫困地区治疗地方病及基本医疗卫生、公共环境卫生所需的基本医疗药品、基本医疗器械、医疗书籍和资料。

其中，"基本医疗药品"是指用于急救、治疗、防疫、消毒、抗菌等用途的药品和人体移植用的器官，但不包括保健药和营养药；"基本医疗器械"是指诊疗器械、手术器械、卫生检测器械、伤残修复器械、防疫防护器械、消毒灭菌器械。

4. 直接用于公共图书馆、公共博物馆、各类职业学校、高中、初中、小学、幼儿园教育的教学仪器、教材、图书、资料和一般学习用品。

其中，"公共图书馆和公共博物馆"是指经省级以上文化行政管理部门认定、向社会开放的县(市)级以上单位管理的公益性图书馆或经省级以上文物行政管理部门认定、向公众开放的县(市)级以上单位管理的各类公益性博物馆；"教学仪器"是指《扶贫、慈善性捐赠物资免征进口税收暂行办法》规定的学校、幼儿园专用于教学的检验、观察、计量、演示用的仪器和器具；"一般学习用品"是指《扶贫、慈善性捐赠物资免征进口税收暂行办法》规定的学校、幼儿园教学和学生专用的文具、教具、婴幼儿玩具、标本、模型、切片、各类学习软件、实验室用器皿和试剂、学生服装(含鞋帽)和书包等。

5. 直接用于环境保护的专用仪器。具体是指环保系统专用的空气质量与污染源废气监测仪器及治理设备、环境水质与污水监测仪器及治理设备、环境污染事故应急监测仪器、固体废物监测仪器及处置设备、辐射防护与电磁辐射监测仪器及设备、生态保护监测仪器及设备、噪声及振动监测仪器和实验室通用分析仪器及设备。

6. 经国务院批准的其他直接用于扶贫、慈善事业的物资。

上述物资不包括国家停止减免税的20种商品、汽车、生产性设备、生产性原材料及半成品等。

捐赠物资应为新品，在捐赠物资内不得夹带有害环境、公共卫生和社会道德及政治渗透等违禁物品。

(三)本征免性质不适用：

1. 无偿援助物资，征免性质代码"201"。

2. 残疾人专用品、残疾人专用设备及专用生产设备，征免性质代码"413"。

●进口抗艾滋病病毒药品

进口抗艾滋病病毒药品指对卫生部委托进口的抗艾滋病病毒药物免征进口关税和进口环节增值税政策。

本征免性质代码"803"，简称"抗艾滋病药品"。

●享受进口税收优惠政策和进口种子（苗）、种畜（禽）、鱼种（苗）和种用野生动植物种源

享受进口税收优惠政策的进口种子（苗）、种畜（禽）、鱼种（苗）和种用野生动植物种源指根据规定进口种子（苗）、种畜（禽）、鱼种（苗）和种用野生动植物种源免征进口环节增值税政策。

本征免性质代码"811"，简称"种苗种畜"。

●中央储备粮油免征进口环节增值税政策

中央储备粮油免征进口环节增值税政策指对中储粮总公司及其子公司在免税进口额度范围内进口的粮油，予以免征进口环节增值税。

本征免性质代码"818"，简称"中央储备粮油"。

●进口科研教学用图书资料

一、定义及代码

进口科研教学用图书资料指根据规定对中国图书进出口（集团）总公司等7家图书进出口公司为科研单位、大专院校进口用于科研、教学的图书、文献、报刊及其他资料（包括只读光盘、缩微平片、胶卷、地球资料卫星照片、科技和教学声像制品）免征进口环节增值税。

本征免性质代码"819"，简称"科教图书"。

二、适用范围

享受该项进口税收优惠政策的企业为中国图书进出口（集团）总公司及其具有独立法人资格的子公司、中国经济图书进出口公司、中国教育图书进出口公司、中国出版对外贸易总公司、北京中科进出口有限责任公司、中国科技资料进出口总公司和中国国际图书贸易集团有限公司等7家图书进出口公司。

●经核准的航空公司进口维修用航空器材

一、定义及代码

经核准的航空公司进口维修用航空器材是指经国务院批准，由民航总局确认的营运国际和港澳航线的国内航空公司进口的维修用航空器材。

本征免性质代码"888"，简称"航材减免"。

二、适用范围

(一)本征免性质仅限经国务院批准，由民航总局确认的营运国际和港澳航线的国内航空公司。

(二)进口维修用航空器材限于用于维修飞机机载设备及其零部件所进口的航空器材，以及维修飞机所必需的消耗材料，包括：

1. 发动机及其零部件、附件。

2. 辅助动力装置(APU)及其零部件、附件。

3. 起落架及其零部件、附件。

4. 其他飞机零部件、附件。

5. 维修飞机所必需的润滑油、油漆。

6. 上述设备、装置和附件送境外维修时所更换的零部件及附件。

进口维修用的飞机驾驶舱内的设备及其零部件，以及固定安装在飞机上且为飞行和载客、载货运输所必需的设备及其零部件(例如，飞机上的液晶显示屏、机上用照明灯具、飞机轮胎等)，属于可享受进口税收优惠政策的商品范围。但移动式餐车等非固定安装在飞机上的物品不属于减税商品范围。

●国务院特准减免税的进出口货物

一、定义及代码

国务院特准减免税的进出口货物指经国务院特案批准予以减免税的进出口货物，

本征免性质代码"898"，简称"国批减免"。

二、适用范围

本征免性质仅限国务院特案批准予以减免税的特殊行业或进出口货物，如国家计划内进口的化肥、饲料、图书资料、种子(苗)、种畜(禽)、鱼苗和非盈利性种用野生动植物、航空公司进口或租赁的飞机等。

●例外减免税进出口货物

一、定义及代码

例外减免税进出口货物指无法归入以上各类列名征免性质的减免税进出口货物。

本征免性质代码"999"，简称"例外减免"。

二、管理规定

(一)按海关总署文件或通知的具体内容执行。

(二)减免税办理程序

申请减免税的企业或单位持批准文件和其他有关单证，到所在地海关办理减免税审批手续。

海关核发"进出口货物征免税证明"，进出口地海关凭以办理货物的减免税手续。

征减免税方式代码表

征减免税方式代码	征减免税方式名称	征减免税方式代码	征减免税方式名称	征减免税方式代码	征减免税方式名称
1	照章征税	4	特案	7	保函
2	折半征税	5	随征免性质	8	折半补税
3	全免	6	保证金	9	全额退税

征减免税方式代码表说明

征减免税方式是指进出口货物征税、减税、免税或特案处理的方式。

一、征减免税方式的分类

征减免税方式分为照章征税、折半征税、全免、特案减免、随征免性质、保证金、保证函、折半补税，各种方式分别用不同的代码标定。

二、征减免税方式代码说明

（一）征减免税方式分为照章征税，折半征税、全免、特案、随征免性质、保证金、保函、折半补税及出口全额退税九种。

（二）征减免税方式代码表说明

照章征税：代码“1”，进出口货物依照法定税率计征各类税、费。

折半征税：代码“2”，依照海关签发的“进出口货物征免税证明”或海关总署的通知，对进出口货物依照法定税率折半征收税款。

全免：代码“3”，依照海关签发的“进出口货物征免税证明”或其他有关规定，对进出口货物免征关税和增值税，消费税是否免征依批文规定办理。

特案：代码“4”，依照海关签发的“进出口货物征免税证明”或其他有关规定所规定的税率或完税价计征关税、增值税和消费税。

随征免性质：代码“5”，用于特定监管方式进出口的货物按特殊计税公式或税率计征关税、增值税和消费税。

保证金：代码“6”：经海关准予担保放行的货物收取保证金。

保证函：代码“7”，经海关准予担保放行的货物凭保证函办理。

运输方式代码表

运输方式代码	运输方式名称	运输方式代码	运输方式名称
0	非保税区	8	保税仓库
1	监管仓库	9	其它运输
2	水路运输	H	边境特殊海关作业区
3	铁路运输	T	综合实验区
4	公路运输	W	物流中心
5	航空运输	X	物流园区
6	邮件运输	Y	保税港区
7	保税区	Z	出口加工区

运输方式代码表说明

一、定义

运输方式包括实际运输方式和海关规定的特殊运输方式，前者指货物实际进出境的运输方式，按进出境所使用的运输工具分类；后者指货物无实际进出境的运输方式，按货物在境内的流向分类。

二、运输方式分类说明

(一)水路运输：代码“2” ，指利用船舶在国内外港口之间，通过固定的航区和航线进行货物运输的一种方式。

(二)铁路运输：代码“3” ，指利用铁路承担进出口货物运输的一种方式。

(三)公路运输：代码“4” ，指利用汽车承担进出口货物运输的一种方式。

(四)航空运输：代码“5” ，指利用航空器承运进出口货物的一种方式。

(五)邮件运输：代码“6” ，指通过邮局寄运货物进出口的一种方式。

(六)其他运输：代码 “9” ，除上述几种运输方式以外的货物进出口运输方式。如利用人扛、驮畜、输油管道、输水管道和输电网等方式进出口货物的运输方式。

(七)用于标志境内进出和退回保税区或保税仓库等区域的运输方式代码如下：

非保税区：代码“0”，指境内非保税区运入保税区和保税区退区(退运境内)货物。

监管仓库：代码“1”，指境内存入出口监管仓和出口监管仓退仓货物。

保税区：代码“7”，指保税区运往境内非保税区货物。

保税仓库：代码“8”，指保税仓库转内销货物。

边境特殊海关作业区：代码“H”，指境内运入深港西部通道港方口岸区的货物。

综合实验区：代码“T”，用于横琴新区或平潭综合实验区区内企业按选择性征关税的货物和上述区域与境内区外间经指定申报通道往来的货物(即二线区外申报时使用)。横琴新区与平潭综合实验区与境外之间进出的货物、与境内特殊监管区域或保税监管场所间流转的保税货物，以及区内加工企业与区外加工企业间往来的保税货物，其报关单或备案清单的运输方式应按《海关总署关于修订<中华人民共和国海关进出口货物报关单填制规范>的公告》（公告〔2009〕6 号）和《海关总署关于海关特殊监管区域管理问题的公告》（公告〔2010〕22 号）申报。

物流中心：代码“W”，指从境内运入保税物流中心或从保税物流中心运往境内非保税物流中心的货物。

物流园区：代码“X”，指从境内运入保税物流园区或从园区运往境内的货物。

保税港区：代码”Y”，指从保税港区(不包括直通港区)运往区外和区外运入保税港区的货物。

出口加工区：代码“Z”指出口加工区运往境内加工区外和区外运入出口加工区的货物。

关区代码表

关区代码	关区名称	关区简称	关区代码	关区名称	关区简称
0000	海关总署/全部关区	海关总署	0403	唐山海关	唐山海关
0100	北京关区	北京关区	0404	廊坊海关	廊坊海关
0101	机场单证	机场单证	0405	保定海关	保定海关
0102	京监管处	京监管处	0406	石家庄海关驻邯郸办事处	石关邯办
0103	京关展览	京关展览	0407	秦加工区	秦加工区
0104	京一处	京一处	0408	中华人民共和国沧州海关	沧州海关
0105	京二处	京二处	0409	廊坊海关驻出口加工区办事处	廊加工区
0106	京关关税	京关关税	0410	石家庄海关驻机场办事处	石机场办
0107	机场库区	机场库区	0411	中华人民共和国张家口海关	张家口关
0108	京通关处	京通关处	0412	石家庄海关驻曹妃甸港区办事处	石关曹办
0109	机场旅检	机场旅检	0413	邢台海关	邢台海关
0110	平谷海关	平谷海关	0414	曹妃甸综合保税区	曹综保区
0111	京五里店	京五里店	0500	太原海关	太原海关
0112	京邮办处	京邮办处	0501	并关监管	并关监管
0113	京中关村	京中关村	0502	太原机场海关	并机场关
0114	京国际局	京国际局	0503	大同海关	大同海关
0115	京东郊站	京东郊站	0504	侯马海关	侯马海关
0116	京信	京信	0505	山西方略保税物流中心	方略物流
0117	京开发区	京开发区	0506	太原武宿综合保税区	太原综保
0118	十八里店	十八里店	0600	满洲里关	满洲里关
0119	机场物流	机场物流	0601	海拉尔关	海拉尔关
0121	京稽查处	京稽查处	0602	额尔古纳	额尔古纳
0123	机场调技	机场调技	0603	满十八里	满十八里
0124	北京站	北京站	0604	满赤峰办	满赤峰办
0125	西客站	西客站	0605	满通辽办	满通辽办
0126	京加工区	京加工区	0606	满哈沙特	满哈沙特
0127	京快件	京快件	0607	满室韦	满室韦
0128	京顺义办	京顺义办	0608	满互贸区	满互贸区
0129	北京海关天竺综合保税区	京关天竺	0609	满铁路	满铁路
0130	北京亦庄保税物流中心	亦庄物流	0610	满市区	满市区
0200	天津关区	天津关区	0611	满洲里海关驻西郊机场办事处	满关机办
0201	天津海关	天津海关	0700	呼特关区	呼特关区
0202	新港海关	新港海关	0701	呼和浩特	呼和浩特
0203	津开发区	津开发区	0702	二连海关	二连海关
0204	东港海关	东港海关	0703	包头海关	包头海关
0205	津塘沽办	津塘沽办	0704	呼关邮办	呼关邮办
0206	津驻邮办	津驻邮办	0705	二连公路	二连公路
0207	津机场办	津机场办	0706	包头海关驻国际集装箱中转站办事处	包头箱站
0208	津保税区	津保税区	0707	额济纳海关	额济纳关
0209	蓟县海关	蓟县海关	0708	乌拉特海关	乌拉特关
0210	武清海关	武清海关	0709	满都拉口岸	满达口岸
0211	津加工区	津加工区	0710	东乌海关	东乌海关
0212	天津保税物流园区	津物流园	0711	呼和浩特海关驻白塔机场办事处	呼关机办
0213	天津东疆保税港区	天津东疆	0712	呼和浩特海关驻出口加工区办事处	呼加工区
0214	天津滨海新区综合保税区	津滨综保	0713	鄂尔多斯海关	鄂尔多斯
0215	天津机场海关快件监管中心	津机快件	0800	沈阳关区	沈阳关区
0216	天津经济技术开发区保税物流中心	津开物流	0801	沈阳海关	沈阳海关
0217	天津东疆保税港区海关（港区）	东疆港区	0802	锦州海关	锦州海关
0218	静海海关	静海海关	0803	沈驻邮办	沈驻邮办
0220	津关税处	津关税处	0804	沈驻抚顺	沈驻抚顺
0400	石家庄区	石家庄区	0805	沈开发区	沈开发区
0401	石家庄关	石家庄关	0806	沈驻辽阳	沈驻辽阳
0402	秦皇岛关	秦皇岛关	0807	沈机场办	沈机场办

关区代码	关区名称	关区简称	关区代码	关区名称	关区简称
0808	沈阳综合保税区海关	沈综保区	1559	延吉邮办	延吉邮办
0809	沈阳国际快件监管中心	沈快件	1569	延吉海关驻机场办事处	延吉机办
0810	葫芦岛关	葫芦岛关	1591	长春邮办	长春邮办
0811	沈阳海关驻辽宁沈阳出口加工区办事处	辽沈加区	1593	长白邮办	长白邮办
0812	沈阳海关驻张士出口加工区办事处	沈张出加	1595	图们邮办	图们邮办
0813	沈阳保税物流中心	沈阳物流	1596	集安邮办	集安邮办
0900	大连海关	大连海关	1900	哈尔滨区	哈尔滨区
0901	大连港湾海关	大连港湾	1901	哈尔滨关	哈尔滨关
0902	大连机场	大连机场	1902	绥关铁路	绥关铁路
0903	连开发区	连开发区	1903	黑河海关	黑河海关
0904	连加工区	连加工区	1904	同江海关	同江海关
0905	大窑湾海关驻北良港办事处	窑北良办	1905	佳木斯关	佳木斯关
0906	连保税区	连保税区	1906	牡丹江关	牡丹江关
0907	大连保税物流园区	连物流园	1907	东宁海关	东宁海关
0908	连大窑湾	连大窑湾	1908	逊克海关	逊克海关
0909	大连邮办	大连邮办	1909	齐齐哈尔	齐齐哈尔
0910	大连大窑湾保税港区	连保税港	1910	大庆海关	大庆海关
0912	大连国际快件监管中心	大连快件	1911	密山海关	密山海关
0915	庄河海关	庄河海关	1912	虎林海关	虎林海关
0917	大连海关驻旅顺办事处	大连旅办	1913	富锦海关	富锦海关
0930	丹东海关	丹东海关	1914	抚远海关	抚远海关
0931	大连海关驻本溪办事处	大连本办	1915	漠河海关	漠河海关
0932	太平湾海关	丹太平湾	1916	萝北海关	萝北海关
0940	营口海关	营口海关	1917	嘉荫海关	嘉荫海关
0941	营口海关驻盘锦办事处	营盘锦办	1918	饶河海关	饶河海关
0950	鲅鱼圈关	鲅鱼圈关	1919	哈内陆港	哈内陆港
0951	营口港保税物流中心	营港物流	1920	哈开发区	哈开发区
0960	大东港关	大东港关	1921	黑龙江绥芬河综合保税区	绥综保区
0980	鞍山海关	鞍山海关	1922	哈关邮办	哈关邮办
1500	长春关区	长春关区	1923	哈关车办	哈关车办
1501	长春海关	长春海关	1924	哈关机办	哈关机办
1502	长开发区	长开发区	1925	绥关公路	绥关公路
1503	长白海关	长白海关	2200	上海海关	上海海关
1504	临江海关	临江海关	2201	浦江海关	浦江海关
1505	图们海关	图们海关	2202	吴淞海关	吴淞海关
1506	集安海关	集安海关	2203	沪机场关	沪机场关
1507	珲春海关	珲春海关	2204	闵开发区	闵开发区
1508	吉林海关	吉林海关	2205	沪车站办	沪车站办
1509	延吉海关	延吉海关	2206	沪邮局办	沪邮局办
1510	长春兴隆综合保税区	长春综保	2207	沪稽查处	沪稽查处
1511	长春机办	长春机办	2208	宝山海关	宝山海关
1515	图们车办	图们车办	2209	龙吴海关	龙吴海关
1516	集海关村	集海关村	2210	浦东海关	浦东海关
1517	珲长岭子	珲长岭子	2211	卢湾监管	卢湾监管
1518	吉林海关驻车站办事处	吉关车办	2212	奉贤海关	奉贤海关
1519	延吉三合	延吉三合	2213	莘庄海关	莘庄海关
1521	一汽场站	一汽场站	2214	漕河泾发	漕河泾发
1525	图们桥办	图们桥办	2215	上海海关驻上海世博会园区监管服务中心	世博中心
1526	集安青石	集安青石	2216	上海浦东机场综合保税区	浦机综保
1527	珲春圈河	珲春圈河	2217	嘉定海关	嘉定海关
1529	延吉南坪	延吉南坪	2218	外高桥关	外高桥关
1531	长春东站	长春东站	2219	杨浦监管	杨浦监管
1537	珲沙坨子	珲沙坨子	2220	金山海关	金山海关
1539	延开山屯	延开山屯	2221	松江海关	松江海关
1547	珲加工区	珲加工区	2222	青浦海关	青浦海关
1549	延古城里	延古城里	2223	南汇海关	南汇海关
1557	珲春海关驻车站办事处	珲春车办	2224	崇明海关	崇明海关

关区代码	关区名称	关区简称	关区代码	关区名称	关区简称
2225	外港海关	外港海关	2332	锡锡山办	锡锡山办
2226	贸易网点	贸易网点	2333	南通关办	南通关办
2227	普陀区站	普陀区站	2335	昆山加工	昆山加工
2228	长宁区站	长宁区站	2336	苏园加工	苏园加工
2229	航交办	航交办	2337	连开发办	连开发办
2230	徐汇区站	徐汇区站	2338	苏关邮办	苏关邮办
2231	洋山海关驻市内报关点	洋山市内	2339	南通海关驻出口加工区办事处	南通加工
2232	嘉定海关驻出口加工区办事处	嘉定出口	2340	无锡海关驻出口加工区办事处	无锡加工
2233	浦东机场	浦东机场	2341	连云港海关驻连云港出口加工区办事处	连关加工
2234	沪钻交所	沪钻交所	2342	南京海关驻江苏南京出口加工区办事处	南京加工
2235	松江加工	松江加工	2343	南京海关驻江苏南京出口加工区（南区）办事处	宁南加工
2236	洋山海关驻芦潮港铁路集装箱中心站监管点	洋山芦潮	2344	苏州海关驻苏州高新区出口加工区办事处	苏高加工
2237	上海松江出口加工区 B 区	松江 B 区	2345	镇江海关驻镇江出口加工区办事处	镇江加工
2238	上海青浦出口加工区	青浦加工	2346	苏州工业园区海关保税物流中心	苏园物流
2239	上海闵行出口加工区	闵行加工	2347	苏州工业园区海关驻苏州工业园区出口加工区B区办事处	苏园B区
2240	上海漕河泾出口加工区	漕河泾加	2348	张家港保税物流园区	张物流园
2241	沪业一处	沪业一处	2349	南京海关驻邮局办事处	宁关邮办
2242	沪业二处	沪业二处	2350	苏州高新区保税物流中心（B型）	苏高物流
2243	沪业三处	沪业三处	2351	南京海关驻江宁经济技术开发区办事处	江宁办
2244	上海快件	上海快件	2352	南京龙潭保税物流中心(B型)	龙潭物流
2245	沪金桥办	沪金桥办	2353	常州海关驻出口加工区办事处	常关出加
2246	上海保税物流园区	保税物流	2354	扬州海关驻出口加工区办事处	扬关出加
2247	上海海关驻化学工业区办事处	沪化工区	2355	常熟海关驻出口加工区办事处	常熟出加
2248	洋山海关（港区）	洋山港区	2356	吴江海关驻出口加工区办事处	吴江出加
2249	洋山海关（保税）	洋山保税	2357	常州海关驻武进办事处	常关武办
2300	南京海关	南京海关	2358	苏州工业园综合保税区	苏园保税
2301	连云港关	连云港关	2359	苏州海关驻吴中出口加工区办事处	吴中出加
2302	南通海关	南通海关	2360	盐城海关驻大丰港办事处	盐关港办
2303	苏州海关	苏州海关	2361	淮安海关驻出口加工区办事处	淮关出加
2304	无锡海关	无锡海关	2362	江阴保税物流中心	澄关物流
2305	张家港关	张家港关	2363	太仓保税物流中心	太仓物流
2306	常州海关	常州海关	2364	江苏武进出口加工区	武进出加
2307	镇江海关	镇江海关	2365	张家港保税港区	张保税港
2308	新生圩关	新生圩关	2366	中华人民共和国宿迁海关	宿迁海关
2309	盐城海关	盐城海关	2367	泰州海关驻出口加工区办事处	泰出加区
2310	扬州海关	扬州海关	2368	苏州高新技术产业开发区综合保税区	苏高综保
2311	徐州海关	徐州海关	2369	昆山综合保税区	昆山综保
2312	江阴海关	江阴海关	2370	连云港保税物流中心	连关物流
2313	张保税区	张保税区	2371	盐城海关驻机场办事处	盐机场办
2314	苏工业区	苏工业区	2372	盐城综合保税区	盐城综保
2315	淮安海关	淮安海关	2373	淮安综合保税区	淮安综保
2316	泰州海关	泰州海关	2374	无锡高新区综合保税区	锡高综保
2317	禄口机办	禄口机办	2375	靖江海关	靖江海关
2318	南京现场	南京现场	2900	杭州关区	杭州关区
2319	如皋海关	如皋海关	2901	杭州海关	杭州海关
2320	无锡海关驻机场办事处	锡关机办	2903	温州海关	温州海关
2321	常溧阳办	常溧阳办	2904	舟山海关	舟山海关
2322	镇丹阳办	镇丹阳办	2905	台州海关	台州海关
2323	金陵海关	金陵海关	2906	绍兴海关	绍兴海关
2324	常熟海关	常熟海关	2907	湖州海关	湖州海关
2325	昆山海关	昆山海关	2908	嘉兴海关	嘉兴海关
2326	吴江海关	吴江海关	2909	杭经开关	杭经开关
2327	太仓海关	太仓海关	2910	杭州萧山机场海关	杭州机场
2328	苏吴县办	苏吴县办	2911	杭关邮办	杭关邮办
2329	通启东办	通启东办	2912	杭关萧办	杭关萧办
2330	泰州海关驻泰兴办事处	泰泰兴办	2915	丽水海关	丽水海关
2331	锡宜兴办	锡宜兴办	2916	杭州萧山机场海关快件监管中心	杭州快件

关区代码	关区名称	关区简称	关区代码	关区名称	关区简称
2917	衢州海关	衢州海关	3308	池州海关	池州海关
2918	杭关余办	杭关余办	3309	滁州海关	滁州海关
2919	杭富阳办	杭富阳办	3310	合肥现场	合肥现场
2920	金华海关	金华海关	3311	合肥海关驻新桥机场办事处	合肥机场
2921	义乌海关	义乌海关	3312	芜湖海关驻出口加工区办事处	芜关加办
2922	金华海关驻永康办事处	金关永办	3313	合肥出口加工区	合关加办
2928	杭州跨境电子商务海关监管中心	杭关电商	3500	福州关区	福州关区
2931	温关邮办	温关邮办	3501	马尾海关	马尾海关
2932	温经开关	温经开关	3502	福清海关	福清海关
2933	温关机办	温关机办	3503	宁德海关	宁德海关
2934	温关鳌办	温关鳌办	3504	三明海关	三明海关
2935	温州海关驻瑞安办事处	温关瑞办	3505	福保税区	福保税区
2936	温州海关驻乐清办事处	温关乐办	3506	莆田海关	莆田海关
2941	舟山海关驻嵊泗办事处	舟关嵊办	3507	福关机办	福关机办
2942	舟山海关金塘监管科	舟关金塘	3508	福州新港	福州新港
2943	舟山海关驻舟山港综合保税区办事处	舟关综保	3509	福关邮办	福关邮办
2951	台州海关驻临海办事处	台关临办	3510	南平海关	南平海关
2952	台州海关驻温岭办事处	台关温办	3511	武夷山关	武夷山关
2953	台州海关驻玉环办事处	台关玉办	3512	黄岐对台小额贸易监管点	黄岐监管
2961	绍兴海关驻上虞办事处	绍关虞办	3513	福现业处	福现业处
2962	绍兴海关驻诸暨办事处	绍关诸办	3520	福州出口加工区海关	福州加工
2963	绍兴海关驻新嵊办事处	绍关新办	3521	福清出口加工区海关	福清加工
2981	嘉关乍办	嘉关乍办	3522	福州保税物流园区	福物流园
2982	嘉兴海关驻嘉善办事处	嘉关善办	3700	厦门关区	厦门关区
2983	嘉兴海关驻出口加工区办事处	嘉兴加工	3701	厦门海关	厦门海关
2984	嘉兴海关驻海宁办事处	嘉关宁办	3702	泉州海关	泉州海关
2985	嘉兴海关驻桐乡办事处	嘉兴桐办	3703	漳州海关	漳州海关
2986	嘉兴海关驻出口加工区（B）区办事处	嘉加B区	3704	东山海关	东山海关
2991	杭州经济技术开发区海关驻出口加工区办事处	杭加工区	3705	泉州海关驻石狮办事处	泉石狮办
2992	杭州保税物流中心（B型）	杭州物流	3706	龙岩海关	龙岩海关
3100	宁波关区	宁波关区	3707	泉州海关驻肖厝办事处	泉肖厝办
3101	宁波海关	宁波海关	3708	厦门海沧保税港区港口功能区	海沧港区
3102	镇海海关	镇海海关	3709	厦门海沧保税港区保税加工物流功能区	海沧保税
3103	甬开发区	甬开发区	3710	厦高崎办	厦高崎办
3104	北仑海关	北仑海关	3711	厦门东渡海关	东渡海关
3105	甬保税区	甬保税区	3712	厦海沧办	厦海沧办
3106	大榭海关	大榭海关	3713	厦驻邮办	厦驻邮办
3107	甬驻余办	甬驻余办	3714	象屿保税	象屿保税
3108	甬驻慈办	甬驻慈办	3715	高崎机场海关	机场海关
3109	宁波机场海关	甬机场关	3716	厦同安办	厦同安办
3110	象山海关	象山海关	3717	象屿保税物流园区	厦物流园
3111	宁波保税区海关驻出口加工区办事处	甬加工区	3718	泉州出口加工区	泉州加工
3112	宁波保税物流园区	甬物流区	3719	厦门加工	厦门加工
3113	浙江慈溪出口加工区	慈加工区	3720	厦门火炬（翔安）保税物流中心	厦门物流
3114	宁波海关驻鄞州办事处	甬驻鄞办	3722	厦门海关驻同安办事处大嶝监管科	大嶝监管
3115	宁波海关驻鄞州办事处栎社保税物流中心	栎社物流	3723	泉州海关驻晋江办事处	泉晋江办
3116	宁波梅山保税港区港口功能区	梅山港区	3724	厦门海关驻国际邮轮港办事处	邮轮办
3117	宁波梅山保税港区保税加工物流功能区	梅山保税	3777	厦稽查处	厦稽查处
3118	宁波栎社国际机场快件监管中心	宁波快件	3788	厦侦查局	厦侦查局
3300	合肥海关	合肥海关	4000	南昌关区	南昌关区
3301	芜湖海关	芜湖海关	4001	南昌海关	南昌海关
3302	安庆海关	安庆海关	4002	九江海关	九江海关
3303	马鞍山海关	马鞍山关	4003	赣州海关	赣州海关
3304	黄山海关	黄山海关	4004	景德镇关	景德镇关
3305	蚌埠海关	蚌埠海关	4005	吉安海关	吉安海关
3306	铜陵海关	铜陵海关	4006	昌北机办	昌北机办
3307	阜阳海关	阜阳海关	4007	南昌海关驻高新技术产业开发区办事处	洪关高新

关区代码	关区名称	关区简称	关区代码	关区名称	关区简称
4008	南昌海关驻龙南办事处	洪关龙南	4249	潍坊海关驻出口加工区办事处	潍加工区
4009	新余海关	新余海关	4250	青岛西海岸出口加工区	青西加区
4010	九江海关驻出口加工区办事处	浔关区办	4251	淄博保税物流中心	淄博物流
4011	南昌海关驻出口加工区办事处	洪关区办	4253	日照保税物流中心	日照物流
4012	赣州海关驻出口加工区办事处	虔关区办	4254	青岛保税物流中心	青岛物流
4013	南昌海关驻上饶办事处	洪关上饶	4255	潍坊海关驻寿光办事处	潍寿光办
4014	南昌保税物流中心	南昌物流	4258	青岛前湾保税港区	青保税港
4015	井冈山出口加工区	吉井加工	4300	济南海关	济南海关
4200	青岛海关	青岛海关	4301	现场业务处	现场业务
4201	烟台海关	烟台海关	4302	济南海关驻机场办事处	济机场办
4202	日照海关	日照海关	4303	济南海关驻出口加工区办事处	济加工区
4203	龙口海关	龙口海关	4305	济南海关驻邮局办事处	济邮局办
4204	威海海关	威海海关	4310	潍坊海关	潍坊海关
4205	济南海关	济南海关	4311	潍诸城办	潍诸城办
4206	潍坊海关	潍坊海关	4312	潍坊海关驻出口加工区办事处	潍加工区
4207	淄博海关	淄博海关	4313	潍坊海关驻寿光办事处	潍寿光办
4208	烟台海关驻出口加工区B区办事处	烟加B区	4320	淄博海关	淄博海关
4209	荣成海关	荣成海关	4321	淄博保税物流中心	淄博物流
4210	青保税区	青保税区	4330	泰安海关	泰安海关
4211	济宁海关	济宁海关	4341	济南海关驻机场办事处快件现场	济关快件
4212	泰安海关	泰安海关	4350	东营海关	东营海关
4213	临沂海关	临沂海关	4360	济南海关驻聊城办事处	济聊城办
4214	青前湾港	青前湾港	4370	德州海关	德州海关
4215	青菏泽办	青菏泽办	4380	济南海关驻滨州办事处	济滨州办
4216	东营海关	东营海关	4390	济南海关驻莱芜办事处	济莱芜办
4217	青枣庄办	青枣庄办	4600	郑州关区	郑州关区
4218	青开发区	青开发区	4601	郑州海关	郑州海关
4219	蓬莱海关	蓬莱海关	4602	洛阳海关	洛阳海关
4220	青机场关	青机场关	4603	南阳海关	南阳海关
4221	烟机场办	烟机场办	4604	郑州机办	郑州机办
4222	莱州海关	莱州海关	4605	郑州邮办	郑州邮办
4223	青邮局办	青邮局办	4606	郑铁东办	郑铁东办
4224	龙长岛办	龙长岛办	4607	安阳海关	安阳海关
4225	威开发区	威开发区	4608	郑州海关驻出口加工区办事处	郑加工区
4226	青岛海关驻聊城办事处	青聊城办	4609	郑州海关驻商丘办事处	郑关商办
4227	青岛大港	青岛大港	4610	周口海关	周口海关
4228	烟关快件	烟关快件	4611	河南保税物流中心	河南物流
4229	德州海关	德州海关	4612	郑州新郑综合保税区	新郑综保
4230	青岛保税物流园区	青物流园	4613	郑州海关航空进出境快件监管中心	郑关快件
4231	烟开发区	烟开发区	4614	焦作海关	焦作海关
4232	日岚山办	日岚山办	4615	三门峡海关	三门峡关
4233	济南海关驻机场办事处	济机场办	4616	新乡海关	新乡海关
4234	济南海关驻出口加工区办事处	济加工区	4700	武汉海关	武汉海关
4235	济南海关驻邮局办事处	济邮局办	4701	宜昌海关	宜昌海关
4236	荣成海关驻龙眼港办事处	荣龙眼办	4702	荆州海关	荆州海关
4237	现场业务处	现场业务	4703	襄阳海关	襄阳海关
4238	威海关驻威海邮局办事处	威海快件	4704	黄石海关	黄石海关
4239	潍诸城办	潍诸城办	4705	武汉沌口	武汉沌口
4240	青岛海关快件监管中心	青关快件	4706	宜三峡办	宜三峡办
4241	烟加工区	烟加工区	4707	鄂加工区	鄂加工区
4242	威加工区	威加工区	4708	武汉海关现场业务处	武业务处
4243	济宁海关驻曲阜办事处	济曲阜办	4709	武汉海关驻江汉办事处东西湖保税物流中心	武江物流
4244	青岛海关驻滨州办事处	青滨州办	4710	武关货管	武关货管
4245	烟台海关驻邮局办事处	烟台邮办	4711	武关江岸	武关江岸
4246	青加工区	青加工区	4712	武关机场	武关机场
4247	威海海关驻机场办事处	威机场办	4713	武关邮办	武关邮办
4248	青岛海关驻莱芜办事处	青莱芜办	4716	十堰海关	十堰海关

关区代码	关区名称	关区简称	关区代码	关区名称	关区简称
4718	武汉东湖新技术开发区海关	东湖海关	5146	亚运物资通关服务中心	穗亚运会
4719	武汉东湖综合保税区	东湖综保	5147	穗邮办监	穗邮办监
4900	长沙关区	长沙关区	5148	穗大郎站	穗大郎站
4901	衡阳海关	衡阳海关	5149	大铲海关	大铲海关
4902	岳阳海关	岳阳海关	5150	顺德海关	顺德海关
4903	长沙海关驻郴州办事处	湘关郴办	5151	顺德海关加工贸易监管科	顺德保税
4904	常德海关	常德海关	5152	顺德食出	顺德食出
4905	长沙海关	长沙海关	5153	顺德车场	顺德车场
4906	株洲海关	株洲海关	5154	北窖车场	北窖车场
4907	韶山海关	韶山海关	5155	顺德旅检	顺德旅检
4908	湘关机办	湘关机办	5157	顺德陈村港澳货柜车检查场	陈村车场
4909	株洲海关驻醴陵办事处	株关醴办	5158	顺德勒流	顺德勒流
4910	长沙海关驻郴州出口加工区办事处	郴加工区	5160	番禺海关	番禺海关
4911	衡阳海关永州监管组	衡关永办	5161	沙湾车场	沙湾车场
4913	长沙金霞保税物流中心	金霞物流	5162	番禺旅检	番禺旅检
4914	张家界海关	张家界关	5163	番禺货柜	番禺货柜
5000	广东分署	广东分署	5164	番禺船舶	番禺船舶
5100	广州海关	广州海关	5165	南沙旅检	南沙旅检
5101	内港新风	内港新风	5166	广州南沙保税港区	南沙保税
5103	清远海关	清远海关	5167	南沙货港	南沙货港
5104	清远英德	清远英德	5168	广东南沙出口加工区	南沙加工
5105	广州海关现场业务处	广州现场	5169	南沙海关	南沙海关
5106	南沙海关小虎监管点	南沙小虎	5170	肇庆海关	肇庆海关
5107	肇庆高新区大旺进出境货运车辆检查场	肇庆大旺	5171	肇庆高要	肇庆高要
5108	肇庆德庆	肇庆德庆	5172	肇庆车场	肇庆车场
5109	内港滘心	内港滘心	5173	肇庆新港	肇庆新港
5110	南海海关	南海海关	5174	肇庆旅检	肇庆旅检
5111	南海官窑	南海官窑	5175	肇庆码头	肇庆码头
5112	南海九江	南海九江	5176	肇庆四会	肇庆四会
5113	南海北村	南海北村	5177	肇庆三榕	肇庆三榕
5114	南海平洲	南海平洲	5178	云浮海关	云浮海关
5116	南海业务	南海业务	5179	罗定海关	罗定海关
5117	桂江货柜车场	桂江车场	5180	佛山海关	佛山海关
5118	平洲旅检	平洲旅检	5181	高明海关	高明海关
5119	南海三山	南海三山	5182	佛山澜石	佛山澜石
5120	广州内港	广州内港	5183	三水码头	三水码头
5121	内港芳村	内港芳村	5184	佛山窖口	佛山窖口
5122	内港洲嘴	内港洲嘴	5185	佛山海关快件监管现场	佛山快件
5123	内港四仓	内港四仓	5186	佛山保税	佛山保税
5125	从化海关	从化海关	5187	佛山车场	佛山车场
5126	内港赤航	内港赤航	5188	佛山火车	佛山火车
5130	广州萝岗	广州萝岗	5189	佛山新港	佛山新港
5131	花都海关	花都海关	5190	韶关海关	韶关海关
5132	花都码头	花都码头	5191	韶关乐昌	韶关乐昌
5133	萝岗石牌	萝岗石牌	5192	三水海关	三水海关
5134	穗保税处	穗保税处	5193	三水车场	三水车场
5135	广州海关现场业务处驻市政务中心监管点	穗现场处	5194	三水港	三水港
5136	穗统计处	穗统计处	5195	审单中心	审单中心
5137	穗价格处	穗价格处	5196	云浮新港	云浮新港
5138	高明食出	高明食出	5197	广州联邦快递亚太转运中心	转运中心
5139	穗监管处	穗监管处	5198	穗河源关	穗河源关
5140	穗关税处	穗关税处	5199	穗技术处	穗技术处
5141	广州机场	广州机场	5200	黄埔关区	黄埔关区
5142	民航快件	民航快件	5201	黄埔老港海关	埔老港关
5143	广州车站	广州车站	5202	黄埔新港海关	埔新港关
5144	穗州头咀	穗州头咀	5203	新塘海关	新塘海关
5145	广州邮办	广州邮办	5204	东莞海关	东莞海关

关区代码	关区名称	关区简称	关区代码	关区名称	关区简称
5205	太平海关	太平海关	5342	深红海办	深红海办
5206	惠州海关	惠州海关	5343	深圳盐田港保税物流园区	深盐物流
5207	黄埔海关驻凤岗办事处	埔凤岗办	5344	惠州港海关驻大亚湾石化区办事处	惠石化办
5208	黄埔海关驻广州经济技术开发区办事处(广州保税区海关)	埔开发区	5345	深圳湾海关	深圳湾关
5210	埔红海办	埔红海办	5346	深圳机场海关快件监管中心	深机快件
5211	河源海关	河源海关	5348	大铲湾海关	深关大铲
5212	新沙海关	新沙海关	5349	深圳前海湾保税港区口岸作业区	前海港区
5213	黄埔海关驻长安办事处	埔长安办	5350	大运物资通关服务中心	大运通关
5214	黄埔海关驻常平办事处	埔常平办	5351	深圳前海湾保税港区保税功能区	前海保税
5216	黄埔海关驻沙田办事处	埔沙田办	5700	拱北关区	拱北关区
5217	东莞海关寮步车检场	寮步车场	5701	拱稽查处	拱稽查处
5218	新塘海关江龙车检场	江龙车场	5710	拱关闸办	拱关闸办
5219	广州保税物流园区	埔物流园	5720	中山海关	中山海关
5220	东莞保税物流中心（B型）	东莞物流	5721	中山港	中山港
5221	新塘车检场	新塘车场	5724	中石岐办	中石岐办
5300	深圳海关	深圳海关	5725	坦洲货场	坦洲货场
5301	皇岗海关	皇岗海关	5726	中山保税物流中心	中山物流
5302	罗湖海关	罗湖海关	5727	中小榄办	中小榄办
5303	沙头角关	沙头角关	5728	中山海关驻神湾港办事处	神湾办
5304	蛇口海关	蛇口海关	5729	中山国际快件监管中心	中山快件
5305	深关现场	深关现场	5730	拱香洲办	拱香洲办
5306	笋岗海关	笋岗海关	5740	湾仔海关	湾仔海关
5307	南头海关	南头海关	5741	湾仔船舶	湾仔船舶
5308	沙湾海关	沙湾海关	5750	九洲海关	九洲海关
5309	布吉海关	布吉海关	5760	拱白石办	拱白石办
5310	淡水办	淡水办	5770	斗门海关	斗门海关
5311	深关车站	深关车站	5771	斗井岸办	斗井岸办
5312	深监管处	深监管处	5772	斗平沙办	斗平沙办
5313	深调查局	深调查局	5780	高栏海关	高栏海关
5314	深关邮办	深关邮办	5790	拱监管处	拱监管处
5315	惠东海关	惠东海关	5791	珠澳跨境工业区珠海园区海关办事机构	拱跨工区
5316	大鹏海关	大鹏海关	5792	拱保税区	拱保税区
5317	深关机场	深关机场	5793	万山海关	万山海关
5318	梅林海关	梅林海关	5794	万山海关桂山中途监管站	桂山中途
5319	同乐海关	同乐海关	5795	横琴海关	横琴海关
5320	文锦渡关	文锦渡关	5796	澳门大学新校区临时监管区	澳大校区
5321	福保税关	福保税关	5798	拱行监邮	拱行监邮
5322	沙保税关	沙保税关	5799	拱行监处	拱行监处
5323	深审单处	深审单处	6000	汕头海关	汕头海关
5324	深审价办	深审价办	6001	汕关货一	汕关货一
5325	深关税处	深关税处	6002	汕关货二	汕关货二
5326	深数统处	深数统处	6003	汕关行邮	汕关行邮
5327	深法规处	深法规处	6004	汕关机场	汕关机场
5328	深规范处	深规范处	6006	汕关保税	汕关保税
5329	深保税处	深保税处	6007	汕关业务	汕关业务
5330	盐保税关	盐保税关	6008	汕保税区	汕保税区
5331	三门岛办	三门岛办	6009	汕关邮包	汕关邮包
5332	深财务处	深财务处	6011	揭阳海关	揭阳海关
5333	深侦查局	深侦查局	6012	汕关普宁	汕关普宁
5334	深稽查处	深稽查处	6013	澄海海关	澄海海关
5335	深技术处	深技术处	6014	广澳海关	广澳海关
5336	深办公室	深办公室	6015	南澳海关	南澳海关
5337	大亚湾核	大亚湾核	6018	汕关惠来	汕关惠来
5338	惠州港关	惠州港关	6019	汕关联成	汕关联成
5339	深加工区	深加工区	6020	汕关港口	汕关港口
5340	深关特办	深关特办	6021	潮州海关	潮州海关
5341	深惠州关	深惠州关	6022	饶平海关	饶平海关

关区代码	关区名称	关区简称	关区代码	关区名称	关区简称
6023	潮州海润快件监管中心	饶平快件	6867	鹤山稽查	鹤山稽查
6028	潮阳海关	潮阳海关	6870	阳江海关	阳江海关
6031	汕尾海关	汕尾海关	6871	阳江港	阳江港
6032	汕关海城	汕关海城	6872	阳江车场	阳江车场
6033	汕关陆丰	汕关陆丰	6877	阳江稽查	阳江稽查
6038	汕头海关外砂快件监管中心	汕关快件	7200	南宁关区	南宁关区
6041	梅州海关	梅州海关	7201	邕州海关	邕州海关
6042	梅州兴宁	梅州兴宁	7202	北海海关	北海海关
6400	海口关区	海口关区	7203	梧州海关	梧州海关
6401	海口港海关	海口港	7204	桂林海关	桂林海关
6402	三亚海关	三亚海关	7205	柳州海关	柳州海关
6403	八所海关	八所海关	7206	防城海关	防城海关
6404	洋浦经济开发区海关	洋浦区关	7207	东兴海关	东兴海关
6405	海保税区	海保税区	7208	凭祥海关	凭祥海关
6406	清澜海关	清澜海关	7209	贵港海关	贵港海关
6407	美兰机场	美兰机场	7210	水口海关	水口海关
6408	洋浦保税港区海关	洋浦港区	7211	龙邦海关	龙邦海关
6409	海口综合保税区海关	海口综保	7212	钦州海关	钦州海关
6410	马村港监管点	马村监管	7213	桂林机办	桂林机办
6411	海口海关现场业务处	海口现场	7214	北海海关驻出口加工区办事处	北海加工
6700	湛江关区	湛江关区	7215	广西钦州保税港区	南关钦保
6701	湛江海关	湛江海关	7216	南宁保税物流中心	南宁物流
6702	茂名海关	茂名海关	7217	广西钦州保税港（口岸）	钦保口岸
6703	徐闻海关	徐闻海关	7218	南宁海关驻玉林办事处	玉林办
6704	湛江南油	湛江南油	7219	广西凭祥综合保税区	南凭综保
6705	湛江水东	湛江水东	7900	成都关区	成都关区
6706	湛江吴川	湛江吴川	7901	成都海关	成都海关
6707	湛江廉江	湛江廉江	7902	成都双流机场海关	蓉机场关
6708	湛江高州	湛江高州	7903	乐山海关	乐山海关
6709	湛江信宜	湛江信宜	7904	攀枝花关	攀枝花关
6710	东海岛组	东海岛组	7905	绵阳海关	绵阳海关
6711	霞山海关	霞山海关	7906	成关邮办	成关邮办
6712	湛江霞海	湛江霞海	7907	成都自贡	成都自贡
6713	湛江机场	湛江机场	7908	成都加工	成都加工
6714	湛江博贺	湛江博贺	7909	成都公路国际物流中心监管场站	公路场站
6715	湛江进出境快件监管中心	湛江快件	7910	成都双流机场海关非邮政快件监管点	蓉机快件
6800	江门关区	江门关区	7911	成都海关驻泸州办事处	泸州办
6810	江门海关	江门海关	7912	成都海关驻宜宾办事处	宜宾办
6811	江门高沙	江门高沙	7913	成都海关驻南充办事处	南充办
6812	江门外海	江门外海	7914	绵阳出口加工区	绵阳出口
6813	江门旅检	江门旅检	7915	成都保税物流中心（B型）	成都物流
6816	江门市进出境货运车辆检查场	江门车场	7916	成都高新综合保税区	成都综保
6817	江门保税	江门保税	7919	成都空港海关	成都空港
6820	新会海关	新会海关	8000	重庆关区	重庆关区
6821	新会港	新会港	8001	重庆海关	重庆海关
6827	新会稽查	新会稽查	8002	南坪开发	南坪开发
6830	台山海关	台山海关	8003	重庆机办	重庆机办
6831	台公益港	台公益港	8004	重庆邮办	重庆邮办
6837	台山稽查	台山稽查	8005	万州海关	万州海关
6840	开平海关	开平海关	8006	重庆东站	重庆东站
6841	开平码头	开平码头	8007	九龙坡港	九龙坡港
6847	开平稽查	开平稽查	8008	渝加工区	渝加工区
6850	恩平海关	恩平海关	8009	重庆海关驻涪陵办事处	渝涪陵办
6851	恩平港	恩平港	8010	重庆两路寸滩保税港区水港功能区	寸滩水港
6857	恩平稽查	恩平稽查	8011	重庆两路寸滩保税港区空港功能区	两路空港
6860	鹤山海关	鹤山海关	8012	重庆两路寸滩保税港区保税加工物流功能区	重庆保税
6861	鹤山码头	鹤山码头	8013	重庆西永综合保税区	西永综保

关区代码	关区名称	关区简称	关区代码	关区名称	关区简称
8014	重庆西永海关	西永海关	9003	宝鸡海关	宝鸡海关
8300	贵阳海关	贵阳海关	9004	西安海关邮局办事处	西关邮办
8301	贵阳总关	贵阳总关	9005	陕西西安出口加工区A区	陕加工A
8302	贵阳海关驻机场办事处	贵关机办	9006	陕西西安出口加工区B区	陕加工B
8303	中华人民共和国遵义海关	遵义海关	9007	西安综合保税区	西安综保
8600	昆明关区	昆明关区	9008	西安高新综合保税区	高新综保
8601	昆明海关	昆明海关	9009	西安高新综合保税区口岸作业区	西安高新
8602	畹町海关	畹町海关	9400	乌关区	乌关区
8603	瑞丽海关	瑞丽海关	9401	乌鲁木齐海关现场业务处	乌关现场
8604	章凤海关	章凤海关	9402	霍尔果斯	霍尔果斯
8605	盈江海关	盈江海关	9403	吐尔尕特	吐尔尕特
8606	孟连海关	孟连海关	9404	阿拉山口	阿拉山口
8607	南伞海关	南伞海关	9405	塔城海关	塔城海关
8608	孟定海关	孟定海关	9406	伊宁海关	伊宁海关
8609	打洛海关	打洛海关	9407	吉木乃办	吉木乃办
8610	腾冲海关	腾冲海关	9408	喀什海关	喀什海关
8611	沧源海关	沧源海关	9409	红其拉甫	红其拉甫
8612	勐腊海关	勐腊海关	9410	乌鲁木齐海关隶属阿勒泰海关	阿勒泰关
8613	河口海关	河口海关	9411	塔克什肯	塔克什肯
8614	金水河关	金水河关	9412	乌拉斯太	乌拉斯太
8615	天保海关	天保海关	9413	老爷庙	老爷庙
8616	田蓬海关	田蓬海关	9414	红山嘴	红山嘴
8617	大理海关	大理海关	9415	伊尔克什	伊尔克什
8618	芒市海关	芒市海关	9416	库尔勒办	库尔勒办
8619	保山监管	保山监管	9417	乌鲁木齐机场海关	乌机场关
8620	昆明机场	昆明机场	9418	乌鲁木齐海关驻出口加工区办事处	乌加工区
8621	昆明邮办	昆明邮办	9419	都拉塔海关	都拉塔关
8622	西双版纳	西双版纳	9420	乌鲁木齐海关驻车站办事处	乌关车办
8623	昆丽江办	昆丽江办	9421	霍尔果斯国际边境合作中心海关	霍中心A
8624	思茅海关	思茅海关	9422	石河子海关	石河子关
8625	河口海关驻山腰办事处	河口山腰	9500	兰州关区	兰州关区
8626	六库监管	六库监管	9501	兰州海关	兰州海关
8627	昆明海关现场业务处开发区监管科	昆明高新	9502	酒泉海关	酒泉海关
8628	云南昆明出口加工区	昆明加工	9503	甘肃机场集团空港国际物流中心海关监管组	兰州空港
8800	拉萨海关	拉萨海关	9505	兰州海关驻天水监管组	天水监管
8801	聂拉木关	聂拉木关	9600	银川海关	银川海关
8802	日喀则关	日喀则关	9601	银川海关业务现场	银川现场
8803	狮泉河关	狮泉河关	9602	银川海关驻机场办事处	银机办
8804	拉萨机办	拉萨机办	9603	银川海关驻惠农监管组	惠农监管
8805	拉萨现场	拉萨现场	9604	银川综合保税区	银川综保
8808	吉隆海关	吉隆海关	9700	西宁关区	西宁关区
9000	西安关区	西安关区	9701	西宁海关现场	西宁海关
9001	西安综合保税区口岸作业区	西安陆港	9900	政法司	政法司
9002	咸阳机场	咸阳机场			

关区代码表说明

一、关区代码表用于填报进出口报关单的进出口口岸海关的名称。

关区代码表由两部分组成，即关区代码和关区名称。

关区代码由四位数字组成，前两位采用海关统计的直属海关关别代码，后两位为隶属海关的代码。关区名称即各口岸海关中文名称。

二、使用关区代码时应注意的问题

代码表中只有直属海关关别和代码的，可以填报直属海关名称和代码（见例 1）；如果有隶属海关关别和代码，则必须填报隶属海关关别和代码（见例 2）。

例 1：在太原海关办理货物进出口报关手续，本栏目可填报“太原海关”，代码“0050”。

例 2：在上海浦江海关办理货物进出口报关手续，本栏目不得填报“上海海关”、代码“2200”，必须填报“上海浦江海关”、代码“2201”。

国内地区代码表

国内地区代码	国内地区名称	国内地区性质标记	国内地区代码	国内地区名称	国内地区性质标记	国内地区代码	国内地区名称	国内地区性质标记
11013	中关村国家自主创新示范区(东城园)		12089	滨海新区(汉沽)	2	15023	包头高新技术产业开发区	B
11019	东城区	9	12099	滨海新区(大港)	2	15029	包头其他	
11023	中关村国家自主创新示范区(西城园)		12106	天津滨海新区综合保税区	6	15039	乌海	
11029	西城区	9	12109	东丽区	2	15049	赤峰	
11039	崇文区	9	12119	西青区	2	15059	二连	2
11049	宣武区	9	12129	津南区	2	15069	满洲里	2
11053	中关村国家自主创新示范区(朝阳园)	B	12139	北辰区	2	15079	呼伦贝尔盟	
11059	朝阳区	9	12149	宁河县	2	15089	哲里木盟	
11063	中关村国家自主创新示范区(丰台园)	B	12159	武清县	2	15099	兴安盟	
11069	丰台区	9	12169	静海县	2	15109	乌兰察布盟	
11073	中关村国家自主创新示范区(石景山园)		12179	宝坻县	2	15119	巴彦淖尔市	
11079	石景山	9	12189	蓟县	2	15129	伊克昭盟	
11083	中关村国家自主创新示范区(海淀园)	B	12909	天津其他	2	15139	阿拉善盟	
11089	海淀区其他	9	13013	石家庄高新技术产业开发实验区	B	15149	锡林郭勒盟	
11093	中关村国家自主创新示范区(门头沟园)		13019	石家庄其他	2	15909	内蒙古其他	
11099	门头沟	9	13029	唐山		21012	沈阳经济技术开发区	3
11103	中关村国家自主创新示范区(房山园)		13032	秦皇岛经济技术开发区	3	21013	沈阳南湖科技开发区	B
11109	房山	9	13035	河北秦皇岛出口加工区	2	21015	辽宁沈阳、张士出口加工区	
11113	中关村国家自主创新示范区(顺义园)		13039	秦皇岛其他	2	21016	沈阳综合保税区	
11115	北京天竺出口加工区		13049	邯郸		21019	沈阳其他	
11116	北京天竺综合保税区		13059	邢台		21022	大连经济技术开发区	3
11119	顺义	9	13063	保定高新技术产业开发区	B	21023	大连高新技术产业园区	B
11123	中关村国家自主创新示范区(昌平园)	B	13069	保定其他		21024	大连大窑湾保税区	A
11129	昌平	9	13079	张家口		21025	辽宁大连出口加工区	
11132	北京经济技术开发区	3	13089	承德		21026	大窑湾保税港区	
11133	中关村国家自主创新示范区(大兴-亦庄园)	B	13099	沧州		21027	大连保税物流园区	2
11139	大兴其他	9	13105	河北廊坊出口加工区		21029	大连其他	2
1113W	北京亦庄保税物流中心		13109	廊坊		21033	鞍山高新技术产业开发区	B
11143	中关村国家自主创新示范区(通州园)		13119	衡水		21039	鞍山其他	
11149	通县	9	13129	武安		21049	抚顺	
11153	中关村国家自主创新示范区(怀柔园)		13909	河北其他		21059	本溪	
11159	怀柔	9	14012	山西太原经济技术开发区	3	21069	丹东	
11163	中关村国家自主创新示范区(平谷园)		14013	太原高新技术产业开发区	B	21079	锦州	
11169	平谷	9	14016	太原武宿综合保税区		21089	营口	
11173	中关村国家自主创新示范区(延庆园)		14019	太原其他	2	2108W	营口港保税物流中心	
11179	延庆	9	14022	大同经济技术开发区	2	21099	阜新	
11183	中关村国家自主创新示范区(密云园)		14029	大同		21109	辽阳	
11189	密云	9	14039	阳泉		21119	盘锦	
11909	北京其他	9	14049	长治		21129	铁岭	
12019	和平区	2	14059	晋城		21139	朝阳	
12029	河东区	2	14069	朔州		21149	葫芦岛市	
12039	河西区	2	14079	雁北		21159	瓦房店	
12043	天津新技术产业园区	B	14089	忻州		21169	海城	
12049	南开区其他	2	14099	吕梁		21179	兴城	
12059	河北区	2	14102	晋中经济技术开发区	2	21189	铁法	
12069	红桥区	2	14109	晋中		21199	北票	
12072	天津经济技术开发区	3	14119	临汾		21209	开源	
12074	天津港保税区	A	1411W	山西方略保税物流中心		21909	辽宁其他	
12075	天津出口加工区		14129	运城		22012	长春经济技术开发区	3
12076	天津东疆保税港区	2	14139	古交		22013	长春南湖—南岭新技术产业园区	B
12077	天津保税物流园	2	14909	山西其他		22016	长春兴隆综合保税区	
12079	滨海新区(塘沽其他)	2	15015	内蒙古呼和浩特出口加工区		22019	长春其他	2
1207W	天津经济技术开发区保税物流中心		15019	呼和浩特		22023	吉林高新技术产业开发区	B

国内地区代码	国内地区名称	国内地区性质标记	国内地区代码	国内地区名称	国内地区性质标记	国内地区代码	国内地区名称	国内地区性质标记
22029	吉林其他		31112	上海闵行经济技术开发区	2	32115	江苏镇江出口加工区	
22039	四平		31113	上海浦江高科技园区	B	32119	镇江	
22049	辽源		31115	上海漕河泾出口加工区	2	32125	江苏泰州出口加工区	
22059	通化		31119	闵行其他	2	32129	泰州	
22069	白山		31129	宝山	2	32139	仪征	
22075	吉林珲春出口加工区		31145	上海嘉定出口加工区	2	32145	江苏常熟出口加工区	
22079	珲春	2	31149	嘉定	2	32149	常熟	
22089	图们		31159	川沙	2	32154	江苏张家港保税区	A
22099	白城		31162	上海闵行经济技术开发区（临港新城）	3	32156	张家港保税港区	
22109	延边		31166	洋山保税港区	2	32157	张家港保税物流园	
22119	公主岭		31169	南汇	2	32159	张家港其他	
22129	梅河口		31175	上海闵行出口加工区	2	32169	江阴	
22139	集安		31179	奉贤	2	3216W	江阴保税物流中心	
22149	桦甸		31185	上海松江出口加工区		32179	宿迁	
22159	九台		31189	松江	2	32189	丹阳	
22169	蛟河		31199	金山	2	32199	东台	
22179	松原		31205	上海青浦出口加工区	2	32209	兴化	
22189	延吉市		31209	青浦	2	32229	宜兴	
22909	吉林其他		31219	崇明	2	32235	江苏昆山出口加工区	
23012	哈尔滨经济技术开发区	3	31222	上海浦东新区	3	32236	昆山综合保税区	
23013	哈尔滨高技术开发区	B	31224	上海外高桥保税区	A	32239	昆山	
23019	哈尔滨其他	2	31225	上海金桥出口加工区南区		32249	启东	
23029	齐齐哈尔		31226	上海浦东机场综合保税区	2	32255	江苏吴江出口加工区	
23039	鸡西		31227	上海保税物流园区	2	32259	吴江市	
23049	鹤岗		31229	浦东其他	2	32269	太仓市	
23059	双鸭山		31909	上海其他	2	3226W	太仓保税物流中心	
23063	大庆高新技术产业开发区	B	32013	南京浦口高新技术外向型开发区	B	32909	江苏其他	
23069	大庆其他		32015	江苏南京出口加工区		33012	杭州经济技术开发区	3
23079	伊春		32019	南京其他		33013	杭州高新技术产业开发区	B
23089	佳木斯		3201W	南京龙潭港保税物流中心		33015	浙江杭州出口加工区	
23099	七台河		32023	无锡高新技术产业开发区	B	33019	杭州其他	
23109	牡丹江		32025	江苏无锡出口加工区		33022	宁波经济技术开发区	3
23119	黑河	2	32026	无锡高新区综合保税区		33023	宁波高新技术产业开发区	3
23126	绥芬河综合保税区		32029	无锡其他		33024	宁波北仑港保税区	A
23129	绥芬河	2	32039	徐州		33025	浙江宁波出口加工区	2
23139	松花江		32043	常州高新技术产业开发区	B	33026	宁波梅山保税港区	2
23149	绥化		32045	江苏常州出口加工区		33027	宁波保税物流园	2
23159	大兴安岭		32049	常州其他		33029	宁波其他	2
23169	阿城		32052	苏州工业园区	3	3302W	宁波栎社保税物流中心	
23179	同江		32053	苏州高新技术产业开发区	B	33032	温州经济技术开发区	3
23189	富锦		32055	江苏苏州工业园区加工区		33039	温州其他	2
23199	铁力		32056	苏州工业园综合保税区 苏州高新综保区		33045	浙江嘉兴出口加工区	
23209	密山		32059	苏州其他		33049	嘉兴	
23909	黑龙江其他		32062	南通经济技术开发区	3	33059	湖州	
31019	黄浦	2	32065	江苏南通出口加工区		33069	绍兴	
31029	南市	2	32069	南通其他	2	33072	金华经济技术开发区	3
31039	卢湾	2	32072	连云港经济技术开发区	3	33079	金华	
31043	上海漕河泾新技术开发区	B	32075	江苏连云港出口加工区	2	33089	衢州	
31049	徐汇其他	2	32079	连云港其他	2	33096	舟山港综合保税区	
31052	上海经济技术开发区	3	3207W	连云港保税物流中心		33099	舟山	
31059	长宁	2	32085	江苏省淮安出口加工区		33109	丽水	
31069	静安	2	32086	淮安综合保税区		33119	台州	
31079	普陀	2	32089	淮安市		33129	余姚	
3107W	上海西北物流园区保税物流中心		32096	盐城综合保税区		33139	海宁	
31089	闸北	2	32099	盐城		33149	兰溪	
31099	虹口	2	32105	江苏扬州出口加工区		33159	瑞安	
31109	杨浦	2	32109	扬州		33169	萧山	

国内地区代码	国内地区名称	国内地区性质标记	国内地区代码	国内地区名称	国内地区性质标记	国内地区代码	国内地区名称	国内地区性质标记
3316W	杭州保税物流中心		3502W	厦门火炬（翔安）保税物流中心		37062	烟台经济技术开发区	3
33179	江山		35039	莆田	8	37065	山东烟台出口加工区	
33189	义乌		35049	三明		37069	烟台其他	2
33199	东阳		35055	福建泉州出口加工区	8	37073	潍坊高新技术产业开发区	B
33205	浙江慈溪出口加工区		35059	泉州	8	37075	山东潍坊出口加工区	
33209	慈溪		35069	漳州	8	37079	潍坊其他	
33219	奉化		35079	南平	8	37089	济宁	
33229	诸暨		35089	宁德	8	37099	泰安	
33239	黄岩		35099	龙岩	8	37103	威海火炬高技术产业开发区	B
33909	浙江其他		35109	永安	8	37105	山东威海出口加工区	
34012	合肥经济技术开发区	3	35119	石狮	8	37109	威海其他	
34013	合肥科技工业园区	B	35128	平潭综合试验区	8	37119	日照	
34015	安徽合肥出口加工区	5	35129	平潭		3711W	日照保税物流中心	
34019	合肥其他	2	35909	福建其他	8	37129	惠民	
34022	芜湖经济技术开发区	3	36012	南昌经济技术开发区	3	37139	德州	
34023	芜湖高新技术产业开发区		36013	南昌高新技术产业开发区	B	37149	聊城	
34025	安徽芜湖出口加工区		36015	江西南昌出口加工区		37159	临沂	
34029	芜湖其他	2	36019	南昌其他		37169	菏泽	
34033	蚌埠高新技术产业开发区		3601W	南昌保税物流中心		37179	青州	
34039	蚌埠		36023	景德镇高新技术产业开发区	B	37189	龙口	
34042	安徽淮南经济技术开发区		36029	景德镇		37199	曲阜	
34049	淮南		36032	萍乡经济技术开发区	3	37209	莱芜	
34052	马鞍山经济技术开发区	3	36039	萍乡		37219	新泰	
34053	马鞍山慈湖高新技术产业开发区		36042	九江经济技术开发区	3	37229	胶州	
34059	马鞍山		36045	江西九江出口加工区	2	37239	诸城	
34069	淮北		36049	九江	2	37249	莱阳	
34072	铜陵经济技术开发区	3	36053	新余高新技术产业开发区	B	37259	滕州	
34079	铜陵		36059	新余		37269	文登	
34082	安庆经济技术开发区	3	36069	鹰潭		37279	荣城	
34089	安庆		36072	赣州经济技术开发区	3	37289	即墨	
34099	黄山		36075	江西赣州出口加工区		37299	平度	
34109	阜阳		36079	赣州		37909	山东其他	
34119	宿州		36089	宜春		41012	郑州经济技术开发区	2
34122	滁州经济技术开发区	3	36092	上饶经济技术开发区	3	41013	郑州高新技术开发区	B
34129	滁州		36099	上饶		41015	河南郑州出口加工区	
34132	安徽六安经济技术开发区		36102	井冈山经济技术开发区	3	41016	新郑综合保税区	
34139	六安		36105	井冈山出口加工区		41018	郑州航空港经济综合实验区	
34142	安徽宁国经济技术开发区		36109	吉安		41019	郑州其他	2
34149	宣城		36119	抚州		4101W	河南保税物流中心	
34159	巢湖		36129	瑞昌		41029	开封	
34162	池州经济技术开发区	3	36909	江西其他		41033	洛阳高新技术产业开发区	B
34169	池州		37013	济南高新技术产业开发区	B	41039	洛阳其他	
34179	亳州		37015	山东济南出口加工区		41049	平顶山	
34909	安徽其他		37019	济南其他		41059	安阳	
35012	福州经济技术开发区	3	37022	青岛经济技术开发区	3	41069	鹤壁	
35013	福州科技园区	B	37023	青岛高新技术产业开发区	B	41079	新乡	
35014	福建马尾保税区	A	37024	青岛保税区	A	41089	焦作	
35015	福建福州、福清出口加工区	8	37025	山东青岛出口加工区		41099	濮阳	
35017	福州保税物流园区	2	37026	青岛前湾保税港区	2	41109	许昌	
35019	福州其他	2	37027	青岛保税物流园	2	41119	漯河	
35021	厦门特区	1	37029	青岛其他	2	41129	三门峡	
35023	厦门火炬高技术产业开发区	B	3702W	青岛保税物流中心		41139	商丘	
35024	厦门象屿保税区	A	37033	淄博高新技术产业开发区	B	41149	周口	
35025	福建厦门出口加工区		37039	淄博		41159	驻马店	
35026	厦门海沧保税港区		3703W	淄博保税物流中心		41169	南阳	
35027	厦门象屿保税物流园	1	37049	枣庄		41179	信阳	
35029	厦门其他	2	37059	东营		41189	义马	

国内地区代码	国内地区名称	国内地区性质标记	国内地区代码	国内地区名称	国内地区性质标记	国内地区代码	国内地区名称	国内地区性质标记
41199	汝州		43199	津市		45013	南宁高新技术产业开发区	B
41209	济源		43909	湖南其他		45019	南宁其他	2
41219	禹州		44012	广州经济技术开发区	3	4501W	南宁保税物流中心	
41229	卫辉		44013	广州天河高新技术产业开发区	B	45029	柳州	
41239	辉县		44014	广州保税区	A	45033	桂林高新技术产业开发区	B
41249	泌阳		44015	广东广州出口加工区		45039	桂林其他	
41909	河南其他		44017	广州保税物流园区	7	45049	梧州	
42012	武汉经济技术开发区	3	44019	广州其他	2	45055	广西北海出口加工区	
42013	武汉东湖新技术开发区	B	44029	韶关	7	45059	北海	2
42015	湖北武汉出口加工区		44031	深圳特区	1	45069	玉林	
42016	武汉东湖综合保税区		44033	深圳科技工业园	B	45079	百色	
42019	武汉其他	2	44034	福田盐田沙头角保税区	A	45089	河池	
4201W	武汉东西湖保税物流中心		44035	广东深圳出口加工区		45096	广西钦州保税港区	
42022	黄石经济技术开发区	3	44036	深圳前海湾保税港区		45099	钦州	
42029	黄石		44037	深圳盐田保税物流园	1	45106	广西凭祥综合保税区	
42039	十堰		44039	深圳其他	7	45109	凭祥	2
42049	沙市		4403W	深圳机场保税物流中心		45119	东兴	2
42059	宜昌		44041	珠海特区	1	45129	防城港市	
42062	襄阳经济技术开发区	3	44043	珠海高新技术产业开发区	B	45139	贵港市	
42063	襄阳高新技术产业开发区	B	44044	珠海保税区	A	45149	崇左	
42069	襄阳其他		44045	珠澳跨境工业区珠海园区	7	45159	来宾	
42079	鄂州		44048	珠海横琴新区		45169	贺州	
42089	荆门		44049	珠海其他	7	45909	广西其他	
42099	黄冈		44051	汕头特区	1	46011	海口	1
42109	孝感		44054	汕头保税区	A	46013	海南国际科技园区	B
42119	咸宁		44059	汕头其他	7	46014	海南海口保税区	A
42122	荆州经济技术开发区	3	44063	佛山高新技术产业开发区	B	46016	海口综合保税区	1
42129	荆州		44069	佛山其他	7	46021	三亚	5
42139	郧阳		44079	江门	7	46031	三沙	
42149	鄂西		44082	湛江经济技术开发区	3	46041	五指山	
42159	随州		44089	湛江其他	2	46051	琼海	
42169	老河口		44099	茂名	7	46061	儋州	
42179	枣阳		44129	肇庆	7	46062	洋浦经济开发区	
42189	神农架		44133	惠州高新技术产业开发区	B	46066	洋浦保税港区	
42909	湖北其他		44139	惠州其他	7	46071	文昌	
43013	长沙科技开发区	B	44149	梅州	7	46081	万宁	
43019	长沙其他	2	44159	汕尾	7	46091	东方	
4301W	长沙金霞保税物流中心		44169	河源	7	46101	定安	
43023	株州高新技术产业开发区	B	44179	阳江	7	46111	屯昌	
43029	株州其他		44189	清远	7	46121	澄迈	
43039	湘潭		44199	东莞	7	46131	临高	
43049	衡阳		4419W	东莞保税物流中心		46141	白沙	
43059	邵阳		44203	中山火炬高技术产业开发区	B	46151	昌江	
43069	岳阳	2	44209	中山其他	7	46161	乐东	
43079	常德		4420W	中山保税物流中心		46171	陵水	
43089	张家界		44219	潮州	7	46181	保亭	
43099	益阳		44229	顺德	7	46191	琼中	
43109	娄底		44235	广东南沙出口加工区	7	46901	海南其他	1
43115	湖南郴州出口加工区		44236	广州南沙保税港区		46902	海南洋浦经济技术开发区	3
43119	郴州		44239	番禺	7	46906	海南洋浦保税港区	5
43129	永州		44249	揭阳	7	50012	万州经济技术开发区	2
43139	怀化		44289	南海	7	50019	万州区	
43149	湘西		44299	云浮市	7	50029	涪陵区	
43159	醴陵		4430	南沙新区		50039	渝中区	
43169	湘乡		44306	广州南沙保税港区		50049	大渡口区	
43179	耒阳		44309	南沙其他		50052	重庆两江新区江北区	3
43189	汨罗		44909	广东其他	7	50056	重庆两路寸滩保税港区（水港）	

国内地区代码	国内地区名称	国内地区性质标记	国内地区代码	国内地区名称	国内地区性质标记	国内地区代码	国内地区名称	国内地区性质标记
50059	江北区		51082	广元经济技术开发区		53909	云南其他	
50066	重庆西永综合保税区		51089	广元		54019	拉萨	6
50069	沙坪坝区		51099	遂宁		54029	昌都	6
50073	重庆高新技术产业开发区	B	51109	内江		54039	山南	6
50079	九龙坡区		51119	乐山		54049	日喀则	6
50082	重庆经济技术开发区	3	51142	宜宾临港经济开发区		54059	那曲	6
50089	南岸区		51149	宜宾		54069	阿里	6
50092	重庆两江新区北碚区	3	51159	南充		54079	林芝	6
50099	北碚区		51169	达县		54909	西藏其他	6
50109	万盛区		51179	雅安		61012	陕西航天经济技术开发区	
50119	双桥区		51189	阿坝		61013	西安新技术产业开发区	B
50122	重庆两江新区渝北区	3	51199	甘孜		61015	陕西西安出口加工区	
50125	重庆出口加工区		51209	凉山		61016	西安综合保税区和西安高新综合保税区	
50126	重庆两路寸滩保税港区（空港）		51229	广汉		61019	西安其他	2
50129	渝北区		51239	江油		61029	铜川	
50139	巴南区		51249	都江堰		61033	宝鸡高新技术产业开发区	B
50212	长寿经济技术开发区	2	51259	峨眉山		61039	宝鸡其他	
50219	长寿县		51269	资阳		61049	咸阳	
50229	綦江区		51279	眉山		61059	渭南	
50239	潼南县		51289	广安		61062	汉中经济技术开发区	
50249	铜梁县		51299	巴中		61069	汉中	
50259	大足区		51909	四川其他		61079	安康	
50269	荣昌县		52013	贵阳高新技术产业开发区	B	61089	商洛	
50279	璧山县		52019	贵阳其他	2	61099	延安	
50289	梁平县		52029	六盘水		61109	榆林	
50299	城口县		52039	遵义		61909	陕西其他	
50309	丰都县		52049	铜仁		62013	兰州宁卧庄新技术产业开发区	B
50319	垫江县		52059	黔西南		62019	兰州其他	2
50329	武隆县		52069	毕节		62029	嘉峪关	
50339	忠县		52079	安顺		62039	金昌	
50349	开县		52089	黔东南		62049	白银	
50359	云阳县		52099	黔南		62059	天水	
50369	奉节县		52909	贵州其他		62069	酒泉	
50379	巫山县		53012	昆明经济技术开发区	3	62079	张掖	
50389	巫溪县		53013	昆明高新技术产业开发区	B	62089	武威	
50399	黔江		53015	云南昆明出口加工区		62099	定西	
50409	石柱土家族自治县		53019	昆明其他		62109	陇南	
50419	秀山土家族苗族自治县		53029	东川		62119	平凉	
50429	酉阳土家族苗族自治县		53039	昭通		62129	庆阳	
50439	彭水苗族土家族自治县		53042	曲靖经济技术开发区	3	62139	临夏	
50819	江津区		53049	曲靖		62149	甘南	
50829	合川区		53059	楚雄		62909	甘肃其他	
50839	永川区		53069	玉溪		63012	西宁经济技术开发区	3
50849	南川区		53079	红河		63013	青海高新技术产业开发区	B
51012	成都经济技术开发区	3	53089	文山		63019	西宁	2
51013	成都高新技术产业开发区	B	53099	普洱		63029	海东	
51015	四川成都出口加工区		53109	西双版纳		63039	海北	
51016	成都高新综合保税区		53119	大理		63049	黄南	
51019	成都其他	2	53129	保山		63059	海南	
51039	自贡		53139	德宏		63069	果洛	
51049	攀枝花		53149	丽江		63079	玉树	
51059	泸州		53159	怒江		63089	海西	
51069	德阳		53169	迪庆		63909	青海其他	
51072	绵阳经济技术开发区		53179	临沧		64012	银川经济技术开发区	3
51073	绵阳高新技术产业开发区	B	53189	畹町	2	64016	银川综合保税区	
51075	四川绵阳出口加工区		53199	瑞丽	2	64019	银川	2
51079	绵阳其他		53209	河口	2	64029	石嘴山	

国内地区代码	国内地区名称	国内地区性质标记	国内地区代码	国内地区名称	国内地区性质标记	国内地区代码	国内地区名称	国内地区性质标记
64039	吴中		65029	克拉玛依	9	65109	塔城	2
64049	固原		65039	博乐	9	65119	阿勒泰	9
64059	中卫		65049	巴音	9	65122	石河子经济技术开发区	3
64909	宁夏其他		65059	阿克苏	9	65129	石河子	9
65012	乌鲁木齐经济技术开发区	3	65069	克孜	9	65219	吐鲁番	9
65013	乌鲁木齐高新技术产业开发区	B	65079	喀什	9	65229	哈密	9
65015	新疆乌鲁木齐出口加工区	9	65089	和田	9	65239	昌吉回族自治州	9
65019	乌鲁木齐其他	9	65099	伊宁	9	65909	新疆其他	9

国内地区代码表说明

国内地区代码表用于填报进出口报关单的境内目的地和境内货源地。

国内地区代码表由5位数字组成：

(一)第一至四位为行政区划代码：

1.第一、二位表示省、自治区、直辖市。

例如：北京市11、广东省44

2.第三、四位表示省辖市(地区、省直辖行政单位)，包括省会城市、计划单列城市、沿海开放城市。

例如：北京市东城区1101、广州市4401、深圳市4403。

(二)第五位为省辖市(地区、省直辖行政单位)经济区划代码：

代码“1”：经济特区，如：深圳市44031、44030，厦门市35021。

代码“2”：经济技术开发区，包括上海浦东新区、海南洋浦经济开发区。

代码“3”：高新技术产业开发区。

代码“4”：保税区。

代码“5”：出口加工区。

代码“6”：保税港区。

代码“7”：保税物流园区。

代码“9”：其他地区。

结汇方式代码表

结汇方式代码	结汇方式名称	结汇方式代码	结汇方式名称	结汇方式代码	结汇方式名称
1	信汇	4	付款交单	7	先出后结
2	电汇	5	承兑交单	8	先结后出
3	票汇	6	信用证	9	其他

结汇方式代码表说明

一、定义

结汇方式是出口货物发货人或其代理通过银行收结外汇的方式。

二、结汇方式代码表结构及说明

(一)结汇方式代码表由两部分组成，即结汇方式代码和结汇方式名称。

(二)结汇方式代码分为汇付、托收、信用证和其他。

1．汇付包括：

(1)信汇：代码“1”，指买方将贷款交给进口地银行，由银行开具付款委托书，邮寄出口地银行，委托其向卖方付款。

(2)电汇：代码“2”，指进口地银行应买方申请，直接用电报发出付款委托书，委托出口地银行向卖方付款。

(3)票汇：代码“3”，指买方向进口地银行购买银行汇票径寄卖方，由卖方或其指定的人持票向出口地有关银行取款。

汇付从时间上分预付和后付。预付即卖方装运货物前，买方先将货款汇结卖方;后付即卖方先交货，在买方收到货物或单据后才汇付货款。

2.托收包括：

(1)付款交单(D/P)：代码“4”，指卖方托收时指示托收行，只有在买方付清货款时才交出单据。

(2)承兑交单(D/A)：代码“5”，指买方承兑汇票后即可取得单据，提取货物，待汇票到期时才付贷款。

3．信用证(L/C)：代码“6”，是银行在买卖双方之间保证付款的凭证。银行根据买方的申请书，向卖方开出保证付款的信用证，即只要卖方提交符合信用证要求的单据，银行就保证付款。

4．先出后结：代码“7”。

5．先结后出：代码“8”。

6．其他：代码“9”，指除上述以外的结汇方式。

监管证件代码表

监管证件代码	监管证件名称	监管证件代码	监管证件名称	监管证件代码	监管证件名称
1	进口许可证	G	两用物项和技术出口许可证(定向)	W	麻醉药品进出口准许证
2	两用物项和技术进口许可证	H	港澳 OPA 纺织品证明	X	有毒化学品环境管理放行通知单
3	两用物项和技术出口许可证	I	精神药物进(出)口准许证	Y	原产地证明
4	出口许可证	J	黄金及其制品进出口准许证或批件	Z	音像制品进口批准单或节目提取单
5	纺织品临时出口许可证	K	深加工结转申请表	c	内销征税联系单
6	旧机电产品禁止进口	L	药品进出口准许证	e	关税配额外优惠税率进口棉花配额证
7	自动进口许可证	M	密码产品和设备进口许可证	h	核增核扣表
8	禁止出口商品	O	自动进口许可证(新旧机电产品)	q	国别关税配额证明
9	禁止进口商品	P	固体废物进口许可证	r	预归类标志
A	入境货物通关单	Q	进口药品通关单	s	适用 ITA 税率的商品用途认定证明
B	出境货物通关单	R	进口兽药通关单	t	关税配额证明
D	出/入境货物通关单(毛坯钻石用)	S	进出口农药登记证明	v	自动进口许可证(加工贸易)
E	濒危物种允许出口证明书	T	银行调运现钞进出境许可证	x	出口许可证(加工贸易)
F	濒危物种允许进口证明书	U	合法捕捞产品通关证明	y	出口许可证(边境小额贸易)

监管证件代码表说明

一、定义

监管证件名称代码是海关依据我国外贸法律、法规及规章，为便于实施计算机系统管理和便捷通关需求，对实行进出口许可证件管理的货物在海关管理环节须验核的各种进出口许可证件分类标志。其总和称为监管证件名称代码表。

二、监管证件名称代码表结构

监管证件名称代码表由两部分组成，即监管证件代码和监管证件名称。例如：代码“1”，为进口许可证，如果某一商品编号后注有监管证件“1”，则说明在一般贸易项下进口该种商品需申领进口许可证。

三、监管证件名称代码说明

(一)代码“1”——进口许可证：指商务部配额许可证事务局或其授权机关签发的进口许可证。

(二)代码“2”——两用物项和技术进口许可证：指列入《两用物项和技术进口许可证管理目录》的商品，进口时由商务部签发两用物项和技术进口许可证。

(三)代码“3”——两用物项和技术出口许可证：根据商务部会同海关总署联合发布《敏感物项和技术出口许可证暂行管理办法》及《敏感物项和技术出口许可证管理目录》，凭商务部签发的敏感物项和技术出口批复到商务部授权的发证机构领取敏感物项和技术出口许可证。

(四)代码“4”——出口许可证：指商务部配额许可证事务局或其授权机关签发的出口许可证。

(五)代码“6”——旧机电产品禁止进口：商品编码后面有此代码的商品，其旧品禁止进口。

(六)代码“7”——自动进口许可证或重要工业品证明：指进口商品实行自动进口许可管理，由商务部及其授权机构按职责分工签发自动进口许可证。

(七)代吗“8”——禁止出口商品：指商务院授权商务部门会同有关部门，依照《中华人民共和国对外贸易法》等有关法律法规，制定、调整并公布的禁止出口货物目录所列商品。商品编码后有此代码的商品禁止出口。

(八)代码“9”——禁止进口商品：指国务院授权商务部门会同有关部门，依照《中华人民共和国对外贸易法》等有关法律法规，制定、调整并公布的禁止进口货物目录所列商品。商品编码后有此代码的商品禁止进口。

(九)代码“A”——入境货物通关单：指国家质量监督检验检疫机构根据《中华人民共和国进出口商品检验法》、《中华人民共和国动植物检疫法》和《中华人民共和国食品卫生法》等有关法律、法规，对列入《出入境检验检疫机构实施检验检疫的进出境商品目录》的进口商品签发的入境货物通关单。

(十)代码“B”——出境货物通关单：指国家质量监督检验检疫机构根据《中华人民共和国进出口商品检验法》、《中华人民共和国动植物检疫法》和《中华人民共和国食品卫生法》等有关法律、法规，对列入《出入境检验检疫机构实施检验检疫的进出境商品目录》的进口商品签发的出境货物通关单。

(十一)代码“D”——出/入境货物通关单：为履行我国国际义务，制止“冲突钻石”非法交易，国家质检总局、海关总署等六部委联合发布 2002 年第 132 号公告，对毛坯钻石进口实施管理，毛坯钻石进出口时，授权检验检疫机构签发出 / 入境货物通关单。

(十二)代码“E”——濒危物种出口允许证：指根据《中华人民共和国野生动物保护法》及相关法律法规，对列入《国家重点保护野生动物名录》货物，出口时由国家濒危物种进出口管理办公室或其办事机构签发允许出口证明书。

(十三)代码“F”——濒危物种进口允许证：指根据《中华人民共和国野生动物保护法》及相关法律法规，对列入《国家重点保护野生动物名录》货物，进口时由国家濒危物种进出口管理办公室或其办事机构签发允许进口证明书。

(十四)代码“G”——易制毒化学品定向出口许可证：指列

入《向特定国家(地区)出口易制毒化学品管理目录》的商品，向特定国家出口时由商务部签发易制毒化学品定向出口许可证。

(十五)代码“I”——精神药物进(出)口准许证：根据《中华人民共和国药品管理法》和国务院《精神药品管理办法》及相关法律法规，国家对精神药品的进(出)口实行进(出)口准许证管理制度。

对列入《精神药品管制品种目录》的商品，国家食品药品监督管理局核发精神药品进(出)口准许证或携带麻醉药品、精神药品证明。

(十六)代码“J”——黄金及其制品进出口准许证或批件：指根据《中华人民共和国金银管理条例》及相关法律法规，对进出口黄金及其制品，由中国人民银行签发的准许进出境证件。

(十七)代码“K”——深加工结转申请表，由所在地海关签发

(十八)代码“L”——药品进(出)口准许证：根据《中华人民共和国反兴奋剂条例》，国家食品药品监督管理部门依法对列入兴奋剂目录的蛋白同化制剂、肽类激素等供医疗使用的兴奋剂实施进出口管理，签发准予进(出)口的许可证件。

(十九)代码“M”——密码产品和设备进口许可证：根据《商用密码管理条例》，对列入《密码产品和含有密码技术的设备进口管理目录》的商品，由国家密码管理局签发进口许可证件。

(二十)代码“O”——自动进口许可证(新旧机电产品)：根据商务部、海关总署、国家质检总局 2001 年第 10 号令《机电产品进口管理办法》和《机电产品自动进口许可管理实施细则》，进口实行自动进口许可管理的机电产品，进口单位应当在办理海关报关手续前，向商务部或地方外经贸主管机构、部门机电办申领自动进口许可证。

(二十一)代码“P”——进口废物批准证书：根据《中华人民共和国固体废物污染环境防治法》和《废物进口环境保护管理暂行规定》及相关法律法规，对列入《国家限制进口的可用做原料的废物目录》的进口商品，由国家环境保护部签发进口废物批准证书。

(二十二)代码“Q”——进口药品通关单：根据《中华人民共和国药品管理法》及相关法律法规，对列入《进口药品管理目录》的药品，国家食品药品监督管理局及其授权机构签发进口药品通关单。

(二十三)代码“R”——进口兽药通关单：根据《兽药管理条例》，农业部或兽药进口口岸所在地省级人民政府兽医行政管理部门对列入《进口兽药管理目录》的进口兽药实施监督管理，签发准予进口的许可证件。

(二十四)代码“S”——进出口农药登记证明：根据《农药管理条例》及有关法律法规，《中华人民共和国进出口农药登记证明管理名录》和《中华人民共和国进出口列入事先知情同意程序(PIC)农药登记证明管理名录》的商品，进出口时，农业部签发进出口农药登记证明。

(二十五)代码“T”——银行调运外币现钞进出境许可证：指国家外汇管理局和中国人民银行根据《银行调运外币现钞进出境管理规定》等法律、法规，对允许进出境的外币和人民币现钞签发的许可证件。

(二十六)代码“U”——合法捕捞产品通关证明：进口“实施合法捕捞证明的水产品清单”所列的鱼类，由农业部签发“合法捕捞产品通关证明”。

(二十七)代码“W”——麻醉药品进出口准许证：根据《中华人民共和国药品管理法》和国务院《麻醉药品管理办法》及相关法律法规，国家对麻醉药品的进(出)口实行进(出)口准许证管理制度。

对列入“麻醉药品管制品种目录”的商品，国家食品药品监督管理局核发麻醉药品进(出)口准许证或携带麻醉药品、精神药品证明。

(二十八)代码“X”——有毒化学品环境管理放行通知单：指列入《中国严格限制的有毒化学品名录》的进出口化学品，由国家环境保护部签发的放行通知单。

(二十九)代码“Y”——原产地证明：是指受惠国政府指定部门签发的证明该货物原产于该国的证明文书。

(三十)代码“Z”——进口音像制品批准单或节目提取单：指国家实行进口管理的音像制品，由文化部签发的文化部进口音像制品批准单或广播电影电视总局及其授权部门签发的进口广播电影电视节目带(片)提取单。

(三十一)代码“e”——关税配额外优惠关税税率进口棉花配额证：指对于一定数量的关税配额外报关进口的棉花，按“暂定优惠关税税率”征收进口关税，由国家发展改革委授权机构出具关税配额外优惠关税税率进口棉花配额证。

(三十二)代码“c”——内销征税联系单，由所在地海关签发。

(三十三)代码“q”——国别关税配额证明：进口原产于新西兰并享受协定税率的羊毛或毛条时，应单独向海关申报，并按照海关总署令第 175 号规定提交原产地证明文件和商务部及其授权机构签发的在备注栏注明“新西兰羊毛、毛条国别配额”字样的农产品进口关税配额证，该证简称“国别关税配额证明”。

(三十四)代码“r”——预归类标志，由所在地海关关税部门签发.

(三十五)代码“s”——适用 ITA 税率的商品用途认定证明，由所在地海关关税部门签发.

(三十六)代码“t”——关税配额证明：指列入实施《关税配额目录》的商品，进口时由商务部签发关税配额证明。

(三十七)代码“v”——自动进口许可证(加工贸易)：适用于加工贸易方式下自动进口许可证管理的商品。

(三十八)代码“x”——出口许可证(加工贸易)：适用于加工贸易方式下出口许可证管理的商品。

(三十九)代码“y”——出口许可证：边境小额贸易项下需凭出口许可证办理有关手续。

用途代码表

用途代码	用 途	用途代码	用途	用途代码	用途
01	外贸自营内销	05	加工返销	09	作价提供
02	特区内销	06	借用	10	货样,广告品
03	其它内销	07	收保证金	11	其它
04	企业自用	08	免费提供	13	以产顶进

用途代码表说明

一、定义

指进口货物的实际用途，以此对征免税和监管条件进行辅助检查和处理。

二、用途分类代码及说明

(一)外贸自营内销：代码“01”，指有外贸进出口经营权的企业，在其经营范围内以正常方式成交的进口货物。

(二)特区内销：代码“02”，指特区内有外贸进出口经营权的企业在其经营范围内进口在特区内销售的货物。

(三)其他内销：代码“03”，指进料加工转内销部分、来料加工转内销货物及外商投资企业进口供加工内销产品的料件。

(四)企业自用：代码“04”，指进口供本单位(企业)自用的货物，如外商投资企业及特区内的企业、事业和机关单位进口自用的机器设备等。

(五)加工返销：代码“05”，指来料加工、进料加工、补偿贸易和外商投资企业为履行产品出口合同从国外进口料件，用于在国内加工后返销到境外。

(六)借用:代码“06”，指从境外租借进口，在规定的使用期满后退运出境外的进口货物，如租赁贸易进口货物。

(七)收保证金:代码“07”，指由担保人向海关缴纳现金的一种担保形式。

(八)免费提供:代码“08”，指免费提供的进口货物，如无偿援助、捐赠、礼品等进口货物。

(九)作价提供:代码“09”，指我方与外商签订合同(协议)，规定由外商作价提供进口的货物，事后由我方支付或从我方出口货物款中或出口加工成品的加工费中扣除，如来料加工贸易进口设备等。

(十)货样、广告品:代码“10”，指进口专供订货参考的货物样品及用以宣传有关商品内容的广告宣传品。

(十一)其他:代码“11”，指用途代码表中未具体列名的其他用途。

(十二)以产顶进：代码“13”，指经国家有关经贸部门审批，对目前国内尚无法加工生产，需在境外购买的商品，可准许在境内的三资企业购买以替代进口。

企业性质代码表

企业性质代码	企业性质简称	企业性质代码	企业性质简称
1	国有	6	私营
2	合作	7	个体工商户
3	合资	8	报关
4	独资	9	其他
5	集体		

货币代码表

货币代码	货币符号	货币名称	货币代码	货币符号	货币名称	货币代码	货币符号	货币名称
110	HKD	港币	300	EUR	欧元	318	FIM	芬兰马克
116	JPY	日本元	302	DKK	丹麦克朗	326	NOK	挪威克朗
121	MOP	澳门元	303	GBP	英镑	330	SEK	瑞典克朗
129	PHP	菲律宾比索	304	DEM	德国马克	331	CHF	瑞士法郎
132	SGD	新加坡元	305	FRF	法国法郎	501	CAD	加拿大元
133	KRW	韩国圆	307	ITL	意大利里拉	502	USD	美元
136	THB	泰国铢	312	ESP	西班牙比赛塔	601	AUD	澳大利亚元
142	CNY	人民币	315	ATS	奥地利先令	609	NZD	新西兰元

成交方式代码表

成交方式代码	成交方式名称	成交方式代码	成交方式名称
1	CIF	4	C&I
2	C&F	5	市场价
3	FOB	6	垫仓

计量单位代码表

计量单位代码	计量单位名称	计量单位代码	计量单位名称	计量单位代码	计量单位名称
001	台	028	株	054	千个
002	座	029	井	055	亿支
003	辆	030	米	056	亿个
004	艘	031	盘	057	万套
005	架	032	平方米	058	千张
006	套	033	立方米	059	万张
007	个	034	筒	060	千伏安
008	只	035	千克	061	千瓦
009	头	036	克	062	千瓦时
010	张	037	盆	063	千升
011	件	038	万个	067	英尺
012	支	039	具	070	吨
013	枝	040	百副	071	长吨
014	根	041	百支	072	短吨
015	条	042	百把	073	司马担
016	把	043	百个	074	司马斤
017	块	044	百片	075	斤
018	卷	045	刀	076	磅
019	副	046	疋	077	担
020	片	047	公担	078	英担
021	组	048	扇	079	短担
022	份	049	百枝	080	两
023	幅	050	千只	081	市担
025	双	051	千块	083	盎司
026	对	052	千盒	084	克拉
027	棵	053	千枝	085	市尺

计量单位代码	计量单位名称	计量单位代码	计量单位名称	计量单位代码	计量单位名称
086	码	120	箱	135	捆
088	英寸	121	批	136	袋
089	寸	122	罐	139	粒
095	升	123	桶	140	盒
096	毫升	124	扎	141	合
097	英加仑	125	包	142	瓶
098	美加仑	126	箩	143	千支
099	立方英尺	127	打	144	万双
101	立方尺	128	筐	145	万粒
110	平方码	129	罗	146	千粒
111	平方英尺	130	匹	147	千米
112	平方尺	131	册	148	千英尺
115	英制马力	132	本	149	百万贝可
116	公制马力	133	发	163	部
118	令	134	枚	164	亿株

国别(地区)代码表

国家（地区）代码	国际标准英文简称	中文国家（地区）名称	英文国家（地区）名称	优惠/普通税率标记	船舶吨税优/普标记
101	AFG	阿富汗	Afghanistan	L	H
102	BHR	巴林	Bahrian	L	H
103	BGD	孟加拉国	Bangladesh	L	L
104	BTN	不丹	Bhutan	H	H
105	BRN	文莱	Brunei	L	H
106	MMR	缅甸	Myanmar	L	H
107	KHM	柬埔寨	Cambodia	L	H
108	CYP	塞浦路斯	Cyprus	L	L
109	PRK	朝鲜	Korea, DPR	L	L
110	HKG	香港	Hong Kong	L	L
111	IND	印度	India	L	L
112	IDN	印度尼西亚	Indonesia	L	L
113	IRN	伊朗	Iran	L	L
114	IRQ	伊拉克	Iraq	L	H
115	ISR	以色列	Israel	L	L
116	JPN	日本	Japan	L	L
117	JOR	约旦	Jordan	L	H
118	KWT	科威特	Kuwait	L	H
119	LAO	老挝	Lao PDR	L	H
120	LBN	黎巴嫩	Lebanon	L	L
121	MAC	澳门	Macau	L	L
122	MYS	马来西亚	Malaysia	L	L
123	MDV	马尔代夫	Maldives	L	H
124	MNG	蒙古	Mongolia	L	L
125	NPL	尼泊尔联邦民主共和国	Nepal, FDR	L	H
126	OMN	阿曼	Oman	L	L
127	PAK	巴基斯坦	Pakistan	L	L
128	PSE	巴勒斯坦	Palestine	H	H
129	PHL	菲律宾	Philippines	L	L
130	QAT	卡塔尔	Qatar	L	H
131	SAU	沙特阿拉伯	Saudi Arabia	L	H
132	SGP	新加坡	Singapore	L	L
133	KOR	韩国	Korea, Rep.	L	L
134	LKA	斯里兰卡	Sri Lanka	L	L
135	SYR	叙利亚	Syrian Arab Republic	L	H

国家（地区）代码	国际标准英文简称	中文国家（地区）名称	英文国家（地区）名称	优惠 / 普通税率标记	船舶吨税优/普标记
136	THA	泰国	Thailand	L	L
137	TUR	土耳其	Turkey	L	L
138	ARE	阿联酋	United Arab Emirates	L	H
139	YEM	也门	Yemen	L	L
141	NVM	越南	Viet Nam	L	L
142	CHN	中国	China	L	L
143	TWN	台澎金马关税区	Taiwan, Prov.of China	L	H
144	TLS	东帝汶	Timor-Leste	L	H
145	KAZ	哈萨克斯坦	Kazakhstan	L	H
146	KGZ	吉尔吉斯斯坦	Kyrgyzstan	L	H
147	TJK	塔吉克斯坦	Tajikistan	L	H
148	TKM	土库曼斯坦	Turkmenistan	L	H
149	UZB	乌兹别克斯坦	Uzbekistan	L	H
199		亚洲其他国家(地区)	Oth. Asia nes		
201	DZA	阿尔及利亚	Algeria	L	L
202	AGO	安哥拉	Angola	L	H
203	BEN	贝宁	Benin	L	H
204	BWA	博茨瓦纳	Botswana	L	H
205	BDI	布隆迪	Burundi	L	H
206	CMR	喀麦隆	Cameroon	L	H
207		加那利群岛	Canary Islands	H	H
208	CPV	佛得角	Cape Verde	L	H
209	CAF	中非	Central African Republic.	L	H
210		塞卜泰(休达)	Ceuta	H	H
211	TCD	乍得	Chad	L	H
212	COM	科摩罗	Comoros	H	H
213	COG	刚果(布)	Congo	L	L
214	DJI	吉布提	Djibouti	L	H
215	EGY	埃及	Egypt	L	L
216	GNQ	赤道几内亚	Equatorial Guinea	L	H
217	ETH	埃塞俄比亚	Ethiopia	L	L
218	GAB	加蓬	Gabon	L	H
219	GMB	冈比亚	Gambia	L	H
220	GHA	加纳	Ghana	L	L
221	GIN	几内亚	Guinea	L	H
222	GNB	几内亚比绍	Guinea-Bissau	L	H
223	CIV	科特迪瓦	Cote d'lvoire	L	H
224	KEN	肯尼亚	Kenya	L	L
225	LBR	利比里亚	Liberia	L	H
226	LBY	利比亚	Libyan Arab Jamahiriya	L	H
227	MDG	马达加斯加	Madagascar	L	H
228	MWI	马拉维	Malawi	L	H
229	MLI	马里	Mali	L	H
230	MRT	毛里塔尼亚	Mauritania	L	H
231	MUS	毛里求斯	Mauritius	L	H
232	MAR	摩洛哥	Morocco	L	L
233	MOZ	莫桑比克	Mozambique	L	H
234	NAM	纳米比亚	Namibia	L	H
235	NER	尼日尔	Niger	L	H
236	NGA	尼日利亚	Nigeria	L	H
237	REU	留尼汪	Reunion	H	H
238	RWA	卢旺达	Rwanda	L	H
239	STP	圣多美和普林西比	Sao Tome and Principe	H	H
240	SEN	塞内加尔	Senegal	L	H
241	SYC	塞舌尔	Seychelles	H	H
242	SLE	塞拉利昂	Sierra Leone	L	H

国家（地区）代码	国际标准英文简称	中文国家（地区）名称	英文国家（地区）名称	优惠/普通税率标记	船舶吨税优/普标记
243	SOM	索马里	Somalia	L	H
244	ZAF	南非	South Africa	L	L
245	ESH	西撒哈拉	Western Sahara	H	H
246	SDN	苏丹	Sudan	L	L
247	TZA	坦桑尼亚	Tanzania	L	H
248	TGO	多哥	Togo	L	H
249	TUN	突尼斯	Tunisia	L	L
250	UGA	乌干达	Uganda	L	H
251	BFA	布基纳法索	Burkina Faso	L	H
252	COD	刚果(金)	Congo, DR	L	L
253	ZMB	赞比亚	Zambia	L	H
254	ZWE	津巴布韦	Zimbabwe	L	H
255	LSO	莱索托	Lesotho	L	H
256		梅利利亚	Melilla	H	H
257	SWZ	斯威士兰	Swaziland	L	H
258	ERI	厄立特里亚	Eritrea	L	H
259	MYT	马约特	Mayotte	L	H
260		南苏丹共和国	Republic of South Sudan	H	H
299		非洲其他国家(地区)	Oth. Afr. nes		
301	BEL	比利时	Belgium	L	L
302	DNK	丹麦	Denmark	L	L
303	GBR	英国	United Kingdom	L	L
304	DEU	德国	Germany	L	L
305	FRA	法国	France	L	L
306	IRL	爱尔兰	Ireland	L	L
307	ITA	意大利	Italy	L	L
308	LUX	卢森堡	Luxembourg	L	L
309	NLD	荷兰	Netherlands	L	L
310	GRC	希腊	Greece	L	L
311	PRT	葡萄牙	Portugal	L	L
312	ESP	西班牙	Spain	L	L
313	ALB	阿尔巴尼亚	Albania	L	L
314	AND	安道尔	Andorra	H	H
315	AUT	奥地利	Austria	L	L
316	BGR	保加利亚	Bulgaria	L	L
318	FIN	芬兰	Finland	L	L
320	GIB	直布罗陀	Gibraltar	H	L
321	HUN	匈牙利	Hungary	L	L
322	ISL	冰岛	Iceland	L	H
323	LIE	列支敦士登	Liechtenstein	L	H
324	MLT	马耳他	Malta	L	L
325	MCO	摩纳哥	Monaco	L	H
326	NOR	挪威	Norway	L	L
327	POL	波兰	Poland	L	L
328	ROM	罗马尼亚	Romania	L	L
329	SMR	圣马力诺	San Marino	L	H
330	SWE	瑞典	Sweden	L	L
331	CHE	瑞士	Switzerland	L	H
334	EST	爱沙尼亚	Estonia	L	L
335	LVA	拉脱维亚	Latvia	L	L
336	LTU	立陶宛	Lithuania	L	L
337	GEO	格鲁吉亚	Georgia	L	L
338	ARM	亚美尼亚	Armenia	L	H
339	AZE	阿塞拜疆	Azerbai jan	L	H
340	BLR	白俄罗斯	Belarus	L	H
343	MDA	摩尔多瓦	Moldova	L	H
344	RUS	俄罗斯联邦	Russian Federation	L	L

国家（地区）代码	国际标准英文简称	中文国家（地区）名称	英文国家（地区）名称	优惠 / 普通税率标记	船舶吨税优/普标记
347	UKR	乌克兰	Ukraine	L	L
349		塞尔维亚和黑山		H	H
350	SVN	斯洛文尼亚	Slovenia	L	L
351	HRV	克罗地亚	Croatia	L	L
352	CZE	捷克	Czech Republic	L	L
353	SVK	斯洛伐克	Slovakia	L	L
354	MKD	前南马其顿	Macedonia, FYR	L	H
355	BIH	波黑	Bosnia and Hercegovina	L	H
356	VAT	梵蒂冈城国	Vatican City State	H	H
357	FRO	法罗群岛	Faroe Islands	L	H
358	SRB	塞尔维亚	Serbia	L	H
359	MNE	黑山	Montenegro	L	H
399		欧洲其他国家(地区)	Oth. Eur. nes		
401	ATG	安提瓜和巴布达	Antigua & Barbuda	L	H
402	ARG	阿根廷	Argentina	L	L
403	ABW	阿鲁巴	Aruba	H	H
404	BHS	巴哈马	Bahamas	H	L
405	BRB	巴巴多斯	Barbados	L	H
406	BLZ	伯利兹	Belize	L	H
408	BOL	多民族玻利维亚国	Estado Plurinacional de Bolivia	L	H
409		博内尔	Bonaire	H	H
410	BRA	巴西	Brazil	L	L
411	CYM	开曼群岛	Cayman Islands	H	L
412	CHL	智利	Chile	L	L
413	COL	哥伦比亚	Colombia	L	H
414	DMA	多米尼克	Dominica	L	H
415	CRI	哥斯达黎加	Costa Rica	L	H
416	CUB	古巴	Cuba	L	L
417		库腊索岛	Curacao	H	H
418	DOM	多米尼加共和国	Dominican Republic	L	H
419	ECU	厄瓜多尔	Ecuador	L	H
420	GUF	法属圭亚那	French Guiana	H	H
421	GRD	格林纳达	Grenada	L	H
422	GLP	瓜德罗普	Guadeloupe	H	H
423	GTM	危地马拉	Guatemala	L	H
424	GUY	圭亚那	Guyana	L	H
425	HTI	海地	Haiti	L	H
426	HND	洪都拉斯	Honduras	L	H
427	JAM	牙买加	Jamaica	L	H
428	MTQ	马提尼克	Martinique	H	H
429	MEX	墨西哥	Mexico	L	L
430	MSR	蒙特塞拉特	Montserrat	H	H
431	NIC	尼加拉瓜	Nicaragua	L	H
432	PAN	巴拿马	Panama	L	H
433	PRY	巴拉圭	Paraguay	L	H
434	PER	秘鲁	Peru	L	L
435	PRI	波多黎各	Puerto Rico	L	H
436		萨巴	Saba	H	H
437	LCA	圣卢西亚	Saint Lucia	L	H
438		圣马丁岛	Saint Martin Islands	H	H
439	VCT	圣文森特和格林纳丁斯	Saint Vincent and Grenadines	L	H
440	SLV	萨尔瓦多	El Salvador	H	H
441	SUR	苏里南	Suriname	L	H
442	TTO	特立尼达和多巴哥	Trinidad and Tobago	L	H
443	TCA	特克斯和凯科斯群岛	Turks and Caicos Islands	H	H

国家（地区）代码	国际标准英文简称	中文国家（地区）名称	英文国家（地区）名称	优惠/普通税率标记	船舶吨税优/普标记
444	URY	乌拉圭	Uruguay	L	H
445	VEN	委内瑞拉	Venezuela	L	H
446	VGB	英属维尔京群岛	Virgin Islands, British	H	H
447	KNA	圣其茨和尼维斯	Saint Kitts and Nevis	L	H
448	SPM	圣皮埃尔和密克隆	Saint.Pierre and Miquelon	L	H
449	ANT	荷属安地列斯	Netherlands Antilles	H	H
499		拉丁美洲其他国家(地区)	Oth. L.Amer. nes		
501	CAN	加拿大	Canada	L	L
502	USA	美国	United States	L	L
503	GRL	格陵兰	Greenland	L	H
504	BMU	百慕大	Bermuda	H	L
599		北美洲其他国家(地区)	Oth. N.Amer. nes		
601	AUS	澳大利亚	Australia	L	H
602	COK	库克群岛	Cook Islands	L	H
603	FJI	斐济	Fiji	L	H
604		盖比群岛	Gambier Islands	H	H
605		马克萨斯群岛	Marquesas Islands	H	H
606	NRU	瑙鲁	Nauru	H	H
607	NCL	新喀里多尼亚	New Caledonia	L	H
608	VUT	瓦努阿图	Vanuatu	L	H
609	NZL	新西兰	New Zealand	L	L
610	NFK	诺福克岛	Norfolk Island	H	H
611	PNG	巴布亚新几内亚	Papua New Guinea	L	H
612		社会群岛	Society Islands	H	H
613	SLB	所罗门群岛	Solomon Islands	L	H
614	TON	汤加	Tonga	L	H
615		土阿莫土群岛	Tuamotu Islands	H	H
616		土布艾群岛	Tubai Islands	H	H
617	WSM	萨摩亚	Samoa	L	H
618	KIR	基里巴斯	Kiribati	H	H
619	TUV	图瓦卢	Tuvalu	H	H
620	FSM	密克罗尼西亚联邦	Micronesia, Fs	L	H
621	MHL	马绍尔群岛	Marshall Islands	H	H
622	PLW	帕劳	Palau	H	H
623	PYF	法属波利尼西亚	French Polynesia	L	H
625	WLF	瓦利斯和浮图纳	Wallis and Futuna	L	H
699		大洋洲其他国家(地区)	Oth. Ocean. nes		
701		国(地)别不详	Countries(reg.) unknown	H	H
702		联合国及机构和国际组织	UN and oth. Int'l org.		
999		中性包装原产国别	Conutries of Neutral Package	H	H

地区性质代码表

地区性质代码	地区性质名称	地区性质代码	地区性质名称
1	经济特区	7	广东省
2	沿海开放城市	8	福建省
3	经济技术开发区	9	北京市、新疆
4	经济开放区	A	保税工业区
5	海南省	B	新技术开发园区
6	西藏自治区		

第五部分　海关进出口商品规范申报目录

目　录

第一类 活动物；动物产品

第一章 活动物

税则号列	商品名称	申报要素(A:归类要素 B:价格要素 C:审单及其他要素)及说明举例
01.01	马、驴、骡:	A:1.品名;2.是否改良种用。B:3.品种
01.02	牛:	A:1.品名;2.是否改良种用
0103.1000	-改良种用	A:1.品名;2.是否改良种用
	-其他	A:1.品名;2.个体重量
01.04	绵羊、山羊:	A:1.品名;2.是否改良种用
0104.1010	---改良种用	例:改良种用绵羊
0104.1090	---其他	例:活绵羊
0104.2010	---改良种用	例:改良种用山羊
0104.2090	---其他	例:活山羊
01.05	家禽，即鸡、鸭、鹅、火鸡及珍珠鸡:	A:1.品名;2.是否改良种用;3.个体重量。例:不包括其他活禽(如鹧鸪、野鸡、鸽、野鸭、大雁)(税目 01.06)
01.06	其他活动物:	
	-哺乳动物:	A:1.品名;2.是否改良种用
	---改良种用	A:1.品名;2.是否改良种用
0106.2020	---食用	A:1.品名;2.用途(食用)
0106.2090	---其他	A:1.品名
	--猛禽:	A:1.品名;2.是否改良种用
	--鹦形目（包括普通鹦鹉、长尾鹦鹉、金刚鹦鹉及美冠鹦鹉）:	A:1.品名;2.是否改良种用
	--鸵鸟；鸸鹋:	A:1.品名;2.是否改良种用
0106.3910	---改良种用	A:1.品名;2.是否改良种用
	---食用	A:1.品名;2.用途(食用)
0106.3990	---其他	A:1.品名
	-昆虫:	A:1.品名;2.是否改良种用
	-其他:	A:1.品名;2.是否改良种用

第二章 肉及食用杂碎

[注解]

本章中的“鲜的”包括运输途中用盐临时保藏的肉及杂碎；“冷的”即产品温度一般降至0℃左右，但未冻结的；“冻的”即冷却到产品的冰点以下，使产品全部冻结的。

税则号列	商品名称	申报要素(A:归类要素 B:价格要素 C:审单及其他要素)及说明举例
02.01	鲜、冷牛肉:	A:1.品名;2.制作或保存方法(鲜、冷);3.加工方法(整头及半头、带骨或去骨等)。B:4.牛肉部位（如眼肉、腱子肉等）;5.包装规格
02.02	冻牛肉:	A:1.品名;2.制作或保存方法(冻);3.加工方法(整头及半头、带骨或去骨等)。B:4. 牛肉部位（如眼肉、腱子肉等）;5.包装规格
02.03	鲜、冷、冻猪肉:	A:1.品名;2.制作或保存方法(鲜、冷、冻);3.加工方法(整头及半头、带骨或去骨等)。B:4.包装规格
02.04	鲜、冷、冻绵羊肉或山羊肉:	A:1.品名;2.制作或保存方法(鲜、冷、冻);3.加工方法(整头及半头、带骨或去骨等)
02.05	鲜、冷、冻马、驴、骡肉:	A:1.品名;2.制作或保存方法(鲜、冷、冻)
02.06	鲜、冷、冻牛、猪、绵羊、山羊、马、驴、骡的食用杂碎:	A:1.品名;2.制作或保存方法(鲜、冷、冻);3.种类(舌、肝、心管、板筋等)。B:4.包装规格
0207.1100	--整只,鲜或冷的	A:1.品名;2.制作或保存方法(鲜、冷);3.加工方法(整只、带骨或去骨等)。B:4.厂号（名称或号码，饲养场或加工厂）; 5.品牌
0207.1200	--整只,冻的	A:1.品名;2.制作或保存方法(冻);3.加工方法(整只、带骨或去骨等)。B:4.厂号（名称或号码，饲养场或加工厂）; 5.品牌
	--块及杂碎，鲜或冷的:	A:1.品名;2.制作或保存方法(鲜、冷);3.加工方法(整只、带骨或去骨等)。B:4.厂号（名称或号码，饲养场或加工厂）; 5.品牌
	---块:	A:1.品名;2.制作或保存方法(冻);3.加工方法(整只、带骨或去骨等)。B:4.厂号（名称或号码，饲养场或加工厂）; 5.品牌
0207.1421	----翼(不包括翼尖)	A:1.品名;2.制作或保存方法(冻);3.加工方法(整只、带骨或去骨等)。B:4.厂号（名称或号码，饲养场或加工厂）; 5.品牌

税则号列	商品名称	申报要素(A:归类要素 B:价格要素 C:审单及其他要素)及说明举例
0207.1422	----鸡爪	A: 1. 品名; 2. 制作或保存方法(冻); 3. 加工方法(整只、带骨或去骨等) 。B: 4. 厂号(名称或号码, 饲养场或加工厂); 5. 品牌; 6. 规格(个体重量)
0207.1429	----其他	A: 1. 品名; 2. 制作或保存方法(冻); 3. 加工方法(整只、带骨或去骨等); 4. 种类(心、肝等)。B: 5. 厂号(名称或号码, 饲养场或加工厂); 6. 品牌
0207.2400	—整只, 鲜或冷的	A: 1. 品名; 2. 制作或保存方法(鲜、冷); 3. 加工方法(整只、带骨或去骨等)
0207.2500	—整只, 冻的	A: 1. 品名; 2. 制作或保存方法(冻); 3. 加工方法(整只、带骨或去骨等)
0207.2600	—块及杂碎, 鲜或冷的	A: 1. 品名; 2. 制作或保存方法(鲜、冷); 3. 加工方法(整只、带骨或去骨等); 4. 杂碎请列明具体种类
0207.2700	--块及杂碎, 冻的	A: 1. 品名; 2. 制作或保存方法(冻); 3. 加工方法(整只、带骨或去骨等); 4. 杂碎请列明具体种类
0207.4100	--整只, 鲜或冷的	A: 1. 品名; 2. 制作或保存方法(鲜、冷); 3. 加工方法(整只)
0207.4200	--整只, 冻的	A: 1. 品名; 2. 制作或保存方法(冻); 3. 加工方法(整只)
0207.4300	--肥肝, 鲜或冷的	A: 1. 品名; 2. 制作或保存方法(鲜、冷)
0207.4400	--其他, 鲜或冷的	A: 1. 品名; 2. 制作或保存方法(鲜、冷); 3. 加工方法(带骨或去骨等); 4. 杂碎请列明具体种类
0207.4500	--其他, 冻的	A: 1. 品名; 2. 制作或保存方法(冻); 3. 加工方法(带骨或去骨等); 4. 杂碎请列明具体种类
0207.5100	--整只, 鲜或冷的	A: 1. 品名; 2. 制作或保存方法(鲜、冷); 3. 加工方法(整只)
0207.5200	--整只, 冻的	A: 1. 品名; 2. 制作或保存方法(冻); 3. 加工方法(整只)
0207.5300	--肥肝, 鲜或冷的	A: 1. 品名; 2. 制作或保存方法(鲜、冷)
0207.5400	--其他, 鲜或冷的	A: 1. 品名; 2. 制作或保存方法(鲜、冷); 3. 加工方法(带骨或去骨等); 4. 杂碎请列明具体种类
0207.5500	--其他, 冻的	A: 1. 品名; 2. 制作或保存方法(冻); 3. 加工方法(带骨或去骨等); 4. 杂碎请列明具体种类
0207.6000	-珍珠鸡	A: 1. 品名; 2. 制作或保存方法(鲜、冷、冻); 3. 加工方法(整只、带骨或去骨等); 4. 杂碎请列明具体种类
0208.1010	---鲜、冷兔肉, 兔头除外	A: 1. 品名; 2. 制作或保存方法(鲜、冷)。B: 3. 包装规格
0208.1020	---冻兔肉, 兔头除外	A: 1. 品名; 2. 制作或保存方法(冻)。B: 3. 包装规格
0208.1090	---其他	A: 1. 品名; 2. 制作或保存方法(鲜、冷、冻); 3. 杂碎请列明具体种类及用途。B: 4. 包装规格
0208.3000	-灵长目的	A: 1. 品名; 2. 制作或保存方法(鲜、冷、冻); 3. 杂碎请列明具体种类及用途。B: 4. 包装规格
0208.4000	-鲸、海豚及鼠海豚(鲸目哺乳动物)的; 海牛及儒艮(海牛目哺乳动物)的; 海豹、海狮及海象(鳍足亚目哺乳动物)的	A: 1. 品名; 2. 制作或保存方法(鲜、冷、冻); 3. 杂碎请列明具体种类及用途。B: 4. 包装规格
0208.5000	-爬行动物(包括蛇及龟鳖)的	A: 1. 品名; 2. 制作或保存方法(鲜、冷、冻); 3. 杂碎请列明具体种类及用途。B: 4. 包装规格
0208.6000	-骆驼及其他骆驼科动物的	A: 1. 品名; 2. 制作或保存方法(鲜、冷、冻); 3. 杂碎请列明具体种类及用途。B: 4. 包装规格
	-其他:	A: 1. 品名; 2. 制作或保存方法(鲜、冷、冻); 3. 杂碎请列明具体种类及用途。B: 4. 包装规格
02.09	未炼制或用其他方法提取的不带瘦肉的肥猪肉、猪脂肪及家禽脂肪, 鲜、冷、冻、干、熏、盐腌或盐渍的:	A: 1. 品名; 2. 制作或保存方法(未炼制、未提取脂肪, 干、熏、盐腌、盐渍等)。例: 不包括经炼制或用其他方法提取的脂肪(税目 15.01); 不包括海生哺乳动物的脂肪(第十五章)
02.10	肉及食用杂碎, 干、熏、盐腌或盐渍的; 可供食用的肉或杂碎的细粉、粗粉:	例: 不包括未炼制或用其他方法提取的不带瘦肉的肥猪肉、猪脂肪或家禽脂肪(税目 02.09); 不包括不合适供人食用的肉或杂碎的粗粉或细粉(税目 23.01)
	-猪肉:	A: 1. 品名; 2. 制作或保存方法(带骨、腿肉、腹肉、干、熏、盐腌、盐渍等)
0210.2000	-牛肉	A: 1. 品名; 2. 制作或保存方法(干、熏、盐腌、盐渍等)
	-其他, 包括可供食用的肉或杂碎的细粉、粗粉:	A: 1. 品名; 2. 用途; 3. 制作或保存方法(干、熏、盐腌、盐渍等); 4. 杂碎请列明具体种类

第三章　鱼、甲壳动物、软体动物及其他水生无脊椎动物

[注解]

本章所称"冷"指产品的温度一般降至0℃左右, 但产品尚未冻结的; "冻"指温度降至产品的冰点以下, 使产品全部冻结的; "观赏鱼"指因其色彩或形态特殊而通常养于水族箱中以供观赏的活鱼; "鱼片"指顺鱼脊骨平切的长条肉片。

税则号列	商品名称	申报要素(A:归类要素 B:价格要素 C:审单及其他要素)及说明举例
03.01	活鱼:	
	-观赏鱼:	A:1.品名;2.用途(观赏用);3.状态(活);4.拉丁名称
0301.9110	---鱼苗	A:1.品名;2.状态(活);3.是否为鱼苗;4.拉丁名称
0301.9190	---其他	A:1.品名;2.状态(活);3.拉丁名称
0301.9210	---鱼苗	A:1.品名;2.状态(活);3.是否为鱼苗;4.拉丁名称
0301.9290	---其他	A:1.品名;2.状态(活);3.拉丁名称
0301.9310	---鱼苗	A:1.品名;2.状态(活);3.是否为鱼苗;4.拉丁名称
0301.9390	---其他	A:1.品名;2.状态(活);3.拉丁名称
0301.9410	---鱼苗	A:1.品名;2.状态(活);3.是否为鱼苗;4.拉丁名称
	---其他	A:1.品名;2.状态(活);3.拉丁名称
0301.9510	---鱼苗	A:1.品名;2.状态(活);3.是否为鱼苗;4.拉丁名称
0301.9590	---其他	A:1.品名;2.状态(活);3.拉丁名称
	---鱼苗:	A:1.品名;2.状态(活);3.是否为鱼苗;4.拉丁名称
	---其他:	A:1.品名;2.状态(活);3.拉丁名称
03.02	鲜、冷鱼,但税目03.04的鱼片及其他鱼肉除外:	例:不包括鱼片及其他鱼肉(税目03.04)
	-鲑科鱼,但鱼肝及鱼卵除外:	A:1.品名;2.制作或保存方法(鲜、冷);3. 拉丁名称。B:4.个体重量[如1000~2000克/条(块)等]
	-比目鱼,但鱼肝及鱼卵除外:	A:1.品名;2.制作或保存方法(鲜、冷);3. 拉丁名称。B:4.个体重量[如1000~2000克/条(块)等]
	-金枪鱼(金枪鱼属)、鲣鱼或狐鲣(鲣),但鱼肝及鱼卵除外:	A:1.品名;2.制作或保存方法(鲜、冷);3. 拉丁名称。B:4.个体重量[如1000~2000克/条(块)等]
	-鲱鱼(大西洋鲱鱼、太平洋鲱鱼)、鳀鱼(鳀属)、沙丁鱼(沙丁鱼、沙瑙鱼属)、小沙丁鱼属、黍鲱或西鲱、鲭鱼〔大西洋鲭、澳洲鲭(鲐)、日本鲭(鲐)〕、对称竹荚鱼、新西兰竹荚鱼及竹荚鱼(竹荚鱼属)、军曹鱼及剑鱼,但鱼肝及鱼卵除外:	A:1.品名;2.制作或保存方法(鲜、冷);3. 拉丁名称。B:4.个体重量[如1000~2000克/条(块)等]
	-犀鳕科、多丝真鳕科、鳕科、长尾鳕科、黑鳕科、无须鳕科、深海鳕科及南极鳕科鱼,但鱼肝及鱼卵除外:	A:1.品名;2.制作或保存方法(鲜、冷);3. 拉丁名称。B:4.个体重量[如1000~2000克/条(块)等]
	-罗非鱼(口孵非鲫属)、鲶鱼((鱼芒)鲶属、鲶属、胡鲶属、真鮰属)、鲤科鱼(西鲤、黑鲫、草鱼、鲢属、鲮属、青鱼)、鳗鱼(鳗鲡属)、尼罗河鲈鱼(尼罗尖吻鲈)及黑鱼(鳢属),但鱼肝及鱼卵除外:	A:1.品名;2.制作或保存方法(鲜、冷);3. 拉丁名称。B:4.个体重量[如1000~2000克/条(块)等]
	-其他鱼,但鱼肝及鱼卵除外:	A:1.品名;2.制作或保存方法(鲜、冷);3. 拉丁名称。B:4.个体重量[如1000~2000克/条(块)等]
0302.9000	-鱼肝及鱼卵	A:1.品名;2.制作或保存方法(鲜、冷);3.拉丁名称
03.03	冻鱼,但税目03.04的鱼片及其他鱼肉除外:	例:不包括鱼片及其他鱼肉(税目03.04)
	-鲑科鱼,但鱼肝及鱼卵除外:	A:1.品名;2.制作或保存方法(冻);3. 拉丁名称。B:4.个体重量[如1000~2000克/条(块)等]
	-罗非鱼(口孵非鲫属)、鲶鱼((鱼芒)鲶属、鲶属、胡鲶属、真鮰属)、鲤科鱼(西鲤、黑鲫、草鱼、鲢属、鲮属、青鱼)、鳗鱼(鳗鲡属)、尼罗河鲈鱼(尼罗尖吻鲈)及黑鱼(鳢属),但鱼肝及鱼卵除外:	A:1.品名;2.制作或保存方法(冻);3. 拉丁名称。B:4.个体重量[如1000~2000克/条(块)等]
	-比目鱼(鲽科、鲆科、舌鳎科、鳎科、菱鲆科、刺鲆科),但鱼肝及鱼卵除外:	A:1.品名;2.制作或保存方法(冻);3. 拉丁名称。B:4.个体重量[如1000~2000克/条(块)等]
	-金枪鱼(金枪鱼属)、鲣鱼或狐鲣(鲣),但鱼肝及鱼卵除外:	A:1.品名;2.制作或保存方法(冻);3. 拉丁名称。B:4.个体重量[如1000~2000克/条(块)等]
	-鲱鱼(大西洋鲱鱼、太平洋鲱鱼)、沙丁鱼(沙丁鱼、沙瑙鱼属)、小沙丁鱼属、黍鲱或西鲱、鲭鱼〔大西洋鲭、澳洲鲭(鲐)、日本鲭(鲐)〕、对称竹荚鱼、新西兰竹荚鱼及竹荚鱼(竹荚鱼属)、军曹鱼及剑鱼,但鱼肝及鱼卵除外:	A:1.品名;2.制作或保存方法(冻);3. 拉丁名称。B:4.个体重量[如1000~2000克/条(块)等]

税则号列	商品名称	申报要素(A:归类要素 B:价格要素 C:审单及其他要素)及说明举例
	-犀鳕科、多丝真鳕科、鳕科、长尾鳕科、黑鳕科、无须鳕科、深海鳕科及南极鳕科鱼，但鱼肝及鱼卵除外:	A:1.品名;2.制作或保存方法(冻);3. 拉丁名称。B:4.个体重量[如1000~2000克/条(块)等]
	-其他鱼，但鱼肝及鱼卵除外:	A:1.品名;2.制作或保存方法(冻);3. 拉丁名称。B:4.个体重量[如1000~2000克/条(块)等]
0303.9000	-鱼肝及鱼卵	A:1.品名;2.制作或保存方法(冻);3.拉丁名称
03.04	鲜、冷、冻鱼片及其他鱼肉(不论是否绞碎):	
	-鲜或冷的罗非鱼(口孵非鲫属)、鲶鱼((鱼芒)鲶属、鲶属、胡鲶属、真鮰属)、鲤科鱼(西鲤、黑鲫、草鱼、鲢属、鳙属、青鱼)、鳗鱼(鳗鲡属)、尼罗河鲈鱼(尼罗尖吻鲈)及黑鱼(鳢属)的鱼片:	A:1.品名;2.制作或保存方法(鲜、冷);3. 拉丁名称。B:4.规格[克重/片(块)等]
	-鲜或冷的其他鱼片:	A:1.品名;2.制作或保存方法(鲜、冷);3. 拉丁名称。B:4.规格[克重/片(块)等]
	-其他，鲜或冷的:	A:1.品名;2.制作或保存方法(鲜、冷);3. 拉丁名称。B:4.规格[克重/片(块)等]
0304.6100	--罗非鱼(口孵非鲫属)	A:1.品名;2.制作或保存方法(冻);3. 拉丁名称。B:4.规格[克重/片(块)等]
	---叉尾鮰鱼(真鮰属):	A:1.品名;2.制作或保存方法(冻);3. 拉丁名称。B:4.规格[克重/片(块)等]
0304.6290	---其他	A:1.品名;2.制作或保存方法(冻);3. 拉丁名称。B:4.规格[克重/片(块)等];5.是否带头、脏、皮、刺、鳞、鳍
0304.6300	--尼罗河鲈鱼(尼罗尖吻鲈)	A:1.品名;2.制作或保存方法(冻);3. 拉丁名称。B:4.规格[克重/片(块)等];5.是否带头、脏、皮、刺、鳞、鳍
0304.6900	--其他	A:1.品名;2.制作或保存方法(冻);3. 拉丁名称。B:4.规格[克重/片(块)等];5.是否带头、脏、皮、刺、鳞、鳍
	-冻的犀鳕科、多丝真鳕科、鳕科、长尾鳕科、黑鳕科、无须鳕科、深海鳕科及南极鳕科鱼的鱼片:	A:1.品名;2.制作或保存方法(冻);3. 拉丁名称。B:4.规格[克重/片(块)等];5.是否带头、脏、皮、刺、鳞、鳍
0304.8100	--大麻哈鱼〔红大麻哈鱼、细磷大麻哈鱼、大麻哈鱼(种)、大鳞大麻哈鱼、银大麻哈鱼、马苏大麻哈鱼、玫瑰大麻哈鱼〕、大西洋鲑鱼及多瑙哲罗鱼	A:1.品名;2.制作或保存方法(冻);3. 拉丁名称。B:4.规格[克重/片(块)等];5.是否带头、脏、皮、刺、鳞、鳍
0304.8200	--鳟鱼(河鳟、虹鳟、克拉克大麻哈鱼、阿瓜大麻哈鱼、吉雨大麻哈鱼、亚利桑那大麻哈鱼、金腹大麻哈鱼)	A:1.品名;2.制作或保存方法(冻);3. 拉丁名称。B:4.规格[克重/片(块)等];5.是否带头、脏、皮、刺、鳞、鳍
0304.8300	--比目鱼(鲽科、鲆科、舌鳎科、鳎科、菱鲆科、刺鲆科)	A:1.品名;2.制作或保存方法(冻);3. 拉丁名称。B:4.规格[克重/片(块)等];5.是否带头、脏、皮、刺、鳞、鳍
0304.8400	--剑鱼	A:1.品名;2.制作或保存方法(冻);3. 拉丁名称。B:4.规格[克重/片(块)等]
0304.8500	--南极犬牙鱼(南极犬牙鱼属)	A:1.品名;2.制作或保存方法(冻);3. 拉丁名称。B:4.规格[克重/片(块)等]
0304.8600	--鲱鱼(大西洋鲱鱼、太平洋鲱鱼)	A:1.品名;2.制作或保存方法(冻);3. 拉丁名称。B:4.规格[克重/片(块)等];5.是否带头、脏、皮、刺、鳞、鳍
0304.8700	--金枪鱼(金枪鱼属)、鲣鱼或狐鲣(鲣)	A:1.品名;2.制作或保存方法(冻);3. 拉丁名称。B:4.规格[克重/片(块)等];5.是否带头、脏、皮、刺、鳞、鳍
0304.8900	--其他	A:1.品名;2.制作或保存方法(冻);3. 拉丁名称。B:4.规格[克重/片(块)等];5.是否带头、脏、皮、刺、鳞、鳍
	-其他，冻的:	A:1.品名;2.制作或保存方法(冻);3. 拉丁名称。B:4.规格[克重/片(块)等]
0305.1000	-适合供人食用的鱼的细粉、粗粉及团粒	A:1.品名;2.用途;3.拉丁名称
0305.2000	-干、熏、盐腌或盐渍的鱼肝及鱼卵	A:1.品名;2.制作或保存方法(干、熏、盐腌、盐渍);3.拉丁名称
	-干、盐腌或盐渍的鱼片，但熏制的除外:	A:1.品名;2.制作或保存方法(干、盐腌、盐渍);3.拉丁名称
	-熏鱼，包括鱼片，但食用杂碎除外:	A:1.品名;2.制作或保存方法(熏);3.拉丁名称
	-干鱼(不包括食用杂碎)，不论是否盐腌，但熏制的除外:	A:1.品名;2.制作或保存方法(干);3.拉丁名称
	-盐腌及盐渍的鱼(不包括食用杂碎)，但干或熏制的除外:	A:1.品名;2.制作或保存方法(盐腌、盐渍);3.拉丁名称

税则号列	商品名称	申报要素(A:归类要素 B:价格要素 C:审单及其他要素)及说明举例
	-鱼鳍、鱼头、鱼尾、鱼鳔及其他可食用杂碎:	A: 1. 品名; 2. 用途; 3. 拉丁名称
0306.1100	--岩礁虾和其他龙虾(真龙虾属、龙虾属、岩龙虾属)	A: 1. 品名; 2. 制作或保存方法(冻); 3. 状态(带壳、去壳); 4. 拉丁名称。B: 5. 个体重量; 6. 包装规格
0306.1200	--螯龙虾(螯龙虾属)	A: 1. 品名; 2. 制作或保存方法(冻); 3. 状态(带壳、去壳); 4. 拉丁名称。B: 5. 个体重量; 6. 包装规格
	--蟹:	A: 1. 品名; 2. 制作或保存方法(冻); 3. 状态(带壳、去壳); 4. 拉丁名称。B: 5. 个体重量; 6. 包装规格
0306.1500	--挪威海螯虾	A: 1. 品名; 2. 制作或保存方法(冻); 3. 状态(带壳、去壳); 4. 拉丁名称。B: 5. 个体重量; 6. 包装规格
	--冷水小虾及对虾(长额虾属、褐虾):	A: 1. 品名; 2. 制作或保存方法(冷水); 3. 状态(带壳、去壳); 4. 拉丁名称。B: 5. 规格(如 41~50 个/磅); 6. 包装规格
	--其他小虾及对虾:	A: 1. 品名; 2. 制作或保存方法(冻); 3. 状态(带壳、去壳); 4. 拉丁名称。B: 5. 规格(如 41~50 个/磅); 6. 包装规格
	--其他,包括适合供人食用的甲壳动物的细粉、粗粉及团粒:	A: 1. 品名; 2. 制作或保存方法(冻)
0306.2110	---种苗	A: 1. 品名; 2. 是否为种苗; 3. 拉丁名称
0306.2190	---其他	A: 1. 品名; 2. 制作或保存方法(活、鲜、冷、干等); 3. 状态(带壳、去壳); 4. 拉丁名称。B: 5. 个体重量; 6. 包装规格
0306.2210	---种苗	A: 1. 品名; 2. 是否为种苗; 3. 拉丁名称
0306.2290	---其他	A: 1. 品名; 2. 制作或保存方法(活、鲜、冷、干等); 3. 状态(带壳、去壳); 4. 拉丁名称
0306.2410	---种苗	A: 1. 品名; 2. 是否为种苗; 3. 拉丁名称
	---其他:	A: 1. 品名; 2. 制作或保存方法(活、鲜、冷、干等); 3. 状态(带壳、去壳); 4. 拉丁名称。B: 5. 个体重量; 6. 包装规格
0306.2510	---种苗	A: 1. 品名; 2. 是否为种苗; 3. 拉丁名称
0306.2590	---其他:	A: 1. 品名; 2. 制作或保存方法(活、鲜、冷、干等); 3. 状态(带壳、去壳); 4. 拉丁名称。B: 5. 个体重量; 6. 包装规格
0306.2610	---种苗	A: 1. 品名; 2. 是否为种苗; 3. 拉丁名称
0306.2620	---鲜、冷对虾	A: 1. 品名; 2. 制作或保存方法(活、鲜、冷、干等); 3. 状态(带壳、去壳); 4. 拉丁名称。B: 5. 个体重量; 6. 包装规格
0306.2690	---其他	A: 1. 品名; 2. 制作或保存方法(活、鲜、冷、干等); 3. 状态(带壳、去壳); 4. 拉丁名称。B: 5. 个体重量; 6. 包装规格
0306.2710	---种苗	A: 1. 品名; 2. 是否为种苗; 3. 拉丁名称
0306.2720	---鲜、冷对虾	A: 1. 品名; 2. 制作或保存方法(活、鲜、冷、干等); 3. 状态(带壳、去壳); 4. 拉丁名称。B: 5. 个体重量; 6. 包装规格
0306.2790	---其他	A: 1. 品名; 2. 制作或保存方法(活、鲜、冷、干等); 3. 状态(带壳、去壳); 4. 拉丁名称。B: 5. 个体重量; 6. 包装规格
0306.2910	---种苗	A: 1. 品名; 2. 是否为种苗
0306.2990	---其他	A: 1. 品名; 2. 制作或保存方法(活、鲜、冷、干等)
0307.1110	---种苗	A: 1. 品名; 2. 是否为种苗; 3. 拉丁名称
0307.1190	---其他	A: 1. 品名; 2. 制作或保存方法(活、鲜、冷等); 3. 状态(带壳、去壳); 4. 拉丁名称。B: 5. 个体重量; 6. 包装规格
0307.1900	--其他	A: 1. 品名; 2. 制作或保存方法(干、盐腌、盐渍等); 3. 状态(带壳、去壳); 4. 拉丁名称。B: 5. 个体重量; 6. 包装规格
0307.2110	---种苗	A: 1. 品名; 2. 是否为种苗; 3. 拉丁名称
0307.2190	---其他	A: 1. 品名; 2. 制作或保存方法(活、鲜、冷); 3. 状态(带壳、去壳); 4. 拉丁名称。B: 5. 个体重量; 6. 包装规格
0307.2900	--其他	A: 1. 品名; 2. 制作或保存方法(干、盐腌、盐渍等); 3. 状态(带壳、去壳); 4. 拉丁名称。B: 5. 个体重量; 6. 包装规格
0307.3110	---种苗	A: 1. 品名; 2. 是否为种苗; 3. 拉丁名称
0307.3190	---其他	A: 1. 品名; 2. 制作或保存方法(活、鲜、冷等); 3. 状态(带壳、去壳); 4. 拉丁名称。B: 5. 个体重量; 6. 包装规格
0307.3900	--其他	A: 1. 品名; 2. 制作或保存方法(干、盐腌、盐渍等); 3. 状态(带壳、去壳); 4. 拉丁名称。B: 5. 个体重量; 6. 包装规格
0307.4110	---种苗	A: 1. 品名; 2. 是否为种苗; 3. 拉丁名称
0307.4190	---其他	A: 1. 品名; 2. 制作或保存方法(活、鲜、冷); 3. 拉丁名称。B: 4. 个体重量; 5. 包装规格

税则号列	商品名称	申报要素(A:归类要素 B:价格要素 C:审单及其他要素)及说明举例
0307.4900	--其他	A: 1.品名; 2 制作或保存方法(干、盐腌、盐渍等) 3.拉丁名称。B: 4.个体重量; 5.包装规格
0307.5100	—活、鲜或冷的	A: 1.品名; 2.制作或保存方法(活、鲜、冷); 3.拉丁名称。B: 4.个体重量; 5.包装规格
0307.5900	—其他	A: 1.品名; 2.制作或保存方法(干、盐腌、盐渍等); 3.拉丁名称。B: 4.个体重量; 5.包装规格
0307.6010	---种苗	A: 1 品名; 2.是否为种苗; 3.拉丁名称
0307.6090	---其他	A: 1 品名; 2.制作或保存方法(活、鲜、冷、冻、干、盐腌、盐渍等); 3.拉丁名称。B: 4.个体重量; 5.包装规格
0307.7110	---种苗	A: 1.品名; 2.是否为种苗; 3.拉丁名称
	---其他:	A: 1.品名; 2.制作或保存方法(活、鲜、冷); 3.拉丁名称。
	--其他:	A: 1.品名; 2.制作或保存方法(活、鲜、冷); 3.拉丁名称。
0307.8110	---种苗	A: 1.品名; 2.是否为种苗; 3.拉丁名称
0307.8190	---其他	A: 1.品名; 2.制作或保存方法(活、鲜、冷); 3.拉丁名称。
0307.8900	--其他	A: 1.品名; 2.制作或保存方法(冻、干、盐腌、盐渍等); 3.拉丁名称
0307.9110	---种苗	A: 1.品名; 2.是否为种苗; 3.拉丁名称
0307.9190	---其他:	A: 1.品名; 2.制作或保存方法(活、鲜、冷); 3.拉丁名称。
0307.9900	--其他	A: 1.品名; 2.制作或保存方法(冻、干、盐腌、盐渍等); 3.拉丁名称
0308.1110	---种苗	A: 1.品名; 2.种苗请注明个体长度、尾数/千克等
0308.1190	---其他	A: 1.品名; 2.制作或保存方法(活、鲜、冷)
0308.1900	--其他	A: 1.品名; 2.制作或保存方法(冻、干、盐腌、盐渍等); 3.是否经水煮。B: 4.包装规格
0308.2110	---种苗	A: 1.品名; 2.种苗请注明个体长度、尾数/千克等
0308.2190	---其他	A: 1.品名; 2.制作或保存方法(活、鲜、冷)
0308.2900	--其他	A: 1.品名; 2.制作或保存方法(冻、干、盐腌、盐渍等)。B: 3.包装规格
0308.3011	----种苗	A: 1.品名; 2.种苗请注明个体长度、尾数/千克等
0308.3019	----其他	A: 1.品名; 2.制作或保存方法(活、鲜、冷)
0308.3090	---其他	A: 1.品名; 2.制作或保存方法(冻、干、盐腌、盐渍等)。B: 3.包装规格
0308.9011	----种苗	A: 1.品名; 2.种苗请注明个体长度、尾数/千克等
0308.9012	----沙蚕，种苗除外	A: 1.品名; 2.制作或保存方法(活、鲜、冷)
0308.9019	----其他	A: 1.品名; 2.制作或保存方法(活、鲜、冷)
0308.9090	---其他	A: 1.品名; 2.制作或保存方法(冻、干、盐腌、盐渍等)。B: 3.包装规格

第四章　乳品；蛋品；天然蜂蜜；其他食用动物产品

税则号列	商品名称	申报要素(A:归类要素 B:价格要素 C:审单及其他要素)及说明举例
04.01	未浓缩及未加糖或其他甜物质的乳及奶油:	A: 1.品名; 2.制作或保存方法(未浓缩及未加糖或其他甜物质); 3.脂肪含量(按重量计); 4.成分含量。B: 5.包装规格(如1升/盒); 6.品牌
04.02	浓缩、加糖或其他甜物质的乳及奶油:	A: 1.品名; 2.制作或保存方法(浓缩及加糖或其他甜物质); 3.外观(粉状、粒状等); 4.脂肪含量(按重量计); 5.成分含量。B: 6.包装规格(如 25 千克/包); 7. 品牌
04.03	酪乳、结块的乳及奶油、酸乳、酸乳酒及其他发酵或酸化的乳和奶油，不论是否浓缩、加糖、加其他甜物质、加香料、加水果、加坚果或加可可:	A: 1.品名; 2.制作或保存方法(发酵、酸化、浓缩、加糖及其他甜物质、香料等); 3.成分含量。B: 4.包装规格; 5.品牌
0404.1000	-乳清及改性乳清，不论是否浓缩、加糖或其他甜物质	A: 1.品名; 2.用途; 3.制作或保存方法(浓缩、加糖及其他甜物质); 4.成分含量。B: 5.品牌。例: 美女牌低蛋白乳清粉(饲料用)蛋白 3%、乳糖 80%、灰粉 9%、脂肪 0.2%、其他 2.8%、水分 5%
0404.9000	-其他	A: 1.品名; 2.成分含量。例: 该子目仅指其他税目未列名的含天然乳的产品
04.05	黄油及其他从乳中提取的脂和油；乳酱:	A: 1.品名; 2.成分含量。B: 3.包装规格; 4.品牌。例: 安佳牌无盐黄油乳脂含量 85%(25 千克/箱)
0406.1000	-鲜乳酪(未熟化或未固化的)，包括乳清乳酪；凝乳	A: 1.品名; 2.制作或保存方法(未熟化、未固化等); 3.成分含量。B: 4.品牌
0406.2000	-各种磨碎或粉化的乳酪	A: 1.品名; 2.制作或保存方法(未熟化、未固化等); 3.乳脂含量。B: 4.包装规格; 5.品牌
0406.3000	-经加工的乳酪，但磨碎或粉化的除外	A: 1.品名; 2.制作或保存方法(未熟化、未固化等); 3.成分含量。B: 4.包装规格; 5.品牌
0406.4000	-蓝纹乳酪和娄地青霉生产的带有纹理的其他乳酪	A: 1.品名; 2.制作或保存方法(熟化、固化、磨碎或粉化等); 3.成分含量; 4.是否带蓝纹或娄地青霉生产的带有纹理。B: 5.包装规格; 6.品牌

税则号列	商品名称	申报要素(A:归类要素 B:价格要素 C:审单及其他要素)及说明举例
0406.9000	-其他乳酪	A:1.品名;2.制作或保存方法(熟化、固化、磨碎或粉化等); 3.成分含量。B:4.包装规格 5.品牌
04.07	带壳禽蛋，鲜、腌制或煮过的:	
	-孵化用受精禽蛋:	A:1.品名;2.是否孵化用受精禽蛋
	-其他鲜蛋:	A:1.品名;2.制作或保存方法(鲜、带壳)
	-其他:	A:1.品名;2.制作或保存方法(鲜、带壳、腌制、煮过)
04.08	去壳禽蛋及蛋黄，鲜、干、冻、蒸过或水煮、制成型或用其他方法保藏的，不论是否加糖或其他甜物质:	A:1.品名;2.制作或保存方法(鲜、冻、干、去壳、蒸、水煮、制成型等)
04.09	天然蜂蜜:	A:1.品名;2.来源(天然)。B:3.品牌。例:不包括人造蜜及天然蜜和人造蜜的混合制品(税目17.02)
04.10	其他税目未列名的食用动物产品:	例:不包括海龟蛋油(税目 15.06);不包括液态或干制的动物血，不论是否可供食用(税目 05.11 或税目 30.02)
0410.0010	---燕窝	A:1.品名;2.用途(食用)。B:3.品种(燕子的品种);4.外形(燕盏或燕碎，燕条等);5.含水量
0410.0041	----鲜蜂王浆	A:1.品名;2.制作或保存方法(鲜)。B:3.品牌
0410.0042	----鲜蜂王浆粉	A:1.品名;2.制作或保存方法(鲜);3.外观(粉)。B:4.品牌
0410.0043	----蜂花粉	A:1.品名;2.外观(粉)。B:3.品牌
0410.0049	----其他	A:1.品名。B:2.品牌
0410.0090	---其他	A:1.品名;2.用途(食用)

第五章　其他动物产品

[注解]

本章所称“填充用羽毛”是指家禽(特别是鹅或鸭)、鸽子、鹧鸪或类似禽类的羽毛，但粗大的翼毛或尾毛及分级时摒弃的粗大的羽毛除外;“羽绒”，主要指鹅或鸭毛中最为细小、柔软的绒毛，它与羽毛的区别在于没有硬羽轴。

税则号列	商品名称	申报要素(A:归类要素 B:价格要素 C:审单及其他要素)及说明举例
05.01	未经加工的人发，不论是否洗涤;废人发:	A:1.品名;2.是否经加工。例:不包括经过简单洗涤以外加工(如稀疏、染色、漂白、卷曲或为制作假发进行加工)的人发及已按发根和发梢整理的人发(税目 67.03)
05.02	猪鬃、猪毛;獾毛及其他制刷用兽毛;上述鬃毛的废料:	例:不包括成束或成簇的鬃毛(税目 96.03)
	-猪鬃、猪毛及其废料:	A:1.品名
	-其他:	A:1.品名;2.用途(制刷用)
05.04	整个或切块的动物(鱼除外)的肠、膀胱及胃，鲜、冷、冻、干、熏、盐腌或盐渍的:	
	---肠衣:	A:1.品名;2.制作或保存方法(鲜、冷、冻、干、熏、盐腌、盐渍)
0504.0021	----冷、冻的鸡肫	A:1.品名;2.制作或保存方法(冷、冻)。B:3.品牌
0504.0029	----其他	A:1.品名;2.制作或保存方法(鲜、冷、冻、干、熏、盐腌、盐渍)
0504.0090	---其他	A:1.品名;2.制作或保存方法(鲜、冷、冻、干、熏、盐腌、盐渍)
0505.1000	-填充用羽毛; 羽绒	A:1.品名;2.用途;3.制作或保存方法(仅经洗涤、消毒或为了保藏而做过处理)。B:4.绒份; 5.羽毛长度
	-其他:	A:1.品名;2.用途;3.制作或保存方法(仅经洗涤、消毒或为了保藏而做过处理)
0506.1000	-经酸处理的骨胶原及骨	A:1.品名;2.处理方法(未经加工或经脱脂等)
0506.9011	----含牛羊成分的	A:1.品名;2.成分;3.处理方法(未经加工或经脱脂等);4.外观(粉末)5.是否废料
0506.9019	----其他	A:1.品名;2.处理方法(未经加工或经脱脂等)
0506.9090	---其他	A:1.品名;2.处理方法(未经加工或经脱脂等);3.是否脱胶
05.07	兽牙、龟壳、鲸须、鲸须毛、角、鹿角、蹄、甲、爪及喙，未经加工或仅简单整理但未切割成形;上述产品的粉末及废料:	A:1.品名;2.处理方法(未经加工或经脱脂等);3.是否为粉末及废料
05.08	珊瑚及类似品，未经加工或仅简单整理但未经进一步加工;软体动物壳、甲壳动物壳、棘皮动物壳、墨鱼骨，未经加工或仅简单整理但未切割成形，上述壳、骨的粉末及废料:	A:1.品名;2.处理方法(未经加工或经脱脂等);3.是否为粉末及废料
05.10	龙涎香、海狸香、灵猫香及麝香;斑蝥;胆汁，不论是否干制;供配制药用的腺	A:1.品名;2.制作或保存方法(鲜、冷、冻、干或用其他方法暂时保藏)。例:不包括胆汁精及制成干片后用安瓿封装的蛇或蜂的毒液(税目 30.01)

税则号列	商品名称	申报要素(A:归类要素 B:价格要素 C:审单及其他要素)及说明举例
	仫及其他动物产品，鲜、冷、冻或用其他方法暂时保藏的:	
05.11	其他税目未列名的动物产品；不适合供人食用的第一章或第三章的死动物:	例:不包括食用鱼卵及食用鱼肝(第三章)；不包括虫胶片、原胶、梗胶及其他虫胶(税目13.01)
0511.1000	-牛的精液	A:1.品名
0511.9111	----受精鱼卵	A:1.品名
0511.9119	----其他	A:1.品名;2.用途
0511.9190	---其他	A:1.品名;2.用途
0511.9910	---动物精液(牛的精液除外)	A:1.品名
0511.9920	---动物胚胎	A:1.品名
0511.9930	---蚕种	A:1.品名
0511.9940	---马毛及废马毛，不论是否制成有或无衬垫的毛片	A:1.品名
0511.9990	---其他	A:1.品名;2.用途

第二类　植物产品

第六章　活树及其他活植物；鳞茎、根及类似品；插花及装饰用簇叶

[注解]

本章所称“树、灌木”包括具有木质梗的藤本植物(例如，葡萄、杂交草莓、悬钩子属植物、猕猴桃树)及其带根插枝。

税则号列	商品名称	申报要素(A:归类要素 B:价格要素 C:审单及其他要素)及说明举例
06.01	鳞茎、块茎、块根、球茎、根颈及根茎，休眠、生长或开花的；菊苣植物及其根，但税目12.12的根除外:	A:1.品名;2.状态(休眠、生长、开花);3.种类(球茎、块茎、鳞茎、块根等);4.是否种用。例:不包括第七章的某些鳞茎、块茎、块根、球茎、根茎及根颈(如洋葱、青葱、大蒜、马铃薯、洋蓟)；不包括生姜(税目09.10)
0602.1000	-无根插枝及接穗	A:1.品名;2.栽培方法(无根插枝、接穗等)
0602.2010	---种用苗木	A:1.品名;2.是否种用
0602.2090	---其他	A:1.品名
0602.3010	---种用	A:1.品名;2.是否种用
0602.3090	---其他	A:1.品名
0602.4010	---种用	A:1.品名;2.是否种用
0602.4090	---其他	A:1.品名
0602.9010	---蘑菇菌丝	A:1.品名
0602.9091	----种用苗木	A:1.品名;2.是否种用
0602.9092	----兰花	A:1.品名
0602.9093	----菊花	A:1.品名
0602.9094	----百合	A:1.品名
0602.9095	----康乃馨	A:1.品名
0602.9099	----其他	A:1.品名
06.03	制花束或装饰用的插花及花蕾，鲜、干、染色、漂白、浸渍或用其他方法处理的:	A:1.品名;2.用途(制花束或装饰用);3.制作或保存方法(鲜、干、染色、漂白、浸渍等)。例:不包括主要用作香料、药料、杀虫、杀菌或类似用途的花、花瓣及花蕾，如果其报验时的状态已不适合制花束或作装饰用(税目12.11)；不包括税目97.01的拼贴画及类似的装饰板
06.04	制花束或装饰用的不带花及花蕾的植物枝、叶或其他部分、草、苔藓及地衣，鲜、干、染色、漂白、浸渍或用其他方法处理的:	A:1.品名;2.用途(制花束或装饰用);3.制作或保存方法(鲜且不带花及花蕾、干、染色、漂白、浸渍等)。例:不包括主要用作香料、药料、杀虫、杀菌或类似用途的植物及其部分品(包括草、苔藓及地衣)或供编结用的植物及其部分品，如果其报验时的状态已不适合制花束或作装饰用(税目12.11或14.01)；不包括税目97.01的拼贴画及类似的装饰板

第七章　食用蔬菜、根及块茎

[注解]

本章所称“冷藏”，是指产品的温度一般已降至0℃左右，但未冻结。然而，某些产品，例如，马铃薯，当温度降至并维持在10℃时，也可视作“冷藏”。“冷冻”，是指产品已冷却到本身冰点以下并且已经全部冻结。

税则号列	商品名称	申报要素(A:归类要素 B:价格要素 C:审单及其他要素)及说明举例
07.01	鲜或冷藏的马铃薯:	A:1.品名;2.制作或保存方法(鲜、冷);3.是否种用。例:种用马铃薯

税则号列	商品名称	申报要素(A:归类要素 B:价格要素 C:审单及其他要素)及说明举例
07.02	鲜或冷藏的番茄:	A:1.品名;2.制作或保存方法(鲜、冷)。例:鲜番茄
07.03	鲜或冷藏的洋葱、青葱、大蒜、韭葱及其他葱属蔬菜:	A:1.品名;2.制作或保存方法(鲜、冷)。例:本税目仅包括葱属蔬菜;例:鲜蒜头
07.04	鲜或冷藏的卷心菜、菜花、球茎甘蓝、羽衣甘蓝及类似的食用芥菜类蔬菜:	A:1.品名;2.制作或保存方法(鲜、冷)。例:冷藏菜花
07.05	鲜或冷藏的莴苣及菊苣:	A:1.品名;2.制作或保存方法(鲜、冷)。例:不包括菊苣植物及菊苣根(税目06.01或12.12)
07.06	鲜或冷藏的胡萝卜、萝卜、色拉甜菜根、婆罗门参、块根芹、小萝卜及类似的食用根茎:	A:1.品名;2.制作或保存方法(鲜、冷)。例:冷藏胡萝卜
07.07	鲜或冷藏的黄瓜及小黄瓜:	A:1.品名;2.制作或保存方法(鲜、冷)。例:鲜黄瓜
07.08	鲜或冷藏的豆类蔬菜,不论是否脱荚:	A:1.品名;2.制作或保存方法(鲜、冷)。例:不包括大豆(税目12.01)
07.09	鲜或冷藏的其他蔬菜:	A:1.品名;2.制作或保存方法(鲜、冷)。例:不包括荸荠属植物的可食用球茎(税目07.14)
07.10	冷冻蔬菜(不论是否蒸煮):	例:冷冻马铃薯
0710.1000	-马铃薯	A:1.品名;2.制作或保存方法(冻)
	-豆类蔬菜,不论是否脱荚:	A:1.品名;2.制作或保存方法(冻)
0710.3000	-菠菜	A:1.品名;2.制作或保存方法(冻)
0710.4000	-甜玉米	A:1.品名;2.制作或保存方法(冻)
	-其他蔬菜:	A:1.品名;2.制作或保存方法(冻)
0710.9000	-什锦蔬菜	A:1.品名;2.制作或保存方法(冻);3.种类
07.11	暂时保藏(例如,使用二氧化硫气体、盐水、亚硫酸水或其他防腐液)的蔬菜,但不适于直接食用的:	A:1.品名;2.用途(不适于直接食用);3.制作或保存方法(用盐水、二氧化硫气体、亚硫酸水或其他防腐液)。例:盐水松茸(不适于直接食用)
07.12	干蔬菜,整个、切块、切片、破碎或制成粉状,但未经进一步加工的:	A:1.品名;2.制作或保存方法(干制,包括脱水、蒸干或冻干)
0713.1010	---种用	A:1.品名;2.制作或保存方法(干制且脱荚);3.是否种用
0713.1090	---其他	A:1.品名;2.制作或保存方法(干制且脱荚)。B:3.品种(黄豌豆、青豌豆、白豌豆等)
	-鹰嘴豆:	A:1.品名;2.制作或保存方法(干制且脱荚);3.是否种用
	-豇豆属及菜豆属:	A:1.品名;2.制作或保存方法(干制且脱荚);3.是否种用
	-扁豆:	A:1.品名;2.制作或保存方法(干制且脱荚);3.是否种用
	-蚕豆:	A:1.品名;2.制作或保存方法(干制且脱荚);3.是否种用
	-木豆(木豆属):	A:1.品名;2.制作或保存方法(干制且脱荚);3.是否种用
	-其他:	A:1.品名;2.制作或保存方法(干制且脱荚);3.是否种用
07.14	鲜、冷、冻或干的木薯、竹芋、兰科植物块茎、菊芋、甘薯及含有高淀粉或菊粉的类似根茎,不论是否切片或制成团粒;西谷茎髓:	A:1.品名;2.制作或保存方法(鲜、冷、冻、干);3.是否种用。例:干木薯

第八章　食用水果及坚果;柑橘属水果或甜瓜的果皮

[注解]

本章所称"冷藏",是指产品的温度一般降至0℃左右,但未冻结的。但是有些产品(例如,甜瓜及某些柑橘属果实),其温度降至并维持在10℃时,也可视作"冷藏";所称"冷冻",是指温度降至产品的冰点以下,产品已全部冻结。

税则号列	商品名称	申报要素(A:归类要素 B:价格要素 C:审单及其他要素)及说明举例
08.01	鲜或干的椰子、巴西果及腰果,不论是否去壳或去皮:	例:不包括用于榨取椰子油而不适合供人食用的干椰肉(税目12.03)
	-椰子:	A:1.品名;2.制作或保存方法[鲜、干、未去内壳(内果皮)、去壳];3.是否种用
	-巴西果:	A:1.品名;2.制作或保存方法(鲜、干、未去壳、去壳)
0801.3100	--未去壳	A:1.品名;2.制作或保存方法(鲜、干、未去壳、去壳)
0801.3200	--去壳	A:1.品名;2.制作或保存方法(鲜、干、未去壳、去壳)。B:3.等级
08.02	鲜或干的其他坚果,不论是否去壳或去皮:	例:不包括花生(税目12.02);不包括焙炒的花生或花生酱(税目20.08);不包括核桃壳及杏仁壳(税目14.04)
	-扁桃仁:	A:1.品名;2.制作或保存方法(鲜、干、未去壳、去壳)
	-榛子:	A:1.品名;2.制作或保存方法(鲜、干、未去壳、去壳)。B:3.品种
	-核桃:	A:1.品名;2.制作或保存方法(鲜、干、未去壳、去壳)。B:3.品种

税则号列	商品名称	申报要素(A:归类要素 B:价格要素 C:审单及其他要素)及说明举例
	-栗子:	A: 1. 品名; 2. 制作或保存方法(鲜、干、未去壳、去壳)
	-阿月浑子果(开心果):	A: 1. 品名; 2. 制作或保存方法(鲜、干、未去壳、去壳)
	-马卡达姆坚果(夏威夷果):	A: 1. 品名; 2. 制作或保存方法(鲜、干、未去壳、去壳); 3. 是否种用。B: 4. 签约日期
0802.7000	-可乐果(可乐果属)	A: 1. 品名; 2. 制作或保存方法(鲜、干、未去壳、去壳)
0802.8000	-槟榔果	A: 1. 品名; 2. 制作或保存方法(鲜、干、未去壳、去壳)
	-其他:	A: 1. 品名; 2. 制作或保存方法(鲜、干、未去壳、去壳)
08.03	鲜或干的香蕉，包括芭蕉:	A: 1. 品名; 2. 制作或保存方法(鲜、干)。B: 3. 干制方法(脱水、蒸干或冻干); 4. 种类(大香蕉、焦仔、皇帝蕉等); 5. 等级(A 级、B 级、C 级等); 6. 品牌
0804.1000	-椰枣	A: 1. 品名; 2. 制作或保存方法(鲜、干)。B: 3. 等级
0804.2000	-无花果	A: 1. 品名; 2. 制作或保存方法(鲜、干)。B: 3. 等级
0804.3000	-菠萝	A: 1. 品名; 2. 制作或保存方法(鲜、干)。B: 3. 种类(如青菠萝、金菠萝等); 4. 等级
0804.4000	-鳄梨	A: 1. 品名; 2. 制作或保存方法(鲜、干)。B: 3. 等级
	-番石榴、芒果及山竹果:	A: 1. 品名; 2. 制作或保存方法(鲜、干)。B: 3. 等级
08.05	鲜或干的柑橘属水果	例: 不包括柑橘皮(税目 08.14)
0805.1000	-橙	A: 1. 品名; 2. 制作或保存方法(鲜、干)。B: 3. 种类(脐橙、夏橙等); 4. 等级; 5. 品牌
	-柑橘; 杂交柑橘:	A: 1. 品名; 2. 制作或保存方法(鲜、干)。B: 3. 等级
0805.4000	-葡萄柚, 包括柚	A: 1. 品名; 2. 制作或保存方法(鲜、干)。B: 3. 等级
0805.5000	-柠檬及酸橙	A: 1. 品名; 2. 制作或保存方法(鲜、干)。B: 3. 等级; 4. 品牌
0805.9000	-其他	A: 1. 品名; 2. 制作或保存方法(鲜、干)。B: 3. 等级
0806.1000	-鲜的	A: 1. 品名; 2. 制作或保存方法(鲜)。B: 3. 种类; 4. 等级; 5. 品牌
0806.2000	-干的	A: 1. 品名; 2. 制作或保存方法(干)。B: 3. 等级; 4. 品牌
0807.1100	--西瓜	A: 1. 品名; 2. 制作或保存方法(鲜)。B: 3. 等级; 4. 品牌
	--其他:	A: 1. 品名; 2. 制作或保存方法(鲜)。B: 3. 等级
0807.2000	-木瓜	A: 1. 品名; 2. 制作或保存方法(鲜)。B: 3. 等级; 4. 品牌
0808.1000	-苹果	A: 1. 品名; 2. 制作或保存方法(鲜)。B: 3. 种类(蛇果、加纳果、青苹果、富士等); 4. 等级; 5. 品牌
	-梨:	A: 1. 品名; 2. 制作或保存方法(鲜)。B: 3. 等级
0808.4000	-榅桲	A: 1. 品名; 2. 制作或保存方法(鲜)。B: 3. 等级
08.09	鲜的杏、樱桃、桃(包括油桃)、梅及李:	A: 1. 品名; 2. 制作或保存方法(鲜)。B: 3. 等级
0810.1000	-草莓	A: 1. 品名; 2. 制作或保存方法(鲜)。B: 3. 等级
0810.2000	-木莓、黑莓、桑葚及罗甘莓	A: 1. 品名; 2. 制作或保存方法(鲜)。B: 3. 等级
0810.3000	-黑、白或红的穗醋栗(加仑子)及醋栗	A: 1. 品名; 2. 制作或保存方法(鲜)。B: 3. 等级
0810.4000	-蔓越橘及越橘	A: 1. 品名; 2. 制作或保存方法(鲜)。B: 3. 等级
0810.5000	-猕猴桃	A: 1. 品名; 2. 制作或保存方法(鲜)。B: 3. 种类(金奇异果、青奇异果等); 4. 等级
0810.6000	-榴莲	A: 1. 品名; 2. 制作或保存方法(鲜)。B: 3. 等级; 4. 品牌
0810.7000	-柿子	A: 1. 品名; 2. 制作或保存方法(鲜)。B: 3. 等级
	-其他:	A: 1. 品名; 2. 制作或保存方法(鲜)。B: 3. 等级
08.11	冷冻水果及坚果，不论是否蒸煮、加糖或其他甜物质	例: 冷冻未去壳栗子
0811.1000	-草莓	A: 1. 品名; 2. 制作或保存方法(冻)
0811.2000	-木莓、黑莓、桑葚、罗甘莓，黑、白或红的穗醋栗(加仑子)及醋栗	A: 1. 品名; 2. 制作或保存方法(冻)
0811.9010	---栗子, 未去壳	A: 1. 品名; 2. 制作或保存方法(冻、未去壳)
0811.9090	---其他	A: 1. 品名; 2. 制作或保存方法(冻)
08.12	暂时保藏(例如，使用二氧化硫气体、盐水、亚硫酸水或其他防腐液)的水果及坚果，但不适于直接食用的:	A: 1. 品名; 2. 用途(不适于直接食用); 3. 制作或保存方法(用盐水、二氧化硫气体、亚硫酸水或其他防腐液)。例: 盐水保藏樱桃(不适于直接食用)
08.13	税目 08.01 至 08.06 以外的干果; 本章的什锦坚果或干果	例: 本税目仅包括税目 08.01 至 08.06 以外的干果
0813.1000	-杏	A: 1. 品名; 2. 制作或保存方法(干)
0813.2000	-梅及李	A: 1. 品名; 2. 制作或保存方法(干)
0813.3000	-苹果	A: 1. 品名; 2. 制作或保存方法(干)
0813.4010	---龙眼干、肉	A: 1. 品名; 2. 制作或保存方法(干)。B: 3. 等级
0813.4020	---柿饼	A: 1. 品名; 2. 制作或保存方法(干)

税则号列	商品名称	申报要素(A:归类要素 B:价格要素 C:审单及其他要素)及说明举例
0813.4030	---红枣	A:1.品名;2.制作或保存方法(干)
0813.4040	---荔枝干	A:1.品名;2.制作或保存方法(干);3.加工程度(去壳、未去壳)
0813.4090	---其他	A:1.品名;2.制作或保存方法(干)
0813.5000	-本章的什锦坚果或干果	A:1.品名;2.制作或保存方法(干);3.种类
08.14	柑橘属水果或甜瓜(包括西瓜)的果皮,鲜、冻、干或用盐水、亚硫酸水或其他防腐液暂时保藏的:	A:1.品名;2.制作或保存方法(鲜、冻、干,用盐水、亚硫酸水或其他防腐液暂时保藏的)。例:不包括果皮粉(税目 11.06);不包括蜜饯果皮(税目 20.06)

第九章　咖啡、茶、马黛茶及调味香料

税则号列	商品名称	申报要素(A:归类要素 B:价格要素 C:审单及其他要素)及说明举例
09.01	咖啡,不论是否焙炒或浸除咖啡碱;咖啡豆荚及咖啡豆皮;含咖啡的咖啡代用品	例:不包括不含咖啡的焙炒咖啡代用品(税目 21.01);不包括咖啡蜡(税目 15.21);不包括咖啡碱,即咖啡中的生物碱(税目 29.39)
0901.1100	--未浸除咖啡碱	A:1.品名;2.制作或保存方法(豆、粉等,未焙炒且未浸除咖啡碱)
0901.1200	--已浸除咖啡碱	A:1.品名;2.制作或保存方法(豆、粉等,未焙炒且已浸除咖啡碱)
0901.2100	--未浸除咖啡碱	A:1.品名;2.制作或保存方法(豆、粉等,已焙炒且未浸除咖啡碱)
0901.2200	--已浸除咖啡碱	A:1.品名;2.制作或保存方法(豆、粉等,已焙炒且已浸除咖啡碱)
0901.9010	---咖啡豆荚及咖啡豆皮	A:1.品名;2.种类(咖啡豆荚或豆皮)
0901.9020	---含咖啡的咖啡代用品	A:1.品名;2.成分
09.02	茶,不论是否加香料:	A:1.品名;2.制作或保存方法(未发酵、半发酵、发酵);3.内包装每件净重。B:4.品牌
09.03	马黛茶:	A:1.品名
09.04	胡椒;辣椒干及辣椒粉:	A:1.品名;2.制作或保存方法(未磨、已磨、干、粉)
09.05	香子兰豆:	A:1.品名;2.加工方法(未磨、已磨)。例:不包括香草油树脂(人们有时误称为香草香膏或香草浸膏)(税目 13.02);不包括香草糖(税目 17.01 或 17.02);不包括香草醛(香草的香素)(税目 29.12)
09.06	肉桂及肉桂花:	A:1.品名;2.加工方法(未磨、已磨)
09.07	丁香(母丁香、公丁香及丁香梗):	A:1.品名;2.加工方法(未磨、已磨)。例:不包括丁香树皮及树叶(税目 12.11)
09.08	肉豆蔻、肉豆蔻衣及豆蔻:	A:1.品名;2.加工方法(未磨、已磨)
09.09	茴芹子、八角茴香、小茴香子、芫荽子、枯茗子及蒿子;杜松果:	A:1.品名;2.加工方法(未磨、已磨)。例:八角茴香
09.10	姜、番红花、姜黄、麝香草、月桂叶、咖喱及其他调味香料:	
	-姜	A:1.品名;2.加工方法(未磨、已磨)
0910.2000	-番红花	A:1.品名
0910.3000	-姜黄	A:1.品名
	-其他调味香料:	A:1.品名;2.成分含量

第十章　谷　物

税则号列	商品名称	申报要素(A:归类要素 B:价格要素 C:审单及其他要素)及说明举例
10.01	小麦及混合麦:	A:1.品名;2.是否种用;3.是否硬粒;4.种类(白麦、红麦、冬麦、春麦)
10.02	黑麦:	A:1.品名;2.是否种用。例:不包括有麦角寄生的黑麦(税目 12.11)
10.03	大麦:	A:1.品名;2.是否种用。例:不包括烘焙大麦(咖啡代用品)(税目 21.01);不包括在烘焙过程中从发芽麦粒分出来的麦芽新芽及其他酿造废料(粮食、啤酒花等的渣滓)(税目 23.03)
10.04	燕麦:	A:1.品名;2.是否种用。例:种用燕麦
10.05	玉米:	A:1.品名;2.是否种用。例:本税目所称"种用",仅包括由本国主管部门认可作为播种用的玉米
1006.1011	----籼米	A:1.品名;2.种类(籼米);3.是否种用。B:4.包装规格
1006.1019	----其他	A:1.品名;2.种类(香米、巴吞米、白米、糯米等);3.是否种用。B:4.包装规格
1006.1091	----籼米	A:1.品名;2.种类(籼米)。B:3.包装规格
1006.1099	----其他	A:1.品名;2.种类(香米、巴吞米、白米、糯米等)。B:3.包装规格
1006.2010	---籼米	A:1.品名;2.种类(籼米);3.制作或保存方法(糙米)。B:4.包装规格
1006.2090	---其他	A:1.品名;2.种类(香米、巴吞米、白米、糯米等);3.制作或保存方法(糙米)。B:4.包装规格
1006.3010	---籼米	A:1.品名;2.种类(籼米)。B:3.包装规格
1006.3090	---其他	A:1.品名;2.种类(香米、巴吞米、白米、糯米等)。B:3.包装规格

税则号列	商品名称	申报要素(A:归类要素 B:价格要素 C:审单及其他要素)及说明举例
1006.4010	---籼米	A: 1.品名; 2.种类(籼米)。B: 3.包装规格
1006.4090	---其他	A: 1.品名; 2.种类(香米、籼米、巴吞米、白米、糯米等)。B: 3.包装规格
10.07	食用高粱:	A: 1.品名; 2.用途(食用); 3.是否种用。B: 4.包装规格。例: 不包括饲料高粱及草高粱(税目 12.14)、甜高粱(税目 12.12)、帚用高粱(税目 14.03)
10.08	荞麦、谷子及加那利草子; 其他谷物:	A: 1.品名; 2.是否种用。B: 3.包装规格

第十一章　制粉工业产品；麦芽；淀粉；菊粉；面筋

税则号列	商品名称	申报要素(A:归类要素 B:价格要素 C:审单及其他要素)及说明举例
11.01	小麦或混合麦的细粉:	A: 1.品名; 2.状态(细粉)。例: 不包括掺有可可的细粉[按重量计全脱脂可可含量在 40%及以上的(税目 18.06), 低于 40%的(税目 19.01)]
11.02	其他谷物细粉, 但小麦或混合麦的细粉除外:	A: 1.品名; 2.种类(玉米、籼米等); 3. 状态(细粉)。例: 不包括掺有可可的细粉[按重量计全脱脂可可含量在 40%及以上的(税目 18.06), 低于 40%的(税目 19.02)]
11.03	谷物的粗粒、粗粉及团粒:	A: 1.品名; 2.种类(小麦、玉米、燕麦等); 3. 状态(粗粒、粗粉、团粒等)
11.04	经其他加工的谷物(例如, 去壳、滚压、制片、制成粒状、切片或粗磨), 但税目 10.06 的稻谷、大米除外; 谷物胚芽, 整粒、滚压、制片或磨碎的:	A: 1.品名; 2.种类(燕麦、大麦、小麦等); 3.制作或保存方法(去壳、滚压、制片等)
1104.3000	-谷物胚芽, 整粒、滚压、制片或磨碎的	例: 不包括谷物胚芽提取油类后的残渣(税目 23.06)
11.05	马铃薯的细粉、粗粉、粉末、粉片、颗粒及团粒:	A: 1.品名; 2. 状态(细粉、粗粉、粉末、粉片、颗粒及团粒)。例: 不包括马铃薯淀粉(税目 11.08); 不包括仅简单干燥、脱水或蒸干但未进一步加工的马铃薯(税目 07.12); 不包括马铃薯淀粉制得的珍粉代用品(税目 19.03)
11.06	用税目 07.13 的干豆或税目 07.14 的西谷茎髓及植物根茎、块茎制成的细粉、粗粉及粉末; 用第八章的产品制成的细粉、粗粉及粉末:	A: 1.品名; 2.种类(豌豆、鹰嘴豆等); 3.状态(细粉、粗粉、粉末)
1106.1000	-用税目 07.13 的干豆制成的	例: 仅用税目 07.13 的干豆制成; 不包括未脱脂大豆细粉(税目 12.08); 不包括以蔬菜细粉或粗粉为基料的汤料(不论液状、固体或粉状)(税目 21.04)
1106.2000	-用税目 07.14 的西谷茎髓及植物根茎、块茎制成的	例: 仅用税目 07.14 所列产品制成
1106.3000	-用第八章的产品制成的	例: 仅用第八章的产品制成; 不包括西谷茎髓(税目 07.14); 不包括名为珍粉的食品(税目 19.03)
11.07	麦芽, 不论是否焙制:	A: 1.品名; 2.制作或保存方法(未焙制、已焙制)。例: 未焙制麦芽
11.08	淀粉; 菊粉:	例: 不包括制成香粉及盥洗用品的淀粉(第三十三章); 不包括以淀粉为基料的胶(税目 35.05 或 35.06); 不包括用淀粉制成的上光料或浆料(税目 38.09); 不包括分离淀粉所得的离析支链淀粉及离析直链淀粉(税目 39.13)
1108.1100	--小麦淀粉	A: 1.品名; 2.种类(小麦淀粉)
1108.1200	--玉米淀粉	A: 1.品名; 2.种类(玉米淀粉)
1108.1300	--马铃薯淀粉	A: 1.品名; 2.种类(马铃薯淀粉)
1108.1400	--木薯淀粉	A: 1.品名; 2.种类(木薯淀粉)
1108.1900	--其他	A: 1.品名; 2.种类(大米淀粉、竹芋淀粉等)
1108.2000	-菊粉	A: 1.品名
11.09	面筋, 不论是否干制:	A: 1.品名。例: 不包括加有面筋的营养面粉(税目 11.01); 不包括做胶用或做纺织工业上光料或浆料用的面筋(税目 35.06 或 38.09)

第十二章　含油子仁及果实；杂项子仁及果实；工业用或药用植物；稻草、秸秆及饲料

税则号列	商品名称	申报要素(A:归类要素 B:价格要素 C:审单及其他要素)及说明举例
12.01	大豆, 不论是否破碎:	例: 不包括作为咖啡代用品的烘焙大豆(税目 21.01)
1201.1000	-种用	A: 1.品名; 2.种类(黄大豆、黑大豆、青大豆等); 3.是否种用
1201.9010	---黄大豆	A: 1.品名; 2.种类(黄大豆)。B: 3.蛋白含量; 4.油含量; 5.升贴水
1201.9020	---黑大豆	A: 1.品名; 2.种类(黑大豆)
1201.9030	---青大豆	A: 1.品名; 2.种类(青大豆)
1201.9090	---其他	A: 1.品名; 2.种类
12.02	未焙炒或未烹煮的花生, 不论是否去壳或破碎:	A: 1.品名; 2.制作或保存方法(未去壳、去壳、未焙炒、未烹煮); 3.是否种用 例: 本税目仅指未焙炒或未烹煮的

税则号列	商品名称	申报要素(A:归类要素 B:价格要素 C:审单及其他要素)及说明举例
12.03	干椰子肉:	A:1.品名;2.用途(榨油用)。例:不包括供人食用的干椰丝(税目 08.01)
12.04	亚麻子,不论是否破碎:	A:1.品名
12.05	油菜子,不论是否破碎:	例:种用低芥子酸油菜子
1205.1010	---种用	A:1.品名;2.是否种用。B:3.芥子酸含量及所得固体成分每克葡萄糖苷酸(酯)含量
1205.1090	---其他	A:1.品名。B:2.芥子酸含量及所得固体成分每克葡萄糖苷酸(酯)含量
1205.9010	---种用	A:1.品名;2.是否种用
1205.9090	---其他	A:1.品名
1206.0010	---种用	A:1.品名;2.是否种用 例:种用葵花子
1206.0090	---其他	A:1.品名
12.07	其他含油子仁及果实,不论是否破碎:	A:1.品名;2.是否种用
1207.2100	---种用	例:种用棉子
12.08	含油子仁或果实的细粉及粗粉,但芥子粉除外:	A:1.品名;2. 状态(细粉、粗粉)。例:不包括花生酱(税目 20.08);不包括芥子细粉及粗粉,不论是否脱脂、调制(税目 21.03)
12.09	种植用的种子、果实及孢子:	A:1.品名;2.用途(种植用)
12.10	鲜或干的啤酒花,不论是否研磨或制成团粒;蛇麻腺:	A:1.品名;2.制作或保存方法(鲜、干、未研磨、研磨、未制成团粒等) 例:不包括啤酒花浸膏(税目 13.02);不包括废啤酒花(税目 23.03);不包括蛇麻精油(税目 33.01)
12.11	主要用作香料、药料、杀虫、杀菌或类似用途的植物或这些植物的某部分(包括子仁及果实),鲜或干的,不论是否切割、压碎或研磨成粉:	A:1.品名;2.用途(作香料、药料、杀虫、杀菌等类似用途);3.制作或保存方法(鲜、干)。例:不包括制成一定剂量或零售包装的
12.12	鲜、冷、冻或干的刺槐豆、海草及其他藻类、甜菜及甘蔗,不论是否碾磨;主要供人食用的其他税目未列名的果核、果仁及植物产品(包括未焙制的菊苣根):	例:不包括作为胶粘剂或增稠剂的刺槐豆胚乳粉(税目 13.02);不包括琼脂及角叉藻胶(税目 13.02);不包括已死的单细胞藻类(税目 21.02);不包括蔗渣,即甘蔗榨汁后剩下的纤维部分(税目 23.03);不包括作为咖啡代用品的烘焙菊苣根(税目 21.01),不包括其他未烘焙菊苣根(税目 06.01);不包括雕刻用的果核(例如,椰枣核)(税目 14.04)及烘焙果仁(一般作为咖啡代用品)(税目 21.01)
	-海草及其他藻类:	A:1.品名;2.制作或保存方法(鲜、冷、冻、干等);3.状态(整条或切片);4.拉丁名称
1212.9100	--甜菜	A:1.品名;2.制作或保存方法(鲜、冷、冻等)
1212.9200	--刺槐豆	A:1.品名;2.制作或保存方法(鲜、冷、冻等)
1212.9300	--甘蔗	A:1.品名;2.制作或保存方法(鲜、冷、冻等)
1212.9400	--菊苣根	A:1.品名;2.制作或保存方法(鲜、冷、冻等)
	--其他:	A:1.品名;2.用途(主要供人食用)
12.13	未经处理的谷类植物的茎、秆及谷壳,不论是否切碎、碾磨、挤压或制成团粒:	A:1.品名;2.制作或保存方法(切碎、碾磨、挤压等);3.加工程度(未经处理)。例:不包括已净、漂白或染色的谷粒植物草、秆(税目 14.01)
12.14	芜菁甘蓝、饲料甜菜、饲料用根、干草、紫苜蓿、三叶草、驴喜豆、饲料羽衣甘蓝、羽扇豆、巢菜及类似饲料,不论是否制成团粒:	例:不包括谷类植物的草、秆及壳(税目 12.03);不包括虽然用作动物饲料,但并非专为饲养动物而种植的植物产品(如甜菜、胡萝卜叶及玉米叶)(税目 23.08);不包括配制的动物饲料(如甜饲料)(税目 23.09)
1214.1000	-紫苜蓿粗粉及团粒	A:1.品名;2.状态(粗粉及团粒等)
1214.9000	-其他	A:1.品名

第十三章　虫胶;树胶、树脂及其他植物液、汁

税则号列	商品名称	申报要素(A:归类要素 B:价格要素 C:审单及其他要素)及说明举例
13.01	虫胶;天然树胶、树脂、树胶脂及油树脂(例如,香树脂):	例:不包括接触空气即硬化成为一种抗性薄膜的某些东方树木的树液(名为"日本漆"、"中国漆"等)(税目 13.02);不包括琥珀(税目 25.30);不包括虫胶染料,即从虫胶提取的色料(税目 32.03);不包括香膏(从本税目物质中提取的)及提取的油树脂(税目 33.01);不包括妥尔油(有时称为"液体松香")(税目 38.03);不包括松节油(税目 38.05)
1301.2000	-阿拉伯胶	A:1.品名。B:2.用途(食品、饮料、制药等)
	-其他:	A:1.品名
13.02	植物液汁及浸膏;果胶、果胶酸盐及果胶酸酯;从植物产品制得的琼脂、其他胶液及增稠剂,不论是否改性:	例:不包括麦精(税目 19.01);不包括烟草精(税目 24.03);不包括樟脑(税目 29.14);不包括甘草甜及甘草酸(税目 29.38);不包括做血型试剂用的浸膏(税目 30.06);不包括鞣料膏(税目 32.01);不包括染料膏(税目 32.03);不包括天然橡胶、巴拉塔胶、古塔波胶、银胶菊胶,糖胶树胶及类似天然树胶(税目 40.01);不包括藻酸及藻酸盐(税目 39.13)

税则号列	商品名称	申报要素(A:归类要素 B:价格要素 C:审单及其他要素)及说明举例
1302.1100	--鸦片	A:1.品名;2.制作或保存方法(液汁、浸膏、粉末)
1302.1200	--甘草的	A:1.品名;2.制作或保存方法(液汁、浸膏、粉末)
1302.1300	--啤酒花的	A:1.品名;2.制作或保存方法(液汁、浸膏、粉末);3.请注明有效成分含量(α酸等)
	--其他:	A:1.品名;2.制作或保存方法(液汁、浸膏、粉末)
1302.2000	-果胶、果胶酸盐及果胶酸酯	A:1.品名。B:2.用途(食品用、医药用)
1302.3100	--琼脂	A:1.品名。B:2.等级(食品级、医药级等)
1302.3200	--从刺槐豆、刺槐豆子或瓜尔豆制得的胶液及增稠剂,不论是否改性	A:1.品名;2.来源
1302.3911	----卡拉胶	A:1.品名。B:2.种类(卡帕胶、阿欧塔胶、莱姆达胶等);3.用途(乳品、肉类、水、糖果、果冻、甜品)
1302.3912	----褐藻胶	A:1.品名。B:2.用途
1302.3919	----其他	A:1.品名。B:2.用途
1302.3990	---其他	A:1.品名;2.来源。B:3.用途

第十四章　编结用植物材料;其他植物产品

税则号列	商品名称	申报要素(A:归类要素 B:价格要素 C:审单及其他要素)及说明举例
14.01	主要作编结用的植物材料(例如,竹、藤、芦苇、灯芯草、柳条、酒椰叶,已净、漂白或染色的谷类植物的茎秆,椴树皮):	例:不包括木片条(税目44.04)
1401.1000	-竹	A:1.品名;2.用途(主要作编结用)
1401.2000	-藤	A:1.品名;2.用途(主要作编结用)。B:3.种类;4.请注明加工程度(去皮或未去皮);5.直径;6.长度
	-其他:	A:1.品名;2.用途(主要作编结用)
1404.2000	-棉短绒	A:1.品名;2.纤维长度 例:不包括棉絮,药用的或医疗、外科、牙科或兽医用零售包装的(税目30.05);不包括其他棉絮胎(税目56.01)
1404.9010	---主要供染料、鞣料用的植物原料	A:1.品名;2.用途(主要供染料或鞣料用) 例:不包括植物鞣料膏及鞣酸,包括水苹没食子酸(税目32.01);不包括染料木及其他染料植物浸膏(税目32.03)
1404.9090	---其他	A:1.品名

第三类　动、植物油、脂及其分解产品;精制的食用油脂;动、植物蜡

第十五章　动、植物油、脂及其分解产品;精制的食用油脂;动、植物蜡

[注解]

本章税目15.04及15.06至15.15所称分离的主要方法指通过压榨、倾析、冬化及过滤进行干分离、溶剂分离、借助表面活性剂分离。

税则号列	商品名称	申报要素(A:归类要素 B:价格要素 C:审单及其他要素)及说明举例
15.01	猪脂肪(包括已炼制的猪油)及家禽脂肪,但税目02.09及15.03的货品除外:	A:1.品名。 例:不包括未炼制或用其他方法提取的不带瘦肉的肥猪肉、猪脂肪及家禽脂肪(税目02.09);不包括猪油硬脂及液体猪油(税目15.03);不包括人造猪油(税目15.17)
15.02	牛、羊脂肪,但税目15.03的货品除外:	A:1.品名;2.加工程度(干、熏、盐腌、盐渍、已炼制等)。B:3.是否含瘦肉。例:不包括税目15.03的货品,例:油硬脂、食用或非食用脂油(税目15.03);不包括马脂(税目15.06)
15.03	猪油硬脂、液体猪油、油硬脂、食用或非食用脂油,未经乳化、混合或其他方法制作:	A:1.品名;2.加工程度(未经乳化、混合或其他方法制作)
1504.1000	-鱼肝油及其分离品	A:1.品名;2.成分含量;3.加工程度(未经化学改性)。B:4.饲料用的鱼油、脂及其分离品请注明是否精炼;5.保健用鱼油请注明DHA+EPA浓度
1504.2000	-除鱼肝油以外的鱼油、脂及其分离品	A:1.品名;2.成分含量;3.加工程度(未经化学改性)。B:4.饲料用的鱼油、脂及其分离品请注明是否精炼;5.保健用鱼油请注明DHA+EPA浓度
1504.3000	-海生哺乳动物的油、脂及其分离品	A:1.品名;2.成分含量;3.加工程度(未经化学改性)
15.05	羊毛脂及从羊毛脂制得的脂肪物质(包括纯净的羊毛脂):	A:1.品名。 例:不包括羊毛脂残渣(税目15.22)

税则号列	商品名称	申报要素(A:归类要素 B:价格要素 C:审单及其他要素)及说明举例
15.06	其他动物油、脂及其分离品，不论是否精制，但未经化学改性:	A: 1.品名; 2.加工程度(未经化学改性)。例: 不包括猪脂肪及家禽脂肪(税目02.09或15.01); 不包括牛、绵羊或山羊脂肪(税目15.02); 不包括鱼或海生哺乳动物的油、脂及其分离品(税目15.04); 不包括主要同吡啶基组成的产品(通称为骨焦油，有时也称骨油)(税目38.24)
15.07	豆油及其分离品，不论是否精制，但未经化学改性:	A: 1.品名; 2.加工方法(初榨、精制); 3.加工程度(未经化学改性)
1507.1000	-初榨的,不论是否脱胶	例: 初榨豆油(未经化学改性)
15.08	花生油及其分离品，不论是否精制，但未经化学改性:	A: 1.品名; 2.加工方法(初榨、精制); 3.加工程度(未经化学改性)
1508.9000	-其他	例: 精制花生油(未经化学改性)
15.09	油橄榄油及其分离品，不论是否精制，但未经化学改性:	A: 1.品名; 2.加工方法(初榨、精制); 3.加工程度(未经化学改性)。B: 4.包装规格; 5.品牌; 6.酸度; 7.产区。 例: 不包括橄榄渣油及油橄榄油与橄榄渣油的混合油(税目 15.10); 不包括从橄榄油中制取的再酯化油(税目15.16)
15.10	其他橄榄油及其分离品，不论是否精制，但未经化学改性，包括掺有税目15.09的油或分离品的混合物:	A: 1.品名; 2.加工程度(未经化学改性)。B: 3.包装规格; 4.品牌。 例: 包括掺有税目15.09的油或分离品的混合物; 橄榄油(未经化学改性)
1511.1000	-初榨的	A: 1.品名; 2.加工方法(初榨); 3.加工程度(未经化学改性)
1511.9010	---棕榈液油(熔点19℃~24℃)	A: 1.品名; 2.加工程度(未经化学改性); 3.熔点。B: 4.包装方式; 5.规格
1511.9020	---棕榈硬脂(熔点44℃~56℃)	A: 1.品名; 2.加工程度(未经化学改性); 3.熔点。B: 4.包装规格
1511.9090	---其他	A: 1.品名; 2.加工方法(精制); 3.加工程度(未经化学改性)。B: 4.包装规格
15.12	葵花油、红花油或棉子油及其分离品，不论是否精制，但未经化学改性:	A: 1.品名; 2.加工方法(初榨、精制); 3.加工程度(未经化学改性)
1512.1100	--初榨的	例: 初榨葵花油(未经化学改性)
15.13	椰子油、棕榈仁油或巴巴苏棕榈果油及其分离品，不论是否精制，但未经化学改性:	A: 1.品名; 2.加工方法(初榨、精制); 3.加工程度(未经化学改性)
1513.1100	--初榨的	例: 初榨椰子油(未经化学改性)
1514.1100	--初榨的	A: 1.品名; 2.加工方法(初榨); 3.加工程度(未经化学改性)。B: 4.芥子酸含量。 例: 初榨低芥子酸菜子油(未经化学改性)
1514.1900	--其他	A: 1.品名; 2.加工方法(精制); 3.加工程度(未经化学改性)。B: 4.芥子酸含量及所得固体成分每克葡萄糖苷酸(酯)含量
1514.9110	---菜子油	A: 1.品名; 2.加工方法(初榨); 3.加工程度(未经化学改性)
1514.9190	---芥子油	A: 1.品名; 2.加工方法(初榨); 3.加工程度(未经化学改性)
1514.9900	--其他	A: 1.品名; 2.加工方法(精制); 3.加工程度(未经化学改性)
1515.1100	--初榨的	A: 1.品名; 2.加工方法(初榨); 3.加工程度(未经化学改性)
1515.1900	--其他	A: 1.品名; 2.加工方法(精制); 3.加工程度(未经化学改性)
1515.2100	--初榨的	A: 1.品名; 2.加工方法(初榨); 3.加工程度(未经化学改性)
1515.2900	--其他	A: 1.品名; 2.加工方法(精制); 3.加工程度(未经化学改性)
1515.3000	-蓖麻油及其分离品	A: 1.品名; 2.加工方法(初榨、精制); 3.加工程度(未经化学改性)
1515.5000	-芝麻油及其分离品	A: 1.品名; 2.加工方法(初榨、精制); 3.加工程度(未经化学改性)。B: 4.包装规格
	-其他:	A: 1.品名; 2.加工方法(初榨、精制); 3.加工程度(未经化学改性)
1515.9030	---桐油及其分离品	例: 精制桐油(未经化学改性)
15.16	动、植物油、脂及其分离品，全部或部分氢化、相互酯化、再酯化或反油酸化，不论是否精制，但未经进一步加工:	A: 1.品名; 2.加工方法(全部或部分氢化、相互酯化、再酯化或反油酸化)
1517.1000	-人造黄油,但不包括液态的	A: 1.品名; 2.制作或保存方法（氢化、乳化、搅拌等）。B: 3.加工原料(动物油脂、植物油脂); 4.品牌
1517.9010	---起酥油	A: 1.品名; 2.成分含量; 3.用途(食用)。B: 4.加工原料(豆油、菜子油、棕榈油等); 5.品牌
1517.9090	---其他	A: 1.品名; 2.成分含量; 3.用途(食用)。B: 4.加工原料(动物油脂、植物油脂); 5.品牌
15.18	动、植物油、脂及其分离品，经过熟炼、氧化、脱水、硫化、吹制或在真空、惰性气体中加热聚合及用其他化学方法改性的，但税目15.16的产品除外; 本章各种油、脂及其分离品混合制成的其他税目未列名的非食用油、脂或制品:	A: 1.品名; 2.成分含量; 3.加工方法(经熟炼、氧化、脱水、硫化、吹制等)。例: 不包括氢化、相互酯化、再酯化或反油酸化的油、脂(税目15.16); 不包括配制的动物饲料(税目 23.09); 不包括磺化油(即用硫酸处理过的油)(税目34.02)
15.20	粗甘油; 甘油水及甘油碱液:	A: 1.品名; 2.甘油含量。 例: 纯度在95%及以上(以干燥产品的重量计)的

税则号列	商品名称	申报要素（A:归类要素 B:价格要素 C:审单及其他要素）及说明举例
		甘油归入税目 29.05；制成药品或加有药料的甘油归入税目 30.03 或 30.04
15.21	植物蜡（甘油三酯除外）、蜂蜡、其他虫蜡及鲸蜡，不论是否精制或着色：	例：不包括蜂箱用的人造蜡蜂房（税目 96.02）；不包括鲸蜡油，不论是天然的或是通过分离鲸蜡精制的（税目 15.04）
1521.1000	-植物蜡	A：1.品名；2.成分。 例：不包括植物蜡的混合物；不包括与动物蜡、矿物蜡或人造蜡混合的植物蜡；不包括与脂肪、树脂、矿物或其他材料（颜料除外）混合的植物蜡
	-其他：	A：1.品名
15.22	油鞣回收脂；加工处理油脂物质及动、植物蜡所剩的残渣：	A：1.品名；2.来源。 例：不包括仅经氧化或聚合的鱼油（税目 15.18）；不包括磺化油（税目 34.02）；不包括脂化皮革用的制剂（税目 34.03）；不包括从已炼制的猪脂肪或其他动物脂肪中所得的脂渣及膜渣（税目 23.01）

第四类 食品；饮料、酒及醋；烟草、烟草及烟草代用品的制品

第十六章 肉、鱼、甲壳动物、软体动物及其他水生无脊椎动物的制品

税则号列	商品名称	申报要素（A:归类要素 B:价格要素 C:审单及其他要素）及说明举例
1601.0010	---用天然肠衣做外包装的香肠及类似产品	A：1.品名；2 是否用天然肠衣做外包装。B：3.包装规格
1601.0020	---其他香肠及类似产品	A：1.品名。B 2.包装规格
1601.0030	---用香肠制成的食品	A：1.品名。B 2.包装规格
1602.1000	-均化食品	A：1.品名。B 2.包装规格
1602.2000	-动物肝	A：1.品名；2.制作或保存方法（煮、蒸、烤、煎、炸、炒等）。B：3.包装规格。例：不包括包馅面食（饺子等），以肉或食用杂碎做馅的（税目 19.02）；不包括调味汁及其制品、混合调味品（税目 21.03）；不包括汤料及其制品、均化混合食品（税目 21.04）
	-税目 01.05 的家禽的：	例：不包括包馅面食（饺子等），以肉或食用杂碎做馅的（税目 19.02）；不包括调味汁及其制品、混合调味品（税目 21.03）；不包括汤料及其制品、均化混合食品（税目 21.04）
1602.3100	--火鸡的	A：1.品名；2.制作或保存方法（煮、蒸、烤、煎、炸、炒等）。B：3.包装规格
1602.3210	---罐头	A：1.品名；2.制作或保存方法（煮、蒸、烤、煎、炸、炒等）。B：3.包装规格；4.品牌
	---其他：	A：1.品名；2.制作或保存方法（煮、蒸、烤、煎、炸、炒等）。B：3.包装规格
1602.3910	---罐头	A：1.品名；2.制作或保存方法（煮、蒸、烤、煎、炸、炒等）。B：3.包装规格；4.品牌
	---其他：	A：1.品名；2.制作或保存方法（煮、蒸、烤、煎、炸、炒等）。B：3.包装规格
	-猪的：	例：不包括包馅面食（饺子等），以肉或食用杂碎做馅的（税目 19.02）；不包括调味汁及其制品、混合调味品（税目 21.03）；不包括汤料及其制品、均化混合食品（税目 21.04）
1602.4100	--后腿及其肉块	A：1.品名；2.制作或保存方法（煮、蒸、烤、煎、炸、炒等）。B：3.包装规格
1602.4200	--前腿及其肉块	A：1.品名；2.制作或保存方法（煮、蒸、烤、煎、炸、炒等）。B：3.包装规格
1602.4910	---罐头	A：1.品名；2.制作或保存方法（煮、蒸、烤、煎、炸、炒等）。B：3.包装规格；4.品牌
1602.4990	---其他	A：1.品名；2.制作或保存方法（煮、蒸、烤、煎、炸、炒等）。B：3.包装规格
1602.5010	---罐头	A：1.品名；2.制作或保存方法（煮、蒸、烤、煎、炸、炒等）。B：3.包装规格；4.品牌
1602.5090	---其他	A：1.品名；2.制作或保存方法（煮、蒸、烤、煎、炸、炒等）。B：3.包装规格
1602.9010	---罐头	A：1.品名；2.制作或保存方法（煮、蒸、烤、煎、炸、炒等）。B：3.包装规格；4.品牌
1602.9090	---其他	A：1.品名；2.制作或保存方法（煮、蒸、烤、煎、炸、炒等）。B：3.包装规格
16.03	肉、鱼、甲壳动物、软体动物或其他水生无脊椎动物的精及汁：	A：1.品名；2.制作或保存方法（精、汁）。B：3.包装规格。 例：不包括胨及胨化品（税目 35.04）
16.04	制作或保藏的鱼；鲟鱼子酱及鱼卵制的鲟鱼子酱代用品：	例：不包括鱼精及鱼汁（税目 16.03）；不包括鱼馅面食（税目 19.02）；不包括调味汁及其制品、混合调味料（税目 21.03）；不包括汤料及其制品和均化混合食品（税目 21.04）
	-鱼，整条或切块，但未绞碎：	A：1.品名；2.制作或保存方法（整条或切块、非整条或切块、烤、煎、炸等）。B：3.包装规格
	-其他制作或保藏的鱼：	A：1.品名；2.制作或保存方法（整条或切块、非整条或切块、烤、煎、炸等）。

税则号列	商品名称	申报要素(A:归类要素 B:价格要素 C:审单及其他要素)及说明举例
		B: 3. 包装规格
	-鲟鱼子酱及鲟鱼子酱代用品	A: 1. 品名; 2. 包装规格。B: 3. 品牌
1605.1000	-蟹	A: 1. 品名; 2. 制作或保存方法(烤、煎、炸等)。B: 3. 包装规格
	-小虾及对虾	A: 1. 品名; 2. 制作或保存方法(烤、煎、炸等); 3. 是否非密封包装。B: 4. 包装规格
1605.3000	-龙虾	A: 1. 品名; 2. 制作或保存方法(烤、煎、炸等)。B: 3. 包装规格
	-其他甲壳动物:	A: 1. 品名; 2. 制作或保存方法(烤、煎、炸等)。B: 3. 包装规格
	-软体动物:	A: 1. 品名; 2. 制作或保存方法(烤、煎、炸等)。B: 3. 包装规格
	-其他水生无脊椎动物:	A: 1. 品名; 2. 制作或保存方法(烤、煎、炸等)。B: 3. 包装规格

第十七章　糖及糖食

税则号列	商品名称	申报要素(A:归类要素 B:价格要素 C:审单及其他要素)及说明举例
17.01	固体甘蔗糖、甜菜糖及化学纯蔗糖:	
	-未加香料或着色剂的原糖:	A: 1. 品名; 2. 加工方法(未加香料或着色剂)。B: 3. 按重量计干燥状态的糖含量对应的旋光度
1701.9100	--加有香料或着色剂	A: 1. 品名; 2. 加工方法(加香料或着色剂)
	--其他:	A: 1. 品名
17.02	其他固体糖，包括化学纯乳糖、麦芽糖、葡萄糖及果糖; 未加香料或着色剂的糖浆; 人造蜜，不论是否掺有天然蜂蜜; 焦糖:	例: 不包括加香料或着色剂的糖浆(税目 21.06)
	-乳糖及乳糖浆:	A: 1. 品名; 2. 按重量计干燥无水乳糖的含量
1702.2000	-槭糖及槭糖浆	A: 1. 品名
1702.3000	-葡萄糖及葡萄糖浆，不含果糖或按重量计干燥状态的果糖含量在20%以下	A: 1. 品名; 2. 按重量计干燥状态的果糖含量。B: 3. 用途(食用、医用)
1702.4000	-葡萄糖及葡萄糖浆，按重量计干燥状态的果糖含量在20%及以上，但在50%以下	A: 1. 品名; 2. 按重量计干燥状态的果糖含量
1702.5000	-化学纯果糖	A: 1. 品名; 2. 按重量计干燥状态的果糖含量
1702.6000	-其他果糖及果糖浆，按重量计干燥状态的果糖含量在50%以上	A: 1. 品名; 2. 种类(高果糖浆、高果糖晶体、低聚酯果糖等); 3. 按重量计干燥状态的果糖含量。B: 4. 用途(食用、医用)
1702.9000	-其他，包括转化糖	A: 1. 品名; 2. 成分含量
17.03	制糖后所剩的糖蜜:	A: 1. 品名; 2. 原料
17.04	不含可可的糖食(包括白巧克力):	例: 不包括含蔗糖重量在 10%及以下的甘草精(未制成糖果的)(税目 13.02); 不包括含可可糖食(可可脂在此不视为可可)(税目 18.06); 不包括糖渍蔬菜、果实、果皮等的糖食(税目 20.06); 不包括果酱、果子冻等(税目 20.07); 不包括含替代糖的合成甜味剂(例如，山梨醇)的糖果、口香糖及类似品(主要供糖尿病患者用)，加有大量脂肪，有时还加有乳、果仁的糖膏，不适合供直接制糖食的(税目 21.06)
1704.1000	-口香糖，不论是否裹糖	A: 1. 品名; 2. 成分。B: 3. 包装规格; 4. 品牌
1704.9000	-其他	A: 1. 品名。B: 2. 包装规格; 3. 品牌

第十八章　可可及可可制品

[注解]

本章所称“夹心”，包括用巧克力包裹，中心有馅(例如，用奶油、糖壳、干椰子肉、水果、果子膏、酒、蛋白杏仁糖果、坚果、牛轧糖、焦糖或上述产品的混合物做馅)的粒、块、条状食品。谷物、水果或坚果(不论是否成块)嵌于整个巧克力当中的实心块状或条状巧克力，不视为“夹心”。

税则号列	商品名称	申报要素(A:归类要素 B:价格要素 C:审单及其他要素)及说明举例
18.01	整颗或破碎的可可豆，生的或焙炒的:	A: 1. 品名; 2. 制作或保存方法(整颗或破碎的、生的或焙炒的)
18.02	可可荚、壳、皮及废料:	A: 1. 品名
18.03	可可膏，不论是否脱脂:	A: 1. 品名; 2. 可可脂含量
18.04	可可脂、可可油:	A: 1. 品名
18.05	未加糖或其他甜物质的可可粉:	A: 1. 品名; 2. 制作或保存方法(粉末状、未加糖或其他甜物质); 3. 可可脂含量。B: 4. 包装规格。例: 不包括含有仅作为药物赋形剂或载体可可粉的药品(税目 30.03 或 30.04)

税则号列	商品名称	申报要素(A:归类要素 B:价格要素 C:审单及其他要素)及说明举例
18.06	巧克力及其他含可可的食品:	例:不包括白巧克力(由可可脂、糖及奶粉组成)(税目 17.04);不包括裹巧克力的饼干及其他烘焙糕饼(税目 19.05)
1806.1000	-加糖或其他甜物质的可可粉	A:1.品名;2.制作或保存方法(粉末状、加糖或其他甜物质);3.容器包装或内包装每件净重。B:4.品牌
1806.2000	-其他重量超过 2 千克的块状或条状含可可食品,或液状、膏状、粉状、粒状或其他散装形状的含可可食品,容器包装或内包装每件净重超过 2 千克的	A:1.品名;2.成分含量;3.形状(条状、块状等);4.容器包装或内包装每件净重。B:5.品牌
	-其他块状或条状的含可可食品:	A:1.品名;2.成分含量;3.形状(条状、块状等);4.容器包装或内包装每件净重;5.是否夹心。B:6.品牌
1806.9000	-其他	A:1.品名;2.成分含量;3.容器包装或内包装每件净重。B:4.品牌

第十九章　谷物、粮食粉、淀粉或乳的制品；糕饼点心

税则号列	商品名称	申报要素(A:归类要素 B:价格要素 C:审单及其他要素)及说明举例
	-供婴幼儿食用的零售包装食品	A:1.品名;2.成分含量;3.用途(供婴幼儿食用)。B:4.包装规格;5.品牌
1901.2000	-供烘焙税目 19.05 所列面包、糕饼用的调制品及面团	A:1.品名;2.成分含量;3.用途(供烘焙面包、糕饼等用)。B:4.包装规格
1901.9000	-其他	A:1.品名;2.成分含量。B:3.包装规格。例:不包括用牛奶做基料的冰淇淋及其他冰制食品(税目 21.05)
19.02	面食，不论是否煮熟、包馅(肉馅或其他馅)或其他方法制作,例如,通心粉、面条、汤团、馄饨、饺子、奶油面卷;古斯古斯面食，不论是否制作:	例:不包括带面食的汤料及其制品(税目 21.04)
	-生的面食，未包馅或未经其他方法制作:	A:1.品名;2.成分含量;3.制作或保存方法(生的、未包馅或未经其他方法加工)
1902.2000	-包馅面食,不论是否烹煮或经其他方法制作	A:1.品名;2.成分;3 制作或保存方法(包馅或经其他方法加工)
1902.3010	---米粉干	A:1.品名;2.成分含量
1902.3020	---粉丝	A:1.品名;2.成分含量
1902.3030	---即食或快熟面条	A:1.品名;2.种类(即食面条、快熟面条);3.成分含量。B:4.包装规格;5.品牌
1902.3090	---其他	A:1.品名;2.成分含量。B:3.包装规格;4.品牌
1902.4000	-古斯古斯面食	A:1.品名;2.成分含量
19.03	珍粉及淀粉制成的珍粉代用品,片、粒、珠、粉或类似形状的:	A:1.品名;2.成分。B:3.包装规格
1904.1000	-谷物或谷物产品经膨化或烘炒制成的食品	A:1.品名;2.制作或保存方法(膨化或烘炒)。B:3.包装规格
1904.2000	-未烘炒谷物片制成的食品及未烘炒的谷物片与烘炒的谷物片或膨化的谷物混合制成的食品	A:1.品名;2.制作或保存方法(未烘炒、未烘炒与烘炒或膨化混合)。B:3.包装规格
1904.3000	-碾碎的干小麦	A:1.品名;2.制作或保存方法(干、碾碎)。B:3.包装规格
1904.9000	-其他	A:1.品名;2.制作或保存方法(经过预煮或经其他方法制作)。B:3.包装规格。例:玉米除外
19.05	面包、糕点、饼干及其他烘焙糕饼，不论是否含可可;圣餐饼、装药空囊、封缄、糯米纸及类似制品:	A:1.品名。B:2.包装规格;3.品牌

第二十章　蔬菜、水果、坚果或植物其他部分的制品

税则号列	商品名称	申报要素(A:归类要素 B:价格要素 C:审单及其他要素)及说明举例
20.01	蔬菜、水果、坚果及植物的其他食用部分，用醋或醋酸制作或保藏的:	A:1.品名;2.制作方法(用醋或醋酸制作或保藏)。B:3.包装规格。例:不包括用面粉制的糕点; 例:果馅饼(税目 19.05)
20.02	番茄,用醋或醋酸以外的其他方法制作或保藏的:	例:不包括番茄沙司及其他番茄调味汁(税目 21.03);不包括番茄汤料及其制品(税目 21.04)
2002.1010	---罐头	A:1.品名;2.制作或保存方法(整个、切片等)。B:3.包装规格; 4.品牌
2002.1090	---其他	A:1.品名;2.制作或保存方法(整个、切片等)。B:3.包装规格

税则号列	商品名称	申报要素(A:归类要素 B:价格要素 C:审单及其他要素)及说明举例
	---番茄酱罐头:	A: 1. 品名; 2. 包装规格(重量/罐)。B: 3. 品牌
2002.9090	---其他	A: 1. 品名; 2. 制作或保存方法(绞碎等); 3. 包装规格
20.03	蘑菇及块菌,用醋或醋酸以外的其他方法制作或保藏的:	A: 1. 品名; 2. 制作方法。B: 3. 包装规格; 4. 品牌
20.04	其他冷冻蔬菜,用醋或醋酸以外的其他方法制作或保藏的,但税目 20.06 的产品除外:	A: 1. 品名; 2. 制作或保存方法（冻等）。B: 3. 包装规格。例: 税目 20.06 的产品除外
2005.1000	-均化蔬菜	A: 1. 品名; 2. 制作或保存方法(未冷冻等)。B: 3. 包装规格
2005.2000	-马铃薯	A: 1. 品名; 2. 制作或保存方法(未冷冻等)。B: 3. 包装规格
2005.4000	-豌豆	A: 1. 品名; 2. 制作或保存方法(未冷冻等)。B: 3. 包装规格
	---脱荚的:	A: 1. 品名; 2. 制作或保存方法(未冷冻等); 3. 是否脱荚。B: 4. 包装规格
	--其他:	A: 1. 品名; 2. 制作或保存方法(未冷冻等)。B: 3. 包装规格; 4. 品牌
	-芦笋:	A: 1. 品名; 2. 制作或保存方法(未冷冻等)。B: 3. 包装规格; 4. 品牌
2005.7000	-油橄榄	A: 1. 品名; 2. 制作或保存方法(未冷冻等)。B: 3. 包装规格
2005.8000	-甜玉米	A: 1. 品名; 2. 制作或保存方法(未冷冻等)。B: 3. 包装规格
2005.9110	---竹笋罐头	A: 1. 品名; 2. 制作或保存方法(未冷冻等)。B: 3. 包装规格; 4. 品牌
2005.9190	---其他	A: 1. 品名; 2. 制作或保存方法(未冷冻等)。B: 3. 包装规格
2005.9920	---蚕豆罐头	A: 1. 品名; 2. 制作或保存方法(未冷冻等)。B: 3. 包装规格; 4. 品牌
2005.9940	---榨菜	A: 1. 品名; 2. 制作或保存方法(未冷冻等)。B: 3. 包装规格
2005.9950	---咸蕨菜	A: 1. 品名; 2. 制作或保存方法(未冷冻等)。B: 3. 包装规格
2005.9960	---咸藠头	A: 1. 品名; 2. 制作或保存方法(未冷冻等)。B: 3. 包装规格
	---其他:	A: 1. 品名; 2. 制作或保存方法(未冷冻等)。B: 3. 包装规格
20.06	糖渍蔬菜、水果、坚果、果皮及植物的其他部分(沥干、糖渍或裹糖的):	A: 1. 品名; 2. 制作或保存方法(沥干、糖渍、裹糖)。B: 3. 包装规格
20.07	烹煮的果酱、果冻、柑橘酱、果泥及果膏，不论是否加糖或其他甜物质:	A: 1. 品名; 2. 制作或保存方法(烹煮)。B: 3. 包装规格; 4. 品牌
	-其他:	例: 不包括用明胶、糖及果汁或人造果精制成的餐用果冻(税目 21.06)
20.08	用其他方法制作或保藏的其他税目未列名水果、坚果及植物的其他食用部分,不论是否加酒、加糖或其他甜物质:	A: 1. 品名; 2. 制作或保存方法。B: 3. 包装规格; 4. 品牌
20.09	未发酵及未加酒精的水果汁(包括酿酒葡萄汁)、蔬菜汁，不论是否加糖或其他甜物质:	A: 1. 品名; 2. 成分含量; 3. 白利糖度值; 4. 浓缩果汁请注明浓缩倍数; 5. 制作或保存方法(是否经过发酵、是否添加酒精，以及冷冻、非冷冻、混合等); 6. 储藏温度。B: 7. 包装规格; 8. 品牌。例: 不包括半发酵的酿酒葡萄汁，不论其发酵是否已经中止，以及加酒精的未发酵酿酒葡萄汁，如果按容量计酒精浓度已超过 0.5%的(税目 22.04)
2009.1100	--冷冻的	例: 包括保存温度在-18℃及以下的未冻结浓缩澄汁

第二十一章　杂项食品

税则号列	商品名称	申报要素(A:归类要素 B:价格要素 C:审单及其他要素)及说明举例
21.01	咖啡、茶、马黛茶的浓缩精汁及以其为基本成分或以咖啡、茶、马黛茶为基本成分的制品; 烘焙菊苣和其他烘焙咖啡代用品及其浓缩精汁:	A: 1. 品名; 2. 成分含量。B: 3. 包装规格; 4. 品牌。例: 不包括含任何比例咖啡的烘焙咖啡代用品(税目 09.01); 不包括加香料的茶(税目 09.02); 不包括焦糖(焦糖化的糖蜜及糖)(税目 17.02)
21.02	酵母(活性或非活性); 已死的其他单细胞微生物(不包括税目 30.02 的疫苗); 发酵粉:	例: 不包括自发谷物细粉, 例如, 加有发酵粉的细粉(税目 11.01 或 11.02); 不包括自溶酵母(税目 21.06); 不包括培养微生物(酵母除外)及疫苗(税目 30.02); 不包括酶(淀粉酶、胃朊酶、粗制凝乳酶等)(税目 35.07)
2102.1000	-活性酵母	A: 1. 品名; 2. 是否活性酵母。B: 3. 包装规格; 4. 品牌
2102.2000	-非活性酵母; 已死的其他单细胞微生物	A: 1. 品名; 2. 是否活性酵母; 3. 是否已死的单细胞微生物。B: 4. 包装规格; 5. 品牌
2102.3000	-发酵粉	A: 1. 品名。B: 2. 包装规格; 3. 品牌
21.03	调味汁及其制品; 混合调味品; 芥子粉及其调制品:	例: 不包括芥子(税目 12.07); 不包括固定芥子油(税目 15.14); 不包括芥子油饼，即从芥子提取固定油后所剩的产品(税目 23.06); 不包括芥子精油(税目 33.01)
2103.1000	-酱油	A: 1. 品名; 2. 成分。B: 3. 包装规格; 4. 品牌
2103.2000	-番茄沙司及其他番茄调味汁	A: 1. 品名; 2. 成分。B: 3. 包装规格; 4. 品牌
2103.3000	-芥子粉及其调制品	A: 1. 品名; 2. 成分。B: 3. 包装规格; 4. 品牌
2103.9010	---味精	A: 1. 品名; 2. 成分。B: 3. 包装规格; 4. 品牌

税则号列	商品名称	申报要素(A:[illegible]
2103.9020	---别特酒，按体积计酒精含量44.2%~49.2%，按重量计含1.5%~6%的香料、各种配料以及4%~10%的糖	A:1.品名;2.成[illegible]包装规格;4.品[illegible]
2103.9090	---其他	A:1.品名;2.成[illegible]
21.04	汤料及其制品;均化混合食品:	A:1.品名;2.[illegible]
2104.1000	-汤料及其制品	例:不包括干[illegible]细粉、粗粉[illegible]
21.05	冰淇淋及其他冰制食品，不论是否含可可:	A:1.品名。[illegible]
21.06	其他税目未列名的食品:	例:不包括[illegible]30.03或3[illegible]
2106.1000	-浓缩蛋白质及组织化蛋白质	A:1.品名;[illegible]
2106.9010	---制造碳酸饮料的浓缩物	A:1.品名;2.成分含量[illegible]
2106.9020	---制造饮料用的复合酒精制品	A:1.品名;2.成分含量。B:3.包装规格;[illegible]
2106.9030	---蜂王浆制剂	A:1.品名;2.成分含量。B:3.包装规格;4.品牌
2106.9040	---椰子汁	A:1.品名;2.成分含量;3.是否可直接饮用。B:4.包装规格;5.品牌
2106.9050	---海豹油胶囊	A:1.品名;2.成分含量。B:3.包装规格;4.品牌
2106.9090	---其他	A:1.品名;2.成分含量。B:3.包装规格;4.品牌

第二十二章　饮料、酒及醋

税则号列	商品名称	申报要素(A:归类要素 B:价格要素 C:审单及其他要素)及说明举例
22.01	未加糖或其他甜物质及未加味的水，包括天然或人造矿泉水及汽水;冰及雪:	例:不包括"碳酸雪"或"干冰"(即固体二氧化碳)(税目28.11)
	-矿泉水及汽水:	A:1.品名。B:2.包装规格;3.品牌
2201.9010	---天然水	A:1.品名;2.加工程度(未加糖或其他甜物质及未加味);3.来源(天然)。B:4.包装规格;5.品牌
2201.9090	---其他	A:1.品名;2.加工程度(未加糖或其他甜物质及未加味)。B:3.包装规格;4.品牌
22.02	加味、加糖或其他甜物质的水，包括矿泉水及汽水，其他无酒精饮料，但不包括税目20.09的水果汁或蔬菜汁:	例:不包括税目20.09的水果汁或蔬菜汁;不包括含可可、水果或香料的液状酸乳及其他发酵或酸化乳及奶油(税目04.03);不包括水果汁及蔬菜汁，不论是否用作饮料(税目20.09)
2202.1000	-加味、加糖或其他甜物质的水，包括矿泉水及汽水	A:1.品名;2.加工程度(加糖、加味或其他甜物质)。B:3.包装规格;4.品牌
2202.9000	-其他	A:1.品名;2.成分。B:3.包装规格;4.品牌
22.03	麦芽酿造的啤酒:	A:1.品名(中文及外文名称);2.是否麦芽酿造;3.酒精含量。B:4.麦芽浓度;5.包装规格;6.品牌(中文及外文名称)
22.04	鲜葡萄酿造的酒，包括加酒精的;税目20.09以外的酿酒葡萄汁:	例:不包括未发酵或按容量计酒精浓度不超过0.5%的葡萄汁，不论其是否浓缩(税目20.09)
2204.1000	-汽酒	A:1.品名(中文及外文名称);2.种类(汽酒);3.加工方法(鲜葡萄酿造);4.酒精含量。B:5.级别;6.年份(没有年份的申报无年份);7.产区(中文及外文名称);8.酒庄名(中文及外文名称);9.葡萄品种(中文及外文名称);10.包装规格;11.品牌(中文及外文名称)
	-其他酒;加酒精抑制发酵的酿酒葡萄汁:	A:1.品名(中文及外文名称);2.加工方法(鲜葡萄酿造);3.酒精浓度。B:4.级别;5.年份(没有年份的申报无年份);6.产区(中文及外文名称);7.酒庄名(中文及外文名称);8.葡萄品种(中文及外文名称);9.包装规格(单位包装规格×每箱单位数);10.品牌(中文及外文名称)
2204.3000	-其他酿酒葡萄汁	A:1.品名(中文及外文名称);2.种类(酿酒葡萄汁)。B:3.包装规格;4.品牌(中文及外文名称)
22.05	味美思酒及其他加植物或香料的用鲜葡萄酿造的酒:	A:1.品名(中文及外文名称);2.加工方法(鲜葡萄酿造、加植物或香料)。B:3.包装规格;4.品牌(中文及外文名称)
2206.0010	---黄酒	A:1.品名(中文及外文名称);2.加工方法(发酵、混合)。B:3.包装规格;4.品牌(中文及外文名称)
2206.0090	---其他发酵饮料	A:1.品名(中文及外文名称);2.成分含量;3.加工方法(发酵、混合);4.酒精浓度。B:5.包装规格;6.品牌(中文及外文名称);7.年份;8.等级
22.07	未改性乙醇，按容量计酒精浓度在80%及以上;任何浓度的改性乙醇及其他酒精:	A:1.品名(中文及外文名称);2.加工方法(未改性、改性);3.酒精浓度。B:4.品牌(中文及外文名称)。例:不包括以酒精为基料的固体或半固体燃料(通常作为"固体酒精"出售)(税目36.06)

		⋯说要素 B:价格要素 C:审单及其他要素)及说明举例
	⋯的烈性酒	A: 1. 品名（中文及外文名称）; 2. 原料; 3. 酒精浓度。B: 4. 包装规格; 5. 品牌（中文及外文名称）; 6. 级别; 7. 产地
		A: 1. 品名（中文及外文名称）; 2. 原料; 3. 酒精浓度。B: 4. 包装规格; 5. 品牌（中文及外文名称）; 6. 产地
	⋯及蒸馏已发酵甘蔗产品制得⋯他烈性酒	A: 1. 品名（中文及外文名称）; 2. 原料; 3. 酒精浓度。B: 4. 包装规格; 5. 品牌（中文及外文名称）
	⋯松子酒	A: 1. 品名（中文及外文名称）; 2. 原料; 3. 酒精浓度。B: 4. 包装规格; 5. 品牌（中文及外文名称）
	-伏特加酒	A: 1. 品名（中文及外文名称）; 2. 原料; 3. 酒精浓度。B: 4. 包装规格; 5. 品牌（中文及外文名称）
⋯00	-利口酒及柯迪尔酒	A: 1. 品名（中文及外文名称）; 2. 原料; 3. 酒精浓度。B: 4. 包装规格; 5. 品牌（中文及外文名称）
⋯08.9010	---龙舌兰酒	A: 1. 品名（中文及外文名称）; 2. 原料; 3. 酒精浓度。B: 4. 包装规格; 5. 品牌（中文及外文名称）
2208.9020	---白酒	A: 1. 品名; 2. 原料; 3. 酒精浓度。B: 4. 包装规格; 5. 品牌
2208.9090	---其他	A: 1. 品名（中文及外文名称）; 2. 原料; 3. 酒精浓度。B: 4. 包装规格; 5. 品牌（中文及外文名称）
22.09	醋及用醋酸制得的醋代用品:	A: 1. 品名（中文及外文名称）; 2. 醋酸浓度。B: 3. 包装规格; 4. 品牌（中文及外文名称）。例: 不包括盥洗用品(税目 33.04)

第二十三章　食品工业的残渣及废料；配制的动物饲料

[注解]

制成的饲料添加剂种类有：氨基酸添加剂、维生素添加剂、矿物元素添加剂、药物饲料添加剂、饲用酶制剂、饲料酸化剂、饲料保存剂等。

税则号列	商品名称	申报要素(A:归类要素 B:价格要素 C:审单及其他要素)及说明举例
23.01	不适于供人食用的肉、杂碎、鱼、甲壳动物、软体动物或其他水生无脊椎动物的渣粉及团粒; 油渣:	例: 包括供人食用的油渣
	-肉、杂碎的渣粉及团粒; 油渣:	A: 1. 品名; 2. 成分含量(蛋白质含量等); 3. 用途(不适合供人食用); 4. 状态(渣粉、团粒)
2301.2010	---饲料用鱼粉	A: 1. 品名; 2. 成分含量(蛋白质含量等); 3. 用途(不适合供人食用); 4. 状态(渣粉、团粒); 5. 种类（红、白鱼粉　)
2301.2090	---其他	A: 1. 品名; 2. 成分含量(蛋白质含量等); 3. 用途(不适合供人食用); 4. 状态(渣粉、团粒)
23.02	谷物或豆类植物在筛、碾或其他加工过程中所产生的糠、麸及其他残渣，不论是否制成团粒:	A: 1. 品名; 2. 成分含量(蛋白质含量等); 3. 种类(玉米的、小麦的等)。例: 不包括谷物脱粒时产生的谷壳(税目 12.13)
23.03	制造淀粉过程中的残渣及类似的残渣，甜菜渣、甘蔗渣及制糖过程中的其他残渣，酿造及蒸馏过程中的糟粕及残渣，不论是否制成团粒:	A: 1. 品名; 2. 成分含量(蛋白质含量等); 3. 种类; 4. 是否配制。例: 不包括提取或精炼糖所剩的糖蜜(税目 17.03); 不包括非活性酵母或废酵母(税目 21.02); 不包括焚烧并洗涤甜菜糖蜜残渣所得的粗钾盐(税目 26.21); 不包括蔗渣浆(税目 47.06)
23.04	提炼豆油所得的油渣饼及其他固体残渣，不论是否碾磨或制成团粒:	A: 1. 品名; 2. 成分含量(蛋白质含量等); 3. 原料。例: 不包括油脚(税目 15.22); 不包括通过去除脱脂大豆粉的某些成分制得的浓缩蛋白质(用作食品添加剂)及改善了组织结构的大豆粉(税目 21.06)
23.05	提炼花生油所得的油渣饼及其他固体残渣，不论是否碾磨或制成团粒:	A: 1. 品名; 2. 成分含量(蛋白质含量等); 3. 原料
23.06	税目 23.04 或 23.05 以外的提炼植物油脂所得的油渣饼及其他固体残渣，不论是否碾磨或制成团粒:	A: 1. 品名; 2. 成分含量(蛋白质含量等); 3. 原料
23.07	葡萄酒渣; 粗酒石:	A: 1. 品名。例: 不包括酒石(税目 29.18)
23.08	动物饲料用的其他税目未列名的植物原料、废料、残渣及副产品，不论是否制成团粒:	A: 1. 品名; 2. 成分含量(蛋白质含量等); 3. 用途(饲料用)
23.09	配制的动物饲料:	
	-零售包装的狗食或猫食:	A: 1. 品名; 2. 成分含量; 3. 用途(狗食、猫食等); 4. 加工方法(配制的); 5. 包装规格。B: 6. 品牌
	-其他:	A: 1. 品名; 2. 成分含量; 3. 加工方法(配制的); 4. 包装规格。B: 5. 品牌

第二十四章　烟草、烟草及烟草代用品的制品

税则号列	商品名称	申报要素(A:归类要素 B:价格要素 C:审单及其他要素)及说明举例
24.01	烟草;烟草废料:	例:包括烟草废料
	-未去梗的烟草:	A:1.品名;2.加工方法(未去梗);
	-部分或全部去梗的烟草:	A:1.品名;2.加工方法(去梗、部分去梗)
2401.3000	-烟草废料	A:1.品名;2.是否废料
24.02	烟草或烟草代用品制成的雪茄烟及卷烟:	A:1.品名;2.种类(卷烟、雪茄烟);3.来源(烟草制或烟草代用品制)。B:4.品牌
24.03	其他烟草及烟草代用品的制品;“均化”或“再造”烟草;烟草精汁:	
	-供吸用的烟草,不论是否含有任何比例的烟草代用品:	A:1.品名;2.用途(吸用等)
2403.9100	--“均化”或“再造”烟草	A:1.品名;2.加工方法(均化、再造)
2403.9900	--其他	A:1.品名;2.是否烟草精汁

第五类　矿产品

第二十五章　盐;硫磺;泥土及石料;石膏料、石灰及水泥

[注解]

1.“加工方法”指改变原材料、毛坯或半成品的形状、尺寸、性质或表面状态,使之达到规定要求的各种形状的方法。

2.本章“成分含量”是指:“成分”指商品所构成的部分或要素,一般指所含物质的种类;“含量”一般指所含物质的数量。

税则号列	商品名称	申报要素(A:归类要素 B:价格要素 C:审单及其他要素)及说明举例
25.01	盐(包括精制盐及变性盐)及纯氯化钠,不论是否为水溶液,也不论是否添加抗结块剂或松散剂;海水:	A:1.品名;2.成分(是否添加其他成分);3.外观;4.包装;5.是否食用盐。例:不包括加调料的盐(税目21.03)、氯化钠光学元件(税目90.01)、培养氯化钠晶体≥2.5克/颗(税目38.24)
25.02	未焙烧的黄铁矿:	A:1.品名;2.加工方法(焙烧、未焙烧)。例:未焙烧黄铁矿
25.03	各种硫磺,但升华硫磺、沉淀硫磺及胶态硫磺除外:	A:1.品名;2.包装;3.加工工艺。B:4.状态(液态、固态、粉状、块状);5.成分含量。例:不包括升华硫磺、沉淀硫磺、胶态硫磺(税目28.02);例:硫磺(液体罐装)
25.04	天然石墨:	A:1.品名;2.用途;3.外观(粉末、鳞片、块等);4.来源(是否天然);5.是否球化加工。B:6.石墨含量;7.细度指标(细度、鳞片大小)
25.05	各种天然砂,不论是否着色,但第二十六章的含金属矿砂除外:	A:1.品名;2.用途;3.来源(如海砂、湖砂或河砂等)。例:不包括第二十六章的金属砂、焦油砂、沥青砂。例:天然石英砂(玻璃工业用)
25.06	石英(天然砂除外);石英岩,不论是否粗加修整或仅用锯或其他方法切割成矩形(包括正方形)的板、块:	A:1.品名;2.加工方法(天然状态、粗加修整、简单切割等);3.外观。例:不包括宝石半宝石及制品(第七十一章)
25.07	高岭土及类似土,不论是否煅烧:	A:1.品名;2.成分;3.是否活化。B:4.用途;5.外观;6.加工方法(是否煅烧);7.白度;8.细度。例:不包括含高岭土的砂(税目25.05)
2508.1000	-膨润土	A:1.品名;2.种类;3.外观;4.是否活化。B:5.用途;6.蒙脱石成分含量
2508.3000	-耐火黏土	A:1.品名;2.外观;3.是否活化。B:4.氧化铝含量;5.级别;6.是否含有添加剂或改性。例:如级别:耐火级或研磨级
2508.4000	-其他黏土	A:1.品名;2.外观;3.是否活化。B:4.氧化铝含量;5.级别;6.是否含有添加剂或改性。例:不包括税目25.30的颜料土、活性黏土(税目38.02)、膨胀黏土(税目68.06)
2508.5000	-红柱石、蓝晶石及硅线石	A:1.品名;2.种类;3.外观;4.是否活化。B:5.用途
2508.6000	-富铝红柱石	A:1.品名;2.种类;3.外观;4.是否活化。B:5.用途
2508.7000	-火泥及第纳斯土	A:1.品名;2.种类;3.外观;4.是否活化。B:5.用途
25.09	白垩:	A:1.品名。例:不包括磷酸白垩(税目25.10)、法国白垩或威尼斯白垩(税目25.26)
25.10	天然磷酸钙、天然磷酸铝钙及磷酸盐白垩:	例:不包括超出清除杂质范围的煅烧或进一步热处理的产品(第三十一章)
2510.1010	---磷灰石	A:1.品名;2.加工方法(是否碾磨及其他进一步加工);3.成分(磷灰石、天然磷酸钙、天然磷酸铝钙及磷酸盐白垩);4.来源。B:5.注明五氧化二磷含量
2510.1090	---其他	A:1.品名;2.加工方法(是否碾磨及其他进一步加工);3.成分(磷灰石、天然磷酸钙、天然磷酸铝钙及磷酸盐白垩)。B:4.注明五氧化二磷含量
2510.2010	---磷灰石	A:1.品名;2.加工方法(是否碾磨及其他进一步加工);3.成分(磷灰石、天然磷酸钙、天然磷酸铝钙及磷酸盐白垩);4.来源。B:5.注明五氧化二磷含量
2510.2090	---其他	A:1.品名;2.加工方法(是否碾磨及其他进一步加工);3.成分(磷灰石、天然磷酸钙、天然磷酸铝钙及磷酸盐白垩)。B:4.注明五氧化二磷含量

税则号列	商品名称	申报要素(A:归类要素 B:价格要素 C:审单及其他要素)及说明举例
2511.1000	-天然硫酸钡(重晶石)	A: 1.品名; 2.加工方法。B: 3.级别(钻井级/化工级/涂料级等)
2511.2000	-天然碳酸钡(毒重石)	A: 1.品名; 2.加工方法
25.12	硅质化石粗粉(例如,各种硅藻土)及类似的硅质土,不论是否煅烧,其表观比重不超过1:	A: 1.品名; 2.用途; 3.外观; 4.是否活化; 5.表观比重。B: 6.品牌; 7.种类; 8.是否改性; 9.二氧化硅含量。例: 不包括活性硅藻土(税目 38.02)
2513.1000	-浮石	A: 1.品名; 2.加工方法(如天然原状、破碎); 3.外观。B: 4.用途
2513.2000	-刚玉岩、天然刚玉砂、天然石榴石及其他天然磨料	A: 1.品名; 2.种类(刚玉岩、天然刚玉砂、天然石榴石、天然磨料等)。例: 不包括其他税目列名的磨料(税目 25.17 等)
25.14	板岩,不论是否粗加修整或仅用锯或其他方法切割成矩形(包括正方形)的板、块:	A: 1.品名; 2.用途; 3.加工方法(天然原状、粗加修整、锯、割等); 4.外观。例: 不包括铺屋顶、饰墙面及防潮用的板石(税目 68.03)
25.15	大理石、石灰华及其他石灰质碑用或建筑用石,表现比重为 2.5 及以上,蜡石,不论是否粗加修整或仅用锯或其他方法切割成矩形(包括正方形)的板、块:	
	-大理石及石灰华:	A: 1.品名; 2.加工方法(天然原状、粗加修整、锯、割等); 3.外观; 4.表现比重。B: 5.体积或面积数量(立方米数或平方米数); 6.花色品种的中英文名称; 7.规格(长宽高)
2515.2000	-其他石灰质碑用或建筑用石;蜡石	A: 1.品名; 2.加工方法(天然原状、粗加修整、锯、割等); 3.外观; 4.除蜡石外要注明表观比重
25.16	花岗岩、斑岩、玄武岩、砂岩以及其他碑用或建筑用石,不论是否粗加修整或仅用锯或其他方法切割成矩形(包括正方形)的板、块:	
	-花岗岩:	A: 1.品名; 2.加工方法(天然原状、粗加修整、锯、割等); 3.外观。B: 4.体积或面积数量(立方米数或平方米数); 5.花色的中英文名称(如埃及金线米黄等); 6.规格(长宽高)
2516.2000	-砂岩	A: 1.品名; 2.加工方法(天然原状、粗加修整、锯、割等); 3.外观。B: 4.体积或面积数量(立方米数或平方米数); 5.花色的中英文名称(如埃及金线米黄等); 6.规格(长宽高)
2516.9000	-其他碑用或建筑用石	A: 1.品名; 2.用途; 3.加工方法(天然原状、粗加修整、锯、割等); 4.外观。例: 不包括第七十一章的宝石及半宝石、用于印刷业的石灰石(通称为石印石,税目 25.30)
2517.1000	-通常作混凝土粒料、铺路、铁道路基或其他路基用的卵石、砾石及碎石,圆石子及燧石,不论是否热处理	A: 1.品名; 2.用途; 3.外观。例: 不包括切成块的燧石、人工磨圆的卵石。例: 碎石(用作混凝土粒料,不规则小块状)
2517.2000	-矿渣、浮渣及类似的工业残渣,不论是否混有子目 2517.10 所列的材料	A: 1.品名; 2.用途; 3.外观; 4.来源(是否矿渣、浮渣、残渣等)。例: 矿渣(铺路用、矿砂浮选所剩、粉末颗粒混合物)
2517.3000	-沥青碎石	A: 1.品名; 2.用途; 3.外观。例: 大理石粉末
	-税目 25.15 及 25.16 所列各种石料的碎粒、碎屑及粉末,不论是否热处理:	A: 1.品名; 2.外观
25.18	白云石,不论是否煅烧或烧结、粗加修整或仅用锯或其他方法切割成矩形(包括正方形)的板、块;夯混白云石:	A: 1.品名; 2.加工方法(夯混、是否煅烧或烧结、粗加修整、锯、割等); 3.外观。例: 白云石(经过煅烧,不规则块状,粉末颗粒混合物)
25.19	天然碳酸镁(菱镁矿);熔凝镁氧矿;烧结镁氧矿,不论烧结前是否加入少量其他氧化物;其他氧化镁,不论是否纯净:	A: 1.品名; 2.加工方法; 3.成分含量; 4.外观(粉末、粒状、块状等)。B: 5.粉状请注明细度,粒状请注明直径
	---其他:	例: 不包括氧化镁光学元件(税目 90.01)、培养氧化镁晶体≥2.5 克/颗(税目 38.24)。例: 化学纯氧化镁(MgO 含量 99.9%)
25.20	生石膏;硬石膏;熟石膏(由煅烧的生石膏或硫酸钙构成),不论是否着色,也不论是否带有少量促凝剂或缓凝剂:	A: 1.品名; 2.用途(是否牙科用或其他用途)。B: 3.来源。例: 熟石膏(牙科用)
25.21	石灰石助熔剂;通常用于制造石灰或水泥的石灰石及其他钙质石:	A: 1.品名; 2.用途。例: 石灰石(制造石灰用)
25.22	生石灰、熟石灰及水硬石灰,但税目 28.25 的氧化钙及氢氧化钙除外:	A: 1.品名。例: 生石灰
25.23	硅酸盐水泥、矾土水泥、矿渣水泥、富硫酸盐水泥及类似的水凝水泥,不论是否着色,包括水泥熟料:	A: 1.品名; 2.用途。例: 不包括耐火水泥及灰泥(税目 38.16)、非耐火的灰泥及混凝土(税目 38.24)、英国水泥或干固水泥(税目 25.20)等。例: 水泥熟料
25.24	石棉:	A: 1.品名; 2.外观; 3.是否青石棉; 4.是否长纤维。B: 5.型号。例: 不包括人工染色、梳理等进一步加工的(税目 68.12)。例: 青石棉(长纤维)

税则号列	商品名称	申报要素(A:归类要素 B:价格要素 C:审单及其他要素)及说明举例
25.25	云母，包括云母片;云母废料:	A:1.品名;2.用途;3.外观。例:不包括切割或冲模成型、黏合的、复制的
25.26	天然冻石，不论是否粗加修整或仅用锯或其他方法切割成矩形(包括正方形)的板、块;滑石:	例:天然滑石粉
	-未破碎及未研粉:	A:1.品名;2.加工方法(天然原状、粗加修整、简单切割、是否破碎)
2526.2010	---冻石	A:1.品名;2.加工方法(天然原状、粗加修整、简单切割、是否破碎)
2526.2020	---滑石	A:1.品名;2.加工方法(天然原状、粗加修整、简单切割、是否破碎)。B:3.白度
2528.0010	-天然硼砂及其精矿(不论是否煅烧)	A:1.品名。例:不包括精制硼砂(税目 28.40); 例:白硼钙石
2528.0090	-其他	A:1.品名;2.成分含量。例:不包括所含硼酸干重超过 85%的硼酸(税目 28.10)
2529.1000	-长石	A:1.品名;2.用途;3.外观。例:不包括第七十一章的宝石及半宝石
	-萤石:	A:1.品名;2 用途;3.外观;4.氟化钙含量。例:不包括第七十一章的宝石及半宝石
2529.3000	-白榴石;霞石及霞石正长岩	A:1.品名;2.用途;3.外观。例:不包括第七十二章的宝石及半宝石
25.30	其他税目未列名的矿产品:	例:不包括第七十二章的宝石及半宝石
2530.1010	---绿泥石	A:1.品名;2.用途;3.加工方法(天然开采、简单破碎、磨粉、未膨胀等);4.外观;5.成分含量。B:6.白度
2530.1020	---蛭石及珍珠岩	A:1.品名;2.用途;3.加工方法(天然开采、简单破碎、磨粉、未膨胀等);4.外观;5.成分含量
2530.2000	-硫镁矾矿及泻盐矿(天然硫酸镁)	A:1.品名;2.用途;3.加工方法(天然开采、简单破碎、磨粉、未膨胀等);4.外观;5.成分含量
2530.9010	---矿物性药材	A:1.品名;2.用途;3.加工方法(天然开采、简单破碎、磨粉、未膨胀等);4.外观;5.成分含量
2530.9020	---稀土金属矿	A:1.品名;2.用途;3.加工方法(天然开采、简单破碎、磨粉、未膨胀等);4.外观;5.成分含量。C:6.稀土元素的重量百分比，以［A］表示
	---其他:	A:1.品名;2.用途;3.加工方法(天然开采、简单破碎、磨粉、未膨胀等);4.外观;5.成分含量

第二十六章　矿砂、矿渣及矿灰

［注解］

1．“加工方法”指改变原材料、毛坯或半成品的形状、尺寸、性质或表面状态，使之达到规定要求的各种形状的方法。

2．本章“成分含量”是指:“成分”指商品所构成的部分或要素，一般指所含物质的种类;“含量”一般指所含物质的数量。

3．对于本章的“成分含量”要尽量申报出所有的成分及含量，若无法确定，要申报出主要成分及其含量。

税则号列	商品名称	申报要素(A:归类要素 B:价格要素 C:审单及其他要素)及说明举例
26.01	铁矿砂及其精矿，包括焙烧黄铁矿:	例:不包括做颜料用的精细研磨的(第三十二章)。例:铁矿砂(已烧结，Fe:20%，黑色粉末，炼铁用)
	--未烧结:	A:1.品名;2.用途;3.加工方法;4.外观;5.成分含量;6.平均粒度。B:7.来源(矿区名称); 8.签约日期
2601.1200	--已烧结	A:1.品名;2.用途;3.加工方法;4.外观;5.成分含量。B:6.来源(矿区名称);7.签约日期
2601.2000	-焙烧黄铁矿	A:1.品名;2.用途;3.加工方法;4.外观;5.成分含量。B:6.来源(矿区名称);7.签约日期
26.02	锰矿砂及其精矿，包括以干重计含锰量在 20%及以上的锰铁矿及其精矿:	A:1.品名;2.用途;3.加工方法;4.外观;5.成分含量。B:6.来源(矿区名称);7.签约日期。例:不包括用于干电池的软锰矿(税目 25.30)。例:锰矿砂(Mn:21%，天然，黑色粉末，炼锰)
26.03	铜矿砂及其精矿:	A:1.品名;2.加工方法;3.外观;4.成分含量。B:5.含水率;6.来源(矿区名称); 7.签约日期。例:铜精矿(Cu:25%，天然，黑色粉末)
26.04	镍矿砂及其精矿:	A:1.品名;2.加工方法;3.外观;4.成分含量。B:5.来源(矿区名称); 6.签约日期。例:镍矿砂(Ni:1.5%，天然，黑色粉末)
26.05	钴矿砂及其精矿:	A:1.品名;2.加工方法; 3.外观; 4.主要伴生矿物元素含量。B:5.用途;6.来源(矿区名称); 7.签约日期。例:钴精矿(Co:20%，天然，黑色粉末)
26.06	铝矿砂及其精矿:	A 1.品名;2.加工方法;3.外观;4.成分含量。B:5.来源(矿区名称); 6.签约日期。例:铝矿砂(Al:30%，天然，黑色粉末)
26.07	铅矿砂及其精矿:	A:1.品名;2.加工方法;3.外观;4.成分含量。B:5.来源(矿区名称); 6.签约日期。例:铅精矿(Pb:20%，天然，黑色粉末)
26.08	锌矿砂及其精矿:	A:1.品名;2.加工方法;3.外观;4.成分含量。B:5.来源(矿区名称); 6.

税则号列	商品名称	申报要素(A:归类要素 B:价格要素 C:审单及其他要素)及说明举例
		签约日期。例:锌精矿(Zn: 20%，天然，黑色粉末)
26.09	锡矿砂及其精矿:	A: 1.品名; 2.加工方法; 3.外观; 4.成分含量。B: 5.来源（矿区名称）; 6.签约日期。例:锡精矿(Sn: 15%，天然，黑色粉末)
26.10	铬矿砂及其精矿:	A: 1.品名; 2.加工方法; 3.外观; 4.成分含量。B: 5.来源（矿区名称）; 6.签约日期。例:铬精矿(Cr: 15%，天然，黑色粉末)
26.11	钨矿砂及其精矿:	A: 1.品名; 2.加工方法; 3.外观; 4.成分含量。B: 5.来源（矿区名称）; 6.签约日期。例:钨精矿(W: 15%，天然，黑色粉末)
26.12	铀或钍矿砂及其精矿:	例:铀精矿(U: 5%，天然，黑色粉末)
2612.1000	-铀矿砂及其精矿	A: 1.品名; 2.加工方法; 3.外观; 4.成分含量; 5.种类(独居矿、钍石等)。B: 6.来源（矿区名称）; 7.签约日期
2612.2000	-钍矿砂及其精矿	A: 1.品名; 2.加工方法; 3.外观; 4.成分含量; 5.种类(独居矿、钍石等)。B: 6.来源（矿区名称）; 7.签约日期。C: 8.稀土元素的重量百分比，以[A]表示
26.13	钼矿砂及其精矿:	A: 1.品名; 2.加工方法; 3.外观; 4.成分含量。B: 5.来源（矿区名称）; 6.签约日期。例:不包括用作润滑剂的辉钼矿(税目25.30)。例:钼精矿(已焙烧，Mo: 20%，黑色粉末，炼钼)
26.14	钛矿砂及其精矿:	A: 1.品名; 2.加工方法; 3.外观; 4.成分含量。B: 5.来源（矿区名称）; 6.签约日期。例:不包括用作颜料的钛矿粉末(第三十二章)。例:钛精矿(Ti: 20%，天然，黑色粉末，炼钛)
26.15	铌、钽、钒或锆矿砂及其精矿:	例:不包括搪瓷生产上做遮光料的微化锆砂(税目 25.30)。例:钒精矿(V: 20%，天然，黑色粉末，炼钒)
2615.1000	-锆矿砂及其精矿	A: 1.品名; 2.加工方法; 3.外观; 4.成分含量; 5.粒度; 6.用途。B: 7.来源（矿区名称）; 8.签约日期
	-其他:	A: 1.品名; 2.加工方法; 3.外观; 4.成分含量。B: 5.来源（矿区名称）; 6.签约日期
26.16	贵金属矿砂及其精矿:	A: 1.品名; 2.加工方法; 3.外观; 4.成分含量。B: 5.来源（矿区名称）; 6.签约日期。例:金精矿(Au: 15克/吨，天然，黑色粉末，炼金)
26.17	其他矿砂及其精矿:	A: 1.品名; 2.加工方法; 3.外观; 4.成分含量。B: 5.来源（矿区名称）; 6.签约日期。例:锑精矿(Sb: 15%，天然，黑色粉末，炼锑)
26.18	冶炼钢铁所产生的粒状熔渣(熔渣砂):	A: 1.品名; 2.用途; 3.加工方法; 4.外观; 5.成分含量。B: 6.来源。例:不包括泡沫矿渣、矿渣棉(税目68.06)、矿渣水泥(税目25.23)
26.19	冶炼钢铁所产生的熔渣、浮渣(粒状熔渣除外)、氧化皮及其他废料:	A: 1.品名; 2.用途; 3.加工方法; 4.外观; 5.成分含量。B: 6.来源。例:不包括经破碎并粗略分级的筑路熔渣(税目25.17)
26.20	含有金属、砷及其化合物的矿渣、矿灰及残渣(冶炼钢铁所产生的灰、渣除外):	A: 1.品名; 2.用途; 3.加工方法; 4.外观; 5.成分含量。B: 6.来源。例:不包括冶炼钢铁所产生的
26.21	其他矿渣及矿灰，包括海藻灰(海草灰); 焚化城市垃圾所产生的灰、渣:	A: 1.品名; 2.用途; 3.加工方法; 4.外观。B: 5.来源。例:稻壳灰(烧稻壳而得，黑色粉末，隔音用)

第二十七章 矿物燃料、矿物油及其蒸馏产品；沥青物质；矿物蜡

[注解]

1．“加工方法”指改变原材料、毛坯或半成品的形状、尺寸、性质或表面状态，使之达到规定要求的各种形状的方法。

2．本章“成分含量”是指:“成分”指商品所构成的部分或要素，一般指所含物质的种类;“含量”一般指所含物质的数量。

3．对于本章“成分含量”在有些情况下，部分商品要求的成分、含量只要能明确归类即可。如税目 27.07 的杂酚油可以注明“主要成分为酚类和酚酯类”，再如税目27.15的稀释沥青可以申报“沥青 70%，溶剂 30%”。

税则号列	商品名称	申报要素(A:归类要素 B:价格要素 C:审单及其他要素)及说明举例
27.01	煤; 煤砖、煤球及用煤制成的类似固体燃料:	例:不包括黑玉(税目 25.30)、褐煤(税目 27.02)、焦炭及半焦炭(税目27.04)
2701.1100	--无烟煤	A: 1.品名; 2.外观; 3.挥发物含量; 4.热值（统一使用“恒湿无灰基高位发热量”指标）。B: 5.灰分; 6.含硫量; 7.含水量
2701.1210	---炼焦煤	A: 1.品名; 2.外观; 3.挥发物含量; 4.角质层最大厚度; 5.粘结指数。B: 6.灰分; 7.含硫量; 8.含水量
2701.1290	---其他	A: 1.品名; 2.外观; 3.挥发物含量; 4.热值（统一使用“恒湿无灰基高位发热量”指标）。B: 5.灰分; 6.含硫量; 7.含水量
2701.1900	--其他煤	A: 1.品名; 2.外观; 3.挥发物含量; 4.热值（统一使用“恒湿无灰基高位发热量”指标）。B: 5.灰分; 6.含硫量; 7.含水量
2701.2000	-煤砖、煤球及用煤制成的类似固体燃料	A: 1.品名; 2.外观; 3.挥发物含量; 4.等级; 5 热值（统一使用“恒湿无灰基高位发热量”指标）。B: 6.灰分; 7.含硫量; 8.含水量

税则号列	商品名称	申报要素(A:归类要素 B:价格要素 C:审单及其他要素)及说明举例
27.02	褐煤,不论是否制成型,但不包括黑玉:	例:不包括黑玉(税目25.30);例:褐煤(粉末颗粒混合物,不是黑玉)
2702.1000	-褐煤,不论是否粉化,但未制成型	A:1.品名;2.外观;3.是否黑玉;4.热值(统一使用"恒湿无灰基高位发热量"指标)。B:5.透光率;6.含水量
2702.2000	-制成型的褐煤	A:1.品名;2.外观;3.是否黑玉。B:4.透光率;5.含水量
27.03	泥煤(包括肥料用泥煤),不论是否制成型:	A:1.品名;2.外观;3.来源
27.04	煤、褐煤或泥煤制成的焦炭及半焦炭,不论是否制成型;甑炭:	例:不包括电气用甑炭制品(税目85.45);例:焦炭(由褐煤制得,燃料用)
2704.0010	---焦炭或半焦炭	A:1.品名;2.用途;3.来源。B:4.挥发物含量;5.气孔率;6.含磷量;7.灰分;8.粒度;9.含水量;10.含硫量
2704.0090	---其他	A:1.品名;2.用途;3.来源
27.05	煤气、水煤气、炉煤气及类似气体,但石油气及其他烃类气除外:	A:1.品名;2.来源。例:不包括石油气及其他烃类气体(税目27.11)
27.06	从煤、褐煤或泥煤蒸馏所得的焦油及其他矿物焦油,不论是否脱水或部分蒸馏,包括再造焦油:	A:1.品名;2.外观;3.来源;4.成分含量。例:不包括木焦油(税目38.07)。例:焦油(由煤蒸馏而得)
2707.1000	-粗苯	A:1.品名;2.成分含量。例:粗甲苯(甲苯含量93%)
2707.2000	-粗甲苯	A:1.品名;2.成分含量。例:粗二甲苯(二甲苯含量94%)
2707.3000	-粗二甲苯	A:1.品名;2.成分含量
2707.4000	-萘	A:1.品名;2.成分含量(以美国标准实验方法D86为准,250℃时);3.结晶点。B:4.外观。例:不包括混合烷基苯、混合烷基萘(税目38.17)。例:芳烃混合物(主要为苯、甲苯和二甲苯,用D86方法250℃蒸馏出芳烃85%)
2707.5000	-其他芳烃混合物,温度在250℃时蒸馏出的芳烃含量以体积计(包括损耗)在65%及以上(以美国标准试验法D86为准)	A:1.品名;2.成分含量;3.250℃蒸馏出芳烃体积含量;4.馏程。
	-其他:	A:1.品名;2.成分含量
27.08	从煤焦油或其他矿物焦油所得的沥青及沥青焦:	A:1.品名;2.外观;3.来源
27.09	石油原油及从沥青矿物提取的原油:	A:1.品名;2.种类;3.密度或API度;4.若为凝析油需注明
27.10	石油及从沥青矿物提取的油类,但原油除外;以上述油为基本成分(按重量计不低于70%)的其他税目未列名制品;废油:	
	--轻油及其制品:	例:参考相关标准提供技术指标,如:【标准号】GB484-1993【中文标题】车用汽油,【标准号】GB1787-1988【中文标题】航空汽油,中国石化集团公司出口标准SINOPEC002-1987,【标准号】SH0004-1990【中文标题】橡胶工业用溶剂油,【标准号】SH0005-1990【中文标题】油漆工业用溶剂油,【标准号】GB16629-1996【中文标题】6号抽提溶剂油,【标准号】GB1922-1988【中文标题】溶剂油
2710.1210	---车用汽油及航空汽油	A:1.品名;2.馏程;3.硫成分含量
2710.1220	---石脑油	A:1.品名;2.馏程
2710.1230	---橡胶溶剂油、油漆溶剂油、抽提溶剂油	A:1.品名;2.馏程;3.用途。B:4.品牌;5.型号;6.包装规格
2710.1291	----壬烯	A:1.品名;2.成分含量
2710.1299	----其他	A:1.品名;2.馏程;3.成分含量
	---煤油馏分:	A:1.品名;2.馏程
2710.1922	----5~7号燃料油	A:1.品名;2.馏程;3.运动黏度指标(100℃);4.硫含量;5水和沉淀物含量;6闪点(5号轻、5号重、6号燃料油注明闭口闪点,7号燃料油注明开口闪点);7.灰分含量
2710.1923	----柴油	A:1.品名;2.馏程;3.硫含量
2710.1929	----其他	A:1.品名;2.馏程
2710.1991	----润滑油	A:1.品名;2.用途; 3.从石油或沥青提取矿物油类的百分比含量。 B:4.品牌; 5.型号; 6.包装规格
2710.1992	----润滑脂	A:1.品名;2.用途; 3.从石油或沥青提取矿物油类的百分比含量。 B:4.品牌; 5.型号; 6.包装规格
2710.1993	----润滑油基础油	A:1.品名;2.用途。B:3.品牌;4.型号;5.包装规格
2710.1994	----液体石蜡和重质液体石蜡	A:1.品名。B:2.包装规格
2710.1999	----其他	A:1.品名。B:2.包装规格
2710.2000	-石油及从沥青矿物提取的油类(但原油除外)以及以上述油为基本成分(按重量计不低于70%)的其他税目未列名制品,含有生物柴油,但废油除外	A:1.品名;2.用途;3.成分;4.从石油或沥青提取矿物油类的百分比含量

税则号列	商品名称	申报要素(A:归类要素 B:价格要素 C:审单及其他要素)及说明举例
	-废油:	A: 1. 品名; 2. 来源
27.11	石油气及其他烃类气:	A: 1. 品名; 2. 状态(液化或气态); 3. 成分含量。B: 4. 包装容器容积; 5. 加工方法(压力货、冷冻货等)
2712.1000	-凡士林	A: 1. 品名 2. 用途; 3. 是否零售包装。例: 不包括零售包装的适于作护肤用的凡士林(税目 33.04)
2712.2000	-石蜡,按重量计含油量小于 0.75%	A: 1. 品名; 2. 加工方法; 3. 外观; 4. 来源; 5. 含油量
	-其他:	A: 1. 品名; 2. 成分
27.13	石油焦、石油沥青及其他石油或从沥青矿物提取的油类的残渣:	
	-石油焦:	A: 1. 品名; 2. 用途; 3. 加工方法(是否煅烧); 4. 外观; 5. 含硫量
2713.2000	-石油沥青	A: 1. 品名; 2. 针入度; 3. 用途; 4. 加工方法(是否煅烧); 5. 外观。B: 6. 品牌; 7. 包装类型(桶装、散装等); 8. 含蜡量; 9. 签约日期
2713.9000	-其他石油或从沥青矿物提取的油类的残渣	A: 1. 品名; 2. 用途; 3. 加工方法(是否煅烧); 4. 外观
27.14	天然沥青(地沥青)、沥青页岩、油页岩及焦油砂; 沥青岩:	A: 1. 品名; 2. 用途; 3. 加工方法; 4. 外观; 5. 成分含量(沥青、水)
27.15	以天然沥青(地沥青)、石油沥青、矿物焦油或矿物焦油沥青为基本成分的沥青混合物(例如, 沥青胶粘剂、稀释沥青):	A: 1. 品名; 2. 用途; 3. 加工方法; 4. 外观; 5. 成分含量
27.16	电力:	A: 1. 品名

第六类 化学工业及其相关工业的产品

第二十八章 无机化学品; 贵金属、稀土金属、放射性元素及其同位素的有机及无机化合物

[注解]

1. “加工方法”指改变原材料、毛坯或半成品的形状、尺寸、性质或表面状态，使之达到规定要求的各种形状的方法。
2. 本章“成分含量”是指:“成分”指商品所构成的部分或要素，一般指所含物质的种类;“含量”一般指所含物质的数量。
3. 所注明的“包装”内容要足以判断是否为零售包装。

税则号列	商品名称	申报要素(A:归类要素 B:价格要素 C:审单及其他要素)及说明举例
28.01	氟、氯、溴及碘:	A: 1. 品名。B: 2. 包装。例: 碘溶液(50 千克/桶)
28.02	升华硫磺、沉淀硫磺、胶态硫磺:	A: 1. 品名。B: 2. 包装。例: 胶态硫磺(50 千克/袋)
28.03	碳(炭黑及其他税目未列名的其他形态的碳):	A: 1. 品名; 2. 来源; 3. 有无活性; 4. 细度。B: 5. 包装 6. 型号; 7. 品牌。例: 不包括石墨、木炭、动物炭黑、活性碳; 例: 植物炭黑(无活性, 60 目, N550, 60 千克/袋)
2804.1000	-氢	A: 1. 品名。例: 氢气
	-稀有气体:	A: 1. 品名。例: 氩气
2804.3000	-氮	A: 1. 品名。例: 氮气
2804.4000	-氧	A: 1. 品名。例: 氧气
2804.5000	-硼; 碲	A: 1. 品名
	---经掺杂用于电子工业的直径在 7.5 厘米及以上的单晶硅棒:	A: 1. 品名; 2. 用途(用于电子工业等); 3. 加工方法(经掺杂等); 4. 成分含量; 5. 技术指标(直径)
2804.6120	---经掺杂用于电子工业的其他单晶硅棒	A: 1. 品名; 2. 用途(用于电子工业等); 3. 加工方法(经掺杂等); 4. 成分含量; 5. 技术指标(直径)
2804.6190	---其他	A: 1. 品名; 2. 用途; 3. 加工方法(经掺杂等); 4. 成分含量; 5. 外观(多晶硅碎料、块料或锅底料、头尾料等); 6. 电阻率; 7. 是否需清洗
2804.6900	--其他	A: 1. 品名; 2. 用途; 3. 加工方法(经掺杂等); 4. 成分含量。B: 5. 牌号
	-磷:	B: 1. 品名; 2. 成分含量
2804.8000	-砷	A: 1. 品名。例: 黄砷
	-硒:	A: 1. 品名; 2. 用途(用于电子工业等); 3. 加工方法(经掺杂等); 4. 成分含量。B: 5. 包装。例: 不包括已切割圆片状或类似形状的(税目 38.18)、胶态悬浮硒(第三十章)
2805.1100	--钠	A: 1. 品名。B: 2. 包装
2805.1200	--钙	A: 1. 品名。B: 2. 是否高纯度钙; 3. 包装
2805.1900	--其他	A: 1. 品名。B: 2. 包装

税则号列	商品名称	申报要素(A:归类要素 B:价格要素 C:审单及其他要素)及说明举例
	-稀土金属、钪及钇,不论是否相互混合或相互熔合:	A:1.品名;2.混合稀土应注明各组分含量。B:3.是否电池级的稀土金属、钪及钇;4.包装。C:5.稀土元素的重量百分比,以[A]表示
2805.4000	-汞	A:1.品名。B:2.包装
28.06	氯化氢(盐酸);氯磺酸:	A:1.品名。2.成分含量
28.07	硫酸;发烟硫酸:	A:1.品名;2.用途;3.成分含量。 B:4.加工工艺(如回收硫酸;硫磺硫酸;硫矿硫酸)
28.08	硝酸;磺硝酸:	A:1.品名;2.成分含量
28.09	五氧化二磷;磷酸;多磷酸,不论是否已有化学定义:	A:1.品名;2.成分含量
28.10	硼的氧化物;硼酸:	A:1.品名;2.成分含量
2811.1100	--氟化氢(氢氟酸)	A:1.品名;2.成分含量。B:3.包装(槽罐集装箱、塑料桶等)
	--其他:	A:1.品名;2.成分含量
2811.2100	--二氧化碳	A:1.品名;2.成分含量;3.用途
	--二氧化硅	A:1.品名;2.成分含量;3.用途;4.是否经过表面处理。B:5.品牌;6.外观;7.加工工艺;8.细度;9.型号
2811.2900	--其他	A:1.品名
28.12	非金属卤化物及卤氧化物:	A:1.品名。例:氯化亚砜
28.13	非金属硫化物;商品三硫化二磷:	A:1.品名。例:二硫化硅
28.14	氨及氨水:	A:1.品名;2.氨含量
28.15	氢氧化钠(烧碱);氢氧化钾(苛性钾);过氧化钠及过氧化钾:	A:1.品名;2.成分含量;3.用途;4.外观
28.16	氢氧化镁及过氧化镁;锶或钡的氧化物、氢氧化物及过氧化物:	A:1.品名。例:氧化钡
28.17	氧化锌及过氧化锌:	A:1.品名;2.用途;3.天然的请注明。例:不包括天然氧化锌(税目26.08)
2818.1010	---棕刚玉	A:1.品名;2.成分含量;3.用途;4.外观;5.晶型;6.莫氏硬度
2818.1090	---其他	A:1.品名;2.成分含量;3.用途;4.外观;5.晶型
2818.2000	-氧化铝,但人造刚玉除外	A:1.品名;2.用途;3.外观;4.成分含量
2818.3000	-氢氧化铝	A:1.品名;2.外观;3.成分含量
2819.1000	-三氧化铬	A:1.品名;2.成分含量
2819.9000	-其他	A:1.品名
28.20	锰的氧化物:	A:1.品名;2.成分含量
2821.1000	-铁的氧化物及氢氧化物	A:1.品名;2.成分含量
2821.2000	-土色料	A:1.品名;2.铁按三氧化二铁计含量
28.22	钴的氧化物及氢氧化物;商品氧化钴:	A:1.品名。例:不包括天然水合氧化钴(税目26.05);例:氧化钴
28.23	钛的氧化物:	A:1.品名;2.与其他物质混合请注明。B:3.经表面处理的请注明
28.24	铅的氧化物;铅丹及铅橙:	A:1.品名。例:铅丹
2825.1010	---水合肼	A:1.品名;2 水合肼含量。例:水合肼(含量98%)
2825.1020	---硫酸羟胺	A:1.品名
2825.1090	---其他	A:1 品名
	-锂的氧化物及氢氧化物:	A:1.品名
	-钒的氧化物及氢氧化物:	A:1.品名
2825.4000	-镍的氧化物及氢氧化物	A:1.品名
2825.5000	-铜的氧化物及氢氧化物	A:1.品名
2825.6000	-锗的氧化物及二氧化锆	A:1.品名
2825.7000	-钼的氧化物及氢氧化物	A:1.品名
2825.8000	-锑的氧化物	A:1.品名
2825.9011	----钨酸	A:1.品名
2825.9012	----三氧化钨	A:1.品名。B:2.状态(粉末);3.外观(淡黄色);4.粒度;5.杂质含量
2825.9019	----其他	A:1.品名
	---铋的氧化物及氢氧化物:	A:1.品名
	---锡的氧化物及氢氧化物:	A:1.品名
	---铌的氧化物及氢氧化物:	A:1.品名
2825.9090	---其他	A:1.品名
2826.1210	---无水氟化铝	A:1.品名;2.氟质量分数;3.铝质量分数;4.烧碱量;5.松装密度
2826.1290	---其他	A:1.品名
	--其他:	A:1.品名
2826.3000	-六氟铝酸钠(人造冰晶石)	A:1.品名
	-其他:	A:1.品名
28.27	氯化物、氯氧化物及氢氧基氯化物;溴化物及溴氧化物;碘化物及碘氧化物:	

税则号列	商品名称	申报要素(A:归类要素 B:价格要素 C:审单及其他要素)及说明举例
	-氯化铵:	A: 1. 品名; 2. 用途。B: 3. 外观(粉状、颗粒)
2827.2000	-氯化钙	A: 1. 品名
	-其他氯化物:	A: 1. 品名。例: 不包括纯氯化钠及纯氯化钾
	-氯氧化物及氢氧基氯化物:	A: 1. 品名
	-溴化物及溴氧化物:	A: 1. 品名
2827.6000	-碘化物及碘氧化物	A: 1. 品名
28.28	次氯酸盐; 商品次氯酸钙; 亚氯酸盐; 次溴酸盐:	A: 1. 品名。例: 次氯酸钙
28.29	氯酸盐及高氯酸盐; 溴酸盐及过溴酸盐; 碘酸盐及高碘酸盐:	
	-氯酸盐:	A: 1. 品名
2829.9000	-其他	A: 1. 品名。B: 2. 如为高氯酸铵请注明粒度
28.30	硫化物; 多硫化物, 不论是否已有化学定义:	A: 1. 品名。例: 不包括红锑(税目 38.24)。例: 硫化钠
28.31	连二亚硫酸盐及次硫酸盐:	A: 1. 品名。例: 连二亚硫酸钠
28.32	亚硫酸盐; 硫代硫酸盐:	A: 1. 品名。例: 亚硫酸钠
28.33	硫酸盐; 矾; 过硫酸盐:	A: 1. 品名。例: 硫酸镁
28.34	亚硝酸盐; 硝酸盐:	例: 不包括硝酸铵、硝酸钠(第三十一章)
2834.1000	-亚硝酸盐	A: 1. 品名
	--硝酸钾:	A: 1. 品名; 2. 肥料用硝酸钾请注明
	--其他:	A: 1. 品名
28.35	次磷酸盐、亚磷酸盐及磷酸盐; 多磷酸盐, 不论是否已有化学定义:	例: 不包括磷酸一铵、磷酸二铵(税目 31.05)
2835.1000	-次磷酸盐及亚磷酸盐	A: 1. 品名
2835.2200	--磷酸一钠及磷酸二钠	A: 1. 品名
2835.2400	--钾的磷酸盐	A: 1. 品名
	--正磷酸氢钙(磷酸二钙):	A: 1. 品名; 2. 正磷酸氢钙请注明氟含量; 3. 用途(饲料、食品等)
2835.2600	--其他磷酸钙	A: 1. 品名
	--其他:	A: 1. 品名
	-多磷酸盐:	A: 1. 品名; 2. 用途(饲料、食品等)
2836.2000	-碳酸钠(纯碱)	A: 1. 品名
2836.3000	-碳酸氢钠(小苏打)	A: 1. 品名
2836.4000	-钾的碳酸盐	A: 1. 品名
2836.5000	-碳酸钙	A: 1. 品名; 2. 成分含量; 3. 用途。B: 4. 品牌
2836.6000	-碳酸钡	A: 1. 品名
	-其他:	A: 1. 品名
28.37	氰化物、氧氰化物及氰络合物:	A: 1. 品名; 2. 成分含量。B: 3. 包装。例: 不包括非金属氰化物(税目 28.51)
28.39	硅酸盐; 商品碱金属硅酸盐:	A: 1. 品名。例: 硅酸钠
28.40	硼酸盐及过硼酸盐:	A: 1. 品名。例: 四硼酸钠
28.41	金属酸盐及过金属酸盐:	例: 不包括发光钨酸盐(税目 32.06)
2841.3000	-重铬酸钠	A: 1. 品名; 2. 外观
2841.5000	-其他铬酸盐及重铬酸盐; 过铬酸盐	A: 1. 品名; 2. 外观
	-亚锰酸盐、锰酸盐及高锰酸盐:	A: 1. 品名; 2. 外观
	-钼酸盐:	A: 1. 品名; 2. 外观
2841.8010	---仲钨酸铵	A: 1. 品名; 2. 外观。B: 3. 含量(WO_3含量); 4. 杂质含量
2841.8020	---钨酸钠	A: 1. 品名; 2. 外观
2841.8030	---钨酸钙	A: 1. 品名; 2. 外观
2841.8040	---偏钨酸铵	A: 1. 品名; 2. 外观。B: 3. 含量(WO_3含量); 4. 杂质含量
2841.8090	---其他	A: 1. 品名; 2. 外观
2841.9000	-其他	A: 1. 品名; 2. 外观
28.42	其他无机酸盐或过氧酸盐(包括不论是否已有化学定义的硅铝酸盐), 但叠氮化物除外:	A: 1. 品名。B: 2. 包装。例: 硅铝酸钠(20 千克/瓶)
28.43	胶态贵金属; 贵金属的无机或有机化合物, 不论是否已有化学定义; 贵金属汞齐:	A: 1. 品名。B: 2. 包装。例: 硝酸银(20 千克/瓶)
28.44	放射性化学元素及放射性同位素(包括可裂变或可转换的化学元素及同位素)及其化合物; 含上述产品的混合物及残渣:	A: 1. 品名。例: 铀

税则号列	商品名称	申报要素(A:归类要素 B:价格要素 C:审单及其他要素)及说明举例
28.45	税目 28.44 以外的同位素;这些同位素的无机或有机化合物,不论是否已有化学定义:	A: 1. 品名。例: 重水
28.46	稀土金属、钇、钪及其混合物的无机或有机化合物:	
	-铈的化合物:	A: 1. 品名。C: 2. 稀土元素的重量百分比,以[A]表示
	---氧化稀土(氧化铈除外)	A: 1. 品名。C: 2. 稀土元素的重量百分比,以[A]表示
2846.9021	----氯化铽	A: 1. 品名。C: 2. 稀土元素的重量百分比,以[A]表示
2846.9022	----氯化镝	A: 1. 品名。C: 2. 稀土元素的重量百分比,以[A]表示
2846.9023	----氯化镧	A: 1. 品名。C: 2. 稀土元素的重量百分比,以[A]表示
2846.9024	----氯化钕	A: 1. 品名。C: 2. 稀土元素的重量百分比,以[A]表示
2846.9025	----氯化镨	A: 1. 品名。C: 2. 稀土元素的重量百分比,以[A]表示
2846.9026	----氯化钇	A: 1. 品名。C: 2. 稀土元素的重量百分比,以[A]表示
2846.9028	----混合氯化稀土	A: 1. 品名; 2. 成分含量。C: 3. 稀土元素的重量百分比,以[A]表示
2846.9029	----其他	A: 1. 品名; 2. 成分含量。C: 3. 稀土元素的重量百分比,以[A]表示
	---氟化稀土:	A: 1. 品名; 2. 成分含量。C: 3. 稀土元素的重量百分比,以[A]表示
	---碳酸稀土:	A: 1. 品名; 2. 成分含量。C: 3. 稀土元素的重量百分比,以[A]表示
	---其他	A: 1. 品名; 2. 成分含量。C: 3. 稀土元素的重量百分比,以[A]表示
28.47	过氧化氢,不论是否用尿素固化:	A: 1. 品名; 2. 成分含量; 3. 包装。例: 不包括制成一定剂量或零售形状或包装的(税目 30.04)。例: 过氧化氢(50 千克/桶,含量 90%)
28.48	磷化物,不论是否已有化学定义,但不包括磷铁:	A: 1. 品名; 2. 铜母合金请注明磷的重量百分比
28.49	碳化物,不论是否已有化学定义:	A: 1. 品名; 2. 成分含量。 B: 3. 品牌; 4. 型号; 5. 外观; 6. 用途; 7. 碳化钨请注明粒度
28.50	氢化物、氮化物、叠氮化物、硅化物及硼化物,不论是否已有化学定义,但可归入税目 28.49 的碳化物除外:	A: 1. 品名。例: 硼化氮
28.52	汞的无机或有机化合物,不论是否已有化学定义,汞齐除外:	A: 1. 品名; 2. 成分含量
2853.0010	---饮用蒸馏水	A: 1. 品名; 2. 水请注明用途。B: 3. 包装
2853.0020	---氯化氰	A: 1. 品名。B: 2. 包装
2853.0030	---镍钴锰氢氧化物	A: 1. 品名
2853.0090	---其他	A: 1. 品名

第二十九章　有机化学品

[注解]

1."加工方法"指改变原材料、毛坯或半成品的形状、尺寸、性质或表面状态,使之达到规定要求的各种形状的方法。

2. 本章"成分含量"是指:"成分"指商品所构成的部分或要素,一般指所含物质的种类;"含量"一般指所含物质的数量。

3. 所注明的"包装"内容要足以判断是否为零售包装。

4. 本章商品需要申报的品名包括标准命名法名称或工商业通用俗称。

5. 化学结构式和 CAS 号对本章商品的海关管理非常重要。由于报关单的书写限制,在本目录中没有对化学结构式和 CAS 号的要求,但在实际通关中,企业要用其他的方式向海关提供商品的化学结构式和 CAS 号。

税则号列	商品名称	申报要素(A:归类要素 B:价格要素 C:审单及其他要素)及说明举例
29.01	无环烃:	A: 1. 品名; 2. 成分含量; 3. 用途; 4. 用作气体燃料的应报明包装容器容积。B: 5. 散装货物应报明。例: 丁烷,丁烷含量 99%,用于气体燃料,350 毫升罐装
29.02	环烃:	
	-环烷烃、环烯及环萜烯:	A: 1. 品名; 2. 成分含量
2902.2000	-苯	A: 1. 品名; 2. 成分含量
2902.3000	-甲苯	A: 1. 品名; 2. 成分含量
	-二甲苯:	A: 1. 品名; 2. 成分含量
2902.5000	-苯乙烯	A: 1. 品名; 2. 成分含量
2902.6000	-乙苯	A: 1. 品名; 2. 成分含量
2902.7000	-异丙基苯	A: 1. 品名; 2. 成分含量
2902.9010	---四氢萘	A: 1. 品名; 2. 成分含量
2902.9020	---精萘	A: 1. 品名; 2. 成分含量; 3. 结晶温度
2902.9030	---十二烷基苯	A: 1. 品名; 2. 成分含量

税则号列	商品名称	申报要素(A:归类要素 B:价格要素 C:审单及其他要素)及说明举例
2902.9040	---4-(4′-烷基环己基)环己基乙烯	A:1.品名;2.成分含量
2902.9090	---其他	A:1.品名;2.成分含量
29.03	烃的卤化衍生物:	A:1.品名;2.成分含量;3.用途
29.04	烃的磺化、硝化或亚硝化衍生物,不论是否卤化:	A:1.品名;2.成分含量;3.用途
29.05	无环醇及其卤化、磺化、硝化或亚硝化衍生物:	A:1.品名;2.成分含量;3.用途。B:4.包装
29.06	环醇及其卤化、磺化、硝化或亚硝化衍生物:	A:1.品名;2.成分含量;3.用途
29.07	酚;酚醇:	A:1.品名;2.成分含量;3.用途
29.08	酚及酚醇的卤化、磺化、硝化或亚硝化衍生物:	A:1.品名;2.成分含量;3.用途
29.09	醚、醚醇、醚酚、醚醇酚、过氧化醇、过氧化醚、过氧化酮(不论是否已有化学定义)及其卤化、磺化、硝化或亚硝化衍生物:	A:1.品名;2.成分含量;3.用途
29.10	三节环环氧化物、环氧醇、环氧酚、环氧醚及其卤化、磺化、硝化或亚硝化衍生物:	A:1.品名;2.成分含量;3.用途
29.11	缩醛及半缩醛,不论是否含有其他含氧基,及其卤化、磺化、硝化或亚硝化衍生物:	A:1.品名;2.成分含量;3.用途
29.12	醛,不论是否含有其他含氧基;环聚醛;多聚甲醛:	A:1.品名;2.成分含量;3.用途;4.四聚甲醛报明外观
29.13	税目29.12所列产品的卤化、磺化、硝化或亚硝化衍生物:	A:1.品名;2.成分含量;3.用途
29.14	酮及醌,不论是否含有其他含氧基,及其卤化、磺化、硝化或亚硝化衍生物:	A:1.品名;2.成分含量;3.用途。B:4.丙酮报明包装
29.15	饱和无环一元羧酸及其酸酐、酰卤化物、过氧化物和过氧酸以及它们的卤化、磺化、硝化或亚硝化衍生物:	A:1.品名;2.成分含量;3.用途
29.16	不饱和无环一元羧酸、环一元羧酸及其酸酐、酰卤化物、过氧化物和过氧酸以及它们的卤化、磺化、硝化或亚硝化衍生物:	A:1.品名;2.成分含量;3.用途。B:4.丙烯酸、丙烯酸盐或酯应报明包装
29.17	多元羧酸及其酸酐、酰卤化物、过氧化物和过氧酸以及它们的卤化、磺化、硝化或亚硝化衍生物:	A:1.品名;2.成分含量;3.用途 4.对苯二甲酸请注明4-CBA值;5.对苯二甲酸请注明P-TL酸值;6.对苯二甲酸请注明色度;7.对苯二甲酸请注明水分
29.18	含附加含氧基的羧酸及其酸酐、酰卤化物、过氧化物和过氧酸以及它们的卤化、磺化、硝化或亚硝化衍生物:	A:1.品名;2.成分含量;3.用途
29.19	磷酸酯及其盐,包括乳磷酸盐,以及它们的卤化、磺化、硝化或亚硝化衍生物:	A:1.品名;2.成分含量;3.用途
29.20	其他非金属无机酸酯(不包括卤化氢的酯)及其盐以及它们的卤化、磺化、硝化或亚硝化衍生物:	A:1.品名;2.成分含量;3.用途
29.21	氨基化合物:	A:1.品名;2.成分含量;3.用途
29.22	含氧基氨基化合物:	A:1.品名;2.成分含量;3.用途;4.乙醇胺及其盐应报明色度。 B:5.乙醇胺及其盐应报明包装
29.23	季铵盐及季铵碱;卵磷脂及其他磷氨基类脂,不论是否已有化学定义:	A:1.品名;2.成分含量;3.用途
29.24	羧基酰胺基化合物;碳酸酰胺基化合物:	A:1.品名;2.成分含量;3.用途。B:4.包装
29.25	羧基酰亚胺化合物(包括糖精及其盐)及亚胺基化合物:	A:1.品名;2.成分含量;3.用途
29.26	腈基化合物:	A:1.品名;2.成分含量;3.用途
29.27	重氮化合物、偶氮化合物及氧化偶氮化合物:	A:1.品名;2.成分含量;3.用途
29.28	肼(联氨)及胲(羟胺)的有机衍生物:	A:1.品名;2.成分含量;3.用途
29.29	其他含氮基化合物:	A:1.品名;2.成分含量;3.用途
29.30	有机硫化合物:	A:1.品名;2.成分含量;3.用途

税则号列	商品名称	申报要素(A:归类要素 B:价格要素 C:审单及其他要素)及说明举例
29.31	其他有机-无机化合物:	A: 1. 品名; 2. 成分含量; 3. 用途
29.32	仅含氧杂原子的杂环化合物:	A: 1. 品名; 2. 成分含量; 3. 用途
29.33	仅含氮杂原子的杂环化合物:	A: 1. 品名; 2. 成分含量; 3. 用途; 4. 乌洛托品请注明外观。B: 5. 6-己内酰胺请注明外观; 6. 签约日期
29.34	核酸及其盐，不论是否已有化学定义；其他杂环化合物:	A: 1. 品名; 2. 成分含量; 3. 用途
29.35	磺(酰)胺:	A: 1. 品名; 2. 成分含量; 3. 用途
29.36	天然或合成再制的维生素原和维生素(包括天然浓缩物)及其主要用作维生素的衍生物，上述产品的混合物，不论是否溶于溶剂:	A: 1. 品名; 2. 成分含量; 3. 用途; 4. 包装
29.37	天然或合成再制的激素、前列腺素、血栓烷和白细胞三烯以及它们的衍生物和结构类似物，包括主要用作激素的改性链多肽	A: 1. 品名; 2. 成分含量; 3. 用途; 4. 包装
29.38	天然或合成再制的苷(配糖物)及其盐、醚、酯和其他衍生物:	A: 1. 品名; 2. 成分含量; 3. 用途 4. 来源
29.39	天然或合成再制的生物碱及其盐、醚、酯和其他衍生物:	A: 1. 品名; 2. 成分含量; 3. 用途 4. 来源
29.40	化学纯糖，但蔗糖、乳糖、麦芽糖、葡萄糖及果糖除外；糖醚、糖缩醛和糖酯及其盐，但不包括税目 29.37、29.38 及 29.39 的产品:	A: 1. 品名; 2. 成分含量
29.41	抗菌素:	A: 1. 品名; 2. 包装
29.42	其他有机化合物:	A: 1. 品名; 2. 成分含量

第三十章　药品

[注解]

1. “加工方法”指改变原材料、毛坯或半成品的形状、尺寸、性质或表面状态，使之达到规定要求的各种形状的方法。
2. 本章“成分含量”是指：“成分”指商品所构成的部分或要素，一般指所含物质的种类；“含量”一般指所含物质的数量。
3. 所注明的“包装”内容要足以判断是否为零售包装。
4. 对于本章“成分含量”在有些情况下，部分商品的成分、含量只要能满足海关管理即可。

税则号列	商品名称	申报要素(A:归类要素 B:价格要素 C:审单及其他要素)及说明举例
30.01	已干燥的器官疗法用腺体及其他器官，不论是否制成粉末；器官疗法用腺体、其他器官及其分泌物的提取物；肝素及其盐；其他供治疗或预防疾病用的其他税目未列名的人体或动物制品:	A: 1. 品名; 2. 用途; 3. 加工工艺。B: 4. 品牌（英文）; 5. 型号
30.02	人血；治病、防病或诊断用的动物血制品；抗血清、其他血份及免疫制品，不论是否修饰或通过生物工艺加工制得；疫苗、毒素、培养微生物(不包括酵母)及类似产品:	A: 1. 品名; 2. 用途; 3. 加工工艺。B: 4. 品牌; 5. 型号; 6. 包装规格
30.03	两种或两种以上成分混合而成的治病或防病用药品(不包括税目 30.02、30.05 或 30.06 的货品)，未配定剂量或制成零售包装:	A: 1. 品名; 2. 用途; 3. 成分含量; 4. 是否配定剂量或零售包装。B: 5. 品牌; 6. 型号
30.04	由混合或非混合产品构成的治病或防病用药品(不包括税目 30.02、30.05 或 30.06 的货品)，已配定剂量(包括制成皮肤摄入形式的)或制成零售包装:	A: 1. 品名; 2. 用途; 3. 成分; 4. 是否配定剂量或零售包装。B: 5. 品牌
30.05	软填料、纱布、绷带及类似物品(例如，敷料、橡皮膏、泥罨剂)，经过药物浸涂或制成零售包装供医疗、外科、牙科或兽医用:	A: 1. 品名; 2. 用途; 3. 成分; 4. 是否经过药物浸涂或制成零售包装。B: 5. 品牌; 6. 型号

税则号列	商品名称	申报要素(A:归类要素 B:价格要素 C:审单及其他要素)及说明举例
3006.1000	-无菌外科肠线、类似的无菌缝合材料(包括外科或牙科用无菌可吸收缝线)及外伤创口闭合用的无菌粘合胶布;无菌昆布及无菌昆布塞条;外科或牙科用无菌吸收性止血材料;外科或牙科用无菌抗粘连阻隔材料,不论是否可吸收	A:1.品名;2.用途。B:3.包装。4.品牌;5.型号
3006.2000	-血型试剂	A:1.品名;2.用途;3.成分。B:4.品牌;5.型号
3006.3000	-X光检验造影剂;用于病人的诊断试剂	A:1.品名;2.用途;3.成分。B:4.品牌;5.型号
3006.4000	-牙科粘固剂及其他牙科填料;骨骼粘固剂	A:1.品名;2.用途;3.成分。B:4.品牌;5.型号
3006.5000	-急救药箱、药包	A:1.品名;2.组成(指箱或包中的药品、器具等)。B:3.品牌;4.型号。例:不包括医生用较复杂的医药包。例:急救药箱(组成:双氧水、碘酊、红汞、山金车花酊剂、少量敷料、药膏、剪刀、镊子)
	-以激素、税目29.37其他产品或杀精子剂为基本成分的化学避孕药物:	A:1.品名;2.用途;3.成分。B:4.品牌;5.型号
3006.7000	-专用于人类或兽药的凝胶制品,作为外科手术或体检时躯体部位的润滑剂,或者作为躯体和医疗器械之间的耦合剂	A:1.品名;2.用途;3.成分。B:4.品牌;5.型号
3006.9100	--可确定用于造口术的用具	A:1.品名;2.用途。B:3.品牌;4.型号
3006.9200	--废药物	A:1.品名

第三十一章　肥料

[注解]

1.“加工方法”指改变原材料、毛坯或半成品的形状、尺寸、性质或表面状态，使之达到规定要求的各种形状的方法。

2. 本章“成分含量”是指:“成分”指商品所构成的部分或要素，一般指所含物质的种类;“含量”一般指所含物质的数量。

3. 对于本章“成分含量”在有些情况下，部分商品的成分、含量只要能满足海关管理即可。

税则号列	商品名称	申报要素(A:归类要素 B:价格要素 C:审单及其他要素)及说明举例
31.01	动物或植物肥料,不论是否相互混合或经化学处理;动植物产品经混合或化学处理制成的肥料:	A:1.品名;2.用途;3.加工工艺;4.外观;5.包装件重;6.是否经过化学处理或与化学肥料混合。B:7.品牌;8.型号。例:不包括天然与化学肥料的混合物(税目31.05)
31.02	矿物氮肥及化学氮肥:	A:1.品名;2.每包重量。B:3.总氮含量;4.品牌;5.型号;6.成分含量
31.03	矿物磷肥及化学磷肥:	A:1.品名;2.每包重量。B:3.总磷含量;4.品牌;5.型号
31.04	矿物钾肥及化学钾肥:	A:1.品名;2.每包重量。B:3.总钾含量(以氧化物计);4.品牌;5.型号
31.05	含氮、磷、钾中两种或三种肥效元素的矿物肥料或化学肥料;其他肥料;制成片及类似形状或每包毛重不超过10千克的本章各项货品:	A:1.品名;2.成分含量;3.包装件重。B:4.总氮含量、总磷含量、总钾(以氧化物计)含量;5.品牌;6.型号

第三十二章　鞣料浸膏及染料浸膏;鞣酸及其衍生物;染料、颜料及其他着色料;油漆及清漆;油灰及其他类似胶粘剂;墨水、油墨

[注解]

1. 本章“成分含量”是指:“成分”指商品所构成的部分或要素，一般指所含物质的种类;“含量”一般指所含物质的数量。

2. 所注明的“包装”内容要足以判断是否为零售包装。

3，对于本章“成分含量”在有些情况下，部分商品的成分、含量只要能满足海关管理即可。

税则号列	商品名称	申报要素(A:归类要素 B:价格要素 C:审单及其他要素)及说明举例
32.01	植物鞣料浸膏;鞣酸及其盐、醚、酯和其他衍生物:	A:1.品名;2.用途;3.加工工艺。B:4.品牌;5.型号
32.02	有机合成鞣料;无机鞣料;鞣料制剂,不论是否含有天然鞣料;预鞣用酶制剂:	A:1.品名;2.成分含量;3.规格型号。B:4.品牌;5.包装规格
32.03	动植物质着色料(包括染料浸膏,但动物炭黑除外),不论是否已有化学定义;	A:1.品名;2.用途;3.加工工艺。B:4.包装;5.品牌;6.型号;7.成分含量

税则号列	商品名称	申报要素(A:归类要素 B:价格要素 C:审单及其他要素)及说明举例
	本章注释三所述的以动植物质着色料为基本成分的制品:	
32.04	有机合成着色料,不论是否已有化学定义;本章注释三所述的以有机合成着色料为基本成分的制品;用作荧光增白剂或发光体的有机合成产品,不论是否已有化学定义:	A:1.品名;2.成分含量;3.用途;4.染料须报明种类。B:5.包装; 6.品牌;7.型号
32.05	色淀;本章注释三所述的以色淀为基本成分的制品:	A:1.品名;2.成分。B:3.包装;4.品牌;5.型号
3206.1110	---钛白粉	A:1.品名;2.成分含量;3.用途。 B:4.包装;5.型号;6.品牌;7.如果加入放射性盐，请注明放射性比度; 8.级别; 9.签约日期
3206.1190	---其他	A:1.品名;2.成分含量;3.用途。 B:4.包装;5.规格型号;6.品牌;7.如果加入放射性盐，请注明放射性比度
3206.1900	--其他	A:1.品名;2.成分含量;3.用途。 B:4.包装;5.规格型号;6.品牌;7.如果加入放射性盐，请注明放射性比度
3206.2000	-以铬化合物为基本成分的颜料及制品	A:1.品名;2.成分含量;3.用途。 B:4.包装;5.规格型号;6.品牌;7.如果加入放射性盐，请注明放射性比度
	-其他着色料及其他制品:	A:1.品名;2.成分含量;3.用途。 B:4.包装;5.规格型号;6.品牌;7.如果加入放射性盐，请注明放射性比度
3206.5000	-用作发光体的无机产品	A:1.品名;2.成分含量;3.用途。 B:4.包装;5.规格型号;6.品牌;7.如果加入放射性盐，请注明放射性比度。C:8.稀土元素的重量百分比，以[A]表示
32.07	陶瓷、搪瓷及玻璃工业用的调制颜料、遮光剂、着色剂、珐琅和釉料、釉底料(泥釉)、光瓷釉以及类似产品;搪瓷玻璃料及其他玻璃,呈粉、粒或粉片状的:	A:1.品名;2.用途;3.外观;4.成分含量。B:5.包装;6.品牌;7.型号
32.08	以合成聚合物或化学改性天然聚合物为基本成分的油漆及清漆(包括瓷漆及大漆),分散于或溶于非水介质的;本章注释四所述的溶液:	A:1.品名;2.成分含量;3.用途;4.是否分散于或溶于非水介质。B:5.包装;6.品牌;7.型号
32.09	以合成聚合物或化学改性天然聚合物为基本成分的油漆及清漆(包括瓷漆及大漆), 分散于或溶于水介质的:	A:1.品名;2.成分含量;3.用途。B:4.包装;5.品牌;6.型号
32.10	其他油漆及清漆(包括瓷漆、大漆及水浆涂料);加工皮革用的水性颜料:	A:1.品名;2.成分含量;3.用途。B:4.包装;5.品牌;6.型号
32.11	配制的催干剂:	A:1.品名;2.成分含量;3.用途。B:4.包装;5.品牌;6.型号
3212.1000	-压印箔	A:1.品名;2.成分含量;3.用途。B:4.包装;5.外观;6.品牌;7.规格;8.加工工艺
3212.9000	-其他	A:1.品名;2.成分含量;3.用途。B:4.包装;5.外观;6.品牌
32.13	艺术家、学生和广告美工用的颜料、调色料、文娱颜料及类似品,片状、管装、罐装、瓶装、扁盒装以及类似形状或包装的:	A:1.品名;2.用途;3.包装。B:4.品牌;5.型号;6.是否成套
32.14	安装玻璃用油灰、接缝用油灰、树脂胶泥、嵌缝胶及其他类似胶粘剂;漆工用填料;非耐火涂面制剂,涂门面、内墙、地板、天花板等用:	A:1.品名;2.成分含量;3.用途;4.包装。B:5.品牌;6.型号
32.15	印刷油墨、书写或绘图墨水及其他墨料，不论是否固体或浓缩:	
	-印刷油墨:	A:1.品名;2.用途;3.包装;4.颜色;5.成分含量;6.是否具有曝光显影功能
	-其他:	A:1.品名;2.用途;3.包装;4.成分含量;5.颜色

第三十三章　精油及香膏；芳香料制品及化妆盥洗品

[注解]

1. 本章“成分含量”是指:“成分”指商品所构成的部分或要素，一般指所含物质的种类;“含量”一般指所含物质的数量。
2. 所注明的“包装”内容要足以判断是否为零售包装。
3. 对于本章“成分含量”在有些情况下，部分商品的成分、含量只要能满足海关管理即可。

税则号列	商品名称	申报要素(A:归类要素 B:价格要素 C:审单及其他要素)及说明举例
33.01	精油(无萜或含萜),包括浸膏及净油;香膏;提取的油树脂;用花香吸取法或浸渍法制成的含浓缩精油的脂肪、固定油、蜡及类似品;精油脱萜时所得的萜烯副产品;精油水馏液及水溶液:	A:1.品名;2.用途;3.加工工艺。B:4.包装;5.品牌;6.型号;7.成分含量

税则号列	商品名称	申报要素(A:归类要素 B:价格要素 C:审单及其他要素)及说明举例
33.02	工业原料用的芳香物质的混合物及以一种或多种芳香物质为基本成分的混合物(包括酒精溶液);生产饮料用的以芳香物质为基本成分的其他制品:	
	-食品或饮料工业用:	A:1.品名;2.成分;3.用途;4.酒精含量。B:5.品牌;6.型号
3302.9000	-其他	A:1.品名;2.成分;3.用途。B:4.品牌;5.型号
33.03	香水及花露水:	A:1.品名;2.包装。B:3.品牌
33.04	美容品或化妆品及护肤品(药品除外),包括防晒油或晒黑油;指(趾)甲化妆品:	A:1.品名;2.用途;3.包装。B:4.品牌;5.规格
33.05	护发品:	A:1.品名;2.用途;3.包装。B:4.品牌
33.06	口腔及牙齿清洁剂,包括假牙模膏及粉;清洁牙缝用的纱线(牙线),单独零售包装的:	A:1.品名;2.用途;3.包装。B:4.品牌
33.07	剃须用制剂、人体除臭剂、沐浴用制剂、脱毛剂和其他税目未列名的芳香料制品及化妆盥洗品;室内除臭剂,不论是否加香水或消毒剂:	A:1.品名;2.用途;3.包装。B:4.品牌

第三十四章 肥皂、有机表面活性剂、洗涤剂、润滑剂、人造蜡、调制蜡、光洁剂、蜡烛及类似品、塑型用膏、“牙科用蜡”及牙科用熟石膏制剂

[注解]

1. 本章“成分含量”是指:“成分”指商品所构成的部分或要素,一般指所含物质的种类;“含量”一般指所含物质的数量。
2. 所注明的“包装”内容要足以判断是否为零售包装。
3. 对于本章“成分含量”在有些情况下,部分商品的成分、含量只要能满足海关管理即可。

税则号列	商品名称	申报要素(A:归类要素 B:价格要素 C:审单及其他要素)及说明举例
3401.1100	--盥洗用(包括含有药物的产品)	A:1.品名;2.成分含量;3.外观;4.包装。B:5.品牌;6.型号
3401.1910	---洗衣皂	A:1.品名;2.成分含量;3.外观;4.包装。B:5.品牌;6.型号
3401.1990	---其他	A:1.品名;2.成分含量;3.外观;4.包装;5.浸渍物的成分。B:6.品牌;7.型号
3401.2000	-其他形状的肥皂	A:1.品名;2.成分含量;3.外观;4.包装。B:5.品牌;6.型号
3401.3000	-洁肤用的有机表面活性产品及制剂,液状或膏状并制成零售包装的,不论是否含有肥皂	A:1.品名;2.成分含量;3.外观;4.包装。5.品牌;6.型号
34.02	有机表面活性剂(肥皂除外);表面活性剂制品、洗涤剂(包括助洗剂)及清洁剂,不论是否含有肥皂,但税目34.01的产品除外:	
	-有机表面活性剂,不论是否零售包装:	A:1.品名;2.种类(阳离子、阴离子、非离子、两性等);3.成分。B:4.品牌;5.型号
	-零售包装的制品:	A:1.品名;2.用途;3.是否零售包装;4.成分。B:5.品牌;6.型号。例:洗衣粉(每袋450克,主要成分为烷基苯磺酸钠、非离子活性剂、硅酸钠、硅酸镁、过硼酸钠、增白剂等)
3402.9000	-其他	A:1.品名;2.用途;3.是否零售包装;4.成分。例:洗衣粉(每袋50千克,主要成分为烷基苯磺酸钠、非离子活性剂、硅酸钠、硅酸镁、过硼酸钠、增白剂等)
34.03	润滑剂(包括以润滑剂为基本成分的切削油制剂、螺栓或螺母松开剂、防锈或防腐蚀制剂及脱模剂)及用于纺织材料、皮革、毛皮或其他材料油脂处理的制剂,但不包括以石油或从沥青矿物提取的油类为基本成分(按重量计不低于70%)的制剂:	A:1.品名;2.用途;3.成分;4.矿物油含量;5.包装规格
34.04	人造蜡及调制蜡:	A:1.品名;2.用途;3.外观;4.成分。B:5.品牌;6.型号
34.05	鞋靴、家具、地板、车身、玻璃或金属用的光洁剂、擦洗膏、去污粉及类似制品(包括用这类制剂浸渍、涂面或包覆的纸、絮胎、毡呢、无纺织物、泡沫塑料或海绵橡胶),但不包括税目34.04的蜡:	A:1.品名;2.用途;3.成分。B:4.品牌;5.型号
34.06	各种蜡烛及类似品:	A:1.品名;2.成分。B:3.品牌;4.型号
34.07	塑型用膏,包括供儿童娱乐用的在内;通称为“牙科用蜡”或“牙科造形膏”的制品,成套、零售包装或制成片状、马蹄形、条状及类似形状的;以熟石膏(煅烧石膏或硫酸钙)为基本成分的牙科用其他制品:	A:1.品名;2.用途;3.外观;4.包装;5.成分含量。B:6.品牌;7.型号

第三十五章 蛋白类物质；改性淀粉；胶；酶

[注解]

1. 本章“成分含量”是指：“成分”指商品所构成的部分或要素，一般指所含物质的种类；“含量”一般指所含物质的数量。
2. 对于本章“成分含量”在有些情况下，部分商品的成分、含量只要能满足海关管理即可。

税则号列	商品名称	申报要素(A:归类要素 B:价格要素 C:审单及其他要素)及说明举例
35.01	酪蛋白、酪蛋白酸盐及其他酪蛋白衍生物；酪蛋白胶：	A: 1. 品名; 2. 包装。B: 3. 品牌; 4. 型号; 5. 用途
35.02	白蛋白(包括按重量计干质成分的乳清蛋白含量超过 80%的两种或两种以上的乳清蛋白浓缩物)、白蛋白盐及其他白蛋白衍生物：	A: 1. 品名; 2. 用途; 3. 外观; 4. 成分含量。 例: 白蛋白(用于制药，白色粉末，白蛋白含量 90%)
35.03	明胶(包括长方形、正方形明胶薄片，不论是否表面加工或着色)及其衍生物；鱼鳔胶；其他动物胶，但不包括税目 35.01 的酪蛋白胶：	A: 1. 品名; 2. 用途; 3. 外观; 4. 包装。例: 明胶(用于配制食品，透明薄片，每包 10 千克)
35.04	蛋白胨及其衍生物；其他税目未列名的蛋白质及其衍生物；皮粉，不论是否加入铬矾：	A: 1. 品名; 2. 用途; 3. 来源; 4. 包装; 5. 蛋白质含量
35.05	糊精及其他改性淀粉(例如，预凝化淀粉或酯化淀粉)；以淀粉、糊精或其他改性淀粉为基本成分的胶：	A: 1. 品名; 2. 用途; 3. 还原糖含量; 4. 包装。5. 品牌; 6. 型号
35.06	其他税目未列名的调制胶及其他调制黏合剂；适于作胶或黏合剂用的产品，零售包装每件净重不超过 1 千克：	A: 1. 品名; 2. 用途; 3. 包装; 4. 成分。B: 5. 品牌; 6. 型号
35.07	酶；其他税目未列名的酶制品：	A: 1. 品名; 2. 用途; 3. 种类

第三十六章 炸药；烟火制品；火柴；引火合金；易燃材料制品

[注解]

1. 本章“成分”指商品所构成的部分或要素，一般指所含物质的种类。
2. 对于本章“成分”在有些情况下，部分商品的成分只要能满足海关管理即可。

税则号列	商品名称	申报要素(A:归类要素 B:价格要素 C:审单及其他要素)及说明举例
36.01	发射药：	A: 1. 品名; 2. 成分。 例: 黑色火药(主要成分为硝酸钾、硫、木炭)
36.02	配制炸药，但发射药除外：	A: 1. 品名; 2. 成分。 例: 喷妥莱炸药(主要成分为三硝基甲苯、四硝基赤藓醇、蜡、聚合黏合剂等)
36.03	安全导火索；导爆索；火帽或雷管；引爆器；电雷管：	A: 1. 品名。 例: 雷管
36.04	烟花、爆竹、信号弹、降雨火箭、浓雾信号弹及其他烟火制品：	A: 1. 品名。 例: 烟花
36.05	火柴，但税目 36.04 的烟火制品除外：	A: 1. 品名。 例: 火柴
3606.1000	-直接灌注香烟打火机及类似打火器用的液体燃料或液化气体燃料，其包装容器的容积不超过 300 立方厘米	A: 1. 品名; 2. 用途; 3. 包装容器的容积
	---铈铁及其他引火合金：	A: 1. 品名; 2. 用途; 3. 外观。C: 4. 稀土元素的重量百分比，以[A]表示
3606.9090	---其他	A: 1. 品名; 2. 用途; 3. 外观

第三十七章 照相及电影用品

[注解]

1. 本章所称“规格尺寸”一般指长和宽。
2. 本章“成分含量”是指：“成分”指商品所构成的部分或要素，一般指所含物质的种类；“含量”一般指所含物质的数量。

税则号列	商品名称	申报要素(A:归类要素 B:价格要素 C:审单及其他要素)及说明举例
37.01	未曝光的摄影感光硬片及平面软片，用纸、纸板及纺织物以外任何材料制成；未曝光的一次成像感光平片，不论是否分装：	A: 1. 品名; 2. 用途; 3. 材质; 4. 是否成卷; 5. 是否一次成像; 6. 规格尺寸(白边+涂布面积)。B: 7. 品牌; 8. 型号

税则号列	商品名称	申报要素(A:归类要素 B:价格要素 C:审单及其他要素)及说明举例
37.02	成卷的未曝光摄影感光胶片,用纸、纸板及纺织物以外任何材料制成;未曝光的一次成像感光卷片:	A:1.品名;2.用途;3.材质;4.是否成卷;5.是否一次成像;6.规格尺寸(白边+涂布面积)。B:7.品牌;8.型号
37.03	未曝光的摄影感光纸、纸板及纺织物:	A:1.品名;2.用途;3.是否成卷;4.规格尺寸。B:5.品牌;6.型号
37.04	已曝光未冲洗的摄影硬片、软片、纸、纸板及纺织物:	A:1.品名;2.用途;3.规格尺寸。B:4.品牌
37.05	已曝光已冲洗的摄影硬片及软片,但电影胶片除外:	A:1.品名;2.用途;3.规格尺寸。B:4.品牌
37.06	已曝光已冲洗的电影胶片,不论是否配有声道或仅有声道:	A:1.品名;2.用途;3.规格尺寸。B:4.品牌
37.07	摄影用化学制剂(不包括上光漆、胶水、黏合剂及类似制剂);摄影用未混合产品,定量包装或零售包装可立即使用的:	A:1.品名;2.用途;3.包装;4.成分。B:5.品牌;6.型号

第三十八章　杂项化学产品

[注解]

1. 本章“成分含量”是指:“成分”指商品所构成的部分或要素,一般指所含物质的种类;“含量”一般指所含物质的数量。
2. 所注明的“包装”内容要足以判断是否为零售包装。
3. 对于本章“成分含量”在有些情况下,部分商品的成分、含量只要能满足海关管理即可。

税则号列	商品名称	申报要素(A:归类要素 B:价格要素 C:审单及其他要素)及说明举例
38.01	人造石墨;胶态或半胶态石墨;以石墨或其他碳为基本成分的糊状、块状、板状制品或半制品:	A:1.品名;2.用途;3.状态;4.加工工艺;5.成分含量。B:6.品牌;7.型号。C:8.规格
3802.1010	---木质的	A:1.品名;2.用途;3.来源;4.包装。B:5.干品填充密度
3802.1090	---其他	A:1.品名;2.用途;3.来源;4.包装
3802.9000	-其他	A:1.品名;2.用途;3.来源;4.包装
38.03	妥尔油,不论是否精炼:	A:1.品名;2.用途。 例:不包括皂化妥尔油;例:妥尔油(用于制路面乳胶)
38.04	木浆残余碱液,不论是否浓缩、脱糖或经化学处理,包括木素磺酸盐,但不包括税目38.03的妥尔油:	A:1.品名。 例:不包括妥尔油。例:木素磺酸盐
38.05	脂松节油、木松节油和硫酸盐松节油及其他萜烯油,用蒸馏或其他方法从针叶木制得;粗制二聚戊烯;亚硫酸盐松节油及其他粗制对异丙基苯甲烷;以α萜品醇为基本成分的松油:	A:1.品名;2.用途;3.成分;4.二聚戊烯、萜烯烃、萜品醇及水合萜品请注明含量。 例:不包括松节油(税目33.01)、松香油(税目38.06)。例:粗制二聚戊烯(用于溶剂,通过分馏木松节油制得)
38.06	松香和树脂酸及其衍生物;松香精及松香油;再熔胶:	A:1.品名;2.来源。 例:松香(蒸馏松树渗出物制得)
38.07	木焦油;精制木焦油;木杂酚油;粗木精;植物沥青;以松香、树脂酸或植物沥青为基本成分的啤酒桶沥青及类似制品:	A:1.品名;2.用途。 例:粗木精(用作乙醇变性剂)
38.08	杀虫剂、杀鼠剂、杀菌剂、除草剂、抗萌剂、植物生长调节剂、消毒剂及类似产品,零售形状、零售包装或制成制剂及成品(例如,经硫磺处理的带子、杀虫灯芯、蜡烛及捕蝇纸):	A:1.品名;2.用途;3.成分含量;4.包装。B:5.品牌;6.型号
38.09	纺织、造纸、制革及类似工业用的其他税目未列名的整理剂、染料加速着色或固色助剂及其他产品和制剂(例如,修整剂及媒染剂):	A:1.品名;2.用途;3.成分。B:4.品牌;5.型号
38.10	金属表面酸洗剂;焊接用的焊剂及其他辅助剂;金属及其他材料制成的焊粉或焊膏;作焊条芯子或焊条涂料用的制品:	A:1.品名;2.用途;3.成分。B:4.品牌;5.型号
38.11	抗震剂、抗氧剂、防胶剂、黏度改良剂、防腐蚀制剂及其他配制添加剂,用于矿物油(包括汽油)或与矿物油同样用途的其他液体:	A:1.品名;2.包装;3.用途;4.成分。B:5.品牌;6.型号

税则号列	商品名称	申报要素(A:归类要素 B:价格要素 C:审单及其他要素)及说明举例
38.12	配制的橡胶促进剂;其他税目未列名的橡胶或塑料用复合增塑剂;橡胶或塑料用抗氧制剂及其他复合稳定剂:	A:1.品名;2.用途;3.成分。B:4.品牌;5.型号
38.13	灭火器的装配药;已装药的灭火弹:	A:1.品名;2.用途;3.成分。例:灭火器的调配药(主要成分为碳酸氢钙,含有少量甘草浸膏)
38.14	其他税目未列名的有机复合溶剂及稀释剂;除漆剂:	A:1.品名;2.用途;3.成分。B:4.品牌;5.型号
38.15	其他税目未列名的反应引发剂、反应促进剂、催化剂:	A:1.品名;2.用途(如促进某某聚合物的聚合等);3.成分含量
38.16	耐火的水泥、灰泥、混凝土及类似耐火混合制品,但税目38.01的产品除外:	A:1.品名;2.用途;3.成分
38.17	混合烷基苯及混合烷基萘,但税目27.07及29.02的货品除外:	A:1.品名;2.用途;3.成分
38.18	经掺杂用于电子工业的化学元素,已切成圆片、薄片或类似形状;经掺杂用于电子工业的化合物:	
	---直径在7.5厘米及以上的单晶硅切片:	A:1.品名;2.用途;3.外观;4.成分;5.单晶硅切片请注明直径;6.包装;7.加工程度
3818.0090	---其他	A:1.品名;2.用途;3.外观;4.成分;5.包装;6.加工程度
38.19	闸用液压油及其他液压传动用液体,不含石油或从沥青矿物提取的油类,或者按重量计石油或从沥青矿物提取的油类含量低于70%:	A:1.品名;2.用途;3.成分;4.矿物油含量。B:5.品牌;6.型号
38.20	防冻剂及解冻剂:	A:1.品名;2.用途;3.成分。B:4.品牌;5.型号
38.21	制成的供微生物(包括病毒及类似品)或植物细胞、人体细胞、动物细胞生长或维持用的培养基:	A:1.品名;2.用途;3.成分
38.22	附于衬背上的诊断或实验用试剂及不论是否附于衬背上的诊断或实验用配制试剂,但税目30.02及30.06的货品除外;检定参照物:	A:1.品名;2.用途;3.包装;4.成分(区分衬背和试剂来说明举例);5.是否血源筛查用诊断试剂
38.23	工业用单羧脂肪酸;精炼所得的酸性油;工业用脂肪醇:	A:1.品名;2.成分含量;3.来源(动植物油脂等);4.加工程度(是否经过皂化、水解)。B:5.品牌;6.型号
3824.1000	-铸模及铸芯用黏合剂	A:1.品名;2.用途;3.成分含量。B:4.品牌;5.型号。例:铸模及铸芯用黏合剂(用于铸模及铸芯的黏合,主要成分为松香、亚麻子油、植物粘质、糊精、糖蜜)
3824.3000	-自身混合或与金属黏合剂混合的未烧结金属碳化物	A:1.品名;2.用途;3.成分含量。B:4.品牌;5.型号。例:未烧结碳化钼(主要成分为碳化钼、金属黏合剂)
	-水泥、灰泥及混凝土用添加剂:	A:1.品名;2.用途;3.成分含量。B:4.品牌;5.型号。例:混凝土防水剂(主要成分为氯化铁、硅酸钠、粉煤灰、硅灰、硅藻土)
3824.5000	-非耐火的灰泥及混凝土	A:1.品名;2.用途;3.成分含量。B:4.品牌;5.型号。例:非耐火的混凝土(主要成分为CaO、SiO_2、Al_2O_3等)
3824.6000	-子目2905.44以外的山梨醇	A:1.品名;2.用途;3.外观;4.来源;5.成分含量。B:6.品牌;7.型号
	-含有甲烷、乙烷或丙烷的卤化衍生物的混合物:	A:1.品名;2.用途;3.成分含量。B:4.品牌;5.型号
	-含环氧乙烷(氧化乙烯)、多溴联苯(PBBs)、多氯联苯(PCBs)、多氯三联苯(PCTs)或三(2,3-二溴丙基)磷酸酯的混合物及制品:	A:1.品名;2.用途;3.成分含量。B:4.品牌;5.型号
3824.9010	---杂醇油	A:1.品名;2.用途;3.成分含量;4.包装。B:5.品牌;6.型号
3824.9020	---除墨剂、蜡纸改正液及类似品	A:1.品名;2.用途;3.成分含量;4.包装。B:5.品牌;6.型号
3824.9030	---增炭剂	A:1.品名;2.用途;3.成分含量;4.包装。B:5.品牌;6.型号
3824.9091	----按重量计含滑石50%以上的混合物	A:1.品名;2.用途;3.成分含量;4.包装。B:5.品牌;6.型号
3824.9092	----按重量计含氧化镁70%以上的混合物	A:1.品名;2.用途;3.成分含量;4.包装。B:5.品牌;6.型号
3824.9093	----表层包覆钴化合物的氢氧化镍(掺杂碳)	A:1.品名;2.用途;3.成分含量;4.包装。B:5.品牌;6.型号
3824.9099	----其他	A:1.品名;2.用途;3.成分含量;4.包装。B:5.品牌;6.型号。C:7.稀土元素的重量百分比,以[A]表示
38.25	其他税目未列名的化学工业及其相关工业的副产品;城市垃圾;下水道淤泥;本章注释六所规定的其他废物:	A:1.品名;2.用途;3.来源。例:城市垃圾(收集家庭废物而得,用于分拣回收)

税则号列	商品名称	申报要素(A:归类要素 B:价格要素 C:审单及其他要素)及说明举例
38.26	生物柴油及其混合物，不含或含有按重量计低于 70%的石油或从沥青矿物提取的油类:	A: 1. 品名; 2. 用途; 3. 成分含量; 4. 从石油或沥青提取矿物油类的百分比含量

第七类　塑料及其制品；橡胶及其制品

第三十九章　塑料及其制品

［注解］

1. 本章“成分含量”是指：“成分”指商品所构成的部分或要素，一般指所含物质的种类；“含量”一般指所含物质的数量。

2. 第三十九章的多数产品需要注明成分、含量、单体种类、单体比例，这是明确归类的需要。在实际申报中只要申报的内容能明确归类即可。如“聚乙烯”就可以不用申报单体含量，而“乙烯-丙烯聚合物”就必须申报乙烯单体和丙烯单体的含量。

3. 本章商品需要申报的品名包括标准命名法名称或工商业通用俗称

税则号列	商品名称	申报要素(A:归类要素 B:价格要素 C:审单及其他要素)及说明举例
3901.1000	-聚乙烯，比重<0.94	A: 1. 品名; 2. 外观; 3. 成分含量; 4. 单体单元的种类和比例; 5. 是否为线型; 6. 比重。B: 7. 级别; 8. 品牌; 9. 型号; 10. 签约日期; 11. 用途
3901.2000	-聚乙烯，比重≥0.94	A: 1. 品名; 2. 外观; 3. 成分含量; 4. 单体单元的种类和比例; 5. 比重。B: 6. 级别; 7. 品牌; 8. 型号; 9. 签约日期; 10. 用途
3901.3000	-乙烯-乙酸乙烯酯共聚物	A: 1. 品名; 2. 外观; 3. 成分含量; 4. 单体单元的种类和比例。B: 5. 级别; 6. 品牌; 7. 型号; 8. 签约日期; 9. 生产厂商; 10. 牌号; 11. 用途
	-其他:	A: 1. 品名; 2. 外观; 3. 成分含量; 4. 单体单元的种类和比例。B: 5. 级别; 6. 品牌; 7. 型号; 8. 签约日期; 9. 用途
39.02	初级形状的丙烯或其他烯烃聚合物:	A: 1. 品名; 2. 外观; 3. 成分含量; 4. 单体单元的种类和比例。B: 5. 级别; 6. 品牌; 7. 型号; 8. 签约日期; 9. 用途
39.03	初级形状的苯乙烯聚合物:	
	-聚苯乙烯:	A: 1. 品名; 2. 外观; 3. 聚苯乙烯请注明是否为可发性的; 4. 成分含量; 5. 单体单元的种类和比例。B: 6. 级别; 7. 品牌; 8. 型号; 9. 签约日期; 10. 用途
3903.2000	-苯乙烯-丙烯腈(SAN)共聚物	A: 1. 品名; 2. 外观; 3. 成分含量; 4. 单体单元的种类和比例。B: 5. 品牌; 6. 型号; 7. 签约日期; 8. 用途
	-丙烯腈-丁二烯-苯乙烯(ABS)共聚物:	A: 1. 品名; 2. 外观; 3. 成分含量; 4. 单体单元的种类和比例; 5. 是否改性。B: 6. 级别; 7. 品牌; 8. 型号; 9. 签约日期; 10. 用途
3903.9000	-其他	A: 1. 品名; 2. 外观; 3. 成分含量; 4. 单体单元的种类和比例。B: 5. 品牌; 6. 型号; 7. 签约日期; 8. 用途
39.04	初级形状的氯乙烯或其他卤化烯烃聚合物	
	-聚氯乙烯，未掺其他物质:	A: 1. 品名; 2. 外观; 3. 聚氯乙烯请注明是否已塑化; 4. 聚氯乙烯请注明是否掺有其他物质; 5. 成分含量; 6. 单体单元的种类和比例。B: 7. 品牌; 8. 型号; 9. 签约日期; 10. 用途
	-其他聚氯乙烯:	A: 1. 品名; 2. 外观; 3. 聚氯乙烯请注明是否已塑化; 4. 聚氯乙烯请注明是否掺有其他物质; 5. 成分含量; 6. 单体单元的种类和比例。B: 7. 品牌; 8. 型号; 9. 签约日期; 10. 用途
3904.3000	-氯乙烯-乙酸乙烯酯共聚物	A: 1. 品名; 2. 外观; 3. 成分含量; 4. 单体单元的种类和比例。B: 5. 品牌; 6. 型号; 7. 签约日期; 8. 用途
3904.4000	-其他氯乙烯共聚物	A: 1. 品名; 2. 外观; 3. 成分含量; 4. 单体单元的种类和比例。B: 5. 品牌; 6. 型号; 7. 签约日期; 8. 用途
3904.5000	-偏二氯乙烯聚合物	A: 1. 品名; 2. 外观; 3. 成分含量; 4. 单体单元的种类和比例。B: 5. 品牌; 6. 型号; 7. 签约日期; 8. 用途
	-氟聚合物:	A: 1. 品名; 2. 外观; 3. 成分含量; 4. 单体单元的种类和比例。B: 5. 品牌; 6. 型号; 7. 签约日期; 8. 用途
3904.9000	-其他	A: 1. 品名; 2. 外观; 3. 成分含量; 4. 单体单元的种类和比例。B: 5. 品牌; 6. 型号; 7. 签约日期; 8. 用途
39.05	初级形状的乙酸乙烯酯或其他乙烯酯聚合物；初级形状的其他乙烯基聚合物:	A: 1. 品名; 2. 外观; 3. 成分含量; 4. 单体单元的种类和比例。B: 5. 品牌; 6. 型号; 7. 签约日期; 8. 用途
39.06	初级形状的丙烯酸聚合物:	A: 1. 品名; 2. 外观; 3. 成分含量; 4. 单体单元的种类和比例。B: 5. 品牌; 6. 型号; 7. 签约日期; 8. 用途
39.07	初级形状的聚缩醛、其他聚醚及环氧树脂；初级形状的聚碳酸酯、醇酸树脂、聚烯丙基酯及其他聚酯:	
	-聚缩醛:	A: 1. 品名; 2. 外观; 3. 成分含量; 4. 单体单元的种类和比例。B: 5. 品牌; 6. 型号; 7. 签约日期; 8. 用途

税则号列	商品名称	申报要素(A:归类要素 B:价格要素 C:审单及其他要素)及说明举例
	-其他聚醚:	A: 1. 品名; 2. 外观; 3. 成分含量; 4. 单体单元的种类和比例。B: 5. 品牌; 6. 型号; 7. 签约日期
3907.3000	-环氧树脂	A: 1. 品名; 2. 外观; 3. 成分含量; 4. 单体单元的种类和比例。B: 5. 品牌; 6. 型号; 7. 签约日期
3907.4000	-聚碳酸酯	A: 1. 品名; 2. 外观; 3. 成分含量; 4. 单体单元的种类和比例。B: 5. 品牌; 6. 型号; 7. 签约日期
3907.5000	-醇酸树脂	A: 1. 品名; 2. 外观; 3. 成分含量; 4. 单体单元的种类和比例。B: 5. 品牌; 6. 型号; 7. 用途
	-聚对苯二甲酸乙二酯:	A: 1. 品名; 2. 外观; 3. 是否切片; 4. 成分含量; 5. 单体单元的种类和比例; 6. 黏度。B: 7. 级别; 8. 品牌; 9. 型号; 10. 签约日期
3907.7000	-聚乳酸	A: 1. 品名; 2. 外观; 3. 成分含量; 4. 单体单元的种类和比例。B: 5. 品牌; 6. 型号; 7. 签约日期; 8. 用途
	-其他聚酯:	A: 1. 品名; 2. 外观; 3. 是否饱和; 4. 成分含量; 5. 单体单元的种类和比例。B: 6. 品牌; 7. 型号; 8. 签约日期
39.08	初级形状的聚酰胺:	A: 1. 品名; 2. 外观; 3. 是否切片; 4. 成分含量; 5. 单体单元的种类和比例。B: 6. 级别; 7. 品牌; 8. 型号; 9. 签约日期; 10. 用途
39.09	初级形状的氨基树脂、酚醛树脂及聚亚氨酯类:	A: 1. 品名; 2. 外观; 3. 成分含量; 4. 单体单元的种类和比例。B: 5. 品牌; 6. 型号; 7. 签约日期; 8. 用途
39.10	初级形状的聚硅氧烷:	A: 1. 品名; 2. 用途; 3. 外观; 4. 是否溶于水; 5. 成分含量。B: 6. 品牌; 7. 型号; 8. 签约日期
3911.1000	-石油树脂、苯并呋喃树脂、茚树脂、苯并呋喃-茚树脂及多萜树脂	A: 1. 品名; 2. 外观; 3. 成分含量。B: 4. 品牌; 5. 型号; 6. 签约日期; 7. 用途
3911.9000	-其他	A: 1. 品名; 2. 外观; 3. 成分含量; 4. 单体单元的种类和比例。B: 5. 品牌; 6. 型号; 7. 签约日期; 8. 用途
39.12	初级形状的其他税目未列明的纤维素及其化学衍生物:	
	-乙酸纤维素:	A: 1. 品名; 2. 外观; 3. 是否塑化; 4. 成分含量。B: 5. 品牌; 6. 型号; 7. 签约日期; 8. 用途
3912.2000	-硝酸纤维素(包括胶棉)	A: 1. 品名; 2. 外观; 3. 成分含量。B: 4. 品牌; 5. 型号; 6. 签约日期; 7. 用途
	-纤维素醚:	A: 1. 品名; 2. 外观; 3. 成分含量。B: 4. 品牌; 5. 型号; 6. 签约日期; 7. 用途
3912.9000	-其他	A: 1. 品名; 2. 外观; 3. 成分含量。B: 4. 品牌; 5. 型号; 6. 签约日期; 7. 用途
39.13	初级形状的其他税目未列名的天然聚合物(例如,藻酸)及改性天然聚合物(例如,硬化蛋白、天然橡胶的化学衍生物):	A: 1. 品名; 2. 外观; 3. 来源; 4. 成分含量。B: 5. 品牌; 6. 型号; 7. 签约日期; 8. 用途
39.14	初级形状的离子交换剂,以税目 39.01 至 39.13 的聚合物为基本成分的:	A: 1. 品名; 2. 用途; 3. 外观; 4. 成分。B: 5. 品牌; 6. 型号; 7. 签约日期; 8. 级别; 9. 阴离子还是阳离子还是两性
39.15	塑料的废碎料及下脚料:	A: 1. 品名; 2. 外观(颜色、尺寸); 3. 来源; 4. 成分; 5. 是否已经破坏性处理。B: 6. 如为成卷,需注明是否带有轴心。例: 废聚乙烯膜,20~40 厘米成卷,带轴心白色薄膜,纵切破坏性处理
39.16	塑料制的单丝(截面直径超过 1 毫米)、条、杆、型材及异型材,不论是否经表面加工,但未经其他加工:	A: 1. 品名; 2. 外观; 3. 成分; 4. 单丝请注明截面直径。B: 5. 品牌; 6. 型号; 7. 生产厂商; 8. 用途
3917.1000	-硬化蛋白或纤维素材料制的人造肠衣(香肠用肠衣)	A: 1. 品名; 2. 成分; 3. 用途。B: 4. 品牌; 5. 型号; 6. 生产厂商
	-硬管:	A: 1. 品名; 2. 成分。B: 3. 品牌; 4. 型号; 5. 生产厂商; 6 用途
	-其他管:	A: 1. 品名; 2. 成分; 3. 是否装有附件; 4. 最小爆破压力。B: 5. 品牌; 6. 型号; 7. 生产厂商; 8. 用途
3917.4000	-管子附件	A: 1. 品名; 2. 材质 例: 硬聚氯乙烯变接头
39.18	块状或成卷的塑料铺地制品,不论是否胶粘; 本章注释九所规定的塑料糊墙品:	A: 1. 品名; 2. 成分。B: 3. 品牌; 4. 型号; 5. 用途
39.19	自粘的塑料板、片、膜、箔、带、扁条及其他扁平形状材料,不论是否成卷:	A: 1. 品名; 2. 用途; 3. 外观(板、片、膜、箔、带、扁条); 4. 是否成卷; 5. 是否自粘; 6. 成分含量; 7. 规格尺寸。B: 8. 品牌; 9. 型号
39.20	其他非塑料泡沫的板、片、膜、箔及扁条,未用其他材料强化、层压、支撑或用类似方法合制:	
	-乙烯聚合物制:	A: 1. 品名; 2. 用途; 3. 外观; 4. 是否与其他材料合制; 5. 成分; 6. 规格尺寸; 7. 是否非泡沫。B: 8. 品牌; 9. 型号
	-丙烯聚合物制:	A: 1. 品名; 2. 用途; 3. 外观; 4. 是否与其他材料合制; 5. 成分; 6. 规格尺寸; 7. 是否非泡沫。B: 8. 品牌; 9. 型号
3920.3000	-苯乙烯聚合物制	A: 1. 品名; 2. 用途; 3. 外观; 4. 是否与其他材料合制; 5. 成分; 6. 规格尺寸; 7. 是否非泡沫。B: 8. 品牌; 9. 型号

税则号列	商品名称	申报要素(A:归类要素 B:价格要素 C:审单及其他要素)及说明举例
	-氯乙烯聚合物制:	A: 1. 品名; 2. 用途; 3. 外观; 4. 是否与其他材料合制; 5. 成分; 6. 规格尺寸; 7. PVC 制品请注明增塑剂含量; 8. 是否非泡沫。B: 9. 品牌; 10. 型号
	-丙烯酸聚合物制:	A: 1. 品名; 2. 用途; 3. 外观; 4. 是否与其他材料合制; 5. 成分; 6. 规格尺寸; 7. 是否非泡沫。B: 8. 品牌; 9. 型号
	-聚碳酸酯、醇酸树脂、聚烯丙酯或其他聚酯制:	A: 1. 品名; 2. 用途; 3. 外观; 4. 是否与其他材料合制; 5. 成分; 6. 规格尺寸; 7. 是否非泡沫。B: 8. 品牌; 9. 型号
	-纤维素及其化学衍生物制:	A: 1. 品名; 2. 用途; 3. 外观; 4. 是否与其他材料合制; 5. 成分; 6. 规格尺寸; 7. 是否非泡沫。B: 8. 品牌; 9. 型号
	-其他塑料制:	A: 1. 品名; 2. 用途; 3. 外观; 4. 是否与其他材料合制; 5. 成分; 6. 规格尺寸; 7. 是否非泡沫。B: 8. 品牌; 9. 型号
39.21	其他塑料板、片、膜、箔、扁条:	A: 1. 品名; 2. 成分 3. 外观; 4. 是否与其他材料合制; 5. 泡沫塑料请注明; 6. 用途; 7. 规格尺寸。B: 8. 品牌; 9. 型号
39.22	塑料浴缸、淋浴盘、洗涤槽、盥洗盆、坐浴盆、便盆、马桶座圈及盖、抽水箱及类似卫生洁具:	A: 1. 品名; 2. 用途; 3. 材质。B: 4. 品牌; 5. 型号
39.23	供运输或包装货物用的塑料制品; 塑料制的塞子、盖子及类似品	A: 1. 品名; 2. 用途; 3. 材质。B: 4. 品牌; 5. 型号
39.24	塑料制的餐具、厨房用具、其他家庭用具及卫生或盥洗用具:	A: 1. 品名; 2. 用途; 3. 材质。B: 4. 品牌; 5. 型号
39.25	其他税目未列名的建筑用塑料制品:	A: 1. 品名; 2. 用途; 3. 塑料制囤、柜、罐、桶及类似容器请注明容积; 4. 材质。B: 5. 品牌
39.26	其他塑料制品及税目 39.01 至 39.14 所列其他材料的制品:	A: 1. 品名; 2. 用途; 3. 材质。B: 4. 品牌; 5. 型号

第四十章　橡胶及其制品

[注解]

1. 本章“成分含量”是指:“成分”指商品所构成的部分或要素，一般指所含物质的种类;“含量”一般指所含物质的数量。
2. 本章的一些产品需要注明成分、含量、单体种类、单体比例，这是明确归类的需要。在实际申报中只要申报的内容能明确归类即可。
3. 本章商品需要申报的品名包括标准命名法名称或工商业通用俗称。

税则号列	商品名称	申报要素(A:归类要素 B:价格要素 C:审单及其他要素)及说明举例
40.01	天然橡胶、巴拉塔胶、古塔波胶、银胶菊胶、糖胶树胶及类似的天然树胶，初级形状或板、片、带:	A: 1. 品名; 2. 外观; 3. 型号; 4. 包装。B: 5. 签约日期
40.02	合成橡胶及从油类提取的油膏，初级形状或板、片、带; 税目 40.01 所列产品与本税目所列产品的混合物，初级形成或板、片、带:	
	--胶乳:	A: 1. 品名; 2. 用途; 3. 外观; 4. 成分含量。B: 5. 签约日期; 6. 品牌; 7. 型号
	--其他:	A: 1. 品名; 2. 用途; 3. 外观; 4. 丁苯橡胶请注明是否充油、热塑; 5. 成分含量。B: 6. 签约日期; 7. 品牌; 8. 型号
	-丁二烯橡胶(BR):	A: 1. 品名; 2. 用途; 3. 外观; 4. 成分含量。B: 5. 签约日期; 6. 品牌; 7. 型号
	-异丁烯-异戊二烯(丁基)橡胶(IIR); 卤代丁基橡胶(CIIR 或 BIIR):	A: 1. 品名; 2. 用途; 3. 外观; 4. 成分含量。B: 5. 签约日期; 6. 品牌; 7. 型号
	-氯丁二烯(氯丁)橡胶(CR):	A: 1. 品名; 2. 用途; 3. 外观; 4. 成分含量。B: 5. 签约日期; 6. 品牌; 7. 型号
	-丁腈橡胶(NBR):	A: 1. 品名; 2. 用途; 3. 外观; 4. 成分含量。B: 5. 签约日期; 6. 品牌; 7. 型号
	-异戊二烯橡胶(IR)	A: 1. 品名; 2. 用途; 3. 外观; 4. 成分含量。B: 5. 签约日期; 6. 品牌; 7. 型号
	-乙丙非共轭二烯橡胶(EPDM):	A: 1. 品名; 2. 用途; 3. 外观; 4. 成分含量。B: 5. 签约日期; 6. 品牌; 7. 型号
4002.8000	-税目 40.01 所列产品与本税目所列产品的混合物	A: 1. 品名; 2. 用途; 3. 外观; 4. 成分含量。B: 5. 签约日期; 6. 品牌; 7. 型号
	-其他:	A: 1. 品名; 2. 用途; 3. 外观; 4. 成分含量。B: 5. 签约日期; 6. 品牌; 7. 型号
40.03	再生橡胶，初级形状或板、片、带:	A: 1. 品名; 2. 外观; 3. 来源
40.04	橡胶(硬质橡胶除外)的废碎料、下脚料及其粉、粒:	A: 1. 品名; 2. 外观; 3. 来源; 4. 水分; 5. 杂质。B: 6. 干胶含量
40.05	未硫化的复合橡胶，初级形状或板、片、带:	A: 1. 品名; 2. 外观; 3. 硫化的请注明; 4. 成分。B: 5. 签约日期; 6. 品牌; 7. 型号。 例: 未硫化复合橡胶(成分为丁苯橡胶、炭黑，黑色有弹性的片状固体)
40.06	其他形状(例如，杆、管或型材及异型材)的未硫化橡胶及未硫化橡胶制品(例如，盘、环):	A: 1. 品名; 2. 用途; 3. 外观。B: 4. 材质; 5. 品牌; 6. 型号。 例: 未硫化的丁腈橡胶密封圈(用于机械设备的密封，黑色有弹性的环)
40.07	硫化橡胶线及绳:	A: 1. 品名; 2. 外观; 3. 截面尺寸。B: 4. 材质; 5. 品牌; 6. 型号。 例: 硫化丁二

税则号列	商品名称	申报要素(A:归类要素 B:价格要素 C:审单及其他要素)及说明举例
		烯橡胶线(黑色有弹性单股线;截面尺寸 4.5 毫米)
40.08	硫化橡胶(硬质橡胶除外)制的板、片、带、杆或型材及异型材:	A: 1. 品名; 2. 外观; 3. 是否海绵橡胶; 4. 规格尺寸; 5. 是否硫化。B: 6. 材质; 7. 品牌; 8. 型号。 例: 软质硫化的橡胶片(海绵橡胶制, 红色多孔性高弹性片状固体, 厚度 2 毫米, 长度 1 米, 宽度 50 厘米)
40.09	硫化橡胶(硬质橡胶除外)制的管子,不论是否装有附件(例如, 接头、肘管、法兰):	A: 1. 品名; 2. 用途; 3. 外观; 4. 材质构成(是否加强或与其他材料合制); 5. 是否装有附件。B: 6. 品牌; 7. 型号。 例: 未装附件、未加强和未与其他材料合制的软质硫化的橡胶管
40.10	硫化橡胶制的传动带或输送带及带料:	
	-输送带及带料:	A: 1. 品名; 2. 用途; 3. 外观; 4. 材质结构(是否加强或与其他材料合制); 5. 加强材料要注明; 6. 规格尺寸。B: 7. 品牌; 8. 型号。
4010.3100	--梯形截面的环形传动带(三角带),V形肋状的,外周长超过 60 厘米,但不超过 180 厘米	A: 1. 品名; 2. 用途; 3. 外观; 4. 材质结构(是否加强或与其他材料合制); 5. 加强材料要注明; 6. 规格尺寸(外周长); 7. 截面形状。B: 8. 品牌
4010.3200	--梯形截面的环形传动带(三角带),外周长超过60厘米,但不超过180厘米,V形肋状的除外	A: 1. 品名; 2. 用途; 3. 外观; 4. 材质结构(是否加强或与其他材料合制); 5. 加强材料要注明; 6. 规格尺寸(外周长); 7. 截面形状。B: 8. 品牌
4010.3300	--梯形截面的环形传动带(三角带),V形肋状的,外周长超过 180 厘米,但不超过 240 厘米	A: 1. 品名; 2. 用途; 3. 外观; 4. 材质结构(是否加强或与其他材料合制); 5. 加强材料要注明; 6. 规格尺寸(外周长); 7. 截面形状。B: 8. 品牌
4010.3400	--梯形截面的环形传动带(三角带),外周长超过 180 厘米,但不超过 240 厘米,V 形肋状的除外	A: 1. 品名; 2. 用途; 3. 外观; 4. 材质结构(是否加强或与其他材料合制); 5. 加强材料要注明; 6. 规格尺寸(外周长); 7. 截面形状。B: 8. 品牌
4010.3500	--环形同步带,外周长超过 60 厘米,但不超过 150 厘米	A: 1. 品名; 2. 用途; 3. 外观; 4. 材质结构(是否加强或与其他材料合制); 5. 加强材料要注明; 6. 规格尺寸(外周长)。B: 7. 品牌
4010.3600	--环形同步带,外周长超过 150 厘米,但不超过 198 厘米	A: 1. 品名; 2. 用途; 3. 外观; 4. 材质结构(是否加强或与其他材料合制); 5. 加强材料要注明; 6. 规格尺寸(外周长)。B: 7. 品牌
4010.3900	--其他	A: 1. 品名; 2. 用途; 3. 外观; 4. 材质结构(是否加强或与其他材料合制); 5. 加强材料要注明; 6. 规格尺寸(外周长); 7. 截面形状。B: 8. 品牌
40.11	新的充气橡胶轮胎:	A: 1. 品名; 2. 用途; 3. 规格型号; 4. 辋圈尺寸; 5. 胎面花纹; 6. 断面宽度。B: 7. 品牌; 8. 速度等级
40.12	翻新的或旧的充气橡胶轮胎; 实心或半实心橡胶轮胎、橡胶胎面及橡胶轮胎衬带:	A: 1. 品名; 2. 用途; 3. 是否实心; 4. 充气轮胎请注明翻新或旧的。B: 5. 品牌; 6. 型号
40.13	橡胶内胎:	A: 1. 品名; 2. 用途。B: 3. 品牌
40.14	硫化橡胶(硬质橡胶除外)制的卫生及医疗用品(包括奶嘴),不论是否装有硬质橡胶制的附件:	A: 1. 品名; 2. 用途。B: 3. 品牌
40.15	硫化橡胶(硬质橡胶除外)制的衣着用品及附件(包括分指手套、连指手套及露指手套):	例: 不包括橡胶线与纺织材料合制的衣着用品及附件(第六十一或第六十二章)
4015.1100	--外科用	A: 1. 品名; 2. 用途。B: 3. 品牌
4015.1900	--其他	A: 1. 品名; 2. 用途。B: 3. 品牌; 4. 成分(含胶率); 5. 规格型号(S、M、XL 等)
	-其他:	A: 1. 品名; 2. 用途。B: 3. 品牌
40.16	硫化橡胶(硬质橡胶除外)的其他制品:	A: 1. 品名; 2. 用途(其中垫圈、垫片等类似品是否密封用); 3. 材质(海绵橡胶、硫化橡胶等)。B: 4. 品牌; 5. 型号
40.17	各种形状的硬质橡胶(例如, 纯硬质胶), 包括废碎料; 硬质橡胶制品:	A: 1. 品名; 2. 外观; 3. 成分

第八类　生皮、皮革、毛皮及其制品；鞍具及挽具；旅行用品、手提包及类似容器；动物肠线（蚕胶丝除外）制品

第四十一章　生皮(毛皮除外)及皮革

[注解]

油鞣皮革是通过用鱼油或动物油反复鞣制，然后加热烘干或晾干，用碱水洗去余油，最后清洁皮张的表面，并用浮石或其他磨料进行磨里加工制得。这样鞣制的皮革通常采用正面起绒除去粒层的绵羊或羔羊肉面剖层皮来做原料；漆皮，即涂有一层清漆或大漆，或在皮革表面覆盖一层塑料膜的皮革。这种皮革的表面光亮宛如镜面；层压漆皮，商业上称为特种漆革，这种皮革的表面覆盖了一层塑料片，其厚度超过 0.15 毫米，但不超过总厚度的一半，并且与漆皮一样有着镜面般的光洁表面；镀金属皮革，即表面涂有或覆盖金属(例如，银、金、青铜或铝)粉末或箔的皮革；本章所称“坯革”，包括在干燥前经复鞣、染色或加油(加脂)的皮；经鞣

制或鞣制后进一步加工的皮张在贸易上称为“皮革”。鞣制后经干燥的皮革称为“坯革”。

税则号列	商品名称	申报要素(A:归类要素 B:价格要素 C:审单及其他要素)及说明举例
41.01	生牛皮(包括水牛皮)、生马皮(鲜的、盐渍的、干的、石灰浸渍的、浸酸的或以其他方法保藏,但未鞣制、未经羊皮纸化处理或进一步加工的),不论是否去毛或剖层:	A:1.品名;2.制作或保存方法(鲜、干、盐渍、石灰浸渍、浸酸、未鞣制、退鞣处理);3.状态(整张/半张,是否去肉修边等);4.平均每张重量。B:5.种类(公牛、未育/已育母牛、奶牛、阉牛、小牛、死牛、马);6.产区(如澳大利亚维多利亚、新南威尔士等)。例:本税目仅指生皮。例:牛皮、盐干、整张臀部烙印、阉牛、厚度0.5~1毫米、平均每张64~66磅、一级
41.02	绵羊或羔羊生皮(鲜的、盐渍的、干的、石灰浸渍的、浸酸的或经其他方法保藏,但未鞣制、未经羊皮纸化处理或进一步加工的),不论是否带毛或剖层,但本章注释一(三)所述不包括的生皮除外:	A:1.品名;2.制作或保存方法(鲜、干、盐渍、石灰浸渍、浸酸、未鞣制、退鞣处理);3.种类(羔羊、绵羊);4.状态(带毛、不带毛)。B:5.规格(毛长);6.请注明平方英尺数/张;7.等级;8.用途(毛革一体、制革)。例:本税目仅指生皮
41.03	其他生皮(鲜的、盐渍的、干的、石灰浸渍的、浸酸的或以其他方法保藏,但未鞣制、未经羊皮纸化处理或进一步加工的),不论是否去毛或剖层,但本章注释一(二)或(三)所述不包括的生皮除外:	A:1.品名;2.制作或保存方法(鲜、干、盐渍、石灰浸渍、浸酸、未鞣制、退鞣处理);3.种类(山羊、猪、爬行动物等)。B:4.是否源于野生动物;5.规格(面积或重量)
41.04	经鞣制的不带毛牛皮(包括水牛皮)、马皮及其坯革,不论是否剖层,但未经进一步加工:	A:1.品名;2.制作或保存方法(干、鞣制无毛、表面是否涂覆、涂覆何种物质);3.状态(湿,如蓝湿,整张/半张/背皮/头颈等)。B:4.种类(公牛、母牛、奶牛、阉牛、马);5.是否源于野生动物;6.规格(厚度、平均尺寸及平均重量);7.品种(全粒面未剖层或粒面剖层);8.用途;9.级别(头层皮TR1/2/3,二层皮A/B/C/D级)
41.05	经鞣制的不带毛绵羊或羔羊皮革及其坯革,不论是否剖层,但未经进一步加工:	A:1.品名;2.制作或保存方法(干、鞣制无毛);3.种类(羔羊、绵羊);4.状态(湿,如蓝湿)。B:5.是否源于野生动物;6.规格(厚度、张幅)
41.06	经鞣制的其他不带毛动物皮及其坯革,不论是否剖层,但未经进一步加工:	A:1.品名;2.制作或保存方法(干、鞣制无毛);3.种类(如爬行动物、小山羊);4.状态(湿)。B:5.是否源于野生动物;6.规格(厚度、张幅)
41.07	经鞣制或半硝处理后进一步加工的牛皮革(包括水牛皮革)或马皮革,包括羊皮纸化处理的皮革,不论是否剖层,但税目41.14的皮革除外:	
	--全粒面未剖层革:	A:1.品名;2.制作或保存方法(表面是否涂覆、涂覆何种物质);3.种类(牛、马);4.状态(整张,无毛全粒面未剖层或无毛粒面剖层、二层牛皮)。B:5.规格(厚度、平均面积);6.颜色
	--粒面剖层革:	A:1.品名;2.制作或保存方法(表面是否涂覆、涂覆何种物质);3.种类(牛、马);4.状态(整张,无毛全粒面未剖层或无毛粒面剖层、二层牛皮)。B:5.规格(厚度、平均面积);6.颜色
4107.1910	---机器带用	A:1.品名;2.制作或保存方法(表面是否涂覆、涂覆何种物质);3.种类(牛、马);4.状态(整张,无毛全粒面未剖层或无毛粒面剖层、二层牛皮);5.用途(机器带用)。B:6.规格(厚度、平均面积);7.颜色
4107.1990	---其他	A:1.品名;2.制作或保存方法(表面是否涂覆、涂覆何种物质);3.种类(牛、马);4.状态(整张,无毛全粒面未剖层或无毛粒面剖层、二层牛皮)。B:5.规格(厚度、平均面积);6.颜色
4107.9100	--全粒面未剖层革	A:1.品名;2.制作或保存方法(表面是否涂覆、涂覆何种物质);3.种类(牛、马);4.状态(半张,无毛全粒面未剖层或无毛粒面剖层、二层牛皮)。B:5.规格(厚度、平均面积);6.颜色
4107.9200	--粒面剖层革	A:1.品名;2.制作或保存方法(表面是否涂覆、涂覆何种物质);3.种类(牛、马);4.状态(半张,无毛全粒面未剖层或无毛粒面剖层、二层牛皮);B:5.规格(厚度、平均面积);6.颜色
4107.9910	---机器带用	A:1.品名;2.制作或保存方法(表面是否涂覆、涂覆何种物质);3.种类(牛、马);4.状态(半张,无毛全粒面未剖层或无毛粒面剖层、二层牛皮)。5.用途(机器带用);B:6.规格(厚度、平均面积);7.颜色
4107.9990	---其他	A:1.品名;2.制作或保存方法(表面是否涂覆、涂覆何种物质);3.种类(牛、马);4.状态(半张,无毛全粒面未剖层或无毛粒面剖层、二层牛皮)。B:5.规格(厚度、平均面积);6.颜色
41.12	经鞣制或半硝处理后进一步加工的不带毛的绵羊或羔羊皮革,包括羊皮纸化处理的皮革,不论是否剖层,但税目41.14的皮革除外:	A:1.品名;2.种类;3.状态(无毛全粒面或无毛羊皮纸化等)。B:4.规格(厚度及面积);5.颜色
41.13	经鞣制或半硝处理后进一步加工的不带毛的其他动物皮革,包括羊皮纸化处理的皮革,不论是否剖层,但税目	A:1.品名;2.制作或保存方法;3.状态(无毛全粒面)。B:4.规格(厚度);5.请注明平方英尺数/张

税则号列	商品名称	申报要素(A:归类要素 B:价格要素 C:审单及其他要素)及说明举例
	41.14 的皮革除外:	
41.14	油鞣皮革(包括结合鞣制的油鞣皮革);漆皮及层压漆皮;镀金属皮革:	A:1.品名;2.制作或保存方法(漆皮、镀金属)。B:3.规格(厚度);4.请注明平方英尺数/张
4115.1000	-以皮革或皮革纤维为基本成分的再生皮革,成块、成张或成条的,不论是否成卷	A:1.品名;2.制作或保存方法(再生);3.状态(块、张、条、卷、边角料、粉末)。B:4.规格(厚度)
4115.2000	-皮革或再生皮革的边角废料,不适宜作皮革制品用;皮革粉末	A:1.品名;2.状态(块、张、条、卷、边角料、粉末);3.用途。B:4.规格(厚度、面积);5 是否经过筛选

第四十二章　皮革制品;鞍具及挽具;旅行用品、手提包及类似容器;动物肠线(蚕胶丝除外)制品

[注解]

本章所称“运动包”,包括高尔夫球袋、体操袋、网球拍提袋、滑雪袋和钓鱼袋。本章所称“首饰盒”,不仅包括为存放首饰而专门设计的盒子,也包括其形状和配件专门适于盛装一件或多件首饰的各种规格的类似有盖容器,不论是否装有铰链或扣件。它们一般用纺织材料衬里。这些容器盛装首饰后可一同展示及出售,适于长期使用。本章所称“食品或饮料保温包”,包括在运输或临时保存期间保持食物及饮料温度用的可重复使用的保温包。

税则号列	商品名称	申报要素(A:归类要素 B:价格要素 C:审单及其他要素)及说明举例
42.01	各种材料制成的鞍具及挽具(包括缰绳、挽绳、护膝垫、口套、鞍褥、马褡裢、狗外套及类似品),适合各种动物用:	A:1.品名;2.材质
4202.1110	---衣箱	A:1.品名;2.种类(衣箱、提箱、小手袋等);3.表面材质(塑料、纺织物等)。B:4.品牌及款号
4202.1190	---其他	A:1.品名;2.表面材质(塑料、纺织物等)。B:3.品牌及款号
	--以塑料或纺织材料作面:	A:1.品名;2.种类(衣箱、提箱、小手袋等);3.表面材质(塑料、纺织物等)。B:4.品牌及款号
4202.1900	--其他	A:1.品名;2.种类(衣箱、提箱、小手袋等);3.表面材质(塑料、纺织物等)。B:4.品牌及款号
	-手提包,不论是否有背带,包括无把手的:	A:1.品名;2.种类(衣箱、提箱、小手袋等);3.表面材质(塑料、纺织物等)。B:4.品牌及款号
	-通常置于口袋或手提包内的物品:	A:1.品名;2.种类(钱夹、钱包、手机套等适放在口袋、手提袋内);3.表面材质(塑料、纺织物等)。B:4.品牌及款号
	-其他	A:1.品名;2.种类(衣箱、提箱、小手袋等);3.表面材质(塑料、纺织物等)。B:4.品牌及款号
4203.1000	-衣服	A:1.品名;2.材质(皮革或再生皮革);3.衣服种类。B:4 是否源于野生动物;5.品牌及款号
	-手套,包括连指或露指的:	A:1.品名;2.用途(专供运动用、劳保用等);3.材质(皮革或再生皮革)
	-腰带及子弹带:	A:1.品名;2.材质(皮革或再生皮革)
4203.4000	-其他衣着附件	A:1.品名;2.材质(皮革或再生皮革)
4205.0010	---坐具套	A:1.品名;2.材质(皮革或再生皮革)
4205.0020	---机器、机械器具或其他专门技术用途的	A:1.品名;2.用途(机械、技术用等);3.材质(皮革或再生皮革)
4205.0090	---其他	A:1.品名;2.用途;3.材质(皮革或再生皮革)
42.06	肠线(蚕胶丝除外)、肠膜、膀胱或筋腱制品:	A:1.品名。例:蚕胶丝应归入税目 50.06;不包括税目 30.06 的货品

第四十三章　毛皮、人造毛皮及其制品

[注解]

本章所称“人造毛皮”,是指将毛、发或其他纤维(包括绳绒纱线的纤维)粘附或缝合于皮革、织物或其他材料上以仿充毛皮的材料,但不包括有时也被人称为“毛皮织物”的纺织或针织长毛绒织物(一般归入税目 58.01 或 60.01),也不包括“加毛”毛皮,即额外插毛的真毛皮。

税则号列	商品名称	申报要素(A:归类要素 B:价格要素 C:审单及其他要素)及说明举例
43.01	生毛皮(包括适合加工皮货用的头、尾、爪及其他块、片),但税目 41.01、41.02 或 41.03 的生皮除外:	例:明显不能做皮货用的毛皮的废料应归入税目 05.11;不包括税目 41.01、41.02、41.03 的生皮
4301.1000	-整张水貂皮,不论是否带头、尾或爪	A:1.品名;2.种类(中国羔羊、波斯羔羊、狐皮、兔皮等);3.状态(生毛皮);4.外观(整张、头、尾、爪等)。B:5.品种(深棕、黑十字等);6.性别(公、母);7.尺寸(50 号、40 号等);8.颜色;9.质量(皇冠、等外);10.是否来自拍卖会及拍卖会日期

税则号列	商品名称	申报要素(A:归类要素 B:价格要素 C:审单及其他要素)及说明举例
4301.3000	-下列羔羊的整张毛皮,不论是否带头、尾或爪:阿斯特拉罕、喀拉科尔、波斯羔羊及类似羔羊、印度、中国或蒙古羔羊	A:1.品名;2.种类(中国羔羊、波斯羔羊、狐皮、兔皮等);3.状态(生毛皮);4.外观(整张、头、尾、爪等)
4301.6000	-整张狐皮,不论是否带头、尾或爪	A:1.品名;2.种类(中国羔羊、波斯羔羊、狐皮、兔皮等);3.状态(生毛皮);4.外观(整张、头、尾、爪等)。B:5.品种(蓝狐、蓝霜狐皮等);6.尺寸(50号、40号等);7.颜色(深、浅);8.质量(世家皇冠、世家级);9.是否来自拍卖会及拍卖会日期
4301.8010	---兔皮	A:1.品名;2.种类(中国羔羊、波斯羔羊、狐皮、兔皮等);3.状态(生毛皮);4.外观(整张、头、尾、爪等)。B:5颜色(白色、黑色等)
4301.8090	---其他	A:1.品名;2.种类(中国羔羊、波斯羔羊、狐皮、兔皮等);3.状态(生毛皮);4.外观(整张、头、尾、爪等)
	-适合加工皮货用的头、尾、爪及其他块、片:	A:1.品名;2.种类(中国羔羊、波斯羔羊、狐皮、兔皮等);3.状态(生毛皮);4.外观(整张、头、尾、爪等)
4302.1100	--水貂皮	A:1.品名;2.种类(中国羔羊、波斯羔羊、狐皮、兔皮等);3.制作或保存方法(鞣制未缝制或已缝制毛皮);4.外观(整张、头、尾、爪等)。B:5.品种(深棕、黑十字等);6.性别(公、母);7.尺寸(50号、40号等);8.颜色;9.质量(皇冠、等外);10.是否来自拍卖会及拍卖会日期
4302.1910	---灰鼠皮、白鼬皮、其他貂皮、狐皮、水獭皮、旱獭皮及猞猁皮	A:1.品名;2.种类(中国羔羊、波斯羔羊、狐皮、兔皮等);3.制作或保存方法(鞣制未缝制或已缝制毛皮);4.外观(整张、头、尾、爪等)。B:5.品种(蓝狐、蓝霜狐皮等);6.尺寸(50号、40号等);7.颜色(深、浅);8.质量(世家皇冠、世家级);9.是否来自拍卖会及拍卖会日期
4302.1920	---兔皮	A:1.品名;2.种类(中国羔羊、波斯羔羊、狐皮、兔皮等);3.制作或保存方法(鞣制未缝制或已缝制毛皮);4.外观(整张、头、尾、爪等)。B:5.规格
4302.1930	---下列羔羊皮:阿斯特拉罕、喀拉科尔、波斯羔羊及类似羔羊,印度、中国或蒙古羔羊	A:1.品名;2.种类(中国羔羊、波斯羔羊、狐皮、兔皮等);3.制作或保存方法(鞣制未缝制或已缝制毛皮);4.外观(整张、头、尾、爪等)。B:5.规格
4302.1990	---其他	A:1.品名;2.种类(中国羔羊、波斯羔羊、狐皮、兔皮等);3.制作或保存方法(鞣制未缝制或已缝制毛皮);4.外观(整张、头、尾、爪等)。B:5.规格
4302.2000	-未缝制的头、尾、爪及其他块、片	A:1.品名;2.种类(中国羔羊、波斯羔羊、狐皮、兔皮等);3.制作或保存方法(鞣制未缝制或已缝制毛皮);4.外观(整张、头、尾、爪等)。B:5.规格
	-已缝制的整张毛皮及其块、片:	A:1.品名;2.种类(中国羔羊、波斯羔羊、狐皮、兔皮等);3.制作或保存方法(鞣制未缝制或已缝制毛皮);4.外观(整张、头、尾、爪等)。B:5.规格
43.03	毛皮制的衣服、衣着附件及其他物品:	A:1.品名;2.材质(里、外);3.衣服种类
43.04	人造毛皮及其制品:	A:1.品名;2.材质(人造毛皮)

第九类　木及木制品;木炭;软木及软木制品;稻草、秸秆、针茅或其他编结材料制品;篮筐及柳条编结品

第四十四章　木及木制品;木炭

[注解]

"品名"项应填报植物学名;本章所称"强化木",是指经过化学或物理方法处理(对于多层粘合木材,其处理应超出一般黏合需要),从而增加了密度或硬度并改善了机械强度、抗化学或抗电性能的木材;本章所称"木",也包括竹及其他木质材料。

税则号列	商品名称	申报要素(A:归类要素 B:价格要素 C:审单及其他要素)及说明举例
44.01	薪柴(圆木段、块、枝、成捆或类似形状);木片或木粒;锯末、木废料及碎片,不论是否粘结成圆木段、块、片或类似形状:	例:涂有树脂或以其他方法制成点火物的木及木废料归入税目36.06
4401.1000	-薪柴(圆木段、块、枝、成捆或类似形状)	A:1.品名;2.种类(中文及拉丁学名);3.外观(圆木段、块、枝、成捆或类似形状等)
	-木片或木粒:	A:1.品名;2.种类(中文及拉丁学名);3.外观(木片、粒等)
4401.3100	--木屑棒	A:1.品名;2.外观(棒);3.规格(直径×长度)
4401.3900	--其他	A:1.品名;2.外观(末、废料、碎片等)
44.02	木炭(包括果壳炭及果核炭),不论是否结块:	例:与香料混合后制成片状或其他形状的木炭归入税目33.07;活性碳归入税目38.02;绘图用木炭(炭笔)归入税目96.09
4402.1000	-竹的	A:1.品名;2.材质
4402.9000	-其他	A:1.品名;2.材质。B:3.碳含量;4.挥发份
4403.1000	-用油漆、着色剂、杂酚油或其他防腐剂处理	A:1.品名;2.种类(中文及拉丁学名);3.加工方法(用油漆、着色剂等防腐剂处理等)。B:4.直径;5.长度

税则号列	商品名称	申报要素(A:归类要素 B:价格要素 C:审单及其他要素)及说明举例
	-其他，针叶木的:	A: 1. 品名; 2. 种类（中文及拉丁学名）。B: 3. 直径; 4. 长度; 5. 级别（锯材级、切片级等）
	-其他，本章子目注释二所列的热带木的:	A: 1. 品名; 2. 种类（中文及拉丁学名）。B: 3. 直径; 4. 长度; 5. 级别（锯材级、切片级等）
	-其他:	A: 1. 品名; 2. 种类（中文及拉丁学名）。B: 3. 直径; 4. 长度; 5. 级别（锯材级、切片级等）
44.04	箍木; 木劈条; 已削尖但未经纵锯的木桩; 粗加修整但未经车圆、弯曲或其他方式加工的木棒，适合制手杖、伞柄、工具把柄及类似品; 木片条及类似品:	A: 1. 品名; 2. 种类（中文及拉丁学名）; 3. 外观(棒状、条状等)
44.05	木丝; 木粉:	A: 1. 品名; 2. 外观(丝及粉)
44.06	铁道及电车道枕木:	A: 1. 品名; 2. 加工方法(是否浸渍); 3. 规格(长×宽×高)
44.07	经纵锯、纵切、刨切或旋切的木材，不论是否刨平、砂光或端部接合，厚度超过6毫米:	
	-针叶木:	A: 1. 品名; 2. 种类（中文及拉丁学名）; 3. 加工方法(经纵锯、纵切、刨切或旋切加工、端部接合); 4. 规格(长×宽×高)。B: 5. 等级
	-本章子目注释二所列的热带木:	A: 1. 品名; 2. 种类（中文及拉丁学名）; 3. 加工方法(经纵锯、纵切、刨切或旋切加工、端部接合); 4. 规格(长×宽×高)。B: 5. 等级
4407.9100	--栎木(橡木)	A: 1. 品名; 2. 种类（中文及拉丁学名）; 3. 加工方法(经纵锯、纵切、刨切或旋切加工、端部接合); 4. 规格(长×宽×高)。B: 5. 等级
4407.9200	--山毛榉木	A: 1. 品名; 2. 种类（中文及拉丁学名）; 3. 加工方法(经纵锯、纵切、刨切或旋切加工、端部接合); 4. 规格(长×宽×高)。B: 5. 等级; 6. 毛边板或直边板请注明
4407.9300	--枫木	A: 1. 品名; 2. 种类（中文及拉丁学名）; 3. 加工方法(经纵锯、纵切、刨切或旋切加工、端部接合); 4. 规格(长×宽×高)。B: 5. 等级
4407.9400	--樱桃木	A: 1. 品名; 2. 种类（中文及拉丁学名）; 3. 加工方法(经纵锯、纵切、刨切或旋切加工、端部接合); 4. 规格(长×宽×高)。B: 5. 等级
4407.9500	--白蜡木	A: 1. 品名; 2. 种类（中文及拉丁学名）; 3. 加工方法(经纵锯、纵切、刨切或旋切加工、端部接合); 4. 规格(长×宽×高)。B: 5. 等级
	--其他	A: 1. 品名; 2. 种类（中文及拉丁学名）; 3. 加工方法(经纵锯、纵切、刨切或旋切加工、端部接合); 4. 规格(长×宽×高)。B: 5. 等级
44.08	饰面用单板(包括刨切积层木获得的单板)、制胶合板或类似多层板用单板以及其他经纵锯、刨切或旋切的木材，不论是否刨平、砂光、拼接或端部结合，厚度不超过6毫米:	A: 1. 品名; 2. 用途(饰面用等); 3. 种类(树种名称); 4. 外观(单板); 5. 规格(厚度×宽度×长度); 6. 加工工艺(纵锯、刨切、旋切等)。B: 7. 请注明立方米数或平方米数
44.09	任何一边、端或面制成连续形状(舌榫、槽榫、半槽榫、斜角、V形接头、珠榫、缘饰、刨圆及类似形状)的木材(包括未装拼的拼花地板用板条及缘板)，不论其任意一边或面是否刨平、砂光或端部接合:	A: 1. 品名; 2. 种类(中文及拉丁学名); 3. 外观(舌榫、槽榫、半槽榫等); 4. 规格(厚度×宽度×长度); 5. 加工工艺
44.10	碎料板、定向刨花板(OSB)及类似板(例如，华夫板)，木或其他木质材料制，不论是否用树脂或其他有机黏合剂黏合:	A: 1. 品名; 2. 材质(木质或类似木质材料)。B: 3. 请注明立方米数或平方米数 例: 用水泥、石膏或其他无机黏合物质粘聚而成的木质材料板归入税目68.08
44.11	木纤维板或者其他木质材料纤维板，不论是否用树脂或其他有机黏合剂黏合:	
	-中密度纤维板(MDF):	A: 1. 品名; 2. 加工方法(是否经机械加工或盖面、干法、湿法等); 3. 密度; 4. 厚度; 5. 请注明是否辐射松制。B: 6. 请注明立方米数或平方米数
	-其他:	A: 1. 品名; 2. 加工方法(是否经机械加工或盖面、干法、湿法等); 3. 密度; 4. 请注明是否辐射松制。B: 5. 请注明立方米数或平方米数
44.12	胶合板、单板饰面板及类似的多层板:	A: 1. 品名; 2. 每层材质及树种名称; 3. 单层厚度; 4. 规格(厚度×宽度×长度); 5. 加工工艺。B: 6. 请注明立方米数或平方米数;
44.13	强化木，成块、板、条或异型的:	A: 1. 品名; 2. 加工方法(压缩、浸渍等); 3. 外观(块、板、条、异型)
44.14	木制的画框、相框、镜框及类似品:	A: 1. 品名; 2. 材质(木制); 3. 种类（中文及拉丁学名）。例: 镶框玻璃镜归入税目70.09
44.15	包装木箱、木盒、板条箱、圆桶及类似的包装容器; 木制电缆卷筒; 木托板、箱形托盘及其他装载用木板; 木制的托盘护框:	A: 1. 品名; 2. 材质(木制); 3. 种类（中文及拉丁学名）。例: 经特殊设计，装备适于一种或多种运输方式的集装箱归入税目86.09
44.16	木制大桶、琵琶桶、盆和其他木制箍桶及其零件，包括桶板:	A: 1. 品名; 2. 材质(木制); 3. 种类（单一材质申报中文及拉丁学名）

税则号列	商品名称	申报要素(A:归类要素 B:价格要素 C:审单及其他要素)及说明举例
44.17	木制的工具、工具支架、工具柄、扫帚及刷子的身及柄;木制鞋靴楦及楦头:	A:1.品名;2.材质(木制);3.种类(单一材质申报中文及拉丁学名)
44.18	建筑用木工制品,包括蜂窝结构木镶板、已装拼的地板、木瓦及盖屋板:	
	-窗、法兰西式(落地)窗及其框架:	A:1.品名;2.用途(建筑用);3.材质(木制);4.种类(中文及拉丁学名)
4418.2000	-门及其框架和门槛	A:1.品名;2.用途(建筑用);3.材质(木制);4.种类(中文及拉丁学名);5.规格
4418.4000	-水泥构件的模板	A:1.品名;2.用途(建筑用);3.材质(木制);4.种类(中文及拉丁学名);5.规格
4418.5000	-木瓦及盖屋板	A:1.品名;2.用途(建筑用);3.材质(木制);4.种类(中文及拉丁学名);5.规格
4418.6000	-柱及梁	A:1.品名;2.材质(木制);3.种类(中文及拉丁学名、柱、梁);4.规格
	-已装拼的地板:	A:1.品名;2.加工方法(已装拼);3.材质(木制等);4.种类(中文及拉丁学名、马赛克地板、多层地板等);5.规格
	-其他:	A:1.品名;2.用途(建筑用);3.材质(木制等);4.种类(中文及拉丁学名)
4419.0031	----木制	A:1.品名;2.材质(木制);3.是否是一次性产品
4419.0032	----竹制	A:1.品名;2.材质(竹制);3.是否是一次性产品
	---其他:	A:1.品名;2.材质(木制);3.种类(中文及拉丁学名)
44.20	镶嵌木(包括细工镶嵌木);装珠宝或刀具用的木制盒子和小匣子及类似品;木制小雕像及其他装饰品;第九十四章以外的木制家具:	A:1.品名;2.材质(木制);3.种类(单一材质申报中文及拉丁学名)。例:盛装乐器或枪支的木制箱、盒及包有皮革或再生皮革、纸或纸板、钢纸、塑料片或纺织材料的护套、箱、盒及类似容器归入税目42.02
44.21	其他木制品:	例:枪托及其他武器零件归入税目93.05
4421.1000	-衣架	A:1.品名;2.材质(木制);3.种类(单一材质申报中文及拉丁学名)
4421.9010	---卷轴、纡子、筒管、缝纫用线轴及类似品	A:1.品名;2.材质(木制);3.种类(单一材质申报中文及拉丁学名)
4421.9021	----木制	A:1.品名;2.材质(木制);3.种类(单一材质申报中文及拉丁学名、圆签、圆棒、冰果棒、压舌片等);4.是否是一次性产品;5.尺寸(长、宽、厚、直径等)
4421.9022	----竹制	A:1.品名;2.材质(竹制);3.种类(单一材质申报中文及拉丁学名、圆签、圆棒、冰果棒、压舌片等);4.是否是一次性产品
4421.9090	---其他	A:1.品名;2.材质(木制);3.种类(单一材质申报中文及拉丁学名)

第四十五章　软木及软木制品

税则号列	商品名称	申报要素(A:归类要素 B:价格要素 C:审单及其他要素)及说明举例
4501.1000	-未加工或简单加工的天然软木	A:1.品名;2.材质(天然软木);3.加工程度(未加工、简单加工等)
	-其他:	A:1.品名;2.状态(碎的、粒状的或粉状的);3.是否是废料
45.02	天然软木,除去表皮或粗切成方形,或成长方块、正方块、板、片或条状(包括做塞子用的方块坯料):	A:1.品名;2.材质(天然软木);3.加工方法(经除去表皮或粗切成方形等加工);4.外观(块、板、片或条状等)
45.03	天然软木制品:	A:1.品名;2.材质(天然软木);3.规格。B:4.等级
45.04	压制软木(不论是否使用黏合剂压成)及其制品:	A:1.品名;2.材质(压制软木);3.外观(块、板、片等形状)

第四十六章　稻草、秸秆、针茅或其他编结材料制品;篮筐及柳条编结品

[注解]

本章所称“编结材料”,是指其状态或形状适于编结、交织或类似加工的材料,包括稻草、秸秆、柳条、竹、灯芯草、芦苇、木片条、其他植物材料扁条(例如,树皮条、狭叶、酒椰叶纤维或其他从阔叶获取的条)、未纺的天然纺织纤维、塑料单丝及扁条、纸带,但不包括皮革、再生皮革、毡呢或无纺织物的扁条、人发、马毛、纺织粗纱或纱线以及第五十四章的单丝和扁条。

税则号列	商品名称	申报要素(A:归类要素 B:价格要素 C:审单及其他要素)及说明举例
46.01	用编结材料编成的缏条及类似产品,不论是否缝合成宽条;平行连结或编织的成片编结材料、缏条或类似的编结材料产品,不论是否制成品(例如,席子、席料、帘子):	A:1.品名;2.材质(竹、藤、稻草等)

税则号列	商品名称	申报要素(A:归类要素 B:价格要素 C:审单及其他要素)及说明举例
46.02	用编结材料直接编成或用税目 46.01 所列货品制成的篮筐、柳条编结品及其他制品；丝瓜络制品：	A: 1. 品名；2. 材质（竹、藤、草、玉米皮、柳条等）

第十类　木浆及其他纤维状纤维素浆；回收（废碎）纸或纸板；纸、纸板及其制品

第四十七章　木浆及其他纤维状纤维素浆；回收（废碎）纸或纸板

[注解]

本章所称“化学木浆，溶解级”，是指温度在20℃时浸入含18%氢氧化钠的苛性碱溶液内，1小时后，按重量计含有92%及以上的不溶级分的碱木浆或硫酸盐木浆，或者含有 88%及以上的不溶级分的亚硫酸盐木浆。对于亚硫酸盐木浆，按重量计灰分含量不得超过0.15%。

税则号列	商品名称	申报要素(A:归类要素 B:价格要素 C:审单及其他要素)及说明举例
47.01	机械木浆：	A: 1. 品名（机械木浆）。B: 2. 品牌；3. 签约日期
47.02	化学木浆，溶解级：	A: 1. 品名（溶解级化学木浆）。B: 2. 品牌；3. 签约日期
47.03	碱木浆或硫酸盐木浆，但溶解级的除外：	A: 1. 品名；2. 材质（针叶木、非针叶木）；3. 加工方法（漂白、未漂白、半漂白）。B: 4. 水分含量；5. 品牌；6. 签约日期
47.04	亚硫酸盐木浆，但溶解级的除外：	A: 1. 品名；2. 材质（针叶木、非针叶木）；3. 加工方法（漂白、未漂白、半漂白）。B: 4. 水分含量；5. 品牌
47.05	用机械和化学联合制浆法制得的木浆：	A: 1. 品名；2. 加工方法（用机械和化学联合制浆法）。B: 3. 水分含量；4. 品牌
4706.1000	-棉短绒纸浆	A: 1. 品名；2. 种类（棉短绒）
4706.2000	-从回收（废碎）纸或纸板提取的纤维浆	A: 1. 品名；2. 来源（从回收纸或纸板提取的）
4706.3000	-其他，竹浆	A: 1. 品名；2. 来源（从回收纸或纸板提取的）
	-其他：	A: 1. 品名；2. 材质（草浆等）；3. 加工方法（机械、化学、半化学）
4707.1000	-未漂白的牛皮纸或纸板及瓦楞纸或纸板的	A: 1. 品名；2. 种类（未漂白废牛皮纸、废瓦楞纸）；3. 状态（废碎）。B: 4. 产地标准及标号（美废、欧废、港废等）；5. 签约日期。例：以未漂白的牛皮纸及瓦楞纸或纸板为主。例：美废 5、11、12、13、15、16、19、20、21 号；欧废 A4、A5、A6
4707.2000	-主要由漂白化学木浆制成未经本体染色的其他纸和纸板的	A: 1. 品名；2. 种类（未漂白废牛皮纸、废报纸等）；3. 状态（废碎）。B: 4. 产地标准及标号（美废、欧废、港废等）；5. 签约日期。例：以漂白化学木浆的纸及纸板为主。例：废无尘纸、废卫生纸、废滤纸、废标签纸；美废 30、37、40、42 号
4707.3000	-主要由机械浆制成的纸或纸板（例如，报纸、杂志及类似印刷品）的	A: 1. 品名；2. 种类（未漂白废牛皮纸、废报纸等）；3. 状态（废碎）。B: 4. 产地标准及标号（美废、欧废、港废等）；5. 签约日期。例：以机械浆制的纸及纸板（如：报纸、杂志等）为主。例：美废 2、6、7、8、9、10、23 号；欧废 A7、A8、A9、A10 号
4707.9000	-其他，包括未分选的废碎品	A: 1. 品名；2. 种类（未漂白废牛皮纸、废报纸等）。B: 3. 产地标准及标号（美废、欧废、港废等）；4. 签约日期。例：美废 3；欧废 A2；废纸尿裤

第四十八章　纸及纸板；纸浆、纸或纸板制品

税则号列	商品名称	申报要素(A:归类要素 B:价格要素 C:审单及其他要素)及说明举例
48.01	成卷或成张的新闻纸：	A: 1. 品名；2. 规格（成条、成卷的宽度或成张的边长、每平方米克重）。B: 3. 机械或化学—机械法制得的纤维含量；4. 粗糙度；5. 签约日期
48.02	书写、印刷或类似用途的未经涂布的纸及纸板、未打孔的穿孔卡片及穿孔纸带纸，成卷或成张矩形（包括正方形），任何尺寸，但税目 48.01 或 48.03 的纸除外；手工制纸及纸板：	
	-手工制纸及纸板：	A: 1. 品名；2. 用途；3. 种类；4. 加工程度（未涂布、未染面等）；5. 规格（成条、成卷的宽度或成张的边长、每平方米克重）。B: 6. 签约日期
	-光敏、热敏、电敏纸及纸板的原纸和原纸板：	A: 1. 品名；2. 用途；3. 种类；4. 加工程度（未涂布、未染面等）；5. 规格（成条、成卷的宽度或成张的边长、每平方米克重）。B: 6. 签约日期
4802.4000	-壁纸原纸	A: 1. 品名；2. 用途；3. 种类；4. 加工程度（未涂布、未染面等）；5. 规格（成条、成卷的宽度或成张的边长、每平方米克重）。B: 6. 签约日期
	-其他纸及纸板，不含用机械或化学-机械方法制得的纤维或所含前述纤维不超过全部纤维重量的 10%：	A: 1. 品名；2. 用途（书写、印刷等用）；3. 种类；4. 加工程度（未涂布、未染面等）；5. 规格（成条、成卷的宽度或成张的边长、每平方米克重）；6. 纤维种类和含量。B: 7. 签约日期
	-其他纸及纸板，所含用机械或化学-机械方法制得的纤维超过全部纤维重量的 10%：	A: 1. 品名；2. 用途（书写、印刷等用）；3. 种类；4. 加工程度（未涂布、未染面等）；5. 规格（成条、成卷的宽度或成张的边长、每平方米克重）；6. 纤维种类和含量。B: 7. 签约日期

税则号列	商品名称	申报要素(A:归类要素 B:价格要素 C:审单及其他要素)及说明举例
48.03	卫生纸、面巾纸、餐巾纸以及家庭或卫生用的类似纸、纤维素絮纸和纤维素纤维网纸，不论是否起纹、压花、打孔、染面、饰面或印花，成卷或成张的:	A: 1. 品名; 2. 种类(卫生纸、面巾纸等类似纸); 3. 规格(成条、成卷的宽度或成张的边长) 。B: 4. 签约日期
48.04	成卷或成长的未经涂布的牛皮纸及纸板，但不包括税目 48.02 或 48.03 的货品:	
	-牛皮挂面纸:	A: 1. 品名; 2. 种类(牛皮挂面纸、袋用牛皮纸等); 3. 加工程度(未漂白、漂白、未涂布); 4. 规格(成条、成卷的宽度或成张的边长、每平方米克重); 5. 纤维种类和含量; 6. 请注明耐破度、紧度、横向环压指数、横向耐折度。B: 7. 品牌; 8. 签约日期
	-袋用牛皮纸:	A: 1. 品名; 2. 种类(牛皮挂面纸、袋用牛皮纸等); 3. 加工程度(未漂白、漂白、未涂布); 4. 规格(成条、成卷的宽度或成张的边长、每平方米克重); 5. 纤维种类和含量; 6. 请注明缪伦耐破度、横向伸长率、纵向伸长率。B: 7. 品牌; 8. 签约日期
4804.3100	--未漂白	A: 1. 品名; 2. 种类; 3. 加工程度(未漂白、漂白、未涂布); 4. 规格(成条、成卷的宽度或成张的边长、每平方米克重); 5. 纤维种类和含量; 6. 请注明耐破度、紧度、横向环压指数、横向耐折度。B: 7 品牌; 8. 签约日期
4804.3900	--其他	A: 1. 品名; 2. 种类(耐磨纸原纸); 3. 加工程度(未漂白、漂白、未涂布); 4. 规格(成条、成卷的宽度或成张的边长、每平方米克重); 5. 纤维种类和含量。B: 6. 品牌; 7. 签约日期
4804.4100	--未漂白	A: 1. 品名; 2. 种类; 3. 加工程度(未漂白、漂白、未涂布); 4. 规格(成条、成卷的宽度或成张的边长、每平方米克重); 5. 纤维种类和含量; 6. 请注明耐破度、紧度、横向环压指数、横向耐折度。B: 7. 品牌; 8. 签约日期
4804.4200	--本体均匀漂白,所含用化学方法制得的木纤维超过全部纤维重量的 95%	A: 1. 品名; 2. 种类; 3. 加工程度(未漂白、漂白、水体均匀漂白、未涂布); 4. 规格(成条、成卷的宽度或成张的边长、每平方米克重); 5. 纤维种类和含量; 6. 请注明耐破度、紧度、横向环压指数、横向耐折度。B: 7. 品牌; 8. 签约日期
4804.4900	--其他	A: 1. 品名; 2. 种类; 3. 加工程度(未漂白、漂白、未涂布); 4. 规格(成条、成卷的宽度或成张的边长、每平方米克重); 5. 纤维种类和含量; 6. 请注明耐破度、紧度、横向环压指数、横向耐折度。B: 7. 品牌; 8. 签约日期
4804.5100	--未漂白	A: 1. 品名; 2. 种类; 3. 加工程度(未漂白、漂白、未涂布); 4. 规格(成条、成卷的宽度或成张的边长、每平方米克重); 5. 纤维种类和含量; 6. 请注明耐破度、紧度、横向环压指数、横向耐折度。B: 7. 品牌; 8. 签约日期
4804.5200	--本体均匀漂白,所含用化学方法制得的木纤维超过全部纤维重量的 95%	A: 1. 品名; 2. 种类; 3. 加工程度(未漂白、漂白、水体均匀漂白、未涂布); 4. 规格(成条、成卷的宽度或成张的边长、每平方米克重); 5. 纤维种类和含量; 6. 请注明耐破度、紧度、横向环压指数、横向耐折度。B: 7. 品牌; 8. 签约日期
4804.5900	--其他	A: 1. 品名; 2. 种类; 3. 加工程度(未漂白、漂白、未涂布); 4. 规格(成条、成卷的宽度或成张的边长、每平方米克重); 5. 纤维种类和含量; 6. 请注明耐破度、紧度、横向环压指数、横向耐折度。B: 7. 品牌; 8. 签约日期
48.05	成卷或成张的其他未经涂布的纸及纸板，加工程度不超过本章注释三所列范围:	
	-瓦楞原纸:	A: 1. 品名; 2. 种类; 3. 加工程度(未涂布); 4. 规格(成条、成卷的宽度或成张的边长、每平方米克重); 5. 纤维种类和含量。B: 6. 签约日期
	-强韧箱纸板(再生挂面纸板):	A: 1. 品名; 2. 种类; 3. 加工程度(未涂布); 4. 规格(成条、成卷的宽度或成张的边长、每平方米克重)。B: 5. 签约日期
4805.3000	-亚硫酸盐包装纸	A: 1. 品名; 2. 种类; 3. 加工程度(未涂布); 4. 规格(成条、成卷的宽度或成张的边长、每平方米克重)。B: 5. 签约日期
4805.4000	-滤纸及纸板	A: 1. 品名; 2. 种类; 3. 加工程度(未涂布); 4. 规格(成条、成卷的宽度或成张的边长、每平方米克重)。B: 5. 签约日期
4805.5000	-毡纸及纸板	A: 1. 品名; 2. 种类; 3. 加工程度(未涂布); 4. 规格(成条、成卷的宽度或成张的边长、每平方米克重)。B: 5. 签约日期
	-其他:	A: 1. 品名; 2. 种类; 3. 加工程度(未涂布); 4. 规格(成条、成卷的宽度或成张的边长、每平方米克重)。B: 5. 签约日期
4806.1000	-植物羊皮纸	A: 1. 品名; 2. 种类; 3. 规格(成条、成卷的宽度或成张的边长)。B: 4. 签约日期
4806.2000	-防油纸	A: 1. 品名; 2. 种类; 3. 规格(成条、成卷的宽度或成张的边长)。B: 4. 签约日期
4806.3000	-描图纸	A: 1. 品名; 2. 种类; 3. 规格(成条、成卷的宽度或成张的边长)。B: 4. 签约日期
4806.4000	-高光泽透明或半透明纸	A: 1. 品名; 2. 种类; 3. 规格(成卷的宽度或成张的边长)。B: 4. 签约日期

税则号列	商品名称	申报要素(A:归类要素 B:价格要素 C:审单及其他要素)及说明举例
48.07	成卷或成张的复合纸及纸板(用黏合剂黏合各层纸或纸板制成),未经表面涂布或未浸渍,不论内层是否有加强材料:	A:1.品名;2.加工方法(黏合多层);3.加工程度(未经表面涂布或未浸渍);4.规格(成条、成卷的宽度或成张的边长)。B:5.签约日期
4808.1000	-瓦楞纸及纸板,不论是否穿孔	A:1.品名;2.种类(瓦楞纸、皱纹牛皮纸等);3.规格(成条、成卷的宽度或成张的边长)。B:4.签约日期
4808.4000	-皱纹牛皮纸,不论是否压花或穿孔	A:1.品名;2.用途;3.种类;4.规格(成条、成卷的宽度或成张的边长)。B:5.签约日期
4808.9000	-其他	A:1.品名;2.用途;3.种类;4.规格(成条、成卷的宽度或成张的边长)。B:5.签约日期
48.09	复写纸、自印复写纸及其他拷贝或转印纸(包括涂布或浸渍的油印蜡纸或胶印版纸),不论是否印制,成卷或成张的:	例:压印箔归入税目 32.12
4809.2000	-自印复写纸	A:1.品名;2.种类(自印复写纸);3.加工程度(涂布或浸渍);4.规格(成条、成卷的宽度或成张的边长)。B:5.签约日期
4809.9000	-其他	A:1.品名;2.种类(复写纸、拷贝纸等);3.加工程度(涂布或浸渍);4.规格(成条、成卷的宽度或成张的边长)。B:5.签约日期
48.10	成卷或成张矩形(包括正方形)的任何尺寸的单面或双面涂布高岭土或其他无机物质(不论是否加黏合剂)的纸及纸板,但未涂布其他涂料,不论是否染面、饰面或印花:	例:用诊断或实验室试剂浸渍的纸条归入税目 38.22;砂纸或纸板归入税目 68.05;用纸或纸板衬底的云母(云母粉除外)归入税目 68.14
	-书写、印刷或类似用途的纸及纸板,不含用机械或化学—机械方法制得的纤维或所含前述纤维不超过全部纤维重量的10%:	A:1.品名;2.用途(书写、印刷等);3.种类(牛皮纸、白板纸、双面、单面等);4.状态(成卷或张等);5.加工程度(单面或双面涂布无机物、漂白);6.规格(宽度或边长、每平方米克重);7.纤维种类和含量。B:8.签约日期
	-书写、印刷或类似用途的纸及纸板,所含用机械或化学—机械方法制得的纤维超过全部纤维重量的10%:	A:1.品名;2.用途(书写、印刷等);3.种类(牛皮纸、白板纸、双面、单面等);4.状态(成卷或张等);5.加工程度(单面或双面涂布无机物、漂白);6.规格(宽度或边长、每平方米克重);7.纤维种类和含量。B:8.签约日期
	-牛皮纸及纸板,但书写、印刷或类似用途的除外:	A:1.品名;2.用途(书写、印刷等);3.种类(牛皮纸、白板纸、双面、单面等);4.状态(成卷或张等);5.加工程度(单面或双面涂布无机物、漂白);6.规格(宽度或边长、每平方米克重);7.纤维种类和含量。B:8.签约日期
	-其他纸及纸板:	A:1.品名;2.用途(书写、印刷等);3.种类(牛皮纸、白板纸、双面、单面等);4.状态(成卷或张等);5.加工程度(单面或双面涂布无机物、漂白);6.规格(宽度或边长、每平方米克重、各纤维含量)。B:7.签约日期
48.11	成卷或成张矩形(包括正方形)的任何尺寸的经涂布、浸渍、覆面、染面、饰面或印花的纸、纸板、纤维素絮纸及纤维素纤维网纸,但税目 48.03、49.09或48.10的货品除外:	A:1.品名;2.种类;3.加工程度(涂布、浸渍、饰面、漂白等);4.规格(成条等、浸渍或涂布物、每平方米克重) 例:用肥皂或洗涤剂浸渍、覆盖或涂布的纸及纤维素絮纸归入税目 34.01;用光洁剂、擦光膏或类似制剂浸渍、覆盖或涂布的纸及纤维素絮纸归入税目 34.05;石蕊试纸、极谱纸及其他用诊断或实验室试剂浸渍的纸归入税目 38.22;用纸板做基并以柏油或类似材料完全包裹或双面覆盖的屋面归入税目 68.07
48.12	纸浆制的滤块、滤板及滤片:	A:1.品名;2.材质(纸浆制);3.外观(块、板、片) 例:仅压制成片或板状的棉短绒归入税目 14.04
4813.1000	-成小本或管状	A:1.品名;2.规格(如成小本或管状、宽度)
4813.2000	-宽度不超过5厘米成卷的	A:1.品名;2.规格(成卷、宽度)
4813.9000	-其他	A:1.品名;2.规格(宽度等)
48.14	壁纸及类似品;窗用透明纸:	例:外观近似窗用透明的转印纸(移画印花纸)归入税目 49.08;纸基纺织糊墙品归入税目 59.05;用纸衬背的铝箔糊墙品归入税目 76.07
4814.2000	-用塑料涂面或盖面的壁纸及类似品,起纹、压花、着色、印刷图案或经其他装饰	A:1.品名;2.加工程度(用木粒或草粒、塑料、编结材料等饰面、涂面)
4814.9000	-其他	A:1.品名;2.加工程度(用木粒或草粒、塑料、编结材料等饰面、涂面);3.是否为窗用透明纸
4816.2000	-自印复写纸	A:1.品名;2.种类(自印复写纸、热敏转印纸等);3.规格(成条、成卷的宽度或成张的边长)
4816.9010	---热敏转印纸	A:1.品名;2.种类(自印复写纸、热敏转印纸等);3.规格(成条、成卷的宽度或成张的边长)
4816.9090	---其他	A:1.品名;2.种类(复写纸、拷贝纸、转印纸、油印蜡纸、胶版纸等);3.规格(成条、成卷的宽度或成张的边长)
48.17	纸或纸板制的信封、封缄信片、素色明信片及通信卡片;纸或纸板制的盒子、袋子及夹子,内装各种纸制文具:	A:1.品名;2.材质(纸制) 例:税号 4817.3000 的产品必须内装各种纸制文具;印有或用其他方式赋予正在流通的邮票的信封、明信片及信卡等归入税目 49.07;供特殊用途的印刷信件及类似物品,例如,即期票据、搬迁通知、

税则号列	商品名称	申报要素(A:归类要素 B:价格要素 C:审单及其他要素)及说明举例
		广告信，包括需要手工填写的上述物品归入税目 49.11;印有图画的首日封及集邮大型张:未附邮票的归入税目 49.11;附有邮票的归入税目 97.04
48.18	卫生纸及类似纸、家庭或卫生用纤维素絮纸及纤维素纤维网纸,成卷宽度不超过 36 厘米或切成一定尺寸或形状的;纸浆、纸、纤维素絮纸或纤维素纤维网纸制的手帕、面巾、台布、餐巾、床单及类似的家庭、卫生或医院用品、衣服及衣着附件:	A: 1. 品名; 2. 用途（家庭、卫生、医院用等）; 3. 材质（纸制）; 4. 种类（卫生纸、纸台布等）; 5. 规格（成条、成卷的宽度或成张的边长）
4819.1000	-瓦楞纸或纸板制的箱、盒、匣	A: 1. 品名; 2. 材质; 3. 规格; 4. 是否瓦楞纸制
4819.2000	-非瓦楞纸或纸板制的可折叠箱、盒、匣	A: 1. 品名; 2. 材质; 3. 规格; 4. 是否可折叠
4819.3000	-底宽 40 厘米及以上的纸袋	A: 1. 品名; 2. 材质; 3. 规格
4819.4000	-其他纸袋,包括锥形袋	A: 1. 品名; 2. 材质; 3. 规格
4819.5000	-其他包装容器,包括唱片套	A: 1. 品名; 2. 材质; 3. 规格
4819.6000	-办公室、商店及类似场所使用的卷宗盒、信件盘、存储盒及类似品	A: 1. 品名; 2. 材质; 3. 规格
48.20	纸或纸板制的登记本、账本、笔记本、订货本、收据本、信笺本、记事本、日记本及类似品、练习本、吸墨纸本、活动封面(活页及非活页)、文件夹、卷宗皮、多联商业表格纸、页间夹有复写纸的本及其他文具用品;纸或纸板制的样品簿、粘贴簿及书籍封面:	A: 1. 品名; 2. 材质。例: 支票簿归入税目 49.07;空白的联券旅行票据归入税目 49.11
48.21	纸或纸板制的各种标签，不论是否印制:	A: 1. 品名; 2. 材质; 3. 加工程度(印制、非印制)。例: 捕蝇纸归入税目 38.08;纸制太阳伞归入税目 66.01;人造花、簇叶、果实及其部分品归入税目 67.02
4822.1000	-纺织纱线用	A: 1. 品名; 2. 用途(纺织纱线用等); 3. 材质(纸制)
4822.9000	-其他	A: 1. 品名; 2. 用途; 3. 材质(纸制)
4823.2000	-滤纸及纸板	A: 1. 品名; 2. 材质(纸制); 3. 规格(切成一定尺寸或形状、边长、宽度)
4823.4000	-已印制的自动记录器用打印纸卷、纸张及纸盘	A: 1. 品名; 2. 用途(已印制的自动记录器用等); 3. 材质(纸制); 4. 规格(切成一定尺寸或形状、边长、宽度)
4823.6100	--竹浆纸或纸板制的	A: 1. 品名; 2. 材质(竹浆纸制); 3. 种类(盘、碟、盆、杯等)。B: 4. 规格
	--其他	A: 1. 品名; 2. 材质; 3. 种类(盘、碟、盆、杯等)。B: 4. 规格
4823.7000	-压制或模制纸浆制品	A: 1. 品名; 2. 加工方法(压制、模制); 3. 材质(纸浆制); 4. 规格(切成一定尺寸或形状、边长、宽度)
4823.9010	---以纸或纸板为底制成的铺地制品	A: 1. 品名; 2. 用途; 3. 材质(以纸或纸板为底制成); 4. 规格
4823.9020	---神纸及类似用品	A: 1. 品名; 2. 材质(纸制); 3. 规格(切成一定尺寸或形状、边长、宽度)
4823.9030	---纸扇	A: 1. 品名; 2. 材质(纸制); 3. 规格(切成一定尺寸或形状、边长、宽度)
4823.9090	---其他	A: 1. 品名; 2. 材质(纸制); 3. 规格(切成一定尺寸或形状、边长、宽度)

第四十九章　书籍、报纸、印刷图画及其他印刷品；手稿、打字稿及设计图纸

税则号列	商品名称	申报要素(A:归类要素 B:价格要素 C:审单及其他要素)及说明举例
49.01	书籍、小册子、散页印刷品及类似印刷品，不论是否单张:	A: 1. 品名; 2. 种类(字典、百科全书等); 3. 状态(成册、单张)。例: 载有文字或图案以供复制并按序号装订的拷贝纸及转印纸归入税目 48.16
49.02	报纸、杂志及期刊，不论有无插图或广告材料:	A: 1. 品名; 2. 出版周期(日刊、周刊等)。例: 由旧报纸、旧杂志或旧期刊构成的废纸归入税目 47.07
49.03	儿童图画书、绘画或涂色书:	A: 1. 品名; 2. 用途(儿童用); 3. 种类(图画书、绘画或涂色书)
49.04	乐谱原稿或印本，不论是否装订或印有插图:	A: 1. 品名; 2. 种类(原稿或印本等)
4905.1000	-地球仪、天体仪	A: 1. 品名
	-其他:	A: 1. 品名; 2. 状态(成册、非成册)。例: 浮雕地图、详图及地球仪，不论是否印制，归入税目 90.23
49.06	手绘的建筑、工程、工业、商业、地形或类似用途的设计图纸原稿;手稿;用感光纸照相复印或用复写纸誊写的上述物品复制件:	A: 1. 品名; (设计图纸原稿或手稿及其复制件)
4907.0010	---邮票	A: 1. 品名; B: 2. 外观(新的); 3. 种类（小型张、四方联等）
4907.0020	---钞票	A: 1. 品名; B: 2. 外观(新的)
4907.0030	---证券凭证	A: 1. 品名; 2. 种类(证券、特许权等)
4907.0090	---其他	A: 1. 品名; 2. 种类(证券、特许权等)

税则号列	商品名称	申报要素(A:归类要素 B:价格要素 C:审单及其他要素)及说明举例
49.08	转印贴花纸(移画印花法用图案纸):	A:1.品名;2.加工方法(釉转印等)
49.09	印刷或有图画的明信片;印有个人问候、祝贺、通告的卡片,不论是否有图画、带信封或饰边:	A:1.品名;2.加工方法(印刷或有图画等)
49.10	印刷的各种日历,包括日历芯:	A:1.品名。例:包括日历芯;又有日历又可记日记的记事本(包括所谓约会日历本)归入税目48.20
49.11	其他印刷品,包括印刷的图片及照片:	例:照相软片或硬片的负片或正片归入税目 37.05;在一面印有图画、文字的装饰性玻璃镜,不论是否镶框归入税目70.09或70.13;带磁条的印刷卡归入税目85.23或85.24;带电子集成电路的印刷卡("智能"卡)归入税目85.42;印刷的邻近卡及牌归入税目85.43,不论这些产品是否带磁条
	-商业广告品、商品目录及类似印刷品:	A:1.品名;2.用途(有商业价值、无商业价值等)
4911.9100	--图片、设计图样及照片	A:1.品名;2.用途(有商业价值、无商业价值等)
	--其他	A:1.品名;2.材质;3.用途(有商业价值、无商业价值等)。B:4.印刷内容

第十一类 纺织原料及纺织制品

第五十章 蚕丝

[注解]

1. 加工方法:对纤维纱线产品仅指梳理工艺,即粗疏或精梳;对织物则指染整方法(漂白、练白) 以及织造方法(机织物)。
2. 用途:仅指丝线是否用于零售或蚕茧是否适于缫丝。
3. 规格型号:丝线列明细度支数;织物列明幅宽;混纺产品列明丝含量。
4. 纱线的表示:70s/2指由两支70英支的单纱捻制的股线。

税则号列	商品名称	申报要素(A:归类要素 B:价格要素 C:审单及其他要素)及说明举例
50.01	适于缫丝的蚕茧:	A:1.品名;2.用途(用于缫丝);3.种类
5002.0011	----厂丝	A:1.品名;2.种类(桑蚕厂丝);3.是否加捻
5002.0012	----土丝	A:1.品名;2.种类(桑蚕土丝);3.是否加捻
5002.0013	----双宫丝	A:1.品名;2.种类(桑蚕双宫丝);3.是否加捻
5002.0019	----其他	A:1.品名;2.种类;3.是否加捻
5002.0020	---柞蚕丝	A:1.品名;2.种类(柞蚕丝);3.是否加捻
5002.0090	---其他	A:1.品名;2.种类;3.是否加捻
50.03	废丝(包括不适于缫丝的蚕茧、废纱及回收纤维):	A:1.品名;2.是否梳理 例:本税目指不适于缫丝的废丝
50.04	丝纱线(绢纺纱线除外),非供零售用:	A:1.品名;2.是否供零售用 例:绢纺纱线除外(归入税目50.05),不包括税目56.04的丝质仿肠线
50.05	绢纺纱线,非供零售用:	A:1.品名;2.种类(绢纺纱线等);3.是否供零售用;4.成分含量 例:不包括税目56.04的丝质仿肠线
50.06	丝纱线及绢纺纱线,供零售用;蚕胶丝:	A:1.品名;2.种类(绢纺纱线、蚕胶丝、丝纱线、绸纱线);3.包装(供零售用);4.成分含量 例:不包括税目56.04的丝质仿肠线、税目30.06的消毒蚕胶丝
50.07	丝或绢丝机织物:	A:1.品名;2.种类(绸丝、桑蚕丝、绢丝、柞蚕丝等);3.织造方法(机织物);4.染整方法(漂白、未漂白、色织);5.成分含量;6.幅宽;7.每平方米克重

第五十一章 羊毛、动物细毛或粗毛;马毛纱线及其机织物

[注解]

1. 加工方法:对纤维原料指梳理工艺,即粗疏或精梳及脱脂、处理;对织物则指梳理工艺(粗疏或精梳) 以及织造方法(机织物)。
2. 用途:仅指纱线是否用于零售。
3. 品名:应具体列出产品行业名称、种类,如剪羊毛、碳化羊毛、脱脂羊毛、兔毛、动物细毛、粗毛马毛织物等。
4. 规格型号:丝线列明细度支数;织物列明幅宽;混纺产品列明成分含量,每平方米重量(克/平方米)。

税则号列	商品名称	申报要素(A:归类要素 B:价格要素 C:审单及其他要素)及说明举例
5101.1100	--剪羊毛	A:1.品名,2.加工程度(含脂、脱脂、碳化等)。B:3.剪羊毛请注明细度(微米数);4.剪羊毛请注明长度;5.剪羊毛请注明草杂含量。例:T107,7.7MIC,45英寸的灰褪毛,草杂含量2%
5101.1900	--其他	A 1.品名;2.加工程度(未梳、含脂、脱脂、碳化等)

税则号列	商品名称	申报要素(A:归类要素 B:价格要素 C:审单及其他要素)及说明举例
5101.2100	--剪羊毛	A: 1. 品名; 2. 加工程度(未梳、含脂、脱脂、碳化等)。B: 3. 剪羊毛请注明细度(微米数); 4. 剪羊毛请注明长度; 5. 剪羊毛请注明草杂含量
5101.2900	--其他	A: 1. 品名; 2. 加工程度(未梳、含脂、脱脂、碳化等)
5101.3000	-碳化羊毛	A: 1. 品名; 2. 加工程度(未梳、含脂、脱脂、碳化等)
5102.1100	--喀什米尔山羊的	A: 1. 品名; 2. 种类(未梳理的兔毛、喀什米尔山羊毛、山羊绒、骆驼毛)
5102.1910	---兔毛	A: 1. 品名; 2. 种类(未梳理的兔毛、喀什米尔山羊毛、山羊绒、骆驼毛)
5102.1920	---其他山羊绒	A: 1. 品名; 2. 种类(未梳理的兔毛、喀什米尔山羊毛、山羊绒、骆驼毛)。B: 3. 其他山羊绒请注明颜色; 4. 其他山羊绒请注明纤维长度; 5. 其他山羊绒请注明含绒率
5102.1930	---骆驼毛、骆驼绒	A: 1. 品名; 2. 种类(未梳理的兔毛、喀什米尔山羊毛、山羊绒、骆驼毛)
5102.1990	---其他	A: 1. 品名; 2. 种类(未梳理的兔毛、喀什米尔山羊毛、山羊绒、骆驼毛)
5102.2000	-粗毛	A: 1. 品名; 2. 种类(未梳理的兔毛、喀什米尔山羊毛、山羊绒、骆驼毛)
51.03	羊毛或动物细毛或粗毛的废料, 包括废纱线, 但不包括回收纤维:	例: 废料不包括回收纤维(税目 51.04)
	-羊毛或动物细毛的落毛	A: 1. 品名; 2. 种类(羊毛落毛、动物细毛或粗毛废料)
5103.2010	---羊毛废料	A: 1. 品名; 2. 种类(羊毛落毛、动物细毛或粗毛废料)
5103.2090	---其他	A: 1. 品名; 2. 种类(羊毛落毛、动物细毛或粗毛废料)。B: 3. 是否濒危野生
5103.3000	-动物粗毛废料	A: 1. 品名; 2. 种类(羊毛落毛、动物细毛或粗毛废料)
51.04	羊毛及动物细毛或粗毛的回收纤维:	A: 1. 品名; 2. 种类(源于羊毛、动物粗、细毛等的回收纤维)
5105.1000	-粗梳羊毛	A: 1. 品名; 2. 种类(羊毛条、羊毛片毛、兔毛、喀什米尔山羊毛); 3. 梳理方法(粗梳或精梳)
5105.2100	--精梳片毛	A: 1. 品名; 2. 种类(羊毛条、羊毛片毛、兔毛、喀什米尔山羊毛); 3. 梳理方法(粗梳或精梳)
5105.2900	--其他	A: 1. 品名; 2. 种类(羊毛条、羊毛片毛、兔毛、喀什米尔山羊毛); 3. 梳理方法(粗梳或精梳)。B: 4. 其他精梳羊毛请注明支数; 5. 其他精梳羊毛请注明细度
	-已梳动物细毛:	A: 1. 品名; 2. 种类(羊毛条、羊毛片毛、兔毛、喀什米尔山羊毛); 3. 梳理方法(粗梳或精梳)
5105.4000	-已梳动物粗毛	A: 1. 品名; 2. 种类(羊毛条、羊毛片毛、兔毛、喀什米尔山羊毛); 3. 梳理方法(粗梳或精梳)
51.06	粗梳羊毛纱线, 非供零售用:	A: 1. 品名; 2. 梳理方法(粗疏); 3. 是否供零售用; 4. 成分含量
51.07	精梳羊毛纱线, 非供零售用:	A: 1. 品名; 2. 梳理方法(精梳羊毛纱线); 3. 是否供零售用; 4. 成分含量
51.08	动物细毛(粗梳或精梳)纱线, 非供零售用:	A: 1. 品名; 2. 梳理方法(精梳羊毛纱线); 3. 是否供零售用; 4. 成分含量
51.09	羊毛或动物细毛的纱线, 供零售用:	A: 1. 品名; 2. 种类(羊毛等); 3. 是否供零售用; 4. 成分含量
51.10	动物粗毛或马毛的纱线(包括马毛粗松螺旋花线), 不论是否供零售用:	A: 1. 品名; 2. 种类(马毛等粗毛纱线); 3. 成分含量
51.11	粗梳羊毛或粗梳动物细毛的机织物:	A: 1. 品名; 2. 种类(羊毛、驼马毛、美洲驼毛等); 3. 织造方法(机织); 4. 梳理方法(粗梳); 5. 成分含量; 6. 幅宽; 7. 每平方米克重
51.12	精梳羊毛或精梳动物细毛的机织物:	A: 1. 品名; 2. 种类(羊毛、驼马毛、美洲驼毛等); 3. 织造方法(机织); 4. 梳理方法(精梳); 5. 成分含量; 6. 幅宽; 7. 每平方米克重
51.13	动物粗毛或马毛的机织物:	A: 1. 品名; 2. 种类(马毛等); 3. 织造方法(机织); 4. 成分含量; 5. 幅宽; 6. 每平方米克重

第五十二章　棉花

[注解]

1. 纱线细度的换算: 1 特=1000 / 公支数=0.1111×旦数=590.5 / 英支数。
2. 截面或表观宽度: 截面宽度一般指圆形或类似形状单丝, 表观宽度一般指扁形单丝。

税则号列	商品名称	申报要素(A:归类要素 B:价格要素 C:审单及其他要素)及说明举例
52.01	未梳的棉花:	A: 1. 品名; 2. 是否梳理; 3. 纤维长度。B: 4. 等级
5202.1000	-废棉纱线(包括废棉线)	A: 1. 品名; 2. 来源(废棉线、回收纤维等); 3. 成分含量; 4. 废棉纱线请注明长度; 5. 颜色
5202.9100	--回收纤维	A: 1. 品名; 2. 来源(废棉线、回收纤维等); 3. 成分含量
5202.9900	--其他	A: 1. 品名; 2. 来源(废棉线、回收纤维等); 3. 成分含量; 4. 棉种类(包括精落、抄斩、车肚、统破籽、回丝等)
52.03	已梳的棉花:	A: 1. 品名; 2. 是否梳理; 3. 纤维长度; 4. 是否经过细纱工序
52.04	棉制缝纫线, 不论是否供零售用:	A: 1. 品名; 2. 是否供零售用; 3. 成分含量; 4. 纱线细度; 5. 每只重量; 6. 是否上浆; 7. 终捻捻向
52.05	棉纱线(缝纫线除外), 按重量计含棉量在 85%及以上, 非供零售用:	A: 1. 品名; 2. 梳理方法(粗梳、精梳); 3. 纱线形态(单纱、股线或缆线); 4. 是否供零售用; 5. 成分含量; 6. 纱线细度。B: 7. 品牌; 8. 加工工艺

税则号列	商品名称	申报要素(A:归类要素 B:价格要素 C:审单及其他要素)及说明举例
52.06	棉纱线（缝纫线除外），按重量计含棉量在85%以下，非供零售用:	A: 1. 品名; 2. 梳理方法(粗梳、精梳); 3. 纱线形态(单纱、股线或缆线); 4. 是否供零售用; 5. 成分含量; 6. 纱线细度;
52.07	棉纱线(缝纫线除外)，供零售用:	A: 1. 品名; 2. 是否供零售用; 3. 成分含量。例: 缝纫线除外
52.08	棉机织物，按重量计含棉量在85%及以上，每平方米重量不超过200克:	A: 1. 品名; 2. 织造方法(机织物); 3. 染整方法(漂白、未漂白、色织、染色、印花等); 4. 组织结构(平纹、斜纹等); 5. 成分含量; 6. 幅宽; 7. 每平方米克重。B: 8. 品牌
52.09	棉机织物，按重量计含棉量在85%及以上，每平方米重量超过200克:	A: 1. 品名; 2. 织造方法(机织物); 3. 染整方法(漂白、未漂白、色织、染色、印花等); 4. 组织结构(平纹、斜纹等); 5. 成分含量; 6. 幅宽; 7. 每平方米克重。B: 8. 品牌
52.10	棉机织物，按重量计含棉量在85%以下，主要或仅与化学纤维混纺，每平方米重量不超过200克:	A: 1. 品名; 2. 织造方法(机织物); 3. 染整方法(漂白、未漂白、色织、染色、印花等); 4. 组织结构(平纹、斜纹等); 5. 注明与其混纺的化纤是长丝还是短纤; 6. 成分含量; 7. 幅宽; 8. 每平方米克重。B: 9. 品牌
52.11	棉机织物，按重量计含棉量在85%及以下，每平方米重量超过200克:	A: 1. 品名; 2. 织造方法(机织物); 3. 染整方法(漂白、未漂白、色织、染色、印花等); 4. 组织结构(平纹、斜纹等); 5. 注明与其混纺的化纤是长丝还是短纤; 6. 成分含量; 7. 幅宽; 8. 每平方米克重。B: 9. 品牌
52.12	其他棉机织物:	A: 1. 品名; 2. 织造方法(机织物); 3. 染整方法(漂白、未漂白、色织、染色、印花等); 4. 组织结构(平纹、斜纹等); 5. 成分含量; 6. 幅宽; 7. 每平方米克重。B: 8. 品牌

第五十三章　其他植物纺织纤维；纸纱线及其机织物

[注解]

1. 韧皮纤维种类与来源：亚麻、大麻、黄麻、洋麻、苘麻、西沙尔麻、海地大麻、美洲龙舌兰纤维、椰壳纤维。

2. 亚麻等韧皮纤维的一般加工过程：生麻-沤制麻-打或麻-棉花麻纤维-栉梳。

税则号列	商品名称	申报要素(A:归类要素 B:价格要素 C:审单及其他要素)及说明举例
5301.1000	-生的或经沤制的亚麻	A: 1. 品名; 2. 加工程度(生的、经沤制、破开或打成栉梳、回收等)
5301.2100	--破开的或打成的	A: 1. 品名; 2. 加工程度(生的、经沤制、破开或打成栉梳、回收等)。B: 3. 可纺支数; 4. 长度
5301.2900	--其他	A: 1. 品名; 2. 加工程度(生的、经沤制、破开或打成栉梳、回收等)
5301.3000	-亚麻短纤及废麻	A: 1. 品名; 2. 加工程度(生的、经沤制、破开或打成栉梳、回收等); 3. 是否为短纤或废麻; 4. 种类(二粗、机械短麻、落麻)
5302.1000	-生的或经沤制的大麻	A: 1. 品名; 2. 加工程度(生的、沤制的)
5302.9000	-其他	A: 1. 品名; 2. 加工程度(生的、沤制的); 3. 是否为短纤或废麻
5303.1000	-生的或经沤制的黄麻及其他纺织用韧皮纤维	A: 1. 品名; 2. 种类(黄麻、洋麻、苘麻等); 3. 加工程度(未纺制的、生的或沤制的)
5303.9000	-其他	A: 1. 品名; 2. 种类(黄麻、洋麻、苘麻等); 3. 加工程度(未纺制的、生的或沤制的); 4. 是否为短纤或废麻
5305.0011	----生的	A: 1. 品名; 2. 种类(椰壳纤维、蕉麻、苎麻等); 3. 加工程度(生的或经加工但未纺制的)
5305.0012	----经加工但未纺制的	A: 1. 品名; 2. 种类（椰壳纤维、蕉麻、苎麻等）; 3. 加工程度（生的或经加工但未纺制的）
5305.0013	----短纤及废料	A: 1. 品名; 2. 种类(椰壳纤维、蕉麻、苎麻等); 3. 加工程度(生的或经加工但未纺制的); 4. 是否为短纤或废麻
5305.0019	----其他	A: 1. 品名; 2. 种类(椰壳纤维、蕉麻、苎麻等); 3. 加工程度(生的或经加工但未纺制的)
5305.0020	---蕉麻	A: 1. 品名; 2. 种类(椰壳纤维、蕉麻、苎麻等); 3. 加工程度(生的或经加工但未纺制的)
	---其他:	A: 1. 品名; 2. 种类(椰壳纤维、蕉麻、苎麻等); 3. 加工程度(生的或经加工但未纺制的); 4. 是否为短纤或废麻
53.06	亚麻纱线:	A: 1. 品名; 2. 纱线形态(单纱、股线或缆线)。B: 3. 细度
53.07	黄麻纱线或税目53.03的其他纺织用韧皮纤维纱线:	A: 1. 品名; 2. 种类(黄麻、洋麻、苘麻等); 3. 纱线形态(单纱、股线或缆线)。B: 4. 细度
5308.1000	-椰壳纤维纱线	A: 1. 品名; 2. 种类(椰壳纤维纱线、大麻纱线、苎麻纱线、纸纱线等); 3. 成分含量。B: 4. 细度
5308.2000	-大麻纱线	A: 1. 品名; 2. 种类(椰壳纤维纱线、大麻纱线、苎麻纱线、纸纱线等); 3. 成分含量。B: 4. 细度
	---苎麻纱线:	A: 1. 品名; 2. 种类(椰壳纤维纱线、大麻纱线、苎麻纱线、纸纱线等); 3. 染整方法(漂白、未漂白、色织); 4. 成分含量。B: 5. 细度
	---其他:	A: 1. 品名; 2. 种类(椰壳纤维纱线、大麻纱线、苎麻纱线、纸纱线等); 3. 成分含量。B: 4. 细度

税则号列	商品名称	申报要素(A:归类要素 B:价格要素 C:审单及其他要素)及说明举例
53.09	亚麻机织物:	A:1.品名;2.织造方法(机织);3.染整方法(漂白、未漂白、色织);4.成分含量;5.幅宽;6.每平方米克重
53.10	黄麻或税目53.03的其他纺织用韧皮纤维机织物:	A:1.品名;2.种类(黄麻、洋麻、菽麻等);3.织造方法(机织);4.染整工艺(漂白、未漂白、色织);5.成分含量;6.幅宽;7.每平方米克重
53.11	其他纺织用植物纤维机织物;纸纱线机织物:	A:1.品名;2.种类(黄麻、洋麻、菽麻等);3.织造方法(机织);4.染整工艺(漂白、未漂白、色织);5.成分含量;6.幅宽;7.每平方米克重

第五十四章　化学纤维长丝;化学纤维纺织材料制扁条及类似品

税则号列	商品名称	申报要素(A:归类要素 B:价格要素 C:审单及其他要素)及说明举例
54.01	化学纤维长丝纺制的缝纫线,不论是否供零售用:	A:1.品名;2.是否供零售用; 3.纤维成分(聚酯等);4.每只重量;5.是否上浆;6.终捻捻向
54.02	合成纤维长丝纱线(缝纫线除外)非供零售用,包括细度在67分特以下的合成纤维单丝:	
	-尼龙或其他聚酰胺纺制的高强力纱:	A:1.品名;2.种类(高强力纱或变形纱线等);3.纱线形态(单纱、股线或缆线);4.是否供零售用;5.纤维成分(聚酯等);6.纱线细度
5402.2000	-聚酯高强力纱	A:1.品名;2.种类(高强力纱或变形纱线等);3.纱线形态(单纱、股线或缆线);4.是否供零售用;5.纤维成分(聚酯等);6.纱线细度
	-变形纱线:	A:1.品名;2.种类(高强力纱或变形纱线等);3.纱线形态(单纱、股线或缆线);4.是否供零售用;5.纤维成分(聚酯等);6.纱线细度
	--弹性纱线:	A:1.品名;2.种类(高强力纱或变形纱线等);3.纱线形态(单纱、股线或缆线);4.高强纱请注明用途;5.是否供零售用;6.纤维成分(聚酯等);7.纱线细度;8.是否加捻(如加捻请注明捻度)
	--其他,尼龙或其他聚酰胺纱线:	A:1.品名;2.种类(高强力纱或变形纱线等);3.纱线形态(单纱、股线或缆线);4.高强纱请注明用途;5.是否供零售用;6.纤维成分(聚酯等);7.纱线细度;8.是否加捻(如加捻请注明捻度)
5402.4600	--其他,部分定向聚酯纱线	A:1.品名;2.种类(高强力纱或变形纱线等);3.纱线形态(单纱、股线或缆线);4.高强纱请注明用途;5.是否供零售用;6.纤维成分(聚酯等);7.纱线细度;8.是否加捻(如加捻请注明捻度)
5402.4700	--其他,聚酯纱线	A:1.品名;2.种类(高强力纱或变形纱线等);3.纱线形态(单纱、股线或缆线);4.高强纱请注明用途;5.是否供零售用;6.纤维成分(聚酯等);7.纱线细度;8.是否加捻(如加捻请注明捻度)
5402.4800	--其他,聚丙烯纱线	A:1.品名;2.种类(高强力纱或变形纱线等);3.纱线形态(单纱、股线或缆线);4.高强纱请注明用途;5.是否供零售用;6.纤维成分(聚酯等);7.纱线细度;8.是否加捻(如加捻请注明捻度)
5402.4910	---断裂强度大于等于22cN/dtex,且初始模量大于等于750cN/dtex的聚乙烯纱线	A:1.品名;2.种类(高强力纱或变形纱线等);3.纱线形态(单纱、股线或缆线);4.高强纱请注明用途;5.是否供零售用;6.纤维成分(聚酯等);7.纱线细度;8.是否加捻(如加捻请注明捻度);9.断裂强度
5402.4990	---其他	A:1.品名;2.种类(高强力纱或变形纱线等);3.纱线形态(单纱、股线或缆线);4.高强纱请注明用途;5.是否供零售用;6.纤维成分(聚酯等);7.纱线细度;8.是否加捻(如加捻请注明捻度)
	--尼龙或其他聚酰胺纱线:	A:1.品名;2.种类(高强力纱或变形纱线等);3.纱线形态(单纱、股线或缆线);4.是否供零售用;5.纤维成分(聚酯等);6.纱线细度;7.是否加捻(如加捻请注明捻度)
5402.5200	--聚酯纱线	A:1.品名;2.种类(高强力纱或变形纱线等);3.纱线形态(单纱、股线或缆线);4.是否供零售用;5.纤维成分(聚酯等);6.纱线细度;7.是否加捻(如加捻请注明捻度)
5402.5910	---聚丙烯纱线	A:1.品名;2.种类(高强力纱或变形纱线等);3.纱线形态(单纱、股线或缆线);4.是否供零售用;5.纤维成分(聚酯等);6.纱线细度;7.是否加捻(如加捻请注明捻度)
5402.5920	---断裂强度大于等于22cN/dtex,且初始模量大于等于750cN/dtex的聚乙烯纱线	A:1.品名;2.种类(高强力纱或变形纱线等);3.纱线形态(单纱、股线或缆线);4.是否供零售用;5.纤维成分(聚酯等);6.纱线细度;7.是否加捻(如加捻请注明捻度);8.断裂强度
5402.5990	---其他	A:1.品名;2.种类(高强力纱或变形纱线等);3.纱线形态(单纱、股线或缆线);4.是否供零售用;5.纤维成分(聚酯等);6.纱线细度;7.是否加捻(如加捻请注明捻度)
	-其他纱线(多股纱线或缆线):	A:1.品名;2.种类(高强力纱或变形纱线等);3.纱线形态(单纱、股线或缆线);4.是否供零售用;5.纤维成分(聚酯等);6.纱线细度

税则号列	商品名称	申报要素(A:归类要素 B:价格要素 C:审单及其他要素)及说明举例
54.03	人造纤维长丝纱线(缝纫线除外),非供零售用,包括细度在67分特以下的人造纤维单丝:	A:1.品名;2.种类(高强力纱或变形纱线等);3.纱线形态(单纱、股线或缆线);4.是否供零售用;5.纤维成分(如粘胶等);6.纱线细度;7.纱线捻度;8.高强力纱需注明断裂强度(单位:厘牛顿/特克斯);9.股数
54.04	截面尺寸不超过1毫米,细度在67分特及以上的合成纤维单丝;表观宽度不超过5毫米的合成纤维纺织材料制扁条及类似品(例如,人造草):	A:1.品名;2.种类(单丝、扁条等);3.纤维成分;4.单丝细度或扁条表观宽度
54.05	截面尺寸不超过1毫米,细度在67分特及以上的人造纤维单丝;表观宽度不超过5毫米的人造纤维纺织材料制扁条及类似品(例如,人造草):	A:1.品名;2.种类(单丝、扁条等);3.纤维成分;4.单丝细度或扁条表观宽度
54.06	化学纤维长丝纱线(缝纫线除外),供零售用:	A:1.品名;2.包装(供零售用);3.纤维成分
54.07	合成纤维长丝纱线的机织物,包括税目54.04所列材料的机织物:	
	-尼龙或其他聚酰胺高强力纱、聚酯高强力纱纺制的机织物:	A:1.品名;2.织造方法(机织、平行纱层叠黏合);3.染整方法(漂白、色织、染色等);4.组织结构(平纹、斜纹、缎纹等);5.成分含量;6.幅宽;7.每平方米克重;8.是否为高强力纱。B:9.品牌
5407.2000	-扁条及类似品的机织物	A:1.品名;2.织造方法(机织、平行纱层叠黏合);3.染整方法(漂白、色织、染色等);4.组织结构(平纹、斜纹、缎纹等);5.成分含量;6.幅宽;7.每平方米克重。B:8.品牌
5407.3000	-第十一类注释九所列的机织物	A:1.品名;2.织造方法(机织、平行纱层叠黏合);3.染整方法(漂白、色织、染色等);4.组织结构(平纹、斜纹、缎纹等);5.成分含量;6.幅宽;7.每平方米克重。B:8 品牌
	-其他机织物,按重量计尼龙或其他聚酰胺长丝含量在85%及以上:	A:1.品名;2.织造方法(机织、平行纱层叠黏合);3.染整方法(漂白、色织、染色等);4.组织结构(平纹、斜纹、缎纹等);5.成分含量;6.幅宽;7.每平方米克重。B:8.品牌
	-其他机织物,按重量计聚酯变形长丝含量在85%及以上:	A:1.品名;2.织造方法(机织、平行纱层叠黏合);3.染整方法(漂白、色织、染色等);4.组织结构(平纹、斜纹、缎纹等);5.成分含量(聚酯变形长丝等成分及含量);6.幅宽;7.每平方米克重。B:8.品牌
	-其他机织物,按重量计聚酯长丝含量在85%及以上:	A:1.品名;2.织造方法(机织、平行纱层叠黏合);3.染整方法(漂白、色织、染色等);4.组织结构(平纹、斜纹、缎纹等);5.成分含量;6.幅宽;7.每平方米克重。B:8.品牌
	-其他机织物,按重量计其他合成纤维长丝含量在85%及以上:	A:1.品名;2.织造方法(机织、平行纱层叠黏合);3.染整方法(漂白、色织、染色等);4.组织结构(平纹、斜纹、缎纹等);5.成分含量;6.幅宽;7.每平方米克重。B:8.品牌
	-其他机织物,按重量计其他合成纤维长丝含量在85%以下,主要或仅与棉混纺:	A:1.品名;2.织造方法(机织、平行纱层叠黏合);3.染整方法(漂白、色织、染色等);4.组织结构(平纹、斜纹、缎纹等);5.成分含量;6.幅宽;7.每平方米克重。B:8.品牌
	-其他机织物:	A:1.品名;2.织造方法(机织、平行纱层叠黏合);3.染整方法(漂白、色织、染色等);4.组织结构(平纹、斜纹、缎纹等);5.成分含量;6.幅宽;7.每平方米克重。B:8.品牌
54.08	人造纤维长丝纱线的机织物,包括税目54.05所列材料的机织物:	A:1.品名;2.织造方法(机织、平行纱层叠黏合);3.染整方法(漂白、色织、染色等);4.组织结构(平纹、斜纹、缎纹等);5.成分含量;6.幅宽;7.每平方米克重。B:8.品牌

第五十五章　化学纤维短纤

[注解]

混纺纱线织物的归类原理:

1．按制成该物品的纤维品种、性质先归入相对应的章。

2．按该物品所属的加工程度归入该章的前、中或后的商品编码中。

3．由两种或两种以上的纺织材料混合制成的物品,应按重量比例最大的那种材料归类,当没有一种纺织材料的重量比例较大时,应按可归入有关商品编码中最后一个商品编码所列的纺织材料归类。

税则号列	商品名称	申报要素(A:归类要素 B:价格要素 C:审单及其他要素)及说明举例
55.01	合成纤维长丝丝束:	A:1.品名;2.纤维成分;3.单丝细度;4.丝束长度;5.丝束捻度;6.丝束总细度
55.02	人造纤维长丝丝束:	A:1.品名;2.纤维成分;3.单丝细度;4.丝束长度;5.丝束捻度;6.丝束总细度
55.03	合成纤维短纤,未梳或未经其他纺前加工:	A:1.品名;2.加工程度(未梳、未经纺前加工);3.纤维成分;4.长度;5.细度

税则号列	商品名称	申报要素(A:归类要素 B:价格要素 C:审单及其他要素)及说明举例
55.04	人造纤维短纤，未梳或未经其他纺前加工:	A: 1.品名; 2.加工程度(未梳、未经纺前加工); 3.人造纤维种类; 4.细度; 5.长度
55.05	化学纤维废料(包括落棉、废纱及回收纤维):	A: 1.品名; 2.来源(落绵、废纱、回收纤维); 3.纤维成分; 4.颜色(白色、杂色等)
55.06	合成纤维短纤，已梳或经其他纺前加工:	A: 1.品名; 2.加工程度(已梳、经纺前加工); 3.纤维成分
55.07	人造纤维短纤，已梳或经其他纺前加工:	A: 1.品名; 2.加工程度(已梳、经纺前加工); 3.纤维成分
55.08	化学纤维短纤纺制的缝纫线，不论是否供零售用:	A: 1.品名; 2.成分含量; 3.纱线细度; 4.每只重量; 5.是否上浆; 6.终捻捻向; 7.是否供零售用
55.09	合成纤维短纤纺制的纱线(缝纫线除外)，非供零售用:	A: 1.品名; 2.种类(单纱、股线、缆线); 3.是否供零售用; 4.成分含量; 5.纱线细度; 6.股线注明股数
55.10	人造纤维短纤纺制的纱线(缝纫线除外)，非供零售用:	A: 1.品名; 2.种类(单纱、股线、缆线); 3.是否供零售用; 4.成分含量; 5.纱线细度; 6.股线注明股数
55.11	化学纤维短纤纺制的纱线(缝纫线除外)，供零售用:	A: 1.品名; 2.种类(单纱、股线、缆线); 3.是否供零售用; 4.成分含量; 5.纱线细度
55.12	合成纤维短纤纺制的机织物，按重量计合成纤维短纤含量在85%及以上:	A: 1.品名; 2.织造方法(机织); 3.染整方法(漂白、未漂白、色织、染色等); 4.组织结构(平纹、斜纹、缎纹等); 5.成分含量; 6.幅宽; 7.每平方米克重。B: 8.品牌
55.13	合成纤维短纤纺制的机织物，按重量计合成纤维短纤含量在85%以下，主要或仅与棉混纺，每平方米重量不超过170克:	A: 1.品名; 2.种类(单纱、股线、缆线); 3.织造方法(机织); 4.染整方法(漂白、未漂白、色织、染色等); 5.组织结构(平纹、斜纹、缎纹等); 6.成分含量; 7.幅宽; 8.每平方米克重。B: 9.品牌
55.14	合成纤维短纤纺制的机织物，按重量计合成纤维短纤含量在85%以下，主要或仅与棉混纺，每平方米重量超过170克:	A: 1.品名; 2.织造方法(机织); 3.染整方法(漂白、未漂白、色织、染色等); 4.组织结构(平纹、斜纹、缎纹等); 5.成分含量; 6.幅宽; 7.每平方米克重。B: 8.品牌
55.15	合成纤维短纤纺制的其他机织物:	A: 1.品名; 2.织造方法(机织); 3.染整方法(漂白、未漂白、色织、染色等); 4.组织结构(平纹、斜纹、缎纹等); 5.成分含量; 6.幅宽; 7.每平方米克重。B: 8.品牌
55.16	人造纤维短纤纺制的机织物:	A: 1.品名; 2.织造方法(机织); 3.染整方法(漂白、未漂白、色织、染色等); 4.组织结构(平纹、斜纹、缎纹等); 5.成分含量; 6.幅宽; 7.每平方米克重。B: 8.品牌

第五十六章　絮胎、毡呢及无纺织物；特种纱线；线、绳、索、缆及其制品

[注解]

1. 无纺织物与普通絮胎的主要区别：无纺织物一般按照整张网或薄片的厚度和宽度将纤维或长丝黏合起来。
2. 无纺织物与纸、纸板的主要区别：无纺织物的纤维一般在生产过程中未被融化掉。

税则号列	商品名称	申报要素(A:归类要素 B:价格要素 C:审单及其他要素)及说明举例
56.01	纺织材料絮胎及其制品；长度不超过5毫米的纺织纤维(纤维屑)、纤维粉末及球结	
	-絮胎；其他絮胎制品:	A: 1.品名; 2.纤维成分(如棉制)
5601.3000	-纤维屑、纤维粉末及球结	A: 1.品名; 2.状态(纤维屑、球结)
56.02	毡呢，不论是否浸渍、涂布、包覆或层压:	A: 1.品名; 2.加工方法(针刺缝编、涂布、浸渍、层压、包覆等); 3.纤维成分含量
5603.1110	---经浸渍、涂布、包覆或层压	A: 1.品名; 2.加工方法(涂布、浸渍、层压、包覆等); 3.是否化学纤维长丝制; 4.每平方米克重; 5.成分含量。B: 6.用途
5603.1190	---其他	A: 1.品名; 2.加工方法; 3.化学纤维长丝制应注明; 4.每平方米克重; 5.成分含量。B: 6.用途
	--每平方米重量超过25克，但不超过70克:	A: 1.品名; 2.加工方法(涂布、浸渍、层压、包覆等); 3.是否化学纤维长丝制; 4.每平方米克重; 5.成分含量。B: 6.用途
	--每平方米重量超过70克，但不超过150克:	A: 1.品名; 2.加工方法(涂布、浸渍、层压、包覆等); 3.是否化学纤维长丝制; 4.每平方米克重; 5.成分含量。B: 6.用途
5603.1410	---经浸渍、涂布、包覆或层压	A: 1.品名; 2.加工方法(涂布、浸渍、层压、包覆等); 3.是否化学纤维长丝制; 4.每平方米克重; 5.成分含量。B: 6.用途
5603.1490	---其他	A: 1.品名; 2.加工方法; 3.化学纤维长丝制应注明; 4.每平方米克重; 5.成分含量。B: 6.用途
5603.9110	---经浸渍、涂布、包覆或层压	A: 1.品名; 2.加工方法(涂布、浸渍、层压、包覆等); 3.每平方米克重; 4.成分含量。B: 5.用途
5603.9190	---其他	A: 1.品名; 2.加工方法; 3.每平方米克重; 4.成分及含量。B: 5.用途
5603.9210	---经浸渍、涂布、包覆或层压	A: 1.品名; 2.加工方法(涂布、浸渍、层压、包覆等); 3.每平方米克重; 4.成分含量。B: 5.用途

税则号列	商品名称	申报要素(A:归类要素 B:价格要素 C:审单及其他要素)及说明举例
5603.9290	---其他	A:1.品名;2.加工方法;3.每平方米克重;4.成分及含量。B:5.用途
5603.9310	---经浸渍、涂布、包覆或层压	A:1.品名;2.加工方法(涂布、浸渍、层压、包覆等);3.每平方米克重;4.成分含量。B:5.用途
5603.9390	---其他	A:1.品名;2.加工方法;3.每平方米克重;4.成分及含量。B:5.用途
5603.9410	---经浸渍、涂布、包覆或层压	A:1.品名;2.加工方法(涂布、浸渍、层压、包覆等);3.每平方米克重;4.成分含量。B:5.用途
5603.9490	---其他	A:1.品名;2.加工方法;3.每平方米克重;4.成分含量。B:5.用途
56.04	用纺织材料包覆的橡胶线及绳;用橡胶或塑料浸渍、涂布、包覆或套裹的纺织纱线及税目54.04或54.05的扁条及类似品:	A:1.品名;2.加工方法(浸渍、涂布或包覆等);3.内层材质;4.外层材质
56.05	含金属纱线,不论是否螺旋花线,由纺织纱线或税目54.04或54.05的扁条及类似品与金属线、扁条或粉末混合制得或用金属包覆制得:	A:1.品名;2.含金属纱线;3.成分含量
5606.0000	粗松螺旋花线,税目54.04或54.05的扁条及类似品制的螺旋花线(税目56.05的货品及马毛粗松螺旋花线除外);绳绒线(包括植绒绳绒线);纵行起圈纱线	A:1.品名;2.种类(绳绒及粗松花线、纵行起圈纱线等)
5607.2100	--包扎用绳	A:1.品名;2.用途(包扎用等);3.纤维成分
5607.2900	--其他	A:1.品名;2.纤维成分
5607.4100	--包扎用绳	A:1.品名;2.用途(包扎用等);3.纤维成分
5607.4900	--其他	A:1.品名;2.纤维成分
5607.5000	-其他合成纤维纺制	A:1.品名;2.纤维成分;3.是否编织
	-其他:	A:1.品名;2.纤维成分
5608.1100	--制成的渔网	A:1.品名;2.用途(渔网、购物网等);3.纤维成分;4.成网方式(结制)
5608.1900	--其他	A:1.品名;2.用途(渔网、购物网等);3.纤维成分
5608.9000	-其他	A:1.品名;2.用途(渔网、购物网等);3.纤维成分
56.09	用纱线、税目54.04或54.05的扁条及类似品或线、绳、索、缆制成的其他税目未列名物品:	A:1.品名;2.用途;3.纤维成分

第五十七章 地毯及纺织材料的其他铺地制品

税则号列	商品名称	申报要素(A:归类要素 B:价格要素 C:审单及其他要素)及说明举例
57.01	结织栽绒地毯及纺织材料的其他结织栽绒铺地制品,不论是否制成的:	A:1.品名;2.织造方法(栽绒、手织等);3.是否为铺地制品;4.纤维成分;5.规格尺寸
5702.1000	-“开来姆”、“苏麦克”、“卡拉马尼”及类似的手织地毯	A:1.品名;2.织造方法(机织、手织等);3.纤维成分;4.规格尺寸
5702.2000	-椰壳纤维制的铺地制品	A:1.品名;2.织造方法(栽绒、手织等);3.是否为铺地制品;4.纤维成分;5.规格尺寸
	-其他起绒结构的铺地制品,未制成的:	A:1.品名;2.织造方法(栽绒、手织等);3.是否为铺地制品;4.纤维成分;5.规格尺寸
	-其他起绒结构的铺地制品,制成的:	A:1.品名;2.织造方法(栽绒、手织等);3.是否为铺地制品;4.纤维成分;5.规格尺寸
	-其他非起绒结构的铺地制品,未制成的:	A:1.品名;2.织造方法(栽绒、手织等);3.是否为铺地制品;4.纤维成分;5.规格尺寸
	-其他非起绒结构的铺地制品,制成的:	A:1.品名;2.织造方法(栽绒、手织等);3.是否为铺地制品;4.纤维成分;5.规格尺寸
57.03	簇绒地毯及纺织材料的其他簇绒铺地制品,不论是否制成的:	A:1.品名;2.织造方法(簇绒);3.是否为铺地制品;4.纤维成分;5.规格尺寸
57.04	毡呢地毯及纺织材料的其他毡呢铺地制品,未簇绒或未植绒,不论是否制成的:	A:1.品名;2.织造方法(毡呢);3.是否为铺地制品;4.纤维成分;5.规格尺寸(最大表面面积)
57.05	其他地毯及纺织材料的其他铺地制品,不论是否制成的:	A:1.品名;2.是否为铺地制品;3.纤维成分;4.是否含有膨润土;5.规格尺寸

第五十八章　特种机织物；簇绒织物；花边；装饰毯；装饰带；刺绣品

[注解]

“被褥状纺织制品”一般指一层胎料缝合一层织物或两层织物夹一层胎料，但缝合主要起绗缝的特征，图案不构成刺绣品的特征。

税则号列	商品名称	申报要素(A:归类要素 B:价格要素 C:审单及其他要素)及说明举例
5801.1000	-羊毛或动物细毛制	A:1.品名;2.织造方法(机织);3.幅宽;4.纤维成分
5801.2100	--不割绒的纬起绒织物	A:1.品名;2.织造方法(机织);3.起绒方式(经起绒、纬起绒或绳绒);4.幅宽;5.纤维成分
5801.2200	--割绒的灯芯绒	A:1.品名;2.织造方法(机织);3.割绒请注明;4.幅宽;5.纤维成分
5801.2300	--其他纬起绒织物	A:1.品名;2.织造方法(机织);3.起绒方式(经起绒、纬起绒或绳绒);4.幅宽;5.纤维成分
5801.2600	--绳绒织物	A:1.品名;2.织造方法(机织);3.起绒方式(经起绒、纬起绒或绳绒);4.幅宽;5.纤维成分
5801.2710	---不割绒的（棱纹绸）	A:1.品名;2.织造方法(机织);3.起绒方式(经起绒、纬起绒或绳绒);4.幅宽;5.纤维成分
5801.2720	---割绒的	A:1.品名;2.织造方法(机织);3.起绒方式(经起绒、纬起绒或绳绒);4.是否为割绒;5. 幅宽;6.纤维成分
5801.3100	--不割绒的纬起绒织物	A:1.品名;2.织造方法(机织);3.起绒方式(经起绒、纬起绒或绳绒);4.幅宽;5.纤维成分
5801.3200	--割绒的灯芯绒	A:1.品名; 2.织造方法(机织); 3.起绒方式(经起绒、纬起绒或绳绒); 4.是否为割绒; 5.幅宽; 6.纤维成分
5801.3300	--其他纬起绒织物	A:1.品名; 2.织造方法（机织）; 3.起绒方式（经起绒、纬起绒或绳绒）; 4.幅宽; 5.纤维成分
5801.3600	--绳绒织物	A:1.品名; 2.织造方法（机织）; 3.起绒方式（经起绒、纬起绒或绳绒）; 4.幅宽; 5.纤维成分
5801.3710	---不割绒的（棱纹绸）	A:1.品名; 2.织造方法（机织）; 3.起绒方式（经起绒、纬起绒或绳绒）; 4.幅宽; 5.纤维成分
5801.3720	---割绒的	A:1.品名; 2.织造方法(机织); 3.起绒方式(经起绒、纬起绒或绳绒); 4.是否为割绒; 5.幅宽; 6.纤维成分
5801.9010	---丝及绢丝制	A:1.品名; 2.织造方法（机织）; 3.幅宽; 4.纤维成分
5801.9090	---其他	A:1.品名; 2.织造方法（机织）; 3.起绒方式（经起绒、纬起绒或绳绒）; 4.幅宽; 5.纤维成分
5802.1100	--未漂白	A:1.品名; 2.织造方法（机织）; 3.起绒方式（簇绒或毛圈）; 4.是否漂白; 5.幅宽; 6.纤维成分
5802.1900	--其他	A:1.品名; 2.织造方法（机织）; 3.起绒方式（簇绒或毛圈）; 4.幅宽; 5.纤维成分
	-其他纺织材料制的毛巾织物及类似的毛圈机织物:	A:1.品名; 2.织造方法（机织）; 3.起绒方式（簇绒或毛圈）; 4.幅宽; 5.纤维成分
	-簇绒织物:	A:1.品名; 2.织造方法（机织）; 3.起绒方式（簇绒或毛圈）; 4.幅宽; 5.纤维成分
58.03	纱罗，但税目 58.06 的狭幅织物除外:	A:1.品名; 2.组织结构（纱罗）; 3.幅宽; 4.纤维成分
58.04	网眼薄纱及其他网眼织物，但不包括机织物、针织物或钩编织物；成卷、成条或成小块图案的花边，但税目 60.02 至 60.06 的织物除外:	A:1.品名; 2.种类（网眼、花边）; 3.织造方法（机制、手工制）; 4.幅宽; 5.纤维成分
58.05	“哥白林”、“弗朗德”、“奥步生”、“波威”及类似式样的手织装饰毯，以及手工针绣嵌花装饰毯(例如，小针脚或十字绣)，不论是否制成的:	A:1.品名; 2.用途（装饰用）; 3.种类（手工针绣嵌花装饰毯等）; 4.幅宽; 5.纤维成分
58.06	狭幅机织物，但税目 58.07 的货品除外；用黏合剂黏合制成的有经纱而无纬纱的狭幅织物（包扎匹头用带）:	
	-起绒机织物(包括毛巾织物及类似的毛圈织物)及绳绒织物:	A:1.品名; 2.织造方法（机织）; 3.起绒方式（毛巾、绳绒等）; 4.成分含量; 5.幅宽
5806.2000	-按重量计弹性纱线或橡胶线含量在5%及以上的其他机织物	A:1.品名; 2.织造方法（机织）; 3.成分含量; 4.幅宽
	-其他机织物:	A:1.品名; 2.织造方法（机织）; 3.成分含量; 4.幅宽
	-用黏合剂黏合制成的有经纱而无纬纱的织物(包扎匹头用带):	A:1.品名; 2.织造方法（机织）; 3.成分含量; 4.幅宽
58.07	非绣制的纺织材料制标签、徽章及类似品，成匹、成条或裁成一定形状或尺寸:	A:1.品名; 2.织造方法（机织、针织等）; 3.成分含量; 4.幅宽; 5.刺绣请注明。例:包括除刺绣以外的各种纺织材料制的标签
58.08	成匹的编带；非绣制的成匹装饰带，但针织或钩编的除外；流苏、绒球及类似品:	A:1.品名; 2.规格（成匹）; 3.幅宽; 4.成分含量 例:针织和钩编除外
58.09	其他税目未列名的金属线机织物及税	A:1.品名; 2.用途（衣着、装饰等）; 3.织造方法（金属线或含金属纱线

税则号列	商品名称	申报要素(A:归类要素 B:价格要素 C:审单及其他要素)及说明举例
	目 56.05 所列含金属纱线的机织物，用于衣着、装饰及类似用途:	机织）；4.幅宽；5.成分含量
58.10	成匹、成条或成小块图案的刺绣品:	A:1.品名；2.织造方法（刺绣）；3.是否见底布；4.成分含量 例:刺绣品归入税目 58.10
58.11	用一层或几层纺织材料与胎料经绗缝或其他方法组合制成的被褥状纺织品，但税目 58.10 的刺绣品除外:	A:1.品名；2.成分含量

第五十九章　浸渍、涂布、包覆或层压的纺织物；工业用纺织制品

税则号列	商品名称	申报要素(A:归类要素 B:价格要素 C:审单及其他要素)及说明举例
59.01	用胶或淀粉物质涂布的纺织物，作书籍封面及类似用途的;描图布;制成的油画布;作帽里的硬衬布及类似硬挺纺织物:	A:1.品名；2.用途；3.处理工艺及材质（涂布、浸渍、层压）；4.成分含量
59.02	尼龙或其他聚酰胺、聚酯或粘胶纤维高强力纱制的帘子布:	A:1.品名；2.成分含量；3.是否高强力纱制
59.03	用塑料浸渍、涂布、包覆或层压的纺织物，但税目 59.02 的货品除外:	A:1.品名；2.处理方法（涂布、浸渍、层压等）；3.塑料种类；4.成分含量
59.04	列诺伦(亚麻油地毡)，不论是否剪切成形;以织物为底布经涂布或覆面的铺地制品，不论是否剪切成形:	A:1.品名
59.05	糊墙织物:	A:1.品名；2.是否糊墙用；3.是否为纸衬背；4.幅宽；5.表面层纤维成分含量
59.06	用橡胶处理的纺织物，但税目 59.02 的货物除外:	
	-宽度不超过 20 厘米的胶粘带:	A:1.品名；2.织造方法（机织、针织、钩编等）；3.处理材料（橡胶）；4.是否是胶粘带、绝缘带；5.幅宽
5906.9100	--针织或钩编的	A:1.品名；2.织造方法（机织、针织、钩编等）；3.处理材料（橡胶）；4.幅宽
5906.9910	---绝缘布或带	A:1.品名；2.织造方法（机织、针织、钩编等）；3.处理材料（橡胶）；4.是否是胶粘带、绝缘带；5.幅宽
5906.9990	---其他	A:1.品名；2.织造方法（机织、针织、钩编等）；3.处理材料（橡胶）；4.幅宽
5907.0010	---绝缘布或带	A:1.品名；2.处理材料；3.是否为绝缘带
5907.0020	---已绘制画布	A:1.品名；2.是否为已绘制画布;3.处理材料
5907.0090	---其他	A:1.品名；2.处理材料
59.08	用纺织材料机织、编结或针织而成的灯芯、炉芯、打火机芯、烛芯或类似品;煤气灯纱筒及纱罩，不论是否浸渍:	A:1.品名；2.用途
59.09	纺织材料制的水龙软管及类似的管子，不论有无其他材料作衬里、护套或附件:	A:1.品名；2.纤维成分
59.10	纺织材料制的传动带或输送带及带料，不论是否用塑料浸渍、涂布、包覆或层压，也不论是否用金属或其他材料加强:	A:1.品名；2.纤维成分；3.厚度
59.11	本章注释七所规定的作专门技术用途的纺织产品及制品:	
	-用橡胶、皮革或其他材料涂布、包覆或层压的作针布用的纺织物、毡呢及毡呢衬里机织物，以及作专门技术用途的类似织物，包括用橡胶浸渍的、用于包覆纺锤(织轴)的狭幅丝绒织物:	A:1.品名；2.用途
5911.2000	-筛布，不论是否制成的	A:1.品名；2.纤维成分含量
	-环状或装有联接装置的纺织物及毡呢，用于造纸机器或类似机器(例如，制浆机或制石棉水泥的机器):	A:1.品名；2.用途；3.是否为环状或有连接装置的纺织物或毡呢；4.每平方米克重
5911.4000	-用于榨油机器或类似机器的滤布，包括人发制滤布	A:1.品名；2.用途
5911.9000	-其他	A:1.品名；2.用途

第六十章　针织物及钩编织物

税则号列	商品名称	申报要素(A:归类要素 B:价格要素 C:审单及其他要素)及说明举例
6001.1000	-“长毛绒”织物	A:1.品名;2.织造方法(针织或钩编);3.起绒方法(毛圈或长毛绒);4.幅宽;5.纤维成分含量
	-毛圈绒头织物:	A:1.品名;2.织造方法(针织或钩编);3.起绒方法(毛圈或长毛绒);4.幅宽;5.纤维成分含量
	-其他:	A:1.品名;2.织造方法(针织或钩编);3.幅宽;4.纤维成分含量
60.02	宽度不超过 30 厘米，按重量计弹性纱线或橡胶线含量在 5%及以上的针织物或钩编织物,但税目 60.01 的货品除外:	A:1.品名;2.织造方法(针织或钩编);3.成分含量;4.幅宽
60.03	宽度不超过 30 厘米的针织物或钩编织物,但税目 60.01 或 60.02 的货品除外:	A:1.品名;2.织造方法(针织或钩编);3.成分含量;4.幅宽
60.04	宽度超过 30 厘米，按重量计弹性纱线或橡胶线含量在 5%及以上的针织物或钩编织物，但税目 60.01 的货品除外:	A:1.品名;2.织造方法(针织或钩编);3.成分含量;4.幅宽
60.05	经编针织物(包括由花边针织机织成的),但税目 60.01 至 60.04 的货品除外:	A:1.品名;2.织造方法(针织、经编);3.染整方法(色织、染色、漂白等);4.成分含量;5.幅宽
60.06	其他针织或钩编织物:	A:1.品名;2.织造方法(针织或钩编);3.染整方法(色织、染色、漂白等);4.成分含量;5.幅宽

第六十一章　针织或钩编的服装及衣着附件

税则号列	商品名称	申报要素(A:归类要素 B:价格要素 C:审单及其他要素)及说明举例
61.01	针织或钩编的男式大衣、短大衣、斗篷、短斗篷、带风帽的防寒短上衣(包括滑雪短上衣)、防风衣、防风短上衣及类似品，但税目 61.03 的货品除外:	A:1.品名;2.织造方法(针织或钩编);3.种类(防风大衣、短大衣、斗篷等);4.类别（男式）;5.成分含量。B:6.品牌
61.02	针织或钩编的女式大衣、短大衣、斗篷、短斗篷、带风帽的防寒短上衣(包括滑雪短上衣)、防风衣、防风短上衣及类似品，但税目 61.04 的货品除外:	A:1.品名;2.织造方法(针织或钩编);3.种类(防风大衣、短大衣、斗篷等);4.类别（女式）;5.成分含量。B:6.品牌
61.03	针织或钩编的男式西服套装、便服套装、上衣、长裤、护胸背带工装裤、马裤及短裤(游泳裤除外):	A:1.品名;2.织造方法(针织或钩编);3.种类(防风大衣、短大衣、斗篷等);4.类别（男式）;5.成分含量。B:6.品牌。例:游泳裤除外(税目 61.12)
61.04	针织或钩编的女式西服套装、便服套装、上衣、连衣裙、裙子、裙裤、长裤、护胸背带工装裤、马裤及短裤(游泳服除外):	A:1.品名;2.织造方法(针织或钩编);3.种类(西服、便服套装、上衣、长裤、马裤、工装裤等);4.类别（女式）;5.成分含量。B:6.品牌。例:游泳服除外(税目 61.12)
61.05	针织或钩编的男衬衫:	A:1.品名;2.织造方法(针织或钩编);3.种类(衬衫);4.类别（男式）;5.成分含量。B:6.品牌。例:包括男童游戏套装衬衫
61.06	针织或钩编的女衬衫:	A:1.品名;2.织造方法(针织或钩编);3.种类(衬衫);4.类别（女式）;5.成分含量。B:6.品牌。例:包括女童游戏套装衬衫
61.07	针织或钩编的男式内裤、三角裤、长睡衣、睡衣裤、浴衣、晨衣及类似品:	A:1.品名;2.织造方法(针织或钩编);3.种类(内衣、内裤等);4.类别（男式）;5.成分含量。B:6.品牌
61.08	针织或钩编的女式长衬裙、衬裙、三角裤、短衬裤、睡衣、睡衣裤、浴衣、晨衣及类似品:	A:1.品名;2.织造方法(针织或钩编);3.种类(内衣、内裤等);4.类别（女式）;5.成分含量。B:6.品牌
61.09	针织或钩编的T恤衫、汗衫及其他内衣背心:	A:1.品名;2.织造方法(针织或钩编);3.种类(T 恤衫、汗衫等);4.类别(男式、女式);5.成分含量。B:6.品牌
61.10	针织或钩编的套头衫、开襟衫、背心及类似品:	A:1.品名;2.织造方法(针织、钩编，是否为起绒);3.种类(套头衫、开襟衫、背心等);4.类别(男式、女式);5.成分含量。B:6.品牌。例:包括“儿童游戏套装”
61.11	针织或钩编的婴儿服装及衣着附件:	A:1.品名;2.织造方法(针织或钩编);3.种类(外衣、雨衣等);4.类别(婴儿);5.成分含量;6.尺寸（衣长及裤长）。B:7.品牌。例:婴儿身长不超过 86 厘米
61.12	针织或钩编的运动服、滑雪服及游泳服:	A:1.品名;2.织造方法(针织或钩编);3.种类(运动套装、运动装、滑雪服、游泳服);4.类别(男式、女式);5.成分含量。B:6.品牌

税则号列	商品名称	申报要素(A:归类要素 B:价格要素 C:审单及其他要素)及说明举例
61.13	用税目 59.03、59.06 或 59.07 的针织物或钩编织物制成的服装:	A: 1. 品名; 2. 织造方法(针织或钩编); 3. 种类(上衣、长裤、短裤等); 4. 类别(男式、女式); 5. 处理材料(塑料、橡胶); 6. 成分含量。B: 7. 品牌
61.14	针织或钩编的其他服装:	A: 1. 品名; 2. 织造方法(针织或钩编); 3. 种类(连身衣、夏服、水洗服、无袖罩衫等); 4. 类别(男式、女式、儿童); 5. 成分含量。B: 6. 品牌
6115.1000	-渐紧压袜类(例如,用以治疗静脉曲张的长统袜)	A: 1. 品名; 2. 织造方法(针织或钩编); 3. 用途。B: 4. 品牌
6115.2100	--每根单丝细度在 67 分特以下的合成纤维制	A: 1. 品名; 2. 织造方法(针织或钩编); 3. 种类(连裤袜、统袜、矫正袜); 4. 成分含量; 5. 单丝细度。B: 6. 品牌
6115.2200	--每根单丝细度在 67 分特及以上的合成纤维制	A: 1. 品名; 2. 织造方法(针织或钩编); 3. 种类(连裤袜、统袜、矫正袜); 4. 成分含量; 5. 单丝细度。B: 6. 品牌
	--其他纺织材料制:	A: 1. 品名; 2. 织造方法(针织或钩编); 3. 种类(连裤袜、统袜、矫正袜); 4. 成分含量。B: 5. 品牌
6115.3000	-女式长统袜及中统袜,每根单丝细度在 67 分特以下	A: 1. 品名; 2. 织造方法(针织或钩编); 3. 种类(连裤袜、统袜、矫正袜); 4. 类别(女式); 5. 是否为女士统袜; 6. 成分含量; 7. 单丝细度。B: 8. 品牌
6115.9400	--羊毛或动物细毛制	A: 1. 品名; 2. 织造方法(针织或钩编); 3. 种类(连裤袜、统袜、矫正袜); 4. 成分含量; 5. 单丝细度。B: 6. 品牌
6115.9500	--棉制	A: 1. 品名; 2. 织造方法(针织或钩编); 3. 种类(连裤袜、统袜、矫正袜); 4. 成分含量; 5. 单丝细度。B: 6. 品牌
6115.9600	--合成纤维制	A: 1. 品名; 2. 织造方法(针织或钩编); 3. 种类(连裤袜、统袜、矫正袜); 4. 类别(男式、女式); 5. 是否为女士统袜; 6. 成分含量; 7. 单丝细度。B: 8. 品牌
6115.9900	--其他纺织材料制	A: 1. 品名; 2. 织造方法(针织或钩编); 3. 种类(连裤袜、统袜、矫正袜); 4. 类别(男式、女式); 5. 是否为女士统袜; 6. 成分含量; 7. 单丝细度。B: 8. 品牌
61.16	针织或钩编的分指手套、连指手套及露指手套:	A: 1. 品名; 2. 织造方法(针织或钩编); 3. 处理材料(塑料、橡胶); 4. 成分含量。B: 5. 品牌
61.17	其他制成的针织或钩编的衣着附件;服装或衣着附件的针织或钩编的零件:	
	-披巾、头巾、围巾、披纱、面纱及类似品:	A: 1. 品名; 2. 织造方法(针织或钩编); 3. 成分含量。B: 4. 品牌
	-其他附件:	A: 1. 品名; 2. 织造方法(针织或钩编); 3. 成分含量。B: 4. 品牌
6117.9000	-零件	A: 1. 品名; 2. 织造方法(针织或钩编); 3. 成分含量

第六十二章 非针织或非钩编的服装及衣着附件

[注解]

1. 本章基本上为非针织非钩编织物,如机织、无纺等,但税目 62.12 与 62.17 除外。

2. 本章"衬衣及仿男式女衬衣"指人体上身穿着并从领口处全开襟或半开襟的长袖或短袖衣服;"罩衫"也是上半身穿的,但可以无袖,领口处也可以不开襟。

税则号列	商品名称	申报要素(A:归类要素 B:价格要素 C:审单及其他要素)及说明举例
62.01	男式大衣、短大衣、斗篷、短斗篷、带风帽的防寒短上衣(包括滑雪短上衣)、防风衣、防风短上衣及类似品,但税目 62.03 的货品除外:	A: 1. 品名; 2. 织造方法(机织等); 3. 种类(防风大衣、短大衣、斗篷等); 4. 类别(男式); 5. 成分含量。B: 6. 品牌
62.02	女式大衣、短大衣、斗篷、短斗篷、带风帽的防寒短上衣(包括滑雪短上衣)、防风衣、防风短上衣及类似品,但税目 62.04 的货品除外:	A: 1. 品名; 2. 织造方法(机织等); 3. 种类(防风大衣、短大衣、斗篷等); 4. 类别(女式); 5. 成分含量。B: 6. 品牌
62.03	男式西服套装、便服套装、上衣、长裤、护胸背带工装裤、马裤及短裤(游泳裤除外):	A: 1. 品名; 2 织造方法(机织等); 3. 种类(西服、便服套装、上衣、长裤、马裤、工装裤等); 4. 类别(男式); 5. 成分含量。B: 6. 品牌。例: 游泳裤除外(税目 62.11)
62.04	女式西服套装、便服套装、上衣、连衣裙、裙子、裙裤、长裤、护胸背带工装裤、马裤及短裤(游泳服除外):	A: 1. 品名; 2. 织造方法(机织等); 3. 种类(西服、便服套装、上衣、长裤、马裤、工装裤等); 4. 类别(女式); 5. 成分含量。B: 6. 品牌。例: 游泳服除外(税目 62.11)
62.05	男衬衫:	A: 1. 品名; 2. 织造方法(机织等); 3. 种类(衬衫); 4. 类别(男式); 5. 成分含量。6. 品牌。例: 包括男童游戏套装衬衫
62.06	女衬衫:	A: 1. 品名; 2. 织造方法(机织等); 3. 种类(衬衫); 4. 类别(女式); 5. 成分含量。B: 6. 品牌。例: 包括女童游戏套装衬衫
62.07	男式背心及其他内衣、内裤、三角裤、长睡衣、睡衣裤、浴衣、晨衣及类似品:	A: 1. 品名; 2. 织造方法(机织等); 3. 种类(内衣、内裤等); 4. 类别(男式); 5. 成分含量。B: 6. 品牌
62.08	女式背心及其他内衣、长衬裙、衬裙、三角裤、短衬裤、睡衣、睡衣裤、浴衣、	A: 1. 品名; 2. 织造方法(机织等); 3. 种类(内衣、内裤等); 4. 类别(女式); 5. 成分含量。B: 6. 品牌

税则号列	商品名称	申报要素(A:归类要素 B:价格要素 C:审单及其他要素)及说明举例
	晨衣及类似品:	
62.09	婴儿服装及衣着附件:	A:1.品名;2.织造方法(机织等);3.种类(外衣、雨衣等);4.类别(婴儿);5.成分含量;6.尺寸(衣长及裤长)。B:7.品牌。例:婴儿身长不超过86厘米
62.10	用税目56.02、56.03、59.03、59.06或59.07的织物制成的服装:	
	-用税目56.02或56.03的织物制成的服装:	A:1.品名;2.织造方法(机织等);3.种类(上衣、长裤、短裤等);4.类别(男式、女士);5.成分含量。B:6.品牌
6210.2000	-子目6201.11至6201.19所列类型的其他服装	A:1.品名;2.织造方法(机织等);3.种类(上衣、长裤、短裤等);4.类别(男式、女式);5.处理材料(塑料、橡胶);6.成分含量。B:7.品牌
6210.3000	-子目6202.11至6202.19所列类型的其他服装	A:1.品名;2.织造方法(机织等);3.种类(上衣、长裤、短裤等);4.类别(男式、女式);5.处理材料(塑料、橡胶);6.成分含量。B:7.品牌
6210.4000	-其他男式服装	A:1.品名;2.织造方法(机织等);3.种类(上衣、长裤、短裤等);4.类别(男式);5.处理材料(塑料、橡胶);6.成分含量。B:7.品牌
6210.5000	-其他女式服装	A:1.品名;2.织造方法(机织等);3.种类(上衣、长裤、短裤等);4.类别(女式);5.处理材料(塑料、橡胶);6.成分含量。B:7.品牌
62.11	运动服、滑雪服及游泳服;其他服装:	A:1.品名;2.织造方法(机织等);3.种类(连身衣、夏服、水洗服、无袖罩衫等);4.类别(男式、女式、儿童);5.成分含量。B:6.品牌
62.12	胸罩、束腰带、紧身胸衣、吊裤带、吊袜带、束袜带和类似品及其零件,不论是否针织或钩编的:	A:1.品名;2.种类(胸罩、腹带、束腰胸衣、吊袜带、吊裤带等);3.成分含量。B:4.品牌。例:不论针织或钩编
62.13	手帕:	A:1.品名;2.织造方法(机织、刺绣、非刺绣);3.成分含量;4.尺寸。B:5.品牌
62.14	披巾、领巾、围巾、披纱、面纱及类似品:	A:1.品名;2.织造方法(机织等);3.成分含量。B:4.品牌
62.15	领带及领结:	A:1.品名;2.织造方法(机织等);3.成分含量。B:4.品牌
62.16	分指手套、连指手套及露指手套:	A:1.品名;2.织造方法(机织等);3.是否浸渍(塑料或橡胶);4.是否为运动手套;5.成分含量。B:6.品牌
62.17	其他制成的衣着附件;服装或衣着附件的零件,但税目62.12的货品除外:	A:1.品名;2.成分含量;3.织造方法。B:4.品牌。例:包括非裁切成形的标签、徽章、纹章、军衔、符号等(裁切制成的归入税目58.07,小块图案刺绣品归入税目58.10)

第六十三章　其他纺织制成品;成套物品;旧衣着及旧纺织品;碎织物

[注解]

税目63.07其他制成品,例如,经某些加工(如缝边、挖领口等) 的针织物片,准备用于制衣,但还未加工成服装。税目63.07还包括服装裁剪样,一般用硬帆布(纸制服装裁样与纸制服装)。此外还包括:服装袋(轻便衣橱)、旗帜(含三角旗及横幅、)、卫生巾(税目56.01的物品除外)以及其他符合第十一类注释七“制成品”定义,但又不归入第十一类其他税目的成段织物制品,例如,门窗用的织物制挡风帘。

税则号列	商品名称	申报要素(A:归类要素 B:价格要素 C:审单及其他要素)及说明举例
63.01	毯子及旅行毯:	A:1.品名;2.种类(毯子、旅行毯、电暖毯);3.成分含量
63.02	床上、餐桌、盥洗及厨房用的织物制品:	A:1.品名;2.用途(床上用品、餐桌用、盥洗用、厨房用);3.织造方法(针织、钩编、机织、手工、刺绣、毛圈等);4.成分含量
63.03	窗帘(包括帷帘)及帐幔;帘帷或床帷:	A:1.品名;2.种类(窗帘、帘帷、帐幔、床帷);3.织造方法(针织、钩编、机织等);4.成分含量
63.04	其他装饰用织物制品,但税目94.04的货品除外:	例:包括蚊帐
	-床罩:	A:1.品名;2.织造方法(针织、钩编、机织、手工、刺绣等);3.成分含量
	-其他:	A:1.品名;2.是否装饰用;3.织造方法(针织、钩编、机织、手工、刺绣等);4.成分含量
63.05	货物包装用袋:	A:1.品名;2.种类(包装袋);3.成分含量
63.06	油苫布、天篷及遮阳篷;帐篷;风帆;野营用品:	A:1.品名;2.种类(油苫布、天篷、遮阳篷、风帆、野营用品);3.成分含量
63.07	其他制成品、包括服装裁剪样:	A:1.品名;2.种类(擦光布、抹布、安全带、救生衣、标签等);3.成分含量
63.08	由机织物及纱线构成的零售包装成套物品,不论是否带附件,用以制作小地毯、装饰毯、绣花台布、餐巾或类似的纺织物品:	A:1.品名;2.是否为零售包装。例:仅指机织物和纱线制
63.09	旧衣物:	A:1.品名;2.是否为旧
63.10	纺织材料的新的或旧的碎织物及废线、绳、索、缆及其制品:	A:1.品名;2.是否经分拣;3.成分含量

第十二类 鞋、帽、伞、杖、鞭及其零件；已加工的羽毛及其制品；人造花；人发制品

第六十四章 鞋靴、护腿和类似品及其零件

税则号列	商品名称	申报要素(A:归类要素 B:价格要素 C:审单及其他要素)及说明举例
64.01	橡胶或塑料制外底及鞋面的防水鞋靴，其鞋面不是用缝、铆、钉、旋、塞或类似方法固定在鞋面上的:	
	-装有金属防护鞋头的鞋靴:	A: 1.品名; 2.款式(高统、装金属护头等); 3.鞋面材料; 4.鞋底材料。B: 5.品牌
	-其他鞋靴:	A: 1.品名; 2.款式(高统等); 3.鞋面材料; 4.鞋底材料。B: 5.品牌
64.02	橡胶或塑料制外底及鞋面的其他鞋靴:	A: 1.品名; 2.款式(高统等); 3.鞋面材料; 4.鞋底材料。B: 5.品牌
64.03	橡胶、塑料、皮革或再生皮革制外底，皮革制鞋面的鞋靴:	
	-运动鞋靴:	A: 1.品名; 2.款式(高统等); 3.鞋面材料; 4.鞋底材料。B: 5.品牌
6403.2000	-皮革制外底，由交叉于脚背并绕大脚趾的皮革条带构成鞋面的鞋	A: 1.品名; 2.款式(高统、装金属护头等); 3.鞋面材料; 4.鞋底材料。B: 5.品牌
6403.4000	-装有金属防护鞋头的其他鞋靴	A: 1.品名; 2.款式(高统、装金属护头等); 3.鞋面材料; 4.鞋底材料。B: 5.品牌
	-皮革制外底的其他鞋靴:	A: 1.品名; 2.款式(是否过踝或过小腿); 3.鞋面材料; 4.鞋底材料; 5.内底长度。B: 6.品牌
	-其他鞋靴:	A: 1.品名; 2.款式(是否过踝或过小腿); 3.鞋面材料; 4.鞋底材料; 5.内底长度。B: 6.品牌
64.04	橡胶、塑料、皮革或再生皮革制外底，用纺织材料制鞋面的鞋靴:	A: 1.品名; 2.款式(高统等); 3.鞋面材料; 4.鞋底材料。B: 5.品牌
64.05	其他鞋靴:	A: 1.品名; 2.款式; 3.鞋面材料; 4.鞋底材料。B: 5.品牌
64.06	鞋靴零件(包括鞋面，不论是否带有除外底以外的其他鞋底); 活动式鞋内底、跟垫及类似品; 护腿、裹腿和类似品及其零件:	A: 1.品名; 2.材质; 3.加工程度(是否已成型)

第六十五章 帽类及其零件

税则号列	商品名称	申报要素(A:归类要素 B:价格要素 C:审单及其他要素)及说明举例
65.01	毡呢制的帽坯、帽身及帽兜，未楦制成形，也未加帽边; 毡呢制的圆帽片及制帽用的毡呢筒(包括裁开的毡呢筒):	A: 1.品名; 2.材质(毡呢)。B: 3.品牌
65.02	编结的帽坯或用任何材料的条带拼制而成的帽坯，未楦制成形，也未加帽边、衬里或装饰物:	A: 1.品名; 2.材质; 3.制作工艺(编结、拼制)。B: 4.品牌
65.04	编结帽或用任何材料的条带拼制而成的帽类，不论有无衬里或装饰物:	A: 1.品名 2.制作工艺(编结、拼制)。B: 3.品牌
6505.0010	---发网	A: 1.品名; 2.成分含量。B: 3.品牌
6505.0020	---钩编的帽类	A: 1.品名; 2.制作工艺(针织、钩编、手工等); 3.成分含量。B: 4.品牌
6505.0091	----用税目65.01的帽身、帽兜或圆帽片制成的毡呢帽类，无论有无衬里或装饰物	A 1.品名; 2.材质(毡呢); 3.成分含量。B: 4.品牌
6505.0099	---其他	A: 1.品名; 2.制作工艺(针织、钩编、手工等); 3.成分含量; 4.材质。B: 5.品牌
65.06	其他帽类，不论有无衬里或装饰物:	A: 1.品名; 2.材质。B: 3.品牌
65.07	帽圈、帽衬、帽套、帽帮、帽骨架、帽舌及帽颏带:	A: 1.品名; 2.材质

第六十六章 雨伞、阳伞、手杖、鞭子、马鞭及其零件

税则号列	商品名称	申报要素(A:归类要素 B:价格要素 C:审单及其他要素)及说明举例
6601.1000	-庭园用伞及类似伞	A: 1.品名; 2.款式
	-其他:	A: 1.品名; 2.款式。B: 3.品牌
66.02	手杖、带座手杖、鞭子、马鞭及类似品:	A: 1.品名; 2.材质
66.03	税目66.01或66.02所列物品的零件及装饰品:	A: 1.品名; 2.材质

第六十七章 已加工羽毛、羽绒及其制品；人造花；人发制品

税则号列	商品名称	申报要素(A:归类要素 B:价格要素 C:审单及其他要素)及说明举例
67.01	带羽毛或羽绒的鸟皮及鸟体其他部分、羽毛、部分羽毛、羽绒及其制品(税目05.05 的货品和经加工的羽管及羽轴除外):	A:1.品名;2.加工程度
67.02	人造花、叶、果实及其零件;用人造花、叶或果实制成的物品:	A:1.品名;2.制作材料(塑料丝等)
67.03	经梳理、稀疏、脱色或其他方法加工的人发;做假发及类似品用的羊毛、其他动物毛或其他纺织材料:	A:1.品名;2.加工程度(经梳理、脱色等);3.制作材料
67.04	人发、动物毛或纺织材料制的假发、假胡须、假眉毛、假睫毛及类似品;其他税目未列名的人发制品:	A:1.品名;2.加工程度(经梳理、脱色等);3.制作材料

第十三类 石料、石膏、水泥、石棉、云母及类似材料的制品；陶瓷产品；玻璃及其制品

第六十八章 石料、石膏、水泥、石棉、云母及类似材料的制品

税则号列	商品名称	申报要素(A:归类要素 B:价格要素 C:审单及其他要素)及说明举例
68.01	天然石料(不包括板岩)制的长方砌石、路缘石、扁平石:	A:1.品名;2.种类(长方砌石、扁平石、路缘石)3.材质
68.02	已加工的碑石或建筑用石(不包括板岩)及其制品,但税目 68.01 的货品除外;天然石料(包括板岩)制的镶嵌石(马赛克)及类似品,不论是否有衬背;天然石料(包括板岩)制的人工染色石粒、石片及石粉:	A:1.品名;2.用途(用于建筑可直接使用);3.材质(大理石、花岗岩);4.加工程度(切、锯、抛光及是否石刻等);5.尺寸(最大表面积的最大边长)
68.03	已加工的板岩及板岩或粘聚板岩的制品:	A:1.品名;2.加工程度;3.材质
6804.1000	-碾磨或磨浆用石磨、石碾	A:1.品名;2.用途(碾磨或磨浆、磨光用等);3.材质(石料、粘聚合成料等);4.是否装支架
	-其他石磨、石碾、砂轮及类似品:	A:1.品名;2.用途(碾磨或磨浆、磨光用等);3.材质(石料、粘聚合成料等);4.是否装支架。B:5.品牌
6804.3010	---琢磨油石	A:1.品名;2.用途(碾磨或磨浆、磨光用等);3.材质(石料、粘聚合成料等);4.是否装支架
6804.3090	---其他	A:1.品名;2.用途(碾磨或磨浆、磨光用等);3.材质(石料、粘聚合成料等);4.是否装支架;5.是否手用磨
68.05	砂布、砂纸及以其他材料为底的类似品,不论是否裁切、缝合或用其他方法加工成形:	A:1.品名; 2.基底材料; 3.砂粒材质; 4.是否涂层(如有,请申报材质)。B:5.品牌; 6.型号; 7.尺寸。例:包括裁剪、缝合加工而成的
68.06	矿渣棉、岩石棉及类似的矿质棉;页状蛭石、膨胀粘土、泡沫矿渣及类似的膨胀矿物材料;具有隔热、隔音或吸音性能的矿物材料的混合物及制品,但税目68.11、68.12 或第六十九章的货品除外:	例:不包括粒状矿渣(税目 26.18)
	-矿渣棉、岩石棉及类似的矿质棉(包括其相互混合物),块状、成片或成卷	A:1.品名;2.材质(矿物纤维等);3.形状;4.含有石棉纤维的要注明其含量
6806.2000	-页状蛭石、膨胀黏土、泡沫矿渣及类似的膨胀矿物材料(包括其相互混合物)	A:1.品名;2.材质(页状蛭石、膨胀粘土、泡沫矿渣等);3.形状;4.含有石棉纤维的要注明其含量
6806.9000	-其他	A:1.品名;2.材质;3.形状;4.含有石棉纤维的要注明其含量
68.07	沥青或类似原料(例如,石油沥青或煤焦油沥青)的制品:	A:1.品名; 2.形状。例:不包括用焦油、沥青等涂布、浸渍或覆盖的纸(税目 48.11)和纺织物(第五十六章或五十九章)、石棉加沥青制品(税目68.11)等

税则号列	商品名称	申报要素(A:归类要素 B:价格要素 C:审单及其他要素)及说明举例
68.08	镶板、平板、瓦、砖及类似品，用水泥、石膏及其他矿物黏合材料黏合植物纤维、稻草、刨花、木片屑、木粉、锯末或木废料制成	A:1.品名;2.种类(镶板、平板瓦、砖等);3.原料(稻草、刨花等);4.粘料(水泥、石膏等矿物性黏合材料)
68.09	石膏制品及以石膏为基本成分的混合材料制品:	A:1.品名;2.加工方法(是否装饰、经贴面或加强等);3.是否未经装饰,仅用纸或纸板贴面或加强的;4.成分含量。例:不包括石膏骨折绷带(税目30.05)和夹板(税目 90.21);专供示范用的模型(税目 90.23);裁缝用人体模型(税目96.18)等
68.10	水泥、混凝土或人造石制品，不论是否加强:	A:1.品名;2.用途(铁道用等);3.种类(砖、瓦、管及建筑构件钢筋混凝土板等);4.材料(水泥、混凝土、人造石)。例:不包括破碎混凝土块
68.11	石棉水泥、纤维素水泥或类似材料的制品:	A:1.品名;2.种类(砖、瓦、管、板等);3.材料(石棉水泥、纤维素水泥等)
68.12	已加工的石棉纤维;以石棉为基本成分或以石棉和碳酸镁为基本成分的混合物;上述混合物或石棉的制品(例如，纱线、机织物、服装、帽类、鞋靴、衬垫)，不论是否加强，但税目 68.11 或 68.13 的货品除外:	A:1.品名;2.种类(纱线、机织物、服装、鞋帽、衬垫等);3.材料(石棉纤维、石棉)
68.13	以石棉、其他矿物质或纤维素为基本成分的未装配摩擦材料及其制品(例如，片、卷、带、盘、圈、垫及扇形)，适于作制动器、离合器及类似品，不论是否与织物或其他材料结合而成:	A:1.品名;2.材质;3.种类(片、卷、带、闸衬、闸垫、扇形等)。例:指未装配的摩擦材料及制品
68.14	已加工的云母及其制品，包括粘聚或复制的云母，不论是否附于纸、纸板或其他材料上:	A:1.品名;2.材质(云母);3.形状(板、片、带等);4.是否粘聚或复制的。例:仅指已加工的云母及制品
68.15	其他税目未列名的石制品及其他矿物制品(包括碳纤维及其制品和泥煤制品):	例:石墨、碳精制品仅指非电器用，电器用应归入税目 85.45
6815.1000	-非电器用的石墨或其他碳精制品	A:1.品名;2.材质;3.用途
6815.2000	-泥煤制品	A:1.品名;2.材质
6815.9100	--含有菱镁矿、白云石或铬铁矿的	A:1.品名;2.材质
6815.9920	---碳纤维	A:1.品名;2.材质
6815.9931	----碳布	A:1.品名;2.材质
6815.9932	----碳纤维预浸料	A:1.品名;2.材质
6815.9939	----其他	A:1.品名;2.材质;3.碳纤维纱线请注明碳含量、比模量和比极限抗拉强度
6815.9940	---玄武岩纤维及其制品	A:1.品名;2.材质
6815.9990	---其他	A:1.品名;2.材质;

第六十九章　陶瓷产品

税则号列	商品名称	申报要素(A:归类要素 B:价格要素 C:审单及其他要素)及说明举例
69.01	硅质化石粉(例如，各种硅藻土)或类似硅土制的砖、块、瓦及其他陶瓷制品:	A:1.品名;2.材质(硅质化石粉、硅藻土或类似硅土等);3.种类(砖、瓦等)
69.02	耐火砖、块、瓦及类似耐火陶瓷建材制品，但硅质化石粉及类似硅土制的除外:	A:1.品名;2.种类(耐火砖、瓦、块等);3.成分含量。B:4.耐火温度。例:本税目指耐火、耐火陶瓷建材制品，不包括硅质化石粉或类似硅土制
69.03	其他耐火陶瓷制品(例如，甑、坩埚、马弗罩、喷管、栓塞、支架、烤钵、管子、护套及棒条)，但硅质化石粉及类似硅土制的除外:	A:1.品名;2.种类(坩埚、支架、马弗罩等);3.成分含量。B:4.耐火温度。例:不包括耐火陶瓷建筑材料制品、硅质化石粉或类似硅土制
69.04	陶瓷制建筑用砖、铺地砖、支撑或填充用砖及类似品:	A:1.品名;2.种类(建筑用砖、地面砖等)。例:本税目指非耐火陶瓷
69.05	屋顶瓦、烟囱罩、通风帽、烟囱衬壁、建筑装饰物及其他建筑用陶瓷制品:	A:1.品名;2.种类(屋顶瓦、烟囱罩等)
69.06	陶瓷套管、导管、槽管及管子附件:	A:1.品名;2.种类(套管、导管、槽管等)
69.07	未上釉的陶瓷贴面砖、铺面砖、包括炉面砖及墙面砖;未上釉的陶瓷镶嵌砖(马赛克)及类似品，不论是否有衬背:	A:1.品名;2.种类(贴面砖、铺面砖、马赛克等);3.尺寸(最大表面积的最大边长)。例:本税目指未上釉的

税则号列	商品名称	申报要素(A:归类要素 B:价格要素 C:审单及其他要素)及说明举例
69.08	上釉的陶瓷贴面砖、铺面砖,包括炉面砖及墙面砖;上釉的陶瓷镶嵌砖(马赛克)及类似品,不论是否有衬背:	A:1.品名;2.种类(贴面砖、铺面砖、马赛克等);3.尺寸(最大表面积的最大边长)。例:本税目指上釉的
69.09	实验室、化学或其他专门技术用途的陶瓷器;农业用陶瓷槽、缸及类似容器;通常供运输及盛装货物用的陶瓷罐、坛及类似品:	A:1.品名;2.用途(实验室用、化学、农业用等);3.种类(瓷制、陶制);4.莫氏硬度
69.10	陶瓷洗涤槽、脸盆、脸盆座、浴缸、坐浴盆、抽水马桶、水箱、小便池及类似的固定卫生设备:	A:1.品名;2.材质(瓷制、陶制)。B:3.品牌;4.规格型号
69.11	瓷餐具、厨房器具及其他家用或盥洗用瓷器:	A:1.品名;2.材质(瓷制、陶制);3.种类(餐具、厨房器具等)。B:4.品牌
69.12	陶餐具、厨房器具及其他家用或盥洗用陶器:	A:1.品名;2.材质(瓷制、陶制);3.种类(餐具、厨房器具等)。B:4.品牌
69.13	塑像及其他装饰用陶瓷制品:	A:1.品名;2.材质(瓷制、陶制);3.用途
69.14	其他陶瓷制品:	A:1.品名;2.材质(瓷制、陶制);3.用途

第七十章　玻璃及其制品

[注解]

1.“品名”是指货品的具体商业名称。

2.“用途”是指货品在出入境后的应用场合或下游产品。

3.“加工方法”是指货品在出入境前的加工工艺或制造方法。

4.“材质”是指货品按《税则》中的材质分类原则所确定的具体材料种类。

5.“形状”是指货品按《税则》中的形状定义描述所确定的外观形状。

税则号列	商品名称	申报要素(A:归类要素 B:价格要素 C:审单及其他要素)及说明举例
70.01	碎玻璃及废玻璃;玻璃块料:	A:1.品名;2.用途;4.状态(废、碎、块料)
7002.1000	-玻璃球	A:1.品名;2.用途;3.直径
7002.2010	---光导纤维预制棒	A:1.品名;2.用途(光导纤维预制棒等)。B:3.光导纤维预制棒请注明规格型号; 4. 品牌
7002.2090	---其他	A:1.品名;2.用途(光导纤维预制棒等)。B:3.光导纤维预制棒请注明规格型号
	--熔融石英或其他熔融硅石制:	A:1.品名;2.用途(光导纤维用、光通信用等);3.材质(熔融石英、熔融硅石等);4.级别(波导级)。B:5.外径
7002.3200	--温度在 0℃至 300℃时线膨胀系数不超过 5×10^{-6}/开尔文的其他玻璃制	A:1.品名;2.用途(光导纤维用、光通信用等);3.材质(熔融石英、熔融硅石等);4.线膨胀系数。B:5.级别(波导级);6.外径
7002.3900	--其他	A:1.品名;2.用途(光导纤维用、光通信用等);3.材质(熔融石英、熔融硅石等);4.线膨胀系数。B:5.级别(波导级);6.外径
7003.1200	--整块着色、不透明、镀色或具有吸收、反射或非反射层的	A:1.品名;2.用途;3.加工方法(整块着色、具有吸收层等);4.状态(是否夹丝);5.形状(板、片、型材、异型材);6.工艺(铸制或轧制)
7003.1900	--其他	A:1.品名;2.用途;3.状态(是否夹丝);4.形状(板、片、型材、异型材);5.工艺(铸制或轧制)
7003.2000	-夹丝玻璃板、片	A:1.品名;2.用途;3.状态(是否夹丝);4.形状(板、片、型材、异型材);5.工艺(铸制或轧制)
7003.3000	-型材及异型材	A:1.品名;2.用途;3.状态(是否夹丝);4.形状(板、片、型材、异型材);5.工艺(铸制或轧制)
7004.2000	-整块着色、不透明、镀色或具有吸收、反射或非反射层的	A:1.品名;2.用途;3.加工方法(整块着色、具有吸收层等);4.状态(是否经过表面加工);5.形状(板、片);6.工艺(拉制或吹制)
7004.9000	-其他玻璃	A:1.品名;2.用途;3.状态(是否经过表面加工);4.形状(板、片);5.工艺(拉制或吹制)
7005.1000	-具有吸收、反射或非反射层的非夹丝玻璃	A:1.品名;2.用途;3.加工方法(具有吸收、反射或非反射层的);4.状态(是否夹丝);5.形状(板、片);6.工艺(浮法、表面研磨、抛光)
7005.2100	--整块着色、不透明、镀色或仅表面研磨的	A:1.品名;2.用途;3.加工方法(整块着色、不透明、镀色等);4.状态(是否夹丝);5.形状(板、片);6.工艺(浮法、表面研磨、抛光)
7005.2900	--其他	A:1.品名;2.用途;3.状态(是否夹丝);4.形状(板、片);5.工艺(浮法、表面研磨、抛光)
7005.3000	-夹丝玻璃	A:1.品名;2.用途;3.状态(是否夹丝);4.形状(板、片);5.工艺(浮法、表面研磨、抛光)

税则号列	商品名称	申报要素(A:归类要素 B:价格要素 C:审单及其他要素)及说明举例
70.06	经弯曲、磨边、镂刻、钻孔、涂珐琅或其他加工的税目 70.03、70.04 或 70.05 的玻璃，但未用其他材料镶框或装配:	A: 1. 品名; 2. 用途; 3. 加工方法(经弯曲、磨边、镂刻、钻孔、涂珐琅等); 4. 状态(未用其他材料镶框或装配); 5. 形状(板、片、型材、异型材)
70.07	钢化或层压玻璃制的安全玻璃:	A: 1. 品名; 2. 用途(车辆、航空器、航天器、船舶); 3. 加工方法(钢化、层压)。B: 4. 品牌
70.08	多层隔温、隔音玻璃组件:	A: 1. 品名; 2. 用途(隔温、隔音); 3. 类型(中空、真空等); 4. 层数。B: 5. 品牌
7009.1000	-车辆后视镜	A: 1. 品名; 2. 用途(车辆后视用等); 3. 加工方法(未经光学加工)
	-其他:	A: 1. 品名; 2. 用途(车辆后视用等); 3. 加工方法(未经光学加工); 4. 是否镶框
70.10	玻璃制的坛、瓶、缸、罐、安瓿及其他容器，用于运输或盛装货物; 玻璃制保藏罐; 玻璃塞、盖及类似的封口器:	A: 1. 品名; 2. 用途(用于运输或盛装货物); 3. 容积
70.11	制灯泡、阴极射线管及类似品用的未封口玻璃外壳(包括玻璃泡及管)及其玻璃零件，但未装有配件:	A: 1. 品名; 2. 用途(制灯泡、阴极射线管等); 3. 加工方法(用荧光物质衬里、未封口、无配件等)
7013.1000	-玻璃陶瓷制	A: 1. 品名; 2. 用途(供餐桌、厨房、盥洗室、办公室、室内装饰用); 3. 材质(玻璃陶瓷、铅晶质玻璃等); 4. 器皿种类(杯等)
	-杯子，但玻璃陶瓷制的除外:	A: 1. 品名; 2. 用途(供餐桌、厨房、盥洗室、办公室、室内装饰用); 3. 材质(玻璃陶瓷、铅晶质玻璃等); 4. 器皿种类(杯等); 5. 型号或生产厂商; 6. 平脚还是高脚杯; 7. 规格。B: 8. 品牌
	-其他杯子，但玻璃陶瓷制的除外:	A: 1. 品名; 2. 用途(供餐桌、厨房、盥洗室、办公室、室内装饰用); 3. 材质(玻璃陶瓷、铅晶质玻璃等); 4. 器皿种类(杯等); 5. 型号或生产厂商; 6. 平脚还是高脚杯; 7. 规格。B: 8. 品牌
	-餐桌或厨房用玻璃器皿(不包括杯子)，但玻璃陶瓷制的除外:	A: 1. 品名; 2. 用途(供餐桌、厨房、盥洗室、办公室、室内装饰用); 3. 材质(玻璃陶瓷、铅晶质玻璃等); 4. 器皿种类(杯等); 5. 线膨胀系数
	-其他玻璃器:	A: 1. 品名; 2. 用途(供餐桌、厨房、盥洗室、办公室、室内装饰用); 3. 材质(玻璃陶瓷、铅晶质玻璃等); 4. 器皿种类(杯等)
7014.0010	---光学仪器用光学元件毛坯	A: 1. 品名; 2. 用途(具体列明用于光学仪器名称); 3. 形状、尺寸及外观; 4. 是否经光学加工。例: 凸透镜玻璃毛坯，用于制作相机镜头的凸透镜，圆形表面为双球面，直径 52 毫米，外观为半透明，未经过光学加工。
7014.0090	---其他	A: 1. 品名; 2. 用途(是否用于光学仪器); 3. 形状、尺寸及外观; 4. 是否经光学加工
7015.1010	---变色镜片坯件	A: 1. 品名; 2. 用途(用于制造眼镜等); 3. 加工方法(未经光学加工); 4. 形状(弧面、弯曲、凹形、扇形等); 5. 元件种类(视力矫正玻璃毛坯等); 6. 特殊功能(变色等)
7015.1090	---其他	A: 1. 品名; 2. 用途(用于制造眼镜等); 3. 加工方法(未经光学加工); 4. 形状(弧面、弯曲、凹形、扇形等); 5. 元件种类(视力矫正玻璃毛坯等)
7015.9010	---钟表玻璃	A: 1. 品名; 2. 用途(用于制造钟表等); 3. 加工方法(未经光学加工); 4. 形状(弧面、弯曲、凹形、扇形等); 5. 元件种类(视力矫正玻璃毛坯等)
7015.9020	---平光变色镜片坯件	A: 1. 品名; 2. 用途(用于制造眼镜等); 3. 加工方法(未经光学加工); 4. 形状(弧面、弯曲、凹形、扇形等); 5. 元件种类(视力矫正玻璃毛坯等); 6. 特殊功能(变色等)
7015.9090	---其他	A: 1. 品名; 2. 用途(用于制造眼镜等); 3. 加工方法(未经光学加工); 4. 形状(弧面、弯曲、凹形、扇形等); 5. 元件种类(视力矫正玻璃毛坯等)
70.16	建筑用压制或模制的铺面用玻璃块、砖、片、瓦及其他制品，不论是否夹丝; 供镶嵌或类似装饰用的玻璃马赛克及其他小件玻璃品，不论是否有衬背; 花饰铅条窗玻璃及类似品; 多孔或泡沫玻璃块、板、片及类似品:	A: 1. 品名; 2. 用途(建筑铺面用); 3. 加工方法(压制、模制等); 4. 制品种类(马赛克、花饰铅条窗玻璃、铺面砖、块、片等)
70.17	实验室、卫生及配药用的玻璃器，不论有无刻度或标量:	A: 1. 品名; 2. 用途(实验室、卫生、配药用); 3. 材质(熔融石英、熔融硅石); 4. 器皿种类(量筒等); 5. 线膨胀系数
70.18	玻璃珠、仿珍珠、仿宝石或仿半宝石和类似小件玻璃品及其制品，但仿首饰除外; 玻璃假眼，但医用假眼除外; 灯工方法制作的玻璃塑像及其他玻璃装饰品，但仿首饰除外; 直径不超过 1 毫米的微型玻璃球:	A: 1. 品名; 2. 用途(装饰用等); 3. 加工方法(灯工方法等); 4. 玻璃球的直径; 5. 材质(钙钠玻璃、铅晶玻璃等)。B: 6. 品牌; 7. 型号
70.19	玻璃纤维(包括玻璃棉)及其制品(例如，玻璃纤维纱线及其织物):	

税则号列	商品名称	申报要素(A:归类要素 B:价格要素 C:审单及其他要素)及说明举例
	-梳条、粗纱、纱线及短切纤维:	A: 1. 品名; 2. 材质(玻璃纤维制); 3. 种类(梳条、粗纱、纱线、短纤); 4. 长度
	-薄片(巴厘纱)、纤维网、席、垫、板及类似无纺产品:	A: 1. 品名; 2. 材质(玻璃纤维制); 3. 种类(席、薄片、纤维网、垫、板等)
7019.4000	-粗纱机织物	A: 1. 品名; 2. 材质(玻璃纤维制); 3. 织造方法(机织); 4. 纱线类型(粗纱)
7019.5100	--宽度不超过30厘米的	A: 1. 品名; 2. 材质(玻璃纤维制); 3. 织造方法(机织); 4. 纱线类型(细纱等); 5. 幅宽
7019.5200	--宽度超过30厘米的长丝平纹织物,每平方米重量不超过250克,单根纱线细度不超过136特克斯	A: 1. 品名; 2. 材质(玻璃纤维制); 3. 织造方法(机织); 4. 纱线类型(细纱等); 5. 幅宽; 6. 每平方米克重; 7. 单纱细度。B: 8. 标称厚度
7019.5900	--其他	A: 1. 品名; 2. 材质(玻璃纤维制); 3. 织造方法(机织); 4. 纱线类型(细纱等); 5. 幅宽; 6. 每平方米克重; 7. 单纱细度
7019.9010	---玻璃棉及其制品	A: 1. 品名; 2. 用途; 3. 材质(玻璃棉制)
7019.9021	----每平方米重量小于450克	A: 1. 品名; 2. 用途; 3. 材质(玻璃纤维布浸胶); 4. 每平方米重量
7019.9029	----其他	A: 1. 品名; 2. 用途; 3. 材质(玻璃纤维布浸胶); 4. 每平方米重量
7019.9090	---其他	A: 1. 品名; 2. 用途; 3. 材质(玻璃纤维制)
7020.0011	----导电玻璃	A: 1. 品名; 2. 用途; 3. 材质(玻璃制)。B: 4. 导电层材质、电阻值
7020.0012	----绝缘子用玻璃伞盘	A: 1. 品名; 2. 用途; 3. 材质(玻璃制)
7020.0013	----熔融石英或其他熔融硅石制	A: 1. 品名; 2. 用途; 3. 材质(熔融石英或其他熔融硅石制)
7020.0019	----其他	A: 1. 品名; 2. 用途; 3. 材质(玻璃制)
	---其他:	A: 1. 品名; 2. 用途; 3. 材质(玻璃制)

第十四类　天然或养殖珍珠、宝石或半宝石、贵金属、包贵金属及其制品；仿首饰；硬币

第七十一章　天然或养殖珍珠、宝石或半宝石、贵金属、包贵金属及其制品；仿首饰；硬币

[注解]

1. “品名”是指货品的具体商业名称。
2. “用途”是指货品在出入境后的应用场合或下游产品。
3. “加工方法”是指货品在出入境前的加工工艺或制造方法。
4. “材质”是指货品按《税则》中的材质分类原则所确定的具体材料种类。
5. “形状”是指货品按《税则》中的形状定义描述所确定的外观形状。

税则号列	商品名称	申报要素(A:归类要素 B:价格要素 C:审单及其他要素)及说明举例
71.01	天然或养殖珍珠,不论是否加工或分级,但未成串或镶嵌;天然或养殖珍珠,为便于运输而暂穿成串:	A: 1. 品名; 2. 种类(黑珍珠等); 3. 加工程度(打孔、未加工等); 4. 状态(未成串、未镶嵌等); 5. 来源(天然、养殖); 6. 等级
71.02	钻石,不论是否加工,但未镶嵌:	A: 1. 品名; 2. 用途; 3. 加工程度(未加工、经简单锯开、劈开、粗磨等); 4. 来源(天然)
7103.1000	-未加工或经简单锯开或粗制成形	A: 1. 品名; 2. 种类(红宝石、蓝宝石、祖母绿、翡翠等); 3. 加工程度(未加工,经简单锯开、粗制成形); 4. 状态(未成串、未镶嵌等); 5. 来源(天然); 6. 等级。B: 7. 矿物学名; 8. 规格; 9. 化学成分; 10. 缅甸公盘成交需申报玉石编号、件数、重量
	-经其他加工:	A: 1. 品名; 2. 种类(红宝石、蓝宝石、祖母绿、翡翠等); 3. 加工程度(未加工,经简单锯开、粗制成形); 4. 状态(未成串、未镶嵌等); 5. 来源(天然); 6. 等级。B: 7. 矿物学名; 8. 规格; 9. 化学成分
71.04	合成或再造的宝石或半宝石,不论是否加工或分级,但未成串或镶嵌的;未分级的合成或再造的宝石或半宝石,为便于运输而暂穿成串:	A: 1. 品名; 2. 用途; 3. 种类(压电石英等); 4. 加工程度(经简单锯开、粗制成形); 5. 状态(未成串、未镶嵌等); 6. 来源(合成、再造)
71.05	天然或合成的宝石或半宝石的粉末:	A: 1. 品名; 2. 种类(压电石英等); 3. 加工程度(经简单锯开、粗制成形); 4. 状态(未成串、未镶嵌等); 5. 来源(合成、再造)
71.06	银(包括镀金、镀铂的银),未锻造、半制成或粉末状:	
	-银粉:	A: 1. 品名; 2. 形状(粉末); 3. 材质(纯银、银合金、镀金、镀铂); 4. 加工程度(未锻造、半制成); 5. 纯度; 6. 平均粒径
	-其他:	A: 1. 品名; 2. 形状(粉末); 3. 材质(纯银、银合金、镀金、镀铂); 4. 加工程度(未锻造、半制成); 5. 纯度

税则号列	商品名称	申报要素(A:归类要素 B:价格要素 C:审单及其他要素)及说明举例
71.07	以贱金属为底的包银材料:	A:1.品名;2.基底材质(铜等)
71.08	金(包括镀铂的金),未锻造、半制成或粉末状:	A:1.品名;2.形状(粉末);3.材质(纯金、金合金、镀铂);4.纯度;5.加工程度(未锻造、半制成);6.货币用请注明用途
71.09	以贱金属或银为底的包金材料:	A:1.品名;2.基底材质(铜、银等)
71.10	铂,未锻造、半制成或粉末状:	A:1.品名;2.形状(粉末); 3.材质(铂、钯、铑、铱、锇、钌); 4.加工程度(未锻造,板、片等)
71.11	以贱金属、银或金为底的包铂材料:	A:1.品名;2.基底材质(铜、银、金等)
71.12	贵金属或包贵金属的废碎料;含有贵金属或贵金属化合物的其他废碎料,主要用于回收贵金属:	A:1.品名;2.状态(废碎料、灰);3.来源(由破碎含有贵金属的电路板而得等);4.贵金属的成分含量
71.13	贵金属或包贵金属制的首饰及其零件:	A:1.品名;2.材质(铂、金、银等);3.加工方法(镶嵌宝石、包金、包银等);4.首饰种类(戒指等)
71.14	贵金属或包贵金属制的金银器及其零件:	A:1.品名;2.种类(餐具等);3.材质(铂、金、银等);4.加工方法(包金、镀金等)
71.15	贵金属或包贵金属的其他制品:	A:1.品名;2.用途(工业用、实验室用等);3.种类(坩埚等);4.形状(格栅形状等);5.材质(铂等)
71.16	用天然或养殖珍珠、宝石或半宝石(天然、合成或再造)制成的物品:	A:1.品名;2.种类(手镯等);3.材质(养殖珍珠、天然珍珠、宝石、半宝石)
71.17	仿首饰:	A:1.品名;2.种类(袖扣、饰扣、手镯等);3.材质;4.加工方法(镀贵金属等)。B:5.品牌
71.18	硬币:	A:1.品名;2.用途(法定货币、非法定货币);3.材质(铜制等)

第十五类　贱金属及其制品

第七十二章　钢铁

[注解]

1.“品名”是指货品的具体商业名称。

2.“用途”是指货品在出入境后的应用场合或下游产品。

3.“加工方法”是指货品在出入境前的加工工艺或制造方法。

4.“材质”是指货品按《税则》中的材质分类原则所确定的具体材料种类。

5.“形状”是指货品按《税则》中的形状定义描述所确定的外观形状。

税则号列	商品名称	申报要素(A:归类要素 B:价格要素 C:审单及其他要素)及说明举例
72.01	生铁及镜铁,锭、块或其他初级形状:	A:1.品名;2.形状(锭、块等);3.材质(生铁、镜铁);4.成分含量(铁、碳、铬、锰、磷、硅的含量)
72.02	铁合金	
	-锰铁:	A:1.品名;2.材质(锰铁、硅铁、铬铁、镍铁等);3.成分含量(铁含量及合金元素的含量);4.碳含量
	-硅铁:	A:1.品名;2.材质(锰铁、硅铁、铬铁、镍铁等);3.成分含量(铁含量及合金元素的含量)
7202.3000	-硅锰铁	A:1.品名;2.材质(锰铁、硅铁、铬铁、镍铁等);3.成分含量(铁含量及合金元素的含量)
	-铬铁:	A:1.品名;2.材质(锰铁、硅铁、铬铁、镍铁等);3.成分含量(铁含量及合金元素的含量)
7202.5000	-硅铬铁	A:1.品名;2.材质(锰铁、硅铁、铬铁、镍铁等);3.成分含量(铁含量及合金元素的含量)
7202.6000	-镍铁	A:1.品名;2.材质(锰铁、硅铁、铬铁、镍铁等);3.成分含量(铁含量及合金元素的含量)
7202.7000	-钼铁	A:1.品名;2.材质(锰铁、硅铁、铬铁、镍铁等);3.成分含量(铁含量及合金元素的含量)
	-钨铁及硅钨铁:	A:1.品名;2.材质(锰铁、硅铁、铬铁、镍铁等);3.成分含量(铁含量及合金元素的含量)
7202.9100	--钛铁及硅钛铁	A:1.品名; 2.材质(锰铁、硅铁、铬铁、镍铁等); 3.成分含量(铁含量及合金元素的含量)
	--钒铁:	A:1.品名; 2.材质(锰铁、硅铁、铬铁、镍铁等); 3.成分含量(铁含量及合金元素的含量)

税则号列	商品名称	申报要素(A:归类要素 B:价格要素 C:审单及其他要素)及说明举例
7202.9300	--铌铁	A:1.品名；2.材质（锰铁、硅铁、铬铁、镍铁等）；3.成分含量(铁含量及合金元素的含量)
	--其他:	A:1.品名；2.材质（锰铁、硅铁、铬铁、镍铁等）；3.成分含量(铁含量及合金元素的含量)。C:4.稀土元素的重量百分比，以[A]表示
72.03	直接从铁矿还原所得的铁产品及其他海绵铁产品，块、团、团粒及类似形状；按重量计纯度在99.94%级以上的铁，块、团、团粒及类似形状:	A:1.品名；2.形状(块、团、团粒等)；3.来源(是直接从铁矿还原所得还是海锦铁产品)；4.成分含量(铁、碳、合金元素、非合金元素的含量)
7204.1000	-铸铁废碎料	A:1.品名；2.用途(供再熔炼钢用)；3.形状(废碎、切割、压缩成包或板、条状等)；4.材质(铸铁、合金钢、不锈钢等)；5.来源(机械加工产生、由破碎何种钢铁制品而得)；6.是否汽车压件、废五金电器
7204.2100	--不锈钢废碎料	A:1.品名；2.用途(供再熔炼钢用)；3.形状(废碎、切割、压缩成包或板、条状等)；4.材质(铸铁、合金钢、不锈钢等)；5.来源(机械加工产生、由破碎何种钢铁制品而得)；6.是否汽车压件、废五金电器。B:7.钢号
7204.3000	-镀锡钢铁废碎料	A:1.品名；2.用途(供再熔炼钢用)；3.形状(废碎、切割、压缩成包或板、条状等)；4.材质(铸铁、合金钢、不锈钢等)；5.来源(机械加工产生、由破碎何种钢铁制品而得)；6.是否汽车压件、废五金电器
7204.4100	--车、刨、铣、磨、锯、锉、剪、冲加工过程中产生的废料，不论是否成捆	A:1.品名；2.用途(供再熔炼钢用)；3.形状(废碎、切割、压缩成包或板、条状等)；4.材质(铸铁、合金钢、不锈钢等)；5.来源(机械加工产生、由破碎何种钢铁制品而得)；6.是否汽车压件、废五金电器
7204.4900	--其他	A:1.品名；2.用途(供再熔炼钢用)；3.形状(废碎、切割、压缩成包或板、条状等)；4.材质(铸铁、合金钢、不锈钢等)；5.来源(机械加工产生、由破碎何种钢铁制品而得)；6.是否汽车压件、废五金电器。C:7. 稀土元素的重量百分比，以[A]表示
7204.5000	-供再熔的碎料钢铁锭	A:1.品名；2.用途(供再熔炼钢用)；3.形状(废碎、切割、压缩成包或板、条状等)；4.材质(铸铁、合金钢、不锈钢等)；5.来源(机械加工产生、由破碎何种钢铁制品而得)；6.是否汽车压件、废五金电器
7205.1000	-颗粒	A:1.品名；2.形状(颗粒、粉末)；3.材质(生铁、镜铁、合金钢等)；4.成分含量(铁、碳、合金元素、非合金元素的含量)；5.粒度。C:6.稀土元素的重量百分比，以[A]表示
7205.2100	--合金钢的	A:1.品名；2.形状(颗粒、粉末)；3.材质(生铁、镜铁、合金钢等)；4.成分含量(铁、碳、合金元素、非合金元素的含量)；5.粒度。C:6.稀土元素的重量百分比，以[A]表示
7205.2900	--其他	A:1.品名；2.形状(颗粒、粉末)；3.材质(生铁、镜铁、合金钢等)；4.成分含量(铁、碳、合金元素、非合金元素的含量)；5.粒度
72.06	铁及非合金钢，锭状或其他初级形状（税目72.03的铁除外）:	A:1.品名；2.形状(方锭、其他初级形状等)；3.材质(铁、非合金钢)；4.成分含量(铁、碳、合金元素、非合金元素的含量)
7207.1100	--矩形(包括正方形)截面，宽度小于厚度的两倍	A:1.品名；2.形状(大方坯、小方坯等)；3.材质(铁、非合金钢)；4.加工方法(初轧、粗锻等)；5.成分含量(铁、碳、合金元素、非合金元素的含量)；6.截面形状(正方形等)；7.截面尺寸
7207.1200	--其他矩形(正方形除外)截面的	A:1.品名；2.形状(大方坯、小方坯等)；3.材质(铁、非合金钢)；4.加工方法(初轧、粗锻等)；5.成分含量(铁、碳、合金元素、非合金元素的含量)；6.截面形状(正方形等)；7.截面尺寸
7207.1900	--其他	A:1.品名；2.形状(大方坯、小方坯等)；3.材质(铁、非合金钢)；4.加工方法(初轧、粗锻等)；5.成分含量(铁、碳、合金元素、非合金元素的含量)；6.截面形状(正方形等)
7207.2000	-按重量计含碳量在0.25%及以上	A:1.品名；2.形状(大方坯、小方坯等)；3.材质(铁、非合金钢)；4.加工方法(初轧、粗锻等)；5.成分含量(铁、碳、合金元素、非合金元素的含量)；6.截面形状(正方形等)
72.08	宽度在600毫米及以上的铁或非合金钢平板轧材，经热轧，但未经包覆、镀层或涂层:	A:1.品名；2.形状(平板、卷板)；3.材质(铁、非合金钢)；4.加工方法(热轧等)；5.加工程度(酸洗、轧有花纹、未包覆、未镀层、未涂层等)；6.成分含量(铁、碳、合金元素、非合金元素的含量)；7.规格(板材的厚度、宽度)；8.技术参数(屈服强度)。B:9.钢号
72.09	宽度在600毫米及以上的铁或非合金钢平板轧材，经冷轧，但未经包覆、镀层或涂层:	A:1.品名；2.形状(平板、卷板)；3.材质(铁、非合金钢)；4.加工方法(冷轧)；5.加工程度(未包覆、未镀层、未涂层等)；6.成分含量(铁、碳、合金元素、非合金元素的含量)；7.规格(板材的厚度、宽度)；8.技术参数(屈服强度)。B:9.钢号
72.10	宽度在600毫米及以上的铁或非合金钢平板轧材，经包覆、镀层或涂层:	A:1.品名；2.形状(平板、卷板)；3.材质(铁、非合金钢)；4.加工方法(经包覆、经镀层、经涂层)；5.成分含量(铁、碳、合金元素、非合金元素的含量)；6.规格(板材的厚度、宽度)；7.涂层种类(锡、铅、电镀锌、涂锌

税则号列	商品名称	申报要素(A:归类要素 B:价格要素 C:审单及其他要素)及说明举例
		等);8.涂层厚度(0.5毫米等)。B:9.钢号
72.11	宽度小于600毫米的铁或非合金钢平板轧材,但未经包覆、镀层或涂层:	A:1.品名;2.形状(平板、卷板);3.材质(铁、非合金钢);4.加工方法(热轧、冷轧、未包覆、未镀层、未涂层等);5.成分含量(铁、碳、合金元素、非合金元素的含量);6.规格(板材的厚度、宽度)。B:7.钢号
72.12	宽度小于600毫米的铁或非合金钢平板轧材,经包覆、镀层或涂层:	A:1.品名;2.形状(平板、卷板);3.材质(铁、非合金钢);4.加工方法(热轧、冷轧、经包覆、经镀层、经涂层);5.成分含量(铁、碳、合金元素、非合金元素的含量);6.规格(板材的厚度、宽度);7.涂层种类(锡、铅、电镀锌、涂锌等)
7213.1000	-带有轧制过程中产生的凹痕、凸缘、槽沟及其他变形的	A:1.品名;2.形状(条、杆);3.材质(铁、非合金钢);4.加工方法(热轧);5.状态(不规则盘卷、带有凹痕、凸缘等);6.成分含量(合金元素、非合金元素的含量);7.规格(条、杆的直径)
7213.2000	-其他,易切削钢制	A:1.品名;2.形状(条、杆);3.材质(易切削钢);4.加工方法(热轧);5.状态(不规则盘卷、不带有凹痕、凸缘等);6.成分含量(合金元素、非合金元素的含量);7.规格(条、杆的直径)
	-其他:	A:1.品名;2.形状(条、杆);3.材质(铁、非合金钢);4.加工方法(热轧);5.状态(不规则盘卷);6.成分含量(合金元素、非合金元素的含量);7.截面形状;8.规格(圆形截面需报条、杆的直径)
7214.1000	-锻造的	A:1.品名;2.形状(条、杆);3.材质(铁、非合金钢);4.加工方法(锻造);5.成分含量(合金元素、非合金元素的含量);6.规格(条、杆的直径);7.截面形状(圆形、矩形、正方形等)
7214.2000	-带有轧制过程中产生的凹痕、凸缘、槽沟或其他变形以及轧制后扭曲的	A:1.品名;2.形状(条、杆);3.材质(铁、非合金钢);4.加工方法(热轧、热拉拔、热挤压);5.状态(带有轧制产生的变形或轧制后扭曲的);6.成分含量(合金元素、非合金元素的含量);7.规格(条、杆的直径);8.截面形状(正方形等)。B:9.钢号
7214.3000	-其他,易切削钢制	A:1.品名;2.形状(条、杆);3.材质(易切削钢);4.加工方法(热轧、热拉拔、热挤压);5.成分含量(合金元素、非合金元素的含量);6.状态(不带有轧制产生的变形或轧制后扭曲的);7.规格(条、杆的直径);8.截面形状(正方形等)
	-其他:	A:1.品名;2.形状(条、杆);3.材质(铁、非合金钢);4.加工方法(热轧、热拉拔、热挤压);5.成分含量(合金元素、非合金元素的含量);6.状态(不带有轧制产生的变形或轧制后扭曲的);7.规格(条、杆的直径);8.截面形状(正方形等)
72.15	铁及非合金钢的其他条、杆:	A:1.品名;2.形状(条、杆);3.材质(铁、非合金钢);4.加工方法(热加工、冷加工);5.加工程度;6.成分含量(铁、碳、合金元素、非合金元素的含量);7.规格(条、杆的直径);8.易切削钢请注明
72.16	铁或非合金钢的角材、型材及异型材:	A:1.品名;2.形状(槽钢、角钢、工字钢、H形钢等);3.材质(铁、非合金钢);4.加工方法(热轧、热拉拔、热挤压、冷加工、平板轧材冷弯成形);5.加工程度(例如,打孔、冲孔、扭绞、涂层等);6.成分含量(合金元素、非合金元素的含量);7.规格(型材的截面高度)
72.17	铁丝或非合金钢丝:	A:1.品名;2.形状(丝);3.材质(铁、非合金钢);4.加工方法(镀层、涂层);5.成分含量(铁、碳、合金元素、非合金元素的含量);6.涂层种类(锌、铜等);7.直径;8.状态(盘卷等)
72.18	不锈钢,锭状或其他初级形状;不锈钢半制成品:	A:1.品名;2.形状(方锭等);3.材质(不锈钢);4.截面形状(正方形等)。B:5.钢号
72.19	不锈钢平板轧材,宽度在600毫米及以上:	A:1.品名;2.形状(卷板、平板等);3.材质(不锈钢);4.加工方法(热轧、冷轧);5.加工程度;6.成分含量;7.规格(板材的厚度、宽度)。B:8.钢号
72.20	不锈钢平板轧材,宽度小于600毫米:	A:1.品名;2.形状(卷板、平板等);3.材质(不锈钢);4.加工方法(热轧、冷轧);5.加工程度;6.成分含量(铁、碳、铬及合金元素、非合金元素的含量);7.规格(板材的厚度、宽度)。B:8.钢号
72.21	不规则盘卷的不锈钢热轧条、杆:	A:1.品名;2.形状(条、杆);3.材质(不锈钢);4.加工方法(热轧);5.状态(不规则盘卷);6.成分含量(铁、碳、铬及合金元素、非合金元素的含量)。B:7.钢号;8.直径
72.22	不锈钢其他条、杆;不锈钢角材、型材及异型材:	A:1.品名;2.形状(条、杆、角材、型材、异型材);3.材质(不锈钢);4.加工方法(热轧、热拉拔、热挤压、冷成形、冷加工);5.成分含量(铁、碳、铬及合金元素、非合金元素的含量);6.截面形状(圆形、方形等)。B:7.钢号
72.23	不锈钢丝:	A:1.品名;2.形状(丝);3.材质(不锈钢);4.加工方法(镀层、涂层);5.成分含量(铁、碳、铬及合金元素、非合金元素的含量)。B:6.直径;7.钢号

税则号列	商品名称	申报要素(A:归类要素 B:价格要素 C:审单及其他要素)及说明举例
7224.1000	-锭状及其他初级形状	A: 1. 品名; 2. 形状(方锭等); 3. 材质(硅锰钢等); 4. 成分含量(铁、碳及合金元素、非合金元素的含量)。B: 5. 钢号
	-其他:	A: 1. 品名; 2. 形状(方锭等); 3. 材质(硅锰钢等); 4. 成分含量(铁、碳及合金元素、非合金元素的含量); 5. 粗铸锻件坯请注明单件重量。B: 6. 钢号
72.25	其他合金钢平板轧材, 宽度在600毫米及以上:	
	-硅电钢制:	A: 1. 品名; 2. 形状(平板、卷材); 3. 材质(硅电钢、高速钢等, 取向性硅电钢请注明); 4. 加工方法(热轧、冷轧、镀层、涂层); 5. 成分含量(铁、碳、合金元素、非合金元素的含量); 6. 规格(板材的厚度、宽度)。B: 7. 钢号
7225.3000	-其他卷材, 除热轧外未经进一步加工	A: 1. 品名; 2. 形状(平板、卷材); 3. 材质(硅电钢、高速钢等, 取向性硅电钢请注明); 4. 加工方法(热轧、冷轧、镀层、涂层); 5. 成分含量(铁、碳、合金元素、非合金元素的含量); 6. 规格(板材的厚度、宽度)。B: 7. 钢号
7225.4000	-其他非卷材, 除热轧外未经进一步加工	A: 1. 品名; 2. 形状(平板、卷材); 3. 材质(硅电钢、高速钢等, 取向性硅电钢请注明); 4. 加工方法(热轧、冷轧、镀层、涂层); 5. 成分含量(铁、碳、合金元素、非合金元素的含量); 6. 规格(板材的厚度、宽度)。B: 7. 钢号
7225.5000	-其他, 除冷轧外未经进一步加工	A: 1. 品名; 2. 形状(平板、卷材); 3. 材质(硅电钢、高速钢等, 取向性硅电钢请注明); 4. 加工方法(热轧、冷轧、镀层、涂层); 5. 成分含量(铁、碳、合金元素、非合金元素的含量); 6. 规格(板材的厚度、宽度)。B: 7. 钢号
	-其他:	A: 1. 品名; 2. 形状(平板、卷材); 3. 材质(硅电钢、高速钢等, 取向性硅电钢请注明); 4. 加工方法(热轧、冷轧、镀层、涂层); 5. 成分含量(铁、碳、合金元素、非合金元素的含量); 6. 规格(板材的厚度、宽度); 7. 涂层种类(电镀锌、涂锌等) 。B: 8. 钢号
72.26	其他合金钢平板轧材, 宽度小于600毫米:	
	-硅电钢制:	A: 1. 品名; 2. 形状(平板、卷材); 3. 材质(硅电钢、高速钢等, 取向性硅电钢请注明); 4. 加工方法(热轧、冷轧、镀层、涂层); 5. 成分含量(铁、碳、合金元素、非合金元素的含量); 6. 规格(板材的厚度、宽度) 。B: 7. 钢号
7226.2000	-高速钢制	A: 1. 品名; 2. 形状(平板、卷材); 3. 材质(硅电钢、高速钢等, 取向性硅电钢请注明); 4. 加工方法(热轧、冷轧、镀层、涂层); 5. 成分含量(铁、碳、合金元素、非合金元素的含量); 6. 规格(板材的厚度、宽度) 。B: 7. 钢号
	-其他:	A: 1. 品名; 2. 形状(平板、卷材); 3. 材质(硅电钢、高速钢等, 取向性硅电钢请注明); 4. 加工方法(热轧、冷轧、镀层、涂层); 5. 成分含量(铁、碳、合金元素、非合金元素的含量); 6. 规格(板材的厚度、宽度); 7. 涂层种类(电镀锌、涂锌等)。B: 8. 钢号
72.27	不规则盘卷的其他合金钢热轧条、杆:	A: 1. 品名; 2. 形状(条、杆); 3. 材质(高速钢、硅锰钢等); 4. 加工方法(热轧); 5. 状态(不规则盘卷); 6. 成分含量(铁、碳、合金元素、非合金元素的含量)。B: 7. 钢号
7228.1000	-高速钢条、杆	A: 1. 品名; 2. 用途(适用场所或下游产品); 3. 形状(条、杆、角材、型材、异型材); 4. 材质(高速钢、硅锰钢等); 5. 加工方法(热轧、热拉拔、热挤压、冷成形、冷加工); 6. 成分含量(铁、碳、合金元素、非合金元素的含量)。B: 7. 钢号
7228.2000	-硅锰钢条、杆	A: 1. 品名; 2. 用途(适用场所或下游产品); 3. 形状(条、杆、角材、型材、异型材); 4. 材质(高速钢、硅锰钢等); 5. 加工方法(热轧、热拉拔、热挤压、冷成形、冷加工); 6. 成分含量(铁、碳、合金元素、非合金元素的含量)。B: 7. 钢号
	-其他条、杆, 除热轧、热拉拔或热挤压外未经进一步加工	A: 1. 品名; 2. 用途(适用场所或下游产品); 3. 形状(条、杆、角材、型材、异型材); 4. 材质(高速钢、硅锰钢等); 5. 加工方法(热轧、热拉拔、热挤压、冷成形、冷加工); 6. 成分含量(铁、碳、合金元素、非合金元素的含量)。B: 7. 钢号
7228.4000	-其他条、杆, 除锻造外未经进一步加工	A: 1. 品名; 2. 用途(适用场所或下游产品); 3. 形状(条、杆、角材、型材、异型材); 4. 材质(高速钢、硅锰钢等); 5. 加工方法(热轧、热拉拔、热挤压、冷成形、冷加工); 6. 成分含量(铁、碳、合金元素、非合金元素的含量)。B: 7. 钢号
7228.5000	-其他条、杆, 除冷成形或冷加工外未经进一步加工	A: 1. 品名; 2. 用途(适用场所或下游产品); 3. 形状(条、杆、角材、型材、异型材); 4. 材质(高速钢、硅锰钢等); 5. 加工方法(热轧、热拉拔、热挤压、冷成形、冷加工); 6. 成分含量(铁、碳、合金元素、非合金元素的含量)。B: 7. 钢号
7228.6000	-其他条、杆	A: 1. 品名; 2. 用途(适用场所或下游产品); 3. 形状(条、杆、角材、型材、异型材); 4. 材质(高速钢、硅锰钢等); 5. 加工方法(热轧、热拉拔、热挤压、冷成形、冷加工); 6. 成分含量(铁、碳、合金元素、非合金元素的含量)。B: 7. 钢号
7228.7010	---履带板型钢	A: 1. 品名; 2. 用途(适用场所或下游产品); 3. 形状(条、杆、角材、型材、异型材); 4. 材质(高速钢、硅锰钢等); 5. 加工方法(热轧、热拉拔、热挤压、冷成形、冷加工); 6. 成分含量(铁、碳、合金元素、非合金元素的含量); 7. 空心钻钢需额外申报最大外形尺寸和最大内孔尺寸。B: 8. 钢号
7228.7090	---其他	A: 1. 品名; 2. 用途(适用场所或下游产品); 3. 形状(条、杆、角材、型材、异型材); 4. 材质(高速钢、硅锰钢等); 5. 加工方法(热轧、热拉拔、热挤压、冷

税则号列	商品名称	申报要素(A:归类要素 B:价格要素 C:审单及其他要素)及说明举例
		成形、冷加工);6.成分含量(铁、碳、合金元素、非合金元素的含量)。B:7.钢号
7228.8000	-空心钻钢	A:1.品名;2.用途(适用场所或下游产品);3.形状(条、杆、角材、型材、异型材);4.材质(高速钢、硅锰钢等);5.加工方法(热轧、热拉拔、热挤压、冷成形、冷加工);6.成分含量(铁、碳、合金元素、非合金元素的含量);7.空心钻钢需额外申报最大外形尺寸和最大内孔尺寸。B:8.钢号
72.29	其他合金钢丝:	A:1.品名;2.形状(丝);3.材质(高速钢、硅锰钢等);4.加工方法(镀层、涂层);5.成分含量(铁、碳、合金元素、非合金元素的含量);6.用途。B:7.钢号

第七十三章　钢铁制品

[注解]

1．"品名"是指货品的具体商业名称。

2．"用途"是指货品在出入境后的应用场合或下游产品。

3．"加工方法"是指货品在出入境前的加工工艺或制造方法。

4．"材质"是指货品按《税则》中的材质分类原则所确定的具体材料种类。

5．"形状"是指货品按《税则》中的形状定义描述所确定的外观形状。

税则号列	商品名称	申报要素(A:归类要素 B:价格要素 C:审单及其他要素)及说明举例
73.01	钢铁板桩,不论是否钻孔、打眼或组装;焊接的钢铁角材、型材及异型材:	A:1.品名;2.形状(板桩、焊接的角材、型材、异型材);3.材质(铁、非合金钢、不锈钢、合金钢)。B:4.加工方法(冷轧、热轧等);5.规格(截面尺寸)
73.02	铁道及电车道铺轨用钢铁材料(钢轨、护轨、齿轨、道岔尖轨、辙叉、尖轨拉杆及其他岔道段体、轨枕、鱼尾板、轨座、轨座楔、钢轨垫板、钢轨夹、底板、固定板及其他专门用于连接或加固路轨的材料):	A:1.品名;2.用途(铁道及电车道铺轨用等);3.材质(铁、非合金钢、不锈钢、合金钢);4.制品种类(钢轨、轨枕、岔道段体等)
73.03	铸铁管及空心异型材:	A:1.品名;2.规格(管的内径);3.形状(圆形截面管、空心异型材);4.材质(铸铁)
73.04	无缝钢铁管及空心异型材(铸铁的除外):	A:1.品名;2.规格(管的外径);3.用途(锅炉用、石油或天然气钻探用等);4.形状(管、空心异型材);5.材质(铁、非合金钢、不锈钢、合金钢);6.加工方法(冷拔、冷轧、热扎等);7.种类(无缝管)
73.05	其他圆形截面钢铁管(例如,焊、铆及用类似方法接合的管),外径超过406.4毫米:	A:1.品名;2.规格(管的外径);3.用途(石油或天然气管道用等);4.材质(铁、非合金钢、不锈钢、合金钢);5.种类(焊接管);6.加工方法(铆、纵向焊、埋弧焊);7.截面形状(圆形)
73.06	其他钢铁管及空心异型材(例如,辊缝、焊、铆及类似方法接合的):	A:1.品名;2.规格(圆管的外径、壁厚);3.用途(石油或天然气管道用);4.材质(铁、非合金钢、不锈钢、合金钢);5.种类(焊接管);6.加工方法(铆、纵向焊、埋弧焊);7.截面形状(圆形、方形或椭圆形等)
73.07	钢铁管子附件(例如,接头、肘管、管套):	A:1.品名;2.用途(用于管子之间连通);3.材质(铁、非合金钢、不锈钢、合金钢);4.种类(法兰、管套、十字接头、对焊件等);5.加工方法(铸造、锻造等)
73.08	钢铁结构体(税目94.06的活动房屋除外)及其部件(例如,桥梁及桥梁体段、闸门、塔楼、格构杆、屋顶、屋顶框架、门窗及其框架、门槛、百叶窗、栏杆、支柱及立柱);上述结构体用的已加工钢铁板、杆、角材、型材、异型材、管子及类似品:	A:1.品名;2.用途(支撑用等);3.材质(钢铁);4.种类(门窗、立柱、塔楼、脚手架、桥梁体段等)
73.09	盛装物料用的钢铁囤、柜、罐、桶及类似容器(装压缩气体或液化气体的除外),容积超过300升,不论是否衬里或隔热,但无机械或热力装置:	A:1.品名;2.用途(盛装液体用等);3.材质(钢铁);4.种类(罐、桶等);5.规格(容积);6.是否装有机械或热力装置
73.10	盛装物料用的钢铁柜、桶、罐、听、盒及类似容器(装压缩气体或液化气体的除外),容积不超过300升,不论是否衬里或隔热,但无机械或热力装置:	A:1.品名;2.用途(盛装液体用等);3.材质(钢铁);4.种类(罐、桶等);5.加工方法(焊边接合、卷边接合等);6.规格(容积);7.是否装有机械或热力装置
73.11	装压缩气体或液化气体用的钢铁容器:	A:1.品名;2.用途(压缩气体或液化气体用、零售包装用等);3.材质(钢铁);4.种类(罐、桶等)
73.12	非绝缘的钢铁绞股线、绳、缆、编带、吊索及类似品:	A:1.品名;2.材质(钢铁);3.制品种类(绞股线、吊索、绳等);4.注明"非绝缘"。

税则号列	商品名称	申报要素(A:归类要素 B:价格要素 C:审单及其他要素)及说明举例
73.13	带刺钢铁丝;围篱用的钢铁绞带或单股扁丝(不论是否带刺)及松绞的双股丝:	A:1.品名;2.用途(围篱用);3.材质(钢铁);4.种类(带刺钢铁丝、绞带、单股扁丝、松绞的双股丝);5.截面尺寸
73.14	钢铁丝制的布(包括环形带)、网、篱、格栅;网眼钢铁板:	A:1.品名;2.用途(工业用等);3.材质(铁、非合金钢、不锈钢、合金钢);4.种类(网、篱、格栅等);5.加工方法(镀锌、涂锌、涂塑等);6.规格(网眼尺寸、丝的截面尺寸)
73.15	钢铁链及其零件:	A:1.品名;2.用途(自行车用、摩托车用等);3.材质(钢铁);4.种类(铰接链、滚子链、日字环节链等)
73.16	钢铁锚、多爪锚及其零件:	A:1.品名;2.材质(钢铁);3.种类(钢铁锚、多爪锚等)
73.17	钢铁制的钉、平头钉、图钉、波纹钉、U形钉(税目 83.05 的货品除外)及类似品,不论钉头是否用其他材料制成,但不包括铜头钉:	A:1.品名;2.材质(钢铁);3.种类(图钉、U形钉、平头钉、波纹钉等)。例:铜头的钉归入税目 74.15
7318.1100	--方头螺钉	A:1.品名;2.材质(钢铁);3. 螺钉种类(方头);B:4.品牌; 5.规格型号
7318.1200	--其他木螺钉	A:1.品名;2.材质(钢铁)。B:3.品牌; 4.规格型号
7318.1300	--钩头螺钉及环头螺钉	A:1.品名;2.材质(钢铁)。B:3.品牌; 4.规格型号
7318.1400	--自攻螺钉	A:1.品名;2.材质(钢铁);3.螺钉种类(钩头、环头) B:4.品牌; 5.规格型号
7318.1510	---抗拉强度在800兆帕及以上的	A:1.品名;2.材质(钢铁);3.种类(螺钉、螺母、垫圈、铆钉、销等);4.抗拉强度。B:5.品牌; 6.规格型号
7318.1590	---其他	A:1.品名;2.材质(钢铁);3.种类(螺钉、螺母、垫圈、铆钉、销等);4.抗拉强度。B:5.品牌; 6.规格型号
7318.1600	--螺母	A:1.品名;2.材质(钢铁)。B:3.品牌; 4.规格型号
7318.1900	--其他	A:1.品名;2.材质(钢铁);3.种类(螺钉、螺母、垫圈、铆钉、销等);4.螺钉请注明种类(方头、钩头、环头等)。B:5.品牌; 6.规格型号
	-无螺纹制品:	A:1.品名;2.材质(钢铁)。B:3.品牌; 4.规格型号
73.19	钢铁制手工缝针、编织针、引针、钩针、刺绣穿孔锥及类似制品;其他税目未列名的钢铁制安全别针及其他别针:	A:1.品名;2.材质(钢铁);3.种类(缝针、织补针、刺绣针、别针等)
73.20	钢铁制弹簧及弹簧片:	A:1.品名;2.用途(汽车用、铁道车辆用等);3.材质(钢铁);4.种类(片簧、螺旋弹簧等)
73.21	非电热的钢铁制家用炉、灶(包括附有集中供暖用的热水锅的炉)、烤肉架、烤炉、煤气灶、加热板和类似非电热的家用器具及其零件:	A:1.品名;2.材质(钢铁);3.种类(煤油炉、煤气灶、烤肉架、烤炉等);4.原理(非电热);5.燃料种类(液体、固体、气体燃料)。B:6.品牌; 7.型号
73.22	非电热的钢铁制集中供暖用散热器及其零件;非电热的钢铁制空气加热器、暖气分布器(包括可分布新鲜空气或调节空气的)及其零件,装有电动风扇或鼓风机:	A:1.品名;2.用途(集中供暖用等);3.材质(钢铁);4.种类(散热器、空气加热器、暖气分布器等);5.原理(非电热);6.是否装有电动风扇或鼓风机
73.23	餐桌、厨房或其他家用钢铁器具及其零件;钢铁丝绒;钢铁制擦锅器、洗刷擦光用的块垫、手套及类似品:	A:1.品名;2.用途(厨房用、餐桌用等);3.材质(铁、非合金钢、不锈钢、合金钢);4.种类(水壶、煎锅等);5.加工方法(已搪瓷、未搪瓷)。B:6.品牌
73.24	钢铁制卫生器具及其零件:	A:1.品名;2.用途(卫生间用等);3.材质(铁、非合金钢、不锈钢、合金钢);4.种类(脸盆、浴缸等);5.加工方法(已搪瓷、未搪瓷)。B:6.品牌
73.25	其他钢铁铸造制品:	A:1.品名;2.用途(工业用、非工业用、研磨机用等);3.材质(无可锻性铸铁等);4.种类(井盖、研磨球等)
73.26	其他钢铁制品:	A:1.品名;2.用途(工业用、非工业用);3.材质(钢铁);4.种类(捕鼠器、香烟盒等);5.加工方法(锻造、冲压等)

第七十四章　铜及其制品

[注解]

1."品名"是指货品的具体商业名称。

2."用途"是指货品在出入境后的应用场合或下游产品。

3."加工方法"是指货品在出入境前的加工工艺或制造方法。

4."材质"是指货品按《税则》中的材质分类原则所确定的具体材料种类。

5."形状"是指货品按《税则》中的形状定义描述所确定的外观形状。

税则号列	商品名称	申报要素(A:归类要素 B:价格要素 C:审单及其他要素)及说明举例
74.01	铜锍;沉积铜(泥铜):	A:1.品名;2.材质(铜锍、沉积铜);3.来源;4.成分含量(铜化合物的含量)。

税则号列	商品名称	申报要素(A:归类要素 B:价格要素 C:审单及其他要素)及说明举例
		例:铜锍颗粒(熔炼硫化铜矿而得),含硫化铜40%、硫化铁30%
74.02	未精炼铜;电解精炼用的铜阳极:	A:1.品名;2.成分含量(铜的含量及黄金含量);3.形状(块状、粉末等);4.材质(未精炼铜);5.用途(电解精炼用等)
74.03	未锻轧的精炼铜及铜合金:	例:未锻轧精炼铜锭,含铜99.9%
	--阴极及阴极型材:	A:1.品名;2.形状(型材、线锭、坯段等);3.材质(精炼铜、黄铜、青铜、白铜等);4.加工方法(未锻轧等);5.成分含量(铜及合金元素的含量)。B:6.定价日期; 7.签约日期; 8.定价方式
7403.1200	--线锭	A:1.品名;2.形状(型材、线锭、坯段等);3.材质(精炼铜、黄铜、青铜、白铜等);4.加工方法(未锻轧等);5.成分含量(铜及合金元素的含量)
7403.1300	--坯段	A:1.品名;2.形状(型材、线锭、坯段等);3.材质(精炼铜、黄铜、青铜、白铜等);4.加工方法(未锻轧等);5.成分含量(铜及合金元素的含量)
7403.1900	--其他	A:1.品名;2.形状(型材、线锭、坯段等);3.材质(精炼铜、黄铜、青铜、白铜等);4.加工方法(未锻轧等);5.成分含量(铜及合金元素的含量)
	-铜合金:	A:1.品名;2.形状(型材、线锭、坯段等);3.材质(精炼铜、黄铜、青铜、白铜等);4.加工方法(未锻轧等);5.成分含量(铜及合金元素的含量)
74.04	铜废碎料:	A:1.品名;2.用途(供回收铜用);3.材质(铜);4.状态(废、碎、管、板、线、棒、边角料等);5.来源(废的电机、电线、电缆、五金等);6.成分含量(回收金属的含量)。B:7.包装形式
74.05	铜母合金:	A:1.品名;2.用途(用作炼铜的添加剂);3.形状(粒状等);4.材质(铜母合金);5.成分含量(铜、磷的含量)。例:铬铜粉(用作炼铜的添加剂),含铜40%,不含磷
74.06	铜粉及片状粉末:	A:1.品名;2.用途(用作电镀基底、金属颜料等);3.形状(片状粉末、非片状粉末);4.材质(精炼铜、黄铜、青铜、白铜等);5.成分含量(铜及合金元素的含量);6.粒度。例:非片状精炼铜粉(用作电镀基料),含铜99.9%
74.07	铜条、杆、型材及异型材:	例:精炼铜杆,含铜99.9%
	-精炼铜制:	A:1.品名;2.形状(条、杆、型材、异型材);3.材质(精炼铜、黄铜、青铜、白铜等);4.成分含量(铜及合金元素的含量)
7407.2111	----直线度不大于0.5毫米/米	A:1.品名;2.形状(条、杆、型材、异型材);3.材质(精炼铜、黄铜、青铜、白铜等);4.成分含量(铜及合金元素的含量); 5.直线度
7407.2119	----其他	A:1.品名;2.形状(条、杆、型材、异型材);3.材质(精炼铜、黄铜、青铜、白铜等);4.成分含量(铜及合金元素的含量)
7407.2190	---其他	A:1.品名;2.形状(条、杆、型材、异型材);3.材质(精炼铜、黄铜、青铜、白铜等);4.成分含量(铜及合金元素的含量)
7407.2900	--其他	A:1.品名;2.形状(条、杆、型材、异型材);3.材质(精炼铜、黄铜、青铜、白铜等);4.成分含量(铜及合金元素的含量)
74.08	铜丝:	A:1.品名;2.形状(丝);3.材质(精炼铜、黄铜、青铜、白铜等);4.成分含量(铜及合金元素的含量);5.规格(丝的最大截面尺寸)。例:精炼铜丝,含铜99.9%,直径4毫米
74.09	铜板、片及带,厚度超过0.15毫米:	A:1.品名;2.形状(板、片、带);3.材质(精炼铜、黄铜、青铜、白铜等);4.状态(盘卷、平板等);5.成分含量(铜及合金元素的含量);6.规格(长×宽×厚)。
74.10	铜箔(不论是否印花或用纸、纸板、塑料或类似材料衬背),厚度(衬背除外)不超过0.15毫米:	A:1.品名;2.形状(箔);3.材质(精炼铜、黄铜、青铜、白铜等);4.状态(有无衬背);5.成分含量(铜及合金元素的含量);6.规格(整体厚度、铜箔厚度、长度、宽度);7.用途。B:8.品牌;9.牌号;10.种类(压延铜箔、电解铜箔、刚性覆铜板、柔性覆铜板);11.覆铜板的铜箔层数;12.基材材质(纸基、玻璃布基、复合基、环保型基等);13.生产厂商;14.介电常数
74.11	铜管:	A:1.品名;2.材质(精炼铜、黄铜、青铜、白铜等);3.成分含量(铜及合金元素的含量);4.外径;5.有无螺纹或翅片。B:6.用途
74.12	铜制管子附件(例如,接头、肘管、管套):	A:1.品名;2.用途(用于管子之间连通);3.材质(精炼铜、黄铜、青铜、白铜等);4.种类(接头、肘管、管套);5.成分含量(铜及合金元素的含量)。例:精炼铜制管接头,含铜99.9%
74.13	非绝缘的铜丝绞股线、缆、编带及类似品:	A:1.品名;2.材质(铜);3.种类(绞股线、缆、编带等); 4.注明"非绝缘"。例:非绝缘的铜丝绞股线
74.15	铜制或钢铁制带铜头的钉、平头钉、图钉、U形钉(税目83.05的货品除外)及类似品;铜制螺钉、螺栓、螺母、钩头螺钉、铆钉、销、开尾销、垫圈(包括弹簧垫圈)及类似品:	A:1.品名;2.材质(铜);3.种类(图钉、U形钉、螺钉、螺母、垫圈、铆钉等)。例:铜制螺母
74.18	餐桌、厨房或其他家用铜制器具及其零件;铜制刷锅器、洗刷擦光用的块垫、手套及类似品;铜制卫生器具及其零件:	例:铜制水壶(厨房用)

税则号列	商品名称	申报要素(A:归类要素 B:价格要素 C:审单及其他要素)及说明举例
7418.1010	---擦锅器及洗刷、擦光用的块垫、手套及类似品	A: 1.品名; 2.用途(厨房用、餐桌用、卫生用等); 3.材质(铜); 4.种类(水壶、煎锅等)。B: 5.品牌
7418.1020	---非电热的铜制家用烹饪器具及其零件	A: 1.品名; 2.材质(铜); 3.种类(煤油炉、煤气灶等); 4.原理(非电热)。B: 5.品牌
7418.1090	---其他	A: 1.品名; 2.用途(厨房用、餐桌用、卫生用等); 3.材质(铜); 4.种类(水壶、煎锅等)。B: 5.品牌
7418.2000	-卫生器具及其零件	A: 1.品名; 2.用途(厨房用、餐桌用、卫生用等); 3.材质(铜); 4.种类(水壶、煎锅等)。B: 5.品牌
7419.1000	-链条及其零件	A: 1.品名; 2.用途(工业用、非工业用); 3.材质(铜); 4.种类(链条、容器等); 5.加工方法(锻造、冲压等)
	--铸造、模压、冲压或锻造,但未经进一步加工的:	A: 1.品名; 2.用途(工业用、非工业用); 3.材质(铜); 4.种类(链条、容器等); 5.加工方法(锻造、冲压等)
7419.9920	---铜弹簧	A: 1.品名; 2.材质(铜); 3.种类(片簧、螺旋弹簧等)
7419.9930	---铜丝制的布(包括环形带)	A: 1.品名; 2.材质(铜); 3.种类
7419.9940	---铜丝制的网、格栅、网眼铜板	A: 1.品名; 2.材质(铜); 3.种类(网、格栅、网眼铜板等)
7419.9950	---非电热的铜制家用供暖器具及其零件	A: 1.品名; 2.材质(铜); 3.种类; 4.原理(非电热)
	---其他:	A: 1.品名; 2.用途(工业用、非工业用); 3.材质(铜); 4.种类(链条、容器等); 5.加工方法(锻造、冲压等)

第七十五章　镍及其制品

[注解]

1."品名"是指货品的具体商业名称。

2."用途"是指货品在出入境后的应用场合或下游产品。

3."加工方法"是指货品在出入境前的加工工艺或制造方法。

4."材质"是指货品按《税则》中的材质分类原则所确定的具体材料种类。

5."形状"是指货品按《税则》中的形状定义描述所确定的外观形状。

税则号列	商品名称	申报要素(A:归类要素 B:价格要素 C:审单及其他要素)及说明举例
75.01	镍锍、氧化镍烧结物及镍冶炼的其他中间产品:	A: 1.品名; 2.材质(镍锍、氧化镍烧结物等); 3.来源; 4.成分含量(镍化合物的含量)。例: 镍锍颗粒(熔炼硫化镍矿而得),含硫化镍40%
75.02	未锻轧镍:	A: 1.品名; 2.形状(锭、块等); 3.材质(非合金镍、镍合金); 4.加工方法(未锻轧); 5.成分含量(镍及合金元素的含量)。例: 未锻轧非合金镍锭,含镍99.9%
75.03	镍废碎料:	A: 1.品名; 2.用途(供回收镍用); 3.状态(废、碎); 4.来源(非合金镍、镍合金的废碎料); 5.成分含量(镍及合金元素的含量)。例: 镍废碎料(供回收镍用),含镍80%
75.04	镍粉及片状粉末:	A: 1.品名; 2.形状(片状粉末、非片状粉末); 3.材质(非合金镍、镍合金); 4.成分含量(镍及合金元素的含量); 5.粒度。例: 非片状非合金镍粉(用作硬质合金的黏合剂),含镍99.9%,颗粒直径600微米
75.05	镍条、杆、型材及异型材或丝:	例: 非合金镍杆,含镍99.9%
	-条、杆、型材及异型材:	A: 1.品名; 2.形状(条、杆、型材、异型材、丝); 3.材质(非合金镍、镍合金); 4.成分含量(镍及合金元素的含量)
	-丝:	A: 1.品名; 2.形状(条、杆、型材、异型材、丝); 3.材质(非合金镍、镍合金); 4.成分含量(镍及合金元素的含量); 5.丝的直径
75.06	镍板、片、带、箔:	A: 1.品名; 2.形状(板、片、带、箔); 3.材质(非合金镍、镍合金); 4.成分含量(镍及合金元素的含量)。B. 5.规格(长×宽×厚)
75.07	镍管及管子附件(例如,接头、肘管、管套):	A: 1.品名; 2.用途(用于管子之间连通); 3.材质(非合金镍、镍合金); 4.种类(管、接头、肘管、管套等); 5.成分含量(镍及合金元素的含量)。例: 非合金镍制管接头(用于管子之间连通),含镍99.9%
75.08	其他镍制品:	A: 1.品名; 2.用途(电镀用、工业用、非工业用); 3.材质(非合金镍、镍合金); 4.种类(网、篮、格栅等)。例: 镍网(工业用)

第七十六章　铝及其制品

[注解]

1."品名"是指货品的具体商业名称。

2."用途"是指货品在出入境后的应用场合或下游产品。

3．“加工方法”是指货品在出入境前的加工工艺或制造方法。

4．“材质”是指货品按《税则》中的材质分类原则所确定的具体材料种类。

5．“形状”是指货品按《税则》中的形状定义描述所确定的外观形状。

税则号列	商品名称	申报要素(A:归类要素 B:价格要素 C:审单及其他要素)及说明举例
76.01	未锻轧铝:	A:1.品名;2.形状(锭、块);3.材质(非合金铝、铝合金);4.加工方法(未锻轧或铸造、烧结等);5.成分含量(铝及合金元素的含量)
76.02	铝废碎料:	A:1.品名;2.用途(供回收铝用);3.状态(废、碎、板、管、线、边角料等);4.来源(废电线、废电缆、废五金电器等);5.成分含量(回收金属的含量)。B:6.包装形式。例:废铝管（供回收铝用），含铝80%
76.03	铝粉及片状粉末:	A:1.品名;2.形状(片状粉末、非片状粉末);3.材质(非合金铝、铝合金);4.成分含量(铝的含量);5.粒度。例:非片状非合金铝粉(用作硬质合金的黏合剂)，含铝99.9%，颗粒直径600微米
76.04	铝条、杆、型材及异型材:	A:1.品名;2.形状(条、杆、型材、异型材);3.材质(非合金铝、铝合金);4.成分含量(铝及合金元素的含量);5.型材、异型材请注明是否空心;6.铝合金条、杆请注明截面周长;7.柱形实心体铝合金请注明20℃时的极限抗拉强度。B:8.牌号
76.05	铝丝:	A:1.品名;2.形状(丝);3.材质(非合金铝、铝合金);4.成分含量(铝及合金元素的含量);5.规格(丝的最大截面尺寸)。例:非合金铝丝，含铝99.9%，直径4毫米
76.06	铝板、片及带，厚度超过0.2毫米:	A:1.品名;2.形状(矩形等);3.材质(非合金铝、铝合金);4.状态(板、片、带);5.成分含量(铝及合金元素的含量);6.规格(长×宽×厚)。B:7.品牌（中英文）;8.用途;9.牌号
76.07	铝箔(不论是否印花或用纸、纸板、塑料或类似材料衬背)，厚度(衬背除外)不超过0.2毫米:	A:1.品名;2.形状(箔);3.材质(铝);4.状态(有无衬背、衬背材料);5.规格(长×宽×厚);6.加工方法（轧制等）;7.加工程度（是否进一步加工）
76.08	铝管:	A:1.品名;2.材质(非合金铝、铝合金);3.种类(管);4.成分含量(铝及合金元素的含量);5.管壁厚度、管壁外径、孔眼直径、管材长度。例:非合金铝管，含铝99.9%
76.09	铝制管子附件(例如，接头、肘管、管套):	A:1.品名;2.用途;3.材质(非合金铝、铝合金);4.种类(接头、肘管、管套)。例:铝制管接头(用于管子之间连通)
76.10	铝制结构体(税目94.06的活动房屋除外)及其部件(例如，桥梁及桥梁体段、塔、格构杆、屋顶、屋顶框架、门窗及其框架、门槛、栏杆、支柱及立柱);上述结构体用的已加工铝板、杆、型材、异型材、管子及类似品:	A:1.品名;2.材质(铝);3.种类(门窗、门槛、塔楼、桥梁体段等);4.加工方法(铆接、栓接、钻孔、弯曲等)。例:铝合金制窗框(经钻孔)
76.11	盛装物料用的铝制囤、柜、罐、桶及类似容器(装压缩气体或液化气体的除外)，容积超过300升，不论是否衬里或隔热，但无机械或热力装置:	A:1.品名;2.用途(盛装液体用等);3.材质(铝);4.种类(罐、桶等);5.规格(容积)。B:6.品牌。例:本税目不包括装有机械或热力装置的。例:铝桶(盛装液体用)，容积400升
76.12	盛装物料用的铝制桶、罐、听、盒及类似容器，包括软管容器及硬管容器(装压缩气体或液化气体的除外)，容积不超过300升，不论是否衬里或隔热，但无机械或热力装置:	A:1.品名;2.用途(盛装液体用等);3.材质(铝);4.种类(罐、桶等);5.规格(容积)。B:6.品牌。例:本税目不包括有机械或热力装置的。例:铝制易拉罐(盛装液体用)，容积100升
76.13	装压缩气体或液化气体用的铝制容器:	A:1.品名;2.用途(盛装液体用等);3.材质(铝);4.种类(罐、桶等);5.规格(容积)。B:6.品牌。例:铝桶(盛装压缩气体用，且零售包装用，无机械或热力装置)
76.14	非绝缘的铝制绞股线、缆、编带及类似品:	A:1.品名;2.材质(铝);3.种类(绞股线、缆、编带等);4.状态(非绝缘);5.带钢芯请注明 例:非绝缘的铝丝绞股线(带钢芯)
76.15	餐桌、厨房或其他家用铝制器具及其零件;铝制擦锅器、洗刷擦光用的块垫，手套及类似品;铝制卫生器具及其零件:	A:1.品名;2.用途(厨房用、餐桌用、卫生用等);3.材质(铝);4.种类(水壶、煎锅等)。例:铝制水壶(厨房用)
76.16	其他铝制品:	A:1.品名;2.用途(工业用、非工业用);3.材质(铝);4.种类(图钉、螺钉、布、网、篱等)。例:铝制螺母(工业用)

第七十八章　铅及其制品

[注解]

1.“品名”是指货品的具体商业名称。

2.“用途”是指货品在出入境后的应用场合或下游产品。

3.“加工方法”是指货品在出入境前的加工工艺或制造方法。

4.“材质”是指货品按《税则》中的材质分类原则所确定的具体材料种类。

5.“形状”是指货品按《税则》中的形状定义描述所确定的外观形状。

税则号列	商品名称	申报要素(A:归类要素 B:价格要素 C:审单及其他要素)及说明举例
78.01	未锻轧铅:	A:1.品名;2.形状(锭、块);3.材质(精炼铅、铅合金);4.加工方法(未锻轧);5.成分含量(铅及合金元素的含量)。例:未锻轧精炼铅锭,含铅99.9%
78.02	铅废碎料:	A:1.品名;2.用途(供回收铅用);3.材质(铅);4.状态(废、碎);5.来源(精炼铅、铅合金的废碎料);6.成分含量(铅的含量)。例:铅废碎料(供回收铅用),含铅80%
78.04	铅板、片、带、箔;铅粉及片状粉末:	A:1.品名;2.形状(板、片、带、箔、粉末及片状粉末);3.材质(铅);4.规格(板、箔的厚度);5.粒度。例:铅板,厚度1毫米
7806.0010	---铅条、杆、型材及异型材或丝	A:1.品名;2.形状(条、杆、型材、异型材、丝);3.材质(铅)
7806.0090	---其他	A:1.品名;2.用途(工业用、非工业用);3.材质(铅);4.种类(容器、铅坠等)

第七十九章　锌及其制品

[注解]

1.“品名”是指货品的具体商业名称。

2.“用途”是指货品在出入境后的应用场合或下游产品。

3.“加工方法”是指货品在出入境前的加工工艺或制造方法。

4.“材质”是指货品按《税则》中的材质分类原则所确定的具体材料种类。

5.“形状”是指货品按《税则》中的形状定义描述所确定的外观形状。

税则号列	商品名称	申报要素(A:归类要素 B:价格要素 C:审单及其他要素)及说明举例
79.01	未锻轧锌:	A:1.品名;2.形状(锭、块);3.材质(非合金锌、锌合金);4.加工方法(未锻轧);5.成分含量(锌及合金元素的含量)。例:未锻轧非合金锌锭,含锌99.9%
79.02	锌废碎料:	A:1.品名;2.用途(供回收锌用);3.状态(废、碎);4.来源(精炼锌、锌合金的废碎料);5.成分含量(锌的含量)。例:锌废碎料(供回收锌用),含锌80%
79.03	锌末、锌粉及片状粉末:	A:1.品名;2.用途(用作硬质合金的黏合剂);3.形状(片状粉末、非片状粉末);4.材质(锌);5.成分含量(锌的含量);6.粒度。例:非片状锌粉(用作硬质合金的黏合剂),含锌99.9%,颗粒直径600微米
79.04	锌条、杆、型材及异型材或丝:	A:1.品名;2.形状(条、杆、型材、异型材、丝);3.材质(锌)。例:锌杆
79.05	锌板、片、带、箔:	A:1.品名;2.形状(矩形等);3.材质(锌等);4.状态(板、片、带);5.成分含量(锌及合金元素的含量);6.规格(长×宽×厚)。B:7.品牌(中英文);8.用途;9.加工程度(是否经表面处理剂处理方法和所用材料)
79.07	其他锌制品:	A:1.品名;2.用途;3.材质(锌);4.种类(管、接头、肘管、管套等)。例:锌制容器(非工业用)

第八十章　锡及其制品

税则号列	商品名称	申报要素(A:归类要素 B:价格要素 C:审单及其他要素)及说明举例
80.01	未锻轧锡:	A:1.品名;2.形状(锭、块、粒);3.材质(非合金锡、锡合金);4.加工方法(未锻轧);5.成分含量(锡及合金元素的含量)。例:未锻轧非合金锡锭,含锡99.9%
80.02	锡废碎料:	A:1.品名;2.用途(供回收锡用);3.状态(废、碎);4.来源(非合金锡、锡合金的废碎料);5.成分含量(锡的含量)。例:锡废碎料(供回收锡用),含锡80%
80.03	锡条、杆、型材及异型材或丝:	A:1.品名;2.形状(条、杆、型材、异型材、丝);3.材质(锡);4.状态(是否带焊剂)。例:锡杆
8007.0020	---锡板、片及带,厚度超过0.2毫米	A:1.品名;2.形状(板、片、带);3.规格(长、宽、厚);4.材质(锡);5.状态(有无衬背、衬背材料)。例:锡制牙膏软管(非工业用)
8007.0030	---锡箔(不论是否印花或用纸、纸板、	A:1.品名;2.形状(箔、粉末);3.材质(锡);4.状态(有无衬背、衬背材

税则号列	商品名称	申报要素(A:归类要素 B:价格要素 C:审单及其他要素)及说明举例
	塑料或类似材料衬背),厚度(衬背除外)不超过0.2毫米;锡粉及片状粉末	料);5.规格(锡箔长×宽×厚、粉末粒度)
8007.0040	---锡管及管子附件(例如,接头、肘管、管套)	A:1.品名;2.用途(用于管子之间连通);3.材质(锡);4.种类(接头、肘管、管套等)
8007.0090	---其他	A:1.品名;2.材质(锡); 3.种类

第八十一章 其他贱金属、金属陶瓷及其制品

[注解]

1.“品名”是指货品的具体商业名称。

2.“用途”是指货品在出入境后的应用场合或下游产品。

3.“加工方法”是指货品在出入境前的加工工艺或制造方法。

4.“材质”是指货品按《税则》中的材质分类原则所确定的具体材料种类。

5.“形状”是指货品按《税则》中的形状定义描述所确定的外观形状。

税则号列	商品名称	申报要素(A:归类要素 B:价格要素 C:审单及其他要素)及说明举例
81.01	钨及其制品,包括废碎料:	例:未锻轧钨锭,含钨99.9%
8101.1000	-粉末	A:1.品名;2.形状(粉末);3.材质(钨);4.成分含量(钨的含量);5.粒度;6.粉末请注明细度
8101.9400	--未锻轧钨,包括简单烧结而成的条、杆	A:1.品名;2.形状(条、杆等);3.材质(钨);4.加工方法(未锻轧、简单烧结等)
8101.9600	--丝	A:1.品名;2.形状(丝);3.材质(钨)
8101.9700	--废碎料	A:1.品名;2.用途(供回收钨用);3.材质(钨);4.状态(废、碎);5.来源
	--其他:	A:1.品名;2.形状(条、杆、型材、异型材、板、片、带、箔);3.材质(钨、钨合金);4.加工方法(锻轧);5.用途;6.成分含量。B:7.每个重量;8.圆柱形请注明是否空心、内径
81.02	钼及其制品,包括废碎料:	例:未锻轧钼锭,含钼99.9%
8102.1000	-粉末	A:1.品名;2.形状(粉末);3.材质(钼);4.粉末请注明细度
8102.9400	--未锻轧钼,包括简单烧结而成的条、杆	A:1.品名;2.形状(条、杆);3.材质(钼);4.加工方法(未锻轧、简单烧结等)
8102.9500	--条、杆,但简单烧结而成的除外;型材及异型材,板、片、带、箔	A:1.品名;2.形状(条、杆、型材、异型材、板、片、带、箔);3.材质(钼、钼合金);4.加工方法(锻轧)
8102.9600	--丝	A:1.品名;2.形状(丝);3.材质(钼)
8102.9700	--废碎料	A:1.品名;2.用途(供回收钼用);3.材质(钼);4.来源
8102.9900	--其他	A:1.品名;2.材质(钼);3.种类
81.03	钽及其制品,包括废碎料:	
	-未锻轧钽,包括简单烧结而成的条、杆;粉末:	A:1.品名;2.形状(粉末、条、杆、型材、异型材、板、片、带、箔);3.材质(钽、钽合金);4.加工方法(锻轧、未锻轧、简单烧结等);5.状态(废、碎);6.成分含量(钽的含量);7.粉末需申报松装密度
8103.3000	-废碎料	A:1.品名;2.形状(粉末、条、杆、型材、异型材、板、片、带、箔);3.材质(钽、钽合金); 4.加工方法(锻轧、未锻轧、简单烧结等);5.状态(废、碎);6.成分含量(钽的含量)
	-其他:	A:1.品名;2.形状(粉末、条、杆、型材、异型材、板、片、带、箔);3.材质(钽、钽合金);4.加工方法(锻轧、未锻轧、简单烧结等);5.状态(废、碎);6.成分含量(钽的含量);7.丝需申报直径
81.04	镁及其制品,包括废碎料:	
	-未锻轧镁:	A:1.品名;2.材质(镁);3.加工方法(未锻轧);4.成分含量(镁的含量);5.粉末粒度。例:未锻轧镁锭,含镁99.9%
8104.2000	-废碎料	A:1.品名;2.用途(供回收镁用);3.状态(废、碎);4.来源
8104.3000	-锉屑、车屑及颗粒,已按规格分级的;粉末	A:1.品名;2.形状(粉末等);3.材质(镁);4.来源(锉屑、车屑等);5.成分含量(镁的含量);6.粒度
	-其他:	A:1.品名;2.材质(镁);3加工方法(锻轧等)
81.05	钴锍及其他冶炼钴时所得的中间产品;钴及其制品,包括废碎料:	A:1.品名;2.形状(粉末、条、杆、型材、异型材、板、片、带、箔);3.材质(钴、钴合金、钴锍);4.加工方法(锻轧、未锻轧);5.状态(废、碎);6.成分含量(以干基钴为标准);7.粉末粒度。例:未锻轧钴锭,含钴99.9%
81.06	铋及其制品,包括废碎料:	A:1.品名;2.形状(粉末、条、杆、型材、异型材、板、片、带、箔);3.材质(铋、铋合金);4.加工方法(锻轧、未锻轧);5.状态(废、碎);6.成分含量(铋的含量)。例:未锻轧铋锭,含铋99.9%

税则号列	商品名称	申报要素(A:归类要素 B:价格要素 C:审单及其他要素)及说明举例
81.07	镉及其制品，包括废碎料:	A:1.品名;2.形状(粉末、条、杆、型材、异型材、板、片、带、箔);3.材质(镉、镉合金);4.加工方法(锻轧、未锻轧);5.状态(废、碎)。例:未锻轧镉锭，含镉99.9%
81.08	钛及其制品，包括废碎料:	
	-未锻轧钛;粉末:	A:1.品名;2.形状(粉末、杆等);3.材质(钛);4.加工方法(未锻轧);5.成分含量(钛的含量);6.粉末粒度。例:未锻轧钛锭，含钛99.9%
8108.3000	-废碎料	A:1.品名;2.用途(供回收钛用);3.状态(废、碎);4.来源
	-其他:	A:1.品名;2.形状(条、杆、型材、异型材、板、片、带、箔等);3.材质(钛);4.种类;5.加工方法(未锻轧);6.板、片、带、箔的厚度
81.09	锆及其制品，包括废碎料:	A:1.品名;2.形状(粉末、条、杆、型材、异型材、板、片、带、箔);3.材质(锆、锆合金);4.加工方法(未锻轧等);5.状态(废、碎);6.成分含量(锆的含量);7.粉末粒度。例:粉末须申报细度。例:未锻轧锆锭，含锆99.9%
81.10	锑及其制品，包括废碎料:	A:1.品名;2.形状(粉末、条、杆、型材、异型材、板、片、带、箔);3.材质(锑、锑合金);4..加工方法(未锻轧等);5.状态(废、碎);6.成分含量(锑的含量);7.粉末粒度。例:未锻轧锑锭，含锑99.9%
81.11	锰及其制品，包括废碎料:	A:1.品名;2.形状(粉末、条、杆、型材、异型材、板、片、带、箔);3.材质(锰、锰合金);4.加工方法(未锻轧、锻压、模压等);5.状态(废、碎);6.成分含量(锰的含量);7.粉末粒度
81.12	铍、铬、锗、钒、镓、铪、铟、铌、铼、铊及其制品，包括废碎料:	A:1.品名;2.形状(粉末、条、杆、型材、异型材、板、片、带、箔);3.材质(铍、铬等贱金属及其合金);4.加工方法(未锻轧等);5.状态(废、碎);6.成分含量;7.粉末粒度
81.13	金属陶瓷及其制品，包括废碎料:	A:1.品名;2.材质(金属陶瓷); 3.状态(废、碎)。例:金属陶瓷制防热套

第八十二章　贱金属工具、器具、利口器、餐匙、餐叉及其零件

[注解]

1.“品名”是指货品的具体商业名称。
2.“用途”是指货品在出入境后的应用场合或下游产品。
3.“加工方法”是指货品在出入境前的加工工艺或制造方法。
4.“材质”是指货品按《税则》中的材质分类原则所确定的具体材料种类。
5.“形状”是指货品按《税则》中的形状定义描述所确定的外观形状。

税则号列	商品名称	申报要素(A:归类要素 B:价格要素 C:审单及其他要素)及说明举例
82.01	锹、铲、镐、锄、叉及耙;斧子、钩刀及类似砍伐工具;各种修枝用剪刀;镰刀、秣刀、树篱剪、伐木楔子及其他农业、园艺或林业用手工工具:	A:1.品名;2.用途(砍伐用、修枝用等);3.材质(合金钢制等);4.种类(锹、铲、剪等);5.式样(单手操作等)。B:6.品牌
82.02	手工锯;各种锯的锯片(包括切条、切槽或无齿锯片):	A:1.品名;2.用途(加工金属用等);3.材质(合金钢制等);4.种类(手工锯、带锯片、圆锯片、直锯片等);5.圆锯片带有钢制工作部件请注明。B:6.品牌
82.03	钢锉、木锉、钳子(包括剪钳)、镊子、白铁剪、切管器、螺栓切头器、打孔冲子及类似手工工具:	A:1.品名;2.用途(锉木材用等);3.材质(合金钢制等);4.种类(锉、钳子、镊子等)。B:5.品牌
82.04	手动扳手及扳钳(包括转矩扳手，但不包括丝锥扳手);可互换的扳手套筒，不论是否带手柄:	A:1.品名;2.材质(合金钢制等);3.种类(扳手、扳钳、扳手套筒等);4.式样(固定的、可调的)。B:5.品牌
82.05	其他税目未列名的手工工具(包括玻璃刀);喷灯;台钳、夹钳及类似品,但作为机床附件或零件的除外;砧;轻便锻炉;带支架的手摇或脚踏砂轮:	A:1.品名;2.用途(家用等);3.材质(合金钢制等);4.种类(锤子、螺丝刀等);5.是否成套。B:6.品牌
82.06	由税目82.02至82.05中两个或多个税目所列工具组成的零售包装成套货品:	A:1.品名;2.材质(合金钢制等);3.包含的种类(扳手、钳子、螺丝刀等);4.是否零售包装成套。B:5.品牌
82.07	手工工具(不论是否有动力装置)及机床(例如，锻压、冲压、攻丝、钻孔、镗孔、铰孔及铣削、车削或上螺丝用的机器)的可互换工具，包括金属拉拔或挤压用模以及凿岩或钻探工具:	A:1.品名;2.用途(钻探、铣削、锻压、镗孔用等);3.材质(合金钢制等);4.种类(锻模、铣刀等);5.带有工作部件请注明材质(金属陶瓷、金刚石等)。B:6.品牌

税则号列	商品名称	申报要素(A:归类要素 B:价格要素 C:审单及其他要素)及说明举例
82.08	机器或机械器具的刀及刀片:	A: 1.品名; 2.用途(金属加工用、木器加工用等); 3.材质(不锈钢制等); 4.种类(机器用刀片等); 5.是否经镀或涂层。B: 6.品牌
8209.0010	---板	A: 1.品名; 2.用途(工具用); 3.材质(金属陶瓷制); 4.种类(板、杆、刀头等); 5.是否装配。B: 6.品牌
8209.0021	----晶粒度小于0.8微米的	A: 1.品名; 2.用途(工具用); 3.材质(金属陶瓷制); 4.种类(板、杆、刀头等); 5.是否装配; 6.晶粒度。B: 7.品牌
8209.0029	----其他	A: 1.品名; 2.用途(工具用); 3.材质(金属陶瓷制); 4.种类(板、杆、刀头等); 5.是否装配。B: 6.品牌
8209.0030	---刀头	A: 1.品名; 2.用途(工具用); 3.材质(金属陶瓷制); 4.种类(板、杆、刀头等); 5.是否装配。B: 6.品牌
8209.0090	---其他	A: 1.品名; 2.用途(工具用); 3.材质(金属陶瓷制); 4.种类(板、杆、刀头等); 5.是否装配。B: 6.品牌
82.10	用于加工或调制食品或饮料的手动机械器具,重量不超过10千克:	A: 1.品名; 2.用途(加工食品用等); 3.材质(不锈钢制等); 4.种类(绞肉机、榨汁机等); 5.原理(手动); 6.单件重量。B: 7.品牌
82.11	有刃口的刀及其刀片,不论是否有锯齿(包括整枝刀),但税目82.08的刀除外:	A: 1.品名; 2.材质(不锈钢制等); 3.状态(有刃口); 4.种类(餐刀、折叠刀等); 5.式样(刃面固定、可换刃面); 6.是否成套。B: 7.品牌
82.12	剃刀及其刀片(包括未分开的刀片条):	A: 1.品名; 2.材质(不锈钢制等); 3.种类(剃刀、安全刀片等)。B: 4.品牌
82.13	剪刀、裁缝剪刀及类似品、剪刀片:	A: 1.品名; 2.用途(裁缝用等); 3.材质(不锈钢制等); 4.种类(剪刀、剪刀片等)。B: 5.品牌
82.14	其他利口器(例如,理发推剪、屠刀、砍骨刀、切肉刀、切菜刀、裁纸刀);修指甲及修脚用具(包括指甲锉):	A: 1.品名; 2.材质(不锈钢制等); 3.种类(裁纸刀、指甲锉、手动理发推剪、切菜刀等)。B: 4.品牌
82.15	餐匙、餐叉、长柄勺、漏勺、糕点夹、鱼刀、黄油刀、糖块夹及类似的厨房或餐桌用具:	A: 1.品名; 2.用途(餐桌、厨房用); 3.材质(不锈钢制等); 4.种类(餐叉、漏勺等); 5.是否镀贵金属; 6.是否成套。B: 7.品牌

第八十三章　贱金属杂项制品

[注解]

1.“品名”是指货品的具体商业名称。

2.“用途”是指货品在出入境后的应用场合或下游产品。

3.“加工方法”是指货品在出入境前的加工工艺或制造方法。

4.“材质”是指货品按《税则》中的材质分类原则所确定的具体材料种类。

5.“形状”是指货品按《税则》中的形状定义描述所确定的外观形状。

税则号列	商品名称	申报要素(A:归类要素 B:价格要素 C:审单及其他要素)及说明举例
83.01	贱金属制的锁(钥匙锁、数码锁及电动锁);贱金属制带锁的扣环及扣环框架;上述锁的贱金属制钥匙:	A: 1.品名; 2.用途(机动车用、家具用等); 3.材质(不锈钢制等); 4.种类(钥匙锁、数码锁、电动锁、钥匙等)。B: 5.品牌
8302.1000	-铰链(折叶)	A: 1.品名; 2.用途(机动车用、家具用等); 3.材质(不锈钢制等); 4.种类(铰链、自动闭门器等)。B: 5.品牌
8302.2000	-小脚轮	A: 1.品名; 2.用途(机动车用、家具用等); 3.材质(不锈钢制等); 4.种类(铰链、自动闭门器等); 5.直径; 6.所装轮或胎的宽度。B: 7.品牌
8302.3000	-机动车辆用的其他附件及架座	A: 1.品名; 2.用途(机动车用、家具用等); 3.材质(不锈钢制等); 4.种类(铰链、自动闭门器等)。B: 5.品牌
	-其他附件及架座:	A: 1.品名; 2.用途(机动车用、家具用等); 3.材质(不锈钢制等); 4.种类(铰链、自动闭门器等)。B: 5.品牌
8302.5000	-帽架、帽钩、托架及类似品	A: 1.品名; 2.用途(机动车用、家具用等); 3.材质(不锈钢制等); 4.种类(铰链、自动闭门器等)。B: 5.品牌
8302.6000	-自动闭门器	A: 1.品名; 2.用途(机动车用、家具用等); 3.材质(不锈钢制等); 4.种类(铰链、自动闭门器等)。B: 5.品牌
83.03	装甲或加强的贱金属制保险箱、保险柜及保险库的门和带锁保险储存橱、钱箱、契约箱及类似品:	A: 1.品名; 2.材质(不锈钢制等); 3.种类(保险箱、保险柜、保险库的门等)。B: 4.品牌
83.04	贱金属制的档案柜、卡片索引柜、文件	A: 1.品名; 2.用途(办公室用); 3.材质(不锈钢制等); 4.种类(档案柜、卡片

税则号列	商品名称	申报要素(A:归类要素 B:价格要素 C:审单及其他要素)及说明举例
	盘、文件篮、笔盘、公章架及类似的办公用具,但税目 94.03 的办公室家具除外:	索引柜、文件盘等);5.式样(非落地)。B:6.品牌
83.05	活页夹、卷宗夹的贱金属附件,贱金属制的信夹、信角、文件夹、索引标签及类似的办公用品;贱金属制的成条订书钉(例如,供办公室、室内装饰或包装用):	A:1.品名;2.用途(办公室用、室内装饰或包装用);3.材质(不锈钢制等);4.种类(活页夹、宗卷夹、成条订书钉等)。B:5.品牌
83.06	非电动的贱金属铃、钟、锣及类似品;贱金属雕塑像及其他装饰品;贱金属相框或画框及类似框架;贱金属镜子:	A:1.品名;2.材质(不锈钢制等);3.种类(铃、钟、锣、雕塑像、相框、画框等);4.是否镀贵金属;5.铃、钟、锣请注明非电动。B:6.品牌
83.07	贱金属软管,不论是否有附件:	A:1.品名;2.材质(钢铁制、其他贱金属制);3.种类(软管)。B:4.品牌
83.08	贱金属制的扣、钩、环、眼及类似品,用于衣着、鞋靴、天篷、提包、旅行用品或其他制品;贱金属制的管形铆钉及开口铆钉;贱金属制的珠子及亮晶片:	A:1.品名;2.用途(用于衣服、提包上等);3.材质(不锈钢制等);4.种类(扣、钩、环、铆钉等)。B:5.品牌
83.09	贱金属制的塞子、盖子(包括冠形瓶塞、螺口盖及倒水塞)、瓶帽、螺口塞、塞子帽、封志及其他包装用附件:	A:1.品名;2.形状(冠形、圆形等);3.材质(不锈钢制等);4.种类(塞子、盖子等)。B:5.品牌
83.10	贱金属制的标志牌、铭牌、地名牌及类似品,号码、字母及类似标志,但税目 94.05 的货品除外:	A:1.品名;2.用途(汽车用等);3.材质(不锈钢制、贱金属种类等);4.种类(标志、铭牌等)。B:5.品牌
83.11	贱金属或硬质合金制的丝、条、管、板、电极及类似品,以焊剂涂面或以焊剂为芯,用于焊接或沉积金属、硬质合金;贱金属粉粘聚而成的丝或条,供金属喷镀用:	A:1.品名;2.用途(电弧焊用、气焊用、钎焊用等);3.材质(贱金属、硬质合金制);4.种类(电极、焊条、焊丝等);5.状态(以焊剂涂面、以焊剂为芯)。B:6.品牌

第十六类　机器、机械器具、电气设备及其零件;录音机及放声机、电视图像、声音的录制和重放设备及其零件、附件

第八十四章　核反应堆、锅炉、机器、机械器具及其零件

税则号列	商品名称	申报要素(A:归类要素 B:价格要素 C:审单及其他要素)及说明举例
8401.1000	-核反应堆	A:1.品名。B:2.用途;3.品牌;4.型号
8401.2000	-同位素分离机器、装置及其零件	A:1.品名;2.用途。B:3.品牌;4.型号
	-未辐照燃料元件(释热元件):	A:1.品名。B:2.用途;3.品牌;4.型号
	-核反应堆零件:	A:1.品名; 2.用途(适用机型)。B:3.品牌;4.型号
84.02	蒸汽锅炉(能产生低压水蒸气的集中供暖用的热水锅炉除外);过热水锅炉:	
	-蒸汽锅炉:	A:1.品名;2.用途;3.构造方式;4.蒸发量。B:5.品牌; 6.型号
8402.2000	-过热水锅炉	A:1.品名;2.用途;3.温度。B:4.品牌; 5.型号
8402.9000	-零件	A:1.品名;2.用途(适用机型)。B:3.品牌;4.型号
8403.1010	---家用型	A:1.品名;2.用途。B:3.品牌;4.型号;5.是否装有循环装置;6.功率;7.温度
8403.1090	---其他	A:1.品名;2.用途。B:3.品牌;4.型号;5.温度
8403.9000	-零件	A:1.品名;2.用途(适用机型)。B:3.品牌;4.型号
84.04	品目 84.02 或 84.03 所列锅炉的辅助设备(例如,节热器、过热器、除灰器、气体回收器);水蒸汽或其他蒸汽动力装置的冷凝器:	
	-税目 84.02 或 84.03 所列锅炉的辅助设备:	A:1.品名;2.用途。B:3.品牌
8404.2000	-水蒸气或其他蒸汽动力装置的冷凝器	A:1.品名;2.用途。B:3.品牌
	-零件:	A:1.品名;2.用途(适用机型)。B:3.品牌;4.型号
8405.1000	-煤气发生器,不论有无净化器;乙炔发生器及类似的水解气体发生器,不论有无净化器	A:1.品名;2.品牌。B:3.型号

税则号列	商品名称	申报要素(A:归类要素 B:价格要素 C:审单及其他要素)及说明举例
8405.9000	-零件	A: 1.品名; 2.用途(适用机型)。B: 3.品牌; 4.型号
8406.1000	-船舶动力用汽轮机	A: 1.品名; 2.用途。B: 3.品牌; 4.型号; 5.输出功率
	-其他汽轮机:	A: 1.品名; 2.用途; 3.输出功率。B: 4.品牌; 5.型号
8406.9000	-零件	A: 1.品名; 2.用途(适用机型)。B: 3.品牌; 4.型号
84.07	点燃往复式或旋转式活塞内燃发动机:	
	-航空器发动机:	A: 1.品名; 2.用途; 3.输出功率。B: 4.品牌; 5.型号; 6.燃料类型
8407.2100	--舷外发动机	A: 1.品名; 2 用途; 3.发动机安装位置(舷外或舷内)。B: 4.品牌; 5.型号; 6.燃料类型 7.功率
8407.2900	--其他	A: 1.品名; 2.用途; 3.发动机安装位置(舷外或舷内)。B: 4.品牌; 5.型号; 6.燃料类型; 7.是否提供主动力; 8.功率
	-用于第八十七章所列车辆的往复式活塞发动机:	A: 1.品名; 2.用途; 3.排气量; 4.成套散件或毛坯请注明; 5.燃料类型; 6.状态(成品、半成品、成套散件); 7.生产件的通用零件编号后加注"/TY"; 8.成套散件装配后完整品的零部件的编号; B: 9.品牌; 10.型号; 11.零件完整编号并在前加注"S/"、"W/"或"WF/"之一(生产件填报"S/"品牌和适用的整车厂牌一致的维修件填报"W/",品牌和适用的整车厂牌不一致的维修件的填报"WF/")
	-其他发动机:	A: 1.品名; 2.用途; 3.燃料类型。B: 4.品牌; 5.型号; 6.转速
8408.1000	-船舶发动机	A: 1.品名; 2.用途。B: 3.品牌; 4.型号; 5.输出功率
	-用于第八十七章所列车辆的发动机:	A: 1.品名; 2.用途; 3.输出功率; 4.成套散件或毛坯请注明; 5.生产件的通用零件编号后加注"/TY"; 6.成套散件装配后完整品的零部件的编号。B: 7.品牌; 8.型号; 9.零件完整编号并在前加注"S/"、"W/"或"WF/"之一(生产件填报"S/"品牌和适用的整车厂牌一致的维修件填报"W/",品牌和适用的整车厂牌不一致的维修件的填报"WF/")
	-其他发动机:	A: 1.品名; 2.用途; 3.输出功率。B: 4.品牌; 5.型号; 6.转速
84.09	专用于或主要用于税目 84.07 或 84.08 所列发动机的零件:	A: 1.品名; 2.适用何种用途发动机(如飞机用、船舶用等); 3.适用发动机的类型(点燃式/压燃式)。B: 4.品牌; 5.零件号
8410.1100	--功率不超过 1000 千瓦	A: 1.品名; 2.功率。B: 3.品牌; 4.型号
8410.1200	--功率超过 1000 千瓦,但不超过 10000 千瓦	A: 1.品名; 2.功率。B: 3.品牌; 4.型号
	--功率超过 10000 千瓦:	A: 1.品名; 2.功率; 3.工作方式。B: 4.品牌; 5.型号
8410.9010	---调节器	A: 1.品名。B: 2.品牌; 3.原理; 4.型号
8410.9090	---其他	A: 1.品名。B: 2.品牌; 3.型号
84.11	涡轮喷气发动机、涡轮螺桨发动机及其他燃气轮机:	
	-涡轮喷气发动机:	A: 1.品名; 2.原理; 3.推力。B: 4.品牌; 5.型号
	-涡轮螺桨发动机:	A: 1.品名; 2.原理; 3.功率。B: 4.品牌; 5.型号
	-其他燃气轮机:	A: 1.品名; 2.原理; 3.功率。B: 4.品牌; 5.型号
	-零件:	A: 1.品名; 2.用途(适用机型)。B: 3.品牌; 4.型号
84.12	其他发动机及动力装置:	
	-喷气发动机,但涡轮喷气发动机除外:	A: 1.品名; 2.用途; 3.原理。B: 4.品牌; 5.型号
	-液压动力装置:	A: 1.品名; 2.原理。B: 3.用途; 4.品牌; 5.型号
	-气压动力装置:	A: 1.品名; 2.原理。B: 3.用途; 4.品牌; 5.型号
8412.8000	-其他	A: 1.品名; 2.原理。B: 3.用途; 4.品牌; 5.型号
	-零件:	A: 1.品名; 2.用途(适用机型)。B: 3.品牌; 4.型号
84.13	液体泵,不论是否装有计量装置;液体提升机:	
	-装有或可装计量装置的泵:	A: 1.品名; 2.用途; 3.是否装有或可装计量装置。B: 4.品牌; 5.型号
8413.2000	-手泵,但子目 8413.11 或 8413.19 的货品除外	A: 1.品名; 2.是否手动。B: 3.品牌; 4.型号
	-活塞式内燃发动机用的燃油泵、润滑油泵或冷却剂泵:	A: 1.品名; 2.用途(是否为活塞式内燃发动机用); 3.适用发动机的输出功率。B: 4.品牌; 5.型号。例:活塞式内燃发动机用燃油泵,发动机输出功率 180 千瓦,品牌 MXS,型号 X-1
8413.4000	-混凝土泵	A: 1.品名; 2.用途。B: 3.品牌; 4.型号
	-其他往复式排液泵	A: 1.品名; 2.驱动方式; 3.原理(往复式、回转式、离心式等)。B: 4.用途; 5.品牌; 6.型号
	-其他回转式排液泵:	A: 1.品名; 2.驱动方式; 3.原理(往复式、回转式、离心式等)。B: 4.用途; 5.品牌; 6.型号
	-其他离心泵:	A: 1.品名 2.驱动方式; 3.原理(往复式、回转式、离心式等); 4.转速。B: 5.用途 6.品牌; 7.型号
	-其他泵;液体提升机:	A: 1.品名。B: 2.用途; 3.品牌; 4.型号; 5.原理(柱塞式、齿轮式、螺杆式等)

税则号列	商品名称	申报要素(A:归类要素 B:价格要素 C:审单及其他要素)及说明举例
	-零件:	A: 1. 品名; 2. 用途(适用机型)。B: 3. 品牌; 4. 型号。例: 燃油泵用泵体, 无品牌、型号
8414.1000	-真空泵	A: 1. 品名。B: 2. 用途; 3. 品牌; 4. 型号; 5. 性能(抽气能力)
8414.2000	-手动或脚踏式空气泵	A: 1. 品名; 2. 是否手动或脚踏。B: 3. 品牌; 4. 型号
	-用于制冷设备的压缩机:	A: 1. 品名; 2. 用途; 3. 驱动方式; 4. 额定功率。B: 5. 品牌; 6. 型号
8414.4000	-装在拖车底盘上的空气压缩机	A: 1. 品名; 2. 用途。B: 3. 品牌; 4. 型号
	-风机、风扇:	A: 1. 品名; 2. 用途; 3. 安装方式(如吊扇、落地扇、壁扇等); 4. 输出功率。B: 5. 品牌; 6. 型号
	-罩的平面最大边长不超过120厘米的通风罩或循环气罩:	A: 1. 品名; 2. 罩的平面最大边长。B: 3. 品牌; 4. 型号
8414.8010	---燃气轮机用的自由活塞式发生器	A: 1. 品名; 2. 用途。B: 3. 品牌; 4. 型号
8414.8020	---二氧化碳压缩机	A: 1. 品名; 2. 用途。B: 3. 品牌; 4. 型号
8414.8030	---发动机用增压器	A: 1. 品名; 2. 用途。B: 3. 品牌; 4. 型号; 5. 压力比
8414.8090	---其他	A: 1. 品名; 2. 用途。B: 3. 品牌; 4. 型号
	-零件:	A: 1. 品名; 2. 用途(适用机型)。B: 3. 品牌; 4. 型号; 5. 材质。例: 窗式空调器用压缩机外壳, 塑料制, 无品牌、型号
8415.1010	---独立式	A: 1. 品名; 2. 是否窗式或壁式安装; 3. 是否为独立式或分体式。B: 4. 品牌; 5. 型号
	---分体式:	A: 1. 品名; 2. 是否窗式或壁式安装; 3. 是否为独立式或分体式; 4. 制冷量。B: 5. 品牌; 6. 型号。例: 空调器(分体壁式), 品牌格力, 制冷量2000大卡, 型号RS0232
8415.2000	-机动车辆上供人使用的	A: 1. 品名; 2. 用途。B: 3. 品牌; 4. 型号
	--装有一个制冷装置及冷热循环换向阀(可逆式热泵)的:	A: 1. 品名; 2 是否装有制冷装置; 3. 是否装有冷热换向阀; 4. 制冷量。B: 5. 品牌; 6. 型号
	--其他, 装有制冷装置的:	A: 1. 品名; 2 是否装有制冷装置; 3. 是否装有冷热换向阀; 4. 制冷量。B: 5. 品牌; 6. 型号
8415.8300	--未装有制冷装置的	A: 1. 品名。B: 2. 品牌; 3. 结构; 4. 型号
	-零件:	A: 1. 品名; 2. 用途(适用机型); 3. 适用机型制冷量(以"大卡/时"计)。B: 4. 品牌; 5. 型号
8416.1000	-使用液体燃料的炉用燃烧器	A: 1. 品名; 2. 用途; 3. 燃料类型。B: 4. 品牌; 5. 型号
	-其他炉用燃烧器, 包括复式燃烧器:	A: 1. 品名; 2. 用途; 3. 燃料类型。B: 4. 品牌; 5. 型号
8416.3000	-机械加煤机, 包括其机械炉箅、机械出灰器及类似装置	A: 1. 品名; 2. 用途。B: 3. 品牌;
8416.9000	-零件	A: 1. 品名; 2. 用途(适用机型)。B: 3. 品牌; 4. 型号
8417.1000	-矿砂、黄铁矿或金属的焙烧、熔化或其他热处理用炉及烘箱	A: 1. 品名; 2. 用途; 3. 加热方式。B: 4. 品牌; 5. 型号
8417.2000	-面包房用烤炉及烘箱, 包括做饼干用的	A: 1. 品名; 2. 用途; 3. 加热方式。B: 4. 品牌; 5. 型号
	-其他:	A: 1. 品名; 2. 用途; 3. 加热方式。B: 4. 品牌; 5. 型号
	-零件:	A: 1. 品名; 2. 用途(适用机型)。B: 3. 品牌; 4. 型号
84.18	电气或非电气的冷藏箱、冷冻箱及其他制冷设备; 热泵, 但品目84.15的空气调节器除外:	
	-冷藏—冷冻组合机, 各自装有单独外门的:	A: 1. 品名; 2. 结构[冷藏—冷冻组合机(各自装有单独外门的)]; 3. 容积。B: 4. 品牌; 5. 型号
	-家用型冷藏箱:	A: 1. 品名; 2. 用途(是否家用); 3. 原理; 4. 容积。B: 5. 品牌; 6. 型号
	-柜式冷冻箱, 容积不超过800升:	A: 1. 品名; 2. 容积; 3. 最低制冷温度; 4. 是否柜式。B: 5. 品牌; 6. 型号
	-立式冷冻箱, 容积不超过900升:	A: 1. 品名; 2. 结构(是否为立式); 3. 容积; 4. 最低制冷温度。B: 5. 品牌; 6. 型号
8418.5000	-装有冷藏或冷冻装置的其他设备(柜、箱、展示台、陈列箱及类似品), 用于存储及展示	A: 1. 品名; 2. 用途。B: 3. 品牌; 4. 型号; 5. 容积; 6. 最低制冷温度
	-其他制冷设备; 热泵:	A: 1. 品名; 2. 原理(是否为压缩式)。B: 3. 品牌; 4. 型号
	-零件:	A: 1. 品名; 2. 用途(适用机型); 3. 适用机型的制冷温度和容积。4. 品牌; 5. 型号。例: 立式冷冻箱箱门, 无品牌、型号, 制冷温度-30摄氏度, 容积460升
84.19	利用温度变化处理材料的机器、装置及类似的实验室设备, 例如, 加热、烹煮、烘炒、蒸馏、精馏、消毒、灭菌、汽蒸、干燥、蒸发、气化、冷凝、冷却的机器设备, 不论是否电热的(不包括品目85.14的炉, 烘箱及其他设备), 但家用的除外; 非电热的快速热水器或贮备式热水器:	
	-非电热的快速热水器或贮备式热水器:	A: 1. 品名; 2. 原理; 3. 加热方式。B: 4. 用途; 5. 品牌; 6. 型号

税则号列	商品名称	申报要素(A:归类要素 B:价格要素 C:审单及其他要素)及说明举例
8419.2000	-医用或实验室用消毒器具	A: 1.品名; 2.用途。B: 3.品牌; 4.型号
	-干燥器:	A: 1.品名; 2.用途; 3.干燥材质。B: 4.品牌; 5.型号
	-蒸馏或精馏设备:	A: 1.品名; 2.用途。B: 3.品牌; 4.型号; 5.原理
8419.5000	-热交换装置:	A: 1.品名。E: 2.用途; 3.品牌; 4.型号
	---制氧机:	A: 1.品名; 2.用途; 3.制氧量。B: 4.品牌; 5.型号
8419.6090	---其他	A: 1.品名; 2.用途。B: 3.品牌; 4.型号
	-其他机器设备:	A: 1.品名; 2.用途。B: 3.品牌; 4.型号
	-零件:	A: 1.品名; 2.用途(适用机型)。B: 3.品牌; 4.型号
8420.1000	-砑光机或其他滚压机器	A: 1.品名; 2.用途。B: 3.品牌; 4.型号
	-零件:	A: 1.品名; 2.用途(适用机型)。B: 3.品牌; 4.型号
8421.1100	--奶油分离器	A: 1.品名; 2.用途; 3.原理。B: 4.品牌; 5.型号
	--干衣机:	A: 1.品名; 2.用途; 3.原理; 4.干衣量。B: 5.品牌; 6.型号
	--其他:	A: 1.品名; 2.用途; 3.原理。B: 4.品牌; 5.型号
	--过滤或净化水用:	A: 1.品名; 2.用途。B: 3.品牌; 4.型号; 5.原理; 6.单位时间水处理量
8421.2200	--过滤或净化饮料(水除外)用	A: 1.品名; 2.用途; 3.原理。B: 4.品牌; 5.型号
8421.2300	--内燃发动机的滤油器	A: 1.品名; 2.用途; 3.原理。B: 4.品牌; 5.型号
	--其他:	A: 1.品名; 2.用途; 3.原理。B: 4.品牌; 5.型号
8421.3100	--内燃发动机的进气过滤器	A: 1.品名; 2.用途; 3.原理。B: 4.品牌; 5.型号
	--其他:	A: 1.品名; 2.用途; 3.原理。B: 4.品牌; 5.型号; 6.额定功率(非电动的不需注明额定功率)
	-零件:	A: 1.品名; 2.用途(适用机型)。B: 3.品牌; 4.型号
84.22	洗碟机;瓶子及其他容器的洗涤或干燥机器;瓶、罐、箱、袋或其他容器装填、封口、密封、贴标签的机器;瓶、罐、管、筒或类似容器的包封机器;其他包装或打包机器(包括热缩包装机器);饮料充气机:	
	-洗碟机:	A: 1.品名。B: 2.品牌; 3.型号。例: 飞利浦家用洗碟机,型号 TX098
8422.2000	-瓶子或其他容器的洗涤或干燥机器	A: 1.品名; 2.用途。B: 3.品牌; 4.型号
	-瓶、罐、箱、袋或其他容器的装填、封口、密封、贴标签的机器;瓶、罐、管、筒或类似容器的包封机器;饮料充气机:	A: 1.品名; 2 用途。B: 3.品牌; 4.型号
8422.4000	-其他包装或打包机器(包括热缩包装机器)	A: 1.品名; 2.用途; B: 3.品牌; 4.型号
	-零件:	A: 1.品名; 2.用途(适用机型); B: 3.品牌; 4.型号。例: 家用洗碟机碟架,无品牌、型号
8423.1000	-体重计,包括婴儿秤;家用秤	A: 1.品名; 2.用途。B: 3.品牌; 4.型号
	-输送带上连续称货的秤:	A: 1.品名; 2.用途; 3.原理。B: 4.品牌; 5.型号
	-恒定秤、物料定量装袋或装容器用的秤,包括库秤:	A: 1.品名; 2.用途。B: 3.品牌; 4.型号
	-其他衡器:	A: 1.品名; 2.用途; 3.原理; 4.最大称量。B: 5.品牌; 6.型号
8423.9000	-衡器用的各种砝码、秤砣;衡器的零件	A: 1.品名; 2.用途(适用机型)。B: 3.品牌; 4.型号
8424.1000	-灭火器,不论是否装药	A: 1.品名; 2.用途; B: 3.品牌; 4.型号
8424.2000	-喷枪及类似器具	A: 1.品名。B: 2.用途; 3.品牌; 4.喷射材料; 5.型号
8424.3000	-喷气机、喷砂机及类似的喷射机器	A: 1.品名; 2.喷射材料。B: 3.用途; 4.品牌; 5.型号
	-其他器具:	A: 1.品名; 2.用途。B: 3.品牌; 4.喷射材料; 5.型号
	-零件:	A: 1.品名; 2.用途(适用机型)。B: 3.品牌; 4.型号
84.25	滑车及提升机,但倒卸式提升机除外;卷扬机及绞盘;千斤顶:	A: 1.品名; 2.用途; 3.驱动方式。B: 4.品牌; 5.型号; 6.最大提升高度(距离); 7.最大提升重量
84.26	船用桅杆式起重机;起重机,包括缆式起重机;移动式吊运架、跨运车及装有起重机的工作车:	A: 1.品名; 2.用途; 3.结构类型。B: 4.品牌; 5.型号
84.27	叉车;其他装有升降或搬运装置的工作车:	A: 1.品名; 2.用途; 3.推进方式。B: 4.品牌; 5.型号; 6.最大提升高度(距离); 7.最大提升重量
8428.1010	---载客电梯	A: 1.品名; 2.用途。B: 3.品牌; 4.型号; 5.提升速度; 6.停层数; 7.载重量
8428.1090	---其他	A: 1.品名; 2.用途; B: 3.品牌; 4.型号
8428.2000	-气压升降机及输送机	A: 1.品名; 2.驱动方式。B: 3.品牌 4.型号
	-其他用于连续运送货物或材料的升降机及输送机:	A: 1.品名; 2.用途; 3.运送方式; 4.工作构件类型(斗式、带式等)。B: 5.品牌; 6.型号
8428.4000	-自动梯及自动人行道	A: 1.品名。B: 2.品牌; 3.型号
	-缆车、座式升降机、滑雪拉索、索道用牵引装置:	A: 1.品名; 2.用途; 3.原理; 4.结构类型. B: 5.品牌; 6.型号
	-其他机械:	A: 1.品名; 2.用途。B: 3.品牌; 4.型号

税则号列	商品名称	申报要素(A:归类要素 B:价格要素 C:审单及其他要素)及说明举例
84.29	机动推土机、侧铲推土机、筑路机、平地机、铲运机、机械铲、挖掘机、机铲装载机、捣固机械及压路机:	
	-推土机及侧铲推土机:	A: 1.品名; 2.行走装置类型(轮胎式、履带式等); 3.发动机输出功率。B: 4.品牌; 5. 是否自推进; 6.型号; 7.机械重量
	-筑路机及平地机:	A: 1.品名; 2.是否自推进; 3.发动机输出功率。B: 4.品牌; 5.型号
	-铲运机:	A: 1.品名; 2.是否自推进; 3.斗容量。B: 4.品牌; 5.型号
	-捣固机械及压路机:	A: 1.品名; 2.原理; 3.是否自推进; 4.机重。B: 5.品牌; 6.型号
8429.5100	--前铲装载机	A: 1.品名; 2. 是否自推进。B: 3.品牌; 4.行走装置类型(轮胎式、履带式等); 5.型号
	---挖掘机:	A: 1.品名; 2.行走装置类型(轮胎式、履带式等); 3.是否自推进; 4.是否上部结构可旋转360度。B: 5.品牌; 6.型号; 7.斗容量; 8.功率; 9.机重
8429.5290	---其他	A: 1.品名; 2.是否自推进; 3.是否上部结构可旋转360度。B: 4.品牌; 5. 行走装置类型(轮胎式、履带式等); 6.型号
8429.5900	--其他	A: 1.品名; 2.是否自推进。3.品牌; 4.行走装置类型(轮胎式、履带式等)5.型号; 6.斗容量; 7.功率; 8.机重
8430.1000	-打桩机及拔桩机	A: 1.品名。B: 2.品牌; 3.型号
8430.2000	-扫雪机及吹雪机	A: 1.品名。B: 2.品牌; 3.型号; 4.是否为自推进
	-采截煤机、凿岩机及隧道掘进机:	A: 1.品名; 2.是否自推进。B: 3.品牌; 4.型号。例: 三菱牌自推进隧道掘进机, 型号WD6532
	---石油及天然气钻探机	A: 1.品名; 2.用途; 3.是否自推进; 4.钻探深度。B: 5.品牌; 6.型号
8430.4121	----钻探深度在6000米及以上的	A: 1.品名; 2.用途; 3. 是否自推进; 4. 钻探深度。B: 5.品牌; 6.型号
8430.4122	----钻探深度在6000米以下的履带式自推进钻机	A: 1.品名; 2.用途; 3. 是否自推进; 4. 钻探深度。B: 5.品牌; 6.型号; 7.机身号; 8.钻头直径; 9.机身重量
8430.4129	----钻探深度在6000米以下的其他钻探机	A: 1.品名; 2.用途; 3.是否自推进; 4.钻探深度。B: 5.品牌; 6.型号
8430.4190	---其他	A: 1.品名; 2.用途; 3.是否自推进; 4.钻探深度。B: 5.品牌; 6.型号
8430.4900	--其他	A: 1.品名; 2.用途; 3.是否自推进; 4.钻探深度。B: 5.品牌; 6.型号
	-其他自推进机械:	A: 1.品名; 2.用途; 3.是否自推进; 4.牙轮直径。B: 5.品牌; 6.型号
	-其他非自推进机械:	A: 1.品名; 2.用途; 3.是否自推进; 4.钻筒直径。B: 5.品牌; 6.型号
84.31	专用于或主要用于税目84.25至84.30所列机械的零件:	A: 1.品名; 2.用途(适用机型)。B: 3.品牌; 4.型号。例: 挖掘机用挖斗, 无品牌、型号
8432.1000	-犁	A: 1.品名。B: 2.用途; 3.品牌; 4.型号
	-耙、松土机、中耕机、除草机及耕耘机:	A: 1.品名; 2.用途。B: 3.品牌; 4.型号
	-播种机、种植机及移植机	A: 1.品名; 2.用途。B: 3.品牌; 4.型号
8432.4000	-施肥机	A: 1.品名; 2.用途。B: 3.品牌; 4.型号
	-其他机械:	A: 1.品名; 2.用途。B: 3.品牌; 4.型号
8432.9000	-零件	A: 1.品名; 2.用途(适用机型)。B: 3.品牌; 4.型号
84.33	收割机、脱粒机, 包括草料打包机; 割草机; 蛋类、水果或其他农产品的清洁、分选、分级机器, 但品目84.37的机器除外:	
	-草坪、公园或运动场地用的割草机:	A: 1.品名; 2.用途; 3.驱动方式; 4.切割装置的旋转类型。B: 5.品牌; 6.型号
8433.2000	-其他割草机, 包括牵引装置用的刀具杆	A: 1.品名; 2.用途。B: 3.品牌; 4.型号
8433.3000	-其他干草切割、翻晒机器	A: 1.品名。B: 2.品牌; 3.型号
8433.4000	-草料打包机, 包括收集打包机	A: 1.品名。B: 2.品牌; 3.型号
8433.5100	--联合收割机	A: 1.品名; 2.用途。B: 3.品牌; 4.型号; 5.功率
8433.5200	--其他脱粒机	A: 1.品名; 2.用途。B: 3.品牌; 4.型号
8433.5300	--根茎或块茎收获机	A: 1.品名; 2.用途。B: 3.品牌; 4.型号; 5.功率
	--其他:	A: 1.品名; 2.用途。B: 3.品牌; 4.型号; 5.功率
8433.6000	-蛋类、水果或其他农产品的清洁、分选、分级机器	A: 1.品名; 2.用途。B: 3.品牌; 4.型号
	-零件:	A: 1.品名; 2.用途(适用机型)。B: 3.品牌; 4.型号
8434.1000	-挤奶机	A: 1.品名; 2.用途。B: 3.品牌; 4.型号
8434.2000	-乳品加工机器	A: 1.品名; 2.用途。B: 3.品牌; 4.型号
8434.9000	-零件	A: 1.品名; 2.用途(适用机型)。B: 3.品牌; 4.型号
8435.1000	-机器	A: 1.品名; 2.用途。B: 3.品牌; 4.型号
8435.9000	-零件	A: 1.品名; 2.用途(适用型号)。B: 3.品牌; 4.型号
8436.1000	-动物饲料配制机	A: 1.品名; 2.用途。B: 3.品牌; 4.型号
	-家禽饲养用的机器; 家禽孵卵器及育雏器:	A: 1.品名; 2.用途。B: 3.品牌; 4.型号

税则号列	商品名称	申报要素(A:归类要素 B:价格要素 C:审单及其他要素)及说明举例
8436.8000	-其他机器	A: 1. 品名; 2. 用途。B: 3. 品牌; 4. 型号
	-零件:	A: 1. 品名; 2. 用途(适用机型)。B: 3. 品牌; 4. 型号
84.37	种子、谷物或干豆的清洁、分选或分级机器；谷物磨粉业加工机器或谷物、干豆加工机器，但农业用机器除外:	
	-种子、谷物或干豆的清洁、分选或分级机器:	A: 1. 品名; 2. 用途。B: 3. 品牌; 4. 型号
8437.8000	-其他机器	A: 1. 品名; 2. 用途。B: 3. 品牌; 4. 型号
8437.9000	-零件	A: 1. 品名; 2. 用途(适用机型)。B: 3. 品牌; 4. 型号
8438.1000	-糕点加工机器及生产通心粉、面条或类似产品的机器	A: 1. 品名; 2. 用途。B: 3. 品牌; 4. 型号
8438.2000	-生产糖果、可可粉、巧克力的机器	A: 1. 品名; 2. 用途。B: 3. 品牌; 4. 型号
8438.3000	-制糖机器	A: 1. 品名; 2. 用途。B: 3. 品牌; 4. 型号
8438.4000	-酿酒机器	A: 1. 品名; 2. 用途。B: 3. 品牌; 4. 型号
8438.5000	-肉类或家禽加工机器	A: 1. 品名; 2. 用途。B: 3. 品牌; 4. 型号
8438.6000	-水果、坚果或蔬菜加工机器	A: 1. 品名; 2. 用途。B: 3. 品牌; 4. 型号
8438.8000	-其他机器	A: 1. 品名; 2. 用途。B: 3. 品牌; 4. 型号
8438.9000	-零件	A: 1. 品名; 2. 用途(适用机型)。B: 3. 品牌; 4. 型号
8439.1000	-制造纤维素纸浆的机器	A: 1. 品名; 2. 用途。B: 3. 品牌; 4. 型号
8439.2000	-纸或纸板的抄造机器	A: 1. 品名; 2. 用途。B: 3. 品牌; 4. 型号
8439.3000	-纸或纸板的整理机器	A: 1. 品名; 2. 用途。B: 3. 品牌; 4. 型号
	-零件:	A: 1. 品名; 2. 用途(适用机型)。B: 3. 品牌; 4. 型号
84.40	书本装订书器，包括锁线订书机:	
	-机器:	A: 1. 品名; 2. 用途。B: 3. 品牌; 4. 型号
8440.9000	-零件	A: 1. 品名; 2. 用途(适用机型)。B: 3. 品牌; 4. 型号
8441.1000	-切纸机	A: 1. 品名; 2. 用途。B: 3. 品牌; 4. 型号
8441.2000	-制造包、袋或信封的机器	A: 1. 品名; 2. 用途。B: 3. 品牌; 4. 型号
	-制造箱、盒、管、桶或类似容器的机器，但模制成型机器除外:	A: 1. 品名; 2. 用途。B: 3. 品牌; 4. 型号
8441.4000	-纸浆、纸或纸板制品模制成型机器	A: 1. 品名; 2. 用途。B: 3. 品牌; 4. 型号
	-其他机器:	A: 1. 品名; 2. 用途。B: 3. 品牌; 4. 型号
	-零件:	A: 1. 品名; 2. 用途(适用机型)。B: 3. 品牌; 4. 型号
84.42	制版用的机器、器具及设备(品目 84.56 至 84.65 的机床除外)；印刷用版(片)、滚筒及其他印刷部件；制成供印刷用(例如，刨平、压纹或抛光)的板(片)、滚筒及石板:	
	-机器、器具及设备:	A: 1. 品名; 2 用途; 3. 原理; B: 4. 品牌; 5. 型号
8442.4000	-上述机器、器具及设备的零件	A: 1. 品名; 2 用途(适用机型)。B: 3. 品牌; 4. 型号
8442.5000	-印刷用版(片)、滚筒及其他印刷部件；制成供印刷用(例如，刨平、压纹或抛光)的板(片)、滚筒及石板	A: 1. 品名; 2. 用途; 3. 原理。B: 4. 品牌; 5. 型号
84.43	用品目 84.42 的印刷用版(片)、滚筒及其他印刷部件进行印刷的机器；其他印刷(打印机)、复印机及传真机，不论是否组合式；上述机器的零件及附件:	
	-用税目 84.42 的印刷用版(片)、滚筒及其他印刷部件进行印刷的机器:	A: 1. 品名; 2. 用途; 3. 原理; 4. 进料方式; 5. 片尺寸。B: 6. 品牌; 7. 型号
	--具有印刷(打印)、复印或传真中两种及以上功能的机器，可与自动数据处理设备或网络连接:	A: 1. 品名; 2. 原理; 3. 功能。B: 4. 品牌; 5. 型号
	---专用于税目 84.71 所列设备的打印机:	A: 1. 品名; 2. 用途(是否专用于税目 84.71 所列设备); 3. 原理。B: 4. 品牌; 5. 型号; 6. 打印幅宽; 7. 打印速度
	---数字式印刷设备:	A: 1. 品名; 2. 用途; 3. 原理。B: 4. 品牌。5. 型号
8443.3290	----其他	A: 1. 品名; 2. 用途; 3. 原理。B: 4. 品牌; 5. 型号
	--其他:	A: 1. 品名; 2. 用途(是否专用于税目 84.71 所列设备); 3. 原理。B: 4. 品牌; 5. 型号
	-零件及附件:	A: 1. 品名; 2. 用途(适用机型)。B: 3. 品牌; 4. 型号
84.44	化学纺织纤维挤压、拉伸、变形或切割机器:	A: 1. 品名; 2. 用途。B: 3. 品牌; 4. 型号
84.45	纺织纤维的预处理机器；纺纱机，并线机、加捻机及其他生产纺织纱线的机器；摇纱机、络纱机(包括卷纬机)及处理税目 84.46 或 84.47 所列机器用的纺织纱线的机器:	A: 1. 品名; 2. 用途; 3. 原理。B: 4. 品牌; 5. 型号
84.46	织机:	A: 1. 品名; 2. 用途; 3. 原理; 4. 织物宽度。B: 5. 品牌; 6. 型号

税则号列	商品名称	申报要素(A:归类要素 B:价格要素 C:审单及其他要素)及说明举例
84.47	针织机、缝编机及制粗松螺旋花线、网眼薄纱、花边、刺绣品、装饰带、编织带或网的机器及簇绒机:	
	-圆型针织机:	A: 1. 品名; 2. 圆筒直径。B: 3. 品牌; 4. 型号
	-平型针织机; 缝编机:	A: 1. 品名; 2. 原理。B: 3. 品牌; 4. 型号; 5. 幅宽
	-其他:	A: 1. 品名; 2. 原理。B: 3. 品牌; 4. 型号
84.48	税目 84.44、84.45、84.46 或 84.47 所列机器的辅助机器(例如，多臂机、提花机、自停装置及换梭装置); 专用于或主要用于税目 84.44、84.45、84.46 或 84.47 所列机器的零件、附件(例如，锭子、锭壳、钢丝针布、梳、喷丝头、梭子、综丝、综框、针织机用针):	A: 1. 品名; 2. 用途(适用机型)。B: 3. 品牌; 4. 型号。例: 织机用综框，无品牌、型号
84.49	成匹、成形的毡呢或无纺织物制造或整理机器，包括制毡呢帽机器; 帽模:	A: 1. 品名; 2. 原理。B: 3. 品牌; 4. 型号
84.50	家用型或洗衣房用洗衣机，包括洗涤干燥两用机:	
	-干衣量不超过 10 千克的洗衣机:	A: 1. 品名; 2. 原理; 3. 是否全自动; 4. 干衣量。B: 5. 品牌; 6. 型号
	-干衣量超过 10 千克的洗衣机	A: 1. 品名; 2. 原理; 3. 是否全自动; 4. 干衣量。B: 5. 品牌; 6. 型号
	-零件:	A: 1. 品名; 2. 用途(适用机型)。B: 3. 品牌; 4. 型号
8451.1000	-干洗机	A: 1. 品名; 2. 用途。B: 3. 品牌; 4. 型号; 5. 衣容量(千克)
	-干燥机:	A: 1. 品名; 2. 用途; 3. 干衣量。B: 4. 品牌; 5. 型号
8451.3000	-熨烫机及挤压机(包括熔压机)	A: 1. 品名; 2. 用途。B: 3. 品牌; 4. 型号
8451.4000	-洗涤、漂白或染色机器	A: 1. 品名; 2. 用途。B: 3. 品牌; 4. 型号
8451.5000	-纺织物的卷绕、退绕、折叠、剪切或剪齿边机器	A: 1. 品名; 2. 用途。B: 3. 品牌; 4. 型号
8451.8000	-其他机器	A: 1. 品名; 2. 用途。B: 3. 品牌; 4. 型号
8451.9000	-零件	A: 1. 品名; 2. 用途(适用机型)。B: 3. 品牌; 4. 型号
84.52	缝纫机，但品目 84.40 的锁线订书机除外; 缝纫机专用的特制家具、底座及罩盖; 缝纫机针:	
	-家用型缝纫机:	A: 1. 品名; 2. 用途; 3. 是否手动。B: 4. 品牌; 5. 型号
	-其他缝纫机:	A: 1. 品名; 2. 用途; 3. 是否自动。B: 4. 品牌; 5. 型号
8452.3000	-缝纫机针	A: 1. 品名; 2. 用途。B: 3. 品牌; 4. 型号
	-缝纫机专用的特制家具、底座和罩盖及其零件; 缝纫机的其他零件:	A: 1. 品名; 2. 用途(适用机型)。B: 3. 品牌; 4. 型号
8453.1000	-生皮、皮革的处理、鞣制或加工机器	A: 1. 品名; 2. 用途。B: 3. 品牌; 4. 型号
8453.2000	-鞋靴制作或修理机器	A: 1. 品名; 2. 用途。B: 3. 品牌; 4. 型号
8453.8000	-其他机器	A: 1. 品名; 2. 用途。B: 3. 品牌; 4. 型号
8453.9000	-零件	A: 1. 品名; 2. 用途(适用机型)。B: 3. 品牌; 4. 型号
8454.1000	-转炉	A: 1. 品名; 2. 用途。B: 3. 品牌; 4. 型号
	-锭模及浇包:	A: 1. 品名; 2. 用途。B: 3. 品牌; 4. 型号
	-铸造机:	A: 1. 品名; 2. 用途。B: 3. 品牌; 4. 型号
	-零件:	A: 1. 品名; 2. 用途(适用机型)。B: 3. 品牌; 4. 型号
84.55	金属轧机及其轧辊:	
	-轧管机:	A: 1. 品名; 2. 用途; 3. 加工方式; B: 4. 品牌; 5. 型号
	-其他轧机:	A: 1. 品名; 2. 用途; 3. 加工方式。B: 4. 品牌; 5. 型号
8455.3000	-轧机用轧辊	A: 1. 品名; 2. 用途(适用机型)。B: 3. 品牌; 4. 型号; 5. 规格(轧辊长度、辊身直径、辊颈直径)
8455.9000	-其他零件	A: 1. 品名; 2. 用途(适用机型)。B: 3. 品牌; 4. 型号
8456.1000	-用激光、其他光或光子束处理的	A: 1. 品名; 2. 功能; 3. 加工方式。B: 4. 品牌; 5. 型号
8456.2000	-用超声波处理的	A: 1. 品名; 2. 功能; 3. 加工方式。B: 4. 品牌; 5. 型号
	-用放电处理的:	A: 1. 品名; 2. 控制方式; 3. 功能; 4. 加工方式。B: 5. 品牌; 6. 型号
	-其他:	A: 1. 品名; 2. 控制方式; 3. 功能; 4. 加工方式。B: 5. 品牌; 6. 型号
84.57	加工金属的加工中心、单工位组合机床及多工位组合机床:	
	-加工中心:	A: 1. 品名; 2. 用途; 3. 功能(如金属钻、镗、铣等); 4. 可加装刀库注明刀库容量及选配件; 5. 是否可自动换刀。B: 6. 品牌; 7. 型号。例: 立式加工中心，金属钻、铣，带刀库(12 件)，可自动换刀，永进牌，型号 YCM-MV66A
8457.2000	-单工位组合机床	A: 1. 品名; 2. 用途; 3. 功能(如金属钻、镗、铣等); 4. 加工工位数; 5: 动力头个数。B: 6. 品牌; 7. 型号
8457.3000	-多工位组合机床	A: 1. 品名; 2. 用途; 3. 功能(如金属钻、镗、铣等); 4. 加工工位数; 5: 动力头个数。B: 6. 品牌; 7. 型号

税则号列	商品名称	申报要素(A:归类要素 B:价格要素 C:审单及其他要素)及说明举例
84.58	切削金属的车床(包括车削中心):	A: 1. 品名; 2. 用途; 3. 控制方式; 4. 主轴方向(垂直或水平)。B: 5. 品牌; 6. 型号
8459.1000	-直线移动式动力头机床	A: 1. 品名; 2. 用途; 3. 功能; 4. 动力头移动方式。B: 5. 品牌; 6. 控制方式; 7. 型号; 8. 可加装刀库注明刀库容及量及选配件
	-其他钻床:	A: 1. 品名; 2. 用途; 3. 功能; 4. 控制方式。B: 5. 品牌; 6. 型号
	-其他镗铣机床:	A: 1. 品名; 2. 用途; 3. 功能; 4. 控制方式。B: 5. 品牌; 6. 型号
	-其他镗床:	A: 1. 品名; 2. 用途; 3. 功能; 4. 控制方式。B: 5. 品牌; 6. 型号
	-升降台式铣床:	A: 1. 品名; 2. 用途; 3. 功能; 4. 控制方式; 5. 是否为升降台式。B: 6. 品牌; 7. 型号
	-其他铣床:	A: 1. 品名; 2. 用途; 3. 功能; 4. 控制方式; 5. 是否为龙门式。B: 6. 品牌; 7. 型号
8459.7000	-其他攻丝机床	A: 1. 品名; 2. 用途; 3. 功能。B: 4. 品牌; 5. 控制方式; 6. 型号
84.60	用磨石、磨料或抛光材料对金属或金属陶瓷进行去毛刺、刃磨、磨削、珩磨、研磨、抛光或其他精加工机床,但品目 84.61 的切齿机、齿轮磨床或齿轮精加工机床除外:	
	-平面磨床,在任一坐标的定位精度至少是 0.01 毫米:	A: 1. 品名; 2. 用途; 3. 控制方式; 4. 坐标定位精度。B: 5. 品牌; 6. 型号
	-其他磨床,在任一坐标的定位精度至少是 0.01 毫米:	A: 1. 品名; 2. 用途; 3. 控制方式; 4. 坐标定位精度; 5. 结构类型(内圆、外圆等)。B: 6. 品牌; 7. 型号
	-刃磨(工具或刀具)机床:	A: 1. 品名; 2. 用途; 3. 控制方式。B: 4. 品牌; 5. 型号
	-珩磨或研磨机床:	A: 1. 品名; 2. 用途。B: 3. 品牌; 4. 型号
	-其他:	A: 1. 品名; 2. 用途。B: 3. 品牌; 4. 型号
84.61	切削金属或金属陶瓷的刨床、牛头刨床、插床、拉床、切齿机、齿轮磨床或齿轮精加工机床、锯床、切断机及其他税目未列名的切削机床:	
	-牛头刨床或插床:	A: 1. 品名; 2. 用途; 3.. 功能; 4. 结构类型。B: 5. 品牌; 6. 型号
8461.3000	-拉床	A: 1. 品名; 2. 用途; 3. 功能; 4. 结构类型; B: 5. 品牌; 6. 型号
	-切齿机、齿轮磨床或齿轮精加工机床:	A: 1. 品名; 2. 用途; 3. 控制方式; 4. 功能。B: 5. 品牌; 6. 型号
8461.5000	-锯床或切断机	A: 1. 品名; 2. 用途; 3. 功能。B: 4. 品牌; 5. 型号
	-其他:	A: 1. 品名; 2. 用途; 3. 功能; 。4. 结构类型。B: 5. 品牌; 6. 型号
84.62	加工金属的锻造(包括模锻)或冲压机床;加工金属的弯曲、折叠、矫直、矫平、剪切、冲孔或开槽机床;其他加工金属或硬质合金的压力机:	
	-锻造(包括模锻)或冲压机床及锻锤:	A: 1. 品名; 2. 用途; 3. 功能; 4. 控制方式。B: 5. 品牌; 6. 型号
	-弯曲、折叠、矫直或矫平机床:	A: 1. 品名; 2. 用途; 3. 功能; 4. 控制方式。B: 5. 品牌; 6. 型号
	-剪切机床,但冲剪两用机除外:	A: 1. 品名; 2. 用途; 3. 功能; 4. 控制方式。B: 5. 品牌; 6. 型号
	-冲孔或开槽机床,包括冲剪两用机:	A: 1. 品名; 2. 用途; 3. 功能; 4. 控制方式。B: 5. 品牌; 6. 型号
	-其他:	A: 1. 品名; 2. 用途; 3. 功能; 4. 加工方式(弯曲、折叠、卷曲等)。B: 5. 品牌; 6. 型号
84.63	金属或金属陶瓷的其他非切削加工机床:	A: 1. 品名; 2. 用途; 3. 功能。B: 4. 品牌; 5. 型号
84.64	石料、陶瓷、混凝土、石棉水泥或类似矿物材料的加工机床、玻璃冷加工机床:	A: 1. 品名; 2. 用途; 3. 功能; 4. 加工材料。B: 5. 品牌; 6. 型号
84.65	木材、软木、骨、硬质橡胶、硬质塑料或类似硬质材料的加工机床(包括用打钉或打 U 形钉、胶粘或其他方法组合前述材料的机器):	A: 1. 品名; 2. 用途; 3. 功能; 4. 加工材料。B: 5. 品牌; 6. 型号
84.66	专用于或主要用于税目 84.56 至 84.65 所列机器的零件、附件,包括工件或工具的夹具、自启扳牙切头、分度头及其他专用于机床的附件;各种手提工具的工具夹具:	A: 1. 品名; 2 用途(适用机型)。B: 3. 品牌; 4. 型号
84.67	手提式风动或液压工具及本身装有电动或非电动动力装置的手提式工具:	
	-风动的:	A: 1. 品名; 2. 驱动方式; 3. 是否为手提式。B: 4. 品牌; 5. 型号
	-本身装有电动动力装置的:	A: 1. 品名; 2. 驱动方式; 3. 是否为手提式。B: 4. 品牌; 5. 型号
	-其他工具:	A: 1 品名; 2. 驱动方式; 3. 是否为手提式。B: 4. 品牌; 5. 型号
	-零件:	A: 1. 品名; 2. 用途(适用机型)。B: 3. 品牌; 4. 型号
8468.1000	-手提喷焊器	A: 1. 品名; 2. 原理; 3. 是否为手提式。B: 4. 品牌; 5. 型号
8468.2000	-其他气体焊接或表面回火机器及装置	A: 1. 品名; 2. 原理; 3. 是否为手提式。B: 4. 品牌; 5. 型号
8468.8000	-其他机器及装置	A: 1. 品名; 2. 原理; 3. 是否为手提式。B: 4. 品牌; 5. 型号
8468.9000	-零件	A: 1. 品名; 2. 用途(适用机型)。B: 3. 品牌; 4. 型号
84.69	打字机,但税目 84.43 的打印机除外;	A: 1. 品名; 2. 驱动方式。B: 3. 品牌; 4. 型号

税则号列	商品名称	申报要素(A:归类要素 B:价格要素 C:审单及其他要素)及说明举例
	文字处理机:	
8470.1000	-不需外接电源的电子计算器及具有计算功能的袖珍式数据记录、重现及显示机器	A:1.品名;2.是否需外接电源。B:3.品牌; 4.型号。例:东芝电子计算器(不需外接电源的),型号WQX-9
	-其他电子计算器:	A:1.品名;2.是否有打印装置。B:3.品牌; 4.型号
8470.3000	-其他计算机器	A:1.品名。B:2.品牌;3.型号
	-现金出纳机:	A:1.品名;2.用途。B:3.品牌;4.型号
8470.9000	-其他	A:1.品名;2.用途。B:3.品牌;4.型号
84.71	自动数据处理设备及其部件;其他税目未列明的磁性或光学阅读机、将数据以代码形式转录到数据记录媒体的机器及处理这些数据的机器:	
	-重量不超过10千克的便携数字式自动数据处理设备,至少由一个中央处理部件、一个键盘及一个显示器组成	A:1.品名;2.机型;3.配置(系统组成部件)。B:4.品牌; 5.型号
	--同一机壳内至少有一个中央处理部件及一个输入和输出部件,不论是否组合式:	A:1.品名;2.机型;3.配置(系统组成部件)。B:4.品牌; 5.型号 6.操作系统
	--其他,以系统形式进口或出口的:	A:1.品名;2.机型;3.配置(系统组成部件); 4.是否以系统形式报验。B:5.品牌; 6.型号; 7.操作系统
	-子目8471.41或8471.49所列以外的处理部件,不论是否在同一机壳内有一个或两个下列部件存储部件、输入部件、输出部件:	A:1.品名;2.机型;3.配置(系统组成部件)。B:4.品牌; 5.型号; 6.操作系统; 7.用途
8471.6040	---巨型机、大型机、中型机及小型机用终端	A:1.品名。B:2.品牌;3.型号
8471.6050	---扫描仪	A:1.品名。B:2.品牌;3.型号
8471.6060	---数字化仪	A:1.品名。B:2.品牌;3.型号
	---键盘、鼠标器:	A:1.品名。B:2.品牌;3.机型;4.型号;5.连接方式(有线、无线)
8471.6090	---其他	A:1.品名。B:2.品牌;3.型号
8471.7010	---硬盘驱动器	A:1.品名。B:2.品牌;3.型号;4.硬盘容量及缓存容量;5.转速
8471.7020	---软盘驱动器	A:1.品名。B:2.品牌;3.型号
8471.7030	---光盘驱动器	A:1.品名。B:2.品牌;3.型号。例:HP牌光盘驱动器,型号SOHC-4832K,CD-ROM,48X,不带刻录功能
8471.7090	---其他	A:1.品名。B:2.品牌;3.型号
8471.8000	-自动数据处理设备的其他部件	A:1.品名。B:2.品牌;3.型号
8471.9000	-其他	A:1.品名。B:2.品牌;3.型号
8472.1000	-胶版复印机、油印机	A:1.品名;2.用途。B:3.品牌;4.型号
	-信件分类或折叠机或信件装封机、信件开封或闭封机,粘贴或盖销邮票机:	A:1.品名;2.用途。B:3.品牌;4.型号
8472.9010	---自动柜员机	A:1.品名;2.用途(存款、取款、存取款一体机等)。B:3.品牌;4.型号;5.配置; 6.安装方式(穿墙式等)
	---装订用机器:	A:1.品名;2.用途。B:3.品牌;4.型号
8472.9030	---碎纸机	A:1.品名;2.用途。B:3.品牌;4.型号
8472.9040	---地址印写机及地址铭牌压印机	A:1.品名;2.用途。B:3.品牌;4.型号
8472.9090	---其他	A:1.品名;2.用途。B:3.品牌;4.型号
84.73	专用于或主要用于税目84.69至84.72所列机器的零件、附件(罩套、提箱及类似品除外):	A:1.品名;2.用途(适用机型)。B:3.品牌;4.型号。例:软盘驱动器用盘架,无品牌、型号
8474.1000	-分类、筛选、分离或洗涤机器	A:1.品名;2.用途。B:3.品牌;4.型号
	-破碎或磨粉机器:	A:1.品名;2.用途;3.原理。B:4.品牌; 5.型号
	-混合或搅拌机器:	A:1.品名;2.用途。B:3.品牌;4.型号
	-其他机器:	A:1.品名;2.用途;3.原理。B:4.品牌; 5.型号
8474.9000	-零件	A:1.品名;2.用途(适用机型)。3.品牌;4.型号
8475.1000	-白炽灯泡、灯管、放电灯管、电子管、闪光灯泡及类似品的封装机器	A:1.品名;2.用途。B:3.品牌;4.型号
	-玻璃或玻璃制品的制造或热加工机器:	A:1.品名;2.用途。B:3.品牌;4.型号
8475.9000	-零件	A:1.品名;2.用途(适用机型)。B:3.品牌;4.型号
84.76	自动售货机(例如,出售邮票、香烟、食品或饮料的机器),包括钱币兑换机:	

税则号列	商品名称	申报要素(A:归类要素 B:价格要素 C:审单及其他要素)及说明举例
	-饮料自动销售机:	A: 1. 品名; 2. 供应商品种类; 3. 是否装有加热或制冷装置。B: 4. 品牌; 5. 型号
	-其他机器:	A: 1. 品名; 2. 供应商品种类; 3. 是否装有加热或制冷装置。B: 4. 品牌; 5. 型号
8476.9000	-零件	A: 1. 品名; 2. 用途(适用机型)。B: 3. 品牌; 4. 型号
84.77	本章其他税目未列名的橡胶或塑料及其产品的加工机器:	
	-注射机:	A: 1. 品名; 2. 用途; 3. 功能。B: 4. 品牌; 5. 型号; 6. 合模力
	-挤出机:	A: 1. 品名; 2. 用途; 3. 功能。B: 4. 品牌; 5. 型号
	-吹塑机	A: 1. 品名; 2. 用途; 3. 功能。B: 4. 品牌; 5. 型号
	-真空模塑机器及其他热成型机器:	A: 1. 品名; 2. 用途; 3. 功能。B: 4. 品牌; 5. 型号
	-其他模塑或成型机器:	A: 1. 品名; 2. 用途; 3. 功能。B: 4. 品牌; 5. 型号
8477.8000	-其他机器	A: 1. 品名; 2. 用途。B: 3. 品牌; 4. 型号
8477.9000	-零件	A: 1. 品名; 2. 用途(适用机型)。B: 3. 品牌; 4. 型号
8478.1000	-机器	A: 1. 品名; 2. 用途。B: 3. 品牌; 4. 型号
8478.9000	-零件	A: 1. 品名; 2. 用途(适用机型)。B: 3. 品牌; 4. 型号
84.79	本章其他税目未列名的具有独立功能的机器及机械器具:	
	-公共工程用机器:	A: 1. 品名; 2. 用途; 3. 功能。B: 4. 品牌; 5. 型号
8479.2000	-提取、加工动物油脂或植物固定油脂的机器	A: 1. 品名; 2. 用途; 3. 功能。B: 4. 品牌; 5. 型号
8479.3000	-木碎料板或木纤维板的挤压机及其他木材或软木处理机	A: 1. 品名; 2. 用途; 3. 功能。B: 4. 品牌; 5. 型号
8479.4000	-绳或缆的制造机器	A: 1. 品名; 2. 用途; 3. 功能。B: 4. 品牌; 5. 型号
	-未列名工业用机器人:	A: 1. 品名; 2. 用途; 3. 功能。B: 4. 品牌; 5. 型号
8479.6000	-蒸发式空气冷却器	A: 1. 品名; 2. 用途; 3. 功能。B: 4. 品牌; 5. 型号
	-旅客登机（船）桥:	A: 1. 品名; 2. 用途; 3. 功能。B: 4. 品牌; 5. 型号
	-其他机器及机械器具:	A: 1. 品名; 2. 用途; 3. 功能。B: 4. 品牌; 5. 型号
	-零件:	A: 1. 品名; 2. 用途(适用机型)。B: 3. 品牌; 4. 型号
8480.1000	-金属铸造用型箱	A: 1. 品名; 2. 用途; 3. 适用材料。B: 4. 品牌; 5. 型号
8480.2000	-型模底板	A: 1. 品名; 2. 用途; 3. 适用材料。B: 4. 品牌; 5. 型号
8480.3000	-阳模	A: 1. 品名; 2. 用途; 3. 适用材料。B: 4. 品牌; 5. 型号
	-金属、硬质合金用型模:	A: 1. 品名; 2. 用途; 3. 适用材料。B: 4. 品牌; 5. 型号; 6. 原理
8480.5000	-玻璃用型模	A: 1. 品名; 2. 用途; 3. 适用材料。B: 4. 品牌; 5. 型号
8480.6000	-矿物材料用型模	A: 1. 品名; 2. 用途; 3. 适用材料。B: 4. 品牌; 5. 型号
	-塑料或橡胶用型模:	A: 1. 品名; 2. 用途; 3. 适用材料。B: 4. 品牌; 5. 型号; 6. 原理
8481.1000	-减压阀	A: 1. 品名; 2. 用途。B: 3. 品牌; 4. 型号
	-油压或气压传动阀:	A: 1. 品名; 2. 用途。B: 3. 品牌; 4. 型号
8481.3000	-止回阀	A: 1. 品名; 2. 用途。B: 3. 品牌; 4. 型号
8481.4000	-安全阀或溢流阀	A: 1. 品名; 2. 用途。B: 3. 品牌; 4. 型号
	---换向阀:	A: 1. 品名; 2. 用途 3. 是否电磁式。B: 4. 品牌; 5. 型号
	---流量阀:	A: 1. 品名; 2. 用途。B: 3. 品牌; 4. 型号
8481.8040	---其他阀门	A: 1. 品名; 2. 用途。B: 3. 品牌; 4. 型号
8481.8090	---其他	A: 1. 品名; 2. 用途。B: 3. 品牌; 4. 型号
	-零件:	A: 1. 品名; 2. 用途（适用机型）。B: 3. 品牌; 4. 型号
84.82	滚珠轴承:	
	-滚珠轴承:	A: 1. 品名; 2. 结构类型; 3. 用途。B: 4. 品牌; 5. 型号
8482.2000	-锥形滚子轴承, 包括锥形滚子组件	A: 1. 品名; 2. 结构类型; 3. 用途。B: 4. 品牌; 5. 型号
8482.3000	-鼓形滚子轴承	A: 1. 品名; 2. 结构类型; 3. 用途。B: 4. 品牌; 5. 型号
8482.4000	-滚针轴承	A: 1. 品名; 2. 结构类型; 3. 用途。B: 4. 品牌; 5. 型号
8482.5000	-其他圆柱形滚子轴承	A: 1. 品名; 2. 结构类型; 3. 用途。B: 4. 品牌; 5. 型号
8482.8000	-其他, 包括球、柱混合轴承	A: 1. 品名; 2. 结构类型; 3. 用途。B: 4. 品牌; 5. 型号
8482.9100	--滚珠、滚针及滚柱:	A: 1. 品名; 2. 用途（适用机型）; 3. 直径（包括最大、最小及标称直径）。B: 4. 品牌; 5. 型号
8482.9900	--其他	A: 1. 品名; 2. 用途（适用机型）。B: 3. 品牌; 4. 型号
84.83	传动轴（包括凸轮轴及曲柄轴）及曲柄; 轴承座及滑动轴承; 齿轮及齿轮传动装置; 滚珠或滚子螺杆传动装置; 齿轮箱及其他变速装置, 包括扭矩变换器; 飞轮及滑轮, 包括滑轮组; 离合器及联轴器（包括万向节）:	
	-传动轴(包括凸轮轴及曲柄轴)及曲柄:	A: 1. 品名; 2. 用途。B: 3. 品牌; 4. 型号
8483.2000	-装有滚珠或滚子轴承的轴承座	A: 1. 品名; 2. 注明是否装有滚珠或滚子轴承; 3. 用途。B: 4. 品牌; 5. 型号
8483.3000	-未装有滚珠或滚子轴承的轴承座; 滑动轴承	A: 1. 品名; 2. 如为轴承座需注明是否带有滚珠或滚子轴承; 3. 用途。B: 4. 品牌; 5. 型号
	-齿轮及齿轮传动装置, 但单独报验的	A: 1. 品名; 2. 原理。3. 用途。B: 4. 品牌; 5. 型号

税则号列	商品名称	申报要素(A:归类要素 B:价格要素 C:审单及其他要素)及说明举例
	带齿的轮、链轮及其他传动元件除外;滚珠或滚子螺杆传动装置;齿轮箱及其他变速装置,包括扭矩变换器:	
8483.5000	-飞轮及滑轮,包括滑轮组	A:1.品名; 2.用途。B:3.品牌;4.型号
8483.6000	-离合器及联轴器(包括万向节)	A:1.品名;2.用途。B:3.品牌;4.型号
8483.9000	-单独报验的带齿的轮、链轮及其他传动元件;零件	A:1.品名; 2.用途。B:3.品牌;4.型号
8484.1000	-密封垫或类似接合衬垫,用金属片与其他材料制成或用双层或多层金属片制成	A:1.品名。2.组成材料。B:3.品牌; 4.型号
8484.2000	-机械密封件	A:1.品名;2.结构。B:3.品牌; 4.型号
8484.9000	-其他	A:1.品名;2.各自构成材料;3.是否成套包装。B:4.品牌;5.型号
84.86	专用于或主要用于制造半导体单晶柱或晶圆、半导体器件、集成电路或平板显示器的机器及装置;本章注释九(三)规定的机器及装置;零件及附件:	
	-制造单晶柱或圆片用的机器及装置:	A:1.品名;2.用途;3.功能。B:4.品牌;5.型号
	-制造半导体器件或集成电路用的机器及装置:	A:1.品名;2.用途;3.功能。B:4.品牌;5.型号
	-制造平板显示器用的机器及装置:	A:1.品名;2.用途;3.功能。B:4.品牌;5.型号
	-本章注释九(三)规定的机器及装置:	A:1.品名;2.用途;3.功能。B:4.品牌;5.型号
	-零件及附件:	A:1.品名;2.用途(适用机型)。B:3.品牌;4.型号
84.87	本章其他税目未列名的机器零件,不具有电气接插件、绝缘体、线圈、触点或其他电气器材特征的:	A:1.品名;2.用途(适用机型)。B:3.品牌;4.型号

第八十五章　电机、电气设备及其零件;录音机及放声机、电视图像、声音的录制和重放设备及其零件、附件

税则号列	商品名称	申报要素(A:归类要素 B:价格要素 C:审单及其他要素)及说明举例
8501.1010	---玩具用	A:1.品名;2.用途;3.输出功率。B:4.品牌; 5.型号
	---其他:	A:1.品名;2.用途;3.输出功率; 4.机座尺寸。B:5.品牌; 6.型号
8501.2000	-交直流两用电动机,输出功率超过37.5瓦	A:1.品名;2.用途;3.是否为交直流两用;4.输出功率。B:5.品牌; 6.型号
	-其他直流电动机;直流发电机:	A:1.品名;2.是否为直流;3.输出功率。B:4.品牌; 5.型号
8501.4000	-其他单相交流电动机	A:1.品名;2.是否为单相交流;3.输出功率。B:4.品牌; 5.型号
	-其他多相交流电动机:	A:1.品名;2.输出功率; 3.是否为多相电动机。B:4.品牌; 5.型号
	-交流发电机:	A:1.品名;2.用途;3.是否为交流;4.输出功率。B:5.品牌; 6.型号
85.02	发电机组及旋转式变流机:	A:1.品名;2.组成原动机类型;3.输出功率。B:4.品牌; 5.型号
85.03	专用于或主要用于税目85.01或85.02所列机器的零件:	A:1.品名;2.用途(适用机型)。B:3.品牌;4.型号
85.04	变压器、静止式变流器(例如,整流器)及电感器:	
	-放电灯或放电管用镇流器:	A:1.品名;2.用途。B:3.品牌;4.型号
	-液体介质变压器:	A:1.品名;2.额定容量;3.是否为液体介质。B:4.品牌; 5.型号
	-其他变压器:	A:1.品名;2.额定容量;3.是否为液体介质。B:4.品牌; 5.型号
	---稳压电源:	A:1.品名;2.用途;3.类型(交流稳压电源或直流稳压电源);4.功率;5.精度。B:6.品牌; 7.型号
8504.4020	---不间断供电电源	A:1.品名;2.功率。B:3.品牌; 4.型号
8504.4030	---逆变器	A:1.品名;2.功率。B:3.品牌; 4.型号
8504.4091	----具有变流功能的半导体模块	A:1.品名;2.用途;3.是否封装。B:4.品牌; 5.型号
8504.4099	----其他	A:1.品名; 2.用途; 3.功率。B:4.品牌; 5.型号
8504.5000	-其他电感器	A:1.品名;2.用途。B:3.品牌;4.型号
	-零件:	A:1.品名;2.用途(适用机型)。B:3.品牌;4.型号
8505.1110	---稀土的	A:1.品名; 2.用途; 3.材质。B:4.品牌; 5.型号。C:6.稀土元素的重量百分比以[A]表示
8505.1190	---其他	A:1.品名; 2.用途; 3.材质。B:4.品牌; 5.型号
8505.1900	--其他	A:1.品名; 2.用途; 3.材质。B:4.品牌; 5.型号

税则号列	商品名称	申报要素(A:归类要素 B:价格要素 C:审单及其他要素)及说明举例
8505.2000	-电磁联轴节、离合器及制动器	A: 1.品名; 2.用途。B: 3.品牌; 4.型号
	-其他，包括零件:	A: 1.品名; 2.用途; 3.原理。B: 4.品牌 5.型号
8506.1011	----扣式	A: 1.品名; 2.用途; 3.材质; 4.形状。B: 5.品牌; 6.型号; 7.容量; 8.是否含汞
8506.1012	----圆柱形	A: 1.品名; 2.用途; 3.材质; 4.形状。B: 5.品牌; 6.型号; 7.容量; 8.是否含汞
8506.1019	----其他	A: 1.品名; 2.用途; 3.材质。B: 4.品牌; 5.型号; 6.容量; 7.是否含汞
8506.1090	---其他	A: 1.品名; 2.用途; 3.材质。B: 4.品牌; 5.型号; 6.容量; 7.是否含汞
8506.3000	-氧化汞的	A: 1.品名; 2.用途; 3.材质。B: 4.品牌; 5.型号; 6.容量; 7.是否含汞
8506.4000	-氧化银的	A: 1.品名; 2.用途; 3.材质。B: 4.品牌; 5.型号; 6.容量; 7.是否含汞
8506.5000	-锂的	A: 1.品名; 2.用途; 3.材质。B: 4.品牌; 5.型号; 6.容量; 7.是否含汞
8506.6000	-锌空气的	A: 1.品名; 2.用途; 3.材质。B: 4.品牌; 5.型号; 6.容量; 7.是否含汞
8506.8000	-其他原电池及原电池组	A: 1.品名; 2.用途; 3.材质。B: 4.品牌; 5.型号; 6.容量; 7.是否含汞
	-零件:	A: 1.品名; 2.用途(适用机型)。B: 3.品牌; 4.型号
8507.1000	-铅酸蓄电池，用于启动活塞式发动机	A: 1.品名; 2.用途; 3.材质。B: 4.品牌; 5.型号; 6.容量; 7.是否含汞; 8.额定电压
8507.2000	-其他铅酸蓄电池	A: 1.品名; 2.用途; 3.材质。B: 4.品牌; 5.型号; 6.容量; 7.是否含汞; 8.额定电压
8507.3000	-镍镉蓄电池	A: 1.品名; 2.用途; 3.材质。B: 4.品牌; 5.型号; 6.容量; 7.是否含汞; 8.额定电压
8507.4000	-镍铁蓄电池	A: 1.品名; 2.用途; 3.材质。B: 4.品牌; 5.型号; 6.容量; 7.是否含汞; 8.额定电压
8507.5000	-镍氢蓄电池	A: 1.品名; 2.用途; 3.材质。B: 4.品牌; 5.型号; 6.容量; 7.是否含汞; 8.额定电压
8507.6000	-锂离子蓄电池	A: 1.品名; 2.用途; 3.材质。B: 4.品牌; 5.型号; 6.容量; 7.是否含汞; 8.额定电压
	-其他蓄电池:	A: 1.品名; 2.用途; 3.材质。B: 4.品牌; 5.型号; 6.容量; 7.是否含汞; 8.额定电压
	-零件:	A: 1.品名; 2.用途（适用机型）。B: 3.品牌; 4.型号
85.08	真空吸尘器:	
	-电动的:	A: 1.品名; 2.驱动方式; 3.集尘器容积。B: 4.品牌; 5.型号; 6.功率
8508.6000	-其他真空吸尘器	A: 1.品名; 2.驱动方式。B: 3.品牌; 4.型号
	-零件:	A: 1.品名; 2.用途(适用机型)。B: 3.品牌; 4.型号
85.09	家用电动器具，税目85.08的真空吸尘器除外:	
	-食品研磨机及搅拌器；水果或蔬菜的榨汁器:	A: 1.品名; 2.用途; 3.机重; 4.功率。B: 5.品牌; 6.型号
	-其他器具:	A: 1.品名; 2.用途; 3.机重; 4.功率。B: 5.品牌; 6.型号
8509.9000	-零件	A: 1.品名; 2.用途（适用机型）。B: 3.品牌; 4.型号
8510.1000	-剃须刀	A: 1.品名; 2.用途。B: 3.品牌; 4.型号
8510.2000	-毛发推剪	A: 1.品名; 2.用途。B: 3.品牌; 4.型号
8510.3000	-脱毛器	A: 1.品名; 2.用途。B: 3.品牌; 4.型号
8510.9000	-零件	A: 1.品名; 2.用途(适用机型)。B: 3.品牌; 4.型号
8511.1000	-火花塞	A: 1.品名; 2.用途; 3.功能; 4.生产件的通用零件编号后加注“/TY”; 5.成套散件装配后完整品的零部件的编号。B: 6.品牌; 7.型号; 8.零部件完整编号并在前加注“S/”、“W/”或“WF/”之一（生产件填报“S/”，品牌和适用的整车厂牌一致的维修件填报“W/”，品牌和适用的整车厂牌不一致的维修件的填报“WF/”）
	-点火磁电机；永磁直流发电机；磁飞轮:	A: 1.品名; 2.用途; 3.功能。B: 4.品牌; 5.型号
	-分电器；点火线圈:	A: 1.品名; 2.用途; 3.功能。B: 4.品牌; 5.型号
8511.4010	---机车、航空器及船舶用	A: 1.品名; 2.用途; 3.功能。B: 4.品牌; 5.型号
	---其他:	A: 1.品名; 2.用途; 3.功能; 4.适用发动机的输出功率。B: 5.品牌; 6.型号
	-其他发电机:	A: 1.品名; 2.用途; 3.功能。B: 4.品牌; 5.型号
8511.8000	-其他装置	A: 1.品名; 2.用途; 3.功能。B: 4.品牌; 5.型号
	-零件:	A: 1.品名; 2.用途(适用机型)。B: 3.品牌; 4.型号
8512.1000	-自行车用照明或视觉信号装置	A: 1.品名; 2.用途; 3.功能。B: 4.品牌; 5.型号
8512.2010	---机动车辆用照明装置	A: 1.品名; 2.用途; 3.功能; 4.生产件的通用零件编号后加注“/TY”; 5.成套散件装配后完整品的零部件的编号。B: 6.品牌; 7.型号; 8.零部件完整编号并在前加注“S/”、“W/”或“WF/”之一（生产件填报“S/”，品牌和适用的整车厂牌一致的维修件填报“W/”，品牌和适用的整车厂牌不一致的维修件的填报“WF/”）
8512.2090	---其他	A: 1.品名; 2.用途; 3.功能。B: 4.品牌; 5.型号
	-音响信号装置:	A: 1.品名; 2.用途; 3.功能。B: 4.品牌 5.型号
8512.4000	-风挡刮水器、除霜器及去雾器	A: 1.品名; 2.用途。B: 3.品牌; 4.型号
8512.9000	-零件	A: 1.品名; 2.用途(适用机型)。B: 3.品牌; 4.型号
85.13	自供能源（例如，使用二电池、蓄电池、永磁发电机）的手提式电灯，但税目85.12的照明装置除外:	
	-灯:	A: 1.品名; 2.是否手提式。B: 3.品牌; 4.型号
	-零件:	A: 1.品名; 2.用途(适用机型)。B: 3.品牌; 4.型号
85.14	工业或实验室用电炉及电烘箱(包括通过感应或介质损耗工作的)；工业或实验室用其他通过感应或介质损耗对材	

税则号列	商品名称	申报要素(A:归类要素 B:价格要素 C:审单及其他要素)及说明举例
	料进行热处理的设备:	
	-电阻加热的炉及烘箱:	A: 1. 品名; 2. 用途; 3. 加热原理。B: 4. 品牌; 5. 型号
8514.2000	-通过感应或介质损耗工作的炉及烘箱	A: 1. 品名; 2. 用途; 3. 加热原理。B: 4. 品牌; 5. 型号
8514.3000	-其他炉及烘箱	A: 1. 品名; 2. 用途; 3. 加热原理。B: 4. 品牌; 5. 型号
8514.4000	-其他通过感应或介质损耗对材料进行热处理的设备	A: 1. 品名; 2. 用途; 3. 加热原理。B: 4. 品牌; 5. 型号
	-零件:	A: 1. 品名; 2. 用途(适用机型)。B: 3. 品牌; 4. 型号
85.15	电气(包括电热气体)、激光、其他光、光子束、超声波、电子束、磁脉冲或等离子弧焊接机器及装置,不论是否兼有切割功能;用于热喷金属或金属陶瓷的电气机器及装置:	
	-钎焊机器及装置:	A: 1. 品名; 2. 原理。B: 3. 品牌; 4. 型号
	-电阻焊接机器及装置:	A: 1. 品名; 2. 原理; 3. 是否为全自动或半自动。B: 4. 品牌; 5. 型号
	-电弧(包括等离子弧)焊接机器及装置:	A: 1. 品名; 2. 原理; 3. 是否为全自动或半自动。B: 4. 品牌; 5. 型号
	-其他机器及装置:	A: 1. 品名; 2. 原理。B: 3. 品牌; 4. 型号
8515.9000	-零件	A: 1. 品名; 2. 用途(适用机型)。B: 3. 品牌; 4. 型号
8516.1010	---储存式电热水器	A: 1. 品名; 2. 用途; 3. 加热原理。B: 4. 品牌; 5. 型号; 6. 容量
8516.1020	---即热式电热水器	A: 1. 品名; 2. 用途; 3. 加热原理。B: 4. 品牌; 5. 型号
8516.1090	---其他	A: 1. 品名; 2. 用途; 3. 加热原理。B: 4. 品牌; 5. 型号
	-电气空间加热器及土壤加热器:	A: 1. 品名; 2. 用途; 3. 加热原理。B: 4. 品牌; 5. 型号
	-电热的理发器具及干手器:	A: 1. 品名; 2. 用途; 3. 加热原理。B: 4. 品牌; 5. 型号
8516.4000	-电熨斗	A: 1. 品名; 2. 用途; 3. 加热原理。B: 4. 品牌; 5. 型号
8516.5000	-微波炉	A: 1. 品名; 2. 用途; 3. 加热原理。B: 4. 品牌; 5. 型号
	-其他炉;电锅、电热板、加热环、烧烤炉及烘烤器:	A: 1. 品名; 2. 用途; 3. 加热原理。B: 4. 品牌; 5. 型号
	-其他电热器具:	A: 1. 品名; 2. 用途; 3. 加热原理。B: 4. 品牌; 5. 型号
8516.8000	-加热电阻器	A: 1. 品名; 2. 用途。B: 3. 品牌; 4. 型号
	-零件:	A: 1. 品名; 2. 用途(适用机型)。B: 3. 品牌; 4. 型号
85.17	电话机,包括用于蜂窝网络或其他无线网络的电话机;其他发送或接收声音、图像或其他数据用的设备,包括有线或无线网络(例如,局域网或广域网)的通信设备,品目84.43、85.25、85.27或85.28的发送或接收设备除外:	
	-电话机,包括蜂窝网络或其他无线网络的电话机:	A: 1. 品名; 2. 用途; 3. 适用网络种类(蜂窝网络、无线网络、有线网络、以太网等)。B: 4. 品牌; 5. 型号; 6. 是否加密
8517.1100	--无绳电话机	例: 西门子家用无绳加密电话机, 型号601i
	--基站:	A: 1. 品名; 2. 用途。B: 3. 品牌; 4. 型号; 5. 是否加密
	---数字式程控电话或电报交换机:	A: 1. 品名; 2. 用途; 3. 控制方式; 4. 处理信号的类型。B: 5. 型号
	---光通讯设备:	A: 1. 品名; 2. 用途; 3. 通讯方式。B: 4. 品牌; 5. 型号; 6. 是否加密
	---其他有线数字通信设备:	A: 1. 品名; 2. 用途; 3. 通讯方式。B: 4. 品牌; 5. 型号
	---其他:	A: 1. 品名; 2. 用途; 3. 功能。B: 4. 品牌; 5. 型号
	--其他:	A: 1. 品名; 2. 用途。B: 3. 品牌; 4. 型号
	-零件:	A: 1. 品名; 2. 用途(适用机型); 3. 组成部件; B: 4. 品牌; 5. 型号
8518.1000	-传声器(麦克风)及其座架	A: 1. 品名。B: 2. 品牌; 3. 型号
8518.2100	--单喇叭音箱	A: 1. 品名; 2. 结构类型(是否有箱体); 3. 额定功率; 4. 用途。B: 5. 品牌; 6. 型号
8518.2200	--多喇叭音箱	A: 1. 品名; 2. 结构类型(是否有箱体); 3. 额定功率; 4. 用途。B: 5. 品牌; 6. 型号; 7. 喇叭数量和尺寸
8518.2900	--其他	A: 1. 品名; 2. 结构类型(是否有箱体); 3. 额定功率; 4. 用途。B: 5. 品牌; 6. 型号
8518.3000	-耳机及耳塞机,不论是否装有传声器,以及由传声器及一个或多个扬声器组成的组合机	A: 1. 品名。B: 2. 品牌; 3. 型号
8518.4000	-音频扩大器	A: 1. 品名。B: 2. 品牌; 3. 型号
8518.5000	-电气扩音机组	A: 1. 品名; 2. 组成部件。B: 3. 品牌; 4. 型号
8518.9000	-零件	A: 1. 品名; 2. 用途(适用机型)。B: 3. 品牌; 4. 型号
8519.2000	-用硬币、钞票、银行卡、代币或其他支付方式使其工作的设备	A: 1. 品名; 2. 支付方式。B: 3. 品牌; 4. 型号
8519.3000	-唱机转盘(唱机唱盘)	A: 1. 品名。B: 2. 品牌; 3. 型号
8519.5000	-电话应答机	A: 1. 品名。B: 2. 品牌; 3. 型号
	-其他设备:	A: 1. 品名; 2. 使用媒介。B: 3. 品牌; 4. 型号
85.21	视频信号录制或重放设备,不论是否装有高频调谐器:	
	-磁带型:	A: 1. 品名; 2. 用途; 3. 使用媒介。B: 4. 品牌; 5. 型号

税则号列	商品名称	申报要素(A:归类要素 B:价格要素 C:审单及其他要素)及说明举例
	-其他:	A: 1. 品名; 2. 使用媒介; 3. 类型。B: 4. 品牌 5. 型号
8521.9012	----数字化视频光盘（DVD）	例: 松下 DVD 播放机，型号 S98
85.22	专用于或主要用于税目 85.19 至 85.21 所列设备的零件、附件:	A: 1. 品名; 2. 用途(适用机型)。B: 3. 品牌; 4. 型号
85.23	录制声音或其他信息用的圆盘、磁带、固态非易失性数据存储器件、“智能卡”及其他媒体，不论是否已录制，包括供复制圆盘用的母片及母带，但不包括第三十七章的产品:	
	--磁条卡:	A: 1. 品名; 2. 用途; 3. 是否录制。B: 4. 品牌; 5. 型号; 6. 录制内容类型
	--磁盘:	A: 1. 品名; 2. 用途; 3. 是否录制。B: 4. 品牌; 5. 型号; 6. 录制内容类型
	---磁带:	A: 1. 品名; 2. 用途; 3. 是否录制; 4. 磁带宽度。B: 5. 品牌; 6. 型号; 7. 录制内容类型
8523.2990	---其他	A: 1. 品名; 2. 用途; 3. 是否录制。B: 4. 品牌; 5. 型号; 6. 录制内容类型
	-光学媒体:	A: 1. 品名; 2. 用途; 3. 是否录制; 4. 录制内容类型。B: 5. 品牌; 6. 型号; 7. 存储容量; 8. 读取速度
	--固态非易失性存储器件（闪速存储器）:	A: 1. 品名; 2. 用途; 3. 是否录制。B: 4. 品牌; 5. 型号; 6. 容量
	--“智能卡”:	A: 1. 品名; 2. 用途; 3. 是否录制。B: 4. 品牌; 5. 型号; 6. 是否加密
	--其他:	A: 1. 品名; 2. 用途; 3. 是否录制。B: 4. 品牌; 5. 型号
	-其他:	A: 1. 品名; 2. 用途; 3. 是否录制。B: 4. 品牌; 5. 型号
8525.5000	-发送设备	A: 1. 品名; 2. 用途。B: 3. 品牌; 4. 型号
	-装有接收装置的发送设备:	A: 1. 品名; 2. 用途; 3. 结构组成。B: 4. 品牌; 5. 型号
	--电视摄像机:	A: 1. 品名; 2. 用途。B: 3. 品牌; 4. 型号
8525.8021	----特种用途的	A: 1. 品名; 2. 用途。B: 3. 品牌; 4. 型号
8525.8022	----非特种用途的，单镜头反光型	A: 1. 品名; 2. 用途。B: 3. 品牌; 4. 型号
8525.8025	----非特种用途的，其他可换镜头的	A: 1. 品名; 2. 用途。B: 3. 品牌; 4. 型号
8525.8029	----非特种用途的，其他类型	A: 1. 品名; 2. 用途。B: 3. 品牌; 4. 型号; 5. 像素
	---视频摄录一体机:	A: 1. 品名; 2. 用途。B: 3. 品牌; 4. 型号
85.26	雷达设备、无线电导航设备及无线电遥控设备:	
	-雷达设备:	A: 1. 品名; 2. 用途。B: 3. 品牌; 4. 型号
	--无线电导航设备:	A: 1. 品名; 2. 用途。B: 3. 品牌; 4. 型号
8526.9200	--无线电遥控设备	A: 1. 品名; 2. 用途。B: 3. 品牌; 4. 型号; 5. 控制距离
85.27	无线电广播接收设备，不论是否与声音的录制、重放装置或时钟组合在同一机壳内:	
	-不需外接电源的无线电收音机:	A: 1. 品名; 2. 使用媒介(是否为盒式磁带); 3. 是否需外接电源。B: 4. 品牌; 5. 型号; 6. 外形尺寸
	-需外接电源的汽车用无线电收音机:	A: 1. 品名; 2. 用途; 3. 结构组成。B: 4. 品牌; 5. 型号
	-其他:	A: 1. 品名; 2. 用途。B: 3. 品牌; 4. 型号
8528.4100	--专用于或主要用于税目 84.71 的自动数据处理系统的	A: 1. 品名; 2. 用途; 3. 显示原理; 4. 显示屏幕尺寸; 5. 接口类型(包括接口电路)。B: 6 品牌; 7. 型号
	--其他:	A: 1. 品名; 2. 用途; 3. 显示原理; 4. 显示屏幕尺寸。B: 5. 品牌; 6. 型号
8528.5110	---液晶的	A: 1. 品名; 2. 用途; 3. 显示原理; 4. 显示屏幕尺寸; 5. 接口类型(包括接口电路); 6. 构成（是否带标记板、解码板或高频头板等信号处理板）。B: 7. 品牌; 8. 型号
8528.5190	---其他	A: 1. 品名; 2. 用途; 3. 显示原理; 4. 显示屏幕尺寸; 5. 接口类型(包括接口电路)。B: 6. 品牌; 7. 型号
8528.5910	---彩色的	A: 1. 品名; 2. 用途; 3. 显示原理; 4. 显示屏幕尺寸。B: 5. 品牌; 6. 型号; 7. 最高分辨率
8528.5990	---单色的	A: 1. 品名; 2. 用途; 3. 显示原理; 4. 显示屏幕尺寸。B: 5. 品牌; 6. 型号
8528.6100	--专用于或主要用于税目 84.71 的自动数据处理系统的:	A: 1. 品名; 2. 用途; 3. 显示原理; 4. 接口类型(包括接口电路)。B: 5. 品牌; 6. 型号; 7. 亮度
	--其他:	A: 1. 品名; 2. 用途; 3. 显示原理; 4. 接口类型(包括接口电路)。B: 5. 品牌; 6. 型号; 7. 亮度
	--在设计上不带视频显示器或屏幕的:	A: 1. 品名; 2. 用途; 3. 是否带显示屏。B: 4. 品牌; 5. 型号
	--其他，彩色的:	A: 1. 品名; 2. 用途; 3. 显示原理; 4. 显示屏幕尺寸。B: 5. 品牌; 6. 型号
8528.7300	--其他，单色的	A: 1. 品名; 2. 用途; 3. 显示原理; 4. 显示屏幕尺寸。B: 5. 品牌; 6. 型号
85.29	专用于或主要用于税目 85.25 至 85.28 所列装置或设备的零件:	
	-各种天线或天线反射器及其零件:	A: 1. 品名; 2. 用途（适用机型）。B: 3. 品牌; 4. 型号
8529.9010	---电视发送、差转设备及卫星电视地面接收转播设备用	A: 1. 品名; 2. 用途（适用机型）。B: 3. 品牌; 4. 型号
8529.9041	----特种用途的	A: 1. 品名; 2. 用途（适用机型）。B: 3. 品牌; 4. 型号

税则号列	商品名称	申报要素(A:归类要素 B:价格要素 C:审单及其他要素)及说明举例
8529.9042	----非特种用途的取像模块	A: 1.品名; 2.用途(适用机型); 3.是否带有数字信号处理电路。B: 4.品牌; 5.型号
8529.9049	----其他	A: 1.品名; 2.用途(适用机型)。B: 3.品牌; 4.型号
8529.9050	---雷达设备及无线电导航设备用	A: 1.品名; 2.用途(适用机型)。B: 3.品牌; 4.型号
8529.9060	---无线电收音机及其组合机用	A: 1.品名; 2.用途(适用机型)。B: 3.品牌; 4.型号
	---电视接收机用(高频调谐器除外):	A: 1.品名; 2.用途(适用机型)。B: 3.品牌; 4.型号
8529.9090	---其他	A: 1.品名; 2.用途(适用机型)。B: 3.品牌; 4.型号
8530.1000	-铁道或电车道用的设备	A: 1.品名; 2.用途。B: 3.品牌; 4.型号
8530.8000	-其他设备	A: 1.品名; 2.用途。B: 3.品牌; 4.型号
8530.9000	-零件	A: 1.品名; 2.用途(适用机型)。B: 3.品牌; 4.型号
8531.1000	-防盗或防火报警器及类似装置	A: 1.品名; 2.用途。B: 3.品牌; 4.型号; 5.工作原理
8531.2000	-装有液晶装置(LCD)或发光二极管(LED)的显示板	A: 1.品名; 2.用途; 3.显示原理。B: 4.品牌; 5.型号
	-其他装置:	A: 1.品名; 2.用途。B: 3.品牌; 4.型号
	-零件:	A: 1.品名; 2.用途(适用机型)。B: 3.品牌; 4.型号
8532.1000	-固定电容器,用于50/60赫兹电路,其额定无功功率不低于0.5千瓦(电力电容器)	A: 1.品名; 2.用途; 3.额定无功功率; 4.适用频率。B: 5.品牌; 6.型号
	-其他固定电容器:	A: 1.品名; 2.结构类型(单层; 多层等); 3.介质类型。B: 4.品牌; 5.型号
8532.3000	-可变或可调(微调)电容器	A: 1.品名; 2.是否可变、可调。B: 3.品牌; 4.型号
	-零件:	A: 1.品名; 2.用途(适用机型)。B: 3.品牌; 4.型号
8533.1000	-固定碳质电阻器,合成或薄膜式	A: 1.品名; 2.结构类型; 3.介质。B: 4.品牌; 5.型号
	-其他固定电阻器:	A: 1.品名; 2.额定功率。B: 3.品牌; 4.型号
	-线绕可变电阻器,包括变阻器及电位器:	A: 1.品名; 2.额定功率。B: 3.品牌; 4.型号
8533.4000	-其他可变电阻器,包括变阻器及电位器	A: 1.品名。B: 2.品牌; 3.型号
8533.9000	-零件	A: 1.品名; 2.用途(适用机型)。B: 3.品牌; 4.型号
85.34	印刷电路:	A: 1.品名; 2.电路层数。B: 3.品牌; 4.型号
85.35	电路的开关、保护或连接用的电气装置(例如,开关、熔断器、避雷器、电压限幅器、电涌抑制器、插头及其他连接器、接线盒),用于电压超过1000伏的线路:	A: 1.品名; 2.用途; 3.电压。B: 4.品牌; 5.型号
8536.1000	-熔断器	A: 1.品名; 2.用途; 3.电压。B: 4.品牌; 5.型号
8536.2000	-自动断路器	A: 1.品名; 2.用途; 3.电压。B: 4.品牌; 5.型号
8536.3000	-其他电路保护装置	A: 1.品名; 2.用途; 3.电压。B: 4.品牌; 5.型号
	-继电器:	A: 1.品名; 2.用途; 3.电压。B: 4.品牌; 5.型号
8536.5000	-其他开关	A: 1.品名; 2.用途; 3.电压。B: 4.品牌; 5.型号
	-灯座、插头及插座:	A: 1.品名; 2.用途; 3.电压。B: 4.品牌; 5.型号
8536.7000	-光导纤维、光导纤维束或光缆用连接器	A: 1.品名; 2.用途。B: 3.品牌; 4.型号
	-其他装置	A: 1.品名; 2.用途; 3.电压。B: 4.品牌; 5.型号
85.37	用于电气控制或电力分配的盘、板、台、柜及其他基座,装有两个或多个税目85.35或85.36所列的装置,包括装有第九十章所列的仪器或装置,以及数控装置,但税目85.17的交换机除外:	A: 1.品名; 2.用途; 3.原理; 4电压。B: 5.品牌; 6.型号
85.38	专用于或主要用于税目85.35、85.36或85.37所列装置的零件:	A: 1.品名; 2.用途(适用机型)。B: 3.品牌; 4.型号
8539.1000	-封闭式聚光灯	A: 1.品名; 2.用途; 3.类型。B: 4.品牌; 5.型号
	--卤钨灯:	A: 1.品名; 2.用途; 3.类型。B: 4.品牌; 5.型号
	--其他灯,功率不超过200瓦,但额定电压超过100伏:	A: 1.品名; 2.用途; 3.类型; 4.功率; 5.额定电压。B: 6.品牌; 7.型号
	--其他:	A: 1.品名; 2.用途; 3.类型; 4.功率; 5.额定电压。B: 6.品牌; 7.型号
	-放电灯管,但紫外线灯管除外:	A: 1.品名; 2.用途; 3.类型。B: 4.品牌; 5.型号
	-紫外线灯管或红外线灯泡;弧光灯:	A: 1.品名; 2.用途; 3.类型。B: 4.品牌; 5.型号
8539.9000	-零件	A: 1.品名; 2.用途(适用机型)。B: 3.品牌; 4.型号
85.40	热电子管、冷阴极管或光阴极管(例如,真空管或充气管、汞弧整流管、阴极射线管、电视摄像管):	

税则号列	商品名称	申报要素(A:归类要素 B:价格要素 C:审单及其他要素)及说明举例
	-阴极射线电视显像管，包括视频监视器用阴极射线管:	A: 1. 品名; 2. 原理。B: 3. 品牌; 4. 型号
	-电视摄像管; 变像管及图像增强管; 其他光阴极管:	A: 1. 品名; 2. 用途。B: 3. 品牌; 4. 型号
8540.4010	-彩色的数据/图形显示管, 屏幕荧光点间距小于 0.4 毫米	A: 1. 品名; 2. 是否彩色; 3. 荧光点距。B: 4. 品牌; 5. 型号
8540.4020	---单色的数据/图形显示管	A: 1. 品名; 2. 是否单色; 3. 荧光点距。B: 4. 品牌; 5. 型号
	-其他阴极射线管:	A: 1. 品名; 2. 用途; 3. 类型。B: 4. 品牌; 5. 型号
	-微波管(例如，磁控管、速调管、行波管、返波管)，但不包括栅控管:	A: 1. 品名; 2. 用途; 3. 类型。B: 4. 品牌; 5. 型号
	-其他管:	A: 1. 品名; 2. 用途; 3. 类型。B: 4. 品牌; 5. 型号
	-零件:	A: 1. 品名; 2. 用途(适用机型)。B: 3. 品牌; 4. 型号
8541.1000	-二极管, 但光敏二极管或发光二极管除外	A: 1. 品名。B: 2. 品牌; 3. 型号
	-晶体管，但光敏晶体管除外:	A: 1. 品名; 2. 耗散功率。B: 3. 品牌; 4. 型号
8541.3000	-半导体开关元件、两端交流开关元件及三端双向可控硅开关元件, 但光敏器件除外	A: 1. 品名; 2. 类型; 3. 是否由多个半导体元件构成。B: 4. 品牌; 5. 型号
8541.4010	---发光二极管	A: 1. 品名。B: 2. 品牌; 3. 型号
8541.4020	---太阳能电池	A: 1. 品名; 2. 额定功率。B: 3. 品牌; 4. 型号; 5. 转换效率
8541.4090	---其他	A: 1. 品名。B: 2. 品牌; 3. 型号
8541.5000	-其他半导体器件	A: 1. 品名; 2. 类型; 3. 是否由多个半导体元件构成。B: 4. 品牌; 5. 型号
8541.6000	-已装配的压电晶体	A: 1. 品名; 2. 是否已装配。B: 3. 品牌; 4. 型号
8541.9000	-零件	A: 1. 品名; 2. 用途(适用机型)。B: 3. 品牌; 4. 型号
85.42	集成电路:	
	-集成电路:	A: 1. 品名; 2. 用途; 3. 功能。B: 4. 品牌; 5. 型号
8542.9000	-零件	A: 1. 品名; 2. 用途(适用机型)。B: 3. 品牌; 4. 型号
8543.1000	-粒子加速器	A: 1. 品名; 2. 用途; 3. 功能。B: 4. 品牌; 5. 型号
	-信号发生器:	A: 1. 品名; 2. 用途; 3. 功能; 4. 输出信号频率范围。B: 5. 品牌; 6. 型号
8543.3000	-电镀、电解或电泳设备及装置	A: 1. 品名; 2. 用途; 3. 功能。B: 4. 品牌; 5. 型号
	-其他设备及装置	A: 1. 品名; 2. 用途; 3. 功能。B: 4. 品牌; 5. 型号
	-零件:	A: 1. 品名; 2. 用途(适用机型)。B: 3. 品牌; 4. 型号
85.44	绝缘(包括漆包或阳极化处理)电线、电缆(包括同轴电缆)及其他绝缘电导体，不论是否有接头；由每根被覆光纤组成的光缆，不论是否与电导体装配或装有接头:	
	-绕组电线:	A: 1. 品名; 2. 用途; 3. 材质。B: 4. 品牌; 5. 型号
8544.2000	-同轴电缆及其他同轴电导体	A: 1. 品名; 2. 用途; 3. 结构类型(同轴、有接头等)。B: 4. 品牌; 5. 型号
	-车辆、航空器、船舶用点火布线组及其他布线组:	A: 1. 品名; 2. 用途; 3. 结构类型(有接头等)。B: 4. 品牌; 5. 型号; 6. 额定电压
	-其他电导体，额定电压不超过 1000 伏:	A: 1. 品名; 2. 用途; 3. 结构类型(有接头等)。B: 4. 品牌; 5. 型号; 6. 额定电压
	-其他电导体，额定电压超过1000伏:	A: 1. 品名; 2. 用途; 3. 结构类型(有接头等)。B: 4. 品牌; 5. 型号; 6. 额定电压
8544.7000	-光缆	A: 1. 品名; 2. 是否每根光纤被覆。B: 3. 品牌; 4. 型号
85.45	碳电极、碳刷、灯碳棒、电池碳棒及电气设备用的其他石墨或碳精制品，不论是否带金属:	A: 1. 品名; 2. 用途; 3. 材质。B: 4. 品牌; 5. 型号
85.46	各种材料制的绝缘子:	A: 1. 品名; 2. 用途; 3. 材质。B: 4. 品牌; 5. 型号
85.47	电气机器、器具或设备用的绝缘零件，除了为装配需要而在模制时装入的小金属零件(例如，螺纹孔)以外，全部用绝缘材料制成，但税目 85.46 的绝缘子除外；内衬绝缘材料的贱金属制线路导管及其接头:	A: 1. 品名; 2. 用途; 3. 材质。B: 4. 品牌; 5. 型号
85.48	原电池、原电池组及蓄电池的废碎料；废原电池、废原电池组及废蓄电池；机器或设备的本章其他税目未列名的电气零件:	A: 1. 品名; 2. 用途。B: 3. 品牌; 4. 型号

第十七类　车辆、航空器、船舶及有关运输设备

第八十六章　铁道及电车道机车、车辆及其零件；铁道及电车道轨道固定装置及其零件、附件；各种机械（包括电动机械）交通信号设备

税则号列	商品名称	申报要素(A:归类要素 B:价格要素 C:审单及其他要素)及说明举例
86.01	铁道电力机车，由外部电力或蓄电池驱动:	A: 1. 品名; 2. 用途; 3. 驱动装置类型; 4. 控制装置类型。B: 5. 品牌; 6. 型号
86.02	其他铁道机车；机车煤水车	
	-柴油电力机车:	A: 1. 品名; 2. 用途; 3. 驱动装置类型; 4. 控制装置类型。B: 5. 品牌; 6. 型号
8602.9000	-其他	A: 1. 品名; 2. 用途; 3. 驱动装置类型。B: 4. 品牌; 5. 型号
86.03	铁道及电车道用的机动客车、货车、敞车，但税目 86.04 的货品除外:	A: 1. 品名; 2. 用途; 3. 驱动装置类型。B: 4. 品牌; 5. 型号
86.04	铁道及电车道用的维修或服务车，不论是否机动（例如，工场车、起重机车、道砟捣固车、轨道校正车、检验车及查道车）:	A: 1. 品名; 2. 用途; 3. 类型。B: 4. 品牌; 5. 型号
86.05	铁道及电车道用的非机动客车；行李车、邮政车和其他铁道及电车道用的非机动特殊用途车辆（税目 86.04 的货品除外）:	A: 1. 品名; 2. 用途; 3. 类型。B: 4. 品牌; 5. 型号
86.06	铁道及电车道用的非机动有篷及无篷货车:	A: 1. 品名; 2. 用途; 3. 类型; 4. 结构。B: 5. 品牌; 6. 型号
86.07	铁道及电车道机车或其他车辆的零件:	A: 1. 品名; 2. 用途（适用车型）。B: 3. 品牌; 4. 型号
86.08	铁道及电车道轨道固定装置及其附件；供铁道、电车道、道路、内河航道、停车场、港口或机场用的机械（包括电动机械）信号、安全或交通管理设备；上述货品的零件:	A: 1. 品名; 2. 用途。B: 3. 品牌; 4. 型号
86.09	集装箱（包括运输液体的集装箱），经特殊设计、装备适用于各种运输方式:	A: 1. 品名; 2. 类型（公路等）; 3. 规格尺寸。B: 4. 品牌

第八十七章　车辆及其零件、附件，但铁道及电车道车辆除外

税则号列	商品名称	申报要素(A:归类要素 B:价格要素 C:审单及其他要素)及说明举例
8701.1000	-手扶拖拉机	A: 1. 品名。B: 2. 品牌; 3. 型号
8701.2000	-半挂车用的公路牵引车	A: 1. 品名; 2. 用途。B: 3. 品牌; 4. 型号
8701.3000	-履带式牵引车、拖拉机	A: 1. 品名。B: 2. 品牌; 3. 结构类型; 4. 型号
	-其他:	A: 1. 品名; 2. 结构类型; 3. 功率。B: 4. 用途; 5. 品牌; 6. 型号
8702.1020	---机坪客车	A: 1. 品名; 2. 发动机类型（柴油、半柴油、汽油等）; 3. 成套散件请注明。B: 4. 厂牌（如与签注名称相同可省略）; 5. 签注名称; 6. 排气量（毫升）; 7. 规格型号
	---其他:	A: 1. 品名; 2. 发动机类型（柴油、半柴油、汽油等）; 3. 成套散件请注明; 4. 座位数。B: 5. 厂牌（如与签注名称相同可省略）; 6. 签注名称; 7. 排气量（毫升）; 8. 规格型号
	-其他:	A: 1. 品名; 2. 发动机类型（柴油、半柴油、汽油等）; 3. 成套散件请注明; 4. 座位数。B: 5. 厂牌（如与签注名称相同可省略）; 6. 签注名称; 7. 排气量（毫升）; 8. 规格型号
8703.1011	----全地形车	A: 1. 品名; 2. 发动机类型（柴油、半柴油、汽油等）; 3. 成套散件请注明; 4. 座位数。B: 5. 厂牌（如与签注名称相同可省略）; 6. 签注名称; 7. 排气量（毫升）; 8. 规格型号
8703.1019	----其他	A: 1. 品名; 2. 发动机类型（柴油、半柴油、汽油等）; 3. 成套散件请注明; 4. 排气量（毫升）。B: 5. 厂牌（如与签注名称相同可省略）; 6. 签注名称; 7. 规格型号
8703.1090	---其他	A: 1. 品名; 2. 发动机类型（柴油、半柴油、汽油等）; 3. 成套散件请注明; 4. 排气量（毫升）。B: 5. 厂牌（如与签注名称相同可省略）; 6. 签注名称; 7. 规格型号
	-装有点燃往复式活塞内燃发动机的其他车辆:	A: 1. 品名; 2. 发动机类型（柴油、半柴油、汽油等）; 3. 成套散件请注明; 4. 座位数。B: 5. 厂牌（如与签注名称相同可省略）; 6. 签注名称; 7. 排气量（毫升）; 8. 规格型号

税则号列	商品名称	申报要素(A:归类要素 B:价格要素 C:审单及其他要素)及说明举例
	-装有压燃式活塞内燃发动机（柴油或半柴油发动机）的其他车辆:	A: 1. 品名; 2. 发动机类型（柴油、半柴油、汽油等）; 3. 成套散件请注明; 4. 座位数。B: 5. 厂牌（如与签注名称相同可省略）; 6. 签注名称; 7. 排气量（毫升）; 8. 规格型号
8703.9000	-其他	A: 1. 品名; 2. 发动机类型(柴油、半柴油、汽油等); 3. 成套散件请注明; 4. 座位数。B: 5. 厂牌(如与签注名称相同可省略); 6. 签注名称; 7. 排气量(毫升); 8. 规格型号
8704.1030	---电动轮货运自卸车	A: 1. 品名; 2. 用途; 3. 是否为电动轮。B: 4. 品牌(厂牌); 5. 型号
8704.1090	---其他	A: 1. 品名; 2. 用途; 3. 是否为电动轮; 4. 发动机类型(柴油、半柴油、汽油等)。B: 5. 品牌(厂牌); 6. 型号;
	-装有压燃式活塞内燃发动机（柴油或半柴油发动机）的其他货车:	A: 1. 品名; 2. 发动机类型(柴油、半柴油、汽油等); 3. 车辆总重。B: 4. 品牌(厂牌); 5. 型号
	-装有点燃式活塞内燃发动机的其他货车:	A: 1. 品名; 2. 发动机类型(柴油、半柴油、汽油等); 3. 车辆总重。B: 4. 品牌(厂牌); 5. 型号
8704.9000	-其他	A: 1. 品名; 2. 发动机类型(柴油、半柴油、汽油等); 3. 车辆总重。B: 4. 品牌(厂牌); 5. 型号
87.05	特殊用途的机动车辆（例如，抢修车、起重车、救火车、混凝土搅拌车、道路清洁车、喷洒车、流动工场车及流动放射线检查车），但主要用于载人或运货的车辆除外:	
	-起重车:	A: 1. 品名; 2. 作业范围(全路面等); 3. 最大起重重量。B: 4. 品牌(厂牌); 5. 型号
8705.2000	-钻探车	A: 1. 品名。B: 2. 用途; 3. 品牌; 4. 型号
	-救火车:	A: 1. 品名; 2. 固定安装配置。B: 3. 品牌; 4. 型号
8705.4000	-混凝土搅拌车	A: 1. 品名; 2. 固定安装配置。B: 3. 品牌; 4. 型号
	-其他:	A: 1. 品名; 2. 用途; 3. 固定安装配置。B: 4. 品牌(厂牌); 5. 型号
8706.0010	---非公路用自卸车底盘	A: 1. 品名; 2. 适用车型。B: 3. 品牌; 4. 型号
	---货车底盘:	A: 1. 品名; 2. 适用车型; 3. 车辆总重量; 4. 是否带驾驶室。B: 5. 品牌; 6. 型号
8706.0030	---大型客车底盘	A: 1. 品名; 2. 适用车型; 3. 是否带驾驶室。B: 4. 品牌; 5. 型号
8706.0040	---汽车起重机底盘	A: 1. 品名; 2. 适用车型; 3. 是否带驾驶室。B: 4. 品牌; 5. 型号
8706.0090	---其他	A: 1. 品名; 2. 适用车型。B: 3. 品牌; 4. 型号
87.07	机动车辆的车身(包括驾驶室)，税目87.01至87.05所列车辆用:	A: 1. 品名; 2. 适用车型。B: 3. 品牌; 4. 型号
8708.1000	-缓冲器(保险杠)及其零件	A: 1. 品名; 2. 成套散件或毛坯请注明; 3. 生产件的通用零件编号后加注“/TY”; 4. 成套散件装配后完整品的零部件的编号。B: 5. 品牌; 6. 适用车型; 7. 型号; 8. 零部件完整编号并在前加注“S/”、“W/”或“WF/”之一（生产件填报“S/”，品牌和适用的整车厂牌一致的维修件填报“W/”，品牌和适用的整车厂牌不一致的维修件的填报“WF/”）
8708.2100	--坐椅安全带	A: 1. 品名; 2. 成套散件或毛坯请注明; 3. 生产件的通用零件编号后加注“/TY”; 4. 成套散件装配后完整品的零部件的编号。B: 5. 品牌; 6. 适用车型; 7. 型号; 8. 零部件完整编号并在前加注“S/”、“W/”或“WF/”之一（生产件填报“S/”，品牌和适用的整车厂牌一致的维修件填报“W/”，品牌和适用的整车厂牌不一致的维修件的填报“WF/”）
8708.2930	---车窗玻璃升降器	A: 1. 品名; 2. 成套散件或毛坯请注明; 3. 生产件的通用零件编号后加注“/TY”; 4. 成套散件装配后完整品的零部件的编号。B: 5. 品牌; 6. 适用车型; 7. 型号; 8. 零部件完整编号并在前加注“S/”、“W/”或“WF/”之一（生产件填报“S/”，品牌和适用的整车厂牌一致的维修件填报“W/”，品牌和适用的整车厂牌不一致的维修件的填报“WF/”）
8708.2941	----电动的	A: 1. 品名; 2. 成套散件或毛坯请注明; 3. 生产件的通用零件编号后加注“/TY”; 4. 成套散件装配后完整品的零部件的编号。B: 5. 品牌; 6. 适用车型; 7. 型号; 8. 零部件完整编号并在前加注“S/”、“W/”或“WF/”之一（生产件填报“S/”，品牌和适用的整车厂牌一致的维修件填报“W/”，品牌和适用的整车厂牌不一致的维修件的填报“WF/”）
8708.2942	----手动的	A: 1. 品名。B: 2. 品牌; 3. 适用车型; 4. 型号
	---其他车身覆盖件:	A: 1. 品名。B: 2. 品牌; 3. 适用车型; 4. 型号
8708.2990	---其他	A: 1. 品名。B: 2. 品牌; 3. 适用车型; 4. 型号
	-制动器、助力制动器及其零件:	A: 1. 品名; 2. 适用车型; 3. 成套散件或毛坯请注明; 4. 生产件的通用零件编号后加注“/TY”; 5. 成套散件装配后完整品的零部件的编号。B: 6. 品牌; 7. 型号; 8. 零部件完整编号并在前加注“S/”、“W/”或“WF/”之一（生产件填报“S/”，品牌和适用的整车厂牌一致的维修件填报“W/”，品牌和适用的整车厂牌不一致的维修件的填报“WF/”）
8708.4010	---税目87.01所列车辆用	A: 1. 品名 2. 适用车型; 3. 成套散件或毛坯请注明; 4. 生产件的通用零件编

税则号列	商品名称	申报要素(A:归类要素 B:价格要素 C:审单及其他要素)及说明举例
		号后加注“/TY”;5.成套散件装配后完整品的零部件的编号。B:6.品牌; 7.型号; 8.零部件完整编号并在前加注“S/”、“W/”或“WF/”之一(生产件填报“S/”,品牌和适用的整车厂牌一致的维修件填报“W/”,品牌和适用的整车厂牌不一致的维修件的填报“WF/”)
8708.4020	---税号 8702.1091 及 8702.9010 所列车辆用	A:1.品名;2.适用车型;3.成套散件或毛坯请注明;4.生产件的通用零件编号后加注“/TY”;5.成套散件装配后完整品的零部件的编号。B:6.品牌; 7.型号; 8.零部件完整编号并在前加注“S/”、“W/”或“WF/”之一(生产件填报“S/”,品牌和适用的整车厂牌一致的维修件填报“W/”,品牌和适用的整车厂牌不一致的维修件的填报“WF/”); 9.座位数
8708.4030	---税号 8704.1030 及 8704.1090 所列车辆用	A:1.品名;2.适用车型;3.成套散件或毛坯请注明;4.生产件的通用零件编号后加注“/TY”;5.成套散件装配后完整品的零部件的编号。B:6.品牌;7.扭矩; 8.型号; 9.零部件完整编号并在前加注“S/”、“W/”或“WF/”之一(生产件填报“S/”,品牌和适用的整车厂牌一致的维修件填报“W/”,品牌和适用的整车厂牌不一致的维修件的填报“WF/”)
8708.4040	---税号 8704.2100、8704.2230、8704.3100 及 8704.3230 所列车辆用	A:1.品名;2.适用车型;3.成套散件或毛坯请注明;4.生产件的通用零件编号后加注“/TY”;5.成套散件装配后完整品的零部件的编号。B:6.品牌;7.扭矩; 8.型号; 9.零部件完整编号并在前加注“S/”、“W/”或“WF/”之一(生产件填报“S/”,品牌和适用的整车厂牌一致的维修件填报“W/”,品牌和适用的整车厂牌不一致的维修件的填报“WF/”)
8708.4050	---税号 8704.2240、8704.2300 及 8704.3240 所列车辆用	A:1.品名;2.适用车型;3.成套散件或毛坯请注明;4.生产件的通用零件编号后加注“/TY”;5.成套散件装配后完整品的零部件的编号。B:6.品牌;7.扭矩; 8.型号; 9.零部件完整编号并在前加注“S/”、“W/”或“WF/”之一(生产件填报“S/”,品牌和适用的整车厂牌一致的维修件填报“W/”,品牌和适用的整车厂牌不一致的维修件的填报“WF/”)
8708.4060	---税目 87.05 所列车辆用	A:1.品名;2.适用车型;3.成套散件或毛坯请注明;4.生产件的通用零件编号后加注“/TY”;5.成套散件装配后完整品的零部件的编号。B:6.品牌;7.扭矩; 8.型号; 9.零部件完整编号并在前加注“S/”、“W/”或“WF/”之一(生产件填报“S/”,品牌和适用的整车厂牌一致的维修件填报“W/”,品牌和适用的整车厂牌不一致的维修件的填报“WF/”)
	---其他:	A:1.品名;2.适用车型;3.原理(是否为 4 挡及 4 挡以下); 4.成套散件或毛坯请注明;5.生产件的通用零件编号后加注“/TY”;6.成套散件装配后完整品的零部件的编号。B:7.品牌; 8.扭矩; 9.型号; 10.零部件完整编号并在前加注“S/”、“W/”或“WF/”之一(生产件填报“S/”,品牌和适用的整车厂牌一致的维修件填报“W/”,品牌和适用的整车厂牌不一致的维修件的填报“WF/”)
8708.5071	----税目 87.01 所列车辆用	A:1.品名;2.适用车型;3.传动部件;4.驱动位置;5.轴荷;6.成套散件或毛坯请注明;7.生产件的通用零件编号后加注“/TY”;8.成套散件装配后完整品的零部件的编号。B:9.品牌; 10.型号; 11.零部件完整编号并在前加注“S/”、“W/”或“WF/”之一(生产件填报“S/”,品牌和适用的整车厂牌一致的维修件填报“W/”,品牌和适用的整车厂牌不一致的维修件的填报“WF/”)
8708.5072	----税号 8702.1091 及 8702.9010 所列车辆用	A:1.品名;2.适用车型;3.传动部件;4.驱动位置;5.轴荷;6.成套散件或毛坯请注明;7.生产件的通用零件编号后加注“/TY”;8.成套散件装配后完整品的零部件的编号。B:9.品牌; 10.型号; 11.零部件完整编号并在前加注“S/”、“W/”或“WF/”之一(生产件填报“S/”,品牌和适用的整车厂牌一致的维修件填报“W/”,品牌和适用的整车厂牌不一致的维修件的填报“WF/”)
8708.5073	----税号 8704.1030 及 8704.1090 所列车辆用	A:1.品名;2.适用车型;3.传动部件;4.驱动位置;5.轴荷;6.成套散件或毛坯请注明;7.生产件的通用零件编号后加注“/TY”;8.成套散件装配后完整品的零部件的编号。B:9.品牌; 10.型号; 11.零部件完整编号并在前加注“S/”、“W/”或“WF/”之一(生产件填报“S/”,品牌和适用的整车厂牌一致的维修件填报“W/”,品牌和适用的整车厂牌不一致的维修件的填报“WF/”)
8708.5074	----税号 8704.2100、8704.2230、8704.3100 及 8704.3230 所列车辆用	A:1.品名;2.适用车型;3.传动部件;4.驱动位置;5.成套散件或毛坯请注明;6.生产件的通用零件编号后加注“/TY”;7.成套散件装配后完整品的零部件的编号。B:8.品牌; 9.型号; 10.零部件完整编号并在前加注“S/”、“W/”或“WF/”之一(生产件填报“S/”,品牌和适用的整车厂牌一致的维修件填报“W/”,品牌和适用的整车厂牌不一致的维修件的填报“WF/”)
8708.5075	----税号 8704.2240、8704.2300 及	A:1.品名;2.适用车型;3.传动部件;4.驱动位置;5.成套散件或毛坯请注

税则号列	商品名称	申报要素(A:归类要素 B:价格要素 C:审单及其他要素)及说明举例
	8704.3240 所列车辆用	明;6.生产件的通用零件编号后加注“/TY”;7.成套散件装配后完整品的零部件的编号。B:8.品牌;9.型号;10.零部件完整编号并在前加注“S/”、“W/”或“WF/”之一(生产件填报“S/”,品牌和适用的整车厂牌一致的维修件填报“W/”,品牌和适用的整车厂牌不一致的维修件的填报“WF/”)
8708.5076	----税目 87.05 所列车辆用	A:1.品名;2.适用车型;3.传动部件;4.驱动位置;5.成套散件或毛坯请注明;6.生产件的通用零件编号后加注“/TY”;7.成套散件装配后完整品的零部件的编号。B:8.品牌;9.型号;10.零部件完整编号并在前加注“S/”、“W/”或“WF/”之一(生产件填报“S/”,品牌和适用的整车厂牌一致的维修件填报“W/”,品牌和适用的整车厂牌不一致的维修件的填报“WF/”)
8708.5079	----其他	A:1.品名;2.适用车型;3.传动部件;4.成套散件或毛坯请注明;5.生产件的通用零件编号后加注“/TY”;6.成套散件装配后完整品的零部件的编号。B:7.品牌;8.型号;9.零部件完整编号并在前加注“S/”、“W/”或“WF/”之一(生产件填报“S/”,品牌和适用的整车厂牌一致的维修件填报“W/”,品牌和适用的整车厂牌不一致的维修件的填报“WF/”)
	---非驱动桥及其零件:	A:1.品名;2.适用车型;3.传动部件;4.成套散件或毛坯请注明;5.生产件的通用零件编号后加注“/TY”;6.成套散件装配后完整品的零部件的编号。B:7.品牌;8.型号;9.零部件完整编号并在前加注“S/”、“W/”或“WF/”之一(生产件填报“S/”,品牌和适用的整车厂牌一致的维修件填报“W/”,品牌和适用的整车厂牌不一致的维修件的填报“WF/”)
	-车轮及其零件、附件:	A:1.品名;2.适用车型;3.成套散件或毛坯请注明;4.生产件的通用零件编号后加注“/TY”;5.成套散件装配后完整品的零部件的编号。B:6.品牌;7.型号;8.零部件完整编号并在前加注“S/”、“W/”或“WF/”之一(生产件填报“S/”,品牌和适用的整车厂牌一致的维修件填报“W/”,品牌和适用的整车厂牌不一致的维修件的填报“WF/”)
	-悬挂系统及其零件(包括减震器):	A:1.品名;2.适用车型;3.成套散件或毛坯请注明;4.生产件的通用零件编号后加注“/TY”;5.成套散件装配后完整品的零部件的编号。B:6.品牌;7.型号;8.零部件完整编号并在前加注“S/”、“W/”或“WF/”之一(生产件填报“S/”,品牌和适用的整车厂牌一致的维修件填报“W/”,品牌和适用的整车厂牌不一致的维修件的填报“WF/”)
	--散热器及其零件:	A:1.品名;2.适用车型;3.成套散件或毛坯请注明;4.生产件的通用零件编号后加注“/TY”;5.成套散件装配后完整品的零部件的编号。B:6.品牌;7.型号;8.零部件完整编号并在前加注“S/”、“W/”或“WF/”之一(生产件填报“S/”,品牌和适用的整车厂牌一致的维修件填报“W/”,品牌和适用的整车厂牌不一致的维修件的填报“WF/”)
8708.9200	--消声器(消音器)、排气管及其零件	A:1.品名;2.适用车型;3.成套散件或毛坯请注明;4.生产件的通用零件编号后加注“/TY”;5.成套散件装配后完整品的零部件的编号。B:6.品牌;7.型号;8.零部件完整编号并在前加注“S/”、“W/”或“WF/”之一(生产件填报“S/”,品牌和适用的整车厂牌一致的维修件填报“W/”,品牌和适用的整车厂牌不一致的维修件的填报“WF/”)
	--离合器及其零件:	A:1.品名;2.适用车型;3.成套散件或毛坯请注明;4.生产件的通用零件编号后加注“/TY”;5.成套散件装配后完整品的零部件的编号。B:6.品牌;7.型号;8.零部件完整编号并在前加注“S/”、“W/”或“WF/”之一(生产件填报“S/”,品牌和适用的整车厂牌一致的维修件填报“W/”,品牌和适用的整车厂牌不一致的维修件的填报“WF/”)
8708.9410	---税目 87.01 所列车辆用	A:1.品名;2.适用车型;3.成套散件或毛坯请注明;4.生产件的通用零件编号后加注“/TY”;5.成套散件装配后完整品的零部件的编号。B:6.品牌;7.型号;8.零部件完整编号并在前加注“S/”、“W/”或“WF/”之一(生产件填报“S/”,品牌和适用的整车厂牌一致的维修件填报“W/”,品牌和适用的整车厂牌不一致的维修件的填报“WF/”)
8708.9420	---税号 8702.1091 及 8702.9010 所列车辆用	A:1.品名;2.适用车型;3.成套散件或毛坯请注明;4.生产件的通用零件编号后加注“/TY”;5.成套散件装配后完整品的零部件的编号;6.座位数。B:7.品牌;8.型号;9.零部件完整编号并在前加注“S/”、“W/”或“WF/”之一(生产件填报“S/”,品牌和适用的整车厂牌一致的维修件填报“W/”,品牌和适用的整车厂牌不一致的维修件的填报“WF/”)
8708.9430	---税号 8704.1030 及 8704.1090 所列车辆用	A:1.品名;2.适用车型;3.成套散件或毛坯请注明;4.生产件的通用零件编号后加注“/TY”;5.成套散件装配后完整品的零部件的编号。B:6.品牌;7.型号;8.零部件完整编号并在前加注“S/”、“W/”或“WF/”之一(生产件填报“S/”,品牌和适用的整车厂牌一致的维修件填报“W/”,品牌和适用的整车厂牌不一致的维修件的填报“WF/”)

税则号列	商品名称	申报要素(A:归类要素 B:价格要素 C:审单及其他要素)及说明举例
8708.9440	---税号 8704.2100、8704.2230、8704.3100及8704.3230所列车辆用	A:1.品名;2.适用车型;3.成套散件或毛坯请注明;4.生产件的通用零件编号后加注"/TY";5.成套散件装配后完整品的零部件的编号。B:6.品牌;7.型号;8.零部件完整编号并在前加注"S/"、"W/"或"WF/"之一(生产件填报"S/",品牌和适用的整车厂牌一致的维修件填报"W/",品牌和适用的整车厂牌不一致的维修件的填报"WF/")
8708.9450	---税号 8704.2240、8704.2300及8704.3240所列车辆用	A:1.品名;2.适用车型;3.成套散件或毛坯请注明;4.生产件的通用零件编号后加注"/TY";5.成套散件装配后完整品的零部件的编号。B:6.品牌;7.型号;8.零部件完整编号并在前加注"S/"、"W/"或"WF/"之一(生产件填报"S/",品牌和适用的整车厂牌一致的维修件填报"W/",品牌和适用的整车厂牌不一致的维修件的填报"WF/")
8708.9460	---税目87.05所列车辆用转向器	A:1.品名;2.适用车型;3.成套散件或毛坯请注明;4.生产件的通用零件编号后加注"/TY";5.成套散件装配后完整品的零部件的编号。B:6.品牌;7.型号;8.零部件完整编号并在前加注"S/"、"W/"或"WF/"之一(生产件填报"S/",品牌和适用的整车厂牌一致的维修件填报"W/",品牌和适用的整车厂牌不一致的维修件的填报"WF/")
8708.9490	---其他	A:1.品名;2.适用车型;3.成套散件或毛坯请注明;4.生产件的通用零件编号后加注"/TY";5.成套散件装配后完整品的零部件的编号。B:6.品牌;7.型号;8.零部件完整编号并在前加注"S/"、"W/"或"WF/"之一(生产件填报"S/",品牌和适用的整车厂牌一致的维修件填报"W/",品牌和适用的整车厂牌不一致的维修件的填报"WF/")
8708.9500	--带充气系统的安全气囊及其零件	A:1.品名;2.适用车型;3.成套散件或毛坯请注明;4.生产件的通用零件编号后加注"/TY";5.成套散件装配后完整品的零部件的编号。B:6.品牌;7.型号;8.零部件完整编号并在前加注"S/"、"W/"或"WF/"之一(生产件填报"S/",品牌和适用的整车厂牌一致的维修件填报"W/",品牌和适用的整车厂牌不一致的维修件的填报"WF/")
8708.9910	---税目87.01所列车辆用	A:1.品名;2.适用车型。B:3.品牌;4.型号
8708.9921	----车架	A:1.品名;2.适用车型;3.成套散件或毛坯请注明;4.生产件的通用零件编号后加注"/TY";5.成套散件装配后完整品的零部件的编号。B:6.品牌;7.型号;8.零部件完整编号并在前加注"S/"、"W/"或"WF/"之一(生产件填报"S/",品牌和适用的整车厂牌一致的维修件填报"W/",品牌和适用的整车厂牌不一致的维修件的填报"WF/")
8708.9929	----其他	A:1.品名;2.适用车型;3.座位数。B:4.品牌;5.型号
8708.9931	----车架	A:1.品名;2.适用车型;3.成套散件或毛坯请注明;4.生产件的通用零件编号后加注"/TY";5.成套散件装配后完整品的零部件的编号。B:6.品牌;7.型号;8.零部件完整编号并在前加注"S/"、"W/"或"WF/"之一(生产件填报"S/",品牌和适用的整车厂牌一致的维修件填报"W/",品牌和适用的整车厂牌不一致的维修件的填报"WF/")
8708.9939	----其他	A:1.品名;2.适用车型。B:3.品牌;4.型号
8708.9941	----车架	A:1.品名;2.适用车型;3.成套散件或毛坯请注明;4.生产件的通用零件编号后加注"/TY";5.成套散件装配后完整品的零部件的编号。B:6.品牌;7.型号;8.零部件完整编号并在前加注"S/"、"W/"或"WF/"之一(生产件填报"S/",品牌和适用的整车厂牌一致的维修件填报"W/",品牌和适用的整车厂牌不一致的维修件的填报"WF/")
8708.9949	----其他	A:1.品名;2.适用车型。B:3.品牌;4.型号
8708.9951	----车架	A:1.品名;2.适用车型;3.成套散件或毛坯请注明;4.生产件的通用零件编号后加注"/TY";5.成套散件装配后完整品的零部件的编号。B:6.品牌;7.型号;8.零部件完整编号并在前加注"S/"、"W/"或"WF/"之一(生产件填报"S/",品牌和适用的整车厂牌一致的维修件填报"W/",品牌和适用的整车厂牌不一致的维修件的填报"WF/")
8708.9959	----其他	A:1.品名;2.适用车型。B:3.品牌;4.型号
8708.9960	---税目87.05所列车辆用	A:1.品名;2.适用车型。B:3.品牌;4.型号
8708.9991	----车架	A:1.品名;2.适用车型;3.成套散件或毛坯请注明;4.生产件的通用零件编号后加注"/TY";5.成套散件装配后完整品的零部件的编号。B:6.品牌;7.型号;8.零部件完整编号并在前加注"S/"、"W/"或"WF/"之一(生产件填报"S/",品牌和适用的整车厂牌一致的维修件填报"W/",品牌和适用的整车厂牌不一致的维修件的填报"WF/")
8708.9992	----传动轴	A:1.品名;2.适用车型。B:3.品牌;4.型号
8708.9999	----其他	A:1.品名;2.适用车型。B:3.品牌;4.型号

税则号列	商品名称	申报要素(A:归类要素 B:价格要素 C:审单及其他要素)及说明举例
87.09	短距离运输货物的机动车辆，未装有提升或搬运设备，用于工厂、仓库、码头或机场；火车站台上用的牵引车；上述车辆的零件:	
	-车辆:	A: 1. 品名; 2. 发动机类型; 3. 适用场所。B: 4. 品牌; 5. 型号; 6. 技术参数(最高时速、转弯半径等)
8709.9000	-零件	A: 1. 品名; 2. 用途(适用车型)。B: 3. 品牌; 4. 型号
87.10	坦克及其他机动装甲战斗车辆，不论是否装有武器；上述车辆的零件:	A: 1. 品名。B: 2. 品牌; 3. 型号
8711.1000	-装有往复式活塞内燃发动机，气缸容量(排气量)不超过50毫升	A: 1. 品名; 2. 发动机类型; 3. 排气量。B: 4. 品牌; 5. 型号
	-装有往复式活塞内燃发动机，气缸容量(排气量)超过50毫升，但不超过250毫升:	A: 1. 品名; 2. 发动机类型; 3. 排气量。B: 4. 品牌; 5. 型号
	-装有往复式活塞内燃发动机，气缸容量(排气量)超过250毫升，但不超过500毫升:	A: 1. 品名; 2. 发动机类型; 3. 排气量。B: 4. 品牌; 5. 型号
8711.4000	-装有往复式活塞内燃发动机，气缸容量(排气量)超过500毫升，但不超过800毫升	A: 1. 品名; 2. 发动机类型; 3. 排气量。B: 4. 品牌; 5. 型号
8711.5000	-装有往复式活塞内燃发动机，气缸容量(排气量)超过800毫升	A: 1. 品名; 2. 发动机类型; 3. 排气量。B: 4. 品牌; 5. 型号
8711.9010	---电动及电动助力的	A: 1. 品名; 2. 发动机类型。B: 3. 品牌; 4. 型号
8711.9090	---其他	A: 1. 品名; 2. 发动机类型; 3. 排气量。B: 4. 品牌; 5. 型号
87.12	自行车及其他非机动脚踏车(包括运货三轮脚踏车):	A: 1. 品名; 2. 用途; 3. 轮径。B: 4. 品牌; 5. 型号
87.13	残疾人用车，不论是否机动或其他机械驱动:	A: 1. 品名; 2. 用途; 3. 驱动方式。B: 4. 品牌; 5. 型号
87.14	零件、附件，税目87.11至87.13所列车辆用:	A: 1. 品名; 2. 用途（适用车型）。B: 3. 品牌; 4. 型号
87.15	婴孩车及其零件:	A: 1. 品名; 2. 适用车型。B: 3. 品牌
8716.1000	-供居住或野营用厢式挂车及半挂车	A: 1. 品名; 2. 用途; 3. 类型。B: 4. 品牌; 5. 型号
8716.2000	-农用自装或自卸式挂车及半挂车	A: 1. 品名; 2. 用途; 3. 类型。B: 4. 品牌; 5. 型号
	-其他货运挂车及半挂车:	A: 1. 品名; 2. 用途; 3. 类型。B: 4. 品牌; 5. 型号
8716.4000	-其他挂车及半挂车	A: 1. 品名。B: 2. 品牌; 3. 型号
8716.8000	-其他车辆	A: 1. 品名。B: 2. 品牌; 3. 型号
8716.9000	-零件	A: 1. 品名; 2. 用途(适用车型)。B: 3. 品牌; 4. 型号

第八十八章　航空器、航天器及其零件

税则号列	商品名称	申报要素(A:归类要素 B:价格要素 C:审单及其他要素)及说明举例
88.01	气球及飞艇；滑翔机、悬挂滑翔机及其他无动力航空器:	A: 1. 品名 2. 用途。B: 3. 品牌; 4. 型号
88.02	其他航空器（例如，直升机、飞机）；航天器(包括卫星)及其运载工具、亚轨道运载工具:	
	-直升机:	A: 1. 品名 2. 用途; 3. 类型; 4. 空载重量。B: 5. 品牌; 6. 型号
8802.2000	-飞机及其他航空器，空载重量不超过2000千克	A: 1. 品名; 2. 用途; 3. 类型; 4. 空载重量。B: 5. 品牌; 6. 型号
8802.3000	-飞机及其他航空器，空载重量超过2000千克，但不超过15000千克	A: 1. 品名; 2. 用途; 3. 类型; 4. 空载重量。B: 5. 品牌; 6. 型号
8802.4010	---空载重量超过15000千克，但不超过45000千克	A 1. 品名; 2. 用途; 3. 类型; 4. 空载重量。B: 5. 品牌; 6. 型号
8802.4020	---空载重量超过45000千克	A: 1. 品名; 2. 用途; 3. 类型; 4. 空载重量。B: 5. 品牌; 6. 型号
8802.6000	-航天器(包括卫星)及其运载工具、亚轨道运载工具	A: 1. 品名。B: 2. 品牌; 3. 型号
88.03	税目88.01或88.02所列货品的零件:	A: 1. 品名; 2. 用途（适用机型）。B: 3. 品牌; 4. 型号
88.04	降落伞(包括可操纵降落伞及滑翔伞)、旋翼降落伞及其零件、附件:	A: 1. 品名; 2. 用途（适用机型）。B: 3. 品牌; 4. 型号
88.05	航空器的发射装置、甲板停机装置或类似装置和地面飞行训练器及其零件:	A: 1. 品名; 2. 用途（适用机型）。B: 3. 品牌; 4. 型号

第八十九章　船舶及浮动结构体

税则号列	商品名称	申报要素(A:归类要素 B:价格要素 C:审单及其他要素)及说明举例
89.01	巡航船、游览船、渡船、货船、驳船及类似的客运或货运船舶:	
	-巡航船、游览船及主要用于客运的类似船舶;各式渡船:	A:1.品名;2.驱动方式。B:3.品牌;4.型号;5.最高时速
	---成品油船:	A:1.品名;2.用途;3.载重量。B:4.品牌;5.型号
	---原油船:	A:1.品名;2.用途;3.载重量。B:4.品牌;5.型号
	---液化石油气船:	A:1.品名;2.用途;3.容积。B:4.品牌;5.型号
	---液化天然气船:	A:1.品名;2.用途;3.容积。B:4.品牌;5.型号
8901.2090	---其他	A:1.品名;2.用途;3.载重量。B:4.品牌;5.型号
8901.3000	-冷藏船,但子目8901.20的船舶除外	A:1.品名。B:2.品牌;3.型号
	---机动集装箱船:	A:1.品名;2.用途;3.可载标准集装箱数。B:4.品牌;5.型号
	---机动滚装船:	A:1.品名;2.用途;3.载重量。B:4.品牌;5.型号
	---机动散货船:	A:1.品名;2.用途;3.载重量。B:4.品牌;5.型号
8901.9050	---机动多用途船	A:1.品名;2.用途。B:3.品牌;4.型号
8901.9080	---其他机动船舶	A:1.品名;2.用途。B:3.品牌;4.型号
8901.9090	---其他非机动船舶	A:1.品名;2.用途。B:3.品牌;4.型号
89.02	捕鱼船;加工船及其他加工保藏鱼类产品的船舶:	A:1.品名;2.用途;3.驱动方式。B:4.品牌;5.型号
8903.1000	-充气的	A:1.品名;2.用途;3.类型;4.发动机安装方式;5.船体长度;6.固定安装配置。B:7.品牌;8.型号
8903.9100	--帆船,不论是否装有辅助发动机	A:1.品名;2.用途;3.类型;4.发动机安装方式;5.船体长度。B:6.品牌;7.型号
8903.9200	--汽艇,但装有舷外发动机的除外	A:1.品名;2.用途;3.类型;4.发动机安装方式;5.船体长度。B:6.品牌;7.型号
8903.9900	--其他	A:1.品名;2.用途;3.类型;4.船体长度;5.固定安装配置。B:6.品牌;7.型号
89.04	拖轮及顶推船:	A:1.品名;2.功能。B:3.品牌;4.型号
8905.1000	-挖泥船	A:1.品名;2.用途。B:3.品牌;4.型号
8905.2000	-浮动或潜水式钻探或生产平台	A:1.品名;2.用途。B:3.品牌;4.型号
	-其他:	A:1.品名;2.用途;3.结构。B:4.品牌;5.型号
89.06	其他船舶,包括军舰及救生船,但划艇除外:	A:1.品名;2.用途;3.驱动方式。B:4.品牌;5.型号
89.07	其他浮动结构体(例如,筏、柜、潜水箱、浮码头、浮筒及航标):	A:1.品名;2.材质。B:3.品牌;4.型号
89.08	供拆卸的船舶及其他浮动结构体:	A:1.品名;2.轻吨数(不包括非金属固定压载在内的空船重量);3.船型(如油轮、客船、驳船、集装箱船等)

第十八类　光学、照相、电影、计量、检验、医疗或外科用仪器及设备、精密仪器及设备;钟表;乐器;上述物品的零件、附件

第九十章　光学、照相、电影、计量、检验、医疗或外科用仪器及设备、精密仪器及设备;上述物品的零件、附件

税则号列	商品名称	申报要素(A:归类要素 B:价格要素 C:审单及其他要素)及说明举例
9001.1000	-光导纤维、光导纤维束及光缆	A:1.品名;2.结构;3.用途。B:4.品牌;5.型号
9001.2000	-偏振材料制的片及板	A:1.品名;2.用途;3.材质;4.形状(片、板等)。B:5.品牌; 6.型号
9001.3000	-隐形眼镜片	A:1.品名。B:2.品牌;3.型号
	-玻璃制眼镜片:	A:1.品名;2.材质;3.类型(变色等)。B:4.品牌; 5.型号
	-其他材料制眼镜片:	A:1.品名;2.材质;3.类型(变色等)。B:4.品牌; 5.型号
	-其他:	A:1.品名;2.用途(适用机型);3.材质。B:4.品牌; 5.型号
90.02	已装配的各种材料制透镜、棱镜、反射镜及其他光学元件,作为仪器或装置的零件、配件,但未经光学加工的玻璃制上述元件除外:	A:1.品名;2.用途(适用机型);3.是否已装配。B:4.品牌; 5.型号
90.03	眼镜架及其零件:	A:1.品名;2.材质。B:3.品牌;4.型号

税则号列	商品名称	申报要素(A:归类要素 B:价格要素 C:审单及其他要素)及说明举例
90.04	矫正视力、保护眼睛或其他用途的眼镜、挡风镜及类似品:	A: 1.品名; 2.用途; 3.类型(变色等)。B: 4.品牌; 5.型号
9005.1000	-双筒望远镜	A: 1.品名; 2.用途; 3.是否双筒。B: 4.品牌; 5.型号
	-其他仪器:	A: 1.品名; 2.用途。B: 3.品牌; 4.型号
	-零件、附件(包括座架):	A: 1.品名; 2.用途(适用机型)。B: 3.品牌; 4.型号
90.06	照相机(电影摄影机除外);照相闪光灯装置及闪光灯泡,但税目85.39的放电灯泡除外:	
	-制版照相机:	A: 1.品名; 2.用途; 3.原理。B: 4.品牌; 5.型号
9006.3000	-水下、航空测量或体内器官检查用的特种照相机;法庭或犯罪学用的比较照相机	A: 1.品名; 2.用途; 3.原理。B: 4.品牌; 5.型号
9006.4000	--一次成像照相机	A: 1.品名; 2.用途; 3.原理。B: 4.品牌; 5.型号
9006.5100	--通过镜头取景[单镜头反光式(SLR)],使用胶片宽度不超过35毫米	A: 1.品名; 2.用途; 3.原理; 4.胶片宽度。B: 5.品牌; 6.型号
	--其他,使用胶片宽度小于35毫米:	A: 1.品名; 2.用途; 3.原理; 4.胶片宽度。B: 5.品牌; 6.型号
9006.5300	--其他,使用胶片宽度为35毫米	A: 1.品名; 2.用途; 3.原理; 4.胶片宽度。B: 5.品牌; 6.型号
	--其他	A: 1.品名; 2.用途; 3.原理。B: 4.品牌; 5.型号
	-照相闪光灯装置及闪光灯泡:	A: 1.品名; 2.用途; 3.原理。B: 4.品牌; 5.型号
	-零件、附件:	A: 1.品名; 2.用途(适用机型)。B: 3.品牌; 4.型号
90.07	电影摄像机、放映机、不论是否带有声音的录制或重放装置:	
	-摄影机:	A: 1.品名; 2.用途; 3.原理; 4.胶片宽度; 5.摄影速度。B: 6.品牌; 7.型号
	-放映机:	A: 1.品名; 2.用途; 3.原理。B: 4.品牌; 5.型号
	-零件、附件:	A: 1.品名; 2.用途(适用机型)。B: 3.品牌; 4.型号
9008.5010	---幻灯机	A: 1.品名; 2.用途。B: 3.品牌; 4.型号
9008.5020	---缩微胶卷、缩微胶片或其他缩微品的阅读机,不论是否可以进行复制	A: 1.品名; 2.用途。B: 3.品牌; 4.型号
	---其他影像投影仪:	A: 1.品名; 2.用途; 3.原理。B: 4.品牌; 5.型号
9008.5040	---照片(电影片除外)放大机及缩片机	A: 1.品名; 2.用途。B: 3.品牌; 4.型号
	-零件、附件:	A: 1.品名; 2.用途(适用机型)。B: 3.品牌; 4.型号
90.10	本章其他税目未列名的照相(包括电影)洗印用装置及设备;负片显示器;银幕及其他投影屏幕:	
	-照相(包括电影)胶卷或成卷感光纸的自动显影装置及设备或将已冲洗胶卷自动曝光到成卷感光纸上的装置及设备:	A: 1.品名; 2.用途; 3.原理。B: 4.品牌; 5.型号
	-照相(包括电影)洗印用其他装置和设备;负片显示器:	A: 1.品名; 2.用途; 3.原理。B: 4.品牌; 5.型号
9010.6000	-银幕及其他投影屏幕	A: 1.品名; 2.用途。B: 3.品牌; 4.型号
	-零件、附件:	A: 1.品名; 2.用途(适用机型)。B: 3.品牌; 4.型号
9011.1000	-立体显微镜	A: 1.品名; 2.用途; 3.原理。B: 4.品牌; 5.型号; 6.倍数
9011.2000	-显微照相、显微电影摄影及显微投影用的其他显微镜	A: 1.品名; 2.用途; 3.原理。B: 4.品牌; 5.型号; 6.倍数
9011.8000	-其他显微镜	A: 1.品名; 2.用途; 3.原理。B: 4.品牌; 5.型号; 6.倍数
9011.9000	-零件、附件	A: 1.品名; 2.用途(适用机型)。B: 3.品牌; 4.型号
9012.1000	-显微镜,但光学显微镜除外;衍射设备	A: 1.品名; 2.用途; 3.原理。B: 4.品牌; 5.型号
9012.9000	-零件、附件	A: 1.品名; 2.用途(适用机型)。B: 3.品牌; 4.型号
9013.1000	-武器用望远镜瞄准具;潜望镜式望远镜;作为本章或第十六类的机器、设备、仪器或器具部件的望远镜	A: 1.品名; 2.用途。B: 3.品牌; 4.型号
9013.2000	-激光器,但激光二极管除外	A: 1.品名; 2.用途; 3.原理。B: 4.品牌; 5.型号
9013.8010	---放大镜	A: 1.品名; 2.用途; 3.原理。B: 4.品牌; 5.型号
9013.8020	---光学门眼	A: 1.品名; 2.用途; 3.原理。B: 4.品牌; 5.型号
9013.8030	---液晶显示板	A: 1.品名; 2.用途; 3.原理(是否为液晶); 4.尺寸。B: 5.品牌; 6.型号
9013.8090	---其他	A: 1.品名; 2.用途; 3.原理。B: 4.品牌; 5.型号
	-零件、附件:	A: 1.品名; 2.用途(适用机型)。B: 3.品牌; 4.型号
9014.1000	-定向罗盘	A: 1.品名; 2.用途; 3.原理。B: 4.品牌; 5.型号
	-航空或航天导航仪器及装置(罗盘除外):	A: 1.品名; 2.用途。B: 3.品牌; 4.型号
9014.8000	-其他仪器及装置	A: 1.品名; 2.用途; 3.原理。B: 4.品牌; 5.型号
	-零件、附件:	A: 1.品名; 2.用途(适用机型)。B: 3.品牌; 4.型号
9015.1000	-测距仪	A: 1.品名; 2.用途; 3.原理。B: 4.品牌; 5.型号
9015.2000	-经纬仪及视距仪	A: 1.品名; 2.用途; 3.原理。B: 4.品牌; 5.型号

税则号列	商品名称	申报要素(A:归类要素 B:价格要素 C:审单及其他要素)及说明举例
9015.3000	-水平仪	A:1.品名;2.用途;3.原理。B:4.品牌; 5.型号
9015.4000	-摄影测量用仪器及装置	A:1.品名;2.用途;3.原理。B:4.品牌; 5.型号
9015.8000	-其他仪器及装置	A:1.品名;2.用途;3.原理。B:4.品牌; 5.型号
9015.9000	-零件、附件	A:1.品名;2.用途(适用机型)。B:3.品牌;4.型号
90.16	感量为50毫克或更精密的天平,不论是否带有砝码:	A:1.品名;2.感量。B:3.品牌; 4.型号
9017.1000	-绘图台及绘图机,不论是否自动	A:1.品名;2.用途;3.功能。B:4.品牌; 5.型号
9017.2000	-其他绘图、划线或数学计算器具	A:1.品名;2.用途;3.功能;4.是否手用。B:5.品牌; 6.型号
9017.3000	-千分尺、卡尺及量规	A:1.品名;2.用途;3.功能;4.是否手用。B:5.品牌; 6.型号
9017.8000	-其他仪器及器具	A:1.品名;2.用途;3.功能。B:4.品牌; 5.型号
9017.9000	-零件、附件	A:1.品名;2.用途(适用机型)。B:3.品牌;4.型号
90.18	医疗、外科、牙科或兽医用仪器及器具,包括闪烁扫描装置、其他电气医疗装置及视力检查仪器:	
	-电气诊断装置(包括功能检查或生理参数检查用装置):	A:1.品名; 2.用途; 3.原理。B:4.品牌; 5.型号。例:彩色多普勒超声诊断仪,医疗用,SIEMENS,SONOLINEG60S,2个常规探头
9018.2000	-紫外线及红外线装置	A:1.品名;2.用途;3.原理。B:4.品牌; 5.型号
9018.3100	--注射器,不论是否装有针头	A:1.品名;2.用途。B:3.品牌;4.型号
	--管状金属针头及缝合用针:	A:1.品名;2.用途。B:3.品牌;4.型号
9018.3900	--其他	A:1.品名;2.用途;3.材质。B:4.品牌; 5.型号
9018.4100	--牙钻机,不论是否与其他牙科设备组装在同一底座上	A:1.品名;2.用途。B:3.品牌;4.型号
9018.4910	---装有牙科设备的牙科用椅	A:1.品名;2.用途。B:3.品牌;4.型号
9018.4990	---其他	A:1.品名;2.用途;3.原理。B:4.品牌; 5.型号
9018.5000	-眼科用其他仪器及器具	A:1.品名;2.用途;3.原理。B:4.品牌; 5.型号
9018.9010	---听诊器	A:1.品名;2.用途。B:3.品牌;4.型号
9018.9020	---血压测量仪器及器具	A:1.品名;2.用途;3.原理。B:4.品牌; 5.型号
9018.9030	---内窥镜	A:1.品名;2.用途。B:3.品牌;4.型号。例:KARLSTORZ胆囊切除腹腔镜,20242001型,含三晶片摄像系统、监视器、冷光源
9018.9040	---肾脏透析设备(人工肾)	A:1.品名;2.用途;3.原理。B:4.品牌
9018.9050	---透热疗法设备	A:1.品名;2.用途;3.原理。B:4.品牌
9018.9060	---输血设备	A:1.品名;2.用途。B:3.品牌;4.型号
9018.9070	---麻醉设备	A:1.品名;2.用途。B:3.品牌;4.型号
9018.9080	---宫内节育器	A:1.品名;2.用途。B:3.品牌;4.型号
9018.9090	---其他	A:1.品名;2.用途。B:3.品牌;4.型号
9019.1010	---按摩器具	A:1.品名;2.用途;3.功能。B:4.品牌; 5.型号
9019.1090	---其他	A:1.品名;2.用途;3.功能;4.原理。B:5.品牌; 6.型号
9019.2000	-臭氧治疗器、氧气治疗器、喷雾治疗器、人工呼吸器或其他治疗用呼吸器具	A:1.品名;2.用途;3. 功能。B:4.品牌;5.型号
90.20	其他呼吸器具及防毒面具,但不包括既无机械零件又无可互换过滤器的防护面具:	A:1.品名;2.用途;3.构成;4.有无机械零件或可互换过滤装置。B:5.品牌;6.型号
9021.1000	-矫形或骨折用器具	A:1.品名;2.用途。B:3.品牌;4.材质;5.型号;6.技术参数
	-假牙及牙齿固定件:	A:1.品名。B:2.品牌;3.材质;4.型号
9021.3100	--人造关节	A:1.品名;2.用途; 3.人造关节部位。B:4.品牌; 5.材质; 6.型号
9021.3900	--其他	A:1.品名;2.用途。B:3.品牌;4.材质;5.型号
9021.4000	-助听器,不包括零件、附件	A:1.品名
9021.5000	-心脏起搏器,不包括零件、附件	A:1.品名;2.材质
	-其他	A:1.品名;2.用途;3.原理。B:4.品牌; 5.型号。例1:冠状动脉支架,等离子体技术涂层钛氧化氮,球囊扩张式; 强生CYPHER型; 例2:单叶机械心脏,碳素合金材质,美敦力A4501
9022.1200	--X射线断层检查仪	A:1.品名;2.用途;3.原理。B:4.品牌; 5.型号; 6.排数
9022.1300	--其他,牙科用	A:1.品名;2.用途; 3.原理。B:4.品牌; 5.型号
9022.1400	--其他,医疗、外科或兽医用	A:1.品名;2.用途;3.原理。B:4.品牌; 5.型号
	--其他:	A:1.品名;2.用途;3.原理。B:4.品牌; 5.型号
	-α射线、β射线、γ射线的应用设备,不论是否用于医疗、外科、牙科或兽医,包括射线照相或射线治疗设备:	A:1.品名;2.用途;3.原理。B:4.品牌; 5.型号
9022.3000	-X射线管	A:1.品名;2.用途;3.原理。B:4.品牌; 5.型号
	-其他,包括零件、附件:	A:1.品名;2.用途;3.原理。B:4.品牌; 5.型号
90.23	专供示范(例如,教学或展览)而无其他用途的仪器、装置及模型:	A:1.品名;2.用途。B:3.品牌;4.型号

税则号列	商品名称	申报要素(A:归类要素 B:价格要素 C:审单及其他要素)及说明举例
90.24	各种材料(例如,金属、木材、纺织材料、纸张、塑料)的硬度、强度、压缩性、弹性或其他机械性能的试验机器及器具:	
	-金属材料的试验用机器及器具:	A: 1. 品名; 2. 功能; 3. 试验材料类型。B: 4. 品牌; 5. 型号
9024.8000	-其他机器及器具	A: 1. 品名; 2. 功能; 3. 试验材料类型。B: 4. 品牌; 5. 型号
9024.9000	-零件、附件	A 1. 品名; 2. 用途(适用机型)。B: 3. 品牌; 4. 型号
90.25	记录式或非记录式的液体比重计及类似的浮子式仪器、温度计、高温计、气压计、湿度计、干湿球湿度计及其组合装置:	
	-温度计及高温计,未与其他仪器组合:	A: 1. 品名; 2. 原理; 3. 是否可直接读数。B: 4. 品牌; 5. 型号
9025.8000	-其他仪器	A: 1. 品名; 2. 原理。B: 3. 品牌; 4. 型号
9025.9000	-零件、附件	A: 1. 品名; 2. 用途(适用机型)。B: 3. 品牌; 4. 型号
9026.1000	-测量、检验液体流量或液位的仪器及装置	A: 1. 品名; 2. 功能; 3. 检测对象。B: 4. 品牌; 5. 型号
	-测量、检验压力的仪器及装置:	A: 1. 品名; 2. 功能; 3. 检测对象。B: 4. 品牌; 5. 型号
	-其他仪器及装置	A: 1. 品名; 2. 功能; 3. 检测对象。B: 4. 品牌; 5. 型号
9026.9000	-零件、附件	A: 1. 品名; 2. 用途(适用机型)。B: 3. 品牌; 4. 型号
9027.1000	-气体或烟雾分析仪	A: 1. 品名; 2. 原理; 3. 功能; 4. 检测对象。B: 5. 品牌; 6. 型号
	-色谱仪及电泳仪:	A: 1. 品名; 2. 原理; 3. 功能; 4. 检测对象。B: 5. 品牌; 6. 型号
9027.3000	-使用光学射线(紫外线、可见光、红外线)的分光仪、分光光度计及摄谱仪	A: 1. 品名; 2. 原理; 3. 功能; 4. 检测对象。B: 5. 品牌; 6. 型号
9027.5000	-使用光学射线(紫外线、可见光、红外线)的其他仪器及装置	A: 1. 品名; 2. 原理; 3. 功能; 4. 检测对象。B: 5. 品牌; 6. 型号
	-其他仪器及装置:	A: 1. 品名; 2. 原理; 3. 功能; 4. 检测对象。B: 5. 品牌; 6. 型号
9027.9000	-检镜切片机; 零件、附件	A: 1. 品名; 2. 用途(适用机型)。B: 3. 品牌; 4. 型号
90.28	生产或供应气体、液体、及电力用的计量仪表,包括它们的校准仪表:	
	-气量计:	A: 1. 品名; 2. 用途。B: 3. 品牌; 4. 型号
	-液量计:	A: 1. 品名; 2. 用途。B: 3. 品牌; 4. 型号
	-电量计:	A: 1. 品名; 2. 用途; 3. 原理。B: 4. 品牌; 5. 型号
	-零件、附件:	A: 1. 品名; 2. 用途(适用机型)。B: 3. 品牌; 4. 型号
90.29	转数计、产量计数器、车费计、里程计、步数计及类似仪表;速度计及转速表,品目 90.14 及 90.15 的仪表除外;频闪观测仪:	
	-转数计、产量计数器、车费计、里程计、步数计及类似仪表:	A: 1. 品名; 2. 用途。B: 3. 品牌; 4. 型号
	-速度计及转速表,频闪观测仪:	1. 品名; 2. 用途。B: 3. 品牌; 4. 型号
9029.9000	-零件、附件	A: 1. 品名; 2. 用途(适用机型)。B: 3. 品牌; 4. 型号
9030.1000	-离子射线的测量或检验仪器及装置	A: 1. 品名; 2. 用途; 3. 功能。B: 4. 品牌; 5. 型号
	-示波器:	A: 1. 品名; 2. 用途; 3. 功能; 4. 频率。B: 5. 品牌; 6. 型号
	--万用表,不带记录装置:	A: 1. 品名; 2. 用途; 3. 功能; 4. 量程; 5. 是否带记录装置。B: 6. 品牌; 7. 型号
9030.3200	--万用表,带记录装置	A: 1. 品名; 2. 用途; 3. 功能; 4. 量程; 5. 是否带记录装置。B: 6. 品牌; 7. 型号
9030.3310	---量程在五位半及以下的数字电流表、电压表	A: 1. 品名; 2. 用途; 3. 功能; 4. 量程; 5. 是否带记录装置。B: 6. 品牌; 7. 型号
9030.3320	---电阻测试仪	A: 1. 品名; 2. 用途; 3. 功能; 4. 是否带记录装置。B: 5. 品牌; 6. 型号
9030.3390	---其他	A: 1. 品名; 2. 用途; 3. 功能; 4. 是否带记录装置。B: 5. 品牌; 6. 型号
9030.3900	--其他,带记录装置	A: 1. 品名; 2. 用途; 3. 功能; 4. 是否带记录装置。B: 5. 品牌; 6. 型号
	-通信专用的其他仪器及装置(例如,串音测试器、增益测量仪、失真度表、噪声计):	A: 1. 品名; 2. 用途; 3. 功能; 4. 测试频率。B: 5. 品牌; 6. 型号
	-其他仪器及装置:	A: 1. 品名; 2. 用途; 3. 功能; 4. 是否带记录装置。B: 5. 品牌; 6. 型号
9030.9000	-零件、附件	A: 1. 品名; 2. 用途(适用机型)。B: 3. 品牌; 4. 型号
9031.1000	-机械零件平衡试验机	A: 1. 品名; 2. 用途; 3. 功能。B: 4. 品牌; 5. 型号
9031.2000	-试验台	A: 1. 品名; 2. 用途; 3. 功能。B: 4. 品牌; 5. 型号
	-其他光学仪器及器具:	A: 1. 品名; 2. 用途; 3. 功能。B: 4. 品牌; 5. 型号
	-其他仪器、器具及机器:	A: 1. 品名; 2. 用途; 3. 原理; 4. 功能。B: 5. 品牌; 6. 型号
9031.9000	-零件、附件	A: 1. 品名; 2. 用途(适用机型)。B: 3. 品牌; 4. 型号
9032.1000	-恒温器	A: 1. 品名; 2. 用途; 3. 原理; 4. 功能。B: 5. 品牌; 6. 型号
9032.2000	-恒压器	A: 1. 品名; 2. 用途; 3. 原理; 4. 功能。B: 5. 品牌; 6. 型号
	-其他仪器及装置:	A: 1. 品名; 2. 用途; 3. 原理; 4. 功能。B: 5. 品牌; 6. 型号
9032.9000	-零件、附件	A: 1. 品名; 2. 用途(适用机型)。B: 3. 品牌; 4. 型号
90.33	第九十章所列机器、器具、仪器或装置用的本章其他税目未列名的零件、附件	A: 1. 品名; 2. 用途(适用机型)。B: 3. 品牌; 4. 型号

第九十一章　钟表及其零件

税则号列	商品名称	申报要素(A:归类要素 B:价格要素 C:审单及其他要素)及说明举例
91.01	手表、怀表及其他表，包括秒表，表壳用贵金属或包贵金属制成的:	A: 1.品名; 2.外壳材质(贵金属或包贵金属制); 3.驱动方式(电子、机械、自动、非自动); 4.指示方式(指针、光电)。B: 5.品牌; 6.型号
91.02	手表、怀表及其他表，包括秒表，但税目 91.01 的货品除外:	A: 1.品名; 2.外壳材质(金属制); 3.驱动方式(电子、机械、自动、非自动); 4.指示方式(指针、光电)。B: 5.品牌; 6.型号
91.03	以表芯装成的钟，但不包括税目 91.04 的钟:	A: 1.品名; 2.驱动方式(电子、机械、自动、非自动)。B: 3.品牌; 4.型号
91.04	仪表板钟及车辆、航空器、航天器或船舶用的类似钟:	A: 1.品名; 2.驱动方式(电子、机械、自动、非自动)。B: 3.品牌; 4.型号
91.05	其他钟	
	-闹钟:	A: 1.品名; 2.驱动方式(电子、机械、自动、非自动)。B: 3.品牌; 4.型号
	-挂钟:	A: 1.品名; 2.驱动方式(电子、机械、自动、非自动)。B: 3.品牌; 4.型号
9105.9110	---天文钟	A: 1.品名; 2.用途(车辆、船舶等用)。B: 3.品牌; 4.型号
9105.9190	---其他	A: 1.品名; 2.用途(闹钟、天文钟等); 3.驱动方式(电子、机械)。B: 4.品牌; 5.型号
9105.9900	--其他	A: 1.品名; 2.用途(闹钟、天文钟等); 3.驱动方式(电子、机械)。B: 4.品牌; 5.型号
91.06	时间记录器以及测量、记录或指示时间间隔的装置，装有钟、表机芯或同步电动机的(例如，考勤钟、时刻记录器):	A: 1.品名; 2.用途(闹钟、天文钟等); 3.驱动方式(电子、机械)。B: 4.品牌; 5.型号
91.07	装有钟、表机芯或同步电动机的定时开关:	A: 1.品名; 2.用途(闹钟、天文钟等); 3.驱动方式(电子、机械)。B: 4.品牌; 5.型号
91.08	已组装的完整表芯:	
	-电力驱动的:	A: 1.品名; 2.用途(闹钟、天文钟等); 3.驱动方式(电子、机械); 4.表面尺寸; 5.指示方式。B: 6.品牌
9108.2000	-自动上弦的	A: 1.品名; 2.用途(闹钟、天文钟等); 3.驱动方式(电子、机械); 4.表面尺寸; 5.指示方式。B: 6.品牌
9108.9010	---表面尺寸在 33.8 毫米及以下	A: 1.品名; 2.用途(考勤钟、停车记时表等); 3.驱动方式(电子、机械); 4.表面尺寸。B: 5.品牌
9108.9090	---其他	A: 1.品名; 2.表面尺寸
91.09	已组装的完整钟芯:	A: 1.品名; 2.驱动方式(电子、机械、自动、非自动)。例: 已组装电子闹钟芯
91.10	未组装或部分组装的完整钟、表机芯(机芯套装件); 已组装的不完整钟、表机芯; 未组装的不完整钟、表机芯:	
	-表的:	A: 1.品名; 2.驱动方式(电子、机械、自动、非自动)
	-其他:	A: 1.品名; 2.用途
9111.1000	-贵金属表壳或包贵金属表壳	A: 1.品名; 2.材质; 3.贵金属含量
9111.2000	-贱金属表壳，不论是否镀金或镀银	A: 1.品名; 2.材质
9111.8000	-其他表壳	A: 1.品名; 2.材质
9111.9000	-零件	A: 1.品名; 2.材质
91.12	钟壳和本章所列其他货品的类似外壳及其零件:	A: 1.品名; 2.用途。例: 塑料钟壳
9113.1000	-贵金属或包贵金属制	A: 1.品名; 2.材质(贵金属、贱金属等); 3.贵金属含量
9113.2000	-贱金属制，不论是否镀金或镀银	A: 1.品名; 2.材质(贵金属、贱金属等)
9113.9000	-其他	A: 1.品名; 2.材质(贵金属、贱金属等); 3.是否野生动物皮制
9114.1000	-发条，包括游丝	A: 1.品名; 2.用途。B: 3.材质
9114.3000	-钟面或表面	A: 1.品名。B: 2.材质(贵金属、贱金属等)
9114.4000	-夹板及横担(过桥)	A: 1.品名。B: 2.材质(贵金属、贱金属等)
9114.9010	---宝石轴承	A: 1.品名; 2.用途。B: 3.材质
9114.9090	---其他	A: 1.品名。B: 2.材质(贵金属、贱金属等)

第九十二章　乐器及其零件、附件

税则号列	商品名称	申报要素(A:归类要素 B:价格要素 C:审单及其他要素)及说明举例
92.01	钢琴，包括自动钢琴、拨弦古钢琴及其他键盘弦乐器:	A: 1.品名; 2.有否琴凳。B: 3.产品编码; 4.材质(象牙琴键、贵金属、贱金属等); 5.种类(新旧、竖卧式、是否数码); 6.品牌; 7.型号
92.02	其他弦乐器(例如，吉他、小提琴、竖琴):	A: 1.品名; 2.是否为野生动物皮制。B: 3.用途; 4.规格型号
92.05	管乐器(例如，键盘管风琴、手风琴、	A: 1.品名。B: 2.种类; 3.品牌; 4.规格型号

税则号列	商品名称	申报要素(A:归类要素 B:价格要素 C:审单及其他要素)及说明举例
	单簧管、小号、风笛),但游艺场风琴及手摇风琴除外:	
92.06	打击乐器(例如,鼓、木琴、铙、钹、响板、响葫芦):	A:1.品名;2.是否为野生动物皮制。B:3.用途; 4.品牌;5.规格型号
92.07	通过电产生或扩大声音的乐器(例如,电风琴、电吉他、电手风琴):	A:1.品名。B:2.种类;3.品牌; 4.规格型号
9208.1000	-百音盒	A:1.品名。B:2.种类;3.品牌
9208.9000	-其他	A:1.品名。B:2.品牌
9209.3000	-乐器用的弦	A:1.品名;2.用途(适用乐器类型)。B:3.品牌; 4.材质; 5.规格型号
	-其他:	A:1.品名 2.用途

第十九类 武器、弹药及其零件、附件

第九十三章 武器、弹药及其零件、附件

税则号列	商品名称	申报要素(A:归类要素 B:价格要素 C:审单及其他要素)及说明举例
93.01	军用武器,但左轮手枪、其他手枪及税目93.07的兵器除外:	A:1.品名;2.驱动方式。B:3.型号
93.02	左轮手枪及其他手枪,但税目93.03或93.04的货品除外:	A 1.品名。B:2.型号
93.03	靠爆炸药发射的其他火器及类似装置(例如,运动用猎枪及步枪、前装枪、维利式信号枪及其他专为发射信号弹的装置、发射空包弹的左轮手枪和其他手枪、弩枪式无痛捕杀器、抛缆枪):	A:1.品名。B:2.型号
93.04	其他武器(例如,弹簧枪、气枪、气手枪、警棍),但不包括税目93.07的货品:	A:1.品名。B:2.型号
93.05	税目93.01至93.04所列物品的零件、附件:	A:1.品名。B:2.型号
93.06	炸弹、手榴弹、鱼雷、地雷、水雷、导弹及类似武器及其零件;子弹、其他弹药和射弹及其零件,包括弹丸及弹垫:	A:1.品名。B:2.型号
93.07	剑、短弯刀、刺刀、长矛和类似的武器及其零件;刀鞘、剑鞘:	A:1.品名;2.用途

第二十类 杂项制品

第九十四章 家具;寝具、褥垫、弹簧床垫、软座垫及类似的填充制品;未列名灯具及照明装置;发光标志、发光铭牌及类似品;活动房屋

税则号列	商品名称	申报要素(A:归类要素 B:价格要素 C:审单及其他要素)及说明举例
9401.1000	-飞机用坐具	A:1.品名;2.用途。B:3.品牌
	-机动车辆用坐具:	A:1.品名;2.用途;3.材质。B:4.品牌
9401.3000	-可调高度的转动坐具	A:1.品名;2.用途;3.材质;4.是否可调节、可转动。B:5.品牌
	-能做床用的两用椅,但庭园坐具或野营设备除外:	A:1.品名;2.用途;3.材质;4.是否可做床用。B:5.品牌
	-藤、柳条、竹及类似材料制的坐具:	A:1.品名;2.用途;3.材质。B:4.品牌
	-木框架的其他坐具:	A:1.品名;2.用途;3.材质;4.是否装软垫。B:5.品牌
	-金属框架的其他坐具:	A:1.品名;2.用途;3.材质;4.是否装软垫。B:5.品牌
	-其他坐具:	A:1.品名;2.用途;3.材质。B:4.品牌
	-零件:	A:1.品名;2.用途(适用机型);3.材质
9402.1010	---理发用椅及其零件	A:1.品名;2.用途;3.材质。B:4.品牌
9402.1090	---其他	A:1.品名;2.用途;3.配置附属装置;4.是否带医疗用具。B:5.品牌
9402.9000	-其他	A:1.品名;2.用途;3.配置附属装置;4.是否带医疗用具。B:5.品牌

税则号列	商品名称	申报要素(A:归类要素 B:价格要素 C:审单及其他要素)及说明举例
9403.1000	-办公室用金属家具	A:1.品名;2.用途;3.材质;4.是否办公室用。B:5.品牌; 6.规格
9403.2000	-其他金属家具	A:1.品名;2.用途;3.材质。B:4.品牌;5.规格
9403.3000	-办公室用木家具	A:1.品名;2.用途;3.材质;4.是否办公室用。B:5.品牌;6.规格
9403.4000	-厨房用木家具	A:1.品名;2.用途;3.材质;4.是否厨房用。B:5.品牌; 6.规格
	-卧室用木家具:	A:1.品名;2.用途;3.材质;4.是否卧室用。B:5.品牌; 6.规格
	-其他木家具:	A:1.品名;2.用途;3.材质。B:4.品牌;5.规格
9403.7000	-塑料家具	A:1.品名;2.用途;3.材质。B:4.品牌;5.规格
	-其他材料制的家具,包括藤、柳条、竹或类似材料制的:	A:1.品名;2.用途;3.材质。B:4.品牌;5.规格
9403.9000	-零件	A:1.品名;2.用途;3.材质。B:4.规格
9404.1000	-弹簧床垫	A:1.品名;2.材质(包面及填充物)。B:3.品牌; 4.规格
	-褥垫:	A:1.品名;2.材质(包面及填充物)。B:3.品牌; 4.规格
	-睡袋:	A:1.品名;2.材质(包面及填充物)。B:3.品牌; 4.规格
9404.9010	---羽毛或羽绒填充的	A:1.品名;2.材质(包面及填充物)。B:3.品牌; 4.规格
9404.9020	---兽毛填充的	A:1.品名;2.材质(包面及填充物)。B:3.品牌; 4.规格
9404.9030	---丝棉填充的	A:1.品名;2.材质(包面及填充物)。B:3.品牌; 4.规格
9404.9040	---化纤棉填充的	A:1.品名;2.材质。B:3.品牌; 4.规格
9404.9090	---其他	A:1.品名;2.材质。B:3.品牌; 4.规格
9405.1000	-枝形吊灯及天花板或墙壁上的其他电气照明装置,但不包括公共露天场所或街道上的电气照明装置	A:1.品名;2.材质;3.种类;4.用途。B:5.品牌
9405.2000	-电气的台灯、床头灯或落地灯	A:1.品名;2.材质;3.种类;4.用途。B:5.品牌
9405.3000	-圣诞树用的成套灯具	A:1.品名;2.材质;3.种类;4.用途。B:5.品牌
	-其他电灯及照明装置:	A:1.品名;2.材质;3.种类;4.用途。B:5.品牌
9405.5000	-非电气的灯具及照明装置	A:1.品名;2.材质;3.种类;4.用途。B:5.品牌
9405.6000	-发光标志、发光铭牌及类似品	A:1.品名;2.材质;3.种类;4.用途。B:5.品牌
	-零件:	A:1.品名;2.材质;3.用途
94.06	活动房屋:	A:1.品名;2.材质;3.内部配置; 4.规格(尺寸)

第九十五章　玩具、游戏品、运动用品及其零件、附件

税则号列	商品名称	申报要素(A:归类要素 B:价格要素 C:审单及其他要素)及说明举例
9503.0010	---三轮车、踏板车、踏板汽车和类似的带轮玩具;玩偶车	A:1.品名;2.用途;3.种类。B:4.品牌
	---玩偶,不论是否着装:玩具动物:	A:1.品名;2.用途;3.种类。B:4.品牌
	---缩小(按比例缩小)的全套模型组件,不论是否活动:	A:1.品名;2.用途;3.种类。B:4.品牌
9503.0040	---其他建筑套件及建筑玩具	A:1.品名;2.用途;3.种类。B:4.品牌
9503.0050	---玩具乐器	A:1.品名;2.用途;3.种类。B:4.品牌
9503.0060	---智力玩具	A:1.品名;2.用途;3.种类。B:4.品牌
9503.0081	----组装成套或全套的	A:1.品名;2.用途;3.种类;4.是否成套
9503.0082	----其他带动力装置的玩具及模型	A:1.品名;2.用途;3.种类;4.是否带有动力装置。B:5.品牌
9503.0089	----其他	A:1.品名;2.用途;3.种类。B:4.品牌
9503.0090	---零件、附件	A:1.品名;2.用途;3.种类。B:4.品牌
9504.2000	-各种台球用品及附件	A:1.品名;2.用途。B:3.品牌
9504.3010	---电子游戏机	A:1.品名;2.用途;3.种类。B:4.品牌
9504.3090	---其他	A:1.品名;2.用途。B:3.品牌
9504.4000	-扑克牌	A:1.品名;2.用途。B:3.品牌
	-视频游戏控制器及设备,但子目9504.30的货品除外:	A:1.品名;2.用途;3.种类; 4.是否与电视接收机配套使用。B:5.品牌
9504.9010	---其他电子游戏机	A:1.品名;2.用途;3.种类。B:4.品牌
	---保龄球自动球道设备及器具:	A:1.品名;2.用途;3.种类。B:4.品牌
9504.9030	---中国象棋、国际象棋、跳棋等棋类用品	A:1.品名;2.用途;3.种类。B:4.品牌
9504.9040	---麻将及类似桌上游戏用品	A:1.品名;2.用途;3.种类。B:4.品牌
9504.9090	---其他	A:1.品名;2.用途;3.种类。B:4.品牌
9505.1000	-圣诞节用品	A:1.品名;2.用途。B:3.品牌

税则号列	商品名称	申报要素(A:归类要素 B:价格要素 C:审单及其他要素)及说明举例
9505.9000	-其他	A:1.品名;2.用途;3.种类。B:4.品牌
95.06	一般的体育活动、体操、竞技及其他运动(包括乒乓球运动)或户外游戏用的本章其他品目未列名用品及设备;游泳池或戏水池:	
	-滑雪屐及其他滑雪用具:	A:1.品名;2.用途;3.种类。B:4.品牌;5.型号
	-滑水板、冲浪板、帆板及其他水上运动用具:	A:1.品名;2.用途;3.种类。B:4.品牌;5.型号
	-高尔夫球棍及其他高尔夫球用具:	A:1.品名;2.用途。B:3.品牌;4.型号
	-乒乓球运动用品及器械:	A:1.品名;2.用途;3.种类。B:4.品牌;5.型号
	-网球拍、羽毛球拍或类似的球拍,不论是否装弦:	A:1.品名;2.用途;3.种类。B:4.品牌;5.型号
	-球,但高尔夫球及乒乓球除外:	A:1.品名;2.用途;3.种类。B:4.品牌;5.型号
	-溜冰鞋及旱冰鞋,包括装有冰刀的溜冰靴:	A:1.品名;2.用途;3.种类。B:4.品牌;5.型号
	---一般的体育活动、体操或竞技用品及设备:	A:1.品名;2.用途;3.种类。B:4.品牌;5.型号
9506.9900	--其他	A:1.品名;2.材质。B:3.品牌;4.型号
9507.1000	-钓鱼竿	A:1.品名;2.材质。B:3.品牌;4.型号
9507.2000	-钓鱼钩,不论有无系钩丝	A:1.品名。B:2.品牌;3.型号
9507.3000	-钓线轮	A:1.品名。B:2.品牌;3.型号
9507.9000	-其他	A:1.品名;2.用途。B:3.品牌;4.型号。例:税目56.08货品除外
95.08	旋转木马、秋千、射击用靶及其他游乐场的娱乐设备;流动马戏团及流动动物园;流动剧团:	A:1.品名;2.用途。例:旋转木马;射击用靶

第九十六章 杂项制品

税则号列	商品名称	申报要素(A:归类要素 B:价格要素 C:审单及其他要素)及说明举例
9601.1000	-已加工的兽牙及其制品	A:1.品名;2.材质;3.是否野生动物产品;4.是否已加工。例:野生象牙制的筷子,已加工
9601.9000	-其他	A:1.品名;2.材质;3.加工工艺
9602.0010	---装药用胶囊	A:1.品名。例:不包括税目19.05的装药空囊
9602.0090	---其他	A:1.品名;2.材质;3.加工工艺
96.03	帚、刷(包括作为机器、器具、车辆零件的刷)、非机动的手工操作地板清扫器、拖把及毛掸;供制帚、刷用的成束或成簇的材料;油漆块垫及滚筒;橡皮扫帚(橡皮辊除外):	A:1.品名;2.用途;3.材质。例:机器用钢丝刷;野鸡羽毛掸
96.04	手用粗筛、细筛:	A:1.品名 例:手用粗筛、细筛
96.05	个人梳妆、缝纫或清洁鞋靴、衣服用的成套旅行用具:	A:1.品名;2.组成(内装货品)。例:擦鞋套具(内含棕色、黑色鞋油各1支、鞋擦1个、鞋刷2把,成套盒装)
96.06	钮扣、揿扣、钮扣芯及钮扣和揿扣的其他零件;钮扣坯:	A:1.品名;2.材质;3.种类;4.是否用纺织材料包裹
96.07	拉链及其零件:	A:1.品名;2.材质。例:铜拉链
96.08	圆珠笔;毡尖和其他渗水式笔尖笔及唛头笔;自来水笔、铁笔型自来水笔及其他钢笔;蜡纸铁笔;活动铅笔;钢笔杆、铅笔套及类似的笔套;上述物品的零件(包括帽、夹),但税目96.09的货品除外:	A:1.品名;2.种类。B:3.品牌;4.型号
96.09	铅笔(税目96.08的铅笔除外)、颜色铅笔、铅笔芯、蜡笔、图画碳笔、书写或绘画用粉笔及裁缝划粉:	A:1.品名;2.种类。B:3.品牌;4.型号。例:不包括活动铅笔
96.10	具有书写或绘画面的石板、黑板及类似板,不论是否镶框:	A:1.品名;2.种类。B:3.品牌
96.11	手用日期戳、封缄戳、编号戳及类似印戳(包括标签压印器);手工操作的排字盘及带有排字盘的手印器	A:1.品名;2.用途

税则号列	商品名称	申报要素(A:归类要素 B:价格要素 C:审单及其他要素)及说明举例
96.12	打字机色带或类似色带，已上油或经其他方法处理能着色的，不论是否装轴或装盒;印台，不论是否已加印油或带盒子:	A:1.品名;2.材质。B:3.品牌;4.型号。例:不包括未上有油墨的色带;例:化学纤维制打字机色带，松下kx-8
96.13	香烟打火机和其他打火器(不论是机械的还是电气的)及其零件，但打火石及打火机芯除外:	A:1.品名;2.种类。B:3.型号
9614.0010	---烟斗及烟斗头	A:1.品名;2.材质。B:3.品牌;4.型号
9614.0090	---其他	A:1.品名;2.材质。B:3.品牌。例:野生象牙制的烟嘴，无品牌
96.15	梳子、发夹及类似品;发卡、卷发夹、卷发器或类似品及其零件，但税目85.16的货品除外:	A:1.品名;2.材质。例:牛骨梳，非野生
96.16	香水喷雾器或类似的化妆用喷雾器及其座架、喷头;粉扑及粉拍，施敷脂粉或化妆品用:	A:1.品名;2.用途。例:香水喷雾器
96.17	带壳的保温瓶和其他真空容器及其零件，但玻璃瓶胆除外:	A:1.品名;2.是否带外壳的保温瓶
96.18	裁缝用人体模型及其他人体活动模型;橱窗装饰用的自动模型及其他活动陈列品:	A:1.品名;2.用途;3.材质
9618.0000	裁缝用人体模型及其他人体活动模型;橱窗装饰用的自动模型及其他活动陈列品	例:裁缝用塑料人体模型
96.19	任何材料制的卫生巾(护垫)及止血塞、婴儿尿布及尿布衬里和类似品:	1.品名。B:2.品牌

第二十一类　艺术品、收藏品及古物

第九十七章　艺术品、收藏品及古物

税则号列	商品名称	申报要素(A:归类要素 B:价格要素 C:审单及其他要素)及说明举例
97.01	油画、粉画及其他手绘画,但带有手工绘制及手工描饰的制品或税目49.06的图纸除外;拼贴画及类似装饰板:	A:1.品名;2.是否野生动物产品。B:3.尺寸大小
97.02	雕版画、印制画、石印画的原本:	A:1.品名。B:2.尺寸大小;3.原作者姓名;4.创作年份
97.03	各种材料制的雕塑品原件	A:1.品名;2.用途(如具有商业性质的装饰用雕塑品、个人装饰品及其他具有商业性质的传统手工艺品)。B:3.尺寸大小
97.04	使用过或未使用过的邮票、印花税票、邮戳印记、首日封、邮政信笺(印有邮票的纸品)及类似品，但税目49.07的货品除外:	A:1.品名;2.种类。B:3.指运国(地区)。例:税目49.07的货品除外。例:未使用过的新加坡邮票
97.05	具有动物学、植物学、矿物学、解剖学、历史学、考古学、古生物学、人种学或钱币学意义的收集品及珍藏品:	A:1.品名;2.种类;3.年代;4.是否野生动物产品。例:2～3亿年前的三叶虫化石(注:该例仅限于举例,实为国家禁止出口古文物)
97.06	超过100年的古物:	A:1.品名;2.种类;3.年代;4.是否野生动物产品